This Bible belongs to

I0821309

NIV

Journal the Word®

BIBLE

DOUBLE-COLUMN

NEW INTERNATIONAL VERSION

NIV

Journal the Word®

BIBLE

DOUBLE-COLUMN

Reflect, Journal, or Create Art Next to Your Favorite Verses

ZONDERVAN®

NIV Journal the Word® Bible, Double Column
Published by Zondervan, 2023
Grand Rapids, Michigan, USA

www.Zondervan.com

This Bible was set in the Zondervan NIV Typeface, created at the 2K/DENMARK type foundry.

Library of Congress Catalog Card Number 2015939018

Printed in South Korea

N120712

25 26 27 28 29 30 31 32 33 /SWK/ 22 21 20 19 18 17 16 15 14

A portion of the purchase price of your NIV® Bible is provided to Biblica so together we support the mission of *Transforming lives through God's Word.*

Biblica provides God's Word to people through translation, publishing and Bible engagement in Africa, Asia Pacific, Europe, Latin America, Middle East, and North America. Through its worldwide reach, Biblica engages people with God's Word so that their lives are transformed through a relationship with Jesus Christ.

TABLE OF CONTENTS

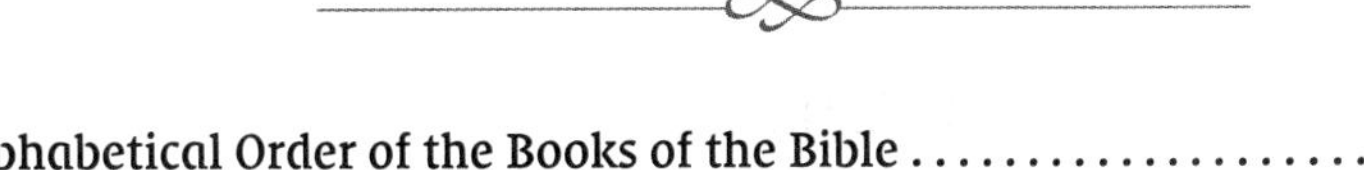

THE OLD TESTAMENT

THE NEW TESTAMENT

ALPHABETICAL ORDER OF THE BOOKS OF THE BIBLE

The books of the New Testament are indicated by *italics.*

PREFACE

The goal of the New International Version (NIV) is to enable English-speaking people from around the world to read and hear God's eternal Word in their own language. Our work as translators is motivated by our conviction that the Bible is God's Word in written form. We believe that the Bible contains the divine answer to the deepest needs of humanity, sheds unique light on our path in a dark world and sets forth the way to our eternal well-being. Out of these deep convictions, we have sought to recreate as far as possible the experience of the original audience — blending transparency to the original text with accessibility for the millions of English speakers around the world. We have prioritized accuracy, clarity and literary quality with the goal of creating a translation suitable for public and private reading, evangelism, teaching, preaching, memorizing and liturgical use. We have also sought to preserve a measure of continuity with the long tradition of translating the Scriptures into English.

The complete NIV Bible was first published in 1978. It was a completely new translation made by over a hundred scholars working directly from the best available Hebrew, Aramaic and Greek texts. The translators came from the United States, Great Britain, Canada, Australia and New Zealand, giving the translation an international scope. They were from many denominations and churches — including Anglican, Assemblies of God, Baptist, Brethren, Christian Reformed, Church of Christ, Evangelical Covenant, Evangelical Free, Lutheran, Mennonite, Methodist, Nazarene, Presbyterian, Wesleyan and others. This breadth of denominational and theological perspective helped to safeguard the translation from sectarian bias. For these reasons, and by the grace of God, the NIV has gained a wide readership in all parts of the English-speaking world.

The work of translating the Bible is never finished. As good as they are, English translations must be regularly updated so that they will continue to communicate accurately the meaning of God's Word. Updates are needed in order to reflect the latest developments in our understanding of the biblical world and its languages and to keep pace with changes in English usage. Recognizing, then, that the NIV would retain its ability to communicate God's Word accurately only if it were regularly updated, the original translators established the Committee on Bible Translation (CBT). The Committee is a self-perpetuating group of biblical scholars charged with keeping abreast of advances in biblical scholarship and changes in English and issuing periodic updates to the NIV. The CBT is an independent, self-governing body and has sole responsibility for the NIV text. The Committee mirrors the original group of translators in its diverse international and denominational makeup and in its unifying commitment to the Bible as God's inspired Word.

In obedience to its mandate, the Committee has issued periodic updates to the NIV. An initial revision was released in 1984. A more thorough revision process was completed in 2005, resulting in the separately published TNIV. The updated NIV you now have in your hands builds on both the original NIV and the TNIV and represents the latest effort of the Committee to articulate God's unchanging Word in the way the original authors might have said it had they been speaking in English to the global English-speaking audience today.

Translation Philosophy

The Committee's translating work has been governed by three widely accepted principles about the way people use words and about the way we understand them.

First, the meaning of words is determined by the way that users of the language actually use them at any given time. For the biblical languages, therefore, the Committee utilizes the best and most recent scholarship on the way Hebrew, Aramaic and Greek words were being used in biblical times. At the same time, the Committee carefully studies the state of modern English. Good translation is like good communication: one must know the target audience so that the appropriate choices can be made about which English words to use to represent the original words of Scripture. From its inception, the NIV has had as its target the general English-speaking population all over the world, the "International" in its title reflecting this concern. The aim of the Committee is to put the Scriptures into natural English that will communicate effectively with the broadest possible audience of English speakers.

Modern technology has enhanced the Committee's ability to choose the right English words to convey the meaning of the original text. The field of computational linguistics harnesses the power of computers to provide broadly applicable and current data about the state of the language. Translators can now access huge databases of modern English to better understand the current meaning and usage of key words. The Committee utilized this resource in preparing the 2011 edition of the NIV. An area of especially rapid and significant change in English is the way certain nouns and pronouns are used to refer to human beings. The Committee therefore requested experts in computational linguistics at Collins Dictionaries to pose some key questions about this usage to its database of English — the largest in the world, with over 4.4 billion words, gathered from several English-speaking countries and including both spoken and written English. (The Collins Study, called "The Development and Use of Gender Language in Contemporary English," can be accessed at *http://www.thenivbible.com/about-the-niv/about-the-2011-edition/*.) The study revealed that the most popular words to describe the human race in modern U.S. English were "humanity," "man" and "mankind." The Committee then used this data in the updated NIV, choosing from among these three words (and occasionally others also) depending on the context.

A related issue creates a larger problem for modern translations: the move away from using the third-person masculine singular pronouns — "he/him/his" — to refer to men and women equally. This usage does persist in some forms of English, and this revision therefore occasionally uses these pronouns in a generic sense. But the tendency, recognized in day-to-day usage and confirmed by the Collins study, is away from the generic use of "he," "him" and "his." In recognition of this shift in language and in an effort to translate into the natural English that people are actually using, this revision of the NIV generally uses other constructions when the biblical text is plainly addressed to men and women equally. The reader will encounter especially frequently a "they," "their" or "them" to express a generic singular idea. Thus, for instance, Mark 8:36 reads: "What good is it for someone to gain the whole world, yet forfeit their soul?" This generic use of the "distributive" or "singular" "they/them/their" has been used for many centuries by respected writers of English and has now become established as standard English, spoken and written, all over the world.

A second linguistic principle that feeds into the Committee's translation work is that meaning is found not in individual words, as vital as they are, but in larger clusters: phrases, clauses, sentences, discourses. Translation is not, as many people think, a matter of word substitution: English word *x* in place of Hebrew word *y*. Translators must first determine the meaning of the words of the biblical languages in the context of the passage and then select English words that accurately communicate that meaning to modern listeners and readers. This means that accurate translation will not always reflect the exact structure of the original language. To be sure, there is debate over the degree to which translators should try to preserve the "form" of the original text in English. From the beginning, the NIV has taken a mediating position on this issue. The manual produced when the translation that became the NIV was first being planned states: "If the Greek or Hebrew syntax has a good parallel in modern English, it should be used. But if there is no good parallel, the English syntax appropriate to the meaning of the original is to be chosen." It is fine, in other words, to carry over the form of the biblical languages into English — but not at the expense of natural expression. The principle that meaning resides in larger clusters of words means that the Committee has not insisted on a "word-for-word" approach to translation. We certainly believe that every word of Scripture is inspired by God and therefore to be carefully studied to determine what God is saying to us. It is for this reason that the Committee labors over every single word of the original texts, working hard to determine how each of those words contributes to what the text is saying. Ultimately, however, it is how these individual words function in combination with other words that determines meaning.

A third linguistic principle guiding the Committee in its translation work is the recognition that words have a spectrum of meaning. It is popular to define a word by using another word, or "gloss," to substitute for it. This substitute word is then sometimes called the "literal" meaning of a word. In fact, however, words have a range of possible meanings. Those meanings will vary depending on the context, and words in one language will usually not occupy the same semantic range as words in another language. The Committee therefore studies each original word of Scripture in its context to identify its meaning in a particular verse and then chooses an appropriate English word (or phrase) to represent it. It is impossible, then, to translate any given Hebrew, Aramaic or Greek word with the same English word all the time. The Committee does try to translate related occurrences of a word in the original languages with the same English word in order to preserve the connection for the English reader. But the Committee generally privileges clear natural meaning over a concern with consistency in rendering particular words.

Textual Basis

For the Old Testament the standard Hebrew text, the Masoretic Text as published in the latest edition of *Biblia Hebraica*, has been used throughout. The Masoretic Text tradition contains marginal notations that offer variant readings. These have sometimes been followed instead of the text itself. Because such instances involve variants within the Masoretic tradition, they have not been indicated in the textual notes. In a few cases, words in the basic consonantal text have been divided differently than in the Masoretic Text. Such cases are usually indicated in the textual footnotes. The Dead Sea Scrolls contain biblical texts that represent an earlier stage of the transmission of the Hebrew text. They have been consulted, as have been the Samaritan Pentateuch and the ancient scribal traditions concerning deliberate textual changes. The translators also consulted the more important early versions. Readings from these versions, the Dead Sea Scrolls and the scribal traditions were occasionally followed where the Masoretic Text seemed doubtful and where accepted principles of textual criticism showed that one or more of these textual witnesses appeared to provide the correct reading. In rare cases, the translators have emended the Hebrew text where it appears to have become corrupted at an even earlier stage of its transmission. These departures from the Masoretic Text are also indicated in the textual footnotes. Sometimes the vowel indicators (which are later additions to the basic consonantal text) found in the Masoretic Text did not, in the judgment of the translators, represent the correct vowels for the original text. Accordingly, some words have been read with a different set of vowels. These instances are usually not indicated in the footnotes.

The Greek text used in translating the New Testament has been an eclectic one, based on the latest editions of the Nestle-Aland/United Bible Societies' Greek New Testament. The translators have made their choices among the variant readings in accordance with widely accepted principles of New Testament textual criticism. Footnotes call attention to places where uncertainty remains.

The New Testament authors, writing in Greek, often quote the Old Testament from its ancient Greek version, the Septuagint. This is one reason why some of the Old Testament quotations in the NIV New Testament are not identical to the corresponding passages in the NIV Old Testament. Such quotations in the New Testament are indicated with the footnote "(see Septuagint)."

Footnotes and Formatting

Footnotes in this version are of several kinds, most of which need no explanation. Those giving alternative translations begin with "Or" and generally introduce the alternative with the last word preceding it in the text, except when it is a single-word alternative. When poetry is quoted in a footnote a slash mark indicates a line division.

It should be noted that references to diseases, minerals, flora and fauna, architectural details, clothing, jewelry, musical instruments and other articles cannot always be identified with precision. Also, linear measurements and measures of capacity can only be approximated (see the Table of Weights and Measures). Although *Selah*, used mainly in the Psalms, is probably a musical term, its meaning is uncertain. Since it may interrupt reading and distract the reader, this word has not been kept in the English text, but every occurrence has been signaled by a footnote.

As an aid to the reader, sectional headings have been inserted. They are not to be regarded as part of the biblical text and are not intended for oral reading. It is the Committee's hope that these headings may prove more helpful to the reader than the traditional chapter divisions, which were introduced long after the Bible was written.

Sometimes the chapter and/or verse numbering in English translations of the Old Testament differs from that found in published Hebrew texts. This is particularly the case in the Psalms, where the traditional titles are included in the Hebrew verse numbering. Such differences are indicated in the footnotes at the bottom of the page. In the New Testament, verse numbers that marked off portions of the traditional English text not supported by the best Greek manuscripts now appear in brackets, with a footnote indicating the text that has been omitted (see, for example, Matthew 17:[21]).

Mark 16:9 – 20 and John 7:53 — 8:11, although long accorded virtually equal status with the rest of the Gospels in which they stand, have a questionable standing in the textual history of the New Testament, as noted in the bracketed annotations with which they are set off. A different typeface has been chosen for these passages to indicate their uncertain status.

Basic formatting of the text, such as lining the poetry, paragraphing (both prose and poetry), setting up of (administrative-like) lists, indenting letters and lengthy prayers within narratives and the insertion of sectional headings, has been the work of the Committee. However, the choice between single-column and double-column formats has been left to the publishers. Also the issuing of "red-letter" editions is a publisher's choice — one that the Committee does not endorse.

The Committee has again been reminded that every human effort is flawed — including this revision of the NIV. We trust, however, that many will find in it an improved representation of the Word of God, through which they hear his call to faith in our Lord Jesus Christ and to service in his kingdom. We offer this version of the Bible to him in whose name and for whose glory it has been made.

The Committee on Bible Translation

OLD TESTAMENT

GENESIS

The Beginning

1 In the beginning God created
the heavens and the earth. 2 Now
the earth was formless and empty,
darkness was over the surface of the
deep, and the Spirit of God was hovering over the waters.

3 And God said, "Let there be light," and
there was light. 4 God saw that the
light was good, and he separated
the light from the darkness. 5 God
called the light "day," and the darkness he called "night." And there
was evening, and there was morning — the first day.
6 And God said, "Let there be a vault between the waters to separate water
from water." 7 So God made the vault
and separated the water under the
vault from the water above it. And
it was so. 8 God called the vault "sky."
And there was evening, and there
was morning — the second day.
9 And God said, "Let the water under the
sky be gathered to one place, and let
dry ground appear." And it was so.
10 God called the dry ground "land,"
and the gathered waters he called
"seas." And God saw that it was good.
11 Then God said, "Let the land
produce vegetation: seed-bearing
plants and trees on the land that
bear fruit with seed in it, according to their various kinds." And it
was so. 12 The land produced vegetation: plants bearing seed according to their kinds and trees bearing
fruit with seed in it according to
their kinds. And God saw that it was
good. 13 And there was evening, and
there was morning — the third day.
14 And God said, "Let there be lights in the
vault of the sky to separate the day
from the night, and let them serve as
signs to mark sacred times, and days
and years, 15 and let them be lights in
the vault of the sky to give light on
the earth." And it was so. 16 God made
two great lights — the greater light
to govern the day and the lesser light
to govern the night. He also made
the stars. 17 God set them in the vault
of the sky to give light on the earth,
18 to govern the day and the night,
and to separate light from darkness.
And God saw that it was good. 19 And
there was evening, and there was
morning — the fourth day.
20 And God said, "Let the water teem
with living creatures, and let birds
fly above the earth across the vault
of the sky." 21 So God created the
great creatures of the sea and every
living thing with which the water
teems and that moves about in it,
according to their kinds, and every
winged bird according to its kind.
And God saw that it was good. 22 God
blessed them and said, "Be fruitful
and increase in number and fill the
water in the seas, and let the birds
increase on the earth." 23 And there
was evening, and there was morning — the fifth day.
24 And God said, "Let the land produce
living creatures according to their
kinds: the livestock, the creatures
that move along the ground, and
the wild animals, each according to
its kind." And it was so. 25 God made
the wild animals according to their
kinds, the livestock according to
their kinds, and all the creatures
that move along the ground according to their kinds. And God saw that
it was good.
26 Then God said, "Let us make
mankind in our image, in our likeness, so that they may rule over the
fish in the sea and the birds in the
sky, over the livestock and all the
wild animals,[a] and over all the creatures that move along the ground."

27 So God created mankind in his own
image,
in the image of God he created them;
male and female he created them.

28 God blessed them and said to
them, "Be fruitful and increase in
number; fill the earth and subdue it.
Rule over the fish in the sea and the
birds in the sky and over every living
creature that moves on the ground."
29 Then God said, "I give you every seed-bearing plant on the face
of the whole earth and every tree

[a] 26 Probable reading of the original Hebrew text (see Syriac); Masoretic Text *the earth*

that has fruit with seed in it. They will be yours for food. 30 And to all the beasts of the earth and all the birds in the sky and all the creatures that move along the ground — everything that has the breath of life in it — I give every green plant for food." And it was so.

31 God saw all that he had made, and it was very good. And there was evening, and there was morning — the sixth day.

2 Thus the heavens and the earth were completed in all their vast array.

2 By the seventh day God had finished the work he had been doing; so on the seventh day he rested from all his work. 3 Then God blessed the seventh day and made it holy, because on it he rested from all the work of creating that he had done.

Adam and Eve

4 This is the account of the heavens and the earth when they were created, when the LORD God made the earth and the heavens.

5 Now no shrub had yet appeared on the earth[a] and no plant had yet sprung up, for the LORD God had not sent rain on the earth and there was no one to work the ground, 6 but streams[b] came up from the earth and watered the whole surface of the ground. 7 Then the LORD God formed a man[c] from the dust of the ground and breathed into his nostrils the breath of life, and the man became a living being.

8 Now the LORD God had planted a garden in the east, in Eden; and there he put the man he had formed. 9 The LORD God made all kinds of trees grow out of the ground — trees that were pleasing to the eye and good for food. In the middle of the garden were the tree of life and the tree of the knowledge of good and evil.

10 A river watering the garden flowed from Eden; from there it was separated into four headwaters. 11 The name of the first is the Pishon; it winds through the entire land of Havilah, where there is gold. 12 (The gold of that land is good; aromatic resin[d] and onyx are also there.) 13 The name of the second river is the Gihon; it winds through the entire land of Cush.[e] 14 The name of the third river is the Tigris; it runs along the east side of Ashur. And the fourth river is the Euphrates.

15 The LORD God took the man and put him in the Garden of Eden to work it and take care of it. 16 And the LORD God commanded the man, "You are free to eat from any tree in the garden; 17 but you must not eat from the tree of the knowledge of good and evil, for when you eat from it you will certainly die."

18 The LORD God said, "It is not good for the man to be alone. I will make a helper suitable for him."

19 Now the LORD God had formed out of the ground all the wild animals and all the birds in the sky. He brought them to the man to see what he would name them; and whatever the man called each living creature, that was its name. 20 So the man gave names to all the livestock, the birds in the sky and all the wild animals.

But for Adam[f] no suitable helper was found. 21 So the LORD God caused the man to fall into a deep sleep; and while he was sleeping, he took one of the man's ribs[g] and then closed up the place with flesh. 22 Then the LORD God made a woman from the rib[h] he had taken out of the man, and he brought her to the man.

23 The man said,

"This is now bone of my bones
and flesh of my flesh;
she shall be called 'woman,'
for she was taken out of man."

24 That is why a man leaves his father and mother and is united to his wife, and they become one flesh.

25 Adam and his wife were both naked, and they felt no shame.

The Fall

3 Now the serpent was more crafty than any of the wild animals the LORD God had made. He said to the woman, "Did God really say, 'You must not eat from any tree in the garden'?"

2 The woman said to the serpent, "We may eat fruit from the trees in the garden, 3 but God did say, 'You must not eat fruit from the tree that is in the middle of the garden, and you must not touch it, or you will die.'"

4 "You will not certainly die," the serpent said to the woman. 5 "For God knows that when you eat from it your eyes will be opened, and you will be like God, knowing good and evil."

[a] 5 Or *land*; also in verse 6 [b] 6 Or *mist* [c] 7 The Hebrew for *man (adam)* sounds like and may be related to the Hebrew for *ground (adamah)*; it is also the name *Adam* (see verse 20).
[d] 12 Or *good; pearls* [e] 13 Possibly southeast Mesopotamia [f] 20 Or *the man* [g] 21 Or *took part of the man's side* [h] 22 Or *part*

6When the woman saw that the fruit
of the tree was good for food and pleasing to the eye, and also desirable for
gaining wisdom, she took some and ate
it. She also gave some to her husband,
who was with her, and he ate it. 7Then
the eyes of both of them were opened,
and they realized they were naked; so
they sewed fig leaves together and made
coverings for themselves.

8Then the man and his wife heard the
sound of the LORD God as he was walking
in the garden in the cool of the day, and
they hid from the LORD God among the
trees of the garden. 9But the LORD God
called to the man, "Where are you?"

10He answered, "I heard you in the
garden, and I was afraid because I was
naked; so I hid."

11And he said, "Who told you that you
were naked? Have you eaten from the tree
that I commanded you not to eat from?"

12The man said, "The woman you put
here with me—she gave me some fruit
from the tree, and I ate it."

13Then the LORD God said to the woman, "What is this you have done?"

The woman said, "The serpent deceived me, and I ate."

14So the LORD God said to the serpent,
"Because you have done this,

"Cursed are you above all livestock
and all wild animals!
You will crawl on your belly
and you will eat dust
all the days of your life.
15And I will put enmity
between you and the woman,
and between your offspring[a] and
hers;
he will crush[b] your head,
and you will strike his heel."

16To the woman he said,

"I will make your pains in
childbearing very severe;
with painful labor you will give
birth to children.
Your desire will be for your husband,
and he will rule over you."

17To Adam he said, "Because you listened to your wife and ate fruit from the
tree about which I commanded you, 'You
must not eat from it,'

"Cursed is the ground because of you;
through painful toil you will eat
food from it
all the days of your life.
18It will produce thorns and thistles for
you,
and you will eat the plants of the
field.
19By the sweat of your brow
you will eat your food
until you return to the ground,
since from it you were taken;
for dust you are
and to dust you will return."

20Adam[c] named his wife Eve,[d] because
she would become the mother of all the
living.

21The LORD God made garments of
skin for Adam and his wife and clothed
them. 22And the LORD God said, "The man
has now become like one of us, knowing
good and evil. He must not be allowed to
reach out his hand and take also from
the tree of life and eat, and live forever."
23So the LORD God banished him from
the Garden of Eden to work the ground
from which he had been taken. 24After he
drove the man out, he placed on the east
side[e] of the Garden of Eden cherubim
and a flaming sword flashing back and
forth to guard the way to the tree of life.

Cain and Abel

4 Adam[c] made love to his wife Eve,
and she became pregnant and gave
birth to Cain.[f] She said, "With the help of
the LORD I have brought forth[g] a man."
2Later she gave birth to his brother Abel.

Now Abel kept flocks, and Cain
worked the soil. 3In the course of time
Cain brought some of the fruits of the
soil as an offering to the LORD. 4And Abel
also brought an offering—fat portions
from some of the firstborn of his flock.
The LORD looked with favor on Abel
and his offering, 5but on Cain and his
offering he did not look with favor. So
Cain was very angry, and his face was
downcast.

6Then the LORD said to Cain, "Why are
you angry? Why is your face downcast? 7If
you do what is right, will you not be accepted? But if you do not do what is right,
sin is crouching at your door; it desires to
have you, but you must rule over it."

8Now Cain said to his brother Abel,
"Let's go out to the field."[h] While they
were in the field, Cain attacked his
brother Abel and killed him.

9Then the LORD said to Cain, "Where is
your brother Abel?"

[a] 15 Or *seed* [b] 15 Or *strike* [c] 20,1 Or *The man* [d] 20 *Eve* probably means *living.* [e] 24 Or *placed in front* [f] 1 *Cain* sounds like the Hebrew for *brought forth* or *acquired.* [g] 1 Or *have acquired* [h] 8 Samaritan Pentateuch, Septuagint, Vulgate and Syriac; Masoretic Text does not have *"Let's go out to the field."*

"I don't know," he replied. "Am I my
brother's keeper?"
10 The LORD said, "What have you
done? Listen! Your brother's blood cries
out to me from the ground. 11 Now you
are under a curse and driven from the
ground, which opened its mouth to receive your brother's blood from your
hand. 12 When you work the ground, it
will no longer yield its crops for you. You
will be a restless wanderer on the earth."
13 Cain said to the LORD, "My punishment is more than I can bear. 14 Today
you are driving me from the land, and I
will be hidden from your presence; I will
be a restless wanderer on the earth, and
whoever finds me will kill me."
15 But the LORD said to him, "Not so[a];
anyone who kills Cain will suffer vengeance seven times over." Then the LORD
put a mark on Cain so that no one who
found him would kill him. 16 So Cain went
out from the LORD's presence and lived
in the land of Nod,[b] east of Eden.
17 Cain made love to his wife, and she
became pregnant and gave birth to
Enoch. Cain was then building a city,
and he named it after his son Enoch. 18 To
Enoch was born Irad, and Irad was the
father of Mehujael, and Mehujael was
the father of Methushael, and Methushael was the father of Lamech.
19 Lamech married two women, one
named Adah and the other Zillah.
20 Adah gave birth to Jabal; he was the
father of those who live in tents and
raise livestock. 21 His brother's name was
Jubal; he was the father of all who play
stringed instruments and pipes. 22 Zillah
also had a son, Tubal-Cain, who forged
all kinds of tools out of[c] bronze and iron.
Tubal-Cain's sister was Naamah.
23 Lamech said to his wives,

"Adah and Zillah, listen to me;
  wives of Lamech, hear my words.
I have killed a man for wounding me,
  a young man for injuring me.
24 If Cain is avenged seven times,
  then Lamech seventy-seven times."

25 Adam made love to his wife again,
and she gave birth to a son and named
him Seth,[d] saying, "God has granted me
another child in place of Abel, since Cain
killed him." 26 Seth also had a son, and he
named him Enosh.
At that time people began to call on[e]
the name of the LORD.

From Adam to Noah

5 This is the written account of Adam's
family line.

When God created mankind, he made
them in the likeness of God. 2 He created them male and female and blessed
them. And he named them "Mankind"[f]
when they were created.
3 When Adam had lived 130 years, he
had a son in his own likeness, in his own
image; and he named him Seth. 4 After
Seth was born, Adam lived 800 years
and had other sons and daughters. 5 Altogether, Adam lived a total of 930 years,
and then he died.
6 When Seth had lived 105 years, he became the father[g] of Enosh. 7 After he became the father of Enosh, Seth lived 807
years and had other sons and daughters. 8 Altogether, Seth lived a total of 912
years, and then he died.
9 When Enosh had lived 90 years, he
became the father of Kenan. 10 After he
became the father of Kenan, Enosh lived
815 years and had other sons and daughters. 11 Altogether, Enosh lived a total of
905 years, and then he died.
12 When Kenan had lived 70 years, he
became the father of Mahalalel. 13 After
he became the father of Mahalalel, Kenan lived 840 years and had other sons
and daughters. 14 Altogether, Kenan
lived a total of 910 years, and then he
died.
15 When Mahalalel had lived 65 years,
he became the father of Jared. 16 After he
became the father of Jared, Mahalalel
lived 830 years and had other sons and
daughters. 17 Altogether, Mahalalel lived
a total of 895 years, and then he died.
18 When Jared had lived 162 years,
he became the father of Enoch. 19 After
he became the father of Enoch, Jared
lived 800 years and had other sons and
daughters. 20 Altogether, Jared lived a
total of 962 years, and then he died.
21 When Enoch had lived 65 years, he
became the father of Methuselah. 22 After he became the father of Methuselah,
Enoch walked faithfully with God 300
years and had other sons and daughters. 23 Altogether, Enoch lived a total of
365 years. 24 Enoch walked faithfully with
God; then he was no more, because God
took him away.
25 When Methuselah had lived 187
years, he became the father of Lamech.

[a] *15* Septuagint, Vulgate and Syriac; Hebrew *Very well* [b] *16* *Nod* means *wandering* (see verses 12 and 14). [c] *22* Or *who instructed all who work in* [d] *25* *Seth* probably means *granted.* [e] *26* Or *to proclaim* [f] *2* Hebrew *adam* [g] *6* *Father* may mean *ancestor;* also in verses 7-26.

26After he became the father of Lamech,
Methuselah lived 782 years and had other sons and daughters. 27Altogether, Methuselah lived a total of 969 years, and
then he died.

28When Lamech had lived 182 years,
he had a son. 29He named him Noah[a]
and said, "He will comfort us in the labor and painful toil of our hands caused
by the ground the LORD has cursed."
30After Noah was born, Lamech lived 595
years and had other sons and daughters.
31Altogether, Lamech lived a total of 777
years, and then he died.

32After Noah was 500 years old, he became the father of Shem, Ham and Japheth.

Wickedness in the World

6 When human beings began to increase in number on the earth and
daughters were born to them, 2the sons
of God saw that the daughters of humans were beautiful, and they married
any of them they chose. 3Then the LORD
said, "My Spirit will not contend with[b]
humans forever, for they are mortal[c];
their days will be a hundred and twenty years."

4The Nephilim were on the earth in
those days — and also afterward — when
the sons of God went to the daughters of
humans and had children by them. They
were the heroes of old, men of renown.

5The LORD saw how great the wickedness of the human race had become on
the earth, and that every inclination of
the thoughts of the human heart was
only evil all the time. 6The LORD regretted that he had made human beings
on the earth, and his heart was deeply
troubled. 7So the LORD said, "I will wipe
from the face of the earth the human
race I have created — and with them
the animals, the birds and the creatures
that move along the ground — for I regret that I have made them." 8But Noah
found favor in the eyes of the LORD.

Noah and the Flood

9This is the account of Noah and his
family.

Noah was a righteous man, blameless
among the people of his time, and he
walked faithfully with God. 10Noah had
three sons: Shem, Ham and Japheth.

11Now the earth was corrupt in God's
sight and was full of violence. 12God saw
how corrupt the earth had become, for
all the people on earth had corrupted
their ways. 13So God said to Noah, "I am
going to put an end to all people, for the
earth is filled with violence because of
them. I am surely going to destroy both
them and the earth. 14So make yourself
an ark of cypress[d] wood; make rooms in
it and coat it with pitch inside and out.
15This is how you are to build it: The ark is
to be three hundred cubits long, fifty cubits wide and thirty cubits high.[e] 16Make
a roof for it, leaving below the roof an
opening one cubit[f] high all around.[g] Put
a door in the side of the ark and make
lower, middle and upper decks. 17I am
going to bring floodwaters on the earth
to destroy all life under the heavens, every creature that has the breath of life in
it. Everything on earth will perish. 18But
I will establish my covenant with you,
and you will enter the ark — you and
your sons and your wife and your sons'
wives with you. 19You are to bring into
the ark two of all living creatures, male
and female, to keep them alive with you.
20Two of every kind of bird, of every kind
of animal and of every kind of creature
that moves along the ground will come
to you to be kept alive. 21You are to take
every kind of food that is to be eaten
and store it away as food for you and for
them."

22Noah did everything just as God
commanded him.

7 The LORD then said to Noah, "Go into
the ark, you and your whole family,
because I have found you righteous in
this generation. 2Take with you seven
pairs of every kind of clean animal, a
male and its mate, and one pair of every kind of unclean animal, a male and
its mate, 3and also seven pairs of every
kind of bird, male and female, to keep
their various kinds alive throughout the
earth. 4Seven days from now I will send
rain on the earth for forty days and forty nights, and I will wipe from the face
of the earth every living creature I have
made."

5And Noah did all that the LORD commanded him.

6Noah was six hundred years old when
the floodwaters came on the earth. 7And
Noah and his sons and his wife and his

[a] *29 Noah* sounds like the Hebrew for *comfort.* [b] *3* Or *My spirit will not remain in* [c] *3* Or *corrupt* [d] *14* The meaning of the Hebrew for this word is uncertain. [e] *15* That is, about 450 feet long, 75 feet wide and 45 feet high or about 135 meters long, 23 meters wide and 14 meters high [f] *16* That is, about 18 inches or about 45 centimeters [g] *16* The meaning of the Hebrew for this clause is uncertain.

sons' wives entered the ark to escape the waters of the flood. 8Pairs of clean and unclean animals, of birds and of all creatures that move along the ground, 9male and female, came to Noah and entered the ark, as God had commanded Noah. 10And after the seven days the floodwaters came on the earth.

11In the six hundredth year of Noah's life, on the seventeenth day of the second month — on that day all the springs of the great deep burst forth, and the floodgates of the heavens were opened. 12And rain fell on the earth forty days and forty nights.

13On that very day Noah and his sons, Shem, Ham and Japheth, together with his wife and the wives of his three sons, entered the ark. 14They had with them every wild animal according to its kind, all livestock according to their kinds, every creature that moves along the ground according to its kind and every bird according to its kind, everything with wings. 15Pairs of all creatures that have the breath of life in them came to Noah and entered the ark. 16The animals going in were male and female of every living thing, as God had commanded Noah. Then the LORD shut him in.

17For forty days the flood kept coming on the earth, and as the waters increased they lifted the ark high above the earth. 18The waters rose and increased greatly on the earth, and the ark floated on the surface of the water. 19They rose greatly on the earth, and all the high mountains under the entire heavens were covered. 20The waters rose and covered the mountains to a depth of more than fifteen cubits.[a,b] 21Every living thing that moved on land perished — birds, livestock, wild animals, all the creatures that swarm over the earth, and all mankind. 22Everything on dry land that had the breath of life in its nostrils died. 23Every living thing on the face of the earth was wiped out; people and animals and the creatures that move along the ground and the birds were wiped from the earth. Only Noah was left, and those with him in the ark.

24The waters flooded the earth for a hundred and fifty days.

8 But God remembered Noah and all the wild animals and the livestock that were with him in the ark, and he sent a wind over the earth, and the waters receded. 2Now the springs of the deep and the floodgates of the heavens had been closed, and the rain had stopped falling from the sky. 3The water receded steadily from the earth. At the end of the hundred and fifty days the water had gone down, 4and on the seventeenth day of the seventh month the ark came to rest on the mountains of Ararat. 5The waters continued to recede until the tenth month, and on the first day of the tenth month the tops of the mountains became visible.

6After forty days Noah opened a window he had made in the ark 7and sent out a raven, and it kept flying back and forth until the water had dried up from the earth. 8Then he sent out a dove to see if the water had receded from the surface of the ground. 9But the dove could find nowhere to perch because there was water over all the surface of the earth; so it returned to Noah in the ark. He reached out his hand and took the dove and brought it back to himself in the ark. 10He waited seven more days and again sent out the dove from the ark. 11When the dove returned to him in the evening, there in its beak was a freshly plucked olive leaf! Then Noah knew that the water had receded from the earth. 12He waited seven more days and sent the dove out again, but this time it did not return to him.

13By the first day of the first month of Noah's six hundred and first year, the water had dried up from the earth. Noah then removed the covering from the ark and saw that the surface of the ground was dry. 14By the twenty-seventh day of the second month the earth was completely dry.

15Then God said to Noah, 16"Come out of the ark, you and your wife and your sons and their wives. 17Bring out every kind of living creature that is with you — the birds, the animals, and all the creatures that move along the ground — so they can multiply on the earth and be fruitful and increase in number on it."

18So Noah came out, together with his sons and his wife and his sons' wives. 19All the animals and all the creatures that move along the ground and all the birds — everything that moves on land — came out of the ark, one kind after another.

20Then Noah built an altar to the LORD and, taking some of all the clean animals and clean birds, he sacrificed burnt

[a] *20* That is, about 23 feet or about 6.8 meters [b] *20* Or *rose more than fifteen cubits, and the mountains were covered*

offerings on it. 21The LORD smelled the
pleasing aroma and said in his heart:
"Never again will I curse the ground because of humans, even though[a] every inclination of the human heart is evil from
childhood. And never again will I destroy all living creatures, as I have done.

22"As long as the earth endures,
seedtime and harvest,
cold and heat,
summer and winter,
day and night
will never cease."

God's Covenant With Noah

9 Then God blessed Noah and his sons,
saying to them, "Be fruitful and increase in number and fill the earth. 2The
fear and dread of you will fall on all the
beasts of the earth, and on all the birds
in the sky, on every creature that moves
along the ground, and on all the fish in
the sea; they are given into your hands.
3Everything that lives and moves about
will be food for you. Just as I gave you
the green plants, I now give you everything.

4"But you must not eat meat that has
its lifeblood still in it. 5And for your lifeblood I will surely demand an accounting. I will demand an accounting from
every animal. And from each human being, too, I will demand an accounting for
the life of another human being.

6"Whoever sheds human blood,
by humans shall their blood be
shed;
for in the image of God
has God made mankind.

7As for you, be fruitful and increase in
number; multiply on the earth and increase upon it."

8Then God said to Noah and to his sons
with him: 9"I now establish my covenant
with you and with your descendants after you 10and with every living creature
that was with you — the birds, the livestock and all the wild animals, all those
that came out of the ark with you — every living creature on earth. 11I establish
my covenant with you: Never again will
all life be destroyed by the waters of a
flood; never again will there be a flood
to destroy the earth."

12And God said, "This is the sign of the
covenant I am making between me and
you and every living creature with you, a
covenant for all generations to come: 13I
have set my rainbow in the clouds, and it
will be the sign of the covenant between
me and the earth. 14Whenever I bring
clouds over the earth and the rainbow
appears in the clouds, 15I will remember
my covenant between me and you and
all living creatures of every kind. Never again will the waters become a flood
to destroy all life. 16Whenever the rainbow appears in the clouds, I will see it
and remember the everlasting covenant
between God and all living creatures of
every kind on the earth."

17So God said to Noah, "This is the sign
of the covenant I have established between me and all life on the earth."

The Sons of Noah

18The sons of Noah who came out of
the ark were Shem, Ham and Japheth.
(Ham was the father of Canaan.) 19These
were the three sons of Noah, and from
them came the people who were scattered over the whole earth.

20Noah, a man of the soil, proceeded[b]
to plant a vineyard. 21When he drank
some of its wine, he became drunk and
lay uncovered inside his tent. 22Ham, the
father of Canaan, saw his father naked
and told his two brothers outside. 23But
Shem and Japheth took a garment and
laid it across their shoulders; then they
walked in backward and covered their
father's naked body. Their faces were
turned the other way so that they would
not see their father naked.

24When Noah awoke from his wine
and found out what his youngest son
had done to him, 25he said,

"Cursed be Canaan!
The lowest of slaves
will he be to his brothers."

26He also said,

"Praise be to the LORD, the God of
Shem!
May Canaan be the slave of Shem.
27May God extend Japheth's[c] territory;
may Japheth live in the tents of
Shem,
and may Canaan be the slave of
Japheth."

28After the flood Noah lived 350 years.
29Noah lived a total of 950 years, and
then he died.

[a] 21 Or *humans, for* [b] 20 Or *soil, was the first* [c] 27 *Japheth* sounds like the Hebrew for *extend.*

The Table of Nations

10 This is the account of Shem, Ham and Japheth, Noah's sons, who themselves had sons after the flood.

The Japhethites

2 The sons[a] of Japheth:
Gomer, Magog, Madai, Javan, Tubal, Meshek and Tiras.
3 The sons of Gomer:
Ashkenaz, Riphath and Togarmah.
4 The sons of Javan:
Elishah, Tarshish, the Kittites and the Rodanites.[b] 5(From these the maritime peoples spread out into their territories by their clans within their nations, each with its own language.)

The Hamites

6 The sons of Ham:
Cush, Egypt, Put and Canaan.
7 The sons of Cush:
Seba, Havilah, Sabtah, Raamah and Sabteka.
The sons of Raamah:
Sheba and Dedan.

8 Cush was the father[c] of Nimrod, who became a mighty warrior on the earth. 9 He was a mighty hunter before the LORD; that is why it is said, "Like Nimrod, a mighty hunter before the LORD." 10 The first centers of his kingdom were Babylon, Uruk, Akkad and Kalneh, in[d] Shinar.[e] 11 From that land he went to Assyria, where he built Nineveh, Rehoboth Ir,[f] Calah 12 and Resen, which is between Nineveh and Calah—which is the great city.

13 Egypt was the father of
the Ludites, Anamites, Lehabites, Naphtuhites, 14 Pathrusites, Kasluhites (from whom the Philistines came) and Caphtorites.
15 Canaan was the father of
Sidon his firstborn,[g] and of the Hittites, 16 Jebusites, Amorites, Girgashites, 17 Hivites, Arkites, Sinites, 18 Arvadites, Zemarites and Hamathites.

Later the Canaanite clans scattered 19 and the borders of Canaan reached from Sidon toward Gerar as far as Gaza, and then toward Sodom, Gomorrah, Admah and Zeboyim, as far as Lasha.

20 These are the sons of Ham by their clans and languages, in their territories and nations.

The Semites

21 Sons were also born to Shem, whose older brother was[h] Japheth; Shem was the ancestor of all the sons of Eber.

22 The sons of Shem:
Elam, Ashur, Arphaxad, Lud and Aram.
23 The sons of Aram:
Uz, Hul, Gether and Meshek.[i]
24 Arphaxad was the father of[j] Shelah, and Shelah the father of Eber.
25 Two sons were born to Eber:
One was named Peleg,[k] because in his time the earth was divided; his brother was named Joktan.
26 Joktan was the father of
Almodad, Sheleph, Hazarmaveth, Jerah, 27 Hadoram, Uzal, Diklah, 28 Obal, Abimael, Sheba, 29 Ophir, Havilah and Jobab. All these were sons of Joktan.

30 The region where they lived stretched from Mesha toward Sephar, in the eastern hill country.

31 These are the sons of Shem by their clans and languages, in their territories and nations.

32 These are the clans of Noah's sons, according to their lines of descent, within their nations. From these the nations spread out over the earth after the flood.

The Tower of Babel

11 Now the whole world had one language and a common speech. 2 As people moved eastward,[l] they found a plain in Shinar[e] and settled there.

3 They said to each other, "Come, let's make bricks and bake them thoroughly." They used brick instead of stone, and tar for mortar. 4 Then they said, "Come, let us build ourselves a city, with a tower that reaches to the heavens, so that we may make a name for ourselves; otherwise we will be scattered over the face of the whole earth."

[a] 2 *Sons* may mean *descendants* or *successors* or *nations*; also in verses 3, 4, 6, 7, 20-23, 29 and 31. [b] 4 Some manuscripts of the Masoretic Text and Samaritan Pentateuch (see also Septuagint and 1 Chron. 1:7); most manuscripts of the Masoretic Text *Dodanites* [c] 8 *Father* may mean *ancestor* or *predecessor* or *founder*; also in verses 13, 15, 24 and 26. [d] 10 Or *Uruk and Akkad—all of them in* [e] 10,2 That is, Babylonia [f] 11 Or *Nineveh with its city squares* [g] 15 Or *of the Sidonians, the foremost* [h] 21 Or *Shem, the older brother of* [i] 23 See Septuagint and 1 Chron. 1:17; Hebrew *Mash.* [j] 24 Hebrew; Septuagint *father of Cainan, and Cainan was the father of* [k] 25 *Peleg* means *division.* [l] 2 Or *from the east*; or *in the east*

5But the LORD came down to see the
city and the tower the people were building. 6The LORD said, "If as one people
speaking the same language they have
begun to do this, then nothing they plan
to do will be impossible for them. 7Come,
let us go down and confuse their language so they will not understand each
other."
8So the LORD scattered them from
there over all the earth, and they stopped
building the city. 9That is why it was
called Babel[a] — because there the LORD
confused the language of the whole
world. From there the LORD scattered
them over the face of the whole earth.

From Shem to Abram

10This is the account of Shem's family line.

Two years after the flood, when Shem
was 100 years old, he became the father[b]
of Arphaxad. 11And after he became the
father of Arphaxad, Shem lived 500
years and had other sons and daughters.
12When Arphaxad had lived 35 years,
he became the father of Shelah. 13And
after he became the father of Shelah,
Arphaxad lived 403 years and had other
sons and daughters.[c]
14When Shelah had lived 30 years, he
became the father of Eber. 15And after
he became the father of Eber, Shelah
lived 403 years and had other sons and
daughters.
16When Eber had lived 34 years, he
became the father of Peleg. 17And after he became the father of Peleg, Eber
lived 430 years and had other sons and
daughters.
18When Peleg had lived 30 years, he
became the father of Reu. 19And after he
became the father of Reu, Peleg lived 209
years and had other sons and daughters.
20When Reu had lived 32 years, he
became the father of Serug. 21And after he became the father of Serug, Reu
lived 207 years and had other sons and
daughters.
22When Serug had lived 30 years, he
became the father of Nahor. 23And after
he became the father of Nahor, Serug
lived 200 years and had other sons and
daughters.
24When Nahor had lived 29 years, he
became the father of Terah. 25And after
he became the father of Terah, Nahor
lived 119 years and had other sons and
daughters.
26After Terah had lived 70 years, he
became the father of Abram, Nahor and
Haran.

Abram's Family

27This is the account of Terah's family line.

Terah became the father of Abram,
Nahor and Haran. And Haran became
the father of Lot. 28While his father Terah was still alive, Haran died in Ur of
the Chaldeans, in the land of his birth.
29Abram and Nahor both married. The
name of Abram's wife was Sarai, and
the name of Nahor's wife was Milkah;
she was the daughter of Haran, the father of both Milkah and Iskah. 30Now
Sarai was childless because she was not
able to conceive.
31Terah took his son Abram, his grandson Lot son of Haran, and his daughter-
in-law Sarai, the wife of his son Abram,
and together they set out from Ur of the
Chaldeans to go to Canaan. But when
they came to Harran, they settled there.
32Terah lived 205 years, and he died in
Harran.

The Call of Abram

12 The LORD had said to Abram, "Go
from your country, your people and
your father's household to the land I will
show you.

2 "I will make you into a great nation,
   and I will bless you;
I will make your name great,
   and you will be a blessing.[d]
3 I will bless those who bless you,
   and whoever curses you I will
      curse;
and all peoples on earth
   will be blessed through you."[e]

4So Abram went, as the LORD had told
him; and Lot went with him. Abram was
seventy-five years old when he set out
from Harran. 5He took his wife Sarai, his
nephew Lot, all the possessions they had
accumulated and the people they had

[a] 9 That is, Babylon; *Babel* sounds like the Hebrew for *confused.* [b] 10 *Father* may mean *ancestor;* also in verses 11-25. [c] 12,13 Hebrew; Septuagint (see also Luke 3:35, 36 and note at Gen. 10:24) *35 years, he became the father of Cainan. 13And after he became the father of Cainan, Arphaxad lived 430 years and had other sons and daughters, and then he died. When Cainan had lived 130 years, he became the father of Shelah. And after he became the father of Shelah, Cainan lived 330 years and had other sons and daughters* [d] 2 Or *be seen as blessed* [e] 3 Or *earth / will use your name in blessings* (see 48:20)

acquired in Harran, and they set out for the land of Canaan, and they arrived there.

6Abram traveled through the land as far as the site of the great tree of Moreh at Shechem. At that time the Canaanites were in the land. 7The LORD appeared to Abram and said, "To your offspring[a] I will give this land." So he built an altar there to the LORD, who had appeared to him.

8From there he went on toward the hills east of Bethel and pitched his tent, with Bethel on the west and Ai on the east. There he built an altar to the LORD and called on the name of the LORD.

9Then Abram set out and continued toward the Negev.

Abram in Egypt

10Now there was a famine in the land, and Abram went down to Egypt to live there for a while because the famine was severe. 11As he was about to enter Egypt, he said to his wife Sarai, "I know what a beautiful woman you are. 12When the Egyptians see you, they will say, 'This is his wife.' Then they will kill me but will let you live. 13Say you are my sister, so that I will be treated well for your sake and my life will be spared because of you."

14When Abram came to Egypt, the Egyptians saw that Sarai was a very beautiful woman. 15And when Pharaoh's officials saw her, they praised her to Pharaoh, and she was taken into his palace. 16He treated Abram well for her sake, and Abram acquired sheep and cattle, male and female donkeys, male and female servants, and camels.

17But the LORD inflicted serious diseases on Pharaoh and his household because of Abram's wife Sarai. 18So Pharaoh summoned Abram. "What have you done to me?" he said. "Why didn't you tell me she was your wife? 19Why did you say, 'She is my sister,' so that I took her to be my wife? Now then, here is your wife. Take her and go!" 20Then Pharaoh gave orders about Abram to his men, and they sent him on his way, with his wife and everything he had.

Abram and Lot Separate

13 So Abram went up from Egypt to the Negev, with his wife and everything he had, and Lot went with him. 2Abram had become very wealthy in livestock and in silver and gold.

3From the Negev he went from place to place until he came to Bethel, to the place between Bethel and Ai where his tent had been earlier 4and where he had first built an altar. There Abram called on the name of the LORD.

5Now Lot, who was moving about with Abram, also had flocks and herds and tents. 6But the land could not support them while they stayed together, for their possessions were so great that they were not able to stay together. 7And quarreling arose between Abram's herders and Lot's. The Canaanites and Perizzites were also living in the land at that time.

8So Abram said to Lot, "Let's not have any quarreling between you and me, or between your herders and mine, for we are close relatives. 9Is not the whole land before you? Let's part company. If you go to the left, I'll go to the right; if you go to the right, I'll go to the left."

10Lot looked around and saw that the whole plain of the Jordan toward Zoar was well watered, like the garden of the LORD, like the land of Egypt. (This was before the LORD destroyed Sodom and Gomorrah.) 11So Lot chose for himself the whole plain of the Jordan and set out toward the east. The two men parted company: 12Abram lived in the land of Canaan, while Lot lived among the cities of the plain and pitched his tents near Sodom. 13Now the people of Sodom were wicked and were sinning greatly against the LORD.

14The LORD said to Abram after Lot had parted from him, "Look around from where you are, to the north and south, to the east and west. 15All the land that you see I will give to you and your offspring[b] forever. 16I will make your offspring like the dust of the earth, so that if anyone could count the dust, then your offspring could be counted. 17Go, walk through the length and breadth of the land, for I am giving it to you."

18So Abram went to live near the great trees of Mamre at Hebron, where he pitched his tents. There he built an altar to the LORD.

Abram Rescues Lot

14 At the time when Amraphel was king of Shinar,[c] Arioch king of Ellasar, Kedorlaomer king of Elam and Tidal king of Goyim, 2these kings went to war against Bera king of Sodom, Birsha king of Gomorrah, Shinab king of Admah, Shemeber king of Zeboyim, and the king of Bela (that is, Zoar). 3All these latter kings joined forces in the Valley of Siddim (that is, the Dead Sea Valley). 4For

[a] 7 Or *seed* [b] 15 Or *seed*; also in verse 16 [c] 1 That is, Babylonia; also in verse 9

twelve years they had been subject to
Kedorlaomer, but in the thirteenth year
they rebelled.
5 In the fourteenth year, Kedorlaomer
and the kings allied with him went out
and defeated the Rephaites in Ashteroth
Karnaim, the Zuzites in Ham, the Emites
in Shaveh Kiriathaim 6 and the Horites in
the hill country of Seir, as far as El Paran
near the desert. 7 Then they turned back
and went to En Mishpat (that is, Kadesh),
and they conquered the whole territory
of the Amalekites, as well as the Amorites who were living in Hazezon Tamar.
8 Then the king of Sodom, the king of
Gomorrah, the king of Admah, the king
of Zeboyim and the king of Bela (that is,
Zoar) marched out and drew up their battle lines in the Valley of Siddim 9 against
Kedorlaomer king of Elam, Tidal king of
Goyim, Amraphel king of Shinar and Arioch king of Ellasar — four kings against
five. 10 Now the Valley of Siddim was full
of tar pits, and when the kings of Sodom
and Gomorrah fled, some of the men fell
into them and the rest fled to the hills.
11 The four kings seized all the goods of
Sodom and Gomorrah and all their food;
then they went away. 12 They also carried
off Abram's nephew Lot and his possessions, since he was living in Sodom.
13 A man who had escaped came and
reported this to Abram the Hebrew. Now
Abram was living near the great trees of
Mamre the Amorite, a brother[a] of Eshkol and Aner, all of whom were allied
with Abram. 14 When Abram heard that
his relative had been taken captive, he
called out the 318 trained men born in
his household and went in pursuit as far
as Dan. 15 During the night Abram divided his men to attack them and he routed
them, pursuing them as far as Hobah,
north of Damascus. 16 He recovered all
the goods and brought back his relative
Lot and his possessions, together with
the women and the other people.
17 After Abram returned from defeating Kedorlaomer and the kings allied
with him, the king of Sodom came out
to meet him in the Valley of Shaveh (that
is, the King's Valley).
18 Then Melchizedek king of Salem
brought out bread and wine. He was
priest of God Most High, 19 and he blessed
Abram, saying,

"Blessed be Abram by God Most High,
Creator of heaven and earth.
20 And praise be to God Most High,
who delivered your enemies into
your hand."

Then Abram gave him a tenth of everything.
21 The king of Sodom said to Abram,
"Give me the people and keep the goods
for yourself."
22 But Abram said to the king of Sodom, "With raised hand I have sworn an
oath to the LORD, God Most High, Creator
of heaven and earth, 23 that I will accept
nothing belonging to you, not even a
thread or the strap of a sandal, so that
you will never be able to say, 'I made
Abram rich.' 24 I will accept nothing but
what my men have eaten and the share
that belongs to the men who went with
me — to Aner, Eshkol and Mamre. Let
them have their share."

The LORD's Covenant With Abram

15 After this, the word of the LORD
came to Abram in a vision:

"Do not be afraid, Abram.
I am your shield,[b]
your very great reward.[c]"

2 But Abram said, "Sovereign LORD,
what can you give me since I remain
childless and the one who will inherit[d]
my estate is Eliezer of Damascus?" 3 And
Abram said, "You have given me no children; so a servant in my household will
be my heir."
4 Then the word of the LORD came to
him: "This man will not be your heir, but
a son who is your own flesh and blood
will be your heir." 5 He took him outside and said, "Look up at the sky and
count the stars — if indeed you can count
them." Then he said to him, "So shall
your offspring[e] be."
6 Abram believed the LORD, and he
credited it to him as righteousness.
7 He also said to him, "I am the LORD,
who brought you out of Ur of the Chaldeans to give you this land to take possession of it."
8 But Abram said, "Sovereign LORD,
how can I know that I will gain possession of it?"
9 So the LORD said to him, "Bring me
a heifer, a goat and a ram, each three
years old, along with a dove and a young
pigeon."
10 Abram brought all these to him, cut
them in two and arranged the halves
opposite each other; the birds, however,
he did not cut in half. 11 Then birds of prey

[a] *13* Or *a relative*; or *an ally* [b] *1* Or *sovereign* [c] *1* Or *shield; / your reward will be very great*
[d] *2* The meaning of the Hebrew for this phrase is uncertain. [e] *5* Or *seed*

came down on the carcasses, but Abram drove them away.

12 As the sun was setting, Abram fell into a deep sleep, and a thick and dreadful darkness came over him. 13 Then the LORD said to him, "Know for certain that for four hundred years your descendants will be strangers in a country not their own and that they will be enslaved and mistreated there. 14 But I will punish the nation they serve as slaves, and afterward they will come out with great possessions. 15 You, however, will go to your ancestors in peace and be buried at a good old age. 16 In the fourth generation your descendants will come back here, for the sin of the Amorites has not yet reached its full measure."

17 When the sun had set and darkness had fallen, a smoking firepot with a blazing torch appeared and passed between the pieces. 18 On that day the LORD made a covenant with Abram and said, "To your descendants I give this land, from the Wadi[a] of Egypt to the great river, the Euphrates — 19 the land of the Kenites, Kenizzites, Kadmonites, 20 Hittites, Perizzites, Rephaites, 21 Amorites, Canaanites, Girgashites and Jebusites."

Hagar and Ishmael

16 Now Sarai, Abram's wife, had borne him no children. But she had an Egyptian slave named Hagar; 2 so she said to Abram, "The LORD has kept me from having children. Go, sleep with my slave; perhaps I can build a family through her."

Abram agreed to what Sarai said. 3 So after Abram had been living in Canaan ten years, Sarai his wife took her Egyptian slave Hagar and gave her to her husband to be his wife. 4 He slept with Hagar, and she conceived.

When she knew she was pregnant, she began to despise her mistress. 5 Then Sarai said to Abram, "You are responsible for the wrong I am suffering. I put my slave in your arms, and now that she knows she is pregnant, she despises me. May the LORD judge between you and me."

6 "Your slave is in your hands," Abram said. "Do with her whatever you think best." Then Sarai mistreated Hagar; so she fled from her.

7 The angel of the LORD found Hagar near a spring in the desert; it was the spring that is beside the road to Shur. 8 And he said, "Hagar, slave of Sarai, where have you come from, and where are you going?"

"I'm running away from my mistress Sarai," she answered.

9 Then the angel of the LORD told her, "Go back to your mistress and submit to her." 10 The angel added, "I will increase your descendants so much that they will be too numerous to count."

11 The angel of the LORD also said to her:

"You are now pregnant
and you will give birth to a son.
You shall name him Ishmael,[b]
for the LORD has heard of your misery.
12 He will be a wild donkey of a man;
his hand will be against everyone
and everyone's hand against him,
and he will live in hostility
toward[c] all his brothers."

13 She gave this name to the LORD who spoke to her: "You are the God who sees me," for she said, "I have now seen[d] the One who sees me." 14 That is why the well was called Beer Lahai Roi[e]; it is still there, between Kadesh and Bered.

15 So Hagar bore Abram a son, and Abram gave the name Ishmael to the son she had borne. 16 Abram was eighty-six years old when Hagar bore him Ishmael.

The Covenant of Circumcision

17 When Abram was ninety-nine years old, the LORD appeared to him and said, "I am God Almighty[f]; walk before me faithfully and be blameless. 2 Then I will make my covenant between me and you and will greatly increase your numbers."

3 Abram fell facedown, and God said to him, 4 "As for me, this is my covenant with you: You will be the father of many nations. 5 No longer will you be called Abram[g]; your name will be Abraham,[h] for I have made you a father of many nations. 6 I will make you very fruitful; I will make nations of you, and kings will come from you. 7 I will establish my covenant as an everlasting covenant between me and you and your descendants after you for the generations to come, to be your God and the God of your descendants after you. 8 The whole

[a] 18 Or *river* [b] 11 *Ishmael* means *God hears.* [c] 12 Or *live to the east / of* [d] 13 Or *seen the back of* [e] 14 *Beer Lahai Roi* means *well of the Living One who sees me.* [f] 1 Hebrew *El-Shaddai* [g] 5 *Abram* means *exalted father.* [h] 5 *Abraham* probably means *father of many.*

land of Canaan, where you now reside as
a foreigner, I will give as an everlasting
possession to you and your descendants
after you; and I will be their God."
9 Then God said to Abraham, "As for
you, you must keep my covenant, you
and your descendants after you for the
generations to come. 10 This is my covenant with you and your descendants
after you, the covenant you are to keep:
Every male among you shall be circumcised. 11 You are to undergo circumcision,
and it will be the sign of the covenant between me and you. 12 For the generations
to come every male among you who is
eight days old must be circumcised, including those born in your household
or bought with money from a foreigner — those who are not your offspring.
13 Whether born in your household or
bought with your money, they must be
circumcised. My covenant in your flesh is
to be an everlasting covenant. 14 Any uncircumcised male, who has not been circumcised in the flesh, will be cut off from
his people; he has broken my covenant."
15 God also said to Abraham, "As for Sarai your wife, you are no longer to call
her Sarai; her name will be Sarah. 16 I will
bless her and will surely give you a son
by her. I will bless her so that she will be
the mother of nations; kings of peoples
will come from her."
17 Abraham fell facedown; he laughed
and said to himself, "Will a son be born
to a man a hundred years old? Will Sarah bear a child at the age of ninety?"
18 And Abraham said to God, "If only Ishmael might live under your blessing!"
19 Then God said, "Yes, but your wife
Sarah will bear you a son, and you will
call him Isaac.[a] I will establish my covenant with him as an everlasting covenant for his descendants after him.
20 And as for Ishmael, I have heard you:
I will surely bless him; I will make him
fruitful and will greatly increase his
numbers. He will be the father of twelve
rulers, and I will make him into a great
nation. 21 But my covenant I will establish with Isaac, whom Sarah will bear to
you by this time next year." 22 When he
had finished speaking with Abraham,
God went up from him.
23 On that very day Abraham took his
son Ishmael and all those born in his
household or bought with his money,
every male in his household, and circumcised them, as God told him. 24 Abraham was ninety-nine years old when he
was circumcised, 25 and his son Ishmael
was thirteen; 26 Abraham and his son
Ishmael were both circumcised on that
very day. 27 And every male in Abraham's
household, including those born in his
household or bought from a foreigner,
was circumcised with him.

The Three Visitors

18 The LORD appeared to Abraham
near the great trees of Mamre
while he was sitting at the entrance to
his tent in the heat of the day. 2 Abraham
looked up and saw three men standing
nearby. When he saw them, he hurried
from the entrance of his tent to meet
them and bowed low to the ground.
3 He said, "If I have found favor in your
eyes, my lord,[b] do not pass your servant
by. 4 Let a little water be brought, and
then you may all wash your feet and rest
under this tree. 5 Let me get you something to eat, so you can be refreshed and
then go on your way — now that you
have come to your servant."
"Very well," they answered, "do as you
say."
6 So Abraham hurried into the tent to
Sarah. "Quick," he said, "get three seahs[c]
of the finest flour and knead it and bake
some bread."
7 Then he ran to the herd and selected a choice, tender calf and gave it to a
servant, who hurried to prepare it. 8 He
then brought some curds and milk and
the calf that had been prepared, and set
these before them. While they ate, he
stood near them under a tree.
9 "Where is your wife Sarah?" they
asked him.
"There, in the tent," he said.
10 Then one of them said, "I will surely
return to you about this time next year,
and Sarah your wife will have a son."
Now Sarah was listening at the entrance to the tent, which was behind him.
11 Abraham and Sarah were already very
old, and Sarah was past the age of childbearing. 12 So Sarah laughed to herself as
she thought, "After I am worn out and my
lord is old, will I now have this pleasure?"
13 Then the LORD said to Abraham,
"Why did Sarah laugh and say, 'Will I
really have a child, now that I am old?'
14 Is anything too hard for the LORD? I will
return to you at the appointed time next
year, and Sarah will have a son."
15 Sarah was afraid, so she lied and
said, "I did not laugh."
But he said, "Yes, you did laugh."

[a] 19 *Isaac* means *he laughs.* [b] 3 Or *eyes, Lord* [c] 6 That is, probably about 36 pounds or
about 16 kilograms

Abraham Pleads for Sodom

16 When the men got up to leave, they looked down toward Sodom, and Abraham walked along with them to see them on their way. 17 Then the LORD said, "Shall I hide from Abraham what I am about to do? 18 Abraham will surely become a great and powerful nation, and all nations on earth will be blessed through him.[a] 19 For I have chosen him, so that he will direct his children and his household after him to keep the way of the LORD by doing what is right and just, so that the LORD will bring about for Abraham what he has promised him."

20 Then the LORD said, "The outcry against Sodom and Gomorrah is so great and their sin so grievous 21 that I will go down and see if what they have done is as bad as the outcry that has reached me. If not, I will know."

22 The men turned away and went toward Sodom, but Abraham remained standing before the LORD.[b] 23 Then Abraham approached him and said: "Will you sweep away the righteous with the wicked? 24 What if there are fifty righteous people in the city? Will you really sweep it away and not spare[c] the place for the sake of the fifty righteous people in it? 25 Far be it from you to do such a thing—to kill the righteous with the wicked, treating the righteous and the wicked alike. Far be it from you! Will not the Judge of all the earth do right?"

26 The LORD said, "If I find fifty righteous people in the city of Sodom, I will spare the whole place for their sake."

27 Then Abraham spoke up again: "Now that I have been so bold as to speak to the Lord, though I am nothing but dust and ashes, 28 what if the number of the righteous is five less than fifty? Will you destroy the whole city for lack of five people?"

"If I find forty-five there," he said, "I will not destroy it."

29 Once again he spoke to him, "What if only forty are found there?"

He said, "For the sake of forty, I will not do it."

30 Then he said, "May the Lord not be angry, but let me speak. What if only thirty can be found there?"

He answered, "I will not do it if I find thirty there."

31 Abraham said, "Now that I have been so bold as to speak to the Lord, what if only twenty can be found there?"

He said, "For the sake of twenty, I will not destroy it."

32 Then he said, "May the Lord not be angry, but let me speak just once more. What if only ten can be found there?"

He answered, "For the sake of ten, I will not destroy it."

33 When the LORD had finished speaking with Abraham, he left, and Abraham returned home.

Sodom and Gomorrah Destroyed

19 The two angels arrived at Sodom in the evening, and Lot was sitting in the gateway of the city. When he saw them, he got up to meet them and bowed down with his face to the ground. 2 "My lords," he said, "please turn aside to your servant's house. You can wash your feet and spend the night and then go on your way early in the morning."

"No," they answered, "we will spend the night in the square."

3 But he insisted so strongly that they did go with him and entered his house. He prepared a meal for them, baking bread without yeast, and they ate. 4 Before they had gone to bed, all the men from every part of the city of Sodom—both young and old—surrounded the house. 5 They called to Lot, "Where are the men who came to you tonight? Bring them out to us so that we can have sex with them."

6 Lot went outside to meet them and shut the door behind him 7 and said, "No, my friends. Don't do this wicked thing. 8 Look, I have two daughters who have never slept with a man. Let me bring them out to you, and you can do what you like with them. But don't do anything to these men, for they have come under the protection of my roof."

9 "Get out of our way," they replied. "This fellow came here as a foreigner, and now he wants to play the judge! We'll treat you worse than them." They kept bringing pressure on Lot and moved forward to break down the door.

10 But the men inside reached out and pulled Lot back into the house and shut the door. 11 Then they struck the men who were at the door of the house, young and old, with blindness so that they could not find the door.

12 The two men said to Lot, "Do you have anyone else here—sons-in-law, sons or daughters, or anyone else in the city who belongs to you? Get them out of here, 13 because we are going to

[a] 18 Or *will use his name in blessings* (see 48:20) [b] 22 Masoretic Text; an ancient Hebrew scribal tradition *but the LORD remained standing before Abraham* [c] 24 Or *forgive*; also in verse 26

destroy this place. The outcry to the LORD against its people is so great that he has sent us to destroy it."

14 So Lot went out and spoke to his sons-in-law, who were pledged to marry[a] his daughters. He said, "Hurry and get out of this place, because the LORD is about to destroy the city!" But his sons-in-law thought he was joking.

15 With the coming of dawn, the angels urged Lot, saying, "Hurry! Take your wife and your two daughters who are here, or you will be swept away when the city is punished."

16 When he hesitated, the men grasped his hand and the hands of his wife and of his two daughters and led them safely out of the city, for the LORD was merciful to them. 17 As soon as they had brought them out, one of them said, "Flee for your lives! Don't look back, and don't stop anywhere in the plain! Flee to the mountains or you will be swept away!"

18 But Lot said to them, "No, my lords,[b] please! 19 Your[c] servant has found favor in your[c] eyes, and you[c] have shown great kindness to me in sparing my life. But I can't flee to the mountains; this disaster will overtake me, and I'll die. 20 Look, here is a town near enough to run to, and it is small. Let me flee to it — it is very small, isn't it? Then my life will be spared."

21 He said to him, "Very well, I will grant this request too; I will not overthrow the town you speak of. 22 But flee there quickly, because I cannot do anything until you reach it." (That is why the town was called Zoar.[d])

23 By the time Lot reached Zoar, the sun had risen over the land. 24 Then the LORD rained down burning sulfur on Sodom and Gomorrah — from the LORD out of the heavens. 25 Thus he overthrew those cities and the entire plain, destroying all those living in the cities — and also the vegetation in the land. 26 But Lot's wife looked back, and she became a pillar of salt.

27 Early the next morning Abraham got up and returned to the place where he had stood before the LORD. 28 He looked down toward Sodom and Gomorrah, toward all the land of the plain, and he saw dense smoke rising from the land, like smoke from a furnace.

29 So when God destroyed the cities of the plain, he remembered Abraham, and he brought Lot out of the catastrophe that overthrew the cities where Lot had lived.

Lot and His Daughters

30 Lot and his two daughters left Zoar and settled in the mountains, for he was afraid to stay in Zoar. He and his two daughters lived in a cave. 31 One day the older daughter said to the younger, "Our father is old, and there is no man around here to give us children — as is the custom all over the earth. 32 Let's get our father to drink wine and then sleep with him and preserve our family line through our father."

33 That night they got their father to drink wine, and the older daughter went in and slept with him. He was not aware of it when she lay down or when she got up.

34 The next day the older daughter said to the younger, "Last night I slept with my father. Let's get him to drink wine again tonight, and you go in and sleep with him so we can preserve our family line through our father." 35 So they got their father to drink wine that night also, and the younger daughter went in and slept with him. Again he was not aware of it when she lay down or when she got up.

36 So both of Lot's daughters became pregnant by their father. 37 The older daughter had a son, and she named him Moab[e]; he is the father of the Moabites of today. 38 The younger daughter also had a son, and she named him Ben-Ammi[f]; he is the father of the Ammonites[g] of today.

Abraham and Abimelek

20 Now Abraham moved on from there into the region of the Negev and lived between Kadesh and Shur. For a while he stayed in Gerar, 2 and there Abraham said of his wife Sarah, "She is my sister." Then Abimelek king of Gerar sent for Sarah and took her.

3 But God came to Abimelek in a dream one night and said to him, "You are as good as dead because of the woman you have taken; she is a married woman."

4 Now Abimelek had not gone near her, so he said, "Lord, will you destroy an innocent nation? 5 Did he not say to me, 'She is my sister,' and didn't she also say, 'He is my brother'? I have done this with a clear conscience and clean hands."

6 Then God said to him in the dream, "Yes, I know you did this with a clear conscience, and so I have kept you from sinning against me. That is why I did not

[a] 14 Or *were married to* [b] 18 Or *No, Lord*; or *No, my lord* [c] 19 The Hebrew is singular.
[d] 22 *Zoar* means *small.* [e] 37 *Moab* sounds like the Hebrew for *from father.* [f] 38 *Ben-Ammi* means *son of my father's people.* [g] 38 Hebrew *Bene-Ammon*

let you touch her. [7]Now return the man's wife, for he is a prophet, and he will pray for you and you will live. But if you do not return her, you may be sure that you and all who belong to you will die."

[8]Early the next morning Abimelek summoned all his officials, and when he told them all that had happened, they were very much afraid. [9]Then Abimelek called Abraham in and said, "What have you done to us? How have I wronged you that you have brought such great guilt upon me and my kingdom? You have done things to me that should never be done." [10]And Abimelek asked Abraham, "What was your reason for doing this?"

[11]Abraham replied, "I said to myself, 'There is surely no fear of God in this place, and they will kill me because of my wife.' [12]Besides, she really is my sister, the daughter of my father though not of my mother; and she became my wife. [13]And when God had me wander from my father's household, I said to her, 'This is how you can show your love to me: Everywhere we go, say of me, "He is my brother."'"

[14]Then Abimelek brought sheep and cattle and male and female slaves and gave them to Abraham, and he returned Sarah his wife to him. [15]And Abimelek said, "My land is before you; live wherever you like."

[16]To Sarah he said, "I am giving your brother a thousand shekels[a] of silver. This is to cover the offense against you before all who are with you; you are completely vindicated."

[17]Then Abraham prayed to God, and God healed Abimelek, his wife and his female slaves so they could have children again, [18]for the LORD had kept all the women in Abimelek's household from conceiving because of Abraham's wife Sarah.

The Birth of Isaac

21 Now the LORD was gracious to Sarah as he had said, and the LORD did for Sarah what he had promised. [2]Sarah became pregnant and bore a son to Abraham in his old age, at the very time God had promised him. [3]Abraham gave the name Isaac[b] to the son Sarah bore him. [4]When his son Isaac was eight days old, Abraham circumcised him, as God commanded him. [5]Abraham was a hundred years old when his son Isaac was born to him.

[6]Sarah said, "God has brought me laughter, and everyone who hears about this will laugh with me." [7]And she added, "Who would have said to Abraham that Sarah would nurse children? Yet I have borne him a son in his old age."

Hagar and Ishmael Sent Away

[8]The child grew and was weaned, and on the day Isaac was weaned Abraham held a great feast. [9]But Sarah saw that the son whom Hagar the Egyptian had borne to Abraham was mocking, [10]and she said to Abraham, "Get rid of that slave woman and her son, for that woman's son will never share in the inheritance with my son Isaac."

[11]The matter distressed Abraham greatly because it concerned his son. [12]But God said to him, "Do not be so distressed about the boy and your slave woman. Listen to whatever Sarah tells you, because it is through Isaac that your offspring[c] will be reckoned. [13]I will make the son of the slave into a nation also, because he is your offspring."

[14]Early the next morning Abraham took some food and a skin of water and gave them to Hagar. He set them on her shoulders and then sent her off with the boy. She went on her way and wandered in the Desert of Beersheba.

[15]When the water in the skin was gone, she put the boy under one of the bushes. [16]Then she went off and sat down about a bowshot away, for she thought, "I cannot watch the boy die." And as she sat there, she[d] began to sob.

[17]God heard the boy crying, and the angel of God called to Hagar from heaven and said to her, "What is the matter, Hagar? Do not be afraid; God has heard the boy crying as he lies there. [18]Lift the boy up and take him by the hand, for I will make him into a great nation."

[19]Then God opened her eyes and she saw a well of water. So she went and filled the skin with water and gave the boy a drink.

[20]God was with the boy as he grew up. He lived in the desert and became an archer. [21]While he was living in the Desert of Paran, his mother got a wife for him from Egypt.

The Treaty at Beersheba

[22]At that time Abimelek and Phicol the commander of his forces said to Abraham, "God is with you in everything you

[a] 16 That is, about 25 pounds or about 12 kilograms [b] 3 *Isaac* means *he laughs.* [c] 12 Or *seed*
[d] 16 Hebrew; Septuagint *the child*

do. 23Now swear to me here before God that you will not deal falsely with me or my children or my descendants. Show to me and the country where you now reside as a foreigner the same kindness I have shown to you."

24Abraham said, "I swear it."

25Then Abraham complained to Abimelek about a well of water that Abimelek's servants had seized. 26But Abimelek said, "I don't know who has done this. You did not tell me, and I heard about it only today."

27So Abraham brought sheep and cattle and gave them to Abimelek, and the two men made a treaty. 28Abraham set apart seven ewe lambs from the flock, 29and Abimelek asked Abraham, "What is the meaning of these seven ewe lambs you have set apart by themselves?"

30He replied, "Accept these seven lambs from my hand as a witness that I dug this well."

31So that place was called Beersheba,[a] because the two men swore an oath there.

32After the treaty had been made at Beersheba, Abimelek and Phicol the commander of his forces returned to the land of the Philistines. 33Abraham planted a tamarisk tree in Beersheba, and there he called on the name of the LORD, the Eternal God. 34And Abraham stayed in the land of the Philistines for a long time.

Abraham Tested

22 Some time later God tested Abraham. He said to him, "Abraham!"

"Here I am," he replied.

2Then God said, "Take your son, your only son, whom you love — Isaac — and go to the region of Moriah. Sacrifice him there as a burnt offering on a mountain I will show you."

3Early the next morning Abraham got up and loaded his donkey. He took with him two of his servants and his son Isaac. When he had cut enough wood for the burnt offering, he set out for the place God had told him about. 4On the third day Abraham looked up and saw the place in the distance. 5He said to his servants, "Stay here with the donkey while I and the boy go over there. We will worship and then we will come back to you."

6Abraham took the wood for the burnt offering and placed it on his son Isaac, and he himself carried the fire and the knife. As the two of them went on together, 7Isaac spoke up and said to his father Abraham, "Father?"

"Yes, my son?" Abraham replied.

"The fire and wood are here," Isaac said, "but where is the lamb for the burnt offering?"

8Abraham answered, "God himself will provide the lamb for the burnt offering, my son." And the two of them went on together.

9When they reached the place God had told him about, Abraham built an altar there and arranged the wood on it. He bound his son Isaac and laid him on the altar, on top of the wood. 10Then he reached out his hand and took the knife to slay his son. 11But the angel of the LORD called out to him from heaven, "Abraham! Abraham!"

"Here I am," he replied.

12"Do not lay a hand on the boy," he said. "Do not do anything to him. Now I know that you fear God, because you have not withheld from me your son, your only son."

13Abraham looked up and there in a thicket he saw a ram[b] caught by its horns. He went over and took the ram and sacrificed it as a burnt offering instead of his son. 14So Abraham called that place The LORD Will Provide. And to this day it is said, "On the mountain of the LORD it will be provided."

15The angel of the LORD called to Abraham from heaven a second time 16and said, "I swear by myself, declares the LORD, that because you have done this and have not withheld your son, your only son, 17I will surely bless you and make your descendants as numerous as the stars in the sky and as the sand on the seashore. Your descendants will take possession of the cities of their enemies, 18and through your offspring[c] all nations on earth will be blessed,[d] because you have obeyed me."

19Then Abraham returned to his servants, and they set off together for Beersheba. And Abraham stayed in Beersheba.

Nahor's Sons

20Some time later Abraham was told, "Milkah is also a mother; she has borne sons to your brother Nahor: 21Uz the

[a] 31 *Beersheba* can mean *well of seven* and *well of the oath.* [b] 13 Many manuscripts of the Masoretic Text, Samaritan Pentateuch, Septuagint and Syriac; most manuscripts of the Masoretic Text *a ram behind him* [c] 18 Or *seed* [d] 18 Or *and all nations on earth will use the name of your offspring in blessings* (see 48:20)

firstborn, Buz his brother, Kemuel (the father of Aram), 22Kesed, Hazo, Pildash, Jidlaph and Bethuel." 23Bethuel became the father of Rebekah. Milkah bore these eight sons to Abraham's brother Nahor. 24His concubine, whose name was Reumah, also had sons: Tebah, Gaham, Tahash and Maakah.

The Death of Sarah

23 Sarah lived to be a hundred and twenty-seven years old. 2She died at Kiriath Arba (that is, Hebron) in the land of Canaan, and Abraham went to mourn for Sarah and to weep over her.

3Then Abraham rose from beside his dead wife and spoke to the Hittites.[a] He said, 4"I am a foreigner and stranger among you. Sell me some property for a burial site here so I can bury my dead."

5The Hittites replied to Abraham, 6"Sir, listen to us. You are a mighty prince among us. Bury your dead in the choicest of our tombs. None of us will refuse you his tomb for burying your dead."

7Then Abraham rose and bowed down before the people of the land, the Hittites. 8He said to them, "If you are willing to let me bury my dead, then listen to me and intercede with Ephron son of Zohar on my behalf 9so he will sell me the cave of Machpelah, which belongs to him and is at the end of his field. Ask him to sell it to me for the full price as a burial site among you."

10Ephron the Hittite was sitting among his people and he replied to Abraham in the hearing of all the Hittites who had come to the gate of his city. 11"No, my lord," he said. "Listen to me; I give[b] you the field, and I give[b] you the cave that is in it. I give[b] it to you in the presence of my people. Bury your dead."

12Again Abraham bowed down before the people of the land 13and he said to Ephron in their hearing, "Listen to me, if you will. I will pay the price of the field. Accept it from me so I can bury my dead there."

14Ephron answered Abraham, 15"Listen to me, my lord; the land is worth four hundred shekels[c] of silver, but what is that between you and me? Bury your dead."

16Abraham agreed to Ephron's terms and weighed out for him the price he had named in the hearing of the Hittites: four hundred shekels of silver, according to the weight current among the merchants.

17So Ephron's field in Machpelah near Mamre—both the field and the cave in it, and all the trees within the borders of the field—was deeded 18to Abraham as his property in the presence of all the Hittites who had come to the gate of the city. 19Afterward Abraham buried his wife Sarah in the cave in the field of Machpelah near Mamre (which is at Hebron) in the land of Canaan. 20So the field and the cave in it were deeded to Abraham by the Hittites as a burial site.

Isaac and Rebekah

24 Abraham was now very old, and the LORD had blessed him in every way. 2He said to the senior servant in his household, the one in charge of all that he had, "Put your hand under my thigh. 3I want you to swear by the LORD, the God of heaven and the God of earth, that you will not get a wife for my son from the daughters of the Canaanites, among whom I am living, 4but will go to my country and my own relatives and get a wife for my son Isaac."

5The servant asked him, "What if the woman is unwilling to come back with me to this land? Shall I then take your son back to the country you came from?"

6"Make sure that you do not take my son back there," Abraham said. 7"The LORD, the God of heaven, who brought me out of my father's household and my native land and who spoke to me and promised me on oath, saying, 'To your offspring[d] I will give this land'—he will send his angel before you so that you can get a wife for my son from there. 8If the woman is unwilling to come back with you, then you will be released from this oath of mine. Only do not take my son back there." 9So the servant put his hand under the thigh of his master Abraham and swore an oath to him concerning this matter.

10Then the servant left, taking with him ten of his master's camels loaded with all kinds of good things from his master. He set out for Aram Naharaim[e] and made his way to the town of Nahor. 11He had the camels kneel down near the well outside the town; it was toward evening, the time the women go out to draw water.

12Then he prayed, "LORD, God of my master Abraham, make me successful today, and show kindness to my master Abraham. 13See, I am standing beside

[a] 3 Or *the descendants of Heth*; also in verses 5, 7, 10, 16, 18 and 20 [b] 11 Or *sell* [c] 15 That is, about 10 pounds or about 4.6 kilograms [d] 7 Or *seed* [e] 10 That is, Northwest Mesopotamia

this spring, and the daughters of the
townspeople are coming out to draw water. 14May it be that when I say to a young
woman, 'Please let down your jar that I
may have a drink,' and she says, 'Drink,
and I'll water your camels too'—let her
be the one you have chosen for your servant Isaac. By this I will know that you
have shown kindness to my master."

15Before he had finished praying, Rebekah came out with her jar on her
shoulder. She was the daughter of Bethuel son of Milkah, who was the wife of
Abraham's brother Nahor. 16The woman
was very beautiful, a virgin; no man had
ever slept with her. She went down to the
spring, filled her jar and came up again.

17The servant hurried to meet her and
said, "Please give me a little water from
your jar."

18"Drink, my lord," she said, and quickly lowered the jar to her hands and gave
him a drink.

19After she had given him a drink,
she said, "I'll draw water for your camels too, until they have had enough to
drink." 20So she quickly emptied her jar
into the trough, ran back to the well to
draw more water, and drew enough for
all his camels. 21Without saying a word,
the man watched her closely to learn
whether or not the LORD had made his
journey successful.

22When the camels had finished drinking, the man took out a gold nose ring
weighing a beka[a] and two gold bracelets
weighing ten shekels.[b] 23Then he asked,
"Whose daughter are you? Please tell
me, is there room in your father's house
for us to spend the night?"

24She answered him, "I am the daughter of Bethuel, the son that Milkah bore
to Nahor." 25And she added, "We have
plenty of straw and fodder, as well as
room for you to spend the night."

26Then the man bowed down and
worshiped the LORD, 27saying, "Praise
be to the LORD, the God of my master
Abraham, who has not abandoned his
kindness and faithfulness to my master.
As for me, the LORD has led me on the
journey to the house of my master's relatives."

28The young woman ran and told her
mother's household about these things.
29Now Rebekah had a brother named Laban, and he hurried out to the man at
the spring. 30As soon as he had seen the
nose ring, and the bracelets on his sister's arms, and had heard Rebekah tell
what the man said to her, he went out
to the man and found him standing by
the camels near the spring. 31"Come, you
who are blessed by the LORD," he said.
"Why are you standing out here? I have
prepared the house and a place for the
camels."

32So the man went to the house, and
the camels were unloaded. Straw and
fodder were brought for the camels, and
water for him and his men to wash their
feet. 33Then food was set before him, but
he said, "I will not eat until I have told
you what I have to say."

"Then tell us," Laban said.

34So he said, "I am Abraham's servant.
35The LORD has blessed my master abundantly, and he has become wealthy. He
has given him sheep and cattle, silver
and gold, male and female servants, and
camels and donkeys. 36My master's wife
Sarah has borne him a son in her old
age, and he has given him everything
he owns. 37And my master made me
swear an oath, and said, 'You must not
get a wife for my son from the daughters
of the Canaanites, in whose land I live,
38but go to my father's family and to my
own clan, and get a wife for my son.'

39"Then I asked my master, 'What if
the woman will not come back with me?'

40"He replied, 'The LORD, before whom
I have walked faithfully, will send his
angel with you and make your journey a
success, so that you can get a wife for my
son from my own clan and from my father's family. 41You will be released from
my oath if, when you go to my clan, they
refuse to give her to you—then you will
be released from my oath.'

42"When I came to the spring today, I
said, 'LORD, God of my master Abraham,
if you will, please grant success to the
journey on which I have come. 43See, I am
standing beside this spring. If a young
woman comes out to draw water and I
say to her, "Please let me drink a little
water from your jar," 44and if she says to
me, "Drink, and I'll draw water for your
camels too," let her be the one the LORD
has chosen for my master's son.'

45"Before I finished praying in my
heart, Rebekah came out, with her jar
on her shoulder. She went down to the
spring and drew water, and I said to her,
'Please give me a drink.'

46"She quickly lowered her jar from
her shoulder and said, 'Drink, and I'll
water your camels too.' So I drank, and
she watered the camels also.

[a] *22* That is, about 1/5 ounce or about 5.7 grams

[b] *22* That is, about 4 ounces or about 115 grams

47“I asked her, ‘Whose daughter are
you?’
“She said, ‘The daughter of Bethuel
son of Nahor, whom Milkah bore to him.’
“Then I put the ring in her nose and
the bracelets on her arms, 48and I bowed
down and worshiped the LORD. I praised
the LORD, the God of my master Abraham, who had led me on the right road
to get the granddaughter of my master’s brother for his son. 49Now if you will
show kindness and faithfulness to my
master, tell me; and if not, tell me, so I
may know which way to turn.”
50Laban and Bethuel answered, “This
is from the LORD; we can say nothing to
you one way or the other. 51Here is Rebekah; take her and go, and let her become the wife of your master’s son, as
the LORD has directed.”
52When Abraham’s servant heard
what they said, he bowed down to the
ground before the LORD. 53Then the servant brought out gold and silver jewelry
and articles of clothing and gave them
to Rebekah; he also gave costly gifts to
her brother and to her mother. 54Then he
and the men who were with him ate and
drank and spent the night there.
When they got up the next morning,
he said, “Send me on my way to my master.”
55But her brother and her mother replied, “Let the young woman remain with us ten days or so; then you[a]
may go.”
56But he said to them, “Do not detain
me, now that the LORD has granted success to my journey. Send me on my way
so I may go to my master.”
57Then they said, “Let’s call the young
woman and ask her about it.” 58So they
called Rebekah and asked her, “Will you
go with this man?”
“I will go,” she said.
59So they sent their sister Rebekah on
her way, along with her nurse and Abraham’s servant and his men. 60And they
blessed Rebekah and said to her,

“Our sister, may you increase
  to thousands upon thousands;
may your offspring possess
  the cities of their enemies.”

61Then Rebekah and her attendants
got ready and mounted the camels and
went back with the man. So the servant
took Rebekah and left.
62Now Isaac had come from Beer Lahai Roi, for he was living in the Negev.
63He went out to the field one evening to
meditate,[b] and as he looked up, he saw
camels approaching. 64Rebekah also
looked up and saw Isaac. She got down
from her camel 65and asked the servant,
“Who is that man in the field coming to
meet us?”
“He is my master,” the servant answered. So she took her veil and covered
herself.
66Then the servant told Isaac all he
had done. 67Isaac brought her into the
tent of his mother Sarah, and he married
Rebekah. So she became his wife, and he
loved her; and Isaac was comforted after
his mother’s death.

The Death of Abraham

25 Abraham had taken another wife,
whose name was Keturah. 2She
bore him Zimran, Jokshan, Medan, Midian, Ishbak and Shuah. 3Jokshan was
the father of Sheba and Dedan; the descendants of Dedan were the Ashurites,
the Letushites and the Leummites. 4The
sons of Midian were Ephah, Epher, Hanok, Abida and Eldaah. All these were
descendants of Keturah.
5Abraham left everything he owned to
Isaac. 6But while he was still living, he
gave gifts to the sons of his concubines
and sent them away from his son Isaac
to the land of the east.
7Abraham lived a hundred and seventy-
five years. 8Then Abraham breathed
his last and died at a good old age, an
old man and full of years; and he was
gathered to his people. 9His sons Isaac
and Ishmael buried him in the cave of
Machpelah near Mamre, in the field of
Ephron son of Zohar the Hittite, 10the
field Abraham had bought from the Hittites.[c] There Abraham was buried with
his wife Sarah. 11After Abraham’s death,
God blessed his son Isaac, who then lived
near Beer Lahai Roi.

Ishmael’s Sons

12This is the account of the family line
of Abraham’s son Ishmael, whom Sarah’s slave, Hagar the Egyptian, bore to
Abraham.
13These are the names of the sons of
Ishmael, listed in the order of their birth:
Nebaioth the firstborn of Ishmael, Kedar, Adbeel, Mibsam, 14Mishma, Dumah,

[a] 55 Or *she* [b] 63 The meaning of the Hebrew for this word is uncertain. [c] 10 Or *the descendants of Heth*

Massa, 15Hadad, Tema, Jetur, Naphish
and Kedemah. 16These were the sons of
Ishmael, and these are the names of the
twelve tribal rulers according to their
settlements and camps. 17Ishmael lived
a hundred and thirty-seven years. He
breathed his last and died, and he was
gathered to his people. 18His descendants
settled in the area from Havilah to Shur,
near the eastern border of Egypt, as you
go toward Ashur. And they lived in hostility toward[a] all the tribes related to them.

Jacob and Esau

19This is the account of the family line
of Abraham's son Isaac.

Abraham became the father of Isaac,
20and Isaac was forty years old when he
married Rebekah daughter of Bethuel
the Aramean from Paddan Aram[b] and
sister of Laban the Aramean.
21Isaac prayed to the LORD on behalf of
his wife, because she was childless. The
LORD answered his prayer, and his wife
Rebekah became pregnant. 22The babies
jostled each other within her, and she
said, "Why is this happening to me?" So
she went to inquire of the LORD.
23The LORD said to her,

"Two nations are in your womb,
and two peoples from within you
will be separated;
one people will be stronger than the
other,
and the older will serve the
younger."

24When the time came for her to give
birth, there were twin boys in her womb.
25The first to come out was red, and his
whole body was like a hairy garment; so
they named him Esau.[c] 26After this, his
brother came out, with his hand grasping Esau's heel; so he was named Jacob.[d]
Isaac was sixty years old when Rebekah
gave birth to them.
27The boys grew up, and Esau became
a skillful hunter, a man of the open
country, while Jacob was content to stay
at home among the tents. 28Isaac, who
had a taste for wild game, loved Esau,
but Rebekah loved Jacob.
29Once when Jacob was cooking some
stew, Esau came in from the open country, famished. 30He said to Jacob, "Quick,
let me have some of that red stew! I'm
famished!" (That is why he was also
called Edom.[e])
31Jacob replied, "First sell me your
birthright."
32"Look, I am about to die," Esau said.
"What good is the birthright to me?"
33But Jacob said, "Swear to me first."
So he swore an oath to him, selling his
birthright to Jacob.
34Then Jacob gave Esau some bread
and some lentil stew. He ate and drank,
and then got up and left.
So Esau despised his birthright.

Isaac and Abimelek

26 Now there was a famine in the
land — besides the previous famine in Abraham's time — and Isaac went
to Abimelek king of the Philistines in
Gerar. 2The LORD appeared to Isaac and
said, "Do not go down to Egypt; live in
the land where I tell you to live. 3Stay in
this land for a while, and I will be with
you and will bless you. For to you and
your descendants I will give all these
lands and will confirm the oath I swore
to your father Abraham. 4I will make
your descendants as numerous as the
stars in the sky and will give them all
these lands, and through your offspring[f]
all nations on earth will be blessed,[g] 5be-
cause Abraham obeyed me and did everything I required of him, keeping my
commands, my decrees and my instructions." 6So Isaac stayed in Gerar.
7When the men of that place asked
him about his wife, he said, "She is my
sister," because he was afraid to say, "She
is my wife." He thought, "The men of this
place might kill me on account of Rebekah, because she is beautiful."
8When Isaac had been there a long
time, Abimelek king of the Philistines
looked down from a window and saw
Isaac caressing his wife Rebekah. 9So
Abimelek summoned Isaac and said,
"She is really your wife! Why did you say,
'She is my sister'?"
Isaac answered him, "Because I
thought I might lose my life on account
of her."
10Then Abimelek said, "What is this
you have done to us? One of the men
might well have slept with your wife, and
you would have brought guilt upon us."
11So Abimelek gave orders to all the
people: "Anyone who harms this man or
his wife shall surely be put to death."
12Isaac planted crops in that land and
the same year reaped a hundredfold,

[a] 18 Or *lived to the east of* [b] 20 That is, Northwest Mesopotamia [c] 25 *Esau* may mean *hairy.*
[d] 26 *Jacob* means *he grasps the heel,* a Hebrew idiom for *he deceives.* [e] 30 *Edom* means *red.*
[f] 4 Or *seed* [g] 4 Or *and all nations on earth will use the name of your offspring in blessings* (see 48:20)

because the LORD blessed him. 13The
man became rich, and his wealth continued to grow until he became very
wealthy. 14He had so many flocks and
herds and servants that the Philistines
envied him. 15So all the wells that his father's servants had dug in the time of his
father Abraham, the Philistines stopped
up, filling them with earth.

16Then Abimelek said to Isaac, "Move
away from us; you have become too
powerful for us."

17So Isaac moved away from there and
encamped in the Valley of Gerar, where
he settled. 18Isaac reopened the wells
that had been dug in the time of his father Abraham, which the Philistines had
stopped up after Abraham died, and he
gave them the same names his father
had given them.

19Isaac's servants dug in the valley and
discovered a well of fresh water there.
20But the herders of Gerar quarreled
with those of Isaac and said, "The water is ours!" So he named the well Esek,[a]
because they disputed with him. 21Then
they dug another well, but they quarreled over that one also; so he named it
Sitnah.[b] 22He moved on from there and
dug another well, and no one quarreled
over it. He named it Rehoboth,[c] saying,
"Now the LORD has given us room and
we will flourish in the land."

23From there he went up to Beersheba.
24That night the LORD appeared to him
and said, "I am the God of your father
Abraham. Do not be afraid, for I am with
you; I will bless you and will increase the
number of your descendants for the sake
of my servant Abraham."

25Isaac built an altar there and called
on the name of the LORD. There he
pitched his tent, and there his servants
dug a well.

26Meanwhile, Abimelek had come to
him from Gerar, with Ahuzzath his personal adviser and Phicol the commander
of his forces. 27Isaac asked them, "Why
have you come to me, since you were
hostile to me and sent me away?"

28They answered, "We saw clearly that
the LORD was with you; so we said, 'There
ought to be a sworn agreement between
us'—between us and you. Let us make
a treaty with you 29that you will do us
no harm, just as we did not harm you
but always treated you well and sent
you away peacefully. And now you are
blessed by the LORD."

30Isaac then made a feast for them,
and they ate and drank. 31Early the next
morning the men swore an oath to each
other. Then Isaac sent them on their
way, and they went away peacefully.

32That day Isaac's servants came and
told him about the well they had dug.
They said, "We've found water!" 33He
called it Shibah,[d] and to this day the
name of the town has been Beersheba.[e]

Jacob Takes Esau's Blessing

34When Esau was forty years old, he
married Judith daughter of Beeri the
Hittite, and also Basemath daughter of
Elon the Hittite. 35They were a source of
grief to Isaac and Rebekah.

27 When Isaac was old and his eyes
were so weak that he could no longer see, he called for Esau his older son
and said to him, "My son."

"Here I am," he answered.

2Isaac said, "I am now an old man and
don't know the day of my death. 3Now
then, get your equipment—your quiver
and bow—and go out to the open country to hunt some wild game for me. 4Pre-
pare me the kind of tasty food I like and
bring it to me to eat, so that I may give
you my blessing before I die."

5Now Rebekah was listening as Isaac
spoke to his son Esau. When Esau left
for the open country to hunt game and
bring it back, 6Rebekah said to her son
Jacob, "Look, I overheard your father say
to your brother Esau, 7'Bring me some
game and prepare me some tasty food to
eat, so that I may give you my blessing
in the presence of the LORD before I die.'
8Now, my son, listen carefully and do
what I tell you: 9Go out to the flock and
bring me two choice young goats, so I
can prepare some tasty food for your father, just the way he likes it. 10Then take
it to your father to eat, so that he may
give you his blessing before he dies."

11Jacob said to Rebekah his mother,
"But my brother Esau is a hairy man
while I have smooth skin. 12What if my
father touches me? I would appear to be
tricking him and would bring down a
curse on myself rather than a blessing."

13His mother said to him, "My son, let
the curse fall on me. Just do what I say;
go and get them for me."

14So he went and got them and brought
them to his mother, and she prepared
some tasty food, just the way his father
liked it. 15Then Rebekah took the best

[a] 20 *Esek* means *dispute.* [b] 21 *Sitnah* means *opposition.* [c] 22 *Rehoboth* means *room.*
[d] 33 *Shibah* can mean *oath* or *seven.* [e] 33 *Beersheba* can mean *well of the oath* and *well of seven.*

clothes of Esau her older son, which she
had in the house, and put them on her
younger son Jacob. 16She also covered his
hands and the smooth part of his neck
with the goatskins. 17Then she handed
to her son Jacob the tasty food and the
bread she had made.

18He went to his father and said, "My
father."

"Yes, my son," he answered. "Who is it?"

19Jacob said to his father, "I am Esau
your firstborn. I have done as you told me.
Please sit up and eat some of my game, so
that you may give me your blessing."

20Isaac asked his son, "How did you
find it so quickly, my son?"

"The LORD your God gave me success,"
he replied.

21Then Isaac said to Jacob, "Come
near so I can touch you, my son, to know
whether you really are my son Esau or
not."

22Jacob went close to his father Isaac,
who touched him and said, "The voice
is the voice of Jacob, but the hands are
the hands of Esau." 23He did not recognize him, for his hands were hairy like
those of his brother Esau; so he proceeded to bless him. 24"Are you really my son
Esau?" he asked.

"I am," he replied.

25Then he said, "My son, bring me
some of your game to eat, so that I may
give you my blessing."

Jacob brought it to him and he ate;
and he brought some wine and he
drank. 26Then his father Isaac said to
him, "Come here, my son, and kiss me."

27So he went to him and kissed him.
When Isaac caught the smell of his
clothes, he blessed him and said,

"Ah, the smell of my son
is like the smell of a field
that the LORD has blessed.
28 May God give you heaven's dew
and earth's richness —
an abundance of grain and new
wine.
29 May nations serve you
and peoples bow down to you.
Be lord over your brothers,
and may the sons of your mother
bow down to you.
May those who curse you be cursed
and those who bless you be
blessed."

30After Isaac finished blessing him,
and Jacob had scarcely left his father's
presence, his brother Esau came in from
hunting. 31He too prepared some tasty
food and brought it to his father. Then
he said to him, "My father, please sit up
and eat some of my game, so that you
may give me your blessing."

32His father Isaac asked him, "Who are
you?"

"I am your son," he answered, "your
firstborn, Esau."

33Isaac trembled violently and said,
"Who was it, then, that hunted game
and brought it to me? I ate it just before
you came and I blessed him — and indeed he will be blessed!"

34When Esau heard his father's words,
he burst out with a loud and bitter cry
and said to his father, "Bless me — me
too, my father!"

35But he said, "Your brother came deceitfully and took your blessing."

36Esau said, "Isn't he rightly named
Jacob[a]? This is the second time he has
taken advantage of me: He took my
birthright, and now he's taken my blessing!" Then he asked, "Haven't you reserved any blessing for me?"

37Isaac answered Esau, "I have made
him lord over you and have made all his
relatives his servants, and I have sustained him with grain and new wine. So
what can I possibly do for you, my son?"

38Esau said to his father, "Do you have
only one blessing, my father? Bless me
too, my father!" Then Esau wept aloud.

39His father Isaac answered him,

"Your dwelling will be
away from the earth's richness,
away from the dew of heaven
above.
40 You will live by the sword
and you will serve your brother.
But when you grow restless,
you will throw his yoke
from off your neck."

41Esau held a grudge against Jacob because of the blessing his father had giv-
en him. He said to himself, "The days of
mourning for my father are near; then I
will kill my brother Jacob."

42When Rebekah was told what her
older son Esau had said, she sent for
her younger son Jacob and said to
him, "Your brother Esau is planning to
avenge himself by killing you. 43Now
then, my son, do what I say: Flee at once
to my brother Laban in Harran. 44Stay
with him for a while until your brother's
fury subsides. 45When your brother is no
longer angry with you and forgets what

[a] 36 *Jacob* means *he grasps the heel,* a Hebrew idiom for *he takes advantage of* or *he deceives.*

you did to him, I'll send word for you to
come back from there. Why should I lose
both of you in one day?"
46Then Rebekah said to Isaac, "I'm dis-
gusted with living because of these Hittite women. If Jacob takes a wife from
among the women of this land, from
Hittite women like these, my life will not
be worth living."
28 So Isaac called for Jacob and
blessed him. Then he commanded
him: "Do not marry a Canaanite woman.
2Go at once to Paddan Aram,[a] to the house
of your mother's father Bethuel. Take
a wife for yourself there, from among
the daughters of Laban, your mother's
brother. 3May God Almighty[b] bless you
and make you fruitful and increase your
numbers until you become a community
of peoples. 4May he give you and your descendants the blessing given to Abraham,
so that you may take possession of the
land where you now reside as a foreigner, the land God gave to Abraham." 5Then
Isaac sent Jacob on his way, and he went
to Paddan Aram, to Laban son of Bethuel the Aramean, the brother of Rebekah,
who was the mother of Jacob and Esau.
6Now Esau learned that Isaac had
blessed Jacob and had sent him to Paddan Aram to take a wife from there,
and that when he blessed him he commanded him, "Do not marry a Canaanite woman," 7and that Jacob had obeyed
his father and mother and had gone to
Paddan Aram. 8Esau then realized how
displeasing the Canaanite women were
to his father Isaac; 9so he went to Ishmael and married Mahalath, the sister of
Nebaioth and daughter of Ishmael son
of Abraham, in addition to the wives he
already had.

Jacob's Dream at Bethel

10Jacob left Beersheba and set out for
Harran. 11When he reached a certain
place, he stopped for the night because
the sun had set. Taking one of the stones
there, he put it under his head and lay
down to sleep. 12He had a dream in which
he saw a stairway resting on the earth,
with its top reaching to heaven, and the
angels of God were ascending and descending on it. 13There above it[c] stood the
LORD, and he said: "I am the LORD, the
God of your father Abraham and the God
of Isaac. I will give you and your descendants the land on which you are lying.
14Your descendants will be like the dust
of the earth, and you will spread out to
the west and to the east, to the north and
to the south. All peoples on earth will be
blessed through you and your offspring.[d]
15I am with you and will watch over you
wherever you go, and I will bring you
back to this land. I will not leave you until
I have done what I have promised you."
16When Jacob awoke from his sleep,
he thought, "Surely the LORD is in this
place, and I was not aware of it." 17He
was afraid and said, "How awesome is
this place! This is none other than the
house of God; this is the gate of heaven."
18Early the next morning Jacob took
the stone he had placed under his head
and set it up as a pillar and poured oil
on top of it. 19He called that place Bethel,[e] though the city used to be called Luz.
20Then Jacob made a vow, saying, "If
God will be with me and will watch over
me on this journey I am taking and will
give me food to eat and clothes to wear
21so that I return safely to my father's
household, then the LORD[f] will be my
God 22and[g] this stone that I have set up
as a pillar will be God's house, and of all
that you give me I will give you a tenth."

Jacob Arrives in Paddan Aram

29 Then Jacob continued on his journey and came to the land of the
eastern peoples. 2There he saw a well in
the open country, with three flocks of
sheep lying near it because the flocks
were watered from that well. The stone
over the mouth of the well was large.
3When all the flocks were gathered there,
the shepherds would roll the stone away
from the well's mouth and water the
sheep. Then they would return the stone
to its place over the mouth of the well.
4Jacob asked the shepherds, "My
brothers, where are you from?"
"We're from Harran," they replied.
5He said to them, "Do you know Laban, Nahor's grandson?"
"Yes, we know him," they answered.
6Then Jacob asked them, "Is he well?"
"Yes, he is," they said, "and here comes
his daughter Rachel with the sheep."
7"Look," he said, "the sun is still high; it
is not time for the flocks to be gathered.
Water the sheep and take them back to
pasture."

[a] 2 That is, Northwest Mesopotamia; also in verses 5, 6 and 7 [b] 3 Hebrew *El-Shaddai* [c] 13 Or *There beside him* [d] 14 *Or will use your name and the name of your offspring in blessings* (see 48:20) [e] 19 *Bethel* means *house of God.* [f] 20,21 Or *Since God . . . father's household, the LORD* [g] 21,22 Or *household, and the LORD will be my God, 22then*

8 "We can't," they replied, "until all the
flocks are gathered and the stone has
been rolled away from the mouth of the
well. Then we will water the sheep."
9 While he was still talking with them,
Rachel came with her father's sheep, for
she was a shepherd. 10 When Jacob saw
Rachel daughter of his uncle Laban,
and Laban's sheep, he went over and
rolled the stone away from the mouth of
the well and watered his uncle's sheep.
11 Then Jacob kissed Rachel and began to
weep aloud. 12 He had told Rachel that he
was a relative of her father and a son of
Rebekah. So she ran and told her father.
13 As soon as Laban heard the news
about Jacob, his sister's son, he hurried to meet him. He embraced him
and kissed him and brought him to his
home, and there Jacob told him all these
things. 14 Then Laban said to him, "You
are my own flesh and blood."

Jacob Marries Leah and Rachel

After Jacob had stayed with him for
a whole month, 15 Laban said to him,
"Just because you are a relative of mine,
should you work for me for nothing? Tell
me what your wages should be."
16 Now Laban had two daughters; the
name of the older was Leah, and the
name of the younger was Rachel. 17 Leah
had weak[a] eyes, but Rachel had a lovely
figure and was beautiful. 18 Jacob was in
love with Rachel and said, "I'll work for
you seven years in return for your younger daughter Rachel."
19 Laban said, "It's better that I give
her to you than to some other man. Stay
here with me." 20 So Jacob served seven
years to get Rachel, but they seemed
like only a few days to him because of
his love for her.
21 Then Jacob said to Laban, "Give me
my wife. My time is completed, and I
want to make love to her."
22 So Laban brought together all the
people of the place and gave a feast.
23 But when evening came, he took his
daughter Leah and brought her to Jacob,
and Jacob made love to her. 24 And Laban
gave his servant Zilpah to his daughter
as her attendant.
25 When morning came, there was
Leah! So Jacob said to Laban, "What is
this you have done to me? I served you
for Rachel, didn't I? Why have you deceived me?"
26 Laban replied, "It is not our custom
here to give the younger daughter in
marriage before the older one. 27 Finish
this daughter's bridal week; then we will
give you the younger one also, in return
for another seven years of work."
28 And Jacob did so. He finished the
week with Leah, and then Laban gave
him his daughter Rachel to be his wife.
29 Laban gave his servant Bilhah to his
daughter Rachel as her attendant. 30 Jacob made love to Rachel also, and his
love for Rachel was greater than his love
for Leah. And he worked for Laban another seven years.

Jacob's Children

31 When the LORD saw that Leah was
not loved, he enabled her to conceive,
but Rachel remained childless. 32 Leah
became pregnant and gave birth to a
son. She named him Reuben,[b] for she
said, "It is because the LORD has seen my
misery. Surely my husband will love me
now."
33 She conceived again, and when she
gave birth to a son she said, "Because
the LORD heard that I am not loved, he
gave me this one too." So she named him
Simeon.[c]
34 Again she conceived, and when she
gave birth to a son she said, "Now at last
my husband will become attached to me,
because I have borne him three sons." So
he was named Levi.[d]
35 She conceived again, and when she
gave birth to a son she said, "This time I
will praise the LORD." So she named him
Judah.[e] Then she stopped having children.
30 When Rachel saw that she was not
bearing Jacob any children, she
became jealous of her sister. So she said
to Jacob, "Give me children, or I'll die!"
2 Jacob became angry with her and
said, "Am I in the place of God, who has
kept you from having children?"
3 Then she said, "Here is Bilhah, my
servant. Sleep with her so that she can
bear children for me and I too can build
a family through her."
4 So she gave him her servant Bilhah
as a wife. Jacob slept with her, 5 and she
became pregnant and bore him a son.
6 Then Rachel said, "God has vindicated
me; he has listened to my plea and giv-
en me a son." Because of this she named
him Dan.[f]

[a] 17 Or *delicate* [b] 32 *Reuben* sounds like the Hebrew for *he has seen my misery*; the name means *see, a son.* [c] 33 *Simeon* probably means *one who hears.* [d] 34 *Levi* sounds like and may be derived from the Hebrew for *attached.* [e] 35 *Judah* sounds like and may be derived from the Hebrew for *praise.* [f] 6 *Dan* here means *he has vindicated.*

7Rachel's servant Bilhah conceived
again and bore Jacob a second son.
8Then Rachel said, "I have had a great
struggle with my sister, and I have won."
So she named him Naphtali.[a]
9When Leah saw that she had stopped
having children, she took her servant
Zilpah and gave her to Jacob as a wife.
10Leah's servant Zilpah bore Jacob a son.
11Then Leah said, "What good fortune!"[b]
So she named him Gad.[c]
12Leah's servant Zilpah bore Jacob a
second son. 13Then Leah said, "How happy I am! The women will call me happy."
So she named him Asher.[d]
14During wheat harvest, Reuben went
out into the fields and found some
mandrake plants, which he brought to
his mother Leah. Rachel said to Leah,
"Please give me some of your son's mandrakes."
15But she said to her, "Wasn't it enough
that you took away my husband? Will
you take my son's mandrakes too?"
"Very well," Rachel said, "he can sleep
with you tonight in return for your son's
mandrakes."
16So when Jacob came in from the fields
that evening, Leah went out to meet
him. "You must sleep with me," she said.
"I have hired you with my son's mandrakes." So he slept with her that night.
17God listened to Leah, and she became pregnant and bore Jacob a fifth
son. 18Then Leah said, "God has rewarded me for giving my servant to my husband." So she named him Issachar.[e]
19Leah conceived again and bore Jacob a sixth son. 20Then Leah said, "God
has presented me with a precious gift.
This time my husband will treat me
with honor, because I have borne him
six sons." So she named him Zebulun.[f]
21Some time later she gave birth to a
daughter and named her Dinah.
22Then God remembered Rachel; he
listened to her and enabled her to conceive. 23She became pregnant and gave
birth to a son and said, "God has taken
away my disgrace." 24She named him
Joseph,[g] and said, "May the LORD add to
me another son."

Jacob's Flocks Increase

25After Rachel gave birth to Joseph,
Jacob said to Laban, "Send me on my
way so I can go back to my own homeland. 26Give me my wives and children,
for whom I have served you, and I will
be on my way. You know how much work
I've done for you."
27But Laban said to him, "If I have
found favor in your eyes, please stay.
I have learned by divination that the
LORD has blessed me because of you."
28He added, "Name your wages, and I
will pay them."
29Jacob said to him, "You know how I
have worked for you and how your livestock has fared under my care. 30The little you had before I came has increased
greatly, and the LORD has blessed you
wherever I have been. But now, when
may I do something for my own household?"
31"What shall I give you?" he asked.
"Don't give me anything," Jacob replied. "But if you will do this one thing
for me, I will go on tending your flocks
and watching over them: 32Let me go
through all your flocks today and remove from them every speckled or spotted sheep, every dark-colored lamb and
every spotted or speckled goat. They will
be my wages. 33And my honesty will testify for me in the future, whenever you
check on the wages you have paid me.
Any goat in my possession that is not
speckled or spotted, or any lamb that is
not dark-colored, will be considered stolen."
34"Agreed," said Laban. "Let it be as
you have said." 35That same day he removed all the male goats that were
streaked or spotted, and all the speckled or spotted female goats (all that had
white on them) and all the dark-colored
lambs, and he placed them in the care of
his sons. 36Then he put a three-day journey between himself and Jacob, while
Jacob continued to tend the rest of Laban's flocks.
37Jacob, however, took fresh-cut
branches from poplar, almond and plane
trees and made white stripes on them by
peeling the bark and exposing the white
inner wood of the branches. 38Then he
placed the peeled branches in all the
watering troughs, so that they would be
directly in front of the flocks when they
came to drink. When the flocks were in
heat and came to drink, 39they mated
in front of the branches. And they bore
young that were streaked or speckled or

[a] 8 *Naphtali* means *my struggle.* [b] 11 Or *"A troop is coming!"* [c] 11 *Gad* can mean *good fortune* or *a troop.* [d] 13 *Asher* means *happy.* [e] 18 *Issachar* sounds like the Hebrew for *reward.* [f] 20 *Zebulun* probably means *honor.* [g] 24 *Joseph* means *may he add.*

spotted. 40Jacob set apart the young of
the flock by themselves, but made the
rest face the streaked and dark-colored
animals that belonged to Laban. Thus
he made separate flocks for himself and
did not put them with Laban's animals.
41Whenever the stronger females were
in heat, Jacob would place the branches in the troughs in front of the animals
so they would mate near the branches,
42but if the animals were weak, he would
not place them there. So the weak animals went to Laban and the strong ones
to Jacob. 43In this way the man grew exceedingly prosperous and came to own
large flocks, and female and male servants, and camels and donkeys.

Jacob Flees From Laban

31 Jacob heard that Laban's sons were
saying, "Jacob has taken everything our father owned and has gained
all this wealth from what belonged to
our father." 2And Jacob noticed that Laban's attitude toward him was not what
it had been.

3Then the LORD said to Jacob, "Go back
to the land of your fathers and to your
relatives, and I will be with you."

4So Jacob sent word to Rachel and
Leah to come out to the fields where his
flocks were. 5He said to them, "I see that
your father's attitude toward me is not
what it was before, but the God of my father has been with me. 6You know that
I've worked for your father with all my
strength, 7yet your father has cheated me
by changing my wages ten times. However, God has not allowed him to harm
me. 8If he said, 'The speckled ones will
be your wages,' then all the flocks gave
birth to speckled young; and if he said,
'The streaked ones will be your wages,'
then all the flocks bore streaked young.
9So God has taken away your father's
livestock and has given them to me.

10"In breeding season I once had a
dream in which I looked up and saw
that the male goats mating with the
flock were streaked, speckled or spotted. 11The angel of God said to me in the
dream, 'Jacob.' I answered, 'Here I am.'
12And he said, 'Look up and see that all
the male goats mating with the flock are
streaked, speckled or spotted, for I have
seen all that Laban has been doing to
you. 13I am the God of Bethel, where you
anointed a pillar and where you made a
vow to me. Now leave this land at once
and go back to your native land.'"

14Then Rachel and Leah replied, "Do
we still have any share in the inheritance of our father's estate? 15Does he
not regard us as foreigners? Not only has
he sold us, but he has used up what was
paid for us. 16Surely all the wealth that
God took away from our father belongs
to us and our children. So do whatever
God has told you."

17Then Jacob put his children and his
wives on camels, 18and he drove all his
livestock ahead of him, along with all
the goods he had accumulated in Paddan Aram,[a] to go to his father Isaac in
the land of Canaan.

19When Laban had gone to shear his
sheep, Rachel stole her father's household gods. 20Moreover, Jacob deceived
Laban the Aramean by not telling him
he was running away. 21So he fled with
all he had, crossed the Euphrates River,
and headed for the hill country of Gilead.

Laban Pursues Jacob

22On the third day Laban was told that
Jacob had fled. 23Taking his relatives
with him, he pursued Jacob for seven
days and caught up with him in the hill
country of Gilead. 24Then God came to
Laban the Aramean in a dream at night
and said to him, "Be careful not to say
anything to Jacob, either good or bad."

25Jacob had pitched his tent in the
hill country of Gilead when Laban overtook him, and Laban and his relatives
camped there too. 26Then Laban said
to Jacob, "What have you done? You've
deceived me, and you've carried off my
daughters like captives in war. 27Why
did you run off secretly and deceive
me? Why didn't you tell me, so I could
send you away with joy and singing to
the music of timbrels and harps? 28You
didn't even let me kiss my grandchildren and my daughters goodbye. You
have done a foolish thing. 29I have the
power to harm you; but last night the
God of your father said to me, 'Be careful not to say anything to Jacob, either
good or bad.' 30Now you have gone off
because you longed to return to your father's household. But why did you steal
my gods?"

31Jacob answered Laban, "I was afraid,
because I thought you would take your
daughters away from me by force. 32But
if you find anyone who has your gods,
that person shall not live. In the presence
of our relatives, see for yourself whether there is anything of yours here with

[a] *18* That is, Northwest Mesopotamia

me; and if so, take it." Now Jacob did not
know that Rachel had stolen the gods.
33So Laban went into Jacob's tent and
into Leah's tent and into the tent of the
two female servants, but he found nothing. After he came out of Leah's tent, he
entered Rachel's tent. 34Now Rachel had
taken the household gods and put them
inside her camel's saddle and was sitting
on them. Laban searched through everything in the tent but found nothing.
35Rachel said to her father, "Don't be
angry, my lord, that I cannot stand up
in your presence; I'm having my period."
So he searched but could not find the
household gods.
36Jacob was angry and took Laban to
task. "What is my crime?" he asked Laban. "How have I wronged you that you
hunt me down? 37Now that you have
searched through all my goods, what
have you found that belongs to your
household? Put it here in front of your
relatives and mine, and let them judge
between the two of us.
38"I have been with you for twenty
years now. Your sheep and goats have
not miscarried, nor have I eaten rams
from your flocks. 39I did not bring you
animals torn by wild beasts; I bore the
loss myself. And you demanded payment from me for whatever was stolen
by day or night. 40This was my situation:
The heat consumed me in the daytime
and the cold at night, and sleep fled
from my eyes. 41It was like this for the
twenty years I was in your household. I
worked for you fourteen years for your
two daughters and six years for your
flocks, and you changed my wages ten
times. 42If the God of my father, the God
of Abraham and the Fear of Isaac, had
not been with me, you would surely have
sent me away empty-handed. But God
has seen my hardship and the toil of my
hands, and last night he rebuked you."
43Laban answered Jacob, "The women
are my daughters, the children are my
children, and the flocks are my flocks. All
you see is mine. Yet what can I do today
about these daughters of mine, or about
the children they have borne? 44Come
now, let's make a covenant, you and I,
and let it serve as a witness between us."
45So Jacob took a stone and set it up as
a pillar. 46He said to his relatives, "Gather some stones." So they took stones and
piled them in a heap, and they ate there
by the heap. 47Laban called it Jegar Sahadutha, and Jacob called it Galeed.[a]
48Laban said, "This heap is a witness
between you and me today." That is why
it was called Galeed. 49It was also called
Mizpah,[b] because he said, "May the LORD
keep watch between you and me when
we are away from each other. 50If you
mistreat my daughters or if you take
any wives besides my daughters, even
though no one is with us, remember that
God is a witness between you and me."
51Laban also said to Jacob, "Here is
this heap, and here is this pillar I have
set up between you and me. 52This heap
is a witness, and this pillar is a witness,
that I will not go past this heap to your
side to harm you and that you will not
go past this heap and pillar to my side to
harm me. 53May the God of Abraham and
the God of Nahor, the God of their father,
judge between us."
So Jacob took an oath in the name of
the Fear of his father Isaac. 54He offered
a sacrifice there in the hill country and
invited his relatives to a meal. After they
had eaten, they spent the night there.
55Early the next morning Laban kissed
his grandchildren and his daughters and
blessed them. Then he left and returned
home.[c]

Jacob Prepares to Meet Esau

32[d] Jacob also went on his way, and
the angels of God met him. 2When
Jacob saw them, he said, "This is the
camp of God!" So he named that place
Mahanaim.[e]
3Jacob sent messengers ahead of
him to his brother Esau in the land of
Seir, the country of Edom. 4He instructed them: "This is what you are to say to
my lord Esau: 'Your servant Jacob says, I
have been staying with Laban and have
remained there till now. 5I have cattle
and donkeys, sheep and goats, male and
female servants. Now I am sending this
message to my lord, that I may find favor in your eyes.'"
6When the messengers returned to Jacob, they said, "We went to your brother
Esau, and now he is coming to meet you,
and four hundred men are with him."
7In great fear and distress Jacob divided the people who were with him
into two groups,[f] and the flocks and
herds and camels as well. 8He thought,

[a] 47 The Aramaic *Jegar Sahadutha* and the Hebrew *Galeed* both mean *witness heap.*
[b] 49 *Mizpah* means *watchtower.* [c] 55 In Hebrew texts this verse (31:55) is numbered 32:1.
[d] In Hebrew texts 32:1-32 is numbered 32:2-33. [e] 2 *Mahanaim* means *two camps.* [f] 7 Or
camps

"If Esau comes and attacks one group,[a]
the group[a] that is left may escape."
9Then Jacob prayed, "O God of my father Abraham, God of my father Isaac,
LORD, you who said to me, 'Go back to
your country and your relatives, and I
will make you prosper,' 10I am unworthy
of all the kindness and faithfulness you
have shown your servant. I had only my
staff when I crossed this Jordan, but now
I have become two camps. 11Save me, I
pray, from the hand of my brother Esau,
for I am afraid he will come and attack
me, and also the mothers with their children. 12But you have said, 'I will surely
make you prosper and will make your
descendants like the sand of the sea,
which cannot be counted.'"
13He spent the night there, and from
what he had with him he selected a gift
for his brother Esau: 14two hundred female goats and twenty male goats, two
hundred ewes and twenty rams, 15thirty
female camels with their young, forty
cows and ten bulls, and twenty female
donkeys and ten male donkeys. 16He put
them in the care of his servants, each
herd by itself, and said to his servants,
"Go ahead of me, and keep some space
between the herds."
17He instructed the one in the lead:
"When my brother Esau meets you and
asks, 'Who do you belong to, and where
are you going, and who owns all these
animals in front of you?' 18then you are
to say, 'They belong to your servant Jacob. They are a gift sent to my lord Esau,
and he is coming behind us.'"
19He also instructed the second, the
third and all the others who followed the
herds: "You are to say the same thing to
Esau when you meet him. 20And be sure
to say, 'Your servant Jacob is coming behind us.'" For he thought, "I will pacify
him with these gifts I am sending on
ahead; later, when I see him, perhaps he
will receive me." 21So Jacob's gifts went
on ahead of him, but he himself spent
the night in the camp.

Jacob Wrestles With God

22That night Jacob got up and took
his two wives, his two female servants
and his eleven sons and crossed the
ford of the Jabbok. 23After he had sent
them across the stream, he sent over
all his possessions. 24So Jacob was left
alone, and a man wrestled with him till
daybreak. 25When the man saw that he
could not overpower him, he touched the
socket of Jacob's hip so that his hip was
wrenched as he wrestled with the man.
26Then the man said, "Let me go, for it
is daybreak."
But Jacob replied, "I will not let you go
unless you bless me."
27The man asked him, "What is your
name?"
"Jacob," he answered.
28Then the man said, "Your name will
no longer be Jacob, but Israel,[b] because
you have struggled with God and with
humans and have overcome."
29Jacob said, "Please tell me your
name."
But he replied, "Why do you ask my
name?" Then he blessed him there.
30So Jacob called the place Peniel,[c]
saying, "It is because I saw God face to
face, and yet my life was spared."
31The sun rose above him as he passed
Peniel,[d] and he was limping because of
his hip. 32Therefore to this day the Israelites do not eat the tendon attached to
the socket of the hip, because the socket of Jacob's hip was touched near the
tendon.

Jacob Meets Esau

33 Jacob looked up and there was
Esau, coming with his four hundred men; so he divided the children
among Leah, Rachel and the two female
servants. 2He put the female servants
and their children in front, Leah and her
children next, and Rachel and Joseph in
the rear. 3He himself went on ahead and
bowed down to the ground seven times
as he approached his brother.
4But Esau ran to meet Jacob and embraced him; he threw his arms around
his neck and kissed him. And they wept.
5Then Esau looked up and saw the wom-
en and children. "Who are these with
you?" he asked.
Jacob answered, "They are the children God has graciously given your servant."
6Then the female servants and their
children approached and bowed down.
7Next, Leah and her children came and
bowed down. Last of all came Joseph
and Rachel, and they too bowed down.
8Esau asked, "What's the meaning of
all these flocks and herds I met?"
"To find favor in your eyes, my lord,"
he said.
9But Esau said, "I already have plenty, my brother. Keep what you have for
yourself."

[a] 8 Or *camp* [b] 28 *Israel* probably means *he struggles with God.* [c] 30 *Peniel* means *face of God.* [d] 31 Hebrew *Penuel*, a variant of *Peniel*

10"No, please!" said Jacob. "If I have found favor in your eyes, accept this gift from me. For to see your face is like seeing the face of God, now that you have received me favorably. 11Please accept the present that was brought to you, for God has been gracious to me and I have all I need." And because Jacob insisted, Esau accepted it.

12Then Esau said, "Let us be on our way; I'll accompany you."

13But Jacob said to him, "My lord knows that the children are tender and that I must care for the ewes and cows that are nursing their young. If they are driven hard just one day, all the animals will die. 14So let my lord go on ahead of his servant, while I move along slowly at the pace of the flocks and herds before me and the pace of the children, until I come to my lord in Seir."

15Esau said, "Then let me leave some of my men with you."

"But why do that?" Jacob asked. "Just let me find favor in the eyes of my lord."

16So that day Esau started on his way back to Seir. 17Jacob, however, went to Sukkoth, where he built a place for himself and made shelters for his livestock. That is why the place is called Sukkoth.[a]

18After Jacob came from Paddan Aram,[b] he arrived safely at the city of Shechem in Canaan and camped within sight of the city. 19For a hundred pieces of silver,[c] he bought from the sons of Hamor, the father of Shechem, the plot of ground where he pitched his tent. 20There he set up an altar and called it El Elohe Israel.[d]

Dinah and the Shechemites

34 Now Dinah, the daughter Leah had borne to Jacob, went out to visit the women of the land. 2When Shechem son of Hamor the Hivite, the ruler of that area, saw her, he took her and raped her. 3His heart was drawn to Dinah daughter of Jacob; he loved the young woman and spoke tenderly to her. 4And Shechem said to his father Hamor, "Get me this girl as my wife."

5When Jacob heard that his daughter Dinah had been defiled, his sons were in the fields with his livestock; so he did nothing about it until they came home.

6Then Shechem's father Hamor went out to talk with Jacob. 7Meanwhile, Jacob's sons had come in from the fields as soon as they heard what had happened. They were shocked and furious, because Shechem had done an outrageous thing in[e] Israel by sleeping with Jacob's daughter — a thing that should not be done.

8But Hamor said to them, "My son Shechem has his heart set on your daughter. Please give her to him as his wife. 9Intermarry with us; give us your daughters and take our daughters for yourselves. 10You can settle among us; the land is open to you. Live in it, trade[f] in it, and acquire property in it."

11Then Shechem said to Dinah's father and brothers, "Let me find favor in your eyes, and I will give you whatever you ask. 12Make the price for the bride and the gift I am to bring as great as you like, and I'll pay whatever you ask me. Only give me the young woman as my wife."

13Because their sister Dinah had been defiled, Jacob's sons replied deceitfully as they spoke to Shechem and his father Hamor. 14They said to them, "We can't do such a thing; we can't give our sister to a man who is not circumcised. That would be a disgrace to us. 15We will enter into an agreement with you on one condition only: that you become like us by circumcising all your males. 16Then we will give you our daughters and take your daughters for ourselves. We'll settle among you and become one people with you. 17But if you will not agree to be circumcised, we'll take our sister and go."

18Their proposal seemed good to Hamor and his son Shechem. 19The young man, who was the most honored of all his father's family, lost no time in doing what they said, because he was delighted with Jacob's daughter. 20So Hamor and his son Shechem went to the gate of their city to speak to the men of their city. 21"These men are friendly toward us," they said. "Let them live in our land and trade in it; the land has plenty of room for them. We can marry their daughters and they can marry ours. 22But the men will agree to live with us as one people only on the condition that our males be circumcised, as they themselves are. 23Won't their livestock, their property and all their other animals become ours? So let us agree to their terms, and they will settle among us."

[a] *17 Sukkoth* means *shelters.* [b] *18* That is, Northwest Mesopotamia [c] *19* Hebrew *hundred kesitahs;* a kesitah was a unit of money of unknown weight and value. [d] *20 El Elohe Israel* can mean *El is the God of Israel* or *mighty is the God of Israel.* [e] *7* Or *against* [f] *10* Or *move about freely;* also in verse 21

24 All the men who went out of the city
gate agreed with Hamor and his son
Shechem, and every male in the city was
circumcised.
25 Three days later, while all of them
were still in pain, two of Jacob's sons,
Simeon and Levi, Dinah's brothers, took
their swords and attacked the unsuspecting city, killing every male. 26 They
put Hamor and his son Shechem to the
sword and took Dinah from Shechem's
house and left. 27 The sons of Jacob came
upon the dead bodies and looted the
city where[a] their sister had been defiled.
28 They seized their flocks and herds and
donkeys and everything else of theirs
in the city and out in the fields. 29 They
carried off all their wealth and all their
women and children, taking as plunder
everything in the houses.
30 Then Jacob said to Simeon and Levi,
"You have brought trouble on me by
making me obnoxious to the Canaanites
and Perizzites, the people living in this
land. We are few in number, and if they
join forces against me and attack me, I
and my household will be destroyed."
31 But they replied, "Should he have
treated our sister like a prostitute?"

Jacob Returns to Bethel

35 Then God said to Jacob, "Go up to
Bethel and settle there, and build
an altar there to God, who appeared to
you when you were fleeing from your
brother Esau."
2 So Jacob said to his household and
to all who were with him, "Get rid of the
foreign gods you have with you, and purify yourselves and change your clothes.
3 Then come, let us go up to Bethel, where
I will build an altar to God, who answered me in the day of my distress and
who has been with me wherever I have
gone." 4 So they gave Jacob all the foreign
gods they had and the rings in their ears,
and Jacob buried them under the oak at
Shechem. 5 Then they set out, and the terror of God fell on the towns all around
them so that no one pursued them.
6 Jacob and all the people with him
came to Luz (that is, Bethel) in the land of
Canaan. 7 There he built an altar, and he
called the place El Bethel,[b] because it was
there that God revealed himself to him
when he was fleeing from his brother.
8 Now Deborah, Rebekah's nurse, died
and was buried under the oak outside
Bethel. So it was named Allon Bakuth.[c]
9 After Jacob returned from Paddan
Aram,[d] God appeared to him again and
blessed him. 10 God said to him, "Your
name is Jacob,[e] but you will no longer be
called Jacob; your name will be Israel.[f]"
So he named him Israel.
11 And God said to him, "I am God Almighty[g]; be fruitful and increase in
number. A nation and a community of
nations will come from you, and kings
will be among your descendants. 12 The
land I gave to Abraham and Isaac I also
give to you, and I will give this land to
your descendants after you." 13 Then God
went up from him at the place where he
had talked with him.
14 Jacob set up a stone pillar at the
place where God had talked with him,
and he poured out a drink offering on
it; he also poured oil on it. 15 Jacob called
the place where God had talked with him
Bethel.[h]

The Deaths of Rachel and Isaac

16 Then they moved on from Bethel.
While they were still some distance from
Ephrath, Rachel began to give birth and
had great difficulty. 17 And as she was
having great difficulty in childbirth, the
midwife said to her, "Don't despair, for
you have another son." 18 As she breathed
her last — for she was dying — she
named her son Ben-Oni.[i] But his father
named him Benjamin.[j]
19 So Rachel died and was buried on
the way to Ephrath (that is, Bethlehem).
20 Over her tomb Jacob set up a pillar,
and to this day that pillar marks Rachel's tomb.
21 Israel moved on again and pitched
his tent beyond Migdal Eder. 22 While Israel was living in that region, Reuben
went in and slept with his father's concubine Bilhah, and Israel heard of it.

Jacob had twelve sons:
23 The sons of Leah:
Reuben the firstborn of Jacob,
Simeon, Levi, Judah, Issachar
and Zebulun.
24 The sons of Rachel:
Joseph and Benjamin.
25 The sons of Rachel's servant Bilhah:
Dan and Naphtali.

[a] 27 Or *because* [b] 7 *El Bethel* means *God of Bethel.* [c] 8 *Allon Bakuth* means *oak of weeping.*
[d] 9 That is, Northwest Mesopotamia; also in verse 26 [e] 10 *Jacob* means *he grasps the heel,* a
Hebrew idiom for *he deceives.* [f] 10 *Israel* probably means *he struggles with God.*
[g] 11 Hebrew *El-Shaddai* [h] 15 *Bethel* means *house of God.* [i] 18 *Ben-Oni* means *son of my
trouble.* [j] 18 *Benjamin* means *son of my right hand.*

26 The sons of Leah's servant Zilpah:
Gad and Asher.
These were the sons of Jacob, who
were born to him in Paddan Aram.

27 Jacob came home to his father Isaac
in Mamre, near Kiriath Arba (that is, Hebron), where Abraham and Isaac had
stayed. 28 Isaac lived a hundred and
eighty years. 29 Then he breathed his last
and died and was gathered to his people,
old and full of years. And his sons Esau
and Jacob buried him.

Esau's Descendants

36 This is the account of the family
line of Esau (that is, Edom).

2 Esau took his wives from the
women of Canaan: Adah daughter
of Elon the Hittite, and Oholibamah
daughter of Anah and granddaughter of Zibeon the Hivite — 3 also Basemath daughter of Ishmael and sister of Nebaioth.

4 Adah bore Eliphaz to Esau, Basemath bore Reuel, 5 and Oholibamah
bore Jeush, Jalam and Korah. These
were the sons of Esau, who were
born to him in Canaan.

6 Esau took his wives and sons
and daughters and all the members
of his household, as well as his livestock and all his other animals and
all the goods he had acquired in Canaan, and moved to a land some
distance from his brother Jacob.
7 Their possessions were too great
for them to remain together; the
land where they were staying could
not support them both because of
their livestock. 8 So Esau (that is,
Edom) settled in the hill country of
Seir.

9 This is the account of the family line
of Esau the father of the Edomites in the
hill country of Seir.

10 These are the names of Esau's sons:
Eliphaz, the son of Esau's wife
Adah, and Reuel, the son of Esau's
wife Basemath.
11 The sons of Eliphaz:
Teman, Omar, Zepho, Gatam and
Kenaz.
12 Esau's son Eliphaz also had a concubine named Timna, who bore
him Amalek. These were grandsons of Esau's wife Adah.
13 The sons of Reuel:
Nahath, Zerah, Shammah and
Mizzah. These were grandsons of
Esau's wife Basemath.
14 The sons of Esau's wife Oholibamah daughter of Anah and granddaughter of Zibeon, whom she bore
to Esau:
Jeush, Jalam and Korah.

15 These were the chiefs among Esau's
descendants:
The sons of Eliphaz the firstborn of
Esau:
Chiefs Teman, Omar, Zepho, Kenaz, 16 Korah,[a] Gatam and Amalek. These were the chiefs descended from Eliphaz in Edom;
they were grandsons of Adah.
17 The sons of Esau's son Reuel:
Chiefs Nahath, Zerah, Shammah
and Mizzah. These were the chiefs
descended from Reuel in Edom;
they were grandsons of Esau's
wife Basemath.
18 The sons of Esau's wife Oholibamah:
Chiefs Jeush, Jalam and Korah.
These were the chiefs descended from Esau's wife Oholibamah
daughter of Anah.

19 These were the sons of Esau (that is,
Edom), and these were their chiefs.

20 These were the sons of Seir the Horite, who were living in the region:
Lotan, Shobal, Zibeon, Anah, 21 Dishon, Ezer and Dishan. These sons
of Seir in Edom were Horite chiefs.
22 The sons of Lotan:
Hori and Homam.[b] Timna was
Lotan's sister.
23 The sons of Shobal:
Alvan, Manahath, Ebal, Shepho
and Onam.
24 The sons of Zibeon:
Aiah and Anah. This is the Anah
who discovered the hot springs[c]
in the desert while he was grazing
the donkeys of his father Zibeon.
25 The children of Anah:
Dishon and Oholibamah daughter of Anah.
26 The sons of Dishon[d]:
Hemdan, Eshban, Ithran and Keran.
27 The sons of Ezer:
Bilhan, Zaavan and Akan.
28 The sons of Dishan:
Uz and Aran.

[a] *16* Masoretic Text; Samaritan Pentateuch (also verse 11 and 1 Chron. 1:36) does not have *Korah*. [b] *22* Hebrew *Hemam*, a variant of *Homam* (see 1 Chron. 1:39) [c] *24* Vulgate; Syriac *discovered water*; the meaning of the Hebrew for this word is uncertain. [d] *26* Hebrew *Dishan*, a variant of *Dishon*

29 These were the Horite chiefs:
Lotan, Shobal, Zibeon, Anah, 30 Dishon, Ezer and Dishan. These were
the Horite chiefs, according to
their divisions, in the land of Seir.

The Rulers of Edom

31 These were the kings who reigned in
Edom before any Israelite king reigned:
32 Bela son of Beor became king of
Edom. His city was named Dinhabah.
33 When Bela died, Jobab son of Zerah
from Bozrah succeeded him as
king.
34 When Jobab died, Husham from the
land of the Temanites succeeded
him as king.
35 When Husham died, Hadad son of
Bedad, who defeated Midian in
the country of Moab, succeeded
him as king. His city was named
Avith.
36 When Hadad died, Samlah from
Masrekah succeeded him as king.
37 When Samlah died, Shaul from Rehoboth on the river succeeded
him as king.
38 When Shaul died, Baal-Hanan son
of Akbor succeeded him as king.
39 When Baal-Hanan son of Akbor
died, Hadad[a] succeeded him as
king. His city was named Pau,
and his wife's name was Mehetabel daughter of Matred, the
daughter of Me-Zahab.

40 These were the chiefs descended
from Esau, by name, according to their
clans and regions:
Timna, Alvah, Jetheth, 41 Oholibamah, Elah, Pinon, 42 Kenaz, Teman, Mibzar, 43 Magdiel and Iram.
These were the chiefs of Edom,
according to their settlements in
the land they occupied.

This is the family line of Esau, the father of the Edomites.

Joseph's Dreams

37 Jacob lived in the land where his
father had stayed, the land of
Canaan.

2 This is the account of Jacob's family
line.

Joseph, a young man of seventeen,
was tending the flocks with his brothers,
the sons of Bilhah and the sons of Zilpah,
his father's wives, and he brought their
father a bad report about them.

3 Now Israel loved Joseph more than
any of his other sons, because he had
been born to him in his old age; and he
made an ornate[b] robe for him. 4 When his
brothers saw that their father loved him
more than any of them, they hated him
and could not speak a kind word to him.

5 Joseph had a dream, and when he
told it to his brothers, they hated him
all the more. 6 He said to them, "Listen
to this dream I had: 7 We were binding
sheaves of grain out in the field when
suddenly my sheaf rose and stood upright, while your sheaves gathered
around mine and bowed down to it."

8 His brothers said to him, "Do you intend to reign over us? Will you actually rule us?" And they hated him all the
more because of his dream and what he
had said.

9 Then he had another dream, and he
told it to his brothers. "Listen," he said,
"I had another dream, and this time the
sun and moon and eleven stars were
bowing down to me."

10 When he told his father as well as his
brothers, his father rebuked him and said,
"What is this dream you had? Will your
mother and I and your brothers actually
come and bow down to the ground before
you?" 11 His brothers were jealous of him,
but his father kept the matter in mind.

Joseph Sold by His Brothers

12 Now his brothers had gone to graze
their father's flocks near Shechem, 13 and
Israel said to Joseph, "As you know, your
brothers are grazing the flocks near Shechem. Come, I am going to send you to
them."

"Very well," he replied.

14 So he said to him, "Go and see if all
is well with your brothers and with the
flocks, and bring word back to me." Then
he sent him off from the Valley of Hebron.

When Joseph arrived at Shechem, 15 a
man found him wandering around in
the fields and asked him, "What are you
looking for?"

16 He replied, "I'm looking for my
brothers. Can you tell me where they are
grazing their flocks?"

17 "They have moved on from here," the
man answered. "I heard them say, 'Let's
go to Dothan.'"

[a] 39 Many manuscripts of the Masoretic Text, Samaritan Pentateuch and Syriac (see also 1 Chron. 1:50); most manuscripts of the Masoretic Text *Hadar* [b] 3 The meaning of the Hebrew for this word is uncertain; also in verses 23 and 32.

So Joseph went after his brothers and
found them near Dothan. 18But they
saw him in the distance, and before he
reached them, they plotted to kill him.
19"Here comes that dreamer!" they
said to each other. 20"Come now, let's
kill him and throw him into one of these
cisterns and say that a ferocious animal devoured him. Then we'll see what
comes of his dreams."
21When Reuben heard this, he tried to
rescue him from their hands. "Let's not
take his life," he said. 22"Don't shed any
blood. Throw him into this cistern here in
the wilderness, but don't lay a hand on
him." Reuben said this to rescue him from
them and take him back to his father.
23So when Joseph came to his brothers,
they stripped him of his robe — the ornate robe he was wearing — 24and they
took him and threw him into the cistern.
The cistern was empty; there was no water in it.
25As they sat down to eat their meal,
they looked up and saw a caravan of
Ishmaelites coming from Gilead. Their
camels were loaded with spices, balm
and myrrh, and they were on their way
to take them down to Egypt.
26Judah said to his brothers, "What will
we gain if we kill our brother and cover
up his blood? 27Come, let's sell him to the
Ishmaelites and not lay our hands on
him; after all, he is our brother, our own
flesh and blood." His brothers agreed.
28So when the Midianite merchants
came by, his brothers pulled Joseph up
out of the cistern and sold him for twenty shekels[a] of silver to the Ishmaelites,
who took him to Egypt.
29When Reuben returned to the cistern and saw that Joseph was not there,
he tore his clothes. 30He went back to his
brothers and said, "The boy isn't there!
Where can I turn now?"
31Then they got Joseph's robe, slaughtered a goat and dipped the robe in the
blood. 32They took the ornate robe back
to their father and said, "We found this.
Examine it to see whether it is your son's
robe."
33He recognized it and said, "It is my
son's robe! Some ferocious animal has
devoured him. Joseph has surely been
torn to pieces."
34Then Jacob tore his clothes, put
on sackcloth and mourned for his son
many days. 35All his sons and daughters
came to comfort him, but he refused to
be comforted. "No," he said, "I will continue to mourn until I join my son in the
grave." So his father wept for him.
36Meanwhile, the Midianites[b] sold Joseph in Egypt to Potiphar, one of Pharaoh's officials, the captain of the guard.

Judah and Tamar

38 At that time, Judah left his brothers and went down to stay with a
man of Adullam named Hirah. 2There
Judah met the daughter of a Canaanite
man named Shua. He married her and
made love to her; 3she became pregnant
and gave birth to a son, who was named
Er. 4She conceived again and gave birth
to a son and named him Onan. 5She gave
birth to still another son and named him
Shelah. It was at Kezib that she gave
birth to him.
6Judah got a wife for Er, his firstborn,
and her name was Tamar. 7But Er, Judah's firstborn, was wicked in the LORD's
sight; so the LORD put him to death.
8Then Judah said to Onan, "Sleep with
your brother's wife and fulfill your duty
to her as a brother-in-law to raise up offspring for your brother." 9But Onan knew
that the child would not be his; so whenever he slept with his brother's wife, he
spilled his semen on the ground to keep
from providing offspring for his brother.
10What he did was wicked in the LORD's
sight; so the LORD put him to death also.
11Judah then said to his daughter-
in-law Tamar, "Live as a widow in your
father's household until my son Shelah
grows up." For he thought, "He may die
too, just like his brothers." So Tamar
went to live in her father's household.
12After a long time Judah's wife, the
daughter of Shua, died. When Judah had
recovered from his grief, he went up to
Timnah, to the men who were shearing
his sheep, and his friend Hirah the Adullamite went with him.
13When Tamar was told, "Your father-
in-law is on his way to Timnah to shear
his sheep," 14she took off her widow's
clothes, covered herself with a veil to disguise herself, and then sat down at the
entrance to Enaim, which is on the road
to Timnah. For she saw that, though Shelah had now grown up, she had not been
given to him as his wife.
15When Judah saw her, he thought she
was a prostitute, for she had covered
her face. 16Not realizing that she was his
daughter-in-law, he went over to her by

[a] *28* That is, about 8 ounces or about 230 grams [b] *36* Samaritan Pentateuch, Septuagint, Vulgate and Syriac (see also verse 28); Masoretic Text *Medanites*

the roadside and said, "Come now, let
me sleep with you."
"And what will you give me to sleep
with you?" she asked.
17"I'll send you a young goat from my
flock," he said.
"Will you give me something as a
pledge until you send it?" she asked.
18He said, "What pledge should I give
you?"
"Your seal and its cord, and the staff
in your hand," she answered. So he gave
them to her and slept with her, and she
became pregnant by him. 19After she left,
she took off her veil and put on her widow's clothes again.
20Meanwhile Judah sent the young goat
by his friend the Adullamite in order to
get his pledge back from the woman, but
he did not find her. 21He asked the men
who lived there, "Where is the shrine prostitute who was beside the road at Enaim?"
"There hasn't been any shrine prostitute here," they said.
22So he went back to Judah and said,
"I didn't find her. Besides, the men who
lived there said, 'There hasn't been any
shrine prostitute here.' "
23Then Judah said, "Let her keep what
she has, or we will become a laughingstock. After all, I did send her this young
goat, but you didn't find her."
24About three months later Judah was
told, "Your daughter-in-law Tamar is
guilty of prostitution, and as a result she
is now pregnant."
Judah said, "Bring her out and have
her burned to death!"
25As she was being brought out, she
sent a message to her father-in-law.
"I am pregnant by the man who owns
these," she said. And she added, "See if
you recognize whose seal and cord and
staff these are."
26Judah recognized them and said,
"She is more righteous than I, since I
wouldn't give her to my son Shelah." And
he did not sleep with her again.
27When the time came for her to give
birth, there were twin boys in her womb.
28As she was giving birth, one of them
put out his hand; so the midwife took
a scarlet thread and tied it on his wrist
and said, "This one came out first." 29But
when he drew back his hand, his brother came out, and she said, "So this is
how you have broken out!" And he was
named Perez.[a] 30Then his brother, who
had the scarlet thread on his wrist, came
out. And he was named Zerah.[b]

Joseph and Potiphar's Wife

39 Now Joseph had been taken down
to Egypt. Potiphar, an Egyptian
who was one of Pharaoh's officials, the
captain of the guard, bought him from
the Ishmaelites who had taken him
there.
2The LORD was with Joseph so that he
prospered, and he lived in the house of
his Egyptian master. 3When his master
saw that the LORD was with him and
that the LORD gave him success in everything he did, 4Joseph found favor in
his eyes and became his attendant. Potiphar put him in charge of his household,
and he entrusted to his care everything
he owned. 5From the time he put him in
charge of his household and of all that
he owned, the LORD blessed the household of the Egyptian because of Joseph.
The blessing of the LORD was on everything Potiphar had, both in the house
and in the field. 6So Potiphar left everything he had in Joseph's care; with
Joseph in charge, he did not concern
himself with anything except the food
he ate.
Now Joseph was well-built and handsome, 7and after a while his master's
wife took notice of Joseph and said,
"Come to bed with me!"
8But he refused. "With me in charge,"
he told her, "my master does not concern
himself with anything in the house; everything he owns he has entrusted to
my care. 9No one is greater in this house
than I am. My master has withheld nothing from me except you, because you
are his wife. How then could I do such
a wicked thing and sin against God?"
10And though she spoke to Joseph day
after day, he refused to go to bed with
her or even be with her.
11One day he went into the house to
attend to his duties, and none of the
household servants was inside. 12She
caught him by his cloak and said, "Come
to bed with me!" But he left his cloak in
her hand and ran out of the house.
13When she saw that he had left his
cloak in her hand and had run out of
the house, 14she called her household
servants. "Look," she said to them, "this
Hebrew has been brought to us to make
sport of us! He came in here to sleep with
me, but I screamed. 15When he heard me
scream for help, he left his cloak beside
me and ran out of the house."
16She kept his cloak beside her until
his master came home. 17Then she told

[a] 29 *Perez* means *breaking out.* [b] 30 *Zerah* can mean *scarlet* or *brightness.*

him this story: "That Hebrew slave you brought us came to me to make sport of me. 18But as soon as I screamed for help, he left his cloak beside me and ran out of the house."

19When his master heard the story his wife told him, saying, "This is how your slave treated me," he burned with anger. 20Joseph's master took him and put him in prison, the place where the king's prisoners were confined.

But while Joseph was there in the prison, 21the LORD was with him; he showed him kindness and granted him favor in the eyes of the prison warden. 22So the warden put Joseph in charge of all those held in the prison, and he was made responsible for all that was done there. 23The warden paid no attention to anything under Joseph's care, because the LORD was with Joseph and gave him success in whatever he did.

The Cupbearer and the Baker

40 Some time later, the cupbearer and the baker of the king of Egypt offended their master, the king of Egypt. 2Pharaoh was angry with his two officials, the chief cupbearer and the chief baker, 3and put them in custody in the house of the captain of the guard, in the same prison where Joseph was confined. 4The captain of the guard assigned them to Joseph, and he attended them.

After they had been in custody for some time, 5each of the two men — the cupbearer and the baker of the king of Egypt, who were being held in prison — had a dream the same night, and each dream had a meaning of its own.

6When Joseph came to them the next morning, he saw that they were dejected. 7So he asked Pharaoh's officials who were in custody with him in his master's house, "Why do you look so sad today?"

8"We both had dreams," they answered, "but there is no one to interpret them."

Then Joseph said to them, "Do not interpretations belong to God? Tell me your dreams."

9So the chief cupbearer told Joseph his dream. He said to him, "In my dream I saw a vine in front of me, 10and on the vine were three branches. As soon as it budded, it blossomed, and its clusters ripened into grapes. 11Pharaoh's cup was in my hand, and I took the grapes, squeezed them into Pharaoh's cup and put the cup in his hand."

12"This is what it means," Joseph said to him. "The three branches are three days. 13Within three days Pharaoh will lift up your head and restore you to your position, and you will put Pharaoh's cup in his hand, just as you used to do when you were his cupbearer. 14But when all goes well with you, remember me and show me kindness; mention me to Pharaoh and get me out of this prison. 15I was forcibly carried off from the land of the Hebrews, and even here I have done nothing to deserve being put in a dungeon."

16When the chief baker saw that Joseph had given a favorable interpretation, he said to Joseph, "I too had a dream: On my head were three baskets of bread.[a] 17In the top basket were all kinds of baked goods for Pharaoh, but the birds were eating them out of the basket on my head."

18"This is what it means," Joseph said. "The three baskets are three days. 19Within three days Pharaoh will lift off your head and impale your body on a pole. And the birds will eat away your flesh."

20Now the third day was Pharaoh's birthday, and he gave a feast for all his officials. He lifted up the heads of the chief cupbearer and the chief baker in the presence of his officials: 21He restored the chief cupbearer to his position, so that he once again put the cup into Pharaoh's hand — 22but he impaled the chief baker, just as Joseph had said to them in his interpretation.

23The chief cupbearer, however, did not remember Joseph; he forgot him.

Pharaoh's Dreams

41 When two full years had passed, Pharaoh had a dream: He was standing by the Nile, 2when out of the river there came up seven cows, sleek and fat, and they grazed among the reeds. 3After them, seven other cows, ugly and gaunt, came up out of the Nile and stood beside those on the riverbank. 4And the cows that were ugly and gaunt ate up the seven sleek, fat cows. Then Pharaoh woke up.

5He fell asleep again and had a second dream: Seven heads of grain, healthy and good, were growing on a single stalk. 6After them, seven other heads of grain sprouted — thin and scorched by the east wind. 7The thin heads of grain swallowed up the seven healthy, full heads. Then Pharaoh woke up; it had been a dream.

[a] 16 Or *three wicker baskets*

8In the morning his mind was troubled, so he sent for all the magicians and
wise men of Egypt. Pharaoh told them
his dreams, but no one could interpret
them for him.
9Then the chief cupbearer said to
Pharaoh, "Today I am reminded of my
shortcomings. 10Pharaoh was once angry
with his servants, and he imprisoned me
and the chief baker in the house of the
captain of the guard. 11Each of us had a
dream the same night, and each dream
had a meaning of its own. 12Now a young
Hebrew was there with us, a servant of
the captain of the guard. We told him
our dreams, and he interpreted them for
us, giving each man the interpretation
of his dream. 13And things turned out exactly as he interpreted them to us: I was
restored to my position, and the other
man was impaled."
14So Pharaoh sent for Joseph, and he
was quickly brought from the dungeon.
When he had shaved and changed his
clothes, he came before Pharaoh.
15Pharaoh said to Joseph, "I had a
dream, and no one can interpret it. But I
have heard it said of you that when you
hear a dream you can interpret it."
16"I cannot do it," Joseph replied to
Pharaoh, "but God will give Pharaoh the
answer he desires."
17Then Pharaoh said to Joseph, "In my
dream I was standing on the bank of the
Nile, 18when out of the river there came
up seven cows, fat and sleek, and they
grazed among the reeds. 19After them,
seven other cows came up — scrawny
and very ugly and lean. I had never seen
such ugly cows in all the land of Egypt.
20The lean, ugly cows ate up the seven
fat cows that came up first. 21But even
after they ate them, no one could tell
that they had done so; they looked just
as ugly as before. Then I woke up.
22"In my dream I saw seven heads
of grain, full and good, growing on a
single stalk. 23After them, seven other heads sprouted — withered and thin
and scorched by the east wind. 24The thin
heads of grain swallowed up the seven
good heads. I told this to the magicians,
but none of them could explain it to me."
25Then Joseph said to Pharaoh, "The
dreams of Pharaoh are one and the
same. God has revealed to Pharaoh what
he is about to do. 26The seven good cows
are seven years, and the seven good
heads of grain are seven years; it is one
and the same dream. 27The seven lean,
ugly cows that came up afterward are
seven years, and so are the seven worthless heads of grain scorched by the east
wind: They are seven years of famine.
28"It is just as I said to Pharaoh: God
has shown Pharaoh what he is about to
do. 29Seven years of great abundance are
coming throughout the land of Egypt,
30but seven years of famine will follow
them. Then all the abundance in Egypt
will be forgotten, and the famine will
ravage the land. 31The abundance in the
land will not be remembered, because
the famine that follows it will be so severe. 32The reason the dream was given
to Pharaoh in two forms is that the matter has been firmly decided by God, and
God will do it soon.
33"And now let Pharaoh look for a discerning and wise man and put him in
charge of the land of Egypt. 34Let Pharaoh appoint commissioners over the
land to take a fifth of the harvest of
Egypt during the seven years of abundance. 35They should collect all the food
of these good years that are coming and
store up the grain under the authority of
Pharaoh, to be kept in the cities for food.
36This food should be held in reserve for
the country, to be used during the sev-
en years of famine that will come upon
Egypt, so that the country may not be ruined by the famine."
37The plan seemed good to Pharaoh
and to all his officials. 38So Pharaoh
asked them, "Can we find anyone like
this man, one in whom is the spirit of
God[a]?"
39Then Pharaoh said to Joseph, "Since
God has made all this known to you,
there is no one so discerning and wise
as you. 40You shall be in charge of my
palace, and all my people are to submit
to your orders. Only with respect to the
throne will I be greater than you."

Joseph in Charge of Egypt

41So Pharaoh said to Joseph, "I hereby
put you in charge of the whole land of
Egypt." 42Then Pharaoh took his signet
ring from his finger and put it on Joseph's finger. He dressed him in robes of
fine linen and put a gold chain around
his neck. 43He had him ride in a chariot
as his second-in-command,[b] and people
shouted before him, "Make way[c]!" Thus
he put him in charge of the whole land
of Egypt.

[a] 38 Or *of the gods* [b] 43 Or *in the chariot of his second-in-command*; or *in his second chariot*
[c] 43 Or *Bow down*

44Then Pharaoh said to Joseph, "I am Pharaoh, but without your word no one will lift hand or foot in all Egypt." 45Pharaoh gave Joseph the name Zaphenath-Paneah and gave him Asenath daughter of Potiphera, priest of On,[a] to be his wife. And Joseph went throughout the land of Egypt.

46Joseph was thirty years old when he entered the service of Pharaoh king of Egypt. And Joseph went out from Pharaoh's presence and traveled throughout Egypt. 47During the seven years of abundance the land produced plentifully. 48Joseph collected all the food produced in those seven years of abundance in Egypt and stored it in the cities. In each city he put the food grown in the fields surrounding it. 49Joseph stored up huge quantities of grain, like the sand of the sea; it was so much that he stopped keeping records because it was beyond measure.

50Before the years of famine came, two sons were born to Joseph by Asenath daughter of Potiphera, priest of On. 51Joseph named his firstborn Manasseh[b] and said, "It is because God has made me forget all my trouble and all my father's household." 52The second son he named Ephraim[c] and said, "It is because God has made me fruitful in the land of my suffering."

53The seven years of abundance in Egypt came to an end, 54and the seven years of famine began, just as Joseph had said. There was famine in all the other lands, but in the whole land of Egypt there was food. 55When all Egypt began to feel the famine, the people cried to Pharaoh for food. Then Pharaoh told all the Egyptians, "Go to Joseph and do what he tells you."

56When the famine had spread over the whole country, Joseph opened all the storehouses and sold grain to the Egyptians, for the famine was severe throughout Egypt. 57And all the world came to Egypt to buy grain from Joseph, because the famine was severe everywhere.

Joseph's Brothers Go to Egypt

42 When Jacob learned that there was grain in Egypt, he said to his sons, "Why do you just keep looking at each other?" 2He continued, "I have heard that there is grain in Egypt. Go down there and buy some for us, so that we may live and not die."

3Then ten of Joseph's brothers went down to buy grain from Egypt. 4But Jacob did not send Benjamin, Joseph's brother, with the others, because he was afraid that harm might come to him. 5So Israel's sons were among those who went to buy grain, for there was famine in the land of Canaan also.

6Now Joseph was the governor of the land, the person who sold grain to all its people. So when Joseph's brothers arrived, they bowed down to him with their faces to the ground. 7As soon as Joseph saw his brothers, he recognized them, but he pretended to be a stranger and spoke harshly to them. "Where do you come from?" he asked.

"From the land of Canaan," they replied, "to buy food."

8Although Joseph recognized his brothers, they did not recognize him. 9Then he remembered his dreams about them and said to them, "You are spies! You have come to see where our land is unprotected."

10"No, my lord," they answered. "Your servants have come to buy food. 11We are all the sons of one man. Your servants are honest men, not spies."

12"No!" he said to them. "You have come to see where our land is unprotected."

13But they replied, "Your servants were twelve brothers, the sons of one man, who lives in the land of Canaan. The youngest is now with our father, and one is no more."

14Joseph said to them, "It is just as I told you: You are spies! 15And this is how you will be tested: As surely as Pharaoh lives, you will not leave this place unless your youngest brother comes here. 16Send one of your number to get your brother; the rest of you will be kept in prison, so that your words may be tested to see if you are telling the truth. If you are not, then as surely as Pharaoh lives, you are spies!" 17And he put them all in custody for three days.

18On the third day, Joseph said to them, "Do this and you will live, for I fear God: 19If you are honest men, let one of your brothers stay here in prison, while the rest of you go and take grain back for your starving households. 20But you must bring your youngest brother to me, so that your words may be verified and that you may not die." This they proceeded to do.

21They said to one another, "Surely we are being punished because of our

[a] 45 That is, Heliopolis; also in verse 50 [b] 51 *Manasseh* sounds like and may be derived from the Hebrew for *forget.* [c] 52 *Ephraim* sounds like the Hebrew for *twice fruitful.*

brother. We saw how distressed he was
when he pleaded with us for his life, but
we would not listen; that's why this distress has come on us."
22Reuben replied, "Didn't I tell you not
to sin against the boy? But you wouldn't
listen! Now we must give an accounting
for his blood." 23They did not realize that
Joseph could understand them, since he
was using an interpreter.
24He turned away from them and began to weep, but then came back and
spoke to them again. He had Simeon
taken from them and bound before their
eyes.
25Joseph gave orders to fill their bags
with grain, to put each man's silver back
in his sack, and to give them provisions
for their journey. After this was done for
them, 26they loaded their grain on their
donkeys and left.
27At the place where they stopped for
the night one of them opened his sack
to get feed for his donkey, and he saw
his silver in the mouth of his sack. 28"My
silver has been returned," he said to his
brothers. "Here it is in my sack."
Their hearts sank and they turned to
each other trembling and said, "What is
this that God has done to us?"
29When they came to their father Jacob in the land of Canaan, they told him
all that had happened to them. They
said, 30"The man who is lord over the
land spoke harshly to us and treated us
as though we were spying on the land.
31But we said to him, 'We are honest
men; we are not spies. 32We were twelve
brothers, sons of one father. One is no
more, and the youngest is now with our
father in Canaan.'
33"Then the man who is lord over the
land said to us, 'This is how I will know
whether you are honest men: Leave one
of your brothers here with me, and take
food for your starving households and
go. 34But bring your youngest brother to
me so I will know that you are not spies
but honest men. Then I will give your
brother back to you, and you can trade[a]
in the land.'"
35As they were emptying their sacks,
there in each man's sack was his pouch
of silver! When they and their father saw
the money pouches, they were frightened. 36Their father Jacob said to them,
"You have deprived me of my children.
Joseph is no more and Simeon is no
more, and now you want to take Benjamin. Everything is against me!"
37Then Reuben said to his father, "You
may put both of my sons to death if I do
not bring him back to you. Entrust him
to my care, and I will bring him back."
38But Jacob said, "My son will not
go down there with you; his brother is
dead and he is the only one left. If harm
comes to him on the journey you are taking, you will bring my gray head down to
the grave in sorrow."

The Second Journey to Egypt

43 Now the famine was still severe in
the land. 2So when they had eat-
en all the grain they had brought from
Egypt, their father said to them, "Go
back and buy us a little more food."
3But Judah said to him, "The man
warned us solemnly, 'You will not see my
face again unless your brother is with
you.' 4If you will send our brother along
with us, we will go down and buy food
for you. 5But if you will not send him, we
will not go down, because the man said
to us, 'You will not see my face again unless your brother is with you.'"
6Israel asked, "Why did you bring this
trouble on me by telling the man you
had another brother?"
7They replied, "The man questioned us
closely about ourselves and our family.
'Is your father still living?' he asked us.
'Do you have another brother?' We simply answered his questions. How were we
to know he would say, 'Bring your brother down here'?"
8Then Judah said to Israel his father, "Send the boy along with me and
we will go at once, so that we and you
and our children may live and not die.
9I myself will guarantee his safety; you
can hold me personally responsible for
him. If I do not bring him back to you
and set him here before you, I will bear
the blame before you all my life. 10As it
is, if we had not delayed, we could have
gone and returned twice."
11Then their father Israel said to them,
"If it must be, then do this: Put some of the
best products of the land in your bags and
take them down to the man as a gift—a
little balm and a little honey, some spices
and myrrh, some pistachio nuts and almonds. 12Take double the amount of silver
with you, for you must return the silver
that was put back into the mouths of your
sacks. Perhaps it was a mistake. 13Take
your brother also and go back to the man
at once. 14And may God Almighty[b] grant
you mercy before the man so that he will

[a] 34 Or *move about freely* [b] 14 Hebrew *El-Shaddai*

let your other brother and Benjamin come
back with you. As for me, if I am bereaved,
I am bereaved."
15So the men took the gifts and double the amount of silver, and Benjamin
also. They hurried down to Egypt and
presented themselves to Joseph. 16When
Joseph saw Benjamin with them, he said
to the steward of his house, "Take these
men to my house, slaughter an animal
and prepare a meal; they are to eat with
me at noon."
17The man did as Joseph told him and
took the men to Joseph's house. 18Now
the men were frightened when they
were taken to his house. They thought,
"We were brought here because of the
silver that was put back into our sacks
the first time. He wants to attack us and
overpower us and seize us as slaves and
take our donkeys."
19So they went up to Joseph's steward
and spoke to him at the entrance to the
house. 20"We beg your pardon, our lord,"
they said, "we came down here the first
time to buy food. 21But at the place where
we stopped for the night we opened our
sacks and each of us found his silver —
the exact weight — in the mouth of his
sack. So we have brought it back with us.
22We have also brought additional silver
with us to buy food. We don't know who
put our silver in our sacks."
23"It's all right," he said. "Don't be
afraid. Your God, the God of your father,
has given you treasure in your sacks; I
received your silver." Then he brought
Simeon out to them.
24The steward took the men into Joseph's house, gave them water to wash
their feet and provided fodder for their
donkeys. 25They prepared their gifts for
Joseph's arrival at noon, because they
had heard that they were to eat there.
26When Joseph came home, they presented to him the gifts they had brought
into the house, and they bowed down before him to the ground. 27He asked them
how they were, and then he said, "How
is your aged father you told me about?
Is he still living?"
28They replied, "Your servant our father is still alive and well." And they
bowed down, prostrating themselves
before him.
29As he looked about and saw his
brother Benjamin, his own mother's son,
he asked, "Is this your youngest brother,
the one you told me about?" And he said,
"God be gracious to you, my son." 30Deep-
ly moved at the sight of his brother, Joseph hurried out and looked for a place
to weep. He went into his private room
and wept there.
31After he had washed his face, he
came out and, controlling himself, said,
"Serve the food."
32They served him by himself, the
brothers by themselves, and the Egyptians who ate with him by themselves,
because Egyptians could not eat with Hebrews, for that is detestable to Egyptians.
33The men had been seated before him in
the order of their ages, from the firstborn
to the youngest; and they looked at each
other in astonishment. 34When portions
were served to them from Joseph's table, Benjamin's portion was five times as
much as anyone else's. So they feasted
and drank freely with him.

A Silver Cup in a Sack

44 Now Joseph gave these instructions to the steward of his house:
"Fill the men's sacks with as much food
as they can carry, and put each man's silver in the mouth of his sack. 2Then put
my cup, the silver one, in the mouth of the
youngest one's sack, along with the silver
for his grain." And he did as Joseph said.
3As morning dawned, the men were
sent on their way with their donkeys.
4They had not gone far from the city
when Joseph said to his steward, "Go
after those men at once, and when you
catch up with them, say to them, 'Why
have you repaid good with evil? 5Isn't
this the cup my master drinks from and
also uses for divination? This is a wicked
thing you have done.'"
6When he caught up with them, he repeated these words to them. 7But they
said to him, "Why does my lord say such
things? Far be it from your servants to
do anything like that! 8We even brought
back to you from the land of Canaan the
silver we found inside the mouths of our
sacks. So why would we steal silver or
gold from your master's house? 9If any
of your servants is found to have it, he
will die; and the rest of us will become
my lord's slaves."
10"Very well, then," he said, "let it be as
you say. Whoever is found to have it will
become my slave; the rest of you will be
free from blame."
11Each of them quickly lowered his
sack to the ground and opened it. 12Then
the steward proceeded to search, beginning with the oldest and ending with
the youngest. And the cup was found in
Benjamin's sack. 13At this, they tore their
clothes. Then they all loaded their donkeys and returned to the city.

14 Joseph was still in the house when
Judah and his brothers came in, and
they threw themselves to the ground before him. 15 Joseph said to them, "What
is this you have done? Don't you know
that a man like me can find things out
by divination?"
16 "What can we say to my lord?" Judah
replied. "What can we say? How can we
prove our innocence? God has uncovered your servants' guilt. We are now my
lord's slaves — we ourselves and the one
who was found to have the cup."
17 But Joseph said, "Far be it from me
to do such a thing! Only the man who
was found to have the cup will become
my slave. The rest of you, go back to your
father in peace."
18 Then Judah went up to him and said:
"Pardon your servant, my lord, let me
speak a word to my lord. Do not be angry
with your servant, though you are equal
to Pharaoh himself. 19 My lord asked
his servants, 'Do you have a father or a
brother?' 20 And we answered, 'We have
an aged father, and there is a young son
born to him in his old age. His brother is
dead, and he is the only one of his mother's sons left, and his father loves him.'
21 "Then you said to your servants,
'Bring him down to me so I can see him
for myself.' 22 And we said to my lord,
'The boy cannot leave his father; if he
leaves him, his father will die.' 23 But you
told your servants, 'Unless your youngest
brother comes down with you, you will
not see my face again.' 24 When we went
back to your servant my father, we told
him what my lord had said.
25 "Then our father said, 'Go back and
buy a little more food.' 26 But we said, 'We
cannot go down. Only if our youngest
brother is with us will we go. We cannot
see the man's face unless our youngest
brother is with us.'
27 "Your servant my father said to us,
'You know that my wife bore me two
sons. 28 One of them went away from me,
and I said, "He has surely been torn to
pieces." And I have not seen him since.
29 If you take this one from me too and
harm comes to him, you will bring my
gray head down to the grave in misery.'
30 "So now, if the boy is not with us
when I go back to your servant my father, and if my father, whose life is closely bound up with the boy's life, 31 sees that
the boy isn't there, he will die. Your servants will bring the gray head of our father down to the grave in sorrow. 32 Your
servant guaranteed the boy's safety to
my father. I said, 'If I do not bring him
back to you, I will bear the blame before
you, my father, all my life!'
33 "Now then, please let your servant
remain here as my lord's slave in place
of the boy, and let the boy return with his
brothers. 34 How can I go back to my father if the boy is not with me? No! Do not
let me see the misery that would come
on my father."

Joseph Makes Himself Known

45 Then Joseph could no longer control himself before all his attendants, and he cried out, "Have everyone
leave my presence!" So there was no
one with Joseph when he made himself
known to his brothers. 2 And he wept so
loudly that the Egyptians heard him,
and Pharaoh's household heard about it.
3 Joseph said to his brothers, "I am Joseph! Is my father still living?" But his
brothers were not able to answer him, because they were terrified at his presence.
4 Then Joseph said to his brothers,
"Come close to me." When they had done
so, he said, "I am your brother Joseph, the
one you sold into Egypt! 5 And now, do not
be distressed and do not be angry with
yourselves for selling me here, because it
was to save lives that God sent me ahead
of you. 6 For two years now there has been
famine in the land, and for the next five
years there will be no plowing and reap-
ing. 7 But God sent me ahead of you to preserve for you a remnant on earth and to
save your lives by a great deliverance.[a]
8 "So then, it was not you who sent me
here, but God. He made me father to
Pharaoh, lord of his entire household
and ruler of all Egypt. 9 Now hurry back
to my father and say to him, 'This is what
your son Joseph says: God has made me
lord of all Egypt. Come down to me;
don't delay. 10 You shall live in the region
of Goshen and be near me — you, your
children and grandchildren, your flocks
and herds, and all you have. 11 I will provide for you there, because five years of
famine are still to come. Otherwise you
and your household and all who belong
to you will become destitute.'
12 "You can see for yourselves, and so
can my brother Benjamin, that it is really I who am speaking to you. 13 Tell my
father about all the honor accorded me
in Egypt and about everything you have
seen. And bring my father down here
quickly."

[a] 7 Or *save you as a great band of survivors*

14Then he threw his arms around his
brother Benjamin and wept, and Benjamin embraced him, weeping. 15And he
kissed all his brothers and wept over them.
Afterward his brothers talked with him.

16When the news reached Phar-
aoh's palace that Joseph's brothers had
come, Pharaoh and all his officials were
pleased. 17Pharaoh said to Joseph, "Tell
your brothers, 'Do this: Load your animals and return to the land of Canaan,
18and bring your father and your families back to me. I will give you the best of
the land of Egypt and you can enjoy the
fat of the land.'

19"You are also directed to tell them,
'Do this: Take some carts from Egypt
for your children and your wives, and
get your father and come. 20Never mind
about your belongings, because the best
of all Egypt will be yours.'"

21So the sons of Israel did this. Joseph
gave them carts, as Pharaoh had commanded, and he also gave them provisions for their journey. 22To each of them
he gave new clothing, but to Benjamin
he gave three hundred shekels[a] of silver and five sets of clothes. 23And this is
what he sent to his father: ten donkeys
loaded with the best things of Egypt,
and ten female donkeys loaded with
grain and bread and other provisions for
his journey. 24Then he sent his brothers
away, and as they were leaving he said
to them, "Don't quarrel on the way!"

25So they went up out of Egypt and
came to their father Jacob in the land of
Canaan. 26They told him, "Joseph is still
alive! In fact, he is ruler of all Egypt."
Jacob was stunned; he did not believe
them. 27But when they told him everything Joseph had said to them, and
when he saw the carts Joseph had sent to
carry him back, the spirit of their father
Jacob revived. 28And Israel said, "I'm
convinced! My son Joseph is still alive. I
will go and see him before I die."

Jacob Goes to Egypt

46 So Israel set out with all that was
his, and when he reached Beersheba, he offered sacrifices to the God of
his father Isaac.

2And God spoke to Israel in a vision at
night and said, "Jacob! Jacob!"

"Here I am," he replied.

3"I am God, the God of your father,"
he said. "Do not be afraid to go down to
Egypt, for I will make you into a great
nation there. 4I will go down to Egypt
with you, and I will surely bring you
back again. And Joseph's own hand will
close your eyes."

5Then Jacob left Beersheba, and Israel's sons took their father Jacob and their
children and their wives in the carts that
Pharaoh had sent to transport him. 6So
Jacob and all his offspring went to Egypt,
taking with them their livestock and the
possessions they had acquired in Canaan.
7Jacob brought with him to Egypt his sons
and grandsons and his daughters and
granddaughters — all his offspring.

8These are the names of the sons of
Israel (Jacob and his descendants) who
went to Egypt:

Reuben the firstborn of Jacob.
9 The sons of Reuben:
Hanok, Pallu, Hezron and Karmi.
10 The sons of Simeon:
Jemuel, Jamin, Ohad, Jakin, Zohar and Shaul the son of a Canaanite woman.
11 The sons of Levi:
Gershon, Kohath and Merari.
12 The sons of Judah:
Er, Onan, Shelah, Perez and Zerah
(but Er and Onan had died in the
land of Canaan).
The sons of Perez:
Hezron and Hamul.
13 The sons of Issachar:
Tola, Puah,[b] Jashub[c] and Shimron.
14 The sons of Zebulun:
Sered, Elon and Jahleel.

15These were the sons Leah bore to Jacob in Paddan Aram,[d] besides his daughter Dinah. These sons and daughters of
his were thirty-three in all.

16 The sons of Gad:
Zephon,[e] Haggi, Shuni, Ezbon, Eri,
Arodi and Areli.
17 The sons of Asher:
Imnah, Ishvah, Ishvi and Beriah.
Their sister was Serah.
The sons of Beriah:
Heber and Malkiel.

18These were the children born to Jacob by Zilpah, whom Laban had given to
his daughter Leah — sixteen in all.

[a] *22* That is, about 7 1/2 pounds or about 3.5 kilograms [b] *13* Samaritan Pentateuch and Syriac (see also 1 Chron. 7:1); Masoretic Text *Puvah* [c] *13* Samaritan Pentateuch and some Septuagint manuscripts (see also Num. 26:24 and 1 Chron. 7:1); Masoretic Text *Iob* [d] *15* That is, Northwest Mesopotamia [e] *16* Samaritan Pentateuch and Septuagint (see also Num. 26:15); Masoretic Text *Ziphion*

19 The sons of Jacob's wife Rachel:
Joseph and Benjamin. 20 In Egypt,
Manasseh and Ephraim were
born to Joseph by Asenath daughter of Potiphera, priest of On.[a]
21 The sons of Benjamin:
Bela, Beker, Ashbel, Gera, Naaman, Ehi, Rosh, Muppim, Huppim
and Ard.
22 These were the sons of Rachel who
were born to Jacob — fourteen in all.

23 The son of Dan:
Hushim.
24 The sons of Naphtali:
Jahziel, Guni, Jezer and Shillem.
25 These were the sons born to Jacob
by Bilhah, whom Laban had given to his
daughter Rachel — seven in all.

26 All those who went to Egypt with Jacob — those who were his direct descendants, not counting his sons' wives —
numbered sixty-six persons. 27 With the
two sons[b] who had been born to Joseph
in Egypt, the members of Jacob's family, which went to Egypt, were seventy[c]
in all.

28 Now Jacob sent Judah ahead of him
to Joseph to get directions to Goshen.
When they arrived in the region of Goshen, 29 Joseph had his chariot made
ready and went to Goshen to meet his father Israel. As soon as Joseph appeared
before him, he threw his arms around
his father[d] and wept for a long time.
30 Israel said to Joseph, "Now I am
ready to die, since I have seen for myself
that you are still alive."
31 Then Joseph said to his brothers
and to his father's household, "I will go
up and speak to Pharaoh and will say
to him, 'My brothers and my father's
household, who were living in the land
of Canaan, have come to me. 32 The men
are shepherds; they tend livestock, and
they have brought along their flocks and
herds and everything they own.' 33 When
Pharaoh calls you in and asks, 'What is
your occupation?' 34 you should answer,
'Your servants have tended livestock
from our boyhood on, just as our fathers
did.' Then you will be allowed to settle in
the region of Goshen, for all shepherds
are detestable to the Egyptians."
47 Joseph went and told Pharaoh,
"My father and brothers, with
their flocks and herds and everything
they own, have come from the land of
Canaan and are now in Goshen." 2 He
chose five of his brothers and presented
them before Pharaoh.
3 Pharaoh asked the brothers, "What is
your occupation?"
"Your servants are shepherds," they
replied to Pharaoh, "just as our fathers
were." 4 They also said to him, "We have
come to live here for a while, because
the famine is severe in Canaan and
your servants' flocks have no pasture.
So now, please let your servants settle in
Goshen."
5 Pharaoh said to Joseph, "Your father
and your brothers have come to you,
6 and the land of Egypt is before you; settle your father and your brothers in the
best part of the land. Let them live in
Goshen. And if you know of any among
them with special ability, put them in
charge of my own livestock."
7 Then Joseph brought his father Jacob
in and presented him before Pharaoh.
After Jacob blessed[e] Pharaoh, 8 Pharaoh
asked him, "How old are you?"
9 And Jacob said to Pharaoh, "The
years of my pilgrimage are a hundred
and thirty. My years have been few and
difficult, and they do not equal the years
of the pilgrimage of my fathers." 10 Then
Jacob blessed[f] Pharaoh and went out
from his presence.
11 So Joseph settled his father and his
brothers in Egypt and gave them property in the best part of the land, the district of Rameses, as Pharaoh directed.
12 Joseph also provided his father and his
brothers and all his father's household
with food, according to the number of
their children.

Joseph and the Famine

13 There was no food, however, in the
whole region because the famine was
severe; both Egypt and Canaan wasted
away because of the famine. 14 Joseph
collected all the money that was to be
found in Egypt and Canaan in payment
for the grain they were buying, and he
brought it to Pharaoh's palace. 15 When
the money of the people of Egypt and
Canaan was gone, all Egypt came to Joseph and said, "Give us food. Why should
we die before your eyes? Our money is all
gone."
16 "Then bring your livestock," said Joseph. "I will sell you food in exchange
for your livestock, since your money is

[a] 20 That is, Heliopolis [b] 27 Hebrew; Septuagint *the nine children* [c] 27 Hebrew (see also Exodus 1:5 and note); Septuagint (see also Acts 7:14) *seventy-five* [d] 29 Hebrew *around him* [e] 7 Or *greeted* [f] 10 Or *said farewell to*

gone." 17So they brought their livestock to Joseph, and he gave them food in exchange for their horses, their sheep and goats, their cattle and donkeys. And he brought them through that year with food in exchange for all their livestock.

18When that year was over, they came to him the following year and said, "We cannot hide from our lord the fact that since our money is gone and our livestock belongs to you, there is nothing left for our lord except our bodies and our land. 19Why should we perish before your eyes—we and our land as well? Buy us and our land in exchange for food, and we with our land will be in bondage to Pharaoh. Give us seed so that we may live and not die, and that the land may not become desolate."

20So Joseph bought all the land in Egypt for Pharaoh. The Egyptians, one and all, sold their fields, because the famine was too severe for them. The land became Pharaoh's, 21and Joseph reduced the people to servitude,[a] from one end of Egypt to the other. 22However, he did not buy the land of the priests, because they received a regular allotment from Pharaoh and had food enough from the allotment Pharaoh gave them. That is why they did not sell their land.

23Joseph said to the people, "Now that I have bought you and your land today for Pharaoh, here is seed for you so you can plant the ground. 24But when the crop comes in, give a fifth of it to Pharaoh. The other four-fifths you may keep as seed for the fields and as food for yourselves and your households and your children."

25"You have saved our lives," they said. "May we find favor in the eyes of our lord; we will be in bondage to Pharaoh."

26So Joseph established it as a law concerning land in Egypt—still in force today—that a fifth of the produce belongs to Pharaoh. It was only the land of the priests that did not become Pharaoh's.

27Now the Israelites settled in Egypt in the region of Goshen. They acquired property there and were fruitful and increased greatly in number.

28Jacob lived in Egypt seventeen years, and the years of his life were a hundred and forty-seven. 29When the time drew near for Israel to die, he called for his son Joseph and said to him, "If I have found favor in your eyes, put your hand under my thigh and promise that you will show me kindness and faithfulness. Do not bury me in Egypt, 30but when I rest with my fathers, carry me out of Egypt and bury me where they are buried."

"I will do as you say," he said.

31"Swear to me," he said. Then Joseph swore to him, and Israel worshiped as he leaned on the top of his staff.[b]

Manasseh and Ephraim

48 Some time later Joseph was told, "Your father is ill." So he took his two sons Manasseh and Ephraim along with him. 2When Jacob was told, "Your son Joseph has come to you," Israel rallied his strength and sat up on the bed.

3Jacob said to Joseph, "God Almighty[c] appeared to me at Luz in the land of Canaan, and there he blessed me 4and said to me, 'I am going to make you fruitful and increase your numbers. I will make you a community of peoples, and I will give this land as an everlasting possession to your descendants after you.'

5"Now then, your two sons born to you in Egypt before I came to you here will be reckoned as mine; Ephraim and Manasseh will be mine, just as Reuben and Simeon are mine. 6Any children born to you after them will be yours; in the territory they inherit they will be reckoned under the names of their brothers. 7As I was returning from Paddan,[d] to my sorrow Rachel died in the land of Canaan while we were still on the way, a little distance from Ephrath. So I buried her there beside the road to Ephrath" (that is, Bethlehem).

8When Israel saw the sons of Joseph, he asked, "Who are these?"

9"They are the sons God has given me here," Joseph said to his father.

Then Israel said, "Bring them to me so I may bless them."

10Now Israel's eyes were failing because of old age, and he could hardly see. So Joseph brought his sons close to him, and his father kissed them and embraced them.

11Israel said to Joseph, "I never expected to see your face again, and now God has allowed me to see your children too."

12Then Joseph removed them from Israel's knees and bowed down with his face to the ground. 13And Joseph took both of them, Ephraim on his right

[a] 21 Samaritan Pentateuch and Septuagint (see also Vulgate); Masoretic Text *and he moved the people into the cities* [b] 31 Or *Israel bowed down at the head of his bed* [c] 3 Hebrew *El-Shaddai*
[d] 7 That is, Northwest Mesopotamia

toward Israel's left hand and Manasseh
on his left toward Israel's right hand,
and brought them close to him. 14 But Israel reached out his right hand and put
it on Ephraim's head, though he was the
younger, and crossing his arms, he put
his left hand on Manasseh's head, even
though Manasseh was the firstborn.
15 Then he blessed Joseph and said,

"May the God before whom my fathers
Abraham and Isaac walked
faithfully,
the God who has been my shepherd
all my life to this day,
16 the Angel who has delivered me from
all harm
— may he bless these boys.
May they be called by my name
and the names of my fathers
Abraham and Isaac,
and may they increase greatly
on the earth."

17 When Joseph saw his father placing
his right hand on Ephraim's head he was
displeased; so he took hold of his father's
hand to move it from Ephraim's head to
Manasseh's head. 18 Joseph said to him,
"No, my father, this one is the firstborn;
put your right hand on his head."
19 But his father refused and said, "I
know, my son, I know. He too will become a people, and he too will become
great. Nevertheless, his younger brother
will be greater than he, and his descendants will become a group of nations."
20 He blessed them that day and said,

"In your[a] name will Israel pronounce
this blessing:
'May God make you like Ephraim
and Manasseh.'"

So he put Ephraim ahead of Manasseh.
21 Then Israel said to Joseph, "I am
about to die, but God will be with you[b]
and take you[b] back to the land of your[b]
fathers. 22 And to you I give one more
ridge of land[c] than to your brothers, the
ridge I took from the Amorites with my
sword and my bow."

Jacob Blesses His Sons

49 Then Jacob called for his sons and
said: "Gather around so I can tell
you what will happen to you in days to
come.

2 "Assemble and listen, sons of Jacob;
listen to your father Israel.

3 "Reuben, you are my firstborn,
my might, the first sign of my
strength,
excelling in honor, excelling in
power.
4 Turbulent as the waters, you will no
longer excel,
for you went up onto your father's
bed,
onto my couch and defiled it.

5 "Simeon and Levi are brothers —
their swords[d] are weapons of
violence.
6 Let me not enter their council,
let me not join their assembly,
for they have killed men in their
anger
and hamstrung oxen as they
pleased.
7 Cursed be their anger, so fierce,
and their fury, so cruel!
I will scatter them in Jacob
and disperse them in Israel.

8 "Judah,[e] your brothers will praise
you;
your hand will be on the neck of
your enemies;
your father's sons will bow down to
you.
9 You are a lion's cub, Judah;
you return from the prey, my son.
Like a lion he crouches and lies down,
like a lioness — who dares to rouse
him?
10 The scepter will not depart from
Judah,
nor the ruler's staff from between
his feet,[f]
until he to whom it belongs[g] shall
come
and the obedience of the nations
shall be his.
11 He will tether his donkey to a vine,
his colt to the choicest branch;
he will wash his garments in wine,
his robes in the blood of grapes.
12 His eyes will be darker than wine,
his teeth whiter than milk.[h]

13 "Zebulun will live by the seashore
and become a haven for ships;
his border will extend toward
Sidon.

[a] *20* The Hebrew is singular. [b] *21* The Hebrew is plural. [c] *22* The Hebrew for *ridge of land* is identical with the place name Shechem. [d] *5* The meaning of the Hebrew for this word is uncertain. [e] *8* *Judah* sounds like and may be derived from the Hebrew for *praise.* [f] *10* Or *from his descendants* [g] *10* Or *to whom tribute belongs*; the meaning of the Hebrew for this phrase is uncertain. [h] *12* Or *will be dull from wine, / his teeth white from milk*

14 "Issachar is a rawboned[a] donkey
lying down among the sheep pens.[b]
15 When he sees how good is his resting place
and how pleasant is his land,
he will bend his shoulder to the burden
and submit to forced labor.

16 "Dan[c] will provide justice for his people
as one of the tribes of Israel.
17 Dan will be a snake by the roadside,
a viper along the path,
that bites the horse's heels
so that its rider tumbles backward.

18 "I look for your deliverance, LORD.

19 "Gad[d] will be attacked by a band of raiders,
but he will attack them at their heels.

20 "Asher's food will be rich;
he will provide delicacies fit for a king.

21 "Naphtali is a doe set free
that bears beautiful fawns.[e]

22 "Joseph is a fruitful vine,
a fruitful vine near a spring,
whose branches climb over a wall.[f]
23 With bitterness archers attacked him;
they shot at him with hostility.
24 But his bow remained steady,
his strong arms stayed[g] limber,
because of the hand of the Mighty One of Jacob,
because of the Shepherd, the Rock of Israel,
25 because of your father's God, who helps you,
because of the Almighty,[h] who blesses you
with blessings of the skies above,
blessings of the deep springs below,
blessings of the breast and womb.
26 Your father's blessings are greater
than the blessings of the ancient mountains,
than[i] the bounty of the age-old hills.
Let all these rest on the head of Joseph,
on the brow of the prince among[j] his brothers.

27 "Benjamin is a ravenous wolf;
in the morning he devours the prey,
in the evening he divides the plunder."

28 All these are the twelve tribes of Israel, and this is what their father said to
them when he blessed them, giving each
the blessing appropriate to him.

The Death of Jacob

29 Then he gave them these instructions: "I am about to be gathered to
my people. Bury me with my fathers in
the cave in the field of Ephron the Hittite, 30 the cave in the field of Machpelah,
near Mamre in Canaan, which Abraham
bought along with the field as a burial
place from Ephron the Hittite. 31 There
Abraham and his wife Sarah were buried, there Isaac and his wife Rebekah
were buried, and there I buried Leah.
32 The field and the cave in it were bought
from the Hittites.[k]"

33 When Jacob had finished giving instructions to his sons, he drew his feet up
into the bed, breathed his last and was
gathered to his people.

50 Joseph threw himself on his father and wept over him and kissed
him. 2 Then Joseph directed the physicians in his service to embalm his father
Israel. So the physicians embalmed him,
3 taking a full forty days, for that was
the time required for embalming. And
the Egyptians mourned for him seventy days.

4 When the days of mourning had
passed, Joseph said to Pharaoh's court,
"If I have found favor in your eyes, speak
to Pharaoh for me. Tell him, 5 'My father
made me swear an oath and said, "I am
about to die; bury me in the tomb I dug
for myself in the land of Canaan." Now
let me go up and bury my father; then I
will return.'"

6 Pharaoh said, "Go up and bury your
father, as he made you swear to do."

7 So Joseph went up to bury his father.
All Pharaoh's officials accompanied
him — the dignitaries of his court and all
the dignitaries of Egypt — 8 besides all
the members of Joseph's household and
his brothers and those belonging to his
father's household. Only their children

[a] 14 Or *strong* [b] 14 Or *the campfires*; or *the saddlebags* [c] 16 *Dan* here means *he provides justice.* [d] 19 *Gad* sounds like the Hebrew for *attack* and also for *band of raiders.* [e] 21 Or *free; / he utters beautiful words* [f] 22 Or *Joseph is a wild colt, / a wild colt near a spring, / a wild donkey on a terraced hill* [g] 23,24 Or *archers will attack . . . will shoot . . . will remain . . . will stay* [h] 25 Hebrew *Shaddai* [i] 26 Or *of my progenitors, / as great as* [j] 26 Or *of the one separated from* [k] 32 Or *the descendants of Heth*

and their flocks and herds were left in
Goshen. 9Chariots and horsemen[a] also
went up with him. It was a very large
company.
10When they reached the threshing
floor of Atad, near the Jordan, they la-
mented loudly and bitterly; and there
Joseph observed a seven-day period
of mourning for his father. 11When the
Canaanites who lived there saw the
mourning at the threshing floor of Atad,
they said, "The Egyptians are holding a
solemn ceremony of mourning." That is
why that place near the Jordan is called
Abel Mizraim.[b]
12So Jacob's sons did as he had commanded them: 13They carried him to
the land of Canaan and buried him in
the cave in the field of Machpelah, near
Mamre, which Abraham had bought
along with the field as a burial place
from Ephron the Hittite. 14After burying
his father, Joseph returned to Egypt, together with his brothers and all the others who had gone with him to bury his
father.

Joseph Reassures His Brothers

15When Joseph's brothers saw that
their father was dead, they said, "What
if Joseph holds a grudge against us and
pays us back for all the wrongs we did to
him?" 16So they sent word to Joseph, saying, "Your father left these instructions
before he died: 17'This is what you are to
say to Joseph: I ask you to forgive your
brothers the sins and the wrongs they
committed in treating you so badly.' Now
please forgive the sins of the servants of
the God of your father." When their message came to him, Joseph wept.
18His brothers then came and threw
themselves down before him. "We are
your slaves," they said.
19But Joseph said to them, "Don't be
afraid. Am I in the place of God? 20You
intended to harm me, but God intended
it for good to accomplish what is now
being done, the saving of many lives.
21So then, don't be afraid. I will provide
for you and your children." And he reas-
sured them and spoke kindly to them.

The Death of Joseph

22Joseph stayed in Egypt, along with
all his father's family. He lived a hundred and ten years 23and saw the third
generation of Ephraim's children. Also
the children of Makir son of Manasseh
were placed at birth on Joseph's knees.[c]
24Then Joseph said to his brothers,
"I am about to die. But God will surely
come to your aid and take you up out
of this land to the land he promised
on oath to Abraham, Isaac and Jacob."
25And Joseph made the Israelites swear
an oath and said, "God will surely come
to your aid, and then you must carry my
bones up from this place."
26So Joseph died at the age of a hundred and ten. And after they embalmed
him, he was placed in a coffin in Egypt.

[a] 9 Or *charioteers* [b] 11 *Abel Mizraim* means *mourning of the Egyptians.* [c] 23 That is, were counted as his

EXODUS

The Israelites Oppressed

1 These are the names of the sons of Israel who went to Egypt with Jacob, each with his family: 2 Reuben, Simeon, Levi and Judah; 3 Issachar, Zebulun and Benjamin; 4 Dan and Naphtali; Gad and Asher. 5 The descendants of Jacob numbered seventy[a] in all; Joseph was already in Egypt.

6 Now Joseph and all his brothers and all that generation died, 7 but the Israelites were exceedingly fruitful; they multiplied greatly, increased in numbers and became so numerous that the land was filled with them.

8 Then a new king, to whom Joseph meant nothing, came to power in Egypt. 9 "Look," he said to his people, "the Israelites have become far too numerous for us. 10 Come, we must deal shrewdly with them or they will become even more numerous and, if war breaks out, will join our enemies, fight against us and leave the country."

11 So they put slave masters over them to oppress them with forced labor, and they built Pithom and Rameses as store cities for Pharaoh. 12 But the more they were oppressed, the more they multiplied and spread; so the Egyptians came to dread the Israelites 13 and worked them ruthlessly. 14 They made their lives bitter with harsh labor in brick and mortar and with all kinds of work in the fields; in all their harsh labor the Egyptians worked them ruthlessly.

15 The king of Egypt said to the Hebrew midwives, whose names were Shiphrah and Puah, 16 "When you are helping the Hebrew women during childbirth on the delivery stool, if you see that the baby is a boy, kill him; but if it is a girl, let her live." 17 The midwives, however, feared God and did not do what the king of Egypt had told them to do; they let the boys live. 18 Then the king of Egypt summoned the midwives and asked them, "Why have you done this? Why have you let the boys live?"

19 The midwives answered Pharaoh, "Hebrew women are not like Egyptian women; they are vigorous and give birth before the midwives arrive."

20 So God was kind to the midwives and the people increased and became even more numerous. 21 And because the midwives feared God, he gave them families of their own.

22 Then Pharaoh gave this order to all his people: "Every Hebrew boy that is born you must throw into the Nile, but let every girl live."

The Birth of Moses

2 Now a man of the tribe of Levi married a Levite woman, 2 and she became pregnant and gave birth to a son. When she saw that he was a fine child, she hid him for three months. 3 But when she could hide him no longer, she got a papyrus basket[b] for him and coated it with tar and pitch. Then she placed the child in it and put it among the reeds along the bank of the Nile. 4 His sister stood at a distance to see what would happen to him.

5 Then Pharaoh's daughter went down to the Nile to bathe, and her attendants were walking along the riverbank. She saw the basket among the reeds and sent her female slave to get it. 6 She opened it and saw the baby. He was crying, and she felt sorry for him. "This is one of the Hebrew babies," she said.

7 Then his sister asked Pharaoh's daughter, "Shall I go and get one of the Hebrew women to nurse the baby for you?"

8 "Yes, go," she answered. So the girl went and got the baby's mother. 9 Pharaoh's daughter said to her, "Take this baby and nurse him for me, and I will pay you." So the woman took the baby and nursed him. 10 When the child grew older, she took him to Pharaoh's daughter and he became her son. She named him Moses,[c] saying, "I drew him out of the water."

Moses Flees to Midian

11 One day, after Moses had grown up, he went out to where his own people were and watched them at their hard labor. He saw an Egyptian beating a Hebrew, one of his own people. 12 Looking this way and that and seeing no one, he killed the Egyptian and hid him in the sand. 13 The next

[a] *5* Masoretic Text (see also Gen. 46:27); Dead Sea Scrolls and Septuagint (see also Acts 7:14 and note at Gen. 46:27) *seventy-five* [b] *3* The Hebrew can also mean *ark*, as in Gen. 6:14.
[c] *10* *Moses* sounds like the Hebrew for *draw out*.

day he went out and saw two Hebrews fighting. He asked the one in the wrong, "Why are you hitting your fellow Hebrew?"

14 The man said, "Who made you ruler and judge over us? Are you thinking of killing me as you killed the Egyptian?" Then Moses was afraid and thought, "What I did must have become known."

15 When Pharaoh heard of this, he tried to kill Moses, but Moses fled from Pharaoh and went to live in Midian, where he sat down by a well. 16 Now a priest of Midian had seven daughters, and they came to draw water and fill the troughs to water their father's flock. 17 Some shepherds came along and drove them away, but Moses got up and came to their rescue and watered their flock.

18 When the girls returned to Reuel their father, he asked them, "Why have you returned so early today?"

19 They answered, "An Egyptian rescued us from the shepherds. He even drew water for us and watered the flock."

20 "And where is he?" Reuel asked his daughters. "Why did you leave him? Invite him to have something to eat."

21 Moses agreed to stay with the man, who gave his daughter Zipporah to Moses in marriage. 22 Zipporah gave birth to a son, and Moses named him Gershom,[a] saying, "I have become a foreigner in a foreign land."

23 During that long period, the king of Egypt died. The Israelites groaned in their slavery and cried out, and their cry for help because of their slavery went up to God. 24 God heard their groaning and he remembered his covenant with Abraham, with Isaac and with Jacob. 25 So God looked on the Israelites and was concerned about them.

Moses and the Burning Bush

3 Now Moses was tending the flock of Jethro his father-in-law, the priest of Midian, and he led the flock to the far side of the wilderness and came to Horeb, the mountain of God. 2 There the angel of the LORD appeared to him in flames of fire from within a bush. Moses saw that though the bush was on fire it did not burn up. 3 So Moses thought, "I will go over and see this strange sight — why the bush does not burn up."

4 When the LORD saw that he had gone over to look, God called to him from within the bush, "Moses! Moses!"

And Moses said, "Here I am."

5 "Do not come any closer," God said. "Take off your sandals, for the place where you are standing is holy ground." 6 Then he said, "I am the God of your father,[b] the God of Abraham, the God of Isaac and the God of Jacob." At this, Moses hid his face, because he was afraid to look at God.

7 The LORD said, "I have indeed seen the misery of my people in Egypt. I have heard them crying out because of their slave drivers, and I am concerned about their suffering. 8 So I have come down to rescue them from the hand of the Egyptians and to bring them up out of that land into a good and spacious land, a land flowing with milk and honey — the home of the Canaanites, Hittites, Amorites, Perizzites, Hivites and Jebusites. 9 And now the cry of the Israelites has reached me, and I have seen the way the Egyptians are oppressing them. 10 So now, go. I am sending you to Pharaoh to bring my people the Israelites out of Egypt."

11 But Moses said to God, "Who am I that I should go to Pharaoh and bring the Israelites out of Egypt?"

12 And God said, "I will be with you. And this will be the sign to you that it is I who have sent you: When you have brought the people out of Egypt, you[c] will worship God on this mountain."

13 Moses said to God, "Suppose I go to the Israelites and say to them, 'The God of your fathers has sent me to you,' and they ask me, 'What is his name?' Then what shall I tell them?"

14 God said to Moses, "I AM WHO I AM.[d] This is what you are to say to the Israelites: 'I AM has sent me to you.'"

15 God also said to Moses, "Say to the Israelites, 'The LORD,[e] the God of your fathers — the God of Abraham, the God of Isaac and the God of Jacob — has sent me to you.'

"This is my name forever,
the name you shall call me
from generation to generation.

16 "Go, assemble the elders of Israel and say to them, 'The LORD, the God of your fathers — the God of Abraham, Isaac and Jacob — appeared to me and said: I have watched over you and have seen what has been done to you in Egypt. 17 And I have promised to bring you up out of your misery in Egypt into the land of the Canaanites, Hittites, Amorites, Perizzites, Hivites and Jebusites — a land flowing with milk and honey.'

[a] *22 Gershom* sounds like the Hebrew for *a foreigner there.* [b] *6* Masoretic Text; Samaritan Pentateuch (see Acts 7:32) *fathers* [c] *12* The Hebrew is plural. [d] *14* Or *I WILL BE WHAT I WILL BE*
[e] *15* The Hebrew for *LORD* sounds like and may be related to the Hebrew for *I AM* in verse 14.

[18]"The elders of Israel will listen to you.
Then you and the elders are to go to the
king of Egypt and say to him, 'The LORD,
the God of the Hebrews, has met with us.
Let us take a three-day journey into the
wilderness to offer sacrifices to the LORD
our God.' [19]But I know that the king of
Egypt will not let you go unless a mighty
hand compels him. [20]So I will stretch out
my hand and strike the Egyptians with all
the wonders that I will perform among
them. After that, he will let you go.

[21]"And I will make the Egyptians favorably disposed toward this people,
so that when you leave you will not go
empty-handed. [22]Every woman is to ask
her neighbor and any woman living in
her house for articles of silver and gold
and for clothing, which you will put on
your sons and daughters. And so you will
plunder the Egyptians."

Signs for Moses

4 Moses answered, "What if they do
not believe me or listen to me and
say, 'The LORD did not appear to you'?"

[2]Then the LORD said to him, "What is
that in your hand?"

"A staff," he replied.

[3]The LORD said, "Throw it on the
ground."

Moses threw it on the ground and
it became a snake, and he ran from it.
[4]Then the LORD said to him, "Reach out
your hand and take it by the tail." So
Moses reached out and took hold of the
snake and it turned back into a staff in
his hand. [5]"This," said the LORD, "is so
that they may believe that the LORD, the
God of their fathers — the God of Abraham, the God of Isaac and the God of Jacob — has appeared to you."

[6]Then the LORD said, "Put your hand
inside your cloak." So Moses put his hand
into his cloak, and when he took it out,
the skin was leprous[a] — it had become as
white as snow.

[7]"Now put it back into your cloak," he
said. So Moses put his hand back into his
cloak, and when he took it out, it was restored, like the rest of his flesh.

[8]Then the LORD said, "If they do not
believe you or pay attention to the first
sign, they may believe the second. [9]But
if they do not believe these two signs or
listen to you, take some water from the
Nile and pour it on the dry ground. The
water you take from the river will become blood on the ground."

[10]Moses said to the LORD, "Pardon
your servant, Lord. I have never been eloquent, neither in the past nor since you
have spoken to your servant. I am slow
of speech and tongue."

[11]The LORD said to him, "Who gave human beings their mouths? Who makes
them deaf or mute? Who gives them
sight or makes them blind? Is it not I,
the LORD? [12]Now go; I will help you speak
and will teach you what to say."

[13]But Moses said, "Pardon your servant, Lord. Please send someone else."

[14]Then the LORD's anger burned
against Moses and he said, "What about
your brother, Aaron the Levite? I know
he can speak well. He is already on his
way to meet you, and he will be glad to
see you. [15]You shall speak to him and put
words in his mouth; I will help both of
you speak and will teach you what to do.
[16]He will speak to the people for you, and
it will be as if he were your mouth and
as if you were God to him. [17]But take this
staff in your hand so you can perform
the signs with it."

Moses Returns to Egypt

[18]Then Moses went back to Jethro his
father-in-law and said to him, "Let me
return to my own people in Egypt to see
if any of them are still alive."

Jethro said, "Go, and I wish you well."

[19]Now the LORD had said to Moses in
Midian, "Go back to Egypt, for all those
who wanted to kill you are dead." [20]So
Moses took his wife and sons, put them
on a donkey and started back to Egypt.
And he took the staff of God in his hand.

[21]The LORD said to Moses, "When you
return to Egypt, see that you perform
before Pharaoh all the wonders I have
given you the power to do. But I will
harden his heart so that he will not let
the people go. [22]Then say to Pharaoh,
'This is what the LORD says: Israel is my
firstborn son, [23]and I told you, "Let my
son go, so he may worship me." But you
refused to let him go; so I will kill your
firstborn son.'"

[24]At a lodging place on the way, the
LORD met Moses[b] and was about to kill
him. [25]But Zipporah took a flint knife, cut
off her son's foreskin and touched Moses' feet with it.[c] "Surely you are a bridegroom of blood to me," she said. [26]So the
LORD let him alone. (At that time she
said "bridegroom of blood," referring to
circumcision.)

[a] *6* The Hebrew word for *leprous* was used for various diseases affecting the skin.
[b] *24* Hebrew *him* [c] *25* The meaning of the Hebrew for this clause is uncertain.

27The LORD said to Aaron, "Go into
the wilderness to meet Moses." So he
met Moses at the mountain of God and
kissed him. 28Then Moses told Aaron everything the LORD had sent him to say,
and also about all the signs he had commanded him to perform.
29Moses and Aaron brought together all
the elders of the Israelites, 30and Aaron
told them everything the LORD had said
to Moses. He also performed the signs before the people, 31and they believed. And
when they heard that the LORD was concerned about them and had seen their
misery, they bowed down and worshiped.

Bricks Without Straw

5 Afterward Moses and Aaron went to
Pharaoh and said, "This is what the
LORD, the God of Israel, says: 'Let my
people go, so that they may hold a festival to me in the wilderness.'"
2Pharaoh said, "Who is the LORD, that
I should obey him and let Israel go? I do
not know the LORD and I will not let Israel go."
3Then they said, "The God of the Hebrews has met with us. Now let us take
a three-day journey into the wilderness
to offer sacrifices to the LORD our God, or
he may strike us with plagues or with the
sword."
4But the king of Egypt said, "Moses
and Aaron, why are you taking the people away from their labor? Get back to
your work!" 5Then Pharaoh said, "Look,
the people of the land are now numerous, and you are stopping them from
working."
6That same day Pharaoh gave this order to the slave drivers and overseers in
charge of the people: 7"You are no longer
to supply the people with straw for making bricks; let them go and gather their
own straw. 8But require them to make
the same number of bricks as before;
don't reduce the quota. They are lazy;
that is why they are crying out, 'Let us go
and sacrifice to our God.' 9Make the work
harder for the people so that they keep
working and pay no attention to lies."
10Then the slave drivers and the overseers went out and said to the people,
"This is what Pharaoh says: 'I will not
give you any more straw. 11Go and get
your own straw wherever you can find it,
but your work will not be reduced at all.'"
12So the people scattered all over Egypt to
gather stubble to use for straw. 13The slave
drivers kept pressing them, saying, "Complete the work required of you for each
day, just as when you had straw." 14And
Pharaoh's slave drivers beat the Israelite
overseers they had appointed, demanding, "Why haven't you met your quota of
bricks yesterday or today, as before?"
15Then the Israelite overseers went
and appealed to Pharaoh: "Why have
you treated your servants this way?
16Your servants are given no straw, yet
we are told, 'Make bricks!' Your servants
are being beaten, but the fault is with
your own people."
17Pharaoh said, "Lazy, that's what you
are — lazy! That is why you keep saying, 'Let us go and sacrifice to the LORD.'
18Now get to work. You will not be giv-
en any straw, yet you must produce your
full quota of bricks."
19The Israelite overseers realized they
were in trouble when they were told, "You
are not to reduce the number of bricks required of you for each day." 20When they
left Pharaoh, they found Moses and Aaron waiting to meet them, 21and they said,
"May the LORD look on you and judge
you! You have made us obnoxious to
Pharaoh and his officials and have put a
sword in their hand to kill us."

God Promises Deliverance

22Moses returned to the LORD and
said, "Why, Lord, why have you brought
trouble on this people? Is this why you
sent me? 23Ever since I went to Pharaoh
to speak in your name, he has brought
trouble on this people, and you have not
rescued your people at all."
6 Then the LORD said to Moses, "Now
you will see what I will do to Pharaoh: Because of my mighty hand he will
let them go; because of my mighty hand
he will drive them out of his country."
2God also said to Moses, "I am the
LORD. 3I appeared to Abraham, to Isaac
and to Jacob as God Almighty,[a] but by
my name the LORD[b] I did not make myself fully known to them. 4I also established my covenant with them to give
them the land of Canaan, where they
resided as foreigners. 5Moreover, I have
heard the groaning of the Israelites,
whom the Egyptians are enslaving, and
I have remembered my covenant.
6"Therefore, say to the Israelites: 'I am
the LORD, and I will bring you out from
under the yoke of the Egyptians. I will
free you from being slaves to them, and
I will redeem you with an outstretched
arm and with mighty acts of judgment.

[a] 3 Hebrew *El-Shaddai* [b] 3 See note at 3:15.

7 I will take you as my own people, and I
will be your God. Then you will know that
I am the LORD your God, who brought you
out from under the yoke of the Egyptians. 8 And I will bring you to the land I
swore with uplifted hand to give to Abraham, to Isaac and to Jacob. I will give it
to you as a possession. I am the LORD.' "
9 Moses reported this to the Israelites,
but they did not listen to him because of
their discouragement and harsh labor.
10 Then the LORD said to Moses, 11 "Go,
tell Pharaoh king of Egypt to let the Israelites go out of his country."
12 But Moses said to the LORD, "If the Israelites will not listen to me, why would
Pharaoh listen to me, since I speak with
faltering lips[a]?"

Family Record of Moses and Aaron

13 Now the LORD spoke to Moses and
Aaron about the Israelites and Pharaoh
king of Egypt, and he commanded them
to bring the Israelites out of Egypt.
14 These were the heads of their
families[b]:

The sons of Reuben the firstborn
son of Israel were Hanok and Pallu,
Hezron and Karmi. These were the
clans of Reuben.
15 The sons of Simeon were Jemuel, Jamin, Ohad, Jakin, Zohar and
Shaul the son of a Canaanite woman. These were the clans of Simeon.
16 These were the names of the
sons of Levi according to their records: Gershon, Kohath and Merari.
Levi lived 137 years.
17 The sons of Gershon, by clans,
were Libni and Shimei.
18 The sons of Kohath were Amram, Izhar, Hebron and Uzziel. Kohath lived 133 years.
19 The sons of Merari were Mahli
and Mushi.
These were the clans of Levi according to their records.
20 Amram married his father's sister Jochebed, who bore him Aaron
and Moses. Amram lived 137 years.
21 The sons of Izhar were Korah,
Nepheg and Zikri.
22 The sons of Uzziel were Mishael,
Elzaphan and Sithri.
23 Aaron married Elisheba, daughter of Amminadab and sister of
Nahshon, and she bore him Nadab
and Abihu, Eleazar and Ithamar.
24 The sons of Korah were Assir,
Elkanah and Abiasaph. These were
the Korahite clans.
25 Eleazar son of Aaron married
one of the daughters of Putiel, and
she bore him Phinehas.

These were the heads of the Levite families, clan by clan.
26 It was this Aaron and Moses to whom
the LORD said, "Bring the Israelites out
of Egypt by their divisions." 27 They were
the ones who spoke to Pharaoh king of
Egypt about bringing the Israelites out
of Egypt — this same Moses and Aaron.

Aaron to Speak for Moses

28 Now when the LORD spoke to Moses in Egypt, 29 he said to him, "I am the
LORD. Tell Pharaoh king of Egypt everything I tell you."
30 But Moses said to the LORD, "Since
I speak with faltering lips, why would
Pharaoh listen to me?"
7 Then the LORD said to Moses, "See, I
have made you like God to Pharaoh,
and your brother Aaron will be your
prophet. 2 You are to say everything I
command you, and your brother Aaron is to tell Pharaoh to let the Israelites
go out of his country. 3 But I will harden
Pharaoh's heart, and though I multiply my signs and wonders in Egypt, 4 he
will not listen to you. Then I will lay my
hand on Egypt and with mighty acts of
judgment I will bring out my divisions,
my people the Israelites. 5 And the Egyptians will know that I am the LORD when
I stretch out my hand against Egypt and
bring the Israelites out of it."
6 Moses and Aaron did just as the LORD
commanded them. 7 Moses was eighty
years old and Aaron eighty-three when
they spoke to Pharaoh.

Aaron's Staff Becomes a Snake

8 The LORD said to Moses and Aaron,
9 "When Pharaoh says to you, 'Perform
a miracle,' then say to Aaron, 'Take your
staff and throw it down before Pharaoh,'
and it will become a snake."
10 So Moses and Aaron went to Pharaoh and did just as the LORD commanded. Aaron threw his staff down in front of
Pharaoh and his officials, and it became
a snake. 11 Pharaoh then summoned wise
men and sorcerers, and the Egyptian magicians also did the same things by their
secret arts: 12 Each one threw down his staff

[a] 12 Hebrew *I am uncircumcised of lips;* also in verse 30 [b] 14 The Hebrew for *families* here and in verse 25 refers to units larger than clans.

and it became a snake. But Aaron's staff
swallowed up their staffs. 13Yet Pharaoh's
heart became hard and he would not listen to them, just as the LORD had said.

The Plague of Blood

14Then the LORD said to Moses, "Pharaoh's heart is unyielding; he refuses to
let the people go. 15Go to Pharaoh in the
morning as he goes out to the river. Confront him on the bank of the Nile, and
take in your hand the staff that was
changed into a snake. 16Then say to him,
'The LORD, the God of the Hebrews, has
sent me to say to you: Let my people go,
so that they may worship me in the wilderness. But until now you have not listened. 17This is what the LORD says: By
this you will know that I am the LORD:
With the staff that is in my hand I will
strike the water of the Nile, and it will be
changed into blood. 18The fish in the Nile
will die, and the river will stink; the Egyptians will not be able to drink its water.'"

19The LORD said to Moses, "Tell Aaron, 'Take your staff and stretch out your
hand over the waters of Egypt — over the
streams and canals, over the ponds and
all the reservoirs — and they will turn to
blood.' Blood will be everywhere in Egypt,
even in vessels[a] of wood and stone."

20Moses and Aaron did just as the
LORD had commanded. He raised his
staff in the presence of Pharaoh and
his officials and struck the water of the
Nile, and all the water was changed into
blood. 21The fish in the Nile died, and the
river smelled so bad that the Egyptians
could not drink its water. Blood was everywhere in Egypt.

22But the Egyptian magicians did the
same things by their secret arts, and
Pharaoh's heart became hard; he would
not listen to Moses and Aaron, just as the
LORD had said. 23Instead, he turned and
went into his palace, and did not take
even this to heart. 24And all the Egyptians dug along the Nile to get drinking
water, because they could not drink the
water of the river.

The Plague of Frogs

25Seven days passed after the LORD
8[b] struck the Nile. 1Then the LORD said
to Moses, "Go to Pharaoh and say to
him, 'This is what the LORD says: Let my
people go, so that they may worship me.
2If you refuse to let them go, I will send
a plague of frogs on your whole country.
3The Nile will teem with frogs. They will
come up into your palace and your bedroom and onto your bed, into the houses
of your officials and on your people, and
into your ovens and kneading troughs.
4The frogs will come up on you and your
people and all your officials.'"

5Then the LORD said to Moses, "Tell
Aaron, 'Stretch out your hand with your
staff over the streams and canals and
ponds, and make frogs come up on the
land of Egypt.'"

6So Aaron stretched out his hand over
the waters of Egypt, and the frogs came
up and covered the land. 7But the magicians did the same things by their secret
arts; they also made frogs come up on
the land of Egypt.

8Pharaoh summoned Moses and Aaron and said, "Pray to the LORD to take
the frogs away from me and my people,
and I will let your people go to offer sacrifices to the LORD."

9Moses said to Pharaoh, "I leave to you
the honor of setting the time for me to
pray for you and your officials and your
people that you and your houses may be
rid of the frogs, except for those that remain in the Nile."

10"Tomorrow," Pharaoh said.

Moses replied, "It will be as you say, so
that you may know there is no one like
the LORD our God. 11The frogs will leave
you and your houses, your officials and
your people; they will remain only in the
Nile."

12After Moses and Aaron left Pharaoh,
Moses cried out to the LORD about the
frogs he had brought on Pharaoh. 13And
the LORD did what Moses asked. The
frogs died in the houses, in the courtyards and in the fields. 14They were piled
into heaps, and the land reeked of them.
15But when Pharaoh saw that there was
relief, he hardened his heart and would
not listen to Moses and Aaron, just as the
LORD had said.

The Plague of Gnats

16Then the LORD said to Moses, "Tell
Aaron, 'Stretch out your staff and strike
the dust of the ground,' and throughout
the land of Egypt the dust will become
gnats." 17They did this, and when Aaron stretched out his hand with the staff
and struck the dust of the ground, gnats
came on people and animals. All the
dust throughout the land of Egypt became gnats. 18But when the magicians

[a] *19* Or *even on their idols* [b] In Hebrew texts 8:1-4 is numbered 7:26-29, and 8:5-32 is numbered 8:1-28.

tried to produce gnats by their secret arts, they could not.

Since the gnats were on people and animals everywhere, 19 the magicians said to Pharaoh, "This is the finger of God." But Pharaoh's heart was hard and he would not listen, just as the LORD had said.

The Plague of Flies

20 Then the LORD said to Moses, "Get up early in the morning and confront Pharaoh as he goes to the river and say to him, 'This is what the LORD says: Let my people go, so that they may worship me. 21 If you do not let my people go, I will send swarms of flies on you and your officials, on your people and into your houses. The houses of the Egyptians will be full of flies; even the ground will be covered with them.

22 "'But on that day I will deal differently with the land of Goshen, where my people live; no swarms of flies will be there, so that you will know that I, the LORD, am in this land. 23 I will make a distinction[a] between my people and your people. This sign will occur tomorrow.'"

24 And the LORD did this. Dense swarms of flies poured into Pharaoh's palace and into the houses of his officials; throughout Egypt the land was ruined by the flies.

25 Then Pharaoh summoned Moses and Aaron and said, "Go, sacrifice to your God here in the land."

26 But Moses said, "That would not be right. The sacrifices we offer the LORD our God would be detestable to the Egyptians. And if we offer sacrifices that are detestable in their eyes, will they not stone us? 27 We must take a three-day journey into the wilderness to offer sacrifices to the LORD our God, as he commands us."

28 Pharaoh said, "I will let you go to offer sacrifices to the LORD your God in the wilderness, but you must not go very far. Now pray for me."

29 Moses answered, "As soon as I leave you, I will pray to the LORD, and tomorrow the flies will leave Pharaoh and his officials and his people. Only let Pharaoh be sure that he does not act deceitfully again by not letting the people go to offer sacrifices to the LORD."

30 Then Moses left Pharaoh and prayed to the LORD, 31 and the LORD did what Moses asked. The flies left Pharaoh and his officials and his people; not a fly remained. 32 But this time also Pharaoh hardened his heart and would not let the people go.

The Plague on Livestock

9 Then the LORD said to Moses, "Go to Pharaoh and say to him, 'This is what the LORD, the God of the Hebrews, says: "Let my people go, so that they may worship me." 2 If you refuse to let them go and continue to hold them back, 3 the hand of the LORD will bring a terrible plague on your livestock in the field — on your horses, donkeys and camels and on your cattle, sheep and goats. 4 But the LORD will make a distinction between the livestock of Israel and that of Egypt, so that no animal belonging to the Israelites will die.'"

5 The LORD set a time and said, "Tomorrow the LORD will do this in the land." 6 And the next day the LORD did it: All the livestock of the Egyptians died, but not one animal belonging to the Israelites died. 7 Pharaoh investigated and found that not even one of the animals of the Israelites had died. Yet his heart was unyielding and he would not let the people go.

The Plague of Boils

8 Then the LORD said to Moses and Aaron, "Take handfuls of soot from a furnace and have Moses toss it into the air in the presence of Pharaoh. 9 It will become fine dust over the whole land of Egypt, and festering boils will break out on people and animals throughout the land."

10 So they took soot from a furnace and stood before Pharaoh. Moses tossed it into the air, and festering boils broke out on people and animals. 11 The magicians could not stand before Moses because of the boils that were on them and on all the Egyptians. 12 But the LORD hardened Pharaoh's heart and he would not listen to Moses and Aaron, just as the LORD had said to Moses.

The Plague of Hail

13 Then the LORD said to Moses, "Get up early in the morning, confront Pharaoh and say to him, 'This is what the LORD, the God of the Hebrews, says: Let my people go, so that they may worship me, 14 or this time I will send the full force of my plagues against you and against your officials and your people, so you may know that there is no one like me in all the earth. 15 For by now I could have stretched out my hand and struck you and your people with a plague that would have wiped you off the earth. 16 But I have

[a] *23* Septuagint and Vulgate; Hebrew *will put a deliverance*

raised you up[a] for this very purpose, that
I might show you my power and that my
name might be proclaimed in all the
earth. 17You still set yourself against my
people and will not let them go. 18There-
fore, at this time tomorrow I will send the
worst hailstorm that has ever fallen on
Egypt, from the day it was founded till
now. 19Give an order now to bring your
livestock and everything you have in the
field to a place of shelter, because the
hail will fall on every person and animal
that has not been brought in and is still
out in the field, and they will die.' "

20Those officials of Pharaoh who
feared the word of the LORD hurried to
bring their slaves and their livestock inside. 21But those who ignored the word of
the LORD left their slaves and livestock
in the field.

22Then the LORD said to Moses,
"Stretch out your hand toward the sky
so that hail will fall all over Egypt — on
people and animals and on everything
growing in the fields of Egypt." 23When
Moses stretched out his staff toward the
sky, the LORD sent thunder and hail, and
lightning flashed down to the ground.
So the LORD rained hail on the land of
Egypt; 24hail fell and lightning flashed
back and forth. It was the worst storm
in all the land of Egypt since it had become a nation. 25Throughout Egypt hail
struck everything in the fields — both
people and animals; it beat down everything growing in the fields and stripped
every tree. 26The only place it did not hail
was the land of Goshen, where the Israelites were.

27Then Pharaoh summoned Moses and
Aaron. "This time I have sinned," he said
to them. "The LORD is in the right, and I
and my people are in the wrong. 28Pray
to the LORD, for we have had enough
thunder and hail. I will let you go; you
don't have to stay any longer."

29Moses replied, "When I have gone
out of the city, I will spread out my hands
in prayer to the LORD. The thunder will
stop and there will be no more hail,
so you may know that the earth is the
LORD's. 30But I know that you and your
officials still do not fear the LORD God."

31(The flax and barley were destroyed,
since the barley had headed and the flax
was in bloom. 32The wheat and spelt,
however, were not destroyed, because
they ripen later.)

33Then Moses left Pharaoh and went
out of the city. He spread out his hands
toward the LORD; the thunder and hail
stopped, and the rain no longer poured
down on the land. 34When Pharaoh saw
that the rain and hail and thunder had
stopped, he sinned again: He and his officials hardened their hearts. 35So Pharaoh's heart was hard and he would not
let the Israelites go, just as the LORD had
said through Moses.

The Plague of Locusts

10 Then the LORD said to Moses, "Go
to Pharaoh, for I have hardened
his heart and the hearts of his officials so
that I may perform these signs of mine
among them 2that you may tell your
children and grandchildren how I dealt
harshly with the Egyptians and how I
performed my signs among them, and
that you may know that I am the LORD."

3So Moses and Aaron went to Pharaoh
and said to him, "This is what the LORD,
the God of the Hebrews, says: 'How long
will you refuse to humble yourself before
me? Let my people go, so that they may
worship me. 4If you refuse to let them go,
I will bring locusts into your country tomorrow. 5They will cover the face of the
ground so that it cannot be seen. They
will devour what little you have left after the hail, including every tree that
is growing in your fields. 6They will fill
your houses and those of all your officials and all the Egyptians — something
neither your parents nor your ancestors
have ever seen from the day they settled
in this land till now.' " Then Moses turned
and left Pharaoh.

7Pharaoh's officials said to him, "How
long will this man be a snare to us? Let
the people go, so that they may worship
the LORD their God. Do you not yet realize that Egypt is ruined?"

8Then Moses and Aaron were brought
back to Pharaoh. "Go, worship the LORD
your God," he said. "But tell me who will
be going."

9Moses answered, "We will go with our
young and our old, with our sons and
our daughters, and with our flocks and
herds, because we are to celebrate a festival to the LORD."

10Pharaoh said, "The LORD be with
you — if I let you go, along with your
women and children! Clearly you are
bent on evil.[b] 11No! Have only the men go
and worship the LORD, since that's what
you have been asking for." Then Moses
and Aaron were driven out of Pharaoh's
presence.

[a] 16 Or *have spared you* [b] 10 Or *Be careful, trouble is in store for you!*

12And the LORD said to Moses, "Stretch out your hand over Egypt so that locusts swarm over the land and devour everything growing in the fields, everything left by the hail."

13So Moses stretched out his staff over Egypt, and the LORD made an east wind blow across the land all that day and all that night. By morning the wind had brought the locusts; 14they invaded all Egypt and settled down in every area of the country in great numbers. Never before had there been such a plague of locusts, nor will there ever be again. 15They covered all the ground until it was black. They devoured all that was left after the hail — everything growing in the fields and the fruit on the trees. Nothing green remained on tree or plant in all the land of Egypt.

16Pharaoh quickly summoned Moses and Aaron and said, "I have sinned against the LORD your God and against you. 17Now forgive my sin once more and pray to the LORD your God to take this deadly plague away from me."

18Moses then left Pharaoh and prayed to the LORD. 19And the LORD changed the wind to a very strong west wind, which caught up the locusts and carried them into the Red Sea.[a] Not a locust was left anywhere in Egypt. 20But the LORD hardened Pharaoh's heart, and he would not let the Israelites go.

The Plague of Darkness

21Then the LORD said to Moses, "Stretch out your hand toward the sky so that darkness spreads over Egypt — darkness that can be felt." 22So Moses stretched out his hand toward the sky, and total darkness covered all Egypt for three days. 23No one could see anyone else or move about for three days. Yet all the Israelites had light in the places where they lived.

24Then Pharaoh summoned Moses and said, "Go, worship the LORD. Even your women and children may go with you; only leave your flocks and herds behind."

25But Moses said, "You must allow us to have sacrifices and burnt offerings to present to the LORD our God. 26Our livestock too must go with us; not a hoof is to be left behind. We have to use some of them in worshiping the LORD our God, and until we get there we will not know what we are to use to worship the LORD."

27But the LORD hardened Pharaoh's heart, and he was not willing to let them go. 28Pharaoh said to Moses, "Get out of my sight! Make sure you do not appear before me again! The day you see my face you will die."

29"Just as you say," Moses replied. "I will never appear before you again."

The Plague on the Firstborn

11 Now the LORD had said to Moses, "I will bring one more plague on Pharaoh and on Egypt. After that, he will let you go from here, and when he does, he will drive you out completely. 2Tell the people that men and women alike are to ask their neighbors for articles of silver and gold." 3(The LORD made the Egyptians favorably disposed toward the people, and Moses himself was highly regarded in Egypt by Pharaoh's officials and by the people.)

4So Moses said, "This is what the LORD says: 'About midnight I will go throughout Egypt. 5Every firstborn son in Egypt will die, from the firstborn son of Pharaoh, who sits on the throne, to the firstborn son of the female slave, who is at her hand mill, and all the firstborn of the cattle as well. 6There will be loud wailing throughout Egypt — worse than there has ever been or ever will be again. 7But among the Israelites not a dog will bark at any person or animal.' Then you will know that the LORD makes a distinction between Egypt and Israel. 8All these officials of yours will come to me, bowing down before me and saying, 'Go, you and all the people who follow you!' After that I will leave." Then Moses, hot with anger, left Pharaoh.

9The LORD had said to Moses, "Pharaoh will refuse to listen to you — so that my wonders may be multiplied in Egypt." 10Moses and Aaron performed all these wonders before Pharaoh, but the LORD hardened Pharaoh's heart, and he would not let the Israelites go out of his country.

The Passover and the Festival of Unleavened Bread

12 The LORD said to Moses and Aaron in Egypt, 2"This month is to be for you the first month, the first month of your year. 3Tell the whole community of Israel that on the tenth day of this month each man is to take a lamb[b] for his family, one for each household. 4If any household is too small for a whole

[a] 19 Or *the Sea of Reeds* [b] 3 The Hebrew word can mean *lamb* or *kid*; also in verse 4.

lamb, they must share one with their nearest neighbor, having taken into account the number of people there are. You are to determine the amount of lamb needed in accordance with what each person will eat. 5The animals you choose must be year-old males without defect, and you may take them from the sheep or the goats. 6Take care of them until the fourteenth day of the month, when all the members of the community of Israel must slaughter them at twilight. 7Then they are to take some of the blood and put it on the sides and tops of the doorframes of the houses where they eat the lambs. 8That same night they are to eat the meat roasted over the fire, along with bitter herbs, and bread made without yeast. 9Do not eat the meat raw or boiled in water, but roast it over a fire — with the head, legs and internal organs. 10Do not leave any of it till morning; if some is left till morning, you must burn it. 11This is how you are to eat it: with your cloak tucked into your belt, your sandals on your feet and your staff in your hand. Eat it in haste; it is the LORD's Passover.

12"On that same night I will pass through Egypt and strike down every firstborn of both people and animals, and I will bring judgment on all the gods of Egypt. I am the LORD. 13The blood will be a sign for you on the houses where you are, and when I see the blood, I will pass over you. No destructive plague will touch you when I strike Egypt.

14"This is a day you are to commemorate; for the generations to come you shall celebrate it as a festival to the LORD — a lasting ordinance. 15For seven days you are to eat bread made without yeast. On the first day remove the yeast from your houses, for whoever eats anything with yeast in it from the first day through the seventh must be cut off from Israel. 16On the first day hold a sacred assembly, and another one on the seventh day. Do no work at all on these days, except to prepare food for everyone to eat; that is all you may do.

17"Celebrate the Festival of Unleavened Bread, because it was on this very day that I brought your divisions out of Egypt. Celebrate this day as a lasting ordinance for the generations to come. 18In the first month you are to eat bread made without yeast, from the evening of the fourteenth day until the evening of the twenty-first day. 19For seven days no yeast is to be found in your houses. And anyone, whether foreigner or native-born, who eats anything with yeast in it must be cut off from the community of Israel. 20Eat nothing made with yeast. Wherever you live, you must eat unleavened bread."

21Then Moses summoned all the elders of Israel and said to them, "Go at once and select the animals for your families and slaughter the Passover lamb. 22Take a bunch of hyssop, dip it into the blood in the basin and put some of the blood on the top and on both sides of the doorframe. None of you shall go out of the door of your house until morning. 23When the LORD goes through the land to strike down the Egyptians, he will see the blood on the top and sides of the doorframe and will pass over that doorway, and he will not permit the destroyer to enter your houses and strike you down.

24"Obey these instructions as a lasting ordinance for you and your descendants. 25When you enter the land that the LORD will give you as he promised, observe this ceremony. 26And when your children ask you, 'What does this ceremony mean to you?' 27then tell them, 'It is the Passover sacrifice to the LORD, who passed over the houses of the Israelites in Egypt and spared our homes when he struck down the Egyptians.'" Then the people bowed down and worshiped. 28The Israelites did just what the LORD commanded Moses and Aaron.

29At midnight the LORD struck down all the firstborn in Egypt, from the firstborn of Pharaoh, who sat on the throne, to the firstborn of the prisoner, who was in the dungeon, and the firstborn of all the livestock as well. 30Pharaoh and all his officials and all the Egyptians got up during the night, and there was loud wailing in Egypt, for there was not a house without someone dead.

The Exodus

31During the night Pharaoh summoned Moses and Aaron and said, "Up! Leave my people, you and the Israelites! Go, worship the LORD as you have requested. 32Take your flocks and herds, as you have said, and go. And also bless me."

33The Egyptians urged the people to hurry and leave the country. "For otherwise," they said, "we will all die!" 34So the people took their dough before the yeast was added, and carried it on their shoulders in kneading troughs wrapped in clothing. 35The Israelites did as Moses instructed and asked the Egyptians for articles of silver and gold and for clothing. 36The LORD had made the Egyptians favorably disposed toward the people, and they gave them what they asked for; so they plundered the Egyptians.

37The Israelites journeyed from Rameses to Sukkoth. There were about six hundred thousand men on foot, besides women and children. 38Many other people went up with them, and also large droves of livestock, both flocks and herds. 39With the dough the Israelites had brought from Egypt, they baked loaves of unleavened bread. The dough was without yeast because they had been driven out of Egypt and did not have time to prepare food for themselves.

40Now the length of time the Israelite people lived in Egypt[a] was 430 years. 41At the end of the 430 years, to the very day, all the LORD's divisions left Egypt. 42Because the LORD kept vigil that night to bring them out of Egypt, on this night all the Israelites are to keep vigil to honor the LORD for the generations to come.

Passover Restrictions

43The LORD said to Moses and Aaron, "These are the regulations for the Passover meal:

"No foreigner may eat it. 44Any slave you have bought may eat it after you have circumcised him, 45but a temporary resident or a hired worker may not eat it.

46"It must be eaten inside the house; take none of the meat outside the house. Do not break any of the bones. 47The whole community of Israel must celebrate it.

48"A foreigner residing among you who wants to celebrate the LORD's Passover must have all the males in his household circumcised; then he may take part like one born in the land. No uncircumcised male may eat it. 49The same law applies both to the native-born and to the foreigner residing among you."

50All the Israelites did just what the LORD had commanded Moses and Aaron. 51And on that very day the LORD brought the Israelites out of Egypt by their divisions.

Consecration of the Firstborn

13 The LORD said to Moses, 2"Consecrate to me every firstborn male. The first offspring of every womb among the Israelites belongs to me, whether human or animal."

3Then Moses said to the people, "Commemorate this day, the day you came out of Egypt, out of the land of slavery, because the LORD brought you out of it with a mighty hand. Eat nothing containing yeast. 4Today, in the month of Aviv, you are leaving. 5When the LORD brings you into the land of the Canaanites, Hittites, Amorites, Hivites and Jebusites — the land he swore to your ancestors to give you, a land flowing with milk and honey — you are to observe this ceremony in this month: 6For seven days eat bread made without yeast and on the seventh day hold a festival to the LORD. 7Eat unleavened bread during those seven days; nothing with yeast in it is to be seen among you, nor shall any yeast be seen anywhere within your borders. 8On that day tell your son, 'I do this because of what the LORD did for me when I came out of Egypt.' 9This observance will be for you like a sign on your hand and a reminder on your forehead that this law of the LORD is to be on your lips. For the LORD brought you out of Egypt with his mighty hand. 10You must keep this ordinance at the appointed time year after year.

11"After the LORD brings you into the land of the Canaanites and gives it to you, as he promised on oath to you and your ancestors, 12you are to give over to the LORD the first offspring of every womb. All the firstborn males of your livestock belong to the LORD. 13Redeem with a lamb every firstborn donkey, but if you do not redeem it, break its neck. Redeem every firstborn among your sons.

14"In days to come, when your son asks you, 'What does this mean?' say to him, 'With a mighty hand the LORD brought us out of Egypt, out of the land of slavery. 15When Pharaoh stubbornly refused to let us go, the LORD killed the firstborn of both people and animals in Egypt. This is why I sacrifice to the LORD the first male offspring of every womb and redeem each of my firstborn sons.' 16And it will be like a sign on your hand and a symbol on your forehead that the LORD brought us out of Egypt with his mighty hand."

Crossing the Sea

17When Pharaoh let the people go, God did not lead them on the road through the Philistine country, though that was shorter. For God said, "If they face war,

[a] 40 Masoretic Text; Samaritan Pentateuch and Septuagint *Egypt and Canaan*

they might change their minds and return to Egypt." 18So God led the people
around by the desert road toward the
Red Sea.[a] The Israelites went up out of
Egypt ready for battle.
19Moses took the bones of Joseph with
him because Joseph had made the Israelites swear an oath. He had said, "God
will surely come to your aid, and then
you must carry my bones up with you
from this place."[b]
20After leaving Sukkoth they camped
at Etham on the edge of the desert. 21By
day the LORD went ahead of them in a
pillar of cloud to guide them on their
way and by night in a pillar of fire to
give them light, so that they could travel by day or night. 22Neither the pillar
of cloud by day nor the pillar of fire by
night left its place in front of the people.
14 Then the LORD said to Moses, 2"Tell
the Israelites to turn back and encamp near Pi Hahiroth, between Migdol and the sea. They are to encamp by
the sea, directly opposite Baal Zephon.
3Pharaoh will think, 'The Israelites are
wandering around the land in confusion, hemmed in by the desert.' 4And
I will harden Pharaoh's heart, and he
will pursue them. But I will gain glory
for myself through Pharaoh and all his
army, and the Egyptians will know that
I am the LORD." So the Israelites did this.
5When the king of Egypt was told that
the people had fled, Pharaoh and his officials changed their minds about them
and said, "What have we done? We have
let the Israelites go and have lost their
services!" 6So he had his chariot made
ready and took his army with him.
7He took six hundred of the best chariots, along with all the other chariots
of Egypt, with officers over all of them.
8The LORD hardened the heart of Pharaoh king of Egypt, so that he pursued the
Israelites, who were marching out boldly. 9The Egyptians — all Pharaoh's horses
and chariots, horsemen[c] and troops —
pursued the Israelites and overtook
them as they camped by the sea near Pi
Hahiroth, opposite Baal Zephon.
10As Pharaoh approached, the Israelites looked up, and there were the Egyptians, marching after them. They were
terrified and cried out to the LORD. 11They
said to Moses, "Was it because there were
no graves in Egypt that you brought
us to the desert to die? What have you
done to us by bringing us out of Egypt?
12Didn't we say to you in Egypt, 'Leave
us alone; let us serve the Egyptians'? It
would have been better for us to serve
the Egyptians than to die in the desert!"
13Moses answered the people, "Do
not be afraid. Stand firm and you will
see the deliverance the LORD will bring
you today. The Egyptians you see today
you will never see again. 14The LORD will
fight for you; you need only to be still."
15Then the LORD said to Moses, "Why
are you crying out to me? Tell the Israelites to move on. 16Raise your staff and
stretch out your hand over the sea to divide the water so that the Israelites can
go through the sea on dry ground. 17I
will harden the hearts of the Egyptians
so that they will go in after them. And
I will gain glory through Pharaoh and
all his army, through his chariots and
his horsemen. 18The Egyptians will know
that I am the LORD when I gain glory
through Pharaoh, his chariots and his
horsemen."
19Then the angel of God, who had
been traveling in front of Israel's army,
withdrew and went behind them. The
pillar of cloud also moved from in front
and stood behind them, 20coming between the armies of Egypt and Israel.
Throughout the night the cloud brought
darkness to the one side and light to the
other side; so neither went near the other all night long.
21Then Moses stretched out his hand
over the sea, and all that night the LORD
drove the sea back with a strong east
wind and turned it into dry land. The
waters were divided, 22and the Israelites
went through the sea on dry ground,
with a wall of water on their right and
on their left.
23The Egyptians pursued them, and
all Pharaoh's horses and chariots and
horsemen followed them into the sea.
24During the last watch of the night the
LORD looked down from the pillar of fire
and cloud at the Egyptian army and
threw it into confusion. 25He jammed[d]
the wheels of their chariots so that they
had difficulty driving. And the Egyptians
said, "Let's get away from the Israelites!
The LORD is fighting for them against
Egypt."
26Then the LORD said to Moses, "Stretch
out your hand over the sea so that the
waters may flow back over the Egyptians
and their chariots and horsemen." 27Mo-
ses stretched out his hand over the sea,

[a] *18* Or *the Sea of Reeds* [b] *19* See Gen. 50:25. [c] *9* Or *charioteers*; also in verses 17, 18, 23, 26 and 28 [d] *25* See Samaritan Pentateuch, Septuagint and Syriac; Masoretic Text *removed*

and at daybreak the sea went back to
its place. The Egyptians were fleeing toward[a] it, and the LORD swept them into
the sea. 28 The water flowed back and
covered the chariots and horsemen—
the entire army of Pharaoh that had followed the Israelites into the sea. Not one
of them survived.

29 But the Israelites went through the
sea on dry ground, with a wall of water
on their right and on their left. 30 That day
the LORD saved Israel from the hands of
the Egyptians, and Israel saw the Egyptians lying dead on the shore. 31 And when
the Israelites saw the mighty hand of the
LORD displayed against the Egyptians,
the people feared the LORD and put their
trust in him and in Moses his servant.

The Song of Moses and Miriam

15 Then Moses and the Israelites sang
this song to the LORD:

"I will sing to the LORD,
for he is highly exalted.
Both horse and driver
he has hurled into the sea.

2 "The LORD is my strength and my
defense[b];
he has become my salvation.
He is my God, and I will praise him,
my father's God, and I will exalt
him.
3 The LORD is a warrior;
the LORD is his name.
4 Pharaoh's chariots and his army
he has hurled into the sea.
The best of Pharaoh's officers
are drowned in the Red Sea.[c]
5 The deep waters have covered them;
they sank to the depths like a
stone.
6 Your right hand, LORD,
was majestic in power.
Your right hand, LORD,
shattered the enemy.

7 "In the greatness of your majesty
you threw down those who
opposed you.
You unleashed your burning anger;
it consumed them like stubble.
8 By the blast of your nostrils
the waters piled up.
The surging waters stood up like a
wall;
the deep waters congealed in the
heart of the sea.
9 The enemy boasted,
'I will pursue, I will overtake them.
I will divide the spoils;
I will gorge myself on them.
I will draw my sword
and my hand will destroy them.'
10 But you blew with your breath,
and the sea covered them.
They sank like lead
in the mighty waters.
11 Who among the gods
is like you, LORD?
Who is like you—
majestic in holiness,
awesome in glory,
working wonders?

12 "You stretch out your right hand,
and the earth swallows your
enemies.
13 In your unfailing love you will lead
the people you have redeemed.
In your strength you will guide them
to your holy dwelling.
14 The nations will hear and tremble;
anguish will grip the people of
Philistia.
15 The chiefs of Edom will be terrified,
the leaders of Moab will be seized
with trembling,
the people[d] of Canaan will melt away;
16 terror and dread will fall on them.
By the power of your arm
they will be as still as a stone—
until your people pass by, LORD,
until the people you bought[e]
pass by.
17 You will bring them in and plant
them
on the mountain of your
inheritance—
the place, LORD, you made for your
dwelling,
the sanctuary, Lord, your hands
established.

18 "The LORD reigns
for ever and ever."

19 When Pharaoh's horses, chariots and
horsemen[f] went into the sea, the LORD
brought the waters of the sea back over
them, but the Israelites walked through
the sea on dry ground. 20 Then Miriam
the prophet, Aaron's sister, took a timbrel in her hand, and all the women followed her, with timbrels and dancing.
21 Miriam sang to them:

"Sing to the LORD,
for he is highly exalted.
Both horse and driver
he has hurled into the sea."

[a] 27 Or *from* [b] 2 Or *song* [c] 4 Or *the Sea of Reeds*; also in verse 22 [d] 15 Or *rulers* [e] 16 Or *created* [f] 19 Or *charioteers*

The Waters of Marah and Elim

22Then Moses led Israel from the Red
Sea and they went into the Desert of
Shur. For three days they traveled in the
desert without finding water. 23When
they came to Marah, they could not
drink its water because it was bitter.
(That is why the place is called Marah.[a])
24So the people grumbled against Moses,
saying, "What are we to drink?"

25Then Moses cried out to the LORD,
and the LORD showed him a piece of
wood. He threw it into the water, and the
water became fit to drink.

There the LORD issued a ruling and instruction for them and put them to the
test. 26He said, "If you listen carefully to
the LORD your God and do what is right in his eyes, if you pay attention to his commands and keep all his decrees, I will not bring on you any of the diseases I brought on the Egyptians, for I am the LORD, who heals you."

27Then they came to Elim, where there
were twelve springs and seventy palm trees, and they camped there near the water.

Manna and Quail

16 The whole Israelite community set out from Elim and came to the Desert of Sin, which is between Elim and Sinai, on the fifteenth day of the second month after they had come out of
Egypt. 2In the desert the whole commu-
nity grumbled against Moses and Aaron.
3The Israelites said to them, "If only we had died by the LORD's hand in Egypt! There we sat around pots of meat and ate all the food we wanted, but you have brought us out into this desert to starve this entire assembly to death."

4Then the LORD said to Moses, "I will rain down bread from heaven for you. The people are to go out each day and gather enough for that day. In this way I will test them and see whether they will
follow my instructions. 5On the sixth day
they are to prepare what they bring in, and that is to be twice as much as they gather on the other days."

6So Moses and Aaron said to all the Israelites, "In the evening you will know that it was the LORD who brought you
out of Egypt, 7and in the morning you
will see the glory of the LORD, because he has heard your grumbling against him. Who are we, that you should grumble against us?" 8Moses also said, "You
will know that it was the LORD when he gives you meat to eat in the evening and all the bread you want in the morning, because he has heard your grumbling against him. Who are we? You are not grumbling against us, but against the LORD."

9Then Moses told Aaron, "Say to the entire Israelite community, 'Come before the LORD, for he has heard your grumbling.'"

10While Aaron was speaking to the whole Israelite community, they looked toward the desert, and there was the glory of the LORD appearing in the cloud.

11The LORD said to Moses, 12"I have
heard the grumbling of the Israelites. Tell them, 'At twilight you will eat meat, and in the morning you will be filled with bread. Then you will know that I am the LORD your God.'"

13That evening quail came and covered the camp, and in the morning there
was a layer of dew around the camp.
14When the dew was gone, thin flakes
like frost on the ground appeared on the
desert floor. 15When the Israelites saw it,
they said to each other, "What is it?" For they did not know what it was.

Moses said to them, "It is the bread the
LORD has given you to eat. 16This is what
the LORD has commanded: 'Everyone is to gather as much as they need. Take an omer[b] for each person you have in your tent.'"

17The Israelites did as they were told;
some gathered much, some little. 18And
when they measured it by the omer, the one who gathered much did not have too much, and the one who gathered little did not have too little. Everyone had gathered just as much as they needed.

19Then Moses said to them, "No one is to keep any of it until morning."

20However, some of them paid no attention to Moses; they kept part of it until morning, but it was full of maggots and began to smell. So Moses was angry with them.

21Each morning everyone gathered as
much as they needed, and when the sun
grew hot, it melted away. 22On the sixth
day, they gathered twice as much — two omers[c] for each person — and the leaders of the community came and reported
this to Moses. 23He said to them, "This is
what the LORD commanded: 'Tomorrow is to be a day of sabbath rest, a holy sabbath to the LORD. So bake what you want

[a] 23 *Marah* means *bitter.* [b] 16 That is, possibly about 3 pounds or about 1.4 kilograms; also in verses 18, 32, 33 and 36 [c] 22 That is, possibly about 6 pounds or about 2.8 kilograms

to bake and boil what you want to boil. Save whatever is left and keep it until morning.' "

24 So they saved it until morning, as Moses commanded, and it did not stink or get maggots in it. 25 "Eat it today," Moses said, "because today is a sabbath to the LORD. You will not find any of it on the ground today. 26 Six days you are to gather it, but on the seventh day, the Sabbath, there will not be any."

27 Nevertheless, some of the people went out on the seventh day to gather it, but they found none. 28 Then the LORD said to Moses, "How long will you[a] refuse to keep my commands and my instructions? 29 Bear in mind that the LORD has given you the Sabbath; that is why on the sixth day he gives you bread for two days. Everyone is to stay where they are on the seventh day; no one is to go out." 30 So the people rested on the seventh day.

31 The people of Israel called the bread manna.[b] It was white like coriander seed and tasted like wafers made with honey. 32 Moses said, "This is what the LORD has commanded: 'Take an omer of manna and keep it for the generations to come, so they can see the bread I gave you to eat in the wilderness when I brought you out of Egypt.' "

33 So Moses said to Aaron, "Take a jar and put an omer of manna in it. Then place it before the LORD to be kept for the generations to come."

34 As the LORD commanded Moses, Aaron put the manna with the tablets of the covenant law, so that it might be preserved. 35 The Israelites ate manna forty years, until they came to a land that was settled; they ate manna until they reached the border of Canaan.

36 (An omer is one-tenth of an ephah.)

Water From the Rock

17 The whole Israelite community set out from the Desert of Sin, traveling from place to place as the LORD commanded. They camped at Rephidim, but there was no water for the people to drink. 2 So they quarreled with Moses and said, "Give us water to drink."

Moses replied, "Why do you quarrel with me? Why do you put the LORD to the test?"

3 But the people were thirsty for water there, and they grumbled against Moses. They said, "Why did you bring us up out of Egypt to make us and our children and livestock die of thirst?"

4 Then Moses cried out to the LORD, "What am I to do with these people? They are almost ready to stone me."

5 The LORD answered Moses, "Go out in front of the people. Take with you some of the elders of Israel and take in your hand the staff with which you struck the Nile, and go. 6 I will stand there before you by the rock at Horeb. Strike the rock, and water will come out of it for the people to drink." So Moses did this in the sight of the elders of Israel. 7 And he called the place Massah[c] and Meribah[d] because the Israelites quarreled and because they tested the LORD saying, "Is the LORD among us or not?"

The Amalekites Defeated

8 The Amalekites came and attacked the Israelites at Rephidim. 9 Moses said to Joshua, "Choose some of our men and go out to fight the Amalekites. Tomorrow I will stand on top of the hill with the staff of God in my hands."

10 So Joshua fought the Amalekites as Moses had ordered, and Moses, Aaron and Hur went to the top of the hill. 11 As long as Moses held up his hands, the Israelites were winning, but whenever he lowered his hands, the Amalekites were winning. 12 When Moses' hands grew tired, they took a stone and put it under him and he sat on it. Aaron and Hur held his hands up — one on one side, one on the other — so that his hands remained steady till sunset. 13 So Joshua overcame the Amalekite army with the sword.

14 Then the LORD said to Moses, "Write this on a scroll as something to be remembered and make sure that Joshua hears it, because I will completely blot out the name of Amalek from under heaven."

15 Moses built an altar and called it The LORD is my Banner. 16 He said, "Because hands were lifted up against[e] the throne of the LORD,[f] the LORD will be at war against the Amalekites from generation to generation."

Jethro Visits Moses

18 Now Jethro, the priest of Midian and father-in-law of Moses, heard of everything God had done for Moses and for his people Israel, and how the LORD had brought Israel out of Egypt.

[a] 28 The Hebrew is plural. [b] 31 *Manna* sounds like the Hebrew for *What is it?* (see verse 15). [c] 7 *Massah* means *testing.* [d] 7 *Meribah* means *quarreling.* [e] 16 Or *to* [f] 16 The meaning of the Hebrew for this clause is uncertain.

2After Moses had sent away his wife Zipporah, his father-in-law Jethro received her 3and her two sons. One son was named Gershom,[a] for Moses said, "I have become a foreigner in a foreign land"; 4and the other was named Eliezer,[b] for he said, "My father's God was my helper; he saved me from the sword of Pharaoh."

5Jethro, Moses' father-in-law, together with Moses' sons and wife, came to him in the wilderness, where he was camped near the mountain of God. 6Jethro had sent word to him, "I, your father-in-law Jethro, am coming to you with your wife and her two sons."

7So Moses went out to meet his father-in-law and bowed down and kissed him. They greeted each other and then went into the tent. 8Moses told his father-in-law about everything the LORD had done to Pharaoh and the Egyptians for Israel's sake and about all the hardships they had met along the way and how the LORD had saved them.

9Jethro was delighted to hear about all the good things the LORD had done for Israel in rescuing them from the hand of the Egyptians. 10He said, "Praise be to the LORD, who rescued you from the hand of the Egyptians and of Pharaoh, and who rescued the people from the hand of the Egyptians. 11Now I know that the LORD is greater than all other gods, for he did this to those who had treated Israel arrogantly." 12Then Jethro, Moses' father-in-law, brought a burnt offering and other sacrifices to God, and Aaron came with all the elders of Israel to eat a meal with Moses' father-in-law in the presence of God.

13The next day Moses took his seat to serve as judge for the people, and they stood around him from morning till evening. 14When his father-in-law saw all that Moses was doing for the people, he said, "What is this you are doing for the people? Why do you alone sit as judge, while all these people stand around you from morning till evening?"

15Moses answered him, "Because the people come to me to seek God's will. 16Whenever they have a dispute, it is brought to me, and I decide between the parties and inform them of God's decrees and instructions."

17Moses' father-in-law replied, "What you are doing is not good. 18You and these people who come to you will only wear yourselves out. The work is too heavy for you; you cannot handle it alone. 19Listen now to me and I will give you some advice, and may God be with you. You must be the people's representative before God and bring their disputes to him. 20Teach them his decrees and instructions, and show them the way they are to live and how they are to behave. 21But select capable men from all the people — men who fear God, trustworthy men who hate dishonest gain — and appoint them as officials over thousands, hundreds, fifties and tens. 22Have them serve as judges for the people at all times, but have them bring every difficult case to you; the simple cases they can decide themselves. That will make your load lighter, because they will share it with you. 23If you do this and God so commands, you will be able to stand the strain, and all these people will go home satisfied."

24Moses listened to his father-in-law and did everything he said. 25He chose capable men from all Israel and made them leaders of the people, officials over thousands, hundreds, fifties and tens. 26They served as judges for the people at all times. The difficult cases they brought to Moses, but the simple ones they decided themselves.

27Then Moses sent his father-in-law on his way, and Jethro returned to his own country.

At Mount Sinai

19 On the first day of the third month after the Israelites left Egypt — on that very day — they came to the Desert of Sinai. 2After they set out from Rephidim, they entered the Desert of Sinai, and Israel camped there in the desert in front of the mountain.

3Then Moses went up to God, and the LORD called to him from the mountain and said, "This is what you are to say to the descendants of Jacob and what you are to tell the people of Israel: 4'You yourselves have seen what I did to Egypt, and how I carried you on eagles' wings and brought you to myself. 5Now if you obey me fully and keep my covenant, then out of all nations you will be my treasured possession. Although the whole earth is mine, 6you[c] will be for me a kingdom of priests and a holy nation.' These are the words you are to speak to the Israelites."

[a] 3 *Gershom* sounds like the Hebrew for *a foreigner there.* [b] 4 *Eliezer* means *my God is helper.*
[c] 5,6 Or *possession, for the whole earth is mine.* 6*You*

7So Moses went back and summoned
the elders of the people and set before
them all the words the LORD had commanded him to speak. 8The people all
responded together, "We will do everything the LORD has said." So Moses
brought their answer back to the LORD.

9The LORD said to Moses, "I am going
to come to you in a dense cloud, so that
the people will hear me speaking with
you and will always put their trust in
you." Then Moses told the LORD what the
people had said.

10And the LORD said to Moses, "Go to
the people and consecrate them today
and tomorrow. Have them wash their
clothes 11and be ready by the third day,
because on that day the LORD will come
down on Mount Sinai in the sight of all
the people. 12Put limits for the people
around the mountain and tell them, 'Be
careful that you do not approach the
mountain or touch the foot of it. Whoever touches the mountain is to be put
to death. 13They are to be stoned or shot
with arrows; not a hand is to be laid on
them. No person or animal shall be permitted to live.' Only when the ram's horn
sounds a long blast may they approach
the mountain."

14After Moses had gone down the
mountain to the people, he consecrated them, and they washed their clothes.
15Then he said to the people, "Prepare
yourselves for the third day. Abstain
from sexual relations."

16On the morning of the third day
there was thunder and lightning, with
a thick cloud over the mountain, and
a very loud trumpet blast. Everyone in
the camp trembled. 17Then Moses led
the people out of the camp to meet with
God, and they stood at the foot of the
mountain. 18Mount Sinai was covered
with smoke, because the LORD descended on it in fire. The smoke billowed up
from it like smoke from a furnace, and
the whole mountain[a] trembled violently.
19As the sound of the trumpet grew louder and louder, Moses spoke and the voice
of God answered him.[b]

20The LORD descended to the top of
Mount Sinai and called Moses to the
top of the mountain. So Moses went up
21and the LORD said to him, "Go down
and warn the people so they do not force
their way through to see the LORD and
many of them perish. 22Even the priests,
who approach the LORD, must consecrate themselves, or the LORD will break
out against them."

23Moses said to the LORD, "The people
cannot come up Mount Sinai, because
you yourself warned us, 'Put limits
around the mountain and set it apart
as holy.' "

24The LORD replied, "Go down and
bring Aaron up with you. But the priests
and the people must not force their way
through to come up to the LORD, or he
will break out against them."

25So Moses went down to the people
and told them.

The Ten Commandments

20 And God spoke all these words:

2"I am the LORD your God, who
brought you out of Egypt, out
of the land of slavery.

3"You shall have no other gods before[c] me.

4"You shall not make for yourself
an image in the form of anything in heaven above or on
the earth beneath or in the waters below. 5You shall not bow
down to them or worship them;
for I, the LORD your God, am a
jealous God, punishing the children for the sin of the parents
to the third and fourth generation of those who hate me, 6but
showing love to a thousand
generations of those who love
me and keep my command-
ments.

7"You shall not misuse the name of
the LORD your God, for the LORD
will not hold anyone guiltless
who misuses his name.

8"Remember the Sabbath day by
keeping it holy. 9Six days you
shall labor and do all your
work, 10but the seventh day
is a sabbath to the LORD your
God. On it you shall not do any
work, neither you, nor your son
or daughter, nor your male or
female servant, nor your animals, nor any foreigner residing in your towns. 11For in six
days the LORD made the heavens and the earth, the sea, and
all that is in them, but he rested on the seventh day. Therefore the LORD blessed the Sabbath day and made it holy.

[a] 18 Most Hebrew manuscripts; a few Hebrew manuscripts and Septuagint *and all the people*
[b] 19 Or *and God answered him with thunder* [c] 3 Or *besides*

12 "Honor your father and your mother, so that you may live long in
the land the LORD your God is
giving you.
13 "You shall not murder.
14 "You shall not commit adultery.
15 "You shall not steal.
16 "You shall not give false testimony
against your neighbor.
17 "You shall not covet your neighbor's
house. You shall not covet your
neighbor's wife, or his male or
female servant, his ox or donkey, or anything that belongs
to your neighbor."

18 When the people saw the thunder
and lightning and heard the trumpet
and saw the mountain in smoke, they
trembled with fear. They stayed at a distance 19 and said to Moses, "Speak to us
yourself and we will listen. But do not
have God speak to us or we will die."
20 Moses said to the people, "Do not be
afraid. God has come to test you, so that
the fear of God will be with you to keep
you from sinning."
21 The people remained at a distance,
while Moses approached the thick darkness where God was.

Idols and Altars

22 Then the LORD said to Moses, "Tell
the Israelites this: 'You have seen for
yourselves that I have spoken to you
from heaven: 23 Do not make any gods to
be alongside me; do not make for yourselves gods of silver or gods of gold.
24 " 'Make an altar of earth for me and
sacrifice on it your burnt offerings and
fellowship offerings, your sheep and
goats and your cattle. Wherever I cause
my name to be honored, I will come to
you and bless you. 25 If you make an altar of stones for me, do not build it with
dressed stones, for you will defile it if you
use a tool on it. 26 And do not go up to my
altar on steps, or your private parts may
be exposed.'

21 "These are the laws you are to set
before them:

Hebrew Servants

2 "If you buy a Hebrew servant, he is
to serve you for six years. But in the seventh year, he shall go free, without paying anything. 3 If he comes alone, he is to
go free alone; but if he has a wife when
he comes, she is to go with him. 4 If his
master gives him a wife and she bears
him sons or daughters, the woman and
her children shall belong to her master,
and only the man shall go free.
5 "But if the servant declares, 'I love my
master and my wife and children and
do not want to go free,' 6 then his master must take him before the judges.[a] He
shall take him to the door or the doorpost and pierce his ear with an awl. Then
he will be his servant for life.
7 "If a man sells his daughter as a servant, she is not to go free as male servants do. 8 If she does not please the
master who has selected her for himself,[b] he must let her be redeemed. He
has no right to sell her to foreigners, because he has broken faith with her. 9 If he
selects her for his son, he must grant her
the rights of a daughter. 10 If he marries
another woman, he must not deprive the
first one of her food, clothing and marital rights. 11 If he does not provide her
with these three things, she is to go free,
without any payment of money.

Personal Injuries

12 "Anyone who strikes a person with a
fatal blow is to be put to death. 13 However, if it is not done intentionally, but God
lets it happen, they are to flee to a place
I will designate. 14 But if anyone schemes
and kills someone deliberately, that person is to be taken from my altar and put
to death.
15 "Anyone who attacks[c] their father or
mother is to be put to death.
16 "Anyone who kidnaps someone is to
be put to death, whether the victim has
been sold or is still in the kidnapper's
possession.
17 "Anyone who curses their father or
mother is to be put to death.
18 "If people quarrel and one person
hits another with a stone or with their
fist[d] and the victim does not die but is
confined to bed, 19 the one who struck the
blow will not be held liable if the other
can get up and walk around outside
with a staff; however, the guilty party
must pay the injured person for any loss
of time and see that the victim is completely healed.
20 "Anyone who beats their male or female slave with a rod must be punished
if the slave dies as a direct result, 21 but
they are not to be punished if the slave
recovers after a day or two, since the
slave is their property.

[a] 6 Or *before God* [b] 8 Or *master so that he does not choose her* [c] 15 Or *kills* [d] 18 Or *with a tool*

22“If people are fighting and hit a pregnant woman and she gives birth prematurely[a] but there is no serious injury, the offender must be fined whatever the woman’s husband demands and the court allows. 23But if there is serious injury, you are to take life for life, 24eye for eye, tooth for tooth, hand for hand, foot for foot, 25burn for burn, wound for wound, bruise for bruise.

26“An owner who hits a male or female slave in the eye and destroys it must let the slave go free to compensate for the eye. 27And an owner who knocks out the tooth of a male or female slave must let the slave go free to compensate for the tooth.

28“If a bull gores a man or woman to death, the bull is to be stoned to death, and its meat must not be eaten. But the owner of the bull will not be held responsible. 29If, however, the bull has had the habit of goring and the owner has been warned but has not kept it penned up and it kills a man or woman, the bull is to be stoned and its owner also is to be put to death. 30However, if payment is demanded, the owner may redeem his life by the payment of whatever is demanded. 31This law also applies if the bull gores a son or daughter. 32If the bull gores a male or female slave, the owner must pay thirty shekels[b] of silver to the master of the slave, and the bull is to be stoned to death.

33“If anyone uncovers a pit or digs one and fails to cover it and an ox or a donkey falls into it, 34the one who opened the pit must pay the owner for the loss and take the dead animal in exchange.

35“If anyone’s bull injures someone else’s bull and it dies, the two parties are to sell the live one and divide both the money and the dead animal equally. 36However, if it was known that the bull had the habit of goring, yet the owner did not keep it penned up, the owner must pay, animal for animal, and take the dead animal in exchange.

Protection of Property

22[c] “Whoever steals an ox or a sheep and slaughters it or sells it must pay back five head of cattle for the ox and four sheep for the sheep.

2“If a thief is caught breaking in at night and is struck a fatal blow, the defender is not guilty of bloodshed; 3but if it happens after sunrise, the defender is guilty of bloodshed.

“Anyone who steals must certainly make restitution, but if they have nothing, they must be sold to pay for their theft. 4If the stolen animal is found alive in their possession — whether ox or donkey or sheep — they must pay back double.

5“If anyone grazes their livestock in a field or vineyard and lets them stray and they graze in someone else’s field, the offender must make restitution from the best of their own field or vineyard.

6“If a fire breaks out and spreads into thornbushes so that it burns shocks of grain or standing grain or the whole field, the one who started the fire must make restitution.

7“If anyone gives a neighbor silver or goods for safekeeping and they are stolen from the neighbor’s house, the thief, if caught, must pay back double. 8But if the thief is not found, the owner of the house must appear before the judges, and they must[d] determine whether the owner of the house has laid hands on the other person’s property. 9In all cases of illegal possession of an ox, a donkey, a sheep, a garment, or any other lost property about which somebody says, ‘This is mine,’ both parties are to bring their cases before the judges.[e] The one whom the judges declare[f] guilty must pay back double to the other.

10“If anyone gives a donkey, an ox, a sheep or any other animal to their neighbor for safekeeping and it dies or is injured or is taken away while no one is looking, 11the issue between them will be settled by the taking of an oath before the LORD that the neighbor did not lay hands on the other person’s property. The owner is to accept this, and no restitution is required. 12But if the animal was stolen from the neighbor, restitution must be made to the owner. 13If it was torn to pieces by a wild animal, the neighbor shall bring in the remains as evidence and shall not be required to pay for the torn animal.

14“If anyone borrows an animal from their neighbor and it is injured or dies while the owner is not present, they must make restitution. 15But if the owner is with the animal, the borrower will not have to pay. If the animal was hired, the money paid for the hire covers the loss.

[a] 22 Or *she has a miscarriage* [b] 32 That is, about 12 ounces or about 345 grams [c] In Hebrew texts 22:1 is numbered 21:37, and 22:2-31 is numbered 22:1-30. [d] 8 Or *before God, and he will* [e] 9 Or *before God* [f] 9 Or *whom God declares*

Social Responsibility

16“If a man seduces a virgin who is not
pledged to be married and sleeps with
her, he must pay the bride-price, and she
shall be his wife. 17If her father absolutely refuses to give her to him, he must still
pay the bride-price for virgins.

18“Do not allow a sorceress to live.

19“Anyone who has sexual relations
with an animal is to be put to death.

20“Whoever sacrifices to any god other
than the LORD must be destroyed.[a]

21“Do not mistreat or oppress a foreigner, for you were foreigners in Egypt.

22“Do not take advantage of the widow
or the fatherless. 23If you do and they cry
out to me, I will certainly hear their cry.
24My anger will be aroused, and I will kill
you with the sword; your wives will become widows and your children fatherless.

25“If you lend money to one of my people among you who is needy, do not treat
it like a business deal; charge no interest. 26If you take your neighbor’s cloak as
a pledge, return it by sunset, 27because
that cloak is the only covering your
neighbor has. What else can they sleep
in? When they cry out to me, I will hear,
for I am compassionate.

28“Do not blaspheme God[b] or curse the
ruler of your people.

29“Do not hold back offerings from
your granaries or your vats.[c]

“You must give me the firstborn of
your sons. 30Do the same with your cattle
and your sheep. Let them stay with their
mothers for seven days, but give them to
me on the eighth day.

31“You are to be my holy people. So do
not eat the meat of an animal torn by
wild beasts; throw it to the dogs.

Laws of Justice and Mercy

23 “Do not spread false reports. Do
not help a guilty person by being
a malicious witness.

2“Do not follow the crowd in doing
wrong. When you give testimony in a
lawsuit, do not pervert justice by siding
with the crowd, 3and do not show favoritism to a poor person in a lawsuit.

4“If you come across your enemy’s ox
or donkey wandering off, be sure to return it. 5If you see the donkey of someone who hates you fallen down under its
load, do not leave it there; be sure you
help them with it.

6“Do not deny justice to your poor people in their lawsuits. 7Have nothing to
do with a false charge and do not put an
innocent or honest person to death, for I
will not acquit the guilty.

8“Do not accept a bribe, for a bribe
blinds those who see and twists the
words of the innocent.

9“Do not oppress a foreigner; you yourselves know how it feels to be foreigners,
because you were foreigners in Egypt.

Sabbath Laws

10“For six years you are to sow your
fields and harvest the crops, 11but during the seventh year let the land lie
unplowed and unused. Then the poor
among your people may get food from
it, and the wild animals may eat what is
left. Do the same with your vineyard and
your olive grove.

12“Six days do your work, but on the
seventh day do not work, so that your ox
and your donkey may rest, and so that
the slave born in your household and
the foreigner living among you may be
refreshed.

13“Be careful to do everything I have
said to you. Do not invoke the names of
other gods; do not let them be heard on
your lips.

The Three Annual Festivals

14“Three times a year you are to celebrate a festival to me.

15“Celebrate the Festival of Unleavened Bread; for seven days eat bread
made without yeast, as I commanded
you. Do this at the appointed time in
the month of Aviv, for in that month you
came out of Egypt.

“No one is to appear before me empty-
handed.

16“Celebrate the Festival of Harvest
with the firstfruits of the crops you sow
in your field.

“Celebrate the Festival of Ingathering
at the end of the year, when you gather
in your crops from the field.

17“Three times a year all the men are
to appear before the Sovereign LORD.

18“Do not offer the blood of a sacrifice to
me along with anything containing yeast.

“The fat of my festival offerings must
not be kept until morning.

19“Bring the best of the firstfruits of your
soil to the house of the LORD your God.

“Do not cook a young goat in its mother’s milk.

[a] *20* The Hebrew term refers to the irrevocable giving over of things or persons to the LORD, often by totally destroying them. [b] *28* Or *Do not revile the judges* [c] *29* The meaning of the Hebrew for this phrase is uncertain.

God's Angel to Prepare the Way

20“See, I am sending an angel ahead of
you to guard you along the way and to
bring you to the place I have prepared.
21Pay attention to him and listen to what
he says. Do not rebel against him; he will
not forgive your rebellion, since my Name
is in him. 22If you listen carefully to what
he says and do all that I say, I will be an
enemy to your enemies and will oppose
those who oppose you. 23My angel will go
ahead of you and bring you into the land
of the Amorites, Hittites, Perizzites, Canaanites, Hivites and Jebusites, and I will
wipe them out. 24Do not bow down before
their gods or worship them or follow their
practices. You must demolish them and
break their sacred stones to pieces. 25Wor-
ship the LORD your God, and his blessing
will be on your food and water. I will take
away sickness from among you, 26and
none will miscarry or be barren in your
land. I will give you a full life span.

27“I will send my terror ahead of you
and throw into confusion every nation
you encounter. I will make all your enemies turn their backs and run. 28I will
send the hornet ahead of you to drive
the Hivites, Canaanites and Hittites out
of your way. 29But I will not drive them
out in a single year, because the land
would become desolate and the wild animals too numerous for you. 30Little by
little I will drive them out before you,
until you have increased enough to take
possession of the land.

31“I will establish your borders from
the Red Sea[a] to the Mediterranean Sea,[b]
and from the desert to the Euphrates
River. I will give into your hands the
people who live in the land, and you
will drive them out before you. 32Do not
make a covenant with them or with their
gods. 33Do not let them live in your land
or they will cause you to sin against me,
because the worship of their gods will
certainly be a snare to you.”

The Covenant Confirmed

24 Then the LORD said to Moses,
“Come up to the LORD, you and
Aaron, Nadab and Abihu, and seventy
of the elders of Israel. You are to worship at a distance, 2but Moses alone is
to approach the LORD; the others must
not come near. And the people may not
come up with him.”

3When Moses went and told the people all the LORD's words and laws, they
responded with one voice, “Everything
the LORD has said we will do.” 4Moses
then wrote down everything the LORD
had said.

He got up early the next morning and
built an altar at the foot of the mountain
and set up twelve stone pillars representing the twelve tribes of Israel. 5Then he
sent young Israelite men, and they offered burnt offerings and sacrificed young
bulls as fellowship offerings to the LORD.
6Moses took half of the blood and put it
in bowls, and the other half he splashed
against the altar. 7Then he took the Book
of the Covenant and read it to the people.
They responded, “We will do everything
the LORD has said; we will obey.”

8Moses then took the blood, sprinkled
it on the people and said, “This is the
blood of the covenant that the LORD has
made with you in accordance with all
these words.”

9Moses and Aaron, Nadab and Abihu,
and the seventy elders of Israel went up
10and saw the God of Israel. Under his
feet was something like a pavement
made of lapis lazuli, as bright blue as
the sky. 11But God did not raise his hand
against these leaders of the Israelites;
they saw God, and they ate and drank.

12The LORD said to Moses, “Come up to
me on the mountain and stay here, and I
will give you the tablets of stone with the
law and commandments I have written
for their instruction.”

13Then Moses set out with Joshua his
aide, and Moses went up on the mountain of God. 14He said to the elders, “Wait
here for us until we come back to you.
Aaron and Hur are with you, and anyone
involved in a dispute can go to them.”

15When Moses went up on the mountain, the cloud covered it, 16and the glory
of the LORD settled on Mount Sinai. For
six days the cloud covered the mountain, and on the seventh day the LORD
called to Moses from within the cloud.
17To the Israelites the glory of the LORD
looked like a consuming fire on top of
the mountain. 18Then Moses entered the
cloud as he went on up the mountain.
And he stayed on the mountain forty
days and forty nights.

Offerings for the Tabernacle

25 The LORD said to Moses, 2“Tell the
Israelites to bring me an offering.
You are to receive the offering for me
from everyone whose heart prompts
them to give. 3These are the offerings
you are to receive from them: gold, silver

[a] 31 Or *the Sea of Reeds* [b] 31 Hebrew *to the Sea of the Philistines*

and bronze; 4blue, purple and scarlet yarn and fine linen; goat hair; 5ram skins dyed red and another type of durable leather[a]; acacia wood; 6olive oil for the light; spices for the anointing oil and for the fragrant incense; 7and onyx stones and other gems to be mounted on the ephod and breastpiece.

8"Then have them make a sanctuary for me, and I will dwell among them. 9Make this tabernacle and all its furnishings exactly like the pattern I will show you.

The Ark

10"Have them make an ark[b] of acacia wood — two and a half cubits long, a cubit and a half wide, and a cubit and a half high.[c] 11Overlay it with pure gold, both inside and out, and make a gold molding around it. 12Cast four gold rings for it and fasten them to its four feet, with two rings on one side and two rings on the other. 13Then make poles of acacia wood and overlay them with gold. 14Insert the poles into the rings on the sides of the ark to carry it. 15The poles are to remain in the rings of this ark; they are not to be removed. 16Then put in the ark the tablets of the covenant law, which I will give you.

17"Make an atonement cover of pure gold — two and a half cubits long and a cubit and a half wide. 18And make two cherubim out of hammered gold at the ends of the cover. 19Make one cherub on one end and the second cherub on the other; make the cherubim of one piece with the cover, at the two ends. 20The cherubim are to have their wings spread upward, overshadowing the cover with them. The cherubim are to face each other, looking toward the cover. 21Place the cover on top of the ark and put in the ark the tablets of the covenant law that I will give you. 22There, above the cover between the two cherubim that are over the ark of the covenant law, I will meet with you and give you all my commands for the Israelites.

The Table

23"Make a table of acacia wood — two cubits long, a cubit wide and a cubit and a half high.[d] 24Overlay it with pure gold and make a gold molding around it. 25Also make around it a rim a handbreadth[e] wide and put a gold molding on the rim. 26Make four gold rings for the table and fasten them to the four corners, where the four legs are. 27The rings are to be close to the rim to hold the poles used in carrying the table. 28Make the poles of acacia wood, overlay them with gold and carry the table with them. 29And make its plates and dishes of pure gold, as well as its pitchers and bowls for the pouring out of offerings. 30Put the bread of the Presence on this table to be before me at all times.

The Lampstand

31"Make a lampstand of pure gold. Hammer out its base and shaft, and make its flowerlike cups, buds and blossoms of one piece with them. 32Six branches are to extend from the sides of the lampstand — three on one side and three on the other. 33Three cups shaped like almond flowers with buds and blossoms are to be on one branch, three on the next branch, and the same for all six branches extending from the lampstand. 34And on the lampstand there are to be four cups shaped like almond flowers with buds and blossoms. 35One bud shall be under the first pair of branches extending from the lampstand, a second bud under the second pair, and a third bud under the third pair — six branches in all. 36The buds and branches shall all be of one piece with the lampstand, hammered out of pure gold.

37"Then make its seven lamps and set them up on it so that they light the space in front of it. 38Its wick trimmers and trays are to be of pure gold. 39A talent[f] of pure gold is to be used for the lampstand and all these accessories. 40See that you make them according to the pattern shown you on the mountain.

The Tabernacle

26 "Make the tabernacle with ten curtains of finely twisted linen and blue, purple and scarlet yarn, with cherubim woven into them by a skilled worker. 2All the curtains are to be the same size — twenty-eight cubits long and four cubits wide.[g] 3Join five of the curtains together, and do the same with the other five.

[a] *5* Possibly the hides of large aquatic mammals [b] *10* That is, a chest [c] *10* That is, about 3 3/4 feet long and 2 1/4 feet wide and high or about 1.1 meters long and 68 centimeters wide and high; similarly in verse 17 [d] *23* That is, about 3 feet long, 1 1/2 feet wide and 2 1/4 feet high or about 90 centimeters long, 45 centimeters wide and 68 centimeters high [e] *25* That is, about 3 inches or about 7.5 centimeters [f] *39* That is, about 75 pounds or about 34 kilograms
[g] *2* That is, about 42 feet long and 6 feet wide or about 13 meters long and 1.8 meters wide

4Make loops of blue material along the edge of the end curtain in one set, and do the same with the end curtain in the other set. 5Make fifty loops on one curtain and fifty loops on the end curtain of the other set, with the loops opposite each other. 6Then make fifty gold clasps and use them to fasten the curtains together so that the tabernacle is a unit.

7"Make curtains of goat hair for the tent over the tabernacle — eleven altogether. 8All eleven curtains are to be the same size — thirty cubits long and four cubits wide.[a] 9Join five of the curtains together into one set and the other six into another set. Fold the sixth curtain double at the front of the tent. 10Make fifty loops along the edge of the end curtain in one set and also along the edge of the end curtain in the other set. 11Then make fifty bronze clasps and put them in the loops to fasten the tent together as a unit. 12As for the additional length of the tent curtains, the half curtain that is left over is to hang down at the rear of the tabernacle. 13The tent curtains will be a cubit[b] longer on both sides; what is left will hang over the sides of the tabernacle so as to cover it. 14Make for the tent a covering of ram skins dyed red, and over that a covering of the other durable leather.[c]

15"Make upright frames of acacia wood for the tabernacle. 16Each frame is to be ten cubits long and a cubit and a half wide,[d] 17with two projections set parallel to each other. Make all the frames of the tabernacle in this way. 18Make twenty frames for the south side of the tabernacle 19and make forty silver bases to go under them — two bases for each frame, one under each projection. 20For the other side, the north side of the tabernacle, make twenty frames 21and forty silver bases — two under each frame. 22Make six frames for the far end, that is, the west end of the tabernacle, 23and make two frames for the corners at the far end. 24At these two corners they must be double from the bottom all the way to the top and fitted into a single ring; both shall be like that. 25So there will be eight frames and sixteen silver bases — two under each frame.

26"Also make crossbars of acacia wood: five for the frames on one side of the tabernacle, 27five for those on the other side, and five for the frames on the west, at the far end of the tabernacle. 28The center crossbar is to extend from end to end at the middle of the frames. 29Overlay the frames with gold and make gold rings to hold the crossbars. Also overlay the crossbars with gold.

30"Set up the tabernacle according to the plan shown you on the mountain.

31"Make a curtain of blue, purple and scarlet yarn and finely twisted linen, with cherubim woven into it by a skilled worker. 32Hang it with gold hooks on four posts of acacia wood overlaid with gold and standing on four silver bases. 33Hang the curtain from the clasps and place the ark of the covenant law behind the curtain. The curtain will separate the Holy Place from the Most Holy Place. 34Put the atonement cover on the ark of the covenant law in the Most Holy Place. 35Place the table outside the curtain on the north side of the tabernacle and put the lampstand opposite it on the south side.

36"For the entrance to the tent make a curtain of blue, purple and scarlet yarn and finely twisted linen — the work of an embroiderer. 37Make gold hooks for this curtain and five posts of acacia wood overlaid with gold. And cast five bronze bases for them.

The Altar of Burnt Offering

27 "Build an altar of acacia wood, three cubits[e] high; it is to be square, five cubits long and five cubits wide.[f] 2Make a horn at each of the four corners, so that the horns and the altar are of one piece, and overlay the altar with bronze. 3Make all its utensils of bronze — its pots to remove the ashes, and its shovels, sprinkling bowls, meat forks and firepans. 4Make a grating for it, a bronze network, and make a bronze ring at each of the four corners of the network. 5Put it under the ledge of the altar so that it is halfway up the altar. 6Make poles of acacia wood for the altar and overlay them with bronze. 7The poles are to be inserted into the rings so they will be on two sides of the altar when it is carried. 8Make the altar hollow, out of boards. It is to be made just as you were shown on the mountain.

[a] *8* That is, about 45 feet long and 6 feet wide or about 13.5 meters long and 1.8 meters wide
[b] *13* That is, about 18 inches or about 45 centimeters [c] *14* Possibly the hides of large aquatic mammals (see 25:5) [d] *16* That is, about 15 feet long and 2 1/4 feet wide or about 4.5 meters long and 68 centimeters wide [e] *1* That is, about 4 1/2 feet or about 1.4 meters [f] *1* That is, about 7 1/2 feet or about 2.3 meters long and wide

The Courtyard

9“Make a courtyard for the tabernacle. The south side shall be a hundred
cubits[a] long and is to have curtains of
finely twisted linen, 10with twenty posts
and twenty bronze bases and with silver hooks and bands on the posts. 11The
north side shall also be a hundred cubits
long and is to have curtains, with twenty
posts and twenty bronze bases and with
silver hooks and bands on the posts.
12“The west end of the courtyard shall
be fifty cubits[b] wide and have curtains,
with ten posts and ten bases. 13On the
east end, toward the sunrise, the courtyard shall also be fifty cubits wide. 14Cur-
tains fifteen cubits[c] long are to be on one
side of the entrance, with three posts
and three bases, 15and curtains fifteen
cubits long are to be on the other side,
with three posts and three bases.
16“For the entrance to the courtyard,
provide a curtain twenty cubits[d] long, of
blue, purple and scarlet yarn and finely
twisted linen — the work of an embroiderer — with four posts and four bases.
17All the posts around the courtyard are to
have silver bands and hooks, and bronze
bases. 18The courtyard shall be a hundred
cubits long and fifty cubits wide,[e] with
curtains of finely twisted linen five cubits[f]
high, and with bronze bases. 19All the other articles used in the service of the tabernacle, whatever their function, including
all the tent pegs for it and those for the
courtyard, are to be of bronze.

Oil for the Lampstand

20“Command the Israelites to bring
you clear oil of pressed olives for the
light so that the lamps may be kept
burning. 21In the tent of meeting, outside
the curtain that shields the ark of the
covenant law, Aaron and his sons are to
keep the lamps burning before the LORD
from evening till morning. This is to be
a lasting ordinance among the Israelites
for the generations to come.

The Priestly Garments

28 “Have Aaron your brother brought
to you from among the Israelites,
along with his sons Nadab and Abihu,
Eleazar and Ithamar, so they may serve
me as priests. 2Make sacred garments for
your brother Aaron to give him dignity
and honor. 3Tell all the skilled workers to
whom I have given wisdom in such matters that they are to make garments for
Aaron, for his consecration, so he may
serve me as priest. 4These are the garments they are to make: a breastpiece,
an ephod, a robe, a woven tunic, a turban and a sash. They are to make these
sacred garments for your brother Aaron
and his sons, so they may serve me as
priests. 5Have them use gold, and blue,
purple and scarlet yarn, and fine linen.

The Ephod

6“Make the ephod of gold, and of blue,
purple and scarlet yarn, and of finely twisted linen — the work of skilled
hands. 7It is to have two shoulder pieces
attached to two of its corners, so it can
be fastened. 8Its skillfully woven waistband is to be like it — of one piece with
the ephod and made with gold, and with
blue, purple and scarlet yarn, and with
finely twisted linen.
9“Take two onyx stones and engrave
on them the names of the sons of Israel
10in the order of their birth — six names
on one stone and the remaining six on
the other. 11Engrave the names of the
sons of Israel on the two stones the way a
gem cutter engraves a seal. Then mount
the stones in gold filigree settings 12and
fasten them on the shoulder pieces of the
ephod as memorial stones for the sons of
Israel. Aaron is to bear the names on his
shoulders as a memorial before the LORD.
13Make gold filigree settings 14and two
braided chains of pure gold, like a rope,
and attach the chains to the settings.

The Breastpiece

15“Fashion a breastpiece for making
decisions — the work of skilled hands.
Make it like the ephod: of gold, and of
blue, purple and scarlet yarn, and of finely twisted linen. 16It is to be square — a
span[g] long and a span wide — and folded double. 17Then mount four rows of
precious stones on it. The first row shall
be carnelian, chrysolite and beryl; 18the
second row shall be turquoise, lapis lazuli and emerald; 19the third row shall be
jacinth, agate and amethyst; 20the fourth
row shall be topaz, onyx and jasper.[h]

[a] *9* That is, about 150 feet or about 45 meters; also in verse 11 [b] *12* That is, about 75 feet or about 23 meters; also in verse 13 [c] *14* That is, about 23 feet or about 6.8 meters; also in verse 15 [d] *16* That is, about 30 feet or about 9 meters [e] *18* That is, about 150 feet long and 75 feet wide or about 45 meters long and 23 meters wide [f] *18* That is, about 7 1/2 feet or about 2.3 meters [g] *16* That is, about 9 inches or about 23 centimeters [h] *20* The precise identification of some of these precious stones is uncertain.

Mount them in gold filigree settings.
[21]There are to be twelve stones, one for
each of the names of the sons of Israel,
each engraved like a seal with the name
of one of the twelve tribes.
[22]"For the breastpiece make braided
chains of pure gold, like a rope. [23]Make
two gold rings for it and fasten them to
two corners of the breastpiece. [24]Fasten
the two gold chains to the rings at the
corners of the breastpiece, [25]and the other ends of the chains to the two settings,
attaching them to the shoulder pieces
of the ephod at the front. [26]Make two
gold rings and attach them to the other two corners of the breastpiece on the
inside edge next to the ephod. [27]Make
two more gold rings and attach them
to the bottom of the shoulder pieces on
the front of the ephod, close to the seam
just above the waistband of the ephod.
[28]The rings of the breastpiece are to be
tied to the rings of the ephod with blue
cord, connecting it to the waistband, so
that the breastpiece will not swing out
from the ephod.
[29]"Whenever Aaron enters the Holy
Place, he will bear the names of the sons
of Israel over his heart on the breastpiece of decision as a continuing memorial before the LORD. [30]Also put the Urim
and the Thummim in the breastpiece, so
they may be over Aaron's heart whenever he enters the presence of the LORD.
Thus Aaron will always bear the means
of making decisions for the Israelites
over his heart before the LORD.

Other Priestly Garments

[31]"Make the robe of the ephod entirely of blue cloth, [32]with an opening for
the head in its center. There shall be a
woven edge like a collar[a] around this
opening, so that it will not tear. [33]Make
pomegranates of blue, purple and scarlet yarn around the hem of the robe,
with gold bells between them. [34]The gold
bells and the pomegranates are to alternate around the hem of the robe. [35]Aaron must wear it when he ministers. The
sound of the bells will be heard when he
enters the Holy Place before the LORD
and when he comes out, so that he will
not die.
[36]"Make a plate of pure gold and engrave on it as on a seal: HOLY TO THE
LORD. [37]Fasten a blue cord to it to attach
it to the turban; it is to be on the front of
the turban. [38]It will be on Aaron's forehead, and he will bear the guilt involved
in the sacred gifts the Israelites consecrate, whatever their gifts may be. It will
be on Aaron's forehead continually so
that they will be acceptable to the LORD.
[39]"Weave the tunic of fine linen and
make the turban of fine linen. The sash
is to be the work of an embroiderer.
[40]Make tunics, sashes and caps for Aaron's sons to give them dignity and honor. [41]After you put these clothes on your
brother Aaron and his sons, anoint and
ordain them. Consecrate them so they
may serve me as priests.
[42]"Make linen undergarments as a
covering for the body, reaching from the
waist to the thigh. [43]Aaron and his sons
must wear them whenever they enter
the tent of meeting or approach the altar to minister in the Holy Place, so that
they will not incur guilt and die.
"This is to be a lasting ordinance for
Aaron and his descendants.

Consecration of the Priests

29 "This is what you are to do to consecrate them, so they may serve
me as priests: Take a young bull and two
rams without defect. [2]And from the finest wheat flour make round loaves without yeast, thick loaves without yeast and
with olive oil mixed in, and thin loaves
without yeast and brushed with olive
oil. [3]Put them in a basket and present
them along with the bull and the two
rams. [4]Then bring Aaron and his sons to
the entrance to the tent of meeting and
wash them with water. [5]Take the garments and dress Aaron with the tunic,
the robe of the ephod, the ephod itself
and the breastpiece. Fasten the ephod
on him by its skillfully woven waistband. [6]Put the turban on his head and
attach the sacred emblem to the turban.
[7]Take the anointing oil and anoint him
by pouring it on his head. [8]Bring his sons
and dress them in tunics [9]and fasten
caps on them. Then tie sashes on Aaron
and his sons.[b] The priesthood is theirs by
a lasting ordinance.
"Then you shall ordain Aaron and his
sons.
[10]"Bring the bull to the front of the tent
of meeting, and Aaron and his sons shall
lay their hands on its head. [11]Slaughter
it in the LORD's presence at the entrance
to the tent of meeting. [12]Take some of
the bull's blood and put it on the horns
of the altar with your finger, and pour
out the rest of it at the base of the altar.
[13]Then take all the fat on the internal

[a] *32* The meaning of the Hebrew for this word is uncertain. [b] *9* Hebrew; Septuagint *on them*

organs, the long lobe of the liver, and
both kidneys with the fat on them, and
burn them on the altar. 14But burn the
bull's flesh and its hide and its intestines
outside the camp. It is a sin offering.[a]

15"Take one of the rams, and Aaron
and his sons shall lay their hands on its
head. 16Slaughter it and take the blood
and splash it against the sides of the altar. 17Cut the ram into pieces and wash
the internal organs and the legs, putting
them with the head and the other pieces.
18Then burn the entire ram on the altar.
It is a burnt offering to the LORD, a pleasing aroma, a food offering presented to
the LORD.

19"Take the other ram, and Aaron
and his sons shall lay their hands on
its head. 20Slaughter it, take some of
its blood and put it on the lobes of the
right ears of Aaron and his sons, on the
thumbs of their right hands, and on the
big toes of their right feet. Then splash
blood against the sides of the altar.
21And take some blood from the altar
and some of the anointing oil and sprinkle it on Aaron and his garments and
on his sons and their garments. Then he
and his sons and their garments will be
consecrated.

22"Take from this ram the fat, the fat
tail, the fat on the internal organs, the
long lobe of the liver, both kidneys with
the fat on them, and the right thigh.
(This is the ram for the ordination.)
23From the basket of bread made without yeast, which is before the LORD, take
one round loaf, one thick loaf with olive oil mixed in, and one thin loaf. 24Put
all these in the hands of Aaron and his
sons and have them wave them before
the LORD as a wave offering. 25Then take
them from their hands and burn them
on the altar along with the burnt offering for a pleasing aroma to the LORD,
a food offering presented to the LORD.
26After you take the breast of the ram for
Aaron's ordination, wave it before the
LORD as a wave offering, and it will be
your share.

27"Consecrate those parts of the ordination ram that belong to Aaron and
his sons: the breast that was waved and
the thigh that was presented. 28This is
always to be the perpetual share from
the Israelites for Aaron and his sons. It
is the contribution the Israelites are to
make to the LORD from their fellowship
offerings.

29"Aaron's sacred garments will belong to his descendants so that they can
be anointed and ordained in them. 30The
son who succeeds him as priest and
comes to the tent of meeting to minister
in the Holy Place is to wear them seven
days.

31"Take the ram for the ordination and
cook the meat in a sacred place. 32At the
entrance to the tent of meeting, Aaron
and his sons are to eat the meat of the
ram and the bread that is in the basket. 33They are to eat these offerings by
which atonement was made for their ordination and consecration. But no one
else may eat them, because they are
sacred. 34And if any of the meat of the
ordination ram or any bread is left over
till morning, burn it up. It must not be
eaten, because it is sacred.

35"Do for Aaron and his sons everything I have commanded you, taking
seven days to ordain them. 36Sacrifice a
bull each day as a sin offering to make
atonement. Purify the altar by making
atonement for it, and anoint it to consecrate it. 37For seven days make atonement for the altar and consecrate it.
Then the altar will be most holy, and
whatever touches it will be holy.

38"This is what you are to offer on the
altar regularly each day: two lambs
a year old. 39Offer one in the morning
and the other at twilight. 40With the
first lamb offer a tenth of an ephah[b] of
the finest flour mixed with a quarter of
a hin[c] of oil from pressed olives, and a
quarter of a hin of wine as a drink offering. 41Sacrifice the other lamb at twilight with the same grain offering and
its drink offering as in the morning — a
pleasing aroma, a food offering presented to the LORD.

42"For the generations to come this
burnt offering is to be made regularly at
the entrance to the tent of meeting, before the LORD. There I will meet you and
speak to you; 43there also I will meet with
the Israelites, and the place will be consecrated by my glory.

44"So I will consecrate the tent of
meeting and the altar and will consecrate Aaron and his sons to serve me
as priests. 45Then I will dwell among
the Israelites and be their God. 46They
will know that I am the LORD their God,
who brought them out of Egypt so that I
might dwell among them. I am the LORD
their God.

[a] 14 Or *purification offering*; also in verse 36 [b] 40 That is, probably about 3 1/2 pounds or about 1.6 kilograms [c] 40 That is, probably about 1 quart or about 1 liter

The Altar of Incense

30 "Make an altar of acacia wood for burning incense. 2It is to be square, a cubit long and a cubit wide, and two cubits high[a] — its horns of one piece with it. 3Overlay the top and all the sides and the horns with pure gold, and make a gold molding around it. 4Make two gold rings for the altar below the molding — two on each of the opposite sides — to hold the poles used to carry it. 5Make the poles of acacia wood and overlay them with gold. 6Put the altar in front of the curtain that shields the ark of the covenant law — before the atonement cover that is over the tablets of the covenant law — where I will meet with you.

7"Aaron must burn fragrant incense on the altar every morning when he tends the lamps. 8He must burn incense again when he lights the lamps at twilight so incense will burn regularly before the LORD for the generations to come. 9Do not offer on this altar any other incense or any burnt offering or grain offering, and do not pour a drink offering on it. 10Once a year Aaron shall make atonement on its horns. This annual atonement must be made with the blood of the atoning sin offering[b] for the generations to come. It is most holy to the LORD."

Atonement Money

11Then the LORD said to Moses, 12"When you take a census of the Israelites to count them, each one must pay the LORD a ransom for his life at the time he is counted. Then no plague will come on them when you number them. 13Each one who crosses over to those already counted is to give a half shekel,[c] according to the sanctuary shekel, which weighs twenty gerahs. This half shekel is an offering to the LORD. 14All who cross over, those twenty years old or more, are to give an offering to the LORD. 15The rich are not to give more than a half shekel and the poor are not to give less when you make the offering to the LORD to atone for your lives. 16Receive the atonement money from the Israelites and use it for the service of the tent of meeting. It will be a memorial for the Israelites before the LORD, making atonement for your lives."

Basin for Washing

17Then the LORD said to Moses, 18"Make a bronze basin, with its bronze stand, for washing. Place it between the tent of meeting and the altar, and put water in it. 19Aaron and his sons are to wash their hands and feet with water from it. 20Whenever they enter the tent of meeting, they shall wash with water so that they will not die. Also, when they approach the altar to minister by presenting a food offering to the LORD, 21they shall wash their hands and feet so that they will not die. This is to be a lasting ordinance for Aaron and his descendants for the generations to come."

Anointing Oil

22Then the LORD said to Moses, 23"Take the following fine spices: 500 shekels[d] of liquid myrrh, half as much (that is, 250 shekels) of fragrant cinnamon, 250 shekels[e] of fragrant calamus, 24500 shekels of cassia — all according to the sanctuary shekel — and a hin[f] of olive oil. 25Make these into a sacred anointing oil, a fragrant blend, the work of a perfumer. It will be the sacred anointing oil. 26Then use it to anoint the tent of meeting, the ark of the covenant law, 27the table and all its articles, the lampstand and its accessories, the altar of incense, 28the altar of burnt offering and all its utensils, and the basin with its stand. 29You shall consecrate them so they will be most holy, and whatever touches them will be holy.

30"Anoint Aaron and his sons and consecrate them so they may serve me as priests. 31Say to the Israelites, 'This is to be my sacred anointing oil for the generations to come. 32Do not pour it on anyone else's body and do not make any other oil using the same formula. It is sacred, and you are to consider it sacred. 33Whoever makes perfume like it and puts it on anyone other than a priest must be cut off from their people.' "

Incense

34Then the LORD said to Moses, "Take fragrant spices — gum resin, onycha and galbanum — and pure frankincense, all in equal amounts, 35and make a fragrant blend of incense, the work of a perfumer. It is to be salted and pure and sacred. 36Grind some of it to powder and place it

[a] *2* That is, about 1 1/2 feet long and wide and 3 feet high or about 45 centimeters long and wide and 90 centimeters high [b] *10* Or *purification offering* [c] *13* That is, about 1/5 ounce or about 5.8 grams; also in verse 15 [d] *23* That is, about 12 1/2 pounds or about 5.8 kilograms; also in verse 24 [e] *23* That is, about 6 1/4 pounds or about 2.9 kilograms [f] *24* That is, probably about 1 gallon or about 3.8 liters

in front of the ark of the covenant law in the tent of meeting, where I will meet with you. It shall be most holy to you. [37]Do not make any incense with this formula for yourselves; consider it holy to the LORD. [38]Whoever makes incense like it to enjoy its fragrance must be cut off from their people."

Bezalel and Oholiab

31 Then the LORD said to Moses, [2]"See, I have chosen Bezalel son of Uri, the son of Hur, of the tribe of Judah, [3]and I have filled him with the Spirit of God, with wisdom, with understanding, with knowledge and with all kinds of skills — [4]to make artistic designs for work in gold, silver and bronze, [5]to cut and set stones, to work in wood, and to engage in all kinds of crafts. [6]Moreover, I have appointed Oholiab son of Ahisamak, of the tribe of Dan, to help him. Also I have given ability to all the skilled workers to make everything I have commanded you: [7]the tent of meeting, the ark of the covenant law with the atonement cover on it, and all the other furnishings of the tent — [8]the table and its articles, the pure gold lampstand and all its accessories, the altar of incense, [9]the altar of burnt offering and all its utensils, the basin with its stand — [10]and also the woven garments, both the sacred garments for Aaron the priest and the garments for his sons when they serve as priests, [11]and the anointing oil and fragrant incense for the Holy Place. They are to make them just as I commanded you."

The Sabbath

[12]Then the LORD said to Moses, [13]"Say to the Israelites, 'You must observe my Sabbaths. This will be a sign between me and you for the generations to come, so you may know that I am the LORD, who makes you holy.

[14]" 'Observe the Sabbath, because it is holy to you. Anyone who desecrates it is to be put to death; those who do any work on that day must be cut off from their people. [15]For six days work is to be done, but the seventh day is a day of sabbath rest, holy to the LORD. Whoever does any work on the Sabbath day is to be put to death. [16]The Israelites are to observe the Sabbath, celebrating it for the generations to come as a lasting covenant. [17]It will be a sign between me and the Israelites forever, for in six days the LORD made the heavens and the earth, and on the seventh day he rested and was refreshed.' "

[18]When the LORD finished speaking to Moses on Mount Sinai, he gave him the two tablets of the covenant law, the tablets of stone inscribed by the finger of God.

The Golden Calf

32 When the people saw that Moses was so long in coming down from the mountain, they gathered around Aaron and said, "Come, make us gods[a] who will go before us. As for this fellow Moses who brought us up out of Egypt, we don't know what has happened to him."

[2]Aaron answered them, "Take off the gold earrings that your wives, your sons and your daughters are wearing, and bring them to me." [3]So all the people took off their earrings and brought them to Aaron. [4]He took what they handed him and made it into an idol cast in the shape of a calf, fashioning it with a tool. Then they said, "These are your gods,[b] Israel, who brought you up out of Egypt."

[5]When Aaron saw this, he built an altar in front of the calf and announced, "Tomorrow there will be a festival to the LORD." [6]So the next day the people rose early and sacrificed burnt offerings and presented fellowship offerings. Afterward they sat down to eat and drink and got up to indulge in revelry.

[7]Then the LORD said to Moses, "Go down, because your people, whom you brought up out of Egypt, have become corrupt. [8]They have been quick to turn away from what I commanded them and have made themselves an idol cast in the shape of a calf. They have bowed down to it and sacrificed to it and have said, 'These are your gods, Israel, who brought you up out of Egypt.'

[9]"I have seen these people," the LORD said to Moses, "and they are a stiff-necked people. [10]Now leave me alone so that my anger may burn against them and that I may destroy them. Then I will make you into a great nation."

[11]But Moses sought the favor of the LORD his God. "LORD," he said, "why should your anger burn against your people, whom you brought out of Egypt with great power and a mighty hand? [12]Why should the Egyptians say, 'It was with evil intent that he brought them out, to kill them in the mountains and

[a] *1* Or *a god*; also in verses 23 and 31 [b] *4* Or *This is your god*; also in verse 8

to wipe them off the face of the earth'?
Turn from your fierce anger; relent and
do not bring disaster on your people.
13Remember your servants Abraham,
Isaac and Israel, to whom you swore by
your own self: 'I will make your descendants as numerous as the stars in the
sky and I will give your descendants all
this land I promised them, and it will be
their inheritance forever.'" 14Then the
LORD relented and did not bring on his
people the disaster he had threatened.

15Moses turned and went down the
mountain with the two tablets of the
covenant law in his hands. They were
inscribed on both sides, front and back.
16The tablets were the work of God; the
writing was the writing of God, engraved
on the tablets.

17When Joshua heard the noise of
the people shouting, he said to Moses,
"There is the sound of war in the camp."

18Moses replied:

"It is not the sound of victory,
it is not the sound of defeat;
it is the sound of singing that I
hear."

19When Moses approached the camp
and saw the calf and the dancing, his
anger burned and he threw the tablets
out of his hands, breaking them to pieces at the foot of the mountain. 20And he
took the calf the people had made and
burned it in the fire; then he ground it
to powder, scattered it on the water and
made the Israelites drink it.

21He said to Aaron, "What did these
people do to you, that you led them into
such great sin?"

22"Do not be angry, my lord," Aaron
answered. "You know how prone these
people are to evil. 23They said to me,
'Make us gods who will go before us. As
for this fellow Moses who brought us up
out of Egypt, we don't know what has
happened to him.' 24So I told them, 'Whoever has any gold jewelry, take it off.'
Then they gave me the gold, and I threw
it into the fire, and out came this calf!"

25Moses saw that the people were running wild and that Aaron had let them
get out of control and so become a
laughingstock to their enemies. 26So he
stood at the entrance to the camp and
said, "Whoever is for the LORD, come to
me." And all the Levites rallied to him.

27Then he said to them, "This is what
the LORD, the God of Israel, says: 'Each
man strap a sword to his side. Go back
and forth through the camp from one
end to the other, each killing his brother and friend and neighbor.'" 28The Levites did as Moses commanded, and that
day about three thousand of the people
died. 29Then Moses said, "You have been
set apart to the LORD today, for you were
against your own sons and brothers, and
he has blessed you this day."

30The next day Moses said to the peo-
ple, "You have committed a great sin.
But now I will go up to the LORD; perhaps
I can make atonement for your sin."

31So Moses went back to the LORD and
said, "Oh, what a great sin these people
have committed! They have made themselves gods of gold. 32But now, please forgive their sin — but if not, then blot me
out of the book you have written."

33The LORD replied to Moses, "Whoever has sinned against me I will blot out
of my book. 34Now go, lead the people to
the place I spoke of, and my angel will
go before you. However, when the time
comes for me to punish, I will punish
them for their sin."

35And the LORD struck the people with
a plague because of what they did with
the calf Aaron had made.

33 Then the LORD said to Moses,
"Leave this place, you and the
people you brought up out of Egypt, and
go up to the land I promised on oath to
Abraham, Isaac and Jacob, saying, 'I
will give it to your descendants.' 2I will
send an angel before you and drive out
the Canaanites, Amorites, Hittites, Perizzites, Hivites and Jebusites. 3Go up to the
land flowing with milk and honey. But I
will not go with you, because you are a
stiff-necked people and I might destroy
you on the way."

4When the people heard these dis-
tressing words, they began to mourn
and no one put on any ornaments. 5For
the LORD had said to Moses, "Tell the Israelites, 'You are a stiff-necked people. If
I were to go with you even for a moment,
I might destroy you. Now take off your
ornaments and I will decide what to do
with you.'" 6So the Israelites stripped off
their ornaments at Mount Horeb.

The Tent of Meeting

7Now Moses used to take a tent and
pitch it outside the camp some distance
away, calling it the "tent of meeting."
Anyone inquiring of the LORD would go
to the tent of meeting outside the camp.
8And whenever Moses went out to the
tent, all the people rose and stood at
the entrances to their tents, watching
Moses until he entered the tent. 9As Moses went into the tent, the pillar of cloud

would come down and stay at the entrance, while the LORD spoke with Moses. 10 Whenever the people saw the pillar of cloud standing at the entrance to
the tent, they all stood and worshiped,
each at the entrance to their tent. 11 The
LORD would speak to Moses face to face,
as one speaks to a friend. Then Moses
would return to the camp, but his young
aide Joshua son of Nun did not leave the
tent.

Moses and the Glory of the LORD

12 Moses said to the LORD, "You have
been telling me, 'Lead these people,' but
you have not let me know whom you will
send with me. You have said, 'I know you
by name and you have found favor with
me.' 13 If you are pleased with me, teach
me your ways so I may know you and
continue to find favor with you. Remember that this nation is your people."

14 The LORD replied, "My Presence will
go with you, and I will give you rest."

15 Then Moses said to him, "If your
Presence does not go with us, do not
send us up from here. 16 How will anyone
know that you are pleased with me and
with your people unless you go with us?
What else will distinguish me and your
people from all the other people on the
face of the earth?"

17 And the LORD said to Moses, "I will do
the very thing you have asked, because
I am pleased with you and I know you
by name."

18 Then Moses said, "Now show me your
glory."

19 And the LORD said, "I will cause all
my goodness to pass in front of you,
and I will proclaim my name, the LORD,
in your presence. I will have mercy on
whom I will have mercy, and I will have
compassion on whom I will have compassion. 20 But," he said, "you cannot
see my face, for no one may see me and
live."

21 Then the LORD said, "There is a place
near me where you may stand on a rock.
22 When my glory passes by, I will put you
in a cleft in the rock and cover you with
my hand until I have passed by. 23 Then
I will remove my hand and you will see
my back; but my face must not be seen."

The New Stone Tablets

34 The LORD said to Moses, "Chisel
out two stone tablets like the first
ones, and I will write on them the words
that were on the first tablets, which you
broke. 2 Be ready in the morning, and
then come up on Mount Sinai. Present
yourself to me there on top of the mountain. 3 No one is to come with you or be
seen anywhere on the mountain; not
even the flocks and herds may graze in
front of the mountain."

4 So Moses chiseled out two stone tablets like the first ones and went up Mount
Sinai early in the morning, as the LORD
had commanded him; and he carried
the two stone tablets in his hands. 5 Then
the LORD came down in the cloud and
stood there with him and proclaimed
his name, the LORD. 6 And he passed in
front of Moses, proclaiming, "The LORD,
the LORD, the compassionate and gracious God, slow to anger, abounding in
love and faithfulness, 7 maintaining love
to thousands, and forgiving wickedness,
rebellion and sin. Yet he does not leave
the guilty unpunished; he punishes the
children and their children for the sin of
the parents to the third and fourth generation."

8 Moses bowed to the ground at once
and worshiped. 9 "Lord," he said, "if I
have found favor in your eyes, then let
the Lord go with us. Although this is a
stiff-necked people, forgive our wickedness and our sin, and take us as your inheritance."

10 Then the LORD said: "I am making a
covenant with you. Before all your people I will do wonders never before done
in any nation in all the world. The people
you live among will see how awesome
is the work that I, the LORD, will do for
you. 11 Obey what I command you today.
I will drive out before you the Amorites,
Canaanites, Hittites, Perizzites, Hivites
and Jebusites. 12 Be careful not to make
a treaty with those who live in the land
where you are going, or they will be a
snare among you. 13 Break down their altars, smash their sacred stones and cut
down their Asherah poles.[a] 14 Do not worship any other god, for the LORD, whose
name is Jealous, is a jealous God.

15 "Be careful not to make a treaty with
those who live in the land; for when they
prostitute themselves to their gods and
sacrifice to them, they will invite you
and you will eat their sacrifices. 16 And
when you choose some of their daughters as wives for your sons and those
daughters prostitute themselves to their
gods, they will lead your sons to do the
same.

17 "Do not make any idols.

[a] *13* That is, wooden symbols of the goddess Asherah

18"Celebrate the Festival of Unleavened Bread. For seven days eat bread made without yeast, as I commanded you. Do this at the appointed time in the month of Aviv, for in that month you came out of Egypt.

19"The first offspring of every womb belongs to me, including all the firstborn males of your livestock, whether from herd or flock. 20Redeem the firstborn donkey with a lamb, but if you do not redeem it, break its neck. Redeem all your firstborn sons.

"No one is to appear before me empty-handed.

21"Six days you shall labor, but on the seventh day you shall rest; even during the plowing season and harvest you must rest.

22"Celebrate the Festival of Weeks with the firstfruits of the wheat harvest, and the Festival of Ingathering at the turn of the year.[a] 23Three times a year all your men are to appear before the Sovereign LORD, the God of Israel. 24I will drive out nations before you and enlarge your territory, and no one will covet your land when you go up three times each year to appear before the LORD your God.

25"Do not offer the blood of a sacrifice to me along with anything containing yeast, and do not let any of the sacrifice from the Passover Festival remain until morning.

26"Bring the best of the firstfruits of your soil to the house of the LORD your God.

"Do not cook a young goat in its mother's milk."

27Then the LORD said to Moses, "Write down these words, for in accordance with these words I have made a covenant with you and with Israel." 28Moses was there with the LORD forty days and forty nights without eating bread or drinking water. And he wrote on the tablets the words of the covenant — the Ten Commandments.

The Radiant Face of Moses

29When Moses came down from Mount Sinai with the two tablets of the covenant law in his hands, he was not aware that his face was radiant because he had spoken with the LORD. 30When Aaron and all the Israelites saw Moses, his face was radiant, and they were afraid to come near him. 31But Moses called to them; so Aaron and all the leaders of the community came back to him, and he spoke to them. 32Afterward all the Israelites came near him, and he gave them all the commands the LORD had given him on Mount Sinai.

33When Moses finished speaking to them, he put a veil over his face. 34But whenever he entered the LORD's presence to speak with him, he removed the veil until he came out. And when he came out and told the Israelites what he had been commanded, 35they saw that his face was radiant. Then Moses would put the veil back over his face until he went in to speak with the LORD.

Sabbath Regulations

35 Moses assembled the whole Israelite community and said to them, "These are the things the LORD has commanded you to do: 2For six days, work is to be done, but the seventh day shall be your holy day, a day of sabbath rest to the LORD. Whoever does any work on it is to be put to death. 3Do not light a fire in any of your dwellings on the Sabbath day."

Materials for the Tabernacle

4Moses said to the whole Israelite community, "This is what the LORD has commanded: 5From what you have, take an offering for the LORD. Everyone who is willing is to bring to the LORD an offering of gold, silver and bronze; 6blue, purple and scarlet yarn and fine linen; goat hair; 7ram skins dyed red and another type of durable leather[b]; acacia wood; 8olive oil for the light; spices for the anointing oil and for the fragrant incense; 9and onyx stones and other gems to be mounted on the ephod and breastpiece.

10"All who are skilled among you are to come and make everything the LORD has commanded: 11the tabernacle with its tent and its covering, clasps, frames, crossbars, posts and bases; 12the ark with its poles and the atonement cover and the curtain that shields it; 13the table with its poles and all its articles and the bread of the Presence; 14the lampstand that is for light with its accessories, lamps and oil for the light; 15the altar of incense with its poles, the anointing oil and the fragrant incense; the curtain for the doorway at the entrance to the tabernacle; 16the altar of burnt offering with its bronze grating, its poles and all its utensils; the bronze basin with its stand; 17the curtains of the courtyard

[a] *22* That is, in the autumn [b] *7* Possibly the hides of large aquatic mammals; also in verse 23

with its posts and bases, and the curtain for the entrance to the courtyard; 18the tent pegs for the tabernacle and for the courtyard, and their ropes; 19the woven garments worn for ministering in the sanctuary — both the sacred garments for Aaron the priest and the garments for his sons when they serve as priests."

20Then the whole Israelite community withdrew from Moses' presence, 21and everyone who was willing and whose heart moved them came and brought an offering to the LORD for the work on the tent of meeting, for all its service, and for the sacred garments. 22All who were willing, men and women alike, came and brought gold jewelry of all kinds: brooches, earrings, rings and ornaments. They all presented their gold as a wave offering to the LORD. 23Everyone who had blue, purple or scarlet yarn or fine linen, or goat hair, ram skins dyed red or the other durable leather brought them. 24Those presenting an offering of silver or bronze brought it as an offering to the LORD, and everyone who had acacia wood for any part of the work brought it. 25Every skilled woman spun with her hands and brought what she had spun — blue, purple or scarlet yarn or fine linen. 26And all the women who were willing and had the skill spun the goat hair. 27The leaders brought onyx stones and other gems to be mounted on the ephod and breastpiece. 28They also brought spices and olive oil for the light and for the anointing oil and for the fragrant incense. 29All the Israelite men and women who were willing brought to the LORD freewill offerings for all the work the LORD through Moses had commanded them to do.

Bezalel and Oholiab

30Then Moses said to the Israelites, "See, the LORD has chosen Bezalel son of Uri, the son of Hur, of the tribe of Judah, 31and he has filled him with the Spirit of God, with wisdom, with understanding, with knowledge and with all kinds of skills — 32to make artistic designs for work in gold, silver and bronze, 33to cut and set stones, to work in wood and to engage in all kinds of artistic crafts. 34And he has given both him and Oholiab son of Ahisamak, of the tribe of Dan, the ability to teach others. 35He has filled them with skill to do all kinds of work as engravers, designers, embroiderers in blue, purple and scarlet yarn and fine linen, and weavers — all of them skilled workers and designers.

36 1So Bezalel, Oholiab and every skilled person to whom the LORD has given skill and ability to know how to carry out all the work of constructing the sanctuary are to do the work just as the LORD has commanded."

2Then Moses summoned Bezalel and Oholiab and every skilled person to whom the LORD had given ability and who was willing to come and do the work. 3They received from Moses all the offerings the Israelites had brought to carry out the work of constructing the sanctuary. And the people continued to bring freewill offerings morning after morning. 4So all the skilled workers who were doing all the work on the sanctuary left what they were doing 5and said to Moses, "The people are bringing more than enough for doing the work the LORD commanded to be done."

6Then Moses gave an order and they sent this word throughout the camp: "No man or woman is to make anything else as an offering for the sanctuary." And so the people were restrained from bringing more, 7because what they already had was more than enough to do all the work.

The Tabernacle

8All those who were skilled among the workers made the tabernacle with ten curtains of finely twisted linen and blue, purple and scarlet yarn, with cherubim woven into them by expert hands. 9All the curtains were the same size — twenty-eight cubits long and four cubits wide.[a] 10They joined five of the curtains together and did the same with the other five. 11Then they made loops of blue material along the edge of the end curtain in one set, and the same was done with the end curtain in the other set. 12They also made fifty loops on one curtain and fifty loops on the end curtain of the other set, with the loops opposite each other. 13Then they made fifty gold clasps and used them to fasten the two sets of curtains together so that the tabernacle was a unit.

14They made curtains of goat hair for the tent over the tabernacle — eleven altogether. 15All eleven curtains were the same size — thirty cubits long and four cubits wide.[b] 16They joined five of the curtains into one set and the other six into another set. 17Then they made fifty loops along the edge of the end curtain

[a] *9* That is, about 42 feet long and 6 feet wide or about 13 meters long and 1.8 meters wide
[b] *15* That is, about 45 feet long and 6 feet wide or about 14 meters long and 1.8 meters wide

in one set and also along the edge of the
end curtain in the other set. [18]They made
fifty bronze clasps to fasten the tent together as a unit. [19]Then they made for
the tent a covering of ram skins dyed
red, and over that a covering of the other durable leather.[a]

[20]They made upright frames of acacia
wood for the tabernacle. [21]Each frame
was ten cubits long and a cubit and a
half wide,[b] [22]with two projections set
parallel to each other. They made all
the frames of the tabernacle in this way.
[23]They made twenty frames for the south
side of the tabernacle [24]and made forty
silver bases to go under them — two bases for each frame, one under each projection. [25]For the other side, the north
side of the tabernacle, they made twenty
frames [26]and forty silver bases — two under each frame. [27]They made six frames
for the far end, that is, the west end of
the tabernacle, [28]and two frames were
made for the corners of the tabernacle
at the far end. [29]At these two corners the
frames were double from the bottom
all the way to the top and fitted into a
single ring; both were made alike. [30]So
there were eight frames and sixteen silver bases — two under each frame.

[31]They also made crossbars of acacia
wood: five for the frames on one side of
the tabernacle, [32]five for those on the
other side, and five for the frames on
the west, at the far end of the tabernacle. [33]They made the center crossbar so
that it extended from end to end at the
middle of the frames. [34]They overlaid the
frames with gold and made gold rings
to hold the crossbars. They also overlaid
the crossbars with gold.

[35]They made the curtain of blue, purple and scarlet yarn and finely twisted
linen, with cherubim woven into it by a
skilled worker. [36]They made four posts
of acacia wood for it and overlaid them
with gold. They made gold hooks for
them and cast their four silver bases.
[37]For the entrance to the tent they made
a curtain of blue, purple and scarlet yarn
and finely twisted linen — the work of an
embroiderer; [38]and they made five posts
with hooks for them. They overlaid the
tops of the posts and their bands with
gold and made their five bases of bronze.

The Ark

37 Bezalel made the ark of acacia
wood — two and a half cubits long,
a cubit and a half wide, and a cubit and a
half high.[c] [2]He overlaid it with pure gold,
both inside and out, and made a gold
molding around it. [3]He cast four gold
rings for it and fastened them to its four
feet, with two rings on one side and two
rings on the other. [4]Then he made poles
of acacia wood and overlaid them with
gold. [5]And he inserted the poles into the
rings on the sides of the ark to carry it.

[6]He made the atonement cover of
pure gold — two and a half cubits long
and a cubit and a half wide. [7]Then he
made two cherubim out of hammered
gold at the ends of the cover. [8]He made
one cherub on one end and the second
cherub on the other; at the two ends he
made them of one piece with the cover.
[9]The cherubim had their wings spread
upward, overshadowing the cover with
them. The cherubim faced each other,
looking toward the cover.

The Table

[10]They[d] made the table of acacia
wood — two cubits long, a cubit wide
and a cubit and a half high.[e] [11]Then they
overlaid it with pure gold and made
a gold molding around it. [12]They also
made around it a rim a handbreadth[f]
wide and put a gold molding on the rim.
[13]They cast four gold rings for the table
and fastened them to the four corners,
where the four legs were. [14]The rings
were put close to the rim to hold the
poles used in carrying the table. [15]The
poles for carrying the table were made
of acacia wood and were overlaid with
gold. [16]And they made from pure gold
the articles for the table — its plates and
dishes and bowls and its pitchers for the
pouring out of drink offerings.

The Lampstand

[17]They made the lampstand of pure
gold. They hammered out its base and
shaft, and made its flowerlike cups,
buds and blossoms of one piece with
them. [18]Six branches extended from the
sides of the lampstand — three on one
side and three on the other. [19]Three cups
shaped like almond flowers with buds

[a] *19* Possibly the hides of large aquatic mammals (see 35:7) [b] *21* That is, about 15 feet long and 2 1/4 feet wide or about 4.5 meters long and 68 centimeters wide [c] *1* That is, about 3 3/4 feet long and 2 1/4 feet wide and high or about 1.1 meters long and 68 centimeters wide and high; similarly in verse 6 [d] *10* Or *He*; also in verses 11-29 [e] *10* That is, about 3 feet long, 1 1/2 feet wide and 2 1/4 feet high or about 90 centimeters long, 45 centimeters wide and 68 centimeters high [f] *12* That is, about 3 inches or about 7.5 centimeters

and blossoms were on one branch, three on the next branch and the same for all six branches extending from the lampstand. 20And on the lampstand were four cups shaped like almond flowers with buds and blossoms. 21One bud was under the first pair of branches extending from the lampstand, a second bud under the second pair, and a third bud under the third pair — six branches in all. 22The buds and the branches were all of one piece with the lampstand, hammered out of pure gold.

23They made its seven lamps, as well as its wick trimmers and trays, of pure gold. 24They made the lampstand and all its accessories from one talent[a] of pure gold.

The Altar of Incense

25They made the altar of incense out of acacia wood. It was square, a cubit long and a cubit wide and two cubits high[b] — its horns of one piece with it. 26They overlaid the top and all the sides and the horns with pure gold, and made a gold molding around it. 27They made two gold rings below the molding — two on each of the opposite sides — to hold the poles used to carry it. 28They made the poles of acacia wood and overlaid them with gold.

29They also made the sacred anointing oil and the pure, fragrant incense — the work of a perfumer.

The Altar of Burnt Offering

38 They[c] built the altar of burnt offering of acacia wood, three cubits[d] high; it was square, five cubits long and five cubits wide.[e] 2They made a horn at each of the four corners, so that the horns and the altar were of one piece, and they overlaid the altar with bronze. 3They made all its utensils of bronze — its pots, shovels, sprinkling bowls, meat forks and firepans. 4They made a grating for the altar, a bronze network, to be under its ledge, halfway up the altar. 5They cast bronze rings to hold the poles for the four corners of the bronze grating. 6They made the poles of acacia wood and overlaid them with bronze. 7They inserted the poles into the rings so they would be on the sides of the altar for carrying it. They made it hollow, out of boards.

The Basin for Washing

8They made the bronze basin and its bronze stand from the mirrors of the women who served at the entrance to the tent of meeting.

The Courtyard

9Next they made the courtyard. The south side was a hundred cubits[f] long and had curtains of finely twisted linen, 10with twenty posts and twenty bronze bases, and with silver hooks and bands on the posts. 11The north side was also a hundred cubits long and had twenty posts and twenty bronze bases, with silver hooks and bands on the posts.

12The west end was fifty cubits[g] wide and had curtains, with ten posts and ten bases, with silver hooks and bands on the posts. 13The east end, toward the sunrise, was also fifty cubits wide. 14Curtains fifteen cubits[h] long were on one side of the entrance, with three posts and three bases, 15and curtains fifteen cubits long were on the other side of the entrance to the courtyard, with three posts and three bases. 16All the curtains around the courtyard were of finely twisted linen. 17The bases for the posts were bronze. The hooks and bands on the posts were silver, and their tops were overlaid with silver; so all the posts of the courtyard had silver bands.

18The curtain for the entrance to the courtyard was made of blue, purple and scarlet yarn and finely twisted linen — the work of an embroiderer. It was twenty cubits[i] long and, like the curtains of the courtyard, five cubits[j] high, 19with four posts and four bronze bases. Their hooks and bands were silver, and their tops were overlaid with silver. 20All the tent pegs of the tabernacle and of the surrounding courtyard were bronze.

The Materials Used

21These are the amounts of the materials used for the tabernacle, the tabernacle of the covenant law, which were recorded at Moses' command by the Levites under the direction of Ithamar son of Aaron, the priest. 22(Bezalel son of Uri, the son of Hur, of the tribe of Judah, made everything the LORD commanded Moses; 23with him was Oholiab son of Ahisamak, of the

[a] *24* That is, about 75 pounds or about 34 kilograms [b] *25* That is, about 1 1/2 feet long and wide and 3 feet high or about 45 centimeters long and wide and 90 centimeters high [c] *1* Or *He*; also in verses 2-9 [d] *1* That is, about 4 1/2 feet or about 1.4 meters [e] *1* That is, about 7 1/2 feet or about 2.3 meters long and wide [f] *9* That is, about 150 feet or about 45 meters [g] *12* That is, about 75 feet or about 23 meters [h] *14* That is, about 22 feet or about 6.8 meters [i] *18* That is, about 30 feet or about 9 meters [j] *18* That is, about 7 1/2 feet or about 2.3 meters

tribe of Dan — an engraver and designer, and an embroiderer in blue, purple and scarlet yarn and fine linen.) 24 The total amount of the gold from the wave offering used for all the work on the sanctuary was 29 talents and 730 shekels,[a] according to the sanctuary shekel.

25 The silver obtained from those of the community who were counted in the census was 100 talents[b] and 1,775 shekels,[c] according to the sanctuary shekel — 26 one beka per person, that is, half a shekel,[d] according to the sanctuary shekel, from everyone who had crossed over to those counted, twenty years old or more, a total of 603,550 men. 27 The 100 talents of silver were used to cast the bases for the sanctuary and for the curtain — 100 bases from the 100 talents, one talent for each base. 28 They used the 1,775 shekels to make the hooks for the posts, to overlay the tops of the posts, and to make their bands.

29 The bronze from the wave offering was 70 talents and 2,400 shekels.[e] 30 They used it to make the bases for the entrance to the tent of meeting, the bronze altar with its bronze grating and all its utensils, 31 the bases for the surrounding courtyard and those for its entrance and all the tent pegs for the tabernacle and those for the surrounding courtyard.

The Priestly Garments

39 From the blue, purple and scarlet yarn they made woven garments for ministering in the sanctuary. They also made sacred garments for Aaron, as the LORD commanded Moses.

The Ephod

2 They[f] made the ephod of gold, and of blue, purple and scarlet yarn, and of finely twisted linen. 3 They hammered out thin sheets of gold and cut strands to be worked into the blue, purple and scarlet yarn and fine linen — the work of skilled hands. 4 They made shoulder pieces for the ephod, which were attached to two of its corners, so it could be fastened. 5 Its skillfully woven waistband was like it — of one piece with the ephod and made with gold, and with blue, purple and scarlet yarn, and with finely twisted linen, as the LORD commanded Moses.

6 They mounted the onyx stones in gold filigree settings and engraved them like a seal with the names of the sons of Israel. 7 Then they fastened them on the shoulder pieces of the ephod as memorial stones for the sons of Israel, as the LORD commanded Moses.

The Breastpiece

8 They fashioned the breastpiece — the work of a skilled craftsman. They made it like the ephod: of gold, and of blue, purple and scarlet yarn, and of finely twisted linen. 9 It was square — a span[g] long and a span wide — and folded double. 10 Then they mounted four rows of precious stones on it. The first row was carnelian, chrysolite and beryl; 11 the second row was turquoise, lapis lazuli and emerald; 12 the third row was jacinth, agate and amethyst; 13 the fourth row was topaz, onyx and jasper.[h] They were mounted in gold filigree settings. 14 There were twelve stones, one for each of the names of the sons of Israel, each engraved like a seal with the name of one of the twelve tribes.

15 For the breastpiece they made braided chains of pure gold, like a rope. 16 They made two gold filigree settings and two gold rings, and fastened the rings to two of the corners of the breastpiece. 17 They fastened the two gold chains to the rings at the corners of the breastpiece, 18 and the other ends of the chains to the two settings, attaching them to the shoulder pieces of the ephod at the front. 19 They made two gold rings and attached them to the other two corners of the breastpiece on the inside edge next to the ephod. 20 Then they made two more gold rings and attached them to the bottom of the shoulder pieces on the front of the ephod, close to the seam just above the waistband of the ephod. 21 They tied the rings of the breastpiece to the rings of the ephod with blue cord, connecting it to the waistband so that the breastpiece would not swing out from the ephod — as the LORD commanded Moses.

Other Priestly Garments

22 They made the robe of the ephod entirely of blue cloth — the work of a weaver — 23 with an opening in the center of

[a] *24* The weight of the gold was a little over a ton or about 1 metric ton. [b] *25* That is, about 3 3/4 tons or about 3.4 metric tons; also in verse 27 [c] *25* That is, about 44 pounds or about 20 kilograms; also in verse 28 [d] *26* That is, about 1/5 ounce or about 5.7 grams [e] *29* The weight of the bronze was about 2 1/2 tons or about 2.4 metric tons. [f] *2* Or *He*; also in verses 7, 8 and 22 [g] *9* That is, about 9 inches or about 23 centimeters [h] *13* The precise identification of some of these precious stones is uncertain.

the robe like the opening of a collar,[a] and
a band around this opening, so that it
would not tear. 24They made pomegranates of blue, purple and scarlet yarn and
finely twisted linen around the hem of
the robe. 25And they made bells of pure
gold and attached them around the hem
between the pomegranates. 26The bells
and pomegranates alternated around
the hem of the robe to be worn for ministering, as the LORD commanded Moses.
27For Aaron and his sons, they made
tunics of fine linen — the work of a
weaver — 28and the turban of fine linen,
the linen caps and the undergarments
of finely twisted linen. 29The sash was
made of finely twisted linen and blue,
purple and scarlet yarn — the work of an
embroiderer — as the LORD commanded
Moses.
30They made the plate, the sacred emblem, out of pure gold and engraved on
it, like an inscription on a seal: HOLY TO
THE LORD. 31Then they fastened a blue
cord to it to attach it to the turban, as
the LORD commanded Moses.

Moses Inspects the Tabernacle

32So all the work on the tabernacle,
the tent of meeting, was completed.
The Israelites did everything just as the
LORD commanded Moses. 33Then they
brought the tabernacle to Moses: the
tent and all its furnishings, its clasps,
frames, crossbars, posts and bases; 34the
covering of ram skins dyed red and the
covering of another durable leather[b]
and the shielding curtain; 35the ark of
the covenant law with its poles and the
atonement cover; 36the table with all its
articles and the bread of the Presence;
37the pure gold lampstand with its row
of lamps and all its accessories, and the
olive oil for the light; 38the gold altar,
the anointing oil, the fragrant incense,
and the curtain for the entrance to the
tent; 39the bronze altar with its bronze
grating, its poles and all its utensils; the
basin with its stand; 40the curtains of
the courtyard with its posts and bases,
and the curtain for the entrance to the
courtyard; the ropes and tent pegs for
the courtyard; all the furnishings for the
tabernacle, the tent of meeting; 41and
the woven garments worn for ministering in the sanctuary, both the sacred
garments for Aaron the priest and the
garments for his sons when serving as
priests.
42The Israelites had done all the work
just as the LORD had commanded Moses.
43Moses inspected the work and saw that
they had done it just as the LORD had
commanded. So Moses blessed them.

Setting Up the Tabernacle

40 Then the LORD said to Moses:
2"Set up the tabernacle, the tent
of meeting, on the first day of the first
month. 3Place the ark of the covenant
law in it and shield the ark with the curtain. 4Bring in the table and set out what
belongs on it. Then bring in the lampstand and set up its lamps. 5Place the
gold altar of incense in front of the ark
of the covenant law and put the curtain
at the entrance to the tabernacle.
6"Place the altar of burnt offering in
front of the entrance to the tabernacle,
the tent of meeting; 7place the basin between the tent of meeting and the altar
and put water in it. 8Set up the courtyard
around it and put the curtain at the entrance to the courtyard.
9"Take the anointing oil and anoint
the tabernacle and everything in it; consecrate it and all its furnishings, and it
will be holy. 10Then anoint the altar of
burnt offering and all its utensils; consecrate the altar, and it will be most holy.
11Anoint the basin and its stand and consecrate them.
12"Bring Aaron and his sons to the entrance to the tent of meeting and wash
them with water. 13Then dress Aaron in
the sacred garments, anoint him and
consecrate him so he may serve me as
priest. 14Bring his sons and dress them in
tunics. 15Anoint them just as you anointed their father, so they may serve me
as priests. Their anointing will be to a
priesthood that will continue throughout their generations." 16Moses did everything just as the LORD commanded him.
17So the tabernacle was set up on the
first day of the first month in the second
year. 18When Moses set up the tabernacle, he put the bases in place, erected the
frames, inserted the crossbars and set up
the posts. 19Then he spread the tent over
the tabernacle and put the covering over
the tent, as the LORD commanded him.
20He took the tablets of the covenant
law and placed them in the ark, attached the poles to the ark and put
the atonement cover over it. 21Then he
brought the ark into the tabernacle and
hung the shielding curtain and shielded

[a] *23* The meaning of the Hebrew for this word is uncertain. [b] *34* Possibly the hides of large aquatic mammals

the ark of the covenant law, as the LORD
commanded him.
22Moses placed the table in the tent of
meeting on the north side of the tabernacle outside the curtain 23and set out
the bread on it before the LORD, as the
LORD commanded him.
24He placed the lampstand in the tent
of meeting opposite the table on the
south side of the tabernacle 25and set up
the lamps before the LORD, as the LORD
commanded him.
26Moses placed the gold altar in the
tent of meeting in front of the curtain
27and burned fragrant incense on it, as
the LORD commanded him.
28Then he put up the curtain at the entrance to the tabernacle. 29He set the altar of burnt offering near the entrance to
the tabernacle, the tent of meeting, and
offered on it burnt offerings and grain
offerings, as the LORD commanded him.
30He placed the basin between the tent
of meeting and the altar and put water in
it for washing, 31and Moses and Aaron and
his sons used it to wash their hands and
feet. 32They washed whenever they entered the tent of meeting or approached
the altar, as the LORD commanded Moses.
33Then Moses set up the courtyard
around the tabernacle and altar and
put up the curtain at the entrance to the
courtyard. And so Moses finished the
work.

The Glory of the LORD

34Then the cloud covered the tent of
meeting, and the glory of the LORD filled
the tabernacle. 35Moses could not enter
the tent of meeting because the cloud
had settled on it, and the glory of the
LORD filled the tabernacle.
36In all the travels of the Israelites,
whenever the cloud lifted from above
the tabernacle, they would set out; 37but
if the cloud did not lift, they did not set
out — until the day it lifted. 38So the
cloud of the LORD was over the tabernacle by day, and fire was in the cloud
by night, in the sight of all the Israelites
during all their travels.

LEVITICUS

The Burnt Offering

1 The LORD called to Moses and spoke
to him from the tent of meeting. He
said, 2"Speak to the Israelites and say to
them: 'When anyone among you brings
an offering to the LORD, bring as your offering an animal from either the herd or
the flock.

3" 'If the offering is a burnt offering
from the herd, you are to offer a male
without defect. You must present it at
the entrance to the tent of meeting so
that it will be acceptable to the LORD.
4You are to lay your hand on the head of
the burnt offering, and it will be accepted on your behalf to make atonement
for you. 5You are to slaughter the young
bull before the LORD, and then Aaron's
sons the priests shall bring the blood
and splash it against the sides of the altar at the entrance to the tent of meeting. 6You are to skin the burnt offering
and cut it into pieces. 7The sons of Aaron
the priest are to put fire on the altar and
arrange wood on the fire. 8Then Aaron's
sons the priests shall arrange the pieces,
including the head and the fat, on the
wood that is burning on the altar. 9You
are to wash the internal organs and the
legs with water, and the priest is to burn
all of it on the altar. It is a burnt offering, a food offering, an aroma pleasing
to the LORD.

10" 'If the offering is a burnt offering
from the flock, from either the sheep or
the goats, you are to offer a male without defect. 11You are to slaughter it at
the north side of the altar before the
LORD, and Aaron's sons the priests shall
splash its blood against the sides of the
altar. 12You are to cut it into pieces, and
the priest shall arrange them, including
the head and the fat, on the wood that is
burning on the altar. 13You are to wash
the internal organs and the legs with
water, and the priest is to bring all of
them and burn them on the altar. It is
a burnt offering, a food offering, an aroma pleasing to the LORD.

14" 'If the offering to the LORD is a
burnt offering of birds, you are to offer
a dove or a young pigeon. 15The priest
shall bring it to the altar, wring off the
head and burn it on the altar; its blood
shall be drained out on the side of the
altar. 16He is to remove the crop and the
feathers[a] and throw them down east of
the altar where the ashes are. 17He shall
tear it open by the wings, not dividing
it completely, and then the priest shall
burn it on the wood that is burning on
the altar. It is a burnt offering, a food offering, an aroma pleasing to the LORD.

The Grain Offering

2 " 'When anyone brings a grain offering to the LORD, their offering is to be
of the finest flour. They are to pour olive
oil on it, put incense on it 2and take it to
Aaron's sons the priests. The priest shall
take a handful of the flour and oil, together with all the incense, and burn this
as a memorial[b] portion on the altar, a
food offering, an aroma pleasing to the
LORD. 3The rest of the grain offering belongs to Aaron and his sons; it is a most
holy part of the food offerings presented
to the LORD.

4" 'If you bring a grain offering baked
in an oven, it is to consist of the finest
flour: either thick loaves made without
yeast and with olive oil mixed in or thin
loaves made without yeast and brushed
with olive oil. 5If your grain offering is
prepared on a griddle, it is to be made of
the finest flour mixed with oil, and without yeast. 6Crumble it and pour oil on it;
it is a grain offering. 7If your grain offering is cooked in a pan, it is to be made of
the finest flour and some olive oil. 8Bring
the grain offering made of these things
to the LORD; present it to the priest, who
shall take it to the altar. 9He shall take
out the memorial portion from the grain
offering and burn it on the altar as a
food offering, an aroma pleasing to the
LORD. 10The rest of the grain offering belongs to Aaron and his sons; it is a most
holy part of the food offerings presented
to the LORD.

11" 'Every grain offering you bring to
the LORD must be made without yeast, for
you are not to burn any yeast or honey
in a food offering presented to the LORD.
12You may bring them to the LORD as an
offering of the firstfruits, but they are not

[a] *16* Or *crop with its contents*; the meaning of the Hebrew for this word is uncertain. [b] *2* Or *representative*; also in verses 9 and 16

to be offered on the altar as a pleasing aroma. 13Season all your grain offerings with salt. Do not leave the salt of the covenant of your God out of your grain offerings; add salt to all your offerings.

14" 'If you bring a grain offering of firstfruits to the LORD, offer crushed heads of new grain roasted in the fire. 15Put oil and incense on it; it is a grain offering. 16The priest shall burn the memorial portion of the crushed grain and the oil, together with all the incense, as a food offering presented to the LORD.

The Fellowship Offering

3 " 'If your offering is a fellowship offering, and you offer an animal from the herd, whether male or female, you are to present before the LORD an animal without defect. 2You are to lay your hand on the head of your offering and slaughter it at the entrance to the tent of meeting. Then Aaron's sons the priests shall splash the blood against the sides of the altar. 3From the fellowship offering you are to bring a food offering to the LORD: the internal organs and all the fat that is connected to them, 4both kidneys with the fat on them near the loins, and the long lobe of the liver, which you will remove with the kidneys. 5Then Aaron's sons are to burn it on the altar on top of the burnt offering that is lying on the burning wood; it is a food offering, an aroma pleasing to the LORD.

6" 'If you offer an animal from the flock as a fellowship offering to the LORD, you are to offer a male or female without defect. 7If you offer a lamb, you are to present it before the LORD, 8lay your hand on its head and slaughter it in front of the tent of meeting. Then Aaron's sons shall splash its blood against the sides of the altar. 9From the fellowship offering you are to bring a food offering to the LORD: its fat, the entire fat tail cut off close to the backbone, the internal organs and all the fat that is connected to them, 10both kidneys with the fat on them near the loins, and the long lobe of the liver, which you will remove with the kidneys. 11The priest shall burn them on the altar as a food offering presented to the LORD.

12" 'If your offering is a goat, you are to present it before the LORD, 13lay your hand on its head and slaughter it in front of the tent of meeting. Then Aaron's sons shall splash its blood against the sides of the altar. 14From what you offer you are to present this food offering to the LORD: the internal organs and all the fat that is connected to them, 15both kidneys with the fat on them near the loins, and the long lobe of the liver, which you will remove with the kidneys. 16The priest shall burn them on the altar as a food offering, a pleasing aroma. All the fat is the LORD's.

17" 'This is a lasting ordinance for the generations to come, wherever you live: You must not eat any fat or any blood.' "

The Sin Offering

4 The LORD said to Moses, 2"Say to the Israelites: 'When anyone sins unintentionally and does what is forbidden in any of the LORD's commands —

3" 'If the anointed priest sins, bringing guilt on the people, he must bring to the LORD a young bull without defect as a sin offering[a] for the sin he has committed. 4He is to present the bull at the entrance to the tent of meeting before the LORD. He is to lay his hand on its head and slaughter it there before the LORD. 5Then the anointed priest shall take some of the bull's blood and carry it into the tent of meeting. 6He is to dip his finger into the blood and sprinkle some of it seven times before the LORD, in front of the curtain of the sanctuary. 7The priest shall then put some of the blood on the horns of the altar of fragrant incense that is before the LORD in the tent of meeting. The rest of the bull's blood he shall pour out at the base of the altar of burnt offering at the entrance to the tent of meeting. 8He shall remove all the fat from the bull of the sin offering — all the fat that is connected to the internal organs, 9both kidneys with the fat on them near the loins, and the long lobe of the liver, which he will remove with the kidneys — 10just as the fat is removed from the ox[b] sacrificed as a fellowship offering. Then the priest shall burn them on the altar of burnt offering. 11But the hide of the bull and all its flesh, as well as the head and legs, the internal organs and the intestines — 12that is, all the rest of the bull — he must take outside the camp to a place ceremonially clean, where the ashes are thrown, and burn it there in a wood fire on the ash heap.

13" 'If the whole Israelite community sins unintentionally and does what is forbidden in any of the LORD's commands,

[a] *3* Or *purification offering*; here and throughout this chapter [b] *10* The Hebrew word can refer to either male or female.

even though the community is unaware
of the matter, when they realize their
guilt 14and the sin they committed becomes known, the assembly must bring
a young bull as a sin offering and present it before the tent of meeting. 15The
elders of the community are to lay their
hands on the bull's head before the LORD,
and the bull shall be slaughtered before
the LORD. 16Then the anointed priest is
to take some of the bull's blood into the
tent of meeting. 17He shall dip his finger
into the blood and sprinkle it before the
LORD seven times in front of the curtain.
18He is to put some of the blood on the
horns of the altar that is before the LORD
in the tent of meeting. The rest of the
blood he shall pour out at the base of the
altar of burnt offering at the entrance to
the tent of meeting. 19He shall remove
all the fat from it and burn it on the altar, 20and do with this bull just as he did
with the bull for the sin offering. In this
way the priest will make atonement for
the community, and they will be forgiv-
en. 21Then he shall take the bull outside
the camp and burn it as he burned the
first bull. This is the sin offering for the
community.

22" 'When a leader sins unintentionally and does what is forbidden in any
of the commands of the LORD his God,
when he realizes his guilt 23and the sin
he has committed becomes known, he
must bring as his offering a male goat
without defect. 24He is to lay his hand on
the goat's head and slaughter it at the
place where the burnt offering is slaughtered before the LORD. It is a sin offering.
25Then the priest shall take some of the
blood of the sin offering with his finger
and put it on the horns of the altar of
burnt offering and pour out the rest of
the blood at the base of the altar. 26He
shall burn all the fat on the altar as he
burned the fat of the fellowship offering.
In this way the priest will make atonement for the leader's sin, and he will be
forgiven.

27" 'If any member of the community sins unintentionally and does what
is forbidden in any of the LORD's commands, when they realize their guilt
28and the sin they have committed becomes known, they must bring as their
offering for the sin they committed a
female goat without defect. 29They are
to lay their hand on the head of the sin
offering and slaughter it at the place of
the burnt offering. 30Then the priest is
to take some of the blood with his finger and put it on the horns of the altar
of burnt offering and pour out the rest of
the blood at the base of the altar. 31They
shall remove all the fat, just as the fat
is removed from the fellowship offering,
and the priest shall burn it on the altar
as an aroma pleasing to the LORD. In this
way the priest will make atonement for
them, and they will be forgiven.

32" 'If someone brings a lamb as their
sin offering, they are to bring a female
without defect. 33They are to lay their
hand on its head and slaughter it for a
sin offering at the place where the burnt
offering is slaughtered. 34Then the priest
shall take some of the blood of the sin
offering with his finger and put it on the
horns of the altar of burnt offering and
pour out the rest of the blood at the base
of the altar. 35They shall remove all the
fat, just as the fat is removed from the
lamb of the fellowship offering, and the
priest shall burn it on the altar on top of
the food offerings presented to the LORD.
In this way the priest will make atonement for them for the sin they have committed, and they will be forgiven.

5 " 'If anyone sins because they do not
speak up when they hear a public
charge to testify regarding something
they have seen or learned about, they
will be held responsible.

2" 'If anyone becomes aware that they
are guilty — if they unwittingly touch
anything ceremonially unclean (whether the carcass of an unclean animal, wild
or domestic, or of any unclean creature
that moves along the ground) and they
are unaware that they have become unclean, but then they come to realize their
guilt; 3or if they touch human uncleanness (anything that would make them
unclean) even though they are unaware
of it, but then they learn of it and realize
their guilt; 4or if anyone thoughtlessly
takes an oath to do anything, whether
good or evil (in any matter one might
carelessly swear about) even though they
are unaware of it, but then they learn of
it and realize their guilt — 5when anyone becomes aware that they are guilty
in any of these matters, they must confess in what way they have sinned. 6As a
penalty for the sin they have committed,
they must bring to the LORD a female
lamb or goat from the flock as a sin offering[a]; and the priest shall make atonement for them for their sin.

[a] 6 Or *purification offering*; here and throughout this chapter

7“ ‘Anyone who cannot afford a lamb is
to bring two doves or two young pigeons
to the LORD as a penalty for their sin —
one for a sin offering and the other for a
burnt offering. 8They are to bring them
to the priest, who shall first offer the
one for the sin offering. He is to wring
its head from its neck, not dividing it
completely, 9and is to splash some of the
blood of the sin offering against the side
of the altar; the rest of the blood must
be drained out at the base of the altar.
It is a sin offering. 10The priest shall then
offer the other as a burnt offering in the
prescribed way and make atonement for
them for the sin they have committed,
and they will be forgiven.

11“ ‘If, however, they cannot afford two
doves or two young pigeons, they are to
bring as an offering for their sin a tenth
of an ephah[a] of the finest flour for a sin
offering. They must not put olive oil or
incense on it, because it is a sin offering.
12They are to bring it to the priest, who
shall take a handful of it as a memorial[b]
portion and burn it on the altar on top of
the food offerings presented to the LORD.
It is a sin offering. 13In this way the priest
will make atonement for them for any
of these sins they have committed, and
they will be forgiven. The rest of the offering will belong to the priest, as in the
case of the grain offering.’ ”

The Guilt Offering

14The LORD said to Moses: 15“When
anyone is unfaithful to the LORD by sinning unintentionally in regard to any of
the LORD’s holy things, they are to bring
to the LORD as a penalty a ram from
the flock, one without defect and of the
proper value in silver, according to the
sanctuary shekel.[c] It is a guilt offering.
16They must make restitution for what
they have failed to do in regard to the
holy things, pay an additional penalty
of a fifth of its value and give it all to the
priest. The priest will make atonement
for them with the ram as a guilt offering,
and they will be forgiven.

17“If anyone sins and does what is forbidden in any of the LORD’s commands,
even though they do not know it, they
are guilty and will be held responsible.
18They are to bring to the priest as a guilt
offering a ram from the flock, one without defect and of the proper value. In this
way the priest will make atonement for
them for the wrong they have committed
unintentionally, and they will be forgiv-
en. 19It is a guilt offering; they have been
guilty of[d] wrongdoing against the LORD.”

6[e] The LORD said to Moses: 2“If anyone
sins and is unfaithful to the LORD by
deceiving a neighbor about something
entrusted to them or left in their care or
about something stolen, or if they cheat
their neighbor, 3or if they find lost property and lie about it, or if they swear falsely about any such sin that people may
commit — 4when they sin in any of these
ways and realize their guilt, they must
return what they have stolen or taken
by extortion, or what was entrusted to
them, or the lost property they found, 5or
whatever it was they swore falsely about.
They must make restitution in full, add
a fifth of the value to it and give it all to
the owner on the day they present their
guilt offering. 6And as a penalty they
must bring to the priest, that is, to the
LORD, their guilt offering, a ram from the
flock, one without defect and of the proper value. 7In this way the priest will make
atonement for them before the LORD, and
they will be forgiven for any of the things
they did that made them guilty.”

The Burnt Offering

8The LORD said to Moses: 9“Give Aaron
and his sons this command: ‘These are
the regulations for the burnt offering:
The burnt offering is to remain on the
altar hearth throughout the night, till
morning, and the fire must be kept burning on the altar. 10The priest shall then
put on his linen clothes, with linen undergarments next to his body, and shall
remove the ashes of the burnt offering
that the fire has consumed on the altar
and place them beside the altar. 11Then
he is to take off these clothes and put
on others, and carry the ashes outside
the camp to a place that is ceremonially
clean. 12The fire on the altar must be kept
burning; it must not go out. Every morning the priest is to add firewood and arrange the burnt offering on the fire and
burn the fat of the fellowship offerings
on it. 13The fire must be kept burning on
the altar continuously; it must not go out.

The Grain Offering

14“ ‘These are the regulations for the
grain offering: Aaron’s sons are to bring
it before the LORD, in front of the altar.

[a] *11* That is, probably about 3 1/2 pounds or about 1.6 kilograms [b] *12* Or *representative*
[c] *15* That is, about 2/5 ounce or about 12 grams [d] *19* Or *offering; atonement has been made for their*
[e] In Hebrew texts 6:1-7 is numbered 5:20-26, and 6:8-30 is numbered 6:1-23.

15 The priest is to take a handful of the
finest flour and some olive oil, together
with all the incense on the grain offering, and burn the memorial[a] portion
on the altar as an aroma pleasing to
the LORD. 16 Aaron and his sons shall eat
the rest of it, but it is to be eaten without yeast in the sanctuary area; they
are to eat it in the courtyard of the tent
of meeting. 17 It must not be baked with
yeast; I have given it as their share of
the food offerings presented to me. Like
the sin offering[b] and the guilt offering,
it is most holy. 18 Any male descendant of
Aaron may eat it. For all generations to
come it is his perpetual share of the food
offerings presented to the LORD. Whatever touches them will become holy.[c]' "

19 The LORD also said to Moses, 20 "This
is the offering Aaron and his sons are
to bring to the LORD on the day he[d] is
anointed: a tenth of an ephah[e] of the finest flour as a regular grain offering, half
of it in the morning and half in the evening. 21 It must be prepared with oil on a
griddle; bring it well-mixed and present
the grain offering broken[f] in pieces as an
aroma pleasing to the LORD. 22 The son
who is to succeed him as anointed priest
shall prepare it. It is the LORD's perpetual share and is to be burned completely.
23 Every grain offering of a priest shall be
burned completely; it must not be eat-
en."

The Sin Offering

24 The LORD said to Moses, 25 "Say to
Aaron and his sons: 'These are the regulations for the sin offering: The sin offering is to be slaughtered before the LORD
in the place the burnt offering is slaughtered; it is most holy. 26 The priest who offers it shall eat it; it is to be eaten in the
sanctuary area, in the courtyard of the
tent of meeting. 27 Whatever touches any
of the flesh will become holy, and if any
of the blood is spattered on a garment,
you must wash it in the sanctuary area.
28 The clay pot the meat is cooked in must
be broken; but if it is cooked in a bronze
pot, the pot is to be scoured and rinsed
with water. 29 Any male in a priest's family may eat it; it is most holy. 30 But any
sin offering whose blood is brought into
the tent of meeting to make atonement
in the Holy Place must not be eaten; it
must be burned up.

The Guilt Offering

7 " 'These are the regulations for the
guilt offering, which is most holy:
2 The guilt offering is to be slaughtered
in the place where the burnt offering
is slaughtered, and its blood is to be
splashed against the sides of the altar.
3 All its fat shall be offered: the fat tail
and the fat that covers the internal organs, 4 both kidneys with the fat on them
near the loins, and the long lobe of the
liver, which is to be removed with the
kidneys. 5 The priest shall burn them on
the altar as a food offering presented
to the LORD. It is a guilt offering. 6 Any
male in a priest's family may eat it, but
it must be eaten in the sanctuary area;
it is most holy.

7 " 'The same law applies to both the
sin offering[g] and the guilt offering: They
belong to the priest who makes atonement with them. 8 The priest who offers
a burnt offering for anyone may keep its
hide for himself. 9 Every grain offering
baked in an oven or cooked in a pan or
on a griddle belongs to the priest who offers it, 10 and every grain offering, whether mixed with olive oil or dry, belongs
equally to all the sons of Aaron.

The Fellowship Offering

11 " 'These are the regulations for the
fellowship offering anyone may present
to the LORD:

12 " 'If they offer it as an expression
of thankfulness, then along with this
thank offering they are to offer thick
loaves made without yeast and with olive oil mixed in, thin loaves made without yeast and brushed with oil, and thick
loaves of the finest flour well-kneaded
and with oil mixed in. 13 Along with
their fellowship offering of thanksgiving they are to present an offering with
thick loaves of bread made with yeast.
14 They are to bring one of each kind as
an offering, a contribution to the LORD;
it belongs to the priest who splashes the
blood of the fellowship offering against
the altar. 15 The meat of their fellowship
offering of thanksgiving must be eaten
on the day it is offered; they must leave
none of it till morning.

16 " 'If, however, their offering is the result of a vow or is a freewill offering, the
sacrifice shall be eaten on the day they
offer it, but anything left over may be

[a] *15* Or *representative* [b] *17* Or *purification offering*; also in verses 25 and 30 [c] *18* Or *Whoever touches them must be holy*; similarly in verse 27 [d] *20* Or *each* [e] *20* That is, probably about 3 1/2 pounds or about 1.6 kilograms [f] *21* The meaning of the Hebrew for this word is uncertain. [g] *7* Or *purification offering*; also in verse 37

eaten on the next day. 17Any meat of the
sacrifice left over till the third day must
be burned up. 18If any meat of the fellowship offering is eaten on the third day, the
one who offered it will not be accepted. It
will not be reckoned to their credit, for it
has become impure; the person who eats
any of it will be held responsible.

19" 'Meat that touches anything ceremonially unclean must not be eaten; it
must be burned up. As for other meat,
anyone ceremonially clean may eat it.
20But if anyone who is unclean eats any
meat of the fellowship offering belonging to the LORD, they must be cut off
from their people. 21Anyone who touches
something unclean — whether human
uncleanness or an unclean animal or
any unclean creature that moves along
the ground[a] — and then eats any of the
meat of the fellowship offering belonging to the LORD must be cut off from
their people.' "

Eating Fat and Blood Forbidden

22The LORD said to Moses, 23"Say to the
Israelites: 'Do not eat any of the fat of
cattle, sheep or goats. 24The fat of an animal found dead or torn by wild animals
may be used for any other purpose, but
you must not eat it. 25Anyone who eats
the fat of an animal from which a food
offering may be[b] presented to the LORD
must be cut off from their people. 26And
wherever you live, you must not eat the
blood of any bird or animal. 27Anyone
who eats blood must be cut off from
their people.' "

The Priests' Share

28The LORD said to Moses, 29"Say to the
Israelites: 'Anyone who brings a fellowship offering to the LORD is to bring part
of it as their sacrifice to the LORD. 30With
their own hands they are to present the
food offering to the LORD; they are to
bring the fat, together with the breast,
and wave the breast before the LORD as a
wave offering. 31The priest shall burn the
fat on the altar, but the breast belongs to
Aaron and his sons. 32You are to give the
right thigh of your fellowship offerings
to the priest as a contribution. 33The son
of Aaron who offers the blood and the
fat of the fellowship offering shall have
the right thigh as his share. 34From the
fellowship offerings of the Israelites, I
have taken the breast that is waved and
the thigh that is presented and have
given them to Aaron the priest and his
sons as their perpetual share from the
Israelites.' "

35This is the portion of the food offerings presented to the LORD that were allotted to Aaron and his sons on the day
they were presented to serve the LORD as
priests. 36On the day they were anointed,
the LORD commanded that the Israelites give this to them as their perpetual
share for the generations to come.

37These, then, are the regulations for
the burnt offering, the grain offering,
the sin offering, the guilt offering, the
ordination offering and the fellowship
offering, 38which the LORD gave Moses
at Mount Sinai in the Desert of Sinai on
the day he commanded the Israelites to
bring their offerings to the LORD.

The Ordination of Aaron and His Sons

8 The LORD said to Moses, 2"Bring Aaron and his sons, their garments,
the anointing oil, the bull for the sin
offering,[c] the two rams and the basket
containing bread made without yeast,
3and gather the entire assembly at the
entrance to the tent of meeting." 4Moses
did as the LORD commanded him, and
the assembly gathered at the entrance
to the tent of meeting.

5Moses said to the assembly, "This is
what the LORD has commanded to be
done." 6Then Moses brought Aaron and
his sons forward and washed them with
water. 7He put the tunic on Aaron, tied
the sash around him, clothed him with
the robe and put the ephod on him. He
also fastened the ephod with a decora-
tive waistband, which he tied around
him. 8He placed the breastpiece on him
and put the Urim and Thummim in the
breastpiece. 9Then he placed the turban
on Aaron's head and set the gold plate,
the sacred emblem, on the front of it, as
the LORD commanded Moses.

10Then Moses took the anointing oil
and anointed the tabernacle and everything in it, and so consecrated them. 11He
sprinkled some of the oil on the altar
seven times, anointing the altar and all
its utensils and the basin with its stand,
to consecrate them. 12He poured some of
the anointing oil on Aaron's head and
anointed him to consecrate him. 13Then
he brought Aaron's sons forward, put

[a] 21 A few Hebrew manuscripts, Samaritan Pentateuch, Syriac and Targum (see 5:2); most Hebrew manuscripts *any unclean, detestable thing* [b] 25 Or *offering is* [c] 2 Or *purification offering*; also in verse 14

tunics on them, tied sashes around them
and fastened caps on them, as the LORD
commanded Moses.
14He then presented the bull for the
sin offering, and Aaron and his sons
laid their hands on its head. 15Moses
slaughtered the bull and took some of
the blood, and with his finger he put it
on all the horns of the altar to purify the
altar. He poured out the rest of the blood
at the base of the altar. So he consecrated it to make atonement for it. 16Moses
also took all the fat around the internal
organs, the long lobe of the liver, and
both kidneys and their fat, and burned
it on the altar. 17But the bull with its hide
and its flesh and its intestines he burned
up outside the camp, as the LORD commanded Moses.
18He then presented the ram for the
burnt offering, and Aaron and his sons
laid their hands on its head. 19Then Moses slaughtered the ram and splashed the
blood against the sides of the altar. 20He
cut the ram into pieces and burned the
head, the pieces and the fat. 21He washed
the internal organs and the legs with
water and burned the whole ram on the
altar. It was a burnt offering, a pleasing
aroma, a food offering presented to the
LORD, as the LORD commanded Moses.
22He then presented the other ram,
the ram for the ordination, and Aaron and his sons laid their hands on its
head. 23Moses slaughtered the ram and
took some of its blood and put it on the
lobe of Aaron's right ear, on the thumb
of his right hand and on the big toe of
his right foot. 24Moses also brought Aaron's sons forward and put some of the
blood on the lobes of their right ears, on
the thumbs of their right hands and on
the big toes of their right feet. Then he
splashed blood against the sides of the
altar. 25After that, he took the fat, the fat
tail, all the fat around the internal organs, the long lobe of the liver, both kidneys and their fat and the right thigh.
26And from the basket of bread made
without yeast, which was before the
LORD, he took one thick loaf, one thick
loaf with olive oil mixed in, and one thin
loaf, and he put these on the fat portions
and on the right thigh. 27He put all these
in the hands of Aaron and his sons, and
they waved them before the LORD as a
wave offering. 28Then Moses took them
from their hands and burned them on
the altar on top of the burnt offering as
an ordination offering, a pleasing aroma, a food offering presented to the
LORD. 29Moses also took the breast, which
was his share of the ordination ram, and
waved it before the LORD as a wave offering, as the LORD commanded Moses.
30Then Moses took some of the anointing oil and some of the blood from the
altar and sprinkled them on Aaron and
his garments and on his sons and their
garments. So he consecrated Aaron and
his garments and his sons and their garments.
31Moses then said to Aaron and his
sons, "Cook the meat at the entrance to
the tent of meeting and eat it there with
the bread from the basket of ordination
offerings, as I was commanded: 'Aaron
and his sons are to eat it.' 32Then burn
up the rest of the meat and the bread.
33Do not leave the entrance to the tent of
meeting for seven days, until the days of
your ordination are completed, for your
ordination will last seven days. 34What
has been done today was commanded
by the LORD to make atonement for you.
35You must stay at the entrance to the
tent of meeting day and night for seven
days and do what the LORD requires, so
you will not die; for that is what I have
been commanded."
36So Aaron and his sons did everything
the LORD commanded through Moses.

The Priests Begin Their Ministry

9 On the eighth day Moses summoned
Aaron and his sons and the elders
of Israel. 2He said to Aaron, "Take a bull
calf for your sin offering[a] and a ram for
your burnt offering, both without defect,
and present them before the LORD. 3Then
say to the Israelites: 'Take a male goat
for a sin offering, a calf and a lamb —
both a year old and without defect — for
a burnt offering, 4and an ox[b] and a ram
for a fellowship offering to sacrifice before the LORD, together with a grain offering mixed with olive oil. For today the
LORD will appear to you.' "
5They took the things Moses commanded to the front of the tent of meeting, and the entire assembly came near
and stood before the LORD. 6Then Moses
said, "This is what the LORD has commanded you to do, so that the glory of
the LORD may appear to you."
7Moses said to Aaron, "Come to the
altar and sacrifice your sin offering
and your burnt offering and make

[a] 2 Or *purification offering*; here and throughout this chapter to either male or female; also in verses 18 and 19.
[b] 4 The Hebrew word can refer

atonement for yourself and the people; sacrifice the offering that is for the people and make atonement for them, as the LORD has commanded."

8So Aaron came to the altar and slaughtered the calf as a sin offering for himself. 9His sons brought the blood to him, and he dipped his finger into the blood and put it on the horns of the altar; the rest of the blood he poured out at the base of the altar. 10On the altar he burned the fat, the kidneys and the long lobe of the liver from the sin offering, as the LORD commanded Moses; 11the flesh and the hide he burned up outside the camp.

12Then he slaughtered the burnt offering. His sons handed him the blood, and he splashed it against the sides of the altar. 13They handed him the burnt offering piece by piece, including the head, and he burned them on the altar. 14He washed the internal organs and the legs and burned them on top of the burnt offering on the altar.

15Aaron then brought the offering that was for the people. He took the goat for the people's sin offering and slaughtered it and offered it for a sin offering as he did with the first one.

16He brought the burnt offering and offered it in the prescribed way. 17He also brought the grain offering, took a handful of it and burned it on the altar in addition to the morning's burnt offering.

18He slaughtered the ox and the ram as the fellowship offering for the people. His sons handed him the blood, and he splashed it against the sides of the altar. 19But the fat portions of the ox and the ram — the fat tail, the layer of fat, the kidneys and the long lobe of the liver — 20these they laid on the breasts, and then Aaron burned the fat on the altar. 21Aaron waved the breasts and the right thigh before the LORD as a wave offering, as Moses commanded.

22Then Aaron lifted his hands toward the people and blessed them. And having sacrificed the sin offering, the burnt offering and the fellowship offering, he stepped down.

23Moses and Aaron then went into the tent of meeting. When they came out, they blessed the people; and the glory of the LORD appeared to all the people. 24Fire came out from the presence of the LORD and consumed the burnt offering and the fat portions on the altar. And when all the people saw it, they shouted for joy and fell facedown.

The Death of Nadab and Abihu

10 Aaron's sons Nadab and Abihu took their censers, put fire in them and added incense; and they offered unauthorized fire before the LORD, contrary to his command. 2So fire came out from the presence of the LORD and consumed them, and they died before the LORD. 3Moses then said to Aaron, "This is what the LORD spoke of when he said:

"'Among those who approach me
I will be proved holy;
in the sight of all the people
I will be honored.'"

Aaron remained silent.

4Moses summoned Mishael and Elzaphan, sons of Aaron's uncle Uzziel, and said to them, "Come here; carry your cousins outside the camp, away from the front of the sanctuary." 5So they came and carried them, still in their tunics, outside the camp, as Moses ordered.

6Then Moses said to Aaron and his sons Eleazar and Ithamar, "Do not let your hair become unkempt[a] and do not tear your clothes, or you will die and the LORD will be angry with the whole community. But your relatives, all the Israelites, may mourn for those the LORD has destroyed by fire. 7Do not leave the entrance to the tent of meeting or you will die, because the LORD's anointing oil is on you." So they did as Moses said.

8Then the LORD said to Aaron, 9"You and your sons are not to drink wine or other fermented drink whenever you go into the tent of meeting, or you will die. This is a lasting ordinance for the generations to come, 10so that you can distinguish between the holy and the common, between the unclean and the clean, 11and so you can teach the Israelites all the decrees the LORD has given them through Moses."

12Moses said to Aaron and his remaining sons, Eleazar and Ithamar, "Take the grain offering left over from the food offerings prepared without yeast and presented to the LORD and eat it beside the altar, for it is most holy. 13Eat it in the sanctuary area, because it is your share and your sons' share of the food offerings presented to the LORD; for so I have been commanded. 14But you and your sons and your daughters may eat the breast that was waved and the thigh that was presented. Eat them in a ceremonially clean place; they have been given to you and your children as your

[a] 6 Or *Do not uncover your heads*

share of the Israelites' fellowship offerings. [15]The thigh that was presented
and the breast that was waved must be
brought with the fat portions of the food
offerings, to be waved before the LORD as
a wave offering. This will be the perpetual share for you and your children, as the
LORD has commanded."
[16]When Moses inquired about the goat
of the sin offering[a] and found that it had
been burned up, he was angry with Eleazar and Ithamar, Aaron's remaining
sons, and asked, [17]"Why didn't you eat
the sin offering in the sanctuary area?
It is most holy; it was given to you to
take away the guilt of the community
by making atonement for them before
the LORD. [18]Since its blood was not tak-
en into the Holy Place, you should have
eaten the goat in the sanctuary area, as
I commanded."
[19]Aaron replied to Moses, "Today they
sacrificed their sin offering and their
burnt offering before the LORD, but such
things as this have happened to me.
Would the LORD have been pleased if I
had eaten the sin offering today?" [20]When
Moses heard this, he was satisfied.

Clean and Unclean Food

11 The LORD said to Moses and Aaron, [2]"Say to the Israelites: 'Of all
the animals that live on land, these are
the ones you may eat: [3]You may eat any
animal that has a divided hoof and that
chews the cud.
[4]" 'There are some that only chew the
cud or only have a divided hoof, but you
must not eat them. The camel, though
it chews the cud, does not have a divided hoof; it is ceremonially unclean for
you. [5]The hyrax, though it chews the
cud, does not have a divided hoof; it is
unclean for you. [6]The rabbit, though it
chews the cud, does not have a divided
hoof; it is unclean for you. [7]And the pig,
though it has a divided hoof, does not
chew the cud; it is unclean for you. [8]You
must not eat their meat or touch their
carcasses; they are unclean for you.
[9]" 'Of all the creatures living in the water of the seas and the streams you may
eat any that have fins and scales. [10]But
all creatures in the seas or streams that
do not have fins and scales—whether among all the swarming things or
among all the other living creatures in
the water—you are to regard as unclean. [11]And since you are to regard them
as unclean, you must not eat their meat;
you must regard their carcasses as unclean. [12]Anything living in the water that
does not have fins and scales is to be regarded as unclean by you.
[13]" 'These are the birds you are to regard as unclean and not eat because
they are unclean: the eagle,[b] the vulture,
the black vulture, [14]the red kite, any kind
of black kite, [15]any kind of raven, [16]the
horned owl, the screech owl, the gull, any
kind of hawk, [17]the little owl, the cormo-
rant, the great owl, [18]the white owl, the
desert owl, the osprey, [19]the stork, any
kind of heron, the hoopoe and the bat.
[20]" 'All flying insects that walk on all
fours are to be regarded as unclean by
you. [21]There are, however, some flying
insects that walk on all fours that you
may eat: those that have jointed legs
for hopping on the ground. [22]Of these
you may eat any kind of locust, katydid,
cricket or grasshopper. [23]But all other flying insects that have four legs you are to
regard as unclean.
[24]" 'You will make yourselves unclean
by these; whoever touches their carcasses will be unclean till evening. [25]Whoev-
er picks up one of their carcasses must
wash their clothes, and they will be unclean till evening.
[26]" 'Every animal that does not have a
divided hoof or that does not chew the
cud is unclean for you; whoever touches the carcass of any of them will be unclean. [27]Of all the animals that walk on
all fours, those that walk on their paws
are unclean for you; whoever touches
their carcasses will be unclean till evening. [28]Anyone who picks up their carcasses must wash their clothes, and they
will be unclean till evening. These animals are unclean for you.
[29]" 'Of the animals that move along the
ground, these are unclean for you: the
weasel, the rat, any kind of great lizard,
[30]the gecko, the monitor lizard, the wall
lizard, the skink and the chameleon. [31]Of
all those that move along the ground,
these are unclean for you. Whoever
touches them when they are dead will be
unclean till evening. [32]When one of them
dies and falls on something, that article,
whatever its use, will be unclean, whether it is made of wood, cloth, hide or sackcloth. Put it in water; it will be unclean
till evening, and then it will be clean. [33]If
one of them falls into a clay pot, everything in it will be unclean, and you must

[a] *16* Or *purification offering*; also in verses 17 and 19 [b] *13* The precise identification of some of the birds, insects and animals in this chapter is uncertain.

break the pot. 34Any food you are allowed to eat that has come into contact with water from any such pot is unclean, and any liquid that is drunk from such a pot is unclean. 35Anything that one of their carcasses falls on becomes unclean; an oven or cooking pot must be broken up. They are unclean, and you are to regard them as unclean. 36A spring, however, or a cistern for collecting water remains clean, but anyone who touches one of these carcasses is unclean. 37If a carcass falls on any seeds that are to be planted, they remain clean. 38But if water has been put on the seed and a carcass falls on it, it is unclean for you.

39" 'If an animal that you are allowed to eat dies, anyone who touches its carcass will be unclean till evening. 40Anyone who eats some of its carcass must wash their clothes, and they will be unclean till evening. Anyone who picks up the carcass must wash their clothes, and they will be unclean till evening.

41" 'Every creature that moves along the ground is to be regarded as unclean; it is not to be eaten. 42You are not to eat any creature that moves along the ground, whether it moves on its belly or walks on all fours or on many feet; it is unclean. 43Do not defile yourselves by any of these creatures. Do not make yourselves unclean by means of them or be made unclean by them. 44I am the LORD your God; consecrate yourselves and be holy, because I am holy. Do not make yourselves unclean by any creature that moves along the ground. 45I am the LORD, who brought you up out of Egypt to be your God; therefore be holy, because I am holy.

46" 'These are the regulations concerning animals, birds, every living thing that moves about in the water and every creature that moves along the ground. 47You must distinguish between the unclean and the clean, between living creatures that may be eaten and those that may not be eaten.' "

Purification After Childbirth

12 The LORD said to Moses, 2"Say to the Israelites: 'A woman who becomes pregnant and gives birth to a son will be ceremonially unclean for seven days, just as she is unclean during her monthly period. 3On the eighth day the boy is to be circumcised. 4Then the woman must wait thirty-three days to be purified from her bleeding. She must not touch anything sacred or go to the sanctuary until the days of her purification are over. 5If she gives birth to a daughter, for two weeks the woman will be unclean, as during her period. Then she must wait sixty-six days to be purified from her bleeding.

6" 'When the days of her purification for a son or daughter are over, she is to bring to the priest at the entrance to the tent of meeting a year-old lamb for a burnt offering and a young pigeon or a dove for a sin offering.[a] 7He shall offer them before the LORD to make atonement for her, and then she will be ceremonially clean from her flow of blood.

" 'These are the regulations for the woman who gives birth to a boy or a girl. 8But if she cannot afford a lamb, she is to bring two doves or two young pigeons, one for a burnt offering and the other for a sin offering. In this way the priest will make atonement for her, and she will be clean.' "

Regulations About Defiling Skin Diseases

13 The LORD said to Moses and Aaron, 2"When anyone has a swelling or a rash or a shiny spot on their skin that may be a defiling skin disease,[b] they must be brought to Aaron the priest or to one of his sons[c] who is a priest. 3The priest is to examine the sore on the skin, and if the hair in the sore has turned white and the sore appears to be more than skin deep, it is a defiling skin disease. When the priest examines that person, he shall pronounce them ceremonially unclean. 4If the shiny spot on the skin is white but does not appear to be more than skin deep and the hair in it has not turned white, the priest is to isolate the affected person for seven days. 5On the seventh day the priest is to examine them, and if he sees that the sore is unchanged and has not spread in the skin, he is to isolate them for another seven days. 6On the seventh day the priest is to examine them again, and if the sore has faded and has not spread in the skin, the priest shall pronounce them clean; it is only a rash. They must wash their clothes, and they will be clean. 7But if the rash does spread in their skin after they have shown themselves to the

[a] 6 Or *purification offering*; also in verse 8 [b] 2 The Hebrew word for *defiling skin disease*, traditionally translated "leprosy," was used for various diseases affecting the skin; here and throughout verses 3-46. [c] 2 Or *descendants*

priest to be pronounced clean, they must appear before the priest again. 8The priest is to examine that person, and if the rash has spread in the skin, he shall pronounce them unclean; it is a defiling skin disease.

9"When anyone has a defiling skin disease, they must be brought to the priest. 10The priest is to examine them, and if there is a white swelling in the skin that has turned the hair white and if there is raw flesh in the swelling, 11it is a chronic skin disease and the priest shall pronounce them unclean. He is not to isolate them, because they are already unclean.

12"If the disease breaks out all over their skin and, so far as the priest can see, it covers all the skin of the affected person from head to foot, 13the priest is to examine them, and if the disease has covered their whole body, he shall pronounce them clean. Since it has all turned white, they are clean. 14But whenever raw flesh appears on them, they will be unclean. 15When the priest sees the raw flesh, he shall pronounce them unclean. The raw flesh is unclean; they have a defiling disease. 16If the raw flesh changes and turns white, they must go to the priest. 17The priest is to examine them, and if the sores have turned white, the priest shall pronounce the affected person clean; then they will be clean.

18"When someone has a boil on their skin and it heals, 19and in the place where the boil was, a white swelling or reddish-white spot appears, they must present themselves to the priest. 20The priest is to examine it, and if it appears to be more than skin deep and the hair in it has turned white, the priest shall pronounce that person unclean. It is a defiling skin disease that has broken out where the boil was. 21But if, when the priest examines it, there is no white hair in it and it is not more than skin deep and has faded, then the priest is to isolate them for seven days. 22If it is spreading in the skin, the priest shall pronounce them unclean; it is a defiling disease. 23But if the spot is unchanged and has not spread, it is only a scar from the boil, and the priest shall pronounce them clean.

24"When someone has a burn on their skin and a reddish-white or white spot appears in the raw flesh of the burn, 25the priest is to examine the spot, and if the hair in it has turned white, and it appears to be more than skin deep, it is a defiling disease that has broken out in the burn. The priest shall pronounce them unclean; it is a defiling skin disease. 26But if the priest examines it and there is no white hair in the spot and if it is not more than skin deep and has faded, then the priest is to isolate them for seven days. 27On the seventh day the priest is to examine that person, and if it is spreading in the skin, the priest shall pronounce them unclean; it is a defiling skin disease. 28If, however, the spot is unchanged and has not spread in the skin but has faded, it is a swelling from the burn, and the priest shall pronounce them clean; it is only a scar from the burn.

29"If a man or woman has a sore on their head or chin, 30the priest is to examine the sore, and if it appears to be more than skin deep and the hair in it is yellow and thin, the priest shall pronounce them unclean; it is a defiling skin disease on the head or chin. 31But if, when the priest examines the sore, it does not seem to be more than skin deep and there is no black hair in it, then the priest is to isolate the affected person for seven days. 32On the seventh day the priest is to examine the sore, and if it has not spread and there is no yellow hair in it and it does not appear to be more than skin deep, 33then the man or woman must shave themselves, except for the affected area, and the priest is to keep them isolated another seven days. 34On the seventh day the priest is to examine the sore, and if it has not spread in the skin and appears to be no more than skin deep, the priest shall pronounce them clean. They must wash their clothes, and they will be clean. 35But if the sore does spread in the skin after they are pronounced clean, 36the priest is to examine them, and if he finds that the sore has spread in the skin, he does not need to look for yellow hair; they are unclean. 37If, however, the sore is unchanged so far as the priest can see, and if black hair has grown in it, the affected person is healed. They are clean, and the priest shall pronounce them clean.

38"When a man or woman has white spots on the skin, 39the priest is to examine them, and if the spots are dull white, it is a harmless rash that has broken out on the skin; they are clean.

40"A man who has lost his hair and is bald is clean. 41If he has lost his hair from the front of his scalp and has a bald forehead, he is clean. 42But if he has a reddish-white sore on his bald head or forehead, it is a defiling disease breaking out on his head or forehead. 43The priest is to examine him, and if the swollen sore on his head or forehead is reddish-white like a defiling skin disease, 44the man is diseased and is unclean. The priest shall pronounce him unclean because of the sore on his head.

45"Anyone with such a defiling disease must wear torn clothes, let their hair be unkempt,[a] cover the lower part of their face and cry out, 'Unclean! Unclean!' 46As long as they have the disease they remain unclean. They must live alone; they must live outside the camp.

Regulations About Defiling Molds

47"As for any fabric that is spoiled with a defiling mold — any woolen or linen clothing, 48any woven or knitted material of linen or wool, any leather or anything made of leather — 49if the affected area in the fabric, the leather, the woven or knitted material, or any leather article, is greenish or reddish, it is a defiling mold and must be shown to the priest. 50The priest is to examine the affected area and isolate the article for seven days. 51On the seventh day he is to examine it, and if the mold has spread in the fabric, the woven or knitted material, or the leather, whatever its use, it is a persistent defiling mold; the article is unclean. 52He must burn the fabric, the woven or knitted material of wool or linen, or any leather article that has been spoiled; because the defiling mold is persistent, the article must be burned.

53"But if, when the priest examines it, the mold has not spread in the fabric, the woven or knitted material, or the leather article, 54he shall order that the spoiled article be washed. Then he is to isolate it for another seven days. 55After the article has been washed, the priest is to examine it again, and if the mold has not changed its appearance, even though it has not spread, it is unclean. Burn it, no matter which side of the fabric has been spoiled. 56If, when the priest examines it, the mold has faded after the article has been washed, he is to tear the spoiled part out of the fabric, the leather, or the woven or knitted material. 57But if it reappears in the fabric, in the woven or knitted material, or in the leather article, it is a spreading mold; whatever has the mold must be burned. 58Any fabric, woven or knitted material, or any leather article that has been washed and is rid of the mold, must be washed again. Then it will be clean."

59These are the regulations concerning defiling molds in woolen or linen clothing, woven or knitted material, or any leather article, for pronouncing them clean or unclean.

Cleansing From Defiling Skin Diseases

14 The LORD said to Moses, 2"These are the regulations for any diseased person at the time of their ceremonial cleansing, when they are brought to the priest: 3The priest is to go outside the camp and examine them. If they have been healed of their defiling skin disease,[b] 4the priest shall order that two live clean birds and some cedar wood, scarlet yarn and hyssop be brought for the person to be cleansed. 5Then the priest shall order that one of the birds be killed over fresh water in a clay pot. 6He is then to take the live bird and dip it, together with the cedar wood, the scarlet yarn and the hyssop, into the blood of the bird that was killed over the fresh water. 7Seven times he shall sprinkle the one to be cleansed of the defiling disease, and then pronounce them clean. After that, he is to release the live bird in the open fields.

8"The person to be cleansed must wash their clothes, shave off all their hair and bathe with water; then they will be ceremonially clean. After this they may come into the camp, but they must stay outside their tent for seven days. 9On the seventh day they must shave off all their hair; they must shave their head, their beard, their eyebrows and the rest of their hair. They must wash their clothes and bathe themselves with water, and they will be clean.

10"On the eighth day they must bring two male lambs and one ewe lamb a year old, each without defect, along with three-tenths of an ephah[c] of the finest flour mixed with olive oil for a grain offering, and one log[d] of oil. 11The priest who pronounces them clean shall present both the one to be cleansed and their offerings before the LORD at the entrance to the tent of meeting.

12"Then the priest is to take one of the male lambs and offer it as a guilt

[a] *45* Or *clothes, uncover their head* [b] *3* The Hebrew word for *defiling skin disease,* traditionally translated "leprosy," was used for various diseases affecting the skin; also in verses 7, 32, 54 and 57. [c] *10* That is, probably about 11 pounds or about 5 kilograms [d] *10* That is, about 1/3 quart or about 0.3 liter; also in verses 12, 15, 21 and 24

offering, along with the log of oil; he
shall wave them before the LORD as a
wave offering. 13He is to slaughter the
lamb in the sanctuary area where the
sin offering[a] and the burnt offering are
slaughtered. Like the sin offering, the
guilt offering belongs to the priest; it is
most holy. 14The priest is to take some of
the blood of the guilt offering and put it
on the lobe of the right ear of the one to
be cleansed, on the thumb of their right
hand and on the big toe of their right
foot. 15The priest shall then take some of
the log of oil, pour it in the palm of his
own left hand, 16dip his right forefinger
into the oil in his palm, and with his finger sprinkle some of it before the LORD
seven times. 17The priest is to put some of
the oil remaining in his palm on the lobe
of the right ear of the one to be cleansed,
on the thumb of their right hand and on
the big toe of their right foot, on top of
the blood of the guilt offering. 18The rest
of the oil in his palm the priest shall put
on the head of the one to be cleansed
and make atonement for them before
the LORD.

19"Then the priest is to sacrifice the sin
offering and make atonement for the
one to be cleansed from their uncleanness. After that, the priest shall slaughter the burnt offering 20and offer it on
the altar, together with the grain offering, and make atonement for them, and
they will be clean.

21"If, however, they are poor and cannot afford these, they must take one
male lamb as a guilt offering to be
waved to make atonement for them,
together with a tenth of an ephah[b] of
the finest flour mixed with olive oil for
a grain offering, a log of oil, 22and two
doves or two young pigeons, such as they
can afford, one for a sin offering and the
other for a burnt offering.

23"On the eighth day they must bring
them for their cleansing to the priest
at the entrance to the tent of meeting,
before the LORD. 24The priest is to take
the lamb for the guilt offering, together
with the log of oil, and wave them before
the LORD as a wave offering. 25He shall
slaughter the lamb for the guilt offering and take some of its blood and put it
on the lobe of the right ear of the one to
be cleansed, on the thumb of their right
hand and on the big toe of their right
foot. 26The priest is to pour some of the
oil into the palm of his own left hand,
27and with his right forefinger sprinkle some of the oil from his palm sev-
en times before the LORD. 28Some of the
oil in his palm he is to put on the same
places he put the blood of the guilt offering — on the lobe of the right ear of
the one to be cleansed, on the thumb of
their right hand and on the big toe of
their right foot. 29The rest of the oil in
his palm the priest shall put on the head
of the one to be cleansed, to make atonement for them before the LORD. 30Then
he shall sacrifice the doves or the young
pigeons, such as the person can afford,
31one as a sin offering and the other as
a burnt offering, together with the grain
offering. In this way the priest will make
atonement before the LORD on behalf of
the one to be cleansed."

32These are the regulations for anyone
who has a defiling skin disease and who
cannot afford the regular offerings for
their cleansing.

Cleansing From Defiling Molds

33The LORD said to Moses and Aaron,
34"When you enter the land of Canaan,
which I am giving you as your possession, and I put a spreading mold in a
house in that land, 35the owner of the
house must go and tell the priest, 'I
have seen something that looks like a
defiling mold in my house.' 36The priest
is to order the house to be emptied before he goes in to examine the mold, so
that nothing in the house will be pronounced unclean. After this the priest
is to go in and inspect the house. 37He is
to examine the mold on the walls, and
if it has greenish or reddish depressions
that appear to be deeper than the surface of the wall, 38the priest shall go out
the doorway of the house and close it up
for seven days. 39On the seventh day the
priest shall return to inspect the house.
If the mold has spread on the walls, 40he
is to order that the contaminated stones
be torn out and thrown into an unclean
place outside the town. 41He must have
all the inside walls of the house scraped
and the material that is scraped off
dumped into an unclean place outside
the town. 42Then they are to take other stones to replace these and take new
clay and plaster the house.

43"If the defiling mold reappears in
the house after the stones have been
torn out and the house scraped and plastered, 44the priest is to go and examine it

[a] *13* Or *purification offering*; also in verses 19, 22 and 31 [b] *21* That is, probably about 3 1/2 pounds or about 1.6 kilograms

and, if the mold has spread in the house, it is a persistent defiling mold; the house is unclean. 45 It must be torn down—its stones, timbers and all the plaster—and taken out of the town to an unclean place.

46 "Anyone who goes into the house while it is closed up will be unclean till evening. 47 Anyone who sleeps or eats in the house must wash their clothes.

48 "But if the priest comes to examine it and the mold has not spread after the house has been plastered, he shall pronounce the house clean, because the defiling mold is gone. 49 To purify the house he is to take two birds and some cedar wood, scarlet yarn and hyssop. 50 He shall kill one of the birds over fresh water in a clay pot. 51 Then he is to take the cedar wood, the hyssop, the scarlet yarn and the live bird, dip them into the blood of the dead bird and the fresh water, and sprinkle the house seven times. 52 He shall purify the house with the bird's blood, the fresh water, the live bird, the cedar wood, the hyssop and the scarlet yarn. 53 Then he is to release the live bird in the open fields outside the town. In this way he will make atonement for the house, and it will be clean."

54 These are the regulations for any defiling skin disease, for a sore, 55 for defiling molds in fabric or in a house, 56 and for a swelling, a rash or a shiny spot, 57 to determine when something is clean or unclean.

These are the regulations for defiling skin diseases and defiling molds.

Discharges Causing Uncleanness

15 The LORD said to Moses and Aaron, 2 "Speak to the Israelites and say to them: 'When any man has an unusual bodily discharge, such a discharge is unclean. 3 Whether it continues flowing from his body or is blocked, it will make him unclean. This is how his discharge will bring about uncleanness:

4 " 'Any bed the man with a discharge lies on will be unclean, and anything he sits on will be unclean. 5 Anyone who touches his bed must wash their clothes and bathe with water, and they will be unclean till evening. 6 Whoever sits on anything that the man with a discharge sat on must wash their clothes and bathe with water, and they will be unclean till evening.

7 " 'Whoever touches the man who has a discharge must wash their clothes and bathe with water, and they will be unclean till evening.

8 " 'If the man with the discharge spits on anyone who is clean, they must wash their clothes and bathe with water, and they will be unclean till evening.

9 " 'Everything the man sits on when riding will be unclean, 10 and whoever touches any of the things that were under him will be unclean till evening; whoever picks up those things must wash their clothes and bathe with water, and they will be unclean till evening.

11 " 'Anyone the man with a discharge touches without rinsing his hands with water must wash their clothes and bathe with water, and they will be unclean till evening.

12 " 'A clay pot that the man touches must be broken, and any wooden article is to be rinsed with water.

13 " 'When a man is cleansed from his discharge, he is to count off seven days for his ceremonial cleansing; he must wash his clothes and bathe himself with fresh water, and he will be clean. 14 On the eighth day he must take two doves or two young pigeons and come before the LORD to the entrance to the tent of meeting and give them to the priest. 15 The priest is to sacrifice them, the one for a sin offering[a] and the other for a burnt offering. In this way he will make atonement before the LORD for the man because of his discharge.

16 " 'When a man has an emission of semen, he must bathe his whole body with water, and he will be unclean till evening. 17 Any clothing or leather that has semen on it must be washed with water, and it will be unclean till evening. 18 When a man has sexual relations with a woman and there is an emission of semen, both of them must bathe with water, and they will be unclean till evening.

19 " 'When a woman has her regular flow of blood, the impurity of her monthly period will last seven days, and anyone who touches her will be unclean till evening.

20 " 'Anything she lies on during her period will be unclean, and anything she sits on will be unclean. 21 Anyone who touches her bed will be unclean; they must wash their clothes and bathe with water, and they will be unclean till evening. 22 Anyone who touches anything she sits on will be unclean; they must wash their clothes and bathe with water, and they will be unclean till evening.

[a] 15 Or *purification offering;* also in verse 30

23Whether it is the bed or anything she
was sitting on, when anyone touches it,
they will be unclean till evening.
24" 'If a man has sexual relations with
her and her monthly flow touches him,
he will be unclean for seven days; any
bed he lies on will be unclean.
25" 'When a woman has a discharge of
blood for many days at a time other than
her monthly period or has a discharge
that continues beyond her period, she
will be unclean as long as she has the
discharge, just as in the days of her period. 26Any bed she lies on while her discharge continues will be unclean, as is
her bed during her monthly period, and
anything she sits on will be unclean, as
during her period. 27Anyone who touches them will be unclean; they must wash
their clothes and bathe with water, and
they will be unclean till evening.
28" 'When she is cleansed from her discharge, she must count off seven days,
and after that she will be ceremonially
clean. 29On the eighth day she must take
two doves or two young pigeons and
bring them to the priest at the entrance
to the tent of meeting. 30The priest is to
sacrifice one for a sin offering and the
other for a burnt offering. In this way
he will make atonement for her before
the LORD for the uncleanness of her discharge.
31" 'You must keep the Israelites separate from things that make them
unclean, so they will not die in their
uncleanness for defiling my dwelling
place,[a] which is among them.' "
32These are the regulations for a man
with a discharge, for anyone made unclean by an emission of semen, 33for
a woman in her monthly period, for a
man or a woman with a discharge, and
for a man who has sexual relations with
a woman who is ceremonially unclean.

The Day of Atonement

16 The LORD spoke to Moses after
the death of the two sons of Aaron who died when they approached the
LORD. 2The LORD said to Moses: "Tell your
brother Aaron that he is not to come
whenever he chooses into the Most Holy
Place behind the curtain in front of the
atonement cover on the ark, or else he
will die. For I will appear in the cloud
over the atonement cover.
3"This is how Aaron is to enter the
Most Holy Place: He must first bring a
young bull for a sin offering[b] and a ram
for a burnt offering. 4He is to put on the
sacred linen tunic, with linen undergarments next to his body; he is to tie
the linen sash around him and put on
the linen turban. These are sacred garments; so he must bathe himself with
water before he puts them on. 5From the
Israelite community he is to take two
male goats for a sin offering and a ram
for a burnt offering.
6"Aaron is to offer the bull for his own
sin offering to make atonement for himself and his household. 7Then he is to
take the two goats and present them before the LORD at the entrance to the tent
of meeting. 8He is to cast lots for the two
goats — one lot for the LORD and the other for the scapegoat.[c] 9Aaron shall bring
the goat whose lot falls to the LORD and
sacrifice it for a sin offering. 10But the
goat chosen by lot as the scapegoat shall
be presented alive before the LORD to be
used for making atonement by sending
it into the wilderness as a scapegoat.
11"Aaron shall bring the bull for his
own sin offering to make atonement for
himself and his household, and he is to
slaughter the bull for his own sin offering. 12He is to take a censer full of burning coals from the altar before the LORD
and two handfuls of finely ground fragrant incense and take them behind the
curtain. 13He is to put the incense on the
fire before the LORD, and the smoke of
the incense will conceal the atonement
cover above the tablets of the covenant
law, so that he will not die. 14He is to take
some of the bull's blood and with his finger sprinkle it on the front of the atonement cover; then he shall sprinkle some
of it with his finger seven times before
the atonement cover.
15"He shall then slaughter the goat for
the sin offering for the people and take
its blood behind the curtain and do with
it as he did with the bull's blood: He shall
sprinkle it on the atonement cover and
in front of it. 16In this way he will make
atonement for the Most Holy Place because of the uncleanness and rebellion
of the Israelites, whatever their sins
have been. He is to do the same for the
tent of meeting, which is among them
in the midst of their uncleanness. 17No
one is to be in the tent of meeting from
the time Aaron goes in to make atonement in the Most Holy Place until he
comes out, having made atonement for

[a] *31* Or *my tabernacle* [b] *3* Or *purification offering*; here and throughout this chapter
[c] *8* The meaning of the Hebrew for this word is uncertain; also in verses 10 and 26.

himself, his household and the whole community of Israel.

18"Then he shall come out to the altar that is before the LORD and make atonement for it. He shall take some of the bull's blood and some of the goat's blood and put it on all the horns of the altar. 19He shall sprinkle some of the blood on it with his finger seven times to cleanse it and to consecrate it from the uncleanness of the Israelites.

20"When Aaron has finished making atonement for the Most Holy Place, the tent of meeting and the altar, he shall bring forward the live goat. 21He is to lay both hands on the head of the live goat and confess over it all the wickedness and rebellion of the Israelites—all their sins—and put them on the goat's head. He shall send the goat away into the wilderness in the care of someone appointed for the task. 22The goat will carry on itself all their sins to a remote place; and the man shall release it in the wilderness.

23"Then Aaron is to go into the tent of meeting and take off the linen garments he put on before he entered the Most Holy Place, and he is to leave them there. 24He shall bathe himself with water in the sanctuary area and put on his regular garments. Then he shall come out and sacrifice the burnt offering for himself and the burnt offering for the people, to make atonement for himself and for the people. 25He shall also burn the fat of the sin offering on the altar.

26"The man who releases the goat as a scapegoat must wash his clothes and bathe himself with water; afterward he may come into the camp. 27The bull and the goat for the sin offerings, whose blood was brought into the Most Holy Place to make atonement, must be taken outside the camp; their hides, flesh and intestines are to be burned up. 28The man who burns them must wash his clothes and bathe himself with water; afterward he may come into the camp.

29"This is to be a lasting ordinance for you: On the tenth day of the seventh month you must deny yourselves[a] and not do any work—whether native-born or a foreigner residing among you—30because on this day atonement will be made for you, to cleanse you. Then, before the LORD, you will be clean from all your sins. 31It is a day of sabbath rest, and you must deny yourselves; it is a lasting ordinance. 32The priest who is anointed and ordained to succeed his father as high priest is to make atonement. He is to put on the sacred linen garments 33and make atonement for the Most Holy Place, for the tent of meeting and the altar, and for the priests and all the members of the community.

34"This is to be a lasting ordinance for you: Atonement is to be made once a year for all the sins of the Israelites."

And it was done, as the LORD commanded Moses.

Eating Blood Forbidden

17 The LORD said to Moses, 2"Speak to Aaron and his sons and to all the Israelites and say to them: 'This is what the LORD has commanded: 3Any Israelite who sacrifices an ox,[b] a lamb or a goat in the camp or outside of it 4instead of bringing it to the entrance to the tent of meeting to present it as an offering to the LORD in front of the tabernacle of the LORD—that person shall be considered guilty of bloodshed; they have shed blood and must be cut off from their people. 5This is so the Israelites will bring to the LORD the sacrifices they are now making in the open fields. They must bring them to the priest, that is, to the LORD, at the entrance to the tent of meeting and sacrifice them as fellowship offerings. 6The priest is to splash the blood against the altar of the LORD at the entrance to the tent of meeting and burn the fat as an aroma pleasing to the LORD. 7They must no longer offer any of their sacrifices to the goat idols[c] to whom they prostitute themselves. This is to be a lasting ordinance for them and for the generations to come.'

8"Say to them: 'Any Israelite or any foreigner residing among them who offers a burnt offering or sacrifice 9and does not bring it to the entrance to the tent of meeting to sacrifice it to the LORD must be cut off from the people of Israel.

10" 'I will set my face against any Israelite or any foreigner residing among them who eats blood, and I will cut them off from the people. 11For the life of a creature is in the blood, and I have given it to you to make atonement for yourselves on the altar; it is the blood that makes atonement for one's life.[d] 12Therefore I say to the Israelites, "None of you may eat blood, nor may any foreigner residing among you eat blood."

[a] 29 Or *must fast*; also in verse 31 [b] 3 The Hebrew word can refer to either male or female.
[c] 7 Or *the demons* [d] 11 Or *atonement by the life in the blood*

13“ ‘Any Israelite or any foreigner residing among you who hunts any animal or
bird that may be eaten must drain out
the blood and cover it with earth, 14be-
cause the life of every creature is its
blood. That is why I have said to the Israelites, “You must not eat the blood of
any creature, because the life of every
creature is its blood; anyone who eats it
must be cut off.”
15“ ‘Anyone, whether native-born or
foreigner, who eats anything found
dead or torn by wild animals must wash
their clothes and bathe with water, and
they will be ceremonially unclean till
evening; then they will be clean. 16But
if they do not wash their clothes and
bathe themselves, they will be held responsible.’ ”

Unlawful Sexual Relations

18 The LORD said to Moses, 2“Speak
to the Israelites and say to them:
‘I am the LORD your God. 3You must not
do as they do in Egypt, where you used to
live, and you must not do as they do in
the land of Canaan, where I am bringing
you. Do not follow their practices. 4You
must obey my laws and be careful to follow my decrees. I am the LORD your God.
5Keep my decrees and laws, for the person who obeys them will live by them. I
am the LORD.
6“ ‘No one is to approach any close relative to have sexual relations. I am the
LORD.
7“ ‘Do not dishonor your father by having sexual relations with your mother.
She is your mother; do not have relations with her.
8“ ‘Do not have sexual relations with
your father’s wife; that would dishonor
your father.
9“ ‘Do not have sexual relations with
your sister, either your father’s daughter
or your mother’s daughter, whether she
was born in the same home or elsewhere.
10“ ‘Do not have sexual relations with
your son’s daughter or your daughter’s
daughter; that would dishonor you.
11“ ‘Do not have sexual relations with
the daughter of your father’s wife, born
to your father; she is your sister.
12“ ‘Do not have sexual relations with
your father’s sister; she is your father’s
close relative.
13“ ‘Do not have sexual relations with
your mother’s sister, because she is your
mother’s close relative.
14“ ‘Do not dishonor your father’s
brother by approaching his wife to have
sexual relations; she is your aunt.
15“ ‘Do not have sexual relations with
your daughter-in-law. She is your son’s
wife; do not have relations with her.
16“ ‘Do not have sexual relations with
your brother’s wife; that would dishonor
your brother.
17“ ‘Do not have sexual relations with
both a woman and her daughter. Do not
have sexual relations with either her
son’s daughter or her daughter’s daughter; they are her close relatives. That is
wickedness.
18“ ‘Do not take your wife’s sister as a
rival wife and have sexual relations with
her while your wife is living.
19“ ‘Do not approach a woman to have
sexual relations during the uncleanness
of her monthly period.
20“ ‘Do not have sexual relations with
your neighbor’s wife and defile yourself
with her.
21“ ‘Do not give any of your children to
be sacrificed to Molek, for you must not
profane the name of your God. I am the
LORD.
22“ ‘Do not have sexual relations with
a man as one does with a woman; that
is detestable.
23“ ‘Do not have sexual relations with
an animal and defile yourself with it. A
woman must not present herself to an
animal to have sexual relations with it;
that is a perversion.
24“ ‘Do not defile yourselves in any of
these ways, because this is how the nations that I am going to drive out before
you became defiled. 25Even the land was
defiled; so I punished it for its sin, and
the land vomited out its inhabitants.
26But you must keep my decrees and my
laws. The native-born and the foreigners residing among you must not do any
of these detestable things, 27for all these
things were done by the people who lived
in the land before you, and the land became defiled. 28And if you defile the land,
it will vomit you out as it vomited out the
nations that were before you.
29“ ‘Everyone who does any of these
detestable things — such persons must
be cut off from their people. 30Keep my
requirements and do not follow any of
the detestable customs that were practiced before you came and do not defile
yourselves with them. I am the LORD
your God.’ ”

Various Laws

19 The LORD said to Moses, 2“Speak to
the entire assembly of Israel and
say to them: ‘Be holy because I, the LORD
your God, am holy.

3“‘Each of you must respect your mother and father, and you must observe my
Sabbaths. I am the LORD your God.
4“‘Do not turn to idols or make metal
gods for yourselves. I am the LORD your
God.
5“‘When you sacrifice a fellowship offering to the LORD, sacrifice it in such a
way that it will be accepted on your behalf. 6It shall be eaten on the day you
sacrifice it or on the next day; anything
left over until the third day must be
burned up. 7If any of it is eaten on the
third day, it is impure and will not be accepted. 8Whoever eats it will be held responsible because they have desecrated
what is holy to the LORD; they must be
cut off from their people.
9“‘When you reap the harvest of your
land, do not reap to the very edges of
your field or gather the gleanings of your
harvest. 10Do not go over your vineyard a
second time or pick up the grapes that
have fallen. Leave them for the poor and
the foreigner. I am the LORD your God.
11“‘Do not steal.
“‘Do not lie.
“‘Do not deceive one another.
12“‘Do not swear falsely by my name
and so profane the name of your God. I
am the LORD.
13“‘Do not defraud or rob your neighbor.
“‘Do not hold back the wages of a
hired worker overnight.
14“‘Do not curse the deaf or put a
stumbling block in front of the blind, but
fear your God. I am the LORD.
15“‘Do not pervert justice; do not show
partiality to the poor or favoritism to the
great, but judge your neighbor fairly.
16“‘Do not go about spreading slander
among your people.
“‘Do not do anything that endangers
your neighbor’s life. I am the LORD.
17“‘Do not hate a fellow Israelite in
your heart. Rebuke your neighbor frank-
ly so you will not share in their guilt.
18“‘Do not seek revenge or bear a
grudge against anyone among your people, but love your neighbor as yourself. I
am the LORD.
19“‘Keep my decrees.
“‘Do not mate different kinds of animals.
“‘Do not plant your field with two
kinds of seed.
“‘Do not wear clothing woven of two
kinds of material.
20“‘If a man sleeps with a female
slave who is promised to another man
but who has not been ransomed or giv-
en her freedom, there must be due punishment.[a] Yet they are not to be put to
death, because she had not been freed.
21The man, however, must bring a ram to
the entrance to the tent of meeting for a
guilt offering to the LORD. 22With the ram
of the guilt offering the priest is to make
atonement for him before the LORD for
the sin he has committed, and his sin
will be forgiven.
23“‘When you enter the land and plant
any kind of fruit tree, regard its fruit as
forbidden.[b] For three years you are to
consider it forbidden[b]; it must not be
eaten. 24In the fourth year all its fruit
will be holy, an offering of praise to the
LORD. 25But in the fifth year you may eat
its fruit. In this way your harvest will be
increased. I am the LORD your God.
26“‘Do not eat any meat with the blood
still in it.
“‘Do not practice divination or seek
omens.
27“‘Do not cut the hair at the sides of
your head or clip off the edges of your
beard.
28“‘Do not cut your bodies for the dead
or put tattoo marks on yourselves. I am
the LORD.
29“‘Do not degrade your daughter by
making her a prostitute, or the land will
turn to prostitution and be filled with
wickedness.
30“‘Observe my Sabbaths and have
reverence for my sanctuary. I am the
LORD.
31“‘Do not turn to mediums or seek out
spiritists, for you will be defiled by them.
I am the LORD your God.
32“‘Stand up in the presence of the
aged, show respect for the elderly and
revere your God. I am the LORD.
33“‘When a foreigner resides among
you in your land, do not mistreat them.
34The foreigner residing among you
must be treated as your native-born.
Love them as yourself, for you were foreigners in Egypt. I am the LORD your
God.
35“‘Do not use dishonest standards
when measuring length, weight or
quantity. 36Use honest scales and honest
weights, an honest ephah[c] and an honest hin.[d] I am the LORD your God, who
brought you out of Egypt.
37“‘Keep all my decrees and all my
laws and follow them. I am the LORD.’”

[a] 20 Or *be an inquiry* [b] 23 Hebrew *uncircumcised* [c] 36 An ephah was a dry measure having the capacity of about 3/5 of a bushel or about 22 liters. [d] 36 A hin was a liquid measure having the capacity of about 1 gallon or about 3.8 liters.

Punishments for Sin

20 The LORD said to Moses, 2“Say
to the Israelites: ‘Any Israelite
or any foreigner residing in Israel who
sacrifices any of his children to Molek is
to be put to death. The members of the
community are to stone him. 3I myself
will set my face against him and will
cut him off from his people; for by sacrificing his children to Molek, he has
defiled my sanctuary and profaned my
holy name. 4If the members of the community close their eyes when that man
sacrifices one of his children to Molek
and if they fail to put him to death, 5I
myself will set my face against him and
his family and will cut them off from
their people together with all who follow him in prostituting themselves to
Molek.
6“ ‘I will set my face against anyone
who turns to mediums and spiritists
to prostitute themselves by following
them, and I will cut them off from their
people.
7“ ‘Consecrate yourselves and be holy,
because I am the LORD your God. 8Keep
my decrees and follow them. I am the
LORD, who makes you holy.
9“ ‘Anyone who curses their father or
mother is to be put to death. Because
they have cursed their father or mother,
their blood will be on their own head.
10“ ‘If a man commits adultery with
another man’s wife — with the wife of
his neighbor — both the adulterer and
the adulteress are to be put to death.
11“ ‘If a man has sexual relations with
his father’s wife, he has dishonored his
father. Both the man and the woman are
to be put to death; their blood will be on
their own heads.
12“ ‘If a man has sexual relations with
his daughter-in-law, both of them are to
be put to death. What they have done is
a perversion; their blood will be on their
own heads.
13“ ‘If a man has sexual relations with
a man as one does with a woman, both
of them have done what is detestable.
They are to be put to death; their blood
will be on their own heads.
14“ ‘If a man marries both a woman
and her mother, it is wicked. Both he and
they must be burned in the fire, so that
no wickedness will be among you.
15“ ‘If a man has sexual relations with
an animal, he is to be put to death, and
you must kill the animal.
16“ ‘If a woman approaches an animal
to have sexual relations with it, kill both
the woman and the animal. They are to
be put to death; their blood will be on
their own heads.
17“ ‘If a man marries his sister, the
daughter of either his father or his
mother, and they have sexual relations,
it is a disgrace. They are to be publicly
removed from their people. He has dishonored his sister and will be held responsible.
18“ ‘If a man has sexual relations with
a woman during her monthly period, he
has exposed the source of her flow, and
she has also uncovered it. Both of them
are to be cut off from their people.
19“ ‘Do not have sexual relations with
the sister of either your mother or your
father, for that would dishonor a close
relative; both of you would be held responsible.
20“ ‘If a man has sexual relations with
his aunt, he has dishonored his uncle.
They will be held responsible; they will
die childless.
21“ ‘If a man marries his brother’s wife,
it is an act of impurity; he has dishonored his brother. They will be childless.
22“ ‘Keep all my decrees and laws and
follow them, so that the land where I
am bringing you to live may not vomit
you out. 23You must not live according to
the customs of the nations I am going
to drive out before you. Because they did
all these things, I abhorred them. 24But I
said to you, “You will possess their land;
I will give it to you as an inheritance,
a land flowing with milk and honey.” I
am the LORD your God, who has set you
apart from the nations.
25“ ‘You must therefore make a distinction between clean and unclean animals
and between unclean and clean birds.
Do not defile yourselves by any animal
or bird or anything that moves along the
ground — those that I have set apart as
unclean for you. 26You are to be holy to
me because I, the LORD, am holy, and I
have set you apart from the nations to
be my own.
27“ ‘A man or woman who is a medium
or spiritist among you must be put to
death. You are to stone them; their blood
will be on their own heads.’ ”

Rules for Priests

21 The LORD said to Moses, “Speak to
the priests, the sons of Aaron, and
say to them: ‘A priest must not make
himself ceremonially unclean for any
of his people who die, 2except for a close
relative, such as his mother or father,
his son or daughter, his brother, 3or an
unmarried sister who is dependent on

him since she has no husband—for her he may make himself unclean. 4He must not make himself unclean for people related to him by marriage,[a] and so defile himself.

5"'Priests must not shave their heads or shave off the edges of their beards or cut their bodies. 6They must be holy to their God and must not profane the name of their God. Because they present the food offerings to the LORD, the food of their God, they are to be holy.

7"'They must not marry women defiled by prostitution or divorced from their husbands, because priests are holy to their God. 8Regard them as holy, because they offer up the food of your God. Consider them holy, because I the LORD am holy—I who make you holy.

9"'If a priest's daughter defiles herself by becoming a prostitute, she disgraces her father; she must be burned in the fire.

10"'The high priest, the one among his brothers who has had the anointing oil poured on his head and who has been ordained to wear the priestly garments, must not let his hair become unkempt[b] or tear his clothes. 11He must not enter a place where there is a dead body. He must not make himself unclean, even for his father or mother, 12nor leave the sanctuary of his God or desecrate it, because he has been dedicated by the anointing oil of his God. I am the LORD.

13"'The woman he marries must be a virgin. 14He must not marry a widow, a divorced woman, or a woman defiled by prostitution, but only a virgin from his own people, 15so that he will not defile his offspring among his people. I am the LORD, who makes him holy.'"

16The LORD said to Moses, 17"Say to Aaron: 'For the generations to come none of your descendants who has a defect may come near to offer the food of his God. 18No man who has any defect may come near: no man who is blind or lame, disfigured or deformed; 19no man with a crippled foot or hand, 20or who is a hunchback or a dwarf, or who has any eye defect, or who has festering or running sores or damaged testicles. 21No descendant of Aaron the priest who has any defect is to come near to present the food offerings to the LORD. He has a defect; he must not come near to offer the food of his God. 22He may eat the most holy food of his God, as well as the holy food; 23yet because of his defect, he must not go near the curtain or approach the altar, and so desecrate my sanctuary. I am the LORD, who makes them holy.'"

24So Moses told this to Aaron and his sons and to all the Israelites.

22 The LORD said to Moses, 2"Tell Aaron and his sons to treat with respect the sacred offerings the Israelites consecrate to me, so they will not profane my holy name. I am the LORD.

3"Say to them: 'For the generations to come, if any of your descendants is ceremonially unclean and yet comes near the sacred offerings that the Israelites consecrate to the LORD, that person must be cut off from my presence. I am the LORD.

4"'If a descendant of Aaron has a defiling skin disease[c] or a bodily discharge, he may not eat the sacred offerings until he is cleansed. He will also be unclean if he touches something defiled by a corpse or by anyone who has an emission of semen, 5or if he touches any crawling thing that makes him unclean, or any person who makes him unclean, whatever the uncleanness may be. 6The one who touches any such thing will be unclean till evening. He must not eat any of the sacred offerings unless he has bathed himself with water. 7When the sun goes down, he will be clean, and after that he may eat the sacred offerings, for they are his food. 8He must not eat anything found dead or torn by wild animals, and so become unclean through it. I am the LORD.

9"'The priests are to perform my service in such a way that they do not become guilty and die for treating it with contempt. I am the LORD, who makes them holy.

10"'No one outside a priest's family may eat the sacred offering, nor may the guest of a priest or his hired worker eat it. 11But if a priest buys a slave with money, or if slaves are born in his household, they may eat his food. 12If a priest's daughter marries anyone other than a priest, she may not eat any of the sacred contributions. 13But if a priest's daughter becomes a widow or is divorced, yet has no children, and she returns to live in her father's household as in her youth, she may eat her father's food. No unauthorized person, however, may eat it.

[a] 4 Or *unclean as a leader among his people* [b] 10 Or *not uncover his head* [c] 4 The Hebrew word for *defiling skin disease*, traditionally translated "leprosy," was used for various diseases affecting the skin.

14“ ‘Anyone who eats a sacred offering
by mistake must make restitution to the
priest for the offering and add a fifth
of the value to it. 15The priests must not
desecrate the sacred offerings the Israelites present to the LORD 16by allowing
them to eat the sacred offerings and so
bring upon them guilt requiring payment. I am the LORD, who makes them
holy.’ ”

Unacceptable Sacrifices

17The LORD said to Moses, 18“Speak to
Aaron and his sons and to all the Israelites and say to them: ‘If any of you —
whether an Israelite or a foreigner residing in Israel — presents a gift for a
burnt offering to the LORD, either to fulfill a vow or as a freewill offering, 19you
must present a male without defect
from the cattle, sheep or goats in order
that it may be accepted on your behalf.
20Do not bring anything with a defect,
because it will not be accepted on your
behalf. 21When anyone brings from the
herd or flock a fellowship offering to the
LORD to fulfill a special vow or as a freewill offering, it must be without defect or
blemish to be acceptable. 22Do not offer
to the LORD the blind, the injured or the
maimed, or anything with warts or festering or running sores. Do not place any
of these on the altar as a food offering
presented to the LORD. 23You may, however, present as a freewill offering an ox[a]
or a sheep that is deformed or stunted,
but it will not be accepted in fulfillment
of a vow. 24You must not offer to the LORD
an animal whose testicles are bruised,
crushed, torn or cut. You must not do
this in your own land, 25and you must
not accept such animals from the hand
of a foreigner and offer them as the food
of your God. They will not be accepted on
your behalf, because they are deformed
and have defects.’ ”

26The LORD said to Moses, 27“When
a calf, a lamb or a goat is born, it is to
remain with its mother for seven days.
From the eighth day on, it will be acceptable as a food offering presented to
the LORD. 28Do not slaughter a cow or a
sheep and its young on the same day.

29“When you sacrifice a thank offering to the LORD, sacrifice it in such a way
that it will be accepted on your behalf.
30It must be eaten that same day; leave
none of it till morning. I am the LORD.

31“Keep my commands and follow
them. I am the LORD. 32Do not profane
my holy name, for I must be acknowledged as holy by the Israelites. I am the
LORD, who made you holy 33and who
brought you out of Egypt to be your God.
I am the LORD.”

The Appointed Festivals

23 The LORD said to Moses, 2“Speak
to the Israelites and say to them:
‘These are my appointed festivals, the
appointed festivals of the LORD, which
you are to proclaim as sacred assemblies.

The Sabbath

3“ ‘There are six days when you may
work, but the seventh day is a day of
sabbath rest, a day of sacred assembly.
You are not to do any work; wherever
you live, it is a sabbath to the LORD.

The Passover and the Festival of Unleavened Bread

4“ ‘These are the LORD’s appointed festivals, the sacred assemblies you are to
proclaim at their appointed times: 5The
LORD’s Passover begins at twilight on
the fourteenth day of the first month.
6On the fifteenth day of that month the
LORD’s Festival of Unleavened Bread begins; for seven days you must eat bread
made without yeast. 7On the first day
hold a sacred assembly and do no regular work. 8For seven days present a food
offering to the LORD. And on the seventh
day hold a sacred assembly and do no
regular work.’ ”

Offering the Firstfruits

9The LORD said to Moses, 10“Speak to
the Israelites and say to them: ‘When
you enter the land I am going to give
you and you reap its harvest, bring to
the priest a sheaf of the first grain you
harvest. 11He is to wave the sheaf before
the LORD so it will be accepted on your
behalf; the priest is to wave it on the day
after the Sabbath. 12On the day you wave
the sheaf, you must sacrifice as a burnt
offering to the LORD a lamb a year old
without defect, 13together with its grain
offering of two-tenths of an ephah[b] of
the finest flour mixed with olive oil — a
food offering presented to the LORD, a
pleasing aroma — and its drink offering of a quarter of a hin[c] of wine. 14You
must not eat any bread, or roasted or
new grain, until the very day you bring

[a] *23* The Hebrew word can refer to either male or female. [b] *13* That is, probably about 7 pounds or about 3.2 kilograms; also in verse 17 [c] *13* That is, about 1 quart or about 1 liter

this offering to your God. This is to be a lasting ordinance for the generations to come, wherever you live.

The Festival of Weeks

15“ ‘From the day after the Sabbath, the day you brought the sheaf of the wave offering, count off seven full weeks. 16Count off fifty days up to the day after the seventh Sabbath, and then present an offering of new grain to the LORD. 17From wherever you live, bring two loaves made of two-tenths of an ephah of the finest flour, baked with yeast, as a wave offering of firstfruits to the LORD. 18Present with this bread seven male lambs, each a year old and without defect, one young bull and two rams. They will be a burnt offering to the LORD, together with their grain offerings and drink offerings — a food offering, an aroma pleasing to the LORD. 19Then sacrifice one male goat for a sin offering[a] and two lambs, each a year old, for a fellowship offering. 20The priest is to wave the two lambs before the LORD as a wave offering, together with the bread of the firstfruits. They are a sacred offering to the LORD for the priest. 21On that same day you are to proclaim a sacred assembly and do no regular work. This is to be a lasting ordinance for the generations to come, wherever you live.

22“ ‘When you reap the harvest of your land, do not reap to the very edges of your field or gather the gleanings of your harvest. Leave them for the poor and for the foreigner residing among you. I am the LORD your God.’ ”

The Festival of Trumpets

23The LORD said to Moses, 24“Say to the Israelites: ‘On the first day of the seventh month you are to have a day of sabbath rest, a sacred assembly commemorated with trumpet blasts. 25Do no regular work, but present a food offering to the LORD.’ ”

The Day of Atonement

26The LORD said to Moses, 27“The tenth day of this seventh month is the Day of Atonement. Hold a sacred assembly and deny yourselves,[b] and present a food offering to the LORD. 28Do not do any work on that day, because it is the Day of Atonement, when atonement is made for you before the LORD your God. 29Those who do not deny themselves on that day must be cut off from their people. 30I will destroy from among their people anyone who does any work on that day. 31You shall do no work at all. This is to be a lasting ordinance for the generations to come, wherever you live. 32It is a day of sabbath rest for you, and you must deny yourselves. From the evening of the ninth day of the month until the following evening you are to observe your sabbath.”

The Festival of Tabernacles

33The LORD said to Moses, 34“Say to the Israelites: ‘On the fifteenth day of the seventh month the LORD’s Festival of Tabernacles begins, and it lasts for seven days. 35The first day is a sacred assembly; do no regular work. 36For seven days present food offerings to the LORD, and on the eighth day hold a sacred assembly and present a food offering to the LORD. It is the closing special assembly; do no regular work.

37(“ ‘These are the LORD’s appointed festivals, which you are to proclaim as sacred assemblies for bringing food offerings to the LORD — the burnt offerings and grain offerings, sacrifices and drink offerings required for each day. 38These offerings are in addition to those for the LORD’s Sabbaths and[c] in addition to your gifts and whatever you have vowed and all the freewill offerings you give to the LORD.)

39“ ‘So beginning with the fifteenth day of the seventh month, after you have gathered the crops of the land, celebrate the festival to the LORD for seven days; the first day is a day of sabbath rest, and the eighth day also is a day of sabbath rest. 40On the first day you are to take branches from luxuriant trees — from palms, willows and other leafy trees — and rejoice before the LORD your God for seven days. 41Celebrate this as a festival to the LORD for seven days each year. This is to be a lasting ordinance for the generations to come; celebrate it in the seventh month. 42Live in temporary shelters for seven days: All native-born Israelites are to live in such shelters 43so your descendants will know that I had the Israelites live in temporary shelters when I brought them out of Egypt. I am the LORD your God.’ ”

44So Moses announced to the Israelites the appointed festivals of the LORD.

[a] 19 Or *purification offering* [b] 27 Or *and fast*; similarly in verses 29 and 32 [c] 38 Or *These festivals are in addition to the LORD’s Sabbaths, and these offerings are*

Olive Oil and Bread Set Before the LORD

24 The LORD said to Moses, 2“Command the Israelites to bring you clear oil of pressed olives for the light so that the lamps may be kept burning continually. 3Outside the curtain that shields the ark of the covenant law in the tent of meeting, Aaron is to tend the lamps before the LORD from evening till morning, continually. This is to be a lasting ordinance for the generations to come. 4The lamps on the pure gold lampstand before the LORD must be tended continually.

5“Take the finest flour and bake twelve loaves of bread, using two-tenths of an ephah[a] for each loaf. 6Arrange them in two stacks, six in each stack, on the table of pure gold before the LORD. 7By each stack put some pure incense as a memorial[b] portion to represent the bread and to be a food offering presented to the LORD. 8This bread is to be set out before the LORD regularly, Sabbath after Sabbath, on behalf of the Israelites, as a lasting covenant. 9It belongs to Aaron and his sons, who are to eat it in the sanctuary area, because it is a most holy part of their perpetual share of the food offerings presented to the LORD.”

A Blasphemer Put to Death

10Now the son of an Israelite mother and an Egyptian father went out among the Israelites, and a fight broke out in the camp between him and an Israelite. 11The son of the Israelite woman blasphemed the Name with a curse; so they brought him to Moses. (His mother’s name was Shelomith, the daughter of Dibri the Danite.) 12They put him in custody until the will of the LORD should be made clear to them.

13Then the LORD said to Moses: 14“Take the blasphemer outside the camp. All those who heard him are to lay their hands on his head, and the entire assembly is to stone him. 15Say to the Israelites: ‘Anyone who curses their God will be held responsible; 16anyone who blasphemes the name of the LORD is to be put to death. The entire assembly must stone them. Whether foreigner or native-born, when they blaspheme the Name they are to be put to death.

17“ ‘Anyone who takes the life of a human being is to be put to death. 18Anyone who takes the life of someone’s animal must make restitution — life for life. 19Anyone who injures their neighbor is to be injured in the same manner: 20fracture for fracture, eye for eye, tooth for tooth. The one who has inflicted the injury must suffer the same injury. 21Whoever kills an animal must make restitution, but whoever kills a human being is to be put to death. 22You are to have the same law for the foreigner and the native-born. I am the LORD your God.’ ”

23Then Moses spoke to the Israelites, and they took the blasphemer outside the camp and stoned him. The Israelites did as the LORD commanded Moses.

The Sabbath Year

25 The LORD said to Moses at Mount Sinai, 2“Speak to the Israelites and say to them: ‘When you enter the land I am going to give you, the land itself must observe a sabbath to the LORD. 3For six years sow your fields, and for six years prune your vineyards and gather their crops. 4But in the seventh year the land is to have a year of sabbath rest, a sabbath to the LORD. Do not sow your fields or prune your vineyards. 5Do not reap what grows of itself or harvest the grapes of your untended vines. The land is to have a year of rest. 6Whatever the land yields during the sabbath year will be food for you — for yourself, your male and female servants, and the hired worker and temporary resident who live among you, 7as well as for your livestock and the wild animals in your land. Whatever the land produces may be eaten.

The Year of Jubilee

8“ ‘Count off seven sabbath years — seven times seven years — so that the seven sabbath years amount to a period of forty-nine years. 9Then have the trumpet sounded everywhere on the tenth day of the seventh month; on the Day of Atonement sound the trumpet throughout your land. 10Consecrate the fiftieth year and proclaim liberty throughout the land to all its inhabitants. It shall be a jubilee for you; each of you is to return to your family property and to your own clan. 11The fiftieth year shall be a jubilee for you; do not sow and do not reap what grows of itself or harvest the untended vines. 12For it is a jubilee and is to be holy for you; eat only what is taken directly from the fields.

13“ ‘In this Year of Jubilee everyone is to return to their own property.

[a] 5 That is, probably about 7 pounds or about 3.2 kilograms [b] 7 Or *representative*

14“ ‘If you sell land to any of your own
people or buy land from them, do not
take advantage of each other. 15You are
to buy from your own people on the basis
of the number of years since the Jubilee.
And they are to sell to you on the basis
of the number of years left for harvesting crops. 16When the years are many,
you are to increase the price, and when
the years are few, you are to decrease the
price, because what is really being sold
to you is the number of crops. 17Do not
take advantage of each other, but fear
your God. I am the LORD your God.

18“ ‘Follow my decrees and be careful
to obey my laws, and you will live safely
in the land. 19Then the land will yield its
fruit, and you will eat your fill and live
there in safety. 20You may ask, “What
will we eat in the seventh year if we do
not plant or harvest our crops?” 21I will
send you such a blessing in the sixth
year that the land will yield enough for
three years. 22While you plant during
the eighth year, you will eat from the old
crop and will continue to eat from it until the harvest of the ninth year comes in.

23“ ‘The land must not be sold permanently, because the land is mine and
you reside in my land as foreigners and
strangers. 24Throughout the land that
you hold as a possession, you must provide for the redemption of the land.

25“ ‘If one of your fellow Israelites becomes poor and sells some of their property, their nearest relative is to come
and redeem what they have sold. 26If,
however, there is no one to redeem it
for them but later on they prosper and
acquire sufficient means to redeem it
themselves, 27they are to determine the
value for the years since they sold it and
refund the balance to the one to whom
they sold it; they can then go back to
their own property. 28But if they do not
acquire the means to repay, what was
sold will remain in the possession of the
buyer until the Year of Jubilee. It will be
returned in the Jubilee, and they can
then go back to their property.

29“ ‘Anyone who sells a house in a
walled city retains the right of redemption a full year after its sale. During
that time the seller may redeem it. 30If
it is not redeemed before a full year
has passed, the house in the walled city
shall belong permanently to the buyer
and the buyer's descendants. It is not to
be returned in the Jubilee. 31But houses
in villages without walls around them
are to be considered as belonging to the
open country. They can be redeemed,
and they are to be returned in the Jubilee.

32“ ‘The Levites always have the right
to redeem their houses in the Levitical
towns, which they possess. 33So the property of the Levites is redeemable — that
is, a house sold in any town they hold —
and is to be returned in the Jubilee,
because the houses in the towns of the
Levites are their property among the Israelites. 34But the pastureland belonging
to their towns must not be sold; it is their
permanent possession.

35“ ‘If any of your fellow Israelites become poor and are unable to support
themselves among you, help them as
you would a foreigner and stranger, so
they can continue to live among you.
36Do not take interest or any profit from
them, but fear your God, so that they
may continue to live among you. 37You
must not lend them money at interest
or sell them food at a profit. 38I am the
LORD your God, who brought you out of
Egypt to give you the land of Canaan
and to be your God.

39“ ‘If any of your fellow Israelites
become poor and sell themselves to
you, do not make them work as slaves.
40They are to be treated as hired workers or temporary residents among you;
they are to work for you until the Year
of Jubilee. 41Then they and their children
are to be released, and they will go back
to their own clans and to the property of
their ancestors. 42Because the Israelites
are my servants, whom I brought out of
Egypt, they must not be sold as slaves.
43Do not rule over them ruthlessly, but
fear your God.

44“ ‘Your male and female slaves are
to come from the nations around you;
from them you may buy slaves. 45You
may also buy some of the temporary residents living among you and members
of their clans born in your country, and
they will become your property. 46You
can bequeath them to your children as
inherited property and can make them
slaves for life, but you must not rule over
your fellow Israelites ruthlessly.

47“ ‘If a foreigner residing among you
becomes rich and any of your fellow
Israelites become poor and sell themselves to the foreigner or to a member
of the foreigner's clan, 48they retain the
right of redemption after they have sold
themselves. One of their relatives may
redeem them: 49An uncle or a cousin
or any blood relative in their clan may
redeem them. Or if they prosper, they
may redeem themselves. 50They and

their buyer are to count the time from
the year they sold themselves up to the
Year of Jubilee. The price for their release is to be based on the rate paid to
a hired worker for that number of years.
51If many years remain, they must pay
for their redemption a larger share of
the price paid for them. 52If only a few
years remain until the Year of Jubilee,
they are to compute that and pay for
their redemption accordingly. 53They are
to be treated as workers hired from year
to year; you must see to it that those to
whom they owe service do not rule over
them ruthlessly.
54“ ‘Even if someone is not redeemed
in any of these ways, they and their children are to be released in the Year of Jubilee, 55for the Israelites belong to me as
servants. They are my servants, whom I
brought out of Egypt. I am the LORD your
God.

Reward for Obedience

26 “ ‘Do not make idols or set up an
image or a sacred stone for yourselves, and do not place a carved stone
in your land to bow down before it. I am
the LORD your God.
2“ ‘Observe my Sabbaths and have reverence for my sanctuary. I am the LORD.
3“ ‘If you follow my decrees and are
careful to obey my commands, 4I will
send you rain in its season, and the
ground will yield its crops and the trees
their fruit. 5Your threshing will continue
until grape harvest and the grape harvest will continue until planting, and
you will eat all the food you want and
live in safety in your land.
6“ ‘I will grant peace in the land, and
you will lie down and no one will make
you afraid. I will remove wild beasts
from the land, and the sword will not
pass through your country. 7You will
pursue your enemies, and they will fall
by the sword before you. 8Five of you will
chase a hundred, and a hundred of you
will chase ten thousand, and your enemies will fall by the sword before you.
9“ ‘I will look on you with favor and
make you fruitful and increase your
numbers, and I will keep my covenant
with you. 10You will still be eating last
year’s harvest when you will have to
move it out to make room for the new. 11I
will put my dwelling place[a] among you,
and I will not abhor you. 12I will walk
among you and be your God, and you
will be my people. 13I am the LORD your
God, who brought you out of Egypt so
that you would no longer be slaves to the
Egyptians; I broke the bars of your yoke
and enabled you to walk with heads held
high.

Punishment for Disobedience

14“ ‘But if you will not listen to me and
carry out all these commands, 15and if
you reject my decrees and abhor my laws
and fail to carry out all my commands
and so violate my covenant, 16then I will
do this to you: I will bring on you sudden terror, wasting diseases and fever
that will destroy your sight and sap your
strength. You will plant seed in vain, because your enemies will eat it. 17I will set
my face against you so that you will be
defeated by your enemies; those who
hate you will rule over you, and you will
flee even when no one is pursuing you.
18“ ‘If after all this you will not listen to
me, I will punish you for your sins seven
times over. 19I will break down your stubborn pride and make the sky above you
like iron and the ground beneath you
like bronze. 20Your strength will be spent
in vain, because your soil will not yield
its crops, nor will the trees of your land
yield their fruit.
21“ ‘If you remain hostile toward me
and refuse to listen to me, I will multiply your afflictions seven times over, as
your sins deserve. 22I will send wild animals against you, and they will rob you
of your children, destroy your cattle and
make you so few in number that your
roads will be deserted.
23“ ‘If in spite of these things you do
not accept my correction but continue
to be hostile toward me, 24I myself will
be hostile toward you and will afflict
you for your sins seven times over. 25And
I will bring the sword on you to avenge
the breaking of the covenant. When you
withdraw into your cities, I will send a
plague among you, and you will be giv-
en into enemy hands. 26When I cut off
your supply of bread, ten women will be
able to bake your bread in one oven, and
they will dole out the bread by weight.
You will eat, but you will not be satisfied.
27“ ‘If in spite of this you still do not
listen to me but continue to be hostile
toward me, 28then in my anger I will
be hostile toward you, and I myself will
punish you for your sins seven times
over. 29You will eat the flesh of your sons
and the flesh of your daughters. 30I will
destroy your high places, cut down your

[a] 11 Or *my tabernacle*

incense altars and pile your dead bodies[a] on the lifeless forms of your idols, and I will abhor you. 31I will turn your cities into ruins and lay waste your sanctuaries, and I will take no delight in the pleasing aroma of your offerings. 32I myself will lay waste the land, so that your enemies who live there will be appalled. 33I will scatter you among the nations and will draw out my sword and pursue you. Your land will be laid waste, and your cities will lie in ruins. 34Then the land will enjoy its sabbath years all the time that it lies desolate and you are in the country of your enemies; then the land will rest and enjoy its sabbaths. 35All the time that it lies desolate, the land will have the rest it did not have during the sabbaths you lived in it.

36" 'As for those of you who are left, I will make their hearts so fearful in the lands of their enemies that the sound of a windblown leaf will put them to flight. They will run as though fleeing from the sword, and they will fall, even though no one is pursuing them. 37They will stumble over one another as though fleeing from the sword, even though no one is pursuing them. So you will not be able to stand before your enemies. 38You will perish among the nations; the land of your enemies will devour you. 39Those of you who are left will waste away in the lands of their enemies because of their sins; also because of their ancestors' sins they will waste away.

40" 'But if they will confess their sins and the sins of their ancestors — their unfaithfulness and their hostility toward me, 41which made me hostile toward them so that I sent them into the land of their enemies — then when their uncircumcised hearts are humbled and they pay for their sin, 42I will remember my covenant with Jacob and my covenant with Isaac and my covenant with Abraham, and I will remember the land. 43For the land will be deserted by them and will enjoy its sabbaths while it lies desolate without them. They will pay for their sins because they rejected my laws and abhorred my decrees. 44Yet in spite of this, when they are in the land of their enemies, I will not reject them or abhor them so as to destroy them completely, breaking my covenant with them. I am the LORD their God. 45But for their sake I will remember the covenant with their ancestors whom I brought out of Egypt in the sight of the nations to be their God. I am the LORD.' "

46These are the decrees, the laws and the regulations that the LORD established at Mount Sinai between himself and the Israelites through Moses.

Redeeming What Is the LORD's

27 The LORD said to Moses, 2"Speak to the Israelites and say to them: 'If anyone makes a special vow to dedicate a person to the LORD by giving the equivalent value, 3set the value of a male between the ages of twenty and sixty at fifty shekels[b] of silver, according to the sanctuary shekel[c]; 4for a female, set her value at thirty shekels[d]; 5for a person between the ages of five and twenty, set the value of a male at twenty shekels[e] and of a female at ten shekels[f]; 6for a person between one month and five years, set the value of a male at five shekels[g] of silver and that of a female at three shekels[h] of silver; 7for a person sixty years old or more, set the value of a male at fifteen shekels[i] and of a female at ten shekels. 8If anyone making the vow is too poor to pay the specified amount, the person being dedicated is to be presented to the priest, who will set the value according to what the one making the vow can afford.

9" 'If what they vowed is an animal that is acceptable as an offering to the LORD, such an animal given to the LORD becomes holy. 10They must not exchange it or substitute a good one for a bad one, or a bad one for a good one; if they should substitute one animal for another, both it and the substitute become holy. 11If what they vowed is a ceremonially unclean animal — one that is not acceptable as an offering to the LORD — the animal must be presented to the priest, 12who will judge its quality as good or bad. Whatever value the priest then sets, that is what it will be. 13If the owner wishes to redeem the animal, a fifth must be added to its value.

14" 'If anyone dedicates their house as something holy to the LORD, the priest

[a] *30* Or *your funeral offerings* [b] *3* That is, about 1 1/4 pounds or about 575 grams; also in verse 16 [c] *3* That is, about 2/5 ounce or about 12 grams; also in verse 25 [d] *4* That is, about 12 ounces or about 345 grams [e] *5* That is, about 8 ounces or about 230 grams [f] *5* That is, about 4 ounces or about 115 grams; also in verse 7 [g] *6* That is, about 2 ounces or about 58 grams [h] *6* That is, about 1 1/4 ounces or about 35 grams [i] *7* That is, about 6 ounces or about 175 grams

will judge its quality as good or bad.
Whatever value the priest then sets, so
it will remain. 15 If the one who dedicates
their house wishes to redeem it, they
must add a fifth to its value, and the
house will again become theirs.

16 " 'If anyone dedicates to the LORD
part of their family land, its value is to
be set according to the amount of seed
required for it — fifty shekels of silver to
a homer[a] of barley seed. 17 If they dedicate a field during the Year of Jubilee,
the value that has been set remains.
18 But if they dedicate a field after the Jubilee, the priest will determine the value
according to the number of years that remain until the next Year of Jubilee, and
its set value will be reduced. 19 If the one
who dedicates the field wishes to redeem
it, they must add a fifth to its value, and
the field will again become theirs. 20 If,
however, they do not redeem the field,
or if they have sold it to someone else, it
can never be redeemed. 21 When the field
is released in the Jubilee, it will become
holy, like a field devoted to the LORD; it
will become priestly property.

22 " 'If anyone dedicates to the LORD a
field they have bought, which is not part
of their family land, 23 the priest will determine its value up to the Year of Jubilee, and the owner must pay its value
on that day as something holy to the
LORD. 24 In the Year of Jubilee the field
will revert to the person from whom it
was bought, the one whose land it was.
25 Every value is to be set according to the
sanctuary shekel, twenty gerahs to the
shekel.

26 " 'No one, however, may dedicate
the firstborn of an animal, since the
firstborn already belongs to the LORD;
whether an ox[b] or a sheep, it is the
LORD's. 27 If it is one of the unclean animals, it may be bought back at its set
value, adding a fifth of the value to it.
If it is not redeemed, it is to be sold at
its set value.

28 " 'But nothing that a person owns
and devotes[c] to the LORD — whether a
human being or an animal or family
land — may be sold or redeemed; everything so devoted is most holy to the
LORD.

29 " 'No person devoted to destruction[d]
may be ransomed; they are to be put to
death.

30 " 'A tithe of everything from the land,
whether grain from the soil or fruit from
the trees, belongs to the LORD; it is holy
to the LORD. 31 Whoever would redeem
any of their tithe must add a fifth of the
value to it. 32 Every tithe of the herd and
flock — every tenth animal that passes
under the shepherd's rod — will be holy
to the LORD. 33 No one may pick out the
good from the bad or make any substitution. If anyone does make a substitution, both the animal and its substitute
become holy and cannot be redeemed.' "

34 These are the commands the LORD
gave Moses at Mount Sinai for the Israelites.

[a] *16* That is, probably about 300 pounds or about 135 kilograms [b] *26* The Hebrew word can refer to either male or female. [c] *28* The Hebrew term refers to the irrevocable giving over of things or persons to the LORD. [d] *29* The Hebrew term refers to the irrevocable giving over of things or persons to the LORD, often by totally destroying them.

NUMBERS

The Census

1 The LORD spoke to Moses in the tent
of meeting in the Desert of Sinai on
the first day of the second month of the
second year after the Israelites came out
of Egypt. He said: 2 “Take a census of the
whole Israelite community by their clans
and families, listing every man by name,
one by one. 3 You and Aaron are to count
according to their divisions all the men
in Israel who are twenty years old or
more and able to serve in the army. 4 One
man from each tribe, each of them the
head of his family, is to help you. 5 These
are the names of the men who are to assist you:

from Reuben, Elizur son of Shedeur;
6 from Simeon, Shelumiel son of Zurishaddai;
7 from Judah, Nahshon son of Amminadab;
8 from Issachar, Nethanel son of
Zuar;
9 from Zebulun, Eliab son of Helon;
10 from the sons of Joseph:
from Ephraim, Elishama son of
Ammihud;
from Manasseh, Gamaliel son of
Pedahzur;
11 from Benjamin, Abidan son of Gideoni;
12 from Dan, Ahiezer son of Ammishaddai;
13 from Asher, Pagiel son of Okran;
14 from Gad, Eliasaph son of Deuel;
15 from Naphtali, Ahira son of Enan.”

16 These were the men appointed from
the community, the leaders of their ancestral tribes. They were the heads of the
clans of Israel.

17 Moses and Aaron took these men
whose names had been specified, 18 and
they called the whole community together on the first day of the second
month. The people registered their ancestry by their clans and families, and
the men twenty years old or more were
listed by name, one by one, 19 as the LORD
commanded Moses. And so he counted
them in the Desert of Sinai:

20 From the descendants of Reuben
the firstborn son of Israel:
All the men twenty years old or
more who were able to serve in
the army were listed by name,
one by one, according to the records of their clans and families.
21 The number from the tribe of
Reuben was 46,500.

22 From the descendants of Simeon:
All the men twenty years old or
more who were able to serve in
the army were counted and listed
by name, one by one, according
to the records of their clans and
families. 23 The number from the
tribe of Simeon was 59,300.

24 From the descendants of Gad:
All the men twenty years old or
more who were able to serve in
the army were listed by name,
according to the records of their
clans and families. 25 The number
from the tribe of Gad was 45,650.

26 From the descendants of Judah:
All the men twenty years old or
more who were able to serve in
the army were listed by name,
according to the records of their
clans and families. 27 The number from the tribe of Judah was
74,600.

28 From the descendants of Issachar:
All the men twenty years old or
more who were able to serve in
the army were listed by name,
according to the records of their
clans and families. 29 The number from the tribe of Issachar was
54,400.

30 From the descendants of Zebulun:
All the men twenty years old or
more who were able to serve in
the army were listed by name,
according to the records of their
clans and families. 31 The number from the tribe of Zebulun was
57,400.

32 From the sons of Joseph:
From the descendants of Ephraim:
All the men twenty years old or
more who were able to serve in
the army were listed by name,
according to the records of their
clans and families. 33 The number
from the tribe of Ephraim was
40,500.

[34] From the descendants of Manasseh:
All the men twenty years old or more who were able to serve in the army were listed by name, according to the records of their clans and families. [35] The number from the tribe of Manasseh was 32,200.

[36] From the descendants of Benjamin:
All the men twenty years old or more who were able to serve in the army were listed by name, according to the records of their clans and families. [37] The number from the tribe of Benjamin was 35,400.

[38] From the descendants of Dan:
All the men twenty years old or more who were able to serve in the army were listed by name, according to the records of their clans and families. [39] The number from the tribe of Dan was 62,700.

[40] From the descendants of Asher:
All the men twenty years old or more who were able to serve in the army were listed by name, according to the records of their clans and families. [41] The number from the tribe of Asher was 41,500.

[42] From the descendants of Naphtali:
All the men twenty years old or more who were able to serve in the army were listed by name, according to the records of their clans and families. [43] The number from the tribe of Naphtali was 53,400.

[44] These were the men counted by Moses and Aaron and the twelve leaders of Israel, each one representing his family. [45] All the Israelites twenty years old or more who were able to serve in Israel's army were counted according to their families. [46] The total number was 603,550.

[47] The ancestral tribe of the Levites, however, was not counted along with the others. [48] The LORD had said to Moses: [49] "You must not count the tribe of Levi or include them in the census of the other Israelites. [50] Instead, appoint the Levites to be in charge of the tabernacle of the covenant law — over all its furnishings and everything belonging to it. They are to carry the tabernacle and all its furnishings; they are to take care of it and encamp around it. [51] Whenever the tabernacle is to move, the Levites are to take it down, and whenever the tabernacle is to be set up, the Levites shall do it. Anyone else who approaches it is to be put to death. [52] The Israelites are to set up their tents by divisions, each of them in their own camp under their standard. [53] The Levites, however, are to set up their tents around the tabernacle of the covenant law so that my wrath will not fall on the Israelite community. The Levites are to be responsible for the care of the tabernacle of the covenant law."

[54] The Israelites did all this just as the LORD commanded Moses.

The Arrangement of the Tribal Camps

2 The LORD said to Moses and Aaron: [2] "The Israelites are to camp around the tent of meeting some distance from it, each of them under their standard and holding the banners of their family."

[3] On the east, toward the sunrise, the divisions of the camp of Judah are to encamp under their standard. The leader of the people of Judah is Nahshon son of Amminadab. [4] His division numbers 74,600.

[5] The tribe of Issachar will camp next to them. The leader of the people of Issachar is Nethanel son of Zuar. [6] His division numbers 54,400.

[7] The tribe of Zebulun will be next. The leader of the people of Zebulun is Eliab son of Helon. [8] His division numbers 57,400.

[9] All the men assigned to the camp of Judah, according to their divisions, number 186,400. They will set out first.

[10] On the south will be the divisions of the camp of Reuben under their standard. The leader of the people of Reuben is Elizur son of Shedeur. [11] His division numbers 46,500.

[12] The tribe of Simeon will camp next to them. The leader of the people of Simeon is Shelumiel son of Zurishaddai. [13] His division numbers 59,300.

[14] The tribe of Gad will be next. The leader of the people of Gad is Eliasaph son of Deuel.[a] [15] His division numbers 45,650.

[16] All the men assigned to the camp of Reuben, according to their divisions, number 151,450. They will set out second.

[a] *14* Many manuscripts of the Masoretic Text, Samaritan Pentateuch and Vulgate (see also 1:14); most manuscripts of the Masoretic Text *Reuel*

17 Then the tent of meeting and the camp of the Levites will set out in the middle of the camps. They will set out in the same order as they encamp, each in their own place under their standard.

18 On the west will be the divisions of the camp of Ephraim under their standard. The leader of the people of Ephraim is Elishama son of Ammihud. 19 His division numbers 40,500.

20 The tribe of Manasseh will be next to them. The leader of the people of Manasseh is Gamaliel son of Pedahzur. 21 His division numbers 32,200.

22 The tribe of Benjamin will be next. The leader of the people of Benjamin is Abidan son of Gideoni. 23 His division numbers 35,400.

24 All the men assigned to the camp of Ephraim, according to their divisions, number 108,100. They will set out third.

25 On the north will be the divisions of the camp of Dan under their standard. The leader of the people of Dan is Ahiezer son of Ammishaddai. 26 His division numbers 62,700.

27 The tribe of Asher will camp next to them. The leader of the people of Asher is Pagiel son of Okran. 28 His division numbers 41,500.

29 The tribe of Naphtali will be next. The leader of the people of Naphtali is Ahira son of Enan. 30 His division numbers 53,400.

31 All the men assigned to the camp of Dan number 157,600. They will set out last, under their standards.

32 These are the Israelites, counted according to their families. All the men in the camps, by their divisions, number 603,550. 33 The Levites, however, were not counted along with the other Israelites, as the LORD commanded Moses.

34 So the Israelites did everything the LORD commanded Moses; that is the way they encamped under their standards, and that is the way they set out, each of them with their clan and family.

The Levites

3 This is the account of the family of Aaron and Moses at the time the LORD spoke to Moses at Mount Sinai.

2 The names of the sons of Aaron were Nadab the firstborn and Abihu, Eleazar and Ithamar. 3 Those were the names of Aaron's sons, the anointed priests, who were ordained to serve as priests. 4 Nadab and Abihu, however, died before the LORD when they made an offering with unauthorized fire before him in the Desert of Sinai. They had no sons, so Eleazar and Ithamar served as priests during the lifetime of their father Aaron.

5 The LORD said to Moses, 6 "Bring the tribe of Levi and present them to Aaron the priest to assist him. 7 They are to perform duties for him and for the whole community at the tent of meeting by doing the work of the tabernacle. 8 They are to take care of all the furnishings of the tent of meeting, fulfilling the obligations of the Israelites by doing the work of the tabernacle. 9 Give the Levites to Aaron and his sons; they are the Israelites who are to be given wholly to him.[a] 10 Appoint Aaron and his sons to serve as priests; anyone else who approaches the sanctuary is to be put to death."

11 The LORD also said to Moses, 12 "I have taken the Levites from among the Israelites in place of the first male offspring of every Israelite woman. The Levites are mine, 13 for all the firstborn are mine. When I struck down all the firstborn in Egypt, I set apart for myself every firstborn in Israel, whether human or animal. They are to be mine. I am the LORD."

14 The LORD said to Moses in the Desert of Sinai, 15 "Count the Levites by their families and clans. Count every male a month old or more." 16 So Moses counted them, as he was commanded by the word of the LORD.

17 These were the names of the sons of Levi:
Gershon, Kohath and Merari.
18 These were the names of the Gershonite clans:
Libni and Shimei.
19 The Kohathite clans:
Amram, Izhar, Hebron and Uzziel.
20 The Merarite clans:
Mahli and Mushi.

These were the Levite clans, according to their families.

21 To Gershon belonged the clans of the Libnites and Shimeites; these were the Gershonite clans. 22 The number of all the males a month old or more who were counted was 7,500. 23 The Gershonite

[a] 9 Most manuscripts of the Masoretic Text; some manuscripts of the Masoretic Text, Samaritan Pentateuch and Septuagint (see also 8:16) *to me*

clans were to camp on the west, behind the tabernacle. 24 The leader of the families of the Gershonites was Eliasaph son of Lael. 25 At the tent of meeting the Gershonites were responsible for the care of the tabernacle and tent, its coverings, the curtain at the entrance to the tent of meeting, 26 the curtains of the courtyard, the curtain at the entrance to the courtyard surrounding the tabernacle and altar, and the ropes — and everything related to their use.

27 To Kohath belonged the clans of the Amramites, Izharites, Hebronites and Uzzielites; these were the Kohathite clans. 28 The number of all the males a month old or more was 8,600.[a] The Kohathites were responsible for the care of the sanctuary. 29 The Kohathite clans were to camp on the south side of the tabernacle. 30 The leader of the families of the Kohathite clans was Elizaphan son of Uzziel. 31 They were responsible for the care of the ark, the table, the lampstand, the altars, the articles of the sanctuary used in ministering, the curtain, and everything related to their use. 32 The chief leader of the Levites was Eleazar son of Aaron, the priest. He was appointed over those who were responsible for the care of the sanctuary.

33 To Merari belonged the clans of the Mahlites and the Mushites; these were the Merarite clans. 34 The number of all the males a month old or more who were counted was 6,200. 35 The leader of the families of the Merarite clans was Zuriel son of Abihail; they were to camp on the north side of the tabernacle. 36 The Merarites were appointed to take care of the frames of the tabernacle, its crossbars, posts, bases, all its equipment, and everything related to their use, 37 as well as the posts of the surrounding courtyard with their bases, tent pegs and ropes.

38 Moses and Aaron and his sons were to camp to the east of the tabernacle, toward the sunrise, in front of the tent of meeting. They were responsible for the care of the sanctuary on behalf of the Israelites. Anyone else who approached the sanctuary was to be put to death.

39 The total number of Levites counted at the LORD's command by Moses and Aaron according to their clans, including every male a month old or more, was 22,000.

40 The LORD said to Moses, "Count all the firstborn Israelite males who are a month old or more and make a list of their names. 41 Take the Levites for me in place of all the firstborn of the Israelites, and the livestock of the Levites in place of all the firstborn of the livestock of the Israelites. I am the LORD."

42 So Moses counted all the firstborn of the Israelites, as the LORD commanded him. 43 The total number of firstborn males a month old or more, listed by name, was 22,273.

44 The LORD also said to Moses, 45 "Take the Levites in place of all the firstborn of Israel, and the livestock of the Levites in place of their livestock. The Levites are to be mine. I am the LORD. 46 To redeem the 273 firstborn Israelites who exceed the number of the Levites, 47 collect five shekels[b] for each one, according to the sanctuary shekel, which weighs twenty gerahs. 48 Give the money for the redemption of the additional Israelites to Aaron and his sons."

49 So Moses collected the redemption money from those who exceeded the number redeemed by the Levites. 50 From the firstborn of the Israelites he collected silver weighing 1,365 shekels,[c] according to the sanctuary shekel. 51 Moses gave the redemption money to Aaron and his sons, as he was commanded by the word of the LORD.

The Kohathites

4 The LORD said to Moses and Aaron: 2 "Take a census of the Kohathite branch of the Levites by their clans and families. 3 Count all the men from thirty to fifty years of age who come to serve in the work at the tent of meeting.

4 "This is the work of the Kohathites at the tent of meeting: the care of the most holy things. 5 When the camp is to move, Aaron and his sons are to go in and take down the shielding curtain and put it over the ark of the covenant law. 6 Then they are to cover the curtain with a durable leather,[d] spread a cloth of solid blue over that and put the poles in place.

7 "Over the table of the Presence they are to spread a blue cloth and put on it the plates, dishes and bowls, and the jars

[a] *28* Hebrew; some Septuagint manuscripts *8,300* [b] *47* That is, about 2 ounces or about 58 grams [c] *50* That is, about 35 pounds or about 16 kilograms [d] *6* Possibly the hides of large aquatic mammals; also in verses 8, 10, 11, 12, 14 and 25

for drink offerings; the bread that is continually there is to remain on it. 8They
are to spread a scarlet cloth over them,
cover that with the durable leather and
put the poles in place.
9"They are to take a blue cloth and
cover the lampstand that is for light, together with its lamps, its wick trimmers
and trays, and all its jars for the olive oil
used to supply it. 10Then they are to wrap
it and all its accessories in a covering of
the durable leather and put it on a carrying frame.
11"Over the gold altar they are to
spread a blue cloth and cover that with
the durable leather and put the poles in
place.
12"They are to take all the articles used
for ministering in the sanctuary, wrap
them in a blue cloth, cover that with the
durable leather and put them on a carrying frame.
13"They are to remove the ashes from
the bronze altar and spread a purple
cloth over it. 14Then they are to place on
it all the utensils used for ministering at
the altar, including the firepans, meat
forks, shovels and sprinkling bowls. Over
it they are to spread a covering of the durable leather and put the poles in place.
15"After Aaron and his sons have finished covering the holy furnishings and
all the holy articles, and when the camp
is ready to move, only then are the Kohathites to come and do the carrying.
But they must not touch the holy things
or they will die. The Kohathites are to
carry those things that are in the tent of
meeting.
16"Eleazar son of Aaron, the priest, is
to have charge of the oil for the light, the
fragrant incense, the regular grain offering and the anointing oil. He is to be in
charge of the entire tabernacle and everything in it, including its holy furnishings and articles."
17The LORD said to Moses and Aaron,
18"See that the Kohathite tribal clans are
not destroyed from among the Levites.
19So that they may live and not die when
they come near the most holy things, do
this for them: Aaron and his sons are to
go into the sanctuary and assign to each
man his work and what he is to carry.
20But the Kohathites must not go in to
look at the holy things, even for a moment, or they will die."

The Gershonites

21The LORD said to Moses, 22"Take a
census also of the Gershonites by their
families and clans. 23Count all the men
from thirty to fifty years of age who
come to serve in the work at the tent of
meeting.
24"This is the service of the Gershonite
clans in their carrying and their other
work: 25They are to carry the curtains of
the tabernacle, that is, the tent of meeting, its covering and its outer covering
of durable leather, the curtains for the
entrance to the tent of meeting, 26the
curtains of the courtyard surrounding
the tabernacle and altar, the curtain for
the entrance to the courtyard, the ropes
and all the equipment used in the service of the tent. The Gershonites are to
do all that needs to be done with these
things. 27All their service, whether carrying or doing other work, is to be done
under the direction of Aaron and his
sons. You shall assign to them as their
responsibility all they are to carry. 28This
is the service of the Gershonite clans at
the tent of meeting. Their duties are to
be under the direction of Ithamar son of
Aaron, the priest.

The Merarites

29"Count the Merarites by their clans
and families. 30Count all the men from
thirty to fifty years of age who come to
serve in the work at the tent of meeting.
31As part of all their service at the tent,
they are to carry the frames of the tabernacle, its crossbars, posts and bases,
32as well as the posts of the surrounding
courtyard with their bases, tent pegs,
ropes, all their equipment and everything related to their use. Assign to each
man the specific things he is to carry.
33This is the service of the Merarite clans
as they work at the tent of meeting under the direction of Ithamar son of Aaron, the priest."

The Numbering of the Levite Clans

34Moses, Aaron and the leaders of the
community counted the Kohathites by
their clans and families. 35All the men
from thirty to fifty years of age who
came to serve in the work at the tent of
meeting, 36counted by clans, were 2,750.
37This was the total of all those in the
Kohathite clans who served at the tent
of meeting. Moses and Aaron counted
them according to the LORD's command
through Moses.
38The Gershonites were counted by
their clans and families. 39All the men
from thirty to fifty years of age who
came to serve in the work at the tent of
meeting, 40counted by their clans and
families, were 2,630. 41This was the total

of those in the Gershonite clans who served at the tent of meeting. Moses and Aaron counted them according to the LORD's command.

42The Merarites were counted by their clans and families. 43All the men from thirty to fifty years of age who came to serve in the work at the tent of meeting, 44counted by their clans, were 3,200. 45This was the total of those in the Merarite clans. Moses and Aaron counted them according to the LORD's command through Moses.

46So Moses, Aaron and the leaders of Israel counted all the Levites by their clans and families. 47All the men from thirty to fifty years of age who came to do the work of serving and carrying the tent of meeting 48numbered 8,580. 49At the LORD's command through Moses, each was assigned his work and told what to carry.

Thus they were counted, as the LORD commanded Moses.

The Purity of the Camp

5 The LORD said to Moses, 2"Command the Israelites to send away from the camp anyone who has a defiling skin disease[a] or a discharge of any kind, or who is ceremonially unclean because of a dead body. 3Send away male and female alike; send them outside the camp so they will not defile their camp, where I dwell among them." 4The Israelites did so; they sent them outside the camp. They did just as the LORD had instructed Moses.

Restitution for Wrongs

5The LORD said to Moses, 6"Say to the Israelites: 'Any man or woman who wrongs another in any way[b] and so is unfaithful to the LORD is guilty 7and must confess the sin they have committed. They must make full restitution for the wrong they have done, add a fifth of the value to it and give it all to the person they have wronged. 8But if that person has no close relative to whom restitution can be made for the wrong, the restitution belongs to the LORD and must be given to the priest, along with the ram with which atonement is made for the wrongdoer. 9All the sacred contributions the Israelites bring to a priest will belong to him. 10Sacred things belong to their owners, but what they give to the priest will belong to the priest.' "

The Test for an Unfaithful Wife

11Then the LORD said to Moses, 12"Speak to the Israelites and say to them: 'If a man's wife goes astray and is unfaithful to him 13so that another man has sexual relations with her, and this is hidden from her husband and her impurity is undetected (since there is no witness against her and she has not been caught in the act), 14and if feelings of jealousy come over her husband and he suspects his wife and she is impure — or if he is jealous and suspects her even though she is not impure — 15then he is to take his wife to the priest. He must also take an offering of a tenth of an ephah[c] of barley flour on her behalf. He must not pour olive oil on it or put incense on it, because it is a grain offering for jealousy, a reminder-offering to draw attention to wrongdoing.

16" 'The priest shall bring her and have her stand before the LORD. 17Then he shall take some holy water in a clay jar and put some dust from the tabernacle floor into the water. 18After the priest has had the woman stand before the LORD, he shall loosen her hair and place in her hands the reminder-offering, the grain offering for jealousy, while he himself holds the bitter water that brings a curse. 19Then the priest shall put the woman under oath and say to her, "If no other man has had sexual relations with you and you have not gone astray and become impure while married to your husband, may this bitter water that brings a curse not harm you. 20But if you have gone astray while married to your husband and you have made yourself impure by having sexual relations with a man other than your husband" — 21here the priest is to put the woman under this curse — "may the LORD cause you to become a curse[d] among your people when he makes your womb miscarry and your abdomen swell. 22May this water that brings a curse enter your body so that your abdomen swells or your womb miscarries."

" 'Then the woman is to say, "Amen. So be it."

[a] *2* The Hebrew word for *defiling skin disease*, traditionally translated "leprosy," was used for various diseases affecting the skin. [b] *6* Or *woman who commits any wrong common to mankind* [c] *15* That is, probably about 3 1/2 pounds or about 1.6 kilograms [d] *21* That is, may he cause your name to be used in cursing (see Jer. 29:22); or, may others see that you are cursed; similarly in verse 27.

23“‘The priest is to write these curses on a scroll and then wash them off into the bitter water. 24He shall make the woman drink the bitter water that brings a curse, and this water that brings a curse and causes bitter suffering will enter her. 25The priest is to take from her hands the grain offering for jealousy, wave it before the LORD and bring it to the altar. 26The priest is then to take a handful of the grain offering as a memorial[a] offering and burn it on the altar; after that, he is to have the woman drink the water. 27If she has made herself impure and been unfaithful to her husband, this will be the result: When she is made to drink the water that brings a curse and causes bitter suffering, it will enter her, her abdomen will swell and her womb will miscarry, and she will become a curse. 28If, however, the woman has not made herself impure, but is clean, she will be cleared of guilt and will be able to have children.

29“‘This, then, is the law of jealousy when a woman goes astray and makes herself impure while married to her husband, 30or when feelings of jealousy come over a man because he suspects his wife. The priest is to have her stand before the LORD and is to apply this entire law to her. 31The husband will be innocent of any wrongdoing, but the woman will bear the consequences of her sin.’ ”

The Nazirite

6 The LORD said to Moses, 2“Speak to the Israelites and say to them: ‘If a man or woman wants to make a special vow, a vow of dedication to the LORD as a Nazirite, 3they must abstain from wine and other fermented drink and must not drink vinegar made from wine or other fermented drink. They must not drink grape juice or eat grapes or raisins. 4As long as they remain under their Nazirite vow, they must not eat anything that comes from the grapevine, not even the seeds or skins.

5“‘During the entire period of their Nazirite vow, no razor may be used on their head. They must be holy until the period of their dedication to the LORD is over; they must let their hair grow long.

6“‘Throughout the period of their dedication to the LORD, the Nazirite must not go near a dead body. 7Even if their own father or mother or brother or sister dies, they must not make themselves ceremonially unclean on account of them, because the symbol of their dedication to God is on their head. 8Throughout the period of their dedication, they are consecrated to the LORD.

9“‘If someone dies suddenly in the Nazirite’s presence, thus defiling the hair that symbolizes their dedication, they must shave their head on the seventh day—the day of their cleansing. 10Then on the eighth day they must bring two doves or two young pigeons to the priest at the entrance to the tent of meeting. 11The priest is to offer one as a sin offering[b] and the other as a burnt offering to make atonement for the Nazirite because they sinned by being in the presence of the dead body. That same day they are to consecrate their head again. 12They must rededicate themselves to the LORD for the same period of dedication and must bring a year-old male lamb as a guilt offering. The previous days do not count, because they became defiled during their period of dedication.

13“‘Now this is the law of the Nazirite when the period of their dedication is over. They are to be brought to the entrance to the tent of meeting. 14There they are to present their offerings to the LORD: a year-old male lamb without defect for a burnt offering, a year-old ewe lamb without defect for a sin offering, a ram without defect for a fellowship offering, 15together with their grain offerings and drink offerings, and a basket of bread made with the finest flour and without yeast—thick loaves with olive oil mixed in, and thin loaves brushed with olive oil.

16“‘The priest is to present all these before the LORD and make the sin offering and the burnt offering. 17He is to present the basket of unleavened bread and is to sacrifice the ram as a fellowship offering to the LORD, together with its grain offering and drink offering.

18“‘Then at the entrance to the tent of meeting, the Nazirite must shave off the hair that symbolizes their dedication. They are to take the hair and put it in the fire that is under the sacrifice of the fellowship offering.

19“‘After the Nazirite has shaved off the hair that symbolizes their dedication, the priest is to place in their hands a boiled shoulder of the ram, and one thick loaf and one thin loaf from the basket, both made without yeast. 20The priest shall then wave these before the LORD as a wave offering; they are holy

[a] 26 Or *representative* [b] 11 Or *purification offering*; also in verses 14 and 16

and belong to the priest, together with
the breast that was waved and the thigh
that was presented. After that, the Nazirite may drink wine.
21“ ‘This is the law of the Nazirite who
vows offerings to the LORD in accordance
with their dedication, in addition to
whatever else they can afford. They must
fulfill the vows they have made, according to the law of the Nazirite.’ ”

The Priestly Blessing

22The LORD said to Moses, 23“Tell Aaron
and his sons, ‘This is how you are to bless
the Israelites. Say to them:

24“ ‘ “The LORD bless you
and keep you;
25the LORD make his face shine on you
and be gracious to you;
26the LORD turn his face toward you
and give you peace.” ’

27“So they will put my name on the Israelites, and I will bless them.”

Offerings at the Dedication of the Tabernacle

7 When Moses finished setting up the
tabernacle, he anointed and consecrated it and all its furnishings. He also
anointed and consecrated the altar and
all its utensils. 2Then the leaders of Israel, the heads of families who were the
tribal leaders in charge of those who
were counted, made offerings. 3They
brought as their gifts before the LORD
six covered carts and twelve oxen — an
ox from each leader and a cart from every two. These they presented before the
tabernacle.
4The LORD said to Moses, 5“Accept
these from them, that they may be used
in the work at the tent of meeting. Give
them to the Levites as each man’s work
requires.”
6So Moses took the carts and oxen and
gave them to the Levites. 7He gave two
carts and four oxen to the Gershonites,
as their work required, 8and he gave four
carts and eight oxen to the Merarites, as
their work required. They were all under
the direction of Ithamar son of Aaron,
the priest. 9But Moses did not give any
to the Kohathites, because they were to
carry on their shoulders the holy things,
for which they were responsible.
10When the altar was anointed, the
leaders brought their offerings for its
dedication and presented them before
the altar. 11For the LORD had said to Moses, “Each day one leader is to bring his
offering for the dedication of the altar.”

12The one who brought his offering on
the first day was Nahshon son of Amminadab of the tribe of Judah.
13His offering was one silver plate
weighing a hundred and thirty
shekels[a] and one silver sprinkling
bowl weighing seventy shekels,[b]
both according to the sanctuary
shekel, each filled with the finest flour mixed with olive oil as
a grain offering; 14one gold dish
weighing ten shekels,[c] filled with
incense; 15one young bull, one ram
and one male lamb a year old for a
burnt offering; 16one male goat for
a sin offering[d]; 17and two oxen, five
rams, five male goats and five male
lambs a year old to be sacrificed as
a fellowship offering. This was the
offering of Nahshon son of Amminadab.

18On the second day Nethanel son of
Zuar, the leader of Issachar, brought his
offering.
19The offering he brought was one
silver plate weighing a hundred
and thirty shekels and one silver
sprinkling bowl weighing seventy shekels, both according to the
sanctuary shekel, each filled with
the finest flour mixed with olive oil
as a grain offering; 20one gold dish
weighing ten shekels, filled with
incense; 21one young bull, one ram
and one male lamb a year old for a
burnt offering; 22one male goat for
a sin offering; 23and two oxen, five
rams, five male goats and five male
lambs a year old to be sacrificed as
a fellowship offering. This was the
offering of Nethanel son of Zuar.

24On the third day, Eliab son of Helon,
the leader of the people of Zebulun,
brought his offering.
25His offering was one silver plate
weighing a hundred and thirty
shekels and one silver sprinkling
bowl weighing seventy shekels,
both according to the sanctuary
shekel, each filled with the finest flour mixed with olive oil as

[a] *13* That is, about 3 1/4 pounds or about 1.5 kilograms; also elsewhere in this chapter
[b] *13* That is, about 1 3/4 pounds or about 800 grams; also elsewhere in this chapter [c] *14* That is, about 4 ounces or about 115 grams; also elsewhere in this chapter [d] *16* Or *purification offering*; also elsewhere in this chapter

a grain offering; 26one gold dish
weighing ten shekels, filled with
incense; 27one young bull, one ram
and one male lamb a year old for a
burnt offering; 28one male goat for
a sin offering; 29and two oxen, five
rams, five male goats and five male
lambs a year old to be sacrificed as
a fellowship offering. This was the
offering of Eliab son of Helon.

30On the fourth day Elizur son of Shedeur, the leader of the people of Reuben,
brought his offering.

31His offering was one silver plate
weighing a hundred and thirty
shekels and one silver sprinkling
bowl weighing seventy shekels,
both according to the sanctuary
shekel, each filled with the finest flour mixed with olive oil as
a grain offering; 32one gold dish
weighing ten shekels, filled with
incense; 33one young bull, one ram
and one male lamb a year old for a
burnt offering; 34one male goat for
a sin offering; 35and two oxen, five
rams, five male goats and five male
lambs a year old to be sacrificed as
a fellowship offering. This was the
offering of Elizur son of Shedeur.

36On the fifth day Shelumiel son of Zurishaddai, the leader of the people of Simeon, brought his offering.

37His offering was one silver plate
weighing a hundred and thirty
shekels and one silver sprinkling
bowl weighing seventy shekels, both
according to the sanctuary shekel, each filled with the finest flour
mixed with olive oil as a grain offering; 38one gold dish weighing ten
shekels, filled with incense; 39one
young bull, one ram and one male
lamb a year old for a burnt offering;
40one male goat for a sin offering;
41and two oxen, five rams, five male
goats and five male lambs a year
old to be sacrificed as a fellowship
offering. This was the offering of
Shelumiel son of Zurishaddai.

42On the sixth day Eliasaph son of Deuel,
the leader of the people of Gad, brought
his offering.

43His offering was one silver plate
weighing a hundred and thirty
shekels and one silver sprinkling
bowl weighing seventy shekels,
both according to the sanctuary
shekel, each filled with the finest flour mixed with olive oil as
a grain offering; 44one gold dish
weighing ten shekels, filled with
incense; 45one young bull, one ram
and one male lamb a year old for a
burnt offering; 46one male goat for
a sin offering; 47and two oxen, five
rams, five male goats and five male
lambs a year old to be sacrificed as
a fellowship offering. This was the
offering of Eliasaph son of Deuel.

48On the seventh day Elishama son of
Ammihud, the leader of the people of
Ephraim, brought his offering.

49His offering was one silver plate
weighing a hundred and thirty
shekels and one silver sprinkling
bowl weighing seventy shekels,
both according to the sanctuary
shekel, each filled with the finest flour mixed with olive oil as
a grain offering; 50one gold dish
weighing ten shekels, filled with
incense; 51one young bull, one ram
and one male lamb a year old for a
burnt offering; 52one male goat for
a sin offering; 53and two oxen, five
rams, five male goats and five male
lambs a year old to be sacrificed as
a fellowship offering. This was the
offering of Elishama son of Ammihud.

54On the eighth day Gamaliel son of Pedahzur, the leader of the people of Manasseh, brought his offering.

55His offering was one silver plate
weighing a hundred and thirty
shekels and one silver sprinkling
bowl weighing seventy shekels, both
according to the sanctuary shekel, each filled with the finest flour
mixed with olive oil as a grain offering; 56one gold dish weighing ten
shekels, filled with incense; 57one
young bull, one ram and one male
lamb a year old for a burnt offering;
58one male goat for a sin offering;
59and two oxen, five rams, five male
goats and five male lambs a year
old to be sacrificed as a fellowship
offering. This was the offering of
Gamaliel son of Pedahzur.

60On the ninth day Abidan son of Gideoni, the leader of the people of Benjamin,
brought his offering.

61His offering was one silver plate
weighing a hundred and thirty
shekels and one silver sprinkling
bowl weighing seventy shekels,
both according to the sanctuary
shekel, each filled with the finest flour mixed with olive oil as
a grain offering; 62one gold dish

weighing ten shekels, filled with incense; 63 one young bull, one ram and one male lamb a year old for a burnt offering; 64 one male goat for a sin offering; 65 and two oxen, five rams, five male goats and five male lambs a year old to be sacrificed as a fellowship offering. This was the offering of Abidan son of Gideoni.

66 On the tenth day Ahiezer son of Ammishaddai, the leader of the people of Dan, brought his offering.

67 His offering was one silver plate weighing a hundred and thirty shekels and one silver sprinkling bowl weighing seventy shekels, both according to the sanctuary shekel, each filled with the finest flour mixed with olive oil as a grain offering; 68 one gold dish weighing ten shekels, filled with incense; 69 one young bull, one ram and one male lamb a year old for a burnt offering; 70 one male goat for a sin offering; 71 and two oxen, five rams, five male goats and five male lambs a year old to be sacrificed as a fellowship offering. This was the offering of Ahiezer son of Ammishaddai.

72 On the eleventh day Pagiel son of Okran, the leader of the people of Asher, brought his offering.

73 His offering was one silver plate weighing a hundred and thirty shekels and one silver sprinkling bowl weighing seventy shekels, both according to the sanctuary shekel, each filled with the finest flour mixed with olive oil as a grain offering; 74 one gold dish weighing ten shekels, filled with incense; 75 one young bull, one ram and one male lamb a year old for a burnt offering; 76 one male goat for a sin offering; 77 and two oxen, five rams, five male goats and five male lambs a year old to be sacrificed as a fellowship offering. This was the offering of Pagiel son of Okran.

78 On the twelfth day Ahira son of Enan, the leader of the people of Naphtali, brought his offering.

79 His offering was one silver plate weighing a hundred and thirty shekels and one silver sprinkling bowl weighing seventy shekels, both according to the sanctuary shekel, each filled with the finest flour mixed with olive oil as a grain offering; 80 one gold dish weighing ten shekels, filled with incense; 81 one young bull, one ram and one male lamb a year old for a burnt offering; 82 one male goat for a sin offering; 83 and two oxen, five rams, five male goats and five male lambs a year old to be sacrificed as a fellowship offering. This was the offering of Ahira son of Enan.

84 These were the offerings of the Israelite leaders for the dedication of the altar when it was anointed: twelve silver plates, twelve silver sprinkling bowls and twelve gold dishes. 85 Each silver plate weighed a hundred and thirty shekels, and each sprinkling bowl seventy shekels. Altogether, the silver dishes weighed two thousand four hundred shekels,[a] according to the sanctuary shekel. 86 The twelve gold dishes filled with incense weighed ten shekels each, according to the sanctuary shekel. Altogether, the gold dishes weighed a hundred and twenty shekels.[b] 87 The total number of animals for the burnt offering came to twelve young bulls, twelve rams and twelve male lambs a year old, together with their grain offering. Twelve male goats were used for the sin offering. 88 The total number of animals for the sacrifice of the fellowship offering came to twenty-four oxen, sixty rams, sixty male goats and sixty male lambs a year old. These were the offerings for the dedication of the altar after it was anointed.

89 When Moses entered the tent of meeting to speak with the LORD, he heard the voice speaking to him from between the two cherubim above the atonement cover on the ark of the covenant law. In this way the LORD spoke to him.

Setting Up the Lamps

8 The LORD said to Moses, 2 "Speak to Aaron and say to him, 'When you set up the lamps, see that all seven light up the area in front of the lampstand.' "

3 Aaron did so; he set up the lamps so that they faced forward on the lampstand, just as the LORD commanded Moses. 4 This is how the lampstand was made: It was made of hammered gold — from its base to its blossoms. The lampstand was made exactly like the pattern the LORD had shown Moses.

[a] *85* That is, about 60 pounds or about 28 kilograms [b] *86* That is, about 3 pounds or about 1.4 kilograms

The Setting Apart of the Levites

5The LORD said to Moses: 6"Take the
Levites from among all the Israelites
and make them ceremonially clean. 7To
purify them, do this: Sprinkle the water
of cleansing on them; then have them
shave their whole bodies and wash their
clothes. And so they will purify themselves. 8Have them take a young bull
with its grain offering of the finest flour
mixed with olive oil; then you are to take
a second young bull for a sin offering.[a]
9Bring the Levites to the front of the tent
of meeting and assemble the whole Israelite community. 10You are to bring
the Levites before the LORD, and the Israelites are to lay their hands on them.
11Aaron is to present the Levites before
the LORD as a wave offering from the Israelites, so that they may be ready to do
the work of the LORD.

12"Then the Levites are to lay their
hands on the heads of the bulls, using
one for a sin offering to the LORD and
the other for a burnt offering, to make
atonement for the Levites. 13Have the Levites stand in front of Aaron and his sons
and then present them as a wave offering to the LORD. 14In this way you are to
set the Levites apart from the other Israelites, and the Levites will be mine.

15"After you have purified the Levites
and presented them as a wave offering,
they are to come to do their work at the
tent of meeting. 16They are the Israelites
who are to be given wholly to me. I have
taken them as my own in place of the
firstborn, the first male offspring from
every Israelite woman. 17Every firstborn
male in Israel, whether human or animal, is mine. When I struck down all the
firstborn in Egypt, I set them apart for
myself. 18And I have taken the Levites in
place of all the firstborn sons in Israel.
19From among all the Israelites, I have
given the Levites as gifts to Aaron and
his sons to do the work at the tent of
meeting on behalf of the Israelites and
to make atonement for them so that no
plague will strike the Israelites when
they go near the sanctuary."

20Moses, Aaron and the whole Israelite community did with the Levites just
as the LORD commanded Moses. 21The
Levites purified themselves and washed
their clothes. Then Aaron presented
them as a wave offering before the LORD
and made atonement for them to purify them. 22After that, the Levites came
to do their work at the tent of meeting
under the supervision of Aaron and his
sons. They did with the Levites just as the
LORD commanded Moses.

23The LORD said to Moses, 24"This applies to the Levites: Men twenty-five
years old or more shall come to take part
in the work at the tent of meeting, 25but
at the age of fifty, they must retire from
their regular service and work no longer.
26They may assist their brothers in performing their duties at the tent of meeting, but they themselves must not do the
work. This, then, is how you are to assign
the responsibilities of the Levites."

The Passover

9 The LORD spoke to Moses in the
Desert of Sinai in the first month
of the second year after they came out
of Egypt. He said, 2"Have the Israelites
celebrate the Passover at the appointed
time. 3Celebrate it at the appointed time,
at twilight on the fourteenth day of this
month, in accordance with all its rules
and regulations."

4So Moses told the Israelites to celebrate the Passover, 5and they did so in
the Desert of Sinai at twilight on the
fourteenth day of the first month. The
Israelites did everything just as the LORD
commanded Moses.

6But some of them could not celebrate
the Passover on that day because they
were ceremonially unclean on account
of a dead body. So they came to Moses
and Aaron that same day 7and said to
Moses, "We have become unclean because of a dead body, but why should
we be kept from presenting the LORD's
offering with the other Israelites at the
appointed time?"

8Moses answered them, "Wait until I
find out what the LORD commands concerning you."

9Then the LORD said to Moses, 10"Tell
the Israelites: 'When any of you or your
descendants are unclean because of a
dead body or are away on a journey, they
are still to celebrate the LORD's Passover,
11but they are to do it on the fourteenth
day of the second month at twilight.
They are to eat the lamb, together with
unleavened bread and bitter herbs.
12They must not leave any of it till morning or break any of its bones. When they
celebrate the Passover, they must follow
all the regulations. 13But if anyone who
is ceremonially clean and not on a journey fails to celebrate the Passover, they
must be cut off from their people for not

[a] 8 Or *purification offering*; also in verse 12

presenting the LORD's offering at the appointed time. They will bear the consequences of their sin.

14"'A foreigner residing among you is also to celebrate the LORD's Passover in accordance with its rules and regulations. You must have the same regulations for both the foreigner and the native-born.'"

The Cloud Above the Tabernacle

15On the day the tabernacle, the tent of the covenant law, was set up, the cloud covered it. From evening till morning the cloud above the tabernacle looked like fire. 16That is how it continued to be; the cloud covered it, and at night it looked like fire. 17Whenever the cloud lifted from above the tent, the Israelites set out; wherever the cloud settled, the Israelites encamped. 18At the LORD's command the Israelites set out, and at his command they encamped. As long as the cloud stayed over the tabernacle, they remained in camp. 19When the cloud remained over the tabernacle a long time, the Israelites obeyed the LORD's order and did not set out. 20Sometimes the cloud was over the tabernacle only a few days; at the LORD's command they would encamp, and then at his command they would set out. 21Sometimes the cloud stayed only from evening till morning, and when it lifted in the morning, they set out. Whether by day or by night, whenever the cloud lifted, they set out. 22Whether the cloud stayed over the tabernacle for two days or a month or a year, the Israelites would remain in camp and not set out; but when it lifted, they would set out. 23At the LORD's command they encamped, and at the LORD's command they set out. They obeyed the LORD's order, in accordance with his command through Moses.

The Silver Trumpets

10 The LORD said to Moses: 2"Make two trumpets of hammered silver, and use them for calling the community together and for having the camps set out. 3When both are sounded, the whole community is to assemble before you at the entrance to the tent of meeting. 4If only one is sounded, the leaders — the heads of the clans of Israel — are to assemble before you. 5When a trumpet blast is sounded, the tribes camping on the east are to set out. 6At the sounding of a second blast, the camps on the south are to set out. The blast will be the signal for setting out. 7To gather the assembly, blow the trumpets, but not with the signal for setting out.

8"The sons of Aaron, the priests, are to blow the trumpets. This is to be a lasting ordinance for you and the generations to come. 9When you go into battle in your own land against an enemy who is oppressing you, sound a blast on the trumpets. Then you will be remembered by the LORD your God and rescued from your enemies. 10Also at your times of rejoicing — your appointed festivals and New Moon feasts — you are to sound the trumpets over your burnt offerings and fellowship offerings, and they will be a memorial for you before your God. I am the LORD your God."

The Israelites Leave Sinai

11On the twentieth day of the second month of the second year, the cloud lifted from above the tabernacle of the covenant law. 12Then the Israelites set out from the Desert of Sinai and traveled from place to place until the cloud came to rest in the Desert of Paran. 13They set out, this first time, at the LORD's command through Moses.

14The divisions of the camp of Judah went first, under their standard. Nahshon son of Amminadab was in command. 15Nethanel son of Zuar was over the division of the tribe of Issachar, 16and Eliab son of Helon was over the division of the tribe of Zebulun. 17Then the tabernacle was taken down, and the Gershonites and Merarites, who carried it, set out.

18The divisions of the camp of Reuben went next, under their standard. Elizur son of Shedeur was in command. 19Shelumiel son of Zurishaddai was over the division of the tribe of Simeon, 20and Eliasaph son of Deuel was over the division of the tribe of Gad. 21Then the Kohathites set out, carrying the holy things. The tabernacle was to be set up before they arrived.

22The divisions of the camp of Ephraim went next, under their standard. Elishama son of Ammihud was in command. 23Gamaliel son of Pedahzur was over the division of the tribe of Manasseh, 24and Abidan son of Gideoni was over the division of the tribe of Benjamin.

25Finally, as the rear guard for all the units, the divisions of the camp of Dan set out under their standard. Ahiezer son of Ammishaddai was in command. 26Pagiel son of Okran was over the division of the tribe of Asher, 27and Ahira son of Enan was over the division of the tribe of

Naphtali. 28This was the order of march
for the Israelite divisions as they set out.
29Now Moses said to Hobab son of Reuel the Midianite, Moses' father-in-law,
"We are setting out for the place about
which the LORD said, 'I will give it to you.'
Come with us and we will treat you well,
for the LORD has promised good things
to Israel."
30He answered, "No, I will not go; I am
going back to my own land and my own
people."
31But Moses said, "Please do not leave
us. You know where we should camp in
the wilderness, and you can be our eyes.
32If you come with us, we will share with
you whatever good things the LORD
gives us."
33So they set out from the mountain
of the LORD and traveled for three days.
The ark of the covenant of the LORD went
before them during those three days to
find them a place to rest. 34The cloud of
the LORD was over them by day when
they set out from the camp.
35Whenever the ark set out, Moses said,

"Rise up, LORD!
May your enemies be scattered;
may your foes flee before you."

36Whenever it came to rest, he said,

"Return, LORD,
to the countless thousands of
Israel."

Fire From the LORD

11 Now the people complained about
their hardships in the hearing of
the LORD, and when he heard them his
anger was aroused. Then fire from the
LORD burned among them and consumed some of the outskirts of the
camp. 2When the people cried out to Moses, he prayed to the LORD and the fire
died down. 3So that place was called Taberah,[a] because fire from the LORD had
burned among them.

Quail From the LORD

4The rabble with them began to crave
other food, and again the Israelites
started wailing and said, "If only we had
meat to eat! 5We remember the fish we
ate in Egypt at no cost — also the cucum-
bers, melons, leeks, onions and garlic.
6But now we have lost our appetite; we
never see anything but this manna!"
7The manna was like coriander seed
and looked like resin. 8The people went
around gathering it, and then ground
it in a hand mill or crushed it in a mortar. They cooked it in a pot or made it
into loaves. And it tasted like something
made with olive oil. 9When the dew settled on the camp at night, the manna
also came down.
10Moses heard the people of every
family wailing at the entrance to their
tents. The LORD became exceedingly angry, and Moses was troubled. 11He asked
the LORD, "Why have you brought this
trouble on your servant? What have I
done to displease you that you put the
burden of all these people on me? 12Did
I conceive all these people? Did I give
them birth? Why do you tell me to carry them in my arms, as a nurse carries
an infant, to the land you promised on
oath to their ancestors? 13Where can I
get meat for all these people? They keep
wailing to me, 'Give us meat to eat!' 14I
cannot carry all these people by myself;
the burden is too heavy for me. 15If this
is how you are going to treat me, please
go ahead and kill me — if I have found
favor in your eyes — and do not let me
face my own ruin."
16The LORD said to Moses: "Bring me
seventy of Israel's elders who are known
to you as leaders and officials among
the people. Have them come to the tent
of meeting, that they may stand there
with you. 17I will come down and speak
with you there, and I will take some of
the power of the Spirit that is on you and
put it on them. They will share the burden of the people with you so that you
will not have to carry it alone.
18"Tell the people: 'Consecrate yourselves in preparation for tomorrow,
when you will eat meat. The LORD heard
you when you wailed, "If only we had
meat to eat! We were better off in Egypt!"
Now the LORD will give you meat, and
you will eat it. 19You will not eat it for just
one day, or two days, or five, ten or twenty days, 20but for a whole month — until it comes out of your nostrils and you
loathe it — because you have rejected
the LORD, who is among you, and have
wailed before him, saying, "Why did we
ever leave Egypt?"'"
21But Moses said, "Here I am among
six hundred thousand men on foot, and
you say, 'I will give them meat to eat
for a whole month!' 22Would they have
enough if flocks and herds were slaughtered for them? Would they have enough
if all the fish in the sea were caught for
them?"
23The LORD answered Moses, "Is the

[a] 3 *Taberah* means *burning.*

LORD's arm too short? Now you will see whether or not what I say will come true for you."

24 So Moses went out and told the people what the LORD had said. He brought together seventy of their elders and had them stand around the tent. 25 Then the LORD came down in the cloud and spoke with him, and he took some of the power of the Spirit that was on him and put it on the seventy elders. When the Spirit rested on them, they prophesied—but did not do so again.

26 However, two men, whose names were Eldad and Medad, had remained in the camp. They were listed among the elders, but did not go out to the tent. Yet the Spirit also rested on them, and they prophesied in the camp. 27 A young man ran and told Moses, "Eldad and Medad are prophesying in the camp."

28 Joshua son of Nun, who had been Moses' aide since youth, spoke up and said, "Moses, my lord, stop them!"

29 But Moses replied, "Are you jealous for my sake? I wish that all the LORD's people were prophets and that the LORD would put his Spirit on them!" 30 Then Moses and the elders of Israel returned to the camp.

31 Now a wind went out from the LORD and drove quail in from the sea. It scattered them up to two cubits[a] deep all around the camp, as far as a day's walk in any direction. 32 All that day and night and all the next day the people went out and gathered quail. No one gathered less than ten homers.[b] Then they spread them out all around the camp. 33 But while the meat was still between their teeth and before it could be consumed, the anger of the LORD burned against the people, and he struck them with a severe plague. 34 Therefore the place was named Kibroth Hattaavah,[c] because there they buried the people who had craved other food.

35 From Kibroth Hattaavah the people traveled to Hazeroth and stayed there.

Miriam and Aaron Oppose Moses

12 Miriam and Aaron began to talk against Moses because of his Cushite wife, for he had married a Cushite. 2 "Has the LORD spoken only through Moses?" they asked. "Hasn't he also spoken through us?" And the LORD heard this.

3 (Now Moses was a very humble man, more humble than anyone else on the face of the earth.)

4 At once the LORD said to Moses, Aaron and Miriam, "Come out to the tent of meeting, all three of you." So the three of them went out. 5 Then the LORD came down in a pillar of cloud; he stood at the entrance to the tent and summoned Aaron and Miriam. When the two of them stepped forward, 6 he said, "Listen to my words:

"When there is a prophet among you,
I, the LORD, reveal myself to them
in visions,
I speak to them in dreams.
7 But this is not true of my servant
Moses;
he is faithful in all my house.
8 With him I speak face to face,
clearly and not in riddles;
he sees the form of the LORD.
Why then were you not afraid
to speak against my servant
Moses?"

9 The anger of the LORD burned against them, and he left them.

10 When the cloud lifted from above the tent, Miriam's skin was leprous[d]—it became as white as snow. Aaron turned toward her and saw that she had a defiling skin disease, 11 and he said to Moses, "Please, my lord, I ask you not to hold against us the sin we have so foolishly committed. 12 Do not let her be like a stillborn infant coming from its mother's womb with its flesh half eaten away."

13 So Moses cried out to the LORD, "Please, God, heal her!"

14 The LORD replied to Moses, "If her father had spit in her face, would she not have been in disgrace for seven days? Confine her outside the camp for seven days; after that she can be brought back." 15 So Miriam was confined outside the camp for seven days, and the people did not move on till she was brought back.

16 After that, the people left Hazeroth and encamped in the Desert of Paran.

Exploring Canaan

13 The LORD said to Moses, 2 "Send some men to explore the land of Canaan, which I am giving to the Israelites. From each ancestral tribe send one of its leaders."

3 So at the LORD's command Moses sent

[a] *31* That is, about 3 feet or about 90 centimeters [b] *32* That is, possibly about 1 3/4 tons or about 1.6 metric tons [c] *34* *Kibroth Hattaavah* means *graves of craving.* [d] *10* The Hebrew for *leprous* was used for various diseases affecting the skin.

them out from the Desert of Paran. All
of them were leaders of the Israelites.
4These are their names:

from the tribe of Reuben, Shammua son of Zakkur;
5from the tribe of Simeon, Shaphat son of Hori;
6from the tribe of Judah, Caleb son of Jephunneh;
7from the tribe of Issachar, Igal son of Joseph;
8from the tribe of Ephraim, Hoshea son of Nun;
9from the tribe of Benjamin, Palti son of Raphu;
10from the tribe of Zebulun, Gaddiel son of Sodi;
11from the tribe of Manasseh (a tribe of Joseph), Gaddi son of Susi;
12from the tribe of Dan, Ammiel son of Gemalli;
13from the tribe of Asher, Sethur son of Michael;
14from the tribe of Naphtali, Nahbi son of Vophsi;
15from the tribe of Gad, Geuel son of Maki.

16These are the names of the men Moses
sent to explore the land. (Moses gave Hoshea son of Nun the name Joshua.)
17When Moses sent them to explore Canaan, he said, "Go up through the Negev
and on into the hill country. 18See what
the land is like and whether the people
who live there are strong or weak, few
or many. 19What kind of land do they
live in? Is it good or bad? What kind of
towns do they live in? Are they unwalled
or fortified? 20How is the soil? Is it fertile
or poor? Are there trees in it or not? Do
your best to bring back some of the fruit
of the land." (It was the season for the
first ripe grapes.)
21So they went up and explored the
land from the Desert of Zin as far as Rehob, toward Lebo Hamath. 22They went
up through the Negev and came to Hebron, where Ahiman, Sheshai and Talmai, the descendants of Anak, lived. (Hebron had been built seven years before
Zoan in Egypt.) 23When they reached the
Valley of Eshkol,[a] they cut off a branch
bearing a single cluster of grapes. Two of
them carried it on a pole between them,
along with some pomegranates and figs.
24That place was called the Valley of Eshkol because of the cluster of grapes the
Israelites cut off there. 25At the end of
forty days they returned from exploring
the land.

Report on the Exploration

26They came back to Moses and Aaron and the whole Israelite community
at Kadesh in the Desert of Paran. There
they reported to them and to the whole
assembly and showed them the fruit of
the land. 27They gave Moses this account:
"We went into the land to which you sent
us, and it does flow with milk and honey! Here is its fruit. 28But the people who
live there are powerful, and the cities
are fortified and very large. We even saw
descendants of Anak there. 29The Amalekites live in the Negev; the Hittites,
Jebusites and Amorites live in the hill
country; and the Canaanites live near
the sea and along the Jordan."
30Then Caleb silenced the people before Moses and said, "We should go up
and take possession of the land, for we
can certainly do it."
31But the men who had gone up with
him said, "We can't attack those people;
they are stronger than we are." 32And
they spread among the Israelites a bad
report about the land they had explored.
They said, "The land we explored devours those living in it. All the people we
saw there are of great size. 33We saw the
Nephilim there (the descendants of Anak
come from the Nephilim). We seemed
like grasshoppers in our own eyes, and
we looked the same to them."

The People Rebel

14 That night all the members of the
community raised their voices and
wept aloud. 2All the Israelites grumbled
against Moses and Aaron, and the whole
assembly said to them, "If only we had
died in Egypt! Or in this wilderness! 3Why
is the LORD bringing us to this land only
to let us fall by the sword? Our wives
and children will be taken as plunder.
Wouldn't it be better for us to go back
to Egypt?" 4And they said to each other,
"We should choose a leader and go back
to Egypt."
5Then Moses and Aaron fell facedown
in front of the whole Israelite assembly gathered there. 6Joshua son of Nun
and Caleb son of Jephunneh, who were
among those who had explored the
land, tore their clothes 7and said to the
entire Israelite assembly, "The land we
passed through and explored is exceedingly good. 8If the LORD is pleased with
us, he will lead us into that land, a land
flowing with milk and honey, and will
give it to us. 9Only do not rebel against

[a] *23 Eshkol* means *cluster*; also in verse 24.

the LORD. And do not be afraid of the
people of the land, because we will devour them. Their protection is gone, but
the LORD is with us. Do not be afraid of
them."
10But the whole assembly talked about
stoning them. Then the glory of the LORD
appeared at the tent of meeting to all
the Israelites. 11The LORD said to Moses,
"How long will these people treat me
with contempt? How long will they refuse to believe in me, in spite of all the
signs I have performed among them? 12I
will strike them down with a plague and
destroy them, but I will make you into a
nation greater and stronger than they."
13Moses said to the LORD, "Then the
Egyptians will hear about it! By your
power you brought these people up from
among them. 14And they will tell the
inhabitants of this land about it. They
have already heard that you, LORD, are
with these people and that you, LORD,
have been seen face to face, that your
cloud stays over them, and that you go
before them in a pillar of cloud by day
and a pillar of fire by night. 15If you put
all these people to death, leaving none
alive, the nations who have heard this
report about you will say, 16'The LORD
was not able to bring these people into
the land he promised them on oath, so
he slaughtered them in the wilderness.'
17"Now may the Lord's strength be displayed, just as you have declared: 18'The
LORD is slow to anger, abounding in love
and forgiving sin and rebellion. Yet he
does not leave the guilty unpunished;
he punishes the children for the sin of
the parents to the third and fourth generation.' 19In accordance with your great
love, forgive the sin of these people, just
as you have pardoned them from the
time they left Egypt until now."
20The LORD replied, "I have forgiven
them, as you asked. 21Nevertheless, as
surely as I live and as surely as the glory of the LORD fills the whole earth, 22not
one of those who saw my glory and the
signs I performed in Egypt and in the
wilderness but who disobeyed me and
tested me ten times — 23not one of them
will ever see the land I promised on
oath to their ancestors. No one who has
treated me with contempt will ever see
it. 24But because my servant Caleb has
a different spirit and follows me wholeheartedly, I will bring him into the land
he went to, and his descendants will inherit it. 25Since the Amalekites and the
Canaanites are living in the valleys, turn
back tomorrow and set out toward the
desert along the route to the Red Sea.[a]"
26The LORD said to Moses and Aaron:
27"How long will this wicked community grumble against me? I have heard
the complaints of these grumbling Israelites. 28So tell them, 'As surely as I
live, declares the LORD, I will do to you
the very thing I heard you say: 29In this
wilderness your bodies will fall — every
one of you twenty years old or more who
was counted in the census and who has
grumbled against me. 30Not one of you
will enter the land I swore with uplifted
hand to make your home, except Caleb
son of Jephunneh and Joshua son of
Nun. 31As for your children that you said
would be taken as plunder, I will bring
them in to enjoy the land you have rejected. 32But as for you, your bodies will
fall in this wilderness. 33Your children
will be shepherds here for forty years,
suffering for your unfaithfulness, until
the last of your bodies lies in the wilderness. 34For forty years — one year for
each of the forty days you explored the
land — you will suffer for your sins and
know what it is like to have me against
you.' 35I, the LORD, have spoken, and I
will surely do these things to this whole
wicked community, which has banded together against me. They will meet
their end in this wilderness; here they
will die."
36So the men Moses had sent to explore the land, who returned and made
the whole community grumble against
him by spreading a bad report about
it — 37these men who were responsible for spreading the bad report about
the land were struck down and died of
a plague before the LORD. 38Of the men
who went to explore the land, only Joshua son of Nun and Caleb son of Jephunneh survived.
39When Moses reported this to all the
Israelites, they mourned bitterly. 40Ear-
ly the next morning they set out for the
highest point in the hill country, saying, "Now we are ready to go up to the
land the LORD promised. Surely we have
sinned!"
41But Moses said, "Why are you dis-
obeying the LORD's command? This will
not succeed! 42Do not go up, because the
LORD is not with you. You will be defeated by your enemies, 43for the Amalekites
and the Canaanites will face you there.
Because you have turned away from the

[a] 25 *Or the Sea of Reeds*

LORD, he will not be with you and you will fall by the sword."

44 Nevertheless, in their presumption they went up toward the highest point in the hill country, though neither Moses nor the ark of the LORD's covenant moved from the camp. 45 Then the Amalekites and the Canaanites who lived in that hill country came down and attacked them and beat them down all the way to Hormah.

Supplementary Offerings

15 The LORD said to Moses, 2 "Speak to the Israelites and say to them: 'After you enter the land I am giving you as a home 3 and you present to the LORD food offerings from the herd or the flock, as an aroma pleasing to the LORD — whether burnt offerings or sacrifices, for special vows or freewill offerings or festival offerings — 4 then the person who brings an offering shall present to the LORD a grain offering of a tenth of an ephah[a] of the finest flour mixed with a quarter of a hin[b] of olive oil. 5 With each lamb for the burnt offering or the sacrifice, prepare a quarter of a hin of wine as a drink offering.

6 " 'With a ram prepare a grain offering of two-tenths of an ephah[c] of the finest flour mixed with a third of a hin[d] of olive oil, 7 and a third of a hin of wine as a drink offering. Offer it as an aroma pleasing to the LORD.

8 " 'When you prepare a young bull as a burnt offering or sacrifice, for a special vow or a fellowship offering to the LORD, 9 bring with the bull a grain offering of three-tenths of an ephah[e] of the finest flour mixed with half a hin[f] of olive oil, 10 and also bring half a hin of wine as a drink offering. This will be a food offering, an aroma pleasing to the LORD. 11 Each bull or ram, each lamb or young goat, is to be prepared in this manner. 12 Do this for each one, for as many as you prepare.

13 " 'Everyone who is native-born must do these things in this way when they present a food offering as an aroma pleasing to the LORD. 14 For the generations to come, whenever a foreigner or anyone else living among you presents a food offering as an aroma pleasing to the LORD, they must do exactly as you do. 15 The community is to have the same rules for you and for the foreigner residing among you; this is a lasting ordinance for the generations to come. You and the foreigner shall be the same before the LORD: 16 The same laws and regulations will apply both to you and to the foreigner residing among you.' "

17 The LORD said to Moses, 18 "Speak to the Israelites and say to them: 'When you enter the land to which I am taking you 19 and you eat the food of the land, present a portion as an offering to the LORD. 20 Present a loaf from the first of your ground meal and present it as an offering from the threshing floor. 21 Throughout the generations to come you are to give this offering to the LORD from the first of your ground meal.

Offerings for Unintentional Sins

22 " 'Now if you as a community unintentionally fail to keep any of these commands the LORD gave Moses — 23 any of the LORD's commands to you through him, from the day the LORD gave them and continuing through the generations to come — 24 and if this is done unintentionally without the community being aware of it, then the whole community is to offer a young bull for a burnt offering as an aroma pleasing to the LORD, along with its prescribed grain offering and drink offering, and a male goat for a sin offering.[g] 25 The priest is to make atonement for the whole Israelite community, and they will be forgiven, for it was not intentional and they have presented to the LORD for their wrong a food offering and a sin offering. 26 The whole Israelite community and the foreigners residing among them will be forgiven, because all the people were involved in the unintentional wrong.

27 " 'But if just one person sins unintentionally, that person must bring a year-old female goat for a sin offering. 28 The priest is to make atonement before the LORD for the one who erred by sinning unintentionally, and when atonement has been made, that person will be forgiven. 29 One and the same law applies to everyone who sins unintentionally, whether a native-born Israelite or a foreigner residing among you.

30 " 'But anyone who sins defiantly,

[a] 4 That is, probably about 3 1/2 pounds or about 1.6 kilograms [b] 4 That is, about 1 quart or about 1 liter; also in verse 5 [c] 6 That is, probably about 7 pounds or about 3.2 kilograms [d] 6 That is, about 1 1/3 quarts or about 1.3 liters; also in verse 7 [e] 9 That is, probably about 11 pounds or about 5 kilograms [f] 9 That is, about 2 quarts or about 1.9 liters; also in verse 10 [g] 24 Or *purification offering*; also in verses 25 and 27

whether native-born or foreigner, blasphemes the LORD and must be cut off
from the people of Israel. 31Because they
have despised the LORD's word and broken his commands, they must surely be
cut off; their guilt remains on them.' "

The Sabbath-Breaker Put to Death

32While the Israelites were in the wilderness, a man was found gathering
wood on the Sabbath day. 33Those who
found him gathering wood brought him
to Moses and Aaron and the whole assembly, 34and they kept him in custody,
because it was not clear what should
be done to him. 35Then the LORD said to
Moses, "The man must die. The whole
assembly must stone him outside the
camp." 36So the assembly took him outside the camp and stoned him to death,
as the LORD commanded Moses.

Tassels on Garments

37The LORD said to Moses, 38"Speak to
the Israelites and say to them: 'Throughout the generations to come you are to
make tassels on the corners of your garments, with a blue cord on each tassel.
39You will have these tassels to look at
and so you will remember all the commands of the LORD, that you may obey
them and not prostitute yourselves
by chasing after the lusts of your own
hearts and eyes. 40Then you will remember to obey all my commands and will be
consecrated to your God. 41I am the LORD
your God, who brought you out of Egypt
to be your God. I am the LORD your God.' "

Korah, Dathan and Abiram

16 Korah son of Izhar, the son of Kohath, the son of Levi, and certain
Reubenites — Dathan and Abiram, sons
of Eliab, and On son of Peleth — became
insolent[a] 2and rose up against Moses.
With them were 250 Israelite men, well-
known community leaders who had
been appointed members of the council.
3They came as a group to oppose Moses
and Aaron and said to them, "You have
gone too far! The whole community is
holy, every one of them, and the LORD
is with them. Why then do you set yourselves above the LORD's assembly?"
4When Moses heard this, he fell facedown. 5Then he said to Korah and all
his followers: "In the morning the LORD
will show who belongs to him and who
is holy, and he will have that person
come near him. The man he chooses he
will cause to come near him. 6You, Korah, and all your followers are to do this:
Take censers 7and tomorrow put burning coals and incense in them before
the LORD. The man the LORD chooses will
be the one who is holy. You Levites have
gone too far!"
8Moses also said to Korah, "Now listen, you Levites! 9Isn't it enough for you
that the God of Israel has separated you
from the rest of the Israelite community and brought you near himself to do
the work at the LORD's tabernacle and to
stand before the community and minister to them? 10He has brought you and
all your fellow Levites near himself, but
now you are trying to get the priesthood
too. 11It is against the LORD that you and
all your followers have banded together.
Who is Aaron that you should grumble
against him?"
12Then Moses summoned Dathan and
Abiram, the sons of Eliab. But they said,
"We will not come! 13Isn't it enough that
you have brought us up out of a land
flowing with milk and honey to kill us in
the wilderness? And now you also want
to lord it over us! 14Moreover, you haven't
brought us into a land flowing with milk
and honey or given us an inheritance
of fields and vineyards. Do you want to
treat these men like slaves[b]? No, we will
not come!"
15Then Moses became very angry and
said to the LORD, "Do not accept their
offering. I have not taken so much as a
donkey from them, nor have I wronged
any of them."
16Moses said to Korah, "You and all
your followers are to appear before the
LORD tomorrow — you and they and
Aaron. 17Each man is to take his censer
and put incense in it — 250 censers in
all — and present it before the LORD. You
and Aaron are to present your censers
also." 18So each of them took his censer,
put burning coals and incense in it, and
stood with Moses and Aaron at the entrance to the tent of meeting. 19When Korah had gathered all his followers in opposition to them at the entrance to the
tent of meeting, the glory of the LORD
appeared to the entire assembly. 20The
LORD said to Moses and Aaron, 21"Separate yourselves from this assembly so I
can put an end to them at once."
22But Moses and Aaron fell facedown
and cried out, "O God, the God who gives

[a] 1 Or *Peleth — took men these men*
[b] 14 Or *to deceive these men*; Hebrew *Will you gouge out the eyes of these men*

breath to all living things, will you be angry with the entire assembly when only one man sins?"

23Then the LORD said to Moses, 24"Say to the assembly, 'Move away from the tents of Korah, Dathan and Abiram.'"

25Moses got up and went to Dathan and Abiram, and the elders of Israel followed him. 26He warned the assembly, "Move back from the tents of these wicked men! Do not touch anything belonging to them, or you will be swept away because of all their sins." 27So they moved away from the tents of Korah, Dathan and Abiram. Dathan and Abiram had come out and were standing with their wives, children and little ones at the entrances to their tents.

28Then Moses said, "This is how you will know that the LORD has sent me to do all these things and that it was not my idea: 29If these men die a natural death and suffer the fate of all mankind, then the LORD has not sent me. 30But if the LORD brings about something totally new, and the earth opens its mouth and swallows them, with everything that belongs to them, and they go down alive into the realm of the dead, then you will know that these men have treated the LORD with contempt."

31As soon as he finished saying all this, the ground under them split apart 32and the earth opened its mouth and swallowed them and their households, and all those associated with Korah, together with their possessions. 33They went down alive into the realm of the dead, with everything they owned; the earth closed over them, and they perished and were gone from the community. 34At their cries, all the Israelites around them fled, shouting, "The earth is going to swallow us too!"

35And fire came out from the LORD and consumed the 250 men who were offering the incense.

36The LORD said to Moses, 37"Tell Eleazar son of Aaron, the priest, to remove the censers from the charred remains and scatter the coals some distance away, for the censers are holy— 38the censers of the men who sinned at the cost of their lives. Hammer the censers into sheets to overlay the altar, for they were presented before the LORD and have become holy. Let them be a sign to the Israelites."

39So Eleazar the priest collected the bronze censers brought by those who had been burned to death, and he had them hammered out to overlay the altar, 40as the LORD directed him through Moses. This was to remind the Israelites that no one except a descendant of Aaron should come to burn incense before the LORD, or he would become like Korah and his followers.

41The next day the whole Israelite community grumbled against Moses and Aaron. "You have killed the LORD's people," they said.

42But when the assembly gathered in opposition to Moses and Aaron and turned toward the tent of meeting, suddenly the cloud covered it and the glory of the LORD appeared. 43Then Moses and Aaron went to the front of the tent of meeting, 44and the LORD said to Moses, 45"Get away from this assembly so I can put an end to them at once." And they fell facedown.

46Then Moses said to Aaron, "Take your censer and put incense in it, along with burning coals from the altar, and hurry to the assembly to make atonement for them. Wrath has come out from the LORD; the plague has started." 47So Aaron did as Moses said, and ran into the midst of the assembly. The plague had already started among the people, but Aaron offered the incense and made atonement for them. 48He stood between the living and the dead, and the plague stopped. 49But 14,700 people died from the plague, in addition to those who had died because of Korah. 50Then Aaron returned to Moses at the entrance to the tent of meeting, for the plague had stopped.[a]

The Budding of Aaron's Staff

17[b] The LORD said to Moses, 2"Speak to the Israelites and get twelve staffs from them, one from the leader of each of their ancestral tribes. Write the name of each man on his staff. 3On the staff of Levi write Aaron's name, for there must be one staff for the head of each ancestral tribe. 4Place them in the tent of meeting in front of the ark of the covenant law, where I meet with you. 5The staff belonging to the man I choose will sprout, and I will rid myself of this constant grumbling against you by the Israelites."

6So Moses spoke to the Israelites, and their leaders gave him twelve staffs, one for the leader of each of their ancestral tribes, and Aaron's staff was among them. 7Moses placed the staffs before the LORD in the tent of the covenant law.

[a] 50 In Hebrew texts 16:36-50 is numbered 17:1-15.

[b] In Hebrew texts 17:1-13 is numbered 17:16-28.

8The next day Moses entered the tent
and saw that Aaron's staff, which represented the tribe of Levi, had not only
sprouted but had budded, blossomed
and produced almonds. 9Then Moses brought out all the staffs from the
LORD's presence to all the Israelites. They
looked at them, and each of the leaders
took his own staff.

10The LORD said to Moses, "Put back
Aaron's staff in front of the ark of the
covenant law, to be kept as a sign to the
rebellious. This will put an end to their
grumbling against me, so that they will
not die." 11Moses did just as the LORD
commanded him.

12The Israelites said to Moses, "We will
die! We are lost, we are all lost! 13Anyone
who even comes near the tabernacle of
the LORD will die. Are we all going to
die?"

Duties of Priests and Levites

18 The LORD said to Aaron, "You, your
sons and your family are to bear
the responsibility for offenses connected with the sanctuary, and you and your
sons alone are to bear the responsibility
for offenses connected with the priesthood. 2Bring your fellow Levites from
your ancestral tribe to join you and assist you when you and your sons minister before the tent of the covenant law.
3They are to be responsible to you and
are to perform all the duties of the tent,
but they must not go near the furnishings of the sanctuary or the altar. Otherwise both they and you will die. 4They
are to join you and be responsible for
the care of the tent of meeting — all the
work at the tent — and no one else may
come near where you are.

5"You are to be responsible for the care
of the sanctuary and the altar, so that
my wrath will not fall on the Israelites
again. 6I myself have selected your fellow Levites from among the Israelites
as a gift to you, dedicated to the LORD
to do the work at the tent of meeting.
7But only you and your sons may serve
as priests in connection with everything
at the altar and inside the curtain. I am
giving you the service of the priesthood
as a gift. Anyone else who comes near
the sanctuary is to be put to death."

Offerings for Priests and Levites

8Then the LORD said to Aaron, "I myself have put you in charge of the offerings presented to me; all the holy offerings the Israelites give me I give to you
and your sons as your portion, your perpetual share. 9You are to have the part of
the most holy offerings that is kept from
the fire. From all the gifts they bring me
as most holy offerings, whether grain or
sin[a] or guilt offerings, that part belongs
to you and your sons. 10Eat it as something most holy; every male shall eat it.
You must regard it as holy.

11"This also is yours: whatever is set
aside from the gifts of all the wave offerings of the Israelites. I give this to
you and your sons and daughters as
your perpetual share. Everyone in your
household who is ceremonially clean
may eat it.

12"I give you all the finest olive oil and
all the finest new wine and grain they
give the LORD as the firstfruits of their
harvest. 13All the land's firstfruits that
they bring to the LORD will be yours. Everyone in your household who is ceremonially clean may eat it.

14"Everything in Israel that is devoted[b]
to the LORD is yours. 15The first offspring
of every womb, both human and animal, that is offered to the LORD is yours.
But you must redeem every firstborn
son and every firstborn male of unclean
animals. 16When they are a month old,
you must redeem them at the redemption price set at five shekels[c] of silver,
according to the sanctuary shekel, which
weighs twenty gerahs.

17"But you must not redeem the firstborn of a cow, a sheep or a goat; they are
holy. Splash their blood against the altar and burn their fat as a food offering,
an aroma pleasing to the LORD. 18Their
meat is to be yours, just as the breast of
the wave offering and the right thigh
are yours. 19Whatever is set aside from
the holy offerings the Israelites present
to the LORD I give to you and your sons
and daughters as your perpetual share.
It is an everlasting covenant of salt before the LORD for both you and your offspring."

20The LORD said to Aaron, "You will
have no inheritance in their land, nor
will you have any share among them;
I am your share and your inheritance
among the Israelites.

21"I give to the Levites all the tithes in
Israel as their inheritance in return for
the work they do while serving at the tent
of meeting. 22From now on the Israelites

[a] *9* Or *purification* [b] *14* The Hebrew term refers to the irrevocable giving over of things or persons to the LORD. [c] *16* That is, about 2 ounces or about 58 grams

must not go near the tent of meeting, or they will bear the consequences of their sin and will die. 23It is the Levites who are to do the work at the tent of meeting and bear the responsibility for any offenses they commit against it. This is a lasting ordinance for the generations to come. They will receive no inheritance among the Israelites. 24Instead, I give to the Levites as their inheritance the tithes that the Israelites present as an offering to the LORD. That is why I said concerning them: 'They will have no inheritance among the Israelites.'"

25The LORD said to Moses, 26"Speak to the Levites and say to them: 'When you receive from the Israelites the tithe I give you as your inheritance, you must present a tenth of that tithe as the LORD's offering. 27Your offering will be reckoned to you as grain from the threshing floor or juice from the winepress. 28In this way you also will present an offering to the LORD from all the tithes you receive from the Israelites. From these tithes you must give the LORD's portion to Aaron the priest. 29You must present as the LORD's portion the best and holiest part of everything given to you.'

30"Say to the Levites: 'When you present the best part, it will be reckoned to you as the product of the threshing floor or the winepress. 31You and your households may eat the rest of it anywhere, for it is your wages for your work at the tent of meeting. 32By presenting the best part of it you will not be guilty in this matter; then you will not defile the holy offerings of the Israelites, and you will not die.'"

The Water of Cleansing

19 The LORD said to Moses and Aaron: 2"This is a requirement of the law that the LORD has commanded: Tell the Israelites to bring you a red heifer without defect or blemish and that has never been under a yoke. 3Give it to Eleazar the priest; it is to be taken outside the camp and slaughtered in his presence. 4Then Eleazar the priest is to take some of its blood on his finger and sprinkle it seven times toward the front of the tent of meeting. 5While he watches, the heifer is to be burned — its hide, flesh, blood and intestines. 6The priest is to take some cedar wood, hyssop and scarlet wool and throw them onto the burning heifer. 7After that, the priest must wash his clothes and bathe himself with water. He may then come into the camp, but he will be ceremonially unclean till evening. 8The man who burns it must also wash his clothes and bathe with water, and he too will be unclean till evening.

9"A man who is clean shall gather up the ashes of the heifer and put them in a ceremonially clean place outside the camp. They are to be kept by the Israelite community for use in the water of cleansing; it is for purification from sin. 10The man who gathers up the ashes of the heifer must also wash his clothes, and he too will be unclean till evening. This will be a lasting ordinance both for the Israelites and for the foreigners residing among them.

11"Whoever touches a human corpse will be unclean for seven days. 12They must purify themselves with the water on the third day and on the seventh day; then they will be clean. But if they do not purify themselves on the third and seventh days, they will not be clean. 13If they fail to purify themselves after touching a human corpse, they defile the LORD's tabernacle. They must be cut off from Israel. Because the water of cleansing has not been sprinkled on them, they are unclean; their uncleanness remains on them.

14"This is the law that applies when a person dies in a tent: Anyone who enters the tent and anyone who is in it will be unclean for seven days, 15and every open container without a lid fastened on it will be unclean.

16"Anyone out in the open who touches someone who has been killed with a sword or someone who has died a natural death, or anyone who touches a human bone or a grave, will be unclean for seven days.

17"For the unclean person, put some ashes from the burned purification offering into a jar and pour fresh water over them. 18Then a man who is ceremonially clean is to take some hyssop, dip it in the water and sprinkle the tent and all the furnishings and the people who were there. He must also sprinkle anyone who has touched a human bone or a grave or anyone who has been killed or anyone who has died a natural death. 19The man who is clean is to sprinkle those who are unclean on the third and seventh days, and on the seventh day he is to purify them. Those who are being cleansed must wash their clothes and bathe with water, and that evening they will be clean. 20But if those who are unclean do not purify themselves, they must be cut off from the community, because they have defiled the sanctuary of the LORD. The water of cleansing has not been sprinkled on them, and they are unclean. [21]This is a lasting ordinance for them.

"The man who sprinkles the water of cleansing must also wash his clothes, and anyone who touches the water of cleansing will be unclean till evening. [22]Anything that an unclean person touches becomes unclean, and anyone who touches it becomes unclean till evening."

Water From the Rock

20 In the first month the whole Israelite community arrived at the Desert of Zin, and they stayed at Kadesh. There Miriam died and was buried.

[2]Now there was no water for the community, and the people gathered in opposition to Moses and Aaron. [3]They quarreled with Moses and said, "If only we had died when our brothers fell dead before the LORD! [4]Why did you bring the LORD's community into this wilderness, that we and our livestock should die here? [5]Why did you bring us up out of Egypt to this terrible place? It has no grain or figs, grapevines or pomegranates. And there is no water to drink!"

[6]Moses and Aaron went from the assembly to the entrance to the tent of meeting and fell facedown, and the glory of the LORD appeared to them. [7]The LORD said to Moses, [8]"Take the staff, and you and your brother Aaron gather the assembly together. Speak to that rock before their eyes and it will pour out its water. You will bring water out of the rock for the community so they and their livestock can drink."

[9]So Moses took the staff from the LORD's presence, just as he commanded him. [10]He and Aaron gathered the assembly together in front of the rock and Moses said to them, "Listen, you rebels, must we bring you water out of this rock?" [11]Then Moses raised his arm and struck the rock twice with his staff. Water gushed out, and the community and their livestock drank.

[12]But the LORD said to Moses and Aaron, "Because you did not trust in me enough to honor me as holy in the sight of the Israelites, you will not bring this community into the land I give them."

[13]These were the waters of Meribah,[a] where the Israelites quarreled with the LORD and where he was proved holy among them.

Edom Denies Israel Passage

[14]Moses sent messengers from Kadesh to the king of Edom, saying:

> "This is what your brother Israel says: You know about all the hardships that have come on us. [15]Our ancestors went down into Egypt, and we lived there many years. The Egyptians mistreated us and our ancestors, [16]but when we cried out to the LORD, he heard our cry and sent an angel and brought us out of Egypt.
>
> "Now we are here at Kadesh, a town on the edge of your territory. [17]Please let us pass through your country. We will not go through any field or vineyard, or drink water from any well. We will travel along the King's Highway and not turn to the right or to the left until we have passed through your territory."

[18]But Edom answered:

> "You may not pass through here; if you try, we will march out and attack you with the sword."

[19]The Israelites replied:

> "We will go along the main road, and if we or our livestock drink any of your water, we will pay for it. We only want to pass through on foot — nothing else."

[20]Again they answered:

> "You may not pass through."

Then Edom came out against them with a large and powerful army. [21]Since Edom refused to let them go through their territory, Israel turned away from them.

The Death of Aaron

[22]The whole Israelite community set out from Kadesh and came to Mount Hor. [23]At Mount Hor, near the border of Edom, the LORD said to Moses and Aaron, [24]"Aaron will be gathered to his people. He will not enter the land I give the Israelites, because both of you rebelled against my command at the waters of Meribah. [25]Get Aaron and his son Eleazar and take them up Mount Hor. [26]Remove Aaron's garments and put them on his son Eleazar, for Aaron will be gathered to his people; he will die there."

[27]Moses did as the LORD commanded: They went up Mount Hor in the sight of

[a] 13 *Meribah* means *quarreling*.

the whole community. 28Moses removed
Aaron's garments and put them on his
son Eleazar. And Aaron died there on
top of the mountain. Then Moses and
Eleazar came down from the mountain, 29and when the whole community
learned that Aaron had died, all the Israelites mourned for him thirty days.

Arad Destroyed

21 When the Canaanite king of Arad,
who lived in the Negev, heard that
Israel was coming along the road to Ath-
arim, he attacked the Israelites and captured some of them. 2Then Israel made
this vow to the LORD: "If you will deliver these people into our hands, we will
totally destroy[a] their cities." 3The LORD
listened to Israel's plea and gave the Canaanites over to them. They completely
destroyed them and their towns; so the
place was named Hormah.[b]

The Bronze Snake

4They traveled from Mount Hor along
the route to the Red Sea,[c] to go around
Edom. But the people grew impatient on
the way; 5they spoke against God and
against Moses, and said, "Why have you
brought us up out of Egypt to die in the
wilderness? There is no bread! There is
no water! And we detest this miserable
food!"

6Then the LORD sent venomous snakes
among them; they bit the people and
many Israelites died. 7The people came
to Moses and said, "We sinned when we
spoke against the LORD and against you.
Pray that the LORD will take the snakes
away from us." So Moses prayed for the
people.

8The LORD said to Moses, "Make a
snake and put it up on a pole; anyone
who is bitten can look at it and live." 9So
Moses made a bronze snake and put it
up on a pole. Then when anyone was bitten by a snake and looked at the bronze
snake, they lived.

The Journey to Moab

10The Israelites moved on and camped
at Oboth. 11Then they set out from Oboth
and camped in Iye Abarim, in the wilderness that faces Moab toward the sunrise.
12From there they moved on and camped
in the Zered Valley. 13They set out from
there and camped alongside the Arnon,
which is in the wilderness extending into
Amorite territory. The Arnon is the border of Moab, between Moab and the Amorites. 14That is why the Book of the Wars
of the LORD says:

". . . Zahab[d] in Suphah and the
ravines,
the Arnon 15and[e] the slopes of the
ravines
that lead to the settlement of Ar
and lie along the border of Moab."

16From there they continued on to Beer,
the well where the LORD said to Moses,
"Gather the people together and I will
give them water."

17Then Israel sang this song:

"Spring up, O well!
Sing about it,
18 about the well that the princes dug,
that the nobles of the people
sank—
the nobles with scepters and
staffs."

Then they went from the wilderness to
Mattanah, 19from Mattanah to Nahaliel, from Nahaliel to Bamoth, 20and from
Bamoth to the valley in Moab where the
top of Pisgah overlooks the wasteland.

Defeat of Sihon and Og

21Israel sent messengers to say to Sihon king of the Amorites:

22"Let us pass through your country. We will not turn aside into any
field or vineyard, or drink water
from any well. We will travel along
the King's Highway until we have
passed through your territory."

23But Sihon would not let Israel pass
through his territory. He mustered his
entire army and marched out into the
wilderness against Israel. When he
reached Jahaz, he fought with Israel.
24Israel, however, put him to the sword
and took over his land from the Arnon
to the Jabbok, but only as far as the Ammonites, because their border was fortified. 25Israel captured all the cities of the
Amorites and occupied them, including
Heshbon and all its surrounding settlements. 26Heshbon was the city of Sihon
king of the Amorites, who had fought
against the former king of Moab and
had taken from him all his land as far
as the Arnon.

[a] 2 The Hebrew term refers to the irrevocable giving over of things or persons to the LORD, often by totally destroying them; also in verse 3. [b] 3 *Hormah* means *destruction.* [c] 4 Or *the Sea of Reeds* [d] 14 Septuagint; Hebrew *Waheb* [e] 14,15 Or *"I have been given from Suphah and the ravines / of the Arnon 15to*

[27]That is why the poets say:

"Come to Heshbon and let it be rebuilt;
let Sihon's city be restored.

28 "Fire went out from Heshbon,
a blaze from the city of Sihon.
It consumed Ar of Moab,
the citizens of Arnon's heights.
29 Woe to you, Moab!
You are destroyed, people of
Chemosh!
He has given up his sons as fugitives
and his daughters as captives
to Sihon king of the Amorites.

30 "But we have overthrown them;
Heshbon's dominion has been
destroyed all the way to Dibon.
We have demolished them as far as
Nophah,
which extends to Medeba."

[31]So Israel settled in the land of the
Amorites.
[32]After Moses had sent spies to Jazer,
the Israelites captured its surrounding
settlements and drove out the Amorites
who were there. [33]Then they turned and
went up along the road toward Bashan,
and Og king of Bashan and his whole
army marched out to meet them in battle at Edrei.
[34]The LORD said to Moses, "Do not be
afraid of him, for I have delivered him
into your hands, along with his whole
army and his land. Do to him what you
did to Sihon king of the Amorites, who
reigned in Heshbon."
[35]So they struck him down, together
with his sons and his whole army, leaving them no survivors. And they took
possession of his land.

Balak Summons Balaam

22 Then the Israelites traveled to the
plains of Moab and camped along
the Jordan across from Jericho.
[2]Now Balak son of Zippor saw all that
Israel had done to the Amorites, [3]and
Moab was terrified because there were
so many people. Indeed, Moab was filled
with dread because of the Israelites.
[4]The Moabites said to the elders of
Midian, "This horde is going to lick up
everything around us, as an ox licks up
the grass of the field."
So Balak son of Zippor, who was king
of Moab at that time, [5]sent messengers
to summon Balaam son of Beor, who
was at Pethor, near the Euphrates River,
in his native land. Balak said:

"A people has come out of Egypt;
they cover the face of the land and
have settled next to me. [6]Now come
and put a curse on these people, because they are too powerful for me.
Perhaps then I will be able to defeat them and drive them out of the
land. For I know that whoever you
bless is blessed, and whoever you
curse is cursed."

[7]The elders of Moab and Midian left,
taking with them the fee for divination.
When they came to Balaam, they told
him what Balak had said.
[8]"Spend the night here," Balaam said
to them, "and I will report back to you
with the answer the LORD gives me." So
the Moabite officials stayed with him.
[9]God came to Balaam and asked,
"Who are these men with you?"
[10]Balaam said to God, "Balak son of
Zippor, king of Moab, sent me this message: [11]'A people that has come out of
Egypt covers the face of the land. Now
come and put a curse on them for me.
Perhaps then I will be able to fight them
and drive them away.'"
[12]But God said to Balaam, "Do not go
with them. You must not put a curse on
those people, because they are blessed."
[13]The next morning Balaam got up
and said to Balak's officials, "Go back to
your own country, for the LORD has refused to let me go with you."
[14]So the Moabite officials returned
to Balak and said, "Balaam refused to
come with us."
[15]Then Balak sent other officials, more
numerous and more distinguished than
the first. [16]They came to Balaam and
said:

"This is what Balak son of Zippor says: Do not let anything keep
you from coming to me, [17]because I
will reward you handsomely and do
whatever you say. Come and put a
curse on these people for me."

[18]But Balaam answered them, "Even if
Balak gave me all the silver and gold in
his palace, I could not do anything great
or small to go beyond the command of
the LORD my God. [19]Now spend the night
here so that I can find out what else the
LORD will tell me."
[20]That night God came to Balaam and
said, "Since these men have come to
summon you, go with them, but do only
what I tell you."

Balaam's Donkey

[21]Balaam got up in the morning, saddled his donkey and went with the Moabite officials. [22]But God was very angry

when he went, and the angel of the LORD
stood in the road to oppose him. Balaam was riding on his donkey, and his
two servants were with him. 23When the
donkey saw the angel of the LORD standing in the road with a drawn sword in his
hand, it turned off the road into a field.
Balaam beat it to get it back on the road.
24Then the angel of the LORD stood in a
narrow path through the vineyards, with
walls on both sides. 25When the donkey
saw the angel of the LORD, it pressed
close to the wall, crushing Balaam's foot
against it. So he beat the donkey again.
26Then the angel of the LORD moved
on ahead and stood in a narrow place
where there was no room to turn, either to the right or to the left. 27When
the donkey saw the angel of the LORD, it
lay down under Balaam, and he was angry and beat it with his staff. 28Then the
LORD opened the donkey's mouth, and
it said to Balaam, "What have I done
to you to make you beat me these three
times?"
29Balaam answered the donkey, "You
have made a fool of me! If only I had a
sword in my hand, I would kill you right
now."
30The donkey said to Balaam, "Am I
not your own donkey, which you have
always ridden, to this day? Have I been
in the habit of doing this to you?"

"No," he said.
31Then the LORD opened Balaam's eyes,
and he saw the angel of the LORD standing in the road with his sword drawn. So
he bowed low and fell facedown.
32The angel of the LORD asked him,
"Why have you beaten your donkey
these three times? I have come here to
oppose you because your path is a reckless one before me.[a] 33The donkey saw
me and turned away from me these
three times. If it had not turned away, I
would certainly have killed you by now,
but I would have spared it."
34Balaam said to the angel of the
LORD, "I have sinned. I did not realize
you were standing in the road to oppose
me. Now if you are displeased, I will go
back."
35The angel of the LORD said to Balaam, "Go with the men, but speak only
what I tell you." So Balaam went with
Balak's officials.
36When Balak heard that Balaam was
coming, he went out to meet him at the
Moabite town on the Arnon border, at
the edge of his territory. 37Balak said to
Balaam, "Did I not send you an urgent
summons? Why didn't you come to me?
Am I really not able to reward you?"
38"Well, I have come to you now," Balaam replied. "But I can't say whatever I
please. I must speak only what God puts
in my mouth."
39Then Balaam went with Balak to
Kiriath Huzoth. 40Balak sacrificed cattle and sheep, and gave some to Balaam
and the officials who were with him.
41The next morning Balak took Balaam
up to Bamoth Baal, and from there he
could see the outskirts of the Israelite
camp.

Balaam's First Message

23 Balaam said, "Build me seven altars here, and prepare seven bulls
and seven rams for me." 2Balak did as
Balaam said, and the two of them offered a bull and a ram on each altar.
3Then Balaam said to Balak, "Stay
here beside your offering while I go
aside. Perhaps the LORD will come to
meet with me. Whatever he reveals to
me I will tell you." Then he went off to a
barren height.
4God met with him, and Balaam said,
"I have prepared seven altars, and on
each altar I have offered a bull and a
ram."
5The LORD put a word in Balaam's
mouth and said, "Go back to Balak and
give him this word."
6So he went back to him and found
him standing beside his offering, with
all the Moabite officials. 7Then Balaam
spoke his message:

"Balak brought me from Aram,
the king of Moab from the eastern
mountains.
'Come,' he said, 'curse Jacob for me;
come, denounce Israel.'
8How can I curse
those whom God has not cursed?
How can I denounce
those whom the LORD has not
denounced?
9From the rocky peaks I see them,
from the heights I view them.
I see a people who live apart
and do not consider themselves
one of the nations.
10Who can count the dust of Jacob
or number even a fourth of Israel?
Let me die the death of the righteous,
and may my final end be like
theirs!"

11Balak said to Balaam, "What have
you done to me? I brought you to curse

[a] 32 The meaning of the Hebrew for this clause is uncertain.

my enemies, but you have done nothing
but bless them!"
12 He answered, "Must I not speak what
the LORD puts in my mouth?"

Balaam's Second Message

13 Then Balak said to him, "Come with
me to another place where you can see
them; you will not see them all but only
the outskirts of their camp. And from
there, curse them for me." 14 So he took
him to the field of Zophim on the top of
Pisgah, and there he built seven altars
and offered a bull and a ram on each
altar.
15 Balaam said to Balak, "Stay here beside your offering while I meet with him
over there."
16 The LORD met with Balaam and put
a word in his mouth and said, "Go back
to Balak and give him this word."
17 So he went to him and found him
standing beside his offering, with the
Moabite officials. Balak asked him,
"What did the LORD say?"
18 Then he spoke his message:

"Arise, Balak, and listen;
hear me, son of Zippor.
19 God is not human, that he should lie,
not a human being, that he should
change his mind.
Does he speak and then not act?
Does he promise and not fulfill?
20 I have received a command to bless;
he has blessed, and I cannot
change it.

21 "No misfortune is seen in Jacob,
no misery observed[a] in Israel.
The LORD their God is with them;
the shout of the King is among
them.
22 God brought them out of Egypt;
they have the strength of a wild ox.
23 There is no divination against[b] Jacob,
no evil omens against[b] Israel.
It will now be said of Jacob
and of Israel, 'See what God has
done!'
24 The people rise like a lioness;
they rouse themselves like a lion
that does not rest till it devours its
prey
and drinks the blood of its
victims."

25 Then Balak said to Balaam, "Neither
curse them at all nor bless them at all!"
26 Balaam answered, "Did I not tell you
I must do whatever the LORD says?"

Balaam's Third Message

27 Then Balak said to Balaam, "Come,
let me take you to another place. Perhaps it will please God to let you curse
them for me from there." 28 And Balak
took Balaam to the top of Peor, overlooking the wasteland.
29 Balaam said, "Build me seven altars
here, and prepare seven bulls and sev-
en rams for me." 30 Balak did as Balaam
had said, and offered a bull and a ram
on each altar.

24 Now when Balaam saw that it
pleased the LORD to bless Israel,
he did not resort to divination as at other times, but turned his face toward the
wilderness. 2 When Balaam looked out
and saw Israel encamped tribe by tribe,
the Spirit of God came on him 3 and he
spoke his message:

"The prophecy of Balaam son of Beor,
the prophecy of one whose eye sees
clearly,
4 the prophecy of one who hears the
words of God,
who sees a vision from the
Almighty,[c]
who falls prostrate, and whose eyes
are opened:

5 "How beautiful are your tents, Jacob,
your dwelling places, Israel!

6 "Like valleys they spread out,
like gardens beside a river,
like aloes planted by the LORD,
like cedars beside the waters.
7 Water will flow from their buckets;
their seed will have abundant
water.

"Their king will be greater than Agag;
their kingdom will be exalted.

8 "God brought them out of Egypt;
they have the strength of a wild ox.
They devour hostile nations
and break their bones in pieces;
with their arrows they pierce them.
9 Like a lion they crouch and lie down,
like a lioness — who dares to rouse
them?

"May those who bless you be blessed
and those who curse you be
cursed!"

10 Then Balak's anger burned against
Balaam. He struck his hands together
and said to him, "I summoned you to
curse my enemies, but you have blessed
them these three times. 11 Now leave at

[a] *21* Or *He has not looked on Jacob's offenses / or on the wrongs found* [b] *23* Or *in* [c] *4* Hebrew *Shaddai;* also in verse 16

once and go home! I said I would reward
you handsomely, but the LORD has kept
you from being rewarded."
12 Balaam answered Balak, "Did I not
tell the messengers you sent me, 13 'Even
if Balak gave me all the silver and gold
in his palace, I could not do anything of
my own accord, good or bad, to go beyond the command of the LORD — and
I must say only what the LORD says'?
14 Now I am going back to my people,
but come, let me warn you of what this
people will do to your people in days to
come."

Balaam's Fourth Message

15 Then he spoke his message:

"The prophecy of Balaam son of Beor,
  the prophecy of one whose eye sees
    clearly,
16 the prophecy of one who hears the
    words of God,
  who has knowledge from the Most
    High,
who sees a vision from the Almighty,
  who falls prostrate, and whose eyes
    are opened:

17 "I see him, but not now;
  I behold him, but not near.
A star will come out of Jacob;
  a scepter will rise out of Israel.
He will crush the foreheads of Moab,
  the skulls[a] of[b] all the people of
    Sheth.[c]
18 Edom will be conquered;
  Seir, his enemy, will be conquered,
  but Israel will grow strong.
19 A ruler will come out of Jacob
  and destroy the survivors of the
    city."

Balaam's Fifth Message

20 Then Balaam saw Amalek and spoke
his message:

"Amalek was first among the nations,
  but their end will be utter
    destruction."

Balaam's Sixth Message

21 Then he saw the Kenites and spoke
his message:

"Your dwelling place is secure,
  your nest is set in a rock;
22 yet you Kenites will be destroyed
  when Ashur takes you captive."

Balaam's Seventh Message

23 Then he spoke his message:

"Alas! Who can live when God does
    this?[d]
24 Ships will come from the shores of
    Cyprus;
they will subdue Ashur and Eber,
  but they too will come to ruin."

25 Then Balaam got up and returned
home, and Balak went his own way.

Moab Seduces Israel

25 While Israel was staying in
Shittim, the men began to indulge
in sexual immorality with Moabite
women, 2 who invited them to the sacrifices to their gods. The people ate the
sacrificial meal and bowed down before
these gods. 3 So Israel yoked themselves
to the Baal of Peor. And the LORD's anger
burned against them.
4 The LORD said to Moses, "Take all the
leaders of these people, kill them and
expose them in broad daylight before
the LORD, so that the LORD's fierce anger
may turn away from Israel."
5 So Moses said to Israel's judges, "Each
of you must put to death those of your
people who have yoked themselves to
the Baal of Peor."
6 Then an Israelite man brought into
the camp a Midianite woman right before
the eyes of Moses and the whole assembly
of Israel while they were weeping at the
entrance to the tent of meeting. 7 When
Phinehas son of Eleazar, the son of Aaron,
the priest, saw this, he left the assembly,
took a spear in his hand 8 and followed
the Israelite into the tent. He drove the
spear into both of them, right through
the Israelite man and into the woman's
stomach. Then the plague against the Israelites was stopped; 9 but those who died
in the plague numbered 24,000.
10 The LORD said to Moses, 11 "Phinehas son of Eleazar, the son of Aaron, the
priest, has turned my anger away from
the Israelites. Since he was as zealous for
my honor among them as I am, I did not
put an end to them in my zeal. 12 Therefore tell him I am making my covenant
of peace with him. 13 He and his descendants will have a covenant of a lasting
priesthood, because he was zealous for
the honor of his God and made atonement for the Israelites."

[a] 17 Samaritan Pentateuch (see also Jer. 48:45); the meaning of the word in the Masoretic Text is uncertain. [b] 17 Or possibly *Moab, / batter* [c] 17 Or *all the noisy boasters* [d] 23 Masoretic Text; with a different word division of the Hebrew *The people from the islands will gather from the north.*

14The name of the Israelite who was
killed with the Midianite woman was
Zimri son of Salu, the leader of a Sime-
onite family. 15And the name of the Midianite woman who was put to death was
Kozbi daughter of Zur, a tribal chief of a
Midianite family.

16The LORD said to Moses, 17"Treat the
Midianites as enemies and kill them.
18They treated you as enemies when they
deceived you in the Peor incident involving their sister Kozbi, the daughter of a
Midianite leader, the woman who was
killed when the plague came as a result
of that incident."

The Second Census

26 After the plague the LORD said to
Moses and Eleazar son of Aaron,
the priest, 2"Take a census of the whole
Israelite community by families — all
those twenty years old or more who are
able to serve in the army of Israel." 3So
on the plains of Moab by the Jordan
across from Jericho, Moses and Eleazar
the priest spoke with them and said,
4"Take a census of the men twenty years
old or more, as the LORD commanded
Moses."

These were the Israelites who came out of Egypt:

5The descendants of Reuben, the firstborn son of Israel, were:
through Hanok, the Hanokite clan;
through Pallu, the Palluite clan;
6through Hezron, the Hezronite clan;
through Karmi, the Karmite clan.
7These were the clans of Reuben; those numbered were 43,730.

8The son of Pallu was Eliab, 9and the
sons of Eliab were Nemuel, Dathan and
Abiram. The same Dathan and Abiram
were the community officials who rebelled against Moses and Aaron and
were among Korah's followers when
they rebelled against the LORD. 10The
earth opened its mouth and swallowed
them along with Korah, whose followers died when the fire devoured the 250
men. And they served as a warning sign.
11The line of Korah, however, did not die
out.

12The descendants of Simeon by their clans were:
through Nemuel, the Nemuelite clan;
through Jamin, the Jaminite clan;
through Jakin, the Jakinite clan;
13through Zerah, the Zerahite clan;
through Shaul, the Shaulite clan.
14These were the clans of Simeon; those numbered were 22,200.

15The descendants of Gad by their clans were:
through Zephon, the Zephonite clan;
through Haggi, the Haggite clan;
through Shuni, the Shunite clan;
16through Ozni, the Oznite clan;
through Eri, the Erite clan;
17through Arodi,[a] the Arodite clan;
through Areli, the Arelite clan.
18These were the clans of Gad; those numbered were 40,500.

19Er and Onan were sons of Judah, but they died in Canaan.
20The descendants of Judah by their clans were:
through Shelah, the Shelanite clan;
through Perez, the Perezite clan;
through Zerah, the Zerahite clan.
21The descendants of Perez were:
through Hezron, the Hezronite clan;
through Hamul, the Hamulite clan.
22These were the clans of Judah; those numbered were 76,500.

23The descendants of Issachar by their clans were:
through Tola, the Tolaite clan;
through Puah, the Puite[b] clan;
24through Jashub, the Jashubite clan;
through Shimron, the Shimronite clan.
25These were the clans of Issachar; those numbered were 64,300.

26The descendants of Zebulun by their clans were:
through Sered, the Seredite clan;
through Elon, the Elonite clan;
through Jahleel, the Jahleelite clan.
27These were the clans of Zebulun; those numbered were 60,500.

28The descendants of Joseph by their clans through Manasseh and Ephraim were:

29The descendants of Manasseh:
through Makir, the Makirite clan (Makir was the father of Gilead);
through Gilead, the Gileadite clan.
30These were the descendants of Gilead:
through Iezer, the Iezerite clan;
through Helek, the Helekite clan;

[a] 17 Samaritan Pentateuch and Syriac (see also Gen. 46:16); Masoretic Text *Arod*
[b] 23 Samaritan Pentateuch, Septuagint, Vulgate and Syriac (see also 1 Chron. 7:1); Masoretic Text *through Puvah, the Punite*

31 through Asriel, the Asrielite clan;
through Shechem, the Shechemite clan;
32 through Shemida, the Shemidaite clan;
through Hepher, the Hepherite clan.
33 (Zelophehad son of Hepher had no sons; he had only daughters, whose names were Mahlah, Noah, Hoglah, Milkah and Tirzah.)
34 These were the clans of Manasseh; those numbered were 52,700.

35 These were the descendants of Ephraim by their clans:
through Shuthelah, the Shuthelahite clan;
through Beker, the Bekerite clan;
through Tahan, the Tahanite clan.
36 These were the descendants of Shuthelah:
through Eran, the Eranite clan.
37 These were the clans of Ephraim; those numbered were 32,500.

These were the descendants of Joseph by their clans.

38 The descendants of Benjamin by their clans were:
through Bela, the Belaite clan;
through Ashbel, the Ashbelite clan;
through Ahiram, the Ahiramite clan;
39 through Shupham,[a] the Shuphamite clan;
through Hupham, the Huphamite clan.
40 The descendants of Bela through Ard and Naaman were:
through Ard,[b] the Ardite clan;
through Naaman, the Naamite clan.
41 These were the clans of Benjamin; those numbered were 45,600.

42 These were the descendants of Dan by their clans:
through Shuham, the Shuhamite clan.
These were the clans of Dan: 43 All of them were Shuhamite clans; and those numbered were 64,400.

44 The descendants of Asher by their clans were:
through Imnah, the Imnite clan;
through Ishvi, the Ishvite clan;
through Beriah, the Beriite clan;
45 and through the descendants of Beriah:
through Heber, the Heberite clan;
through Malkiel, the Malkielite clan.
46 (Asher had a daughter named Serah.)
47 These were the clans of Asher; those numbered were 53,400.

48 The descendants of Naphtali by their clans were:
through Jahzeel, the Jahzeelite clan;
through Guni, the Gunite clan;
49 through Jezer, the Jezerite clan;
through Shillem, the Shillemite clan.
50 These were the clans of Naphtali; those numbered were 45,400.

51 The total number of the men of Israel was 601,730.

52 The LORD said to Moses, 53 "The land
is to be allotted to them as an inheritance based on the number of names.
54 To a larger group give a larger inheritance, and to a smaller group a smaller one; each is to receive its inheritance
according to the number of those listed.
55 Be sure that the land is distributed by
lot. What each group inherits will be according to the names for its ancestral
tribe. 56 Each inheritance is to be distributed by lot among the larger and smaller groups."

57 These were the Levites who were counted by their clans:
through Gershon, the Gershonite clan;
through Kohath, the Kohathite clan;
through Merari, the Merarite clan.
58 These also were Levite clans:
the Libnite clan,
the Hebronite clan,
the Mahlite clan,
the Mushite clan,
the Korahite clan.
(Kohath was the forefather of Amram; 59 the name of Amram's wife
was Jochebed, a descendant of
Levi, who was born to the Levites[c]
in Egypt. To Amram she bore Aaron, Moses and their sister Miriam.
60 Aaron was the father of Nadab
and Abihu, Eleazar and Ithamar.

[a] 39 A few manuscripts of the Masoretic Text, Samaritan Pentateuch, Vulgate and Syriac (see also Septuagint); most manuscripts of the Masoretic Text *Shephupham* [b] 40 Samaritan Pentateuch and Vulgate (see also Septuagint); Masoretic Text does not have *through Ard.*
[c] 59 Or *Jochebed, a daughter of Levi, who was born to Levi*

61 But Nadab and Abihu died when they made an offering before the LORD with unauthorized fire.)

62 All the male Levites a month old or more numbered 23,000. They were not counted along with the other Israelites because they received no inheritance among them.

63 These are the ones counted by Moses and Eleazar the priest when they counted the Israelites on the plains of Moab by the Jordan across from Jericho. 64 Not one of them was among those counted by Moses and Aaron the priest when they counted the Israelites in the Desert of Sinai. 65 For the LORD had told those Israelites they would surely die in the wilderness, and not one of them was left except Caleb son of Jephunneh and Joshua son of Nun.

Zelophehad's Daughters

27 The daughters of Zelophehad son of Hepher, the son of Gilead, the son of Makir, the son of Manasseh, belonged to the clans of Manasseh son of Joseph. The names of the daughters were Mahlah, Noah, Hoglah, Milkah and Tirzah. They came forward 2 and stood before Moses, Eleazar the priest, the leaders and the whole assembly at the entrance to the tent of meeting and said, 3 "Our father died in the wilderness. He was not among Korah's followers, who banded together against the LORD, but he died for his own sin and left no sons. 4 Why should our father's name disappear from his clan because he had no son? Give us property among our father's relatives."

5 So Moses brought their case before the LORD, 6 and the LORD said to him, 7 "What Zelophehad's daughters are saying is right. You must certainly give them property as an inheritance among their father's relatives and give their father's inheritance to them.

8 "Say to the Israelites, 'If a man dies and leaves no son, give his inheritance to his daughter. 9 If he has no daughter, give his inheritance to his brothers. 10 If he has no brothers, give his inheritance to his father's brothers. 11 If his father had no brothers, give his inheritance to the nearest relative in his clan, that he may possess it. This is to have the force of law for the Israelites, as the LORD commanded Moses.' "

Joshua to Succeed Moses

12 Then the LORD said to Moses, "Go up this mountain in the Abarim Range and see the land I have given the Israelites. 13 After you have seen it, you too will be gathered to your people, as your brother Aaron was, 14 for when the community rebelled at the waters in the Desert of Zin, both of you disobeyed my command to honor me as holy before their eyes." (These were the waters of Meribah Kadesh, in the Desert of Zin.)

15 Moses said to the LORD, 16 "May the LORD, the God who gives breath to all living things, appoint someone over this community 17 to go out and come in before them, one who will lead them out and bring them in, so the LORD's people will not be like sheep without a shepherd."

18 So the LORD said to Moses, "Take Joshua son of Nun, a man in whom is the spirit of leadership,[a] and lay your hand on him. 19 Have him stand before Eleazar the priest and the entire assembly and commission him in their presence. 20 Give him some of your authority so the whole Israelite community will obey him. 21 He is to stand before Eleazar the priest, who will obtain decisions for him by inquiring of the Urim before the LORD. At his command he and the entire community of the Israelites will go out, and at his command they will come in."

22 Moses did as the LORD commanded him. He took Joshua and had him stand before Eleazar the priest and the whole assembly. 23 Then he laid his hands on him and commissioned him, as the LORD instructed through Moses.

Daily Offerings

28 The LORD said to Moses, 2 "Give this command to the Israelites and say to them: 'Make sure that you present to me at the appointed time my food offerings, as an aroma pleasing to me.' 3 Say to them: 'This is the food offering you are to present to the LORD: two lambs a year old without defect, as a regular burnt offering each day. 4 Offer one lamb in the morning and the other at twilight, 5 together with a grain offering of a tenth of an ephah[b] of the finest flour mixed with a quarter of a hin[c] of oil from pressed olives. 6 This is the regular burnt offering instituted at Mount Sinai as a pleasing aroma, a food offering presented to the LORD. 7 The accompanying

[a] *18* Or *the Spirit* [b] *5* That is, probably about 3 1/2 pounds or about 1.6 kilograms; also in verses 13, 21 and 29 [c] *5* That is, about 1 quart or about 1 liter; also in verses 7 and 14

drink offering is to be a quarter of a hin of fermented drink with each lamb. Pour out the drink offering to the LORD at the sanctuary. 8Offer the second lamb at twilight, along with the same kind of grain offering and drink offering that you offer in the morning. This is a food offering, an aroma pleasing to the LORD.

Sabbath Offerings

9" 'On the Sabbath day, make an offering of two lambs a year old without defect, together with its drink offering and a grain offering of two-tenths of an ephah[a] of the finest flour mixed with olive oil. 10This is the burnt offering for every Sabbath, in addition to the regular burnt offering and its drink offering.

Monthly Offerings

11" 'On the first of every month, present to the LORD a burnt offering of two young bulls, one ram and seven male lambs a year old, all without defect. 12With each bull there is to be a grain offering of three-tenths of an ephah[b] of the finest flour mixed with oil; with the ram, a grain offering of two-tenths of an ephah of the finest flour mixed with oil; 13and with each lamb, a grain offering of a tenth of an ephah of the finest flour mixed with oil. This is for a burnt offering, a pleasing aroma, a food offering presented to the LORD. 14With each bull there is to be a drink offering of half a hin[c] of wine; with the ram, a third of a hin[d]; and with each lamb, a quarter of a hin. This is the monthly burnt offering to be made at each new moon during the year. 15Besides the regular burnt offering with its drink offering, one male goat is to be presented to the LORD as a sin offering.[e]

The Passover

16" 'On the fourteenth day of the first month the LORD's Passover is to be held. 17On the fifteenth day of this month there is to be a festival; for seven days eat bread made without yeast. 18On the first day hold a sacred assembly and do no regular work. 19Present to the LORD a food offering consisting of a burnt offering of two young bulls, one ram and seven male lambs a year old, all without defect. 20With each bull offer a grain offering of three-tenths of an ephah of the finest flour mixed with oil; with the ram, two-tenths; 21and with each of the seven lambs, one-tenth. 22Include one male goat as a sin offering to make atonement for you. 23Offer these in addition to the regular morning burnt offering. 24In this way present the food offering every day for seven days as an aroma pleasing to the LORD; it is to be offered in addition to the regular burnt offering and its drink offering. 25On the seventh day hold a sacred assembly and do no regular work.

The Festival of Weeks

26" 'On the day of firstfruits, when you present to the LORD an offering of new grain during the Festival of Weeks, hold a sacred assembly and do no regular work. 27Present a burnt offering of two young bulls, one ram and seven male lambs a year old as an aroma pleasing to the LORD. 28With each bull there is to be a grain offering of three-tenths of an ephah of the finest flour mixed with oil; with the ram, two-tenths; 29and with each of the seven lambs, one-tenth. 30Include one male goat to make atonement for you. 31Offer these together with their drink offerings, in addition to the regular burnt offering and its grain offering. Be sure the animals are without defect.

The Festival of Trumpets

29 " 'On the first day of the seventh month hold a sacred assembly and do no regular work. It is a day for you to sound the trumpets. 2As an aroma pleasing to the LORD, offer a burnt offering of one young bull, one ram and seven male lambs a year old, all without defect. 3With the bull offer a grain offering of three-tenths of an ephah[f] of the finest flour mixed with olive oil; with the ram, two-tenths[g]; 4and with each of the seven lambs, one-tenth.[h] 5Include one male goat as a sin offering[i] to make atonement for you. 6These are in addition to the monthly and daily burnt offerings with their grain offerings and drink offerings as specified. They are food offerings presented to the LORD, a pleasing aroma.

[a] *9* That is, probably about 7 pounds or about 3.2 kilograms; also in verses 12, 20 and 28
[b] *12* That is, probably about 11 pounds or about 5 kilograms; also in verses 20 and 28
[c] *14* That is, about 2 quarts or about 1.9 liters
[d] *14* That is, about 1 1/3 quarts or about 1.3 liters
[e] *15* Or *purification offering*; also in verse 22
[f] *3* That is, probably about 11 pounds or about 5 kilograms; also in verses 9 and 14
[g] *3* That is, probably about 7 pounds or about 3.2 kilograms; also in verses 9 and 14
[h] *4* That is, probably about 3 1/2 pounds or about 1.6 kilograms; also in verses 10 and 15
[i] *5* Or *purification offering*; also elsewhere in this chapter

The Day of Atonement

7“ ‘On the tenth day of this seventh
month hold a sacred assembly. You must
deny yourselves[a] and do no work. 8Pre-
sent as an aroma pleasing to the LORD
a burnt offering of one young bull, one
ram and seven male lambs a year old,
all without defect. 9With the bull offer
a grain offering of three-tenths of an
ephah of the finest flour mixed with oil;
with the ram, two-tenths; 10and with
each of the seven lambs, one-tenth. 11In-
clude one male goat as a sin offering, in
addition to the sin offering for atonement and the regular burnt offering
with its grain offering, and their drink
offerings.

The Festival of Tabernacles

12“ ‘On the fifteenth day of the seventh
month, hold a sacred assembly and do
no regular work. Celebrate a festival to
the LORD for seven days. 13Present as an
aroma pleasing to the LORD a food offering consisting of a burnt offering of thirteen young bulls, two rams and fourteen
male lambs a year old, all without defect. 14With each of the thirteen bulls offer a grain offering of three-tenths of an
ephah of the finest flour mixed with oil;
with each of the two rams, two-tenths;
15and with each of the fourteen lambs,
one-tenth. 16Include one male goat as
a sin offering, in addition to the regular burnt offering with its grain offering
and drink offering.

17“ ‘On the second day offer twelve
young bulls, two rams and fourteen
male lambs a year old, all without defect. 18With the bulls, rams and lambs,
offer their grain offerings and drink offerings according to the number specified. 19Include one male goat as a sin offering, in addition to the regular burnt
offering with its grain offering, and their
drink offerings.

20“ ‘On the third day offer eleven bulls,
two rams and fourteen male lambs a
year old, all without defect. 21With the
bulls, rams and lambs, offer their grain
offerings and drink offerings according
to the number specified. 22Include one
male goat as a sin offering, in addition
to the regular burnt offering with its
grain offering and drink offering.

23“ ‘On the fourth day offer ten bulls,
two rams and fourteen male lambs a
year old, all without defect. 24With the
bulls, rams and lambs, offer their grain
offerings and drink offerings according
to the number specified. 25Include one
male goat as a sin offering, in addition
to the regular burnt offering with its
grain offering and drink offering.

26“ ‘On the fifth day offer nine bulls,
two rams and fourteen male lambs a
year old, all without defect. 27With the
bulls, rams and lambs, offer their grain
offerings and drink offerings according
to the number specified. 28Include one
male goat as a sin offering, in addition
to the regular burnt offering with its
grain offering and drink offering.

29“ ‘On the sixth day offer eight bulls,
two rams and fourteen male lambs a
year old, all without defect. 30With the
bulls, rams and lambs, offer their grain
offerings and drink offerings according
to the number specified. 31Include one
male goat as a sin offering, in addition
to the regular burnt offering with its
grain offering and drink offering.

32“ ‘On the seventh day offer seven
bulls, two rams and fourteen male lambs
a year old, all without defect. 33With the
bulls, rams and lambs, offer their grain
offerings and drink offerings according
to the number specified. 34Include one
male goat as a sin offering, in addition
to the regular burnt offering with its
grain offering and drink offering.

35“ ‘On the eighth day hold a closing
special assembly and do no regular
work. 36Present as an aroma pleasing to
the LORD a food offering consisting of a
burnt offering of one bull, one ram and
seven male lambs a year old, all without
defect. 37With the bull, the ram and the
lambs, offer their grain offerings and
drink offerings according to the number
specified. 38Include one male goat as a
sin offering, in addition to the regular
burnt offering with its grain offering
and drink offering.

39“ ‘In addition to what you vow and
your freewill offerings, offer these to the
LORD at your appointed festivals: your
burnt offerings, grain offerings, drink
offerings and fellowship offerings.’ ”

40Moses told the Israelites all that the
LORD commanded him.[b]

Vows

30[c] Moses said to the heads of the
tribes of Israel: “This is what the
LORD commands: 2When a man makes a
vow to the LORD or takes an oath to ob-
ligate himself by a pledge, he must not

[a] 7 Or *must fast* [b] *40* In Hebrew texts this verse (29:40) is numbered 30:1. [c] In Hebrew texts 30:1-16 is numbered 30:2-17.

break his word but must do everything he said.

3"When a young woman still living in her father's household makes a vow to the LORD or obligates herself by a pledge 4and her father hears about her vow or pledge but says nothing to her, then all her vows and every pledge by which she obligated herself will stand. 5But if her father forbids her when he hears about it, none of her vows or the pledges by which she obligated herself will stand; the LORD will release her because her father has forbidden her.

6"If she marries after she makes a vow or after her lips utter a rash promise by which she obligates herself 7and her husband hears about it but says nothing to her, then her vows or the pledges by which she obligated herself will stand. 8But if her husband forbids her when he hears about it, he nullifies the vow that obligates her or the rash promise by which she obligates herself, and the LORD will release her.

9"Any vow or obligation taken by a widow or divorced woman will be binding on her.

10"If a woman living with her husband makes a vow or obligates herself by a pledge under oath 11and her husband hears about it but says nothing to her and does not forbid her, then all her vows or the pledges by which she obligated herself will stand. 12But if her husband nullifies them when he hears about them, then none of the vows or pledges that came from her lips will stand. Her husband has nullified them, and the LORD will release her. 13Her husband may confirm or nullify any vow she makes or any sworn pledge to deny herself.[a] 14But if her husband says nothing to her about it from day to day, then he confirms all her vows or the pledges binding on her. He confirms them by saying nothing to her when he hears about them. 15If, however, he nullifies them some time after he hears about them, then he must bear the consequences of her wrongdoing."

16These are the regulations the LORD gave Moses concerning relationships between a man and his wife, and between a father and his young daughter still living at home.

Vengeance on the Midianites

31 The LORD said to Moses, 2"Take vengeance on the Midianites for the Israelites. After that, you will be gathered to your people."

3So Moses said to the people, "Arm some of your men to go to war against the Midianites so that they may carry out the LORD's vengeance on them. 4Send into battle a thousand men from each of the tribes of Israel." 5So twelve thousand men armed for battle, a thousand from each tribe, were supplied from the clans of Israel. 6Moses sent them into battle, a thousand from each tribe, along with Phinehas son of Eleazar, the priest, who took with him articles from the sanctuary and the trumpets for signaling.

7They fought against Midian, as the LORD commanded Moses, and killed every man. 8Among their victims were Evi, Rekem, Zur, Hur and Reba — the five kings of Midian. They also killed Balaam son of Beor with the sword. 9The Israelites captured the Midianite women and children and took all the Midianite herds, flocks and goods as plunder. 10They burned all the towns where the Midianites had settled, as well as all their camps. 11They took all the plunder and spoils, including the people and animals, 12and brought the captives, spoils and plunder to Moses and Eleazar the priest and the Israelite assembly at their camp on the plains of Moab, by the Jordan across from Jericho.

13Moses, Eleazar the priest and all the leaders of the community went to meet them outside the camp. 14Moses was angry with the officers of the army — the commanders of thousands and commanders of hundreds — who returned from the battle.

15"Have you allowed all the women to live?" he asked them. 16"They were the ones who followed Balaam's advice and enticed the Israelites to be unfaithful to the LORD in the Peor incident, so that a plague struck the LORD's people. 17Now kill all the boys. And kill every woman who has slept with a man, 18but save for yourselves every girl who has never slept with a man.

19"Anyone who has killed someone or touched someone who was killed must stay outside the camp seven days. On the third and seventh days you must purify yourselves and your captives. 20Purify every garment as well as everything made of leather, goat hair or wood."

21Then Eleazar the priest said to the soldiers who had gone into battle, "This is what is required by the law that the LORD gave Moses: 22Gold, silver, bronze, iron, tin, lead 23and anything else that can withstand fire must be put through

[a] 13 Or *to fast*

the fire, and then it will be clean. But it must also be purified with the water of cleansing. And whatever cannot withstand fire must be put through that water. 24On the seventh day wash your clothes and you will be clean. Then you may come into the camp."

Dividing the Spoils

25The LORD said to Moses, 26"You and Eleazar the priest and the family heads of the community are to count all the people and animals that were captured. 27Divide the spoils equally between the soldiers who took part in the battle and the rest of the community. 28From the soldiers who fought in the battle, set apart as tribute for the LORD one out of every five hundred, whether people, cattle, donkeys or sheep. 29Take this tribute from their half share and give it to Eleazar the priest as the LORD's part. 30From the Israelites' half, select one out of every fifty, whether people, cattle, donkeys, sheep or other animals. Give them to the Levites, who are responsible for the care of the LORD's tabernacle." 31So Moses and Eleazar the priest did as the LORD commanded Moses.

32The plunder remaining from the spoils that the soldiers took was 675,000 sheep, 3372,000 cattle, 3461,000 donkeys 35and 32,000 women who had never slept with a man.

36The half share of those who fought in the battle was:

337,500 sheep, 37of which the tribute for the LORD was 675;
3836,000 cattle, of which the tribute for the LORD was 72;
3930,500 donkeys, of which the tribute for the LORD was 61;
4016,000 people, of whom the tribute for the LORD was 32.

41Moses gave the tribute to Eleazar the priest as the LORD's part, as the LORD commanded Moses.

42The half belonging to the Israelites, which Moses set apart from that of the fighting men — 43the community's half — was 337,500 sheep, 4436,000 cattle, 4530,500 donkeys 46and 16,000 people. 47From the Israelites' half, Moses selected one out of every fifty people and animals, as the LORD commanded him, and gave them to the Levites, who were responsible for the care of the LORD's tabernacle.

48Then the officers who were over the units of the army — the commanders of thousands and commanders of hundreds — went to Moses 49and said to him, "Your servants have counted the soldiers under our command, and not one is missing. 50So we have brought as an offering to the LORD the gold articles each of us acquired — armlets, bracelets, signet rings, earrings and necklaces — to make atonement for ourselves before the LORD."

51Moses and Eleazar the priest accepted from them the gold — all the crafted articles. 52All the gold from the commanders of thousands and commanders of hundreds that Moses and Eleazar presented as a gift to the LORD weighed 16,750 shekels.[a] 53Each soldier had taken plunder for himself. 54Moses and Eleazar the priest accepted the gold from the commanders of thousands and commanders of hundreds and brought it into the tent of meeting as a memorial for the Israelites before the LORD.

The Transjordan Tribes

32 The Reubenites and Gadites, who had very large herds and flocks, saw that the lands of Jazer and Gilead were suitable for livestock. 2So they came to Moses and Eleazar the priest and to the leaders of the community, and said, 3"Ataroth, Dibon, Jazer, Nimrah, Heshbon, Elealeh, Sebam, Nebo and Beon — 4the land the LORD subdued before the people of Israel — are suitable for livestock, and your servants have livestock. 5If we have found favor in your eyes," they said, "let this land be given to your servants as our possession. Do not make us cross the Jordan."

6Moses said to the Gadites and Reubenites, "Should your fellow Israelites go to war while you sit here? 7Why do you discourage the Israelites from crossing over into the land the LORD has given them? 8This is what your fathers did when I sent them from Kadesh Barnea to look over the land. 9After they went up to the Valley of Eshkol and viewed the land, they discouraged the Israelites from entering the land the LORD had given them. 10The LORD's anger was aroused that day and he swore this oath: 11'Because they have not followed me wholeheartedly, not one of those who were twenty years old or more when they came up out of Egypt will see the land I promised on oath to Abraham, Isaac and Jacob — 12not one except Caleb son of Jephunneh

[a] *52* That is, about 420 pounds or about 190 kilograms

the Kenizzite and Joshua son of Nun, for
they followed the LORD wholeheartedly.'
13The LORD's anger burned against Israel
and he made them wander in the wilderness forty years, until the whole generation of those who had done evil in his
sight was gone.
14"And here you are, a brood of sinners,
standing in the place of your fathers and
making the LORD even more angry with
Israel. 15If you turn away from following
him, he will again leave all this people in
the wilderness, and you will be the cause
of their destruction."
16Then they came up to him and said,
"We would like to build pens here for our
livestock and cities for our women and
children. 17But we will arm ourselves
for battle[a] and go ahead of the Israelites until we have brought them to their
place. Meanwhile our women and children will live in fortified cities, for protection from the inhabitants of the land.
18We will not return to our homes until
each of the Israelites has received their
inheritance. 19We will not receive any
inheritance with them on the other side
of the Jordan, because our inheritance
has come to us on the east side of the
Jordan."
20Then Moses said to them, "If you
will do this — if you will arm yourselves
before the LORD for battle 21and if all of
you who are armed cross over the Jordan
before the LORD until he has driven his
enemies out before him — 22then when
the land is subdued before the LORD, you
may return and be free from your obligation to the LORD and to Israel. And
this land will be your possession before
the LORD.
23"But if you fail to do this, you will be
sinning against the LORD; and you may
be sure that your sin will find you out.
24Build cities for your women and children, and pens for your flocks, but do
what you have promised."
25The Gadites and Reubenites said
to Moses, "We your servants will do as
our lord commands. 26Our children and
wives, our flocks and herds will remain
here in the cities of Gilead. 27But your
servants, every man who is armed for
battle, will cross over to fight before the
LORD, just as our lord says."
28Then Moses gave orders about them
to Eleazar the priest and Joshua son of
Nun and to the family heads of the Israelite tribes. 29He said to them, "If the
Gadites and Reubenites, every man
armed for battle, cross over the Jordan
with you before the LORD, then when the
land is subdued before you, you must
give them the land of Gilead as their
possession. 30But if they do not cross over
with you armed, they must accept their
possession with you in Canaan."
31The Gadites and Reubenites answered, "Your servants will do what the
LORD has said. 32We will cross over before
the LORD into Canaan armed, but the
property we inherit will be on this side
of the Jordan."
33Then Moses gave to the Gadites, the
Reubenites and the half-tribe of Manasseh son of Joseph the kingdom of Sihon
king of the Amorites and the kingdom
of Og king of Bashan — the whole land
with its cities and the territory around
them.
34The Gadites built up Dibon, Ataroth,
Aroer, 35Atroth Shophan, Jazer, Jogbehah, 36Beth Nimrah and Beth Haran
as fortified cities, and built pens for
their flocks. 37And the Reubenites rebuilt Heshbon, Elealeh and Kiriathaim,
38as well as Nebo and Baal Meon (these
names were changed) and Sibmah. They
gave names to the cities they rebuilt.
39The descendants of Makir son of Manasseh went to Gilead, captured it and
drove out the Amorites who were there.
40So Moses gave Gilead to the Makirites,
the descendants of Manasseh, and they
settled there. 41Jair, a descendant of Manasseh, captured their settlements and
called them Havvoth Jair.[b] 42And Nobah
captured Kenath and its surrounding
settlements and called it Nobah after
himself.

Stages in Israel's Journey

33 Here are the stages in the journey of the Israelites when they
came out of Egypt by divisions under
the leadership of Moses and Aaron. 2At
the LORD's command Moses recorded the
stages in their journey. This is their journey by stages:

3The Israelites set out from Rameses on the fifteenth day of the first
month, the day after the Passover.
They marched out defiantly in full
view of all the Egyptians, 4who were
burying all their firstborn, whom
the LORD had struck down among
them; for the LORD had brought
judgment on their gods.
5The Israelites left Rameses and
camped at Sukkoth.

[a] 17 Septuagint; Hebrew *will be quick to arm ourselves*
[b] 41 Or *them the settlements of Jair*

6 They left Sukkoth and camped
at Etham, on the edge of the desert.
7 They left Etham, turned back to
Pi Hahiroth, to the east of Baal Zephon, and camped near Migdol.
8 They left Pi Hahiroth[a] and
passed through the sea into the desert, and when they had traveled for
three days in the Desert of Etham,
they camped at Marah.
9 They left Marah and went to
Elim, where there were twelve
springs and seventy palm trees, and
they camped there.
10 They left Elim and camped by
the Red Sea.[b]
11 They left the Red Sea and
camped in the Desert of Sin.
12 They left the Desert of Sin and
camped at Dophkah.
13 They left Dophkah and camped
at Alush.
14 They left Alush and camped at
Rephidim, where there was no water for the people to drink.
15 They left Rephidim and camped
in the Desert of Sinai.
16 They left the Desert of Sinai and
camped at Kibroth Hattaavah.
17 They left Kibroth Hattaavah and
camped at Hazeroth.
18 They left Hazeroth and camped
at Rithmah.
19 They left Rithmah and camped
at Rimmon Perez.
20 They left Rimmon Perez and
camped at Libnah.
21 They left Libnah and camped at
Rissah.
22 They left Rissah and camped at
Kehelathah.
23 They left Kehelathah and
camped at Mount Shepher.
24 They left Mount Shepher and
camped at Haradah.
25 They left Haradah and camped
at Makheloth.
26 They left Makheloth and
camped at Tahath.
27 They left Tahath and camped at
Terah.
28 They left Terah and camped at
Mithkah.
29 They left Mithkah and camped
at Hashmonah.
30 They left Hashmonah and
camped at Moseroth.
31 They left Moseroth and camped
at Bene Jaakan.
32 They left Bene Jaakan and
camped at Hor Haggidgad.
33 They left Hor Haggidgad and
camped at Jotbathah.
34 They left Jotbathah and camped
at Abronah.
35 They left Abronah and camped
at Ezion Geber.
36 They left Ezion Geber and
camped at Kadesh, in the Desert of
Zin.
37 They left Kadesh and camped at
Mount Hor, on the border of Edom.
38 At the LORD's command Aaron the
priest went up Mount Hor, where
he died on the first day of the fifth
month of the fortieth year after the
Israelites came out of Egypt. 39 Aaron was a hundred and twenty-three
years old when he died on Mount
Hor.
40 The Canaanite king of Arad,
who lived in the Negev of Canaan,
heard that the Israelites were coming.
41 They left Mount Hor and
camped at Zalmonah.
42 They left Zalmonah and camped
at Punon.
43 They left Punon and camped at
Oboth.
44 They left Oboth and camped at
Iye Abarim, on the border of Moab.
45 They left Iye Abarim and
camped at Dibon Gad.
46 They left Dibon Gad and
camped at Almon Diblathaim.
47 They left Almon Diblathaim and
camped in the mountains of Abarim, near Nebo.
48 They left the mountains of Abarim and camped on the plains of
Moab by the Jordan across from Jericho. 49 There on the plains of Moab
they camped along the Jordan from
Beth Jeshimoth to Abel Shittim.

50 On the plains of Moab by the Jordan
across from Jericho the LORD said to Moses, 51 "Speak to the Israelites and say to
them: 'When you cross the Jordan into
Canaan, 52 drive out all the inhabitants
of the land before you. Destroy all their
carved images and their cast idols, and
demolish all their high places. 53 Take
possession of the land and settle in it,
for I have given you the land to possess.
54 Distribute the land by lot, according
to your clans. To a larger group give

[a] *8* Many manuscripts of the Masoretic Text, Samaritan Pentateuch and Vulgate; most manuscripts of the Masoretic Text *left from before Hahiroth* [b] *10* Or *the Sea of Reeds*; also in verse 11

a larger inheritance, and to a smaller group a smaller one. Whatever falls to them by lot will be theirs. Distribute it according to your ancestral tribes.

55 " 'But if you do not drive out the inhabitants of the land, those you allow to remain will become barbs in your eyes and thorns in your sides. They will give you trouble in the land where you will live. 56 And then I will do to you what I plan to do to them.' "

Boundaries of Canaan

34 The LORD said to Moses, 2 "Command the Israelites and say to them: 'When you enter Canaan, the land that will be allotted to you as an inheritance is to have these boundaries:

3 " 'Your southern side will include some of the Desert of Zin along the border of Edom. Your southern boundary will start in the east from the southern end of the Dead Sea, 4 cross south of Scorpion Pass, continue on to Zin and go south of Kadesh Barnea. Then it will go to Hazar Addar and over to Azmon, 5 where it will turn, join the Wadi of Egypt and end at the Mediterranean Sea.

6 " 'Your western boundary will be the coast of the Mediterranean Sea. This will be your boundary on the west.

7 " 'For your northern boundary, run a line from the Mediterranean Sea to Mount Hor 8 and from Mount Hor to Lebo Hamath. Then the boundary will go to Zedad, 9 continue to Ziphron and end at Hazar Enan. This will be your boundary on the north.

10 " 'For your eastern boundary, run a line from Hazar Enan to Shepham. 11 The boundary will go down from Shepham to Riblah on the east side of Ain and continue along the slopes east of the Sea of Galilee.[a] 12 Then the boundary will go down along the Jordan and end at the Dead Sea.

" 'This will be your land, with its boundaries on every side.' "

13 Moses commanded the Israelites: "Assign this land by lot as an inheritance. The LORD has ordered that it be given to the nine and a half tribes, 14 because the families of the tribe of Reuben, the tribe of Gad and the half-tribe of Manasseh have received their inheritance. 15 These two and a half tribes have received their inheritance east of the Jordan across from Jericho, toward the sunrise."

16 The LORD said to Moses, 17 "These are the names of the men who are to assign the land for you as an inheritance: Eleazar the priest and Joshua son of Nun. 18 And appoint one leader from each tribe to help assign the land. 19 These are their names:

Caleb son of Jephunneh,
  from the tribe of Judah;
20 Shemuel son of Ammihud,
  from the tribe of Simeon;
21 Elidad son of Kislon,
  from the tribe of Benjamin;
22 Bukki son of Jogli,
  the leader from the tribe of Dan;
23 Hanniel son of Ephod,
  the leader from the tribe of Manasseh son of Joseph;
24 Kemuel son of Shiphtan,
  the leader from the tribe of Ephraim son of Joseph;
25 Elizaphan son of Parnak,
  the leader from the tribe of Zebulun;
26 Paltiel son of Azzan,
  the leader from the tribe of Issachar;
27 Ahihud son of Shelomi,
  the leader from the tribe of Asher;
28 Pedahel son of Ammihud,
  the leader from the tribe of Naphtali."

29 These are the men the LORD commanded to assign the inheritance to the Israelites in the land of Canaan.

Towns for the Levites

35 On the plains of Moab by the Jordan across from Jericho, the LORD said to Moses, 2 "Command the Israelites to give the Levites towns to live in from the inheritance the Israelites will possess. And give them pasturelands around the towns. 3 Then they will have towns to live in and pasturelands for the cattle they own and all their other animals.

4 "The pasturelands around the towns that you give the Levites will extend a thousand cubits[b] from the town wall. 5 Outside the town, measure two thousand cubits[c] on the east side, two thousand on the south side, two thousand on the west and two thousand on the north, with the town in the center. They will have this area as pastureland for the towns.

Cities of Refuge

6 "Six of the towns you give the Levites will be cities of refuge, to which a person

[a] 11 Hebrew *Kinnereth* [b] 4 That is, about 1,500 feet or about 450 meters [c] 5 That is, about 3,000 feet or about 900 meters

who has killed someone may flee. In addition, give them forty-two other towns.
7In all you must give the Levites forty-
eight towns, together with their pasturelands. 8The towns you give the Levites
from the land the Israelites possess are
to be given in proportion to the inheritance of each tribe: Take many towns
from a tribe that has many, but few from
one that has few."

9Then the LORD said to Moses: 10"Speak
to the Israelites and say to them: 'When
you cross the Jordan into Canaan, 11select
some towns to be your cities of refuge,
to which a person who has killed someone accidentally may flee. 12They will
be places of refuge from the avenger, so
that anyone accused of murder may not
die before they stand trial before the assembly. 13These six towns you give will be
your cities of refuge. 14Give three on this
side of the Jordan and three in Canaan
as cities of refuge. 15These six towns will
be a place of refuge for Israelites and for
foreigners residing among them, so that
anyone who has killed another accidentally can flee there.

16" 'If anyone strikes someone a fatal
blow with an iron object, that person is
a murderer; the murderer is to be put to
death. 17Or if anyone is holding a stone
and strikes someone a fatal blow with
it, that person is a murderer; the murderer is to be put to death. 18Or if anyone
is holding a wooden object and strikes
someone a fatal blow with it, that person is a murderer; the murderer is to
be put to death. 19The avenger of blood
shall put the murderer to death; when
the avenger comes upon the murderer,
the avenger shall put the murderer to
death. 20If anyone with malice aforethought shoves another or throws something at them intentionally so that they
die 21or if out of enmity one person hits
another with their fist so that the other
dies, that person is to be put to death;
that person is a murderer. The avenger
of blood shall put the murderer to death
when they meet.

22" 'But if without enmity someone
suddenly pushes another or throws
something at them unintentionally 23or,
without seeing them, drops on them a
stone heavy enough to kill them, and
they die, then since that other person
was not an enemy and no harm was intended, 24the assembly must judge between the accused and the avenger of
blood according to these regulations.
25The assembly must protect the one
accused of murder from the avenger of
blood and send the accused back to the
city of refuge to which they fled. The accused must stay there until the death of
the high priest, who was anointed with
the holy oil.

26" 'But if the accused ever goes outside the limits of the city of refuge to
which they fled 27and the avenger of
blood finds them outside the city, the
avenger of blood may kill the accused
without being guilty of murder. 28The
accused must stay in the city of refuge
until the death of the high priest; only
after the death of the high priest may
they return to their own property.

29" 'This is to have the force of law
for you throughout the generations to
come, wherever you live.

30" 'Anyone who kills a person is to be
put to death as a murderer only on the
testimony of witnesses. But no one is to
be put to death on the testimony of only
one witness.

31" 'Do not accept a ransom for the life
of a murderer, who deserves to die. They
are to be put to death.

32" 'Do not accept a ransom for anyone
who has fled to a city of refuge and so
allow them to go back and live on their
own land before the death of the high
priest.

33" 'Do not pollute the land where you
are. Bloodshed pollutes the land, and
atonement cannot be made for the land
on which blood has been shed, except by
the blood of the one who shed it. 34Do not
defile the land where you live and where
I dwell, for I, the LORD, dwell among the
Israelites.' "

Inheritance of Zelophehad's Daughters

36 The family heads of the clan of
Gilead son of Makir, the son of Manasseh, who were from the clans of the
descendants of Joseph, came and spoke
before Moses and the leaders, the heads
of the Israelite families. 2They said,
"When the LORD commanded my lord
to give the land as an inheritance to the
Israelites by lot, he ordered you to give
the inheritance of our brother Zelophehad to his daughters. 3Now suppose they
marry men from other Israelite tribes;
then their inheritance will be taken
from our ancestral inheritance and added to that of the tribe they marry into.
And so part of the inheritance allotted
to us will be taken away. 4When the Year
of Jubilee for the Israelites comes, their
inheritance will be added to that of the
tribe into which they marry, and their

property will be taken from the tribal
inheritance of our ancestors."
5Then at the LORD's command Moses
gave this order to the Israelites: "What
the tribe of the descendants of Joseph
is saying is right. 6This is what the LORD
commands for Zelophehad's daughters:
They may marry anyone they please as
long as they marry within their father's
tribal clan. 7No inheritance in Israel is to
pass from one tribe to another, for every
Israelite shall keep the tribal inheritance
of their ancestors. 8Every daughter who
inherits land in any Israelite tribe must
marry someone in her father's tribal
clan, so that every Israelite will possess
the inheritance of their ancestors. 9No
inheritance may pass from one tribe to
another, for each Israelite tribe is to keep
the land it inherits."
10So Zelophehad's daughters did as the
LORD commanded Moses. 11Zelophehad's
daughters — Mahlah, Tirzah, Hoglah,
Milkah and Noah — married their cousins on their father's side. 12They married
within the clans of the descendants of
Manasseh son of Joseph, and their inheritance remained in their father's
tribe and clan.

13These are the commands and regulations the LORD gave through Moses to
the Israelites on the plains of Moab by
the Jordan across from Jericho.

DEUTERONOMY

The Command to Leave Horeb

1 These are the words Moses spoke to all Israel in the wilderness east of the Jordan — that is, in the Arabah — opposite Suph, between Paran and Tophel, Laban, Hazeroth and Dizahab. 2(It takes eleven days to go from Horeb to Kadesh Barnea by the Mount Seir road.)

3In the fortieth year, on the first day of the eleventh month, Moses proclaimed to the Israelites all that the LORD had commanded him concerning them. 4This was after he had defeated Sihon king of the Amorites, who reigned in Heshbon, and at Edrei had defeated Og king of Bashan, who reigned in Ashtaroth.

5East of the Jordan in the territory of Moab, Moses began to expound this law, saying:

6The LORD our God said to us at Horeb, "You have stayed long enough at this mountain. 7Break camp and advance into the hill country of the Amorites; go to all the neighboring peoples in the Arabah, in the mountains, in the western foothills, in the Negev and along the coast, to the land of the Canaanites and to Lebanon, as far as the great river, the Euphrates. 8See, I have given you this land. Go in and take possession of the land the LORD swore he would give to your fathers — to Abraham, Isaac and Jacob — and to their descendants after them."

The Appointment of Leaders

9At that time I said to you, "You are too heavy a burden for me to carry alone. 10The LORD your God has increased your numbers so that today you are as numerous as the stars in the sky. 11May the LORD, the God of your ancestors, increase you a thousand times and bless you as he has promised! 12But how can I bear your problems and your burdens and your disputes all by myself? 13Choose some wise, understanding and respected men from each of your tribes, and I will set them over you."

14You answered me, "What you propose to do is good."

15So I took the leading men of your tribes, wise and respected men, and appointed them to have authority over you — as commanders of thousands, of hundreds, of fifties and of tens and as tribal officials. 16And I charged your judges at that time, "Hear the disputes between your people and judge fairly, whether the case is between two Israelites or between an Israelite and a foreigner residing among you. 17Do not show partiality in judging; hear both small and great alike. Do not be afraid of anyone, for judgment belongs to God. Bring me any case too hard for you, and I will hear it." 18And at that time I told you everything you were to do.

Spies Sent Out

19Then, as the LORD our God commanded us, we set out from Horeb and went toward the hill country of the Amorites through all that vast and dreadful wilderness that you have seen, and so we reached Kadesh Barnea. 20Then I said to you, "You have reached the hill country of the Amorites, which the LORD our God is giving us. 21See, the LORD your God has given you the land. Go up and take possession of it as the LORD, the God of your ancestors, told you. Do not be afraid; do not be discouraged."

22Then all of you came to me and said, "Let us send men ahead to spy out the land for us and bring back a report about the route we are to take and the towns we will come to."

23The idea seemed good to me; so I selected twelve of you, one man from each tribe. 24They left and went up into the hill country, and came to the Valley of Eshkol and explored it. 25Taking with them some of the fruit of the land, they brought it down to us and reported, "It is a good land that the LORD our God is giving us."

Rebellion Against the LORD

26But you were unwilling to go up; you rebelled against the command of the LORD your God. 27You grumbled in your tents and said, "The LORD hates us; so he brought us out of Egypt to deliver us into the hands of the Amorites to destroy us. 28Where can we go? Our brothers have made our hearts melt in fear. They say, 'The people are stronger and taller than we are; the cities are large, with walls up to the sky. We even saw the Anakites there.'"

[29]Then I said to you, "Do not be terrified; do not be afraid of them. [30]The LORD your God, who is going before you, will fight for you, as he did for you in Egypt, before your very eyes, [31]and in the wilderness. There you saw how the LORD your God carried you, as a father carries his son, all the way you went until you reached this place."

[32]In spite of this, you did not trust in the LORD your God, [33]who went ahead of you on your journey, in fire by night and in a cloud by day, to search out places for you to camp and to show you the way you should go.

[34]When the LORD heard what you said, he was angry and solemnly swore: [35]"No one from this evil generation shall see the good land I swore to give your ancestors, [36]except Caleb son of Jephunneh. He will see it, and I will give him and his descendants the land he set his feet on, because he followed the LORD wholeheartedly."

[37]Because of you the LORD became angry with me also and said, "You shall not enter it, either. [38]But your assistant, Joshua son of Nun, will enter it. Encourage him, because he will lead Israel to inherit it. [39]And the little ones that you said would be taken captive, your children who do not yet know good from bad — they will enter the land. I will give it to them and they will take possession of it. [40]But as for you, turn around and set out toward the desert along the route to the Red Sea.[a]"

[41]Then you replied, "We have sinned against the LORD. We will go up and fight, as the LORD our God commanded us." So every one of you put on his weapons, thinking it easy to go up into the hill country.

[42]But the LORD said to me, "Tell them, 'Do not go up and fight, because I will not be with you. You will be defeated by your enemies.'"

[43]So I told you, but you would not listen. You rebelled against the LORD's command and in your arrogance you marched up into the hill country. [44]The Amorites who lived in those hills came out against you; they chased you like a swarm of bees and beat you down from Seir all the way to Hormah. [45]You came back and wept before the LORD, but he paid no attention to your weeping and turned a deaf ear to you. [46]And so you stayed in Kadesh many days — all the time you spent there.

[a] *40,1* Or *the Sea of Reeds*

Wanderings in the Wilderness

2 Then we turned back and set out toward the wilderness along the route to the Red Sea,[a] as the LORD had directed me. For a long time we made our way around the hill country of Seir.

[2]Then the LORD said to me, [3]"You have made your way around this hill country long enough; now turn north. [4]Give the people these orders: 'You are about to pass through the territory of your relatives the descendants of Esau, who live in Seir. They will be afraid of you, but be very careful. [5]Do not provoke them to war, for I will not give you any of their land, not even enough to put your foot on. I have given Esau the hill country of Seir as his own. [6]You are to pay them in silver for the food you eat and the water you drink.'"

[7]The LORD your God has blessed you in all the work of your hands. He has watched over your journey through this vast wilderness. These forty years the LORD your God has been with you, and you have not lacked anything.

[8]So we went on past our relatives the descendants of Esau, who live in Seir. We turned from the Arabah road, which comes up from Elath and Ezion Geber, and traveled along the desert road of Moab.

[9]Then the LORD said to me, "Do not harass the Moabites or provoke them to war, for I will not give you any part of their land. I have given Ar to the descendants of Lot as a possession."

[10](The Emites used to live there — a people strong and numerous, and as tall as the Anakites. [11]Like the Anakites, they too were considered Rephaites, but the Moabites called them Emites. [12]Horites used to live in Seir, but the descendants of Esau drove them out. They destroyed the Horites from before them and settled in their place, just as Israel did in the land the LORD gave them as their possession.)

[13]And the LORD said, "Now get up and cross the Zered Valley." So we crossed the valley.

[14]Thirty-eight years passed from the time we left Kadesh Barnea until we crossed the Zered Valley. By then, that entire generation of fighting men had perished from the camp, as the LORD had sworn to them. [15]The LORD's hand was against them until he had completely eliminated them from the camp.

[16]Now when the last of these fighting

men among the people had died, 17the
LORD said to me, 18"Today you are to pass
by the region of Moab at Ar. 19When you
come to the Ammonites, do not harass
them or provoke them to war, for I will
not give you possession of any land belonging to the Ammonites. I have given
it as a possession to the descendants of
Lot."

20(That too was considered a land of
the Rephaites, who used to live there;
but the Ammonites called them Zam-
zummites. 21They were a people strong
and numerous, and as tall as the Anakites. The LORD destroyed them from
before the Ammonites, who drove them
out and settled in their place. 22The LORD
had done the same for the descendants
of Esau, who lived in Seir, when he destroyed the Horites from before them.
They drove them out and have lived in
their place to this day. 23And as for the
Avvites who lived in villages as far as
Gaza, the Caphtorites coming out from
Caphtor[a] destroyed them and settled in
their place.)

Defeat of Sihon King of Heshbon

24"Set out now and cross the Arnon
Gorge. See, I have given into your hand
Sihon the Amorite, king of Heshbon, and
his country. Begin to take possession of
it and engage him in battle. 25This very
day I will begin to put the terror and fear
of you on all the nations under heaven.
They will hear reports of you and will
tremble and be in anguish because of
you."

26From the Desert of Kedemoth I sent
messengers to Sihon king of Heshbon offering peace and saying, 27"Let us pass
through your country. We will stay on
the main road; we will not turn aside to
the right or to the left. 28Sell us food to
eat and water to drink for their price in
silver. Only let us pass through on foot —
29as the descendants of Esau, who live in
Seir, and the Moabites, who live in Ar,
did for us — until we cross the Jordan
into the land the LORD our God is giving
us." 30But Sihon king of Heshbon refused
to let us pass through. For the LORD your
God had made his spirit stubborn and
his heart obstinate in order to give him
into your hands, as he has now done.

31The LORD said to me, "See, I have
begun to deliver Sihon and his country
over to you. Now begin to conquer and
possess his land."

32When Sihon and all his army came
out to meet us in battle at Jahaz, 33the
LORD our God delivered him over to us
and we struck him down, together with
his sons and his whole army. 34At that
time we took all his towns and completely destroyed[b] them — men, women
and children. We left no survivors. 35But
the livestock and the plunder from the
towns we had captured we carried off
for ourselves. 36From Aroer on the rim
of the Arnon Gorge, and from the town
in the gorge, even as far as Gilead, not
one town was too strong for us. The LORD
our God gave us all of them. 37But in accordance with the command of the LORD
our God, you did not encroach on any of
the land of the Ammonites, neither the
land along the course of the Jabbok nor
that around the towns in the hills.

Defeat of Og King of Bashan

3 Next we turned and went up along
the road toward Bashan, and Og king
of Bashan with his whole army marched
out to meet us in battle at Edrei. 2The
LORD said to me, "Do not be afraid of
him, for I have delivered him into your
hands, along with his whole army and
his land. Do to him what you did to Sihon king of the Amorites, who reigned
in Heshbon."

3So the LORD our God also gave into
our hands Og king of Bashan and all his
army. We struck them down, leaving no
survivors. 4At that time we took all his
cities. There was not one of the sixty cities that we did not take from them — the
whole region of Argob, Og's kingdom in
Bashan. 5All these cities were fortified
with high walls and with gates and
bars, and there were also a great many
unwalled villages. 6We completely destroyed[b] them, as we had done with Sihon king of Heshbon, destroying[b] every
city — men, women and children. 7But
all the livestock and the plunder from
their cities we carried off for ourselves.

8So at that time we took from these
two kings of the Amorites the territory east of the Jordan, from the Arnon
Gorge as far as Mount Hermon. 9(Hermon is called Sirion by the Sidonians;
the Amorites call it Senir.) 10We took all
the towns on the plateau, and all Gilead, and all Bashan as far as Salekah and
Edrei, towns of Og's kingdom in Bashan.
11(Og king of Bashan was the last of the
Rephaites. His bed was decorated with

[a] *23* That is, Crete [b] *34,6* The Hebrew term refers to the irrevocable giving over of things or persons to the LORD, often by totally destroying them.

iron and was more than nine cubits long and four cubits wide.[a] It is still in Rabbah of the Ammonites.)

Division of the Land

12Of the land that we took over at that time, I gave the Reubenites and the Gadites the territory north of Aroer by the Arnon Gorge, including half the hill country of Gilead, together with its towns. 13The rest of Gilead and also all of Bashan, the kingdom of Og, I gave to the half-tribe of Manasseh. (The whole region of Argob in Bashan used to be known as a land of the Rephaites. 14Jair, a descendant of Manasseh, took the whole region of Argob as far as the border of the Geshurites and the Maakathites; it was named after him, so that to this day Bashan is called Havvoth Jair.[b]) 15And I gave Gilead to Makir. 16But to the Reubenites and the Gadites I gave the territory extending from Gilead down to the Arnon Gorge (the middle of the gorge being the border) and out to the Jabbok River, which is the border of the Ammonites. 17Its western border was the Jordan in the Arabah, from Kinnereth to the Sea of the Arabah (that is, the Dead Sea), below the slopes of Pisgah.

18I commanded you at that time: "The LORD your God has given you this land to take possession of it. But all your able-bodied men, armed for battle, must cross over ahead of the other Israelites. 19However, your wives, your children and your livestock (I know you have much livestock) may stay in the towns I have given you, 20until the LORD gives rest to your fellow Israelites as he has to you, and they too have taken over the land that the LORD your God is giving them across the Jordan. After that, each of you may go back to the possession I have given you."

Moses Forbidden to Cross the Jordan

21At that time I commanded Joshua: "You have seen with your own eyes all that the LORD your God has done to these two kings. The LORD will do the same to all the kingdoms over there where you are going. 22Do not be afraid of them; the LORD your God himself will fight for you."

23At that time I pleaded with the LORD: 24"Sovereign LORD, you have begun to show to your servant your greatness and your strong hand. For what god is there in heaven or on earth who can do the deeds and mighty works you do? 25Let me go over and see the good land beyond the Jordan — that fine hill country and Lebanon."

26But because of you the LORD was angry with me and would not listen to me. "That is enough," the LORD said. "Do not speak to me anymore about this matter. 27Go up to the top of Pisgah and look west and north and south and east. Look at the land with your own eyes, since you are not going to cross this Jordan. 28But commission Joshua, and encourage and strengthen him, for he will lead this people across and will cause them to inherit the land that you will see." 29So we stayed in the valley near Beth Peor.

Obedience Commanded

4 Now, Israel, hear the decrees and laws I am about to teach you. Follow them so that you may live and may go in and take possession of the land the LORD, the God of your ancestors, is giving you. 2Do not add to what I command you and do not subtract from it, but keep the commands of the LORD your God that I give you.

3You saw with your own eyes what the LORD did at Baal Peor. The LORD your God destroyed from among you everyone who followed the Baal of Peor, 4but all of you who held fast to the LORD your God are still alive today.

5See, I have taught you decrees and laws as the LORD my God commanded me, so that you may follow them in the land you are entering to take possession of it. 6Observe them carefully, for this will show your wisdom and understanding to the nations, who will hear about all these decrees and say, "Surely this great nation is a wise and understanding people." 7What other nation is so great as to have their gods near them the way the LORD our God is near us whenever we pray to him? 8And what other nation is so great as to have such righteous decrees and laws as this body of laws I am setting before you today?

9Only be careful, and watch yourselves closely so that you do not forget the things your eyes have seen or let them fade from your heart as long as you live. Teach them to your children and to their children after them. 10Remember the day you stood before the LORD your God at Horeb, when he said to me, "Assemble the people before me to hear my words

[a] *11* That is, about 14 feet long and 6 feet wide or about 4 meters long and 1.8 meters wide
[b] *14* Or *called the settlements of Jair*

so that they may learn to revere me as long as they live in the land and may teach them to their children." 11 You came near and stood at the foot of the mountain while it blazed with fire to the very heavens, with black clouds and deep darkness. 12 Then the LORD spoke to you out of the fire. You heard the sound of words but saw no form; there was only a voice. 13 He declared to you his covenant, the Ten Commandments, which he commanded you to follow and then wrote them on two stone tablets. 14 And the LORD directed me at that time to teach you the decrees and laws you are to follow in the land that you are crossing the Jordan to possess.

Idolatry Forbidden

15 You saw no form of any kind the day the LORD spoke to you at Horeb out of the fire. Therefore watch yourselves very carefully, 16 so that you do not become corrupt and make for yourselves an idol, an image of any shape, whether formed like a man or a woman, 17 or like any animal on earth or any bird that flies in the air, 18 or like any creature that moves along the ground or any fish in the waters below. 19 And when you look up to the sky and see the sun, the moon and the stars — all the heavenly array — do not be enticed into bowing down to them and worshiping things the LORD your God has apportioned to all the nations under heaven. 20 But as for you, the LORD took you and brought you out of the iron-smelting furnace, out of Egypt, to be the people of his inheritance, as you now are.

21 The LORD was angry with me because of you, and he solemnly swore that I would not cross the Jordan and enter the good land the LORD your God is giving you as your inheritance. 22 I will die in this land; I will not cross the Jordan; but you are about to cross over and take possession of that good land. 23 Be careful not to forget the covenant of the LORD your God that he made with you; do not make for yourselves an idol in the form of anything the LORD your God has forbidden. 24 For the LORD your God is a consuming fire, a jealous God.

25 After you have had children and grandchildren and have lived in the land a long time — if you then become corrupt and make any kind of idol, doing evil in the eyes of the LORD your God and arousing his anger, 26 I call the heavens and the earth as witnesses against you this day that you will quickly perish from the land that you are crossing the Jordan to possess. You will not live there long but will certainly be destroyed. 27 The LORD will scatter you among the peoples, and only a few of you will survive among the nations to which the LORD will drive you. 28 There you will worship man-made gods of wood and stone, which cannot see or hear or eat or smell. 29 But if from there you seek the LORD your God, you will find him if you seek him with all your heart and with all your soul. 30 When you are in distress and all these things have happened to you, then in later days you will return to the LORD your God and obey him. 31 For the LORD your God is a merciful God; he will not abandon or destroy you or forget the covenant with your ancestors, which he confirmed to them by oath.

The LORD Is God

32 Ask now about the former days, long before your time, from the day God created human beings on the earth; ask from one end of the heavens to the other. Has anything so great as this ever happened, or has anything like it ever been heard of? 33 Has any other people heard the voice of God[a] speaking out of fire, as you have, and lived? 34 Has any god ever tried to take for himself one nation out of another nation, by testings, by signs and wonders, by war, by a mighty hand and an outstretched arm, or by great and awesome deeds, like all the things the LORD your God did for you in Egypt before your very eyes?

35 You were shown these things so that you might know that the LORD is God; besides him there is no other. 36 From heaven he made you hear his voice to discipline you. On earth he showed you his great fire, and you heard his words from out of the fire. 37 Because he loved your ancestors and chose their descendants after them, he brought you out of Egypt by his Presence and his great strength, 38 to drive out before you nations greater and stronger than you and to bring you into their land to give it to you for your inheritance, as it is today.

39 Acknowledge and take to heart this day that the LORD is God in heaven above and on the earth below. There is no other. 40 Keep his decrees and commands, which I am giving you today, so that it may go well with you and your

[a] 33 Or *of a god*

children after you and that you may live
long in the land the LORD your God gives
you for all time.

Cities of Refuge

41 Then Moses set aside three cities east
of the Jordan, 42 to which anyone who
had killed a person could flee if they had
unintentionally killed a neighbor without malice aforethought. They could flee
into one of these cities and save their
life. 43 The cities were these: Bezer in the
wilderness plateau, for the Reubenites;
Ramoth in Gilead, for the Gadites; and
Golan in Bashan, for the Manassites.

Introduction to the Law

44 This is the law Moses set before the
Israelites. 45 These are the stipulations,
decrees and laws Moses gave them when
they came out of Egypt 46 and were in the
valley near Beth Peor east of the Jordan,
in the land of Sihon king of the Amorites, who reigned in Heshbon and was
defeated by Moses and the Israelites as
they came out of Egypt. 47 They took possession of his land and the land of Og
king of Bashan, the two Amorite kings
east of the Jordan. 48 This land extended from Aroer on the rim of the Arnon
Gorge to Mount Sirion[a] (that is, Hermon),
49 and included all the Arabah east of the
Jordan, as far as the Dead Sea,[b] below
the slopes of Pisgah.

The Ten Commandments

5 Moses summoned all Israel and said:
Hear, Israel, the decrees and laws
I declare in your hearing today. Learn
them and be sure to follow them. 2 The
LORD our God made a covenant with
us at Horeb. 3 It was not with our ancestors[c] that the LORD made this covenant,
but with us, with all of us who are alive
here today. 4 The LORD spoke to you face
to face out of the fire on the mountain.
5 (At that time I stood between the LORD
and you to declare to you the word of the
LORD, because you were afraid of the fire
and did not go up the mountain.) And
he said:

6 "I am the LORD your God, who
brought you out of Egypt, out
of the land of slavery.

7 "You shall have no other gods before[d] me.

8 "You shall not make for yourself
an image in the form of anything in heaven above or on
the earth beneath or in the
waters below. 9 You shall not
bow down to them or worship
them; for I, the LORD your God,
am a jealous God, punishing
the children for the sin of the
parents to the third and fourth
generation of those who hate
me, 10 but showing love to a
thousand generations of those
who love me and keep my commandments.

11 "You shall not misuse the name of
the LORD your God, for the LORD
will not hold anyone guiltless
who misuses his name.

12 "Observe the Sabbath day by keeping it holy, as the LORD your
God has commanded you. 13 Six
days you shall labor and do all
your work, 14 but the seventh
day is a sabbath to the LORD
your God. On it you shall not do
any work, neither you, nor your
son or daughter, nor your male
or female servant, nor your ox,
your donkey or any of your animals, nor any foreigner residing in your towns, so that your
male and female servants may
rest, as you do. 15 Remember
that you were slaves in Egypt
and that the LORD your God
brought you out of there with
a mighty hand and an out-
stretched arm. Therefore the
LORD your God has commanded you to observe the Sabbath
day.

16 "Honor your father and your mother, as the LORD your God has
commanded you, so that you
may live long and that it may
go well with you in the land the
LORD your God is giving you.

17 "You shall not murder.

18 "You shall not commit adultery.

19 "You shall not steal.

20 "You shall not give false testimony
against your neighbor.

21 "You shall not covet your neighbor's
wife. You shall not set your desire on your neighbor's house
or land, his male or female
servant, his ox or donkey, or
anything that belongs to your
neighbor."

22 These are the commandments the

[a] 48 Syriac (see also 3:9); Hebrew *Siyon* [b] 49 Hebrew *the Sea of the Arabah* [c] 3 Or *not only with our parents* [d] 7 Or *besides*

LORD proclaimed in a loud voice to your whole assembly there on the mountain from out of the fire, the cloud and the deep darkness; and he added nothing more. Then he wrote them on two stone tablets and gave them to me.

23 When you heard the voice out of the darkness, while the mountain was ablaze with fire, all the leaders of your tribes and your elders came to me. 24 And you said, "The LORD our God has shown us his glory and his majesty, and we have heard his voice from the fire. Today we have seen that a person can live even if God speaks with them. 25 But now, why should we die? This great fire will consume us, and we will die if we hear the voice of the LORD our God any longer. 26 For what mortal has ever heard the voice of the living God speaking out of fire, as we have, and survived? 27 Go near and listen to all that the LORD our God says. Then tell us whatever the LORD our God tells you. We will listen and obey."

28 The LORD heard you when you spoke to me, and the LORD said to me, "I have heard what this people said to you. Everything they said was good. 29 Oh, that their hearts would be inclined to fear me and keep all my commands always, so that it might go well with them and their children forever!

30 "Go, tell them to return to their tents. 31 But you stay here with me so that I may give you all the commands, decrees and laws you are to teach them to follow in the land I am giving them to possess."

32 So be careful to do what the LORD your God has commanded you; do not turn aside to the right or to the left. 33 Walk in obedience to all that the LORD your God has commanded you, so that you may live and prosper and prolong your days in the land that you will possess.

Love the LORD Your God

6 These are the commands, decrees and laws the LORD your God directed me to teach you to observe in the land that you are crossing the Jordan to possess, 2 so that you, your children and their children after them may fear the LORD your God as long as you live by keeping all his decrees and commands that I give you, and so that you may enjoy long life. 3 Hear, Israel, and be careful to obey so that it may go well with you and that you may increase greatly in a land flowing with milk and honey, just as the LORD, the God of your ancestors, promised you.

4 Hear, O Israel: The LORD our God, the LORD is one.[a] 5 Love the LORD your God with all your heart and with all your soul and with all your strength. 6 These commandments that I give you today are to be on your hearts. 7 Impress them on your children. Talk about them when you sit at home and when you walk along the road, when you lie down and when you get up. 8 Tie them as symbols on your hands and bind them on your foreheads. 9 Write them on the doorframes of your houses and on your gates.

10 When the LORD your God brings you into the land he swore to your fathers, to Abraham, Isaac and Jacob, to give you — a land with large, flourishing cities you did not build, 11 houses filled with all kinds of good things you did not provide, wells you did not dig, and vineyards and olive groves you did not plant — then when you eat and are satisfied, 12 be careful that you do not forget the LORD, who brought you out of Egypt, out of the land of slavery.

13 Fear the LORD your God, serve him only and take your oaths in his name. 14 Do not follow other gods, the gods of the peoples around you; 15 for the LORD your God, who is among you, is a jealous God and his anger will burn against you, and he will destroy you from the face of the land. 16 Do not put the LORD your God to the test as you did at Massah. 17 Be sure to keep the commands of the LORD your God and the stipulations and decrees he has given you. 18 Do what is right and good in the LORD's sight, so that it may go well with you and you may go in and take over the good land the LORD promised on oath to your ancestors, 19 thrusting out all your enemies before you, as the LORD said.

20 In the future, when your son asks you, "What is the meaning of the stipulations, decrees and laws the LORD our God has commanded you?" 21 tell him: "We were slaves of Pharaoh in Egypt, but the LORD brought us out of Egypt with a mighty hand. 22 Before our eyes the LORD sent signs and wonders — great and terrible — on Egypt and Pharaoh and his whole household. 23 But he brought us out from there to bring us in and give us the land he promised on oath to our ancestors. 24 The LORD commanded us

[a] 4 Or *The LORD our God is one LORD*; or *The LORD is our God, the LORD is one*; or *The LORD is our God, the LORD alone*

to obey all these decrees and to fear the LORD our God, so that we might always prosper and be kept alive, as is the case today. 25And if we are careful to obey all this law before the LORD our God, as he has commanded us, that will be our righteousness."

Driving Out the Nations

7 When the LORD your God brings you into the land you are entering to possess and drives out before you many nations — the Hittites, Girgashites, Amorites, Canaanites, Perizzites, Hivites and Jebusites, seven nations larger and stronger than you — 2and when the LORD your God has delivered them over to you and you have defeated them, then you must destroy them totally.[a] Make no treaty with them, and show them no mercy. 3Do not intermarry with them. Do not give your daughters to their sons or take their daughters for your sons, 4for they will turn your children away from following me to serve other gods, and the LORD's anger will burn against you and will quickly destroy you. 5This is what you are to do to them: Break down their altars, smash their sacred stones, cut down their Asherah poles[b] and burn their idols in the fire. 6For you are a people holy to the LORD your God. The LORD your God has chosen you out of all the peoples on the face of the earth to be his people, his treasured possession.

7The LORD did not set his affection on you and choose you because you were more numerous than other peoples, for you were the fewest of all peoples. 8But it was because the LORD loved you and kept the oath he swore to your ancestors that he brought you out with a mighty hand and redeemed you from the land of slavery, from the power of Pharaoh king of Egypt. 9Know therefore that the LORD your God is God; he is the faithful God, keeping his covenant of love to a thousand generations of those who love him and keep his commandments. 10But

those who hate him he will repay to
their face by destruction;
he will not be slow to repay to their
face those who hate him.

11Therefore, take care to follow the commands, decrees and laws I give you today.

12If you pay attention to these laws and are careful to follow them, then the LORD your God will keep his covenant of love with you, as he swore to your ancestors. 13He will love you and bless you and increase your numbers. He will bless the fruit of your womb, the crops of your land — your grain, new wine and olive oil — the calves of your herds and the lambs of your flocks in the land he swore to your ancestors to give you. 14You will be blessed more than any other people; none of your men or women will be childless, nor will any of your livestock be without young. 15The LORD will keep you free from every disease. He will not inflict on you the horrible diseases you knew in Egypt, but he will inflict them on all who hate you. 16You must destroy all the peoples the LORD your God gives over to you. Do not look on them with pity and do not serve their gods, for that will be a snare to you.

17You may say to yourselves, "These nations are stronger than we are. How can we drive them out?" 18But do not be afraid of them; remember well what the LORD your God did to Pharaoh and to all Egypt. 19You saw with your own eyes the great trials, the signs and wonders, the mighty hand and outstretched arm, with which the LORD your God brought you out. The LORD your God will do the same to all the peoples you now fear. 20Moreover, the LORD your God will send the hornet among them until even the survivors who hide from you have perished. 21Do not be terrified by them, for the LORD your God, who is among you, is a great and awesome God. 22The LORD your God will drive out those nations before you, little by little. You will not be allowed to eliminate them all at once, or the wild animals will multiply around you. 23But the LORD your God will deliver them over to you, throwing them into great confusion until they are destroyed. 24He will give their kings into your hand, and you will wipe out their names from under heaven. No one will be able to stand up against you; you will destroy them. 25The images of their gods you are to burn in the fire. Do not covet the silver and gold on them, and do not take it for yourselves, or you will be ensnared by it, for it is detestable to the LORD your God. 26Do not bring a detestable thing into your house or you, like it, will be set apart for destruction. Regard it as vile and utterly detest it, for it is set apart for destruction.

[a] *2* The Hebrew term refers to the irrevocable giving over of things or persons to the LORD, often by totally destroying them; also in verse 26. [b] *5* That is, wooden symbols of the goddess Asherah; here and elsewhere in Deuteronomy

Do Not Forget the LORD

8 Be careful to follow every command I am giving you today, so that you may live and increase and may enter and possess the land the LORD promised on oath to your ancestors. 2Remember how the LORD your God led you all the way in the wilderness these forty years, to humble and test you in order to know what was in your heart, whether or not you would keep his commands. 3He humbled you, causing you to hunger and then feeding you with manna, which neither you nor your ancestors had known, to teach you that man does not live on bread alone but on every word that comes from the mouth of the LORD. 4Your clothes did not wear out and your feet did not swell during these forty years. 5Know then in your heart that as a man disciplines his son, so the LORD your God disciplines you.

6Observe the commands of the LORD your God, walking in obedience to him and revering him. 7For the LORD your God is bringing you into a good land — a land with brooks, streams, and deep springs gushing out into the valleys and hills; 8a land with wheat and barley, vines and fig trees, pomegranates, olive oil and honey; 9a land where bread will not be scarce and you will lack nothing; a land where the rocks are iron and you can dig copper out of the hills.

10When you have eaten and are satisfied, praise the LORD your God for the good land he has given you. 11Be careful that you do not forget the LORD your God, failing to observe his commands, his laws and his decrees that I am giving you this day. 12Otherwise, when you eat and are satisfied, when you build fine houses and settle down, 13and when your herds and flocks grow large and your silver and gold increase and all you have is multiplied, 14then your heart will become proud and you will forget the LORD your God, who brought you out of Egypt, out of the land of slavery. 15He led you through the vast and dreadful wilderness, that thirsty and waterless land, with its venomous snakes and scorpions. He brought you water out of hard rock. 16He gave you manna to eat in the wilderness, something your ancestors had never known, to humble and test you so that in the end it might go well with you. 17You may say to yourself, "My power and the strength of my hands have produced this wealth for me." 18But remember the LORD your God, for it is he who gives you the ability to produce wealth, and so confirms his covenant, which he swore to your ancestors, as it is today.

19If you ever forget the LORD your God and follow other gods and worship and bow down to them, I testify against you today that you will surely be destroyed. 20Like the nations the LORD destroyed before you, so you will be destroyed for not obeying the LORD your God.

Not Because of Israel's Righteousness

9 Hear, Israel: You are now about to cross the Jordan to go in and dispossess nations greater and stronger than you, with large cities that have walls up to the sky. 2The people are strong and tall — Anakites! You know about them and have heard it said: "Who can stand up against the Anakites?" 3But be assured today that the LORD your God is the one who goes across ahead of you like a devouring fire. He will destroy them; he will subdue them before you. And you will drive them out and annihilate them quickly, as the LORD has promised you.

4After the LORD your God has driven them out before you, do not say to yourself, "The LORD has brought me here to take possession of this land because of my righteousness." No, it is on account of the wickedness of these nations that the LORD is going to drive them out before you. 5It is not because of your righteousness or your integrity that you are going in to take possession of their land; but on account of the wickedness of these nations, the LORD your God will drive them out before you, to accomplish what he swore to your fathers, to Abraham, Isaac and Jacob. 6Understand, then, that it is not because of your righteousness that the LORD your God is giving you this good land to possess, for you are a stiff-necked people.

The Golden Calf

7Remember this and never forget how you aroused the anger of the LORD your God in the wilderness. From the day you left Egypt until you arrived here, you have been rebellious against the LORD. 8At Horeb you aroused the LORD's wrath so that he was angry enough to destroy you. 9When I went up on the mountain to receive the tablets of stone, the tablets of the covenant that the LORD had made with you, I stayed on the mountain forty days and forty nights; I ate no bread and drank no water. 10The LORD gave me two stone tablets inscribed by the finger

of God. On them were all the commandments the LORD proclaimed to you on
the mountain out of the fire, on the day
of the assembly.
[11]At the end of the forty days and forty
nights, the LORD gave me the two stone
tablets, the tablets of the covenant.
[12]Then the LORD told me, "Go down from
here at once, because your people whom
you brought out of Egypt have become
corrupt. They have turned away quickly
from what I commanded them and have
made an idol for themselves."
[13]And the LORD said to me, "I have seen
this people, and they are a stiff-necked
people indeed! [14]Let me alone, so that
I may destroy them and blot out their
name from under heaven. And I will
make you into a nation stronger and
more numerous than they."
[15]So I turned and went down from the
mountain while it was ablaze with fire.
And the two tablets of the covenant were
in my hands. [16]When I looked, I saw that
you had sinned against the LORD your
God; you had made for yourselves an
idol cast in the shape of a calf. You had
turned aside quickly from the way that
the LORD had commanded you. [17]So I
took the two tablets and threw them out
of my hands, breaking them to pieces
before your eyes.
[18]Then once again I fell prostrate before the LORD for forty days and forty nights; I ate no bread and drank no
water, because of all the sin you had
committed, doing what was evil in the
LORD's sight and so arousing his anger.
[19]I feared the anger and wrath of the
LORD, for he was angry enough with
you to destroy you. But again the LORD
listened to me. [20]And the LORD was angry enough with Aaron to destroy him,
but at that time I prayed for Aaron too.
[21]Also I took that sinful thing of yours,
the calf you had made, and burned it in
the fire. Then I crushed it and ground it
to powder as fine as dust and threw the
dust into a stream that flowed down the
mountain.
[22]You also made the LORD angry at
Taberah, at Massah and at Kibroth Hattaavah.
[23]And when the LORD sent you out
from Kadesh Barnea, he said, "Go up and
take possession of the land I have given
you." But you rebelled against the command of the LORD your God. You did not
trust him or obey him. [24]You have been
rebellious against the LORD ever since I
have known you.
[25]I lay prostrate before the LORD those
forty days and forty nights because the
LORD had said he would destroy you. [26]I
prayed to the LORD and said, "Sovereign
LORD, do not destroy your people, your
own inheritance that you redeemed by
your great power and brought out of
Egypt with a mighty hand. [27]Remember
your servants Abraham, Isaac and Jacob. Overlook the stubbornness of this
people, their wickedness and their sin.
[28]Otherwise, the country from which you
brought us will say, 'Because the LORD
was not able to take them into the land
he had promised them, and because he
hated them, he brought them out to put
them to death in the wilderness.' [29]But
they are your people, your inheritance
that you brought out by your great power and your outstretched arm."

Tablets Like the First Ones

10 At that time the LORD said to me,
"Chisel out two stone tablets like
the first ones and come up to me on the
mountain. Also make a wooden ark.[a]
[2]I will write on the tablets the words
that were on the first tablets, which you
broke. Then you are to put them in the
ark."
[3]So I made the ark out of acacia wood
and chiseled out two stone tablets like
the first ones, and I went up on the
mountain with the two tablets in my
hands. [4]The LORD wrote on these tablets what he had written before, the Ten
Commandments he had proclaimed to
you on the mountain, out of the fire, on
the day of the assembly. And the LORD
gave them to me. [5]Then I came back
down the mountain and put the tablets
in the ark I had made, as the LORD commanded me, and they are there now.
[6](The Israelites traveled from the
wells of Bene Jaakan to Moserah. There
Aaron died and was buried, and Eleazar
his son succeeded him as priest. [7]From
there they traveled to Gudgodah and
on to Jotbathah, a land with streams of
water. [8]At that time the LORD set apart
the tribe of Levi to carry the ark of the
covenant of the LORD, to stand before
the LORD to minister and to pronounce
blessings in his name, as they still do
today. [9]That is why the Levites have no
share or inheritance among their fellow
Israelites; the LORD is their inheritance,
as the LORD your God told them.)
[10]Now I had stayed on the mountain
forty days and forty nights, as I did

[a] 1 That is, a chest

the first time, and the LORD listened to me at this time also. It was not his will to destroy you. 11"Go," the LORD said to me, "and lead the people on their way, so that they may enter and possess the land I swore to their ancestors to give them."

Fear the LORD

12And now, Israel, what does the LORD your God ask of you but to fear the LORD your God, to walk in obedience to him, to love him, to serve the LORD your God with all your heart and with all your soul, 13and to observe the LORD's commands and decrees that I am giving you today for your own good?

14To the LORD your God belong the heavens, even the highest heavens, the earth and everything in it. 15Yet the LORD set his affection on your ancestors and loved them, and he chose you, their descendants, above all the nations — as it is today. 16Circumcise your hearts, therefore, and do not be stiff-necked any longer. 17For the LORD your God is God of gods and Lord of lords, the great God, mighty and awesome, who shows no partiality and accepts no bribes. 18He defends the cause of the fatherless and the widow, and loves the foreigner residing among you, giving them food and clothing. 19And you are to love those who are foreigners, for you yourselves were foreigners in Egypt. 20Fear the LORD your God and serve him. Hold fast to him and take your oaths in his name. 21He is the one you praise; he is your God, who performed for you those great and awesome wonders you saw with your own eyes. 22Your ancestors who went down into Egypt were seventy in all, and now the LORD your God has made you as numerous as the stars in the sky.

Love and Obey the LORD

11 Love the LORD your God and keep his requirements, his decrees, his laws and his commands always. 2Remember today that your children were not the ones who saw and experienced the discipline of the LORD your God: his majesty, his mighty hand, his outstretched arm; 3the signs he performed and the things he did in the heart of Egypt, both to Pharaoh king of Egypt and to his whole country; 4what he did to the Egyptian army, to its horses and chariots, how he overwhelmed them with the waters of the Red Sea[a] as they were pursuing you, and how the LORD brought lasting ruin on them. 5It was not your children who saw what he did for you in the wilderness until you arrived at this place, 6and what he did to Dathan and Abiram, sons of Eliab the Reubenite, when the earth opened its mouth right in the middle of all Israel and swallowed them up with their households, their tents and every living thing that belonged to them. 7But it was your own eyes that saw all these great things the LORD has done.

8Observe therefore all the commands I am giving you today, so that you may have the strength to go in and take over the land that you are crossing the Jordan to possess, 9and so that you may live long in the land the LORD swore to your ancestors to give to them and their descendants, a land flowing with milk and honey. 10The land you are entering to take over is not like the land of Egypt, from which you have come, where you planted your seed and irrigated it by foot as in a vegetable garden. 11But the land you are crossing the Jordan to take possession of is a land of mountains and valleys that drinks rain from heaven. 12It is a land the LORD your God cares for; the eyes of the LORD your God are continually on it from the beginning of the year to its end.

13So if you faithfully obey the commands I am giving you today — to love the LORD your God and to serve him with all your heart and with all your soul — 14then I will send rain on your land in its season, both autumn and spring rains, so that you may gather in your grain, new wine and olive oil. 15I will provide grass in the fields for your cattle, and you will eat and be satisfied.

16Be careful, or you will be enticed to turn away and worship other gods and bow down to them. 17Then the LORD's anger will burn against you, and he will shut up the heavens so that it will not rain and the ground will yield no produce, and you will soon perish from the good land the LORD is giving you. 18Fix these words of mine in your hearts and minds; tie them as symbols on your hands and bind them on your foreheads. 19Teach them to your children, talking about them when you sit at home and when you walk along the road, when you lie down and when you get up. 20Write them on the doorframes of your houses and on your gates, 21so that your days and the days of your children may be

[a] 4 *Or the Sea of Reeds*

many in the land the LORD swore to give your ancestors, as many as the days that the heavens are above the earth.

22If you carefully observe all these commands I am giving you to follow — to love the LORD your God, to walk in obedience to him and to hold fast to him — 23then the LORD will drive out all these nations before you, and you will dispossess nations larger and stronger than you. 24Every place where you set your foot will be yours: Your territory will extend from the desert to Lebanon, and from the Euphrates River to the Mediterranean Sea. 25No one will be able to stand against you. The LORD your God, as he promised you, will put the terror and fear of you on the whole land, wherever you go.

26See, I am setting before you today a blessing and a curse — 27the blessing if you obey the commands of the LORD your God that I am giving you today; 28the curse if you disobey the commands of the LORD your God and turn from the way that I command you today by following other gods, which you have not known. 29When the LORD your God has brought you into the land you are entering to possess, you are to proclaim on Mount Gerizim the blessings, and on Mount Ebal the curses. 30As you know, these mountains are across the Jordan, westward, toward the setting sun, near the great trees of Moreh, in the territory of those Canaanites living in the Arabah in the vicinity of Gilgal. 31You are about to cross the Jordan to enter and take possession of the land the LORD your God is giving you. When you have taken it over and are living there, 32be sure that you obey all the decrees and laws I am setting before you today.

The One Place of Worship

12 These are the decrees and laws you must be careful to follow in the land that the LORD, the God of your ancestors, has given you to possess — as long as you live in the land. 2Destroy completely all the places on the high mountains, on the hills and under every spreading tree, where the nations you are dispossessing worship their gods. 3Break down their altars, smash their sacred stones and burn their Asherah poles in the fire; cut down the idols of their gods and wipe out their names from those places.

4You must not worship the LORD your God in their way. 5But you are to seek the place the LORD your God will choose from among all your tribes to put his Name there for his dwelling. To that place you must go; 6there bring your burnt offerings and sacrifices, your tithes and special gifts, what you have vowed to give and your freewill offerings, and the firstborn of your herds and flocks. 7There, in the presence of the LORD your God, you and your families shall eat and shall rejoice in everything you have put your hand to, because the LORD your God has blessed you.

8You are not to do as we do here today, everyone doing as they see fit, 9since you have not yet reached the resting place and the inheritance the LORD your God is giving you. 10But you will cross the Jordan and settle in the land the LORD your God is giving you as an inheritance, and he will give you rest from all your enemies around you so that you will live in safety. 11Then to the place the LORD your God will choose as a dwelling for his Name — there you are to bring everything I command you: your burnt offerings and sacrifices, your tithes and special gifts, and all the choice possessions you have vowed to the LORD. 12And there rejoice before the LORD your God — you, your sons and daughters, your male and female servants, and the Levites from your towns who have no allotment or inheritance of their own. 13Be careful not to sacrifice your burnt offerings anywhere you please. 14Offer them only at the place the LORD will choose in one of your tribes, and there observe everything I command you.

15Nevertheless, you may slaughter your animals in any of your towns and eat as much of the meat as you want, as if it were gazelle or deer, according to the blessing the LORD your God gives you. Both the ceremonially unclean and the clean may eat it. 16But you must not eat the blood; pour it out on the ground like water. 17You must not eat in your own towns the tithe of your grain and new wine and olive oil, or the firstborn of your herds and flocks, or whatever you have vowed to give, or your freewill offerings or special gifts. 18Instead, you are to eat them in the presence of the LORD your God at the place the LORD your God will choose — you, your sons and daughters, your male and female servants, and the Levites from your towns — and you are to rejoice before the LORD your God in everything you put your hand to. 19Be careful not to neglect the Levites as long as you live in your land.

20When the LORD your God has enlarged

your territory as he promised you, and you crave meat and say, "I would like some meat," then you may eat as much of it as you want. 21 If the place where the LORD your God chooses to put his Name is too far away from you, you may slaughter animals from the herds and flocks the LORD has given you, as I have commanded you, and in your own towns you may eat as much of them as you want. 22 Eat them as you would gazelle or deer. Both the ceremonially unclean and the clean may eat. 23 But be sure you do not eat the blood, because the blood is the life, and you must not eat the life with the meat. 24 You must not eat the blood; pour it out on the ground like water. 25 Do not eat it, so that it may go well with you and your children after you, because you will be doing what is right in the eyes of the LORD.

26 But take your consecrated things and whatever you have vowed to give, and go to the place the LORD will choose. 27 Present your burnt offerings on the altar of the LORD your God, both the meat and the blood. The blood of your sacrifices must be poured beside the altar of the LORD your God, but you may eat the meat. 28 Be careful to obey all these regulations I am giving you, so that it may always go well with you and your children after you, because you will be doing what is good and right in the eyes of the LORD your God.

29 The LORD your God will cut off before you the nations you are about to invade and dispossess. But when you have driven them out and settled in their land, 30 and after they have been destroyed before you, be careful not to be ensnared by inquiring about their gods, saying, "How do these nations serve their gods? We will do the same." 31 You must not worship the LORD your God in their way, because in worshiping their gods, they do all kinds of detestable things the LORD hates. They even burn their sons and daughters in the fire as sacrifices to their gods.

32 See that you do all I command you; do not add to it or take away from it.[a]

Worshiping Other Gods

13[b] If a prophet, or one who foretells by dreams, appears among you and announces to you a sign or wonder, 2 and if the sign or wonder spoken of takes place, and the prophet says, "Let us follow other gods" (gods you have not known) "and let us worship them," 3 you must not listen to the words of that prophet or dreamer. The LORD your God is testing you to find out whether you love him with all your heart and with all your soul. 4 It is the LORD your God you must follow, and him you must revere. Keep his commands and obey him; serve him and hold fast to him. 5 That prophet or dreamer must be put to death for inciting rebellion against the LORD your God, who brought you out of Egypt and redeemed you from the land of slavery. That prophet or dreamer tried to turn you from the way the LORD your God commanded you to follow. You must purge the evil from among you.

6 If your very own brother, or your son or daughter, or the wife you love, or your closest friend secretly entices you, saying, "Let us go and worship other gods" (gods that neither you nor your ancestors have known, 7 gods of the peoples around you, whether near or far, from one end of the land to the other), 8 do not yield to them or listen to them. Show them no pity. Do not spare them or shield them. 9 You must certainly put them to death. Your hand must be the first in putting them to death, and then the hands of all the people. 10 Stone them to death, because they tried to turn you away from the LORD your God, who brought you out of Egypt, out of the land of slavery. 11 Then all Israel will hear and be afraid, and no one among you will do such an evil thing again.

12 If you hear it said about one of the towns the LORD your God is giving you to live in 13 that troublemakers have arisen among you and have led the people of their town astray, saying, "Let us go and worship other gods" (gods you have not known), 14 then you must inquire, probe and investigate it thoroughly. And if it is true and it has been proved that this detestable thing has been done among you, 15 you must certainly put to the sword all who live in that town. You must destroy it completely,[c] both its people and its livestock. 16 You are to gather all the plunder of the town into the middle of the public square and completely burn the town and all its plunder as a whole burnt offering to the LORD your God. That town is to remain a ruin forever, never to be rebuilt, 17 and none of

[a] *32* In Hebrew texts this verse (12:32) is numbered 13:1. [b] In Hebrew texts 13:1-18 is numbered 13:2-19. [c] *15* The Hebrew term refers to the irrevocable giving over of things or persons to the LORD, often by totally destroying them.

the condemned things[a] are to be found
in your hands. Then the LORD will turn
from his fierce anger, will show you mercy, and will have compassion on you. He
will increase your numbers, as he promised on oath to your ancestors— 18be-
cause you obey the LORD your God by
keeping all his commands that I am giving you today and doing what is right in
his eyes.

Clean and Unclean Food

14 You are the children of the LORD
your God. Do not cut yourselves
or shave the front of your heads for the
dead, 2for you are a people holy to the
LORD your God. Out of all the peoples on
the face of the earth, the LORD has chosen you to be his treasured possession.

3Do not eat any detestable thing.
4These are the animals you may eat:
the ox, the sheep, the goat, 5the deer, the
gazelle, the roe deer, the wild goat, the
ibex, the antelope and the mountain
sheep.[b] 6You may eat any animal that
has a divided hoof and that chews the
cud. 7However, of those that chew the
cud or that have a divided hoof you may
not eat the camel, the rabbit or the hyrax. Although they chew the cud, they
do not have a divided hoof; they are ceremonially unclean for you. 8The pig is
also unclean; although it has a divided
hoof, it does not chew the cud. You are
not to eat their meat or touch their carcasses.

9Of all the creatures living in the water, you may eat any that has fins and
scales. 10But anything that does not have
fins and scales you may not eat; for you
it is unclean.

11You may eat any clean bird. 12But
these you may not eat: the eagle, the
vulture, the black vulture, 13the red kite,
the black kite, any kind of falcon, 14any
kind of raven, 15the horned owl, the
screech owl, the gull, any kind of hawk,
16the little owl, the great owl, the white
owl, 17the desert owl, the osprey, the cor-
morant, 18the stork, any kind of heron,
the hoopoe and the bat.

19All flying insects are unclean to you;
do not eat them. 20But any winged creature that is clean you may eat.

21Do not eat anything you find already
dead. You may give it to the foreigner
residing in any of your towns, and they
may eat it, or you may sell it to any other foreigner. But you are a people holy to
the LORD your God.

Do not cook a young goat in its mother's milk.

Tithes

22Be sure to set aside a tenth of all that
your fields produce each year. 23Eat the
tithe of your grain, new wine and olive oil, and the firstborn of your herds
and flocks in the presence of the LORD
your God at the place he will choose as
a dwelling for his Name, so that you
may learn to revere the LORD your God
always. 24But if that place is too distant
and you have been blessed by the LORD
your God and cannot carry your tithe
(because the place where the LORD will
choose to put his Name is so far away),
25then exchange your tithe for silver,
and take the silver with you and go to
the place the LORD your God will choose.
26Use the silver to buy whatever you like:
cattle, sheep, wine or other fermented
drink, or anything you wish. Then you
and your household shall eat there in
the presence of the LORD your God and
rejoice. 27And do not neglect the Levites
living in your towns, for they have no allotment or inheritance of their own.

28At the end of every three years, bring
all the tithes of that year's produce and
store it in your towns, 29so that the Levites (who have no allotment or inheritance of their own) and the foreigners,
the fatherless and the widows who live
in your towns may come and eat and
be satisfied, and so that the LORD your
God may bless you in all the work of your
hands.

The Year for Canceling Debts

15 At the end of every seven years you
must cancel debts. 2This is how it
is to be done: Every creditor shall cancel any loan they have made to a fellow
Israelite. They shall not require payment
from anyone among their own people,
because the LORD's time for canceling
debts has been proclaimed. 3You may
require payment from a foreigner, but
you must cancel any debt your fellow Israelite owes you. 4However, there need
be no poor people among you, for in the
land the LORD your God is giving you to
possess as your inheritance, he will richly bless you, 5if only you fully obey the
LORD your God and are careful to follow

[a] *17* The Hebrew term refers to the irrevocable giving over of things or persons to the LORD, often by totally destroying them. [b] *5* The precise identification of some of the birds and animals in this chapter is uncertain.

all these commands I am giving you today. 6 For the LORD your God will bless you as he has promised, and you will lend to many nations but will borrow from none. You will rule over many nations but none will rule over you.

7 If anyone is poor among your fellow Israelites in any of the towns of the land the LORD your God is giving you, do not be hardhearted or tightfisted toward them. 8 Rather, be openhanded and freely lend them whatever they need. 9 Be careful not to harbor this wicked thought: "The seventh year, the year for canceling debts, is near," so that you do not show ill will toward the needy among your fellow Israelites and give them nothing. They may then appeal to the LORD against you, and you will be found guilty of sin. 10 Give generously to them and do so without a grudging heart; then because of this the LORD your God will bless you in all your work and in everything you put your hand to. 11 There will always be poor people in the land. Therefore I command you to be openhanded toward your fellow Israelites who are poor and needy in your land.

Freeing Servants

12 If any of your people — Hebrew men or women — sell themselves to you and serve you six years, in the seventh year you must let them go free. 13 And when you release them, do not send them away empty-handed. 14 Supply them liberally from your flock, your threshing floor and your winepress. Give to them as the LORD your God has blessed you. 15 Remember that you were slaves in Egypt and the LORD your God redeemed you. That is why I give you this command today.

16 But if your servant says to you, "I do not want to leave you," because he loves you and your family and is well off with you, 17 then take an awl and push it through his earlobe into the door, and he will become your servant for life. Do the same for your female servant.

18 Do not consider it a hardship to set your servant free, because their service to you these six years has been worth twice as much as that of a hired hand. And the LORD your God will bless you in everything you do.

The Firstborn Animals

19 Set apart for the LORD your God every firstborn male of your herds and flocks. Do not put the firstborn of your cows to work, and do not shear the firstborn of your sheep. 20 Each year you and your family are to eat them in the presence of the LORD your God at the place he will choose. 21 If an animal has a defect, is lame or blind, or has any serious flaw, you must not sacrifice it to the LORD your God. 22 You are to eat it in your own towns. Both the ceremonially unclean and the clean may eat it, as if it were gazelle or deer. 23 But you must not eat the blood; pour it out on the ground like water.

The Passover

16 Observe the month of Aviv and celebrate the Passover of the LORD your God, because in the month of Aviv he brought you out of Egypt by night. 2 Sacrifice as the Passover to the LORD your God an animal from your flock or herd at the place the LORD will choose as a dwelling for his Name. 3 Do not eat it with bread made with yeast, but for seven days eat unleavened bread, the bread of affliction, because you left Egypt in haste — so that all the days of your life you may remember the time of your departure from Egypt. 4 Let no yeast be found in your possession in all your land for seven days. Do not let any of the meat you sacrifice on the evening of the first day remain until morning.

5 You must not sacrifice the Passover in any town the LORD your God gives you 6 except in the place he will choose as a dwelling for his Name. There you must sacrifice the Passover in the evening, when the sun goes down, on the anniversary[a] of your departure from Egypt. 7 Roast it and eat it at the place the LORD your God will choose. Then in the morning return to your tents. 8 For six days eat unleavened bread and on the seventh day hold an assembly to the LORD your God and do no work.

The Festival of Weeks

9 Count off seven weeks from the time you begin to put the sickle to the standing grain. 10 Then celebrate the Festival of Weeks to the LORD your God by giving a freewill offering in proportion to the blessings the LORD your God has given you. 11 And rejoice before the LORD your God at the place he will choose as a dwelling for his Name — you, your sons and daughters, your male and female servants, the Levites in your towns, and

[a] 6 Or *down, at the time of day*

the foreigners, the fatherless and the
widows living among you. [12]Remember
that you were slaves in Egypt, and follow
carefully these decrees.

The Festival of Tabernacles

[13]Celebrate the Festival of Tabernacles
for seven days after you have gathered
the produce of your threshing floor and
your winepress. [14]Be joyful at your festival — you, your sons and daughters,
your male and female servants, and the
Levites, the foreigners, the fatherless
and the widows who live in your towns.
[15]For seven days celebrate the festival to
the LORD your God at the place the LORD
will choose. For the LORD your God will
bless you in all your harvest and in all
the work of your hands, and your joy will
be complete.

[16]Three times a year all your men
must appear before the LORD your God
at the place he will choose: at the Festival of Unleavened Bread, the Festival of
Weeks and the Festival of Tabernacles.
No one should appear before the LORD
empty-handed: [17]Each of you must bring
a gift in proportion to the way the LORD
your God has blessed you.

Judges

[18]Appoint judges and officials for each
of your tribes in every town the LORD
your God is giving you, and they shall
judge the people fairly. [19]Do not pervert
justice or show partiality. Do not accept
a bribe, for a bribe blinds the eyes of the
wise and twists the words of the innocent. [20]Follow justice and justice alone,
so that you may live and possess the
land the LORD your God is giving you.

Worshiping Other Gods

[21]Do not set up any wooden Asherah
pole beside the altar you build to the
LORD your God, [22]and do not erect a sacred stone, for these the LORD your God
hates.

17 Do not sacrifice to the LORD your
God an ox or a sheep that has any
defect or flaw in it, for that would be detestable to him.

[2]If a man or woman living among you
in one of the towns the LORD gives you is
found doing evil in the eyes of the LORD
your God in violation of his covenant,
[3]and contrary to my command has worshiped other gods, bowing down to them
or to the sun or the moon or the stars in
the sky, [4]and this has been brought to
your attention, then you must investigate it thoroughly. If it is true and it has
been proved that this detestable thing
has been done in Israel, [5]take the man
or woman who has done this evil deed
to your city gate and stone that person
to death. [6]On the testimony of two or
three witnesses a person is to be put to
death, but no one is to be put to death on
the testimony of only one witness. [7]The
hands of the witnesses must be the first
in putting that person to death, and then
the hands of all the people. You must
purge the evil from among you.

Law Courts

[8]If cases come before your courts that
are too difficult for you to judge — whether bloodshed, lawsuits or assaults — take
them to the place the LORD your God will
choose. [9]Go to the Levitical priests and to
the judge who is in office at that time.
Inquire of them and they will give you
the verdict. [10]You must act according to
the decisions they give you at the place
the LORD will choose. Be careful to do
everything they instruct you to do. [11]Act
according to whatever they teach you
and the decisions they give you. Do not
turn aside from what they tell you, to the
right or to the left. [12]Anyone who shows
contempt for the judge or for the priest
who stands ministering there to the
LORD your God is to be put to death. You
must purge the evil from Israel. [13]All the
people will hear and be afraid, and will
not be contemptuous again.

The King

[14]When you enter the land the LORD
your God is giving you and have taken
possession of it and settled in it, and you
say, “Let us set a king over us like all the
nations around us,” [15]be sure to appoint
over you a king the LORD your God chooses. He must be from among your fellow
Israelites. Do not place a foreigner over
you, one who is not an Israelite. [16]The
king, moreover, must not acquire great
numbers of horses for himself or make
the people return to Egypt to get more
of them, for the LORD has told you, “You
are not to go back that way again.” [17]He
must not take many wives, or his heart
will be led astray. He must not accumu-
late large amounts of silver and gold.

[18]When he takes the throne of his
kingdom, he is to write for himself on a
scroll a copy of this law, taken from that
of the Levitical priests. [19]It is to be with
him, and he is to read it all the days of
his life so that he may learn to revere
the LORD his God and follow carefully all
the words of this law and these decrees

20 and not consider himself better than his fellow Israelites and turn from the law to the right or to the left. Then he and his descendants will reign a long time over his kingdom in Israel.

Offerings for Priests and Levites

18 The Levitical priests—indeed, the whole tribe of Levi—are to have no allotment or inheritance with Israel. They shall live on the food offerings presented to the LORD, for that is their inheritance. 2 They shall have no inheritance among their fellow Israelites; the LORD is their inheritance, as he promised them.

3 This is the share due the priests from the people who sacrifice a bull or a sheep: the shoulder, the internal organs and the meat from the head. 4 You are to give them the firstfruits of your grain, new wine and olive oil, and the first wool from the shearing of your sheep, 5 for the LORD your God has chosen them and their descendants out of all your tribes to stand and minister in the LORD's name always.

6 If a Levite moves from one of your towns anywhere in Israel where he is living, and comes in all earnestness to the place the LORD will choose, 7 he may minister in the name of the LORD his God like all his fellow Levites who serve there in the presence of the LORD. 8 He is to share equally in their benefits, even though he has received money from the sale of family possessions.

Occult Practices

9 When you enter the land the LORD your God is giving you, do not learn to imitate the detestable ways of the nations there. 10 Let no one be found among you who sacrifices their son or daughter in the fire, who practices divination or sorcery, interprets omens, engages in witchcraft, 11 or casts spells, or who is a medium or spiritist or who consults the dead. 12 Anyone who does these things is detestable to the LORD; because of these same detestable practices the LORD your God will drive out those nations before you. 13 You must be blameless before the LORD your God.

The Prophet

14 The nations you will dispossess listen to those who practice sorcery or divination. But as for you, the LORD your God has not permitted you to do so. 15 The LORD your God will raise up for you a prophet like me from among you, from your fellow Israelites. You must listen to him. 16 For this is what you asked of the LORD your God at Horeb on the day of the assembly when you said, "Let us not hear the voice of the LORD our God nor see this great fire anymore, or we will die."

17 The LORD said to me: "What they say is good. 18 I will raise up for them a prophet like you from among their fellow Israelites, and I will put my words in his mouth. He will tell them everything I command him. 19 I myself will call to account anyone who does not listen to my words that the prophet speaks in my name. 20 But a prophet who presumes to speak in my name anything I have not commanded, or a prophet who speaks in the name of other gods, is to be put to death."

21 You may say to yourselves, "How can we know when a message has not been spoken by the LORD?" 22 If what a prophet proclaims in the name of the LORD does not take place or come true, that is a message the LORD has not spoken. That prophet has spoken presumptuously, so do not be alarmed.

Cities of Refuge

19 When the LORD your God has destroyed the nations whose land he is giving you, and when you have driven them out and settled in their towns and houses, 2 then set aside for yourselves three cities in the land the LORD your God is giving you to possess. 3 Determine the distances involved and divide into three parts the land the LORD your God is giving you as an inheritance, so that a person who kills someone may flee for refuge to one of these cities.

4 This is the rule concerning anyone who kills a person and flees there for safety—anyone who kills a neighbor unintentionally, without malice aforethought. 5 For instance, a man may go into the forest with his neighbor to cut wood, and as he swings his ax to fell a tree, the head may fly off and hit his neighbor and kill him. That man may flee to one of these cities and save his life. 6 Otherwise, the avenger of blood might pursue him in a rage, overtake him if the distance is too great, and kill him even though he is not deserving of death, since he did it to his neighbor without malice aforethought. 7 This is why I command you to set aside for yourselves three cities.

8 If the LORD your God enlarges your territory, as he promised on oath to your ancestors, and gives you the whole land

he promised them, 9because you carefully follow all these laws I command you today — to love the LORD your God and to walk always in obedience to him — then you are to set aside three more cities. 10Do this so that innocent blood will not be shed in your land, which the LORD your God is giving you as your inheritance, and so that you will not be guilty of bloodshed.

11But if out of hate someone lies in wait, assaults and kills a neighbor, and then flees to one of these cities, 12the killer shall be sent for by the town elders, be brought back from the city, and be handed over to the avenger of blood to die. 13Show no pity. You must purge from Israel the guilt of shedding innocent blood, so that it may go well with you.

14Do not move your neighbor's boundary stone set up by your predecessors in the inheritance you receive in the land the LORD your God is giving you to possess.

Witnesses

15One witness is not enough to convict anyone accused of any crime or offense they may have committed. A matter must be established by the testimony of two or three witnesses.

16If a malicious witness takes the stand to accuse someone of a crime, 17the two people involved in the dispute must stand in the presence of the LORD before the priests and the judges who are in office at the time. 18The judges must make a thorough investigation, and if the witness proves to be a liar, giving false testimony against a fellow Israelite, 19then do to the false witness as that witness intended to do to the other party. You must purge the evil from among you. 20The rest of the people will hear of this and be afraid, and never again will such an evil thing be done among you. 21Show no pity: life for life, eye for eye, tooth for tooth, hand for hand, foot for foot.

Going to War

20 When you go to war against your enemies and see horses and chariots and an army greater than yours, do not be afraid of them, because the LORD your God, who brought you up out of Egypt, will be with you. 2When you are about to go into battle, the priest shall come forward and address the army. 3He shall say: "Hear, Israel: Today you are going into battle against your enemies. Do not be fainthearted or afraid; do not panic or be terrified by them. 4For the LORD your God is the one who goes with you to fight for you against your enemies to give you victory."

5The officers shall say to the army: "Has anyone built a new house and not yet begun to live in it? Let him go home, or he may die in battle and someone else may begin to live in it. 6Has anyone planted a vineyard and not begun to enjoy it? Let him go home, or he may die in battle and someone else enjoy it. 7Has anyone become pledged to a woman and not married her? Let him go home, or he may die in battle and someone else marry her." 8Then the officers shall add, "Is anyone afraid or fainthearted? Let him go home so that his fellow soldiers will not become disheartened too." 9When the officers have finished speaking to the army, they shall appoint commanders over it.

10When you march up to attack a city, make its people an offer of peace. 11If they accept and open their gates, all the people in it shall be subject to forced labor and shall work for you. 12If they refuse to make peace and they engage you in battle, lay siege to that city. 13When the LORD your God delivers it into your hand, put to the sword all the men in it. 14As for the women, the children, the livestock and everything else in the city, you may take these as plunder for yourselves. And you may use the plunder the LORD your God gives you from your enemies. 15This is how you are to treat all the cities that are at a distance from you and do not belong to the nations nearby.

16However, in the cities of the nations the LORD your God is giving you as an inheritance, do not leave alive anything that breathes. 17Completely destroy[a] them — the Hittites, Amorites, Canaanites, Perizzites, Hivites and Jebusites — as the LORD your God has commanded you. 18Otherwise, they will teach you to follow all the detestable things they do in worshiping their gods, and you will sin against the LORD your God.

19When you lay siege to a city for a long time, fighting against it to capture it, do not destroy its trees by putting an ax to them, because you can eat their fruit. Do not cut them down. Are the trees people, that you should besiege them?[b] 20However, you may cut down

[a] 17 The Hebrew term refers to the irrevocable giving over of things or persons to the LORD, often by totally destroying them. [b] 19 Or *down to use in the siege, for the fruit trees are for the benefit of people.*

trees that you know are not fruit trees and use them to build siege works until the city at war with you falls.

Atonement for an Unsolved Murder

21 If someone is found slain, lying in a field in the land the LORD your God is giving you to possess, and it is not known who the killer was, 2your elders and judges shall go out and measure the distance from the body to the neighboring towns. 3Then the elders of the town nearest the body shall take a heifer that has never been worked and has never worn a yoke 4and lead it down to a valley that has not been plowed or planted and where there is a flowing stream. There in the valley they are to break the heifer's neck. 5The Levitical priests shall step forward, for the LORD your God has chosen them to minister and to pronounce blessings in the name of the LORD and to decide all cases of dispute and assault. 6Then all the elders of the town nearest the body shall wash their hands over the heifer whose neck was broken in the valley, 7and they shall declare: "Our hands did not shed this blood, nor did our eyes see it done. 8Accept this atonement for your people Israel, whom you have redeemed, LORD, and do not hold your people guilty of the blood of an innocent person." Then the bloodshed will be atoned for, 9and you will have purged from yourselves the guilt of shedding innocent blood, since you have done what is right in the eyes of the LORD.

Marrying a Captive Woman

10When you go to war against your enemies and the LORD your God delivers them into your hands and you take captives, 11if you notice among the captives a beautiful woman and are attracted to her, you may take her as your wife. 12Bring her into your home and have her shave her head, trim her nails 13and put aside the clothes she was wearing when captured. After she has lived in your house and mourned her father and mother for a full month, then you may go to her and be her husband and she shall be your wife. 14If you are not pleased with her, let her go wherever she wishes. You must not sell her or treat her as a slave, since you have dishonored her.

The Right of the Firstborn

15If a man has two wives, and he loves one but not the other, and both bear him sons but the firstborn is the son of the wife he does not love, 16when he wills his property to his sons, he must not give the rights of the firstborn to the son of the wife he loves in preference to his actual firstborn, the son of the wife he does not love. 17He must acknowledge the son of his unloved wife as the firstborn by giving him a double share of all he has. That son is the first sign of his father's strength. The right of the firstborn belongs to him.

A Rebellious Son

18If someone has a stubborn and rebellious son who does not obey his father and mother and will not listen to them when they discipline him, 19his father and mother shall take hold of him and bring him to the elders at the gate of his town. 20They shall say to the elders, "This son of ours is stubborn and rebellious. He will not obey us. He is a glutton and a drunkard." 21Then all the men of his town are to stone him to death. You must purge the evil from among you. All Israel will hear of it and be afraid.

Various Laws

22If someone guilty of a capital offense is put to death and their body is exposed on a pole, 23you must not leave the body hanging on the pole overnight. Be sure to bury it that same day, because anyone who is hung on a pole is under God's curse. You must not desecrate the land the LORD your God is giving you as an inheritance.

22 If you see your fellow Israelite's ox or sheep straying, do not ignore it but be sure to take it back to its owner. 2If they do not live near you or if you do not know who owns it, take it home with you and keep it until they come looking for it. Then give it back. 3Do the same if you find their donkey or cloak or anything else they have lost. Do not ignore it.

4If you see your fellow Israelite's donkey or ox fallen on the road, do not ignore it. Help the owner get it to its feet.

5A woman must not wear men's clothing, nor a man wear women's clothing, for the LORD your God detests anyone who does this.

6If you come across a bird's nest beside the road, either in a tree or on the ground, and the mother is sitting on the young or on the eggs, do not take the mother with the young. 7You may take the young, but be sure to let the mother go, so that it may go well with you and you may have a long life.

8When you build a new house, make
a parapet around your roof so that you
may not bring the guilt of bloodshed on
your house if someone falls from the roof.
9Do not plant two kinds of seed in your
vineyard; if you do, not only the crops
you plant but also the fruit of the vineyard will be defiled.[a]
10Do not plow with an ox and a donkey
yoked together.
11Do not wear clothes of wool and linen
woven together.
12Make tassels on the four corners of
the cloak you wear.

Marriage Violations

13If a man takes a wife and, after sleeping with her, dislikes her 14and slanders
her and gives her a bad name, saying,
"I married this woman, but when I approached her, I did not find proof of her
virginity," 15then the young woman's father and mother shall bring to the town
elders at the gate proof that she was a
virgin. 16Her father will say to the elders,
"I gave my daughter in marriage to this
man, but he dislikes her. 17Now he has
slandered her and said, 'I did not find
your daughter to be a virgin.' But here
is the proof of my daughter's virginity."
Then her parents shall display the cloth
before the elders of the town, 18and the
elders shall take the man and punish
him. 19They shall fine him a hundred
shekels[b] of silver and give them to the
young woman's father, because this man
has given an Israelite virgin a bad name.
She shall continue to be his wife; he must
not divorce her as long as he lives.
20If, however, the charge is true and
no proof of the young woman's virginity
can be found, 21she shall be brought to
the door of her father's house and there
the men of her town shall stone her to
death. She has done an outrageous thing
in Israel by being promiscuous while still
in her father's house. You must purge the
evil from among you.
22If a man is found sleeping with another man's wife, both the man who
slept with her and the woman must die.
You must purge the evil from Israel.
23If a man happens to meet in a town
a virgin pledged to be married and he
sleeps with her, 24you shall take both of
them to the gate of that town and stone
them to death — the young woman because she was in a town and did not
scream for help, and the man because he
violated another man's wife. You must
purge the evil from among you.
25But if out in the country a man happens to meet a young woman pledged to
be married and rapes her, only the man
who has done this shall die. 26Do nothing to the woman; she has committed no
sin deserving death. This case is like that
of someone who attacks and murders a
neighbor, 27for the man found the young
woman out in the country, and though
the betrothed woman screamed, there
was no one to rescue her.
28If a man happens to meet a virgin
who is not pledged to be married and
rapes her and they are discovered, 29he
shall pay her father fifty shekels[c] of silver. He must marry the young woman,
for he has violated her. He can never divorce her as long as he lives.
30A man is not to marry his father's
wife; he must not dishonor his father's
bed.[d]

Exclusion From the Assembly

23 [e] No one who has been emasculat-
ed by crushing or cutting may enter the assembly of the LORD.
2No one born of a forbidden marriage[f]
nor any of their descendants may enter
the assembly of the LORD, not even in the
tenth generation.
3No Ammonite or Moabite or any of
their descendants may enter the assembly of the LORD, not even in the tenth
generation. 4For they did not come to
meet you with bread and water on your
way when you came out of Egypt, and
they hired Balaam son of Beor from Pethor in Aram Naharaim[g] to pronounce
a curse on you. 5However, the LORD your
God would not listen to Balaam but
turned the curse into a blessing for you,
because the LORD your God loves you.
6Do not seek a treaty of friendship with
them as long as you live.
7Do not despise an Edomite, for the
Edomites are related to you. Do not despise an Egyptian, because you resided
as foreigners in their country. 8The third
generation of children born to them may
enter the assembly of the LORD.

Uncleanness in the Camp

9When you are encamped against
your enemies, keep away from everything impure. 10If one of your men is

[a] 9 Or *be forfeited to the sanctuary* [b] 19 That is, about 2 1/2 pounds or about 1.2 kilograms
[c] 29 That is, about 1 1/4 pounds or about 575 grams [d] 30 In Hebrew texts this verse (22:30) is
numbered 23:1. [e] In Hebrew texts 23:1-25 is numbered 23:2-26. [f] 2 Or *one of illegitimate birth*
[g] 4 That is, Northwest Mesopotamia

unclean because of a nocturnal emission, he is to go outside the camp and stay there. 11But as evening approaches he is to wash himself, and at sunset he may return to the camp.

12Designate a place outside the camp where you can go to relieve yourself. 13As part of your equipment have something to dig with, and when you relieve yourself, dig a hole and cover up your excrement. 14For the LORD your God moves about in your camp to protect you and to deliver your enemies to you. Your camp must be holy, so that he will not see among you anything indecent and turn away from you.

Miscellaneous Laws

15If a slave has taken refuge with you, do not hand them over to their master. 16Let them live among you wherever they like and in whatever town they choose. Do not oppress them.

17No Israelite man or woman is to become a shrine prostitute. 18You must not bring the earnings of a female prostitute or of a male prostitute[a] into the house of the LORD your God to pay any vow, because the LORD your God detests them both.

19Do not charge a fellow Israelite interest, whether on money or food or anything else that may earn interest. 20You may charge a foreigner interest, but not a fellow Israelite, so that the LORD your God may bless you in everything you put your hand to in the land you are entering to possess.

21If you make a vow to the LORD your God, do not be slow to pay it, for the LORD your God will certainly demand it of you and you will be guilty of sin. 22But if you refrain from making a vow, you will not be guilty. 23Whatever your lips utter you must be sure to do, because you made your vow freely to the LORD your God with your own mouth.

24If you enter your neighbor's vineyard, you may eat all the grapes you want, but do not put any in your basket. 25If you enter your neighbor's grainfield, you may pick kernels with your hands, but you must not put a sickle to their standing grain.

24 If a man marries a woman who becomes displeasing to him because he finds something indecent about her, and he writes her a certificate of divorce, gives it to her and sends her from his house, 2and if after she leaves his house she becomes the wife of another man, 3and her second husband dislikes her and writes her a certificate of divorce, gives it to her and sends her from his house, or if he dies, 4then her first husband, who divorced her, is not allowed to marry her again after she has been defiled. That would be detestable in the eyes of the LORD. Do not bring sin upon the land the LORD your God is giving you as an inheritance.

5If a man has recently married, he must not be sent to war or have any other duty laid on him. For one year he is to be free to stay at home and bring happiness to the wife he has married.

6Do not take a pair of millstones — not even the upper one — as security for a debt, because that would be taking a person's livelihood as security.

7If someone is caught kidnapping a fellow Israelite and treating or selling them as a slave, the kidnapper must die. You must purge the evil from among you.

8In cases of defiling skin diseases,[b] be very careful to do exactly as the Levitical priests instruct you. You must follow carefully what I have commanded them. 9Remember what the LORD your God did to Miriam along the way after you came out of Egypt.

10When you make a loan of any kind to your neighbor, do not go into their house to get what is offered to you as a pledge. 11Stay outside and let the neighbor to whom you are making the loan bring the pledge out to you. 12If the neighbor is poor, do not go to sleep with their pledge in your possession. 13Return their cloak by sunset so that your neighbor may sleep in it. Then they will thank you, and it will be regarded as a righteous act in the sight of the LORD your God.

14Do not take advantage of a hired worker who is poor and needy, whether that worker is a fellow Israelite or a foreigner residing in one of your towns. 15Pay them their wages each day before sunset, because they are poor and are counting on it. Otherwise they may cry to the LORD against you, and you will be guilty of sin.

16Parents are not to be put to death for their children, nor children put to death for their parents; each will die for their own sin.

17Do not deprive the foreigner or the fatherless of justice, or take the cloak of

[a] 18 Hebrew *of a dog* [b] 8 The Hebrew word for *defiling skin diseases,* traditionally translated "leprosy," was used for various diseases affecting the skin.

the widow as a pledge. 18 Remember that you were slaves in Egypt and the LORD your God redeemed you from there. That is why I command you to do this.

19 When you are harvesting in your field and you overlook a sheaf, do not go back to get it. Leave it for the foreigner, the fatherless and the widow, so that the LORD your God may bless you in all the work of your hands. 20 When you beat the olives from your trees, do not go over the branches a second time. Leave what remains for the foreigner, the fatherless and the widow. 21 When you harvest the grapes in your vineyard, do not go over the vines again. Leave what remains for the foreigner, the fatherless and the widow. 22 Remember that you were slaves in Egypt. That is why I command you to do this.

25 When people have a dispute, they are to take it to court and the judges will decide the case, acquitting the innocent and condemning the guilty. 2 If the guilty person deserves to be beaten, the judge shall make them lie down and have them flogged in his presence with the number of lashes the crime deserves, 3 but the judge must not impose more than forty lashes. If the guilty party is flogged more than that, your fellow Israelite will be degraded in your eyes.

4 Do not muzzle an ox while it is treading out the grain.

5 If brothers are living together and one of them dies without a son, his widow must not marry outside the family. Her husband's brother shall take her and marry her and fulfill the duty of a brother-in-law to her. 6 The first son she bears shall carry on the name of the dead brother so that his name will not be blotted out from Israel.

7 However, if a man does not want to marry his brother's wife, she shall go to the elders at the town gate and say, "My husband's brother refuses to carry on his brother's name in Israel. He will not fulfill the duty of a brother-in-law to me." 8 Then the elders of his town shall summon him and talk to him. If he persists in saying, "I do not want to marry her," 9 his brother's widow shall go up to him in the presence of the elders, take off one of his sandals, spit in his face and say, "This is what is done to the man who will not build up his brother's family line." 10 That man's line shall be known in Israel as The Family of the Unsandaled.

11 If two men are fighting and the wife of one of them comes to rescue her husband from his assailant, and she reaches out and seizes him by his private parts, 12 you shall cut off her hand. Show her no pity.

13 Do not have two differing weights in your bag — one heavy, one light. 14 Do not have two differing measures in your house — one large, one small. 15 You must have accurate and honest weights and measures, so that you may live long in the land the LORD your God is giving you. 16 For the LORD your God detests anyone who does these things, anyone who deals dishonestly.

17 Remember what the Amalekites did to you along the way when you came out of Egypt. 18 When you were weary and worn out, they met you on your journey and attacked all who were lagging behind; they had no fear of God. 19 When the LORD your God gives you rest from all the enemies around you in the land he is giving you to possess as an inheritance, you shall blot out the name of Amalek from under heaven. Do not forget!

Firstfruits and Tithes

26 When you have entered the land the LORD your God is giving you as an inheritance and have taken possession of it and settled in it, 2 take some of the firstfruits of all that you produce from the soil of the land the LORD your God is giving you and put them in a basket. Then go to the place the LORD your God will choose as a dwelling for his Name 3 and say to the priest in office at the time, "I declare today to the LORD your God that I have come to the land the LORD swore to our ancestors to give us." 4 The priest shall take the basket from your hands and set it down in front of the altar of the LORD your God. 5 Then you shall declare before the LORD your God: "My father was a wandering Aramean, and he went down into Egypt with a few people and lived there and became a great nation, powerful and numerous. 6 But the Egyptians mistreated us and made us suffer, subjecting us to harsh labor. 7 Then we cried out to the LORD, the God of our ancestors, and the LORD heard our voice and saw our misery, toil and oppression. 8 So the LORD brought us out of Egypt with a mighty hand and an outstretched arm, with great terror and with signs and wonders. 9 He brought us to this place and gave us this land, a land flowing with milk and honey; 10 and now I bring the firstfruits of the soil that you, LORD, have given me." Place the basket before the LORD your God and bow down

before him. [11]Then you and the Levites
and the foreigners residing among you
shall rejoice in all the good things the
LORD your God has given to you and
your household.
[12]When you have finished setting
aside a tenth of all your produce in the
third year, the year of the tithe, you
shall give it to the Levite, the foreigner, the fatherless and the widow, so
that they may eat in your towns and be
satisfied. [13]Then say to the LORD your
God: "I have removed from my house
the sacred portion and have given it
to the Levite, the foreigner, the fatherless and the widow, according to all you
commanded. I have not turned aside
from your commands nor have I forgotten any of them. [14]I have not eaten
any of the sacred portion while I was in
mourning, nor have I removed any of it
while I was unclean, nor have I offered
any of it to the dead. I have obeyed the
LORD my God; I have done everything
you commanded me. [15]Look down from
heaven, your holy dwelling place, and
bless your people Israel and the land
you have given us as you promised on
oath to our ancestors, a land flowing
with milk and honey."

Follow the LORD's Commands

[16]The LORD your God commands you
this day to follow these decrees and
laws; carefully observe them with all
your heart and with all your soul. [17]You
have declared this day that the LORD is
your God and that you will walk in obedience to him, that you will keep his
decrees, commands and laws — that
you will listen to him. [18]And the LORD
has declared this day that you are his
people, his treasured possession as he
promised, and that you are to keep all
his commands. [19]He has declared that
he will set you in praise, fame and honor
high above all the nations he has made
and that you will be a people holy to the
LORD your God, as he promised.

The Altar on Mount Ebal

27 Moses and the elders of Israel
commanded the people: "Keep
all these commands that I give you today. [2]When you have crossed the Jordan
into the land the LORD your God is giving you, set up some large stones and
coat them with plaster. [3]Write on them
all the words of this law when you have
crossed over to enter the land the LORD
your God is giving you, a land flowing
with milk and honey, just as the LORD,
the God of your ancestors, promised you.
[4]And when you have crossed the Jordan,
set up these stones on Mount Ebal, as I
command you today, and coat them
with plaster. [5]Build there an altar to the
LORD your God, an altar of stones. Do not
use any iron tool on them. [6]Build the
altar of the LORD your God with field-
stones and offer burnt offerings on it to
the LORD your God. [7]Sacrifice fellowship
offerings there, eating them and rejoicing in the presence of the LORD your
God. [8]And you shall write very clearly
all the words of this law on these stones
you have set up."

Curses From Mount Ebal

[9]Then Moses and the Levitical priests
said to all Israel, "Be silent, Israel, and
listen! You have now become the people
of the LORD your God. [10]Obey the LORD
your God and follow his commands and
decrees that I give you today."
[11]On the same day Moses commanded
the people:
[12]When you have crossed the Jordan,
these tribes shall stand on Mount Gerizim to bless the people: Simeon, Levi,
Judah, Issachar, Joseph and Benjamin.
[13]And these tribes shall stand on Mount
Ebal to pronounce curses: Reuben, Gad,
Asher, Zebulun, Dan and Naphtali.
[14]The Levites shall recite to all the people of Israel in a loud voice:

[15]"Cursed is anyone who makes
an idol — a thing detestable to the
LORD, the work of skilled hands —
and sets it up in secret."
Then all the people shall
say, "Amen!"
[16]"Cursed is anyone who dishonors their father or mother."
Then all the people shall
say, "Amen!"
[17]"Cursed is anyone who moves
their neighbor's boundary stone."
Then all the people shall
say, "Amen!"
[18]"Cursed is anyone who leads the
blind astray on the road."
Then all the people shall
say, "Amen!"
[19]"Cursed is anyone who withholds justice from the foreigner, the
fatherless or the widow."
Then all the people shall
say, "Amen!"
[20]"Cursed is anyone who sleeps
with his father's wife, for he dishonors his father's bed."
Then all the people shall
say, "Amen!"

21“Cursed is anyone who has sexual relations with any animal.”
Then all the people shall
say, “Amen!”
22“Cursed is anyone who sleeps
with his sister, the daughter of his
father or the daughter of his mother.”
Then all the people shall
say, “Amen!”
23“Cursed is anyone who sleeps
with his mother-in-law.”
Then all the people shall
say, “Amen!”
24“Cursed is anyone who kills
their neighbor secretly.”
Then all the people shall
say, “Amen!”
25“Cursed is anyone who accepts
a bribe to kill an innocent person.”
Then all the people shall
say, “Amen!”
26“Cursed is anyone who does not
uphold the words of this law by carrying them out.”
Then all the people shall
say, “Amen!”

Blessings for Obedience

28 If you fully obey the LORD your
God and carefully follow all his
commands I give you today, the LORD
your God will set you high above all the
nations on earth. 2All these blessings will
come on you and accompany you if you
obey the LORD your God:

3You will be blessed in the city
and blessed in the country.
4The fruit of your womb will be
blessed, and the crops of your land
and the young of your livestock—
the calves of your herds and the
lambs of your flocks.
5Your basket and your kneading
trough will be blessed.
6You will be blessed when you
come in and blessed when you go
out.

7The LORD will grant that the enemies
who rise up against you will be defeated
before you. They will come at you from
one direction but flee from you in seven.
8The LORD will send a blessing on your
barns and on everything you put your
hand to. The LORD your God will bless
you in the land he is giving you.
9The LORD will establish you as his
holy people, as he promised you on oath,
if you keep the commands of the LORD
your God and walk in obedience to him.
10Then all the peoples on earth will see
that you are called by the name of the
LORD, and they will fear you. 11The LORD
will grant you abundant prosperity—in
the fruit of your womb, the young of your
livestock and the crops of your ground—
in the land he swore to your ancestors to
give you.
12The LORD will open the heavens, the
storehouse of his bounty, to send rain
on your land in season and to bless all
the work of your hands. You will lend
to many nations but will borrow from
none. 13The LORD will make you the
head, not the tail. If you pay attention
to the commands of the LORD your God
that I give you this day and carefully follow them, you will always be at the top,
never at the bottom. 14Do not turn aside
from any of the commands I give you today, to the right or to the left, following
other gods and serving them.

Curses for Disobedience

15However, if you do not obey the LORD
your God and do not carefully follow all
his commands and decrees I am giving
you today, all these curses will come on
you and overtake you:

16You will be cursed in the city
and cursed in the country.
17Your basket and your kneading
trough will be cursed.
18The fruit of your womb will be
cursed, and the crops of your land,
and the calves of your herds and the
lambs of your flocks.
19You will be cursed when you
come in and cursed when you go
out.

20The LORD will send on you curses,
confusion and rebuke in everything you
put your hand to, until you are destroyed
and come to sudden ruin because of the
evil you have done in forsaking him.[a]
21The LORD will plague you with diseases until he has destroyed you from the
land you are entering to possess. 22The
LORD will strike you with wasting disease, with fever and inflammation, with
scorching heat and drought, with blight
and mildew, which will plague you until you perish. 23The sky over your head
will be bronze, the ground beneath you
iron. 24The LORD will turn the rain of
your country into dust and powder; it
will come down from the skies until you
are destroyed.

[a] 20 Hebrew *me*

25The LORD will cause you to be defeated before your enemies. You will come at
them from one direction but flee from
them in seven, and you will become a
thing of horror to all the kingdoms on
earth. 26Your carcasses will be food for
all the birds and the wild animals, and
there will be no one to frighten them
away. 27The LORD will afflict you with the
boils of Egypt and with tumors, festering sores and the itch, from which you
cannot be cured. 28The LORD will afflict
you with madness, blindness and confusion of mind. 29At midday you will grope
about like a blind person in the dark. You
will be unsuccessful in everything you
do; day after day you will be oppressed
and robbed, with no one to rescue you.

30You will be pledged to be married to
a woman, but another will take her and
rape her. You will build a house, but you
will not live in it. You will plant a vineyard, but you will not even begin to enjoy its fruit. 31Your ox will be slaughtered
before your eyes, but you will eat none
of it. Your donkey will be forcibly taken
from you and will not be returned. Your
sheep will be given to your enemies, and
no one will rescue them. 32Your sons and
daughters will be given to another nation, and you will wear out your eyes
watching for them day after day, powerless to lift a hand. 33A people that you do
not know will eat what your land and labor produce, and you will have nothing
but cruel oppression all your days. 34The
sights you see will drive you mad. 35The
LORD will afflict your knees and legs
with painful boils that cannot be cured,
spreading from the soles of your feet to
the top of your head.

36The LORD will drive you and the king
you set over you to a nation unknown
to you or your ancestors. There you will
worship other gods, gods of wood and
stone. 37You will become a thing of horror, a byword and an object of ridicule
among all the peoples where the LORD
will drive you.

38You will sow much seed in the field
but you will harvest little, because locusts will devour it. 39You will plant vineyards and cultivate them but you will
not drink the wine or gather the grapes,
because worms will eat them. 40You will
have olive trees throughout your country but you will not use the oil, because
the olives will drop off. 41You will have
sons and daughters but you will not keep
them, because they will go into captivity. 42Swarms of locusts will take over all
your trees and the crops of your land.

43The foreigners who reside among
you will rise above you higher and higher, but you will sink lower and lower.
44They will lend to you, but you will not
lend to them. They will be the head, but
you will be the tail.

45All these curses will come on you.
They will pursue you and overtake you
until you are destroyed, because you did
not obey the LORD your God and observe
the commands and decrees he gave you.
46They will be a sign and a wonder to you
and your descendants forever. 47Because
you did not serve the LORD your God joyfully and gladly in the time of prosperity,
48therefore in hunger and thirst, in nakedness and dire poverty, you will serve
the enemies the LORD sends against you.
He will put an iron yoke on your neck until he has destroyed you.

49The LORD will bring a nation against
you from far away, from the ends of the
earth, like an eagle swooping down,
a nation whose language you will not
understand, 50a fierce-looking nation
without respect for the old or pity for
the young. 51They will devour the young
of your livestock and the crops of your
land until you are destroyed. They will
leave you no grain, new wine or olive oil,
nor any calves of your herds or lambs of
your flocks until you are ruined. 52They
will lay siege to all the cities throughout
your land until the high fortified walls in
which you trust fall down. They will besiege all the cities throughout the land
the LORD your God is giving you.

53Because of the suffering your enemy
will inflict on you during the siege, you
will eat the fruit of the womb, the flesh
of the sons and daughters the LORD your
God has given you. 54Even the most gentle and sensitive man among you will
have no compassion on his own brother or the wife he loves or his surviving
children, 55and he will not give to one
of them any of the flesh of his children
that he is eating. It will be all he has left
because of the suffering your enemy
will inflict on you during the siege of all
your cities. 56The most gentle and sensitive woman among you — so sensitive
and gentle that she would not venture
to touch the ground with the sole of her
foot — will begrudge the husband she
loves and her own son or daughter 57the
afterbirth from her womb and the children she bears. For in her dire need she
intends to eat them secretly because of
the suffering your enemy will inflict on
you during the siege of your cities.

58If you do not carefully follow all the

words of this law, which are written in
this book, and do not revere this glorious and awesome name — the LORD
your God — 59the LORD will send fearful
plagues on you and your descendants,
harsh and prolonged disasters, and severe and lingering illnesses. 60He will
bring on you all the diseases of Egypt
that you dreaded, and they will cling to
you. 61The LORD will also bring on you
every kind of sickness and disaster not
recorded in this Book of the Law, until
you are destroyed. 62You who were as
numerous as the stars in the sky will be
left but few in number, because you did
not obey the LORD your God. 63Just as it
pleased the LORD to make you prosper
and increase in number, so it will please
him to ruin and destroy you. You will be
uprooted from the land you are entering
to possess.

64Then the LORD will scatter you
among all nations, from one end of the
earth to the other. There you will worship other gods — gods of wood and
stone, which neither you nor your ancestors have known. 65Among those nations
you will find no repose, no resting place
for the sole of your foot. There the LORD
will give you an anxious mind, eyes weary with longing, and a despairing heart.
66You will live in constant suspense,
filled with dread both night and day,
never sure of your life. 67In the morning
you will say, "If only it were evening!"
and in the evening, "If only it were
morning!" — because of the terror that
will fill your hearts and the sights that
your eyes will see. 68The LORD will send
you back in ships to Egypt on a journey
I said you should never make again.
There you will offer yourselves for sale to
your enemies as male and female slaves,
but no one will buy you.

Renewal of the Covenant

29[a] These are the terms of the covenant the LORD commanded Mo-
ses to make with the Israelites in Moab,
in addition to the covenant he had made
with them at Horeb.

2Moses summoned all the Israelites
and said to them:

Your eyes have seen all that the LORD
did in Egypt to Pharaoh, to all his officials and to all his land. 3With your own
eyes you saw those great trials, those
signs and great wonders. 4But to this day
the LORD has not given you a mind that
understands or eyes that see or ears that
hear. 5Yet the LORD says, "During the forty years that I led you through the wilderness, your clothes did not wear out,
nor did the sandals on your feet. 6You
ate no bread and drank no wine or other
fermented drink. I did this so that you
might know that I am the LORD your
God."

7When you reached this place, Sihon
king of Heshbon and Og king of Bashan came out to fight against us, but
we defeated them. 8We took their land
and gave it as an inheritance to the Reubenites, the Gadites and the half-tribe of
Manasseh.

9Carefully follow the terms of this covenant, so that you may prosper in everything you do. 10All of you are standing
today in the presence of the LORD your
God — your leaders and chief men, your
elders and officials, and all the other men of Israel, 11together with your
children and your wives, and the foreigners living in your camps who chop
your wood and carry your water. 12You
are standing here in order to enter into
a covenant with the LORD your God, a
covenant the LORD is making with you
this day and sealing with an oath, 13to
confirm you this day as his people, that
he may be your God as he promised you
and as he swore to your fathers, Abraham, Isaac and Jacob. 14I am making
this covenant, with its oath, not only
with you 15who are standing here with
us today in the presence of the LORD our
God but also with those who are not here
today.

16You yourselves know how we lived
in Egypt and how we passed through
the countries on the way here. 17You saw
among them their detestable images
and idols of wood and stone, of silver
and gold. 18Make sure there is no man or
woman, clan or tribe among you today
whose heart turns away from the LORD
our God to go and worship the gods of
those nations; make sure there is no
root among you that produces such bitter poison.

19When such a person hears the words
of this oath and they invoke a blessing
on themselves, thinking, "I will be safe,
even though I persist in going my own
way," they will bring disaster on the watered land as well as the dry. 20The LORD
will never be willing to forgive them; his
wrath and zeal will burn against them.
All the curses written in this book will
fall on them, and the LORD will blot out

[a] In Hebrew texts 29:1 is numbered 28:69, and 29:2-29 is numbered 29:1-28.

their names from under heaven. 21The
LORD will single them out from all the
tribes of Israel for disaster, according to
all the curses of the covenant written in
this Book of the Law.
22Your children who follow you in later generations and foreigners who come
from distant lands will see the calamities that have fallen on the land and
the diseases with which the LORD has
afflicted it. 23The whole land will be a
burning waste of salt and sulfur — nothing planted, nothing sprouting, no vegetation growing on it. It will be like the
destruction of Sodom and Gomorrah,
Admah and Zeboyim, which the LORD
overthrew in fierce anger. 24All the nations will ask: "Why has the LORD done
this to this land? Why this fierce, burning anger?"
25And the answer will be: "It is because
this people abandoned the covenant of
the LORD, the God of their ancestors, the
covenant he made with them when he
brought them out of Egypt. 26They went
off and worshiped other gods and bowed
down to them, gods they did not know,
gods he had not given them. 27There-
fore the LORD's anger burned against
this land, so that he brought on it all the
curses written in this book. 28In furious
anger and in great wrath the LORD uprooted them from their land and thrust
them into another land, as it is now."
29The secret things belong to the LORD
our God, but the things revealed belong
to us and to our children forever, that we
may follow all the words of this law.

Prosperity After Turning to the LORD

30 When all these blessings and curses I have set before you come on
you and you take them to heart wherever the LORD your God disperses you
among the nations, 2and when you and
your children return to the LORD your
God and obey him with all your heart
and with all your soul according to everything I command you today, 3then
the LORD your God will restore your fortunes[a] and have compassion on you and
gather you again from all the nations
where he scattered you. 4Even if you
have been banished to the most distant
land under the heavens, from there the
LORD your God will gather you and bring
you back. 5He will bring you to the land
that belonged to your ancestors, and
you will take possession of it. He will
make you more prosperous and numerous than your ancestors. 6The LORD your
God will circumcise your hearts and the
hearts of your descendants, so that you
may love him with all your heart and
with all your soul, and live. 7The LORD
your God will put all these curses on your
enemies who hate and persecute you.
8You will again obey the LORD and follow
all his commands I am giving you today.
9Then the LORD your God will make you
most prosperous in all the work of your
hands and in the fruit of your womb, the
young of your livestock and the crops of
your land. The LORD will again delight
in you and make you prosperous, just as
he delighted in your ancestors, 10if you
obey the LORD your God and keep his
commands and decrees that are written
in this Book of the Law and turn to the
LORD your God with all your heart and
with all your soul.

The Offer of Life or Death

11Now what I am commanding you today is not too difficult for you or beyond
your reach. 12It is not up in heaven, so
that you have to ask, "Who will ascend
into heaven to get it and proclaim it to
us so we may obey it?" 13Nor is it beyond
the sea, so that you have to ask, "Who
will cross the sea to get it and proclaim
it to us so we may obey it?" 14No, the word
is very near you; it is in your mouth and
in your heart so you may obey it.
15See, I set before you today life and
prosperity, death and destruction. 16For
I command you today to love the LORD
your God, to walk in obedience to him,
and to keep his commands, decrees and
laws; then you will live and increase, and
the LORD your God will bless you in the
land you are entering to possess.
17But if your heart turns away and you
are not obedient, and if you are drawn
away to bow down to other gods and
worship them, 18I declare to you this day
that you will certainly be destroyed. You
will not live long in the land you are
crossing the Jordan to enter and possess.
19This day I call the heavens and the
earth as witnesses against you that I
have set before you life and death, blessings and curses. Now choose life, so that
you and your children may live 20and
that you may love the LORD your God,
listen to his voice, and hold fast to him.
For the LORD is your life, and he will give
you many years in the land he swore to
give to your fathers, Abraham, Isaac and
Jacob.

[a] 3 Or *will bring you back from captivity*

Joshua to Succeed Moses

31 Then Moses went out and spoke these words to all Israel: 2"I am now a hundred and twenty years old and I am no longer able to lead you. The LORD has said to me, 'You shall not cross the Jordan.' 3The LORD your God himself will cross over ahead of you. He will destroy these nations before you, and you will take possession of their land. Joshua also will cross over ahead of you, as the LORD said. 4And the LORD will do to them what he did to Sihon and Og, the kings of the Amorites, whom he destroyed along with their land. 5The LORD will deliver them to you, and you must do to them all that I have commanded you. 6Be strong and courageous. Do not be afraid or terrified because of them, for the LORD your God goes with you; he will never leave you nor forsake you."

7Then Moses summoned Joshua and said to him in the presence of all Israel, "Be strong and courageous, for you must go with this people into the land that the LORD swore to their ancestors to give them, and you must divide it among them as their inheritance. 8The LORD himself goes before you and will be with you; he will never leave you nor forsake you. Do not be afraid; do not be discouraged."

Public Reading of the Law

9So Moses wrote down this law and gave it to the Levitical priests, who carried the ark of the covenant of the LORD, and to all the elders of Israel. 10Then Moses commanded them: "At the end of every seven years, in the year for canceling debts, during the Festival of Tabernacles, 11when all Israel comes to appear before the LORD your God at the place he will choose, you shall read this law before them in their hearing. 12Assemble the people — men, women and children, and the foreigners residing in your towns — so they can listen and learn to fear the LORD your God and follow carefully all the words of this law. 13Their children, who do not know this law, must hear it and learn to fear the LORD your God as long as you live in the land you are crossing the Jordan to possess."

Israel's Rebellion Predicted

14The LORD said to Moses, "Now the day of your death is near. Call Joshua and present yourselves at the tent of meeting, where I will commission him." So Moses and Joshua came and presented themselves at the tent of meeting.

15Then the LORD appeared at the tent in a pillar of cloud, and the cloud stood over the entrance to the tent. 16And the LORD said to Moses: "You are going to rest with your ancestors, and these people will soon prostitute themselves to the foreign gods of the land they are entering. They will forsake me and break the covenant I made with them. 17And in that day I will become angry with them and forsake them; I will hide my face from them, and they will be destroyed. Many disasters and calamities will come on them, and in that day they will ask, 'Have not these disasters come on us because our God is not with us?' 18And I will certainly hide my face in that day because of all their wickedness in turning to other gods.

19"Now write down this song and teach it to the Israelites and have them sing it, so that it may be a witness for me against them. 20When I have brought them into the land flowing with milk and honey, the land I promised on oath to their ancestors, and when they eat their fill and thrive, they will turn to other gods and worship them, rejecting me and breaking my covenant. 21And when many disasters and calamities come on them, this song will testify against them, because it will not be forgotten by their descendants. I know what they are disposed to do, even before I bring them into the land I promised them on oath." 22So Moses wrote down this song that day and taught it to the Israelites.

23The LORD gave this command to Joshua son of Nun: "Be strong and courageous, for you will bring the Israelites into the land I promised them on oath, and I myself will be with you."

24After Moses finished writing in a book the words of this law from beginning to end, 25he gave this command to the Levites who carried the ark of the covenant of the LORD: 26"Take this Book of the Law and place it beside the ark of the covenant of the LORD your God. There it will remain as a witness against you. 27For I know how rebellious and stiff-necked you are. If you have been rebellious against the LORD while I am still alive and with you, how much more will you rebel after I die! 28Assemble before me all the elders of your tribes and all your officials, so that I can speak these words in their hearing and call the heavens and the earth to testify against them. 29For I know that after my death you are sure to become utterly corrupt and to turn from the way I have commanded you. In days to come, disaster will fall on you because you will do evil in the sight of the LORD and arouse his anger by what your hands have made."

The Song of Moses

30 And Moses recited the words of this song from beginning to end in the hearing of the whole assembly of Israel:

32 Listen, you heavens, and I will speak;
hear, you earth, the words of my mouth.
2 Let my teaching fall like rain
and my words descend like dew,
like showers on new grass,
like abundant rain on tender plants.

3 I will proclaim the name of the LORD.
Oh, praise the greatness of our God!
4 He is the Rock, his works are perfect,
and all his ways are just.
A faithful God who does no wrong,
upright and just is he.

5 They are corrupt and not his children;
to their shame they are a warped and crooked generation.
6 Is this the way you repay the LORD,
you foolish and unwise people?
Is he not your Father, your Creator,[a]
who made you and formed you?

7 Remember the days of old;
consider the generations long past.
Ask your father and he will tell you,
your elders, and they will explain to you.
8 When the Most High gave the nations their inheritance,
when he divided all mankind,
he set up boundaries for the peoples
according to the number of the sons of Israel.[b]
9 For the LORD's portion is his people,
Jacob his allotted inheritance.

10 In a desert land he found him,
in a barren and howling waste.
He shielded him and cared for him;
he guarded him as the apple of his eye,
11 like an eagle that stirs up its nest
and hovers over its young,
that spreads its wings to catch them
and carries them aloft.
12 The LORD alone led him;
no foreign god was with him.
13 He made him ride on the heights of the land
and fed him with the fruit of the fields.
He nourished him with honey from the rock,
and with oil from the flinty crag,
14 with curds and milk from herd and flock
and with fattened lambs and goats,
with choice rams of Bashan
and the finest kernels of wheat.
You drank the foaming blood of the grape.

15 Jeshurun[c] grew fat and kicked;
filled with food, they became heavy and sleek.
They abandoned the God who made them
and rejected the Rock their Savior.
16 They made him jealous with their foreign gods
and angered him with their detestable idols.
17 They sacrificed to false gods, which are not God—
gods they had not known,
gods that recently appeared,
gods your ancestors did not fear.
18 You deserted the Rock, who fathered you;
you forgot the God who gave you birth.

19 The LORD saw this and rejected them
because he was angered by his sons and daughters.
20 "I will hide my face from them," he said,
"and see what their end will be;
for they are a perverse generation,
children who are unfaithful.
21 They made me jealous by what is no god
and angered me with their worthless idols.
I will make them envious by those who are not a people;
I will make them angry by a nation that has no understanding.
22 For a fire will be kindled by my wrath,
one that burns down to the realm of the dead below.
It will devour the earth and its harvests
and set afire the foundations of the mountains.

23 "I will heap calamities on them
and spend my arrows against them.

[a] 6 Or *Father, who bought you* [b] 8 Masoretic Text; Dead Sea Scrolls (see also Septuagint) *sons of God* [c] 15 *Jeshurun* means *the upright one,* that is, Israel.

24 I will send wasting famine against
them,
consuming pestilence and deadly
plague;
I will send against them the fangs of
wild beasts,
the venom of vipers that glide in
the dust.
25 In the street the sword will make
them childless;
in their homes terror will reign.
The young men and young women
will perish,
the infants and those with gray
hair.
26 I said I would scatter them
and erase their name from human
memory,
27 but I dreaded the taunt of the enemy,
lest the adversary misunderstand
and say, 'Our hand has triumphed;
the LORD has not done all this.'"
28 They are a nation without sense,
there is no discernment in them.
29 If only they were wise and would
understand this
and discern what their end will be!
30 How could one man chase a
thousand,
or two put ten thousand to flight,
unless their Rock had sold them,
unless the LORD had given them
up?
31 For their rock is not like our Rock,
as even our enemies concede.
32 Their vine comes from the vine of
Sodom
and from the fields of Gomorrah.
Their grapes are filled with poison,
and their clusters with bitterness.
33 Their wine is the venom of serpents,
the deadly poison of cobras.
34 "Have I not kept this in reserve
and sealed it in my vaults?
35 It is mine to avenge; I will repay.
In due time their foot will slip;
their day of disaster is near
and their doom rushes upon them."
36 The LORD will vindicate his people
and relent concerning his servants
when he sees their strength is gone
and no one is left, slave or free.[a]
37 He will say: "Now where are their
gods,
the rock they took refuge in,
38 the gods who ate the fat of their
sacrifices
and drank the wine of their drink
offerings?
Let them rise up to help you!
Let them give you shelter!
39 "See now that I myself am he!
There is no god besides me.
I put to death and I bring to life,
I have wounded and I will heal,
and no one can deliver out of my
hand.
40 I lift my hand to heaven and
solemnly swear:
As surely as I live forever,
41 when I sharpen my flashing sword
and my hand grasps it in
judgment,
I will take vengeance on my
adversaries
and repay those who hate me.
42 I will make my arrows drunk with
blood,
while my sword devours flesh:
the blood of the slain and the
captives,
the heads of the enemy leaders."
43 Rejoice, you nations, with his
people,[b,c]
for he will avenge the blood of his
servants;
he will take vengeance on his
enemies
and make atonement for his land
and people.

44 Moses came with Joshua[d] son of Nun
and spoke all the words of this song in
the hearing of the people. 45 When Moses
finished reciting all these words to all Israel, 46 he said to them, "Take to heart all
the words I have solemnly declared to
you this day, so that you may command
your children to obey carefully all the
words of this law. 47 They are not just idle
words for you — they are your life. By
them you will live long in the land you
are crossing the Jordan to possess."

Moses to Die on Mount Nebo

48 On that same day the LORD told Moses, 49 "Go up into the Abarim Range to
Mount Nebo in Moab, across from Jericho, and view Canaan, the land I am
giving the Israelites as their own possession. 50 There on the mountain that you
have climbed you will die and be gathered to your people, just as your brother Aaron died on Mount Hor and was
gathered to his people. 51 This is because

[a] 36 Or *and they are without a ruler or leader* [b] 43 Or *Make his people rejoice, you nations* [c] 43 Masoretic Text; Dead Sea Scrolls (see also Septuagint) *people, / and let all the angels worship him, /* [d] 44 Hebrew *Hoshea,* a variant of *Joshua*

both of you broke faith with me in the
presence of the Israelites at the waters of
Meribah Kadesh in the Desert of Zin and
because you did not uphold my holiness
among the Israelites. 52 Therefore, you
will see the land only from a distance;
you will not enter the land I am giving
to the people of Israel."

Moses Blesses the Tribes

33 This is the blessing that Moses the
man of God pronounced on the Israelites before his death. 2 He said:

"The LORD came from Sinai
and dawned over them from Seir;
he shone forth from Mount Paran.
He came with[a] myriads of holy ones
from the south, from his mountain slopes.[b]
3 Surely it is you who love the people;
all the holy ones are in your hand.
At your feet they all bow down,
and from you receive instruction,
4 the law that Moses gave us,
the possession of the assembly of Jacob.
5 He was king over Jeshurun[c]
when the leaders of the people assembled,
along with the tribes of Israel.

6 "Let Reuben live and not die,
nor[d] his people be few."

7 And this he said about Judah:

"Hear, LORD, the cry of Judah;
bring him to his people.
With his own hands he defends his cause.
Oh, be his help against his foes!"

8 About Levi he said:

"Your Thummim and Urim belong
to your faithful servant.
You tested him at Massah;
you contended with him at the waters of Meribah.
9 He said of his father and mother,
'I have no regard for them.'
He did not recognize his brothers
or acknowledge his own children,
but he watched over your word
and guarded your covenant.
10 He teaches your precepts to Jacob
and your law to Israel.
He offers incense before you
and whole burnt offerings on your altar.
11 Bless all his skills, LORD,
and be pleased with the work of his hands.
Strike down those who rise against him,
his foes till they rise no more."

12 About Benjamin he said:

"Let the beloved of the LORD rest
secure in him,
for he shields him all day long,
and the one the LORD loves rests
between his shoulders."

13 About Joseph he said:

"May the LORD bless his land
with the precious dew from heaven above
and with the deep waters that lie below;
14 with the best the sun brings forth
and the finest the moon can yield;
15 with the choicest gifts of the ancient mountains
and the fruitfulness of the everlasting hills;
16 with the best gifts of the earth and its fullness
and the favor of him who dwelt in the burning bush.
Let all these rest on the head of Joseph,
on the brow of the prince among[e] his brothers.
17 In majesty he is like a firstborn bull;
his horns are the horns of a wild ox.
With them he will gore the nations,
even those at the ends of the earth.
Such are the ten thousands of Ephraim;
such are the thousands of Manasseh."

18 About Zebulun he said:

"Rejoice, Zebulun, in your going out,
and you, Issachar, in your tents.
19 They will summon peoples to the mountain
and there offer the sacrifices of the righteous;
they will feast on the abundance of the seas,
on the treasures hidden in the sand."

20 About Gad he said:

"Blessed is he who enlarges Gad's domain!
Gad lives there like a lion,
tearing at arm or head.

[a] 2 Or *from* [b] 2 The meaning of the Hebrew for this phrase is uncertain. [c] 5 *Jeshurun* means *the upright one*, that is, Israel; also in verse 26. [d] 6 Or *but let* [e] 16 Or *of the one separated from*

21 He chose the best land for himself;
the leader's portion was kept for him.
When the heads of the people assembled,
he carried out the LORD's righteous will,
and his judgments concerning Israel."

22 About Dan he said:

"Dan is a lion's cub,
springing out of Bashan."

23 About Naphtali he said:

"Naphtali is abounding with the favor of the LORD
and is full of his blessing;
he will inherit southward to the lake."

24 About Asher he said:

"Most blessed of sons is Asher;
let him be favored by his brothers,
and let him bathe his feet in oil.
25 The bolts of your gates will be iron and bronze,
and your strength will equal your days.

26 "There is no one like the God of Jeshurun,
who rides across the heavens to help you
and on the clouds in his majesty.
27 The eternal God is your refuge,
and underneath are the everlasting arms.
He will drive out your enemies before you,
saying, 'Destroy them!'
28 So Israel will live in safety;
Jacob will dwell[a] secure
in a land of grain and new wine,
where the heavens drop dew.
29 Blessed are you, Israel!
Who is like you,
a people saved by the LORD?
He is your shield and helper
and your glorious sword.
Your enemies will cower before you,
and you will tread on their heights."

The Death of Moses

34 Then Moses climbed Mount Nebo
from the plains of Moab to the top
of Pisgah, across from Jericho. There the
LORD showed him the whole land — from
Gilead to Dan, 2all of Naphtali, the territory of Ephraim and Manasseh, all the
land of Judah as far as the Mediterranean Sea, 3the Negev and the whole region from the Valley of Jericho, the City
of Palms, as far as Zoar. 4Then the LORD
said to him, "This is the land I promised
on oath to Abraham, Isaac and Jacob
when I said, 'I will give it to your descendants.' I have let you see it with your
eyes, but you will not cross over into it."
5And Moses the servant of the LORD
died there in Moab, as the LORD had
said. 6He buried him[b] in Moab, in the
valley opposite Beth Peor, but to this
day no one knows where his grave is.
7Moses was a hundred and twenty years
old when he died, yet his eyes were not
weak nor his strength gone. 8The Israelites grieved for Moses in the plains of
Moab thirty days, until the time of weeping and mourning was over.
9Now Joshua son of Nun was filled
with the spirit[c] of wisdom because Moses had laid his hands on him. So the Israelites listened to him and did what the
LORD had commanded Moses.
10Since then, no prophet has risen in
Israel like Moses, whom the LORD knew
face to face, 11who did all those signs
and wonders the LORD sent him to do in
Egypt — to Pharaoh and to all his officials and to his whole land. 12For no one
has ever shown the mighty power or performed the awesome deeds that Moses
did in the sight of all Israel.

[a] 28 Septuagint; Hebrew *Jacob's spring is* [b] 6 Or *He was buried* [c] 9 Or *Spirit*

JOSHUA

Joshua Installed as Leader

1 After the death of Moses the servant
of the LORD, the LORD said to Joshua
son of Nun, Moses' aide: 2"Moses my servant is dead. Now then, you and all these
people, get ready to cross the Jordan
River into the land I am about to give to
them — to the Israelites. 3I will give you
every place where you set your foot, as
I promised Moses. 4Your territory will
extend from the desert to Lebanon, and
from the great river, the Euphrates — all
the Hittite country — to the Mediterranean Sea in the west. 5No one will be
able to stand against you all the days of
your life. As I was with Moses, so I will
be with you; I will never leave you nor
forsake you. 6Be strong and courageous,
because you will lead these people to inherit the land I swore to their ancestors
to give them.

7"Be strong and very courageous. Be
careful to obey all the law my servant
Moses gave you; do not turn from it to
the right or to the left, that you may be
successful wherever you go. 8Keep this
Book of the Law always on your lips;
meditate on it day and night, so that you
may be careful to do everything written
in it. Then you will be prosperous and successful. 9Have I not commanded you? Be
strong and courageous. Do not be afraid;
do not be discouraged, for the LORD your
God will be with you wherever you go."

10So Joshua ordered the officers of the
people: 11"Go through the camp and tell
the people, 'Get your provisions ready.
Three days from now you will cross the
Jordan here to go in and take possession
of the land the LORD your God is giving
you for your own.'"

12But to the Reubenites, the Gadites
and the half-tribe of Manasseh, Joshua
said, 13"Remember the command that
Moses the servant of the LORD gave you
after he said, 'The LORD your God will
give you rest by giving you this land.'
14Your wives, your children and your
livestock may stay in the land that Moses gave you east of the Jordan, but all
your fighting men, ready for battle,
must cross over ahead of your fellow Israelites. You are to help them 15until the
LORD gives them rest, as he has done for
you, and until they too have taken possession of the land the LORD your God is
giving them. After that, you may go back
and occupy your own land, which Moses
the servant of the LORD gave you east of
the Jordan toward the sunrise."

16Then they answered Joshua, "Whatever you have commanded us we will
do, and wherever you send us we will go.
17Just as we fully obeyed Moses, so we
will obey you. Only may the LORD your
God be with you as he was with Moses.
18Whoever rebels against your word and
does not obey it, whatever you may command them, will be put to death. Only be
strong and courageous!"

Rahab and the Spies

2 Then Joshua son of Nun secretly sent
two spies from Shittim. "Go, look over
the land," he said, "especially Jericho."
So they went and entered the house of
a prostitute named Rahab and stayed
there.

2The king of Jericho was told, "Look,
some of the Israelites have come here
tonight to spy out the land." 3So the king
of Jericho sent this message to Rahab:
"Bring out the men who came to you and
entered your house, because they have
come to spy out the whole land."

4But the woman had taken the two
men and hidden them. She said, "Yes,
the men came to me, but I did not know
where they had come from. 5At dusk,
when it was time to close the city gate,
they left. I don't know which way they
went. Go after them quickly. You may
catch up with them." 6(But she had tak-
en them up to the roof and hidden them
under the stalks of flax she had laid out
on the roof.) 7So the men set out in pursuit of the spies on the road that leads
to the fords of the Jordan, and as soon
as the pursuers had gone out, the gate
was shut.

8Before the spies lay down for the
night, she went up on the roof 9and said
to them, "I know that the LORD has giv-
en you this land and that a great fear
of you has fallen on us, so that all who
live in this country are melting in fear
because of you. 10We have heard how the
LORD dried up the water of the Red Sea[a]

[a] 10 Or *the Sea of Reeds*

for you when you came out of Egypt, and
what you did to Sihon and Og, the two
kings of the Amorites east of the Jordan, whom you completely destroyed.[a]
11When we heard of it, our hearts melted in fear and everyone's courage failed
because of you, for the LORD your God is
God in heaven above and on the earth
below.

12"Now then, please swear to me by the
LORD that you will show kindness to my
family, because I have shown kindness
to you. Give me a sure sign 13that you will
spare the lives of my father and mother,
my brothers and sisters, and all who belong to them — and that you will save us
from death."

14"Our lives for your lives!" the men assured her. "If you don't tell what we are
doing, we will treat you kindly and faithfully when the LORD gives us the land."

15So she let them down by a rope
through the window, for the house she
lived in was part of the city wall. 16She
said to them, "Go to the hills so the pursuers will not find you. Hide yourselves
there three days until they return, and
then go on your way."

17Now the men had said to her, "This
oath you made us swear will not be
binding on us 18unless, when we enter
the land, you have tied this scarlet cord
in the window through which you let us
down, and unless you have brought your
father and mother, your brothers and
all your family into your house. 19If any
of them go outside your house into the
street, their blood will be on their own
heads; we will not be responsible. As for
those who are in the house with you,
their blood will be on our head if a hand
is laid on them. 20But if you tell what we
are doing, we will be released from the
oath you made us swear."

21"Agreed," she replied. "Let it be as
you say."

So she sent them away, and they departed. And she tied the scarlet cord in
the window.

22When they left, they went into the
hills and stayed there three days, until the pursuers had searched all along
the road and returned without finding
them. 23Then the two men started back.
They went down out of the hills, forded
the river and came to Joshua son of Nun
and told him everything that had happened to them. 24They said to Joshua,
"The LORD has surely given the whole
land into our hands; all the people are
melting in fear because of us."

Crossing the Jordan

3 Early in the morning Joshua and all
the Israelites set out from Shittim
and went to the Jordan, where they
camped before crossing over. 2After
three days the officers went throughout
the camp, 3giving orders to the people:
"When you see the ark of the covenant
of the LORD your God, and the Levitical
priests carrying it, you are to move out
from your positions and follow it. 4Then
you will know which way to go, since you
have never been this way before. But
keep a distance of about two thousand
cubits[b] between you and the ark; do not
go near it."

5Joshua told the people, "Consecrate
yourselves, for tomorrow the LORD will
do amazing things among you."

6Joshua said to the priests, "Take up
the ark of the covenant and pass on
ahead of the people." So they took it up
and went ahead of them.

7And the LORD said to Joshua, "Today
I will begin to exalt you in the eyes of all
Israel, so they may know that I am with
you as I was with Moses. 8Tell the priests
who carry the ark of the covenant:
'When you reach the edge of the Jordan's
waters, go and stand in the river.' "

9Joshua said to the Israelites, "Come
here and listen to the words of the LORD
your God. 10This is how you will know
that the living God is among you and
that he will certainly drive out before
you the Canaanites, Hittites, Hivites,
Perizzites, Girgashites, Amorites and
Jebusites. 11See, the ark of the covenant
of the Lord of all the earth will go into
the Jordan ahead of you. 12Now then,
choose twelve men from the tribes of Israel, one from each tribe. 13And as soon
as the priests who carry the ark of the
LORD — the Lord of all the earth — set
foot in the Jordan, its waters flowing
downstream will be cut off and stand up
in a heap."

14So when the people broke camp to
cross the Jordan, the priests carrying the
ark of the covenant went ahead of them.
15Now the Jordan is at flood stage all
during harvest. Yet as soon as the priests
who carried the ark reached the Jordan
and their feet touched the water's edge,
16the water from upstream stopped flowing. It piled up in a heap a great distance

[a] *10* The Hebrew term refers to the irrevocable giving over of things or persons to the LORD, often by totally destroying them. [b] *4* That is, about 3,000 feet or about 900 meters

away, at a town called Adam in the vicinity of Zarethan, while the water flowing down to the Sea of the Arabah (that
is, the Dead Sea) was completely cut off.
So the people crossed over opposite Jericho. 17 The priests who carried the ark of
the covenant of the LORD stopped in the
middle of the Jordan and stood on dry
ground, while all Israel passed by until the whole nation had completed the
crossing on dry ground.

4 When the whole nation had finished
crossing the Jordan, the LORD said
to Joshua, 2 "Choose twelve men from
among the people, one from each tribe,
3 and tell them to take up twelve stones
from the middle of the Jordan, from
right where the priests are standing,
and carry them over with you and put
them down at the place where you stay
tonight."

4 So Joshua called together the twelve
men he had appointed from the Israelites, one from each tribe, 5 and said
to them, "Go over before the ark of the
LORD your God into the middle of the Jordan. Each of you is to take up a stone on
his shoulder, according to the number of
the tribes of the Israelites, 6 to serve as
a sign among you. In the future, when
your children ask you, 'What do these
stones mean?' 7 tell them that the flow
of the Jordan was cut off before the
ark of the covenant of the LORD. When
it crossed the Jordan, the waters of the
Jordan were cut off. These stones are to
be a memorial to the people of Israel forever."

8 So the Israelites did as Joshua commanded them. They took twelve stones
from the middle of the Jordan, according to the number of the tribes of the
Israelites, as the LORD had told Joshua;
and they carried them over with them to
their camp, where they put them down.
9 Joshua set up the twelve stones that
had been[a] in the middle of the Jordan
at the spot where the priests who carried
the ark of the covenant had stood. And
they are there to this day.

10 Now the priests who carried the ark
remained standing in the middle of
the Jordan until everything the LORD
had commanded Joshua was done by
the people, just as Moses had directed
Joshua. The people hurried over, 11 and
as soon as all of them had crossed, the
ark of the LORD and the priests came to
the other side while the people watched.
12 The men of Reuben, Gad and the half-
tribe of Manasseh crossed over, ready
for battle, in front of the Israelites, as
Moses had directed them. 13 About forty
thousand armed for battle crossed over
before the LORD to the plains of Jericho
for war.

14 That day the LORD exalted Joshua in
the sight of all Israel; and they stood in
awe of him all the days of his life, just as
they had stood in awe of Moses.

15 Then the LORD said to Joshua,
16 "Command the priests carrying the
ark of the covenant law to come up out
of the Jordan."

17 So Joshua commanded the priests,
"Come up out of the Jordan."

18 And the priests came up out of the
river carrying the ark of the covenant of
the LORD. No sooner had they set their
feet on the dry ground than the waters
of the Jordan returned to their place and
ran at flood stage as before.

19 On the tenth day of the first month
the people went up from the Jordan and
camped at Gilgal on the eastern border
of Jericho. 20 And Joshua set up at Gilgal
the twelve stones they had taken out of
the Jordan. 21 He said to the Israelites,
"In the future when your descendants
ask their parents, 'What do these stones
mean?' 22 tell them, 'Israel crossed the
Jordan on dry ground.' 23 For the LORD
your God dried up the Jordan before you
until you had crossed over. The LORD
your God did to the Jordan what he had
done to the Red Sea[b] when he dried it
up before us until we had crossed over.
24 He did this so that all the peoples of the
earth might know that the hand of the
LORD is powerful and so that you might
always fear the LORD your God."

5 Now when all the Amorite kings west
of the Jordan and all the Canaanite
kings along the coast heard how the
LORD had dried up the Jordan before the
Israelites until they[c] had crossed over,
their hearts melted in fear and they no
longer had the courage to face the Israelites.

Circumcision and Passover at Gilgal

2 At that time the LORD said to Joshua,
"Make flint knives and circumcise the
Israelites again." 3 So Joshua made flint
knives and circumcised the Israelites at
Gibeath Haaraloth.[d]

4 Now this is why he did so: All those
who came out of Egypt — all the men

[a] 9 Or *Joshua also set up twelve stones* [b] 23 Or *the Sea of Reeds* [c] 1 Another textual tradition *we* [d] 3 *Gibeath Haaraloth* means *the hill of foreskins.*

of military age — died in the wilderness on the way after leaving Egypt. 5All the people that came out had been circumcised, but all the people born in the wilderness during the journey from Egypt had not. 6The Israelites had moved about in the wilderness forty years until all the men who were of military age when they left Egypt had died, since they had not obeyed the LORD. For the LORD had sworn to them that they would not see the land he had solemnly promised their ancestors to give us, a land flowing with milk and honey. 7So he raised up their sons in their place, and these were the ones Joshua circumcised. They were still uncircumcised because they had not been circumcised on the way. 8And after the whole nation had been circumcised, they remained where they were in camp until they were healed.

9Then the LORD said to Joshua, "Today I have rolled away the reproach of Egypt from you." So the place has been called Gilgal[a] to this day.

10On the evening of the fourteenth day of the month, while camped at Gilgal on the plains of Jericho, the Israelites celebrated the Passover. 11The day after the Passover, that very day, they ate some of the produce of the land: unleavened bread and roasted grain. 12The manna stopped the day after[b] they ate this food from the land; there was no longer any manna for the Israelites, but that year they ate the produce of Canaan.

The Fall of Jericho

13Now when Joshua was near Jericho, he looked up and saw a man standing in front of him with a drawn sword in his hand. Joshua went up to him and asked, "Are you for us or for our enemies?"

14"Neither," he replied, "but as commander of the army of the LORD I have now come." Then Joshua fell facedown to the ground in reverence, and asked him, "What message does my Lord[c] have for his servant?"

15The commander of the LORD's army replied, "Take off your sandals, for the place where you are standing is holy." And Joshua did so.

6 Now the gates of Jericho were securely barred because of the Israelites. No one went out and no one came in.

2Then the LORD said to Joshua, "See, I have delivered Jericho into your hands, along with its king and its fighting men. 3March around the city once with all the armed men. Do this for six days. 4Have seven priests carry trumpets of rams' horns in front of the ark. On the seventh day, march around the city seven times, with the priests blowing the trumpets. 5When you hear them sound a long blast on the trumpets, have the whole army give a loud shout; then the wall of the city will collapse and the army will go up, everyone straight in."

6So Joshua son of Nun called the priests and said to them, "Take up the ark of the covenant of the LORD and have seven priests carry trumpets in front of it." 7And he ordered the army, "Advance! March around the city, with an armed guard going ahead of the ark of the LORD."

8When Joshua had spoken to the people, the seven priests carrying the seven trumpets before the LORD went forward, blowing their trumpets, and the ark of the LORD's covenant followed them. 9The armed guard marched ahead of the priests who blew the trumpets, and the rear guard followed the ark. All this time the trumpets were sounding. 10But Joshua had commanded the army, "Do not give a war cry, do not raise your voices, do not say a word until the day I tell you to shout. Then shout!" 11So he had the ark of the LORD carried around the city, circling it once. Then the army returned to camp and spent the night there.

12Joshua got up early the next morning and the priests took up the ark of the LORD. 13The seven priests carrying the seven trumpets went forward, marching before the ark of the LORD and blowing the trumpets. The armed men went ahead of them and the rear guard followed the ark of the LORD, while the trumpets kept sounding. 14So on the second day they marched around the city once and returned to the camp. They did this for six days.

15On the seventh day, they got up at daybreak and marched around the city seven times in the same manner, except that on that day they circled the city seven times. 16The seventh time around, when the priests sounded the trumpet blast, Joshua commanded the army, "Shout! For the LORD has given you the city! 17The city and all that is in it are to be devoted[d] to the LORD. Only Rahab the

[a] 9 *Gilgal* sounds like the Hebrew for *roll.* [b] 12 Or *the day* [c] 14 Or *lord* [d] 17 The Hebrew term refers to the irrevocable giving over of things or persons to the LORD, often by totally destroying them; also in verses 18 and 21.

prostitute and all who are with her in her house shall be spared, because she hid the spies we sent. 18But keep away from the devoted things, so that you will not bring about your own destruction by taking any of them. Otherwise you will make the camp of Israel liable to destruction and bring trouble on it. 19All the silver and gold and the articles of bronze and iron are sacred to the LORD and must go into his treasury."

20When the trumpets sounded, the army shouted, and at the sound of the trumpet, when the men gave a loud shout, the wall collapsed; so everyone charged straight in, and they took the city. 21They devoted the city to the LORD and destroyed with the sword every living thing in it — men and women, young and old, cattle, sheep and donkeys.

22Joshua said to the two men who had spied out the land, "Go into the prostitute's house and bring her out and all who belong to her, in accordance with your oath to her." 23So the young men who had done the spying went in and brought out Rahab, her father and mother, her brothers and sisters and all who belonged to her. They brought out her entire family and put them in a place outside the camp of Israel.

24Then they burned the whole city and everything in it, but they put the silver and gold and the articles of bronze and iron into the treasury of the LORD's house. 25But Joshua spared Rahab the prostitute, with her family and all who belonged to her, because she hid the men Joshua had sent as spies to Jericho — and she lives among the Israelites to this day.

26At that time Joshua pronounced this solemn oath: "Cursed before the LORD is the one who undertakes to rebuild this city, Jericho:

"At the cost of his firstborn son
  he will lay its foundations;
at the cost of his youngest
  he will set up its gates."

27So the LORD was with Joshua, and his fame spread throughout the land.

Achan's Sin

7 But the Israelites were unfaithful in regard to the devoted things[a]; Achan son of Karmi, the son of Zimri,[b] the son of Zerah, of the tribe of Judah, took some of them. So the LORD's anger burned against Israel.

2Now Joshua sent men from Jericho to Ai, which is near Beth Aven to the east of Bethel, and told them, "Go up and spy out the region." So the men went up and spied out Ai.

3When they returned to Joshua, they said, "Not all the army will have to go up against Ai. Send two or three thousand men to take it and do not weary the whole army, for only a few people live there." 4So about three thousand went up; but they were routed by the men of Ai, 5who killed about thirty-six of them. They chased the Israelites from the city gate as far as the stone quarries and struck them down on the slopes. At this the hearts of the people melted in fear and became like water.

6Then Joshua tore his clothes and fell facedown to the ground before the ark of the LORD, remaining there till evening. The elders of Israel did the same, and sprinkled dust on their heads. 7And Joshua said, "Alas, Sovereign LORD, why did you ever bring this people across the Jordan to deliver us into the hands of the Amorites to destroy us? If only we had been content to stay on the other side of the Jordan! 8Pardon your servant, Lord. What can I say, now that Israel has been routed by its enemies? 9The Canaanites and the other people of the country will hear about this and they will surround us and wipe out our name from the earth. What then will you do for your own great name?"

10The LORD said to Joshua, "Stand up! What are you doing down on your face? 11Israel has sinned; they have violated my covenant, which I commanded them to keep. They have taken some of the devoted things; they have stolen, they have lied, they have put them with their own possessions. 12That is why the Israelites cannot stand against their enemies; they turn their backs and run because they have been made liable to destruction. I will not be with you anymore unless you destroy whatever among you is devoted to destruction.

13"Go, consecrate the people. Tell them, 'Consecrate yourselves in preparation for tomorrow; for this is what the LORD, the God of Israel, says: There are devoted things among you, Israel. You cannot

[a] *1* The Hebrew term refers to the irrevocable giving over of things or persons to the LORD, often by totally destroying them; also in verses 11, 12, 13 and 15. [b] *1* See Septuagint and 1 Chron. 2:6; Hebrew *Zabdi*; also in verses 17 and 18.

stand against your enemies until you remove them.

14"'In the morning, present yourselves tribe by tribe. The tribe the LORD chooses shall come forward clan by clan; the clan the LORD chooses shall come forward family by family; and the family the LORD chooses shall come forward man by man. 15Whoever is caught with the devoted things shall be destroyed by fire, along with all that belongs to him. He has violated the covenant of the LORD and has done an outrageous thing in Israel!'"

16Early the next morning Joshua had Israel come forward by tribes, and Judah was chosen. 17The clans of Judah came forward, and the Zerahites were chosen. He had the clan of the Zerahites come forward by families, and Zimri was chosen. 18Joshua had his family come forward man by man, and Achan son of Karmi, the son of Zimri, the son of Zerah, of the tribe of Judah, was chosen.

19Then Joshua said to Achan, "My son, give glory to the LORD, the God of Israel, and honor him. Tell me what you have done; do not hide it from me."

20Achan replied, "It is true! I have sinned against the LORD, the God of Israel. This is what I have done: 21When I saw in the plunder a beautiful robe from Babylonia,[a] two hundred shekels[b] of silver and a bar of gold weighing fifty shekels,[c] I coveted them and took them. They are hidden in the ground inside my tent, with the silver underneath."

22So Joshua sent messengers, and they ran to the tent, and there it was, hidden in his tent, with the silver underneath. 23They took the things from the tent, brought them to Joshua and all the Israelites and spread them out before the LORD.

24Then Joshua, together with all Israel, took Achan son of Zerah, the silver, the robe, the gold bar, his sons and daughters, his cattle, donkeys and sheep, his tent and all that he had, to the Valley of Achor. 25Joshua said, "Why have you brought this trouble on us? The LORD will bring trouble on you today."

Then all Israel stoned him, and after they had stoned the rest, they burned them. 26Over Achan they heaped up a large pile of rocks, which remains to this day. Then the LORD turned from his fierce anger. Therefore that place has been called the Valley of Achor[d] ever since.

Ai Destroyed

8 Then the LORD said to Joshua, "Do not be afraid; do not be discouraged. Take the whole army with you, and go up and attack Ai. For I have delivered into your hands the king of Ai, his people, his city and his land. 2You shall do to Ai and its king as you did to Jericho and its king, except that you may carry off their plunder and livestock for yourselves. Set an ambush behind the city."

3So Joshua and the whole army moved out to attack Ai. He chose thirty thousand of his best fighting men and sent them out at night 4with these orders: "Listen carefully. You are to set an ambush behind the city. Don't go very far from it. All of you be on the alert. 5I and all those with me will advance on the city, and when the men come out against us, as they did before, we will flee from them. 6They will pursue us until we have lured them away from the city, for they will say, 'They are running away from us as they did before.' So when we flee from them, 7you are to rise up from ambush and take the city. The LORD your God will give it into your hand. 8When you have taken the city, set it on fire. Do what the LORD has commanded. See to it; you have my orders."

9Then Joshua sent them off, and they went to the place of ambush and lay in wait between Bethel and Ai, to the west of Ai—but Joshua spent that night with the people.

10Early the next morning Joshua mustered his army, and he and the leaders of Israel marched before them to Ai. 11The entire force that was with him marched up and approached the city and arrived in front of it. They set up camp north of Ai, with the valley between them and the city. 12Joshua had taken about five thousand men and set them in ambush between Bethel and Ai, to the west of the city. 13So the soldiers took up their positions—with the main camp to the north of the city and the ambush to the west of it. That night Joshua went into the valley.

14When the king of Ai saw this, he and all the men of the city hurried out early in the morning to meet Israel in battle at a certain place overlooking the Arabah. But he did not know that an ambush had been set against him behind the city. 15Joshua and all Israel let themselves be driven back before them, and they fled

[a] *21* Hebrew *Shinar* [b] *21* That is, about 5 pounds or about 2.3 kilograms [c] *21* That is, about 1 1/4 pounds or about 575 grams [d] *26* *Achor* means *trouble.*

toward the wilderness. 16All the men of
Ai were called to pursue them, and they
pursued Joshua and were lured away
from the city. 17Not a man remained in
Ai or Bethel who did not go after Israel.
They left the city open and went in pursuit of Israel.
18Then the LORD said to Joshua, "Hold
out toward Ai the javelin that is in your
hand, for into your hand I will deliver the city." So Joshua held out toward
the city the javelin that was in his hand.
19As soon as he did this, the men in the
ambush rose quickly from their position and rushed forward. They entered
the city and captured it and quickly set
it on fire.
20The men of Ai looked back and saw
the smoke of the city rising up into the
sky, but they had no chance to escape
in any direction; the Israelites who had
been fleeing toward the wilderness had
turned back against their pursuers. 21For
when Joshua and all Israel saw that the
ambush had taken the city and that
smoke was going up from it, they turned
around and attacked the men of Ai.
22Those in the ambush also came out of
the city against them, so that they were
caught in the middle, with Israelites on
both sides. Israel cut them down, leaving them neither survivors nor fugitives.
23But they took the king of Ai alive and
brought him to Joshua.
24When Israel had finished killing all
the men of Ai in the fields and in the wilderness where they had chased them,
and when every one of them had been
put to the sword, all the Israelites returned to Ai and killed those who were
in it. 25Twelve thousand men and wom-
en fell that day — all the people of Ai.
26For Joshua did not draw back the hand
that held out his javelin until he had destroyed[a] all who lived in Ai. 27But Israel
did carry off for themselves the livestock
and plunder of this city, as the LORD had
instructed Joshua.
28So Joshua burned Ai[b] and made
it a permanent heap of ruins, a desolate place to this day. 29He impaled the
body of the king of Ai on a pole and left
it there until evening. At sunset, Joshua
ordered them to take the body from the
pole and throw it down at the entrance
of the city gate. And they raised a large
pile of rocks over it, which remains to
this day.

The Covenant Renewed at Mount Ebal

30Then Joshua built on Mount Ebal an
altar to the LORD, the God of Israel, 31as
Moses the servant of the LORD had commanded the Israelites. He built it according to what is written in the Book of the
Law of Moses — an altar of uncut stones,
on which no iron tool had been used. On
it they offered to the LORD burnt offerings and sacrificed fellowship offerings.
32There, in the presence of the Israelites,
Joshua wrote on stones a copy of the law
of Moses. 33All the Israelites, with their
elders, officials and judges, were standing on both sides of the ark of the covenant of the LORD, facing the Levitical
priests who carried it. Both the foreigners living among them and the native-
born were there. Half of the people stood
in front of Mount Gerizim and half of
them in front of Mount Ebal, as Moses
the servant of the LORD had formerly
commanded when he gave instructions
to bless the people of Israel.
34Afterward, Joshua read all the words
of the law — the blessings and the curses — just as it is written in the Book of the
Law. 35There was not a word of all that
Moses had commanded that Joshua did
not read to the whole assembly of Israel,
including the women and children, and
the foreigners who lived among them.

The Gibeonite Deception

9 Now when all the kings west of the
Jordan heard about these things —
the kings in the hill country, in the western foothills, and along the entire coast
of the Mediterranean Sea as far as Lebanon (the kings of the Hittites, Amorites,
Canaanites, Perizzites, Hivites and Jebusites) — 2they came together to wage
war against Joshua and Israel.
3However, when the people of Gibeon
heard what Joshua had done to Jericho
and Ai, 4they resorted to a ruse: They
went as a delegation whose donkeys
were loaded[c] with worn-out sacks and
old wineskins, cracked and mended.
5They put worn and patched sandals on
their feet and wore old clothes. All the
bread of their food supply was dry and
moldy. 6Then they went to Joshua in the
camp at Gilgal and said to him and the
Israelites, "We have come from a distant
country; make a treaty with us."

[a] 26 The Hebrew term refers to the irrevocable giving over of things or persons to the LORD, often by totally destroying them. [b] 28 *Ai* means *the ruin.* [c] 4 Most Hebrew manuscripts; some Hebrew manuscripts, Vulgate and Syriac (see also Septuagint) *They prepared provisions and loaded their donkeys*

7The Israelites said to the Hivites, "But
perhaps you live near us, so how can we
make a treaty with you?"
8"We are your servants," they said to
Joshua.
But Joshua asked, "Who are you and
where do you come from?"
9They answered: "Your servants have
come from a very distant country because of the fame of the LORD your God.
For we have heard reports of him: all
that he did in Egypt, 10and all that he
did to the two kings of the Amorites east
of the Jordan — Sihon king of Heshbon,
and Og king of Bashan, who reigned in
Ashtaroth. 11And our elders and all those
living in our country said to us, 'Take
provisions for your journey; go and meet
them and say to them, "We are your servants; make a treaty with us."' 12This
bread of ours was warm when we packed
it at home on the day we left to come to
you. But now see how dry and moldy it
is. 13And these wineskins that we filled
were new, but see how cracked they are.
And our clothes and sandals are worn
out by the very long journey."
14The Israelites sampled their provisions but did not inquire of the LORD.
15Then Joshua made a treaty of peace
with them to let them live, and the leaders of the assembly ratified it by oath.
16Three days after they made the treaty with the Gibeonites, the Israelites
heard that they were neighbors, living
near them. 17So the Israelites set out
and on the third day came to their cities: Gibeon, Kephirah, Beeroth and Kiriath Jearim. 18But the Israelites did not
attack them, because the leaders of the
assembly had sworn an oath to them by
the LORD, the God of Israel.
The whole assembly grumbled against
the leaders, 19but all the leaders answered, "We have given them our oath
by the LORD, the God of Israel, and we
cannot touch them now. 20This is what
we will do to them: We will let them live,
so that God's wrath will not fall on us for
breaking the oath we swore to them."
21They continued, "Let them live, but let
them be woodcutters and water carriers
in the service of the whole assembly." So
the leaders' promise to them was kept.
22Then Joshua summoned the Gibeonites and said, "Why did you deceive us
by saying, 'We live a long way from you,'
while actually you live near us? 23You are
now under a curse: You will never be released from service as woodcutters and
water carriers for the house of my God."
24They answered Joshua, "Your servants were clearly told how the LORD
your God had commanded his servant
Moses to give you the whole land and to
wipe out all its inhabitants from before
you. So we feared for our lives because
of you, and that is why we did this. 25We
are now in your hands. Do to us whatever seems good and right to you."
26So Joshua saved them from the Israelites, and they did not kill them. 27That
day he made the Gibeonites woodcutters
and water carriers for the assembly, to
provide for the needs of the altar of the
LORD at the place the LORD would choose.
And that is what they are to this day.

The Sun Stands Still

10 Now Adoni-Zedek king of Jerusalem heard that Joshua had taken
Ai and totally destroyed[a] it, doing to Ai
and its king as he had done to Jericho
and its king, and that the people of Gibeon had made a treaty of peace with Israel and had become their allies. 2He and
his people were very much alarmed at
this, because Gibeon was an important
city, like one of the royal cities; it was
larger than Ai, and all its men were good
fighters. 3So Adoni-Zedek king of Jerusalem appealed to Hoham king of Hebron,
Piram king of Jarmuth, Japhia king of
Lachish and Debir king of Eglon. 4"Come
up and help me attack Gibeon," he said,
"because it has made peace with Joshua
and the Israelites."
5Then the five kings of the Amorites —
the kings of Jerusalem, Hebron, Jarmuth, Lachish and Eglon — joined forces. They moved up with all their troops
and took up positions against Gibeon
and attacked it.
6The Gibeonites then sent word to
Joshua in the camp at Gilgal: "Do not
abandon your servants. Come up to us
quickly and save us! Help us, because all
the Amorite kings from the hill country
have joined forces against us."
7So Joshua marched up from Gilgal
with his entire army, including all the
best fighting men. 8The LORD said to
Joshua, "Do not be afraid of them; I have
given them into your hand. Not one of
them will be able to withstand you."
9After an all-night march from Gilgal, Joshua took them by surprise. 10The
LORD threw them into confusion before

[a] 1 The Hebrew term refers to the irrevocable giving over of things or persons to the LORD, often by totally destroying them; also in verses 28, 35, 37, 39 and 40.

Israel, so Joshua and the Israelites defeated them completely at Gibeon. Israel pursued them along the road going up to Beth Horon and cut them down all the way to Azekah and Makkedah. 11 As they fled before Israel on the road down from Beth Horon to Azekah, the LORD hurled large hailstones down on them, and more of them died from the hail than were killed by the swords of the Israelites.

12 On the day the LORD gave the Amorites over to Israel, Joshua said to the LORD in the presence of Israel:

"Sun, stand still over Gibeon,
and you, moon, over the Valley of Aijalon."
13 So the sun stood still,
and the moon stopped,
till the nation avenged itself on[a] its enemies,

as it is written in the Book of Jashar.

The sun stopped in the middle of the sky and delayed going down about a full day. 14 There has never been a day like it before or since, a day when the LORD listened to a human being. Surely the LORD was fighting for Israel!

15 Then Joshua returned with all Israel to the camp at Gilgal.

Five Amorite Kings Killed

16 Now the five kings had fled and hidden in the cave at Makkedah. 17 When Joshua was told that the five kings had been found hiding in the cave at Makkedah, 18 he said, "Roll large rocks up to the mouth of the cave, and post some men there to guard it. 19 But don't stop; pursue your enemies! Attack them from the rear and don't let them reach their cities, for the LORD your God has given them into your hand."

20 So Joshua and the Israelites defeated them completely, but a few survivors managed to reach their fortified cities. 21 The whole army then returned safely to Joshua in the camp at Makkedah, and no one uttered a word against the Israelites.

22 Joshua said, "Open the mouth of the cave and bring those five kings out to me." 23 So they brought the five kings out of the cave — the kings of Jerusalem, Hebron, Jarmuth, Lachish and Eglon. 24 When they had brought these kings to Joshua, he summoned all the men of Israel and said to the army commanders who had come with him, "Come here and put your feet on the necks of these kings." So they came forward and placed their feet on their necks.

25 Joshua said to them, "Do not be afraid; do not be discouraged. Be strong and courageous. This is what the LORD will do to all the enemies you are going to fight." 26 Then Joshua put the kings to death and exposed their bodies on five poles, and they were left hanging on the poles until evening.

27 At sunset Joshua gave the order and they took them down from the poles and threw them into the cave where they had been hiding. At the mouth of the cave they placed large rocks, which are there to this day.

Southern Cities Conquered

28 That day Joshua took Makkedah. He put the city and its king to the sword and totally destroyed everyone in it. He left no survivors. And he did to the king of Makkedah as he had done to the king of Jericho.

29 Then Joshua and all Israel with him moved on from Makkedah to Libnah and attacked it. 30 The LORD also gave that city and its king into Israel's hand. The city and everyone in it Joshua put to the sword. He left no survivors there. And he did to its king as he had done to the king of Jericho.

31 Then Joshua and all Israel with him moved on from Libnah to Lachish; he took up positions against it and attacked it. 32 The LORD gave Lachish into Israel's hands, and Joshua took it on the second day. The city and everyone in it he put to the sword, just as he had done to Libnah. 33 Meanwhile, Horam king of Gezer had come up to help Lachish, but Joshua defeated him and his army — until no survivors were left.

34 Then Joshua and all Israel with him moved on from Lachish to Eglon; they took up positions against it and attacked it. 35 They captured it that same day and put it to the sword and totally destroyed everyone in it, just as they had done to Lachish.

36 Then Joshua and all Israel with him went up from Eglon to Hebron and attacked it. 37 They took the city and put it to the sword, together with its king, its villages and everyone in it. They left no survivors. Just as at Eglon, they totally destroyed it and everyone in it.

38 Then Joshua and all Israel with him turned around and attacked Debir.

[a] 13 Or *nation triumphed over*

39They took the city, its king and its villages, and put them to the sword. Everyone in it they totally destroyed. They left no survivors. They did to Debir and its king as they had done to Libnah and its king and to Hebron.

40So Joshua subdued the whole region, including the hill country, the Negev, the western foothills and the mountain slopes, together with all their kings. He left no survivors. He totally destroyed all who breathed, just as the LORD, the God of Israel, had commanded. 41Joshua subdued them from Kadesh Barnea to Gaza and from the whole region of Goshen to Gibeon. 42All these kings and their lands Joshua conquered in one campaign, because the LORD, the God of Israel, fought for Israel.

43Then Joshua returned with all Israel to the camp at Gilgal.

Northern Kings Defeated

11 When Jabin king of Hazor heard of this, he sent word to Jobab king of Madon, to the kings of Shimron and Akshaph, 2and to the northern kings who were in the mountains, in the Arabah south of Kinnereth, in the western foothills and in Naphoth Dor on the west; 3to the Canaanites in the east and west; to the Amorites, Hittites, Perizzites and Jebusites in the hill country; and to the Hivites below Hermon in the region of Mizpah. 4They came out with all their troops and a large number of horses and chariots — a huge army, as numerous as the sand on the seashore. 5All these kings joined forces and made camp together at the Waters of Merom to fight against Israel.

6The LORD said to Joshua, "Do not be afraid of them, because by this time tomorrow I will hand all of them, slain, over to Israel. You are to hamstring their horses and burn their chariots."

7So Joshua and his whole army came against them suddenly at the Waters of Merom and attacked them, 8and the LORD gave them into the hand of Israel. They defeated them and pursued them all the way to Greater Sidon, to Misrephoth Maim, and to the Valley of Mizpah on the east, until no survivors were left. 9Joshua did to them as the LORD had directed: He hamstrung their horses and burned their chariots.

10At that time Joshua turned back and captured Hazor and put its king to the sword. (Hazor had been the head of all these kingdoms.) 11Everyone in it they put to the sword. They totally destroyed[a] them, not sparing anyone that breathed, and he burned Hazor itself.

12Joshua took all these royal cities and their kings and put them to the sword. He totally destroyed them, as Moses the servant of the LORD had commanded. 13Yet Israel did not burn any of the cities built on their mounds — except Hazor, which Joshua burned. 14The Israelites carried off for themselves all the plunder and livestock of these cities, but all the people they put to the sword until they completely destroyed them, not sparing anyone that breathed. 15As the LORD commanded his servant Moses, so Moses commanded Joshua, and Joshua did it; he left nothing undone of all that the LORD commanded Moses.

16So Joshua took this entire land: the hill country, all the Negev, the whole region of Goshen, the western foothills, the Arabah and the mountains of Israel with their foothills, 17from Mount Halak, which rises toward Seir, to Baal Gad in the Valley of Lebanon below Mount Hermon. He captured all their kings and put them to death. 18Joshua waged war against all these kings for a long time. 19Except for the Hivites living in Gibeon, not one city made a treaty of peace with the Israelites, who took them all in battle. 20For it was the LORD himself who hardened their hearts to wage war against Israel, so that he might destroy them totally, exterminating them without mercy, as the LORD had commanded Moses.

21At that time Joshua went and destroyed the Anakites from the hill country: from Hebron, Debir and Anab, from all the hill country of Judah, and from all the hill country of Israel. Joshua totally destroyed them and their towns. 22No Anakites were left in Israelite territory; only in Gaza, Gath and Ashdod did any survive.

23So Joshua took the entire land, just as the LORD had directed Moses, and he gave it as an inheritance to Israel according to their tribal divisions. Then the land had rest from war.

List of Defeated Kings

12 These are the kings of the land whom the Israelites had defeated and whose territory they took over east

[a] 11 The Hebrew term refers to the irrevocable giving over of things or persons to the LORD, often by totally destroying them; also in verses 12, 20 and 21.

of the Jordan, from the Arnon Gorge to
Mount Hermon, including all the eastern
side of the Arabah:

2 Sihon king of the Amorites, who
reigned in Heshbon.
He ruled from Aroer on the rim of
the Arnon Gorge — from the middle of the gorge — to the Jabbok
River, which is the border of the
Ammonites. This included half
of Gilead. 3 He also ruled over the
eastern Arabah from the Sea of
Galilee[a] to the Sea of the Arabah
(that is, the Dead Sea), to Beth
Jeshimoth, and then southward
below the slopes of Pisgah.

4 And the territory of Og king of Bashan, one of the last of the Rephaites, who reigned in Ashtaroth and
Edrei.
5 He ruled over Mount Hermon,
Salekah, all of Bashan to the border of the people of Geshur and
Maakah, and half of Gilead to the
border of Sihon king of Heshbon.

6 Moses, the servant of the LORD, and
the Israelites conquered them. And Moses the servant of the LORD gave their
land to the Reubenites, the Gadites and
the half-tribe of Manasseh to be their
possession.
7 Here is a list of the kings of the land
that Joshua and the Israelites conquered
on the west side of the Jordan, from Baal
Gad in the Valley of Lebanon to Mount
Halak, which rises toward Seir. Joshua
gave their lands as an inheritance to the
tribes of Israel according to their tribal
divisions. 8 The lands included the hill
country, the western foothills, the Arabah, the mountain slopes, the wilderness
and the Negev. These were the lands of
the Hittites, Amorites, Canaanites, Perizzites, Hivites and Jebusites. These were
the kings:

9 the king of Jericho one
the king of Ai (near Bethel) one
10 the king of Jerusalem one
the king of Hebron one
11 the king of Jarmuth one
the king of Lachish one
12 the king of Eglon one
the king of Gezer one
13 the king of Debir one
the king of Geder one
14 the king of Hormah one
the king of Arad one
15 the king of Libnah one
the king of Adullam one
16 the king of Makkedah one
the king of Bethel one
17 the king of Tappuah one
the king of Hepher one
18 the king of Aphek one
the king of Lasharon one
19 the king of Madon one
the king of Hazor one
20 the king of Shimron Meron one
the king of Akshaph one
21 the king of Taanach one
the king of Megiddo one
22 the king of Kedesh one
the king of Jokneam in Carmel one
23 the king of Dor (in Naphoth Dor) one
the king of Goyim in Gilgal one
24 the king of Tirzah one
thirty-one kings in all.

Land Still to Be Taken

13 When Joshua had grown old, the
LORD said to him, "You are now
very old, and there are still very large
areas of land to be taken over.

2 "This is the land that remains: all
the regions of the Philistines and
Geshurites, 3 from the Shihor River
on the east of Egypt to the territory of Ekron on the north, all of it
counted as Canaanite though held
by the five Philistine rulers in Gaza,
Ashdod, Ashkelon, Gath and Ekron;
the territory of the Avvites 4 on the
south; all the land of the Canaanites, from Arah of the Sidonians as
far as Aphek and the border of the
Amorites; 5 the area of Byblos; and
all Lebanon to the east, from Baal
Gad below Mount Hermon to Lebo
Hamath.

6 "As for all the inhabitants of the
mountain regions from Lebanon to Misrephoth Maim, that is, all the Sidonians,
I myself will drive them out before the
Israelites. Be sure to allocate this land
to Israel for an inheritance, as I have instructed you, 7 and divide it as an inheritance among the nine tribes and half of
the tribe of Manasseh."

Division of the Land East of the Jordan

8 The other half of Manasseh,[b] the Reubenites and the Gadites had received the
inheritance that Moses had given them
east of the Jordan, as he, the servant of
the LORD, had assigned it to them.

[a] 3 Hebrew *Kinnereth* [b] 8 Hebrew *With it* (that is, with the other half of Manasseh)

9It extended from Aroer on the rim
of the Arnon Gorge, and from the
town in the middle of the gorge,
and included the whole plateau of
Medeba as far as Dibon, 10and all
the towns of Sihon king of the Amorites, who ruled in Heshbon, out
to the border of the Ammonites. 11It
also included Gilead, the territory of
the people of Geshur and Maakah,
all of Mount Hermon and all Bashan as far as Salekah — 12that is,
the whole kingdom of Og in Bashan,
who had reigned in Ashtaroth and
Edrei. (He was the last of the Rephaites.) Moses had defeated them and
taken over their land. 13But the Israelites did not drive out the people
of Geshur and Maakah, so they continue to live among the Israelites to
this day.

14But to the tribe of Levi he gave no inheritance, since the food offerings presented to the LORD, the God of Israel, are
their inheritance, as he promised them.
15This is what Moses had given to the
tribe of Reuben, according to its clans:

16The territory from Aroer on the
rim of the Arnon Gorge, and from
the town in the middle of the gorge,
and the whole plateau past Medeba
17to Heshbon and all its towns on
the plateau, including Dibon, Bamoth Baal, Beth Baal Meon, 18Jahaz,
Kedemoth, Mephaath, 19Kiriathaim,
Sibmah, Zereth Shahar on the hill in
the valley, 20Beth Peor, the slopes of
Pisgah, and Beth Jeshimoth — 21all
the towns on the plateau and the
entire realm of Sihon king of the
Amorites, who ruled at Heshbon.
Moses had defeated him and the
Midianite chiefs, Evi, Rekem, Zur,
Hur and Reba — princes allied with
Sihon — who lived in that country.
22In addition to those slain in battle,
the Israelites had put to the sword
Balaam son of Beor, who practiced
divination. 23The boundary of the
Reubenites was the bank of the Jordan. These towns and their villages
were the inheritance of the Reubenites, according to their clans.

24This is what Moses had given to the
tribe of Gad, according to its clans:

25The territory of Jazer, all the towns
of Gilead and half the Ammonite
country as far as Aroer, near Rabbah; 26and from Heshbon to Ramath Mizpah and Betonim, and
from Mahanaim to the territory of
Debir; 27and in the valley, Beth Ha-
ram, Beth Nimrah, Sukkoth and Zaphon with the rest of the realm of
Sihon king of Heshbon (the east side
of the Jordan, the territory up to the
end of the Sea of Galilee[a]). 28These
towns and their villages were the
inheritance of the Gadites, according to their clans.

29This is what Moses had given to the
half-tribe of Manasseh, that is, to half
the family of the descendants of Manasseh, according to its clans:

30The territory extending from Mahanaim and including all of Bashan, the entire realm of Og king
of Bashan — all the settlements of
Jair in Bashan, sixty towns, 31half
of Gilead, and Ashtaroth and Edrei
(the royal cities of Og in Bashan).
This was for the descendants of Makir son of Manasseh — for half of
the sons of Makir, according to their
clans.

32This is the inheritance Moses had
given when he was in the plains of Moab
across the Jordan east of Jericho. 33But to
the tribe of Levi, Moses had given no inheritance; the LORD, the God of Israel, is
their inheritance, as he promised them.

Division of the Land West of the Jordan

14 Now these are the areas the Israelites received as an inheritance in
the land of Canaan, which Eleazar the
priest, Joshua son of Nun and the heads
of the tribal clans of Israel allotted to
them. 2Their inheritances were assigned
by lot to the nine and a half tribes, as
the LORD had commanded through Moses. 3Moses had granted the two and a
half tribes their inheritance east of the
Jordan but had not granted the Levites
an inheritance among the rest, 4for Joseph's descendants had become two
tribes — Manasseh and Ephraim. The
Levites received no share of the land but
only towns to live in, with pasturelands
for their flocks and herds. 5So the Israelites divided the land, just as the LORD
had commanded Moses.

Allotment for Caleb

6Now the people of Judah approached
Joshua at Gilgal, and Caleb son of

a 27 Hebrew *Kinnereth*

Jephunneh the Kenizzite said to him,
"You know what the LORD said to Moses
the man of God at Kadesh Barnea about
you and me. 7I was forty years old when
Moses the servant of the LORD sent me
from Kadesh Barnea to explore the land.
And I brought him back a report according to my convictions, 8but my fellow Israelites who went up with me made the
hearts of the people melt in fear. I, however, followed the LORD my God wholeheartedly. 9So on that day Moses swore to me,
'The land on which your feet have walked
will be your inheritance and that of your
children forever, because you have followed the LORD my God wholeheartedly.'[a]

10"Now then, just as the LORD promised, he has kept me alive for forty-five
years since the time he said this to Moses, while Israel moved about in the wilderness. So here I am today, eighty-five
years old! 11I am still as strong today as
the day Moses sent me out; I'm just as
vigorous to go out to battle now as I was
then. 12Now give me this hill country that
the LORD promised me that day. You
yourself heard then that the Anakites
were there and their cities were large
and fortified, but, the LORD helping me,
I will drive them out just as he said."

13Then Joshua blessed Caleb son of Jephunneh and gave him Hebron as his
inheritance. 14So Hebron has belonged
to Caleb son of Jephunneh the Kenizzite
ever since, because he followed the LORD,
the God of Israel, wholeheartedly. 15(Hebron used to be called Kiriath Arba after
Arba, who was the greatest man among
the Anakites.)

Then the land had rest from war.

Allotment for Judah

15 The allotment for the tribe of Judah, according to its clans, extended down to the territory of Edom, to the
Desert of Zin in the extreme south.

2Their southern boundary started
from the bay at the southern end of
the Dead Sea, 3crossed south of Scorpion Pass, continued on to Zin and
went over to the south of Kadesh
Barnea. Then it ran past Hezron up
to Addar and curved around to Kar-
ka. 4It then passed along to Azmon
and joined the Wadi of Egypt, ending at the Mediterranean Sea. This
is their[b] southern boundary.

5The eastern boundary is the
Dead Sea as far as the mouth of the
Jordan.

The northern boundary started from the bay of the sea at the
mouth of the Jordan, 6went up to
Beth Hoglah and continued north of
Beth Arabah to the Stone of Bohan
son of Reuben. 7The boundary then
went up to Debir from the Valley of
Achor and turned north to Gilgal,
which faces the Pass of Adummim
south of the gorge. It continued
along to the waters of En Shemesh
and came out at En Rogel. 8Then it
ran up the Valley of Ben Hinnom
along the southern slope of the Jebusite city (that is, Jerusalem). From
there it climbed to the top of the hill
west of the Hinnom Valley at the
northern end of the Valley of Rephaim. 9From the hilltop the boundary headed toward the spring of
the waters of Nephtoah, came out
at the towns of Mount Ephron and
went down toward Baalah (that is,
Kiriath Jearim). 10Then it curved
westward from Baalah to Mount
Seir, ran along the northern slope
of Mount Jearim (that is, Kesalon),
continued down to Beth Shemesh
and crossed to Timnah. 11It went to
the northern slope of Ekron, turned
toward Shikkeron, passed along to
Mount Baalah and reached Jabne-
el. The boundary ended at the sea.

12The western boundary is the
coastline of the Mediterranean Sea.

These are the boundaries around the
people of Judah by their clans.

13In accordance with the LORD's command to him, Joshua gave to Caleb son
of Jephunneh a portion in Judah — Kiriath Arba, that is, Hebron. (Arba was the
forefather of Anak.) 14From Hebron Caleb
drove out the three Anakites — Sheshai,
Ahiman and Talmai, the sons of Anak.
15From there he marched against the
people living in Debir (formerly called
Kiriath Sepher). 16And Caleb said, "I will
give my daughter Aksah in marriage to
the man who attacks and captures Kiriath Sepher." 17Othniel son of Kenaz, Caleb's brother, took it; so Caleb gave his
daughter Aksah to him in marriage.

18One day when she came to Othniel,
she urged him[c] to ask her father for a
field. When she got off her donkey, Caleb
asked her, "What can I do for you?"

19She replied, "Do me a special favor.
Since you have given me land in the
Negev, give me also springs of water."

[a] *9* Deut. 1:36 [b] *4* Septuagint; Hebrew *your* [c] *18* Hebrew and some Septuagint manuscripts; other Septuagint manuscripts (see also note at Judges 1:14) *Othniel, he urged her*

So Caleb gave her the upper and lower
springs.

20This is the inheritance of the tribe of
Judah, according to its clans:

21The southernmost towns of the tribe of
Judah in the Negev toward the boundary of Edom were:

Kabzeel, Eder, Jagur, 22Kinah,
Dimonah, Adadah, 23Kedesh, Hazor, Ithnan, 24Ziph, Telem, Bealoth,
25Hazor Hadattah, Kerioth Hezron
(that is, Hazor), 26Amam, Shema,
Moladah, 27Hazar Gaddah, Hesh-
mon, Beth Pelet, 28Hazar Shual, Beersheba, Biziothiah, 29Baalah, Iyim,
Ezem, 30Eltolad, Kesil, Hormah,
31Ziklag, Madmannah, Sansannah,
32Lebaoth, Shilhim, Ain and Rimmon — a total of twenty-nine towns
and their villages.

33In the western foothills:

Eshtaol, Zorah, Ashnah, 34Zanoah,
En Gannim, Tappuah, Enam, 35Jar-
muth, Adullam, Sokoh, Azekah,
36Shaaraim, Adithaim and Gederah
(or Gederothaim)[a] — fourteen towns
and their villages.

37Zenan, Hadashah, Migdal Gad,
38Dilean, Mizpah, Joktheel, 39La-
chish, Bozkath, Eglon, 40Kabbon,
Lahmas, Kitlish, 41Gederoth, Beth
Dagon, Naamah and Makkedah —
sixteen towns and their villages.

42Libnah, Ether, Ashan, 43Iphtah,
Ashnah, Nezib, 44Keilah, Akzib and
Mareshah — nine towns and their
villages.

45Ekron, with its surrounding settlements and villages; 46west of Ekron, all that were in the vicinity of
Ashdod, together with their villages; 47Ashdod, its surrounding settlements and villages; and Gaza, its
settlements and villages, as far as
the Wadi of Egypt and the coastline
of the Mediterranean Sea.

48In the hill country:

Shamir, Jattir, Sokoh, 49Dannah,
Kiriath Sannah (that is, Debir),
50Anab, Eshtemoh, Anim, 51Goshen,
Holon and Giloh — eleven towns
and their villages.

52Arab, Dumah, Eshan, 53Janim,
Beth Tappuah, Aphekah, 54Humtah,
Kiriath Arba (that is, Hebron) and
Zior — nine towns and their villages.

55Maon, Carmel, Ziph, Juttah,
56Jezreel, Jokdeam, Zanoah, 57Kain,
Gibeah and Timnah — ten towns
and their villages.

58Halhul, Beth Zur, Gedor, 59Maa-
rath, Beth Anoth and Eltekon — six
towns and their villages.[b]

60Kiriath Baal (that is, Kiriath Jearim) and Rabbah — two towns and
their villages.

61In the wilderness:

Beth Arabah, Middin, Sekakah,
62Nibshan, the City of Salt and En
Gedi — six towns and their villages.

63Judah could not dislodge the Jebusites, who were living in Jerusalem; to
this day the Jebusites live there with the
people of Judah.

Allotment for Ephraim and Manasseh

16 The allotment for Joseph began at the Jordan, east of
the springs of Jericho, and went
up from there through the desert
into the hill country of Bethel. 2It
went on from Bethel (that is, Luz),[c]
crossed over to the territory of the
Arkites in Ataroth, 3descended westward to the territory of the Japhle-
tites as far as the region of Lower
Beth Horon and on to Gezer, ending
at the Mediterranean Sea.
4So Manasseh and Ephraim, the descendants of Joseph, received their inheritance.

5This was the territory of Ephraim, according to its clans:

The boundary of their inheritance went from Ataroth Addar in
the east to Upper Beth Horon 6and
continued to the Mediterranean
Sea. From Mikmethath on the north
it curved eastward to Taanath Shiloh, passing by it to Janoah on
the east. 7Then it went down from
Janoah to Ataroth and Naarah,
touched Jericho and came out at
the Jordan. 8From Tappuah the border went west to the Kanah Ravine
and ended at the Mediterranean
Sea. This was the inheritance of the
tribe of the Ephraimites, according
to its clans. 9It also included all the
towns and their villages that were
set aside for the Ephraimites within
the inheritance of the Manassites.
10They did not dislodge the Canaanites
living in Gezer; to this day the Canaanites live among the people of Ephraim
but are required to do forced labor.

[a] 36 Or *Gederah and Gederothaim* [b] 59 The Septuagint adds another district of eleven towns, including Tekoa and Ephrathah (Bethlehem). [c] 2 Septuagint; Hebrew *Bethel to Luz*

17 This was the allotment for the tribe
of Manasseh as Joseph's firstborn,
that is, for Makir, Manasseh's firstborn.
Makir was the ancestor of the Gileadites,
who had received Gilead and Bashan because the Makirites were great soldiers.
2So this allotment was for the rest of the
people of Manasseh — the clans of Abiezer, Helek, Asriel, Shechem, Hepher and
Shemida. These are the other male descendants of Manasseh son of Joseph by
their clans.
3Now Zelophehad son of Hepher,
the son of Gilead, the son of Makir, the
son of Manasseh, had no sons but only
daughters, whose names were Mahlah,
Noah, Hoglah, Milkah and Tirzah. 4They
went to Eleazar the priest, Joshua son
of Nun, and the leaders and said, "The
LORD commanded Moses to give us an
inheritance among our relatives." So
Joshua gave them an inheritance along
with the brothers of their father, according to the LORD's command. 5Manasseh's
share consisted of ten tracts of land besides Gilead and Bashan east of the Jordan, 6because the daughters of the tribe
of Manasseh received an inheritance
among the sons. The land of Gilead belonged to the rest of the descendants of
Manasseh.
7The territory of Manasseh extended from Asher to Mikmethath
east of Shechem. The boundary ran
southward from there to include the
people living at En Tappuah. 8(Manasseh had the land of Tappuah,
but Tappuah itself, on the boundary of Manasseh, belonged to the
Ephraimites.) 9Then the boundary
continued south to the Kanah Ravine. There were towns belonging
to Ephraim lying among the towns
of Manasseh, but the boundary of
Manasseh was the northern side of
the ravine and ended at the Mediterranean Sea. 10On the south the
land belonged to Ephraim, on the
north to Manasseh. The territory of
Manasseh reached the Mediterranean Sea and bordered Asher on the
north and Issachar on the east.
11Within Issachar and Asher, Manasseh also had Beth Shan, Ibleam
and the people of Dor, Endor, Taanach and Megiddo, together with
their surrounding settlements (the
third in the list is Naphoth[a]).
12Yet the Manassites were not able to
occupy these towns, for the Canaanites
were determined to live in that region.
13However, when the Israelites grew
stronger, they subjected the Canaanites
to forced labor but did not drive them
out completely.
14The people of Joseph said to Joshua, "Why have you given us only one
allotment and one portion for an inheritance? We are a numerous people, and
the LORD has blessed us abundantly."
15"If you are so numerous," Joshua
answered, "and if the hill country of
Ephraim is too small for you, go up into
the forest and clear land for yourselves
there in the land of the Perizzites and
Rephaites."
16The people of Joseph replied, "The
hill country is not enough for us, and
all the Canaanites who live in the plain
have chariots fitted with iron, both those
in Beth Shan and its settlements and
those in the Valley of Jezreel."
17But Joshua said to the tribes of Joseph — to Ephraim and Manasseh —
"You are numerous and very powerful.
You will have not only one allotment
18but the forested hill country as well.
Clear it, and its farthest limits will be
yours; though the Canaanites have chariots fitted with iron and though they are
strong, you can drive them out."

Division of the Rest of the Land

18 The whole assembly of the Israelites gathered at Shiloh and set up
the tent of meeting there. The country
was brought under their control, 2but
there were still seven Israelite tribes who
had not yet received their inheritance.
3So Joshua said to the Israelites: "How
long will you wait before you begin to
take possession of the land that the
LORD, the God of your ancestors, has giv-
en you? 4Appoint three men from each
tribe. I will send them out to make a survey of the land and to write a description of it, according to the inheritance of
each. Then they will return to me. 5You
are to divide the land into seven parts.
Judah is to remain in its territory on the
south and the tribes of Joseph in their
territory on the north. 6After you have
written descriptions of the seven parts
of the land, bring them here to me and
I will cast lots for you in the presence of
the LORD our God. 7The Levites, however, do not get a portion among you, because the priestly service of the LORD is
their inheritance. And Gad, Reuben and
the half-tribe of Manasseh have already

[a] *11* That is, Naphoth Dor

received their inheritance on the east side of the Jordan. Moses the servant of the LORD gave it to them."

8As the men started on their way to map out the land, Joshua instructed them, "Go and make a survey of the land and write a description of it. Then return to me, and I will cast lots for you here at Shiloh in the presence of the LORD." 9So the men left and went through the land. They wrote its description on a scroll, town by town, in seven parts, and returned to Joshua in the camp at Shiloh. 10Joshua then cast lots for them in Shiloh in the presence of the LORD, and there he distributed the land to the Israelites according to their tribal divisions.

Allotment for Benjamin

11The first lot came up for the tribe of Benjamin according to its clans. Their allotted territory lay between the tribes of Judah and Joseph:

12On the north side their boundary began at the Jordan, passed the northern slope of Jericho and headed west into the hill country, coming out at the wilderness of Beth Aven. 13From there it crossed to the south slope of Luz (that is, Bethel) and went down to Ataroth Addar on the hill south of Lower Beth Horon.

14From the hill facing Beth Horon on the south the boundary turned south along the western side and came out at Kiriath Baal (that is, Kiriath Jearim), a town of the people of Judah. This was the western side.

15The southern side began at the outskirts of Kiriath Jearim on the west, and the boundary came out at the spring of the waters of Nephtoah. 16The boundary went down to the foot of the hill facing the Valley of Ben Hinnom, north of the Valley of Rephaim. It continued down the Hinnom Valley along the southern slope of the Jebusite city and so to En Rogel. 17It then curved north, went to En Shemesh, continued to Geliloth, which faces the Pass of Adummim, and ran down to the Stone of Bohan son of Reuben. 18It continued to the northern slope of Beth Arabah[a] and on down into the Arabah. 19It then went to the northern slope of Beth Hoglah and came out at the northern bay of the Dead Sea, at the mouth of the Jordan in the south. This was the southern boundary.

20The Jordan formed the boundary on the eastern side.

These were the boundaries that marked out the inheritance of the clans of Benjamin on all sides.

21The tribe of Benjamin, according to its clans, had the following towns:

Jericho, Beth Hoglah, Emek Keziz, 22Beth Arabah, Zemaraim, Bethel, 23Avvim, Parah, Ophrah, 24Kephar Ammoni, Ophni and Geba — twelve towns and their villages.

25Gibeon, Ramah, Beeroth, 26Mizpah, Kephirah, Mozah, 27Rekem, Irpeel, Taralah, 28Zelah, Haeleph, the Jebusite city (that is, Jerusalem), Gibeah and Kiriath — fourteen towns and their villages.

This was the inheritance of Benjamin for its clans.

Allotment for Simeon

19 The second lot came out for the tribe of Simeon according to its clans. Their inheritance lay within the territory of Judah. 2It included:

Beersheba (or Sheba),[b] Moladah, 3Hazar Shual, Balah, Ezem, 4Eltolad, Bethul, Hormah, 5Ziklag, Beth Markaboth, Hazar Susah, 6Beth Lebaoth and Sharuhen — thirteen towns and their villages;

7Ain, Rimmon, Ether and Ashan — four towns and their villages — 8and all the villages around these towns as far as Baalath Beer (Ramah in the Negev).

This was the inheritance of the tribe of the Simeonites, according to its clans. 9The inheritance of the Simeonites was taken from the share of Judah, because Judah's portion was more than they needed. So the Simeonites received their inheritance within the territory of Judah.

Allotment for Zebulun

10The third lot came up for Zebulun according to its clans:

The boundary of their inheritance went as far as Sarid. 11Going west it ran to Maralah, touched Dabbesheth, and extended to the ravine near Jokneam. 12It turned east from Sarid toward the sunrise

[a] *18* Septuagint; Hebrew *slope facing the Arabah*

[b] *2* Or *Beersheba, Sheba*; 1 Chron. 4:28 does not have *Sheba*.

to the territory of Kisloth Tabor and
went on to Daberath and up to Japhia. 13Then it continued eastward
to Gath Hepher and Eth Kazin; it
came out at Rimmon and turned
toward Neah. 14There the boundary
went around on the north to Han-
nathon and ended at the Valley of
Iphtah El. 15Included were Kattath,
Nahalal, Shimron, Idalah and Bethlehem. There were twelve towns
and their villages.
16These towns and their villages were the
inheritance of Zebulun, according to its
clans.

Allotment for Issachar

17The fourth lot came out for Issachar
according to its clans. 18Their territory
included:
Jezreel, Kesulloth, Shunem,
19Hapharaim, Shion, Anaharath,
20Rabbith, Kishion, Ebez, 21Remeth,
En Gannim, En Haddah and Beth
Pazzez. 22The boundary touched
Tabor, Shahazumah and Beth Shemesh, and ended at the Jordan.
There were sixteen towns and their
villages.
23These towns and their villages were the
inheritance of the tribe of Issachar, according to its clans.

Allotment for Asher

24The fifth lot came out for the tribe of
Asher according to its clans. 25Their territory included:
Helkath, Hali, Beten, Akshaph,
26Allammelek, Amad and Mishal.
On the west the boundary touched
Carmel and Shihor Libnath. 27It
then turned east toward Beth Dagon, touched Zebulun and the Valley of Iphtah El, and went north to
Beth Emek and Neiel, passing Kabul
on the left. 28It went to Abdon,[a] Rehob, Hammon and Kanah, as far as
Greater Sidon. 29The boundary then
turned back toward Ramah and
went to the fortified city of Tyre,
turned toward Hosah and came
out at the Mediterranean Sea in the
region of Akzib, 30Ummah, Aphek
and Rehob. There were twenty-two
towns and their villages.
31These towns and their villages were the
inheritance of the tribe of Asher, according to its clans.

Allotment for Naphtali

32The sixth lot came out for Naphtali according to its clans:
33Their boundary went from He-
leph and the large tree in Zaanannim, passing Adami Nekeb and Jab-
neel to Lakkum and ending at the
Jordan. 34The boundary ran west
through Aznoth Tabor and came
out at Hukkok. It touched Zebulun on the south, Asher on the west
and the Jordan[b] on the east. 35The
fortified towns were Ziddim, Zer,
Hammath, Rakkath, Kinnereth,
36Adamah, Ramah, Hazor, 37Kedesh,
Edrei, En Hazor, 38Iron, Migdal El,
Horem, Beth Anath and Beth Shemesh. There were nineteen towns
and their villages.
39These towns and their villages were the
inheritance of the tribe of Naphtali, according to its clans.

Allotment for Dan

40The seventh lot came out for the tribe
of Dan according to its clans. 41The territory of their inheritance included:
Zorah, Eshtaol, Ir Shemesh, 42Sha-
alabbin, Aijalon, Ithlah, 43Elon, Timnah, Ekron, 44Eltekeh, Gibbethon,
Baalath, 45Jehud, Bene Berak, Gath
Rimmon, 46Me Jarkon and Rakkon,
with the area facing Joppa.
47(When the territory of the Danites
was lost to them, they went up and attacked Leshem, took it, put it to the
sword and occupied it. They settled in
Leshem and named it Dan after their
ancestor.)
48These towns and their villages were the
inheritance of the tribe of Dan, according to its clans.

Allotment for Joshua

49When they had finished dividing the
land into its allotted portions, the Israelites gave Joshua son of Nun an inheritance among them, 50as the LORD had
commanded. They gave him the town
he asked for — Timnath Serah[c] in the hill
country of Ephraim. And he built up the
town and settled there.
51These are the territories that Eleazar the priest, Joshua son of Nun and the
heads of the tribal clans of Israel assigned
by lot at Shiloh in the presence of the LORD
at the entrance to the tent of meeting. And
so they finished dividing the land.

[a] *28* Some Hebrew manuscripts (see also 21:30); most Hebrew manuscripts *Ebron*
[b] *34* Septuagint; Hebrew *west, and Judah, the Jordan,* [c] *50* Also known as *Timnath Heres* (see Judges 2:9)

Cities of Refuge

20 Then the LORD said to Joshua: 2"Tell the Israelites to designate the cities of refuge, as I instructed you through Moses, 3so that anyone who kills a person accidentally and unintentionally may flee there and find protection from the avenger of blood. 4When they flee to one of these cities, they are to stand in the entrance of the city gate and state their case before the elders of that city. Then the elders are to admit the fugitive into their city and provide a place to live among them. 5If the avenger of blood comes in pursuit, the elders must not surrender the fugitive, because the fugitive killed their neighbor unintentionally and without malice aforethought. 6They are to stay in that city until they have stood trial before the assembly and until the death of the high priest who is serving at that time. Then they may go back to their own home in the town from which they fled."

7So they set apart Kedesh in Galilee in the hill country of Naphtali, Shechem in the hill country of Ephraim, and Kiriath Arba (that is, Hebron) in the hill country of Judah. 8East of the Jordan (on the other side from Jericho) they designated Bezer in the wilderness on the plateau in the tribe of Reuben, Ramoth in Gilead in the tribe of Gad, and Golan in Bashan in the tribe of Manasseh. 9Any of the Israelites or any foreigner residing among them who killed someone accidentally could flee to these designated cities and not be killed by the avenger of blood prior to standing trial before the assembly.

Towns for the Levites

21 Now the family heads of the Levites approached Eleazar the priest, Joshua son of Nun, and the heads of the other tribal families of Israel 2at Shiloh in Canaan and said to them, "The LORD commanded through Moses that you give us towns to live in, with pasturelands for our livestock." 3So, as the LORD had commanded, the Israelites gave the Levites the following towns and pasturelands out of their own inheritance:

4The first lot came out for the Kohathites, according to their clans. The Levites who were descendants of Aaron the priest were allotted thirteen towns from the tribes of Judah, Simeon and Benjamin. 5The rest of Kohath's descendants were allotted ten towns from the clans of the tribes of Ephraim, Dan and half of Manasseh.

6The descendants of Gershon were allotted thirteen towns from the clans of the tribes of Issachar, Asher, Naphtali and the half-tribe of Manasseh in Bashan.

7The descendants of Merari, according to their clans, received twelve towns from the tribes of Reuben, Gad and Zebulun.

8So the Israelites allotted to the Levites these towns and their pasturelands, as the LORD had commanded through Moses.

9From the tribes of Judah and Simeon they allotted the following towns by name 10(these towns were assigned to the descendants of Aaron who were from the Kohathite clans of the Levites, because the first lot fell to them):

11They gave them Kiriath Arba (that is, Hebron), with its surrounding pastureland, in the hill country of Judah. (Arba was the forefather of Anak.) 12But the fields and villages around the city they had given to Caleb son of Jephunneh as his possession.

13So to the descendants of Aaron the priest they gave Hebron (a city of refuge for one accused of murder), Libnah, 14Jattir, Eshtemoa, 15Holon, Debir, 16Ain, Juttah and Beth Shemesh, together with their pasturelands — nine towns from these two tribes.

17And from the tribe of Benjamin they gave them Gibeon, Geba, 18Anathoth and Almon, together with their pasturelands — four towns.

19The total number of towns for the priests, the descendants of Aaron, came to thirteen, together with their pasturelands.

20The rest of the Kohathite clans of the Levites were allotted towns from the tribe of Ephraim:

21In the hill country of Ephraim they were given Shechem (a city of refuge for one accused of murder) and Gezer, 22Kibzaim and Beth Horon, together with their pasturelands — four towns.

23Also from the tribe of Dan they received Eltekeh, Gibbethon, 24Aijalon and Gath Rimmon, together with their pasturelands — four towns.

25From half the tribe of Manasseh they received Taanach and Gath Rimmon, together with their pasturelands — two towns.

26 All these ten towns and their pasturelands were given to the rest of the Kohathite clans.

27 The Levite clans of the Gershonites
were given:
from the half-tribe of Manasseh,
Golan in Bashan (a city of refuge for
one accused of murder) and Be Esh-
terah, together with their pasturelands — two towns;
28 from the tribe of Issachar,
Kishion, Daberath, 29 Jarmuth and
En Gannim, together with their pasturelands — four towns;
30 from the tribe of Asher,
Mishal, Abdon, 31 Helkath and Rehob, together with their pasturelands — four towns;
32 from the tribe of Naphtali,
Kedesh in Galilee (a city of refuge
for one accused of murder), Ham-
moth Dor and Kartan, together with
their pasturelands — three towns.
33 The total number of towns of the Gershonite clans came to thirteen, together
with their pasturelands.

34 The Merarite clans (the rest of the Levites) were given:
from the tribe of Zebulun,
Jokneam, Kartah, 35 Dimnah and
Nahalal, together with their pasturelands — four towns;
36 from the tribe of Reuben,
Bezer, Jahaz, 37 Kedemoth and
Mephaath, together with their pasturelands — four towns;
38 from the tribe of Gad,
Ramoth in Gilead (a city of refuge
for one accused of murder), Mahanaim, 39 Heshbon and Jazer, together with their pasturelands — four
towns in all.
40 The total number of towns allotted to
the Merarite clans, who were the rest of
the Levites, came to twelve.
41 The towns of the Levites in the
territory held by the Israelites were
forty-eight in all, together with their
pasturelands. 42 Each of these towns had
pasturelands surrounding it; this was
true for all these towns.

43 So the LORD gave Israel all the land
he had sworn to give their ancestors,
and they took possession of it and settled there. 44 The LORD gave them rest on
every side, just as he had sworn to their
ancestors. Not one of their enemies with-
stood them; the LORD gave all their enemies into their hands. 45 Not one of all
the LORD's good promises to Israel failed;
every one was fulfilled.

Eastern Tribes Return Home

22 Then Joshua summoned the Reubenites, the Gadites and the half-
tribe of Manasseh 2 and said to them,
"You have done all that Moses the servant of the LORD commanded, and you
have obeyed me in everything I commanded. 3 For a long time now — to this
very day — you have not deserted your
fellow Israelites but have carried out
the mission the LORD your God gave you.
4 Now that the LORD your God has given
them rest as he promised, return to your
homes in the land that Moses the servant
of the LORD gave you on the other side of
the Jordan. 5 But be very careful to keep
the commandment and the law that Moses the servant of the LORD gave you: to
love the LORD your God, to walk in obedience to him, to keep his commands, to
hold fast to him and to serve him with all
your heart and with all your soul."
6 Then Joshua blessed them and sent
them away, and they went to their
homes. 7 (To the half-tribe of Manasseh
Moses had given land in Bashan, and to
the other half of the tribe Joshua gave
land on the west side of the Jordan along
with their fellow Israelites.) When Joshua sent them home, he blessed them,
8 saying, "Return to your homes with
your great wealth — with large herds of
livestock, with silver, gold, bronze and
iron, and a great quantity of clothing —
and divide the plunder from your enemies with your fellow Israelites."
9 So the Reubenites, the Gadites and
the half-tribe of Manasseh left the Israelites at Shiloh in Canaan to return to
Gilead, their own land, which they had
acquired in accordance with the command of the LORD through Moses.
10 When they came to Geliloth near the
Jordan in the land of Canaan, the Reubenites, the Gadites and the half-tribe of
Manasseh built an imposing altar there
by the Jordan. 11 And when the Israelites
heard that they had built the altar on
the border of Canaan at Geliloth near
the Jordan on the Israelite side, 12 the
whole assembly of Israel gathered at
Shiloh to go to war against them.
13 So the Israelites sent Phinehas son
of Eleazar, the priest, to the land of Gilead — to Reuben, Gad and the half-tribe
of Manasseh. 14 With him they sent ten
of the chief men, one from each of the
tribes of Israel, each the head of a family
division among the Israelite clans.
15 When they went to Gilead — to Reuben, Gad and the half-tribe of Manasseh — they said to them: 16 "The whole

assembly of the LORD says: 'How could
you break faith with the God of Israel
like this? How could you turn away from
the LORD and build yourselves an altar
in rebellion against him now? 17Was not
the sin of Peor enough for us? Up to this
very day we have not cleansed ourselves
from that sin, even though a plague fell
on the community of the LORD! 18And are
you now turning away from the LORD?

"'If you rebel against the LORD today, tomorrow he will be angry with the
whole community of Israel. 19If the land
you possess is defiled, come over to the
LORD's land, where the LORD's tabernacle
stands, and share the land with us. But
do not rebel against the LORD or against
us by building an altar for yourselves,
other than the altar of the LORD our God.
20When Achan son of Zerah was unfaithful in regard to the devoted things,[a] did
not wrath come on the whole community of Israel? He was not the only one who
died for his sin.'"

21Then Reuben, Gad and the half-tribe
of Manasseh replied to the heads of the
clans of Israel: 22"The Mighty One, God,
the LORD! The Mighty One, God, the
LORD! He knows! And let Israel know!
If this has been in rebellion or disobedience to the LORD, do not spare us this
day. 23If we have built our own altar to
turn away from the LORD and to offer
burnt offerings and grain offerings, or to
sacrifice fellowship offerings on it, may
the LORD himself call us to account.

24"No! We did it for fear that some day
your descendants might say to ours,
'What do you have to do with the LORD,
the God of Israel? 25The LORD has made
the Jordan a boundary between us and
you — you Reubenites and Gadites! You
have no share in the LORD.' So your descendants might cause ours to stop fearing the LORD.

26"That is why we said, 'Let us get
ready and build an altar — but not for
burnt offerings or sacrifices.' 27On the
contrary, it is to be a witness between
us and you and the generations that follow, that we will worship the LORD at his
sanctuary with our burnt offerings, sacrifices and fellowship offerings. Then in
the future your descendants will not be
able to say to ours, 'You have no share
in the LORD.'

28"And we said, 'If they ever say this
to us, or to our descendants, we will answer: Look at the replica of the LORD's
altar, which our ancestors built, not for
burnt offerings and sacrifices, but as a
witness between us and you.'

29"Far be it from us to rebel against
the LORD and turn away from him today
by building an altar for burnt offerings,
grain offerings and sacrifices, other than
the altar of the LORD our God that stands
before his tabernacle."

30When Phinehas the priest and the
leaders of the community — the heads of
the clans of the Israelites — heard what
Reuben, Gad and Manasseh had to say,
they were pleased. 31And Phinehas son of
Eleazar, the priest, said to Reuben, Gad
and Manasseh, "Today we know that the
LORD is with us, because you have not
been unfaithful to the LORD in this matter. Now you have rescued the Israelites
from the LORD's hand."

32Then Phinehas son of Eleazar, the
priest, and the leaders returned to Canaan from their meeting with the Reubenites and Gadites in Gilead and reported to the Israelites. 33They were glad
to hear the report and praised God. And
they talked no more about going to war
against them to devastate the country
where the Reubenites and the Gadites
lived.

34And the Reubenites and the Gadites
gave the altar this name: A Witness Between Us — that the LORD is God.

Joshua's Farewell to the Leaders

23 After a long time had passed and
the LORD had given Israel rest
from all their enemies around them,
Joshua, by then a very old man, 2sum-
moned all Israel — their elders, leaders,
judges and officials — and said to them:
"I am very old. 3You yourselves have seen
everything the LORD your God has done
to all these nations for your sake; it was
the LORD your God who fought for you.
4Remember how I have allotted as an inheritance for your tribes all the land of
the nations that remain — the nations
I conquered — between the Jordan and
the Mediterranean Sea in the west. 5The
LORD your God himself will push them
out for your sake. He will drive them out
before you, and you will take possession of their land, as the LORD your God
promised you.

6"Be very strong; be careful to obey all
that is written in the Book of the Law of
Moses, without turning aside to the right
or to the left. 7Do not associate with these

[a] 20 The Hebrew term refers to the irrevocable giving over of things or persons to the LORD, often by totally destroying them.

nations that remain among you; do not
invoke the names of their gods or swear
by them. You must not serve them or
bow down to them. 8But you are to hold
fast to the LORD your God, as you have
until now.
9"The LORD has driven out before you
great and powerful nations; to this day
no one has been able to withstand you.
10One of you routs a thousand, because
the LORD your God fights for you, just as
he promised. 11So be very careful to love
the LORD your God.
12"But if you turn away and ally yourselves with the survivors of these nations
that remain among you and if you intermarry with them and associate with
them, 13then you may be sure that the
LORD your God will no longer drive out
these nations before you. Instead, they
will become snares and traps for you,
whips on your backs and thorns in your
eyes, until you perish from this good
land, which the LORD your God has giv-
en you.
14"Now I am about to go the way of all
the earth. You know with all your heart
and soul that not one of all the good
promises the LORD your God gave you
has failed. Every promise has been fulfilled; not one has failed. 15But just as all
the good things the LORD your God has
promised you have come to you, so he
will bring on you all the evil things he
has threatened, until the LORD your God
has destroyed you from this good land
he has given you. 16If you violate the
covenant of the LORD your God, which he
commanded you, and go and serve other
gods and bow down to them, the LORD's
anger will burn against you, and you will
quickly perish from the good land he has
given you."

The Covenant Renewed at Shechem

24 Then Joshua assembled all the
tribes of Israel at Shechem. He
summoned the elders, leaders, judges
and officials of Israel, and they presented themselves before God.
2Joshua said to all the people, "This is
what the LORD, the God of Israel, says:
'Long ago your ancestors, including Terah the father of Abraham and Nahor,
lived beyond the Euphrates River and
worshiped other gods. 3But I took your
father Abraham from the land beyond
the Euphrates and led him throughout
Canaan and gave him many descendants. I gave him Isaac, 4and to Isaac I
gave Jacob and Esau. I assigned the hill
country of Seir to Esau, but Jacob and his
family went down to Egypt.
5" 'Then I sent Moses and Aaron, and
I afflicted the Egyptians by what I did
there, and I brought you out. 6When I
brought your people out of Egypt, you
came to the sea, and the Egyptians pursued them with chariots and horsemen[a]
as far as the Red Sea.[b] 7But they cried
to the LORD for help, and he put darkness between you and the Egyptians; he
brought the sea over them and covered
them. You saw with your own eyes what
I did to the Egyptians. Then you lived in
the wilderness for a long time.
8" 'I brought you to the land of the Amorites who lived east of the Jordan. They
fought against you, but I gave them
into your hands. I destroyed them from
before you, and you took possession
of their land. 9When Balak son of Zippor, the king of Moab, prepared to fight
against Israel, he sent for Balaam son of
Beor to put a curse on you. 10But I would
not listen to Balaam, so he blessed you
again and again, and I delivered you out
of his hand.
11" 'Then you crossed the Jordan and
came to Jericho. The citizens of Jericho
fought against you, as did also the Amorites, Perizzites, Canaanites, Hittites,
Girgashites, Hivites and Jebusites, but I
gave them into your hands. 12I sent the
hornet ahead of you, which drove them
out before you — also the two Amorite
kings. You did not do it with your own
sword and bow. 13So I gave you a land
on which you did not toil and cities you
did not build; and you live in them and
eat from vineyards and olive groves that
you did not plant.'
14"Now fear the LORD and serve him
with all faithfulness. Throw away the
gods your ancestors worshiped beyond
the Euphrates River and in Egypt, and
serve the LORD. 15But if serving the LORD
seems undesirable to you, then choose
for yourselves this day whom you will
serve, whether the gods your ancestors
served beyond the Euphrates, or the
gods of the Amorites, in whose land you
are living. But as for me and my household, we will serve the LORD."
16Then the people answered, "Far be it
from us to forsake the LORD to serve other gods! 17It was the LORD our God himself who brought us and our parents up
out of Egypt, from that land of slavery,
and performed those great signs before

[a] 6 Or *charioteers* [b] 6 Or *the Sea of Reeds*

our eyes. He protected us on our entire journey and among all the nations
through which we traveled. 18 And the
LORD drove out before us all the nations,
including the Amorites, who lived in the
land. We too will serve the LORD, because
he is our God."

19 Joshua said to the people, "You are
not able to serve the LORD. He is a holy
God; he is a jealous God. He will not forgive your rebellion and your sins. 20 If
you forsake the LORD and serve foreign
gods, he will turn and bring disaster on
you and make an end of you, after he
has been good to you."

21 But the people said to Joshua, "No!
We will serve the LORD."

22 Then Joshua said, "You are witnesses against yourselves that you have chosen to serve the LORD."

"Yes, we are witnesses," they replied.

23 "Now then," said Joshua, "throw
away the foreign gods that are among
you and yield your hearts to the LORD,
the God of Israel."

24 And the people said to Joshua, "We
will serve the LORD our God and obey
him."

25 On that day Joshua made a covenant
for the people, and there at Shechem he
reaffirmed for them decrees and laws.
26 And Joshua recorded these things in
the Book of the Law of God. Then he took
a large stone and set it up there under
the oak near the holy place of the LORD.

27 "See!" he said to all the people. "This
stone will be a witness against us. It has
heard all the words the LORD has said to
us. It will be a witness against you if you
are untrue to your God."

28 Then Joshua dismissed the people,
each to their own inheritance.

Buried in the Promised Land

29 After these things, Joshua son of
Nun, the servant of the LORD, died at the
age of a hundred and ten. 30 And they
buried him in the land of his inheritance,
at Timnath Serah[a] in the hill country of
Ephraim, north of Mount Gaash.

31 Israel served the LORD throughout
the lifetime of Joshua and of the elders
who outlived him and who had experienced everything the LORD had done for
Israel.

32 And Joseph's bones, which the Israelites had brought up from Egypt, were
buried at Shechem in the tract of land
that Jacob bought for a hundred pieces
of silver[b] from the sons of Hamor, the father of Shechem. This became the inheritance of Joseph's descendants.

33 And Eleazar son of Aaron died and
was buried at Gibeah, which had been
allotted to his son Phinehas in the hill
country of Ephraim.

[a] 30 Also known as *Timnath Heres* (see Judges 2:9) [b] 32 Hebrew *hundred kesitahs*; a kesitah was a unit of money of unknown weight and value.

JUDGES

Israel Fights the Remaining Canaanites

1 After the death of Joshua, the Israelites asked the LORD, "Who of us is to go
up first to fight against the Canaanites?"
2The LORD answered, "Judah shall
go up; I have given the land into their
hands."
3The men of Judah then said to the
Simeonites their fellow Israelites, "Come
up with us into the territory allotted to
us, to fight against the Canaanites. We in
turn will go with you into yours." So the
Simeonites went with them.
4When Judah attacked, the LORD gave
the Canaanites and Perizzites into their
hands, and they struck down ten thousand men at Bezek. 5It was there that
they found Adoni-Bezek and fought
against him, putting to rout the Canaanites and Perizzites. 6Adoni-Bezek
fled, but they chased him and caught
him, and cut off his thumbs and big toes.
7Then Adoni-Bezek said, "Seventy
kings with their thumbs and big toes cut
off have picked up scraps under my table. Now God has paid me back for what
I did to them." They brought him to Jerusalem, and he died there.
8The men of Judah attacked Jerusalem also and took it. They put the city to
the sword and set it on fire.
9After that, Judah went down to fight
against the Canaanites living in the
hill country, the Negev and the western
foothills. 10They advanced against the
Canaanites living in Hebron (formerly
called Kiriath Arba) and defeated Sheshai, Ahiman and Talmai. 11From there
they advanced against the people living
in Debir (formerly called Kiriath Sepher).
12And Caleb said, "I will give my
daughter Aksah in marriage to the
man who attacks and captures Kiriath
Sepher." 13Othniel son of Kenaz, Caleb's
younger brother, took it; so Caleb gave
his daughter Aksah to him in marriage.
14One day when she came to Othniel,
she urged him[a] to ask her father for a
field. When she got off her donkey, Caleb
asked her, "What can I do for you?"
15She replied, "Do me a special favor.
Since you have given me land in the
Negev, give me also springs of water."
So Caleb gave her the upper and lower
springs.
16The descendants of Moses' father-in-
law, the Kenite, went up from the City of
Palms[b] with the people of Judah to live
among the inhabitants of the Desert of
Judah in the Negev near Arad.
17Then the men of Judah went with
the Simeonites their fellow Israelites
and attacked the Canaanites living in
Zephath, and they totally destroyed[c] the
city. Therefore it was called Hormah.[d]
18Judah also took[e] Gaza, Ashkelon and
Ekron — each city with its territory.
19The LORD was with the men of Judah. They took possession of the hill
country, but they were unable to drive
the people from the plains, because
they had chariots fitted with iron. 20As
Moses had promised, Hebron was giv-
en to Caleb, who drove from it the three
sons of Anak. 21The Benjamites, however, did not drive out the Jebusites, who
were living in Jerusalem; to this day
the Jebusites live there with the Benjamites.
22Now the tribes of Joseph attacked
Bethel, and the LORD was with them.
23When they sent men to spy out Bethel (formerly called Luz), 24the spies saw
a man coming out of the city and they
said to him, "Show us how to get into the
city and we will see that you are treated
well." 25So he showed them, and they put
the city to the sword but spared the man
and his whole family. 26He then went to
the land of the Hittites, where he built a
city and called it Luz, which is its name
to this day.
27But Manasseh did not drive out the
people of Beth Shan or Taanach or Dor or
Ibleam or Megiddo and their surrounding settlements, for the Canaanites were
determined to live in that land. 28When
Israel became strong, they pressed the
Canaanites into forced labor but never
drove them out completely. 29Nor did
Ephraim drive out the Canaanites living

[a] 14 Hebrew; Septuagint and Vulgate *Othniel, he urged her* [b] 16 That is, Jericho [c] 17 The Hebrew term refers to the irrevocable giving over of things or persons to the LORD, often by totally destroying them. [d] 17 *Hormah* means *destruction.* [e] 18 Hebrew; Septuagint *Judah did not take*

in Gezer, but the Canaanites continued
to live there among them. 30Neither did
Zebulun drive out the Canaanites living
in Kitron or Nahalol, so these Canaanites
lived among them, but Zebulun did subject them to forced labor. 31Nor did Asher
drive out those living in Akko or Sidon
or Ahlab or Akzib or Helbah or Aphek
or Rehob. 32The Asherites lived among
the Canaanite inhabitants of the land
because they did not drive them out.
33Neither did Naphtali drive out those
living in Beth Shemesh or Beth Anath;
but the Naphtalites too lived among the
Canaanite inhabitants of the land, and
those living in Beth Shemesh and Beth
Anath became forced laborers for them.
34The Amorites confined the Danites to
the hill country, not allowing them to
come down into the plain. 35And the Amorites were determined also to hold out
in Mount Heres, Aijalon and Shaalbim,
but when the power of the tribes of Joseph increased, they too were pressed
into forced labor. 36The boundary of the
Amorites was from Scorpion Pass to Sela
and beyond.

The Angel of the LORD at Bokim

2 The angel of the LORD went up from
Gilgal to Bokim and said, "I brought
you up out of Egypt and led you into the
land I swore to give to your ancestors.
I said, 'I will never break my covenant
with you, 2and you shall not make a covenant with the people of this land, but
you shall break down their altars.' Yet
you have disobeyed me. Why have you
done this? 3And I have also said, 'I will
not drive them out before you; they will
become traps for you, and their gods will
become snares to you.'"

4When the angel of the LORD had spoken these things to all the Israelites, the
people wept aloud, 5and they called that
place Bokim.[a] There they offered sacrifices to the LORD.

Disobedience and Defeat

6After Joshua had dismissed the Israelites, they went to take possession of
the land, each to their own inheritance.
7The people served the LORD throughout
the lifetime of Joshua and of the elders
who outlived him and who had seen all
the great things the LORD had done for
Israel.

8Joshua son of Nun, the servant of the
LORD, died at the age of a hundred and
ten. 9And they buried him in the land of
his inheritance, at Timnath Heres[b] in the
hill country of Ephraim, north of Mount
Gaash.

10After that whole generation had
been gathered to their ancestors, another generation grew up who knew neither
the LORD nor what he had done for Israel. 11Then the Israelites did evil in the
eyes of the LORD and served the Baals.
12They forsook the LORD, the God of their
ancestors, who had brought them out of
Egypt. They followed and worshiped various gods of the peoples around them.
They aroused the LORD's anger 13because
they forsook him and served Baal and
the Ashtoreths. 14In his anger against Israel the LORD gave them into the hands
of raiders who plundered them. He sold
them into the hands of their enemies
all around, whom they were no longer
able to resist. 15Whenever Israel went
out to fight, the hand of the LORD was
against them to defeat them, just as he
had sworn to them. They were in great
distress.

16Then the LORD raised up judges,[c] who
saved them out of the hands of these
raiders. 17Yet they would not listen to
their judges but prostituted themselves
to other gods and worshiped them. They
quickly turned from the ways of their
ancestors, who had been obedient to
the LORD's commands. 18Whenever the
LORD raised up a judge for them, he was
with the judge and saved them out of
the hands of their enemies as long as
the judge lived; for the LORD relented
because of their groaning under those
who oppressed and afflicted them. 19But
when the judge died, the people returned to ways even more corrupt than
those of their ancestors, following other
gods and serving and worshiping them.
They refused to give up their evil practices and stubborn ways.

20Therefore the LORD was very angry with Israel and said, "Because this
nation has violated the covenant I ordained for their ancestors and has not
listened to me, 21I will no longer drive
out before them any of the nations Joshua left when he died. 22I will use them
to test Israel and see whether they will
keep the way of the LORD and walk in it
as their ancestors did." 23The LORD had
allowed those nations to remain; he did
not drive them out at once by giving
them into the hands of Joshua.

[a] *5 Bokim* means *weepers.* [b] *9* Also known as *Timnath Serah* (see Joshua 19:50 and 24:30)
[c] *16* Or *leaders;* similarly in verses 17-19

3 These are the nations the LORD left to test all those Israelites who had not experienced any of the wars in Canaan 2(he did this only to teach warfare to the descendants of the Israelites who had not had previous battle experience): 3the five rulers of the Philistines, all the Canaanites, the Sidonians, and the Hivites living in the Lebanon mountains from Mount Baal Hermon to Lebo Hamath. 4They were left to test the Israelites to see whether they would obey the LORD's commands, which he had given their ancestors through Moses.

5The Israelites lived among the Canaanites, Hittites, Amorites, Perizzites, Hivites and Jebusites. 6They took their daughters in marriage and gave their own daughters to their sons, and served their gods.

Othniel

7The Israelites did evil in the eyes of the LORD; they forgot the LORD their God and served the Baals and the Asherahs. 8The anger of the LORD burned against Israel so that he sold them into the hands of Cushan-Rishathaim king of Aram Naharaim,[a] to whom the Israelites were subject for eight years. 9But when they cried out to the LORD, he raised up for them a deliverer, Othniel son of Kenaz, Caleb's younger brother, who saved them. 10The Spirit of the LORD came on him, so that he became Israel's judge[b] and went to war. The LORD gave Cushan-Rishathaim king of Aram into the hands of Othniel, who overpowered him. 11So the land had peace for forty years, until Othniel son of Kenaz died.

Ehud

12Again the Israelites did evil in the eyes of the LORD, and because they did this evil the LORD gave Eglon king of Moab power over Israel. 13Getting the Ammonites and Amalekites to join him, Eglon came and attacked Israel, and they took possession of the City of Palms.[c] 14The Israelites were subject to Eglon king of Moab for eighteen years.

15Again the Israelites cried out to the LORD, and he gave them a deliverer — Ehud, a left-handed man, the son of Gera the Benjamite. The Israelites sent him with tribute to Eglon king of Moab. 16Now Ehud had made a double-edged sword about a cubit[d] long, which he strapped to his right thigh under his clothing. 17He presented the tribute to Eglon king of Moab, who was a very fat man. 18After Ehud had presented the tribute, he sent on their way those who had carried it. 19But on reaching the stone images near Gilgal he himself went back to Eglon and said, "Your Majesty, I have a secret message for you."

The king said to his attendants, "Leave us!" And they all left.

20Ehud then approached him while he was sitting alone in the upper room of his palace[e] and said, "I have a message from God for you." As the king rose from his seat, 21Ehud reached with his left hand, drew the sword from his right thigh and plunged it into the king's belly. 22Even the handle sank in after the blade, and his bowels discharged. Ehud did not pull the sword out, and the fat closed in over it. 23Then Ehud went out to the porch[f]; he shut the doors of the upper room behind him and locked them.

24After he had gone, the servants came and found the doors of the upper room locked. They said, "He must be relieving himself in the inner room of the palace." 25They waited to the point of embarrassment, but when he did not open the doors of the room, they took a key and unlocked them. There they saw their lord fallen to the floor, dead.

26While they waited, Ehud got away. He passed by the stone images and escaped to Seirah. 27When he arrived there, he blew a trumpet in the hill country of Ephraim, and the Israelites went down with him from the hills, with him leading them.

28"Follow me," he ordered, "for the LORD has given Moab, your enemy, into your hands." So they followed him down and took possession of the fords of the Jordan that led to Moab; they allowed no one to cross over. 29At that time they struck down about ten thousand Moabites, all vigorous and strong; not one escaped. 30That day Moab was made subject to Israel, and the land had peace for eighty years.

Shamgar

31After Ehud came Shamgar son of Anath, who struck down six hundred Philistines with an oxgoad. He too saved Israel.

[a] *8* That is, Northwest Mesopotamia [b] *10* Or *leader* [c] *13* That is, Jericho [d] *16* That is, about 18 inches or about 45 centimeters [e] *20* The meaning of the Hebrew for this word is uncertain; also in verse 24. [f] *23* The meaning of the Hebrew for this word is uncertain.

Deborah

4 Again the Israelites did evil in the eyes of the LORD, now that Ehud was dead. 2 So the LORD sold them into the hands of Jabin king of Canaan, who reigned in Hazor. Sisera, the commander of his army, was based in Harosheth Haggoyim. 3 Because he had nine hundred chariots fitted with iron and had cruelly oppressed the Israelites for twenty years, they cried to the LORD for help.

4 Now Deborah, a prophet, the wife of Lappidoth, was leading[a] Israel at that time. 5 She held court under the Palm of Deborah between Ramah and Bethel in the hill country of Ephraim, and the Israelites went up to her to have their disputes decided. 6 She sent for Barak son of Abinoam from Kedesh in Naphtali and said to him, "The LORD, the God of Israel, commands you: 'Go, take with you ten thousand men of Naphtali and Zebulun and lead them up to Mount Tabor. 7 I will lead Sisera, the commander of Jabin's army, with his chariots and his troops to the Kishon River and give him into your hands.'"

8 Barak said to her, "If you go with me, I will go; but if you don't go with me, I won't go."

9 "Certainly I will go with you," said Deborah. "But because of the course you are taking, the honor will not be yours, for the LORD will deliver Sisera into the hands of a woman." So Deborah went with Barak to Kedesh. 10 There Barak summoned Zebulun and Naphtali, and ten thousand men went up under his command. Deborah also went up with him.

11 Now Heber the Kenite had left the other Kenites, the descendants of Hobab, Moses' brother-in-law,[b] and pitched his tent by the great tree in Zaanannim near Kedesh.

12 When they told Sisera that Barak son of Abinoam had gone up to Mount Tabor, 13 Sisera summoned from Harosheth Haggoyim to the Kishon River all his men and his nine hundred chariots fitted with iron.

14 Then Deborah said to Barak, "Go! This is the day the LORD has given Sisera into your hands. Has not the LORD gone ahead of you?" So Barak went down Mount Tabor, with ten thousand men following him. 15 At Barak's advance, the LORD routed Sisera and all his chariots and army by the sword, and Sisera got down from his chariot and fled on foot. 16 Barak pursued the chariots and army as far as Harosheth Haggoyim, and all Sisera's troops fell by the sword; not a man was left. 17 Sisera, meanwhile, fled on foot to the tent of Jael, the wife of Heber the Kenite, because there was an alliance between Jabin king of Hazor and the family of Heber the Kenite.

18 Jael went out to meet Sisera and said to him, "Come, my lord, come right in. Don't be afraid." So he entered her tent, and she covered him with a blanket.

19 "I'm thirsty," he said. "Please give me some water." She opened a skin of milk, gave him a drink, and covered him up.

20 "Stand in the doorway of the tent," he told her. "If someone comes by and asks you, 'Is anyone in there?' say 'No.'"

21 But Jael, Heber's wife, picked up a tent peg and a hammer and went quietly to him while he lay fast asleep, exhausted. She drove the peg through his temple into the ground, and he died.

22 Just then Barak came by in pursuit of Sisera, and Jael went out to meet him. "Come," she said, "I will show you the man you're looking for." So he went in with her, and there lay Sisera with the tent peg through his temple — dead.

23 On that day God subdued Jabin king of Canaan before the Israelites. 24 And the hand of the Israelites pressed harder and harder against Jabin king of Canaan until they destroyed him.

The Song of Deborah

5 On that day Deborah and Barak son of Abinoam sang this song:

2 "When the princes in Israel take the lead,
when the people willingly offer themselves —
praise the LORD!

3 "Hear this, you kings! Listen, you rulers!
I, even I, will sing to[c] the LORD;
I will praise the LORD, the God of Israel, in song.

4 "When you, LORD, went out from Seir,
when you marched from the land of Edom,
the earth shook, the heavens poured,
the clouds poured down water.
5 The mountains quaked before the LORD, the One of Sinai,
before the LORD, the God of Israel.

6 "In the days of Shamgar son of Anath,

[a] 4 Traditionally *judging* [b] 11 Or *father-in-law* [c] 3 Or *of*

in the days of Jael, the highways
were abandoned;
travelers took to winding paths.
7 Villagers in Israel would not fight;
they held back until I, Deborah,
arose,
until I arose, a mother in Israel.
8 God chose new leaders
when war came to the city gates,
but not a shield or spear was seen
among forty thousand in Israel.
9 My heart is with Israel's princes,
with the willing volunteers among
the people.
Praise the LORD!

10 "You who ride on white donkeys,
sitting on your saddle blankets,
and you who walk along the road,
consider 11 the voice of the singers[a] at
the watering places.
They recite the victories of the
LORD,
the victories of his villagers in
Israel.

"Then the people of the LORD
went down to the city gates.
12 'Wake up, wake up, Deborah!
Wake up, wake up, break out in
song!
Arise, Barak!
Take captive your captives, son of
Abinoam.'

13 "The remnant of the nobles came
down;
the people of the LORD came down
to me against the mighty.
14 Some came from Ephraim, whose
roots were in Amalek;
Benjamin was with the people who
followed you.
From Makir captains came down,
from Zebulun those who bear a
commander's[a] staff.
15 The princes of Issachar were with
Deborah;
yes, Issachar was with Barak,
sent under his command into the
valley.
In the districts of Reuben
there was much searching of heart.
16 Why did you stay among the sheep
pens[b]
to hear the whistling for the flocks?
In the districts of Reuben
there was much searching of heart.
17 Gilead stayed beyond the Jordan.
And Dan, why did he linger by the
ships?
Asher remained on the coast
and stayed in his coves.
18 The people of Zebulun risked their
very lives;
so did Naphtali on the terraced
fields.

19 "Kings came, they fought,
the kings of Canaan fought.
At Taanach, by the waters of Megiddo,
they took no plunder of silver.
20 From the heavens the stars fought,
from their courses they fought
against Sisera.
21 The river Kishon swept them away,
the age-old river, the river Kishon.
March on, my soul; be strong!
22 Then thundered the horses' hooves —
galloping, galloping go his mighty
steeds.
23 'Curse Meroz,' said the angel of the
LORD.
'Curse its people bitterly,
because they did not come to help the
LORD,
to help the LORD against the
mighty.'

24 "Most blessed of women be Jael,
the wife of Heber the Kenite,
most blessed of tent-dwelling
women.
25 He asked for water, and she gave him
milk;
in a bowl fit for nobles she brought
him curdled milk.
26 Her hand reached for the tent peg,
her right hand for the workman's
hammer.
She struck Sisera, she crushed his
head,
she shattered and pierced his
temple.
27 At her feet he sank,
he fell; there he lay.
At her feet he sank, he fell;
where he sank, there he fell —
dead.

28 "Through the window peered Sisera's
mother;
behind the lattice she cried out,
'Why is his chariot so long in coming?
Why is the clatter of his chariots
delayed?'
29 The wisest of her ladies answer her;
indeed, she keeps saying to herself,
30 'Are they not finding and dividing the
spoils:
a woman or two for each man,

[a] 11,14 The meaning of the Hebrew for this word is uncertain. [b] 16 Or *the campfires*; or *the saddlebags*

colorful garments as plunder for
Sisera,
colorful garments embroidered,
highly embroidered garments for my
neck —
all this as plunder?'

31"So may all your enemies perish,
LORD!
But may all who love you be like
the sun
when it rises in its strength."
Then the land had peace forty years.

Gideon

6 The Israelites did evil in the eyes of
the LORD, and for seven years he gave
them into the hands of the Midianites.
2Because the power of Midian was so oppressive, the Israelites prepared shelters
for themselves in mountain clefts, caves
and strongholds. 3Whenever the Israelites planted their crops, the Midianites,
Amalekites and other eastern peoples
invaded the country. 4They camped on
the land and ruined the crops all the
way to Gaza and did not spare a living
thing for Israel, neither sheep nor cattle
nor donkeys. 5They came up with their
livestock and their tents like swarms of
locusts. It was impossible to count them
or their camels; they invaded the land to
ravage it. 6Midian so impoverished the
Israelites that they cried out to the LORD
for help.
7When the Israelites cried out to the
LORD because of Midian, 8he sent them
a prophet, who said, "This is what the
LORD, the God of Israel, says: I brought
you up out of Egypt, out of the land of
slavery. 9I rescued you from the hand of
the Egyptians. And I delivered you from
the hand of all your oppressors; I drove
them out before you and gave you their
land. 10I said to you, 'I am the LORD your
God; do not worship the gods of the Amorites, in whose land you live.' But you
have not listened to me."
11The angel of the LORD came and sat
down under the oak in Ophrah that belonged to Joash the Abiezrite, where his
son Gideon was threshing wheat in a
winepress to keep it from the Midianites.
12When the angel of the LORD appeared
to Gideon, he said, "The LORD is with you,
mighty warrior."
13"Pardon me, my lord," Gideon replied, "but if the LORD is with us, why has
all this happened to us? Where are all his
wonders that our ancestors told us about
when they said, 'Did not the LORD bring
us up out of Egypt?' But now the LORD
has abandoned us and given us into the
hand of Midian."
14The LORD turned to him and said,
"Go in the strength you have and save
Israel out of Midian's hand. Am I not
sending you?"
15"Pardon me, my lord," Gideon replied, "but how can I save Israel? My clan
is the weakest in Manasseh, and I am the
least in my family."
16The LORD answered, "I will be with
you, and you will strike down all the
Midianites, leaving none alive."
17Gideon replied, "If now I have found
favor in your eyes, give me a sign that
it is really you talking to me. 18Please do
not go away until I come back and bring
my offering and set it before you."
And the LORD said, "I will wait until
you return."
19Gideon went inside, prepared a
young goat, and from an ephah[a] of
flour he made bread without yeast. Putting the meat in a basket and its broth in
a pot, he brought them out and offered
them to him under the oak.
20The angel of God said to him, "Take
the meat and the unleavened bread,
place them on this rock, and pour out
the broth." And Gideon did so. 21Then the
angel of the LORD touched the meat and
the unleavened bread with the tip of the
staff that was in his hand. Fire flared
from the rock, consuming the meat and
the bread. And the angel of the LORD disappeared. 22When Gideon realized that it
was the angel of the LORD, he exclaimed,
"Alas, Sovereign LORD! I have seen the
angel of the LORD face to face!"
23But the LORD said to him, "Peace! Do
not be afraid. You are not going to die."
24So Gideon built an altar to the LORD
there and called it The LORD Is Peace. To
this day it stands in Ophrah of the Abiezrites.
25That same night the LORD said to
him, "Take the second bull from your
father's herd, the one seven years old.[b]
Tear down your father's altar to Baal
and cut down the Asherah pole[c] beside
it. 26Then build a proper kind of[d] altar
to the LORD your God on the top of this
height. Using the wood of the Asherah
pole that you cut down, offer the second[e]
bull as a burnt offering."

[a] *19* That is, probably about 36 pounds or about 16 kilograms [b] *25* Or *Take a full-grown, mature bull from your father's herd* [c] *25* That is, a wooden symbol of the goddess Asherah; also in verses 26, 28 and 30 [d] *26* Or *build with layers of stone an* [e] *26* Or *full-grown*; also in verse 28

27 So Gideon took ten of his servants
and did as the LORD told him. But because he was afraid of his family and
the townspeople, he did it at night rather than in the daytime.
28 In the morning when the people of
the town got up, there was Baal's altar,
demolished, with the Asherah pole beside it cut down and the second bull sacrificed on the newly built altar!
29 They asked each other, "Who did
this?"

When they carefully investigated, they
were told, "Gideon son of Joash did it."
30 The people of the town demanded of
Joash, "Bring out your son. He must die,
because he has broken down Baal's altar
and cut down the Asherah pole beside it."
31 But Joash replied to the hostile crowd
around him, "Are you going to plead Baal's cause? Are you trying to save him?
Whoever fights for him shall be put to
death by morning! If Baal really is a god,
he can defend himself when someone
breaks down his altar." 32 So because Gideon broke down Baal's altar, they gave
him the name Jerub-Baal[a] that day, saying, "Let Baal contend with him."
33 Now all the Midianites, Amalekites
and other eastern peoples joined forces
and crossed over the Jordan and camped
in the Valley of Jezreel. 34 Then the Spirit of
the LORD came on Gideon, and he blew a
trumpet, summoning the Abiezrites to follow him. 35 He sent messengers throughout Manasseh, calling them to arms, and
also into Asher, Zebulun and Naphtali, so
that they too went up to meet them.
36 Gideon said to God, "If you will save
Israel by my hand as you have promised— 37 look, I will place a wool fleece
on the threshing floor. If there is dew
only on the fleece and all the ground is
dry, then I will know that you will save
Israel by my hand, as you said." 38 And
that is what happened. Gideon rose early
the next day; he squeezed the fleece and
wrung out the dew—a bowlful of water.
39 Then Gideon said to God, "Do not be
angry with me. Let me make just one
more request. Allow me one more test
with the fleece, but this time make the
fleece dry and let the ground be covered
with dew." 40 That night God did so. Only
the fleece was dry; all the ground was
covered with dew.

Gideon Defeats the Midianites

7 Early in the morning, Jerub-Baal (that
is, Gideon) and all his men camped at
the spring of Harod. The camp of Midian was north of them in the valley near
the hill of Moreh. 2 The LORD said to Gideon, "You have too many men. I cannot
deliver Midian into their hands, or Israel would boast against me, 'My own
strength has saved me.' 3 Now announce
to the army, 'Anyone who trembles with
fear may turn back and leave Mount Gilead.'" So twenty-two thousand men left,
while ten thousand remained.
4 But the LORD said to Gideon, "There
are still too many men. Take them down
to the water, and I will thin them out for
you there. If I say, 'This one shall go with
you,' he shall go; but if I say, 'This one
shall not go with you,' he shall not go."
5 So Gideon took the men down to the
water. There the LORD told him, "Separate those who lap the water with their
tongues as a dog laps from those who
kneel down to drink." 6 Three hundred of
them drank from cupped hands, lapping
like dogs. All the rest got down on their
knees to drink.
7 The LORD said to Gideon, "With the
three hundred men that lapped I will
save you and give the Midianites into
your hands. Let all the others go home."
8 So Gideon sent the rest of the Israelites
home but kept the three hundred, who
took over the provisions and trumpets
of the others.

Now the camp of Midian lay below
him in the valley. 9 During that night the
LORD said to Gideon, "Get up, go down
against the camp, because I am going
to give it into your hands. 10 If you are
afraid to attack, go down to the camp
with your servant Purah 11 and listen to
what they are saying. Afterward, you
will be encouraged to attack the camp."
So he and Purah his servant went down
to the outposts of the camp. 12 The Midianites, the Amalekites and all the other
eastern peoples had settled in the valley,
thick as locusts. Their camels could no
more be counted than the sand on the
seashore.
13 Gideon arrived just as a man was
telling a friend his dream. "I had a
dream," he was saying. "A round loaf
of barley bread came tumbling into the
Midianite camp. It struck the tent with
such force that the tent overturned and
collapsed."
14 His friend responded, "This can be
nothing other than the sword of Gideon
son of Joash, the Israelite. God has given
the Midianites and the whole camp into
his hands."

[a] 32 *Jerub-Baal* probably means *let Baal contend.*

15When Gideon heard the dream and its interpretation, he bowed down and worshiped. He returned to the camp of Israel and called out, "Get up! The LORD has given the Midianite camp into your hands." 16Dividing the three hundred men into three companies, he placed trumpets and empty jars in the hands of all of them, with torches inside.

17"Watch me," he told them. "Follow my lead. When I get to the edge of the camp, do exactly as I do. 18When I and all who are with me blow our trumpets, then from all around the camp blow yours and shout, 'For the LORD and for Gideon.'"

19Gideon and the hundred men with him reached the edge of the camp at the beginning of the middle watch, just after they had changed the guard. They blew their trumpets and broke the jars that were in their hands. 20The three companies blew the trumpets and smashed the jars. Grasping the torches in their left hands and holding in their right hands the trumpets they were to blow, they shouted, "A sword for the LORD and for Gideon!" 21While each man held his position around the camp, all the Midianites ran, crying out as they fled.

22When the three hundred trumpets sounded, the LORD caused the men throughout the camp to turn on each other with their swords. The army fled to Beth Shittah toward Zererah as far as the border of Abel Meholah near Tabbath. 23Israelites from Naphtali, Asher and all Manasseh were called out, and they pursued the Midianites. 24Gideon sent messengers throughout the hill country of Ephraim, saying, "Come down against the Midianites and seize the waters of the Jordan ahead of them as far as Beth Barah."

So all the men of Ephraim were called out and they seized the waters of the Jordan as far as Beth Barah. 25They also captured two of the Midianite leaders, Oreb and Zeeb. They killed Oreb at the rock of Oreb, and Zeeb at the winepress of Zeeb. They pursued the Midianites and brought the heads of Oreb and Zeeb to Gideon, who was by the Jordan.

Zebah and Zalmunna

8 Now the Ephraimites asked Gideon, "Why have you treated us like this? Why didn't you call us when you went to fight Midian?" And they challenged him vigorously.

2But he answered them, "What have I accomplished compared to you? Aren't the gleanings of Ephraim's grapes better than the full grape harvest of Abiezer? 3God gave Oreb and Zeeb, the Midianite leaders, into your hands. What was I able to do compared to you?" At this, their resentment against him subsided.

4Gideon and his three hundred men, exhausted yet keeping up the pursuit, came to the Jordan and crossed it. 5He said to the men of Sukkoth, "Give my troops some bread; they are worn out, and I am still pursuing Zebah and Zalmunna, the kings of Midian."

6But the officials of Sukkoth said, "Do you already have the hands of Zebah and Zalmunna in your possession? Why should we give bread to your troops?"

7Then Gideon replied, "Just for that, when the LORD has given Zebah and Zalmunna into my hand, I will tear your flesh with desert thorns and briers."

8From there he went up to Peniel[a] and made the same request of them, but they answered as the men of Sukkoth had. 9So he said to the men of Peniel, "When I return in triumph, I will tear down this tower."

10Now Zebah and Zalmunna were in Karkor with a force of about fifteen thousand men, all that were left of the armies of the eastern peoples; a hundred and twenty thousand swordsmen had fallen. 11Gideon went up by the route of the nomads east of Nobah and Jogbehah and attacked the unsuspecting army. 12Zebah and Zalmunna, the two kings of Midian, fled, but he pursued them and captured them, routing their entire army.

13Gideon son of Joash then returned from the battle by the Pass of Heres. 14He caught a young man of Sukkoth and questioned him, and the young man wrote down for him the names of the seventy-seven officials of Sukkoth, the elders of the town. 15Then Gideon came and said to the men of Sukkoth, "Here are Zebah and Zalmunna, about whom you taunted me by saying, 'Do you already have the hands of Zebah and Zalmunna in your possession? Why should we give bread to your exhausted men?'" 16He took the elders of the town and taught the men of Sukkoth a lesson by punishing them with desert thorns and briers. 17He also pulled down the tower of Peniel and killed the men of the town.

18Then he asked Zebah and Zalmunna, "What kind of men did you kill at Tabor?"

[a] *8* Hebrew *Penuel*, a variant of *Peniel*; also in verses 9 and 17

"Men like you," they answered, "each
one with the bearing of a prince."
19Gideon replied, "Those were my
brothers, the sons of my own mother.
As surely as the LORD lives, if you had
spared their lives, I would not kill you."
20Turning to Jether, his oldest son, he
said, "Kill them!" But Jether did not draw
his sword, because he was only a boy and
was afraid.
21Zebah and Zalmunna said, "Come,
do it yourself. 'As is the man, so is his
strength.'" So Gideon stepped forward
and killed them, and took the ornaments off their camels' necks.

Gideon's Ephod

22The Israelites said to Gideon, "Rule
over us — you, your son and your grandson — because you have saved us from
the hand of Midian."
23But Gideon told them, "I will not rule
over you, nor will my son rule over you.
The LORD will rule over you." 24And he
said, "I do have one request, that each of
you give me an earring from your share
of the plunder." (It was the custom of the
Ishmaelites to wear gold earrings.)
25They answered, "We'll be glad to give
them." So they spread out a garment,
and each of them threw a ring from his
plunder onto it. 26The weight of the gold
rings he asked for came to seventeen
hundred shekels,[a] not counting the ornaments, the pendants and the purple
garments worn by the kings of Midian
or the chains that were on their camels'
necks. 27Gideon made the gold into an
ephod, which he placed in Ophrah, his
town. All Israel prostituted themselves
by worshiping it there, and it became a
snare to Gideon and his family.

Gideon's Death

28Thus Midian was subdued before
the Israelites and did not raise its head
again. During Gideon's lifetime, the land
had peace forty years.
29Jerub-Baal son of Joash went back
home to live. 30He had seventy sons of
his own, for he had many wives. 31His
concubine, who lived in Shechem, also
bore him a son, whom he named Abimelek. 32Gideon son of Joash died at a good
old age and was buried in the tomb of
his father Joash in Ophrah of the Abiezrites.
33No sooner had Gideon died than the
Israelites again prostituted themselves
to the Baals. They set up Baal-Berith as
their god 34and did not remember the
LORD their God, who had rescued them
from the hands of all their enemies on
every side. 35They also failed to show any
loyalty to the family of Jerub-Baal (that
is, Gideon) in spite of all the good things
he had done for them.

Abimelek

9 Abimelek son of Jerub-Baal went to
his mother's brothers in Shechem
and said to them and to all his mother's
clan, 2"Ask all the citizens of Shechem,
'Which is better for you: to have all seventy of Jerub-Baal's sons rule over you,
or just one man?' Remember, I am your
flesh and blood."
3When the brothers repeated all this
to the citizens of Shechem, they were inclined to follow Abimelek, for they said,
"He is related to us." 4They gave him seventy shekels[b] of silver from the temple
of Baal-Berith, and Abimelek used it to
hire reckless scoundrels, who became his
followers. 5He went to his father's home
in Ophrah and on one stone murdered
his seventy brothers, the sons of Jerub-Baal. But Jotham, the youngest son of
Jerub-Baal, escaped by hiding. 6Then all
the citizens of Shechem and Beth Millo
gathered beside the great tree at the pillar in Shechem to crown Abimelek king.
7When Jotham was told about this, he
climbed up on the top of Mount Gerizim
and shouted to them, "Listen to me, citizens of Shechem, so that God may listen
to you. 8One day the trees went out to
anoint a king for themselves. They said
to the olive tree, 'Be our king.'
9"But the olive tree answered, 'Should
I give up my oil, by which both gods and
humans are honored, to hold sway over
the trees?'
10"Next, the trees said to the fig tree,
'Come and be our king.'
11"But the fig tree replied, 'Should I
give up my fruit, so good and sweet, to
hold sway over the trees?'
12"Then the trees said to the vine,
'Come and be our king.'
13"But the vine answered, 'Should I
give up my wine, which cheers both
gods and humans, to hold sway over the
trees?'
14"Finally all the trees said to the
thornbush, 'Come and be our king.'
15"The thornbush said to the trees, 'If
you really want to anoint me king over

[a] *26* That is, about 43 pounds or about 20 kilograms [b] *4* That is, about 1 3/4 pounds or about 800 grams

you, come and take refuge in my shade; but if not, then let fire come out of the thornbush and consume the cedars of Lebanon!'

16 "Have you acted honorably and in good faith by making Abimelek king? Have you been fair to Jerub-Baal and his family? Have you treated him as he deserves? 17 Remember that my father fought for you and risked his life to rescue you from the hand of Midian. 18 But today you have revolted against my father's family. You have murdered his seventy sons on a single stone and have made Abimelek, the son of his female slave, king over the citizens of Shechem because he is related to you. 19 So have you acted honorably and in good faith toward Jerub-Baal and his family today? If you have, may Abimelek be your joy, and may you be his, too! 20 But if you have not, let fire come out from Abimelek and consume you, the citizens of Shechem and Beth Millo, and let fire come out from you, the citizens of Shechem and Beth Millo, and consume Abimelek!"

21 Then Jotham fled, escaping to Beer, and he lived there because he was afraid of his brother Abimelek.

22 After Abimelek had governed Israel three years, 23 God stirred up animosity between Abimelek and the citizens of Shechem so that they acted treacherously against Abimelek. 24 God did this in order that the crime against Jerub-Baal's seventy sons, the shedding of their blood, might be avenged on their brother Abimelek and on the citizens of Shechem, who had helped him murder his brothers. 25 In opposition to him these citizens of Shechem set men on the hilltops to ambush and rob everyone who passed by, and this was reported to Abimelek.

26 Now Gaal son of Ebed moved with his clan into Shechem, and its citizens put their confidence in him. 27 After they had gone out into the fields and gathered the grapes and trodden them, they held a festival in the temple of their god. While they were eating and drinking, they cursed Abimelek. 28 Then Gaal son of Ebed said, "Who is Abimelek, and why should we Shechemites be subject to him? Isn't he Jerub-Baal's son, and isn't Zebul his deputy? Serve the family of Hamor, Shechem's father! Why should we serve Abimelek? 29 If only this people were under my command! Then I would get rid of him. I would say to Abimelek, 'Call out your whole army!'"[a]

30 When Zebul the governor of the city heard what Gaal son of Ebed said, he was very angry. 31 Under cover he sent messengers to Abimelek, saying, "Gaal son of Ebed and his clan have come to Shechem and are stirring up the city against you. 32 Now then, during the night you and your men should come and lie in wait in the fields. 33 In the morning at sunrise, advance against the city. When Gaal and his men come out against you, seize the opportunity to attack them."

34 So Abimelek and all his troops set out by night and took up concealed positions near Shechem in four companies. 35 Now Gaal son of Ebed had gone out and was standing at the entrance of the city gate just as Abimelek and his troops came out from their hiding place.

36 When Gaal saw them, he said to Zebul, "Look, people are coming down from the tops of the mountains!"

Zebul replied, "You mistake the shadows of the mountains for men."

37 But Gaal spoke up again: "Look, people are coming down from the central hill,[b] and a company is coming from the direction of the diviners' tree."

38 Then Zebul said to him, "Where is your big talk now, you who said, 'Who is Abimelek that we should be subject to him?' Aren't these the men you ridiculed? Go out and fight them!"

39 So Gaal led out[c] the citizens of Shechem and fought Abimelek. 40 Abimelek chased him all the way to the entrance of the gate, and many were killed as they fled. 41 Then Abimelek stayed in Arumah, and Zebul drove Gaal and his clan out of Shechem.

42 The next day the people of Shechem went out to the fields, and this was reported to Abimelek. 43 So he took his men, divided them into three companies and set an ambush in the fields. When he saw the people coming out of the city, he rose to attack them. 44 Abimelek and the companies with him rushed forward to a position at the entrance of the city gate. Then two companies attacked those in the fields and struck them down. 45 All that day Abimelek pressed his attack against the city until he had captured it and killed its people. Then he destroyed the city and scattered salt over it.

46 On hearing this, the citizens in the tower of Shechem went into the stronghold of the temple of El-Berith. 47 When Abimelek heard that they had assembled there, 48 he and all his men went up

[a] 29 Septuagint; Hebrew *him." Then he said to Abimelek, "Call out your whole army!"* [b] 37 The Hebrew for this phrase means *the navel of the earth.* [c] 39 Or *Gaal went out in the sight of*

Mount Zalmon. He took an ax and cut
off some branches, which he lifted to
his shoulders. He ordered the men with
him, "Quick! Do what you have seen me
do!" 49So all the men cut branches and
followed Abimelek. They piled them
against the stronghold and set it on fire
with the people still inside. So all the
people in the tower of Shechem, about
a thousand men and women, also died.
50Next Abimelek went to Thebez and
besieged it and captured it. 51Inside
the city, however, was a strong tower,
to which all the men and women — all
the people of the city — had fled. They
had locked themselves in and climbed
up on the tower roof. 52Abimelek went
to the tower and attacked it. But as he
approached the entrance to the tower
to set it on fire, 53a woman dropped an
upper millstone on his head and cracked
his skull.
54Hurriedly he called to his armor-
bearer, "Draw your sword and kill me,
so that they can't say, 'A woman killed
him.'" So his servant ran him through,
and he died. 55When the Israelites saw
that Abimelek was dead, they went
home.
56Thus God repaid the wickedness that
Abimelek had done to his father by murdering his seventy brothers. 57God also
made the people of Shechem pay for all
their wickedness. The curse of Jotham
son of Jerub-Baal came on them.

Tola

10 After the time of Abimelek, a man
of Issachar named Tola son of
Puah, the son of Dodo, rose to save Israel. He lived in Shamir, in the hill country
of Ephraim. 2He led[a] Israel twenty-three
years; then he died, and was buried in
Shamir.

Jair

3He was followed by Jair of Gilead,
who led Israel twenty-two years. 4He
had thirty sons, who rode thirty donkeys.
They controlled thirty towns in Gilead,
which to this day are called Havvoth
Jair.[b] 5When Jair died, he was buried in
Kamon.

Jephthah

6Again the Israelites did evil in the
eyes of the LORD. They served the Baals and the Ashtoreths, and the gods
of Aram, the gods of Sidon, the gods of
Moab, the gods of the Ammonites and
the gods of the Philistines. And because
the Israelites forsook the LORD and no
longer served him, 7he became angry
with them. He sold them into the hands
of the Philistines and the Ammonites,
8who that year shattered and crushed
them. For eighteen years they oppressed
all the Israelites on the east side of the
Jordan in Gilead, the land of the Amorites. 9The Ammonites also crossed the
Jordan to fight against Judah, Benjamin and Ephraim; Israel was in great
distress. 10Then the Israelites cried out
to the LORD, "We have sinned against
you, forsaking our God and serving the
Baals."
11The LORD replied, "When the Egyptians, the Amorites, the Ammonites,
the Philistines, 12the Sidonians, the Amalekites and the Maonites[c] oppressed
you and you cried to me for help, did I
not save you from their hands? 13But
you have forsaken me and served other
gods, so I will no longer save you. 14Go
and cry out to the gods you have chosen.
Let them save you when you are in trouble!"
15But the Israelites said to the LORD,
"We have sinned. Do with us whatever you think best, but please rescue us
now." 16Then they got rid of the foreign
gods among them and served the LORD.
And he could bear Israel's misery no longer.
17When the Ammonites were called to
arms and camped in Gilead, the Israelites assembled and camped at Mizpah.
18The leaders of the people of Gilead said
to each other, "Whoever will take the
lead in attacking the Ammonites will be
head over all who live in Gilead."
11 Jephthah the Gileadite was a
mighty warrior. His father was Gilead; his mother was a prostitute. 2Gilead's
wife also bore him sons, and when they
were grown up, they drove Jephthah
away. "You are not going to get any inheritance in our family," they said, "because you are the son of another woman." 3So Jephthah fled from his brothers
and settled in the land of Tob, where a
gang of scoundrels gathered around him
and followed him.
4Some time later, when the Ammonites were fighting against Israel, 5the elders of Gilead went to get Jephthah from
the land of Tob. 6"Come," they said, "be
our commander, so we can fight the Ammonites."

[a] 2 Traditionally *judged*; also in verse 3 [b] 4 Or *called the settlements of Jair* [c] 12 Hebrew; some Septuagint manuscripts *Midianites*

7 Jephthah said to them, "Didn't you hate me and drive me from my father's house? Why do you come to me now, when you're in trouble?"

8 The elders of Gilead said to him, "Nevertheless, we are turning to you now; come with us to fight the Ammonites, and you will be head over all of us who live in Gilead."

9 Jephthah answered, "Suppose you take me back to fight the Ammonites and the LORD gives them to me — will I really be your head?"

10 The elders of Gilead replied, "The LORD is our witness; we will certainly do as you say." 11 So Jephthah went with the elders of Gilead, and the people made him head and commander over them. And he repeated all his words before the LORD in Mizpah.

12 Then Jephthah sent messengers to the Ammonite king with the question: "What do you have against me that you have attacked my country?"

13 The king of the Ammonites answered Jephthah's messengers, "When Israel came up out of Egypt, they took away my land from the Arnon to the Jabbok, all the way to the Jordan. Now give it back peaceably."

14 Jephthah sent back messengers to the Ammonite king, 15 saying:

"This is what Jephthah says: Israel did not take the land of Moab or the land of the Ammonites. 16 But when they came up out of Egypt, Israel went through the wilderness to the Red Sea[a] and on to Kadesh. 17 Then Israel sent messengers to the king of Edom, saying, 'Give us permission to go through your country,' but the king of Edom would not listen. They sent also to the king of Moab, and he refused. So Israel stayed at Kadesh.

18 "Next they traveled through the wilderness, skirted the lands of Edom and Moab, passed along the eastern side of the country of Moab, and camped on the other side of the Arnon. They did not enter the territory of Moab, for the Arnon was its border.

19 "Then Israel sent messengers to Sihon king of the Amorites, who ruled in Heshbon, and said to him, 'Let us pass through your country to our own place.' 20 Sihon, however, did not trust Israel[b] to pass through his territory. He mustered all his troops and encamped at Jahaz and fought with Israel.

21 "Then the LORD, the God of Israel, gave Sihon and his whole army into Israel's hands, and they defeated them. Israel took over all the land of the Amorites who lived in that country, 22 capturing all of it from the Arnon to the Jabbok and from the desert to the Jordan.

23 "Now since the LORD, the God of Israel, has driven the Amorites out before his people Israel, what right have you to take it over? 24 Will you not take what your god Chemosh gives you? Likewise, whatever the LORD our God has given us, we will possess. 25 Are you any better than Balak son of Zippor, king of Moab? Did he ever quarrel with Israel or fight with them? 26 For three hundred years Israel occupied Heshbon, Aroer, the surrounding settlements and all the towns along the Arnon. Why didn't you retake them during that time? 27 I have not wronged you, but you are doing me wrong by waging war against me. Let the LORD, the Judge, decide the dispute this day between the Israelites and the Ammonites."

28 The king of Ammon, however, paid no attention to the message Jephthah sent him.

29 Then the Spirit of the LORD came on Jephthah. He crossed Gilead and Manasseh, passed through Mizpah of Gilead, and from there he advanced against the Ammonites. 30 And Jephthah made a vow to the LORD: "If you give the Ammonites into my hands, 31 whatever comes out of the door of my house to meet me when I return in triumph from the Ammonites will be the LORD's, and I will sacrifice it as a burnt offering."

32 Then Jephthah went over to fight the Ammonites, and the LORD gave them into his hands. 33 He devastated twenty towns from Aroer to the vicinity of Minnith, as far as Abel Keramim. Thus Israel subdued Ammon.

34 When Jephthah returned to his home in Mizpah, who should come out to meet him but his daughter, dancing to the sound of timbrels! She was an only child. Except for her he had neither son nor daughter. 35 When he saw her, he tore his clothes and cried, "Oh no, my daughter! You have brought me down and I am devastated. I have made a vow to the LORD that I cannot break."

[a] 16 Or *the Sea of Reeds* [b] 20 Or *however, would not make an agreement for Israel*

36"My father," she replied, "you have
given your word to the LORD. Do to me
just as you promised, now that the LORD
has avenged you of your enemies, the
Ammonites. 37But grant me this one request," she said. "Give me two months to
roam the hills and weep with my friends,
because I will never marry."
38"You may go," he said. And he let her
go for two months. She and her friends
went into the hills and wept because
she would never marry. 39After the two
months, she returned to her father, and
he did to her as he had vowed. And she
was a virgin.
From this comes the Israelite tradition
40that each year the young women of Israel go out for four days to commemorate
the daughter of Jephthah the Gileadite.

Jephthah and Ephraim

12 The Ephraimite forces were called
out, and they crossed over to Zaphon. They said to Jephthah, "Why did
you go to fight the Ammonites without
calling us to go with you? We're going to
burn down your house over your head."
2Jephthah answered, "I and my people were engaged in a great struggle
with the Ammonites, and although I
called, you didn't save me out of their
hands. 3When I saw that you wouldn't
help, I took my life in my hands and
crossed over to fight the Ammonites,
and the LORD gave me the victory over
them. Now why have you come up today
to fight me?"
4Jephthah then called together the
men of Gilead and fought against Ephraim. The Gileadites struck them down because the Ephraimites had said, "You
Gileadites are renegades from Ephraim
and Manasseh." 5The Gileadites captured
the fords of the Jordan leading to Ephraim, and whenever a survivor of Ephraim
said, "Let me cross over," the men of Gilead asked him, "Are you an Ephraimite?"
If he replied, "No," 6they said, "All right,
say 'Shibboleth.'" If he said, "Sibboleth,"
because he could not pronounce the
word correctly, they seized him and killed
him at the fords of the Jordan. Forty-
two thousand Ephraimites were killed at
that time.
7Jephthah led[a] Israel six years. Then
Jephthah the Gileadite died and was
buried in a town in Gilead.

Ibzan, Elon and Abdon

8After him, Ibzan of Bethlehem led
Israel. 9He had thirty sons and thirty
daughters. He gave his daughters away
in marriage to those outside his clan,
and for his sons he brought in thirty
young women as wives from outside his
clan. Ibzan led Israel seven years. 10Then
Ibzan died and was buried in Bethlehem.
11After him, Elon the Zebulunite led Israel ten years. 12Then Elon died and was
buried in Aijalon in the land of Zebulun.
13After him, Abdon son of Hillel, from
Pirathon, led Israel. 14He had forty sons
and thirty grandsons, who rode on seventy donkeys. He led Israel eight years.
15Then Abdon son of Hillel died and was
buried at Pirathon in Ephraim, in the hill
country of the Amalekites.

The Birth of Samson

13 Again the Israelites did evil in the
eyes of the LORD, so the LORD delivered them into the hands of the Philistines for forty years.
2A certain man of Zorah, named Manoah, from the clan of the Danites, had
a wife who was childless, unable to give
birth. 3The angel of the LORD appeared
to her and said, "You are barren and
childless, but you are going to become
pregnant and give birth to a son. 4Now
see to it that you drink no wine or other fermented drink and that you do not
eat anything unclean. 5You will become
pregnant and have a son whose head is
never to be touched by a razor because
the boy is to be a Nazirite, dedicated to
God from the womb. He will take the
lead in delivering Israel from the hands
of the Philistines."
6Then the woman went to her husband and told him, "A man of God came
to me. He looked like an angel of God,
very awesome. I didn't ask him where
he came from, and he didn't tell me his
name. 7But he said to me, 'You will become pregnant and have a son. Now
then, drink no wine or other fermented
drink and do not eat anything unclean,
because the boy will be a Nazirite of
God from the womb until the day of his
death.'"
8Then Manoah prayed to the LORD:
"Pardon your servant, Lord. I beg you to
let the man of God you sent to us come
again to teach us how to bring up the
boy who is to be born."
9God heard Manoah, and the angel
of God came again to the woman while
she was out in the field; but her husband
Manoah was not with her. 10The woman
hurried to tell her husband, "He's here!

[a] 7 Traditionally *judged*; also in verses 8-14

The man who appeared to me the other day!"
11Manoah got up and followed his wife.
When he came to the man, he said, "Are
you the man who talked to my wife?"
"I am," he said.
12So Manoah asked him, "When your
words are fulfilled, what is to be the rule
that governs the boy's life and work?"
13The angel of the LORD answered,
"Your wife must do all that I have told
her. 14She must not eat anything that
comes from the grapevine, nor drink
any wine or other fermented drink nor
eat anything unclean. She must do everything I have commanded her."
15Manoah said to the angel of the
LORD, "We would like you to stay until
we prepare a young goat for you."
16The angel of the LORD replied, "Even
though you detain me, I will not eat any
of your food. But if you prepare a burnt
offering, offer it to the LORD." (Manoah
did not realize that it was the angel of
the LORD.)
17Then Manoah inquired of the angel of the LORD, "What is your name, so
that we may honor you when your word
comes true?"
18He replied, "Why do you ask my
name? It is beyond understanding.[a]"
19Then Manoah took a young goat, together with the grain offering, and sacrificed it on a rock to the LORD. And the
LORD did an amazing thing while Manoah and his wife watched: 20As the flame
blazed up from the altar toward heav-
en, the angel of the LORD ascended in
the flame. Seeing this, Manoah and his
wife fell with their faces to the ground.
21When the angel of the LORD did not
show himself again to Manoah and his
wife, Manoah realized that it was the angel of the LORD.
22"We are doomed to die!" he said to
his wife. "We have seen God!"
23But his wife answered, "If the LORD
had meant to kill us, he would not have
accepted a burnt offering and grain offering from our hands, nor shown us all
these things or now told us this."
24The woman gave birth to a boy and
named him Samson. He grew and the
LORD blessed him, 25and the Spirit of the
LORD began to stir him while he was in Mahaneh Dan, between Zorah and Eshtaol.

Samson's Marriage

14 Samson went down to Timnah and
saw there a young Philistine woman. 2When he returned, he said to his
father and mother, "I have seen a Philistine woman in Timnah; now get her for
me as my wife."
3His father and mother replied, "Isn't
there an acceptable woman among your
relatives or among all our people? Must
you go to the uncircumcised Philistines
to get a wife?"
But Samson said to his father, "Get her
for me. She's the right one for me." 4(His
parents did not know that this was from
the LORD, who was seeking an occasion
to confront the Philistines; for at that
time they were ruling over Israel.)
5Samson went down to Timnah together with his father and mother. As
they approached the vineyards of Timnah, suddenly a young lion came roaring toward him. 6The Spirit of the LORD
came powerfully upon him so that he
tore the lion apart with his bare hands
as he might have torn a young goat. But
he told neither his father nor his mother
what he had done. 7Then he went down
and talked with the woman, and he liked
her.
8Some time later, when he went back
to marry her, he turned aside to look
at the lion's carcass, and in it he saw
a swarm of bees and some honey. 9He
scooped out the honey with his hands
and ate as he went along. When he re-
joined his parents, he gave them some,
and they too ate it. But he did not tell
them that he had taken the honey from
the lion's carcass.
10Now his father went down to see the
woman. And there Samson held a feast,
as was customary for young men. 11When
the people saw him, they chose thirty
men to be his companions.
12"Let me tell you a riddle," Samson
said to them. "If you can give me the answer within the seven days of the feast, I
will give you thirty linen garments and
thirty sets of clothes. 13If you can't tell me
the answer, you must give me thirty lin-
en garments and thirty sets of clothes."
"Tell us your riddle," they said. "Let's
hear it."
14He replied,

"Out of the eater, something to eat;
out of the strong, something
sweet."

For three days they could not give the
answer.
15On the fourth[b] day, they said to Samson's wife, "Coax your husband into
explaining the riddle for us, or we will

[a] 18 Or *is wonderful* [b] 15 Some Septuagint manuscripts and Syriac; Hebrew *seventh*

burn you and your father's household to
death. Did you invite us here to steal our
property?"
16 Then Samson's wife threw herself on
him, sobbing, "You hate me! You don't
really love me. You've given my people
a riddle, but you haven't told me the answer."
"I haven't even explained it to my
father or mother," he replied, "so why
should I explain it to you?" 17 She cried
the whole seven days of the feast. So on
the seventh day he finally told her, because she continued to press him. She in
turn explained the riddle to her people.
18 Before sunset on the seventh day the
men of the town said to him,

"What is sweeter than honey?
  What is stronger than a lion?"

Samson said to them,

"If you had not plowed with my
    heifer,
  you would not have solved my
    riddle."

19 Then the Spirit of the LORD came
powerfully upon him. He went down to
Ashkelon, struck down thirty of their
men, stripped them of everything and
gave their clothes to those who had explained the riddle. Burning with anger,
he returned to his father's home. 20 And
Samson's wife was given to one of his
companions who had attended him at
the feast.

Samson's Vengeance on the Philistines

15 Later on, at the time of wheat harvest, Samson took a young goat
and went to visit his wife. He said, "I'm
going to my wife's room." But her father
would not let him go in.
2 "I was so sure you hated her," he said,
"that I gave her to your companion. Isn't
her younger sister more attractive? Take
her instead."
3 Samson said to them, "This time I
have a right to get even with the Philistines; I will really harm them." 4 So
he went out and caught three hundred
foxes and tied them tail to tail in pairs.
He then fastened a torch to every pair
of tails, 5 lit the torches and let the foxes
loose in the standing grain of the Philistines. He burned up the shocks and
standing grain, together with the vineyards and olive groves.
6 When the Philistines asked, "Who did
this?" they were told, "Samson, the Tim-
nite's son-in-law, because his wife was
given to his companion."
So the Philistines went up and burned
her and her father to death. 7 Samson
said to them, "Since you've acted like
this, I swear that I won't stop until I
get my revenge on you." 8 He attacked
them viciously and slaughtered many of
them. Then he went down and stayed in
a cave in the rock of Etam.
9 The Philistines went up and camped
in Judah, spreading out near Lehi. 10 The
people of Judah asked, "Why have you
come to fight us?"
"We have come to take Samson prisoner," they answered, "to do to him as he
did to us."
11 Then three thousand men from Judah went down to the cave in the rock of
Etam and said to Samson, "Don't you realize that the Philistines are rulers over
us? What have you done to us?"
He answered, "I merely did to them
what they did to me."
12 They said to him, "We've come to tie
you up and hand you over to the Philistines."
Samson said, "Swear to me that you
won't kill me yourselves."
13 "Agreed," they answered. "We will
only tie you up and hand you over to
them. We will not kill you." So they bound
him with two new ropes and led him up
from the rock. 14 As he approached Lehi,
the Philistines came toward him shouting. The Spirit of the LORD came powerfully upon him. The ropes on his arms
became like charred flax, and the bind-
ings dropped from his hands. 15 Finding a
fresh jawbone of a donkey, he grabbed it
and struck down a thousand men.
16 Then Samson said,

"With a donkey's jawbone
  I have made donkeys of them.[a]
With a donkey's jawbone
  I have killed a thousand men."

17 When he finished speaking, he threw
away the jawbone; and the place was
called Ramath Lehi.[b]
18 Because he was very thirsty, he cried
out to the LORD, "You have given your
servant this great victory. Must I now
die of thirst and fall into the hands of
the uncircumcised?" 19 Then God opened
up the hollow place in Lehi, and water
came out of it. When Samson drank, his

[a] 16 Or *made a heap or two*; the Hebrew for *donkey* sounds like the Hebrew for *heap*.
[b] 17 *Ramath Lehi* means *jawbone hill*.

strength returned and he revived. So the
spring was called En Hakkore,[a] and it is
still there in Lehi.
20 Samson led[b] Israel for twenty years
in the days of the Philistines.

Samson and Delilah

16 One day Samson went to Gaza,
where he saw a prostitute. He went
in to spend the night with her. 2 The people of Gaza were told, "Samson is here!"
So they surrounded the place and lay in
wait for him all night at the city gate.
They made no move during the night,
saying, "At dawn we'll kill him."
3 But Samson lay there only until the
middle of the night. Then he got up and
took hold of the doors of the city gate, together with the two posts, and tore them
loose, bar and all. He lifted them to his
shoulders and carried them to the top of
the hill that faces Hebron.
4 Some time later, he fell in love with
a woman in the Valley of Sorek whose
name was Delilah. 5 The rulers of the
Philistines went to her and said, "See if
you can lure him into showing you the
secret of his great strength and how we
can overpower him so we may tie him
up and subdue him. Each one of us will
give you eleven hundred shekels[c] of silver."
6 So Delilah said to Samson, "Tell me
the secret of your great strength and
how you can be tied up and subdued."
7 Samson answered her, "If anyone
ties me with seven fresh bowstrings that
have not been dried, I'll become as weak
as any other man."
8 Then the rulers of the Philistines
brought her seven fresh bowstrings
that had not been dried, and she tied
him with them. 9 With men hidden in
the room, she called to him, "Samson,
the Philistines are upon you!" But he
snapped the bowstrings as easily as a
piece of string snaps when it comes close
to a flame. So the secret of his strength
was not discovered.
10 Then Delilah said to Samson, "You
have made a fool of me; you lied to me.
Come now, tell me how you can be tied."
11 He said, "If anyone ties me securely with new ropes that have never been
used, I'll become as weak as any other
man."
12 So Delilah took new ropes and tied
him with them. Then, with men hidden
in the room, she called to him, "Samson,
the Philistines are upon you!" But he
snapped the ropes off his arms as if they
were threads.
13 Delilah then said to Samson, "All this
time you have been making a fool of me
and lying to me. Tell me how you can be
tied."
He replied, "If you weave the seven
braids of my head into the fabric on
the loom and tighten it with the pin, I'll
become as weak as any other man." So
while he was sleeping, Delilah took the
seven braids of his head, wove them into
the fabric 14 and[d] tightened it with the
pin.
Again she called to him, "Samson,
the Philistines are upon you!" He awoke
from his sleep and pulled up the pin and
the loom, with the fabric.
15 Then she said to him, "How can you
say, 'I love you,' when you won't confide
in me? This is the third time you have
made a fool of me and haven't told me
the secret of your great strength." 16 With
such nagging she prodded him day after
day until he was sick to death of it.
17 So he told her everything. "No razor
has ever been used on my head," he said,
"because I have been a Nazirite dedicated to God from my mother's womb. If my
head were shaved, my strength would
leave me, and I would become as weak
as any other man."
18 When Delilah saw that he had told
her everything, she sent word to the rulers of the Philistines, "Come back once
more; he has told me everything." So the
rulers of the Philistines returned with
the silver in their hands. 19 After putting
him to sleep on her lap, she called for
someone to shave off the seven braids of
his hair, and so began to subdue him.[e]
And his strength left him.
20 Then she called, "Samson, the Philistines are upon you!"
He awoke from his sleep and thought,
"I'll go out as before and shake myself
free." But he did not know that the LORD
had left him.
21 Then the Philistines seized him,
gouged out his eyes and took him down
to Gaza. Binding him with bronze shackles, they set him to grinding grain in the
prison. 22 But the hair on his head began
to grow again after it had been shaved.

[a] 19 *En Hakkore* means *caller's spring.* [b] 20 Traditionally *judged* [c] 5 That is, about 28 pounds or about 13 kilograms [d] 13,14 Some Septuagint manuscripts; Hebrew *replied, "I can if you weave the seven braids of my head into the fabric on the loom." 14 So she* [e] 19 Hebrew; some Septuagint manuscripts *and he began to weaken*

The Death of Samson

23 Now the rulers of the Philistines assembled to offer a great sacrifice to Dagon their god and to celebrate, saying, "Our god has delivered Samson, our enemy, into our hands."

24 When the people saw him, they praised their god, saying,

"Our god has delivered our enemy
into our hands,
the one who laid waste our land
and multiplied our slain."

25 While they were in high spirits, they shouted, "Bring out Samson to entertain us." So they called Samson out of the prison, and he performed for them.

When they stood him among the pillars, 26 Samson said to the servant who held his hand, "Put me where I can feel the pillars that support the temple, so that I may lean against them." 27 Now the temple was crowded with men and women; all the rulers of the Philistines were there, and on the roof were about three thousand men and women watching Samson perform. 28 Then Samson prayed to the LORD, "Sovereign LORD, remember me. Please, God, strengthen me just once more, and let me with one blow get revenge on the Philistines for my two eyes." 29 Then Samson reached toward the two central pillars on which the temple stood. Bracing himself against them, his right hand on the one and his left hand on the other, 30 Samson said, "Let me die with the Philistines!" Then he pushed with all his might, and down came the temple on the rulers and all the people in it. Thus he killed many more when he died than while he lived.

31 Then his brothers and his father's whole family went down to get him. They brought him back and buried him between Zorah and Eshtaol in the tomb of Manoah his father. He had led[a] Israel twenty years.

Micah's Idols

17 Now a man named Micah from the hill country of Ephraim 2 said to his mother, "The eleven hundred shekels[b] of silver that were taken from you and about which I heard you utter a curse — I have that silver with me; I took it."

Then his mother said, "The LORD bless you, my son!"

3 When he returned the eleven hundred shekels of silver to his mother, she said, "I solemnly consecrate my silver to the LORD for my son to make an image overlaid with silver. I will give it back to you."

4 So after he returned the silver to his mother, she took two hundred shekels[c] of silver and gave them to a silversmith, who used them to make the idol. And it was put in Micah's house.

5 Now this man Micah had a shrine, and he made an ephod and some household gods and installed one of his sons as his priest. 6 In those days Israel had no king; everyone did as they saw fit.

7 A young Levite from Bethlehem in Judah, who had been living within the clan of Judah, 8 left that town in search of some other place to stay. On his way[d] he came to Micah's house in the hill country of Ephraim.

9 Micah asked him, "Where are you from?"

"I'm a Levite from Bethlehem in Judah," he said, "and I'm looking for a place to stay."

10 Then Micah said to him, "Live with me and be my father and priest, and I'll give you ten shekels[e] of silver a year, your clothes and your food." 11 So the Levite agreed to live with him, and the young man became like one of his sons to him. 12 Then Micah installed the Levite, and the young man became his priest and lived in his house. 13 And Micah said, "Now I know that the LORD will be good to me, since this Levite has become my priest."

The Danites Settle in Laish

18 In those days Israel had no king. And in those days the tribe of the Danites was seeking a place of their own where they might settle, because they had not yet come into an inheritance among the tribes of Israel. 2 So the Danites sent five of their leading men from Zorah and Eshtaol to spy out the land and explore it. These men represented all the Danites. They told them, "Go, explore the land."

So they entered the hill country of Ephraim and came to the house of Micah, where they spent the night. 3 When they were near Micah's house, they recognized the voice of the young Levite; so they turned in there and asked him, "Who brought you here? What are you doing in this place? Why are you here?"

[a] 31 Traditionally *judged* [b] 2 That is, about 28 pounds or about 13 kilograms [c] 4 That is, about 5 pounds or about 2.3 kilograms [d] 8 Or *To carry on his profession* [e] 10 That is, about 4 ounces or about 115 grams

4He told them what Micah had done for him, and said, "He has hired me and I am his priest."

5Then they said to him, "Please inquire of God to learn whether our journey will be successful."

6The priest answered them, "Go in peace. Your journey has the LORD's approval."

7So the five men left and came to Laish, where they saw that the people were living in safety, like the Sidonians, at peace and secure. And since their land lacked nothing, they were prosperous.[a] Also, they lived a long way from the Sidonians and had no relationship with anyone else.[b]

8When they returned to Zorah and Eshtaol, their fellow Danites asked them, "How did you find things?"

9They answered, "Come on, let's attack them! We have seen the land, and it is very good. Aren't you going to do something? Don't hesitate to go there and take it over. 10When you get there, you will find an unsuspecting people and a spacious land that God has put into your hands, a land that lacks nothing whatever."

11Then six hundred men of the Danites, armed for battle, set out from Zorah and Eshtaol. 12On their way they set up camp near Kiriath Jearim in Judah. This is why the place west of Kiriath Jearim is called Mahaneh Dan[c] to this day. 13From there they went on to the hill country of Ephraim and came to Micah's house.

14Then the five men who had spied out the land of Laish said to their fellow Danites, "Do you know that one of these houses has an ephod, some household gods and an image overlaid with silver? Now you know what to do." 15So they turned in there and went to the house of the young Levite at Micah's place and greeted him. 16The six hundred Danites, armed for battle, stood at the entrance of the gate. 17The five men who had spied out the land went inside and took the idol, the ephod and the household gods while the priest and the six hundred armed men stood at the entrance of the gate.

18When the five men went into Micah's house and took the idol, the ephod and the household gods, the priest said to them, "What are you doing?"

19They answered him, "Be quiet! Don't say a word. Come with us, and be our father and priest. Isn't it better that you serve a tribe and clan in Israel as priest rather than just one man's household?" 20The priest was very pleased. He took the ephod, the household gods and the idol and went along with the people. 21Putting their little children, their livestock and their possessions in front of them, they turned away and left.

22When they had gone some distance from Micah's house, the men who lived near Micah were called together and overtook the Danites. 23As they shouted after them, the Danites turned and said to Micah, "What's the matter with you that you called out your men to fight?"

24He replied, "You took the gods I made, and my priest, and went away. What else do I have? How can you ask, 'What's the matter with you?' "

25The Danites answered, "Don't argue with us, or some of the men may get angry and attack you, and you and your family will lose your lives." 26So the Danites went their way, and Micah, seeing that they were too strong for him, turned around and went back home.

27Then they took what Micah had made, and his priest, and went on to Laish, against a people at peace and secure. They attacked them with the sword and burned down their city. 28There was no one to rescue them because they lived a long way from Sidon and had no relationship with anyone else. The city was in a valley near Beth Rehob.

The Danites rebuilt the city and settled there. 29They named it Dan after their ancestor Dan, who was born to Israel — though the city used to be called Laish. 30There the Danites set up for themselves the idol, and Jonathan son of Gershom, the son of Moses,[d] and his sons were priests for the tribe of Dan until the time of the captivity of the land. 31They continued to use the idol Micah had made, all the time the house of God was in Shiloh.

A Levite and His Concubine

19 In those days Israel had no king. Now a Levite who lived in a remote area in the hill country of Ephraim took a concubine from Bethlehem in Judah. 2But she was unfaithful to him. She left

[a] 7 The meaning of the Hebrew for this clause is uncertain. [b] 7 Hebrew; some Septuagint manuscripts *with the Arameans* [c] 12 *Mahaneh Dan* means *Dan's camp.* [d] 30 Many Hebrew manuscripts, some Septuagint manuscripts and Vulgate; many other Hebrew manuscripts and some other Septuagint manuscripts *Manasseh*

him and went back to her parents' home
in Bethlehem, Judah. After she had been
there four months, 3her husband went
to her to persuade her to return. He had
with him his servant and two donkeys.
She took him into her parents' home,
and when her father saw him, he gladly welcomed him. 4His father-in-law,
the woman's father, prevailed on him
to stay; so he remained with him three
days, eating and drinking, and sleeping
there.

5On the fourth day they got up early
and he prepared to leave, but the woman's father said to his son-in-law, "Refresh yourself with something to eat;
then you can go." 6So the two of them
sat down to eat and drink together. Afterward the woman's father said, "Please
stay tonight and enjoy yourself." 7And
when the man got up to go, his father-
in-law persuaded him, so he stayed there
that night. 8On the morning of the fifth
day, when he rose to go, the woman's
father said, "Refresh yourself. Wait till
afternoon!" So the two of them ate together.

9Then when the man, with his concubine and his servant, got up to leave, his
father-in-law, the woman's father, said,
"Now look, it's almost evening. Spend
the night here; the day is nearly over.
Stay and enjoy yourself. Early tomorrow morning you can get up and be on
your way home." 10But, unwilling to stay
another night, the man left and went toward Jebus (that is, Jerusalem), with his
two saddled donkeys and his concubine.

11When they were near Jebus and the
day was almost gone, the servant said to
his master, "Come, let's stop at this city
of the Jebusites and spend the night."

12His master replied, "No. We won't go
into any city whose people are not Israelites. We will go on to Gibeah." 13He added, "Come, let's try to reach Gibeah or Ramah and spend the night in one of those
places." 14So they went on, and the sun
set as they neared Gibeah in Benjamin.
15There they stopped to spend the night.
They went and sat in the city square, but
no one took them in for the night.

16That evening an old man from the
hill country of Ephraim, who was living
in Gibeah (the inhabitants of the place
were Benjamites), came in from his
work in the fields. 17When he looked and
saw the traveler in the city square, the
old man asked, "Where are you going?
Where did you come from?"

18He answered, "We are on our way
from Bethlehem in Judah to a remote
area in the hill country of Ephraim
where I live. I have been to Bethlehem in
Judah and now I am going to the house
of the LORD.[a] No one has taken me in for
the night. 19We have both straw and fodder for our donkeys and bread and wine
for ourselves your servants — me, the
woman and the young man with us. We
don't need anything."

20"You are welcome at my house," the
old man said. "Let me supply whatever
you need. Only don't spend the night
in the square." 21So he took him into his
house and fed his donkeys. After they
had washed their feet, they had something to eat and drink.

22While they were enjoying themselves, some of the wicked men of the
city surrounded the house. Pounding on
the door, they shouted to the old man
who owned the house, "Bring out the
man who came to your house so we can
have sex with him."

23The owner of the house went outside
and said to them, "No, my friends, don't
be so vile. Since this man is my guest,
don't do this outrageous thing. 24Look,
here is my virgin daughter, and his concubine. I will bring them out to you now,
and you can use them and do to them
whatever you wish. But as for this man,
don't do such an outrageous thing."

25But the men would not listen to him.
So the man took his concubine and sent
her outside to them, and they raped her
and abused her throughout the night,
and at dawn they let her go. 26At daybreak the woman went back to the house
where her master was staying, fell down
at the door and lay there until daylight.

27When her master got up in the morning and opened the door of the house
and stepped out to continue on his way,
there lay his concubine, fallen in the
doorway of the house, with her hands on
the threshold. 28He said to her, "Get up;
let's go." But there was no answer. Then
the man put her on his donkey and set
out for home.

29When he reached home, he took a
knife and cut up his concubine, limb by
limb, into twelve parts and sent them
into all the areas of Israel. 30Everyone
who saw it was saying to one another,
"Such a thing has never been seen or
done, not since the day the Israelites
came up out of Egypt. Just imagine! We
must do something! So speak up!"

[a] *18* Hebrew, Vulgate, Syriac and Targum; Septuagint *going home*

The Israelites Punish the Benjamites

20 Then all Israel from Dan to Beersheba and from the land of Gilead
came together as one and assembled before the LORD in Mizpah. 2The leaders of
all the people of the tribes of Israel took
their places in the assembly of God's people, four hundred thousand men armed
with swords. 3(The Benjamites heard
that the Israelites had gone up to Mizpah.) Then the Israelites said, "Tell us
how this awful thing happened."

4So the Levite, the husband of the
murdered woman, said, "I and my concubine came to Gibeah in Benjamin to
spend the night. 5During the night the
men of Gibeah came after me and surrounded the house, intending to kill me.
They raped my concubine, and she died.
6I took my concubine, cut her into pieces
and sent one piece to each region of Israel's inheritance, because they committed
this lewd and outrageous act in Israel.
7Now, all you Israelites, speak up and tell
me what you have decided to do."

8All the men rose up together as one,
saying, "None of us will go home. No, not
one of us will return to his house. 9But
now this is what we'll do to Gibeah: We'll
go up against it in the order decided by
casting lots. 10We'll take ten men out of
every hundred from all the tribes of Israel, and a hundred from a thousand, and
a thousand from ten thousand, to get
provisions for the army. Then, when the
army arrives at Gibeah[a] in Benjamin, it
can give them what they deserve for this
outrageous act done in Israel." 11So all
the Israelites got together and united as
one against the city.

12The tribes of Israel sent messengers
throughout the tribe of Benjamin, saying, "What about this awful crime that
was committed among you? 13Now turn
those wicked men of Gibeah over to us
so that we may put them to death and
purge the evil from Israel."

But the Benjamites would not listen to
their fellow Israelites. 14From their towns
they came together at Gibeah to fight
against the Israelites. 15At once the Benjamites mobilized twenty-six thousand
swordsmen from their towns, in addition to seven hundred able young men
from those living in Gibeah. 16Among all
these soldiers there were seven hundred
select troops who were left-handed, each
of whom could sling a stone at a hair
and not miss.

17Israel, apart from Benjamin, mustered four hundred thousand swordsmen, all of them fit for battle.

18The Israelites went up to Bethel[b] and
inquired of God. They said, "Who of us
is to go up first to fight against the Benjamites?"

The LORD replied, "Judah shall go
first."

19The next morning the Israelites
got up and pitched camp near Gibeah.
20The Israelites went out to fight the
Benjamites and took up battle positions
against them at Gibeah. 21The Benjamites came out of Gibeah and cut down
twenty-two thousand Israelites on the
battlefield that day. 22But the Israelites
encouraged one another and again took
up their positions where they had stationed themselves the first day. 23The
Israelites went up and wept before the
LORD until evening, and they inquired
of the LORD. They said, "Shall we go up
again to fight against the Benjamites,
our fellow Israelites?"

The LORD answered, "Go up against
them."

24Then the Israelites drew near to Benjamin the second day. 25This time, when
the Benjamites came out from Gibeah
to oppose them, they cut down another
eighteen thousand Israelites, all of them
armed with swords.

26Then all the Israelites, the whole
army, went up to Bethel, and there they
sat weeping before the LORD. They fasted that day until evening and presented
burnt offerings and fellowship offerings
to the LORD. 27And the Israelites inquired
of the LORD. (In those days the ark of the
covenant of God was there, 28with Phinehas son of Eleazar, the son of Aaron,
ministering before it.) They asked, "Shall
we go up again to fight against the Benjamites, our fellow Israelites, or not?"

The LORD responded, "Go, for tomorrow I will give them into your hands."

29Then Israel set an ambush around
Gibeah. 30They went up against the Benjamites on the third day and took up positions against Gibeah as they had done
before. 31The Benjamites came out to
meet them and were drawn away from
the city. They began to inflict casualties
on the Israelites as before, so that about
thirty men fell in the open field and on
the roads — the one leading to Bethel
and the other to Gibeah. 32While the Benjamites were saying, "We are defeating

[a] *10* One Hebrew manuscript; most Hebrew manuscripts *Geba*, a variant of *Gibeah* [b] *18* Or *to the house of God*; also in verse 26

them as before," the Israelites were saying, "Let's retreat and draw them away from the city to the roads."

33 All the men of Israel moved from their places and took up positions at Baal Tamar, and the Israelite ambush charged out of its place on the west[a] of Gibeah.[b] 34 Then ten thousand of Israel's able young men made a frontal attack on Gibeah. The fighting was so heavy that the Benjamites did not realize how near disaster was. 35 The LORD defeated Benjamin before Israel, and on that day the Israelites struck down 25,100 Benjamites, all armed with swords. 36 Then the Benjamites saw that they were beaten.

Now the men of Israel had given way before Benjamin, because they relied on the ambush they had set near Gibeah. 37 Those who had been in ambush made a sudden dash into Gibeah, spread out and put the whole city to the sword. 38 The Israelites had arranged with the ambush that they should send up a great cloud of smoke from the city, 39 and then the Israelites would counterattack.

The Benjamites had begun to inflict casualties on the Israelites (about thirty), and they said, "We are defeating them as in the first battle." 40 But when the column of smoke began to rise from the city, the Benjamites turned and saw the whole city going up in smoke. 41 Then the Israelites counterattacked, and the Benjamites were terrified, because they realized that disaster had come on them. 42 So they fled before the Israelites in the direction of the wilderness, but they could not escape the battle. And the Israelites who came out of the towns cut them down there. 43 They surrounded the Benjamites, chased them and easily[c] overran them in the vicinity of Gibeah on the east. 44 Eighteen thousand Benjamites fell, all of them valiant fighters. 45 As they turned and fled toward the wilderness to the rock of Rimmon, the Israelites cut down five thousand men along the roads. They kept pressing after the Benjamites as far as Gidom and struck down two thousand more.

46 On that day twenty-five thousand Benjamite swordsmen fell, all of them valiant fighters. 47 But six hundred of them turned and fled into the wilderness to the rock of Rimmon, where they stayed four months. 48 The men of Israel went back to Benjamin and put all the towns to the sword, including the animals and everything else they found. All the towns they came across they set on fire.

Wives for the Benjamites

21 The men of Israel had taken an oath at Mizpah: "Not one of us will give his daughter in marriage to a Benjamite."

2 The people went to Bethel,[d] where they sat before God until evening, raising their voices and weeping bitterly. 3 "LORD, God of Israel," they cried, "why has this happened to Israel? Why should one tribe be missing from Israel today?"

4 Early the next day the people built an altar and presented burnt offerings and fellowship offerings.

5 Then the Israelites asked, "Who from all the tribes of Israel has failed to assemble before the LORD?" For they had taken a solemn oath that anyone who failed to assemble before the LORD at Mizpah was to be put to death.

6 Now the Israelites grieved for the tribe of Benjamin, their fellow Israelites. "Today one tribe is cut off from Israel," they said. 7 "How can we provide wives for those who are left, since we have taken an oath by the LORD not to give them any of our daughters in marriage?" 8 Then they asked, "Which one of the tribes of Israel failed to assemble before the LORD at Mizpah?" They discovered that no one from Jabesh Gilead had come to the camp for the assembly. 9 For when they counted the people, they found that none of the people of Jabesh Gilead were there.

10 So the assembly sent twelve thousand fighting men with instructions to go to Jabesh Gilead and put to the sword those living there, including the women and children. 11 "This is what you are to do," they said. "Kill every male and every woman who is not a virgin." 12 They found among the people living in Jabesh Gilead four hundred young women who had never slept with a man, and they took them to the camp at Shiloh in Canaan.

13 Then the whole assembly sent an offer of peace to the Benjamites at the rock of Rimmon. 14 So the Benjamites returned at that time and were given the women of Jabesh Gilead who had been spared. But there were not enough for all of them.

[a] *33* Some Septuagint manuscripts and Vulgate; the meaning of the Hebrew for this word is uncertain. [b] *33* Hebrew *Geba*, a variant of *Gibeah* [c] *43* The meaning of the Hebrew for this word is uncertain. [d] *2* Or *to the house of God*

[15]The people grieved for Benjamin, because the LORD had made a gap in the tribes of Israel. [16]And the elders of the assembly said, "With the women of Benjamin destroyed, how shall we provide wives for the men who are left? [17]The Benjamite survivors must have heirs," they said, "so that a tribe of Israel will not be wiped out. [18]We can't give them our daughters as wives, since we Israelites have taken this oath: 'Cursed be anyone who gives a wife to a Benjamite.' [19]But look, there is the annual festival of the LORD in Shiloh, which lies north of Bethel, east of the road that goes from Bethel to Shechem, and south of Lebonah."

[20]So they instructed the Benjamites, saying, "Go and hide in the vineyards [21]and watch. When the young women of Shiloh come out to join in the dancing, rush from the vineyards and each of you seize one of them to be your wife. Then return to the land of Benjamin. [22]When their fathers or brothers complain to us, we will say to them, 'Do us the favor of helping them, because we did not get wives for them during the war. You will not be guilty of breaking your oath because you did not give your daughters to them.'"

[23]So that is what the Benjamites did. While the young women were dancing, each man caught one and carried her off to be his wife. Then they returned to their inheritance and rebuilt the towns and settled in them.

[24]At that time the Israelites left that place and went home to their tribes and clans, each to his own inheritance.

[25]In those days Israel had no king; everyone did as they saw fit.

RUTH

Naomi Loses Her Husband and Sons

1 In the days when the judges ruled,[a]
there was a famine in the land. So a
man from Bethlehem in Judah, together with his wife and two sons, went to
live for a while in the country of Moab.
2The man's name was Elimelek, his wife's
name was Naomi, and the names of his
two sons were Mahlon and Kilion. They
were Ephrathites from Bethlehem, Judah.
And they went to Moab and lived there.

3Now Elimelek, Naomi's husband,
died, and she was left with her two sons.
4They married Moabite women, one
named Orpah and the other Ruth. After they had lived there about ten years,
5both Mahlon and Kilion also died, and
Naomi was left without her two sons and
her husband.

Naomi and Ruth Return to Bethlehem

6When Naomi heard in Moab that the
LORD had come to the aid of his people
by providing food for them, she and her
daughters-in-law prepared to return
home from there. 7With her two daughters-
in-law she left the place where she had
been living and set out on the road that
would take them back to the land of
Judah.

8Then Naomi said to her two daughters-
in-law, "Go back, each of you, to your
mother's home. May the LORD show you
kindness, as you have shown kindness to
your dead husbands and to me. 9May the
LORD grant that each of you will find rest
in the home of another husband."

Then she kissed them goodbye and
they wept aloud 10and said to her, "We
will go back with you to your people."

11But Naomi said, "Return home, my
daughters. Why would you come with
me? Am I going to have any more sons,
who could become your husbands? 12Re-
turn home, my daughters; I am too old to
have another husband. Even if I thought
there was still hope for me — even if I
had a husband tonight and then gave
birth to sons — 13would you wait until
they grew up? Would you remain unmarried for them? No, my daughters. It is
more bitter for me than for you, because
the LORD's hand has turned against me!"

14At this they wept aloud again. Then
Orpah kissed her mother-in-law goodbye, but Ruth clung to her.

15"Look," said Naomi, "your sister-in-
law is going back to her people and her
gods. Go back with her."

16But Ruth replied, "Don't urge me
to leave you or to turn back from you.
Where you go I will go, and where you
stay I will stay. Your people will be my
people and your God my God. 17Where
you die I will die, and there I will be buried. May the LORD deal with me, be it
ever so severely, if even death separates
you and me." 18When Naomi realized
that Ruth was determined to go with her,
she stopped urging her.

19So the two women went on until
they came to Bethlehem. When they arrived in Bethlehem, the whole town was
stirred because of them, and the women
exclaimed, "Can this be Naomi?"

20"Don't call me Naomi,[b]" she told
them. "Call me Mara,[c] because the Almighty[d] has made my life very bitter. 21I
went away full, but the LORD has brought
me back empty. Why call me Naomi? The
LORD has afflicted[e] me; the Almighty has
brought misfortune upon me."

22So Naomi returned from Moab accompanied by Ruth the Moabite, her
daughter-in-law, arriving in Bethlehem
as the barley harvest was beginning.

Ruth Meets Boaz in the Grain Field

2 Now Naomi had a relative on her
husband's side, a man of standing
from the clan of Elimelek, whose name
was Boaz.

2And Ruth the Moabite said to Naomi,
"Let me go to the fields and pick up the
leftover grain behind anyone in whose
eyes I find favor."

Naomi said to her, "Go ahead, my
daughter." 3So she went out, entered a
field and began to glean behind the harvesters. As it turned out, she was working in a field belonging to Boaz, who was
from the clan of Elimelek.

4Just then Boaz arrived from Bethlehem and greeted the harvesters, "The
LORD be with you!"

[a] 1 Traditionally *judged* [b] 20 *Naomi* means *pleasant.* [c] 20 *Mara* means *bitter.*
[d] 20 Hebrew *Shaddai;* also in verse 21 [e] 21 Or *has testified against*

"The LORD bless you!" they answered.

5Boaz asked the overseer of his harvesters, "Who does that young woman belong to?"

6The overseer replied, "She is the Moabite who came back from Moab with Naomi. 7She said, 'Please let me glean and gather among the sheaves behind the harvesters.' She came into the field and has remained here from morning till now, except for a short rest in the shelter."

8So Boaz said to Ruth, "My daughter, listen to me. Don't go and glean in another field and don't go away from here. Stay here with the women who work for me. 9Watch the field where the men are harvesting, and follow along after the women. I have told the men not to lay a hand on you. And whenever you are thirsty, go and get a drink from the water jars the men have filled."

10At this, she bowed down with her face to the ground. She asked him, "Why have I found such favor in your eyes that you notice me — a foreigner?"

11Boaz replied, "I've been told all about what you have done for your mother-in-law since the death of your husband — how you left your father and mother and your homeland and came to live with a people you did not know before. 12May the LORD repay you for what you have done. May you be richly rewarded by the LORD, the God of Israel, under whose wings you have come to take refuge."

13"May I continue to find favor in your eyes, my lord," she said. "You have put me at ease by speaking kindly to your servant — though I do not have the standing of one of your servants."

14At mealtime Boaz said to her, "Come over here. Have some bread and dip it in the wine vinegar."

When she sat down with the harvesters, he offered her some roasted grain. She ate all she wanted and had some left over. 15As she got up to glean, Boaz gave orders to his men, "Let her gather among the sheaves and don't reprimand her. 16Even pull out some stalks for her from the bundles and leave them for her to pick up, and don't rebuke her."

17So Ruth gleaned in the field until evening. Then she threshed the barley she had gathered, and it amounted to about an ephah.[a] 18She carried it back to town, and her mother-in-law saw how much she had gathered. Ruth also brought out and gave her what she had left over after she had eaten enough.

19Her mother-in-law asked her, "Where did you glean today? Where did you work? Blessed be the man who took notice of you!"

Then Ruth told her mother-in-law about the one at whose place she had been working. "The name of the man I worked with today is Boaz," she said.

20"The LORD bless him!" Naomi said to her daughter-in-law. "He has not stopped showing his kindness to the living and the dead." She added, "That man is our close relative; he is one of our guardian-redeemers.[b]"

21Then Ruth the Moabite said, "He even said to me, 'Stay with my workers until they finish harvesting all my grain.'"

22Naomi said to Ruth her daughter-in-law, "It will be good for you, my daughter, to go with the women who work for him, because in someone else's field you might be harmed."

23So Ruth stayed close to the women of Boaz to glean until the barley and wheat harvests were finished. And she lived with her mother-in-law.

Ruth and Boaz at the Threshing Floor

3 One day Ruth's mother-in-law Naomi said to her, "My daughter, I must find a home[c] for you, where you will be well provided for. 2Now Boaz, with whose women you have worked, is a relative of ours. Tonight he will be winnowing barley on the threshing floor. 3Wash, put on perfume, and get dressed in your best clothes. Then go down to the threshing floor, but don't let him know you are there until he has finished eating and drinking. 4When he lies down, note the place where he is lying. Then go and uncover his feet and lie down. He will tell you what to do."

5"I will do whatever you say," Ruth answered. 6So she went down to the threshing floor and did everything her mother-in-law told her to do.

7When Boaz had finished eating and drinking and was in good spirits, he went over to lie down at the far end of the grain pile. Ruth approached quietly, uncovered his feet and lay down. 8In the middle of the night something startled the man; he turned — and there was a woman lying at his feet!

[a] *17* That is, probably about 30 pounds or about 13 kilograms [b] *20* The Hebrew word for *guardian-redeemer* is a legal term for one who has the obligation to redeem a relative in serious difficulty (see Lev. 25:25-55). [c] *1* Hebrew *find rest* (see 1:9)

9"Who are you?" he asked.
"I am your servant Ruth," she said.
"Spread the corner of your garment over
me, since you are a guardian-redeemer[a]
of our family."
10"The LORD bless you, my daughter,"
he replied. "This kindness is greater than
that which you showed earlier: You have
not run after the younger men, whether rich or poor. 11And now, my daughter,
don't be afraid. I will do for you all you
ask. All the people of my town know
that you are a woman of noble character. 12Although it is true that I am a
guardian-redeemer of our family, there
is another who is more closely related
than I. 13Stay here for the night, and in
the morning if he wants to do his duty as
your guardian-redeemer, good; let him
redeem you. But if he is not willing, as
surely as the LORD lives I will do it. Lie
here until morning."
14So she lay at his feet until morning,
but got up before anyone could be recognized; and he said, "No one must know
that a woman came to the threshing
floor."
15He also said, "Bring me the shawl
you are wearing and hold it out." When
she did so, he poured into it six measures
of barley and placed the bundle on her.
Then he[b] went back to town.
16When Ruth came to her mother-in-
law, Naomi asked, "How did it go, my
daughter?"
Then she told her everything Boaz
had done for her 17and added, "He gave
me these six measures of barley, saying,
'Don't go back to your mother-in-law
empty-handed.'"
18Then Naomi said, "Wait, my daughter, until you find out what happens. For
the man will not rest until the matter is
settled today."

Boaz Marries Ruth

4 Meanwhile Boaz went up to the town
gate and sat down there just as the
guardian-redeemer[c] he had mentioned
came along. Boaz said, "Come over here,
my friend, and sit down." So he went
over and sat down.
2Boaz took ten of the elders of the
town and said, "Sit here," and they
did so. 3Then he said to the guardian-
redeemer, "Naomi, who has come back
from Moab, is selling the piece of land
that belonged to our relative Elimelek.
4I thought I should bring the matter to
your attention and suggest that you buy
it in the presence of these seated here
and in the presence of the elders of my
people. If you will redeem it, do so. But if
you[d] will not, tell me, so I will know. For
no one has the right to do it except you,
and I am next in line."
"I will redeem it," he said.
5Then Boaz said, "On the day you buy
the land from Naomi, you also acquire
Ruth the Moabite, the[e] dead man's widow, in order to maintain the name of the
dead with his property."
6At this, the guardian-redeemer said,
"Then I cannot redeem it because I
might endanger my own estate. You redeem it yourself. I cannot do it."
7(Now in earlier times in Israel, for the
redemption and transfer of property to
become final, one party took off his sandal and gave it to the other. This was the
method of legalizing transactions in Israel.)
8So the guardian-redeemer said to
Boaz, "Buy it yourself." And he removed
his sandal.
9Then Boaz announced to the elders
and all the people, "Today you are witnesses that I have bought from Naomi
all the property of Elimelek, Kilion and
Mahlon. 10I have also acquired Ruth the
Moabite, Mahlon's widow, as my wife, in
order to maintain the name of the dead
with his property, so that his name will
not disappear from among his family or
from his hometown. Today you are witnesses!"
11Then the elders and all the people
at the gate said, "We are witnesses. May
the LORD make the woman who is coming into your home like Rachel and Leah,
who together built up the family of Israel. May you have standing in Ephrathah
and be famous in Bethlehem. 12Through
the offspring the LORD gives you by this
young woman, may your family be
like that of Perez, whom Tamar bore to
Judah."

[a] 9 The Hebrew word for *guardian-redeemer* is a legal term for one who has the obligation to redeem a relative in serious difficulty (see Lev. 25:25-55); also in verses 12 and 13. [b] 15 Most Hebrew manuscripts; many Hebrew manuscripts, Vulgate and Syriac *she* [c] 1 The Hebrew word for *guardian-redeemer* is a legal term for one who has the obligation to redeem a relative in serious difficulty (see Lev. 25:25-55); also in verses 3, 6, 8 and 14. [d] 4 Many Hebrew manuscripts, Septuagint, Vulgate and Syriac; most Hebrew manuscripts *he* [e] 5 Vulgate and Syriac; Hebrew (see also Septuagint) *Naomi and from Ruth the Moabite, you acquire the*

Naomi Gains a Son

[13]So Boaz took Ruth and she became
his wife. When he made love to her, the
Lord enabled her to conceive, and she
gave birth to a son. [14]The women said to
Naomi: "Praise be to the Lord, who this
day has not left you without a guardian-
redeemer. May he become famous
throughout Israel! [15]He will renew your
life and sustain you in your old age. For
your daughter-in-law, who loves you and
who is better to you than seven sons, has
given him birth."

[16]Then Naomi took the child in her
arms and cared for him. [17]The women
living there said, "Naomi has a son!"
And they named him Obed. He was the
father of Jesse, the father of David.

The Genealogy of David

[18]This, then, is the family line of Perez:

Perez was the father of Hezron,
[19] Hezron the father of Ram,
Ram the father of Amminadab,
[20] Amminadab the father of Nahshon,
Nahshon the father of Salmon,[a]
[21] Salmon the father of Boaz,
Boaz the father of Obed,
[22] Obed the father of Jesse,
and Jesse the father of David.

[a] *20* A few Hebrew manuscripts, some Septuagint manuscripts and Vulgate (see also verse 21 and Septuagint of 1 Chron. 2:11); most Hebrew manuscripts *Salma*

1 SAMUEL

The Birth of Samuel

1 There was a certain man from Ramathaim, a Zuphite[a] from the hill
country of Ephraim, whose name was
Elkanah son of Jeroham, the son of Elihu, the son of Tohu, the son of Zuph, an
Ephraimite. 2 He had two wives; one was
called Hannah and the other Peninnah.
Peninnah had children, but Hannah had
none.

3 Year after year this man went up
from his town to worship and sacrifice
to the LORD Almighty at Shiloh, where
Hophni and Phinehas, the two sons of
Eli, were priests of the LORD. 4 Whenever the day came for Elkanah to sacrifice, he would give portions of the meat
to his wife Peninnah and to all her sons
and daughters. 5 But to Hannah he gave
a double portion because he loved her,
and the LORD had closed her womb. 6 Because the LORD had closed Hannah's
womb, her rival kept provoking her in
order to irritate her. 7 This went on year
after year. Whenever Hannah went up
to the house of the LORD, her rival provoked her till she wept and would not
eat. 8 Her husband Elkanah would say
to her, "Hannah, why are you weeping?
Why don't you eat? Why are you down-
hearted? Don't I mean more to you than
ten sons?"

9 Once when they had finished eating
and drinking in Shiloh, Hannah stood
up. Now Eli the priest was sitting on
his chair by the doorpost of the LORD's
house. 10 In her deep anguish Hannah
prayed to the LORD, weeping bitterly.
11 And she made a vow, saying, "LORD
Almighty, if you will only look on your
servant's misery and remember me, and
not forget your servant but give her a
son, then I will give him to the LORD for
all the days of his life, and no razor will
ever be used on his head."

12 As she kept on praying to the LORD,
Eli observed her mouth. 13 Hannah was
praying in her heart, and her lips were
moving but her voice was not heard. Eli
thought she was drunk 14 and said to her,
"How long are you going to stay drunk?
Put away your wine."

15 "Not so, my lord," Hannah replied,
"I am a woman who is deeply troubled.
I have not been drinking wine or beer;
I was pouring out my soul to the LORD.
16 Do not take your servant for a wicked
woman; I have been praying here out of
my great anguish and grief."

17 Eli answered, "Go in peace, and may
the God of Israel grant you what you
have asked of him."

18 She said, "May your servant find favor in your eyes." Then she went her way
and ate something, and her face was no
longer downcast.

19 Early the next morning they arose
and worshiped before the LORD and then
went back to their home at Ramah. Elkanah made love to his wife Hannah, and
the LORD remembered her. 20 So in the
course of time Hannah became pregnant and gave birth to a son. She named
him Samuel,[b] saying, "Because I asked
the LORD for him."

Hannah Dedicates Samuel

21 When her husband Elkanah went
up with all his family to offer the annual sacrifice to the LORD and to fulfill his
vow, 22 Hannah did not go. She said to
her husband, "After the boy is weaned,
I will take him and present him before
the LORD, and he will live there always."[c]

23 "Do what seems best to you," her
husband Elkanah told her. "Stay here
until you have weaned him; only may
the LORD make good his[d] word." So the
woman stayed at home and nursed her
son until she had weaned him.

24 After he was weaned, she took the
boy with her, young as he was, along
with a three-year-old bull,[e] an ephah[f]
of flour and a skin of wine, and brought
him to the house of the LORD at Shiloh.
25 When the bull had been sacrificed, they
brought the boy to Eli, 26 and she said to
him, "Pardon me, my lord. As surely as
you live, I am the woman who stood
here beside you praying to the LORD.

[a] *1* See Septuagint and 1 Chron. 6:26-27,33-35; or *from Ramathaim Zuphim.* [b] *20* *Samuel* sounds like the Hebrew for *heard by God.* [c] *22* Masoretic Text; Dead Sea Scrolls *always. I have dedicated him as a Nazirite — all the days of his life."* [d] *23* Masoretic Text; Dead Sea Scrolls, Septuagint and Syriac *your* [e] *24* Dead Sea Scrolls, Septuagint and Syriac; Masoretic Text *with three bulls* [f] *24* That is, probably about 36 pounds or about 16 kilograms

27 I prayed for this child, and the LORD
has granted me what I asked of him.
28 So now I give him to the LORD. For his
whole life he will be given over to the
LORD." And he worshiped the LORD there.

Hannah's Prayer

2 Then Hannah prayed and said:

"My heart rejoices in the LORD;
  in the LORD my horn[a] is lifted high.
My mouth boasts over my enemies,
  for I delight in your deliverance.

2 "There is no one holy like the LORD;
  there is no one besides you;
  there is no Rock like our God.

3 "Do not keep talking so proudly
  or let your mouth speak such
    arrogance,
for the LORD is a God who knows,
  and by him deeds are weighed.

4 "The bows of the warriors are broken,
  but those who stumbled are armed
    with strength.
5 Those who were full hire themselves
    out for food,
  but those who were hungry are
    hungry no more.
She who was barren has borne seven
    children,
  but she who has had many sons
    pines away.

6 "The LORD brings death and makes
    alive;
  he brings down to the grave and
    raises up.
7 The LORD sends poverty and wealth;
  he humbles and he exalts.
8 He raises the poor from the dust
  and lifts the needy from the ash
    heap;
he seats them with princes
  and has them inherit a throne of
    honor.

"For the foundations of the earth are
    the LORD's;
  on them he has set the world.
9 He will guard the feet of his faithful
    servants,
  but the wicked will be silenced in
    the place of darkness.

"It is not by strength that one
    prevails;
10 those who oppose the LORD will be
    broken.
The Most High will thunder from
    heaven;
  the LORD will judge the ends of the
    earth.

"He will give strength to his king
  and exalt the horn of his anointed."

11 Then Elkanah went home to Ramah,
but the boy ministered before the LORD
under Eli the priest.

Eli's Wicked Sons

12 Eli's sons were scoundrels; they had
no regard for the LORD. 13 Now it was
the practice of the priests that, whenever any of the people offered a sacrifice, the priest's servant would come
with a three-pronged fork in his hand
while the meat was being boiled 14 and
would plunge the fork into the pan or
kettle or caldron or pot. Whatever the
fork brought up the priest would take
for himself. This is how they treated
all the Israelites who came to Shiloh.
15 But even before the fat was burned,
the priest's servant would come and
say to the person who was sacrificing,
"Give the priest some meat to roast; he
won't accept boiled meat from you, but
only raw."

16 If the person said to him, "Let the fat
be burned first, and then take whatever you want," the servant would answer,
"No, hand it over now; if you don't, I'll
take it by force."

17 This sin of the young men was very
great in the LORD's sight, for they[b] were
treating the LORD's offering with contempt.

18 But Samuel was ministering before
the LORD — a boy wearing a linen ephod.
19 Each year his mother made him a little
robe and took it to him when she went
up with her husband to offer the annual
sacrifice. 20 Eli would bless Elkanah and
his wife, saying, "May the LORD give you
children by this woman to take the place
of the one she prayed for and gave to[c]
the LORD." Then they would go home.
21 And the LORD was gracious to Hannah;
she gave birth to three sons and two
daughters. Meanwhile, the boy Samuel
grew up in the presence of the LORD.

22 Now Eli, who was very old, heard
about everything his sons were doing
to all Israel and how they slept with the
women who served at the entrance to
the tent of meeting. 23 So he said to them,
"Why do you do such things? I hear from

[a] *1 Horn* here symbolizes strength; also in verse 10. [b] *17* Dead Sea Scrolls and Septuagint; Masoretic Text *people* [c] *20* Dead Sea Scrolls; Masoretic Text *and asked from*

all the people about these wicked deeds
of yours. 24No, my sons; the report I hear
spreading among the LORD's people is
not good. 25If one person sins against another, God[a] may mediate for the offender; but if anyone sins against the LORD,
who will intercede for them?" His sons,
however, did not listen to their father's
rebuke, for it was the LORD's will to put
them to death.
26And the boy Samuel continued to
grow in stature and in favor with the
LORD and with people.

Prophecy Against the House of Eli

27Now a man of God came to Eli and
said to him, "This is what the LORD says:
'Did I not clearly reveal myself to your
ancestor's family when they were in
Egypt under Pharaoh? 28I chose your
ancestor out of all the tribes of Israel
to be my priest, to go up to my altar, to
burn incense, and to wear an ephod in
my presence. I also gave your ancestor's
family all the food offerings presented
by the Israelites. 29Why do you[b] scorn my
sacrifice and offering that I prescribed
for my dwelling? Why do you honor your
sons more than me by fattening yourselves on the choice parts of every offering made by my people Israel?'
30"Therefore the LORD, the God of Israel, declares: 'I promised that members
of your family would minister before
me forever.' But now the LORD declares:
'Far be it from me! Those who honor me
I will honor, but those who despise me
will be disdained. 31The time is coming
when I will cut short your strength and
the strength of your priestly house, so
that no one in it will reach old age, 32and
you will see distress in my dwelling. Although good will be done to Israel, no
one in your family line will ever reach
old age. 33Every one of you that I do not
cut off from serving at my altar I will
spare only to destroy your sight and sap
your strength, and all your descendants
will die in the prime of life.
34" 'And what happens to your two
sons, Hophni and Phinehas, will be a
sign to you — they will both die on the
same day. 35I will raise up for myself a
faithful priest, who will do according
to what is in my heart and mind. I will
firmly establish his priestly house, and
they will minister before my anointed
one always. 36Then everyone left in your
family line will come and bow down before him for a piece of silver and a loaf
of bread and plead, "Appoint me to
some priestly office so I can have food
to eat." ' "

The LORD Calls Samuel

3 The boy Samuel ministered before
the LORD under Eli. In those days the
word of the LORD was rare; there were
not many visions.
2One night Eli, whose eyes were becoming so weak that he could barely
see, was lying down in his usual place.
3The lamp of God had not yet gone out,
and Samuel was lying down in the house
of the LORD, where the ark of God was.
4Then the LORD called Samuel.
Samuel answered, "Here I am." 5And
he ran to Eli and said, "Here I am; you
called me."
But Eli said, "I did not call; go back
and lie down." So he went and lay down.
6Again the LORD called, "Samuel!" And
Samuel got up and went to Eli and said,
"Here I am; you called me."
"My son," Eli said, "I did not call; go
back and lie down."
7Now Samuel did not yet know the
LORD: The word of the LORD had not yet
been revealed to him.
8A third time the LORD called, "Samuel!" And Samuel got up and went to Eli
and said, "Here I am; you called me."
Then Eli realized that the LORD was
calling the boy. 9So Eli told Samuel, "Go
and lie down, and if he calls you, say,
'Speak, LORD, for your servant is listening.' " So Samuel went and lay down in
his place.
10The LORD came and stood there, calling as at the other times, "Samuel! Samuel!"
Then Samuel said, "Speak, for your
servant is listening."
11And the LORD said to Samuel: "See,
I am about to do something in Israel
that will make the ears of everyone who
hears about it tingle. 12At that time I will
carry out against Eli everything I spoke
against his family — from beginning to
end. 13For I told him that I would judge
his family forever because of the sin he
knew about; his sons blasphemed God,[c]
and he failed to restrain them. 14There-
fore I swore to the house of Eli, 'The guilt
of Eli's house will never be atoned for by
sacrifice or offering.' "
15Samuel lay down until morning and
then opened the doors of the house of

[a] 25 Or *the judges* [b] 29 The Hebrew is plural. [c] 13 An ancient Hebrew scribal tradition (see also Septuagint); Masoretic Text *sons made themselves contemptible*

the LORD. He was afraid to tell Eli the vision, 16but Eli called him and said, "Samuel, my son."
Samuel answered, "Here I am."
17"What was it he said to you?" Eli
asked. "Do not hide it from me. May God
deal with you, be it ever so severely, if
you hide from me anything he told you."
18So Samuel told him everything, hiding
nothing from him. Then Eli said, "He is
the LORD; let him do what is good in his
eyes."
19The LORD was with Samuel as he
grew up, and he let none of Samuel's
words fall to the ground. 20And all Israel
from Dan to Beersheba recognized that
Samuel was attested as a prophet of the
LORD. 21The LORD continued to appear at
Shiloh, and there he revealed himself to
Samuel through his word.
4 And Samuel's word came to all Israel.

The Philistines Capture the Ark

Now the Israelites went out to fight
against the Philistines. The Israelites
camped at Ebenezer, and the Philistines
at Aphek. 2The Philistines deployed their
forces to meet Israel, and as the battle
spread, Israel was defeated by the Philistines, who killed about four thousand
of them on the battlefield. 3When the
soldiers returned to camp, the elders of
Israel asked, "Why did the LORD bring
defeat on us today before the Philistines? Let us bring the ark of the LORD's
covenant from Shiloh, so that he may go
with us and save us from the hand of our
enemies."
4So the people sent men to Shiloh,
and they brought back the ark of the
covenant of the LORD Almighty, who is
enthroned between the cherubim. And
Eli's two sons, Hophni and Phinehas,
were there with the ark of the covenant
of God.
5When the ark of the LORD's covenant
came into the camp, all Israel raised
such a great shout that the ground
shook. 6Hearing the uproar, the Philistines asked, "What's all this shouting in
the Hebrew camp?"
When they learned that the ark of
the LORD had come into the camp, 7the
Philistines were afraid. "A god has[a]
come into the camp," they said. "Oh no!
Nothing like this has happened before.
8We're doomed! Who will deliver us from
the hand of these mighty gods? They are
the gods who struck the Egyptians with
all kinds of plagues in the wilderness.
9Be strong, Philistines! Be men, or you
will be subject to the Hebrews, as they
have been to you. Be men, and fight!"
10So the Philistines fought, and the Israelites were defeated and every man
fled to his tent. The slaughter was very
great; Israel lost thirty thousand foot
soldiers. 11The ark of God was captured,
and Eli's two sons, Hophni and Phinehas, died.

Death of Eli

12That same day a Benjamite ran from
the battle line and went to Shiloh with
his clothes torn and dust on his head.
13When he arrived, there was Eli sitting on his chair by the side of the road,
watching, because his heart feared for
the ark of God. When the man entered
the town and told what had happened,
the whole town sent up a cry.
14Eli heard the outcry and asked,
"What is the meaning of this uproar?"
The man hurried over to Eli, 15who was
ninety-eight years old and whose eyes
had failed so that he could not see. 16He
told Eli, "I have just come from the battle
line; I fled from it this very day."
Eli asked, "What happened, my son?"
17The man who brought the news replied, "Israel fled before the Philistines,
and the army has suffered heavy losses.
Also your two sons, Hophni and Phinehas, are dead, and the ark of God has
been captured."
18When he mentioned the ark of God,
Eli fell backward off his chair by the side
of the gate. His neck was broken and he
died, for he was an old man, and he was
heavy. He had led[b] Israel forty years.
19His daughter-in-law, the wife of
Phinehas, was pregnant and near the
time of delivery. When she heard the
news that the ark of God had been captured and that her father-in-law and
her husband were dead, she went into
labor and gave birth, but was overcome
by her labor pains. 20As she was dying,
the women attending her said, "Don't
despair; you have given birth to a son."
But she did not respond or pay any attention.
21She named the boy Ichabod,[c] saying,
"The Glory has departed from Israel" —
because of the capture of the ark of God
and the deaths of her father-in-law and
her husband. 22She said, "The Glory has
departed from Israel, for the ark of God
has been captured."

[a] 7 Or "*Gods have* (see Septuagint) [b] 18 Traditionally *judged* [c] 21 *Ichabod* means *no glory.*

The Ark in Ashdod and Ekron

5 After the Philistines had captured
the ark of God, they took it from Ebenezer to Ashdod. 2Then they carried
the ark into Dagon's temple and set it
beside Dagon. 3When the people of Ashdod rose early the next day, there was
Dagon, fallen on his face on the ground
before the ark of the LORD! They took Dagon and put him back in his place. 4But
the following morning when they rose,
there was Dagon, fallen on his face on
the ground before the ark of the LORD!
His head and hands had been broken off
and were lying on the threshold; only his
body remained. 5That is why to this day
neither the priests of Dagon nor any others who enter Dagon's temple at Ashdod
step on the threshold.

6The LORD's hand was heavy on the
people of Ashdod and its vicinity; he
brought devastation on them and afflicted them with tumors.[a] 7When the
people of Ashdod saw what was happening, they said, "The ark of the god of Israel must not stay here with us, because
his hand is heavy on us and on Dagon
our god." 8So they called together all the
rulers of the Philistines and asked them,
"What shall we do with the ark of the
god of Israel?"

They answered, "Have the ark of the
god of Israel moved to Gath." So they
moved the ark of the God of Israel.

9But after they had moved it, the
LORD's hand was against that city,
throwing it into a great panic. He afflicted the people of the city, both young and
old, with an outbreak of tumors.[b] 10So
they sent the ark of God to Ekron.

As the ark of God was entering Ekron, the people of Ekron cried out, "They
have brought the ark of the god of Israel
around to us to kill us and our people."
11So they called together all the rulers of
the Philistines and said, "Send the ark of
the god of Israel away; let it go back to
its own place, or it[c] will kill us and our
people." For death had filled the city
with panic; God's hand was very heavy
on it. 12Those who did not die were afflicted with tumors, and the outcry of
the city went up to heaven.

The Ark Returned to Israel

6 When the ark of the LORD had been
in Philistine territory seven months,
2the Philistines called for the priests and
the diviners and said, "What shall we do
with the ark of the LORD? Tell us how we
should send it back to its place."

3They answered, "If you return the ark
of the god of Israel, do not send it back
to him without a gift; by all means send
a guilt offering to him. Then you will be
healed, and you will know why his hand
has not been lifted from you."

4The Philistines asked, "What guilt offering should we send to him?"

They replied, "Five gold tumors and
five gold rats, according to the number
of the Philistine rulers, because the same
plague has struck both you and your rulers. 5Make models of the tumors and of
the rats that are destroying the country,
and give glory to Israel's god. Perhaps
he will lift his hand from you and your
gods and your land. 6Why do you harden
your hearts as the Egyptians and Pharaoh did? When Israel's god dealt harshly
with them, did they not send the Israelites out so they could go on their way?

7"Now then, get a new cart ready, with
two cows that have calved and have
never been yoked. Hitch the cows to the
cart, but take their calves away and pen
them up. 8Take the ark of the LORD and
put it on the cart, and in a chest beside
it put the gold objects you are sending
back to him as a guilt offering. Send it
on its way, 9but keep watching it. If it
goes up to its own territory, toward Beth
Shemesh, then the LORD has brought this
great disaster on us. But if it does not,
then we will know that it was not his
hand that struck us but that it happened
to us by chance."

10So they did this. They took two such
cows and hitched them to the cart and
penned up their calves. 11They placed the
ark of the LORD on the cart and along
with it the chest containing the gold rats
and the models of the tumors. 12Then the
cows went straight up toward Beth Shemesh, keeping on the road and lowing
all the way; they did not turn to the right
or to the left. The rulers of the Philistines
followed them as far as the border of
Beth Shemesh.

13Now the people of Beth Shemesh
were harvesting their wheat in the valley,
and when they looked up and saw the
ark, they rejoiced at the sight. 14The cart
came to the field of Joshua of Beth Shemesh, and there it stopped beside a large
rock. The people chopped up the wood
of the cart and sacrificed the cows as a
burnt offering to the LORD. 15The Levites

[a] 6 Hebrew; Septuagint and Vulgate *tumors. And rats appeared in their land, and there was death and destruction throughout the city* [b] 9 Or *with tumors in the groin* (see Septuagint) [c] 11 Or *he*

took down the ark of the LORD, together
with the chest containing the gold objects, and placed them on the large rock.
On that day the people of Beth Shemesh
offered burnt offerings and made sacrifices to the LORD. 16The five rulers of the
Philistines saw all this and then returned
that same day to Ekron.

17These are the gold tumors the Philistines sent as a guilt offering to the
LORD—one each for Ashdod, Gaza, Ashkelon, Gath and Ekron. 18And the number of the gold rats was according to the
number of Philistine towns belonging to
the five rulers—the fortified towns with
their country villages. The large rock on
which the Levites set the ark of the LORD
is a witness to this day in the field of
Joshua of Beth Shemesh.

19But God struck down some of the
inhabitants of Beth Shemesh, putting
seventy[a] of them to death because they
looked into the ark of the LORD. The people mourned because of the heavy blow
the LORD had dealt them. 20And the people of Beth Shemesh asked, "Who can
stand in the presence of the LORD, this
holy God? To whom will the ark go up
from here?"

21Then they sent messengers to the
people of Kiriath Jearim, saying, "The
Philistines have returned the ark of the
LORD. Come down and take it up to your
7 town." 1So the men of Kiriath Jearim
came and took up the ark of the LORD.
They brought it to Abinadab's house on
the hill and consecrated Eleazar his son
to guard the ark of the LORD. 2The ark remained at Kiriath Jearim a long time—
twenty years in all.

Samuel Subdues the Philistines at Mizpah

Then all the people of Israel turned
back to the LORD. 3So Samuel said to all
the Israelites, "If you are returning to
the LORD with all your hearts, then rid
yourselves of the foreign gods and the
Ashtoreths and commit yourselves to
the LORD and serve him only, and he will
deliver you out of the hand of the Philistines." 4So the Israelites put away their
Baals and Ashtoreths, and served the
LORD only.

5Then Samuel said, "Assemble all Israel at Mizpah, and I will intercede
with the LORD for you." 6When they had
assembled at Mizpah, they drew water and poured it out before the LORD.
On that day they fasted and there they
confessed, "We have sinned against the
LORD." Now Samuel was serving as leader[b] of Israel at Mizpah.

7When the Philistines heard that Israel
had assembled at Mizpah, the rulers of
the Philistines came up to attack them.
When the Israelites heard of it, they were
afraid because of the Philistines. 8They
said to Samuel, "Do not stop crying out
to the LORD our God for us, that he may
rescue us from the hand of the Philistines." 9Then Samuel took a suckling
lamb and sacrificed it as a whole burnt
offering to the LORD. He cried out to the
LORD on Israel's behalf, and the LORD answered him.

10While Samuel was sacrificing the
burnt offering, the Philistines drew near
to engage Israel in battle. But that day
the LORD thundered with loud thunder
against the Philistines and threw them
into such a panic that they were routed
before the Israelites. 11The men of Israel
rushed out of Mizpah and pursued the
Philistines, slaughtering them along the
way to a point below Beth Kar.

12Then Samuel took a stone and set it
up between Mizpah and Shen. He named
it Ebenezer,[c] saying, "Thus far the LORD
has helped us."

13So the Philistines were subdued and
they stopped invading Israel's territory.
Throughout Samuel's lifetime, the hand
of the LORD was against the Philistines.
14The towns from Ekron to Gath that the
Philistines had captured from Israel
were restored to Israel, and Israel delivered the neighboring territory from the
hands of the Philistines. And there was
peace between Israel and the Amorites.

15Samuel continued as Israel's leader all the days of his life. 16From year to
year he went on a circuit from Bethel to
Gilgal to Mizpah, judging Israel in all
those places. 17But he always went back
to Ramah, where his home was, and
there he also held court for Israel. And
he built an altar there to the LORD.

Israel Asks for a King

8 When Samuel grew old, he appointed his sons as Israel's leaders.[d] 2The
name of his firstborn was Joel and the
name of his second was Abijah, and they
served at Beersheba. 3But his sons did
not follow his ways. They turned aside

[a] 19 A few Hebrew manuscripts; most Hebrew manuscripts and Septuagint *50,070*
[b] 6 Traditionally *judge*; also in verse 15 [c] 12 *Ebenezer* means *stone of help*.
[d] 1 Traditionally *judges*

after dishonest gain and accepted bribes and perverted justice.

4So all the elders of Israel gathered together and came to Samuel at Ramah. 5They said to him, "You are old, and your sons do not follow your ways; now appoint a king to lead[a] us, such as all the other nations have."

6But when they said, "Give us a king to lead us," this displeased Samuel; so he prayed to the LORD. 7And the LORD told him: "Listen to all that the people are saying to you; it is not you they have rejected, but they have rejected me as their king. 8As they have done from the day I brought them up out of Egypt until this day, forsaking me and serving other gods, so they are doing to you. 9Now listen to them; but warn them solemnly and let them know what the king who will reign over them will claim as his rights."

10Samuel told all the words of the LORD to the people who were asking him for a king. 11He said, "This is what the king who will reign over you will claim as his rights: He will take your sons and make them serve with his chariots and horses, and they will run in front of his chariots. 12Some he will assign to be commanders of thousands and commanders of fifties, and others to plow his ground and reap his harvest, and still others to make weapons of war and equipment for his chariots. 13He will take your daughters to be perfumers and cooks and bakers. 14He will take the best of your fields and vineyards and olive groves and give them to his attendants. 15He will take a tenth of your grain and of your vintage and give it to his officials and attendants. 16Your male and female servants and the best of your cattle[b] and donkeys he will take for his own use. 17He will take a tenth of your flocks, and you yourselves will become his slaves. 18When that day comes, you will cry out for relief from the king you have chosen, but the LORD will not answer you in that day."

19But the people refused to listen to Samuel. "No!" they said. "We want a king over us. 20Then we will be like all the other nations, with a king to lead us and to go out before us and fight our battles."

21When Samuel heard all that the people said, he repeated it before the LORD. 22The LORD answered, "Listen to them and give them a king."

Then Samuel said to the Israelites, "Everyone go back to your own town."

Samuel Anoints Saul

9 There was a Benjamite, a man of standing, whose name was Kish son of Abiel, the son of Zeror, the son of Bekorath, the son of Aphiah of Benjamin. 2Kish had a son named Saul, as handsome a young man as could be found anywhere in Israel, and he was a head taller than anyone else.

3Now the donkeys belonging to Saul's father Kish were lost, and Kish said to his son Saul, "Take one of the servants with you and go and look for the donkeys." 4So he passed through the hill country of Ephraim and through the area around Shalisha, but they did not find them. They went on into the district of Shaalim, but the donkeys were not there. Then he passed through the territory of Benjamin, but they did not find them.

5When they reached the district of Zuph, Saul said to the servant who was with him, "Come, let's go back, or my father will stop thinking about the donkeys and start worrying about us."

6But the servant replied, "Look, in this town there is a man of God; he is highly respected, and everything he says comes true. Let's go there now. Perhaps he will tell us what way to take."

7Saul said to his servant, "If we go, what can we give the man? The food in our sacks is gone. We have no gift to take to the man of God. What do we have?"

8The servant answered him again. "Look," he said, "I have a quarter of a shekel[c] of silver. I will give it to the man of God so that he will tell us what way to take." 9(Formerly in Israel, if someone went to inquire of God, they would say, "Come, let us go to the seer," because the prophet of today used to be called a seer.)

10"Good," Saul said to his servant. "Come, let's go." So they set out for the town where the man of God was.

11As they were going up the hill to the town, they met some young women coming out to draw water, and they asked them, "Is the seer here?"

12"He is," they answered. "He's ahead of you. Hurry now; he has just come to our town today, for the people have a sacrifice at the high place. 13As soon as you enter the town, you will find him before he goes up to the high place to eat. The people will not begin eating until he comes, because he must bless the sacrifice; afterward, those who are invited

[a] 5 Traditionally *judge*; also in verses 6 and 20
[b] 16 Septuagint; Hebrew *young men*
[c] 8 That is, about 1/10 ounce or about 3 grams

will eat. Go up now; you should find him about this time."

14 They went up to the town, and as they were entering it, there was Samuel, coming toward them on his way up to the high place.

15 Now the day before Saul came, the LORD had revealed this to Samuel: 16 "About this time tomorrow I will send you a man from the land of Benjamin. Anoint him ruler over my people Israel; he will deliver them from the hand of the Philistines. I have looked on my people, for their cry has reached me."

17 When Samuel caught sight of Saul, the LORD said to him, "This is the man I spoke to you about; he will govern my people."

18 Saul approached Samuel in the gateway and asked, "Would you please tell me where the seer's house is?"

19 "I am the seer," Samuel replied. "Go up ahead of me to the high place, for today you are to eat with me, and in the morning I will send you on your way and will tell you all that is in your heart. 20 As for the donkeys you lost three days ago, do not worry about them; they have been found. And to whom is all the desire of Israel turned, if not to you and your whole family line?"

21 Saul answered, "But am I not a Benjamite, from the smallest tribe of Israel, and is not my clan the least of all the clans of the tribe of Benjamin? Why do you say such a thing to me?"

22 Then Samuel brought Saul and his servant into the hall and seated them at the head of those who were invited — about thirty in number. 23 Samuel said to the cook, "Bring the piece of meat I gave you, the one I told you to lay aside."

24 So the cook took up the thigh with what was on it and set it in front of Saul. Samuel said, "Here is what has been kept for you. Eat, because it was set aside for you for this occasion from the time I said, 'I have invited guests.'" And Saul dined with Samuel that day.

25 After they came down from the high place to the town, Samuel talked with Saul on the roof of his house. 26 They rose about daybreak, and Samuel called to Saul on the roof, "Get ready, and I will send you on your way." When Saul got ready, he and Samuel went outside together. 27 As they were going down to the edge of the town, Samuel said to Saul, "Tell the servant to go on ahead of us" — and the servant did so — "but you stay here for a while, so that I may give you a message from God."

10 Then Samuel took a flask of olive oil and poured it on Saul's head and kissed him, saying, "Has not the LORD anointed you ruler over his inheritance?[a] 2 When you leave me today, you will meet two men near Rachel's tomb, at Zelzah on the border of Benjamin. They will say to you, 'The donkeys you set out to look for have been found. And now your father has stopped thinking about them and is worried about you. He is asking, "What shall I do about my son?"'

3 "Then you will go on from there until you reach the great tree of Tabor. Three men going up to worship God at Bethel will meet you there. One will be carrying three young goats, another three loaves of bread, and another a skin of wine. 4 They will greet you and offer you two loaves of bread, which you will accept from them.

5 "After that you will go to Gibeah of God, where there is a Philistine outpost. As you approach the town, you will meet a procession of prophets coming down from the high place with lyres, timbrels, pipes and harps being played before them, and they will be prophesying. 6 The Spirit of the LORD will come powerfully upon you, and you will prophesy with them; and you will be changed into a different person. 7 Once these signs are fulfilled, do whatever your hand finds to do, for God is with you.

8 "Go down ahead of me to Gilgal. I will surely come down to you to sacrifice burnt offerings and fellowship offerings, but you must wait seven days until I come to you and tell you what you are to do."

Saul Made King

9 As Saul turned to leave Samuel, God changed Saul's heart, and all these signs were fulfilled that day. 10 When he and his servant arrived at Gibeah, a procession of prophets met him; the Spirit of God came powerfully upon him, and he joined in their prophesying. 11 When all those who had formerly known him saw him prophesying with the prophets, they asked each other, "What is this that has happened to the son of Kish? Is Saul also among the prophets?"

12 A man who lived there answered, "And who is their father?" So it became a

[a] 1 Hebrew; Septuagint and Vulgate *over his people Israel? You will reign over the LORD's people and save them from the power of their enemies round about. And this will be a sign to you that the LORD has anointed you ruler over his inheritance:*

saying: "Is Saul also among the prophets?" 13After Saul stopped prophesying, he went to the high place.

14Now Saul's uncle asked him and his servant, "Where have you been?"

"Looking for the donkeys," he said. "But when we saw they were not to be found, we went to Samuel."

15Saul's uncle said, "Tell me what Samuel said to you."

16Saul replied, "He assured us that the donkeys had been found." But he did not tell his uncle what Samuel had said about the kingship.

17Samuel summoned the people of Israel to the LORD at Mizpah 18and said to them, "This is what the LORD, the God of Israel, says: 'I brought Israel up out of Egypt, and I delivered you from the power of Egypt and all the kingdoms that oppressed you.' 19But you have now rejected your God, who saves you out of all your disasters and calamities. And you have said, 'No, appoint a king over us.' So now present yourselves before the LORD by your tribes and clans."

20When Samuel had all Israel come forward by tribes, the tribe of Benjamin was taken by lot. 21Then he brought forward the tribe of Benjamin, clan by clan, and Matri's clan was taken. Finally Saul son of Kish was taken. But when they looked for him, he was not to be found. 22So they inquired further of the LORD, "Has the man come here yet?"

And the LORD said, "Yes, he has hidden himself among the supplies."

23They ran and brought him out, and as he stood among the people he was a head taller than any of the others. 24Samuel said to all the people, "Do you see the man the LORD has chosen? There is no one like him among all the people."

Then the people shouted, "Long live the king!"

25Samuel explained to the people the rights and duties of kingship. He wrote them down on a scroll and deposited it before the LORD. Then Samuel dismissed the people to go to their own homes.

26Saul also went to his home in Gibeah, accompanied by valiant men whose hearts God had touched. 27But some scoundrels said, "How can this fellow save us?" They despised him and brought him no gifts. But Saul kept silent.

Saul Rescues the City of Jabesh

11 Nahash[a] the Ammonite went up and besieged Jabesh Gilead. And all the men of Jabesh said to him, "Make a treaty with us, and we will be subject to you."

2But Nahash the Ammonite replied, "I will make a treaty with you only on the condition that I gouge out the right eye of every one of you and so bring disgrace on all Israel."

3The elders of Jabesh said to him, "Give us seven days so we can send messengers throughout Israel; if no one comes to rescue us, we will surrender to you."

4When the messengers came to Gibeah of Saul and reported these terms to the people, they all wept aloud. 5Just then Saul was returning from the fields, behind his oxen, and he asked, "What is wrong with everyone? Why are they weeping?" Then they repeated to him what the men of Jabesh had said.

6When Saul heard their words, the Spirit of God came powerfully upon him, and he burned with anger. 7He took a pair of oxen, cut them into pieces, and sent the pieces by messengers throughout Israel, proclaiming, "This is what will be done to the oxen of anyone who does not follow Saul and Samuel." Then the terror of the LORD fell on the people, and they came out together as one. 8When Saul mustered them at Bezek, the men of Israel numbered three hundred thousand and those of Judah thirty thousand.

9They told the messengers who had come, "Say to the men of Jabesh Gilead, 'By the time the sun is hot tomorrow, you will be rescued.'" When the messengers went and reported this to the men of Jabesh, they were elated. 10They said to the Ammonites, "Tomorrow we will surrender to you, and you can do to us whatever you like."

11The next day Saul separated his men into three divisions; during the last watch of the night they broke into the camp of the Ammonites and slaughtered them until the heat of the day. Those who survived were scattered, so that no two of them were left together.

[a] *1* Masoretic Text; Dead Sea Scrolls *gifts. Now Nahash king of the Ammonites oppressed the Gadites and Reubenites severely. He gouged out all their right eyes and struck terror and dread in Israel. Not a man remained among the Israelites beyond the Jordan whose right eye was not gouged out by Nahash king of the Ammonites, except that seven thousand men fled from the Ammonites and entered Jabesh Gilead. About a month later,* [1]*Nahash*

Saul Confirmed as King

12 The people then said to Samuel, "Who was it that asked, 'Shall Saul reign over us?' Turn these men over to us so that we may put them to death."

13 But Saul said, "No one will be put to death today, for this day the LORD has rescued Israel."

14 Then Samuel said to the people, "Come, let us go to Gilgal and there renew the kingship." 15 So all the people went to Gilgal and made Saul king in the presence of the LORD. There they sacrificed fellowship offerings before the LORD, and Saul and all the Israelites held a great celebration.

Samuel's Farewell Speech

12 Samuel said to all Israel, "I have listened to everything you said to me and have set a king over you. 2 Now you have a king as your leader. As for me, I am old and gray, and my sons are here with you. I have been your leader from my youth until this day. 3 Here I stand. Testify against me in the presence of the LORD and his anointed. Whose ox have I taken? Whose donkey have I taken? Whom have I cheated? Whom have I oppressed? From whose hand have I accepted a bribe to make me shut my eyes? If I have done any of these things, I will make it right."

4 "You have not cheated or oppressed us," they replied. "You have not taken anything from anyone's hand."

5 Samuel said to them, "The LORD is witness against you, and also his anointed is witness this day, that you have not found anything in my hand."

"He is witness," they said.

6 Then Samuel said to the people, "It is the LORD who appointed Moses and Aaron and brought your ancestors up out of Egypt. 7 Now then, stand here, because I am going to confront you with evidence before the LORD as to all the righteous acts performed by the LORD for you and your ancestors.

8 "After Jacob entered Egypt, they cried to the LORD for help, and the LORD sent Moses and Aaron, who brought your ancestors out of Egypt and settled them in this place.

9 "But they forgot the LORD their God; so he sold them into the hand of Sisera, the commander of the army of Hazor, and into the hands of the Philistines and the king of Moab, who fought against them. 10 They cried out to the LORD and said, 'We have sinned; we have forsaken the LORD and served the Baals and the Ashtoreths. But now deliver us from the hands of our enemies, and we will serve you.' 11 Then the LORD sent Jerub-Baal,[a] Barak,[b] Jephthah and Samuel,[c] and he delivered you from the hands of your enemies all around you, so that you lived in safety.

12 "But when you saw that Nahash king of the Ammonites was moving against you, you said to me, 'No, we want a king to rule over us' — even though the LORD your God was your king. 13 Now here is the king you have chosen, the one you asked for; see, the LORD has set a king over you. 14 If you fear the LORD and serve and obey him and do not rebel against his commands, and if both you and the king who reigns over you follow the LORD your God — good! 15 But if you do not obey the LORD, and if you rebel against his commands, his hand will be against you, as it was against your ancestors.

16 "Now then, stand still and see this great thing the LORD is about to do before your eyes! 17 Is it not wheat harvest now? I will call on the LORD to send thunder and rain. And you will realize what an evil thing you did in the eyes of the LORD when you asked for a king."

18 Then Samuel called on the LORD, and that same day the LORD sent thunder and rain. So all the people stood in awe of the LORD and of Samuel.

19 The people all said to Samuel, "Pray to the LORD your God for your servants so that we will not die, for we have added to all our other sins the evil of asking for a king."

20 "Do not be afraid," Samuel replied. "You have done all this evil; yet do not turn away from the LORD, but serve the LORD with all your heart. 21 Do not turn away after useless idols. They can do you no good, nor can they rescue you, because they are useless. 22 For the sake of his great name the LORD will not reject his people, because the LORD was pleased to make you his own. 23 As for me, far be it from me that I should sin against the LORD by failing to pray for you. And I will teach you the way that is good and right. 24 But be sure to fear the LORD and serve him faithfully with all your heart; consider what great things he has done for you. 25 Yet if you persist in doing evil, both you and your king will perish."

[a] *11* Also called *Gideon* [b] *11* Some Septuagint manuscripts and Syriac; Hebrew *Bedan*
[c] *11* Hebrew; some Septuagint manuscripts and Syriac *Samson*

Samuel Rebukes Saul

13 Saul was thirty[a] years old when he
became king, and he reigned over
Israel forty-[b] two years.
2Saul chose three thousand men from
Israel; two thousand were with him at
Mikmash and in the hill country of Bethel, and a thousand were with Jonathan
at Gibeah in Benjamin. The rest of the
men he sent back to their homes.
3Jonathan attacked the Philistine outpost at Geba, and the Philistines heard
about it. Then Saul had the trumpet
blown throughout the land and said,
"Let the Hebrews hear!" 4So all Israel
heard the news: "Saul has attacked the
Philistine outpost, and now Israel has
become obnoxious to the Philistines."
And the people were summoned to join
Saul at Gilgal.
5The Philistines assembled to fight Israel, with three thousand[c] chariots, six
thousand charioteers, and soldiers as
numerous as the sand on the seashore.
They went up and camped at Mikmash,
east of Beth Aven. 6When the Israelites
saw that their situation was critical and
that their army was hard pressed, they
hid in caves and thickets, among the
rocks, and in pits and cisterns. 7Some
Hebrews even crossed the Jordan to the
land of Gad and Gilead.
Saul remained at Gilgal, and all the
troops with him were quaking with fear.
8He waited seven days, the time set by
Samuel; but Samuel did not come to Gilgal, and Saul's men began to scatter. 9So
he said, "Bring me the burnt offering
and the fellowship offerings." And Saul
offered up the burnt offering. 10Just as
he finished making the offering, Samuel
arrived, and Saul went out to greet him.
11"What have you done?" asked Samuel.
Saul replied, "When I saw that the
men were scattering, and that you did
not come at the set time, and that the
Philistines were assembling at Mikmash, 12I thought, 'Now the Philistines
will come down against me at Gilgal,
and I have not sought the LORD's favor.'
So I felt compelled to offer the burnt offering."
13"You have done a foolish thing,"
Samuel said. "You have not kept the
command the LORD your God gave you;
if you had, he would have established
your kingdom over Israel for all time.
14But now your kingdom will not endure;
the LORD has sought out a man after his
own heart and appointed him ruler of
his people, because you have not kept
the LORD's command."
15Then Samuel left Gilgal[d] and went up
to Gibeah in Benjamin, and Saul counted
the men who were with him. They numbered about six hundred.

Israel Without Weapons

16Saul and his son Jonathan and the
men with them were staying in Gibeah[e] in Benjamin, while the Philistines
camped at Mikmash. 17Raiding parties
went out from the Philistine camp in
three detachments. One turned toward
Ophrah in the vicinity of Shual, 18an-
other toward Beth Horon, and the third
toward the borderland overlooking the
Valley of Zeboyim facing the wilderness.
19Not a blacksmith could be found in
the whole land of Israel, because the
Philistines had said, "Otherwise the Hebrews will make swords or spears!" 20So
all Israel went down to the Philistines to
have their plow points, mattocks, axes
and sickles[f] sharpened. 21The price was
two-thirds of a shekel[g] for sharpening
plow points and mattocks, and a third of
a shekel[h] for sharpening forks and axes
and for repointing goads.
22So on the day of the battle not a
soldier with Saul and Jonathan had a
sword or spear in his hand; only Saul
and his son Jonathan had them.

Jonathan Attacks the Philistines

23Now a detachment of Philistines had
14 gone out to the pass at Mikmash.
1One day Jonathan son of Saul said
to his young armor-bearer, "Come, let's
go over to the Philistine outpost on the
other side." But he did not tell his father.
2Saul was staying on the outskirts of
Gibeah under a pomegranate tree in
Migron. With him were about six hundred men, 3among whom was Ahijah,
who was wearing an ephod. He was a
son of Ichabod's brother Ahitub son of
Phinehas, the son of Eli, the LORD's priest

[a] 1 A few late manuscripts of the Septuagint; Hebrew does not have *thirty.* [b] 1 Probable reading of the original Hebrew text (see Acts 13:21); Masoretic Text does not have *forty-*.
[c] 5 Some Septuagint manuscripts and Syriac; Hebrew *thirty thousand* [d] 15 Hebrew; Septuagint *Gilgal and went his way; the rest of the people went after Saul to meet the army, and they went out of Gilgal* [e] 16 Two Hebrew manuscripts; most Hebrew manuscripts *Geba,* a variant of *Gibeah* [f] 20 Septuagint; Hebrew *plow points* [g] 21 That is, about 1/4 ounce or about 8 grams [h] 21 That is, about 1/8 ounce or about 4 grams

in Shiloh. No one was aware that Jonathan had left.
4On each side of the pass that Jonathan intended to cross to reach the Philistine outpost was a cliff; one was called
Bozez and the other Seneh. 5One cliff
stood to the north toward Mikmash, the
other to the south toward Geba.
6Jonathan said to his young armor-
bearer, "Come, let's go over to the outpost
of those uncircumcised men. Perhaps the
LORD will act in our behalf. Nothing can
hinder the LORD from saving, whether by
many or by few."
7"Do all that you have in mind," his
armor-bearer said. "Go ahead; I am with
you heart and soul."
8Jonathan said, "Come on, then; we
will cross over toward them and let them
see us. 9If they say to us, 'Wait there until
we come to you,' we will stay where we
are and not go up to them. 10But if they
say, 'Come up to us,' we will climb up, because that will be our sign that the LORD
has given them into our hands."
11So both of them showed themselves
to the Philistine outpost. "Look!" said
the Philistines. "The Hebrews are crawling out of the holes they were hiding in."
12The men of the outpost shouted to Jonathan and his armor-bearer, "Come up
to us and we'll teach you a lesson."
So Jonathan said to his armor-bearer,
"Climb up after me; the LORD has given
them into the hand of Israel."
13Jonathan climbed up, using his
hands and feet, with his armor-
bearer right behind him. The Philistines
fell before Jonathan, and his armor-
bearer followed and killed behind him.
14In that first attack Jonathan and his
armor-bearer killed some twenty men
in an area of about half an acre.

Israel Routs the Philistines

15Then panic struck the whole army—
those in the camp and field, and those in
the outposts and raiding parties—and
the ground shook. It was a panic sent by
God.[a]
16Saul's lookouts at Gibeah in Benjamin saw the army melting away in all
directions. 17Then Saul said to the men
who were with him, "Muster the forces
and see who has left us." When they did,
it was Jonathan and his armor-bearer
who were not there.
18Saul said to Ahijah, "Bring the ark of
God." (At that time it was with the Israelites.)[b] 19While Saul was talking to the
priest, the tumult in the Philistine camp
increased more and more. So Saul said
to the priest, "Withdraw your hand."
20Then Saul and all his men assembled and went to the battle. They found
the Philistines in total confusion, striking each other with their swords. 21Those
Hebrews who had previously been with
the Philistines and had gone up with
them to their camp went over to the Israelites who were with Saul and Jonathan.
22When all the Israelites who had hidden in the hill country of Ephraim heard
that the Philistines were on the run, they
joined the battle in hot pursuit. 23So on
that day the LORD saved Israel, and the
battle moved on beyond Beth Aven.

Jonathan Eats Honey

24Now the Israelites were in distress
that day, because Saul had bound the
people under an oath, saying, "Cursed
be anyone who eats food before evening
comes, before I have avenged myself on
my enemies!" So none of the troops tasted food.
25The entire army entered the woods,
and there was honey on the ground.
26When they went into the woods, they
saw the honey oozing out; yet no one
put his hand to his mouth, because they
feared the oath. 27But Jonathan had not
heard that his father had bound the people with the oath, so he reached out the
end of the staff that was in his hand and
dipped it into the honeycomb. He raised
his hand to his mouth, and his eyes
brightened.[c] 28Then one of the soldiers
told him, "Your father bound the army
under a strict oath, saying, 'Cursed be
anyone who eats food today!' That is
why the men are faint."
29Jonathan said, "My father has made
trouble for the country. See how my eyes
brightened when I tasted a little of this
honey. 30How much better it would have
been if the men had eaten today some
of the plunder they took from their enemies. Would not the slaughter of the Philistines have been even greater?"
31That day, after the Israelites had
struck down the Philistines from Mikmash to Aijalon, they were exhausted.
32They pounced on the plunder and, taking sheep, cattle and calves, they butchered them on the ground and ate them,
together with the blood. 33Then someone
said to Saul, "Look, the men are sinning

[a] 15 Or *a terrible panic* [b] 18 Hebrew; Septuagint *"Bring the ephod." (At that time he wore the ephod before the Israelites.)* [c] 27 Or *his strength was renewed*; similarly in verse 29

against the LORD by eating meat that
has blood in it."
"You have broken faith," he said. "Roll
a large stone over here at once." 34Then
he said, "Go out among the men and tell
them, 'Each of you bring me your cattle
and sheep, and slaughter them here and
eat them. Do not sin against the LORD by
eating meat with blood still in it.'"
So everyone brought his ox that night
and slaughtered it there. 35Then Saul
built an altar to the LORD; it was the first
time he had done this.
36Saul said, "Let us go down and pursue the Philistines by night and plunder
them till dawn, and let us not leave one
of them alive."
"Do whatever seems best to you," they
replied.
But the priest said, "Let us inquire of
God here."
37So Saul asked God, "Shall I go down
and pursue the Philistines? Will you give
them into Israel's hand?" But God did
not answer him that day.
38Saul therefore said, "Come here, all
you who are leaders of the army, and let
us find out what sin has been committed today. 39As surely as the LORD who
rescues Israel lives, even if the guilt lies
with my son Jonathan, he must die." But
not one of them said a word.
40Saul then said to all the Israelites,
"You stand over there; I and Jonathan
my son will stand over here."
"Do what seems best to you," they replied.
41Then Saul prayed to the LORD, the
God of Israel, "Why have you not answered your servant today? If the fault
is in me or my son Jonathan, respond
with Urim, but if the men of Israel are at
fault,[a] respond with Thummim." Jonathan and Saul were taken by lot, and the
men were cleared. 42Saul said, "Cast the
lot between me and Jonathan my son."
And Jonathan was taken.
43Then Saul said to Jonathan, "Tell me
what you have done."
So Jonathan told him, "I tasted a little
honey with the end of my staff. And now
I must die!"
44Saul said, "May God deal with me,
be it ever so severely, if you do not die,
Jonathan."
45But the men said to Saul, "Should
Jonathan die — he who has brought
about this great deliverance in Israel?
Never! As surely as the LORD lives, not a
hair of his head will fall to the ground,
for he did this today with God's help." So
the men rescued Jonathan, and he was
not put to death.
46Then Saul stopped pursuing the Philistines, and they withdrew to their own
land.
47After Saul had assumed rule over Israel, he fought against their enemies on
every side: Moab, the Ammonites, Edom,
the kings[b] of Zobah, and the Philistines.
Wherever he turned, he inflicted punishment on them.[c] 48He fought valiantly
and defeated the Amalekites, delivering
Israel from the hands of those who had
plundered them.

Saul's Family

49Saul's sons were Jonathan, Ishvi
and Malki-Shua. The name of his older daughter was Merab, and that of the
younger was Michal. 50His wife's name
was Ahinoam daughter of Ahimaaz. The
name of the commander of Saul's army
was Abner son of Ner, and Ner was Saul's
uncle. 51Saul's father Kish and Abner's father Ner were sons of Abiel.
52All the days of Saul there was bitter
war with the Philistines, and whenever
Saul saw a mighty or brave man, he took
him into his service.

The LORD Rejects Saul as King

15 Samuel said to Saul, "I am the one
the LORD sent to anoint you king
over his people Israel; so listen now to
the message from the LORD. 2This is what
the LORD Almighty says: 'I will punish
the Amalekites for what they did to Israel when they waylaid them as they
came up from Egypt. 3Now go, attack the
Amalekites and totally destroy[d] all that
belongs to them. Do not spare them; put
to death men and women, children and
infants, cattle and sheep, camels and
donkeys.'"
4So Saul summoned the men and mustered them at Telaim — two hundred
thousand foot soldiers and ten thousand from Judah. 5Saul went to the city
of Amalek and set an ambush in the ravine. 6Then he said to the Kenites, "Go
away, leave the Amalekites so that I do
not destroy you along with them; for you
showed kindness to all the Israelites when

[a] *41* Septuagint; Hebrew does not have *"Why . . . at fault.* [b] *47* Masoretic Text; Dead Sea Scrolls and Septuagint *king* [c] *47* Hebrew; Septuagint *he was victorious* [d] *3* The Hebrew term refers to the irrevocable giving over of things or persons to the LORD, often by totally destroying them; also in verses 8, 9, 15, 18, 20 and 21.

they came up out of Egypt." So the Kenites
moved away from the Amalekites.
[7]Then Saul attacked the Amalekites
all the way from Havilah to Shur, near
the eastern border of Egypt. [8]He took
Agag king of the Amalekites alive, and
all his people he totally destroyed with
the sword. [9]But Saul and the army
spared Agag and the best of the sheep
and cattle, the fat calves[a] and lambs —
everything that was good. These they
were unwilling to destroy completely,
but everything that was despised and
weak they totally destroyed.
[10]Then the word of the LORD came to
Samuel: [11]"I regret that I have made Saul
king, because he has turned away from
me and has not carried out my instructions."
Samuel was angry, and he cried
out to the LORD all that night.
[12]Early in the morning Samuel got up
and went to meet Saul, but he was told,
"Saul has gone to Carmel. There he has
set up a monument in his own honor and
has turned and gone on down to Gilgal."
[13]When Samuel reached him, Saul
said, "The LORD bless you! I have carried
out the LORD's instructions."
[14]But Samuel said, "What then is this
bleating of sheep in my ears? What is
this lowing of cattle that I hear?"
[15]Saul answered, "The soldiers brought
them from the Amalekites; they spared
the best of the sheep and cattle to sacrifice
to the LORD your God, but we totally
destroyed the rest."
[16]"Enough!" Samuel said to Saul. "Let
me tell you what the LORD said to me last
night."
"Tell me," Saul replied.
[17]Samuel said, "Although you were
once small in your own eyes, did you not
become the head of the tribes of Israel?
The LORD anointed you king over Israel.
[18]And he sent you on a mission, saying,
'Go and completely destroy those wicked
people, the Amalekites; wage war
against them until you have wiped them
out.' [19]Why did you not obey the LORD?
Why did you pounce on the plunder and
do evil in the eyes of the LORD?"
[20]"But I did obey the LORD," Saul said.
"I went on the mission the LORD assigned
me. I completely destroyed the Amalekites
and brought back Agag their king.
[21]The soldiers took sheep and cattle from
the plunder, the best of what was devoted
to God, in order to sacrifice them to
the LORD your God at Gilgal."
[22]But Samuel replied:

"Does the LORD delight in burnt
offerings and sacrifices
as much as in obeying the LORD?
To obey is better than sacrifice,
and to heed is better than the fat of
rams.
[23]For rebellion is like the sin of
divination,
and arrogance like the evil of
idolatry.
Because you have rejected the word
of the LORD,
he has rejected you as king."

[24]Then Saul said to Samuel, "I have
sinned. I violated the LORD's command
and your instructions. I was afraid of the
men and so I gave in to them. [25]Now I beg
you, forgive my sin and come back with
me, so that I may worship the LORD."
[26]But Samuel said to him, "I will not
go back with you. You have rejected the
word of the LORD, and the LORD has rejected
you as king over Israel!"
[27]As Samuel turned to leave, Saul
caught hold of the hem of his robe, and
it tore. [28]Samuel said to him, "The LORD
has torn the kingdom of Israel from you
today and has given it to one of your
neighbors — to one better than you. [29]He
who is the Glory of Israel does not lie or
change his mind; for he is not a human
being, that he should change his mind."
[30]Saul replied, "I have sinned. But
please honor me before the elders of my
people and before Israel; come back with
me, so that I may worship the LORD your
God." [31]So Samuel went back with Saul,
and Saul worshiped the LORD.
[32]Then Samuel said, "Bring me Agag
king of the Amalekites."
Agag came to him in chains.[b] And he
thought, "Surely the bitterness of death
is past."
[33]But Samuel said,

"As your sword has made women
childless,
so will your mother be childless
among women."

And Samuel put Agag to death before
the LORD at Gilgal.
[34]Then Samuel left for Ramah, but Saul
went up to his home in Gibeah of Saul.
[35]Until the day Samuel died, he did not
go to see Saul again, though Samuel
mourned for him. And the LORD regretted
that he had made Saul king over Israel.

[a] 9 Or *the grown bulls*; the meaning of the Hebrew for this phrase is uncertain. [b] 32 The meaning of the Hebrew for this phrase is uncertain.

Samuel Anoints David

16 The LORD said to Samuel, "How
long will you mourn for Saul, since
I have rejected him as king over Israel?
Fill your horn with oil and be on your
way; I am sending you to Jesse of Bethlehem. I have chosen one of his sons to
be king."
2But Samuel said, "How can I go? If
Saul hears about it, he will kill me."
The LORD said, "Take a heifer with you
and say, 'I have come to sacrifice to the
LORD.' 3Invite Jesse to the sacrifice, and
I will show you what to do. You are to
anoint for me the one I indicate."
4Samuel did what the LORD said. When
he arrived at Bethlehem, the elders of
the town trembled when they met him.
They asked, "Do you come in peace?"
5Samuel replied, "Yes, in peace; I have
come to sacrifice to the LORD. Consecrate yourselves and come to the sacrifice with me." Then he consecrated Jesse and his sons and invited them to the
sacrifice.
6When they arrived, Samuel saw Eliab
and thought, "Surely the LORD's anointed stands here before the LORD."
7But the LORD said to Samuel, "Do not
consider his appearance or his height,
for I have rejected him. The LORD does
not look at the things people look at.
People look at the outward appearance,
but the LORD looks at the heart."
8Then Jesse called Abinadab and had
him pass in front of Samuel. But Samuel
said, "The LORD has not chosen this one
either." 9Jesse then had Shammah pass
by, but Samuel said, "Nor has the LORD
chosen this one." 10Jesse had seven of
his sons pass before Samuel, but Samuel
said to him, "The LORD has not chosen
these." 11So he asked Jesse, "Are these all
the sons you have?"
"There is still the youngest," Jesse answered. "He is tending the sheep."
Samuel said, "Send for him; we will
not sit down until he arrives."
12So he sent for him and had him
brought in. He was glowing with health
and had a fine appearance and handsome features.
Then the LORD said, "Rise and anoint
him; this is the one."
13So Samuel took the horn of oil and
anointed him in the presence of his
brothers, and from that day on the Spirit of the LORD came powerfully upon David. Samuel then went to Ramah.

David in Saul's Service

14Now the Spirit of the LORD had departed from Saul, and an evil[a] spirit
from the LORD tormented him.
15Saul's attendants said to him, "See,
an evil spirit from God is tormenting you.
16Let our lord command his servants here
to search for someone who can play the
lyre. He will play when the evil spirit from
God comes on you, and you will feel better."
17So Saul said to his attendants, "Find
someone who plays well and bring him
to me."
18One of the servants answered, "I
have seen a son of Jesse of Bethlehem
who knows how to play the lyre. He is a
brave man and a warrior. He speaks well
and is a fine-looking man. And the LORD
is with him."
19Then Saul sent messengers to Jesse
and said, "Send me your son David, who
is with the sheep." 20So Jesse took a donkey loaded with bread, a skin of wine
and a young goat and sent them with
his son David to Saul.
21David came to Saul and entered his
service. Saul liked him very much, and
David became one of his armor-bearers.
22Then Saul sent word to Jesse, saying,
"Allow David to remain in my service,
for I am pleased with him."
23Whenever the spirit from God came
on Saul, David would take up his lyre
and play. Then relief would come to Saul;
he would feel better, and the evil spirit
would leave him.

David and Goliath

17 Now the Philistines gathered their
forces for war and assembled at
Sokoh in Judah. They pitched camp at
Ephes Dammim, between Sokoh and
Azekah. 2Saul and the Israelites assembled and camped in the Valley of Elah
and drew up their battle line to meet the
Philistines. 3The Philistines occupied one
hill and the Israelites another, with the
valley between them.
4A champion named Goliath, who
was from Gath, came out of the Philistine camp. His height was six cubits and
a span.[b] 5He had a bronze helmet on his
head and wore a coat of scale armor of
bronze weighing five thousand shekels[c];
6on his legs he wore bronze greaves, and a
bronze javelin was slung on his back. 7His
spear shaft was like a weaver's rod, and its
iron point weighed six hundred shekels.[d]
His shield bearer went ahead of him.

[a] 14 Or *and a harmful*; similarly in verses 15, 16 and 23 [b] 4 That is, about 9 feet 9 inches or about 3 meters [c] 5 That is, about 125 pounds or about 58 kilograms [d] 7 That is, about 15 pounds or about 6.9 kilograms

8Goliath stood and shouted to the
ranks of Israel, "Why do you come out
and line up for battle? Am I not a Philistine, and are you not the servants of
Saul? Choose a man and have him come
down to me. 9If he is able to fight and
kill me, we will become your subjects;
but if I overcome him and kill him, you
will become our subjects and serve us."
10Then the Philistine said, "This day I
defy the armies of Israel! Give me a man
and let us fight each other." 11On hearing
the Philistine's words, Saul and all the
Israelites were dismayed and terrified.

12Now David was the son of an Eph-
rathite named Jesse, who was from
Bethlehem in Judah. Jesse had eight
sons, and in Saul's time he was very old.
13Jesse's three oldest sons had followed
Saul to the war: The firstborn was Eliab; the second, Abinadab; and the third,
Shammah. 14David was the youngest.
The three oldest followed Saul, 15but David went back and forth from Saul to
tend his father's sheep at Bethlehem.

16For forty days the Philistine came
forward every morning and evening and
took his stand.

17Now Jesse said to his son David,
"Take this ephah[a] of roasted grain and
these ten loaves of bread for your brothers and hurry to their camp. 18Take along
these ten cheeses to the commander of
their unit. See how your brothers are and
bring back some assurance[b] from them.
19They are with Saul and all the men
of Israel in the Valley of Elah, fighting
against the Philistines."

20Early in the morning David left the
flock in the care of a shepherd, loaded
up and set out, as Jesse had directed. He
reached the camp as the army was going
out to its battle positions, shouting the
war cry. 21Israel and the Philistines were
drawing up their lines facing each other. 22David left his things with the keeper
of supplies, ran to the battle lines and
asked his brothers how they were. 23As he
was talking with them, Goliath, the Philistine champion from Gath, stepped out
from his lines and shouted his usual de-
fiance, and David heard it. 24Whenever
the Israelites saw the man, they all fled
from him in great fear.

25Now the Israelites had been saying,
"Do you see how this man keeps coming out? He comes out to defy Israel. The
king will give great wealth to the man
who kills him. He will also give him his
daughter in marriage and will exempt
his family from taxes in Israel."

26David asked the men standing near
him, "What will be done for the man who
kills this Philistine and removes this disgrace from Israel? Who is this uncircumcised Philistine that he should defy the
armies of the living God?"

27They repeated to him what they had
been saying and told him, "This is what
will be done for the man who kills him."

28When Eliab, David's oldest brother,
heard him speaking with the men, he
burned with anger at him and asked,
"Why have you come down here? And
with whom did you leave those few
sheep in the wilderness? I know how
conceited you are and how wicked your
heart is; you came down only to watch
the battle."

29"Now what have I done?" said David.
"Can't I even speak?" 30He then turned
away to someone else and brought up
the same matter, and the men answered
him as before. 31What David said was
overheard and reported to Saul, and
Saul sent for him.

32David said to Saul, "Let no one lose
heart on account of this Philistine; your
servant will go and fight him."

33Saul replied, "You are not able to go
out against this Philistine and fight him;
you are only a young man, and he has
been a warrior from his youth."

34But David said to Saul, "Your servant has been keeping his father's sheep.
When a lion or a bear came and carried
off a sheep from the flock, 35I went after
it, struck it and rescued the sheep from
its mouth. When it turned on me, I seized
it by its hair, struck it and killed it. 36Your
servant has killed both the lion and the
bear; this uncircumcised Philistine will
be like one of them, because he has defied the armies of the living God. 37The
LORD who rescued me from the paw of
the lion and the paw of the bear will rescue me from the hand of this Philistine."

Saul said to David, "Go, and the LORD
be with you."

38Then Saul dressed David in his own
tunic. He put a coat of armor on him
and a bronze helmet on his head. 39Da-
vid fastened on his sword over the tunic
and tried walking around, because he
was not used to them.

"I cannot go in these," he said to Saul,
"because I am not used to them." So he
took them off. 40Then he took his staff in

[a] 17 That is, probably about 36 pounds or about 16 kilograms [b] 18 Or *some token*; or *some pledge of spoils*

his hand, chose five smooth stones from
the stream, put them in the pouch of his
shepherd's bag and, with his sling in his
hand, approached the Philistine.
41Meanwhile, the Philistine, with his
shield bearer in front of him, kept coming closer to David. 42He looked David
over and saw that he was little more
than a boy, glowing with health and
handsome, and he despised him. 43He
said to David, "Am I a dog, that you come
at me with sticks?" And the Philistine
cursed David by his gods. 44"Come here,"
he said, "and I'll give your flesh to the
birds and the wild animals!"
45David said to the Philistine, "You
come against me with sword and spear
and javelin, but I come against you in
the name of the LORD Almighty, the God
of the armies of Israel, whom you have
defied. 46This day the LORD will deliver
you into my hands, and I'll strike you
down and cut off your head. This very
day I will give the carcasses of the Philistine army to the birds and the wild
animals, and the whole world will know
that there is a God in Israel. 47All those
gathered here will know that it is not by
sword or spear that the LORD saves; for
the battle is the LORD's, and he will give
all of you into our hands."
48As the Philistine moved closer to attack him, David ran quickly toward the
battle line to meet him. 49Reaching into
his bag and taking out a stone, he slung
it and struck the Philistine on the forehead. The stone sank into his forehead,
and he fell facedown on the ground.
50So David triumphed over the Philistine with a sling and a stone; without a
sword in his hand he struck down the
Philistine and killed him.
51David ran and stood over him. He
took hold of the Philistine's sword and
drew it from the sheath. After he killed
him, he cut off his head with the sword.
When the Philistines saw that their
hero was dead, they turned and ran.
52Then the men of Israel and Judah
surged forward with a shout and pursued the Philistines to the entrance of
Gath[a] and to the gates of Ekron. Their
dead were strewn along the Shaaraim
road to Gath and Ekron. 53When the Israelites returned from chasing the Philistines, they plundered their camp.
54David took the Philistine's head and
brought it to Jerusalem; he put the Philistine's weapons in his own tent.
55As Saul watched David going out to
meet the Philistine, he said to Abner,
commander of the army, "Abner, whose
son is that young man?"
Abner replied, "As surely as you live,
Your Majesty, I don't know."
56The king said, "Find out whose son
this young man is."
57As soon as David returned from killing the Philistine, Abner took him and
brought him before Saul, with David still
holding the Philistine's head.
58"Whose son are you, young man?"
Saul asked him.
David said, "I am the son of your servant Jesse of Bethlehem."

Saul's Growing Fear of David

18 After David had finished talking
with Saul, Jonathan became one
in spirit with David, and he loved him
as himself. 2From that day Saul kept David with him and did not let him return
home to his family. 3And Jonathan made
a covenant with David because he loved
him as himself. 4Jonathan took off the
robe he was wearing and gave it to David, along with his tunic, and even his
sword, his bow and his belt.
5Whatever mission Saul sent him
on, David was so successful that Saul
gave him a high rank in the army. This
pleased all the troops, and Saul's officers
as well.
6When the men were returning home
after David had killed the Philistine, the
women came out from all the towns of
Israel to meet King Saul with singing
and dancing, with joyful songs and with
timbrels and lyres. 7As they danced, they
sang:

"Saul has slain his thousands,
and David his tens of thousands."

8Saul was very angry; this refrain displeased him greatly. "They have credited David with tens of thousands," he
thought, "but me with only thousands.
What more can he get but the kingdom?" 9And from that time on Saul kept
a close eye on David.
10The next day an evil[b] spirit from God
came forcefully on Saul. He was prophesying in his house, while David was
playing the lyre, as he usually did. Saul
had a spear in his hand 11and he hurled
it, saying to himself, "I'll pin David to the
wall." But David eluded him twice.
12Saul was afraid of David, because the
LORD was with David but had departed
from Saul. 13So he sent David away from

[a] 52 Some Septuagint manuscripts; Hebrew *of a valley* [b] 10 Or *a harmful*

him and gave him command over a thousand men, and David led the troops in their campaigns. [14]In everything he did he had great success, because the LORD was with him. [15]When Saul saw how successful he was, he was afraid of him. [16]But all Israel and Judah loved David, because he led them in their campaigns.

[17]Saul said to David, "Here is my older daughter Merab. I will give her to you in marriage; only serve me bravely and fight the battles of the LORD." For Saul said to himself, "I will not raise a hand against him. Let the Philistines do that!"

[18]But David said to Saul, "Who am I, and what is my family or my clan in Israel, that I should become the king's son-in-law?" [19]So[a] when the time came for Merab, Saul's daughter, to be given to David, she was given in marriage to Adriel of Meholah.

[20]Now Saul's daughter Michal was in love with David, and when they told Saul about it, he was pleased. [21]"I will give her to him," he thought, "so that she may be a snare to him and so that the hand of the Philistines may be against him." So Saul said to David, "Now you have a second opportunity to become my son-in-law."

[22]Then Saul ordered his attendants: "Speak to David privately and say, 'Look, the king likes you, and his attendants all love you; now become his son-in-law.'"

[23]They repeated these words to David. But David said, "Do you think it is a small matter to become the king's son-in-law? I'm only a poor man and little known."

[24]When Saul's servants told him what David had said, [25]Saul replied, "Say to David, 'The king wants no other price for the bride than a hundred Philistine foreskins, to take revenge on his enemies.'" Saul's plan was to have David fall by the hands of the Philistines.

[26]When the attendants told David these things, he was pleased to become the king's son-in-law. So before the allotted time elapsed, [27]David took his men with him and went out and killed two hundred Philistines and brought back their foreskins. They counted out the full number to the king so that David might become the king's son-in-law. Then Saul gave him his daughter Michal in marriage.

[28]When Saul realized that the LORD was with David and that his daughter Michal loved David, [29]Saul became still more afraid of him, and he remained his enemy the rest of his days.

[30]The Philistine commanders continued to go out to battle, and as often as they did, David met with more success than the rest of Saul's officers, and his name became well known.

Saul Tries to Kill David

19 Saul told his son Jonathan and all the attendants to kill David. But Jonathan had taken a great liking to David [2]and warned him, "My father Saul is looking for a chance to kill you. Be on your guard tomorrow morning; go into hiding and stay there. [3]I will go out and stand with my father in the field where you are. I'll speak to him about you and will tell you what I find out."

[4]Jonathan spoke well of David to Saul his father and said to him, "Let not the king do wrong to his servant David; he has not wronged you, and what he has done has benefited you greatly. [5]He took his life in his hands when he killed the Philistine. The LORD won a great victory for all Israel, and you saw it and were glad. Why then would you do wrong to an innocent man like David by killing him for no reason?"

[6]Saul listened to Jonathan and took this oath: "As surely as the LORD lives, David will not be put to death."

[7]So Jonathan called David and told him the whole conversation. He brought him to Saul, and David was with Saul as before.

[8]Once more war broke out, and David went out and fought the Philistines. He struck them with such force that they fled before him.

[9]But an evil[b] spirit from the LORD came on Saul as he was sitting in his house with his spear in his hand. While David was playing the lyre, [10]Saul tried to pin him to the wall with his spear, but David eluded him as Saul drove the spear into the wall. That night David made good his escape.

[11]Saul sent men to David's house to watch it and to kill him in the morning. But Michal, David's wife, warned him, "If you don't run for your life tonight, tomorrow you'll be killed." [12]So Michal let David down through a window, and he fled and escaped. [13]Then Michal took an idol and laid it on the bed, covering it with a garment and putting some goats' hair at the head.

[a] 19 Or *However,* [b] 9 Or *But a harmful*

14 When Saul sent the men to capture
David, Michal said, "He is ill."
15 Then Saul sent the men back to see
David and told them, "Bring him up to
me in his bed so that I may kill him."
16 But when the men entered, there was
the idol in the bed, and at the head was
some goats' hair.
17 Saul said to Michal, "Why did you
deceive me like this and send my enemy
away so that he escaped?"
Michal told him, "He said to me, 'Let
me get away. Why should I kill you?' "
18 When David had fled and made his
escape, he went to Samuel at Ramah
and told him all that Saul had done to
him. Then he and Samuel went to Naioth
and stayed there. 19 Word came to Saul:
"David is in Naioth at Ramah"; 20 so he
sent men to capture him. But when they
saw a group of prophets prophesying,
with Samuel standing there as their
leader, the Spirit of God came on Saul's
men, and they also prophesied. 21 Saul
was told about it, and he sent more men,
and they prophesied too. Saul sent men
a third time, and they also prophesied.
22 Finally, he himself left for Ramah and
went to the great cistern at Seku. And he
asked, "Where are Samuel and David?"
"Over in Naioth at Ramah," they said.
23 So Saul went to Naioth at Ramah.
But the Spirit of God came even on him,
and he walked along prophesying until he came to Naioth. 24 He stripped off
his garments, and he too prophesied in
Samuel's presence. He lay naked all that
day and all that night. This is why people
say, "Is Saul also among the prophets?"

David and Jonathan

20 Then David fled from Naioth at
Ramah and went to Jonathan
and asked, "What have I done? What is
my crime? How have I wronged your father, that he is trying to kill me?"
2 "Never!" Jonathan replied. "You are
not going to die! Look, my father doesn't
do anything, great or small, without letting me know. Why would he hide this
from me? It isn't so!"
3 But David took an oath and said,
"Your father knows very well that I have
found favor in your eyes, and he has said
to himself, 'Jonathan must not know this
or he will be grieved.' Yet as surely as the
LORD lives and as you live, there is only
a step between me and death."
4 Jonathan said to David, "Whatever
you want me to do, I'll do for you."
5 So David said, "Look, tomorrow is the
New Moon feast, and I am supposed to
dine with the king; but let me go and
hide in the field until the evening of the
day after tomorrow. 6 If your father miss-
es me at all, tell him, 'David earnestly
asked my permission to hurry to Bethlehem, his hometown, because an annual sacrifice is being made there for his
whole clan.' 7 If he says, 'Very well,' then
your servant is safe. But if he loses his
temper, you can be sure that he is determined to harm me. 8 As for you, show
kindness to your servant, for you have
brought him into a covenant with you
before the LORD. If I am guilty, then kill
me yourself! Why hand me over to your
father?"
9 "Never!" Jonathan said. "If I had the
least inkling that my father was determined to harm you, wouldn't I tell you?"
10 David asked, "Who will tell me if
your father answers you harshly?"
11 "Come," Jonathan said, "let's go out
into the field." So they went there together.
12 Then Jonathan said to David, "I
swear by the LORD, the God of Israel, that
I will surely sound out my father by this
time the day after tomorrow! If he is favorably disposed toward you, will I not
send you word and let you know? 13 But
if my father intends to harm you, may
the LORD deal with Jonathan, be it ever
so severely, if I do not let you know and
send you away in peace. May the LORD
be with you as he has been with my father. 14 But show me unfailing kindness
like the LORD's kindness as long as I live,
so that I may not be killed, 15 and do not
ever cut off your kindness from my family—not even when the LORD has cut off
every one of David's enemies from the
face of the earth."
16 So Jonathan made a covenant with
the house of David, saying, "May the
LORD call David's enemies to account."
17 And Jonathan had David reaffirm his
oath out of love for him, because he
loved him as he loved himself.
18 Then Jonathan said to David, "Tomorrow is the New Moon feast. You will
be missed, because your seat will be
empty. 19 The day after tomorrow, toward
evening, go to the place where you hid
when this trouble began, and wait by the
stone Ezel. 20 I will shoot three arrows to
the side of it, as though I were shooting
at a target. 21 Then I will send a boy and
say, 'Go, find the arrows.' If I say to him,
'Look, the arrows are on this side of you;
bring them here,' then come, because,
as surely as the LORD lives, you are safe;
there is no danger. 22 But if I say to the

boy, 'Look, the arrows are beyond you,' then you must go, because the LORD has sent you away. 23And about the matter you and I discussed — remember, the LORD is witness between you and me forever."

24So David hid in the field, and when the New Moon feast came, the king sat down to eat. 25He sat in his customary place by the wall, opposite Jonathan,[a] and Abner sat next to Saul, but David's place was empty. 26Saul said nothing that day, for he thought, "Something must have happened to David to make him ceremonially unclean — surely he is unclean." 27But the next day, the second day of the month, David's place was empty again. Then Saul said to his son Jonathan, "Why hasn't the son of Jesse come to the meal, either yesterday or today?"

28Jonathan answered, "David earnestly asked me for permission to go to Bethlehem. 29He said, 'Let me go, because our family is observing a sacrifice in the town and my brother has ordered me to be there. If I have found favor in your eyes, let me get away to see my brothers.' That is why he has not come to the king's table."

30Saul's anger flared up at Jonathan and he said to him, "You son of a perverse and rebellious woman! Don't I know that you have sided with the son of Jesse to your own shame and to the shame of the mother who bore you? 31As long as the son of Jesse lives on this earth, neither you nor your kingdom will be established. Now send someone to bring him to me, for he must die!"

32"Why should he be put to death? What has he done?" Jonathan asked his father. 33But Saul hurled his spear at him to kill him. Then Jonathan knew that his father intended to kill David.

34Jonathan got up from the table in fierce anger; on that second day of the feast he did not eat, because he was grieved at his father's shameful treatment of David.

35In the morning Jonathan went out to the field for his meeting with David. He had a small boy with him, 36and he said to the boy, "Run and find the arrows I shoot." As the boy ran, he shot an arrow beyond him. 37When the boy came to the place where Jonathan's arrow had fallen, Jonathan called out after him, "Isn't the arrow beyond you?" 38Then he shouted, "Hurry! Go quickly! Don't stop!" The boy picked up the arrow and returned to his master. 39(The boy knew nothing about all this; only Jonathan and David knew.) 40Then Jonathan gave his weapons to the boy and said, "Go, carry them back to town."

41After the boy had gone, David got up from the south side of the stone and bowed down before Jonathan three times, with his face to the ground. Then they kissed each other and wept together — but David wept the most.

42Jonathan said to David, "Go in peace, for we have sworn friendship with each other in the name of the LORD, saying, 'The LORD is witness between you and me, and between your descendants and my descendants forever.'" Then David left, and Jonathan went back to the town.[b]

David at Nob

21 [c] David went to Nob, to Ahimelek the priest. Ahimelek trembled when he met him, and asked, "Why are you alone? Why is no one with you?"

2David answered Ahimelek the priest, "The king sent me on a mission and said to me, 'No one is to know anything about the mission I am sending you on.' As for my men, I have told them to meet me at a certain place. 3Now then, what do you have on hand? Give me five loaves of bread, or whatever you can find."

4But the priest answered David, "I don't have any ordinary bread on hand; however, there is some consecrated bread here — provided the men have kept themselves from women."

5David replied, "Indeed women have been kept from us, as usual whenever[d] I set out. The men's bodies are holy even on missions that are not holy. How much more so today!" 6So the priest gave him the consecrated bread, since there was no bread there except the bread of the Presence that had been removed from before the LORD and replaced by hot bread on the day it was taken away.

7Now one of Saul's servants was there that day, detained before the LORD; he was Doeg the Edomite, Saul's chief shepherd.

8David asked Ahimelek, "Don't you have a spear or a sword here? I haven't brought my sword or any other weapon, because the king's mission was urgent."

[a] 25 Septuagint; Hebrew *wall. Jonathan arose*
[b] 42 In Hebrew texts this sentence (20:42b) is numbered 21:1.
[c] In Hebrew texts 21:1-15 is numbered 21:2-16.
[d] 5 Or *from us in the past few days since*

9The priest replied, "The sword of Goliath the Philistine, whom you killed in
the Valley of Elah, is here; it is wrapped
in a cloth behind the ephod. If you want
it, take it; there is no sword here but that
one."
David said, "There is none like it; give
it to me."

David at Gath

10That day David fled from Saul and
went to Achish king of Gath. 11But the
servants of Achish said to him, "Isn't this
David, the king of the land? Isn't he the
one they sing about in their dances:

"'Saul has slain his thousands,
and David his tens of thousands'?"

12David took these words to heart and
was very much afraid of Achish king of
Gath. 13So he pretended to be insane in
their presence; and while he was in their
hands he acted like a madman, making
marks on the doors of the gate and letting saliva run down his beard.
14Achish said to his servants, "Look at
the man! He is insane! Why bring him to
me? 15Am I so short of madmen that you
have to bring this fellow here to carry on
like this in front of me? Must this man
come into my house?"

David at Adullam and Mizpah

22 David left Gath and escaped to the
cave of Adullam. When his brothers and his father's household heard
about it, they went down to him there.
2All those who were in distress or in debt
or discontented gathered around him,
and he became their commander. About
four hundred men were with him.
3From there David went to Mizpah
in Moab and said to the king of Moab,
"Would you let my father and mother come and stay with you until I learn
what God will do for me?" 4So he left
them with the king of Moab, and they
stayed with him as long as David was in
the stronghold.
5But the prophet Gad said to David,
"Do not stay in the stronghold. Go into
the land of Judah." So David left and
went to the forest of Hereth.

Saul Kills the Priests of Nob

6Now Saul heard that David and his
men had been discovered. And Saul was
seated, spear in hand, under the tamarisk tree on the hill at Gibeah, with all
his officials standing at his side. 7He said
to them, "Listen, men of Benjamin! Will
the son of Jesse give all of you fields and
vineyards? Will he make all of you commanders of thousands and commanders
of hundreds? 8Is that why you have all
conspired against me? No one tells me
when my son makes a covenant with the
son of Jesse. None of you is concerned
about me or tells me that my son has incited my servant to lie in wait for me, as
he does today."
9But Doeg the Edomite, who was
standing with Saul's officials, said, "I
saw the son of Jesse come to Ahimelek
son of Ahitub at Nob. 10Ahimelek inquired of the LORD for him; he also gave
him provisions and the sword of Goliath
the Philistine."
11Then the king sent for the priest
Ahimelek son of Ahitub and all the men
of his family, who were the priests at
Nob, and they all came to the king. 12Saul
said, "Listen now, son of Ahitub."
"Yes, my lord," he answered.
13Saul said to him, "Why have you
conspired against me, you and the son
of Jesse, giving him bread and a sword
and inquiring of God for him, so that he
has rebelled against me and lies in wait
for me, as he does today?"
14Ahimelek answered the king, "Who
of all your servants is as loyal as David,
the king's son-in-law, captain of your
bodyguard and highly respected in your
household? 15Was that day the first time
I inquired of God for him? Of course not!
Let not the king accuse your servant or
any of his father's family, for your servant knows nothing at all about this
whole affair."
16But the king said, "You will surely
die, Ahimelek, you and your whole family."
17Then the king ordered the guards at
his side: "Turn and kill the priests of the
LORD, because they too have sided with
David. They knew he was fleeing, yet
they did not tell me."
But the king's officials were unwilling
to raise a hand to strike the priests of the
LORD.
18The king then ordered Doeg, "You
turn and strike down the priests."
So Doeg the Edomite turned and
struck them down. That day he killed
eighty-five men who wore the linen
ephod. 19He also put to the sword Nob,
the town of the priests, with its men and
women, its children and infants, and its
cattle, donkeys and sheep.
20But one son of Ahimelek son of Ahitub, named Abiathar, escaped and fled
to join David. 21He told David that Saul
had killed the priests of the LORD. 22Then

David said to Abiathar, "That day, when Doeg the Edomite was there, I knew he would be sure to tell Saul. I am responsible for the death of your whole family. 23Stay with me; don't be afraid. The man who wants to kill you is trying to kill me too. You will be safe with me."

David Saves Keilah

23 When David was told, "Look, the Philistines are fighting against Keilah and are looting the threshing floors," 2he inquired of the LORD, saying, "Shall I go and attack these Philistines?"

The LORD answered him, "Go, attack the Philistines and save Keilah."

3But David's men said to him, "Here in Judah we are afraid. How much more, then, if we go to Keilah against the Philistine forces!"

4Once again David inquired of the LORD, and the LORD answered him, "Go down to Keilah, for I am going to give the Philistines into your hand." 5So David and his men went to Keilah, fought the Philistines and carried off their livestock. He inflicted heavy losses on the Philistines and saved the people of Keilah. 6(Now Abiathar son of Ahimelek had brought the ephod down with him when he fled to David at Keilah.)

Saul Pursues David

7Saul was told that David had gone to Keilah, and he said, "God has delivered him into my hands, for David has imprisoned himself by entering a town with gates and bars." 8And Saul called up all his forces for battle, to go down to Keilah to besiege David and his men.

9When David learned that Saul was plotting against him, he said to Abiathar the priest, "Bring the ephod." 10David said, "LORD, God of Israel, your servant has heard definitely that Saul plans to come to Keilah and destroy the town on account of me. 11Will the citizens of Keilah surrender me to him? Will Saul come down, as your servant has heard? LORD, God of Israel, tell your servant."

And the LORD said, "He will."

12Again David asked, "Will the citizens of Keilah surrender me and my men to Saul?"

And the LORD said, "They will."

13So David and his men, about six hundred in number, left Keilah and kept moving from place to place. When Saul was told that David had escaped from Keilah, he did not go there.

14David stayed in the wilderness strongholds and in the hills of the Desert of Ziph. Day after day Saul searched for him, but God did not give David into his hands.

15While David was at Horesh in the Desert of Ziph, he learned that[a] Saul had come out to take his life. 16And Saul's son Jonathan went to David at Horesh and helped him find strength in God. 17"Don't be afraid," he said. "My father Saul will not lay a hand on you. You will be king over Israel, and I will be second to you. Even my father Saul knows this." 18The two of them made a covenant before the LORD. Then Jonathan went home, but David remained at Horesh.

19The Ziphites went up to Saul at Gibeah and said, "Is not David hiding among us in the strongholds at Horesh, on the hill of Hakilah, south of Jeshimon? 20Now, Your Majesty, come down whenever it pleases you to do so, and we will be responsible for giving him into your hands."

21Saul replied, "The LORD bless you for your concern for me. 22Go and get more information. Find out where David usually goes and who has seen him there. They tell me he is very crafty. 23Find out about all the hiding places he uses and come back to me with definite information. Then I will go with you; if he is in the area, I will track him down among all the clans of Judah."

24So they set out and went to Ziph ahead of Saul. Now David and his men were in the Desert of Maon, in the Arabah south of Jeshimon. 25Saul and his men began the search, and when David was told about it, he went down to the rock and stayed in the Desert of Maon. When Saul heard this, he went into the Desert of Maon in pursuit of David.

26Saul was going along one side of the mountain, and David and his men were on the other side, hurrying to get away from Saul. As Saul and his forces were closing in on David and his men to capture them, 27a messenger came to Saul, saying, "Come quickly! The Philistines are raiding the land." 28Then Saul broke off his pursuit of David and went to meet the Philistines. That is why they call this place Sela Hammahlekoth.[b] 29And David went up from there and lived in the strongholds of En Gedi.[c]

[a] 15 Or *he was afraid because* [b] 28 *Sela Hammahlekoth* means *rock of parting.* [c] 29 In Hebrew texts this verse (23:29) is numbered 24:1.

David Spares Saul's Life

24 [a] After Saul returned from pursuing the Philistines, he was told,
"David is in the Desert of En Gedi." 2So
Saul took three thousand able young
men from all Israel and set out to look
for David and his men near the Crags of
the Wild Goats.
3He came to the sheep pens along the
way; a cave was there, and Saul went in
to relieve himself. David and his men
were far back in the cave. 4The men said,
"This is the day the LORD spoke of when
he said[b] to you, 'I will give your enemy
into your hands for you to deal with as
you wish.'" Then David crept up unnoticed and cut off a corner of Saul's robe.
5Afterward, David was conscience-
stricken for having cut off a corner of
his robe. 6He said to his men, "The LORD
forbid that I should do such a thing to
my master, the LORD's anointed, or lay
my hand on him; for he is the anointed
of the LORD." 7With these words David
sharply rebuked his men and did not
allow them to attack Saul. And Saul left
the cave and went his way.
8Then David went out of the cave and
called out to Saul, "My lord the king!"
When Saul looked behind him, David
bowed down and prostrated himself with
his face to the ground. 9He said to Saul,
"Why do you listen when men say, 'David is bent on harming you'? 10This day
you have seen with your own eyes how
the LORD delivered you into my hands
in the cave. Some urged me to kill you,
but I spared you; I said, 'I will not lay
my hand on my lord, because he is the
LORD's anointed.' 11See, my father, look at
this piece of your robe in my hand! I cut
off the corner of your robe but did not kill
you. See that there is nothing in my hand
to indicate that I am guilty of wrongdoing or rebellion. I have not wronged you,
but you are hunting me down to take
my life. 12May the LORD judge between
you and me. And may the LORD avenge
the wrongs you have done to me, but
my hand will not touch you. 13As the old
saying goes, 'From evildoers come evil
deeds,' so my hand will not touch you.
14"Against whom has the king of Israel come out? Who are you pursuing? A
dead dog? A flea? 15May the LORD be our
judge and decide between us. May he
consider my cause and uphold it; may
he vindicate me by delivering me from
your hand."
16When David finished saying this,
Saul asked, "Is that your voice, David
my son?" And he wept aloud. 17"You are
more righteous than I," he said. "You
have treated me well, but I have treated you badly. 18You have just now told
me about the good you did to me; the
LORD delivered me into your hands, but
you did not kill me. 19When a man finds
his enemy, does he let him get away unharmed? May the LORD reward you well
for the way you treated me today. 20I
know that you will surely be king and
that the kingdom of Israel will be established in your hands. 21Now swear to me
by the LORD that you will not kill off my
descendants or wipe out my name from
my father's family."
22So David gave his oath to Saul. Then
Saul returned home, but David and his
men went up to the stronghold.

David, Nabal and Abigail

25 Now Samuel died, and all Israel
assembled and mourned for him;
and they buried him at his home in Ramah. Then David moved down into the
Desert of Paran.[c]
2A certain man in Maon, who had
property there at Carmel, was very
wealthy. He had a thousand goats and
three thousand sheep, which he was
shearing in Carmel. 3His name was Nabal and his wife's name was Abigail. She
was an intelligent and beautiful woman,
but her husband was surly and mean in
his dealings — he was a Calebite.
4While David was in the wilderness, he
heard that Nabal was shearing sheep. 5So
he sent ten young men and said to them,
"Go up to Nabal at Carmel and greet him
in my name. 6Say to him: 'Long life to
you! Good health to you and your household! And good health to all that is yours!
7"'Now I hear that it is sheep-shearing
time. When your shepherds were with
us, we did not mistreat them, and the
whole time they were at Carmel nothing of theirs was missing. 8Ask your own
servants and they will tell you. Therefore
be favorable toward my men, since we
come at a festive time. Please give your
servants and your son David whatever
you can find for them.'"
9When David's men arrived, they gave
Nabal this message in David's name.
Then they waited.
10Nabal answered David's servants,
"Who is this David? Who is this son of

[a] In Hebrew texts 24:1-22 is numbered 24:2-23. [b] 4 Or *"Today the LORD is saying* [c] 1 Hebrew and some Septuagint manuscripts; other Septuagint manuscripts *Maon*

Jesse? Many servants are breaking away from their masters these days. 11 Why should I take my bread and water, and the meat I have slaughtered for my shearers, and give it to men coming from who knows where?"

12 David's men turned around and went back. When they arrived, they reported every word. 13 David said to his men, "Each of you strap on your sword!" So they did, and David strapped his on as well. About four hundred men went up with David, while two hundred stayed with the supplies.

14 One of the servants told Abigail, Nabal's wife, "David sent messengers from the wilderness to give our master his greetings, but he hurled insults at them. 15 Yet these men were very good to us. They did not mistreat us, and the whole time we were out in the fields near them nothing was missing. 16 Night and day they were a wall around us the whole time we were herding our sheep near them. 17 Now think it over and see what you can do, because disaster is hanging over our master and his whole household. He is such a wicked man that no one can talk to him."

18 Abigail acted quickly. She took two hundred loaves of bread, two skins of wine, five dressed sheep, five seahs[a] of roasted grain, a hundred cakes of raisins and two hundred cakes of pressed figs, and loaded them on donkeys. 19 Then she told her servants, "Go on ahead; I'll follow you." But she did not tell her husband Nabal.

20 As she came riding her donkey into a mountain ravine, there were David and his men descending toward her, and she met them. 21 David had just said, "It's been useless — all my watching over this fellow's property in the wilderness so that nothing of his was missing. He has paid me back evil for good. 22 May God deal with David,[b] be it ever so severely, if by morning I leave alive one male of all who belong to him!"

23 When Abigail saw David, she quickly got off her donkey and bowed down before David with her face to the ground. 24 She fell at his feet and said: "Pardon your servant, my lord, and let me speak to you; hear what your servant has to say. 25 Please pay no attention, my lord, to that wicked man Nabal. He is just like his name — his name means Fool, and folly goes with him. And as for me, your servant, I did not see the men my lord sent. 26 And now, my lord, as surely as the LORD your God lives and as you live, since the LORD has kept you from bloodshed and from avenging yourself with your own hands, may your enemies and all who are intent on harming my lord be like Nabal. 27 And let this gift, which your servant has brought to my lord, be given to the men who follow you.

28 "Please forgive your servant's presumption. The LORD your God will certainly make a lasting dynasty for my lord, because you fight the LORD's battles, and no wrongdoing will be found in you as long as you live. 29 Even though someone is pursuing you to take your life, the life of my lord will be bound securely in the bundle of the living by the LORD your God, but the lives of your enemies he will hurl away as from the pocket of a sling. 30 When the LORD has fulfilled for my lord every good thing he promised concerning him and has appointed him ruler over Israel, 31 my lord will not have on his conscience the staggering burden of needless bloodshed or of having avenged himself. And when the LORD your God has brought my lord success, remember your servant."

32 David said to Abigail, "Praise be to the LORD, the God of Israel, who has sent you today to meet me. 33 May you be blessed for your good judgment and for keeping me from bloodshed this day and from avenging myself with my own hands. 34 Otherwise, as surely as the LORD, the God of Israel, lives, who has kept me from harming you, if you had not come quickly to meet me, not one male belonging to Nabal would have been left alive by daybreak."

35 Then David accepted from her hand what she had brought him and said, "Go home in peace. I have heard your words and granted your request."

36 When Abigail went to Nabal, he was in the house holding a banquet like that of a king. He was in high spirits and very drunk. So she told him nothing at all until daybreak. 37 Then in the morning, when Nabal was sober, his wife told him all these things, and his heart failed him and he became like a stone. 38 About ten days later, the LORD struck Nabal and he died.

39 When David heard that Nabal was dead, he said, "Praise be to the LORD, who has upheld my cause against Nabal

[a] *18* That is, probably about 60 pounds or about 27 kilograms [b] *22* Some Septuagint manuscripts; Hebrew *with David's enemies*

for treating me with contempt. He has kept his servant from doing wrong and has brought Nabal's wrongdoing down on his own head."

Then David sent word to Abigail, asking her to become his wife. 40His servants went to Carmel and said to Abigail, "David has sent us to you to take you to become his wife."

41She bowed down with her face to the ground and said, "I am your servant and am ready to serve you and wash the feet of my lord's servants." 42Abigail quickly got on a donkey and, attended by her five female servants, went with David's messengers and became his wife. 43David had also married Ahinoam of Jezreel, and they both were his wives. 44But Saul had given his daughter Michal, David's wife, to Paltiel[a] son of Laish, who was from Gallim.

David Again Spares Saul's Life

26 The Ziphites went to Saul at Gibeah and said, "Is not David hiding on the hill of Hakilah, which faces Jeshimon?"

2So Saul went down to the Desert of Ziph, with his three thousand select Israelite troops, to search there for David. 3Saul made his camp beside the road on the hill of Hakilah facing Jeshimon, but David stayed in the wilderness. When he saw that Saul had followed him there, 4he sent out scouts and learned that Saul had definitely arrived.

5Then David set out and went to the place where Saul had camped. He saw where Saul and Abner son of Ner, the commander of the army, had lain down. Saul was lying inside the camp, with the army encamped around him.

6David then asked Ahimelek the Hittite and Abishai son of Zeruiah, Joab's brother, "Who will go down into the camp with me to Saul?"

"I'll go with you," said Abishai.

7So David and Abishai went to the army by night, and there was Saul, lying asleep inside the camp with his spear stuck in the ground near his head. Abner and the soldiers were lying around him.

8Abishai said to David, "Today God has delivered your enemy into your hands. Now let me pin him to the ground with one thrust of the spear; I won't strike him twice."

9But David said to Abishai, "Don't destroy him! Who can lay a hand on the LORD's anointed and be guiltless? 10As surely as the LORD lives," he said, "the LORD himself will strike him, or his time will come and he will die, or he will go into battle and perish. 11But the LORD forbid that I should lay a hand on the LORD's anointed. Now get the spear and water jug that are near his head, and let's go."

12So David took the spear and water jug near Saul's head, and they left. No one saw or knew about it, nor did anyone wake up. They were all sleeping, because the LORD had put them into a deep sleep.

13Then David crossed over to the other side and stood on top of the hill some distance away; there was a wide space between them. 14He called out to the army and to Abner son of Ner, "Aren't you going to answer me, Abner?"

Abner replied, "Who are you who calls to the king?"

15David said, "You're a man, aren't you? And who is like you in Israel? Why didn't you guard your lord the king? Someone came to destroy your lord the king. 16What you have done is not good. As surely as the LORD lives, you and your men must die, because you did not guard your master, the LORD's anointed. Look around you. Where are the king's spear and water jug that were near his head?"

17Saul recognized David's voice and said, "Is that your voice, David my son?"

David replied, "Yes it is, my lord the king." 18And he added, "Why is my lord pursuing his servant? What have I done, and what wrong am I guilty of? 19Now let my lord the king listen to his servant's words. If the LORD has incited you against me, then may he accept an offering. If, however, people have done it, may they be cursed before the LORD! They have driven me today from my share in the LORD's inheritance and have said, 'Go, serve other gods.' 20Now do not let my blood fall to the ground far from the presence of the LORD. The king of Israel has come out to look for a flea — as one hunts a partridge in the mountains."

21Then Saul said, "I have sinned. Come back, David my son. Because you considered my life precious today, I will not try to harm you again. Surely I have acted like a fool and have been terribly wrong."

22"Here is the king's spear," David answered. "Let one of your young men come over and get it. 23The LORD rewards

[a] 44 Hebrew *Palti*, a variant of *Paltiel*

everyone for their righteousness and
faithfulness. The LORD delivered you into
my hands today, but I would not lay a
hand on the LORD's anointed. [24]As surely
as I valued your life today, so may the
LORD value my life and deliver me from
all trouble."
[25]Then Saul said to David, "May you be
blessed, David my son; you will do great
things and surely triumph."
So David went on his way, and Saul returned home.

David Among the Philistines

27 But David thought to himself, "One
of these days I will be destroyed by
the hand of Saul. The best thing I can do
is to escape to the land of the Philistines.
Then Saul will give up searching for me
anywhere in Israel, and I will slip out of
his hand."
[2]So David and the six hundred men
with him left and went over to Achish
son of Maok king of Gath. [3]David and his
men settled in Gath with Achish. Each
man had his family with him, and David had his two wives: Ahinoam of Jezreel and Abigail of Carmel, the widow of
Nabal. [4]When Saul was told that David
had fled to Gath, he no longer searched
for him.
[5]Then David said to Achish, "If I have
found favor in your eyes, let a place be assigned to me in one of the country towns,
that I may live there. Why should your
servant live in the royal city with you?"
[6]So on that day Achish gave him Ziklag, and it has belonged to the kings of
Judah ever since. [7]David lived in Philistine territory a year and four months.
[8]Now David and his men went up and
raided the Geshurites, the Girzites and
the Amalekites. (From ancient times
these peoples had lived in the land extending to Shur and Egypt.) [9]Whenever
David attacked an area, he did not leave
a man or woman alive, but took sheep
and cattle, donkeys and camels, and
clothes. Then he returned to Achish.
[10]When Achish asked, "Where did you
go raiding today?" David would say,
"Against the Negev of Judah" or "Against
the Negev of Jerahmeel" or "Against the
Negev of the Kenites." [11]He did not leave
a man or woman alive to be brought to
Gath, for he thought, "They might inform on us and say, 'This is what David
did.'" And such was his practice as long
as he lived in Philistine territory. [12]Achish
trusted David and said to himself, "He
has become so obnoxious to his people,
the Israelites, that he will be my servant
for life."

28 In those days the Philistines gathered their forces to fight against
Israel. Achish said to David, "You must
understand that you and your men will
accompany me in the army."
[2]David said, "Then you will see for
yourself what your servant can do."
Achish replied, "Very well, I will make
you my bodyguard for life."

Saul and the Medium at Endor

[3]Now Samuel was dead, and all Israel had mourned for him and buried him
in his own town of Ramah. Saul had expelled the mediums and spiritists from
the land.
[4]The Philistines assembled and came
and set up camp at Shunem, while Saul
gathered all Israel and set up camp at
Gilboa. [5]When Saul saw the Philistine
army, he was afraid; terror filled his
heart. [6]He inquired of the LORD, but the
LORD did not answer him by dreams or
Urim or prophets. [7]Saul then said to his
attendants, "Find me a woman who is a
medium, so I may go and inquire of her."
"There is one in Endor," they said.
[8]So Saul disguised himself, putting on
other clothes, and at night he and two
men went to the woman. "Consult a spirit for me," he said, "and bring up for me
the one I name."
[9]But the woman said to him, "Surely
you know what Saul has done. He has
cut off the mediums and spiritists from
the land. Why have you set a trap for my
life to bring about my death?"
[10]Saul swore to her by the LORD, "As
surely as the LORD lives, you will not be
punished for this."
[11]Then the woman asked, "Whom shall
I bring up for you?"
"Bring up Samuel," he said.
[12]When the woman saw Samuel, she
cried out at the top of her voice and said
to Saul, "Why have you deceived me?
You are Saul!"
[13]The king said to her, "Don't be afraid.
What do you see?"
The woman said, "I see a ghostly figure[a] coming up out of the earth."
[14]"What does he look like?" he asked.
"An old man wearing a robe is coming
up," she said.
Then Saul knew it was Samuel, and
he bowed down and prostrated himself
with his face to the ground.

[a] 13 Or *see spirits*; or *see gods*

15Samuel said to Saul, "Why have you
disturbed me by bringing me up?"
"I am in great distress," Saul said.
"The Philistines are fighting against me,
and God has departed from me. He no
longer answers me, either by prophets or
by dreams. So I have called on you to tell
me what to do."
16Samuel said, "Why do you consult
me, now that the LORD has departed from you and become your enemy?
17The LORD has done what he predicted
through me. The LORD has torn the kingdom out of your hands and given it to
one of your neighbors — to David. 18Be-
cause you did not obey the LORD or carry
out his fierce wrath against the Amalekites, the LORD has done this to you today.
19The LORD will deliver both Israel and
you into the hands of the Philistines, and
tomorrow you and your sons will be with
me. The LORD will also give the army of
Israel into the hands of the Philistines."
20Immediately Saul fell full length on
the ground, filled with fear because of
Samuel's words. His strength was gone,
for he had eaten nothing all that day
and all that night.
21When the woman came to Saul and
saw that he was greatly shaken, she
said, "Look, your servant has obeyed
you. I took my life in my hands and did
what you told me to do. 22Now please listen to your servant and let me give you
some food so you may eat and have the
strength to go on your way."
23He refused and said, "I will not eat."
But his men joined the woman in urging him, and he listened to them. He
got up from the ground and sat on the
couch.
24The woman had a fattened calf at the
house, which she butchered at once. She
took some flour, kneaded it and baked
bread without yeast. 25Then she set it before Saul and his men, and they ate. That
same night they got up and left.

Achish Sends David Back to Ziklag

29 The Philistines gathered all
their forces at Aphek, and Israel camped by the spring in Jezreel. 2As
the Philistine rulers marched with their
units of hundreds and thousands, David and his men were marching at the
rear with Achish. 3The commanders of
the Philistines asked, "What about these
Hebrews?"
Achish replied, "Is this not David, who
was an officer of Saul king of Israel?
He has already been with me for over a
year, and from the day he left Saul until
now, I have found no fault in him."
4But the Philistine commanders were
angry with Achish and said, "Send the
man back, that he may return to the
place you assigned him. He must not
go with us into battle, or he will turn
against us during the fighting. How better could he regain his master's favor
than by taking the heads of our own
men? 5Isn't this the David they sang
about in their dances:

"'Saul has slain his thousands,
and David his tens of thousands'?"

6So Achish called David and said to
him, "As surely as the LORD lives, you
have been reliable, and I would be
pleased to have you serve with me in the
army. From the day you came to me until today, I have found no fault in you,
but the rulers don't approve of you. 7Now
turn back and go in peace; do nothing to
displease the Philistine rulers."
8"But what have I done?" asked David. "What have you found against your
servant from the day I came to you until now? Why can't I go and fight against
the enemies of my lord the king?"
9Achish answered, "I know that you
have been as pleasing in my eyes as an
angel of God; nevertheless, the Philistine
commanders have said, 'He must not go
up with us into battle.' 10Now get up early, along with your master's servants
who have come with you, and leave in
the morning as soon as it is light."
11So David and his men got up early in
the morning to go back to the land of the
Philistines, and the Philistines went up
to Jezreel.

David Destroys the Amalekites

30 David and his men reached Ziklag
on the third day. Now the Amalekites had raided the Negev and Ziklag.
They had attacked Ziklag and burned it,
2and had taken captive the women and
everyone else in it, both young and old.
They killed none of them, but carried
them off as they went on their way.
3When David and his men reached
Ziklag, they found it destroyed by fire
and their wives and sons and daughters
taken captive. 4So David and his men
wept aloud until they had no strength
left to weep. 5David's two wives had been
captured — Ahinoam of Jezreel and Abigail, the widow of Nabal of Carmel. 6Da-
vid was greatly distressed because the
men were talking of stoning him; each
one was bitter in spirit because of his

sons and daughters. But David found strength in the LORD his God.

7 Then David said to Abiathar the priest, the son of Ahimelek, "Bring me the ephod." Abiathar brought it to him, 8 and David inquired of the LORD, "Shall I pursue this raiding party? Will I overtake them?"

"Pursue them," he answered. "You will certainly overtake them and succeed in the rescue."

9 David and the six hundred men with him came to the Besor Valley, where some stayed behind. 10 Two hundred of them were too exhausted to cross the valley, but David and the other four hundred continued the pursuit.

11 They found an Egyptian in a field and brought him to David. They gave him water to drink and food to eat— 12 part of a cake of pressed figs and two cakes of raisins. He ate and was revived, for he had not eaten any food or drunk any water for three days and three nights.

13 David asked him, "Who do you belong to? Where do you come from?"

He said, "I am an Egyptian, the slave of an Amalekite. My master abandoned me when I became ill three days ago. 14 We raided the Negev of the Kerethites, some territory belonging to Judah and the Negev of Caleb. And we burned Ziklag."

15 David asked him, "Can you lead me down to this raiding party?"

He answered, "Swear to me before God that you will not kill me or hand me over to my master, and I will take you down to them."

16 He led David down, and there they were, scattered over the countryside, eating, drinking and reveling because of the great amount of plunder they had taken from the land of the Philistines and from Judah. 17 David fought them from dusk until the evening of the next day, and none of them got away, except four hundred young men who rode off on camels and fled. 18 David recovered everything the Amalekites had taken, including his two wives. 19 Nothing was missing: young or old, boy or girl, plunder or anything else they had taken. David brought everything back. 20 He took all the flocks and herds, and his men drove them ahead of the other livestock, saying, "This is David's plunder."

21 Then David came to the two hundred men who had been too exhausted to follow him and who were left behind at the Besor Valley. They came out to meet David and the men with him. As David and his men approached, he asked them how they were. 22 But all the evil men and troublemakers among David's followers said, "Because they did not go out with us, we will not share with them the plunder we recovered. However, each man may take his wife and children and go."

23 David replied, "No, my brothers, you must not do that with what the LORD has given us. He has protected us and delivered into our hands the raiding party that came against us. 24 Who will listen to what you say? The share of the man who stayed with the supplies is to be the same as that of him who went down to the battle. All will share alike." 25 David made this a statute and ordinance for Israel from that day to this.

26 When David reached Ziklag, he sent some of the plunder to the elders of Judah, who were his friends, saying, "Here is a gift for you from the plunder of the LORD's enemies."

27 David sent it to those who were in Bethel, Ramoth Negev and Jattir; 28 to those in Aroer, Siphmoth, Eshtemoa 29 and Rakal; to those in the towns of the Jerahmeelites and the Kenites; 30 to those in Hormah, Bor Ashan, Athak 31 and Hebron; and to those in all the other places where he and his men had roamed.

Saul Takes His Life

31 Now the Philistines fought against Israel; the Israelites fled before them, and many fell dead on Mount Gilboa. 2 The Philistines were in hot pursuit of Saul and his sons, and they killed his sons Jonathan, Abinadab and Malki-Shua. 3 The fighting grew fierce around Saul, and when the archers overtook him, they wounded him critically.

4 Saul said to his armor-bearer, "Draw your sword and run me through, or these uncircumcised fellows will come and run me through and abuse me."

But his armor-bearer was terrified and would not do it; so Saul took his own sword and fell on it. 5 When the armor-bearer saw that Saul was dead, he too fell on his sword and died with him. 6 So Saul and his three sons and his armor-bearer and all his men died together that same day.

7 When the Israelites along the valley and those across the Jordan saw that the Israelite army had fled and that Saul and his sons had died, they abandoned their towns and fled. And the Philistines came and occupied them.

8 The next day, when the Philistines

came to strip the dead, they found Saul
and his three sons fallen on Mount Gilboa. 9They cut off his head and stripped
off his armor, and they sent messengers
throughout the land of the Philistines to
proclaim the news in the temple of their
idols and among their people. 10They
put his armor in the temple of the Ashtoreths and fastened his body to the wall
of Beth Shan.

11When the people of Jabesh Gilead
heard what the Philistines had done to
Saul, 12all their valiant men marched
through the night to Beth Shan. They
took down the bodies of Saul and his
sons from the wall of Beth Shan and
went to Jabesh, where they burned
them. 13Then they took their bones and
buried them under a tamarisk tree at Jabesh, and they fasted seven days.

2 SAMUEL

David Hears of Saul's Death

1 After the death of Saul, David returned from striking down the Amalekites and stayed in Ziklag two days.
2On the third day a man arrived from
Saul's camp with his clothes torn and
dust on his head. When he came to David, he fell to the ground to pay him
honor.

3"Where have you come from?" David
asked him.

He answered, "I have escaped from
the Israelite camp."

4"What happened?" David asked.
"Tell me."

"The men fled from the battle," he replied. "Many of them fell and died. And
Saul and his son Jonathan are dead."

5Then David said to the young man
who brought him the report, "How do
you know that Saul and his son Jonathan are dead?"

6"I happened to be on Mount Gilboa,"
the young man said, "and there was Saul,
leaning on his spear, with the chariots
and their drivers in hot pursuit. 7When he
turned around and saw me, he called out
to me, and I said, 'What can I do?'

8"He asked me, 'Who are you?'

"'An Amalekite,' I answered.

9"Then he said to me, 'Stand here
by me and kill me! I'm in the throes of
death, but I'm still alive.'

10"So I stood beside him and killed
him, because I knew that after he had
fallen he could not survive. And I took
the crown that was on his head and the
band on his arm and have brought them
here to my lord."

11Then David and all the men with him
took hold of their clothes and tore them.
12They mourned and wept and fasted till
evening for Saul and his son Jonathan,
and for the army of the LORD and for the
nation of Israel, because they had fallen
by the sword.

13David said to the young man who
brought him the report, "Where are you
from?"

"I am the son of a foreigner, an Amalekite," he answered.

14David asked him, "Why weren't you
afraid to lift your hand to destroy the
LORD's anointed?"

15Then David called one of his men
and said, "Go, strike him down!" So he
struck him down, and he died. 16For David had said to him, "Your blood be on
your own head. Your own mouth testified against you when you said, 'I killed
the LORD's anointed.'"

David's Lament for Saul and Jonathan

17David took up this lament concerning Saul and his son Jonathan, 18and
he ordered that the people of Judah be
taught this lament of the bow (it is written in the Book of Jashar):

19 "A gazelle[a] lies slain on your heights, Israel.
How the mighty have fallen!

20 "Tell it not in Gath,
proclaim it not in the streets of Ashkelon,
lest the daughters of the Philistines be glad,
lest the daughters of the uncircumcised rejoice.

21 "Mountains of Gilboa,
may you have neither dew nor rain,
may no showers fall on your terraced fields.[b]
For there the shield of the mighty was despised,
the shield of Saul — no longer rubbed with oil.

22 "From the blood of the slain,
from the flesh of the mighty,
the bow of Jonathan did not turn back,
the sword of Saul did not return unsatisfied.
23 Saul and Jonathan —
in life they were loved and admired,
and in death they were not parted.
They were swifter than eagles,
they were stronger than lions.

24 "Daughters of Israel,
weep for Saul,
who clothed you in scarlet and finery,
who adorned your garments with ornaments of gold.

[a] 19 *Gazelle* here symbolizes a human dignitary.
[b] 21 Or / *nor fields that yield grain for offerings*

25 "How the mighty have fallen in
battle!
Jonathan lies slain on your
heights.
26 I grieve for you, Jonathan my
brother;
you were very dear to me.
Your love for me was wonderful,
more wonderful than that of
women.

27 "How the mighty have fallen!
The weapons of war have
perished!"

David Anointed King Over Judah

2 In the course of time, David inquired
of the LORD. "Shall I go up to one of
the towns of Judah?" he asked.
The LORD said, "Go up."
David asked, "Where shall I go?"
"To Hebron," the LORD answered.
2So David went up there with his two
wives, Ahinoam of Jezreel and Abigail,
the widow of Nabal of Carmel. 3David also
took the men who were with him, each
with his family, and they settled in Hebron
and its towns. 4Then the men of Judah
came to Hebron, and there they anointed
David king over the tribe of Judah.
When David was told that it was the
men from Jabesh Gilead who had buried
Saul, 5he sent messengers to them to say
to them, "The LORD bless you for showing this kindness to Saul your master by
burying him. 6May the LORD now show
you kindness and faithfulness, and I too
will show you the same favor because
you have done this. 7Now then, be strong
and brave, for Saul your master is dead,
and the people of Judah have anointed
me king over them."

War Between the Houses of David and Saul

8Meanwhile, Abner son of Ner, the
commander of Saul's army, had taken
Ish-Bosheth son of Saul and brought him
over to Mahanaim. 9He made him king
over Gilead, Ashuri and Jezreel, and also
over Ephraim, Benjamin and all Israel.
10Ish-Bosheth son of Saul was forty
years old when he became king over Israel, and he reigned two years. The tribe
of Judah, however, remained loyal to
David. 11The length of time David was
king in Hebron over Judah was seven
years and six months.
12Abner son of Ner, together with the
men of Ish-Bosheth son of Saul, left Mahanaim and went to Gibeon. 13Joab son
of Zeruiah and David's men went out
and met them at the pool of Gibeon. One
group sat down on one side of the pool
and one group on the other side.
14Then Abner said to Joab, "Let's have
some of the young men get up and fight
hand to hand in front of us."
"All right, let them do it," Joab said.
15So they stood up and were counted off — twelve men for Benjamin and
Ish-Bosheth son of Saul, and twelve for
David. 16Then each man grabbed his opponent by the head and thrust his dagger into his opponent's side, and they fell
down together. So that place in Gibeon
was called Helkath Hazzurim.[a]
17The battle that day was very fierce,
and Abner and the Israelites were defeated by David's men.
18The three sons of Zeruiah were there:
Joab, Abishai and Asahel. Now Asahel
was as fleet-footed as a wild gazelle.
19He chased Abner, turning neither to the
right nor to the left as he pursued him.
20Abner looked behind him and asked,
"Is that you, Asahel?"
"It is," he answered.
21Then Abner said to him, "Turn aside
to the right or to the left; take on one
of the young men and strip him of his
weapons." But Asahel would not stop
chasing him.
22Again Abner warned Asahel, "Stop
chasing me! Why should I strike you
down? How could I look your brother
Joab in the face?"
23But Asahel refused to give up the
pursuit; so Abner thrust the butt of his
spear into Asahel's stomach, and the
spear came out through his back. He fell
there and died on the spot. And every
man stopped when he came to the place
where Asahel had fallen and died.
24But Joab and Abishai pursued Abner,
and as the sun was setting, they came to
the hill of Ammah, near Giah on the way
to the wasteland of Gibeon. 25Then the
men of Benjamin rallied behind Abner.
They formed themselves into a group
and took their stand on top of a hill.
26Abner called out to Joab, "Must the
sword devour forever? Don't you realize
that this will end in bitterness? How long
before you order your men to stop pursuing their fellow Israelites?"
27Joab answered, "As surely as God
lives, if you had not spoken, the men
would have continued pursuing them
until morning."

[a] 16 *Helkath Hazzurim* means *field of daggers* or *field of hostilities.*

28 So Joab blew the trumpet, and all
the troops came to a halt; they no longer pursued Israel, nor did they fight
anymore.
29 All that night Abner and his men
marched through the Arabah. They
crossed the Jordan, continued through
the morning hours[a] and came to Mahanaim.
30 Then Joab stopped pursuing Abner
and assembled the whole army. Besides
Asahel, nineteen of David's men were
found missing. 31 But David's men had
killed three hundred and sixty Benjamites who were with Abner. 32 They took
Asahel and buried him in his father's
tomb at Bethlehem. Then Joab and his
men marched all night and arrived at
Hebron by daybreak.

3 The war between the house of Saul
and the house of David lasted a long
time. David grew stronger and stronger,
while the house of Saul grew weaker and
weaker.

2 Sons were born to David in Hebron:
His firstborn was Amnon the son
of Ahinoam of Jezreel;
3 his second, Kileab the son of Abigail the widow of Nabal of Carmel;
the third, Absalom the son of Maakah daughter of Talmai king of
Geshur;
4 the fourth, Adonijah the son of
Haggith;
the fifth, Shephatiah the son of
Abital;
5 and the sixth, Ithream the son of
David's wife Eglah.
These were born to David in Hebron.

Abner Goes Over to David

6 During the war between the house of
Saul and the house of David, Abner had
been strengthening his own position in
the house of Saul. 7 Now Saul had had
a concubine named Rizpah daughter
of Aiah. And Ish-Bosheth said to Abner,
"Why did you sleep with my father's concubine?"
8 Abner was very angry because of
what Ish-Bosheth said. So he answered,
"Am I a dog's head — on Judah's side?
This very day I am loyal to the house of
your father Saul and to his family and
friends. I haven't handed you over to
David. Yet now you accuse me of an offense involving this woman! 9 May God
deal with Abner, be it ever so severely,
if I do not do for David what the LORD
promised him on oath 10 and transfer the
kingdom from the house of Saul and establish David's throne over Israel and
Judah from Dan to Beersheba." 11 Ish-
Bosheth did not dare to say another word
to Abner, because he was afraid of him.
12 Then Abner sent messengers on his
behalf to say to David, "Whose land is it?
Make an agreement with me, and I will
help you bring all Israel over to you."
13 "Good," said David. "I will make an
agreement with you. But I demand one
thing of you: Do not come into my presence unless you bring Michal daughter
of Saul when you come to see me." 14 Then
David sent messengers to Ish-Bosheth
son of Saul, demanding, "Give me my
wife Michal, whom I betrothed to myself for the price of a hundred Philistine
foreskins."
15 So Ish-Bosheth gave orders and had
her taken away from her husband Paltiel son of Laish. 16 Her husband, however,
went with her, weeping behind her all
the way to Bahurim. Then Abner said to
him, "Go back home!" So he went back.
17 Abner conferred with the elders of Israel and said, "For some time you have
wanted to make David your king. 18 Now
do it! For the LORD promised David, 'By
my servant David I will rescue my people
Israel from the hand of the Philistines
and from the hand of all their enemies.'"
19 Abner also spoke to the Benjamites
in person. Then he went to Hebron to
tell David everything that Israel and
the whole tribe of Benjamin wanted to
do. 20 When Abner, who had twenty men
with him, came to David at Hebron, David prepared a feast for him and his men.
21 Then Abner said to David, "Let me go at
once and assemble all Israel for my lord
the king, so that they may make a covenant with you, and that you may rule
over all that your heart desires." So David
sent Abner away, and he went in peace.

Joab Murders Abner

22 Just then David's men and Joab returned from a raid and brought with
them a great deal of plunder. But Abner was no longer with David in Hebron,
because David had sent him away, and
he had gone in peace. 23 When Joab and
all the soldiers with him arrived, he was
told that Abner son of Ner had come to
the king and that the king had sent him
away and that he had gone in peace.
24 So Joab went to the king and said,
"What have you done? Look, Abner came

[a] *29* See Septuagint; the meaning of the Hebrew for this phrase is uncertain.

to you. Why did you let him go? Now he is gone! 25You know Abner son of Ner; he came to deceive you and observe your movements and find out everything you are doing."

26Joab then left David and sent messengers after Abner, and they brought him back from the cistern at Sirah. But David did not know it. 27Now when Abner returned to Hebron, Joab took him aside into an inner chamber, as if to speak with him privately. And there, to avenge the blood of his brother Asahel, Joab stabbed him in the stomach, and he died.

28Later, when David heard about this, he said, "I and my kingdom are forever innocent before the LORD concerning the blood of Abner son of Ner. 29May his blood fall on the head of Joab and on his whole family! May Joab's family never be without someone who has a running sore or leprosy[a] or who leans on a crutch or who falls by the sword or who lacks food."

30(Joab and his brother Abishai murdered Abner because he had killed their brother Asahel in the battle at Gibeon.)

31Then David said to Joab and all the people with him, "Tear your clothes and put on sackcloth and walk in mourning in front of Abner." King David himself walked behind the bier. 32They buried Abner in Hebron, and the king wept aloud at Abner's tomb. All the people wept also.

33The king sang this lament for Abner:

"Should Abner have died as the
lawless die?
34 Your hands were not bound,
your feet were not fettered.
You fell as one falls before the
wicked."

And all the people wept over him again.

35Then they all came and urged David to eat something while it was still day; but David took an oath, saying, "May God deal with me, be it ever so severely, if I taste bread or anything else before the sun sets!"

36All the people took note and were pleased; indeed, everything the king did pleased them. 37So on that day all the people there and all Israel knew that the king had no part in the murder of Abner son of Ner.

38Then the king said to his men, "Do you not realize that a commander and a great man has fallen in Israel this day? 39And today, though I am the anointed king, I am weak, and these sons of Zeruiah are too strong for me. May the LORD repay the evildoer according to his evil deeds!"

Ish-Bosheth Murdered

4 When Ish-Bosheth son of Saul heard that Abner had died in Hebron, he lost courage, and all Israel became alarmed. 2Now Saul's son had two men who were leaders of raiding bands. One was named Baanah and the other Rekab; they were sons of Rimmon the Beerothite from the tribe of Benjamin—Beeroth is considered part of Benjamin, 3because the people of Beeroth fled to Gittaim and have resided there as foreigners to this day.

4(Jonathan son of Saul had a son who was lame in both feet. He was five years old when the news about Saul and Jonathan came from Jezreel. His nurse picked him up and fled, but as she hurried to leave, he fell and became disabled. His name was Mephibosheth.)

5Now Rekab and Baanah, the sons of Rimmon the Beerothite, set out for the house of Ish-Bosheth, and they arrived there in the heat of the day while he was taking his noonday rest. 6They went into the inner part of the house as if to get some wheat, and they stabbed him in the stomach. Then Rekab and his brother Baanah slipped away.

7They had gone into the house while he was lying on the bed in his bedroom. After they stabbed and killed him, they cut off his head. Taking it with them, they traveled all night by way of the Arabah. 8They brought the head of Ish-Bosheth to David at Hebron and said to the king, "Here is the head of Ish-Bosheth son of Saul, your enemy, who tried to kill you. This day the LORD has avenged my lord the king against Saul and his offspring."

9David answered Rekab and his brother Baanah, the sons of Rimmon the Beerothite, "As surely as the LORD lives, who has delivered me out of every trouble, 10when someone told me, 'Saul is dead,' and thought he was bringing good news, I seized him and put him to death in Ziklag. That was the reward I gave him for his news! 11How much more—when wicked men have killed an innocent man in his own house and on his own bed—should I not now demand his blood from your hand and rid the earth of you!"

[a] 29 The Hebrew for *leprosy* was used for various diseases affecting the skin.

12 So David gave an order to his men, and they killed them. They cut off their hands and feet and hung the bodies by the pool in Hebron. But they took the head of Ish-Bosheth and buried it in Abner's tomb at Hebron.

David Becomes King Over Israel

5 All the tribes of Israel came to David at Hebron and said, "We are your own flesh and blood. 2 In the past, while Saul was king over us, you were the one who led Israel on their military campaigns. And the LORD said to you, 'You will shepherd my people Israel, and you will become their ruler.' "

3 When all the elders of Israel had come to King David at Hebron, the king made a covenant with them at Hebron before the LORD, and they anointed David king over Israel.

4 David was thirty years old when he became king, and he reigned forty years. 5 In Hebron he reigned over Judah seven years and six months, and in Jerusalem he reigned over all Israel and Judah thirty-three years.

David Conquers Jerusalem

6 The king and his men marched to Jerusalem to attack the Jebusites, who lived there. The Jebusites said to David, "You will not get in here; even the blind and the lame can ward you off." They thought, "David cannot get in here." 7 Nevertheless, David captured the fortress of Zion — which is the City of David.

8 On that day David had said, "Anyone who conquers the Jebusites will have to use the water shaft to reach those 'lame and blind' who are David's enemies.[a]" That is why they say, "The 'blind and lame' will not enter the palace."

9 David then took up residence in the fortress and called it the City of David. He built up the area around it, from the terraces[b] inward. 10 And he became more and more powerful, because the LORD God Almighty was with him.

11 Now Hiram king of Tyre sent envoys to David, along with cedar logs and carpenters and stonemasons, and they built a palace for David. 12 Then David knew that the LORD had established him as king over Israel and had exalted his kingdom for the sake of his people Israel.

13 After he left Hebron, David took more concubines and wives in Jerusalem, and more sons and daughters were born to him. 14 These are the names of the children born to him there: Shammua, Shobab, Nathan, Solomon, 15 Ibhar, Elishua, Nepheg, Japhia, 16 Elishama, Eliada and Eliphelet.

David Defeats the Philistines

17 When the Philistines heard that David had been anointed king over Israel, they went up in full force to search for him, but David heard about it and went down to the stronghold. 18 Now the Philistines had come and spread out in the Valley of Rephaim; 19 so David inquired of the LORD, "Shall I go and attack the Philistines? Will you deliver them into my hands?"

The LORD answered him, "Go, for I will surely deliver the Philistines into your hands."

20 So David went to Baal Perazim, and there he defeated them. He said, "As waters break out, the LORD has broken out against my enemies before me." So that place was called Baal Perazim.[c] 21 The Philistines abandoned their idols there, and David and his men carried them off.

22 Once more the Philistines came up and spread out in the Valley of Rephaim; 23 so David inquired of the LORD, and he answered, "Do not go straight up, but circle around behind them and attack them in front of the poplar trees. 24 As soon as you hear the sound of marching in the tops of the poplar trees, move quickly, because that will mean the LORD has gone out in front of you to strike the Philistine army." 25 So David did as the LORD commanded him, and he struck down the Philistines all the way from Gibeon[d] to Gezer.

The Ark Brought to Jerusalem

6 David again brought together all the able young men of Israel — thirty thousand. 2 He and all his men went to Baalah[e] in Judah to bring up from there the ark of God, which is called by the Name,[f] the name of the LORD Almighty, who is enthroned between the cherubim on the ark. 3 They set the ark of God on a new cart and brought it from the house of Abinadab, which was on the hill. Uzzah and Ahio, sons of Abinadab, were guiding the new cart 4 with the ark of

[a] 8 Or *are hated by David* [b] 9 Or *the Millo* [c] 20 *Baal Perazim* means *the lord who breaks out.* [d] 25 Septuagint (see also 1 Chron. 14:16); Hebrew *Geba* [e] 2 That is, Kiriath Jearim (see 1 Chron. 13:6) [f] 2 Hebrew; Septuagint and Vulgate do not have *the Name.*

God on it,[a] and Ahio was walking in front
of it. 5David and all Israel were celebrating with all their might before the LORD,
with castanets,[b] harps, lyres, timbrels,
sistrums and cymbals.
6When they came to the threshing
floor of Nakon, Uzzah reached out and
took hold of the ark of God, because the
oxen stumbled. 7The LORD's anger burned
against Uzzah because of his irreverent
act; therefore God struck him down, and
he died there beside the ark of God.
8Then David was angry because the
LORD's wrath had broken out against Uzzah, and to this day that place is called
Perez Uzzah.[c]
9David was afraid of the LORD that day
and said, "How can the ark of the LORD
ever come to me?" 10He was not willing
to take the ark of the LORD to be with
him in the City of David. Instead, he took
it to the house of Obed-Edom the Gittite.
11The ark of the LORD remained in the
house of Obed-Edom the Gittite for three
months, and the LORD blessed him and
his entire household.
12Now King David was told, "The LORD
has blessed the household of Obed-Edom
and everything he has, because of the
ark of God." So David went to bring up
the ark of God from the house of Obed-
Edom to the City of David with rejoicing.
13When those who were carrying the ark
of the LORD had taken six steps, he sacrificed a bull and a fattened calf. 14Wear-
ing a linen ephod, David was dancing
before the LORD with all his might,
15while he and all Israel were bringing
up the ark of the LORD with shouts and
the sound of trumpets.
16As the ark of the LORD was entering
the City of David, Michal daughter of
Saul watched from a window. And when
she saw King David leaping and dancing before the LORD, she despised him in
her heart.
17They brought the ark of the LORD
and set it in its place inside the tent that
David had pitched for it, and David sacrificed burnt offerings and fellowship
offerings before the LORD. 18After he had
finished sacrificing the burnt offerings
and fellowship offerings, he blessed
the people in the name of the LORD Almighty. 19Then he gave a loaf of bread,
a cake of dates and a cake of raisins to
each person in the whole crowd of Israelites, both men and women. And all the
people went to their homes.
20When David returned home to bless
his household, Michal daughter of Saul
came out to meet him and said, "How
the king of Israel has distinguished himself today, going around half-naked in
full view of the slave girls of his servants
as any vulgar fellow would!"
21David said to Michal, "It was before
the LORD, who chose me rather than your
father or anyone from his house when he
appointed me ruler over the LORD's people Israel — I will celebrate before the
LORD. 22I will become even more undig-
nified than this, and I will be humiliated
in my own eyes. But by these slave girls
you spoke of, I will be held in honor."
23And Michal daughter of Saul had no
children to the day of her death.

God's Promise to David

7 After the king was settled in his palace and the LORD had given him rest
from all his enemies around him, 2he
said to Nathan the prophet, "Here I am,
living in a house of cedar, while the ark
of God remains in a tent."
3Nathan replied to the king, "Whatever you have in mind, go ahead and do it,
for the LORD is with you."
4But that night the word of the LORD
came to Nathan, saying:

> 5"Go and tell my servant David,
> 'This is what the LORD says: Are you
> the one to build me a house to dwell
> in? 6I have not dwelt in a house from
> the day I brought the Israelites up
> out of Egypt to this day. I have been
> moving from place to place with a
> tent as my dwelling. 7Wherever I
> have moved with all the Israelites,
> did I ever say to any of their rulers
> whom I commanded to shepherd
> my people Israel, "Why have you not
> built me a house of cedar?"'
> 8"Now then, tell my servant
> David, 'This is what the LORD Al-
> mighty says: I took you from the
> pasture, from tending the flock,
> and appointed you ruler over my
> people Israel. 9I have been with
> you wherever you have gone, and I
> have cut off all your enemies from
> before you. Now I will make your
> name great, like the names of the
> greatest men on earth. 10And I will

[a] 3,4 Dead Sea Scrolls and some Septuagint manuscripts; Masoretic Text *cart* [4]*and they brought it with the ark of God from the house of Abinadab, which was on the hill* [b] 5 Masoretic Text; Dead Sea Scrolls and Septuagint (see also 1 Chron. 13:8) *songs* [c] 8 *Perez Uzzah* means *outbreak against Uzzah.*

provide a place for my people Israel and will plant them so that they
can have a home of their own and
no longer be disturbed. Wicked people will not oppress them anymore,
as they did at the beginning 11and
have done ever since the time I appointed leaders[a] over my people Israel. I will also give you rest from all
your enemies.
"'The LORD declares to you that
the LORD himself will establish a
house for you: 12When your days are
over and you rest with your ancestors, I will raise up your offspring
to succeed you, your own flesh and
blood, and I will establish his kingdom. 13He is the one who will build
a house for my Name, and I will establish the throne of his kingdom
forever. 14I will be his father, and
he will be my son. When he does
wrong, I will punish him with a rod
wielded by men, with floggings inflicted by human hands. 15But my
love will never be taken away from
him, as I took it away from Saul,
whom I removed from before you.
16Your house and your kingdom will
endure forever before me[b]; your
throne will be established forever.'"

17Nathan reported to David all the
words of this entire revelation.

David's Prayer

18Then King David went in and sat before the LORD, and he said:

"Who am I, Sovereign LORD, and
what is my family, that you have
brought me this far? 19And as if this
were not enough in your sight, Sovereign LORD, you have also spoken
about the future of the house of
your servant — and this decree, Sovereign LORD, is for a mere human![c]
20"What more can David say to
you? For you know your servant,
Sovereign LORD. 21For the sake of
your word and according to your
will, you have done this great thing
and made it known to your servant.
22"How great you are, Sovereign
LORD! There is no one like you, and
there is no God but you, as we have
heard with our own ears. 23And who
is like your people Israel — the one
nation on earth that God went out
to redeem as a people for himself,
and to make a name for himself,
and to perform great and awesome
wonders by driving out nations and
their gods from before your people,
whom you redeemed from Egypt?[d]
24You have established your people
Israel as your very own forever, and
you, LORD, have become their God.
25"And now, LORD God, keep forever the promise you have made concerning your servant and his house.
Do as you promised, 26so that your
name will be great forever. Then
people will say, 'The LORD Almighty
is God over Israel!' And the house of
your servant David will be established in your sight.
27"LORD Almighty, God of Israel,
you have revealed this to your servant, saying, 'I will build a house
for you.' So your servant has found
courage to pray this prayer to you.
28Sovereign LORD, you are God! Your
covenant is trustworthy, and you
have promised these good things
to your servant. 29Now be pleased
to bless the house of your servant,
that it may continue forever in your
sight; for you, Sovereign LORD, have
spoken, and with your blessing
the house of your servant will be
blessed forever."

David's Victories

8 In the course of time, David defeated the Philistines and subdued them,
and he took Metheg Ammah from the
control of the Philistines.
2David also defeated the Moabites. He
made them lie down on the ground and
measured them off with a length of cord.
Every two lengths of them were put to
death, and the third length was allowed
to live. So the Moabites became subject
to David and brought him tribute.
3Moreover, David defeated Hadadezer son of Rehob, king of Zobah, when
he went to restore his monument at[e]
the Euphrates River. 4David captured
a thousand of his chariots, seven thousand charioteers[f] and twenty thousand
foot soldiers. He hamstrung all but a
hundred of the chariot horses.

[a] 11 Traditionally *judges* [b] 16 Some Hebrew manuscripts and Septuagint; most Hebrew manuscripts *you* [c] 19 Or *for the human race* [d] 23 See Septuagint and 1 Chron. 17:21; Hebrew *wonders for your land and before your people, whom you redeemed from Egypt, from the nations and their gods.* [e] 3 Or *his control along* [f] 4 Septuagint (see also Dead Sea Scrolls and 1 Chron. 18:4); Masoretic Text *captured seventeen hundred of his charioteers*

5When the Arameans of Damascus
came to help Hadadezer king of Zobah,
David struck down twenty-two thousand
of them. 6He put garrisons in the Aramean kingdom of Damascus, and the
Arameans became subject to him and
brought tribute. The LORD gave David
victory wherever he went.
7David took the gold shields that belonged to the officers of Hadadezer and
brought them to Jerusalem. 8From Tebah[a] and Berothai, towns that belonged
to Hadadezer, King David took a great
quantity of bronze.
9When Tou[b] king of Hamath heard
that David had defeated the entire army
of Hadadezer, 10he sent his son Joram[c]
to King David to greet him and congratulate him on his victory in battle over
Hadadezer, who had been at war with
Tou. Joram brought with him articles of
silver, of gold and of bronze.
11King David dedicated these articles to
the LORD, as he had done with the silver
and gold from all the nations he had subdued: 12Edom[d] and Moab, the Ammonites
and the Philistines, and Amalek. He also
dedicated the plunder taken from Hadadezer son of Rehob, king of Zobah.
13And David became famous after he
returned from striking down eighteen
thousand Edomites[e] in the Valley of Salt.
14He put garrisons throughout Edom,
and all the Edomites became subject
to David. The LORD gave David victory
wherever he went.

David's Officials

15David reigned over all Israel, doing
what was just and right for all his people. 16Joab son of Zeruiah was over the
army; Jehoshaphat son of Ahilud was recorder; 17Zadok son of Ahitub and Ahimelek son of Abiathar were priests; Seraiah
was secretary; 18Benaiah son of Jehoiada
was over the Kerethites and Pelethites;
and David's sons were priests.[f]

David and Mephibosheth

9 David asked, "Is there anyone still
left of the house of Saul to whom I
can show kindness for Jonathan's sake?"
2Now there was a servant of Saul's
household named Ziba. They summoned
him to appear before David, and the
king said to him, "Are you Ziba?"
"At your service," he replied.
3The king asked, "Is there no one still
alive from the house of Saul to whom I
can show God's kindness?"
Ziba answered the king, "There is still
a son of Jonathan; he is lame in both
feet."
4"Where is he?" the king asked.
Ziba answered, "He is at the house of
Makir son of Ammiel in Lo Debar."
5So King David had him brought from
Lo Debar, from the house of Makir son
of Ammiel.
6When Mephibosheth son of Jonathan, the son of Saul, came to David, he
bowed down to pay him honor.
David said, "Mephibosheth!"
"At your service," he replied.
7"Don't be afraid," David said to him,
"for I will surely show you kindness for
the sake of your father Jonathan. I will
restore to you all the land that belonged
to your grandfather Saul, and you will
always eat at my table."
8Mephibosheth bowed down and said,
"What is your servant, that you should
notice a dead dog like me?"
9Then the king summoned Ziba, Saul's
steward, and said to him, "I have given
your master's grandson everything that
belonged to Saul and his family. 10You
and your sons and your servants are to
farm the land for him and bring in the
crops, so that your master's grandson
may be provided for. And Mephibosheth,
grandson of your master, will always eat
at my table." (Now Ziba had fifteen sons
and twenty servants.)
11Then Ziba said to the king, "Your servant will do whatever my lord the king
commands his servant to do." So Mephibosheth ate at David's[g] table like one
of the king's sons.
12Mephibosheth had a young son
named Mika, and all the members of
Ziba's household were servants of Mephibosheth. 13And Mephibosheth lived in
Jerusalem, because he always ate at the
king's table; he was lame in both feet.

David Defeats the Ammonites

10 In the course of time, the king of
the Ammonites died, and his son
Hanun succeeded him as king. 2David
thought, "I will show kindness to Hanun

[a] *8* See some Septuagint manuscripts (see also 1 Chron. 18:8); Hebrew *Betah.* [b] *9* Hebrew *Toi,* a variant of *Tou;* also in verse 10 [c] *10* A variant of *Hadoram* [d] *12* Some Hebrew manuscripts, Septuagint and Syriac (see also 1 Chron. 18:11); most Hebrew manuscripts *Aram* [e] *13* A few Hebrew manuscripts, Septuagint and Syriac (see also 1 Chron. 18:12); most Hebrew manuscripts *Aram* (that is, Arameans) [f] *18* Or *were chief officials* (see Septuagint and Targum; see also 1 Chron. 18:17) [g] *11* Septuagint; Hebrew *my*

son of Nahash, just as his father showed kindness to me." So David sent a delegation to express his sympathy to Hanun concerning his father.

When David's men came to the land of the Ammonites, 3the Ammonite commanders said to Hanun their lord, "Do you think David is honoring your father by sending envoys to you to express sympathy? Hasn't David sent them to you only to explore the city and spy it out and overthrow it?" 4So Hanun seized David's envoys, shaved off half of each man's beard, cut off their garments at the buttocks, and sent them away.

5When David was told about this, he sent messengers to meet the men, for they were greatly humiliated. The king said, "Stay at Jericho till your beards have grown, and then come back."

6When the Ammonites realized that they had become obnoxious to David, they hired twenty thousand Aramean foot soldiers from Beth Rehob and Zobah, as well as the king of Maakah with a thousand men, and also twelve thousand men from Tob.

7On hearing this, David sent Joab out with the entire army of fighting men. 8The Ammonites came out and drew up in battle formation at the entrance of their city gate, while the Arameans of Zobah and Rehob and the men of Tob and Maakah were by themselves in the open country.

9Joab saw that there were battle lines in front of him and behind him; so he selected some of the best troops in Israel and deployed them against the Arameans. 10He put the rest of the men under the command of Abishai his brother and deployed them against the Ammonites. 11Joab said, "If the Arameans are too strong for me, then you are to come to my rescue; but if the Ammonites are too strong for you, then I will come to rescue you. 12Be strong, and let us fight bravely for our people and the cities of our God. The LORD will do what is good in his sight."

13Then Joab and the troops with him advanced to fight the Arameans, and they fled before him. 14When the Ammonites realized that the Arameans were fleeing, they fled before Abishai and went inside the city. So Joab returned from fighting the Ammonites and came to Jerusalem.

15After the Arameans saw that they had been routed by Israel, they regrouped. 16Hadadezer had Arameans brought from beyond the Euphrates River; they went to Helam, with Shobak the commander of Hadadezer's army leading them.

17When David was told of this, he gathered all Israel, crossed the Jordan and went to Helam. The Arameans formed their battle lines to meet David and fought against him. 18But they fled before Israel, and David killed seven hundred of their charioteers and forty thousand of their foot soldiers.[a] He also struck down Shobak the commander of their army, and he died there. 19When all the kings who were vassals of Hadadezer saw that they had been routed by Israel, they made peace with the Israelites and became subject to them.

So the Arameans were afraid to help the Ammonites anymore.

David and Bathsheba

11 In the spring, at the time when kings go off to war, David sent Joab out with the king's men and the whole Israelite army. They destroyed the Ammonites and besieged Rabbah. But David remained in Jerusalem.

2One evening David got up from his bed and walked around on the roof of the palace. From the roof he saw a woman bathing. The woman was very beautiful, 3and David sent someone to find out about her. The man said, "She is Bathsheba, the daughter of Eliam and the wife of Uriah the Hittite." 4Then David sent messengers to get her. She came to him, and he slept with her. (Now she was purifying herself from her monthly uncleanness.) Then she went back home. 5The woman conceived and sent word to David, saying, "I am pregnant."

6So David sent this word to Joab: "Send me Uriah the Hittite." And Joab sent him to David. 7When Uriah came to him, David asked him how Joab was, how the soldiers were and how the war was going. 8Then David said to Uriah, "Go down to your house and wash your feet." So Uriah left the palace, and a gift from the king was sent after him. 9But Uriah slept at the entrance to the palace with all his master's servants and did not go down to his house.

10David was told, "Uriah did not go home." So he asked Uriah, "Haven't you just come from a military campaign? Why didn't you go home?"

[a] *18* Some Septuagint manuscripts (see also 1 Chron. 19:18); Hebrew *horsemen*

11Uriah said to David, "The ark and Israel and Judah are staying in tents,[a] and my commander Joab and my lord's men are camped in the open country. How could I go to my house to eat and drink and make love to my wife? As surely as you live, I will not do such a thing!"

12Then David said to him, "Stay here one more day, and tomorrow I will send you back." So Uriah remained in Jerusalem that day and the next. 13At David's invitation, he ate and drank with him, and David made him drunk. But in the evening Uriah went out to sleep on his mat among his master's servants; he did not go home.

14In the morning David wrote a letter to Joab and sent it with Uriah. 15In it he wrote, "Put Uriah out in front where the fighting is fiercest. Then withdraw from him so he will be struck down and die."

16So while Joab had the city under siege, he put Uriah at a place where he knew the strongest defenders were. 17When the men of the city came out and fought against Joab, some of the men in David's army fell; moreover, Uriah the Hittite died.

18Joab sent David a full account of the battle. 19He instructed the messenger: "When you have finished giving the king this account of the battle, 20the king's anger may flare up, and he may ask you, 'Why did you get so close to the city to fight? Didn't you know they would shoot arrows from the wall? 21Who killed Abimelek son of Jerub-Besheth[b]? Didn't a woman drop an upper millstone on him from the wall, so that he died in Thebez? Why did you get so close to the wall?' If he asks you this, then say to him, 'Moreover, your servant Uriah the Hittite is dead.'"

22The messenger set out, and when he arrived he told David everything Joab had sent him to say. 23The messenger said to David, "The men overpowered us and came out against us in the open, but we drove them back to the entrance of the city gate. 24Then the archers shot arrows at your servants from the wall, and some of the king's men died. Moreover, your servant Uriah the Hittite is dead."

25David told the messenger, "Say this to Joab: 'Don't let this upset you; the sword devours one as well as another. Press the attack against the city and destroy it.' Say this to encourage Joab."

26When Uriah's wife heard that her husband was dead, she mourned for him. 27After the time of mourning was over, David had her brought to his house, and she became his wife and bore him a son. But the thing David had done displeased the LORD.

Nathan Rebukes David

12 The LORD sent Nathan to David. When he came to him, he said, "There were two men in a certain town, one rich and the other poor. 2The rich man had a very large number of sheep and cattle, 3but the poor man had nothing except one little ewe lamb he had bought. He raised it, and it grew up with him and his children. It shared his food, drank from his cup and even slept in his arms. It was like a daughter to him.

4"Now a traveler came to the rich man, but the rich man refrained from taking one of his own sheep or cattle to prepare a meal for the traveler who had come to him. Instead, he took the ewe lamb that belonged to the poor man and prepared it for the one who had come to him."

5David burned with anger against the man and said to Nathan, "As surely as the LORD lives, the man who did this must die! 6He must pay for that lamb four times over, because he did such a thing and had no pity."

7Then Nathan said to David, "You are the man! This is what the LORD, the God of Israel, says: 'I anointed you king over Israel, and I delivered you from the hand of Saul. 8I gave your master's house to you, and your master's wives into your arms. I gave you all Israel and Judah. And if all this had been too little, I would have given you even more. 9Why did you despise the word of the LORD by doing what is evil in his eyes? You struck down Uriah the Hittite with the sword and took his wife to be your own. You killed him with the sword of the Ammonites. 10Now, therefore, the sword will never depart from your house, because you despised me and took the wife of Uriah the Hittite to be your own.'

11"This is what the LORD says: 'Out of your own household I am going to bring calamity on you. Before your very eyes I will take your wives and give them to one who is close to you, and he will sleep with your wives in broad daylight. 12You did it in secret, but I will do this thing in broad daylight before all Israel.'"

13Then David said to Nathan, "I have sinned against the LORD."

[a] 11 Or *staying at Sukkoth* [b] 21 Also known as *Jerub-Baal* (that is, Gideon)

Nathan replied, "The LORD has taken away your sin. You are not going to die. 14But because by doing this you have shown utter contempt for[a] the LORD, the son born to you will die."

15After Nathan had gone home, the LORD struck the child that Uriah's wife had borne to David, and he became ill. 16David pleaded with God for the child. He fasted and spent the nights lying in sackcloth[b] on the ground. 17The elders of his household stood beside him to get him up from the ground, but he refused, and he would not eat any food with them.

18On the seventh day the child died. David's attendants were afraid to tell him that the child was dead, for they thought, "While the child was still living, he wouldn't listen to us when we spoke to him. How can we now tell him the child is dead? He may do something desperate."

19David noticed that his attendants were whispering among themselves, and he realized the child was dead. "Is the child dead?" he asked.

"Yes," they replied, "he is dead."

20Then David got up from the ground. After he had washed, put on lotions and changed his clothes, he went into the house of the LORD and worshiped. Then he went to his own house, and at his request they served him food, and he ate.

21His attendants asked him, "Why are you acting this way? While the child was alive, you fasted and wept, but now that the child is dead, you get up and eat!"

22He answered, "While the child was still alive, I fasted and wept. I thought, 'Who knows? The LORD may be gracious to me and let the child live.' 23But now that he is dead, why should I go on fasting? Can I bring him back again? I will go to him, but he will not return to me."

24Then David comforted his wife Bathsheba, and he went to her and made love to her. She gave birth to a son, and they named him Solomon. The LORD loved him; 25and because the LORD loved him, he sent word through Nathan the prophet to name him Jedidiah.[c]

26Meanwhile Joab fought against Rabbah of the Ammonites and captured the royal citadel. 27Joab then sent messengers to David, saying, "I have fought against Rabbah and taken its water supply. 28Now muster the rest of the troops and besiege the city and capture it. Otherwise I will take the city, and it will be named after me."

29So David mustered the entire army and went to Rabbah, and attacked and captured it. 30David took the crown from their king's[d] head, and it was placed on his own head. It weighed a talent[e] of gold, and it was set with precious stones. David took a great quantity of plunder from the city 31and brought out the people who were there, consigning them to labor with saws and with iron picks and axes, and he made them work at brickmaking.[f] David did this to all the Ammonite towns. Then he and his entire army returned to Jerusalem.

Amnon and Tamar

13 In the course of time, Amnon son of David fell in love with Tamar, the beautiful sister of Absalom son of David.

2Amnon became so obsessed with his sister Tamar that he made himself ill. She was a virgin, and it seemed impossible for him to do anything to her.

3Now Amnon had an adviser named Jonadab son of Shimeah, David's brother. Jonadab was a very shrewd man. 4He asked Amnon, "Why do you, the king's son, look so haggard morning after morning? Won't you tell me?"

Amnon said to him, "I'm in love with Tamar, my brother Absalom's sister."

5"Go to bed and pretend to be ill," Jonadab said. "When your father comes to see you, say to him, 'I would like my sister Tamar to come and give me something to eat. Let her prepare the food in my sight so I may watch her and then eat it from her hand.'"

6So Amnon lay down and pretended to be ill. When the king came to see him, Amnon said to him, "I would like my sister Tamar to come and make some special bread in my sight, so I may eat from her hand."

7David sent word to Tamar at the palace: "Go to the house of your brother Amnon and prepare some food for him." 8So Tamar went to the house of her brother Amnon, who was lying down. She took some dough, kneaded it, made the bread in his sight and baked it. 9Then she took the pan and served him the bread, but he refused to eat.

[a] *14* An ancient Hebrew scribal tradition; Masoretic Text *for the enemies of* [b] *16* Dead Sea Scrolls and Septuagint; Masoretic Text does not have *in sackcloth.* [c] *25* *Jedidiah* means *loved by the LORD.* [d] *30* Or *from Milkom's* (that is, Molek's) [e] *30* That is, about 75 pounds or about 34 kilograms [f] *31* The meaning of the Hebrew for this clause is uncertain.

"Send everyone out of here," Amnon said. So everyone left him. 10Then
Amnon said to Tamar, "Bring the food
here into my bedroom so I may eat
from your hand." And Tamar took the
bread she had prepared and brought it
to her brother Amnon in his bedroom.
11But when she took it to him to eat, he
grabbed her and said, "Come to bed with
me, my sister."

12"No, my brother!" she said to him.
"Don't force me! Such a thing should not
be done in Israel! Don't do this wicked
thing. 13What about me? Where could I get
rid of my disgrace? And what about you?
You would be like one of the wicked fools
in Israel. Please speak to the king; he will
not keep me from being married to you."
14But he refused to listen to her, and since
he was stronger than she, he raped her.

15Then Amnon hated her with intense
hatred. In fact, he hated her more than
he had loved her. Amnon said to her,
"Get up and get out!"

16"No!" she said to him. "Sending me
away would be a greater wrong than
what you have already done to me."

But he refused to listen to her. 17He
called his personal servant and said,
"Get this woman out of my sight and
bolt the door after her." 18So his servant
put her out and bolted the door after her.
She was wearing an ornate[a] robe, for
this was the kind of garment the virgin
daughters of the king wore. 19Tamar put
ashes on her head and tore the ornate
robe she was wearing. She put her hands
on her head and went away, weeping
aloud as she went.

20Her brother Absalom said to her,
"Has that Amnon, your brother, been
with you? Be quiet for now, my sister; he
is your brother. Don't take this thing to
heart." And Tamar lived in her brother
Absalom's house, a desolate woman.

21When King David heard all this, he
was furious. 22And Absalom never said a
word to Amnon, either good or bad; he
hated Amnon because he had disgraced
his sister Tamar.

Absalom Kills Amnon

23Two years later, when Absalom's
sheepshearers were at Baal Hazor near
the border of Ephraim, he invited all the
king's sons to come there. 24Absalom
went to the king and said, "Your servant
has had shearers come. Will the king and
his attendants please join me?"

25"No, my son," the king replied. "All
of us should not go; we would only be a
burden to you." Although Absalom urged
him, he still refused to go but gave him
his blessing.

26Then Absalom said, "If not, please
let my brother Amnon come with us."

The king asked him, "Why should he
go with you?" 27But Absalom urged him,
so he sent with him Amnon and the rest
of the king's sons.

28Absalom ordered his men, "Listen!
When Amnon is in high spirits from
drinking wine and I say to you, 'Strike
Amnon down,' then kill him. Don't be
afraid. Haven't I given you this order?
Be strong and brave." 29So Absalom's
men did to Amnon what Absalom had
ordered. Then all the king's sons got up,
mounted their mules and fled.

30While they were on their way, the
report came to David: "Absalom has
struck down all the king's sons; not one
of them is left." 31The king stood up, tore
his clothes and lay down on the ground;
and all his attendants stood by with
their clothes torn.

32But Jonadab son of Shimeah, David's
brother, said, "My lord should not think
that they killed all the princes; only Amnon is dead. This has been Absalom's
express intention ever since the day Amnon raped his sister Tamar. 33My lord the
king should not be concerned about the
report that all the king's sons are dead.
Only Amnon is dead."

34Meanwhile, Absalom had fled.

Now the man standing watch looked
up and saw many people on the road
west of him, coming down the side of
the hill. The watchman went and told
the king, "I see men in the direction of
Horonaim, on the side of the hill."[b]

35Jonadab said to the king, "See, the
king's sons have come; it has happened
just as your servant said."

36As he finished speaking, the king's
sons came in, wailing loudly. The king,
too, and all his attendants wept very bitterly.

37Absalom fled and went to Talmai
son of Ammihud, the king of Geshur. But
King David mourned many days for his
son.

38After Absalom fled and went to Geshur, he stayed there three years. 39And
King David longed to go to Absalom, for
he was consoled concerning Amnon's
death.

[a] *18* The meaning of the Hebrew for this word is uncertain; also in verse 19. [b] *34* Septuagint; Hebrew does not have this sentence.

Absalom Returns to Jerusalem

14 Joab son of Zeruiah knew that the
king's heart longed for Absalom.
2So Joab sent someone to Tekoa and had
a wise woman brought from there. He
said to her, "Pretend you are in mourning. Dress in mourning clothes, and
don't use any cosmetic lotions. Act like a
woman who has spent many days grieving for the dead. 3Then go to the king
and speak these words to him." And Joab
put the words in her mouth.
4When the woman from Tekoa went[a]
to the king, she fell with her face to the
ground to pay him honor, and she said,
"Help me, Your Majesty!"
5The king asked her, "What is troubling you?"
She said, "I am a widow; my husband
is dead. 6I your servant had two sons.
They got into a fight with each other in
the field, and no one was there to separate them. One struck the other and killed
him. 7Now the whole clan has risen up
against your servant; they say, 'Hand over
the one who struck his brother down, so
that we may put him to death for the life
of his brother whom he killed; then we
will get rid of the heir as well.' They would
put out the only burning coal I have left,
leaving my husband neither name nor
descendant on the face of the earth."
8The king said to the woman, "Go
home, and I will issue an order in your
behalf."
9But the woman from Tekoa said to
him, "Let my lord the king pardon me
and my family, and let the king and his
throne be without guilt."
10The king replied, "If anyone says
anything to you, bring them to me, and
they will not bother you again."
11She said, "Then let the king invoke
the LORD his God to prevent the avenger
of blood from adding to the destruction,
so that my son will not be destroyed."
"As surely as the LORD lives," he said,
"not one hair of your son's head will fall
to the ground."
12Then the woman said, "Let your servant speak a word to my lord the king."
"Speak," he replied.
13The woman said, "Why then have
you devised a thing like this against the
people of God? When the king says this,
does he not convict himself, for the king
has not brought back his banished son?
14Like water spilled on the ground, which
cannot be recovered, so we must die. But
that is not what God desires; rather, he
devises ways so that a banished person
does not remain banished from him.
15"And now I have come to say this
to my lord the king because the people have made me afraid. Your servant
thought, 'I will speak to the king; perhaps he will grant his servant's request.
16Perhaps the king will agree to deliver
his servant from the hand of the man
who is trying to cut off both me and my
son from God's inheritance.'
17"And now your servant says, 'May the
word of my lord the king secure my inheritance, for my lord the king is like an
angel of God in discerning good and evil.
May the LORD your God be with you.'"
18Then the king said to the woman,
"Don't keep from me the answer to what
I am going to ask you."
"Let my lord the king speak," the
woman said.
19The king asked, "Isn't the hand of
Joab with you in all this?"
The woman answered, "As surely as
you live, my lord the king, no one can
turn to the right or to the left from anything my lord the king says. Yes, it was
your servant Joab who instructed me to
do this and who put all these words into
the mouth of your servant. 20Your servant Joab did this to change the present
situation. My lord has wisdom like that
of an angel of God — he knows everything that happens in the land."
21The king said to Joab, "Very well, I
will do it. Go, bring back the young man
Absalom."
22Joab fell with his face to the ground
to pay him honor, and he blessed the
king. Joab said, "Today your servant
knows that he has found favor in your
eyes, my lord the king, because the king
has granted his servant's request."
23Then Joab went to Geshur and
brought Absalom back to Jerusalem.
24But the king said, "He must go to his
own house; he must not see my face." So
Absalom went to his own house and did
not see the face of the king.
25In all Israel there was not a man
so highly praised for his handsome appearance as Absalom. From the top of
his head to the sole of his foot there was
no blemish in him. 26Whenever he cut
the hair of his head — he used to cut his
hair once a year because it became too
heavy for him — he would weigh it, and
its weight was two hundred shekels[b] by
the royal standard.

[a] 4 Many Hebrew manuscripts, Septuagint, Vulgate and Syriac; most Hebrew manuscripts *spoke*
[b] 26 That is, about 5 pounds or about 2.3 kilograms

27 Three sons and a daughter were
born to Absalom. His daughter's name
was Tamar, and she became a beautiful
woman.
28 Absalom lived two years in Jerusalem without seeing the king's face.
29 Then Absalom sent for Joab in order to
send him to the king, but Joab refused to
come to him. So he sent a second time,
but he refused to come. 30 Then he said
to his servants, "Look, Joab's field is next
to mine, and he has barley there. Go and
set it on fire." So Absalom's servants set
the field on fire.
31 Then Joab did go to Absalom's house,
and he said to him, "Why have your servants set my field on fire?"
32 Absalom said to Joab, "Look, I sent
word to you and said, 'Come here so I
can send you to the king to ask, "Why
have I come from Geshur? It would be
better for me if I were still there!"' Now
then, I want to see the king's face, and if
I am guilty of anything, let him put me
to death."
33 So Joab went to the king and told
him this. Then the king summoned Absalom, and he came in and bowed down
with his face to the ground before the
king. And the king kissed Absalom.

Absalom's Conspiracy

15 In the course of time, Absalom provided himself with a chariot and
horses and with fifty men to run ahead
of him. 2 He would get up early and stand
by the side of the road leading to the
city gate. Whenever anyone came with a
complaint to be placed before the king
for a decision, Absalom would call out
to him, "What town are you from?" He
would answer, "Your servant is from one
of the tribes of Israel." 3 Then Absalom
would say to him, "Look, your claims are
valid and proper, but there is no representative of the king to hear you." 4 And
Absalom would add, "If only I were appointed judge in the land! Then everyone who has a complaint or case could
come to me and I would see that they
receive justice."
5 Also, whenever anyone approached
him to bow down before him, Absalom
would reach out his hand, take hold of
him and kiss him. 6 Absalom behaved
in this way toward all the Israelites who
came to the king asking for justice, and so
he stole the hearts of the people of Israel.
7 At the end of four[a] years, Absalom
said to the king, "Let me go to Hebron
and fulfill a vow I made to the LORD.
8 While your servant was living at Geshur
in Aram, I made this vow: 'If the LORD
takes me back to Jerusalem, I will worship the LORD in Hebron.[b]'"
9 The king said to him, "Go in peace."
So he went to Hebron.
10 Then Absalom sent secret messengers throughout the tribes of Israel to
say, "As soon as you hear the sound of
the trumpets, then say, 'Absalom is king
in Hebron.'" 11 Two hundred men from
Jerusalem had accompanied Absalom.
They had been invited as guests and
went quite innocently, knowing nothing
about the matter. 12 While Absalom was
offering sacrifices, he also sent for Ahithophel the Gilonite, David's counselor, to
come from Giloh, his hometown. And so
the conspiracy gained strength, and Absalom's following kept on increasing.

David Flees

13 A messenger came and told David,
"The hearts of the people of Israel are
with Absalom."
14 Then David said to all his officials
who were with him in Jerusalem, "Come!
We must flee, or none of us will escape
from Absalom. We must leave immediately, or he will move quickly to overtake
us and bring ruin on us and put the city
to the sword."
15 The king's officials answered him,
"Your servants are ready to do whatever
our lord the king chooses."
16 The king set out, with his entire
household following him; but he left ten
concubines to take care of the palace.
17 So the king set out, with all the people
following him, and they halted at the
edge of the city. 18 All his men marched
past him, along with all the Kerethites
and Pelethites; and all the six hundred
Gittites who had accompanied him from
Gath marched before the king.
19 The king said to Ittai the Gittite,
"Why should you come along with us?
Go back and stay with King Absalom.
You are a foreigner, an exile from your
homeland. 20 You came only yesterday.
And today shall I make you wander
about with us, when I do not know where
I am going? Go back, and take your people with you. May the LORD show you
kindness and faithfulness."[c]

[a] 7 Some Septuagint manuscripts, Syriac and Josephus; Hebrew *forty* [b] 8 Some Septuagint manuscripts; Hebrew does not have *in Hebron.* [c] 20 Septuagint; Hebrew *May kindness and faithfulness be with you*

21 But Ittai replied to the king, "As surely as the LORD lives, and as my lord the king lives, wherever my lord the king may be, whether it means life or death, there will your servant be."

22 David said to Ittai, "Go ahead, march on." So Ittai the Gittite marched on with all his men and the families that were with him.

23 The whole countryside wept aloud as all the people passed by. The king also crossed the Kidron Valley, and all the people moved on toward the wilderness.

24 Zadok was there, too, and all the Levites who were with him were carrying the ark of the covenant of God. They set down the ark of God, and Abiathar offered sacrifices until all the people had finished leaving the city.

25 Then the king said to Zadok, "Take the ark of God back into the city. If I find favor in the LORD's eyes, he will bring me back and let me see it and his dwelling place again. 26 But if he says, 'I am not pleased with you,' then I am ready; let him do to me whatever seems good to him."

27 The king also said to Zadok the priest, "Do you understand? Go back to the city with my blessing. Take your son Ahimaaz with you, and also Abiathar's son Jonathan. You and Abiathar return with your two sons. 28 I will wait at the fords in the wilderness until word comes from you to inform me." 29 So Zadok and Abiathar took the ark of God back to Jerusalem and stayed there.

30 But David continued up the Mount of Olives, weeping as he went; his head was covered and he was barefoot. All the people with him covered their heads too and were weeping as they went up. 31 Now David had been told, "Ahithophel is among the conspirators with Absalom." So David prayed, "LORD, turn Ahithophel's counsel into foolishness."

32 When David arrived at the summit, where people used to worship God, Hushai the Arkite was there to meet him, his robe torn and dust on his head. 33 David said to him, "If you go with me, you will be a burden to me. 34 But if you return to the city and say to Absalom, 'Your Majesty, I will be your servant; I was your father's servant in the past, but now I will be your servant,' then you can help me by frustrating Ahithophel's advice. 35 Won't the priests Zadok and Abiathar be there with you? Tell them anything you hear in the king's palace. 36 Their two sons, Ahimaaz son of Zadok and Jonathan son of Abiathar, are there with them. Send them to me with anything you hear."

37 So Hushai, David's confidant, arrived at Jerusalem as Absalom was entering the city.

David and Ziba

16 When David had gone a short distance beyond the summit, there was Ziba, the steward of Mephibosheth, waiting to meet him. He had a string of donkeys saddled and loaded with two hundred loaves of bread, a hundred cakes of raisins, a hundred cakes of figs and a skin of wine.

2 The king asked Ziba, "Why have you brought these?"

Ziba answered, "The donkeys are for the king's household to ride on, the bread and fruit are for the men to eat, and the wine is to refresh those who become exhausted in the wilderness."

3 The king then asked, "Where is your master's grandson?"

Ziba said to him, "He is staying in Jerusalem, because he thinks, 'Today the Israelites will restore to me my grandfather's kingdom.'"

4 Then the king said to Ziba, "All that belonged to Mephibosheth is now yours."

"I humbly bow," Ziba said. "May I find favor in your eyes, my lord the king."

Shimei Curses David

5 As King David approached Bahurim, a man from the same clan as Saul's family came out from there. His name was Shimei son of Gera, and he cursed as he came out. 6 He pelted David and all the king's officials with stones, though all the troops and the special guard were on David's right and left. 7 As he cursed, Shimei said, "Get out, get out, you murderer, you scoundrel! 8 The LORD has repaid you for all the blood you shed in the household of Saul, in whose place you have reigned. The LORD has given the kingdom into the hands of your son Absalom. You have come to ruin because you are a murderer!"

9 Then Abishai son of Zeruiah said to the king, "Why should this dead dog curse my lord the king? Let me go over and cut off his head."

10 But the king said, "What does this have to do with you, you sons of Zeruiah? If he is cursing because the LORD said to him, 'Curse David,' who can ask, 'Why do you do this?'"

11 David then said to Abishai and all his officials, "My son, my own flesh and blood, is trying to kill me. How much

more, then, this Benjamite! Leave him alone; let him curse, for the LORD has told him to. 12It may be that the LORD will look upon my misery and restore to me his covenant blessing instead of his curse today."

13So David and his men continued along the road while Shimei was going along the hillside opposite him, cursing as he went and throwing stones at him and showering him with dirt. 14The king and all the people with him arrived at their destination exhausted. And there he refreshed himself.

The Advice of Ahithophel and Hushai

15Meanwhile, Absalom and all the men of Israel came to Jerusalem, and Ahithophel was with him. 16Then Hushai the Arkite, David's confidant, went to Absalom and said to him, "Long live the king! Long live the king!"

17Absalom said to Hushai, "So this is the love you show your friend? If he's your friend, why didn't you go with him?"

18Hushai said to Absalom, "No, the one chosen by the LORD, by these people, and by all the men of Israel — his I will be, and I will remain with him. 19Furthermore, whom should I serve? Should I not serve the son? Just as I served your father, so I will serve you."

20Absalom said to Ahithophel, "Give us your advice. What should we do?"

21Ahithophel answered, "Sleep with your father's concubines whom he left to take care of the palace. Then all Israel will hear that you have made yourself obnoxious to your father, and the hands of everyone with you will be more resolute." 22So they pitched a tent for Absalom on the roof, and he slept with his father's concubines in the sight of all Israel.

23Now in those days the advice Ahithophel gave was like that of one who inquires of God. That was how both David and Absalom regarded all of Ahithophel's advice.

17 Ahithophel said to Absalom, "I would[a] choose twelve thousand men and set out tonight in pursuit of David. 2I would attack him while he is weary and weak. I would strike him with terror, and then all the people with him will flee. I would strike down only the king 3and bring all the people back to you. The death of the man you seek will mean the return of all; all the people will be unharmed." 4This plan seemed good to Absalom and to all the elders of Israel.

5But Absalom said, "Summon also Hushai the Arkite, so we can hear what he has to say as well." 6When Hushai came to him, Absalom said, "Ahithophel has given this advice. Should we do what he says? If not, give us your opinion."

7Hushai replied to Absalom, "The advice Ahithophel has given is not good this time. 8You know your father and his men; they are fighters, and as fierce as a wild bear robbed of her cubs. Besides, your father is an experienced fighter; he will not spend the night with the troops. 9Even now, he is hidden in a cave or some other place. If he should attack your troops first,[b] whoever hears about it will say, 'There has been a slaughter among the troops who follow Absalom.' 10Then even the bravest soldier, whose heart is like the heart of a lion, will melt with fear, for all Israel knows that your father is a fighter and that those with him are brave.

11"So I advise you: Let all Israel, from Dan to Beersheba — as numerous as the sand on the seashore — be gathered to you, with you yourself leading them into battle. 12Then we will attack him wherever he may be found, and we will fall on him as dew settles on the ground. Neither he nor any of his men will be left alive. 13If he withdraws into a city, then all Israel will bring ropes to that city, and we will drag it down to the valley until not so much as a pebble is left."

14Absalom and all the men of Israel said, "The advice of Hushai the Arkite is better than that of Ahithophel." For the LORD had determined to frustrate the good advice of Ahithophel in order to bring disaster on Absalom.

15Hushai told Zadok and Abiathar, the priests, "Ahithophel has advised Absalom and the elders of Israel to do such and such, but I have advised them to do so and so. 16Now send a message at once and tell David, 'Do not spend the night at the fords in the wilderness; cross over without fail, or the king and all the people with him will be swallowed up.'"

17Jonathan and Ahimaaz were staying at En Rogel. A female servant was to go and inform them, and they were to go and tell King David, for they could not risk being seen entering the city. 18But a young man saw them and told Absalom. So the two of them left at once and went to the house of a man in Bahurim.

[a] *1* Or *Let me* [b] *9* Or *When some of the men fall at the first attack*

He had a well in his courtyard, and they
climbed down into it. 19His wife took
a covering and spread it out over the
opening of the well and scattered grain
over it. No one knew anything about it.
20When Absalom's men came to the
woman at the house, they asked, "Where
are Ahimaaz and Jonathan?"

The woman answered them, "They
crossed over the brook."[a] The men
searched but found no one, so they returned to Jerusalem.

21After they had gone, the two climbed
out of the well and went to inform King
David. They said to him, "Set out and
cross the river at once; Ahithophel has
advised such and such against you."
22So David and all the people with him
set out and crossed the Jordan. By daybreak, no one was left who had not
crossed the Jordan.

23When Ahithophel saw that his advice had not been followed, he saddled
his donkey and set out for his house in
his hometown. He put his house in order
and then hanged himself. So he died and
was buried in his father's tomb.

Absalom's Death

24David went to Mahanaim, and Absalom crossed the Jordan with all the men
of Israel. 25Absalom had appointed Amasa over the army in place of Joab. Amasa was the son of Jether,[b] an Ishmaelite[c]
who had married Abigail,[d] the daughter of Nahash and sister of Zeruiah the
mother of Joab. 26The Israelites and Absalom camped in the land of Gilead.

27When David came to Mahanaim,
Shobi son of Nahash from Rabbah of the
Ammonites, and Makir son of Ammiel
from Lo Debar, and Barzillai the Gileadite from Rogelim 28brought bedding
and bowls and articles of pottery. They
also brought wheat and barley, flour and
roasted grain, beans and lentils,[e] 29hon-
ey and curds, sheep, and cheese from
cows' milk for David and his people to
eat. For they said, "The people have become exhausted and hungry and thirsty
in the wilderness."

18 David mustered the men who were
with him and appointed over them
commanders of thousands and commanders of hundreds. 2David sent out
his troops, a third under the command
of Joab, a third under Joab's brother
Abishai son of Zeruiah, and a third under Ittai the Gittite. The king told the
troops, "I myself will surely march out
with you."

3But the men said, "You must not go
out; if we are forced to flee, they won't
care about us. Even if half of us die, they
won't care; but you are worth ten thousand of us.[f] It would be better now for
you to give us support from the city."

4The king answered, "I will do whatever seems best to you."

So the king stood beside the gate
while all his men marched out in units
of hundreds and of thousands. 5The king
commanded Joab, Abishai and Ittai, "Be
gentle with the young man Absalom for
my sake." And all the troops heard the
king giving orders concerning Absalom
to each of the commanders.

6David's army marched out of the city
to fight Israel, and the battle took place
in the forest of Ephraim. 7There Israel's
troops were routed by David's men, and
the casualties that day were great—
twenty thousand men. 8The battle
spread out over the whole countryside,
and the forest swallowed up more men
that day than the sword.

9Now Absalom happened to meet
David's men. He was riding his mule,
and as the mule went under the thick
branches of a large oak, Absalom's hair
got caught in the tree. He was left hanging in midair, while the mule he was riding kept on going.

10When one of the men saw what had
happened, he told Joab, "I just saw Absalom hanging in an oak tree."

11Joab said to the man who had told
him this, "What! You saw him? Why
didn't you strike him to the ground right
there? Then I would have had to give
you ten shekels[g] of silver and a warrior's
belt."

12But the man replied, "Even if a thousand shekels[h] were weighed out into
my hands, I would not lay a hand on
the king's son. In our hearing the king
commanded you and Abishai and Ittai,
'Protect the young man Absalom for my

[a] 20 Or *"They passed by the sheep pen toward the water."* [b] 25 Hebrew *Ithra*, a variant of *Jether* [c] 25 Some Septuagint manuscripts (see also 1 Chron. 2:17); Hebrew and other Septuagint manuscripts *Israelite* [d] 25 Hebrew *Abigal*, a variant of *Abigail* [e] 28 Most Septuagint manuscripts and Syriac; Hebrew *lentils, and roasted grain* [f] 3 Two Hebrew manuscripts, some Septuagint manuscripts and Vulgate; most Hebrew manuscripts *care; for now there are ten thousand like us* [g] 11 That is, about 4 ounces or about 115 grams [h] 12 That is, about 25 pounds or about 12 kilograms

sake.[a] 13 And if I had put my life in jeopardy[b] — and nothing is hidden from the king — you would have kept your distance from me."

14 Joab said, "I'm not going to wait like this for you." So he took three javelins in his hand and plunged them into Absalom's heart while Absalom was still alive in the oak tree. 15 And ten of Joab's armor-bearers surrounded Absalom, struck him and killed him.

16 Then Joab sounded the trumpet, and the troops stopped pursuing Israel, for Joab halted them. 17 They took Absalom, threw him into a big pit in the forest and piled up a large heap of rocks over him. Meanwhile, all the Israelites fled to their homes.

18 During his lifetime Absalom had taken a pillar and erected it in the King's Valley as a monument to himself, for he thought, "I have no son to carry on the memory of my name." He named the pillar after himself, and it is called Absalom's Monument to this day.

David Mourns

19 Now Ahimaaz son of Zadok said, "Let me run and take the news to the king that the LORD has vindicated him by delivering him from the hand of his enemies."

20 "You are not the one to take the news today," Joab told him. "You may take the news another time, but you must not do so today, because the king's son is dead."

21 Then Joab said to a Cushite, "Go, tell the king what you have seen." The Cushite bowed down before Joab and ran off.

22 Ahimaaz son of Zadok again said to Joab, "Come what may, please let me run behind the Cushite."

But Joab replied, "My son, why do you want to go? You don't have any news that will bring you a reward."

23 He said, "Come what may, I want to run."

So Joab said, "Run!" Then Ahimaaz ran by way of the plain[c] and outran the Cushite.

24 While David was sitting between the inner and outer gates, the watchman went up to the roof of the gateway by the wall. As he looked out, he saw a man running alone. 25 The watchman called out to the king and reported it.

The king said, "If he is alone, he must have good news." And the runner came closer and closer.

26 Then the watchman saw another runner, and he called down to the gatekeeper, "Look, another man running alone!"

The king said, "He must be bringing good news, too."

27 The watchman said, "It seems to me that the first one runs like Ahimaaz son of Zadok."

"He's a good man," the king said. "He comes with good news."

28 Then Ahimaaz called out to the king, "All is well!" He bowed down before the king with his face to the ground and said, "Praise be to the LORD your God! He has delivered up those who lifted their hands against my lord the king."

29 The king asked, "Is the young man Absalom safe?"

Ahimaaz answered, "I saw great confusion just as Joab was about to send the king's servant and me, your servant, but I don't know what it was."

30 The king said, "Stand aside and wait here." So he stepped aside and stood there.

31 Then the Cushite arrived and said, "My lord the king, hear the good news! The LORD has vindicated you today by delivering you from the hand of all who rose up against you."

32 The king asked the Cushite, "Is the young man Absalom safe?"

The Cushite replied, "May the enemies of my lord the king and all who rise up to harm you be like that young man."

33 The king was shaken. He went up to the room over the gateway and wept. As he went, he said: "O my son Absalom! My son, my son Absalom! If only I had died instead of you — O Absalom, my son, my son!"[d]

19[e] Joab was told, "The king is weeping and mourning for Absalom." 2 And for the whole army the victory that day was turned into mourning, because on that day the troops heard it said, "The king is grieving for his son." 3 The men stole into the city that day as men steal in who are ashamed when they flee from battle. 4 The king covered his face and cried aloud, "O my son Absalom! O Absalom, my son, my son!"

5 Then Joab went into the house to the king and said, "Today you have

[a] 12 A few Hebrew manuscripts, Septuagint, Vulgate and Syriac; most Hebrew manuscripts may be translated *Absalom, whoever you may be.* [b] 13 Or *Otherwise, if I had acted treacherously toward him* [c] 23 That is, the plain of the Jordan [d] 33 In Hebrew texts this verse (18:33) is numbered 19:1. [e] In Hebrew texts 19:1-43 is numbered 19:2-44.

humiliated all your men, who have just saved your life and the lives of your sons and daughters and the lives of your wives and concubines. 6You love those who hate you and hate those who love you. You have made it clear today that the commanders and their men mean nothing to you. I see that you would be pleased if Absalom were alive today and all of us were dead. 7Now go out and encourage your men. I swear by the LORD that if you don't go out, not a man will be left with you by nightfall. This will be worse for you than all the calamities that have come on you from your youth till now."

8So the king got up and took his seat in the gateway. When the men were told, "The king is sitting in the gateway," they all came before him.

Meanwhile, the Israelites had fled to their homes.

David Returns to Jerusalem

9Throughout the tribes of Israel, all the people were arguing among themselves, saying, "The king delivered us from the hand of our enemies; he is the one who rescued us from the hand of the Philistines. But now he has fled the country to escape from Absalom; 10and Absalom, whom we anointed to rule over us, has died in battle. So why do you say nothing about bringing the king back?"

11King David sent this message to Zadok and Abiathar, the priests: "Ask the elders of Judah, 'Why should you be the last to bring the king back to his palace, since what is being said throughout Israel has reached the king at his quarters? 12You are my relatives, my own flesh and blood. So why should you be the last to bring back the king?' 13And say to Amasa, 'Are you not my own flesh and blood? May God deal with me, be it ever so severely, if you are not the commander of my army for life in place of Joab.'"

14He won over the hearts of the men of Judah so that they were all of one mind. They sent word to the king, "Return, you and all your men." 15Then the king returned and went as far as the Jordan.

Now the men of Judah had come to Gilgal to go out and meet the king and bring him across the Jordan. 16Shimei son of Gera, the Benjamite from Bahurim, hurried down with the men of Judah to meet King David. 17With him were a thousand Benjamites, along with Ziba, the steward of Saul's household, and his fifteen sons and twenty servants. They rushed to the Jordan, where the king was. 18They crossed at the ford to take the king's household over and to do whatever he wished.

When Shimei son of Gera crossed the Jordan, he fell prostrate before the king 19and said to him, "May my lord not hold me guilty. Do not remember how your servant did wrong on the day my lord the king left Jerusalem. May the king put it out of his mind. 20For I your servant know that I have sinned, but today I have come here as the first from the tribes of Joseph to come down and meet my lord the king."

21Then Abishai son of Zeruiah said, "Shouldn't Shimei be put to death for this? He cursed the LORD's anointed."

22David replied, "What does this have to do with you, you sons of Zeruiah? What right do you have to interfere? Should anyone be put to death in Israel today? Don't I know that today I am king over Israel?" 23So the king said to Shimei, "You shall not die." And the king promised him on oath.

24Mephibosheth, Saul's grandson, also went down to meet the king. He had not taken care of his feet or trimmed his mustache or washed his clothes from the day the king left until the day he returned safely. 25When he came from Jerusalem to meet the king, the king asked him, "Why didn't you go with me, Mephibosheth?"

26He said, "My lord the king, since I your servant am lame, I said, 'I will have my donkey saddled and will ride on it, so I can go with the king.' But Ziba my servant betrayed me. 27And he has slandered your servant to my lord the king. My lord the king is like an angel of God; so do whatever you wish. 28All my grandfather's descendants deserved nothing but death from my lord the king, but you gave your servant a place among those who eat at your table. So what right do I have to make any more appeals to the king?"

29The king said to him, "Why say more? I order you and Ziba to divide the land."

30Mephibosheth said to the king, "Let him take everything, now that my lord the king has returned home safely."

31Barzillai the Gileadite also came down from Rogelim to cross the Jordan with the king and to send him on his way from there. 32Now Barzillai was very old, eighty years of age. He had provided for the king during his stay in Mahanaim, for he was a very wealthy man. 33The king said to Barzillai, "Cross over with me and stay with me in Jerusalem, and I will provide for you."

34But Barzillai answered the king,
"How many more years will I live, that I
should go up to Jerusalem with the king?
35I am now eighty years old. Can I tell the
difference between what is enjoyable and
what is not? Can your servant taste what
he eats and drinks? Can I still hear the
voices of male and female singers? Why
should your servant be an added burden
to my lord the king? 36Your servant will
cross over the Jordan with the king for a
short distance, but why should the king
reward me in this way? 37Let your servant
return, that I may die in my own town
near the tomb of my father and mother. But here is your servant Kimham. Let
him cross over with my lord the king. Do
for him whatever you wish."

38The king said, "Kimham shall cross
over with me, and I will do for him whatever you wish. And anything you desire
from me I will do for you."

39So all the people crossed the Jordan,
and then the king crossed over. The king
kissed Barzillai and bid him farewell,
and Barzillai returned to his home.

40When the king crossed over to Gilgal,
Kimham crossed with him. All the troops
of Judah and half the troops of Israel
had taken the king over.

41Soon all the men of Israel were coming to the king and saying to him, "Why
did our brothers, the men of Judah, steal
the king away and bring him and his
household across the Jordan, together
with all his men?"

42All the men of Judah answered the
men of Israel, "We did this because the
king is closely related to us. Why are you
angry about it? Have we eaten any of the
king's provisions? Have we taken anything for ourselves?"

43Then the men of Israel answered the
men of Judah, "We have ten shares in
the king; so we have a greater claim on
David than you have. Why then do you
treat us with contempt? Weren't we the
first to speak of bringing back our king?"

But the men of Judah pressed their
claims even more forcefully than the
men of Israel.

Sheba Rebels Against David

20 Now a troublemaker named Sheba son of Bikri, a Benjamite, happened to be there. He sounded the trumpet and shouted,

"We have no share in David,
no part in Jesse's son!
Every man to his tent, Israel!"

2So all the men of Israel deserted David to follow Sheba son of Bikri. But the
men of Judah stayed by their king all the
way from the Jordan to Jerusalem.

3When David returned to his palace in
Jerusalem, he took the ten concubines
he had left to take care of the palace
and put them in a house under guard.
He provided for them but had no sexual
relations with them. They were kept in
confinement till the day of their death,
living as widows.

4Then the king said to Amasa, "Summon the men of Judah to come to me
within three days, and be here yourself."
5But when Amasa went to summon Judah, he took longer than the time the
king had set for him.

6David said to Abishai, "Now Sheba
son of Bikri will do us more harm than
Absalom did. Take your master's men
and pursue him, or he will find fortified
cities and escape from us."[a] 7So Joab's
men and the Kerethites and Pelethites
and all the mighty warriors went out
under the command of Abishai. They
marched out from Jerusalem to pursue
Sheba son of Bikri.

8While they were at the great rock
in Gibeon, Amasa came to meet them.
Joab was wearing his military tunic,
and strapped over it at his waist was a
belt with a dagger in its sheath. As he
stepped forward, it dropped out of its
sheath.

9Joab said to Amasa, "How are you,
my brother?" Then Joab took Amasa by the beard with his right hand to
kiss him. 10Amasa was not on his guard
against the dagger in Joab's hand, and
Joab plunged it into his belly, and his intestines spilled out on the ground. Without being stabbed again, Amasa died.
Then Joab and his brother Abishai pursued Sheba son of Bikri.

11One of Joab's men stood beside Amasa and said, "Whoever favors Joab,
and whoever is for David, let him follow Joab!" 12Amasa lay wallowing in his
blood in the middle of the road, and the
man saw that all the troops came to a
halt there. When he realized that everyone who came up to Amasa stopped, he
dragged him from the road into a field
and threw a garment over him. 13Af-
ter Amasa had been removed from the
road, everyone went on with Joab to pursue Sheba son of Bikri.

14Sheba passed through all the tribes of
Israel to Abel Beth Maakah and through

[a] 6 Or *and do us serious injury*

the entire region of the Bikrites,[a] who gathered together and followed him. 15All the troops with Joab came and besieged Sheba in Abel Beth Maakah. They built a siege ramp up to the city, and it stood against the outer fortifications. While they were battering the wall to bring it down, 16a wise woman called from the city, "Listen! Listen! Tell Joab to come here so I can speak to him." 17He went toward her, and she asked, "Are you Joab?"

"I am," he answered.

She said, "Listen to what your servant has to say."

"I'm listening," he said.

18She continued, "Long ago they used to say, 'Get your answer at Abel,' and that settled it. 19We are the peaceful and faithful in Israel. You are trying to destroy a city that is a mother in Israel. Why do you want to swallow up the LORD's inheritance?"

20"Far be it from me!" Joab replied, "Far be it from me to swallow up or destroy! 21That is not the case. A man named Sheba son of Bikri, from the hill country of Ephraim, has lifted up his hand against the king, against David. Hand over this one man, and I'll withdraw from the city."

The woman said to Joab, "His head will be thrown to you from the wall."

22Then the woman went to all the people with her wise advice, and they cut off the head of Sheba son of Bikri and threw it to Joab. So he sounded the trumpet, and his men dispersed from the city, each returning to his home. And Joab went back to the king in Jerusalem.

David's Officials

23Joab was over Israel's entire army; Benaiah son of Jehoiada was over the Kerethites and Pelethites; 24Adoniram[b] was in charge of forced labor; Jehoshaphat son of Ahilud was recorder; 25Sheva was secretary; Zadok and Abiathar were priests; 26and Ira the Jairite[c] was David's priest.

The Gibeonites Avenged

21 During the reign of David, there was a famine for three successive years; so David sought the face of the LORD. The LORD said, "It is on account of Saul and his blood-stained house; it is because he put the Gibeonites to death."

2The king summoned the Gibeonites and spoke to them. (Now the Gibeonites were not a part of Israel but were survivors of the Amorites; the Israelites had sworn to spare them, but Saul in his zeal for Israel and Judah had tried to annihilate them.) 3David asked the Gibeonites, "What shall I do for you? How shall I make atonement so that you will bless the LORD's inheritance?"

4The Gibeonites answered him, "We have no right to demand silver or gold from Saul or his family, nor do we have the right to put anyone in Israel to death."

"What do you want me to do for you?" David asked.

5They answered the king, "As for the man who destroyed us and plotted against us so that we have been decimated and have no place anywhere in Israel, 6let seven of his male descendants be given to us to be killed and their bodies exposed before the LORD at Gibeah of Saul—the LORD's chosen one."

So the king said, "I will give them to you."

7The king spared Mephibosheth son of Jonathan, the son of Saul, because of the oath before the LORD between David and Jonathan son of Saul. 8But the king took Armoni and Mephibosheth, the two sons of Aiah's daughter Rizpah, whom she had borne to Saul, together with the five sons of Saul's daughter Merab,[d] whom she had borne to Adriel son of Barzillai the Meholathite. 9He handed them over to the Gibeonites, who killed them and exposed their bodies on a hill before the LORD. All seven of them fell together; they were put to death during the first days of the harvest, just as the barley harvest was beginning.

10Rizpah daughter of Aiah took sackcloth and spread it out for herself on a rock. From the beginning of the harvest till the rain poured down from the heavens on the bodies, she did not let the birds touch them by day or the wild animals by night. 11When David was told what Aiah's daughter Rizpah, Saul's concubine, had done, 12he went and took the bones of Saul and his son Jonathan from the citizens of Jabesh Gilead. (They had stolen their bodies from the public square at Beth Shan, where the Philistines had hung them after they struck Saul down on Gilboa.) 13David brought the bones of Saul and his son Jonathan from there,

[a] *14* See Septuagint and Vulgate; Hebrew *Berites*. [b] *24* Some Septuagint manuscripts (see also 1 Kings 4:6 and 5:14); Hebrew *Adoram* [c] *26* Hebrew; some Septuagint manuscripts and Syriac (see also 23:38) *Ithrite* [d] *8* Two Hebrew manuscripts, some Septuagint manuscripts and Syriac (see also 1 Samuel 18:19); most Hebrew and Septuagint manuscripts *Michal*

and the bones of those who had been
killed and exposed were gathered up.
14They buried the bones of Saul and
his son Jonathan in the tomb of Saul's
father Kish, at Zela in Benjamin, and did
everything the king commanded. After
that, God answered prayer in behalf of
the land.

Wars Against the Philistines

15Once again there was a battle between the Philistines and Israel. David
went down with his men to fight against
the Philistines, and he became exhausted. 16And Ishbi-Benob, one of the descendants of Rapha, whose bronze spear-
head weighed three hundred shekels[a]
and who was armed with a new sword,
said he would kill David. 17But Abishai
son of Zeruiah came to David's rescue;
he struck the Philistine down and killed
him. Then David's men swore to him,
saying, "Never again will you go out
with us to battle, so that the lamp of Israel will not be extinguished."
18In the course of time, there was another battle with the Philistines, at Gob.
At that time Sibbekai the Hushathite
killed Saph, one of the descendants of
Rapha.
19In another battle with the Philistines
at Gob, Elhanan son of Jair[b] the Bethle-
hemite killed the brother of[c] Goliath the
Gittite, who had a spear with a shaft like
a weaver's rod.
20In still another battle, which took
place at Gath, there was a huge man
with six fingers on each hand and six
toes on each foot — twenty-four in all. He
also was descended from Rapha. 21When
he taunted Israel, Jonathan son of Shimeah, David's brother, killed him.
22These four were descendants of Rapha in Gath, and they fell at the hands
of David and his men.

David's Song of Praise

22 David sang to the LORD the words
of this song when the LORD delivered him from the hand of all his enemies and from the hand of Saul. 2He
said:

"The LORD is my rock, my fortress and
my deliverer;
3 my God is my rock, in whom I take
refuge,
my shield[d] and the horn[e] of my
salvation.
He is my stronghold, my refuge and
my savior —
from violent people you save me.

4"I called to the LORD, who is worthy of
praise,
and have been saved from my
enemies.
5The waves of death swirled about me;
the torrents of destruction
overwhelmed me.
6The cords of the grave coiled around
me;
the snares of death confronted me.

7"In my distress I called to the LORD;
I called out to my God.
From his temple he heard my voice;
my cry came to his ears.
8The earth trembled and quaked,
the foundations of the heavens[f]
shook;
they trembled because he was
angry.
9Smoke rose from his nostrils;
consuming fire came from his
mouth,
burning coals blazed out of it.
10He parted the heavens and came
down;
dark clouds were under his feet.
11He mounted the cherubim and flew;
he soared[g] on the wings of the wind.
12He made darkness his canopy around
him —
the dark[h] rain clouds of the sky.
13Out of the brightness of his presence
bolts of lightning blazed forth.
14The LORD thundered from heaven;
the voice of the Most High
resounded.
15He shot his arrows and scattered the
enemy,
with great bolts of lightning he
routed them.
16The valleys of the sea were exposed
and the foundations of the earth
laid bare
at the rebuke of the LORD,
at the blast of breath from his
nostrils.

17"He reached down from on high and
took hold of me;
he drew me out of deep waters.

[a] *16* That is, about 7 1/2 pounds or about 3.5 kilograms [b] *19* See 1 Chron. 20:5; Hebrew *Jaare-Oregim.* [c] *19* See 1 Chron. 20:5; Hebrew does not have *the brother of.* [d] *3* Or *sovereign* [e] *3* *Horn* here symbolizes strength. [f] *8* Hebrew; Vulgate and Syriac (see also Psalm 18:7) *mountains* [g] *11* Many Hebrew manuscripts (see also Psalm 18:10); most Hebrew manuscripts *appeared* [h] *12* Septuagint (see also Psalm 18:11); Hebrew *massed*

18 He rescued me from my powerful
enemy,
from my foes, who were too strong
for me.
19 They confronted me in the day of my
disaster,
but the LORD was my support.
20 He brought me out into a spacious
place;
he rescued me because he
delighted in me.

21 "The LORD has dealt with me
according to my righteousness;
according to the cleanness of my
hands he has rewarded me.
22 For I have kept the ways of the LORD;
I am not guilty of turning from my
God.
23 All his laws are before me;
I have not turned away from his
decrees.
24 I have been blameless before him
and have kept myself from sin.
25 The LORD has rewarded me according
to my righteousness,
according to my cleanness[a] in his
sight.

26 "To the faithful you show yourself
faithful,
to the blameless you show yourself
blameless,
27 to the pure you show yourself pure,
but to the devious you show
yourself shrewd.
28 You save the humble,
but your eyes are on the haughty to
bring them low.
29 You, LORD, are my lamp;
the LORD turns my darkness into
light.
30 With your help I can advance against
a troop[b];
with my God I can scale a wall.

31 "As for God, his way is perfect:
The LORD's word is flawless;
he shields all who take refuge in
him.
32 For who is God besides the LORD?
And who is the Rock except our God?
33 It is God who arms me with strength[c]
and keeps my way secure.
34 He makes my feet like the feet of a
deer;
he causes me to stand on the
heights.
35 He trains my hands for battle;
my arms can bend a bow of bronze.
36 You make your saving help my shield;
your help has made[d] me great.
37 You provide a broad path for my feet,
so that my ankles do not give way.

38 "I pursued my enemies and crushed
them;
I did not turn back till they were
destroyed.
39 I crushed them completely, and they
could not rise;
they fell beneath my feet.
40 You armed me with strength for
battle;
you humbled my adversaries
before me.
41 You made my enemies turn their
backs in flight,
and I destroyed my foes.
42 They cried for help, but there was no
one to save them —
to the LORD, but he did not answer.
43 I beat them as fine as the dust of the
earth;
I pounded and trampled them like
mud in the streets.

44 "You have delivered me from the
attacks of the peoples;
you have preserved me as the head
of nations.
People I did not know now serve me,
45 foreigners cower before me;
as soon as they hear of me, they
obey me.
46 They all lose heart;
they come trembling[e] from their
strongholds.

47 "The LORD lives! Praise be to my Rock!
Exalted be my God, the Rock, my
Savior!
48 He is the God who avenges me,
who puts the nations under me,
49 who sets me free from my enemies.
You exalted me above my foes;
from a violent man you rescued me.
50 Therefore I will praise you, LORD,
among the nations;
I will sing the praises of your name.

51 "He gives his king great victories;
he shows unfailing kindness to his
anointed,
to David and his descendants
forever."

[a] 25 Hebrew; Septuagint and Vulgate (see also Psalm 18:24) *to the cleanness of my hands* [b] 30 Or *can run through a barricade* [c] 33 Dead Sea Scrolls, some Septuagint manuscripts, Vulgate and Syriac (see also Psalm 18:32); Masoretic Text *who is my strong refuge* [d] 36 Dead Sea Scrolls; Masoretic Text *shield; / you stoop down to make* [e] 46 Some Septuagint manuscripts and Vulgate (see also Psalm 18:45); Masoretic Text *they arm themselves*

David's Last Words

23 These are the last words of David:

"The inspired utterance of David son of Jesse,
the utterance of the man exalted by the Most High,
the man anointed by the God of Jacob,
the hero of Israel's songs:

2 "The Spirit of the LORD spoke through me;
his word was on my tongue.
3 The God of Israel spoke,
the Rock of Israel said to me:
'When one rules over people in righteousness,
when he rules in the fear of God,
4 he is like the light of morning at sunrise
on a cloudless morning,
like the brightness after rain
that brings grass from the earth.'

5 "If my house were not right with God,
surely he would not have made with me an everlasting covenant,
arranged and secured in every part;
surely he would not bring to fruition my salvation
and grant me my every desire.
6 But evil men are all to be cast aside like thorns,
which are not gathered with the hand.
7 Whoever touches thorns
uses a tool of iron or the shaft of a spear;
they are burned up where they lie."

David's Mighty Warriors

8 These are the names of David's
mighty warriors:
Josheb-Basshebeth,[a] a Tahkemonite,[b]
was chief of the Three; he raised his
spear against eight hundred men, whom
he killed[c] in one encounter.
9 Next to him was Eleazar son of Dodai
the Ahohite. As one of the three mighty
warriors, he was with David when they
taunted the Philistines gathered at Pas
Dammim[d] for battle. Then the Israelites
retreated, 10 but Eleazar stood his ground
and struck down the Philistines till his
hand grew tired and froze to the sword.
The LORD brought about a great victory
that day. The troops returned to Eleazar,
but only to strip the dead.
11 Next to him was Shammah son of
Agee the Hararite. When the Philistines
banded together at a place where there
was a field full of lentils, Israel's troops
fled from them. 12 But Shammah took
his stand in the middle of the field. He
defended it and struck the Philistines
down, and the LORD brought about a
great victory.
13 During harvest time, three of the
thirty chief warriors came down to David at the cave of Adullam, while a band
of Philistines was encamped in the Valley of Rephaim. 14 At that time David was
in the stronghold, and the Philistine garrison was at Bethlehem. 15 David longed
for water and said, "Oh, that someone
would get me a drink of water from the
well near the gate of Bethlehem!" 16 So
the three mighty warriors broke through
the Philistine lines, drew water from the
well near the gate of Bethlehem and carried it back to David. But he refused to
drink it; instead, he poured it out before
the LORD. 17 "Far be it from me, LORD, to
do this!" he said. "Is it not the blood of
men who went at the risk of their lives?"
And David would not drink it.
Such were the exploits of the three
mighty warriors.
18 Abishai the brother of Joab son
of Zeruiah was chief of the Three.[e] He
raised his spear against three hundred
men, whom he killed, and so he became
as famous as the Three. 19 Was he not
held in greater honor than the Three? He
became their commander, even though
he was not included among them.
20 Benaiah son of Jehoiada, a valiant
fighter from Kabzeel, performed great
exploits. He struck down Moab's two
mightiest warriors. He also went down
into a pit on a snowy day and killed a
lion. 21 And he struck down a huge Egyptian. Although the Egyptian had a spear
in his hand, Benaiah went against him
with a club. He snatched the spear from
the Egyptian's hand and killed him with
his own spear. 22 Such were the exploits
of Benaiah son of Jehoiada; he too was

[a] *8* Hebrew; some Septuagint manuscripts suggest *Ish-Bosheth*, that is, *Esh-Baal* (see also 1 Chron. 11:11 *Jashobeam*). [b] *8* Probably a variant of *Hakmonite* (see 1 Chron. 11:11) [c] *8* Some Septuagint manuscripts (see also 1 Chron. 11:11); Hebrew and other Septuagint manuscripts *Three; it was Adino the Eznite who killed eight hundred men* [d] *9* See 1 Chron. 11:13; Hebrew *gathered there.* [e] *18* Most Hebrew manuscripts (see also 1 Chron. 11:20); two Hebrew manuscripts and Syriac *Thirty*

as famous as the three mighty warriors.
23 He was held in greater honor than any
of the Thirty, but he was not included
among the Three. And David put him in
charge of his bodyguard.

24 Among the Thirty were:
Asahel the brother of Joab,
Elhanan son of Dodo from Bethle-
hem,
25 Shammah the Harodite,
Elika the Harodite,
26 Helez the Paltite,
Ira son of Ikkesh from Tekoa,
27 Abiezer from Anathoth,
Sibbekai[a] the Hushathite,
28 Zalmon the Ahohite,
Maharai the Netophathite,
29 Heled[b] son of Baanah the Netophathite,
Ithai son of Ribai from Gibeah in
Benjamin,
30 Benaiah the Pirathonite,
Hiddai[c] from the ravines of Gaash,
31 Abi-Albon the Arbathite,
Azmaveth the Barhumite,
32 Eliahba the Shaalbonite,
the sons of Jashen,
Jonathan 33 son of[d] Shammah the
Hararite,
Ahiam son of Sharar[e] the Hararite,
34 Eliphelet son of Ahasbai the
Maakathite,
Eliam son of Ahithophel the
Gilonite,
35 Hezro the Carmelite,
Paarai the Arbite,
36 Igal son of Nathan from Zobah,
the son of Hagri,[f]
37 Zelek the Ammonite,
Naharai the Beerothite, the armor-
bearer of Joab son of Zeruiah,
38 Ira the Ithrite,
Gareb the Ithrite
39 and Uriah the Hittite.
There were thirty-seven in all.

David Enrolls the Fighting Men

24 Again the anger of the LORD
burned against Israel, and he incited David against them, saying, "Go
and take a census of Israel and Judah."
2 So the king said to Joab and the army
commanders[g] with him, "Go throughout
the tribes of Israel from Dan to Beersheba and enroll the fighting men, so that I
may know how many there are."
3 But Joab replied to the king, "May
the LORD your God multiply the troops a
hundred times over, and may the eyes of
my lord the king see it. But why does my
lord the king want to do such a thing?"
4 The king's word, however, overruled
Joab and the army commanders; so they
left the presence of the king to enroll the
fighting men of Israel.
5 After crossing the Jordan, they
camped near Aroer, south of the town in
the gorge, and then went through Gad
and on to Jazer. 6 They went to Gilead
and the region of Tahtim Hodshi, and
on to Dan Jaan and around toward Sidon. 7 Then they went toward the fortress
of Tyre and all the towns of the Hivites
and Canaanites. Finally, they went on to
Beersheba in the Negev of Judah.
8 After they had gone through the entire land, they came back to Jerusalem
at the end of nine months and twenty
days.
9 Joab reported the number of the fighting men to the king: In Israel there were
eight hundred thousand able-bodied
men who could handle a sword, and in
Judah five hundred thousand.
10 David was conscience-stricken after
he had counted the fighting men, and he
said to the LORD, "I have sinned greatly in what I have done. Now, LORD, I beg
you, take away the guilt of your servant.
I have done a very foolish thing."
11 Before David got up the next morning, the word of the LORD had come to
Gad the prophet, David's seer: 12 "Go and
tell David, 'This is what the LORD says:
I am giving you three options. Choose
one of them for me to carry out against
you.'"
13 So Gad went to David and said to
him, "Shall there come on you three[h]
years of famine in your land? Or three
months of fleeing from your enemies
while they pursue you? Or three days of
plague in your land? Now then, think it
over and decide how I should answer the
one who sent me."

[a] 27 Some Septuagint manuscripts (see also 21:18; 1 Chron. 11:29); Hebrew *Mebunnai* [b] 29 Some Hebrew manuscripts and Vulgate (see also 1 Chron. 11:30); most Hebrew manuscripts *Heleb* [c] 30 Hebrew; some Septuagint manuscripts (see also 1 Chron. 11:32) *Hurai* [d] 33 Some Septuagint manuscripts (see also 1 Chron. 11:34); Hebrew does not have *son of.* [e] 33 Hebrew; some Septuagint manuscripts (see also 1 Chron. 11:35) *Sakar* [f] 36 Some Septuagint manuscripts (see also 1 Chron. 11:38); Hebrew *Haggadi* [g] 2 Septuagint (see also verse 4 and 1 Chron. 21:2); Hebrew *Joab the army commander* [h] 13 Septuagint (see also 1 Chron. 21:12); Hebrew *seven*

14 David said to Gad, "I am in deep distress. Let us fall into the hands of the LORD, for his mercy is great; but do not let me fall into human hands."

15 So the LORD sent a plague on Israel from that morning until the end of the time designated, and seventy thousand of the people from Dan to Beersheba died. 16 When the angel stretched out his hand to destroy Jerusalem, the LORD relented concerning the disaster and said to the angel who was afflicting the people, "Enough! Withdraw your hand." The angel of the LORD was then at the threshing floor of Araunah the Jebusite.

17 When David saw the angel who was striking down the people, he said to the LORD, "I have sinned; I, the shepherd,[a] have done wrong. These are but sheep. What have they done? Let your hand fall on me and my family."

David Builds an Altar

18 On that day Gad went to David and said to him, "Go up and build an altar to the LORD on the threshing floor of Araunah the Jebusite." 19 So David went up, as the LORD had commanded through Gad. 20 When Araunah looked and saw the king and his officials coming toward him, he went out and bowed down before the king with his face to the ground.

21 Araunah said, "Why has my lord the king come to his servant?"

"To buy your threshing floor," David answered, "so I can build an altar to the LORD, that the plague on the people may be stopped."

22 Araunah said to David, "Let my lord the king take whatever he wishes and offer it up. Here are oxen for the burnt offering, and here are threshing sledges and ox yokes for the wood. 23 Your Majesty, Araunah[b] gives all this to the king." Araunah also said to him, "May the LORD your God accept you."

24 But the king replied to Araunah, "No, I insist on paying you for it. I will not sacrifice to the LORD my God burnt offerings that cost me nothing."

So David bought the threshing floor and the oxen and paid fifty shekels[c] of silver for them. 25 David built an altar to the LORD there and sacrificed burnt offerings and fellowship offerings. Then the LORD answered his prayer in behalf of the land, and the plague on Israel was stopped.

[a] 17 Dead Sea Scrolls and Septuagint; Masoretic Text does not have *the shepherd.* [b] 23 Some Hebrew manuscripts and Septuagint; most Hebrew manuscripts *King Araunah* [c] 24 That is, about 1 1/4 pounds or about 575 grams

1 KINGS

Adonijah Sets Himself Up as King

1 When King David was very old, he
could not keep warm even when they
put covers over him. 2So his attendants
said to him, "Let us look for a young virgin to serve the king and take care of
him. She can lie beside him so that our
lord the king may keep warm."
3Then they searched throughout Israel
for a beautiful young woman and found
Abishag, a Shunammite, and brought
her to the king. 4The woman was very
beautiful; she took care of the king and
waited on him, but the king had no sexual relations with her.
5Now Adonijah, whose mother was
Haggith, put himself forward and said,
"I will be king." So he got chariots and
horses[a] ready, with fifty men to run
ahead of him. 6(His father had never rebuked him by asking, "Why do you behave as you do?" He was also very handsome and was born next after Absalom.)
7Adonijah conferred with Joab son of
Zeruiah and with Abiathar the priest,
and they gave him their support. 8But
Zadok the priest, Benaiah son of Jehoiada, Nathan the prophet, Shimei and Rei
and David's special guard did not join
Adonijah.
9Adonijah then sacrificed sheep, cattle and fattened calves at the Stone of
Zoheleth near En Rogel. He invited all
his brothers, the king's sons, and all the
royal officials of Judah, 10but he did not
invite Nathan the prophet or Benaiah or
the special guard or his brother Solomon.
11Then Nathan asked Bathsheba, Solomon's mother, "Have you not heard
that Adonijah, the son of Haggith, has
become king, and our lord David knows
nothing about it? 12Now then, let me advise you how you can save your own life
and the life of your son Solomon. 13Go in
to King David and say to him, 'My lord
the king, did you not swear to me your
servant: "Surely Solomon your son shall
be king after me, and he will sit on my
throne"? Why then has Adonijah become
king?' 14While you are still there talking
to the king, I will come in and add my
word to what you have said."
15So Bathsheba went to see the aged
king in his room, where Abishag the
Shunammite was attending him. 16Bath-
sheba bowed down, prostrating herself
before the king.
"What is it you want?" the king asked.
17She said to him, "My lord, you yourself swore to me your servant by the
LORD your God: 'Solomon your son shall
be king after me, and he will sit on my
throne.' 18But now Adonijah has become
king, and you, my lord the king, do not
know about it. 19He has sacrificed great
numbers of cattle, fattened calves, and
sheep, and has invited all the king's
sons, Abiathar the priest and Joab the
commander of the army, but he has
not invited Solomon your servant. 20My
lord the king, the eyes of all Israel are
on you, to learn from you who will sit
on the throne of my lord the king after
him. 21Otherwise, as soon as my lord the
king is laid to rest with his ancestors, I
and my son Solomon will be treated as
criminals."
22While she was still speaking with the
king, Nathan the prophet arrived. 23And
the king was told, "Nathan the prophet
is here." So he went before the king and
bowed with his face to the ground.
24Nathan said, "Have you, my lord
the king, declared that Adonijah shall
be king after you, and that he will sit on
your throne? 25Today he has gone down
and sacrificed great numbers of cattle,
fattened calves, and sheep. He has invited all the king's sons, the commanders of the army and Abiathar the priest.
Right now they are eating and drinking
with him and saying, 'Long live King
Adonijah!' 26But me your servant, and
Zadok the priest, and Benaiah son of
Jehoiada, and your servant Solomon
he did not invite. 27Is this something my
lord the king has done without letting
his servants know who should sit on the
throne of my lord the king after him?"

David Makes Solomon King

28Then King David said, "Call in Bathsheba." So she came into the king's presence and stood before him.
29The king then took an oath: "As surely as the LORD lives, who has delivered
me out of every trouble, 30I will surely
carry out this very day what I swore to

[a] 5 Or *charioteers*

you by the LORD, the God of Israel: Solomon your son shall be king after me, and
he will sit on my throne in my place."
31Then Bathsheba bowed down with
her face to the ground, prostrating herself before the king, and said, "May my
lord King David live forever!"
32King David said, "Call in Zadok the
priest, Nathan the prophet and Benaiah
son of Jehoiada." When they came before
the king, 33he said to them: "Take your
lord's servants with you and have Solomon my son mount my own mule and
take him down to Gihon. 34There have
Zadok the priest and Nathan the prophet anoint him king over Israel. Blow the
trumpet and shout, 'Long live King Solomon!' 35Then you are to go up with him,
and he is to come and sit on my throne
and reign in my place. I have appointed
him ruler over Israel and Judah."
36Benaiah son of Jehoiada answered
the king, "Amen! May the LORD, the God
of my lord the king, so declare it. 37As the
LORD was with my lord the king, so may
he be with Solomon to make his throne
even greater than the throne of my lord
King David!"
38So Zadok the priest, Nathan the
prophet, Benaiah son of Jehoiada, the
Kerethites and the Pelethites went down
and had Solomon mount King David's
mule, and they escorted him to Gihon.
39Zadok the priest took the horn of oil
from the sacred tent and anointed Solomon. Then they sounded the trumpet
and all the people shouted, "Long live
King Solomon!" 40And all the people
went up after him, playing pipes and rejoicing greatly, so that the ground shook
with the sound.
41Adonijah and all the guests who
were with him heard it as they were finishing their feast. On hearing the sound
of the trumpet, Joab asked, "What's the
meaning of all the noise in the city?"
42Even as he was speaking, Jonathan
son of Abiathar the priest arrived. Adonijah said, "Come in. A worthy man like
you must be bringing good news."
43"Not at all!" Jonathan answered.
"Our lord King David has made Solomon
king. 44The king has sent with him Zadok
the priest, Nathan the prophet, Benaiah
son of Jehoiada, the Kerethites and the
Pelethites, and they have put him on
the king's mule, 45and Zadok the priest
and Nathan the prophet have anointed
him king at Gihon. From there they have
gone up cheering, and the city resounds
with it. That's the noise you hear. 46More-
over, Solomon has taken his seat on the
royal throne. 47Also, the royal officials
have come to congratulate our lord King
David, saying, 'May your God make Solomon's name more famous than yours
and his throne greater than yours!' And
the king bowed in worship on his bed
48and said, 'Praise be to the LORD, the
God of Israel, who has allowed my eyes
to see a successor on my throne today.'"
49At this, all Adonijah's guests rose in
alarm and dispersed. 50But Adonijah, in
fear of Solomon, went and took hold of
the horns of the altar. 51Then Solomon
was told, "Adonijah is afraid of King Solomon and is clinging to the horns of the
altar. He says, 'Let King Solomon swear
to me today that he will not put his servant to death with the sword.'"
52Solomon replied, "If he shows himself to be worthy, not a hair of his head
will fall to the ground; but if evil is found
in him, he will die." 53Then King Solomon
sent men, and they brought him down
from the altar. And Adonijah came and
bowed down to King Solomon, and Solomon said, "Go to your home."

David's Charge to Solomon

2 When the time drew near for David
to die, he gave a charge to Solomon
his son.
2"I am about to go the way of all the
earth," he said. "So be strong, act like a
man, 3and observe what the LORD your
God requires: Walk in obedience to him,
and keep his decrees and commands,
his laws and regulations, as written in
the Law of Moses. Do this so that you
may prosper in all you do and wherever you go 4and that the LORD may keep
his promise to me: 'If your descendants
watch how they live, and if they walk
faithfully before me with all their heart
and soul, you will never fail to have a
successor on the throne of Israel.'
5"Now you yourself know what Joab
son of Zeruiah did to me — what he
did to the two commanders of Israel's
armies, Abner son of Ner and Amasa
son of Jether. He killed them, shedding
their blood in peacetime as if in battle,
and with that blood he stained the belt
around his waist and the sandals on his
feet. 6Deal with him according to your
wisdom, but do not let his gray head go
down to the grave in peace.
7"But show kindness to the sons of
Barzillai of Gilead and let them be
among those who eat at your table. They
stood by me when I fled from your brother Absalom.
8"And remember, you have with you

Shimei son of Gera, the Benjamite from
Bahurim, who called down bitter curses on me the day I went to Mahanaim.
When he came down to meet me at the
Jordan, I swore to him by the LORD: 'I
will not put you to death by the sword.'
9 But now, do not consider him innocent.
You are a man of wisdom; you will know
what to do to him. Bring his gray head
down to the grave in blood."
10 Then David rested with his ancestors
and was buried in the City of David. 11 He
had reigned forty years over Israel —
seven years in Hebron and thirty-three
in Jerusalem. 12 So Solomon sat on the
throne of his father David, and his rule
was firmly established.

Solomon's Throne Established

13 Now Adonijah, the son of Haggith,
went to Bathsheba, Solomon's mother.
Bathsheba asked him, "Do you come
peacefully?"
He answered, "Yes, peacefully." 14 Then
he added, "I have something to say to
you."
"You may say it," she replied.
15 "As you know," he said, "the kingdom
was mine. All Israel looked to me as their
king. But things changed, and the kingdom has gone to my brother; for it has
come to him from the LORD. 16 Now I have
one request to make of you. Do not refuse me."
"You may make it," she said.
17 So he continued, "Please ask King
Solomon — he will not refuse you — to
give me Abishag the Shunammite as my
wife."
18 "Very well," Bathsheba replied, "I will
speak to the king for you."
19 When Bathsheba went to King Solomon to speak to him for Adonijah,
the king stood up to meet her, bowed
down to her and sat down on his throne.
He had a throne brought for the king's
mother, and she sat down at his right
hand.
20 "I have one small request to make of
you," she said. "Do not refuse me."
The king replied, "Make it, my mother;
I will not refuse you."
21 So she said, "Let Abishag the Shunammite be given in marriage to your
brother Adonijah."
22 King Solomon answered his mother,
"Why do you request Abishag the Shunammite for Adonijah? You might as
well request the kingdom for him — after all, he is my older brother — yes, for
him and for Abiathar the priest and Joab
son of Zeruiah!"
23 Then King Solomon swore by the
LORD: "May God deal with me, be it ever
so severely, if Adonijah does not pay
with his life for this request! 24 And now,
as surely as the LORD lives — he who has
established me securely on the throne of
my father David and has founded a dynasty for me as he promised — Adonijah
shall be put to death today!" 25 So King
Solomon gave orders to Benaiah son of
Jehoiada, and he struck down Adonijah
and he died.
26 To Abiathar the priest the king said,
"Go back to your fields in Anathoth. You
deserve to die, but I will not put you to
death now, because you carried the ark
of the Sovereign LORD before my father
David and shared all my father's hardships." 27 So Solomon removed Abiathar
from the priesthood of the LORD, fulfilling the word the LORD had spoken at Shiloh about the house of Eli.
28 When the news reached Joab, who
had conspired with Adonijah though not
with Absalom, he fled to the tent of the
LORD and took hold of the horns of the
altar. 29 King Solomon was told that Joab
had fled to the tent of the LORD and was
beside the altar. Then Solomon ordered
Benaiah son of Jehoiada, "Go, strike him
down!"
30 So Benaiah entered the tent of the
LORD and said to Joab, "The king says,
'Come out!' "
But he answered, "No, I will die here."
Benaiah reported to the king, "This is
how Joab answered me."
31 Then the king commanded Benaiah, "Do as he says. Strike him down
and bury him, and so clear me and my
whole family of the guilt of the innocent
blood that Joab shed. 32 The LORD will repay him for the blood he shed, because
without my father David knowing it he
attacked two men and killed them with
the sword. Both of them — Abner son of
Ner, commander of Israel's army, and
Amasa son of Jether, commander of
Judah's army — were better men and
more upright than he. 33 May the guilt of
their blood rest on the head of Joab and
his descendants forever. But on David
and his descendants, his house and his
throne, may there be the LORD's peace
forever."
34 So Benaiah son of Jehoiada went up
and struck down Joab and killed him,
and he was buried at his home out in
the country. 35 The king put Benaiah son
of Jehoiada over the army in Joab's position and replaced Abiathar with Zadok
the priest.

36Then the king sent for Shimei and
said to him, "Build yourself a house in
Jerusalem and live there, but do not go
anywhere else. 37The day you leave and
cross the Kidron Valley, you can be sure
you will die; your blood will be on your
own head."
38Shimei answered the king, "What
you say is good. Your servant will do as
my lord the king has said." And Shimei
stayed in Jerusalem for a long time.
39But three years later, two of Shimei's
slaves ran off to Achish son of Maakah,
king of Gath, and Shimei was told, "Your
slaves are in Gath." 40At this, he saddled
his donkey and went to Achish at Gath
in search of his slaves. So Shimei went
away and brought the slaves back from
Gath.
41When Solomon was told that Shimei had gone from Jerusalem to Gath and
had returned, 42the king summoned
Shimei and said to him, "Did I not make
you swear by the LORD and warn you, 'On
the day you leave to go anywhere else,
you can be sure you will die'? At that
time you said to me, 'What you say is
good. I will obey.' 43Why then did you not
keep your oath to the LORD and obey the
command I gave you?"
44The king also said to Shimei, "You
know in your heart all the wrong you
did to my father David. Now the LORD
will repay you for your wrongdoing.
45But King Solomon will be blessed, and
David's throne will remain secure before
the LORD forever."
46Then the king gave the order to Benaiah son of Jehoiada, and he went out
and struck Shimei down and he died.
The kingdom was now established in
Solomon's hands.

Solomon Asks for Wisdom

3 Solomon made an alliance with
Pharaoh king of Egypt and married
his daughter. He brought her to the City
of David until he finished building his
palace and the temple of the LORD, and
the wall around Jerusalem. 2The people, however, were still sacrificing at the
high places, because a temple had not
yet been built for the Name of the LORD.
3Solomon showed his love for the LORD
by walking according to the instructions
given him by his father David, except
that he offered sacrifices and burned incense on the high places.
4The king went to Gibeon to offer sacrifices, for that was the most important
high place, and Solomon offered a thousand burnt offerings on that altar. 5At
Gibeon the LORD appeared to Solomon
during the night in a dream, and God
said, "Ask for whatever you want me to
give you."
6Solomon answered, "You have shown
great kindness to your servant, my father David, because he was faithful to
you and righteous and upright in heart.
You have continued this great kindness
to him and have given him a son to sit
on his throne this very day.
7"Now, LORD my God, you have made
your servant king in place of my father
David. But I am only a little child and do
not know how to carry out my duties.
8Your servant is here among the people you have chosen, a great people, too
numerous to count or number. 9So give
your servant a discerning heart to govern your people and to distinguish between right and wrong. For who is able
to govern this great people of yours?"
10The Lord was pleased that Solomon
had asked for this. 11So God said to him,
"Since you have asked for this and not
for long life or wealth for yourself, nor
have asked for the death of your enemies but for discernment in adminis-
tering justice, 12I will do what you have
asked. I will give you a wise and discerning heart, so that there will never have
been anyone like you, nor will there ever
be. 13Moreover, I will give you what you
have not asked for — both wealth and
honor — so that in your lifetime you will
have no equal among kings. 14And if you
walk in obedience to me and keep my
decrees and commands as David your
father did, I will give you a long life."
15Then Solomon awoke — and he realized it had been a dream.
He returned to Jerusalem, stood before the ark of the Lord's covenant and
sacrificed burnt offerings and fellowship
offerings. Then he gave a feast for all his
court.

A Wise Ruling

16Now two prostitutes came to the king
and stood before him. 17One of them
said, "Pardon me, my lord. This woman
and I live in the same house, and I had a
baby while she was there with me. 18The
third day after my child was born, this
woman also had a baby. We were alone;
there was no one in the house but the
two of us.
19"During the night this woman's
son died because she lay on him. 20So
she got up in the middle of the night
and took my son from my side while I
your servant was asleep. She put him

by her breast and put her dead son by my breast. 21The next morning, I got up to nurse my son — and he was dead! But when I looked at him closely in the morning light, I saw that it wasn't the son I had borne."

22The other woman said, "No! The living one is my son; the dead one is yours."

But the first one insisted, "No! The dead one is yours; the living one is mine." And so they argued before the king.

23The king said, "This one says, 'My son is alive and your son is dead,' while that one says, 'No! Your son is dead and mine is alive.' "

24Then the king said, "Bring me a sword." So they brought a sword for the king. 25He then gave an order: "Cut the living child in two and give half to one and half to the other."

26The woman whose son was alive was deeply moved out of love for her son and said to the king, "Please, my lord, give her the living baby! Don't kill him!"

But the other said, "Neither I nor you shall have him. Cut him in two!"

27Then the king gave his ruling: "Give the living baby to the first woman. Do not kill him; she is his mother."

28When all Israel heard the verdict the king had given, they held the king in awe, because they saw that he had wisdom from God to administer justice.

Solomon's Officials and Governors

4 So King Solomon ruled over all Israel. 2And these were his chief officials:

Azariah son of Zadok — the priest;
3Elihoreph and Ahijah, sons of Shisha — secretaries;
Jehoshaphat son of Ahilud — recorder;
4Benaiah son of Jehoiada — commander in chief;
Zadok and Abiathar — priests;
5Azariah son of Nathan — in charge of the district governors;
Zabud son of Nathan — a priest and adviser to the king;
6Ahishar — palace administrator;
Adoniram son of Abda — in charge of forced labor.

7Solomon had twelve district governors over all Israel, who supplied provisions for the king and the royal household. Each one had to provide supplies for one month in the year. 8These are their names:

Ben-Hur — in the hill country of Ephraim;
9Ben-Deker — in Makaz, Shaalbim, Beth Shemesh and Elon Bethhanan;
10Ben-Hesed — in Arubboth (Sokoh and all the land of Hepher were his);
11Ben-Abinadab — in Naphoth Dor (he was married to Taphath daughter of Solomon);
12Baana son of Ahilud — in Taanach and Megiddo, and in all of Beth Shan next to Zarethan below Jezreel, from Beth Shan to Abel Meholah across to Jokmeam;
13Ben-Geber — in Ramoth Gilead (the settlements of Jair son of Manasseh in Gilead were his, as well as the region of Argob in Bashan and its sixty large walled cities with bronze gate bars);
14Ahinadab son of Iddo — in Mahanaim;
15Ahimaaz — in Naphtali (he had married Basemath daughter of Solomon);
16Baana son of Hushai — in Asher and in Aloth;
17Jehoshaphat son of Paruah — in Issachar;
18Shimei son of Ela — in Benjamin;
19Geber son of Uri — in Gilead (the country of Sihon king of the Amorites and the country of Og king of Bashan). He was the only governor over the district.

Solomon's Daily Provisions

20The people of Judah and Israel were as numerous as the sand on the seashore; they ate, they drank and they were happy. 21And Solomon ruled over all the kingdoms from the Euphrates River to the land of the Philistines, as far as the border of Egypt. These countries brought tribute and were Solomon's subjects all his life.

22Solomon's daily provisions were thirty cors[a] of the finest flour and sixty cors[b] of meal, 23ten head of stall-fed cattle, twenty of pasture-fed cattle and a hundred sheep and goats, as well as deer, gazelles, roebucks and choice fowl. 24For he ruled over all the kingdoms west of the Euphrates River, from Tiphsah to Gaza, and had peace on all sides. 25During Solomon's lifetime Judah and Israel, from Dan to Beersheba, lived in safety,

[a] 22 That is, probably about 5 1/2 tons or about 5 metric tons [b] 22 That is, probably about 11 tons or about 10 metric tons

everyone under their own vine and under their own fig tree.

26 Solomon had four[a] thousand stalls for chariot horses, and twelve thousand horses.[b]

27 The district governors, each in his month, supplied provisions for King Solomon and all who came to the king's table. They saw to it that nothing was lacking. 28 They also brought to the proper place their quotas of barley and straw for the chariot horses and the other horses.

Solomon's Wisdom

29 God gave Solomon wisdom and very great insight, and a breadth of understanding as measureless as the sand on the seashore. 30 Solomon's wisdom was greater than the wisdom of all the people of the East, and greater than all the wisdom of Egypt. 31 He was wiser than anyone else, including Ethan the Ezrahite — wiser than Heman, Kalkol and Darda, the sons of Mahol. And his fame spread to all the surrounding nations. 32 He spoke three thousand proverbs and his songs numbered a thousand and five. 33 He spoke about plant life, from the cedar of Lebanon to the hyssop that grows out of walls. He also spoke about animals and birds, reptiles and fish. 34 From all nations people came to listen to Solomon's wisdom, sent by all the kings of the world, who had heard of his wisdom.[c]

Preparations for Building the Temple

5[d] When Hiram king of Tyre heard that Solomon had been anointed king to succeed his father David, he sent his envoys to Solomon, because he had always been on friendly terms with David. 2 Solomon sent back this message to Hiram:

> 3 "You know that because of the wars waged against my father David from all sides, he could not build a temple for the Name of the LORD his God until the LORD put his enemies under his feet. 4 But now the LORD my God has given me rest on every side, and there is no adversary or disaster. 5 I intend, therefore, to build a temple for the Name of the LORD my God, as the LORD told my father David, when he said, 'Your son whom I will put on the throne in your place will build the temple for my Name.'
>
> 6 "So give orders that cedars of Lebanon be cut for me. My men will work with yours, and I will pay you for your men whatever wages you set. You know that we have no one so skilled in felling timber as the Sidonians."

7 When Hiram heard Solomon's message, he was greatly pleased and said, "Praise be to the LORD today, for he has given David a wise son to rule over this great nation."

8 So Hiram sent word to Solomon:

> "I have received the message you sent me and will do all you want in providing the cedar and juniper logs. 9 My men will haul them down from Lebanon to the Mediterranean Sea, and I will float them as rafts by sea to the place you specify. There I will separate them and you can take them away. And you are to grant my wish by providing food for my royal household."

10 In this way Hiram kept Solomon supplied with all the cedar and juniper logs he wanted, 11 and Solomon gave Hiram twenty thousand cors[e] of wheat as food for his household, in addition to twenty thousand baths[f,g] of pressed olive oil. Solomon continued to do this for Hiram year after year. 12 The LORD gave Solomon wisdom, just as he had promised him. There were peaceful relations between Hiram and Solomon, and the two of them made a treaty.

13 King Solomon conscripted laborers from all Israel — thirty thousand men. 14 He sent them off to Lebanon in shifts of ten thousand a month, so that they spent one month in Lebanon and two months at home. Adoniram was in charge of the forced labor. 15 Solomon had seventy thousand carriers and eighty thousand stonecutters in the hills, 16 as well as thirty-three hundred[h] foremen who supervised the project and directed the workers. 17 At the king's command they removed from the quarry large blocks of high-grade stone to provide a foundation of dressed stone for the temple. 18 The craftsmen of Solomon and Hiram and workers from Byblos cut and prepared the timber and stone for the building of the temple.

[a] *26* Some Septuagint manuscripts (see also 2 Chron. 9:25); Hebrew *forty* [b] *26* Or *charioteers*
[c] *34* In Hebrew texts 4:21-34 is numbered 5:1-14. [d] In Hebrew texts 5:1-18 is numbered 5:15-32.
[e] *11* That is, probably about 3,600 tons or about 3,250 metric tons [f] *11* Septuagint (see also 2 Chron. 2:10); Hebrew *twenty cors* [g] *11* That is, about 120,000 gallons or about 440,000 liters
[h] *16* Hebrew; some Septuagint manuscripts (see also 2 Chron. 2:2,18) *thirty-six hundred*

Solomon Builds the Temple

6 In the four hundred and eightieth[a] year after the Israelites came out of Egypt, in the fourth year of Solomon's reign over Israel, in the month of Ziv, the second month, he began to build the temple of the LORD.

2The temple that King Solomon built for the LORD was sixty cubits long, twenty wide and thirty high.[b] 3The portico at the front of the main hall of the temple extended the width of the temple, that is twenty cubits,[c] and projected ten cubits[d] from the front of the temple. 4He made narrow windows high up in the temple walls. 5Against the walls of the main hall and inner sanctuary he built a structure around the building, in which there were side rooms. 6The lowest floor was five cubits[e] wide, the middle floor six cubits[f] and the third floor seven.[g] He made offset ledges around the outside of the temple so that nothing would be inserted into the temple walls.

7In building the temple, only blocks dressed at the quarry were used, and no hammer, chisel or any other iron tool was heard at the temple site while it was being built.

8The entrance to the lowest[h] floor was on the south side of the temple; a stairway led up to the middle level and from there to the third. 9So he built the temple and completed it, roofing it with beams and cedar planks. 10And he built the side rooms all along the temple. The height of each was five cubits, and they were attached to the temple by beams of cedar.

11The word of the LORD came to Solomon: 12"As for this temple you are building, if you follow my decrees, observe my laws and keep all my commands and obey them, I will fulfill through you the promise I gave to David your father. 13And I will live among the Israelites and will not abandon my people Israel."

14So Solomon built the temple and completed it. 15He lined its interior walls with cedar boards, paneling them from the floor of the temple to the ceiling, and covered the floor of the temple with planks of juniper. 16He partitioned off twenty cubits at the rear of the temple with cedar boards from floor to ceiling to form within the temple an inner sanctuary, the Most Holy Place. 17The main hall in front of this room was forty cubits[i] long. 18The inside of the temple was cedar, carved with gourds and open flowers. Everything was cedar; no stone was to be seen.

19He prepared the inner sanctuary within the temple to set the ark of the covenant of the LORD there. 20The inner sanctuary was twenty cubits long, twenty wide and twenty high. He overlaid the inside with pure gold, and he also overlaid the altar of cedar. 21Solomon covered the inside of the temple with pure gold, and he extended gold chains across the front of the inner sanctuary, which was overlaid with gold. 22So he overlaid the whole interior with gold. He also overlaid with gold the altar that belonged to the inner sanctuary.

23For the inner sanctuary he made a pair of cherubim out of olive wood, each ten cubits high. 24One wing of the first cherub was five cubits long, and the other wing five cubits — ten cubits from wing tip to wing tip. 25The second cherub also measured ten cubits, for the two cherubim were identical in size and shape. 26The height of each cherub was ten cubits. 27He placed the cherubim inside the innermost room of the temple, with their wings spread out. The wing of one cherub touched one wall, while the wing of the other touched the other wall, and their wings touched each other in the middle of the room. 28He overlaid the cherubim with gold.

29On the walls all around the temple, in both the inner and outer rooms, he carved cherubim, palm trees and open flowers. 30He also covered the floors of both the inner and outer rooms of the temple with gold.

31For the entrance to the inner sanctuary he made doors out of olive wood that were one fifth of the width of the sanctuary. 32And on the two olive-wood doors he carved cherubim, palm trees and open flowers, and overlaid the cherubim and palm trees with hammered gold. 33In the same way, for the entrance to the main hall he made doorframes out of olive wood that were one fourth of the width of the hall. 34He also made two doors out of juniper wood, each

[a] *1* Hebrew; Septuagint *four hundred and fortieth* [b] *2* That is, about 90 feet long, 30 feet wide and 45 feet high or about 27 meters long, 9 meters wide and 14 meters high [c] *3* That is, about 30 feet or about 9 meters; also in verses 16 and 20 [d] *3* That is, about 15 feet or about 4.5 meters; also in verses 23-26 [e] *6* That is, about 7 1/2 feet or about 2.3 meters; also in verses 10 and 24 [f] *6* That is, about 9 feet or about 2.7 meters [g] *6* That is, about 11 feet or about 3.2 meters [h] *8* Septuagint; Hebrew *middle* [i] *17* That is, about 60 feet or about 18 meters

having two leaves that turned in sockets. 35 He carved cherubim, palm trees and open flowers on them and overlaid them with gold hammered evenly over the carvings.

36 And he built the inner courtyard of three courses of dressed stone and one course of trimmed cedar beams.

37 The foundation of the temple of the LORD was laid in the fourth year, in the month of Ziv. 38 In the eleventh year in the month of Bul, the eighth month, the temple was finished in all its details according to its specifications. He had spent seven years building it.

Solomon Builds His Palace

7 It took Solomon thirteen years, however, to complete the construction of his palace. 2 He built the Palace of the Forest of Lebanon a hundred cubits long, fifty wide and thirty high,[a] with four rows of cedar columns supporting trimmed cedar beams. 3 It was roofed with cedar above the beams that rested on the columns — forty-five beams, fifteen to a row. 4 Its windows were placed high in sets of three, facing each other. 5 All the doorways had rectangular frames; they were in the front part in sets of three, facing each other.[b]

6 He made a colonnade fifty cubits long and thirty wide.[c] In front of it was a portico, and in front of that were pillars and an overhanging roof.

7 He built the throne hall, the Hall of Justice, where he was to judge, and he covered it with cedar from floor to ceiling.[d] 8 And the palace in which he was to live, set farther back, was similar in design. Solomon also made a palace like this hall for Pharaoh's daughter, whom he had married.

9 All these structures, from the outside to the great courtyard and from foundation to eaves, were made of blocks of high-grade stone cut to size and smoothed on their inner and outer faces. 10 The foundations were laid with large stones of good quality, some measuring ten cubits[e] and some eight.[f] 11 Above were high-grade stones, cut to size, and cedar beams. 12 The great courtyard was surrounded by a wall of three courses of dressed stone and one course of trimmed cedar beams, as was the inner courtyard of the temple of the LORD with its portico.

The Temple's Furnishings

13 King Solomon sent to Tyre and brought Huram,[g] 14 whose mother was a widow from the tribe of Naphtali and whose father was from Tyre and a skilled craftsman in bronze. Huram was filled with wisdom, with understanding and with knowledge to do all kinds of bronze work. He came to King Solomon and did all the work assigned to him.

15 He cast two bronze pillars, each eighteen cubits high and twelve cubits in circumference.[h] 16 He also made two capitals of cast bronze to set on the tops of the pillars; each capital was five cubits[i] high. 17 A network of interwoven chains adorned the capitals on top of the pillars, seven for each capital. 18 He made pomegranates in two rows[j] encircling each network to decorate the capitals on top of the pillars.[k] He did the same for each capital. 19 The capitals on top of the pillars in the portico were in the shape of lilies, four cubits[l] high. 20 On the capitals of both pillars, above the bowl-shaped part next to the network, were the two hundred pomegranates in rows all around. 21 He erected the pillars at the portico of the temple. The pillar to the south he named Jakin[m] and the one to the north Boaz.[n] 22 The capitals on top were in the shape of lilies. And so the work on the pillars was completed.

23 He made the Sea of cast metal, circular in shape, measuring ten cubits from rim to rim and five cubits high. It took a line of thirty cubits[o] to measure around it. 24 Below the rim, gourds encircled it — ten to a cubit. The gourds were cast in two rows in one piece with the Sea.

[a] *2* That is, about 150 feet long, 75 feet wide and 45 feet high or about 45 meters long, 23 meters wide and 14 meters high [b] *5* The meaning of the Hebrew for this verse is uncertain.
[c] *6* That is, about 75 feet long and 45 feet wide or about 23 meters long and 14 meters wide
[d] *7* Vulgate and Syriac; Hebrew *floor* [e] *10* That is, about 15 feet or about 4.5 meters; also in verse 23 [f] *10* That is, about 12 feet or about 3.6 meters [g] *13* Hebrew *Hiram*, a variant of *Huram*; also in verses 40 and 45 [h] *15* That is, about 27 feet high and 18 feet in circumference or about 8.1 meters high and 5.4 meters in circumference [i] *16* That is, about 7 1/2 feet or about 2.3 meters; also in verse 23 [j] *18* Two Hebrew manuscripts and Septuagint; most Hebrew manuscripts *made the pillars, and there were two rows* [k] *18* Many Hebrew manuscripts and Syriac; most Hebrew manuscripts *pomegranates* [l] *19* That is, about 6 feet or about 1.8 meters; also in verse 38 [m] *21* *Jakin* probably means *he establishes.* [n] *21* *Boaz* probably means *in him is strength.* [o] *23* That is, about 45 feet or about 14 meters

25The Sea stood on twelve bulls, three
facing north, three facing west, three
facing south and three facing east. The
Sea rested on top of them, and their
hindquarters were toward the center. 26It
was a handbreadth[a] in thickness, and its
rim was like the rim of a cup, like a lily
blossom. It held two thousand baths.[b]

27He also made ten movable stands of
bronze; each was four cubits long, four
wide and three high.[c] 28This is how the
stands were made: They had side panels
attached to uprights. 29On the panels between the uprights were lions, bulls and
cherubim — and on the uprights as well.
Above and below the lions and bulls were
wreaths of hammered work. 30Each stand
had four bronze wheels with bronze axles, and each had a basin resting on four
supports, cast with wreaths on each side.
31On the inside of the stand there was an
opening that had a circular frame one
cubit[d] deep. This opening was round,
and with its basework it measured a cubit and a half.[e] Around its opening there
was engraving. The panels of the stands
were square, not round. 32The four wheels
were under the panels, and the axles of
the wheels were attached to the stand.
The diameter of each wheel was a cubit
and a half. 33The wheels were made like
chariot wheels; the axles, rims, spokes
and hubs were all of cast metal.

34Each stand had four handles, one on
each corner, projecting from the stand.
35At the top of the stand there was a circular band half a cubit[f] deep. The supports and panels were attached to the top
of the stand. 36He engraved cherubim,
lions and palm trees on the surfaces of
the supports and on the panels, in every
available space, with wreaths all around.
37This is the way he made the ten stands.
They were all cast in the same molds and
were identical in size and shape.

38He then made ten bronze basins,
each holding forty baths[g] and measuring four cubits across, one basin to go on
each of the ten stands. 39He placed five of
the stands on the south side of the temple and five on the north. He placed the
Sea on the south side, at the southeast
corner of the temple. 40He also made the
pots[h] and shovels and sprinkling bowls.

So Huram finished all the work he
had undertaken for King Solomon in the
temple of the LORD:

41the two pillars;
the two bowl-shaped capitals on top
of the pillars;
the two sets of network decorating
the two bowl-shaped capitals on
top of the pillars;
42the four hundred pomegranates for
the two sets of network (two rows
of pomegranates for each network decorating the bowl-shaped
capitals on top of the pillars);
43the ten stands with their ten basins;
44the Sea and the twelve bulls under it;
45the pots, shovels and sprinkling
bowls.

All these objects that Huram made
for King Solomon for the temple of the
LORD were of burnished bronze. 46The
king had them cast in clay molds in the
plain of the Jordan between Sukkoth
and Zarethan. 47Solomon left all these
things unweighed, because there were
so many; the weight of the bronze was
not determined.

48Solomon also made all the furnishings that were in the LORD's temple:

the golden altar;
the golden table on which was the
bread of the Presence;
49the lampstands of pure gold (five on
the right and five on the left, in
front of the inner sanctuary);
the gold floral work and lamps and
tongs;
50the pure gold basins, wick trimmers, sprinkling bowls, dishes
and censers;
and the gold sockets for the doors
of the innermost room, the Most
Holy Place, and also for the doors
of the main hall of the temple.

51When all the work King Solomon
had done for the temple of the LORD was
finished, he brought in the things his
father David had dedicated — the silver and gold and the furnishings — and
he placed them in the treasuries of the
LORD's temple.

[a] *26* That is, about 3 inches or about 7.5 centimeters [b] *26* That is, about 12,000 gallons or about 44,000 liters; the Septuagint does not have this sentence. [c] *27* That is, about 6 feet long and wide and about 4 1/2 feet high or about 1.8 meters long and wide and 1.4 meters high [d] *31* That is, about 18 inches or about 45 centimeters [e] *31* That is, about 2 1/4 feet or about 68 centimeters; also in verse 32 [f] *35* That is, about 9 inches or about 23 centimeters [g] *38* That is, about 240 gallons or about 880 liters [h] *40* Many Hebrew manuscripts, Septuagint, Syriac and Vulgate (see also verse 45 and 2 Chron. 4:11); many other Hebrew manuscripts *basins*

The Ark Brought to the Temple

8 Then King Solomon summoned into
his presence at Jerusalem the elders
of Israel, all the heads of the tribes and
the chiefs of the Israelite families, to
bring up the ark of the LORD's covenant
from Zion, the City of David. 2All the Israelites came together to King Solomon
at the time of the festival in the month
of Ethanim, the seventh month.
3When all the elders of Israel had arrived, the priests took up the ark, 4and
they brought up the ark of the LORD and
the tent of meeting and all the sacred
furnishings in it. The priests and Levites
carried them up, 5and King Solomon
and the entire assembly of Israel that
had gathered about him were before
the ark, sacrificing so many sheep and
cattle that they could not be recorded or
counted.
6The priests then brought the ark of
the LORD's covenant to its place in the
inner sanctuary of the temple, the Most
Holy Place, and put it beneath the wings
of the cherubim. 7The cherubim spread
their wings over the place of the ark
and overshadowed the ark and its carrying poles. 8These poles were so long
that their ends could be seen from the
Holy Place in front of the inner sanctuary, but not from outside the Holy Place;
and they are still there today. 9There was
nothing in the ark except the two stone
tablets that Moses had placed in it at
Horeb, where the LORD made a covenant
with the Israelites after they came out of
Egypt.
10When the priests withdrew from the
Holy Place, the cloud filled the temple of
the LORD. 11And the priests could not perform their service because of the cloud,
for the glory of the LORD filled his temple.
12Then Solomon said, "The LORD has
said that he would dwell in a dark cloud;
13I have indeed built a magnificent temple for you, a place for you to dwell forever."
14While the whole assembly of Israel was standing there, the king turned
around and blessed them. 15Then he
said:

"Praise be to the LORD, the God of
Israel, who with his own hand has
fulfilled what he promised with his
own mouth to my father David. For
he said, 16'Since the day I brought
my people Israel out of Egypt, I
have not chosen a city in any tribe
of Israel to have a temple built so
that my Name might be there, but
I have chosen David to rule my people Israel.'
17"My father David had it in his
heart to build a temple for the
Name of the LORD, the God of Israel. 18But the LORD said to my father David, 'You did well to have it
in your heart to build a temple for
my Name. 19Nevertheless, you are
not the one to build the temple,
but your son, your own flesh and
blood—he is the one who will build
the temple for my Name.'
20"The LORD has kept the promise he made: I have succeeded David my father and now I sit on the
throne of Israel, just as the LORD
promised, and I have built the temple for the Name of the LORD, the
God of Israel. 21I have provided a
place there for the ark, in which is
the covenant of the LORD that he
made with our ancestors when he
brought them out of Egypt."

Solomon's Prayer of Dedication

22Then Solomon stood before the altar
of the LORD in front of the whole assembly of Israel, spread out his hands toward heaven 23and said:

"LORD, the God of Israel, there is
no God like you in heaven above
or on earth below—you who keep
your covenant of love with your servants who continue wholeheartedly in your way. 24You have kept your
promise to your servant David my
father; with your mouth you have
promised and with your hand you
have fulfilled it—as it is today.
25"Now LORD, the God of Israel,
keep for your servant David my father the promises you made to him
when you said, 'You shall never fail
to have a successor to sit before me
on the throne of Israel, if only your
descendants are careful in all they
do to walk before me faithfully as
you have done.' 26And now, God of
Israel, let your word that you promised your servant David my father
come true.
27"But will God really dwell on
earth? The heavens, even the highest heaven, cannot contain you.
How much less this temple I have
built! 28Yet give attention to your
servant's prayer and his plea for
mercy, LORD my God. Hear the cry
and the prayer that your servant is

praying in your presence this day. 29May your eyes be open toward this temple night and day, this place of which you said, 'My Name shall be there,' so that you will hear the prayer your servant prays toward this place. 30Hear the supplication of your servant and of your people Israel when they pray toward this place. Hear from heaven, your dwelling place, and when you hear, forgive.

31"When anyone wrongs their neighbor and is required to take an oath and they come and swear the oath before your altar in this temple, 32then hear from heaven and act. Judge between your servants, condemning the guilty by bringing down on their heads what they have done, and vindicating the innocent by treating them in accordance with their innocence.

33"When your people Israel have been defeated by an enemy because they have sinned against you, and when they turn back to you and give praise to your name, praying and making supplication to you in this temple, 34then hear from heaven and forgive the sin of your people Israel and bring them back to the land you gave to their ancestors.

35"When the heavens are shut up and there is no rain because your people have sinned against you, and when they pray toward this place and give praise to your name and turn from their sin because you have afflicted them, 36then hear from heaven and forgive the sin of your servants, your people Israel. Teach them the right way to live, and send rain on the land you gave your people for an inheritance.

37"When famine or plague comes to the land, or blight or mildew, locusts or grasshoppers, or when an enemy besieges them in any of their cities, whatever disaster or disease may come, 38and when a prayer or plea is made by anyone among your people Israel — being aware of the afflictions of their own hearts, and spreading out their hands toward this temple — 39then hear from heaven, your dwelling place. Forgive and act; deal with everyone according to all they do, since you know their hearts (for you alone know every human heart), 40so that they will fear you all the time they live in the land you gave our ancestors.

41"As for the foreigner who does not belong to your people Israel but has come from a distant land because of your name — 42for they will hear of your great name and your mighty hand and your outstretched arm — when they come and pray toward this temple, 43then hear from heaven, your dwelling place. Do whatever the foreigner asks of you, so that all the peoples of the earth may know your name and fear you, as do your own people Israel, and may know that this house I have built bears your Name.

44"When your people go to war against their enemies, wherever you send them, and when they pray to the LORD toward the city you have chosen and the temple I have built for your Name, 45then hear from heaven their prayer and their plea, and uphold their cause.

46"When they sin against you — for there is no one who does not sin — and you become angry with them and give them over to their enemies, who take them captive to their own lands, far away or near; 47and if they have a change of heart in the land where they are held captive, and repent and plead with you in the land of their captors and say, 'We have sinned, we have done wrong, we have acted wickedly'; 48and if they turn back to you with all their heart and soul in the land of their enemies who took them captive, and pray to you toward the land you gave their ancestors, toward the city you have chosen and the temple I have built for your Name; 49then from heaven, your dwelling place, hear their prayer and their plea, and uphold their cause. 50And forgive your people, who have sinned against you; forgive all the offenses they have committed against you, and cause their captors to show them mercy; 51for they are your people and your inheritance, whom you brought out of Egypt, out of that iron-smelting furnace.

52"May your eyes be open to your servant's plea and to the plea of your people Israel, and may you listen to them whenever they cry out to you. 53For you singled them out from all the nations of the world to be your own inheritance, just as you declared through your servant Moses when you, Sovereign LORD, brought our ancestors out of Egypt."

[54]When Solomon had finished all these prayers and supplications to the LORD, he rose from before the altar of the LORD, where he had been kneeling with his hands spread out toward heaven. [55]He stood and blessed the whole assembly of Israel in a loud voice, saying:

[56]"Praise be to the LORD, who has given rest to his people Israel just as he promised. Not one word has failed of all the good promises he gave through his servant Moses. [57]May the LORD our God be with us as he was with our ancestors; may he never leave us nor forsake us. [58]May he turn our hearts to him, to walk in obedience to him and keep the commands, decrees and laws he gave our ancestors. [59]And may these words of mine, which I have prayed before the LORD, be near to the LORD our God day and night, that he may uphold the cause of his servant and the cause of his people Israel according to each day's need, [60]so that all the peoples of the earth may know that the LORD is God and that there is no other. [61]And may your hearts be fully committed to the LORD our God, to live by his decrees and obey his commands, as at this time."

The Dedication of the Temple

[62]Then the king and all Israel with him offered sacrifices before the LORD. [63]Solomon offered a sacrifice of fellowship offerings to the LORD: twenty-two thousand cattle and a hundred and twenty thousand sheep and goats. So the king and all the Israelites dedicated the temple of the LORD.

[64]On that same day the king consecrated the middle part of the courtyard in front of the temple of the LORD, and there he offered burnt offerings, grain offerings and the fat of the fellowship offerings, because the bronze altar that stood before the LORD was too small to hold the burnt offerings, the grain offerings and the fat of the fellowship offerings.

[65]So Solomon observed the festival at that time, and all Israel with him — a vast assembly, people from Lebo Hamath to the Wadi of Egypt. They celebrated it before the LORD our God for seven days and seven days more, fourteen days in all. [66]On the following day he sent the people away. They blessed the king and then went home, joyful and glad in heart for all the good things the LORD had done for his servant David and his people Israel.

The LORD Appears to Solomon

9 When Solomon had finished building the temple of the LORD and the royal palace, and had achieved all he had desired to do, [2]the LORD appeared to him a second time, as he had appeared to him at Gibeon. [3]The LORD said to him:

"I have heard the prayer and plea you have made before me; I have consecrated this temple, which you have built, by putting my Name there forever. My eyes and my heart will always be there.

[4]"As for you, if you walk before me faithfully with integrity of heart and uprightness, as David your father did, and do all I command and observe my decrees and laws, [5]I will establish your royal throne over Israel forever, as I promised David your father when I said, 'You shall never fail to have a successor on the throne of Israel.'

[6]"But if you[a] or your descendants turn away from me and do not observe the commands and decrees I have given you[a] and go off to serve other gods and worship them, [7]then I will cut off Israel from the land I have given them and will reject this temple I have consecrated for my Name. Israel will then become a byword and an object of ridicule among all peoples. [8]This temple will become a heap of rubble. All[b] who pass by will be appalled and will scoff and say, 'Why has the LORD done such a thing to this land and to this temple?' [9]People will answer, 'Because they have forsaken the LORD their God, who brought their ancestors out of Egypt, and have embraced other gods, worshiping and serving them — that is why the LORD brought all this disaster on them.'"

[a] *6* The Hebrew is plural. [b] *8* See some Septuagint manuscripts, Old Latin, Syriac, Arabic and Targum; Hebrew *And though this temple is now imposing, all*

Solomon's Other Activities

10 At the end of twenty years, during which Solomon built these two buildings — the temple of the LORD and the royal palace — 11 King Solomon gave twenty towns in Galilee to Hiram king of Tyre, because Hiram had supplied him with all the cedar and juniper and gold he wanted. 12 But when Hiram went from Tyre to see the towns that Solomon had given him, he was not pleased with them. 13 "What kind of towns are these you have given me, my brother?" he asked. And he called them the Land of Kabul,[a] a name they have to this day. 14 Now Hiram had sent to the king 120 talents[b] of gold.

15 Here is the account of the forced labor King Solomon conscripted to build the LORD's temple, his own palace, the terraces,[c] the wall of Jerusalem, and Hazor, Megiddo and Gezer. 16 (Pharaoh king of Egypt had attacked and captured Gezer. He had set it on fire. He killed its Canaanite inhabitants and then gave it as a wedding gift to his daughter, Solomon's wife. 17 And Solomon rebuilt Gezer.) He built up Lower Beth Horon, 18 Baalath, and Tadmor[d] in the desert, within his land, 19 as well as all his store cities and the towns for his chariots and for his horses[e] — whatever he desired to build in Jerusalem, in Lebanon and throughout all the territory he ruled.

20 There were still people left from the Amorites, Hittites, Perizzites, Hivites and Jebusites (these peoples were not Israelites). 21 Solomon conscripted the descendants of all these peoples remaining in the land — whom the Israelites could not exterminate[f] — to serve as slave labor, as it is to this day. 22 But Solomon did not make slaves of any of the Israelites; they were his fighting men, his government officials, his officers, his captains, and the commanders of his chariots and charioteers. 23 They were also the chief officials in charge of Solomon's projects — 550 officials supervising those who did the work.

24 After Pharaoh's daughter had come up from the City of David to the palace Solomon had built for her, he constructed the terraces.

25 Three times a year Solomon sacrificed burnt offerings and fellowship offerings on the altar he had built for the LORD, burning incense before the LORD along with them, and so fulfilled the temple obligations.

26 King Solomon also built ships at Ezion Geber, which is near Elath in Edom, on the shore of the Red Sea.[g] 27 And Hiram sent his men — sailors who knew the sea — to serve in the fleet with Solomon's men. 28 They sailed to Ophir and brought back 420 talents[h] of gold, which they delivered to King Solomon.

The Queen of Sheba Visits Solomon

10 When the queen of Sheba heard about the fame of Solomon and his relationship to the LORD, she came to test Solomon with hard questions. 2 Arriving at Jerusalem with a very great caravan — with camels carrying spices, large quantities of gold, and precious stones — she came to Solomon and talked with him about all that she had on her mind. 3 Solomon answered all her questions; nothing was too hard for the king to explain to her. 4 When the queen of Sheba saw all the wisdom of Solomon and the palace he had built, 5 the food on his table, the seating of his officials, the attending servants in their robes, his cupbearers, and the burnt offerings he made at[i] the temple of the LORD, she was overwhelmed.

6 She said to the king, "The report I heard in my own country about your achievements and your wisdom is true. 7 But I did not believe these things until I came and saw with my own eyes. Indeed, not even half was told me; in wisdom and wealth you have far exceeded the report I heard. 8 How happy your people must be! How happy your officials, who continually stand before you and hear your wisdom! 9 Praise be to the LORD your God, who has delighted in you and placed you on the throne of Israel. Because of the LORD's eternal love for Israel, he has made you king to maintain justice and righteousness."

10 And she gave the king 120 talents[b] of gold, large quantities of spices, and precious stones. Never again were so many spices brought in as those the queen of Sheba gave to King Solomon.

11 (Hiram's ships brought gold from Ophir; and from there they brought

[a] *13* *Kabul* sounds like the Hebrew for *good-for-nothing.* [b] *14,10* That is, about 4 1/2 tons or about 4 metric tons [c] *15* Or *the Millo*; also in verse 24 [d] *18* The Hebrew may also be read *Tamar.* [e] *19* Or *charioteers* [f] *21* The Hebrew term refers to the irrevocable giving over of things or persons to the LORD, often by totally destroying them. [g] *26* Or *the Sea of Reeds* [h] *28* That is, about 16 tons or about 14 metric tons [i] *5* Or *the ascent by which he went up to*

great cargoes of almugwood[a] and precious stones. 12The king used the almugwood to make supports[b] for the temple
of the LORD and for the royal palace,
and to make harps and lyres for the musicians. So much almugwood has never
been imported or seen since that day.)
13King Solomon gave the queen of Sheba all she desired and asked for, besides
what he had given her out of his royal
bounty. Then she left and returned with
her retinue to her own country.

Solomon's Splendor

14The weight of the gold that Solomon
received yearly was 666 talents,[c] 15not
including the revenues from merchants
and traders and from all the Arabian
kings and the governors of the territories.
16King Solomon made two hundred
large shields of hammered gold; six
hundred shekels[d] of gold went into each
shield. 17He also made three hundred
small shields of hammered gold, with
three minas[e] of gold in each shield. The
king put them in the Palace of the Forest
of Lebanon.
18Then the king made a great throne
covered with ivory and overlaid with
fine gold. 19The throne had six steps, and
its back had a rounded top. On both sides
of the seat were armrests, with a lion
standing beside each of them. 20Twelve
lions stood on the six steps, one at either
end of each step. Nothing like it had ever
been made for any other kingdom. 21All
King Solomon's goblets were gold, and
all the household articles in the Palace
of the Forest of Lebanon were pure gold.
Nothing was made of silver, because
silver was considered of little value in
Solomon's days. 22The king had a fleet
of trading ships[f] at sea along with the
ships of Hiram. Once every three years it
returned, carrying gold, silver and ivory,
and apes and baboons.
23King Solomon was greater in riches
and wisdom than all the other kings of
the earth. 24The whole world sought audience with Solomon to hear the wisdom
God had put in his heart. 25Year after year,
everyone who came brought a gift — articles of silver and gold, robes, weapons
and spices, and horses and mules.
26Solomon accumulated chariots and
horses; he had fourteen hundred chariots and twelve thousand horses,[g] which
he kept in the chariot cities and also with
him in Jerusalem. 27The king made silver
as common in Jerusalem as stones, and
cedar as plentiful as sycamore-fig trees
in the foothills. 28Solomon's horses were
imported from Egypt and from Kue[h] —
the royal merchants purchased them
from Kue at the current price. 29They imported a chariot from Egypt for six hundred shekels of silver, and a horse for a
hundred and fifty.[i] They also exported
them to all the kings of the Hittites and
of the Arameans.

Solomon's Wives

11 King Solomon, however, loved
many foreign women besides Pharaoh's daughter — Moabites, Ammonites,
Edomites, Sidonians and Hittites. 2They
were from nations about which the LORD
had told the Israelites, "You must not intermarry with them, because they will
surely turn your hearts after their gods."
Nevertheless, Solomon held fast to them
in love. 3He had seven hundred wives of
royal birth and three hundred concubines,
and his wives led him astray. 4As Solomon
grew old, his wives turned his heart after
other gods, and his heart was not fully devoted to the LORD his God, as the heart of
David his father had been. 5He followed
Ashtoreth the goddess of the Sidonians,
and Molek the detestable god of the Ammonites. 6So Solomon did evil in the eyes
of the LORD; he did not follow the LORD
completely, as David his father had done.
7On a hill east of Jerusalem, Solomon
built a high place for Chemosh the detestable god of Moab, and for Molek the
detestable god of the Ammonites. 8He
did the same for all his foreign wives,
who burned incense and offered sacrifices to their gods.
9The LORD became angry with Solomon because his heart had turned away
from the LORD, the God of Israel, who
had appeared to him twice. 10Although
he had forbidden Solomon to follow
other gods, Solomon did not keep the
LORD's command. 11So the LORD said to
Solomon, "Since this is your attitude and
you have not kept my covenant and my

[a] *11* Probably a variant of *algumwood*; also in verse 12 [b] *12* The meaning of the Hebrew for this word is uncertain. [c] *14* That is, about 25 tons or about 23 metric tons [d] *16* That is, about 15 pounds or about 6.9 kilograms; also in verse 29 [e] *17* That is, about 3 3/4 pounds or about 1.7 kilograms; or perhaps reference is to double minas, that is, about 7 1/2 pounds or about 3.5 kilograms. [f] *22* Hebrew *of ships of Tarshish* [g] *26* Or *charioteers* [h] *28* Probably *Cilicia* [i] *29* That is, about 3 3/4 pounds or about 1.7 kilograms

decrees, which I commanded you, I will
most certainly tear the kingdom away
from you and give it to one of your sub-
ordinates. 12Nevertheless, for the sake of
David your father, I will not do it during your lifetime. I will tear it out of the
hand of your son. 13Yet I will not tear the
whole kingdom from him, but will give
him one tribe for the sake of David my
servant and for the sake of Jerusalem,
which I have chosen."

Solomon's Adversaries

14Then the LORD raised up against Solomon an adversary, Hadad the Edomite,
from the royal line of Edom. 15Earlier
when David was fighting with Edom,
Joab the commander of the army, who
had gone up to bury the dead, had struck
down all the men in Edom. 16Joab and
all the Israelites stayed there for six
months, until they had destroyed all the
men in Edom. 17But Hadad, still only a
boy, fled to Egypt with some Edomite officials who had served his father. 18They
set out from Midian and went to Paran.
Then taking people from Paran with
them, they went to Egypt, to Pharaoh
king of Egypt, who gave Hadad a house
and land and provided him with food.

19Pharaoh was so pleased with Hadad
that he gave him a sister of his own wife,
Queen Tahpenes, in marriage. 20The sister of Tahpenes bore him a son named
Genubath, whom Tahpenes brought
up in the royal palace. There Genubath
lived with Pharaoh's own children.

21While he was in Egypt, Hadad heard
that David rested with his ancestors and
that Joab the commander of the army
was also dead. Then Hadad said to Pharaoh, "Let me go, that I may return to my
own country."

22"What have you lacked here that you
want to go back to your own country?"
Pharaoh asked.

"Nothing," Hadad replied, "but do let
me go!"

23And God raised up against Solomon
another adversary, Rezon son of Eliada,
who had fled from his master, Hadadezer king of Zobah. 24When David destroyed Zobah's army, Rezon gathered
a band of men around him and became
their leader; they went to Damascus,
where they settled and took control.
25Rezon was Israel's adversary as long
as Solomon lived, adding to the trouble caused by Hadad. So Rezon ruled in
Aram and was hostile toward Israel.

Jeroboam Rebels Against Solomon

26Also, Jeroboam son of Nebat rebelled against the king. He was one of
Solomon's officials, an Ephraimite from
Zeredah, and his mother was a widow
named Zeruah.

27Here is the account of how he rebelled against the king: Solomon had
built the terraces[a] and had filled in the
gap in the wall of the city of David his
father. 28Now Jeroboam was a man of
standing, and when Solomon saw how
well the young man did his work, he put
him in charge of the whole labor force of
the tribes of Joseph.

29About that time Jeroboam was going
out of Jerusalem, and Ahijah the prophet of Shiloh met him on the way, wearing a new cloak. The two of them were
alone out in the country, 30and Ahijah
took hold of the new cloak he was wearing and tore it into twelve pieces. 31Then
he said to Jeroboam, "Take ten pieces for
yourself, for this is what the LORD, the
God of Israel, says: 'See, I am going to
tear the kingdom out of Solomon's hand
and give you ten tribes. 32But for the sake
of my servant David and the city of Jerusalem, which I have chosen out of all the
tribes of Israel, he will have one tribe. 33I
will do this because they have[b] forsaken
me and worshiped Ashtoreth the goddess of the Sidonians, Chemosh the god
of the Moabites, and Molek the god of
the Ammonites, and have not walked in
obedience to me, nor done what is right
in my eyes, nor kept my decrees and laws
as David, Solomon's father, did.

34" 'But I will not take the whole kingdom out of Solomon's hand; I have made
him ruler all the days of his life for the
sake of David my servant, whom I chose
and who obeyed my commands and decrees. 35I will take the kingdom from his
son's hands and give you ten tribes. 36I will
give one tribe to his son so that David my
servant may always have a lamp before
me in Jerusalem, the city where I chose to
put my Name. 37However, as for you, I will
take you, and you will rule over all that
your heart desires; you will be king over
Israel. 38If you do whatever I command
you and walk in obedience to me and do
what is right in my eyes by obeying my
decrees and commands, as David my servant did, I will be with you. I will build you
a dynasty as enduring as the one I built
for David and will give Israel to you. 39I
will humble David's descendants because
of this, but not forever.' "

[a] 27 Or *the Millo* [b] 33 Hebrew; Septuagint, Vulgate and Syriac *because he has*

40 Solomon tried to kill Jeroboam, but Jeroboam fled to Egypt, to Shishak the king, and stayed there until Solomon's death.

Solomon's Death

41 As for the other events of Solomon's reign — all he did and the wisdom he displayed — are they not written in the book of the annals of Solomon? 42 Solomon reigned in Jerusalem over all Israel forty years. 43 Then he rested with his ancestors and was buried in the city of David his father. And Rehoboam his son succeeded him as king.

Israel Rebels Against Rehoboam

12 Rehoboam went to Shechem, for all Israel had gone there to make him king. 2 When Jeroboam son of Nebat heard this (he was still in Egypt, where he had fled from King Solomon), he returned from[a] Egypt. 3 So they sent for Jeroboam, and he and the whole assembly of Israel went to Rehoboam and said to him: 4 "Your father put a heavy yoke on us, but now lighten the harsh labor and the heavy yoke he put on us, and we will serve you."

5 Rehoboam answered, "Go away for three days and then come back to me." So the people went away.

6 Then King Rehoboam consulted the elders who had served his father Solomon during his lifetime. "How would you advise me to answer these people?" he asked.

7 They replied, "If today you will be a servant to these people and serve them and give them a favorable answer, they will always be your servants."

8 But Rehoboam rejected the advice the elders gave him and consulted the young men who had grown up with him and were serving him. 9 He asked them, "What is your advice? How should we answer these people who say to me, 'Lighten the yoke your father put on us'?"

10 The young men who had grown up with him replied, "These people have said to you, 'Your father put a heavy yoke on us, but make our yoke lighter.' Now tell them, 'My little finger is thicker than my father's waist. 11 My father laid on you a heavy yoke; I will make it even heavier. My father scourged you with whips; I will scourge you with scorpions.'"

12 Three days later Jeroboam and all the people returned to Rehoboam, as the king had said, "Come back to me in three days." 13 The king answered the people harshly. Rejecting the advice given him by the elders, 14 he followed the advice of the young men and said, "My father made your yoke heavy; I will make it even heavier. My father scourged you with whips; I will scourge you with scorpions." 15 So the king did not listen to the people, for this turn of events was from the LORD, to fulfill the word the LORD had spoken to Jeroboam son of Nebat through Ahijah the Shilonite.

16 When all Israel saw that the king refused to listen to them, they answered the king:

"What share do we have in David,
  what part in Jesse's son?
To your tents, Israel!
  Look after your own house, David!"

So the Israelites went home. 17 But as for the Israelites who were living in the towns of Judah, Rehoboam still ruled over them.

18 King Rehoboam sent out Adoniram,[b] who was in charge of forced labor, but all Israel stoned him to death. King Rehoboam, however, managed to get into his chariot and escape to Jerusalem. 19 So Israel has been in rebellion against the house of David to this day.

20 When all the Israelites heard that Jeroboam had returned, they sent and called him to the assembly and made him king over all Israel. Only the tribe of Judah remained loyal to the house of David.

21 When Rehoboam arrived in Jerusalem, he mustered all Judah and the tribe of Benjamin — a hundred and eighty thousand able young men — to go to war against Israel and to regain the kingdom for Rehoboam son of Solomon.

22 But this word of God came to Shemaiah the man of God: 23 "Say to Rehoboam son of Solomon king of Judah, to all Judah and Benjamin, and to the rest of the people, 24 'This is what the LORD says: Do not go up to fight against your brothers, the Israelites. Go home, every one of you, for this is my doing.'" So they obeyed the word of the LORD and went home again, as the LORD had ordered.

Golden Calves at Bethel and Dan

25 Then Jeroboam fortified Shechem in the hill country of Ephraim and lived there. From there he went out and built up Peniel.[c]

[a] 2 Or *he remained in* [b] 18 Some Septuagint manuscripts and Syriac (see also 4:6 and 5:14); Hebrew *Adoram* [c] 25 Hebrew *Penuel,* a variant of *Peniel*

26 Jeroboam thought to himself, "The kingdom will now likely revert to the house of David. 27 If these people go up to offer sacrifices at the temple of the LORD in Jerusalem, they will again give their allegiance to their lord, Rehoboam king of Judah. They will kill me and return to King Rehoboam."

28 After seeking advice, the king made two golden calves. He said to the people, "It is too much for you to go up to Jerusalem. Here are your gods, Israel, who brought you up out of Egypt." 29 One he set up in Bethel, and the other in Dan. 30 And this thing became a sin; the people came to worship the one at Bethel and went as far as Dan to worship the other.[a]

31 Jeroboam built shrines on high places and appointed priests from all sorts of people, even though they were not Levites. 32 He instituted a festival on the fifteenth day of the eighth month, like the festival held in Judah, and offered sacrifices on the altar. This he did in Bethel, sacrificing to the calves he had made. And at Bethel he also installed priests at the high places he had made. 33 On the fifteenth day of the eighth month, a month of his own choosing, he offered sacrifices on the altar he had built at Bethel. So he instituted the festival for the Israelites and went up to the altar to make offerings.

The Man of God From Judah

13 By the word of the LORD a man of God came from Judah to Bethel, as Jeroboam was standing by the altar to make an offering. 2 By the word of the LORD he cried out against the altar: "Altar, altar! This is what the LORD says: 'A son named Josiah will be born to the house of David. On you he will sacrifice the priests of the high places who make offerings here, and human bones will be burned on you.'" 3 That same day the man of God gave a sign: "This is the sign the LORD has declared: The altar will be split apart and the ashes on it will be poured out."

4 When King Jeroboam heard what the man of God cried out against the altar at Bethel, he stretched out his hand from the altar and said, "Seize him!" But the hand he stretched out toward the man shriveled up, so that he could not pull it back. 5 Also, the altar was split apart and its ashes poured out according to the sign given by the man of God by the word of the LORD.

6 Then the king said to the man of God, "Intercede with the LORD your God and pray for me that my hand may be restored." So the man of God interceded with the LORD, and the king's hand was restored and became as it was before.

7 The king said to the man of God, "Come home with me for a meal, and I will give you a gift."

8 But the man of God answered the king, "Even if you were to give me half your possessions, I would not go with you, nor would I eat bread or drink water here. 9 For I was commanded by the word of the LORD: 'You must not eat bread or drink water or return by the way you came.'" 10 So he took another road and did not return by the way he had come to Bethel.

11 Now there was a certain old prophet living in Bethel, whose sons came and told him all that the man of God had done there that day. They also told their father what he had said to the king. 12 Their father asked them, "Which way did he go?" And his sons showed him which road the man of God from Judah had taken. 13 So he said to his sons, "Saddle the donkey for me." And when they had saddled the donkey for him, he mounted it 14 and rode after the man of God. He found him sitting under an oak tree and asked, "Are you the man of God who came from Judah?"

"I am," he replied.

15 So the prophet said to him, "Come home with me and eat."

16 The man of God said, "I cannot turn back and go with you, nor can I eat bread or drink water with you in this place. 17 I have been told by the word of the LORD: 'You must not eat bread or drink water there or return by the way you came.'"

18 The old prophet answered, "I too am a prophet, as you are. And an angel said to me by the word of the LORD: 'Bring him back with you to your house so that he may eat bread and drink water.'" (But he was lying to him.) 19 So the man of God returned with him and ate and drank in his house.

20 While they were sitting at the table, the word of the LORD came to the old prophet who had brought him back. 21 He cried out to the man of God who had come from Judah, "This is what the LORD says: 'You have defied the word of the LORD and have not kept the command the LORD your God gave you. 22 You came

[a] 30 Probable reading of the original Hebrew text; Masoretic Text *people went to the one as far as Dan*

back and ate bread and drank water in
the place where he told you not to eat or
drink. Therefore your body will not be
buried in the tomb of your ancestors.'"

23 When the man of God had finished
eating and drinking, the prophet who
had brought him back saddled his donkey for him. 24 As he went on his way, a
lion met him on the road and killed him,
and his body was left lying on the road,
with both the donkey and the lion standing beside it. 25 Some people who passed
by saw the body lying there, with the lion
standing beside the body, and they went
and reported it in the city where the old
prophet lived.

26 When the prophet who had brought
him back from his journey heard of it,
he said, "It is the man of God who defied
the word of the LORD. The LORD has given
him over to the lion, which has mauled
him and killed him, as the word of the
LORD had warned him."

27 The prophet said to his sons, "Saddle the donkey for me," and they did so.
28 Then he went out and found the body
lying on the road, with the donkey and
the lion standing beside it. The lion had
neither eaten the body nor mauled the
donkey. 29 So the prophet picked up the
body of the man of God, laid it on the
donkey, and brought it back to his own
city to mourn for him and bury him.
30 Then he laid the body in his own tomb,
and they mourned over him and said,
"Alas, my brother!"

31 After burying him, he said to his
sons, "When I die, bury me in the grave
where the man of God is buried; lay my
bones beside his bones. 32 For the message he declared by the word of the LORD
against the altar in Bethel and against
all the shrines on the high places in the
towns of Samaria will certainly come
true."

33 Even after this, Jeroboam did not
change his evil ways, but once more appointed priests for the high places from
all sorts of people. Anyone who wanted
to become a priest he consecrated for
the high places. 34 This was the sin of the
house of Jeroboam that led to its downfall and to its destruction from the face
of the earth.

Ahijah's Prophecy Against Jeroboam

14 At that time Abijah son of Jeroboam became ill, 2 and Jeroboam
said to his wife, "Go, disguise yourself,
so you won't be recognized as the wife of
Jeroboam. Then go to Shiloh. Ahijah the
prophet is there — the one who told me
I would be king over this people. 3 Take
ten loaves of bread with you, some cakes
and a jar of honey, and go to him. He will
tell you what will happen to the boy." 4 So
Jeroboam's wife did what he said and
went to Ahijah's house in Shiloh.

Now Ahijah could not see; his sight
was gone because of his age. 5 But the
LORD had told Ahijah, "Jeroboam's wife
is coming to ask you about her son, for
he is ill, and you are to give her such and
such an answer. When she arrives, she
will pretend to be someone else."

6 So when Ahijah heard the sound of
her footsteps at the door, he said, "Come
in, wife of Jeroboam. Why this pretense?
I have been sent to you with bad news.
7 Go, tell Jeroboam that this is what the
LORD, the God of Israel, says: 'I raised
you up from among the people and appointed you ruler over my people Israel.
8 I tore the kingdom away from the house
of David and gave it to you, but you have
not been like my servant David, who
kept my commands and followed me
with all his heart, doing only what was
right in my eyes. 9 You have done more
evil than all who lived before you. You
have made for yourself other gods, idols
made of metal; you have aroused my anger and turned your back on me.

10 " 'Because of this, I am going to bring
disaster on the house of Jeroboam. I will
cut off from Jeroboam every last male in
Israel — slave or free.[a] I will burn up the
house of Jeroboam as one burns dung,
until it is all gone. 11 Dogs will eat those
belonging to Jeroboam who die in the
city, and the birds will feed on those who
die in the country. The LORD has spoken!'

12 "As for you, go back home. When you
set foot in your city, the boy will die. 13 All
Israel will mourn for him and bury him.
He is the only one belonging to Jeroboam who will be buried, because he is
the only one in the house of Jeroboam
in whom the LORD, the God of Israel, has
found anything good.

14 "The LORD will raise up for himself
a king over Israel who will cut off the
family of Jeroboam. Even now this is
beginning to happen.[b] 15 And the LORD
will strike Israel, so that it will be like
a reed swaying in the water. He will uproot Israel from this good land that he
gave to their ancestors and scatter them

[a] *10* Or *Israel — every ruler or leader* [b] *14* The meaning of the Hebrew for this sentence is uncertain.

beyond the Euphrates River, because
they aroused the LORD's anger by making Asherah poles.[a] 16 And he will give
Israel up because of the sins Jeroboam
has committed and has caused Israel to
commit."
17 Then Jeroboam's wife got up and
left and went to Tirzah. As soon as she
stepped over the threshold of the house,
the boy died. 18 They buried him, and all
Israel mourned for him, as the LORD had
said through his servant the prophet
Ahijah.
19 The other events of Jeroboam's reign,
his wars and how he ruled, are written in
the book of the annals of the kings of Israel. 20 He reigned for twenty-two years
and then rested with his ancestors. And
Nadab his son succeeded him as king.

Rehoboam King of Judah

21 Rehoboam son of Solomon was king
in Judah. He was forty-one years old
when he became king, and he reigned
seventeen years in Jerusalem, the city
the LORD had chosen out of all the tribes
of Israel in which to put his Name. His
mother's name was Naamah; she was an
Ammonite.
22 Judah did evil in the eyes of the
LORD. By the sins they committed they
stirred up his jealous anger more than
those who were before them had done.
23 They also set up for themselves high
places, sacred stones and Asherah poles
on every high hill and under every
spreading tree. 24 There were even male
shrine prostitutes in the land; the people
engaged in all the detestable practices of
the nations the LORD had driven out before the Israelites.
25 In the fifth year of King Rehoboam,
Shishak king of Egypt attacked Jerusalem. 26 He carried off the treasures of the
temple of the LORD and the treasures of
the royal palace. He took everything,
including all the gold shields Solomon
had made. 27 So King Rehoboam made
bronze shields to replace them and assigned these to the commanders of the
guard on duty at the entrance to the royal palace. 28 Whenever the king went to
the LORD's temple, the guards bore the
shields, and afterward they returned
them to the guardroom.
29 As for the other events of Rehoboam's reign, and all he did, are they not
written in the book of the annals of the
kings of Judah? 30 There was continual
warfare between Rehoboam and Jeroboam. 31 And Rehoboam rested with his
ancestors and was buried with them in
the City of David. His mother's name was
Naamah; she was an Ammonite. And
Abijah[b] his son succeeded him as king.

Abijah King of Judah

15 In the eighteenth year of the reign
of Jeroboam son of Nebat, Abijah[c]
became king of Judah, 2 and he reigned
in Jerusalem three years. His mother's
name was Maakah daughter of Abishalom.[d]
3 He committed all the sins his father
had done before him; his heart was not
fully devoted to the LORD his God, as the
heart of David his forefather had been.
4 Nevertheless, for David's sake the LORD
his God gave him a lamp in Jerusalem
by raising up a son to succeed him and
by making Jerusalem strong. 5 For David
had done what was right in the eyes of
the LORD and had not failed to keep any
of the LORD's commands all the days of
his life — except in the case of Uriah the
Hittite.
6 There was war between Abijah[e] and
Jeroboam throughout Abijah's lifetime.
7 As for the other events of Abijah's reign,
and all he did, are they not written in the
book of the annals of the kings of Judah?
There was war between Abijah and Jeroboam. 8 And Abijah rested with his ancestors and was buried in the City of David.
And Asa his son succeeded him as king.

Asa King of Judah

9 In the twentieth year of Jeroboam
king of Israel, Asa became king of Judah,
10 and he reigned in Jerusalem forty-one
years. His grandmother's name was Maakah daughter of Abishalom.
11 Asa did what was right in the eyes of
the LORD, as his father David had done.
12 He expelled the male shrine prostitutes from the land and got rid of all
the idols his ancestors had made. 13 He
even deposed his grandmother Maakah
from her position as queen mother, because she had made a repulsive image

[a] *15* That is, wooden symbols of the goddess Asherah; here and elsewhere in 1 Kings
[b] *31* Some Hebrew manuscripts and Septuagint (see also 2 Chron. 12:16); most Hebrew manuscripts *Abijam*
[c] *1* Some Hebrew manuscripts and Septuagint (see also 2 Chron. 12:16); most Hebrew manuscripts *Abijam*; also in verses 7 and 8
[d] *2* A variant of *Absalom*; also in verse 10
[e] *6* Some Hebrew manuscripts and Syriac *Abijam* (that is, Abijah); most Hebrew manuscripts *Rehoboam*

for the worship of Asherah. Asa cut it
down and burned it in the Kidron Valley.
14 Although he did not remove the high
places, Asa's heart was fully committed
to the LORD all his life. 15 He brought into
the temple of the LORD the silver and
gold and the articles that he and his father had dedicated.
16 There was war between Asa and
Baasha king of Israel throughout their
reigns. 17 Baasha king of Israel went up
against Judah and fortified Ramah to
prevent anyone from leaving or entering
the territory of Asa king of Judah.
18 Asa then took all the silver and gold
that was left in the treasuries of the
LORD's temple and of his own palace.
He entrusted it to his officials and sent
them to Ben-Hadad son of Tabrimmon,
the son of Hezion, the king of Aram, who
was ruling in Damascus. 19 "Let there be
a treaty between me and you," he said,
"as there was between my father and
your father. See, I am sending you a gift
of silver and gold. Now break your treaty with Baasha king of Israel so he will
withdraw from me."
20 Ben-Hadad agreed with King Asa
and sent the commanders of his forces against the towns of Israel. He conquered Ijon, Dan, Abel Beth Maakah and
all Kinnereth in addition to Naphtali.
21 When Baasha heard this, he stopped
building Ramah and withdrew to Tirzah. 22 Then King Asa issued an order to
all Judah — no one was exempt — and
they carried away from Ramah the
stones and timber Baasha had been using there. With them King Asa built up
Geba in Benjamin, and also Mizpah.
23 As for all the other events of Asa's
reign, all his achievements, all he did and
the cities he built, are they not written in
the book of the annals of the kings of Judah? In his old age, however, his feet became diseased. 24 Then Asa rested with his
ancestors and was buried with them in
the city of his father David. And Jehoshaphat his son succeeded him as king.

Nadab King of Israel

25 Nadab son of Jeroboam became king
of Israel in the second year of Asa king
of Judah, and he reigned over Israel two
years. 26 He did evil in the eyes of the
LORD, following the ways of his father
and committing the same sin his father
had caused Israel to commit.
27 Baasha son of Ahijah from the tribe
of Issachar plotted against him, and he
struck him down at Gibbethon, a Philistine town, while Nadab and all Israel
were besieging it. 28 Baasha killed Nadab
in the third year of Asa king of Judah
and succeeded him as king.
29 As soon as he began to reign, he
killed Jeroboam's whole family. He
did not leave Jeroboam anyone that
breathed, but destroyed them all, according to the word of the LORD given
through his servant Ahijah the Shilonite. 30 This happened because of the
sins Jeroboam had committed and had
caused Israel to commit, and because he
aroused the anger of the LORD, the God
of Israel.
31 As for the other events of Nadab's
reign, and all he did, are they not written in the book of the annals of the kings
of Israel? 32 There was war between Asa
and Baasha king of Israel throughout
their reigns.

Baasha King of Israel

33 In the third year of Asa king of Judah, Baasha son of Ahijah became king
of all Israel in Tirzah, and he reigned
twenty-four years. 34 He did evil in the
eyes of the LORD, following the ways of
Jeroboam and committing the same sin
Jeroboam had caused Israel to commit.
16 Then the word of the LORD came
to Jehu son of Hanani concerning
Baasha: 2 "I lifted you up from the dust
and appointed you ruler over my people
Israel, but you followed the ways of Jeroboam and caused my people Israel to sin
and to arouse my anger by their sins. 3 So
I am about to wipe out Baasha and his
house, and I will make your house like
that of Jeroboam son of Nebat. 4 Dogs
will eat those belonging to Baasha who
die in the city, and birds will feed on
those who die in the country."
5 As for the other events of Baasha's
reign, what he did and his achievements, are they not written in the book
of the annals of the kings of Israel? 6 Baasha rested with his ancestors and was
buried in Tirzah. And Elah his son succeeded him as king.
7 Moreover, the word of the LORD came
through the prophet Jehu son of Hanani
to Baasha and his house, because of all
the evil he had done in the eyes of the
LORD, arousing his anger by the things he
did, becoming like the house of Jeroboam — and also because he destroyed it.

Elah King of Israel

8 In the twenty-sixth year of Asa king
of Judah, Elah son of Baasha became
king of Israel, and he reigned in Tirzah
two years.

9 Zimri, one of his officials, who had
command of half his chariots, plotted
against him. Elah was in Tirzah at the
time, getting drunk in the home of Arza,
the palace administrator at Tirzah.
10 Zimri came in, struck him down and
killed him in the twenty-seventh year
of Asa king of Judah. Then he succeeded
him as king.
11 As soon as he began to reign and was
seated on the throne, he killed off Baasha's whole family. He did not spare a single male, whether relative or friend. 12 So
Zimri destroyed the whole family of Baasha, in accordance with the word of the
LORD spoken against Baasha through the
prophet Jehu — 13 because of all the sins
Baasha and his son Elah had committed
and had caused Israel to commit, so that
they aroused the anger of the LORD, the
God of Israel, by their worthless idols.
14 As for the other events of Elah's
reign, and all he did, are they not written in the book of the annals of the kings
of Israel?

Zimri King of Israel

15 In the twenty-seventh year of Asa king
of Judah, Zimri reigned in Tirzah seven
days. The army was encamped near Gibbethon, a Philistine town. 16 When the Israelites in the camp heard that Zimri had
plotted against the king and murdered
him, they proclaimed Omri, the commander of the army, king over Israel that
very day there in the camp. 17 Then Omri
and all the Israelites with him withdrew
from Gibbethon and laid siege to Tirzah.
18 When Zimri saw that the city was taken,
he went into the citadel of the royal palace and set the palace on fire around him.
So he died, 19 because of the sins he had
committed, doing evil in the eyes of the
LORD and following the ways of Jeroboam
and committing the same sin Jeroboam
had caused Israel to commit.
20 As for the other events of Zimri's
reign, and the rebellion he carried out,
are they not written in the book of the
annals of the kings of Israel?

Omri King of Israel

21 Then the people of Israel were split
into two factions; half supported Tibni son of Ginath for king, and the other
half supported Omri. 22 But Omri's followers proved stronger than those of Tibni
son of Ginath. So Tibni died and Omri
became king.
23 In the thirty-first year of Asa king of
Judah, Omri became king of Israel, and
he reigned twelve years, six of them in
Tirzah. 24 He bought the hill of Samaria
from Shemer for two talents[a] of silver
and built a city on the hill, calling it Samaria, after Shemer, the name of the
former owner of the hill.
25 But Omri did evil in the eyes of the
LORD and sinned more than all those before him. 26 He followed completely the
ways of Jeroboam son of Nebat, committing the same sin Jeroboam had caused
Israel to commit, so that they aroused
the anger of the LORD, the God of Israel,
by their worthless idols.
27 As for the other events of Omri's
reign, what he did and the things he
achieved, are they not written in the
book of the annals of the kings of Israel? 28 Omri rested with his ancestors and
was buried in Samaria. And Ahab his son
succeeded him as king.

Ahab Becomes King of Israel

29 In the thirty-eighth year of Asa king
of Judah, Ahab son of Omri became king
of Israel, and he reigned in Samaria
over Israel twenty-two years. 30 Ahab son
of Omri did more evil in the eyes of the
LORD than any of those before him. 31 He
not only considered it trivial to commit
the sins of Jeroboam son of Nebat, but he
also married Jezebel daughter of Ethbaal
king of the Sidonians, and began to serve
Baal and worship him. 32 He set up an altar for Baal in the temple of Baal that he
built in Samaria. 33 Ahab also made an
Asherah pole and did more to arouse the
anger of the LORD, the God of Israel, than
did all the kings of Israel before him.
34 In Ahab's time, Hiel of Bethel rebuilt
Jericho. He laid its foundations at the
cost of his firstborn son Abiram, and he
set up its gates at the cost of his youngest son Segub, in accordance with the
word of the LORD spoken by Joshua son
of Nun.

Elijah Announces a Great Drought

17 Now Elijah the Tishbite, from Tish-
be[b] in Gilead, said to Ahab, "As the
LORD, the God of Israel, lives, whom I
serve, there will be neither dew nor rain
in the next few years except at my word."

Elijah Fed by Ravens

2 Then the word of the LORD came to
Elijah: 3 "Leave here, turn eastward and
hide in the Kerith Ravine, east of the
Jordan. 4 You will drink from the brook,

[a] 24 That is, about 150 pounds or about 68 kilograms [b] 1 Or *Tishbite, of the settlers*

and I have directed the ravens to supply you with food there."

5 So he did what the LORD had told him. He went to the Kerith Ravine, east of the Jordan, and stayed there. 6 The ravens brought him bread and meat in the morning and bread and meat in the evening, and he drank from the brook.

Elijah and the Widow at Zarephath

7 Some time later the brook dried up because there had been no rain in the land. 8 Then the word of the LORD came to him: 9 "Go at once to Zarephath in the region of Sidon and stay there. I have directed a widow there to supply you with food." 10 So he went to Zarephath. When he came to the town gate, a widow was there gathering sticks. He called to her and asked, "Would you bring me a little water in a jar so I may have a drink?" 11 As she was going to get it, he called, "And bring me, please, a piece of bread."

12 "As surely as the LORD your God lives," she replied, "I don't have any bread — only a handful of flour in a jar and a little olive oil in a jug. I am gathering a few sticks to take home and make a meal for myself and my son, that we may eat it — and die."

13 Elijah said to her, "Don't be afraid. Go home and do as you have said. But first make a small loaf of bread for me from what you have and bring it to me, and then make something for yourself and your son. 14 For this is what the LORD, the God of Israel, says: 'The jar of flour will not be used up and the jug of oil will not run dry until the day the LORD sends rain on the land.' "

15 She went away and did as Elijah had told her. So there was food every day for Elijah and for the woman and her family. 16 For the jar of flour was not used up and the jug of oil did not run dry, in keeping with the word of the LORD spoken by Elijah.

17 Some time later the son of the woman who owned the house became ill. He grew worse and worse, and finally stopped breathing. 18 She said to Elijah, "What do you have against me, man of God? Did you come to remind me of my sin and kill my son?"

19 "Give me your son," Elijah replied. He took him from her arms, carried him to the upper room where he was staying, and laid him on his bed. 20 Then he cried out to the LORD, "LORD my God, have you brought tragedy even on this widow I am staying with, by causing her son to die?" 21 Then he stretched himself out on the boy three times and cried out to the LORD, "LORD my God, let this boy's life return to him!"

22 The LORD heard Elijah's cry, and the boy's life returned to him, and he lived. 23 Elijah picked up the child and carried him down from the room into the house. He gave him to his mother and said, "Look, your son is alive!"

24 Then the woman said to Elijah, "Now I know that you are a man of God and that the word of the LORD from your mouth is the truth."

Elijah and Obadiah

18 After a long time, in the third year, the word of the LORD came to Elijah: "Go and present yourself to Ahab, and I will send rain on the land." 2 So Elijah went to present himself to Ahab.

Now the famine was severe in Samaria, 3 and Ahab had summoned Obadiah, his palace administrator. (Obadiah was a devout believer in the LORD. 4 While Jezebel was killing off the LORD's prophets, Obadiah had taken a hundred prophets and hidden them in two caves, fifty in each, and had supplied them with food and water.) 5 Ahab had said to Obadiah, "Go through the land to all the springs and valleys. Maybe we can find some grass to keep the horses and mules alive so we will not have to kill any of our animals." 6 So they divided the land they were to cover, Ahab going in one direction and Obadiah in another.

7 As Obadiah was walking along, Elijah met him. Obadiah recognized him, bowed down to the ground, and said, "Is it really you, my lord Elijah?"

8 "Yes," he replied. "Go tell your master, 'Elijah is here.' "

9 "What have I done wrong," asked Obadiah, "that you are handing your servant over to Ahab to be put to death? 10 As surely as the LORD your God lives, there is not a nation or kingdom where my master has not sent someone to look for you. And whenever a nation or kingdom claimed you were not there, he made them swear they could not find you. 11 But now you tell me to go to my master and say, 'Elijah is here.' 12 I don't know where the Spirit of the LORD may carry you when I leave you. If I go and tell Ahab and he doesn't find you, he will kill me. Yet I your servant have worshiped the LORD since my youth. 13 Haven't you heard, my lord, what I did while Jezebel was killing the prophets of the LORD? I hid a hundred of the LORD's prophets in two caves, fifty in each, and

supplied them with food and water.
[14]And now you tell me to go to my master
and say, 'Elijah is here.' He will kill me!"

[15]Elijah said, "As the LORD Almighty
lives, whom I serve, I will surely present
myself to Ahab today."

Elijah on Mount Carmel

[16]So Obadiah went to meet Ahab and
told him, and Ahab went to meet Elijah.
[17]When he saw Elijah, he said to him, "Is
that you, you troubler of Israel?"

[18]"I have not made trouble for Israel,"
Elijah replied. "But you and your father's
family have. You have abandoned the
LORD's commands and have followed the
Baals. [19]Now summon the people from
all over Israel to meet me on Mount Carmel. And bring the four hundred and fifty prophets of Baal and the four hundred
prophets of Asherah, who eat at Jezebel's
table."

[20]So Ahab sent word throughout all
Israel and assembled the prophets on
Mount Carmel. [21]Elijah went before the
people and said, "How long will you waver between two opinions? If the LORD is
God, follow him; but if Baal is God, follow him."

But the people said nothing.

[22]Then Elijah said to them, "I am the
only one of the LORD's prophets left, but
Baal has four hundred and fifty prophets. [23]Get two bulls for us. Let Baal's
prophets choose one for themselves,
and let them cut it into pieces and put
it on the wood but not set fire to it. I will
prepare the other bull and put it on the
wood but not set fire to it. [24]Then you call
on the name of your god, and I will call
on the name of the LORD. The god who
answers by fire — he is God."

Then all the people said, "What you
say is good."

[25]Elijah said to the prophets of Baal,
"Choose one of the bulls and prepare
it first, since there are so many of you.
Call on the name of your god, but do not
light the fire." [26]So they took the bull given them and prepared it.

Then they called on the name of Baal
from morning till noon. "Baal, answer
us!" they shouted. But there was no response; no one answered. And they
danced around the altar they had made.

[27]At noon Elijah began to taunt them.
"Shout louder!" he said. "Surely he is a
god! Perhaps he is deep in thought, or
busy, or traveling. Maybe he is sleeping and must be awakened." [28]So they
shouted louder and slashed themselves
with swords and spears, as was their
custom, until their blood flowed. [29]Midday passed, and they continued their
frantic prophesying until the time for
the evening sacrifice. But there was no
response, no one answered, no one paid
attention.

[30]Then Elijah said to all the people,
"Come here to me." They came to him,
and he repaired the altar of the LORD,
which had been torn down. [31]Elijah
took twelve stones, one for each of the
tribes descended from Jacob, to whom
the word of the LORD had come, saying,
"Your name shall be Israel." [32]With the
stones he built an altar in the name of
the LORD, and he dug a trench around it
large enough to hold two seahs[a] of seed.
[33]He arranged the wood, cut the bull into
pieces and laid it on the wood. Then he
said to them, "Fill four large jars with
water and pour it on the offering and on
the wood."

[34]"Do it again," he said, and they did
it again.

"Do it a third time," he ordered, and
they did it the third time. [35]The water ran
down around the altar and even filled
the trench.

[36]At the time of sacrifice, the prophet Elijah stepped forward and prayed:
"LORD, the God of Abraham, Isaac and
Israel, let it be known today that you are
God in Israel and that I am your servant
and have done all these things at your
command. [37]Answer me, LORD, answer
me, so these people will know that you,
LORD, are God, and that you are turning
their hearts back again."

[38]Then the fire of the LORD fell and
burned up the sacrifice, the wood, the
stones and the soil, and also licked up
the water in the trench.

[39]When all the people saw this, they
fell prostrate and cried, "The LORD — he
is God! The LORD — he is God!"

[40]Then Elijah commanded them,
"Seize the prophets of Baal. Don't let
anyone get away!" They seized them,
and Elijah had them brought down
to the Kishon Valley and slaughtered
there.

[41]And Elijah said to Ahab, "Go, eat and
drink, for there is the sound of a heavy
rain." [42]So Ahab went off to eat and
drink, but Elijah climbed to the top of
Carmel, bent down to the ground and
put his face between his knees.

[a] *32* That is, probably about 24 pounds or about 11 kilograms

43“Go and look toward the sea,” he told
his servant. And he went up and looked.
“There is nothing there,” he said.
Seven times Elijah said, “Go back.”
44The seventh time the servant reported, “A cloud as small as a man’s hand is
rising from the sea.”
So Elijah said, “Go and tell Ahab,
‘Hitch up your chariot and go down before the rain stops you.’ ”
45Meanwhile, the sky grew black with
clouds, the wind rose, a heavy rain
started falling and Ahab rode off to Jezreel. 46The power of the LORD came on
Elijah and, tucking his cloak into his
belt, he ran ahead of Ahab all the way
to Jezreel.

Elijah Flees to Horeb

19 Now Ahab told Jezebel everything
Elijah had done and how he had
killed all the prophets with the sword.
2So Jezebel sent a messenger to Elijah
to say, “May the gods deal with me, be
it ever so severely, if by this time tomorrow I do not make your life like that of
one of them.”
3Elijah was afraid[a] and ran for his life.
When he came to Beersheba in Judah, he
left his servant there, 4while he himself
went a day’s journey into the wilderness.
He came to a broom bush, sat down under it and prayed that he might die. “I
have had enough, LORD,” he said. “Take
my life; I am no better than my ancestors.” 5Then he lay down under the bush
and fell asleep.
All at once an angel touched him
and said, “Get up and eat.” 6He looked
around, and there by his head was some
bread baked over hot coals, and a jar of
water. He ate and drank and then lay
down again.
7The angel of the LORD came back a
second time and touched him and said,
“Get up and eat, for the journey is too
much for you.” 8So he got up and ate
and drank. Strengthened by that food,
he traveled forty days and forty nights
until he reached Horeb, the mountain
of God. 9There he went into a cave and
spent the night.

The LORD Appears to Elijah

And the word of the LORD came to
him: “What are you doing here, Elijah?”
10He replied, “I have been very zealous for the LORD God Almighty. The Israelites have rejected your covenant, torn
down your altars, and put your prophets
to death with the sword. I am the only
one left, and now they are trying to kill
me too.”
11The LORD said, “Go out and stand
on the mountain in the presence of the
LORD, for the LORD is about to pass by.”
Then a great and powerful wind tore
the mountains apart and shattered the
rocks before the LORD, but the LORD was
not in the wind. After the wind there
was an earthquake, but the LORD was
not in the earthquake. 12After the earthquake came a fire, but the LORD was
not in the fire. And after the fire came
a gentle whisper. 13When Elijah heard
it, he pulled his cloak over his face and
went out and stood at the mouth of the
cave.
Then a voice said to him, “What are
you doing here, Elijah?”
14He replied, “I have been very zealous
for the LORD God Almighty. The Israelites have rejected your covenant, torn
down your altars, and put your prophets
to death with the sword. I am the only
one left, and now they are trying to kill
me too.”
15The LORD said to him, “Go back the
way you came, and go to the Desert of
Damascus. When you get there, anoint
Hazael king over Aram. 16Also, anoint
Jehu son of Nimshi king over Israel,
and anoint Elisha son of Shaphat from
Abel Meholah to succeed you as prophet.
17Jehu will put to death any who escape
the sword of Hazael, and Elisha will put
to death any who escape the sword of
Jehu. 18Yet I reserve seven thousand in
Israel — all whose knees have not bowed
down to Baal and whose mouths have
not kissed him.”

The Call of Elisha

19So Elijah went from there and found
Elisha son of Shaphat. He was plowing
with twelve yoke of oxen, and he himself
was driving the twelfth pair. Elijah went
up to him and threw his cloak around
him. 20Elisha then left his oxen and ran
after Elijah. “Let me kiss my father and
mother goodbye,” he said, “and then I
will come with you.”
“Go back,” Elijah replied. “What have
I done to you?”
21So Elisha left him and went back. He
took his yoke of oxen and slaughtered
them. He burned the plowing equipment
to cook the meat and gave it to the people, and they ate. Then he set out to follow Elijah and became his servant.

[a] 3 Or *Elijah saw*

Ben-Hadad Attacks Samaria

20 Now Ben-Hadad king of Aram mustered his entire army. Accompanied by thirty-two kings with their horses and chariots, he went up and besieged Samaria and attacked it. 2He sent messengers into the city to Ahab king of Israel, saying, "This is what Ben-Hadad says: 3'Your silver and gold are mine, and the best of your wives and children are mine.'"

4The king of Israel answered, "Just as you say, my lord the king. I and all I have are yours."

5The messengers came again and said, "This is what Ben-Hadad says: 'I sent to demand your silver and gold, your wives and your children. 6But about this time tomorrow I am going to send my officials to search your palace and the houses of your officials. They will seize everything you value and carry it away.'"

7The king of Israel summoned all the elders of the land and said to them, "See how this man is looking for trouble! When he sent for my wives and my children, my silver and my gold, I did not refuse him."

8The elders and the people all answered, "Don't listen to him or agree to his demands."

9So he replied to Ben-Hadad's messengers, "Tell my lord the king, 'Your servant will do all you demanded the first time, but this demand I cannot meet.'" They left and took the answer back to Ben-Hadad.

10Then Ben-Hadad sent another message to Ahab: "May the gods deal with me, be it ever so severely, if enough dust remains in Samaria to give each of my men a handful."

11The king of Israel answered, "Tell him: 'One who puts on his armor should not boast like one who takes it off.'"

12Ben-Hadad heard this message while he and the kings were drinking in their tents,[a] and he ordered his men: "Prepare to attack." So they prepared to attack the city.

Ahab Defeats Ben-Hadad

13Meanwhile a prophet came to Ahab king of Israel and announced, "This is what the LORD says: 'Do you see this vast army? I will give it into your hand today, and then you will know that I am the LORD.'"

14"But who will do this?" asked Ahab.

The prophet replied, "This is what the LORD says: 'The junior officers under the provincial commanders will do it.'"

"And who will start the battle?" he asked.

The prophet answered, "You will."

15So Ahab summoned the 232 junior officers under the provincial commanders. Then he assembled the rest of the Israelites, 7,000 in all. 16They set out at noon while Ben-Hadad and the 32 kings allied with him were in their tents getting drunk. 17The junior officers under the provincial commanders went out first.

Now Ben-Hadad had dispatched scouts, who reported, "Men are advancing from Samaria."

18He said, "If they have come out for peace, take them alive; if they have come out for war, take them alive."

19The junior officers under the provincial commanders marched out of the city with the army behind them 20and each one struck down his opponent. At that, the Arameans fled, with the Israelites in pursuit. But Ben-Hadad king of Aram escaped on horseback with some of his horsemen. 21The king of Israel advanced and overpowered the horses and chariots and inflicted heavy losses on the Arameans.

22Afterward, the prophet came to the king of Israel and said, "Strengthen your position and see what must be done, because next spring the king of Aram will attack you again."

23Meanwhile, the officials of the king of Aram advised him, "Their gods are gods of the hills. That is why they were too strong for us. But if we fight them on the plains, surely we will be stronger than they. 24Do this: Remove all the kings from their commands and replace them with other officers. 25You must also raise an army like the one you lost—horse for horse and chariot for chariot—so we can fight Israel on the plains. Then surely we will be stronger than they." He agreed with them and acted accordingly.

26The next spring Ben-Hadad mustered the Arameans and went up to Aphek to fight against Israel. 27When the Israelites were also mustered and given provisions, they marched out to meet them. The Israelites camped opposite them like two small flocks of goats, while the Arameans covered the countryside.

28The man of God came up and told the king of Israel, "This is what the LORD says: 'Because the Arameans think the

[a] *12* Or *in Sukkoth;* also in verse 16

LORD is a god of the hills and not a god of
the valleys, I will deliver this vast army
into your hands, and you will know that
I am the LORD.'"
29For seven days they camped opposite
each other, and on the seventh day the
battle was joined. The Israelites inflicted
a hundred thousand casualties on the
Aramean foot soldiers in one day. 30The
rest of them escaped to the city of Aphek,
where the wall collapsed on twenty-
seven thousand of them. And Ben-Hadad
fled to the city and hid in an inner room.
31His officials said to him, "Look, we
have heard that the kings of Israel are
merciful. Let us go to the king of Israel
with sackcloth around our waists and
ropes around our heads. Perhaps he will
spare your life."
32Wearing sackcloth around their
waists and ropes around their heads,
they went to the king of Israel and said,
"Your servant Ben-Hadad says: 'Please
let me live.'"
The king answered, "Is he still alive?
He is my brother."
33The men took this as a good sign and
were quick to pick up his word. "Yes, your
brother Ben-Hadad!" they said.
"Go and get him," the king said. When
Ben-Hadad came out, Ahab had him
come up into his chariot.
34"I will return the cities my father
took from your father," Ben-Hadad offered. "You may set up your own market
areas in Damascus, as my father did in
Samaria."
Ahab said, "On the basis of a treaty I
will set you free." So he made a treaty
with him, and let him go.

A Prophet Condemns Ahab

35By the word of the LORD one of the
company of the prophets said to his
companion, "Strike me with your weapon," but he refused.
36So the prophet said, "Because you
have not obeyed the LORD, as soon as
you leave me a lion will kill you." And
after the man went away, a lion found
him and killed him.
37The prophet found another man and
said, "Strike me, please." So the man
struck him and wounded him. 38Then
the prophet went and stood by the road
waiting for the king. He disguised himself with his headband down over his
eyes. 39As the king passed by, the prophet
called out to him, "Your servant went into
the thick of the battle, and someone came
to me with a captive and said, 'Guard this
man. If he is missing, it will be your life
for his life, or you must pay a talent[a] of
silver.' 40While your servant was busy here
and there, the man disappeared."
"That is your sentence," the king of Israel said. "You have pronounced it yourself."
41Then the prophet quickly removed
the headband from his eyes, and the
king of Israel recognized him as one of
the prophets. 42He said to the king, "This
is what the LORD says: 'You have set free
a man I had determined should die.[b]
Therefore it is your life for his life, your
people for his people.'" 43Sullen and angry, the king of Israel went to his palace
in Samaria.

Naboth's Vineyard

21 Some time later there was an incident involving a vineyard belonging to Naboth the Jezreelite. The vineyard was in Jezreel, close to the palace of
Ahab king of Samaria. 2Ahab said to Naboth, "Let me have your vineyard to use
for a vegetable garden, since it is close
to my palace. In exchange I will give you
a better vineyard or, if you prefer, I will
pay you whatever it is worth."
3But Naboth replied, "The LORD forbid
that I should give you the inheritance of
my ancestors."
4So Ahab went home, sullen and angry
because Naboth the Jezreelite had said,
"I will not give you the inheritance of my
ancestors." He lay on his bed sulking and
refused to eat.
5His wife Jezebel came in and asked
him, "Why are you so sullen? Why won't
you eat?"
6He answered her, "Because I said to
Naboth the Jezreelite, 'Sell me your vineyard; or if you prefer, I will give you another vineyard in its place.' But he said, 'I
will not give you my vineyard.'"
7Jezebel his wife said, "Is this how you
act as king over Israel? Get up and eat!
Cheer up. I'll get you the vineyard of Naboth the Jezreelite."
8So she wrote letters in Ahab's name,
placed his seal on them, and sent them
to the elders and nobles who lived in Naboth's city with him. 9In those letters she
wrote:

"Proclaim a day of fasting and seat
Naboth in a prominent place among
the people. 10But seat two scoundrels

[a] *39* That is, about 75 pounds or about 34 kilograms [b] *42* The Hebrew term refers to the irrevocable giving over of things or persons to the LORD, often by totally destroying them.

opposite him and have them bring
charges that he has cursed both God
and the king. Then take him out and
stone him to death."

11So the elders and nobles who lived
in Naboth's city did as Jezebel directed
in the letters she had written to them.
12They proclaimed a fast and seated Naboth in a prominent place among the
people. 13Then two scoundrels came and
sat opposite him and brought charges
against Naboth before the people, saying, "Naboth has cursed both God and
the king." So they took him outside the
city and stoned him to death. 14Then
they sent word to Jezebel: "Naboth has
been stoned to death."

15As soon as Jezebel heard that Naboth
had been stoned to death, she said to
Ahab, "Get up and take possession of the
vineyard of Naboth the Jezreelite that he
refused to sell you. He is no longer alive,
but dead." 16When Ahab heard that Naboth was dead, he got up and went down
to take possession of Naboth's vineyard.

17Then the word of the LORD came to
Elijah the Tishbite: 18"Go down to meet
Ahab king of Israel, who rules in Samaria. He is now in Naboth's vineyard, where
he has gone to take possession of it. 19Say
to him, 'This is what the LORD says: Have
you not murdered a man and seized his
property?' Then say to him, 'This is what
the LORD says: In the place where dogs
licked up Naboth's blood, dogs will lick
up your blood — yes, yours!' "

20Ahab said to Elijah, "So you have
found me, my enemy!"

"I have found you," he answered, "because you have sold yourself to do evil in
the eyes of the LORD. 21He says, 'I am going to bring disaster on you. I will wipe
out your descendants and cut off from
Ahab every last male in Israel — slave or
free.[a] 22I will make your house like that
of Jeroboam son of Nebat and that of
Baasha son of Ahijah, because you have
aroused my anger and have caused Israel to sin.'

23"And also concerning Jezebel the
LORD says: 'Dogs will devour Jezebel by
the wall of[b] Jezreel.'

24"Dogs will eat those belonging to
Ahab who die in the city, and the birds
will feed on those who die in the country."

25(There was never anyone like Ahab,
who sold himself to do evil in the eyes of
the LORD, urged on by Jezebel his wife.
26He behaved in the vilest manner by
going after idols, like the Amorites the
LORD drove out before Israel.)

27When Ahab heard these words, he
tore his clothes, put on sackcloth and
fasted. He lay in sackcloth and went
around meekly.

28Then the word of the LORD came to
Elijah the Tishbite: 29"Have you noticed
how Ahab has humbled himself before
me? Because he has humbled himself, I
will not bring this disaster in his day, but
I will bring it on his house in the days of
his son."

Micaiah Prophesies Against Ahab

22 For three years there was no war
between Aram and Israel. 2But
in the third year Jehoshaphat king of
Judah went down to see the king of Israel. 3The king of Israel had said to his
officials, "Don't you know that Ramoth
Gilead belongs to us and yet we are doing nothing to retake it from the king of
Aram?"

4So he asked Jehoshaphat, "Will you
go with me to fight against Ramoth Gilead?"

Jehoshaphat replied to the king of Israel, "I am as you are, my people as your
people, my horses as your horses." 5But
Jehoshaphat also said to the king of Israel, "First seek the counsel of the LORD."

6So the king of Israel brought together the prophets — about four hundred
men — and asked them, "Shall I go to
war against Ramoth Gilead, or shall I
refrain?"

"Go," they answered, "for the Lord will
give it into the king's hand."

7But Jehoshaphat asked, "Is there no
longer a prophet of the LORD here whom
we can inquire of?"

8The king of Israel answered Jehoshaphat, "There is still one prophet through
whom we can inquire of the LORD, but I
hate him because he never prophesies
anything good about me, but always
bad. He is Micaiah son of Imlah."

"The king should not say such a
thing," Jehoshaphat replied.

9So the king of Israel called one of his
officials and said, "Bring Micaiah son of
Imlah at once."

10Dressed in their royal robes, the
king of Israel and Jehoshaphat king of
Judah were sitting on their thrones at
the threshing floor by the entrance of
the gate of Samaria, with all the prophets prophesying before them. 11Now

[a] 21 Or *Israel — every ruler or leader* [b] 23 Most Hebrew manuscripts; a few Hebrew manuscripts, Vulgate and Syriac (see also 2 Kings 9:26) *the plot of ground at*

Zedekiah son of Kenaanah had made
iron horns and he declared, "This is what
the LORD says: 'With these you will gore
the Arameans until they are destroyed.' "
12 All the other prophets were prophesying the same thing. "Attack Ramoth Gilead and be victorious," they said, "for the
LORD will give it into the king's hand."
13 The messenger who had gone to
summon Micaiah said to him, "Look, the
other prophets without exception are predicting success for the king. Let your word
agree with theirs, and speak favorably."
14 But Micaiah said, "As surely as the
LORD lives, I can tell him only what the
LORD tells me."
15 When he arrived, the king asked him,
"Micaiah, shall we go to war against Ramoth Gilead, or not?"
"Attack and be victorious," he answered, "for the LORD will give it into the
king's hand."
16 The king said to him, "How many
times must I make you swear to tell me
nothing but the truth in the name of the
LORD?"
17 Then Micaiah answered, "I saw all
Israel scattered on the hills like sheep
without a shepherd, and the LORD said,
'These people have no master. Let each
one go home in peace.' "
18 The king of Israel said to Jehoshaphat, "Didn't I tell you that he never
prophesies anything good about me, but
only bad?"
19 Micaiah continued, "Therefore hear
the word of the LORD: I saw the LORD
sitting on his throne with all the multitudes of heaven standing around him
on his right and on his left. 20 And the
LORD said, 'Who will entice Ahab into attacking Ramoth Gilead and going to his
death there?'
"One suggested this, and another that.
21 Finally, a spirit came forward, stood before the LORD and said, 'I will entice him.'
22 " 'By what means?' the LORD asked.
" 'I will go out and be a deceiving spirit
in the mouths of all his prophets,' he said.
" 'You will succeed in enticing him,'
said the LORD. 'Go and do it.'
23 "So now the LORD has put a deceiving spirit in the mouths of all these
prophets of yours. The LORD has decreed
disaster for you."
24 Then Zedekiah son of Kenaanah
went up and slapped Micaiah in the
face. "Which way did the spirit from[a] the
LORD go when he went from me to speak
to you?" he asked.
25 Micaiah replied, "You will find out on
the day you go to hide in an inner room."
26 The king of Israel then ordered,
"Take Micaiah and send him back to
Amon the ruler of the city and to Joash
the king's son 27 and say, 'This is what the
king says: Put this fellow in prison and
give him nothing but bread and water
until I return safely.' "
28 Micaiah declared, "If you ever return
safely, the LORD has not spoken through
me." Then he added, "Mark my words, all
you people!"

Ahab Killed at Ramoth Gilead

29 So the king of Israel and Jehoshaphat king of Judah went up to Ramoth
Gilead. 30 The king of Israel said to Jehoshaphat, "I will enter the battle in disguise, but you wear your royal robes." So
the king of Israel disguised himself and
went into battle.
31 Now the king of Aram had ordered
his thirty-two chariot commanders, "Do
not fight with anyone, small or great,
except the king of Israel." 32 When the
chariot commanders saw Jehoshaphat,
they thought, "Surely this is the king of
Israel." So they turned to attack him, but
when Jehoshaphat cried out, 33 the chariot commanders saw that he was not the
king of Israel and stopped pursuing him.
34 But someone drew his bow at random and hit the king of Israel between
the sections of his armor. The king told
his chariot driver, "Wheel around and
get me out of the fighting. I've been
wounded." 35 All day long the battle
raged, and the king was propped up in
his chariot facing the Arameans. The
blood from his wound ran onto the floor
of the chariot, and that evening he died.
36 As the sun was setting, a cry spread
through the army: "Every man to his
town. Every man to his land!"
37 So the king died and was brought
to Samaria, and they buried him there.
38 They washed the chariot at a pool in
Samaria (where the prostitutes bathed),[b]
and the dogs licked up his blood, as the
word of the LORD had declared.
39 As for the other events of Ahab's
reign, including all he did, the palace
he built and adorned with ivory, and the
cities he fortified, are they not written
in the book of the annals of the kings of
Israel? 40 Ahab rested with his ancestors.
And Ahaziah his son succeeded him as
king.

[a] 24 Or *Spirit of* [b] 38 Or *Samaria and cleaned the weapons*

Jehoshaphat King of Judah

41 Jehoshaphat son of Asa became king of Judah in the fourth year of Ahab king of Israel. 42 Jehoshaphat was thirty-five years old when he became king, and he reigned in Jerusalem twenty-five years. His mother's name was Azubah daughter of Shilhi. 43 In everything he followed the ways of his father Asa and did not stray from them; he did what was right in the eyes of the LORD. The high places, however, were not removed, and the people continued to offer sacrifices and burn incense there.[a] 44 Jehoshaphat was also at peace with the king of Israel.

45 As for the other events of Jehoshaphat's reign, the things he achieved and his military exploits, are they not written in the book of the annals of the kings of Judah? 46 He rid the land of the rest of the male shrine prostitutes who remained there even after the reign of his father Asa. 47 There was then no king in Edom; a provincial governor ruled.

48 Now Jehoshaphat built a fleet of trading ships[b] to go to Ophir for gold, but they never set sail—they were wrecked at Ezion Geber. 49 At that time Ahaziah son of Ahab said to Jehoshaphat, "Let my men sail with yours," but Jehoshaphat refused.

50 Then Jehoshaphat rested with his ancestors and was buried with them in the city of David his father. And Jehoram his son succeeded him as king.

Ahaziah King of Israel

51 Ahaziah son of Ahab became king of Israel in Samaria in the seventeenth year of Jehoshaphat king of Judah, and he reigned over Israel two years. 52 He did evil in the eyes of the LORD, because he followed the ways of his father and mother and of Jeroboam son of Nebat, who caused Israel to sin. 53 He served and worshiped Baal and aroused the anger of the LORD, the God of Israel, just as his father had done.

[a] 43 In Hebrew texts this sentence (22:43b) is numbered 22:44, and 22:44-53 is numbered 22:45-54. [b] 48 Hebrew *of ships of Tarshish*

2 KINGS

The LORD's Judgment on Ahaziah

1 After Ahab's death, Moab rebelled
against Israel. 2Now Ahaziah had
fallen through the lattice of his upper
room in Samaria and injured himself.
So he sent messengers, saying to them,
"Go and consult Baal-Zebub, the god of
Ekron, to see if I will recover from this
injury."
3But the angel of the LORD said to Elijah the Tishbite, "Go up and meet the
messengers of the king of Samaria and
ask them, 'Is it because there is no God
in Israel that you are going off to consult
Baal-Zebub, the god of Ekron?' 4There-
fore this is what the LORD says: 'You will
not leave the bed you are lying on. You
will certainly die!'" So Elijah went.
5When the messengers returned to
the king, he asked them, "Why have you
come back?"
6"A man came to meet us," they replied. "And he said to us, 'Go back to the
king who sent you and tell him, "This is
what the LORD says: Is it because there
is no God in Israel that you are sending
messengers to consult Baal-Zebub, the
god of Ekron? Therefore you will not
leave the bed you are lying on. You will
certainly die!"'"
7The king asked them, "What kind of
man was it who came to meet you and
told you this?"
8They replied, "He had a garment of
hair[a] and had a leather belt around his
waist."
The king said, "That was Elijah the
Tishbite."
9Then he sent to Elijah a captain with
his company of fifty men. The captain
went up to Elijah, who was sitting on the
top of a hill, and said to him, "Man of
God, the king says, 'Come down!'"
10Elijah answered the captain, "If I am
a man of God, may fire come down from
heaven and consume you and your fifty men!" Then fire fell from heaven and
consumed the captain and his men.
11At this the king sent to Elijah another
captain with his fifty men. The captain
said to him, "Man of God, this is what the
king says, 'Come down at once!'"
12"If I am a man of God," Elijah replied,
"may fire come down from heaven and
consume you and your fifty men!" Then
the fire of God fell from heaven and consumed him and his fifty men.
13So the king sent a third captain with
his fifty men. This third captain went up
and fell on his knees before Elijah. "Man
of God," he begged, "please have respect
for my life and the lives of these fifty
men, your servants! 14See, fire has fall-
en from heaven and consumed the first
two captains and all their men. But now
have respect for my life!"
15The angel of the LORD said to Elijah,
"Go down with him; do not be afraid of
him." So Elijah got up and went down
with him to the king.
16He told the king, "This is what the
LORD says: Is it because there is no God
in Israel for you to consult that you have
sent messengers to consult Baal-Zebub,
the god of Ekron? Because you have
done this, you will never leave the bed
you are lying on. You will certainly die!"
17So he died, according to the word of the
LORD that Elijah had spoken.
Because Ahaziah had no son, Joram[b]
succeeded him as king in the second
year of Jehoram son of Jehoshaphat
king of Judah. 18As for all the other
events of Ahaziah's reign, and what he
did, are they not written in the book of
the annals of the kings of Israel?

Elijah Taken Up to Heaven

2 When the LORD was about to take
Elijah up to heaven in a whirlwind,
Elijah and Elisha were on their way from
Gilgal. 2Elijah said to Elisha, "Stay here;
the LORD has sent me to Bethel."
But Elisha said, "As surely as the LORD
lives and as you live, I will not leave
you." So they went down to Bethel.
3The company of the prophets at Bethel came out to Elisha and asked, "Do you
know that the LORD is going to take your
master from you today?"
"Yes, I know," Elisha replied, "so be
quiet."
4Then Elijah said to him, "Stay here,
Elisha; the LORD has sent me to Jericho."
And he replied, "As surely as the LORD
lives and as you live, I will not leave
you." So they went to Jericho.

[a] 8 Or *He was a hairy man* [b] 17 Hebrew *Jehoram,* a variant of *Joram*

5 The company of the prophets at Jericho went up to Elisha and asked him, "Do you know that the LORD is going to take your master from you today?"

"Yes, I know," he replied, "so be quiet."

6 Then Elijah said to him, "Stay here; the LORD has sent me to the Jordan."

And he replied, "As surely as the LORD lives and as you live, I will not leave you." So the two of them walked on.

7 Fifty men from the company of the prophets went and stood at a distance, facing the place where Elijah and Elisha had stopped at the Jordan. 8 Elijah took his cloak, rolled it up and struck the water with it. The water divided to the right and to the left, and the two of them crossed over on dry ground.

9 When they had crossed, Elijah said to Elisha, "Tell me, what can I do for you before I am taken from you?"

"Let me inherit a double portion of your spirit," Elisha replied.

10 "You have asked a difficult thing," Elijah said, "yet if you see me when I am taken from you, it will be yours — otherwise, it will not."

11 As they were walking along and talking together, suddenly a chariot of fire and horses of fire appeared and separated the two of them, and Elijah went up to heaven in a whirlwind. 12 Elisha saw this and cried out, "My father! My father! The chariots and horsemen of Israel!" And Elisha saw him no more. Then he took hold of his garment and tore it in two.

13 Elisha then picked up Elijah's cloak that had fallen from him and went back and stood on the bank of the Jordan. 14 He took the cloak that had fallen from Elijah and struck the water with it. "Where now is the LORD, the God of Elijah?" he asked. When he struck the water, it divided to the right and to the left, and he crossed over.

15 The company of the prophets from Jericho, who were watching, said, "The spirit of Elijah is resting on Elisha." And they went to meet him and bowed to the ground before him. 16 "Look," they said, "we your servants have fifty able men. Let them go and look for your master. Perhaps the Spirit of the LORD has picked him up and set him down on some mountain or in some valley."

"No," Elisha replied, "do not send them."

17 But they persisted until he was too embarrassed to refuse. So he said, "Send them." And they sent fifty men, who searched for three days but did not find him. 18 When they returned to Elisha, who was staying in Jericho, he said to them, "Didn't I tell you not to go?"

Healing of the Water

19 The people of the city said to Elisha, "Look, our lord, this town is well situated, as you can see, but the water is bad and the land is unproductive."

20 "Bring me a new bowl," he said, "and put salt in it." So they brought it to him.

21 Then he went out to the spring and threw the salt into it, saying, "This is what the LORD says: 'I have healed this water. Never again will it cause death or make the land unproductive.'" 22 And the water has remained pure to this day, according to the word Elisha had spoken.

Elisha Is Jeered

23 From there Elisha went up to Bethel. As he was walking along the road, some boys came out of the town and jeered at him. "Get out of here, baldy!" they said. "Get out of here, baldy!" 24 He turned around, looked at them and called down a curse on them in the name of the LORD. Then two bears came out of the woods and mauled forty-two of the boys. 25 And he went on to Mount Carmel and from there returned to Samaria.

Moab Revolts

3 Joram[a] son of Ahab became king of Israel in Samaria in the eighteenth year of Jehoshaphat king of Judah, and he reigned twelve years. 2 He did evil in the eyes of the LORD, but not as his father and mother had done. He got rid of the sacred stone of Baal that his father had made. 3 Nevertheless he clung to the sins of Jeroboam son of Nebat, which he had caused Israel to commit; he did not turn away from them.

4 Now Mesha king of Moab raised sheep, and he had to pay the king of Israel a tribute of a hundred thousand lambs and the wool of a hundred thousand rams. 5 But after Ahab died, the king of Moab rebelled against the king of Israel. 6 So at that time King Joram set out from Samaria and mobilized all Israel. 7 He also sent this message to Jehoshaphat king of Judah: "The king of Moab has rebelled against me. Will you go with me to fight against Moab?"

"I will go with you," he replied. "I am as you are, my people as your people, my horses as your horses."

[a] 1 Hebrew *Jehoram*, a variant of *Joram*; also in verse 6

8“By what route shall we attack?” he
asked.
“Through the Desert of Edom,” he answered.
9So the king of Israel set out with the
king of Judah and the king of Edom. After a roundabout march of seven days,
the army had no more water for themselves or for the animals with them.
10“What!” exclaimed the king of Israel.
“Has the LORD called us three kings together only to deliver us into the hands
of Moab?”
11But Jehoshaphat asked, “Is there no
prophet of the LORD here, through whom
we may inquire of the LORD?”
An officer of the king of Israel answered, “Elisha son of Shaphat is here.
He used to pour water on the hands of
Elijah.[a]”
12Jehoshaphat said, “The word of the
LORD is with him.” So the king of Israel
and Jehoshaphat and the king of Edom
went down to him.
13Elisha said to the king of Israel, “Why
do you want to involve me? Go to the
prophets of your father and the prophets of your mother.”
“No,” the king of Israel answered,
“because it was the LORD who called us
three kings together to deliver us into
the hands of Moab.”
14Elisha said, “As surely as the LORD Almighty lives, whom I serve, if I did not
have respect for the presence of Jehoshaphat king of Judah, I would not pay any
attention to you. 15But now bring me a
harpist.”
While the harpist was playing, the
hand of the LORD came on Elisha 16and
he said, “This is what the LORD says: I
will fill this valley with pools of water.
17For this is what the LORD says: You will
see neither wind nor rain, yet this valley
will be filled with water, and you, your
cattle and your other animals will drink.
18This is an easy thing in the eyes of the
LORD; he will also deliver Moab into your
hands. 19You will overthrow every fortified city and every major town. You will
cut down every good tree, stop up all the
springs, and ruin every good field with
stones.”
20The next morning, about the time for
offering the sacrifice, there it was — water flowing from the direction of Edom!
And the land was filled with water.
21Now all the Moabites had heard that
the kings had come to fight against
them; so every man, young and old, who
could bear arms was called up and stationed on the border. 22When they got up
early in the morning, the sun was shining on the water. To the Moabites across
the way, the water looked red — like
blood. 23“That’s blood!” they said. “Those
kings must have fought and slaughtered
each other. Now to the plunder, Moab!”
24But when the Moabites came to the
camp of Israel, the Israelites rose up and
fought them until they fled. And the Israelites invaded the land and slaughtered the Moabites. 25They destroyed
the towns, and each man threw a stone
on every good field until it was covered.
They stopped up all the springs and cut
down every good tree. Only Kir Hareseth
was left with its stones in place, but men
armed with slings surrounded it and attacked it.
26When the king of Moab saw that the
battle had gone against him, he took
with him seven hundred swordsmen to
break through to the king of Edom, but
they failed. 27Then he took his firstborn
son, who was to succeed him as king, and
offered him as a sacrifice on the city wall.
The fury against Israel was great; they
withdrew and returned to their own land.

The Widow’s Olive Oil

4 The wife of a man from the company of the prophets cried out to Elisha,
“Your servant my husband is dead, and
you know that he revered the LORD. But
now his creditor is coming to take my
two boys as his slaves.”
2Elisha replied to her, “How can I help
you? Tell me, what do you have in your
house?”
“Your servant has nothing there at
all,” she said, “except a small jar of olive oil.”
3Elisha said, “Go around and ask all
your neighbors for empty jars. Don’t ask
for just a few. 4Then go inside and shut
the door behind you and your sons. Pour
oil into all the jars, and as each is filled,
put it to one side.”
5She left him and shut the door behind
her and her sons. They brought the jars
to her and she kept pouring. 6When all
the jars were full, she said to her son,
“Bring me another one.”
But he replied, “There is not a jar left.”
Then the oil stopped flowing.
7She went and told the man of God,
and he said, “Go, sell the oil and pay
your debts. You and your sons can live
on what is left.”

[a] *11* That is, he was Elijah’s personal servant.

The Shunammite's Son Restored to Life

8 One day Elisha went to Shunem. And
a well-to-do woman was there, who urged
him to stay for a meal. So whenever he
came by, he stopped there to eat. 9 She
said to her husband, "I know that this
man who often comes our way is a holy
man of God. 10 Let's make a small room on
the roof and put in it a bed and a table,
a chair and a lamp for him. Then he can
stay there whenever he comes to us."
11 One day when Elisha came, he went
up to his room and lay down there. 12 He
said to his servant Gehazi, "Call the Shunammite." So he called her, and she
stood before him. 13 Elisha said to him,
"Tell her, 'You have gone to all this trouble for us. Now what can be done for
you? Can we speak on your behalf to the
king or the commander of the army?'"
She replied, "I have a home among my
own people."
14 "What can be done for her?" Elisha
asked.
Gehazi said, "She has no son, and her
husband is old."
15 Then Elisha said, "Call her." So he
called her, and she stood in the doorway.
16 "About this time next year," Elisha said,
"you will hold a son in your arms."
"No, my lord!" she objected. "Please,
man of God, don't mislead your servant!"
17 But the woman became pregnant,
and the next year about that same time
she gave birth to a son, just as Elisha had
told her.
18 The child grew, and one day he went
out to his father, who was with the reapers. 19 He said to his father, "My head! My
head!"
His father told a servant, "Carry him to
his mother." 20 After the servant had lifted him up and carried him to his mother, the boy sat on her lap until noon, and
then he died. 21 She went up and laid him
on the bed of the man of God, then shut
the door and went out.
22 She called her husband and said,
"Please send me one of the servants and
a donkey so I can go to the man of God
quickly and return."
23 "Why go to him today?" he asked.
"It's not the New Moon or the Sabbath."
"That's all right," she said.
24 She saddled the donkey and said to
her servant, "Lead on; don't slow down
for me unless I tell you." 25 So she set out
and came to the man of God at Mount
Carmel.
When he saw her in the distance, the
man of God said to his servant Gehazi,
"Look! There's the Shunammite! 26 Run to
meet her and ask her, 'Are you all right?
Is your husband all right? Is your child
all right?'"
"Everything is all right," she said.
27 When she reached the man of God at
the mountain, she took hold of his feet.
Gehazi came over to push her away, but
the man of God said, "Leave her alone!
She is in bitter distress, but the LORD has
hidden it from me and has not told me
why."
28 "Did I ask you for a son, my lord?"
she said. "Didn't I tell you, 'Don't raise
my hopes'?"
29 Elisha said to Gehazi, "Tuck your
cloak into your belt, take my staff in your
hand and run. Don't greet anyone you
meet, and if anyone greets you, do not
answer. Lay my staff on the boy's face."
30 But the child's mother said, "As surely as the LORD lives and as you live, I will
not leave you." So he got up and followed
her.
31 Gehazi went on ahead and laid the
staff on the boy's face, but there was no
sound or response. So Gehazi went back
to meet Elisha and told him, "The boy
has not awakened."
32 When Elisha reached the house,
there was the boy lying dead on his
couch. 33 He went in, shut the door on
the two of them and prayed to the LORD.
34 Then he got on the bed and lay on the
boy, mouth to mouth, eyes to eyes, hands
to hands. As he stretched himself out on
him, the boy's body grew warm. 35 Elisha
turned away and walked back and forth
in the room and then got on the bed and
stretched out on him once more. The
boy sneezed seven times and opened his
eyes.
36 Elisha summoned Gehazi and said,
"Call the Shunammite." And he did.
When she came, he said, "Take your son."
37 She came in, fell at his feet and bowed
to the ground. Then she took her son and
went out.

Death in the Pot

38 Elisha returned to Gilgal and there
was a famine in that region. While the
company of the prophets was meeting
with him, he said to his servant, "Put
on the large pot and cook some stew for
these prophets."
39 One of them went out into the fields
to gather herbs and found a wild vine
and picked as many of its gourds as his
garment could hold. When he returned,
he cut them up into the pot of stew,
though no one knew what they were.

40 The stew was poured out for the men,
but as they began to eat it, they cried
out, "Man of God, there is death in the
pot!" And they could not eat it.
41 Elisha said, "Get some flour." He put
it into the pot and said, "Serve it to the
people to eat." And there was nothing
harmful in the pot.

Feeding of a Hundred

42 A man came from Baal Shalishah,
bringing the man of God twenty loaves
of barley bread baked from the first ripe
grain, along with some heads of new
grain. "Give it to the people to eat," Elisha said.
43 "How can I set this before a hundred
men?" his servant asked.
But Elisha answered, "Give it to the
people to eat. For this is what the LORD
says: 'They will eat and have some left
over.'" 44 Then he set it before them, and
they ate and had some left over, according to the word of the LORD.

Naaman Healed of Leprosy

5 Now Naaman was commander of the
army of the king of Aram. He was a
great man in the sight of his master and
highly regarded, because through him
the LORD had given victory to Aram. He
was a valiant soldier, but he had leprosy.[a]
2 Now bands of raiders from Aram had
gone out and had taken captive a young
girl from Israel, and she served Naaman's wife. 3 She said to her mistress, "If
only my master would see the prophet
who is in Samaria! He would cure him
of his leprosy."
4 Naaman went to his master and told
him what the girl from Israel had said.
5 "By all means, go," the king of Aram replied. "I will send a letter to the king of
Israel." So Naaman left, taking with him
ten talents[b] of silver, six thousand shekels[c] of gold and ten sets of clothing. 6 The
letter that he took to the king of Israel
read: "With this letter I am sending my
servant Naaman to you so that you may
cure him of his leprosy."
7 As soon as the king of Israel read the
letter, he tore his robes and said, "Am I
God? Can I kill and bring back to life?
Why does this fellow send someone to
me to be cured of his leprosy? See how
he is trying to pick a quarrel with me!"
8 When Elisha the man of God heard
that the king of Israel had torn his
robes, he sent him this message: "Why
have you torn your robes? Have the man
come to me and he will know that there
is a prophet in Israel." 9 So Naaman went
with his horses and chariots and stopped
at the door of Elisha's house. 10 Elisha
sent a messenger to say to him, "Go,
wash yourself seven times in the Jordan,
and your flesh will be restored and you
will be cleansed."
11 But Naaman went away angry and
said, "I thought that he would surely
come out to me and stand and call on
the name of the LORD his God, wave his
hand over the spot and cure me of my
leprosy. 12 Are not Abana and Pharpar,
the rivers of Damascus, better than all
the waters of Israel? Couldn't I wash in
them and be cleansed?" So he turned
and went off in a rage.
13 Naaman's servants went to him
and said, "My father, if the prophet
had told you to do some great thing,
would you not have done it? How much
more, then, when he tells you, 'Wash
and be cleansed'!" 14 So he went down
and dipped himself in the Jordan seven
times, as the man of God had told him,
and his flesh was restored and became
clean like that of a young boy.
15 Then Naaman and all his attendants
went back to the man of God. He stood
before him and said, "Now I know that
there is no God in all the world except in
Israel. So please accept a gift from your
servant."
16 The prophet answered, "As surely as
the LORD lives, whom I serve, I will not
accept a thing." And even though Naaman urged him, he refused.
17 "If you will not," said Naaman,
"please let me, your servant, be given as
much earth as a pair of mules can carry,
for your servant will never again make
burnt offerings and sacrifices to any other god but the LORD. 18 But may the LORD
forgive your servant for this one thing:
When my master enters the temple of
Rimmon to bow down and he is leaning on my arm and I have to bow there
also — when I bow down in the temple
of Rimmon, may the LORD forgive your
servant for this."
19 "Go in peace," Elisha said.
After Naaman had traveled some distance, 20 Gehazi, the servant of Elisha the
man of God, said to himself, "My master

[a] *1* The Hebrew for *leprosy* was used for various diseases affecting the skin; also in verses 3, 6, 7, 11 and 27. [b] *5* That is, about 750 pounds or about 340 kilograms [c] *5* That is, about 150 pounds or about 69 kilograms

was too easy on Naaman, this Aramean, by not accepting from him what he
brought. As surely as the LORD lives, I
will run after him and get something
from him."
21So Gehazi hurried after Naaman.
When Naaman saw him running toward him, he got down from the chariot
to meet him. "Is everything all right?"
he asked.
22"Everything is all right," Gehazi answered. "My master sent me to say, 'Two
young men from the company of the
prophets have just come to me from
the hill country of Ephraim. Please give
them a talent[a] of silver and two sets of
clothing.'"
23"By all means, take two talents,"
said Naaman. He urged Gehazi to accept
them, and then tied up the two talents
of silver in two bags, with two sets of
clothing. He gave them to two of his servants, and they carried them ahead of
Gehazi. 24When Gehazi came to the hill,
he took the things from the servants and
put them away in the house. He sent the
men away and they left.
25When he went in and stood before
his master, Elisha asked him, "Where
have you been, Gehazi?"
"Your servant didn't go anywhere,"
Gehazi answered.
26But Elisha said to him, "Was not
my spirit with you when the man got
down from his chariot to meet you? Is
this the time to take money or to accept
clothes — or olive groves and vineyards,
or flocks and herds, or male and female
slaves? 27Naaman's leprosy will cling to
you and to your descendants forever."
Then Gehazi went from Elisha's presence and his skin was leprous — it had
become as white as snow.

An Axhead Floats

6 The company of the prophets said
to Elisha, "Look, the place where we
meet with you is too small for us. 2Let us
go to the Jordan, where each of us can
get a pole; and let us build a place there
for us to meet."
And he said, "Go."
3Then one of them said, "Won't you
please come with your servants?"
"I will," Elisha replied. 4And he went
with them.
They went to the Jordan and began
to cut down trees. 5As one of them was
cutting down a tree, the iron axhead fell
into the water. "Oh no, my lord!" he cried
out. "It was borrowed!"
6The man of God asked, "Where did
it fall?" When he showed him the place,
Elisha cut a stick and threw it there, and
made the iron float. 7"Lift it out," he said.
Then the man reached out his hand and
took it.

Elisha Traps Blinded Arameans

8Now the king of Aram was at war
with Israel. After conferring with his officers, he said, "I will set up my camp in
such and such a place."
9The man of God sent word to the king
of Israel: "Beware of passing that place,
because the Arameans are going down
there." 10So the king of Israel checked
on the place indicated by the man of
God. Time and again Elisha warned the
king, so that he was on his guard in such
places.
11This enraged the king of Aram. He
summoned his officers and demanded
of them, "Tell me! Which of us is on the
side of the king of Israel?"
12"None of us, my lord the king,"
said one of his officers, "but Elisha, the
prophet who is in Israel, tells the king of
Israel the very words you speak in your
bedroom."
13"Go, find out where he is," the king
ordered, "so I can send men and capture
him." The report came back: "He is in Dothan." 14Then he sent horses and chariots
and a strong force there. They went by
night and surrounded the city.
15When the servant of the man of
God got up and went out early the next
morning, an army with horses and chariots had surrounded the city. "Oh no, my
lord! What shall we do?" the servant
asked.
16"Don't be afraid," the prophet answered. "Those who are with us are more
than those who are with them."
17And Elisha prayed, "Open his eyes,
LORD, so that he may see." Then the LORD
opened the servant's eyes, and he looked
and saw the hills full of horses and chariots of fire all around Elisha.
18As the enemy came down toward
him, Elisha prayed to the LORD, "Strike
this army with blindness." So he struck
them with blindness, as Elisha had
asked.
19Elisha told them, "This is not the road
and this is not the city. Follow me, and I
will lead you to the man you are looking
for." And he led them to Samaria.
20After they entered the city, Elisha
said, "LORD, open the eyes of these men

[a] 22 That is, about 75 pounds or about 34 kilograms

so they can see." Then the LORD opened
their eyes and they looked, and there
they were, inside Samaria.
21When the king of Israel saw them, he
asked Elisha, "Shall I kill them, my father? Shall I kill them?"
22"Do not kill them," he answered.
"Would you kill those you have captured
with your own sword or bow? Set food
and water before them so that they may
eat and drink and then go back to their
master." 23So he prepared a great feast
for them, and after they had finished
eating and drinking, he sent them away,
and they returned to their master. So the
bands from Aram stopped raiding Israel's territory.

Famine in Besieged Samaria

24Some time later, Ben-Hadad king
of Aram mobilized his entire army and
marched up and laid siege to Samaria.
25There was a great famine in the city;
the siege lasted so long that a donkey's
head sold for eighty shekels[a] of silver,
and a quarter of a cab[b] of seed pods[c] for
five shekels.[d]
26As the king of Israel was passing by
on the wall, a woman cried to him, "Help
me, my lord the king!"
27The king replied, "If the LORD does
not help you, where can I get help for
you? From the threshing floor? From
the winepress?" 28Then he asked her,
"What's the matter?"
She answered, "This woman said to me,
'Give up your son so we may eat him today, and tomorrow we'll eat my son.' 29So
we cooked my son and ate him. The next
day I said to her, 'Give up your son so we
may eat him,' but she had hidden him."
30When the king heard the woman's
words, he tore his robes. As he went
along the wall, the people looked, and
they saw that, under his robes, he had
sackcloth on his body. 31He said, "May
God deal with me, be it ever so severely,
if the head of Elisha son of Shaphat remains on his shoulders today!"
32Now Elisha was sitting in his house,
and the elders were sitting with him. The
king sent a messenger ahead, but before he arrived, Elisha said to the elders,
"Don't you see how this murderer is sending someone to cut off my head? Look,
when the messenger comes, shut the
door and hold it shut against him. Is not
the sound of his master's footsteps behind him?" 33While he was still talking to
them, the messenger came down to him.
The king said, "This disaster is from
the LORD. Why should I wait for the LORD
any longer?"
7 Elisha replied, "Hear the word of the
LORD. This is what the LORD says:
About this time tomorrow, a seah[e] of the
finest flour will sell for a shekel[f] and two
seahs[g] of barley for a shekel at the gate
of Samaria."
2The officer on whose arm the king
was leaning said to the man of God,
"Look, even if the LORD should open the
floodgates of the heavens, could this
happen?"
"You will see it with your own eyes,"
answered Elisha, "but you will not eat
any of it!"

The Siege Lifted

3Now there were four men with leprosy[h] at the entrance of the city gate. They
said to each other, "Why stay here until we die? 4If we say, 'We'll go into the
city'—the famine is there, and we will
die. And if we stay here, we will die. So
let's go over to the camp of the Arameans and surrender. If they spare us, we
live; if they kill us, then we die."
5At dusk they got up and went to
the camp of the Arameans. When they
reached the edge of the camp, no one
was there, 6for the Lord had caused the
Arameans to hear the sound of chariots
and horses and a great army, so that
they said to one another, "Look, the king
of Israel has hired the Hittite and Egyptian kings to attack us!" 7So they got up
and fled in the dusk and abandoned
their tents and their horses and donkeys.
They left the camp as it was and ran for
their lives.
8The men who had leprosy reached
the edge of the camp, entered one of the
tents and ate and drank. Then they took
silver, gold and clothes, and went off and
hid them. They returned and entered another tent and took some things from it
and hid them also.
9Then they said to each other, "What
we're doing is not right. This is a day of

[a] *25* That is, about 2 pounds or about 920 grams [b] *25* That is, probably about 1/4 pound or about 100 grams [c] *25* Or *of doves' dung* [d] *25* That is, about 2 ounces or about 58 grams
[e] *1* That is, probably about 12 pounds or about 5.5 kilograms of flour; also in verses 16 and 18
[f] *1* That is, about 2/5 ounce or about 12 grams; also in verses 16 and 18 [g] *1* That is, probably about 20 pounds or about 9 kilograms of barley; also in verses 16 and 18 [h] *3* The Hebrew for *leprosy* was used for various diseases affecting the skin; also in verse 8.

good news and we are keeping it to ourselves. If we wait until daylight, punishment will overtake us. Let's go at once and report this to the royal palace."

10 So they went and called out to the city gatekeepers and told them, "We went into the Aramean camp and no one was there — not a sound of anyone — only tethered horses and donkeys, and the tents left just as they were." 11 The gatekeepers shouted the news, and it was reported within the palace.

12 The king got up in the night and said to his officers, "I will tell you what the Arameans have done to us. They know we are starving; so they have left the camp to hide in the countryside, thinking, 'They will surely come out, and then we will take them alive and get into the city.'"

13 One of his officers answered, "Have some men take five of the horses that are left in the city. Their plight will be like that of all the Israelites left here — yes, they will only be like all these Israelites who are doomed. So let us send them to find out what happened."

14 So they selected two chariots with their horses, and the king sent them after the Aramean army. He commanded the drivers, "Go and find out what has happened." 15 They followed them as far as the Jordan, and they found the whole road strewn with the clothing and equipment the Arameans had thrown away in their headlong flight. So the messengers returned and reported to the king. 16 Then the people went out and plundered the camp of the Arameans. So a seah of the finest flour sold for a shekel, and two seahs of barley sold for a shekel, as the LORD had said.

17 Now the king had put the officer on whose arm he leaned in charge of the gate, and the people trampled him in the gateway, and he died, just as the man of God had foretold when the king came down to his house. 18 It happened as the man of God had said to the king: "About this time tomorrow, a seah of the finest flour will sell for a shekel and two seahs of barley for a shekel at the gate of Samaria."

19 The officer had said to the man of God, "Look, even if the LORD should open the floodgates of the heavens, could this happen?" The man of God had replied, "You will see it with your own eyes, but you will not eat any of it!" 20 And that is exactly what happened to him, for the people trampled him in the gateway, and he died.

The Shunammite's Land Restored

8 Now Elisha had said to the woman whose son he had restored to life, "Go away with your family and stay for a while wherever you can, because the LORD has decreed a famine in the land that will last seven years." 2 The woman proceeded to do as the man of God said. She and her family went away and stayed in the land of the Philistines seven years.

3 At the end of the seven years she came back from the land of the Philistines and went to appeal to the king for her house and land. 4 The king was talking to Gehazi, the servant of the man of God, and had said, "Tell me about all the great things Elisha has done." 5 Just as Gehazi was telling the king how Elisha had restored the dead to life, the woman whose son Elisha had brought back to life came to appeal to the king for her house and land.

Gehazi said, "This is the woman, my lord the king, and this is her son whom Elisha restored to life." 6 The king asked the woman about it, and she told him.

Then he assigned an official to her case and said to him, "Give back everything that belonged to her, including all the income from her land from the day she left the country until now."

Hazael Murders Ben-Hadad

7 Elisha went to Damascus, and Ben-Hadad king of Aram was ill. When the king was told, "The man of God has come all the way up here," 8 he said to Hazael, "Take a gift with you and go to meet the man of God. Consult the LORD through him; ask him, 'Will I recover from this illness?'"

9 Hazael went to meet Elisha, taking with him as a gift forty camel-loads of all the finest wares of Damascus. He went in and stood before him, and said, "Your son Ben-Hadad king of Aram has sent me to ask, 'Will I recover from this illness?'"

10 Elisha answered, "Go and say to him, 'You will certainly recover.' Nevertheless,[a] the LORD has revealed to me that he will in fact die." 11 He stared at him with a fixed gaze until Hazael was embarrassed. Then the man of God began to weep.

12 "Why is my lord weeping?" asked Hazael.

"Because I know the harm you will do to the Israelites," he answered. "You will set fire to their fortified places, kill

[a] 10 The Hebrew may also be read *Go and say, 'You will certainly not recover,' for.*

their young men with the sword, dash
their little children to the ground, and
rip open their pregnant women."
13 Hazael said, "How could your servant,
a mere dog, accomplish such a feat?"
"The LORD has shown me that you will
become king of Aram," answered Elisha.
14 Then Hazael left Elisha and returned
to his master. When Ben-Hadad asked,
"What did Elisha say to you?" Hazael replied, "He told me that you would
certainly recover." 15 But the next day he
took a thick cloth, soaked it in water and
spread it over the king's face, so that
he died. Then Hazael succeeded him as
king.

Jehoram King of Judah

16 In the fifth year of Joram son of
Ahab king of Israel, when Jehoshaphat
was king of Judah, Jehoram son of Jehoshaphat began his reign as king of
Judah. 17 He was thirty-two years old
when he became king, and he reigned in
Jerusalem eight years. 18 He followed the
ways of the kings of Israel, as the house
of Ahab had done, for he married a
daughter of Ahab. He did evil in the eyes
of the LORD. 19 Nevertheless, for the sake
of his servant David, the LORD was not
willing to destroy Judah. He had promised to maintain a lamp for David and
his descendants forever.
20 In the time of Jehoram, Edom rebelled against Judah and set up its own
king. 21 So Jehoram[a] went to Zair with all
his chariots. The Edomites surrounded
him and his chariot commanders, but
he rose up and broke through by night;
his army, however, fled back home. 22 To
this day Edom has been in rebellion
against Judah. Libnah revolted at the
same time.
23 As for the other events of Jehoram's
reign, and all he did, are they not written in the book of the annals of the kings
of Judah? 24 Jehoram rested with his ancestors and was buried with them in the
City of David. And Ahaziah his son succeeded him as king.

Ahaziah King of Judah

25 In the twelfth year of Joram son of
Ahab king of Israel, Ahaziah son of Jehoram king of Judah began to reign.
26 Ahaziah was twenty-two years old
when he became king, and he reigned in
Jerusalem one year. His mother's name
was Athaliah, a granddaughter of Omri
king of Israel. 27 He followed the ways
of the house of Ahab and did evil in the
eyes of the LORD, as the house of Ahab
had done, for he was related by marriage to Ahab's family.
28 Ahaziah went with Joram son of Ahab
to war against Hazael king of Aram at
Ramoth Gilead. The Arameans wounded
Joram; 29 so King Joram returned to Jezreel to recover from the wounds the Arameans had inflicted on him at Ramoth[b] in
his battle with Hazael king of Aram.
Then Ahaziah son of Jehoram king of
Judah went down to Jezreel to see Joram son of Ahab, because he had been
wounded.

Jehu Anointed King of Israel

9 The prophet Elisha summoned a
man from the company of the prophets and said to him, "Tuck your cloak
into your belt, take this flask of olive
oil with you and go to Ramoth Gilead.
2 When you get there, look for Jehu son
of Jehoshaphat, the son of Nimshi. Go to
him, get him away from his companions
and take him into an inner room. 3 Then
take the flask and pour the oil on his
head and declare, 'This is what the LORD
says: I anoint you king over Israel.' Then
open the door and run; don't delay!"
4 So the young prophet went to Ramoth
Gilead. 5 When he arrived, he found the
army officers sitting together. "I have a
message for you, commander," he said.
"For which of us?" asked Jehu.
"For you, commander," he replied.
6 Jehu got up and went into the house.
Then the prophet poured the oil on Jehu's head and declared, "This is what
the LORD, the God of Israel, says: 'I
anoint you king over the LORD's people
Israel. 7 You are to destroy the house of
Ahab your master, and I will avenge the
blood of my servants the prophets and
the blood of all the LORD's servants shed
by Jezebel. 8 The whole house of Ahab
will perish. I will cut off from Ahab every last male in Israel — slave or free.[c]
9 I will make the house of Ahab like the
house of Jeroboam son of Nebat and
like the house of Baasha son of Ahijah.
10 As for Jezebel, dogs will devour her on
the plot of ground at Jezreel, and no one
will bury her.'" Then he opened the door
and ran.
11 When Jehu went out to his fellow
officers, one of them asked him, "Is everything all right? Why did this maniac
come to you?"

[a] *21* Hebrew *Joram,* a variant of *Jehoram;* also in verses 23 and 24 [b] *29* Hebrew *Ramah,* a variant of *Ramoth* [c] *8* Or *Israel — every ruler or leader*

"You know the man and the sort of
things he says," Jehu replied.
12"That's not true!" they said. "Tell us."
Jehu said, "Here is what he told me:
'This is what the LORD says: I anoint you
king over Israel.'"
13They quickly took their cloaks and
spread them under him on the bare
steps. Then they blew the trumpet and
shouted, "Jehu is king!"

Jehu Kills Joram and Ahaziah

14So Jehu son of Jehoshaphat, the son
of Nimshi, conspired against Joram.
(Now Joram and all Israel had been defending Ramoth Gilead against Hazael
king of Aram, 15but King Joram[a] had
returned to Jezreel to recover from the
wounds the Arameans had inflicted on
him in the battle with Hazael king of
Aram.) Jehu said, "If you desire to make
me king, don't let anyone slip out of the
city to go and tell the news in Jezreel."
16Then he got into his chariot and rode
to Jezreel, because Joram was resting
there and Ahaziah king of Judah had
gone down to see him.
17When the lookout standing on the
tower in Jezreel saw Jehu's troops approaching, he called out, "I see some
troops coming."
"Get a horseman," Joram ordered.
"Send him to meet them and ask, 'Do
you come in peace?'"
18The horseman rode off to meet Jehu
and said, "This is what the king says: 'Do
you come in peace?'"
"What do you have to do with peace?"
Jehu replied. "Fall in behind me."
The lookout reported, "The messenger has reached them, but he isn't coming back."
19So the king sent out a second horseman. When he came to them he said,
"This is what the king says: 'Do you come
in peace?'"
Jehu replied, "What do you have to do
with peace? Fall in behind me."
20The lookout reported, "He has
reached them, but he isn't coming back
either. The driving is like that of Jehu son
of Nimshi — he drives like a maniac."
21"Hitch up my chariot," Joram ordered. And when it was hitched up, Joram king of Israel and Ahaziah king of
Judah rode out, each in his own chariot,
to meet Jehu. They met him at the plot of
ground that had belonged to Naboth the
Jezreelite. 22When Joram saw Jehu he
asked, "Have you come in peace, Jehu?"
"How can there be peace," Jehu replied, "as long as all the idolatry and
witchcraft of your mother Jezebel
abound?"
23Joram turned about and fled, calling
out to Ahaziah, "Treachery, Ahaziah!"
24Then Jehu drew his bow and shot Joram between the shoulders. The arrow
pierced his heart and he slumped down
in his chariot. 25Jehu said to Bidkar, his
chariot officer, "Pick him up and throw
him on the field that belonged to Naboth the Jezreelite. Remember how you
and I were riding together in chariots
behind Ahab his father when the LORD
spoke this prophecy against him: 26'Yesterday I saw the blood of Naboth and the
blood of his sons, declares the LORD, and
I will surely make you pay for it on this
plot of ground, declares the LORD.'[b] Now
then, pick him up and throw him on that
plot, in accordance with the word of the
LORD."
27When Ahaziah king of Judah saw
what had happened, he fled up the
road to Beth Haggan.[c] Jehu chased him,
shouting, "Kill him too!" They wounded
him in his chariot on the way up to Gur
near Ibleam, but he escaped to Megiddo
and died there. 28His servants took him
by chariot to Jerusalem and buried him
with his ancestors in his tomb in the City
of David. 29(In the eleventh year of Joram son of Ahab, Ahaziah had become
king of Judah.)

Jezebel Killed

30Then Jehu went to Jezreel. When
Jezebel heard about it, she put on eye
makeup, arranged her hair and looked
out of a window. 31As Jehu entered the
gate, she asked, "Have you come in
peace, you Zimri, you murderer of your
master?"[d]
32He looked up at the window and
called out, "Who is on my side? Who?"
Two or three eunuchs looked down at
him. 33"Throw her down!" Jehu said. So
they threw her down, and some of her
blood spattered the wall and the horses
as they trampled her underfoot.
34Jehu went in and ate and drank.
"Take care of that cursed woman," he
said, "and bury her, for she was a king's
daughter." 35But when they went out
to bury her, they found nothing except

[a] *15* Hebrew *Jehoram*, a variant of *Joram*; also in verses 17 and 21-24 [b] *26* See 1 Kings 21:19.
[c] *27* Or *fled by way of the garden house* [d] *31* Or *"Was there peace for Zimri, who murdered his master?"*

her skull, her feet and her hands. 36They went back and told Jehu, who said, "This is the word of the LORD that he spoke through his servant Elijah the Tishbite: On the plot of ground at Jezreel dogs will devour Jezebel's flesh.[a] 37Jezebel's body will be like dung on the ground in the plot at Jezreel, so that no one will be able to say, 'This is Jezebel.'"

Ahab's Family Killed

10 Now there were in Samaria seventy sons of the house of Ahab. So Jehu wrote letters and sent them to Samaria: to the officials of Jezreel,[b] to the elders and to the guardians of Ahab's children. He said, 2"You have your master's sons with you and you have chariots and horses, a fortified city and weapons. Now as soon as this letter reaches you, 3choose the best and most worthy of your master's sons and set him on his father's throne. Then fight for your master's house."

4But they were terrified and said, "If two kings could not resist him, how can we?"

5So the palace administrator, the city governor, the elders and the guardians sent this message to Jehu: "We are your servants and we will do anything you say. We will not appoint anyone as king; you do whatever you think best."

6Then Jehu wrote them a second letter, saying, "If you are on my side and will obey me, take the heads of your master's sons and come to me in Jezreel by this time tomorrow."

Now the royal princes, seventy of them, were with the leading men of the city, who were rearing them. 7When the letter arrived, these men took the princes and slaughtered all seventy of them. They put their heads in baskets and sent them to Jehu in Jezreel. 8When the messenger arrived, he told Jehu, "They have brought the heads of the princes."

Then Jehu ordered, "Put them in two piles at the entrance of the city gate until morning."

9The next morning Jehu went out. He stood before all the people and said, "You are innocent. It was I who conspired against my master and killed him, but who killed all these? 10Know, then, that not a word the LORD has spoken against the house of Ahab will fail. The LORD has done what he announced through his servant Elijah." 11So Jehu killed everyone in Jezreel who remained of the house of Ahab, as well as all his chief men, his close friends and his priests, leaving him no survivor.

12Jehu then set out and went toward Samaria. At Beth Eked of the Shepherds, 13he met some relatives of Ahaziah king of Judah and asked, "Who are you?"

They said, "We are relatives of Ahaziah, and we have come down to greet the families of the king and of the queen mother."

14"Take them alive!" he ordered. So they took them alive and slaughtered them by the well of Beth Eked — forty-two of them. He left no survivor.

15After he left there, he came upon Jehonadab son of Rekab, who was on his way to meet him. Jehu greeted him and said, "Are you in accord with me, as I am with you?"

"I am," Jehonadab answered.

"If so," said Jehu, "give me your hand." So he did, and Jehu helped him up into the chariot. 16Jehu said, "Come with me and see my zeal for the LORD." Then he had him ride along in his chariot.

17When Jehu came to Samaria, he killed all who were left there of Ahab's family; he destroyed them, according to the word of the LORD spoken to Elijah.

Servants of Baal Killed

18Then Jehu brought all the people together and said to them, "Ahab served Baal a little; Jehu will serve him much. 19Now summon all the prophets of Baal, all his servants and all his priests. See that no one is missing, because I am going to hold a great sacrifice for Baal. Anyone who fails to come will no longer live." But Jehu was acting deceptively in order to destroy the servants of Baal.

20Jehu said, "Call an assembly in honor of Baal." So they proclaimed it. 21Then he sent word throughout Israel, and all the servants of Baal came; not one stayed away. They crowded into the temple of Baal until it was full from one end to the other. 22And Jehu said to the keeper of the wardrobe, "Bring robes for all the servants of Baal." So he brought out robes for them.

23Then Jehu and Jehonadab son of Rekab went into the temple of Baal. Jehu said to the servants of Baal, "Look around and see that no one who serves the LORD is here with you — only servants of Baal." 24So they went in to make sacrifices and burnt offerings. Now Jehu had posted eighty men outside with this

[a] *36* See 1 Kings 21:23. [b] *1* Hebrew; some Septuagint manuscripts and Vulgate *of the city*

warning: "If one of you lets any of the
men I am placing in your hands escape,
it will be your life for his life."
25As soon as Jehu had finished making
the burnt offering, he ordered the guards
and officers: "Go in and kill them; let
no one escape." So they cut them down
with the sword. The guards and officers
threw the bodies out and then entered
the inner shrine of the temple of Baal.
26They brought the sacred stone out of
the temple of Baal and burned it. 27They
demolished the sacred stone of Baal and
tore down the temple of Baal, and people have used it for a latrine to this day.
28So Jehu destroyed Baal worship in
Israel. 29However, he did not turn away
from the sins of Jeroboam son of Nebat,
which he had caused Israel to commit —
the worship of the golden calves at Bethel and Dan.
30The LORD said to Jehu, "Because you
have done well in accomplishing what is
right in my eyes and have done to the
house of Ahab all I had in mind to do,
your descendants will sit on the throne
of Israel to the fourth generation." 31Yet
Jehu was not careful to keep the law of
the LORD, the God of Israel, with all his
heart. He did not turn away from the
sins of Jeroboam, which he had caused
Israel to commit.
32In those days the LORD began to reduce the size of Israel. Hazael overpowered the Israelites throughout their territory 33east of the Jordan in all the land
of Gilead (the region of Gad, Reuben and
Manasseh), from Aroer by the Arnon
Gorge through Gilead to Bashan.
34As for the other events of Jehu's
reign, all he did, and all his achievements, are they not written in the book
of the annals of the kings of Israel?
35Jehu rested with his ancestors and
was buried in Samaria. And Jehoahaz
his son succeeded him as king. 36The
time that Jehu reigned over Israel in Samaria was twenty-eight years.

Athaliah and Joash

11 When Athaliah the mother of Ahaziah saw that her son was dead, she
proceeded to destroy the whole royal
family. 2But Jehosheba, the daughter
of King Jehoram[a] and sister of Ahaziah, took Joash son of Ahaziah and stole
him away from among the royal princes,
who were about to be murdered. She put
him and his nurse in a bedroom to hide
him from Athaliah; so he was not killed.
3He remained hidden with his nurse
at the temple of the LORD for six years
while Athaliah ruled the land.
4In the seventh year Jehoiada sent for
the commanders of units of a hundred,
the Carites and the guards and had them
brought to him at the temple of the LORD.
He made a covenant with them and put
them under oath at the temple of the
LORD. Then he showed them the king's
son. 5He commanded them, saying, "This
is what you are to do: You who are in the
three companies that are going on duty
on the Sabbath — a third of you guarding the royal palace, 6a third at the Sur
Gate, and a third at the gate behind the
guard, who take turns guarding the temple — 7and you who are in the other two
companies that normally go off Sabbath
duty are all to guard the temple for the
king. 8Station yourselves around the
king, each of you with weapon in hand.
Anyone who approaches your ranks[b] is
to be put to death. Stay close to the king
wherever he goes."
9The commanders of units of a hundred did just as Jehoiada the priest ordered. Each one took his men — those
who were going on duty on the Sabbath
and those who were going off duty — and
came to Jehoiada the priest. 10Then he
gave the commanders the spears and
shields that had belonged to King David
and that were in the temple of the LORD.
11The guards, each with weapon in hand,
stationed themselves around the king —
near the altar and the temple, from the
south side to the north side of the temple.
12Jehoiada brought out the king's son
and put the crown on him; he presented
him with a copy of the covenant and proclaimed him king. They anointed him,
and the people clapped their hands and
shouted, "Long live the king!"
13When Athaliah heard the noise made
by the guards and the people, she went
to the people at the temple of the LORD.
14She looked and there was the king,
standing by the pillar, as the custom
was. The officers and the trumpeters
were beside the king, and all the people
of the land were rejoicing and blowing
trumpets. Then Athaliah tore her robes
and called out, "Treason! Treason!"
15Jehoiada the priest ordered the commanders of units of a hundred, who
were in charge of the troops: "Bring
her out between the ranks[c] and put to

[a] 2 Hebrew *Joram,* a variant of *Jehoram* [b] 8 Or *approaches the precincts* [c] 15 Or *out from the precincts*

the sword anyone who follows her." For the priest had said, "She must not be put to death in the temple of the LORD." 16So they seized her as she reached the place where the horses enter the palace grounds, and there she was put to death.

17Jehoiada then made a covenant between the LORD and the king and people that they would be the LORD's people. He also made a covenant between the king and the people. 18All the people of the land went to the temple of Baal and tore it down. They smashed the altars and idols to pieces and killed Mattan the priest of Baal in front of the altars.

Then Jehoiada the priest posted guards at the temple of the LORD. 19He took with him the commanders of hundreds, the Carites, the guards and all the people of the land, and together they brought the king down from the temple of the LORD and went into the palace, entering by way of the gate of the guards. The king then took his place on the royal throne. 20All the people of the land rejoiced, and the city was calm, because Athaliah had been slain with the sword at the palace.

21Joash[a] was seven years old when he began to reign.[b]

Joash Repairs the Temple

12[c] In the seventh year of Jehu, Joash[d] became king, and he reigned in Jerusalem forty years. His mother's name was Zibiah; she was from Beersheba. 2Joash did what was right in the eyes of the LORD all the years Jehoiada the priest instructed him. 3The high places, however, were not removed; the people continued to offer sacrifices and burn incense there.

4Joash said to the priests, "Collect all the money that is brought as sacred offerings to the temple of the LORD—the money collected in the census, the money received from personal vows and the money brought voluntarily to the temple. 5Let every priest receive the money from one of the treasurers, then use it to repair whatever damage is found in the temple."

6But by the twenty-third year of King Joash the priests still had not repaired the temple. 7Therefore King Joash summoned Jehoiada the priest and the other priests and asked them, "Why aren't you repairing the damage done to the temple? Take no more money from your treasurers, but hand it over for repairing the temple." 8The priests agreed that they would not collect any more money from the people and that they would not repair the temple themselves.

9Jehoiada the priest took a chest and bored a hole in its lid. He placed it beside the altar, on the right side as one enters the temple of the LORD. The priests who guarded the entrance put into the chest all the money that was brought to the temple of the LORD. 10Whenever they saw that there was a large amount of money in the chest, the royal secretary and the high priest came, counted the money that had been brought into the temple of the LORD and put it into bags. 11When the amount had been determined, they gave the money to the men appointed to supervise the work on the temple. With it they paid those who worked on the temple of the LORD—the carpenters and builders, 12the masons and stonecutters. They purchased timber and blocks of dressed stone for the repair of the temple of the LORD, and met all the other expenses of restoring the temple.

13The money brought into the temple was not spent for making silver basins, wick trimmers, sprinkling bowls, trumpets or any other articles of gold or silver for the temple of the LORD; 14it was paid to the workers, who used it to repair the temple. 15They did not require an accounting from those to whom they gave the money to pay the workers, because they acted with complete honesty. 16The money from the guilt offerings and sin offerings[e] was not brought into the temple of the LORD; it belonged to the priests.

17About this time Hazael king of Aram went up and attacked Gath and captured it. Then he turned to attack Jerusalem. 18But Joash king of Judah took all the sacred objects dedicated by his predecessors—Jehoshaphat, Jehoram and Ahaziah, the kings of Judah—and the gifts he himself had dedicated and all the gold found in the treasuries of the temple of the LORD and of the royal palace, and he sent them to Hazael king of Aram, who then withdrew from Jerusalem.

19As for the other events of the reign of Joash, and all he did, are they not written in the book of the annals of the kings of Judah? 20His officials conspired

[a] *21* Hebrew *Jehoash,* a variant of *Joash* [b] *21* In Hebrew texts this verse (11:21) is numbered 12:1. [c] In Hebrew texts 12:1-21 is numbered 12:2-22. [d] *1* Hebrew *Jehoash,* a variant of *Joash;* also in verses 2, 4, 6, 7 and 18 [e] *16* Or *purification offerings*

against him and assassinated him at
Beth Millo, on the road down to Silla.
21The officials who murdered him were
Jozabad son of Shimeath and Jehozabad
son of Shomer. He died and was buried
with his ancestors in the City of David.
And Amaziah his son succeeded him as
king.

Jehoahaz King of Israel

13 In the twenty-third year of Joash
son of Ahaziah king of Judah, Jehoahaz son of Jehu became king of Israel in Samaria, and he reigned seventeen years. 2He did evil in the eyes of the
LORD by following the sins of Jeroboam
son of Nebat, which he had caused Israel to commit, and he did not turn away
from them. 3So the LORD's anger burned
against Israel, and for a long time he
kept them under the power of Hazael
king of Aram and Ben-Hadad his son.
4Then Jehoahaz sought the LORD's favor, and the LORD listened to him, for he
saw how severely the king of Aram was
oppressing Israel. 5The LORD provided
a deliverer for Israel, and they escaped
from the power of Aram. So the Israelites lived in their own homes as they had
before. 6But they did not turn away from
the sins of the house of Jeroboam, which
he had caused Israel to commit; they
continued in them. Also, the Asherah
pole[a] remained standing in Samaria.
7Nothing had been left of the army
of Jehoahaz except fifty horsemen, ten
chariots and ten thousand foot soldiers,
for the king of Aram had destroyed the
rest and made them like the dust at
threshing time.
8As for the other events of the reign
of Jehoahaz, all he did and his achievements, are they not written in the book
of the annals of the kings of Israel? 9Je-
hoahaz rested with his ancestors and
was buried in Samaria. And Jehoash[b]
his son succeeded him as king.

Jehoash King of Israel

10In the thirty-seventh year of Joash
king of Judah, Jehoash son of Jehoahaz
became king of Israel in Samaria, and
he reigned sixteen years. 11He did evil
in the eyes of the LORD and did not turn
away from any of the sins of Jeroboam
son of Nebat, which he had caused Israel
to commit; he continued in them.
12As for the other events of the reign
of Jehoash, all he did and his achievements, including his war against Amaziah king of Judah, are they not written
in the book of the annals of the kings of
Israel? 13Jehoash rested with his ancestors, and Jeroboam succeeded him on
the throne. Jehoash was buried in Samaria with the kings of Israel.
14Now Elisha had been suffering from
the illness from which he died. Jehoash
king of Israel went down to see him and
wept over him. "My father! My father!"
he cried. "The chariots and horsemen of
Israel!"
15Elisha said, "Get a bow and some arrows," and he did so. 16"Take the bow in
your hands," he said to the king of Israel. When he had taken it, Elisha put his
hands on the king's hands.
17"Open the east window," he said, and
he opened it. "Shoot!" Elisha said, and
he shot. "The LORD's arrow of victory, the
arrow of victory over Aram!" Elisha declared. "You will completely destroy the
Arameans at Aphek."
18Then he said, "Take the arrows,"
and the king took them. Elisha told
him, "Strike the ground." He struck it
three times and stopped. 19The man of
God was angry with him and said, "You
should have struck the ground five or
six times; then you would have defeated Aram and completely destroyed it.
But now you will defeat it only three
times."
20Elisha died and was buried.
Now Moabite raiders used to enter the
country every spring. 21Once while some
Israelites were burying a man, suddenly they saw a band of raiders; so they
threw the man's body into Elisha's tomb.
When the body touched Elisha's bones,
the man came to life and stood up on
his feet.
22Hazael king of Aram oppressed Israel throughout the reign of Jehoahaz.
23But the LORD was gracious to them and
had compassion and showed concern for
them because of his covenant with Abraham, Isaac and Jacob. To this day he has
been unwilling to destroy them or banish them from his presence.
24Hazael king of Aram died, and Ben-
Hadad his son succeeded him as king.
25Then Jehoash son of Jehoahaz recap-
tured from Ben-Hadad son of Hazael the
towns he had taken in battle from his
father Jehoahaz. Three times Jehoash
defeated him, and so he recovered the
Israelite towns.

[a] 6 That is, a wooden symbol of the goddess Asherah; here and elsewhere in 2 Kings
[b] 9 Hebrew *Joash*, a variant of *Jehoash*; also in verses 12-14 and 25

Amaziah King of Judah

14 In the second year of Jehoash[a] son of Jehoahaz king of Israel, Amaziah son of Joash king of Judah began to reign. 2He was twenty-five years old when he became king, and he reigned in Jerusalem twenty-nine years. His mother's name was Jehoaddan; she was from Jerusalem. 3He did what was right in the eyes of the LORD, but not as his father David had done. In everything he followed the example of his father Joash. 4The high places, however, were not removed; the people continued to offer sacrifices and burn incense there.

5After the kingdom was firmly in his grasp, he executed the officials who had murdered his father the king. 6Yet he did not put the children of the assassins to death, in accordance with what is written in the Book of the Law of Moses where the LORD commanded: "Parents are not to be put to death for their children, nor children put to death for their parents; each will die for their own sin."[b]

7He was the one who defeated ten thousand Edomites in the Valley of Salt and captured Sela in battle, calling it Joktheel, the name it has to this day.

8Then Amaziah sent messengers to Jehoash son of Jehoahaz, the son of Jehu, king of Israel, with the challenge: "Come, let us face each other in battle."

9But Jehoash king of Israel replied to Amaziah king of Judah: "A thistle in Lebanon sent a message to a cedar in Lebanon, 'Give your daughter to my son in marriage.' Then a wild beast in Lebanon came along and trampled the thistle underfoot. 10You have indeed defeated Edom and now you are arrogant. Glory in your victory, but stay at home! Why ask for trouble and cause your own downfall and that of Judah also?"

11Amaziah, however, would not listen, so Jehoash king of Israel attacked. He and Amaziah king of Judah faced each other at Beth Shemesh in Judah. 12Judah was routed by Israel, and every man fled to his home. 13Jehoash king of Israel captured Amaziah king of Judah, the son of Joash, the son of Ahaziah, at Beth Shemesh. Then Jehoash went to Jerusalem and broke down the wall of Jerusalem from the Ephraim Gate to the Corner Gate—a section about four hundred cubits long.[c] 14He took all the gold and silver and all the articles found in the temple of the LORD and in the treasuries of the royal palace. He also took hostages and returned to Samaria.

15As for the other events of the reign of Jehoash, what he did and his achievements, including his war against Amaziah king of Judah, are they not written in the book of the annals of the kings of Israel? 16Jehoash rested with his ancestors and was buried in Samaria with the kings of Israel. And Jeroboam his son succeeded him as king.

17Amaziah son of Joash king of Judah lived for fifteen years after the death of Jehoash son of Jehoahaz king of Israel. 18As for the other events of Amaziah's reign, are they not written in the book of the annals of the kings of Judah?

19They conspired against him in Jerusalem, and he fled to Lachish, but they sent men after him to Lachish and killed him there. 20He was brought back by horse and was buried in Jerusalem with his ancestors, in the City of David.

21Then all the people of Judah took Azariah,[d] who was sixteen years old, and made him king in place of his father Amaziah. 22He was the one who rebuilt Elath and restored it to Judah after Amaziah rested with his ancestors.

Jeroboam II King of Israel

23In the fifteenth year of Amaziah son of Joash king of Judah, Jeroboam son of Jehoash king of Israel became king in Samaria, and he reigned forty-one years. 24He did evil in the eyes of the LORD and did not turn away from any of the sins of Jeroboam son of Nebat, which he had caused Israel to commit. 25He was the one who restored the boundaries of Israel from Lebo Hamath to the Dead Sea,[e] in accordance with the word of the LORD, the God of Israel, spoken through his servant Jonah son of Amittai, the prophet from Gath Hepher.

26The LORD had seen how bitterly everyone in Israel, whether slave or free, was suffering;[f] there was no one to help them. 27And since the LORD had not said he would blot out the name of Israel from under heaven, he saved them by the hand of Jeroboam son of Jehoash.

28As for the other events of Jeroboam's reign, all he did, and his military achievements, including how he recovered for Israel both Damascus and Hamath, which had belonged to Judah, are

[a] *1* Hebrew *Joash,* a variant of *Jehoash;* also in verses 13, 23 and 27 [b] *6* Deut. 24:16 [c] *13* That is, about 600 feet or about 180 meters [d] *21* Also called *Uzziah* [e] *25* Hebrew *the Sea of the Arabah* [f] *26* Or *Israel was suffering. They were without a ruler or leader, and*

they not written in the book of the annals of the kings of Israel? 29 Jeroboam rested with his ancestors, the kings of Israel. And Zechariah his son succeeded him as king.

Azariah King of Judah

15 In the twenty-seventh year of Jeroboam king of Israel, Azariah[a] son of Amaziah king of Judah began to reign. 2 He was sixteen years old when he became king, and he reigned in Jerusalem fifty-two years. His mother's name was Jekoliah; she was from Jerusalem. 3 He did what was right in the eyes of the LORD, just as his father Amaziah had done. 4 The high places, however, were not removed; the people continued to offer sacrifices and burn incense there.

5 The LORD afflicted the king with leprosy[b] until the day he died, and he lived in a separate house.[c] Jotham the king's son had charge of the palace and governed the people of the land.

6 As for the other events of Azariah's reign, and all he did, are they not written in the book of the annals of the kings of Judah? 7 Azariah rested with his ancestors and was buried near them in the City of David. And Jotham his son succeeded him as king.

Zechariah King of Israel

8 In the thirty-eighth year of Azariah king of Judah, Zechariah son of Jeroboam became king of Israel in Samaria, and he reigned six months. 9 He did evil in the eyes of the LORD, as his predecessors had done. He did not turn away from the sins of Jeroboam son of Nebat, which he had caused Israel to commit.

10 Shallum son of Jabesh conspired against Zechariah. He attacked him in front of the people,[d] assassinated him and succeeded him as king. 11 The other events of Zechariah's reign are written in the book of the annals of the kings of Israel. 12 So the word of the LORD spoken to Jehu was fulfilled: "Your descendants will sit on the throne of Israel to the fourth generation."[e]

Shallum King of Israel

13 Shallum son of Jabesh became king in the thirty-ninth year of Uzziah king of Judah, and he reigned in Samaria one month. 14 Then Menahem son of Gadi went from Tirzah up to Samaria. He attacked Shallum son of Jabesh in Samaria, assassinated him and succeeded him as king.

15 The other events of Shallum's reign, and the conspiracy he led, are written in the book of the annals of the kings of Israel.

16 At that time Menahem, starting out from Tirzah, attacked Tiphsah and everyone in the city and its vicinity, because they refused to open their gates. He sacked Tiphsah and ripped open all the pregnant women.

Menahem King of Israel

17 In the thirty-ninth year of Azariah king of Judah, Menahem son of Gadi became king of Israel, and he reigned in Samaria ten years. 18 He did evil in the eyes of the LORD. During his entire reign he did not turn away from the sins of Jeroboam son of Nebat, which he had caused Israel to commit.

19 Then Pul[f] king of Assyria invaded the land, and Menahem gave him a thousand talents[g] of silver to gain his support and strengthen his own hold on the kingdom. 20 Menahem exacted this money from Israel. Every wealthy person had to contribute fifty shekels[h] of silver to be given to the king of Assyria. So the king of Assyria withdrew and stayed in the land no longer.

21 As for the other events of Menahem's reign, and all he did, are they not written in the book of the annals of the kings of Israel? 22 Menahem rested with his ancestors. And Pekahiah his son succeeded him as king.

Pekahiah King of Israel

23 In the fiftieth year of Azariah king of Judah, Pekahiah son of Menahem became king of Israel in Samaria, and he reigned two years. 24 Pekahiah did evil in the eyes of the LORD. He did not turn away from the sins of Jeroboam son of Nebat, which he had caused Israel to commit. 25 One of his chief officers, Pekah son of Remaliah, conspired against him. Taking fifty men of Gilead with him, he assassinated Pekahiah, along with Argob and Arieh, in the citadel of the royal palace at Samaria. So Pekah killed Pekahiah and succeeded him as king.

[a] *1* Also called *Uzziah;* also in verses 6, 7, 8, 17, 23 and 27 [b] *5* The Hebrew for *leprosy* was used for various diseases affecting the skin. [c] *5* Or *in a house where he was relieved of responsibilities* [d] *10* Hebrew; some Septuagint manuscripts *in Ibleam* [e] *12* 2 Kings 10:30 [f] *19* Also called *Tiglath-Pileser* [g] *19* That is, about 38 tons or about 34 metric tons [h] *20* That is, about 1 1/4 pounds or about 575 grams

26The other events of Pekahiah's reign,
and all he did, are written in the book of
the annals of the kings of Israel.

Pekah King of Israel

27In the fifty-second year of Azariah
king of Judah, Pekah son of Remaliah
became king of Israel in Samaria, and he
reigned twenty years. 28He did evil in the
eyes of the LORD. He did not turn away
from the sins of Jeroboam son of Nebat,
which he had caused Israel to commit.
29In the time of Pekah king of Israel,
Tiglath-Pileser king of Assyria came and
took Ijon, Abel Beth Maakah, Janoah,
Kedesh and Hazor. He took Gilead and
Galilee, including all the land of Naphtali, and deported the people to Assyria. 30Then Hoshea son of Elah conspired
against Pekah son of Remaliah. He attacked and assassinated him, and then
succeeded him as king in the twentieth
year of Jotham son of Uzziah.
31As for the other events of Pekah's
reign, and all he did, are they not written in the book of the annals of the kings
of Israel?

Jotham King of Judah

32In the second year of Pekah son of
Remaliah king of Israel, Jotham son of
Uzziah king of Judah began to reign.
33He was twenty-five years old when he
became king, and he reigned in Jerusalem sixteen years. His mother's name
was Jerusha daughter of Zadok. 34He did
what was right in the eyes of the LORD,
just as his father Uzziah had done. 35The
high places, however, were not removed;
the people continued to offer sacrifices
and burn incense there. Jotham rebuilt
the Upper Gate of the temple of the LORD.
36As for the other events of Jotham's
reign, and what he did, are they not
written in the book of the annals of the
kings of Judah? 37(In those days the LORD
began to send Rezin king of Aram and
Pekah son of Remaliah against Judah.)
38Jotham rested with his ancestors and
was buried with them in the City of David, the city of his father. And Ahaz his
son succeeded him as king.

Ahaz King of Judah

16 In the seventeenth year of Pekah
son of Remaliah, Ahaz son of Jotham king of Judah began to reign.
2Ahaz was twenty years old when he
became king, and he reigned in Jerusalem sixteen years. Unlike David his father, he did not do what was right in the
eyes of the LORD his God. 3He followed
the ways of the kings of Israel and even
sacrificed his son in the fire, engaging in
the detestable practices of the nations
the LORD had driven out before the Israelites. 4He offered sacrifices and burned
incense at the high places, on the hilltops and under every spreading tree.
5Then Rezin king of Aram and Pekah
son of Remaliah king of Israel marched
up to fight against Jerusalem and besieged Ahaz, but they could not overpower him. 6At that time, Rezin king of
Aram recovered Elath for Aram by driving out the people of Judah. Edomites
then moved into Elath and have lived
there to this day.
7Ahaz sent messengers to say to Tiglath-
Pileser king of Assyria, "I am your servant
and vassal. Come up and save me out of
the hand of the king of Aram and of the
king of Israel, who are attacking me."
8And Ahaz took the silver and gold found
in the temple of the LORD and in the treasuries of the royal palace and sent it as
a gift to the king of Assyria. 9The king of
Assyria complied by attacking Damascus
and capturing it. He deported its inhabitants to Kir and put Rezin to death.
10Then King Ahaz went to Damascus
to meet Tiglath-Pileser king of Assyria.
He saw an altar in Damascus and sent
to Uriah the priest a sketch of the altar,
with detailed plans for its construction.
11So Uriah the priest built an altar in accordance with all the plans that King
Ahaz had sent from Damascus and
finished it before King Ahaz returned.
12When the king came back from Damascus and saw the altar, he approached it
and presented offerings[a] on it. 13He offered up his burnt offering and grain
offering, poured out his drink offering,
and splashed the blood of his fellowship
offerings against the altar. 14As for the
bronze altar that stood before the LORD,
he brought it from the front of the temple — from between the new altar and
the temple of the LORD — and put it on
the north side of the new altar.
15King Ahaz then gave these orders to
Uriah the priest: "On the large new altar,
offer the morning burnt offering and the
evening grain offering, the king's burnt
offering and his grain offering, and the
burnt offering of all the people of the
land, and their grain offering and their
drink offering. Splash against this altar
the blood of all the burnt offerings and
sacrifices. But I will use the bronze altar

[a] 12 Or *and went up*

for seeking guidance." 16 And Uriah the priest did just as King Ahaz had ordered.

17 King Ahaz cut off the side panels and removed the basins from the movable stands. He removed the Sea from the bronze bulls that supported it and set it on a stone base. 18 He took away the Sabbath canopy[a] that had been built at the temple and removed the royal entryway outside the temple of the LORD, in deference to the king of Assyria.

19 As for the other events of the reign of Ahaz, and what he did, are they not written in the book of the annals of the kings of Judah? 20 Ahaz rested with his ancestors and was buried with them in the City of David. And Hezekiah his son succeeded him as king.

Hoshea Last King of Israel

17 In the twelfth year of Ahaz king of Judah, Hoshea son of Elah became king of Israel in Samaria, and he reigned nine years. 2 He did evil in the eyes of the LORD, but not like the kings of Israel who preceded him.

3 Shalmaneser king of Assyria came up to attack Hoshea, who had been Shalmaneser's vassal and had paid him tribute. 4 But the king of Assyria discovered that Hoshea was a traitor, for he had sent envoys to So[b] king of Egypt, and he no longer paid tribute to the king of Assyria, as he had done year by year. Therefore Shalmaneser seized him and put him in prison. 5 The king of Assyria invaded the entire land, marched against Samaria and laid siege to it for three years. 6 In the ninth year of Hoshea, the king of Assyria captured Samaria and deported the Israelites to Assyria. He settled them in Halah, in Gozan on the Habor River and in the towns of the Medes.

Israel Exiled Because of Sin

7 All this took place because the Israelites had sinned against the LORD their God, who had brought them up out of Egypt from under the power of Pharaoh king of Egypt. They worshiped other gods 8 and followed the practices of the nations the LORD had driven out before them, as well as the practices that the kings of Israel had introduced. 9 The Israelites secretly did things against the LORD their God that were not right. From watchtower to fortified city they built themselves high places in all their towns. 10 They set up sacred stones and Asherah poles on every high hill and under every spreading tree. 11 At every high place they burned incense, as the nations whom the LORD had driven out before them had done. They did wicked things that aroused the LORD's anger. 12 They worshiped idols, though the LORD had said, "You shall not do this."[c] 13 The LORD warned Israel and Judah through all his prophets and seers: "Turn from your evil ways. Observe my commands and decrees, in accordance with the entire Law that I commanded your ancestors to obey and that I delivered to you through my servants the prophets."

14 But they would not listen and were as stiff-necked as their ancestors, who did not trust in the LORD their God. 15 They rejected his decrees and the covenant he had made with their ancestors and the statutes he had warned them to keep. They followed worthless idols and themselves became worthless. They imitated the nations around them although the LORD had ordered them, "Do not do as they do."

16 They forsook all the commands of the LORD their God and made for themselves two idols cast in the shape of calves, and an Asherah pole. They bowed down to all the starry hosts, and they worshiped Baal. 17 They sacrificed their sons and daughters in the fire. They practiced divination and sought omens and sold themselves to do evil in the eyes of the LORD, arousing his anger.

18 So the LORD was very angry with Israel and removed them from his presence. Only the tribe of Judah was left, 19 and even Judah did not keep the commands of the LORD their God. They followed the practices Israel had introduced. 20 Therefore the LORD rejected all the people of Israel; he afflicted them and gave them into the hands of plunderers, until he thrust them from his presence.

21 When he tore Israel away from the house of David, they made Jeroboam son of Nebat their king. Jeroboam enticed Israel away from following the LORD and caused them to commit a great sin. 22 The Israelites persisted in all the sins of Jeroboam and did not turn away from them 23 until the LORD removed them from his presence, as he had warned through all his servants the prophets. So the people of Israel were taken from their homeland into exile in Assyria, and they are still there.

[a] *18* Or *the dais of his throne* (see Septuagint)
[c] *12* Exodus 20:4,5
[b] *4* *So* is probably an abbreviation for *Osorkon*.

Samaria Resettled

24The king of Assyria brought people
from Babylon, Kuthah, Avva, Hamath
and Sepharvaim and settled them in the
towns of Samaria to replace the Israelites. They took over Samaria and lived
in its towns. 25When they first lived there,
they did not worship the LORD; so he
sent lions among them and they killed
some of the people. 26It was reported
to the king of Assyria: "The people you
deported and resettled in the towns of
Samaria do not know what the god of
that country requires. He has sent lions
among them, which are killing them off,
because the people do not know what he
requires."
27Then the king of Assyria gave this
order: "Have one of the priests you took
captive from Samaria go back to live
there and teach the people what the
god of the land requires." 28So one of the
priests who had been exiled from Samaria came to live in Bethel and taught
them how to worship the LORD.
29Nevertheless, each national group
made its own gods in the several towns
where they settled, and set them up in
the shrines the people of Samaria had
made at the high places. 30The people
from Babylon made Sukkoth Benoth,
those from Kuthah made Nergal, and
those from Hamath made Ashima; 31the
Avvites made Nibhaz and Tartak, and
the Sepharvites burned their children
in the fire as sacrifices to Adrammelek
and Anammelek, the gods of Sepharvaim. 32They worshiped the LORD, but they
also appointed all sorts of their own
people to officiate for them as priests
in the shrines at the high places. 33They
worshiped the LORD, but they also served
their own gods in accordance with the
customs of the nations from which they
had been brought.
34To this day they persist in their former practices. They neither worship the
LORD nor adhere to the decrees and regulations, the laws and commands that
the LORD gave the descendants of Jacob,
whom he named Israel. 35When the LORD
made a covenant with the Israelites, he
commanded them: "Do not worship any
other gods or bow down to them, serve
them or sacrifice to them. 36But the LORD,
who brought you up out of Egypt with
mighty power and outstretched arm, is
the one you must worship. To him you
shall bow down and to him offer sacrifices. 37You must always be careful to
keep the decrees and regulations, the
laws and commands he wrote for you.
Do not worship other gods. 38Do not forget the covenant I have made with you,
and do not worship other gods. 39Rather,
worship the LORD your God; it is he who
will deliver you from the hand of all your
enemies."
40They would not listen, however,
but persisted in their former practices.
41Even while these people were worshiping the LORD, they were serving their
idols. To this day their children and
grandchildren continue to do as their
ancestors did.

Hezekiah King of Judah

18 In the third year of Hoshea son of
Elah king of Israel, Hezekiah son
of Ahaz king of Judah began to reign.
2He was twenty-five years old when he
became king, and he reigned in Jerusalem twenty-nine years. His mother's
name was Abijah[a] daughter of Zechariah. 3He did what was right in the eyes
of the LORD, just as his father David
had done. 4He removed the high places,
smashed the sacred stones and cut down
the Asherah poles. He broke into pieces
the bronze snake Moses had made, for
up to that time the Israelites had been
burning incense to it. (It was called Nehushtan.[b])
5Hezekiah trusted in the LORD, the
God of Israel. There was no one like him
among all the kings of Judah, either before him or after him. 6He held fast to the
LORD and did not stop following him; he
kept the commands the LORD had given
Moses. 7And the LORD was with him; he
was successful in whatever he undertook. He rebelled against the king of
Assyria and did not serve him. 8From
watchtower to fortified city, he defeated the Philistines, as far as Gaza and its
territory.
9In King Hezekiah's fourth year, which
was the seventh year of Hoshea son of
Elah king of Israel, Shalmaneser king
of Assyria marched against Samaria
and laid siege to it. 10At the end of three
years the Assyrians took it. So Samaria
was captured in Hezekiah's sixth year,
which was the ninth year of Hoshea king
of Israel. 11The king of Assyria deported
Israel to Assyria and settled them in Halah, in Gozan on the Habor River and
in towns of the Medes. 12This happened

[a] 2 Hebrew *Abi*, a variant of *Abijah* [b] 4 *Nehushtan* sounds like the Hebrew for both *bronze* and *snake*.

because they had not obeyed the LORD their God, but had violated his covenant — all that Moses the servant of the LORD commanded. They neither listened to the commands nor carried them out.

13 In the fourteenth year of King Hezekiah's reign, Sennacherib king of Assyria attacked all the fortified cities of Judah and captured them. 14 So Hezekiah king of Judah sent this message to the king of Assyria at Lachish: "I have done wrong. Withdraw from me, and I will pay whatever you demand of me." The king of Assyria exacted from Hezekiah king of Judah three hundred talents[a] of silver and thirty talents[b] of gold. 15 So Hezekiah gave him all the silver that was found in the temple of the LORD and in the treasuries of the royal palace.

16 At this time Hezekiah king of Judah stripped off the gold with which he had covered the doors and doorposts of the temple of the LORD, and gave it to the king of Assyria.

Sennacherib Threatens Jerusalem

17 The king of Assyria sent his supreme commander, his chief officer and his field commander with a large army, from Lachish to King Hezekiah at Jerusalem. They came up to Jerusalem and stopped at the aqueduct of the Upper Pool, on the road to the Washerman's Field. 18 They called for the king; and Eliakim son of Hilkiah the palace administrator, Shebna the secretary, and Joah son of Asaph the recorder went out to them.

19 The field commander said to them, "Tell Hezekiah:

"'This is what the great king, the king of Assyria, says: On what are you basing this confidence of yours? 20 You say you have the counsel and the might for war — but you speak only empty words. On whom are you depending, that you rebel against me? 21 Look, I know you are depending on Egypt, that splintered reed of a staff, which pierces the hand of anyone who leans on it! Such is Pharaoh king of Egypt to all who depend on him. 22 But if you say to me, "We are depending on the LORD our God" — isn't he the one whose high places and altars Hezekiah removed, saying to Judah and Jerusalem, "You must worship before this altar in Jerusalem"?

23 "'Come now, make a bargain with my master, the king of Assyria: I will give you two thousand horses — if you can put riders on them! 24 How can you repulse one officer of the least of my master's officials, even though you are depending on Egypt for chariots and horsemen[c]? 25 Furthermore, have I come to attack and destroy this place without word from the LORD? The LORD himself told me to march against this country and destroy it.'"

26 Then Eliakim son of Hilkiah, and Shebna and Joah said to the field commander, "Please speak to your servants in Aramaic, since we understand it. Don't speak to us in Hebrew in the hearing of the people on the wall."

27 But the commander replied, "Was it only to your master and you that my master sent me to say these things, and not to the people sitting on the wall — who, like you, will have to eat their own excrement and drink their own urine?"

28 Then the commander stood and called out in Hebrew, "Hear the word of the great king, the king of Assyria! 29 This is what the king says: Do not let Hezekiah deceive you. He cannot deliver you from my hand. 30 Do not let Hezekiah persuade you to trust in the LORD when he says, 'The LORD will surely deliver us; this city will not be given into the hand of the king of Assyria.'

31 "Do not listen to Hezekiah. This is what the king of Assyria says: Make peace with me and come out to me. Then each of you will eat fruit from your own vine and fig tree and drink water from your own cistern, 32 until I come and take you to a land like your own — a land of grain and new wine, a land of bread and vineyards, a land of olive trees and honey. Choose life and not death!

"Do not listen to Hezekiah, for he is misleading you when he says, 'The LORD will deliver us.' 33 Has the god of any nation ever delivered his land from the hand of the king of Assyria? 34 Where are the gods of Hamath and Arpad? Where are the gods of Sepharvaim, Hena and Ivvah? Have they rescued Samaria from my hand? 35 Who of all the gods of these countries has been able to save his land from me? How then can the LORD deliver Jerusalem from my hand?"

36 But the people remained silent and said nothing in reply, because the king had commanded, "Do not answer him."

[a] *14* That is, about 11 tons or about 10 metric tons [b] *14* That is, about 1 ton or about 1 metric ton [c] *24* Or *charioteers*

37 Then Eliakim son of Hilkiah the palace administrator, Shebna the secretary,
and Joah son of Asaph the recorder went
to Hezekiah, with their clothes torn, and
told him what the field commander had
said.

Jerusalem's Deliverance Foretold

19 When King Hezekiah heard this,
he tore his clothes and put on
sackcloth and went into the temple of
the LORD. 2 He sent Eliakim the palace
administrator, Shebna the secretary and
the leading priests, all wearing sackcloth, to the prophet Isaiah son of Amoz.
3 They told him, "This is what Hezekiah
says: This day is a day of distress and
rebuke and disgrace, as when children
come to the moment of birth and there
is no strength to deliver them. 4 It may be
that the LORD your God will hear all the
words of the field commander, whom his
master, the king of Assyria, has sent to
ridicule the living God, and that he will
rebuke him for the words the LORD your
God has heard. Therefore pray for the
remnant that still survives."

5 When King Hezekiah's officials came
to Isaiah, 6 Isaiah said to them, "Tell your
master, 'This is what the LORD says: Do
not be afraid of what you have heard —
those words with which the underlings
of the king of Assyria have blasphemed
me. 7 Listen! When he hears a certain report, I will make him want to return to
his own country, and there I will have
him cut down with the sword.' "

8 When the field commander heard
that the king of Assyria had left Lachish,
he withdrew and found the king fighting
against Libnah.

9 Now Sennacherib received a report
that Tirhakah, the king of Cush,[a] was
marching out to fight against him. So he
again sent messengers to Hezekiah with
this word: 10 "Say to Hezekiah king of Judah: Do not let the god you depend on
deceive you when he says, 'Jerusalem will
not be given into the hands of the king
of Assyria.' 11 Surely you have heard what
the kings of Assyria have done to all the
countries, destroying them completely.
And will you be delivered? 12 Did the gods
of the nations that were destroyed by my
predecessors deliver them — the gods of
Gozan, Harran, Rezeph and the people
of Eden who were in Tel Assar? 13 Where is
the king of Hamath or the king of Arpad?
Where are the kings of Lair, Sepharvaim,
Hena and Ivvah?"

Hezekiah's Prayer

14 Hezekiah received the letter from the
messengers and read it. Then he went up
to the temple of the LORD and spread it
out before the LORD. 15 And Hezekiah
prayed to the LORD: "LORD, the God of Israel, enthroned between the cherubim,
you alone are God over all the kingdoms
of the earth. You have made heaven and
earth. 16 Give ear, LORD, and hear; open
your eyes, LORD, and see; listen to the
words Sennacherib has sent to ridicule
the living God.

17 "It is true, LORD, that the Assyrian
kings have laid waste these nations and
their lands. 18 They have thrown their
gods into the fire and destroyed them,
for they were not gods but only wood
and stone, fashioned by human hands.
19 Now, LORD our God, deliver us from his
hand, so that all the kingdoms of the
earth may know that you alone, LORD,
are God."

Isaiah Prophesies Sennacherib's Fall

20 Then Isaiah son of Amoz sent a message to Hezekiah: "This is what the LORD,
the God of Israel, says: I have heard your
prayer concerning Sennacherib king of
Assyria. 21 This is the word that the LORD
has spoken against him:

" 'Virgin Daughter Zion
  despises you and mocks you.
Daughter Jerusalem
  tosses her head as you flee.
22 Who is it you have ridiculed and
    blasphemed?
  Against whom have you raised
    your voice
and lifted your eyes in pride?
  Against the Holy One of Israel!
23 By your messengers
  you have ridiculed the Lord.
And you have said,
  "With my many chariots
I have ascended the heights of the
    mountains,
  the utmost heights of Lebanon.
I have cut down its tallest cedars,
  the choicest of its junipers.
I have reached its remotest parts,
  the finest of its forests.
24 I have dug wells in foreign lands
  and drunk the water there.
With the soles of my feet
  I have dried up all the streams of
    Egypt."

25 " 'Have you not heard?
  Long ago I ordained it.

[a] 9 That is, the upper Nile region

In days of old I planned it;
now I have brought it to pass,
that you have turned fortified cities
into piles of stone.
26 Their people, drained of power,
are dismayed and put to shame.
They are like plants in the field,
like tender green shoots,
like grass sprouting on the roof,
scorched before it grows up.

27 " 'But I know where you are
and when you come and go
and how you rage against me.
28 Because you rage against me
and because your insolence has
reached my ears,
I will put my hook in your nose
and my bit in your mouth,
and I will make you return
by the way you came.'

29 "This will be the sign for you, Hezekiah:

"This year you will eat what grows by
itself,
and the second year what springs
from that.
But in the third year sow and reap,
plant vineyards and eat their fruit.
30 Once more a remnant of the kingdom
of Judah
will take root below and bear fruit
above.
31 For out of Jerusalem will come a
remnant,
and out of Mount Zion a band of
survivors.

"The zeal of the LORD Almighty will accomplish this.

32 "Therefore this is what the LORD says
concerning the king of Assyria:

" 'He will not enter this city
or shoot an arrow here.
He will not come before it with shield
or build a siege ramp against it.
33 By the way that he came he will
return;
he will not enter this city,
declares the LORD.
34 I will defend this city and save it,
for my sake and for the sake of
David my servant.' "

35 That night the angel of the LORD
went out and put to death a hundred
and eighty-five thousand in the Assyrian camp. When the people got up the
next morning — there were all the dead
bodies! 36 So Sennacherib king of Assyria
broke camp and withdrew. He returned
to Nineveh and stayed there.

37 One day, while he was worshiping
in the temple of his god Nisrok, his sons
Adrammelek and Sharezer killed him
with the sword, and they escaped to the
land of Ararat. And Esarhaddon his son
succeeded him as king.

Hezekiah's Illness

20 In those days Hezekiah became ill
and was at the point of death. The
prophet Isaiah son of Amoz went to him
and said, "This is what the LORD says:
Put your house in order, because you are
going to die; you will not recover."

2 Hezekiah turned his face to the wall
and prayed to the LORD, 3 "Remember,
LORD, how I have walked before you
faithfully and with wholehearted devotion and have done what is good in your
eyes." And Hezekiah wept bitterly.

4 Before Isaiah had left the middle
court, the word of the LORD came to him:
5 "Go back and tell Hezekiah, the ruler of
my people, 'This is what the LORD, the
God of your father David, says: I have
heard your prayer and seen your tears; I
will heal you. On the third day from now
you will go up to the temple of the LORD.
6 I will add fifteen years to your life. And
I will deliver you and this city from the
hand of the king of Assyria. I will defend
this city for my sake and for the sake of
my servant David.' "

7 Then Isaiah said, "Prepare a poultice
of figs." They did so and applied it to the
boil, and he recovered.

8 Hezekiah had asked Isaiah, "What
will be the sign that the LORD will heal
me and that I will go up to the temple
of the LORD on the third day from now?"

9 Isaiah answered, "This is the LORD's
sign to you that the LORD will do what
he has promised: Shall the shadow go
forward ten steps, or shall it go back ten
steps?"

10 "It is a simple matter for the shadow
to go forward ten steps," said Hezekiah.
"Rather, have it go back ten steps."

11 Then the prophet Isaiah called on the
LORD, and the LORD made the shadow go
back the ten steps it had gone down on
the stairway of Ahaz.

Envoys From Babylon

12 At that time Marduk-Baladan son
of Baladan king of Babylon sent Hezekiah letters and a gift, because he had
heard of Hezekiah's illness. 13 Hezekiah
received the envoys and showed them
all that was in his storehouses — the silver, the gold, the spices and the fine olive
oil — his armory and everything found

among his treasures. There was nothing
in his palace or in all his kingdom that
Hezekiah did not show them.
[14]Then Isaiah the prophet went to
King Hezekiah and asked, "What did
those men say, and where did they come
from?"
"From a distant land," Hezekiah replied. "They came from Babylon."
[15]The prophet asked, "What did they
see in your palace?"
"They saw everything in my palace,"
Hezekiah said. "There is nothing among
my treasures that I did not show them."
[16]Then Isaiah said to Hezekiah, "Hear
the word of the LORD: [17]The time will
surely come when everything in your
palace, and all that your predecessors
have stored up until this day, will be
carried off to Babylon. Nothing will be
left, says the LORD. [18]And some of your
descendants, your own flesh and blood
who will be born to you, will be taken
away, and they will become eunuchs in
the palace of the king of Babylon."
[19]"The word of the LORD you have spoken is good," Hezekiah replied. For he
thought, "Will there not be peace and
security in my lifetime?"
[20]As for the other events of Hezekiah's
reign, all his achievements and how he
made the pool and the tunnel by which
he brought water into the city, are they
not written in the book of the annals of
the kings of Judah? [21]Hezekiah rested
with his ancestors. And Manasseh his
son succeeded him as king.

Manasseh King of Judah

21 Manasseh was twelve years old
when he became king, and he
reigned in Jerusalem fifty-five years.
His mother's name was Hephzibah. [2]He
did evil in the eyes of the LORD, following the detestable practices of the nations the LORD had driven out before
the Israelites. [3]He rebuilt the high places
his father Hezekiah had destroyed; he
also erected altars to Baal and made
an Asherah pole, as Ahab king of Israel had done. He bowed down to all the
starry hosts and worshiped them. [4]He
built altars in the temple of the LORD, of
which the LORD had said, "In Jerusalem
I will put my Name." [5]In the two courts
of the temple of the LORD, he built altars
to all the starry hosts. [6]He sacrificed his
own son in the fire, practiced divination,
sought omens, and consulted mediums
and spiritists. He did much evil in the
eyes of the LORD, arousing his anger.
[7]He took the carved Asherah pole he
had made and put it in the temple, of
which the LORD had said to David and
to his son Solomon, "In this temple and
in Jerusalem, which I have chosen out
of all the tribes of Israel, I will put my
Name forever. [8]I will not again make the
feet of the Israelites wander from the
land I gave their ancestors, if only they
will be careful to do everything I commanded them and will keep the whole
Law that my servant Moses gave them."
[9]But the people did not listen. Manasseh
led them astray, so that they did more
evil than the nations the LORD had destroyed before the Israelites.
[10]The LORD said through his servants
the prophets: [11]"Manasseh king of Judah
has committed these detestable sins. He
has done more evil than the Amorites
who preceded him and has led Judah
into sin with his idols. [12]Therefore this is
what the LORD, the God of Israel, says: I
am going to bring such disaster on Jerusalem and Judah that the ears of everyone who hears of it will tingle. [13]I will
stretch out over Jerusalem the measuring line used against Samaria and the
plumb line used against the house of
Ahab. I will wipe out Jerusalem as one
wipes a dish, wiping it and turning it upside down. [14]I will forsake the remnant
of my inheritance and give them into
the hands of enemies. They will be looted and plundered by all their enemies;
[15]they have done evil in my eyes and
have aroused my anger from the day
their ancestors came out of Egypt until
this day."
[16]Moreover, Manasseh also shed so
much innocent blood that he filled Jerusalem from end to end — besides the sin
that he had caused Judah to commit, so
that they did evil in the eyes of the LORD.
[17]As for the other events of Manasseh's
reign, and all he did, including the sin
he committed, are they not written in
the book of the annals of the kings of
Judah? [18]Manasseh rested with his ancestors and was buried in his palace garden, the garden of Uzza. And Amon his
son succeeded him as king.

Amon King of Judah

[19]Amon was twenty-two years old
when he became king, and he reigned in
Jerusalem two years. His mother's name
was Meshullemeth daughter of Haruz;
she was from Jotbah. [20]He did evil in the
eyes of the LORD, as his father Manasseh
had done. [21]He followed completely the
ways of his father, worshiping the idols
his father had worshiped, and bowing

down to them. 22He forsook the LORD, the
God of his ancestors, and did not walk in
obedience to him.
23Amon's officials conspired against
him and assassinated the king in his
palace. 24Then the people of the land
killed all who had plotted against King
Amon, and they made Josiah his son
king in his place.
25As for the other events of Amon's
reign, and what he did, are they not written in the book of the annals of the kings
of Judah? 26He was buried in his tomb in
the garden of Uzza. And Josiah his son
succeeded him as king.

The Book of the Law Found

22 Josiah was eight years old when
he became king, and he reigned
in Jerusalem thirty-one years. His mother's name was Jedidah daughter of Adaiah; she was from Bozkath. 2He did what
was right in the eyes of the LORD and followed completely the ways of his father
David, not turning aside to the right or
to the left.
3In the eighteenth year of his reign,
King Josiah sent the secretary, Shaphan
son of Azaliah, the son of Meshullam,
to the temple of the LORD. He said: 4"Go
up to Hilkiah the high priest and have
him get ready the money that has been
brought into the temple of the LORD,
which the doorkeepers have collected
from the people. 5Have them entrust it
to the men appointed to supervise the
work on the temple. And have these men
pay the workers who repair the temple
of the LORD — 6the carpenters, the builders and the masons. Also have them purchase timber and dressed stone to repair
the temple. 7But they need not account
for the money entrusted to them, because they are honest in their dealings."
8Hilkiah the high priest said to Shaphan the secretary, "I have found the
Book of the Law in the temple of the
LORD." He gave it to Shaphan, who read
it. 9Then Shaphan the secretary went
to the king and reported to him: "Your
officials have paid out the money that
was in the temple of the LORD and have
entrusted it to the workers and supervisors at the temple." 10Then Shaphan
the secretary informed the king, "Hilkiah the priest has given me a book." And
Shaphan read from it in the presence of
the king.
11When the king heard the words of the
Book of the Law, he tore his robes. 12He
gave these orders to Hilkiah the priest,
Ahikam son of Shaphan, Akbor son of
Micaiah, Shaphan the secretary and
Asaiah the king's attendant: 13"Go and
inquire of the LORD for me and for the
people and for all Judah about what is
written in this book that has been found.
Great is the LORD's anger that burns
against us because those who have gone
before us have not obeyed the words of
this book; they have not acted in accordance with all that is written there concerning us."
14Hilkiah the priest, Ahikam, Akbor,
Shaphan and Asaiah went to speak to
the prophet Huldah, who was the wife of
Shallum son of Tikvah, the son of Harhas, keeper of the wardrobe. She lived in
Jerusalem, in the New Quarter.
15She said to them, "This is what the
LORD, the God of Israel, says: Tell the
man who sent you to me, 16'This is what
the LORD says: I am going to bring disaster on this place and its people, according to everything written in the book the
king of Judah has read. 17Because they
have forsaken me and burned incense
to other gods and aroused my anger by
all the idols their hands have made,[a] my
anger will burn against this place and
will not be quenched.' 18Tell the king of
Judah, who sent you to inquire of the
LORD, 'This is what the LORD, the God of
Israel, says concerning the words you
heard: 19Because your heart was responsive and you humbled yourself before
the LORD when you heard what I have
spoken against this place and its people — that they would become a curse[b]
and be laid waste — and because you
tore your robes and wept in my presence,
I also have heard you, declares the LORD.
20Therefore I will gather you to your ancestors, and you will be buried in peace.
Your eyes will not see all the disaster I
am going to bring on this place.'"
So they took her answer back to the
king.

Josiah Renews the Covenant

23 Then the king called together all
the elders of Judah and Jerusalem. 2He went up to the temple of the
LORD with the people of Judah, the inhabitants of Jerusalem, the priests and
the prophets — all the people from the
least to the greatest. He read in their
hearing all the words of the Book of the

[a] 17 Or *by everything they have done* [b] 19 That is, their names would be used in cursing (see Jer. 29:22); or, others would see that they are cursed.

Covenant, which had been found in the
temple of the LORD. 3The king stood by
the pillar and renewed the covenant in
the presence of the LORD — to follow the
LORD and keep his commands, statutes
and decrees with all his heart and all his
soul, thus confirming the words of the
covenant written in this book. Then all
the people pledged themselves to the
covenant.

4The king ordered Hilkiah the high
priest, the priests next in rank and the
doorkeepers to remove from the temple
of the LORD all the articles made for Baal
and Asherah and all the starry hosts.
He burned them outside Jerusalem in
the fields of the Kidron Valley and took
the ashes to Bethel. 5He did away with
the idolatrous priests appointed by the
kings of Judah to burn incense on the
high places of the towns of Judah and
on those around Jerusalem — those
who burned incense to Baal, to the sun
and moon, to the constellations and to
all the starry hosts. 6He took the Asherah pole from the temple of the LORD to
the Kidron Valley outside Jerusalem and
burned it there. He ground it to powder
and scattered the dust over the graves of
the common people. 7He also tore down
the quarters of the male shrine prostitutes that were in the temple of the
LORD, the quarters where women did
weaving for Asherah.

8Josiah brought all the priests from
the towns of Judah and desecrated the
high places, from Geba to Beersheba,
where the priests had burned incense.
He broke down the gateway at the entrance of the Gate of Joshua, the city
governor, which was on the left of the
city gate. 9Although the priests of the
high places did not serve at the altar of
the LORD in Jerusalem, they ate unleavened bread with their fellow priests.

10He desecrated Topheth, which was
in the Valley of Ben Hinnom, so no one
could use it to sacrifice their son or
daughter in the fire to Molek. 11He removed from the entrance to the temple
of the LORD the horses that the kings of
Judah had dedicated to the sun. They
were in the court[a] near the room of an
official named Nathan-Melek. Josiah
then burned the chariots dedicated to
the sun.

12He pulled down the altars the kings
of Judah had erected on the roof near
the upper room of Ahaz, and the altars
Manasseh had built in the two courts
of the temple of the LORD. He removed
them from there, smashed them to pieces and threw the rubble into the Kidron
Valley. 13The king also desecrated the
high places that were east of Jerusalem on the south of the Hill of Corruption — the ones Solomon king of Israel
had built for Ashtoreth the vile goddess
of the Sidonians, for Chemosh the vile
god of Moab, and for Molek the detestable god of the people of Ammon. 14Jo-
siah smashed the sacred stones and cut
down the Asherah poles and covered the
sites with human bones.

15Even the altar at Bethel, the high
place made by Jeroboam son of Nebat,
who had caused Israel to sin — even that
altar and high place he demolished. He
burned the high place and ground it to
powder, and burned the Asherah pole
also. 16Then Josiah looked around, and
when he saw the tombs that were there
on the hillside, he had the bones removed from them and burned on the
altar to defile it, in accordance with the
word of the LORD proclaimed by the man
of God who foretold these things.

17The king asked, "What is that tomb-
stone I see?"

The people of the city said, "It marks
the tomb of the man of God who came
from Judah and pronounced against the
altar of Bethel the very things you have
done to it."

18"Leave it alone," he said. "Don't
let anyone disturb his bones." So they
spared his bones and those of the prophet who had come from Samaria.

19Just as he had done at Bethel, Josiah
removed all the shrines at the high places that the kings of Israel had built in the
towns of Samaria and that had aroused
the LORD's anger. 20Josiah slaughtered
all the priests of those high places on
the altars and burned human bones on
them. Then he went back to Jerusalem.

21The king gave this order to all the
people: "Celebrate the Passover to the
LORD your God, as it is written in this
Book of the Covenant." 22Neither in the
days of the judges who led Israel nor in
the days of the kings of Israel and the
kings of Judah had any such Passover
been observed. 23But in the eighteenth
year of King Josiah, this Passover was
celebrated to the LORD in Jerusalem.

24Furthermore, Josiah got rid of the
mediums and spiritists, the household

[a] *11* The meaning of the Hebrew for this word is uncertain.

gods, the idols and all the other detestable things seen in Judah and Jerusalem. This he did to fulfill the requirements of the law written in the book that Hilkiah the priest had discovered in the temple of the LORD. 25 Neither before nor after Josiah was there a king like him who turned to the LORD as he did — with all his heart and with all his soul and with all his strength, in accordance with all the Law of Moses.

26 Nevertheless, the LORD did not turn away from the heat of his fierce anger, which burned against Judah because of all that Manasseh had done to arouse his anger. 27 So the LORD said, "I will remove Judah also from my presence as I removed Israel, and I will reject Jerusalem, the city I chose, and this temple, about which I said, 'My Name shall be there.'[a]"

28 As for the other events of Josiah's reign, and all he did, are they not written in the book of the annals of the kings of Judah?

29 While Josiah was king, Pharaoh Necho king of Egypt went up to the Euphrates River to help the king of Assyria. King Josiah marched out to meet him in battle, but Necho faced him and killed him at Megiddo. 30 Josiah's servants brought his body in a chariot from Megiddo to Jerusalem and buried him in his own tomb. And the people of the land took Jehoahaz son of Josiah and anointed him and made him king in place of his father.

Jehoahaz King of Judah

31 Jehoahaz was twenty-three years old when he became king, and he reigned in Jerusalem three months. His mother's name was Hamutal daughter of Jeremiah; she was from Libnah. 32 He did evil in the eyes of the LORD, just as his predecessors had done. 33 Pharaoh Necho put him in chains at Riblah in the land of Hamath so that he might not reign in Jerusalem, and he imposed on Judah a levy of a hundred talents[b] of silver and a talent[c] of gold. 34 Pharaoh Necho made Eliakim son of Josiah king in place of his father Josiah and changed Eliakim's name to Jehoiakim. But he took Jehoahaz and carried him off to Egypt, and there he died. 35 Jehoiakim paid Pharaoh Necho the silver and gold he demanded. In order to do so, he taxed the land and exacted the silver and gold from the people of the land according to their assessments.

Jehoiakim King of Judah

36 Jehoiakim was twenty-five years old when he became king, and he reigned in Jerusalem eleven years. His mother's name was Zebidah daughter of Pedaiah; she was from Rumah. 37 And he did evil in the eyes of the LORD, just as his predecessors had done.

24 During Jehoiakim's reign, Nebuchadnezzar king of Babylon invaded the land, and Jehoiakim became his vassal for three years. But then he turned against Nebuchadnezzar and rebelled. 2 The LORD sent Babylonian,[d] Aramean, Moabite and Ammonite raiders against him to destroy Judah, in accordance with the word of the LORD proclaimed by his servants the prophets. 3 Surely these things happened to Judah according to the LORD's command, in order to remove them from his presence because of the sins of Manasseh and all he had done, 4 including the shedding of innocent blood. For he had filled Jerusalem with innocent blood, and the LORD was not willing to forgive.

5 As for the other events of Jehoiakim's reign, and all he did, are they not written in the book of the annals of the kings of Judah? 6 Jehoiakim rested with his ancestors. And Jehoiachin his son succeeded him as king.

7 The king of Egypt did not march out from his own country again, because the king of Babylon had taken all his territory, from the Wadi of Egypt to the Euphrates River.

Jehoiachin King of Judah

8 Jehoiachin was eighteen years old when he became king, and he reigned in Jerusalem three months. His mother's name was Nehushta daughter of Elnathan; she was from Jerusalem. 9 He did evil in the eyes of the LORD, just as his father had done.

10 At that time the officers of Nebuchadnezzar king of Babylon advanced on Jerusalem and laid siege to it, 11 and Nebuchadnezzar himself came up to the city while his officers were besieging it. 12 Jehoiachin king of Judah, his mother, his attendants, his nobles and his officials all surrendered to him.

In the eighth year of the reign of the king of Babylon, he took Jehoiachin prisoner. 13 As the LORD had declared, Nebuchadnezzar removed the treasures from the temple of the LORD and from the

[a] *27* 1 Kings 8:29 [b] *33* That is, about 3 3/4 tons or about 3.4 metric tons [c] *33* That is, about 75 pounds or about 34 kilograms [d] *2* Or *Chaldean*

royal palace, and cut up the gold articles
that Solomon king of Israel had made
for the temple of the LORD. 14He carried
all Jerusalem into exile: all the officers
and fighting men, and all the skilled
workers and artisans — a total of ten
thousand. Only the poorest people of the
land were left.
15Nebuchadnezzar took Jehoiachin
captive to Babylon. He also took from
Jerusalem to Babylon the king's mother, his wives, his officials and the prominent people of the land. 16The king of
Babylon also deported to Babylon the
entire force of seven thousand fighting
men, strong and fit for war, and a thousand skilled workers and artisans. 17He
made Mattaniah, Jehoiachin's uncle,
king in his place and changed his name
to Zedekiah.

Zedekiah King of Judah

18Zedekiah was twenty-one years old
when he became king, and he reigned
in Jerusalem eleven years. His mother's
name was Hamutal daughter of Jeremiah; she was from Libnah. 19He did evil in
the eyes of the LORD, just as Jehoiakim
had done. 20It was because of the LORD's
anger that all this happened to Jerusalem and Judah, and in the end he thrust
them from his presence.

The Fall of Jerusalem

Now Zedekiah rebelled against the
king of Babylon.

25 So in the ninth year of Zedekiah's
reign, on the tenth day of the tenth
month, Nebuchadnezzar king of Babylon marched against Jerusalem with
his whole army. He encamped outside
the city and built siege works all around
it. 2The city was kept under siege until
the eleventh year of King Zedekiah.
3By the ninth day of the fourth[a] month
the famine in the city had become so severe that there was no food for the people to eat. 4Then the city wall was broken through, and the whole army fled at
night through the gate between the two
walls near the king's garden, though the
Babylonians[b] were surrounding the city.
They fled toward the Arabah,[c] 5but the
Babylonian[d] army pursued the king and
overtook him in the plains of Jericho. All
his soldiers were separated from him
and scattered, 6and he was captured.

He was taken to the king of Babylon at
Riblah, where sentence was pronounced
on him. 7They killed the sons of Zedekiah before his eyes. Then they put out his
eyes, bound him with bronze shackles
and took him to Babylon.
8On the seventh day of the fifth month,
in the nineteenth year of Nebuchadnezzar king of Babylon, Nebuzaradan
commander of the imperial guard, an
official of the king of Babylon, came to
Jerusalem. 9He set fire to the temple of
the LORD, the royal palace and all the
houses of Jerusalem. Every important
building he burned down. 10The whole
Babylonian army under the commander of the imperial guard broke down the
walls around Jerusalem. 11Nebuzaradan
the commander of the guard carried into
exile the people who remained in the
city, along with the rest of the populace
and those who had deserted to the king
of Babylon. 12But the commander left behind some of the poorest people of the
land to work the vineyards and fields.
13The Babylonians broke up the bronze
pillars, the movable stands and the
bronze Sea that were at the temple of
the LORD and they carried the bronze to
Babylon. 14They also took away the pots,
shovels, wick trimmers, dishes and all
the bronze articles used in the temple
service. 15The commander of the imperial guard took away the censers and
sprinkling bowls — all that were made
of pure gold or silver.
16The bronze from the two pillars, the
Sea and the movable stands, which Solomon had made for the temple of the
LORD, was more than could be weighed.
17Each pillar was eighteen cubits[e] high.
The bronze capital on top of one pillar
was three cubits[f] high and was decorated with a network and pomegranates of
bronze all around. The other pillar, with
its network, was similar.
18The commander of the guard took as
prisoners Seraiah the chief priest, Zephaniah the priest next in rank and the
three doorkeepers. 19Of those still in the
city, he took the officer in charge of the
fighting men, and five royal advisers.
He also took the secretary who was chief
officer in charge of conscripting the people of the land and sixty of the conscripts
who were found in the city. 20Nebuzara-
dan the commander took them all and

[a] 3 Probable reading of the original Hebrew text (see Jer. 52:6); Masoretic Text does not have *fourth.* [b] 4 Or *Chaldeans*; also in verses 13, 25 and 26 [c] 4 Or *the Jordan Valley* [d] 5 Or *Chaldean*; also in verses 10 and 24 [e] 17 That is, about 27 feet or about 8.1 meters [f] 17 That is, about 4 1/2 feet or about 1.4 meters

brought them to the king of Babylon at
Riblah. 21 There at Riblah, in the land of
Hamath, the king had them executed.

So Judah went into captivity, away
from her land.

22 Nebuchadnezzar king of Babylon
appointed Gedaliah son of Ahikam, the
son of Shaphan, to be over the people he
had left behind in Judah. 23 When all the
army officers and their men heard that
the king of Babylon had appointed Gedaliah as governor, they came to Gedaliah
at Mizpah — Ishmael son of Nethaniah,
Johanan son of Kareah, Seraiah son of
Tanhumeth the Netophathite, Jaazaniah the son of the Maakathite, and their
men. 24 Gedaliah took an oath to reassure
them and their men. "Do not be afraid of
the Babylonian officials," he said. "Settle down in the land and serve the king
of Babylon, and it will go well with you."

25 In the seventh month, however, Ishmael son of Nethaniah, the son of Elishama, who was of royal blood, came with
ten men and assassinated Gedaliah and
also the men of Judah and the Babylonians who were with him at Mizpah.
26 At this, all the people from the least
to the greatest, together with the army
officers, fled to Egypt for fear of the Babylonians.

Jehoiachin Released

27 In the thirty-seventh year of the exile
of Jehoiachin king of Judah, in the year
Awel-Marduk became king of Babylon,
he released Jehoiachin king of Judah
from prison. He did this on the twenty-
seventh day of the twelfth month. 28 He
spoke kindly to him and gave him a
seat of honor higher than those of the
other kings who were with him in Babylon. 29 So Jehoiachin put aside his prison clothes and for the rest of his life ate
regularly at the king's table. 30 Day by
day the king gave Jehoiachin a regular
allowance as long as he lived.

1 CHRONICLES

Historical Records From Adam to Abraham

To Noah's Sons

1 Adam, Seth, Enosh, 2 Kenan, Mahalalel, Jared, 3 Enoch, Methuselah, Lamech, Noah.

4 The sons of Noah:[a]
Shem, Ham and Japheth.

The Japhethites

5 The sons[b] of Japheth:
Gomer, Magog, Madai, Javan, Tubal, Meshek and Tiras.
6 The sons of Gomer:
Ashkenaz, Riphath[c] and Togarmah.
7 The sons of Javan:
Elishah, Tarshish, the Kittites and the Rodanites.

The Hamites

8 The sons of Ham:
Cush, Egypt, Put and Canaan.
9 The sons of Cush:
Seba, Havilah, Sabta, Raamah and Sabteka.
The sons of Raamah:
Sheba and Dedan.
10 Cush was the father[d] of
Nimrod, who became a mighty warrior on earth.
11 Egypt was the father of
the Ludites, Anamites, Lehabites, Naphtuhites, 12 Pathrusites, Kasluhites (from whom the Philistines came) and Caphtorites.
13 Canaan was the father of
Sidon his firstborn,[e] and of the Hittites, 14 Jebusites, Amorites, Girgashites, 15 Hivites, Arkites, Sinites, 16 Arvadites, Zemarites and Hamathites.

The Semites

17 The sons of Shem:
Elam, Ashur, Arphaxad, Lud and Aram.
The sons of Aram:[f]
Uz, Hul, Gether and Meshek.
18 Arphaxad was the father of Shelah,
and Shelah the father of Eber.
19 Two sons were born to Eber:
One was named Peleg,[g] because in his time the earth was divided; his brother was named Joktan.
20 Joktan was the father of
Almodad, Sheleph, Hazarmaveth, Jerah, 21 Hadoram, Uzal, Diklah, 22 Obal,[h] Abimael, Sheba, 23 Ophir, Havilah and Jobab. All these were sons of Joktan.

24 Shem, Arphaxad,[i] Shelah,
25 Eber, Peleg, Reu,
26 Serug, Nahor, Terah
27 and Abram (that is, Abraham).

The Family of Abraham

28 The sons of Abraham:
Isaac and Ishmael.

Descendants of Hagar

29 These were their descendants:
Nebaioth the firstborn of Ishmael, Kedar, Adbeel, Mibsam, 30 Mishma, Dumah, Massa, Hadad, Tema, 31 Jetur, Naphish and Kedemah. These were the sons of Ishmael.

Descendants of Keturah

32 The sons born to Keturah, Abraham's concubine:
Zimran, Jokshan, Medan, Midian, Ishbak and Shuah.
The sons of Jokshan:
Sheba and Dedan.
33 The sons of Midian:
Ephah, Epher, Hanok, Abida and Eldaah.
All these were descendants of Keturah.

[a] 4 Septuagint; Hebrew does not have this line. [b] 5 *Sons* may mean *descendants* or *successors* or *nations*; also in verses 6-9, 17 and 23. [c] 6 Many Hebrew manuscripts and Vulgate (see also Septuagint and Gen. 10:3); most Hebrew manuscripts *Diphath* [d] 10 *Father* may mean *ancestor* or *predecessor* or *founder*; also in verses 11, 13, 18 and 20. [e] 13 Or *of the Sidonians, the foremost* [f] 17 One Hebrew manuscript and some Septuagint manuscripts (see also Gen. 10:23); most Hebrew manuscripts do not have this line. [g] 19 *Peleg* means *division.* [h] 22 Some Hebrew manuscripts and Syriac (see also Gen. 10:28); most Hebrew manuscripts *Ebal* [i] 24 Hebrew; some Septuagint manuscripts *Arphaxad, Cainan* (see also note at Gen. 11:10)

Descendants of Sarah

34 Abraham was the father of Isaac.
The sons of Isaac:
Esau and Israel.

Esau's Sons

35 The sons of Esau:
Eliphaz, Reuel, Jeush, Jalam and Korah.
36 The sons of Eliphaz:
Teman, Omar, Zepho,[a] Gatam and Kenaz;
by Timna: Amalek.[b]
37 The sons of Reuel:
Nahath, Zerah, Shammah and Mizzah.

The People of Seir in Edom

38 The sons of Seir:
Lotan, Shobal, Zibeon, Anah, Dishon, Ezer and Dishan.
39 The sons of Lotan:
Hori and Homam. Timna was Lotan's sister.
40 The sons of Shobal:
Alvan,[c] Manahath, Ebal, Shepho and Onam.
The sons of Zibeon:
Aiah and Anah.
41 The son of Anah:
Dishon.
The sons of Dishon:
Hemdan,[d] Eshban, Ithran and Keran.
42 The sons of Ezer:
Bilhan, Zaavan and Akan.[e]
The sons of Dishan[f]:
Uz and Aran.

The Rulers of Edom

43 These were the kings who reigned in Edom before any Israelite king reigned:
Bela son of Beor, whose city was named Dinhabah.
44 When Bela died, Jobab son of Zerah from Bozrah succeeded him as king.
45 When Jobab died, Husham from the land of the Temanites succeeded him as king.
46 When Husham died, Hadad son of Bedad, who defeated Midian in the country of Moab, succeeded him as king. His city was named Avith.
47 When Hadad died, Samlah from Masrekah succeeded him as king.
48 When Samlah died, Shaul from Rehoboth on the river[g] succeeded him as king.
49 When Shaul died, Baal-Hanan son of Akbor succeeded him as king.
50 When Baal-Hanan died, Hadad succeeded him as king. His city was named Pau,[h] and his wife's name was Mehetabel daughter of Matred, the daughter of Me-Zahab.
51 Hadad also died.

The chiefs of Edom were:
Timna, Alvah, Jetheth, 52 Oholibamah, Elah, Pinon, 53 Kenaz, Teman, Mibzar, 54 Magdiel and Iram.
These were the chiefs of Edom.

Israel's Sons

2 These were the sons of Israel:
Reuben, Simeon, Levi, Judah, Issachar, Zebulun, 2 Dan, Joseph, Benjamin, Naphtali, Gad and Asher.

Judah

To Hezron's Sons

3 The sons of Judah:
Er, Onan and Shelah. These three were born to him by a Canaanite woman, the daughter of Shua. Er, Judah's firstborn, was wicked in the LORD's sight; so the LORD put him to death. 4 Judah's daughter-in-law Tamar bore Perez and Zerah to Judah. He had five sons in all.

5 The sons of Perez:
Hezron and Hamul.
6 The sons of Zerah:
Zimri, Ethan, Heman, Kalkol and Darda[i]—five in all.

[a] 36 Many Hebrew manuscripts, some Septuagint manuscripts and Syriac (see also Gen. 36:11); most Hebrew manuscripts *Zephi* [b] 36 Some Septuagint manuscripts (see also Gen. 36:12); Hebrew *Gatam, Kenaz, Timna and Amalek* [c] 40 Many Hebrew manuscripts and some Septuagint manuscripts (see also Gen. 36:23); most Hebrew manuscripts *Alian* [d] 41 Many Hebrew manuscripts and some Septuagint manuscripts (see also Gen. 36:26); most Hebrew manuscripts *Hamran* [e] 42 Many Hebrew and Septuagint manuscripts (see also Gen. 36:27); most Hebrew manuscripts *Zaavan, Jaakan* [f] 42 See Gen. 36:28; Hebrew *Dishon*, a variant of *Dishan* [g] 48 Possibly the Euphrates [h] 50 Many Hebrew manuscripts, some Septuagint manuscripts, Vulgate and Syriac (see also Gen. 36:39); most Hebrew manuscripts *Pai* [i] 6 Many Hebrew manuscripts, some Septuagint manuscripts and Syriac (see also 1 Kings 4:31); most Hebrew manuscripts *Dara*

7 The son of Karmi:
Achar,[a] who brought trouble on Israel by violating the ban on taking devoted things.[b]
8 The son of Ethan:
Azariah.
9 The sons born to Hezron were:
Jerahmeel, Ram and Caleb.[c]

From Ram Son of Hezron

10 Ram was the father of
Amminadab, and Amminadab the father of Nahshon, the leader of the people of Judah.
11 Nahshon was the father of Salmon,[d]
Salmon the father of Boaz,
12 Boaz the father of Obed and Obed the father of Jesse.
13 Jesse was the father of
Eliab his firstborn; the second son was Abinadab, the third Shimea,
14 the fourth Nethanel, the fifth Raddai,
15 the sixth Ozem and the seventh David.
16 Their sisters were Zeruiah and Abigail. Zeruiah's three sons were Abishai, Joab and Asahel.
17 Abigail was the mother of Amasa, whose father was Jether the Ishmaelite.

Caleb Son of Hezron

18 Caleb son of Hezron had children by his wife Azubah (and by Jerioth). These were her sons: Jesher, Shobab and Ardon.
19 When Azubah died, Caleb married Ephrath, who bore him Hur.
20 Hur was the father of Uri, and Uri the father of Bezalel.
21 Later, Hezron, when he was sixty years old, married the daughter of Makir the father of Gilead. He made love to her, and she bore him Segub.
22 Segub was the father of Jair, who controlled twenty-three towns in Gilead.
23 (But Geshur and Aram captured Havvoth Jair,[e] as well as Kenath with its surrounding settlements — sixty towns.) All these were descendants of Makir the father of Gilead.

24 After Hezron died in Caleb Ephrathah, Abijah the wife of Hezron bore him Ashhur the father[f] of Tekoa.

Jerahmeel Son of Hezron

25 The sons of Jerahmeel the firstborn of Hezron:
Ram his firstborn, Bunah, Oren, Ozem and[g] Ahijah.
26 Jerahmeel had another wife, whose name was Atarah; she was the mother of Onam.
27 The sons of Ram the firstborn of Jerahmeel:
Maaz, Jamin and Eker.
28 The sons of Onam:
Shammai and Jada.
The sons of Shammai:
Nadab and Abishur.
29 Abishur's wife was named Abihail, who bore him Ahban and Molid.
30 The sons of Nadab:
Seled and Appaim. Seled died without children.
31 The son of Appaim:
Ishi, who was the father of Sheshan.
Sheshan was the father of Ahlai.
32 The sons of Jada, Shammai's brother:
Jether and Jonathan. Jether died without children.
33 The sons of Jonathan:
Peleth and Zaza.
These were the descendants of Jerahmeel.
34 Sheshan had no sons — only daughters.
He had an Egyptian servant named Jarha.
35 Sheshan gave his daughter in marriage to his servant Jarha, and she bore him Attai.
36 Attai was the father of Nathan,
Nathan the father of Zabad,
37 Zabad the father of Ephlal,
Ephlal the father of Obed,
38 Obed the father of Jehu,
Jehu the father of Azariah,
39 Azariah the father of Helez,
Helez the father of Eleasah,
40 Eleasah the father of Sismai,
Sismai the father of Shallum,
41 Shallum the father of Jekamiah,
and Jekamiah the father of Elishama.

The Clans of Caleb

42 The sons of Caleb the brother of Jerahmeel:
Mesha his firstborn, who was the father of Ziph, and his son Mareshah,[h] who was the father of Hebron.

[a] 7 *Achar* means *trouble*; *Achar* is called *Achan* in Joshua. [b] 7 The Hebrew term refers to the irrevocable giving over of things or persons to the LORD, often by totally destroying them. [c] 9 Hebrew *Kelubai*, a variant of *Caleb* [d] 11 Septuagint (see also Ruth 4:21); Hebrew *Salma* [e] 23 Or *captured the settlements of Jair* [f] 24 *Father* may mean *civic leader* or *military leader*; also in verses 42, 45, 49-52 and possibly elsewhere. [g] 25 Or *Oren and Ozem, by* [h] 42 The meaning of the Hebrew for this phrase is uncertain.

43 The sons of Hebron:
Korah, Tappuah, Rekem and Shema. 44 Shema was the father of Raham, and Raham the father of Jorkeam. Rekem was the father of Shammai. 45 The son of Shammai was Maon, and Maon was the father of Beth Zur.
46 Caleb's concubine Ephah was the mother of Haran, Moza and Gazez. Haran was the father of Gazez.
47 The sons of Jahdai:
Regem, Jotham, Geshan, Pelet, Ephah and Shaaph.
48 Caleb's concubine Maakah was the mother of Sheber and Tirhanah.
49 She also gave birth to Shaaph
the father of Madmannah and to Sheva the father of Makbenah and Gibea. Caleb's daughter was Aksah.
50 These were the descen-
dants of Caleb.

The sons of Hur the firstborn of Ephrathah:
Shobal the father of Kiriath Jearim,
51 Salma the father of Bethlehem, and Hareph the father of Beth Gader.
52 The descendants of Shobal the father of Kiriath Jearim were:
Haroeh, half the Manahathites,
53 and the clans of Kiriath Jearim: the Ithrites, Puthites, Shumathites and Mishraites. From these descended the Zorathites and Eshtaolites.
54 The descendants of Salma:
Bethlehem, the Netophathites, Atroth Beth Joab, half the Manahathites, the Zorites,
55 and the clans of scribes[a] who lived at Jabez: the Tirathites, Shimeathites and Sucathites. These are the Kenites who came from Hammath, the father of the Rekabites.[b]

The Sons of David

3 These were the sons of David born to him in Hebron:
The firstborn was Amnon the son of Ahinoam of Jezreel;
the second, Daniel the son of Abigail of Carmel;
2 the third, Absalom the son of Maakah daughter of Talmai king of Geshur;
the fourth, Adonijah the son of Haggith;
3 the fifth, Shephatiah the son of Abital;
and the sixth, Ithream, by his wife Eglah.
4 These six were born to David in Hebron, where he reigned seven years and six months.
David reigned in Jerusalem thirty-three years,
5 and these were the children born
to him there:
Shammua,[c] Shobab, Nathan and Solomon. These four were by Bathsheba[d] daughter of Ammiel.
6 There were also Ibhar, Elishua,[e] Eliphelet,
7 Nogah, Nepheg,
Japhia,
8 Elishama, Eliada and Eliphelet — nine in all.
9 All these
were the sons of David, besides his sons by his concubines. And Tamar was their sister.

The Kings of Judah

10 Solomon's son was Rehoboam,
Abijah his son,
Asa his son,
Jehoshaphat his son,
11 Jehoram[f] his son,
Ahaziah his son,
Joash his son,
12 Amaziah his son,
Azariah his son,
Jotham his son,
13 Ahaz his son,
Hezekiah his son,
Manasseh his son,
14 Amon his son,
Josiah his son.
15 The sons of Josiah:
Johanan the firstborn,
Jehoiakim the second son,
Zedekiah the third,
Shallum the fourth.
16 The successors of Jehoiakim:
Jehoiachin[g] his son,
and Zedekiah.

The Royal Line After the Exile

17 The descendants of Jehoiachin the captive:
Shealtiel his son,
18 Malkiram,
Pedaiah, Shenazzar, Jekamiah, Hoshama and Nedabiah.
19 The sons of Pedaiah:
Zerubbabel and Shimei.

[a] 55 Or *of the Sopherites* [b] 55 Or *father of Beth Rekab* [c] 5 Hebrew *Shimea*, a variant of *Shammua* [d] 5 One Hebrew manuscript and Vulgate (see also Septuagint and 2 Samuel 11:3); most Hebrew manuscripts *Bathshua* [e] 6 Two Hebrew manuscripts (see also 2 Samuel 5:15 and 1 Chron. 14:5); most Hebrew manuscripts *Elishama* [f] 11 Hebrew *Joram*, a variant of *Jehoram* [g] 16 Hebrew *Jeconiah*, a variant of *Jehoiachin*; also in verse 17

The sons of Zerubbabel:
Meshullam and Hananiah.
Shelomith was their sister.
20 There were also five others:
Hashubah, Ohel, Berekiah, Hasadiah and Jushab-Hesed.
21 The descendants of Hananiah:
Pelatiah and Jeshaiah, and the sons of Rephaiah, of Arnan, of Obadiah and of Shekaniah.
22 The descendants of Shekaniah:
Shemaiah and his sons:
Hattush, Igal, Bariah, Neariah and Shaphat — six in all.
23 The sons of Neariah:
Elioenai, Hizkiah and Azrikam — three in all.
24 The sons of Elioenai:
Hodaviah, Eliashib, Pelaiah, Akkub, Johanan, Delaiah and Anani — seven in all.

Other Clans of Judah

4 The descendants of Judah:
Perez, Hezron, Karmi, Hur and Shobal.
2 Reaiah son of Shobal was the father of Jahath, and Jahath the father of Ahumai and Lahad. These were the clans of the Zorathites.
3 These were the sons[a] of Etam:
Jezreel, Ishma and Idbash. Their sister was named Hazzelelponi.
4 Penuel was the father of Gedor, and Ezer the father of Hushah.
These were the descendants of Hur, the firstborn of Ephrathah and father[b] of Bethlehem.
5 Ashhur the father of Tekoa had two wives, Helah and Naarah.
6 Naarah bore him Ahuzzam, Hepher, Temeni and Haahashtari. These were the descendants of Naarah.
7 The sons of Helah:
Zereth, Zohar, Ethnan, 8 and Koz, who was the father of Anub and Hazzobebah and of the clans of Aharhel son of Harum.

9 Jabez was more honorable than his
brothers. His mother had named him Jabez,[c] saying, "I gave birth to him in pain."
10 Jabez cried out to the God of Israel, "Oh,
that you would bless me and enlarge my
territory! Let your hand be with me, and
keep me from harm so that I will be free
from pain." And God granted his request.

11 Kelub, Shuhah's brother, was the father of Mehir, who was the father of Eshton. 12 Eshton was the father of Beth Rapha, Paseah and Tehinnah the father of Ir Nahash.[d] These were the men of Rekah.

13 The sons of Kenaz:
Othniel and Seraiah.
The sons of Othniel:
Hathath and Meonothai.[e] 14 Meonothai was the father of Ophrah.
Seraiah was the father of Joab,
the father of Ge Harashim.[f] It was called this because its people were skilled workers.
15 The sons of Caleb son of Jephunneh:
Iru, Elah and Naam.
The son of Elah:
Kenaz.
16 The sons of Jehallelel:
Ziph, Ziphah, Tiria and Asarel.
17 The sons of Ezrah:
Jether, Mered, Epher and Jalon. One of Mered's wives gave birth to Miriam, Shammai and Ishbah the father of Eshtemoa. 18 (His wife from the tribe of Judah gave birth to Jered the father of Gedor, Heber the father of Soko, and Jekuthiel the father of Zanoah.) These were the children of Pharaoh's daughter Bithiah, whom Mered had married.
19 The sons of Hodiah's wife, the sister of Naham:
the father of Keilah the Garmite, and Eshtemoa the Maakathite.
20 The sons of Shimon:
Amnon, Rinnah, Ben-Hanan and Tilon.
The descendants of Ishi:
Zoheth and Ben-Zoheth.
21 The sons of Shelah son of Judah:
Er the father of Lekah, Laadah the father of Mareshah and the clans of the linen workers at Beth Ashbea, 22 Jokim, the men of Kozeba, and Joash and Saraph, who ruled in Moab and Jashubi Lehem. (These records are from ancient times.) 23 They were the potters who lived at Netaim and Gederah; they stayed there and worked for the king.

[a] 3 Some Septuagint manuscripts (see also Vulgate); Hebrew *father* [b] 4 *Father* may mean *civic leader* or *military leader*; also in verses 12, 14, 17, 18 and possibly elsewhere. [c] 9 *Jabez* sounds like the Hebrew for *pain.* [d] 12 Or *of the city of Nahash* [e] 13 Some Septuagint manuscripts and Vulgate; Hebrew does not have *and Meonothai.* [f] 14 *Ge Harashim* means *valley of skilled workers.*

Simeon

24 The descendants of Simeon:
Nemuel, Jamin, Jarib, Zerah and
Shaul;
25 Shallum was Shaul's son, Mibsam
his son and Mishma his son.
26 The descendants of Mishma:
Hammuel his son, Zakkur his son
and Shimei his son.

27 Shimei had sixteen sons and six
daughters, but his brothers did not have
many children; so their entire clan did
not become as numerous as the people of Judah. 28 They lived in Beersheba,
Moladah, Hazar Shual, 29 Bilhah, Ezem,
Tolad, 30 Bethuel, Hormah, Ziklag, 31 Beth
Markaboth, Hazar Susim, Beth Biri and
Shaaraim. These were their towns until
the reign of David. 32 Their surrounding
villages were Etam, Ain, Rimmon, Token
and Ashan — five towns — 33 and all the
villages around these towns as far as
Baalath.[a] These were their settlements.
And they kept a genealogical record.

34 Meshobab, Jamlech, Joshah son of
Amaziah, 35 Joel, Jehu son of Josh-
ibiah, the son of Seraiah, the son
of Asiel, 36 also Elioenai, Jaakobah,
Jeshohaiah, Asaiah, Adiel, Jesimiel,
Benaiah, 37 and Ziza son of Shiphi,
the son of Allon, the son of Jedaiah,
the son of Shimri, the son of Shemaiah.

38 The men listed above by name were
leaders of their clans. Their families increased greatly, 39 and they went to the
outskirts of Gedor to the east of the valley in search of pasture for their flocks.
40 They found rich, good pasture, and
the land was spacious, peaceful and
quiet. Some Hamites had lived there
formerly.

41 The men whose names were listed
came in the days of Hezekiah king of Judah. They attacked the Hamites in their
dwellings and also the Meunites who
were there and completely destroyed[b]
them, as is evident to this day. Then they
settled in their place, because there was
pasture for their flocks. 42 And five hundred of these Simeonites, led by Pelatiah,
Neariah, Rephaiah and Uzziel, the sons
of Ishi, invaded the hill country of Seir.
43 They killed the remaining Amalekites
who had escaped, and they have lived
there to this day.

Reuben

5 The sons of Reuben the firstborn of
Israel (he was the firstborn, but when
he defiled his father's marriage bed,
his rights as firstborn were given to the
sons of Joseph son of Israel; so he could
not be listed in the genealogical record
in accordance with his birthright, 2 and
though Judah was the strongest of his
brothers and a ruler came from him,
the rights of the firstborn belonged to
Joseph) — 3 the sons of Reuben the firstborn of Israel:
Hanok, Pallu, Hezron and Karmi.
4 The descendants of Joel:
Shemaiah his son, Gog his son,
Shimei his son, 5 Micah his son,
Reaiah his son, Baal his son,
6 and Beerah his son, whom Tiglath-
Pileser[c] king of Assyria took into
exile. Beerah was a leader of the
Reubenites.
7 Their relatives by clans, listed according to their genealogical records:
Jeiel the chief, Zechariah, 8 and
Bela son of Azaz, the son of Shema, the son of Joel. They settled
in the area from Aroer to Nebo
and Baal Meon. 9 To the east they
occupied the land up to the edge
of the desert that extends to the
Euphrates River, because their
livestock had increased in Gilead.
10 During Saul's reign they waged
war against the Hagrites, who were
defeated at their hands; they occupied the dwellings of the Hagrites
throughout the entire region east
of Gilead.

Gad

11 The Gadites lived next to them in
Bashan, as far as Salekah:
12 Joel was the chief, Shapham the
second, then Janai and Shaphat,
in Bashan.
13 Their relatives, by families, were:
Michael, Meshullam, Sheba, Jo-
rai, Jakan, Zia and Eber — seven
in all.
14 These were the sons of Abihail
son of Huri, the son of Jaroah, the
son of Gilead, the son of Michael,
the son of Jeshishai, the son of
Jahdo, the son of Buz.
15 Ahi son of Abdiel, the son of Guni,
was head of their family.

[a] *33* Some Septuagint manuscripts (see also Joshua 19:8); Hebrew *Baal* [b] *41* The Hebrew term refers to the irrevocable giving over of things or persons to the LORD, often by totally destroying them. [c] *6* Hebrew *Tilgath-Pilneser,* a variant of *Tiglath-Pileser;* also in verse 26

16 The Gadites lived in Gilead, in Bashan and its outlying villages,
and on all the pasturelands of
Sharon as far as they extended.
17 All these were entered in the genealogical records during the reigns of Jotham king of Judah and Jeroboam king
of Israel.

18 The Reubenites, the Gadites and the
half-tribe of Manasseh had 44,760 men
ready for military service — able-bodied
men who could handle shield and sword,
who could use a bow, and who were
trained for battle. 19 They waged war
against the Hagrites, Jetur, Naphish and
Nodab. 20 They were helped in fighting
them, and God delivered the Hagrites
and all their allies into their hands, because they cried out to him during the
battle. He answered their prayers, because they trusted in him. 21 They seized
the livestock of the Hagrites — fifty thousand camels, two hundred fifty thousand sheep and two thousand donkeys.
They also took one hundred thousand
people captive, 22 and many others fell
slain, because the battle was God's. And
they occupied the land until the exile.

The Half-Tribe of Manasseh

23 The people of the half-tribe of Manasseh were numerous; they settled in
the land from Bashan to Baal Hermon,
that is, to Senir (Mount Hermon).
24 These were the heads of their families: Epher, Ishi, Eliel, Azriel, Jeremiah,
Hodaviah and Jahdiel. They were brave
warriors, famous men, and heads of their
families. 25 But they were unfaithful to
the God of their ancestors and prostituted themselves to the gods of the peoples
of the land, whom God had destroyed before them. 26 So the God of Israel stirred
up the spirit of Pul king of Assyria (that
is, Tiglath-Pileser king of Assyria), who
took the Reubenites, the Gadites and the
half-tribe of Manasseh into exile. He took
them to Halah, Habor, Hara and the river
of Gozan, where they are to this day.

Levi

6 [a] The sons of Levi:
Gershon, Kohath and Merari.
2 The sons of Kohath:
Amram, Izhar, Hebron and Uzziel.
3 The children of Amram:
Aaron, Moses and Miriam.
The sons of Aaron:
Nadab, Abihu, Eleazar and Ithamar.
4 Eleazar was the father of Phinehas,
Phinehas the father of Abishua,
5 Abishua the father of Bukki,
Bukki the father of Uzzi,
6 Uzzi the father of Zerahiah,
Zerahiah the father of Meraioth,
7 Meraioth the father of Amariah,
Amariah the father of Ahitub,
8 Ahitub the father of Zadok,
Zadok the father of Ahimaaz,
9 Ahimaaz the father of Azariah,
Azariah the father of Johanan,
10 Johanan the father of Azariah (it
was he who served as priest in the
temple Solomon built in Jerusalem),
11 Azariah the father of Amariah,
Amariah the father of Ahitub,
12 Ahitub the father of Zadok,
Zadok the father of Shallum,
13 Shallum the father of Hilkiah,
Hilkiah the father of Azariah,
14 Azariah the father of Seraiah,
and Seraiah the father of Jozadak.[b]
15 Jozadak was deported when the
LORD sent Judah and Jerusalem
into exile by the hand of Nebuchadnezzar.

16 The sons of Levi:
Gershon,[c] Kohath and Merari.
17 These are the names of the sons of
Gershon:
Libni and Shimei.
18 The sons of Kohath:
Amram, Izhar, Hebron and Uzziel.
19 The sons of Merari:
Mahli and Mushi.
These are the clans of the Levites
listed according to their fathers:
20 Of Gershon:
Libni his son, Jahath his son,
Zimmah his son, 21 Joah his son,
Iddo his son, Zerah his son
and Jeatherai his son.
22 The descendants of Kohath:
Amminadab his son, Korah his son,
Assir his son, 23 Elkanah his son,
Ebiasaph his son, Assir his son,
24 Tahath his son, Uriel his son,
Uzziah his son and Shaul his son.
25 The descendants of Elkanah:
Amasai, Ahimoth,
26 Elkanah his son,[d] Zophai his son,
Nahath his son, 27 Eliab his son,

[a] In Hebrew texts 6:1-15 is numbered 5:27-41, and 6:16-81 is numbered 6:1-66. [b] *14* Hebrew *Jehozadak*, a variant of *Jozadak*; also in verse 15 [c] *16* Hebrew *Gershom*, a variant of *Gershon*; also in verses 17, 20, 43, 62 and 71 [d] *26* Some Hebrew manuscripts, Septuagint and Syriac; most Hebrew manuscripts *Ahimoth* [26]*and Elkanah. The sons of Elkanah:*

Jeroham his son, Elkanah his son
and Samuel his son.[a]
28 The sons of Samuel:
Joel[b] the firstborn
and Abijah the second son.
29 The descendants of Merari:
Mahli, Libni his son,
Shimei his son, Uzzah his son,
30 Shimea his son, Haggiah his son
and Asaiah his son.

The Temple Musicians

31 These are the men David put in charge
of the music in the house of the LORD after
the ark came to rest there. 32 They ministered with music before the tabernacle,
the tent of meeting, until Solomon built
the temple of the LORD in Jerusalem. They
performed their duties according to the
regulations laid down for them.
33 Here are the men who served, together with their sons:
From the Kohathites:
Heman, the musician,
the son of Joel, the son of Samuel,
34 the son of Elkanah, the son of Jeroham,
the son of Eliel, the son of Toah,
35 the son of Zuph, the son of Elkanah,
the son of Mahath, the son of
Amasai,
36 the son of Elkanah, the son of Joel,
the son of Azariah, the son of
Zephaniah,
37 the son of Tahath, the son of Assir,
the son of Ebiasaph, the son of
Korah,
38 the son of Izhar, the son of Kohath,
the son of Levi, the son of Israel;
39 and Heman's associate Asaph, who
served at his right hand:
Asaph son of Berekiah, the son of
Shimea,
40 the son of Michael, the son of Ba-
aseiah,[c]
the son of Malkijah, 41 the son of
Ethni,
the son of Zerah, the son of Adaiah,
42 the son of Ethan, the son of Zimmah,
the son of Shimei, 43 the son of Jahath,
the son of Gershon, the son of
Levi;
44 and from their associates, the Merarites, at his left hand:
Ethan son of Kishi, the son of
Abdi,
the son of Malluk, 45 the son of
Hashabiah,
the son of Amaziah, the son of
Hilkiah,
46 the son of Amzi, the son of Bani,
the son of Shemer, 47 the son of
Mahli,
the son of Mushi, the son of Merari,
the son of Levi.

48 Their fellow Levites were assigned
to all the other duties of the tabernacle,
the house of God. 49 But Aaron and his descendants were the ones who presented
offerings on the altar of burnt offering
and on the altar of incense in connection
with all that was done in the Most Holy
Place, making atonement for Israel, in
accordance with all that Moses the servant of God had commanded.
50 These were the descendants of Aaron:
Eleazar his son, Phinehas his son,
Abishua his son, 51 Bukki his son,
Uzzi his son, Zerahiah his son,
52 Meraioth his son, Amariah his
son,
Ahitub his son, 53 Zadok his son
and Ahimaaz his son.

54 These were the locations of their settlements allotted as their territory (they
were assigned to the descendants of Aaron who were from the Kohathite clan,
because the first lot was for them):
55 They were given Hebron in Judah with its surrounding pasturelands. 56 But the fields and villages
around the city were given to Caleb
son of Jephunneh.
57 So the descendants of Aaron
were given Hebron (a city of refuge), and Libnah,[d] Jattir, Eshtemoa,
58 Hilen, Debir, 59 Ashan, Juttah[e] and
Beth Shemesh, together with their
pasturelands. 60 And from the tribe
of Benjamin they were given Gibeon,[f] Geba, Alemeth and Anathoth,
together with their pasturelands.
The total number of towns distributed among the Kohathite clans
came to thirteen.

[a] *27* Some Septuagint manuscripts (see also 1 Samuel 1:19,20 and 1 Chron. 6:33,34); Hebrew does not have *and Samuel his son.* [b] *28* Some Septuagint manuscripts and Syriac (see also 1 Samuel 8:2 and 1 Chron. 6:33); Hebrew does not have *Joel.* [c] *40* Most Hebrew manuscripts; some Hebrew manuscripts, one Septuagint manuscript and Syriac *Maaseiah* [d] *57* See Joshua 21:13; Hebrew *given the cities of refuge: Hebron, Libnah.* [e] *59* Syriac (see also Septuagint and Joshua 21:16); Hebrew does not have *Juttah.* [f] *60* See Joshua 21:17; Hebrew does not have *Gibeon.*

61 The rest of Kohath's descendants
were allotted ten towns from the clans
of half the tribe of Manasseh.
62 The descendants of Gershon, clan by
clan, were allotted thirteen towns from
the tribes of Issachar, Asher and Naphtali, and from the part of the tribe of Manasseh that is in Bashan.
63 The descendants of Merari, clan by
clan, were allotted twelve towns from
the tribes of Reuben, Gad and Zebulun.
64 So the Israelites gave the Levites
these towns and their pasturelands.
65 From the tribes of Judah, Simeon and
Benjamin they allotted the previously
named towns.
66 Some of the Kohathite clans were
given as their territory towns from the
tribe of Ephraim.

67 In the hill country of Ephraim
they were given Shechem (a city of
refuge), and Gezer,[a] 68 Jokmeam, Beth
Horon, 69 Aijalon and Gath Rimmon,
together with their pasturelands.
70 And from half the tribe of Manasseh the Israelites gave Aner and Bile-
am, together with their pasturelands,
to the rest of the Kohathite clans.

71 The Gershonites received the following:
From the clan of the half-tribe of
Manasseh
they received Golan in Bashan
and also Ashtaroth, together with
their pasturelands;
72 from the tribe of Issachar
they received Kedesh, Daberath,
73 Ramoth and Anem, together
with their pasturelands;
74 from the tribe of Asher
they received Mashal, Abdon,
75 Hukok and Rehob, together with
their pasturelands;
76 and from the tribe of Naphtali
they received Kedesh in Galilee,
Hammon and Kiriathaim, together with their pasturelands.

77 The Merarites (the rest of the Levites) received the following:
From the tribe of Zebulun
they received Jokneam, Kartah,[b]
Rimmono and Tabor, together
with their pasturelands;
78 from the tribe of Reuben across the
Jordan east of Jericho
they received Bezer in the wilderness, Jahzah, 79 Kedemoth and
Mephaath, together with their
pasturelands;
80 and from the tribe of Gad
they received Ramoth in Gilead,
Mahanaim, 81 Heshbon and Jazer,
together with their pasturelands.

Issachar

7 The sons of Issachar:
Tola, Puah, Jashub and Shimron — four in all.
2 The sons of Tola:
Uzzi, Rephaiah, Jeriel, Jahmai,
Ibsam and Samuel — heads of
their families. During the reign
of David, the descendants of Tola
listed as fighting men in their genealogy numbered 22,600.
3 The son of Uzzi:
Izrahiah.
The sons of Izrahiah:
Michael, Obadiah, Joel and Ishiah. All five of them were chiefs.
4 According to their family genealogy, they had 36,000 men ready
for battle, for they had many
wives and children.
5 The relatives who were fighting
men belonging to all the clans of
Issachar, as listed in their genealogy, were 87,000 in all.

Benjamin

6 Three sons of Benjamin:
Bela, Beker and Jediael.
7 The sons of Bela:
Ezbon, Uzzi, Uzziel, Jerimoth and
Iri, heads of families — five in all.
Their genealogical record listed
22,034 fighting men.
8 The sons of Beker:
Zemirah, Joash, Eliezer, Elioenai, Omri, Jeremoth, Abijah, Anathoth and Alemeth. All these
were the sons of Beker. 9 Their genealogical record listed the heads
of families and 20,200 fighting
men.
10 The son of Jediael:
Bilhan.
The sons of Bilhan:
Jeush, Benjamin, Ehud, Kenaanah, Zethan, Tarshish and Ahish-
ahar. 11 All these sons of Jediael
were heads of families. There
were 17,200 fighting men ready
to go out to war.
12 The Shuppites and Huppites were
the descendants of Ir, and the Hu-
shites[c] the descendants of Aher.

[a] 67 See Joshua 21:21; Hebrew *given the cities of refuge: Shechem, Gezer.* [b] 77 See Septuagint and Joshua 21:34; Hebrew does not have *Jokneam, Kartah.* [c] 12 Or *Ir. The sons of Dan: Hushim,* (see Gen. 46:23); Hebrew does not have *The sons of Dan.*

Naphtali

13 The sons of Naphtali:
Jahziel, Guni, Jezer and Shillem[a] — the descendants of Bilhah.

Manasseh

14 The descendants of Manasseh:
Asriel was his descendant through his Aramean concubine. She gave birth to Makir the father
of Gilead. 15 Makir took a wife from among the Huppites and Shuppites. His sister's name was Maakah.
Another descendant was named Zelophehad, who had only daughters.
16 Makir's wife Maakah gave birth to a son and named him Peresh. His brother was named Sheresh, and his sons were Ulam and Rakem.
17 The son of Ulam:
Bedan.
These were the sons of Gilead son of Makir, the son of Manasseh.
18 His sister Hammoleketh gave birth to Ishhod, Abiezer and Mahlah.
19 The sons of Shemida were:
Ahian, Shechem, Likhi and Aniam.

Ephraim

20 The descendants of Ephraim:
Shuthelah, Bered his son,
Tahath his son, Eleadah his son,
Tahath his son, 21 Zabad his son
and Shuthelah his son.
Ezer and Elead were killed by the native-born men of Gath, when they went down to seize their livestock.
22 Their father Ephraim mourned for them many days, and his relatives came to comfort him.
23 Then he made love to his wife again, and she became pregnant and gave birth to a son. He named him Beriah,[b] because there had been misfortune in his family.
24 His daughter was Sheerah, who built Lower and Upper Beth Horon as well as Uzzen Sheerah.
25 Rephah was his son, Resheph his son,[c]
Telah his son, Tahan his son,
26 Ladan his son, Ammihud his son,
Elishama his son, 27 Nun his son
and Joshua his son.

28 Their lands and settlements included Bethel and its surrounding villages, Naaran to the east, Gezer and its villages to the west, and Shechem and its villages all the way to Ayyah and its villages.
29 Along the borders of Manasseh were Beth Shan, Taanach, Megiddo and Dor, together with their villages. The descendants of Joseph son of Israel lived in these towns.

Asher

30 The sons of Asher:
Imnah, Ishvah, Ishvi and Beriah.
Their sister was Serah.
31 The sons of Beriah:
Heber and Malkiel, who was the father of Birzaith.
32 Heber was the father of Japhlet, Shomer and Hotham and of their sister Shua.
33 The sons of Japhlet:
Pasak, Bimhal and Ashvath.
These were Japhlet's sons.
34 The sons of Shomer:
Ahi, Rohgah,[d] Hubbah and Aram.
35 The sons of his brother Helem:
Zophah, Imna, Shelesh and Amal.
36 The sons of Zophah:
Suah, Harnepher, Shual, Beri, Imrah,
37 Bezer, Hod, Shamma, Shilshah, Ithran[e] and Beera.
38 The sons of Jether:
Jephunneh, Pispah and Ara.
39 The sons of Ulla:
Arah, Hanniel and Rizia.
40 All these were descendants of Asher — heads of families, choice men, brave warriors and outstanding leaders. The number of men ready for battle, as listed in their genealogy, was 26,000.

The Genealogy of Saul the Benjamite

8 Benjamin was the father of Bela his firstborn,
Ashbel the second son, Aharah the third,
2 Nohah the fourth and Rapha the fifth.
3 The sons of Bela were:
Addar, Gera, Abihud,[f] 4 Abishua,
Naaman, Ahoah, 5 Gera, Shephuphan and Huram.
6 These were the descendants of Ehud, who were heads of families of those living in Geba and were deported to Manahath:

[a] 13 Some Hebrew and Septuagint manuscripts (see also Gen. 46:24 and Num. 26:49); most Hebrew manuscripts *Shallum* [b] 23 *Beriah* sounds like the Hebrew for *misfortune.*
[c] 25 Some Septuagint manuscripts; Hebrew does not have *his son.* [d] 34 Or *of his brother Shomer: Rohgah* [e] 37 Possibly a variant of *Jether* [f] 3 Or *Gera the father of Ehud*

7 Naaman, Ahijah, and Gera, who
deported them and who was the
father of Uzza and Ahihud.
8 Sons were born to Shaharaim in
Moab after he had divorced his
wives Hushim and Baara. 9 By his
wife Hodesh he had Jobab, Zib-
ia, Mesha, Malkam, 10 Jeuz, Sakia
and Mirmah. These were his sons,
heads of families. 11 By Hushim he
had Abitub and Elpaal.
12 The sons of Elpaal:
Eber, Misham, Shemed (who built
Ono and Lod with its surrounding
villages), 13 and Beriah and Shema, who were heads of families
of those living in Aijalon and who
drove out the inhabitants of Gath.
14 Ahio, Shashak, Jeremoth, 15 Zebadiah, Arad, Eder, 16 Michael, Ishpah
and Joha were the sons of Beriah.
17 Zebadiah, Meshullam, Hizki, Heber,
18 Ishmerai, Izliah and Jobab were
the sons of Elpaal.
19 Jakim, Zikri, Zabdi, 20 Elienai, Zillethai, Eliel, 21 Adaiah, Beraiah and
Shimrath were the sons of Shimei.
22 Ishpan, Eber, Eliel, 23 Abdon, Zikri,
Hanan, 24 Hananiah, Elam, An-
thothijah, 25 Iphdeiah and Penuel
were the sons of Shashak.
26 Shamsherai, Shehariah, Athaliah,
27 Jaareshiah, Elijah and Zikri
were the sons of Jeroham.
28 All these were heads of families,
chiefs as listed in their genealogy, and
they lived in Jerusalem.

29 Jeiel[a] the father[b] of Gibeon lived in
Gibeon.
His wife's name was Maakah,
30 and his firstborn son was Abdon, followed by Zur, Kish, Baal,
Ner,[c] Nadab, 31 Gedor, Ahio, Zeker
32 and Mikloth, who was the father
of Shimeah. They too lived near
their relatives in Jerusalem.
33 Ner was the father of Kish, Kish the
father of Saul, and Saul the father
of Jonathan, Malki-Shua, Abinadab and Esh-Baal.[d]
34 The son of Jonathan:
Merib-Baal,[e] who was the father
of Micah.
35 The sons of Micah:
Pithon, Melek, Tarea and Ahaz.
36 Ahaz was the father of Jehoaddah, Jehoaddah was the father
of Alemeth, Azmaveth and Zimri,
and Zimri was the father of Moza.
37 Moza was the father of Binea;
Raphah was his son, Eleasah his
son and Azel his son.
38 Azel had six sons, and these were
their names:
Azrikam, Bokeru, Ishmael, She-
ariah, Obadiah and Hanan. All
these were the sons of Azel.
39 The sons of his brother Eshek:
Ulam his firstborn, Jeush the second son and Eliphelet the third.
40 The sons of Ulam were brave
warriors who could handle the
bow. They had many sons and
grandsons — 150 in all.
All these were the descendants of
Benjamin.

9 All Israel was listed in the genealogies recorded in the book of the
kings of Israel and Judah. They were
taken captive to Babylon because of
their unfaithfulness.

The People in Jerusalem

2 Now the first to resettle on their own
property in their own towns were some
Israelites, priests, Levites and temple
servants.
3 Those from Judah, from Benjamin,
and from Ephraim and Manasseh who
lived in Jerusalem were:
4 Uthai son of Ammihud, the son of
Omri, the son of Imri, the son of
Bani, a descendant of Perez son of
Judah.
5 Of the Shelanites[f]:
Asaiah the firstborn and his sons.
6 Of the Zerahites:
Jeuel.
The people from Judah numbered 690.
7 Of the Benjamites:
Sallu son of Meshullam, the son of
Hodaviah, the son of Hassenuah;
8 Ibneiah son of Jeroham; Elah son
of Uzzi, the son of Mikri; and Meshullam son of Shephatiah, the
son of Reuel, the son of Ibnijah.
9 The people from Benjamin, as
listed in their genealogy, numbered 956. All these men were
heads of their families.
10 Of the priests:
Jedaiah; Jehoiarib; Jakin;

[a] 29 Some Septuagint manuscripts (see also 9:35); Hebrew does not have *Jeiel.* [b] 29 *Father* may mean *civic leader* or *military leader.* [c] 30 Some Septuagint manuscripts (see also 9:36); Hebrew does not have *Ner.* [d] 33 Also known as *Ish-Bosheth* [e] 34 Also known as *Mephibosheth* [f] 5 See Num. 26:20; Hebrew *Shilonites.*

11 Azariah son of Hilkiah, the son of
Meshullam, the son of Zadok, the
son of Meraioth, the son of Ahitub, the official in charge of the
house of God;
12 Adaiah son of Jeroham, the son
of Pashhur, the son of Malkijah;
and Maasai son of Adiel, the son
of Jahzerah, the son of Meshullam, the son of Meshillemith, the
son of Immer.
13 The priests, who were heads of
families, numbered 1,760. They
were able men, responsible for
ministering in the house of God.
14 Of the Levites:
Shemaiah son of Hasshub, the
son of Azrikam, the son of Hashabiah, a Merarite; 15 Bakbakkar,
Heresh, Galal and Mattaniah son
of Mika, the son of Zikri, the son
of Asaph; 16 Obadiah son of Shemaiah, the son of Galal, the son
of Jeduthun; and Berekiah son
of Asa, the son of Elkanah, who
lived in the villages of the Netophathites.
17 The gatekeepers:
Shallum, Akkub, Talmon, Ahiman
and their fellow Levites, Shallum
their chief 18 being stationed at the
King's Gate on the east, up to the
present time. These were the gatekeepers belonging to the camp of
the Levites. 19 Shallum son of Kore,
the son of Ebiasaph, the son of
Korah, and his fellow gatekeepers from his family (the Korahites)
were responsible for guarding the
thresholds of the tent just as their
ancestors had been responsible
for guarding the entrance to the
dwelling of the LORD. 20 In earlier
times Phinehas son of Eleazar was
the official in charge of the gatekeepers, and the LORD was with
him. 21 Zechariah son of Meshelemiah was the gatekeeper at the
entrance to the tent of meeting.
22 Altogether, those chosen to be gatekeepers at the thresholds numbered 212.
They were registered by genealogy in
their villages. The gatekeepers had been
assigned to their positions of trust by David and Samuel the seer. 23 They and their
descendants were in charge of guarding
the gates of the house of the LORD — the
house called the tent of meeting. 24 The
gatekeepers were on the four sides: east,
west, north and south. 25 Their fellow Levites in their villages had to come from
time to time and share their duties for
seven-day periods. 26 But the four princi-
pal gatekeepers, who were Levites, were
entrusted with the responsibility for the
rooms and treasuries in the house of God.
27 They would spend the night stationed
around the house of God, because they
had to guard it; and they had charge of
the key for opening it each morning.
28 Some of them were in charge of the
articles used in the temple service; they
counted them when they were brought
in and when they were taken out. 29 Others were assigned to take care of the
furnishings and all the other articles
of the sanctuary, as well as the special
flour and wine, and the olive oil, incense
and spices. 30 But some of the priests
took care of mixing the spices. 31 A Levite named Mattithiah, the firstborn son
of Shallum the Korahite, was entrusted
with the responsibility for baking the offering bread. 32 Some of the Kohathites,
their fellow Levites, were in charge of
preparing for every Sabbath the bread
set out on the table.
33 Those who were musicians, heads of
Levite families, stayed in the rooms of
the temple and were exempt from other
duties because they were responsible for
the work day and night.
34 All these were heads of Levite families, chiefs as listed in their genealogy,
and they lived in Jerusalem.

The Genealogy of Saul

35 Jeiel the father[a] of Gibeon lived in
Gibeon.
His wife's name was Maakah,
36 and his firstborn son was Abdon, followed by Zur, Kish, Baal,
Ner, Nadab, 37 Gedor, Ahio, Zechariah and Mikloth. 38 Mikloth was
the father of Shimeam. They too
lived near their relatives in Jerusalem.
39 Ner was the father of Kish, Kish the
father of Saul, and Saul the father
of Jonathan, Malki-Shua, Abinadab and Esh-Baal.[b]
40 The son of Jonathan:
Merib-Baal,[c] who was the father
of Micah.
41 The sons of Micah:
Pithon, Melek, Tahrea and Ahaz.[d]

[a] 35 *Father* may mean *civic leader* or *military leader.* [b] 39 Also known as *Ish-Bosheth*
[c] 40 Also known as *Mephibosheth* [d] 41 Vulgate and Syriac (see also Septuagint and 8:35); Hebrew does not have *and Ahaz.*

42 Ahaz was the father of Jadah, Jadah[a] was the father of Alemeth,
Azmaveth and Zimri, and Zimri
was the father of Moza. 43 Moza
was the father of Binea; Rephaiah was his son, Eleasah his son
and Azel his son.
44 Azel had six sons, and these were
their names:
Azrikam, Bokeru, Ishmael, Shea-
riah, Obadiah and Hanan. These
were the sons of Azel.

Saul Takes His Life

10 Now the Philistines fought against
Israel; the Israelites fled before
them, and many fell dead on Mount Gilboa. 2 The Philistines were in hot pursuit
of Saul and his sons, and they killed his
sons Jonathan, Abinadab and Malki-
Shua. 3 The fighting grew fierce around
Saul, and when the archers overtook
him, they wounded him.
4 Saul said to his armor-bearer, "Draw
your sword and run me through, or these
uncircumcised fellows will come and
abuse me."
But his armor-bearer was terrified and
would not do it; so Saul took his own
sword and fell on it. 5 When the armor-
bearer saw that Saul was dead, he too
fell on his sword and died. 6 So Saul and
his three sons died, and all his house
died together.
7 When all the Israelites in the valley
saw that the army had fled and that Saul
and his sons had died, they abandoned
their towns and fled. And the Philistines
came and occupied them.
8 The next day, when the Philistines
came to strip the dead, they found Saul
and his sons fallen on Mount Gilboa.
9 They stripped him and took his head
and his armor, and sent messengers
throughout the land of the Philistines
to proclaim the news among their idols
and their people. 10 They put his armor in
the temple of their gods and hung up his
head in the temple of Dagon.
11 When all the inhabitants of Jabesh
Gilead heard what the Philistines had
done to Saul, 12 all their valiant men went
and took the bodies of Saul and his sons
and brought them to Jabesh. Then they
buried their bones under the great tree
in Jabesh, and they fasted seven days.
13 Saul died because he was unfaithful
to the LORD; he did not keep the word of
the LORD and even consulted a medium
for guidance, 14 and did not inquire of the
LORD. So the LORD put him to death and
turned the kingdom over to David son of
Jesse.

David Becomes King Over Israel

11 All Israel came together to David at
Hebron and said, "We are your own
flesh and blood. 2 In the past, even while
Saul was king, you were the one who led
Israel on their military campaigns. And
the LORD your God said to you, 'You will
shepherd my people Israel, and you will
become their ruler.'"
3 When all the elders of Israel had
come to King David at Hebron, he made
a covenant with them at Hebron before
the LORD, and they anointed David king
over Israel, as the LORD had promised
through Samuel.

David Conquers Jerusalem

4 David and all the Israelites marched
to Jerusalem (that is, Jebus). The Jebusites who lived there 5 said to David, "You
will not get in here." Nevertheless, David
captured the fortress of Zion — which is
the City of David.
6 David had said, "Whoever leads the
attack on the Jebusites will become
commander in chief." Joab son of Zeruiah went up first, and so he received the
command.
7 David then took up residence in the
fortress, and so it was called the City of
David. 8 He built up the city around it,
from the terraces[b] to the surrounding
wall, while Joab restored the rest of the
city. 9 And David became more and more
powerful, because the LORD Almighty
was with him.

David's Mighty Warriors

10 These were the chiefs of David's
mighty warriors — they, together with
all Israel, gave his kingship strong support to extend it over the whole land, as
the LORD had promised — 11 this is the list
of David's mighty warriors:
Jashobeam,[c] a Hakmonite, was chief
of the officers[d]; he raised his spear
against three hundred men, whom he
killed in one encounter.
12 Next to him was Eleazar son of Dodai the Ahohite, one of the three mighty
warriors. 13 He was with David at Pas
Dammim when the Philistines gathered

[a] *42* Some Hebrew manuscripts and Septuagint (see also 8:36); most Hebrew manuscripts *Jarah, Jarah* [b] *8* Or *the Millo* [c] *11* Possibly a variant of *Jashob-Baal* [d] *11* Or *Thirty*; some Septuagint manuscripts *Three* (see also 2 Samuel 23:8)

there for battle. At a place where there
was a field full of barley, the troops fled
from the Philistines. [14]But they took their
stand in the middle of the field. They
defended it and struck the Philistines
down, and the LORD brought about a
great victory.

[15]Three of the thirty chiefs came down
to David to the rock at the cave of Adullam, while a band of Philistines was encamped in the Valley of Rephaim. [16]At
that time David was in the stronghold,
and the Philistine garrison was at Bethlehem. [17]David longed for water and
said, "Oh, that someone would get me
a drink of water from the well near the
gate of Bethlehem!" [18]So the Three broke
through the Philistine lines, drew water
from the well near the gate of Bethlehem and carried it back to David. But he
refused to drink it; instead, he poured
it out to the LORD. [19]"God forbid that I
should do this!" he said. "Should I drink
the blood of these men who went at the
risk of their lives?" Because they risked
their lives to bring it back, David would
not drink it.

Such were the exploits of the three
mighty warriors.

[20]Abishai the brother of Joab was chief
of the Three. He raised his spear against
three hundred men, whom he killed,
and so he became as famous as the
Three. [21]He was doubly honored above
the Three and became their commander, even though he was not included
among them.

[22]Benaiah son of Jehoiada, a valiant
fighter from Kabzeel, performed great
exploits. He struck down Moab's two
mightiest warriors. He also went down
into a pit on a snowy day and killed a
lion. [23]And he struck down an Egyptian
who was five cubits[a] tall. Although the
Egyptian had a spear like a weaver's rod
in his hand, Benaiah went against him
with a club. He snatched the spear from
the Egyptian's hand and killed him with
his own spear. [24]Such were the exploits
of Benaiah son of Jehoiada; he too was
as famous as the three mighty warriors.
[25]He was held in greater honor than any
of the Thirty, but he was not included
among the Three. And David put him in
charge of his bodyguard.

[26]The mighty warriors were:
Asahel the brother of Joab,
Elhanan son of Dodo from Bethlehem,
[27]Shammoth the Harorite,
Helez the Pelonite,
[28]Ira son of Ikkesh from Tekoa,
Abiezer from Anathoth,
[29]Sibbekai the Hushathite,
Ilai the Ahohite,
[30]Maharai the Netophathite,
Heled son of Baanah the Netophathite,
[31]Ithai son of Ribai from Gibeah in Benjamin,
Benaiah the Pirathonite,
[32]Hurai from the ravines of Gaash,
Abiel the Arbathite,
[33]Azmaveth the Baharumite,
Eliahba the Shaalbonite,
[34]the sons of Hashem the Gizonite,
Jonathan son of Shagee the Hararite,
[35]Ahiam son of Sakar the Hararite,
Eliphal son of Ur,
[36]Hepher the Mekerathite,
Ahijah the Pelonite,
[37]Hezro the Carmelite,
Naarai son of Ezbai,
[38]Joel the brother of Nathan,
Mibhar son of Hagri,
[39]Zelek the Ammonite,
Naharai the Berothite, the armor-bearer of Joab son of Zeruiah,
[40]Ira the Ithrite,
Gareb the Ithrite,
[41]Uriah the Hittite,
Zabad son of Ahlai,
[42]Adina son of Shiza the Reubenite, who was chief of the Reubenites, and the thirty with him,
[43]Hanan son of Maakah,
Joshaphat the Mithnite,
[44]Uzzia the Ashterathite,
Shama and Jeiel the sons of Hotham the Aroerite,
[45]Jediael son of Shimri,
his brother Joha the Tizite,
[46]Eliel the Mahavite,
Jeribai and Joshaviah the sons of Elnaam,
Ithmah the Moabite,
[47]Eliel, Obed and Jaasiel the Mezobaite.

Warriors Join David

12 These were the men who came to
David at Ziklag, while he was banished from the presence of Saul son of
Kish (they were among the warriors who
helped him in battle; [2]they were armed
with bows and were able to shoot arrows or to sling stones right-handed or

[a] *23* That is, about 7 feet 6 inches or about 2.3 meters

left-handed; they were relatives of Saul from the tribe of Benjamin):

[3]Ahiezer their chief and Joash the sons of Shemaah the Gibeathite; Jeziel and Pelet the sons of Azmaveth; Berakah, Jehu the Anathothite, [4]and Ishmaiah the Gibeonite, a mighty warrior among the Thirty, who was a leader of the Thirty; Jeremiah, Jahaziel, Johanan, Jozabad the Gederathite,[a] [5]Eluzai, Jerimoth, Bealiah, Shemariah and Shephatiah the Haruphite; [6]Elkanah, Ishiah, Azarel, Joezer and Jashobeam the Korahites; [7]and Joelah and Zebadiah the sons of Jeroham from Gedor.

[8]Some Gadites defected to David at his stronghold in the wilderness. They were brave warriors, ready for battle and able to handle the shield and spear. Their faces were the faces of lions, and they were as swift as gazelles in the mountains.

9 Ezer was the chief,
Obadiah the second in command, Eliab the third,
10 Mishmannah the fourth, Jeremiah the fifth,
11 Attai the sixth, Eliel the seventh,
12 Johanan the eighth, Elzabad the ninth,
13 Jeremiah the tenth and Makbannai the eleventh.

[14]These Gadites were army commanders; the least was a match for a hundred, and the greatest for a thousand. [15]It was they who crossed the Jordan in the first month when it was overflowing all its banks, and they put to flight everyone living in the valleys, to the east and to the west.

[16]Other Benjamites and some men from Judah also came to David in his stronghold. [17]David went out to meet them and said to them, "If you have come to me in peace to help me, I am ready for you to join me. But if you have come to betray me to my enemies when my hands are free from violence, may the God of our ancestors see it and judge you."

[18]Then the Spirit came on Amasai, chief of the Thirty, and he said:

"We are yours, David!
We are with you, son of Jesse!
Success, success to you,
and success to those who help you,
for your God will help you."

So David received them and made them leaders of his raiding bands.

[19]Some of the tribe of Manasseh defected to David when he went with the Philistines to fight against Saul. (He and his men did not help the Philistines because, after consultation, their rulers sent him away. They said, "It will cost us our heads if he deserts to his master Saul.") [20]When David went to Ziklag, these were the men of Manasseh who defected to him: Adnah, Jozabad, Jediael, Michael, Jozabad, Elihu and Zillethai, leaders of units of a thousand in Manasseh. [21]They helped David against raiding bands, for all of them were brave warriors, and they were commanders in his army. [22]Day after day men came to help David, until he had a great army, like the army of God.[b]

Others Join David at Hebron

[23]These are the numbers of the men armed for battle who came to David at Hebron to turn Saul's kingdom over to him, as the LORD had said:

24 from Judah, carrying shield and spear — 6,800 armed for battle;
25 from Simeon, warriors ready for battle — 7,100;
26 from Levi — 4,600, [27]including Jehoiada, leader of the family of Aaron, with 3,700 men, [28]and Zadok, a brave young warrior, with 22 officers from his family;
29 from Benjamin, Saul's tribe — 3,000, most of whom had remained loyal to Saul's house until then;
30 from Ephraim, brave warriors, famous in their own clans — 20,800;
31 from half the tribe of Manasseh, designated by name to come and make David king — 18,000;
32 from Issachar, men who understood the times and knew what Israel should do — 200 chiefs, with all their relatives under their command;
33 from Zebulun, experienced soldiers prepared for battle with every type of weapon, to help David with undivided loyalty — 50,000;
34 from Naphtali — 1,000 officers, together with 37,000 men carrying shields and spears;
35 from Dan, ready for battle — 28,600;
36 from Asher, experienced soldiers prepared for battle — 40,000;

[a] 4 In Hebrew texts the second half of this verse (*Jeremiah . . . Gederathite*) is numbered 12:5, and 12:5-40 is numbered 12:6-41. [b] 22 Or *a great and mighty army*

37 and from east of the Jordan, from
Reuben, Gad and the half-tribe of
Manasseh, armed with every type
of weapon — 120,000.
38 All these were fighting men who
volunteered to serve in the ranks. They
came to Hebron fully determined to
make David king over all Israel. All the
rest of the Israelites were also of one
mind to make David king. 39 The men
spent three days there with David, eating and drinking, for their families had
supplied provisions for them. 40 Also,
their neighbors from as far away as Issachar, Zebulun and Naphtali came bringing food on donkeys, camels, mules and
oxen. There were plentiful supplies of
flour, fig cakes, raisin cakes, wine, olive
oil, cattle and sheep, for there was joy in
Israel.

Bringing Back the Ark

13 David conferred with each of his
officers, the commanders of thousands and commanders of hundreds.
2 He then said to the whole assembly
of Israel, "If it seems good to you and
if it is the will of the LORD our God, let
us send word far and wide to the rest of
our people throughout the territories of
Israel, and also to the priests and Levites who are with them in their towns
and pasturelands, to come and join us.
3 Let us bring the ark of our God back to
us, for we did not inquire of[a] it[b] during
the reign of Saul." 4 The whole assembly agreed to do this, because it seemed
right to all the people.
5 So David assembled all Israel, from
the Shihor River in Egypt to Lebo Hamath, to bring the ark of God from Kiriath Jearim. 6 David and all Israel went
to Baalah of Judah (Kiriath Jearim) to
bring up from there the ark of God the
LORD, who is enthroned between the
cherubim — the ark that is called by the
Name.
7 They moved the ark of God from
Abinadab's house on a new cart, with
Uzzah and Ahio guiding it. 8 David and
all the Israelites were celebrating with
all their might before God, with songs
and with harps, lyres, timbrels, cymbals
and trumpets.
9 When they came to the threshing
floor of Kidon, Uzzah reached out his
hand to steady the ark, because the oxen
stumbled. 10 The LORD's anger burned
against Uzzah, and he struck him down
because he had put his hand on the ark.
So he died there before God.
11 Then David was angry because the
LORD's wrath had broken out against Uzzah, and to this day that place is called
Perez Uzzah.[c]
12 David was afraid of God that day and
asked, "How can I ever bring the ark of
God to me?" 13 He did not take the ark to
be with him in the City of David. Instead,
he took it to the house of Obed-Edom the
Gittite. 14 The ark of God remained with
the family of Obed-Edom in his house for
three months, and the LORD blessed his
household and everything he had.

David's House and Family

14 Now Hiram king of Tyre sent messengers to David, along with cedar
logs, stonemasons and carpenters to
build a palace for him. 2 And David knew
that the LORD had established him as
king over Israel and that his kingdom
had been highly exalted for the sake of
his people Israel.
3 In Jerusalem David took more wives
and became the father of more sons and
daughters. 4 These are the names of the
children born to him there: Shammua,
Shobab, Nathan, Solomon, 5 Ibhar, Elishua, Elpelet, 6 Nogah, Nepheg, Japhia,
7 Elishama, Beeliada[d] and Eliphelet.

David Defeats the Philistines

8 When the Philistines heard that David had been anointed king over all Israel, they went up in full force to search for
him, but David heard about it and went
out to meet them. 9 Now the Philistines
had come and raided the Valley of Rephaim; 10 so David inquired of God: "Shall
I go and attack the Philistines? Will you
deliver them into my hands?"
The LORD answered him, "Go, I will deliver them into your hands."
11 So David and his men went up to
Baal Perazim, and there he defeated
them. He said, "As waters break out, God
has broken out against my enemies by
my hand." So that place was called Baal
Perazim.[e] 12 The Philistines had abandoned their gods there, and David gave
orders to burn them in the fire.
13 Once more the Philistines raided the
valley; 14 so David inquired of God again,
and God answered him, "Do not go directly after them, but circle around them
and attack them in front of the poplar
trees. 15 As soon as you hear the sound of

[a] 3 Or *we neglected* [b] 3 Or *him* [c] 11 *Perez Uzzah* means *outbreak against Uzzah.*
[d] 7 A variant of *Eliada* [e] 11 *Baal Perazim* means *the lord who breaks out.*

marching in the tops of the poplar trees,
move out to battle, because that will
mean God has gone out in front of you
to strike the Philistine army.” 16 So David
did as God commanded him, and they
struck down the Philistine army, all the
way from Gibeon to Gezer.
17 So David’s fame spread throughout
every land, and the LORD made all the
nations fear him.

The Ark Brought to Jerusalem

15 After David had constructed buildings for himself in the City of David, he prepared a place for the ark of
God and pitched a tent for it. 2 Then David said, “No one but the Levites may
carry the ark of God, because the LORD
chose them to carry the ark of the LORD
and to minister before him forever.”
3 David assembled all Israel in Jerusalem to bring up the ark of the LORD
to the place he had prepared for it. 4 He
called together the descendants of Aaron
and the Levites:
5 From the descendants of Kohath,
Uriel the leader and 120 relatives;
6 from the descendants of Merari,
Asaiah the leader and 220 relatives;
7 from the descendants of Gershon,[a]
Joel the leader and 130 relatives;
8 from the descendants of Elizaphan,
Shemaiah the leader and 200 relatives;
9 from the descendants of Hebron,
Eliel the leader and 80 relatives;
10 from the descendants of Uzziel,
Amminadab the leader and 112
relatives.
11 Then David summoned Zadok and
Abiathar the priests, and Uriel, Asaiah,
Joel, Shemaiah, Eliel and Amminadab
the Levites. 12 He said to them, “You are
the heads of the Levitical families; you
and your fellow Levites are to consecrate yourselves and bring up the ark of
the LORD, the God of Israel, to the place
I have prepared for it. 13 It was because
you, the Levites, did not bring it up the
first time that the LORD our God broke
out in anger against us. We did not inquire of him about how to do it in the
prescribed way.” 14 So the priests and Levites consecrated themselves in order to
bring up the ark of the LORD, the God of
Israel. 15 And the Levites carried the ark
of God with the poles on their shoulders,
as Moses had commanded in accordance
with the word of the LORD.
16 David told the leaders of the Levites to
appoint their fellow Levites as musicians
to make a joyful sound with musical instruments: lyres, harps and cymbals.
17 So the Levites appointed Heman son
of Joel; from his relatives, Asaph son of
Berekiah; and from their relatives the
Merarites, Ethan son of Kushaiah; 18 and
with them their relatives next in rank:
Zechariah,[b] Jaaziel, Shemiramoth, Jehiel, Unni, Eliab, Benaiah, Maaseiah,
Mattithiah, Eliphelehu, Mikneiah, Obed-
Edom and Jeiel,[c] the gatekeepers.
19 The musicians Heman, Asaph and
Ethan were to sound the bronze cymbals;
20 Zechariah, Jaaziel,[d] Shemiramoth, Jehiel, Unni, Eliab, Maaseiah and Benaiah
were to play the lyres according to *alamoth*,[e] 21 and Mattithiah, Eliphelehu, Mikneiah, Obed-Edom, Jeiel and Azaziah were
to play the harps, directing according to
sheminith.[e] 22 Kenaniah the head Levite
was in charge of the singing; that was his
responsibility because he was skillful at it.
23 Berekiah and Elkanah were to be
doorkeepers for the ark. 24 Shebaniah,
Joshaphat, Nethanel, Amasai, Zechariah, Benaiah and Eliezer the priests were
to blow trumpets before the ark of God.
Obed-Edom and Jehiah were also to be
doorkeepers for the ark.
25 So David and the elders of Israel and
the commanders of units of a thousand
went to bring up the ark of the covenant
of the LORD from the house of Obed-
Edom, with rejoicing. 26 Because God
had helped the Levites who were carrying the ark of the covenant of the LORD,
seven bulls and seven rams were sacrificed. 27 Now David was clothed in a robe
of fine linen, as were all the Levites who
were carrying the ark, and as were the
musicians, and Kenaniah, who was in
charge of the singing of the choirs. David
also wore a linen ephod. 28 So all Israel
brought up the ark of the covenant of the
LORD with shouts, with the sounding of
rams’ horns and trumpets, and of cymbals, and the playing of lyres and harps.
29 As the ark of the covenant of the
LORD was entering the City of David, Michal daughter of Saul watched from a
window. And when she saw King David
dancing and celebrating, she despised
him in her heart.

[a] *7* Hebrew *Gershom*, a variant of *Gershon* [b] *18* Three Hebrew manuscripts and most Septuagint manuscripts (see also verse 20 and 16:5); most Hebrew manuscripts *Zechariah son and* or *Zechariah, Ben and* [c] *18* Hebrew; Septuagint (see also verse 21) *Jeiel and Azaziah*
[d] *20* See verse 18; Hebrew *Aziel*, a variant of *Jaaziel*. [e] *20,21* Probably a musical term

Ministering Before the Ark

16 They brought the ark of God and
set it inside the tent that David had
pitched for it, and they presented burnt
offerings and fellowship offerings before
God. 2 After David had finished sacrificing the burnt offerings and fellowship
offerings, he blessed the people in the
name of the LORD. 3 Then he gave a loaf of
bread, a cake of dates and a cake of raisins to each Israelite man and woman.

4 He appointed some of the Levites to
minister before the ark of the LORD, to
extol,[a] thank, and praise the LORD, the
God of Israel: 5 Asaph was the chief, and
next to him in rank were Zechariah, then
Jaaziel,[b] Shemiramoth, Jehiel, Mattithiah, Eliab, Benaiah, Obed-Edom and Jeiel. They were to play the lyres and harps,
Asaph was to sound the cymbals, 6 and
Benaiah and Jahaziel the priests were to
blow the trumpets regularly before the
ark of the covenant of God.

7 That day David first appointed Asaph
and his associates to give praise to the
LORD in this manner:

8 Give praise to the LORD, proclaim his name;
make known among the nations what he has done.
9 Sing to him, sing praise to him;
tell of all his wonderful acts.
10 Glory in his holy name;
let the hearts of those who seek the LORD rejoice.
11 Look to the LORD and his strength;
seek his face always.

12 Remember the wonders he has done,
his miracles, and the judgments he pronounced,
13 you his servants, the descendants of Israel,
his chosen ones, the children of Jacob.
14 He is the LORD our God;
his judgments are in all the earth.

15 He remembers[c] his covenant forever,
the promise he made, for a thousand generations,
16 the covenant he made with Abraham,
the oath he swore to Isaac.
17 He confirmed it to Jacob as a decree,
to Israel as an everlasting covenant:
18 "To you I will give the land of Canaan
as the portion you will inherit."

19 When they were but few in number,
few indeed, and strangers in it,
20 they[d] wandered from nation to nation,
from one kingdom to another.
21 He allowed no one to oppress them;
for their sake he rebuked kings:
22 "Do not touch my anointed ones;
do my prophets no harm."

23 Sing to the LORD, all the earth;
proclaim his salvation day after day.
24 Declare his glory among the nations,
his marvelous deeds among all peoples.
25 For great is the LORD and most worthy of praise;
he is to be feared above all gods.
26 For all the gods of the nations are idols,
but the LORD made the heavens.
27 Splendor and majesty are before him;
strength and joy are in his dwelling place.

28 Ascribe to the LORD, all you families of nations,
ascribe to the LORD glory and strength.
29 Ascribe to the LORD the glory due his name;
bring an offering and come before him.
Worship the LORD in the splendor of his[e] holiness.
30 Tremble before him, all the earth!
The world is firmly established; it cannot be moved.

31 Let the heavens rejoice, let the earth be glad;
let them say among the nations,
"The LORD reigns!"
32 Let the sea resound, and all that is in it;
let the fields be jubilant, and everything in them!
33 Let the trees of the forest sing,
let them sing for joy before the LORD,
for he comes to judge the earth.

34 Give thanks to the LORD, for he is good;
his love endures forever.

[a] 4 Or *petition*; or *invoke* [b] 5 See 15:18,20; Hebrew *Jeiel*, possibly another name for *Jaaziel*.
[c] 15 Some Septuagint manuscripts (see also Psalm 105:8); Hebrew *Remember*
[d] 18-20 One Hebrew manuscript, Septuagint and Vulgate (see also Psalm 105:12); most Hebrew manuscripts *inherit*, / [19]*though you are but few in number, / few indeed, and strangers in it."* / [20]*They* [e] 29 Or *LORD with the splendor of*

35Cry out, "Save us, God our Savior;
gather us and deliver us from the
nations,
that we may give thanks to your holy
name,
and glory in your praise."
36Praise be to the LORD, the God of Israel,
from everlasting to everlasting.

Then all the people said "Amen" and
"Praise the LORD."

37David left Asaph and his associates
before the ark of the covenant of the
LORD to minister there regularly, according to each day's requirements. 38He also
left Obed-Edom and his sixty-eight associates to minister with them. Obed-Edom
son of Jeduthun, and also Hosah, were
gatekeepers.
39David left Zadok the priest and his
fellow priests before the tabernacle of
the LORD at the high place in Gibeon
40to present burnt offerings to the LORD
on the altar of burnt offering regularly, morning and evening, in accordance
with everything written in the Law of the
LORD, which he had given Israel. 41With
them were Heman and Jeduthun and
the rest of those chosen and designated by name to give thanks to the LORD,
"for his love endures forever." 42Heman
and Jeduthun were responsible for the
sounding of the trumpets and cymbals
and for the playing of the other instruments for sacred song. The sons of Jeduthun were stationed at the gate.
43Then all the people left, each for
their own home, and David returned
home to bless his family.

God's Promise to David

17 After David was settled in his palace, he said to Nathan the prophet,
"Here I am, living in a house of cedar,
while the ark of the covenant of the LORD
is under a tent."
2Nathan replied to David, "Whatever
you have in mind, do it, for God is with
you."
3But that night the word of God came
to Nathan, saying:

4"Go and tell my servant David,
'This is what the LORD says: You
are not the one to build me a house
to dwell in. 5I have not dwelt in a
house from the day I brought Israel
up out of Egypt to this day. I have
moved from one tent site to another,
from one dwelling place to another.
6Wherever I have moved with all the
Israelites, did I ever say to any of
their leaders[a] whom I commanded
to shepherd my people, "Why have
you not built me a house of cedar?"'
7"Now then, tell my servant David, 'This is what the LORD Almighty
says: I took you from the pasture,
from tending the flock, and appointed you ruler over my people
Israel. 8I have been with you wherever you have gone, and I have cut
off all your enemies from before
you. Now I will make your name
like the names of the greatest men
on earth. 9And I will provide a place
for my people Israel and will plant
them so that they can have a home
of their own and no longer be disturbed. Wicked people will not oppress them anymore, as they did at
the beginning 10and have done ever
since the time I appointed leaders
over my people Israel. I will also
subdue all your enemies.
"'I declare to you that the LORD
will build a house for you: 11When
your days are over and you go to be
with your ancestors, I will raise up
your offspring to succeed you, one
of your own sons, and I will establish his kingdom. 12He is the one who
will build a house for me, and I will
establish his throne forever. 13I will
be his father, and he will be my son.
I will never take my love away from
him, as I took it away from your
predecessor. 14I will set him over my
house and my kingdom forever; his
throne will be established forever.'"

15Nathan reported to David all the
words of this entire revelation.

David's Prayer

16Then King David went in and sat before the LORD, and he said:

"Who am I, LORD God, and what
is my family, that you have brought
me this far? 17And as if this were not
enough in your sight, my God, you
have spoken about the future of the
house of your servant. You, LORD
God, have looked on me as though I
were the most exalted of men.
18"What more can David say to
you for honoring your servant? For
you know your servant, 19LORD. For
the sake of your servant and according to your will, you have done this
great thing and made known all
these great promises.

[a] 6 Traditionally *judges*; also in verse 10

20“There is no one like you, LORD, and there is no God but you, as we have heard with our own ears. 21And who is like your people Israel—the one nation on earth whose God went out to redeem a people for himself, and to make a name for yourself, and to perform great and awesome wonders by driving out nations from before your people, whom you redeemed from Egypt? 22You made your people Israel your very own forever, and you, LORD, have become their God.

23“And now, LORD, let the promise you have made concerning your servant and his house be established forever. Do as you promised, 24so that it will be established and that your name will be great forever. Then people will say, ‘The LORD Almighty, the God over Israel, is Israel’s God!’ And the house of your servant David will be established before you.

25“You, my God, have revealed to your servant that you will build a house for him. So your servant has found courage to pray to you. 26You, LORD, are God! You have promised these good things to your servant. 27Now you have been pleased to bless the house of your servant, that it may continue forever in your sight; for you, LORD, have blessed it, and it will be blessed forever.”

David’s Victories

18 In the course of time, David defeated the Philistines and subdued them, and he took Gath and its surrounding villages from the control of the Philistines.

2David also defeated the Moabites, and they became subject to him and brought him tribute.

3Moreover, David defeated Hadadezer king of Zobah, in the vicinity of Hamath, when he went to set up his monument at[a] the Euphrates River. 4David captured a thousand of his chariots, seven thousand charioteers and twenty thousand foot soldiers. He hamstrung all but a hundred of the chariot horses.

5When the Arameans of Damascus came to help Hadadezer king of Zobah, David struck down twenty-two thousand of them. 6He put garrisons in the Aramean kingdom of Damascus, and the Arameans became subject to him and brought him tribute. The LORD gave David victory wherever he went.

7David took the gold shields carried by the officers of Hadadezer and brought them to Jerusalem. 8From Tebah[b] and Kun, towns that belonged to Hadadezer, David took a great quantity of bronze, which Solomon used to make the bronze Sea, the pillars and various bronze articles.

9When Tou king of Hamath heard that David had defeated the entire army of Hadadezer king of Zobah, 10he sent his son Hadoram to King David to greet him and congratulate him on his victory in battle over Hadadezer, who had been at war with Tou. Hadoram brought all kinds of articles of gold, of silver and of bronze.

11King David dedicated these articles to the LORD, as he had done with the silver and gold he had taken from all these nations: Edom and Moab, the Ammonites and the Philistines, and Amalek.

12Abishai son of Zeruiah struck down eighteen thousand Edomites in the Valley of Salt. 13He put garrisons in Edom, and all the Edomites became subject to David. The LORD gave David victory wherever he went.

David’s Officials

14David reigned over all Israel, doing what was just and right for all his people. 15Joab son of Zeruiah was over the army; Jehoshaphat son of Ahilud was recorder; 16Zadok son of Ahitub and Ahimelek[c] son of Abiathar were priests; Shavsha was secretary; 17Benaiah son of Jehoiada was over the Kerethites and Pelethites; and David’s sons were chief officials at the king’s side.

David Defeats the Ammonites

19 In the course of time, Nahash king of the Ammonites died, and his son succeeded him as king. 2David thought, “I will show kindness to Hanun son of Nahash, because his father showed kindness to me.” So David sent a delegation to express his sympathy to Hanun concerning his father.

When David’s envoys came to Hanun in the land of the Ammonites to express sympathy to him, 3the Ammonite commanders said to Hanun, “Do you think David is honoring your father by sending envoys to you to express sympathy?

[a] 3 Or *to restore his control over* [b] 8 Hebrew *Tibhath*, a variant of *Tebah* [c] 16 Some Hebrew manuscripts, Vulgate and Syriac (see also 2 Samuel 8:17); most Hebrew manuscripts *Abimelek*

Haven't his envoys come to you only to explore and spy out the country and overthrow it?" 4So Hanun seized David's envoys, shaved them, cut off their garments at the buttocks, and sent them away.

5When someone came and told David about the men, he sent messengers to meet them, for they were greatly humiliated. The king said, "Stay at Jericho till your beards have grown, and then come back."

6When the Ammonites realized that they had become obnoxious to David, Hanun and the Ammonites sent a thousand talents[a] of silver to hire chariots and charioteers from Aram Naharaim,[b] Aram Maakah and Zobah. 7They hired thirty-two thousand chariots and charioteers, as well as the king of Maakah with his troops, who came and camped near Medeba, while the Ammonites were mustered from their towns and moved out for battle.

8On hearing this, David sent Joab out with the entire army of fighting men. 9The Ammonites came out and drew up in battle formation at the entrance to their city, while the kings who had come were by themselves in the open country.

10Joab saw that there were battle lines in front of him and behind him; so he selected some of the best troops in Israel and deployed them against the Arameans. 11He put the rest of the men under the command of Abishai his brother, and they were deployed against the Ammonites. 12Joab said, "If the Arameans are too strong for me, then you are to rescue me; but if the Ammonites are too strong for you, then I will rescue you. 13Be strong, and let us fight bravely for our people and the cities of our God. The LORD will do what is good in his sight."

14Then Joab and the troops with him advanced to fight the Arameans, and they fled before him. 15When the Ammonites realized that the Arameans were fleeing, they too fled before his brother Abishai and went inside the city. So Joab went back to Jerusalem.

16After the Arameans saw that they had been routed by Israel, they sent messengers and had Arameans brought from beyond the Euphrates River, with Shophak the commander of Hadadezer's army leading them.

17When David was told of this, he gathered all Israel and crossed the Jordan; he advanced against them and formed his battle lines opposite them. David formed his lines to meet the Arameans in battle, and they fought against him. 18But they fled before Israel, and David killed seven thousand of their charioteers and forty thousand of their foot soldiers. He also killed Shophak the commander of their army.

19When the vassals of Hadadezer saw that they had been routed by Israel, they made peace with David and became subject to him.

So the Arameans were not willing to help the Ammonites anymore.

The Capture of Rabbah

20 In the spring, at the time when kings go off to war, Joab led out the armed forces. He laid waste the land of the Ammonites and went to Rabbah and besieged it, but David remained in Jerusalem. Joab attacked Rabbah and left it in ruins. 2David took the crown from the head of their king[c] — its weight was found to be a talent[d] of gold, and it was set with precious stones — and it was placed on David's head. He took a great quantity of plunder from the city 3and brought out the people who were there, consigning them to labor with saws and with iron picks and axes. David did this to all the Ammonite towns. Then David and his entire army returned to Jerusalem.

War With the Philistines

4In the course of time, war broke out with the Philistines, at Gezer. At that time Sibbekai the Hushathite killed Sippai, one of the descendants of the Rephaites, and the Philistines were subjugated.

5In another battle with the Philistines, Elhanan son of Jair killed Lahmi the brother of Goliath the Gittite, who had a spear with a shaft like a weaver's rod.

6In still another battle, which took place at Gath, there was a huge man with six fingers on each hand and six toes on each foot — twenty-four in all. He also was descended from Rapha. 7When he taunted Israel, Jonathan son of Shimea, David's brother, killed him.

8These were descendants of Rapha in Gath, and they fell at the hands of David and his men.

[a] 6 That is, about 38 tons or about 34 metric tons [b] 6 That is, Northwest Mesopotamia
[c] 2 Or *of Milkom*, that is, Molek [d] 2 That is, about 75 pounds or about 34 kilograms

David Counts the Fighting Men

21 Satan rose up against Israel and
incited David to take a census of Israel. 2So David said to Joab and the commanders of the troops, "Go and count the
Israelites from Beersheba to Dan. Then
report back to me so that I may know
how many there are."
3But Joab replied, "May the LORD multiply his troops a hundred times over. My
lord the king, are they not all my lord's
subjects? Why does my lord want to do
this? Why should he bring guilt on Israel?"
4The king's word, however, overruled
Joab; so Joab left and went throughout
Israel and then came back to Jerusalem.
5Joab reported the number of the fighting men to David: In all Israel there were
one million one hundred thousand men
who could handle a sword, including
four hundred and seventy thousand in
Judah.
6But Joab did not include Levi and
Benjamin in the numbering, because
the king's command was repulsive to
him. 7This command was also evil in the
sight of God; so he punished Israel.
8Then David said to God, "I have
sinned greatly by doing this. Now, I beg
you, take away the guilt of your servant.
I have done a very foolish thing."
9The LORD said to Gad, David's seer,
10"Go and tell David, 'This is what the
LORD says: I am giving you three options. Choose one of them for me to carry
out against you.'"
11So Gad went to David and said to
him, "This is what the LORD says: 'Take
your choice: 12three years of famine,
three months of being swept away[a] before your enemies, with their swords
overtaking you, or three days of the
sword of the LORD—days of plague in
the land, with the angel of the LORD rav-
aging every part of Israel.' Now then,
decide how I should answer the one who
sent me."
13David said to Gad, "I am in deep distress. Let me fall into the hands of the
LORD, for his mercy is very great; but do
not let me fall into human hands."
14So the LORD sent a plague on Israel, and seventy thousand men of Israel fell dead. 15And God sent an angel to
destroy Jerusalem. But as the angel was
doing so, the LORD saw it and relented
concerning the disaster and said to the
angel who was destroying the people,
"Enough! Withdraw your hand." The angel of the LORD was then standing at the
threshing floor of Araunah[b] the Jebusite.
16David looked up and saw the angel
of the LORD standing between heaven
and earth, with a drawn sword in his
hand extended over Jerusalem. Then
David and the elders, clothed in sackcloth, fell facedown.
17David said to God, "Was it not I who
ordered the fighting men to be counted?
I, the shepherd,[c] have sinned and done
wrong. These are but sheep. What have
they done? LORD my God, let your hand
fall on me and my family, but do not let
this plague remain on your people."

David Builds an Altar

18Then the angel of the LORD ordered
Gad to tell David to go up and build an
altar to the LORD on the threshing floor
of Araunah the Jebusite. 19So David went
up in obedience to the word that Gad
had spoken in the name of the LORD.
20While Araunah was threshing
wheat, he turned and saw the angel; his
four sons who were with him hid themselves. 21Then David approached, and
when Araunah looked and saw him, he
left the threshing floor and bowed down
before David with his face to the ground.
22David said to him, "Let me have the
site of your threshing floor so I can build
an altar to the LORD, that the plague on
the people may be stopped. Sell it to me
at the full price."
23Araunah said to David, "Take it! Let
my lord the king do whatever pleases
him. Look, I will give the oxen for the
burnt offerings, the threshing sledges for
the wood, and the wheat for the grain offering. I will give all this."
24But King David replied to Araunah,
"No, I insist on paying the full price. I
will not take for the LORD what is yours,
or sacrifice a burnt offering that costs
me nothing."
25So David paid Araunah six hundred
shekels[d] of gold for the site. 26David built
an altar to the LORD there and sacrificed
burnt offerings and fellowship offerings.
He called on the LORD, and the LORD answered him with fire from heaven on the
altar of burnt offering.
27Then the LORD spoke to the angel, and he put his sword back into its

[a] 12 Hebrew; Septuagint and Vulgate (see also 2 Samuel 24:13) *of fleeing* [b] 15 Hebrew *Ornan*, a variant of *Araunah*; also in verses 18-28 [c] 17 Probable reading of the original Hebrew text (see 2 Samuel 24:17 and note); Masoretic Text does not have *the shepherd*. [d] 25 That is, about 15 pounds or about 6.9 kilograms

sheath. 28At that time, when David saw
that the LORD had answered him on the
threshing floor of Araunah the Jebusite,
he offered sacrifices there. 29The tabernacle of the LORD, which Moses had
made in the wilderness, and the altar of
burnt offering were at that time on the
high place at Gibeon. 30But David could
not go before it to inquire of God, because he was afraid of the sword of the
angel of the LORD.

22 Then David said, "The house of the
LORD God is to be here, and also
the altar of burnt offering for Israel."

Preparations for the Temple

2So David gave orders to assemble the
foreigners residing in Israel, and from
among them he appointed stonecutters
to prepare dressed stone for building
the house of God. 3He provided a large
amount of iron to make nails for the
doors of the gateways and for the fit-
tings, and more bronze than could be
weighed. 4He also provided more cedar
logs than could be counted, for the Sidonians and Tyrians had brought large
numbers of them to David.

5David said, "My son Solomon is young
and inexperienced, and the house to be
built for the LORD should be of great
magnificence and fame and splendor in
the sight of all the nations. Therefore I
will make preparations for it." So David
made extensive preparations before his
death.

6Then he called for his son Solomon
and charged him to build a house for
the LORD, the God of Israel. 7David said
to Solomon: "My son, I had it in my
heart to build a house for the Name of
the LORD my God. 8But this word of the
LORD came to me: 'You have shed much
blood and have fought many wars. You
are not to build a house for my Name,
because you have shed much blood on
the earth in my sight. 9But you will have
a son who will be a man of peace and
rest, and I will give him rest from all his
enemies on every side. His name will be
Solomon,[a] and I will grant Israel peace
and quiet during his reign. 10He is the
one who will build a house for my Name.
He will be my son, and I will be his father. And I will establish the throne of his
kingdom over Israel forever.'

11"Now, my son, the LORD be with you,
and may you have success and build the
house of the LORD your God, as he said
you would. 12May the LORD give you discretion and understanding when he puts
you in command over Israel, so that you
may keep the law of the LORD your God.
13Then you will have success if you are
careful to observe the decrees and laws
that the LORD gave Moses for Israel. Be
strong and courageous. Do not be afraid
or discouraged.

14"I have taken great pains to provide
for the temple of the LORD a hundred
thousand talents[b] of gold, a million talents[c] of silver, quantities of bronze and
iron too great to be weighed, and wood
and stone. And you may add to them.
15You have many workers: stonecutters,
masons and carpenters, as well as those
skilled in every kind of work 16in gold
and silver, bronze and iron — craftsmen
beyond number. Now begin the work,
and the LORD be with you."

17Then David ordered all the leaders
of Israel to help his son Solomon. 18He
said to them, "Is not the LORD your God
with you? And has he not granted you
rest on every side? For he has given the
inhabitants of the land into my hands,
and the land is subject to the LORD and
to his people. 19Now devote your heart
and soul to seeking the LORD your God.
Begin to build the sanctuary of the LORD
God, so that you may bring the ark of
the covenant of the LORD and the sacred articles belonging to God into the
temple that will be built for the Name
of the LORD."

The Levites

23 When David was old and full of
years, he made his son Solomon
king over Israel.

2He also gathered together all the
leaders of Israel, as well as the priests
and Levites. 3The Levites thirty years
old or more were counted, and the total
number of men was thirty-eight thousand. 4David said, "Of these, twenty-four
thousand are to be in charge of the work
of the temple of the LORD and six thousand are to be officials and judges. 5Four
thousand are to be gatekeepers and four
thousand are to praise the LORD with the
musical instruments I have provided for
that purpose."

6David separated the Levites into divisions corresponding to the sons of Levi:
Gershon, Kohath and Merari.

[a] 9 *Solomon* sounds like and may be derived from the Hebrew for *peace.* [b] 14 That is, about 3,750 tons or about 3,400 metric tons [c] 14 That is, about 37,500 tons or about 34,000 metric tons

Gershonites

[7]Belonging to the Gershonites:
Ladan and Shimei.
[8]The sons of Ladan:
Jehiel the first, Zetham and Joel — three in all.
[9]The sons of Shimei:
Shelomoth, Haziel and Haran — three in all.
These were the heads of the families of Ladan.
[10]And the sons of Shimei:
Jahath, Ziza,[a] Jeush and Beriah.
These were the sons of Shimei — four in all.
[11]Jahath was the first and Ziza the second, but Jeush and Beriah did not have many sons; so they were counted as one family with one assignment.

Kohathites

[12]The sons of Kohath:
Amram, Izhar, Hebron and Uzziel — four in all.
[13]The sons of Amram:
Aaron and Moses.
Aaron was set apart, he and his descendants forever, to consecrate the most holy things, to offer sacrifices before the LORD, to minister before him and to pronounce blessings in his name forever.
[14]The sons of Moses the man of God were counted as part of the tribe of Levi.
[15]The sons of Moses:
Gershom and Eliezer.
[16]The descendants of Gershom:
Shubael was the first.
[17]The descendants of Eliezer:
Rehabiah was the first.
Eliezer had no other sons, but the sons of Rehabiah were very numerous.
[18]The sons of Izhar:
Shelomith was the first.
[19]The sons of Hebron:
Jeriah the first, Amariah the second, Jahaziel the third and Jekameam the fourth.
[20]The sons of Uzziel:
Micah the first and Ishiah the second.

Merarites

[21]The sons of Merari:
Mahli and Mushi.
The sons of Mahli:
Eleazar and Kish.
[22]Eleazar died without having sons: he had only daughters. Their cousins, the sons of Kish, married them.
[23]The sons of Mushi:
Mahli, Eder and Jerimoth — three in all.

[24]These were the descendants of Levi by their families — the heads of families as they were registered under their names and counted individually, that is, the workers twenty years old or more who served in the temple of the LORD.
[25]For David had said, "Since the LORD,
the God of Israel, has granted rest to his people and has come to dwell in Jerusalem forever,
[26]the Levites no longer need to carry the tabernacle or any of the articles used in its service."
[27]According to
the last instructions of David, the Levites were counted from those twenty years old or more.
[28]The duty of the Levites was to help Aaron's descendants in the service of the temple of the LORD: to be in charge of the courtyards, the side rooms, the purification of all sacred things and the performance of other duties at the house of God.
[29]They were in charge of the bread
set out on the table, the special flour for the grain offerings, the thin loaves made without yeast, the baking and the mixing, and all measurements of quantity and size.
[30]They were also to stand
every morning to thank and praise the LORD. They were to do the same in the evening
[31]and whenever burnt offerings
were presented to the LORD on the Sabbaths, at the New Moon feasts and at the appointed festivals. They were to serve before the LORD regularly in the proper number and in the way prescribed for them.
[32]And so the Levites carried out their responsibilities for the tent of meeting, for the Holy Place and, under their relatives the descendants of Aaron, for the service of the temple of the LORD.

The Divisions of Priests

24 These were the divisions of the descendants of Aaron:
The sons of Aaron were Nadab, Abihu, Eleazar and Ithamar.
[2]But Nadab
and Abihu died before their father did, and they had no sons; so Eleazar and Ithamar served as the priests.
[3]With the
help of Zadok a descendant of Eleazar and Ahimelek a descendant of Ithamar,

[a] *10* One Hebrew manuscript, Septuagint and Vulgate (see also verse 11); most Hebrew manuscripts *Zina*

David separated them into divisions
for their appointed order of ministering. 4 A larger number of leaders were
found among Eleazar's descendants
than among Ithamar's, and they were
divided accordingly: sixteen heads of
families from Eleazar's descendants and
eight heads of families from Ithamar's
descendants. 5 They divided them impartially by casting lots, for there were
officials of the sanctuary and officials of
God among the descendants of both Eleazar and Ithamar.

6 The scribe Shemaiah son of Nethanel, a Levite, recorded their names in the
presence of the king and of the officials:
Zadok the priest, Ahimelek son of Abiathar and the heads of families of the
priests and of the Levites — one family
being taken from Eleazar and then one
from Ithamar.

7 The first lot fell to Jehoiarib,
the second to Jedaiah,
8 the third to Harim,
the fourth to Seorim,
9 the fifth to Malkijah,
the sixth to Mijamin,
10 the seventh to Hakkoz,
the eighth to Abijah,
11 the ninth to Jeshua,
the tenth to Shekaniah,
12 the eleventh to Eliashib,
the twelfth to Jakim,
13 the thirteenth to Huppah,
the fourteenth to Jeshebeab,
14 the fifteenth to Bilgah,
the sixteenth to Immer,
15 the seventeenth to Hezir,
the eighteenth to Happizzez,
16 the nineteenth to Pethahiah,
the twentieth to Jehezkel,
17 the twenty-first to Jakin,
the twenty-second to Gamul,
18 the twenty-third to Delaiah
and the twenty-fourth to Maaziah.

19 This was their appointed order of ministering when they entered the temple of the LORD, according to the regulations prescribed for them by their ancestor Aaron, as the LORD, the God of Israel, had commanded him.

The Rest of the Levites

20 As for the rest of the descendants of Levi:
from the sons of Amram: Shubael;
from the sons of Shubael: Jehdeiah.
21 As for Rehabiah, from his sons:
Ishiah was the first.
22 From the Izharites: Shelomoth;
from the sons of Shelomoth: Jahath.
23 The sons of Hebron: Jeriah the first,[a]
Amariah the second, Jahaziel the third and Jekameam the fourth.
24 The son of Uzziel: Micah;
from the sons of Micah: Shamir.
25 The brother of Micah: Ishiah;
from the sons of Ishiah: Zechariah.
26 The sons of Merari: Mahli and Mushi.
The son of Jaaziah: Beno.
27 The sons of Merari:
from Jaaziah: Beno, Shoham, Zakkur and Ibri.
28 From Mahli: Eleazar, who had no sons.
29 From Kish: the son of Kish:
Jerahmeel.
30 And the sons of Mushi: Mahli, Eder and Jerimoth.

These were the Levites, according to
their families. 31 They also cast lots, just
as their relatives the descendants of
Aaron did, in the presence of King David
and of Zadok, Ahimelek, and the heads
of families of the priests and of the Levites. The families of the oldest brother were treated the same as those of the youngest.

The Musicians

25 David, together with the commanders of the army, set apart some of the sons of Asaph, Heman and Jeduthun for the ministry of prophesying, accompanied by harps, lyres and cymbals. Here is the list of the men who performed this service:

2 From the sons of Asaph:
Zakkur, Joseph, Nethaniah and Asarelah. The sons of Asaph were under the supervision of Asaph, who prophesied under the king's supervision.
3 As for Jeduthun, from his sons:
Gedaliah, Zeri, Jeshaiah, Shimei,[b] Hashabiah and Mattithiah, six in all, under the supervision of their father Jeduthun, who prophesied, using the harp in thanking and praising the LORD.

[a] *23* Two Hebrew manuscripts and some Septuagint manuscripts (see also 23:19); most Hebrew manuscripts *The sons of Jeriah:* [b] *3* One Hebrew manuscript and some Septuagint manuscripts (see also verse 17); most Hebrew manuscripts do not have *Shimei.*

4 As for Heman, from his sons:
Bukkiah, Mattaniah, Uzziel, Shubael and Jerimoth; Hananiah, Hanani, Eliathah, Giddalti and Romamti-Ezer; Joshbekashah, Mallothi, Hothir
and Mahazioth. 5 (All these were sons
of Heman the king's seer. They were given him through the promises of God to exalt him. God gave Heman fourteen sons and three daughters.)

6 All these men were under the supervision of their father for the music of the temple of the LORD, with cymbals, lyres and harps, for the ministry at the house of God.

Asaph, Jeduthun and Heman were under the supervision of the king. 7 Along
with their relatives — all of them trained and skilled in music for the LORD — they
numbered 288. 8 Young and old alike,
teacher as well as student, cast lots for their duties.

9 The first lot, which was for Asaph, fell to Joseph,
his sons and relatives[a] 12[b]
the second to Gedaliah,
him and his relatives and sons 12
10 the third to Zakkur,
his sons and relatives 12
11 the fourth to Izri,[c]
his sons and relatives 12
12 the fifth to Nethaniah,
his sons and relatives 12
13 the sixth to Bukkiah,
his sons and relatives 12
14 the seventh to Jesarelah,[d]
his sons and relatives 12
15 the eighth to Jeshaiah,
his sons and relatives 12
16 the ninth to Mattaniah,
his sons and relatives 12
17 the tenth to Shimei,
his sons and relatives 12
18 the eleventh to Azarel,[e]
his sons and relatives 12
19 the twelfth to Hashabiah,
his sons and relatives 12
20 the thirteenth to Shubael,
his sons and relatives 12
21 the fourteenth to Mattithiah,
his sons and relatives 12
22 the fifteenth to Jerimoth,
his sons and relatives 12
23 the sixteenth to Hananiah,
his sons and relatives 12
24 the seventeenth to Joshbekashah,
his sons and relatives 12
25 the eighteenth to Hanani,
his sons and relatives 12
26 the nineteenth to Mallothi,
his sons and relatives 12
27 the twentieth to Eliathah,
his sons and relatives 12
28 the twenty-first to Hothir,
his sons and relatives 12
29 the twenty-second to Giddalti,
his sons and relatives 12
30 the twenty-third to Mahazioth,
his sons and relatives 12
31 the twenty-fourth to Romamti-Ezer,
his sons and relatives 12.

The Gatekeepers

26 The divisions of the gatekeepers:

From the Korahites: Meshelemiah son of Kore, one of the sons of Asaph.
2 Meshelemiah had sons:
Zechariah the firstborn,
Jediael the second,
Zebadiah the third,
Jathniel the fourth,
3 Elam the fifth,
Jehohanan the sixth
and Eliehoenai the seventh.
4 Obed-Edom also had sons:
Shemaiah the firstborn,
Jehozabad the second,
Joah the third,
Sakar the fourth,
Nethanel the fifth,
5 Ammiel the sixth,
Issachar the seventh
and Peullethai the eighth.
(For God had blessed Obed-Edom.)

6 Obed-Edom's son Shemaiah also had sons, who were leaders in their father's family because they
were very capable men. 7 The sons
of Shemaiah: Othni, Rephael, Obed and Elzabad; his relatives Elihu and Semakiah were also
able men. 8 All these were descendants of Obed-Edom; they and their sons and their relatives were capable men with the strength to do the work — descendants of Obed-Edom, 62 in all.
9 Meshelemiah had sons and relatives, who were able men — 18 in all.

[a] 9 See Septuagint; Hebrew does not have *his sons and relatives.* [b] 9 See the total in verse 7; Hebrew does not have *twelve.* [c] 11 A variant of *Zeri* [d] 14 A variant of *Asarelah* [e] 18 A variant of *Uzziel*

10 Hosah the Merarite had sons: Shimri
the first (although he was not the
firstborn, his father had appointed him the first), 11 Hilkiah the second, Tabaliah the third and Zechariah the fourth. The sons and
relatives of Hosah were 13 in all.

12 These divisions of the gatekeepers,
through their leaders, had duties for
ministering in the temple of the LORD,
just as their relatives had. 13 Lots were
cast for each gate, according to their
families, young and old alike.

14 The lot for the East Gate fell to Shelemiah.[a] Then lots were cast for his son
Zechariah, a wise counselor, and the lot
for the North Gate fell to him. 15 The lot
for the South Gate fell to Obed-Edom,
and the lot for the storehouse fell to his
sons. 16 The lots for the West Gate and the
Shalleketh Gate on the upper road fell to
Shuppim and Hosah.

Guard was alongside of guard: 17 There
were six Levites a day on the east, four a
day on the north, four a day on the south
and two at a time at the storehouse. 18 As
for the court[b] to the west, there were four
at the road and two at the court[b] itself.

19 These were the divisions of the gatekeepers who were descendants of Korah
and Merari.

The Treasurers and Other Officials

20 Their fellow Levites were[c] in charge
of the treasuries of the house of God and
the treasuries for the dedicated things.

21 The descendants of Ladan, who were
Gershonites through Ladan and who
were heads of families belonging to Ladan the Gershonite, were Jehieli, 22 the
sons of Jehieli, Zetham and his brother
Joel. They were in charge of the treasuries of the temple of the LORD.

23 From the Amramites, the Izharites,
the Hebronites and the Uzzielites:

24 Shubael, a descendant of Gershom
son of Moses, was the official in
charge of the treasuries. 25 His relatives through Eliezer: Rehabiah his
son, Jeshaiah his son, Joram his
son, Zikri his son and Shelomith
his son. 26 Shelomith and his relatives were in charge of all the treasuries for the things dedicated by
King David, by the heads of families who were the commanders
of thousands and commanders of
hundreds, and by the other army
commanders. 27 Some of the plunder taken in battle they dedicated
for the repair of the temple of the
LORD. 28 And everything dedicated
by Samuel the seer and by Saul son
of Kish, Abner son of Ner and Joab
son of Zeruiah, and all the other
dedicated things were in the care
of Shelomith and his relatives.

29 From the Izharites: Kenaniah and
his sons were assigned duties
away from the temple, as officials
and judges over Israel.

30 From the Hebronites: Hashabiah
and his relatives — seventeen
hundred able men — were responsible in Israel west of the Jordan for all the work of the LORD
and for the king's service. 31 As for
the Hebronites, Jeriah was their
chief according to the genealogical records of their families. In
the fortieth year of David's reign
a search was made in the records,
and capable men among the Hebronites were found at Jazer in
Gilead. 32 Jeriah had twenty-seven
hundred relatives, who were able
men and heads of families, and
King David put them in charge of
the Reubenites, the Gadites and
the half-tribe of Manasseh for every matter pertaining to God and
for the affairs of the king.

Army Divisions

27 This is the list of the Israelites —
heads of families, commanders
of thousands and commanders of hundreds, and their officers, who served the
king in all that concerned the army divisions that were on duty month by month
throughout the year. Each division consisted of 24,000 men.

2 In charge of the first division, for the
first month, was Jashobeam son of
Zabdiel. There were 24,000 men in
his division. 3 He was a descendant
of Perez and chief of all the army officers for the first month.

4 In charge of the division for the second month was Dodai the Ahohite;
Mikloth was the leader of his division. There were 24,000 men in his
division.

5 The third army commander, for the
third month, was Benaiah son of Jehoiada the priest. He was chief and
there were 24,000 men in his division.

[a] *14* A variant of *Meshelemiah* [b] *18* The meaning of the Hebrew for this word is uncertain.
[c] *20* Septuagint; Hebrew *As for the Levites, Ahijah was*

6This was the Benaiah who was a mighty warrior among the Thirty and was over the Thirty. His son Ammizabad was in charge of his division.

7 The fourth, for the fourth month, was Asahel the brother of Joab; his son Zebadiah was his successor. There were 24,000 men in his division.

8 The fifth, for the fifth month, was the commander Shamhuth the Izrahite. There were 24,000 men in his division.

9 The sixth, for the sixth month, was Ira the son of Ikkesh the Tekoite. There were 24,000 men in his division.

10 The seventh, for the seventh month, was Helez the Pelonite, an Ephraimite. There were 24,000 men in his division.

11 The eighth, for the eighth month, was Sibbekai the Hushathite, a Zerahite. There were 24,000 men in his division.

12 The ninth, for the ninth month, was Abiezer the Anathothite, a Benjamite. There were 24,000 men in his division.

13 The tenth, for the tenth month, was Maharai the Netophathite, a Zerahite. There were 24,000 men in his division.

14 The eleventh, for the eleventh month, was Benaiah the Pirathonite, an Ephraimite. There were 24,000 men in his division.

15 The twelfth, for the twelfth month, was Heldai the Netophathite, from the family of Othniel. There were 24,000 men in his division.

Leaders of the Tribes

16 The leaders of the tribes of Israel:

over the Reubenites: Eliezer son of Zikri;
over the Simeonites: Shephatiah son of Maakah;
17 over Levi: Hashabiah son of Kemuel;
over Aaron: Zadok;
18 over Judah: Elihu, a brother of David;
over Issachar: Omri son of Michael;
19 over Zebulun: Ishmaiah son of Obadiah;
over Naphtali: Jerimoth son of Azriel;
20 over the Ephraimites: Hoshea son of Azaziah;
over half the tribe of Manasseh: Joel son of Pedaiah;
21 over the half-tribe of Manasseh in Gilead: Iddo son of Zechariah;
over Benjamin: Jaasiel son of Abner;
22 over Dan: Azarel son of Jeroham.

These were the leaders of the tribes of Israel.

23David did not take the number of the
men twenty years old or less, because
the LORD had promised to make Israel as
numerous as the stars in the sky. 24Joab
son of Zeruiah began to count the men
but did not finish. God's wrath came on
Israel on account of this numbering, and
the number was not entered in the book[a]
of the annals of King David.

The King's Overseers

25Azmaveth son of Adiel was in charge of the royal storehouses.

Jonathan son of Uzziah was in charge of the storehouses in the outlying districts, in the towns, the villages and the watchtowers.

26Ezri son of Kelub was in charge of the workers who farmed the land.

27Shimei the Ramathite was in charge of the vineyards.

Zabdi the Shiphmite was in charge of the produce of the vineyards for the wine vats.

28Baal-Hanan the Gederite was in charge of the olive and sycamore-fig trees in the western foothills.

Joash was in charge of the supplies of olive oil.

29Shitrai the Sharonite was in charge of the herds grazing in Sharon.

Shaphat son of Adlai was in charge of the herds in the valleys.

30Obil the Ishmaelite was in charge of the camels.

Jehdeiah the Meronothite was in charge of the donkeys.

31Jaziz the Hagrite was in charge of the flocks.

All these were the officials in charge of King David's property.

32Jonathan, David's uncle, was a counselor, a man of insight and a scribe. Jehiel son of Hakmoni took care of the king's sons.

33Ahithophel was the king's counselor.
Hushai the Arkite was the king's confidant. 34Ahithophel was succeeded by Jehoiada son of Benaiah and by Abiathar.
Joab was the commander of the royal army.

David's Plans for the Temple

28 David summoned all the officials of Israel to assemble at Jerusalem: the officers over the tribes, the commanders of the divisions in the service of the

[a] 24 Septuagint; Hebrew *number*

king, the commanders of thousands and
commanders of hundreds, and the officials in charge of all the property and livestock belonging to the king and his sons,
together with the palace officials, the warriors and all the brave fighting men.
2King David rose to his feet and said:
"Listen to me, my fellow Israelites, my
people. I had it in my heart to build a
house as a place of rest for the ark of the
covenant of the LORD, for the footstool
of our God, and I made plans to build it.
3But God said to me, 'You are not to build
a house for my Name, because you are a
warrior and have shed blood.'
4"Yet the LORD, the God of Israel, chose
me from my whole family to be king over
Israel forever. He chose Judah as leader,
and from the tribe of Judah he chose my
family, and from my father's sons he was
pleased to make me king over all Israel.
5Of all my sons — and the LORD has given
me many — he has chosen my son Solomon to sit on the throne of the kingdom
of the LORD over Israel. 6He said to me:
'Solomon your son is the one who will
build my house and my courts, for I have
chosen him to be my son, and I will be
his father. 7I will establish his kingdom
forever if he is unswerving in carrying
out my commands and laws, as is being
done at this time.'
8"So now I charge you in the sight
of all Israel and of the assembly of the
LORD, and in the hearing of our God: Be
careful to follow all the commands of
the LORD your God, that you may possess this good land and pass it on as an
inheritance to your descendants forever.
9"And you, my son Solomon, acknowledge the God of your father, and serve
him with wholehearted devotion and
with a willing mind, for the LORD searches every heart and understands every
desire and every thought. If you seek
him, he will be found by you; but if you
forsake him, he will reject you forever.
10Consider now, for the LORD has chosen
you to build a house as the sanctuary. Be
strong and do the work."
11Then David gave his son Solomon
the plans for the portico of the temple,
its buildings, its storerooms, its upper
parts, its inner rooms and the place of
atonement. 12He gave him the plans of
all that the Spirit had put in his mind
for the courts of the temple of the LORD
and all the surrounding rooms, for the
treasuries of the temple of God and for
the treasuries for the dedicated things.
13He gave him instructions for the divisions of the priests and Levites, and for
all the work of serving in the temple of
the LORD, as well as for all the articles to
be used in its service. 14He designated the
weight of gold for all the gold articles to
be used in various kinds of service, and
the weight of silver for all the silver articles to be used in various kinds of service:
15the weight of gold for the gold lampstands and their lamps, with the weight
for each lampstand and its lamps; and
the weight of silver for each silver lampstand and its lamps, according to the use
of each lampstand; 16the weight of gold
for each table for consecrated bread; the
weight of silver for the silver tables; 17the
weight of pure gold for the forks, sprinkling bowls and pitchers; the weight of
gold for each gold dish; the weight of silver for each silver dish; 18and the weight
of the refined gold for the altar of incense. He also gave him the plan for the
chariot, that is, the cherubim of gold that
spread their wings and overshadow the
ark of the covenant of the LORD.
19"All this," David said, "I have in writing as a result of the LORD's hand on me,
and he enabled me to understand all the
details of the plan."
20David also said to Solomon his son,
"Be strong and courageous, and do the
work. Do not be afraid or discouraged,
for the LORD God, my God, is with you.
He will not fail you or forsake you until
all the work for the service of the temple
of the LORD is finished. 21The divisions
of the priests and Levites are ready for
all the work on the temple of God, and
every willing person skilled in any craft
will help you in all the work. The officials
and all the people will obey your every
command."

Gifts for Building the Temple

29 Then King David said to the whole
assembly: "My son Solomon, the
one whom God has chosen, is young and
inexperienced. The task is great, because
this palatial structure is not for man but
for the LORD God. 2With all my resources I
have provided for the temple of my God —
gold for the gold work, silver for the silver,
bronze for the bronze, iron for the iron
and wood for the wood, as well as onyx
for the settings, turquoise,[a] stones of various colors, and all kinds of fine stone and
marble — all of these in large quantities.
3Besides, in my devotion to the temple of
my God I now give my personal treasures
of gold and silver for the temple of my
God, over and above everything I have

[a] *2* The meaning of the Hebrew for this word is uncertain.

provided for this holy temple: 4three thousand talents[a] of gold (gold of Ophir) and
seven thousand talents[b] of refined silver, for the overlaying of the walls of the
buildings, 5for the gold work and the silver
work, and for all the work to be done by
the craftsmen. Now, who is willing to consecrate themselves to the LORD today?"
6Then the leaders of families, the officers of the tribes of Israel, the commanders of thousands and commanders of
hundreds, and the officials in charge of
the king's work gave willingly. 7They gave
toward the work on the temple of God five
thousand talents[c] and ten thousand darics[d] of gold, ten thousand talents[e] of silver, eighteen thousand talents[f] of bronze
and a hundred thousand talents[g] of iron.
8Anyone who had precious stones gave
them to the treasury of the temple of the
LORD in the custody of Jehiel the Gershonite. 9The people rejoiced at the willing response of their leaders, for they had giv-
en freely and wholeheartedly to the LORD.
David the king also rejoiced greatly.

David's Prayer

10David praised the LORD in the presence of the whole assembly, saying,

"Praise be to you, LORD,
the God of our father Israel,
from everlasting to everlasting.
11 Yours, LORD, is the greatness and the power
and the glory and the majesty and the splendor,
for everything in heaven and earth is yours.
Yours, LORD, is the kingdom;
you are exalted as head over all.
12 Wealth and honor come from you;
you are the ruler of all things.
In your hands are strength and power
to exalt and give strength to all.
13 Now, our God, we give you thanks,
and praise your glorious name.

14"But who am I, and who are my people, that we should be able to give as generously as this? Everything comes from
you, and we have given you only what
comes from your hand. 15We are foreigners and strangers in your sight, as were all
our ancestors. Our days on earth are like
a shadow, without hope. 16LORD our God,
all this abundance that we have provided for building you a temple for your Holy
Name comes from your hand, and all of it
belongs to you. 17I know, my God, that you
test the heart and are pleased with integrity. All these things I have given willingly
and with honest intent. And now I have
seen with joy how willingly your people
who are here have given to you. 18LORD,
the God of our fathers Abraham, Isaac and
Israel, keep these desires and thoughts in
the hearts of your people forever, and keep
their hearts loyal to you. 19And give my
son Solomon the wholehearted devotion
to keep your commands, statutes and decrees and to do everything to build the palatial structure for which I have provided."
20Then David said to the whole assembly, "Praise the LORD your God." So they
all praised the LORD, the God of their
fathers; they bowed down, prostrating
themselves before the LORD and the king.

Solomon Acknowledged as King

21The next day they made sacrifices
to the LORD and presented burnt offerings to him: a thousand bulls, a thousand rams and a thousand male lambs,
together with their drink offerings, and
other sacrifices in abundance for all Israel. 22They ate and drank with great joy
in the presence of the LORD that day.
Then they acknowledged Solomon son
of David as king a second time, anointing
him before the LORD to be ruler and Zadok to be priest. 23So Solomon sat on the
throne of the LORD as king in place of his
father David. He prospered and all Israel
obeyed him. 24All the officers and warriors,
as well as all of King David's sons, pledged
their submission to King Solomon.
25The LORD highly exalted Solomon in
the sight of all Israel and bestowed on
him royal splendor such as no king over
Israel ever had before.

The Death of David

26David son of Jesse was king over all
Israel. 27He ruled over Israel forty years—
seven in Hebron and thirty-three in Jerusalem. 28He died at a good old age, having enjoyed long life, wealth and honor.
His son Solomon succeeded him as king.
29As for the events of King David's reign,
from beginning to end, they are written in
the records of Samuel the seer, the records
of Nathan the prophet and the records of
Gad the seer, 30together with the details
of his reign and power, and the circumstances that surrounded him and Israel
and the kingdoms of all the other lands.

[a] 4 That is, about 110 tons or about 100 metric tons [b] 4 That is, about 260 tons or about 235 metric tons [c] 7 That is, about 190 tons or about 170 metric tons [d] 7 That is, about 185 pounds or about 84 kilograms [e] 7 That is, about 380 tons or about 340 metric tons [f] 7 That is, about 675 tons or about 610 metric tons [g] 7 That is, about 3,800 tons or about 3,400 metric tons

2 CHRONICLES

Solomon Asks for Wisdom

1 Solomon son of David established himself firmly over his kingdom, for the LORD his God was with him and made him exceedingly great.

2 Then Solomon spoke to all Israel — to the commanders of thousands and commanders of hundreds, to the judges and to all the leaders in Israel, the heads of families — 3 and Solomon and the whole assembly went to the high place at Gibeon, for God's tent of meeting was there, which Moses the LORD's servant had made in the wilderness. 4 Now David had brought up the ark of God from Kiriath Jearim to the place he had prepared for it, because he had pitched a tent for it in Jerusalem. 5 But the bronze altar that Bezalel son of Uri, the son of Hur, had made was in Gibeon in front of the tabernacle of the LORD; so Solomon and the assembly inquired of him there. 6 Solomon went up to the bronze altar before the LORD in the tent of meeting and offered a thousand burnt offerings on it.

7 That night God appeared to Solomon and said to him, "Ask for whatever you want me to give you."

8 Solomon answered God, "You have shown great kindness to David my father and have made me king in his place. 9 Now, LORD God, let your promise to my father David be confirmed, for you have made me king over a people who are as numerous as the dust of the earth. 10 Give me wisdom and knowledge, that I may lead this people, for who is able to govern this great people of yours?"

11 God said to Solomon, "Since this is your heart's desire and you have not asked for wealth, possessions or honor, nor for the death of your enemies, and since you have not asked for a long life but for wisdom and knowledge to govern my people over whom I have made you king, 12 therefore wisdom and knowledge will be given you. And I will also give you wealth, possessions and honor, such as no king who was before you ever had and none after you will have."

13 Then Solomon went to Jerusalem from the high place at Gibeon, from before the tent of meeting. And he reigned over Israel.

14 Solomon accumulated chariots and horses; he had fourteen hundred chariots and twelve thousand horses,[a] which he kept in the chariot cities and also with him in Jerusalem. 15 The king made silver and gold as common in Jerusalem as stones, and cedar as plentiful as sycamore-fig trees in the foothills. 16 Solomon's horses were imported from Egypt and from Kue[b] — the royal merchants purchased them from Kue at the current price. 17 They imported a chariot from Egypt for six hundred shekels[c] of silver, and a horse for a hundred and fifty.[d] They also exported them to all the kings of the Hittites and of the Arameans.

Preparations for Building the Temple

2[e] Solomon gave orders to build a temple for the Name of the LORD and a royal palace for himself. 2 He conscripted 70,000 men as carriers and 80,000 as stonecutters in the hills and 3,600 as foremen over them.

3 Solomon sent this message to Hiram[f] king of Tyre:

> "Send me cedar logs as you did for my father David when you sent him cedar to build a palace to live in. 4 Now I am about to build a temple for the Name of the LORD my God and to dedicate it to him for burning fragrant incense before him, for setting out the consecrated bread regularly, and for making burnt offerings every morning and evening and on the Sabbaths, at the New Moons and at the appointed festivals of the LORD our God. This is a lasting ordinance for Israel.
>
> 5 "The temple I am going to build will be great, because our God is greater than all other gods. 6 But who is able to build a temple for him, since the heavens, even the highest heavens, cannot contain him? Who then am I to build a temple for him, except as a place to burn sacrifices before him?

[a] 14 Or *charioteers* [b] 16 Probably Cilicia [c] 17 That is, about 15 pounds or about 6.9 kilograms [d] 17 That is, about 3 3/4 pounds or about 1.7 kilograms [e] In Hebrew texts 2:1 is numbered 1:18, and 2:2-18 is numbered 2:1-17. [f] 3 Hebrew *Huram*, a variant of *Hiram*; also in verses 11 and 12

7"Send me, therefore, a man skilled
to work in gold and silver, bronze
and iron, and in purple, crimson and
blue yarn, and experienced in the art
of engraving, to work in Judah and
Jerusalem with my skilled workers,
whom my father David provided.
8"Send me also cedar, juniper and
algum[a] logs from Lebanon, for I
know that your servants are skilled
in cutting timber there. My servants
will work with yours 9to provide me
with plenty of lumber, because the
temple I build must be large and
magnificent. 10I will give your servants, the woodsmen who cut the
timber, twenty thousand cors[b] of
ground wheat, twenty thousand
cors[c] of barley, twenty thousand
baths[d] of wine and twenty thousand baths of olive oil."

11Hiram king of Tyre replied by letter
to Solomon:

"Because the LORD loves his people, he has made you their king."

12And Hiram added:

"Praise be to the LORD, the God of
Israel, who made heaven and earth!
He has given King David a wise son,
endowed with intelligence and discernment, who will build a temple
for the LORD and a palace for himself.
13"I am sending you Huram-Abi,
a man of great skill, 14whose mother was from Dan and whose father
was from Tyre. He is trained to work
in gold and silver, bronze and iron,
stone and wood, and with purple
and blue and crimson yarn and fine
linen. He is experienced in all kinds
of engraving and can execute any
design given to him. He will work
with your skilled workers and with
those of my lord, David your father.
15"Now let my lord send his servants the wheat and barley and the
olive oil and wine he promised, 16and
we will cut all the logs from Lebanon
that you need and will float them as
rafts by sea down to Joppa. You can
then take them up to Jerusalem."

17Solomon took a census of all the foreigners residing in Israel, after the census his father David had taken; and they
were found to be 153,600. 18He assigned
70,000 of them to be carriers and 80,000
to be stonecutters in the hills, with 3,600
foremen over them to keep the people
working.

Solomon Builds the Temple

3 Then Solomon began to build the
temple of the LORD in Jerusalem on
Mount Moriah, where the LORD had appeared to his father David. It was on the
threshing floor of Araunah[e] the Jebusite,
the place provided by David. 2He began
building on the second day of the second
month in the fourth year of his reign.
3The foundation Solomon laid for
building the temple of God was sixty cubits long and twenty cubits wide[f] (using
the cubit of the old standard). 4The portico at the front of the temple was twenty cubits[g] long across the width of the
building and twenty[h] cubits high.
He overlaid the inside with pure gold.
5He paneled the main hall with juniper
and covered it with fine gold and decorated it with palm tree and chain designs. 6He adorned the temple with precious stones. And the gold he used was
gold of Parvaim. 7He overlaid the ceiling
beams, doorframes, walls and doors
of the temple with gold, and he carved
cherubim on the walls.
8He built the Most Holy Place, its
length corresponding to the width of the
temple — twenty cubits long and twenty
cubits wide. He overlaid the inside with
six hundred talents[i] of fine gold. 9The
gold nails weighed fifty shekels.[j] He also
overlaid the upper parts with gold.
10For the Most Holy Place he made a
pair of sculptured cherubim and overlaid them with gold. 11The total wing-
span of the cherubim was twenty cubits.
One wing of the first cherub was five
cubits[k] long and touched the temple
wall, while its other wing, also five cubits long, touched the wing of the other cherub. 12Similarly one wing of the
second cherub was five cubits long and
touched the other temple wall, and its

[a] *8* Probably a variant of *almug* [b] *10* That is, probably about 3,600 tons or about 3,200 metric tons of wheat [c] *10* That is, probably about 3,000 tons or about 2,700 metric tons of barley [d] *10* That is, about 120,000 gallons or about 440,000 liters [e] *1* Hebrew *Ornan*, a variant of *Araunah* [f] *3* That is, about 90 feet long and 30 feet wide or about 27 meters long and 9 meters wide [g] *4* That is, about 30 feet or about 9 meters; also in verses 8, 11 and 13
[h] *4* Some Septuagint and Syriac manuscripts; Hebrew *and a hundred and twenty* [i] *8* That is, about 23 tons or about 21 metric tons [j] *9* That is, about 1 1/4 pounds or about 575 grams
[k] *11* That is, about 7 1/2 feet or about 2.3 meters; also in verse 15

other wing, also five cubits long, touched
the wing of the first cherub. 13 The wings
of these cherubim extended twenty cubits. They stood on their feet, facing the
main hall.[a]

14 He made the curtain of blue, purple
and crimson yarn and fine linen, with
cherubim worked into it.

15 For the front of the temple he made
two pillars, which together were thirty-
five cubits[b] long, each with a capital
five cubits high. 16 He made interwoven
chains[c] and put them on top of the pillars. He also made a hundred pomegranates and attached them to the chains.
17 He erected the pillars in the front of the
temple, one to the south and one to the
north. The one to the south he named Jakin[d] and the one to the north Boaz.[e]

The Temple's Furnishings

4 He made a bronze altar twenty cubits long, twenty cubits wide and ten
cubits high.[f] 2 He made the Sea of cast
metal, circular in shape, measuring ten
cubits from rim to rim and five cubits[g]
high. It took a line of thirty cubits[h] to
measure around it. 3 Below the rim, figures of bulls encircled it — ten to a cubit.[i]
The bulls were cast in two rows in one
piece with the Sea.

4 The Sea stood on twelve bulls, three
facing north, three facing west, three
facing south and three facing east. The
Sea rested on top of them, and their
hindquarters were toward the center. 5 It
was a handbreadth[j] in thickness, and its
rim was like the rim of a cup, like a lily
blossom. It held three thousand baths.[k]

6 He then made ten basins for washing
and placed five on the south side and
five on the north. In them the things
to be used for the burnt offerings were
rinsed, but the Sea was to be used by the
priests for washing.

7 He made ten gold lampstands according to the specifications for them
and placed them in the temple, five on
the south side and five on the north.

8 He made ten tables and placed them
in the temple, five on the south side and
five on the north. He also made a hundred gold sprinkling bowls.

9 He made the courtyard of the priests,
and the large court and the doors for
the court, and overlaid the doors with
bronze. 10 He placed the Sea on the south
side, at the southeast corner.

11 And Huram also made the pots and
shovels and sprinkling bowls.

So Huram finished the work he had
undertaken for King Solomon in the
temple of God:

12 the two pillars;
the two bowl-shaped capitals on top of the pillars;
the two sets of network decorating the two bowl-shaped capitals on top of the pillars;
13 the four hundred pomegranates for the two sets of network (two rows of pomegranates for each network, decorating the bowl-shaped capitals on top of the pillars);
14 the stands with their basins;
15 the Sea and the twelve bulls under it;
16 the pots, shovels, meat forks and all related articles.

All the objects that Huram-Abi made for
King Solomon for the temple of the LORD
were of polished bronze. 17 The king had
them cast in clay molds in the plain of the
Jordan between Sukkoth and Zarethan.[l]
18 All these things that Solomon made
amounted to so much that the weight of
the bronze could not be calculated.

19 Solomon also made all the furnishings that were in God's temple:

the golden altar;
the tables on which was the bread of the Presence;
20 the lampstands of pure gold with their lamps, to burn in front of the inner sanctuary as prescribed;
21 the gold floral work and lamps and tongs (they were solid gold);
22 the pure gold wick trimmers, sprinkling bowls, dishes and censers; and the gold doors of the temple: the inner doors to the Most Holy Place and the doors of the main hall.

[a] 13 Or *facing inward* [b] 15 That is, about 53 feet or about 16 meters [c] 16 Or possibly *made chains in the inner sanctuary*; the meaning of the Hebrew for this phrase is uncertain.
[d] 17 *Jakin* probably means *he establishes.* [e] 17 *Boaz* probably means *in him is strength.*
[f] 1 That is, about 30 feet long and wide and 15 feet high or about 9 meters long and wide and 4.5 meters high [g] 2 That is, about 7 1/2 feet or about 2.3 meters [h] 2 That is, about 45 feet or about 14 meters [i] 3 That is, about 18 inches or about 45 centimeters [j] 5 That is, about 3 inches or about 7.5 centimeters [k] 5 That is, about 18,000 gallons or about 66,000 liters
[l] 17 Hebrew *Zeredatha,* a variant of *Zarethan*

5 When all the work Solomon had done for the temple of the LORD was finished, he brought in the things his father David had dedicated — the silver and gold and all the furnishings — and he placed them in the treasuries of God's temple.

The Ark Brought to the Temple

2Then Solomon summoned to Jerusalem the elders of Israel, all the heads of the tribes and the chiefs of the Israelite families, to bring up the ark of the LORD's covenant from Zion, the City of David. 3And all the Israelites came together to the king at the time of the festival in the seventh month.

4When all the elders of Israel had arrived, the Levites took up the ark, 5and they brought up the ark and the tent of meeting and all the sacred furnishings in it. The Levitical priests carried them up; 6and King Solomon and the entire assembly of Israel that had gathered about him were before the ark, sacrificing so many sheep and cattle that they could not be recorded or counted.

7The priests then brought the ark of the LORD's covenant to its place in the inner sanctuary of the temple, the Most Holy Place, and put it beneath the wings of the cherubim. 8The cherubim spread their wings over the place of the ark and covered the ark and its carrying poles. 9These poles were so long that their ends, extending from the ark, could be seen from in front of the inner sanctuary, but not from outside the Holy Place; and they are still there today. 10There was nothing in the ark except the two tablets that Moses had placed in it at Horeb, where the LORD made a covenant with the Israelites after they came out of Egypt.

11The priests then withdrew from the Holy Place. All the priests who were there had consecrated themselves, regardless of their divisions. 12All the Levites who were musicians — Asaph, Heman, Jeduthun and their sons and relatives — stood on the east side of the altar, dressed in fine linen and playing cymbals, harps and lyres. They were accompanied by 120 priests sounding trumpets. 13The trumpeters and musicians joined in unison to give praise and thanks to the LORD. Accompanied by trumpets, cymbals and other instruments, the singers raised their voices in praise to the LORD and sang:

"He is good;
  his love endures forever."

Then the temple of the LORD was filled with the cloud, 14and the priests could not perform their service because of the cloud, for the glory of the LORD filled the temple of God.

6 Then Solomon said, "The LORD has said that he would dwell in a dark cloud; 2I have built a magnificent temple for you, a place for you to dwell forever."

3While the whole assembly of Israel was standing there, the king turned around and blessed them. 4Then he said:

"Praise be to the LORD, the God of Israel, who with his hands has fulfilled what he promised with his mouth to my father David. For he said, 5'Since the day I brought my people out of Egypt, I have not chosen a city in any tribe of Israel to have a temple built so that my Name might be there, nor have I chosen anyone to be ruler over my people Israel. 6But now I have chosen Jerusalem for my Name to be there, and I have chosen David to rule my people Israel.'

7"My father David had it in his heart to build a temple for the Name of the LORD, the God of Israel. 8But the LORD said to my father David, 'You did well to have it in your heart to build a temple for my Name. 9Nevertheless, you are not the one to build the temple, but your son, your own flesh and blood — he is the one who will build the temple for my Name.'

10"The LORD has kept the promise he made. I have succeeded David my father and now I sit on the throne of Israel, just as the LORD promised, and I have built the temple for the Name of the LORD, the God of Israel. 11There I have placed the ark, in which is the covenant of the LORD that he made with the people of Israel."

Solomon's Prayer of Dedication

12Then Solomon stood before the altar of the LORD in front of the whole assembly of Israel and spread out his hands. 13Now he had made a bronze platform, five cubits long, five cubits wide and three cubits high,[a] and had placed it in the center of the outer court. He stood on the platform and then knelt down before

[a] *13* That is, about 7 1/2 feet long and wide and 4 1/2 feet high or about 2.3 meters long and wide and 1.4 meters high

the whole assembly of Israel and spread out his hands toward heaven. 14He said:

"LORD, the God of Israel, there is no God like you in heaven or on earth — you who keep your covenant of love with your servants who continue wholeheartedly in your way. 15You have kept your promise to your servant David my father; with your mouth you have promised and with your hand you have fulfilled it — as it is today.

16"Now, LORD, the God of Israel, keep for your servant David my father the promises you made to him when you said, 'You shall never fail to have a successor to sit before me on the throne of Israel, if only your descendants are careful in all they do to walk before me according to my law, as you have done.' 17And now, LORD, the God of Israel, let your word that you promised your servant David come true.

18"But will God really dwell on earth with humans? The heavens, even the highest heavens, cannot contain you. How much less this temple I have built! 19Yet, LORD my God, give attention to your servant's prayer and his plea for mercy. Hear the cry and the prayer that your servant is praying in your presence. 20May your eyes be open toward this temple day and night, this place of which you said you would put your Name there. May you hear the prayer your servant prays toward this place. 21Hear the supplications of your servant and of your people Israel when they pray toward this place. Hear from heaven, your dwelling place; and when you hear, forgive.

22"When anyone wrongs their neighbor and is required to take an oath and they come and swear the oath before your altar in this temple, 23then hear from heaven and act. Judge between your servants, condemning the guilty and bringing down on their heads what they have done, and vindicating the innocent by treating them in accordance with their innocence.

24"When your people Israel have been defeated by an enemy because they have sinned against you and when they turn back and give praise to your name, praying and making supplication before you in this temple, 25then hear from heaven and forgive the sin of your people Israel and bring them back to the land you gave to them and their ancestors.

26"When the heavens are shut up and there is no rain because your people have sinned against you, and when they pray toward this place and give praise to your name and turn from their sin because you have afflicted them, 27then hear from heaven and forgive the sin of your servants, your people Israel. Teach them the right way to live, and send rain on the land you gave your people for an inheritance.

28"When famine or plague comes to the land, or blight or mildew, locusts or grasshoppers, or when enemies besiege them in any of their cities, whatever disaster or disease may come, 29and when a prayer or plea is made by anyone among your people Israel — being aware of their afflictions and pains, and spreading out their hands toward this temple — 30then hear from heaven, your dwelling place. Forgive, and deal with everyone according to all they do, since you know their hearts (for you alone know the human heart), 31so that they will fear you and walk in obedience to you all the time they live in the land you gave our ancestors.

32"As for the foreigner who does not belong to your people Israel but has come from a distant land because of your great name and your mighty hand and your outstretched arm — when they come and pray toward this temple, 33then hear from heaven, your dwelling place. Do whatever the foreigner asks of you, so that all the peoples of the earth may know your name and fear you, as do your own people Israel, and may know that this house I have built bears your Name.

34"When your people go to war against their enemies, wherever you send them, and when they pray to you toward this city you have chosen and the temple I have built for your Name, 35then hear from heaven their prayer and their plea, and uphold their cause.

36"When they sin against you — for there is no one who does not sin — and you become angry with them and give them over to the

enemy, who takes them captive to
a land far away or near; 37and if
they have a change of heart in the
land where they are held captive,
and repent and plead with you in
the land of their captivity and say,
'We have sinned, we have done
wrong and acted wickedly'; 38and if
they turn back to you with all their
heart and soul in the land of their
captivity where they were taken,
and pray toward the land you gave
their ancestors, toward the city you
have chosen and toward the temple
I have built for your Name; 39then
from heaven, your dwelling place,
hear their prayer and their pleas,
and uphold their cause. And forgive your people, who have sinned
against you.
40"Now, my God, may your eyes be
open and your ears attentive to the
prayers offered in this place.

41"Now arise, LORD God, and come
to your resting place,
you and the ark of your might.
May your priests, LORD God, be
clothed with salvation,
may your faithful people
rejoice in your goodness.
42LORD God, do not reject your
anointed one.
Remember the great love
promised to David your
servant."

The Dedication of the Temple

7 When Solomon finished praying, fire
came down from heaven and consumed the burnt offering and the sacrifices, and the glory of the LORD filled the
temple. 2The priests could not enter the
temple of the LORD because the glory of
the LORD filled it. 3When all the Israelites
saw the fire coming down and the glory
of the LORD above the temple, they knelt
on the pavement with their faces to the
ground, and they worshiped and gave
thanks to the LORD, saying,

"He is good;
his love endures forever."

4Then the king and all the people offered
sacrifices before the LORD. 5And King Solomon offered a sacrifice of twenty-two
thousand head of cattle and a hundred
and twenty thousand sheep and goats.
So the king and all the people dedicated the temple of God. 6The priests took
their positions, as did the Levites with
the LORD's musical instruments, which
King David had made for praising the
LORD and which were used when he gave
thanks, saying, "His love endures forever." Opposite the Levites, the priests blew
their trumpets, and all the Israelites
were standing.
7Solomon consecrated the middle part
of the courtyard in front of the temple
of the LORD, and there he offered burnt
offerings and the fat of the fellowship offerings, because the bronze altar he had
made could not hold the burnt offerings,
the grain offerings and the fat portions.
8So Solomon observed the festival at
that time for seven days, and all Israel with him — a vast assembly, people
from Lebo Hamath to the Wadi of Egypt.
9On the eighth day they held an assembly, for they had celebrated the dedication of the altar for seven days and the
festival for seven days more. 10On the
twenty-third day of the seventh month
he sent the people to their homes, joyful
and glad in heart for the good things the
LORD had done for David and Solomon
and for his people Israel.

The LORD Appears to Solomon

11When Solomon had finished the temple of the LORD and the royal palace, and
had succeeded in carrying out all he had
in mind to do in the temple of the LORD
and in his own palace, 12the LORD appeared to him at night and said:

"I have heard your prayer and
have chosen this place for myself as
a temple for sacrifices.
13"When I shut up the heavens so
that there is no rain, or command
locusts to devour the land or send
a plague among my people, 14if my
people, who are called by my name,
will humble themselves and pray
and seek my face and turn from
their wicked ways, then I will hear
from heaven, and I will forgive
their sin and will heal their land.
15Now my eyes will be open and my
ears attentive to the prayers offered
in this place. 16I have chosen and
consecrated this temple so that my
Name may be there forever. My eyes
and my heart will always be there.
17"As for you, if you walk before
me faithfully as David your father
did, and do all I command, and observe my decrees and laws, 18I will
establish your royal throne, as I
covenanted with David your father
when I said, 'You shall never fail to
have a successor to rule over Israel.'

19"But if you[a] turn away and forsake the decrees and commands
I have given you[a] and go off to
serve other gods and worship them,
20then I will uproot Israel from my
land, which I have given them, and
will reject this temple I have consecrated for my Name. I will make it
a byword and an object of ridicule
among all peoples. 21This temple
will become a heap of rubble. All[b]
who pass by will be appalled and
say, 'Why has the LORD done such a
thing to this land and to this temple?' 22People will answer, 'Because
they have forsaken the LORD, the
God of their ancestors, who brought
them out of Egypt, and have embraced other gods, worshiping
and serving them — that is why he
brought all this disaster on them.'"

Solomon's Other Activities

8 At the end of twenty years, during
which Solomon built the temple of
the LORD and his own palace, 2Solomon
rebuilt the villages that Hiram[c] had giv-
en him, and settled Israelites in them.
3Solomon then went to Hamath Zobah
and captured it. 4He also built up Tadmor in the desert and all the store cities
he had built in Hamath. 5He rebuilt Upper Beth Horon and Lower Beth Horon as
fortified cities, with walls and with gates
and bars, 6as well as Baalath and all his
store cities, and all the cities for his chariots and for his horses[d] — whatever he desired to build in Jerusalem, in Lebanon
and throughout all the territory he ruled.
7There were still people left from the
Hittites, Amorites, Perizzites, Hivites and
Jebusites (these people were not Israelites). 8Solomon conscripted the descendants of all these people remaining in
the land — whom the Israelites had not
destroyed — to serve as slave labor, as it
is to this day. 9But Solomon did not make
slaves of the Israelites for his work; they
were his fighting men, commanders of
his captains, and commanders of his
chariots and charioteers. 10They were
also King Solomon's chief officials — two
hundred and fifty officials supervising
the men.
11Solomon brought Pharaoh's daughter up from the City of David to the palace he had built for her, for he said, "My
wife must not live in the palace of David
king of Israel, because the places the ark
of the LORD has entered are holy."
12On the altar of the LORD that he had
built in front of the portico, Solomon
sacrificed burnt offerings to the LORD,
13according to the daily requirement for
offerings commanded by Moses for the
Sabbaths, the New Moons and the three
annual festivals — the Festival of Unleavened Bread, the Festival of Weeks
and the Festival of Tabernacles. 14In
keeping with the ordinance of his father
David, he appointed the divisions of the
priests for their duties, and the Levites to
lead the praise and to assist the priests
according to each day's requirement. He
also appointed the gatekeepers by divisions for the various gates, because this
was what David the man of God had ordered. 15They did not deviate from the
king's commands to the priests or to the
Levites in any matter, including that of
the treasuries.
16All Solomon's work was carried out,
from the day the foundation of the temple of the LORD was laid until its completion. So the temple of the LORD was
finished.
17Then Solomon went to Ezion Geber
and Elath on the coast of Edom. 18And
Hiram sent him ships commanded by
his own men, sailors who knew the sea.
These, with Solomon's men, sailed to
Ophir and brought back four hundred
and fifty talents[e] of gold, which they delivered to King Solomon.

The Queen of Sheba Visits Solomon

9 When the queen of Sheba heard of
Solomon's fame, she came to Jerusalem to test him with hard questions. Arriving with a very great caravan — with
camels carrying spices, large quantities
of gold, and precious stones — she came
to Solomon and talked with him about
all she had on her mind. 2Solomon answered all her questions; nothing was
too hard for him to explain to her. 3When
the queen of Sheba saw the wisdom of
Solomon, as well as the palace he had
built, 4the food on his table, the seating
of his officials, the attending servants
in their robes, the cupbearers in their
robes and the burnt offerings he made
at[f] the temple of the LORD, she was overwhelmed.

[a] *19* The Hebrew is plural. [b] *21* See some Septuagint manuscripts, Old Latin, Syriac, Arabic and Targum; Hebrew *And though this temple is now so imposing, all* [c] *2* Hebrew *Huram,* a variant of *Hiram;* also in verse 18 [d] *6* Or *charioteers* [e] *18* That is, about 17 tons or about 15 metric tons [f] *4* Or *and the ascent by which he went up to*

5She said to the king, "The report I
heard in my own country about your
achievements and your wisdom is true.
6But I did not believe what they said until I came and saw with my own eyes.
Indeed, not even half the greatness of
your wisdom was told me; you have far
exceeded the report I heard. 7How happy
your people must be! How happy your officials, who continually stand before you
and hear your wisdom! 8Praise be to the
LORD your God, who has delighted in you
and placed you on his throne as king to
rule for the LORD your God. Because of
the love of your God for Israel and his desire to uphold them forever, he has made
you king over them, to maintain justice
and righteousness."

9Then she gave the king 120 talents[a] of
gold, large quantities of spices, and precious stones. There had never been such
spices as those the queen of Sheba gave
to King Solomon.

10(The servants of Hiram and the servants of Solomon brought gold from
Ophir; they also brought algumwood[b]
and precious stones. 11The king used the
algumwood to make steps for the temple of the LORD and for the royal palace,
and to make harps and lyres for the musicians. Nothing like them had ever been
seen in Judah.)

12King Solomon gave the queen of Sheba all she desired and asked for; he gave
her more than she had brought to him.
Then she left and returned with her retinue to her own country.

Solomon's Splendor

13The weight of the gold that Solomon
received yearly was 666 talents,[c] 14not including the revenues brought in by merchants and traders. Also all the kings of
Arabia and the governors of the territories brought gold and silver to Solomon.

15King Solomon made two hundred
large shields of hammered gold; six
hundred shekels[d] of hammered gold
went into each shield. 16He also made
three hundred small shields of hammered gold, with three hundred shekels[e]
of gold in each shield. The king put them
in the Palace of the Forest of Lebanon.

17Then the king made a great throne
covered with ivory and overlaid with
pure gold. 18The throne had six steps,
and a footstool of gold was attached to
it. On both sides of the seat were armrests, with a lion standing beside each
of them. 19Twelve lions stood on the six
steps, one at either end of each step.
Nothing like it had ever been made for
any other kingdom. 20All King Solomon's
goblets were gold, and all the household
articles in the Palace of the Forest of Lebanon were pure gold. Nothing was made
of silver, because silver was considered of
little value in Solomon's day. 21The king
had a fleet of trading ships[f] manned
by Hiram's[g] servants. Once every three
years it returned, carrying gold, silver
and ivory, and apes and baboons.

22King Solomon was greater in riches and wisdom than all the other kings
of the earth. 23All the kings of the earth
sought audience with Solomon to hear
the wisdom God had put in his heart.
24Year after year, everyone who came
brought a gift — articles of silver and
gold, and robes, weapons and spices,
and horses and mules.

25Solomon had four thousand stalls
for horses and chariots, and twelve
thousand horses,[h] which he kept in the
chariot cities and also with him in Jerusalem. 26He ruled over all the kings from
the Euphrates River to the land of the
Philistines, as far as the border of Egypt.
27The king made silver as common in Jerusalem as stones, and cedar as plentiful as sycamore-fig trees in the foothills.
28Solomon's horses were imported from
Egypt and from all other countries.

Solomon's Death

29As for the other events of Solomon's
reign, from beginning to end, are they
not written in the records of Nathan the
prophet, in the prophecy of Ahijah the
Shilonite and in the visions of Iddo the
seer concerning Jeroboam son of Nebat?
30Solomon reigned in Jerusalem over all
Israel forty years. 31Then he rested with
his ancestors and was buried in the city
of David his father. And Rehoboam his
son succeeded him as king.

Israel Rebels Against Rehoboam

10 Rehoboam went to Shechem, for
all Israel had gone there to make
him king. 2When Jeroboam son of Nebat heard this (he was in Egypt, where
he had fled from King Solomon), he returned from Egypt. 3So they sent for

[a] 9 That is, about 4 1/2 tons or about 4 metric tons [b] 10 Probably a variant of *almugwood* [c] 13 That is, about 25 tons or about 23 metric tons [d] 15 That is, about 15 pounds or about 6.9 kilograms [e] 16 That is, about 7 1/2 pounds or about 3.5 kilograms [f] 21 Hebrew *of ships that could go to Tarshish* [g] 21 Hebrew *Huram,* a variant of *Hiram* [h] 25 Or *charioteers*

Jeroboam, and he and all Israel went to Rehoboam and said to him: 4"Your father put a heavy yoke on us, but now lighten the harsh labor and the heavy yoke he put on us, and we will serve you."

5Rehoboam answered, "Come back to me in three days." So the people went away.

6Then King Rehoboam consulted the elders who had served his father Solomon during his lifetime. "How would you advise me to answer these people?" he asked.

7They replied, "If you will be kind to these people and please them and give them a favorable answer, they will always be your servants."

8But Rehoboam rejected the advice the elders gave him and consulted the young men who had grown up with him and were serving him. 9He asked them, "What is your advice? How should we answer these people who say to me, 'Lighten the yoke your father put on us'?"

10The young men who had grown up with him replied, "The people have said to you, 'Your father put a heavy yoke on us, but make our yoke lighter.' Now tell them, 'My little finger is thicker than my father's waist. 11My father laid on you a heavy yoke; I will make it even heavier. My father scourged you with whips; I will scourge you with scorpions.'"

12Three days later Jeroboam and all the people returned to Rehoboam, as the king had said, "Come back to me in three days." 13The king answered them harshly. Rejecting the advice of the elders, 14he followed the advice of the young men and said, "My father made your yoke heavy; I will make it even heavier. My father scourged you with whips; I will scourge you with scorpions." 15So the king did not listen to the people, for this turn of events was from God, to fulfill the word the LORD had spoken to Jeroboam son of Nebat through Ahijah the Shilonite.

16When all Israel saw that the king refused to listen to them, they answered the king:

"What share do we have in David,
  what part in Jesse's son?
To your tents, Israel!
  Look after your own house, David!"

So all the Israelites went home. 17But as for the Israelites who were living in the towns of Judah, Rehoboam still ruled over them.

18King Rehoboam sent out Adoniram,[a] who was in charge of forced labor, but the Israelites stoned him to death. King Rehoboam, however, managed to get into his chariot and escape to Jerusalem. 19So Israel has been in rebellion against the house of David to this day.

11 When Rehoboam arrived in Jerusalem, he mustered Judah and Benjamin—a hundred and eighty thousand able young men—to go to war against Israel and to regain the kingdom for Rehoboam.

2But this word of the LORD came to Shemaiah the man of God: 3"Say to Rehoboam son of Solomon king of Judah and to all Israel in Judah and Benjamin, 4'This is what the LORD says: Do not go up to fight against your fellow Israelites. Go home, every one of you, for this is my doing.'" So they obeyed the words of the LORD and turned back from marching against Jeroboam.

Rehoboam Fortifies Judah

5Rehoboam lived in Jerusalem and built up towns for defense in Judah: 6Bethlehem, Etam, Tekoa, 7Beth Zur, Soko, Adullam, 8Gath, Mareshah, Ziph, 9Adoraim, Lachish, Azekah, 10Zorah, Aijalon and Hebron. These were fortified cities in Judah and Benjamin. 11He strengthened their defenses and put commanders in them, with supplies of food, olive oil and wine. 12He put shields and spears in all the cities, and made them very strong. So Judah and Benjamin were his.

13The priests and Levites from all their districts throughout Israel sided with him. 14The Levites even abandoned their pasturelands and property and came to Judah and Jerusalem, because Jeroboam and his sons had rejected them as priests of the LORD 15when he appointed his own priests for the high places and for the goat and calf idols he had made. 16Those from every tribe of Israel who set their hearts on seeking the LORD, the God of Israel, followed the Levites to Jerusalem to offer sacrifices to the LORD, the God of their ancestors. 17They strengthened the kingdom of Judah and supported Rehoboam son of Solomon three years, following the ways of David and Solomon during this time.

Rehoboam's Family

18Rehoboam married Mahalath, who was the daughter of David's son Jerimoth and of Abihail, the daughter of Jesse's son Eliab. 19She bore him sons:

[a] 18 Hebrew *Hadoram*, a variant of *Adoniram*

Jeush, Shemariah and Zaham. [20]Then he married Maakah daughter of Absalom, who bore him Abijah, Attai, Ziza and Shelomith. [21]Rehoboam loved Maakah daughter of Absalom more than any of his other wives and concubines. In all, he had eighteen wives and sixty concubines, twenty-eight sons and sixty daughters.

[22]Rehoboam appointed Abijah son of Maakah as crown prince among his brothers, in order to make him king. [23]He acted wisely, dispersing some of his sons throughout the districts of Judah and Benjamin, and to all the fortified cities. He gave them abundant provisions and took many wives for them.

Shishak Attacks Jerusalem

12 After Rehoboam's position as king was established and he had become strong, he and all Israel[a] with him abandoned the law of the LORD. [2]Because they had been unfaithful to the LORD, Shishak king of Egypt attacked Jerusalem in the fifth year of King Rehoboam. [3]With twelve hundred chariots and sixty thousand horsemen and the innumerable troops of Libyans, Sukkites and Cushites[b] that came with him from Egypt, [4]he captured the fortified cities of Judah and came as far as Jerusalem.

[5]Then the prophet Shemaiah came to Rehoboam and to the leaders of Judah who had assembled in Jerusalem for fear of Shishak, and he said to them, "This is what the LORD says, 'You have abandoned me; therefore, I now abandon you to Shishak.'"

[6]The leaders of Israel and the king humbled themselves and said, "The LORD is just."

[7]When the LORD saw that they humbled themselves, this word of the LORD came to Shemaiah: "Since they have humbled themselves, I will not destroy them but will soon give them deliverance. My wrath will not be poured out on Jerusalem through Shishak. [8]They will, however, become subject to him, so that they may learn the difference between serving me and serving the kings of other lands."

[9]When Shishak king of Egypt attacked Jerusalem, he carried off the treasures of the temple of the LORD and the treasures of the royal palace. He took everything, including the gold shields Solomon had made. [10]So King Rehoboam made bronze shields to replace them and assigned these to the commanders of the guard on duty at the entrance to the royal palace. [11]Whenever the king went to the LORD's temple, the guards went with him, bearing the shields, and afterward they returned them to the guardroom.

[12]Because Rehoboam humbled himself, the LORD's anger turned from him, and he was not totally destroyed. Indeed, there was some good in Judah.

[13]King Rehoboam established himself firmly in Jerusalem and continued as king. He was forty-one years old when he became king, and he reigned seventeen years in Jerusalem, the city the LORD had chosen out of all the tribes of Israel in which to put his Name. His mother's name was Naamah; she was an Ammonite. [14]He did evil because he had not set his heart on seeking the LORD.

[15]As for the events of Rehoboam's reign, from beginning to end, are they not written in the records of Shemaiah the prophet and of Iddo the seer that deal with genealogies? There was continual warfare between Rehoboam and Jeroboam. [16]Rehoboam rested with his ancestors and was buried in the City of David. And Abijah his son succeeded him as king.

Abijah King of Judah

13 In the eighteenth year of the reign of Jeroboam, Abijah became king of Judah, [2]and he reigned in Jerusalem three years. His mother's name was Maakah,[c] a daughter[d] of Uriel of Gibeah.

There was war between Abijah and Jeroboam. [3]Abijah went into battle with an army of four hundred thousand able fighting men, and Jeroboam drew up a battle line against him with eight hundred thousand able troops.

[4]Abijah stood on Mount Zemaraim, in the hill country of Ephraim, and said, "Jeroboam and all Israel, listen to me! [5]Don't you know that the LORD, the God of Israel, has given the kingship of Israel to David and his descendants forever by a covenant of salt? [6]Yet Jeroboam son of Nebat, an official of Solomon son of David, rebelled against his master. [7]Some worthless scoundrels gathered around him and opposed Rehoboam son of Solomon when he was young and indecisive and not strong enough to resist them.

[8]"And now you plan to resist the kingdom of the LORD, which is in the hands

[a] *1* That is, Judah, as frequently in 2 Chronicles [b] *3* That is, people from the upper Nile region [c] *2* Most Septuagint manuscripts and Syriac (see also 11:20 and 1 Kings 15:2); Hebrew *Micaiah* [d] *2* Or *granddaughter*

of David's descendants. You are indeed a vast army and have with you the golden calves that Jeroboam made to be your gods. 9But didn't you drive out the priests of the LORD, the sons of Aaron, and the Levites, and make priests of your own as the peoples of other lands do? Whoever comes to consecrate himself with a young bull and seven rams may become a priest of what are not gods.

10"As for us, the LORD is our God, and we have not forsaken him. The priests who serve the LORD are sons of Aaron, and the Levites assist them. 11Every morning and evening they present burnt offerings and fragrant incense to the LORD. They set out the bread on the ceremonially clean table and light the lamps on the gold lampstand every evening. We are observing the requirements of the LORD our God. But you have forsaken him. 12God is with us; he is our leader. His priests with their trumpets will sound the battle cry against you. People of Israel, do not fight against the LORD, the God of your ancestors, for you will not succeed."

13Now Jeroboam had sent troops around to the rear, so that while he was in front of Judah the ambush was behind them. 14Judah turned and saw that they were being attacked at both front and rear. Then they cried out to the LORD. The priests blew their trumpets 15and the men of Judah raised the battle cry. At the sound of their battle cry, God routed Jeroboam and all Israel before Abijah and Judah. 16The Israelites fled before Judah, and God delivered them into their hands. 17Abijah and his troops inflicted heavy losses on them, so that there were five hundred thousand casualties among Israel's able men. 18The Israelites were subdued on that occasion, and the people of Judah were victorious because they relied on the LORD, the God of their ancestors.

19Abijah pursued Jeroboam and took from him the towns of Bethel, Jeshanah and Ephron, with their surrounding villages. 20Jeroboam did not regain power during the time of Abijah. And the LORD struck him down and he died.

21But Abijah grew in strength. He married fourteen wives and had twenty-two sons and sixteen daughters.

22The other events of Abijah's reign, what he did and what he said, are written in the annotations of the prophet Iddo.

14[a] And Abijah rested with his ancestors and was buried in the City of David. Asa his son succeeded him as king, and in his days the country was at peace for ten years.

Asa King of Judah

2Asa did what was good and right in the eyes of the LORD his God. 3He removed the foreign altars and the high places, smashed the sacred stones and cut down the Asherah poles.[b] 4He commanded Judah to seek the LORD, the God of their ancestors, and to obey his laws and commands. 5He removed the high places and incense altars in every town in Judah, and the kingdom was at peace under him. 6He built up the fortified cities of Judah, since the land was at peace. No one was at war with him during those years, for the LORD gave him rest.

7"Let us build up these towns," he said to Judah, "and put walls around them, with towers, gates and bars. The land is still ours, because we have sought the LORD our God; we sought him and he has given us rest on every side." So they built and prospered.

8Asa had an army of three hundred thousand men from Judah, equipped with large shields and with spears, and two hundred and eighty thousand from Benjamin, armed with small shields and with bows. All these were brave fighting men.

9Zerah the Cushite marched out against them with an army of thousands upon thousands and three hundred chariots, and came as far as Mareshah. 10Asa went out to meet him, and they took up battle positions in the Valley of Zephathah near Mareshah.

11Then Asa called to the LORD his God and said, "LORD, there is no one like you to help the powerless against the mighty. Help us, LORD our God, for we rely on you, and in your name we have come against this vast army. LORD, you are our God; do not let mere mortals prevail against you."

12The LORD struck down the Cushites before Asa and Judah. The Cushites fled, 13and Asa and his army pursued them as far as Gerar. Such a great number of Cushites fell that they could not recover; they were crushed before the LORD and his forces. The men of Judah carried off a large amount of plunder. 14They destroyed all the villages around Gerar,

[a] In Hebrew texts 14:1 is numbered 13:23, and 14:2-15 is numbered 14:1-14. [b] 3 That is, wooden symbols of the goddess Asherah; here and elsewhere in 2 Chronicles

for the terror of the LORD had fallen
on them. They looted all these villages, since there was much plunder there.
15They also attacked the camps of the
herders and carried off droves of sheep
and goats and camels. Then they returned to Jerusalem.

Asa's Reform

15 The Spirit of God came on Azariah
son of Oded. 2He went out to meet
Asa and said to him, "Listen to me, Asa
and all Judah and Benjamin. The LORD is
with you when you are with him. If you
seek him, he will be found by you, but if
you forsake him, he will forsake you. 3For
a long time Israel was without the true
God, without a priest to teach and without the law. 4But in their distress they
turned to the LORD, the God of Israel, and
sought him, and he was found by them.
5In those days it was not safe to travel about, for all the inhabitants of the
lands were in great turmoil. 6One nation
was being crushed by another and one
city by another, because God was troubling them with every kind of distress.
7But as for you, be strong and do not give
up, for your work will be rewarded."

8When Asa heard these words and the
prophecy of Azariah son of[a] Oded the
prophet, he took courage. He removed
the detestable idols from the whole
land of Judah and Benjamin and from
the towns he had captured in the hills
of Ephraim. He repaired the altar of the
LORD that was in front of the portico of
the LORD's temple.

9Then he assembled all Judah and
Benjamin and the people from Ephraim, Manasseh and Simeon who had settled among them, for large numbers had
come over to him from Israel when they
saw that the LORD his God was with him.

10They assembled at Jerusalem in
the third month of the fifteenth year of
Asa's reign. 11At that time they sacrificed
to the LORD seven hundred head of cattle and seven thousand sheep and goats
from the plunder they had brought back.
12They entered into a covenant to seek
the LORD, the God of their ancestors, with
all their heart and soul. 13All who would
not seek the LORD, the God of Israel,
were to be put to death, whether small
or great, man or woman. 14They took an
oath to the LORD with loud acclamation,
with shouting and with trumpets and
horns. 15All Judah rejoiced about the
oath because they had sworn it wholeheartedly. They sought God eagerly, and
he was found by them. So the LORD gave
them rest on every side.

16King Asa also deposed his grandmother Maakah from her position as
queen mother, because she had made
a repulsive image for the worship of
Asherah. Asa cut it down, broke it up
and burned it in the Kidron Valley. 17Al-
though he did not remove the high
places from Israel, Asa's heart was fully
committed to the LORD all his life. 18He
brought into the temple of God the silver
and gold and the articles that he and his
father had dedicated.

19There was no more war until the
thirty-fifth year of Asa's reign.

Asa's Last Years

16 In the thirty-sixth year of Asa's
reign Baasha king of Israel went
up against Judah and fortified Ramah
to prevent anyone from leaving or entering the territory of Asa king of Judah.

2Asa then took the silver and gold
out of the treasuries of the LORD's temple and of his own palace and sent it to
Ben-Hadad king of Aram, who was ruling in Damascus. 3"Let there be a treaty
between me and you," he said, "as there
was between my father and your father.
See, I am sending you silver and gold.
Now break your treaty with Baasha king
of Israel so he will withdraw from me."

4Ben-Hadad agreed with King Asa
and sent the commanders of his forces
against the towns of Israel. They conquered Ijon, Dan, Abel Maim[b] and all
the store cities of Naphtali. 5When Baasha heard this, he stopped building
Ramah and abandoned his work. 6Then
King Asa brought all the men of Judah,
and they carried away from Ramah the
stones and timber Baasha had been using. With them he built up Geba and Mizpah.

7At that time Hanani the seer came to
Asa king of Judah and said to him: "Because you relied on the king of Aram and
not on the LORD your God, the army of
the king of Aram has escaped from your
hand. 8Were not the Cushites[c] and Libyans a mighty army with great numbers
of chariots and horsemen[d]? Yet when
you relied on the LORD, he delivered
them into your hand. 9For the eyes of

[a] 8 Vulgate and Syriac (see also Septuagint and verse 1); Hebrew does not have *Azariah son of.*
[b] 4 Also known as *Abel Beth Maakah* [c] 8 That is, people from the upper Nile region [d] 8 Or *charioteers*

the LORD range throughout the earth to
strengthen those whose hearts are fully
committed to him. You have done a foolish thing, and from now on you will be
at war."
10 Asa was angry with the seer because
of this; he was so enraged that he put
him in prison. At the same time Asa brutally oppressed some of the people.
11 The events of Asa's reign, from beginning to end, are written in the book
of the kings of Judah and Israel. 12 In the
thirty-ninth year of his reign Asa was afflicted with a disease in his feet. Though
his disease was severe, even in his illness
he did not seek help from the LORD, but
only from the physicians. 13 Then in the
forty-first year of his reign Asa died and
rested with his ancestors. 14 They buried
him in the tomb that he had cut out for
himself in the City of David. They laid
him on a bier covered with spices and
various blended perfumes, and they
made a huge fire in his honor.

Jehoshaphat King of Judah

17 Jehoshaphat his son succeeded him
as king and strengthened himself
against Israel. 2 He stationed troops in all
the fortified cities of Judah and put garrisons in Judah and in the towns of Ephraim that his father Asa had captured.
3 The LORD was with Jehoshaphat because he followed the ways of his father
David before him. He did not consult the
Baals 4 but sought the God of his father
and followed his commands rather than
the practices of Israel. 5 The LORD established the kingdom under his control;
and all Judah brought gifts to Jehoshaphat, so that he had great wealth and
honor. 6 His heart was devoted to the
ways of the LORD; furthermore, he removed the high places and the Asherah
poles from Judah.
7 In the third year of his reign he sent
his officials Ben-Hail, Obadiah, Zechariah, Nethanel and Micaiah to teach in the
towns of Judah. 8 With them were certain
Levites — Shemaiah, Nethaniah, Zebadiah, Asahel, Shemiramoth, Jehonathan,
Adonijah, Tobijah and Tob-Adonijah —
and the priests Elishama and Jehoram.
9 They taught throughout Judah, taking
with them the Book of the Law of the
LORD; they went around to all the towns
of Judah and taught the people.
10 The fear of the LORD fell on all the
kingdoms of the lands surrounding
Judah, so that they did not go to war
against Jehoshaphat. 11 Some Philistines
brought Jehoshaphat gifts and silver
as tribute, and the Arabs brought him
flocks: seven thousand seven hundred
rams and seven thousand seven hundred goats.
12 Jehoshaphat became more and
more powerful; he built forts and store
cities in Judah 13 and had large supplies
in the towns of Judah. He also kept experienced fighting men in Jerusalem.
14 Their enrollment by families was as
follows:

From Judah, commanders of units
of 1,000:
Adnah the commander, with
300,000 fighting men;
15 next, Jehohanan the commander,
with 280,000;
16 next, Amasiah son of Zikri, who
volunteered himself for the service of the LORD, with 200,000.
17 From Benjamin:
Eliada, a valiant soldier, with
200,000 men armed with bows
and shields;
18 next, Jehozabad, with 180,000
men armed for battle.

19 These were the men who served the
king, besides those he stationed in the
fortified cities throughout Judah.

Micaiah Prophesies Against Ahab

18 Now Jehoshaphat had great
wealth and honor, and he allied
himself with Ahab by marriage. 2 Some
years later he went down to see Ahab in
Samaria. Ahab slaughtered many sheep
and cattle for him and the people with
him and urged him to attack Ramoth
Gilead. 3 Ahab king of Israel asked Jehoshaphat king of Judah, "Will you go
with me against Ramoth Gilead?"
Jehoshaphat replied, "I am as you are,
and my people as your people; we will
join you in the war." 4 But Jehoshaphat
also said to the king of Israel, "First seek
the counsel of the LORD."
5 So the king of Israel brought together
the prophets — four hundred men — and
asked them, "Shall we go to war against
Ramoth Gilead, or shall I not?"
"Go," they answered, "for God will give
it into the king's hand."
6 But Jehoshaphat asked, "Is there no
longer a prophet of the LORD here whom
we can inquire of?"
7 The king of Israel answered Jehoshaphat, "There is still one prophet through
whom we can inquire of the LORD, but I
hate him because he never prophesies
anything good about me, but always
bad. He is Micaiah son of Imlah."

"The king should not say such a
thing," Jehoshaphat replied.
8So the king of Israel called one of his
officials and said, "Bring Micaiah son of
Imlah at once."
9Dressed in their royal robes, the king
of Israel and Jehoshaphat king of Judah were sitting on their thrones at the
threshing floor by the entrance of the
gate of Samaria, with all the prophets
prophesying before them. 10Now Zedekiah son of Kenaanah had made iron
horns, and he declared, "This is what the
LORD says: 'With these you will gore the
Arameans until they are destroyed.'"
11All the other prophets were prophesying the same thing. "Attack Ramoth
Gilead and be victorious," they said,
"for the LORD will give it into the king's
hand."
12The messenger who had gone to
summon Micaiah said to him, "Look,
the other prophets without exception
are predicting success for the king. Let
your word agree with theirs, and speak
favorably."
13But Micaiah said, "As surely as the
LORD lives, I can tell him only what my
God says."
14When he arrived, the king asked him,
"Micaiah, shall we go to war against Ramoth Gilead, or shall I not?"
"Attack and be victorious," he answered, "for they will be given into your
hand."
15The king said to him, "How many
times must I make you swear to tell me
nothing but the truth in the name of the
LORD?"
16Then Micaiah answered, "I saw all
Israel scattered on the hills like sheep
without a shepherd, and the LORD said,
'These people have no master. Let each
one go home in peace.'"
17The king of Israel said to Jehoshaphat, "Didn't I tell you that he never
prophesies anything good about me, but
only bad?"
18Micaiah continued, "Therefore hear
the word of the LORD: I saw the LORD
sitting on his throne with all the multitudes of heaven standing on his right
and on his left. 19And the LORD said, 'Who
will entice Ahab king of Israel into attacking Ramoth Gilead and going to his
death there?'
"One suggested this, and another that.
20Finally, a spirit came forward, stood
before the LORD and said, 'I will entice
him.'
"'By what means?' the LORD asked.
21"'I will go and be a deceiving spirit in
the mouths of all his prophets,' he said.
"'You will succeed in enticing him,'
said the LORD. 'Go and do it.'
22"So now the LORD has put a deceiving spirit in the mouths of these prophets of yours. The LORD has decreed disaster for you."
23Then Zedekiah son of Kenaanah
went up and slapped Micaiah in the
face. "Which way did the spirit from[a] the
LORD go when he went from me to speak
to you?" he asked.
24Micaiah replied, "You will find out
on the day you go to hide in an inner
room."
25The king of Israel then ordered,
"Take Micaiah and send him back to
Amon the ruler of the city and to Joash
the king's son, 26and say, 'This is what
the king says: Put this fellow in prison
and give him nothing but bread and water until I return safely.'"
27Micaiah declared, "If you ever return
safely, the LORD has not spoken through
me." Then he added, "Mark my words, all
you people!"

Ahab Killed at Ramoth Gilead

28So the king of Israel and Jehoshaphat king of Judah went up to Ramoth
Gilead. 29The king of Israel said to Jehoshaphat, "I will enter the battle in disguise, but you wear your royal robes." So
the king of Israel disguised himself and
went into battle.
30Now the king of Aram had ordered
his chariot commanders, "Do not fight
with anyone, small or great, except
the king of Israel." 31When the chariot commanders saw Jehoshaphat, they
thought, "This is the king of Israel." So
they turned to attack him, but Jehoshaphat cried out, and the LORD helped
him. God drew them away from him,
32for when the chariot commanders saw
that he was not the king of Israel, they
stopped pursuing him.
33But someone drew his bow at random and hit the king of Israel between
the breastplate and the scale armor.
The king told the chariot driver, "Wheel
around and get me out of the fighting. I've been wounded." 34All day long
the battle raged, and the king of Israel
propped himself up in his chariot facing the Arameans until evening. Then at
sunset he died.

[a] 23 Or *Spirit of*

19 When Jehoshaphat king of Judah returned safely to his palace in Jerusalem, 2Jehu the seer, the son of Hanani, went out to meet him and said to the king, "Should you help the wicked and love[a] those who hate the LORD? Because of this, the wrath of the LORD is on you. 3There is, however, some good in you, for you have rid the land of the Asherah poles and have set your heart on seeking God."

Jehoshaphat Appoints Judges

4Jehoshaphat lived in Jerusalem, and he went out again among the people from Beersheba to the hill country of Ephraim and turned them back to the LORD, the God of their ancestors. 5He appointed judges in the land, in each of the fortified cities of Judah. 6He told them, "Consider carefully what you do, because you are not judging for mere mortals but for the LORD, who is with you whenever you give a verdict. 7Now let the fear of the LORD be on you. Judge carefully, for with the LORD our God there is no injustice or partiality or bribery."

8In Jerusalem also, Jehoshaphat appointed some of the Levites, priests and heads of Israelite families to administer the law of the LORD and to settle disputes. And they lived in Jerusalem. 9He gave them these orders: "You must serve faithfully and wholeheartedly in the fear of the LORD. 10In every case that comes before you from your people who live in the cities — whether bloodshed or other concerns of the law, commands, decrees or regulations — you are to warn them not to sin against the LORD; otherwise his wrath will come on you and your people. Do this, and you will not sin.

11"Amariah the chief priest will be over you in any matter concerning the LORD, and Zebadiah son of Ishmael, the leader of the tribe of Judah, will be over you in any matter concerning the king, and the Levites will serve as officials before you. Act with courage, and may the LORD be with those who do well."

Jehoshaphat Defeats Moab and Ammon

20 After this, the Moabites and Ammonites with some of the Meunites[b] came to wage war against Jehoshaphat.

2Some people came and told Jehoshaphat, "A vast army is coming against you from Edom,[c] from the other side of the Dead Sea. It is already in Hazezon Tamar" (that is, En Gedi). 3Alarmed, Jehoshaphat resolved to inquire of the LORD, and he proclaimed a fast for all Judah. 4The people of Judah came together to seek help from the LORD; indeed, they came from every town in Judah to seek him.

5Then Jehoshaphat stood up in the assembly of Judah and Jerusalem at the temple of the LORD in the front of the new courtyard 6and said:

> "LORD, the God of our ancestors, are you not the God who is in heaven? You rule over all the kingdoms of the nations. Power and might are in your hand, and no one can withstand you. 7Our God, did you not drive out the inhabitants of this land before your people Israel and give it forever to the descendants of Abraham your friend? 8They have lived in it and have built in it a sanctuary for your Name, saying, 9'If calamity comes upon us, whether the sword of judgment, or plague or famine, we will stand in your presence before this temple that bears your Name and will cry out to you in our distress, and you will hear us and save us.'
>
> 10"But now here are men from Ammon, Moab and Mount Seir, whose territory you would not allow Israel to invade when they came from Egypt; so they turned away from them and did not destroy them. 11See how they are repaying us by coming to drive us out of the possession you gave us as an inheritance. 12Our God, will you not judge them? For we have no power to face this vast army that is attacking us. We do not know what to do, but our eyes are on you."

13All the men of Judah, with their wives and children and little ones, stood there before the LORD.

14Then the Spirit of the LORD came on Jahaziel son of Zechariah, the son of Benaiah, the son of Jeiel, the son of Mattaniah, a Levite and descendant of Asaph, as he stood in the assembly.

15He said: "Listen, King Jehoshaphat and all who live in Judah and Jerusalem! This is what the LORD says to you: 'Do not be afraid or discouraged because of this vast army. For the battle is not yours, but God's. 16Tomorrow march down against them. They will be climbing up by the Pass of Ziz, and you will find them at the end of

[a] *2* Or *and make alliances with* [b] *1* Some Septuagint manuscripts; Hebrew *Ammonites*
[c] *2* One Hebrew manuscript; most Hebrew manuscripts, Septuagint and Vulgate *Aram*

the gorge in the Desert of Jeruel. 17You will
not have to fight this battle. Take up your
positions; stand firm and see the deliverance the LORD will give you, Judah and Jerusalem. Do not be afraid; do not be discouraged. Go out to face them tomorrow,
and the LORD will be with you.'"

18Jehoshaphat bowed down with his
face to the ground, and all the people of
Judah and Jerusalem fell down in worship before the LORD. 19Then some Levites from the Kohathites and Korahites
stood up and praised the LORD, the God
of Israel, with a very loud voice.

20Early in the morning they left for the
Desert of Tekoa. As they set out, Jehoshaphat stood and said, "Listen to me, Judah and people of Jerusalem! Have faith
in the LORD your God and you will be upheld; have faith in his prophets and you
will be successful." 21After consulting the
people, Jehoshaphat appointed men to
sing to the LORD and to praise him for
the splendor of his[a] holiness as they
went out at the head of the army, saying:

"Give thanks to the LORD,
for his love endures forever."

22As they began to sing and praise, the
LORD set ambushes against the men of
Ammon and Moab and Mount Seir who
were invading Judah, and they were defeated. 23The Ammonites and Moabites
rose up against the men from Mount Seir
to destroy and annihilate them. After
they finished slaughtering the men from
Seir, they helped to destroy one another.

24When the men of Judah came to
the place that overlooks the desert and
looked toward the vast army, they saw
only dead bodies lying on the ground;
no one had escaped. 25So Jehoshaphat
and his men went to carry off their plunder, and they found among them a great
amount of equipment and clothing[b] and
also articles of value — more than they
could take away. There was so much
plunder that it took three days to collect it. 26On the fourth day they assembled in the Valley of Berakah, where they
praised the LORD. This is why it is called
the Valley of Berakah[c] to this day.

27Then, led by Jehoshaphat, all the
men of Judah and Jerusalem returned
joyfully to Jerusalem, for the LORD had
given them cause to rejoice over their
enemies. 28They entered Jerusalem and
went to the temple of the LORD with
harps and lyres and trumpets.

29The fear of God came on all the surrounding kingdoms when they heard
how the LORD had fought against the
enemies of Israel. 30And the kingdom of
Jehoshaphat was at peace, for his God
had given him rest on every side.

The End of Jehoshaphat's Reign

31So Jehoshaphat reigned over Judah.
He was thirty-five years old when he became king of Judah, and he reigned in
Jerusalem twenty-five years. His mother's name was Azubah daughter of Shilhi. 32He followed the ways of his father
Asa and did not stray from them; he did
what was right in the eyes of the LORD.
33The high places, however, were not removed, and the people still had not set
their hearts on the God of their ancestors.

34The other events of Jehoshaphat's
reign, from beginning to end, are written in the annals of Jehu son of Hanani, which are recorded in the book of the
kings of Israel.

35Later, Jehoshaphat king of Judah
made an alliance with Ahaziah king of Israel, whose ways were wicked. 36He agreed
with him to construct a fleet of trading
ships.[d] After these were built at Ezion Geber, 37Eliezer son of Dodavahu of Mareshah
prophesied against Jehoshaphat, saying,
"Because you have made an alliance with
Ahaziah, the LORD will destroy what you
have made." The ships were wrecked and
were not able to set sail to trade.[e]

21 Then Jehoshaphat rested with his
ancestors and was buried with
them in the City of David. And Jehoram
his son succeeded him as king. 2Jeho-
ram's brothers, the sons of Jehoshaphat,
were Azariah, Jehiel, Zechariah, Azari-
ahu, Michael and Shephatiah. All these
were sons of Jehoshaphat king of Israel.[f]
3Their father had given them many gifts
of silver and gold and articles of value,
as well as fortified cities in Judah, but he
had given the kingdom to Jehoram because he was his firstborn son.

Jehoram King of Judah

4When Jehoram established himself
firmly over his father's kingdom, he put
all his brothers to the sword along with
some of the officials of Israel. 5Jehoram
was thirty-two years old when he became
king, and he reigned in Jerusalem eight
years. 6He followed the ways of the kings
of Israel, as the house of Ahab had done,

[a] 21 Or *him with the splendor of* [b] 25 Some Hebrew manuscripts and Vulgate; most Hebrew manuscripts *corpses* [c] 26 *Berakah* means *praise.* [d] 36 Hebrew *of ships that could go to Tarshish* [e] 37 Hebrew *sail for Tarshish* [f] 2 That is, Judah, as frequently in 2 Chronicles

for he married a daughter of Ahab. He did evil in the eyes of the LORD. 7Nevertheless, because of the covenant the LORD had made with David, the LORD was not willing to destroy the house of David. He had promised to maintain a lamp for him and his descendants forever.

8In the time of Jehoram, Edom rebelled against Judah and set up its own king. 9So Jehoram went there with his officers and all his chariots. The Edomites surrounded him and his chariot commanders, but he rose up and broke through by night. 10To this day Edom has been in rebellion against Judah.

Libnah revolted at the same time, because Jehoram had forsaken the LORD, the God of his ancestors. 11He had also built high places on the hills of Judah and had caused the people of Jerusalem to prostitute themselves and had led Judah astray.

12Jehoram received a letter from Elijah the prophet, which said:

> "This is what the LORD, the God of your father David, says: 'You have not followed the ways of your father Jehoshaphat or of Asa king of Judah. 13But you have followed the ways of the kings of Israel, and you have led Judah and the people of Jerusalem to prostitute themselves, just as the house of Ahab did. You have also murdered your own brothers, members of your own family, men who were better than you. 14So now the LORD is about to strike your people, your sons, your wives and everything that is yours, with a heavy blow. 15You yourself will be very ill with a lingering disease of the bowels, until the disease causes your bowels to come out.' "

16The LORD aroused against Jehoram the hostility of the Philistines and of the Arabs who lived near the Cushites. 17They attacked Judah, invaded it and carried off all the goods found in the king's palace, together with his sons and wives. Not a son was left to him except Ahaziah,[a] the youngest.

18After all this, the LORD afflicted Jehoram with an incurable disease of the bowels. 19In the course of time, at the end of the second year, his bowels came out because of the disease, and he died in great pain. His people made no funeral fire in his honor, as they had for his predecessors.

20Jehoram was thirty-two years old when he became king, and he reigned in Jerusalem eight years. He passed away, to no one's regret, and was buried in the City of David, but not in the tombs of the kings.

Ahaziah King of Judah

22 The people of Jerusalem made Ahaziah, Jehoram's youngest son, king in his place, since the raiders, who came with the Arabs into the camp, had killed all the older sons. So Ahaziah son of Jehoram king of Judah began to reign.

2Ahaziah was twenty-two[b] years old when he became king, and he reigned in Jerusalem one year. His mother's name was Athaliah, a granddaughter of Omri.

3He too followed the ways of the house of Ahab, for his mother encouraged him to act wickedly. 4He did evil in the eyes of the LORD, as the house of Ahab had done, for after his father's death they became his advisers, to his undoing. 5He also followed their counsel when he went with Joram[c] son of Ahab king of Israel to wage war against Hazael king of Aram at Ramoth Gilead. The Arameans wounded Joram; 6so he returned to Jezreel to recover from the wounds they had inflicted on him at Ramoth[d] in his battle with Hazael king of Aram.

Then Ahaziah[e] son of Jehoram king of Judah went down to Jezreel to see Joram son of Ahab because he had been wounded.

7Through Ahaziah's visit to Joram, God brought about Ahaziah's downfall. When Ahaziah arrived, he went out with Joram to meet Jehu son of Nimshi, whom the LORD had anointed to destroy the house of Ahab. 8While Jehu was executing judgment on the house of Ahab, he found the officials of Judah and the sons of Ahaziah's relatives, who had been attending Ahaziah, and he killed them. 9He then went in search of Ahaziah, and his men captured him while he was hiding in Samaria. He was brought to Jehu and put to death. They buried him, for they said, "He was a son of Jehoshaphat, who sought the LORD with all his heart." So there was no one in the house of Ahaziah powerful enough to retain the kingdom.

[a] *17* Hebrew *Jehoahaz,* a variant of *Ahaziah* [b] *2* Some Septuagint manuscripts and Syriac (see also 2 Kings 8:26); Hebrew *forty-two* [c] *5* Hebrew *Jehoram,* a variant of *Joram;* also in verses 6 and 7 [d] *6* Hebrew *Ramah,* a variant of *Ramoth* [e] *6* Some Hebrew manuscripts, Septuagint, Vulgate and Syriac (see also 2 Kings 8:29); most Hebrew manuscripts *Azariah*

Athaliah and Joash

10 When Athaliah the mother of Ahaziah saw that her son was dead, she proceeded to destroy the whole royal family of the house of Judah. 11 But Jehosheba,[a] the daughter of King Jehoram, took Joash son of Ahaziah and stole him away from among the royal princes who were about to be murdered and put him and his nurse in a bedroom. Because Jehosheba,[a] the daughter of King Jehoram and wife of the priest Jehoiada, was Ahaziah's sister, she hid the child from Athaliah so she could not kill him. 12 He remained hidden with them at the temple of God for six years while Athaliah ruled the land.

23 In the seventh year Jehoiada showed his strength. He made a covenant with the commanders of units of a hundred: Azariah son of Jeroham, Ishmael son of Jehohanan, Azariah son of Obed, Maaseiah son of Adaiah, and Elishaphat son of Zikri. 2 They went throughout Judah and gathered the Levites and the heads of Israelite families from all the towns. When they came to Jerusalem, 3 the whole assembly made a covenant with the king at the temple of God.

Jehoiada said to them, "The king's son shall reign, as the LORD promised concerning the descendants of David. 4 Now this is what you are to do: A third of you priests and Levites who are going on duty on the Sabbath are to keep watch at the doors, 5 a third of you at the royal palace and a third at the Foundation Gate, and all the others are to be in the courtyards of the temple of the LORD. 6 No one is to enter the temple of the LORD except the priests and Levites on duty; they may enter because they are consecrated, but all the others are to observe the LORD's command not to enter.[b] 7 The Levites are to station themselves around the king, each with weapon in hand. Anyone who enters the temple is to be put to death. Stay close to the king wherever he goes."

8 The Levites and all the men of Judah did just as Jehoiada the priest ordered. Each one took his men — those who were going on duty on the Sabbath and those who were going off duty — for Jehoiada the priest had not released any of the divisions. 9 Then he gave the commanders of units of a hundred the spears and the large and small shields that had belonged to King David and that were in the temple of God. 10 He stationed all the men, each with his weapon in his hand, around the king — near the altar and the temple, from the south side to the north side of the temple.

11 Jehoiada and his sons brought out the king's son and put the crown on him; they presented him with a copy of the covenant and proclaimed him king. They anointed him and shouted, "Long live the king!"

12 When Athaliah heard the noise of the people running and cheering the king, she went to them at the temple of the LORD. 13 She looked, and there was the king, standing by his pillar at the entrance. The officers and the trumpeters were beside the king, and all the people of the land were rejoicing and blowing trumpets, and musicians with their instruments were leading the praises. Then Athaliah tore her robes and shouted, "Treason! Treason!"

14 Jehoiada the priest sent out the commanders of units of a hundred, who were in charge of the troops, and said to them: "Bring her out between the ranks[c] and put to the sword anyone who follows her." For the priest had said, "Do not put her to death at the temple of the LORD." 15 So they seized her as she reached the entrance of the Horse Gate on the palace grounds, and there they put her to death.

16 Jehoiada then made a covenant that he, the people and the king[d] would be the LORD's people. 17 All the people went to the temple of Baal and tore it down. They smashed the altars and idols and killed Mattan the priest of Baal in front of the altars.

18 Then Jehoiada placed the oversight of the temple of the LORD in the hands of the Levitical priests, to whom David had made assignments in the temple, to present the burnt offerings of the LORD as written in the Law of Moses, with rejoicing and singing, as David had ordered. 19 He also stationed gatekeepers at the gates of the LORD's temple so that no one who was in any way unclean might enter.

20 He took with him the commanders of hundreds, the nobles, the rulers of the people and all the people of the land and brought the king down from the temple of the LORD. They went into the palace through the Upper Gate and seated the king on the royal throne. 21 All the people of the land rejoiced, and the city was calm, because Athaliah had been slain with the sword.

[a] 11 Hebrew *Jehoshabeath,* a variant of *Jehosheba* [b] 6 *Or are to stand guard where the LORD has assigned them* [c] 14 *Or out from the precincts* [d] 16 *Or covenant between the LORD and the people and the king that they* (see 2 Kings 11:17)

Joash Repairs the Temple

24 Joash was seven years old when he became king, and he reigned in Jerusalem forty years. His mother's name was Zibiah; she was from Beersheba. 2 Joash did what was right in the eyes of the LORD all the years of Jehoiada the priest. 3 Jehoiada chose two wives for him, and he had sons and daughters.

4 Some time later Joash decided to restore the temple of the LORD. 5 He called together the priests and Levites and said to them, "Go to the towns of Judah and collect the money due annually from all Israel, to repair the temple of your God. Do it now." But the Levites did not act at once.

6 Therefore the king summoned Jehoiada the chief priest and said to him, "Why haven't you required the Levites to bring in from Judah and Jerusalem the tax imposed by Moses the servant of the LORD and by the assembly of Israel for the tent of the covenant law?"

7 Now the sons of that wicked woman Athaliah had broken into the temple of God and had used even its sacred objects for the Baals.

8 At the king's command, a chest was made and placed outside, at the gate of the temple of the LORD. 9 A proclamation was then issued in Judah and Jerusalem that they should bring to the LORD the tax that Moses the servant of God had required of Israel in the wilderness. 10 All the officials and all the people brought their contributions gladly, dropping them into the chest until it was full. 11 Whenever the chest was brought in by the Levites to the king's officials and they saw that there was a large amount of money, the royal secretary and the officer of the chief priest would come and empty the chest and carry it back to its place. They did this regularly and collected a great amount of money. 12 The king and Jehoiada gave it to those who carried out the work required for the temple of the LORD. They hired masons and carpenters to restore the LORD's temple, and also workers in iron and bronze to repair the temple.

13 The men in charge of the work were diligent, and the repairs progressed under them. They rebuilt the temple of God according to its original design and reinforced it. 14 When they had finished, they brought the rest of the money to the king and Jehoiada, and with it were made articles for the LORD's temple: articles for the service and for the burnt offerings, and also dishes and other objects of gold and silver. As long as Jehoiada lived, burnt offerings were presented continually in the temple of the LORD.

15 Now Jehoiada was old and full of years, and he died at the age of a hundred and thirty. 16 He was buried with the kings in the City of David, because of the good he had done in Israel for God and his temple.

The Wickedness of Joash

17 After the death of Jehoiada, the officials of Judah came and paid homage to the king, and he listened to them. 18 They abandoned the temple of the LORD, the God of their ancestors, and worshiped Asherah poles and idols. Because of their guilt, God's anger came on Judah and Jerusalem. 19 Although the LORD sent prophets to the people to bring them back to him, and though they testified against them, they would not listen.

20 Then the Spirit of God came on Zechariah son of Jehoiada the priest. He stood before the people and said, "This is what God says: 'Why do you disobey the LORD's commands? You will not prosper. Because you have forsaken the LORD, he has forsaken you.' "

21 But they plotted against him, and by order of the king they stoned him to death in the courtyard of the LORD's temple. 22 King Joash did not remember the kindness Zechariah's father Jehoiada had shown him but killed his son, who said as he lay dying, "May the LORD see this and call you to account."

23 At the turn of the year,[a] the army of Aram marched against Joash; it invaded Judah and Jerusalem and killed all the leaders of the people. They sent all the plunder to their king in Damascus. 24 Although the Aramean army had come with only a few men, the LORD delivered into their hands a much larger army. Because Judah had forsaken the LORD, the God of their ancestors, judgment was executed on Joash. 25 When the Arameans withdrew, they left Joash severely wounded. His officials conspired against him for murdering the son of Jehoiada the priest, and they killed him in his bed. So he died and was buried in the City of David, but not in the tombs of the kings.

26 Those who conspired against him were Zabad,[b] son of Shimeath an Ammonite woman, and Jehozabad, son of Shimrith[c] a Moabite woman. 27 The account of his sons, the many prophecies

[a] *23* Probably in the spring [b] *26* A variant of *Jozabad* [c] *26* A variant of *Shomer*

about him, and the record of the restoration of the temple of God are written
in the annotations on the book of the
kings. And Amaziah his son succeeded
him as king.

Amaziah King of Judah

25 Amaziah was twenty-five years
old when he became king, and he
reigned in Jerusalem twenty-nine years.
His mother's name was Jehoaddan; she
was from Jerusalem. 2He did what was
right in the eyes of the LORD, but not
wholeheartedly. 3After the kingdom was
firmly in his control, he executed the officials who had murdered his father the
king. 4Yet he did not put their children to
death, but acted in accordance with what
is written in the Law, in the Book of Moses,
where the LORD commanded: "Parents
shall not be put to death for their children, nor children be put to death for their
parents; each will die for their own sin."[a]

5Amaziah called the people of Judah
together and assigned them according
to their families to commanders of thousands and commanders of hundreds for
all Judah and Benjamin. He then mustered those twenty years old or more and
found that there were three hundred
thousand men fit for military service,
able to handle the spear and shield. 6He
also hired a hundred thousand fighting
men from Israel for a hundred talents[b]
of silver.

7But a man of God came to him and
said, "Your Majesty, these troops from
Israel must not march with you, for the
LORD is not with Israel — not with any of
the people of Ephraim. 8Even if you go
and fight courageously in battle, God will
overthrow you before the enemy, for God
has the power to help or to overthrow."

9Amaziah asked the man of God, "But
what about the hundred talents I paid
for these Israelite troops?"

The man of God replied, "The LORD
can give you much more than that."

10So Amaziah dismissed the troops
who had come to him from Ephraim and
sent them home. They were furious with
Judah and left for home in a great rage.

11Amaziah then marshaled his
strength and led his army to the Valley
of Salt, where he killed ten thousand
men of Seir. 12The army of Judah also
captured ten thousand men alive, took
them to the top of a cliff and threw them
down so that all were dashed to pieces.

13Meanwhile the troops that Amaziah
had sent back and had not allowed to
take part in the war raided towns belonging to Judah from Samaria to Beth Horon.
They killed three thousand people and
carried off great quantities of plunder.

14When Amaziah returned from
slaughtering the Edomites, he brought
back the gods of the people of Seir. He set
them up as his own gods, bowed down
to them and burned sacrifices to them.
15The anger of the LORD burned against
Amaziah, and he sent a prophet to him,
who said, "Why do you consult this people's gods, which could not save their
own people from your hand?"

16While he was still speaking, the king
said to him, "Have we appointed you an
adviser to the king? Stop! Why be struck
down?"

So the prophet stopped but said, "I
know that God has determined to destroy you, because you have done this
and have not listened to my counsel."

17After Amaziah king of Judah consulted his advisers, he sent this challenge to
Jehoash[c] son of Jehoahaz, the son of
Jehu, king of Israel: "Come, let us face
each other in battle."

18But Jehoash king of Israel replied to
Amaziah king of Judah: "A thistle in Lebanon sent a message to a cedar in Lebanon, 'Give your daughter to my son in
marriage.' Then a wild beast in Lebanon
came along and trampled the thistle
underfoot. 19You say to yourself that you
have defeated Edom, and now you are
arrogant and proud. But stay at home!
Why ask for trouble and cause your own
downfall and that of Judah also?"

20Amaziah, however, would not listen,
for God so worked that he might deliver them into the hands of Jehoash, because they sought the gods of Edom. 21So
Jehoash king of Israel attacked. He and
Amaziah king of Judah faced each other
at Beth Shemesh in Judah. 22Judah was
routed by Israel, and every man fled to
his home. 23Jehoash king of Israel captured Amaziah king of Judah, the son
of Joash, the son of Ahaziah,[d] at Beth
Shemesh. Then Jehoash brought him to
Jerusalem and broke down the wall of
Jerusalem from the Ephraim Gate to the
Corner Gate — a section about four hundred cubits[e] long. 24He took all the gold
and silver and all the articles found in
the temple of God that had been in the

[a] 4 Deut. 24:16 [b] 6 That is, about 3 3/4 tons or about 3.4 metric tons; also in verse 9
[c] 17 Hebrew *Joash*, a variant of *Jehoash*; also in verses 18, 21, 23 and 25 [d] *23* Hebrew *Jehoahaz*, a variant of *Ahaziah* [e] *23* That is, about 600 feet or about 180 meters

care of Obed-Edom, together with the palace treasures and the hostages, and returned to Samaria.

25 Amaziah son of Joash king of Judah lived for fifteen years after the death of Jehoash son of Jehoahaz king of Israel. 26 As for the other events of Amaziah's reign, from beginning to end, are they not written in the book of the kings of Judah and Israel? 27 From the time that Amaziah turned away from following the LORD, they conspired against him in Jerusalem and he fled to Lachish, but they sent men after him to Lachish and killed him there. 28 He was brought back by horse and was buried with his ancestors in the City of Judah.[a]

Uzziah King of Judah

26 Then all the people of Judah took Uzziah,[b] who was sixteen years old, and made him king in place of his father Amaziah. 2 He was the one who rebuilt Elath and restored it to Judah after Amaziah rested with his ancestors.

3 Uzziah was sixteen years old when he became king, and he reigned in Jerusalem fifty-two years. His mother's name was Jekoliah; she was from Jerusalem. 4 He did what was right in the eyes of the LORD, just as his father Amaziah had done. 5 He sought God during the days of Zechariah, who instructed him in the fear[c] of God. As long as he sought the LORD, God gave him success.

6 He went to war against the Philistines and broke down the walls of Gath, Jabneh and Ashdod. He then rebuilt towns near Ashdod and elsewhere among the Philistines. 7 God helped him against the Philistines and against the Arabs who lived in Gur Baal and against the Meunites. 8 The Ammonites brought tribute to Uzziah, and his fame spread as far as the border of Egypt, because he had become very powerful.

9 Uzziah built towers in Jerusalem at the Corner Gate, at the Valley Gate and at the angle of the wall, and he fortified them. 10 He also built towers in the wilderness and dug many cisterns, because he had much livestock in the foothills and in the plain. He had people working his fields and vineyards in the hills and in the fertile lands, for he loved the soil.

11 Uzziah had a well-trained army, ready to go out by divisions according to their numbers as mustered by Jeiel the secretary and Maaseiah the officer under the direction of Hananiah, one of the royal officials. 12 The total number of family leaders over the fighting men was 2,600. 13 Under their command was an army of 307,500 men trained for war, a powerful force to support the king against his enemies. 14 Uzziah provided shields, spears, helmets, coats of armor, bows and slingstones for the entire army. 15 In Jerusalem he made devices invented for use on the towers and on the corner defenses so that soldiers could shoot arrows and hurl large stones from the walls. His fame spread far and wide, for he was greatly helped until he became powerful.

16 But after Uzziah became powerful, his pride led to his downfall. He was unfaithful to the LORD his God, and entered the temple of the LORD to burn incense on the altar of incense. 17 Azariah the priest with eighty other courageous priests of the LORD followed him in. 18 They confronted King Uzziah and said, "It is not right for you, Uzziah, to burn incense to the LORD. That is for the priests, the descendants of Aaron, who have been consecrated to burn incense. Leave the sanctuary, for you have been unfaithful; and you will not be honored by the LORD God."

19 Uzziah, who had a censer in his hand ready to burn incense, became angry. While he was raging at the priests in their presence before the incense altar in the LORD's temple, leprosy[d] broke out on his forehead. 20 When Azariah the chief priest and all the other priests looked at him, they saw that he had leprosy on his forehead, so they hurried him out. Indeed, he himself was eager to leave, because the LORD had afflicted him.

21 King Uzziah had leprosy until the day he died. He lived in a separate house[e]—leprous, and banned from the temple of the LORD. Jotham his son had charge of the palace and governed the people of the land.

22 The other events of Uzziah's reign, from beginning to end, are recorded by the prophet Isaiah son of Amoz. 23 Uzziah rested with his ancestors and was buried near them in a cemetery that belonged to the kings, for people said, "He had leprosy." And Jotham his son succeeded him as king.

[a] *28* Most Hebrew manuscripts; some Hebrew manuscripts, Septuagint, Vulgate and Syriac (see also 2 Kings 14:20) *David* [b] *1* Also called *Azariah* [c] *5* Many Hebrew manuscripts, Septuagint and Syriac; other Hebrew manuscripts *vision* [d] *19* The Hebrew for *leprosy* was used for various diseases affecting the skin; also in verses 20, 21 and 23. [e] *21* Or *in a house where he was relieved of responsibilities*

Jotham King of Judah

27 Jotham was twenty-five years old when he became king, and he reigned in Jerusalem sixteen years. His mother's name was Jerusha daughter of Zadok. 2He did what was right in the eyes of the LORD, just as his father Uzziah had done, but unlike him he did not enter the temple of the LORD. The people, however, continued their corrupt practices. 3Jotham rebuilt the Upper Gate of the temple of the LORD and did extensive work on the wall at the hill of Ophel. 4He built towns in the hill country of Judah and forts and towers in the wooded areas.

5Jotham waged war against the king of the Ammonites and conquered them. That year the Ammonites paid him a hundred talents[a] of silver, ten thousand cors[b] of wheat and ten thousand cors[c] of barley. The Ammonites brought him the same amount also in the second and third years.

6Jotham grew powerful because he walked steadfastly before the LORD his God.

7The other events in Jotham's reign, including all his wars and the other things he did, are written in the book of the kings of Israel and Judah. 8He was twenty-five years old when he became king, and he reigned in Jerusalem sixteen years. 9Jotham rested with his ancestors and was buried in the City of David. And Ahaz his son succeeded him as king.

Ahaz King of Judah

28 Ahaz was twenty years old when he became king, and he reigned in Jerusalem sixteen years. Unlike David his father, he did not do what was right in the eyes of the LORD. 2He followed the ways of the kings of Israel and also made idols for worshiping the Baals. 3He burned sacrifices in the Valley of Ben Hinnom and sacrificed his children in the fire, engaging in the detestable practices of the nations the LORD had driven out before the Israelites. 4He offered sacrifices and burned incense at the high places, on the hilltops and under every spreading tree.

5Therefore the LORD his God delivered him into the hands of the king of Aram. The Arameans defeated him and took many of his people as prisoners and brought them to Damascus.

He was also given into the hands of the king of Israel, who inflicted heavy casualties on him. 6In one day Pekah son of Remaliah killed a hundred and twenty thousand soldiers in Judah—because Judah had forsaken the LORD, the God of their ancestors. 7Zikri, an Ephraimite warrior, killed Maaseiah the king's son, Azrikam the officer in charge of the palace, and Elkanah, second to the king. 8The men of Israel took captive from their fellow Israelites who were from Judah two hundred thousand wives, sons and daughters. They also took a great deal of plunder, which they carried back to Samaria.

9But a prophet of the LORD named Oded was there, and he went out to meet the army when it returned to Samaria. He said to them, "Because the LORD, the God of your ancestors, was angry with Judah, he gave them into your hand. But you have slaughtered them in a rage that reaches to heaven. 10And now you intend to make the men and women of Judah and Jerusalem your slaves. But aren't you also guilty of sins against the LORD your God? 11Now listen to me! Send back your fellow Israelites you have taken as prisoners, for the LORD's fierce anger rests on you."

12Then some of the leaders in Ephraim—Azariah son of Jehohanan, Berekiah son of Meshillemoth, Jehizkiah son of Shallum, and Amasa son of Hadlai—confronted those who were arriving from the war. 13"You must not bring those prisoners here," they said, "or we will be guilty before the LORD. Do you intend to add to our sin and guilt? For our guilt is already great, and his fierce anger rests on Israel."

14So the soldiers gave up the prisoners and plunder in the presence of the officials and all the assembly. 15The men designated by name took the prisoners, and from the plunder they clothed all who were naked. They provided them with clothes and sandals, food and drink, and healing balm. All those who were weak they put on donkeys. So they took them back to their fellow Israelites at Jericho, the City of Palms, and returned to Samaria.

16At that time King Ahaz sent to the kings[d] of Assyria for help. 17The Edomites had again come and attacked Judah and carried away prisoners, 18while

[a] *5* That is, about 3 3/4 tons or about 3.4 metric tons [b] *5* That is, probably about 1,800 tons or about 1,600 metric tons of wheat [c] *5* That is, probably about 1,500 tons or about 1,350 metric tons of barley [d] *16* Most Hebrew manuscripts; one Hebrew manuscript, Septuagint and Vulgate (see also 2 Kings 16:7) *king*

the Philistines had raided towns in the
foothills and in the Negev of Judah.
They captured and occupied Beth Shemesh, Aijalon and Gederoth, as well as
Soko, Timnah and Gimzo, with their
surrounding villages. 19 The LORD had
humbled Judah because of Ahaz king of
Israel,[a] for he had promoted wickedness
in Judah and had been most unfaithful
to the LORD. 20 Tiglath-Pileser[b] king of Assyria came to him, but he gave him trouble instead of help. 21 Ahaz took some of
the things from the temple of the LORD
and from the royal palace and from the
officials and presented them to the king
of Assyria, but that did not help him.

22 In his time of trouble King Ahaz became even more unfaithful to the LORD.
23 He offered sacrifices to the gods of Damascus, who had defeated him; for he
thought, "Since the gods of the kings of
Aram have helped them, I will sacrifice
to them so they will help me." But they
were his downfall and the downfall of
all Israel.

24 Ahaz gathered together the furnishings from the temple of God and
cut them in pieces. He shut the doors
of the LORD's temple and set up altars
at every street corner in Jerusalem. 25 In
every town in Judah he built high places to burn sacrifices to other gods and
aroused the anger of the LORD, the God
of his ancestors.

26 The other events of his reign and
all his ways, from beginning to end, are
written in the book of the kings of Judah
and Israel. 27 Ahaz rested with his ancestors and was buried in the city of Jerusalem, but he was not placed in the tombs
of the kings of Israel. And Hezekiah his
son succeeded him as king.

Hezekiah Purifies the Temple

29 Hezekiah was twenty-five years
old when he became king, and he
reigned in Jerusalem twenty-nine years.
His mother's name was Abijah daughter
of Zechariah. 2 He did what was right in
the eyes of the LORD, just as his father
David had done.

3 In the first month of the first year
of his reign, he opened the doors of the
temple of the LORD and repaired them.
4 He brought in the priests and the Levites, assembled them in the square on
the east side 5 and said: "Listen to me,
Levites! Consecrate yourselves now and
consecrate the temple of the LORD, the
God of your ancestors. Remove all defile-
ment from the sanctuary. 6 Our parents
were unfaithful; they did evil in the eyes
of the LORD our God and forsook him.
They turned their faces away from the
LORD's dwelling place and turned their
backs on him. 7 They also shut the doors
of the portico and put out the lamps.
They did not burn incense or present
any burnt offerings at the sanctuary to
the God of Israel. 8 Therefore, the anger
of the LORD has fallen on Judah and Jerusalem; he has made them an object of
dread and horror and scorn, as you can
see with your own eyes. 9 This is why our
fathers have fallen by the sword and
why our sons and daughters and our
wives are in captivity. 10 Now I intend to
make a covenant with the LORD, the God
of Israel, so that his fierce anger will turn
away from us. 11 My sons, do not be negligent now, for the LORD has chosen you to
stand before him and serve him, to minister before him and to burn incense."

12 Then these Levites set to work:
from the Kohathites,
Mahath son of Amasai and Joel
son of Azariah;
from the Merarites,
Kish son of Abdi and Azariah son
of Jehallelel;
from the Gershonites,
Joah son of Zimmah and Eden
son of Joah;
13 from the descendants of Elizaphan,
Shimri and Jeiel;
from the descendants of Asaph,
Zechariah and Mattaniah;
14 from the descendants of Heman,
Jehiel and Shimei;
from the descendants of Jeduthun,
Shemaiah and Uzziel.

15 When they had assembled their fellow Levites and consecrated themselves,
they went in to purify the temple of the
LORD, as the king had ordered, following
the word of the LORD. 16 The priests went
into the sanctuary of the LORD to purify
it. They brought out to the courtyard of
the LORD's temple everything unclean
that they found in the temple of the LORD.
The Levites took it and carried it out to
the Kidron Valley. 17 They began the consecration on the first day of the first month,
and by the eighth day of the month they
reached the portico of the LORD. For eight
more days they consecrated the temple of
the LORD itself, finishing on the sixteenth
day of the first month.

[a] *19* That is, Judah, as frequently in 2 Chronicles
[b] *20* Hebrew *Tilgath-Pilneser,* a variant of *Tiglath-Pileser*

18 Then they went in to King Hezekiah and reported: "We have purified the entire temple of the LORD, the altar of burnt offering with all its utensils, and the table for setting out the consecrated bread, with all its articles. 19 We have prepared and consecrated all the articles that King Ahaz removed in his unfaithfulness while he was king. They are now in front of the LORD's altar."

20 Early the next morning King Hezekiah gathered the city officials together and went up to the temple of the LORD. 21 They brought seven bulls, seven rams, seven male lambs and seven male goats as a sin offering[a] for the kingdom, for the sanctuary and for Judah. The king commanded the priests, the descendants of Aaron, to offer these on the altar of the LORD. 22 So they slaughtered the bulls, and the priests took the blood and splashed it against the altar; next they slaughtered the rams and splashed their blood against the altar; then they slaughtered the lambs and splashed their blood against the altar. 23 The goats for the sin offering were brought before the king and the assembly, and they laid their hands on them. 24 The priests then slaughtered the goats and presented their blood on the altar for a sin offering to atone for all Israel, because the king had ordered the burnt offering and the sin offering for all Israel.

25 He stationed the Levites in the temple of the LORD with cymbals, harps and lyres in the way prescribed by David and Gad the king's seer and Nathan the prophet; this was commanded by the LORD through his prophets. 26 So the Levites stood ready with David's instruments, and the priests with their trumpets.

27 Hezekiah gave the order to sacrifice the burnt offering on the altar. As the offering began, singing to the LORD began also, accompanied by trumpets and the instruments of David king of Israel. 28 The whole assembly bowed in worship, while the musicians played and the trumpets sounded. All this continued until the sacrifice of the burnt offering was completed.

29 When the offerings were finished, the king and everyone present with him knelt down and worshiped. 30 King Hezekiah and his officials ordered the Levites to praise the LORD with the words of David and of Asaph the seer. So they sang praises with gladness and bowed down and worshiped.

31 Then Hezekiah said, "You have now dedicated yourselves to the LORD. Come and bring sacrifices and thank offerings to the temple of the LORD." So the assembly brought sacrifices and thank offerings, and all whose hearts were willing brought burnt offerings.

32 The number of burnt offerings the assembly brought was seventy bulls, a hundred rams and two hundred male lambs—all of them for burnt offerings to the LORD. 33 The animals consecrated as sacrifices amounted to six hundred bulls and three thousand sheep and goats. 34 The priests, however, were too few to skin all the burnt offerings; so their relatives the Levites helped them until the task was finished and until other priests had been consecrated, for the Levites had been more conscientious in consecrating themselves than the priests had been. 35 There were burnt offerings in abundance, together with the fat of the fellowship offerings and the drink offerings that accompanied the burnt offerings.

So the service of the temple of the LORD was reestablished. 36 Hezekiah and all the people rejoiced at what God had brought about for his people, because it was done so quickly.

Hezekiah Celebrates the Passover

30 Hezekiah sent word to all Israel and Judah and also wrote letters to Ephraim and Manasseh, inviting them to come to the temple of the LORD in Jerusalem and celebrate the Passover to the LORD, the God of Israel. 2 The king and his officials and the whole assembly in Jerusalem decided to celebrate the Passover in the second month. 3 They had not been able to celebrate it at the regular time because not enough priests had consecrated themselves and the people had not assembled in Jerusalem. 4 The plan seemed right both to the king and to the whole assembly. 5 They decided to send a proclamation throughout Israel, from Beersheba to Dan, calling the people to come to Jerusalem and celebrate the Passover to the LORD, the God of Israel. It had not been celebrated in large numbers according to what was written.

6 At the king's command, couriers went throughout Israel and Judah with letters from the king and from his officials, which read:

"People of Israel, return to the LORD, the God of Abraham, Isaac and Israel, that he may return to you who

[a] 21 Or *purification offering*; also in verses 23 and 24

are left, who have escaped from the hand of the kings of Assyria. 7Do not be like your parents and your fellow Israelites, who were unfaithful to the LORD, the God of their ancestors, so that he made them an object of horror, as you see. 8Do not be stiff-necked, as your ancestors were; submit to the LORD. Come to his sanctuary, which he has consecrated forever. Serve the LORD your God, so that his fierce anger will turn away from you. 9If you return to the LORD, then your fellow Israelites and your children will be shown compassion by their captors and will return to this land, for the LORD your God is gracious and compassionate. He will not turn his face from you if you return to him."

10The couriers went from town to town in Ephraim and Manasseh, as far as Zebulun, but people scorned and ridiculed them. 11Nevertheless, some from Asher, Manasseh and Zebulun humbled themselves and went to Jerusalem. 12Also in Judah the hand of God was on the people to give them unity of mind to carry out what the king and his officials had ordered, following the word of the LORD.

13A very large crowd of people assembled in Jerusalem to celebrate the Festival of Unleavened Bread in the second month. 14They removed the altars in Jerusalem and cleared away the incense altars and threw them into the Kidron Valley.

15They slaughtered the Passover lamb on the fourteenth day of the second month. The priests and the Levites were ashamed and consecrated themselves and brought burnt offerings to the temple of the LORD. 16Then they took up their regular positions as prescribed in the Law of Moses the man of God. The priests splashed against the altar the blood handed to them by the Levites. 17Since many in the crowd had not consecrated themselves, the Levites had to kill the Passover lambs for all those who were not ceremonially clean and could not consecrate their lambs[a] to the LORD. 18Although most of the many people who came from Ephraim, Manasseh, Issachar and Zebulun had not purified themselves, yet they ate the Passover, contrary to what was written. But Hezekiah prayed for them, saying, "May the LORD, who is good, pardon everyone 19who sets their heart on seeking God — the LORD, the God of their ancestors — even if they are not clean according to the rules of the sanctuary." 20And the LORD heard Hezekiah and healed the people.

21The Israelites who were present in Jerusalem celebrated the Festival of Unleavened Bread for seven days with great rejoicing, while the Levites and priests praised the LORD every day with resounding instruments dedicated to the LORD.[b]

22Hezekiah spoke encouragingly to all the Levites, who showed good understanding of the service of the LORD. For the seven days they ate their assigned portion and offered fellowship offerings and praised[c] the LORD, the God of their ancestors.

23The whole assembly then agreed to celebrate the festival seven more days; so for another seven days they celebrated joyfully. 24Hezekiah king of Judah provided a thousand bulls and seven thousand sheep and goats for the assembly, and the officials provided them with a thousand bulls and ten thousand sheep and goats. A great number of priests consecrated themselves. 25The entire assembly of Judah rejoiced, along with the priests and Levites and all who had assembled from Israel, including the foreigners who had come from Israel and also those who resided in Judah. 26There was great joy in Jerusalem, for since the days of Solomon son of David king of Israel there had been nothing like this in Jerusalem. 27The priests and the Levites stood to bless the people, and God heard them, for their prayer reached heaven, his holy dwelling place.

31 When all this had ended, the Israelites who were there went out to the towns of Judah, smashed the sacred stones and cut down the Asherah poles. They destroyed the high places and the altars throughout Judah and Benjamin and in Ephraim and Manasseh. After they had destroyed all of them, the Israelites returned to their own towns and to their own property.

Contributions for Worship

2Hezekiah assigned the priests and Levites to divisions — each of them according to their duties as priests or Levites — to offer burnt offerings and fellowship offerings, to minister, to give thanks and to sing praises at the gates of the LORD's dwelling. 3The king contributed from his own possessions for the morning and

[a] 17 *Or consecrate themselves* [b] 21 *Or priests sang to the LORD every day, accompanied by the LORD's instruments of praise* [c] 22 *Or and confessed their sins to*

evening burnt offerings and for the burnt
offerings on the Sabbaths, at the New
Moons and at the appointed festivals as
written in the Law of the LORD. 4He ordered the people living in Jerusalem to
give the portion due the priests and Levites so they could devote themselves to
the Law of the LORD. 5As soon as the order
went out, the Israelites generously gave
the firstfruits of their grain, new wine,
olive oil and honey and all that the fields
produced. They brought a great amount,
a tithe of everything. 6The people of Israel and Judah who lived in the towns of
Judah also brought a tithe of their herds
and flocks and a tithe of the holy things
dedicated to the LORD their God, and they
piled them in heaps. 7They began doing
this in the third month and finished in
the seventh month. 8When Hezekiah and
his officials came and saw the heaps,
they praised the LORD and blessed his
people Israel.

9Hezekiah asked the priests and Levites about the heaps; 10and Azariah the
chief priest, from the family of Zadok,
answered, "Since the people began to
bring their contributions to the temple
of the LORD, we have had enough to eat
and plenty to spare, because the LORD
has blessed his people, and this great
amount is left over."

11Hezekiah gave orders to prepare storerooms in the temple of the LORD, and this
was done. 12Then they faithfully brought
in the contributions, tithes and dedicated
gifts. Konaniah, a Levite, was the overseer
in charge of these things, and his brother
Shimei was next in rank. 13Jehiel, Azaziah,
Nahath, Asahel, Jerimoth, Jozabad, Eliel,
Ismakiah, Mahath and Benaiah were
assistants of Konaniah and Shimei his
brother. All these served by appointment
of King Hezekiah and Azariah the official
in charge of the temple of God.

14Kore son of Imnah the Levite, keeper of the East Gate, was in charge of the
freewill offerings given to God, distributing the contributions made to the LORD
and also the consecrated gifts. 15Eden,
Miniamin, Jeshua, Shemaiah, Amariah
and Shekaniah assisted him faithfully
in the towns of the priests, distributing
to their fellow priests according to their
divisions, old and young alike.

16In addition, they distributed to the
males three years old or more whose
names were in the genealogical records — all who would enter the temple of
the LORD to perform the daily duties of
their various tasks, according to their responsibilities and their divisions. 17And
they distributed to the priests enrolled
by their families in the genealogical records and likewise to the Levites twenty
years old or more, according to their responsibilities and their divisions. 18They
included all the little ones, the wives,
and the sons and daughters of the whole
community listed in these genealogical
records. For they were faithful in consecrating themselves.

19As for the priests, the descendants
of Aaron, who lived on the farmlands
around their towns or in any other
towns, men were designated by name to
distribute portions to every male among
them and to all who were recorded in the
genealogies of the Levites.

20This is what Hezekiah did throughout Judah, doing what was good and
right and faithful before the LORD his
God. 21In everything that he undertook
in the service of God's temple and in obedience to the law and the commands, he
sought his God and worked wholeheartedly. And so he prospered.

Sennacherib Threatens Jerusalem

32 After all that Hezekiah had so
faithfully done, Sennacherib king
of Assyria came and invaded Judah. He
laid siege to the fortified cities, thinking to conquer them for himself. 2When
Hezekiah saw that Sennacherib had
come and that he intended to wage war
against Jerusalem, 3he consulted with
his officials and military staff about
blocking off the water from the springs
outside the city, and they helped him.
4They gathered a large group of people who blocked all the springs and the
stream that flowed through the land.
"Why should the kings[a] of Assyria come
and find plenty of water?" they said.
5Then he worked hard repairing all the
broken sections of the wall and building
towers on it. He built another wall outside that one and reinforced the terraces[b] of the City of David. He also made
large numbers of weapons and shields.

6He appointed military officers over
the people and assembled them before
him in the square at the city gate and
encouraged them with these words: 7"Be
strong and courageous. Do not be afraid
or discouraged because of the king of
Assyria and the vast army with him, for
there is a greater power with us than
with him. 8With him is only the arm of

[a] 4 Hebrew; Septuagint and Syriac *king* [b] 5 Or *the Millo*

flesh, but with us is the LORD our God
to help us and to fight our battles." And
the people gained confidence from what
Hezekiah the king of Judah said.
9Later, when Sennacherib king of Assyria and all his forces were laying siege
to Lachish, he sent his officers to Jerusalem with this message for Hezekiah king
of Judah and for all the people of Judah
who were there:

10"This is what Sennacherib king
of Assyria says: On what are you
basing your confidence, that you
remain in Jerusalem under siege?
11When Hezekiah says, 'The LORD
our God will save us from the hand
of the king of Assyria,' he is misleading you, to let you die of hunger
and thirst. 12Did not Hezekiah himself remove this god's high places
and altars, saying to Judah and Jerusalem, 'You must worship before
one altar and burn sacrifices on it'?
13"Do you not know what I and my
predecessors have done to all the
peoples of the other lands? Were the
gods of those nations ever able to deliver their land from my hand? 14Who
of all the gods of these nations that
my predecessors destroyed has been
able to save his people from me?
How then can your god deliver you
from my hand? 15Now do not let Hezekiah deceive you and mislead you
like this. Do not believe him, for no
god of any nation or kingdom has
been able to deliver his people from
my hand or the hand of my predecessors. How much less will your god
deliver you from my hand!"

16Sennacherib's officers spoke further
against the LORD God and against his
servant Hezekiah. 17The king also wrote
letters ridiculing the LORD, the God of Israel, and saying this against him: "Just
as the gods of the peoples of the other
lands did not rescue their people from
my hand, so the god of Hezekiah will not
rescue his people from my hand." 18Then
they called out in Hebrew to the people
of Jerusalem who were on the wall, to
terrify them and make them afraid in
order to capture the city. 19They spoke
about the God of Jerusalem as they did
about the gods of the other peoples of
the world — the work of human hands.
20King Hezekiah and the prophet Isaiah son of Amoz cried out in prayer to
heaven about this. 21And the LORD sent
an angel, who annihilated all the fighting men and the commanders and officers in the camp of the Assyrian king. So
he withdrew to his own land in disgrace.
And when he went into the temple of his
god, some of his sons, his own flesh and
blood, cut him down with the sword.
22So the LORD saved Hezekiah and the
people of Jerusalem from the hand of
Sennacherib king of Assyria and from
the hand of all others. He took care of
them[a] on every side. 23Many brought offerings to Jerusalem for the LORD and
valuable gifts for Hezekiah king of Judah. From then on he was highly regarded by all the nations.

Hezekiah's Pride, Success and Death

24In those days Hezekiah became ill
and was at the point of death. He prayed
to the LORD, who answered him and
gave him a miraculous sign. 25But Hezekiah's heart was proud and he did not respond to the kindness shown him; therefore the LORD's wrath was on him and on
Judah and Jerusalem. 26Then Hezekiah
repented of the pride of his heart, as did
the people of Jerusalem; therefore the
LORD's wrath did not come on them during the days of Hezekiah.
27Hezekiah had very great wealth and
honor, and he made treasuries for his silver and gold and for his precious stones,
spices, shields and all kinds of valuables.
28He also made buildings to store the
harvest of grain, new wine and olive oil;
and he made stalls for various kinds of
cattle, and pens for the flocks. 29He built
villages and acquired great numbers of
flocks and herds, for God had given him
very great riches.
30It was Hezekiah who blocked the upper outlet of the Gihon spring and chan-
neled the water down to the west side of
the City of David. He succeeded in everything he undertook. 31But when envoys
were sent by the rulers of Babylon to ask
him about the miraculous sign that had
occurred in the land, God left him to test
him and to know everything that was in
his heart.
32The other events of Hezekiah's reign
and his acts of devotion are written
in the vision of the prophet Isaiah son
of Amoz in the book of the kings of Judah and Israel. 33Hezekiah rested with
his ancestors and was buried on the hill
where the tombs of David's descendants
are. All Judah and the people of Jerusalem honored him when he died. And Manasseh his son succeeded him as king.

[a] 22 Hebrew; Septuagint and Vulgate *He gave them rest*

Manasseh King of Judah

33 Manasseh was twelve years old when he became king, and he reigned in Jerusalem fifty-five years. 2He did evil in the eyes of the LORD, following the detestable practices of the nations the LORD had driven out before the Israelites. 3He rebuilt the high places his father Hezekiah had demolished; he also erected altars to the Baals and made Asherah poles. He bowed down to all the starry hosts and worshiped them. 4He built altars in the temple of the LORD, of which the LORD had said, "My Name will remain in Jerusalem forever." 5In both courts of the temple of the LORD, he built altars to all the starry hosts. 6He sacrificed his children in the fire in the Valley of Ben Hinnom, practiced divination and witchcraft, sought omens, and consulted mediums and spiritists. He did much evil in the eyes of the LORD, arousing his anger.

7He took the image he had made and put it in God's temple, of which God had said to David and to his son Solomon, "In this temple and in Jerusalem, which I have chosen out of all the tribes of Israel, I will put my Name forever. 8I will not again make the feet of the Israelites leave the land I assigned to your ancestors, if only they will be careful to do everything I commanded them concerning all the laws, decrees and regulations given through Moses." 9But Manasseh led Judah and the people of Jerusalem astray, so that they did more evil than the nations the LORD had destroyed before the Israelites.

10The LORD spoke to Manasseh and his people, but they paid no attention. 11So the LORD brought against them the army commanders of the king of Assyria, who took Manasseh prisoner, put a hook in his nose, bound him with bronze shackles and took him to Babylon. 12In his distress he sought the favor of the LORD his God and humbled himself greatly before the God of his ancestors. 13And when he prayed to him, the LORD was moved by his entreaty and listened to his plea; so he brought him back to Jerusalem and to his kingdom. Then Manasseh knew that the LORD is God.

14Afterward he rebuilt the outer wall of the City of David, west of the Gihon spring in the valley, as far as the entrance of the Fish Gate and encircling the hill of Ophel; he also made it much higher. He stationed military commanders in all the fortified cities in Judah.

15He got rid of the foreign gods and removed the image from the temple of the LORD, as well as all the altars he had built on the temple hill and in Jerusalem; and he threw them out of the city. 16Then he restored the altar of the LORD and sacrificed fellowship offerings and thank offerings on it, and told Judah to serve the LORD, the God of Israel. 17The people, however, continued to sacrifice at the high places, but only to the LORD their God.

18The other events of Manasseh's reign, including his prayer to his God and the words the seers spoke to him in the name of the LORD, the God of Israel, are written in the annals of the kings of Israel.[a] 19His prayer and how God was moved by his entreaty, as well as all his sins and unfaithfulness, and the sites where he built high places and set up Asherah poles and idols before he humbled himself — all these are written in the records of the seers.[b] 20Manasseh rested with his ancestors and was buried in his palace. And Amon his son succeeded him as king.

Amon King of Judah

21Amon was twenty-two years old when he became king, and he reigned in Jerusalem two years. 22He did evil in the eyes of the LORD, as his father Manasseh had done. Amon worshiped and offered sacrifices to all the idols Manasseh had made. 23But unlike his father Manasseh, he did not humble himself before the LORD; Amon increased his guilt.

24Amon's officials conspired against him and assassinated him in his palace. 25Then the people of the land killed all who had plotted against King Amon, and they made Josiah his son king in his place.

Josiah's Reforms

34 Josiah was eight years old when he became king, and he reigned in Jerusalem thirty-one years. 2He did what was right in the eyes of the LORD and followed the ways of his father David, not turning aside to the right or to the left.

3In the eighth year of his reign, while he was still young, he began to seek the God of his father David. In his twelfth year he began to purge Judah and Jerusalem of high places, Asherah poles and idols. 4Under his direction the altars of the Baals were torn down; he cut to pieces the incense altars that were above

[a] *18* That is, Judah, as frequently in 2 Chronicles

[b] *19* One Hebrew manuscript and Septuagint; most Hebrew manuscripts *of Hozai*

them, and smashed the Asherah poles
and the idols. These he broke to pieces
and scattered over the graves of those
who had sacrificed to them. 5He burned
the bones of the priests on their altars,
and so he purged Judah and Jerusalem.
6In the towns of Manasseh, Ephraim
and Simeon, as far as Naphtali, and in
the ruins around them, 7he tore down
the altars and the Asherah poles and
crushed the idols to powder and cut to
pieces all the incense altars throughout
Israel. Then he went back to Jerusalem.

8In the eighteenth year of Josiah's
reign, to purify the land and the temple, he sent Shaphan son of Azaliah and
Maaseiah the ruler of the city, with Joah
son of Joahaz, the recorder, to repair the
temple of the LORD his God.

9They went to Hilkiah the high priest
and gave him the money that had been
brought into the temple of God, which
the Levites who were the gatekeepers
had collected from the people of Manasseh, Ephraim and the entire remnant of
Israel and from all the people of Judah
and Benjamin and the inhabitants of Jerusalem. 10Then they entrusted it to the
men appointed to supervise the work
on the LORD's temple. These men paid
the workers who repaired and restored
the temple. 11They also gave money to
the carpenters and builders to purchase
dressed stone, and timber for joists and
beams for the buildings that the kings of
Judah had allowed to fall into ruin.

12The workers labored faithfully. Over
them to direct them were Jahath and
Obadiah, Levites descended from Merari, and Zechariah and Meshullam, descended from Kohath. The Levites — all
who were skilled in playing musical instruments — 13had charge of the laborers and supervised all the workers from
job to job. Some of the Levites were secretaries, scribes and gatekeepers.

The Book of the Law Found

14While they were bringing out the
money that had been taken into the temple of the LORD, Hilkiah the priest found
the Book of the Law of the LORD that had
been given through Moses. 15Hilkiah said
to Shaphan the secretary, "I have found
the Book of the Law in the temple of the
LORD." He gave it to Shaphan.

16Then Shaphan took the book to the
king and reported to him: "Your officials
are doing everything that has been committed to them. 17They have paid out the
money that was in the temple of the LORD
and have entrusted it to the supervisors
and workers." 18Then Shaphan the secretary informed the king, "Hilkiah the
priest has given me a book." And Shaphan
read from it in the presence of the king.

19When the king heard the words of
the Law, he tore his robes. 20He gave
these orders to Hilkiah, Ahikam son of
Shaphan, Abdon son of Micah,[a] Shaphan
the secretary and Asaiah the king's attendant: 21"Go and inquire of the LORD
for me and for the remnant in Israel and
Judah about what is written in this book
that has been found. Great is the LORD's
anger that is poured out on us because
those who have gone before us have not
kept the word of the LORD; they have not
acted in accordance with all that is written in this book."

22Hilkiah and those the king had sent
with him[b] went to speak to the prophet
Huldah, who was the wife of Shallum
son of Tokhath,[c] the son of Hasrah,[d]
keeper of the wardrobe. She lived in Jerusalem, in the New Quarter.

23She said to them, "This is what the
LORD, the God of Israel, says: Tell the
man who sent you to me, 24'This is what
the LORD says: I am going to bring disaster on this place and its people — all
the curses written in the book that has
been read in the presence of the king
of Judah. 25Because they have forsaken
me and burned incense to other gods
and aroused my anger by all that their
hands have made,[e] my anger will be
poured out on this place and will not be
quenched.' 26Tell the king of Judah, who
sent you to inquire of the LORD, 'This is
what the LORD, the God of Israel, says
concerning the words you heard: 27Be-
cause your heart was responsive and you
humbled yourself before God when you
heard what he spoke against this place
and its people, and because you humbled yourself before me and tore your
robes and wept in my presence, I have
heard you, declares the LORD. 28Now I
will gather you to your ancestors, and
you will be buried in peace. Your eyes
will not see all the disaster I am going
to bring on this place and on those who
live here.'"

So they took her answer back to the
king.

[a] 20 Also called *Akbor son of Micaiah* [b] 22 One Hebrew manuscript, Vulgate and Syriac; most Hebrew manuscripts do not have *had sent with him.* [c] 22 Also called *Tikvah* [d] 22 Also called *Harhas* [e] 25 Or *by everything they have done*

29Then the king called together all the elders of Judah and Jerusalem. 30He went up to the temple of the LORD with the people of Judah, the inhabitants of Jerusalem, the priests and the Levites — all the people from the least to the greatest. He read in their hearing all the words of the Book of the Covenant, which had been found in the temple of the LORD. 31The king stood by his pillar and renewed the covenant in the presence of the LORD — to follow the LORD and keep his commands, statutes and decrees with all his heart and all his soul, and to obey the words of the covenant written in this book.

32Then he had everyone in Jerusalem and Benjamin pledge themselves to it; the people of Jerusalem did this in accordance with the covenant of God, the God of their ancestors.

33Josiah removed all the detestable idols from all the territory belonging to the Israelites, and he had all who were present in Israel serve the LORD their God. As long as he lived, they did not fail to follow the LORD, the God of their ancestors.

Josiah Celebrates the Passover

35 Josiah celebrated the Passover to the LORD in Jerusalem, and the Passover lamb was slaughtered on the fourteenth day of the first month. 2He appointed the priests to their duties and encouraged them in the service of the LORD's temple. 3He said to the Levites, who instructed all Israel and who had been consecrated to the LORD: "Put the sacred ark in the temple that Solomon son of David king of Israel built. It is not to be carried about on your shoulders. Now serve the LORD your God and his people Israel. 4Prepare yourselves by families in your divisions, according to the instructions written by David king of Israel and by his son Solomon.

5"Stand in the holy place with a group of Levites for each subdivision of the families of your fellow Israelites, the lay people. 6Slaughter the Passover lambs, consecrate yourselves and prepare the lambs for your fellow Israelites, doing what the LORD commanded through Moses."

7Josiah provided for all the lay people who were there a total of thirty thousand lambs and goats for the Passover offerings, and also three thousand cattle — all from the king's own possessions.

8His officials also contributed voluntarily to the people and the priests and Levites. Hilkiah, Zechariah and Jehiel, the officials in charge of God's temple, gave the priests twenty-six hundred Passover offerings and three hundred cattle. 9Also Konaniah along with Shemaiah and Nethanel, his brothers, and Hashabiah, Jeiel and Jozabad, the leaders of the Levites, provided five thousand Passover offerings and five hundred head of cattle for the Levites.

10The service was arranged and the priests stood in their places with the Levites in their divisions as the king had ordered. 11The Passover lambs were slaughtered, and the priests splashed against the altar the blood handed to them, while the Levites skinned the animals. 12They set aside the burnt offerings to give them to the subdivisions of the families of the people to offer to the LORD, as it is written in the Book of Moses. They did the same with the cattle. 13They roasted the Passover animals over the fire as prescribed, and boiled the holy offerings in pots, caldrons and pans and served them quickly to all the people. 14After this, they made preparations for themselves and for the priests, because the priests, the descendants of Aaron, were sacrificing the burnt offerings and the fat portions until nightfall. So the Levites made preparations for themselves and for the Aaronic priests.

15The musicians, the descendants of Asaph, were in the places prescribed by David, Asaph, Heman and Jeduthun the king's seer. The gatekeepers at each gate did not need to leave their posts, because their fellow Levites made the preparations for them.

16So at that time the entire service of the LORD was carried out for the celebration of the Passover and the offering of burnt offerings on the altar of the LORD, as King Josiah had ordered. 17The Israelites who were present celebrated the Passover at that time and observed the Festival of Unleavened Bread for seven days. 18The Passover had not been observed like this in Israel since the days of the prophet Samuel; and none of the kings of Israel had ever celebrated such a Passover as did Josiah, with the priests, the Levites and all Judah and Israel who were there with the people of Jerusalem. 19This Passover was celebrated in the eighteenth year of Josiah's reign.

The Death of Josiah

20After all this, when Josiah had set the temple in order, Necho king of Egypt went up to fight at Carchemish on the Euphrates, and Josiah marched out to meet him in battle. 21But Necho sent messengers to him, saying, "What quarrel is there, king of Judah, between you and me? It is not you I am attacking at this time, but the house with which I am at war. God has told me to hurry; so stop opposing God, who is with me, or he will destroy you."

22Josiah, however, would not turn away from him, but disguised himself to engage him in battle. He would not listen to what Necho had said at God's command but went to fight him on the plain of Megiddo.

23Archers shot King Josiah, and he told his officers, "Take me away; I am badly wounded." 24So they took him out of his chariot, put him in his other chariot and brought him to Jerusalem, where he died. He was buried in the tombs of his ancestors, and all Judah and Jerusalem mourned for him.

25Jeremiah composed laments for Josiah, and to this day all the male and female singers commemorate Josiah in the laments. These became a tradition in Israel and are written in the Laments.

26The other events of Josiah's reign and his acts of devotion in accordance with what is written in the Law of the LORD— 27all the events, from beginning to end, are written in the book of the
36 kings of Israel and Judah. 1And the people of the land took Jehoahaz son of Josiah and made him king in Jerusalem in place of his father.

Jehoahaz King of Judah

2Jehoahaz[a] was twenty-three years old when he became king, and he reigned in Jerusalem three months. 3The king of Egypt dethroned him in Jerusalem and imposed on Judah a levy of a hundred talents[b] of silver and a talent[c] of gold. 4The king of Egypt made Eliakim, a brother of Jehoahaz, king over Judah and Jerusalem and changed Eliakim's name to Jehoiakim. But Necho took Eliakim's brother Jehoahaz and carried him off to Egypt.

Jehoiakim King of Judah

5Jehoiakim was twenty-five years old when he became king, and he reigned in Jerusalem eleven years. He did evil in the eyes of the LORD his God. 6Nebuchadnezzar king of Babylon attacked him and bound him with bronze shackles to take him to Babylon. 7Nebuchadnezzar also took to Babylon articles from the temple of the LORD and put them in his temple[d] there.

8The other events of Jehoiakim's reign, the detestable things he did and all that was found against him, are written in the book of the kings of Israel and Judah. And Jehoiachin his son succeeded him as king.

Jehoiachin King of Judah

9Jehoiachin was eighteen[e] years old when he became king, and he reigned in Jerusalem three months and ten days. He did evil in the eyes of the LORD. 10In the spring, King Nebuchadnezzar sent for him and brought him to Babylon, together with articles of value from the temple of the LORD, and he made Jehoiachin's uncle,[f] Zedekiah, king over Judah and Jerusalem.

Zedekiah King of Judah

11Zedekiah was twenty-one years old when he became king, and he reigned in Jerusalem eleven years. 12He did evil in the eyes of the LORD his God and did not humble himself before Jeremiah the prophet, who spoke the word of the LORD. 13He also rebelled against King Nebuchadnezzar, who had made him take an oath in God's name. He became stiff-necked and hardened his heart and would not turn to the LORD, the God of Israel. 14Furthermore, all the leaders of the priests and the people became more and more unfaithful, following all the detestable practices of the nations and defiling the temple of the LORD, which he had consecrated in Jerusalem.

The Fall of Jerusalem

15The LORD, the God of their ancestors, sent word to them through his messengers again and again, because he had pity on his people and on his dwelling place. 16But they mocked God's messengers, despised his words and scoffed at his prophets until the wrath of the LORD was aroused against his people and there was no remedy. 17He brought up against them the king of the Babylonians,[g] who killed their young men with the sword in the sanctuary, and did not spare young men or young women, the

[a] *2* Hebrew *Joahaz,* a variant of *Jehoahaz;* also in verse 4 [b] *3* That is, about 3 3/4 tons or about 3.4 metric tons [c] *3* That is, about 75 pounds or about 34 kilograms [d] *7* Or *palace*
[e] *9* One Hebrew manuscript, some Septuagint manuscripts and Syriac (see also 2 Kings 24:8); most Hebrew manuscripts *eight* [f] *10* Hebrew *brother,* that is, relative (see 2 Kings 24:17)
[g] *17* Or *Chaldeans*

elderly or the infirm. God gave them all
into the hands of Nebuchadnezzar. [18]He
carried to Babylon all the articles from
the temple of God, both large and small,
and the treasures of the LORD's temple
and the treasures of the king and his officials. [19]They set fire to God's temple and
broke down the wall of Jerusalem; they
burned all the palaces and destroyed everything of value there.

[20]He carried into exile to Babylon the
remnant, who escaped from the sword,
and they became servants to him and
his successors until the kingdom of Persia came to power. [21]The land enjoyed
its sabbath rests; all the time of its desolation it rested, until the seventy years
were completed in fulfillment of the
word of the LORD spoken by Jeremiah.

[22]In the first year of Cyrus king of Persia, in order to fulfill the word of the
LORD spoken by Jeremiah, the LORD
moved the heart of Cyrus king of Persia
to make a proclamation throughout his
realm and also to put it in writing:

[23]"This is what Cyrus king of Persia
says:

"'The LORD, the God of heaven,
has given me all the kingdoms of
the earth and he has appointed me
to build a temple for him at Jerusalem in Judah. Any of his people
among you may go up, and may
the LORD their God be with them.'"

EZRA

Cyrus Helps the Exiles to Return

1 In the first year of Cyrus king of Persia, in order to fulfill the word of the
LORD spoken by Jeremiah, the LORD
moved the heart of Cyrus king of Persia
to make a proclamation throughout his
realm and also to put it in writing:

2 "This is what Cyrus king of Persia
says:
"'The LORD, the God of heaven,
has given me all the kingdoms of
the earth and he has appointed me
to build a temple for him at Jerusalem in Judah. 3 Any of his people
among you may go up to Jerusalem
in Judah and build the temple of the
LORD, the God of Israel, the God who
is in Jerusalem, and may their God
be with them. 4 And in any locality
where survivors may now be living,
the people are to provide them with
silver and gold, with goods and livestock, and with freewill offerings for
the temple of God in Jerusalem.'"

5 Then the family heads of Judah and
Benjamin, and the priests and Levites —
everyone whose heart God had moved —
prepared to go up and build the house of
the LORD in Jerusalem. 6 All their neighbors assisted them with articles of silver
and gold, with goods and livestock, and
with valuable gifts, in addition to all the
freewill offerings.
7 Moreover, King Cyrus brought out
the articles belonging to the temple of
the LORD, which Nebuchadnezzar had
carried away from Jerusalem and had
placed in the temple of his god.[a] 8 Cyrus king of Persia had them brought by
Mithredath the treasurer, who counted
them out to Sheshbazzar the prince of
Judah.
9 This was the inventory:

gold dishes	30
silver dishes	1,000
silver pans[b]	29
10 gold bowls	30
matching silver bowls	410
other articles	1,000

11 In all, there were 5,400 articles of
gold and of silver. Sheshbazzar brought
all these along with the exiles when they
came up from Babylon to Jerusalem.

The List of the Exiles Who Returned

2 Now these are the people of the province who came up from the captivity of the exiles, whom Nebuchadnezzar
king of Babylon had taken captive to
Babylon (they returned to Jerusalem and
Judah, each to their own town, 2 in company with Zerubbabel, Joshua, Nehemiah, Seraiah, Reelaiah, Mordecai, Bilshan,
Mispar, Bigvai, Rehum and Baanah):

The list of the men of the people of
Israel:

3 the descendants of Parosh	2,172
4 of Shephatiah	372
5 of Arah	775
6 of Pahath-Moab (through the line of Jeshua and Joab)	2,812
7 of Elam	1,254
8 of Zattu	945
9 of Zakkai	760
10 of Bani	642
11 of Bebai	623
12 of Azgad	1,222
13 of Adonikam	666
14 of Bigvai	2,056
15 of Adin	454
16 of Ater (through Hezekiah)	98
17 of Bezai	323
18 of Jorah	112
19 of Hashum	223
20 of Gibbar	95

21 the men of Bethlehem	123
22 of Netophah	56
23 of Anathoth	128
24 of Azmaveth	42
25 of Kiriath Jearim,[c] Kephirah and Beeroth	743
26 of Ramah and Geba	621
27 of Mikmash	122
28 of Bethel and Ai	223
29 of Nebo	52
30 of Magbish	156
31 of the other Elam	1,254
32 of Harim	320
33 of Lod, Hadid and Ono	725
34 of Jericho	345
35 of Senaah	3,630

[a] 7 Or *gods* [b] 9 The meaning of the Hebrew for this word is uncertain. [c] 25 See Septuagint (see also Neh. 7:29); Hebrew *Kiriath Arim.*

36 The priests:

the descendants of
Jedaiah (through the
family of Jeshua) 973
37 of Immer 1,052
38 of Pashhur 1,247
39 of Harim 1,017

40 The Levites:

the descendants of Jeshua
and Kadmiel (of the line
of Hodaviah) 74

41 The musicians:

the descendants of Asaph 128

42 The gatekeepers of the temple:

the descendants of
Shallum, Ater, Talmon,
Akkub, Hatita and Shobai 139

43 The temple servants:

the descendants of
Ziha, Hasupha, Tabbaoth,
44 Keros, Siaha, Padon,
45 Lebanah, Hagabah, Akkub,
46 Hagab, Shalmai, Hanan,
47 Giddel, Gahar, Reaiah,
48 Rezin, Nekoda, Gazzam,
49 Uzza, Paseah, Besai,
50 Asnah, Meunim, Nephusim,
51 Bakbuk, Hakupha, Harhur,
52 Bazluth, Mehida, Harsha,
53 Barkos, Sisera, Temah,
54 Neziah and Hatipha

55 The descendants of the servants of
Solomon:

the descendants of
Sotai, Hassophereth, Peruda,
56 Jaala, Darkon, Giddel,
57 Shephatiah, Hattil,
Pokereth-Hazzebaim and Ami

58 The temple servants and the
descendants of the
servants of Solomon 392

59 The following came up from
the towns of Tel Melah, Tel Harsha,
Kerub, Addon and Immer, but they
could not show that their families
were descended from Israel:

60 The descendants of
Delaiah, Tobiah and
Nekoda 652

61 And from among the priests:

The descendants of
Hobaiah, Hakkoz and Barzillai
(a man who had married
a daughter of Barzillai the
Gileadite and was called by
that name).

62 These searched for their family records, but they could not find
them and so were excluded from
the priesthood as unclean. 63 The
governor ordered them not to eat
any of the most sacred food until
there was a priest ministering with
the Urim and Thummim.

64 The whole company numbered
42,360, 65 besides their 7,337 male
and female slaves; and they also
had 200 male and female singers.
66 They had 736 horses, 245 mules,
67 435 camels and 6,720 donkeys.

68 When they arrived at the house
of the LORD in Jerusalem, some of the
heads of the families gave freewill offerings toward the rebuilding of the house
of God on its site. 69 According to their
ability they gave to the treasury for this
work 61,000 darics[a] of gold, 5,000 minas[b] of silver and 100 priestly garments.

70 The priests, the Levites, the musicians, the gatekeepers and the temple
servants settled in their own towns,
along with some of the other people,
and the rest of the Israelites settled in
their towns.

Rebuilding the Altar

3 When the seventh month came and
the Israelites had settled in their
towns, the people assembled together
as one in Jerusalem. 2 Then Joshua son
of Jozadak and his fellow priests and
Zerubbabel son of Shealtiel and his associates began to build the altar of the
God of Israel to sacrifice burnt offerings
on it, in accordance with what is written in the Law of Moses the man of God.
3 Despite their fear of the peoples around
them, they built the altar on its foundation and sacrificed burnt offerings on
it to the LORD, both the morning and
evening sacrifices. 4 Then in accordance
with what is written, they celebrated the
Festival of Tabernacles with the required
number of burnt offerings prescribed for
each day. 5 After that, they presented the
regular burnt offerings, the New Moon
sacrifices and the sacrifices for all the
appointed sacred festivals of the LORD,

[a] 69 That is, about 1,100 pounds or about 500 kilograms [b] 69 That is, about 3 tons or about 2.8 metric tons

as well as those brought as freewill offerings to the LORD. 6On the first day of the seventh month they began to offer burnt offerings to the LORD, though the foundation of the LORD's temple had not yet been laid.

Rebuilding the Temple

7Then they gave money to the masons and carpenters, and gave food and drink and olive oil to the people of Sidon and Tyre, so that they would bring cedar logs by sea from Lebanon to Joppa, as authorized by Cyrus king of Persia.

8In the second month of the second year after their arrival at the house of God in Jerusalem, Zerubbabel son of Shealtiel, Joshua son of Jozadak and the rest of the people (the priests and the Levites and all who had returned from the captivity to Jerusalem) began the work. They appointed Levites twenty years old and older to supervise the building of the house of the LORD. 9Joshua and his sons and brothers and Kadmiel and his sons (descendants of Hodaviah[a]) and the sons of Henadad and their sons and brothers—all Levites—joined together in supervising those working on the house of God.

10When the builders laid the foundation of the temple of the LORD, the priests in their vestments and with trumpets, and the Levites (the sons of Asaph) with cymbals, took their places to praise the LORD, as prescribed by David king of Israel. 11With praise and thanksgiving they sang to the LORD:

"He is good;
his love toward Israel endures
forever."

And all the people gave a great shout of praise to the LORD, because the foundation of the house of the LORD was laid. 12But many of the older priests and Levites and family heads, who had seen the former temple, wept aloud when they saw the foundation of this temple being laid, while many others shouted for joy. 13No one could distinguish the sound of the shouts of joy from the sound of weeping, because the people made so much noise. And the sound was heard far away.

Opposition to the Rebuilding

4 When the enemies of Judah and Benjamin heard that the exiles were building a temple for the LORD, the God of Israel, 2they came to Zerubbabel and to the heads of the families and said, "Let us help you build because, like you, we seek your God and have been sacrificing to him since the time of Esarhaddon king of Assyria, who brought us here."

3But Zerubbabel, Joshua and the rest of the heads of the families of Israel answered, "You have no part with us in building a temple to our God. We alone will build it for the LORD, the God of Israel, as King Cyrus, the king of Persia, commanded us."

4Then the peoples around them set out to discourage the people of Judah and make them afraid to go on building.[b] 5They bribed officials to work against them and frustrate their plans during the entire reign of Cyrus king of Persia and down to the reign of Darius king of Persia.

Later Opposition Under Xerxes and Artaxerxes

6At the beginning of the reign of Xerxes,[c] they lodged an accusation against the people of Judah and Jerusalem.

7And in the days of Artaxerxes king of Persia, Bishlam, Mithredath, Tabeel and the rest of his associates wrote a letter to Artaxerxes. The letter was written in Aramaic script and in the Aramaic language.[d,e]

8Rehum the commanding officer and Shimshai the secretary wrote a letter against Jerusalem to Artaxerxes the king as follows:

9Rehum the commanding officer and Shimshai the secretary, together with the rest of their associates—the judges, officials and administrators over the people from Persia, Uruk and Babylon, the Elamites of Susa, 10and the other people whom the great and honorable Ashurbanipal deported and settled in the city of Samaria and elsewhere in Trans-Euphrates.

11(This is a copy of the letter they sent him.)

To King Artaxerxes,

From your servants in Trans-Euphrates:

12The king should know that the people who came up to us from you have gone to Jerusalem and are rebuilding that rebellious and wicked city. They are restoring the walls and repairing the foundations.

[a] 9 Hebrew *Yehudah,* a variant of *Hodaviah* [b] 4 Or *and troubled them as they built* [c] 6 Hebrew *Ahasuerus* [d] 7 Or *written in Aramaic and translated* [e] 7 The text of 4:8–6:18 is in Aramaic.

13 Furthermore, the king should know that if this city is built and its walls are restored, no more taxes, tribute or duty will be paid, and eventually the royal revenues will suffer.[a] 14 Now since we are under obligation to the palace and it is not proper for us to see the king dishonored, we are sending this message to inform the king, 15 so that a search may be made in the archives of your predecessors. In these records you will find that this city is a rebellious city, troublesome to kings and provinces, a place with a long history of sedition. That is why this city was destroyed. 16 We inform the king that if this city is built and its walls are restored, you will be left with nothing in Trans-Euphrates.

17 The king sent this reply:

To Rehum the commanding officer, Shimshai the secretary and the rest of their associates living in Samaria and elsewhere in Trans-Euphrates:

Greetings.

18 The letter you sent us has been read and translated in my presence. 19 I issued an order and a search was made, and it was found that this city has a long history of revolt against kings and has been a place of rebellion and sedition. 20 Jerusalem has had powerful kings ruling over the whole of Trans-Euphrates, and taxes, tribute and duty were paid to them. 21 Now issue an order to these men to stop work, so that this city will not be rebuilt until I so order. 22 Be careful not to neglect this matter. Why let this threat grow, to the detriment of the royal interests?

23 As soon as the copy of the letter of King Artaxerxes was read to Rehum and Shimshai the secretary and their associates, they went immediately to the Jews in Jerusalem and compelled them by force to stop.

24 Thus the work on the house of God in Jerusalem came to a standstill until the second year of the reign of Darius king of Persia.

Tattenai's Letter to Darius

5 Now Haggai the prophet and Zechariah the prophet, a descendant of Iddo, prophesied to the Jews in Judah and Jerusalem in the name of the God of Israel, who was over them. 2 Then Zerubbabel son of Shealtiel and Joshua son of Jozadak set to work to rebuild the house of God in Jerusalem. And the prophets of God were with them, supporting them.

3 At that time Tattenai, governor of Trans-Euphrates, and Shethar-Bozenai and their associates went to them and asked, "Who authorized you to rebuild this temple and to finish it?" 4 They[b] also asked, "What are the names of those who are constructing this building?" 5 But the eye of their God was watching over the elders of the Jews, and they were not stopped until a report could go to Darius and his written reply be received.

6 This is a copy of the letter that Tattenai, governor of Trans-Euphrates, and Shethar-Bozenai and their associates, the officials of Trans-Euphrates, sent to King Darius. 7 The report they sent him read as follows:

To King Darius:

Cordial greetings.

8 The king should know that we went to the district of Judah, to the temple of the great God. The people are building it with large stones and placing the timbers in the walls. The work is being carried on with diligence and is making rapid progress under their direction.

9 We questioned the elders and asked them, "Who authorized you to rebuild this temple and to finish it?" 10 We also asked them their names, so that we could write down the names of their leaders for your information.

11 This is the answer they gave us:

"We are the servants of the God of heaven and earth, and we are rebuilding the temple that was built many years ago, one that a great king of Israel built and finished. 12 But because our ancestors angered the God of heaven, he gave them into the hands of Nebuchadnezzar the Chaldean, king of Babylon, who destroyed this temple and deported the people to Babylon.

13 "However, in the first year of Cyrus king of Babylon, King Cyrus issued a decree to rebuild this house of God. 14 He even removed from the temple[c] of Babylon the gold and silver articles of the house of God,

[a] *13* The meaning of the Aramaic for this clause is uncertain. [b] *4* See Septuagint; Aramaic *We.* [c] *14* Or *palace*

which Nebuchadnezzar had taken
from the temple in Jerusalem and
brought to the temple[a] in Babylon.
Then King Cyrus gave them to a
man named Sheshbazzar, whom he
had appointed governor, 15and he
told him, 'Take these articles and
go and deposit them in the temple
in Jerusalem. And rebuild the house
of God on its site.'
16"So this Sheshbazzar came and
laid the foundations of the house of
God in Jerusalem. From that day to
the present it has been under construction but is not yet finished."

17Now if it pleases the king, let
a search be made in the royal archives of Babylon to see if King
Cyrus did in fact issue a decree to
rebuild this house of God in Jerusalem. Then let the king send us his
decision in this matter.

The Decree of Darius

6 King Darius then issued an order,
and they searched in the archives
stored in the treasury at Babylon. 2A
scroll was found in the citadel of Ecbata-
na in the province of Media, and this was
written on it:

Memorandum:

3In the first year of King Cyrus,
the king issued a decree concerning
the temple of God in Jerusalem:

Let the temple be rebuilt as a
place to present sacrifices, and let
its foundations be laid. It is to be
sixty cubits[b] high and sixty cubits
wide, 4with three courses of large
stones and one of timbers. The costs
are to be paid by the royal treasury.
5Also, the gold and silver articles of
the house of God, which Nebuchadnezzar took from the temple in Jerusalem and brought to Babylon,
are to be returned to their places in
the temple in Jerusalem; they are
to be deposited in the house of God.

6Now then, Tattenai, governor
of Trans-Euphrates, and Shethar-
Bozenai and you other officials
of that province, stay away from
there. 7Do not interfere with the
work on this temple of God. Let the
governor of the Jews and the Jewish elders rebuild this house of God
on its site.

8Moreover, I hereby decree what
you are to do for these elders of
the Jews in the construction of this
house of God:

Their expenses are to be fully paid
out of the royal treasury, from the
revenues of Trans-Euphrates, so that
the work will not stop. 9Whatever is
needed — young bulls, rams, male
lambs for burnt offerings to the God
of heaven, and wheat, salt, wine and
olive oil, as requested by the priests
in Jerusalem — must be given them
daily without fail, 10so that they
may offer sacrifices pleasing to the
God of heaven and pray for the well-
being of the king and his sons.
11Furthermore, I decree that if
anyone defies this edict, a beam is
to be pulled from their house and
they are to be impaled on it. And for
this crime their house is to be made
a pile of rubble. 12May God, who has
caused his Name to dwell there,
overthrow any king or people who
lifts a hand to change this decree or
to destroy this temple in Jerusalem.
I Darius have decreed it. Let it be
carried out with diligence.

Completion and Dedication of the Temple

13Then, because of the decree King
Darius had sent, Tattenai, governor of
Trans-Euphrates, and Shethar-Bozenai
and their associates carried it out with
diligence. 14So the elders of the Jews continued to build and prosper under the
preaching of Haggai the prophet and
Zechariah, a descendant of Iddo. They
finished building the temple according
to the command of the God of Israel and
the decrees of Cyrus, Darius and Artaxerxes, kings of Persia. 15The temple was
completed on the third day of the month
Adar, in the sixth year of the reign of
King Darius.
16Then the people of Israel — the
priests, the Levites and the rest of the
exiles — celebrated the dedication of the
house of God with joy. 17For the dedication of this house of God they offered a
hundred bulls, two hundred rams, four
hundred male lambs and, as a sin offering[c] for all Israel, twelve male goats, one
for each of the tribes of Israel. 18And they
installed the priests in their divisions
and the Levites in their groups for the
service of God at Jerusalem, according
to what is written in the Book of Moses.

[a] 14 Or *palace* [b] 3 That is, about 90 feet or about 27 meters [c] 17 Or *purification offering*

The Passover

19On the fourteenth day of the first
month, the exiles celebrated the Passover. 20The priests and Levites had purified themselves and were all ceremonially clean. The Levites slaughtered the
Passover lamb for all the exiles, for their
relatives the priests and for themselves.
21So the Israelites who had returned
from the exile ate it, together with all
who had separated themselves from the
unclean practices of their Gentile neighbors in order to seek the LORD, the God
of Israel. 22For seven days they celebrated with joy the Festival of Unleavened
Bread, because the LORD had filled them
with joy by changing the attitude of the
king of Assyria so that he assisted them
in the work on the house of God, the God
of Israel.

Ezra Comes to Jerusalem

7 After these things, during the reign
of Artaxerxes king of Persia, Ezra
son of Seraiah, the son of Azariah, the
son of Hilkiah, 2the son of Shallum, the
son of Zadok, the son of Ahitub, 3the son
of Amariah, the son of Azariah, the son
of Meraioth, 4the son of Zerahiah, the
son of Uzzi, the son of Bukki, 5the son
of Abishua, the son of Phinehas, the son
of Eleazar, the son of Aaron the chief
priest — 6this Ezra came up from Babylon. He was a teacher well versed in the
Law of Moses, which the LORD, the God of
Israel, had given. The king had granted
him everything he asked, for the hand of
the LORD his God was on him. 7Some of
the Israelites, including priests, Levites,
musicians, gatekeepers and temple servants, also came up to Jerusalem in the
seventh year of King Artaxerxes.

8Ezra arrived in Jerusalem in the fifth
month of the seventh year of the king.
9He had begun his journey from Babylon on the first day of the first month,
and he arrived in Jerusalem on the first
day of the fifth month, for the gracious
hand of his God was on him. 10For Ezra
had devoted himself to the study and observance of the Law of the LORD, and to
teaching its decrees and laws in Israel.

King Artaxerxes' Letter to Ezra

11This is a copy of the letter King Artaxerxes had given to Ezra the priest,
a teacher of the Law, a man learned in
matters concerning the commands and
decrees of the LORD for Israel:

12Artaxerxes, king of kings,

To Ezra the priest, teacher of the
Law of the God of heaven:

Greetings.

13Now I decree that any of the Israelites in my kingdom, including
priests and Levites, who volunteer
to go to Jerusalem with you, may
go. 14You are sent by the king and
his seven advisers to inquire about
Judah and Jerusalem with regard
to the Law of your God, which is in
your hand. 15Moreover, you are to
take with you the silver and gold
that the king and his advisers have
freely given to the God of Israel,
whose dwelling is in Jerusalem, 16to-
gether with all the silver and gold
you may obtain from the province
of Babylon, as well as the freewill
offerings of the people and priests
for the temple of their God in Jerusalem. 17With this money be sure to
buy bulls, rams and male lambs,
together with their grain offerings
and drink offerings, and sacrifice
them on the altar of the temple of
your God in Jerusalem.

18You and your fellow Israelites
may then do whatever seems best
with the rest of the silver and gold,
in accordance with the will of your
God. 19Deliver to the God of Jerusalem all the articles entrusted to you
for worship in the temple of your
God. 20And anything else needed for
the temple of your God that you are
responsible to supply, you may provide from the royal treasury.

21Now I, King Artaxerxes, decree
that all the treasurers of Trans-
Euphrates are to provide with diligence whatever Ezra the priest,
the teacher of the Law of the God
of heaven, may ask of you — 22up
to a hundred talents[a] of silver, a
hundred cors[b] of wheat, a hundred
baths[c] of wine, a hundred baths[c]
of olive oil, and salt without limit.
23Whatever the God of heaven has
prescribed, let it be done with diligence for the temple of the God
of heaven. Why should his wrath
fall on the realm of the king and
of his sons? 24You are also to know
that you have no authority to impose taxes, tribute or duty on any
of the priests, Levites, musicians,

[a] *22* That is, about 3 3/4 tons or about 3.4 metric tons [b] *22* That is, probably about 18 tons or about 16 metric tons [c] *22* That is, about 600 gallons or about 2,200 liters

gatekeepers, temple servants or
other workers at this house of God.
25 And you, Ezra, in accordance
with the wisdom of your God,
which you possess, appoint magistrates and judges to administer
justice to all the people of Trans-
Euphrates — all who know the laws
of your God. And you are to teach
any who do not know them. 26 Whoever does not obey the law of your
God and the law of the king must
surely be punished by death, ban-
ishment, confiscation of property,
or imprisonment.[a]

27 Praise be to the LORD, the God of our
ancestors, who has put it into the king's
heart to bring honor to the house of the
LORD in Jerusalem in this way 28 and who
has extended his good favor to me before the king and his advisers and all
the king's powerful officials. Because the
hand of the LORD my God was on me, I
took courage and gathered leaders from
Israel to go up with me.

List of the Family Heads Returning With Ezra

8 These are the family heads and those
registered with them who came up
with me from Babylon during the reign
of King Artaxerxes:

2 of the descendants of Phinehas, Gershom;
of the descendants of Ithamar, Daniel;
of the descendants of David, Hattush 3 of the descendants of Shekaniah;

of the descendants of Parosh, Zechariah, and with him were registered 150 men;
4 of the descendants of Pahath-Moab, Eliehoenai son of Zerahiah, and with him 200 men;
5 of the descendants of Zattu,[b] Shekaniah son of Jahaziel, and with him 300 men;
6 of the descendants of Adin, Ebed son of Jonathan, and with him 50 men;
7 of the descendants of Elam, Jeshaiah son of Athaliah, and with him 70 men;
8 of the descendants of Shephatiah, Zebadiah son of Michael, and with him 80 men;
9 of the descendants of Joab, Obadiah son of Jehiel, and with him 218 men;
10 of the descendants of Bani,[c] Shelomith son of Josiphiah, and with him 160 men;
11 of the descendants of Bebai, Zechariah son of Bebai, and with him 28 men;
12 of the descendants of Azgad, Johanan son of Hakkatan, and with him 110 men;
13 of the descendants of Adonikam, the last ones, whose names were Eliphelet, Jeuel and Shemaiah, and with them 60 men;
14 of the descendants of Bigvai, Uthai and Zakkur, and with them 70 men.

The Return to Jerusalem

15 I assembled them at the canal that
flows toward Ahava, and we camped
there three days. When I checked among
the people and the priests, I found no Levites there. 16 So I summoned Eliezer, Ariel, Shemaiah, Elnathan, Jarib, Elnathan,
Nathan, Zechariah and Meshullam, who
were leaders, and Joiarib and Elnathan, who were men of learning, 17 and I
ordered them to go to Iddo, the leader
in Kasiphia. I told them what to say to
Iddo and his fellow Levites, the temple
servants in Kasiphia, so that they might
bring attendants to us for the house of
our God. 18 Because the gracious hand of
our God was on us, they brought us Sherebiah, a capable man, from the descendants of Mahli son of Levi, the son of Israel, and Sherebiah's sons and brothers,
18 in all; 19 and Hashabiah, together with
Jeshaiah from the descendants of Merari, and his brothers and nephews, 20 in
all. 20 They also brought 220 of the temple servants — a body that David and
the officials had established to assist the
Levites. All were registered by name.
21 There, by the Ahava Canal, I proclaimed a fast, so that we might humble
ourselves before our God and ask him
for a safe journey for us and our children, with all our possessions. 22 I was
ashamed to ask the king for soldiers and
horsemen to protect us from enemies on
the road, because we had told the king,
"The gracious hand of our God is on everyone who looks to him, but his great
anger is against all who forsake him."

[a] *26* The text of 7:12-26 is in Aramaic. [b] *5* Some Septuagint manuscripts (also 1 Esdras 8:32); Hebrew does not have *Zattu.* [c] *10* Some Septuagint manuscripts (also 1 Esdras 8:36); Hebrew does not have *Bani.*

23So we fasted and petitioned our God about this, and he answered our prayer.

24Then I set apart twelve of the leading priests, namely, Sherebiah, Hashabiah and ten of their brothers, 25and I weighed out to them the offering of silver and gold and the articles that the king, his advisers, his officials and all Israel present there had donated for the house of our God. 26I weighed out to them 650 talents[a] of silver, silver articles weighing 100 talents,[b] 100 talents[b] of gold, 2720 bowls of gold valued at 1,000 darics,[c] and two fine articles of polished bronze, as precious as gold.

28I said to them, "You as well as these articles are consecrated to the LORD. The silver and gold are a freewill offering to the LORD, the God of your ancestors. 29Guard them carefully until you weigh them out in the chambers of the house of the LORD in Jerusalem before the leading priests and the Levites and the family heads of Israel." 30Then the priests and Levites received the silver and gold and sacred articles that had been weighed out to be taken to the house of our God in Jerusalem.

31On the twelfth day of the first month we set out from the Ahava Canal to go to Jerusalem. The hand of our God was on us, and he protected us from enemies and bandits along the way. 32So we arrived in Jerusalem, where we rested three days.

33On the fourth day, in the house of our God, we weighed out the silver and gold and the sacred articles into the hands of Meremoth son of Uriah, the priest. Eleazar son of Phinehas was with him, and so were the Levites Jozabad son of Jeshua and Noadiah son of Binnui. 34Everything was accounted for by number and weight, and the entire weight was recorded at that time.

35Then the exiles who had returned from captivity sacrificed burnt offerings to the God of Israel: twelve bulls for all Israel, ninety-six rams, seventy-seven male lambs and, as a sin offering,[d] twelve male goats. All this was a burnt offering to the LORD. 36They also delivered the king's orders to the royal satraps and to the governors of Trans-Euphrates, who then gave assistance to the people and to the house of God.

Ezra's Prayer About Intermarriage

9 After these things had been done, the leaders came to me and said, "The people of Israel, including the priests and the Levites, have not kept themselves separate from the neighboring peoples with their detestable practices, like those of the Canaanites, Hittites, Perizzites, Jebusites, Ammonites, Moabites, Egyptians and Amorites. 2They have taken some of their daughters as wives for themselves and their sons, and have mingled the holy race with the peoples around them. And the leaders and officials have led the way in this unfaithfulness."

3When I heard this, I tore my tunic and cloak, pulled hair from my head and beard and sat down appalled. 4Then everyone who trembled at the words of the God of Israel gathered around me because of this unfaithfulness of the exiles. And I sat there appalled until the evening sacrifice.

5Then, at the evening sacrifice, I rose from my self-abasement, with my tunic and cloak torn, and fell on my knees with my hands spread out to the LORD my God 6and prayed:

"I am too ashamed and disgraced, my God, to lift up my face to you, because our sins are higher than our heads and our guilt has reached to the heavens. 7From the days of our ancestors until now, our guilt has been great. Because of our sins, we and our kings and our priests have been subjected to the sword and captivity, to pillage and humiliation at the hand of foreign kings, as it is today.

8"But now, for a brief moment, the LORD our God has been gracious in leaving us a remnant and giving us a firm place[e] in his sanctuary, and so our God gives light to our eyes and a little relief in our bondage. 9Though we are slaves, our God has not forsaken us in our bondage. He has shown us kindness in the sight of the kings of Persia: He has granted us new life to rebuild the house of our God and repair its ruins, and he has given us a wall of protection in Judah and Jerusalem.

10"But now, our God, what can we say after this? For we have forsaken the commands 11you gave through your servants the prophets when you said: 'The land you are entering to possess is a land polluted by the corruption of its peoples. By their detestable practices they have filled

[a] *26* That is, about 24 tons or about 22 metric tons [b] *26* That is, about 3 3/4 tons or about 3.4 metric tons [c] *27* That is, about 19 pounds or about 8.4 kilograms [d] *35* Or *purification offering* [e] *8* Or *a foothold*

it with their impurity from one end to the other. 12Therefore, do not give your daughters in marriage to their sons or take their daughters for your sons. Do not seek a treaty of friendship with them at any time, that you may be strong and eat the good things of the land and leave it to your children as an everlasting inheritance.'

13"What has happened to us is a result of our evil deeds and our great guilt, and yet, our God, you have punished us less than our sins deserved and have given us a remnant like this. 14Shall we then break your commands again and intermarry with the peoples who commit such detestable practices? Would you not be angry enough with us to destroy us, leaving us no remnant or survivor? 15LORD, the God of Israel, you are righteous! We are left this day as a remnant. Here we are before you in our guilt, though because of it not one of us can stand in your presence."

The People's Confession of Sin

10 While Ezra was praying and confessing, weeping and throwing himself down before the house of God, a large crowd of Israelites — men, women and children — gathered around him. They too wept bitterly. 2Then Shekaniah son of Jehiel, one of the descendants of Elam, said to Ezra, "We have been unfaithful to our God by marrying foreign women from the peoples around us. But in spite of this, there is still hope for Israel. 3Now let us make a covenant before our God to send away all these women and their children, in accordance with the counsel of my lord and of those who fear the commands of our God. Let it be done according to the Law. 4Rise up; this matter is in your hands. We will support you, so take courage and do it."

5So Ezra rose up and put the leading priests and Levites and all Israel under oath to do what had been suggested. And they took the oath. 6Then Ezra withdrew from before the house of God and went to the room of Jehohanan son of Eliashib. While he was there, he ate no food and drank no water, because he continued to mourn over the unfaithfulness of the exiles.

7A proclamation was then issued throughout Judah and Jerusalem for all the exiles to assemble in Jerusalem. 8Anyone who failed to appear within three days would forfeit all his property, in accordance with the decision of the officials and elders, and would himself be expelled from the assembly of the exiles.

9Within the three days, all the men of Judah and Benjamin had gathered in Jerusalem. And on the twentieth day of the ninth month, all the people were sitting in the square before the house of God, greatly distressed by the occasion and because of the rain. 10Then Ezra the priest stood up and said to them, "You have been unfaithful; you have married foreign women, adding to Israel's guilt. 11Now honor[a] the LORD, the God of your ancestors, and do his will. Separate yourselves from the peoples around you and from your foreign wives."

12The whole assembly responded with a loud voice: "You are right! We must do as you say. 13But there are many people here and it is the rainy season; so we cannot stand outside. Besides, this matter cannot be taken care of in a day or two, because we have sinned greatly in this thing. 14Let our officials act for the whole assembly. Then let everyone in our towns who has married a foreign woman come at a set time, along with the elders and judges of each town, until the fierce anger of our God in this matter is turned away from us." 15Only Jonathan son of Asahel and Jahzeiah son of Tikvah, supported by Meshullam and Shabbethai the Levite, opposed this.

16So the exiles did as was proposed. Ezra the priest selected men who were family heads, one from each family division, and all of them designated by name. On the first day of the tenth month they sat down to investigate the cases, 17and by the first day of the first month they finished dealing with all the men who had married foreign women.

Those Guilty of Intermarriage

18Among the descendants of the priests, the following had married foreign women:

From the descendants of Joshua son of Jozadak, and his brothers: Maaseiah, Eliezer, Jarib and Gedaliah. 19(They all gave their hands in pledge to put away their wives, and for their guilt they each presented a ram from the flock as a guilt offering.)

[a] 11 Or *Now make confession to*

20 From the descendants of Immer:
Hanani and Zebadiah.
21 From the descendants of Harim:
Maaseiah, Elijah, Shemaiah, Jehiel and Uzziah.
22 From the descendants of Pashhur:
Elioenai, Maaseiah, Ishmael, Nethanel, Jozabad and Elasah.
23 Among the Levites:

Jozabad, Shimei, Kelaiah (that is, Kelita), Pethahiah, Judah and Eliezer.
24 From the musicians:
Eliashib.
From the gatekeepers:
Shallum, Telem and Uri.
25 And among the other Israelites:

From the descendants of Parosh:
Ramiah, Izziah, Malkijah, Mijamin, Eleazar, Malkijah and Benaiah.
26 From the descendants of Elam:
Mattaniah, Zechariah, Jehiel, Abdi, Jeremoth and Elijah.
27 From the descendants of Zattu:
Elioenai, Eliashib, Mattaniah, Jeremoth, Zabad and Aziza.
28 From the descendants of Bebai:
Jehohanan, Hananiah, Zabbai and Athlai.
29 From the descendants of Bani:
Meshullam, Malluk, Adaiah, Jashub, Sheal and Jeremoth.
30 From the descendants of Pahath-Moab:
Adna, Kelal, Benaiah, Maaseiah, Mattaniah, Bezalel, Binnui and Manasseh.
31 From the descendants of Harim:
Eliezer, Ishijah, Malkijah, Shemaiah, Shimeon,
32 Benjamin, Malluk and Shemariah.
33 From the descendants of Hashum:
Mattenai, Mattattah, Zabad, Eliphelet, Jeremai, Manasseh and Shimei.
34 From the descendants of Bani:
Maadai, Amram, Uel,
35 Benaiah, Bedeiah, Keluhi,
36 Vaniah, Meremoth, Eliashib,
37 Mattaniah, Mattenai and Jaasu.
38 From the descendants of Binnui:[a]
Shimei,
39 Shelemiah, Nathan, Adaiah,
40 Maknadebai, Shashai, Sharai,
41 Azarel, Shelemiah, Shemariah,
42 Shallum, Amariah and Joseph.
43 From the descendants of Nebo:
Jeiel, Mattithiah, Zabad, Zebina, Jaddai, Joel and Benaiah.

44 All these had married foreign women, and some of them had children by these wives.[b]

[a] 37,38 See Septuagint (also 1 Esdras 9:34); Hebrew *Jaasu* [38]*and Bani and Binnui,* [b] 44 Or *and they sent them away with their children*

NEHEMIAH

Nehemiah's Prayer

1 The words of Nehemiah son of Hakaliah:

In the month of Kislev in the twentieth year, while I was in the citadel of
Susa, 2Hanani, one of my brothers, came
from Judah with some other men, and I
questioned them about the Jewish remnant that had survived the exile, and
also about Jerusalem.
3They said to me, "Those who survived
the exile and are back in the province
are in great trouble and disgrace. The
wall of Jerusalem is broken down, and
its gates have been burned with fire."
4When I heard these things, I sat down
and wept. For some days I mourned and
fasted and prayed before the God of
heaven. 5Then I said:

"LORD, the God of heaven, the
great and awesome God, who keeps
his covenant of love with those who
love him and keep his commandments, 6let your ear be attentive and
your eyes open to hear the prayer
your servant is praying before you
day and night for your servants, the
people of Israel. I confess the sins
we Israelites, including myself and
my father's family, have committed
against you. 7We have acted very
wickedly toward you. We have not
obeyed the commands, decrees and
laws you gave your servant Moses.
8"Remember the instruction you
gave your servant Moses, saying, 'If
you are unfaithful, I will scatter you
among the nations, 9but if you return to me and obey my commands,
then even if your exiled people are
at the farthest horizon, I will gather
them from there and bring them to
the place I have chosen as a dwelling for my Name.'
10"They are your servants and
your people, whom you redeemed
by your great strength and your
mighty hand. 11Lord, let your ear be
attentive to the prayer of this your
servant and to the prayer of your
servants who delight in revering
your name. Give your servant success today by granting him favor in
the presence of this man."

I was cupbearer to the king.

Artaxerxes Sends Nehemiah to Jerusalem

2 In the month of Nisan in the twentieth year of King Artaxerxes, when
wine was brought for him, I took the
wine and gave it to the king. I had not
been sad in his presence before, 2so the
king asked me, "Why does your face look
so sad when you are not ill? This can be
nothing but sadness of heart."
I was very much afraid, 3but I said
to the king, "May the king live forever!
Why should my face not look sad when
the city where my ancestors are buried
lies in ruins, and its gates have been destroyed by fire?"
4The king said to me, "What is it you
want?"
Then I prayed to the God of heaven,
5and I answered the king, "If it pleases
the king and if your servant has found
favor in his sight, let him send me to the
city in Judah where my ancestors are
buried so that I can rebuild it."
6Then the king, with the queen sitting
beside him, asked me, "How long will
your journey take, and when will you get
back?" It pleased the king to send me; so
I set a time.
7I also said to him, "If it pleases the
king, may I have letters to the governors
of Trans-Euphrates, so that they will provide me safe-conduct until I arrive in Judah? 8And may I have a letter to Asaph,
keeper of the royal park, so he will give
me timber to make beams for the gates
of the citadel by the temple and for the
city wall and for the residence I will occupy?" And because the gracious hand
of my God was on me, the king granted
my requests. 9So I went to the governors
of Trans-Euphrates and gave them the
king's letters. The king had also sent
army officers and cavalry with me.
10When Sanballat the Horonite and
Tobiah the Ammonite official heard
about this, they were very much disturbed that someone had come to promote the welfare of the Israelites.

Nehemiah Inspects Jerusalem's Walls

11I went to Jerusalem, and after staying there three days 12I set out during
the night with a few others. I had not

told anyone what my God had put in my heart to do for Jerusalem. There were no mounts with me except the one I was riding on.

13 By night I went out through the Valley Gate toward the Jackal[a] Well and the Dung Gate, examining the walls of Jerusalem, which had been broken down, and its gates, which had been destroyed by fire. 14 Then I moved on toward the Fountain Gate and the King's Pool, but there was not enough room for my mount to get through; 15 so I went up the valley by night, examining the wall. Finally, I turned back and reentered through the Valley Gate. 16 The officials did not know where I had gone or what I was doing, because as yet I had said nothing to the Jews or the priests or nobles or officials or any others who would be doing the work.

17 Then I said to them, "You see the trouble we are in: Jerusalem lies in ruins, and its gates have been burned with fire. Come, let us rebuild the wall of Jerusalem, and we will no longer be in disgrace." 18 I also told them about the gracious hand of my God on me and what the king had said to me.

They replied, "Let us start rebuilding." So they began this good work.

19 But when Sanballat the Horonite, Tobiah the Ammonite official and Geshem the Arab heard about it, they mocked and ridiculed us. "What is this you are doing?" they asked. "Are you rebelling against the king?"

20 I answered them by saying, "The God of heaven will give us success. We his servants will start rebuilding, but as for you, you have no share in Jerusalem or any claim or historic right to it."

Builders of the Wall

3 Eliashib the high priest and his fellow priests went to work and rebuilt the Sheep Gate. They dedicated it and set its doors in place, building as far as the Tower of the Hundred, which they dedicated, and as far as the Tower of Hananel. 2 The men of Jericho built the adjoining section, and Zakkur son of Imri built next to them.

3 The Fish Gate was rebuilt by the sons of Hassenaah. They laid its beams and put its doors and bolts and bars in place. 4 Meremoth son of Uriah, the son of Hakkoz, repaired the next section. Next to him Meshullam son of Berekiah, the son of Meshezabel, made repairs, and next to him Zadok son of Baana also made repairs. 5 The next section was repaired by the men of Tekoa, but their nobles would not put their shoulders to the work under their supervisors.[b]

6 The Jeshanah[c] Gate was repaired by Joiada son of Paseah and Meshullam son of Besodeiah. They laid its beams and put its doors with their bolts and bars in place. 7 Next to them, repairs were made by men from Gibeon and Mizpah — Melatiah of Gibeon and Jadon of Meronoth — places under the authority of the governor of Trans-Euphrates. 8 Uzziel son of Harhaiah, one of the goldsmiths, repaired the next section; and Hananiah, one of the perfume-makers, made repairs next to that. They restored Jerusalem as far as the Broad Wall. 9 Rephaiah son of Hur, ruler of a half-district of Jerusalem, repaired the next section. 10 Adjoining this, Jedaiah son of Harumaph made repairs opposite his house, and Hattush son of Hashabneiah made repairs next to him. 11 Malkijah son of Harim and Hasshub son of Pahath-Moab repaired another section and the Tower of the Ovens. 12 Shallum son of Hallohesh, ruler of a half-district of Jerusalem, repaired the next section with the help of his daughters.

13 The Valley Gate was repaired by Hanun and the residents of Zanoah. They rebuilt it and put its doors with their bolts and bars in place. They also repaired a thousand cubits[d] of the wall as far as the Dung Gate.

14 The Dung Gate was repaired by Malkijah son of Rekab, ruler of the district of Beth Hakkerem. He rebuilt it and put its doors with their bolts and bars in place.

15 The Fountain Gate was repaired by Shallun son of Kol-Hozeh, ruler of the district of Mizpah. He rebuilt it, roofing it over and putting its doors and bolts and bars in place. He also repaired the wall of the Pool of Siloam,[e] by the King's Garden, as far as the steps going down from the City of David. 16 Beyond him, Nehemiah son of Azbuk, ruler of a half-district of Beth Zur, made repairs up to a point opposite the tombs[f] of David, as far as the artificial pool and the House of the Heroes.

[a] *13* Or *Serpent* or *Fig* [b] *5* Or *their Lord* or *the governor* [c] *6* Or *Old* [d] *13* That is, about 1,500 feet or about 450 meters [e] *15* Hebrew *Shelah*, a variant of *Shiloah*, that is, Siloam [f] *16* Hebrew; Septuagint, some Vulgate manuscripts and Syriac *tomb*

17 Next to him, the repairs were made
by the Levites under Rehum son of Bani.
Beside him, Hashabiah, ruler of half the
district of Keilah, carried out repairs for
his district. 18 Next to him, the repairs
were made by their fellow Levites under
Binnui[a] son of Henadad, ruler of the other half-district of Keilah. 19 Next to him,
Ezer son of Jeshua, ruler of Mizpah, repaired another section, from a point facing the ascent to the armory as far as the
angle of the wall. 20 Next to him, Baruch
son of Zabbai zealously repaired another
section, from the angle to the entrance
of the house of Eliashib the high priest.
21 Next to him, Meremoth son of Uriah,
the son of Hakkoz, repaired another
section, from the entrance of Eliashib's
house to the end of it.

22 The repairs next to him were made
by the priests from the surrounding region. 23 Beyond them, Benjamin and
Hasshub made repairs in front of their
house; and next to them, Azariah son
of Maaseiah, the son of Ananiah, made
repairs beside his house. 24 Next to him,
Binnui son of Henadad repaired another section, from Azariah's house to the
angle and the corner, 25 and Palal son of
Uzai worked opposite the angle and the
tower projecting from the upper palace
near the court of the guard. Next to him,
Pedaiah son of Parosh 26 and the temple
servants living on the hill of Ophel made
repairs up to a point opposite the Water
Gate toward the east and the projecting
tower. 27 Next to them, the men of Tekoa
repaired another section, from the great
projecting tower to the wall of Ophel.

28 Above the Horse Gate, the priests
made repairs, each in front of his own
house. 29 Next to them, Zadok son of Immer made repairs opposite his house.
Next to him, Shemaiah son of Shekaniah, the guard at the East Gate, made
repairs. 30 Next to him, Hananiah son of
Shelemiah, and Hanun, the sixth son of
Zalaph, repaired another section. Next
to them, Meshullam son of Berekiah
made repairs opposite his living quarters. 31 Next to him, Malkijah, one of the
goldsmiths, made repairs as far as the
house of the temple servants and the
merchants, opposite the Inspection Gate,
and as far as the room above the corner;
32 and between the room above the corner and the Sheep Gate the goldsmiths
and merchants made repairs.

Opposition to the Rebuilding

4 [b] When Sanballat heard that we were
rebuilding the wall, he became angry
and was greatly incensed. He ridiculed
the Jews, 2 and in the presence of his associates and the army of Samaria, he said,
"What are those feeble Jews doing? Will
they restore their wall? Will they offer sacrifices? Will they finish in a day? Can they
bring the stones back to life from those
heaps of rubble — burned as they are?"

3 Tobiah the Ammonite, who was at
his side, said, "What they are building —
even a fox climbing up on it would break
down their wall of stones!"

4 Hear us, our God, for we are despised.
Turn their insults back on their own
heads. Give them over as plunder in a
land of captivity. 5 Do not cover up their
guilt or blot out their sins from your
sight, for they have thrown insults in the
face of[c] the builders.

6 So we rebuilt the wall till all of it
reached half its height, for the people
worked with all their heart.

7 But when Sanballat, Tobiah, the
Arabs, the Ammonites and the people of
Ashdod heard that the repairs to Jerusalem's walls had gone ahead and that the
gaps were being closed, they were very
angry. 8 They all plotted together to come
and fight against Jerusalem and stir up
trouble against it. 9 But we prayed to our
God and posted a guard day and night to
meet this threat.

10 Meanwhile, the people in Judah said,
"The strength of the laborers is giving
out, and there is so much rubble that we
cannot rebuild the wall."

11 Also our enemies said, "Before they
know it or see us, we will be right there
among them and will kill them and put
an end to the work."

12 Then the Jews who lived near them
came and told us ten times over, "Wherever you turn, they will attack us."

13 Therefore I stationed some of the
people behind the lowest points of the
wall at the exposed places, posting them
by families, with their swords, spears
and bows. 14 After I looked things over, I
stood up and said to the nobles, the officials and the rest of the people, "Don't be
afraid of them. Remember the Lord, who
is great and awesome, and fight for your
families, your sons and your daughters,
your wives and your homes."

[a] *18* Two Hebrew manuscripts and Syriac (see also Septuagint and verse 24); most Hebrew manuscripts *Bavvai* [b] In Hebrew texts 4:1-6 is numbered 3:33-38, and 4:7-23 is numbered 4:1-17.
[c] *5* Or *have aroused your anger before*

15When our enemies heard that we were aware of their plot and that God had frustrated it, we all returned to the wall, each to our own work.

16From that day on, half of my men did the work, while the other half were equipped with spears, shields, bows and armor. The officers posted themselves behind all the people of Judah 17who were building the wall. Those who carried materials did their work with one hand and held a weapon in the other, 18and each of the builders wore his sword at his side as he worked. But the man who sounded the trumpet stayed with me.

19Then I said to the nobles, the officials and the rest of the people, "The work is extensive and spread out, and we are widely separated from each other along the wall. 20Wherever you hear the sound of the trumpet, join us there. Our God will fight for us!"

21So we continued the work with half the men holding spears, from the first light of dawn till the stars came out. 22At that time I also said to the people, "Have every man and his helper stay inside Jerusalem at night, so they can serve us as guards by night and as workers by day." 23Neither I nor my brothers nor my men nor the guards with me took off our clothes; each had his weapon, even when he went for water.[a]

Nehemiah Helps the Poor

5 Now the men and their wives raised a great outcry against their fellow Jews. 2Some were saying, "We and our sons and daughters are numerous; in order for us to eat and stay alive, we must get grain."

3Others were saying, "We are mortgaging our fields, our vineyards and our homes to get grain during the famine."

4Still others were saying, "We have had to borrow money to pay the king's tax on our fields and vineyards. 5Although we are of the same flesh and blood as our fellow Jews and though our children are as good as theirs, yet we have to subject our sons and daughters to slavery. Some of our daughters have already been enslaved, but we are powerless, because our fields and our vineyards belong to others."

6When I heard their outcry and these charges, I was very angry. 7I pondered them in my mind and then accused the nobles and officials. I told them, "You are charging your own people interest!" So I called together a large meeting to deal with them 8and said: "As far as possible, we have bought back our fellow Jews who were sold to the Gentiles. Now you are selling your own people, only for them to be sold back to us!" They kept quiet, because they could find nothing to say.

9So I continued, "What you are doing is not right. Shouldn't you walk in the fear of our God to avoid the reproach of our Gentile enemies? 10I and my brothers and my men are also lending the people money and grain. But let us stop charging interest! 11Give back to them immediately their fields, vineyards, olive groves and houses, and also the interest you are charging them — one percent of the money, grain, new wine and olive oil."

12"We will give it back," they said. "And we will not demand anything more from them. We will do as you say."

Then I summoned the priests and made the nobles and officials take an oath to do what they had promised. 13I also shook out the folds of my robe and said, "In this way may God shake out of their house and possessions anyone who does not keep this promise. So may such a person be shaken out and emptied!"

At this the whole assembly said, "Amen," and praised the LORD. And the people did as they had promised.

14Moreover, from the twentieth year of King Artaxerxes, when I was appointed to be their governor in the land of Judah, until his thirty-second year — twelve years — neither I nor my brothers ate the food allotted to the governor. 15But the earlier governors — those preceding me — placed a heavy burden on the people and took forty shekels[b] of silver from them in addition to food and wine. Their assistants also lorded it over the people. But out of reverence for God I did not act like that. 16Instead, I devoted myself to the work on this wall. All my men were assembled there for the work; we[c] did not acquire any land.

17Furthermore, a hundred and fifty Jews and officials ate at my table, as well as those who came to us from the surrounding nations. 18Each day one ox, six choice sheep and some poultry were

[a] *23* The meaning of the Hebrew for this clause is uncertain. [b] *15* That is, about 1 pound or about 460 grams [c] *16* Most Hebrew manuscripts; some Hebrew manuscripts, Septuagint, Vulgate and Syriac *I*

prepared for me, and every ten days an abundant supply of wine of all kinds. In spite of all this, I never demanded the food allotted to the governor, because the demands were heavy on these people.

[19]Remember me with favor, my God, for all I have done for these people.

Further Opposition to the Rebuilding

6 When word came to Sanballat, Tobiah, Geshem the Arab and the rest of our enemies that I had rebuilt the wall and not a gap was left in it — though up to that time I had not set the doors in the gates — [2]Sanballat and Geshem sent me this message: "Come, let us meet together in one of the villages[a] on the plain of Ono."

But they were scheming to harm me; [3]so I sent messengers to them with this reply: "I am carrying on a great project and cannot go down. Why should the work stop while I leave it and go down to you?" [4]Four times they sent me the same message, and each time I gave them the same answer.

[5]Then, the fifth time, Sanballat sent his aide to me with the same message, and in his hand was an unsealed letter [6]in which was written:

> "It is reported among the nations — and Geshem[b] says it is true — that you and the Jews are plotting to revolt, and therefore you are building the wall. Moreover, according to these reports you are about to become their king [7]and have even appointed prophets to make this proclamation about you in Jerusalem: 'There is a king in Judah!' Now this report will get back to the king; so come, let us meet together."

[8]I sent him this reply: "Nothing like what you are saying is happening; you are just making it up out of your head."

[9]They were all trying to frighten us, thinking, "Their hands will get too weak for the work, and it will not be completed."

But I prayed, "Now strengthen my hands."

[10]One day I went to the house of Shemaiah son of Delaiah, the son of Mehetabel, who was shut in at his home. He said, "Let us meet in the house of God, inside the temple, and let us close the temple doors, because men are coming to kill you — by night they are coming to kill you."

[11]But I said, "Should a man like me run away? Or should someone like me go into the temple to save his life? I will not go!" [12]I realized that God had not sent him, but that he had prophesied against me because Tobiah and Sanballat had hired him. [13]He had been hired to intimidate me so that I would commit a sin by doing this, and then they would give me a bad name to discredit me.

[14]Remember Tobiah and Sanballat, my God, because of what they have done; remember also the prophet Noadiah and how she and the rest of the prophets have been trying to intimidate me. [15]So the wall was completed on the twenty-fifth of Elul, in fifty-two days.

Opposition to the Completed Wall

[16]When all our enemies heard about this, all the surrounding nations were afraid and lost their self-confidence, because they realized that this work had been done with the help of our God.

[17]Also, in those days the nobles of Judah were sending many letters to Tobiah, and replies from Tobiah kept coming to them. [18]For many in Judah were under oath to him, since he was son-in-law to Shekaniah son of Arah, and his son Jehohanan had married the daughter of Meshullam son of Berekiah. [19]Moreover, they kept reporting to me his good deeds and then telling him what I said. And Tobiah sent letters to intimidate me.

7 After the wall had been rebuilt and I had set the doors in place, the gatekeepers, the musicians and the Levites were appointed. [2]I put in charge of Jerusalem my brother Hanani, along with Hananiah the commander of the citadel, because he was a man of integrity and feared God more than most people do. [3]I said to them, "The gates of Jerusalem are not to be opened until the sun is hot. While the gatekeepers are still on duty, have them shut the doors and bar them. Also appoint residents of Jerusalem as guards, some at their posts and some near their own houses."

The List of the Exiles Who Returned

[4]Now the city was large and spacious, but there were few people in it, and the houses had not yet been rebuilt. [5]So my God put it into my heart to assemble the nobles, the officials and the common

[a] 2 Or *in Kephirim* [b] 6 Hebrew *Gashmu,* a variant of *Geshem*

people for registration by families. I
found the genealogical record of those
who had been the first to return. This is
what I found written there:

6These are the people of the province who came up from the captivity of the exiles whom Nebuchadnezzar king of Babylon had taken captive (they returned to Jerusalem and Judah, each to his own town, 7in company with Zerubbabel, Joshua, Nehemiah, Azariah, Raamiah, Nahamani, Mordecai, Bilshan, Mispereth, Bigvai, Nehum and Baanah):

The list of the men of Israel:

8 the descendants of Parosh 2,172
9 of Shephatiah 372
10 of Arah 652
11 of Pahath-Moab (through the line of Jeshua and Joab) 2,818
12 of Elam 1,254
13 of Zattu 845
14 of Zakkai 760
15 of Binnui 648
16 of Bebai 628
17 of Azgad 2,322
18 of Adonikam 667
19 of Bigvai 2,067
20 of Adin 655
21 of Ater (through Hezekiah) 98
22 of Hashum 328
23 of Bezai 324
24 of Hariph 112
25 of Gibeon 95
26 the men of Bethlehem and Netophah 188
27 of Anathoth 128
28 of Beth Azmaveth 42
29 of Kiriath Jearim, Kephirah and Beeroth 743
30 of Ramah and Geba 621
31 of Mikmash 122
32 of Bethel and Ai 123
33 of the other Nebo 52
34 of the other Elam 1,254
35 of Harim 320
36 of Jericho 345
37 of Lod, Hadid and Ono 721
38 of Senaah 3,930

39The priests:

the descendants of Jedaiah (through the family of Jeshua) 973
40 of Immer 1,052
41 of Pashhur 1,247
42 of Harim 1,017

43The Levites:

the descendants of Jeshua (through Kadmiel through the line of Hodaviah) 74

44The musicians:

the descendants of Asaph 148

45The gatekeepers:

the descendants of Shallum, Ater, Talmon, Akkub, Hatita and Shobai 138

46The temple servants:

the descendants of
Ziha, Hasupha, Tabbaoth,
47 Keros, Sia, Padon,
48 Lebana, Hagaba, Shalmai,
49 Hanan, Giddel, Gahar,
50 Reaiah, Rezin, Nekoda,
51 Gazzam, Uzza, Paseah,
52 Besai, Meunim, Nephusim,
53 Bakbuk, Hakupha, Harhur,
54 Bazluth, Mehida, Harsha,
55 Barkos, Sisera, Temah,
56 Neziah and Hatipha

57The descendants of the servants of Solomon:

the descendants of
Sotai, Sophereth, Perida,
58 Jaala, Darkon, Giddel,
59 Shephatiah, Hattil,
Pokereth-Hazzebaim and Amon

60 The temple servants and the descendants of the servants of Solomon 392

61The following came up from
the towns of Tel Melah, Tel Harsha,
Kerub, Addon and Immer, but they
could not show that their families
were descended from Israel:

62 the descendants of Delaiah, Tobiah and Nekoda 642

63And from among the priests:

the descendants of Hobaiah, Hakkoz and Barzillai (a man who had married a daughter of Barzillai the Gileadite and was called by that name).

64These searched for their family records, but they could not find
them and so were excluded from the
priesthood as unclean. 65The governor, therefore, ordered them not to
eat any of the most sacred food until
there should be a priest ministering
with the Urim and Thummim.

66The whole company numbered 42,360, 67besides their 7,337 male and female slaves; and they also had 245 male and female singers. 68There were 736 horses, 245 mules,[a] 69435 camels and 6,720 donkeys.

70Some of the heads of the families contributed to the work. The governor gave to the treasury 1,000 darics[b] of gold, 50 bowls and 530 garments for priests. 71Some of the heads of the families gave to the treasury for the work 20,000 darics[c] of gold and 2,200 minas[d] of silver. 72The total given by the rest of the people was 20,000 darics of gold, 2,000 minas[e] of silver and 67 garments for priests.

73The priests, the Levites, the gatekeepers, the musicians and the temple servants, along with certain of the people and the rest of the Israelites, settled in their own towns.

Ezra Reads the Law

When the seventh month came and the Israelites had settled in their towns,

8 1all the people came together as one in the square before the Water Gate. They told Ezra the teacher of the Law to bring out the Book of the Law of Moses, which the LORD had commanded for Israel.

2So on the first day of the seventh month Ezra the priest brought the Law before the assembly, which was made up of men and women and all who were able to understand. 3He read it aloud from daybreak till noon as he faced the square before the Water Gate in the presence of the men, women and others who could understand. And all the people listened attentively to the Book of the Law.

4Ezra the teacher of the Law stood on a high wooden platform built for the occasion. Beside him on his right stood Mattithiah, Shema, Anaiah, Uriah, Hilkiah and Maaseiah; and on his left were Pedaiah, Mishael, Malkijah, Hashum, Hashbaddanah, Zechariah and Meshullam.

5Ezra opened the book. All the people could see him because he was standing above them; and as he opened it, the people all stood up. 6Ezra praised the LORD, the great God; and all the people lifted their hands and responded, "Amen! Amen!" Then they bowed down and worshiped the LORD with their faces to the ground.

7The Levites — Jeshua, Bani, Sherebiah, Jamin, Akkub, Shabbethai, Hodiah, Maaseiah, Kelita, Azariah, Jozabad, Hanan and Pelaiah — instructed the people in the Law while the people were standing there. 8They read from the Book of the Law of God, making it clear[f] and giving the meaning so that the people understood what was being read.

9Then Nehemiah the governor, Ezra the priest and teacher of the Law, and the Levites who were instructing the people said to them all, "This day is holy to the LORD your God. Do not mourn or weep." For all the people had been weeping as they listened to the words of the Law.

10Nehemiah said, "Go and enjoy choice food and sweet drinks, and send some to those who have nothing prepared. This day is holy to our Lord. Do not grieve, for the joy of the LORD is your strength."

11The Levites calmed all the people, saying, "Be still, for this is a holy day. Do not grieve."

12Then all the people went away to eat and drink, to send portions of food and to celebrate with great joy, because they now understood the words that had been made known to them.

13On the second day of the month, the heads of all the families, along with the priests and the Levites, gathered around Ezra the teacher to give attention to the words of the Law. 14They found written in the Law, which the LORD had commanded through Moses, that the Israelites were to live in temporary shelters during the festival of the seventh month 15and that they should proclaim this word and spread it throughout their towns and in Jerusalem: "Go out into the hill country and bring back branches from olive and wild olive trees, and from myrtles, palms and shade trees, to make temporary shelters" — as it is written.[g]

16So the people went out and brought back branches and built themselves temporary shelters on their own roofs, in their courtyards, in the courts of the house of God and in the square by the Water Gate and the one by the Gate of Ephraim. 17The whole company that had

[a] *68* Some Hebrew manuscripts (see also Ezra 2:66); most Hebrew manuscripts do not have this verse. [b] *70* That is, about 19 pounds or about 8.4 kilograms [c] *71* That is, about 375 pounds or about 170 kilograms; also in verse 72 [d] *71* That is, about 1 1/3 tons or about 1.2 metric tons [e] *72* That is, about 1 1/4 tons or about 1.1 metric tons [f] *8* Or *God, translating it* [g] *15* See Lev. 23:37-40.

returned from exile built temporary shelters and lived in them. From the days of Joshua son of Nun until that day, the Israelites had not celebrated it like this. And their joy was very great.

18 Day after day, from the first day to the last, Ezra read from the Book of the Law of God. They celebrated the festival for seven days, and on the eighth day, in accordance with the regulation, there was an assembly.

The Israelites Confess Their Sins

9 On the twenty-fourth day of the same month, the Israelites gathered together, fasting and wearing sackcloth and putting dust on their heads. 2 Those of Israelite descent had separated themselves from all foreigners. They stood in their places and confessed their sins and the sins of their ancestors. 3 They stood where they were and read from the Book of the Law of the LORD their God for a quarter of the day, and spent another quarter in confession and in worshiping the LORD their God. 4 Standing on the stairs of the Levites were Jeshua, Bani, Kadmiel, Shebaniah, Bunni, Sherebiah, Bani and Kenani. They cried out with loud voices to the LORD their God. 5 And the Levites — Jeshua, Kadmiel, Bani, Hashabneiah, Sherebiah, Hodiah, Shebaniah and Pethahiah — said: "Stand up and praise the LORD your God, who is from everlasting to everlasting.[a]"

"Blessed be your glorious name, and may it be exalted above all blessing and praise. 6 You alone are the LORD. You made the heavens, even the highest heavens, and all their starry host, the earth and all that is on it, the seas and all that is in them. You give life to everything, and the multitudes of heaven worship you.

7 "You are the LORD God, who chose Abram and brought him out of Ur of the Chaldeans and named him Abraham. 8 You found his heart faithful to you, and you made a covenant with him to give to his descendants the land of the Canaanites, Hittites, Amorites, Perizzites, Jebusites and Girgashites. You have kept your promise because you are righteous.

9 "You saw the suffering of our ancestors in Egypt; you heard their cry at the Red Sea.[b] 10 You sent signs and wonders against Pharaoh, against all his officials and all the people of his land, for you knew how arrogantly the Egyptians treated them. You made a name for yourself, which remains to this day. 11 You divided the sea before them, so that they passed through it on dry ground, but you hurled their pursuers into the depths, like a stone into mighty waters. 12 By day you led them with a pillar of cloud, and by night with a pillar of fire to give them light on the way they were to take.

13 "You came down on Mount Sinai; you spoke to them from heaven. You gave them regulations and laws that are just and right, and decrees and commands that are good. 14 You made known to them your holy Sabbath and gave them commands, decrees and laws through your servant Moses. 15 In their hunger you gave them bread from heaven and in their thirst you brought them water from the rock; you told them to go in and take possession of the land you had sworn with uplifted hand to give them.

16 "But they, our ancestors, became arrogant and stiff-necked, and they did not obey your commands. 17 They refused to listen and failed to remember the miracles you performed among them. They became stiff-necked and in their rebellion appointed a leader in order to return to their slavery. But you are a forgiving God, gracious and compassionate, slow to anger and abounding in love. Therefore you did not desert them, 18 even when they cast for themselves an image of a calf and said, 'This is your god, who brought you up out of Egypt,' or when they committed awful blasphemies.

19 "Because of your great compassion you did not abandon them in the wilderness. By day the pillar of cloud did not fail to guide them on their path, nor the pillar of fire by night to shine on the way they were to take. 20 You gave your good Spirit to instruct them. You did not withhold your manna from their mouths, and you gave them water for their thirst. 21 For forty years you sustained them in the wilderness; they lacked nothing, their clothes did not wear out nor did their feet become swollen.

[a] 5 Or *God for ever and ever* [b] 9 Or *the Sea of Reeds*

22 “You gave them kingdoms and nations, allotting to them even the remotest frontiers. They took over the country of Sihon[a] king of Heshbon and the country of Og king of Bashan. 23 You made their children as numerous as the stars in the sky, and you brought them into the land that you told their parents to enter and possess. 24 Their children went in and took possession of the land. You subdued before them the Canaanites, who lived in the land; you gave the Canaanites into their hands, along with their kings and the peoples of the land, to deal with them as they pleased. 25 They captured fortified cities and fertile land; they took possession of houses filled with all kinds of good things, wells already dug, vineyards, olive groves and fruit trees in abundance. They ate to the full and were well-nourished; they reveled in your great goodness.

26 “But they were disobedient and rebelled against you; they turned their backs on your law. They killed your prophets, who had warned them in order to turn them back to you; they committed awful blasphemies. 27 So you delivered them into the hands of their enemies, who oppressed them. But when they were oppressed they cried out to you. From heaven you heard them, and in your great compassion you gave them deliverers, who rescued them from the hand of their enemies.

28 “But as soon as they were at rest, they again did what was evil in your sight. Then you abandoned them to the hand of their enemies so that they ruled over them. And when they cried out to you again, you heard from heaven, and in your compassion you delivered them time after time.

29 “You warned them in order to turn them back to your law, but they became arrogant and disobeyed your commands. They sinned against your ordinances, of which you said, ‘The person who obeys them will live by them.’ Stubbornly they turned their backs on you, became stiff-necked and refused to listen. 30 For many years you were patient with them. By your Spirit you warned them through your prophets. Yet they paid no attention, so you gave them into the hands of the neighboring peoples. 31 But in your great mercy you did not put an end to them or abandon them, for you are a gracious and merciful God.

32 “Now therefore, our God, the great God, mighty and awesome, who keeps his covenant of love, do not let all this hardship seem trifling in your eyes — the hardship that has come on us, on our kings and leaders, on our priests and prophets, on our ancestors and all your people, from the days of the kings of Assyria until today. 33 In all that has happened to us, you have remained righteous; you have acted faithfully, while we acted wickedly. 34 Our kings, our leaders, our priests and our ancestors did not follow your law; they did not pay attention to your commands or the statutes you warned them to keep. 35 Even while they were in their kingdom, enjoying your great goodness to them in the spacious and fertile land you gave them, they did not serve you or turn from their evil ways.

36 “But see, we are slaves today, slaves in the land you gave our ancestors so they could eat its fruit and the other good things it produces. 37 Because of our sins, its abundant harvest goes to the kings you have placed over us. They rule over our bodies and our cattle as they please. We are in great distress.

The Agreement of the People

38 “In view of all this, we are making a binding agreement, putting it in writing, and our leaders, our Levites and our priests are affixing their seals to it.”[b]

10[c] Those who sealed it were:

Nehemiah the governor, the son of Hakaliah.

Zedekiah, 2 Seraiah, Azariah, Jeremiah,
3 Pashhur, Amariah, Malkijah,
4 Hattush, Shebaniah, Malluk,
5 Harim, Meremoth, Obadiah,
6 Daniel, Ginnethon, Baruch,
7 Meshullam, Abijah, Mijamin,
8 Maaziah, Bilgai and Shemaiah.
These were the priests.

[a] *22* One Hebrew manuscript and Septuagint; most Hebrew manuscripts *Sihon, that is, the country of the* [b] *38* In Hebrew texts this verse (9:38) is numbered 10:1. [c] In Hebrew texts 10:1-39 is numbered 10:2-40.

9 The Levites:

Jeshua son of Azaniah, Binnui of the sons of Henadad, Kadmiel,
10 and their associates: Shebaniah, Hodiah, Kelita, Pelaiah, Hanan,
11 Mika, Rehob, Hashabiah,
12 Zakkur, Sherebiah, Shebaniah,
13 Hodiah, Bani and Beninu.

14 The leaders of the people:

Parosh, Pahath-Moab, Elam, Zattu, Bani,
15 Bunni, Azgad, Bebai,
16 Adonijah, Bigvai, Adin,
17 Ater, Hezekiah, Azzur,
18 Hodiah, Hashum, Bezai,
19 Hariph, Anathoth, Nebai,
20 Magpiash, Meshullam, Hezir,
21 Meshezabel, Zadok, Jaddua,
22 Pelatiah, Hanan, Anaiah,
23 Hoshea, Hananiah, Hasshub,
24 Hallohesh, Pilha, Shobek,
25 Rehum, Hashabnah, Maaseiah,
26 Ahiah, Hanan, Anan,
27 Malluk, Harim and Baanah.

28 "The rest of the people — priests,
Levites, gatekeepers, musicians,
temple servants and all who separated themselves from the neighboring peoples for the sake of the
Law of God, together with their wives
and all their sons and daughters
who are able to understand — 29 all
these now join their fellow Israelites the nobles, and bind themselves
with a curse and an oath to follow
the Law of God given through Moses
the servant of God and to obey carefully all the commands, regulations
and decrees of the LORD our Lord.

30 "We promise not to give our
daughters in marriage to the peoples around us or take their daughters for our sons.

31 "When the neighboring peoples bring merchandise or grain to
sell on the Sabbath, we will not buy
from them on the Sabbath or on
any holy day. Every seventh year we
will forgo working the land and will
cancel all debts.

32 "We assume the responsibility
for carrying out the commands to
give a third of a shekel[a] each year
for the service of the house of our
God: 33 for the bread set out on the
table; for the regular grain offerings
and burnt offerings; for the offerings
on the Sabbaths, at the New Moon
feasts and at the appointed festivals;
for the holy offerings; for sin offerings[b] to make atonement for Israel;
and for all the duties of the house of
our God.

34 "We — the priests, the Levites
and the people — have cast lots to
determine when each of our families
is to bring to the house of our God at
set times each year a contribution of
wood to burn on the altar of the LORD
our God, as it is written in the Law.

35 "We also assume responsibility for bringing to the house of the
LORD each year the firstfruits of our
crops and of every fruit tree.

36 "As it is also written in the Law,
we will bring the firstborn of our
sons and of our cattle, of our herds
and of our flocks to the house of our
God, to the priests ministering there.

37 "Moreover, we will bring to the
storerooms of the house of our God,
to the priests, the first of our ground
meal, of our grain offerings, of the
fruit of all our trees and of our new
wine and olive oil. And we will bring
a tithe of our crops to the Levites, for
it is the Levites who collect the tithes
in all the towns where we work. 38 A
priest descended from Aaron is to
accompany the Levites when they
receive the tithes, and the Levites
are to bring a tenth of the tithes up
to the house of our God, to the storerooms of the treasury. 39 The people
of Israel, including the Levites, are
to bring their contributions of grain,
new wine and olive oil to the storerooms, where the articles for the
sanctuary and for the ministering
priests, the gatekeepers and the musicians are also kept.

"We will not neglect the house of
our God."

The New Residents of Jerusalem

11 Now the leaders of the people settled in Jerusalem. The rest of the
people cast lots to bring one out of every ten of them to live in Jerusalem, the
holy city, while the remaining nine were
to stay in their own towns. 2 The people
commended all who volunteered to live
in Jerusalem.

3 These are the provincial leaders who
settled in Jerusalem (now some Israelites, priests, Levites, temple servants and
descendants of Solomon's servants lived
in the towns of Judah, each on their own

[a] 32 That is, about 1/8 ounce or about 4 grams [b] 33 Or *purification offerings*

property in the various towns, 4while
other people from both Judah and Benjamin lived in Jerusalem):

From the descendants of Judah:

Athaiah son of Uzziah, the son of
Zechariah, the son of Amariah, the
son of Shephatiah, the son of Mahalalel, a descendant of Perez; 5and
Maaseiah son of Baruch, the son of
Kol-Hozeh, the son of Hazaiah, the
son of Adaiah, the son of Joiarib,
the son of Zechariah, a descendant
of Shelah. 6The descendants of Perez who lived in Jerusalem totaled
468 men of standing.

7From the descendants of Benjamin:

Sallu son of Meshullam, the son of
Joed, the son of Pedaiah, the son of
Kolaiah, the son of Maaseiah, the son
of Ithiel, the son of Jeshaiah, 8and his
followers, Gabbai and Sallai — 928
men. 9Joel son of Zikri was their chief
officer, and Judah son of Hassenuah
was over the New Quarter of the city.

10From the priests:

Jedaiah; the son of Joiarib; Jakin;
11Seraiah son of Hilkiah, the son of
Meshullam, the son of Zadok, the
son of Meraioth, the son of Ahitub,
the official in charge of the house
of God, 12and their associates, who
carried on work for the temple —
822 men; Adaiah son of Jeroham,
the son of Pelaliah, the son of Amzi,
the son of Zechariah, the son of
Pashhur, the son of Malkijah, 13and
his associates, who were heads of
families — 242 men; Amashsai son
of Azarel, the son of Ahzai, the son
of Meshillemoth, the son of Immer,
14and his[a] associates, who were men
of standing — 128. Their chief officer
was Zabdiel son of Haggedolim.

15From the Levites:

Shemaiah son of Hasshub, the son
of Azrikam, the son of Hashabiah,
the son of Bunni; 16Shabbethai and
Jozabad, two of the heads of the Levites, who had charge of the outside
work of the house of God; 17Mattani-
ah son of Mika, the son of Zabdi, the
son of Asaph, the director who led
in thanksgiving and prayer; Bakbukiah, second among his associates;
and Abda son of Shammua, the son
of Galal, the son of Jeduthun. 18The
Levites in the holy city totaled 284.

19The gatekeepers:

Akkub, Talmon and their associates, who kept watch at the gates —
172 men.

20The rest of the Israelites, with the
priests and Levites, were in all the towns
of Judah, each on their ancestral property.
21The temple servants lived on the hill
of Ophel, and Ziha and Gishpa were in
charge of them.
22The chief officer of the Levites in Jerusalem was Uzzi son of Bani, the son of
Hashabiah, the son of Mattaniah, the
son of Mika. Uzzi was one of Asaph's
descendants, who were the musicians
responsible for the service of the house
of God. 23The musicians were under the
king's orders, which regulated their daily activity.
24Pethahiah son of Meshezabel, one of
the descendants of Zerah son of Judah,
was the king's agent in all affairs relat-
ing to the people.
25As for the villages with their fields,
some of the people of Judah lived in Kiriath Arba and its surrounding settlements,
in Dibon and its settlements, in Jekabzeel
and its villages, 26in Jeshua, in Moladah,
in Beth Pelet, 27in Hazar Shual, in Beersheba and its settlements, 28in Ziklag,
in Mekonah and its settlements, 29in En
Rimmon, in Zorah, in Jarmuth, 30Zano-
ah, Adullam and their villages, in Lachish
and its fields, and in Azekah and its settlements. So they were living all the way
from Beersheba to the Valley of Hinnom.
31The descendants of the Benjamites
from Geba lived in Mikmash, Aija, Bethel and its settlements, 32in Anathoth, Nob
and Ananiah, 33in Hazor, Ramah and Gittaim, 34in Hadid, Zeboim and Neballat,
35in Lod and Ono, and in Ge Harashim.
36Some of the divisions of the Levites
of Judah settled in Benjamin.

Priests and Levites

12 These were the priests and Levites
who returned with Zerubbabel son
of Shealtiel and with Joshua:

Seraiah, Jeremiah, Ezra,
2 Amariah, Malluk, Hattush,
3 Shekaniah, Rehum, Meremoth,
4 Iddo, Ginnethon,[b] Abijah,
5 Mijamin,[c] Moadiah, Bilgah,
6 Shemaiah, Joiarib, Jedaiah,
7 Sallu, Amok, Hilkiah and Jedaiah.

[a] 14 Most Septuagint manuscripts; Hebrew *their*
[b] 4 Many Hebrew manuscripts and Vulgate (see also verse 16); most Hebrew manuscripts *Ginnethoi*
[c] 5 A variant of *Miniamin*

These were the leaders of the priests and
their associates in the days of Joshua.
8 The Levites were Jeshua, Binnui, Kadmiel, Sherebiah, Judah, and also Mattaniah, who, together with his associates,
was in charge of the songs of thanksgiving. 9 Bakbukiah and Unni, their associates, stood opposite them in the services.
10 Joshua was the father of Joiakim,
Joiakim the father of Eliashib, Eliashib
the father of Joiada, 11 Joiada the father
of Jonathan, and Jonathan the father of
Jaddua.
12 In the days of Joiakim, these were
the heads of the priestly families:
of Seraiah's family, Meraiah;
of Jeremiah's, Hananiah;
13 of Ezra's, Meshullam;
of Amariah's, Jehohanan;
14 of Malluk's, Jonathan;
of Shekaniah's,[a] Joseph;
15 of Harim's, Adna;
of Meremoth's,[b] Helkai;
16 of Iddo's, Zechariah;
of Ginnethon's, Meshullam;
17 of Abijah's, Zikri;
of Miniamin's and of Moadiah's,
Piltai;
18 of Bilgah's, Shammua;
of Shemaiah's, Jehonathan;
19 of Joiarib's, Mattenai;
of Jedaiah's, Uzzi;
20 of Sallu's, Kallai;
of Amok's, Eber;
21 of Hilkiah's, Hashabiah;
of Jedaiah's, Nethanel.
22 The family heads of the Levites in
the days of Eliashib, Joiada, Johanan
and Jaddua, as well as those of the
priests, were recorded in the reign of
Darius the Persian. 23 The family heads
among the descendants of Levi up to the
time of Johanan son of Eliashib were recorded in the book of the annals. 24 And
the leaders of the Levites were Hashabiah, Sherebiah, Jeshua son of Kadmiel,
and their associates, who stood opposite
them to give praise and thanksgiving,
one section responding to the other, as
prescribed by David the man of God.
25 Mattaniah, Bakbukiah, Obadiah,
Meshullam, Talmon and Akkub were
gatekeepers who guarded the storerooms at the gates. 26 They served in the
days of Joiakim son of Joshua, the son of
Jozadak, and in the days of Nehemiah
the governor and of Ezra the priest, the
teacher of the Law.

Dedication of the Wall of Jerusalem

27 At the dedication of the wall of Jerusalem, the Levites were sought out from
where they lived and were brought to
Jerusalem to celebrate joyfully the dedication with songs of thanksgiving and
with the music of cymbals, harps and
lyres. 28 The musicians also were brought
together from the region around Jerusalem — from the villages of the Netophathites, 29 from Beth Gilgal, and from the
area of Geba and Azmaveth, for the musicians had built villages for themselves
around Jerusalem. 30 When the priests
and Levites had purified themselves ceremonially, they purified the people, the
gates and the wall.
31 I had the leaders of Judah go up on
top of[c] the wall. I also assigned two large
choirs to give thanks. One was to proceed
on top of[d] the wall to the right, toward
the Dung Gate. 32 Hoshaiah and half the
leaders of Judah followed them, 33 along
with Azariah, Ezra, Meshullam, 34 Judah,
Benjamin, Shemaiah, Jeremiah, 35 as well
as some priests with trumpets, and also
Zechariah son of Jonathan, the son of
Shemaiah, the son of Mattaniah, the son
of Micaiah, the son of Zakkur, the son of
Asaph, 36 and his associates — Shemaiah,
Azarel, Milalai, Gilalai, Maai, Nethanel,
Judah and Hanani — with musical instruments prescribed by David the man
of God. Ezra the teacher of the Law led
the procession. 37 At the Fountain Gate
they continued directly up the steps of
the City of David on the ascent to the
wall and passed above the site of David's
palace to the Water Gate on the east.
38 The second choir proceeded in the
opposite direction. I followed them on
top of[e] the wall, together with half the
people — past the Tower of the Ovens to
the Broad Wall, 39 over the Gate of Ephraim, the Jeshanah[f] Gate, the Fish Gate,
the Tower of Hananel and the Tower of
the Hundred, as far as the Sheep Gate. At
the Gate of the Guard they stopped.
40 The two choirs that gave thanks
then took their places in the house of
God; so did I, together with half the officials, 41 as well as the priests — Eliakim,
Maaseiah, Miniamin, Micaiah, Elioenai, Zechariah and Hananiah with their
trumpets — 42 and also Maaseiah, Shemaiah, Eleazar, Uzzi, Jehohanan, Malkijah, Elam and Ezer. The choirs sang

[a] 14 Very many Hebrew manuscripts, some Septuagint manuscripts and Syriac (see also verse 3); most Hebrew manuscripts *Shebaniah's* [b] 15 Some Septuagint manuscripts (see also verse 3); Hebrew *Meraioth's* [c] 31 Or *go alongside* [d] 31 Or *proceed alongside* [e] 38 Or *them alongside* [f] 39 Or *Old*

under the direction of Jezrahiah. 43 And on that day they offered great sacrifices, rejoicing because God had given them great joy. The women and children also rejoiced. The sound of rejoicing in Jerusalem could be heard far away.

44 At that time men were appointed to be in charge of the storerooms for the contributions, firstfruits and tithes. From the fields around the towns they were to bring into the storerooms the portions required by the Law for the priests and the Levites, for Judah was pleased with the ministering priests and Levites. 45 They performed the service of their God and the service of purification, as did also the musicians and gatekeepers, according to the commands of David and his son Solomon. 46 For long ago, in the days of David and Asaph, there had been directors for the musicians and for the songs of praise and thanksgiving to God. 47 So in the days of Zerubbabel and of Nehemiah, all Israel contributed the daily portions for the musicians and the gatekeepers. They also set aside the portion for the other Levites, and the Levites set aside the portion for the descendants of Aaron.

Nehemiah's Final Reforms

13 On that day the Book of Moses was read aloud in the hearing of the people and there it was found written that no Ammonite or Moabite should ever be admitted into the assembly of God, 2 because they had not met the Israelites with food and water but had hired Balaam to call a curse down on them. (Our God, however, turned the curse into a blessing.) 3 When the people heard this law, they excluded from Israel all who were of foreign descent.

4 Before this, Eliashib the priest had been put in charge of the storerooms of the house of our God. He was closely associated with Tobiah, 5 and he had provided him with a large room formerly used to store the grain offerings and incense and temple articles, and also the tithes of grain, new wine and olive oil prescribed for the Levites, musicians and gatekeepers, as well as the contributions for the priests.

6 But while all this was going on, I was not in Jerusalem, for in the thirty-second year of Artaxerxes king of Babylon I had returned to the king. Some time later I asked his permission 7 and came back to Jerusalem. Here I learned about the evil thing Eliashib had done in providing Tobiah a room in the courts of the house of God. 8 I was greatly displeased and threw all Tobiah's household goods out of the room. 9 I gave orders to purify the rooms, and then I put back into them the equipment of the house of God, with the grain offerings and the incense.

10 I also learned that the portions assigned to the Levites had not been given to them, and that all the Levites and musicians responsible for the service had gone back to their own fields. 11 So I rebuked the officials and asked them, "Why is the house of God neglected?" Then I called them together and stationed them at their posts.

12 All Judah brought the tithes of grain, new wine and olive oil into the storerooms. 13 I put Shelemiah the priest, Zadok the scribe, and a Levite named Pedaiah in charge of the storerooms and made Hanan son of Zakkur, the son of Mattaniah, their assistant, because they were considered trustworthy. They were made responsible for distributing the supplies to their fellow Levites.

14 Remember me for this, my God, and do not blot out what I have so faithfully done for the house of my God and its services.

15 In those days I saw people in Judah treading winepresses on the Sabbath and bringing in grain and loading it on donkeys, together with wine, grapes, figs and all other kinds of loads. And they were bringing all this into Jerusalem on the Sabbath. Therefore I warned them against selling food on that day. 16 People from Tyre who lived in Jerusalem were bringing in fish and all kinds of merchandise and selling them in Jerusalem on the Sabbath to the people of Judah. 17 I rebuked the nobles of Judah and said to them, "What is this wicked thing you are doing — desecrating the Sabbath day? 18 Didn't your ancestors do the same things, so that our God brought all this calamity on us and on this city? Now you are stirring up more wrath against Israel by desecrating the Sabbath."

19 When evening shadows fell on the gates of Jerusalem before the Sabbath, I ordered the doors to be shut and not opened until the Sabbath was over. I stationed some of my own men at the gates so that no load could be brought in on the Sabbath day. 20 Once or twice the merchants and sellers of all kinds of goods spent the night outside Jerusalem. 21 But I warned them and said, "Why do you spend the night by the wall? If you do this again, I will arrest you."

From that time on they no longer came on the Sabbath. 22Then I commanded the Levites to purify themselves and go and guard the gates in order to keep the Sabbath day holy.

Remember me for this also, my God, and show mercy to me according to your great love.

23Moreover, in those days I saw men of Judah who had married women from Ashdod, Ammon and Moab. 24Half of their children spoke the language of Ashdod or the language of one of the other peoples, and did not know how to speak the language of Judah. 25I rebuked them and called curses down on them. I beat some of the men and pulled out their hair. I made them take an oath in God's name and said: "You are not to give your daughters in marriage to their sons, nor are you to take their daughters in marriage for your sons or for yourselves. 26Was it not because of marriages like these that Solomon king of Israel sinned? Among the many nations there was no king like him. He was loved by his God, and God made him king over all Israel, but even he was led into sin by foreign women. 27Must we hear now that you too are doing all this terrible wickedness and are being unfaithful to our God by marrying foreign women?"

28One of the sons of Joiada son of Eliashib the high priest was son-in-law to Sanballat the Horonite. And I drove him away from me.

29Remember them, my God, because they defiled the priestly office and the covenant of the priesthood and of the Levites.

30So I purified the priests and the Levites of everything foreign, and assigned them duties, each to his own task. 31I also made provision for contributions of wood at designated times, and for the firstfruits.

Remember me with favor, my God.

ESTHER

Queen Vashti Deposed

1 This is what happened during the
time of Xerxes,[a] the Xerxes who ruled
over 127 provinces stretching from India to Cush[b]: 2At that time King Xerxes
reigned from his royal throne in the citadel of Susa, 3and in the third year of
his reign he gave a banquet for all his
nobles and officials. The military leaders of Persia and Media, the princes, and
the nobles of the provinces were present.
4For a full 180 days he displayed
the vast wealth of his kingdom and
the splendor and glory of his majesty.
5When these days were over, the king
gave a banquet, lasting seven days, in
the enclosed garden of the king's palace,
for all the people from the least to the
greatest who were in the citadel of Susa.
6The garden had hangings of white and
blue linen, fastened with cords of white
linen and purple material to silver rings
on marble pillars. There were couches of
gold and silver on a mosaic pavement of
porphyry, marble, mother-of-pearl and
other costly stones. 7Wine was served
in goblets of gold, each one different
from the other, and the royal wine was
abundant, in keeping with the king's
liberality. 8By the king's command each
guest was allowed to drink with no re-
strictions, for the king instructed all the
wine stewards to serve each man what
he wished.
9Queen Vashti also gave a banquet for
the women in the royal palace of King
Xerxes.
10On the seventh day, when King Xerxes was in high spirits from wine, he
commanded the seven eunuchs who
served him — Mehuman, Biztha, Harbona, Bigtha, Abagtha, Zethar and
Karkas — 11to bring before him Queen
Vashti, wearing her royal crown, in order to display her beauty to the people
and nobles, for she was lovely to look at.
12But when the attendants delivered the
king's command, Queen Vashti refused
to come. Then the king became furious
and burned with anger.
13Since it was customary for the king
to consult experts in matters of law and
justice, he spoke with the wise men who
understood the times 14and were closest
to the king — Karshena, Shethar, Adma-
tha, Tarshish, Meres, Marsena and Memukan, the seven nobles of Persia and
Media who had special access to the king
and were highest in the kingdom.
15"According to law, what must be done
to Queen Vashti?" he asked. "She has not
obeyed the command of King Xerxes
that the eunuchs have taken to her."
16Then Memukan replied in the presence of the king and the nobles, "Queen
Vashti has done wrong, not only against
the king but also against all the nobles
and the peoples of all the provinces of
King Xerxes. 17For the queen's conduct
will become known to all the women,
and so they will despise their husbands
and say, 'King Xerxes commanded
Queen Vashti to be brought before him,
but she would not come.' 18This very
day the Persian and Median women of
the nobility who have heard about the
queen's conduct will respond to all the
king's nobles in the same way. There will
be no end of disrespect and discord.
19"Therefore, if it pleases the king, let
him issue a royal decree and let it be
written in the laws of Persia and Media,
which cannot be repealed, that Vashti
is never again to enter the presence of
King Xerxes. Also let the king give her
royal position to someone else who is
better than she. 20Then when the king's
edict is proclaimed throughout all his
vast realm, all the women will respect
their husbands, from the least to the
greatest."
21The king and his nobles were pleased
with this advice, so the king did as Memukan proposed. 22He sent dispatches to
all parts of the kingdom, to each province in its own script and to each people
in their own language, proclaiming that
every man should be ruler over his own
household, using his native tongue.

Esther Made Queen

2 Later when King Xerxes' fury had
subsided, he remembered Vashti and what she had done and what he
had decreed about her. 2Then the king's
personal attendants proposed, "Let a
search be made for beautiful young virgins for the king. 3Let the king appoint

[a] 1 Hebrew *Ahasuerus*; here and throughout Esther [b] 1 That is, the upper Nile region

commissioners in every province of his realm to bring all these beautiful young women into the harem at the citadel of Susa. Let them be placed under the care of Hegai, the king's eunuch, who is in charge of the women; and let beauty treatments be given to them. 4 Then let the young woman who pleases the king be queen instead of Vashti." This advice appealed to the king, and he followed it.

5 Now there was in the citadel of Susa a Jew of the tribe of Benjamin, named Mordecai son of Jair, the son of Shimei, the son of Kish, 6 who had been carried into exile from Jerusalem by Nebuchadnezzar king of Babylon, among those taken captive with Jehoiachin[a] king of Judah. 7 Mordecai had a cousin named Hadassah, whom he had brought up because she had neither father nor mother. This young woman, who was also known as Esther, had a lovely figure and was beautiful. Mordecai had taken her as his own daughter when her father and mother died.

8 When the king's order and edict had been proclaimed, many young women were brought to the citadel of Susa and put under the care of Hegai. Esther also was taken to the king's palace and entrusted to Hegai, who had charge of the harem. 9 She pleased him and won his favor. Immediately he provided her with her beauty treatments and special food. He assigned to her seven female attendants selected from the king's palace and moved her and her attendants into the best place in the harem.

10 Esther had not revealed her nationality and family background, because Mordecai had forbidden her to do so. 11 Every day he walked back and forth near the courtyard of the harem to find out how Esther was and what was happening to her.

12 Before a young woman's turn came to go in to King Xerxes, she had to complete twelve months of beauty treatments prescribed for the women, six months with oil of myrrh and six with perfumes and cosmetics. 13 And this is how she would go to the king: Anything she wanted was given her to take with her from the harem to the king's palace. 14 In the evening she would go there and in the morning return to another part of the harem to the care of Shaashgaz, the king's eunuch who was in charge of the concubines. She would not return to the king unless he was pleased with her and summoned her by name.

15 When the turn came for Esther (the young woman Mordecai had adopted, the daughter of his uncle Abihail) to go to the king, she asked for nothing other than what Hegai, the king's eunuch who was in charge of the harem, suggested. And Esther won the favor of everyone who saw her. 16 She was taken to King Xerxes in the royal residence in the tenth month, the month of Tebeth, in the seventh year of his reign.

17 Now the king was attracted to Esther more than to any of the other women, and she won his favor and approval more than any of the other virgins. So he set a royal crown on her head and made her queen instead of Vashti. 18 And the king gave a great banquet, Esther's banquet, for all his nobles and officials. He proclaimed a holiday throughout the provinces and distributed gifts with royal liberality.

Mordecai Uncovers a Conspiracy

19 When the virgins were assembled a second time, Mordecai was sitting at the king's gate. 20 But Esther had kept secret her family background and nationality just as Mordecai had told her to do, for she continued to follow Mordecai's instructions as she had done when he was bringing her up.

21 During the time Mordecai was sitting at the king's gate, Bigthana[b] and Teresh, two of the king's officers who guarded the doorway, became angry and conspired to assassinate King Xerxes. 22 But Mordecai found out about the plot and told Queen Esther, who in turn reported it to the king, giving credit to Mordecai. 23 And when the report was investigated and found to be true, the two officials were impaled on poles. All this was recorded in the book of the annals in the presence of the king.

Haman's Plot to Destroy the Jews

3 After these events, King Xerxes honored Haman son of Hammedatha, the Agagite, elevating him and giving him a seat of honor higher than that of all the other nobles. 2 All the royal officials at the king's gate knelt down and paid honor to Haman, for the king had commanded this concerning him. But Mordecai would not kneel down or pay him honor.

3 Then the royal officials at the king's gate asked Mordecai, "Why do you disobey the king's command?" 4 Day after

[a] 6 Hebrew *Jeconiah*, a variant of *Jehoiachin*

[b] 21 Hebrew *Bigthan*, a variant of *Bigthana*

day they spoke to him but he refused
to comply. Therefore they told Haman
about it to see whether Mordecai's behavior would be tolerated, for he had
told them he was a Jew.
5When Haman saw that Mordecai
would not kneel down or pay him hon-
or, he was enraged. 6Yet having learned
who Mordecai's people were, he scorned
the idea of killing only Mordecai. Instead Haman looked for a way to destroy
all Mordecai's people, the Jews, throughout the whole kingdom of Xerxes.
7In the twelfth year of King Xerxes,
in the first month, the month of Nisan,
the *pur* (that is, the lot) was cast in the
presence of Haman to select a day and
month. And the lot fell on[a] the twelfth
month, the month of Adar.
8Then Haman said to King Xerxes,
"There is a certain people dispersed
among the peoples in all the provinces
of your kingdom who keep themselves
separate. Their customs are different
from those of all other people, and they
do not obey the king's laws; it is not in
the king's best interest to tolerate them.
9If it pleases the king, let a decree be issued to destroy them, and I will give ten
thousand talents[b] of silver to the king's
administrators for the royal treasury."
10So the king took his signet ring from
his finger and gave it to Haman son of
Hammedatha, the Agagite, the enemy
of the Jews. 11"Keep the money," the king
said to Haman, "and do with the people
as you please."
12Then on the thirteenth day of the
first month the royal secretaries were
summoned. They wrote out in the script
of each province and in the language of
each people all Haman's orders to the
king's satraps, the governors of the various provinces and the nobles of the various peoples. These were written in the
name of King Xerxes himself and sealed
with his own ring. 13Dispatches were
sent by couriers to all the king's provinces with the order to destroy, kill and
annihilate all the Jews — young and old,
women and children — on a single day,
the thirteenth day of the twelfth month,
the month of Adar, and to plunder their
goods. 14A copy of the text of the edict
was to be issued as law in every province and made known to the people of
every nationality so they would be ready
for that day.
15The couriers went out, spurred on by
the king's command, and the edict was
issued in the citadel of Susa. The king
and Haman sat down to drink, but the
city of Susa was bewildered.

Mordecai Persuades Esther to Help

4 When Mordecai learned of all that
had been done, he tore his clothes,
put on sackcloth and ashes, and went
out into the city, wailing loudly and
bitterly. 2But he went only as far as the
king's gate, because no one clothed in
sackcloth was allowed to enter it. 3In
every province to which the edict and
order of the king came, there was great
mourning among the Jews, with fasting,
weeping and wailing. Many lay in sackcloth and ashes.
4When Esther's eunuchs and female
attendants came and told her about
Mordecai, she was in great distress. She
sent clothes for him to put on instead of
his sackcloth, but he would not accept
them. 5Then Esther summoned Hathak,
one of the king's eunuchs assigned to
attend her, and ordered him to find out
what was troubling Mordecai and why.
6So Hathak went out to Mordecai in
the open square of the city in front of
the king's gate. 7Mordecai told him everything that had happened to him, including the exact amount of money Haman had promised to pay into the royal
treasury for the destruction of the Jews.
8He also gave him a copy of the text of
the edict for their annihilation, which
had been published in Susa, to show to
Esther and explain it to her, and he told
him to instruct her to go into the king's
presence to beg for mercy and plead
with him for her people.
9Hathak went back and reported to
Esther what Mordecai had said. 10Then
she instructed him to say to Mordecai,
11"All the king's officials and the people of the royal provinces know that
for any man or woman who approaches the king in the inner court without
being summoned the king has but one
law: that they be put to death unless the
king extends the gold scepter to them
and spares their lives. But thirty days
have passed since I was called to go to
the king."
12When Esther's words were reported
to Mordecai, 13he sent back this answer:
"Do not think that because you are in the
king's house you alone of all the Jews will
escape. 14For if you remain silent at this

[a] 7 Septuagint; Hebrew does not have *And the lot fell on.* [b] 9 That is, about 375 tons or about 340 metric tons

time, relief and deliverance for the Jews
will arise from another place, but you and
your father's family will perish. And who
knows but that you have come to your
royal position for such a time as this?"
15Then Esther sent this reply to Mordecai: 16"Go, gather together all the Jews
who are in Susa, and fast for me. Do not
eat or drink for three days, night or day.
I and my attendants will fast as you do.
When this is done, I will go to the king,
even though it is against the law. And if
I perish, I perish."
17So Mordecai went away and carried
out all of Esther's instructions.

Esther's Request to the King

5 On the third day Esther put on her
royal robes and stood in the inner
court of the palace, in front of the king's
hall. The king was sitting on his royal
throne in the hall, facing the entrance.
2When he saw Queen Esther standing in
the court, he was pleased with her and
held out to her the gold scepter that was
in his hand. So Esther approached and
touched the tip of the scepter.
3Then the king asked, "What is it,
Queen Esther? What is your request?
Even up to half the kingdom, it will be
given you."
4"If it pleases the king," replied Esther,
"let the king, together with Haman,
come today to a banquet I have prepared for him."
5"Bring Haman at once," the king said,
"so that we may do what Esther asks."
So the king and Haman went to the
banquet Esther had prepared. 6As they
were drinking wine, the king again
asked Esther, "Now what is your petition? It will be given you. And what is
your request? Even up to half the kingdom, it will be granted."
7Esther replied, "My petition and my
request is this: 8If the king regards me
with favor and if it pleases the king to
grant my petition and fulfill my request,
let the king and Haman come tomorrow
to the banquet I will prepare for them.
Then I will answer the king's question."

Haman's Rage Against Mordecai

9Haman went out that day happy and
in high spirits. But when he saw Mordecai at the king's gate and observed that
he neither rose nor showed fear in his
presence, he was filled with rage against
Mordecai. 10Nevertheless, Haman restrained himself and went home.
Calling together his friends and Zeresh, his wife, 11Haman boasted to them
about his vast wealth, his many sons,
and all the ways the king had honored
him and how he had elevated him above
the other nobles and officials. 12"And
that's not all," Haman added. "I'm the
only person Queen Esther invited to accompany the king to the banquet she
gave. And she has invited me along with
the king tomorrow. 13But all this gives
me no satisfaction as long as I see that
Jew Mordecai sitting at the king's gate."
14His wife Zeresh and all his friends
said to him, "Have a pole set up, reaching to a height of fifty cubits,[a] and ask
the king in the morning to have Mordecai impaled on it. Then go with the king
to the banquet and enjoy yourself." This
suggestion delighted Haman, and he
had the pole set up.

Mordecai Honored

6 That night the king could not sleep;
so he ordered the book of the chronicles, the record of his reign, to be brought
in and read to him. 2It was found recorded there that Mordecai had exposed Bigthana and Teresh, two of the king's officers who guarded the doorway, who had
conspired to assassinate King Xerxes.
3"What honor and recognition has
Mordecai received for this?" the king
asked.
"Nothing has been done for him," his
attendants answered.
4The king said, "Who is in the court?"
Now Haman had just entered the outer
court of the palace to speak to the king
about impaling Mordecai on the pole he
had set up for him.
5His attendants answered, "Haman is
standing in the court."
"Bring him in," the king ordered.
6When Haman entered, the king asked
him, "What should be done for the man
the king delights to honor?"
Now Haman thought to himself, "Who
is there that the king would rather hon-
or than me?" 7So he answered the king,
"For the man the king delights to honor,
8have them bring a royal robe the king
has worn and a horse the king has ridden, one with a royal crest placed on its
head. 9Then let the robe and horse be entrusted to one of the king's most noble
princes. Let them robe the man the king
delights to honor, and lead him on the
horse through the city streets, proclaiming before him, 'This is what is done for
the man the king delights to honor!'"

[a] *14* That is, about 75 feet or about 23 meters

10"Go at once," the king commanded
Haman. "Get the robe and the horse and
do just as you have suggested for Mordecai the Jew, who sits at the king's gate.
Do not neglect anything you have rec-
ommended."
11So Haman got the robe and the
horse. He robed Mordecai, and led him
on horseback through the city streets,
proclaiming before him, "This is what
is done for the man the king delights to
honor!"
12Afterward Mordecai returned to the
king's gate. But Haman rushed home,
with his head covered in grief, 13and told
Zeresh his wife and all his friends everything that had happened to him.
His advisers and his wife Zeresh said
to him, "Since Mordecai, before whom
your downfall has started, is of Jewish origin, you cannot stand against
him — you will surely come to ruin!"
14While they were still talking with him,
the king's eunuchs arrived and hurried
Haman away to the banquet Esther had
prepared.

Haman Impaled

7 So the king and Haman went to
Queen Esther's banquet, 2and as they
were drinking wine on the second day,
the king again asked, "Queen Esther,
what is your petition? It will be given
you. What is your request? Even up to
half the kingdom, it will be granted."
3Then Queen Esther answered, "If I have
found favor with you, Your Majesty, and if
it pleases you, grant me my life — this is
my petition. And spare my people — this
is my request. 4For I and my people have
been sold to be destroyed, killed and annihilated. If we had merely been sold as
male and female slaves, I would have
kept quiet, because no such distress would
justify disturbing the king.[a]"
5King Xerxes asked Queen Esther,
"Who is he? Where is he — the man who
has dared to do such a thing?"
6Esther said, "An adversary and enemy! This vile Haman!"
Then Haman was terrified before the
king and queen. 7The king got up in a
rage, left his wine and went out into the
palace garden. But Haman, realizing
that the king had already decided his
fate, stayed behind to beg Queen Esther
for his life.
8Just as the king returned from the
palace garden to the banquet hall, Haman was falling on the couch where Esther was reclining.
The king exclaimed, "Will he even mo-
lest the queen while she is with me in the
house?"
As soon as the word left the king's
mouth, they covered Haman's face.
9Then Harbona, one of the eunuchs attending the king, said, "A pole reaching
to a height of fifty cubits[b] stands by Haman's house. He had it set up for Mordecai, who spoke up to help the king."
The king said, "Impale him on it!" 10So
they impaled Haman on the pole he had
set up for Mordecai. Then the king's fury
subsided.

The King's Edict in Behalf of the Jews

8 That same day King Xerxes gave
Queen Esther the estate of Haman,
the enemy of the Jews. And Mordecai
came into the presence of the king, for
Esther had told how he was related to
her. 2The king took off his signet ring,
which he had reclaimed from Haman,
and presented it to Mordecai. And Esther appointed him over Haman's estate.
3Esther again pleaded with the king,
falling at his feet and weeping. She
begged him to put an end to the evil
plan of Haman the Agagite, which he
had devised against the Jews. 4Then the
king extended the gold scepter to Esther
and she arose and stood before him.
5"If it pleases the king," she said, "and
if he regards me with favor and thinks it
the right thing to do, and if he is pleased
with me, let an order be written overrul-
ing the dispatches that Haman son of
Hammedatha, the Agagite, devised and
wrote to destroy the Jews in all the king's
provinces. 6For how can I bear to see disaster fall on my people? How can I bear
to see the destruction of my family?"
7King Xerxes replied to Queen Esther
and to Mordecai the Jew, "Because Haman attacked the Jews, I have given his
estate to Esther, and they have impaled
him on the pole he set up. 8Now write another decree in the king's name in behalf
of the Jews as seems best to you, and
seal it with the king's signet ring — for
no document written in the king's name
and sealed with his ring can be revoked."
9At once the royal secretaries were
summoned — on the twenty-third day
of the third month, the month of Sivan.
They wrote out all Mordecai's orders to
the Jews, and to the satraps, governors

[a] 4 Or *quiet, but the compensation our adversary offers cannot be compared with the loss the king would suffer* [b] 9 That is, about 75 feet or about 23 meters

and nobles of the 127 provinces stretching
from India to Cush.[a] These orders were
written in the script of each province and
the language of each people and also
to the Jews in their own script and language. 10Mordecai wrote in the name of
King Xerxes, sealed the dispatches with
the king's signet ring, and sent them by
mounted couriers, who rode fast horses
especially bred for the king.
11The king's edict granted the Jews in
every city the right to assemble and protect themselves; to destroy, kill and annihilate the armed men of any nationality or province who might attack them
and their women and children,[b] and to
plunder the property of their enemies.
12The day appointed for the Jews to do
this in all the provinces of King Xerxes
was the thirteenth day of the twelfth
month, the month of Adar. 13A copy of
the text of the edict was to be issued as
law in every province and made known
to the people of every nationality so that
the Jews would be ready on that day to
avenge themselves on their enemies.
14The couriers, riding the royal horses,
went out, spurred on by the king's command, and the edict was issued in the
citadel of Susa.

The Triumph of the Jews

15When Mordecai left the king's presence, he was wearing royal garments
of blue and white, a large crown of gold
and a purple robe of fine linen. And the
city of Susa held a joyous celebration.
16For the Jews it was a time of happiness
and joy, gladness and honor. 17In every
province and in every city to which the
edict of the king came, there was joy and
gladness among the Jews, with feasting
and celebrating. And many people of
other nationalities became Jews because
fear of the Jews had seized them.

9 On the thirteenth day of the twelfth
month, the month of Adar, the edict
commanded by the king was to be carried out. On this day the enemies of the
Jews had hoped to overpower them, but
now the tables were turned and the Jews
got the upper hand over those who hated
them. 2The Jews assembled in their cities
in all the provinces of King Xerxes to attack those determined to destroy them.
No one could stand against them, because the people of all the other nationalities were afraid of them. 3And all the
nobles of the provinces, the satraps, the
governors and the king's administrators
helped the Jews, because fear of Mordecai had seized them. 4Mordecai was
prominent in the palace; his reputation
spread throughout the provinces, and he
became more and more powerful.
5The Jews struck down all their enemies with the sword, killing and destroying them, and they did what they
pleased to those who hated them. 6In
the citadel of Susa, the Jews killed and
destroyed five hundred men. 7They also
killed Parshandatha, Dalphon, Aspatha,
8Poratha, Adalia, Aridatha, 9Parmash-
ta, Arisai, Aridai and Vaizatha, 10the ten
sons of Haman son of Hammedatha, the
enemy of the Jews. But they did not lay
their hands on the plunder.
11The number of those killed in the
citadel of Susa was reported to the king
that same day. 12The king said to Queen
Esther, "The Jews have killed and destroyed five hundred men and the ten
sons of Haman in the citadel of Susa.
What have they done in the rest of the
king's provinces? Now what is your petition? It will be given you. What is your
request? It will also be granted."
13"If it pleases the king," Esther answered, "give the Jews in Susa permission to carry out this day's edict tomorrow also, and let Haman's ten sons be
impaled on poles."
14So the king commanded that this
be done. An edict was issued in Susa,
and they impaled the ten sons of Haman. 15The Jews in Susa came together
on the fourteenth day of the month of
Adar, and they put to death in Susa three
hundred men, but they did not lay their
hands on the plunder.
16Meanwhile, the remainder of the
Jews who were in the king's provinces
also assembled to protect themselves
and get relief from their enemies. They
killed seventy-five thousand of them but
did not lay their hands on the plunder.
17This happened on the thirteenth day
of the month of Adar, and on the fourteenth they rested and made it a day of
feasting and joy.
18The Jews in Susa, however, had assembled on the thirteenth and fourteenth,
and then on the fifteenth they rested and
made it a day of feasting and joy.
19That is why rural Jews — those living in villages — observe the fourteenth
of the month of Adar as a day of joy and
feasting, a day for giving presents to
each other.

[a] 9 That is, the upper Nile region [b] 11 Or *province, together with their women and children, who might attack them;*

Purim Established

20 Mordecai recorded these events, and
he sent letters to all the Jews throughout
the provinces of King Xerxes, near and
far, 21 to have them celebrate annually
the fourteenth and fifteenth days of the
month of Adar 22 as the time when the
Jews got relief from their enemies, and
as the month when their sorrow was
turned into joy and their mourning into
a day of celebration. He wrote them to
observe the days as days of feasting and
joy and giving presents of food to one
another and gifts to the poor.

23 So the Jews agreed to continue the
celebration they had begun, doing what
Mordecai had written to them. 24 For Haman son of Hammedatha, the Agagite,
the enemy of all the Jews, had plotted
against the Jews to destroy them and
had cast the *pur* (that is, the lot) for their
ruin and destruction. 25 But when the
plot came to the king's attention,[a] he issued written orders that the evil scheme
Haman had devised against the Jews
should come back onto his own head,
and that he and his sons should be impaled on poles. 26 (Therefore these days
were called Purim, from the word *pur*.)
Because of everything written in this letter and because of what they had seen
and what had happened to them, 27 the
Jews took it on themselves to establish
the custom that they and their descendants and all who join them should
without fail observe these two days every year, in the way prescribed and at
the time appointed. 28 These days should
be remembered and observed in every
generation by every family, and in every province and in every city. And these
days of Purim should never fail to be
celebrated by the Jews — nor should the
memory of these days die out among
their descendants.

29 So Queen Esther, daughter of Abihail,
along with Mordecai the Jew, wrote with
full authority to confirm this second letter
concerning Purim. 30 And Mordecai sent
letters to all the Jews in the 127 provinces
of Xerxes' kingdom — words of goodwill
and assurance — 31 to establish these days
of Purim at their designated times, as
Mordecai the Jew and Queen Esther had
decreed for them, and as they had established for themselves and their descendants in regard to their times of fasting
and lamentation. 32 Esther's decree confirmed these regulations about Purim,
and it was written down in the records.

The Greatness of Mordecai

10 King Xerxes imposed tribute
throughout the empire, to its distant shores. 2 And all his acts of power
and might, together with a full account
of the greatness of Mordecai, whom the
king had promoted, are they not written
in the book of the annals of the kings
of Media and Persia? 3 Mordecai the Jew
was second in rank to King Xerxes, pre-
eminent among the Jews, and held in
high esteem by his many fellow Jews,
because he worked for the good of his
people and spoke up for the welfare of
all the Jews.

[a] 25 Or *when Esther came before the king*

JOB

Prologue

1 In the land of Uz there lived a man whose name was Job. This man was blameless and upright; he feared God and shunned evil. 2He had seven sons and three daughters, 3and he owned seven thousand sheep, three thousand camels, five hundred yoke of oxen and five hundred donkeys, and had a large number of servants. He was the greatest man among all the people of the East.

4His sons used to hold feasts in their homes on their birthdays, and they would invite their three sisters to eat and drink with them. 5When a period of feasting had run its course, Job would make arrangements for them to be purified. Early in the morning he would sacrifice a burnt offering for each of them, thinking, "Perhaps my children have sinned and cursed God in their hearts." This was Job's regular custom.

6One day the angels[a] came to present themselves before the LORD, and Satan[b] also came with them. 7The LORD said to Satan, "Where have you come from?"

Satan answered the LORD, "From roaming throughout the earth, going back and forth on it."

8Then the LORD said to Satan, "Have you considered my servant Job? There is no one on earth like him; he is blameless and upright, a man who fears God and shuns evil."

9"Does Job fear God for nothing?" Satan replied. 10"Have you not put a hedge around him and his household and everything he has? You have blessed the work of his hands, so that his flocks and herds are spread throughout the land. 11But now stretch out your hand and strike everything he has, and he will surely curse you to your face."

12The LORD said to Satan, "Very well, then, everything he has is in your power, but on the man himself do not lay a finger."

Then Satan went out from the presence of the LORD.

13One day when Job's sons and daughters were feasting and drinking wine at the oldest brother's house, 14a messenger came to Job and said, "The oxen were plowing and the donkeys were grazing nearby, 15and the Sabeans attacked and made off with them. They put the servants to the sword, and I am the only one who has escaped to tell you!"

16While he was still speaking, another messenger came and said, "The fire of God fell from the heavens and burned up the sheep and the servants, and I am the only one who has escaped to tell you!"

17While he was still speaking, another messenger came and said, "The Chaldeans formed three raiding parties and swept down on your camels and made off with them. They put the servants to the sword, and I am the only one who has escaped to tell you!"

18While he was still speaking, yet another messenger came and said, "Your sons and daughters were feasting and drinking wine at the oldest brother's house, 19when suddenly a mighty wind swept in from the desert and struck the four corners of the house. It collapsed on them and they are dead, and I am the only one who has escaped to tell you!"

20At this, Job got up and tore his robe and shaved his head. Then he fell to the ground in worship 21and said:

"Naked I came from my mother's
womb,
and naked I will depart.[c]
The LORD gave and the LORD has
taken away;
may the name of the LORD be
praised."

22In all this, Job did not sin by charging God with wrongdoing.

2 On another day the angels[a] came to present themselves before the LORD, and Satan also came with them to present himself before him. 2And the LORD said to Satan, "Where have you come from?"

Satan answered the LORD, "From roaming throughout the earth, going back and forth on it."

3Then the LORD said to Satan, "Have you considered my servant Job? There is no one on earth like him; he is blameless and upright, a man who fears God and shuns evil. And he still maintains his integrity, though you incited me against him to ruin him without any reason."

[a] 6,1 Hebrew *the sons of God* [b] 6 Hebrew *satan* means *adversary.* [c] 21 Or *will return there*

4“Skin for skin!” Satan replied. “A man
will give all he has for his own life. 5But
now stretch out your hand and strike his
flesh and bones, and he will surely curse
you to your face.”
6The LORD said to Satan, “Very well,
then, he is in your hands; but you must
spare his life.”
7So Satan went out from the presence
of the LORD and afflicted Job with painful
sores from the soles of his feet to the crown
of his head. 8Then Job took a piece of broken pottery and scraped himself with it
as he sat among the ashes.
9His wife said to him, “Are you still
maintaining your integrity? Curse God
and die!”
10He replied, “You are talking like a foolish[a] woman. Shall we accept good from
God, and not trouble?”
In all this, Job did not sin in what he
said.

11When Job’s three friends, Eliphaz the
Temanite, Bildad the Shuhite and Zophar
the Naamathite, heard about all the troubles that had come upon him, they set
out from their homes and met together
by agreement to go and sympathize with
him and comfort him. 12When they saw
him from a distance, they could hardly
recognize him; they began to weep aloud,
and they tore their robes and sprinkled
dust on their heads. 13Then they sat on
the ground with him for seven days and
seven nights. No one said a word to him,
because they saw how great his suffering was.

Job Speaks

3 After this, Job opened his mouth and
cursed the day of his birth. 2He said:

3“May the day of my birth perish,
and the night that said, ‘A boy is
conceived!’
4That day — may it turn to darkness;
may God above not care about it;
may no light shine on it.
5May gloom and utter darkness claim
it once more;
may a cloud settle over it;
may blackness overwhelm it.
6That night — may thick darkness
seize it;
may it not be included among the
days of the year
nor be entered in any of the
months.
7May that night be barren;
may no shout of joy be heard in it.
8May those who curse days[b] curse that
day,
those who are ready to rouse
Leviathan.
9May its morning stars become dark;
may it wait for daylight in vain
and not see the first rays of dawn,
10for it did not shut the doors of the
womb on me
to hide trouble from my eyes.

11“Why did I not perish at birth,
and die as I came from the womb?
12Why were there knees to receive me
and breasts that I might
be nursed?
13For now I would be lying down in
peace;
I would be asleep and at rest
14with kings and rulers of the earth,
who built for themselves places
now lying in ruins,
15with princes who had gold,
who filled their houses with silver.
16Or why was I not hidden away in the
ground like a stillborn child,
like an infant who never saw the
light of day?
17There the wicked cease from turmoil,
and there the weary are at rest.
18Captives also enjoy their ease;
they no longer hear the slave
driver’s shout.
19The small and the great are there,
and the slaves are freed from their
owners.

20“Why is light given to those
in misery,
and life to the bitter of soul,
21to those who long for death that does
not come,
who search for it more than for
hidden treasure,
22who are filled with gladness
and rejoice when they reach the
grave?
23Why is life given to a man
whose way is hidden,
whom God has hedged in?
24For sighing has become my daily
food;
my groans pour out like water.
25What I feared has come upon me;
what I dreaded has happened
to me.
26I have no peace, no quietness;
I have no rest, but only turmoil.”

[a] *10* The Hebrew word rendered *foolish* denotes moral deficiency.
[b] *8* Or *curse the sea*

Eliphaz

4 Then Eliphaz the Temanite replied:

2 "If someone ventures a word with
you, will you be impatient?
But who can keep from speaking?
3 Think how you have instructed many,
how you have strengthened feeble
hands.
4 Your words have supported those who
stumbled;
you have strengthened faltering
knees.
5 But now trouble comes to you, and
you are discouraged;
it strikes you, and you are
dismayed.
6 Should not your piety be your
confidence
and your blameless ways your
hope?

7 "Consider now: Who, being innocent,
has ever perished?
Where were the upright ever
destroyed?
8 As I have observed, those who plow
evil
and those who sow trouble reap it.
9 At the breath of God they perish;
at the blast of his anger they are no
more.
10 The lions may roar and growl,
yet the teeth of the great lions are
broken.
11 The lion perishes for lack of prey,
and the cubs of the lioness are
scattered.

12 "A word was secretly brought to me,
my ears caught a whisper of it.
13 Amid disquieting dreams in the
night,
when deep sleep falls on people,
14 fear and trembling seized me
and made all my bones shake.
15 A spirit glided past my face,
and the hair on my body stood on
end.
16 It stopped,
but I could not tell what it was.
A form stood before my eyes,
and I heard a hushed voice:
17 'Can a mortal be more righteous than
God?
Can even a strong man be more
pure than his Maker?
18 If God places no trust in his servants,
if he charges his angels with error,
19 how much more those who live in
houses of clay,
whose foundations are in the dust,
who are crushed more readily than
a moth!
20 Between dawn and dusk they are
broken to pieces;
unnoticed, they perish forever.
21 Are not the cords of their tent pulled
up,
so that they die without wisdom?'

5 "Call if you will, but who will answer
you?
To which of the holy ones will you
turn?
2 Resentment kills a fool,
and envy slays the simple.
3 I myself have seen a fool taking root,
but suddenly his house was cursed.
4 His children are far from safety,
crushed in court without a
defender.
5 The hungry consume his harvest,
taking it even from among thorns,
and the thirsty pant after his
wealth.
6 For hardship does not spring from the
soil,
nor does trouble sprout from the
ground.
7 Yet man is born to trouble
as surely as sparks fly upward.

8 "But if I were you, I would appeal to
God;
I would lay my cause before him.
9 He performs wonders that cannot be
fathomed,
miracles that cannot be counted.
10 He provides rain for the earth;
he sends water on the countryside.
11 The lowly he sets on high,
and those who mourn are lifted to
safety.
12 He thwarts the plans of the crafty,
so that their hands achieve no
success.
13 He catches the wise in their craftiness,
and the schemes of the wily are
swept away.
14 Darkness comes upon them in the
daytime;
at noon they grope as in the night.
15 He saves the needy from the sword in
their mouth;
he saves them from the clutches of
the powerful.
16 So the poor have hope,
and injustice shuts its mouth.

17 "Blessed is the one whom God corrects;
so do not despise the discipline of
the Almighty.[a]

[a] 17 Hebrew *Shaddai*; here and throughout Job

18 For he wounds, but he also binds up;
he injures, but his hands also heal.
19 From six calamities he will rescue you;
in seven no harm will touch you.
20 In famine he will deliver you from death,
and in battle from the stroke of the sword.
21 You will be protected from the lash of the tongue,
and need not fear when destruction comes.
22 You will laugh at destruction and famine,
and need not fear the wild animals.
23 For you will have a covenant with the stones of the field,
and the wild animals will be at peace with you.
24 You will know that your tent is secure;
you will take stock of your property and find nothing missing.
25 You will know that your children will be many,
and your descendants like the grass of the earth.
26 You will come to the grave in full vigor,
like sheaves gathered in season.

27 "We have examined this, and it is true.
So hear it and apply it to yourself."

Job

6 Then Job replied:

2 "If only my anguish could be weighed
and all my misery be placed on the scales!
3 It would surely outweigh the sand of the seas —
no wonder my words have been impetuous.
4 The arrows of the Almighty are in me,
my spirit drinks in their poison;
God's terrors are marshaled against me.
5 Does a wild donkey bray when it has grass,
or an ox bellow when it has fodder?
6 Is tasteless food eaten without salt,
or is there flavor in the sap of the mallow[a]?
7 I refuse to touch it;
such food makes me ill.

8 "Oh, that I might have my request,
that God would grant what I hope for,
9 that God would be willing to crush me,
to let loose his hand and cut off my life!
10 Then I would still have this consolation —
my joy in unrelenting pain —
that I had not denied the words of the Holy One.

11 "What strength do I have, that I should still hope?
What prospects, that I should be patient?
12 Do I have the strength of stone?
Is my flesh bronze?
13 Do I have any power to help myself,
now that success has been driven from me?

14 "Anyone who withholds kindness from a friend
forsakes the fear of the Almighty.
15 But my brothers are as undependable as intermittent streams,
as the streams that overflow
16 when darkened by thawing ice
and swollen with melting snow,
17 but that stop flowing in the dry season,
and in the heat vanish from their channels.
18 Caravans turn aside from their routes;
they go off into the wasteland and perish.
19 The caravans of Tema look for water,
the traveling merchants of Sheba look in hope.
20 They are distressed, because they had been confident;
they arrive there, only to be disappointed.
21 Now you too have proved to be of no help;
you see something dreadful and are afraid.
22 Have I ever said, 'Give something on my behalf,
pay a ransom for me from your wealth,
23 deliver me from the hand of the enemy,
rescue me from the clutches of the ruthless'?

24 "Teach me, and I will be quiet;
show me where I have been wrong.
25 How painful are honest words!
But what do your arguments prove?
26 Do you mean to correct what I say,
and treat my desperate words as wind?
27 You would even cast lots for the fatherless
and barter away your friend.

[a] *6* The meaning of the Hebrew for this phrase is uncertain.

28 "But now be so kind as to look at me.
Would I lie to your face?
29 Relent, do not be unjust;
reconsider, for my integrity is at stake.[a]
30 Is there any wickedness on my lips?
Can my mouth not discern malice?

7 "Do not mortals have hard service on earth?
Are not their days like those of hired laborers?
2 Like a slave longing for the evening shadows,
or a hired laborer waiting to be paid,
3 so I have been allotted months of futility,
and nights of misery have been assigned to me.
4 When I lie down I think, 'How long before I get up?'
The night drags on, and I toss and turn until dawn.
5 My body is clothed with worms and scabs,
my skin is broken and festering.

6 "My days are swifter than a weaver's shuttle,
and they come to an end without hope.
7 Remember, O God, that my life is but a breath;
my eyes will never see happiness again.
8 The eye that now sees me will see me no longer;
you will look for me, but I will be no more.
9 As a cloud vanishes and is gone,
so one who goes down to the grave does not return.
10 He will never come to his house again;
his place will know him no more.

11 "Therefore I will not keep silent;
I will speak out in the anguish of my spirit,
I will complain in the bitterness of my soul.
12 Am I the sea, or the monster of the deep,
that you put me under guard?
13 When I think my bed will comfort me
and my couch will ease my complaint,
14 even then you frighten me with dreams
and terrify me with visions,
15 so that I prefer strangling and death,
rather than this body of mine.
16 I despise my life; I would not live forever.
Let me alone; my days have no meaning.

17 "What is mankind that you make so much of them,
that you give them so much attention,
18 that you examine them every morning
and test them every moment?
19 Will you never look away from me,
or let me alone even for an instant?
20 If I have sinned, what have I done to you,
you who see everything we do?
Why have you made me your target?
Have I become a burden to you?[b]
21 Why do you not pardon my offenses
and forgive my sins?
For I will soon lie down in the dust;
you will search for me, but I will be no more."

Bildad

8 Then Bildad the Shuhite replied:

2 "How long will you say such things?
Your words are a blustering wind.
3 Does God pervert justice?
Does the Almighty pervert what is right?
4 When your children sinned against him,
he gave them over to the penalty of their sin.
5 But if you will seek God earnestly
and plead with the Almighty,
6 if you are pure and upright,
even now he will rouse himself on your behalf
and restore you to your prosperous state.
7 Your beginnings will seem humble,
so prosperous will your future be.

8 "Ask the former generation
and find out what their ancestors learned,
9 for we were born only yesterday and know nothing,
and our days on earth are but a shadow.
10 Will they not instruct you and tell you?
Will they not bring forth words from their understanding?

[a] 29 Or *my righteousness still stands* [b] 20 A few manuscripts of the Masoretic Text, an ancient Hebrew scribal tradition and Septuagint; most manuscripts of the Masoretic Text *I have become a burden to myself.*

11 Can papyrus grow tall where there is no marsh?
Can reeds thrive without water?
12 While still growing and uncut,
they wither more quickly than grass.
13 Such is the destiny of all who forget God;
so perishes the hope of the godless.
14 What they trust in is fragile[a];
what they rely on is a spider's web.
15 They lean on the web, but it gives way;
they cling to it, but it does not hold.
16 They are like a well-watered plant in the sunshine,
spreading its shoots over the garden;
17 it entwines its roots around a pile of rocks
and looks for a place among the stones.
18 But when it is torn from its spot,
that place disowns it and says, 'I never saw you.'
19 Surely its life withers away,
and[b] from the soil other plants grow.

20 "Surely God does not reject one who is blameless
or strengthen the hands of evildoers.
21 He will yet fill your mouth with laughter
and your lips with shouts of joy.
22 Your enemies will be clothed in shame,
and the tents of the wicked will be no more."

Job

9 Then Job replied:

2 "Indeed, I know that this is true.
But how can mere mortals prove their innocence before God?
3 Though they wished to dispute with him,
they could not answer him one time out of a thousand.
4 His wisdom is profound, his power is vast.
Who has resisted him and come out unscathed?
5 He moves mountains without their knowing it
and overturns them in his anger.
6 He shakes the earth from its place
and makes its pillars tremble.
7 He speaks to the sun and it does not shine;
he seals off the light of the stars.
8 He alone stretches out the heavens
and treads on the waves of the sea.
9 He is the Maker of the Bear[c] and Orion,
the Pleiades and the constellations of the south.
10 He performs wonders that cannot be fathomed,
miracles that cannot be counted.
11 When he passes me, I cannot see him;
when he goes by, I cannot perceive him.
12 If he snatches away, who can stop him?
Who can say to him, 'What are you doing?'
13 God does not restrain his anger;
even the cohorts of Rahab cowered at his feet.

14 "How then can I dispute with him?
How can I find words to argue with him?
15 Though I were innocent, I could not answer him;
I could only plead with my Judge for mercy.
16 Even if I summoned him and he responded,
I do not believe he would give me a hearing.
17 He would crush me with a storm
and multiply my wounds for no reason.
18 He would not let me catch my breath
but would overwhelm me with misery.
19 If it is a matter of strength, he is mighty!
And if it is a matter of justice, who can challenge him[d]?
20 Even if I were innocent, my mouth would condemn me;
if I were blameless, it would pronounce me guilty.

21 "Although I am blameless,
I have no concern for myself;
I despise my own life.
22 It is all the same; that is why I say,
'He destroys both the blameless and the wicked.'
23 When a scourge brings sudden death,
he mocks the despair of the innocent.
24 When a land falls into the hands of the wicked,
he blindfolds its judges.
If it is not he, then who is it?

[a] 14 The meaning of the Hebrew for this word is uncertain. [b] 19 Or *Surely all the joy it has / is that* [c] 9 Or *of Leo* [d] 19 See Septuagint; Hebrew *me.*

25 "My days are swifter than a runner;
they fly away without a glimpse
of joy.
26 They skim past like boats of papyrus,
like eagles swooping down on their
prey.
27 If I say, 'I will forget my complaint,
I will change my expression, and
smile,'
28 I still dread all my sufferings,
for I know you will not hold me
innocent.
29 Since I am already found guilty,
why should I struggle in vain?
30 Even if I washed myself with soap
and my hands with cleansing
powder,
31 you would plunge me into a slime pit
so that even my clothes would
detest me.

32 "He is not a mere mortal like me that
I might answer him,
that we might confront each other
in court.
33 If only there were someone to
mediate between us,
someone to bring us together,
34 someone to remove God's rod from me,
so that his terror would frighten
me no more.
35 Then I would speak up without fear
of him,
but as it now stands with me, I
cannot.

10 "I loathe my very life;
therefore I will give free rein to
my complaint
and speak out in the bitterness of
my soul.
2 I say to God: Do not declare me guilty,
but tell me what charges you have
against me.
3 Does it please you to oppress me,
to spurn the work of your hands,
while you smile on the plans of the
wicked?
4 Do you have eyes of flesh?
Do you see as a mortal sees?
5 Are your days like those of a mortal
or your years like those of a strong
man,
6 that you must search out my faults
and probe after my sin —
7 though you know that I am not guilty
and that no one can rescue me
from your hand?

8 "Your hands shaped me and made me.
Will you now turn and destroy me?
9 Remember that you molded me like
clay.
Will you now turn me to dust
again?
10 Did you not pour me out like milk
and curdle me like cheese,
11 clothe me with skin and flesh
and knit me together with bones
and sinews?
12 You gave me life and showed me
kindness,
and in your providence watched
over my spirit.

13 "But this is what you concealed in
your heart,
and I know that this was in your
mind:
14 If I sinned, you would be watching me
and would not let my offense go
unpunished.
15 If I am guilty — woe to me!
Even if I am innocent, I cannot lift
my head,
for I am full of shame
and drowned in[a] my affliction.
16 If I hold my head high, you stalk me
like a lion
and again display your awesome
power against me.
17 You bring new witnesses against me
and increase your anger toward
me;
your forces come against me wave
upon wave.

18 "Why then did you bring me out of
the womb?
I wish I had died before any eye
saw me.
19 If only I had never come into being,
or had been carried straight from
the womb to the grave!
20 Are not my few days almost over?
Turn away from me so I can have a
moment's joy
21 before I go to the place of no return,
to the land of gloom and utter
darkness,
22 to the land of deepest night,
of utter darkness and disorder,
where even the light is like
darkness."

Zophar

11 Then Zophar the Naamathite replied:

2 "Are all these words to go
unanswered?
Is this talker to be vindicated?

[a] 15 Or *and aware of*

3 Will your idle talk reduce others to silence?
Will no one rebuke you when you mock?
4 You say to God, 'My beliefs are flawless
and I am pure in your sight.'
5 Oh, how I wish that God would speak,
that he would open his lips against you
6 and disclose to you the secrets of wisdom,
for true wisdom has two sides.
Know this: God has even forgotten some of your sin.

7 "Can you fathom the mysteries of God?
Can you probe the limits of the Almighty?
8 They are higher than the heavens above — what can you do?
They are deeper than the depths below — what can you know?
9 Their measure is longer than the earth
and wider than the sea.

10 "If he comes along and confines you in prison
and convenes a court, who can oppose him?
11 Surely he recognizes deceivers;
and when he sees evil, does he not take note?
12 But the witless can no more become wise
than a wild donkey's colt can be born human.[a]

13 "Yet if you devote your heart to him
and stretch out your hands to him,
14 if you put away the sin that is in your hand
and allow no evil to dwell in your tent,
15 then, free of fault, you will lift up your face;
you will stand firm and without fear.
16 You will surely forget your trouble,
recalling it only as waters gone by.
17 Life will be brighter than noonday,
and darkness will become like morning.
18 You will be secure, because there is hope;
you will look about you and take your rest in safety.
19 You will lie down, with no one to make you afraid,
and many will court your favor.
20 But the eyes of the wicked will fail,
and escape will elude them;
their hope will become a dying gasp."

Job 12

12 Then Job replied:

2 "Doubtless you are the only people who matter,
and wisdom will die with you!
3 But I have a mind as well as you;
I am not inferior to you.
Who does not know all these things?

4 "I have become a laughingstock to my friends,
though I called on God and he answered —
a mere laughingstock, though righteous and blameless!
5 Those who are at ease have contempt for misfortune
as the fate of those whose feet are slipping.
6 The tents of marauders are undisturbed,
and those who provoke God are secure —
those God has in his hand.[b]

7 "But ask the animals, and they will teach you,
or the birds in the sky, and they will tell you;
8 or speak to the earth, and it will teach you,
or let the fish in the sea inform you.
9 Which of all these does not know
that the hand of the LORD has done this?
10 In his hand is the life of every creature
and the breath of all mankind.
11 Does not the ear test words
as the tongue tastes food?
12 Is not wisdom found among the aged?
Does not long life bring understanding?

13 "To God belong wisdom and power;
counsel and understanding are his.
14 What he tears down cannot be rebuilt;
those he imprisons cannot be released.
15 If he holds back the waters, there is drought;
if he lets them loose, they devastate the land.

[a] 12 Or *wild donkey can be born tame* [b] 6 Or *those whose god is in their own hand*

16 To him belong strength and insight;
both deceived and deceiver are his.
17 He leads rulers away stripped
and makes fools of judges.
18 He takes off the shackles put on by kings
and ties a loincloth[a] around their waist.
19 He leads priests away stripped
and overthrows officials long established.
20 He silences the lips of trusted advisers
and takes away the discernment of elders.
21 He pours contempt on nobles
and disarms the mighty.
22 He reveals the deep things of darkness
and brings utter darkness into the light.
23 He makes nations great, and destroys them;
he enlarges nations, and disperses them.
24 He deprives the leaders of the earth of their reason;
he makes them wander in a trackless waste.
25 They grope in darkness with no light;
he makes them stagger like drunkards.

13 "My eyes have seen all this,
my ears have heard and understood it.
2 What you know, I also know;
I am not inferior to you.
3 But I desire to speak to the Almighty
and to argue my case with God.
4 You, however, smear me with lies;
you are worthless physicians, all of you!
5 If only you would be altogether silent!
For you, that would be wisdom.
6 Hear now my argument;
listen to the pleas of my lips.
7 Will you speak wickedly on God's behalf?
Will you speak deceitfully for him?
8 Will you show him partiality?
Will you argue the case for God?
9 Would it turn out well if he examined you?
Could you deceive him as you might deceive a mortal?
10 He would surely call you to account
if you secretly showed partiality.
11 Would not his splendor terrify you?
Would not the dread of him fall on you?
12 Your maxims are proverbs of ashes;
your defenses are defenses of clay.

13 "Keep silent and let me speak;
then let come to me what may.
14 Why do I put myself in jeopardy
and take my life in my hands?
15 Though he slay me, yet will I hope in him;
I will surely[b] defend my ways to his face.
16 Indeed, this will turn out for my deliverance,
for no godless person would dare come before him!
17 Listen carefully to what I say;
let my words ring in your ears.
18 Now that I have prepared my case,
I know I will be vindicated.
19 Can anyone bring charges against me?
If so, I will be silent and die.

20 "Only grant me these two things, God,
and then I will not hide from you:
21 Withdraw your hand far from me,
and stop frightening me with your terrors.
22 Then summon me and I will answer,
or let me speak, and you reply to me.
23 How many wrongs and sins have I committed?
Show me my offense and my sin.
24 Why do you hide your face
and consider me your enemy?
25 Will you torment a windblown leaf?
Will you chase after dry chaff?
26 For you write down bitter things against me
and make me reap the sins of my youth.
27 You fasten my feet in shackles;
you keep close watch on all my paths
by putting marks on the soles of my feet.

28 "So man wastes away like something rotten,
like a garment eaten by moths.

14 "Mortals, born of woman,
are of few days and full of trouble.
2 They spring up like flowers and wither away;
like fleeting shadows, they do not endure.
3 Do you fix your eye on them?
Will you bring them[c] before you for judgment?

[a] 18 Or *shackles of kings / and ties a belt* [b] 15 Or *He will surely slay me; I have no hope — / yet I will* [c] 3 Septuagint, Vulgate and Syriac; Hebrew *me*

4 Who can bring what is pure from the impure?
No one!
5 A person's days are determined;
you have decreed the number of his months
and have set limits he cannot exceed.
6 So look away from him and let him alone,
till he has put in his time like a hired laborer.

7 "At least there is hope for a tree:
If it is cut down, it will sprout again,
and its new shoots will not fail.
8 Its roots may grow old in the ground
and its stump die in the soil,
9 yet at the scent of water it will bud
and put forth shoots like a plant.
10 But a man dies and is laid low;
he breathes his last and is no more.
11 As the water of a lake dries up
or a riverbed becomes parched and dry,
12 so he lies down and does not rise;
till the heavens are no more,
people will not awake
or be roused from their sleep.

13 "If only you would hide me in the grave
and conceal me till your anger has passed!
If only you would set me a time
and then remember me!
14 If someone dies, will they live again?
All the days of my hard service
I will wait for my renewal[a] to come.
15 You will call and I will answer you;
you will long for the creature your hands have made.
16 Surely then you will count my steps
but not keep track of my sin.
17 My offenses will be sealed up in a bag;
you will cover over my sin.

18 "But as a mountain erodes and crumbles
and as a rock is moved from its place,
19 as water wears away stones
and torrents wash away the soil,
so you destroy a person's hope.
20 You overpower them once for all, and they are gone;
you change their countenance and send them away.
21 If their children are honored, they do not know it;
if their offspring are brought low, they do not see it.
22 They feel but the pain of their own bodies
and mourn only for themselves."

[a] 14 Or *release*

Eliphaz

15 Then Eliphaz the Temanite replied:

2 "Would a wise person answer with empty notions
or fill their belly with the hot east wind?
3 Would they argue with useless words,
with speeches that have no value?
4 But you even undermine piety
and hinder devotion to God.
5 Your sin prompts your mouth;
you adopt the tongue of the crafty.
6 Your own mouth condemns you, not mine;
your own lips testify against you.

7 "Are you the first man ever born?
Were you brought forth before the hills?
8 Do you listen in on God's council?
Do you have a monopoly on wisdom?
9 What do you know that we do not know?
What insights do you have that we do not have?
10 The gray-haired and the aged are on our side,
men even older than your father.
11 Are God's consolations not enough for you,
words spoken gently to you?
12 Why has your heart carried you away,
and why do your eyes flash,
13 so that you vent your rage against God
and pour out such words from your mouth?

14 "What are mortals, that they could be pure,
or those born of woman, that they could be righteous?
15 If God places no trust in his holy ones,
if even the heavens are not pure in his eyes,
16 how much less mortals, who are vile and corrupt,
who drink up evil like water!

17 "Listen to me and I will explain to you;
let me tell you what I have seen,
18 what the wise have declared,
hiding nothing received from their ancestors
19 (to whom alone the land was given
when no foreigners moved among them):
20 All his days the wicked man suffers torment,
the ruthless man through all the years stored up for him.

21 Terrifying sounds fill his ears;
when all seems well, marauders attack him.
22 He despairs of escaping the realm of darkness;
he is marked for the sword.
23 He wanders about for food like a vulture;
he knows the day of darkness is at hand.
24 Distress and anguish fill him with terror;
troubles overwhelm him, like a king poised to attack,
25 because he shakes his fist at God
and vaunts himself against the Almighty,
26 defiantly charging against him
with a thick, strong shield.

27 "Though his face is covered with fat
and his waist bulges with flesh,
28 he will inhabit ruined towns
and houses where no one lives,
houses crumbling to rubble.
29 He will no longer be rich and his wealth will not endure,
nor will his possessions spread over the land.
30 He will not escape the darkness;
a flame will wither his shoots,
and the breath of God's mouth will carry him away.
31 Let him not deceive himself by trusting what is worthless,
for he will get nothing in return.
32 Before his time he will wither,
and his branches will not flourish.
33 He will be like a vine stripped of its unripe grapes,
like an olive tree shedding its blossoms.
34 For the company of the godless will be barren,
and fire will consume the tents of those who love bribes.
35 They conceive trouble and give birth to evil;
their womb fashions deceit."

Job 16

Then Job replied:

2 "I have heard many things like these;
you are miserable comforters, all of you!
3 Will your long-winded speeches never end?
What ails you that you keep on arguing?
4 I also could speak like you,
if you were in my place;
I could make fine speeches against you
and shake my head at you.
5 But my mouth would encourage you;
comfort from my lips would bring you relief.

6 "Yet if I speak, my pain is not relieved;
and if I refrain, it does not go away.
7 Surely, God, you have worn me out;
you have devastated my entire household.
8 You have shriveled me up — and it has become a witness;
my gauntness rises up and testifies against me.
9 God assails me and tears me in his anger
and gnashes his teeth at me;
my opponent fastens on me his piercing eyes.
10 People open their mouths to jeer at me;
they strike my cheek in scorn
and unite together against me.
11 God has turned me over to the ungodly
and thrown me into the clutches of the wicked.
12 All was well with me, but he shattered me;
he seized me by the neck and crushed me.
He has made me his target;
13 his archers surround me.
Without pity, he pierces my kidneys
and spills my gall on the ground.
14 Again and again he bursts upon me;
he rushes at me like a warrior.

15 "I have sewed sackcloth over my skin
and buried my brow in the dust.
16 My face is red with weeping,
dark shadows ring my eyes;
17 yet my hands have been free of violence
and my prayer is pure.

18 "Earth, do not cover my blood;
may my cry never be laid to rest!
19 Even now my witness is in heaven;
my advocate is on high.
20 My intercessor is my friend[a]
as my eyes pour out tears to God;
21 on behalf of a man he pleads with God
as one pleads for a friend.

22 "Only a few years will pass
before I take the path of no return.

[a] 20 Or *My friends treat me with scorn*

17 [1]My spirit is broken,
my days are cut short,
the grave awaits me.
[2]Surely mockers surround me;
my eyes must dwell on their hostility.

[3]"Give me, O God, the pledge you demand.
Who else will put up security for me?
[4]You have closed their minds to understanding;
therefore you will not let them triumph.
[5]If anyone denounces their friends for reward,
the eyes of their children will fail.

[6]"God has made me a byword to everyone,
a man in whose face people spit.
[7]My eyes have grown dim with grief;
my whole frame is but a shadow.
[8]The upright are appalled at this;
the innocent are aroused against the ungodly.
[9]Nevertheless, the righteous will hold to their ways,
and those with clean hands will grow stronger.

[10]"But come on, all of you, try again!
I will not find a wise man among you.
[11]My days have passed, my plans are shattered.
Yet the desires of my heart
[12]turn night into day;
in the face of the darkness light is near.
[13]If the only home I hope for is the grave,
if I spread out my bed in the realm of darkness,
[14]if I say to corruption, 'You are my father,'
and to the worm, 'My mother' or 'My sister,'
[15]where then is my hope —
who can see any hope for me?
[16]Will it go down to the gates of death?
Will we descend together into the dust?"

Bildad

18 Then Bildad the Shuhite replied:

[2]"When will you end these speeches?
Be sensible, and then we can talk.
[3]Why are we regarded as cattle
and considered stupid in your sight?
[4]You who tear yourself to pieces in your anger,
is the earth to be abandoned for your sake?
Or must the rocks be moved from their place?

[5]"The lamp of a wicked man is snuffed out;
the flame of his fire stops burning.
[6]The light in his tent becomes dark;
the lamp beside him goes out.
[7]The vigor of his step is weakened;
his own schemes throw him down.
[8]His feet thrust him into a net;
he wanders into its mesh.
[9]A trap seizes him by the heel;
a snare holds him fast.
[10]A noose is hidden for him on the ground;
a trap lies in his path.
[11]Terrors startle him on every side
and dog his every step.
[12]Calamity is hungry for him;
disaster is ready for him when he falls.
[13]It eats away parts of his skin;
death's firstborn devours his limbs.
[14]He is torn from the security of his tent
and marched off to the king of terrors.
[15]Fire resides[a] in his tent;
burning sulfur is scattered over his dwelling.
[16]His roots dry up below
and his branches wither above.
[17]The memory of him perishes from the earth;
he has no name in the land.
[18]He is driven from light into the realm of darkness
and is banished from the world.
[19]He has no offspring or descendants among his people,
no survivor where once he lived.
[20]People of the west are appalled at his fate;
those of the east are seized with horror.
[21]Surely such is the dwelling of an evil man;
such is the place of one who does not know God."

Job

19 Then Job replied:

[2]"How long will you torment me
and crush me with words?
[3]Ten times now you have reproached me;
shamelessly you attack me.

[a] 15 Or *Nothing he had remains*

4 If it is true that I have gone astray,
my error remains my concern alone.
5 If indeed you would exalt yourselves
above me
and use my humiliation against me,
6 then know that God has wronged me
and drawn his net around me.

7 "Though I cry, 'Violence!' I get no
response;
though I call for help, there is no
justice.
8 He has blocked my way so I cannot
pass;
he has shrouded my paths in
darkness.
9 He has stripped me of my honor
and removed the crown from my
head.
10 He tears me down on every side till I
am gone;
he uproots my hope like a tree.
11 His anger burns against me;
he counts me among his enemies.
12 His troops advance in force;
they build a siege ramp against me
and encamp around my tent.

13 "He has alienated my family from
me;
my acquaintances are completely
estranged from me.
14 My relatives have gone away;
my closest friends have forgotten
me.
15 My guests and my female servants
count me a foreigner;
they look on me as on a stranger.
16 I summon my servant, but he does
not answer,
though I beg him with my own
mouth.
17 My breath is offensive to my wife;
I am loathsome to my own family.
18 Even the little boys scorn me;
when I appear, they ridicule me.
19 All my intimate friends detest me;
those I love have turned against
me.
20 I am nothing but skin and bones;
I have escaped only by the skin of
my teeth.[a]

21 "Have pity on me, my friends, have
pity,
for the hand of God has struck me.
22 Why do you pursue me as God does?
Will you never get enough of my
flesh?

23 "Oh, that my words were recorded,
that they were written on a scroll,
24 that they were inscribed with an iron
tool on[b] lead,
or engraved in rock forever!
25 I know that my redeemer[c] lives,
and that in the end he will stand on
the earth.[d]
26 And after my skin has been
destroyed,
yet[e] in[f] my flesh I will see God;
27 I myself will see him
with my own eyes — I, and not
another.
How my heart yearns within me!

28 "If you say, 'How we will hound him,
since the root of the trouble lies in
him,[g]'
29 you should fear the sword
yourselves;
for wrath will bring punishment by
the sword,
and then you will know that there
is judgment.[h]"

Zophar

20 Then Zophar the Naamathite replied:

2 "My troubled thoughts prompt me to
answer
because I am greatly disturbed.
3 I hear a rebuke that dishonors me,
and my understanding inspires me
to reply.

4 "Surely you know how it has been
from of old,
ever since mankind[i] was placed on
the earth,
5 that the mirth of the wicked is brief,
the joy of the godless lasts but a
moment.
6 Though the pride of the godless
person reaches to the heavens
and his head touches the clouds,
7 he will perish forever, like his own
dung;
those who have seen him will say,
'Where is he?'
8 Like a dream he flies away, no more
to be found,
banished like a vision of the night.
9 The eye that saw him will not see him
again;
his place will look on him no more.

[a] 20 Or *only by my gums* [b] 24 Or *and* [c] 25 Or *vindicator* [d] 25 Or *on my grave* [e] 26 Or *And after I awake, / though this body has been destroyed, / then* [f] 26 Or *destroyed, / apart from* [g] 28 Many Hebrew manuscripts, Septuagint and Vulgate; most Hebrew manuscripts *me* [h] 29 Or *sword, / that you may come to know the Almighty* [i] 4 Or *Adam*

10 His children must make amends to
the poor;
his own hands must give back his
wealth.
11 The youthful vigor that fills his bones
will lie with him in the dust.

12 "Though evil is sweet in his mouth
and he hides it under his tongue,
13 though he cannot bear to let it go
and lets it linger in his mouth,
14 yet his food will turn sour in his
stomach;
it will become the venom of
serpents within him.
15 He will spit out the riches he
swallowed;
God will make his stomach vomit
them up.
16 He will suck the poison of serpents;
the fangs of an adder will kill him.
17 He will not enjoy the streams,
the rivers flowing with honey and
cream.
18 What he toiled for he must give back
uneaten;
he will not enjoy the profit from his
trading.
19 For he has oppressed the poor and left
them destitute;
he has seized houses he did not
build.

20 "Surely he will have no respite from
his craving;
he cannot save himself by his
treasure.
21 Nothing is left for him to devour;
his prosperity will not endure.
22 In the midst of his plenty, distress will
overtake him;
the full force of misery will come
upon him.
23 When he has filled his belly,
God will vent his burning anger
against him
and rain down his blows on him.
24 Though he flees from an iron
weapon,
a bronze-tipped arrow pierces
him.
25 He pulls it out of his back,
the gleaming point out of his liver.
Terrors will come over him;
26 total darkness lies in wait for his
treasures.
A fire unfanned will consume him
and devour what is left in his tent.
27 The heavens will expose his guilt;
the earth will rise up against him.
28 A flood will carry off his house,
rushing waters[a] on the day of
God's wrath.
29 Such is the fate God allots the wicked,
the heritage appointed for them
by God."

Job

21 Then Job replied:

2 "Listen carefully to my words;
let this be the consolation you give
me.
3 Bear with me while I speak,
and after I have spoken, mock on.

4 "Is my complaint directed to a
human being?
Why should I not be impatient?
5 Look at me and be appalled;
clap your hand over your mouth.
6 When I think about this, I am
terrified;
trembling seizes my body.
7 Why do the wicked live on,
growing old and increasing in
power?
8 They see their children established
around them,
their offspring before their eyes.
9 Their homes are safe and free from
fear;
the rod of God is not on them.
10 Their bulls never fail to breed;
their cows calve and do not
miscarry.
11 They send forth their children as a
flock;
their little ones dance about.
12 They sing to the music of timbrel and
lyre;
they make merry to the sound of
the pipe.
13 They spend their years in prosperity
and go down to the grave in
peace.[b]
14 Yet they say to God, 'Leave us alone!
We have no desire to know your
ways.
15 Who is the Almighty, that we should
serve him?
What would we gain by praying to
him?'
16 But their prosperity is not in their
own hands,
so I stand aloof from the plans of
the wicked.

17 "Yet how often is the lamp of the
wicked snuffed out?

[a] 28 Or *The possessions in his house will be carried off, / washed away* [b] 13 Or *in an instant*

How often does calamity come
upon them,
the fate God allots in his anger?
18 How often are they like straw before
the wind,
like chaff swept away by a gale?
19 It is said, 'God stores up the
punishment of the wicked for
their children.'
Let him repay the wicked, so
that they themselves will
experience it!
20 Let their own eyes see their
destruction;
let them drink the cup of the wrath
of the Almighty.
21 For what do they care about the
families they leave behind
when their allotted months come
to an end?

22 "Can anyone teach knowledge to God,
since he judges even the highest?
23 One person dies in full vigor,
completely secure and at ease,
24 well nourished in body,[a]
bones rich with marrow.
25 Another dies in bitterness of soul,
never having enjoyed anything
good.
26 Side by side they lie in the dust,
and worms cover them both.

27 "I know full well what you are thinking,
the schemes by which you would
wrong me.
28 You say, 'Where now is the house of
the great,
the tents where the wicked lived?'
29 Have you never questioned those who
travel?
Have you paid no regard to their
accounts —
30 that the wicked are spared from the
day of calamity,
that they are delivered from[b] the
day of wrath?
31 Who denounces their conduct to their
face?
Who repays them for what they
have done?
32 They are carried to the grave,
and watch is kept over their tombs.
33 The soil in the valley is sweet to them;
everyone follows after them,
and a countless throng goes[c]
before them.

34 "So how can you console me with
your nonsense?
Nothing is left of your answers but
falsehood!"

Eliphaz

22 Then Eliphaz the Temanite replied:

2 "Can a man be of benefit to God?
Can even a wise person benefit
him?
3 What pleasure would it give
the Almighty if you were
righteous?
What would he gain if your ways
were blameless?

4 "Is it for your piety that he rebukes
you
and brings charges against you?
5 Is not your wickedness great?
Are not your sins endless?
6 You demanded security from your
relatives for no reason;
you stripped people of their
clothing, leaving them naked.
7 You gave no water to the weary
and you withheld food from the
hungry,
8 though you were a powerful man,
owning land —
an honored man, living on it.
9 And you sent widows away empty-
handed
and broke the strength of the
fatherless.
10 That is why snares are all around you,
why sudden peril terrifies you,
11 why it is so dark you cannot see,
and why a flood of water covers
you.

12 "Is not God in the heights of heaven?
And see how lofty are the highest
stars!
13 Yet you say, 'What does God know?
Does he judge through such
darkness?
14 Thick clouds veil him, so he does not
see us
as he goes about in the vaulted
heavens.'
15 Will you keep to the old path
that the wicked have trod?
16 They were carried off before their
time,
their foundations washed away by
a flood.
17 They said to God, 'Leave us alone!
What can the Almighty do to us?'
18 Yet it was he who filled their houses
with good things,
so I stand aloof from the plans of
the wicked.

[a] 24 The meaning of the Hebrew for this word is uncertain. [b] 30 Or *wicked are reserved for the day of calamity, / that they are brought forth to* [c] 33 Or *them, / as a countless throng went*

19 The righteous see their ruin and
rejoice;
the innocent mock them, saying,
20 'Surely our foes are destroyed,
and fire devours their wealth.'

21 "Submit to God and be at peace with
him;
in this way prosperity will come to
you.
22 Accept instruction from his mouth
and lay up his words in your heart.
23 If you return to the Almighty, you will
be restored:
If you remove wickedness far from
your tent
24 and assign your nuggets to the dust,
your gold of Ophir to the rocks in
the ravines,
25 then the Almighty will be your gold,
the choicest silver for you.
26 Surely then you will find delight in
the Almighty
and will lift up your face to God.
27 You will pray to him, and he will hear
you,
and you will fulfill your vows.
28 What you decide on will be done,
and light will shine on your ways.
29 When people are brought low and
you say, 'Lift them up!'
then he will save the downcast.
30 He will deliver even one who is not
innocent,
who will be delivered through the
cleanness of your hands."

Job 23

23 Then Job replied:

2 "Even today my complaint is bitter;
his hand[a] is heavy in spite of[b] my
groaning.
3 If only I knew where to find him;
if only I could go to his dwelling!
4 I would state my case before him
and fill my mouth with arguments.
5 I would find out what he would
answer me,
and consider what he would say to
me.
6 Would he vigorously oppose me?
No, he would not press charges
against me.
7 There the upright can establish their
innocence before him,
and there I would be delivered
forever from my judge.

8 "But if I go to the east, he is not there;
if I go to the west, I do not find him.
9 When he is at work in the north, I do
not see him;
when he turns to the south, I catch
no glimpse of him.
10 But he knows the way that I take;
when he has tested me, I will come
forth as gold.
11 My feet have closely followed his steps;
I have kept to his way without
turning aside.
12 I have not departed from the
commands of his lips;
I have treasured the words of his
mouth more than my daily
bread.

13 "But he stands alone, and who can
oppose him?
He does whatever he pleases.
14 He carries out his decree against me,
and many such plans he still has in
store.
15 That is why I am terrified before him;
when I think of all this, I fear him.
16 God has made my heart faint;
the Almighty has terrified me.
17 Yet I am not silenced by the darkness,
by the thick darkness that covers
my face.

24 "Why does the Almighty not set
times for judgment?
Why must those who know him
look in vain for such days?
2 There are those who move boundary
stones;
they pasture flocks they have
stolen.
3 They drive away the orphan's donkey
and take the widow's ox in pledge.
4 They thrust the needy from the path
and force all the poor of the land
into hiding.
5 Like wild donkeys in the desert,
the poor go about their labor of
foraging food;
the wasteland provides food for
their children.
6 They gather fodder in the fields
and glean in the vineyards of the
wicked.
7 Lacking clothes, they spend the night
naked;
they have nothing to cover
themselves in the cold.
8 They are drenched by mountain rains
and hug the rocks for lack of shelter.
9 The fatherless child is snatched from
the breast;
the infant of the poor is seized for a
debt.

[a] 2 Septuagint and Syriac; Hebrew / *the hand on me* [b] 2 Or *heavy on me in*

[10] Lacking clothes, they go about naked;
they carry the sheaves, but still go hungry.
[11] They crush olives among the terraces[a];
they tread the winepresses, yet suffer thirst.
[12] The groans of the dying rise from the city,
and the souls of the wounded cry out for help.
But God charges no one with wrongdoing.

[13] "There are those who rebel against the light,
who do not know its ways
or stay in its paths.
[14] When daylight is gone, the murderer rises up,
kills the poor and needy,
and in the night steals forth like a thief.
[15] The eye of the adulterer watches for dusk;
he thinks, 'No eye will see me,'
and he keeps his face concealed.
[16] In the dark, thieves break into houses,
but by day they shut themselves in;
they want nothing to do with the light.
[17] For all of them, midnight is their morning;
they make friends with the terrors of darkness.

[18] "Yet they are foam on the surface of the water;
their portion of the land is cursed,
so that no one goes to the vineyards.
[19] As heat and drought snatch away the melted snow,
so the grave snatches away those who have sinned.
[20] The womb forgets them,
the worm feasts on them;
the wicked are no longer remembered
but are broken like a tree.
[21] They prey on the barren and childless woman,
and to the widow they show no kindness.
[22] But God drags away the mighty by his power;
though they become established,
they have no assurance of life.
[23] He may let them rest in a feeling of security,
but his eyes are on their ways.
[24] For a little while they are exalted, and then they are gone;
they are brought low and gathered up like all others;
they are cut off like heads of grain.

[25] "If this is not so, who can prove me false
and reduce my words to nothing?"

Bildad

25 Then Bildad the Shuhite replied:

[2] "Dominion and awe belong to God;
he establishes order in the heights of heaven.
[3] Can his forces be numbered?
On whom does his light not rise?
[4] How then can a mortal be righteous before God?
How can one born of woman be pure?
[5] If even the moon is not bright
and the stars are not pure in his eyes,
[6] how much less a mortal, who is but a maggot—
a human being, who is only a worm!"

Job

26 Then Job replied:

[2] "How you have helped the powerless!
How you have saved the arm that is feeble!
[3] What advice you have offered to one without wisdom!
And what great insight you have displayed!
[4] Who has helped you utter these words?
And whose spirit spoke from your mouth?

[5] "The dead are in deep anguish,
those beneath the waters and all that live in them.
[6] The realm of the dead is naked before God;
Destruction[b] lies uncovered.
[7] He spreads out the northern skies over empty space;
he suspends the earth over nothing.
[8] He wraps up the waters in his clouds,
yet the clouds do not burst under their weight.
[9] He covers the face of the full moon,
spreading his clouds over it.

[a] *11* The meaning of the Hebrew for this word is uncertain. [b] *6* Hebrew *Abaddon*

10 He marks out the horizon on the face of the waters
for a boundary between light and darkness.
11 The pillars of the heavens quake,
aghast at his rebuke.
12 By his power he churned up the sea;
by his wisdom he cut Rahab to pieces.
13 By his breath the skies became fair;
his hand pierced the gliding serpent.
14 And these are but the outer fringe of his works;
how faint the whisper we hear of him!
Who then can understand the thunder of his power?"

Job's Final Word to His Friends

27 And Job continued his discourse:

2 "As surely as God lives, who has denied me justice,
the Almighty, who has made my life bitter,
3 as long as I have life within me,
the breath of God in my nostrils,
4 my lips will not say anything wicked,
and my tongue will not utter lies.
5 I will never admit you are in the right;
till I die, I will not deny my integrity.
6 I will maintain my innocence and never let go of it;
my conscience will not reproach me as long as I live.

7 "May my enemy be like the wicked,
my adversary like the unjust!
8 For what hope have the godless when they are cut off,
when God takes away their life?
9 Does God listen to their cry
when distress comes upon them?
10 Will they find delight in the Almighty?
Will they call on God at all times?

11 "I will teach you about the power of God;
the ways of the Almighty I will not conceal.
12 You have all seen this yourselves.
Why then this meaningless talk?

13 "Here is the fate God allots to the wicked,
the heritage a ruthless man receives from the Almighty:
14 However many his children, their fate is the sword;
his offspring will never have enough to eat.
15 The plague will bury those who survive him,
and their widows will not weep for them.
16 Though he heaps up silver like dust
and clothes like piles of clay,
17 what he lays up the righteous will wear,
and the innocent will divide his silver.
18 The house he builds is like a moth's cocoon,
like a hut made by a watchman.
19 He lies down wealthy, but will do so no more;
when he opens his eyes, all is gone.
20 Terrors overtake him like a flood;
a tempest snatches him away in the night.
21 The east wind carries him off, and he is gone;
it sweeps him out of his place.
22 It hurls itself against him without mercy
as he flees headlong from its power.
23 It claps its hands in derision
and hisses him out of his place."

Interlude: Where Wisdom Is Found

28 There is a mine for silver
and a place where gold is refined.
2 Iron is taken from the earth,
and copper is smelted from ore.
3 Mortals put an end to the darkness;
they search out the farthest recesses
for ore in the blackest darkness.
4 Far from human dwellings they cut a shaft,
in places untouched by human feet;
far from other people they dangle and sway.
5 The earth, from which food comes,
is transformed below as by fire;
6 lapis lazuli comes from its rocks,
and its dust contains nuggets of gold.
7 No bird of prey knows that hidden path,
no falcon's eye has seen it.
8 Proud beasts do not set foot on it,
and no lion prowls there.
9 People assault the flinty rock with their hands
and lay bare the roots of the mountains.
10 They tunnel through the rock;
their eyes see all its treasures.

11 They search[a] the sources of the rivers
and bring hidden things to light.
12 But where can wisdom be found?
Where does understanding dwell?
13 No mortal comprehends its worth;
it cannot be found in the land of the living.
14 The deep says, "It is not in me";
the sea says, "It is not with me."
15 It cannot be bought with the finest gold,
nor can its price be weighed out in silver.
16 It cannot be bought with the gold of Ophir,
with precious onyx or lapis lazuli.
17 Neither gold nor crystal can compare with it,
nor can it be had for jewels of gold.
18 Coral and jasper are not worthy of mention;
the price of wisdom is beyond rubies.
19 The topaz of Cush cannot compare with it;
it cannot be bought with pure gold.

20 Where then does wisdom come from?
Where does understanding dwell?
21 It is hidden from the eyes of every living thing,
concealed even from the birds in the sky.
22 Destruction[b] and Death say,
"Only a rumor of it has reached our ears."
23 God understands the way to it
and he alone knows where it dwells,
24 for he views the ends of the earth
and sees everything under the heavens.
25 When he established the force of the wind
and measured out the waters,
26 when he made a decree for the rain
and a path for the thunderstorm,
27 then he looked at wisdom and appraised it;
he confirmed it and tested it.
28 And he said to the human race,
"The fear of the Lord — that is wisdom,
and to shun evil is understanding."

Job's Final Defense

29 Job continued his discourse:

2 "How I long for the months gone by,
for the days when God watched over me,
3 when his lamp shone on my head
and by his light I walked through darkness!
4 Oh, for the days when I was in my prime,
when God's intimate friendship blessed my house,
5 when the Almighty was still with me
and my children were around me,
6 when my path was drenched with cream
and the rock poured out for me streams of olive oil.

7 "When I went to the gate of the city
and took my seat in the public square,
8 the young men saw me and stepped aside
and the old men rose to their feet;
9 the chief men refrained from speaking
and covered their mouths with their hands;
10 the voices of the nobles were hushed,
and their tongues stuck to the roof of their mouths.
11 Whoever heard me spoke well of me,
and those who saw me commended me,
12 because I rescued the poor who cried for help,
and the fatherless who had none to assist them.
13 The one who was dying blessed me;
I made the widow's heart sing.
14 I put on righteousness as my clothing;
justice was my robe and my turban.
15 I was eyes to the blind
and feet to the lame.
16 I was a father to the needy;
I took up the case of the stranger.
17 I broke the fangs of the wicked
and snatched the victims from their teeth.

18 "I thought, 'I will die in my own house,
my days as numerous as the grains of sand.
19 My roots will reach to the water,
and the dew will lie all night on my branches.
20 My glory will not fade;
the bow will be ever new in my hand.'

21 "People listened to me expectantly,
waiting in silence for my counsel.
22 After I had spoken, they spoke no more;
my words fell gently on their ears.

[a] 11 Septuagint, Aquila and Vulgate; Hebrew *They dam up*
[b] 22 Hebrew *Abaddon*

23 They waited for me as for showers
and drank in my words as the
spring rain.
24 When I smiled at them, they scarcely
believed it;
the light of my face was precious to
them.[a]
25 I chose the way for them and sat as
their chief;
I dwelt as a king among his troops;
I was like one who comforts
mourners.

30 "But now they mock me,
men younger than I,
whose fathers I would have disdained
to put with my sheep dogs.
2 Of what use was the strength of their
hands to me,
since their vigor had gone from
them?
3 Haggard from want and hunger,
they roamed[b] the parched land
in desolate wastelands at night.
4 In the brush they gathered salt herbs,
and their food[c] was the root of the
broom bush.
5 They were banished from human
society,
shouted at as if they were thieves.
6 They were forced to live in the dry
stream beds,
among the rocks and in holes in
the ground.
7 They brayed among the bushes
and huddled in the undergrowth.
8 A base and nameless brood,
they were driven out of the land.

9 "And now those young men mock me
in song;
I have become a byword among
them.
10 They detest me and keep their
distance;
they do not hesitate to spit in my
face.
11 Now that God has unstrung my bow
and afflicted me,
they throw off restraint in my
presence.
12 On my right the tribe[d] attacks;
they lay snares for my feet,
they build their siege ramps
against me.
13 They break up my road;
they succeed in destroying me.
'No one can help him,' they say.
14 They advance as through a gaping
breach;
amid the ruins they come rolling
in.
15 Terrors overwhelm me;
my dignity is driven away as by the
wind,
my safety vanishes like a cloud.

16 "And now my life ebbs away;
days of suffering grip me.
17 Night pierces my bones;
my gnawing pains never rest.
18 In his great power God becomes like
clothing to me[e];
he binds me like the neck of my
garment.
19 He throws me into the mud,
and I am reduced to dust and
ashes.

20 "I cry out to you, God, but you do not
answer;
I stand up, but you merely look at
me.
21 You turn on me ruthlessly;
with the might of your hand you
attack me.
22 You snatch me up and drive me
before the wind;
you toss me about in the storm.
23 I know you will bring me down to
death,
to the place appointed for all the
living.

24 "Surely no one lays a hand on a
broken man
when he cries for help in his
distress.
25 Have I not wept for those in trouble?
Has not my soul grieved for the
poor?
26 Yet when I hoped for good, evil came;
when I looked for light, then came
darkness.
27 The churning inside me never stops;
days of suffering confront me.
28 I go about blackened, but not by the
sun;
I stand up in the assembly and cry
for help.
29 I have become a brother of jackals,
a companion of owls.
30 My skin grows black and peels;
my body burns with fever.
31 My lyre is tuned to mourning,
and my pipe to the sound of
wailing.

[a] *24* The meaning of the Hebrew for this clause is uncertain. [b] *3* Or *gnawed* [c] *4* Or *fuel*
[d] *12* The meaning of the Hebrew for this word is uncertain. [e] *18* Hebrew; Septuagint *power he grasps my clothing*

31 "I made a covenant with my eyes
not to look lustfully at a young
woman.
2 For what is our lot from God above,
our heritage from the Almighty on
high?
3 Is it not ruin for the wicked,
disaster for those who do wrong?
4 Does he not see my ways
and count my every step?

5 "If I have walked with falsehood
or my foot has hurried after
deceit —
6 let God weigh me in honest scales
and he will know that I am
blameless —
7 if my steps have turned from the
path,
if my heart has been led by my
eyes,
or if my hands have been defiled,
8 then may others eat what I have
sown,
and may my crops be uprooted.

9 "If my heart has been enticed by a
woman,
or if I have lurked at my neighbor's
door,
10 then may my wife grind another
man's grain,
and may other men sleep with her.
11 For that would have been wicked,
a sin to be judged.
12 It is a fire that burns to Destruction[a];
it would have uprooted my harvest.

13 "If I have denied justice to any of my
servants,
whether male or female,
when they had a grievance against
me,
14 what will I do when God confronts
me?
What will I answer when called to
account?
15 Did not he who made me in the womb
make them?
Did not the same one form us both
within our mothers?

16 "If I have denied the desires of the
poor
or let the eyes of the widow grow
weary,
17 if I have kept my bread to myself,
not sharing it with the fatherless —
18 but from my youth I reared them as a
father would,
and from my birth I guided the
widow —
19 if I have seen anyone perishing for
lack of clothing,
or the needy without garments,
20 and their hearts did not bless me
for warming them with the fleece
from my sheep,
21 if I have raised my hand against the
fatherless,
knowing that I had influence in
court,
22 then let my arm fall from the
shoulder,
let it be broken off at the joint.
23 For I dreaded destruction from God,
and for fear of his splendor I could
not do such things.

24 "If I have put my trust in gold
or said to pure gold, 'You are my
security,'
25 if I have rejoiced over my great wealth,
the fortune my hands had gained,
26 if I have regarded the sun in its
radiance
or the moon moving in splendor,
27 so that my heart was secretly enticed
and my hand offered them a kiss of
homage,
28 then these also would be sins to be
judged,
for I would have been unfaithful to
God on high.

29 "If I have rejoiced at my enemy's
misfortune
or gloated over the trouble that
came to him —
30 I have not allowed my mouth to sin
by invoking a curse against their
life —
31 if those of my household have never
said,
'Who has not been filled with Job's
meat?' —
32 but no stranger had to spend the
night in the street,
for my door was always open to the
traveler —
33 if I have concealed my sin as people
do,[b]
by hiding my guilt in my heart
34 because I so feared the crowd
and so dreaded the contempt of the
clans
that I kept silent and would not go
outside —

35 ("Oh, that I had someone to hear me!
I sign now my defense — let the
Almighty answer me;
let my accuser put his indictment
in writing.

[a] 12 Hebrew *Abaddon* [b] 33 Or *as Adam did*

36 Surely I would wear it on my
shoulder,
I would put it on like a crown.
37 I would give him an account of my
every step;
I would present it to him as to a
ruler.) —

38 "if my land cries out against me
and all its furrows are wet with
tears,
39 if I have devoured its yield without
payment
or broken the spirit of its tenants,
40 then let briers come up instead of
wheat
and stinkweed instead of barley."

The words of Job are ended.

Elihu

32 So these three men stopped answering Job, because he was righteous
in his own eyes. 2 But Elihu son of Barakel
the Buzite, of the family of Ram, became
very angry with Job for justifying himself rather than God. 3 He was also angry
with the three friends, because they had
found no way to refute Job, and yet had
condemned him.[a] 4 Now Elihu had waited
before speaking to Job because they were
older than he. 5 But when he saw that the
three men had nothing more to say, his
anger was aroused.
6 So Elihu son of Barakel the Buzite said:

"I am young in years,
and you are old;
that is why I was fearful,
not daring to tell you what I know.
7 I thought, 'Age should speak;
advanced years should teach
wisdom.'
8 But it is the spirit[b] in a person,
the breath of the Almighty, that
gives them understanding.
9 It is not only the old[c] who are wise,
not only the aged who understand
what is right.

10 "Therefore I say: Listen to me;
I too will tell you what I know.
11 I waited while you spoke,
I listened to your reasoning;
while you were searching for words,
12 I gave you my full attention.
But not one of you has proved Job
wrong;
none of you has answered his
arguments.
13 Do not say, 'We have found wisdom;
let God, not a man, refute him.'
14 But Job has not marshaled his words
against me,
and I will not answer him with your
arguments.

15 "They are dismayed and have no
more to say;
words have failed them.
16 Must I wait, now that they are silent,
now that they stand there with no
reply?
17 I too will have my say;
I too will tell what I know.
18 For I am full of words,
and the spirit within me compels
me;
19 inside I am like bottled-up wine,
like new wineskins ready to burst.
20 I must speak and find relief;
I must open my lips and reply.
21 I will show no partiality,
nor will I flatter anyone;
22 for if I were skilled in flattery,
my Maker would soon take me
away.

33 "But now, Job, listen to my words;
pay attention to everything I say.
2 I am about to open my mouth;
my words are on the tip of my
tongue.
3 My words come from an upright
heart;
my lips sincerely speak what I
know.
4 The Spirit of God has made me;
the breath of the Almighty gives
me life.
5 Answer me then, if you can;
stand up and argue your case
before me.
6 I am the same as you in God's sight;
I too am a piece of clay.
7 No fear of me should alarm you,
nor should my hand be heavy on
you.

8 "But you have said in my hearing —
I heard the very words —
9 'I am pure, I have done no wrong;
I am clean and free from sin.
10 Yet God has found fault with me;
he considers me his enemy.
11 He fastens my feet in shackles;
he keeps close watch on all my
paths.'

12 "But I tell you, in this you are not
right,
for God is greater than any
mortal.

[a] 3 Masoretic Text; an ancient Hebrew scribal tradition *Job, and so had condemned God*
[b] 8 Or *Spirit*; also in verse 18 [c] 9 Or *many*; or *great*

13 Why do you complain to him
that he responds to no one's words[a]?
14 For God does speak — now one way,
now another —
though no one perceives it.
15 In a dream, in a vision of the night,
when deep sleep falls on people
as they slumber in their beds,
16 he may speak in their ears
and terrify them with warnings,
17 to turn them from wrongdoing
and keep them from pride,
18 to preserve them from the pit,
their lives from perishing by the
sword.[b]

19 "Or someone may be chastened on a
bed of pain
with constant distress in their
bones,
20 so that their body finds food repulsive
and their soul loathes the choicest
meal.
21 Their flesh wastes away to nothing,
and their bones, once hidden, now
stick out.
22 They draw near to the pit,
and their life to the messengers of
death.[c]
23 Yet if there is an angel at their side,
a messenger, one out of a
thousand,
sent to tell them how to be upright,
24 and he is gracious to that person and
says to God,
'Spare them from going down to
the pit;
I have found a ransom for them —
25 let their flesh be renewed like a
child's;
let them be restored as in the days
of their youth' —
26 then that person can pray to God and
find favor with him,
they will see God's face and shout
for joy;
he will restore them to full well-
being.
27 And they will go to others and say,
'I have sinned, I have perverted
what is right,
but I did not get what I deserved.
28 God has delivered me from going
down to the pit,
and I shall live to enjoy the light of
life.'

29 "God does all these things to a
person —
twice, even three times —
30 to turn them back from the pit,
that the light of life may shine on
them.

31 "Pay attention, Job, and listen to me;
be silent, and I will speak.
32 If you have anything to say, answer
me;
speak up, for I want to vindicate
you.
33 But if not, then listen to me;
be silent, and I will teach you
wisdom."

34

Then Elihu said:

2 "Hear my words, you wise men;
listen to me, you men of learning.
3 For the ear tests words
as the tongue tastes food.
4 Let us discern for ourselves what is
right;
let us learn together what is good.

5 "Job says, 'I am innocent,
but God denies me justice.
6 Although I am right,
I am considered a liar;
although I am guiltless,
his arrow inflicts an incurable
wound.'
7 Is there anyone like Job,
who drinks scorn like water?
8 He keeps company with evildoers;
he associates with the wicked.
9 For he says, 'There is no profit
in trying to please God.'

10 "So listen to me, you men of
understanding.
Far be it from God to do evil,
from the Almighty to do wrong.
11 He repays everyone for what they
have done;
he brings on them what their
conduct deserves.
12 It is unthinkable that God would do
wrong,
that the Almighty would pervert
justice.
13 Who appointed him over the earth?
Who put him in charge of the
whole world?
14 If it were his intention
and he withdrew his spirit[d] and
breath,
15 all humanity would perish together
and mankind would return to the
dust.

[a] 13 Or *that he does not answer for any of his actions* [b] 18 Or *from crossing the river* [c] 22 Or *to the place of the dead* [d] 14 Or *Spirit*

16 "If you have understanding, hear this;
listen to what I say.
17 Can someone who hates justice govern?
Will you condemn the just and mighty One?
18 Is he not the One who says to kings, 'You are worthless,'
and to nobles, 'You are wicked,'
19 who shows no partiality to princes
and does not favor the rich over the poor,
for they are all the work of his hands?
20 They die in an instant, in the middle of the night;
the people are shaken and they pass away;
the mighty are removed without human hand.

21 "His eyes are on the ways of mortals;
he sees their every step.
22 There is no deep shadow, no utter darkness,
where evildoers can hide.
23 God has no need to examine people further,
that they should come before him for judgment.
24 Without inquiry he shatters the mighty
and sets up others in their place.
25 Because he takes note of their deeds,
he overthrows them in the night
and they are crushed.
26 He punishes them for their wickedness
where everyone can see them,
27 because they turned from following him
and had no regard for any of his ways.
28 They caused the cry of the poor to come before him,
so that he heard the cry of the needy.
29 But if he remains silent, who can condemn him?
If he hides his face, who can see him?
Yet he is over individual and nation alike,
30 to keep the godless from ruling,
from laying snares for the people.

31 "Suppose someone says to God,
'I am guilty but will offend no more.
32 Teach me what I cannot see;
if I have done wrong, I will not do so again.'
33 Should God then reward you on your terms,
when you refuse to repent?
You must decide, not I;
so tell me what you know.

34 "Men of understanding declare,
wise men who hear me say to me,
35 'Job speaks without knowledge;
his words lack insight.'
36 Oh, that Job might be tested to the utmost
for answering like a wicked man!
37 To his sin he adds rebellion;
scornfully he claps his hands among us
and multiplies his words against God."

35

Then Elihu said:

2 "Do you think this is just?
You say, 'I am in the right, not God.'
3 Yet you ask him, 'What profit is it to me,[a]
and what do I gain by not sinning?'

4 "I would like to reply to you
and to your friends with you.
5 Look up at the heavens and see;
gaze at the clouds so high above you.
6 If you sin, how does that affect him?
If your sins are many, what does that do to him?
7 If you are righteous, what do you give to him,
or what does he receive from your hand?
8 Your wickedness only affects humans like yourself,
and your righteousness only other people.

9 "People cry out under a load of oppression;
they plead for relief from the arm of the powerful.
10 But no one says, 'Where is God my Maker,
who gives songs in the night,
11 who teaches us more than he teaches[b] the beasts of the earth
and makes us wiser than[c] the birds in the sky?'
12 He does not answer when people cry out
because of the arrogance of the wicked.
13 Indeed, God does not listen to their empty plea;
the Almighty pays no attention to it.

[a] 3 Or *you* [b] 10,11 Or *night,* / [11] *who teaches us by* [c] 11 Or *us wise by*

14 How much less, then, will he listen
when you say that you do not see
him,
that your case is before him
and you must wait for him,
15 and further, that his anger never
punishes
and he does not take the least
notice of wickedness.[a]
16 So Job opens his mouth with empty
talk;
without knowledge he multiplies
words."

36 Elihu continued:
2 "Bear with me a little longer and I
will show you
that there is more to be said in
God's behalf.
3 I get my knowledge from afar;
I will ascribe justice to my Maker.
4 Be assured that my words are not
false;
one who has perfect knowledge is
with you.

5 "God is mighty, but despises no one;
he is mighty, and firm in his
purpose.
6 He does not keep the wicked alive
but gives the afflicted their rights.
7 He does not take his eyes off the
righteous;
he enthrones them with kings
and exalts them forever.
8 But if people are bound in chains,
held fast by cords of affliction,
9 he tells them what they have done —
that they have sinned arrogantly.
10 He makes them listen to correction
and commands them to repent of
their evil.
11 If they obey and serve him,
they will spend the rest of their
days in prosperity
and their years in contentment.
12 But if they do not listen,
they will perish by the sword[b]
and die without knowledge.

13 "The godless in heart harbor
resentment;
even when he fetters them, they do
not cry for help.
14 They die in their youth,
among male prostitutes of the
shrines.
15 But those who suffer he delivers in
their suffering;
he speaks to them in their
affliction.

16 "He is wooing you from the jaws of
distress
to a spacious place free from
restriction,
to the comfort of your table laden
with choice food.
17 But now you are laden with the
judgment due the wicked;
judgment and justice have taken
hold of you.
18 Be careful that no one entices you by
riches;
do not let a large bribe turn you
aside.
19 Would your wealth or even all your
mighty efforts
sustain you so you would not be in
distress?
20 Do not long for the night,
to drag people away from their
homes.[c]
21 Beware of turning to evil,
which you seem to prefer to
affliction.

22 "God is exalted in his power.
Who is a teacher like him?
23 Who has prescribed his ways for him,
or said to him, 'You have done
wrong'?
24 Remember to extol his work,
which people have praised in song.
25 All humanity has seen it;
mortals gaze on it from afar.
26 How great is God — beyond our
understanding!
The number of his years is past
finding out.

27 "He draws up the drops of water,
which distill as rain to the streams[d];
28 the clouds pour down their moisture
and abundant showers fall on
mankind.
29 Who can understand how he spreads
out the clouds,
how he thunders from his pavilion?
30 See how he scatters his lightning
about him,
bathing the depths of the sea.
31 This is the way he governs[e] the
nations
and provides food in abundance.
32 He fills his hands with lightning
and commands it to strike its mark.

[a] *15* Symmachus, Theodotion and Vulgate; the meaning of the Hebrew for this word is uncertain. [b] *12* Or *will cross the river* [c] *20* The meaning of the Hebrew for verses 18-20 is uncertain. [d] *27* Or *distill from the mist as rain* [e] *31* Or *nourishes*

33 His thunder announces the coming
storm;
even the cattle make known its
approach.[a]

37 "At this my heart pounds
and leaps from its place.
2 Listen! Listen to the roar of his voice,
to the rumbling that comes from
his mouth.
3 He unleashes his lightning beneath
the whole heaven
and sends it to the ends of the
earth.
4 After that comes the sound of his
roar;
he thunders with his majestic voice.
When his voice resounds,
he holds nothing back.
5 God's voice thunders in marvelous
ways;
he does great things beyond our
understanding.
6 He says to the snow, 'Fall on the
earth,'
and to the rain shower, 'Be a
mighty downpour.'
7 So that everyone he has made may
know his work,
he stops all people from their
labor.[b]
8 The animals take cover;
they remain in their dens.
9 The tempest comes out from its
chamber,
the cold from the driving winds.
10 The breath of God produces ice,
and the broad waters become
frozen.
11 He loads the clouds with moisture;
he scatters his lightning through
them.
12 At his direction they swirl around
over the face of the whole earth
to do whatever he commands
them.
13 He brings the clouds to punish people,
or to water his earth and show his
love.

14 "Listen to this, Job;
stop and consider God's wonders.
15 Do you know how God controls the
clouds
and makes his lightning flash?
16 Do you know how the clouds hang
poised,
those wonders of him who has
perfect knowledge?
17 You who swelter in your clothes
when the land lies hushed under
the south wind,
18 can you join him in spreading out the
skies,
hard as a mirror of cast bronze?

19 "Tell us what we should say to him;
we cannot draw up our case
because of our darkness.
20 Should he be told that I want to
speak?
Would anyone ask to be swallowed
up?
21 Now no one can look at the sun,
bright as it is in the skies
after the wind has swept them
clean.
22 Out of the north he comes in golden
splendor;
God comes in awesome majesty.
23 The Almighty is beyond our reach
and exalted in power;
in his justice and great
righteousness, he does not
oppress.
24 Therefore, people revere him,
for does he not have regard for all
the wise in heart?[c]"

The LORD Speaks

38 Then the LORD spoke to Job out of
the storm. He said:

2 "Who is this that obscures my plans
with words without knowledge?
3 Brace yourself like a man;
I will question you,
and you shall answer me.

4 "Where were you when I laid the
earth's foundation?
Tell me, if you understand.
5 Who marked off its dimensions?
Surely you know!
Who stretched a measuring line
across it?
6 On what were its footings set,
or who laid its cornerstone —
7 while the morning stars sang
together
and all the angels[d] shouted for joy?

8 "Who shut up the sea behind doors
when it burst forth from the womb,
9 when I made the clouds its garment
and wrapped it in thick darkness,
10 when I fixed limits for it
and set its doors and bars in place,

[a] 33 Or *announces his coming — / the One zealous against evil* [b] 7 Or *work, / he fills all people with fear by his power* [c] 24 Or *for he does not have regard for any who think they are wise.*
[d] 7 Hebrew *the sons of God*

11 when I said, 'This far you may come
and no farther;
here is where your proud waves
halt'?
12 "Have you ever given orders to the
morning,
or shown the dawn its place,
13 that it might take the earth by the
edges
and shake the wicked out of it?
14 The earth takes shape like clay under
a seal;
its features stand out like those of
a garment.
15 The wicked are denied their light,
and their upraised arm is broken.

16 "Have you journeyed to the springs of
the sea
or walked in the recesses of the
deep?
17 Have the gates of death been shown
to you?
Have you seen the gates of the
deepest darkness?
18 Have you comprehended the vast
expanses of the earth?
Tell me, if you know all this.

19 "What is the way to the abode of
light?
And where does darkness reside?
20 Can you take them to their places?
Do you know the paths to their
dwellings?
21 Surely you know, for you were already
born!
You have lived so many years!

22 "Have you entered the storehouses of
the snow
or seen the storehouses of the hail,
23 which I reserve for times of trouble,
for days of war and battle?
24 What is the way to the place where
the lightning is dispersed,
or the place where the east winds
are scattered over the earth?
25 Who cuts a channel for the torrents of
rain,
and a path for the thunderstorm,
26 to water a land where no one lives,
an uninhabited desert,
27 to satisfy a desolate wasteland
and make it sprout with grass?
28 Does the rain have a father?
Who fathers the drops of dew?
29 From whose womb comes the ice?
Who gives birth to the frost from
the heavens
30 when the waters become hard as
stone,
when the surface of the deep is
frozen?

31 "Can you bind the chains[a] of the
Pleiades?
Can you loosen Orion's belt?
32 Can you bring forth the constellations
in their seasons[b]
or lead out the Bear[c] with its cubs?
33 Do you know the laws of the heavens?
Can you set up God's[d] dominion
over the earth?

34 "Can you raise your voice to the
clouds
and cover yourself with a flood of
water?
35 Do you send the lightning bolts on
their way?
Do they report to you, 'Here we
are'?
36 Who gives the ibis wisdom[e]
or gives the rooster
understanding?[f]
37 Who has the wisdom to count the
clouds?
Who can tip over the water jars of
the heavens
38 when the dust becomes hard
and the clods of earth stick
together?

39 "Do you hunt the prey for the lioness
and satisfy the hunger of the lions
40 when they crouch in their dens
or lie in wait in a thicket?
41 Who provides food for the raven
when its young cry out to God
and wander about for lack of food?

39 "Do you know when the
mountain goats give birth?
Do you watch when the doe bears
her fawn?
2 Do you count the months till they
bear?
Do you know the time they give
birth?
3 They crouch down and bring forth
their young;
their labor pains are ended.
4 Their young thrive and grow strong
in the wilds;
they leave and do not return.

5 "Who let the wild donkey go free?
Who untied its ropes?

[a] 31 Septuagint; Hebrew *beauty* [b] 32 Or *the morning star in its season* [c] 32 Or *out Leo* [d] 33 Or *their* [e] 36 That is, wisdom about the flooding of the Nile [f] 36 That is, understanding of when to crow; the meaning of the Hebrew for this verse is uncertain.

6 I gave it the wasteland as its home,
the salt flats as its habitat.
7 It laughs at the commotion in the town;
it does not hear a driver's shout.
8 It ranges the hills for its pasture
and searches for any green thing.

9 "Will the wild ox consent to serve you?
Will it stay by your manger at night?
10 Can you hold it to the furrow with a harness?
Will it till the valleys behind you?
11 Will you rely on it for its great strength?
Will you leave your heavy work to it?
12 Can you trust it to haul in your grain
and bring it to your threshing floor?

13 "The wings of the ostrich flap joyfully,
though they cannot compare
with the wings and feathers of the stork.
14 She lays her eggs on the ground
and lets them warm in the sand,
15 unmindful that a foot may crush them,
that some wild animal may trample them.
16 She treats her young harshly, as if they were not hers;
she cares not that her labor was in vain,
17 for God did not endow her with wisdom
or give her a share of good sense.
18 Yet when she spreads her feathers to run,
she laughs at horse and rider.

19 "Do you give the horse its strength
or clothe its neck with a flowing mane?
20 Do you make it leap like a locust,
striking terror with its proud snorting?
21 It paws fiercely, rejoicing in its strength,
and charges into the fray.
22 It laughs at fear, afraid of nothing;
it does not shy away from the sword.
23 The quiver rattles against its side,
along with the flashing spear and lance.
24 In frenzied excitement it eats up the ground;
it cannot stand still when the trumpet sounds.
25 At the blast of the trumpet it snorts, 'Aha!'
It catches the scent of battle from afar,
the shout of commanders and the battle cry.

26 "Does the hawk take flight by your wisdom
and spread its wings toward the south?
27 Does the eagle soar at your command
and build its nest on high?
28 It dwells on a cliff and stays there at night;
a rocky crag is its stronghold.
29 From there it looks for food;
its eyes detect it from afar.
30 Its young ones feast on blood,
and where the slain are, there it is."

40 The LORD said to Job:

2 "Will the one who contends with the Almighty correct him?
Let him who accuses God answer him!"

3 Then Job answered the LORD:

4 "I am unworthy — how can I reply to you?
I put my hand over my mouth.
5 I spoke once, but I have no answer —
twice, but I will say no more."

6 Then the LORD spoke to Job out of the storm:

7 "Brace yourself like a man;
I will question you,
and you shall answer me.

8 "Would you discredit my justice?
Would you condemn me to justify yourself?
9 Do you have an arm like God's,
and can your voice thunder like his?
10 Then adorn yourself with glory and splendor,
and clothe yourself in honor and majesty.
11 Unleash the fury of your wrath,
look at all who are proud and bring them low,
12 look at all who are proud and humble them,
crush the wicked where they stand.
13 Bury them all in the dust together;
shroud their faces in the grave.
14 Then I myself will admit to you
that your own right hand can save you.

15 "Look at Behemoth,
which I made along with you
and which feeds on grass like an ox.
16 What strength it has in its loins,
what power in the muscles of its
belly!
17 Its tail sways like a cedar;
the sinews of its thighs are close-
knit.
18 Its bones are tubes of bronze,
its limbs like rods of iron.
19 It ranks first among the works of God,
yet its Maker can approach it with
his sword.
20 The hills bring it their produce,
and all the wild animals play
nearby.
21 Under the lotus plants it lies,
hidden among the reeds in the
marsh.
22 The lotuses conceal it in their shadow;
the poplars by the stream surround
it.
23 A raging river does not alarm it;
it is secure, though the Jordan
should surge against its mouth.
24 Can anyone capture it by the eyes,
or trap it and pierce its nose?

41[a] "Can you pull in Leviathan with
a fishhook
or tie down its tongue with a rope?
2 Can you put a cord through its nose
or pierce its jaw with a hook?
3 Will it keep begging you for mercy?
Will it speak to you with gentle
words?
4 Will it make an agreement with you
for you to take it as your slave for
life?
5 Can you make a pet of it like a bird
or put it on a leash for the young
women in your house?
6 Will traders barter for it?
Will they divide it up among the
merchants?
7 Can you fill its hide with harpoons
or its head with fishing spears?
8 If you lay a hand on it,
you will remember the struggle
and never do it again!
9 Any hope of subduing it is false;
the mere sight of it is overpowering.
10 No one is fierce enough to rouse it.
Who then is able to stand against
me?
11 Who has a claim against me that I
must pay?
Everything under heaven belongs
to me.
12 "I will not fail to speak of Leviathan's
limbs,
its strength and its graceful form.
13 Who can strip off its outer coat?
Who can penetrate its double coat
of armor[b]?
14 Who dares open the doors of its
mouth,
ringed about with fearsome teeth?
15 Its back has[c] rows of shields
tightly sealed together;
16 each is so close to the next
that no air can pass between.
17 They are joined fast to one another;
they cling together and cannot be
parted.
18 Its snorting throws out flashes of
light;
its eyes are like the rays of dawn.
19 Flames stream from its mouth;
sparks of fire shoot out.
20 Smoke pours from its nostrils
as from a boiling pot over burning
reeds.
21 Its breath sets coals ablaze,
and flames dart from its mouth.
22 Strength resides in its neck;
dismay goes before it.
23 The folds of its flesh are tightly joined;
they are firm and immovable.
24 Its chest is hard as rock,
hard as a lower millstone.
25 When it rises up, the mighty are
terrified;
they retreat before its thrashing.
26 The sword that reaches it has no
effect,
nor does the spear or the dart or
the javelin.
27 Iron it treats like straw
and bronze like rotten wood.
28 Arrows do not make it flee;
slingstones are like chaff to it.
29 A club seems to it but a piece of straw;
it laughs at the rattling of the lance.
30 Its undersides are jagged potsherds,
leaving a trail in the mud like a
threshing sledge.
31 It makes the depths churn like a
boiling caldron
and stirs up the sea like a pot of
ointment.
32 It leaves a glistening wake behind it;
one would think the deep had
white hair.
33 Nothing on earth is its equal —
a creature without fear.
34 It looks down on all that are haughty;
it is king over all that are proud."

[a] In Hebrew texts 41:1-8 is numbered 40:25-32, and 41:9-34 is numbered 41:1-26.
[b] 13 Septuagint; Hebrew *double bridle* [c] 15 Or *Its pride is its*

Job

42 Then Job replied to the LORD:

2 "I know that you can do all things;
no purpose of yours can be
thwarted.
3 You asked, 'Who is this that obscures
my plans without knowledge?'
Surely I spoke of things I did not
understand,
things too wonderful for me to
know.

4 "You said, 'Listen now, and I will
speak;
I will question you,
and you shall answer me.'
5 My ears had heard of you
but now my eyes have seen you.
6 Therefore I despise myself
and repent in dust and ashes."

Epilogue

7 After the LORD had said these things
to Job, he said to Eliphaz the Temanite, "I
am angry with you and your two friends,
because you have not spoken the truth
about me, as my servant Job has. 8 So now
take seven bulls and seven rams and go to
my servant Job and sacrifice a burnt offering for yourselves. My servant Job will
pray for you, and I will accept his prayer
and not deal with you according to your
folly. You have not spoken the truth about
me, as my servant Job has." 9 So Eliphaz
the Temanite, Bildad the Shuhite and Zophar the Naamathite did what the LORD
told them; and the LORD accepted Job's
prayer.

10 After Job had prayed for his friends,
the LORD restored his fortunes and gave
him twice as much as he had before. 11 All
his brothers and sisters and everyone who
had known him before came and ate with
him in his house. They comforted and consoled him over all the trouble the LORD
had brought on him, and each one gave
him a piece of silver[a] and a gold ring.

12 The LORD blessed the latter part of
Job's life more than the former part. He
had fourteen thousand sheep, six thousand camels, a thousand yoke of oxen and
a thousand donkeys. 13 And he also had
seven sons and three daughters. 14 The first
daughter he named Jemimah, the second Keziah and the third Keren-Happuch.
15 Nowhere in all the land were there found
women as beautiful as Job's daughters,
and their father granted them an inheritance along with their brothers.

16 After this, Job lived a hundred and
forty years; he saw his children and their
children to the fourth generation. 17 And
so Job died, an old man and full of years.

[a] *11* Hebrew *him a kesitah;* a kesitah was a unit of money of unknown weight and value.

PSALMS

BOOK I

Psalms 1–41

Psalm 1

1 Blessed is the one
who does not walk in step with the wicked
or stand in the way that sinners take
or sit in the company of mockers,
2 but whose delight is in the law of the LORD,
and who meditates on his law day and night.
3 That person is like a tree planted by streams of water,
which yields its fruit in season
and whose leaf does not wither—
whatever they do prospers.

4 Not so the wicked!
They are like chaff
that the wind blows away.
5 Therefore the wicked will not stand in the judgment,
nor sinners in the assembly of the righteous.

6 For the LORD watches over the way of the righteous,
but the way of the wicked leads to destruction.

Psalm 2

1 Why do the nations conspire[a]
and the peoples plot in vain?
2 The kings of the earth rise up
and the rulers band together
against the LORD and against his anointed, saying,
3 "Let us break their chains
and throw off their shackles."

4 The One enthroned in heaven laughs;
the Lord scoffs at them.
5 He rebukes them in his anger
and terrifies them in his wrath, saying,
6 "I have installed my king
on Zion, my holy mountain."

7 I will proclaim the LORD's decree:

He said to me, "You are my son;
today I have become your father.
8 Ask me,
and I will make the nations your inheritance,
the ends of the earth your possession.
9 You will break them with a rod of iron[b];
you will dash them to pieces like pottery."

10 Therefore, you kings, be wise;
be warned, you rulers of the earth.
11 Serve the LORD with fear
and celebrate his rule with trembling.
12 Kiss his son, or he will be angry
and your way will lead to your destruction,
for his wrath can flare up in a moment.
Blessed are all who take refuge in him.

Psalm 3[c]

A psalm of David. When he fled from his son Absalom.

1 LORD, how many are my foes!
How many rise up against me!
2 Many are saying of me,
"God will not deliver him."[d]

3 But you, LORD, are a shield around me,
my glory, the One who lifts my head high.
4 I call out to the LORD,
and he answers me from his holy mountain.

5 I lie down and sleep;
I wake again, because the LORD sustains me.
6 I will not fear though tens of thousands
assail me on every side.

7 Arise, LORD!
Deliver me, my God!
Strike all my enemies on the jaw;
break the teeth of the wicked.

8 From the LORD comes deliverance.
May your blessing be on your people.

[a] *1* Hebrew; Septuagint *rage* [b] *9* Or *will rule them with an iron scepter* (see Septuagint and Syriac) [c] In Hebrew texts 3:1-8 is numbered 3:2-9. [d] *2* The Hebrew has *Selah* (a word of uncertain meaning) here and at the end of verses 4 and 8.

Psalm 4[a]

For the director of music. With stringed instruments. A psalm of David.

1 Answer me when I call to you,
my righteous God.
Give me relief from my distress;
have mercy on me and hear my
prayer.

2 How long will you people turn my
glory into shame?
How long will you love delusions
and seek false gods[b]?[c]
3 Know that the LORD has set apart his
faithful servant for himself;
the LORD hears when I call to him.

4 Tremble and[d] do not sin;
when you are on your beds,
search your hearts and be silent.
5 Offer the sacrifices of the righteous
and trust in the LORD.

6 Many, LORD, are asking, "Who will
bring us prosperity?"
Let the light of your face shine on
us.
7 Fill my heart with joy
when their grain and new wine
abound.

8 In peace I will lie down and sleep,
for you alone, LORD,
make me dwell in safety.

Psalm 5[e]

For the director of music. For pipes. A psalm of David.

1 Listen to my words, LORD,
consider my lament.
2 Hear my cry for help,
my King and my God,
for to you I pray.

3 In the morning, LORD, you hear my
voice;
in the morning I lay my requests
before you
and wait expectantly.
4 For you are not a God who is pleased
with wickedness;
with you, evil people are not
welcome.
5 The arrogant cannot stand
in your presence.
You hate all who do wrong;
6 you destroy those who tell lies.
The bloodthirsty and deceitful
you, LORD, detest.
7 But I, by your great love,
can come into your house;
in reverence I bow down
toward your holy temple.

8 Lead me, LORD, in your righteousness
because of my enemies —
make your way straight before me.
9 Not a word from their mouth can be
trusted;
their heart is filled with malice.
Their throat is an open grave;
with their tongues they tell lies.
10 Declare them guilty, O God!
Let their intrigues be their
downfall.
Banish them for their many sins,
for they have rebelled against you.
11 But let all who take refuge in you be
glad;
let them ever sing for joy.
Spread your protection over them,
that those who love your name
may rejoice in you.

12 Surely, LORD, you bless the righteous;
you surround them with your favor
as with a shield.

Psalm 6[f]

For the director of music. With stringed instruments. According to sheminith.[g] *A psalm of David.*

1 LORD, do not rebuke me in your anger
or discipline me in your wrath.
2 Have mercy on me, LORD, for I am
faint;
heal me, LORD, for my bones are in
agony.
3 My soul is in deep anguish.
How long, LORD, how long?

4 Turn, LORD, and deliver me;
save me because of your unfailing
love.
5 Among the dead no one proclaims
your name.
Who praises you from the grave?

6 I am worn out from my groaning.

All night long I flood my bed with
weeping
and drench my couch with tears.
7 My eyes grow weak with sorrow;
they fail because of all my foes.

8 Away from me, all you who do evil,
for the LORD has heard my
weeping.

[a] In Hebrew texts 4:1-8 is numbered 4:2-9. [b] 2 Or *seek lies* [c] 2 The Hebrew has *Selah* (a word of uncertain meaning) here and at the end of verse 4. [d] 4 Or *In your anger* (see Septuagint) [e] In Hebrew texts 5:1-12 is numbered 5:2-13. [f] In Hebrew texts 6:1-10 is numbered 6:2-11. [g] Title: Probably a musical term

[9] The LORD has heard my cry for mercy;
the LORD accepts my prayer.
[10] All my enemies will be overwhelmed
with shame and anguish;
they will turn back and suddenly
be put to shame.

Psalm 7[a]

A shiggaion[b] of David, which he sang to the LORD concerning Cush, a Benjamite.

[1] LORD my God, I take refuge in you;
save and deliver me from all who
pursue me,
[2] or they will tear me apart like a lion
and rip me to pieces with no one to
rescue me.
[3] LORD my God, if I have done this
and there is guilt on my hands —
[4] if I have repaid my ally with evil
or without cause have robbed my
foe —
[5] then let my enemy pursue and
overtake me;
let him trample my life to the
ground
and make me sleep in the dust.[c]

[6] Arise, LORD, in your anger;
rise up against the rage of my
enemies.
Awake, my God; decree justice.
[7] Let the assembled peoples gather
around you,
while you sit enthroned over them
on high.
[8] Let the LORD judge the peoples.
Vindicate me, LORD, according to my
righteousness,
according to my integrity, O Most
High.
[9] Bring to an end the violence of the
wicked
and make the righteous secure —
you, the righteous God
who probes minds and hearts.

[10] My shield[d] is God Most High,
who saves the upright in heart.
[11] God is a righteous judge,
a God who displays his wrath every
day.
[12] If he does not relent,
he[e] will sharpen his sword;
he will bend and string his bow.
[13] He has prepared his deadly weapons;
he makes ready his flaming arrows.
[14] Whoever is pregnant with evil
conceives trouble and gives birth
to disillusionment.
[15] Whoever digs a hole and scoops
it out
falls into the pit they have made.
[16] The trouble they cause recoils on
them;
their violence comes down on their
own heads.

[17] I will give thanks to the LORD because
of his righteousness;
I will sing the praises of the name
of the LORD Most High.

Psalm 8[f]

For the director of music. According to gittith.[g] A psalm of David.

[1] LORD, our Lord,
how majestic is your name in all
the earth!

You have set your glory
in the heavens.
[2] Through the praise of children and
infants
you have established a stronghold
against your enemies,
to silence the foe and the avenger.
[3] When I consider your heavens,
the work of your fingers,
the moon and the stars,
which you have set in place,
[4] what is mankind that you are
mindful of them,
human beings that you care for
them?[h]

[5] You have made them[i] a little lower
than the angels[j]
and crowned them[i] with glory and
honor.
[6] You made them rulers over the works
of your hands;
you put everything under their[k]
feet:
[7] all flocks and herds,
and the animals of the wild,
[8] the birds in the sky,
and the fish in the sea,
all that swim the paths of the seas.

[9] LORD, our Lord,
how majestic is your name in all
the earth!

[a] In Hebrew texts 7:1-17 is numbered 7:2-18. [b] Title: Probably a literary or musical term [c] 5 The Hebrew has *Selah* (a word of uncertain meaning) here. [d] 10 Or *sovereign* [e] 12 Or *If anyone does not repent, / God* [f] In Hebrew texts 8:1-9 is numbered 8:2-10. [g] Title: Probably a musical term [h] 4 Or *what is a human being that you are mindful of him, / a son of man that you care for him?* [i] 5 Or *him* [j] 5 Or *than God* [k] 6 Or *made him ruler . . . ; / . . . his*

Psalm 9[a,b]

For the director of music. To the tune of "The Death of the Son." A psalm of David.

1 I will give thanks to you, LORD, with all my heart;
I will tell of all your wonderful deeds.
2 I will be glad and rejoice in you;
I will sing the praises of your name, O Most High.

3 My enemies turn back;
they stumble and perish before you.
4 For you have upheld my right and my cause,
sitting enthroned as the righteous judge.
5 You have rebuked the nations and destroyed the wicked;
you have blotted out their name for ever and ever.
6 Endless ruin has overtaken my enemies,
you have uprooted their cities;
even the memory of them has perished.

7 The LORD reigns forever;
he has established his throne for judgment.
8 He rules the world in righteousness
and judges the peoples with equity.
9 The LORD is a refuge for the oppressed,
a stronghold in times of trouble.
10 Those who know your name trust in you,
for you, LORD, have never forsaken those who seek you.

11 Sing the praises of the LORD, enthroned in Zion;
proclaim among the nations what he has done.
12 For he who avenges blood remembers;
he does not ignore the cries of the afflicted.

13 LORD, see how my enemies persecute me!
Have mercy and lift me up from the gates of death,
14 that I may declare your praises
in the gates of Daughter Zion,
and there rejoice in your salvation.
15 The nations have fallen into the pit they have dug;
their feet are caught in the net they have hidden.
16 The LORD is known by his acts of justice;
the wicked are ensnared by the work of their hands.[c]
17 The wicked go down to the realm of the dead,
all the nations that forget God.
18 But God will never forget the needy;
the hope of the afflicted will never perish.

19 Arise, LORD, do not let mortals triumph;
let the nations be judged in your presence.
20 Strike them with terror, LORD;
let the nations know they are only mortal.

Psalm 10[a]

1 Why, LORD, do you stand far off?
Why do you hide yourself in times of trouble?

2 In his arrogance the wicked man hunts down the weak,
who are caught in the schemes he devises.
3 He boasts about the cravings of his heart;
he blesses the greedy and reviles the LORD.
4 In his pride the wicked man does not seek him;
in all his thoughts there is no room for God.
5 His ways are always prosperous;
your laws are rejected by[d] him;
he sneers at all his enemies.
6 He says to himself, "Nothing will ever shake me."
He swears, "No one will ever do me harm."

7 His mouth is full of lies and threats;
trouble and evil are under his tongue.
8 He lies in wait near the villages;
from ambush he murders the innocent.
His eyes watch in secret for his victims;
9 like a lion in cover he lies in wait.

[a] Psalms 9 and 10 may originally have been a single acrostic poem in which alternating lines began with the successive letters of the Hebrew alphabet. In the Septuagint they constitute one psalm. [b] In Hebrew texts 9:1-20 is numbered 9:2-21. [c] *16* The Hebrew has *Higgaion* and *Selah* (words of uncertain meaning) here; *Selah* occurs also at the end of verse 20. [d] *5* See Septuagint; Hebrew / *they are haughty, and your laws are far from*

He lies in wait to catch the helpless;
he catches the helpless and drags them off in his net.
10 His victims are crushed, they collapse;
they fall under his strength.
11 He says to himself, "God will never notice;
he covers his face and never sees."

12 Arise, LORD! Lift up your hand, O God.
Do not forget the helpless.
13 Why does the wicked man revile God?
Why does he say to himself,
"He won't call me to account"?
14 But you, God, see the trouble of the afflicted;
you consider their grief and take it in hand.
The victims commit themselves to you;
you are the helper of the fatherless.
15 Break the arm of the wicked man;
call the evildoer to account for his wickedness
that would not otherwise be found out.

16 The LORD is King for ever and ever;
the nations will perish from his land.
17 You, LORD, hear the desire of the afflicted;
you encourage them, and you listen to their cry,
18 defending the fatherless and the oppressed,
so that mere earthly mortals
will never again strike terror.

Psalm 11

For the director of music. Of David.

1 In the LORD I take refuge.
How then can you say to me:
"Flee like a bird to your mountain.
2 For look, the wicked bend their bows;
they set their arrows against the strings
to shoot from the shadows
at the upright in heart.
3 When the foundations are being destroyed,
what can the righteous do?"

4 The LORD is in his holy temple;
the LORD is on his heavenly throne.
He observes everyone on earth;
his eyes examine them.
5 The LORD examines the righteous,
but the wicked, those who love violence,
he hates with a passion.
6 On the wicked he will rain
fiery coals and burning sulfur;
a scorching wind will be their lot.

7 For the LORD is righteous,
he loves justice;
the upright will see his face.

Psalm 12[a]

For the director of music. According to sheminith.[b] *A psalm of David.*

1 Help, LORD, for no one is faithful anymore;
those who are loyal have vanished from the human race.
2 Everyone lies to their neighbor;
they flatter with their lips
but harbor deception in their hearts.

3 May the LORD silence all flattering lips
and every boastful tongue —
4 those who say,
"By our tongues we will prevail;
our own lips will defend us — who is lord over us?"

5 "Because the poor are plundered and the needy groan,
I will now arise," says the LORD.
"I will protect them from those who malign them."
6 And the words of the LORD are flawless,
like silver purified in a crucible,
like gold[c] refined seven times.

7 You, LORD, will keep the needy safe
and will protect us forever from the wicked,
8 who freely strut about
when what is vile is honored by the human race.

Psalm 13[d]

For the director of music. A psalm of David.

1 How long, LORD? Will you forget me forever?
How long will you hide your face from me?
2 How long must I wrestle with my thoughts
and day after day have sorrow in my heart?
How long will my enemy triumph over me?

[a] In Hebrew texts 12:1-8 is numbered 12:2-9. [b] Title: Probably a musical term [c] 6 Probable reading of the original Hebrew text; Masoretic Text *earth* [d] In Hebrew texts 13:1-6 is numbered 13:2-6.

3 Look on me and answer, LORD my God.
Give light to my eyes, or I will sleep in death,
4 and my enemy will say, "I have overcome him,"
and my foes will rejoice when I fall.

5 But I trust in your unfailing love;
my heart rejoices in your salvation.
6 I will sing the LORD's praise,
for he has been good to me.

Psalm 14

For the director of music. Of David.

1 The fool[a] says in his heart,
"There is no God."
They are corrupt, their deeds are vile;
there is no one who does good.

2 The LORD looks down from heaven
on all mankind
to see if there are any who understand,
any who seek God.
3 All have turned away, all have become corrupt;
there is no one who does good,
not even one.

4 Do all these evildoers know nothing?

They devour my people as though eating bread;
they never call on the LORD.
5 But there they are, overwhelmed with dread,
for God is present in the company of the righteous.
6 You evildoers frustrate the plans of the poor,
but the LORD is their refuge.

7 Oh, that salvation for Israel would come out of Zion!
When the LORD restores his people,
let Jacob rejoice and Israel be glad!

Psalm 15

A psalm of David.

1 LORD, who may dwell in your sacred tent?
Who may live on your holy mountain?

2 The one whose walk is blameless,
who does what is righteous,
who speaks the truth from their heart;
3 whose tongue utters no slander,
who does no wrong to a neighbor,
and casts no slur on others;
4 who despises a vile person
but honors those who fear the LORD;
who keeps an oath even when it hurts,
and does not change their mind;
5 who lends money to the poor without interest;
who does not accept a bribe against the innocent.

Whoever does these things
will never be shaken.

Psalm 16

A miktam[b] of David.

1 Keep me safe, my God,
for in you I take refuge.

2 I say to the LORD, "You are my Lord;
apart from you I have no good thing."
3 I say of the holy people who are in the land,
"They are the noble ones in whom is all my delight."
4 Those who run after other gods will suffer more and more.
I will not pour out libations of blood to such gods
or take up their names on my lips.

5 LORD, you alone are my portion and my cup;
you make my lot secure.
6 The boundary lines have fallen for me in pleasant places;
surely I have a delightful inheritance.
7 I will praise the LORD, who counsels me;
even at night my heart instructs me.
8 I keep my eyes always on the LORD.
With him at my right hand, I will not be shaken.

9 Therefore my heart is glad and my tongue rejoices;
my body also will rest secure,
10 because you will not abandon me to the realm of the dead,
nor will you let your faithful[c] one see decay.
11 You make known to me the path of life;
you will fill me with joy in your presence,
with eternal pleasures at your right hand.

[a] *1* The Hebrew words rendered *fool* in Psalms denote one who is morally deficient. [b] Title: Probably a literary or musical term [c] *10* Or *holy*

Psalm 17

A prayer of David.

1 Hear me, LORD, my plea is just;
listen to my cry.
Hear my prayer—
it does not rise from deceitful lips.
2 Let my vindication come from you;
may your eyes see what is right.

3 Though you probe my heart,
though you examine me at night and test me,
you will find that I have planned no evil;
my mouth has not transgressed.
4 Though people tried to bribe me,
I have kept myself from the ways of the violent
through what your lips have commanded.
5 My steps have held to your paths;
my feet have not stumbled.

6 I call on you, my God, for you will answer me;
turn your ear to me and hear my prayer.
7 Show me the wonders of your great love,
you who save by your right hand
those who take refuge in you from their foes.
8 Keep me as the apple of your eye;
hide me in the shadow of your wings
9 from the wicked who are out to destroy me,
from my mortal enemies who surround me.

10 They close up their callous hearts,
and their mouths speak with arrogance.
11 They have tracked me down, they now surround me,
with eyes alert, to throw me to the ground.
12 They are like a lion hungry for prey,
like a fierce lion crouching in cover.

13 Rise up, LORD, confront them, bring them down;
with your sword rescue me from the wicked.
14 By your hand save me from such people, LORD,
from those of this world whose reward is in this life.
May what you have stored up for the wicked fill their bellies;
may their children gorge themselves on it,
and may there be leftovers for their little ones.

15 As for me, I will be vindicated and will see your face;
when I awake, I will be satisfied
with seeing your likeness.

Psalm 18[a]

For the director of music. Of David the servant of the LORD. He sang to the LORD the words of this song when the LORD delivered him from the hand of all his enemies and from the hand of Saul. He said:

1 I love you, LORD, my strength.

2 The LORD is my rock, my fortress and my deliverer;
my God is my rock, in whom I take refuge,
my shield[b] and the horn[c] of my salvation, my stronghold.

3 I called to the LORD, who is worthy of praise,
and I have been saved from my enemies.
4 The cords of death entangled me;
the torrents of destruction overwhelmed me.
5 The cords of the grave coiled around me;
the snares of death confronted me.

6 In my distress I called to the LORD;
I cried to my God for help.
From his temple he heard my voice;
my cry came before him, into his ears.
7 The earth trembled and quaked,
and the foundations of the mountains shook;
they trembled because he was angry.
8 Smoke rose from his nostrils;
consuming fire came from his mouth,
burning coals blazed out of it.
9 He parted the heavens and came down;
dark clouds were under his feet.
10 He mounted the cherubim and flew;
he soared on the wings of the wind.
11 He made darkness his covering, his canopy around him—
the dark rain clouds of the sky.
12 Out of the brightness of his presence clouds advanced,
with hailstones and bolts of lightning.

[a] In Hebrew texts 18:1-50 is numbered 18:2-51. [b] 2 Or *sovereign* [c] 2 *Horn* here symbolizes strength.

[13]The LORD thundered from heaven;
the voice of the Most High resounded.[a]
[14]He shot his arrows and scattered the enemy,
with great bolts of lightning he routed them.
[15]The valleys of the sea were exposed
and the foundations of the earth laid bare
at your rebuke, LORD,
at the blast of breath from your nostrils.

[16]He reached down from on high and took hold of me;
he drew me out of deep waters.
[17]He rescued me from my powerful enemy,
from my foes, who were too strong for me.
[18]They confronted me in the day of my disaster,
but the LORD was my support.
[19]He brought me out into a spacious place;
he rescued me because he delighted in me.

[20]The LORD has dealt with me according to my righteousness;
according to the cleanness of my hands he has rewarded me.
[21]For I have kept the ways of the LORD;
I am not guilty of turning from my God.
[22]All his laws are before me;
I have not turned away from his decrees.
[23]I have been blameless before him
and have kept myself from sin.
[24]The LORD has rewarded me according to my righteousness,
according to the cleanness of my hands in his sight.

[25]To the faithful you show yourself faithful,
to the blameless you show yourself blameless,
[26]to the pure you show yourself pure,
but to the devious you show yourself shrewd.
[27]You save the humble
but bring low those whose eyes are haughty.
[28]You, LORD, keep my lamp burning;
my God turns my darkness into light.
[29]With your help I can advance against a troop[b];
with my God I can scale a wall.

[30]As for God, his way is perfect:
The LORD's word is flawless;
he shields all who take refuge in him.
[31]For who is God besides the LORD?
And who is the Rock except our God?
[32]It is God who arms me with strength
and keeps my way secure.
[33]He makes my feet like the feet of a deer;
he causes me to stand on the heights.
[34]He trains my hands for battle;
my arms can bend a bow of bronze.
[35]You make your saving help my shield,
and your right hand sustains me;
your help has made me great.
[36]You provide a broad path for my feet,
so that my ankles do not give way.

[37]I pursued my enemies and overtook them;
I did not turn back till they were destroyed.
[38]I crushed them so that they could not rise;
they fell beneath my feet.
[39]You armed me with strength for battle;
you humbled my adversaries before me.
[40]You made my enemies turn their backs in flight,
and I destroyed my foes.
[41]They cried for help, but there was no one to save them—
to the LORD, but he did not answer.
[42]I beat them as fine as windblown dust;
I trampled them[c] like mud in the streets.
[43]You have delivered me from the attacks of the people;
you have made me the head of nations.
People I did not know now serve me,
[44]foreigners cower before me;
as soon as they hear of me, they obey me.
[45]They all lose heart;
they come trembling from their strongholds.

[a] *13* Some Hebrew manuscripts and Septuagint (see also 2 Samuel 22:14); most Hebrew manuscripts *resounded, / amid hailstones and bolts of lightning* [b] *29* Or *can run through a barricade* [c] *42* Many Hebrew manuscripts, Septuagint, Syriac and Targum (see also 2 Samuel 22:43); Masoretic Text *I poured them out*

46 The LORD lives! Praise be to my Rock!
Exalted be God my Savior!
47 He is the God who avenges me,
who subdues nations under me,
48 who saves me from my enemies.
You exalted me above my foes;
from a violent man you rescued
me.
49 Therefore I will praise you, LORD,
among the nations;
I will sing the praises of
your name.

50 He gives his king great victories;
he shows unfailing love to his
anointed,
to David and to his descendants
forever.

Psalm 19[a]

For the director of music. A psalm of David.

1 The heavens declare the glory of God;
the skies proclaim the work of his
hands.
2 Day after day they pour forth speech;
night after night they reveal
knowledge.
3 They have no speech, they use no
words;
no sound is heard from them.
4 Yet their voice[b] goes out into all the
earth,
their words to the ends of the
world.
In the heavens God has pitched a tent
for the sun.
5 It is like a bridegroom coming out
of his chamber,
like a champion rejoicing to run his
course.
6 It rises at one end of the heavens
and makes its circuit to the other;
nothing is deprived of its warmth.

7 The law of the LORD is perfect,
refreshing the soul.
The statutes of the LORD are
trustworthy,
making wise the simple.
8 The precepts of the LORD are right,
giving joy to the heart.
The commands of the LORD are
radiant,
giving light to the eyes.
9 The fear of the LORD is pure,
enduring forever.
The decrees of the LORD are firm,
and all of them are righteous.

10 They are more precious than gold,
than much pure gold;
they are sweeter than honey,
than honey from the honeycomb.
11 By them your servant is warned;
in keeping them there is great
reward.
12 But who can discern their own errors?
Forgive my hidden faults.
13 Keep your servant also from willful
sins;
may they not rule over me.
Then I will be blameless,
innocent of great transgression.

14 May these words of my mouth and
this meditation of my heart
be pleasing in your sight,
LORD, my Rock and my Redeemer.

Psalm 20[c]

For the director of music. A psalm of David.

1 May the LORD answer you when you
are in distress;
may the name of the God of Jacob
protect you.
2 May he send you help from the
sanctuary
and grant you support from Zion.
3 May he remember all
your sacrifices
and accept your burnt offerings.[d]
4 May he give you the desire of your
heart
and make all your plans succeed.
5 May we shout for joy over
your victory
and lift up our banners in the
name of our God.

May the LORD grant all your requests.

6 Now this I know:
The LORD gives victory to his
anointed.
He answers him from his heavenly
sanctuary
with the victorious power of his
right hand.
7 Some trust in chariots and some in
horses,
but we trust in the name of the
LORD our God.
8 They are brought to their knees and
fall,
but we rise up and stand firm.
9 LORD, give victory to the king!
Answer us when we call!

[a] In Hebrew texts 19:1-14 is numbered 19:2-15. [b] 4 Septuagint, Jerome and Syriac; Hebrew *measuring line* [c] In Hebrew texts 20:1-9 is numbered 20:2-10. [d] 3 The Hebrew has *Selah* (a word of uncertain meaning) here.

Psalm 21[a]

For the director of music. A psalm of David.

1 The king rejoices in your strength, LORD.
How great is his joy in the victories you give!

2 You have granted him his heart's desire
and have not withheld the request of his lips.[b]
3 You came to greet him with rich blessings
and placed a crown of pure gold on his head.
4 He asked you for life, and you gave it to him —
length of days, for ever and ever.
5 Through the victories you gave, his glory is great;
you have bestowed on him splendor and majesty.
6 Surely you have granted him unending blessings
and made him glad with the joy of your presence.
7 For the king trusts in the LORD;
through the unfailing love of the Most High
he will not be shaken.

8 Your hand will lay hold on all your enemies;
your right hand will seize your foes.
9 When you appear for battle,
you will burn them up as in a blazing furnace.
The LORD will swallow them up in his wrath,
and his fire will consume them.
10 You will destroy their descendants from the earth,
their posterity from mankind.
11 Though they plot evil against you
and devise wicked schemes, they cannot succeed.
12 You will make them turn their backs
when you aim at them with drawn bow.

13 Be exalted in your strength, LORD;
we will sing and praise your might.

Psalm 22[c]

For the director of music. To the tune of "The Doe of the Morning." A psalm of David.

1 My God, my God, why have you forsaken me?
Why are you so far from saving me,
so far from my cries of anguish?
2 My God, I cry out by day, but you do not answer,
by night, but I find no rest.[d]

3 Yet you are enthroned as the Holy One;
you are the one Israel praises.[e]
4 In you our ancestors put their trust;
they trusted and you delivered them.
5 To you they cried out and were saved;
in you they trusted and were not put to shame.

6 But I am a worm and not a man,
scorned by everyone, despised by the people.
7 All who see me mock me;
they hurl insults, shaking their heads.
8 "He trusts in the LORD," they say,
"let the LORD rescue him.
Let him deliver him,
since he delights in him."

9 Yet you brought me out of the womb;
you made me trust in you, even at my mother's breast.
10 From birth I was cast on you;
from my mother's womb you have been my God.

11 Do not be far from me,
for trouble is near
and there is no one to help.

12 Many bulls surround me;
strong bulls of Bashan encircle me.
13 Roaring lions that tear their prey
open their mouths wide against me.
14 I am poured out like water,
and all my bones are out of joint.
My heart has turned to wax;
it has melted within me.
15 My mouth[f] is dried up like a potsherd,
and my tongue sticks to the roof of my mouth;
you lay me in the dust of death.

[a] In Hebrew texts 21:1-13 is numbered 21:2-14. [b] 2 The Hebrew has *Selah* (a word of uncertain meaning) here. [c] In Hebrew texts 22:1-31 is numbered 22:2-32. [d] 2 Or *night, and am not silent* [e] 3 Or *Yet you are holy, / enthroned on the praises of Israel* [f] 15 Probable reading of the original Hebrew text; Masoretic Text *strength*

16 Dogs surround me,
a pack of villains encircles me;
they pierce[a] my hands and my feet.
17 All my bones are on display;
people stare and gloat over me.
18 They divide my clothes among them
and cast lots for my garment.

19 But you, LORD, do not be far from me.
You are my strength; come quickly
to help me.
20 Deliver me from the sword,
my precious life from the power of
the dogs.
21 Rescue me from the mouth of the lions;
save me from the horns of the wild
oxen.

22 I will declare your name to my people;
in the assembly I will praise you.
23 You who fear the LORD, praise him!
All you descendants of Jacob,
honor him!
Revere him, all you descendants of
Israel!
24 For he has not despised or scorned
the suffering of the afflicted one;
he has not hidden his face from him
but has listened to his cry for help.

25 From you comes the theme of my
praise in the great assembly;
before those who fear you[b] I will
fulfill my vows.
26 The poor will eat and be satisfied;
those who seek the LORD will praise
him —
may your hearts live forever!

27 All the ends of the earth
will remember and turn to the
LORD,
and all the families of the nations
will bow down before him,
28 for dominion belongs to the LORD
and he rules over the nations.

29 All the rich of the earth will feast and
worship;
all who go down to the dust will
kneel before him —
those who cannot keep themselves
alive.
30 Posterity will serve him;
future generations will be told
about the Lord.
31 They will proclaim his righteousness,
declaring to a people yet unborn:
He has done it!

Psalm 23

A psalm of David.

1 The LORD is my shepherd, I lack
nothing.
2 He makes me lie down in green
pastures,
he leads me beside quiet waters,
3 he refreshes my soul.
He guides me along the right paths
for his name's sake.
4 Even though I walk
through the darkest valley,[c]
I will fear no evil,
for you are with me;
your rod and your staff,
they comfort me.

5 You prepare a table before me
in the presence of my enemies.
You anoint my head with oil;
my cup overflows.
6 Surely your goodness and love will
follow me
all the days of my life,
and I will dwell in the house
of the LORD
forever.

Psalm 24

Of David. A psalm.

1 The earth is the LORD's, and
everything in it,
the world, and all who live in it;
2 for he founded it on the seas
and established it on the waters.

3 Who may ascend the mountain of the
LORD?
Who may stand in his holy place?
4 The one who has clean hands and a
pure heart,
who does not trust in an idol
or swear by a false god.[d]
5 They will receive blessing from the
LORD
and vindication from God their
Savior.
6 Such is the generation of those who
seek him,
who seek your face, God of Jacob.[e,f]

7 Lift up your heads, you gates;
be lifted up, you ancient doors,
that the King of glory may
come in.

[a] *16* Dead Sea Scrolls and some manuscripts of the Masoretic Text, Septuagint and Syriac; most manuscripts of the Masoretic Text *me, / like a lion* [b] *25* Hebrew *him* [c] *4* Or *the valley of the shadow of death* [d] *4* Or *swear falsely* [e] *6* Two Hebrew manuscripts and Syriac (see also Septuagint); most Hebrew manuscripts *face, Jacob* [f] *6* The Hebrew has *Selah* (a word of uncertain meaning) here and at the end of verse 10.

8 Who is this King of glory?
The LORD strong and mighty,
the LORD mighty in battle.
9 Lift up your heads, you gates;
lift them up, you ancient doors,
that the King of glory may come in.
10 Who is he, this King of glory?
The LORD Almighty —
he is the King of glory.

Psalm 25[a]

Of David.

1 In you, LORD my God,
I put my trust.

2 I trust in you;
do not let me be put to shame,
nor let my enemies triumph over me.
3 No one who hopes in you
will ever be put to shame,
but shame will come on those
who are treacherous without cause.

4 Show me your ways, LORD,
teach me your paths.
5 Guide me in your truth and teach me,
for you are God my Savior,
and my hope is in you all day long.
6 Remember, LORD, your great mercy
and love,
for they are from of old.
7 Do not remember the sins of my youth
and my rebellious ways;
according to your love remember me,
for you, LORD, are good.

8 Good and upright is the LORD;
therefore he instructs sinners in his
ways.
9 He guides the humble in what is right
and teaches them his way.
10 All the ways of the LORD are loving
and faithful
toward those who keep the
demands of his covenant.
11 For the sake of your name, LORD,
forgive my iniquity, though it is
great.

12 Who, then, are those who fear the
LORD?
He will instruct them in the ways
they should choose.[b]
13 They will spend their days in
prosperity,
and their descendants will inherit
the land.
14 The LORD confides in those who fear
him;
he makes his covenant known to
them.
15 My eyes are ever on the LORD,
for only he will release my feet
from the snare.

16 Turn to me and be gracious to me,
for I am lonely and afflicted.
17 Relieve the troubles of my heart
and free me from my anguish.
18 Look on my affliction and my distress
and take away all my sins.
19 See how numerous are my enemies
and how fiercely they hate me!

20 Guard my life and rescue me;
do not let me be put to shame,
for I take refuge in you.
21 May integrity and uprightness
protect me,
because my hope, LORD,[c] is in you.

22 Deliver Israel, O God,
from all their troubles!

Psalm 26

Of David.

1 Vindicate me, LORD,
for I have led a blameless life;
I have trusted in the LORD
and have not faltered.
2 Test me, LORD, and try me,
examine my heart and my mind;
3 for I have always been mindful of
your unfailing love
and have lived in reliance on your
faithfulness.

4 I do not sit with the deceitful,
nor do I associate with hypocrites.
5 I abhor the assembly of evildoers
and refuse to sit with the wicked.
6 I wash my hands in innocence,
and go about your altar, LORD,
7 proclaiming aloud your praise
and telling of all your wonderful
deeds.

8 LORD, I love the house where you live,
the place where your glory dwells.
9 Do not take away my soul along with
sinners,
my life with those who are
bloodthirsty,
10 in whose hands are wicked schemes,
whose right hands are full of
bribes.
11 I lead a blameless life;
deliver me and be merciful to me.

12 My feet stand on level ground;
in the great congregation I will
praise the LORD.

[a] This psalm is an acrostic poem, the verses of which begin with the successive letters of the Hebrew alphabet. [b] *12* Or *ways he chooses* [c] *21* Septuagint; Hebrew does not have *LORD*.

Psalm 27

Of David.

[1]The LORD is my light and my
salvation —
whom shall I fear?
The LORD is the stronghold of my
life —
of whom shall I be afraid?

[2]When the wicked advance against me
to devour[a] me,
it is my enemies and my foes
who will stumble and fall.
[3]Though an army besiege me,
my heart will not fear;
though war break out against me,
even then I will be confident.

[4]One thing I ask from the LORD,
this only do I seek:
that I may dwell in the house
of the LORD
all the days of my life,
to gaze on the beauty of the LORD
and to seek him in his temple.
[5]For in the day of trouble
he will keep me safe in his
dwelling;
he will hide me in the shelter of his
sacred tent
and set me high upon a rock.

[6]Then my head will be exalted
above the enemies who surround
me;
at his sacred tent I will sacrifice with
shouts of joy;
I will sing and make music to the
LORD.

[7]Hear my voice when I call, LORD;
be merciful to me and
answer me.
[8]My heart says of you, "Seek
his face!"
Your face, LORD, I will seek.
[9]Do not hide your face from me,
do not turn your servant away in
anger;
you have been my helper.
Do not reject me or forsake me,
God my Savior.
[10]Though my father and mother
forsake me,
the LORD will receive me.
[11]Teach me your way, LORD;
lead me in a straight path
because of my oppressors.
[12]Do not turn me over to the desire of
my foes,
for false witnesses rise up against
me,
spouting malicious accusations.
[13]I remain confident of this:
I will see the goodness of the LORD
in the land of the living.
[14]Wait for the LORD;
be strong and take heart
and wait for the LORD.

Psalm 28

Of David.

[1]To you, LORD, I call;
you are my Rock,
do not turn a deaf ear to me.
For if you remain silent,
I will be like those who go down
to the pit.
[2]Hear my cry for mercy
as I call to you for help,
as I lift up my hands
toward your Most Holy Place.

[3]Do not drag me away with the wicked,
with those who do evil,
who speak cordially with their
neighbors
but harbor malice in their hearts.
[4]Repay them for their deeds
and for their evil work;
repay them for what their hands have
done
and bring back on them what they
deserve.

[5]Because they have no regard for the
deeds of the LORD
and what his hands have done,
he will tear them down
and never build them up again.

[6]Praise be to the LORD,
for he has heard my cry for mercy.
[7]The LORD is my strength and my
shield;
my heart trusts in him, and he
helps me.
My heart leaps for joy,
and with my song I praise him.

[8]The LORD is the strength of his people,
a fortress of salvation for his
anointed one.
[9]Save your people and bless your
inheritance;
be their shepherd and carry them
forever.

[a] 2 Or *slander*

Psalm 29

A psalm of David.

[1]Ascribe to the LORD, you heavenly
beings,
ascribe to the LORD glory and
strength.
[2]Ascribe to the LORD the glory due his
name;
worship the LORD in the splendor of
his[a] holiness.

[3]The voice of the LORD is over the waters;
the God of glory thunders,
the LORD thunders over the mighty
waters.
[4]The voice of the LORD is powerful;
the voice of the LORD is majestic.
[5]The voice of the LORD breaks the
cedars;
the LORD breaks in pieces the
cedars of Lebanon.
[6]He makes Lebanon leap like a calf,
Sirion[b] like a young wild ox.
[7]The voice of the LORD strikes
with flashes of lightning.
[8]The voice of the LORD shakes the
desert;
the LORD shakes the Desert of
Kadesh.
[9]The voice of the LORD twists the oaks[c]
and strips the forests bare.
And in his temple all cry, "Glory!"

[10]The LORD sits enthroned over the
flood;
the LORD is enthroned as King
forever.
[11]The LORD gives strength to his people;
the LORD blesses his people with
peace.

Psalm 30[d]

A psalm. A song. For the dedication of the temple.[e] Of David.

[1]I will exalt you, LORD,
for you lifted me out of the depths
and did not let my enemies gloat
over me.
[2]LORD my God, I called to you for help,
and you healed me.
[3]You, LORD, brought me up from the
realm of the dead;
you spared me from going down to
the pit.

[4]Sing the praises of the LORD, you his
faithful people;
praise his holy name.
[5]For his anger lasts only a moment,
but his favor lasts a lifetime;
weeping may stay for the night,
but rejoicing comes in the morning.

[6]When I felt secure, I said,
"I will never be shaken."
[7]LORD, when you favored me,
you made my royal mountain[f]
stand firm;
but when you hid your face,
I was dismayed.

[8]To you, LORD, I called;
to the Lord I cried for mercy:
[9]"What is gained if I am silenced,
if I go down to the pit?
Will the dust praise you?
Will it proclaim your faithfulness?
[10]Hear, LORD, and be merciful to me;
LORD, be my help."

[11]You turned my wailing into dancing;
you removed my sackcloth and
clothed me with joy,
[12]that my heart may sing your praises
and not be silent.
LORD my God, I will praise you
forever.

Psalm 31[g]

For the director of music. A psalm of David.

[1]In you, LORD, I have taken refuge;
let me never be put to shame;
deliver me in your righteousness.
[2]Turn your ear to me,
come quickly to my rescue;
be my rock of refuge,
a strong fortress to save me.
[3]Since you are my rock and my
fortress,
for the sake of your name lead and
guide me.
[4]Keep me free from the trap that is set
for me,
for you are my refuge.
[5]Into your hands I commit my spirit;
deliver me, LORD, my faithful God.

[6]I hate those who cling to worthless
idols;
as for me, I trust in the LORD.
[7]I will be glad and rejoice in your love,
for you saw my affliction
and knew the anguish of my soul.
[8]You have not given me into the hands
of the enemy
but have set my feet in a spacious
place.

[a] 2 Or *LORD with the splendor of* [b] 6 That is, Mount Hermon [c] 9 Or *LORD makes the deer give birth* [d] In Hebrew texts 30:1-12 is numbered 30:2-13. [e] Title: Or *palace* [f] 7 That is, Mount Zion
[g] In Hebrew texts 31:1-24 is numbered 31:2-25.

9 Be merciful to me, LORD, for I am in
distress;
my eyes grow weak with sorrow,
my soul and body with grief.
10 My life is consumed by anguish
and my years by groaning;
my strength fails because of my
affliction,[a]
and my bones grow weak.
11 Because of all my enemies,
I am the utter contempt of my
neighbors
and an object of dread to my closest
friends—
those who see me on the street flee
from me.
12 I am forgotten as though I were dead;
I have become like broken pottery.
13 For I hear many whispering,
"Terror on every side!"
They conspire against me
and plot to take my life.

14 But I trust in you, LORD;
I say, "You are my God."
15 My times are in your hands;
deliver me from the hands of my
enemies,
from those who pursue me.
16 Let your face shine on your servant;
save me in your unfailing love.
17 Let me not be put to shame, LORD,
for I have cried out to you;
but let the wicked be put to shame
and be silent in the realm of the
dead.
18 Let their lying lips be silenced,
for with pride and contempt
they speak arrogantly against the
righteous.

19 How abundant are the good things
that you have stored up for those
who fear you,
that you bestow in the sight of all,
on those who take refuge in you.
20 In the shelter of your presence you
hide them
from all human intrigues;
you keep them safe in your dwelling
from accusing tongues.
21 Praise be to the LORD,
for he showed me the wonders of
his love
when I was in a city under siege.
22 In my alarm I said,
"I am cut off from your sight!"
Yet you heard my cry for mercy
when I called to you for help.

23 Love the LORD, all his faithful people!
The LORD preserves those who are
true to him,
but the proud he pays back in full.
24 Be strong and take heart,
all you who hope in the LORD.

Psalm 32

Of David. A maskil.[b]

1 Blessed is the one
whose transgressions are forgiven,
whose sins are covered.
2 Blessed is the one
whose sin the LORD does not count
against them
and in whose spirit is no deceit.

3 When I kept silent,
my bones wasted away
through my groaning all day long.
4 For day and night
your hand was heavy on me;
my strength was sapped
as in the heat of summer.[c]

5 Then I acknowledged my sin to you
and did not cover up my iniquity.
I said, "I will confess
my transgressions to the LORD."
And you forgave
the guilt of my sin.

6 Therefore let all the faithful pray to
you
while you may be found;
surely the rising of the mighty waters
will not reach them.
7 You are my hiding place;
you will protect me from trouble
and surround me with songs of
deliverance.

8 I will instruct you and teach you in
the way you should go;
I will counsel you with my loving
eye on you.
9 Do not be like the horse or the mule,
which have no understanding
but must be controlled by bit and
bridle
or they will not come to you.
10 Many are the woes of the wicked,
but the LORD's unfailing love
surrounds the one who trusts in
him.

11 Rejoice in the LORD and be glad, you
righteous;
sing, all you who are upright in
heart!

[a] *10* Or *guilt* [b] Title: Probably a literary or musical term [c] *4* The Hebrew has *Selah* (a word of uncertain meaning) here and at the end of verses 5 and 7.

Psalm 33

1 Sing joyfully to the LORD, you righteous;
it is fitting for the upright to praise him.
2 Praise the LORD with the harp;
make music to him on the ten-stringed lyre.
3 Sing to him a new song;
play skillfully, and shout for joy.

4 For the word of the LORD is right and true;
he is faithful in all he does.
5 The LORD loves righteousness and justice;
the earth is full of his unfailing love.

6 By the word of the LORD the heavens were made,
their starry host by the breath of his mouth.
7 He gathers the waters of the sea into jars[a];
he puts the deep into storehouses.
8 Let all the earth fear the LORD;
let all the people of the world revere him.
9 For he spoke, and it came to be;
he commanded, and it stood firm.

10 The LORD foils the plans of the nations;
he thwarts the purposes of the peoples.
11 But the plans of the LORD stand firm forever,
the purposes of his heart through all generations.

12 Blessed is the nation whose God is the LORD,
the people he chose for his inheritance.
13 From heaven the LORD looks down
and sees all mankind;
14 from his dwelling place he watches
all who live on earth—
15 he who forms the hearts of all,
who considers everything they do.

16 No king is saved by the size of his army;
no warrior escapes by his great strength.
17 A horse is a vain hope for deliverance;
despite all its great strength it cannot save.
18 But the eyes of the LORD are on those who fear him,
on those whose hope is in his unfailing love,
19 to deliver them from death
and keep them alive in famine.

20 We wait in hope for the LORD;
he is our help and our shield.
21 In him our hearts rejoice,
for we trust in his holy name.
22 May your unfailing love be with us, LORD,
even as we put our hope in you.

Psalm 34[b,c]

Of David. When he pretended to be insane before Abimelek, who drove him away, and he left.

1 I will extol the LORD at all times;
his praise will always be on my lips.
2 I will glory in the LORD;
let the afflicted hear and rejoice.
3 Glorify the LORD with me;
let us exalt his name together.

4 I sought the LORD, and he answered me;
he delivered me from all my fears.
5 Those who look to him are radiant;
their faces are never covered with shame.
6 This poor man called, and the LORD heard him;
he saved him out of all his troubles.
7 The angel of the LORD encamps around those who fear him,
and he delivers them.

8 Taste and see that the LORD is good;
blessed is the one who takes refuge in him.
9 Fear the LORD, you his holy people,
for those who fear him lack nothing.
10 The lions may grow weak and hungry,
but those who seek the LORD lack no good thing.
11 Come, my children, listen to me;
I will teach you the fear of the LORD.
12 Whoever of you loves life
and desires to see many good days,
13 keep your tongue from evil
and your lips from telling lies.
14 Turn from evil and do good;
seek peace and pursue it.

15 The eyes of the LORD are on the righteous,
and his ears are attentive to their cry;

[a] 7 Or *sea as into a heap* [b] This psalm is an acrostic poem, the verses of which begin with the successive letters of the Hebrew alphabet. [c] In Hebrew texts 34:1-22 is numbered 34:2-23.

16 but the face of the LORD is against
those who do evil,
to blot out their name from the
earth.

17 The righteous cry out, and the LORD
hears them;
he delivers them from all their
troubles.
18 The LORD is close to the
brokenhearted
and saves those who are crushed in
spirit.

19 The righteous person may have many
troubles,
but the LORD delivers him from
them all;
20 he protects all his bones,
not one of them will be broken.

21 Evil will slay the wicked;
the foes of the righteous will be
condemned.
22 The LORD will rescue his servants;
no one who takes refuge in him will
be condemned.

Psalm 35

Of David.

1 Contend, LORD, with those who
contend with me;
fight against those who fight
against me.
2 Take up shield and armor;
arise and come to my aid.
3 Brandish spear and javelin[a]
against those who pursue me.
Say to me,
"I am your salvation."

4 May those who seek my life
be disgraced and put to shame;
may those who plot my ruin
be turned back in dismay.
5 May they be like chaff before the
wind,
with the angel of the LORD driving
them away;
6 may their path be dark and slippery,
with the angel of the LORD
pursuing them.

7 Since they hid their net for me
without cause
and without cause dug a pit for me,
8 may ruin overtake them by
surprise —
may the net they hid entangle
them,
may they fall into the pit, to their
ruin.
9 Then my soul will rejoice in the LORD
and delight in his salvation.
10 My whole being will exclaim,
"Who is like you, LORD?
You rescue the poor from those too
strong for them,
the poor and needy from those who
rob them."

11 Ruthless witnesses come forward;
they question me on things I know
nothing about.
12 They repay me evil for good
and leave me like one bereaved.
13 Yet when they were ill, I put on
sackcloth
and humbled myself with fasting.
When my prayers returned to me
unanswered,
14 I went about mourning
as though for my friend or brother.
I bowed my head in grief
as though weeping for my mother.
15 But when I stumbled, they gathered
in glee;
assailants gathered against me
without my knowledge.
They slandered me without
ceasing.
16 Like the ungodly they maliciously
mocked;[b]
they gnashed their teeth at me.

17 How long, Lord, will you look on?
Rescue me from their ravages,
my precious life from these lions.
18 I will give you thanks in the great
assembly;
among the throngs I will praise
you.
19 Do not let those gloat over me
who are my enemies without
cause;
do not let those who hate me without
reason
maliciously wink the eye.
20 They do not speak peaceably,
but devise false accusations
against those who live quietly in
the land.
21 They sneer at me and say, "Aha! Aha!
With our own eyes we have seen it."

22 LORD, you have seen this; do not be
silent.
Do not be far from me, Lord.
23 Awake, and rise to my defense!
Contend for me, my God and Lord.
24 Vindicate me in your righteousness,
LORD my God;
do not let them gloat over me.

[a] 3 Or *and block the way* [b] 16 Septuagint; Hebrew may mean *Like an ungodly circle of mockers,*

25 Do not let them think, "Aha, just what
we wanted!"
or say, "We have swallowed him up."

26 May all who gloat over my distress
be put to shame and confusion;
may all who exalt themselves over
me
be clothed with shame and
disgrace.
27 May those who delight in my
vindication
shout for joy and gladness;
may they always say, "The LORD be
exalted,
who delights in the well-being of
his servant."

28 My tongue will proclaim your
righteousness,
your praises all day long.

Psalm 36[a]

For the director of music. Of David the servant of the LORD.

1 I have a message from God in my
heart
concerning the sinfulness of the
wicked:[b]
There is no fear of God
before their eyes.

2 In their own eyes they flatter
themselves
too much to detect or hate their sin.
3 The words of their mouths are wicked
and deceitful;
they fail to act wisely or do good.
4 Even on their beds they plot evil;
they commit themselves to a sinful
course
and do not reject what is wrong.

5 Your love, LORD, reaches to the
heavens,
your faithfulness to the skies.
6 Your righteousness is like the highest
mountains,
your justice like the great deep.
You, LORD, preserve both people
and animals.
7 How priceless is your unfailing love,
O God!
People take refuge in the shadow of
your wings.
8 They feast on the abundance of your
house;
you give them drink from your
river of delights.
9 For with you is the fountain of life;
in your light we see light.

10 Continue your love to those who
know you,
your righteousness to the upright
in heart.
11 May the foot of the proud not come
against me,
nor the hand of the wicked drive
me away.
12 See how the evildoers lie fallen —
thrown down, not able to rise!

Psalm 37[c]

Of David.

1 Do not fret because of those who are
evil
or be envious of those who do
wrong;
2 for like the grass they will soon
wither,
like green plants they will soon die
away.

3 Trust in the LORD and do good;
dwell in the land and enjoy safe
pasture.
4 Take delight in the LORD,
and he will give you the desires of
your heart.

5 Commit your way to the LORD;
trust in him and he will do this:
6 He will make your righteous reward
shine like the dawn,
your vindication like the noonday
sun.

7 Be still before the LORD
and wait patiently for him;
do not fret when people succeed in
their ways,
when they carry out their wicked
schemes.

8 Refrain from anger and turn from
wrath;
do not fret — it leads only to evil.
9 For those who are evil will be
destroyed,
but those who hope in the LORD will
inherit the land.

10 A little while, and the wicked will be
no more;
though you look for them, they will
not be found.
11 But the meek will inherit the land
and enjoy peace and prosperity.

[a] In Hebrew texts 36:1-12 is numbered 36:2-13. [b] *1* Or *A message from God: The transgression of the wicked / resides in their hearts.* [c] This psalm is an acrostic poem, the stanzas of which begin with the successive letters of the Hebrew alphabet.

12 The wicked plot against the righteous
and gnash their teeth at them;
13 but the Lord laughs at the wicked,
for he knows their day is coming.

14 The wicked draw the sword
and bend the bow
to bring down the poor and needy,
to slay those whose ways are upright.
15 But their swords will pierce their own hearts,
and their bows will be broken.

16 Better the little that the righteous have
than the wealth of many wicked;
17 for the power of the wicked will be broken,
but the LORD upholds the righteous.

18 The blameless spend their days under the LORD's care,
and their inheritance will endure forever.
19 In times of disaster they will not wither;
in days of famine they will enjoy plenty.

20 But the wicked will perish:
Though the LORD's enemies are like the flowers of the field,
they will be consumed, they will go up in smoke.

21 The wicked borrow and do not repay,
but the righteous give generously;
22 those the LORD blesses will inherit the land,
but those he curses will be destroyed.

23 The LORD makes firm the steps
of the one who delights in him;
24 though he may stumble, he will not fall,
for the LORD upholds him with his hand.

25 I was young and now I am old,
yet I have never seen the righteous forsaken
or their children begging bread.
26 They are always generous and lend freely;
their children will be a blessing.[a]

27 Turn from evil and do good;
then you will dwell in the land forever.
28 For the LORD loves the just
and will not forsake his faithful ones.
Wrongdoers will be completely destroyed[b];
the offspring of the wicked will perish.
29 The righteous will inherit the land
and dwell in it forever.
30 The mouths of the righteous utter wisdom,
and their tongues speak what is just.
31 The law of their God is in their hearts;
their feet do not slip.

32 The wicked lie in wait for the righteous,
intent on putting them to death;
33 but the LORD will not leave them in the power of the wicked
or let them be condemned when brought to trial.

34 Hope in the LORD
and keep his way.
He will exalt you to inherit the land;
when the wicked are destroyed, you will see it.

35 I have seen a wicked and ruthless man
flourishing like a luxuriant native tree,
36 but he soon passed away and was no more;
though I looked for him, he could not be found.

37 Consider the blameless, observe the upright;
a future awaits those who seek peace.[c]
38 But all sinners will be destroyed;
there will be no future[d] for the wicked.

39 The salvation of the righteous comes from the LORD;
he is their stronghold in time of trouble.
40 The LORD helps them and delivers them;
he delivers them from the wicked and saves them,
because they take refuge in him.

[a] 26 Or *freely; / the names of their children will be used in blessings* (see Gen. 48:20); or *freely; / others will see that their children are blessed* [b] 28 See Septuagint; Hebrew *They will be protected forever* [c] 37 Or *upright; / those who seek peace will have posterity* [d] 38 Or *posterity*

Psalm 38[a]

A psalm of David. A petition.

1 LORD, do not rebuke me in your anger
or discipline me in your wrath.
2 Your arrows have pierced me,
and your hand has come down on me.
3 Because of your wrath there is no health in my body;
there is no soundness in my bones because of my sin.
4 My guilt has overwhelmed me
like a burden too heavy to bear.

5 My wounds fester and are loathsome
because of my sinful folly.
6 I am bowed down and brought very low;
all day long I go about mourning.
7 My back is filled with searing pain;
there is no health in my body.
8 I am feeble and utterly crushed;
I groan in anguish of heart.

9 All my longings lie open before you, Lord;
my sighing is not hidden from you.
10 My heart pounds, my strength fails me;
even the light has gone from my eyes.
11 My friends and companions avoid me
because of my wounds;
my neighbors stay far away.
12 Those who want to kill me set their traps,
those who would harm me talk of my ruin;
all day long they scheme and lie.

13 I am like the deaf, who cannot hear,
like the mute, who cannot speak;
14 I have become like one who does not hear,
whose mouth can offer no reply.
15 LORD, I wait for you;
you will answer, Lord my God.
16 For I said, "Do not let them gloat
or exalt themselves over me when my feet slip."

17 For I am about to fall,
and my pain is ever with me.
18 I confess my iniquity;
I am troubled by my sin.
19 Many have become my enemies without cause[b];
those who hate me without reason are numerous.
20 Those who repay my good with evil
lodge accusations against me,
though I seek only to do what is good.

21 LORD, do not forsake me;
do not be far from me, my God.
22 Come quickly to help me,
my Lord and my Savior.

Psalm 39[c]

For the director of music. For Jeduthun. A psalm of David.

1 I said, "I will watch my ways
and keep my tongue from sin;
I will put a muzzle on my mouth
while in the presence of the wicked."
2 So I remained utterly silent,
not even saying anything good.
But my anguish increased;
3 my heart grew hot within me.
While I meditated, the fire burned;
then I spoke with my tongue:

4 "Show me, LORD, my life's end
and the number of my days;
let me know how fleeting my life is.
5 You have made my days a mere handbreadth;
the span of my years is as nothing before you.
Everyone is but a breath,
even those who seem secure.[d]

6 "Surely everyone goes around like a mere phantom;
in vain they rush about, heaping up wealth
without knowing whose it will finally be.

7 "But now, Lord, what do I look for?
My hope is in you.
8 Save me from all my transgressions;
do not make me the scorn of fools.
9 I was silent; I would not open my mouth,
for you are the one who has done this.
10 Remove your scourge from me;
I am overcome by the blow of your hand.
11 When you rebuke and discipline anyone for their sin,
you consume their wealth like a moth —
surely everyone is but a breath.

[a] In Hebrew texts 38:1-22 is numbered 38:2-23. [b] *19* One Dead Sea Scrolls manuscript; Masoretic Text *my vigorous enemies* [c] In Hebrew texts 39:1-13 is numbered 39:2-14. [d] *5* The Hebrew has *Selah* (a word of uncertain meaning) here and at the end of verse 11.

12 "Hear my prayer, LORD,
listen to my cry for help;
do not be deaf to my weeping.
I dwell with you as a foreigner,
a stranger, as all my ancestors
were.
13 Look away from me, that I may enjoy
life again
before I depart and am no more."

Psalm 40[a]

For the director of music. Of David. A psalm.

1 I waited patiently for the LORD;
he turned to me and heard my cry.
2 He lifted me out of the slimy pit,
out of the mud and mire;
he set my feet on a rock
and gave me a firm place to stand.
3 He put a new song in my mouth,
a hymn of praise to our God.
Many will see and fear the LORD
and put their trust in him.

4 Blessed is the one
who trusts in the LORD,
who does not look to the proud,
to those who turn aside to false
gods.[b]
5 Many, LORD my God,
are the wonders you have done,
the things you planned for us.
None can compare with you;
were I to speak and tell of your
deeds,
they would be too many to declare.

6 Sacrifice and offering you did not
desire —
but my ears you have opened[c] —
burnt offerings and sin offerings[d]
you did not require.
7 Then I said, "Here I am, I have
come —
it is written about me in the scroll.[e]
8 I desire to do your will, my God;
your law is within my heart."

9 I proclaim your saving acts in the
great assembly;
I do not seal my lips, LORD,
as you know.
10 I do not hide your righteousness in
my heart;
I speak of your faithfulness and
your saving help.
I do not conceal your love and your
faithfulness
from the great assembly.

11 Do not withhold your mercy from me,
LORD;
may your love and faithfulness
always protect me.
12 For troubles without number
surround me;
my sins have overtaken me, and I
cannot see.
They are more than the hairs of my
head,
and my heart fails within me.
13 Be pleased to save me, LORD;
come quickly, LORD, to help me.

14 May all who want to take my life
be put to shame and confusion;
may all who desire my ruin
be turned back in disgrace.
15 May those who say to me, "Aha! Aha!"
be appalled at their own shame.
16 But may all who seek you
rejoice and be glad in you;
may those who long for your saving
help always say,
"The LORD is great!"

17 But as for me, I am poor and needy;
may the Lord think of me.
You are my help and my deliverer;
you are my God, do not delay.

Psalm 41[f]

For the director of music. A psalm of David.

1 Blessed are those who have regard for
the weak;
the LORD delivers them in times of
trouble.
2 The LORD protects and preserves
them —
they are counted among the
blessed in the land —
he does not give them over to the
desire of their foes.
3 The LORD sustains them on their
sickbed
and restores them from their bed of
illness.

4 I said, "Have mercy on me, LORD;
heal me, for I have sinned against
you."
5 My enemies say of me in malice,
"When will he die and his name
perish?"
6 When one of them comes to see me,
he speaks falsely, while his heart
gathers slander;
then he goes out and spreads it
around.

[a] In Hebrew texts 40:1-17 is numbered 40:2-18. [b] 4 Or *to lies* [c] 6 Hebrew; some Septuagint manuscripts *but a body you have prepared for me* [d] 6 Or *purification offerings* [e] 7 Or *come / with the scroll written for me* [f] In Hebrew texts 41:1-13 is numbered 41:2-14.

7 All my enemies whisper together
against me;
they imagine the worst for me,
saying,
8 "A vile disease has afflicted him;
he will never get up from the place
where he lies."
9 Even my close friend,
someone I trusted,
one who shared my bread,
has turned[a] against me.

10 But may you have mercy on me,
LORD;
raise me up, that I may repay
them.
11 I know that you are pleased with me,
for my enemy does not triumph
over me.
12 Because of my integrity you uphold
me
and set me in your presence
forever.

13 Praise be to the LORD, the God of
Israel,
from everlasting to everlasting.
Amen and Amen.

BOOK II

Psalms 42 – 72

Psalm 42[b,c]

For the director of music. A maskil[d] of the Sons of Korah.

1 As the deer pants for streams of
water,
so my soul pants for you, my God.
2 My soul thirsts for God, for the living
God.
When can I go and meet with God?
3 My tears have been my food
day and night,
while people say to me all day long,
"Where is your God?"
4 These things I remember
as I pour out my soul:
how I used to go to the house of God
under the protection of the Mighty
One[e]
with shouts of joy and praise
among the festive throng.

5 Why, my soul, are you downcast?
Why so disturbed within me?
Put your hope in God,
for I will yet praise him,
my Savior and my God.

6 My soul is downcast within me;
therefore I will remember you
from the land of the Jordan,
the heights of Hermon — from
Mount Mizar.
7 Deep calls to deep
in the roar of your waterfalls;
all your waves and breakers
have swept over me.

8 By day the LORD directs his love,
at night his song is with me —
a prayer to the God of my life.

9 I say to God my Rock,
"Why have you forgotten me?
Why must I go about mourning,
oppressed by the enemy?"
10 My bones suffer mortal agony
as my foes taunt me,
saying to me all day long,
"Where is your God?"

11 Why, my soul, are you downcast?
Why so disturbed within me?
Put your hope in God,
for I will yet praise him,
my Savior and my God.

Psalm 43[b]

1 Vindicate me, my God,
and plead my cause
against an unfaithful nation.
Rescue me from those who are
deceitful and wicked.
2 You are God my stronghold.
Why have you rejected me?
Why must I go about mourning,
oppressed by the enemy?
3 Send me your light and your faithful
care,
let them lead me;
let them bring me to your holy
mountain,
to the place where you dwell.
4 Then I will go to the altar of God,
to God, my joy and my delight.
I will praise you with the lyre,
O God, my God.

5 Why, my soul, are you downcast?
Why so disturbed within me?
Put your hope in God,
for I will yet praise him,
my Savior and my God.

[a] 9 Hebrew *has lifted up his heel* [b] In many Hebrew manuscripts Psalms 42 and 43 constitute one psalm. [c] In Hebrew texts 42:1-11 is numbered 42:2-12. [d] Title: Probably a literary or musical term [e] 4 See Septuagint and Syriac; the meaning of the Hebrew for this line is uncertain.

Psalm 44[a]

For the director of music. Of the Sons of Korah. A maskil.[b]

1 We have heard it with our ears, O God;
our ancestors have told us
what you did in their days,
in days long ago.
2 With your hand you drove out the nations
and planted our ancestors;
you crushed the peoples
and made our ancestors flourish.
3 It was not by their sword that they won the land,
nor did their arm bring them victory;
it was your right hand, your arm,
and the light of your face, for you loved them.

4 You are my King and my God,
who decrees[c] victories for Jacob.
5 Through you we push back our enemies;
through your name we trample our foes.
6 I put no trust in my bow,
my sword does not bring me victory;
7 but you give us victory over our enemies,
you put our adversaries to shame.
8 In God we make our boast all day long,
and we will praise your name forever.[d]

9 But now you have rejected and humbled us;
you no longer go out with our armies.
10 You made us retreat before the enemy,
and our adversaries have plundered us.
11 You gave us up to be devoured like sheep
and have scattered us among the nations.
12 You sold your people for a pittance,
gaining nothing from their sale.
13 You have made us a reproach to our neighbors,
the scorn and derision of those around us.
14 You have made us a byword among the nations;
the peoples shake their heads at us.
15 I live in disgrace all day long,
and my face is covered with shame
16 at the taunts of those who reproach and revile me,
because of the enemy, who is bent on revenge.

17 All this came upon us,
though we had not forgotten you;
we had not been false to your covenant.
18 Our hearts had not turned back;
our feet had not strayed from your path.
19 But you crushed us and made us a haunt for jackals;
you covered us over with deep darkness.

20 If we had forgotten the name of our God
or spread out our hands to a foreign god,
21 would not God have discovered it,
since he knows the secrets of the heart?
22 Yet for your sake we face death all day long;
we are considered as sheep to be slaughtered.

23 Awake, Lord! Why do you sleep?
Rouse yourself! Do not reject us forever.
24 Why do you hide your face
and forget our misery and oppression?

25 We are brought down to the dust;
our bodies cling to the ground.
26 Rise up and help us;
rescue us because of your unfailing love.

Psalm 45[e]

For the director of music. To the tune of "Lilies." Of the Sons of Korah. A maskil.[b] *A wedding song.*

1 My heart is stirred by a noble theme
as I recite my verses for the king;
my tongue is the pen of a skillful writer.

2 You are the most excellent of men
and your lips have been anointed with grace,
since God has blessed you forever.

3 Gird your sword on your side, you mighty one;
clothe yourself with splendor and majesty.

[a] In Hebrew texts 44:1-26 is numbered 44:2-27. [b] Title: Probably a literary or musical term [c] 4 Septuagint, Aquila and Syriac; Hebrew *King, O God; / command* [d] 8 The Hebrew has *Selah* (a word of uncertain meaning) here. [e] In Hebrew texts 45:1-17 is numbered 45:2-18.

4 In your majesty ride forth victoriously
in the cause of truth, humility and
justice;
let your right hand achieve
awesome deeds.
5 Let your sharp arrows pierce the
hearts of the king's enemies;
let the nations fall beneath your
feet.
6 Your throne, O God,[a] will last for ever
and ever;
a scepter of justice will be the
scepter of your kingdom.
7 You love righteousness and hate
wickedness;
therefore God, your God, has set
you above your companions
by anointing you with the oil of joy.
8 All your robes are fragrant with
myrrh and aloes and cassia;
from palaces adorned with ivory
the music of the strings makes you
glad.
9 Daughters of kings are among your
honored women;
at your right hand is the royal
bride in gold of Ophir.

10 Listen, daughter, and pay careful
attention:
Forget your people and your
father's house.
11 Let the king be enthralled by your
beauty;
honor him, for he is your lord.
12 The city of Tyre will come with a gift,[b]
people of wealth will seek your
favor.
13 All glorious is the princess within her
chamber;
her gown is interwoven with gold.
14 In embroidered garments she is led
to the king;
her virgin companions follow
her —
those brought to be with her.
15 Led in with joy and gladness,
they enter the palace of the king.

16 Your sons will take the place of your
fathers;
you will make them princes
throughout the land.

17 I will perpetuate your memory
through all generations;
therefore the nations will praise
you for ever and ever.

Psalm 46[c]

For the director of music. Of the Sons of Korah. According to alamoth.[d] *A song.*

1 God is our refuge and strength,
an ever-present help in trouble.
2 Therefore we will not fear, though the
earth give way
and the mountains fall into the
heart of the sea,
3 though its waters roar and foam
and the mountains quake with
their surging.[e]

4 There is a river whose streams make
glad the city of God,
the holy place where the Most High
dwells.
5 God is within her, she will not fall;
God will help her at break of day.
6 Nations are in uproar, kingdoms fall;
he lifts his voice, the earth melts.

7 The LORD Almighty is with us;
the God of Jacob is our fortress.

8 Come and see what the LORD has done,
the desolations he has brought on
the earth.
9 He makes wars cease
to the ends of the earth.
He breaks the bow and shatters the
spear;
he burns the shields[f] with fire.
10 He says, "Be still, and know that I am
God;
I will be exalted among the
nations,
I will be exalted in the earth."

11 The LORD Almighty is with us;
the God of Jacob is our fortress.

Psalm 47[g]

For the director of music. Of the Sons of Korah. A psalm.

1 Clap your hands, all you nations;
shout to God with cries of joy.

2 For the LORD Most High is awesome,
the great King over all the earth.
3 He subdued nations under us,
peoples under our feet.
4 He chose our inheritance for us,
the pride of Jacob, whom he loved.[h]

5 God has ascended amid shouts of joy,
the LORD amid the sounding of
trumpets.

[a] 6 Here the king is addressed as God's representative. [b] 12 Or *A Tyrian robe is among the gifts* [c] In Hebrew texts 46:1-11 is numbered 46:2-12. [d] Title: Probably a musical term [e] 3 The Hebrew has *Selah* (a word of uncertain meaning) here and at the end of verses 7 and 11. [f] 9 Or *chariots* [g] In Hebrew texts 47:1-9 is numbered 47:2-10. [h] 4 The Hebrew has *Selah* (a word of uncertain meaning) here.

6 Sing praises to God, sing praises;
sing praises to our King, sing praises.
7 For God is the King of all the earth;
sing to him a psalm of praise.

8 God reigns over the nations;
God is seated on his holy throne.
9 The nobles of the nations assemble
as the people of the God of Abraham,
for the kings[a] of the earth belong to God;
he is greatly exalted.

Psalm 48[b]

A song. A psalm of the Sons of Korah.

1 Great is the LORD, and most worthy of praise,
in the city of our God, his holy mountain.

2 Beautiful in its loftiness,
the joy of the whole earth,
like the heights of Zaphon[c] is Mount Zion,
the city of the Great King.
3 God is in her citadels;
he has shown himself to be her fortress.

4 When the kings joined forces,
when they advanced together,
5 they saw her and were astounded;
they fled in terror.
6 Trembling seized them there,
pain like that of a woman in labor.
7 You destroyed them like ships of Tarshish
shattered by an east wind.

8 As we have heard,
so we have seen
in the city of the LORD Almighty,
in the city of our God:
God makes her secure
forever.[d]

9 Within your temple, O God,
we meditate on your unfailing love.
10 Like your name, O God,
your praise reaches to the ends of the earth;
your right hand is filled with righteousness.
11 Mount Zion rejoices,
the villages of Judah are glad
because of your judgments.

12 Walk about Zion, go around her,
count her towers,
13 consider well her ramparts,
view her citadels,
that you may tell of them
to the next generation.
14 For this God is our God for ever and ever;
he will be our guide even to the end.

Psalm 49[e]

For the director of music. Of the Sons of Korah. A psalm.

1 Hear this, all you peoples;
listen, all who live in this world,
2 both low and high,
rich and poor alike:
3 My mouth will speak words of wisdom;
the meditation of my heart will give you understanding.
4 I will turn my ear to a proverb;
with the harp I will expound my riddle:

5 Why should I fear when evil days come,
when wicked deceivers surround me—
6 those who trust in their wealth
and boast of their great riches?
7 No one can redeem the life of another
or give to God a ransom for them—
8 the ransom for a life is costly,
no payment is ever enough—
9 so that they should live on forever
and not see decay.
10 For all can see that the wise die,
that the foolish and the senseless also perish,
leaving their wealth to others.
11 Their tombs will remain their houses[f] forever,
their dwellings for endless generations,
though they had[g] named lands after themselves.

12 People, despite their wealth, do not endure;
they are like the beasts that perish.

13 This is the fate of those who trust in themselves,
and of their followers, who approve their sayings.[h]

[a] 9 Or *shields* [b] In Hebrew texts 48:1-14 is numbered 48:2-15. [c] 2 *Zaphon* was the most sacred mountain of the Canaanites. [d] 8 The Hebrew has *Selah* (a word of uncertain meaning) here. [e] In Hebrew texts 49:1-20 is numbered 49:2-21. [f] 11 Septuagint and Syriac; Hebrew *In their thoughts their houses will remain* [g] 11 Or *generations, / for they have* [h] 13 The Hebrew has *Selah* (a word of uncertain meaning) here and at the end of verse 15.

14 They are like sheep and are destined
to die;
death will be their shepherd
(but the upright will prevail over
them in the morning).
Their forms will decay in the grave,
far from their princely mansions.
15 But God will redeem me from the
realm of the dead;
he will surely take me to himself.
16 Do not be overawed when others
grow rich,
when the splendor of their houses
increases;
17 for they will take nothing with them
when they die,
their splendor will not descend
with them.
18 Though while they live they count
themselves blessed —
and people praise you when you
prosper —
19 they will join those who have gone
before them,
who will never again see the light
of life.

20 People who have wealth but lack
understanding
are like the beasts that perish.

Psalm 50

A psalm of Asaph.

1 The Mighty One, God, the LORD,
speaks and summons the earth
from the rising of the sun to where
it sets.
2 From Zion, perfect in beauty,
God shines forth.
3 Our God comes
and will not be silent;
a fire devours before him,
and around him a tempest rages.
4 He summons the heavens above,
and the earth, that he may judge
his people:
5 "Gather to me this consecrated
people,
who made a covenant with me by
sacrifice."
6 And the heavens proclaim his
righteousness,
for he is a God of justice.[a,b]

7 "Listen, my people, and I will speak;
I will testify against you, Israel:
I am God, your God.
8 I bring no charges against you
concerning your sacrifices
or concerning your burnt offerings,
which are ever before me.
9 I have no need of a bull from your
stall
or of goats from your pens,
10 for every animal of the forest
is mine,
and the cattle on a thousand hills.
11 I know every bird in the mountains,
and the insects in the fields are
mine.
12 If I were hungry I would not tell you,
for the world is mine, and all that
is in it.
13 Do I eat the flesh of bulls
or drink the blood of goats?

14 "Sacrifice thank offerings to God,
fulfill your vows to the Most High,
15 and call on me in the day of trouble;
I will deliver you, and you will
honor me."

16 But to the wicked person, God says:

"What right have you to recite my
laws
or take my covenant on your lips?
17 You hate my instruction
and cast my words behind you.
18 When you see a thief, you join with
him;
you throw in your lot with
adulterers.
19 You use your mouth for evil
and harness your tongue to deceit.
20 You sit and testify against your
brother
and slander your own mother's
son.
21 When you did these things and I kept
silent,
you thought I was exactly[c]
like you.
But I now arraign you
and set my accusations before you.

22 "Consider this, you who forget God,
or I will tear you to pieces, with no
one to rescue you:
23 Those who sacrifice thank offerings
honor me,
and to the blameless[d] I will show
my salvation."

[a] 6 With a different word division of the Hebrew; Masoretic Text *for God himself is judge*
[b] 6 The Hebrew has *Selah* (a word of uncertain meaning) here. [c] 21 Or *thought the 'I AM' was*
[d] 23 Probable reading of the original Hebrew text; the meaning of the Masoretic Text for this phrase is uncertain.

Psalm 51[a]

For the director of music. A psalm of David. When the prophet Nathan came to him after David had committed adultery with Bathsheba.

1 Have mercy on me, O God,
according to your unfailing love;
according to your great compassion
blot out my transgressions.
2 Wash away all my iniquity
and cleanse me from my sin.
3 For I know my transgressions,
and my sin is always before me.
4 Against you, you only, have I sinned
and done what is evil in your sight;
so you are right in your verdict
and justified when you judge.
5 Surely I was sinful at birth,
sinful from the time my mother
conceived me.
6 Yet you desired faithfulness even in
the womb;
you taught me wisdom in that
secret place.

7 Cleanse me with hyssop, and I will be
clean;
wash me, and I will be whiter than
snow.
8 Let me hear joy and gladness;
let the bones you have crushed
rejoice.
9 Hide your face from my sins
and blot out all my iniquity.

10 Create in me a pure heart, O God,
and renew a steadfast spirit within
me.
11 Do not cast me from your presence
or take your Holy Spirit from me.
12 Restore to me the joy of your
salvation
and grant me a willing spirit, to
sustain me.

13 Then I will teach transgressors your
ways,
so that sinners will turn back to
you.
14 Deliver me from the guilt of
bloodshed, O God,
you who are God my Savior,
and my tongue will sing of your
righteousness.
15 Open my lips, Lord,
and my mouth will declare your
praise.
16 You do not delight in sacrifice, or I
would bring it;
you do not take pleasure in burnt
offerings.
17 My sacrifice, O God, is[b] a broken
spirit;
a broken and contrite heart
you, God, will not despise.

18 May it please you to prosper Zion,
to build up the walls of Jerusalem.
19 Then you will delight in the sacrifices
of the righteous,
in burnt offerings offered whole;
then bulls will be offered on your
altar.

Psalm 52[c]

For the director of music. A maskil[d] of David. When Doeg the Edomite had gone to Saul and told him: "David has gone to the house of Ahimelek."

1 Why do you boast of evil, you mighty
hero?
Why do you boast all day long,
you who are a disgrace in the eyes
of God?
2 You who practice deceit,
your tongue plots destruction;
it is like a sharpened razor.
3 You love evil rather than good,
falsehood rather than speaking the
truth.[e]
4 You love every harmful word,
you deceitful tongue!

5 Surely God will bring you down to
everlasting ruin:
He will snatch you up and pluck
you from your tent;
he will uproot you from the land of
the living.
6 The righteous will see and fear;
they will laugh at you, saying,
7 "Here now is the man
who did not make God his
stronghold
but trusted in his great wealth
and grew strong by destroying
others!"

8 But I am like an olive tree
flourishing in the house of God;
I trust in God's unfailing love
for ever and ever.
9 For what you have done I will always
praise you
in the presence of your faithful
people.
And I will hope in your name,
for your name is good.

[a] In Hebrew texts 51:1-19 is numbered 51:3-21. [b] 17 Or *The sacrifices of God are* [c] In Hebrew texts 52:1-9 is numbered 52:3-11. [d] Title: Probably a literary or musical term [e] 3 The Hebrew has *Selah* (a word of uncertain meaning) here and at the end of verse 5.

Psalm 53[a]

For the director of music. According to mahalath.[b] *A* maskil[c] *of David.*

1 The fool says in his heart,
"There is no God."
They are corrupt, and their ways are vile;
there is no one who does good.

2 God looks down from heaven
on all mankind
to see if there are any who understand,
any who seek God.
3 Everyone has turned away, all have become corrupt;
there is no one who does good,
not even one.

4 Do all these evildoers know nothing?

They devour my people as though eating bread;
they never call on God.
5 But there they are, overwhelmed with dread,
where there was nothing to dread.
God scattered the bones of those who attacked you;
you put them to shame, for God despised them.

6 Oh, that salvation for Israel would come out of Zion!
When God restores his people,
let Jacob rejoice and Israel be glad!

Psalm 54[d]

For the director of music. With stringed instruments. A maskil[c] *of David. When the Ziphites had gone to Saul and said, "Is not David hiding among us?"*

1 Save me, O God, by your name;
vindicate me by your might.
2 Hear my prayer, O God;
listen to the words of my mouth.

3 Arrogant foes are attacking me;
ruthless people are trying to kill me—
people without regard for God.[e]

4 Surely God is my help;
the Lord is the one who sustains me.

5 Let evil recoil on those who slander me;
in your faithfulness destroy them.

6 I will sacrifice a freewill offering to you;
I will praise your name, LORD, for it is good.
7 You have delivered me from all my troubles,
and my eyes have looked in triumph on my foes.

Psalm 55[f]

For the director of music. With stringed instruments. A maskil[c] *of David.*

1 Listen to my prayer, O God,
do not ignore my plea;
2 hear me and answer me.
My thoughts trouble me and I am distraught
3 because of what my enemy is saying,
because of the threats of the wicked;
for they bring down suffering on me
and assail me in their anger.

4 My heart is in anguish within me;
the terrors of death have fallen on me.
5 Fear and trembling have beset me;
horror has overwhelmed me.
6 I said, "Oh, that I had the wings of a dove!
I would fly away and be at rest.
7 I would flee far away
and stay in the desert;[g]
8 I would hurry to my place of shelter,
far from the tempest and storm."

9 Lord, confuse the wicked, confound their words,
for I see violence and strife in the city.
10 Day and night they prowl about on its walls;
malice and abuse are within it.
11 Destructive forces are at work in the city;
threats and lies never leave its streets.

12 If an enemy were insulting me,
I could endure it;
if a foe were rising against me,
I could hide.
13 But it is you, a man like myself,
my companion, my close friend,

[a] In Hebrew texts 53:1-6 is numbered 53:2-7. [b] Title: Probably a musical term [c] Title: Probably a literary or musical term [d] In Hebrew texts 54:1-7 is numbered 54:3-9. [e] 3 The Hebrew has *Selah* (a word of uncertain meaning) here. [f] In Hebrew texts 55:1-23 is numbered 55:2-24. [g] 7 The Hebrew has *Selah* (a word of uncertain meaning) here and in the middle of verse 19.

[14] with whom I once enjoyed sweet fellowship
at the house of God,
as we walked about
among the worshipers.

[15] Let death take my enemies by surprise;
let them go down alive to the realm of the dead,
for evil finds lodging among them.

[16] As for me, I call to God,
and the LORD saves me.
[17] Evening, morning and noon
I cry out in distress,
and he hears my voice.
[18] He rescues me unharmed
from the battle waged against me,
even though many oppose me.
[19] God, who is enthroned from of old,
who does not change —
he will hear them and humble them,
because they have no fear of God.

[20] My companion attacks his friends;
he violates his covenant.
[21] His talk is smooth as butter,
yet war is in his heart;
his words are more soothing than oil,
yet they are drawn swords.

[22] Cast your cares on the LORD
and he will sustain you;
he will never let
the righteous be shaken.
[23] But you, God, will bring down the wicked
into the pit of decay;
the bloodthirsty and deceitful
will not live out half their days.

But as for me, I trust in you.

Psalm 56[a]

For the director of music. To the tune of "A Dove on Distant Oaks." Of David. A miktam.[b] *When the Philistines had seized him in Gath.*

[1] Be merciful to me, my God,
for my enemies are in hot pursuit;
all day long they press their attack.
[2] My adversaries pursue me all day long;
in their pride many are attacking me.

[3] When I am afraid, I put my trust in you.
[4] In God, whose word I praise —
in God I trust and am not afraid.
What can mere mortals do to me?

[5] All day long they twist my words;
all their schemes are for my ruin.
[6] They conspire, they lurk,
they watch my steps,
hoping to take my life.
[7] Because of their wickedness do not[c] let them escape;
in your anger, God, bring the nations down.

[8] Record my misery;
list my tears on your scroll[d] —
are they not in your record?
[9] Then my enemies will turn back
when I call for help.
By this I will know that God is for me.

[10] In God, whose word I praise,
in the LORD, whose word I praise —
[11] in God I trust and am not afraid.
What can man do to me?

[12] I am under vows to you, my God;
I will present my thank offerings to you.
[13] For you have delivered me from death
and my feet from stumbling,
that I may walk before God
in the light of life.

Psalm 57[e]

For the director of music. To the tune of "Do Not Destroy." Of David. A miktam.[b] *When he had fled from Saul into the cave.*

[1] Have mercy on me, my God, have mercy on me,
for in you I take refuge.
I will take refuge in the shadow of your wings
until the disaster has passed.

[2] I cry out to God Most High,
to God, who vindicates me.
[3] He sends from heaven and saves me,
rebuking those who hotly pursue me —[f]
God sends forth his love and his faithfulness.

[4] I am in the midst of lions;
I am forced to dwell among ravenous beasts —
men whose teeth are spears and arrows,
whose tongues are sharp swords.

[5] Be exalted, O God, above the heavens;
let your glory be over all the earth.

[a] In Hebrew texts 56:1-13 is numbered 56:2-14. [b] Title: Probably a literary or musical term [c] 7 Probable reading of the original Hebrew text; Masoretic Text does not have *do not.* [d] *8* Or *misery; / put my tears in your wineskin* [e] In Hebrew texts 57:1-11 is numbered 57:2-12. [f] *3* The Hebrew has *Selah* (a word of uncertain meaning) here and at the end of verse 6.

6 They spread a net for my feet —
I was bowed down in distress.
They dug a pit in my path —
but they have fallen into it
themselves.

7 My heart, O God, is steadfast,
my heart is steadfast;
I will sing and make music.
8 Awake, my soul!
Awake, harp and lyre!
I will awaken the dawn.

9 I will praise you, Lord, among the
nations;
I will sing of you among the
peoples.
10 For great is your love, reaching to the
heavens;
your faithfulness reaches to the
skies.

11 Be exalted, O God, above the heavens;
let your glory be over all the earth.

Psalm 58[a]

For the director of music. To the tune of "Do Not Destroy." Of David. A miktam.[b]

1 Do you rulers indeed speak justly?
Do you judge people with equity?
2 No, in your heart you devise injustice,
and your hands mete out violence
on the earth.

3 Even from birth the wicked go astray;
from the womb they are wayward,
spreading lies.
4 Their venom is like the venom of a
snake,
like that of a cobra that has
stopped its ears,
5 that will not heed the tune of the
charmer,
however skillful the enchanter may
be.

6 Break the teeth in their mouths,
O God;
LORD, tear out the fangs of those
lions!
7 Let them vanish like water that flows
away;
when they draw the bow, let their
arrows fall short.
8 May they be like a slug that melts
away as it moves along,
like a stillborn child that never sees
the sun.

9 Before your pots can feel the heat of
the thorns —
whether they be green or dry — the
wicked will be swept away.[c]
10 The righteous will be glad when they
are avenged,
when they dip their feet in the
blood of the wicked.
11 Then people will say,
"Surely the righteous still are
rewarded;
surely there is a God who judges
the earth."

Psalm 59[d]

For the director of music. To the tune of "Do Not Destroy." Of David. A miktam.[b] *When Saul had sent men to watch David's house in order to kill him.*

1 Deliver me from my enemies, O God;
be my fortress against those who
are attacking me.
2 Deliver me from evildoers
and save me from those who are
after my blood.

3 See how they lie in wait for me!
Fierce men conspire against me
for no offense or sin of mine, LORD.
4 I have done no wrong, yet they are
ready to attack me.
Arise to help me; look on my plight!
5 You, LORD God Almighty,
you who are the God of Israel,
rouse yourself to punish all the
nations;
show no mercy to wicked traitors.[e]

6 They return at evening,
snarling like dogs,
and prowl about the city.
7 See what they spew from their
mouths —
the words from their lips are sharp
as swords,
and they think, "Who can hear us?"
8 But you laugh at them, LORD;
you scoff at all those nations.

9 You are my strength, I watch for you;
you, God, are my fortress,
10 my God on whom I can rely.

God will go before me
and will let me gloat over those
who slander me.
11 But do not kill them, Lord our shield,[f]
or my people will forget.

[a] In Hebrew texts 58:1-11 is numbered 58:2-12. [b] Title: Probably a literary or musical term
[c] 9 The meaning of the Hebrew for this verse is uncertain. [d] In Hebrew texts 59:1-17 is numbered 59:2-18. [e] 5 The Hebrew has *Selah* (a word of uncertain meaning) here and at the end of verse 13. [f] 11 Or *sovereign*

In your might uproot them
and bring them down.
12 For the sins of their mouths,
for the words of their lips,
let them be caught in their pride.
For the curses and lies they utter,
13 consume them in your wrath,
consume them till they are no more.
Then it will be known to the ends of the earth
that God rules over Jacob.

14 They return at evening,
snarling like dogs,
and prowl about the city.
15 They wander about for food
and howl if not satisfied.
16 But I will sing of your strength,
in the morning I will sing of your love;
for you are my fortress,
my refuge in times of trouble.

17 You are my strength, I sing praise to you;
you, God, are my fortress,
my God on whom I can rely.

Psalm 60[a]

For the director of music. To the tune of "The Lily of the Covenant." A miktam[b] of David. For teaching. When he fought Aram Naharaim[c] and Aram Zobah,[d] and when Joab returned and struck down twelve thousand Edomites in the Valley of Salt.

1 You have rejected us, God, and burst upon us;
you have been angry—now restore us!
2 You have shaken the land and torn it open;
mend its fractures, for it is quaking.
3 You have shown your people desperate times;
you have given us wine that makes us stagger.
4 But for those who fear you, you have raised a banner
to be unfurled against the bow.[e]

5 Save us and help us with your right hand,
that those you love may be delivered.
6 God has spoken from his sanctuary:
"In triumph I will parcel out Shechem
and measure off the Valley of Sukkoth.
7 Gilead is mine, and Manasseh is mine;
Ephraim is my helmet,
Judah is my scepter.
8 Moab is my washbasin,
on Edom I toss my sandal;
over Philistia I shout in triumph."

9 Who will bring me to the fortified city?
Who will lead me to Edom?
10 Is it not you, God, you who have now rejected us
and no longer go out with our armies?
11 Give us aid against the enemy,
for human help is worthless.
12 With God we will gain the victory,
and he will trample down our enemies.

Psalm 61[f]

For the director of music. With stringed instruments. Of David.

1 Hear my cry, O God;
listen to my prayer.

2 From the ends of the earth I call to you,
I call as my heart grows faint;
lead me to the rock that is higher than I.
3 For you have been my refuge,
a strong tower against the foe.

4 I long to dwell in your tent forever
and take refuge in the shelter of your wings.[e]
5 For you, God, have heard my vows;
you have given me the heritage of those who fear your name.

6 Increase the days of the king's life,
his years for many generations.
7 May he be enthroned in God's presence forever;
appoint your love and faithfulness to protect him.

8 Then I will ever sing in praise of your name
and fulfill my vows day after day.

[a] In Hebrew texts 60:1-12 is numbered 60:3-14. [b] Title: Probably a literary or musical term [c] Title: That is, Arameans of Northwest Mesopotamia [d] Title: That is, Arameans of central Syria [e] 4 The Hebrew has *Selah* (a word of uncertain meaning) here. [f] In Hebrew texts 61:1-8 is numbered 61:2-9.

Psalm 62[a]

For the director of music. For Jeduthun. A psalm of David.

1 Truly my soul finds rest in God;
my salvation comes from him.
2 Truly he is my rock and my salvation;
he is my fortress, I will never be shaken.

3 How long will you assault me?
Would all of you throw me down —
this leaning wall, this tottering fence?
4 Surely they intend to topple me
from my lofty place;
they take delight in lies.
With their mouths they bless,
but in their hearts they curse.[b]

5 Yes, my soul, find rest in God;
my hope comes from him.
6 Truly he is my rock and my salvation;
he is my fortress, I will not be shaken.
7 My salvation and my honor depend on God[c];
he is my mighty rock, my refuge.
8 Trust in him at all times, you people;
pour out your hearts to him,
for God is our refuge.

9 Surely the lowborn are but a breath,
the highborn are but a lie.
If weighed on a balance, they are nothing;
together they are only a breath.
10 Do not trust in extortion
or put vain hope in stolen goods;
though your riches increase,
do not set your heart on them.

11 One thing God has spoken,
two things I have heard:
"Power belongs to you, God,
12 and with you, Lord, is unfailing love";
and, "You reward everyone
according to what they have done."

Psalm 63[d]

A psalm of David. When he was in the Desert of Judah.

1 You, God, are my God,
earnestly I seek you;
I thirst for you,
my whole being longs for you,
in a dry and parched land
where there is no water.
2 I have seen you in the sanctuary
and beheld your power and your glory.
3 Because your love is better than life,
my lips will glorify you.
4 I will praise you as long as I live,
and in your name I will lift up my hands.
5 I will be fully satisfied as with the richest of foods;
with singing lips my mouth will praise you.

6 On my bed I remember you;
I think of you through the watches of the night.
7 Because you are my help,
I sing in the shadow of your wings.
8 I cling to you;
your right hand upholds me.

9 Those who want to kill me will be destroyed;
they will go down to the depths of the earth.
10 They will be given over to the sword
and become food for jackals.

11 But the king will rejoice in God;
all who swear by God will glory in him,
while the mouths of liars will be silenced.

Psalm 64[e]

For the director of music. A psalm of David.

1 Hear me, my God, as I voice my complaint;
protect my life from the threat of the enemy.

2 Hide me from the conspiracy of the wicked,
from the plots of evildoers.
3 They sharpen their tongues like swords
and aim cruel words like deadly arrows.
4 They shoot from ambush at the innocent;
they shoot suddenly, without fear.

5 They encourage each other in evil plans,
they talk about hiding their snares;
they say, "Who will see it[f]?"
6 They plot injustice and say,
"We have devised a perfect plan!"
Surely the human mind and heart are cunning.

[a] In Hebrew texts 62:1-12 is numbered 62:2-13. [b] 4 The Hebrew has *Selah* (a word of uncertain meaning) here and at the end of verse 8. [c] 7 Or / *God Most High is my salvation and my honor* [d] In Hebrew texts 63:1-11 is numbered 63:2-12. [e] In Hebrew texts 64:1-10 is numbered 64:2-11. [f] 5 Or *us*

[7] But God will shoot them with his arrows;
they will suddenly be struck down.
[8] He will turn their own tongues against them
and bring them to ruin;
all who see them will shake their heads in scorn.
[9] All people will fear;
they will proclaim the works of God
and ponder what he has done.

[10] The righteous will rejoice in the LORD
and take refuge in him;
all the upright in heart will glory in him!

Psalm 65[a]

For the director of music. A psalm of David. A song.

[1] Praise awaits[b] you, our God, in Zion;
to you our vows will be fulfilled.
[2] You who answer prayer,
to you all people will come.
[3] When we were overwhelmed by sins,
you forgave[c] our transgressions.
[4] Blessed are those you choose
and bring near to live in your courts!
We are filled with the good things of your house,
of your holy temple.

[5] You answer us with awesome and righteous deeds,
God our Savior,
the hope of all the ends of the earth
and of the farthest seas,
[6] who formed the mountains by your power,
having armed yourself with strength,
[7] who stilled the roaring of the seas,
the roaring of their waves,
and the turmoil of the nations.
[8] The whole earth is filled with awe at your wonders;
where morning dawns, where evening fades,
you call forth songs of joy.

[9] You care for the land and water it;
you enrich it abundantly.
The streams of God are filled with water
to provide the people with grain,
for so you have ordained it.[d]
[10] You drench its furrows and level its ridges;
you soften it with showers and bless its crops.
[11] You crown the year with your bounty,
and your carts overflow with abundance.
[12] The grasslands of the wilderness overflow;
the hills are clothed with gladness.
[13] The meadows are covered with flocks
and the valleys are mantled with grain;
they shout for joy and sing.

Psalm 66

For the director of music. A song. A psalm.

[1] Shout for joy to God, all the earth!
[2] Sing the glory of his name;
make his praise glorious.
[3] Say to God, "How awesome are your deeds!
So great is your power
that your enemies cringe before you.
[4] All the earth bows down to you;
they sing praise to you,
they sing the praises of your name."[e]

[5] Come and see what God has done,
his awesome deeds for mankind!
[6] He turned the sea into dry land,
they passed through the waters on foot —
come, let us rejoice in him.
[7] He rules forever by his power,
his eyes watch the nations —
let not the rebellious rise up against him.

[8] Praise our God, all peoples,
let the sound of his praise be heard;
[9] he has preserved our lives
and kept our feet from slipping.
[10] For you, God, tested us;
you refined us like silver.
[11] You brought us into prison
and laid burdens on our backs.
[12] You let people ride over our heads;
we went through fire and water,
but you brought us to a place of abundance.

[13] I will come to your temple with burnt offerings
and fulfill my vows to you —
[14] vows my lips promised and my mouth spoke
when I was in trouble.
[15] I will sacrifice fat animals to you
and an offering of rams;
I will offer bulls and goats.

[a] In Hebrew texts 65:1-13 is numbered 65:2-14. [b] 1 Or *befits*; the meaning of the Hebrew for this word is uncertain. [c] 3 Or *made atonement for* [d] 9 Or *for that is how you prepare the land* [e] 4 The Hebrew has *Selah* (a word of uncertain meaning) here and at the end of verses 7 and 15.

16 Come and hear, all you who fear God;
let me tell you what he has done for me.
17 I cried out to him with my mouth;
his praise was on my tongue.
18 If I had cherished sin in my heart,
the Lord would not have listened;
19 but God has surely listened
and has heard my prayer.
20 Praise be to God,
who has not rejected my prayer
or withheld his love from me!

Psalm 67[a]

For the director of music. With stringed instruments. A psalm. A song.

1 May God be gracious to us and bless us
and make his face shine on us —[b]
2 so that your ways may be known on earth,
your salvation among all nations.

3 May the peoples praise you, God;
may all the peoples praise you.
4 May the nations be glad and sing for joy,
for you rule the peoples with equity
and guide the nations of the earth.
5 May the peoples praise you, God;
may all the peoples praise you.

6 The land yields its harvest;
God, our God, blesses us.
7 May God bless us still,
so that all the ends of the earth will fear him.

Psalm 68[c]

For the director of music. Of David. A psalm. A song.

1 May God arise, may his enemies be scattered;
may his foes flee before him.
2 May you blow them away like smoke —
as wax melts before the fire,
may the wicked perish before God.
3 But may the righteous be glad
and rejoice before God;
may they be happy and joyful.

4 Sing to God, sing in praise of his name,
extol him who rides on the clouds[d];
rejoice before him — his name is the LORD.
5 A father to the fatherless, a defender of widows,
is God in his holy dwelling.
6 God sets the lonely in families,[e]
he leads out the prisoners with singing;
but the rebellious live in a sun-scorched land.

7 When you, God, went out before your people,
when you marched through the wilderness,[f]
8 the earth shook, the heavens poured down rain,
before God, the One of Sinai,
before God, the God of Israel.
9 You gave abundant showers, O God;
you refreshed your weary inheritance.
10 Your people settled in it,
and from your bounty, God, you provided for the poor.

11 The Lord announces the word,
and the women who proclaim it are a mighty throng:
12 "Kings and armies flee in haste;
the women at home divide the plunder.
13 Even while you sleep among the sheep pens,[g]
the wings of my dove are sheathed with silver,
its feathers with shining gold."
14 When the Almighty[h] scattered the kings in the land,
it was like snow fallen on Mount Zalmon.

15 Mount Bashan, majestic mountain,
Mount Bashan, rugged mountain,
16 why gaze in envy, you rugged mountain,
at the mountain where God chooses to reign,
where the LORD himself will dwell forever?
17 The chariots of God are tens of thousands
and thousands of thousands;
the Lord has come from Sinai into his sanctuary.[i]

[a] In Hebrew texts 67:1-7 is numbered 67:2-8. [b] 1 The Hebrew has *Selah* (a word of uncertain meaning) here and at the end of verse 4. [c] In Hebrew texts 68:1-35 is numbered 68:2-36. [d] 4 Or *name, / prepare the way for him who rides through the deserts* [e] 6 Or *the desolate in a homeland* [f] 7 The Hebrew has *Selah* (a word of uncertain meaning) here and at the end of verses 19 and 32. [g] 13 Or *the campfires;* or *the saddlebags* [h] 14 Hebrew *Shaddai* [i] 17 Probable reading of the original Hebrew text; Masoretic Text *Lord is among them at Sinai in holiness*

18 When you ascended on high,
you took many captives;
you received gifts from people,
even from[a] the rebellious —
that you,[b] LORD God, might dwell there.

19 Praise be to the Lord, to God our Savior,
who daily bears our burdens.
20 Our God is a God who saves;
from the Sovereign LORD comes escape from death.
21 Surely God will crush the heads of his enemies,
the hairy crowns of those who go on in their sins.
22 The Lord says, "I will bring them from Bashan;
I will bring them from the depths of the sea,
23 that your feet may wade in the blood of your foes,
while the tongues of your dogs have their share."

24 Your procession, God, has come into view,
the procession of my God and King into the sanctuary.
25 In front are the singers, after them the musicians;
with them are the young women playing the timbrels.
26 Praise God in the great congregation;
praise the LORD in the assembly of Israel.
27 There is the little tribe of Benjamin, leading them,
there the great throng of Judah's princes,
and there the princes of Zebulun and of Naphtali.

28 Summon your power, God[c];
show us your strength, our God, as you have done before.
29 Because of your temple at Jerusalem
kings will bring you gifts.
30 Rebuke the beast among the reeds,
the herd of bulls among the calves of the nations.
Humbled, may the beast bring bars of silver.
Scatter the nations who delight in war.
31 Envoys will come from Egypt;
Cush[d] will submit herself to God.
32 Sing to God, you kingdoms of the earth,
sing praise to the Lord,
33 to him who rides across the highest heavens, the ancient heavens,
who thunders with mighty voice.
34 Proclaim the power of God,
whose majesty is over Israel,
whose power is in the heavens.
35 You, God, are awesome in your sanctuary;
the God of Israel gives power and strength to his people.

Praise be to God!

Psalm 69[e]

For the director of music. To the tune of "Lilies." Of David.

1 Save me, O God,
for the waters have come up to my neck.
2 I sink in the miry depths,
where there is no foothold.
I have come into the deep waters;
the floods engulf me.
3 I am worn out calling for help;
my throat is parched.
My eyes fail,
looking for my God.
4 Those who hate me without reason
outnumber the hairs of my head;
many are my enemies without cause,
those who seek to destroy me.
I am forced to restore
what I did not steal.

5 You, God, know my folly;
my guilt is not hidden from you.

6 Lord, the LORD Almighty,
may those who hope in you
not be disgraced because of me;
God of Israel,
may those who seek you
not be put to shame because of me.
7 For I endure scorn for your sake,
and shame covers my face.
8 I am a foreigner to my own family,
a stranger to my own mother's children;
9 for zeal for your house consumes me,
and the insults of those who insult you fall on me.
10 When I weep and fast,
I must endure scorn;
11 when I put on sackcloth,
people make sport of me.
12 Those who sit at the gate mock me,
and I am the song of the drunkards.

[a] *18* Or *gifts for people, / even* [b] *18* Or *they* [c] *28* Many Hebrew manuscripts, Septuagint and Syriac; most Hebrew manuscripts *Your God has summoned power for you* [d] *31* That is, the upper Nile region [e] In Hebrew texts 69:1-36 is numbered 69:2-37.

13 But I pray to you, LORD,
in the time of your favor;
in your great love, O God,
answer me with your sure salvation.
14 Rescue me from the mire,
do not let me sink;
deliver me from those who hate me,
from the deep waters.
15 Do not let the floodwaters engulf me
or the depths swallow me up
or the pit close its mouth over me.

16 Answer me, LORD, out of the goodness
of your love;
in your great mercy turn to me.
17 Do not hide your face from your
servant;
answer me quickly, for I am in
trouble.
18 Come near and rescue me;
deliver me because of my foes.

19 You know how I am scorned,
disgraced and shamed;
all my enemies are before you.
20 Scorn has broken my heart
and has left me helpless;
I looked for sympathy, but there was
none,
for comforters, but I found none.
21 They put gall in my food
and gave me vinegar for my thirst.

22 May the table set before them become
a snare;
may it become retribution and[a]
a trap.
23 May their eyes be darkened so they
cannot see,
and their backs be bent forever.
24 Pour out your wrath on them;
let your fierce anger overtake
them.
25 May their place be deserted;
let there be no one to dwell in their
tents.
26 For they persecute those you wound
and talk about the pain of those
you hurt.
27 Charge them with crime upon crime;
do not let them share in your
salvation.
28 May they be blotted out of the book
of life
and not be listed with the
righteous.

29 But as for me, afflicted and in pain —
may your salvation, God, protect
me.

30 I will praise God's name in song
and glorify him with thanksgiving.
31 This will please the LORD more than
an ox,
more than a bull with its horns and
hooves.
32 The poor will see and be glad —
you who seek God, may your hearts
live!
33 The LORD hears the needy
and does not despise his captive
people.

34 Let heaven and earth praise him,
the seas and all that move in them,
35 for God will save Zion
and rebuild the cities of Judah.
Then people will settle there and
possess it;
36 the children of his servants will
inherit it,
and those who love his name will
dwell there.

Psalm 70[b]

For the director of music. Of David. A petition.

1 Hasten, O God, to save me;
come quickly, LORD, to help me.

2 May those who want to take my life
be put to shame and confusion;
may all who desire my ruin
be turned back in disgrace.
3 May those who say to me, "Aha! Aha!"
turn back because of their shame.
4 But may all who seek you
rejoice and be glad in you;
may those who long for your saving
help always say,
"The LORD is great!"

5 But as for me, I am poor and needy;
come quickly to me, O God.
You are my help and my deliverer;
LORD, do not delay.

Psalm 71

1 In you, LORD, I have taken refuge;
let me never be put to shame.
2 In your righteousness, rescue me and
deliver me;
turn your ear to me and save me.
3 Be my rock of refuge,
to which I can always go;
give the command to save me,
for you are my rock and my
fortress.
4 Deliver me, my God, from the hand of
the wicked,
from the grasp of those who are
evil and cruel.

[a] *22* Or *snare / and their fellowship become*

[b] In Hebrew texts 70:1-5 is numbered 70:2-6.

5 For you have been my hope,
Sovereign LORD,
my confidence since my youth.
6 From birth I have relied on you;
you brought me forth from my
mother's womb.
I will ever praise you.
7 I have become a sign to many;
you are my strong refuge.
8 My mouth is filled with your praise,
declaring your splendor all day
long.

9 Do not cast me away when I am old;
do not forsake me when my
strength is gone.
10 For my enemies speak against me;
those who wait to kill me conspire
together.
11 They say, "God has forsaken him;
pursue him and seize him,
for no one will rescue him."
12 Do not be far from me, my God;
come quickly, God, to help me.
13 May my accusers perish in shame;
may those who want to harm me
be covered with scorn and disgrace.

14 As for me, I will always have hope;
I will praise you more and more.
15 My mouth will tell of your righteous
deeds,
of your saving acts all day long—
though I know not how to relate
them all.
16 I will come and proclaim your mighty
acts, Sovereign LORD;
I will proclaim your righteous
deeds, yours alone.
17 Since my youth, God, you have taught
me,
and to this day I declare your
marvelous deeds.
18 Even when I am old and gray,
do not forsake me, my God,
till I declare your power to the next
generation,
your mighty acts to all who are to
come.

19 Your righteousness, God, reaches to
the heavens,
you who have done great things.
Who is like you, God?
20 Though you have made me see
troubles,
many and bitter,
you will restore my life again;
from the depths of the earth
you will again bring me up.
21 You will increase my honor
and comfort me once more.

22 I will praise you with the harp
for your faithfulness, my God;
I will sing praise to you with the lyre,
Holy One of Israel.
23 My lips will shout for joy
when I sing praise to you—
I whom you have delivered.
24 My tongue will tell of your righteous
acts
all day long,
for those who wanted to harm me
have been put to shame and
confusion.

Psalm 72

Of Solomon.

1 Endow the king with your justice,
O God,
the royal son with your
righteousness.
2 May he judge your people in
righteousness,
your afflicted ones with justice.

3 May the mountains bring prosperity
to the people,
the hills the fruit of righteousness.
4 May he defend the afflicted among
the people
and save the children of the needy;
may he crush the oppressor.
5 May he endure[a] as long as the sun,
as long as the moon, through all
generations.
6 May he be like rain falling on a mown
field,
like showers watering the earth.
7 In his days may the righteous
flourish
and prosperity abound till the
moon is no more.

8 May he rule from sea to sea
and from the River[b] to the ends of
the earth.
9 May the desert tribes bow before him
and his enemies lick the dust.
10 May the kings of Tarshish and of
distant shores
bring tribute to him.
May the kings of Sheba and Seba
present him gifts.
11 May all kings bow down to him
and all nations serve him.

12 For he will deliver the needy who cry
out,
the afflicted who have no one to
help.
13 He will take pity on the weak and the
needy
and save the needy from death.

[a] 5 Septuagint; Hebrew *You will be feared* [b] 8 That is, the Euphrates

14 He will rescue them from oppression
and violence,
for precious is their blood in his
sight.

15 Long may he live!
May gold from Sheba be given him.
May people ever pray for him
and bless him all day long.
16 May grain abound throughout the
land;
on the tops of the hills may it sway.
May the crops flourish like Lebanon
and thrive[a] like the grass of the
field.
17 May his name endure forever;
may it continue as long as the sun.

Then all nations will be blessed
through him,[b]
and they will call him blessed.

18 Praise be to the LORD God, the God of
Israel,
who alone does marvelous deeds.
19 Praise be to his glorious name
forever;
may the whole earth be filled with
his glory.
Amen and Amen.

20 This concludes the prayers of David
son of Jesse.

BOOK III

Psalms 73 – 89

Psalm 73

A psalm of Asaph.

1 Surely God is good to Israel,
to those who are pure in heart.

2 But as for me, my feet had almost
slipped;
I had nearly lost my foothold.
3 For I envied the arrogant
when I saw the prosperity of the
wicked.

4 They have no struggles;
their bodies are healthy and
strong.[c]
5 They are free from common human
burdens;
they are not plagued by human ills.
6 Therefore pride is their necklace;
they clothe themselves with
violence.
7 From their callous hearts comes
iniquity[d];
their evil imaginations have no
limits.
8 They scoff, and speak with malice;
with arrogance they threaten
oppression.
9 Their mouths lay claim to heaven,
and their tongues take possession
of the earth.
10 Therefore their people turn to them
and drink up waters in
abundance.[e]
11 They say, "How would God know?
Does the Most High know
anything?"

12 This is what the wicked are like —
always free of care, they go on
amassing wealth.

13 Surely in vain I have kept my heart
pure
and have washed my hands in
innocence.
14 All day long I have been afflicted,
and every morning brings new
punishments.

15 If I had spoken out like that,
I would have betrayed your
children.
16 When I tried to understand all this,
it troubled me deeply
17 till I entered the sanctuary of God;
then I understood their final
destiny.

18 Surely you place them on slippery
ground;
you cast them down to ruin.
19 How suddenly are they destroyed,
completely swept away by terrors!
20 They are like a dream when one
awakes;
when you arise, Lord,
you will despise them as fantasies.

21 When my heart was grieved
and my spirit embittered,
22 I was senseless and ignorant;
I was a brute beast before you.

23 Yet I am always with you;
you hold me by my right hand.
24 You guide me with your counsel,
and afterward you will take me
into glory.

[a] *16* Probable reading of the original Hebrew text; Masoretic Text *Lebanon, / from the city* [b] *17* Or *will use his name in blessings* (see Gen. 48:20) [c] *4* With a different word division of the Hebrew; Masoretic Text *struggles at their death; / their bodies are healthy* [d] *7* Syriac (see also Septuagint); Hebrew *Their eyes bulge with fat* [e] *10* The meaning of the Hebrew for this verse is uncertain.

25 Whom have I in heaven but you?
And earth has nothing I desire
besides you.
26 My flesh and my heart may fail,
but God is the strength of my heart
and my portion forever.
27 Those who are far from you will perish;
you destroy all who are unfaithful
to you.
28 But as for me, it is good to be near God.
I have made the Sovereign LORD
my refuge;
I will tell of all your deeds.

Psalm 74

A maskil[a] of Asaph.

1 O God, why have you rejected us
forever?
Why does your anger smolder
against the sheep of your
pasture?
2 Remember the nation you purchased
long ago,
the people of your inheritance,
whom you redeemed —
Mount Zion, where you dwelt.
3 Turn your steps toward these
everlasting ruins,
all this destruction the enemy has
brought on the sanctuary.
4 Your foes roared in the place where
you met with us;
they set up their standards as
signs.
5 They behaved like men wielding axes
to cut through a thicket of trees.
6 They smashed all the carved paneling
with their axes and hatchets.
7 They burned your sanctuary to the
ground;
they defiled the dwelling place of
your Name.
8 They said in their hearts, "We will
crush them completely!"
They burned every place where God
was worshiped in the land.
9 We are given no signs from God;
no prophets are left,
and none of us knows how long
this will be.
10 How long will the enemy mock you,
God?
Will the foe revile your name
forever?
11 Why do you hold back your hand,
your right hand?
Take it from the folds of your
garment and destroy them!
12 But God is my King from long ago;
he brings salvation on the earth.
13 It was you who split open the sea
by your power;
you broke the heads of the monster
in the waters.
14 It was you who crushed the heads
of Leviathan
and gave it as food to the creatures
of the desert.
15 It was you who opened up springs
and streams;
you dried up the ever-flowing
rivers.
16 The day is yours, and yours also the
night;
you established the sun
and moon.
17 It was you who set all the boundaries
of the earth;
you made both summer and
winter.
18 Remember how the enemy has
mocked you, LORD,
how foolish people have reviled
your name.
19 Do not hand over the life of your dove
to wild beasts;
do not forget the lives of your
afflicted people forever.
20 Have regard for your covenant,
because haunts of violence fill the
dark places of the land.
21 Do not let the oppressed retreat in
disgrace;
may the poor and needy praise
your name.
22 Rise up, O God, and defend your
cause;
remember how fools mock you all
day long.
23 Do not ignore the clamor of your
adversaries,
the uproar of your enemies, which
rises continually.

Psalm 75[b]

For the director of music. To the tune of "Do Not Destroy." A psalm of Asaph. A song.

1 We praise you, God,
we praise you, for your Name is
near;
people tell of your wonderful
deeds.
2 You say, "I choose the appointed
time;
it is I who judge with equity.

[a] Title: Probably a literary or musical term [b] In Hebrew texts 75:1-10 is numbered 75:2-11.

[3]When the earth and all its people
quake,
it is I who hold its pillars firm.[a]
[4]To the arrogant I say, 'Boast no more,'
and to the wicked, 'Do not lift up
your horns.[b]
[5]Do not lift your horns against heaven;
do not speak so defiantly.'"

[6]No one from the east or the west
or from the desert can exalt
themselves.
[7]It is God who judges:
He brings one down, he exalts
another.
[8]In the hand of the LORD is a cup
full of foaming wine mixed with
spices;
he pours it out, and all the wicked of
the earth
drink it down to its very dregs.

[9]As for me, I will declare this forever;
I will sing praise to the God of
Jacob,
[10]who says, "I will cut off the horns of
all the wicked,
but the horns of the righteous will
be lifted up."

Psalm 76[c]

For the director of music. With stringed instruments. A psalm of Asaph. A song.

[1]God is renowned in Judah;
in Israel his name is great.
[2]His tent is in Salem,
his dwelling place in Zion.
[3]There he broke the flashing arrows,
the shields and the swords, the
weapons of war.[d]

[4]You are radiant with light,
more majestic than mountains rich
with game.
[5]The valiant lie plundered,
they sleep their last sleep;
not one of the warriors
can lift his hands.
[6]At your rebuke, God of Jacob,
both horse and chariot lie still.

[7]It is you alone who are to be feared.
Who can stand before you when
you are angry?
[8]From heaven you pronounced
judgment,
and the land feared and was quiet—
[9]when you, God, rose up to judge,
to save all the afflicted of the land.
[10]Surely your wrath against mankind
brings you praise,
and the survivors of your wrath are
restrained.[e]

[11]Make vows to the LORD your God and
fulfill them;
let all the neighboring lands
bring gifts to the One to be feared.
[12]He breaks the spirit of rulers;
he is feared by the kings of the
earth.

Psalm 77[f]

For the director of music. For Jeduthun. Of Asaph. A psalm.

[1]I cried out to God for help;
I cried out to God to hear me.
[2]When I was in distress, I sought the
Lord;
at night I stretched out untiring
hands,
and I would not be comforted.

[3]I remembered you, God, and I
groaned;
I meditated, and my spirit grew
faint.[g]
[4]You kept my eyes from closing;
I was too troubled to speak.
[5]I thought about the former days,
the years of long ago;
[6]I remembered my songs in the night.
My heart meditated and my spirit
asked:

[7]"Will the Lord reject forever?
Will he never show his favor again?
[8]Has his unfailing love vanished
forever?
Has his promise failed for all time?
[9]Has God forgotten to be merciful?
Has he in anger withheld his
compassion?"

[10]Then I thought, "To this I will appeal:
the years when the Most High
stretched out his right hand.
[11]I will remember the deeds of the
LORD;
yes, I will remember your miracles
of long ago.
[12]I will consider all your works
and meditate on all your mighty
deeds."

[a] *3* The Hebrew has *Selah* (a word of uncertain meaning) here. [b] *4* *Horns* here symbolize strength; also in verses 5 and 10. [c] In Hebrew texts 76:1-12 is numbered 76:2-13. [d] *3* The Hebrew has *Selah* (a word of uncertain meaning) here and at the end of verse 9. [e] *10* Or *Surely the wrath of mankind brings you praise, / and with the remainder of wrath you arm yourself* [f] In Hebrew texts 77:1-20 is numbered 77:2-21. [g] *3* The Hebrew has *Selah* (a word of uncertain meaning) here and at the end of verses 9 and 15.

13 Your ways, God, are holy.
What god is as great as our God?
14 You are the God who performs miracles;
you display your power among the peoples.
15 With your mighty arm you redeemed your people,
the descendants of Jacob and Joseph.

16 The waters saw you, God,
the waters saw you and writhed;
the very depths were convulsed.
17 The clouds poured down water,
the heavens resounded with thunder;
your arrows flashed back and forth.
18 Your thunder was heard in the whirlwind,
your lightning lit up the world;
the earth trembled and quaked.
19 Your path led through the sea,
your way through the mighty waters,
though your footprints were not seen.

20 You led your people like a flock
by the hand of Moses and Aaron.

Psalm 78

A maskil[a] *of Asaph.*

1 My people, hear my teaching;
listen to the words of my mouth.
2 I will open my mouth with a parable;
I will utter hidden things, things from of old —
3 things we have heard and known,
things our ancestors have told us.
4 We will not hide them from their descendants;
we will tell the next generation
the praiseworthy deeds of the LORD,
his power, and the wonders he has done.
5 He decreed statutes for Jacob
and established the law in Israel,
which he commanded our ancestors
to teach their children,
6 so the next generation would know them,
even the children yet to be born,
and they in turn would tell their children.
7 Then they would put their trust in God
and would not forget his deeds
but would keep his commands.
8 They would not be like their ancestors —
a stubborn and rebellious generation,
whose hearts were not loyal to God,
whose spirits were not faithful to him.

9 The men of Ephraim, though armed with bows,
turned back on the day of battle;
10 they did not keep God's covenant
and refused to live by his law.
11 They forgot what he had done,
the wonders he had shown them.
12 He did miracles in the sight of their ancestors
in the land of Egypt, in the region of Zoan.
13 He divided the sea and led them through;
he made the water stand up like a wall.
14 He guided them with the cloud by day
and with light from the fire all night.
15 He split the rocks in the wilderness
and gave them water as abundant as the seas;
16 he brought streams out of a rocky crag
and made water flow down like rivers.

17 But they continued to sin against him,
rebelling in the wilderness against the Most High.
18 They willfully put God to the test
by demanding the food they craved.
19 They spoke against God;
they said, "Can God really
spread a table in the wilderness?
20 True, he struck the rock,
and water gushed out,
streams flowed abundantly,
but can he also give us bread?
Can he supply meat for his people?"
21 When the LORD heard them, he was furious;
his fire broke out against Jacob,
and his wrath rose against Israel,
22 for they did not believe in God
or trust in his deliverance.
23 Yet he gave a command to the skies above
and opened the doors of the heavens;
24 he rained down manna for the people to eat,
he gave them the grain of heaven.

[a] Title: Probably a literary or musical term

25 Human beings ate the bread of angels;
he sent them all the food they could eat.
26 He let loose the east wind from the heavens
and by his power made the south wind blow.
27 He rained meat down on them like dust,
birds like sand on the seashore.
28 He made them come down inside their camp,
all around their tents.
29 They ate till they were gorged —
he had given them what they craved.
30 But before they turned from what they craved,
even while the food was still in their mouths,
31 God's anger rose against them;
he put to death the sturdiest among them,
cutting down the young men of Israel.

32 In spite of all this, they kept on sinning;
in spite of his wonders, they did not believe.
33 So he ended their days in futility
and their years in terror.
34 Whenever God slew them, they would seek him;
they eagerly turned to him again.
35 They remembered that God was their Rock,
that God Most High was their Redeemer.
36 But then they would flatter him with their mouths,
lying to him with their tongues;
37 their hearts were not loyal to him,
they were not faithful to his covenant.
38 Yet he was merciful;
he forgave their iniquities
and did not destroy them.
Time after time he restrained his anger
and did not stir up his full wrath.
39 He remembered that they were but flesh,
a passing breeze that does not return.

40 How often they rebelled against him in the wilderness
and grieved him in the wasteland!
41 Again and again they put God to the test;
they vexed the Holy One of Israel.
42 They did not remember his power —
the day he redeemed them from the oppressor,
43 the day he displayed his signs in Egypt,
his wonders in the region of Zoan.
44 He turned their river into blood;
they could not drink from their streams.
45 He sent swarms of flies that devoured them,
and frogs that devastated them.
46 He gave their crops to the grasshopper,
their produce to the locust.
47 He destroyed their vines with hail
and their sycamore-figs with sleet.
48 He gave over their cattle to the hail,
their livestock to bolts of lightning.
49 He unleashed against them his hot anger,
his wrath, indignation and hostility —
a band of destroying angels.
50 He prepared a path for his anger;
he did not spare them from death
but gave them over to the plague.
51 He struck down all the firstborn of Egypt,
the firstfruits of manhood in the tents of Ham.
52 But he brought his people out like a flock;
he led them like sheep through the wilderness.
53 He guided them safely, so they were unafraid;
but the sea engulfed their enemies.
54 And so he brought them to the border of his holy land,
to the hill country his right hand had taken.
55 He drove out nations before them
and allotted their lands to them as an inheritance;
he settled the tribes of Israel in their homes.

56 But they put God to the test
and rebelled against the Most High;
they did not keep his statutes.
57 Like their ancestors they were disloyal and faithless,
as unreliable as a faulty bow.
58 They angered him with their high places;
they aroused his jealousy with their idols.
59 When God heard them, he was furious;
he rejected Israel completely.

60 He abandoned the tabernacle of Shiloh,
the tent he had set up among humans.
61 He sent the ark of his might into captivity,
his splendor into the hands of the enemy.
62 He gave his people over to the sword;
he was furious with his inheritance.
63 Fire consumed their young men,
and their young women had no wedding songs;
64 their priests were put to the sword,
and their widows could not weep.

65 Then the Lord awoke as from sleep,
as a warrior wakes from the stupor of wine.
66 He beat back his enemies;
he put them to everlasting shame.
67 Then he rejected the tents of Joseph,
he did not choose the tribe of Ephraim;
68 but he chose the tribe of Judah,
Mount Zion, which he loved.
69 He built his sanctuary like the heights,
like the earth that he established forever.
70 He chose David his servant
and took him from the sheep pens;
71 from tending the sheep he brought him
to be the shepherd of his people Jacob,
of Israel his inheritance.
72 And David shepherded them with integrity of heart;
with skillful hands he led them.

Psalm 79

A psalm of Asaph.

1 O God, the nations have invaded your inheritance;
they have defiled your holy temple,
they have reduced Jerusalem to rubble.
2 They have left the dead bodies of your servants
as food for the birds of the sky,
the flesh of your own people for the animals of the wild.
3 They have poured out blood like water
all around Jerusalem,
and there is no one to bury the dead.
4 We are objects of contempt to our neighbors,
of scorn and derision to those around us.

5 How long, LORD? Will you be angry forever?
How long will your jealousy burn like fire?
6 Pour out your wrath on the nations
that do not acknowledge you,
on the kingdoms
that do not call on your name;
7 for they have devoured Jacob
and devastated his homeland.
8 Do not hold against us the sins of past generations;
may your mercy come quickly to meet us,
for we are in desperate need.
9 Help us, God our Savior,
for the glory of your name;
deliver us and forgive our sins
for your name's sake.
10 Why should the nations say,
"Where is their God?"

Before our eyes, make known among the nations
that you avenge the outpoured blood of your servants.
11 May the groans of the prisoners come before you;
with your strong arm preserve those condemned to die.
12 Pay back into the laps of our neighbors seven times
the contempt they have hurled at you, Lord.
13 Then we your people, the sheep of your pasture,
will praise you forever;
from generation to generation
we will proclaim your praise.

Psalm 80[a]

For the director of music. To the tune of "The Lilies of the Covenant." Of Asaph. A psalm.

1 Hear us, Shepherd of Israel,
you who lead Joseph like a flock.
You who sit enthroned between the cherubim,
shine forth 2 before Ephraim,
Benjamin and Manasseh.
Awaken your might;
come and save us.

3 Restore us, O God;
make your face shine on us,
that we may be saved.

4 How long, LORD God Almighty,
will your anger smolder
against the prayers of your people?

[a] In Hebrew texts 80:1-19 is numbered 80:2-20.

5 You have fed them with the bread of tears;
you have made them drink tears by the bowlful.
6 You have made us an object of derision[a] to our neighbors,
and our enemies mock us.

7 Restore us, God Almighty;
make your face shine on us,
that we may be saved.

8 You transplanted a vine from Egypt;
you drove out the nations and planted it.
9 You cleared the ground for it,
and it took root and filled the land.
10 The mountains were covered with its shade,
the mighty cedars with its branches.
11 Its branches reached as far as the Sea,[b]
its shoots as far as the River.[c]

12 Why have you broken down its walls
so that all who pass by pick its grapes?
13 Boars from the forest ravage it,
and insects from the fields feed on it.
14 Return to us, God Almighty!
Look down from heaven and see!
Watch over this vine,
15 the root your right hand has planted,
the son[d] you have raised up for yourself.

16 Your vine is cut down, it is burned with fire;
at your rebuke your people perish.
17 Let your hand rest on the man at your right hand,
the son of man you have raised up for yourself.
18 Then we will not turn away from you;
revive us, and we will call on your name.

19 Restore us, LORD God Almighty;
make your face shine on us,
that we may be saved.

Psalm 81[e]

For the director of music. According to gittith.[f] *Of Asaph.*

1 Sing for joy to God our strength;
shout aloud to the God of Jacob!
2 Begin the music, strike the timbrel,
play the melodious harp and lyre.
3 Sound the ram's horn at the New Moon,
and when the moon is full, on the day of our festival;
4 this is a decree for Israel,
an ordinance of the God of Jacob.
5 When God went out against Egypt,
he established it as a statute for Joseph.

I heard an unknown voice say:

6 "I removed the burden from their shoulders;
their hands were set free from the basket.
7 In your distress you called and I rescued you,
I answered you out of a thundercloud;
I tested you at the waters of Meribah.[g]
8 Hear me, my people, and I will warn you —
if you would only listen to me, Israel!
9 You shall have no foreign god among you;
you shall not worship any god other than me.
10 I am the LORD your God,
who brought you up out of Egypt.
Open wide your mouth and I will fill it.

11 "But my people would not listen to me;
Israel would not submit to me.
12 So I gave them over to their stubborn hearts
to follow their own devices.

13 "If my people would only listen to me,
if Israel would only follow my ways,
14 how quickly I would subdue their enemies
and turn my hand against their foes!
15 Those who hate the LORD would cringe before him,
and their punishment would last forever.
16 But you would be fed with the finest of wheat;
with honey from the rock I would satisfy you."

[a] 6 Probable reading of the original Hebrew text; Masoretic Text *contention* [b] 11 Probably the Mediterranean [c] 11 That is, the Euphrates [d] 15 Or *branch* [e] In Hebrew texts 81:1-16 is numbered 81:2-17. [f] Title: Probably a musical term [g] 7 The Hebrew has *Selah* (a word of uncertain meaning) here.

Psalm 82

A psalm of Asaph.

1 God presides in the great assembly;
he renders judgment among the "gods":
2 "How long will you[a] defend the unjust
and show partiality to the wicked?[b]
3 Defend the weak and the fatherless;
uphold the cause of the poor and the oppressed.
4 Rescue the weak and the needy;
deliver them from the hand of the wicked.

5 "The 'gods' know nothing, they understand nothing.
They walk about in darkness;
all the foundations of the earth are shaken.

6 "I said, 'You are "gods";
you are all sons of the Most High.'
7 But you will die like mere mortals;
you will fall like every other ruler."

8 Rise up, O God, judge the earth,
for all the nations are your inheritance.

Psalm 83[c]

A song. A psalm of Asaph.

1 O God, do not remain silent;
do not turn a deaf ear,
do not stand aloof, O God.
2 See how your enemies growl,
how your foes rear their heads.
3 With cunning they conspire against your people;
they plot against those you cherish.
4 "Come," they say, "let us destroy them as a nation,
so that Israel's name is remembered no more."

5 With one mind they plot together;
they form an alliance against you —
6 the tents of Edom and the Ishmaelites,
of Moab and the Hagrites,
7 Byblos, Ammon and Amalek,
Philistia, with the people of Tyre.
8 Even Assyria has joined them
to reinforce Lot's descendants.[b]

9 Do to them as you did to Midian,
as you did to Sisera and Jabin at the river Kishon,
10 who perished at Endor
and became like dung on the ground.
11 Make their nobles like Oreb and Zeeb,
all their princes like Zebah and Zalmunna,
12 who said, "Let us take possession
of the pasturelands of God."

13 Make them like tumbleweed, my God,
like chaff before the wind.
14 As fire consumes the forest
or a flame sets the mountains ablaze,
15 so pursue them with your tempest
and terrify them with your storm.
16 Cover their faces with shame, LORD,
so that they will seek your name.

17 May they ever be ashamed and dismayed;
may they perish in disgrace.
18 Let them know that you, whose name is the LORD —
that you alone are the Most High
over all the earth.

Psalm 84[d]

For the director of music. According to gittith.[e] Of the Sons of Korah. A psalm.

1 How lovely is your dwelling place,
LORD Almighty!
2 My soul yearns, even faints,
for the courts of the LORD;
my heart and my flesh cry out
for the living God.
3 Even the sparrow has found a home,
and the swallow a nest for herself,
where she may have her young —
a place near your altar,
LORD Almighty, my King and my God.
4 Blessed are those who dwell in your house;
they are ever praising you.[f]

5 Blessed are those whose strength is in you,
whose hearts are set on pilgrimage.
6 As they pass through the Valley of Baka,
they make it a place of springs;
the autumn rains also cover it with pools.[g]
7 They go from strength to strength,
till each appears before God in Zion.

[a] 2 The Hebrew is plural. [b] 2,8 The Hebrew has *Selah* (a word of uncertain meaning) here. [c] In Hebrew texts 83:1-18 is numbered 83:2-19. [d] In Hebrew texts 84:1-12 is numbered 84:2-13. [e] Title: Probably a musical term [f] 4 The Hebrew has *Selah* (a word of uncertain meaning) here and at the end of verse 8. [g] 6 Or *blessings*

8 Hear my prayer, LORD God Almighty;
listen to me, God of Jacob.
9 Look on our shield,[a] O God;
look with favor on your anointed one.

10 Better is one day in your courts
than a thousand elsewhere;
I would rather be a doorkeeper in the house of my God
than dwell in the tents of the wicked.
11 For the LORD God is a sun and shield;
the LORD bestows favor and honor;
no good thing does he withhold
from those whose walk is blameless.

12 LORD Almighty,
blessed is the one who trusts in you.

Psalm 85[b]

For the director of music. Of the Sons of Korah. A psalm.

1 You, LORD, showed favor to your land;
you restored the fortunes of Jacob.
2 You forgave the iniquity of your people
and covered all their sins.[c]
3 You set aside all your wrath
and turned from your fierce anger.

4 Restore us again, God our Savior,
and put away your displeasure toward us.
5 Will you be angry with us forever?
Will you prolong your anger through all generations?
6 Will you not revive us again,
that your people may rejoice in you?
7 Show us your unfailing love, LORD,
and grant us your salvation.

8 I will listen to what God the LORD says;
he promises peace to his people, his faithful servants —
but let them not turn to folly.
9 Surely his salvation is near those who fear him,
that his glory may dwell in our land.

10 Love and faithfulness meet together;
righteousness and peace kiss each other.
11 Faithfulness springs forth from the earth,
and righteousness looks down from heaven.
12 The LORD will indeed give what is good,
and our land will yield its harvest.
13 Righteousness goes before him
and prepares the way for his steps.

Psalm 86

A prayer of David.

1 Hear me, LORD, and answer me,
for I am poor and needy.
2 Guard my life, for I am faithful to you;
save your servant who trusts in you.
You are my God; 3 have mercy on me, Lord,
for I call to you all day long.
4 Bring joy to your servant, Lord,
for I put my trust in you.

5 You, Lord, are forgiving and good,
abounding in love to all who call to you.
6 Hear my prayer, LORD;
listen to my cry for mercy.
7 When I am in distress, I call to you,
because you answer me.

8 Among the gods there is none like you, Lord;
no deeds can compare with yours.
9 All the nations you have made
will come and worship before you, Lord;
they will bring glory to your name.
10 For you are great and do marvelous deeds;
you alone are God.

11 Teach me your way, LORD,
that I may rely on your faithfulness;
give me an undivided heart,
that I may fear your name.
12 I will praise you, Lord my God, with all my heart;
I will glorify your name forever.
13 For great is your love toward me;
you have delivered me from the depths,
from the realm of the dead.

14 Arrogant foes are attacking me, O God;
ruthless people are trying to kill me —
they have no regard for you.
15 But you, Lord, are a compassionate and gracious God,
slow to anger, abounding in love and faithfulness.

[a] 9 Or *sovereign* [b] In Hebrew texts 85:1-13 is numbered 85:2-14. [c] 2 The Hebrew has *Selah* (a word of uncertain meaning) here.

16 Turn to me and have mercy on me;
show your strength in behalf of your servant;
save me, because I serve you
just as my mother did.
17 Give me a sign of your goodness,
that my enemies may see it and be put to shame,
for you, LORD, have helped me and comforted me.

Psalm 87

Of the Sons of Korah. A psalm. A song.

1 He has founded his city on the holy mountain.
2 The LORD loves the gates of Zion
more than all the other dwellings of Jacob.

3 Glorious things are said of you,
city of God:[a]
4 "I will record Rahab[b] and Babylon
among those who acknowledge me—
Philistia too, and Tyre, along with Cush[c]—
and will say, 'This one was born in Zion.'"[d]
5 Indeed, of Zion it will be said,
"This one and that one were born in her,
and the Most High himself will establish her."
6 The LORD will write in the register of the peoples:
"This one was born in Zion."

7 As they make music they will sing,
"All my fountains are in you."

Psalm 88[e]

A song. A psalm of the Sons of Korah. For the director of music. According to mahalath leannoth.[f] *A* maskil[g] *of Heman the Ezrahite.*

1 LORD, you are the God who saves me;
day and night I cry out to you.
2 May my prayer come before you;
turn your ear to my cry.

3 I am overwhelmed with troubles
and my life draws near to death.
4 I am counted among those who go down to the pit;
I am like one without strength.
5 I am set apart with the dead,
like the slain who lie in the grave,
whom you remember no more,
who are cut off from your care.

6 You have put me in the lowest pit,
in the darkest depths.
7 Your wrath lies heavily on me;
you have overwhelmed me with all your waves.[h]
8 You have taken from me my closest friends
and have made me repulsive to them.
I am confined and cannot escape;
9 my eyes are dim with grief.

I call to you, LORD, every day;
I spread out my hands to you.
10 Do you show your wonders to the dead?
Do their spirits rise up and praise you?
11 Is your love declared in the grave,
your faithfulness in Destruction[i]?
12 Are your wonders known in the place of darkness,
or your righteous deeds in the land of oblivion?

13 But I cry to you for help, LORD;
in the morning my prayer comes before you.
14 Why, LORD, do you reject me
and hide your face from me?

15 From my youth I have suffered and been close to death;
I have borne your terrors and am in despair.
16 Your wrath has swept over me;
your terrors have destroyed me.
17 All day long they surround me like a flood;
they have completely engulfed me.
18 You have taken from me friend and neighbor—
darkness is my closest friend.

Psalm 89[j]

A maskil[g] *of Ethan the Ezrahite.*

1 I will sing of the LORD's great love forever;
with my mouth I will make your faithfulness known
through all generations.

[a] *3* The Hebrew has *Selah* (a word of uncertain meaning) here and at the end of verse 6.
[b] *4* A poetic name for Egypt [c] *4* That is, the upper Nile region [d] *4* Or *"I will record concerning those who acknowledge me: / 'This one was born in Zion.' / Hear this, Rahab and Babylon, / and you too, Philistia, Tyre and Cush."* [e] In Hebrew texts 88:1-18 is numbered 88:2-19.
[f] Title: Possibly a tune, "The Suffering of Affliction" [g] Title: Probably a literary or musical term [h] *7* The Hebrew has *Selah* (a word of uncertain meaning) here and at the end of verse 10.
[i] *11* Hebrew *Abaddon* [j] In Hebrew texts 89:1-52 is numbered 89:2-53.

2 I will declare that your love stands
firm forever,
that you have established your
faithfulness in heaven itself.
3 You said, "I have made a covenant
with my chosen one,
I have sworn to David my servant,
4 'I will establish your line forever
and make your throne firm
through all generations.' "[a]

5 The heavens praise your wonders,
LORD,
your faithfulness too, in the
assembly of the holy ones.
6 For who in the skies above can
compare with the LORD?
Who is like the LORD among the
heavenly beings?
7 In the council of the holy ones God is
greatly feared;
he is more awesome than all who
surround him.
8 Who is like you, LORD God Almighty?
You, LORD, are mighty, and your
faithfulness surrounds you.

9 You rule over the surging sea;
when its waves mount up, you still
them.
10 You crushed Rahab like one of the
slain;
with your strong arm you scattered
your enemies.
11 The heavens are yours, and yours
also the earth;
you founded the world and all that
is in it.
12 You created the north and the south;
Tabor and Hermon sing for joy at
your name.
13 Your arm is endowed with power;
your hand is strong, your right
hand exalted.

14 Righteousness and justice are the
foundation of your throne;
love and faithfulness go before
you.
15 Blessed are those who have learned
to acclaim you,
who walk in the light of your
presence, LORD.
16 They rejoice in your name all day
long;
they celebrate your righteousness.
17 For you are their glory and strength,
and by your favor you exalt our
horn.[b]
18 Indeed, our shield[c] belongs to the
LORD,
our king to the Holy One of Israel.

19 Once you spoke in a vision,
to your faithful people you said:
"I have bestowed strength on a
warrior;
I have raised up a young man from
among the people.
20 I have found David my servant;
with my sacred oil I have anointed
him.
21 My hand will sustain him;
surely my arm will strengthen
him.
22 The enemy will not get the better of
him;
the wicked will not oppress him.
23 I will crush his foes before him
and strike down his adversaries.
24 My faithful love will be with him,
and through my name his horn[d]
will be exalted.
25 I will set his hand over the sea,
his right hand over the rivers.
26 He will call out to me, 'You are my
Father,
my God, the Rock my Savior.'
27 And I will appoint him to be my
firstborn,
the most exalted of the kings of
the earth.
28 I will maintain my love to him
forever,
and my covenant with him will
never fail.
29 I will establish his line forever,
his throne as long as the heavens
endure.

30 "If his sons forsake my law
and do not follow my statutes,
31 if they violate my decrees
and fail to keep my commands,
32 I will punish their sin with the rod,
their iniquity with flogging;
33 but I will not take my love
from him,
nor will I ever betray my
faithfulness.
34 I will not violate my covenant
or alter what my lips have uttered.
35 Once for all, I have sworn by my
holiness —
and I will not lie to David —
36 that his line will continue forever
and his throne endure before me
like the sun;

[a] 4 The Hebrew has *Selah* (a word of uncertain meaning) here and at the end of verses 37, 45 and 48. [b] 17 *Horn* here symbolizes strong one. [c] 18 Or *sovereign* [d] 24 *Horn* here symbolizes strength.

[37] it will be established forever like the
moon,
the faithful witness in the sky."

[38] But you have rejected, you have
spurned,
you have been very angry with
your anointed one.
[39] You have renounced the covenant
with your servant
and have defiled his crown in the
dust.
[40] You have broken through all
his walls
and reduced his strongholds to
ruins.
[41] All who pass by have plundered him;
he has become the scorn of his
neighbors.
[42] You have exalted the right hand of
his foes;
you have made all his enemies
rejoice.
[43] Indeed, you have turned back the
edge of his sword
and have not supported him in
battle.
[44] You have put an end to his splendor
and cast his throne to the ground.
[45] You have cut short the days of his
youth;
you have covered him with a
mantle of shame.

[46] How long, LORD? Will you hide
yourself forever?
How long will your wrath burn like
fire?
[47] Remember how fleeting is my life.
For what futility you have created
all humanity!
[48] Who can live and not see death,
or who can escape the power
of the grave?
[49] Lord, where is your former
great love,
which in your faithfulness you
swore to David?
[50] Remember, Lord, how your servant
has[a] been mocked,
how I bear in my heart the taunts
of all the nations,
[51] the taunts with which your enemies,
LORD, have mocked,
with which they have mocked
every step of your anointed
one.

[52] Praise be to the LORD forever!
Amen and Amen.

[a] 50 Or *your servants have*

BOOK IV

Psalms 90 – 106

Psalm 90

A prayer of Moses the man of God.

[1] Lord, you have been our dwelling place
throughout all generations.
[2] Before the mountains were born
or you brought forth the whole
world,
from everlasting to everlasting you
are God.

[3] You turn people back to dust,
saying, "Return to dust, you
mortals."
[4] A thousand years in your sight
are like a day that has just gone by,
or like a watch in the night.
[5] Yet you sweep people away in the
sleep of death —
they are like the new grass of the
morning:
[6] In the morning it springs up new,
but by evening it is dry and
withered.

[7] We are consumed by your anger
and terrified by your indignation.
[8] You have set our iniquities before you,
our secret sins in the light of your
presence.
[9] All our days pass away under your
wrath;
we finish our years with a moan.
[10] Our days may come to seventy years,
or eighty, if our strength endures;
yet the best of them are but trouble
and sorrow,
for they quickly pass, and we fly
away.
[11] If only we knew the power of your
anger!
Your wrath is as great as the fear
that is your due.
[12] Teach us to number our days,
that we may gain a heart of
wisdom.

[13] Relent, LORD! How long will it be?
Have compassion on your servants.
[14] Satisfy us in the morning with your
unfailing love,
that we may sing for joy and be
glad all our days.
[15] Make us glad for as many days as you
have afflicted us,
for as many years as we have seen
trouble.

16 May your deeds be shown to your
servants,
your splendor to their children.

17 May the favor[a] of the Lord our God
rest on us;
establish the work of our hands
for us —
yes, establish the work of our
hands.

Psalm 91

1 Whoever dwells in the shelter of the
Most High
will rest in the shadow of the
Almighty.[b]
2 I will say of the LORD, "He is my
refuge and my fortress,
my God, in whom I trust."

3 Surely he will save you
from the fowler's snare
and from the deadly pestilence.
4 He will cover you with his feathers,
and under his wings you will find
refuge;
his faithfulness will be your shield
and rampart.
5 You will not fear the terror of night,
nor the arrow that flies by day,
6 nor the pestilence that stalks in the
darkness,
nor the plague that destroys at
midday.
7 A thousand may fall at your side,
ten thousand at your right hand,
but it will not come near you.
8 You will only observe with
your eyes
and see the punishment of the
wicked.

9 If you say, "The LORD is my refuge,"
and you make the Most High your
dwelling,
10 no harm will overtake you,
no disaster will come near your
tent.
11 For he will command his angels
concerning you
to guard you in all your ways;
12 they will lift you up in their hands,
so that you will not strike your foot
against a stone.
13 You will tread on the lion and the
cobra;
you will trample the great lion and
the serpent.

14 "Because he[c] loves me," says the
LORD, "I will rescue him;
I will protect him, for he
acknowledges my name.
15 He will call on me, and I will answer
him;
I will be with him in trouble,
I will deliver him and honor him.
16 With long life I will satisfy him
and show him my salvation."

Psalm 92[d]

A psalm. A song. For the Sabbath day.

1 It is good to praise the LORD
and make music to your name,
O Most High,
2 proclaiming your love in the morning
and your faithfulness at night,
3 to the music of the ten-stringed lyre
and the melody of the harp.

4 For you make me glad by your deeds,
LORD;
I sing for joy at what your hands
have done.
5 How great are your works, LORD,
how profound your thoughts!
6 Senseless people do not know,
fools do not understand,
7 that though the wicked spring up like
grass
and all evildoers flourish,
they will be destroyed forever.

8 But you, LORD, are forever exalted.

9 For surely your enemies, LORD,
surely your enemies will perish;
all evildoers will be scattered.
10 You have exalted my horn[e] like that
of a wild ox;
fine oils have been poured on me.
11 My eyes have seen the defeat of my
adversaries;
my ears have heard the rout of my
wicked foes.

12 The righteous will flourish like a
palm tree,
they will grow like a cedar of
Lebanon;
13 planted in the house of the LORD,
they will flourish in the courts of
our God.
14 They will still bear fruit in old age,
they will stay fresh and green,
15 proclaiming, "The LORD is upright;
he is my Rock, and there is no
wickedness in him."

[a] *17* Or *beauty* [b] *1* Hebrew *Shaddai* [c] *14* That is, probably the king [d] In Hebrew texts 92:1-15 is numbered 92:2-16. [e] *10* *Horn* here symbolizes strength.

Psalm 93

1 The LORD reigns, he is robed in majesty;
the LORD is robed in majesty and armed with strength;
indeed, the world is established, firm and secure.
2 Your throne was established long ago;
you are from all eternity.

3 The seas have lifted up, LORD,
the seas have lifted up their voice;
the seas have lifted up their pounding waves.
4 Mightier than the thunder of the great waters,
mightier than the breakers of the sea —
the LORD on high is mighty.

5 Your statutes, LORD, stand firm;
holiness adorns your house
for endless days.

Psalm 94

1 The LORD is a God who avenges.
O God who avenges, shine forth.
2 Rise up, Judge of the earth;
pay back to the proud what they deserve.
3 How long, LORD, will the wicked,
how long will the wicked be jubilant?

4 They pour out arrogant words;
all the evildoers are full of boasting.
5 They crush your people, LORD;
they oppress your inheritance.
6 They slay the widow and the foreigner;
they murder the fatherless.
7 They say, "The LORD does not see;
the God of Jacob takes no notice."

8 Take notice, you senseless ones among the people;
you fools, when will you become wise?
9 Does he who fashioned the ear not hear?
Does he who formed the eye not see?
10 Does he who disciplines nations not punish?
Does he who teaches mankind lack knowledge?
11 The LORD knows all human plans;
he knows that they are futile.

12 Blessed is the one you discipline, LORD,
the one you teach from your law;
13 you grant them relief from days of trouble,
till a pit is dug for the wicked.
14 For the LORD will not reject his people;
he will never forsake his inheritance.
15 Judgment will again be founded on righteousness,
and all the upright in heart will follow it.

16 Who will rise up for me against the wicked?
Who will take a stand for me against evildoers?
17 Unless the LORD had given me help,
I would soon have dwelt in the silence of death.
18 When I said, "My foot is slipping,"
your unfailing love, LORD, supported me.
19 When anxiety was great within me,
your consolation brought me joy.

20 Can a corrupt throne be allied with you —
a throne that brings on misery by its decrees?
21 The wicked band together against the righteous
and condemn the innocent to death.
22 But the LORD has become my fortress,
and my God the rock in whom I take refuge.
23 He will repay them for their sins
and destroy them for their wickedness;
the LORD our God will destroy them.

Psalm 95

1 Come, let us sing for joy to the LORD;
let us shout aloud to the Rock of our salvation.
2 Let us come before him with thanksgiving
and extol him with music and song.

3 For the LORD is the great God,
the great King above all gods.
4 In his hand are the depths of the earth,
and the mountain peaks belong to him.
5 The sea is his, for he made it,
and his hands formed the dry land.
6 Come, let us bow down in worship,
let us kneel before the LORD our Maker;
7 for he is our God
and we are the people of his pasture,
the flock under his care.

Today, if only you would hear his
voice,
8 "Do not harden your hearts as you did
at Meribah,[a]
as you did that day at Massah[b] in
the wilderness,
9 where your ancestors tested me;
they tried me, though they had
seen what I did.
10 For forty years I was angry with that
generation;
I said, 'They are a people whose
hearts go astray,
and they have not known my ways.'
11 So I declared on oath in my anger,
'They shall never enter my rest.' "

Psalm 96

1 Sing to the LORD a new song;
sing to the LORD, all the earth.
2 Sing to the LORD, praise his name;
proclaim his salvation day after
day.
3 Declare his glory among the nations,
his marvelous deeds among all
peoples.

4 For great is the LORD and most
worthy of praise;
he is to be feared above all gods.
5 For all the gods of the nations are
idols,
but the LORD made the heavens.
6 Splendor and majesty are before him;
strength and glory are in his
sanctuary.

7 Ascribe to the LORD, all you families
of nations,
ascribe to the LORD glory and
strength.
8 Ascribe to the LORD the glory due his
name;
bring an offering and come into his
courts.
9 Worship the LORD in the splendor of
his[c] holiness;
tremble before him, all the earth.
10 Say among the nations, "The LORD
reigns."
The world is firmly established, it
cannot be moved;
he will judge the peoples with
equity.

11 Let the heavens rejoice, let the earth
be glad;
let the sea resound, and all that is
in it.
12 Let the fields be jubilant, and
everything in them;
let all the trees of the forest sing for
joy.
13 Let all creation rejoice before the
LORD, for he comes,
he comes to judge the earth.
He will judge the world in
righteousness
and the peoples in his faithfulness.

Psalm 97

1 The LORD reigns, let the earth be glad;
let the distant shores rejoice.
2 Clouds and thick darkness surround
him;
righteousness and justice are the
foundation of his throne.
3 Fire goes before him
and consumes his foes on every
side.
4 His lightning lights up the world;
the earth sees and trembles.
5 The mountains melt like wax before
the LORD,
before the Lord of all the earth.
6 The heavens proclaim his
righteousness,
and all peoples see his glory.

7 All who worship images are put to
shame,
those who boast in idols —
worship him, all you gods!

8 Zion hears and rejoices
and the villages of Judah are glad
because of your judgments, LORD.
9 For you, LORD, are the Most High over
all the earth;
you are exalted far above all gods.
10 Let those who love the LORD hate evil,
for he guards the lives of his
faithful ones
and delivers them from the hand of
the wicked.
11 Light shines[d] on the righteous
and joy on the upright in heart.
12 Rejoice in the LORD, you who are
righteous,
and praise his holy name.

Psalm 98

A psalm.

1 Sing to the LORD a new song,
for he has done marvelous things;
his right hand and his holy arm
have worked salvation for him.

[a] *8 Meribah* means *quarreling.* [b] *8 Massah* means *testing.* [c] *9* Or *LORD with the splendor of*
[d] *11* One Hebrew manuscript and ancient versions (see also 112:4); most Hebrew manuscripts *Light is sown*

2 The LORD has made his salvation
known
and revealed his righteousness to
the nations.
3 He has remembered his love
and his faithfulness to Israel;
all the ends of the earth have seen
the salvation of our God.

4 Shout for joy to the LORD, all the earth,
burst into jubilant song with music;
5 make music to the LORD with the
harp,
with the harp and the sound of
singing,
6 with trumpets and the blast of the
ram's horn —
shout for joy before the LORD, the
King.

7 Let the sea resound, and everything
in it,
the world, and all who live in it.
8 Let the rivers clap their hands,
let the mountains sing together for
joy;
9 let them sing before the LORD,
for he comes to judge the earth.
He will judge the world in
righteousness
and the peoples with equity.

Psalm 99

1 The LORD reigns,
let the nations tremble;
he sits enthroned between the
cherubim,
let the earth shake.
2 Great is the LORD in Zion;
he is exalted over all the nations.
3 Let them praise your great and
awesome name —
he is holy.

4 The King is mighty, he loves justice —
you have established equity;
in Jacob you have done
what is just and right.
5 Exalt the LORD our God
and worship at his footstool;
he is holy.
6 Moses and Aaron were among his
priests,
Samuel was among those who
called on his name;
they called on the LORD
and he answered them.
7 He spoke to them from the pillar of
cloud;
they kept his statutes and the
decrees he gave them.

8 LORD our God,
you answered them;
you were to Israel a forgiving God,
though you punished their
misdeeds.[a]
9 Exalt the LORD our God
and worship at his holy mountain,
for the LORD our God is holy.

Psalm 100

A psalm. For giving grateful praise.

1 Shout for joy to the LORD, all the
earth.
2 Worship the LORD with gladness;
come before him with joyful songs.
3 Know that the LORD is God.
It is he who made us, and we are his[b];
we are his people, the sheep of his
pasture.

4 Enter his gates with thanksgiving
and his courts with praise;
give thanks to him and praise his
name.
5 For the LORD is good and his love
endures forever;
his faithfulness continues through
all generations.

Psalm 101

Of David. A psalm.

1 I will sing of your love and justice;
to you, LORD, I will sing praise.
2 I will be careful to lead a blameless
life —
when will you come to me?

I will conduct the affairs of my house
with a blameless heart.
3 I will not look with approval
on anything that is vile.

I hate what faithless people do;
I will have no part in it.
4 The perverse of heart shall be far
from me;
I will have nothing to do with what
is evil.

5 Whoever slanders their neighbor in
secret,
I will put to silence;
whoever has haughty eyes and a
proud heart,
I will not tolerate.

6 My eyes will be on the faithful in the
land,
that they may dwell with me;
the one whose walk is blameless
will minister to me.

[a] 8 Or *God, / an avenger of the wrongs done to them*

[b] 3 Or *and not we ourselves*

7 No one who practices deceit
will dwell in my house;
no one who speaks falsely
will stand in my presence.

8 Every morning I will put to silence
all the wicked in the land;
I will cut off every evildoer
from the city of the LORD.

Psalm 102[a]

A prayer of an afflicted person who has grown weak and pours out a lament before the LORD.

1 Hear my prayer, LORD;
let my cry for help come to you.
2 Do not hide your face from me
when I am in distress.
Turn your ear to me;
when I call, answer me quickly.

3 For my days vanish like smoke;
my bones burn like glowing embers.
4 My heart is blighted and withered
like grass;
I forget to eat my food.
5 In my distress I groan aloud
and am reduced to skin and bones.
6 I am like a desert owl,
like an owl among the ruins.
7 I lie awake; I have become
like a bird alone on a roof.
8 All day long my enemies taunt me;
those who rail against me use my
name as a curse.
9 For I eat ashes as my food
and mingle my drink with tears
10 because of your great wrath,
for you have taken me up and
thrown me aside.
11 My days are like the evening shadow;
I wither away like grass.

12 But you, LORD, sit enthroned forever;
your renown endures through all
generations.
13 You will arise and have compassion
on Zion,
for it is time to show favor to her;
the appointed time has come.
14 For her stones are dear to your
servants;
her very dust moves them to pity.
15 The nations will fear the name of the
LORD,
all the kings of the earth will revere
your glory.
16 For the LORD will rebuild Zion
and appear in his glory.
17 He will respond to the prayer of the
destitute;
he will not despise their plea.

18 Let this be written for a future
generation,
that a people not yet created may
praise the LORD:
19 "The LORD looked down from his
sanctuary on high,
from heaven he viewed the earth,
20 to hear the groans of the prisoners
and release those condemned to
death."
21 So the name of the LORD will be
declared in Zion
and his praise in Jerusalem
22 when the peoples and the kingdoms
assemble to worship the LORD.

23 In the course of my life[b] he broke
my strength;
he cut short my days.
24 So I said:
"Do not take me away, my God,
in the midst of my days;
your years go on through all
generations.
25 In the beginning you laid the
foundations of the earth,
and the heavens are the work of
your hands.
26 They will perish, but you remain;
they will all wear out like a
garment.
Like clothing you will change them
and they will be discarded.
27 But you remain the same,
and your years will never end.
28 The children of your servants will live
in your presence;
their descendants will be
established before you."

Psalm 103

Of David.

1 Praise the LORD, my soul;
all my inmost being, praise his
holy name.
2 Praise the LORD, my soul,
and forget not all his benefits—
3 who forgives all your sins
and heals all your diseases,
4 who redeems your life from the pit
and crowns you with love and
compassion,
5 who satisfies your desires with good
things
so that your youth is renewed like
the eagle's.

6 The LORD works righteousness
and justice for all the oppressed.

[a] In Hebrew texts 102:1-28 is numbered 102:2-29.

[b] *23* Or *By his power*

[7]He made known his ways to Moses,
his deeds to the people of Israel:
[8]The LORD is compassionate and gracious,
slow to anger, abounding in love.
[9]He will not always accuse,
nor will he harbor his anger forever;
[10]he does not treat us as our sins deserve
or repay us according to our iniquities.
[11]For as high as the heavens are above the earth,
so great is his love for those who fear him;
[12]as far as the east is from the west,
so far has he removed our transgressions from us.

[13]As a father has compassion on his children,
so the LORD has compassion on those who fear him;
[14]for he knows how we are formed,
he remembers that we are dust.
[15]The life of mortals is like grass,
they flourish like a flower of the field;
[16]the wind blows over it and it is gone,
and its place remembers it no more.
[17]But from everlasting to everlasting
the LORD's love is with those who fear him,
and his righteousness with their children's children —
[18]with those who keep his covenant
and remember to obey his precepts.

[19]The LORD has established his throne in heaven,
and his kingdom rules over all.

[20]Praise the LORD, you his angels,
you mighty ones who do his bidding,
who obey his word.
[21]Praise the LORD, all his heavenly hosts,
you his servants who do his will.
[22]Praise the LORD, all his works
everywhere in his dominion.

Praise the LORD, my soul.

Psalm 104

[1]Praise the LORD, my soul.

LORD my God, you are very great;
you are clothed with splendor and majesty.

[2]The LORD wraps himself in light as with a garment;
he stretches out the heavens like a tent
[3]and lays the beams of his upper chambers on their waters.
He makes the clouds his chariot
and rides on the wings of the wind.
[4]He makes winds his messengers,[a]
flames of fire his servants.

[5]He set the earth on its foundations;
it can never be moved.
[6]You covered it with the watery depths as with a garment;
the waters stood above the mountains.
[7]But at your rebuke the waters fled,
at the sound of your thunder they took to flight;
[8]they flowed over the mountains,
they went down into the valleys,
to the place you assigned for them.
[9]You set a boundary they cannot cross;
never again will they cover the earth.

[10]He makes springs pour water into the ravines;
it flows between the mountains.
[11]They give water to all the beasts of the field;
the wild donkeys quench their thirst.
[12]The birds of the sky nest by the waters;
they sing among the branches.
[13]He waters the mountains from his upper chambers;
the land is satisfied by the fruit of his work.
[14]He makes grass grow for the cattle,
and plants for people to cultivate —
bringing forth food from the earth:
[15]wine that gladdens human hearts,
oil to make their faces shine,
and bread that sustains their hearts.
[16]The trees of the LORD are well watered,
the cedars of Lebanon that he planted.
[17]There the birds make their nests;
the stork has its home in the junipers.
[18]The high mountains belong to the wild goats;
the crags are a refuge for the hyrax.

[a] 4 Or *angels*

19 He made the moon to mark the seasons,
and the sun knows when to go down.
20 You bring darkness, it becomes night,
and all the beasts of the forest prowl.
21 The lions roar for their prey
and seek their food from God.
22 The sun rises, and they steal away;
they return and lie down in their dens.
23 Then people go out to their work,
to their labor until evening.

24 How many are your works, LORD!
In wisdom you made them all;
the earth is full of your creatures.
25 There is the sea, vast and spacious,
teeming with creatures beyond number—
living things both large and small.
26 There the ships go to and fro,
and Leviathan, which you formed to frolic there.

27 All creatures look to you
to give them their food at the proper time.
28 When you give it to them,
they gather it up;
when you open your hand,
they are satisfied with good things.
29 When you hide your face,
they are terrified;
when you take away their breath,
they die and return to the dust.
30 When you send your Spirit,
they are created,
and you renew the face of the ground.

31 May the glory of the LORD endure forever;
may the LORD rejoice in his works—
32 he who looks at the earth, and it trembles,
who touches the mountains, and they smoke.

33 I will sing to the LORD all my life;
I will sing praise to my God as long as I live.
34 May my meditation be pleasing to him,
as I rejoice in the LORD.
35 But may sinners vanish from the earth
and the wicked be no more.

Praise the LORD, my soul.

Praise the LORD.[a]

Psalm 105

1 Give praise to the LORD, proclaim his name;
make known among the nations what he has done.
2 Sing to him, sing praise to him;
tell of all his wonderful acts.
3 Glory in his holy name;
let the hearts of those who seek the LORD rejoice.
4 Look to the LORD and his strength;
seek his face always.

5 Remember the wonders he has done,
his miracles, and the judgments he pronounced,
6 you his servants, the descendants of Abraham,
his chosen ones, the children of Jacob.
7 He is the LORD our God;
his judgments are in all the earth.

8 He remembers his covenant forever,
the promise he made, for a thousand generations,
9 the covenant he made with Abraham,
the oath he swore to Isaac.
10 He confirmed it to Jacob as a decree,
to Israel as an everlasting covenant:
11 "To you I will give the land of Canaan
as the portion you will inherit."

12 When they were but few in number,
few indeed, and strangers in it,
13 they wandered from nation to nation,
from one kingdom to another.
14 He allowed no one to oppress them;
for their sake he rebuked kings:
15 "Do not touch my anointed ones;
do my prophets no harm."

16 He called down famine on the land
and destroyed all their supplies of food;
17 and he sent a man before them—
Joseph, sold as a slave.
18 They bruised his feet with shackles,
his neck was put in irons,
19 till what he foretold came to pass,
till the word of the LORD proved him true.
20 The king sent and released him,
the ruler of peoples set him free.
21 He made him master of his household,
ruler over all he possessed,
22 to instruct his princes as he pleased
and teach his elders wisdom.

[a] 35 Hebrew *Hallelu Yah*; in the Septuagint this line stands at the beginning of Psalm 105.

23 Then Israel entered Egypt;
Jacob resided as a foreigner in the land of Ham.
24 The LORD made his people very fruitful;
he made them too numerous for their foes,
25 whose hearts he turned to hate his people,
to conspire against his servants.
26 He sent Moses his servant,
and Aaron, whom he had chosen.
27 They performed his signs among them,
his wonders in the land of Ham.
28 He sent darkness and made the land dark —
for had they not rebelled against his words?
29 He turned their waters into blood,
causing their fish to die.
30 Their land teemed with frogs,
which went up into the bedrooms of their rulers.
31 He spoke, and there came swarms of flies,
and gnats throughout their country.
32 He turned their rain into hail,
with lightning throughout their land;
33 he struck down their vines and fig trees
and shattered the trees of their country.
34 He spoke, and the locusts came,
grasshoppers without number;
35 they ate up every green thing in their land,
ate up the produce of their soil.
36 Then he struck down all the firstborn in their land,
the firstfruits of all their manhood.
37 He brought out Israel, laden with silver and gold,
and from among their tribes no one faltered.
38 Egypt was glad when they left,
because dread of Israel had fallen on them.

39 He spread out a cloud as a covering,
and a fire to give light at night.
40 They asked, and he brought them quail;
he fed them well with the bread of heaven.
41 He opened the rock, and water gushed out;
it flowed like a river in the desert.
42 For he remembered his holy promise
given to his servant Abraham.
43 He brought out his people with rejoicing,
his chosen ones with shouts of joy;
44 he gave them the lands of the nations,
and they fell heir to what others had toiled for —
45 that they might keep his precepts
and observe his laws.

Praise the LORD.[a]

Psalm 106

1 Praise the LORD.[b]

Give thanks to the LORD, for he is good;
his love endures forever.

2 Who can proclaim the mighty acts of the LORD
or fully declare his praise?
3 Blessed are those who act justly,
who always do what is right.

4 Remember me, LORD, when you show favor to your people,
come to my aid when you save them,
5 that I may enjoy the prosperity of your chosen ones,
that I may share in the joy of your nation
and join your inheritance in giving praise.

6 We have sinned, even as our ancestors did;
we have done wrong and acted wickedly.
7 When our ancestors were in Egypt,
they gave no thought to your miracles;
they did not remember your many kindnesses,
and they rebelled by the sea, the Red Sea.[c]
8 Yet he saved them for his name's sake,
to make his mighty power known.
9 He rebuked the Red Sea, and it dried up;
he led them through the depths as through a desert.
10 He saved them from the hand of the foe;
from the hand of the enemy he redeemed them.
11 The waters covered their adversaries;
not one of them survived.

[a] 45 Hebrew *Hallelu Yah* [b] 1 Hebrew *Hallelu Yah*; also in verse 48 [c] 7 Or *the Sea of Reeds*; also in verses 9 and 22

12 Then they believed his promises
and sang his praise.

13 But they soon forgot what he had done
and did not wait for his plan to
unfold.
14 In the desert they gave in to their
craving;
in the wilderness they put God to
the test.
15 So he gave them what they asked for,
but sent a wasting disease among
them.

16 In the camp they grew envious of
Moses
and of Aaron, who was consecrated
to the LORD.
17 The earth opened up and swallowed
Dathan;
it buried the company of Abiram.
18 Fire blazed among their followers;
a flame consumed the wicked.
19 At Horeb they made a calf
and worshiped an idol cast from
metal.
20 They exchanged their glorious God
for an image of a bull, which eats
grass.
21 They forgot the God who saved them,
who had done great things in Egypt,
22 miracles in the land of Ham
and awesome deeds by the Red Sea.
23 So he said he would destroy them —
had not Moses, his chosen one,
stood in the breach before him
to keep his wrath from destroying
them.

24 Then they despised the pleasant land;
they did not believe his promise.
25 They grumbled in their tents
and did not obey the LORD.
26 So he swore to them with uplifted
hand
that he would make them fall in
the wilderness,
27 make their descendants fall among
the nations
and scatter them throughout the
lands.

28 They yoked themselves to the Baal of
Peor
and ate sacrifices offered to lifeless
gods;
29 they aroused the LORD's anger by
their wicked deeds,
and a plague broke out among them.
30 But Phinehas stood up and
intervened,
and the plague was checked.
31 This was credited to him as
righteousness
for endless generations to come.
32 By the waters of Meribah they
angered the LORD,
and trouble came to Moses because
of them;
33 for they rebelled against the Spirit of
God,
and rash words came from Moses'
lips.[a]

34 They did not destroy the peoples
as the LORD had commanded them,
35 but they mingled with the nations
and adopted their customs.
36 They worshiped their idols,
which became a snare to them.
37 They sacrificed their sons
and their daughters to false gods.
38 They shed innocent blood,
the blood of their sons and
daughters,
whom they sacrificed to the idols of
Canaan,
and the land was desecrated by
their blood.
39 They defiled themselves by what they
did;
by their deeds they prostituted
themselves.

40 Therefore the LORD was angry with
his people
and abhorred his inheritance.
41 He gave them into the hands of the
nations,
and their foes ruled over them.
42 Their enemies oppressed them
and subjected them to their power.
43 Many times he delivered them,
but they were bent on rebellion
and they wasted away in their sin.
44 Yet he took note of their distress
when he heard their cry;
45 for their sake he remembered his
covenant
and out of his great love he
relented.
46 He caused all who held them captive
to show them mercy.

47 Save us, LORD our God,
and gather us from the nations,
that we may give thanks to your holy
name
and glory in your praise.

48 Praise be to the LORD, the God of Israel,
from everlasting to everlasting.

Let all the people say, "Amen!"

Praise the LORD.

[a] *33* Or *against his spirit, / and rash words came from his lips*

BOOK V

Psalms 107 – 150

Psalm 107

1 Give thanks to the LORD, for he is good;
his love endures forever.

2 Let the redeemed of the LORD tell
their story —
those he redeemed from the hand
of the foe,
3 those he gathered from the lands,
from east and west, from north and
south.[a]

4 Some wandered in desert wastelands,
finding no way to a city where they
could settle.
5 They were hungry and thirsty,
and their lives ebbed away.
6 Then they cried out to the LORD in
their trouble,
and he delivered them from their
distress.
7 He led them by a straight way
to a city where they could settle.
8 Let them give thanks to the LORD for
his unfailing love
and his wonderful deeds for
mankind,
9 for he satisfies the thirsty
and fills the hungry with good
things.

10 Some sat in darkness, in utter darkness,
prisoners suffering in iron chains,
11 because they rebelled against God's
commands
and despised the plans of the Most
High.
12 So he subjected them to bitter labor;
they stumbled, and there was no
one to help.
13 Then they cried to the LORD in their
trouble,
and he saved them from their
distress.
14 He brought them out of darkness, the
utter darkness,
and broke away their chains.
15 Let them give thanks to the LORD for
his unfailing love
and his wonderful deeds for
mankind,
16 for he breaks down gates of bronze
and cuts through bars of iron.

17 Some became fools through their
rebellious ways
and suffered affliction because of
their iniquities.
18 They loathed all food
and drew near the gates of death.
19 Then they cried to the LORD in their
trouble,
and he saved them from their
distress.
20 He sent out his word and healed
them;
he rescued them from the grave.
21 Let them give thanks to the LORD for
his unfailing love
and his wonderful deeds for
mankind.
22 Let them sacrifice thank offerings
and tell of his works with songs of
joy.

23 Some went out on the sea in ships;
they were merchants on the mighty
waters.
24 They saw the works of the LORD,
his wonderful deeds in the deep.
25 For he spoke and stirred up a tempest
that lifted high the waves.
26 They mounted up to the heavens and
went down to the depths;
in their peril their courage melted
away.
27 They reeled and staggered like
drunkards;
they were at their wits' end.
28 Then they cried out to the LORD in
their trouble,
and he brought them out of their
distress.
29 He stilled the storm to a whisper;
the waves of the sea[b] were hushed.
30 They were glad when it grew calm,
and he guided them to their
desired haven.
31 Let them give thanks to the LORD for
his unfailing love
and his wonderful deeds for
mankind.
32 Let them exalt him in the assembly of
the people
and praise him in the council of the
elders.

33 He turned rivers into a desert,
flowing springs into thirsty ground,
34 and fruitful land into a salt waste,
because of the wickedness of those
who lived there.
35 He turned the desert into pools of
water
and the parched ground into
flowing springs;
36 there he brought the hungry to live,
and they founded a city where they
could settle.

[a] 3 Hebrew *north and the sea* [b] 29 Dead Sea Scrolls; Masoretic Text / *their waves*

37 They sowed fields and planted vineyards
that yielded a fruitful harvest;
38 he blessed them, and their numbers greatly increased,
and he did not let their herds diminish.

39 Then their numbers decreased, and they were humbled
by oppression, calamity and sorrow;
40 he who pours contempt on nobles
made them wander in a trackless waste.
41 But he lifted the needy out of their affliction
and increased their families like flocks.
42 The upright see and rejoice,
but all the wicked shut their mouths.

43 Let the one who is wise heed these things
and ponder the loving deeds of the LORD.

Psalm 108[a]

A song. A psalm of David.

1 My heart, O God, is steadfast;
I will sing and make music with all my soul.
2 Awake, harp and lyre!
I will awaken the dawn.
3 I will praise you, LORD, among the nations;
I will sing of you among the peoples.
4 For great is your love, higher than the heavens;
your faithfulness reaches to the skies.
5 Be exalted, O God, above the heavens;
let your glory be over all the earth.

6 Save us and help us with your right hand,
that those you love may be delivered.
7 God has spoken from his sanctuary:
"In triumph I will parcel out Shechem
and measure off the Valley of Sukkoth.
8 Gilead is mine, Manasseh is mine;
Ephraim is my helmet,
Judah is my scepter.
9 Moab is my washbasin,
on Edom I toss my sandal;
over Philistia I shout in triumph."

10 Who will bring me to the fortified city?
Who will lead me to Edom?
11 Is it not you, God, you who have rejected us
and no longer go out with our armies?
12 Give us aid against the enemy,
for human help is worthless.
13 With God we will gain the victory,
and he will trample down our enemies.

Psalm 109

For the director of music. Of David. A psalm.

1 My God, whom I praise,
do not remain silent,
2 for people who are wicked and deceitful
have opened their mouths against me;
they have spoken against me with lying tongues.
3 With words of hatred they surround me;
they attack me without cause.
4 In return for my friendship they accuse me,
but I am a man of prayer.
5 They repay me evil for good,
and hatred for my friendship.

6 Appoint someone evil to oppose my enemy;
let an accuser stand at his right hand.
7 When he is tried, let him be found guilty,
and may his prayers condemn him.
8 May his days be few;
may another take his place of leadership.
9 May his children be fatherless
and his wife a widow.
10 May his children be wandering beggars;
may they be driven[b] from their ruined homes.
11 May a creditor seize all he has;
may strangers plunder the fruits of his labor.
12 May no one extend kindness to him
or take pity on his fatherless children.
13 May his descendants be cut off,
their names blotted out from the next generation.
14 May the iniquity of his fathers be remembered before the LORD;
may the sin of his mother never be blotted out.

[a] In Hebrew texts 108:1-13 is numbered 108:2-14.

[b] *10* Septuagint; Hebrew *sought*

15 May their sins always remain before
the LORD,
that he may blot out their name
from the earth.
16 For he never thought of doing a
kindness,
but hounded to death the poor
and the needy and the
brokenhearted.
17 He loved to pronounce a curse —
may it come back on him.
He found no pleasure in blessing —
may it be far from him.
18 He wore cursing as his garment;
it entered into his body like water,
into his bones like oil.
19 May it be like a cloak wrapped about
him,
like a belt tied forever around him.
20 May this be the LORD's payment to my
accusers,
to those who speak evil of me.

21 But you, Sovereign LORD,
help me for your name's sake;
out of the goodness of your love,
deliver me.
22 For I am poor and needy,
and my heart is wounded within me.
23 I fade away like an evening shadow;
I am shaken off like a locust.
24 My knees give way from fasting;
my body is thin and gaunt.
25 I am an object of scorn to my accusers;
when they see me, they shake their
heads.

26 Help me, LORD my God;
save me according to your
unfailing love.
27 Let them know that it is your hand,
that you, LORD, have done it.
28 While they curse, may you bless;
may those who attack me be put to
shame,
but may your servant rejoice.
29 May my accusers be clothed with
disgrace
and wrapped in shame as in a cloak.

30 With my mouth I will greatly extol
the LORD;
in the great throng of worshipers I
will praise him.
31 For he stands at the right hand of the
needy,
to save their lives from those who
would condemn them.

Psalm 110

Of David. A psalm.

1 The LORD says to my lord:[a]
"Sit at my right hand
until I make your enemies
a footstool for your feet."
2 The LORD will extend your mighty
scepter from Zion, saying,
"Rule in the midst of your
enemies!"
3 Your troops will be willing
on your day of battle.
Arrayed in holy splendor,
your young men will come to you
like dew from the morning's womb.[b]

4 The LORD has sworn
and will not change his mind:
"You are a priest forever,
in the order of Melchizedek."

5 The Lord is at your right hand[c];
he will crush kings on the day of his
wrath.
6 He will judge the nations, heaping up
the dead
and crushing the rulers of the
whole earth.
7 He will drink from a brook along the
way,[d]
and so he will lift his head high.

Psalm 111[e]

1 Praise the LORD.[f]

I will extol the LORD with all my heart
in the council of the upright and in
the assembly.

2 Great are the works of the LORD;
they are pondered by all who
delight in them.
3 Glorious and majestic are his deeds,
and his righteousness endures
forever.
4 He has caused his wonders to be
remembered;
the LORD is gracious and
compassionate.
5 He provides food for those who fear
him;
he remembers his covenant forever.

6 He has shown his people the power of
his works,
giving them the lands of other
nations.

[a] 1 Or *Lord* [b] 3 The meaning of the Hebrew for this sentence is uncertain. [c] 5 Or *My lord is at your right hand, LORD* [d] 7 The meaning of the Hebrew for this clause is uncertain. [e] This psalm is an acrostic poem, the lines of which begin with the successive letters of the Hebrew alphabet. [f] 1 Hebrew *Hallelu Yah*

7 The works of his hands are faithful
and just;
all his precepts are trustworthy.
8 They are established for ever and ever,
enacted in faithfulness and
uprightness.
9 He provided redemption for his
people;
he ordained his covenant forever —
holy and awesome is his name.

10 The fear of the LORD is the beginning
of wisdom;
all who follow his precepts have
good understanding.
To him belongs eternal praise.

Psalm 112[a]

1 Praise the LORD.[b]

Blessed are those who fear the LORD,
who find great delight in his
commands.

2 Their children will be mighty in the
land;
the generation of the upright will
be blessed.
3 Wealth and riches are in their houses,
and their righteousness endures
forever.
4 Even in darkness light dawns for the
upright,
for those who are gracious and
compassionate and righteous.
5 Good will come to those who are
generous and lend freely,
who conduct their affairs with
justice.

6 Surely the righteous will never be
shaken;
they will be remembered forever.
7 They will have no fear of bad news;
their hearts are steadfast, trusting
in the LORD.
8 Their hearts are secure, they will have
no fear;
in the end they will look in triumph
on their foes.
9 They have freely scattered their gifts
to the poor,
their righteousness endures forever;
their horn[c] will be lifted high in
honor.

10 The wicked will see and be vexed,
they will gnash their teeth and
waste away;
the longings of the wicked will
come to nothing.

Psalm 113

1 Praise the LORD.[d]

Praise the LORD, you his servants;
praise the name of the LORD.
2 Let the name of the LORD be praised,
both now and forevermore.
3 From the rising of the sun to the place
where it sets,
the name of the LORD is to be
praised.

4 The LORD is exalted over all the
nations,
his glory above the heavens.
5 Who is like the LORD our God,
the One who sits enthroned on high,
6 who stoops down to look
on the heavens and the earth?

7 He raises the poor from the dust
and lifts the needy from the ash
heap;
8 he seats them with princes,
with the princes of his people.
9 He settles the childless woman in her
home
as a happy mother of children.

Praise the LORD.

Psalm 114

1 When Israel came out of Egypt,
Jacob from a people of foreign
tongue,
2 Judah became God's sanctuary,
Israel his dominion.

3 The sea looked and fled,
the Jordan turned back;
4 the mountains leaped like rams,
the hills like lambs.

5 Why was it, sea, that you fled?
Why, Jordan, did you turn back?
6 Why, mountains, did you leap like
rams,
you hills, like lambs?

7 Tremble, earth, at the presence of the
Lord,
at the presence of the God of Jacob,
8 who turned the rock into a pool,
the hard rock into springs of water.

Psalm 115

1 Not to us, LORD, not to us
but to your name be the glory,
because of your love and
faithfulness.

[a] This psalm is an acrostic poem, the lines of which begin with the successive letters of the Hebrew alphabet. [b] *1* Hebrew *Hallelu Yah* [c] *9* *Horn* here symbolizes dignity. [d] *1* Hebrew *Hallelu Yah*; also in verse 9

2 Why do the nations say,
"Where is their God?"
3 Our God is in heaven;
he does whatever pleases him.
4 But their idols are silver and gold,
made by human hands.
5 They have mouths, but cannot speak,
eyes, but cannot see.
6 They have ears, but cannot hear,
noses, but cannot smell.
7 They have hands, but cannot feel,
feet, but cannot walk,
nor can they utter a sound with
their throats.
8 Those who make them will be like
them,
and so will all who trust in them.

9 All you Israelites, trust in the LORD—
he is their help and shield.
10 House of Aaron, trust in the LORD—
he is their help and shield.
11 You who fear him, trust in the LORD—
he is their help and shield.

12 The LORD remembers us and will
bless us:
He will bless his people Israel,
he will bless the house of Aaron,
13 he will bless those who fear the
LORD—
small and great alike.

14 May the LORD cause you to flourish,
both you and your children.
15 May you be blessed by the LORD,
the Maker of heaven and earth.

16 The highest heavens belong to the
LORD,
but the earth he has given to
mankind.
17 It is not the dead who praise the
LORD,
those who go down to the place of
silence;
18 it is we who extol the LORD,
both now and forevermore.

Praise the LORD.[a]

Psalm 116

1 I love the LORD, for he heard my voice;
he heard my cry for mercy.
2 Because he turned his ear to me,
I will call on him as long as I live.

3 The cords of death entangled me,
the anguish of the grave came over
me;
I was overcome by distress and
sorrow.
4 Then I called on the name of the
LORD:
"LORD, save me!"
5 The LORD is gracious and righteous;
our God is full of compassion.
6 The LORD protects the unwary;
when I was brought low, he saved
me.

7 Return to your rest, my soul,
for the LORD has been good to you.

8 For you, LORD, have delivered me
from death,
my eyes from tears,
my feet from stumbling,
9 that I may walk before the LORD
in the land of the living.

10 I trusted in the LORD when I said,
"I am greatly afflicted";
11 in my alarm I said,
"Everyone is a liar."

12 What shall I return to the LORD
for all his goodness to me?

13 I will lift up the cup of salvation
and call on the name of the LORD.
14 I will fulfill my vows to the LORD
in the presence of all his people.

15 Precious in the sight of the LORD
is the death of his faithful servants.
16 Truly I am your servant, LORD;
I serve you just as my mother did;
you have freed me from my chains.

17 I will sacrifice a thank offering to you
and call on the name of the LORD.
18 I will fulfill my vows to the LORD
in the presence of all his people,
19 in the courts of the house of the
LORD—
in your midst, Jerusalem.

Praise the LORD.[a]

Psalm 117

1 Praise the LORD, all you nations;
extol him, all you peoples.
2 For great is his love toward us,
and the faithfulness of the LORD
endures forever.

Praise the LORD.[a]

Psalm 118

1 Give thanks to the LORD, for he is
good;
his love endures forever.

2 Let Israel say:
"His love endures forever."

[a] *18,19,2* Hebrew *Hallelu Yah*

3 Let the house of Aaron say:
"His love endures forever."
4 Let those who fear the LORD say:
"His love endures forever."

5 When hard pressed, I cried to the LORD;
he brought me into a spacious place.
6 The LORD is with me; I will not be afraid.
What can mere mortals do to me?
7 The LORD is with me; he is my helper.
I look in triumph on my enemies.

8 It is better to take refuge in the LORD
than to trust in humans.
9 It is better to take refuge in the LORD
than to trust in princes.
10 All the nations surrounded me,
but in the name of the LORD I cut them down.
11 They surrounded me on every side,
but in the name of the LORD I cut them down.
12 They swarmed around me like bees,
but they were consumed as quickly as burning thorns;
in the name of the LORD I cut them down.
13 I was pushed back and about to fall,
but the LORD helped me.
14 The LORD is my strength and my defense[a];
he has become my salvation.

15 Shouts of joy and victory
resound in the tents of the righteous:
"The LORD's right hand has done mighty things!
16 The LORD's right hand is lifted high;
the LORD's right hand has done mighty things!"
17 I will not die but live,
and will proclaim what the LORD has done.
18 The LORD has chastened me severely,
but he has not given me over to death.
19 Open for me the gates of the righteous;
I will enter and give thanks to the LORD.
20 This is the gate of the LORD
through which the righteous may enter.
21 I will give you thanks, for you answered me;
you have become my salvation.

22 The stone the builders rejected
has become the cornerstone;
23 the LORD has done this,
and it is marvelous in our eyes.
24 The LORD has done it this very day;
let us rejoice today and be glad.

25 LORD, save us!
LORD, grant us success!

26 Blessed is he who comes in the name of the LORD.
From the house of the LORD we bless you.[b]
27 The LORD is God,
and he has made his light shine on us.
With boughs in hand, join in the festal procession
up[c] to the horns of the altar.

28 You are my God, and I will praise you;
you are my God, and I will exalt you.

29 Give thanks to the LORD, for he is good;
his love endures forever.

Psalm 119[d]

א Aleph

1 Blessed are those whose ways are blameless,
who walk according to the law of the LORD.
2 Blessed are those who keep his statutes
and seek him with all their heart—
3 they do no wrong
but follow his ways.
4 You have laid down precepts
that are to be fully obeyed.
5 Oh, that my ways were steadfast
in obeying your decrees!
6 Then I would not be put to shame
when I consider all your commands.
7 I will praise you with an upright heart
as I learn your righteous laws.
8 I will obey your decrees;
do not utterly forsake me.

ב Beth

9 How can a young person stay on the path of purity?
By living according to your word.
10 I seek you with all my heart;
do not let me stray from your commands.
11 I have hidden your word in my heart
that I might not sin against you.

[a] 14 Or *song* [b] 26 The Hebrew is plural. [c] 27 Or *Bind the festal sacrifice with ropes / and take it*
[d] This psalm is an acrostic poem, the stanzas of which begin with successive letters of the Hebrew alphabet; moreover, the verses of each stanza begin with the same letter of the Hebrew alphabet.

12 Praise be to you, LORD;
teach me your decrees.
13 With my lips I recount
all the laws that come from your mouth.
14 I rejoice in following your statutes
as one rejoices in great riches.
15 I meditate on your precepts
and consider your ways.
16 I delight in your decrees;
I will not neglect your word.

ג Gimel

17 Be good to your servant while I live,
that I may obey your word.
18 Open my eyes that I may see
wonderful things in your law.
19 I am a stranger on earth;
do not hide your commands from me.
20 My soul is consumed with longing
for your laws at all times.
21 You rebuke the arrogant, who are accursed,
those who stray from your commands.
22 Remove from me their scorn and contempt,
for I keep your statutes.
23 Though rulers sit together and slander me,
your servant will meditate on your decrees.
24 Your statutes are my delight;
they are my counselors.

ד Daleth

25 I am laid low in the dust;
preserve my life according to your word.
26 I gave an account of my ways and you answered me;
teach me your decrees.
27 Cause me to understand the way of your precepts,
that I may meditate on your wonderful deeds.
28 My soul is weary with sorrow;
strengthen me according to your word.
29 Keep me from deceitful ways;
be gracious to me and teach me your law.
30 I have chosen the way of faithfulness;
I have set my heart on your laws.
31 I hold fast to your statutes, LORD;
do not let me be put to shame.
32 I run in the path of your commands,
for you have broadened my understanding.

ה He

33 Teach me, LORD, the way of your decrees,
that I may follow it to the end.[a]
34 Give me understanding, so that I may keep your law
and obey it with all my heart.
35 Direct me in the path of your commands,
for there I find delight.
36 Turn my heart toward your statutes
and not toward selfish gain.
37 Turn my eyes away from worthless things;
preserve my life according to your word.[b]
38 Fulfill your promise to your servant,
so that you may be feared.
39 Take away the disgrace I dread,
for your laws are good.
40 How I long for your precepts!
In your righteousness preserve my life.

ו Waw

41 May your unfailing love come to me, LORD,
your salvation, according to your promise;
42 then I can answer anyone who taunts me,
for I trust in your word.
43 Never take your word of truth from my mouth,
for I have put my hope in your laws.
44 I will always obey your law,
for ever and ever.
45 I will walk about in freedom,
for I have sought out your precepts.
46 I will speak of your statutes before kings
and will not be put to shame,
47 for I delight in your commands
because I love them.
48 I reach out for your commands, which I love,
that I may meditate on your decrees.

ז Zayin

49 Remember your word to your servant,
for you have given me hope.
50 My comfort in my suffering is this:
Your promise preserves my life.
51 The arrogant mock me unmercifully,
but I do not turn from your law.
52 I remember, LORD, your ancient laws,
and I find comfort in them.

[a] 33 Or *follow it for its reward* [b] 37 Two manuscripts of the Masoretic Text and Dead Sea Scrolls; most manuscripts of the Masoretic Text *life in your way*

53 Indignation grips me because of the
wicked,
who have forsaken your law.
54 Your decrees are the theme of my
song
wherever I lodge.
55 In the night, LORD, I remember your
name,
that I may keep your law.
56 This has been my practice:
I obey your precepts.

ח Heth

57 You are my portion, LORD;
I have promised to obey your
words.
58 I have sought your face with all my
heart;
be gracious to me according to your
promise.
59 I have considered my ways
and have turned my steps to your
statutes.
60 I will hasten and not delay
to obey your commands.
61 Though the wicked bind me with
ropes,
I will not forget your law.
62 At midnight I rise to give you thanks
for your righteous laws.
63 I am a friend to all who fear you,
to all who follow your precepts.
64 The earth is filled with your love,
LORD;
teach me your decrees.

ט Teth

65 Do good to your servant
according to your word, LORD.
66 Teach me knowledge and good
judgment,
for I trust your commands.
67 Before I was afflicted I went astray,
but now I obey your word.
68 You are good, and what you do is
good;
teach me your decrees.
69 Though the arrogant have smeared
me with lies,
I keep your precepts with all my
heart.
70 Their hearts are callous and
unfeeling,
but I delight in your law.
71 It was good for me to be afflicted
so that I might learn your decrees.
72 The law from your mouth is more
precious to me
than thousands of pieces of silver
and gold.

י Yodh

73 Your hands made me and formed me;
give me understanding to learn
your commands.
74 May those who fear you rejoice when
they see me,
for I have put my hope in your
word.
75 I know, LORD, that your laws are
righteous,
and that in faithfulness you have
afflicted me.
76 May your unfailing love be my
comfort,
according to your promise to your
servant.
77 Let your compassion come to me that
I may live,
for your law is my delight.
78 May the arrogant be put to shame for
wronging me without cause;
but I will meditate on your
precepts.
79 May those who fear you turn to me,
those who understand your
statutes.
80 May I wholeheartedly follow your
decrees,
that I may not be put to shame.

כ Kaph

81 My soul faints with longing for your
salvation,
but I have put my hope in your
word.
82 My eyes fail, looking for your
promise;
I say, "When will you comfort me?"
83 Though I am like a wineskin in the
smoke,
I do not forget your decrees.
84 How long must your servant wait?
When will you punish my
persecutors?
85 The arrogant dig pits to trap me,
contrary to your law.
86 All your commands are trustworthy;
help me, for I am being persecuted
without cause.
87 They almost wiped me from the
earth,
but I have not forsaken your
precepts.
88 In your unfailing love preserve
my life,
that I may obey the statutes
of your mouth.

ל Lamedh

89 Your word, LORD, is eternal;
it stands firm in the heavens.

90 Your faithfulness continues through
all generations;
you established the earth, and it
endures.
91 Your laws endure to this day,
for all things serve you.
92 If your law had not been my delight,
I would have perished in my
affliction.
93 I will never forget your precepts,
for by them you have preserved
my life.
94 Save me, for I am yours;
I have sought out your precepts.
95 The wicked are waiting to destroy me,
but I will ponder your statutes.
96 To all perfection I see a limit,
but your commands are boundless.

מ Mem

97 Oh, how I love your law!
I meditate on it all day long.
98 Your commands are always with me
and make me wiser than my
enemies.
99 I have more insight than all my
teachers,
for I meditate on your statutes.
100 I have more understanding than the
elders,
for I obey your precepts.
101 I have kept my feet from every
evil path
so that I might obey your word.
102 I have not departed from your laws,
for you yourself have taught me.
103 How sweet are your words to my taste,
sweeter than honey to my mouth!
104 I gain understanding from your
precepts;
therefore I hate every wrong path.

נ Nun

105 Your word is a lamp for my feet,
a light on my path.
106 I have taken an oath and
confirmed it,
that I will follow your righteous laws.
107 I have suffered much;
preserve my life, LORD, according to
your word.
108 Accept, LORD, the willing praise of my
mouth,
and teach me your laws.
109 Though I constantly take my life in
my hands,
I will not forget your law.
110 The wicked have set a snare for me,
but I have not strayed from your
precepts.
111 Your statutes are my heritage
forever;
they are the joy of my heart.
112 My heart is set on keeping your
decrees
to the very end.[a]

ס Samekh

113 I hate double-minded people,
but I love your law.
114 You are my refuge and my shield;
I have put my hope in your word.
115 Away from me, you evildoers,
that I may keep the commands of
my God!
116 Sustain me, my God, according to
your promise, and I will live;
do not let my hopes be dashed.
117 Uphold me, and I will be delivered;
I will always have regard for your
decrees.
118 You reject all who stray from your
decrees,
for their delusions come to nothing.
119 All the wicked of the earth you
discard like dross;
therefore I love your statutes.
120 My flesh trembles in fear of you;
I stand in awe of your laws.

ע Ayin

121 I have done what is righteous and
just;
do not leave me to my oppressors.
122 Ensure your servant's well-being;
do not let the arrogant oppress me.
123 My eyes fail, looking for your
salvation,
looking for your righteous promise.
124 Deal with your servant according to
your love
and teach me your decrees.
125 I am your servant; give me
discernment
that I may understand your statutes.
126 It is time for you to act, LORD;
your law is being broken.
127 Because I love your commands
more than gold, more than pure
gold,
128 and because I consider all your
precepts right,
I hate every wrong path.

פ Pe

129 Your statutes are wonderful;
therefore I obey them.
130 The unfolding of your words gives
light;
it gives understanding to the simple.

[a] 112 Or *decrees / for their enduring reward*

131 I open my mouth and pant,
longing for your commands.
132 Turn to me and have mercy on me,
as you always do to those who love your name.
133 Direct my footsteps according to your word;
let no sin rule over me.
134 Redeem me from human oppression,
that I may obey your precepts.
135 Make your face shine on your servant
and teach me your decrees.
136 Streams of tears flow from my eyes,
for your law is not obeyed.

צ Tsadhe

137 You are righteous, LORD,
and your laws are right.
138 The statutes you have laid down are righteous;
they are fully trustworthy.
139 My zeal wears me out,
for my enemies ignore your words.
140 Your promises have been thoroughly tested,
and your servant loves them.
141 Though I am lowly and despised,
I do not forget your precepts.
142 Your righteousness is everlasting
and your law is true.
143 Trouble and distress have come upon me,
but your commands give me delight.
144 Your statutes are always righteous;
give me understanding that I may live.

ק Qoph

145 I call with all my heart; answer me, LORD,
and I will obey your decrees.
146 I call out to you; save me
and I will keep your statutes.
147 I rise before dawn and cry for help;
I have put my hope in your word.
148 My eyes stay open through the watches of the night,
that I may meditate on your promises.
149 Hear my voice in accordance with your love;
preserve my life, LORD, according to your laws.
150 Those who devise wicked schemes are near,
but they are far from your law.
151 Yet you are near, LORD,
and all your commands are true.
152 Long ago I learned from your statutes
that you established them to last forever.

ר Resh

153 Look on my suffering and deliver me,
for I have not forgotten your law.
154 Defend my cause and redeem me;
preserve my life according to your promise.
155 Salvation is far from the wicked,
for they do not seek out your decrees.
156 Your compassion, LORD, is great;
preserve my life according to your laws.
157 Many are the foes who persecute me,
but I have not turned from your statutes.
158 I look on the faithless with loathing,
for they do not obey your word.
159 See how I love your precepts;
preserve my life, LORD, in accordance with your love.
160 All your words are true;
all your righteous laws are eternal.

ש Sin and Shin

161 Rulers persecute me without cause,
but my heart trembles at your word.
162 I rejoice in your promise
like one who finds great spoil.
163 I hate and detest falsehood
but I love your law.
164 Seven times a day I praise you
for your righteous laws.
165 Great peace have those who love your law,
and nothing can make them stumble.
166 I wait for your salvation, LORD,
and I follow your commands.
167 I obey your statutes,
for I love them greatly.
168 I obey your precepts and your statutes,
for all my ways are known to you.

ת Taw

169 May my cry come before you, LORD;
give me understanding according to your word.
170 May my supplication come before you;
deliver me according to your promise.
171 May my lips overflow with praise,
for you teach me your decrees.
172 May my tongue sing of your word,
for all your commands are righteous.
173 May your hand be ready to help me,
for I have chosen your precepts.

174 I long for your salvation, LORD,
and your law gives me delight.
175 Let me live that I may praise you,
and may your laws sustain me.
176 I have strayed like a lost sheep.
Seek your servant,
for I have not forgotten your commands.

Psalm 120

A song of ascents.

1 I call on the LORD in my distress,
and he answers me.
2 Save me, LORD,
from lying lips
and from deceitful tongues.

3 What will he do to you,
and what more besides,
you deceitful tongue?
4 He will punish you with a warrior's sharp arrows,
with burning coals of the broom bush.

5 Woe to me that I dwell in Meshek,
that I live among the tents of Kedar!
6 Too long have I lived
among those who hate peace.
7 I am for peace;
but when I speak, they are for war.

Psalm 121

A song of ascents.

1 I lift up my eyes to the mountains —
where does my help come from?
2 My help comes from the LORD,
the Maker of heaven and earth.

3 He will not let your foot slip —
he who watches over you will not slumber;
4 indeed, he who watches over Israel
will neither slumber nor sleep.

5 The LORD watches over you —
the LORD is your shade at your right hand;
6 the sun will not harm you by day,
nor the moon by night.

7 The LORD will keep you from all harm —
he will watch over your life;
8 the LORD will watch over your coming and going
both now and forevermore.

Psalm 122

A song of ascents. Of David.

1 I rejoiced with those who said to me,
"Let us go to the house of the LORD."
2 Our feet are standing
in your gates, Jerusalem.

3 Jerusalem is built like a city
that is closely compacted together.
4 That is where the tribes go up —
the tribes of the LORD —
to praise the name of the LORD
according to the statute given to Israel.
5 There stand the thrones for judgment,
the thrones of the house of David.

6 Pray for the peace of Jerusalem:
"May those who love you be secure.
7 May there be peace within your walls
and security within your citadels."
8 For the sake of my family and friends,
I will say, "Peace be within you."
9 For the sake of the house of the LORD our God,
I will seek your prosperity.

Psalm 123

A song of ascents.

1 I lift up my eyes to you,
to you who sit enthroned in heaven.
2 As the eyes of slaves look to the hand of their master,
as the eyes of a female slave look to the hand of her mistress,
so our eyes look to the LORD our God,
till he shows us his mercy.

3 Have mercy on us, LORD, have mercy on us,
for we have endured no end of contempt.
4 We have endured no end
of ridicule from the arrogant,
of contempt from the proud.

Psalm 124

A song of ascents. Of David.

1 If the LORD had not been on our side —
let Israel say —
2 if the LORD had not been on our side
when people attacked us,
3 they would have swallowed us alive
when their anger flared against us;
4 the flood would have engulfed us,
the torrent would have swept over us,
5 the raging waters
would have swept us away.

6 Praise be to the LORD,
who has not let us be torn by their teeth.
7 We have escaped like a bird
from the fowler's snare;
the snare has been broken,
and we have escaped.
8 Our help is in the name of the LORD,
the Maker of heaven and earth.

Psalm 125

A song of ascents.

[1] Those who trust in the LORD are like
Mount Zion,
which cannot be shaken but
endures forever.
[2] As the mountains surround
Jerusalem,
so the LORD surrounds his people
both now and forevermore.

[3] The scepter of the wicked will not
remain
over the land allotted to the
righteous,
for then the righteous might use
their hands to do evil.

[4] LORD, do good to those who are good,
to those who are upright in heart.
[5] But those who turn to crooked ways
the LORD will banish with the
evildoers.

Peace be on Israel.

Psalm 126

A song of ascents.

[1] When the LORD restored the fortunes
of[a] Zion,
we were like those who dreamed.[b]
[2] Our mouths were filled with laughter,
our tongues with songs of joy.
Then it was said among the nations,
"The LORD has done great things
for them."
[3] The LORD has done great things for us,
and we are filled with joy.

[4] Restore our fortunes,[c] LORD,
like streams in the Negev.
[5] Those who sow with tears
will reap with songs of joy.
[6] Those who go out weeping,
carrying seed to sow,
will return with songs of joy,
carrying sheaves with them.

Psalm 127

A song of ascents. Of Solomon.

[1] Unless the LORD builds the house,
the builders labor in vain.
Unless the LORD watches over the city,
the guards stand watch in vain.
[2] In vain you rise early
and stay up late,
toiling for food to eat —
for he grants sleep to[d] those he loves.

[3] Children are a heritage from the LORD,
offspring a reward from him.
[4] Like arrows in the hands of a warrior
are children born in one's youth.
[5] Blessed is the man
whose quiver is full of them.
They will not be put to shame
when they contend with their
opponents in court.

Psalm 128

A song of ascents.

[1] Blessed are all who fear the LORD,
who walk in obedience to him.
[2] You will eat the fruit of your labor;
blessings and prosperity will be
yours.
[3] Your wife will be like a fruitful vine
within your house;
your children will be like olive shoots
around your table.
[4] Yes, this will be the blessing
for the man who fears the LORD.

[5] May the LORD bless you from Zion;
may you see the prosperity of
Jerusalem
all the days of your life.
[6] May you live to see your children's
children —
peace be on Israel.

Psalm 129

A song of ascents.

[1] "They have greatly oppressed me
from my youth,"
let Israel say;
[2] "they have greatly oppressed me
from my youth,
but they have not gained the
victory over me.
[3] Plowmen have plowed my back
and made their furrows long.
[4] But the LORD is righteous;
he has cut me free from the cords
of the wicked."

[5] May all who hate Zion
be turned back in shame.
[6] May they be like grass on the roof,
which withers before it can grow;
[7] a reaper cannot fill his hands with it,
nor one who gathers fill his arms.
[8] May those who pass by not say to
them,
"The blessing of the LORD be on you;
we bless you in the name of the
LORD."

[a] *1* Or *LORD brought back the captives to* [b] *1* Or *those restored to health* [c] *4* Or *Bring back our captives* [d] *2* Or *eat — / for while they sleep he provides for*

Psalm 130

A song of ascents.

1 Out of the depths I cry to you, LORD;
2 Lord, hear my voice.
Let your ears be attentive
to my cry for mercy.

3 If you, LORD, kept a record of sins,
Lord, who could stand?
4 But with you there is forgiveness,
so that we can, with reverence,
serve you.

5 I wait for the LORD, my whole being
waits,
and in his word I put my hope.
6 I wait for the Lord
more than watchmen wait for the
morning,
more than watchmen wait for the
morning.

7 Israel, put your hope in the LORD,
for with the LORD is unfailing love
and with him is full redemption.
8 He himself will redeem Israel
from all their sins.

Psalm 131

A song of ascents. Of David.

1 My heart is not proud, LORD,
my eyes are not haughty;
I do not concern myself with great
matters
or things too wonderful for me.
2 But I have calmed and quieted myself,
I am like a weaned child with its
mother;
like a weaned child I am content.

3 Israel, put your hope in the LORD
both now and forevermore.

Psalm 132

A song of ascents.

1 LORD, remember David
and all his self-denial.

2 He swore an oath to the LORD,
he made a vow to the Mighty One
of Jacob:
3 "I will not enter my house
or go to my bed,
4 I will allow no sleep to my eyes
or slumber to my eyelids,
5 till I find a place for the LORD,
a dwelling for the Mighty One of
Jacob."

6 We heard it in Ephrathah,
we came upon it in the fields of Jaar:[a]
7 "Let us go to his dwelling place,
let us worship at his footstool,
saying,
8 'Arise, LORD, and come to your resting
place,
you and the ark of your might.
9 May your priests be clothed with your
righteousness;
may your faithful people sing for
joy.' "

10 For the sake of your servant David,
do not reject your anointed one.

11 The LORD swore an oath to David,
a sure oath he will not revoke:
"One of your own descendants
I will place on your throne.
12 If your sons keep my covenant
and the statutes I teach them,
then their sons will sit
on your throne for ever and ever."

13 For the LORD has chosen Zion,
he has desired it for his dwelling,
saying,
14 "This is my resting place for ever and
ever;
here I will sit enthroned, for I have
desired it.
15 I will bless her with abundant
provisions;
her poor I will satisfy with food.
16 I will clothe her priests with
salvation,
and her faithful people will ever
sing for joy.

17 "Here I will make a horn[b] grow for
David
and set up a lamp for my anointed
one.
18 I will clothe his enemies with shame,
but his head will be adorned with a
radiant crown."

Psalm 133

A song of ascents. Of David.

1 How good and pleasant it is
when God's people live together in
unity!

2 It is like precious oil poured on the
head,
running down on the beard,
running down on Aaron's beard,
down on the collar of his robe.
3 It is as if the dew of Hermon
were falling on Mount Zion.
For there the LORD bestows his blessing,
even life forevermore.

[a] 6 Or *heard of it in Ephrathah, / we found it in the fields of Jearim.* (See 1 Chron. 13:5,6) (And no quotation marks around verses 7-9) [b] 17 *Horn* here symbolizes strong one, that is, king.

Psalm 134

A song of ascents.

1 Praise the LORD, all you servants of the LORD
who minister by night in the house of the LORD.
2 Lift up your hands in the sanctuary
and praise the LORD.

3 May the LORD bless you from Zion,
he who is the Maker of heaven and earth.

Psalm 135

1 Praise the LORD.[a]

Praise the name of the LORD;
praise him, you servants of the LORD,
2 you who minister in the house of the LORD,
in the courts of the house of our God.

3 Praise the LORD, for the LORD is good;
sing praise to his name, for that is pleasant.
4 For the LORD has chosen Jacob to be his own,
Israel to be his treasured possession.

5 I know that the LORD is great,
that our Lord is greater than all gods.
6 The LORD does whatever pleases him,
in the heavens and on the earth,
in the seas and all their depths.
7 He makes clouds rise from the ends of the earth;
he sends lightning with the rain
and brings out the wind from his storehouses.

8 He struck down the firstborn of Egypt,
the firstborn of people and animals.
9 He sent his signs and wonders into your midst, Egypt,
against Pharaoh and all his servants.
10 He struck down many nations
and killed mighty kings —
11 Sihon king of the Amorites,
Og king of Bashan,
and all the kings of Canaan —
12 and he gave their land as an inheritance,
an inheritance to his people Israel.

13 Your name, LORD, endures forever,
your renown, LORD, through all generations.
14 For the LORD will vindicate his people
and have compassion on his servants.

15 The idols of the nations are silver and gold,
made by human hands.
16 They have mouths, but cannot speak,
eyes, but cannot see.
17 They have ears, but cannot hear,
nor is there breath in their mouths.
18 Those who make them will be like them,
and so will all who trust in them.

19 All you Israelites, praise the LORD;
house of Aaron, praise the LORD;
20 house of Levi, praise the LORD;
you who fear him, praise the LORD.
21 Praise be to the LORD from Zion,
to him who dwells in Jerusalem.

Praise the LORD.

Psalm 136

1 Give thanks to the LORD, for he is good.
His love endures forever.
2 Give thanks to the God of gods.
His love endures forever.
3 Give thanks to the Lord of lords:
His love endures forever.

4 to him who alone does great wonders,
His love endures forever.
5 who by his understanding made the heavens,
His love endures forever.
6 who spread out the earth upon the waters,
His love endures forever.
7 who made the great lights —
His love endures forever.
8 the sun to govern the day,
His love endures forever.
9 the moon and stars to govern the night;
His love endures forever.

10 to him who struck down the firstborn of Egypt
His love endures forever.
11 and brought Israel out from among them
His love endures forever.
12 with a mighty hand and outstretched arm;
His love endures forever.

[a] *1* Hebrew *Hallelu Yah*; also in verses 3 and 21

13 to him who divided the Red Sea[a]
asunder
His love endures forever.
14 and brought Israel through the midst
of it,
His love endures forever.
15 but swept Pharaoh and his army into
the Red Sea;
His love endures forever.

16 to him who led his people through the
wilderness;
His love endures forever.

17 to him who struck down great kings,
His love endures forever.
18 and killed mighty kings—
His love endures forever.
19 Sihon king of the Amorites
His love endures forever.
20 and Og king of Bashan—
His love endures forever.
21 and gave their land as an inheritance,
His love endures forever.
22 an inheritance to his servant Israel.
His love endures forever.

23 He remembered us in our low estate
His love endures forever.
24 and freed us from our enemies.
His love endures forever.
25 He gives food to every creature.
His love endures forever.

26 Give thanks to the God of heaven.
His love endures forever.

Psalm 137

1 By the rivers of Babylon we sat and
wept
when we remembered Zion.
2 There on the poplars
we hung our harps,
3 for there our captors asked us for songs,
our tormentors demanded songs of
joy;
they said, "Sing us one of the songs
of Zion!"

4 How can we sing the songs of the
LORD
while in a foreign land?
5 If I forget you, Jerusalem,
may my right hand forget its skill.
6 May my tongue cling to the roof of
my mouth
if I do not remember you,
if I do not consider Jerusalem
my highest joy.

7 Remember, LORD, what the Edomites
did
on the day Jerusalem fell.
"Tear it down," they cried,
"tear it down to its foundations!"
8 Daughter Babylon, doomed to
destruction,
happy is the one who repays you
according to what you have done to
us.
9 Happy is the one who seizes your
infants
and dashes them against the rocks.

Psalm 138

Of David.

1 I will praise you, LORD, with all my
heart;
before the "gods" I will sing your
praise.
2 I will bow down toward your holy
temple
and will praise your name
for your unfailing love and your
faithfulness,
for you have so exalted your solemn
decree
that it surpasses your fame.
3 When I called, you answered me;
you greatly emboldened me.

4 May all the kings of the earth praise
you, LORD,
when they hear what you have
decreed.
5 May they sing of the ways of the
LORD,
for the glory of the LORD is great.

6 Though the LORD is exalted, he looks
kindly on the lowly;
though lofty, he sees them from afar.
7 Though I walk in the midst of trouble,
you preserve my life.
You stretch out your hand against the
anger of my foes;
with your right hand you save me.
8 The LORD will vindicate me;
your love, LORD, endures forever—
do not abandon the works of your
hands.

Psalm 139

For the director of music. Of David. A psalm.

1 You have searched me, LORD,
and you know me.
2 You know when I sit and when I rise;
you perceive my thoughts from afar.
3 You discern my going out and my
lying down;
you are familiar with all my ways.
4 Before a word is on my tongue
you, LORD, know it completely.

[a] 13 Or *the Sea of Reeds;* also in verse 15

[5] You hem me in behind and before,
and you lay your hand upon me.
[6] Such knowledge is too wonderful for me,
too lofty for me to attain.

[7] Where can I go from your Spirit?
Where can I flee from your presence?
[8] If I go up to the heavens, you are there;
if I make my bed in the depths, you are there.
[9] If I rise on the wings of the dawn,
if I settle on the far side of the sea,
[10] even there your hand will guide me,
your right hand will hold me fast.
[11] If I say, "Surely the darkness will hide me
and the light become night around me,"
[12] even the darkness will not be dark to you;
the night will shine like the day,
for darkness is as light to you.

[13] For you created my inmost being;
you knit me together in my mother's womb.
[14] I praise you because I am fearfully and wonderfully made;
your works are wonderful,
I know that full well.
[15] My frame was not hidden from you
when I was made in the secret place,
when I was woven together in the depths of the earth.
[16] Your eyes saw my unformed body;
all the days ordained for me were written in your book
before one of them came to be.
[17] How precious to me are your thoughts,[a] God!
How vast is the sum of them!
[18] Were I to count them,
they would outnumber the grains of sand —
when I awake, I am still with you.

[19] If only you, God, would slay the wicked!
Away from me, you who are bloodthirsty!
[20] They speak of you with evil intent;
your adversaries misuse your name.
[21] Do I not hate those who hate you, LORD,
and abhor those who are in rebellion against you?
[22] I have nothing but hatred for them;
I count them my enemies.
[23] Search me, God, and know my heart;
test me and know my anxious thoughts.
[24] See if there is any offensive way in me,
and lead me in the way everlasting.

Psalm 140[b]

For the director of music. A psalm of David.

[1] Rescue me, LORD, from evildoers;
protect me from the violent,
[2] who devise evil plans in their hearts
and stir up war every day.
[3] They make their tongues as sharp as a serpent's;
the poison of vipers is on their lips.[c]

[4] Keep me safe, LORD, from the hands of the wicked;
protect me from the violent,
who devise ways to trip my feet.
[5] The arrogant have hidden a snare for me;
they have spread out the cords of their net
and have set traps for me along my path.

[6] I say to the LORD, "You are my God."
Hear, LORD, my cry for mercy.
[7] Sovereign LORD, my strong deliverer,
you shield my head in the day of battle.
[8] Do not grant the wicked their desires, LORD;
do not let their plans succeed.

[9] Those who surround me proudly rear their heads;
may the mischief of their lips engulf them.
[10] May burning coals fall on them;
may they be thrown into the fire,
into miry pits, never to rise.
[11] May slanderers not be established in the land;
may disaster hunt down the violent.

[12] I know that the LORD secures justice for the poor
and upholds the cause of the needy.
[13] Surely the righteous will praise your name,
and the upright will live in your presence.

[a] *17* Or *How amazing are your thoughts concerning me* [b] In Hebrew texts 140:1-13 is numbered 140:2-14. [c] *3* The Hebrew has *Selah* (a word of uncertain meaning) here and at the end of verses 5 and 8.

Psalm 141

A psalm of David.

1 I call to you, LORD, come quickly to me;
hear me when I call to you.
2 May my prayer be set before you like incense;
may the lifting up of my hands be like the evening sacrifice.

3 Set a guard over my mouth, LORD;
keep watch over the door of my lips.
4 Do not let my heart be drawn to what is evil
so that I take part in wicked deeds
along with those who are evildoers;
do not let me eat their delicacies.
5 Let a righteous man strike me — that is a kindness;
let him rebuke me — that is oil on my head.
My head will not refuse it,
for my prayer will still be against the deeds of evildoers.

6 Their rulers will be thrown down from the cliffs,
and the wicked will learn that my words were well spoken.
7 They will say, "As one plows and breaks up the earth,
so our bones have been scattered at the mouth of the grave."

8 But my eyes are fixed on you, Sovereign LORD;
in you I take refuge — do not give me over to death.
9 Keep me safe from the traps set by evildoers,
from the snares they have laid for me.
10 Let the wicked fall into their own nets,
while I pass by in safety.

Psalm 142[a]

A maskil[b] *of David. When he was in the cave. A prayer.*

1 I cry aloud to the LORD;
I lift up my voice to the LORD for mercy.
2 I pour out before him my complaint;
before him I tell my trouble.

3 When my spirit grows faint within me,
it is you who watch over my way.
In the path where I walk
people have hidden a snare for me.
4 Look and see, there is no one at my right hand;
no one is concerned for me.
I have no refuge;
no one cares for my life.

5 I cry to you, LORD;
I say, "You are my refuge,
my portion in the land of the living."

6 Listen to my cry,
for I am in desperate need;
rescue me from those who pursue me,
for they are too strong for me.
7 Set me free from my prison,
that I may praise your name.
Then the righteous will gather about me
because of your goodness to me.

Psalm 143

A psalm of David.

1 LORD, hear my prayer,
listen to my cry for mercy;
in your faithfulness and righteousness
come to my relief.
2 Do not bring your servant into judgment,
for no one living is righteous before you.
3 The enemy pursues me,
he crushes me to the ground;
he makes me dwell in the darkness
like those long dead.
4 So my spirit grows faint within me;
my heart within me is dismayed.
5 I remember the days of long ago;
I meditate on all your works
and consider what your hands have done.
6 I spread out my hands to you;
I thirst for you like a parched land.[c]

7 Answer me quickly, LORD;
my spirit fails.
Do not hide your face from me
or I will be like those who go down to the pit.
8 Let the morning bring me word of your unfailing love,
for I have put my trust in you.
Show me the way I should go,
for to you I entrust my life.
9 Rescue me from my enemies, LORD,
for I hide myself in you.
10 Teach me to do your will,
for you are my God;
may your good Spirit
lead me on level ground.

[a] In Hebrew texts 142:1-7 is numbered 142:2-8. [b] Title: Probably a literary or musical term
[c] 6 The Hebrew has *Selah* (a word of uncertain meaning) here.

[11] For your name's sake, LORD, preserve
my life;
in your righteousness, bring me out
of trouble.
[12] In your unfailing love, silence my
enemies;
destroy all my foes,
for I am your servant.

Psalm 144

Of David.

[1] Praise be to the LORD my Rock,
who trains my hands for war,
my fingers for battle.
[2] He is my loving God and my fortress,
my stronghold and my deliverer,
my shield, in whom I take refuge,
who subdues peoples[a] under me.

[3] LORD, what are human beings that
you care for them,
mere mortals that you think of
them?
[4] They are like a breath;
their days are like a fleeting
shadow.

[5] Part your heavens, LORD, and come
down;
touch the mountains, so that they
smoke.
[6] Send forth lightning and scatter the
enemy;
shoot your arrows and rout them.
[7] Reach down your hand from on high;
deliver me and rescue me
from the mighty waters,
from the hands of foreigners
[8] whose mouths are full of lies,
whose right hands are deceitful.

[9] I will sing a new song to you, my God;
on the ten-stringed lyre I will make
music to you,
[10] to the One who gives victory to kings,
who delivers his servant David.

From the deadly sword [11] deliver me;
rescue me from the hands of
foreigners
whose mouths are full of lies,
whose right hands are deceitful.

[12] Then our sons in their youth
will be like well-nurtured plants,
and our daughters will be like pillars
carved to adorn a palace.
[13] Our barns will be filled
with every kind of provision.
Our sheep will increase by thousands,
by tens of thousands in our fields;
[14] our oxen will draw heavy loads.[b]
There will be no breaching of walls,
no going into captivity,
no cry of distress in our streets.
[15] Blessed is the people of whom this is
true;
blessed is the people whose God is
the LORD.

Psalm 145[c]

A psalm of praise. Of David.

[1] I will exalt you, my God the King;
I will praise your name for ever and
ever.
[2] Every day I will praise you
and extol your name for ever and
ever.

[3] Great is the LORD and most worthy of
praise;
his greatness no one can fathom.
[4] One generation commends your
works to another;
they tell of your mighty acts.
[5] They speak of the glorious splendor
of your majesty —
and I will meditate on your
wonderful works.[d]
[6] They tell of the power of your
awesome works —
and I will proclaim your great
deeds.
[7] They celebrate your abundant
goodness
and joyfully sing of your
righteousness.

[8] The LORD is gracious and
compassionate,
slow to anger and rich in love.

[9] The LORD is good to all;
he has compassion on all he has
made.
[10] All your works praise you, LORD;
your faithful people extol you.
[11] They tell of the glory of your kingdom
and speak of your might,
[12] so that all people may know of your
mighty acts
and the glorious splendor of your
kingdom.

[a] *2* Many manuscripts of the Masoretic Text, Dead Sea Scrolls, Aquila, Jerome and Syriac; most manuscripts of the Masoretic Text *subdues my people* [b] *14* Or *our chieftains will be firmly established* [c] This psalm is an acrostic poem, the verses of which (including verse 13b) begin with the successive letters of the Hebrew alphabet. [d] *5* Dead Sea Scrolls and Syriac (see also Septuagint); Masoretic Text *On the glorious splendor of your majesty / and on your wonderful works I will meditate*

13 Your kingdom is an everlasting kingdom,
and your dominion endures through all generations.

The LORD is trustworthy in all he promises
and faithful in all he does.[a]
14 The LORD upholds all who fall
and lifts up all who are bowed down.
15 The eyes of all look to you,
and you give them their food at the proper time.
16 You open your hand
and satisfy the desires of every living thing.

17 The LORD is righteous in all his ways
and faithful in all he does.
18 The LORD is near to all who call on him,
to all who call on him in truth.
19 He fulfills the desires of those who fear him;
he hears their cry and saves them.
20 The LORD watches over all who love him,
but all the wicked he will destroy.

21 My mouth will speak in praise of the LORD.
Let every creature praise his holy name
for ever and ever.

Psalm 146

1 Praise the LORD.[b]

Praise the LORD, my soul.

2 I will praise the LORD all my life;
I will sing praise to my God as long as I live.
3 Do not put your trust in princes,
in human beings, who cannot save.
4 When their spirit departs, they return to the ground;
on that very day their plans come to nothing.
5 Blessed are those whose help is the God of Jacob,
whose hope is in the LORD their God.

6 He is the Maker of heaven and earth,
the sea, and everything in them —
he remains faithful forever.
7 He upholds the cause of the oppressed
and gives food to the hungry.
The LORD sets prisoners free,
8 the LORD gives sight to the blind,
the LORD lifts up those who are bowed down,
the LORD loves the righteous.
9 The LORD watches over the foreigner
and sustains the fatherless and the widow,
but he frustrates the ways of the wicked.

10 The LORD reigns forever,
your God, O Zion, for all generations.

Praise the LORD.

Psalm 147

1 Praise the LORD.[c]

How good it is to sing praises to our God,
how pleasant and fitting to praise him!

2 The LORD builds up Jerusalem;
he gathers the exiles of Israel.
3 He heals the brokenhearted
and binds up their wounds.
4 He determines the number of the stars
and calls them each by name.
5 Great is our Lord and mighty in power;
his understanding has no limit.
6 The LORD sustains the humble
but casts the wicked to the ground.

7 Sing to the LORD with grateful praise;
make music to our God on the harp.

8 He covers the sky with clouds;
he supplies the earth with rain
and makes grass grow on the hills.
9 He provides food for the cattle
and for the young ravens when they call.
10 His pleasure is not in the strength of the horse,
nor his delight in the legs of the warrior;
11 the LORD delights in those who fear him,
who put their hope in his unfailing love.

12 Extol the LORD, Jerusalem;
praise your God, Zion.

13 He strengthens the bars of your gates
and blesses your people within you.
14 He grants peace to your borders
and satisfies you with the finest of wheat.

15 He sends his command to the earth;
his word runs swiftly.
16 He spreads the snow like wool
and scatters the frost like ashes.

[a] *13* One manuscript of the Masoretic Text, Dead Sea Scrolls and Syriac (see also Septuagint); most manuscripts of the Masoretic Text do not have the last two lines of verse 13. [b] *1* Hebrew *Hallelu Yah*; also in verse 10 [c] *1* Hebrew *Hallelu Yah*; also in verse 20

17 He hurls down his hail like pebbles.
Who can withstand his icy blast?
18 He sends his word and melts them;
he stirs up his breezes, and the waters flow.

19 He has revealed his word to Jacob,
his laws and decrees to Israel.
20 He has done this for no other nation;
they do not know his laws.[a]

Praise the LORD.

Psalm 148

1 Praise the LORD.[b]

Praise the LORD from the heavens;
praise him in the heights above.
2 Praise him, all his angels;
praise him, all his heavenly hosts.
3 Praise him, sun and moon;
praise him, all you shining stars.
4 Praise him, you highest heavens
and you waters above the skies.

5 Let them praise the name of the LORD,
for at his command they were created,
6 and he established them for ever and ever —
he issued a decree that will never pass away.

7 Praise the LORD from the earth,
you great sea creatures and all ocean depths,
8 lightning and hail, snow and clouds,
stormy winds that do his bidding,
9 you mountains and all hills,
fruit trees and all cedars,
10 wild animals and all cattle,
small creatures and flying birds,
11 kings of the earth and all nations,
you princes and all rulers on earth,
12 young men and women,
old men and children.

13 Let them praise the name of the LORD,
for his name alone is exalted;
his splendor is above the earth and the heavens.
14 And he has raised up for his people a horn,[c]
the praise of all his faithful servants,
of Israel, the people close to his heart.

Praise the LORD.

Psalm 149

1 Praise the LORD.[d]

Sing to the LORD a new song,
his praise in the assembly of his faithful people.

2 Let Israel rejoice in their Maker;
let the people of Zion be glad in their King.
3 Let them praise his name with dancing
and make music to him with timbrel and harp.
4 For the LORD takes delight in his people;
he crowns the humble with victory.
5 Let his faithful people rejoice in this honor
and sing for joy on their beds.

6 May the praise of God be in their mouths
and a double-edged sword in their hands,
7 to inflict vengeance on the nations
and punishment on the peoples,
8 to bind their kings with fetters,
their nobles with shackles of iron,
9 to carry out the sentence written against them —
this is the glory of all his faithful people.

Praise the LORD.

Psalm 150

1 Praise the LORD.[e]

Praise God in his sanctuary;
praise him in his mighty heavens.
2 Praise him for his acts of power;
praise him for his surpassing greatness.
3 Praise him with the sounding of the trumpet,
praise him with the harp and lyre,
4 praise him with timbrel and dancing,
praise him with the strings and pipe,
5 praise him with the clash of cymbals,
praise him with resounding cymbals.

6 Let everything that has breath praise the LORD.

Praise the LORD.

[a] *20* Masoretic Text; Dead Sea Scrolls and Septuagint *nation; / he has not made his laws known to them* [b] *1* Hebrew *Hallelu Yah*; also in verse 14 [c] *14* *Horn* here symbolizes strength.
[d] *1* Hebrew *Hallelu Yah*; also in verse 9 [e] *1* Hebrew *Hallelu Yah*; also in verse 6

PROVERBS

Purpose and Theme

1 The proverbs of Solomon son of David,
king of Israel:

[2] for gaining wisdom and instruction;
for understanding words of insight;
[3] for receiving instruction in prudent behavior,
doing what is right and just and fair;
[4] for giving prudence to those who are simple,[a]
knowledge and discretion to the young —
[5] let the wise listen and add to their learning,
and let the discerning get guidance —
[6] for understanding proverbs and parables,
the sayings and riddles of the wise.[b]

[7] The fear of the LORD is the beginning of knowledge,
but fools[c] despise wisdom and instruction.

Prologue: Exhortations to Embrace Wisdom

Warning Against the Invitation of Sinful Men

[8] Listen, my son, to your father's instruction
and do not forsake your mother's teaching.
[9] They are a garland to grace your head
and a chain to adorn your neck.

[10] My son, if sinful men entice you,
do not give in to them.
[11] If they say, "Come along with us;
let's lie in wait for innocent blood,
let's ambush some harmless soul;
[12] let's swallow them alive, like the grave,
and whole, like those who go down to the pit;
[13] we will get all sorts of valuable things
and fill our houses with plunder;
[14] cast lots with us;
we will all share the loot" —
[15] my son, do not go along with them,
do not set foot on their paths;
[16] for their feet rush into evil,
they are swift to shed blood.
[17] How useless to spread a net
where every bird can see it!
[18] These men lie in wait for their own blood;
they ambush only themselves!
[19] Such are the paths of all who go after ill-gotten gain;
it takes away the life of those who get it.

Wisdom's Rebuke

[20] Out in the open wisdom calls aloud,
she raises her voice in the public square;
[21] on top of the wall[d] she cries out,
at the city gate she makes her speech:

[22] "How long will you who are simple
love your simple ways?
How long will mockers delight in mockery
and fools hate knowledge?
[23] Repent at my rebuke!
Then I will pour out my thoughts to you,
I will make known to you my teachings.
[24] But since you refuse to listen when I call
and no one pays attention when I stretch out my hand,
[25] since you disregard all my advice
and do not accept my rebuke,
[26] I in turn will laugh when disaster strikes you;
I will mock when calamity overtakes you —
[27] when calamity overtakes you like a storm,
when disaster sweeps over you like a whirlwind,
when distress and trouble overwhelm you.

[a] 4 The Hebrew word rendered *simple* in Proverbs denotes a person who is gullible, without moral direction and inclined to evil. [b] 6 Or *understanding a proverb, namely, a parable, / and the sayings of the wise, their riddles* [c] 7 The Hebrew words rendered *fool* in Proverbs, and often elsewhere in the Old Testament, denote a person who is morally deficient. [d] 21 Septuagint; Hebrew / *at noisy street corners*

28 "Then they will call to me but I will
not answer;
they will look for me but will not
find me,
29 since they hated knowledge
and did not choose to fear the
LORD.
30 Since they would not accept my
advice
and spurned my rebuke,
31 they will eat the fruit of their ways
and be filled with the fruit of their
schemes.
32 For the waywardness of the simple
will kill them,
and the complacency of fools will
destroy them;
33 but whoever listens to me will live in
safety
and be at ease, without fear of
harm."

Moral Benefits of Wisdom

2 My son, if you accept my words
and store up my commands within
you,
2 turning your ear to wisdom
and applying your heart to
understanding —
3 indeed, if you call out for insight
and cry aloud for understanding,
4 and if you look for it as for silver
and search for it as for hidden
treasure,
5 then you will understand the fear of
the LORD
and find the knowledge of God.
6 For the LORD gives wisdom;
from his mouth come knowledge
and understanding.
7 He holds success in store for the
upright,
he is a shield to those whose walk is
blameless,
8 for he guards the course of the just
and protects the way of his faithful
ones.

9 Then you will understand what is
right and just
and fair — every good path.
10 For wisdom will enter your heart,
and knowledge will be pleasant to
your soul.
11 Discretion will protect you,
and understanding will guard you.

12 Wisdom will save you from the ways
of wicked men,
from men whose words are
perverse,
13 who have left the straight paths
to walk in dark ways,
14 who delight in doing wrong
and rejoice in the perverseness of
evil,
15 whose paths are crooked
and who are devious in their ways.

16 Wisdom will save you also from the
adulterous woman,
from the wayward woman with her
seductive words,
17 who has left the partner of her youth
and ignored the covenant she
made before God.[a]
18 Surely her house leads down
to death
and her paths to the spirits of the
dead.
19 None who go to her return
or attain the paths of life.

20 Thus you will walk in the ways of the
good
and keep to the paths of the
righteous.
21 For the upright will live in the land,
and the blameless will remain in it;
22 but the wicked will be cut off from the
land,
and the unfaithful will be torn
from it.

Wisdom Bestows Well-Being

3 My son, do not forget my teaching,
but keep my commands in your
heart,
2 for they will prolong your life many
years
and bring you peace and
prosperity.

3 Let love and faithfulness never leave
you;
bind them around your neck,
write them on the tablet of your
heart.
4 Then you will win favor and a good
name
in the sight of God and man.

5 Trust in the LORD with all your heart
and lean not on your own
understanding;
6 in all your ways submit to him,
and he will make your paths
straight.[b]

7 Do not be wise in your own eyes;
fear the LORD and shun evil.
8 This will bring health to your body
and nourishment to your bones.

[a] 17 Or *covenant of her God* [b] 6 Or *will direct your paths*

[9] Honor the LORD with your wealth,
with the firstfruits of all your crops;
[10] then your barns will be filled to overflowing,
and your vats will brim over with new wine.

[11] My son, do not despise the LORD's discipline,
and do not resent his rebuke,
[12] because the LORD disciplines those he loves,
as a father the son he delights in.[a]

[13] Blessed are those who find wisdom,
those who gain understanding,
[14] for she is more profitable than silver
and yields better returns than gold.
[15] She is more precious than rubies;
nothing you desire can compare with her.
[16] Long life is in her right hand;
in her left hand are riches and honor.
[17] Her ways are pleasant ways,
and all her paths are peace.
[18] She is a tree of life to those who take hold of her;
those who hold her fast will be blessed.

[19] By wisdom the LORD laid the earth's foundations,
by understanding he set the heavens in place;
[20] by his knowledge the watery depths were divided,
and the clouds let drop the dew.

[21] My son, do not let wisdom and understanding out of your sight,
preserve sound judgment and discretion;
[22] they will be life for you,
an ornament to grace your neck.
[23] Then you will go on your way in safety,
and your foot will not stumble.
[24] When you lie down, you will not be afraid;
when you lie down, your sleep will be sweet.
[25] Have no fear of sudden disaster
or of the ruin that overtakes the wicked,
[26] for the LORD will be at your side
and will keep your foot from being snared.

[27] Do not withhold good from those to whom it is due,
when it is in your power to act.
[28] Do not say to your neighbor,
"Come back tomorrow and I'll give it to you" —
when you already have it with you.
[29] Do not plot harm against your neighbor,
who lives trustfully near you.
[30] Do not accuse anyone for no reason —
when they have done you no harm.

[31] Do not envy the violent
or choose any of their ways.

[32] For the LORD detests the perverse
but takes the upright into his confidence.
[33] The LORD's curse is on the house of the wicked,
but he blesses the home of the righteous.
[34] He mocks proud mockers
but shows favor to the humble and oppressed.
[35] The wise inherit honor,
but fools get only shame.

Get Wisdom at Any Cost

4 Listen, my sons, to a father's instruction;
pay attention and gain understanding.
[2] I give you sound learning,
so do not forsake my teaching.
[3] For I too was a son to my father,
still tender, and cherished by my mother.
[4] Then he taught me, and he said to me,
"Take hold of my words with all your heart;
keep my commands, and you will live.
[5] Get wisdom, get understanding;
do not forget my words or turn away from them.
[6] Do not forsake wisdom, and she will protect you;
love her, and she will watch over you.
[7] The beginning of wisdom is this: Get[b] wisdom.
Though it cost all you have,[c] get understanding.
[8] Cherish her, and she will exalt you;
embrace her, and she will honor you.
[9] She will give you a garland to grace your head
and present you with a glorious crown."

[a] 12 Hebrew; Septuagint *loves, / and he chastens everyone he accepts as his child* [b] 7 Or *Wisdom is supreme; therefore get* [c] 7 Or *wisdom. / Whatever else you get*

10 Listen, my son, accept what I say,
and the years of your life will be many.
11 I instruct you in the way of wisdom
and lead you along straight paths.
12 When you walk, your steps will not be hampered;
when you run, you will not stumble.
13 Hold on to instruction, do not let it go;
guard it well, for it is your life.
14 Do not set foot on the path of the wicked
or walk in the way of evildoers.
15 Avoid it, do not travel on it;
turn from it and go on your way.
16 For they cannot rest until they do evil;
they are robbed of sleep till they make someone stumble.
17 They eat the bread of wickedness
and drink the wine of violence.

18 The path of the righteous is like the morning sun,
shining ever brighter till the full light of day.
19 But the way of the wicked is like deep darkness;
they do not know what makes them stumble.

20 My son, pay attention to what I say;
turn your ear to my words.
21 Do not let them out of your sight,
keep them within your heart;
22 for they are life to those who find them
and health to one's whole body.
23 Above all else, guard your heart,
for everything you do flows from it.
24 Keep your mouth free of perversity;
keep corrupt talk far from your lips.
25 Let your eyes look straight ahead;
fix your gaze directly before you.
26 Give careful thought to the[a] paths for your feet
and be steadfast in all your ways.
27 Do not turn to the right or the left;
keep your foot from evil.

Warning Against Adultery

5 My son, pay attention to my wisdom,
turn your ear to my words of insight,
2 that you may maintain discretion
and your lips may preserve knowledge.
3 For the lips of the adulterous woman drip honey,
and her speech is smoother than oil;
4 but in the end she is bitter as gall,
sharp as a double-edged sword.
5 Her feet go down to death;
her steps lead straight to the grave.
6 She gives no thought to the way of life;
her paths wander aimlessly, but she does not know it.

7 Now then, my sons, listen to me;
do not turn aside from what I say.
8 Keep to a path far from her,
do not go near the door of her house,
9 lest you lose your honor to others
and your dignity[b] to one who is cruel,
10 lest strangers feast on your wealth
and your toil enrich the house of another.
11 At the end of your life you will groan,
when your flesh and body are spent.
12 You will say, "How I hated discipline!
How my heart spurned correction!
13 I would not obey my teachers
or turn my ear to my instructors.
14 And I was soon in serious trouble
in the assembly of God's people."

15 Drink water from your own cistern,
running water from your own well.
16 Should your springs overflow in the streets,
your streams of water in the public squares?
17 Let them be yours alone,
never to be shared with strangers.
18 May your fountain be blessed,
and may you rejoice in the wife of your youth.
19 A loving doe, a graceful deer—
may her breasts satisfy you always,
may you ever be intoxicated with her love.
20 Why, my son, be intoxicated with another man's wife?
Why embrace the bosom of a wayward woman?

21 For your ways are in full view of the LORD,
and he examines all your paths.
22 The evil deeds of the wicked ensnare them;
the cords of their sins hold them fast.
23 For lack of discipline they will die,
led astray by their own great folly.

[a] 26 Or *Make level* [b] 9 Or *years*

Warnings Against Folly

6 My son, if you have put up security
for your neighbor,
if you have shaken hands in pledge
for a stranger,
2 you have been trapped by what you
said,
ensnared by the words of your
mouth.
3 So do this, my son, to free yourself,
since you have fallen into your
neighbor's hands:
Go — to the point of exhaustion —[a]
and give your neighbor no rest!
4 Allow no sleep to your eyes,
no slumber to your eyelids.
5 Free yourself, like a gazelle from the
hand of the hunter,
like a bird from the snare of the
fowler.

6 Go to the ant, you sluggard;
consider its ways and be wise!
7 It has no commander,
no overseer or ruler,
8 yet it stores its provisions in summer
and gathers its food at harvest.

9 How long will you lie there, you
sluggard?
When will you get up from your
sleep?
10 A little sleep, a little slumber,
a little folding of the hands to rest —
11 and poverty will come on you like a
thief
and scarcity like an armed man.

12 A troublemaker and a villain,
who goes about with a corrupt
mouth,
13 who winks maliciously with his eye,
signals with his feet
and motions with his fingers,
14 who plots evil with deceit in his
heart —
he always stirs up conflict.
15 Therefore disaster will overtake him
in an instant;
he will suddenly be destroyed —
without remedy.

16 There are six things the LORD hates,
seven that are detestable to him:
17 haughty eyes,
a lying tongue,
hands that shed innocent blood,
18 a heart that devises wicked
schemes,
feet that are quick to rush into evil,
19 a false witness who pours out lies
and a person who stirs up
conflict in the community.

Warning Against Adultery

20 My son, keep your father's command
and do not forsake your mother's
teaching.
21 Bind them always on your heart;
fasten them around your neck.
22 When you walk, they will guide you;
when you sleep, they will watch
over you;
when you awake, they will speak
to you.
23 For this command is a lamp,
this teaching is a light,
and correction and instruction
are the way to life,
24 keeping you from your neighbor's
wife,
from the smooth talk of a
wayward woman.

25 Do not lust in your heart after her
beauty
or let her captivate you with her
eyes.

26 For a prostitute can be had for a loaf
of bread,
but another man's wife preys on
your very life.
27 Can a man scoop fire into his lap
without his clothes being burned?
28 Can a man walk on hot coals
without his feet being scorched?
29 So is he who sleeps with another
man's wife;
no one who touches her will go
unpunished.

30 People do not despise a thief if he
steals
to satisfy his hunger when he is
starving.
31 Yet if he is caught, he must pay
sevenfold,
though it costs him all the wealth
of his house.
32 But a man who commits adultery
has no sense;
whoever does so destroys
himself.
33 Blows and disgrace are his lot,
and his shame will never be
wiped away.

34 For jealousy arouses a husband's
fury,
and he will show no mercy when
he takes revenge.
35 He will not accept any compensation;
he will refuse a bribe, however
great it is.

[a] 3 Or *Go and humble yourself,*

Warning Against the Adulterous Woman

7 My son, keep my words
and store up my commands within you.
2 Keep my commands and you will live;
guard my teachings as the apple of your eye.
3 Bind them on your fingers;
write them on the tablet of your heart.
4 Say to wisdom, "You are my sister,"
and to insight, "You are my relative."
5 They will keep you from the adulterous woman,
from the wayward woman with her seductive words.

6 At the window of my house
I looked down through the lattice.
7 I saw among the simple,
I noticed among the young men,
a youth who had no sense.
8 He was going down the street near her corner,
walking along in the direction of her house
9 at twilight, as the day was fading,
as the dark of night set in.

10 Then out came a woman to meet him,
dressed like a prostitute and with crafty intent.
11 (She is unruly and defiant,
her feet never stay at home;
12 now in the street, now in the squares,
at every corner she lurks.)
13 She took hold of him and kissed him
and with a brazen face she said:

14 "Today I fulfilled my vows,
and I have food from my fellowship offering at home.
15 So I came out to meet you;
I looked for you and have found you!
16 I have covered my bed
with colored linens from Egypt.
17 I have perfumed my bed
with myrrh, aloes and cinnamon.
18 Come, let's drink deeply of love till morning;
let's enjoy ourselves with love!
19 My husband is not at home;
he has gone on a long journey.
20 He took his purse filled with money
and will not be home till full moon."

21 With persuasive words she led him astray;
she seduced him with her smooth talk.
22 All at once he followed her
like an ox going to the slaughter,
like a deer[a] stepping into a noose[b]
23 till an arrow pierces his liver,
like a bird darting into a snare,
little knowing it will cost him his life.

24 Now then, my sons, listen to me;
pay attention to what I say.
25 Do not let your heart turn to her ways
or stray into her paths.
26 Many are the victims she has brought down;
her slain are a mighty throng.
27 Her house is a highway to the grave,
leading down to the chambers of death.

Wisdom's Call

8 Does not wisdom call out?
Does not understanding raise her voice?
2 At the highest point along the way,
where the paths meet, she takes her stand;
3 beside the gate leading into the city,
at the entrance, she cries aloud:
4 "To you, O people, I call out;
I raise my voice to all mankind.
5 You who are simple, gain prudence;
you who are foolish, set your hearts on it.[c]
6 Listen, for I have trustworthy things to say;
I open my lips to speak what is right.
7 My mouth speaks what is true,
for my lips detest wickedness.
8 All the words of my mouth are just;
none of them is crooked or perverse.
9 To the discerning all of them are right;
they are upright to those who have found knowledge.
10 Choose my instruction instead of silver,
knowledge rather than choice gold,
11 for wisdom is more precious than rubies,
and nothing you desire can compare with her.

12 "I, wisdom, dwell together with prudence;
I possess knowledge and discretion.
13 To fear the LORD is to hate evil;
I hate pride and arrogance,
evil behavior and perverse speech.

[a] *22* Syriac (see also Septuagint); Hebrew *fool* [b] *22* The meaning of the Hebrew for this line is uncertain. [c] *5* Septuagint; Hebrew *foolish, instruct your minds*

14 Counsel and sound judgment are
mine;
I have insight, I have power.
15 By me kings reign
and rulers issue decrees that are
just;
16 by me princes govern,
and nobles — all who rule on
earth.[a]
17 I love those who love me,
and those who seek me find me.
18 With me are riches and honor,
enduring wealth and prosperity.
19 My fruit is better than fine gold;
what I yield surpasses choice silver.
20 I walk in the way of righteousness,
along the paths of justice,
21 bestowing a rich inheritance on those
who love me
and making their treasuries full.

22 "The LORD brought me forth as the
first of his works,[b,c]
before his deeds of old;
23 I was formed long ages ago,
at the very beginning, when the
world came to be.
24 When there were no watery depths, I
was given birth,
when there were no springs
overflowing with water;
25 before the mountains were settled in
place,
before the hills, I was given birth,
26 before he made the world or its fields
or any of the dust of the earth.
27 I was there when he set the heavens
in place,
when he marked out the horizon
on the face of the deep,
28 when he established the clouds above
and fixed securely the fountains of
the deep,
29 when he gave the sea its boundary
so the waters would not overstep
his command,
and when he marked out the
foundations of the earth.
30 Then I was constantly[d] at his side.
I was filled with delight day after day,
rejoicing always in his presence,
31 rejoicing in his whole world
and delighting in mankind.

32 "Now then, my children, listen to me;
blessed are those who keep my
ways.
33 Listen to my instruction and be wise;
do not disregard it.
34 Blessed are those who listen to me,
watching daily at my doors,
waiting at my doorway.
35 For those who find me find life
and receive favor from the LORD.
36 But those who fail to find me harm
themselves;
all who hate me love death."

Invitations of Wisdom and Folly

9 Wisdom has built her house;
she has set up[e] its seven pillars.
2 She has prepared her meat and
mixed her wine;
she has also set her table.
3 She has sent out her servants, and
she calls
from the highest point of the city,
4 "Let all who are simple come to
my house!"
To those who have no sense she says,
5 "Come, eat my food
and drink the wine I have mixed.
6 Leave your simple ways and you will
live;
walk in the way of insight."

7 Whoever corrects a mocker invites
insults;
whoever rebukes the wicked incurs
abuse.
8 Do not rebuke mockers or they will
hate you;
rebuke the wise and they will love
you.
9 Instruct the wise and they will be
wiser still;
teach the righteous and they will
add to their learning.

10 The fear of the LORD is the beginning
of wisdom,
and knowledge of the Holy One is
understanding.
11 For through wisdom[f] your days will
be many,
and years will be added
to your life.
12 If you are wise, your wisdom will
reward you;
if you are a mocker, you alone will
suffer.

13 Folly is an unruly woman;
she is simple and knows nothing.

[a] 16 Some Hebrew manuscripts and Septuagint; other Hebrew manuscripts *all righteous rulers*
[b] 22 Or *way;* or *dominion*
[c] 22 Or *The LORD possessed me at the beginning of his work;* or *The LORD brought me forth at the beginning of his work*
[d] 30 Or *was the artisan;* or *was a little child*
[e] 1 Septuagint, Syriac and Targum; Hebrew *has hewn out*
[f] 11 Septuagint, Syriac and Targum; Hebrew *me*

14 She sits at the door of her house,
on a seat at the highest point of the city,
15 calling out to those who pass by,
who go straight on their way,
16 "Let all who are simple come to my house!"
To those who have no sense she says,
17 "Stolen water is sweet;
food eaten in secret is delicious!"
18 But little do they know that the dead are there,
that her guests are deep in the realm of the dead.

Proverbs of Solomon

10 The proverbs of Solomon:

A wise son brings joy to his father,
but a foolish son brings grief to his mother.

2 Ill-gotten treasures have no lasting value,
but righteousness delivers from death.

3 The LORD does not let the righteous go hungry,
but he thwarts the craving of the wicked.

4 Lazy hands make for poverty,
but diligent hands bring wealth.

5 He who gathers crops in summer is a prudent son,
but he who sleeps during harvest is a disgraceful son.

6 Blessings crown the head of the righteous,
but violence overwhelms the mouth of the wicked.[a]

7 The name of the righteous is used in blessings,[b]
but the name of the wicked will rot.

8 The wise in heart accept commands,
but a chattering fool comes to ruin.

9 Whoever walks in integrity walks securely,
but whoever takes crooked paths will be found out.

10 Whoever winks maliciously causes grief,
and a chattering fool comes to ruin.

11 The mouth of the righteous is a fountain of life,
but the mouth of the wicked conceals violence.

12 Hatred stirs up conflict,
but love covers over all wrongs.

13 Wisdom is found on the lips of the discerning,
but a rod is for the back of one who has no sense.

14 The wise store up knowledge,
but the mouth of a fool invites ruin.

15 The wealth of the rich is their fortified city,
but poverty is the ruin of the poor.

16 The wages of the righteous is life,
but the earnings of the wicked are sin and death.

17 Whoever heeds discipline shows the way to life,
but whoever ignores correction leads others astray.

18 Whoever conceals hatred with lying lips
and spreads slander is a fool.

19 Sin is not ended by multiplying words,
but the prudent hold their tongues.

20 The tongue of the righteous is choice silver,
but the heart of the wicked is of little value.

21 The lips of the righteous nourish many,
but fools die for lack of sense.

22 The blessing of the LORD brings wealth,
without painful toil for it.

23 A fool finds pleasure in wicked schemes,
but a person of understanding delights in wisdom.

24 What the wicked dread will overtake them;
what the righteous desire will be granted.

25 When the storm has swept by, the wicked are gone,
but the righteous stand firm forever.

26 As vinegar to the teeth and smoke to the eyes,
so are sluggards to those who send them.

27 The fear of the LORD adds length to life,
but the years of the wicked are cut short.

[a] 6 Or *righteous, / but the mouth of the wicked conceals violence* [b] 7 See Gen. 48:20.

28 The prospect of the righteous is joy,
but the hopes of the wicked come to nothing.

29 The way of the LORD is a refuge for the blameless,
but it is the ruin of those who do evil.

30 The righteous will never be uprooted,
but the wicked will not remain in the land.

31 From the mouth of the righteous comes the fruit of wisdom,
but a perverse tongue will be silenced.

32 The lips of the righteous know what finds favor,
but the mouth of the wicked only what is perverse.

11 The LORD detests dishonest scales,
but accurate weights find favor with him.

2 When pride comes, then comes disgrace,
but with humility comes wisdom.

3 The integrity of the upright guides them,
but the unfaithful are destroyed by their duplicity.

4 Wealth is worthless in the day of wrath,
but righteousness delivers from death.

5 The righteousness of the blameless makes their paths straight,
but the wicked are brought down by their own wickedness.

6 The righteousness of the upright delivers them,
but the unfaithful are trapped by evil desires.

7 Hopes placed in mortals die with them;
all the promise of[a] their power comes to nothing.

8 The righteous person is rescued from trouble,
and it falls on the wicked instead.

9 With their mouths the godless destroy their neighbors,
but through knowledge the righteous escape.

10 When the righteous prosper, the city rejoices;
when the wicked perish, there are shouts of joy.

11 Through the blessing of the upright a city is exalted,
but by the mouth of the wicked it is destroyed.

12 Whoever derides their neighbor has no sense,
but the one who has understanding holds their tongue.

13 A gossip betrays a confidence,
but a trustworthy person keeps a secret.

14 For lack of guidance a nation falls,
but victory is won through many advisers.

15 Whoever puts up security for a stranger will surely suffer,
but whoever refuses to shake hands in pledge is safe.

16 A kindhearted woman gains honor,
but ruthless men gain only wealth.

17 Those who are kind benefit themselves,
but the cruel bring ruin on themselves.

18 A wicked person earns deceptive wages,
but the one who sows righteousness reaps a sure reward.

19 Truly the righteous attain life,
but whoever pursues evil finds death.

20 The LORD detests those whose hearts are perverse,
but he delights in those whose ways are blameless.

21 Be sure of this: The wicked will not go unpunished,
but those who are righteous will go free.

22 Like a gold ring in a pig's snout
is a beautiful woman who shows no discretion.

23 The desire of the righteous ends only in good,
but the hope of the wicked only in wrath.

24 One person gives freely, yet gains even more;
another withholds unduly, but comes to poverty.

25 A generous person will prosper;
whoever refreshes others will be refreshed.

[a] 7 Two Hebrew manuscripts; most Hebrew manuscripts, Vulgate, Syriac and Targum *When the wicked die, their hope perishes; / all they expected from*

26 People curse the one who hoards grain,
but they pray God's blessing on the one who is willing to sell.

27 Whoever seeks good finds favor,
but evil comes to one who searches for it.

28 Those who trust in their riches will fall,
but the righteous will thrive like a green leaf.

29 Whoever brings ruin on their family will inherit only wind,
and the fool will be servant to the wise.

30 The fruit of the righteous is a tree of life,
and the one who is wise saves lives.

31 If the righteous receive their due on earth,
how much more the ungodly and the sinner!

12 Whoever loves discipline loves knowledge,
but whoever hates correction is stupid.

2 Good people obtain favor from the LORD,
but he condemns those who devise wicked schemes.

3 No one can be established through wickedness,
but the righteous cannot be uprooted.

4 A wife of noble character is her husband's crown,
but a disgraceful wife is like decay in his bones.

5 The plans of the righteous are just,
but the advice of the wicked is deceitful.

6 The words of the wicked lie in wait for blood,
but the speech of the upright rescues them.

7 The wicked are overthrown and are no more,
but the house of the righteous stands firm.

8 A person is praised according to their prudence,
and one with a warped mind is despised.

9 Better to be a nobody and yet have a servant
than pretend to be somebody and have no food.

10 The righteous care for the needs of their animals,
but the kindest acts of the wicked are cruel.

11 Those who work their land will have abundant food,
but those who chase fantasies have no sense.

12 The wicked desire the stronghold of evildoers,
but the root of the righteous endures.

13 Evildoers are trapped by their sinful talk,
and so the innocent escape trouble.

14 From the fruit of their lips people are filled with good things,
and the work of their hands brings them reward.

15 The way of fools seems right to them,
but the wise listen to advice.

16 Fools show their annoyance at once,
but the prudent overlook an insult.

17 An honest witness tells the truth,
but a false witness tells lies.

18 The words of the reckless pierce like swords,
but the tongue of the wise brings healing.

19 Truthful lips endure forever,
but a lying tongue lasts only a moment.

20 Deceit is in the hearts of those who plot evil,
but those who promote peace have joy.

21 No harm overtakes the righteous,
but the wicked have their fill of trouble.

22 The LORD detests lying lips,
but he delights in people who are trustworthy.

23 The prudent keep their knowledge to themselves,
but a fool's heart blurts out folly.

24 Diligent hands will rule,
but laziness ends in forced labor.

25 Anxiety weighs down the heart,
but a kind word cheers it up.

26 The righteous choose their friends carefully,
but the way of the wicked leads them astray.

27 The lazy do not roast[a] any game,
but the diligent feed on the riches of the hunt.

28 In the way of righteousness there is life;
along that path is immortality.

13 A wise son heeds his father's instruction,
but a mocker does not respond to rebukes.

2 From the fruit of their lips people enjoy good things,
but the unfaithful have an appetite for violence.

3 Those who guard their lips preserve their lives,
but those who speak rashly will come to ruin.

4 A sluggard's appetite is never filled,
but the desires of the diligent are fully satisfied.

5 The righteous hate what is false,
but the wicked make themselves a stench
and bring shame on themselves.

6 Righteousness guards the person of integrity,
but wickedness overthrows the sinner.

7 One person pretends to be rich, yet has nothing;
another pretends to be poor, yet has great wealth.

8 A person's riches may ransom their life,
but the poor cannot respond to threatening rebukes.

9 The light of the righteous shines brightly,
but the lamp of the wicked is snuffed out.

10 Where there is strife, there is pride,
but wisdom is found in those who take advice.

11 Dishonest money dwindles away,
but whoever gathers money little by little makes it grow.

12 Hope deferred makes the heart sick,
but a longing fulfilled is a tree of life.

13 Whoever scorns instruction will pay for it,
but whoever respects a command is rewarded.

14 The teaching of the wise is a fountain of life,
turning a person from the snares of death.

15 Good judgment wins favor,
but the way of the unfaithful leads to their destruction.[b]

16 All who are prudent act with[c] knowledge,
but fools expose their folly.

17 A wicked messenger falls into trouble,
but a trustworthy envoy brings healing.

18 Whoever disregards discipline comes to poverty and shame,
but whoever heeds correction is honored.

19 A longing fulfilled is sweet to the soul,
but fools detest turning from evil.

20 Walk with the wise and become wise,
for a companion of fools suffers harm.

21 Trouble pursues the sinner,
but the righteous are rewarded with good things.

22 A good person leaves an inheritance for their children's children,
but a sinner's wealth is stored up for the righteous.

23 An unplowed field produces food for the poor,
but injustice sweeps it away.

24 Whoever spares the rod hates their children,
but the one who loves their children is careful to discipline them.

25 The righteous eat to their hearts' content,
but the stomach of the wicked goes hungry.

14 The wise woman builds her house,
but with her own hands the foolish one tears hers down.

2 Whoever fears the LORD walks uprightly,
but those who despise him are devious in their ways.

3 A fool's mouth lashes out with pride,
but the lips of the wise protect them.

[a] 27 The meaning of the Hebrew for this word is uncertain. [b] 15 Septuagint and Syriac; the meaning of the Hebrew for this phrase is uncertain. [c] 16 Or *prudent protect themselves through*

[4] Where there are no oxen, the manger
is empty,
but from the strength of an ox
come abundant harvests.

[5] An honest witness does not deceive,
but a false witness pours out lies.

[6] The mocker seeks wisdom and finds
none,
but knowledge comes easily to the
discerning.

[7] Stay away from a fool,
for you will not find knowledge on
their lips.

[8] The wisdom of the prudent is to give
thought to their ways,
but the folly of fools is deception.

[9] Fools mock at making amends for sin,
but goodwill is found among the
upright.

[10] Each heart knows its own bitterness,
and no one else can share its joy.

[11] The house of the wicked will be
destroyed,
but the tent of the upright will
flourish.

[12] There is a way that appears to be right,
but in the end it leads to death.

[13] Even in laughter the heart may ache,
and rejoicing may end in grief.

[14] The faithless will be fully repaid for
their ways,
and the good rewarded for theirs.

[15] The simple believe anything,
but the prudent give thought to
their steps.

[16] The wise fear the LORD and shun evil,
but a fool is hotheaded and yet
feels secure.

[17] A quick-tempered person does foolish
things,
and the one who devises evil
schemes is hated.

[18] The simple inherit folly,
but the prudent are crowned with
knowledge.

[19] Evildoers will bow down in the
presence of the good,
and the wicked at the gates of the
righteous.

[20] The poor are shunned even by their
neighbors,
but the rich have many friends.

[21] It is a sin to despise one's neighbor,
but blessed is the one who is kind
to the needy.

[22] Do not those who plot evil go astray?
But those who plan what is good
find[a] love and faithfulness.

[23] All hard work brings a profit,
but mere talk leads only to poverty.

[24] The wealth of the wise is their crown,
but the folly of fools yields folly.

[25] A truthful witness saves lives,
but a false witness is deceitful.

[26] Whoever fears the LORD has a secure
fortress,
and for their children it will be a
refuge.

[27] The fear of the LORD is a fountain of
life,
turning a person from the snares of
death.

[28] A large population is a king's glory,
but without subjects a prince is
ruined.

[29] Whoever is patient has great
understanding,
but one who is quick-tempered
displays folly.

[30] A heart at peace gives life to the body,
but envy rots the bones.

[31] Whoever oppresses the poor shows
contempt for their Maker,
but whoever is kind to the needy
honors God.

[32] When calamity comes, the wicked are
brought down,
but even in death the righteous
seek refuge in God.

[33] Wisdom reposes in the heart of the
discerning
and even among fools she lets
herself be known.[b]

[34] Righteousness exalts a nation,
but sin condemns any people.

[35] A king delights in a wise servant,
but a shameful servant arouses his
fury.

15 A gentle answer turns away wrath,
but a harsh word stirs up anger.

[2] The tongue of the wise adorns
knowledge,
but the mouth of the fool gushes
folly.

[a] 22 Or *show*
[b] 33 Hebrew; Septuagint and Syriac *discerning / but in the heart of fools she is not known*

[3] The eyes of the LORD are everywhere,
keeping watch on the wicked and the good.

[4] The soothing tongue is a tree of life,
but a perverse tongue crushes the spirit.

[5] A fool spurns a parent's discipline,
but whoever heeds correction shows prudence.

[6] The house of the righteous contains great treasure,
but the income of the wicked brings ruin.

[7] The lips of the wise spread knowledge,
but the hearts of fools are not upright.

[8] The LORD detests the sacrifice of the wicked,
but the prayer of the upright pleases him.

[9] The LORD detests the way of the wicked,
but he loves those who pursue righteousness.

[10] Stern discipline awaits anyone who leaves the path;
the one who hates correction will die.

[11] Death and Destruction[a] lie open before the LORD —
how much more do human hearts!

[12] Mockers resent correction,
so they avoid the wise.

[13] A happy heart makes the face cheerful,
but heartache crushes the spirit.

[14] The discerning heart seeks knowledge,
but the mouth of a fool feeds on folly.

[15] All the days of the oppressed are wretched,
but the cheerful heart has a continual feast.

[16] Better a little with the fear of the LORD
than great wealth with turmoil.

[17] Better a small serving of vegetables with love
than a fattened calf with hatred.

[18] A hot-tempered person stirs up conflict,
but the one who is patient calms a quarrel.

[19] The way of the sluggard is blocked with thorns,
but the path of the upright is a highway.

[20] A wise son brings joy to his father,
but a foolish man despises his mother.

[21] Folly brings joy to one who has no sense,
but whoever has understanding keeps a straight course.

[22] Plans fail for lack of counsel,
but with many advisers they succeed.

[23] A person finds joy in giving an apt reply —
and how good is a timely word!

[24] The path of life leads upward for the prudent
to keep them from going down to the realm of the dead.

[25] The LORD tears down the house of the proud,
but he sets the widow's boundary stones in place.

[26] The LORD detests the thoughts of the wicked,
but gracious words are pure in his sight.

[27] The greedy bring ruin to their households,
but the one who hates bribes will live.

[28] The heart of the righteous weighs its answers,
but the mouth of the wicked gushes evil.

[29] The LORD is far from the wicked,
but he hears the prayer of the righteous.

[30] Light in a messenger's eyes brings joy to the heart,
and good news gives health to the bones.

[31] Whoever heeds life-giving correction
will be at home among the wise.

[32] Those who disregard discipline despise themselves,
but the one who heeds correction gains understanding.

[33] Wisdom's instruction is to fear the LORD,
and humility comes before honor.

[a] *11* Hebrew *Abaddon*

16 To humans belong the plans of the heart,
but from the LORD comes the proper answer of the tongue.

2 All a person's ways seem pure to them,
but motives are weighed by the LORD.

3 Commit to the LORD whatever you do,
and he will establish your plans.

4 The LORD works out everything to its proper end —
even the wicked for a day of disaster.

5 The LORD detests all the proud of heart.
Be sure of this: They will not go unpunished.

6 Through love and faithfulness sin is atoned for;
through the fear of the LORD evil is avoided.

7 When the LORD takes pleasure in anyone's way,
he causes their enemies to make peace with them.

8 Better a little with righteousness
than much gain with injustice.

9 In their hearts humans plan their course,
but the LORD establishes their steps.

10 The lips of a king speak as an oracle,
and his mouth does not betray justice.

11 Honest scales and balances belong to the LORD;
all the weights in the bag are of his making.

12 Kings detest wrongdoing,
for a throne is established through righteousness.

13 Kings take pleasure in honest lips;
they value the one who speaks what is right.

14 A king's wrath is a messenger of death,
but the wise will appease it.

15 When a king's face brightens, it means life;
his favor is like a rain cloud in spring.

16 How much better to get wisdom than gold,
to get insight rather than silver!

17 The highway of the upright avoids evil;
those who guard their ways preserve their lives.

18 Pride goes before destruction,
a haughty spirit before a fall.

19 Better to be lowly in spirit along with the oppressed
than to share plunder with the proud.

20 Whoever gives heed to instruction prospers,[a]
and blessed is the one who trusts in the LORD.

21 The wise in heart are called discerning,
and gracious words promote instruction.[b]

22 Prudence is a fountain of life to the prudent,
but folly brings punishment to fools.

23 The hearts of the wise make their mouths prudent,
and their lips promote instruction.[c]

24 Gracious words are a honeycomb,
sweet to the soul and healing to the bones.

25 There is a way that appears to be right,
but in the end it leads to death.

26 The appetite of laborers works for them;
their hunger drives them on.

27 A scoundrel plots evil,
and on their lips it is like a scorching fire.

28 A perverse person stirs up conflict,
and a gossip separates close friends.

29 A violent person entices their neighbor
and leads them down a path that is not good.

30 Whoever winks with their eye is plotting perversity;
whoever purses their lips is bent on evil.

31 Gray hair is a crown of splendor;
it is attained in the way of righteousness.

[a] 20 Or *whoever speaks prudently finds what is good* [b] 21 Or *words make a person persuasive*
[c] 23 Or *prudent / and make their lips persuasive*

[32] Better a patient person than a
warrior,
one with self-control than one who
takes a city.

[33] The lot is cast into the lap,
but its every decision is from the
LORD.

17 Better a dry crust with peace and
quiet
than a house full of feasting, with
strife.

[2] A prudent servant will rule over a
disgraceful son
and will share the inheritance as
one of the family.

[3] The crucible for silver and the furnace
for gold,
but the LORD tests the heart.

[4] A wicked person listens to deceitful
lips;
a liar pays attention to a
destructive tongue.

[5] Whoever mocks the poor shows
contempt for their Maker;
whoever gloats over disaster will
not go unpunished.

[6] Children's children are a crown to the
aged,
and parents are the pride of their
children.

[7] Eloquent lips are unsuited to a
godless fool —
how much worse lying lips to a
ruler!

[8] A bribe is seen as a charm by the one
who gives it;
they think success will come at
every turn.

[9] Whoever would foster love covers
over an offense,
but whoever repeats the matter
separates close friends.

[10] A rebuke impresses a discerning
person
more than a hundred lashes a fool.

[11] Evildoers foster rebellion against
God;
the messenger of death will be sent
against them.

[12] Better to meet a bear robbed of her
cubs
than a fool bent on folly.

[13] Evil will never leave the house
of one who pays back evil for good.

[14] Starting a quarrel is like breaching a
dam;
so drop the matter before a dispute
breaks out.

[15] Acquitting the guilty and
condemning the innocent —
the LORD detests them both.

[16] Why should fools have money in
hand to buy wisdom,
when they are not able to
understand it?

[17] A friend loves at all times,
and a brother is born for a time of
adversity.

[18] One who has no sense shakes hands
in pledge
and puts up security for a neighbor.

[19] Whoever loves a quarrel loves sin;
whoever builds a high gate invites
destruction.

[20] One whose heart is corrupt does not
prosper;
one whose tongue is perverse falls
into trouble.

[21] To have a fool for a child brings grief;
there is no joy for the parent of a
godless fool.

[22] A cheerful heart is good medicine,
but a crushed spirit dries up the
bones.

[23] The wicked accept bribes in secret
to pervert the course of justice.

[24] A discerning person keeps wisdom in
view,
but a fool's eyes wander to the ends
of the earth.

[25] A foolish son brings grief to his father
and bitterness to the mother who
bore him.

[26] If imposing a fine on the innocent is
not good,
surely to flog honest officials is not
right.

[27] The one who has knowledge uses
words with restraint,
and whoever has understanding is
even-tempered.

[28] Even fools are thought wise if they
keep silent,
and discerning if they hold their
tongues.

18 An unfriendly person pursues
selfish ends
and against all sound judgment
starts quarrels.

2 Fools find no pleasure in understanding
but delight in airing their own opinions.

3 When wickedness comes, so does contempt,
and with shame comes reproach.

4 The words of the mouth are deep waters,
but the fountain of wisdom is a rushing stream.

5 It is not good to be partial to the wicked
and so deprive the innocent of justice.

6 The lips of fools bring them strife,
and their mouths invite a beating.

7 The mouths of fools are their undoing,
and their lips are a snare to their very lives.

8 The words of a gossip are like choice morsels;
they go down to the inmost parts.

9 One who is slack in his work
is brother to one who destroys.

10 The name of the LORD is a fortified tower;
the righteous run to it and are safe.

11 The wealth of the rich is their fortified city;
they imagine it a wall too high to scale.

12 Before a downfall the heart is haughty,
but humility comes before honor.

13 To answer before listening —
that is folly and shame.

14 The human spirit can endure in sickness,
but a crushed spirit who can bear?

15 The heart of the discerning acquires knowledge,
for the ears of the wise seek it out.

16 A gift opens the way
and ushers the giver into the presence of the great.

17 In a lawsuit the first to speak seems right,
until someone comes forward and cross-examines.

18 Casting the lot settles disputes
and keeps strong opponents apart.

19 A brother wronged is more unyielding than a fortified city;
disputes are like the barred gates of a citadel.

20 From the fruit of their mouth a person's stomach is filled;
with the harvest of their lips they are satisfied.

21 The tongue has the power of life and death,
and those who love it will eat its fruit.

22 He who finds a wife finds what is good
and receives favor from the LORD.

23 The poor plead for mercy,
but the rich answer harshly.

24 One who has unreliable friends soon comes to ruin,
but there is a friend who sticks closer than a brother.

19 Better the poor whose walk is blameless
than a fool whose lips are perverse.

2 Desire without knowledge is not good —
how much more will hasty feet miss the way!

3 A person's own folly leads to their ruin,
yet their heart rages against the LORD.

4 Wealth attracts many friends,
but even the closest friend of the poor person deserts them.

5 A false witness will not go unpunished,
and whoever pours out lies will not go free.

6 Many curry favor with a ruler,
and everyone is the friend of one who gives gifts.

7 The poor are shunned by all their relatives —
how much more do their friends avoid them!
Though the poor pursue them with pleading,
they are nowhere to be found.[a]

8 The one who gets wisdom loves life;
the one who cherishes understanding will soon prosper.

[a] 7 The meaning of the Hebrew for this sentence is uncertain.

9 A false witness will not go
unpunished,
and whoever pours out lies will
perish.

10 It is not fitting for a fool to live in
luxury —
how much worse for a slave to rule
over princes!

11 A person's wisdom yields patience;
it is to one's glory to overlook an
offense.

12 A king's rage is like the roar of a lion,
but his favor is like dew on the
grass.

13 A foolish child is a father's ruin,
and a quarrelsome wife is like
the constant dripping of a leaky
roof.

14 Houses and wealth are inherited
from parents,
but a prudent wife is from the
LORD.

15 Laziness brings on deep sleep,
and the shiftless go hungry.

16 Whoever keeps commandments
keeps their life,
but whoever shows contempt for
their ways will die.

17 Whoever is kind to the poor lends to
the LORD,
and he will reward them for what
they have done.

18 Discipline your children, for in that
there is hope;
do not be a willing party to their
death.

19 A hot-tempered person must pay the
penalty;
rescue them, and you will have to
do it again.

20 Listen to advice and accept discipline,
and at the end you will be counted
among the wise.

21 Many are the plans in a person's
heart,
but it is the LORD's purpose that
prevails.

22 What a person desires is unfailing
love[a];
better to be poor than a liar.

23 The fear of the LORD leads to life;
then one rests content, untouched
by trouble.

24 A sluggard buries his hand in the
dish;
he will not even bring it back to his
mouth!

25 Flog a mocker, and the simple will
learn prudence;
rebuke the discerning, and they
will gain knowledge.

26 Whoever robs their father and drives
out their mother
is a child who brings shame and
disgrace.

27 Stop listening to instruction, my son,
and you will stray from the words
of knowledge.

28 A corrupt witness mocks at justice,
and the mouth of the wicked gulps
down evil.

29 Penalties are prepared for mockers,
and beatings for the backs of fools.

20 Wine is a mocker and beer a
brawler;
whoever is led astray by them is
not wise.

2 A king's wrath strikes terror like the
roar of a lion;
those who anger him forfeit their
lives.

3 It is to one's honor to avoid strife,
but every fool is quick to quarrel.

4 Sluggards do not plow in season;
so at harvest time they look but
find nothing.

5 The purposes of a person's heart are
deep waters,
but one who has insight draws
them out.

6 Many claim to have unfailing love,
but a faithful person who can find?

7 The righteous lead blameless lives;
blessed are their children after
them.

8 When a king sits on his throne to
judge,
he winnows out all evil with his
eyes.

9 Who can say, "I have kept my heart
pure;
I am clean and without sin"?

10 Differing weights and differing
measures —
the LORD detests them both.

[a] *22* Or *Greed is a person's shame*

11 Even small children are known by
their actions,
so is their conduct really pure and
upright?

12 Ears that hear and eyes that see —
the LORD has made them both.

13 Do not love sleep or you will grow poor;
stay awake and you will have food
to spare.

14 "It's no good, it's no good!" says the
buyer —
then goes off and boasts about the
purchase.

15 Gold there is, and rubies in
abundance,
but lips that speak knowledge are a
rare jewel.

16 Take the garment of one who puts up
security for a stranger;
hold it in pledge if it is done for an
outsider.

17 Food gained by fraud tastes sweet,
but one ends up with a mouth full
of gravel.

18 Plans are established by seeking
advice;
so if you wage war, obtain
guidance.

19 A gossip betrays a confidence;
so avoid anyone who talks too
much.

20 If someone curses their father or
mother,
their lamp will be snuffed out in
pitch darkness.

21 An inheritance claimed too soon
will not be blessed at the end.

22 Do not say, "I'll pay you back for this
wrong!"
Wait for the LORD, and he will
avenge you.

23 The LORD detests differing weights,
and dishonest scales do not please
him.

24 A person's steps are directed by the
LORD.
How then can anyone understand
their own way?

25 It is a trap to dedicate something
rashly
and only later to consider one's
vows.

26 A wise king winnows out the wicked;
he drives the threshing wheel over
them.

27 The human spirit is[a] the lamp of the
LORD
that sheds light on one's inmost
being.

28 Love and faithfulness keep a king
safe;
through love his throne is made
secure.

29 The glory of young men is their
strength,
gray hair the splendor of the old.

30 Blows and wounds scrub away evil,
and beatings purge the inmost
being.

21 In the LORD's hand the king's heart
is a stream of water
that he channels toward all who
please him.

2 A person may think their own ways
are right,
but the LORD weighs the heart.

3 To do what is right and just
is more acceptable to the LORD
than sacrifice.

4 Haughty eyes and a proud heart —
the unplowed field of the wicked —
produce sin.

5 The plans of the diligent lead to profit
as surely as haste leads to poverty.

6 A fortune made by a lying tongue
is a fleeting vapor and a deadly
snare.[b]

7 The violence of the wicked will drag
them away,
for they refuse to do what is right.

8 The way of the guilty is devious,
but the conduct of the innocent is
upright.

9 Better to live on a corner of the roof
than share a house with a
quarrelsome wife.

10 The wicked crave evil;
their neighbors get no mercy from
them.

11 When a mocker is punished, the
simple gain wisdom;
by paying attention to the wise
they get knowledge.

[a] *27* Or *A person's words are* [b] 6 Some Hebrew manuscripts, Septuagint and Vulgate; most Hebrew manuscripts *vapor for those who seek death*

12 The Righteous One[a] takes note of the
house of the wicked
and brings the wicked to ruin.

13 Whoever shuts their ears to the cry of
the poor
will also cry out and not be
answered.

14 A gift given in secret soothes anger,
and a bribe concealed in the cloak
pacifies great wrath.

15 When justice is done, it brings joy to
the righteous
but terror to evildoers.

16 Whoever strays from the path of
prudence
comes to rest in the company of the
dead.

17 Whoever loves pleasure will become
poor;
whoever loves wine and olive oil
will never be rich.

18 The wicked become a ransom for the
righteous,
and the unfaithful for the upright.

19 Better to live in a desert
than with a quarrelsome and
nagging wife.

20 The wise store up choice food and
olive oil,
but fools gulp theirs down.

21 Whoever pursues righteousness and
love
finds life, prosperity[b] and honor.

22 One who is wise can go up against the
city of the mighty
and pull down the stronghold in
which they trust.

23 Those who guard their mouths and
their tongues
keep themselves from calamity.

24 The proud and arrogant person —
"Mocker" is his name —
behaves with insolent fury.

25 The craving of a sluggard will be the
death of him,
because his hands refuse to work.

26 All day long he craves for more,
but the righteous give without
sparing.

27 The sacrifice of the wicked is
detestable —
how much more so when brought
with evil intent!

28 A false witness will perish,
but a careful listener will testify
successfully.

29 The wicked put up a bold front,
but the upright give thought to
their ways.

30 There is no wisdom, no insight, no plan
that can succeed against the LORD.

31 The horse is made ready for the day
of battle,
but victory rests with the LORD.

22 A good name is more desirable
than great riches;
to be esteemed is better than silver
or gold.

2 Rich and poor have this in common:
The LORD is the Maker of them all.

3 The prudent see danger and take
refuge,
but the simple keep going and pay
the penalty.

4 Humility is the fear of the LORD;
its wages are riches and honor and
life.

5 In the paths of the wicked are snares
and pitfalls,
but those who would preserve their
life stay far from them.

6 Start children off on the way they
should go,
and even when they are old they
will not turn from it.

7 The rich rule over the poor,
and the borrower is slave to the
lender.

8 Whoever sows injustice reaps
calamity,
and the rod they wield in fury will
be broken.

9 The generous will themselves be
blessed,
for they share their food with the
poor.

10 Drive out the mocker, and out goes
strife;
quarrels and insults are ended.

11 One who loves a pure heart and who
speaks with grace
will have the king for a friend.

12 The eyes of the LORD keep watch over
knowledge,
but he frustrates the words of the
unfaithful.

[a] 12 Or *The righteous person* [b] 21 Or *righteousness*

13 The sluggard says, "There's a lion outside!
I'll be killed in the public square!"

14 The mouth of an adulterous woman is a deep pit;
a man who is under the LORD's wrath falls into it.

15 Folly is bound up in the heart of a child,
but the rod of discipline will drive it far away.

16 One who oppresses the poor to increase his wealth
and one who gives gifts to the rich — both come to poverty.

Thirty Sayings of the Wise

Saying 1

17 Pay attention and turn your ear to the sayings of the wise;
apply your heart to what I teach,
18 for it is pleasing when you keep them in your heart
and have all of them ready on your lips.
19 So that your trust may be in the LORD,
I teach you today, even you.
20 Have I not written thirty sayings for you,
sayings of counsel and knowledge,
21 teaching you to be honest and to speak the truth,
so that you bring back truthful reports
to those you serve?

Saying 2

22 Do not exploit the poor because they are poor
and do not crush the needy in court,
23 for the LORD will take up their case
and will exact life for life.

Saying 3

24 Do not make friends with a hot-tempered person,
do not associate with one easily angered,
25 or you may learn their ways
and get yourself ensnared.

Saying 4

26 Do not be one who shakes hands in pledge
or puts up security for debts;
27 if you lack the means to pay,
your very bed will be snatched from under you.

Saying 5

28 Do not move an ancient boundary stone
set up by your ancestors.

Saying 6

29 Do you see someone skilled in their work?
They will serve before kings;
they will not serve before officials of low rank.

Saying 7

23 When you sit to dine with a ruler,
note well what[a] is before you,
2 and put a knife to your throat
if you are given to gluttony.
3 Do not crave his delicacies,
for that food is deceptive.

Saying 8

4 Do not wear yourself out to get rich;
do not trust your own cleverness.
5 Cast but a glance at riches, and they are gone,
for they will surely sprout wings
and fly off to the sky like an eagle.

Saying 9

6 Do not eat the food of a begrudging host,
do not crave his delicacies;
7 for he is the kind of person
who is always thinking about the cost.[b]
"Eat and drink," he says to you,
but his heart is not with you.
8 You will vomit up the little you have eaten
and will have wasted your compliments.

Saying 10

9 Do not speak to fools,
for they will scorn your prudent words.

Saying 11

10 Do not move an ancient boundary stone
or encroach on the fields of the fatherless,
11 for their Defender is strong;
he will take up their case against you.

Saying 12

12 Apply your heart to instruction
and your ears to words of knowledge.

[a] 1 Or *who* [b] 7 Or *for as he thinks within himself, / so he is*; or *for as he puts on a feast, / so he is*

Saying 13

13 Do not withhold discipline from a child;
if you punish them with the rod, they will not die.
14 Punish them with the rod
and save them from death.

Saying 14

15 My son, if your heart is wise,
then my heart will be glad indeed;
16 my inmost being will rejoice
when your lips speak what is right.

Saying 15

17 Do not let your heart envy sinners,
but always be zealous for the fear of the LORD.
18 There is surely a future hope for you,
and your hope will not be cut off.

Saying 16

19 Listen, my son, and be wise,
and set your heart on the right path:
20 Do not join those who drink too much wine
or gorge themselves on meat,
21 for drunkards and gluttons become poor,
and drowsiness clothes them in rags.

Saying 17

22 Listen to your father, who gave you life,
and do not despise your mother when she is old.
23 Buy the truth and do not sell it —
wisdom, instruction and insight as well.
24 The father of a righteous child has great joy;
a man who fathers a wise son rejoices in him.
25 May your father and mother rejoice;
may she who gave you birth be joyful!

Saying 18

26 My son, give me your heart
and let your eyes delight in my ways,
27 for an adulterous woman is a deep pit,
and a wayward wife is a narrow well.
28 Like a bandit she lies in wait
and multiplies the unfaithful among men.

Saying 19

29 Who has woe? Who has sorrow?
Who has strife? Who has complaints?
Who has needless bruises?
Who has bloodshot eyes?
30 Those who linger over wine,
who go to sample bowls of mixed wine.
31 Do not gaze at wine when it is red,
when it sparkles in the cup,
when it goes down smoothly!
32 In the end it bites like a snake
and poisons like a viper.
33 Your eyes will see strange sights,
and your mind will imagine confusing things.
34 You will be like one sleeping on the high seas,
lying on top of the rigging.
35 "They hit me," you will say, "but I'm not hurt!
They beat me, but I don't feel it!
When will I wake up
so I can find another drink?"

Saying 20

24 Do not envy the wicked,
do not desire their company;
2 for their hearts plot violence,
and their lips talk about making trouble.

Saying 21

3 By wisdom a house is built,
and through understanding it is established;
4 through knowledge its rooms are filled
with rare and beautiful treasures.

Saying 22

5 The wise prevail through great power,
and those who have knowledge muster their strength.
6 Surely you need guidance to wage war,
and victory is won through many advisers.

Saying 23

7 Wisdom is too high for fools;
in the assembly at the gate they must not open their mouths.

Saying 24

8 Whoever plots evil
will be known as a schemer.
9 The schemes of folly are sin,
and people detest a mocker.

Saying 25

10 If you falter in a time of trouble,
how small is your strength!
11 Rescue those being led away
to death;
hold back those staggering toward
slaughter.
12 If you say, "But we knew nothing
about this,"
does not he who weighs the heart
perceive it?
Does not he who guards your life
know it?
Will he not repay everyone
according to what they have
done?

Saying 26

13 Eat honey, my son, for it is good;
honey from the comb is sweet to
your taste.
14 Know also that wisdom is like honey
for you:
If you find it, there is a future hope
for you,
and your hope will not be cut off.

Saying 27

15 Do not lurk like a thief near the house
of the righteous,
do not plunder their dwelling
place;
16 for though the righteous fall seven
times, they rise again,
but the wicked stumble when
calamity strikes.

Saying 28

17 Do not gloat when your enemy falls;
when they stumble, do not let your
heart rejoice,
18 or the LORD will see and disapprove
and turn his wrath away from
them.

Saying 29

19 Do not fret because of evildoers
or be envious of the wicked,
20 for the evildoer has no future hope,
and the lamp of the wicked will be
snuffed out.

Saying 30

21 Fear the LORD and the king, my son,
and do not join with rebellious
officials,
22 for those two will send sudden
destruction on them,
and who knows what calamities
they can bring?

Further Sayings of the Wise

23 These also are sayings of the wise:

To show partiality in judging is not
good:
24 Whoever says to the guilty, "You are
innocent,"
will be cursed by peoples and
denounced by nations.
25 But it will go well with those who
convict the guilty,
and rich blessing will come on them.

26 An honest answer
is like a kiss on the lips.

27 Put your outdoor work in order
and get your fields ready;
after that, build your house.

28 Do not testify against your neighbor
without cause —
would you use your lips to mislead?
29 Do not say, "I'll do to them as they
have done to me;
I'll pay them back for what they did."

30 I went past the field of a sluggard,
past the vineyard of someone who
has no sense;
31 thorns had come up everywhere,
the ground was covered with
weeds,
and the stone wall was in ruins.
32 I applied my heart to what I observed
and learned a lesson from what I
saw:
33 A little sleep, a little slumber,
a little folding of the hands to rest —
34 and poverty will come on you like a
thief
and scarcity like an armed man.

More Proverbs of Solomon

25 These are more proverbs of Solomon, compiled by the men of Hezekiah king of Judah:

2 It is the glory of God to conceal a
matter;
to search out a matter is the glory
of kings.
3 As the heavens are high and the
earth is deep,
so the hearts of kings are
unsearchable.

4 Remove the dross from the silver,
and a silversmith can produce a
vessel;
5 remove wicked officials from the
king's presence,
and his throne will be established
through righteousness.

6 Do not exalt yourself in the king's
presence,
and do not claim a place among
his great men;
7 it is better for him to say to you,
"Come up here,"
than for him to humiliate you
before his nobles.

What you have seen with your eyes
8 do not bring[a] hastily to court,
for what will you do in the end
if your neighbor puts you to
shame?

9 If you take your neighbor to court,
do not betray another's confidence,
10 or the one who hears it may shame
you
and the charge against you will
stand.

11 Like apples[b] of gold in settings of
silver
is a ruling rightly given.
12 Like an earring of gold or an
ornament of fine gold
is the rebuke of a wise judge to a
listening ear.

13 Like a snow-cooled drink at harvest
time
is a trustworthy messenger to the
one who sends him;
he refreshes the spirit of his master.
14 Like clouds and wind without rain
is one who boasts of gifts never
given.

15 Through patience a ruler can be
persuaded,
and a gentle tongue can break a
bone.

16 If you find honey, eat just enough—
too much of it, and you will vomit.
17 Seldom set foot in your neighbor's
house—
too much of you, and they will hate
you.

18 Like a club or a sword or a sharp
arrow
is one who gives false testimony
against a neighbor.
19 Like a broken tooth or a lame foot
is reliance on the unfaithful in a
time of trouble.
20 Like one who takes away a garment
on a cold day,
or like vinegar poured on a wound,
is one who sings songs to a heavy
heart.

21 If your enemy is hungry, give him
food to eat;
if he is thirsty, give him water to
drink.
22 In doing this, you will heap burning
coals on his head,
and the LORD will reward you.

23 Like a north wind that brings
unexpected rain
is a sly tongue—which provokes a
horrified look.

24 Better to live on a corner of the roof
than share a house with a
quarrelsome wife.

25 Like cold water to a weary soul
is good news from a distant land.
26 Like a muddied spring or a polluted
well
are the righteous who give way to
the wicked.

27 It is not good to eat too much honey,
nor is it honorable to search out
matters that are too deep.

28 Like a city whose walls are broken
through
is a person who lacks self-control.

26

Like snow in summer or rain in
harvest,
honor is not fitting for a fool.
2 Like a fluttering sparrow or a darting
swallow,
an undeserved curse does not come
to rest.
3 A whip for the horse, a bridle for the
donkey,
and a rod for the backs of fools!
4 Do not answer a fool according to his
folly,
or you yourself will be just
like him.
5 Answer a fool according to his folly,
or he will be wise in his own eyes.
6 Sending a message by the hands of a
fool
is like cutting off one's feet or
drinking poison.
7 Like the useless legs of one who is
lame
is a proverb in the mouth of a fool.
8 Like tying a stone in a sling
is the giving of honor to a fool.
9 Like a thornbush in a drunkard's
hand
is a proverb in the mouth of a fool.
10 Like an archer who wounds at
random
is one who hires a fool or any
passer-by.

[a] 7,8 Or *nobles / on whom you had set your eyes. / [8]Do not go* [b] 11 Or possibly *apricots*

[11] As a dog returns to its vomit,
so fools repeat their folly.
[12] Do you see a person wise in their own eyes?
There is more hope for a fool than for them.

[13] A sluggard says, "There's a lion in the road,
a fierce lion roaming the streets!"
[14] As a door turns on its hinges,
so a sluggard turns on his bed.
[15] A sluggard buries his hand in the dish;
he is too lazy to bring it back to his mouth.
[16] A sluggard is wiser in his own eyes
than seven people who answer discreetly.

[17] Like one who grabs a stray dog by the ears
is someone who rushes into a quarrel not their own.

[18] Like a maniac shooting
flaming arrows of death
[19] is one who deceives their neighbor
and says, "I was only joking!"

[20] Without wood a fire goes out;
without a gossip a quarrel dies down.
[21] As charcoal to embers and as wood to fire,
so is a quarrelsome person for kindling strife.
[22] The words of a gossip are like choice morsels;
they go down to the inmost parts.

[23] Like a coating of silver dross on earthenware
are fervent[a] lips with an evil heart.
[24] Enemies disguise themselves with their lips,
but in their hearts they harbor deceit.
[25] Though their speech is charming, do not believe them,
for seven abominations fill their hearts.
[26] Their malice may be concealed by deception,
but their wickedness will be exposed in the assembly.
[27] Whoever digs a pit will fall into it;
if someone rolls a stone, it will roll back on them.
[28] A lying tongue hates those it hurts,
and a flattering mouth works ruin.

27 Do not boast about tomorrow,
for you do not know what a day may bring.

[2] Let someone else praise you, and not your own mouth;
an outsider, and not your own lips.

[3] Stone is heavy and sand a burden,
but a fool's provocation is heavier than both.

[4] Anger is cruel and fury overwhelming,
but who can stand before jealousy?

[5] Better is open rebuke
than hidden love.

[6] Wounds from a friend can be trusted,
but an enemy multiplies kisses.

[7] One who is full loathes honey from the comb,
but to the hungry even what is bitter tastes sweet.

[8] Like a bird that flees its nest
is anyone who flees from home.

[9] Perfume and incense bring joy to the heart,
and the pleasantness of a friend
springs from their heartfelt advice.

[10] Do not forsake your friend or a friend of your family,
and do not go to your relative's house when disaster strikes you —
better a neighbor nearby than a relative far away.

[11] Be wise, my son, and bring joy to my heart;
then I can answer anyone who treats me with contempt.

[12] The prudent see danger and take refuge,
but the simple keep going and pay the penalty.

[13] Take the garment of one who puts up security for a stranger;
hold it in pledge if it is done for an outsider.

[14] If anyone loudly blesses their neighbor early in the morning,
it will be taken as a curse.

[15] A quarrelsome wife is like the dripping
of a leaky roof in a rainstorm;
[16] restraining her is like restraining the wind
or grasping oil with the hand.

[17] As iron sharpens iron,
so one person sharpens another.

[a] *23* Hebrew; Septuagint *smooth*

18 The one who guards a fig tree will eat
its fruit,
and whoever protects their master
will be honored.

19 As water reflects the face,
so one's life reflects the heart.[a]

20 Death and Destruction[b] are never
satisfied,
and neither are human eyes.

21 The crucible for silver and the furnace
for gold,
but people are tested by their praise.

22 Though you grind a fool in a mortar,
grinding them like grain with a
pestle,
you will not remove their folly from
them.

23 Be sure you know the condition of
your flocks,
give careful attention to your
herds;
24 for riches do not endure forever,
and a crown is not secure for all
generations.
25 When the hay is removed and new
growth appears
and the grass from the hills is
gathered in,
26 the lambs will provide you with
clothing,
and the goats with the price of a
field.
27 You will have plenty of goats' milk to
feed your family
and to nourish your female
servants.

28

The wicked flee though no one
pursues,
but the righteous are as bold as a
lion.

2 When a country is rebellious, it has
many rulers,
but a ruler with discernment and
knowledge maintains order.

3 A ruler[c] who oppresses the poor
is like a driving rain that leaves no
crops.

4 Those who forsake instruction praise
the wicked,
but those who heed it resist them.
5 Evildoers do not understand what is
right,
but those who seek the LORD
understand it fully.

6 Better the poor whose walk is
blameless
than the rich whose ways are
perverse.

7 A discerning son heeds instruction,
but a companion of gluttons
disgraces his father.

8 Whoever increases wealth by taking
interest or profit from the poor
amasses it for another, who will be
kind to the poor.

9 If anyone turns a deaf ear to my
instruction,
even their prayers are detestable.

10 Whoever leads the upright along an
evil path
will fall into their own trap,
but the blameless will receive a
good inheritance.

11 The rich are wise in their own eyes;
one who is poor and discerning
sees how deluded they are.

12 When the righteous triumph, there is
great elation;
but when the wicked rise to power,
people go into hiding.

13 Whoever conceals their sins does not
prosper,
but the one who confesses and
renounces them finds mercy.

14 Blessed is the one who always
trembles before God,
but whoever hardens their heart
falls into trouble.

15 Like a roaring lion or a charging bear
is a wicked ruler over a helpless
people.
16 A tyrannical ruler practices extortion,
but one who hates ill-gotten gain
will enjoy a long reign.

17 Anyone tormented by the guilt of
murder
will seek refuge in the grave;
let no one hold them back.

18 The one whose walk is blameless is
kept safe,
but the one whose ways are
perverse will fall into the pit.[d]

19 Those who work their land will have
abundant food,
but those who chase fantasies will
have their fill of poverty.

[a] 19 Or *so others reflect your heart back to you* [b] 20 Hebrew *Abaddon* [c] 3 Or *A poor person*
[d] 18 Syriac (see Septuagint); Hebrew *into one*

20 A faithful person will be richly
blessed,
but one eager to get rich will not go
unpunished.

21 To show partiality is not good —
yet a person will do wrong for a
piece of bread.

22 The stingy are eager to get rich
and are unaware that poverty
awaits them.

23 Whoever rebukes a person will in the
end gain favor
rather than one who has a
flattering tongue.

24 Whoever robs their father or mother
and says, "It's not wrong,"
is partner to one who destroys.

25 The greedy stir up conflict,
but those who trust in the LORD will
prosper.

26 Those who trust in themselves are
fools,
but those who walk in wisdom are
kept safe.

27 Those who give to the poor will lack
nothing,
but those who close their eyes to
them receive many curses.

28 When the wicked rise to power,
people go into hiding;
but when the wicked perish, the
righteous thrive.

29 Whoever remains stiff-necked
after many rebukes
will suddenly be destroyed —
without remedy.

2 When the righteous thrive, the people
rejoice;
when the wicked rule, the people
groan.

3 A man who loves wisdom brings joy
to his father,
but a companion of prostitutes
squanders his wealth.

4 By justice a king gives a country
stability,
but those who are greedy for[a]
bribes tear it down.

5 Those who flatter their neighbors
are spreading nets for their feet.

6 Evildoers are snared by their own sin,
but the righteous shout for joy and
are glad.

7 The righteous care about justice for
the poor,
but the wicked have no such
concern.

8 Mockers stir up a city,
but the wise turn away anger.

9 If a wise person goes to court with a
fool,
the fool rages and scoffs, and there
is no peace.

10 The bloodthirsty hate a person of
integrity
and seek to kill the upright.

11 Fools give full vent to their rage,
but the wise bring calm in the end.

12 If a ruler listens to lies,
all his officials become wicked.

13 The poor and the oppressor have this
in common:
The LORD gives sight to the eyes of
both.

14 If a king judges the poor with
fairness,
his throne will be established
forever.

15 A rod and a reprimand impart
wisdom,
but a child left undisciplined
disgraces its mother.

16 When the wicked thrive, so does sin,
but the righteous will see their
downfall.

17 Discipline your children, and they will
give you peace;
they will bring you the delights you
desire.

18 Where there is no revelation, people
cast off restraint;
but blessed is the one who heeds
wisdom's instruction.

19 Servants cannot be corrected by mere
words;
though they understand, they will
not respond.

20 Do you see someone who speaks in
haste?
There is more hope for a fool than
for them.

21 A servant pampered from youth
will turn out to be insolent.

22 An angry person stirs up conflict,
and a hot-tempered person
commits many sins.

[a] 4 Or *who give*

23 Pride brings a person low,
but the lowly in spirit gain honor.

24 The accomplices of thieves are their own enemies;
they are put under oath and dare not testify.

25 Fear of man will prove to be a snare,
but whoever trusts in the LORD is kept safe.

26 Many seek an audience with a ruler,
but it is from the LORD that one gets justice.

27 The righteous detest the dishonest;
the wicked detest the upright.

Sayings of Agur

30 The sayings of Agur son of Jakeh — an inspired utterance.

This man's utterance to Ithiel:
"I am weary, God,
but I can prevail.[a]
2 Surely I am only a brute, not a man;
I do not have human understanding.
3 I have not learned wisdom,
nor have I attained to the knowledge of the Holy One.
4 Who has gone up to heaven and come down?
Whose hands have gathered up the wind?
Who has wrapped up the waters in a cloak?
Who has established all the ends of the earth?
What is his name, and what is the name of his son?
Surely you know!

5 "Every word of God is flawless;
he is a shield to those who take refuge in him.
6 Do not add to his words,
or he will rebuke you and prove you a liar.

7 "Two things I ask of you, LORD;
do not refuse me before I die:
8 Keep falsehood and lies far from me;
give me neither poverty nor riches,
but give me only my daily bread.
9 Otherwise, I may have too much and disown you
and say, 'Who is the LORD?'
Or I may become poor and steal,
and so dishonor the name of my God.

10 "Do not slander a servant to their master,
or they will curse you, and you will pay for it.

11 "There are those who curse their fathers
and do not bless their mothers;
12 those who are pure in their own eyes
and yet are not cleansed of their filth;
13 those whose eyes are ever so haughty,
whose glances are so disdainful;
14 those whose teeth are swords
and whose jaws are set with knives
to devour the poor from the earth
and the needy from among mankind.

15 "The leech has two daughters.
'Give! Give!' they cry.

"There are three things that are never satisfied,
four that never say, 'Enough!':
16 the grave, the barren womb,
land, which is never satisfied with water,
and fire, which never says, 'Enough!'

17 "The eye that mocks a father,
that scorns an aged mother,
will be pecked out by the ravens of the valley,
will be eaten by the vultures.

18 "There are three things that are too amazing for me,
four that I do not understand:
19 the way of an eagle in the sky,
the way of a snake on a rock,
the way of a ship on the high seas,
and the way of a man with a young woman.

20 "This is the way of an adulterous woman:
She eats and wipes her mouth
and says, 'I've done nothing wrong.'

21 "Under three things the earth trembles,
under four it cannot bear up:
22 a servant who becomes king,
a godless fool who gets plenty to eat,
23 a contemptible woman who gets married,
and a servant who displaces her mistress.

24 "Four things on earth are small,
yet they are extremely wise:
25 Ants are creatures of little strength,
yet they store up their food in the summer;

[a] 1 With a different word division of the Hebrew; Masoretic Text *utterance to Ithiel, / to Ithiel and Ukal:*

26 hyraxes are creatures of little power,
yet they make their home in the crags;
27 locusts have no king,
yet they advance together in ranks;
28 a lizard can be caught with the hand,
yet it is found in kings' palaces.

29 "There are three things that are stately in their stride,
four that move with stately bearing:
30 a lion, mighty among beasts,
who retreats before nothing;
31 a strutting rooster, a he-goat,
and a king secure against revolt.[a]

32 "If you play the fool and exalt yourself,
or if you plan evil,
clap your hand over your mouth!
33 For as churning cream produces butter,
and as twisting the nose produces blood,
so stirring up anger produces strife."

Sayings of King Lemuel

31 The sayings of King Lemuel — an inspired utterance his mother taught him.

2 Listen, my son! Listen, son of my womb!
Listen, my son, the answer to my prayers!
3 Do not spend your strength[b] on women,
your vigor on those who ruin kings.

4 It is not for kings, Lemuel —
it is not for kings to drink wine,
not for rulers to crave beer,
5 lest they drink and forget what has been decreed,
and deprive all the oppressed of their rights.
6 Let beer be for those who are perishing,
wine for those who are in anguish!
7 Let them drink and forget their poverty
and remember their misery no more.

8 Speak up for those who cannot speak for themselves,
for the rights of all who are destitute.
9 Speak up and judge fairly;
defend the rights of the poor and needy.

Epilogue: The Wife of Noble Character

10 [c]A wife of noble character who can find?
She is worth far more than rubies.
11 Her husband has full confidence in her
and lacks nothing of value.
12 She brings him good, not harm,
all the days of her life.
13 She selects wool and flax
and works with eager hands.
14 She is like the merchant ships,
bringing her food from afar.
15 She gets up while it is still night;
she provides food for her family
and portions for her female servants.
16 She considers a field and buys it;
out of her earnings she plants a vineyard.
17 She sets about her work vigorously;
her arms are strong for her tasks.
18 She sees that her trading is profitable,
and her lamp does not go out at night.
19 In her hand she holds the distaff
and grasps the spindle with her fingers.
20 She opens her arms to the poor
and extends her hands to the needy.
21 When it snows, she has no fear for her household;
for all of them are clothed in scarlet.
22 She makes coverings for her bed;
she is clothed in fine linen and purple.
23 Her husband is respected at the city gate,
where he takes his seat among the elders of the land.
24 She makes linen garments and sells them,
and supplies the merchants with sashes.
25 She is clothed with strength and dignity;
she can laugh at the days to come.
26 She speaks with wisdom,
and faithful instruction is on her tongue.
27 She watches over the affairs of her household
and does not eat the bread of idleness.
28 Her children arise and call her blessed;
her husband also, and he praises her:
29 "Many women do noble things,
but you surpass them all."
30 Charm is deceptive, and beauty is fleeting;
but a woman who fears the LORD is to be praised.
31 Honor her for all that her hands have done,
and let her works bring her praise at the city gate.

[a] *31* The meaning of the Hebrew for this phrase is uncertain. [b] *3* Or *wealth* [c] *10* Verses 10-31 are an acrostic poem, the verses of which begin with the successive letters of the Hebrew alphabet.

ECCLESIASTES

Everything Is Meaningless

1 The words of the Teacher,[a] son of David,
king in Jerusalem:

2 "Meaningless! Meaningless!"
  says the Teacher.
"Utterly meaningless!
  Everything is meaningless."

3 What do people gain from all their
    labors
  at which they toil under the sun?
4 Generations come and generations go,
  but the earth remains forever.
5 The sun rises and the sun sets,
  and hurries back to where it rises.
6 The wind blows to the south
  and turns to the north;
round and round it goes,
  ever returning on its course.
7 All streams flow into the sea,
  yet the sea is never full.
To the place the streams come from,
  there they return again.
8 All things are wearisome,
  more than one can say.
The eye never has enough of seeing,
  nor the ear its fill of hearing.
9 What has been will be again,
  what has been done will be done
    again;
  there is nothing new under the sun.
10 Is there anything of which one can say,
  "Look! This is something new"?
It was here already, long ago;
  it was here before our time.
11 No one remembers the former
    generations,
  and even those yet to come
will not be remembered
  by those who follow them.

Wisdom Is Meaningless

12 I, the Teacher, was king over Israel in
Jerusalem. 13 I applied my mind to study
and to explore by wisdom all that is done
under the heavens. What a heavy burden
God has laid on mankind! 14 I have seen all
the things that are done under the sun;
all of them are meaningless, a chasing
after the wind.

15 What is crooked cannot be
    straightened;
  what is lacking cannot be counted.

16 I said to myself, "Look, I have increased in wisdom more than anyone
who has ruled over Jerusalem before me;
I have experienced much of wisdom and
knowledge." 17 Then I applied myself to
the understanding of wisdom, and also of
madness and folly, but I learned that this,
too, is a chasing after the wind.

18 For with much wisdom comes much
    sorrow;
  the more knowledge, the more grief.

Pleasures Are Meaningless

2 I said to myself, "Come now, I will test
you with pleasure to find out what is
good." But that also proved to be meaningless. 2 "Laughter," I said, "is madness.
And what does pleasure accomplish?" 3 I
tried cheering myself with wine, and embracing folly — my mind still guiding me
with wisdom. I wanted to see what was
good for people to do under the heavens
during the few days of their lives.
4 I undertook great projects: I built houses for myself and planted vineyards. 5 I
made gardens and parks and planted
all kinds of fruit trees in them. 6 I made
reservoirs to water groves of flourishing
trees. 7 I bought male and female slaves
and had other slaves who were born in
my house. I also owned more herds and
flocks than anyone in Jerusalem before
me. 8 I amassed silver and gold for myself,
and the treasure of kings and provinces. I
acquired male and female singers, and a
harem[b] as well — the delights of a man's
heart. 9 I became greater by far than anyone in Jerusalem before me. In all this my
wisdom stayed with me.

10 I denied myself nothing my eyes
    desired;
  I refused my heart no pleasure.
My heart took delight in all my labor,
  and this was the reward for all my
    toil.
11 Yet when I surveyed all that my
    hands had done
  and what I had toiled to achieve,
everything was meaningless, a
    chasing after the wind;
  nothing was gained under the sun.

[a] *1* Or *the leader of the assembly*; also in verses 2 and 12
[b] *8* The meaning of the Hebrew for this phrase is uncertain.

Wisdom and Folly Are Meaningless

12 Then I turned my thoughts to
consider wisdom,
and also madness and folly.
What more can the king's successor do
than what has already been done?
13 I saw that wisdom is better than folly,
just as light is better than darkness.
14 The wise have eyes in their heads,
while the fool walks in the
darkness;
but I came to realize
that the same fate overtakes them
both.

15 Then I said to myself,

"The fate of the fool will overtake me
also.
What then do I gain by being wise?"
I said to myself,
"This too is meaningless."
16 For the wise, like the fool, will not be
long remembered;
the days have already come when
both have been forgotten.
Like the fool, the wise too must die!

Toil Is Meaningless

17 So I hated life, because the work that
is done under the sun was grievous to me.
All of it is meaningless, a chasing after
the wind. 18 I hated all the things I had
toiled for under the sun, because I must
leave them to the one who comes after me.
19 And who knows whether that person will
be wise or foolish? Yet they will have control over all the fruit of my toil into which
I have poured my effort and skill under
the sun. This too is meaningless. 20 So my
heart began to despair over all my toilsome labor under the sun. 21 For a person
may labor with wisdom, knowledge and
skill, and then they must leave all they
own to another who has not toiled for it.
This too is meaningless and a great misfortune. 22 What do people get for all the
toil and anxious striving with which they
labor under the sun? 23 All their days their
work is grief and pain; even at night their
minds do not rest. This too is meaningless.
24 A person can do nothing better than
to eat and drink and find satisfaction
in their own toil. This too, I see, is from
the hand of God, 25 for without him, who
can eat or find enjoyment? 26 To the person who pleases him, God gives wisdom,
knowledge and happiness, but to the sinner he gives the task of gathering and
storing up wealth to hand it over to the
one who pleases God. This too is meaningless, a chasing after the wind.

A Time for Everything

3 There is a time for everything,
and a season for every activity
under the heavens:

2 a time to be born and a time to die,
a time to plant and a time to uproot,
3 a time to kill and a time to heal,
a time to tear down and a time to
build,
4 a time to weep and a time to laugh,
a time to mourn and a time to
dance,
5 a time to scatter stones and a time
to gather them,
a time to embrace and a time to
refrain from embracing,
6 a time to search and a time to give
up,
a time to keep and a time to throw
away,
7 a time to tear and a time to mend,
a time to be silent and a time to
speak,
8 a time to love and a time to hate,
a time for war and a time for peace.

9 What do workers gain from their toil?
10 I have seen the burden God has laid on
the human race. 11 He has made everything beautiful in its time. He has also
set eternity in the human heart; yet[a] no
one can fathom what God has done from
beginning to end. 12 I know that there is
nothing better for people than to be happy
and to do good while they live. 13 That each
of them may eat and drink, and find satisfaction in all their toil — this is the gift
of God. 14 I know that everything God does
will endure forever; nothing can be added
to it and nothing taken from it. God does
it so that people will fear him.

15 Whatever is has already been,
and what will be has been before;
and God will call the past to
account.[b]

16 And I saw something else under
the sun:

In the place of judgment —
wickedness was there,
in the place of justice — wickedness
was there.

17 I said to myself,

"God will bring into judgment
both the righteous and the wicked,
for there will be a time for every
activity,
a time to judge every deed."

[a] 11 Or *also placed ignorance in the human heart, so that* [b] 15 Or *God calls back the past*

18I also said to myself, "As for humans,
God tests them so that they may see
that they are like the animals. 19Surely
the fate of human beings is like that of
the animals; the same fate awaits them
both: As one dies, so dies the other. All
have the same breath[a]; humans have no
advantage over animals. Everything is
meaningless. 20All go to the same place;
all come from dust, and to dust all return.
21Who knows if the human spirit rises upward and if the spirit of the animal goes
down into the earth?"

22So I saw that there is nothing better
for a person than to enjoy their work,
because that is their lot. For who can
bring them to see what will happen
after them?

Oppression, Toil, Friendlessness

4 Again I looked and saw all the oppression that was taking place under the
sun:

I saw the tears of the oppressed —
and they have no comforter;
power was on the side of their
oppressors —
and they have no comforter.
2 And I declared that the dead,
who had already died,
are happier than the living,
who are still alive.
3 But better than both
is the one who has never been born,
who has not seen the evil
that is done under the sun.

4And I saw that all toil and all achieve-
ment spring from one person's envy of
another. This too is meaningless, a chasing after the wind.

5 Fools fold their hands
and ruin themselves.
6 Better one handful with tranquillity
than two handfuls with toil
and chasing after the wind.

7Again I saw something meaningless
under the sun:

8 There was a man all alone;
he had neither son nor brother.
There was no end to his toil,
yet his eyes were not content with
his wealth.
"For whom am I toiling," he asked,
"and why am I depriving myself of
enjoyment?"
This too is meaningless —
a miserable business!

9 Two are better than one,
because they have a good return
for their labor:
10 If either of them falls down,
one can help the other up.
But pity anyone who falls
and has no one to help them up.
11 Also, if two lie down together, they
will keep warm.
But how can one keep warm alone?
12 Though one may be overpowered,
two can defend themselves.
A cord of three strands is not quickly
broken.

Advancement Is Meaningless

13Better a poor but wise youth than an
old but foolish king who no longer knows
how to heed a warning. 14The youth may
have come from prison to the kingship, or
he may have been born in poverty within
his kingdom. 15I saw that all who lived and
walked under the sun followed the youth,
the king's successor. 16There was no end to
all the people who were before them. But
those who came later were not pleased
with the successor. This too is meaningless, a chasing after the wind.

Fulfill Your Vow to God

5[b] Guard your steps when you go to the
house of God. Go near to listen rather
than to offer the sacrifice of fools, who do
not know that they do wrong.

2 Do not be quick with your mouth,
do not be hasty in your heart
to utter anything before God.
God is in heaven
and you are on earth,
so let your words be few.
3 A dream comes when there are many
cares,
and many words mark the speech
of a fool.

4When you make a vow to God, do not
delay to fulfill it. He has no pleasure in
fools; fulfill your vow. 5It is better not to
make a vow than to make one and not
fulfill it. 6Do not let your mouth lead you
into sin. And do not protest to the temple
messenger, "My vow was a mistake." Why
should God be angry at what you say and
destroy the work of your hands? 7Much
dreaming and many words are meaningless. Therefore fear God.

Riches Are Meaningless

8If you see the poor oppressed in a district, and justice and rights denied, do
not be surprised at such things; for one

[a] 19 Or *spirit* [b] In Hebrew texts 5:1 is numbered 4:17, and 5:2-20 is numbered 5:1-19.

official is eyed by a higher one, and over
them both are others higher still. 9 The increase from the land is taken by all; the
king himself profits from the fields.

10 Whoever loves money never has
enough;
whoever loves wealth is never
satisfied with their income.
This too is meaningless.

11 As goods increase,
so do those who consume them.
And what benefit are they to the
owners
except to feast their eyes on them?

12 The sleep of a laborer is sweet,
whether they eat little or much,
but as for the rich, their abundance
permits them no sleep.

13 I have seen a grievous evil under the
sun:

wealth hoarded to the harm of its
owners,
14 or wealth lost through some
misfortune,
so that when they have children
there is nothing left for them to
inherit.
15 Everyone comes naked from their
mother's womb,
and as everyone comes, so they
depart.
They take nothing from their toil
that they can carry in their hands.

16 This too is a grievous evil:

As everyone comes, so they depart,
and what do they gain,
since they toil for the wind?
17 All their days they eat in darkness,
with great frustration, affliction
and anger.

18 This is what I have observed to be
good: that it is appropriate for a person
to eat, to drink and to find satisfaction in
their toilsome labor under the sun during
the few days of life God has given them —
for this is their lot. 19 Moreover, when God
gives someone wealth and possessions,
and the ability to enjoy them, to accept
their lot and be happy in their toil — this is
a gift of God. 20 They seldom reflect on the
days of their life, because God keeps them
occupied with gladness of heart.

6 I have seen another evil under the
sun, and it weighs heavily on mankind: 2 God gives some people wealth,
possessions and honor, so that they lack
nothing their hearts desire, but God does
not grant them the ability to enjoy them,
and strangers enjoy them instead. This is
meaningless, a grievous evil.
3 A man may have a hundred children
and live many years; yet no matter how
long he lives, if he cannot enjoy his prosperity and does not receive proper burial, I
say that a stillborn child is better off than
he. 4 It comes without meaning, it departs
in darkness, and in darkness its name is
shrouded. 5 Though it never saw the sun
or knew anything, it has more rest than
does that man — 6 even if he lives a thousand years twice over but fails to enjoy his
prosperity. Do not all go to the same place?

7 Everyone's toil is for their mouth,
yet their appetite is never satisfied.
8 What advantage have the wise over
fools?
What do the poor gain
by knowing how to conduct
themselves before others?
9 Better what the eye sees
than the roving of the appetite.
This too is meaningless,
a chasing after the wind.

10 Whatever exists has already been
named,
and what humanity is has been
known;
no one can contend
with someone who is stronger.
11 The more the words,
the less the meaning,
and how does that profit anyone?

12 For who knows what is good for a person in life, during the few and meaningless days they pass through like a shadow?
Who can tell them what will happen under
the sun after they are gone?

Wisdom

7 A good name is better than fine
perfume,
and the day of death better than
the day of birth.
2 It is better to go to a house of
mourning
than to go to a house of feasting,
for death is the destiny of everyone;
the living should take this to heart.
3 Frustration is better than laughter,
because a sad face is good for the
heart.
4 The heart of the wise is in the house
of mourning,
but the heart of fools is in the
house of pleasure.
5 It is better to heed the rebuke of a
wise person
than to listen to the song of fools.

[6] Like the crackling of thorns under the pot,
so is the laughter of fools.
This too is meaningless.

[7] Extortion turns a wise person into a fool,
and a bribe corrupts the heart.

[8] The end of a matter is better than its beginning,
and patience is better than pride.
[9] Do not be quickly provoked in your spirit,
for anger resides in the lap of fools.

[10] Do not say, "Why were the old days better than these?"
For it is not wise to ask such questions.

[11] Wisdom, like an inheritance, is a good thing
and benefits those who see the sun.
[12] Wisdom is a shelter
as money is a shelter,
but the advantage of knowledge is this:
Wisdom preserves those who have it.

[13] Consider what God has done:

Who can straighten
what he has made crooked?
[14] When times are good, be happy;
but when times are bad, consider this:
God has made the one
as well as the other.
Therefore, no one can discover
anything about their future.

[15] In this meaningless life of mine I have seen both of these:

the righteous perishing in their righteousness,
and the wicked living long in their wickedness.
[16] Do not be overrighteous,
neither be overwise —
why destroy yourself?
[17] Do not be overwicked,
and do not be a fool —
why die before your time?
[18] It is good to grasp the one
and not let go of the other.
Whoever fears God will avoid all extremes.[a]

[19] Wisdom makes one wise person more powerful
than ten rulers in a city.

[20] Indeed, there is no one on earth who is righteous,
no one who does what is right and never sins.

[21] Do not pay attention to every word people say,
or you may hear your servant cursing you —
[22] for you know in your heart
that many times you yourself have cursed others.

[23] All this I tested by wisdom and I said,

"I am determined to be wise" —
but this was beyond me.
[24] Whatever exists is far off and most profound —
who can discover it?
[25] So I turned my mind to understand,
to investigate and to search out
wisdom and the scheme of things
and to understand the stupidity of wickedness
and the madness of folly.

[26] I find more bitter than death
the woman who is a snare,
whose heart is a trap
and whose hands are chains.
The man who pleases God will escape her,
but the sinner she will ensnare.

[27] "Look," says the Teacher,[b] "this is what I have discovered:

"Adding one thing to another to discover the scheme of things —
[28] while I was still searching
but not finding —
I found one upright man among a thousand,
but not one upright woman among them all.
[29] This only have I found:
God created mankind upright,
but they have gone in search of many schemes."

[8] Who is like the wise?
Who knows the explanation of things?
A person's wisdom brightens their face
and changes its hard appearance.

Obey the King

[2] Obey the king's command, I say, because you took an oath before God. [3] Do not be in a hurry to leave the king's presence. Do not stand up for a bad cause, for he will do whatever he pleases. [4] Since a

[a] 18 Or *will follow them both* [b] 27 Or *the leader of the assembly*

king's word is supreme, who can say to
him, "What are you doing?"

5 Whoever obeys his command will
come to no harm,
and the wise heart will know the
proper time and procedure.
6 For there is a proper time and
procedure for every matter,
though a person may be weighed
down by misery.

7 Since no one knows the future,
who can tell someone else what is
to come?
8 As no one has power over the wind to
contain it,
so[a] no one has power over the time
of their death.
As no one is discharged in time of war,
so wickedness will not release those
who practice it.

9 All this I saw, as I applied my mind to
everything done under the sun. There is
a time when a man lords it over others to
his own[b] hurt. 10 Then too, I saw the wicked
buried — those who used to come and go
from the holy place and receive praise[c]
in the city where they did this. This too is
meaningless.

11 When the sentence for a crime is not
quickly carried out, people's hearts are
filled with schemes to do wrong. 12 Although a wicked person who commits a
hundred crimes may live a long time, I
know that it will go better with those who
fear God, who are reverent before him.
13 Yet because the wicked do not fear God, it
will not go well with them, and their days
will not lengthen like a shadow.

14 There is something else meaningless
that occurs on earth: the righteous who get
what the wicked deserve, and the wicked
who get what the righteous deserve. This
too, I say, is meaningless. 15 So I commend
the enjoyment of life, because there is nothing better for a person under the sun than
to eat and drink and be glad. Then joy will
accompany them in their toil all the days of
the life God has given them under the sun.

16 When I applied my mind to know
wisdom and to observe the labor that is
done on earth — people getting no sleep
day or night — 17 then I saw all that God
has done. No one can comprehend what
goes on under the sun. Despite all their
efforts to search it out, no one can discover
its meaning. Even if the wise claim they
know, they cannot really comprehend it.

A Common Destiny for All

9 So I reflected on all this and concluded
that the righteous and the wise and
what they do are in God's hands, but no
one knows whether love or hate awaits
them. 2 All share a common destiny — the
righteous and the wicked, the good and
the bad,[d] the clean and the unclean, those
who offer sacrifices and those who do not.

As it is with the good,
so with the sinful;
as it is with those who take oaths,
so with those who are afraid to
take them.

3 This is the evil in everything that happens under the sun: The same destiny
overtakes all. The hearts of people, moreover, are full of evil and there is madness
in their hearts while they live, and afterward they join the dead. 4 Anyone who is
among the living has hope[e] — even a live
dog is better off than a dead lion!

5 For the living know that they will die,
but the dead know nothing;
they have no further reward,
and even their name is forgotten.
6 Their love, their hate
and their jealousy have long since
vanished;
never again will they have a part
in anything that happens under
the sun.

7 Go, eat your food with gladness, and
drink your wine with a joyful heart, for
God has already approved what you do.
8 Always be clothed in white, and always
anoint your head with oil. 9 Enjoy life with
your wife, whom you love, all the days of
this meaningless life that God has given
you under the sun — all your meaningless
days. For this is your lot in life and in your
toilsome labor under the sun. 10 Whatever
your hand finds to do, do it with all your
might, for in the realm of the dead, where
you are going, there is neither working
nor planning nor knowledge nor wisdom.

11 I have seen something else under the
sun:

The race is not to the swift
or the battle to the strong,
nor does food come to the wise
or wealth to the brilliant
or favor to the learned;
but time and chance happen to them
all.

[a] 8 Or *over the human spirit to retain it, / and so* [b] 9 Or *to their* [c] 10 Some Hebrew manuscripts and Septuagint (Aquila); most Hebrew manuscripts *and are forgotten*
[d] 2 Septuagint (Aquila), Vulgate and Syriac; Hebrew does not have *and the bad.* [e] 4 Or *What then is to be chosen? With all who live, there is hope*

[12]Moreover, no one knows when their
hour will come:

As fish are caught in a cruel net,
or birds are taken in a snare,
so people are trapped by evil times
that fall unexpectedly upon them.

Wisdom Better Than Folly

[13]I also saw under the sun this example of wisdom that greatly impressed me:
[14]There was once a small city with only a
few people in it. And a powerful king came
against it, surrounded it and built huge
siege works against it. [15]Now there lived
in that city a man poor but wise, and he
saved the city by his wisdom. But nobody
remembered that poor man. [16]So I said,
"Wisdom is better than strength." But the
poor man's wisdom is despised, and his
words are no longer heeded.

[17]The quiet words of the wise are more
to be heeded
than the shouts of a ruler of fools.
[18]Wisdom is better than weapons of
war,
but one sinner destroys much good.

10 As dead flies give perfume a bad
smell,
so a little folly outweighs wisdom
and honor.
[2]The heart of the wise inclines to the
right,
but the heart of the fool to the left.
[3]Even as fools walk along the road,
they lack sense
and show everyone how stupid
they are.
[4]If a ruler's anger rises against you,
do not leave your post;
calmness can lay great offenses
to rest.
[5]There is an evil I have seen under
the sun,
the sort of error that arises from
a ruler:
[6]Fools are put in many high positions,
while the rich occupy the low ones.
[7]I have seen slaves on horseback,
while princes go on foot
like slaves.
[8]Whoever digs a pit may fall into it;
whoever breaks through a wall
may be bitten by a snake.
[9]Whoever quarries stones may be
injured by them;
whoever splits logs may be
endangered by them.
[10]If the ax is dull
and its edge unsharpened,
more strength is needed,
but skill will bring success.
[11]If a snake bites before it is charmed,
the charmer receives no fee.
[12]Words from the mouth of the wise are
gracious,
but fools are consumed by their
own lips.
[13]At the beginning their words are folly;
at the end they are wicked
madness —
[14] and fools multiply words.

No one knows what is coming —
who can tell someone else what
will happen after them?
[15]The toil of fools wearies them;
they do not know the way to town.
[16]Woe to the land whose king was a
servant[a]
and whose princes feast in the
morning.
[17]Blessed is the land whose king is of
noble birth
and whose princes eat at a proper
time —
for strength and not for
drunkenness.
[18]Through laziness, the rafters sag;
because of idle hands, the house
leaks.
[19]A feast is made for laughter,
wine makes life merry,
and money is the answer for
everything.
[20]Do not revile the king even in your
thoughts,
or curse the rich in your bedroom,
because a bird in the sky may carry
your words,
and a bird on the wing may report
what you say.

Invest in Many Ventures

11 Ship your grain across the sea;
after many days you may receive
a return.
[2]Invest in seven ventures, yes, in eight;
you do not know what disaster may
come upon the land.
[3]If clouds are full of water,
they pour rain on the earth.
Whether a tree falls to the south or to
the north,
in the place where it falls, there it
will lie.

[a] 16 Or *king is a child*

4 Whoever watches the wind will not plant;
whoever looks at the clouds will not reap.

5 As you do not know the path of the wind,
or how the body is formed[a] in a mother's womb,
so you cannot understand the work of God,
the Maker of all things.

6 Sow your seed in the morning,
and at evening let your hands not be idle,
for you do not know which will succeed,
whether this or that,
or whether both will do equally well.

Remember Your Creator While Young

7 Light is sweet,
and it pleases the eyes to see the sun.
8 However many years anyone may live,
let them enjoy them all.
But let them remember the days of darkness,
for there will be many.
Everything to come is meaningless.

9 You who are young, be happy while you are young,
and let your heart give you joy in the days of your youth.
Follow the ways of your heart
and whatever your eyes see,
but know that for all these things
God will bring you into judgment.
10 So then, banish anxiety from your heart
and cast off the troubles of your body,
for youth and vigor are meaningless.

12 Remember your Creator
in the days of your youth,
before the days of trouble come
and the years approach when you will say,
"I find no pleasure in them" —
2 before the sun and the light
and the moon and the stars grow dark,
and the clouds return after the rain;
3 when the keepers of the house tremble,
and the strong men stoop,
when the grinders cease because they are few,
and those looking through the windows grow dim;
4 when the doors to the street are closed
and the sound of grinding fades;
when people rise up at the sound of birds,
but all their songs grow faint;
5 when people are afraid of heights
and of dangers in the streets;
when the almond tree blossoms
and the grasshopper drags itself along
and desire no longer is stirred.
Then people go to their eternal home
and mourners go about the streets.

6 Remember him — before the silver cord is severed,
and the golden bowl is broken;
before the pitcher is shattered at the spring,
and the wheel broken at the well,
7 and the dust returns to the ground it came from,
and the spirit returns to God who gave it.

8 "Meaningless! Meaningless!" says the Teacher.[b]
"Everything is meaningless!"

The Conclusion of the Matter

9 Not only was the Teacher wise, but he
also imparted knowledge to the people.
He pondered and searched out and set
in order many proverbs. 10 The Teacher searched to find just the right words,
and what he wrote was upright and true.
11 The words of the wise are like goads,
their collected sayings like firmly embed-
ded nails — given by one shepherd.[c] 12 Be
warned, my son, of anything in addition
to them.

Of making many books there is no end, and much study wearies the body.

13 Now all has been heard;
here is the conclusion of the matter:
Fear God and keep his commandments,
for this is the duty of all mankind.
14 For God will bring every deed into judgment,
including every hidden thing,
whether it is good or evil.

[a] 5 Or *know how life* (or *the spirit*) */ enters the body being formed* [b] 8 Or *the leader of the assembly*; also in verses 9 and 10 [c] 11 Or *Shepherd*

SONG OF SONGS

1 Solomon's Song of Songs.

She[a]

[2]Let him kiss me with the kisses of his mouth —
for your love is more delightful than wine.
[3]Pleasing is the fragrance of your perfumes;
your name is like perfume poured out.
No wonder the young women love you!
[4]Take me away with you — let us hurry!
Let the king bring me into his chambers.

Friends

We rejoice and delight in you[b];
we will praise your love more than wine.

She

How right they are to adore you!

[5]Dark am I, yet lovely,
daughters of Jerusalem,
dark like the tents of Kedar,
like the tent curtains of Solomon.[c]
[6]Do not stare at me because I am dark,
because I am darkened by the sun.
My mother's sons were angry with me
and made me take care of the vineyards;
my own vineyard I had to neglect.
[7]Tell me, you whom I love,
where you graze your flock
and where you rest your sheep at midday.
Why should I be like a veiled woman
beside the flocks of your friends?

Friends

[8]If you do not know, most beautiful of women,
follow the tracks of the sheep
and graze your young goats
by the tents of the shepherds.

He

[9]I liken you, my darling, to a mare
among Pharaoh's chariot horses.
[10]Your cheeks are beautiful with earrings,
your neck with strings of jewels.
[11]We will make you earrings of gold,
studded with silver.

She

[12]While the king was at his table,
my perfume spread its fragrance.
[13]My beloved is to me a sachet of myrrh
resting between my breasts.
[14]My beloved is to me a cluster of henna blossoms
from the vineyards of En Gedi.

He

[15]How beautiful you are, my darling!
Oh, how beautiful!
Your eyes are doves.

She

[16]How handsome you are, my beloved!
Oh, how charming!
And our bed is verdant.

He

[17]The beams of our house are cedars;
our rafters are firs.

She[d]

2 I am a rose[e] of Sharon,
a lily of the valleys.

He

[2]Like a lily among thorns
is my darling among the young women.

She

[3]Like an apple[f] tree among the trees of the forest
is my beloved among the young men.
I delight to sit in his shade,
and his fruit is sweet to my taste.
[4]Let him lead me to the banquet hall,
and let his banner over me be love.
[5]Strengthen me with raisins,
refresh me with apples,
for I am faint with love.

[a] The main male and female speakers (identified primarily on the basis of the gender of the relevant Hebrew forms) are indicated by the captions *He* and *She* respectively. The words of others are marked *Friends*. In some instances the divisions and their captions are debatable.
[b] 4 The Hebrew is masculine singular. [c] 5 Or *Salma* [d] Or *He* [e] 1 Probably a member of the crocus family [f] 3 Or possibly *apricot*; here and elsewhere in Song of Songs

6 His left arm is under my head,
and his right arm embraces me.
7 Daughters of Jerusalem, I charge you
by the gazelles and by the does of the field:
Do not arouse or awaken love
until it so desires.

8 Listen! My beloved!
Look! Here he comes,
leaping across the mountains,
bounding over the hills.
9 My beloved is like a gazelle or a young stag.
Look! There he stands behind our wall,
gazing through the windows,
peering through the lattice.
10 My beloved spoke and said to me,
"Arise, my darling,
my beautiful one, come with me.
11 See! The winter is past;
the rains are over and gone.
12 Flowers appear on the earth;
the season of singing has come,
the cooing of doves
is heard in our land.
13 The fig tree forms its early fruit;
the blossoming vines spread their fragrance.
Arise, come, my darling;
my beautiful one, come with me."

He

14 My dove in the clefts of the rock,
in the hiding places on the mountainside,
show me your face,
let me hear your voice;
for your voice is sweet,
and your face is lovely.
15 Catch for us the foxes,
the little foxes
that ruin the vineyards,
our vineyards that are in bloom.

She

16 My beloved is mine and I am his;
he browses among the lilies.
17 Until the day breaks
and the shadows flee,
turn, my beloved,
and be like a gazelle
or like a young stag
on the rugged hills.[a]

3 All night long on my bed
I looked for the one my heart loves;
I looked for him but did not find him.
2 I will get up now and go about the city,
through its streets and squares;
I will search for the one my heart loves.
So I looked for him but did not find him.
3 The watchmen found me
as they made their rounds in the city.
"Have you seen the one my heart loves?"
4 Scarcely had I passed them
when I found the one my heart loves.
I held him and would not let him go
till I had brought him to my mother's house,
to the room of the one who conceived me.
5 Daughters of Jerusalem, I charge you
by the gazelles and by the does of the field:
Do not arouse or awaken love
until it so desires.

6 Who is this coming up from the wilderness
like a column of smoke,
perfumed with myrrh and incense
made from all the spices of the merchant?
7 Look! It is Solomon's carriage,
escorted by sixty warriors,
the noblest of Israel,
8 all of them wearing the sword,
all experienced in battle,
each with his sword at his side,
prepared for the terrors of the night.
9 King Solomon made for himself the carriage;
he made it of wood from Lebanon.
10 Its posts he made of silver,
its base of gold.
Its seat was upholstered with purple,
its interior inlaid with love.
Daughters of Jerusalem, 11 come out,
and look, you daughters of Zion.
Look[b] on King Solomon wearing a crown,
the crown with which his mother crowned him
on the day of his wedding,
the day his heart rejoiced.

He

4 How beautiful you are, my darling!
Oh, how beautiful!
Your eyes behind your veil are doves.
Your hair is like a flock of goats
descending from the hills of Gilead.

[a] 17 Or *the hills of Bether* [b] 10,11 Or *interior lovingly inlaid / by the daughters of Jerusalem. / [11]Come out, you daughters of Zion, / and look*

2 Your teeth are like a flock of sheep
just shorn,
coming up from the washing.
Each has its twin;
not one of them is alone.
3 Your lips are like a scarlet ribbon;
your mouth is lovely.
Your temples behind your veil
are like the halves of a pomegranate.
4 Your neck is like the tower of David,
built with courses of stone[a];
on it hang a thousand shields,
all of them shields of warriors.
5 Your breasts are like two fawns,
like twin fawns of a gazelle
that browse among the lilies.
6 Until the day breaks
and the shadows flee,
I will go to the mountain of myrrh
and to the hill of incense.
7 You are altogether beautiful, my
darling;
there is no flaw in you.
8 Come with me from Lebanon, my bride,
come with me from Lebanon.
Descend from the crest of Amana,
from the top of Senir, the summit
of Hermon,
from the lions' dens
and the mountain haunts of leopards.
9 You have stolen my heart, my sister,
my bride;
you have stolen my heart
with one glance of your eyes,
with one jewel of your necklace.
10 How delightful is your love, my sister,
my bride!
How much more pleasing is your
love than wine,
and the fragrance of your perfume
more than any spice!
11 Your lips drop sweetness as the
honeycomb, my bride;
milk and honey are under your
tongue.
The fragrance of your garments
is like the fragrance of Lebanon.
12 You are a garden locked up, my sister,
my bride;
you are a spring enclosed, a sealed
fountain.
13 Your plants are an orchard of
pomegranates
with choice fruits,
with henna and nard,
14 nard and saffron,
calamus and cinnamon,
with every kind of incense tree,
with myrrh and aloes
and all the finest spices.
15 You are[b] a garden fountain,
a well of flowing water
streaming down from Lebanon.

She

16 Awake, north wind,
and come, south wind!
Blow on my garden,
that its fragrance may spread
everywhere.
Let my beloved come into his garden
and taste its choice fruits.

He

5 I have come into my garden, my
sister, my bride;
I have gathered my myrrh with my
spice.
I have eaten my honeycomb and my
honey;
I have drunk my wine and my milk.

Friends

Eat, friends, and drink;
drink your fill of love.

She

2 I slept but my heart was awake.
Listen! My beloved is knocking:
"Open to me, my sister, my darling,
my dove, my flawless one.
My head is drenched with dew,
my hair with the dampness of the
night."
3 I have taken off my robe —
must I put it on again?
I have washed my feet —
must I soil them again?
4 My beloved thrust his hand through
the latch-opening;
my heart began to pound for him.
5 I arose to open for my beloved,
and my hands dripped with myrrh,
my fingers with flowing myrrh,
on the handles of the bolt.
6 I opened for my beloved,
but my beloved had left; he was
gone.
My heart sank at his departure.[c]
I looked for him but did not find him.
I called him but he did not answer.
7 The watchmen found me
as they made their rounds in the city.
They beat me, they bruised me;
they took away my cloak,
those watchmen of the walls!
8 Daughters of Jerusalem, I charge you —
if you find my beloved,
what will you tell him?
Tell him I am faint with love.

[a] 4 The meaning of the Hebrew for this phrase is uncertain. [b] 15 Or *I am* (spoken by *She*)
[c] 6 Or *heart had gone out to him when he spoke*

Friends

9 How is your beloved better than others,
most beautiful of women?
How is your beloved better than others,
that you so charge us?

She

10 My beloved is radiant and ruddy,
outstanding among ten thousand.
11 His head is purest gold;
his hair is wavy
and black as a raven.
12 His eyes are like doves
by the water streams,
washed in milk,
mounted like jewels.
13 His cheeks are like beds of spice
yielding perfume.
His lips are like lilies
dripping with myrrh.
14 His arms are rods of gold
set with topaz.
His body is like polished ivory
decorated with lapis lazuli.
15 His legs are pillars of marble
set on bases of pure gold.
His appearance is like Lebanon,
choice as its cedars.
16 His mouth is sweetness itself;
he is altogether lovely.
This is my beloved, this is my friend,
daughters of Jerusalem.

Friends

6 Where has your beloved gone,
most beautiful of women?
Which way did your beloved turn,
that we may look for him with you?

She

2 My beloved has gone down to his garden,
to the beds of spices,
to browse in the gardens
and to gather lilies.
3 I am my beloved's and my beloved is mine;
he browses among the lilies.

He

4 You are as beautiful as Tirzah, my darling,
as lovely as Jerusalem,
as majestic as troops with banners.
5 Turn your eyes from me;
they overwhelm me.
Your hair is like a flock of goats
descending from Gilead.
6 Your teeth are like a flock of sheep
coming up from the washing.
Each has its twin,
not one of them is missing.
7 Your temples behind your veil
are like the halves of a pomegranate.
8 Sixty queens there may be,
and eighty concubines,
and virgins beyond number;
9 but my dove, my perfect one, is unique,
the only daughter of her mother,
the favorite of the one who bore her.
The young women saw her and called her blessed;
the queens and concubines praised her.

Friends

10 Who is this that appears like the dawn,
fair as the moon, bright as the sun,
majestic as the stars in procession?

He

11 I went down to the grove of nut trees
to look at the new growth in the valley,
to see if the vines had budded
or the pomegranates were in bloom.
12 Before I realized it,
my desire set me among the royal chariots of my people.[a]

Friends

13 Come back, come back,
O Shulammite;
come back, come back, that we may gaze on you!

He

Why would you gaze on the Shulammite
as on the dance of Mahanaim?[b]

7[c] How beautiful your sandaled feet,
O prince's daughter!
Your graceful legs are like jewels,
the work of an artist's hands.
2 Your navel is a rounded goblet
that never lacks blended wine.
Your waist is a mound of wheat
encircled by lilies.
3 Your breasts are like two fawns,
like twin fawns of a gazelle.
4 Your neck is like an ivory tower.
Your eyes are the pools of Heshbon
by the gate of Bath Rabbim.

[a] *12* Or *among the chariots of Amminadab*; or *among the chariots of the people of the prince*
[b] *13* In Hebrew texts this verse (6:13) is numbered 7:1. [c] In Hebrew texts 7:1-13 is numbered 7:2-14.

Your nose is like the tower of Lebanon
looking toward Damascus.
5 Your head crowns you like Mount
Carmel.
Your hair is like royal tapestry;
the king is held captive by its
tresses.
6 How beautiful you are and how
pleasing,
my love, with your delights!
7 Your stature is like that of the palm,
and your breasts like clusters of fruit.
8 I said, "I will climb the palm tree;
I will take hold of its fruit."
May your breasts be like clusters of
grapes on the vine,
the fragrance of your breath like
apples,
9 and your mouth like the best wine.

She

May the wine go straight to my
beloved,
flowing gently over lips and teeth.[a]
10 I belong to my beloved,
and his desire is for me.
11 Come, my beloved, let us go to the
countryside,
let us spend the night in the
villages.[b]
12 Let us go early to the vineyards
to see if the vines have budded,
if their blossoms have opened,
and if the pomegranates are in
bloom —
there I will give you my love.
13 The mandrakes send out their
fragrance,
and at our door is every delicacy,
both new and old,
that I have stored up for you, my
beloved.

8 If only you were to me like a brother,
who was nursed at my mother's
breasts!
Then, if I found you outside,
I would kiss you,
and no one would despise me.
2 I would lead you
and bring you to my mother's
house —
she who has taught me.
I would give you spiced wine to drink,
the nectar of my pomegranates.
3 His left arm is under my head
and his right arm embraces me.
4 Daughters of Jerusalem, I charge you:
Do not arouse or awaken love
until it so desires.

Friends

5 Who is this coming up from the
wilderness
leaning on her beloved?

She

Under the apple tree I roused you;
there your mother conceived you,
there she who was in labor gave
you birth.
6 Place me like a seal over your heart,
like a seal on your arm;
for love is as strong as death,
its jealousy[c] unyielding as the
grave.
It burns like blazing fire,
like a mighty flame.[d]
7 Many waters cannot quench love;
rivers cannot sweep it away.
If one were to give
all the wealth of one's house for love,
it[e] would be utterly scorned.

Friends

8 We have a little sister,
and her breasts are not yet grown.
What shall we do for our sister
on the day she is spoken for?
9 If she is a wall,
we will build towers of silver on her.
If she is a door,
we will enclose her with panels of
cedar.

She

10 I am a wall,
and my breasts are like towers.
Thus I have become in his eyes
like one bringing contentment.
11 Solomon had a vineyard in Baal
Hamon;
he let out his vineyard to tenants.
Each was to bring for its fruit
a thousand shekels[f] of silver.
12 But my own vineyard is mine to give;
the thousand shekels are for you,
Solomon,
and two hundred[g] are for those
who tend its fruit.

He

13 You who dwell in the gardens
with friends in attendance,
let me hear your voice!

She

14 Come away, my beloved,
and be like a gazelle
or like a young stag
on the spice-laden mountains.

[a] 9 Septuagint, Aquila, Vulgate and Syriac; Hebrew *lips of sleepers* [b] 11 Or *the henna bushes* [c] 6 Or *ardor* [d] 6 Or *fire, / like the very flame of the LORD* [e] 7 Or *he* [f] 11 That is, about 25 pounds or about 12 kilograms; also in verse 12 [g] 12 That is, about 5 pounds or about 2.3 kilograms

ISAIAH

1 The vision concerning Judah and Jerusalem that Isaiah son of Amoz saw during the reigns of Uzziah, Jotham, Ahaz and Hezekiah, kings of Judah.

A Rebellious Nation

2 Hear me, you heavens! Listen, earth!
For the LORD has spoken:
"I reared children and brought them up,
but they have rebelled against me.
3 The ox knows its master,
the donkey its owner's manger,
but Israel does not know,
my people do not understand."

4 Woe to the sinful nation,
a people whose guilt is great,
a brood of evildoers,
children given to corruption!
They have forsaken the LORD;
they have spurned the Holy One of Israel
and turned their backs on him.

5 Why should you be beaten anymore?
Why do you persist in rebellion?
Your whole head is injured,
your whole heart afflicted.
6 From the sole of your foot to the top of your head
there is no soundness —
only wounds and welts
and open sores,
not cleansed or bandaged
or soothed with olive oil.

7 Your country is desolate,
your cities burned with fire;
your fields are being stripped by foreigners
right before you,
laid waste as when overthrown by strangers.
8 Daughter Zion is left
like a shelter in a vineyard,
like a hut in a cucumber field,
like a city under siege.
9 Unless the LORD Almighty
had left us some survivors,
we would have become like Sodom,
we would have been like Gomorrah.

10 Hear the word of the LORD,
you rulers of Sodom;
listen to the instruction of our God,
you people of Gomorrah!
11 "The multitude of your sacrifices —
what are they to me?" says the LORD.
"I have more than enough of burnt offerings,
of rams and the fat of fattened animals;
I have no pleasure
in the blood of bulls and lambs and goats.
12 When you come to appear before me,
who has asked this of you,
this trampling of my courts?
13 Stop bringing meaningless offerings!
Your incense is detestable to me.
New Moons, Sabbaths and convocations —
I cannot bear your worthless assemblies.
14 Your New Moon feasts and your appointed festivals
I hate with all my being.
They have become a burden to me;
I am weary of bearing them.
15 When you spread out your hands in prayer,
I hide my eyes from you;
even when you offer many prayers,
I am not listening.

Your hands are full of blood!

16 Wash and make yourselves clean.
Take your evil deeds out of my sight;
stop doing wrong.
17 Learn to do right; seek justice.
Defend the oppressed.[a]
Take up the cause of the fatherless;
plead the case of the widow.

18 "Come now, let us settle the matter,"
says the LORD.
"Though your sins are like scarlet,
they shall be as white as snow;
though they are red as crimson,
they shall be like wool.
19 If you are willing and obedient,
you will eat the good things of the land;
20 but if you resist and rebel,
you will be devoured by the sword."
For the mouth of the LORD has spoken.

[a] 17 Or *justice. / Correct the oppressor*

21 See how the faithful city
has become a prostitute!
She once was full of justice;
righteousness used to dwell in her—
but now murderers!
22 Your silver has become dross,
your choice wine is diluted with water.
23 Your rulers are rebels,
partners with thieves;
they all love bribes
and chase after gifts.
They do not defend the cause of the fatherless;
the widow's case does not come before them.
24 Therefore the Lord, the LORD Almighty,
the Mighty One of Israel, declares:
"Ah! I will vent my wrath on my foes
and avenge myself on my enemies.
25 I will turn my hand against you;[a]
I will thoroughly purge away your dross
and remove all your impurities.
26 I will restore your leaders as in days of old,
your rulers as at the beginning.
Afterward you will be called
the City of Righteousness,
the Faithful City."
27 Zion will be delivered with justice,
her penitent ones with righteousness.
28 But rebels and sinners will both be broken,
and those who forsake the LORD will perish.

29 "You will be ashamed because of the sacred oaks
in which you have delighted;
you will be disgraced because of the gardens
that you have chosen.
30 You will be like an oak with fading leaves,
like a garden without water.
31 The mighty man will become tinder
and his work a spark;
both will burn together,
with no one to quench the fire."

The Mountain of the LORD

2 This is what Isaiah son of Amoz saw concerning Judah and Jerusalem:

2 In the last days
the mountain of the LORD's temple will be established
as the highest of the mountains;
it will be exalted above the hills,
and all nations will stream to it.
3 Many peoples will come and say,
"Come, let us go up to the mountain of the LORD,
to the temple of the God of Jacob.
He will teach us his ways,
so that we may walk in his paths."
The law will go out from Zion,
the word of the LORD from Jerusalem.
4 He will judge between the nations
and will settle disputes for many peoples.
They will beat their swords into plowshares
and their spears into pruning hooks.
Nation will not take up sword against nation,
nor will they train for war anymore.
5 Come, descendants of Jacob,
let us walk in the light of the LORD.

The Day of the LORD

6 You, LORD, have abandoned your people,
the descendants of Jacob.
They are full of superstitions from the East;
they practice divination like the Philistines
and embrace pagan customs.
7 Their land is full of silver and gold;
there is no end to their treasures.
Their land is full of horses;
there is no end to their chariots.
8 Their land is full of idols;
they bow down to the work of their hands,
to what their fingers have made.
9 So people will be brought low
and everyone humbled—
do not forgive them.[b]

10 Go into the rocks, hide in the ground
from the fearful presence of the LORD
and the splendor of his majesty!
11 The eyes of the arrogant will be humbled
and human pride brought low;
the LORD alone will be exalted in that day.
12 The LORD Almighty has a day in store
for all the proud and lofty,
for all that is exalted
(and they will be humbled),
13 for all the cedars of Lebanon, tall and lofty,
and all the oaks of Bashan,
14 for all the towering mountains
and all the high hills,

[a] 25 That is, against Jerusalem [b] 9 Or *not raise them up*

15 for every lofty tower
and every fortified wall,
16 for every trading ship[a]
and every stately vessel.
17 The arrogance of man will be brought low
and human pride humbled;
the LORD alone will be exalted in that day,
18 and the idols will totally disappear.

19 People will flee to caves in the rocks
and to holes in the ground
from the fearful presence of the LORD
and the splendor of his majesty,
when he rises to shake the earth.
20 In that day people will throw away
to the moles and bats
their idols of silver and idols of gold,
which they made to worship.
21 They will flee to caverns in the rocks
and to the overhanging crags
from the fearful presence of the LORD
and the splendor of his majesty,
when he rises to shake the earth.

22 Stop trusting in mere humans,
who have but a breath in their nostrils.
Why hold them in esteem?

Judgment on Jerusalem and Judah

3 See now, the Lord,
the LORD Almighty,
is about to take from Jerusalem and Judah
both supply and support:
all supplies of food and all supplies of water,
2 the hero and the warrior,
the judge and the prophet,
the diviner and the elder,
3 the captain of fifty and the man of rank,
the counselor, skilled craftsman
and clever enchanter.

4 "I will make mere youths their officials;
children will rule over them."

5 People will oppress each other —
man against man, neighbor against neighbor.
The young will rise up against the old,
the nobody against the honored.

6 A man will seize one of his brothers
in his father's house, and say,
"You have a cloak, you be our leader;
take charge of this heap of ruins!"
7 But in that day he will cry out,
"I have no remedy.
I have no food or clothing in my house;
do not make me the leader of the people."

8 Jerusalem staggers,
Judah is falling;
their words and deeds are against the LORD,
defying his glorious presence.
9 The look on their faces testifies against them;
they parade their sin like Sodom;
they do not hide it.
Woe to them!
They have brought disaster upon themselves.

10 Tell the righteous it will be well with them,
for they will enjoy the fruit of their deeds.
11 Woe to the wicked!
Disaster is upon them!
They will be paid back
for what their hands have done.

12 Youths oppress my people,
women rule over them.
My people, your guides lead you astray;
they turn you from the path.

13 The LORD takes his place in court;
he rises to judge the people.
14 The LORD enters into judgment
against the elders and leaders of his people:
"It is you who have ruined my vineyard;
the plunder from the poor is in your houses.
15 What do you mean by crushing my people
and grinding the faces of the poor?"
declares the Lord,
the LORD Almighty.

16 The LORD says,
"The women of Zion are haughty,
walking along with outstretched necks,
flirting with their eyes,
strutting along with swaying hips,
with ornaments jingling on their ankles.
17 Therefore the Lord will bring sores on the heads of the women of Zion;
the LORD will make their scalps bald."

[a] 16 Hebrew *every ship of Tarshish*

18 In that day the Lord will snatch away
their finery: the bangles and headbands
and crescent necklaces, 19 the earrings and
bracelets and veils, 20 the headdresses and
anklets and sashes, the perfume bottles
and charms, 21 the signet rings and nose
rings, 22 the fine robes and the capes and
cloaks, the purses 23 and mirrors, and the
linen garments and tiaras and shawls.

24 Instead of fragrance there will be a
stench;
instead of a sash, a rope;
instead of well-dressed hair, baldness;
instead of fine clothing, sackcloth;
instead of beauty, branding.
25 Your men will fall by the sword,
your warriors in battle.
26 The gates of Zion will lament and
mourn;
destitute, she will sit on the ground.

4 1 In that day seven women
will take hold of one man
and say, "We will eat our own food
and provide our own clothes;
only let us be called by your name.
Take away our disgrace!"

The Branch of the LORD

2 In that day the Branch of the LORD will
be beautiful and glorious, and the fruit
of the land will be the pride and glory of
the survivors in Israel. 3 Those who are left
in Zion, who remain in Jerusalem, will be
called holy, all who are recorded among
the living in Jerusalem. 4 The Lord will wash
away the filth of the women of Zion; he will
cleanse the bloodstains from Jerusalem by
a spirit[a] of judgment and a spirit[a] of fire.
5 Then the LORD will create over all of Mount
Zion and over those who assemble there a
cloud of smoke by day and a glow of flaming fire by night; over everything the glory[b]
will be a canopy. 6 It will be a shelter and
shade from the heat of the day, and a refuge
and hiding place from the storm and rain.

The Song of the Vineyard

5 I will sing for the one I love
a song about his vineyard:
My loved one had a vineyard
on a fertile hillside.
2 He dug it up and cleared it of stones
and planted it with the choicest
vines.
He built a watchtower in it
and cut out a winepress as well.
Then he looked for a crop of good
grapes,
but it yielded only bad fruit.

3 "Now you dwellers in Jerusalem and
people of Judah,
judge between me and my
vineyard.
4 What more could have been done for
my vineyard
than I have done for it?
When I looked for good grapes,
why did it yield only bad?
5 Now I will tell you
what I am going to do to my
vineyard:
I will take away its hedge,
and it will be destroyed;
I will break down its wall,
and it will be trampled.
6 I will make it a wasteland,
neither pruned nor cultivated,
and briers and thorns will grow
there.
I will command the clouds
not to rain on it."

7 The vineyard of the LORD Almighty
is the nation of Israel,
and the people of Judah
are the vines he delighted in.
And he looked for justice, but saw
bloodshed;
for righteousness, but heard cries
of distress.

Woes and Judgments

8 Woe to you who add house to house
and join field to field
till no space is left
and you live alone in the land.

9 The LORD Almighty has declared in
my hearing:

"Surely the great houses will become
desolate,
the fine mansions left without
occupants.
10 A ten-acre vineyard will produce only
a bath[c] of wine;
a homer[d] of seed will yield only an
ephah[e] of grain."

11 Woe to those who rise early in the
morning
to run after their drinks,
who stay up late at night
till they are inflamed with wine.
12 They have harps and lyres at their
banquets,
pipes and timbrels and wine,
but they have no regard for the deeds
of the LORD,
no respect for the work of his hands.

[a] 4 Or *the Spirit* [b] 5 Or *over all the glory there* [c] 10 That is, about 6 gallons or about 22 liters
[d] 10 That is, probably about 360 pounds or about 160 kilograms [e] 10 That is, probably about
36 pounds or about 16 kilograms

13 Therefore my people will go into exile
for lack of understanding;
those of high rank will die of hunger
and the common people will be
parched with thirst.
14 Therefore Death expands its jaws,
opening wide its mouth;
into it will descend their nobles and
masses
with all their brawlers
and revelers.
15 So people will be brought low
and everyone humbled,
the eyes of the arrogant humbled.
16 But the LORD Almighty will be exalted
by his justice,
and the holy God will be proved
holy by his righteous acts.
17 Then sheep will graze as in their own
pasture;
lambs will feed[a] among the ruins
of the rich.

18 Woe to those who draw sin along
with cords of deceit,
and wickedness as with cart ropes,
19 to those who say, "Let God hurry;
let him hasten his work
so we may see it.
The plan of the Holy One of Israel —
let it approach, let it come into
view,
so we may know it."

20 Woe to those who call evil good
and good evil,
who put darkness for light
and light for darkness,
who put bitter for sweet
and sweet for bitter.

21 Woe to those who are wise in their
own eyes
and clever in their own sight.

22 Woe to those who are heroes at
drinking wine
and champions at mixing drinks,
23 who acquit the guilty for a bribe,
but deny justice to the innocent.
24 Therefore, as tongues of fire lick up
straw
and as dry grass sinks down in the
flames,
so their roots will decay
and their flowers blow away like
dust;
for they have rejected the law of the
LORD Almighty
and spurned the word of the Holy
One of Israel.

25 Therefore the LORD's anger burns
against his people;
his hand is raised and he strikes
them down.
The mountains shake,
and the dead bodies are like refuse
in the streets.

Yet for all this, his anger is not turned
away,
his hand is still upraised.

26 He lifts up a banner for the distant
nations,
he whistles for those at the ends of
the earth.
Here they come,
swiftly and speedily!
27 Not one of them grows tired or
stumbles,
not one slumbers or sleeps;
not a belt is loosened at the waist,
not a sandal strap is broken.
28 Their arrows are sharp,
all their bows are strung;
their horses' hooves seem like flint,
their chariot wheels like a
whirlwind.
29 Their roar is like that of the lion,
they roar like young lions;
they growl as they seize their prey
and carry it off with no one to
rescue.
30 In that day they will roar over it
like the roaring of the sea.
And if one looks at the land,
there is only darkness and distress;
even the sun will be darkened by
clouds.

Isaiah's Commission

6 In the year that King Uzziah died, I saw
the Lord, high and exalted, seated on
a throne; and the train of his robe filled
the temple. 2 Above him were seraphim,
each with six wings: With two wings they
covered their faces, with two they covered
their feet, and with two they were flying.
3 And they were calling to one another:

"Holy, holy, holy is the LORD
Almighty;
the whole earth is full of his glory."

4 At the sound of their voices the doorposts
and thresholds shook and the temple was
filled with smoke.
5 "Woe to me!" I cried. "I am ruined!
For I am a man of unclean lips, and I
live among a people of unclean lips, and
my eyes have seen the King, the LORD
Almighty."

[a] 17 Septuagint; Hebrew / *strangers will eat*

6Then one of the seraphim flew to me
with a live coal in his hand, which he had
taken with tongs from the altar. 7With it
he touched my mouth and said, "See, this
has touched your lips; your guilt is taken
away and your sin atoned for."
8Then I heard the voice of the Lord saying, "Whom shall I send? And who will
go for us?"
And I said, "Here am I. Send me!"
9He said, "Go and tell this people:

"'Be ever hearing, but never
understanding;
be ever seeing, but never
perceiving.'
10 Make the heart of this people
calloused;
make their ears dull
and close their eyes.[a]
Otherwise they might see with their
eyes,
hear with their ears,
understand with their hearts,
and turn and be healed."

11Then I said, "For how long, Lord?"
And he answered:

"Until the cities lie ruined
and without inhabitant,
until the houses are left deserted
and the fields ruined and ravaged,
12 until the LORD has sent everyone far
away
and the land is utterly forsaken.
13 And though a tenth remains in the
land,
it will again be laid waste.
But as the terebinth and oak
leave stumps when they are cut
down,
so the holy seed will be the stump
in the land."

The Sign of Immanuel

7 When Ahaz son of Jotham, the son of
Uzziah, was king of Judah, King Rezin
of Aram and Pekah son of Remaliah king
of Israel marched up to fight against Jerusalem, but they could not overpower it.
2Now the house of David was told,
"Aram has allied itself with[b] Ephraim";
so the hearts of Ahaz and his people were
shaken, as the trees of the forest are shak-
en by the wind.
3Then the LORD said to Isaiah, "Go out,
you and your son Shear-Jashub,[c] to meet
Ahaz at the end of the aqueduct of the
Upper Pool, on the road to the Launderer's
Field. 4Say to him, 'Be careful, keep calm
and don't be afraid. Do not lose heart
because of these two smoldering stubs of
firewood — because of the fierce anger of
Rezin and Aram and of the son of Remaliah. 5Aram, Ephraim and Remaliah's
son have plotted your ruin, saying, 6"Let
us invade Judah; let us tear it apart and
divide it among ourselves, and make the
son of Tabeel king over it." 7Yet this is what
the Sovereign LORD says:

"'It will not take place,
it will not happen,
8 for the head of Aram is Damascus,
and the head of Damascus is only
Rezin.
Within sixty-five years
Ephraim will be too shattered to
be a people.
9 The head of Ephraim is Samaria,
and the head of Samaria is only
Remaliah's son.
If you do not stand firm in your faith,
you will not stand at all.'"

10Again the LORD spoke to Ahaz, 11"Ask
the LORD your God for a sign, whether in the
deepest depths or in the highest heights."
12But Ahaz said, "I will not ask; I will
not put the LORD to the test."
13Then Isaiah said, "Hear now, you
house of David! Is it not enough to try
the patience of humans? Will you try the
patience of my God also? 14Therefore the
Lord himself will give you[d] a sign: The virgin[e] will conceive and give birth to a son,
and[f] will call him Immanuel.[g] 15He will be
eating curds and honey when he knows
enough to reject the wrong and choose the
right, 16for before the boy knows enough to
reject the wrong and choose the right, the
land of the two kings you dread will be laid
waste. 17The LORD will bring on you and
on your people and on the house of your
father a time unlike any since Ephraim
broke away from Judah — he will bring
the king of Assyria."

Assyria, the LORD's Instrument

18In that day the LORD will whistle for
flies from the Nile delta in Egypt and for
bees from the land of Assyria. 19They will
all come and settle in the steep ravines
and in the crevices in the rocks, on all the

[a] 9,10 Hebrew; Septuagint *'You will be ever hearing, but never understanding; / you will be ever seeing, but never perceiving.' / 10This people's heart has become calloused; / they hardly hear with their ears, / and they have closed their eyes* [b] 2 Or *has set up camp in* [c] 3 *Shear-Jashub* means *a remnant will return.* [d] 14 The Hebrew is plural. [e] 14 Or *young woman* [f] 14 Masoretic Text; Dead Sea Scrolls *son, and he* or *son, and they* [g] 14 *Immanuel* means *God with us.*

thornbushes and at all the water holes.
20 In that day the Lord will use a razor
hired from beyond the Euphrates River — the king of Assyria — to shave your
head and private parts, and to cut off your
beard also. 21 In that day, a person will
keep alive a young cow and two goats.
22 And because of the abundance of the
milk they give, there will be curds to eat.
All who remain in the land will eat curds
and honey. 23 In that day, in every place
where there were a thousand vines worth
a thousand silver shekels,[a] there will be
only briers and thorns. 24 Hunters will go
there with bow and arrow, for the land
will be covered with briers and thorns.
25 As for all the hills once cultivated by the
hoe, you will no longer go there for fear
of the briers and thorns; they will become
places where cattle are turned loose and
where sheep run.

Isaiah and His Children as Signs

8 The LORD said to me, "Take a large
scroll and write on it with an ordinary pen: Maher-Shalal-Hash-Baz."[b] 2 So
I called in Uriah the priest and Zechariah
son of Jeberekiah as reliable witnesses
for me. 3 Then I made love to the proph-
etess, and she conceived and gave birth
to a son. And the LORD said to me, "Name
him Maher-Shalal-Hash-Baz. 4 For before
the boy knows how to say 'My father' or
'My mother,' the wealth of Damascus and
the plunder of Samaria will be carried off
by the king of Assyria."
5 The LORD spoke to me again:

6 "Because this people has rejected
the gently flowing waters of
Shiloah
and rejoices over Rezin
and the son of Remaliah,
7 therefore the Lord is about to bring
against them
the mighty floodwaters of the
Euphrates —
the king of Assyria with all his
pomp.
It will overflow all its channels,
run over all its banks
8 and sweep on into Judah, swirling
over it,
passing through it and reaching up
to the neck.
Its outspread wings will cover the
breadth of your land,
Immanuel[c]!"

9 Raise the war cry,[d] you nations, and
be shattered!
Listen, all you distant lands.
Prepare for battle, and be shattered!
Prepare for battle, and be
shattered!
10 Devise your strategy, but it will be
thwarted;
propose your plan, but it will not
stand,
for God is with us.[e]

11 This is what the LORD says to me with
his strong hand upon me, warning me not
to follow the way of this people:

12 "Do not call conspiracy
everything this people calls a
conspiracy;
do not fear what they fear,
and do not dread it.
13 The LORD Almighty is the one you are
to regard as holy,
he is the one you are to fear,
he is the one you are to dread.
14 He will be a holy place;
for both Israel and Judah he will be
a stone that causes people to stumble
and a rock that makes them fall.
And for the people of Jerusalem he
will be
a trap and a snare.
15 Many of them will stumble;
they will fall and be broken,
they will be snared and captured."

16 Bind up this testimony of warning
and seal up God's instruction
among my disciples.
17 I will wait for the LORD,
who is hiding his face from the
descendants of Jacob.
I will put my trust in him.

18 Here am I, and the children the LORD
has given me. We are signs and symbols
in Israel from the LORD Almighty, who
dwells on Mount Zion.

The Darkness Turns to Light

19 When someone tells you to consult
mediums and spiritists, who whisper and
mutter, should not a people inquire of
their God? Why consult the dead on behalf
of the living? 20 Consult God's instruction
and the testimony of warning. If anyone
does not speak according to this word,
they have no light of dawn. 21 Distressed
and hungry, they will roam through the
land; when they are famished, they will

[a] *23* That is, about 25 pounds or about 12 kilograms [b] *1* *Maher-Shalal-Hash-Baz* means *quick to the plunder, swift to the spoil*; also in verse 3. [c] *8* *Immanuel* means *God with us.* [d] *9* Or *Do your worst* [e] *10* Hebrew *Immanuel*

become enraged and, looking upward, will
curse their king and their God. 22 Then they
will look toward the earth and see only
distress and darkness and fearful gloom,
and they will be thrust into utter darkness.

9[a] Nevertheless, there will be no more
gloom for those who were in distress. In the past he humbled the land
of Zebulun and the land of Naphtali, but
in the future he will honor Galilee of the
nations, by the Way of the Sea, beyond
the Jordan —

2 The people walking in darkness
have seen a great light;
on those living in the land of deep darkness
a light has dawned.
3 You have enlarged the nation
and increased their joy;
they rejoice before you
as people rejoice at the harvest,
as warriors rejoice
when dividing the plunder.
4 For as in the day of Midian's defeat,
you have shattered
the yoke that burdens them,
the bar across their shoulders,
the rod of their oppressor.
5 Every warrior's boot used in battle
and every garment rolled in blood
will be destined for burning,
will be fuel for the fire.
6 For to us a child is born,
to us a son is given,
and the government will be on his shoulders.
And he will be called
Wonderful Counselor, Mighty God,
Everlasting Father, Prince of Peace.
7 Of the greatness of his government
and peace
there will be no end.
He will reign on David's throne
and over his kingdom,
establishing and upholding it
with justice and righteousness
from that time on and forever.
The zeal of the LORD Almighty
will accomplish this.

The LORD's Anger Against Israel

8 The Lord has sent a message against
Jacob;
it will fall on Israel.
9 All the people will know it —
Ephraim and the inhabitants of
Samaria —
who say with pride
and arrogance of heart,
10 "The bricks have fallen down,
but we will rebuild with dressed stone;
the fig trees have been felled,
but we will replace them with cedars."
11 But the LORD has strengthened
Rezin's foes against them
and has spurred their enemies on.
12 Arameans from the east and
Philistines from the west
have devoured Israel with open mouth.

Yet for all this, his anger is not turned away,
his hand is still upraised.

13 But the people have not returned to
him who struck them,
nor have they sought the LORD
Almighty.
14 So the LORD will cut off from Israel
both head and tail,
both palm branch and reed in a single day;
15 the elders and dignitaries are the head,
the prophets who teach lies are the tail.
16 Those who guide this people mislead them,
and those who are guided are led astray.
17 Therefore the Lord will take no
pleasure in the young men,
nor will he pity the fatherless and widows,
for everyone is ungodly and wicked,
every mouth speaks folly.

Yet for all this, his anger is not turned away,
his hand is still upraised.

18 Surely wickedness burns like a fire;
it consumes briers and thorns,
it sets the forest thickets ablaze,
so that it rolls upward in a column
of smoke.
19 By the wrath of the LORD Almighty
the land will be scorched
and the people will be fuel for the fire;
they will not spare one another.
20 On the right they will devour,
but still be hungry;
on the left they will eat,
but not be satisfied.
Each will feed on the flesh of their
own offspring[b]:

[a] In Hebrew texts 9:1 is numbered 8:23, and 9:2-21 is numbered 9:1-20. [b] *20* Or *arm*

21 Manasseh will feed on Ephraim,
and Ephraim on Manasseh;
together they will turn against
Judah.

Yet for all this, his anger is not turned
away,
his hand is still upraised.

10 Woe to those who make unjust
laws,
to those who issue oppressive
decrees,
2 to deprive the poor of their rights
and withhold justice from the
oppressed of my people,
making widows their prey
and robbing the fatherless.
3 What will you do on the day of
reckoning,
when disaster comes from afar?
To whom will you run for help?
Where will you leave your riches?
4 Nothing will remain but to cringe
among the captives
or fall among the slain.

Yet for all this, his anger is not turned
away,
his hand is still upraised.

God's Judgment on Assyria

5 "Woe to the Assyrian, the rod of my
anger,
in whose hand is the club of my
wrath!
6 I send him against a godless nation,
I dispatch him against a people
who anger me,
to seize loot and snatch plunder,
and to trample them down like
mud in the streets.
7 But this is not what he intends,
this is not what he has in mind;
his purpose is to destroy,
to put an end to many nations.
8 'Are not my commanders all kings?'
he says.
9 'Has not Kalno fared like
Carchemish?
Is not Hamath like Arpad,
and Samaria like Damascus?
10 As my hand seized the kingdoms of
the idols,
kingdoms whose images excelled
those of Jerusalem and
Samaria—
11 shall I not deal with Jerusalem and
her images
as I dealt with Samaria and her
idols?'"

12 When the Lord has finished all his
work against Mount Zion and Jerusalem,
he will say, "I will punish the king of Assyria for the willful pride of his heart and
the haughty look in his eyes. 13 For he says:

"'By the strength of my hand I have
done this,
and by my wisdom, because I have
understanding.
I removed the boundaries of nations,
I plundered their treasures;
like a mighty one I subdued[a] their
kings.
14 As one reaches into a nest,
so my hand reached for the wealth
of the nations;
as people gather abandoned eggs,
so I gathered all the countries;
not one flapped a wing,
or opened its mouth to chirp.'"

15 Does the ax raise itself above the
person who swings it,
or the saw boast against the one
who uses it?
As if a rod were to wield the person
who lifts it up,
or a club brandish the one who is
not wood!
16 Therefore, the Lord, the LORD
Almighty,
will send a wasting disease upon
his sturdy warriors;
under his pomp a fire will be kindled
like a blazing flame.
17 The Light of Israel will become a fire,
their Holy One a flame;
in a single day it will burn and
consume
his thorns and his briers.
18 The splendor of his forests and fertile
fields
it will completely destroy,
as when a sick person wastes away.
19 And the remaining trees of his forests
will be so few
that a child could write them down.

The Remnant of Israel

20 In that day the remnant of Israel,
the survivors of Jacob,
will no longer rely on him
who struck them down
but will truly rely on the LORD,
the Holy One of Israel.
21 A remnant will return,[b] a remnant of
Jacob
will return to the Mighty God.

[a] 13 Or *treasures; / I subdued the mighty,* [b] 21 Hebrew *shear-jashub* (see 7:3 and note); also in verse 22

22 Though your people be like the sand
by the sea, Israel,
only a remnant will return.
Destruction has been decreed,
overwhelming and righteous.
23 The Lord, the LORD Almighty, will
carry out
the destruction decreed upon the
whole land.

24 Therefore this is what the Lord, the
LORD Almighty, says:

"My people who live in Zion,
do not be afraid of the Assyrians,
who beat you with a rod
and lift up a club against you, as
Egypt did.
25 Very soon my anger against you will
end
and my wrath will be directed to
their destruction."

26 The LORD Almighty will lash them
with a whip,
as when he struck down Midian at
the rock of Oreb;
and he will raise his staff over the
waters,
as he did in Egypt.
27 In that day their burden will be lifted
from your shoulders,
their yoke from your neck;
the yoke will be broken
because you have grown so fat.[a]

28 They enter Aiath;
they pass through Migron;
they store supplies at Mikmash.
29 They go over the pass, and say,
"We will camp overnight at Geba."
Ramah trembles;
Gibeah of Saul flees.
30 Cry out, Daughter Gallim!
Listen, Laishah!
Poor Anathoth!
31 Madmenah is in flight;
the people of Gebim take cover.
32 This day they will halt at Nob;
they will shake their fist
at the mount of Daughter Zion,
at the hill of Jerusalem.

33 See, the Lord, the LORD Almighty,
will lop off the boughs with great
power.
The lofty trees will be felled,
the tall ones will be brought low.
34 He will cut down the forest thickets
with an ax;
Lebanon will fall before the Mighty
One.

The Branch From Jesse

11 A shoot will come up from the
stump of Jesse;
from his roots a Branch will bear
fruit.
2 The Spirit of the LORD will rest on him —
the Spirit of wisdom and of
understanding,
the Spirit of counsel and of might,
the Spirit of the knowledge and
fear of the LORD —
3 and he will delight in the fear of the
LORD.

He will not judge by what he sees with
his eyes,
or decide by what he hears with his
ears;
4 but with righteousness he will judge
the needy,
with justice he will give decisions
for the poor of the earth.
He will strike the earth with the rod of
his mouth;
with the breath of his lips he will
slay the wicked.
5 Righteousness will be his belt
and faithfulness the sash around
his waist.

6 The wolf will live with the lamb,
the leopard will lie down with the
goat,
the calf and the lion and the
yearling[b] together;
and a little child will lead them.
7 The cow will feed with the bear,
their young will lie down together,
and the lion will eat straw like the
ox.
8 The infant will play near the cobra's
den,
and the young child will put its
hand into the viper's nest.
9 They will neither harm nor destroy
on all my holy mountain,
for the earth will be filled with the
knowledge of the LORD
as the waters cover the sea.

10 In that day the Root of Jesse will stand
as a banner for the peoples; the nations
will rally to him, and his resting place
will be glorious. 11 In that day the Lord
will reach out his hand a second time to
reclaim the surviving remnant of his people from Assyria, from Lower Egypt, from
Upper Egypt, from Cush,[c] from Elam, from
Babylonia,[d] from Hamath and from the
islands of the Mediterranean.

[a] 27 Hebrew; Septuagint *broken / from your shoulders* [b] 6 Hebrew; Septuagint *lion will feed*
[c] 11 That is, the upper Nile region [d] 11 Hebrew *Shinar*

12 He will raise a banner for the nations
and gather the exiles of Israel;
he will assemble the scattered people of Judah
from the four quarters of the earth.
13 Ephraim's jealousy will vanish,
and Judah's enemies[a] will be destroyed;
Ephraim will not be jealous of Judah,
nor Judah hostile toward Ephraim.
14 They will swoop down on the slopes of Philistia to the west;
together they will plunder the people to the east.
They will subdue Edom and Moab,
and the Ammonites will be subject to them.
15 The LORD will dry up
the gulf of the Egyptian sea;
with a scorching wind he will sweep his hand
over the Euphrates River.
He will break it up into seven streams
so that anyone can cross over in sandals.
16 There will be a highway for the remnant of his people
that is left from Assyria,
as there was for Israel
when they came up from Egypt.

Songs of Praise

12 In that day you will say:

"I will praise you, LORD.
Although you were angry with me,
your anger has turned away
and you have comforted me.
2 Surely God is my salvation;
I will trust and not be afraid.
The LORD, the LORD himself, is my strength and my defense[b];
he has become my salvation."
3 With joy you will draw water
from the wells of salvation.

4 In that day you will say:

"Give praise to the LORD, proclaim his name;
make known among the nations what he has done,
and proclaim that his name is exalted.
5 Sing to the LORD, for he has done glorious things;
let this be known to all the world.
6 Shout aloud and sing for joy, people of Zion,
for great is the Holy One of Israel among you."

A Prophecy Against Babylon

13 A prophecy against Babylon that Isaiah son of Amoz saw:

2 Raise a banner on a bare hilltop,
shout to them;
beckon to them
to enter the gates of the nobles.
3 I have commanded those I prepared for battle;
I have summoned my warriors to carry out my wrath —
those who rejoice in my triumph.

4 Listen, a noise on the mountains,
like that of a great multitude!
Listen, an uproar among the kingdoms,
like nations massing together!
The LORD Almighty is mustering
an army for war.
5 They come from faraway lands,
from the ends of the heavens —
the LORD and the weapons of his wrath —
to destroy the whole country.

6 Wail, for the day of the LORD is near;
it will come like destruction from the Almighty.[c]
7 Because of this, all hands will go limp,
every heart will melt with fear.
8 Terror will seize them,
pain and anguish will grip them;
they will writhe like a woman in labor.
They will look aghast at each other,
their faces aflame.

9 See, the day of the LORD is coming
— a cruel day, with wrath and fierce anger —
to make the land desolate
and destroy the sinners within it.
10 The stars of heaven and their constellations
will not show their light.
The rising sun will be darkened
and the moon will not give its light.
11 I will punish the world for its evil,
the wicked for their sins.
I will put an end to the arrogance of the haughty
and will humble the pride of the ruthless.
12 I will make people scarcer than pure gold,
more rare than the gold of Ophir.
13 Therefore I will make the heavens tremble;
and the earth will shake from its place
at the wrath of the LORD Almighty,
in the day of his burning anger.

[a] 13 Or *hostility* [b] 2 Or *song* [c] 6 Hebrew *Shaddai*

14 Like a hunted gazelle,
like sheep without a shepherd,
they will all return to their own people,
they will flee to their native land.
15 Whoever is captured will be thrust through;
all who are caught will fall by the sword.
16 Their infants will be dashed to pieces before their eyes;
their houses will be looted and their wives violated.

17 See, I will stir up against them the Medes,
who do not care for silver
and have no delight in gold.
18 Their bows will strike down the young men;
they will have no mercy on infants,
nor will they look with compassion on children.
19 Babylon, the jewel of kingdoms,
the pride and glory of the Babylonians,[a]
will be overthrown by God
like Sodom and Gomorrah.
20 She will never be inhabited
or lived in through all generations;
there no nomads will pitch their tents,
there no shepherds will rest their flocks.
21 But desert creatures will lie there,
jackals will fill her houses;
there the owls will dwell,
and there the wild goats will leap about.
22 Hyenas will inhabit her strongholds,
jackals her luxurious palaces.
Her time is at hand,
and her days will not be prolonged.

14 The LORD will have compassion on Jacob;
once again he will choose Israel
and will settle them in their own land.
Foreigners will join them
and unite with the descendants of Jacob.
2 Nations will take them
and bring them to their own place.
And Israel will take possession of the nations
and make them male and female servants in the LORD's land.
They will make captives of their captors
and rule over their oppressors.

3 On the day the LORD gives you relief
from your suffering and turmoil and from
the harsh labor forced on you, 4 you will
take up this taunt against the king of
Babylon:

How the oppressor has come to an end!
How his fury[b] has ended!
5 The LORD has broken the rod of the wicked,
the scepter of the rulers,
6 which in anger struck down peoples
with unceasing blows,
and in fury subdued nations
with relentless aggression.
7 All the lands are at rest and at peace;
they break into singing.
8 Even the junipers and the cedars of Lebanon
gloat over you and say,
"Now that you have been laid low,
no one comes to cut us down."
9 The realm of the dead below is all astir
to meet you at your coming;
it rouses the spirits of the departed to greet you —
all those who were leaders in the world;
it makes them rise from their thrones —
all those who were kings over the nations.
10 They will all respond,
they will say to you,
"You also have become weak, as we are;
you have become like us."
11 All your pomp has been brought down to the grave,
along with the noise of your harps;
maggots are spread out beneath you
and worms cover you.
12 How you have fallen from heaven,
morning star, son of the dawn!
You have been cast down to the earth,
you who once laid low the nations!
13 You said in your heart,
"I will ascend to the heavens;
I will raise my throne
above the stars of God;
I will sit enthroned on the mount of assembly,
on the utmost heights of Mount Zaphon.[c]
14 I will ascend above the tops of the clouds;
I will make myself like the Most High."

[a] 19 Or *Chaldeans* [b] 4 Dead Sea Scrolls, Septuagint and Syriac; the meaning of the word in the Masoretic Text is uncertain. [c] 13 Or *of the north*; Zaphon was the most sacred mountain of the Canaanites.

15 But you are brought down to the realm of the dead,
to the depths of the pit.

16 Those who see you stare at you,
they ponder your fate:
"Is this the man who shook the earth
and made kingdoms tremble,
17 the man who made the world a wilderness,
who overthrew its cities
and would not let his captives go home?"

18 All the kings of the nations lie in state,
each in his own tomb.
19 But you are cast out of your tomb
like a rejected branch;
you are covered with the slain,
with those pierced by the sword,
those who descend to the stones of the pit.
Like a corpse trampled underfoot,
20 you will not join them in burial,
for you have destroyed your land
and killed your people.

Let the offspring of the wicked
never be mentioned again.
21 Prepare a place to slaughter his children
for the sins of their ancestors;
they are not to rise to inherit the land
and cover the earth with their cities.

22 "I will rise up against them,"
declares the LORD Almighty.
"I will wipe out Babylon's name and survivors,
her offspring and descendants,"
declares the LORD.
23 "I will turn her into a place for owls
and into swampland;
I will sweep her with the broom of destruction,"
declares the LORD Almighty.

24 The LORD Almighty has sworn,

"Surely, as I have planned, so it will be,
and as I have purposed, so it will happen.
25 I will crush the Assyrian in my land;
on my mountains I will trample him down.
His yoke will be taken from my people,
and his burden removed from their shoulders."

26 This is the plan determined for the whole world;
this is the hand stretched out over all nations.
27 For the LORD Almighty has purposed,
and who can thwart him?
His hand is stretched out, and who can turn it back?

A Prophecy Against the Philistines

28 This prophecy came in the year King Ahaz died:

29 Do not rejoice, all you Philistines,
that the rod that struck you is broken;
from the root of that snake will spring up a viper,
its fruit will be a darting, venomous serpent.
30 The poorest of the poor will find pasture,
and the needy will lie down in safety.
But your root I will destroy by famine;
it will slay your survivors.

31 Wail, you gate! Howl, you city!
Melt away, all you Philistines!
A cloud of smoke comes from the north,
and there is not a straggler in its ranks.
32 What answer shall be given
to the envoys of that nation?
"The LORD has established Zion,
and in her his afflicted people will find refuge."

A Prophecy Against Moab

15 A prophecy against Moab:

Ar in Moab is ruined,
destroyed in a night!
Kir in Moab is ruined,
destroyed in a night!
2 Dibon goes up to its temple,
to its high places to weep;
Moab wails over Nebo and Medeba.
Every head is shaved
and every beard cut off.
3 In the streets they wear sackcloth;
on the roofs and in the public squares
they all wail,
prostrate with weeping.
4 Heshbon and Elealeh cry out,
their voices are heard all the way to Jahaz.
Therefore the armed men of Moab cry out,
and their hearts are faint.

[5] My heart cries out over Moab;
her fugitives flee as far as Zoar,
as far as Eglath Shelishiyah.
They go up the hill to Luhith,
weeping as they go;
on the road to Horonaim
they lament their destruction.
[6] The waters of Nimrim are dried up
and the grass is withered;
the vegetation is gone
and nothing green is left.
[7] So the wealth they have acquired and stored up
they carry away over the Ravine of the Poplars.
[8] Their outcry echoes along the border of Moab;
their wailing reaches as far as Eglaim,
their lamentation as far as Beer Elim.
[9] The waters of Dimon[a] are full of blood,
but I will bring still more upon Dimon[a] —
a lion upon the fugitives of Moab
and upon those who remain in the land.

16 Send lambs as tribute
to the ruler of the land,
from Sela, across the desert,
to the mount of Daughter Zion.
[2] Like fluttering birds
pushed from the nest,
so are the women of Moab
at the fords of the Arnon.

[3] "Make up your mind," Moab says.
"Render a decision.
Make your shadow like night —
at high noon.
Hide the fugitives,
do not betray the refugees.
[4] Let the Moabite fugitives stay with you;
be their shelter from the destroyer."

The oppressor will come to an end,
and destruction will cease;
the aggressor will vanish from the land.
[5] In love a throne will be established;
in faithfulness a man will sit on it —
one from the house[b] of David —
one who in judging seeks justice
and speeds the cause of righteousness.

[6] We have heard of Moab's pride —
how great is her arrogance! —
of her conceit, her pride and her insolence;
but her boasts are empty.
[7] Therefore the Moabites wail,
they wail together for Moab.
Lament and grieve
for the raisin cakes of Kir Hareseth.
[8] The fields of Heshbon wither,
the vines of Sibmah also.
The rulers of the nations
have trampled down the choicest vines,
which once reached Jazer
and spread toward the desert.
Their shoots spread out
and went as far as the sea.[c]
[9] So I weep, as Jazer weeps,
for the vines of Sibmah.
Heshbon and Elealeh,
I drench you with tears!
The shouts of joy over your ripened fruit
and over your harvests have been stilled.
[10] Joy and gladness are taken away
from the orchards;
no one sings or shouts in the vineyards;
no one treads out wine at the presses,
for I have put an end to the shouting.
[11] My heart laments for Moab like a harp,
my inmost being for Kir Hareseth.
[12] When Moab appears at her high place,
she only wears herself out;
when she goes to her shrine to pray,
it is to no avail.

[13] This is the word the LORD has already spoken concerning Moab. [14] But now the LORD says: "Within three years, as a servant bound by contract would count them, Moab's splendor and all her many people will be despised, and her survivors will be very few and feeble."

A Prophecy Against Damascus

17 A prophecy against Damascus:

"See, Damascus will no longer be a city
but will become a heap of ruins.
[2] The cities of Aroer will be deserted
and left to flocks, which will lie down,
with no one to make them afraid.

[a] 9 *Dimon*, a wordplay on *Dibon* (see verse 2), sounds like the Hebrew for *blood*. [b] 5 Hebrew *tent* [c] 8 Probably the Dead Sea

3 The fortified city will disappear from
Ephraim,
and royal power from Damascus;
the remnant of Aram will be
like the glory of the Israelites,"
declares the LORD Almighty.

4 "In that day the glory of Jacob will
fade;
the fat of his body will waste away.
5 It will be as when reapers harvest the
standing grain,
gathering the grain in their arms —
as when someone gleans heads of
grain
in the Valley of Rephaim.
6 Yet some gleanings will remain,
as when an olive tree is beaten,
leaving two or three olives on the
topmost branches,
four or five on the fruitful boughs,"
declares the LORD, the God
of Israel.

7 In that day people will look to their
Maker
and turn their eyes to the Holy One
of Israel.
8 They will not look to the altars,
the work of their hands,
and they will have no regard for the
Asherah poles[a]
and the incense altars their fingers
have made.

9 In that day their strong cities, which
they left because of the Israelites, will be
like places abandoned to thickets and
undergrowth. And all will be desolation.

10 You have forgotten God your Savior;
you have not remembered the
Rock, your fortress.
Therefore, though you set out the
finest plants
and plant imported vines,
11 though on the day you set them out,
you make them grow,
and on the morning when you plant
them, you bring them to bud,
yet the harvest will be as nothing
in the day of disease and incurable
pain.

12 Woe to the many nations that rage —
they rage like the raging sea!
Woe to the peoples who roar —
they roar like the roaring of great
waters!
13 Although the peoples roar like the
roar of surging waters,
when he rebukes them they flee far
away,
driven before the wind like chaff on
the hills,
like tumbleweed before a gale.
14 In the evening, sudden terror!
Before the morning, they are gone!
This is the portion of those who loot us,
the lot of those who plunder us.

A Prophecy Against Cush

18 Woe to the land of whirring
wings[b]
along the rivers of Cush,[c]
2 which sends envoys by sea
in papyrus boats over the water.

Go, swift messengers,
to a people tall and smooth-skinned,
to a people feared far and wide,
an aggressive nation of strange
speech,
whose land is divided by rivers.

3 All you people of the world,
you who live on the earth,
when a banner is raised on the
mountains,
you will see it,
and when a trumpet sounds,
you will hear it.
4 This is what the LORD says to me:
"I will remain quiet and will look
on from my dwelling place,
like shimmering heat in the sunshine,
like a cloud of dew in the heat of
harvest."
5 For, before the harvest, when the
blossom is gone
and the flower becomes a ripening
grape,
he will cut off the shoots with pruning
knives,
and cut down and take away the
spreading branches.
6 They will all be left to the mountain
birds of prey
and to the wild animals;
the birds will feed on them all
summer,
the wild animals all winter.

7 At that time gifts will be brought to the
LORD Almighty

from a people tall and smooth-
skinned,
from a people feared far and wide,
an aggressive nation of strange
speech,
whose land is divided by rivers —

the gifts will be brought to Mount Zion, the
place of the Name of the LORD Almighty.

[a] *8* That is, wooden symbols of the goddess Asherah [b] *1* Or *of locusts* [c] *1* That is, the upper Nile region

A Prophecy Against Egypt

19 A prophecy against Egypt:

See, the LORD rides on a swift cloud
and is coming to Egypt.
The idols of Egypt tremble before him,
and the hearts of the Egyptians melt with fear.

2 "I will stir up Egyptian against Egyptian —
brother will fight against brother,
neighbor against neighbor,
city against city,
kingdom against kingdom.
3 The Egyptians will lose heart,
and I will bring their plans to nothing;
they will consult the idols and the spirits of the dead,
the mediums and the spiritists.
4 I will hand the Egyptians over
to the power of a cruel master,
and a fierce king will rule over them,"
declares the Lord, the LORD Almighty.

5 The waters of the river will dry up,
and the riverbed will be parched and dry.
6 The canals will stink;
the streams of Egypt will dwindle and dry up.
The reeds and rushes will wither,
7 also the plants along the Nile,
at the mouth of the river.
Every sown field along the Nile
will become parched, will blow away and be no more.
8 The fishermen will groan and lament,
all who cast hooks into the Nile;
those who throw nets on the water
will pine away.
9 Those who work with combed flax will despair,
the weavers of fine linen will lose hope.
10 The workers in cloth will be dejected,
and all the wage earners will be sick at heart.

11 The officials of Zoan are nothing but fools;
the wise counselors of Pharaoh give senseless advice.
How can you say to Pharaoh,
"I am one of the wise men,
a disciple of the ancient kings"?
12 Where are your wise men now?
Let them show you and make known
what the LORD Almighty
has planned against Egypt.
13 The officials of Zoan have become fools,
the leaders of Memphis are deceived;
the cornerstones of her peoples
have led Egypt astray.
14 The LORD has poured into them
a spirit of dizziness;
they make Egypt stagger in all that she does,
as a drunkard staggers around in his vomit.
15 There is nothing Egypt can do —
head or tail, palm branch or reed.

16 In that day the Egyptians will become
weaklings. They will shudder with fear at
the uplifted hand that the LORD Almighty
raises against them. 17 And the land of
Judah will bring terror to the Egyptians;
everyone to whom Judah is mentioned
will be terrified, because of what the LORD
Almighty is planning against them.

18 In that day five cities in Egypt will
speak the language of Canaan and swear
allegiance to the LORD Almighty. One of
them will be called the City of the Sun.[a]

19 In that day there will be an altar to the
LORD in the heart of Egypt, and a monument to the LORD at its border. 20 It will be
a sign and witness to the LORD Almighty
in the land of Egypt. When they cry out
to the LORD because of their oppressors,
he will send them a savior and defender,
and he will rescue them. 21 So the LORD will
make himself known to the Egyptians,
and in that day they will acknowledge
the LORD. They will worship with sacrifices
and grain offerings; they will make vows
to the LORD and keep them. 22 The LORD will
strike Egypt with a plague; he will strike
them and heal them. They will turn to the
LORD, and he will respond to their pleas
and heal them.

23 In that day there will be a highway
from Egypt to Assyria. The Assyrians will
go to Egypt and the Egyptians to Assyria.
The Egyptians and Assyrians will worship together. 24 In that day Israel will be
the third, along with Egypt and Assyria,
a blessing[b] on the earth. 25 The LORD Almighty will bless them, saying, "Blessed be
Egypt my people, Assyria my handiwork,
and Israel my inheritance."

[a] 18 Some manuscripts of the Masoretic Text, Dead Sea Scrolls, Symmachus and Vulgate; most manuscripts of the Masoretic Text *City of Destruction* [b] 24 Or *Assyria, whose names will be used in blessings* (see Gen. 48:20); or *Assyria, who will be seen by others as blessed*

A Prophecy Against Egypt and Cush

20 In the year that the supreme commander, sent by Sargon king of
Assyria, came to Ashdod and attacked
and captured it — 2at that time the LORD
spoke through Isaiah son of Amoz. He said
to him, "Take off the sackcloth from your
body and the sandals from your feet."
And he did so, going around stripped and
barefoot.
3Then the LORD said, "Just as my servant
Isaiah has gone stripped and barefoot for
three years, as a sign and portent against
Egypt and Cush,[a] 4so the king of Assyria will lead away stripped and barefoot
the Egyptian captives and Cushite exiles,
young and old, with buttocks bared — to
Egypt's shame. 5Those who trusted in Cush
and boasted in Egypt will be dismayed
and put to shame. 6In that day the people who live on this coast will say, 'See
what has happened to those we relied on,
those we fled to for help and deliverance
from the king of Assyria! How then can
we escape?' "

A Prophecy Against Babylon

21 A prophecy against the Desert by the Sea:

Like whirlwinds sweeping through
the southland,
an invader comes from the desert,
from a land of terror.

2 A dire vision has been shown to me:
The traitor betrays, the looter
takes loot.
Elam, attack! Media, lay siege!
I will bring to an end all the
groaning she caused.

3 At this my body is racked with pain,
pangs seize me, like those of a
woman in labor;
I am staggered by what I hear,
I am bewildered by what I see.
4 My heart falters,
fear makes me tremble;
the twilight I longed for
has become a horror to me.

5 They set the tables,
they spread the rugs,
they eat, they drink!
Get up, you officers,
oil the shields!

6This is what the Lord says to me:

"Go, post a lookout
and have him report what he sees.
7 When he sees chariots
with teams of horses,
riders on donkeys
or riders on camels,
let him be alert,
fully alert."

8 And the lookout[b] shouted,

"Day after day, my lord, I stand on
the watchtower;
every night I stay at my post.
9 Look, here comes a man in a chariot
with a team of horses.
And he gives back the answer:
'Babylon has fallen, has fallen!
All the images of its gods
lie shattered on the ground!' "

10 My people who are crushed on the
threshing floor,
I tell you what I have heard
from the LORD Almighty,
from the God of Israel.

A Prophecy Against Edom

11A prophecy against Dumah[c]:

Someone calls to me from Seir,
"Watchman, what is left of the
night?
Watchman, what is left of the
night?"
12 The watchman replies,
"Morning is coming, but also the
night.
If you would ask, then ask;
and come back yet again."

A Prophecy Against Arabia

13A prophecy against Arabia:

You caravans of Dedanites,
who camp in the thickets
of Arabia,
14 bring water for the thirsty;
you who live in Tema,
bring food for the fugitives.
15 They flee from the sword,
from the drawn sword,
from the bent bow
and from the heat of battle.

16This is what the Lord says to me:
"Within one year, as a servant bound by
contract would count it, all the splendor
of Kedar will come to an end. 17The survivors of the archers, the warriors of Kedar,
will be few." The LORD, the God of Israel,
has spoken.

[a] *3* That is, the upper Nile region; also in verse 5 [b] *8* Dead Sea Scrolls and Syriac; Masoretic Text *A lion* [c] *11* *Dumah*, a wordplay on *Edom*, means *silence* or *stillness*.

A Prophecy About Jerusalem

22 A prophecy against the Valley of Vision:

What troubles you now,
that you have all gone up on the roofs,
2 you town so full of commotion,
you city of tumult and revelry?
Your slain were not killed by the sword,
nor did they die in battle.
3 All your leaders have fled together;
they have been captured without using the bow.
All you who were caught were taken prisoner together,
having fled while the enemy was still far away.
4 Therefore I said, "Turn away from me;
let me weep bitterly.
Do not try to console me
over the destruction of my people."

5 The Lord, the LORD Almighty, has a day
of tumult and trampling and terror
in the Valley of Vision,
a day of battering down walls
and of crying out to the mountains.
6 Elam takes up the quiver,
with her charioteers and horses;
Kir uncovers the shield.
7 Your choicest valleys are full of chariots,
and horsemen are posted at the city gates.

8 The Lord stripped away the defenses of Judah,
and you looked in that day
to the weapons in the Palace of the Forest.
9 You saw that the walls of the City of David
were broken through in many places;
you stored up water
in the Lower Pool.
10 You counted the buildings in Jerusalem
and tore down houses to strengthen the wall.
11 You built a reservoir between the two walls
for the water of the Old Pool,
but you did not look to the One who made it,
or have regard for the One who planned it long ago.

12 The Lord, the LORD Almighty,
called you on that day
to weep and to wail,
to tear out your hair and put on sackcloth.
13 But see, there is joy and revelry,
slaughtering of cattle and killing of sheep,
eating of meat and drinking of wine!
"Let us eat and drink," you say,
"for tomorrow we die!"

14 The LORD Almighty has revealed this
in my hearing: "Till your dying day this
sin will not be atoned for," says the Lord,
the LORD Almighty.

15 This is what the Lord, the LORD Almighty, says:

"Go, say to this steward,
to Shebna the palace administrator:
16 What are you doing here and who gave you permission
to cut out a grave for yourself here,
hewing your grave on the height
and chiseling your resting place in the rock?
17 "Beware, the LORD is about to take firm hold of you
and hurl you away, you mighty man.
18 He will roll you up tightly like a ball
and throw you into a large country.
There you will die
and there the chariots you were so proud of
will become a disgrace to your master's house.
19 I will depose you from your office,
and you will be ousted from your position.

20 "In that day I will summon my servant, Eliakim son of Hilkiah. 21 I will clothe
him with your robe and fasten your sash
around him and hand your authority over
to him. He will be a father to those who
live in Jerusalem and to the people of
Judah. 22 I will place on his shoulder the
key to the house of David; what he opens
no one can shut, and what he shuts no
one can open. 23 I will drive him like a peg
into a firm place; he will become a seat[a]
of honor for the house of his father. 24 All
the glory of his family will hang on him:
its offspring and offshoots — all its lesser vessels, from the bowls to all the jars.

25 "In that day," declares the LORD Almighty, "the peg driven into the firm place
will give way; it will be sheared off and will
fall, and the load hanging on it will be cut
down." The LORD has spoken.

[a] *23* Or *throne*

A Prophecy Against Tyre

23 A prophecy against Tyre:

Wail, you ships of Tarshish!
For Tyre is destroyed
and left without house or harbor.
From the land of Cyprus
word has come to them.

2 Be silent, you people of the island
and you merchants of Sidon,
whom the seafarers have enriched.
3 On the great waters
came the grain of the Shihor;
the harvest of the Nile[a] was the revenue of Tyre,
and she became the marketplace of the nations.

4 Be ashamed, Sidon, and you fortress of the sea,
for the sea has spoken:
"I have neither been in labor nor given birth;
I have neither reared sons nor brought up daughters."
5 When word comes to Egypt,
they will be in anguish at the report from Tyre.

6 Cross over to Tarshish;
wail, you people of the island.
7 Is this your city of revelry,
the old, old city,
whose feet have taken her
to settle in far-off lands?
8 Who planned this against Tyre,
the bestower of crowns,
whose merchants are princes,
whose traders are renowned in the earth?
9 The LORD Almighty planned it,
to bring down her pride in all her splendor
and to humble all who are renowned on the earth.

10 Till[b] your land as they do along the Nile,
Daughter Tarshish,
for you no longer have a harbor.
11 The LORD has stretched out his hand over the sea
and made its kingdoms tremble.
He has given an order concerning Phoenicia
that her fortresses be destroyed.
12 He said, "No more of your reveling,
Virgin Daughter Sidon, now crushed!

"Up, cross over to Cyprus;
even there you will find no rest."
13 Look at the land of the Babylonians,[c]
this people that is now of no account!
The Assyrians have made it
a place for desert creatures;
they raised up their siege towers,
they stripped its fortresses bare
and turned it into a ruin.

14 Wail, you ships of Tarshish;
your fortress is destroyed!

15 At that time Tyre will be forgotten for
seventy years, the span of a king's life.
But at the end of these seventy years, it
will happen to Tyre as in the song of the
prostitute:

16 "Take up a harp, walk through the city,
you forgotten prostitute;
play the harp well, sing many a song,
so that you will be remembered."

17 At the end of seventy years, the LORD
will deal with Tyre. She will return to her
lucrative prostitution and will ply her
trade with all the kingdoms on the face of
the earth. 18 Yet her profit and her earnings
will be set apart for the LORD; they will not
be stored up or hoarded. Her profits will
go to those who live before the LORD, for
abundant food and fine clothes.

The LORD's Devastation of the Earth

24 See, the LORD is going to lay waste the earth
and devastate it;
he will ruin its face
and scatter its inhabitants—
2 it will be the same
for priest as for people,
for the master as for his servant,
for the mistress as for her servant,
for seller as for buyer,
for borrower as for lender,
for debtor as for creditor.
3 The earth will be completely laid waste
and totally plundered.
The LORD has spoken this word.

4 The earth dries up and withers,
the world languishes and withers,
the heavens languish with the earth.
5 The earth is defiled by its people;
they have disobeyed the laws,
violated the statutes
and broken the everlasting covenant.

[a] *2,3* Masoretic Text; Dead Sea Scrolls *Sidon, / who cross over the sea; / your envoys* [3]*are on the great waters. / The grain of the Shihor, / the harvest of the Nile,* [b] *10* Dead Sea Scrolls and some Septuagint manuscripts; Masoretic Text *Go through* [c] *13* Or *Chaldeans*

6 Therefore a curse consumes the earth;
its people must bear their guilt.
Therefore earth's inhabitants are burned up,
and very few are left.
7 The new wine dries up and the vine withers;
all the merrymakers groan.
8 The joyful timbrels are stilled,
the noise of the revelers has stopped,
the joyful harp is silent.
9 No longer do they drink wine with a song;
the beer is bitter to its drinkers.
10 The ruined city lies desolate;
the entrance to every house is barred.
11 In the streets they cry out for wine;
all joy turns to gloom,
all joyful sounds are banished from the earth.
12 The city is left in ruins,
its gate is battered to pieces.
13 So will it be on the earth
and among the nations,
as when an olive tree is beaten,
or as when gleanings are left after the grape harvest.
14 They raise their voices, they shout for joy;
from the west they acclaim the LORD's majesty.
15 Therefore in the east give glory to the LORD;
exalt the name of the LORD, the God of Israel,
in the islands of the sea.
16 From the ends of the earth we hear singing:
"Glory to the Righteous One."
But I said, "I waste away, I waste away!
Woe to me!
The treacherous betray!
With treachery the treacherous betray!"
17 Terror and pit and snare await you,
people of the earth.
18 Whoever flees at the sound of terror
will fall into a pit;
whoever climbs out of the pit
will be caught in a snare.

The floodgates of the heavens are opened,
the foundations of the earth shake.
19 The earth is broken up,
the earth is split asunder,
the earth is violently shaken.
20 The earth reels like a drunkard,
it sways like a hut in the wind;
so heavy upon it is the guilt of its rebellion
that it falls — never to rise again.

21 In that day the LORD will punish
the powers in the heavens above
and the kings on the earth below.
22 They will be herded together
like prisoners bound in a dungeon;
they will be shut up in prison
and be punished[a] after many days.
23 The moon will be dismayed,
the sun ashamed;
for the LORD Almighty will reign
on Mount Zion and in Jerusalem,
and before its elders — with great glory.

Praise to the LORD

25 LORD, you are my God;
I will exalt you and praise your name,
for in perfect faithfulness
you have done wonderful things,
things planned long ago.
2 You have made the city a heap of rubble,
the fortified town a ruin,
the foreigners' stronghold a city no more;
it will never be rebuilt.
3 Therefore strong peoples will honor you;
cities of ruthless nations will revere you.
4 You have been a refuge for the poor,
a refuge for the needy in their distress,
a shelter from the storm
and a shade from the heat.
For the breath of the ruthless
is like a storm driving against a wall
5 and like the heat of the desert.
You silence the uproar of foreigners;
as heat is reduced by the shadow of a cloud,
so the song of the ruthless is stilled.

6 On this mountain the LORD Almighty will prepare
a feast of rich food for all peoples,
a banquet of aged wine —
the best of meats and the finest of wines.
7 On this mountain he will destroy
the shroud that enfolds all peoples,
the sheet that covers all nations;
8 he will swallow up death forever.

[a] 22 Or *released*

The Sovereign LORD will wipe away
the tears
from all faces;
he will remove his people's disgrace
from all the earth.
The LORD has spoken.

9 In that day they will say,

"Surely this is our God;
we trusted in him, and he saved us.
This is the LORD, we trusted in him;
let us rejoice and be glad in his
salvation."

10 The hand of the LORD will rest on this
mountain;
but Moab will be trampled in their
land
as straw is trampled down in the
manure.
11 They will stretch out their hands in it,
as swimmers stretch out their
hands to swim.
God will bring down their pride
despite the cleverness[a] of their
hands.
12 He will bring down your high fortified
walls
and lay them low;
he will bring them down to the
ground,
to the very dust.

A Song of Praise

26 In that day this song will be sung
in the land of Judah:

We have a strong city;
God makes salvation
its walls and ramparts.
2 Open the gates
that the righteous nation may
enter,
the nation that keeps faith.
3 You will keep in perfect peace
those whose minds are steadfast,
because they trust in you.
4 Trust in the LORD forever,
for the LORD, the LORD himself, is
the Rock eternal.
5 He humbles those who dwell on high,
he lays the lofty city low;
he levels it to the ground
and casts it down to the dust.
6 Feet trample it down —
the feet of the oppressed,
the footsteps of the poor.

7 The path of the righteous is level;
you, the Upright One, make the
way of the righteous smooth.
8 Yes, LORD, walking in the way of your
laws,[b]
we wait for you;
your name and renown
are the desire of our hearts.
9 My soul yearns for you in the night;
in the morning my spirit longs for
you.
When your judgments come upon the
earth,
the people of the world learn
righteousness.
10 But when grace is shown to the
wicked,
they do not learn righteousness;
even in a land of uprightness they go
on doing evil
and do not regard the majesty of
the LORD.
11 LORD, your hand is lifted high,
but they do not see it.
Let them see your zeal for your people
and be put to shame;
let the fire reserved for your
enemies consume them.

12 LORD, you establish peace for us;
all that we have accomplished you
have done for us.
13 LORD our God, other lords besides you
have ruled over us,
but your name alone do we honor.
14 They are now dead, they live
no more;
their spirits do not rise.
You punished them and brought
them to ruin;
you wiped out all memory of them.
15 You have enlarged the nation, LORD;
you have enlarged the nation.
You have gained glory for yourself;
you have extended all the borders
of the land.

16 LORD, they came to you in their
distress;
when you disciplined them,
they could barely whisper a
prayer.[c]
17 As a pregnant woman about to give
birth
writhes and cries out in her pain,
so were we in your presence, LORD.
18 We were with child, we writhed in
labor,
but we gave birth to wind.
We have not brought salvation to the
earth,
and the people of the world have
not come to life.

[a] *11* The meaning of the Hebrew for this word is uncertain. [b] *8* Or *judgments* [c] *16* The meaning of the Hebrew for this clause is uncertain.

19 But your dead will live, LORD;
their bodies will rise —
let those who dwell in the dust
wake up and shout for joy —
your dew is like the dew of the morning;
the earth will give birth to her dead.

20 Go, my people, enter your rooms
and shut the doors behind you;
hide yourselves for a little while
until his wrath has passed by.
21 See, the LORD is coming out of his dwelling
to punish the people of the earth for their sins.
The earth will disclose the blood shed on it;
the earth will conceal its slain no longer.

Deliverance of Israel

27 In that day,
the LORD will punish with his sword —
his fierce, great and powerful sword —
Leviathan the gliding serpent,
Leviathan the coiling serpent;
he will slay the monster of the sea.

2 In that day —
"Sing about a fruitful vineyard:
3 I, the LORD, watch over it;
I water it continually.
I guard it day and night
so that no one may harm it.
4 I am not angry.
If only there were briers and thorns confronting me!
I would march against them in battle;
I would set them all on fire.
5 Or else let them come to me for refuge;
let them make peace with me,
yes, let them make peace with me."

6 In days to come Jacob will take root,
Israel will bud and blossom
and fill all the world with fruit.

7 Has the LORD struck her
as he struck down those who struck her?
Has she been killed
as those were killed who killed her?
8 By warfare[a] and exile you contend with her —
with his fierce blast he drives her out,
as on a day the east wind blows.
9 By this, then, will Jacob's guilt be atoned for,
and this will be the full fruit of the removal of his sin:
When he makes all the altar stones
to be like limestone crushed to pieces,
no Asherah poles[b] or incense altars
will be left standing.
10 The fortified city stands desolate,
an abandoned settlement,
forsaken like the wilderness;
there the calves graze,
there they lie down;
they strip its branches bare.
11 When its twigs are dry, they are broken off
and women come and make fires with them.
For this is a people without understanding;
so their Maker has no compassion on them,
and their Creator shows them no favor.

12 In that day the LORD will thresh from
the flowing Euphrates to the Wadi of
Egypt, and you, Israel, will be gathered
up one by one. 13 And in that day a great
trumpet will sound. Those who were
perishing in Assyria and those who were
exiled in Egypt will come and worship
the LORD on the holy mountain in Jerusalem.

Woe to the Leaders of Ephraim and Judah

28 Woe to that wreath, the pride of Ephraim's drunkards,
to the fading flower, his glorious beauty,
set on the head of a fertile valley —
to that city, the pride of those laid low by wine!
2 See, the Lord has one who is powerful and strong.
Like a hailstorm and a destructive wind,
like a driving rain and a flooding downpour,
he will throw it forcefully to the ground.
3 That wreath, the pride of Ephraim's drunkards,
will be trampled underfoot.
4 That fading flower, his glorious beauty,
set on the head of a fertile valley,

[a] *8* See Septuagint; the meaning of the Hebrew for this word is uncertain. [b] *9* That is, wooden symbols of the goddess Asherah

will be like figs ripe before harvest —
as soon as people see them and take them in hand,
they swallow them.

5 In that day the LORD Almighty
will be a glorious crown,
a beautiful wreath
for the remnant of his people.
6 He will be a spirit of justice
to the one who sits in judgment,
a source of strength
to those who turn back the battle at the gate.

7 And these also stagger from wine
and reel from beer:
Priests and prophets stagger from beer
and are befuddled with wine;
they reel from beer,
they stagger when seeing visions,
they stumble when rendering decisions.
8 All the tables are covered with vomit
and there is not a spot without filth.

9 "Who is it he is trying to teach?
To whom is he explaining his message?
To children weaned from their milk,
to those just taken from the breast?
10 For it is:
Do this, do that,
a rule for this, a rule for that[a];
a little here, a little there."

11 Very well then, with foreign lips and strange tongues
God will speak to this people,
12 to whom he said,
"This is the resting place, let the weary rest";
and, "This is the place of repose" —
but they would not listen.
13 So then, the word of the LORD to them will become:
Do this, do that,
a rule for this, a rule for that;
a little here, a little there —
so that as they go they will fall backward;
they will be injured and snared and captured.

14 Therefore hear the word of the LORD,
you scoffers
who rule this people in Jerusalem.
15 You boast, "We have entered into a covenant with death,
with the realm of the dead we have made an agreement.
When an overwhelming scourge sweeps by,
it cannot touch us,
for we have made a lie our refuge
and falsehood[b] our hiding place."

16 So this is what the Sovereign LORD says:

"See, I lay a stone in Zion, a tested stone,
a precious cornerstone for a sure foundation;
the one who relies on it
will never be stricken with panic.
17 I will make justice the measuring line
and righteousness the plumb line;
hail will sweep away your refuge, the lie,
and water will overflow your hiding place.
18 Your covenant with death will be annulled;
your agreement with the realm of the dead will not stand.
When the overwhelming scourge sweeps by,
you will be beaten down by it.
19 As often as it comes it will carry you away;
morning after morning, by day and by night,
it will sweep through."

The understanding of this message
will bring sheer terror.
20 The bed is too short to stretch out on,
the blanket too narrow to wrap around you.
21 The LORD will rise up as he did at Mount Perazim,
he will rouse himself as in the Valley of Gibeon —
to do his work, his strange work,
and perform his task, his alien task.
22 Now stop your mocking,
or your chains will become heavier;
the Lord, the LORD Almighty, has told me
of the destruction decreed against the whole land.

23 Listen and hear my voice;
pay attention and hear what I say.
24 When a farmer plows for planting,
does he plow continually?
Does he keep on breaking up and working the soil?
25 When he has leveled the surface,
does he not sow caraway and scatter cumin?

[a] 10 Hebrew / *sav lasav sav lasav / kav lakav kav lakav* (probably meaningless sounds mimicking the prophet's words); also in verse 13 [b] 15 Or *false gods*

Does he not plant wheat in its place,[a]
barley in its plot,[a]
and spelt in its field?
26 His God instructs him
and teaches him the right way.

27 Caraway is not threshed with a sledge,
nor is the wheel of a cart rolled over cumin;
caraway is beaten out with a rod,
and cumin with a stick.
28 Grain must be ground to make bread;
so one does not go on threshing it forever.
The wheels of a threshing cart may be rolled over it,
but one does not use horses to grind grain.
29 All this also comes from the LORD Almighty,
whose plan is wonderful,
whose wisdom is magnificent.

Woe to David's City

29 Woe to you, Ariel, Ariel,
the city where David settled!
Add year to year
and let your cycle of festivals go on.
2 Yet I will besiege Ariel;
she will mourn and lament,
she will be to me like an altar hearth.[b]
3 I will encamp against you on all sides;
I will encircle you with towers
and set up my siege works against you.
4 Brought low, you will speak from the ground;
your speech will mumble out of the dust.
Your voice will come ghostlike from the earth;
out of the dust your speech will whisper.

5 But your many enemies will become like fine dust,
the ruthless hordes like blown chaff.
Suddenly, in an instant,
6 the LORD Almighty will come
with thunder and earthquake and great noise,
with windstorm and tempest and flames of a devouring fire.
7 Then the hordes of all the nations
that fight against Ariel,
that attack her and her fortress
and besiege her,
will be as it is with a dream,
with a vision in the night—
8 as when a hungry person dreams of eating,
but awakens hungry still;
as when a thirsty person dreams of drinking,
but awakens faint and thirsty still.
So will it be with the hordes of all the nations
that fight against Mount Zion.

9 Be stunned and amazed,
blind yourselves and be sightless;
be drunk, but not from wine,
stagger, but not from beer.
10 The LORD has brought over you a deep sleep:
He has sealed your eyes (the prophets);
he has covered your heads (the seers).

11 For you this whole vision is nothing but
words sealed in a scroll. And if you give
the scroll to someone who can read, and
say, "Read this, please," they will answer,
"I can't; it is sealed." 12 Or if you give the
scroll to someone who cannot read, and
say, "Read this, please," they will answer,
"I don't know how to read."

13 The Lord says:

"These people come near to me with their mouth
and honor me with their lips,
but their hearts are far from me.
Their worship of me
is based on merely human rules
they have been taught.[c]
14 Therefore once more I will astound these people
with wonder upon wonder;
the wisdom of the wise will perish,
the intelligence of the intelligent will vanish."
15 Woe to those who go to great depths
to hide their plans from the LORD,
who do their work in darkness and think,
"Who sees us? Who will know?"
16 You turn things upside down,
as if the potter were thought to be like the clay!
Shall what is formed say to the one who formed it,
"You did not make me"?

[a] *25* The meaning of the Hebrew for this word is uncertain. [b] *2* The Hebrew for *altar hearth* sounds like the Hebrew for *Ariel.* [c] *13* Hebrew; Septuagint *They worship me in vain; / their teachings are merely human rules*

Can the pot say to the potter,
"You know nothing"?

17 In a very short time, will not Lebanon
be turned into a fertile field
and the fertile field seem like a
forest?
18 In that day the deaf will hear the
words of the scroll,
and out of gloom and darkness
the eyes of the blind will see.
19 Once more the humble will rejoice in
the LORD;
the needy will rejoice in the Holy
One of Israel.
20 The ruthless will vanish,
the mockers will disappear,
and all who have an eye for evil
will be cut down —
21 those who with a word make
someone out to be guilty,
who ensnare the defender in court
and with false testimony deprive
the innocent of justice.

22 Therefore this is what the LORD, who
redeemed Abraham, says to the descendants of Jacob:

"No longer will Jacob be ashamed;
no longer will their faces grow pale.
23 When they see among them their
children,
the work of my hands,
they will keep my name holy;
they will acknowledge the holiness
of the Holy One of Jacob,
and will stand in awe of the God of
Israel.
24 Those who are wayward in spirit will
gain understanding;
those who complain will accept
instruction."

Woe to the Obstinate Nation

30 "Woe to the obstinate children,"
declares the LORD,
"to those who carry out plans that are
not mine,
forming an alliance, but not by my
Spirit,
heaping sin upon sin;
2 who go down to Egypt
without consulting me;
who look for help to Pharaoh's
protection,
to Egypt's shade for refuge.
3 But Pharaoh's protection will be to
your shame,
Egypt's shade will bring you
disgrace.
4 Though they have officials in Zoan
and their envoys have arrived in
Hanes,
5 everyone will be put to shame
because of a people useless to
them,
who bring neither help nor
advantage,
but only shame and disgrace."

6 A prophecy concerning the animals
of the Negev:

Through a land of hardship and
distress,
of lions and lionesses,
of adders and darting snakes,
the envoys carry their riches on
donkeys' backs,
their treasures on the humps of
camels,
to that unprofitable nation,
7 to Egypt, whose help is utterly
useless.
Therefore I call her
Rahab the Do-Nothing.

8 Go now, write it on a tablet for them,
inscribe it on a scroll,
that for the days to come
it may be an everlasting witness.
9 For these are rebellious people,
deceitful children,
children unwilling to listen to the
LORD's instruction.
10 They say to the seers,
"See no more visions!"
and to the prophets,
"Give us no more visions of what
is right!
Tell us pleasant things,
prophesy illusions.
11 Leave this way,
get off this path,
and stop confronting us
with the Holy One of Israel!"

12 Therefore this is what the Holy One
of Israel says:

"Because you have rejected this
message,
relied on oppression
and depended on deceit,
13 this sin will become for you
like a high wall, cracked and
bulging,
that collapses suddenly, in an
instant.
14 It will break in pieces like pottery,
shattered so mercilessly
that among its pieces not a fragment
will be found
for taking coals from a hearth
or scooping water out of
a cistern."

15 This is what the Sovereign LORD, the Holy One of Israel, says:

"In repentance and rest is your
salvation,
in quietness and trust is your
strength,
but you would have none of it.
16 You said, 'No, we will flee on horses.'
Therefore you will flee!
You said, 'We will ride off on swift
horses.'
Therefore your pursuers will be
swift!
17 A thousand will flee
at the threat of one;
at the threat of five
you will all flee away,
till you are left
like a flagstaff on a mountaintop,
like a banner on a hill."

18 Yet the LORD longs to be gracious to
you;
therefore he will rise up to show
you compassion.
For the LORD is a God of justice.
Blessed are all who wait for him!

19 People of Zion, who live in Jerusalem,
you will weep no more. How gracious he
will be when you cry for help! As soon as he
hears, he will answer you. 20 Although the
Lord gives you the bread of adversity and
the water of affliction, your teachers will
be hidden no more; with your own eyes
you will see them. 21 Whether you turn to
the right or to the left, your ears will hear a
voice behind you, saying, "This is the way;
walk in it." 22 Then you will desecrate your
idols overlaid with silver and your images
covered with gold; you will throw them
away like a menstrual cloth and say to
them, "Away with you!"

23 He will also send you rain for the seed
you sow in the ground, and the food that
comes from the land will be rich and plentiful. In that day your cattle will graze in
broad meadows. 24 The oxen and donkeys that work the soil will eat fodder and
mash, spread out with fork and shovel.
25 In the day of great slaughter, when the
towers fall, streams of water will flow on
every high mountain and every lofty hill.
26 The moon will shine like the sun, and
the sunlight will be seven times brighter,
like the light of seven full days, when the
LORD binds up the bruises of his people
and heals the wounds he inflicted.

27 See, the Name of the LORD comes
from afar,
with burning anger and dense
clouds of smoke;
his lips are full of wrath,
and his tongue is a consuming fire.
28 His breath is like a rushing torrent,
rising up to the neck.
He shakes the nations in the sieve of
destruction;
he places in the jaws of the peoples
a bit that leads them astray.
29 And you will sing
as on the night you celebrate a holy
festival;
your hearts will rejoice
as when people playing pipes go up
to the mountain of the LORD,
to the Rock of Israel.
30 The LORD will cause people to hear his
majestic voice
and will make them see his arm
coming down
with raging anger and consuming fire,
with cloudburst, thunderstorm and
hail.
31 The voice of the LORD will shatter
Assyria;
with his rod he will strike them
down.
32 Every stroke the LORD lays on them
with his punishing club
will be to the music of timbrels and
harps,
as he fights them in battle with the
blows of his arm.
33 Topheth has long been prepared;
it has been made ready for the
king.
Its fire pit has been made deep and
wide,
with an abundance of fire and
wood;
the breath of the LORD,
like a stream of burning sulfur,
sets it ablaze.

Woe to Those Who Rely on Egypt

31 Woe to those who go down to
Egypt for help,
who rely on horses,
who trust in the multitude of their
chariots
and in the great strength of their
horsemen,
but do not look to the Holy One of
Israel,
or seek help from the LORD.
2 Yet he too is wise and can bring
disaster;
he does not take back his words.
He will rise up against that wicked
nation,
against those who help evildoers.
3 But the Egyptians are mere mortals
and not God;
their horses are flesh and not spirit.

When the LORD stretches out his hand,
those who help will stumble,
those who are helped will fall;
all will perish together.

4 This is what the LORD says to me:

"As a lion growls,
a great lion over its prey—
and though a whole band of shepherds
is called together against it,
it is not frightened by their shouts
or disturbed by their clamor—
so the LORD Almighty will come down
to do battle on Mount Zion and on its heights.
5 Like birds hovering overhead,
the LORD Almighty will shield Jerusalem;
he will shield it and deliver it,
he will 'pass over' it and will rescue it."

6 Return, you Israelites, to the One you
have so greatly revolted against. 7 For in
that day every one of you will reject the
idols of silver and gold your sinful hands
have made.

8 "Assyria will fall by no human sword;
a sword, not of mortals, will devour them.
They will flee before the sword
and their young men will be put to forced labor.
9 Their stronghold will fall because of terror;
at the sight of the battle standard
their commanders will panic,"
declares the LORD,
whose fire is in Zion,
whose furnace is in Jerusalem.

The Kingdom of Righteousness

32 See, a king will reign in righteousness
and rulers will rule with justice.
2 Each one will be like a shelter from the wind
and a refuge from the storm,
like streams of water in the desert
and the shadow of a great rock in a thirsty land.

3 Then the eyes of those who see will no longer be closed,
and the ears of those who hear will listen.
4 The fearful heart will know and understand,
and the stammering tongue will be fluent and clear.
5 No longer will the fool be called noble
nor the scoundrel be highly respected.
6 For fools speak folly,
their hearts are bent on evil:
They practice ungodliness
and spread error concerning the LORD;
the hungry they leave empty
and from the thirsty they withhold water.
7 Scoundrels use wicked methods,
they make up evil schemes
to destroy the poor with lies,
even when the plea of the needy is just.
8 But the noble make noble plans,
and by noble deeds they stand.

The Women of Jerusalem

9 You women who are so complacent,
rise up and listen to me;
you daughters who feel secure,
hear what I have to say!
10 In little more than a year
you who feel secure will tremble;
the grape harvest will fail,
and the harvest of fruit will not come.
11 Tremble, you complacent women;
shudder, you daughters who feel secure!
Strip off your fine clothes
and wrap yourselves in rags.
12 Beat your breasts for the pleasant fields,
for the fruitful vines
13 and for the land of my people,
a land overgrown with thorns and briers—
yes, mourn for all houses of merriment
and for this city of revelry.
14 The fortress will be abandoned,
the noisy city deserted;
citadel and watchtower will become a wasteland forever,
the delight of donkeys, a pasture for flocks,
15 till the Spirit is poured on us from on high,
and the desert becomes a fertile field,
and the fertile field seems like a forest.
16 The LORD's justice will dwell in the desert,
his righteousness live in the fertile field.
17 The fruit of that righteousness will be peace;
its effect will be quietness and confidence forever.

[18] My people will live in peaceful
dwelling places,
in secure homes,
in undisturbed places of rest.
[19] Though hail flattens the forest
and the city is leveled completely,
[20] how blessed you will be,
sowing your seed by every stream,
and letting your cattle and donkeys
range free.

Distress and Help

33 Woe to you, destroyer,
you who have not been destroyed!
Woe to you, betrayer,
you who have not been betrayed!
When you stop destroying,
you will be destroyed;
when you stop betraying,
you will be betrayed.
[2] LORD, be gracious to us;
we long for you.
Be our strength every morning,
our salvation in time of distress.
[3] At the uproar of your army, the
peoples flee;
when you rise up, the nations
scatter.
[4] Your plunder, O nations, is harvested
as by young locusts;
like a swarm of locusts people
pounce on it.
[5] The LORD is exalted, for he dwells on
high;
he will fill Zion with his justice and
righteousness.
[6] He will be the sure foundation for
your times,
a rich store of salvation and
wisdom and knowledge;
the fear of the LORD is the key to
this treasure.[a]
[7] Look, their brave men cry aloud in
the streets;
the envoys of peace weep bitterly.
[8] The highways are deserted,
no travelers are on the roads.
The treaty is broken,
its witnesses[b] are despised,
no one is respected.
[9] The land dries up and wastes away,
Lebanon is ashamed and withers;
Sharon is like the Arabah,
and Bashan and Carmel drop their
leaves.
[10] "Now will I arise," says the LORD.
"Now will I be exalted;
now will I be lifted up.
[11] You conceive chaff,
you give birth to straw;
your breath is a fire that consumes
you.
[12] The peoples will be burned to ashes;
like cut thornbushes they will be
set ablaze."
[13] You who are far away, hear what I
have done;
you who are near, acknowledge my
power!
[14] The sinners in Zion are terrified;
trembling grips the godless:
"Who of us can dwell with the
consuming fire?
Who of us can dwell with
everlasting burning?"
[15] Those who walk righteously
and speak what is right,
who reject gain from extortion
and keep their hands from
accepting bribes,
who stop their ears against plots of
murder
and shut their eyes against
contemplating evil —
[16] they are the ones who will dwell on
the heights,
whose refuge will be the mountain
fortress.
Their bread will be supplied,
and water will not fail them.
[17] Your eyes will see the king in his
beauty
and view a land that stretches afar.
[18] In your thoughts you will ponder the
former terror:
"Where is that chief officer?
Where is the one who took the
revenue?
Where is the officer in charge of the
towers?"
[19] You will see those arrogant people no
more,
people whose speech is obscure,
whose language is strange and
incomprehensible.
[20] Look on Zion, the city of our festivals;
your eyes will see Jerusalem,
a peaceful abode, a tent that will
not be moved;
its stakes will never be pulled up,
nor any of its ropes broken.
[21] There the LORD will be our Mighty
One.
It will be like a place of broad rivers
and streams.
No galley with oars will ride them,
no mighty ship will sail them.

[a] 6 Or *is a treasure from him* [b] 8 Dead Sea Scrolls; Masoretic Text / *the cities*

[22] For the LORD is our judge,
the LORD is our lawgiver,
the LORD is our king;
it is he who will save us.

[23] Your rigging hangs loose:
The mast is not held secure,
the sail is not spread.
Then an abundance of spoils will be divided
and even the lame will carry off plunder.
[24] No one living in Zion will say, "I am ill";
and the sins of those who dwell there will be forgiven.

Judgment Against the Nations

34 Come near, you nations, and listen;
pay attention, you peoples!
Let the earth hear, and all that is in it,
the world, and all that comes out of it!
[2] The LORD is angry with all nations;
his wrath is on all their armies.
He will totally destroy[a] them,
he will give them over to slaughter.
[3] Their slain will be thrown out,
their dead bodies will stink;
the mountains will be soaked with their blood.
[4] All the stars in the sky will be dissolved
and the heavens rolled up like a scroll;
all the starry host will fall
like withered leaves from the vine,
like shriveled figs from the fig tree.

[5] My sword has drunk its fill in the heavens;
see, it descends in judgment on Edom,
the people I have totally destroyed.
[6] The sword of the LORD is bathed in blood,
it is covered with fat—
the blood of lambs and goats,
fat from the kidneys of rams.
For the LORD has a sacrifice in Bozrah
and a great slaughter in the land of Edom.
[7] And the wild oxen will fall with them,
the bull calves and the great bulls.
Their land will be drenched with blood,
and the dust will be soaked with fat.
[8] For the LORD has a day of vengeance,
a year of retribution, to uphold Zion's cause.
[9] Edom's streams will be turned into pitch,
her dust into burning sulfur;
her land will become blazing pitch!
[10] It will not be quenched night or day;
its smoke will rise forever.
From generation to generation it will lie desolate;
no one will ever pass through it again.
[11] The desert owl[b] and screech owl[b] will possess it;
the great owl[b] and the raven will nest there.
God will stretch out over Edom
the measuring line of chaos
and the plumb line of desolation.
[12] Her nobles will have nothing there to be called a kingdom,
all her princes will vanish away.
[13] Thorns will overrun her citadels,
nettles and brambles her strongholds.
She will become a haunt for jackals,
a home for owls.
[14] Desert creatures will meet with hyenas,
and wild goats will bleat to each other;
there the night creatures will also lie down
and find for themselves places of rest.
[15] The owl will nest there and lay eggs,
she will hatch them, and care for her young
under the shadow of her wings;
there also the falcons will gather,
each with its mate.

[16] Look in the scroll of the LORD and read:

None of these will be missing,
not one will lack her mate.
For it is his mouth that has given the order,
and his Spirit will gather them together.
[17] He allots their portions;
his hand distributes them by measure.
They will possess it forever
and dwell there from generation to generation.

[a] *2* The Hebrew term refers to the irrevocable giving over of things or persons to the LORD, often by totally destroying them; also in verse 5. [b] *11* The precise identification of these birds is uncertain.

Joy of the Redeemed

35 The desert and the parched land
will be glad;
the wilderness will rejoice and
blossom.
Like the crocus, 2it will burst into
bloom;
it will rejoice greatly and shout for
joy.
The glory of Lebanon will be given
to it,
the splendor of Carmel and Sharon;
they will see the glory of the LORD,
the splendor of our God.

3 Strengthen the feeble hands,
steady the knees that give way;
4 say to those with fearful hearts,
"Be strong, do not fear;
your God will come,
he will come with vengeance;
with divine retribution
he will come to save you."

5 Then will the eyes of the blind be
opened
and the ears of the deaf
unstopped.
6 Then will the lame leap like a deer,
and the mute tongue shout
for joy.
Water will gush forth in the
wilderness
and streams in the desert.
7 The burning sand will become a pool,
the thirsty ground bubbling
springs.
In the haunts where jackals once lay,
grass and reeds and papyrus will
grow.

8 And a highway will be there;
it will be called the Way
of Holiness;
it will be for those who walk on
that Way.
The unclean will not journey on it;
wicked fools will not go about on it.
9 No lion will be there,
nor any ravenous beast;
they will not be found there.
But only the redeemed will walk
there,
10 and those the LORD has rescued
will return.
They will enter Zion with singing;
everlasting joy will crown their
heads.
Gladness and joy will overtake them,
and sorrow and sighing will flee
away.

Sennacherib Threatens Jerusalem

36 In the fourteenth year of King Hezekiah's reign, Sennacherib king of
Assyria attacked all the fortified cities of
Judah and captured them. 2Then the king
of Assyria sent his field commander with
a large army from Lachish to King Hezekiah at Jerusalem. When the commander stopped at the aqueduct of the Upper
Pool, on the road to the Launderer's Field,
3Eliakim son of Hilkiah the palace administrator, Shebna the secretary, and Joah
son of Asaph the recorder went out to him.
4The field commander said to them,
"Tell Hezekiah:

"'This is what the great king, the
king of Assyria, says: On what are
you basing this confidence of yours?
5You say you have counsel and might
for war—but you speak only empty
words. On whom are you depending,
that you rebel against me? 6Look, I
know you are depending on Egypt,
that splintered reed of a staff, which
pierces the hand of anyone who leans
on it! Such is Pharaoh king of Egypt
to all who depend on him. 7But if
you say to me, "We are depending
on the LORD our God"—isn't he the
one whose high places and altars
Hezekiah removed, saying to Judah
and Jerusalem, "You must worship
before this altar"?

8"'Come now, make a bargain with
my master, the king of Assyria: I will
give you two thousand horses—if
you can put riders on them! 9How
then can you repulse one officer of
the least of my master's officials, even
though you are depending on Egypt
for chariots and horsemen[a]? 10Fur-
thermore, have I come to attack and
destroy this land without the LORD?
The LORD himself told me to march
against this country and destroy it.'"

11Then Eliakim, Shebna and Joah said
to the field commander, "Please speak to
your servants in Aramaic, since we understand it. Don't speak to us in Hebrew
in the hearing of the people on the wall."
12But the commander replied, "Was it
only to your master and you that my master sent me to say these things, and not to
the people sitting on the wall—who, like
you, will have to eat their own excrement
and drink their own urine?"
13Then the commander stood and called
out in Hebrew, "Hear the words of the
great king, the king of Assyria! 14This is

[a] 9 Or *charioteers*

what the king says: Do not let Hezekiah deceive you. He cannot deliver you! 15Do not let Hezekiah persuade you to trust in the LORD when he says, 'The LORD will surely deliver us; this city will not be given into the hand of the king of Assyria.'

16"Do not listen to Hezekiah. This is what the king of Assyria says: Make peace with me and come out to me. Then each of you will eat fruit from your own vine and fig tree and drink water from your own cistern, 17until I come and take you to a land like your own — a land of grain and new wine, a land of bread and vineyards.

18"Do not let Hezekiah mislead you when he says, 'The LORD will deliver us.' Have the gods of any nations ever delivered their lands from the hand of the king of Assyria? 19Where are the gods of Hamath and Arpad? Where are the gods of Sepharvaim? Have they rescued Samaria from my hand? 20Who of all the gods of these countries have been able to save their lands from me? How then can the LORD deliver Jerusalem from my hand?"

21But the people remained silent and said nothing in reply, because the king had commanded, "Do not answer him."

22Then Eliakim son of Hilkiah the palace administrator, Shebna the secretary and Joah son of Asaph the recorder went to Hezekiah, with their clothes torn, and told him what the field commander had said.

Jerusalem's Deliverance Foretold

37 When King Hezekiah heard this, he tore his clothes and put on sackcloth and went into the temple of the LORD. 2He sent Eliakim the palace administrator, Shebna the secretary, and the leading priests, all wearing sackcloth, to the prophet Isaiah son of Amoz. 3They told him, "This is what Hezekiah says: This day is a day of distress and rebuke and disgrace, as when children come to the moment of birth and there is no strength to deliver them. 4It may be that the LORD your God will hear the words of the field commander, whom his master, the king of Assyria, has sent to ridicule the living God, and that he will rebuke him for the words the LORD your God has heard. Therefore pray for the remnant that still survives."

5When King Hezekiah's officials came to Isaiah, 6Isaiah said to them, "Tell your master, 'This is what the LORD says: Do not be afraid of what you have heard — those words with which the underlings of the king of Assyria have blasphemed me. 7Listen! When he hears a certain report, I will make him want to return to his own country, and there I will have him cut down with the sword.'"

8When the field commander heard that the king of Assyria had left Lachish, he withdrew and found the king fighting against Libnah.

9Now Sennacherib received a report that Tirhakah, the king of Cush,[a] was marching out to fight against him. When he heard it, he sent messengers to Hezekiah with this word: 10"Say to Hezekiah king of Judah: Do not let the god you depend on deceive you when he says, 'Jerusalem will not be given into the hands of the king of Assyria.' 11Surely you have heard what the kings of Assyria have done to all the countries, destroying them completely. And will you be delivered? 12Did the gods of the nations that were destroyed by my predecessors deliver them — the gods of Gozan, Harran, Rezeph and the people of Eden who were in Tel Assar? 13Where is the king of Hamath or the king of Arpad? Where are the kings of Lair, Sepharvaim, Hena and Ivvah?"

Hezekiah's Prayer

14Hezekiah received the letter from the messengers and read it. Then he went up to the temple of the LORD and spread it out before the LORD. 15And Hezekiah prayed to the LORD: 16"LORD Almighty, the God of Israel, enthroned between the cherubim, you alone are God over all the kingdoms of the earth. You have made heaven and earth. 17Give ear, LORD, and hear; open your eyes, LORD, and see; listen to all the words Sennacherib has sent to ridicule the living God.

18"It is true, LORD, that the Assyrian kings have laid waste all these peoples and their lands. 19They have thrown their gods into the fire and destroyed them, for they were not gods but only wood and stone, fashioned by human hands. 20Now, LORD our God, deliver us from his hand, so that all the kingdoms of the earth may know that you, LORD, are the only God.[b]"

Sennacherib's Fall

21Then Isaiah son of Amoz sent a message to Hezekiah: "This is what the LORD, the God of Israel, says: Because you have prayed to me concerning Sennacherib king of Assyria, 22this is the word the LORD has spoken against him:

[a] *9* That is, the upper Nile region [b] *20* Dead Sea Scrolls (see also 2 Kings 19:19); Masoretic Text *you alone are the LORD*

"Virgin Daughter Zion
despises and mocks you.
Daughter Jerusalem
tosses her head as you flee.
23 Who is it you have ridiculed and
blasphemed?
Against whom have you raised
your voice
and lifted your eyes in pride?
Against the Holy One of Israel!
24 By your messengers
you have ridiculed the Lord.
And you have said,
'With my many chariots
I have ascended the heights of the
mountains,
the utmost heights of Lebanon.
I have cut down its tallest cedars,
the choicest of its junipers.
I have reached its remotest heights,
the finest of its forests.
25 I have dug wells in foreign lands[a]
and drunk the water there.
With the soles of my feet
I have dried up all the streams of
Egypt.'

26 "Have you not heard?
Long ago I ordained it.
In days of old I planned it;
now I have brought it to pass,
that you have turned fortified cities
into piles of stone.
27 Their people, drained of power,
are dismayed and put to shame.
They are like plants in the field,
like tender green shoots,
like grass sprouting on the roof,
scorched[b] before it grows up.

28 "But I know where you are
and when you come and go
and how you rage against me.
29 Because you rage against me
and because your insolence has
reached my ears,
I will put my hook in your nose
and my bit in your mouth,
and I will make you return
by the way you came.

30 "This will be the sign for you, Hezekiah:

"This year you will eat what grows by
itself,
and the second year what springs
from that.
But in the third year sow and reap,
plant vineyards and eat their fruit.
31 Once more a remnant of the kingdom
of Judah
will take root below and bear fruit
above.
32 For out of Jerusalem will come a
remnant,
and out of Mount Zion a band of
survivors.
The zeal of the LORD Almighty
will accomplish this.

33 "Therefore this is what the LORD says
concerning the king of Assyria:

"He will not enter this city
or shoot an arrow here.
He will not come before it with shield
or build a siege ramp against it.
34 By the way that he came he will
return;
he will not enter this city,"
declares the LORD.
35 "I will defend this city and save it,
for my sake and for the sake of
David my servant!"

36 Then the angel of the LORD went
out and put to death a hundred and
eighty-five thousand in the Assyrian
camp. When the people got up the next
morning — there were all the dead bodies!
37 So Sennacherib king of Assyria broke
camp and withdrew. He returned to Nineveh and stayed there.
38 One day, while he was worshiping
in the temple of his god Nisrok, his sons
Adrammelek and Sharezer killed him
with the sword, and they escaped to the
land of Ararat. And Esarhaddon his son
succeeded him as king.

Hezekiah's Illness

38 In those days Hezekiah became ill
and was at the point of death. The
prophet Isaiah son of Amoz went to him
and said, "This is what the LORD says: Put
your house in order, because you are going
to die; you will not recover."
2 Hezekiah turned his face to the wall
and prayed to the LORD, 3 "Remember,
LORD, how I have walked before you faithfully and with wholehearted devotion and
have done what is good in your eyes." And
Hezekiah wept bitterly.
4 Then the word of the LORD came to Isaiah: 5 "Go and tell Hezekiah, 'This is what
the LORD, the God of your father David,
says: I have heard your prayer and seen
your tears; I will add fifteen years to your
life. 6 And I will deliver you and this city

[a] 25 Dead Sea Scrolls (see also 2 Kings 19:24); Masoretic Text does not have *in foreign lands.*
[b] 27 Some manuscripts of the Masoretic Text, Dead Sea Scrolls and some Septuagint manuscripts (see also 2 Kings 19:26); most manuscripts of the Masoretic Text *roof / and terraced fields*

from the hand of the king of Assyria. I will
defend this city.
7"'This is the LORD's sign to you that
the LORD will do what he has promised:
8I will make the shadow cast by the sun
go back the ten steps it has gone down
on the stairway of Ahaz.'" So the sunlight
went back the ten steps it had gone down.

9A writing of Hezekiah king of Judah
after his illness and recovery:

10 I said, "In the prime of my life
must I go through the gates of death
and be robbed of the rest of my
years?"
11 I said, "I will not again see the LORD
himself
in the land of the living;
no longer will I look on my fellow
man,
or be with those who now dwell in
this world.
12 Like a shepherd's tent my house
has been pulled down and taken
from me.
Like a weaver I have rolled up my life,
and he has cut me off from the loom;
day and night you made an end of
me.
13 I waited patiently till dawn,
but like a lion he broke all my
bones;
day and night you made an end of
me.
14 I cried like a swift or thrush,
I moaned like a mourning dove.
My eyes grew weak as I looked to the
heavens.
I am being threatened; Lord, come
to my aid!"

15 But what can I say?
He has spoken to me, and he
himself has done this.
I will walk humbly all my years
because of this anguish of my soul.
16 Lord, by such things people live;
and my spirit finds life in them too.
You restored me to health
and let me live.
17 Surely it was for my benefit
that I suffered such anguish.
In your love you kept me
from the pit of destruction;
you have put all my sins
behind your back.
18 For the grave cannot praise you,
death cannot sing your praise;
those who go down to the pit
cannot hope for your faithfulness.
19 The living, the living — they praise you,
as I am doing today;
parents tell their children
about your faithfulness.
20 The LORD will save me,
and we will sing with stringed
instruments
all the days of our lives
in the temple of the LORD.

21Isaiah had said, "Prepare a poultice
of figs and apply it to the boil, and he
will recover."
22Hezekiah had asked, "What will be
the sign that I will go up to the temple
of the LORD?"

Envoys From Babylon

39 At that time Marduk-Baladan son
of Baladan king of Babylon sent
Hezekiah letters and a gift, because he had
heard of his illness and recovery. 2Hezeki-
ah received the envoys gladly and showed
them what was in his storehouses — the
silver, the gold, the spices, the fine olive
oil — his entire armory and everything
found among his treasures. There was
nothing in his palace or in all his kingdom
that Hezekiah did not show them.
3Then Isaiah the prophet went to King
Hezekiah and asked, "What did those
men say, and where did they come from?"
"From a distant land," Hezekiah replied.
"They came to me from Babylon."
4The prophet asked, "What did they see
in your palace?"
"They saw everything in my palace,"
Hezekiah said. "There is nothing among
my treasures that I did not show them."
5Then Isaiah said to Hezekiah, "Hear the
word of the LORD Almighty: 6The time will
surely come when everything in your palace, and all that your predecessors have
stored up until this day, will be carried
off to Babylon. Nothing will be left, says
the LORD. 7And some of your descendants,
your own flesh and blood who will be born
to you, will be taken away, and they will
become eunuchs in the palace of the king
of Babylon."
8"The word of the LORD you have spoken
is good," Hezekiah replied. For he thought,
"There will be peace and security in my
lifetime."

Comfort for God's People

40 Comfort, comfort my people,
says your God.
2 Speak tenderly to Jerusalem,
and proclaim to her
that her hard service has been
completed,
that her sin has been paid for,
that she has received from the LORD's
hand
double for all her sins.

3 A voice of one calling:
"In the wilderness prepare
the way for the LORD[a];
make straight in the desert
a highway for our God.[b]
4 Every valley shall be raised up,
every mountain and hill made low;
the rough ground shall become level,
the rugged places a plain.
5 And the glory of the LORD will be
revealed,
and all people will see it together.
For the mouth of the LORD
has spoken."

6 A voice says, "Cry out."
And I said, "What shall I cry?"

"All people are like grass,
and all their faithfulness is like the
flowers of the field.
7 The grass withers and the flowers fall,
because the breath of the LORD
blows on them.
Surely the people are grass.
8 The grass withers and the flowers fall,
but the word of our God endures
forever."

9 You who bring good news to Zion,
go up on a high mountain.
You who bring good news to
Jerusalem,[c]
lift up your voice with a shout,
lift it up, do not be afraid;
say to the towns of Judah,
"Here is your God!"
10 See, the Sovereign LORD comes with
power,
and he rules with a mighty arm.
See, his reward is with him,
and his recompense accompanies
him.
11 He tends his flock like a shepherd:
He gathers the lambs in his arms
and carries them close to his heart;
he gently leads those that have
young.

12 Who has measured the waters in the
hollow of his hand,
or with the breadth of his hand
marked off the heavens?
Who has held the dust of the earth in
a basket,
or weighed the mountains on the
scales
and the hills in a balance?
13 Who can fathom the Spirit[d] of the
LORD,
or instruct the LORD as his counselor?
14 Whom did the LORD consult to
enlighten him,
and who taught him the right way?
Who was it that taught him
knowledge,
or showed him the path of
understanding?

15 Surely the nations are like a drop in a
bucket;
they are regarded as dust on the
scales;
he weighs the islands as though
they were fine dust.
16 Lebanon is not sufficient for altar
fires,
nor its animals enough for burnt
offerings.
17 Before him all the nations are as
nothing;
they are regarded by him as
worthless
and less than nothing.

18 With whom, then, will you compare
God?
To what image will you liken him?
19 As for an idol, a metalworker casts it,
and a goldsmith overlays it with
gold
and fashions silver chains for it.
20 A person too poor to present such an
offering
selects wood that will not rot;
they look for a skilled worker
to set up an idol that will not topple.

21 Do you not know?
Have you not heard?
Has it not been told you from the
beginning?
Have you not understood since the
earth was founded?
22 He sits enthroned above the circle of
the earth,
and its people are like grasshoppers.
He stretches out the heavens like a
canopy,
and spreads them out like a tent to
live in.
23 He brings princes to naught
and reduces the rulers of this world
to nothing.
24 No sooner are they planted,
no sooner are they sown,
no sooner do they take root in the
ground,
than he blows on them and they wither,
and a whirlwind sweeps them
away like chaff.

[a] 3 Or *A voice of one calling in the wilderness: / "Prepare the way for the* LORD [b] 3 Hebrew; Septuagint *make straight the paths of our God* [c] 9 Or *Zion, bringer of good news, / go up on a high mountain. / Jerusalem, bringer of good news* [d] 13 Or *mind*

25 "To whom will you compare me?
Or who is my equal?" says the Holy One.
26 Lift up your eyes and look to the heavens:
Who created all these?
He who brings out the starry host one by one
and calls forth each of them by name.
Because of his great power and mighty strength,
not one of them is missing.

27 Why do you complain, Jacob?
Why do you say, Israel,
"My way is hidden from the LORD;
my cause is disregarded by my God"?
28 Do you not know?
Have you not heard?
The LORD is the everlasting God,
the Creator of the ends of the earth.
He will not grow tired or weary,
and his understanding no one can fathom.
29 He gives strength to the weary
and increases the power of the weak.
30 Even youths grow tired and weary,
and young men stumble and fall;
31 but those who hope in the LORD
will renew their strength.
They will soar on wings like eagles;
they will run and not grow weary,
they will walk and not be faint.

The Helper of Israel

41 "Be silent before me, you islands!
Let the nations renew their strength!
Let them come forward and speak;
let us meet together at the place of judgment.

2 "Who has stirred up one from the east,
calling him in righteousness to his service[a]?
He hands nations over to him
and subdues kings before him.
He turns them to dust with his sword,
to windblown chaff with his bow.
3 He pursues them and moves on unscathed,
by a path his feet have not traveled before.
4 Who has done this and carried it through,
calling forth the generations from the beginning?
I, the LORD—with the first of them
and with the last—I am he."

5 The islands have seen it and fear;
the ends of the earth tremble.
They approach and come forward;
6 they help each other
and say to their companions, "Be strong!"
7 The metalworker encourages the goldsmith,
and the one who smooths with the hammer
spurs on the one who strikes the anvil.
One says of the welding, "It is good."
The other nails down the idol so it will not topple.

8 "But you, Israel, my servant,
Jacob, whom I have chosen,
you descendants of Abraham my friend,
9 I took you from the ends of the earth,
from its farthest corners I called you.
I said, 'You are my servant';
I have chosen you and have not rejected you.
10 So do not fear, for I am with you;
do not be dismayed, for I am your God.
I will strengthen you and help you;
I will uphold you with my righteous right hand.

11 "All who rage against you
will surely be ashamed and disgraced;
those who oppose you
will be as nothing and perish.
12 Though you search for your enemies,
you will not find them.
Those who wage war against you
will be as nothing at all.
13 For I am the LORD your God
who takes hold of your right hand
and says to you, Do not fear;
I will help you.
14 Do not be afraid, you worm Jacob,
little Israel, do not fear,
for I myself will help you," declares the LORD,
your Redeemer, the Holy One of Israel.
15 "See, I will make you into a threshing sledge,
new and sharp, with many teeth.
You will thresh the mountains and crush them,
and reduce the hills to chaff.
16 You will winnow them, the wind will pick them up,
and a gale will blow them away.
But you will rejoice in the LORD
and glory in the Holy One of Israel.

[a] 2 Or *east, / whom victory meets at every step*

17 "The poor and needy search for water,
but there is none;
their tongues are parched with thirst.
But I the LORD will answer them;
I, the God of Israel, will not forsake them.
18 I will make rivers flow on barren heights,
and springs within the valleys.
I will turn the desert into pools of water,
and the parched ground into springs.
19 I will put in the desert
the cedar and the acacia, the myrtle and the olive.
I will set junipers in the wasteland,
the fir and the cypress together,
20 so that people may see and know,
may consider and understand,
that the hand of the LORD has done this,
that the Holy One of Israel has created it.

21 "Present your case," says the LORD.
"Set forth your arguments," says Jacob's King.
22 "Tell us, you idols,
what is going to happen.
Tell us what the former things were,
so that we may consider them
and know their final outcome.
Or declare to us the things to come,
23 tell us what the future holds,
so we may know that you are gods.
Do something, whether good or bad,
so that we will be dismayed and filled with fear.
24 But you are less than nothing
and your works are utterly worthless;
whoever chooses you is detestable.

25 "I have stirred up one from the north,
and he comes —
one from the rising sun who calls on my name.
He treads on rulers as if they were mortar,
as if he were a potter treading the clay.
26 Who told of this from the beginning,
so we could know,
or beforehand, so we could say, 'He was right'?
No one told of this,
no one foretold it,
no one heard any words from you.
27 I was the first to tell Zion, 'Look, here they are!'
I gave to Jerusalem a messenger of good news.
28 I look but there is no one —
no one among the gods to give counsel,
no one to give answer when I ask them.
29 See, they are all false!
Their deeds amount to nothing;
their images are but wind and confusion.

The Servant of the LORD

42 "Here is my servant, whom I uphold,
my chosen one in whom I delight;
I will put my Spirit on him,
and he will bring justice to the nations.
2 He will not shout or cry out,
or raise his voice in the streets.
3 A bruised reed he will not break,
and a smoldering wick he will not snuff out.
In faithfulness he will bring forth justice;
4 he will not falter or be discouraged
till he establishes justice on earth.
In his teaching the islands will put their hope."

5 This is what God the LORD says —
the Creator of the heavens, who stretches them out,
who spreads out the earth with all that springs from it,
who gives breath to its people,
and life to those who walk on it:
6 "I, the LORD, have called you in righteousness;
I will take hold of your hand.
I will keep you and will make you
to be a covenant for the people
and a light for the Gentiles,
7 to open eyes that are blind,
to free captives from prison
and to release from the dungeon
those who sit in darkness.

8 "I am the LORD; that is my name!
I will not yield my glory to another
or my praise to idols.
9 See, the former things have taken place,
and new things I declare;
before they spring into being
I announce them to you."

Song of Praise to the LORD

10 Sing to the LORD a new song,
his praise from the ends of the earth,
you who go down to the sea, and all that is in it,
you islands, and all who live in them.

11 Let the wilderness and its towns raise their voices;
let the settlements where Kedar lives rejoice.
Let the people of Sela sing for joy;
let them shout from the mountaintops.
12 Let them give glory to the LORD
and proclaim his praise in the islands.
13 The LORD will march out like a champion,
like a warrior he will stir up his zeal;
with a shout he will raise the battle cry
and will triumph over his enemies.

14 "For a long time I have kept silent,
I have been quiet and held myself back.
But now, like a woman in childbirth,
I cry out, I gasp and pant.
15 I will lay waste the mountains and hills
and dry up all their vegetation;
I will turn rivers into islands
and dry up the pools.
16 I will lead the blind by ways they have not known,
along unfamiliar paths I will guide them;
I will turn the darkness into light before them
and make the rough places smooth.
These are the things I will do;
I will not forsake them.
17 But those who trust in idols,
who say to images, 'You are our gods,'
will be turned back in utter shame.

Israel Blind and Deaf

18 "Hear, you deaf;
look, you blind, and see!
19 Who is blind but my servant,
and deaf like the messenger I send?
Who is blind like the one in covenant with me,
blind like the servant of the LORD?
20 You have seen many things, but you pay no attention;
your ears are open, but you do not listen."
21 It pleased the LORD
for the sake of his righteousness
to make his law great and glorious.
22 But this is a people plundered and looted,
all of them trapped in pits
or hidden away in prisons.
They have become plunder,
with no one to rescue them;
they have been made loot,
with no one to say, "Send them back."

23 Which of you will listen to this
or pay close attention in time to come?
24 Who handed Jacob over to become loot,
and Israel to the plunderers?
Was it not the LORD,
against whom we have sinned?
For they would not follow his ways;
they did not obey his law.
25 So he poured out on them his burning anger,
the violence of war.
It enveloped them in flames, yet they did not understand;
it consumed them, but they did not take it to heart.

Israel's Only Savior

43 But now, this is what the LORD says —
he who created you, Jacob,
he who formed you, Israel:
"Do not fear, for I have redeemed you;
I have summoned you by name; you are mine.
2 When you pass through the waters,
I will be with you;
and when you pass through the rivers,
they will not sweep over you.
When you walk through the fire,
you will not be burned;
the flames will not set you ablaze.
3 For I am the LORD your God,
the Holy One of Israel, your Savior;
I give Egypt for your ransom,
Cush[a] and Seba in your stead.
4 Since you are precious and honored in my sight,
and because I love you,
I will give people in exchange for you,
nations in exchange for your life.
5 Do not be afraid, for I am with you;
I will bring your children from the east
and gather you from the west.
6 I will say to the north, 'Give them up!'
and to the south, 'Do not hold them back.'
Bring my sons from afar
and my daughters from the ends of the earth —
7 everyone who is called by my name,
whom I created for my glory,
whom I formed and made."

[a] 3 That is, the upper Nile region

8 Lead out those who have eyes but are blind,
who have ears but are deaf.
9 All the nations gather together
and the peoples assemble.
Which of their gods foretold this
and proclaimed to us the former things?
Let them bring in their witnesses to prove they were right,
so that others may hear and say, "It is true."
10 "You are my witnesses," declares the LORD,
"and my servant whom I have chosen,
so that you may know and believe me
and understand that I am he.
Before me no god was formed,
nor will there be one after me.
11 I, even I, am the LORD,
and apart from me there is no savior.
12 I have revealed and saved and proclaimed —
I, and not some foreign god among you.
You are my witnesses," declares the LORD, "that I am God.
13 Yes, and from ancient days I am he.
No one can deliver out of my hand.
When I act, who can reverse it?"

God's Mercy and Israel's Unfaithfulness

14 This is what the LORD says —
your Redeemer, the Holy One of Israel:
"For your sake I will send to Babylon
and bring down as fugitives all the Babylonians,[a]
in the ships in which they took pride.
15 I am the LORD, your Holy One,
Israel's Creator, your King."
16 This is what the LORD says —
he who made a way through the sea,
a path through the mighty waters,
17 who drew out the chariots and horses,
the army and reinforcements together,
and they lay there, never to rise again,
extinguished, snuffed out like a wick:
18 "Forget the former things;
do not dwell on the past.
19 See, I am doing a new thing!
Now it springs up; do you not perceive it?
I am making a way in the wilderness
and streams in the wasteland.
20 The wild animals honor me,
the jackals and the owls,
because I provide water in the wilderness
and streams in the wasteland,
to give drink to my people, my chosen,
21 the people I formed for myself
that they may proclaim my praise.
22 "Yet you have not called on me, Jacob,
you have not wearied yourselves for[b] me, Israel.
23 You have not brought me sheep for burnt offerings,
nor honored me with your sacrifices.
I have not burdened you with grain offerings
nor wearied you with demands for incense.
24 You have not bought any fragrant calamus for me,
or lavished on me the fat of your sacrifices.
But you have burdened me with your sins
and wearied me with your offenses.
25 "I, even I, am he who blots out
your transgressions, for my own sake,
and remembers your sins no more.
26 Review the past for me,
let us argue the matter together;
state the case for your innocence.
27 Your first father sinned;
those I sent to teach you rebelled against me.
28 So I disgraced the dignitaries of your temple;
I consigned Jacob to destruction[c]
and Israel to scorn.

Israel the Chosen

44 "But now listen, Jacob, my servant,
Israel, whom I have chosen.
2 This is what the LORD says —
he who made you, who formed you in the womb,
and who will help you:
Do not be afraid, Jacob, my servant,
Jeshurun,[d] whom I have chosen.

[a] 14 Or *Chaldeans* [b] 22 Or *Jacob; / surely you have grown weary of* [c] 28 The Hebrew term refers to the irrevocable giving over of things or persons to the LORD, often by totally destroying them. [d] 2 *Jeshurun* means *the upright one*, that is, Israel.

3 For I will pour water on the thirsty land,
and streams on the dry ground;
I will pour out my Spirit on your offspring,
and my blessing on your descendants.
4 They will spring up like grass in a meadow,
like poplar trees by flowing streams.
5 Some will say, 'I belong to the LORD';
others will call themselves by the name of Jacob;
still others will write on their hand, 'The LORD's,'
and will take the name Israel.

The LORD, Not Idols

6 "This is what the LORD says —
Israel's King and Redeemer, the LORD Almighty:
I am the first and I am the last;
apart from me there is no God.
7 Who then is like me? Let him proclaim it.
Let him declare and lay out before me
what has happened since I established my ancient people,
and what is yet to come —
yes, let them foretell what will come.
8 Do not tremble, do not be afraid.
Did I not proclaim this and foretell it long ago?
You are my witnesses. Is there any God besides me?
No, there is no other Rock; I know not one."

9 All who make idols are nothing,
and the things they treasure are worthless.
Those who would speak up for them are blind;
they are ignorant, to their own shame.
10 Who shapes a god and casts an idol,
which can profit nothing?
11 People who do that will be put to shame;
such craftsmen are only human beings.
Let them all come together and take their stand;
they will be brought down to terror and shame.

12 The blacksmith takes a tool
and works with it in the coals;
he shapes an idol with hammers,
he forges it with the might of his arm.
He gets hungry and loses his strength;
he drinks no water and grows faint.
13 The carpenter measures with a line
and makes an outline with a marker;
he roughs it out with chisels
and marks it with compasses.
He shapes it in human form,
human form in all its glory,
that it may dwell in a shrine.
14 He cut down cedars,
or perhaps took a cypress or oak.
He let it grow among the trees of the forest,
or planted a pine, and the rain made it grow.
15 It is used as fuel for burning;
some of it he takes and warms himself,
he kindles a fire and bakes bread.
But he also fashions a god and worships it;
he makes an idol and bows down to it.
16 Half of the wood he burns in the fire;
over it he prepares his meal,
he roasts his meat and eats his fill.
He also warms himself and says,
"Ah! I am warm; I see the fire."
17 From the rest he makes a god, his idol;
he bows down to it and worships.
He prays to it and says,
"Save me! You are my god!"
18 They know nothing, they understand nothing;
their eyes are plastered over so they cannot see,
and their minds closed so they cannot understand.
19 No one stops to think,
no one has the knowledge or understanding to say,
"Half of it I used for fuel;
I even baked bread over its coals,
I roasted meat and I ate.
Shall I make a detestable thing from what is left?
Shall I bow down to a block of wood?"
20 Such a person feeds on ashes; a deluded heart misleads him;
he cannot save himself, or say,
"Is not this thing in my right hand a lie?"

21 "Remember these things, Jacob,
for you, Israel, are my servant.
I have made you, you are my servant;
Israel, I will not forget you.

[22] I have swept away your offenses like
a cloud,
your sins like the morning mist.
Return to me,
for I have redeemed you."

[23] Sing for joy, you heavens, for the LORD
has done this;
shout aloud, you earth beneath.
Burst into song, you mountains,
you forests and all your trees,
for the LORD has redeemed Jacob,
he displays his glory in Israel.

Jerusalem to Be Inhabited

[24] "This is what the LORD says —
your Redeemer, who formed you in
the womb:

I am the LORD,
the Maker of all things,
who stretches out the heavens,
who spreads out the earth by
myself,
[25] who foils the signs of false prophets
and makes fools of diviners,
who overthrows the learning of the
wise
and turns it into nonsense,
[26] who carries out the words of his
servants
and fulfills the predictions of his
messengers,

who says of Jerusalem, 'It shall be
inhabited,'
of the towns of Judah, 'They shall
be rebuilt,'
and of their ruins, 'I will restore
them,'
[27] who says to the watery deep, 'Be dry,
and I will dry up your streams,'
[28] who says of Cyrus, 'He is my shepherd
and will accomplish all that I
please;
he will say of Jerusalem, "Let it be
rebuilt,"
and of the temple, "Let its
foundations be laid."'

45 "This is what the LORD says to his
anointed,
to Cyrus, whose right hand I take
hold of
to subdue nations before him
and to strip kings of their armor,
to open doors before him
so that gates will not be shut:
[2] I will go before you
and will level the mountains[a];
I will break down gates of bronze
and cut through bars of iron.
[3] I will give you hidden treasures,
riches stored in secret places,
so that you may know that I am the
LORD,
the God of Israel, who summons
you by name.
[4] For the sake of Jacob my servant,
of Israel my chosen,
I summon you by name
and bestow on you a title of honor,
though you do not acknowledge me.
[5] I am the LORD, and there is no other;
apart from me there is no God.
I will strengthen you,
though you have not
acknowledged me,
[6] so that from the rising of the sun
to the place of its setting
people may know there is none
besides me.
I am the LORD, and there is no
other.
[7] I form the light and create darkness,
I bring prosperity and create
disaster;
I, the LORD, do all these things.

[8] "You heavens above, rain down my
righteousness;
let the clouds shower it down.
Let the earth open wide,
let salvation spring up,
let righteousness flourish with it;
I, the LORD, have created it.

[9] "Woe to those who quarrel with their
Maker,
those who are nothing but
potsherds
among the potsherds on the
ground.
Does the clay say to the potter,
'What are you making?'
Does your work say,
'The potter has no hands'?
[10] Woe to the one who says to a father,
'What have you begotten?'
or to a mother,
'What have you brought to birth?'

[11] "This is what the LORD says —
the Holy One of Israel, and its
Maker:
Concerning things to come,
do you question me about my
children,
or give me orders about the work of
my hands?
[12] It is I who made the earth
and created mankind on it.
My own hands stretched out the
heavens;
I marshaled their starry hosts.

[a] 2 Dead Sea Scrolls and Septuagint; the meaning of the word in the Masoretic Text is uncertain.

13 I will raise up Cyrus[a] in my
righteousness:
I will make all his ways straight.
He will rebuild my city
and set my exiles free,
but not for a price or reward,
says the LORD Almighty."

14 This is what the LORD says:

"The products of Egypt and the
merchandise of Cush,[b]
and those tall Sabeans —
they will come over to you
and will be yours;
they will trudge behind you,
coming over to you in chains.
They will bow down before you
and plead with you, saying,
'Surely God is with you, and there is
no other;
there is no other god.'"

15 Truly you are a God who has been
hiding himself,
the God and Savior of Israel.
16 All the makers of idols will be put to
shame and disgraced;
they will go off into disgrace
together.
17 But Israel will be saved by the LORD
with an everlasting salvation;
you will never be put to shame or
disgraced,
to ages everlasting.

18 For this is what the LORD says —
he who created the heavens,
he is God;
he who fashioned and made the earth,
he founded it;
he did not create it to be empty,
but formed it to be inhabited —
he says:
"I am the LORD,
and there is no other.
19 I have not spoken in secret,
from somewhere in a land of
darkness;
I have not said to Jacob's
descendants,
'Seek me in vain.'
I, the LORD, speak the truth;
I declare what is right.

20 "Gather together and come;
assemble, you fugitives from the
nations.
Ignorant are those who carry about
idols of wood,
who pray to gods that cannot save.
21 Declare what is to be, present it —
let them take counsel together.
Who foretold this long ago,
who declared it from the distant
past?
Was it not I, the LORD?
And there is no God apart from me,
a righteous God and a Savior;
there is none but me.

22 "Turn to me and be saved,
all you ends of the earth;
for I am God, and there is no other.
23 By myself I have sworn,
my mouth has uttered in all integrity
a word that will not be revoked:
Before me every knee will bow;
by me every tongue will swear.
24 They will say of me, 'In the LORD
alone
are deliverance and strength.'"
All who have raged against him
will come to him and be put to
shame.
25 But all the descendants of Israel
will find deliverance in the LORD
and will make their boast in him.

Gods of Babylon

46 Bel bows down, Nebo stoops low;
their idols are borne by beasts of
burden.[c]
The images that are carried about
are burdensome,
a burden for the weary.
2 They stoop and bow down together;
unable to rescue the burden,
they themselves go off into
captivity.

3 "Listen to me, you descendants of
Jacob,
all the remnant of the people of
Israel,
you whom I have upheld since your
birth,
and have carried since you were
born.
4 Even to your old age and gray hairs
I am he, I am he who will sustain
you.
I have made you and I will carry you;
I will sustain you and I will rescue
you.

5 "With whom will you compare me or
count me equal?
To whom will you liken me that we
may be compared?
6 Some pour out gold from their bags
and weigh out silver on the scales;
they hire a goldsmith to make it into
a god,
and they bow down and worship it.

[a] *13* Hebrew *him* [b] *14* That is, the upper Nile region [c] *1* Or *are but beasts and cattle*

[7]They lift it to their shoulders and
carry it;
they set it up in its place, and there
it stands.
From that spot it cannot move.
Even though someone cries out to it,
it cannot answer;
it cannot save them from their
troubles.

[8]"Remember this, keep it in mind,
take it to heart, you rebels.
[9]Remember the former things, those
of long ago;
I am God, and there is no other;
I am God, and there is none like me.
[10]I make known the end from the
beginning,
from ancient times, what is still
to come.
I say, 'My purpose will stand,
and I will do all that I please.'
[11]From the east I summon a bird of prey;
from a far-off land, a man to fulfill
my purpose.
What I have said, that I will bring
about;
what I have planned, that I will do.
[12]Listen to me, you stubborn-hearted,
you who are now far from my
righteousness.
[13]I am bringing my righteousness near,
it is not far away;
and my salvation will not be delayed.
I will grant salvation to Zion,
my splendor to Israel.

The Fall of Babylon

47 "Go down, sit in the dust,
Virgin Daughter Babylon;
sit on the ground without a throne,
queen city of the Babylonians.[a]
No more will you be called
tender or delicate.
[2]Take millstones and grind flour;
take off your veil.
Lift up your skirts, bare your legs,
and wade through the streams.
[3]Your nakedness will be exposed
and your shame uncovered.
I will take vengeance;
I will spare no one."

[4]Our Redeemer — the LORD Almighty
is his name —
is the Holy One of Israel.

[5]"Sit in silence, go into darkness,
queen city of the Babylonians;
no more will you be called
queen of kingdoms.
[6]I was angry with my people
and desecrated my inheritance;
I gave them into your hand,
and you showed them no mercy.
Even on the aged
you laid a very heavy yoke.
[7]You said, 'I am forever —
the eternal queen!'
But you did not consider these things
or reflect on what might happen.

[8]"Now then, listen, you lover of pleasure,
lounging in your security
and saying to yourself,
'I am, and there is none besides me.
I will never be a widow
or suffer the loss of children.'
[9]Both of these will overtake you
in a moment, on a single day:
loss of children and widowhood.
They will come upon you in full
measure,
in spite of your many sorceries
and all your potent spells.
[10]You have trusted in your wickedness
and have said, 'No one sees me.'
Your wisdom and knowledge mislead
you
when you say to yourself,
'I am, and there is none besides me.'
[11]Disaster will come upon you,
and you will not know how to
conjure it away.
A calamity will fall upon you
that you cannot ward off with a
ransom;
a catastrophe you cannot foresee
will suddenly come upon you.

[12]"Keep on, then, with your magic spells
and with your many sorceries,
which you have labored at since
childhood.
Perhaps you will succeed,
perhaps you will cause terror.
[13]All the counsel you have received has
only worn you out!
Let your astrologers come forward,
those stargazers who make
predictions month by month,
let them save you from what is
coming upon you.
[14]Surely they are like stubble;
the fire will burn them up.
They cannot even save themselves
from the power of the flame.
These are not coals for warmth;
this is not a fire to sit by.
[15]That is all they are to you —
these you have dealt with
and labored with since childhood.
All of them go on in their error;
there is not one that can save you.

[a] *1* Or *Chaldeans*; also in verse 5

Stubborn Israel

48 "Listen to this, you descendants of Jacob,
you who are called by the name of Israel
and come from the line of Judah,
you who take oaths in the name of the LORD
and invoke the God of Israel —
but not in truth or righteousness —
2 you who call yourselves citizens of the holy city
and claim to rely on the God of Israel —
the LORD Almighty is his name:
3 I foretold the former things long ago,
my mouth announced them and I made them known;
then suddenly I acted, and they came to pass.
4 For I knew how stubborn you were;
your neck muscles were iron,
your forehead was bronze.
5 Therefore I told you these things long ago;
before they happened I announced them to you
so that you could not say,
'My images brought them about;
my wooden image and metal god ordained them.'
6 You have heard these things; look at them all.
Will you not admit them?

"From now on I will tell you of new things,
of hidden things unknown to you.
7 They are created now, and not long ago;
you have not heard of them before today.
So you cannot say,
'Yes, I knew of them.'
8 You have neither heard nor understood;
from of old your ears have not been open.
Well do I know how treacherous you are;
you were called a rebel from birth.
9 For my own name's sake I delay my wrath;
for the sake of my praise I hold it back from you,
so as not to destroy you completely.
10 See, I have refined you, though not as silver;
I have tested you in the furnace of affliction.
11 For my own sake, for my own sake, I do this.
How can I let myself be defamed?
I will not yield my glory to another.

Israel Freed

12 "Listen to me, Jacob,
Israel, whom I have called:
I am he;
I am the first and I am the last.
13 My own hand laid the foundations of the earth,
and my right hand spread out the heavens;
when I summon them,
they all stand up together.

14 "Come together, all of you, and listen:
Which of the idols has foretold these things?
The LORD's chosen ally
will carry out his purpose against Babylon;
his arm will be against the Babylonians.[a]
15 I, even I, have spoken;
yes, I have called him.
I will bring him,
and he will succeed in his mission.

16 "Come near me and listen to this:

"From the first announcement I have not spoken in secret;
at the time it happens, I am there."

And now the Sovereign LORD has sent me,
endowed with his Spirit.

17 This is what the LORD says —
your Redeemer, the Holy One of Israel:
"I am the LORD your God,
who teaches you what is best for you,
who directs you in the way you should go.
18 If only you had paid attention to my commands,
your peace would have been like a river,
your well-being like the waves of the sea.
19 Your descendants would have been like the sand,
your children like its numberless grains;
their name would never be blotted out
nor destroyed from before me."

[a] 14 Or *Chaldeans*; also in verse 20

20 Leave Babylon,
flee from the Babylonians!
Announce this with shouts of joy
and proclaim it.
Send it out to the ends of the earth;
say, "The LORD has redeemed his
servant Jacob."
21 They did not thirst when he led them
through the deserts;
he made water flow for them from
the rock;
he split the rock
and water gushed out.
22 "There is no peace," says the LORD,
"for the wicked."

The Servant of the LORD

49 Listen to me, you islands;
hear this, you distant nations:
Before I was born the LORD called me;
from my mother's womb he has
spoken my name.
2 He made my mouth like a sharpened
sword,
in the shadow of his hand he hid
me;
he made me into a polished arrow
and concealed me in his quiver.
3 He said to me, "You are my servant,
Israel, in whom I will display my
splendor."
4 But I said, "I have labored in vain;
I have spent my strength for
nothing at all.
Yet what is due me is in the LORD's
hand,
and my reward is with my God."

5 And now the LORD says —
he who formed me in the womb to
be his servant
to bring Jacob back to him
and gather Israel to himself,
for I am[a] honored in the eyes of the
LORD
and my God has been my
strength —
6 he says:
"It is too small a thing for you to be
my servant
to restore the tribes of Jacob
and bring back those of Israel I
have kept.
I will also make you a light for the
Gentiles,
that my salvation may reach to
the ends of the earth."

7 This is what the LORD says —
the Redeemer and Holy One of
Israel —
to him who was despised and
abhorred by the nation,
to the servant of rulers:
"Kings will see you and stand up,
princes will see and bow down,
because of the LORD, who is faithful,
the Holy One of Israel, who has
chosen you."

Restoration of Israel

8 This is what the LORD says:

"In the time of my favor I will answer
you,
and in the day of salvation I will
help you;
I will keep you and will make you
to be a covenant for the people,
to restore the land
and to reassign its desolate
inheritances,
9 to say to the captives, 'Come out,'
and to those in darkness, 'Be free!'

"They will feed beside the roads
and find pasture on every barren
hill.
10 They will neither hunger nor thirst,
nor will the desert heat or the sun
beat down on them.
He who has compassion on them will
guide them
and lead them beside springs of
water.
11 I will turn all my mountains into
roads,
and my highways will be raised up.
12 See, they will come from afar —
some from the north, some from
the west,
some from the region of Aswan.[b]"

13 Shout for joy, you heavens;
rejoice, you earth;
burst into song, you mountains!
For the LORD comforts his people
and will have compassion on his
afflicted ones.

14 But Zion said, "The LORD has forsaken
me,
the Lord has forgotten me."

15 "Can a mother forget the baby at her
breast
and have no compassion on the
child she has borne?
Though she may forget,
I will not forget you!

[a] 5 Or *him, / but Israel would not be gathered; / yet I will be*
[b] 12 Dead Sea Scrolls; Masoretic Text *Sinim*

16 See, I have engraved you on the palms of my hands;
your walls are ever before me.
17 Your children hasten back,
and those who laid you waste depart from you.
18 Lift up your eyes and look around;
all your children gather and come to you.
As surely as I live," declares the LORD,
"you will wear them all as ornaments;
you will put them on, like a bride.

19 "Though you were ruined and made desolate
and your land laid waste,
now you will be too small for your people,
and those who devoured you will be far away.
20 The children born during your bereavement
will yet say in your hearing,
'This place is too small for us;
give us more space to live in.'
21 Then you will say in your heart,
'Who bore me these?
I was bereaved and barren;
I was exiled and rejected.
Who brought these up?
I was left all alone,
but these — where have they come from?' "

22 This is what the Sovereign LORD says:

"See, I will beckon to the nations,
I will lift up my banner to the peoples;
they will bring your sons in their arms
and carry your daughters on their hips.
23 Kings will be your foster fathers,
and their queens your nursing mothers.
They will bow down before you with their faces to the ground;
they will lick the dust at your feet.
Then you will know that I am the LORD;
those who hope in me will not be disappointed."

24 Can plunder be taken from warriors,
or captives be rescued from the fierce[a]?

25 But this is what the LORD says:

"Yes, captives will be taken from warriors,
and plunder retrieved from the fierce;
I will contend with those who contend with you,
and your children I will save.
26 I will make your oppressors eat their own flesh;
they will be drunk on their own blood, as with wine.
Then all mankind will know
that I, the LORD, am your Savior,
your Redeemer, the Mighty One of Jacob."

Israel's Sin and the Servant's Obedience

50 This is what the LORD says:

"Where is your mother's certificate of divorce
with which I sent her away?
Or to which of my creditors
did I sell you?
Because of your sins you were sold;
because of your transgressions your mother was sent away.
2 When I came, why was there no one?
When I called, why was there no one to answer?
Was my arm too short to deliver you?
Do I lack the strength to rescue you?
By a mere rebuke I dry up the sea,
I turn rivers into a desert;
their fish rot for lack of water
and die of thirst.
3 I clothe the heavens with darkness
and make sackcloth its covering."

4 The Sovereign LORD has given me a well-instructed tongue,
to know the word that sustains the weary.
He wakens me morning by morning,
wakens my ear to listen like one being instructed.
5 The Sovereign LORD has opened my ears;
I have not been rebellious,
I have not turned away.
6 I offered my back to those who beat me,
my cheeks to those who pulled out my beard;
I did not hide my face
from mocking and spitting.
7 Because the Sovereign LORD helps me,
I will not be disgraced.
Therefore have I set my face like flint,
and I know I will not be put to shame.

[a] 24 Dead Sea Scrolls, Vulgate and Syriac (see also Septuagint and verse 25); Masoretic Text *righteous*

8 He who vindicates me is near.
Who then will bring charges
against me?
Let us face each other!
Who is my accuser?
Let him confront me!
9 It is the Sovereign LORD who helps me.
Who will condemn me?
They will all wear out like a garment;
the moths will eat them up.

10 Who among you fears the LORD
and obeys the word of his servant?
Let the one who walks in the dark,
who has no light,
trust in the name of the LORD
and rely on their God.
11 But now, all you who light fires
and provide yourselves with
flaming torches,
go, walk in the light of your fires
and of the torches you have set
ablaze.
This is what you shall receive from
my hand:
You will lie down in torment.

Everlasting Salvation for Zion

51 "Listen to me, you who pursue
righteousness
and who seek the LORD:
Look to the rock from which you were
cut
and to the quarry from which you
were hewn;
2 look to Abraham, your father,
and to Sarah, who gave you birth.
When I called him he was only one
man,
and I blessed him and made him
many.
3 The LORD will surely comfort Zion
and will look with compassion on
all her ruins;
he will make her deserts like Eden,
her wastelands like the garden of
the LORD.
Joy and gladness will be found in her,
thanksgiving and the sound of
singing.
4 "Listen to me, my people;
hear me, my nation:
Instruction will go out from me;
my justice will become a light to
the nations.
5 My righteousness draws near
speedily,
my salvation is on the way,
and my arm will bring justice to
the nations.
The islands will look to me
and wait in hope for my arm.
6 Lift up your eyes to the heavens,
look at the earth beneath;
the heavens will vanish like smoke,
the earth will wear out like a
garment
and its inhabitants die like flies.
But my salvation will last forever,
my righteousness will never fail.

7 "Hear me, you who know what is right,
you people who have taken my
instruction to heart:
Do not fear the reproach of mere
mortals
or be terrified by their insults.
8 For the moth will eat them up like a
garment;
the worm will devour them like wool.
But my righteousness will last
forever,
my salvation through all
generations."

9 Awake, awake, arm of the LORD,
clothe yourself with strength!
Awake, as in days gone by,
as in generations of old.
Was it not you who cut Rahab to
pieces,
who pierced that monster through?
10 Was it not you who dried up the sea,
the waters of the great deep,
who made a road in the depths of the
sea
so that the redeemed might cross
over?
11 Those the LORD has rescued will
return.
They will enter Zion with singing;
everlasting joy will crown their
heads.
Gladness and joy will overtake them,
and sorrow and sighing will flee
away.

12 "I, even I, am he who comforts you.
Who are you that you fear mere
mortals,
human beings who are but grass,
13 that you forget the LORD your Maker,
who stretches out the heavens
and who lays the foundations of
the earth,
that you live in constant terror every
day
because of the wrath of the
oppressor,
who is bent on destruction?
For where is the wrath of the
oppressor?
14 The cowering prisoners will soon be
set free;
they will not die in their dungeon,
nor will they lack bread.

[15] For I am the LORD your God,
who stirs up the sea so that its waves roar —
the LORD Almighty is his name.
[16] I have put my words in your mouth
and covered you with the shadow of my hand —
I who set the heavens in place,
who laid the foundations of the earth,
and who say to Zion, 'You are my people.'"

The Cup of the LORD's Wrath

[17] Awake, awake!
Rise up, Jerusalem,
you who have drunk from the hand of the LORD
the cup of his wrath,
you who have drained to its dregs
the goblet that makes people stagger.
[18] Among all the children she bore
there was none to guide her;
among all the children she reared
there was none to take her by the hand.
[19] These double calamities have come upon you —
who can comfort you? —
ruin and destruction, famine and sword —
who can[a] console you?
[20] Your children have fainted;
they lie at every street corner,
like antelope caught in a net.
They are filled with the wrath of the LORD,
with the rebuke of your God.

[21] Therefore hear this, you afflicted one,
made drunk, but not with wine.
[22] This is what your Sovereign LORD says,
your God, who defends his people:
"See, I have taken out of your hand
the cup that made you stagger;
from that cup, the goblet of my wrath,
you will never drink again.
[23] I will put it into the hands of your tormentors,
who said to you,
'Fall prostrate that we may walk on you.'
And you made your back like the ground,
like a street to be walked on."

52 Awake, awake, Zion,
clothe yourself with strength!
Put on your garments of splendor,
Jerusalem, the holy city.
The uncircumcised and defiled
will not enter you again.
[2] Shake off your dust;
rise up, sit enthroned, Jerusalem.
Free yourself from the chains on your neck,
Daughter Zion, now a captive.

[3] For this is what the LORD says:

"You were sold for nothing,
and without money you will be redeemed."

[4] For this is what the Sovereign LORD says:

"At first my people went down to Egypt to live;
lately, Assyria has oppressed them.

[5] "And now what do I have here?" declares the LORD.

"For my people have been taken away for nothing,
and those who rule them mock,[b]"
declares the LORD.
"And all day long
my name is constantly blasphemed.
[6] Therefore my people will know my name;
therefore in that day they will know
that it is I who foretold it.
Yes, it is I."

[7] How beautiful on the mountains
are the feet of those who bring good news,
who proclaim peace,
who bring good tidings,
who proclaim salvation,
who say to Zion,
"Your God reigns!"
[8] Listen! Your watchmen lift up their voices;
together they shout for joy.
When the LORD returns to Zion,
they will see it with their own eyes.
[9] Burst into songs of joy together,
you ruins of Jerusalem,
for the LORD has comforted his people,
he has redeemed Jerusalem.
[10] The LORD will lay bare his holy arm
in the sight of all the nations,
and all the ends of the earth will see
the salvation of our God.

[a] *19* Dead Sea Scrolls, Septuagint, Vulgate and Syriac; Masoretic Text / *how can I* [b] *5* Dead Sea Scrolls and Vulgate; Masoretic Text *wail*

11 Depart, depart, go out from there!
Touch no unclean thing!
Come out from it and be pure,
you who carry the articles of the LORD's house.
12 But you will not leave in haste
or go in flight;
for the LORD will go before you,
the God of Israel will be your rear guard.

The Suffering and Glory of the Servant

13 See, my servant will act wisely[a];
he will be raised and lifted up and highly exalted.
14 Just as there were many who were appalled at him[b] —
his appearance was so disfigured beyond that of any human being
and his form marred beyond human likeness —
15 so he will sprinkle many nations,[c]
and kings will shut their mouths because of him.
For what they were not told, they will see,
and what they have not heard, they will understand.

53 Who has believed our message
and to whom has the arm of the LORD been revealed?
2 He grew up before him like a tender shoot,
and like a root out of dry ground.
He had no beauty or majesty to attract us to him,
nothing in his appearance that we should desire him.
3 He was despised and rejected by mankind,
a man of suffering, and familiar with pain.
Like one from whom people hide their faces
he was despised, and we held him in low esteem.
4 Surely he took up our pain
and bore our suffering,
yet we considered him punished by God,
stricken by him, and afflicted.
5 But he was pierced for our transgressions,
he was crushed for our iniquities;
the punishment that brought us peace was on him,
and by his wounds we are healed.
6 We all, like sheep, have gone astray,
each of us has turned to our own way;
and the LORD has laid on him
the iniquity of us all.

7 He was oppressed and afflicted,
yet he did not open his mouth;
he was led like a lamb to the slaughter,
and as a sheep before its shearers is silent,
so he did not open his mouth.
8 By oppression[d] and judgment he was taken away.
Yet who of his generation protested?
For he was cut off from the land of the living;
for the transgression of my people he was punished.[e]
9 He was assigned a grave with the wicked,
and with the rich in his death,
though he had done no violence,
nor was any deceit in his mouth.

10 Yet it was the LORD's will to crush him
and cause him to suffer,
and though the LORD makes[f] his life an offering for sin,
he will see his offspring and prolong his days,
and the will of the LORD will prosper in his hand.
11 After he has suffered,
he will see the light of life[g] and be satisfied[h];
by his knowledge[i] my righteous servant will justify many,
and he will bear their iniquities.
12 Therefore I will give him a portion among the great,[j]
and he will divide the spoils with the strong,[k]
because he poured out his life unto death,
and was numbered with the transgressors.
For he bore the sin of many,
and made intercession for the transgressors.

[a] 13 Or *will prosper* [b] 14 Hebrew *you* [c] 15 Or *so will many nations be amazed at him* (see also Septuagint) [d] 8 Or *From arrest* [e] 8 Or *generation considered / that he was cut off from the land of the living, / that he was punished for the transgression of my people?* [f] 10 Hebrew *though you make* [g] 11 Dead Sea Scrolls (see also Septuagint); Masoretic Text does not have *the light of life.* [h] 11 Or (with Masoretic Text) *"He will see the fruit of his suffering / and will be satisfied* [i] 11 Or *by knowledge of him* [j] 12 Or *many* [k] 12 Or *numerous*

The Future Glory of Zion

54 "Sing, barren woman,
you who never bore a child;
burst into song, shout for joy,
you who were never in labor;
because more are the children of the desolate woman
than of her who has a husband,"
says the LORD.
2 "Enlarge the place of your tent,
stretch your tent curtains wide,
do not hold back;
lengthen your cords,
strengthen your stakes.
3 For you will spread out to the right and to the left;
your descendants will dispossess nations
and settle in their desolate cities.

4 "Do not be afraid; you will not be put to shame.
Do not fear disgrace; you will not be humiliated.
You will forget the shame of your youth
and remember no more the reproach of your widowhood.
5 For your Maker is your husband —
the LORD Almighty is his name —
the Holy One of Israel is your Redeemer;
he is called the God of all the earth.
6 The LORD will call you back
as if you were a wife deserted and distressed in spirit —
a wife who married young,
only to be rejected," says your God.
7 "For a brief moment I abandoned you,
but with deep compassion I will bring you back.
8 In a surge of anger
I hid my face from you for a moment,
but with everlasting kindness
I will have compassion on you,"
says the LORD your Redeemer.

9 "To me this is like the days of Noah,
when I swore that the waters of Noah would never again cover the earth.
So now I have sworn not to be angry with you,
never to rebuke you again.
10 Though the mountains be shaken
and the hills be removed,
yet my unfailing love for you will not be shaken
nor my covenant of peace be removed,"
says the LORD, who has compassion on you.

11 "Afflicted city, lashed by storms and not comforted,
I will rebuild you with stones of turquoise,[a]
your foundations with lapis lazuli.
12 I will make your battlements of rubies,
your gates of sparkling jewels,
and all your walls of precious stones.
13 All your children will be taught by the LORD,
and great will be their peace.
14 In righteousness you will be established:
Tyranny will be far from you;
you will have nothing to fear.
Terror will be far removed;
it will not come near you.
15 If anyone does attack you, it will not be my doing;
whoever attacks you will surrender to you.

16 "See, it is I who created the blacksmith
who fans the coals into flame
and forges a weapon fit for its work.
And it is I who have created the destroyer to wreak havoc;
17 no weapon forged against you will prevail,
and you will refute every tongue that accuses you.
This is the heritage of the servants of the LORD,
and this is their vindication from me,"
declares the LORD.

Invitation to the Thirsty

55 "Come, all you who are thirsty,
come to the waters;
and you who have no money,
come, buy and eat!
Come, buy wine and milk
without money and without cost.
2 Why spend money on what is not bread,
and your labor on what does not satisfy?
Listen, listen to me, and eat what is good,
and you will delight in the richest of fare.
3 Give ear and come to me;
listen, that you may live.
I will make an everlasting covenant with you,
my faithful love promised to David.

[a] *11* The meaning of the Hebrew for this word is uncertain.

4 See, I have made him a witness to the peoples,
a ruler and commander of the peoples.
5 Surely you will summon nations you know not,
and nations you do not know will come running to you,
because of the LORD your God,
the Holy One of Israel,
for he has endowed you with splendor."

6 Seek the LORD while he may be found;
call on him while he is near.
7 Let the wicked forsake their ways
and the unrighteous their thoughts.
Let them turn to the LORD, and he will have mercy on them,
and to our God, for he will freely pardon.

8 "For my thoughts are not your thoughts,
neither are your ways my ways,"
declares the LORD.
9 "As the heavens are higher than the earth,
so are my ways higher than your ways
and my thoughts than your thoughts.
10 As the rain and the snow
come down from heaven,
and do not return to it
without watering the earth
and making it bud and flourish,
so that it yields seed for the sower
and bread for the eater,
11 so is my word that goes out from my mouth:
It will not return to me empty,
but will accomplish what I desire
and achieve the purpose for which I sent it.
12 You will go out in joy
and be led forth in peace;
the mountains and hills
will burst into song before you,
and all the trees of the field
will clap their hands.
13 Instead of the thornbush will grow the juniper,
and instead of briers the myrtle will grow.
This will be for the LORD's renown,
for an everlasting sign,
that will endure forever."

Salvation for Others

56 This is what the LORD says:

"Maintain justice
and do what is right,
for my salvation is close at hand
and my righteousness will soon be revealed.
2 Blessed is the one who does this—
the person who holds it fast,
who keeps the Sabbath without desecrating it,
and keeps their hands from doing any evil."

3 Let no foreigner who is bound to the LORD say,
"The LORD will surely exclude me from his people."
And let no eunuch complain,
"I am only a dry tree."

4 For this is what the LORD says:

"To the eunuchs who keep my Sabbaths,
who choose what pleases me
and hold fast to my covenant—
5 to them I will give within my temple and its walls
a memorial and a name
better than sons and daughters;
I will give them an everlasting name
that will endure forever.
6 And foreigners who bind themselves to the LORD
to minister to him,
to love the name of the LORD,
and to be his servants,
all who keep the Sabbath without desecrating it
and who hold fast to my covenant—
7 these I will bring to my holy mountain
and give them joy in my house of prayer.
Their burnt offerings and sacrifices
will be accepted on my altar;
for my house will be called
a house of prayer for all nations."
8 The Sovereign LORD declares—
he who gathers the exiles of Israel:
"I will gather still others to them
besides those already gathered."

God's Accusation Against the Wicked

9 Come, all you beasts of the field,
come and devour, all you beasts of the forest!
10 Israel's watchmen are blind,
they all lack knowledge;
they are all mute dogs,
they cannot bark;
they lie around and dream,
they love to sleep.
11 They are dogs with mighty appetites;
they never have enough.

They are shepherds who lack understanding;
they all turn to their own way,
they seek their own gain.
12 "Come," each one cries, "let me get wine!
Let us drink our fill of beer!
And tomorrow will be like today,
or even far better."

57 The righteous perish,
and no one takes it to heart;
the devout are taken away,
and no one understands
that the righteous are taken away
to be spared from evil.
2 Those who walk uprightly
enter into peace;
they find rest as they lie in death.

3 "But you — come here, you children of a sorceress,
you offspring of adulterers and prostitutes!
4 Who are you mocking?
At whom do you sneer
and stick out your tongue?
Are you not a brood of rebels,
the offspring of liars?
5 You burn with lust among the oaks
and under every spreading tree;
you sacrifice your children in the ravines
and under the overhanging crags.
6 The idols among the smooth stones of the ravines are your portion;
indeed, they are your lot.
Yes, to them you have poured out drink offerings
and offered grain offerings.
In view of all this, should I relent?
7 You have made your bed on a high and lofty hill;
there you went up to offer your sacrifices.
8 Behind your doors and your doorposts
you have put your pagan symbols.
Forsaking me, you uncovered your bed,
you climbed into it and opened it wide;
you made a pact with those whose beds you love,
and you looked with lust on their naked bodies.
9 You went to Molek[a] with olive oil
and increased your perfumes.
You sent your ambassadors[b] far away;
you descended to the very realm of the dead!
10 You wearied yourself by such going about,
but you would not say, 'It is hopeless.'
You found renewal of your strength,
and so you did not faint.

11 "Whom have you so dreaded and feared
that you have not been true to me,
and have neither remembered me
nor taken this to heart?
Is it not because I have long been silent
that you do not fear me?
12 I will expose your righteousness and your works,
and they will not benefit you.
13 When you cry out for help,
let your collection of idols save you!
The wind will carry all of them off,
a mere breath will blow them away.
But whoever takes refuge in me
will inherit the land
and possess my holy mountain."

Comfort for the Contrite

14 And it will be said:

"Build up, build up, prepare the road!
Remove the obstacles out of the way of my people."
15 For this is what the high and exalted One says —
he who lives forever, whose name is holy:
"I live in a high and holy place,
but also with the one who is contrite and lowly in spirit,
to revive the spirit of the lowly
and to revive the heart of the contrite.
16 I will not accuse them forever,
nor will I always be angry,
for then they would faint away because of me —
the very people I have created.
17 I was enraged by their sinful greed;
I punished them, and hid my face in anger,
yet they kept on in their willful ways.
18 I have seen their ways, but I will heal them;
I will guide them and restore comfort to Israel's mourners,
19 creating praise on their lips.
Peace, peace, to those far and near,"
says the LORD. "And I will heal them."

[a] 9 Or *to the king* [b] 9 Or *idols*

20 But the wicked are like the tossing sea,
which cannot rest,
whose waves cast up mire and mud.
21 "There is no peace," says my God, "for
the wicked."

True Fasting

58 "Shout it aloud, do not hold back.
Raise your voice like a trumpet.
Declare to my people their rebellion
and to the descendants of Jacob
their sins.
2 For day after day they seek me out;
they seem eager to know my ways,
as if they were a nation that does
what is right
and has not forsaken the
commands of its God.
They ask me for just decisions
and seem eager for God to come
near them.
3 'Why have we fasted,' they say,
'and you have not seen it?
Why have we humbled ourselves,
and you have not noticed?'

"Yet on the day of your fasting, you
do as you please
and exploit all your workers.
4 Your fasting ends in quarreling and
strife,
and in striking each other with
wicked fists.
You cannot fast as you do today
and expect your voice to be heard
on high.
5 Is this the kind of fast I have chosen,
only a day for people to humble
themselves?
Is it only for bowing one's head like a
reed
and for lying in sackcloth and
ashes?
Is that what you call a fast,
a day acceptable to the LORD?
6 "Is not this the kind of fasting I have
chosen:
to loose the chains of injustice
and untie the cords of the yoke,
to set the oppressed free
and break every yoke?
7 Is it not to share your food with the
hungry
and to provide the poor wanderer
with shelter —
when you see the naked, to clothe
them,
and not to turn away from your
own flesh and blood?
8 Then your light will break forth like
the dawn,
and your healing will quickly
appear;
then your righteousness[a] will go
before you,
and the glory of the LORD will be
your rear guard.
9 Then you will call, and the LORD will
answer;
you will cry for help, and he will
say: Here am I.

"If you do away with the yoke of
oppression,
with the pointing finger and
malicious talk,
10 and if you spend yourselves in behalf
of the hungry
and satisfy the needs of the
oppressed,
then your light will rise in the
darkness,
and your night will become like the
noonday.
11 The LORD will guide you always;
he will satisfy your needs in a sun-
scorched land
and will strengthen your frame.
You will be like a well-watered
garden,
like a spring whose waters never
fail.
12 Your people will rebuild the ancient
ruins
and will raise up the age-old
foundations;
you will be called Repairer of Broken
Walls,
Restorer of Streets with Dwellings.
13 "If you keep your feet from breaking
the Sabbath
and from doing as you please on
my holy day,
if you call the Sabbath a delight
and the LORD's holy day honorable,
and if you honor it by not going your
own way
and not doing as you please or
speaking idle words,
14 then you will find your joy in the
LORD,
and I will cause you to ride in
triumph on the heights of the
land
and to feast on the inheritance of
your father Jacob."
For the mouth of the LORD
has spoken.

[a] 8 Or *your righteous One*

Sin, Confession and Redemption

59 Surely the arm of the LORD is not
too short to save,
nor his ear too dull to hear.
2 But your iniquities have separated
you from your God;
your sins have hidden his face from
you,
so that he will not hear.
3 For your hands are stained with blood,
your fingers with guilt.
Your lips have spoken falsely,
and your tongue mutters wicked
things.
4 No one calls for justice;
no one pleads a case with integrity.
They rely on empty arguments, they
utter lies;
they conceive trouble and give
birth to evil.
5 They hatch the eggs of vipers
and spin a spider's web.
Whoever eats their eggs will die,
and when one is broken, an adder
is hatched.
6 Their cobwebs are useless for clothing;
they cannot cover themselves with
what they make.
Their deeds are evil deeds,
and acts of violence are in their
hands.
7 Their feet rush into sin;
they are swift to shed innocent
blood.
They pursue evil schemes;
acts of violence mark their ways.
8 The way of peace they do not know;
there is no justice in their paths.
They have turned them into crooked
roads;
no one who walks along them will
know peace.

9 So justice is far from us,
and righteousness does not reach us.
We look for light, but all is darkness;
for brightness, but we walk in deep
shadows.
10 Like the blind we grope along the wall,
feeling our way like people without
eyes.
At midday we stumble as if it were
twilight;
among the strong, we are like the
dead.
11 We all growl like bears;
we moan mournfully like doves.
We look for justice, but find none;
for deliverance, but it is far away.
12 For our offenses are many in your sight,
and our sins testify against us.
Our offenses are ever with us,
and we acknowledge our iniquities:
13 rebellion and treachery against the
LORD,
turning our backs on our God,
inciting revolt and oppression,
uttering lies our hearts have
conceived.
14 So justice is driven back,
and righteousness stands at a
distance;
truth has stumbled in the streets,
honesty cannot enter.
15 Truth is nowhere to be found,
and whoever shuns evil becomes
a prey.

The LORD looked and was displeased
that there was no justice.
16 He saw that there was no one,
he was appalled that there was no
one to intervene;
so his own arm achieved salvation for
him,
and his own righteousness
sustained him.
17 He put on righteousness as his
breastplate,
and the helmet of salvation on his
head;
he put on the garments of vengeance
and wrapped himself in zeal as in a
cloak.
18 According to what they have done,
so will he repay
wrath to his enemies
and retribution to his foes;
he will repay the islands their due.
19 From the west, people will fear the
name of the LORD,
and from the rising of the sun, they
will revere his glory.
For he will come like a pent-up flood
that the breath of the LORD drives
along.[a]

20 "The Redeemer will come to Zion,
to those in Jacob who repent of
their sins,"
declares the LORD.

21 "As for me, this is my covenant with
them," says the LORD. "My Spirit, who is
on you, will not depart from you, and my
words that I have put in your mouth will
always be on your lips, on the lips of your
children and on the lips of their descendants — from this time on and forever,"
says the LORD.

[a] 19 Or *When enemies come in like a flood, / the Spirit of the LORD will put them to flight*

The Glory of Zion

60 "Arise, shine, for your light has come,
and the glory of the LORD rises upon you.
2 See, darkness covers the earth
and thick darkness is over the peoples,
but the LORD rises upon you
and his glory appears over you.
3 Nations will come to your light,
and kings to the brightness of your dawn.

4 "Lift up your eyes and look about you:
All assemble and come to you;
your sons come from afar,
and your daughters are carried on the hip.
5 Then you will look and be radiant,
your heart will throb and swell with joy;
the wealth on the seas will be brought to you,
to you the riches of the nations will come.
6 Herds of camels will cover your land,
young camels of Midian and Ephah.
And all from Sheba will come,
bearing gold and incense
and proclaiming the praise of the LORD.
7 All Kedar's flocks will be gathered to you,
the rams of Nebaioth will serve you;
they will be accepted as offerings on my altar,
and I will adorn my glorious temple.

8 "Who are these that fly along like clouds,
like doves to their nests?
9 Surely the islands look to me;
in the lead are the ships of Tarshish,[a]
bringing your children from afar,
with their silver and gold,
to the honor of the LORD your God,
the Holy One of Israel,
for he has endowed you with splendor.

10 "Foreigners will rebuild your walls,
and their kings will serve you.
Though in anger I struck you,
in favor I will show you compassion.
11 Your gates will always stand open,
they will never be shut, day or night,
so that people may bring you the wealth of the nations—
their kings led in triumphal procession.
12 For the nation or kingdom that will not serve you will perish;
it will be utterly ruined.

13 "The glory of Lebanon will come to you,
the juniper, the fir and the cypress together,
to adorn my sanctuary;
and I will glorify the place for my feet.
14 The children of your oppressors will come bowing before you;
all who despise you will bow down at your feet
and will call you the City of the LORD,
Zion of the Holy One of Israel.

15 "Although you have been forsaken and hated,
with no one traveling through,
I will make you the everlasting pride
and the joy of all generations.
16 You will drink the milk of nations
and be nursed at royal breasts.
Then you will know that I, the LORD,
am your Savior,
your Redeemer, the Mighty One of Jacob.
17 Instead of bronze I will bring you gold,
and silver in place of iron.
Instead of wood I will bring you bronze,
and iron in place of stones.
I will make peace your governor
and well-being your ruler.
18 No longer will violence be heard in your land,
nor ruin or destruction within your borders,
but you will call your walls Salvation
and your gates Praise.
19 The sun will no more be your light by day,
nor will the brightness of the moon shine on you,
for the LORD will be your everlasting light,
and your God will be your glory.
20 Your sun will never set again,
and your moon will wane no more;
the LORD will be your everlasting light,
and your days of sorrow will end.

[a] 9 Or *the trading ships*

[21] Then all your people will be righteous
and they will possess the land forever.
They are the shoot I have planted,
the work of my hands,
for the display of my splendor.
[22] The least of you will become a thousand,
the smallest a mighty nation.
I am the LORD;
in its time I will do this swiftly."

The Year of the LORD's Favor

61 The Spirit of the Sovereign LORD is on me,
because the LORD has anointed me
to proclaim good news to the poor.
He has sent me to bind up the brokenhearted,
to proclaim freedom for the captives
and release from darkness for the prisoners,[a]
[2] to proclaim the year of the LORD's favor
and the day of vengeance of our God,
to comfort all who mourn,
[3] and provide for those who grieve in Zion —
to bestow on them a crown of beauty
instead of ashes,
the oil of joy
instead of mourning,
and a garment of praise
instead of a spirit of despair.
They will be called oaks of righteousness,
a planting of the LORD
for the display of his splendor.

[4] They will rebuild the ancient ruins
and restore the places long devastated;
they will renew the ruined cities
that have been devastated for generations.
[5] Strangers will shepherd your flocks;
foreigners will work your fields and vineyards.
[6] And you will be called priests of the LORD,
you will be named ministers of our God.
You will feed on the wealth of nations,
and in their riches you will boast.

[7] Instead of your shame
you will receive a double portion,
and instead of disgrace
you will rejoice in your inheritance.
And so you will inherit a double portion in your land,
and everlasting joy will be yours.

[8] "For I, the LORD, love justice;
I hate robbery and wrongdoing.
In my faithfulness I will reward my people
and make an everlasting covenant with them.
[9] Their descendants will be known among the nations
and their offspring among the peoples.
All who see them will acknowledge
that they are a people the LORD has blessed."

[10] I delight greatly in the LORD;
my soul rejoices in my God.
For he has clothed me with garments of salvation
and arrayed me in a robe of his righteousness,
as a bridegroom adorns his head like a priest,
and as a bride adorns herself with her jewels.
[11] For as the soil makes the sprout come up
and a garden causes seeds to grow,
so the Sovereign LORD will make righteousness
and praise spring up before all nations.

Zion's New Name

62 For Zion's sake I will not keep silent,
for Jerusalem's sake I will not remain quiet,
till her vindication shines out like the dawn,
her salvation like a blazing torch.
[2] The nations will see your vindication,
and all kings your glory;
you will be called by a new name
that the mouth of the LORD will bestow.
[3] You will be a crown of splendor in the LORD's hand,
a royal diadem in the hand of your God.
[4] No longer will they call you Deserted,
or name your land Desolate.
But you will be called Hephzibah,[b]
and your land Beulah[c];
for the LORD will take delight in you,
and your land will be married.

[a] 1 Hebrew; Septuagint *the blind* [b] 4 *Hephzibah* means *my delight is in her.* [c] 4 *Beulah* means *married.*

[5] As a young man marries a young
woman,
so will your Builder marry you;
as a bridegroom rejoices over his bride,
so will your God rejoice over you.

[6] I have posted watchmen on your
walls, Jerusalem;
they will never be silent day or
night.
You who call on the LORD,
give yourselves no rest,
[7] and give him no rest till he
establishes Jerusalem
and makes her the praise of the
earth.

[8] The LORD has sworn by his right hand
and by his mighty arm:
"Never again will I give your grain
as food for your enemies,
and never again will foreigners drink
the new wine
for which you have toiled;
[9] but those who harvest it will eat it
and praise the LORD,
and those who gather the grapes will
drink it
in the courts of my sanctuary."

[10] Pass through, pass through the gates!
Prepare the way for the people.
Build up, build up the highway!
Remove the stones.
Raise a banner for the nations.

[11] The LORD has made proclamation
to the ends of the earth:
"Say to Daughter Zion,
'See, your Savior comes!
See, his reward is with him,
and his recompense accompanies
him.'"
[12] They will be called the Holy People,
the Redeemed of the LORD;
and you will be called Sought After,
the City No Longer Deserted.

God's Day of Vengeance and Redemption

63 Who is this coming from Edom,
from Bozrah, with his garments
stained crimson?
Who is this, robed in splendor,
striding forward in the greatness of
his strength?

"It is I, proclaiming victory,
mighty to save."

[2] Why are your garments red,
like those of one treading the
winepress?

[3] "I have trodden the winepress alone;
from the nations no one was with
me.
I trampled them in my anger
and trod them down in my wrath;
their blood spattered my garments,
and I stained all my clothing.
[4] It was for me the day of vengeance;
the year for me to redeem had come.
[5] I looked, but there was no one to help,
I was appalled that no one gave
support;
so my own arm achieved salvation
for me,
and my own wrath sustained me.
[6] I trampled the nations in my anger;
in my wrath I made them drunk
and poured their blood on the
ground."

Praise and Prayer

[7] I will tell of the kindnesses of the LORD,
the deeds for which he is to be
praised,
according to all the LORD has done
for us —
yes, the many good things
he has done for Israel,
according to his compassion and
many kindnesses.
[8] He said, "Surely they are my people,
children who will be true to me";
and so he became their Savior.
[9] In all their distress he too was
distressed,
and the angel of his presence saved
them.[a]
In his love and mercy he redeemed
them;
he lifted them up and carried them
all the days of old.
[10] Yet they rebelled
and grieved his Holy Spirit.
So he turned and became their enemy
and he himself fought against
them.

[11] Then his people recalled[b] the days of
old,
the days of Moses and his people —
where is he who brought them
through the sea,
with the shepherd of his flock?
Where is he who set
his Holy Spirit among them,
[12] who sent his glorious arm of power
to be at Moses' right hand,
who divided the waters before them,
to gain for himself everlasting
renown,

[a] 9 Or *Savior* [9] *in their distress. / It was no envoy or angel / but his own presence that saved them*
[b] 11 Or *But may he recall*

13 who led them through the depths?
Like a horse in open country,
they did not stumble;
14 like cattle that go down to the plain,
they were given rest by the Spirit of the LORD.
This is how you guided your people
to make for yourself a glorious name.

15 Look down from heaven and see,
from your lofty throne, holy and glorious.
Where are your zeal and your might?
Your tenderness and compassion
are withheld from us.
16 But you are our Father,
though Abraham does not know us
or Israel acknowledge us;
you, LORD, are our Father,
our Redeemer from of old is your name.
17 Why, LORD, do you make us wander
from your ways
and harden our hearts so we do not revere you?
Return for the sake of your servants,
the tribes that are your inheritance.
18 For a little while your people
possessed your holy place,
but now our enemies have
trampled down your sanctuary.
19 We are yours from of old;
but you have not ruled over them,
they have not been called[a] by your name.

64 [b] Oh, that you would rend the heavens and come down,
that the mountains would tremble before you!
2 As when fire sets twigs ablaze
and causes water to boil,
come down to make your name
known to your enemies
and cause the nations to quake
before you!
3 For when you did awesome things
that we did not expect,
you came down, and the
mountains trembled before you.
4 Since ancient times no one has heard,
no ear has perceived,
no eye has seen any God besides you,
who acts on behalf of those who
wait for him.
5 You come to the help of those who
gladly do right,
who remember your ways.
But when we continued to sin against them,
you were angry.
How then can we be saved?
6 All of us have become like one who is unclean,
and all our righteous acts are like
filthy rags;
we all shrivel up like a leaf,
and like the wind our sins sweep us away.
7 No one calls on your name
or strives to lay hold of you;
for you have hidden your face from us
and have given us over to[c] our sins.

8 Yet you, LORD, are our Father.
We are the clay, you are the potter;
we are all the work of your hand.
9 Do not be angry beyond measure, LORD;
do not remember our sins forever.
Oh, look on us, we pray,
for we are all your people.
10 Your sacred cities have become a wasteland;
even Zion is a wasteland,
Jerusalem a desolation.
11 Our holy and glorious temple, where
our ancestors praised you,
has been burned with fire,
and all that we treasured lies in ruins.
12 After all this, LORD, will you hold
yourself back?
Will you keep silent and punish us
beyond measure?

Judgment and Salvation

65 "I revealed myself to those who
did not ask for me;
I was found by those who did not
seek me.
To a nation that did not call on my name,
I said, 'Here am I, here am I.'
2 All day long I have held out my hands
to an obstinate people,
who walk in ways not good,
pursuing their own
imaginations —
3 a people who continually provoke me
to my very face,
offering sacrifices in gardens
and burning incense on altars of brick;

[a] 19 Or *We are like those you have never ruled, / like those never called* [b] In Hebrew texts 64:1 is numbered 63:19b, and 64:2-12 is numbered 64:1-11. [c] 7 Septuagint, Syriac and Targum; Hebrew *have made us melt because of*

4 who sit among the graves
and spend their nights keeping
secret vigil;
who eat the flesh of pigs,
and whose pots hold broth of
impure meat;
5 who say, 'Keep away; don't come near
me,
for I am too sacred for you!'
Such people are smoke in my nostrils,
a fire that keeps burning all day.

6 "See, it stands written before me:
I will not keep silent but will pay
back in full;
I will pay it back into their laps—
7 both your sins and the sins of your
ancestors,"
says the LORD.
"Because they burned sacrifices on
the mountains
and defied me on the hills,
I will measure into their laps
the full payment for their former
deeds."

8 This is what the LORD says:

"As when juice is still found in a
cluster of grapes
and people say, 'Don't destroy it,
there is still a blessing in it,'
so will I do in behalf of my servants;
I will not destroy them all.
9 I will bring forth descendants from
Jacob,
and from Judah those who will
possess my mountains;
my chosen people will inherit them,
and there will my servants live.
10 Sharon will become a pasture for
flocks,
and the Valley of Achor a resting
place for herds,
for my people who seek me.

11 "But as for you who forsake the LORD
and forget my holy mountain,
who spread a table for Fortune
and fill bowls of mixed wine for
Destiny,
12 I will destine you for the sword,
and all of you will fall in the
slaughter;
for I called but you did not answer,
I spoke but you did not listen.
You did evil in my sight
and chose what displeases me."

13 Therefore this is what the Sovereign
LORD says:

"My servants will eat,
but you will go hungry;
my servants will drink,
but you will go thirsty;
my servants will rejoice,
but you will be put to shame.
14 My servants will sing
out of the joy of their hearts,
but you will cry out
from anguish of heart
and wail in brokenness of spirit.
15 You will leave your name
for my chosen ones to use in their
curses;
the Sovereign LORD will put you to
death,
but to his servants he will give
another name.
16 Whoever invokes a blessing in the land
will do so by the one true God;
whoever takes an oath in the land
will swear by the one true God.
For the past troubles will be forgotten
and hidden from my eyes.

New Heavens and a New Earth

17 "See, I will create
new heavens and a new earth.
The former things will not be
remembered,
nor will they come to mind.
18 But be glad and rejoice forever
in what I will create,
for I will create Jerusalem to be a
delight
and its people a joy.
19 I will rejoice over Jerusalem
and take delight in my people;
the sound of weeping and of crying
will be heard in it no more.

20 "Never again will there be in it
an infant who lives but a few days,
or an old man who does not live
out his years;
the one who dies at a hundred
will be thought a mere child;
the one who fails to reach[a] a hundred
will be considered accursed.
21 They will build houses and dwell in
them;
they will plant vineyards and eat
their fruit.
22 No longer will they build houses and
others live in them,
or plant and others eat.
For as the days of a tree,
so will be the days of my people;
my chosen ones will long enjoy
the work of their hands.
23 They will not labor in vain,
nor will they bear children doomed
to misfortune;

[a] 20 *Or the sinner who reaches*

for they will be a people blessed by
the LORD,
they and their descendants with
them.
24 Before they call I will answer;
while they are still speaking I will
hear.
25 The wolf and the lamb will feed
together,
and the lion will eat straw like
the ox,
and dust will be the serpent's food.
They will neither harm nor destroy
on all my holy mountain,"
says the LORD.

Judgment and Hope

66 This is what the LORD says:

"Heaven is my throne,
and the earth is my footstool.
Where is the house you will build for
me?
Where will my resting place be?
2 Has not my hand made all these
things,
and so they came into being?"
declares the LORD.

"These are the ones I look on with
favor:
those who are humble and contrite
in spirit,
and who tremble at my word.
3 But whoever sacrifices a bull
is like one who kills a person,
and whoever offers a lamb
is like one who breaks a dog's neck;
whoever makes a grain offering
is like one who presents pig's
blood,
and whoever burns memorial incense
is like one who worships an idol.
They have chosen their own ways,
and they delight in their
abominations;
4 so I also will choose harsh treatment
for them
and will bring on them what they
dread.
For when I called, no one answered,
when I spoke, no one listened.
They did evil in my sight
and chose what displeases me."

5 Hear the word of the LORD,
you who tremble at his word:
"Your own people who hate you,
and exclude you because of my
name, have said,
'Let the LORD be glorified,
that we may see your joy!'
Yet they will be put to shame.
6 Hear that uproar from the city,
hear that noise from the temple!
It is the sound of the LORD
repaying his enemies all they
deserve.

7 "Before she goes into labor,
she gives birth;
before the pains come upon her,
she delivers a son.
8 Who has ever heard of such things?
Who has ever seen things like this?
Can a country be born in a day
or a nation be brought forth in a
moment?
Yet no sooner is Zion in labor
than she gives birth to her children.
9 Do I bring to the moment of birth
and not give delivery?" says the
LORD.
"Do I close up the womb
when I bring to delivery?" says
your God.
10 "Rejoice with Jerusalem and be glad
for her,
all you who love her;
rejoice greatly with her,
all you who mourn over her.
11 For you will nurse and be satisfied
at her comforting breasts;
you will drink deeply
and delight in her overflowing
abundance."

12 For this is what the LORD says:

"I will extend peace to her like a river,
and the wealth of nations like a
flooding stream;
you will nurse and be carried on her
arm
and dandled on her knees.
13 As a mother comforts her child,
so will I comfort you;
and you will be comforted over
Jerusalem."

14 When you see this, your heart will
rejoice
and you will flourish like grass;
the hand of the LORD will be made
known to his servants,
but his fury will be shown to his
foes.
15 See, the LORD is coming with fire,
and his chariots are like a
whirlwind;
he will bring down his anger with
fury,
and his rebuke with flames of fire.
16 For with fire and with his sword
the LORD will execute judgment on
all people,
and many will be those slain by the
LORD.

17"Those who consecrate and purify
themselves to go into the gardens, following one who is among those who eat
the flesh of pigs, rats and other unclean
things — they will meet their end together with the one they follow," declares the
LORD.
18"And I, because of what they have
planned and done, am about to come[a]
and gather the people of all nations and
languages, and they will come and see
my glory.
19"I will set a sign among them, and I
will send some of those who survive to the
nations — to Tarshish, to the Libyans[b] and
Lydians (famous as archers), to Tubal and
Greece, and to the distant islands that have
not heard of my fame or seen my glory.
They will proclaim my glory among the nations. 20And they will bring all your people,
from all the nations, to my holy mountain
in Jerusalem as an offering to the LORD —
on horses, in chariots and wagons, and on
mules and camels," says the LORD. "They
will bring them, as the Israelites bring their
grain offerings, to the temple of the LORD
in ceremonially clean vessels. 21And I will
select some of them also to be priests and
Levites," says the LORD.

22"As the new heavens and the new
earth that I make will endure before
me," declares the LORD, "so will your name
and descendants endure. 23From one New
Moon to another and from one Sabbath to
another, all mankind will come and bow
down before me," says the LORD. 24"And
they will go out and look on the dead bodies of those who rebelled against me; the
worms that eat them will not die, the fire
that burns them will not be quenched, and
they will be loathsome to all mankind."

[a] *18* The meaning of the Hebrew for this clause is uncertain. [b] *19* Some Septuagint manuscripts *Put* (Libyans); Hebrew *Pul*

JEREMIAH

1 The words of Jeremiah son of Hilkiah, one of the priests at Anathoth in
the territory of Benjamin. 2 The word of
the LORD came to him in the thirteenth
year of the reign of Josiah son of Amon
king of Judah, 3 and through the reign of
Jehoiakim son of Josiah king of Judah,
down to the fifth month of the eleventh
year of Zedekiah son of Josiah king of
Judah, when the people of Jerusalem
went into exile.

The Call of Jeremiah

4 The word of the LORD came to me,
saying,

5 "Before I formed you in the womb I
knew[a] you,
before you were born I set you
apart;
I appointed you as a prophet to the
nations."

6 "Alas, Sovereign LORD," I said, "I do
not know how to speak; I am too young."
7 But the LORD said to me, "Do not say, 'I
am too young.' You must go to everyone I
send you to and say whatever I command
you. 8 Do not be afraid of them, for I am
with you and will rescue you," declares
the LORD.
9 Then the LORD reached out his hand
and touched my mouth and said to me, "I
have put my words in your mouth. 10 See,
today I appoint you over nations and
kingdoms to uproot and tear down, to
destroy and overthrow, to build and to
plant."
11 The word of the LORD came to me:
"What do you see, Jeremiah?"
"I see the branch of an almond tree,"
I replied.
12 The LORD said to me, "You have seen
correctly, for I am watching[b] to see that
my word is fulfilled."
13 The word of the LORD came to me
again: "What do you see?"
"I see a pot that is boiling," I answered.
"It is tilting toward us from the north."
14 The LORD said to me, "From the north
disaster will be poured out on all who live
in the land. 15 I am about to summon all
the peoples of the northern kingdoms,"
declares the LORD.

"Their kings will come and set up
their thrones
in the entrance of the gates of
Jerusalem;
they will come against all her
surrounding walls
and against all the towns of Judah.
16 I will pronounce my judgments on my
people
because of their wickedness in
forsaking me,
in burning incense to other gods
and in worshiping what their
hands have made.

17 "Get yourself ready! Stand up and say
to them whatever I command you. Do
not be terrified by them, or I will terrify
you before them. 18 Today I have made
you a fortified city, an iron pillar and a
bronze wall to stand against the whole
land — against the kings of Judah, its
officials, its priests and the people of the
land. 19 They will fight against you but
will not overcome you, for I am with you
and will rescue you," declares the LORD.

Israel Forsakes God

2 The word of the LORD came to me:
2 "Go and proclaim in the hearing of
Jerusalem:

"This is what the LORD says:

"'I remember the devotion of your
youth,
how as a bride you loved me
and followed me through the
wilderness,
through a land not sown.
3 Israel was holy to the LORD,
the firstfruits of his harvest;
all who devoured her were held guilty,
and disaster overtook them,'"
declares the LORD.

4 Hear the word of the LORD, you
descendants of Jacob,
all you clans of Israel.

5 This is what the LORD says:

"What fault did your ancestors find in
me,
that they strayed so far from me?
They followed worthless idols
and became worthless themselves.

[a] 5 Or *chose* [b] 12 The Hebrew for *watching* sounds like the Hebrew for *almond tree.*

6 They did not ask, 'Where is the LORD,
who brought us up out of Egypt
and led us through the barren wilderness,
through a land of deserts and ravines,
a land of drought and utter darkness,
a land where no one travels and no one lives?'
7 I brought you into a fertile land
to eat its fruit and rich produce.
But you came and defiled my land
and made my inheritance detestable.
8 The priests did not ask,
'Where is the LORD?'
Those who deal with the law did not know me;
the leaders rebelled against me.
The prophets prophesied by Baal,
following worthless idols.

9 "Therefore I bring charges against you again,"
declares the LORD.
"And I will bring charges against your children's children.
10 Cross over to the coasts of Cyprus and look,
send to Kedar[a] and observe closely;
see if there has ever been anything like this:
11 Has a nation ever changed its gods?
(Yet they are not gods at all.)
But my people have exchanged their glorious God
for worthless idols.
12 Be appalled at this, you heavens,
and shudder with great horror,"
declares the LORD.
13 "My people have committed two sins:
They have forsaken me,
the spring of living water,
and have dug their own cisterns,
broken cisterns that cannot hold water.
14 Is Israel a servant, a slave by birth?
Why then has he become plunder?
15 Lions have roared;
they have growled at him.
They have laid waste his land;
his towns are burned and deserted.
16 Also, the men of Memphis and Tahpanhes
have cracked your skull.
17 Have you not brought this on yourselves
by forsaking the LORD your God
when he led you in the way?
18 Now why go to Egypt
to drink water from the Nile[b]?
And why go to Assyria
to drink water from the Euphrates?
19 Your wickedness will punish you;
your backsliding will rebuke you.
Consider then and realize
how evil and bitter it is for you
when you forsake the LORD your God
and have no awe of me,"
declares the Lord,
the LORD Almighty.

20 "Long ago you broke off your yoke
and tore off your bonds;
you said, 'I will not serve you!'
Indeed, on every high hill
and under every spreading tree
you lay down as a prostitute.
21 I had planted you like a choice vine
of sound and reliable stock.
How then did you turn against me
into a corrupt, wild vine?
22 Although you wash yourself with soap
and use an abundance of cleansing powder,
the stain of your guilt is still before me,"
declares the Sovereign LORD.
23 "How can you say, 'I am not defiled;
I have not run after the Baals'?
See how you behaved in the valley;
consider what you have done.
You are a swift she-camel
running here and there,
24 a wild donkey accustomed to the desert,
sniffing the wind in her craving —
in her heat who can restrain her?
Any males that pursue her need not tire themselves;
at mating time they will find her.
25 Do not run until your feet are bare
and your throat is dry.
But you said, 'It's no use!
I love foreign gods,
and I must go after them.'

26 "As a thief is disgraced when he is caught,
so the people of Israel are disgraced —
they, their kings and their officials,
their priests and their prophets.
27 They say to wood, 'You are my father,'
and to stone, 'You gave me birth.'
They have turned their backs to me
and not their faces;
yet when they are in trouble, they say,
'Come and save us!'
28 Where then are the gods you made for yourselves?
Let them come if they can save you
when you are in trouble!

[a] *10* In the Syro-Arabian desert [b] *18* Hebrew *Shihor;* that is, a branch of the Nile

For you, Judah, have as many gods
as you have towns.

29 "Why do you bring charges against me?
You have all rebelled against me,"
declares the LORD.
30 "In vain I punished your people;
they did not respond to correction.
Your sword has devoured your
prophets
like a ravenous lion.

31 "You of this generation, consider the
word of the LORD:

"Have I been a desert to Israel
or a land of great darkness?
Why do my people say, 'We are free to
roam;
we will come to you no more'?
32 Does a young woman forget her
jewelry,
a bride her wedding ornaments?
Yet my people have forgotten me,
days without number.
33 How skilled you are at pursuing love!
Even the worst of women can learn
from your ways.
34 On your clothes is found
the lifeblood of the innocent poor,
though you did not catch them
breaking in.
Yet in spite of all this
35 you say, 'I am innocent;
he is not angry with me.'
But I will pass judgment on you
because you say, 'I have not
sinned.'
36 Why do you go about so much,
changing your ways?
You will be disappointed by Egypt
as you were by Assyria.
37 You will also leave that place
with your hands on your head,
for the LORD has rejected those you
trust;
you will not be helped by them.

3 "If a man divorces his wife
and she leaves him and marries
another man,
should he return to her again?
Would not the land be completely
defiled?
But you have lived as a prostitute
with many lovers —
would you now return to me?"
declares the LORD.
2 "Look up to the barren heights and see.
Is there any place where you have
not been ravished?
By the roadside you sat waiting for
lovers,
sat like a nomad in the desert.
You have defiled the land
with your prostitution and
wickedness.
3 Therefore the showers have been
withheld,
and no spring rains have fallen.
Yet you have the brazen look of a
prostitute;
you refuse to blush with shame.
4 Have you not just called to me:
'My Father, my friend from my
youth,
5 will you always be angry?
Will your wrath continue forever?'
This is how you talk,
but you do all the evil you can."

Unfaithful Israel

6 During the reign of King Josiah, the
LORD said to me, "Have you seen what
faithless Israel has done? She has gone
up on every high hill and under every
spreading tree and has committed adultery there. 7 I thought that after she had
done all this she would return to me but
she did not, and her unfaithful sister Judah saw it. 8 I gave faithless Israel her
certificate of divorce and sent her away
because of all her adulteries. Yet I saw
that her unfaithful sister Judah had no
fear; she also went out and committed
adultery. 9 Because Israel's immorality
mattered so little to her, she defiled the
land and committed adultery with stone
and wood. 10 In spite of all this, her unfaithful sister Judah did not return to me
with all her heart, but only in pretense,"
declares the LORD.
11 The LORD said to me, "Faithless Israel
is more righteous than unfaithful Judah.
12 Go, proclaim this message toward the
north:

"'Return, faithless Israel,' declares
the LORD,
'I will frown on you no longer,
for I am faithful,' declares the LORD,
'I will not be angry forever.
13 Only acknowledge your guilt —
you have rebelled against the LORD
your God,
you have scattered your favors to
foreign gods
under every spreading tree,
and have not obeyed me,'"
declares the LORD.

14 "Return, faithless people," declares the
LORD, "for I am your husband. I will choose
you — one from a town and two from a
clan — and bring you to Zion. 15 Then I will
give you shepherds after my own heart,
who will lead you with knowledge and

understanding. 16 In those days, when your
numbers have increased greatly in the
land,” declares the LORD, “people will no
longer say, ‘The ark of the covenant of the
LORD.’ It will never enter their minds or be
remembered; it will not be missed, nor will
another one be made. 17 At that time they
will call Jerusalem The Throne of the LORD,
and all nations will gather in Jerusalem
to honor the name of the LORD. No longer
will they follow the stubbornness of their
evil hearts. 18 In those days the people of
Judah will join the people of Israel, and
together they will come from a northern
land to the land I gave your ancestors as
an inheritance.

19 “I myself said,

“ ‘How gladly would I treat you like
my children
and give you a pleasant land,
the most beautiful inheritance of
any nation.’
I thought you would call me ‘Father’
and not turn away from following
me.
20 But like a woman unfaithful to her
husband,
so you, Israel, have been unfaithful
to me,”
declares the LORD.

21 A cry is heard on the barren heights,
the weeping and pleading of the
people of Israel,
because they have perverted their
ways
and have forgotten the LORD their
God.

22 “Return, faithless people;
I will cure you of backsliding.”

“Yes, we will come to you,
for you are the LORD our God.
23 Surely the idolatrous commotion on
the hills
and mountains is a deception;
surely in the LORD our God
is the salvation of Israel.
24 From our youth shameful gods have
consumed
the fruits of our ancestors’ labor—
their flocks and herds,
their sons and daughters.
25 Let us lie down in our shame,
and let our disgrace cover us.
We have sinned against the LORD our
God,
both we and our ancestors;
from our youth till this day
we have not obeyed the LORD our
God.”

4 “If you, Israel, will return,
then return to me,”
declares the LORD.
“If you put your detestable idols out
of my sight
and no longer go astray,
2 and if in a truthful, just and righteous
way
you swear, ‘As surely as the LORD
lives,’
then the nations will invoke blessings
by him
and in him they will boast.”

3 This is what the LORD says to the people
of Judah and to Jerusalem:

“Break up your unplowed ground
and do not sow among thorns.
4 Circumcise yourselves to the LORD,
circumcise your hearts,
you people of Judah and
inhabitants of Jerusalem,
or my wrath will flare up and burn
like fire
because of the evil you have
done—
burn with no one to quench it.

Disaster From the North

5 “Announce in Judah and proclaim in
Jerusalem and say:
‘Sound the trumpet throughout the
land!’
Cry aloud and say:
‘Gather together!
Let us flee to the fortified cities!’
6 Raise the signal to go to Zion!
Flee for safety without delay!
For I am bringing disaster from the
north,
even terrible destruction.”

7 A lion has come out of his lair;
a destroyer of nations has set out.
He has left his place
to lay waste your land.
Your towns will lie in ruins
without inhabitant.
8 So put on sackcloth,
lament and wail,
for the fierce anger of the LORD
has not turned away from us.

9 “In that day,” declares the LORD,
“the king and the officials will lose
heart,
the priests will be horrified,
and the prophets will be appalled.”

10 Then I said, “Alas, Sovereign LORD! How
completely you have deceived this people
and Jerusalem by saying, ‘You will have
peace,’ when the sword is at our throats!”

[11]At that time this people and Jerusalem will be told, "A scorching wind from
the barren heights in the desert blows
toward my people, but not to winnow or
cleanse; [12]a wind too strong for that comes
from me. Now I pronounce my judgments
against them."

[13] Look! He advances like the clouds,
his chariots come like a whirlwind,
his horses are swifter than eagles.
Woe to us! We are ruined!
[14] Jerusalem, wash the evil from your heart and be saved.
How long will you harbor wicked thoughts?
[15] A voice is announcing from Dan,
proclaiming disaster from the hills of Ephraim.
[16] "Tell this to the nations,
proclaim concerning Jerusalem:
'A besieging army is coming from a distant land,
raising a war cry against the cities of Judah.
[17] They surround her like men guarding a field,
because she has rebelled against me,'"
declares the LORD.
[18] "Your own conduct and actions
have brought this on you.
This is your punishment.
How bitter it is!
How it pierces to the heart!"

[19] Oh, my anguish, my anguish!
I writhe in pain.
Oh, the agony of my heart!
My heart pounds within me,
I cannot keep silent.
For I have heard the sound of the trumpet;
I have heard the battle cry.
[20] Disaster follows disaster;
the whole land lies in ruins.
In an instant my tents are destroyed,
my shelter in a moment.
[21] How long must I see the battle standard
and hear the sound of the trumpet?

[22] "My people are fools;
they do not know me.
They are senseless children;
they have no understanding.
They are skilled in doing evil;
they know not how to do good."

[23] I looked at the earth,
and it was formless and empty;
and at the heavens,
and their light was gone.
[24] I looked at the mountains,
and they were quaking;
all the hills were swaying.
[25] I looked, and there were no people;
every bird in the sky had flown away.
[26] I looked, and the fruitful land was a desert;
all its towns lay in ruins
before the LORD, before his fierce anger.

[27]This is what the LORD says:

"The whole land will be ruined,
though I will not destroy it completely.
[28] Therefore the earth will mourn
and the heavens above grow dark,
because I have spoken and will not relent,
I have decided and will not turn back."

[29] At the sound of horsemen and archers
every town takes to flight.
Some go into the thickets;
some climb up among the rocks.
All the towns are deserted;
no one lives in them.

[30] What are you doing, you devastated one?
Why dress yourself in scarlet
and put on jewels of gold?
Why highlight your eyes with makeup?
You adorn yourself in vain.
Your lovers despise you;
they want to kill you.

[31] I hear a cry as of a woman in labor,
a groan as of one bearing her first child —
the cry of Daughter Zion gasping for breath,
stretching out her hands and saying,
"Alas! I am fainting;
my life is given over to murderers."

Not One Is Upright

5 "Go up and down the streets of Jerusalem,
look around and consider,
search through her squares.
If you can find but one person
who deals honestly and seeks the truth,
I will forgive this city.
[2] Although they say, 'As surely as the LORD lives,'
still they are swearing falsely."

[3] LORD, do not your eyes look for truth?
You struck them, but they felt no pain;
you crushed them, but they refused correction.

They made their faces harder than stone
and refused to repent.
4 I thought, "These are only the poor;
they are foolish,
for they do not know the way of the LORD,
the requirements of their God.
5 So I will go to the leaders
and speak to them;
surely they know the way of the LORD,
the requirements of their God."
But with one accord they too had broken off the yoke
and torn off the bonds.
6 Therefore a lion from the forest will attack them,
a wolf from the desert will ravage them,
a leopard will lie in wait near their towns
to tear to pieces any who venture out,
for their rebellion is great
and their backslidings many.

7 "Why should I forgive you?
Your children have forsaken me
and sworn by gods that are not gods.
I supplied all their needs,
yet they committed adultery
and thronged to the houses of prostitutes.
8 They are well-fed, lusty stallions,
each neighing for another man's wife.
9 Should I not punish them for this?"
declares the LORD.
"Should I not avenge myself
on such a nation as this?

10 "Go through her vineyards and ravage them,
but do not destroy them completely.
Strip off her branches,
for these people do not belong to the LORD.
11 The people of Israel and the people of Judah
have been utterly unfaithful to me,"
declares the LORD.

12 They have lied about the LORD;
they said, "He will do nothing!
No harm will come to us;
we will never see sword or famine.
13 The prophets are but wind
and the word is not in them;
so let what they say be done to them."

14 Therefore this is what the LORD God
Almighty says:

"Because the people have spoken these words,
I will make my words in your mouth a fire
and these people the wood it consumes.
15 People of Israel," declares the LORD,
"I am bringing a distant nation against you —
an ancient and enduring nation,
a people whose language you do not know,
whose speech you do not understand.
16 Their quivers are like an open grave;
all of them are mighty warriors.
17 They will devour your harvests and food,
devour your sons and daughters;
they will devour your flocks and herds,
devour your vines and fig trees.
With the sword they will destroy
the fortified cities in which you trust.

18 "Yet even in those days," declares the
LORD, "I will not destroy you completely.
19 And when the people ask, 'Why has the
LORD our God done all this to us?' you will
tell them, 'As you have forsaken me and
served foreign gods in your own land, so
now you will serve foreigners in a land
not your own.'

20 "Announce this to the descendants of Jacob
and proclaim it in Judah:
21 Hear this, you foolish and senseless people,
who have eyes but do not see,
who have ears but do not hear:
22 Should you not fear me?" declares the LORD.
"Should you not tremble in my presence?
I made the sand a boundary for the sea,
an everlasting barrier it cannot cross.
The waves may roll, but they cannot prevail;
they may roar, but they cannot cross it.
23 But these people have stubborn and rebellious hearts;
they have turned aside and gone away.
24 They do not say to themselves,
'Let us fear the LORD our God,
who gives autumn and spring rains in season,
who assures us of the regular weeks of harvest.'

25 Your wrongdoings have kept these
away;
your sins have deprived you of
good.

26 "Among my people are the wicked
who lie in wait like men who snare
birds
and like those who set traps to
catch people.
27 Like cages full of birds,
their houses are full of deceit;
they have become rich and powerful
28 and have grown fat and sleek.
Their evil deeds have no limit;
they do not seek justice.
They do not promote the case of the
fatherless;
they do not defend the just cause of
the poor.
29 Should I not punish them for this?"
declares the LORD.
"Should I not avenge myself
on such a nation as this?

30 "A horrible and shocking thing
has happened in the land:
31 The prophets prophesy lies,
the priests rule by their own
authority,
and my people love it this way.
But what will you do in the end?

Jerusalem Under Siege

6 "Flee for safety, people of Benjamin!
Flee from Jerusalem!
Sound the trumpet in Tekoa!
Raise the signal over Beth
Hakkerem!
For disaster looms out of the north,
even terrible destruction.
2 I will destroy Daughter Zion,
so beautiful and delicate.
3 Shepherds with their flocks will come
against her;
they will pitch their tents around her,
each tending his own portion."

4 "Prepare for battle against her!
Arise, let us attack at noon!
But, alas, the daylight is fading,
and the shadows of evening grow
long.
5 So arise, let us attack at night
and destroy her fortresses!"

6 This is what the LORD Almighty says:

"Cut down the trees
and build siege ramps against
Jerusalem.
This city must be punished;
it is filled with oppression.
7 As a well pours out its water,
so she pours out her wickedness.
Violence and destruction resound in
her;
her sickness and wounds are ever
before me.
8 Take warning, Jerusalem,
or I will turn away from you
and make your land desolate
so no one can live in it."

9 This is what the LORD Almighty says:

"Let them glean the remnant of Israel
as thoroughly as a vine;
pass your hand over the branches
again,
like one gathering grapes."

10 To whom can I speak and give
warning?
Who will listen to me?
Their ears are closed[a]
so they cannot hear.
The word of the LORD is offensive to
them;
they find no pleasure in it.
11 But I am full of the wrath of the LORD,
and I cannot hold it in.

"Pour it out on the children in the
street
and on the young men gathered
together;
both husband and wife will be caught
in it,
and the old, those weighed down
with years.
12 Their houses will be turned over to
others,
together with their fields and their
wives,
when I stretch out my hand
against those who live in the land,"
declares the LORD.
13 "From the least to the greatest,
all are greedy for gain;
prophets and priests alike,
all practice deceit.
14 They dress the wound of my people
as though it were not serious.
'Peace, peace,' they say,
when there is no peace.
15 Are they ashamed of their detestable
conduct?
No, they have no shame at all;
they do not even know how to
blush.
So they will fall among the fallen;
they will be brought down when I
punish them,"
says the LORD.

[a] 10 Hebrew *uncircumcised*

16 This is what the LORD says:

"Stand at the crossroads and look;
ask for the ancient paths,
ask where the good way is, and walk in it,
and you will find rest for your souls.
But you said, 'We will not walk in it.'
17 I appointed watchmen over you and said,
'Listen to the sound of the trumpet!'
But you said, 'We will not listen.'
18 Therefore hear, you nations;
you who are witnesses,
observe what will happen to them.
19 Hear, you earth:
I am bringing disaster on this people,
the fruit of their schemes,
because they have not listened to my words
and have rejected my law.
20 What do I care about incense from Sheba
or sweet calamus from a distant land?
Your burnt offerings are not acceptable;
your sacrifices do not please me."

21 Therefore this is what the LORD says:

"I will put obstacles before this people.
Parents and children alike will stumble over them;
neighbors and friends will perish."

22 This is what the LORD says:

"Look, an army is coming
from the land of the north;
a great nation is being stirred up
from the ends of the earth.
23 They are armed with bow and spear;
they are cruel and show no mercy.
They sound like the roaring sea
as they ride on their horses;
they come like men in battle formation
to attack you, Daughter Zion."
24 We have heard reports about them,
and our hands hang limp.
Anguish has gripped us,
pain like that of a woman in labor.
25 Do not go out to the fields
or walk on the roads,
for the enemy has a sword,
and there is terror on every side.
26 Put on sackcloth, my people,
and roll in ashes;
mourn with bitter wailing
as for an only son,
for suddenly the destroyer
will come upon us.
27 "I have made you a tester of metals
and my people the ore,
that you may observe
and test their ways.
28 They are all hardened rebels,
going about to slander.
They are bronze and iron;
they all act corruptly.
29 The bellows blow fiercely
to burn away the lead with fire,
but the refining goes on in vain;
the wicked are not purged out.
30 They are called rejected silver,
because the LORD has rejected them."

False Religion Worthless

7 This is the word that came to Jeremiah from the LORD: 2 "Stand at the gate
of the LORD's house and there proclaim
this message:
" 'Hear the word of the LORD, all you
people of Judah who come through these
gates to worship the LORD. 3 This is what
the LORD Almighty, the God of Israel, says:
Reform your ways and your actions, and
I will let you live in this place. 4 Do not
trust in deceptive words and say, "This
is the temple of the LORD, the temple of
the LORD, the temple of the LORD!" 5 If you
really change your ways and your actions
and deal with each other justly, 6 if you do
not oppress the foreigner, the fatherless
or the widow and do not shed innocent
blood in this place, and if you do not follow other gods to your own harm, 7 then I
will let you live in this place, in the land
I gave your ancestors for ever and ever.
8 But look, you are trusting in deceptive
words that are worthless.
9 " 'Will you steal and murder, commit
adultery and perjury,[a] burn incense to
Baal and follow other gods you have not
known, 10 and then come and stand before
me in this house, which bears my Name,
and say, "We are safe" — safe to do all
these detestable things? 11 Has this house,
which bears my Name, become a den of
robbers to you? But I have been watching!
declares the LORD.
12 " 'Go now to the place in Shiloh where
I first made a dwelling for my Name, and
see what I did to it because of the wickedness of my people Israel. 13 While you were
doing all these things, declares the LORD, I

[a] 9 Or *and swear by false gods*

spoke to you again and again, but you did
not listen; I called you, but you did not answer. 14Therefore, what I did to Shiloh I will
now do to the house that bears my Name,
the temple you trust in, the place I gave to
you and your ancestors. 15I will thrust you
from my presence, just as I did all your
fellow Israelites, the people of Ephraim.'

16"So do not pray for this people nor offer any plea or petition for them; do not
plead with me, for I will not listen to you.
17Do you not see what they are doing in
the towns of Judah and in the streets of
Jerusalem? 18The children gather wood,
the fathers light the fire, and the women
knead the dough and make cakes to offer
to the Queen of Heaven. They pour out
drink offerings to other gods to arouse my
anger. 19But am I the one they are provoking? declares the LORD. Are they not rather
harming themselves, to their own shame?

20" 'Therefore this is what the Sovereign
LORD says: My anger and my wrath will be
poured out on this place — on man and
beast, on the trees of the field and on the
crops of your land — and it will burn and
not be quenched.

21" 'This is what the LORD Almighty, the
God of Israel, says: Go ahead, add your
burnt offerings to your other sacrifices
and eat the meat yourselves! 22For when I
brought your ancestors out of Egypt and
spoke to them, I did not just give them commands about burnt offerings and sacrifices,
23but I gave them this command: Obey me,
and I will be your God and you will be my
people. Walk in obedience to all I command
you, that it may go well with you. 24But they
did not listen or pay attention; instead, they
followed the stubborn inclinations of their
evil hearts. They went backward and not
forward. 25From the time your ancestors left
Egypt until now, day after day, again and
again I sent you my servants the prophets. 26But they did not listen to me or pay
attention. They were stiff-necked and did
more evil than their ancestors.'

27"When you tell them all this, they
will not listen to you; when you call to
them, they will not answer. 28Therefore
say to them, 'This is the nation that has
not obeyed the LORD its God or responded
to correction. Truth has perished; it has
vanished from their lips.

29" 'Cut off your hair and throw it away;
take up a lament on the barren heights,
for the LORD has rejected and abandoned
this generation that is under his wrath.

The Valley of Slaughter

30" 'The people of Judah have done evil in
my eyes, declares the LORD. They have set
up their detestable idols in the house that
bears my Name and have defiled it. 31They
have built the high places of Topheth in the
Valley of Ben Hinnom to burn their sons
and daughters in the fire — something I did
not command, nor did it enter my mind.
32So beware, the days are coming, declares
the LORD, when people will no longer call
it Topheth or the Valley of Ben Hinnom,
but the Valley of Slaughter, for they will
bury the dead in Topheth until there is no
more room. 33Then the carcasses of this
people will become food for the birds and
the wild animals, and there will be no one
to frighten them away. 34I will bring an end
to the sounds of joy and gladness and to
the voices of bride and bridegroom in the
towns of Judah and the streets of Jerusalem, for the land will become desolate.

8 " 'At that time, declares the LORD, the
bones of the kings and officials of Judah, the bones of the priests and prophets,
and the bones of the people of Jerusalem
will be removed from their graves. 2They
will be exposed to the sun and the moon
and all the stars of the heavens, which
they have loved and served and which
they have followed and consulted and
worshiped. They will not be gathered up
or buried, but will be like dung lying on
the ground. 3Wherever I banish them, all
the survivors of this evil nation will prefer
death to life, declares the LORD Almighty.'

Sin and Punishment

4"Say to them, 'This is what the LORD
says:

" 'When people fall down, do they not
get up?
When someone turns away, do they
not return?
5Why then have these people turned
away?
Why does Jerusalem always turn
away?
They cling to deceit;
they refuse to return.
6I have listened attentively,
but they do not say what is right.
None of them repent of their
wickedness,
saying, "What have I done?"
Each pursues their own course
like a horse charging into battle.
7Even the stork in the sky
knows her appointed seasons,
and the dove, the swift and the
thrush
observe the time of their
migration.
But my people do not know
the requirements of the LORD.

8 " 'How can you say, "We are wise,
for we have the law of the LORD,"
when actually the lying pen of the scribes
has handled it falsely?
9 The wise will be put to shame;
they will be dismayed and trapped.
Since they have rejected the word of the LORD,
what kind of wisdom do they have?
10 Therefore I will give their wives to other men
and their fields to new owners.
From the least to the greatest,
all are greedy for gain;
prophets and priests alike,
all practice deceit.
11 They dress the wound of my people
as though it were not serious.
"Peace, peace," they say,
when there is no peace.
12 Are they ashamed of their detestable conduct?
No, they have no shame at all;
they do not even know how to blush.
So they will fall among the fallen;
they will be brought down when they are punished,
says the LORD.

13 " 'I will take away their harvest,
declares the LORD.
There will be no grapes on the vine.
There will be no figs on the tree,
and their leaves will wither.
What I have given them
will be taken from them.[a]' "

14 Why are we sitting here?
Gather together!
Let us flee to the fortified cities
and perish there!
For the LORD our God has doomed us to perish
and given us poisoned water to drink,
because we have sinned against him.
15 We hoped for peace
but no good has come,
for a time of healing
but there is only terror.
16 The snorting of the enemy's horses
is heard from Dan;
at the neighing of their stallions
the whole land trembles.
They have come to devour
the land and everything in it,
the city and all who live there.

17 "See, I will send venomous snakes
among you,
vipers that cannot be charmed,
and they will bite you,"
declares the LORD.

18 You who are my Comforter[b] in sorrow,
my heart is faint within me.
19 Listen to the cry of my people
from a land far away:
"Is the LORD not in Zion?
Is her King no longer there?"
"Why have they aroused my anger
with their images,
with their worthless foreign idols?"
20 "The harvest is past,
the summer has ended,
and we are not saved."
21 Since my people are crushed, I am crushed;
I mourn, and horror grips me.
22 Is there no balm in Gilead?
Is there no physician there?
Why then is there no healing
for the wound of my people?

9[c] 1 Oh, that my head were a spring of water
and my eyes a fountain of tears!
I would weep day and night
for the slain of my people.
2 Oh, that I had in the desert
a lodging place for travelers,
so that I might leave my people
and go away from them;
for they are all adulterers,
a crowd of unfaithful people.

3 "They make ready their tongue
like a bow, to shoot lies;
it is not by truth
that they triumph[d] in the land.
They go from one sin to another;
they do not acknowledge me,"
declares the LORD.
4 "Beware of your friends;
do not trust anyone in your clan.
For every one of them is a deceiver,[e]
and every friend a slanderer.
5 Friend deceives friend,
and no one speaks the truth.
They have taught their tongues to lie;
they weary themselves with sinning.
6 You[f] live in the midst of deception;
in their deceit they refuse to acknowledge me,"
declares the LORD.

[a] 13 The meaning of the Hebrew for this sentence is uncertain. [b] 18 The meaning of the Hebrew for this word is uncertain. [c] In Hebrew texts 9:1 is numbered 8:23, and 9:2-26 is numbered 9:1-25. [d] 3 Or *lies; / they are not valiant for truth* [e] 4 Or *a deceiving Jacob* [f] 6 That is, Jeremiah (the Hebrew is singular)

7Therefore this is what the LORD Almighty says:

"See, I will refine and test them,
for what else can I do
because of the sin of my people?
8Their tongue is a deadly arrow;
it speaks deceitfully.
With their mouths they all speak
cordially to their neighbors,
but in their hearts they set traps for
them.
9Should I not punish them for this?"
declares the LORD.
"Should I not avenge myself
on such a nation as this?"

10I will weep and wail for the
mountains
and take up a lament concerning
the wilderness grasslands.
They are desolate and untraveled,
and the lowing of cattle is not
heard.
The birds have all fled
and the animals are gone.

11"I will make Jerusalem a heap of ruins,
a haunt of jackals;
and I will lay waste the towns of
Judah
so no one can live there."

12Who is wise enough to understand
this? Who has been instructed by the LORD
and can explain it? Why has the land been
ruined and laid waste like a desert that
no one can cross?
13The LORD said, "It is because they have
forsaken my law, which I set before them;
they have not obeyed me or followed my
law. 14Instead, they have followed the stubbornness of their hearts; they have followed the Baals, as their ancestors taught
them." 15Therefore this is what the LORD
Almighty, the God of Israel, says: "See, I
will make this people eat bitter food and
drink poisoned water. 16I will scatter them
among nations that neither they nor their
ancestors have known, and I will pursue
them with the sword until I have made
an end of them."

17This is what the LORD Almighty says:

"Consider now! Call for the wailing
women to come;
send for the most skillful of them.
18Let them come quickly
and wail over us
till our eyes overflow with tears
and water streams from our
eyelids.
19The sound of wailing is heard from
Zion:
'How ruined we are!
How great is our shame!
We must leave our land
because our houses are in ruins.'"

20Now, you women, hear the word of
the LORD;
open your ears to the words of his
mouth.
Teach your daughters how to wail;
teach one another a lament.
21Death has climbed in through our
windows
and has entered our fortresses;
it has removed the children from the
streets
and the young men from the public
squares.

22Say, "This is what the LORD declares:

"'Dead bodies will lie
like dung on the open field,
like cut grain behind the reaper,
with no one to gather them.'"

23This is what the LORD says:

"Let not the wise boast of their
wisdom
or the strong boast of their strength
or the rich boast of their riches,
24but let the one who boasts boast
about this:
that they have the understanding
to know me,
that I am the LORD, who exercises
kindness,
justice and righteousness on earth,
for in these I delight,"
declares the LORD.

25"The days are coming," declares the
LORD, "when I will punish all who are
circumcised only in the flesh— 26Egypt,
Judah, Edom, Ammon, Moab and all who
live in the wilderness in distant places.[a]
For all these nations are really uncircumcised, and even the whole house of Israel
is uncircumcised in heart."

God and Idols

10 Hear what the LORD says to you, people of Israel. 2This is what the
LORD says:

"Do not learn the ways of the nations
or be terrified by signs in the
heavens,
though the nations are terrified by
them.

[a] 26 Or *wilderness and who clip the hair by their foreheads*

[3] For the practices of the peoples are worthless;
they cut a tree out of the forest,
and a craftsman shapes it with his chisel.
[4] They adorn it with silver and gold;
they fasten it with hammer and nails
so it will not totter.
[5] Like a scarecrow in a cucumber field,
their idols cannot speak;
they must be carried
because they cannot walk.
Do not fear them;
they can do no harm
nor can they do any good."
[6] No one is like you, LORD;
you are great,
and your name is mighty in power.
[7] Who should not fear you,
King of the nations?
This is your due.
Among all the wise leaders of the nations
and in all their kingdoms,
there is no one like you.
[8] They are all senseless and foolish;
they are taught by worthless wooden idols.
[9] Hammered silver is brought from Tarshish
and gold from Uphaz.
What the craftsman and goldsmith have made
is then dressed in blue and purple —
all made by skilled workers.
[10] But the LORD is the true God;
he is the living God, the eternal King.
When he is angry, the earth trembles;
the nations cannot endure his wrath.

[11] "Tell them this: 'These gods, who did not make the heavens and the earth, will perish from the earth and from under the heavens.'"[a]

[12] But God made the earth by his power;
he founded the world by his wisdom
and stretched out the heavens by his understanding.
[13] When he thunders, the waters in the heavens roar;
he makes clouds rise from the ends of the earth.
He sends lightning with the rain
and brings out the wind from his storehouses.

[14] Everyone is senseless and without knowledge;
every goldsmith is shamed by his idols.
The images he makes are a fraud;
they have no breath in them.
[15] They are worthless, the objects of mockery;
when their judgment comes, they will perish.
[16] He who is the Portion of Jacob is not like these,
for he is the Maker of all things,
including Israel, the people of his inheritance —
the LORD Almighty is his name.

Coming Destruction

[17] Gather up your belongings to leave the land,
you who live under siege.
[18] For this is what the LORD says:
"At this time I will hurl out
those who live in this land;
I will bring distress on them
so that they may be captured."

[19] Woe to me because of my injury!
My wound is incurable!
Yet I said to myself,
"This is my sickness, and I must endure it."
[20] My tent is destroyed;
all its ropes are snapped.
My children are gone from me and are no more;
no one is left now to pitch my tent
or to set up my shelter.
[21] The shepherds are senseless
and do not inquire of the LORD;
so they do not prosper
and all their flock is scattered.
[22] Listen! The report is coming —
a great commotion from the land of the north!
It will make the towns of Judah desolate,
a haunt of jackals.

Jeremiah's Prayer

[23] LORD, I know that people's lives are not their own;
it is not for them to direct their steps.
[24] Discipline me, LORD, but only in due measure —
not in your anger,
or you will reduce me to nothing.

[a] *11* The text of this verse is in Aramaic.

25 Pour out your wrath on the nations
that do not acknowledge you,
on the peoples who do not call on
your name.
For they have devoured Jacob;
they have devoured him completely
and destroyed his homeland.

The Covenant Is Broken

11 This is the word that came to Jeremiah from the LORD: 2"Listen to the
terms of this covenant and tell them to
the people of Judah and to those who live
in Jerusalem. 3Tell them that this is what
the LORD, the God of Israel, says: 'Cursed
is the one who does not obey the terms of
this covenant — 4the terms I commanded
your ancestors when I brought them out of
Egypt, out of the iron-smelting furnace.' I
said, 'Obey me and do everything I command you, and you will be my people,
and I will be your God. 5Then I will fulfill
the oath I swore to your ancestors, to give
them a land flowing with milk and honey' — the land you possess today."

I answered, "Amen, LORD."

6The LORD said to me, "Proclaim all these
words in the towns of Judah and in the
streets of Jerusalem: 'Listen to the terms
of this covenant and follow them. 7From
the time I brought your ancestors up from
Egypt until today, I warned them again
and again, saying, "Obey me." 8But they
did not listen or pay attention; instead,
they followed the stubbornness of their
evil hearts. So I brought on them all the
curses of the covenant I had commanded
them to follow but that they did not keep.'"

9Then the LORD said to me, "There is a
conspiracy among the people of Judah and
those who live in Jerusalem. 10They have
returned to the sins of their ancestors, who
refused to listen to my words. They have
followed other gods to serve them. Both
Israel and Judah have broken the covenant
I made with their ancestors. 11Therefore this
is what the LORD says: 'I will bring on them
a disaster they cannot escape. Although
they cry out to me, I will not listen to them.
12The towns of Judah and the people of
Jerusalem will go and cry out to the gods
to whom they burn incense, but they will
not help them at all when disaster strikes.
13You, Judah, have as many gods as you
have towns; and the altars you have set up
to burn incense to that shameful god Baal
are as many as the streets of Jerusalem.'

14"Do not pray for this people or offer
any plea or petition for them, because I
will not listen when they call to me in the
time of their distress.

15 "What is my beloved doing in my
temple
as she, with many others, works out
her evil schemes?
Can consecrated meat avert your
punishment?
When you engage in your wickedness,
then you rejoice.[a]"

16 The LORD called you a thriving olive
tree
with fruit beautiful in form.
But with the roar of a mighty storm
he will set it on fire,
and its branches will be broken.

17The LORD Almighty, who planted you,
has decreed disaster for you, because the
people of both Israel and Judah have done
evil and aroused my anger by burning
incense to Baal.

Plot Against Jeremiah

18Because the LORD revealed their plot to
me, I knew it, for at that time he showed
me what they were doing. 19I had been like
a gentle lamb led to the slaughter; I did
not realize that they had plotted against
me, saying,

"Let us destroy the tree and its fruit;
let us cut him off from the land of
the living,
that his name be remembered no
more."

20 But you, LORD Almighty, who judge
righteously
and test the heart and mind,
let me see your vengeance on them,
for to you I have committed my
cause.

21Therefore this is what the LORD says
about the people of Anathoth who are
threatening to kill you, saying, "Do not
prophesy in the name of the LORD or you
will die by our hands" — 22therefore this
is what the LORD Almighty says: "I will
punish them. Their young men will die
by the sword, their sons and daughters
by famine. 23Not even a remnant will be
left to them, because I will bring disaster
on the people of Anathoth in the year of
their punishment."

Jeremiah's Complaint

12 You are always righteous, LORD,
when I bring a case before you.
Yet I would speak with you about
your justice:
Why does the way of the wicked
prosper?
Why do all the faithless live at ease?

[a] 15 Or *Could consecrated meat avert your punishment? / Then you would rejoice*

[2]You have planted them, and they
have taken root;
they grow and bear fruit.
You are always on their lips
but far from their hearts.
[3]Yet you know me, LORD;
you see me and test my thoughts
about you.
Drag them off like sheep to be
butchered!
Set them apart for the day of
slaughter!
[4]How long will the land lie parched
and the grass in every field be
withered?
Because those who live in it are
wicked,
the animals and birds have
perished.
Moreover, the people are saying,
"He will not see what happens to us."

God's Answer

[5]"If you have raced with men on foot
and they have worn you out,
how can you compete with horses?
If you stumble[a] in safe country,
how will you manage in the
thickets by[b] the Jordan?
[6]Your relatives, members of your own
family—
even they have betrayed you;
they have raised a loud cry against
you.
Do not trust them,
though they speak well of you.

[7]"I will forsake my house,
abandon my inheritance;
I will give the one I love
into the hands of her enemies.
[8]My inheritance has become to me
like a lion in the forest.
She roars at me;
therefore I hate her.
[9]Has not my inheritance become to me
like a speckled bird of prey
that other birds of prey surround
and attack?
Go and gather all the wild beasts;
bring them to devour.
[10]Many shepherds will ruin my
vineyard
and trample down my field;
they will turn my pleasant field
into a desolate wasteland.
[11]It will be made a wasteland,
parched and desolate before me;
the whole land will be laid waste
because there is no one who cares.
[12]Over all the barren heights in the
desert
destroyers will swarm,
for the sword of the LORD will devour
from one end of the land to the other;
no one will be safe.
[13]They will sow wheat but reap thorns;
they will wear themselves out but
gain nothing.
They will bear the shame of their
harvest
because of the LORD's fierce anger."

[14]This is what the LORD says: "As for all my
wicked neighbors who seize the inheritance
I gave my people Israel, I will uproot them
from their lands and I will uproot the people
of Judah from among them. [15]But after I uproot them, I will again have compassion and
will bring each of them back to their own
inheritance and their own country. [16]And if
they learn well the ways of my people and
swear by my name, saying, 'As surely as the
LORD lives'—even as they once taught my
people to swear by Baal—then they will be
established among my people. [17]But if any
nation does not listen, I will completely
uproot and destroy it," declares the LORD.

A Linen Belt

13 This is what the LORD said to me:
"Go and buy a linen belt and put it
around your waist, but do not let it touch
water." [2]So I bought a belt, as the LORD directed, and put it around my waist.

[3]Then the word of the LORD came to me
a second time: [4]"Take the belt you bought
and are wearing around your waist, and
go now to Perath[c] and hide it there in a
crevice in the rocks." [5]So I went and hid it
at Perath, as the LORD told me.

[6]Many days later the LORD said to me,
"Go now to Perath and get the belt I told
you to hide there." [7]So I went to Perath
and dug up the belt and took it from the
place where I had hidden it, but now it was
ruined and completely useless.

[8]Then the word of the LORD came to
me: [9]"This is what the LORD says: 'In the
same way I will ruin the pride of Judah
and the great pride of Jerusalem. [10]These
wicked people, who refuse to listen to my
words, who follow the stubbornness of
their hearts and go after other gods to
serve and worship them, will be like this
belt—completely useless! [11]For as a belt
is bound around the waist, so I bound all
the people of Israel and all the people of
Judah to me,' declares the LORD, 'to be
my people for my renown and praise and
honor. But they have not listened.'

[a] 5 Or *you feel secure only* [b] 5 Or *the flooding of* [c] 4 Or possibly *to the Euphrates*; similarly in verses 5-7

Wineskins

[12]"Say to them: 'This is what the LORD, the God of Israel, says: Every wineskin should be filled with wine.' And if they say to you, 'Don't we know that every wineskin should be filled with wine?'
[13]then tell them, 'This is what the LORD says: I am going to fill with drunkenness all who live in this land, including the kings who sit on David's throne, the priests, the prophets and all those living in Jerusalem.
[14]I will smash them one against the other, parents and children alike, declares the LORD. I will allow no pity or mercy or compassion to keep me from destroying them.'"

Threat of Captivity

[15]Hear and pay attention,
do not be arrogant,
for the LORD has spoken.
[16]Give glory to the LORD your God
before he brings the darkness,
before your feet stumble
on the darkening hills.
You hope for light,
but he will turn it to utter darkness
and change it to deep gloom.
[17]If you do not listen,
I will weep in secret
because of your pride;
my eyes will weep bitterly,
overflowing with tears,
because the LORD's flock will be taken captive.

[18]Say to the king and to the queen mother,
"Come down from your thrones,
for your glorious crowns
will fall from your heads."
[19]The cities in the Negev will be shut up,
and there will be no one to open them.
All Judah will be carried into exile,
carried completely away.

[20]Look up and see
those who are coming from the north.
Where is the flock that was entrusted to you,
the sheep of which you boasted?
[21]What will you say when the LORD sets over you
those you cultivated as your special allies?
Will not pain grip you
like that of a woman in labor?
[22]And if you ask yourself,
"Why has this happened to me?"—
it is because of your many sins
that your skirts have been torn off
and your body mistreated.
[23]Can an Ethiopian[a] change his skin
or a leopard its spots?
Neither can you do good
who are accustomed to doing evil.

[24]"I will scatter you like chaff
driven by the desert wind.
[25]This is your lot,
the portion I have decreed for you,"
declares the LORD,
"because you have forgotten me
and trusted in false gods.
[26]I will pull up your skirts over your face
that your shame may be seen—
[27]your adulteries and lustful neighings,
your shameless prostitution!
I have seen your detestable acts
on the hills and in the fields.
Woe to you, Jerusalem!
How long will you be unclean?"

Drought, Famine, Sword

14 This is the word of the LORD that came to Jeremiah concerning the drought:

[2]"Judah mourns,
her cities languish;
they wail for the land,
and a cry goes up from Jerusalem.
[3]The nobles send their servants for water;
they go to the cisterns
but find no water.
They return with their jars unfilled;
dismayed and despairing,
they cover their heads.
[4]The ground is cracked
because there is no rain in the land;
the farmers are dismayed
and cover their heads.
[5]Even the doe in the field
deserts her newborn fawn
because there is no grass.
[6]Wild donkeys stand on the barren heights
and pant like jackals;
their eyes fail
for lack of food."

[7]Although our sins testify against us,
do something, LORD, for the sake of your name.
For we have often rebelled;
we have sinned against you.

[a] *23* Hebrew *Cushite* (probably a person from the upper Nile region)

8 You who are the hope of Israel,
its Savior in times of distress,
why are you like a stranger in the land,
like a traveler who stays only a night?
9 Why are you like a man taken by surprise,
like a warrior powerless to save?
You are among us, LORD,
and we bear your name;
do not forsake us!

10 This is what the LORD says about this
people:

"They greatly love to wander;
they do not restrain their feet.
So the LORD does not accept them;
he will now remember their wickedness
and punish them for their sins."

11 Then the LORD said to me, "Do not
pray for the well-being of this people. 12 Although they fast, I will not listen to their
cry; though they offer burnt offerings and
grain offerings, I will not accept them. Instead, I will destroy them with the sword,
famine and plague."
13 But I said, "Alas, Sovereign LORD! The
prophets keep telling them, 'You will not
see the sword or suffer famine. Indeed, I
will give you lasting peace in this place.'"
14 Then the LORD said to me, "The
prophets are prophesying lies in my
name. I have not sent them or appointed them or spoken to them. They are
prophesying to you false visions, divinations, idolatries[a] and the delusions
of their own minds. 15 Therefore this is
what the LORD says about the prophets
who are prophesying in my name: I did
not send them, yet they are saying, 'No
sword or famine will touch this land.'
Those same prophets will perish by sword
and famine. 16 And the people they are
prophesying to will be thrown out into
the streets of Jerusalem because of the
famine and sword. There will be no one
to bury them, their wives, their sons and
their daughters. I will pour out on them
the calamity they deserve.
17 "Speak this word to them:

"'Let my eyes overflow with tears
night and day without ceasing;
for the Virgin Daughter, my people,
has suffered a grievous wound,
a crushing blow.
18 If I go into the country,
I see those slain by the sword;
if I go into the city,
I see the ravages of famine.
Both prophet and priest
have gone to a land they know not.'"

19 Have you rejected Judah completely?
Do you despise Zion?
Why have you afflicted us
so that we cannot be healed?
We hoped for peace
but no good has come,
for a time of healing
but there is only terror.
20 We acknowledge our wickedness, LORD,
and the guilt of our ancestors;
we have indeed sinned against you.
21 For the sake of your name do not
despise us;
do not dishonor your glorious throne.
Remember your covenant with us
and do not break it.
22 Do any of the worthless idols of the
nations bring rain?
Do the skies themselves send down showers?
No, it is you, LORD our God.
Therefore our hope is in you,
for you are the one who does all this.

15 Then the LORD said to me: "Even if
Moses and Samuel were to stand
before me, my heart would not go out
to this people. Send them away from my
presence! Let them go! 2 And if they ask
you, 'Where shall we go?' tell them, 'This
is what the LORD says:

"'Those destined for death, to death;
those for the sword, to the sword;
those for starvation, to starvation;
those for captivity, to captivity.'

3 "I will send four kinds of destroyers
against them," declares the LORD, "the
sword to kill and the dogs to drag away
and the birds and the wild animals to
devour and destroy. 4 I will make them
abhorrent to all the kingdoms of the
earth because of what Manasseh son of
Hezekiah king of Judah did in Jerusalem.

5 "Who will have pity on you,
Jerusalem?
Who will mourn for you?
Who will stop to ask how you are?
6 You have rejected me," declares the
LORD.
"You keep on backsliding.
So I will reach out and destroy you;
I am tired of holding back.

[a] 14 Or *visions, worthless divinations*

7 I will winnow them with a winnowing fork
at the city gates of the land.
I will bring bereavement and destruction on my people,
for they have not changed their ways.
8 I will make their widows more numerous
than the sand of the sea.
At midday I will bring a destroyer
against the mothers of their young men;
suddenly I will bring down on them
anguish and terror.
9 The mother of seven will grow faint
and breathe her last.
Her sun will set while it is still day;
she will be disgraced and humiliated.
I will put the survivors to the sword
before their enemies,"
declares the LORD.

10 Alas, my mother, that you gave me birth,
a man with whom the whole land strives and contends!
I have neither lent nor borrowed,
yet everyone curses me.

11 The LORD said,

"Surely I will deliver you for a good purpose;
surely I will make your enemies plead with you
in times of disaster and times of distress.

12 "Can a man break iron —
iron from the north — or bronze?

13 "Your wealth and your treasures
I will give as plunder, without charge,
because of all your sins
throughout your country.
14 I will enslave you to your enemies
in[a] a land you do not know,
for my anger will kindle a fire
that will burn against you."

15 LORD, you understand;
remember me and care for me.
Avenge me on my persecutors.
You are long-suffering — do not take me away;
think of how I suffer reproach for your sake.
16 When your words came, I ate them;
they were my joy and my heart's delight,
for I bear your name,
LORD God Almighty.
17 I never sat in the company of revelers,
never made merry with them;
I sat alone because your hand was on me
and you had filled me with indignation.
18 Why is my pain unending
and my wound grievous and incurable?
You are to me like a deceptive brook,
like a spring that fails.

19 Therefore this is what the LORD says:

"If you repent, I will restore you
that you may serve me;
if you utter worthy, not worthless, words,
you will be my spokesman.
Let this people turn to you,
but you must not turn to them.
20 I will make you a wall to this people,
a fortified wall of bronze;
they will fight against you
but will not overcome you,
for I am with you
to rescue and save you,"
declares the LORD.
21 "I will save you from the hands of the wicked
and deliver you from the grasp of the cruel."

Day of Disaster

16 Then the word of the LORD came to
me: 2 "You must not marry and have
sons or daughters in this place." 3 For this
is what the LORD says about the sons and
daughters born in this land and about the
women who are their mothers and the
men who are their fathers: 4 "They will
die of deadly diseases. They will not be
mourned or buried but will be like dung
lying on the ground. They will perish by
sword and famine, and their dead bodies
will become food for the birds and the
wild animals."
5 For this is what the LORD says: "Do not
enter a house where there is a funeral
meal; do not go to mourn or show sympathy, because I have withdrawn my blessing, my love and my pity from this people,"
declares the LORD. 6 "Both high and low will
die in this land. They will not be buried or
mourned, and no one will cut themselves

[a] 14 Some Hebrew manuscripts, Septuagint and Syriac (see also 17:4); most Hebrew manuscripts *I will cause your enemies to bring you / into*

or shave their head for the dead. 7No one
will offer food to comfort those who mourn
for the dead — not even for a father or a
mother — nor will anyone give them a
drink to console them.

8"And do not enter a house where there
is feasting and sit down to eat and drink.
9For this is what the LORD Almighty, the
God of Israel, says: Before your eyes and in
your days I will bring an end to the sounds
of joy and gladness and to the voices of
bride and bridegroom in this place.

10"When you tell these people all this
and they ask you, 'Why has the LORD decreed such a great disaster against us?
What wrong have we done? What sin have
we committed against the LORD our God?'
11then say to them, 'It is because your ancestors forsook me,' declares the LORD, 'and
followed other gods and served and worshiped them. They forsook me and did not
keep my law. 12But you have behaved more
wickedly than your ancestors. See how all
of you are following the stubbornness of
your evil hearts instead of obeying me.
13So I will throw you out of this land into a
land neither you nor your ancestors have
known, and there you will serve other gods
day and night, for I will show you no favor.'

14"However, the days are coming," declares the LORD, "when it will no longer
be said, 'As surely as the LORD lives, who
brought the Israelites up out of Egypt,'
15but it will be said, 'As surely as the LORD
lives, who brought the Israelites up out
of the land of the north and out of all the
countries where he had banished them.'
For I will restore them to the land I gave
their ancestors.

16"But now I will send for many fishermen," declares the LORD, "and they will
catch them. After that I will send for many
hunters, and they will hunt them down
on every mountain and hill and from the
crevices of the rocks. 17My eyes are on all
their ways; they are not hidden from me,
nor is their sin concealed from my eyes.
18I will repay them double for their wickedness and their sin, because they have
defiled my land with the lifeless forms
of their vile images and have filled my
inheritance with their detestable idols."

19 LORD, my strength and my fortress,
my refuge in time of distress,
to you the nations will come
from the ends of the earth and say,
"Our ancestors possessed nothing but
false gods,
worthless idols that did them no
good.
20 Do people make their own gods?
Yes, but they are not gods!"

21 "Therefore I will teach them —
this time I will teach them
my power and might.
Then they will know
that my name is the LORD.

17

"Judah's sin is engraved with an
iron tool,
inscribed with a flint point,
on the tablets of their hearts
and on the horns of their altars.
2 Even their children remember
their altars and Asherah poles[a]
beside the spreading trees
and on the high hills.
3 My mountain in the land
and your[b] wealth and all your
treasures
I will give away as plunder,
together with your high places,
because of sin throughout your
country.
4 Through your own fault you will lose
the inheritance I gave you.
I will enslave you to your enemies
in a land you do not know,
for you have kindled my anger,
and it will burn forever."

5This is what the LORD says:

"Cursed is the one who trusts in man,
who draws strength from mere
flesh
and whose heart turns away from
the LORD.
6 That person will be like a bush in the
wastelands;
they will not see prosperity when it
comes.
They will dwell in the parched places
of the desert,
in a salt land where no one lives.

7 "But blessed is the one who trusts in
the LORD,
whose confidence is in him.
8 They will be like a tree planted by the
water
that sends out its roots by the
stream.
It does not fear when heat comes;
its leaves are always green.
It has no worries in a year of drought
and never fails to bear fruit."

9 The heart is deceitful above all things
and beyond cure.
Who can understand it?

[a] *2* That is, wooden symbols of the goddess Asherah [b] *2,3* Or *hills* / [3]*and the mountains of the land. / Your*

10 "I the LORD search the heart
and examine the mind,
to reward each person according to their conduct,
according to what their deeds deserve."

11 Like a partridge that hatches eggs it did not lay
are those who gain riches by unjust means.
When their lives are half gone, their riches will desert them,
and in the end they will prove to be fools.

12 A glorious throne, exalted from the beginning,
is the place of our sanctuary.
13 LORD, you are the hope of Israel;
all who forsake you will be put to shame.
Those who turn away from you will be written in the dust
because they have forsaken the LORD,
the spring of living water.

14 Heal me, LORD, and I will be healed;
save me and I will be saved,
for you are the one I praise.
15 They keep saying to me,
"Where is the word of the LORD?
Let it now be fulfilled!"
16 I have not run away from being your shepherd;
you know I have not desired the day of despair.
What passes my lips is open before you.
17 Do not be a terror to me;
you are my refuge in the day of disaster.
18 Let my persecutors be put to shame,
but keep me from shame;
let them be terrified,
but keep me from terror.
Bring on them the day of disaster;
destroy them with double destruction.

Keeping the Sabbath Day Holy

19 This is what the LORD said to me:
"Go and stand at the Gate of the People,[a]
through which the kings of Judah go in
and out; stand also at all the other gates
of Jerusalem. 20 Say to them, 'Hear the word
of the LORD, you kings of Judah and all
people of Judah and everyone living in
Jerusalem who come through these gates.
21 This is what the LORD says: Be careful not
to carry a load on the Sabbath day or bring
it through the gates of Jerusalem. 22 Do not
bring a load out of your houses or do any
work on the Sabbath, but keep the Sabbath
day holy, as I commanded your ancestors.
23 Yet they did not listen or pay attention;
they were stiff-necked and would not listen
or respond to discipline. 24 But if you are
careful to obey me, declares the LORD, and
bring no load through the gates of this city
on the Sabbath, but keep the Sabbath day
holy by not doing any work on it, 25 then
kings who sit on David's throne will come
through the gates of this city with their
officials. They and their officials will come
riding in chariots and on horses, accompanied by the men of Judah and those
living in Jerusalem, and this city will be
inhabited forever. 26 People will come from
the towns of Judah and the villages around
Jerusalem, from the territory of Benjamin
and the western foothills, from the hill
country and the Negev, bringing burnt offerings and sacrifices, grain offerings and
incense, and bringing thank offerings to
the house of the LORD. 27 But if you do not
obey me to keep the Sabbath day holy by
not carrying any load as you come through
the gates of Jerusalem on the Sabbath day,
then I will kindle an unquenchable fire in
the gates of Jerusalem that will consume
her fortresses.'"

At the Potter's House

18 This is the word that came to Jeremiah from the LORD: 2 "Go down to
the potter's house, and there I will give
you my message." 3 So I went down to the
potter's house, and I saw him working at
the wheel. 4 But the pot he was shaping
from the clay was marred in his hands;
so the potter formed it into another pot,
shaping it as seemed best to him.

5 Then the word of the LORD came to me.
6 He said, "Can I not do with you, Israel,
as this potter does?" declares the LORD.
"Like clay in the hand of the potter, so are
you in my hand, Israel. 7 If at any time I
announce that a nation or kingdom is to
be uprooted, torn down and destroyed,
8 and if that nation I warned repents of
its evil, then I will relent and not inflict
on it the disaster I had planned. 9 And if
at another time I announce that a nation
or kingdom is to be built up and planted,
10 and if it does evil in my sight and does
not obey me, then I will reconsider the
good I had intended to do for it.

11 "Now therefore say to the people of Judah and those living in Jerusalem, 'This is
what the LORD says: Look! I am preparing

[a] 19 Or *Army*

a disaster for you and devising a plan
against you. So turn from your evil ways,
each one of you, and reform your ways and
your actions.' 12But they will reply, 'It's no
use. We will continue with our own plans;
we will all follow the stubbornness of our
evil hearts.'"

13Therefore this is what the LORD says:

"Inquire among the nations:
 Who has ever heard anything like this?
A most horrible thing has been done
 by Virgin Israel.
14Does the snow of Lebanon
 ever vanish from its rocky slopes?
Do its cool waters from distant sources
 ever stop flowing?[a]
15Yet my people have forgotten me;
 they burn incense to worthless idols,
which made them stumble in their ways,
 in the ancient paths.
They made them walk in byways,
 on roads not built up.
16Their land will be an object of horror
 and of lasting scorn;
all who pass by will be appalled
 and will shake their heads.
17Like a wind from the east,
 I will scatter them before their enemies;
I will show them my back and not my face
 in the day of their disaster."

18They said, "Come, let's make plans
against Jeremiah; for the teaching of the
law by the priest will not cease, nor will
counsel from the wise, nor the word from
the prophets. So come, let's attack him
with our tongues and pay no attention
to anything he says."

19Listen to me, LORD;
 hear what my accusers are saying!
20Should good be repaid with evil?
 Yet they have dug a pit for me.
Remember that I stood before you
 and spoke in their behalf
 to turn your wrath away from them.
21So give their children over to famine;
 hand them over to the power of the sword.
Let their wives be made childless and widows;
 let their men be put to death,
 their young men slain by the sword in battle.
22Let a cry be heard from their houses
 when you suddenly bring invaders against them,
for they have dug a pit to capture me
 and have hidden snares for my feet.
23But you, LORD, know
 all their plots to kill me.
Do not forgive their crimes
 or blot out their sins from your sight.
Let them be overthrown before you;
 deal with them in the time of your anger.

19 This is what the LORD says: "Go and
buy a clay jar from a potter. Take
along some of the elders of the people
and of the priests 2and go out to the Valley of Ben Hinnom, near the entrance of
the Potsherd Gate. There proclaim the
words I tell you, 3and say, 'Hear the word
of the LORD, you kings of Judah and people of Jerusalem. This is what the LORD
Almighty, the God of Israel, says: Listen! I
am going to bring a disaster on this place
that will make the ears of everyone who
hears of it tingle. 4For they have forsaken
me and made this a place of foreign gods;
they have burned incense in it to gods
that neither they nor their ancestors nor
the kings of Judah ever knew, and they
have filled this place with the blood of
the innocent. 5They have built the high
places of Baal to burn their children in
the fire as offerings to Baal — something
I did not command or mention, nor did it
enter my mind. 6So beware, the days are
coming, declares the LORD, when people
will no longer call this place Topheth or
the Valley of Ben Hinnom, but the Valley
of Slaughter.

7" 'In this place I will ruin[b] the plans of
Judah and Jerusalem. I will make them
fall by the sword before their enemies,
at the hands of those who want to kill
them, and I will give their carcasses as
food to the birds and the wild animals.
8I will devastate this city and make it an
object of horror and scorn; all who pass
by will be appalled and will scoff because
of all its wounds. 9I will make them eat
the flesh of their sons and daughters, and
they will eat one another's flesh because
their enemies will press the siege so hard
against them to destroy them.'

10"Then break the jar while those who go
with you are watching, 11and say to them,
'This is what the LORD Almighty says: I will
smash this nation and this city just as this

[a] 14 The meaning of the Hebrew for this sentence is uncertain. [b] 7 The Hebrew for *ruin* sounds like the Hebrew for *jar* (see verses 1 and 10).

potter's jar is smashed and cannot be repaired. They will bury the dead in Topheth
until there is no more room. 12This is what
I will do to this place and to those who live
here, declares the LORD. I will make this
city like Topheth. 13The houses in Jerusalem and those of the kings of Judah will
be defiled like this place, Topheth — all the
houses where they burned incense on the
roofs to all the starry hosts and poured out
drink offerings to other gods.'"
14Jeremiah then returned from Topheth,
where the LORD had sent him to prophesy,
and stood in the court of the LORD's temple
and said to all the people, 15"This is what
the LORD Almighty, the God of Israel, says:
'Listen! I am going to bring on this city and
all the villages around it every disaster I
pronounced against them, because they
were stiff-necked and would not listen to
my words.'"

Jeremiah and Pashhur

20 When the priest Pashhur son of
Immer, the official in charge of
the temple of the LORD, heard Jeremiah
prophesying these things, 2he had Jeremiah the prophet beaten and put in the
stocks at the Upper Gate of Benjamin at
the LORD's temple. 3The next day, when
Pashhur released him from the stocks,
Jeremiah said to him, "The LORD's name
for you is not Pashhur, but Terror on Every
Side. 4For this is what the LORD says: 'I will
make you a terror to yourself and to all
your friends; with your own eyes you will
see them fall by the sword of their enemies. I will give all Judah into the hands
of the king of Babylon, who will carry
them away to Babylon or put them to the
sword. 5I will deliver all the wealth of this
city into the hands of their enemies — all
its products, all its valuables and all the
treasures of the kings of Judah. They will
take it away as plunder and carry it off
to Babylon. 6And you, Pashhur, and all
who live in your house will go into exile
to Babylon. There you will die and be buried, you and all your friends to whom you
have prophesied lies.'"

Jeremiah's Complaint

7You deceived[a] me, LORD, and I was deceived[a];
you overpowered me and prevailed.
I am ridiculed all day long;
everyone mocks me.
8Whenever I speak, I cry out
proclaiming violence and destruction.
So the word of the LORD has brought me
insult and reproach all day long.
9But if I say, "I will not mention his word
or speak anymore in his name,"
his word is in my heart like a fire,
a fire shut up in my bones.
I am weary of holding it in;
indeed, I cannot.
10I hear many whispering,
"Terror on every side!
Denounce him! Let's denounce him!"
All my friends
are waiting for me to slip, saying,
"Perhaps he will be deceived;
then we will prevail over him
and take our revenge on him."

11But the LORD is with me like a mighty warrior;
so my persecutors will stumble and not prevail.
They will fail and be thoroughly disgraced;
their dishonor will never be forgotten.
12LORD Almighty, you who examine the righteous
and probe the heart and mind,
let me see your vengeance on them,
for to you I have committed my cause.

13Sing to the LORD!
Give praise to the LORD!
He rescues the life of the needy
from the hands of the wicked.

14Cursed be the day I was born!
May the day my mother bore me not be blessed!
15Cursed be the man who brought my father the news,
who made him very glad, saying,
"A child is born to you — a son!"
16May that man be like the towns
the LORD overthrew without pity.
May he hear wailing in the morning,
a battle cry at noon.
17For he did not kill me in the womb,
with my mother as my grave,
her womb enlarged forever.
18Why did I ever come out of the womb
to see trouble and sorrow
and to end my days in shame?

God Rejects Zedekiah's Request

21 The word came to Jeremiah from
the LORD when King Zedekiah sent
to him Pashhur son of Malkijah and the
priest Zephaniah son of Maaseiah. They

[a] 7 Or *persuaded*

said: 2"Inquire now of the LORD for us
because Nebuchadnezzar[a] king of Babylon is attacking us. Perhaps the LORD
will perform wonders for us as in times
past so that he will withdraw from us."
3But Jeremiah answered them, "Tell
Zedekiah, 4'This is what the LORD, the God
of Israel, says: I am about to turn against
you the weapons of war that are in your
hands, which you are using to fight the
king of Babylon and the Babylonians[b]
who are outside the wall besieging you.
And I will gather them inside this city.
5I myself will fight against you with an
outstretched hand and a mighty arm in
furious anger and in great wrath. 6I will
strike down those who live in this city—
both man and beast—and they will die
of a terrible plague. 7After that, declares
the LORD, I will give Zedekiah king of Judah, his officials and the people in this
city who survive the plague, sword and
famine, into the hands of Nebuchadnezzar king of Babylon and to their enemies
who want to kill them. He will put them
to the sword; he will show them no mercy
or pity or compassion.'
8"Furthermore, tell the people, 'This
is what the LORD says: See, I am setting
before you the way of life and the way
of death. 9Whoever stays in this city will
die by the sword, famine or plague. But
whoever goes out and surrenders to the
Babylonians who are besieging you will
live; they will escape with their lives. 10I
have determined to do this city harm and
not good, declares the LORD. It will be giv-
en into the hands of the king of Babylon,
and he will destroy it with fire.'
11"Moreover, say to the royal house of
Judah, 'Hear the word of the LORD. 12This
is what the LORD says to you, house of
David:

"'Administer justice every morning;
rescue from the hand of the
oppressor
the one who has been robbed,
or my wrath will break out and burn
like fire
because of the evil you have
done—
burn with no one to quench it.
13I am against you, Jerusalem,
you who live above this valley
on the rocky plateau, declares the
LORD—
you who say, "Who can come against
us?
Who can enter our refuge?"
14I will punish you as your deeds
deserve,
declares the LORD.
I will kindle a fire in your forests
that will consume everything
around you.'"

Judgment Against Wicked Kings

22 This is what the LORD says: "Go down
to the palace of the king of Judah
and proclaim this message there: 2'Hear
the word of the LORD to you, king of Judah, you who sit on David's throne—you,
your officials and your people who come
through these gates. 3This is what the
LORD says: Do what is just and right. Rescue from the hand of the oppressor the
one who has been robbed. Do no wrong
or violence to the foreigner, the fatherless
or the widow, and do not shed innocent
blood in this place. 4For if you are careful to carry out these commands, then
kings who sit on David's throne will come
through the gates of this palace, riding in
chariots and on horses, accompanied by
their officials and their people. 5But if you
do not obey these commands, declares the
LORD, I swear by myself that this palace
will become a ruin.'"
6For this is what the LORD says about
the palace of the king of Judah:

"Though you are like Gilead to me,
like the summit of Lebanon,
I will surely make you like a
wasteland,
like towns not inhabited.
7I will send destroyers against you,
each man with his weapons,
and they will cut up your fine cedar
beams
and throw them into the fire.

8"People from many nations will pass
by this city and will ask one another, 'Why
has the LORD done such a thing to this
great city?' 9And the answer will be: 'Because they have forsaken the covenant of
the LORD their God and have worshiped
and served other gods.'"

10Do not weep for the dead king or
mourn his loss;
rather, weep bitterly for him who is
exiled,
because he will never return
nor see his native land again.

11For this is what the LORD says about Shallum[c] son of Josiah, who succeeded his
father as king of Judah but has gone from

[a] 2 Hebrew *Nebuchadrezzar,* of which *Nebuchadnezzar* is a variant; here and often in Jeremiah and Ezekiel [b] 4 Or *Chaldeans;* also in verse 9 [c] 11 Also called *Jehoahaz*

this place: "He will never return. 12He will
die in the place where they have led him
captive; he will not see this land again."

13 "Woe to him who builds his palace by
unrighteousness,
his upper rooms by injustice,
making his own people work for
nothing,
not paying them for their labor.
14 He says, 'I will build myself a great
palace
with spacious upper rooms.'
So he makes large windows in it,
panels it with cedar
and decorates it in red.

15 "Does it make you a king
to have more and more cedar?
Did not your father have food and
drink?
He did what was right and just,
so all went well with him.
16 He defended the cause of the poor
and needy,
and so all went well.
Is that not what it means to know
me?"
declares the LORD.
17 "But your eyes and your heart
are set only on dishonest gain,
on shedding innocent blood
and on oppression and extortion."

18Therefore this is what the LORD says
about Jehoiakim son of Josiah king of
Judah:

"They will not mourn for him:
'Alas, my brother! Alas, my sister!'
They will not mourn for him:
'Alas, my master! Alas, his
splendor!'
19 He will have the burial of a donkey —
dragged away and thrown
outside the gates of Jerusalem."

20 "Go up to Lebanon and cry out,
let your voice be heard in Bashan,
cry out from Abarim,
for all your allies are crushed.
21 I warned you when you felt secure,
but you said, 'I will not listen!'
This has been your way from your
youth;
you have not obeyed me.
22 The wind will drive all your shepherds
away,
and your allies will go into exile.
Then you will be ashamed and
disgraced
because of all your wickedness.
23 You who live in 'Lebanon,[a]'
who are nestled in cedar buildings,
how you will groan when pangs come
upon you,
pain like that of a woman in labor!

24"As surely as I live," declares the LORD,
"even if you, Jehoiachin[b] son of Jehoiakim
king of Judah, were a signet ring on my
right hand, I would still pull you off. 25I will
deliver you into the hands of those who
want to kill you, those you fear — Nebuchadnezzar king of Babylon and the Babylonians.[c] 26I will hurl you and the mother
who gave you birth into another country,
where neither of you was born, and there
you both will die. 27You will never come
back to the land you long to return to."

28 Is this man Jehoiachin a despised,
broken pot,
an object no one wants?
Why will he and his children be
hurled out,
cast into a land they do not know?
29 O land, land, land,
hear the word of the LORD!
30 This is what the LORD says:
"Record this man as if childless,
a man who will not prosper in his
lifetime,
for none of his offspring will prosper,
none will sit on the throne of David
or rule anymore in Judah."

The Righteous Branch

23 "Woe to the shepherds who are destroying and scattering the sheep of
my pasture!" declares the LORD. 2Therefore
this is what the LORD, the God of Israel,
says to the shepherds who tend my people:
"Because you have scattered my flock and
driven them away and have not bestowed
care on them, I will bestow punishment on
you for the evil you have done," declares the
LORD. 3"I myself will gather the remnant
of my flock out of all the countries where I
have driven them and will bring them back
to their pasture, where they will be fruitful
and increase in number. 4I will place shepherds over them who will tend them, and
they will no longer be afraid or terrified,
nor will any be missing," declares the LORD.

5 "The days are coming," declares the
LORD,
"when I will raise up for David[d] a
righteous Branch,
a King who will reign wisely
and do what is just and right in the
land.

[a] 23 That is, the palace in Jerusalem (see 1 Kings 7:2) [b] 24 Hebrew *Koniah*, a variant of *Jehoiachin*; also in verse 28 [c] 25 Or *Chaldeans* [d] 5 Or *up from David's line*

[6] In his days Judah will be saved
and Israel will live in safety.
This is the name by which he will be called:
The LORD Our Righteous Savior.

[7]"So then, the days are coming," declares
the LORD, "when people will no longer say,
'As surely as the LORD lives, who brought
the Israelites up out of Egypt,' [8]but they
will say, 'As surely as the LORD lives, who
brought the descendants of Israel up out
of the land of the north and out of all the
countries where he had banished them.'
Then they will live in their own land."

Lying Prophets

[9]Concerning the prophets:

My heart is broken within me;
all my bones tremble.
I am like a drunken man,
like a strong man overcome by wine,
because of the LORD
and his holy words.
[10] The land is full of adulterers;
because of the curse[a] the land lies parched
and the pastures in the wilderness are withered.
The prophets follow an evil course
and use their power unjustly.
[11] "Both prophet and priest are godless;
even in my temple I find their wickedness,"
declares the LORD.
[12] "Therefore their path will become slippery;
they will be banished to darkness
and there they will fall.
I will bring disaster on them
in the year they are punished,"
declares the LORD.
[13] "Among the prophets of Samaria
I saw this repulsive thing:
They prophesied by Baal
and led my people Israel astray.
[14] And among the prophets of Jerusalem
I have seen something horrible:
They commit adultery and live a lie.
They strengthen the hands of evildoers,
so that not one of them turns from their wickedness.
They are all like Sodom to me;
the people of Jerusalem are like Gomorrah."

[15]Therefore this is what the LORD Almighty says concerning the prophets:

"I will make them eat bitter food
and drink poisoned water,
because from the prophets of Jerusalem
ungodliness has spread throughout the land."

[16]This is what the LORD Almighty says:

"Do not listen to what the prophets are prophesying to you;
they fill you with false hopes.
They speak visions from their own minds,
not from the mouth of the LORD.
[17] They keep saying to those who despise me,
'The LORD says: You will have peace.'
And to all who follow the stubbornness of their hearts
they say, 'No harm will come to you.'
[18] But which of them has stood in the council of the LORD
to see or to hear his word?
Who has listened and heard his word?
[19] See, the storm of the LORD
will burst out in wrath,
a whirlwind swirling down
on the heads of the wicked.
[20] The anger of the LORD will not turn back
until he fully accomplishes
the purposes of his heart.
In days to come
you will understand it clearly.
[21] I did not send these prophets,
yet they have run with their message;
I did not speak to them,
yet they have prophesied.
[22] But if they had stood in my council,
they would have proclaimed my words to my people
and would have turned them from their evil ways
and from their evil deeds.

[23] "Am I only a God nearby,"
declares the LORD,
"and not a God far away?
[24] Who can hide in secret places
so that I cannot see them?"
declares the LORD.
"Do not I fill heaven and earth?"
declares the LORD.

[a] 10 Or *because of these things*

25“I have heard what the prophets say
who prophesy lies in my name. They say,
‘I had a dream! I had a dream!’ 26How long
will this continue in the hearts of these
lying prophets, who prophesy the delusions of their own minds? 27They think the
dreams they tell one another will make my
people forget my name, just as their ancestors forgot my name through Baal worship. 28Let the prophet who has a dream
recount the dream, but let the one who
has my word speak it faithfully. For what
has straw to do with grain?” declares the
LORD. 29“Is not my word like fire,” declares
the LORD, “and like a hammer that breaks
a rock in pieces?
30“Therefore,” declares the LORD, “I
am against the prophets who steal from
one another words supposedly from me.
31Yes,” declares the LORD, “I am against the
prophets who wag their own tongues and
yet declare, ‘The LORD declares.’ 32Indeed,
I am against those who prophesy false
dreams,” declares the LORD. “They tell
them and lead my people astray with their
reckless lies, yet I did not send or appoint
them. They do not benefit these people in
the least,” declares the LORD.

False Prophecy

33“When these people, or a prophet or a
priest, ask you, ‘What is the message from
the LORD?’ say to them, ‘What message?
I will forsake you, declares the LORD.’
34If a prophet or a priest or anyone else
claims, ‘This is a message from the LORD,’
I will punish them and their household.
35This is what each of you keeps saying to
your friends and other Israelites: ‘What
is the LORD’s answer?’ or ‘What has the
LORD spoken?’ 36But you must not mention ‘a message from the LORD’ again,
because each one’s word becomes their
own message. So you distort the words
of the living God, the LORD Almighty,
our God. 37This is what you keep saying
to a prophet: ‘What is the LORD’s answer
to you?’ or ‘What has the LORD spoken?’
38Although you claim, ‘This is a message
from the LORD,’ this is what the LORD says:
You used the words, ‘This is a message
from the LORD,’ even though I told you
that you must not claim, ‘This is a message from the LORD.’ 39Therefore, I will
surely forget you and cast you out of my
presence along with the city I gave to you
and your ancestors. 40I will bring on you
everlasting disgrace — everlasting shame
that will not be forgotten.”

Two Baskets of Figs

24 After Jehoiachin[a] son of Jehoiakim
king of Judah and the officials, the
skilled workers and the artisans of Judah
were carried into exile from Jerusalem
to Babylon by Nebuchadnezzar king of
Babylon, the LORD showed me two baskets of figs placed in front of the temple
of the LORD. 2One basket had very good
figs, like those that ripen early; the other basket had very bad figs, so bad they
could not be eaten.
3Then the LORD asked me, “What do you
see, Jeremiah?”
“Figs,” I answered. “The good ones are
very good, but the bad ones are so bad
they cannot be eaten.”
4Then the word of the LORD came to
me: 5“This is what the LORD, the God of
Israel, says: ‘Like these good figs, I regard
as good the exiles from Judah, whom I
sent away from this place to the land of
the Babylonians.[b] 6My eyes will watch
over them for their good, and I will bring
them back to this land. I will build them
up and not tear them down; I will plant
them and not uproot them. 7I will give
them a heart to know me, that I am the
LORD. They will be my people, and I will
be their God, for they will return to me
with all their heart.
8“ ‘But like the bad figs, which are so bad
they cannot be eaten,’ says the LORD, ‘so
will I deal with Zedekiah king of Judah,
his officials and the survivors from Jerusalem, whether they remain in this land or
live in Egypt. 9I will make them abhorrent
and an offense to all the kingdoms of the
earth, a reproach and a byword, a curse[c]
and an object of ridicule, wherever I banish them. 10I will send the sword, famine
and plague against them until they are
destroyed from the land I gave to them
and their ancestors.’ ”

Seventy Years of Captivity

25 The word came to Jeremiah concerning all the people of Judah in
the fourth year of Jehoiakim son of Josiah
king of Judah, which was the first year of
Nebuchadnezzar king of Babylon. 2So Jeremiah the prophet said to all the people of
Judah and to all those living in Jerusalem:
3For twenty-three years — from the thirteenth year of Josiah son of Amon king
of Judah until this very day — the word
of the LORD has come to me and I have
spoken to you again and again, but you
have not listened.

[a] 1 Hebrew *Jeconiah,* a variant of *Jehoiachin* [b] 5 Or *Chaldeans* [c] 9 That is, their names will be used in cursing (see 29:22); or, others will see that they are cursed.

4And though the LORD has sent all his servants the prophets to you again and again, you have not listened or paid any attention. 5They said, "Turn now, each of you, from your evil ways and your evil practices, and you can stay in the land the LORD gave to you and your ancestors for ever and ever. 6Do not follow other gods to serve and worship them; do not arouse my anger with what your hands have made. Then I will not harm you."

7"But you did not listen to me," declares the LORD, "and you have aroused my anger with what your hands have made, and you have brought harm to yourselves."

8Therefore the LORD Almighty says this: "Because you have not listened to my words, 9I will summon all the peoples of the north and my servant Nebuchadnezzar king of Babylon," declares the LORD, "and I will bring them against this land and its inhabitants and against all the surrounding nations. I will completely destroy[a] them and make them an object of horror and scorn, and an everlasting ruin. 10I will banish from them the sounds of joy and gladness, the voices of bride and bridegroom, the sound of millstones and the light of the lamp. 11This whole country will become a desolate wasteland, and these nations will serve the king of Babylon seventy years.

12"But when the seventy years are fulfilled, I will punish the king of Babylon and his nation, the land of the Babylonians,[b] for their guilt," declares the LORD, "and will make it desolate forever. 13I will bring on that land all the things I have spoken against it, all that are written in this book and prophesied by Jeremiah against all the nations. 14They themselves will be enslaved by many nations and great kings; I will repay them according to their deeds and the work of their hands."

The Cup of God's Wrath

15This is what the LORD, the God of Israel, said to me: "Take from my hand this cup filled with the wine of my wrath and make all the nations to whom I send you drink it. 16When they drink it, they will stagger and go mad because of the sword I will send among them."

17So I took the cup from the LORD's hand and made all the nations to whom he sent me drink it: 18Jerusalem and the towns of Judah, its kings and officials, to make them a ruin and an object of horror and scorn, a curse[c] — as they are today; 19Pharaoh king of Egypt, his attendants, his officials and all his people, 20and all the foreign people there; all the kings of Uz; all the kings of the Philistines (those of Ashkelon, Gaza, Ekron, and the people left at Ashdod); 21Edom, Moab and Ammon; 22all the kings of Tyre and Sidon; the kings of the coastlands across the sea; 23Dedan, Tema, Buz and all who are in distant places[d]; 24all the kings of Arabia and all the kings of the foreign people who live in the wilderness; 25all the kings of Zimri, Elam and Media; 26and all the kings of the north, near and far, one after the other — all the kingdoms on the face of the earth. And after all of them, the king of Sheshak[e] will drink it too.

27"Then tell them, 'This is what the LORD Almighty, the God of Israel, says: Drink, get drunk and vomit, and fall to rise no more because of the sword I will send among you.' 28But if they refuse to take the cup from your hand and drink, tell them, 'This is what the LORD Almighty says: You must drink it! 29See, I am beginning to bring disaster on the city that bears my Name, and will you indeed go unpunished? You will not go unpunished, for I am calling down a sword on all who live on the earth, declares the LORD Almighty.'

30"Now prophesy all these words against them and say to them:

" 'The LORD will roar from on high;
he will thunder from his holy dwelling
and roar mightily against his land.
He will shout like those who tread the grapes,
shout against all who live on the earth.
31 The tumult will resound to the ends of the earth,
for the LORD will bring charges against the nations;
he will bring judgment on all mankind
and put the wicked to the sword,' "
declares the LORD.

32This is what the LORD Almighty says:

"Look! Disaster is spreading
from nation to nation;
a mighty storm is rising
from the ends of the earth."

[a] 9 The Hebrew term refers to the irrevocable giving over of things or persons to the LORD, often by totally destroying them. [b] 12 Or *Chaldeans* [c] 18 That is, their names to be used in cursing (see 29:22); or, to be seen by others as cursed [d] 23 Or *who clip the hair by their foreheads* [e] 26 *Sheshak* is a cryptogram for Babylon.

33 At that time those slain by the LORD
will be everywhere — from one end of
the earth to the other. They will not be
mourned or gathered up or buried, but
will be like dung lying on the ground.

34 Weep and wail, you shepherds;
roll in the dust, you leaders of the
flock.
For your time to be slaughtered has
come;
you will fall like the best of the
rams.[a]
35 The shepherds will have nowhere
to flee,
the leaders of the flock no place
to escape.
36 Hear the cry of the shepherds,
the wailing of the leaders of the
flock,
for the LORD is destroying their
pasture.
37 The peaceful meadows will be laid
waste
because of the fierce anger of
the LORD.
38 Like a lion he will leave his lair,
and their land will become
desolate
because of the sword[b] of the
oppressor
and because of the LORD's fierce
anger.

Jeremiah Threatened With Death

26 Early in the reign of Jehoiakim son
of Josiah king of Judah, this word
came from the LORD: 2 "This is what the
LORD says: Stand in the courtyard of the
LORD's house and speak to all the people
of the towns of Judah who come to worship in the house of the LORD. Tell them
everything I command you; do not omit
a word. 3 Perhaps they will listen and each
will turn from their evil ways. Then I will
relent and not inflict on them the disaster
I was planning because of the evil they
have done. 4 Say to them, 'This is what the
LORD says: If you do not listen to me and
follow my law, which I have set before you,
5 and if you do not listen to the words of my
servants the prophets, whom I have sent
to you again and again (though you have
not listened), 6 then I will make this house
like Shiloh and this city a curse[c] among
all the nations of the earth.' "
7 The priests, the prophets and all the
people heard Jeremiah speak these words
in the house of the LORD. 8 But as soon as
Jeremiah finished telling all the people
everything the LORD had commanded
him to say, the priests, the prophets and
all the people seized him and said, "You
must die! 9 Why do you prophesy in the
LORD's name that this house will be like
Shiloh and this city will be desolate and
deserted?" And all the people crowded
around Jeremiah in the house of the LORD.
10 When the officials of Judah heard
about these things, they went up from
the royal palace to the house of the LORD
and took their places at the entrance of
the New Gate of the LORD's house. 11 Then
the priests and the prophets said to the
officials and all the people, "This man
should be sentenced to death because he
has prophesied against this city. You have
heard it with your own ears!"
12 Then Jeremiah said to all the officials
and all the people: "The LORD sent me to
prophesy against this house and this city
all the things you have heard. 13 Now reform
your ways and your actions and obey the
LORD your God. Then the LORD will relent
and not bring the disaster he has pronounced against you. 14 As for me, I am in
your hands; do with me whatever you think
is good and right. 15 Be assured, however,
that if you put me to death, you will bring
the guilt of innocent blood on yourselves
and on this city and on those who live in
it, for in truth the LORD has sent me to you
to speak all these words in your hearing."
16 Then the officials and all the people
said to the priests and the prophets, "This
man should not be sentenced to death!
He has spoken to us in the name of the
LORD our God."
17 Some of the elders of the land stepped
forward and said to the entire assembly of
people, 18 "Micah of Moresheth prophesied
in the days of Hezekiah king of Judah. He
told all the people of Judah, 'This is what
the LORD Almighty says:

" 'Zion will be plowed like a field,
Jerusalem will become a heap of
rubble,
the temple hill a mound overgrown
with thickets.'[d]

19 "Did Hezekiah king of Judah or anyone
else in Judah put him to death? Did not
Hezekiah fear the LORD and seek his favor?
And did not the LORD relent, so that he
did not bring the disaster he pronounced
against them? We are about to bring a
terrible disaster on ourselves!"

[a] *34* Septuagint; Hebrew *fall and be shattered like fine pottery* [b] *38* Some Hebrew manuscripts and Septuagint (see also 46:16 and 50:16); most Hebrew manuscripts *anger* [c] *6* That is, its name will be used in cursing (see 29:22); or, others will see that it is cursed. [d] *18* Micah 3:12

20(Now Uriah son of Shemaiah from
Kiriath Jearim was another man who
prophesied in the name of the LORD; he
prophesied the same things against this
city and this land as Jeremiah did. 21When
King Jehoiakim and all his officers and
officials heard his words, the king was
determined to put him to death. But Uriah heard of it and fled in fear to Egypt.
22King Jehoiakim, however, sent Elnathan
son of Akbor to Egypt, along with some
other men. 23They brought Uriah out of
Egypt and took him to King Jehoiakim,
who had him struck down with a sword
and his body thrown into the burial place
of the common people.)

24Furthermore, Ahikam son of Shaphan
supported Jeremiah, and so he was not
handed over to the people to be put to
death.

Judah to Serve Nebuchadnezzar

27 Early in the reign of Zedekiah[a] son
of Josiah king of Judah, this word
came to Jeremiah from the LORD: 2This is
what the LORD said to me: "Make a yoke
out of straps and crossbars and put it on
your neck. 3Then send word to the kings
of Edom, Moab, Ammon, Tyre and Sidon
through the envoys who have come to Jerusalem to Zedekiah king of Judah. 4Give
them a message for their masters and say,
'This is what the LORD Almighty, the God
of Israel, says: "Tell this to your masters:
5With my great power and outstretched
arm I made the earth and its people and
the animals that are on it, and I give it to
anyone I please. 6Now I will give all your
countries into the hands of my servant
Nebuchadnezzar king of Babylon; I will
make even the wild animals subject to
him. 7All nations will serve him and his
son and his grandson until the time for
his land comes; then many nations and
great kings will subjugate him.

8" ' "If, however, any nation or kingdom
will not serve Nebuchadnezzar king of
Babylon or bow its neck under his yoke,
I will punish that nation with the sword,
famine and plague, declares the LORD,
until I destroy it by his hand. 9So do not
listen to your prophets, your diviners, your
interpreters of dreams, your mediums or
your sorcerers who tell you, 'You will not
serve the king of Babylon.' 10They prophesy lies to you that will only serve to remove
you far from your lands; I will banish you
and you will perish. 11But if any nation
will bow its neck under the yoke of the
king of Babylon and serve him, I will let
that nation remain in its own land to till
it and to live there, declares the LORD." ' "

12I gave the same message to Zedekiah king of Judah. I said, "Bow your neck
under the yoke of the king of Babylon;
serve him and his people, and you will
live. 13Why will you and your people die by
the sword, famine and plague with which
the LORD has threatened any nation that
will not serve the king of Babylon? 14Do not
listen to the words of the prophets who
say to you, 'You will not serve the king of
Babylon,' for they are prophesying lies to
you. 15'I have not sent them,' declares the
LORD. 'They are prophesying lies in my
name. Therefore, I will banish you and
you will perish, both you and the prophets
who prophesy to you.' "

16Then I said to the priests and all these
people, "This is what the LORD says: Do
not listen to the prophets who say, 'Very
soon now the articles from the LORD's
house will be brought back from Babylon.'
They are prophesying lies to you. 17Do not
listen to them. Serve the king of Babylon,
and you will live. Why should this city become a ruin? 18If they are prophets and
have the word of the LORD, let them plead
with the LORD Almighty that the articles
remaining in the house of the LORD and
in the palace of the king of Judah and
in Jerusalem not be taken to Babylon.
19For this is what the LORD Almighty says
about the pillars, the bronze Sea, the movable stands and the other articles that are
left in this city, 20which Nebuchadnezzar
king of Babylon did not take away when
he carried Jehoiachin[b] son of Jehoiakim
king of Judah into exile from Jerusalem
to Babylon, along with all the nobles of
Judah and Jerusalem — 21yes, this is what
the LORD Almighty, the God of Israel, says
about the things that are left in the house
of the LORD and in the palace of the king
of Judah and in Jerusalem: 22'They will
be taken to Babylon and there they will
remain until the day I come for them,'
declares the LORD. 'Then I will bring them
back and restore them to this place.' "

The False Prophet Hananiah

28 In the fifth month of that same year,
the fourth year, early in the reign of
Zedekiah king of Judah, the prophet Hananiah son of Azzur, who was from Gibeon,
said to me in the house of the LORD in the

[a] *1* A few Hebrew manuscripts and Syriac (see also 27:3,12 and 28:1); most Hebrew manuscripts *Jehoiakim* (Most Septuagint manuscripts do not have this verse.) [b] *20* Hebrew *Jeconiah,* a variant of *Jehoiachin*

presence of the priests and all the people: 2“This is what the LORD Almighty, the God of Israel, says: ‘I will break the yoke of the king of Babylon. 3Within two years I will bring back to this place all the articles of the LORD’s house that Nebuchadnezzar king of Babylon removed from here and took to Babylon. 4I will also bring back to this place Jehoiachin[a] son of Jehoiakim king of Judah and all the other exiles from Judah who went to Babylon,’ declares the LORD, ‘for I will break the yoke of the king of Babylon.’ ”

5Then the prophet Jeremiah replied to the prophet Hananiah before the priests and all the people who were standing in the house of the LORD. 6He said, “Amen! May the LORD do so! May the LORD fulfill the words you have prophesied by bringing the articles of the LORD’s house and all the exiles back to this place from Babylon. 7Nevertheless, listen to what I have to say in your hearing and in the hearing of all the people: 8From early times the prophets who preceded you and me have prophesied war, disaster and plague against many countries and great kingdoms. 9But the prophet who prophesies peace will be recognized as one truly sent by the LORD only if his prediction comes true.”

10Then the prophet Hananiah took the yoke off the neck of the prophet Jeremiah and broke it, 11and he said before all the people, “This is what the LORD says: ‘In the same way I will break the yoke of Nebuchadnezzar king of Babylon off the neck of all the nations within two years.’ ” At this, the prophet Jeremiah went on his way.

12After the prophet Hananiah had broken the yoke off the neck of the prophet Jeremiah, the word of the LORD came to Jeremiah: 13“Go and tell Hananiah, ‘This is what the LORD says: You have broken a wooden yoke, but in its place you will get a yoke of iron. 14This is what the LORD Almighty, the God of Israel, says: I will put an iron yoke on the necks of all these nations to make them serve Nebuchadnezzar king of Babylon, and they will serve him. I will even give him control over the wild animals.’ ”

15Then the prophet Jeremiah said to Hananiah the prophet, “Listen, Hananiah! The LORD has not sent you, yet you have persuaded this nation to trust in lies. 16Therefore this is what the LORD says: ‘I am about to remove you from the face of the earth. This very year you are going to die, because you have preached rebellion against the LORD.’ ”

17In the seventh month of that same year, Hananiah the prophet died.

A Letter to the Exiles

29 This is the text of the letter that the prophet Jeremiah sent from Jerusalem to the surviving elders among the exiles and to the priests, the prophets and all the other people Nebuchadnezzar had carried into exile from Jerusalem to Babylon. 2(This was after King Jehoiachin[a] and the queen mother, the court officials and the leaders of Judah and Jerusalem, the skilled workers and the artisans had gone into exile from Jerusalem.) 3He entrusted the letter to Elasah son of Shaphan and to Gemariah son of Hilkiah, whom Zedekiah king of Judah sent to King Nebuchadnezzar in Babylon. It said:

4This is what the LORD Almighty, the God of Israel, says to all those I carried into exile from Jerusalem to Babylon: 5“Build houses and settle down; plant gardens and eat what they produce. 6Marry and have sons and daughters; find wives for your sons and give your daughters in marriage, so that they too may have sons and daughters. Increase in number there; do not decrease. 7Also, seek the peace and prosperity of the city to which I have carried you into exile. Pray to the LORD for it, because if it prospers, you too will prosper.” 8Yes, this is what the LORD Almighty, the God of Israel, says: “Do not let the prophets and diviners among you deceive you. Do not listen to the dreams you encourage them to have. 9They are prophesying lies to you in my name. I have not sent them,” declares the LORD.

10This is what the LORD says: “When seventy years are completed for Babylon, I will come to you and fulfill my good promise to bring you back to this place. 11For I know the plans I have for you,” declares the LORD, “plans to prosper you and not to harm you, plans to give you hope and a future. 12Then you will call on me and come and pray to me, and I will listen to you. 13You will seek me and find me when you seek me with all your heart. 14I will be found by you,” declares the LORD, “and will bring you back from captivity.[b] I will gather you from all the nations and places where I have banished you,” declares the LORD, “and will bring you back to the place from which I carried you into exile.”

[a] 4,2 Hebrew *Jeconiah,* a variant of *Jehoiachin*

[b] 14 Or *will restore your fortunes*

15 You may say, "The LORD has
raised up prophets for us in Babylon,"
16 but this is what the LORD says about
the king who sits on David's throne
and all the people who remain in this
city, your fellow citizens who did not
go with you into exile — 17 yes, this is
what the LORD Almighty says: "I will
send the sword, famine and plague
against them and I will make them
like figs that are so bad they cannot
be eaten. 18 I will pursue them with the
sword, famine and plague and will
make them abhorrent to all the kingdoms of the earth, a curse[a] and an object of horror, of scorn and reproach,
among all the nations where I drive
them. 19 For they have not listened to
my words," declares the LORD, "words
that I sent to them again and again
by my servants the prophets. And
you exiles have not listened either,"
declares the LORD.
20 Therefore, hear the word of the
LORD, all you exiles whom I have sent
away from Jerusalem to Babylon.
21 This is what the LORD Almighty,
the God of Israel, says about Ahab
son of Kolaiah and Zedekiah son of
Maaseiah, who are prophesying lies
to you in my name: "I will deliver
them into the hands of Nebuchadnezzar king of Babylon, and he will
put them to death before your very
eyes. 22 Because of them, all the exiles
from Judah who are in Babylon will
use this curse: 'May the LORD treat
you like Zedekiah and Ahab, whom
the king of Babylon burned in the
fire.' 23 For they have done outrageous
things in Israel; they have committed
adultery with their neighbors' wives,
and in my name they have uttered
lies — which I did not authorize. I
know it and am a witness to it," declares the LORD.

Message to Shemaiah

24 Tell Shemaiah the Nehelamite, 25 "This
is what the LORD Almighty, the God of
Israel, says: You sent letters in your own
name to all the people in Jerusalem, to
the priest Zephaniah son of Maaseiah,
and to all the other priests. You said to
Zephaniah, 26 'The LORD has appointed you
priest in place of Jehoiada to be in charge
of the house of the LORD; you should put
any maniac who acts like a prophet into
the stocks and neck-irons. 27 So why have
you not reprimanded Jeremiah from Anathoth, who poses as a prophet among
you? 28 He has sent this message to us in
Babylon: It will be a long time. Therefore
build houses and settle down; plant gardens and eat what they produce.'"
29 Zephaniah the priest, however, read
the letter to Jeremiah the prophet. 30 Then
the word of the LORD came to Jeremiah:
31 "Send this message to all the exiles: 'This
is what the LORD says about Shemaiah
the Nehelamite: Because Shemaiah has
prophesied to you, even though I did not
send him, and has persuaded you to trust
in lies, 32 this is what the LORD says: I will
surely punish Shemaiah the Nehelamite
and his descendants. He will have no one
left among this people, nor will he see the
good things I will do for my people, declares the LORD, because he has preached
rebellion against me.'"

Restoration of Israel

30 This is the word that came to Jeremiah from the LORD: 2 "This is what
the LORD, the God of Israel, says: 'Write in
a book all the words I have spoken to you.
3 The days are coming,' declares the LORD,
'when I will bring my people Israel and
Judah back from captivity[b] and restore
them to the land I gave their ancestors
to possess,' says the LORD."
4 These are the words the LORD spoke
concerning Israel and Judah: 5 "This is
what the LORD says:

"'Cries of fear are heard —
terror, not peace.
6 Ask and see:
Can a man bear children?
Then why do I see every strong man
with his hands on his stomach like
a woman in labor,
every face turned deathly pale?
7 How awful that day will be!
No other will be like it.
It will be a time of trouble for Jacob,
but he will be saved out of it.

8 "'In that day,' declares the LORD
Almighty,
'I will break the yoke off their necks
and will tear off their bonds;
no longer will foreigners enslave
them.
9 Instead, they will serve the LORD their
God
and David their king,
whom I will raise up for them.

[a] 18 That is, their names will be used in cursing (see verse 22); or, others will see that they are cursed. [b] 3 Or *will restore the fortunes of my people Israel and Judah*

10 " 'So do not be afraid, Jacob my servant;
do not be dismayed, Israel,'
declares the LORD.
'I will surely save you out of a distant place,
your descendants from the land of their exile.
Jacob will again have peace and security,
and no one will make him afraid.
11 I am with you and will save you,'
declares the LORD.
'Though I completely destroy all the nations
among which I scatter you,
I will not completely destroy you.
I will discipline you but only in due measure;
I will not let you go entirely unpunished.'

12 "This is what the LORD says:

" 'Your wound is incurable,
your injury beyond healing.
13 There is no one to plead your cause,
no remedy for your sore,
no healing for you.
14 All your allies have forgotten you;
they care nothing for you.
I have struck you as an enemy would
and punished you as would the cruel,
because your guilt is so great
and your sins so many.
15 Why do you cry out over your wound,
your pain that has no cure?
Because of your great guilt and many sins
I have done these things to you.

16 " 'But all who devour you will be devoured;
all your enemies will go into exile.
Those who plunder you will be plundered;
all who make spoil of you I will despoil.
17 But I will restore you to health
and heal your wounds,'
declares the LORD,
'because you are called an outcast,
Zion for whom no one cares.'

18 "This is what the LORD says:

" 'I will restore the fortunes of Jacob's tents
and have compassion on his dwellings;
the city will be rebuilt on her ruins,
and the palace will stand in its proper place.
19 From them will come songs of thanksgiving
and the sound of rejoicing.
I will add to their numbers,
and they will not be decreased;
I will bring them honor,
and they will not be disdained.
20 Their children will be as in days of old,
and their community will be established before me;
I will punish all who oppress them.
21 Their leader will be one of their own;
their ruler will arise from among them.
I will bring him near and he will come close to me —
for who is he who will devote himself
to be close to me?'
declares the LORD.
22 " 'So you will be my people,
and I will be your God.' "

23 See, the storm of the LORD
will burst out in wrath,
a driving wind swirling down
on the heads of the wicked.
24 The fierce anger of the LORD will not turn back
until he fully accomplishes
the purposes of his heart.
In days to come
you will understand this.

31 "At that time," declares the LORD, "I
will be the God of all the families of
Israel, and they will be my people."
2 This is what the LORD says:

"The people who survive the sword
will find favor in the wilderness;
I will come to give rest to Israel."

3 The LORD appeared to us in the past,[a]
saying:

"I have loved you with an everlasting love;
I have drawn you with unfailing kindness.
4 I will build you up again,
and you, Virgin Israel, will be rebuilt.
Again you will take up your timbrels
and go out to dance with the joyful.
5 Again you will plant vineyards
on the hills of Samaria;
the farmers will plant them
and enjoy their fruit.
6 There will be a day when watchmen cry out
on the hills of Ephraim,
'Come, let us go up to Zion,
to the LORD our God.' "

[a] 3 Or *LORD has appeared to us from afar*

7This is what the LORD says:

"Sing with joy for Jacob;
shout for the foremost of the nations.
Make your praises heard, and say,
'LORD, save your people,
the remnant of Israel.'
8 See, I will bring them from the land of the north
and gather them from the ends of the earth.
Among them will be the blind and the lame,
expectant mothers and women in labor;
a great throng will return.
9 They will come with weeping;
they will pray as I bring them back.
I will lead them beside streams of water
on a level path where they will not stumble,
because I am Israel's father,
and Ephraim is my firstborn son.

10 "Hear the word of the LORD, you nations;
proclaim it in distant coastlands:
'He who scattered Israel will gather them
and will watch over his flock like a shepherd.'
11 For the LORD will deliver Jacob
and redeem them from the hand of those stronger than they.
12 They will come and shout for joy on the heights of Zion;
they will rejoice in the bounty of the LORD —
the grain, the new wine and the olive oil,
the young of the flocks and herds.
They will be like a well-watered garden,
and they will sorrow no more.
13 Then young women will dance and be glad,
young men and old as well.
I will turn their mourning into gladness;
I will give them comfort and joy instead of sorrow.
14 I will satisfy the priests with abundance,
and my people will be filled with my bounty,"
declares the LORD.

15This is what the LORD says:

"A voice is heard in Ramah,
mourning and great weeping,
Rachel weeping for her children
and refusing to be comforted,
because they are no more."

16This is what the LORD says:

"Restrain your voice from weeping
and your eyes from tears,
for your work will be rewarded,"
declares the LORD.
"They will return from the land of the enemy.
17 So there is hope for your descendants,"
declares the LORD.
"Your children will return to their own land.

18 "I have surely heard Ephraim's moaning:
'You disciplined me like an unruly calf,
and I have been disciplined.
Restore me, and I will return,
because you are the LORD my God.
19 After I strayed,
I repented;
after I came to understand,
I beat my breast.
I was ashamed and humiliated
because I bore the disgrace of my youth.'
20 Is not Ephraim my dear son,
the child in whom I delight?
Though I often speak against him,
I still remember him.
Therefore my heart yearns for him;
I have great compassion for him,"
declares the LORD.

21 "Set up road signs;
put up guideposts.
Take note of the highway,
the road that you take.
Return, Virgin Israel,
return to your towns.
22 How long will you wander,
unfaithful Daughter Israel?
The LORD will create a new thing on earth —
the woman will return to[a] the man."

23This is what the LORD Almighty, the
God of Israel, says: "When I bring them
back from captivity,[b] the people in the
land of Judah and in its towns will once
again use these words: 'The LORD bless
you, you prosperous city, you sacred

[a] 22 Or *will protect* [b] 23 Or *I restore their fortunes*

mountain.' [24]People will live together in
Judah and all its towns — farmers and
those who move about with their flocks.
[25]I will refresh the weary and satisfy the
faint."

[26]At this I awoke and looked around. My
sleep had been pleasant to me.

[27]"The days are coming," declares the
LORD, "when I will plant the kingdoms
of Israel and Judah with the offspring of
people and of animals. [28]Just as I watched
over them to uproot and tear down, and
to overthrow, destroy and bring disaster,
so I will watch over them to build and to
plant," declares the LORD. [29]"In those days
people will no longer say,

'The parents have eaten sour grapes,
and the children's teeth are set on edge.'

[30]Instead, everyone will die for their own
sin; whoever eats sour grapes — their own
teeth will be set on edge.

[31]"The days are coming," declares the LORD,
"when I will make a new covenant
with the people of Israel
and with the people of Judah.
[32]It will not be like the covenant
I made with their ancestors
when I took them by the hand
to lead them out of Egypt,
because they broke my covenant,
though I was a husband to[a] them,[b]"
declares the LORD.
[33]"This is the covenant I will make with the people of Israel
after that time," declares the LORD.
"I will put my law in their minds
and write it on their hearts.
I will be their God,
and they will be my people.
[34]No longer will they teach their neighbor,
or say to one another, 'Know the LORD,'
because they will all know me,
from the least of them to the greatest,"
declares the LORD.
"For I will forgive their wickedness
and will remember their sins no more."

[35]This is what the LORD says,

he who appoints the sun
to shine by day,
who decrees the moon and stars
to shine by night,
who stirs up the sea
so that its waves roar —
the LORD Almighty is his name:
[36]"Only if these decrees vanish from my sight,"
declares the LORD,
"will Israel ever cease
being a nation before me."

[37]This is what the LORD says:

"Only if the heavens above can be measured
and the foundations of the earth below be searched out
will I reject all the descendants of Israel
because of all they have done,"
declares the LORD.

[38]"The days are coming," declares the
LORD, "when this city will be rebuilt for me
from the Tower of Hananel to the Corner
Gate. [39]The measuring line will stretch
from there straight to the hill of Gareb
and then turn to Goah. [40]The whole valley
where dead bodies and ashes are thrown,
and all the terraces out to the Kidron Valley
on the east as far as the corner of the Horse
Gate, will be holy to the LORD. The city will
never again be uprooted or demolished."

Jeremiah Buys a Field

32 This is the word that came to Jeremiah from the LORD in the tenth
year of Zedekiah king of Judah, which was
the eighteenth year of Nebuchadnezzar.
[2]The army of the king of Babylon was then
besieging Jerusalem, and Jeremiah the
prophet was confined in the courtyard
of the guard in the royal palace of Judah.

[3]Now Zedekiah king of Judah had imprisoned him there, saying, "Why do you
prophesy as you do? You say, 'This is what
the LORD says: I am about to give this city
into the hands of the king of Babylon, and
he will capture it. [4]Zedekiah king of Judah
will not escape the Babylonians[c] but will
certainly be given into the hands of the
king of Babylon, and will speak with him
face to face and see him with his own eyes.
[5]He will take Zedekiah to Babylon, where
he will remain until I deal with him, declares the LORD. If you fight against the
Babylonians, you will not succeed.' "

[6]Jeremiah said, "The word of the LORD
came to me: [7]Hanamel son of Shallum
your uncle is going to come to you and
say, 'Buy my field at Anathoth, because
as nearest relative it is your right and
duty to buy it.'

[a] *32* Hebrew; Septuagint and Syriac / *and I turned away from* [b] *32* Or *was their master*
[c] *4* Or *Chaldeans*; also in verses 5, 24, 25, 28, 29 and 43

8“Then, just as the LORD had said, my cousin Hanamel came to me in the courtyard of the guard and said, ‘Buy my field at Anathoth in the territory of Benjamin. Since it is your right to redeem it and possess it, buy it for yourself.’

“I knew that this was the word of the LORD; 9so I bought the field at Anathoth from my cousin Hanamel and weighed out for him seventeen shekels[a] of silver. 10I signed and sealed the deed, had it witnessed, and weighed out the silver on the scales. 11I took the deed of purchase — the sealed copy containing the terms and conditions, as well as the unsealed copy — 12and I gave this deed to Baruch son of Neriah, the son of Mahseiah, in the presence of my cousin Hanamel and of the witnesses who had signed the deed and of all the Jews sitting in the courtyard of the guard.

13“In their presence I gave Baruch these instructions: 14‘This is what the LORD Almighty, the God of Israel, says: Take these documents, both the sealed and unsealed copies of the deed of purchase, and put them in a clay jar so they will last a long time. 15For this is what the LORD Almighty, the God of Israel, says: Houses, fields and vineyards will again be bought in this land.’

16“After I had given the deed of purchase to Baruch son of Neriah, I prayed to the LORD:

17“Ah, Sovereign LORD, you have made the heavens and the earth by your great power and outstretched arm. Nothing is too hard for you. 18You show love to thousands but bring the punishment for the parents’ sins into the laps of their children after them. Great and mighty God, whose name is the LORD Almighty, 19great are your purposes and mighty are your deeds. Your eyes are open to the ways of all mankind; you reward each person according to their conduct and as their deeds deserve. 20You performed signs and wonders in Egypt and have continued them to this day, in Israel and among all mankind, and have gained the renown that is still yours. 21You brought your people Israel out of Egypt with signs and wonders, by a mighty hand and an outstretched arm and with great terror. 22You gave them this land you had sworn to give their ancestors, a land flowing with milk and honey. 23They came in and took possession of it, but they did not obey you or follow your law; they did not do what you commanded them to do. So you brought all this disaster on them.

24“See how the siege ramps are built up to take the city. Because of the sword, famine and plague, the city will be given into the hands of the Babylonians who are attacking it. What you said has happened, as you now see. 25And though the city will be given into the hands of the Babylonians, you, Sovereign LORD, say to me, ‘Buy the field with silver and have the transaction witnessed.’ ”

26Then the word of the LORD came to Jeremiah: 27“I am the LORD, the God of all mankind. Is anything too hard for me? 28Therefore this is what the LORD says: I am about to give this city into the hands of the Babylonians and to Nebuchadnezzar king of Babylon, who will capture it. 29The Babylonians who are attacking this city will come in and set it on fire; they will burn it down, along with the houses where the people aroused my anger by burning incense on the roofs to Baal and by pouring out drink offerings to other gods.

30“The people of Israel and Judah have done nothing but evil in my sight from their youth; indeed, the people of Israel have done nothing but arouse my anger with what their hands have made, declares the LORD. 31From the day it was built until now, this city has so aroused my anger and wrath that I must remove it from my sight. 32The people of Israel and Judah have provoked me by all the evil they have done — they, their kings and officials, their priests and prophets, the people of Judah and those living in Jerusalem. 33They turned their backs to me and not their faces; though I taught them again and again, they would not listen or respond to discipline. 34They set up their vile images in the house that bears my Name and defiled it. 35They built high places for Baal in the Valley of Ben Hinnom to sacrifice their sons and daughters to Molek, though I never commanded — nor did it enter my mind — that they should do such a detestable thing and so make Judah sin.

36“You are saying about this city, ‘By the sword, famine and plague it will be given into the hands of the king of Babylon’; but this is what the LORD, the God of Israel, says: 37I will surely gather them from all the lands where I banish them in my furious anger and great wrath; I will bring

[a] 9 That is, about 7 ounces or about 200 grams

them back to this place and let them live in safety. 38They will be my people, and I will be their God. 39I will give them singleness of heart and action, so that they will always fear me and that all will then go well for them and for their children after them. 40I will make an everlasting covenant with them: I will never stop doing good to them, and I will inspire them to fear me, so that they will never turn away from me. 41I will rejoice in doing them good and will assuredly plant them in this land with all my heart and soul.

42"This is what the LORD says: As I have brought all this great calamity on this people, so I will give them all the prosperity I have promised them. 43Once more fields will be bought in this land of which you say, 'It is a desolate waste, without people or animals, for it has been given into the hands of the Babylonians.' 44Fields will be bought for silver, and deeds will be signed, sealed and witnessed in the territory of Benjamin, in the villages around Jerusalem, in the towns of Judah and in the towns of the hill country, of the western foothills and of the Negev, because I will restore their fortunes,[a] declares the LORD."

Promise of Restoration

33 While Jeremiah was still confined in the courtyard of the guard, the word of the LORD came to him a second time: 2"This is what the LORD says, he who made the earth, the LORD who formed it and established it — the LORD is his name: 3'Call to me and I will answer you and tell you great and unsearchable things you do not know.' 4For this is what the LORD, the God of Israel, says about the houses in this city and the royal palaces of Judah that have been torn down to be used against the siege ramps and the sword 5in the fight with the Babylonians[b]: 'They will be filled with the dead bodies of the people I will slay in my anger and wrath. I will hide my face from this city because of all its wickedness.

6" 'Nevertheless, I will bring health and healing to it; I will heal my people and will let them enjoy abundant peace and security. 7I will bring Judah and Israel back from captivity[c] and will rebuild them as they were before. 8I will cleanse them from all the sin they have committed against me and will forgive all their sins of rebellion against me. 9Then this city will bring me renown, joy, praise and honor before all nations on earth that hear of all the good things I do for it; and they will be in awe and will tremble at the abundant prosperity and peace I provide for it.'

10"This is what the LORD says: 'You say about this place, "It is a desolate waste, without people or animals." Yet in the towns of Judah and the streets of Jerusalem that are deserted, inhabited by neither people nor animals, there will be heard once more 11the sounds of joy and gladness, the voices of bride and bridegroom, and the voices of those who bring thank offerings to the house of the LORD, saying,

"Give thanks to the LORD Almighty,
for the LORD is good;
his love endures forever."

For I will restore the fortunes of the land as they were before,' says the LORD.

12"This is what the LORD Almighty says: 'In this place, desolate and without people or animals — in all its towns there will again be pastures for shepherds to rest their flocks. 13In the towns of the hill country, of the western foothills and of the Negev, in the territory of Benjamin, in the villages around Jerusalem and in the towns of Judah, flocks will again pass under the hand of the one who counts them,' says the LORD.

14" 'The days are coming,' declares the LORD, 'when I will fulfill the good promise I made to the people of Israel and Judah.

15" 'In those days and at that time
I will make a righteous Branch
sprout from David's line;
he will do what is just and right in
the land.
16In those days Judah will be saved
and Jerusalem will live in safety.
This is the name by which it[d] will be
called:
The LORD Our Righteous Savior.'

17For this is what the LORD says: 'David will never fail to have a man to sit on the throne of Israel, 18nor will the Levitical priests ever fail to have a man to stand before me continually to offer burnt offerings, to burn grain offerings and to present sacrifices.' "

19The word of the LORD came to Jeremiah: 20"This is what the LORD says: 'If you can break my covenant with the day and my covenant with the night, so that day and night no longer come at their appointed time, 21then my covenant with David my servant — and my covenant with the Levites who are priests ministering before

[a] 44 Or *will bring them back from captivity* [b] 5 Or *Chaldeans* [c] 7 Or *will restore the fortunes of Judah and Israel* [d] 16 Or *he*

me — can be broken and David will no
longer have a descendant to reign on his
throne. 22I will make the descendants of
David my servant and the Levites who
minister before me as countless as the
stars in the sky and as measureless as the
sand on the seashore.' "
23The word of the LORD came to Jeremiah: 24"Have you not noticed that these
people are saying, 'The LORD has rejected the two kingdoms[a] he chose'? So they
despise my people and no longer regard
them as a nation. 25This is what the LORD
says: 'If I have not made my covenant with
day and night and established the laws
of heaven and earth, 26then I will reject
the descendants of Jacob and David my
servant and will not choose one of his sons
to rule over the descendants of Abraham,
Isaac and Jacob. For I will restore their
fortunes[b] and have compassion on them.' "

Warning to Zedekiah

34 While Nebuchadnezzar king of Babylon and all his army and all the
kingdoms and peoples in the empire he
ruled were fighting against Jerusalem and
all its surrounding towns, this word came
to Jeremiah from the LORD: 2"This is what
the LORD, the God of Israel, says: Go to
Zedekiah king of Judah and tell him, 'This
is what the LORD says: I am about to give
this city into the hands of the king of Babylon, and he will burn it down. 3You will
not escape from his grasp but will surely
be captured and given into his hands. You
will see the king of Babylon with your own
eyes, and he will speak with you face to
face. And you will go to Babylon.
4" 'Yet hear the LORD's promise to you,
Zedekiah king of Judah. This is what the
LORD says concerning you: You will not
die by the sword; 5you will die peacefully.
As people made a funeral fire in honor of
your predecessors, the kings who ruled
before you, so they will make a fire in your
honor and lament, "Alas, master!" I myself
make this promise, declares the LORD.' "
6Then Jeremiah the prophet told all this
to Zedekiah king of Judah, in Jerusalem,
7while the army of the king of Babylon
was fighting against Jerusalem and the
other cities of Judah that were still holding
out — Lachish and Azekah. These were the
only fortified cities left in Judah.

Freedom for Slaves

8The word came to Jeremiah from the
LORD after King Zedekiah had made a covenant with all the people in Jerusalem to
proclaim freedom for the slaves. 9Everyone
was to free their Hebrew slaves, both male
and female; no one was to hold a fellow
Hebrew in bondage. 10So all the officials
and people who entered into this covenant
agreed that they would free their male and
female slaves and no longer hold them in
bondage. They agreed, and set them free.
11But afterward they changed their minds
and took back the slaves they had freed
and enslaved them again.
12Then the word of the LORD came to
Jeremiah: 13"This is what the LORD, the
God of Israel, says: I made a covenant with
your ancestors when I brought them out
of Egypt, out of the land of slavery. I said,
14'Every seventh year each of you must
free any fellow Hebrews who have sold
themselves to you. After they have served
you six years, you must let them go free.'[c]
Your ancestors, however, did not listen to
me or pay attention to me. 15Recently you
repented and did what is right in my sight:
Each of you proclaimed freedom to your
own people. You even made a covenant before me in the house that bears my Name.
16But now you have turned around and
profaned my name; each of you has taken
back the male and female slaves you had
set free to go where they wished. You have
forced them to become your slaves again.
17"Therefore this is what the LORD says:
You have not obeyed me; you have not
proclaimed freedom to your own people.
So I now proclaim 'freedom' for you, declares the LORD — 'freedom' to fall by the
sword, plague and famine. I will make
you abhorrent to all the kingdoms of the
earth. 18Those who have violated my covenant and have not fulfilled the terms of
the covenant they made before me, I will
treat like the calf they cut in two and then
walked between its pieces. 19The leaders of
Judah and Jerusalem, the court officials,
the priests and all the people of the land
who walked between the pieces of the calf,
20I will deliver into the hands of their enemies who want to kill them. Their dead
bodies will become food for the birds and
the wild animals.
21"I will deliver Zedekiah king of Judah
and his officials into the hands of their
enemies who want to kill them, to the
army of the king of Babylon, which has
withdrawn from you. 22I am going to give
the order, declares the LORD, and I will
bring them back to this city. They will fight
against it, take it and burn it down. And
I will lay waste the towns of Judah so no
one can live there."

[a] 24 Or *families* [b] 26 Or *will bring them back from captivity* [c] 14 Deut. 15:12

The Rekabites

35 This is the word that came to Jeremiah from the LORD during the
reign of Jehoiakim son of Josiah king of
Judah: 2"Go to the Rekabite family and
invite them to come to one of the side
rooms of the house of the LORD and give
them wine to drink."
3So I went to get Jaazaniah son of Jeremiah, the son of Habazziniah, and his
brothers and all his sons — the whole
family of the Rekabites. 4I brought them
into the house of the LORD, into the room
of the sons of Hanan son of Igdaliah the
man of God. It was next to the room of the
officials, which was over that of Maaseiah
son of Shallum the doorkeeper. 5Then I set
bowls full of wine and some cups before
the Rekabites and said to them, "Drink
some wine."
6But they replied, "We do not drink
wine, because our forefather Jehonadab[a]
son of Rekab gave us this command: 'Neither you nor your descendants must ever
drink wine. 7Also you must never build
houses, sow seed or plant vineyards; you
must never have any of these things, but
must always live in tents. Then you will
live a long time in the land where you are
nomads.' 8We have obeyed everything our
forefather Jehonadab son of Rekab commanded us. Neither we nor our wives nor
our sons and daughters have ever drunk
wine 9or built houses to live in or had
vineyards, fields or crops. 10We have lived
in tents and have fully obeyed everything
our forefather Jehonadab commanded
us. 11But when Nebuchadnezzar king of
Babylon invaded this land, we said, 'Come,
we must go to Jerusalem to escape the
Babylonian[b] and Aramean armies.' So we
have remained in Jerusalem."
12Then the word of the LORD came to
Jeremiah, saying: 13"This is what the LORD
Almighty, the God of Israel, says: Go and
tell the people of Judah and those living
in Jerusalem, 'Will you not learn a lesson
and obey my words?' declares the LORD.
14'Jehonadab son of Rekab ordered his
descendants not to drink wine and this
command has been kept. To this day they
do not drink wine, because they obey their
forefather's command. But I have spoken
to you again and again, yet you have not
obeyed me. 15Again and again I sent all
my servants the prophets to you. They
said, "Each of you must turn from your
wicked ways and reform your actions;
do not follow other gods to serve them.
Then you will live in the land I have given
to you and your ancestors." But you have
not paid attention or listened to me. 16The
descendants of Jehonadab son of Rekab
have carried out the command their forefather gave them, but these people have
not obeyed me.'
17"Therefore this is what the LORD God
Almighty, the God of Israel, says: 'Listen!
I am going to bring on Judah and on everyone living in Jerusalem every disaster
I pronounced against them. I spoke to
them, but they did not listen; I called to
them, but they did not answer.' "
18Then Jeremiah said to the family of
the Rekabites, "This is what the LORD Almighty, the God of Israel, says: 'You have
obeyed the command of your forefather
Jehonadab and have followed all his instructions and have done everything he
ordered.' 19Therefore this is what the LORD
Almighty, the God of Israel, says: 'Jehonadab son of Rekab will never fail to have
a descendant to serve me.' "

Jehoiakim Burns Jeremiah's Scroll

36 In the fourth year of Jehoiakim son
of Josiah king of Judah, this word
came to Jeremiah from the LORD: 2"Take
a scroll and write on it all the words I have
spoken to you concerning Israel, Judah
and all the other nations from the time I
began speaking to you in the reign of Josiah till now. 3Perhaps when the people of
Judah hear about every disaster I plan to
inflict on them, they will each turn from
their wicked ways; then I will forgive their
wickedness and their sin."
4So Jeremiah called Baruch son of Neriah, and while Jeremiah dictated all the
words the LORD had spoken to him, Baruch
wrote them on the scroll. 5Then Jeremiah
told Baruch, "I am restricted; I am not
allowed to go to the LORD's temple. 6So
you go to the house of the LORD on a day
of fasting and read to the people from
the scroll the words of the LORD that you
wrote as I dictated. Read them to all the
people of Judah who come in from their
towns. 7Perhaps they will bring their petition before the LORD and will each turn
from their wicked ways, for the anger and
wrath pronounced against this people by
the LORD are great."
8Baruch son of Neriah did everything
Jeremiah the prophet told him to do; at
the LORD's temple he read the words of
the LORD from the scroll. 9In the ninth
month of the fifth year of Jehoiakim son
of Josiah king of Judah, a time of fasting
before the LORD was proclaimed for all the

[a] 6 Hebrew *Jonadab*, a variant of *Jehonadab*; here and often in this chapter [b] 11 Or *Chaldean*

people in Jerusalem and those who had come from the towns of Judah. 10From the room of Gemariah son of Shaphan the secretary, which was in the upper courtyard at the entrance of the New Gate of the temple, Baruch read to all the people at the LORD's temple the words of Jeremiah from the scroll.

11When Micaiah son of Gemariah, the son of Shaphan, heard all the words of the LORD from the scroll, 12he went down to the secretary's room in the royal palace, where all the officials were sitting: Elishama the secretary, Delaiah son of Shemaiah, Elnathan son of Akbor, Gemariah son of Shaphan, Zedekiah son of Hananiah, and all the other officials. 13After Micaiah told them everything he had heard Baruch read to the people from the scroll, 14all the officials sent Jehudi son of Nethaniah, the son of Shelemiah, the son of Cushi, to say to Baruch, "Bring the scroll from which you have read to the people and come." So Baruch son of Neriah went to them with the scroll in his hand. 15They said to him, "Sit down, please, and read it to us."

So Baruch read it to them. 16When they heard all these words, they looked at each other in fear and said to Baruch, "We must report all these words to the king." 17Then they asked Baruch, "Tell us, how did you come to write all this? Did Jeremiah dictate it?"

18"Yes," Baruch replied, "he dictated all these words to me, and I wrote them in ink on the scroll."

19Then the officials said to Baruch, "You and Jeremiah, go and hide. Don't let anyone know where you are."

20After they put the scroll in the room of Elishama the secretary, they went to the king in the courtyard and reported everything to him. 21The king sent Jehudi to get the scroll, and Jehudi brought it from the room of Elishama the secretary and read it to the king and all the officials standing beside him. 22It was the ninth month and the king was sitting in the winter apartment, with a fire burning in the firepot in front of him. 23Whenever Jehudi had read three or four columns of the scroll, the king cut them off with a scribe's knife and threw them into the firepot, until the entire scroll was burned in the fire. 24The king and all his attendants who heard all these words showed no fear, nor did they tear their clothes. 25Even though Elnathan, Delaiah and Gemariah urged the king not to burn the scroll, he would not listen to them. 26Instead, the king commanded Jerahmeel, a son of the king, Seraiah son of Azriel and Shelemiah son of Abdeel to arrest Baruch the scribe and Jeremiah the prophet. But the LORD had hidden them.

27After the king burned the scroll containing the words that Baruch had written at Jeremiah's dictation, the word of the LORD came to Jeremiah: 28"Take another scroll and write on it all the words that were on the first scroll, which Jehoiakim king of Judah burned up. 29Also tell Jehoiakim king of Judah, 'This is what the LORD says: You burned that scroll and said, "Why did you write on it that the king of Babylon would certainly come and destroy this land and wipe from it both man and beast?" 30Therefore this is what the LORD says about Jehoiakim king of Judah: He will have no one to sit on the throne of David; his body will be thrown out and exposed to the heat by day and the frost by night. 31I will punish him and his children and his attendants for their wickedness; I will bring on them and those living in Jerusalem and the people of Judah every disaster I pronounced against them, because they have not listened.'"

32So Jeremiah took another scroll and gave it to the scribe Baruch son of Neriah, and as Jeremiah dictated, Baruch wrote on it all the words of the scroll that Jehoiakim king of Judah had burned in the fire. And many similar words were added to them.

Jeremiah in Prison

37 Zedekiah son of Josiah was made king of Judah by Nebuchadnezzar king of Babylon; he reigned in place of Jehoiachin[a] son of Jehoiakim. 2Neither he nor his attendants nor the people of the land paid any attention to the words the LORD had spoken through Jeremiah the prophet.

3King Zedekiah, however, sent Jehukal son of Shelemiah with the priest Zephaniah son of Maaseiah to Jeremiah the prophet with this message: "Please pray to the LORD our God for us."

4Now Jeremiah was free to come and go among the people, for he had not yet been put in prison. 5Pharaoh's army had marched out of Egypt, and when the Babylonians[b] who were besieging Jerusalem heard the report about them, they withdrew from Jerusalem.

6Then the word of the LORD came to Jeremiah the prophet: 7"This is what the LORD, the God of Israel, says: Tell the king of Judah, who sent you to inquire of me,

[a] 1 Hebrew *Koniah*, a variant of *Jehoiachin* [b] 5 Or *Chaldeans*; also in verses 8, 9, 13 and 14

'Pharaoh's army, which has marched out to support you, will go back to its own land, to Egypt. 8Then the Babylonians will return and attack this city; they will capture it and burn it down.'

9"This is what the LORD says: Do not deceive yourselves, thinking, 'The Babylonians will surely leave us.' They will not! 10Even if you were to defeat the entire Babylonian[a] army that is attacking you and only wounded men were left in their tents, they would come out and burn this city down."

11After the Babylonian army had withdrawn from Jerusalem because of Pharaoh's army, 12Jeremiah started to leave the city to go to the territory of Benjamin to get his share of the property among the people there. 13But when he reached the Benjamin Gate, the captain of the guard, whose name was Irijah son of Shelemiah, the son of Hananiah, arrested him and said, "You are deserting to the Babylonians!"

14"That's not true!" Jeremiah said. "I am not deserting to the Babylonians." But Irijah would not listen to him; instead, he arrested Jeremiah and brought him to the officials. 15They were angry with Jeremiah and had him beaten and imprisoned in the house of Jonathan the secretary, which they had made into a prison.

16Jeremiah was put into a vaulted cell in a dungeon, where he remained a long time. 17Then King Zedekiah sent for him and had him brought to the palace, where he asked him privately, "Is there any word from the LORD?"

"Yes," Jeremiah replied, "you will be delivered into the hands of the king of Babylon."

18Then Jeremiah said to King Zedekiah, "What crime have I committed against you or your attendants or this people, that you have put me in prison? 19Where are your prophets who prophesied to you, 'The king of Babylon will not attack you or this land'? 20But now, my lord the king, please listen. Let me bring my petition before you: Do not send me back to the house of Jonathan the secretary, or I will die there."

21King Zedekiah then gave orders for Jeremiah to be placed in the courtyard of the guard and given a loaf of bread from the street of the bakers each day until all the bread in the city was gone. So Jeremiah remained in the courtyard of the guard.

Jeremiah Thrown Into a Cistern

38 Shephatiah son of Mattan, Gedaliah son of Pashhur, Jehukal[b] son of Shelemiah, and Pashhur son of Malkijah heard what Jeremiah was telling all the people when he said, 2"This is what the LORD says: 'Whoever stays in this city will die by the sword, famine or plague, but whoever goes over to the Babylonians[c] will live. They will escape with their lives; they will live.' 3And this is what the LORD says: 'This city will certainly be given into the hands of the army of the king of Babylon, who will capture it.'"

4Then the officials said to the king, "This man should be put to death. He is discouraging the soldiers who are left in this city, as well as all the people, by the things he is saying to them. This man is not seeking the good of these people but their ruin."

5"He is in your hands," King Zedekiah answered. "The king can do nothing to oppose you."

6So they took Jeremiah and put him into the cistern of Malkijah, the king's son, which was in the courtyard of the guard. They lowered Jeremiah by ropes into the cistern; it had no water in it, only mud, and Jeremiah sank down into the mud.

7But Ebed-Melek, a Cushite,[d] an official[e] in the royal palace, heard that they had put Jeremiah into the cistern. While the king was sitting in the Benjamin Gate, 8Ebed-Melek went out of the palace and said to him, 9"My lord the king, these men have acted wickedly in all they have done to Jeremiah the prophet. They have thrown him into a cistern, where he will starve to death when there is no longer any bread in the city."

10Then the king commanded Ebed-Melek the Cushite, "Take thirty men from here with you and lift Jeremiah the prophet out of the cistern before he dies."

11So Ebed-Melek took the men with him and went to a room under the treasury in the palace. He took some old rags and worn-out clothes from there and let them down with ropes to Jeremiah in the cistern. 12Ebed-Melek the Cushite said to Jeremiah, "Put these old rags and worn-out clothes under your arms to pad the ropes." Jeremiah did so, 13and they pulled him up with the ropes and lifted him out of the cistern. And Jeremiah remained in the courtyard of the guard.

[a] *10* Or *Chaldean;* also in verse 11 [b] *1* Hebrew *Jukal,* a variant of *Jehukal* [c] *2* Or *Chaldeans;* also in verses 18, 19 and 23 [d] *7* Probably from the upper Nile region [e] *7* Or *a eunuch*

Zedekiah Questions Jeremiah Again

14Then King Zedekiah sent for Jeremiah
the prophet and had him brought to the
third entrance to the temple of the LORD.
"I am going to ask you something," the
king said to Jeremiah. "Do not hide anything from me."
15Jeremiah said to Zedekiah, "If I give
you an answer, will you not kill me? Even
if I did give you counsel, you would not
listen to me."
16But King Zedekiah swore this oath
secretly to Jeremiah: "As surely as the
LORD lives, who has given us breath, I
will neither kill you nor hand you over to
those who want to kill you."
17Then Jeremiah said to Zedekiah, "This
is what the LORD God Almighty, the God of
Israel, says: 'If you surrender to the officers of the king of Babylon, your life will
be spared and this city will not be burned
down; you and your family will live. 18But
if you will not surrender to the officers of
the king of Babylon, this city will be given
into the hands of the Babylonians and
they will burn it down; you yourself will
not escape from them.'"
19King Zedekiah said to Jeremiah, "I
am afraid of the Jews who have gone over
to the Babylonians, for the Babylonians
may hand me over to them and they will
mistreat me."
20"They will not hand you over," Jeremiah replied. "Obey the LORD by doing
what I tell you. Then it will go well with
you, and your life will be spared. 21But if
you refuse to surrender, this is what the
LORD has revealed to me: 22All the women
left in the palace of the king of Judah will
be brought out to the officials of the king
of Babylon. Those women will say to you:

" 'They misled you and overcame
you —
those trusted friends of yours.
Your feet are sunk in the mud;
your friends have deserted you.'

23"All your wives and children will be
brought out to the Babylonians. You yourself will not escape from their hands but
will be captured by the king of Babylon;
and this city will[a] be burned down."
24Then Zedekiah said to Jeremiah, "Do
not let anyone know about this conversation, or you may die. 25If the officials hear
that I talked with you, and they come to
you and say, 'Tell us what you said to the
king and what the king said to you; do not
hide it from us or we will kill you,' 26then
tell them, 'I was pleading with the king
not to send me back to Jonathan's house
to die there.'"
27All the officials did come to Jeremiah
and question him, and he told them everything the king had ordered him to say.
So they said no more to him, for no one
had heard his conversation with the king.
28And Jeremiah remained in the courtyard of the guard until the day Jerusalem
was captured.

The Fall of Jerusalem

39 This is how Jerusalem was taken:
1In the ninth year of Zedekiah king
of Judah, in the tenth month, Nebuchadnezzar king of Babylon marched against
Jerusalem with his whole army and laid
siege to it. 2And on the ninth day of the
fourth month of Zedekiah's eleventh
year, the city wall was broken through.
3Then all the officials of the king of Babylon came and took seats in the Middle
Gate: Nergal-Sharezer of Samgar, Nebo-
Sarsekim a chief officer, Nergal-Sharezer
a high official and all the other officials
of the king of Babylon. 4When Zedekiah
king of Judah and all the soldiers saw
them, they fled; they left the city at night
by way of the king's garden, through the
gate between the two walls, and headed
toward the Arabah.[b]
5But the Babylonian[c] army pursued
them and overtook Zedekiah in the plains
of Jericho. They captured him and took
him to Nebuchadnezzar king of Babylon
at Riblah in the land of Hamath, where
he pronounced sentence on him. 6There
at Riblah the king of Babylon slaughtered
the sons of Zedekiah before his eyes and
also killed all the nobles of Judah. 7Then
he put out Zedekiah's eyes and bound
him with bronze shackles to take him
to Babylon.
8The Babylonians[d] set fire to the royal
palace and the houses of the people and
broke down the walls of Jerusalem. 9Neb-
uzaradan commander of the imperial
guard carried into exile to Babylon the
people who remained in the city, along
with those who had gone over to him, and
the rest of the people. 10But Nebuzaradan
the commander of the guard left behind
in the land of Judah some of the poor
people, who owned nothing; and at that
time he gave them vineyards and fields.
11Now Nebuchadnezzar king of Babylon
had given these orders about Jeremiah
through Nebuzaradan commander of the

[a] 23 Or *and you will cause this city to* Chaldeans [b] 4 Or *the Jordan Valley* [c] 5 Or *Chaldean* [d] 8 Or

imperial guard: 12“Take him and look after
him; don’t harm him but do for him whatever he asks.” 13So Nebuzaradan the commander of the guard, Nebushazban a chief
officer, Nergal-Sharezer a high official and
all the other officers of the king of Babylon
14sent and had Jeremiah taken out of the
courtyard of the guard. They turned him
over to Gedaliah son of Ahikam, the son
of Shaphan, to take him back to his home.
So he remained among his own people.
15While Jeremiah had been confined
in the courtyard of the guard, the word
of the LORD came to him: 16“Go and tell
Ebed-Melek the Cushite, ‘This is what the
LORD Almighty, the God of Israel, says: I
am about to fulfill my words against this
city — words concerning disaster, not prosperity. At that time they will be fulfilled
before your eyes. 17But I will rescue you on
that day, declares the LORD; you will not be
given into the hands of those you fear. 18I
will save you; you will not fall by the sword
but will escape with your life, because you
trust in me, declares the LORD.’ ”

Jeremiah Freed

40 The word came to Jeremiah from
the LORD after Nebuzaradan
commander of the imperial guard had
released him at Ramah. He had found
Jeremiah bound in chains among all the
captives from Jerusalem and Judah who
were being carried into exile to Babylon.
2When the commander of the guard found
Jeremiah, he said to him, “The LORD your
God decreed this disaster for this place.
3And now the LORD has brought it about;
he has done just as he said he would. All
this happened because you people sinned
against the LORD and did not obey him.
4But today I am freeing you from the
chains on your wrists. Come with me to
Babylon, if you like, and I will look after
you; but if you do not want to, then don’t
come. Look, the whole country lies before
you; go wherever you please.” 5However,
before Jeremiah turned to go,[a] Nebuzaradan added, “Go back to Gedaliah son
of Ahikam, the son of Shaphan, whom
the king of Babylon has appointed over
the towns of Judah, and live with him
among the people, or go anywhere else
you please.”
Then the commander gave him provisions and a present and let him go. 6So
Jeremiah went to Gedaliah son of Ahikam
at Mizpah and stayed with him among the
people who were left behind in the land.

Gedaliah Assassinated

7When all the army officers and their
men who were still in the open country
heard that the king of Babylon had appointed Gedaliah son of Ahikam as governor over the land and had put him in
charge of the men, women and children
who were the poorest in the land and
who had not been carried into exile to
Babylon, 8they came to Gedaliah at Mizpah — Ishmael son of Nethaniah, Johanan and Jonathan the sons of Kareah,
Seraiah son of Tanhumeth, the sons of
Ephai the Netophathite, and Jaazaniah[b] the son of the Maakathite, and their
men. 9Gedaliah son of Ahikam, the son
of Shaphan, took an oath to reassure
them and their men. “Do not be afraid to
serve the Babylonians,[c]” he said. “Settle
down in the land and serve the king of
Babylon, and it will go well with you. 10I
myself will stay at Mizpah to represent
you before the Babylonians who come
to us, but you are to harvest the wine,
summer fruit and olive oil, and put them
in your storage jars, and live in the towns
you have taken over.”
11When all the Jews in Moab, Ammon,
Edom and all the other countries heard
that the king of Babylon had left a remnant in Judah and had appointed Gedaliah son of Ahikam, the son of Shaphan,
as governor over them, 12they all came
back to the land of Judah, to Gedaliah at
Mizpah, from all the countries where they
had been scattered. And they harvested
an abundance of wine and summer fruit.
13Johanan son of Kareah and all the
army officers still in the open country
came to Gedaliah at Mizpah 14and said to
him, “Don’t you know that Baalis king of
the Ammonites has sent Ishmael son of
Nethaniah to take your life?” But Gedaliah son of Ahikam did not believe them.
15Then Johanan son of Kareah said privately to Gedaliah in Mizpah, “Let me go
and kill Ishmael son of Nethaniah, and
no one will know it. Why should he take
your life and cause all the Jews who are
gathered around you to be scattered and
the remnant of Judah to perish?”
16But Gedaliah son of Ahikam said to
Johanan son of Kareah, “Don’t do such a
thing! What you are saying about Ishmael
is not true.”
41 In the seventh month Ishmael son
of Nethaniah, the son of Elishama,
who was of royal blood and had been one
of the king’s officers, came with ten men

[a] 5 Or *Jeremiah answered* [b] 8 Hebrew *Jezaniah*, a variant of *Jaazaniah* [c] 9 Or *Chaldeans*;
also in verse 10

to Gedaliah son of Ahikam at Mizpah.
While they were eating together there,
2Ishmael son of Nethaniah and the ten
men who were with him got up and struck
down Gedaliah son of Ahikam, the son of
Shaphan, with the sword, killing the one
whom the king of Babylon had appointed
as governor over the land. 3Ishmael also
killed all the men of Judah who were with
Gedaliah at Mizpah, as well as the Babylonian[a] soldiers who were there.

4The day after Gedaliah's assassination,
before anyone knew about it, 5eighty men
who had shaved off their beards, torn their
clothes and cut themselves came from
Shechem, Shiloh and Samaria, bringing
grain offerings and incense with them
to the house of the LORD. 6Ishmael son of
Nethaniah went out from Mizpah to meet
them, weeping as he went. When he met
them, he said, "Come to Gedaliah son of
Ahikam." 7When they went into the city,
Ishmael son of Nethaniah and the men
who were with him slaughtered them and
threw them into a cistern. 8But ten of them
said to Ishmael, "Don't kill us! We have
wheat and barley, olive oil and honey,
hidden in a field." So he let them alone
and did not kill them with the others.
9Now the cistern where he threw all the
bodies of the men he had killed along with
Gedaliah was the one King Asa had made
as part of his defense against Baasha king
of Israel. Ishmael son of Nethaniah filled
it with the dead.

10Ishmael made captives of all the rest
of the people who were in Mizpah — the
king's daughters along with all the others who were left there, over whom Nebuzaradan commander of the imperial
guard had appointed Gedaliah son of
Ahikam. Ishmael son of Nethaniah took
them captive and set out to cross over to
the Ammonites.

11When Johanan son of Kareah and
all the army officers who were with him
heard about all the crimes Ishmael son
of Nethaniah had committed, 12they took
all their men and went to fight Ishmael
son of Nethaniah. They caught up with
him near the great pool in Gibeon. 13When
all the people Ishmael had with him saw
Johanan son of Kareah and the army
officers who were with him, they were
glad. 14All the people Ishmael had taken
captive at Mizpah turned and went over
to Johanan son of Kareah. 15But Ishmael
son of Nethaniah and eight of his men
escaped from Johanan and fled to the
Ammonites.

Flight to Egypt

16Then Johanan son of Kareah and all
the army officers who were with him led
away all the people of Mizpah who had
survived, whom Johanan had recovered
from Ishmael son of Nethaniah after Ishmael had assassinated Gedaliah son of
Ahikam — the soldiers, women, children
and court officials he had recovered from
Gibeon. 17And they went on, stopping at
Geruth Kimham near Bethlehem on their
way to Egypt 18to escape the Babylonians.[b]
They were afraid of them because Ishmael
son of Nethaniah had killed Gedaliah son
of Ahikam, whom the king of Babylon
had appointed as governor over the land.

42 Then all the army officers, including
Johanan son of Kareah and Jeza-
niah[c] son of Hoshaiah, and all the people
from the least to the greatest approached
2Jeremiah the prophet and said to him,
"Please hear our petition and pray to the
LORD your God for this entire remnant.
For as you now see, though we were once
many, now only a few are left. 3Pray that
the LORD your God will tell us where we
should go and what we should do."

4"I have heard you," replied Jeremiah
the prophet. "I will certainly pray to the
LORD your God as you have requested; I
will tell you everything the LORD says and
will keep nothing back from you."

5Then they said to Jeremiah, "May
the LORD be a true and faithful witness
against us if we do not act in accordance
with everything the LORD your God sends
you to tell us. 6Whether it is favorable or
unfavorable, we will obey the LORD our
God, to whom we are sending you, so that
it will go well with us, for we will obey the
LORD our God."

7Ten days later the word of the LORD
came to Jeremiah. 8So he called together
Johanan son of Kareah and all the army
officers who were with him and all the
people from the least to the greatest. 9He
said to them, "This is what the LORD, the
God of Israel, to whom you sent me to
present your petition, says: 10'If you stay
in this land, I will build you up and not
tear you down; I will plant you and not
uproot you, for I have relented concerning the disaster I have inflicted on you.
11Do not be afraid of the king of Babylon,
whom you now fear. Do not be afraid of
him, declares the LORD, for I am with you
and will save you and deliver you from
his hands. 12I will show you compassion
so that he will have compassion on you
and restore you to your land.'

[a] 3 Or *Chaldean* [b] 18 Or *Chaldeans* [c] 1 Hebrew; Septuagint (see also 43:2) *Azariah*

13 “However, if you say, ‘We will not stay
in this land,’ and so disobey the LORD your
God, 14 and if you say, ‘No, we will go and
live in Egypt, where we will not see war or
hear the trumpet or be hungry for bread,’
15 then hear the word of the LORD, you remnant of Judah. This is what the LORD Almighty, the God of Israel, says: ‘If you are
determined to go to Egypt and you do go
to settle there, 16 then the sword you fear
will overtake you there, and the famine
you dread will follow you into Egypt, and
there you will die. 17 Indeed, all who are
determined to go to Egypt to settle there
will die by the sword, famine and plague;
not one of them will survive or escape
the disaster I will bring on them.’ 18 This
is what the LORD Almighty, the God of Israel, says: ‘As my anger and wrath have
been poured out on those who lived in
Jerusalem, so will my wrath be poured out
on you when you go to Egypt. You will be
a curse[a] and an object of horror, a curse[a]
and an object of reproach; you will never
see this place again.’

19 “Remnant of Judah, the LORD has told
you, ‘Do not go to Egypt.’ Be sure of this: I
warn you today 20 that you made a fatal
mistake when you sent me to the LORD
your God and said, ‘Pray to the LORD our
God for us; tell us everything he says and
we will do it.’ 21 I have told you today, but
you still have not obeyed the LORD your
God in all he sent me to tell you. 22 So now,
be sure of this: You will die by the sword,
famine and plague in the place where you
want to go to settle.”

43 When Jeremiah had finished telling the people all the words of the
LORD their God — everything the LORD
had sent him to tell them — 2 Azariah son
of Hoshaiah and Johanan son of Kareah
and all the arrogant men said to Jeremiah, “You are lying! The LORD our God has
not sent you to say, ‘You must not go to
Egypt to settle there.’ 3 But Baruch son of
Neriah is inciting you against us to hand
us over to the Babylonians,[b] so they may
kill us or carry us into exile to Babylon.”

4 So Johanan son of Kareah and all the
army officers and all the people disobeyed
the LORD’s command to stay in the land of
Judah. 5 Instead, Johanan son of Kareah
and all the army officers led away all the
remnant of Judah who had come back to
live in the land of Judah from all the nations where they had been scattered. 6 They
also led away all those whom Nebuzaradan commander of the imperial guard
had left with Gedaliah son of Ahikam, the
son of Shaphan — the men, the women,
the children and the king’s daughters.
And they took Jeremiah the prophet and
Baruch son of Neriah along with them.
7 So they entered Egypt in disobedience to
the LORD and went as far as Tahpanhes.

8 In Tahpanhes the word of the LORD
came to Jeremiah: 9 “While the Jews are
watching, take some large stones with
you and bury them in clay in the brick
pavement at the entrance to Pharaoh’s
palace in Tahpanhes. 10 Then say to them,
‘This is what the LORD Almighty, the God
of Israel, says: I will send for my servant
Nebuchadnezzar king of Babylon, and I
will set his throne over these stones I have
buried here; he will spread his royal canopy above them. 11 He will come and attack
Egypt, bringing death to those destined
for death, captivity to those destined for
captivity, and the sword to those destined
for the sword. 12 He will set fire to the temples of the gods of Egypt; he will burn their
temples and take their gods captive. As a
shepherd picks his garment clean of lice, so
he will pick Egypt clean and depart. 13 There
in the temple of the sun[c] in Egypt he will
demolish the sacred pillars and will burn
down the temples of the gods of Egypt.’ ”

Disaster Because of Idolatry

44 This word came to Jeremiah concerning all the Jews living in Lower
Egypt — in Migdol, Tahpanhes and Memphis — and in Upper Egypt: 2 “This is what
the LORD Almighty, the God of Israel, says:
You saw the great disaster I brought on Jerusalem and on all the towns of Judah. Today they lie deserted and in ruins 3 because
of the evil they have done. They aroused my
anger by burning incense to and worshiping other gods that neither they nor you nor
your ancestors ever knew. 4 Again and again
I sent my servants the prophets, who said,
‘Do not do this detestable thing that I hate!’
5 But they did not listen or pay attention;
they did not turn from their wickedness or
stop burning incense to other gods. 6 Therefore, my fierce anger was poured out; it
raged against the towns of Judah and the
streets of Jerusalem and made them the
desolate ruins they are today.

7 “Now this is what the LORD God Almighty, the God of Israel, says: Why bring
such great disaster on yourselves by cutting off from Judah the men and women,
the children and infants, and so leave
yourselves without a remnant? 8 Why

[a] *18* That is, your name will be used in cursing (see 29:22); or, others will see that you are cursed.
[b] *3* Or *Chaldeans* [c] *13* Or *in Heliopolis*

arouse my anger with what your hands have made, burning incense to other gods in Egypt, where you have come to live? You will destroy yourselves and make yourselves a curse[a] and an object of reproach among all the nations on earth. 9Have you forgotten the wickedness committed by your ancestors and by the kings and queens of Judah and the wickedness committed by you and your wives in the land of Judah and the streets of Jerusalem? 10To this day they have not humbled themselves or shown reverence, nor have they followed my law and the decrees I set before you and your ancestors.

11"Therefore this is what the LORD Almighty, the God of Israel, says: I am determined to bring disaster on you and to destroy all Judah. 12I will take away the remnant of Judah who were determined to go to Egypt to settle there. They will all perish in Egypt; they will fall by the sword or die from famine. From the least to the greatest, they will die by sword or famine. They will become a curse and an object of horror, a curse and an object of reproach. 13I will punish those who live in Egypt with the sword, famine and plague, as I punished Jerusalem. 14None of the remnant of Judah who have gone to live in Egypt will escape or survive to return to the land of Judah, to which they long to return and live; none will return except a few fugitives."

15Then all the men who knew that their wives were burning incense to other gods, along with all the women who were present — a large assembly — and all the people living in Lower and Upper Egypt, said to Jeremiah, 16"We will not listen to the message you have spoken to us in the name of the LORD! 17We will certainly do everything we said we would: We will burn incense to the Queen of Heaven and will pour out drink offerings to her just as we and our ancestors, our kings and our officials did in the towns of Judah and in the streets of Jerusalem. At that time we had plenty of food and were well off and suffered no harm. 18But ever since we stopped burning incense to the Queen of Heaven and pouring out drink offerings to her, we have had nothing and have been perishing by sword and famine."

19The women added, "When we burned incense to the Queen of Heaven and poured out drink offerings to her, did not our husbands know that we were making cakes impressed with her image and pouring out drink offerings to her?"

20Then Jeremiah said to all the people, both men and women, who were answering him, 21"Did not the LORD remember and call to mind the incense burned in the towns of Judah and the streets of Jerusalem by you and your ancestors, your kings and your officials and the people of the land? 22When the LORD could no longer endure your wicked actions and the detestable things you did, your land became a curse and a desolate waste without inhabitants, as it is today. 23Because you have burned incense and have sinned against the LORD and have not obeyed him or followed his law or his decrees or his stipulations, this disaster has come upon you, as you now see."

24Then Jeremiah said to all the people, including the women, "Hear the word of the LORD, all you people of Judah in Egypt. 25This is what the LORD Almighty, the God of Israel, says: You and your wives have done what you said you would do when you promised, 'We will certainly carry out the vows we made to burn incense and pour out drink offerings to the Queen of Heaven.'

"Go ahead then, do what you promised! Keep your vows! 26But hear the word of the LORD, all you Jews living in Egypt: 'I swear by my great name,' says the LORD, 'that no one from Judah living anywhere in Egypt will ever again invoke my name or swear, "As surely as the Sovereign LORD lives." 27For I am watching over them for harm, not for good; the Jews in Egypt will perish by sword and famine until they are all destroyed. 28Those who escape the sword and return to the land of Judah from Egypt will be very few. Then the whole remnant of Judah who came to live in Egypt will know whose word will stand — mine or theirs.

29" 'This will be the sign to you that I will punish you in this place,' declares the LORD, 'so that you will know that my threats of harm against you will surely stand.' 30This is what the LORD says: 'I am going to deliver Pharaoh Hophra king of Egypt into the hands of his enemies who want to kill him, just as I gave Zedekiah king of Judah into the hands of Nebuchadnezzar king of Babylon, the enemy who wanted to kill him.' "

A Message to Baruch

45 When Baruch son of Neriah wrote on a scroll the words Jeremiah the prophet dictated in the fourth year of Jehoiakim son of Josiah king of Judah, Jeremiah said this to Baruch: 2"This is

[a] *8* That is, your name will be used in cursing (see 29:22); or, others will see that you are cursed; also in verse 12; similarly in verse 22.

what the LORD, the God of Israel, says to
you, Baruch: 3You said, 'Woe to me! The
LORD has added sorrow to my pain; I am
worn out with groaning and find no rest.'
4But the LORD has told me to say to you,
'This is what the LORD says: I will overthrow what I have built and uproot what
I have planted, throughout the earth.
5Should you then seek great things for
yourself? Do not seek them. For I will bring
disaster on all people, declares the LORD,
but wherever you go I will let you escape
with your life.'"

A Message About Egypt

46 This is the word of the LORD that came to Jeremiah the prophet concerning the nations:

2Concerning Egypt:

This is the message against the army of Pharaoh Necho king of Egypt, which was defeated at Carchemish on the Euphrates River by Nebuchadnezzar king of Babylon in the fourth year of Jehoiakim son of Josiah king of Judah:

3"Prepare your shields, both large and small,
and march out for battle!
4Harness the horses,
mount the steeds!
Take your positions
with helmets on!
Polish your spears,
put on your armor!
5What do I see?
They are terrified,
they are retreating,
their warriors are defeated.
They flee in haste
without looking back,
and there is terror on every side,"
declares the LORD.
6"The swift cannot flee
nor the strong escape.
In the north by the River Euphrates
they stumble and fall.

7"Who is this that rises like the Nile,
like rivers of surging waters?
8Egypt rises like the Nile,
like rivers of surging waters.
She says, 'I will rise and cover the earth;
I will destroy cities and their people.'
9Charge, you horses!
Drive furiously, you charioteers!
March on, you warriors — men of Cush[a]
and Put who carry shields,
men of Lydia who draw the bow.
10But that day belongs to the Lord, the LORD Almighty —
a day of vengeance, for vengeance on his foes.
The sword will devour till it is satisfied,
till it has quenched its thirst with blood.
For the Lord, the LORD Almighty, will offer sacrifice
in the land of the north by the River Euphrates.

11"Go up to Gilead and get balm,
Virgin Daughter Egypt.
But you try many medicines in vain;
there is no healing for you.
12The nations will hear of your shame;
your cries will fill the earth.
One warrior will stumble over another;
both will fall down together."

13This is the message the LORD spoke to Jeremiah the prophet about the coming of Nebuchadnezzar king of Babylon to attack Egypt:

14"Announce this in Egypt, and proclaim it in Migdol;
proclaim it also in Memphis and Tahpanhes:
'Take your positions and get ready,
for the sword devours those around you.'
15Why will your warriors be laid low?
They cannot stand, for the LORD will push them down.
16They will stumble repeatedly;
they will fall over each other.
They will say, 'Get up, let us go back
to our own people and our native lands,
away from the sword of the oppressor.'
17There they will exclaim,
'Pharaoh king of Egypt is only a loud noise;
he has missed his opportunity.'

18"As surely as I live," declares the King,
whose name is the LORD Almighty,
"one will come who is like Tabor among the mountains,
like Carmel by the sea.
19Pack your belongings for exile,
you who live in Egypt,
for Memphis will be laid waste
and lie in ruins without inhabitant.

20"Egypt is a beautiful heifer,
but a gadfly is coming
against her from the north.

[a] 9 That is, the upper Nile region

21 The mercenaries in her ranks
are like fattened calves.
They too will turn and flee together,
they will not stand their ground,
for the day of disaster is coming
upon them,
the time for them to be punished.
22 Egypt will hiss like a fleeing serpent
as the enemy advances in force;
they will come against her with axes,
like men who cut down trees.
23 They will chop down her forest,"
declares the LORD,
"dense though it be.
They are more numerous than
locusts,
they cannot be counted.
24 Daughter Egypt will be put to shame,
given into the hands of the people
of the north."

25 The LORD Almighty, the God of Israel,
says: "I am about to bring punishment
on Amon god of Thebes, on Pharaoh, on
Egypt and her gods and her kings, and on
those who rely on Pharaoh. 26 I will give
them into the hands of those who want
to kill them — Nebuchadnezzar king of
Babylon and his officers. Later, however,
Egypt will be inhabited as in times past,"
declares the LORD.

27 "Do not be afraid, Jacob my servant;
do not be dismayed, Israel.
I will surely save you out of a distant
place,
your descendants from the land
of their exile.
Jacob will again have peace and
security,
and no one will make him
afraid.
28 Do not be afraid, Jacob my servant,
for I am with you," declares the
LORD.
"Though I completely destroy all
the nations
among which I scatter you,
I will not completely destroy you.
I will discipline you but only in due
measure;
I will not let you go entirely
unpunished."

A Message About the Philistines

47 This is the word of the LORD that
came to Jeremiah the prophet concerning the Philistines before Pharaoh
attacked Gaza:

2 This is what the LORD says:

"See how the waters are rising in the
north;
they will become an overflowing
torrent.
They will overflow the land and
everything in it,
the towns and those who live in
them.
The people will cry out;
all who dwell in the land will wail
3 at the sound of the hooves of
galloping steeds,
at the noise of enemy chariots
and the rumble of their wheels.
Parents will not turn to help their
children;
their hands will hang limp.
4 For the day has come
to destroy all the Philistines
and to remove all survivors
who could help Tyre and Sidon.
The LORD is about to destroy the
Philistines,
the remnant from the coasts of
Caphtor.[a]
5 Gaza will shave her head in mourning;
Ashkelon will be silenced.
You remnant on the plain,
how long will you cut yourselves?

6 " 'Alas, sword of the LORD,
how long till you rest?
Return to your sheath;
cease and be still.'
7 But how can it rest
when the LORD has commanded it,
when he has ordered it
to attack Ashkelon and the coast?"

A Message About Moab

48 Concerning Moab:

This is what the LORD Almighty, the God
of Israel, says:

"Woe to Nebo, for it will be ruined.
Kiriathaim will be disgraced and
captured;
the stronghold[b] will be disgraced
and shattered.
2 Moab will be praised no more;
in Heshbon[c] people will plot her
downfall:
'Come, let us put an end to that
nation.'
You, the people of Madmen,[d] will also
be silenced;
the sword will pursue you.

[a] 4 That is, Crete [b] 1 Or *captured; / Misgab* [c] 2 The Hebrew for *Heshbon* sounds like the Hebrew for *plot*. [d] 2 The name of the Moabite town Madmen sounds like the Hebrew for *be silenced*.

3 Cries of anguish arise from Horonaim,
cries of great havoc and destruction.
4 Moab will be broken;
her little ones will cry out.[a]
5 They go up the hill to Luhith,
weeping bitterly as they go;
on the road down to Horonaim
anguished cries over the destruction are heard.
6 Flee! Run for your lives;
become like a bush[b] in the desert.
7 Since you trust in your deeds and riches,
you too will be taken captive,
and Chemosh will go into exile,
together with his priests and officials.
8 The destroyer will come against every town,
and not a town will escape.
The valley will be ruined
and the plateau destroyed,
because the LORD has spoken.
9 Put salt on Moab,
for she will be laid waste[c];
her towns will become desolate,
with no one to live in them.

10 "A curse on anyone who is lax in doing the LORD's work!
A curse on anyone who keeps their sword from bloodshed!

11 "Moab has been at rest from youth,
like wine left on its dregs,
not poured from one jar to another —
she has not gone into exile.
So she tastes as she did,
and her aroma is unchanged.
12 But days are coming,"
declares the LORD,
"when I will send men who pour from pitchers,
and they will pour her out;
they will empty her pitchers
and smash her jars.
13 Then Moab will be ashamed of Chemosh,
as Israel was ashamed
when they trusted in Bethel.

14 "How can you say, 'We are warriors,
men valiant in battle'?
15 Moab will be destroyed and her towns invaded;
her finest young men will go down in the slaughter,"
declares the King, whose name is the LORD Almighty.
16 "The fall of Moab is at hand;
her calamity will come quickly.
17 Mourn for her, all who live around her,
all who know her fame;
say, 'How broken is the mighty scepter,
how broken the glorious staff!'

18 "Come down from your glory
and sit on the parched ground,
you inhabitants of Daughter Dibon,
for the one who destroys Moab
will come up against you
and ruin your fortified cities.
19 Stand by the road and watch,
you who live in Aroer.
Ask the man fleeing and the woman escaping,
ask them, 'What has happened?'
20 Moab is disgraced, for she is shattered.
Wail and cry out!
Announce by the Arnon
that Moab is destroyed.
21 Judgment has come to the plateau —
to Holon, Jahzah and Mephaath,
22 to Dibon, Nebo and Beth Diblathaim,
23 to Kiriathaim, Beth Gamul and Beth Meon,
24 to Kerioth and Bozrah —
to all the towns of Moab, far and near.
25 Moab's horn[d] is cut off;
her arm is broken,"
declares the LORD.

26 "Make her drunk,
for she has defied the LORD.
Let Moab wallow in her vomit;
let her be an object of ridicule.
27 Was not Israel the object of your ridicule?
Was she caught among thieves,
that you shake your head in scorn
whenever you speak of her?
28 Abandon your towns and dwell among the rocks,
you who live in Moab.
Be like a dove that makes its nest
at the mouth of a cave.

29 "We have heard of Moab's pride —
how great is her arrogance! —
of her insolence, her pride, her conceit
and the haughtiness of her heart.
30 I know her insolence but it is futile,"
declares the LORD,
"and her boasts accomplish nothing.

[a] 4 Hebrew; Septuagint / *proclaim it to Zoar* [b] 6 Or *like Aroer* [c] 9 Or *Give wings to Moab, / for she will fly away* [d] 25 *Horn* here symbolizes strength.

31 Therefore I wail over Moab,
for all Moab I cry out,
I moan for the people of Kir Hareseth.
32 I weep for you, as Jazer weeps,
you vines of Sibmah.
Your branches spread as far as the sea[a];
they reached as far as[b] Jazer.
The destroyer has fallen
on your ripened fruit and grapes.
33 Joy and gladness are gone
from the orchards and fields of Moab.
I have stopped the flow of wine from the presses;
no one treads them with shouts of joy.
Although there are shouts,
they are not shouts of joy.

34 "The sound of their cry rises
from Heshbon to Elealeh and Jahaz,
from Zoar as far as Horonaim and Eglath Shelishiyah,
for even the waters of Nimrim are dried up.
35 In Moab I will put an end
to those who make offerings on the high places
and burn incense to their gods,"
declares the LORD.
36 "So my heart laments for Moab like the music of a pipe;
it laments like a pipe for the people of Kir Hareseth.
The wealth they acquired is gone.
37 Every head is shaved
and every beard cut off;
every hand is slashed
and every waist is covered with sackcloth.
38 On all the roofs in Moab
and in the public squares
there is nothing but mourning,
for I have broken Moab
like a jar that no one wants,"
declares the LORD.
39 "How shattered she is! How they wail!
How Moab turns her back in shame!
Moab has become an object of ridicule,
an object of horror to all those around her."

40 This is what the LORD says:

"Look! An eagle is swooping down,
spreading its wings over Moab.
41 Kerioth[c] will be captured
and the strongholds taken.
In that day the hearts of Moab's warriors
will be like the heart of a woman in labor.
42 Moab will be destroyed as a nation
because she defied the LORD.
43 Terror and pit and snare await you,
you people of Moab,"
declares the LORD.
44 "Whoever flees from the terror
will fall into a pit,
whoever climbs out of the pit
will be caught in a snare;
for I will bring on Moab
the year of her punishment,"
declares the LORD.

45 "In the shadow of Heshbon
the fugitives stand helpless,
for a fire has gone out from Heshbon,
a blaze from the midst of Sihon;
it burns the foreheads of Moab,
the skulls of the noisy boasters.
46 Woe to you, Moab!
The people of Chemosh are destroyed;
your sons are taken into exile
and your daughters into captivity.

47 "Yet I will restore the fortunes of Moab
in days to come,"
declares the LORD.

Here ends the judgment on Moab.

A Message About Ammon

49 Concerning the Ammonites:

This is what the LORD says:

"Has Israel no sons?
Has Israel no heir?
Why then has Molek[d] taken possession of Gad?
Why do his people live in its towns?
2 But the days are coming,"
declares the LORD,
"when I will sound the battle cry
against Rabbah of the Ammonites;
it will become a mound of ruins,
and its surrounding villages will be set on fire.
Then Israel will drive out
those who drove her out,"
says the LORD.
3 "Wail, Heshbon, for Ai is destroyed!
Cry out, you inhabitants of Rabbah!
Put on sackcloth and mourn;
rush here and there inside the walls,

[a] 32 Probably the Dead Sea [b] 32 Two Hebrew manuscripts and Septuagint; most Hebrew manuscripts *as far as the Sea of* [c] 41 Or *The cities* [d] 1 Or *their king*; also in verse 3

for Molek will go into exile,
together with his priests and officials.
4 Why do you boast of your valleys,
boast of your valleys so fruitful?
Unfaithful Daughter Ammon,
you trust in your riches and say,
'Who will attack me?'
5 I will bring terror on you
from all those around you,"
declares the Lord,
the LORD Almighty.
"Every one of you will be driven away,
and no one will gather the fugitives.

6 "Yet afterward, I will restore the fortunes of the Ammonites,"
declares the LORD.

A Message About Edom

7 Concerning Edom:

This is what the LORD Almighty says:

"Is there no longer wisdom in Teman?
Has counsel perished from the prudent?
Has their wisdom decayed?
8 Turn and flee, hide in deep caves,
you who live in Dedan,
for I will bring disaster on Esau
at the time when I punish him.
9 If grape pickers came to you,
would they not leave a few grapes?
If thieves came during the night,
would they not steal only as much as they wanted?
10 But I will strip Esau bare;
I will uncover his hiding places,
so that he cannot conceal himself.
His armed men are destroyed,
also his allies and neighbors,
so there is no one to say,
11 'Leave your fatherless children; I will keep them alive.
Your widows too can depend on me.'"

12 This is what the LORD says: "If those
who do not deserve to drink the cup must
drink it, why should you go unpunished?
You will not go unpunished, but must
drink it. 13 I swear by myself," declares the
LORD, "that Bozrah will become a ruin and
a curse,[a] an object of horror and reproach;
and all its towns will be in ruins forever."

14 I have heard a message from the LORD;
an envoy was sent to the nations to say,
"Assemble yourselves to attack it!
Rise up for battle!"

15 "Now I will make you small among the nations,
despised by mankind.
16 The terror you inspire
and the pride of your heart have deceived you,
you who live in the clefts of the rocks,
who occupy the heights of the hill.
Though you build your nest as high as the eagle's,
from there I will bring you down,"
declares the LORD.
17 "Edom will become an object of horror;
all who pass by will be appalled and will scoff
because of all its wounds.
18 As Sodom and Gomorrah were overthrown,
along with their neighboring towns,"
says the LORD,
"so no one will live there;
no people will dwell in it.

19 "Like a lion coming up from Jordan's thickets
to a rich pastureland,
I will chase Edom from its land in an instant.
Who is the chosen one I will appoint for this?
Who is like me and who can challenge me?
And what shepherd can stand against me?"

20 Therefore, hear what the LORD has planned against Edom,
what he has purposed against those who live in Teman:
The young of the flock will be dragged away;
their pasture will be appalled at their fate.
21 At the sound of their fall the earth will tremble;
their cry will resound to the Red Sea.[b]
22 Look! An eagle will soar and swoop down,
spreading its wings over Bozrah.
In that day the hearts of Edom's warriors
will be like the heart of a woman in labor.

A Message About Damascus

23 Concerning Damascus:

"Hamath and Arpad are dismayed,
for they have heard bad news.
They are disheartened,
troubled like[c] the restless sea.

[a] *13* That is, its name will be used in cursing (see 29:22); or, others will see that it is cursed.
[b] *21* Or *the Sea of Reeds* [c] *23* Hebrew *on* or *by*

24 Damascus has become feeble,
she has turned to flee
and panic has gripped her;
anguish and pain have seized her,
pain like that of a woman in labor.
25 Why has the city of renown not been abandoned,
the town in which I delight?
26 Surely, her young men will fall in the streets;
all her soldiers will be silenced in that day,"
declares the LORD Almighty.
27 "I will set fire to the walls of Damascus;
it will consume the fortresses of Ben-Hadad."

A Message About Kedar and Hazor

28 Concerning Kedar and the kingdoms of Hazor, which Nebuchadnezzar king of Babylon attacked:

This is what the LORD says:

"Arise, and attack Kedar
and destroy the people of the East.
29 Their tents and their flocks will be taken;
their shelters will be carried off
with all their goods and camels.
People will shout to them,
'Terror on every side!'

30 "Flee quickly away!
Stay in deep caves, you who live in Hazor,"
declares the LORD.
"Nebuchadnezzar king of Babylon
has plotted against you;
he has devised a plan against you.
31 "Arise and attack a nation at ease,
which lives in confidence,"
declares the LORD,
"a nation that has neither gates nor bars;
its people live far from danger.
32 Their camels will become plunder,
and their large herds will be spoils of war.
I will scatter to the winds those who are in distant places[a]
and will bring disaster on them from every side,"
declares the LORD.
33 "Hazor will become a haunt of jackals,
a desolate place forever.
No one will live there;
no people will dwell in it."

A Message About Elam

34 This is the word of the LORD that came to Jeremiah the prophet concerning Elam, early in the reign of Zedekiah king of Judah:

35 This is what the LORD Almighty says:

"See, I will break the bow of Elam,
the mainstay of their might.
36 I will bring against Elam the four winds
from the four quarters of heaven;
I will scatter them to the four winds,
and there will not be a nation
where Elam's exiles do not go.
37 I will shatter Elam before their foes,
before those who want to kill them;
I will bring disaster on them,
even my fierce anger,"
declares the LORD.
"I will pursue them with the sword
until I have made an end of them.
38 I will set my throne in Elam
and destroy her king and officials,"
declares the LORD.

39 "Yet I will restore the fortunes of Elam
in days to come,"
declares the LORD.

A Message About Babylon

50 This is the word the LORD spoke through Jeremiah the prophet concerning Babylon and the land of the Babylonians[b]:

2 "Announce and proclaim among the nations,
lift up a banner and proclaim it;
keep nothing back, but say,
'Babylon will be captured;
Bel will be put to shame,
Marduk filled with terror.
Her images will be put to shame
and her idols filled with terror.'
3 A nation from the north will attack her
and lay waste her land.
No one will live in it;
both people and animals will flee away.

4 "In those days, at that time,"
declares the LORD,
"the people of Israel and the people of Judah together
will go in tears to seek the LORD their God.
5 They will ask the way to Zion
and turn their faces toward it.

[a] 32 Or *who clip the hair by their foreheads*

[b] 1 Or *Chaldeans*; also in verses 8, 25, 35 and 45

They will come and bind themselves
to the LORD
in an everlasting covenant
that will not be forgotten.

6 "My people have been lost sheep;
their shepherds have led them
astray
and caused them to roam on the
mountains.
They wandered over mountain and
hill
and forgot their own resting place.
7 Whoever found them devoured them;
their enemies said, 'We are not
guilty,
for they sinned against the LORD,
their verdant pasture,
the LORD, the hope of their
ancestors.'

8 "Flee out of Babylon;
leave the land of the Babylonians,
and be like the goats that lead the
flock.
9 For I will stir up and bring against
Babylon
an alliance of great nations from
the land of the north.
They will take up their positions
against her,
and from the north she will be
captured.
Their arrows will be like skilled
warriors
who do not return empty-handed.
10 So Babylonia[a] will be plundered;
all who plunder her will have their
fill,"
declares the LORD.

11 "Because you rejoice and are glad,
you who pillage my inheritance,
because you frolic like a heifer
threshing grain
and neigh like stallions,
12 your mother will be greatly ashamed;
she who gave you birth will be
disgraced.
She will be the least of the nations —
a wilderness, a dry land, a desert.
13 Because of the LORD's anger she will
not be inhabited
but will be completely desolate.
All who pass Babylon will be appalled;
they will scoff because of all her
wounds.

14 "Take up your positions around
Babylon,
all you who draw the bow.
Shoot at her! Spare no arrows,
for she has sinned against the LORD.
15 Shout against her on every side!
She surrenders, her towers fall,
her walls are torn down.
Since this is the vengeance of the LORD,
take vengeance on her;
do to her as she has done to others.
16 Cut off from Babylon the sower,
and the reaper with his sickle at
harvest.
Because of the sword of the oppressor
let everyone return to their own
people,
let everyone flee to their own land.

17 "Israel is a scattered flock
that lions have chased away.
The first to devour them
was the king of Assyria;
the last to crush their bones
was Nebuchadnezzar king of
Babylon."

18 Therefore this is what the LORD Almighty, the God of Israel, says:

"I will punish the king of Babylon
and his land
as I punished the king of Assyria.
19 But I will bring Israel back to their
own pasture,
and they will graze on Carmel and
Bashan;
their appetite will be satisfied
on the hills of Ephraim and Gilead.
20 In those days, at that time,"
declares the LORD,
"search will be made for Israel's guilt,
but there will be none,
and for the sins of Judah,
but none will be found,
for I will forgive the remnant I spare.

21 "Attack the land of Merathaim
and those who live in Pekod.
Pursue, kill and completely destroy[b]
them,"
declares the LORD.
"Do everything I have commanded
you.
22 The noise of battle is in the land,
the noise of great destruction!
23 How broken and shattered
is the hammer of the whole earth!
How desolate is Babylon
among the nations!
24 I set a trap for you, Babylon,
and you were caught before you
knew it;
you were found and captured
because you opposed the LORD.

[a] *10* Or *Chaldea* [b] *21* The Hebrew term refers to the irrevocable giving over of things or persons to the LORD, often by totally destroying them; also in verse 26.

25 The LORD has opened his arsenal
and brought out the weapons of his wrath,
for the Sovereign LORD Almighty has work to do
in the land of the Babylonians.
26 Come against her from afar.
Break open her granaries;
pile her up like heaps of grain.
Completely destroy her
and leave her no remnant.
27 Kill all her young bulls;
let them go down to the slaughter!
Woe to them! For their day has come,
the time for them to be punished.
28 Listen to the fugitives and refugees from Babylon
declaring in Zion
how the LORD our God has taken vengeance,
vengeance for his temple.

29 "Summon archers against Babylon,
all those who draw the bow.
Encamp all around her;
let no one escape.
Repay her for her deeds;
do to her as she has done.
For she has defied the LORD,
the Holy One of Israel.
30 Therefore, her young men will fall in the streets;
all her soldiers will be silenced in that day,"
declares the LORD.
31 "See, I am against you, you arrogant one,"
declares the Lord, the LORD Almighty,
"for your day has come,
the time for you to be punished.
32 The arrogant one will stumble and fall
and no one will help her up;
I will kindle a fire in her towns
that will consume all who are around her."

33 This is what the LORD Almighty says:

"The people of Israel are oppressed,
and the people of Judah as well.
All their captors hold them fast,
refusing to let them go.
34 Yet their Redeemer is strong;
the LORD Almighty is his name.
He will vigorously defend their cause
so that he may bring rest to their land,
but unrest to those who live in Babylon.

35 "A sword against the Babylonians!"
declares the LORD —
"against those who live in Babylon
and against her officials and wise men!
36 A sword against her false prophets!
They will become fools.
A sword against her warriors!
They will be filled with terror.
37 A sword against her horses and chariots
and all the foreigners in her ranks!
They will become weaklings.
A sword against her treasures!
They will be plundered.
38 A drought on[a] her waters!
They will dry up.
For it is a land of idols,
idols that will go mad with terror.

39 "So desert creatures and hyenas will live there,
and there the owl will dwell.
It will never again be inhabited
or lived in from generation to generation.
40 As I overthrew Sodom and Gomorrah
along with their neighboring towns,"
declares the LORD,
"so no one will live there;
no people will dwell in it.

41 "Look! An army is coming from the north;
a great nation and many kings
are being stirred up from the ends of the earth.
42 They are armed with bows and spears;
they are cruel and without mercy.
They sound like the roaring sea
as they ride on their horses;
they come like men in battle formation
to attack you, Daughter Babylon.
43 The king of Babylon has heard reports about them,
and his hands hang limp.
Anguish has gripped him,
pain like that of a woman in labor.
44 Like a lion coming up from Jordan's thickets
to a rich pastureland,
I will chase Babylon from its land in an instant.
Who is the chosen one I will appoint for this?
Who is like me and who can challenge me?
And what shepherd can stand against me?"

[a] 38 Or *A sword against*

45 Therefore, hear what the LORD has
planned against Babylon,
what he has purposed against the
land of the Babylonians:
The young of the flock will be
dragged away;
their pasture will be appalled at
their fate.
46 At the sound of Babylon's capture the
earth will tremble;
its cry will resound among the
nations.

51 This is what the LORD says:

"See, I will stir up the spirit of a
destroyer
against Babylon and the people of
Leb Kamai.[a]
2 I will send foreigners to Babylon
to winnow her and to devastate her
land;
they will oppose her on every side
in the day of her disaster.
3 Let not the archer string his bow,
nor let him put on his armor.
Do not spare her young men;
completely destroy[b] her army.
4 They will fall down slain in Babylon,[c]
fatally wounded in her streets.
5 For Israel and Judah have not been
forsaken
by their God, the LORD Almighty,
though their land[d] is full of guilt
before the Holy One of Israel.

6 "Flee from Babylon!
Run for your lives!
Do not be destroyed because of her
sins.
It is time for the LORD's vengeance;
he will repay her what she deserves.
7 Babylon was a gold cup in the LORD's
hand;
she made the whole earth drunk.
The nations drank her wine;
therefore they have now gone mad.
8 Babylon will suddenly fall and be
broken.
Wail over her!
Get balm for her pain;
perhaps she can be healed.

9 " 'We would have healed Babylon,
but she cannot be healed;
let us leave her and each go to our
own land,
for her judgment reaches to the
skies,
it rises as high as the heavens.'
10 " 'The LORD has vindicated us;
come, let us tell in Zion
what the LORD our God has done.'

11 "Sharpen the arrows,
take up the shields!
The LORD has stirred up the kings of
the Medes,
because his purpose is to destroy
Babylon.
The LORD will take vengeance,
vengeance for his temple.
12 Lift up a banner against the walls of
Babylon!
Reinforce the guard,
station the watchmen,
prepare an ambush!
The LORD will carry out his purpose,
his decree against the people of
Babylon.
13 You who live by many waters
and are rich in treasures,
your end has come,
the time for you to be destroyed.
14 The LORD Almighty has sworn by
himself:
I will surely fill you with troops, as
with a swarm of locusts,
and they will shout in triumph over
you.

15 "He made the earth by his power;
he founded the world by his
wisdom
and stretched out the heavens by
his understanding.
16 When he thunders, the waters in the
heavens roar;
he makes clouds rise from the ends
of the earth.
He sends lightning with the rain
and brings out the wind from his
storehouses.

17 "Everyone is senseless and without
knowledge;
every goldsmith is shamed by his
idols.
The images he makes are a fraud;
they have no breath in them.
18 They are worthless, the objects of
mockery;
when their judgment comes, they
will perish.
19 He who is the Portion of Jacob is not
like these,
for he is the Maker of all things,
including the people of his
inheritance —
the LORD Almighty is his name.

[a] 1 *Leb Kamai* is a cryptogram for Chaldea, that is, Babylonia. [b] 3 The Hebrew term refers to the irrevocable giving over of things or persons to the LORD, often by totally destroying them. [c] 4 Or *Chaldea* [d] 5 Or *Almighty, / and the land of the Babylonians*

20 "You are my war club,
my weapon for battle —
with you I shatter nations,
with you I destroy kingdoms,
21 with you I shatter horse and rider,
with you I shatter chariot and driver,
22 with you I shatter man and woman,
with you I shatter old man and youth,
with you I shatter young man and young woman,
23 with you I shatter shepherd and flock,
with you I shatter farmer and oxen,
with you I shatter governors and officials.

24 "Before your eyes I will repay Babylon
and all who live in Babylonia[a] for all the
wrong they have done in Zion," declares
the LORD.

25 "I am against you, you destroying mountain,
you who destroy the whole earth,"
declares the LORD.
"I will stretch out my hand against you,
roll you off the cliffs,
and make you a burned-out mountain.
26 No rock will be taken from you for a cornerstone,
nor any stone for a foundation,
for you will be desolate forever,"
declares the LORD.

27 "Lift up a banner in the land!
Blow the trumpet among the nations!
Prepare the nations for battle against her;
summon against her these kingdoms:
Ararat, Minni and Ashkenaz.
Appoint a commander against her;
send up horses like a swarm of locusts.
28 Prepare the nations for battle against her —
the kings of the Medes,
their governors and all their officials,
and all the countries they rule.
29 The land trembles and writhes,
for the LORD's purposes against Babylon stand —
to lay waste the land of Babylon
so that no one will live there.
30 Babylon's warriors have stopped fighting;
they remain in their strongholds.
Their strength is exhausted;
they have become weaklings.
Her dwellings are set on fire;
the bars of her gates are broken.
31 One courier follows another
and messenger follows messenger
to announce to the king of Babylon
that his entire city is captured,
32 the river crossings seized,
the marshes set on fire,
and the soldiers terrified."

33 This is what the LORD Almighty, the
God of Israel, says:

"Daughter Babylon is like a threshing floor
at the time it is trampled;
the time to harvest her will soon come."

34 "Nebuchadnezzar king of Babylon
has devoured us,
he has thrown us into confusion,
he has made us an empty jar.
Like a serpent he has swallowed us
and filled his stomach with our delicacies,
and then has spewed us out.
35 May the violence done to our flesh[b] be on Babylon,"
say the inhabitants of Zion.
"May our blood be on those who live in Babylonia,"
says Jerusalem.

36 Therefore this is what the LORD says:

"See, I will defend your cause
and avenge you;
I will dry up her sea
and make her springs dry.
37 Babylon will be a heap of ruins,
a haunt of jackals,
an object of horror and scorn,
a place where no one lives.
38 Her people all roar like young lions,
they growl like lion cubs.
39 But while they are aroused,
I will set out a feast for them
and make them drunk,
so that they shout with laughter —
then sleep forever and not awake,"
declares the LORD.
40 "I will bring them down
like lambs to the slaughter,
like rams and goats.

41 "How Sheshak[c] will be captured,
the boast of the whole earth seized!
How desolate Babylon will be
among the nations!

[a] 24 Or *Chaldea*; also in verse 35 [b] 35 Or *done to us and to our children* [c] 41 *Sheshak* is a cryptogram for Babylon.

42 The sea will rise over Babylon;
its roaring waves will cover her.
43 Her towns will be desolate,
a dry and desert land,
a land where no one lives,
through which no one travels.
44 I will punish Bel in Babylon
and make him spew out what he has swallowed.
The nations will no longer stream to him.
And the wall of Babylon will fall.

45 "Come out of her, my people!
Run for your lives!
Run from the fierce anger of the LORD.
46 Do not lose heart or be afraid
when rumors are heard in the land;
one rumor comes this year, another the next,
rumors of violence in the land
and of ruler against ruler.
47 For the time will surely come
when I will punish the idols of Babylon;
her whole land will be disgraced
and her slain will all lie fallen within her.
48 Then heaven and earth and all that is in them
will shout for joy over Babylon,
for out of the north
destroyers will attack her,"
declares the LORD.

49 "Babylon must fall because of Israel's slain,
just as the slain in all the earth
have fallen because of Babylon.
50 You who have escaped the sword,
leave and do not linger!
Remember the LORD in a distant land,
and call to mind Jerusalem."

51 "We are disgraced,
for we have been insulted
and shame covers our faces,
because foreigners have entered
the holy places of the LORD's house."

52 "But days are coming," declares the LORD,
"when I will punish her idols,
and throughout her land
the wounded will groan.
53 Even if Babylon ascends to the heavens
and fortifies her lofty stronghold,
I will send destroyers against her,"
declares the LORD.

54 "The sound of a cry comes from Babylon,
the sound of great destruction
from the land of the Babylonians.[a]
55 The LORD will destroy Babylon;
he will silence her noisy din.
Waves of enemies will rage like great waters;
the roar of their voices will resound.
56 A destroyer will come against Babylon;
her warriors will be captured,
and their bows will be broken.
For the LORD is a God of retribution;
he will repay in full.
57 I will make her officials and wise men drunk,
her governors, officers and warriors as well;
they will sleep forever and not awake,"
declares the King, whose name is the LORD Almighty.

58 This is what the LORD Almighty says:

"Babylon's thick wall will be leveled
and her high gates set on fire;
the peoples exhaust themselves for nothing,
the nations' labor is only fuel for the flames."

59 This is the message Jeremiah the prophet gave to the staff officer Seraiah son of
Neriah, the son of Mahseiah, when he went
to Babylon with Zedekiah king of Judah in
the fourth year of his reign. 60 Jeremiah had
written on a scroll about all the disasters
that would come upon Babylon — all that
had been recorded concerning Babylon. 61 He
said to Seraiah, "When you get to Babylon,
see that you read all these words aloud.
62 Then say, 'LORD, you have said you will
destroy this place, so that neither people
nor animals will live in it; it will be desolate forever.' 63 When you finish reading
this scroll, tie a stone to it and throw it into
the Euphrates. 64 Then say, 'So will Babylon
sink to rise no more because of the disaster
I will bring on her. And her people will fall.'"

The words of Jeremiah end here.

The Fall of Jerusalem

52 Zedekiah was twenty-one years
old when he became king, and he
reigned in Jerusalem eleven years. His
mother's name was Hamutal daughter
of Jeremiah; she was from Libnah. 2 He
did evil in the eyes of the LORD, just as
Jehoiakim had done. 3 It was because of
the LORD's anger that all this happened
to Jerusalem and Judah, and in the end
he thrust them from his presence.

[a] 54 Or *Chaldeans*

Now Zedekiah rebelled against the king
of Babylon.
4So in the ninth year of Zedekiah's reign,
on the tenth day of the tenth month, Nebuchadnezzar king of Babylon marched
against Jerusalem with his whole army.
They encamped outside the city and built
siege works all around it. 5The city was
kept under siege until the eleventh year
of King Zedekiah.
6By the ninth day of the fourth month
the famine in the city had become so severe
that there was no food for the people to eat.
7Then the city wall was broken through,
and the whole army fled. They left the city
at night through the gate between the two
walls near the king's garden, though the
Babylonians[a] were surrounding the city.
They fled toward the Arabah,[b] 8but the
Babylonian[c] army pursued King Zedekiah
and overtook him in the plains of Jericho.
All his soldiers were separated from him
and scattered, 9and he was captured.
He was taken to the king of Babylon at
Riblah in the land of Hamath, where he
pronounced sentence on him. 10There at
Riblah the king of Babylon killed the sons
of Zedekiah before his eyes; he also killed
all the officials of Judah. 11Then he put out
Zedekiah's eyes, bound him with bronze
shackles and took him to Babylon, where
he put him in prison till the day of his death.
12On the tenth day of the fifth month, in
the nineteenth year of Nebuchadnezzar
king of Babylon, Nebuzaradan commander of the imperial guard, who served the
king of Babylon, came to Jerusalem. 13He
set fire to the temple of the LORD, the royal
palace and all the houses of Jerusalem. Every important building he burned down.
14The whole Babylonian army, under the
commander of the imperial guard, broke
down all the walls around Jerusalem.
15Nebuzaradan the commander of the
guard carried into exile some of the poorest people and those who remained in the
city, along with the rest of the craftsmen[d]
and those who had deserted to the king of
Babylon. 16But Nebuzaradan left behind
the rest of the poorest people of the land
to work the vineyards and fields.
17The Babylonians broke up the bronze
pillars, the movable stands and the bronze
Sea that were at the temple of the LORD
and they carried all the bronze to Babylon.
18They also took away the pots, shovels,
wick trimmers, sprinkling bowls, dishes
and all the bronze articles used in the temple service. 19The commander of the imperial guard took away the basins, censers,
sprinkling bowls, pots, lampstands, dishes
and bowls used for drink offerings—all
that were made of pure gold or silver.
20The bronze from the two pillars, the
Sea and the twelve bronze bulls under it,
and the movable stands, which King Solomon had made for the temple of the LORD,
was more than could be weighed. 21Each
pillar was eighteen cubits high and twelve
cubits in circumference[e]; each was four
fingers thick, and hollow. 22The bronze
capital on top of one pillar was five cubits[f]
high and was decorated with a network
and pomegranates of bronze all around.
The other pillar, with its pomegranates,
was similar. 23There were ninety-six pomegranates on the sides; the total number
of pomegranates above the surrounding
network was a hundred.
24The commander of the guard took as
prisoners Seraiah the chief priest, Zephaniah the priest next in rank and the three
doorkeepers. 25Of those still in the city, he
took the officer in charge of the fighting
men, and seven royal advisers. He also
took the secretary who was chief officer in
charge of conscripting the people of the
land, sixty of whom were found in the city.
26Nebuzaradan the commander took them
all and brought them to the king of Babylon
at Riblah. 27There at Riblah, in the land
of Hamath, the king had them executed.
So Judah went into captivity, away from
her land. 28This is the number of the people Nebuchadnezzar carried into exile:

in the seventh year, 3,023 Jews;
29 in Nebuchadnezzar's eighteenth year,
832 people from Jerusalem;
30 in his twenty-third year,
745 Jews taken into exile by Nebuzaradan the commander of the
imperial guard.
There were 4,600 people in all.

Jehoiachin Released

31In the thirty-seventh year of the exile
of Jehoiachin king of Judah, in the year
Awel-Marduk became king of Babylon, on
the twenty-fifth day of the twelfth month,
he released Jehoiachin king of Judah and
freed him from prison. 32He spoke kindly to him and gave him a seat of honor
higher than those of the other kings who
were with him in Babylon. 33So Jehoiachin
put aside his prison clothes and for the
rest of his life ate regularly at the king's
table. 34Day by day the king of Babylon
gave Jehoiachin a regular allowance as
long as he lived, till the day of his death.

[a] 7 Or *Chaldeans*; also in verse 17 [b] 7 Or *the Jordan Valley* [c] 8 Or *Chaldean*; also in verse 14
[d] 15 Or *the populace* [e] 21 That is, about 27 feet high and 18 feet in circumference or about 8.1 meters high and 5.4 meters in circumference [f] 22 That is, about 7 1/2 feet or about 2.3 meters

LAMENTATIONS

1 [a] How deserted lies the city,
once so full of people!
How like a widow is she,
who once was great among the nations!
She who was queen among the provinces
has now become a slave.

2 Bitterly she weeps at night,
tears are on her cheeks.
Among all her lovers
there is no one to comfort her.
All her friends have betrayed her;
they have become her enemies.

3 After affliction and harsh labor,
Judah has gone into exile.
She dwells among the nations;
she finds no resting place.
All who pursue her have overtaken her
in the midst of her distress.

4 The roads to Zion mourn,
for no one comes to her appointed festivals.
All her gateways are desolate,
her priests groan,
her young women grieve,
and she is in bitter anguish.

5 Her foes have become her masters;
her enemies are at ease.
The LORD has brought her grief
because of her many sins.
Her children have gone into exile,
captive before the foe.

6 All the splendor has departed
from Daughter Zion.
Her princes are like deer
that find no pasture;
in weakness they have fled
before the pursuer.

7 In the days of her affliction and wandering
Jerusalem remembers all the treasures
that were hers in days of old.
When her people fell into enemy hands,
there was no one to help her.
Her enemies looked at her
and laughed at her destruction.

8 Jerusalem has sinned greatly
and so has become unclean.
All who honored her despise her,
for they have all seen her naked;
she herself groans
and turns away.

9 Her filthiness clung to her skirts;
she did not consider her future.
Her fall was astounding;
there was none to comfort her.
"Look, LORD, on my affliction,
for the enemy has triumphed."

10 The enemy laid hands
on all her treasures;
she saw pagan nations
enter her sanctuary—
those you had forbidden
to enter your assembly.

11 All her people groan
as they search for bread;
they barter their treasures for food
to keep themselves alive.
"Look, LORD, and consider,
for I am despised."

12 "Is it nothing to you, all you who pass by?
Look around and see.
Is any suffering like my suffering
that was inflicted on me,
that the LORD brought on me
in the day of his fierce anger?

13 "From on high he sent fire,
sent it down into my bones.
He spread a net for my feet
and turned me back.
He made me desolate,
faint all the day long.

14 "My sins have been bound into a yoke[b];
by his hands they were woven together.
They have been hung on my neck,
and the Lord has sapped my strength.
He has given me into the hands
of those I cannot withstand.

15 "The Lord has rejected
all the warriors in my midst;
he has summoned an army against me
to[c] crush my young men.
In his winepress the Lord has trampled
Virgin Daughter Judah.

[a] This chapter is an acrostic poem, the verses of which begin with the successive letters of the Hebrew alphabet. [b] 14 Most Hebrew manuscripts; many Hebrew manuscripts and Septuagint *He kept watch over my sins* [c] 15 *Or has set a time for me / when he will*

16 "This is why I weep
and my eyes overflow with tears.
No one is near to comfort me,
no one to restore my spirit.
My children are destitute
because the enemy has prevailed."

17 Zion stretches out her hands,
but there is no one to comfort her.
The LORD has decreed for Jacob
that his neighbors become his foes;
Jerusalem has become
an unclean thing among them.

18 "The LORD is righteous,
yet I rebelled against his
command.
Listen, all you peoples;
look on my suffering.
My young men and young women
have gone into exile.

19 "I called to my allies
but they betrayed me.
My priests and my elders
perished in the city
while they searched for food
to keep themselves alive.

20 "See, LORD, how distressed I am!
I am in torment within,
and in my heart I am disturbed,
for I have been most rebellious.
Outside, the sword bereaves;
inside, there is only death.

21 "People have heard my groaning,
but there is no one to comfort me.
All my enemies have heard of my
distress;
they rejoice at what you have done.
May you bring the day you have
announced
so they may become like me.

22 "Let all their wickedness come before
you;
deal with them
as you have dealt with me
because of all my sins.
My groans are many
and my heart is faint."

2[a] How the Lord has covered Daughter
Zion
with the cloud of his anger[b]!
He has hurled down the splendor of
Israel
from heaven to earth;
he has not remembered his footstool
in the day of his anger.

2 Without pity the Lord has swallowed up
all the dwellings of Jacob;
in his wrath he has torn down
the strongholds of Daughter
Judah.
He has brought her kingdom and its
princes
down to the ground in dishonor.

3 In fierce anger he has cut off
every horn[c,d] of Israel.
He has withdrawn his right hand
at the approach of the enemy.
He has burned in Jacob like a
flaming fire
that consumes everything
around it.

4 Like an enemy he has strung his bow;
his right hand is ready.
Like a foe he has slain
all who were pleasing to the eye;
he has poured out his wrath like fire
on the tent of Daughter Zion.

5 The Lord is like an enemy;
he has swallowed up Israel.
He has swallowed up all her palaces
and destroyed her strongholds.
He has multiplied mourning and
lamentation
for Daughter Judah.

6 He has laid waste his dwelling like a
garden;
he has destroyed his place of
meeting.
The LORD has made Zion forget
her appointed festivals and her
Sabbaths;
in his fierce anger he has spurned
both king and priest.

7 The Lord has rejected his altar
and abandoned his sanctuary.
He has given the walls of her palaces
into the hands of the enemy;
they have raised a shout in the house
of the LORD
as on the day of an appointed
festival.

8 The LORD determined to tear down
the wall around Daughter Zion.
He stretched out a measuring line
and did not withhold his hand
from destroying.
He made ramparts and walls lament;
together they wasted away.

9 Her gates have sunk into the ground;
their bars he has broken and
destroyed.

[a] This chapter is an acrostic poem, the verses of which begin with the successive letters of the Hebrew alphabet. [b] 1 Or *How the Lord in his anger / has treated Daughter Zion with contempt*
[c] 3 Or *off / all the strength*; or *every king* [d] 3 *Horn* here symbolizes strength.

Her king and her princes are exiled
among the nations,
the law is no more,
and her prophets no longer find
visions from the LORD.

10 The elders of Daughter Zion
sit on the ground in silence;
they have sprinkled dust on their
heads
and put on sackcloth.
The young women of Jerusalem
have bowed their heads to the
ground.

11 My eyes fail from weeping,
I am in torment within;
my heart is poured out on the ground
because my people are destroyed,
because children and infants faint
in the streets of the city.

12 They say to their mothers,
"Where is bread and wine?"
as they faint like the wounded
in the streets of the city,
as their lives ebb away
in their mothers' arms.

13 What can I say for you?
With what can I compare you,
Daughter Jerusalem?
To what can I liken you,
that I may comfort you,
Virgin Daughter Zion?
Your wound is as deep as the sea.
Who can heal you?

14 The visions of your prophets
were false and worthless;
they did not expose your sin
to ward off your captivity.
The prophecies they gave you
were false and misleading.

15 All who pass your way
clap their hands at you;
they scoff and shake their heads
at Daughter Jerusalem:
"Is this the city that was called
the perfection of beauty,
the joy of the whole earth?"

16 All your enemies open their mouths
wide against you;
they scoff and gnash their teeth
and say, "We have swallowed her
up.
This is the day we have waited for;
we have lived to see it."

17 The LORD has done what he planned;
he has fulfilled his word,
which he decreed long ago.
He has overthrown you without pity,
he has let the enemy gloat over
you,
he has exalted the horn[a] of your
foes.

18 The hearts of the people
cry out to the Lord.
You walls of Daughter Zion,
let your tears flow like a river
day and night;
give yourself no relief,
your eyes no rest.

19 Arise, cry out in the night,
as the watches of the night begin;
pour out your heart like water
in the presence of the Lord.
Lift up your hands to him
for the lives of your children,
who faint from hunger
at every street corner.

20 "Look, LORD, and consider:
Whom have you ever treated like
this?
Should women eat their offspring,
the children they have cared for?
Should priest and prophet be killed
in the sanctuary of the Lord?

21 "Young and old lie together
in the dust of the streets;
my young men and young women
have fallen by the sword.
You have slain them in the day of
your anger;
you have slaughtered them
without pity.

22 "As you summon to a feast day,
so you summoned against me
terrors on every side.
In the day of the LORD's anger
no one escaped or survived;
those I cared for and reared
my enemy has destroyed."

3[b] I am the man who has seen
affliction
by the rod of the LORD's wrath.
2 He has driven me away and made me
walk
in darkness rather than light;
3 indeed, he has turned his hand
against me
again and again, all day long.

[a] 17 *Horn* here symbolizes strength. [b] This chapter is an acrostic poem; the verses of each stanza begin with the successive letters of the Hebrew alphabet, and the verses within each stanza begin with the same letter.

4 He has made my skin and my flesh
grow old
and has broken my bones.
5 He has besieged me and surrounded me
with bitterness and hardship.
6 He has made me dwell in darkness
like those long dead.

7 He has walled me in so I cannot escape;
he has weighed me down with
chains.
8 Even when I call out or cry for help,
he shuts out my prayer.
9 He has barred my way with blocks of
stone;
he has made my paths crooked.

10 Like a bear lying in wait,
like a lion in hiding,
11 he dragged me from the path and
mangled me
and left me without help.
12 He drew his bow
and made me the target for his
arrows.

13 He pierced my heart
with arrows from his quiver.
14 I became the laughingstock of all my
people;
they mock me in song all day long.
15 He has filled me with bitter herbs
and given me gall to drink.

16 He has broken my teeth with gravel;
he has trampled me in the dust.
17 I have been deprived of peace;
I have forgotten what prosperity is.
18 So I say, "My splendor is gone
and all that I had hoped from the
LORD."

19 I remember my affliction and my
wandering,
the bitterness and the gall.
20 I well remember them,
and my soul is downcast within me.
21 Yet this I call to mind
and therefore I have hope:

22 Because of the LORD's great love we
are not consumed,
for his compassions never fail.
23 They are new every morning;
great is your faithfulness.
24 I say to myself, "The LORD is my
portion;
therefore I will wait for him."

25 The LORD is good to those whose hope
is in him,
to the one who seeks him;
26 it is good to wait quietly
for the salvation of the LORD.
27 It is good for a man to bear the yoke
while he is young.

28 Let him sit alone in silence,
for the LORD has laid it on him.
29 Let him bury his face in the dust —
there may yet be hope.
30 Let him offer his cheek to one who
would strike him,
and let him be filled with disgrace.

31 For no one is cast off
by the Lord forever.
32 Though he brings grief, he will show
compassion,
so great is his unfailing love.
33 For he does not willingly bring
affliction
or grief to anyone.

34 To crush underfoot
all prisoners in the land,
35 to deny people their rights
before the Most High,
36 to deprive them of justice —
would not the Lord see such things?

37 Who can speak and have it happen
if the Lord has not decreed it?
38 Is it not from the mouth of the Most
High
that both calamities and good
things come?
39 Why should the living complain
when punished for their sins?

40 Let us examine our ways and test
them,
and let us return to the LORD.
41 Let us lift up our hearts and our
hands
to God in heaven, and say:
42 "We have sinned and rebelled
and you have not forgiven.

43 "You have covered yourself with
anger and pursued us;
you have slain without pity.
44 You have covered yourself with a
cloud
so that no prayer can get through.
45 You have made us scum and refuse
among the nations.

46 "All our enemies have opened their
mouths
wide against us.
47 We have suffered terror and pitfalls,
ruin and destruction."
48 Streams of tears flow from my eyes
because my people are destroyed.

49 My eyes will flow unceasingly,
without relief,
50 until the LORD looks down
from heaven and sees.
51 What I see brings grief to my soul
because of all the women of my city.

52 Those who were my enemies without cause
hunted me like a bird.
53 They tried to end my life in a pit
and threw stones at me;
54 the waters closed over my head,
and I thought I was about to perish.

55 I called on your name, LORD,
from the depths of the pit.
56 You heard my plea: "Do not close your ears
to my cry for relief."
57 You came near when I called you,
and you said, "Do not fear."

58 You, Lord, took up my case;
you redeemed my life.
59 LORD, you have seen the wrong done to me.
Uphold my cause!
60 You have seen the depth of their vengeance,
all their plots against me.

61 LORD, you have heard their insults,
all their plots against me—
62 what my enemies whisper and mutter
against me all day long.
63 Look at them! Sitting or standing,
they mock me in their songs.

64 Pay them back what they deserve, LORD,
for what their hands have done.
65 Put a veil over their hearts,
and may your curse be on them!
66 Pursue them in anger and destroy them
from under the heavens of the LORD.

4 [a] How the gold has lost its luster,
the fine gold become dull!
The sacred gems are scattered
at every street corner.

2 How the precious children of Zion,
once worth their weight in gold,
are now considered as pots of clay,
the work of a potter's hands!

3 Even jackals offer their breasts
to nurse their young,
but my people have become heartless
like ostriches in the desert.

4 Because of thirst the infant's tongue
sticks to the roof of its mouth;
the children beg for bread,
but no one gives it to them.

5 Those who once ate delicacies
are destitute in the streets.
Those brought up in royal purple
now lie on ash heaps.

6 The punishment of my people
is greater than that of Sodom,
which was overthrown in a moment
without a hand turned to help her.

7 Their princes were brighter than snow
and whiter than milk,
their bodies more ruddy than rubies,
their appearance like lapis lazuli.

8 But now they are blacker than soot;
they are not recognized in the streets.
Their skin has shriveled on their bones;
it has become as dry as a stick.

9 Those killed by the sword are better off
than those who die of famine;
racked with hunger, they waste away
for lack of food from the field.

10 With their own hands compassionate women
have cooked their own children,
who became their food
when my people were destroyed.

11 The LORD has given full vent to his wrath;
he has poured out his fierce anger.
He kindled a fire in Zion
that consumed her foundations.

12 The kings of the earth did not believe,
nor did any of the peoples of the world,
that enemies and foes could enter
the gates of Jerusalem.

13 But it happened because of the sins of her prophets
and the iniquities of her priests,
who shed within her
the blood of the righteous.

14 Now they grope through the streets
as if they were blind.
They are so defiled with blood
that no one dares to touch their garments.

15 "Go away! You are unclean!" people cry to them.
"Away! Away! Don't touch us!"
When they flee and wander about,
people among the nations say,
"They can stay here no longer."

[a] This chapter is an acrostic poem, the verses of which begin with the successive letters of the Hebrew alphabet.

[16] The LORD himself has scattered them;
he no longer watches over them.
The priests are shown no honor,
the elders no favor.

[17] Moreover, our eyes failed,
looking in vain for help;
from our towers we watched
for a nation that could not save us.

[18] People stalked us at every step,
so we could not walk in our streets.
Our end was near, our days were numbered,
for our end had come.

[19] Our pursuers were swifter
than eagles in the sky;
they chased us over the mountains
and lay in wait for us in the desert.

[20] The LORD's anointed, our very life breath,
was caught in their traps.
We thought that under his shadow
we would live among the nations.

[21] Rejoice and be glad, Daughter Edom,
you who live in the land of Uz.
But to you also the cup will be passed;
you will be drunk and stripped naked.

[22] Your punishment will end, Daughter Zion;
he will not prolong your exile.
But he will punish your sin, Daughter Edom,
and expose your wickedness.

5 Remember, LORD, what has happened to us;
look, and see our disgrace.
[2] Our inheritance has been turned over to strangers,
our homes to foreigners.
[3] We have become fatherless,
our mothers are widows.
[4] We must buy the water we drink;
our wood can be had only at a price.
[5] Those who pursue us are at our heels;
we are weary and find no rest.
[6] We submitted to Egypt and Assyria
to get enough bread.
[7] Our ancestors sinned and are no more,
and we bear their punishment.
[8] Slaves rule over us,
and there is no one to free us from their hands.
[9] We get our bread at the risk of our lives
because of the sword in the desert.
[10] Our skin is hot as an oven,
feverish from hunger.
[11] Women have been violated in Zion,
and virgins in the towns of Judah.
[12] Princes have been hung up by their hands;
elders are shown no respect.
[13] Young men toil at the millstones;
boys stagger under loads of wood.
[14] The elders are gone from the city gate;
the young men have stopped their music.
[15] Joy is gone from our hearts;
our dancing has turned to mourning.
[16] The crown has fallen from our head.
Woe to us, for we have sinned!
[17] Because of this our hearts are faint,
because of these things our eyes grow dim
[18] for Mount Zion, which lies desolate,
with jackals prowling over it.
[19] You, LORD, reign forever;
your throne endures from generation to generation.
[20] Why do you always forget us?
Why do you forsake us so long?
[21] Restore us to yourself, LORD, that we may return;
renew our days as of old
[22] unless you have utterly rejected us
and are angry with us beyond measure.

EZEKIEL

Ezekiel's Inaugural Vision

1 In my thirtieth year, in the fourth month on the fifth day, while I was among the exiles by the Kebar River, the heavens were opened and I saw visions of God.

2 On the fifth of the month — it was the fifth year of the exile of King Jehoiachin — 3 the word of the LORD came to Ezekiel the priest, the son of Buzi, by the Kebar River in the land of the Babylonians.[a] There the hand of the LORD was on him.

4 I looked, and I saw a windstorm coming out of the north — an immense cloud with flashing lightning and surrounded by brilliant light. The center of the fire looked like glowing metal, 5 and in the fire was what looked like four living creatures. In appearance their form was human, 6 but each of them had four faces and four wings. 7 Their legs were straight; their feet were like those of a calf and gleamed like burnished bronze. 8 Under their wings on their four sides they had human hands. All four of them had faces and wings, 9 and the wings of one touched the wings of another. Each one went straight ahead; they did not turn as they moved.

10 Their faces looked like this: Each of the four had the face of a human being, and on the right side each had the face of a lion, and on the left the face of an ox; each also had the face of an eagle. 11 Such were their faces. They each had two wings spreading out upward, each wing touching that of the creature on either side; and each had two other wings covering its body. 12 Each one went straight ahead. Wherever the spirit would go, they would go, without turning as they went. 13 The appearance of the living creatures was like burning coals of fire or like torches. Fire moved back and forth among the creatures; it was bright, and lightning flashed out of it. 14 The creatures sped back and forth like flashes of lightning.

15 As I looked at the living creatures, I saw a wheel on the ground beside each creature with its four faces. 16 This was the appearance and structure of the wheels: They sparkled like topaz, and all four looked alike. Each appeared to be made like a wheel intersecting a wheel. 17 As they moved, they would go in any one of the four directions the creatures faced; the wheels did not change direction as the creatures went. 18 Their rims were high and awesome, and all four rims were full of eyes all around.

19 When the living creatures moved, the wheels beside them moved; and when the living creatures rose from the ground, the wheels also rose. 20 Wherever the spirit would go, they would go, and the wheels would rise along with them, because the spirit of the living creatures was in the wheels. 21 When the creatures moved, they also moved; when the creatures stood still, they also stood still; and when the creatures rose from the ground, the wheels rose along with them, because the spirit of the living creatures was in the wheels.

22 Spread out above the heads of the living creatures was what looked something like a vault, sparkling like crystal, and awesome. 23 Under the vault their wings were stretched out one toward the other, and each had two wings covering its body. 24 When the creatures moved, I heard the sound of their wings, like the roar of rushing waters, like the voice of the Almighty,[b] like the tumult of an army. When they stood still, they lowered their wings.

25 Then there came a voice from above the vault over their heads as they stood with lowered wings. 26 Above the vault over their heads was what looked like a throne of lapis lazuli, and high above on the throne was a figure like that of a man. 27 I saw that from what appeared to be his waist up he looked like glowing metal, as if full of fire, and that from there down he looked like fire; and brilliant light surrounded him. 28 Like the appearance of a rainbow in the clouds on a rainy day, so was the radiance around him.

This was the appearance of the likeness of the glory of the LORD. When I saw it, I fell facedown, and I heard the voice of one speaking.

Ezekiel's Call to Be a Prophet

2 He said to me, "Son of man,[c] stand up on your feet and I will speak to you." 2 As he spoke, the Spirit came into me and raised me to my feet, and I heard him speaking to me.

[a] 3 Or *Chaldeans* [b] 24 Hebrew *Shaddai* [c] 1 The Hebrew phrase *ben adam* means *human being*. The phrase *son of man* is retained as a form of address here and throughout Ezekiel because of its possible association with "Son of Man" in the New Testament.

3He said: "Son of man, I am sending you
to the Israelites, to a rebellious nation that
has rebelled against me; they and their
ancestors have been in revolt against me
to this very day. 4The people to whom I am
sending you are obstinate and stubborn.
Say to them, 'This is what the Sovereign
LORD says.' 5And whether they listen or
fail to listen — for they are a rebellious
people — they will know that a prophet has
been among them. 6And you, son of man,
do not be afraid of them or their words. Do
not be afraid, though briers and thorns are
all around you and you live among scorpions. Do not be afraid of what they say
or be terrified by them, though they are
a rebellious people. 7You must speak my
words to them, whether they listen or fail
to listen, for they are rebellious. 8But you,
son of man, listen to what I say to you. Do
not rebel like that rebellious people; open
your mouth and eat what I give you."
9Then I looked, and I saw a hand
stretched out to me. In it was a scroll,
10which he unrolled before me. On both
sides of it were written words of lament
and mourning and woe.

3 And he said to me, "Son of man, eat
what is before you, eat this scroll; then
go and speak to the people of Israel." 2So
I opened my mouth, and he gave me the
scroll to eat.
3Then he said to me, "Son of man, eat
this scroll I am giving you and fill your
stomach with it." So I ate it, and it tasted
as sweet as honey in my mouth.
4He then said to me: "Son of man, go
now to the people of Israel and speak my
words to them. 5You are not being sent to a
people of obscure speech and strange language, but to the people of Israel — 6not
to many peoples of obscure speech and
strange language, whose words you cannot understand. Surely if I had sent you
to them, they would have listened to you.
7But the people of Israel are not willing to
listen to you because they are not willing
to listen to me, for all the Israelites are
hardened and obstinate. 8But I will make
you as unyielding and hardened as they
are. 9I will make your forehead like the
hardest stone, harder than flint. Do not be
afraid of them or terrified by them, though
they are a rebellious people."
10And he said to me, "Son of man, listen
carefully and take to heart all the words
I speak to you. 11Go now to your people in
exile and speak to them. Say to them, 'This
is what the Sovereign LORD says,' whether
they listen or fail to listen."
12Then the Spirit lifted me up, and I
heard behind me a loud rumbling sound
as the glory of the LORD rose from the
place where it was standing.[a] 13It was the
sound of the wings of the living creatures brushing against each other and
the sound of the wheels beside them, a
loud rumbling sound. 14The Spirit then
lifted me up and took me away, and I
went in bitterness and in the anger of my
spirit, with the strong hand of the LORD
on me. 15I came to the exiles who lived at
Tel Aviv near the Kebar River. And there,
where they were living, I sat among them
for seven days — deeply distressed.

Ezekiel's Task as Watchman

16At the end of seven days the word of
the LORD came to me: 17"Son of man, I have
made you a watchman for the people of
Israel; so hear the word I speak and give
them warning from me. 18When I say to
a wicked person, 'You will surely die,' and
you do not warn them or speak out to dissuade them from their evil ways in order
to save their life, that wicked person will
die for[b] their sin, and I will hold you accountable for their blood. 19But if you do
warn the wicked person and they do not
turn from their wickedness or from their
evil ways, they will die for their sin; but
you will have saved yourself.
20"Again, when a righteous person turns
from their righteousness and does evil,
and I put a stumbling block before them,
they will die. Since you did not warn them,
they will die for their sin. The righteous
things that person did will not be remembered, and I will hold you accountable
for their blood. 21But if you do warn the
righteous person not to sin and they do
not sin, they will surely live because they
took warning, and you will have saved
yourself."
22The hand of the LORD was on me there,
and he said to me, "Get up and go out to
the plain, and there I will speak to you."
23So I got up and went out to the plain.
And the glory of the LORD was standing
there, like the glory I had seen by the Kebar River, and I fell facedown.
24Then the Spirit came into me and
raised me to my feet. He spoke to me
and said: "Go, shut yourself inside your
house. 25And you, son of man, they will
tie with ropes; you will be bound so that
you cannot go out among the people. 26I
will make your tongue stick to the roof
of your mouth so that you will be silent

[a] *12* Probable reading of the original Hebrew text; Masoretic Text *sound — may the glory of the LORD be praised from his place* [b] *18* Or *in*; also in verses 19 and 20

and unable to rebuke them, for they are
a rebellious people. 27But when I speak to
you, I will open your mouth and you shall
say to them, 'This is what the Sovereign
LORD says.' Whoever will listen let them
listen, and whoever will refuse let them
refuse; for they are a rebellious people.

Siege of Jerusalem Symbolized

4 "Now, son of man, take a block of clay,
put it in front of you and draw the
city of Jerusalem on it. 2Then lay siege
to it: Erect siege works against it, build
a ramp up to it, set up camps against it
and put battering rams around it. 3Then
take an iron pan, place it as an iron wall
between you and the city and turn your
face toward it. It will be under siege, and
you shall besiege it. This will be a sign to
the people of Israel.

4"Then lie on your left side and put the
sin of the people of Israel upon yourself.[a]
You are to bear their sin for the number of
days you lie on your side. 5I have assigned
you the same number of days as the years
of their sin. So for 390 days you will bear
the sin of the people of Israel.

6"After you have finished this, lie down
again, this time on your right side, and
bear the sin of the people of Judah. I have
assigned you 40 days, a day for each year.
7Turn your face toward the siege of Jerusalem and with bared arm prophesy
against her. 8I will tie you up with ropes
so that you cannot turn from one side to
the other until you have finished the days
of your siege.

9"Take wheat and barley, beans and
lentils, millet and spelt; put them in a
storage jar and use them to make bread
for yourself. You are to eat it during the
390 days you lie on your side. 10Weigh out
twenty shekels[b] of food to eat each day
and eat it at set times. 11Also measure out
a sixth of a hin[c] of water and drink it at set
times. 12Eat the food as you would a loaf
of barley bread; bake it in the sight of the
people, using human excrement for fuel."
13The LORD said, "In this way the people
of Israel will eat defiled food among the
nations where I will drive them."

14Then I said, "Not so, Sovereign LORD! I
have never defiled myself. From my youth
until now I have never eaten anything
found dead or torn by wild animals. No
impure meat has ever entered my mouth."

15"Very well," he said, "I will let you bake
your bread over cow dung instead of human excrement."

16He then said to me: "Son of man, I
am about to cut off the food supply in
Jerusalem. The people will eat rationed
food in anxiety and drink rationed water
in despair, 17for food and water will be
scarce. They will be appalled at the sight
of each other and will waste away because
of[d] their sin.

God's Razor of Judgment

5 "Now, son of man, take a sharp sword
and use it as a barber's razor to shave
your head and your beard. Then take a set
of scales and divide up the hair. 2When the
days of your siege come to an end, burn
a third of the hair inside the city. Take
a third and strike it with the sword all
around the city. And scatter a third to the
wind. For I will pursue them with drawn
sword. 3But take a few hairs and tuck
them away in the folds of your garment.
4Again, take a few of these and throw them
into the fire and burn them up. A fire will
spread from there to all Israel.

5"This is what the Sovereign LORD says:
This is Jerusalem, which I have set in the
center of the nations, with countries all
around her. 6Yet in her wickedness she
has rebelled against my laws and decrees more than the nations and countries around her. She has rejected my laws
and has not followed my decrees.

7"Therefore this is what the Sovereign
LORD says: You have been more unruly
than the nations around you and have
not followed my decrees or kept my laws.
You have not even[e] conformed to the standards of the nations around you.

8"Therefore this is what the Sovereign
LORD says: I myself am against you, Jerusalem, and I will inflict punishment on
you in the sight of the nations. 9Because
of all your detestable idols, I will do to
you what I have never done before and
will never do again. 10Therefore in your
midst parents will eat their children, and
children will eat their parents. I will inflict
punishment on you and will scatter all
your survivors to the winds. 11Therefore
as surely as I live, declares the Sovereign
LORD, because you have defiled my sanctuary with all your vile images and detestable practices, I myself will shave you;
I will not look on you with pity or spare
you. 12A third of your people will die of the
plague or perish by famine inside you; a
third will fall by the sword outside your
walls; and a third I will scatter to the winds
and pursue with drawn sword.

[a] 4 Or *upon your side* [b] 10 That is, about 8 ounces or about 230 grams [c] 11 That is, about 2/3 quart or about 0.6 liter [d] 17 Or *away in* [e] 7 Most Hebrew manuscripts; some Hebrew manuscripts and Syriac *You have*

13“Then my anger will cease and my wrath against them will subside, and I will be avenged. And when I have spent my wrath on them, they will know that I the LORD have spoken in my zeal.

14“I will make you a ruin and a reproach among the nations around you, in the sight of all who pass by. 15You will be a reproach and a taunt, a warning and an object of horror to the nations around you when I inflict punishment on you in anger and in wrath and with stinging rebuke. I the LORD have spoken. 16When I shoot at you with my deadly and destructive arrows of famine, I will shoot to destroy you. I will bring more and more famine upon you and cut off your supply of food. 17I will send famine and wild beasts against you, and they will leave you childless. Plague and bloodshed will sweep through you, and I will bring the sword against you. I the LORD have spoken.”

Doom for the Mountains of Israel

6 The word of the LORD came to me: 2“Son of man, set your face against the mountains of Israel; prophesy against them 3and say: ‘You mountains of Israel, hear the word of the Sovereign LORD. This is what the Sovereign LORD says to the mountains and hills, to the ravines and valleys: I am about to bring a sword against you, and I will destroy your high places. 4Your altars will be demolished and your incense altars will be smashed; and I will slay your people in front of your idols. 5I will lay the dead bodies of the Israelites in front of their idols, and I will scatter your bones around your altars. 6Wherever you live, the towns will be laid waste and the high places demolished, so that your altars will be laid waste and devastated, your idols smashed and ruined, your incense altars broken down, and what you have made wiped out. 7Your people will fall slain among you, and you will know that I am the LORD.

8“ ‘But I will spare some, for some of you will escape the sword when you are scattered among the lands and nations. 9Then in the nations where they have been carried captive, those who escape will remember me — how I have been grieved by their adulterous hearts, which have turned away from me, and by their eyes, which have lusted after their idols. They will loathe themselves for the evil they have done and for all their detestable practices. 10And they will know that I am the LORD; I did not threaten in vain to bring this calamity on them.

11“ ‘This is what the Sovereign LORD says: Strike your hands together and stamp your feet and cry out “Alas!” because of all the wicked and detestable practices of the people of Israel, for they will fall by the sword, famine and plague. 12One who is far away will die of the plague, and one who is near will fall by the sword, and anyone who survives and is spared will die of famine. So will I pour out my wrath on them. 13And they will know that I am the LORD, when their people lie slain among their idols around their altars, on every high hill and on all the mountaintops, under every spreading tree and every leafy oak — places where they offered fragrant incense to all their idols. 14And I will stretch out my hand against them and make the land a desolate waste from the desert to Diblah[a] — wherever they live. Then they will know that I am the LORD.’ ”

The End Has Come

7 The word of the LORD came to me: 2“Son of man, this is what the Sovereign LORD says to the land of Israel:

“ ‘The end! The end has come
upon the four corners of the land!
3The end is now upon you,
and I will unleash my anger
against you.
I will judge you according to your
conduct
and repay you for all your
detestable practices.
4I will not look on you with pity;
I will not spare you.
I will surely repay you for your
conduct
and for the detestable practices
among you.

“ ‘Then you will know that I am the LORD.’

5“This is what the Sovereign LORD says:

“ ‘Disaster! Unheard-of[b] disaster!
See, it comes!
6The end has come!
The end has come!
It has roused itself against you.
See, it comes!
7Doom has come upon you,
upon you who dwell in the land.
The time has come! The day is near!
There is panic, not joy, on the
mountains.

[a] *14* Most Hebrew manuscripts; a few Hebrew manuscripts *Riblah* [b] *5* Most Hebrew manuscripts; some Hebrew manuscripts and Syriac *Disaster after*

[8] I am about to pour out my wrath
on you
and spend my anger against you.
I will judge you according to your
conduct
and repay you for all your
detestable practices.
[9] I will not look on you with pity;
I will not spare you.
I will repay you for your conduct
and for the detestable practices
among you.

" 'Then you will know that it is I the LORD who strikes you.

[10] " 'See, the day!
See, it comes!
Doom has burst forth,
the rod has budded,
arrogance has blossomed!
[11] Violence has arisen,[a]
a rod to punish the wicked.
None of the people will be left,
none of that crowd —
none of their wealth,
nothing of value.
[12] The time has come!
The day has arrived!
Let not the buyer rejoice
nor the seller grieve,
for my wrath is on the whole crowd.
[13] The seller will not recover
the property that was sold —
as long as both buyer and seller live.
For the vision concerning the whole
crowd
will not be reversed.
Because of their sins, not one of them
will preserve their life.

[14] " 'They have blown the trumpet,
they have made all things ready,
but no one will go into battle,
for my wrath is on the whole crowd.
[15] Outside is the sword;
inside are plague and famine.
Those in the country
will die by the sword;
those in the city
will be devoured by famine and
plague.
[16] The fugitives who escape
will flee to the mountains.
Like doves of the valleys,
they will all moan,
each for their own sins.
[17] Every hand will go limp;
every leg will be wet with urine.
[18] They will put on sackcloth
and be clothed with terror.
Every face will be covered with shame,
and every head will be shaved.
[19] " 'They will throw their silver into the
streets,
and their gold will be treated as a
thing unclean.
Their silver and gold
will not be able to deliver them
in the day of the LORD's wrath.
It will not satisfy their hunger
or fill their stomachs,
for it has caused them to stumble
into sin.
[20] They took pride in their beautiful
jewelry
and used it to make their
detestable idols.
They made it into vile images;
therefore I will make it a thing
unclean for them.
[21] I will give their wealth as plunder to
foreigners
and as loot to the wicked of the
earth,
who will defile it.
[22] I will turn my face away from the
people,
and robbers will desecrate the
place I treasure.
They will enter it
and will defile it.

[23] " 'Prepare chains!
For the land is full of bloodshed,
and the city is full of violence.
[24] I will bring the most wicked of nations
to take possession of their houses.
I will put an end to the pride of the
mighty,
and their sanctuaries will be
desecrated.
[25] When terror comes,
they will seek peace in vain.
[26] Calamity upon calamity will come,
and rumor upon rumor.
They will go searching for a vision
from the prophet,
priestly instruction in the law will
cease,
the counsel of the elders will come
to an end.
[27] The king will mourn,
the prince will be clothed with
despair,
and the hands of the people of the
land will tremble.
I will deal with them according to
their conduct,
and by their own standards I will
judge them.

" 'Then they will know that I am the LORD.' "

[a] 11 Or *The violent one has become*

Idolatry in the Temple

8 In the sixth year, in the sixth month on
the fifth day, while I was sitting in my
house and the elders of Judah were sitting
before me, the hand of the Sovereign LORD
came on me there. 2 I looked, and I saw
a figure like that of a man.[a] From what
appeared to be his waist down he was like
fire, and from there up his appearance was
as bright as glowing metal. 3 He stretched
out what looked like a hand and took me
by the hair of my head. The Spirit lifted
me up between earth and heaven and in
visions of God he took me to Jerusalem,
to the entrance of the north gate of the
inner court, where the idol that provokes
to jealousy stood. 4 And there before me
was the glory of the God of Israel, as in
the vision I had seen in the plain.
5 Then he said to me, "Son of man, look
toward the north." So I looked, and in the
entrance north of the gate of the altar I
saw this idol of jealousy.
6 And he said to me, "Son of man, do
you see what they are doing — the utterly
detestable things the Israelites are doing
here, things that will drive me far from my
sanctuary? But you will see things that are
even more detestable."
7 Then he brought me to the entrance
to the court. I looked, and I saw a hole
in the wall. 8 He said to me, "Son of man,
now dig into the wall." So I dug into the
wall and saw a doorway there.
9 And he said to me, "Go in and see the
wicked and detestable things they are doing here." 10 So I went in and looked, and I
saw portrayed all over the walls all kinds
of crawling things and unclean animals
and all the idols of Israel. 11 In front of them
stood seventy elders of Israel, and Jaazaniah son of Shaphan was standing among
them. Each had a censer in his hand, and
a fragrant cloud of incense was rising.
12 He said to me, "Son of man, have you
seen what the elders of Israel are doing
in the darkness, each at the shrine of his
own idol? They say, 'The LORD does not
see us; the LORD has forsaken the land.' "
13 Again, he said, "You will see them doing
things that are even more detestable."
14 Then he brought me to the entrance
of the north gate of the house of the LORD,
and I saw women sitting there, mourning
the god Tammuz. 15 He said to me, "Do you
see this, son of man? You will see things
that are even more detestable than this."
16 He then brought me into the inner court
of the house of the LORD, and there at the
entrance to the temple, between the portico
and the altar, were about twenty-five men.
With their backs toward the temple of the
LORD and their faces toward the east, they
were bowing down to the sun in the east.
17 He said to me, "Have you seen this, son
of man? Is it a trivial matter for the people
of Judah to do the detestable things they
are doing here? Must they also fill the land
with violence and continually arouse my
anger? Look at them putting the branch
to their nose! 18 Therefore I will deal with
them in anger; I will not look on them
with pity or spare them. Although they
shout in my ears, I will not listen to them."

Judgment on the Idolaters

9 Then I heard him call out in a loud
voice, "Bring near those who are appointed to execute judgment on the city,
each with a weapon in his hand." 2 And I
saw six men coming from the direction of
the upper gate, which faces north, each
with a deadly weapon in his hand. With
them was a man clothed in linen who had
a writing kit at his side. They came in and
stood beside the bronze altar.
3 Now the glory of the God of Israel went
up from above the cherubim, where it had
been, and moved to the threshold of the
temple. Then the LORD called to the man
clothed in linen who had the writing kit at
his side 4 and said to him, "Go throughout
the city of Jerusalem and put a mark on
the foreheads of those who grieve and
lament over all the detestable things that
are done in it."
5 As I listened, he said to the others, "Follow him through the city and kill, without
showing pity or compassion. 6 Slaughter
the old men, the young men and wom-
en, the mothers and children, but do not
touch anyone who has the mark. Begin
at my sanctuary." So they began with the
old men who were in front of the temple.
7 Then he said to them, "Defile the temple
and fill the courts with the slain. Go!" So
they went out and began killing throughout the city. 8 While they were killing and I
was left alone, I fell facedown, crying out,
"Alas, Sovereign LORD! Are you going to
destroy the entire remnant of Israel in this
outpouring of your wrath on Jerusalem?"
9 He answered me, "The sin of the people
of Israel and Judah is exceedingly great;
the land is full of bloodshed and the city
is full of injustice. They say, 'The LORD has
forsaken the land; the LORD does not see.'
10 So I will not look on them with pity or
spare them, but I will bring down on their
own heads what they have done."
11 Then the man in linen with the writing
kit at his side brought back word, saying,
"I have done as you commanded."

[a] 2 Or *saw a fiery figure*

God's Glory Departs From the Temple

10 I looked, and I saw the likeness of a throne of lapis lazuli above the vault that was over the heads of the cherubim. 2 The LORD said to the man clothed in linen, "Go in among the wheels beneath the cherubim. Fill your hands with burning coals from among the cherubim and scatter them over the city." And as I watched, he went in.

3 Now the cherubim were standing on the south side of the temple when the man went in, and a cloud filled the inner court. 4 Then the glory of the LORD rose from above the cherubim and moved to the threshold of the temple. The cloud filled the temple, and the court was full of the radiance of the glory of the LORD. 5 The sound of the wings of the cherubim could be heard as far away as the outer court, like the voice of God Almighty[a] when he speaks.

6 When the LORD commanded the man in linen, "Take fire from among the wheels, from among the cherubim," the man went in and stood beside a wheel. 7 Then one of the cherubim reached out his hand to the fire that was among them. He took up some of it and put it into the hands of the man in linen, who took it and went out. 8 (Under the wings of the cherubim could be seen what looked like human hands.)

9 I looked, and I saw beside the cherubim four wheels, one beside each of the cherubim; the wheels sparkled like topaz. 10 As for their appearance, the four of them looked alike; each was like a wheel intersecting a wheel. 11 As they moved, they would go in any one of the four directions the cherubim faced; the wheels did not turn about[b] as the cherubim went. The cherubim went in whatever direction the head faced, without turning as they went. 12 Their entire bodies, including their backs, their hands and their wings, were completely full of eyes, as were their four wheels. 13 I heard the wheels being called "the whirling wheels." 14 Each of the cherubim had four faces: One face was that of a cherub, the second the face of a human being, the third the face of a lion, and the fourth the face of an eagle.

15 Then the cherubim rose upward. These were the living creatures I had seen by the Kebar River. 16 When the cherubim moved, the wheels beside them moved; and when the cherubim spread their wings to rise from the ground, the wheels did not leave their side. 17 When the cherubim stood still, they also stood still; and when the cherubim rose, they rose with them, because the spirit of the living creatures was in them.

18 Then the glory of the LORD departed from over the threshold of the temple and stopped above the cherubim. 19 While I watched, the cherubim spread their wings and rose from the ground, and as they went, the wheels went with them. They stopped at the entrance of the east gate of the LORD's house, and the glory of the God of Israel was above them.

20 These were the living creatures I had seen beneath the God of Israel by the Kebar River, and I realized that they were cherubim. 21 Each had four faces and four wings, and under their wings was what looked like human hands. 22 Their faces had the same appearance as those I had seen by the Kebar River. Each one went straight ahead.

God's Sure Judgment on Jerusalem

11 Then the Spirit lifted me up and brought me to the gate of the house of the LORD that faces east. There at the entrance of the gate were twenty-five men, and I saw among them Jaazaniah son of Azzur and Pelatiah son of Benaiah, leaders of the people. 2 The LORD said to me, "Son of man, these are the men who are plotting evil and giving wicked advice in this city. 3 They say, 'Haven't our houses been recently rebuilt? This city is a pot, and we are the meat in it.' 4 Therefore prophesy against them; prophesy, son of man."

5 Then the Spirit of the LORD came on me, and he told me to say: "This is what the LORD says: That is what you are saying, you leaders in Israel, but I know what is going through your mind. 6 You have killed many people in this city and filled its streets with the dead.

7 "Therefore this is what the Sovereign LORD says: The bodies you have thrown there are the meat and this city is the pot, but I will drive you out of it. 8 You fear the sword, and the sword is what I will bring against you, declares the Sovereign LORD. 9 I will drive you out of the city and deliver you into the hands of foreigners and inflict punishment on you. 10 You will fall by the sword, and I will execute judgment on you at the borders of Israel. Then you will know that I am the LORD. 11 This city will not be a pot for you, nor will you be the meat in it; I will execute judgment on you at the borders of Israel. 12 And you will know that I am the LORD, for you have not followed my decrees or kept my laws but have conformed to the standards of the nations around you."

13 Now as I was prophesying, Pelatiah son of Benaiah died. Then I fell facedown and cried out in a loud voice, "Alas, Sovereign LORD! Will you completely destroy the remnant of Israel?"

[a] 5 Hebrew *El-Shaddai* [b] 11 Or *aside*

The Promise of Israel's Return

14The word of the LORD came to me: 15"Son of man, the people of Jerusalem have said of your fellow exiles and all the other Israelites, 'They are far away from the LORD; this land was given to us as our possession.'

16"Therefore say: 'This is what the Sovereign LORD says: Although I sent them far away among the nations and scattered them among the countries, yet for a little while I have been a sanctuary for them in the countries where they have gone.'

17"Therefore say: 'This is what the Sovereign LORD says: I will gather you from the nations and bring you back from the countries where you have been scattered, and I will give you back the land of Israel again.'

18"They will return to it and remove all its vile images and detestable idols. 19I will give them an undivided heart and put a new spirit in them; I will remove from them their heart of stone and give them a heart of flesh. 20Then they will follow my decrees and be careful to keep my laws. They will be my people, and I will be their God. 21But as for those whose hearts are devoted to their vile images and detestable idols, I will bring down on their own heads what they have done, declares the Sovereign LORD."

22Then the cherubim, with the wheels beside them, spread their wings, and the glory of the God of Israel was above them. 23The glory of the LORD went up from within the city and stopped above the mountain east of it. 24The Spirit lifted me up and brought me to the exiles in Babylonia[a] in the vision given by the Spirit of God.

Then the vision I had seen went up from me, 25and I told the exiles everything the LORD had shown me.

The Exile Symbolized

12 The word of the LORD came to me: 2"Son of man, you are living among a rebellious people. They have eyes to see but do not see and ears to hear but do not hear, for they are a rebellious people.

3"Therefore, son of man, pack your belongings for exile and in the daytime, as they watch, set out and go from where you are to another place. Perhaps they will understand, though they are a rebellious people. 4During the daytime, while they watch, bring out your belongings packed for exile. Then in the evening, while they are watching, go out like those who go into exile. 5While they watch, dig through the wall and take your belongings out through it. 6Put them on your shoulder as they are watching and carry them out at dusk. Cover your face so that you cannot see the land, for I have made you a sign to the Israelites."

7So I did as I was commanded. During the day I brought out my things packed for exile. Then in the evening I dug through the wall with my hands. I took my belongings out at dusk, carrying them on my shoulders while they watched.

8In the morning the word of the LORD came to me: 9"Son of man, did not the Israelites, that rebellious people, ask you, 'What are you doing?'

10"Say to them, 'This is what the Sovereign LORD says: This prophecy concerns the prince in Jerusalem and all the Israelites who are there.' 11Say to them, 'I am a sign to you.'

"As I have done, so it will be done to them. They will go into exile as captives.

12"The prince among them will put his things on his shoulder at dusk and leave, and a hole will be dug in the wall for him to go through. He will cover his face so that he cannot see the land. 13I will spread my net for him, and he will be caught in my snare; I will bring him to Babylonia, the land of the Chaldeans, but he will not see it, and there he will die. 14I will scatter to the winds all those around him — his staff and all his troops — and I will pursue them with drawn sword.

15"They will know that I am the LORD, when I disperse them among the nations and scatter them through the countries. 16But I will spare a few of them from the sword, famine and plague, so that in the nations where they go they may acknowledge all their detestable practices. Then they will know that I am the LORD."

17The word of the LORD came to me: 18"Son of man, tremble as you eat your food, and shudder in fear as you drink your water. 19Say to the people of the land: 'This is what the Sovereign LORD says about those living in Jerusalem and in the land of Israel: They will eat their food in anxiety and drink their water in despair, for their land will be stripped of everything in it because of the violence of all who live there. 20The inhabited towns will be laid waste and the land will be desolate. Then you will know that I am the LORD.'"

There Will Be No Delay

21The word of the LORD came to me: 22"Son of man, what is this proverb you have in the land of Israel: 'The days go

[a] 24 Or *Chaldea*

by and every vision comes to nothing'?
23Say to them, 'This is what the Sovereign
LORD says: I am going to put an end to this
proverb, and they will no longer quote it
in Israel.' Say to them, 'The days are near
when every vision will be fulfilled. 24For
there will be no more false visions or flattering divinations among the people of
Israel. 25But I the LORD will speak what I
will, and it shall be fulfilled without delay.
For in your days, you rebellious people,
I will fulfill whatever I say, declares the
Sovereign LORD.' "
26The word of the LORD came to me:
27"Son of man, the Israelites are saying,
'The vision he sees is for many years from
now, and he prophesies about the distant
future.'
28"Therefore say to them, 'This is what
the Sovereign LORD says: None of my
words will be delayed any longer; whatever I say will be fulfilled, declares the
Sovereign LORD.' "

False Prophets Condemned

13 The word of the LORD came to me:
2"Son of man, prophesy against the
prophets of Israel who are now prophesying. Say to those who prophesy out of
their own imagination: 'Hear the word
of the LORD! 3This is what the Sovereign
LORD says: Woe to the foolish[a] prophets
who follow their own spirit and have seen
nothing! 4Your prophets, Israel, are like
jackals among ruins. 5You have not gone
up to the breaches in the wall to repair it
for the people of Israel so that it will stand
firm in the battle on the day of the LORD.
6Their visions are false and their divinations a lie. Even though the LORD has not
sent them, they say, "The LORD declares,"
and expect him to fulfill their words. 7Have
you not seen false visions and uttered lying
divinations when you say, "The LORD declares," though I have not spoken?
8" 'Therefore this is what the Sovereign
LORD says: Because of your false words
and lying visions, I am against you, declares the Sovereign LORD. 9My hand will
be against the prophets who see false
visions and utter lying divinations. They
will not belong to the council of my people or be listed in the records of Israel, nor
will they enter the land of Israel. Then you
will know that I am the Sovereign LORD.
10" 'Because they lead my people astray,
saying, "Peace," when there is no peace,
and because, when a flimsy wall is built,
they cover it with whitewash, 11therefore tell
those who cover it with whitewash that it is
going to fall. Rain will come in torrents, and
I will send hailstones hurtling down, and violent winds will burst forth. 12When the wall
collapses, will people not ask you, "Where is
the whitewash you covered it with?"
13" 'Therefore this is what the Sovereign
LORD says: In my wrath I will unleash a
violent wind, and in my anger hailstones
and torrents of rain will fall with destructive fury. 14I will tear down the wall you
have covered with whitewash and will
level it to the ground so that its foundation will be laid bare. When it[b] falls, you
will be destroyed in it; and you will know
that I am the LORD. 15So I will pour out my
wrath against the wall and against those
who covered it with whitewash. I will say
to you, "The wall is gone and so are those
who whitewashed it, 16those prophets of Israel who prophesied to Jerusalem and saw
visions of peace for her when there was
no peace, declares the Sovereign LORD." '
17"Now, son of man, set your face against
the daughters of your people who prophesy out of their own imagination. Prophesy
against them 18and say, 'This is what the
Sovereign LORD says: Woe to the women
who sew magic charms on all their wrists
and make veils of various lengths for their
heads in order to ensnare people. Will you
ensnare the lives of my people but preserve your own? 19You have profaned me
among my people for a few handfuls of
barley and scraps of bread. By lying to my
people, who listen to lies, you have killed
those who should not have died and have
spared those who should not live.
20" 'Therefore this is what the Sovereign
LORD says: I am against your magic charms
with which you ensnare people like birds
and I will tear them from your arms; I will
set free the people that you ensnare like
birds. 21I will tear off your veils and save
my people from your hands, and they will
no longer fall prey to your power. Then you
will know that I am the LORD. 22Because
you disheartened the righteous with your
lies, when I had brought them no grief, and
because you encouraged the wicked not to
turn from their evil ways and so save their
lives, 23therefore you will no longer see false
visions or practice divination. I will save
my people from your hands. And then you
will know that I am the LORD.' "

Idolaters Condemned

14 Some of the elders of Israel came
to me and sat down in front of me.
2Then the word of the LORD came to me:
3"Son of man, these men have set up idols

[a] 3 Or *wicked* [b] 14 Or *the city*

in their hearts and put wicked stumbling
blocks before their faces. Should I let them
inquire of me at all? 4Therefore speak
to them and tell them, 'This is what the
Sovereign LORD says: When any of the
Israelites set up idols in their hearts and
put a wicked stumbling block before their
faces and then go to a prophet, I the LORD
will answer them myself in keeping with
their great idolatry. 5I will do this to re-
capture the hearts of the people of Israel,
who have all deserted me for their idols.'

6"Therefore say to the people of Israel,
'This is what the Sovereign LORD says: Repent! Turn from your idols and renounce
all your detestable practices!

7" 'When any of the Israelites or any
foreigner residing in Israel separate themselves from me and set up idols in their
hearts and put a wicked stumbling block
before their faces and then go to a prophet
to inquire of me, I the LORD will answer
them myself. 8I will set my face against
them and make them an example and
a byword. I will remove them from my
people. Then you will know that I am the
LORD.

9" 'And if the prophet is enticed to utter a prophecy, I the LORD have enticed
that prophet, and I will stretch out my
hand against him and destroy him from
among my people Israel. 10They will bear
their guilt — the prophet will be as guilty
as the one who consults him. 11Then the
people of Israel will no longer stray from
me, nor will they defile themselves anymore with all their sins. They will be my
people, and I will be their God, declares
the Sovereign LORD.' "

Jerusalem's Judgment Inescapable

12The word of the LORD came to me:
13"Son of man, if a country sins against me
by being unfaithful and I stretch out my
hand against it to cut off its food supply
and send famine upon it and kill its people
and their animals, 14even if these three
men — Noah, Daniel[a] and Job — were in
it, they could save only themselves by
their righteousness, declares the Sovereign LORD.

15"Or if I send wild beasts through that
country and they leave it childless and it
becomes desolate so that no one can pass
through it because of the beasts, 16as surely as I live, declares the Sovereign LORD,
even if these three men were in it, they
could not save their own sons or daughters. They alone would be saved, but the
land would be desolate.

17"Or if I bring a sword against that
country and say, 'Let the sword pass
throughout the land,' and I kill its people and their animals, 18as surely as I live,
declares the Sovereign LORD, even if these
three men were in it, they could not save
their own sons or daughters. They alone
would be saved.

19"Or if I send a plague into that land
and pour out my wrath on it through
bloodshed, killing its people and their
animals, 20as surely as I live, declares the
Sovereign LORD, even if Noah, Daniel and
Job were in it, they could save neither son
nor daughter. They would save only themselves by their righteousness.

21"For this is what the Sovereign LORD
says: How much worse will it be when I
send against Jerusalem my four dreadful judgments — sword and famine and
wild beasts and plague — to kill its men
and their animals! 22Yet there will be
some survivors — sons and daughters
who will be brought out of it. They will
come to you, and when you see their
conduct and their actions, you will be
consoled regarding the disaster I have
brought on Jerusalem — every disaster I
have brought on it. 23You will be consoled
when you see their conduct and their actions, for you will know that I have done
nothing in it without cause, declares the
Sovereign LORD."

Jerusalem as a Useless Vine

15 The word of the LORD came to me:
2"Son of man, how is the wood of a
vine different from that of a branch from
any of the trees in the forest? 3Is wood ever
taken from it to make anything useful? Do
they make pegs from it to hang things on?
4And after it is thrown on the fire as fuel
and the fire burns both ends and chars
the middle, is it then useful for anything?
5If it was not useful for anything when it
was whole, how much less can it be made
into something useful when the fire has
burned it and it is charred?

6"Therefore this is what the Sovereign
LORD says: As I have given the wood of
the vine among the trees of the forest as
fuel for the fire, so will I treat the people
living in Jerusalem. 7I will set my face
against them. Although they have come
out of the fire, the fire will yet consume
them. And when I set my face against
them, you will know that I am the LORD.
8I will make the land desolate because
they have been unfaithful, declares the
Sovereign LORD."

[a] 14 Or *Danel*, a man of renown in ancient literature; also in verse 20

Jerusalem as an Adulterous Wife

16 The word of the LORD came to me:
2“Son of man, confront Jerusalem
with her detestable practices 3and say,
‘This is what the Sovereign LORD says to
Jerusalem: Your ancestry and birth were
in the land of the Canaanites; your father
was an Amorite and your mother a Hittite.
4On the day you were born your cord was
not cut, nor were you washed with water
to make you clean, nor were you rubbed
with salt or wrapped in cloths. 5No one
looked on you with pity or had compassion enough to do any of these things for
you. Rather, you were thrown out into the
open field, for on the day you were born
you were despised.

6“ ‘Then I passed by and saw you kicking about in your blood, and as you lay
there in your blood I said to you, “Live!”[a]
7I made you grow like a plant of the field.
You grew and developed and entered pu-
berty. Your breasts had formed and your
hair had grown, yet you were stark naked.

8“ ‘Later I passed by, and when I looked
at you and saw that you were old enough
for love, I spread the corner of my garment
over you and covered your naked body. I
gave you my solemn oath and entered
into a covenant with you, declares the
Sovereign LORD, and you became mine.

9“ ‘I bathed you with water and washed
the blood from you and put ointments on
you. 10I clothed you with an embroidered
dress and put sandals of fine leather on
you. I dressed you in fine linen and covered you with costly garments. 11I adorned
you with jewelry: I put bracelets on your
arms and a necklace around your neck,
12and I put a ring on your nose, earrings
on your ears and a beautiful crown on
your head. 13So you were adorned with
gold and silver; your clothes were of fine
linen and costly fabric and embroidered
cloth. Your food was honey, olive oil and
the finest flour. You became very beautiful
and rose to be a queen. 14And your fame
spread among the nations on account of
your beauty, because the splendor I had
given you made your beauty perfect, declares the Sovereign LORD.

15“ ‘But you trusted in your beauty and
used your fame to become a prostitute.
You lavished your favors on anyone who
passed by and your beauty became his.
16You took some of your garments to make
gaudy high places, where you carried on
your prostitution. You went to him, and
he possessed your beauty.[b] 17You also took
the fine jewelry I gave you, the jewelry
made of my gold and silver, and you made
for yourself male idols and engaged in
prostitution with them. 18And you took
your embroidered clothes to put on them,
and you offered my oil and incense before
them. 19Also the food I provided for you —
the flour, olive oil and honey I gave you
to eat — you offered as fragrant incense
before them. That is what happened, declares the Sovereign LORD.

20“ ‘And you took your sons and daughters whom you bore to me and sacrificed
them as food to the idols. Was your prostitution not enough? 21You slaughtered my
children and sacrificed them to the idols.
22In all your detestable practices and your
prostitution you did not remember the
days of your youth, when you were naked
and bare, kicking about in your blood.

23“ ‘Woe! Woe to you, declares the Sovereign LORD. In addition to all your other wickedness, 24you built a mound for
yourself and made a lofty shrine in every
public square. 25At every street corner you
built your lofty shrines and degraded your
beauty, spreading your legs with increasing promiscuity to anyone who passed
by. 26You engaged in prostitution with
the Egyptians, your neighbors with large
genitals, and aroused my anger with your
increasing promiscuity. 27So I stretched out
my hand against you and reduced your
territory; I gave you over to the greed of
your enemies, the daughters of the Philistines, who were shocked by your lewd
conduct. 28You engaged in prostitution
with the Assyrians too, because you were
insatiable; and even after that, you still
were not satisfied. 29Then you increased
your promiscuity to include Babylonia,[c]
a land of merchants, but even with this
you were not satisfied.

30“ ‘I am filled with fury against you,[d]
declares the Sovereign LORD, when you
do all these things, acting like a brazen
prostitute! 31When you built your mounds
at every street corner and made your lofty
shrines in every public square, you were
unlike a prostitute, because you scorned
payment.

32“ ‘You adulterous wife! You prefer
strangers to your own husband! 33All prostitutes receive gifts, but you give gifts to all
your lovers, bribing them to come to you
from everywhere for your illicit favors. 34So
in your prostitution you are the opposite

[a] 6 A few Hebrew manuscripts, Septuagint and Syriac; most Hebrew manuscripts repeat *and as you lay there in your blood I said to you, “Live!”* [b] 16 The meaning of the Hebrew for this sentence is uncertain. [c] 29 Or *Chaldea* [d] 30 Or *How feverish is your heart,*

of others; no one runs after you for your
favors. You are the very opposite, for you
give payment and none is given to you.
[35]"'Therefore, you prostitute, hear the
word of the LORD! [36]This is what the Sovereign LORD says: Because you poured
out your lust and exposed your naked
body in your promiscuity with your lovers, and because of all your detestable
idols, and because you gave them your
children's blood, [37]therefore I am going
to gather all your lovers, with whom you
found pleasure, those you loved as well
as those you hated. I will gather them
against you from all around and will strip
you in front of them, and they will see
you stark naked. [38]I will sentence you
to the punishment of women who commit adultery and who shed blood; I will
bring on you the blood vengeance of my
wrath and jealous anger. [39]Then I will
deliver you into the hands of your lovers,
and they will tear down your mounds
and destroy your lofty shrines. They will
strip you of your clothes and take your
fine jewelry and leave you stark naked.
[40]They will bring a mob against you, who
will stone you and hack you to pieces with
their swords. [41]They will burn down your
houses and inflict punishment on you
in the sight of many women. I will put a
stop to your prostitution, and you will no
longer pay your lovers. [42]Then my wrath
against you will subside and my jealous
anger will turn away from you; I will be
calm and no longer angry.
[43]"'Because you did not remember the
days of your youth but enraged me with
all these things, I will surely bring down on
your head what you have done, declares
the Sovereign LORD. Did you not add lewdness to all your other detestable practices?
[44]"'Everyone who quotes proverbs will
quote this proverb about you: "Like mother, like daughter." [45]You are a true daughter of your mother, who despised her husband and her children; and you are a true
sister of your sisters, who despised their
husbands and their children. Your mother
was a Hittite and your father an Amorite.
[46]Your older sister was Samaria, who lived
to the north of you with her daughters;
and your younger sister, who lived to the
south of you with her daughters, was Sodom. [47]You not only followed their ways
and copied their detestable practices, but
in all your ways you soon became more
depraved than they. [48]As surely as I live,
declares the Sovereign LORD, your sister
Sodom and her daughters never did what
you and your daughters have done.
[49]"'Now this was the sin of your sister
Sodom: She and her daughters were arrogant, overfed and unconcerned; they
did not help the poor and needy. [50]They
were haughty and did detestable things
before me. Therefore I did away with
them as you have seen. [51]Samaria did
not commit half the sins you did. You
have done more detestable things than
they, and have made your sisters seem
righteous by all these things you have
done. [52]Bear your disgrace, for you have
furnished some justification for your
sisters. Because your sins were more vile
than theirs, they appear more righteous
than you. So then, be ashamed and bear
your disgrace, for you have made your
sisters appear righteous.
[53]"'However, I will restore the fortunes
of Sodom and her daughters and of Samaria and her daughters, and your fortunes along with them, [54]so that you may
bear your disgrace and be ashamed of all
you have done in giving them comfort.
[55]And your sisters, Sodom with her daughters and Samaria with her daughters, will
return to what they were before; and you
and your daughters will return to what
you were before. [56]You would not even
mention your sister Sodom in the day of
your pride, [57]before your wickedness was
uncovered. Even so, you are now scorned
by the daughters of Edom[a] and all her
neighbors and the daughters of the Philistines — all those around you who despise
you. [58]You will bear the consequences of
your lewdness and your detestable practices, declares the LORD.
[59]"'This is what the Sovereign LORD
says: I will deal with you as you deserve,
because you have despised my oath by
breaking the covenant. [60]Yet I will remember the covenant I made with you in the
days of your youth, and I will establish an
everlasting covenant with you. [61]Then you
will remember your ways and be ashamed
when you receive your sisters, both those
who are older than you and those who are
younger. I will give them to you as daughters, but not on the basis of my covenant
with you. [62]So I will establish my covenant
with you, and you will know that I am the
LORD. [63]Then, when I make atonement for
you for all you have done, you will remember and be ashamed and never again open
your mouth because of your humiliation,
declares the Sovereign LORD.'"

[a] 57 Many Hebrew manuscripts and Syriac; most Hebrew manuscripts, Septuagint and Vulgate *Aram*

Two Eagles and a Vine

17 The word of the LORD came to me:
2"Son of man, set forth an allegory
and tell it to the Israelites as a parable.
3Say to them, 'This is what the Sovereign
LORD says: A great eagle with powerful
wings, long feathers and full plumage of
varied colors came to Lebanon. Taking
hold of the top of a cedar, 4he broke off
its topmost shoot and carried it away to
a land of merchants, where he planted it
in a city of traders.

5" 'He took one of the seedlings of the
land and put it in fertile soil. He planted
it like a willow by abundant water, 6and
it sprouted and became a low, spreading
vine. Its branches turned toward him, but
its roots remained under it. So it became
a vine and produced branches and put
out leafy boughs.

7" 'But there was another great eagle
with powerful wings and full plumage.
The vine now sent out its roots toward
him from the plot where it was planted
and stretched out its branches to him for
water. 8It had been planted in good soil
by abundant water so that it would produce branches, bear fruit and become a
splendid vine.'

9"Say to them, 'This is what the Sovereign LORD says: Will it thrive? Will it not
be uprooted and stripped of its fruit so
that it withers? All its new growth will
wither. It will not take a strong arm or
many people to pull it up by the roots. 10It
has been planted, but will it thrive? Will
it not wither completely when the east
wind strikes it — wither away in the plot
where it grew?' "

11Then the word of the LORD came to
me: 12"Say to this rebellious people, 'Do
you not know what these things mean?'
Say to them: 'The king of Babylon went
to Jerusalem and carried off her king and
her nobles, bringing them back with him
to Babylon. 13Then he took a member of
the royal family and made a treaty with
him, putting him under oath. He also carried away the leading men of the land,
14so that the kingdom would be brought
low, unable to rise again, surviving only
by keeping his treaty. 15But the king rebelled against him by sending his envoys
to Egypt to get horses and a large army.
Will he succeed? Will he who does such
things escape? Will he break the treaty
and yet escape?

16" 'As surely as I live, declares the Sovereign LORD, he shall die in Babylon, in
the land of the king who put him on the
throne, whose oath he despised and whose
treaty he broke. 17Pharaoh with his mighty
army and great horde will be of no help
to him in war, when ramps are built and
siege works erected to destroy many lives.
18He despised the oath by breaking the
covenant. Because he had given his hand
in pledge and yet did all these things, he
shall not escape.

19" 'Therefore this is what the Sovereign LORD says: As surely as I live, I will
repay him for despising my oath and
breaking my covenant. 20I will spread
my net for him, and he will be caught
in my snare. I will bring him to Babylon
and execute judgment on him there because he was unfaithful to me. 21All his
choice troops will fall by the sword, and
the survivors will be scattered to the
winds. Then you will know that I the
LORD have spoken.

22" 'This is what the Sovereign LORD
says: I myself will take a shoot from the
very top of a cedar and plant it; I will break
off a tender sprig from its topmost shoots
and plant it on a high and lofty mountain.
23On the mountain heights of Israel I will
plant it; it will produce branches and bear
fruit and become a splendid cedar. Birds
of every kind will nest in it; they will find
shelter in the shade of its branches. 24All
the trees of the forest will know that I the
LORD bring down the tall tree and make
the low tree grow tall. I dry up the green
tree and make the dry tree flourish.

" 'I the LORD have spoken, and I will
do it.' "

The One Who Sins Will Die

18 The word of the LORD came to me:
2"What do you people mean by quot-
ing this proverb about the land of Israel:

" 'The parents eat sour grapes,
and the children's teeth are set on
edge'?

3"As surely as I live, declares the Sovereign LORD, you will no longer quote this
proverb in Israel. 4For everyone belongs to
me, the parent as well as the child — both
alike belong to me. The one who sins is the
one who will die.

5"Suppose there is a righteous man
who does what is just and right.
6He does not eat at the mountain
shrines
or look to the idols of Israel.
He does not defile his neighbor's wife
or have sexual relations with a
woman during her period.
7He does not oppress anyone,
but returns what he took in pledge
for a loan.

He does not commit robbery
but gives his food to the hungry
and provides clothing for the naked.
8 He does not lend to them at interest
or take a profit from them.
He withholds his hand from doing
wrong
and judges fairly between two
parties.
9 He follows my decrees
and faithfully keeps my laws.
That man is righteous;
he will surely live,
declares the Sovereign LORD.

10 "Suppose he has a violent son, who
sheds blood or does any of these other
things[a] 11 (though the father has done none
of them):

"He eats at the mountain shrines.
He defiles his neighbor's wife.
12 He oppresses the poor and needy.
He commits robbery.
He does not return what he took in
pledge.
He looks to the idols.
He does detestable things.
13 He lends at interest and takes a
profit.

Will such a man live? He will not! Because
he has done all these detestable things,
he is to be put to death; his blood will be
on his own head.

14 "But suppose this son has a son who
sees all the sins his father commits, and
though he sees them, he does not do such
things:

15 "He does not eat at the mountain
shrines
or look to the idols of Israel.
He does not defile his neighbor's wife.
16 He does not oppress anyone
or require a pledge for a loan.
He does not commit robbery
but gives his food to the hungry
and provides clothing for the
naked.
17 He withholds his hand from
mistreating the poor
and takes no interest or profit from
them.
He keeps my laws and follows my
decrees.

He will not die for his father's sin; he will
surely live. 18 But his father will die for
his own sin, because he practiced extortion, robbed his brother and did what was
wrong among his people.

19 "Yet you ask, 'Why does the son not
share the guilt of his father?' Since the
son has done what is just and right and
has been careful to keep all my decrees,
he will surely live. 20 The one who sins is
the one who will die. The child will not
share the guilt of the parent, nor will the
parent share the guilt of the child. The
righteousness of the righteous will be
credited to them, and the wickedness of
the wicked will be charged against them.

21 "But if a wicked person turns away
from all the sins they have committed
and keeps all my decrees and does what is
just and right, that person will surely live;
they will not die. 22 None of the offenses
they have committed will be remembered
against them. Because of the righteous
things they have done, they will live. 23 Do I
take any pleasure in the death of the wicked? declares the Sovereign LORD. Rather,
am I not pleased when they turn from
their ways and live?

24 "But if a righteous person turns from
their righteousness and commits sin and
does the same detestable things the wicked person does, will they live? None of the
righteous things that person has done will
be remembered. Because of the unfaithfulness they are guilty of and because
of the sins they have committed, they
will die.

25 "Yet you say, 'The way of the Lord is
not just.' Hear, you Israelites: Is my way
unjust? Is it not your ways that are unjust? 26 If a righteous person turns from
their righteousness and commits sin, they
will die for it; because of the sin they have
committed they will die. 27 But if a wicked
person turns away from the wickedness
they have committed and does what is
just and right, they will save their life.
28 Because they consider all the offenses
they have committed and turn away from
them, that person will surely live; they
will not die. 29 Yet the Israelites say, 'The
way of the Lord is not just.' Are my ways
unjust, people of Israel? Is it not your ways
that are unjust?

30 "Therefore, you Israelites, I will judge
each of you according to your own ways,
declares the Sovereign LORD. Repent! Turn
away from all your offenses; then sin will
not be your downfall. 31 Rid yourselves of
all the offenses you have committed, and
get a new heart and a new spirit. Why will
you die, people of Israel? 32 For I take no
pleasure in the death of anyone, declares
the Sovereign LORD. Repent and live!

[a] 10 Or *things to a brother*

A Lament Over Israel's Princes

19 "Take up a lament concerning the princes of Israel 2and say:

"'What a lioness was your mother
among the lions!
She lay down among them
and reared her cubs.
3 She brought up one of her cubs,
and he became a strong lion.
He learned to tear the prey
and he became a man-eater.
4 The nations heard about him,
and he was trapped in their pit.
They led him with hooks
to the land of Egypt.

5 "'When she saw her hope unfulfilled,
her expectation gone,
she took another of her cubs
and made him a strong lion.
6 He prowled among the lions,
for he was now a strong lion.
He learned to tear the prey
and he became a man-eater.
7 He broke down[a] their strongholds
and devastated their towns.
The land and all who were in it
were terrified by his roaring.
8 Then the nations came against him,
those from regions round about.
They spread their net for him,
and he was trapped in their pit.
9 With hooks they pulled him into a
cage
and brought him to the king of
Babylon.
They put him in prison,
so his roar was heard no longer
on the mountains of Israel.

10 "'Your mother was like a vine in your
vineyard[b]
planted by the water;
it was fruitful and full of branches
because of abundant water.
11 Its branches were strong,
fit for a ruler's scepter.
It towered high
above the thick foliage,
conspicuous for its height
and for its many branches.
12 But it was uprooted in fury
and thrown to the ground.
The east wind made it shrivel,
it was stripped of its fruit;
its strong branches withered
and fire consumed them.
13 Now it is planted in the desert,
in a dry and thirsty land.
14 Fire spread from one of its main[c]
branches
and consumed its fruit.
No strong branch is left on it
fit for a ruler's scepter.'

"This is a lament and is to be used as a lament."

Rebellious Israel Purged

20 In the seventh year, in the fifth
month on the tenth day, some of
the elders of Israel came to inquire of the
LORD, and they sat down in front of me.
2Then the word of the LORD came to
me: 3"Son of man, speak to the elders of
Israel and say to them, 'This is what the
Sovereign LORD says: Have you come to
inquire of me? As surely as I live, I will
not let you inquire of me, declares the
Sovereign LORD.'
4"Will you judge them? Will you judge
them, son of man? Then confront them
with the detestable practices of their ancestors 5and say to them: 'This is what the
Sovereign LORD says: On the day I chose
Israel, I swore with uplifted hand to the
descendants of Jacob and revealed myself to them in Egypt. With uplifted hand
I said to them, "I am the LORD your God."
6On that day I swore to them that I would
bring them out of Egypt into a land I had
searched out for them, a land flowing with
milk and honey, the most beautiful of all
lands. 7And I said to them, "Each of you,
get rid of the vile images you have set your
eyes on, and do not defile yourselves with
the idols of Egypt. I am the LORD your God."
8"'But they rebelled against me and
would not listen to me; they did not get rid
of the vile images they had set their eyes
on, nor did they forsake the idols of Egypt.
So I said I would pour out my wrath on
them and spend my anger against them
in Egypt. 9But for the sake of my name,
I brought them out of Egypt. I did it to
keep my name from being profaned in
the eyes of the nations among whom they
lived and in whose sight I had revealed
myself to the Israelites. 10Therefore I led
them out of Egypt and brought them into
the wilderness. 11I gave them my decrees
and made known to them my laws, by
which the person who obeys them will
live. 12Also I gave them my Sabbaths as a
sign between us, so they would know that
I the LORD made them holy.
13"'Yet the people of Israel rebelled
against me in the wilderness. They did
not follow my decrees but rejected my

[a] *7* Targum (see Septuagint); Hebrew *He knew* [b] *10* Two Hebrew manuscripts; most Hebrew manuscripts *your blood* [c] *14* Or *from under its*

laws — by which the person who obeys
them will live — and they utterly desecrated my Sabbaths. So I said I would pour out
my wrath on them and destroy them in the
wilderness. 14But for the sake of my name
I did what would keep it from being profaned in the eyes of the nations in whose
sight I had brought them out. 15Also with
uplifted hand I swore to them in the wilderness that I would not bring them into
the land I had given them — a land flowing
with milk and honey, the most beautiful
of all lands — 16because they rejected my
laws and did not follow my decrees and
desecrated my Sabbaths. For their hearts
were devoted to their idols. 17Yet I looked
on them with pity and did not destroy them
or put an end to them in the wilderness.
18I said to their children in the wilderness,
"Do not follow the statutes of your parents
or keep their laws or defile yourselves with
their idols. 19I am the LORD your God; follow
my decrees and be careful to keep my laws.
20Keep my Sabbaths holy, that they may
be a sign between us. Then you will know
that I am the LORD your God."

21" 'But the children rebelled against me:
They did not follow my decrees, they were
not careful to keep my laws, of which I said,
"The person who obeys them will live by
them," and they desecrated my Sabbaths.
So I said I would pour out my wrath on
them and spend my anger against them in
the wilderness. 22But I withheld my hand,
and for the sake of my name I did what
would keep it from being profaned in the
eyes of the nations in whose sight I had
brought them out. 23Also with uplifted hand
I swore to them in the wilderness that I
would disperse them among the nations
and scatter them through the countries,
24because they had not obeyed my laws but
had rejected my decrees and desecrated my
Sabbaths, and their eyes lusted after their
parents' idols. 25So I gave them other statutes that were not good and laws through
which they could not live; 26I defiled them
through their gifts — the sacrifice of every
firstborn — that I might fill them with horror so they would know that I am the LORD.'

27"Therefore, son of man, speak to the
people of Israel and say to them, 'This is
what the Sovereign LORD says: In this also
your ancestors blasphemed me by being
unfaithful to me: 28When I brought them
into the land I had sworn to give them and
they saw any high hill or any leafy tree,
there they offered their sacrifices, made
offerings that aroused my anger, presented their fragrant incense and poured out
their drink offerings. 29Then I said to them:
What is this high place you go to?' " (It is
called Bamah[a] to this day.)

Rebellious Israel Renewed

30"Therefore say to the Israelites: 'This
is what the Sovereign LORD says: Will you
defile yourselves the way your ancestors
did and lust after their vile images? 31When
you offer your gifts — the sacrifice of your
children in the fire — you continue to defile
yourselves with all your idols to this day.
Am I to let you inquire of me, you Israelites? As surely as I live, declares the Sovereign LORD, I will not let you inquire of me.

32" 'You say, "We want to be like the nations, like the peoples of the world, who
serve wood and stone." But what you have
in mind will never happen. 33As surely as
I live, declares the Sovereign LORD, I will
reign over you with a mighty hand and
an outstretched arm and with outpoured
wrath. 34I will bring you from the nations
and gather you from the countries where
you have been scattered — with a mighty
hand and an outstretched arm and with
outpoured wrath. 35I will bring you into the
wilderness of the nations and there, face to
face, I will execute judgment upon you. 36As
I judged your ancestors in the wilderness
of the land of Egypt, so I will judge you, declares the Sovereign LORD. 37I will take note
of you as you pass under my rod, and I will
bring you into the bond of the covenant. 38I
will purge you of those who revolt and rebel
against me. Although I will bring them out
of the land where they are living, yet they
will not enter the land of Israel. Then you
will know that I am the LORD.

39" 'As for you, people of Israel, this is
what the Sovereign LORD says: Go and
serve your idols, every one of you! But
afterward you will surely listen to me and
no longer profane my holy name with your
gifts and idols. 40For on my holy mountain,
the high mountain of Israel, declares the
Sovereign LORD, there in the land all the
people of Israel will serve me, and there I
will accept them. There I will require your
offerings and your choice gifts,[b] along
with all your holy sacrifices. 41I will accept
you as fragrant incense when I bring you
out from the nations and gather you from
the countries where you have been scattered, and I will be proved holy through
you in the sight of the nations. 42Then
you will know that I am the LORD, when I
bring you into the land of Israel, the land
I had sworn with uplifted hand to give to
your ancestors. 43There you will remember

[a] 29 *Bamah* means *high place.* [b] 40 Or *and the gifts of your firstfruits*

your conduct and all the actions by which you have defiled yourselves, and you will loathe yourselves for all the evil you have
done. 44You will know that I am the LORD, when I deal with you for my name's sake and not according to your evil ways and your corrupt practices, you people of Israel, declares the Sovereign LORD.'"

Prophecy Against the South

45The word of the LORD came to me:
46"Son of man, set your face toward the south; preach against the south and prophesy against the forest of the southland.
47Say to the southern forest: 'Hear the word of the LORD. This is what the Sovereign LORD says: I am about to set fire to you, and it will consume all your trees, both green and dry. The blazing flame will not be quenched, and every face from south to north will be scorched
by it. 48Everyone will see that I the LORD have kindled it; it will not be quenched.'"
49Then I said, "Sovereign LORD, they are saying of me, 'Isn't he just telling parables?'"[a]

Babylon as God's Sword of Judgment

21 [b] The word of the LORD came to me:
2"Son of man, set your face against Jerusalem and preach against the sanctuary. Prophesy against the land of Israel
3and say to her: 'This is what the LORD says: I am against you. I will draw my sword from its sheath and cut off from you both the righteous and the wicked.
4Because I am going to cut off the righteous and the wicked, my sword will be unsheathed against everyone from south
to north. 5Then all people will know that I the LORD have drawn my sword from its sheath; it will not return again.'
6"Therefore groan, son of man! Groan before them with broken heart and bitter
grief. 7And when they ask you, 'Why are you groaning?' you shall say, 'Because of the news that is coming. Every heart will melt with fear and every hand go limp; every spirit will become faint and every leg will be wet with urine.' It is coming! It will surely take place, declares the Sovereign LORD."
8The word of the LORD came to me:
9"Son of man, prophesy and say, 'This is what the Lord says:

"'A sword, a sword,
sharpened and polished —
10sharpened for the slaughter,
polished to flash like lightning!

"'Shall we rejoice in the scepter of my royal son? The sword despises every such stick.

11"'The sword is appointed to be polished,
to be grasped with the hand;
it is sharpened and polished,
made ready for the hand of the slayer.
12Cry out and wail, son of man,
for it is against my people;
it is against all the princes of Israel.
They are thrown to the sword
along with my people.
Therefore beat your breast.

13"'Testing will surely come. And what if even the scepter, which the sword despises, does not continue? declares the Sovereign LORD.'

14"So then, son of man, prophesy
and strike your hands together.
Let the sword strike twice,
even three times.
It is a sword for slaughter —
a sword for great slaughter,
closing in on them from every side.
15So that hearts may melt with fear
and the fallen be many,
I have stationed the sword for slaughter[c]
at all their gates.
Look! It is forged to strike like lightning,
it is grasped for slaughter.
16Slash to the right, you sword,
then to the left,
wherever your blade is turned.
17I too will strike my hands together,
and my wrath will subside.
I the LORD have spoken."

18The word of the LORD came to me:
19"Son of man, mark out two roads for the sword of the king of Babylon to take, both starting from the same country. Make a signpost where the road branches off
to the city. 20Mark out one road for the sword to come against Rabbah of the Ammonites and another against Judah
and fortified Jerusalem. 21For the king of Babylon will stop at the fork in the road, at the junction of the two roads, to seek an omen: He will cast lots with arrows, he will consult his idols, he will examine
the liver. 22Into his right hand will come the lot for Jerusalem, where he is to set up battering rams, to give the command to slaughter, to sound the battle cry, to

[a] 49 In Hebrew texts 20:45-49 is numbered 21:1-5. [b] In Hebrew texts 21:1-32 is numbered 21:6-37.
[c] 15 Septuagint; the meaning of the Hebrew for this word is uncertain.

set battering rams against the gates, to
build a ramp and to erect siege works.
23 It will seem like a false omen to those
who have sworn allegiance to him, but
he will remind them of their guilt and
take them captive.
24 "Therefore this is what the Sovereign
LORD says: 'Because you people have
brought to mind your guilt by your open
rebellion, revealing your sins in all that
you do — because you have done this, you
will be taken captive.
25 " 'You profane and wicked prince of
Israel, whose day has come, whose time
of punishment has reached its climax,
26 this is what the Sovereign LORD says:
Take off the turban, remove the crown.
It will not be as it was: The lowly will be
exalted and the exalted will be brought
low. 27 A ruin! A ruin! I will make it a ruin!
The crown will not be restored until he to
whom it rightfully belongs shall come; to
him I will give it.'
28 "And you, son of man, prophesy and
say, 'This is what the Sovereign LORD says
about the Ammonites and their insults:

" 'A sword, a sword,
drawn for the slaughter,
polished to consume
and to flash like lightning!
29 Despite false visions concerning you
and lying divinations about you,
it will be laid on the necks
of the wicked who are to be slain,
whose day has come,
whose time of punishment has
reached its climax.

30 " 'Let the sword return to its sheath.
In the place where you were created,
in the land of your ancestry,
I will judge you.
31 I will pour out my wrath on you
and breathe out my fiery anger
against you;
I will deliver you into the hands of
brutal men,
men skilled in destruction.
32 You will be fuel for the fire,
your blood will be shed in your land,
you will be remembered no more;
for I the LORD have spoken.' "

Judgment on Jerusalem's Sins

22 The word of the LORD came to me:
2 "Son of man, will you judge her? Will
you judge this city of bloodshed? Then confront her with all her detestable practices
3 and say: 'This is what the Sovereign LORD
says: You city that brings on herself doom
by shedding blood in her midst and defiles
herself by making idols, 4 you have become
guilty because of the blood you have shed
and have become defiled by the idols you
have made. You have brought your days
to a close, and the end of your years has
come. Therefore I will make you an object
of scorn to the nations and a laughingstock
to all the countries. 5 Those who are near
and those who are far away will mock you,
you infamous city, full of turmoil.
6 " 'See how each of the princes of Israel who are in you uses his power to shed
blood. 7 In you they have treated father
and mother with contempt; in you they
have oppressed the foreigner and mistreated the fatherless and the widow.
8 You have despised my holy things and
desecrated my Sabbaths. 9 In you are slanderers who are bent on shedding blood;
in you are those who eat at the mountain
shrines and commit lewd acts. 10 In you are
those who dishonor their father's bed; in
you are those who violate women during
their period, when they are ceremonially
unclean. 11 In you one man commits a detestable offense with his neighbor's wife,
another shamefully defiles his daughter-
in-law, and another violates his sister, his
own father's daughter. 12 In you are people
who accept bribes to shed blood; you take
interest and make a profit from the poor.
You extort unjust gain from your neighbors. And you have forgotten me, declares
the Sovereign LORD.
13 " 'I will surely strike my hands together
at the unjust gain you have made and at
the blood you have shed in your midst.
14 Will your courage endure or your hands
be strong in the day I deal with you? I
the LORD have spoken, and I will do it.
15 I will disperse you among the nations
and scatter you through the countries;
and I will put an end to your uncleanness.
16 When you have been defiled[a] in the eyes
of the nations, you will know that I am
the LORD.' "
17 Then the word of the LORD came to
me: 18 "Son of man, the people of Israel
have become dross to me; all of them are
the copper, tin, iron and lead left inside a
furnace. They are but the dross of silver.
19 Therefore this is what the Sovereign
LORD says: 'Because you have all become
dross, I will gather you into Jerusalem.
20 As silver, copper, iron, lead and tin are
gathered into a furnace to be melted with
a fiery blast, so will I gather you in my anger and my wrath and put you inside the

[a] 16 Or *When I have allotted you your inheritance*

city and melt you. 21 I will gather you and I will blow on you with my fiery wrath, and you will be melted inside her. 22 As silver is melted in a furnace, so you will be melted inside her, and you will know that I the LORD have poured out my wrath on you.'"

23 Again the word of the LORD came to me: 24 "Son of man, say to the land, 'You are a land that has not been cleansed or rained on in the day of wrath.' 25 There is a conspiracy of her princes[a] within her like a roaring lion tearing its prey; they devour people, take treasures and precious things and make many widows within her. 26 Her priests do violence to my law and profane my holy things; they do not distinguish between the holy and the common; they teach that there is no difference between the unclean and the clean; and they shut their eyes to the keeping of my Sabbaths, so that I am profaned among them. 27 Her officials within her are like wolves tearing their prey; they shed blood and kill people to make unjust gain. 28 Her prophets whitewash these deeds for them by false visions and lying divinations. They say, 'This is what the Sovereign LORD says' — when the LORD has not spoken. 29 The people of the land practice extortion and commit robbery; they oppress the poor and needy and mistreat the foreigner, denying them justice.

30 "I looked for someone among them who would build up the wall and stand before me in the gap on behalf of the land so I would not have to destroy it, but I found no one. 31 So I will pour out my wrath on them and consume them with my fiery anger, bringing down on their own heads all they have done, declares the Sovereign LORD."

Two Adulterous Sisters

23 The word of the LORD came to me: 2 "Son of man, there were two women, daughters of the same mother. 3 They became prostitutes in Egypt, engaging in prostitution from their youth. In that land their breasts were fondled and their virgin bosoms caressed. 4 The older was named Oholah, and her sister was Oholibah. They were mine and gave birth to sons and daughters. Oholah is Samaria, and Oholibah is Jerusalem.

5 "Oholah engaged in prostitution while she was still mine; and she lusted after her lovers, the Assyrians — warriors 6 clothed in blue, governors and commanders, all of them handsome young men, and mounted horsemen. 7 She gave herself as a prostitute to all the elite of the Assyrians and defiled herself with all the idols of everyone she lusted after. 8 She did not give up the prostitution she began in Egypt, when during her youth men slept with her, caressed her virgin bosom and poured out their lust on her.

9 "Therefore I delivered her into the hands of her lovers, the Assyrians, for whom she lusted. 10 They stripped her naked, took away her sons and daughters and killed her with the sword. She became a byword among women, and punishment was inflicted on her.

11 "Her sister Oholibah saw this, yet in her lust and prostitution she was more depraved than her sister. 12 She too lusted after the Assyrians — governors and commanders, warriors in full dress, mounted horsemen, all handsome young men. 13 I saw that she too defiled herself; both of them went the same way.

14 "But she carried her prostitution still further. She saw men portrayed on a wall, figures of Chaldeans[b] portrayed in red, 15 with belts around their waists and flowing turbans on their heads; all of them looked like Babylonian chariot officers, natives of Chaldea.[c] 16 As soon as she saw them, she lusted after them and sent messengers to them in Chaldea. 17 Then the Babylonians came to her, to the bed of love, and in their lust they defiled her. After she had been defiled by them, she turned away from them in disgust. 18 When she carried on her prostitution openly and exposed her naked body, I turned away from her in disgust, just as I had turned away from her sister. 19 Yet she became more and more promiscuous as she recalled the days of her youth, when she was a prostitute in Egypt. 20 There she lusted after her lovers, whose genitals were like those of donkeys and whose emission was like that of horses. 21 So you longed for the lewdness of your youth, when in Egypt your bosom was caressed and your young breasts fondled.[d]

22 "Therefore, Oholibah, this is what the Sovereign LORD says: I will stir up your lovers against you, those you turned away from in disgust, and I will bring them against you from every side — 23 the Babylonians and all the Chaldeans, the men of Pekod and Shoa and Koa, and all the Assyrians with them, handsome young men, all of them governors and commanders, chariot officers and men of high rank,

[a] *25* Septuagint; Hebrew *prophets* [b] *14* Or *Babylonians* [c] *15* Or *Babylonia*; also in verse 16
[d] *21* Syriac (see also verse 3); Hebrew *caressed because of your young breasts*

all mounted on horses. 24They will come
against you with weapons,[a] chariots and
wagons and with a throng of people; they
will take up positions against you on every side with large and small shields and
with helmets. I will turn you over to them
for punishment, and they will punish you
according to their standards. 25I will direct
my jealous anger against you, and they
will deal with you in fury. They will cut off
your noses and your ears, and those of you
who are left will fall by the sword. They
will take away your sons and daughters,
and those of you who are left will be consumed by fire. 26They will also strip you
of your clothes and take your fine jewelry.
27So I will put a stop to the lewdness and
prostitution you began in Egypt. You will
not look on these things with longing or
remember Egypt anymore.

28"For this is what the Sovereign LORD
says: I am about to deliver you into the
hands of those you hate, to those you
turned away from in disgust. 29They will
deal with you in hatred and take away
everything you have worked for. They will
leave you stark naked, and the shame of
your prostitution will be exposed. Your
lewdness and promiscuity 30have brought
this on you, because you lusted after the
nations and defiled yourself with their
idols. 31You have gone the way of your
sister; so I will put her cup into your hand.

32"This is what the Sovereign LORD says:

"You will drink your sister's cup,
a cup large and deep;
it will bring scorn and derision,
for it holds so much.
33 You will be filled with drunkenness
and sorrow,
the cup of ruin and desolation,
the cup of your sister Samaria.
34 You will drink it and drain it dry
and chew on its pieces —
and you will tear your breasts.

I have spoken, declares the Sovereign
LORD.

35"Therefore this is what the Sovereign
LORD says: Since you have forgotten me
and turned your back on me, you must
bear the consequences of your lewdness
and prostitution."

36The LORD said to me: "Son of man, will
you judge Oholah and Oholibah? Then
confront them with their detestable practices, 37for they have committed adultery
and blood is on their hands. They committed adultery with their idols; they even
sacrificed their children, whom they bore
to me, as food for them. 38They have also
done this to me: At that same time they
defiled my sanctuary and desecrated my
Sabbaths. 39On the very day they sacrificed
their children to their idols, they entered
my sanctuary and desecrated it. That is
what they did in my house.

40"They even sent messengers for men
who came from far away, and when they arrived you bathed yourself for them, applied
eye makeup and put on your jewelry. 41You
sat on an elegant couch, with a table spread
before it on which you had placed the incense and olive oil that belonged to me.

42"The noise of a carefree crowd was
around her; drunkards were brought from
the desert along with men from the rabble, and they put bracelets on the wrists
of the woman and her sister and beautiful
crowns on their heads. 43Then I said about
the one worn out by adultery, 'Now let
them use her as a prostitute, for that is all
she is.' 44And they slept with her. As men
sleep with a prostitute, so they slept with
those lewd women, Oholah and Oholibah.
45But righteous judges will sentence them
to the punishment of women who commit
adultery and shed blood, because they are
adulterous and blood is on their hands.

46"This is what the Sovereign LORD says:
Bring a mob against them and give them
over to terror and plunder. 47The mob will
stone them and cut them down with their
swords; they will kill their sons and daughters and burn down their houses.

48"So I will put an end to lewdness in the
land, that all women may take warning
and not imitate you. 49You will suffer the
penalty for your lewdness and bear the consequences of your sins of idolatry. Then you
will know that I am the Sovereign LORD."

Jerusalem as a Cooking Pot

24 In the ninth year, in the tenth
month on the tenth day, the word
of the LORD came to me: 2"Son of man,
record this date, this very date, because
the king of Babylon has laid siege to Jerusalem this very day. 3Tell this rebellious
people a parable and say to them: 'This is
what the Sovereign LORD says:

" 'Put on the cooking pot; put it on
and pour water into it.
4 Put into it the pieces of meat,
all the choice pieces — the leg and
the shoulder.
Fill it with the best of these bones;
5 take the pick of the flock.
Pile wood beneath it for the bones;
bring it to a boil
and cook the bones in it.

[a] 24 The meaning of the Hebrew for this word is uncertain.

6"'For this is what the Sovereign LORD
says:

"'Woe to the city of bloodshed,
to the pot now encrusted,
whose deposit will not go away!
Take the meat out piece by piece
in whatever order it comes.

7"'For the blood she shed is in her midst:
She poured it on the bare rock;
she did not pour it on the ground,
where the dust would cover it.
8To stir up wrath and take revenge
I put her blood on the bare rock,
so that it would not be covered.

9"'Therefore this is what the Sovereign
LORD says:

"'Woe to the city of bloodshed!
I, too, will pile the wood high.
10So heap on the wood
and kindle the fire.
Cook the meat well,
mixing in the spices;
and let the bones be charred.
11Then set the empty pot on the coals
till it becomes hot and its copper
glows,
so that its impurities may be melted
and its deposit burned away.
12It has frustrated all efforts;
its heavy deposit has not been
removed,
not even by fire.

13"'Now your impurity is lewdness. Because I tried to cleanse you but you would
not be cleansed from your impurity, you
will not be clean again until my wrath
against you has subsided.

14"'I the LORD have spoken. The time has
come for me to act. I will not hold back; I
will not have pity, nor will I relent. You will
be judged according to your conduct and
your actions, declares the Sovereign LORD.'"

Ezekiel's Wife Dies

15The word of the LORD came to me:
16"Son of man, with one blow I am about
to take away from you the delight of your
eyes. Yet do not lament or weep or shed
any tears. 17Groan quietly; do not mourn
for the dead. Keep your turban fastened
and your sandals on your feet; do not
cover your mustache and beard or eat the
customary food of mourners."
18So I spoke to the people in the morning, and in the evening my wife died. The
next morning I did as I had been commanded.
19Then the people asked me, "Won't you
tell us what these things have to do with
us? Why are you acting like this?"
20So I said to them, "The word of the
LORD came to me: 21Say to the people of
Israel, 'This is what the Sovereign LORD
says: I am about to desecrate my sanctuary — the stronghold in which you take
pride, the delight of your eyes, the object
of your affection. The sons and daughters
you left behind will fall by the sword. 22And
you will do as I have done. You will not
cover your mustache and beard or eat the
customary food of mourners. 23You will
keep your turbans on your heads and your
sandals on your feet. You will not mourn or
weep but will waste away because of[a] your
sins and groan among yourselves. 24Ezek-
iel will be a sign to you; you will do just
as he has done. When this happens, you
will know that I am the Sovereign LORD.'
25"And you, son of man, on the day I
take away their stronghold, their joy and
glory, the delight of their eyes, their heart's
desire, and their sons and daughters as
well — 26on that day a fugitive will come
to tell you the news. 27At that time your
mouth will be opened; you will speak with
him and will no longer be silent. So you
will be a sign to them, and they will know
that I am the LORD."

A Prophecy Against Ammon

25 The word of the LORD came to me:
2"Son of man, set your face against
the Ammonites and prophesy against
them. 3Say to them, 'Hear the word of the
Sovereign LORD. This is what the Sovereign
LORD says: Because you said "Aha!" over
my sanctuary when it was desecrated
and over the land of Israel when it was
laid waste and over the people of Judah
when they went into exile, 4therefore I
am going to give you to the people of the
East as a possession. They will set up their
camps and pitch their tents among you;
they will eat your fruit and drink your
milk. 5I will turn Rabbah into a pasture for
camels and Ammon into a resting place
for sheep. Then you will know that I am
the LORD. 6For this is what the Sovereign
LORD says: Because you have clapped your
hands and stamped your feet, rejoicing
with all the malice of your heart against
the land of Israel, 7therefore I will stretch
out my hand against you and give you as
plunder to the nations. I will wipe you out
from among the nations and exterminate
you from the countries. I will destroy you,
and you will know that I am the LORD.'"

[a] 23 Or *away in*

A Prophecy Against Moab

8 "This is what the Sovereign LORD says: 'Because Moab and Seir said, "Look, Judah has become like all the other nations," 9 therefore I will expose the flank of Moab, beginning at its frontier towns — Beth Jeshimoth, Baal Meon and Kiriathaim — the glory of that land. 10 I will give Moab along with the Ammonites to the people of the East as a possession, so that the Ammonites will not be remembered among the nations; 11 and I will inflict punishment on Moab. Then they will know that I am the LORD.' "

A Prophecy Against Edom

12 "This is what the Sovereign LORD says: 'Because Edom took revenge on Judah and became very guilty by doing so, 13 therefore this is what the Sovereign LORD says: I will stretch out my hand against Edom and kill both man and beast. I will lay it waste, and from Teman to Dedan they will fall by the sword. 14 I will take vengeance on Edom by the hand of my people Israel, and they will deal with Edom in accordance with my anger and my wrath; they will know my vengeance, declares the Sovereign LORD.' "

A Prophecy Against Philistia

15 "This is what the Sovereign LORD says: 'Because the Philistines acted in vengeance and took revenge with malice in their hearts, and with ancient hostility sought to destroy Judah, 16 therefore this is what the Sovereign LORD says: I am about to stretch out my hand against the Philistines, and I will wipe out the Kerethites and destroy those remaining along the coast. 17 I will carry out great vengeance on them and punish them in my wrath. Then they will know that I am the LORD, when I take vengeance on them.' "

A Prophecy Against Tyre

26 In the eleventh month of the twelfth[a] year, on the first day of the month, the word of the LORD came to me: 2 "Son of man, because Tyre has said of Jerusalem, 'Aha! The gate to the nations is broken, and its doors have swung open to me; now that she lies in ruins I will prosper,' 3 therefore this is what the Sovereign LORD says: I am against you, Tyre, and I will bring many nations against you, like the sea casting up its waves. 4 They will destroy the walls of Tyre and pull down her towers; I will scrape away her rubble and make her a bare rock. 5 Out in the sea she will become a place to spread fishnets, for I have spoken, declares the Sovereign LORD. She will become plunder for the nations, 6 and her settlements on the mainland will be ravaged by the sword. Then they will know that I am the LORD.

7 "For this is what the Sovereign LORD says: From the north I am going to bring against Tyre Nebuchadnezzar[b] king of Babylon, king of kings, with horses and chariots, with horsemen and a great army. 8 He will ravage your settlements on the mainland with the sword; he will set up siege works against you, build a ramp up to your walls and raise his shields against you. 9 He will direct the blows of his battering rams against your walls and demolish your towers with his weapons. 10 His horses will be so many that they will cover you with dust. Your walls will tremble at the noise of the warhorses, wagons and chariots when he enters your gates as men enter a city whose walls have been broken through. 11 The hooves of his horses will trample all your streets; he will kill your people with the sword, and your strong pillars will fall to the ground. 12 They will plunder your wealth and loot your merchandise; they will break down your walls and demolish your fine houses and throw your stones, timber and rubble into the sea. 13 I will put an end to your noisy songs, and the music of your harps will be heard no more. 14 I will make you a bare rock, and you will become a place to spread fishnets. You will never be rebuilt, for I the LORD have spoken, declares the Sovereign LORD.

15 "This is what the Sovereign LORD says to Tyre: Will not the coastlands tremble at the sound of your fall, when the wounded groan and the slaughter takes place in you? 16 Then all the princes of the coast will step down from their thrones and lay aside their robes and take off their embroidered garments. Clothed with terror, they will sit on the ground, trembling every moment, appalled at you. 17 Then they will take up a lament concerning you and say to you:

" 'How you are destroyed, city of
  renown,
 peopled by men of the sea!
You were a power on the seas,
 you and your citizens;
you put your terror
 on all who lived there.

[a] *1* Probable reading of the original Hebrew text; Masoretic Text does not have *month of the twelfth.* [b] *7* Hebrew *Nebuchadrezzar,* of which *Nebuchadnezzar* is a variant; here and often in Ezekiel and Jeremiah

18 Now the coastlands tremble
on the day of your fall;
the islands in the sea
are terrified at your collapse.'

19"This is what the Sovereign LORD says:
When I make you a desolate city, like cities
no longer inhabited, and when I bring the
ocean depths over you and its vast waters
cover you, 20then I will bring you down
with those who go down to the pit, to the
people of long ago. I will make you dwell
in the earth below, as in ancient ruins,
with those who go down to the pit, and
you will not return or take your place[a] in
the land of the living. 21I will bring you to a
horrible end and you will be no more. You
will be sought, but you will never again
be found, declares the Sovereign LORD."

A Lament Over Tyre

27 The word of the LORD came to me:
2"Son of man, take up a lament concerning Tyre. 3Say to Tyre, situated at the
gateway to the sea, merchant of peoples
on many coasts, 'This is what the Sovereign LORD says:

" 'You say, Tyre,
"I am perfect in beauty."
4 Your domain was on the high seas;
your builders brought your beauty
to perfection.
5 They made all your timbers
of juniper from Senir[b];
they took a cedar from Lebanon
to make a mast for you.
6 Of oaks from Bashan
they made your oars;
of cypress wood[c] from the coasts of
Cyprus
they made your deck, adorned with
ivory.
7 Fine embroidered linen from Egypt
was your sail
and served as your banner;
your awnings were of blue and purple
from the coasts of Elishah.
8 Men of Sidon and Arvad were your
oarsmen;
your skilled men, Tyre, were
aboard as your sailors.
9 Veteran craftsmen of Byblos were on
board
as shipwrights to caulk your seams.
All the ships of the sea and their
sailors
came alongside to trade for your
wares.
10 " 'Men of Persia, Lydia and Put
served as soldiers in your army.
They hung their shields and helmets
on your walls,
bringing you splendor.
11 Men of Arvad and Helek
guarded your walls on every side;
men of Gammad
were in your towers.
They hung their shields around your
walls;
they brought your beauty to
perfection.

12" 'Tarshish did business with you because of your great wealth of goods; they
exchanged silver, iron, tin and lead for
your merchandise.
13" 'Greece, Tubal and Meshek did business with you; they traded human beings
and articles of bronze for your wares.
14" 'Men of Beth Togarmah exchanged
chariot horses, cavalry horses and mules
for your merchandise.
15" 'The men of Rhodes[d] traded with
you, and many coastlands were your customers; they paid you with ivory tusks
and ebony.
16" 'Aram[e] did business with you because
of your many products; they exchanged
turquoise, purple fabric, embroidered
work, fine linen, coral and rubies for your
merchandise.
17" 'Judah and Israel traded with you;
they exchanged wheat from Minnith and
confections,[f] honey, olive oil and balm for
your wares.
18" 'Damascus did business with you
because of your many products and great
wealth of goods. They offered wine from
Helbon, wool from Zahar 19and casks of
wine from Izal in exchange for your wares:
wrought iron, cassia and calamus.
20" 'Dedan traded in saddle blankets
with you.
21" 'Arabia and all the princes of Kedar
were your customers; they did business
with you in lambs, rams and goats.
22" 'The merchants of Sheba and Raamah traded with you; for your merchandise they exchanged the finest of all kinds
of spices and precious stones, and gold.
23" 'Harran, Kanneh and Eden and merchants of Sheba, Ashur and Kilmad traded with you. 24In your marketplace they
traded with you beautiful garments, blue
fabric, embroidered work and multicol-
ored rugs with cords twisted and tightly
knotted.

[a] *20* Septuagint; Hebrew *return, and I will give glory* [b] *5* That is, Mount Hermon
[c] *6* Targum; the Masoretic Text has a different division of the consonants. [d] *15* Septuagint; Hebrew *Dedan* [e] *16* Most Hebrew manuscripts; some Hebrew manuscripts and Syriac *Edom*
[f] *17* The meaning of the Hebrew for this word is uncertain.

25 “ ‘The ships of Tarshish serve
as carriers for your wares.
You are filled with heavy cargo
as you sail the sea.
26 Your oarsmen take you
out to the high seas.
But the east wind will break you to
pieces
far out at sea.
27 Your wealth, merchandise and
wares,
your mariners, sailors and
shipwrights,
your merchants and all your
soldiers,
and everyone else on board
will sink into the heart of the sea
on the day of your shipwreck.
28 The shorelands will quake
when your sailors cry out.
29 All who handle the oars
will abandon their ships;
the mariners and all the sailors
will stand on the shore.
30 They will raise their voice
and cry bitterly over you;
they will sprinkle dust on their heads
and roll in ashes.
31 They will shave their heads because
of you
and will put on sackcloth.
They will weep over you with anguish
of soul
and with bitter mourning.
32 As they wail and mourn over you,
they will take up a lament
concerning you:
“Who was ever silenced like Tyre,
surrounded by the sea?”
33 When your merchandise went out on
the seas,
you satisfied many nations;
with your great wealth and your
wares
you enriched the kings of
the earth.
34 Now you are shattered by the sea
in the depths of the waters;
your wares and all your company
have gone down with you.
35 All who live in the coastlands
are appalled at you;
their kings shudder with horror
and their faces are distorted with
fear.
36 The merchants among the nations
scoff at you;
you have come to a horrible end
and will be no more.’ ”

A Prophecy Against the King of Tyre

28 The word of the LORD came to me:
2 “Son of man, say to the ruler of
Tyre, ‘This is what the Sovereign LORD
says:

“ ‘In the pride of your heart
you say, “I am a god;
I sit on the throne of a god
in the heart of the seas.”
But you are a mere mortal and not
a god,
though you think you are as wise
as a god.
3 Are you wiser than Daniel[a]?
Is no secret hidden from you?
4 By your wisdom and understanding
you have gained wealth for
yourself
and amassed gold and silver
in your treasuries.
5 By your great skill in trading
you have increased your wealth,
and because of your wealth
your heart has grown proud.

6 “ ‘Therefore this is what the Sovereign
LORD says:

“ ‘Because you think you are wise,
as wise as a god,
7 I am going to bring foreigners
against you,
the most ruthless of nations;
they will draw their swords against
your beauty and wisdom
and pierce your shining splendor.
8 They will bring you down to the pit,
and you will die a violent death
in the heart of the seas.
9 Will you then say, “I am a god,”
in the presence of those who kill
you?
You will be but a mortal, not a god,
in the hands of those who slay you.
10 You will die the death of the
uncircumcised
at the hands of foreigners.

I have spoken, declares the Sovereign
LORD.’ ”

11 The word of the LORD came to me:
12 “Son of man, take up a lament concerning the king of Tyre and say to him: ‘This
is what the Sovereign LORD says:

“ ‘You were the seal of perfection,
full of wisdom and perfect in
beauty.
13 You were in Eden,
the garden of God;

[a] 3 Or *Danel*, a man of renown in ancient literature

every precious stone adorned you:
carnelian, chrysolite and emerald,
topaz, onyx and jasper,
lapis lazuli, turquoise and beryl.[a]
Your settings and mountings[b] were made of gold;
on the day you were created they were prepared.
14 You were anointed as a guardian cherub,
for so I ordained you.
You were on the holy mount of God;
you walked among the fiery stones.
15 You were blameless in your ways
from the day you were created
till wickedness was found in you.
16 Through your widespread trade
you were filled with violence,
and you sinned.
So I drove you in disgrace from the mount of God,
and I expelled you, guardian cherub,
from among the fiery stones.
17 Your heart became proud
on account of your beauty,
and you corrupted your wisdom
because of your splendor.
So I threw you to the earth;
I made a spectacle of you before kings.
18 By your many sins and dishonest trade
you have desecrated your sanctuaries.
So I made a fire come out from you,
and it consumed you,
and I reduced you to ashes on the ground
in the sight of all who were watching.
19 All the nations who knew you
are appalled at you;
you have come to a horrible end
and will be no more.' "

A Prophecy Against Sidon

20 The word of the LORD came to me:
21 "Son of man, set your face against Sidon;
prophesy against her 22 and say: 'This is
what the Sovereign LORD says:

" 'I am against you, Sidon,
and among you I will display my glory.
You will know that I am the LORD,
when I inflict punishment on you
and within you am proved to be holy.
23 I will send a plague upon you
and make blood flow in your streets.
The slain will fall within you,
with the sword against you on every side.
Then you will know that I am the LORD.

24 " 'No longer will the people of Israel
have malicious neighbors who are painful briers and sharp thorns. Then they
will know that I am the Sovereign LORD.
25 " 'This is what the Sovereign LORD says:
When I gather the people of Israel from
the nations where they have been scattered, I will be proved holy through them
in the sight of the nations. Then they will
live in their own land, which I gave to
my servant Jacob. 26 They will live there
in safety and will build houses and plant
vineyards; they will live in safety when I
inflict punishment on all their neighbors
who maligned them. Then they will know
that I am the LORD their God.' "

A Prophecy Against Egypt

Judgment on Pharaoh

29 In the tenth year, in the tenth
month on the twelfth day, the word
of the LORD came to me: 2 "Son of man, set
your face against Pharaoh king of Egypt
and prophesy against him and against
all Egypt. 3 Speak to him and say: 'This is
what the Sovereign LORD says:

" 'I am against you, Pharaoh king of Egypt,
you great monster lying among your streams.
You say, "The Nile belongs to me;
I made it for myself."
4 But I will put hooks in your jaws
and make the fish of your streams stick to your scales.
I will pull you out from among your streams,
with all the fish sticking to your scales.
5 I will leave you in the desert,
you and all the fish of your streams.
You will fall on the open field
and not be gathered or picked up.
I will give you as food
to the beasts of the earth and the birds of the sky.

6 Then all who live in Egypt will know that
I am the LORD.

[a] *13* The precise identification of some of these precious stones is uncertain. [b] *13* The meaning of the Hebrew for this phrase is uncertain.

"'You have been a staff of reed for the
people of Israel. 7When they grasped you
with their hands, you splintered and you
tore open their shoulders; when they
leaned on you, you broke and their backs
were wrenched.[a]

8"'Therefore this is what the Sovereign
LORD says: I will bring a sword against you
and kill both man and beast. 9Egypt will
become a desolate wasteland. Then they
will know that I am the LORD.

"'Because you said, "The Nile is mine;
I made it," 10therefore I am against you
and against your streams, and I will make
the land of Egypt a ruin and a desolate
waste from Migdol to Aswan, as far as the
border of Cush.[b] 11The foot of neither man
nor beast will pass through it; no one will
live there for forty years. 12I will make the
land of Egypt desolate among devastated
lands, and her cities will lie desolate forty
years among ruined cities. And I will disperse the Egyptians among the nations
and scatter them through the countries.

13"'Yet this is what the Sovereign LORD
says: At the end of forty years I will gather the Egyptians from the nations where
they were scattered. 14I will bring them
back from captivity and return them to
Upper Egypt, the land of their ancestry.
There they will be a lowly kingdom. 15It
will be the lowliest of kingdoms and will
never again exalt itself above the other
nations. I will make it so weak that it will
never again rule over the nations. 16Egypt
will no longer be a source of confidence
for the people of Israel but will be a reminder of their sin in turning to her for
help. Then they will know that I am the
Sovereign LORD.'"

Nebuchadnezzar's Reward

17In the twenty-seventh year, in the first
month on the first day, the word of the
LORD came to me: 18"Son of man, Nebuchadnezzar king of Babylon drove his
army in a hard campaign against Tyre;
every head was rubbed bare and every
shoulder made raw. Yet he and his army
got no reward from the campaign he led
against Tyre. 19Therefore this is what the
Sovereign LORD says: I am going to give
Egypt to Nebuchadnezzar king of Babylon,
and he will carry off its wealth. He will loot
and plunder the land as pay for his army.
20I have given him Egypt as a reward for
his efforts because he and his army did
it for me, declares the Sovereign LORD.

21"On that day I will make a horn[c] grow
for the Israelites, and I will open your
mouth among them. Then they will know
that I am the LORD."

A Lament Over Egypt

30 The word of the LORD came to me:
2"Son of man, prophesy and say:
'This is what the Sovereign LORD says:

"'Wail and say,
"Alas for that day!"
3For the day is near,
the day of the LORD is near —
a day of clouds,
a time of doom for the nations.
4A sword will come against Egypt,
and anguish will come upon Cush.[d]
When the slain fall in Egypt,
her wealth will be carried away
and her foundations torn down.

5Cush and Libya, Lydia and all Arabia,
Kub and the people of the covenant land
will fall by the sword along with Egypt.

6"'This is what the LORD says:

"'The allies of Egypt will fall
and her proud strength will fail.
From Migdol to Aswan
they will fall by the sword within
her,
declares the Sovereign LORD.
7"'They will be desolate
among desolate lands,
and their cities will lie
among ruined cities.
8Then they will know that I am the
LORD,
when I set fire to Egypt
and all her helpers are crushed.

9"'On that day messengers will go out
from me in ships to frighten Cush out of
her complacency. Anguish will take hold
of them on the day of Egypt's doom, for
it is sure to come.

10"'This is what the Sovereign LORD says:

"'I will put an end to the hordes of
Egypt
by the hand of Nebuchadnezzar
king of Babylon.
11He and his army — the most ruthless
of nations —
will be brought in to destroy the
land.
They will draw their swords against
Egypt
and fill the land with the slain.

[a] 7 Syriac (see also Septuagint and Vulgate); Hebrew *and you caused their backs to stand*
[b] 10 That is, the upper Nile region [c] 21 *Horn* here symbolizes strength. [d] 4 That is, the upper Nile region; also in verses 5 and 9

12 I will dry up the waters of the Nile
and sell the land to an evil nation;
by the hand of foreigners
I will lay waste the land and
everything in it.

I the LORD have spoken.

13 " 'This is what the Sovereign LORD says:

" 'I will destroy the idols
and put an end to the images in
Memphis.
No longer will there be a prince in
Egypt,
and I will spread fear throughout
the land.
14 I will lay waste Upper Egypt,
set fire to Zoan
and inflict punishment on Thebes.
15 I will pour out my wrath on Pelusium,
the stronghold of Egypt,
and wipe out the hordes of Thebes.
16 I will set fire to Egypt;
Pelusium will writhe in agony.
Thebes will be taken by storm;
Memphis will be in constant
distress.
17 The young men of Heliopolis and
Bubastis
will fall by the sword,
and the cities themselves will go
into captivity.
18 Dark will be the day at Tahpanhes
when I break the yoke of Egypt;
there her proud strength will come
to an end.
She will be covered with clouds,
and her villages will go into
captivity.
19 So I will inflict punishment on Egypt,
and they will know that I am the
LORD.' "

Pharaoh's Arms Are Broken

20 In the eleventh year, in the first month
on the seventh day, the word of the LORD
came to me: 21 "Son of man, I have broken
the arm of Pharaoh king of Egypt. It has
not been bound up to be healed or put
in a splint so that it may become strong
enough to hold a sword. 22 Therefore this
is what the Sovereign LORD says: I am
against Pharaoh king of Egypt. I will break
both his arms, the good arm as well as
the broken one, and make the sword fall
from his hand. 23 I will disperse the Egyptians among the nations and scatter them
through the countries. 24 I will strengthen
the arms of the king of Babylon and put
my sword in his hand, but I will break
the arms of Pharaoh, and he will groan
before him like a mortally wounded man.
25 I will strengthen the arms of the king of
Babylon, but the arms of Pharaoh will fall
limp. Then they will know that I am the
LORD, when I put my sword into the hand
of the king of Babylon and he brandish-
es it against Egypt. 26 I will disperse the
Egyptians among the nations and scatter
them through the countries. Then they
will know that I am the LORD."

Pharaoh as a Felled Cedar of Lebanon

31 In the eleventh year, in the third
month on the first day, the word of
the LORD came to me: 2 "Son of man, say to
Pharaoh king of Egypt and to his hordes:

" 'Who can be compared with you in
majesty?
3 Consider Assyria, once a cedar in
Lebanon,
with beautiful branches
overshadowing the forest;
it towered on high,
its top above the thick foliage.
4 The waters nourished it,
deep springs made it grow tall;
their streams flowed
all around its base
and sent their channels
to all the trees of the field.
5 So it towered higher
than all the trees of the field;
its boughs increased
and its branches grew long,
spreading because of abundant
waters.
6 All the birds of the sky
nested in its boughs,
all the animals of the wild
gave birth under its branches;
all the great nations
lived in its shade.
7 It was majestic in beauty,
with its spreading boughs,
for its roots went down
to abundant waters.
8 The cedars in the garden of God
could not rival it,
nor could the junipers
equal its boughs,
nor could the plane trees
compare with its branches —
no tree in the garden of God
could match its beauty.
9 I made it beautiful
with abundant branches,
the envy of all the trees of Eden
in the garden of God.

10 " 'Therefore this is what the Sovereign
LORD says: Because the great cedar towered
over the thick foliage, and because it was
proud of its height, 11 I gave it into the hands

of the ruler of the nations, for him to deal
with according to its wickedness. I cast it
aside, 12 and the most ruthless of foreign
nations cut it down and left it. Its boughs
fell on the mountains and in all the valleys;
its branches lay broken in all the ravines of
the land. All the nations of the earth came
out from under its shade and left it. 13 All
the birds settled on the fallen tree, and all
the wild animals lived among its branches. 14 Therefore no other trees by the waters
are ever to tower proudly on high, lifting
their tops above the thick foliage. No other
trees so well-watered are ever to reach such
a height; they are all destined for death,
for the earth below, among mortals who
go down to the realm of the dead.

15 " 'This is what the Sovereign LORD
says: On the day it was brought down to
the realm of the dead I covered the deep
springs with mourning for it; I held back
its streams, and its abundant waters were
restrained. Because of it I clothed Lebanon with gloom, and all the trees of the
field withered away. 16 I made the nations
tremble at the sound of its fall when I
brought it down to the realm of the dead
to be with those who go down to the pit.
Then all the trees of Eden, the choicest and
best of Lebanon, the well-watered trees,
were consoled in the earth below. 17 They
too, like the great cedar, had gone down
to the realm of the dead, to those killed
by the sword, along with the armed men
who lived in its shade among the nations.

18 " 'Which of the trees of Eden can be
compared with you in splendor and majesty? Yet you, too, will be brought down
with the trees of Eden to the earth below;
you will lie among the uncircumcised,
with those killed by the sword.

" 'This is Pharaoh and all his hordes,
declares the Sovereign LORD.' "

A Lament Over Pharaoh

32 In the twelfth year, in the twelfth
month on the first day, the word of
the LORD came to me: 2 "Son of man, take
up a lament concerning Pharaoh king of
Egypt and say to him:

" 'You are like a lion among the nations;
you are like a monster in the seas
thrashing about in your streams,
churning the water with your feet
and muddying the streams.

3 " 'This is what the Sovereign LORD says:

" 'With a great throng of people
I will cast my net over you,
and they will haul you up in my net.
4 I will throw you on the land
and hurl you on the open field.
I will let all the birds of the sky settle
on you
and all the animals of the wild
gorge themselves on you.
5 I will spread your flesh on the
mountains
and fill the valleys with your
remains.
6 I will drench the land with your
flowing blood
all the way to the mountains,
and the ravines will be filled with
your flesh.
7 When I snuff you out, I will cover the
heavens
and darken their stars;
I will cover the sun with a cloud,
and the moon will not give
its light.
8 All the shining lights in the heavens
I will darken over you;
I will bring darkness over your
land,
declares the Sovereign LORD.
9 I will trouble the hearts of many
peoples
when I bring about your
destruction among the
nations,
among[a] lands you have not known.
10 I will cause many peoples to be
appalled at you,
and their kings will shudder with
horror because of you
when I brandish my sword before
them.
On the day of your downfall
each of them will tremble
every moment for his life.

11 " 'For this is what the Sovereign LORD
says:

" 'The sword of the king of Babylon
will come against you.
12 I will cause your hordes to fall
by the swords of mighty men —
the most ruthless of all nations.
They will shatter the pride of Egypt,
and all her hordes will be
overthrown.
13 I will destroy all her cattle
from beside abundant waters
no longer to be stirred by the foot of
man
or muddied by the hooves of cattle.
14 Then I will let her waters settle
and make her streams flow like oil,
declares the Sovereign LORD.

[a] 9 Hebrew; Septuagint *bring you into captivity among the nations, / to*

15 When I make Egypt desolate
and strip the land of everything in it,
when I strike down all who live there,
then they will know that I am the
LORD.'

16 "This is the lament they will chant
for her. The daughters of the nations will
chant it; for Egypt and all her hordes they
will chant it, declares the Sovereign LORD."

Egypt's Descent Into the Realm of the Dead

17 In the twelfth year, on the fifteenth day
of the month, the word of the LORD came
to me: 18 "Son of man, wail for the hordes
of Egypt and consign to the earth below
both her and the daughters of mighty
nations, along with those who go down
to the pit. 19 Say to them, 'Are you more
favored than others? Go down and be laid
among the uncircumcised.' 20 They will
fall among those killed by the sword. The
sword is drawn; let her be dragged off with
all her hordes. 21 From within the realm
of the dead the mighty leaders will say
of Egypt and her allies, 'They have come
down and they lie with the uncircumcised,
with those killed by the sword.'
22 "Assyria is there with her whole army;
she is surrounded by the graves of all her
slain, all who have fallen by the sword.
23 Their graves are in the depths of the pit
and her army lies around her grave. All
who had spread terror in the land of the
living are slain, fallen by the sword.
24 "Elam is there, with all her hordes
around her grave. All of them are slain,
fallen by the sword. All who had spread
terror in the land of the living went down
uncircumcised to the earth below. They
bear their shame with those who go down
to the pit. 25 A bed is made for her among
the slain, with all her hordes around her
grave. All of them are uncircumcised,
killed by the sword. Because their terror
had spread in the land of the living, they
bear their shame with those who go down
to the pit; they are laid among the slain.
26 "Meshek and Tubal are there, with
all their hordes around their graves. All
of them are uncircumcised, killed by the
sword because they spread their terror in
the land of the living. 27 But they do not lie
with the fallen warriors of old,[a] who went
down to the realm of the dead with their
weapons of war — their swords placed under their heads and their shields[b] resting
on their bones — though these warriors
also had terrorized the land of the living.
28 "You too, Pharaoh, will be broken and
will lie among the uncircumcised, with
those killed by the sword.
29 "Edom is there, her kings and all her
princes; despite their power, they are laid
with those killed by the sword. They lie
with the uncircumcised, with those who
go down to the pit.
30 "All the princes of the north and all
the Sidonians are there; they went down
with the slain in disgrace despite the terror caused by their power. They lie uncircumcised with those killed by the sword
and bear their shame with those who go
down to the pit.
31 "Pharaoh — he and all his army — will
see them and he will be consoled for all
his hordes that were killed by the sword,
declares the Sovereign LORD. 32 Although
I had him spread terror in the land of the
living, Pharaoh and all his hordes will
be laid among the uncircumcised, with
those killed by the sword, declares the
Sovereign LORD."

Renewal of Ezekiel's Call as Watchman

33 The word of the LORD came to me:
2 "Son of man, speak to your people
and say to them: 'When I bring the sword
against a land, and the people of the land
choose one of their men and make him their
watchman, 3 and he sees the sword coming
against the land and blows the trumpet to
warn the people, 4 then if anyone hears the
trumpet but does not heed the warning
and the sword comes and takes their life,
their blood will be on their own head. 5 Since
they heard the sound of the trumpet but
did not heed the warning, their blood will
be on their own head. If they had heeded
the warning, they would have saved themselves. 6 But if the watchman sees the sword
coming and does not blow the trumpet to
warn the people and the sword comes and
takes someone's life, that person's life will
be taken because of their sin, but I will hold
the watchman accountable for their blood.'
7 "Son of man, I have made you a watchman for the people of Israel; so hear the
word I speak and give them warning from
me. 8 When I say to the wicked, 'You wicked person, you will surely die,' and you do
not speak out to dissuade them from their
ways, that wicked person will die for[c] their
sin, and I will hold you accountable for
their blood. 9 But if you do warn the wicked
person to turn from their ways and they
do not do so, they will die for their sin,
though you yourself will be saved.

[a] 27 Septuagint; Hebrew *warriors who were uncircumcised* [b] 27 Probable reading of the original Hebrew text; Masoretic Text *punishment* [c] 8 Or *in*; also in verse 9

10"Son of man, say to the Israelites, 'This is what you are saying: "Our offenses and sins weigh us down, and we are wasting away because of[a] them. How then can we live?"' 11Say to them, 'As surely as I live, declares the Sovereign LORD, I take no pleasure in the death of the wicked, but rather that they turn from their ways and live. Turn! Turn from your evil ways! Why will you die, people of Israel?'

12"Therefore, son of man, say to your people, 'If someone who is righteous disobeys, that person's former righteousness will count for nothing. And if someone who is wicked repents, that person's former wickedness will not bring condemnation. The righteous person who sins will not be allowed to live even though they were formerly righteous.' 13If I tell a righteous person that they will surely live, but then they trust in their righteousness and do evil, none of the righteous things that person has done will be remembered; they will die for the evil they have done. 14And if I say to a wicked person, 'You will surely die,' but they then turn away from their sin and do what is just and right— 15if they give back what they took in pledge for a loan, return what they have stolen, follow the decrees that give life, and do no evil—that person will surely live; they will not die. 16None of the sins that person has committed will be remembered against them. They have done what is just and right; they will surely live.

17"Yet your people say, 'The way of the Lord is not just.' But it is their way that is not just. 18If a righteous person turns from their righteousness and does evil, they will die for it. 19And if a wicked person turns away from their wickedness and does what is just and right, they will live by doing so. 20Yet you Israelites say, 'The way of the Lord is not just.' But I will judge each of you according to your own ways."

Jerusalem's Fall Explained

21In the twelfth year of our exile, in the tenth month on the fifth day, a man who had escaped from Jerusalem came to me and said, "The city has fallen!" 22Now the evening before the man arrived, the hand of the LORD was on me, and he opened my mouth before the man came to me in the morning. So my mouth was opened and I was no longer silent.

23Then the word of the LORD came to me: 24"Son of man, the people living in those ruins in the land of Israel are saying, 'Abraham was only one man, yet he possessed the land. But we are many; surely the land has been given to us as our possession.' 25Therefore say to them, 'This is what the Sovereign LORD says: Since you eat meat with the blood still in it and look to your idols and shed blood, should you then possess the land? 26You rely on your sword, you do detestable things, and each of you defiles his neighbor's wife. Should you then possess the land?'

27"Say this to them: 'This is what the Sovereign LORD says: As surely as I live, those who are left in the ruins will fall by the sword, those out in the country I will give to the wild animals to be devoured, and those in strongholds and caves will die of a plague. 28I will make the land a desolate waste, and her proud strength will come to an end, and the mountains of Israel will become desolate so that no one will cross them. 29Then they will know that I am the LORD, when I have made the land a desolate waste because of all the detestable things they have done.'

30"As for you, son of man, your people are talking together about you by the walls and at the doors of the houses, saying to each other, 'Come and hear the message that has come from the LORD.' 31My people come to you, as they usually do, and sit before you to hear your words, but they do not put them into practice. Their mouths speak of love, but their hearts are greedy for unjust gain. 32Indeed, to them you are nothing more than one who sings love songs with a beautiful voice and plays an instrument well, for they hear your words but do not put them into practice.

33"When all this comes true—and it surely will—then they will know that a prophet has been among them."

The LORD Will Be Israel's Shepherd

34 The word of the LORD came to me: 2"Son of man, prophesy against the shepherds of Israel; prophesy and say to them: 'This is what the Sovereign LORD says: Woe to you shepherds of Israel who only take care of yourselves! Should not shepherds take care of the flock? 3You eat the curds, clothe yourselves with the wool and slaughter the choice animals, but you do not take care of the flock. 4You have not strengthened the weak or healed the sick or bound up the injured. You have not brought back the strays or searched for the lost. You have ruled them harshly and brutally. 5So they were scattered because there was no shepherd, and when they were scattered they became food for all the wild animals. 6My sheep wandered over

[a] 10 Or *away in*

all the mountains and on every high hill.
They were scattered over the whole earth,
and no one searched or looked for them.
7 "'Therefore, you shepherds, hear the
word of the LORD: 8 As surely as I live, declares the Sovereign LORD, because my
flock lacks a shepherd and so has been
plundered and has become food for all
the wild animals, and because my shepherds did not search for my flock but cared
for themselves rather than for my flock,
9 therefore, you shepherds, hear the word
of the LORD: 10 This is what the Sovereign
LORD says: I am against the shepherds
and will hold them accountable for my
flock. I will remove them from tending
the flock so that the shepherds can no
longer feed themselves. I will rescue my
flock from their mouths, and it will no
longer be food for them.
11 "'For this is what the Sovereign LORD
says: I myself will search for my sheep and
look after them. 12 As a shepherd looks after
his scattered flock when he is with them,
so will I look after my sheep. I will rescue
them from all the places where they were
scattered on a day of clouds and darkness.
13 I will bring them out from the nations
and gather them from the countries, and
I will bring them into their own land. I will
pasture them on the mountains of Israel,
in the ravines and in all the settlements
in the land. 14 I will tend them in a good
pasture, and the mountain heights of Israel will be their grazing land. There they
will lie down in good grazing land, and
there they will feed in a rich pasture on the
mountains of Israel. 15 I myself will tend my
sheep and have them lie down, declares
the Sovereign LORD. 16 I will search for the
lost and bring back the strays. I will bind
up the injured and strengthen the weak,
but the sleek and the strong I will destroy.
I will shepherd the flock with justice.
17 "'As for you, my flock, this is what the
Sovereign LORD says: I will judge between
one sheep and another, and between rams
and goats. 18 Is it not enough for you to
feed on the good pasture? Must you also
trample the rest of your pasture with your
feet? Is it not enough for you to drink clear
water? Must you also muddy the rest with
your feet? 19 Must my flock feed on what
you have trampled and drink what you
have muddied with your feet?
20 "'Therefore this is what the Sovereign
LORD says to them: See, I myself will judge
between the fat sheep and the lean sheep.
21 Because you shove with flank and shoulder, butting all the weak sheep with your
horns until you have driven them away, 22 I
will save my flock, and they will no longer
be plundered. I will judge between one
sheep and another. 23 I will place over them
one shepherd, my servant David, and he
will tend them; he will tend them and be
their shepherd. 24 I the LORD will be their
God, and my servant David will be prince
among them. I the LORD have spoken.
25 "'I will make a covenant of peace with
them and rid the land of savage beasts so
that they may live in the wilderness and
sleep in the forests in safety. 26 I will make
them and the places surrounding my hill a
blessing.[a] I will send down showers in season; there will be showers of blessing. 27 The
trees will yield their fruit and the ground
will yield its crops; the people will be secure
in their land. They will know that I am the
LORD, when I break the bars of their yoke
and rescue them from the hands of those
who enslaved them. 28 They will no longer
be plundered by the nations, nor will wild
animals devour them. They will live in
safety, and no one will make them afraid.
29 I will provide for them a land renowned
for its crops, and they will no longer be
victims of famine in the land or bear the
scorn of the nations. 30 Then they will know
that I, the LORD their God, am with them
and that they, the Israelites, are my people,
declares the Sovereign LORD. 31 You are my
sheep, the sheep of my pasture, and I am
your God, declares the Sovereign LORD.'"

A Prophecy Against Edom

35 The word of the LORD came to me:
2 "Son of man, set your face against
Mount Seir; prophesy against it 3 and say:
'This is what the Sovereign LORD says: I am
against you, Mount Seir, and I will stretch
out my hand against you and make you
a desolate waste. 4 I will turn your towns
into ruins and you will be desolate. Then
you will know that I am the LORD.
5 "'Because you harbored an ancient
hostility and delivered the Israelites over
to the sword at the time of their calamity,
the time their punishment reached its climax, 6 therefore as surely as I live, declares
the Sovereign LORD, I will give you over to
bloodshed and it will pursue you. Since
you did not hate bloodshed, bloodshed
will pursue you. 7 I will make Mount Seir a
desolate waste and cut off from it all who
come and go. 8 I will fill your mountains
with the slain; those killed by the sword will
fall on your hills and in your valleys and in

[a] 26 Or *I will cause them and the places surrounding my hill to be named in blessings* (see Gen. 48:20); or *I will cause them and the places surrounding my hill to be seen as blessed*

all your ravines. 9I will make you desolate
forever; your towns will not be inhabited.
Then you will know that I am the LORD.
10"'Because you have said, "These two
nations and countries will be ours and we
will take possession of them," even though
I the LORD was there, 11therefore as surely
as I live, declares the Sovereign LORD, I will
treat you in accordance with the anger
and jealousy you showed in your hatred
of them and I will make myself known
among them when I judge you. 12Then
you will know that I the LORD have heard
all the contemptible things you have said
against the mountains of Israel. You said,
"They have been laid waste and have been
given over to us to devour." 13You boasted
against me and spoke against me without
restraint, and I heard it. 14This is what the
Sovereign LORD says: While the whole
earth rejoices, I will make you desolate.
15Because you rejoiced when the inheritance of Israel became desolate, that is
how I will treat you. You will be desolate,
Mount Seir, you and all of Edom. Then they
will know that I am the LORD.'"

Hope for the Mountains of Israel

36 "Son of man, prophesy to the mountains of Israel and say, 'Mountains
of Israel, hear the word of the LORD. 2This
is what the Sovereign LORD says: The enemy said of you, "Aha! The ancient heights
have become our possession."' 3Therefore
prophesy and say, 'This is what the Sovereign LORD says: Because they ravaged
and crushed you from every side so that
you became the possession of the rest
of the nations and the object of people's
malicious talk and slander, 4therefore,
mountains of Israel, hear the word of the
Sovereign LORD: This is what the Sovereign
LORD says to the mountains and hills, to
the ravines and valleys, to the desolate
ruins and the deserted towns that have
been plundered and ridiculed by the rest
of the nations around you — 5this is what
the Sovereign LORD says: In my burning
zeal I have spoken against the rest of the
nations, and against all Edom, for with
glee and with malice in their hearts they
made my land their own possession so
that they might plunder its pastureland.'
6Therefore prophesy concerning the land
of Israel and say to the mountains and
hills, to the ravines and valleys: 'This is
what the Sovereign LORD says: I speak in
my jealous wrath because you have suffered the scorn of the nations. 7Therefore
this is what the Sovereign LORD says: I
swear with uplifted hand that the nations
around you will also suffer scorn.

8"'But you, mountains of Israel, will
produce branches and fruit for my people Israel, for they will soon come home.
9I am concerned for you and will look on
you with favor; you will be plowed and
sown, 10and I will cause many people to
live on you — yes, all of Israel. The towns
will be inhabited and the ruins rebuilt. 11I
will increase the number of people and
animals living on you, and they will be
fruitful and become numerous. I will settle people on you as in the past and will
make you prosper more than before. Then
you will know that I am the LORD. 12I will
cause people, my people Israel, to live on
you. They will possess you, and you will
be their inheritance; you will never again
deprive them of their children.
13"'This is what the Sovereign LORD
says: Because some say to you, "You devour people and deprive your nation of its
children," 14therefore you will no longer
devour people or make your nation childless, declares the Sovereign LORD. 15No
longer will I make you hear the taunts of
the nations, and no longer will you suffer
the scorn of the peoples or cause your nation to fall, declares the Sovereign LORD.'"

Israel's Restoration Assured

16Again the word of the LORD came to
me: 17"Son of man, when the people of
Israel were living in their own land, they
defiled it by their conduct and their actions. Their conduct was like a woman's
monthly uncleanness in my sight. 18So I
poured out my wrath on them because
they had shed blood in the land and because they had defiled it with their idols.
19I dispersed them among the nations, and
they were scattered through the countries;
I judged them according to their conduct
and their actions. 20And wherever they
went among the nations they profaned my
holy name, for it was said of them, 'These
are the LORD's people, and yet they had to
leave his land.' 21I had concern for my holy
name, which the people of Israel profaned
among the nations where they had gone.
22"Therefore say to the Israelites, 'This
is what the Sovereign LORD says: It is not
for your sake, people of Israel, that I am
going to do these things, but for the sake
of my holy name, which you have profaned among the nations where you have
gone. 23I will show the holiness of my great
name, which has been profaned among
the nations, the name you have profaned
among them. Then the nations will know
that I am the LORD, declares the Sovereign
LORD, when I am proved holy through you
before their eyes.

24“ ‘For I will take you out of the nations;
I will gather you from all the countries and
bring you back into your own land. 25I will
sprinkle clean water on you, and you will be
clean; I will cleanse you from all your impurities and from all your idols. 26I will give
you a new heart and put a new spirit in you;
I will remove from you your heart of stone
and give you a heart of flesh. 27And I will
put my Spirit in you and move you to follow
my decrees and be careful to keep my laws.
28Then you will live in the land I gave your
ancestors; you will be my people, and I will
be your God. 29I will save you from all your
uncleanness. I will call for the grain and
make it plentiful and will not bring famine upon you. 30I will increase the fruit of
the trees and the crops of the field, so that
you will no longer suffer disgrace among
the nations because of famine. 31Then you
will remember your evil ways and wicked
deeds, and you will loathe yourselves for
your sins and detestable practices. 32I want
you to know that I am not doing this for
your sake, declares the Sovereign LORD. Be
ashamed and disgraced for your conduct,
people of Israel!

33“ ‘This is what the Sovereign LORD says:
On the day I cleanse you from all your sins,
I will resettle your towns, and the ruins
will be rebuilt. 34The desolate land will
be cultivated instead of lying desolate in
the sight of all who pass through it. 35They
will say, “This land that was laid waste
has become like the garden of Eden; the
cities that were lying in ruins, desolate
and destroyed, are now fortified and inhabited.” 36Then the nations around you
that remain will know that I the LORD
have rebuilt what was destroyed and have
replanted what was desolate. I the LORD
have spoken, and I will do it.’

37“This is what the Sovereign LORD says:
Once again I will yield to Israel’s plea and
do this for them: I will make their people
as numerous as sheep, 38as numerous
as the flocks for offerings at Jerusalem
during her appointed festivals. So will the
ruined cities be filled with flocks of people.
Then they will know that I am the LORD.”

The Valley of Dry Bones

37 The hand of the LORD was on me,
and he brought me out by the Spirit
of the LORD and set me in the middle of
a valley; it was full of bones. 2He led me
back and forth among them, and I saw a
great many bones on the floor of the valley, bones that were very dry. 3He asked
me, “Son of man, can these bones live?”

I said, “Sovereign LORD, you alone know.”

4Then he said to me, “Prophesy to these
bones and say to them, ‘Dry bones, hear
the word of the LORD! 5This is what the
Sovereign LORD says to these bones: I will
make breath[a] enter you, and you will come
to life. 6I will attach tendons to you and
make flesh come upon you and cover you
with skin; I will put breath in you, and you
will come to life. Then you will know that
I am the LORD.’ ”

7So I prophesied as I was commanded.
And as I was prophesying, there was a
noise, a rattling sound, and the bones
came together, bone to bone. 8I looked,
and tendons and flesh appeared on them
and skin covered them, but there was no
breath in them.

9Then he said to me, “Prophesy to the
breath; prophesy, son of man, and say
to it, ‘This is what the Sovereign LORD
says: Come, breath, from the four winds
and breathe into these slain, that they
may live.’ ” 10So I prophesied as he commanded me, and breath entered them;
they came to life and stood up on their
feet—a vast army.

11Then he said to me: “Son of man, these
bones are the people of Israel. They say,
‘Our bones are dried up and our hope is
gone; we are cut off.’ 12Therefore prophesy
and say to them: ‘This is what the Sovereign LORD says: My people, I am going to
open your graves and bring you up from
them; I will bring you back to the land of
Israel. 13Then you, my people, will know
that I am the LORD, when I open your
graves and bring you up from them. 14I
will put my Spirit in you and you will live,
and I will settle you in your own land. Then
you will know that I the LORD have spoken,
and I have done it, declares the LORD.’ ”

One Nation Under One King

15The word of the LORD came to me:
16“Son of man, take a stick of wood and
write on it, ‘Belonging to Judah and the
Israelites associated with him.’ Then take
another stick of wood, and write on it,
‘Belonging to Joseph (that is, to Ephraim)
and all the Israelites associated with him.’
17Join them together into one stick so that
they will become one in your hand.

18“When your people ask you, ‘Won’t
you tell us what you mean by this?’ 19say
to them, ‘This is what the Sovereign LORD
says: I am going to take the stick of Joseph—which is in Ephraim’s hand—and
of the Israelite tribes associated with him,
and join it to Judah’s stick. I will make
them into a single stick of wood, and they

[a] 5 The Hebrew for this word can also mean *wind* or *spirit* (see verses 6-14).

will become one in my hand.' 20 Hold before their eyes the sticks you have written on 21 and say to them, 'This is what the Sovereign LORD says: I will take the Israelites out of the nations where they have gone. I will gather them from all around and bring them back into their own land. 22 I will make them one nation in the land, on the mountains of Israel. There will be one king over all of them and they will never again be two nations or be divided into two kingdoms. 23 They will no longer defile themselves with their idols and vile images or with any of their offenses, for I will save them from all their sinful backsliding,[a] and I will cleanse them. They will be my people, and I will be their God.

24 " 'My servant David will be king over them, and they will all have one shepherd. They will follow my laws and be careful to keep my decrees. 25 They will live in the land I gave to my servant Jacob, the land where your ancestors lived. They and their children and their children's children will live there forever, and David my servant will be their prince forever. 26 I will make a covenant of peace with them; it will be an everlasting covenant. I will establish them and increase their numbers, and I will put my sanctuary among them forever. 27 My dwelling place will be with them; I will be their God, and they will be my people. 28 Then the nations will know that I the LORD make Israel holy, when my sanctuary is among them forever.' "

The LORD's Great Victory Over the Nations

38 The word of the LORD came to me: 2 "Son of man, set your face against Gog, of the land of Magog, the chief prince of[b] Meshek and Tubal; prophesy against him 3 and say: 'This is what the Sovereign LORD says: I am against you, Gog, chief prince of[c] Meshek and Tubal. 4 I will turn you around, put hooks in your jaws and bring you out with your whole army — your horses, your horsemen fully armed, and a great horde with large and small shields, all of them brandishing their swords. 5 Persia, Cush[d] and Put will be with them, all with shields and helmets, 6 also Gomer with all its troops, and Beth Togarmah from the far north with all its troops — the many nations with you.

7 " 'Get ready; be prepared, you and all the hordes gathered about you, and take command of them. 8 After many days you will be called to arms. In future years you will invade a land that has recovered from war, whose people were gathered from many nations to the mountains of Israel, which had long been desolate. They had been brought out from the nations, and now all of them live in safety. 9 You and all your troops and the many nations with you will go up, advancing like a storm; you will be like a cloud covering the land.

10 " 'This is what the Sovereign LORD says: On that day thoughts will come into your mind and you will devise an evil scheme. 11 You will say, "I will invade a land of unwalled villages; I will attack a peaceful and unsuspecting people — all of them living without walls and without gates and bars. 12 I will plunder and loot and turn my hand against the resettled ruins and the people gathered from the nations, rich in livestock and goods, living at the center of the land.[e]" 13 Sheba and Dedan and the merchants of Tarshish and all her villages[f] will say to you, "Have you come to plunder? Have you gathered your hordes to loot, to carry off silver and gold, to take away livestock and goods and to seize much plunder?" '

14 "Therefore, son of man, prophesy and say to Gog: 'This is what the Sovereign LORD says: In that day, when my people Israel are living in safety, will you not take notice of it? 15 You will come from your place in the far north, you and many nations with you, all of them riding on horses, a great horde, a mighty army. 16 You will advance against my people Israel like a cloud that covers the land. In days to come, Gog, I will bring you against my land, so that the nations may know me when I am proved holy through you before their eyes.

17 " 'This is what the Sovereign LORD says: You are the one I spoke of in former days by my servants the prophets of Israel. At that time they prophesied for years that I would bring you against them. 18 This is what will happen in that day: When Gog attacks the land of Israel, my hot anger will be aroused, declares the Sovereign LORD. 19 In my zeal and fiery wrath I declare that at that time there shall be a great earthquake in the land of Israel. 20 The fish in the sea, the birds in the sky, the beasts of the field, every creature that moves along the ground, and all the people on the face of the earth will tremble at my presence. The mountains

[a] 23 Many Hebrew manuscripts (see also Septuagint); most Hebrew manuscripts *all their dwelling places where they sinned* [b] 2 Or *the prince of Rosh,* [c] 3 Or *Gog, prince of Rosh,* [d] 5 That is, the upper Nile region [e] 12 The Hebrew for this phrase means *the navel of the earth.* [f] 13 Or *her strong lions*

will be overturned, the cliffs will crumble
and every wall will fall to the ground. 21I
will summon a sword against Gog on all
my mountains, declares the Sovereign
LORD. Every man's sword will be against
his brother. 22I will execute judgment on
him with plague and bloodshed; I will
pour down torrents of rain, hailstones
and burning sulfur on him and on his
troops and on the many nations with him.
23And so I will show my greatness and my
holiness, and I will make myself known
in the sight of many nations. Then they
will know that I am the LORD.'

39 "Son of man, prophesy against Gog
and say: 'This is what the Sovereign
LORD says: I am against you, Gog, chief
prince of[a] Meshek and Tubal. 2I will turn
you around and drag you along. I will
bring you from the far north and send you
against the mountains of Israel. 3Then I
will strike your bow from your left hand
and make your arrows drop from your
right hand. 4On the mountains of Israel
you will fall, you and all your troops and
the nations with you. I will give you as food
to all kinds of carrion birds and to the wild
animals. 5You will fall in the open field,
for I have spoken, declares the Sovereign
LORD. 6I will send fire on Magog and on
those who live in safety in the coastlands,
and they will know that I am the LORD.

7" 'I will make known my holy name
among my people Israel. I will no longer
let my holy name be profaned, and the
nations will know that I the LORD am the
Holy One in Israel. 8It is coming! It will
surely take place, declares the Sovereign
LORD. This is the day I have spoken of.

9" 'Then those who live in the towns of
Israel will go out and use the weapons
for fuel and burn them up — the small
and large shields, the bows and arrows,
the war clubs and spears. For seven years
they will use them for fuel. 10They will not
need to gather wood from the fields or
cut it from the forests, because they will
use the weapons for fuel. And they will
plunder those who plundered them and
loot those who looted them, declares the
Sovereign LORD.

11" 'On that day I will give Gog a burial
place in Israel, in the valley of those who
travel east of the Sea. It will block the
way of travelers, because Gog and all his
hordes will be buried there. So it will be
called the Valley of Hamon Gog.[b]

12" 'For seven months the Israelites will
be burying them in order to cleanse the
land. 13All the people of the land will bury
them, and the day I display my glory will
be a memorable day for them, declares the
Sovereign LORD. 14People will be continually employed in cleansing the land. They
will spread out across the land and, along
with others, they will bury any bodies that
are lying on the ground.

" 'After the seven months they will carry out a more detailed search. 15As they
go through the land, anyone who sees a
human bone will leave a marker beside it
until the gravediggers bury it in the Valley
of Hamon Gog, 16near a town called Hamonah.[c] And so they will cleanse the land.'

17"Son of man, this is what the Sovereign LORD says: Call out to every kind of
bird and all the wild animals: 'Assemble
and come together from all around to
the sacrifice I am preparing for you, the
great sacrifice on the mountains of Israel.
There you will eat flesh and drink blood.
18You will eat the flesh of mighty men and
drink the blood of the princes of the earth
as if they were rams and lambs, goats and
bulls — all of them fattened animals from
Bashan. 19At the sacrifice I am preparing
for you, you will eat fat till you are glutted
and drink blood till you are drunk. 20At
my table you will eat your fill of horses
and riders, mighty men and soldiers of
every kind,' declares the Sovereign LORD.

21"I will display my glory among the
nations, and all the nations will see the
punishment I inflict and the hand I lay on
them. 22From that day forward the people
of Israel will know that I am the LORD their
God. 23And the nations will know that the
people of Israel went into exile for their
sin, because they were unfaithful to me. So
I hid my face from them and handed them
over to their enemies, and they all fell by
the sword. 24I dealt with them according
to their uncleanness and their offenses,
and I hid my face from them.

25"Therefore this is what the Sovereign
LORD says: I will now restore the fortunes
of Jacob[d] and will have compassion on all
the people of Israel, and I will be zealous
for my holy name. 26They will forget their
shame and all the unfaithfulness they
showed toward me when they lived in
safety in their land with no one to make
them afraid. 27When I have brought them
back from the nations and have gathered
them from the countries of their enemies,
I will be proved holy through them in the
sight of many nations. 28Then they will
know that I am the LORD their God, for

[a] *1* Or *Gog, prince of Rosh,* [b] *11 Hamon Gog* means *hordes of Gog.* [c] *16 Hamonah* means *horde.* [d] *25* Or *now bring Jacob back from captivity*

though I sent them into exile among the nations, I will gather them to their own land, not leaving any behind. 29I will no longer hide my face from them, for I will pour out my Spirit on the people of Israel, declares the Sovereign LORD."

The Temple Area Restored

40 In the twenty-fifth year of our exile, at the beginning of the year, on the tenth of the month, in the fourteenth year after the fall of the city — on that very day the hand of the LORD was on me and he took me there. 2In visions of God he took me to the land of Israel and set me on a very high mountain, on whose south side were some buildings that looked like a city. 3He took me there, and I saw a man whose appearance was like bronze; he was standing in the gateway with a linen cord and a measuring rod in his hand. 4The man said to me, "Son of man, look carefully and listen closely and pay attention to everything I am going to show you, for that is why you have been brought here. Tell the people of Israel everything you see."

The East Gate to the Outer Court

5I saw a wall completely surrounding the temple area. The length of the measuring rod in the man's hand was six long cubits,[a] each of which was a cubit and a handbreadth. He measured the wall; it was one measuring rod thick and one rod high.

6Then he went to the east gate. He climbed its steps and measured the threshold of the gate; it was one rod deep. 7The alcoves for the guards were one rod long and one rod wide, and the projecting walls between the alcoves were five cubits[b] thick. And the threshold of the gate next to the portico facing the temple was one rod deep.

8Then he measured the portico of the gateway; 9it[c] was eight cubits[d] deep and its jambs were two cubits[e] thick. The portico of the gateway faced the temple.

10Inside the east gate were three alcoves on each side; the three had the same measurements, and the faces of the projecting walls on each side had the same measurements. 11Then he measured the width of the entrance of the gateway; it was ten cubits and its length was thirteen cubits.[f] 12In front of each alcove was a wall one cubit high, and the alcoves were six cubits square. 13Then he measured the gateway from the top of the rear wall of one alcove to the top of the opposite one; the distance was twenty-five cubits[g] from one parapet opening to the opposite one. 14He measured along the faces of the projecting walls all around the inside of the gateway — sixty cubits.[h] The measurement was up to the portico[i] facing the courtyard.[j] 15The distance from the entrance of the gateway to the far end of its portico was fifty cubits.[k] 16The alcoves and the projecting walls inside the gateway were surmounted by narrow parapet openings all around, as was the portico; the openings all around faced inward. The faces of the projecting walls were decorated with palm trees.

The Outer Court

17Then he brought me into the outer court. There I saw some rooms and a pavement that had been constructed all around the court; there were thirty rooms along the pavement. 18It abutted the sides of the gateways and was as wide as they were long; this was the lower pavement. 19Then he measured the distance from the inside of the lower gateway to the outside of the inner court; it was a hundred cubits[l] on the east side as well as on the north.

The North Gate

20Then he measured the length and width of the north gate, leading into the outer court. 21Its alcoves — three on each side — its projecting walls and its portico had the same measurements as those of the first gateway. It was fifty cubits long and twenty-five cubits wide. 22Its openings, its portico and its palm tree decorations had the same measurements as those of the gate facing east. Seven steps led up to it, with its portico opposite them. 23There was a gate to the inner court facing the north gate, just as there was on the east. He measured from one gate to the opposite one; it was a hundred cubits.

[a] *5* That is, about 11 feet or about 3.2 meters; also in verse 12. The long cubit of about 21 inches or about 53 centimeters is the basic unit of measurement of length throughout chapters 40 – 48. [b] *7* That is, about 8 3/4 feet or about 2.7 meters; also in verse 48 [c] *8,9* Many Hebrew manuscripts, Septuagint, Vulgate and Syriac; most Hebrew manuscripts *gateway facing the temple; it was one rod deep. 9Then he measured the portico of the gateway; it* [d] *9* That is, about 14 feet or about 4.2 meters [e] *9* That is, about 3 1/2 feet or about 1 meter [f] *11* That is, about 18 feet wide and 23 feet long or about 5.3 meters wide and 6.9 meters long [g] *13* That is, about 44 feet or about 13 meters; also in verses 21, 25, 29, 30, 33 and 36 [h] *14* That is, about 105 feet or about 32 meters [i] *14* Septuagint; Hebrew *projecting wall* [j] *14* The meaning of the Hebrew for this verse is uncertain. [k] *15* That is, about 88 feet or about 27 meters; also in verses 21, 25, 29, 33 and 36 [l] *19* That is, about 175 feet or about 53 meters; also in verses 23, 27 and 47

The South Gate

[24]Then he led me to the south side and I saw the south gate. He measured its jambs and its portico, and they had the same measurements as the others. [25]The gateway and its portico had narrow openings all around, like the openings of the others. It was fifty cubits long and twenty-five cubits wide. [26]Seven steps led up to it, with its portico opposite them; it had palm tree decorations on the faces of the projecting walls on each side. [27]The inner court also had a gate facing south, and he measured from this gate to the outer gate on the south side; it was a hundred cubits.

The Gates to the Inner Court

[28]Then he brought me into the inner court through the south gate, and he measured the south gate; it had the same measurements as the others. [29]Its alcoves, its projecting walls and its portico had the same measurements as the others. The gateway and its portico had openings all around. It was fifty cubits long and twenty-five cubits wide. [30](The porticoes of the gateways around the inner court were twenty-five cubits wide and five cubits deep.) [31]Its portico faced the outer court; palm trees decorated its jambs, and eight steps led up to it.

[32]Then he brought me to the inner court on the east side, and he measured the gateway; it had the same measurements as the others. [33]Its alcoves, its projecting walls and its portico had the same measurements as the others. The gateway and its portico had openings all around. It was fifty cubits long and twenty-five cubits wide. [34]Its portico faced the outer court; palm trees decorated the jambs on either side, and eight steps led up to it.

[35]Then he brought me to the north gate and measured it. It had the same measurements as the others, [36]as did its alcoves, its projecting walls and its portico, and it had openings all around. It was fifty cubits long and twenty-five cubits wide. [37]Its portico[a] faced the outer court; palm trees decorated the jambs on either side, and eight steps led up to it.

The Rooms for Preparing Sacrifices

[38]A room with a doorway was by the portico in each of the inner gateways, where the burnt offerings were washed. [39]In the portico of the gateway were two tables on each side, on which the burnt offerings, sin offerings[b] and guilt offerings were slaughtered. [40]By the outside wall of the portico of the gateway, near the steps at the entrance of the north gateway were two tables, and on the other side of the steps were two tables. [41]So there were four tables on one side of the gateway and four on the other — eight tables in all — on which the sacrifices were slaughtered. [42]There were also four tables of dressed stone for the burnt offerings, each a cubit and a half long, a cubit and a half wide and a cubit high.[c] On them were placed the utensils for slaughtering the burnt offerings and the other sacrifices. [43]And double-pronged hooks, each a handbreadth[d] long, were attached to the wall all around. The tables were for the flesh of the offerings.

The Rooms for the Priests

[44]Outside the inner gate, within the inner court, were two rooms, one[e] at the side of the north gate and facing south, and another at the side of the south[f] gate and facing north. [45]He said to me, "The room facing south is for the priests who guard the temple, [46]and the room facing north is for the priests who guard the altar. These are the sons of Zadok, who are the only Levites who may draw near to the LORD to minister before him."

[47]Then he measured the court: It was square — a hundred cubits long and a hundred cubits wide. And the altar was in front of the temple.

The New Temple

[48]He brought me to the portico of the temple and measured the jambs of the portico; they were five cubits wide on either side. The width of the entrance was fourteen cubits[g] and its projecting walls were[h] three cubits[i] wide on either side. [49]The portico was twenty cubits[j] wide, and twelve[k] cubits[l] from front to back. It was reached by a flight of stairs,[m] and there were pillars on each side of the jambs.

[a] *37* Septuagint (see also verses 31 and 34); Hebrew *jambs* [b] *39* Or *purification offerings*
[c] *42* That is, about 2 2/3 feet long and wide and 21 inches high or about 80 centimeters long and wide and 53 centimeters high [d] *43* That is, about 3 1/2 inches or about 9 centimeters
[e] *44* Septuagint; Hebrew *were rooms for singers, which were* [f] *44* Septuagint; Hebrew *east*
[g] *48* That is, about 25 feet or about 7.4 meters [h] *48* Septuagint; Hebrew *entrance was*
[i] *48* That is, about 5 1/4 feet or about 1.6 meters [j] *49* That is, about 35 feet or about 11 meters
[k] *49* Septuagint; Hebrew *eleven* [l] *49* That is, about 21 feet or about 6.4 meters
[m] *49* Hebrew; Septuagint *Ten steps led up to it*

41 Then the man brought me to the
main hall and measured the jambs;
the width of the jambs was six cubits[a] on
each side.[b] 2The entrance was ten cubits[c]
wide, and the projecting walls on each
side of it were five cubits[d] wide. He also
measured the main hall; it was forty cubits
long and twenty cubits wide.[e]
3Then he went into the inner sanctuary
and measured the jambs of the entrance;
each was two cubits[f] wide. The entrance
was six cubits wide, and the projecting
walls on each side of it were seven cubits[g]
wide. 4And he measured the length of the
inner sanctuary; it was twenty cubits, and
its width was twenty cubits across the end
of the main hall. He said to me, "This is
the Most Holy Place."
5Then he measured the wall of the temple; it was six cubits thick, and each side
room around the temple was four cubits[h]
wide. 6The side rooms were on three levels,
one above another, thirty on each level.
There were ledges all around the wall of
the temple to serve as supports for the
side rooms, so that the supports were not
inserted into the wall of the temple. 7The
side rooms all around the temple were
wider at each successive level. The structure surrounding the temple was built
in ascending stages, so that the rooms
widened as one went upward. A stairway
went up from the lowest floor to the top
floor through the middle floor.
8I saw that the temple had a raised base
all around it, forming the foundation of
the side rooms. It was the length of the
rod, six long cubits. 9The outer wall of the
side rooms was five cubits thick. The open
area between the side rooms of the temple 10and the priests' rooms was twenty
cubits wide all around the temple. 11There
were entrances to the side rooms from the
open area, one on the north and another
on the south; and the base adjoining the
open area was five cubits wide all around.
12The building facing the temple courtyard on the west side was seventy cubits[i]
wide. The wall of the building was five
cubits thick all around, and its length was
ninety cubits.[j]
13Then he measured the temple; it was
a hundred cubits[k] long, and the temple
courtyard and the building with its walls
were also a hundred cubits long. 14The
width of the temple courtyard on the east,
including the front of the temple, was a
hundred cubits.
15Then he measured the length of the
building facing the courtyard at the rear
of the temple, including its galleries on
each side; it was a hundred cubits.
The main hall, the inner sanctuary and
the portico facing the court, 16as well as the
thresholds and the narrow windows and
galleries around the three of them — everything beyond and including the threshold
was covered with wood. The floor, the wall
up to the windows, and the windows were
covered. 17In the space above the outside of
the entrance to the inner sanctuary and on
the walls at regular intervals all around the
inner and outer sanctuary 18were carved
cherubim and palm trees. Palm trees alternated with cherubim. Each cherub had two
faces: 19the face of a human being toward
the palm tree on one side and the face of
a lion toward the palm tree on the other.
They were carved all around the whole
temple. 20From the floor to the area above
the entrance, cherubim and palm trees
were carved on the wall of the main hall.
21The main hall had a rectangular doorframe, and the one at the front of the Most
Holy Place was similar. 22There was a wood-
en altar three cubits[l] high and two cubits
square[m]; its corners, its base[n] and its sides
were of wood. The man said to me, "This is
the table that is before the LORD." 23Both the
main hall and the Most Holy Place had double doors. 24Each door had two leaves — two
hinged leaves for each door. 25And on the
doors of the main hall were carved cherubim and palm trees like those carved on the
walls, and there was a wooden overhang on
the front of the portico. 26On the sidewalls
of the portico were narrow windows with
palm trees carved on each side. The side
rooms of the temple also had overhangs.

The Rooms for the Priests

42 Then the man led me northward
into the outer court and brought
me to the rooms opposite the temple
courtyard and opposite the outer wall on

[a] 1 That is, about 11 feet or about 3.2 meters; also in verses 3, 5 and 8 [b] 1 One Hebrew manuscript and Septuagint; most Hebrew manuscripts *side, the width of the tent* [c] 2 That is, about 18 feet or about 5.3 meters [d] 2 That is, about 8 3/4 feet or about 2.7 meters; also in verses 9, 11 and 12 [e] 2 That is, about 70 feet long and 35 feet wide or about 21 meters long and 11 meters wide [f] 3 That is, about 3 1/2 feet or about 1.1 meters; also in verse 22 [g] 3 That is, about 12 feet or about 3.7 meters [h] 5 That is, about 7 feet or about 2.1 meters [i] 12 That is, about 123 feet or about 37 meters [j] 12 That is, about 158 feet or about 48 meters [k] 13 That is, about 175 feet or about 53 meters; also in verses 14 and 15 [l] 22 That is, about 5 1/4 feet or about 1.5 meters [m] 22 Septuagint; Hebrew *long* [n] 22 Septuagint; Hebrew *length*

the north side. 2The building whose door faced north was a hundred cubits long and fifty cubits wide.[a] 3Both in the section twenty cubits[b] from the inner court and in the section opposite the pavement of the outer court, gallery faced gallery at the three levels. 4In front of the rooms was an inner passageway ten cubits wide and a hundred cubits[c] long.[d] Their doors were on the north. 5Now the upper rooms were narrower, for the galleries took more space from them than from the rooms on the lower and middle floors of the building. 6The rooms on the top floor had no pillars, as the courts had; so they were smaller in floor space than those on the lower and middle floors. 7There was an outer wall parallel to the rooms and the outer court; it extended in front of the rooms for fifty cubits. 8While the row of rooms on the side next to the outer court was fifty cubits long, the row on the side nearest the sanctuary was a hundred cubits long. 9The lower rooms had an entrance on the east side as one enters them from the outer court.

10On the south side[e] along the length of the wall of the outer court, adjoining the temple courtyard and opposite the outer wall, were rooms 11with a passageway in front of them. These were like the rooms on the north; they had the same length and width, with similar exits and dimensions. Similar to the doorways on the north 12were the doorways of the rooms on the south. There was a doorway at the beginning of the passageway that was parallel to the corresponding wall extending eastward, by which one enters the rooms.

13Then he said to me, "The north and south rooms facing the temple courtyard are the priests' rooms, where the priests who approach the LORD will eat the most holy offerings. There they will put the most holy offerings — the grain offerings, the sin offerings[f] and the guilt offerings — for the place is holy. 14Once the priests enter the holy precincts, they are not to go into the outer court until they leave behind the garments in which they minister, for these are holy. They are to put on other clothes before they go near the places that are for the people."

15When he had finished measuring what was inside the temple area, he led me out by the east gate and measured the area all around: 16He measured the east side with the measuring rod; it was five hundred cubits.[g,h] 17He measured the north side; it was five hundred cubits[i] by the measuring rod. 18He measured the south side; it was five hundred cubits by the measuring rod. 19Then he turned to the west side and measured; it was five hundred cubits by the measuring rod. 20So he measured the area on all four sides. It had a wall around it, five hundred cubits long and five hundred cubits wide, to separate the holy from the common.

God's Glory Returns to the Temple

43 Then the man brought me to the gate facing east, 2and I saw the glory of the God of Israel coming from the east. His voice was like the roar of rushing waters, and the land was radiant with his glory. 3The vision I saw was like the vision I had seen when he[j] came to destroy the city and like the visions I had seen by the Kebar River, and I fell facedown. 4The glory of the LORD entered the temple through the gate facing east. 5Then the Spirit lifted me up and brought me into the inner court, and the glory of the LORD filled the temple.

6While the man was standing beside me, I heard someone speaking to me from inside the temple. 7He said: "Son of man, this is the place of my throne and the place for the soles of my feet. This is where I will live among the Israelites forever. The people of Israel will never again defile my holy name — neither they nor their kings — by their prostitution and the funeral offerings[k] for their kings at their death.[l] 8When they placed their threshold next to my threshold and their doorposts beside my doorposts, with only a wall between me and them, they defiled my holy name by their detestable practices. So I destroyed them in my anger. 9Now let them put away from me their prostitution and the funeral offerings for their kings, and I will live among them forever.

10"Son of man, describe the temple to the people of Israel, that they may be ashamed of their sins. Let them consider its perfection, 11and if they are ashamed of

[a] *2* That is, about 175 feet long and 88 feet wide or about 53 meters long and 27 meters wide
[b] *3* That is, about 35 feet or about 11 meters [c] *4* Septuagint and Syriac; Hebrew *and one cubit*
[d] *4* That is, about 18 feet wide and 175 feet long or about 5.3 meters wide and 53 meters long
[e] *10* Septuagint; Hebrew *Eastward* [f] *13* Or *purification offerings* [g] *16* See Septuagint of verse 17; Hebrew *rods*; also in verses 18 and 19. [h] *16* Five hundred cubits equal about 875 feet or about 265 meters; also in verses 17, 18 and 19. [i] *17* Septuagint; Hebrew *rods* [j] *3* Some Hebrew manuscripts and Vulgate; most Hebrew manuscripts *I* [k] *7* Or *the memorial monuments*; also in verse 9 [l] *7* Or *their high places*

all they have done, make known to them the design of the temple — its arrangement, its exits and entrances — its whole design and all its regulations[a] and laws. Write these down before them so that they may be faithful to its design and follow all its regulations.

12 "This is the law of the temple: All the surrounding area on top of the mountain will be most holy. Such is the law of the temple.

The Great Altar Restored

13 "These are the measurements of the altar in long cubits,[b] that cubit being a cubit and a handbreadth: Its gutter is a cubit deep and a cubit wide, with a rim of one span[c] around the edge. And this is the height of the altar: 14 From the gutter on the ground up to the lower ledge that goes around the altar it is two cubits high, and the ledge is a cubit wide.[d] From this lower ledge to the upper ledge that goes around the altar it is four cubits high, and that ledge is also a cubit wide.[e] 15 Above that, the altar hearth is four cubits high, and four horns project upward from the hearth. 16 The altar hearth is square, twelve cubits[f] long and twelve cubits wide. 17 The upper ledge also is square, fourteen cubits[g] long and fourteen cubits wide. All around the altar is a gutter of one cubit with a rim of half a cubit.[c] The steps of the altar face east."

18 Then he said to me, "Son of man, this is what the Sovereign LORD says: These will be the regulations for sacrificing burnt offerings and splashing blood against the altar when it is built: 19 You are to give a young bull as a sin offering[h] to the Levitical priests of the family of Zadok, who come near to minister before me, declares the Sovereign LORD. 20 You are to take some of its blood and put it on the four horns of the altar and on the four corners of the upper ledge and all around the rim, and so purify the altar and make atonement for it. 21 You are to take the bull for the sin offering and burn it in the designated part of the temple area outside the sanctuary.

22 "On the second day you are to offer a male goat without defect for a sin offering, and the altar is to be purified as it was purified with the bull. 23 When you have finished purifying it, you are to offer a young bull and a ram from the flock, both without defect. 24 You are to offer them before the LORD, and the priests are to sprinkle salt on them and sacrifice them as a burnt offering to the LORD.

25 "For seven days you are to provide a male goat daily for a sin offering; you are also to provide a young bull and a ram from the flock, both without defect. 26 For seven days they are to make atonement for the altar and cleanse it; thus they will dedicate it. 27 At the end of these days, from the eighth day on, the priests are to present your burnt offerings and fellowship offerings on the altar. Then I will accept you, declares the Sovereign LORD."

The Priesthood Restored

44 Then the man brought me back to the outer gate of the sanctuary, the one facing east, and it was shut. 2 The LORD said to me, "This gate is to remain shut. It must not be opened; no one may enter through it. It is to remain shut because the LORD, the God of Israel, has entered through it. 3 The prince himself is the only one who may sit inside the gateway to eat in the presence of the LORD. He is to enter by way of the portico of the gateway and go out the same way."

4 Then the man brought me by way of the north gate to the front of the temple. I looked and saw the glory of the LORD filling the temple of the LORD, and I fell facedown.

5 The LORD said to me, "Son of man, look carefully, listen closely and give attention to everything I tell you concerning all the regulations and instructions regarding the temple of the LORD. Give attention to the entrance to the temple and all the exits of the sanctuary. 6 Say to rebellious Israel, 'This is what the Sovereign LORD says: Enough of your detestable practices, people of Israel! 7 In addition to all your other detestable practices, you brought foreigners uncircumcised in heart and flesh into my sanctuary, desecrating my temple while you offered me food, fat and blood, and you broke my covenant. 8 Instead of carrying out your duty in regard

[a] 11 Some Hebrew manuscripts and Septuagint; most Hebrew manuscripts *regulations and its whole design* [b] 13 That is, about 21 inches or about 53 centimeters; also in verses 14 and 17. The long cubit is the basic unit for linear measurement throughout Ezekiel 40 – 48. [c] 13,17 That is, about 11 inches or about 27 centimeters [d] 14 That is, about 3 1/2 feet high and 1 3/4 feet wide or about 105 centimeters high and 53 centimeters wide [e] 14 That is, about 7 feet high and 1 3/4 feet wide or about 2.1 meters high and 53 centimeters wide [f] 16 That is, about 21 feet or about 6.4 meters [g] 17 That is, about 25 feet or about 7.4 meters [h] 19 Or *purification offering*; also in verses 21, 22 and 25

to my holy things, you put others in charge of my sanctuary. 9This is what the Sovereign LORD says: No foreigner uncircumcised in heart and flesh is to enter my sanctuary, not even the foreigners who live among the Israelites.

10" 'The Levites who went far from me when Israel went astray and who wandered from me after their idols must bear the consequences of their sin. 11They may serve in my sanctuary, having charge of the gates of the temple and serving in it; they may slaughter the burnt offerings and sacrifices for the people and stand before the people and serve them. 12But because they served them in the presence of their idols and made the people of Israel fall into sin, therefore I have sworn with uplifted hand that they must bear the consequences of their sin, declares the Sovereign LORD. 13They are not to come near to serve me as priests or come near any of my holy things or my most holy offerings; they must bear the shame of their detestable practices. 14And I will appoint them to guard the temple for all the work that is to be done in it.

15" 'But the Levitical priests, who are descendants of Zadok and who guarded my sanctuary when the Israelites went astray from me, are to come near to minister before me; they are to stand before me to offer sacrifices of fat and blood, declares the Sovereign LORD. 16They alone are to enter my sanctuary; they alone are to come near my table to minister before me and serve me as guards.

17" 'When they enter the gates of the inner court, they are to wear linen clothes; they must not wear any woolen garment while ministering at the gates of the inner court or inside the temple. 18They are to wear linen turbans on their heads and linen undergarments around their waists. They must not wear anything that makes them perspire. 19When they go out into the outer court where the people are, they are to take off the clothes they have been ministering in and are to leave them in the sacred rooms, and put on other clothes, so that the people are not consecrated through contact with their garments.

20" 'They must not shave their heads or let their hair grow long, but they are to keep the hair of their heads trimmed. 21No priest is to drink wine when he enters the inner court. 22They must not marry widows or divorced women; they may marry only virgins of Israelite descent or widows of priests. 23They are to teach my people the difference between the holy and the common and show them how to distinguish between the unclean and the clean.

24" 'In any dispute, the priests are to serve as judges and decide it according to my ordinances. They are to keep my laws and my decrees for all my appointed festivals, and they are to keep my Sabbaths holy.

25" 'A priest must not defile himself by going near a dead person; however, if the dead person was his father or mother, son or daughter, brother or unmarried sister, then he may defile himself. 26After he is cleansed, he must wait seven days. 27On the day he goes into the inner court of the sanctuary to minister in the sanctuary, he is to offer a sin offering[a] for himself, declares the Sovereign LORD.

28" 'I am to be the only inheritance the priests have. You are to give them no possession in Israel; I will be their possession. 29They will eat the grain offerings, the sin offerings and the guilt offerings; and everything in Israel devoted[b] to the LORD will belong to them. 30The best of all the firstfruits and of all your special gifts will belong to the priests. You are to give them the first portion of your ground meal so that a blessing may rest on your household. 31The priests must not eat anything, whether bird or animal, found dead or torn by wild animals.

Israel Fully Restored

45 " 'When you allot the land as an inheritance, you are to present to the LORD a portion of the land as a sacred district, 25,000 cubits[c] long and 20,000[d] cubits[e] wide; the entire area will be holy. 2Of this, a section 500 cubits[f] square is to be for the sanctuary, with 50 cubits[g] around it for open land. 3In the sacred district, measure off a section 25,000 cubits long and 10,000 cubits[h] wide. In it will be the sanctuary, the Most Holy Place. 4It will be the sacred portion of the land for the priests, who minister in the sanctuary and who draw near to minister before the LORD. It will be a place for their houses

[a] *27* Or *purification offering*; also in verse 29 [b] *29* The Hebrew term refers to the irrevocable giving over of things or persons to the LORD. [c] *1* That is, about 8 miles or about 13 kilometers; also in verses 3, 5 and 6 [d] *1* Septuagint (see also verses 3 and 5 and 48:9); Hebrew *10,000* [e] *1* That is, about 6 1/2 miles or about 11 kilometers [f] *2* That is, about 875 feet or about 265 meters [g] *2* That is, about 88 feet or about 27 meters [h] *3* That is, about 3 1/3 miles or about 5.3 kilometers; also in verse 5

as well as a holy place for the sanctuary. 5An area 25,000 cubits long and 10,000 cubits wide will belong to the Levites, who serve in the temple, as their possession for towns to live in.[a]

6" 'You are to give the city as its property an area 5,000 cubits[b] wide and 25,000 cubits long, adjoining the sacred portion; it will belong to all Israel.

7" 'The prince will have the land bordering each side of the area formed by the sacred district and the property of the city. It will extend westward from the west side and eastward from the east side, running lengthwise from the western to the eastern border parallel to one of the tribal portions. 8This land will be his possession in Israel. And my princes will no longer oppress my people but will allow the people of Israel to possess the land according to their tribes.

9" 'This is what the Sovereign LORD says: You have gone far enough, princes of Israel! Give up your violence and oppression and do what is just and right. Stop dispossessing my people, declares the Sovereign LORD. 10You are to use accurate scales, an accurate ephah[c] and an accurate bath.[d] 11The ephah and the bath are to be the same size, the bath containing a tenth of a homer and the ephah a tenth of a homer; the homer is to be the standard measure for both. 12The shekel[e] is to consist of twenty gerahs. Twenty shekels plus twenty-five shekels plus fifteen shekels equal one mina.[f]

13" 'This is the special gift you are to offer: a sixth of an ephah[g] from each homer of wheat and a sixth of an ephah[h] from each homer of barley. 14The prescribed portion of olive oil, measured by the bath, is a tenth of a bath[i] from each cor (which consists of ten baths or one homer, for ten baths are equivalent to a homer). 15Also one sheep is to be taken from every flock of two hundred from the well-watered pastures of Israel. These will be used for the grain offerings, burnt offerings and fellowship offerings to make atonement for the people, declares the Sovereign LORD. 16All the people of the land will be required to give this special offering to the prince in Israel. 17It will be the duty of the prince to provide the burnt offerings, grain offerings and drink offerings at the festivals, the New Moons and the Sabbaths — at all the appointed festivals of Israel. He will provide the sin offerings,[j] grain offerings, burnt offerings and fellowship offerings to make atonement for the Israelites.

18" 'This is what the Sovereign LORD says: In the first month on the first day you are to take a young bull without defect and purify the sanctuary. 19The priest is to take some of the blood of the sin offering and put it on the doorposts of the temple, on the four corners of the upper ledge of the altar and on the gateposts of the inner court. 20You are to do the same on the seventh day of the month for anyone who sins unintentionally or through ignorance; so you are to make atonement for the temple.

21" 'In the first month on the fourteenth day you are to observe the Passover, a festival lasting seven days, during which you shall eat bread made without yeast. 22On that day the prince is to provide a bull as a sin offering for himself and for all the people of the land. 23Every day during the seven days of the festival he is to provide seven bulls and seven rams without defect as a burnt offering to the LORD, and a male goat for a sin offering. 24He is to provide as a grain offering an ephah for each bull and an ephah for each ram, along with a hin[k] of olive oil for each ephah.

25" 'During the seven days of the festival, which begins in the seventh month on the fifteenth day, he is to make the same provision for sin offerings, burnt offerings, grain offerings and oil.

46 " 'This is what the Sovereign LORD says: The gate of the inner court facing east is to be shut on the six working days, but on the Sabbath day and on the day of the New Moon it is to be opened. 2The prince is to enter from the outside through the portico of the gateway and stand by the gatepost. The priests are to sacrifice his burnt offering and his fellowship offerings. He is to bow down in worship at the threshold of the gateway and then go out, but the gate will not be shut until evening. 3On the Sabbaths and

[a] 5 Septuagint; Hebrew *temple; they will have as their possession 20 rooms* [b] 6 That is, about 1 2/3 miles or about 2.7 kilometers [c] 10 An ephah was a dry measure having the capacity of about 3/5 bushel or about 22 liters. [d] 10 A bath was a liquid measure equaling about 6 gallons or about 22 liters. [e] 12 A shekel weighed about 2/5 ounce or about 12 grams. [f] 12 That is, 60 shekels; the common mina was 50 shekels. Sixty shekels were about 1 1/2 pounds or about 690 grams. [g] 13 That is, probably about 6 pounds or about 2.7 kilograms [h] 13 That is, probably about 5 pounds or about 2.3 kilograms [i] 14 That is, about 2 1/2 quarts or about 2.2 liters [j] 17 Or *purification offerings*; also in verses 19, 22, 23 and 25 [k] 24 That is, about 1 gallon or about 3.8 liters

New Moons the people of the land are
to worship in the presence of the LORD
at the entrance of that gateway. 4The
burnt offering the prince brings to the
LORD on the Sabbath day is to be six male
lambs and a ram, all without defect. 5The
grain offering given with the ram is to be
an ephah,[a] and the grain offering with
the lambs is to be as much as he pleases,
along with a hin[b] of olive oil for each
ephah. 6On the day of the New Moon he
is to offer a young bull, six lambs and a
ram, all without defect. 7He is to provide
as a grain offering one ephah with the
bull, one ephah with the ram, and with
the lambs as much as he wants to give,
along with a hin of oil for each ephah.
8When the prince enters, he is to go in
through the portico of the gateway, and
he is to come out the same way.

9" 'When the people of the land come
before the LORD at the appointed festivals, whoever enters by the north gate to
worship is to go out the south gate; and
whoever enters by the south gate is to go
out the north gate. No one is to return
through the gate by which they entered,
but each is to go out the opposite gate.
10The prince is to be among them, going in
when they go in and going out when they
go out. 11At the feasts and the appointed
festivals, the grain offering is to be an
ephah with a bull, an ephah with a ram,
and with the lambs as much as he pleases, along with a hin of oil for each ephah.

12" 'When the prince provides a freewill
offering to the LORD — whether a burnt
offering or fellowship offerings — the gate
facing east is to be opened for him. He
shall offer his burnt offering or his fellowship offerings as he does on the Sabbath
day. Then he shall go out, and after he has
gone out, the gate will be shut.

13" 'Every day you are to provide a year-
old lamb without defect for a burnt offering to the LORD; morning by morning you
shall provide it. 14You are also to provide
with it morning by morning a grain offering, consisting of a sixth of an ephah[c]
with a third of a hin[d] of oil to moisten the
flour. The presenting of this grain offering
to the LORD is a lasting ordinance. 15So the
lamb and the grain offering and the oil
shall be provided morning by morning
for a regular burnt offering.

16" 'This is what the Sovereign LORD
says: If the prince makes a gift from his
inheritance to one of his sons, it will also
belong to his descendants; it is to be their
property by inheritance. 17If, however, he
makes a gift from his inheritance to one of
his servants, the servant may keep it until
the year of freedom; then it will revert to
the prince. His inheritance belongs to his
sons only; it is theirs. 18The prince must not
take any of the inheritance of the people,
driving them off their property. He is to
give his sons their inheritance out of his
own property, so that not one of my people
will be separated from their property.' "

19Then the man brought me through the
entrance at the side of the gate to the sacred rooms facing north, which belonged
to the priests, and showed me a place at
the western end. 20He said to me, "This is
the place where the priests are to cook the
guilt offering and the sin offering[e] and
bake the grain offering, to avoid bringing
them into the outer court and consecrating the people."

21He then brought me to the outer court
and led me around to its four corners, and
I saw in each corner another court. 22In
the four corners of the outer court were
enclosed[f] courts, forty cubits long and thirty cubits wide;[g] each of the courts in the
four corners was the same size. 23Around
the inside of each of the four courts was
a ledge of stone, with places for fire built
all around under the ledge. 24He said to
me, "These are the kitchens where those
who minister at the temple are to cook
the sacrifices of the people."

The River From the Temple

47 The man brought me back to the
entrance to the temple, and I saw
water coming out from under the threshold of the temple toward the east (for the
temple faced east). The water was coming down from under the south side of
the temple, south of the altar. 2He then
brought me out through the north gate
and led me around the outside to the outer
gate facing east, and the water was trick-
ling from the south side.

3As the man went eastward with a measuring line in his hand, he measured off a
thousand cubits[h] and then led me through
water that was ankle-deep. 4He measured

[a] *5* That is, probably about 35 pounds or about 16 kilograms; also in verses 7 and 11 [b] *5* That is, about 1 gallon or about 3.8 liters; also in verses 7 and 11 [c] *14* That is, probably about 6 pounds or about 2.7 kilograms [d] *14* That is, about 1 1/2 quarts or about 1.3 liters [e] *20* Or *purification offering* [f] *22* The meaning of the Hebrew for this word is uncertain. [g] *22* That is, about 70 feet long and 53 feet wide or about 21 meters long and 16 meters wide [h] *3* That is, about 1,700 feet or about 530 meters

off another thousand cubits and led me
through water that was knee-deep. He
measured off another thousand and led
me through water that was up to the waist.
5He measured off another thousand, but
now it was a river that I could not cross,
because the water had risen and was deep
enough to swim in — a river that no one
could cross. 6He asked me, "Son of man,
do you see this?"

Then he led me back to the bank of the
river. 7When I arrived there, I saw a great
number of trees on each side of the river.
8He said to me, "This water flows toward
the eastern region and goes down into
the Arabah,[a] where it enters the Dead Sea.
When it empties into the sea, the salty
water there becomes fresh. 9Swarms of
living creatures will live wherever the river
flows. There will be large numbers of fish,
because this water flows there and makes
the salt water fresh; so where the river
flows everything will live. 10Fishermen will
stand along the shore; from En Gedi to En
Eglaim there will be places for spreading
nets. The fish will be of many kinds — like
the fish of the Mediterranean Sea. 11But
the swamps and marshes will not become
fresh; they will be left for salt. 12Fruit trees
of all kinds will grow on both banks of the
river. Their leaves will not wither, nor will
their fruit fail. Every month they will bear
fruit, because the water from the sanctuary flows to them. Their fruit will serve for
food and their leaves for healing."

The Boundaries of the Land

13This is what the Sovereign LORD says:
"These are the boundaries of the land that
you will divide among the twelve tribes
of Israel as their inheritance, with two
portions for Joseph. 14You are to divide it
equally among them. Because I swore with
uplifted hand to give it to your ancestors,
this land will become your inheritance.

15"This is to be the boundary of the land:

"On the north side it will run from the
Mediterranean Sea by the Hethlon
road past Lebo Hamath to Zedad,
16Berothah[b] and Sibraim (which lies
on the border between Damascus and
Hamath), as far as Hazer Hattikon,
which is on the border of Hauran.
17The boundary will extend from the
sea to Hazar Enan,[c] along the northern border of Damascus, with the
border of Hamath to the north. This
will be the northern boundary.

18"On the east side the boundary will
run between Hauran and Damascus,
along the Jordan between Gilead and
the land of Israel, to the Dead Sea
and as far as Tamar.[d] This will be the
eastern boundary.

19"On the south side it will run from Tamar as far as the waters of Meribah
Kadesh, then along the Wadi of Egypt
to the Mediterranean Sea. This will
be the southern boundary.

20"On the west side, the Mediterranean
Sea will be the boundary to a point
opposite Lebo Hamath. This will be
the western boundary.

21"You are to distribute this land among
yourselves according to the tribes of Israel.
22You are to allot it as an inheritance for
yourselves and for the foreigners residing among you and who have children.
You are to consider them as native-born
Israelites; along with you they are to be
allotted an inheritance among the tribes
of Israel. 23In whatever tribe a foreigner
resides, there you are to give them their
inheritance," declares the Sovereign LORD.

The Division of the Land

48 "These are the tribes, listed by
name: At the northern frontier,
Dan will have one portion; it will follow
the Hethlon road to Lebo Hamath; Hazar Enan and the northern border of Damascus next to Hamath will be part of its
border from the east side to the west side.

2"Asher will have one portion; it will border the territory of Dan from east to west.

3"Naphtali will have one portion; it will
border the territory of Asher from east
to west.

4"Manasseh will have one portion; it
will border the territory of Naphtali from
east to west.

5"Ephraim will have one portion; it will
border the territory of Manasseh from
east to west.

6"Reuben will have one portion; it will
border the territory of Ephraim from east
to west.

7"Judah will have one portion; it will
border the territory of Reuben from east
to west.

8"Bordering the territory of Judah from
east to west will be the portion you are to
present as a special gift. It will be 25,000
cubits[e] wide, and its length from east to

[a] *8* Or *the Jordan Valley* [b] *15,16* See Septuagint and 48:1; Hebrew *road to go into Zedad,* *16Hamath, Berothah.* [c] *17* Hebrew *Enon,* a variant of *Enan* [d] *18* See Syriac; Hebrew *Israel. You will measure to the Dead Sea.* [e] *8* That is, about 8 miles or about 13 kilometers; also in verses 9, 10, 13, 15, 20 and 21

west will equal one of the tribal portions;
the sanctuary will be in the center of it.
9“The special portion you are to offer
to the LORD will be 25,000 cubits long
and 10,000 cubits[a] wide. 10This will be
the sacred portion for the priests. It will
be 25,000 cubits long on the north side,
10,000 cubits wide on the west side, 10,000
cubits wide on the east side and 25,000 cubits long on the south side. In the center of
it will be the sanctuary of the LORD. 11This
will be for the consecrated priests, the Za-
dokites, who were faithful in serving me
and did not go astray as the Levites did
when the Israelites went astray. 12It will
be a special gift to them from the sacred
portion of the land, a most holy portion,
bordering the territory of the Levites.
13“Alongside the territory of the priests,
the Levites will have an allotment 25,000
cubits long and 10,000 cubits wide. Its
total length will be 25,000 cubits and its
width 10,000 cubits. 14They must not sell
or exchange any of it. This is the best of the
land and must not pass into other hands,
because it is holy to the LORD.
15“The remaining area, 5,000 cubits[b]
wide and 25,000 cubits long, will be for the
common use of the city, for houses and for
pastureland. The city will be in the center
of it 16and will have these measurements:
the north side 4,500 cubits,[c] the south side
4,500 cubits, the east side 4,500 cubits, and
the west side 4,500 cubits. 17The pastureland for the city will be 250 cubits[d] on the
north, 250 cubits on the south, 250 cubits
on the east, and 250 cubits on the west.
18What remains of the area, bordering
on the sacred portion and running the
length of it, will be 10,000 cubits on the
east side and 10,000 cubits on the west
side. Its produce will supply food for the
workers of the city. 19The workers from
the city who farm it will come from all
the tribes of Israel. 20The entire portion
will be a square, 25,000 cubits on each
side. As a special gift you will set aside
the sacred portion, along with the property of the city.
21“What remains on both sides of the
area formed by the sacred portion and
the property of the city will belong to the
prince. It will extend eastward from the
25,000 cubits of the sacred portion to
the eastern border, and westward from
the 25,000 cubits to the western border.
Both these areas running the length of the
tribal portions will belong to the prince,
and the sacred portion with the temple
sanctuary will be in the center of them.
22So the property of the Levites and the
property of the city will lie in the center
of the area that belongs to the prince. The
area belonging to the prince will lie between the border of Judah and the border
of Benjamin.
23“As for the rest of the tribes: Benjamin
will have one portion; it will extend from
the east side to the west side.
24“Simeon will have one portion; it will
border the territory of Benjamin from
east to west.
25“Issachar will have one portion; it
will border the territory of Simeon from
east to west.
26“Zebulun will have one portion; it will
border the territory of Issachar from east
to west.
27“Gad will have one portion; it will border the territory of Zebulun from east
to west.
28“The southern boundary of Gad will
run south from Tamar to the waters of
Meribah Kadesh, then along the Wadi of
Egypt to the Mediterranean Sea.
29“This is the land you are to allot as
an inheritance to the tribes of Israel, and
these will be their portions,” declares the
Sovereign LORD.

The Gates of the New City

30“These will be the exits of the city: Beginning on the north side, which is 4,500
cubits long, 31the gates of the city will be
named after the tribes of Israel. The three
gates on the north side will be the gate of
Reuben, the gate of Judah and the gate
of Levi.
32“On the east side, which is 4,500 cubits long, will be three gates: the gate
of Joseph, the gate of Benjamin and the
gate of Dan.
33“On the south side, which measures
4,500 cubits, will be three gates: the gate
of Simeon, the gate of Issachar and the
gate of Zebulun.
34“On the west side, which is 4,500 cubits
long, will be three gates: the gate of Gad,
the gate of Asher and the gate of Naphtali.
35“The distance all around will be 18,000
cubits.[e]

“And the name of the city from that
time on will be:

THE LORD IS THERE.”

[a] *9* That is, about 3 1/3 miles or about 5.3 kilometers; also in verses 10, 13 and 18 [b] *15* That is, about 1 2/3 miles or about 2.7 kilometers [c] *16* That is, about 1 1/2 miles or about 2.4 kilometers; also in verses 30, 32, 33 and 34 [d] *17* That is, about 440 feet or about 135 meters [e] *35* That is, about 6 miles or about 9.5 kilometers

DANIEL

Daniel's Training in Babylon

1 In the third year of the reign of Jehoiakim king of Judah, Nebuchadnezzar king of Babylon came to Jerusalem and besieged it. 2And the Lord delivered Jehoiakim king of Judah into his hand, along with some of the articles from the temple of God. These he carried off to the temple of his god in Babylonia[a] and put in the treasure house of his god.

3Then the king ordered Ashpenaz, chief of his court officials, to bring into the king's service some of the Israelites from the royal family and the nobility — 4young men without any physical defect, handsome, showing aptitude for every kind of learning, well informed, quick to understand, and qualified to serve in the king's palace. He was to teach them the language and literature of the Babylonians.[b] 5The king assigned them a daily amount of food and wine from the king's table. They were to be trained for three years, and after that they were to enter the king's service.

6Among those who were chosen were some from Judah: Daniel, Hananiah, Mishael and Azariah. 7The chief official gave them new names: to Daniel, the name Belteshazzar; to Hananiah, Shadrach; to Mishael, Meshach; and to Azariah, Abednego.

8But Daniel resolved not to defile himself with the royal food and wine, and he asked the chief official for permission not to defile himself this way. 9Now God had caused the official to show favor and compassion to Daniel, 10but the official told Daniel, "I am afraid of my lord the king, who has assigned your[c] food and drink. Why should he see you looking worse than the other young men your age? The king would then have my head because of you."

11Daniel then said to the guard whom the chief official had appointed over Daniel, Hananiah, Mishael and Azariah, 12"Please test your servants for ten days: Give us nothing but vegetables to eat and water to drink. 13Then compare our appearance with that of the young men who eat the royal food, and treat your servants in accordance with what you see." 14So he agreed to this and tested them for ten days.

15At the end of the ten days they looked healthier and better nourished than any of the young men who ate the royal food. 16So the guard took away their choice food and the wine they were to drink and gave them vegetables instead.

17To these four young men God gave knowledge and understanding of all kinds of literature and learning. And Daniel could understand visions and dreams of all kinds.

18At the end of the time set by the king to bring them into his service, the chief official presented them to Nebuchadnezzar. 19The king talked with them, and he found none equal to Daniel, Hananiah, Mishael and Azariah; so they entered the king's service. 20In every matter of wisdom and understanding about which the king questioned them, he found them ten times better than all the magicians and enchanters in his whole kingdom.

21And Daniel remained there until the first year of King Cyrus.

Nebuchadnezzar's Dream

2 In the second year of his reign, Nebuchadnezzar had dreams; his mind was troubled and he could not sleep. 2So the king summoned the magicians, enchanters, sorcerers and astrologers[d] to tell him what he had dreamed. When they came in and stood before the king, 3he said to them, "I have had a dream that troubles me and I want to know what it means.[e]"

4Then the astrologers answered the king,[f] "May the king live forever! Tell your servants the dream, and we will interpret it."

5The king replied to the astrologers, "This is what I have firmly decided: If you do not tell me what my dream was and interpret it, I will have you cut into pieces and your houses turned into piles of rubble. 6But if you tell me the dream and explain it, you will receive from me gifts and rewards and great honor. So tell me the dream and interpret it for me."

7Once more they replied, "Let the king tell his servants the dream, and we will interpret it."

[a] 2 Hebrew *Shinar* [b] 4 Or *Chaldeans* [c] 10 The Hebrew for *your* and *you* in this verse is plural.
[d] 2 Or *Chaldeans*; also in verses 4, 5 and 10 [e] 3 Or *was* [f] 4 At this point the Hebrew text has *in Aramaic*, indicating that the text from here through the end of chapter 7 is in Aramaic.

8 Then the king answered, "I am certain
that you are trying to gain time, because
you realize that this is what I have firmly
decided: 9 If you do not tell me the dream,
there is only one penalty for you. You have
conspired to tell me misleading and wicked
things, hoping the situation will change.
So then, tell me the dream, and I will know
that you can interpret it for me."

10 The astrologers answered the king,
"There is no one on earth who can do what
the king asks! No king, however great and
mighty, has ever asked such a thing of
any magician or enchanter or astrologer.
11 What the king asks is too difficult. No one
can reveal it to the king except the gods,
and they do not live among humans."

12 This made the king so angry and furious that he ordered the execution of all
the wise men of Babylon. 13 So the decree
was issued to put the wise men to death,
and men were sent to look for Daniel and
his friends to put them to death.

14 When Arioch, the commander of the
king's guard, had gone out to put to death
the wise men of Babylon, Daniel spoke to
him with wisdom and tact. 15 He asked the
king's officer, "Why did the king issue such
a harsh decree?" Arioch then explained
the matter to Daniel. 16 At this, Daniel went
in to the king and asked for time, so that
he might interpret the dream for him.

17 Then Daniel returned to his house and
explained the matter to his friends Hananiah, Mishael and Azariah. 18 He urged
them to plead for mercy from the God of
heaven concerning this mystery, so that
he and his friends might not be executed
with the rest of the wise men of Babylon.
19 During the night the mystery was revealed to Daniel in a vision. Then Daniel
praised the God of heaven 20 and said:

"Praise be to the name of God for ever
and ever;
wisdom and power are his.
21 He changes times and seasons;
he deposes kings and raises up
others.
He gives wisdom to the wise
and knowledge to the discerning.
22 He reveals deep and hidden things;
he knows what lies in darkness,
and light dwells with him.
23 I thank and praise you, God of my
ancestors:
You have given me wisdom and
power,
you have made known to me what we
asked of you,
you have made known to us the
dream of the king."

Daniel Interprets the Dream

24 Then Daniel went to Arioch, whom
the king had appointed to execute the
wise men of Babylon, and said to him,
"Do not execute the wise men of Babylon.
Take me to the king, and I will interpret
his dream for him."

25 Arioch took Daniel to the king at once
and said, "I have found a man among the
exiles from Judah who can tell the king
what his dream means."

26 The king asked Daniel (also called
Belteshazzar), "Are you able to tell me
what I saw in my dream and interpret it?"

27 Daniel replied, "No wise man, enchanter, magician or diviner can explain to the
king the mystery he has asked about,
28 but there is a God in heaven who reveals
mysteries. He has shown King Nebuchadnezzar what will happen in days to come.
Your dream and the visions that passed
through your mind as you were lying in
bed are these:

29 "As Your Majesty was lying there, your
mind turned to things to come, and the
revealer of mysteries showed you what is
going to happen. 30 As for me, this mystery
has been revealed to me, not because I
have greater wisdom than anyone else
alive, but so that Your Majesty may know
the interpretation and that you may understand what went through your mind.

31 "Your Majesty looked, and there before
you stood a large statue — an enormous,
dazzling statue, awesome in appearance.
32 The head of the statue was made of pure
gold, its chest and arms of silver, its belly
and thighs of bronze, 33 its legs of iron, its
feet partly of iron and partly of baked clay.
34 While you were watching, a rock was cut
out, but not by human hands. It struck
the statue on its feet of iron and clay and
smashed them. 35 Then the iron, the clay,
the bronze, the silver and the gold were
all broken to pieces and became like chaff
on a threshing floor in the summer. The
wind swept them away without leaving a
trace. But the rock that struck the statue
became a huge mountain and filled the
whole earth.

36 "This was the dream, and now we will
interpret it to the king. 37 Your Majesty, you
are the king of kings. The God of heaven
has given you dominion and power and
might and glory; 38 in your hands he has
placed all mankind and the beasts of the
field and the birds in the sky. Wherever
they live, he has made you ruler over them
all. You are that head of gold.

39 "After you, another kingdom will arise,
inferior to yours. Next, a third kingdom, one
of bronze, will rule over the whole earth.

40Finally, there will be a fourth kingdom, strong as iron — for iron breaks and smashes everything — and as iron breaks things to pieces, so it will crush and break all the others. 41Just as you saw that the feet and toes were partly of baked clay and partly of iron, so this will be a divided kingdom; yet it will have some of the strength of iron in it, even as you saw iron mixed with clay. 42As the toes were partly iron and partly clay, so this kingdom will be partly strong and partly brittle. 43And just as you saw the iron mixed with baked clay, so the people will be a mixture and will not remain united, any more than iron mixes with clay.

44"In the time of those kings, the God of heaven will set up a kingdom that will never be destroyed, nor will it be left to another people. It will crush all those kingdoms and bring them to an end, but it will itself endure forever. 45This is the meaning of the vision of the rock cut out of a mountain, but not by human hands — a rock that broke the iron, the bronze, the clay, the silver and the gold to pieces.

"The great God has shown the king what will take place in the future. The dream is true and its interpretation is trustworthy."

46Then King Nebuchadnezzar fell prostrate before Daniel and paid him honor and ordered that an offering and incense be presented to him. 47The king said to Daniel, "Surely your God is the God of gods and the Lord of kings and a revealer of mysteries, for you were able to reveal this mystery."

48Then the king placed Daniel in a high position and lavished many gifts on him. He made him ruler over the entire province of Babylon and placed him in charge of all its wise men. 49Moreover, at Daniel's request the king appointed Shadrach, Meshach and Abednego administrators over the province of Babylon, while Daniel himself remained at the royal court.

The Image of Gold and the Blazing Furnace

3 King Nebuchadnezzar made an image of gold, sixty cubits high and six cubits wide,[a] and set it up on the plain of Dura in the province of Babylon. 2He then summoned the satraps, prefects, governors, advisers, treasurers, judges, magistrates and all the other provincial officials to come to the dedication of the image he had set up. 3So the satraps, prefects, governors, advisers, treasurers, judges, magistrates and all the other provincial officials assembled for the dedication of the image that King Nebuchadnezzar had set up, and they stood before it.

4Then the herald loudly proclaimed, "Nations and peoples of every language, this is what you are commanded to do: 5As soon as you hear the sound of the horn, flute, zither, lyre, harp, pipe and all kinds of music, you must fall down and worship the image of gold that King Nebuchadnezzar has set up. 6Whoever does not fall down and worship will immediately be thrown into a blazing furnace."

7Therefore, as soon as they heard the sound of the horn, flute, zither, lyre, harp and all kinds of music, all the nations and peoples of every language fell down and worshiped the image of gold that King Nebuchadnezzar had set up.

8At this time some astrologers[b] came forward and denounced the Jews. 9They said to King Nebuchadnezzar, "May the king live forever! 10Your Majesty has issued a decree that everyone who hears the sound of the horn, flute, zither, lyre, harp, pipe and all kinds of music must fall down and worship the image of gold, 11and that whoever does not fall down and worship will be thrown into a blazing furnace. 12But there are some Jews whom you have set over the affairs of the province of Babylon — Shadrach, Meshach and Abednego — who pay no attention to you, Your Majesty. They neither serve your gods nor worship the image of gold you have set up."

13Furious with rage, Nebuchadnezzar summoned Shadrach, Meshach and Abednego. So these men were brought before the king, 14and Nebuchadnezzar said to them, "Is it true, Shadrach, Meshach and Abednego, that you do not serve my gods or worship the image of gold I have set up? 15Now when you hear the sound of the horn, flute, zither, lyre, harp, pipe and all kinds of music, if you are ready to fall down and worship the image I made, very good. But if you do not worship it, you will be thrown immediately into a blazing furnace. Then what god will be able to rescue you from my hand?"

16Shadrach, Meshach and Abednego replied to him, "King Nebuchadnezzar, we do not need to defend ourselves before you in this matter. 17If we are thrown into the blazing furnace, the God we serve is able to deliver us from it, and he will deliver us[c] from Your Majesty's hand. 18But

[a] *1* That is, about 90 feet high and 9 feet wide or about 27 meters high and 2.7 meters wide
[b] *8* Or *Chaldeans* [c] *17* Or *If the God we serve is able to deliver us, then he will deliver us from the blazing furnace and*

even if he does not, we want you to know,
Your Majesty, that we will not serve your
gods or worship the image of gold you
have set up."
19Then Nebuchadnezzar was furious
with Shadrach, Meshach and Abednego,
and his attitude toward them changed. He
ordered the furnace heated seven times
hotter than usual 20and commanded some
of the strongest soldiers in his army to
tie up Shadrach, Meshach and Abednego and throw them into the blazing furnace. 21So these men, wearing their robes,
trousers, turbans and other clothes, were
bound and thrown into the blazing furnace. 22The king's command was so urgent
and the furnace so hot that the flames of
the fire killed the soldiers who took up
Shadrach, Meshach and Abednego, 23and
these three men, firmly tied, fell into the
blazing furnace.
24Then King Nebuchadnezzar leaped
to his feet in amazement and asked his
advisers, "Weren't there three men that we
tied up and threw into the fire?"
They replied, "Certainly, Your Majesty."
25He said, "Look! I see four men walking around in the fire, unbound and unharmed, and the fourth looks like a son
of the gods."
26Nebuchadnezzar then approached
the opening of the blazing furnace and
shouted, "Shadrach, Meshach and Abednego, servants of the Most High God, come
out! Come here!"
So Shadrach, Meshach and Abednego
came out of the fire, 27and the satraps,
prefects, governors and royal advisers
crowded around them. They saw that the
fire had not harmed their bodies, nor was
a hair of their heads singed; their robes
were not scorched, and there was no smell
of fire on them.
28Then Nebuchadnezzar said, "Praise
be to the God of Shadrach, Meshach and
Abednego, who has sent his angel and
rescued his servants! They trusted in him
and defied the king's command and were
willing to give up their lives rather than
serve or worship any god except their own
God. 29Therefore I decree that the people of
any nation or language who say anything
against the God of Shadrach, Meshach
and Abednego be cut into pieces and their
houses be turned into piles of rubble, for
no other god can save in this way."
30Then the king promoted Shadrach,
Meshach and Abednego in the province
of Babylon.

Nebuchadnezzar's Dream of a Tree

4 [a] King Nebuchadnezzar,

To the nations and peoples of every
language, who live in all the earth:

May you prosper greatly!

2It is my pleasure to tell you about
the miraculous signs and wonders
that the Most High God has performed for me.

3How great are his signs,
how mighty his wonders!
His kingdom is an eternal
kingdom;
his dominion endures from
generation to generation.

4I, Nebuchadnezzar, was at home
in my palace, contented and prosperous. 5I had a dream that made
me afraid. As I was lying in bed,
the images and visions that passed
through my mind terrified me. 6So I
commanded that all the wise men of
Babylon be brought before me to interpret the dream for me. 7When the
magicians, enchanters, astrologers[b]
and diviners came, I told them the
dream, but they could not interpret it
for me. 8Finally, Daniel came into my
presence and I told him the dream.
(He is called Belteshazzar, after the
name of my god, and the spirit of the
holy gods is in him.)
9I said, "Belteshazzar, chief of the
magicians, I know that the spirit of
the holy gods is in you, and no mystery is too difficult for you. Here is my
dream; interpret it for me. 10These
are the visions I saw while lying in
bed: I looked, and there before me
stood a tree in the middle of the land.
Its height was enormous. 11The tree
grew large and strong and its top
touched the sky; it was visible to the
ends of the earth. 12Its leaves were
beautiful, its fruit abundant, and on
it was food for all. Under it the wild
animals found shelter, and the birds
lived in its branches; from it every
creature was fed.
13"In the visions I saw while lying
in bed, I looked, and there before me
was a holy one, a messenger,[c] coming down from heaven. 14He called
in a loud voice: 'Cut down the tree
and trim off its branches; strip off
its leaves and scatter its fruit. Let the

[a] In Aramaic texts 4:1-3 is numbered 3:31-33, and 4:4-37 is numbered 4:1-34. [b] 7 Or *Chaldeans*
[c] 13 Or *watchman*; also in verses 17 and 23

animals flee from under it and the
birds from its branches. 15But let the
stump and its roots, bound with iron
and bronze, remain in the ground, in
the grass of the field.

" 'Let him be drenched with the
dew of heaven, and let him live with
the animals among the plants of the
earth. 16Let his mind be changed from
that of a man and let him be giv-
en the mind of an animal, till seven
times[a] pass by for him.

17" 'The decision is announced by
messengers, the holy ones declare
the verdict, so that the living may
know that the Most High is sovereign over all kingdoms on earth and
gives them to anyone he wishes and
sets over them the lowliest of people.'

18"This is the dream that I, King
Nebuchadnezzar, had. Now, Belteshazzar, tell me what it means, for
none of the wise men in my kingdom
can interpret it for me. But you can,
because the spirit of the holy gods
is in you."

Daniel Interprets the Dream

19Then Daniel (also called Belteshazzar) was greatly perplexed for
a time, and his thoughts terrified
him. So the king said, "Belteshazzar,
do not let the dream or its meaning
alarm you."

Belteshazzar answered, "My lord,
if only the dream applied to your enemies and its meaning to your adversaries! 20The tree you saw, which
grew large and strong, with its top
touching the sky, visible to the whole
earth, 21with beautiful leaves and
abundant fruit, providing food for
all, giving shelter to the wild animals, and having nesting places in
its branches for the birds — 22Your
Majesty, you are that tree! You have
become great and strong; your greatness has grown until it reaches the
sky, and your dominion extends to
distant parts of the earth.

23"Your Majesty saw a holy one, a
messenger, coming down from heav-
en and saying, 'Cut down the tree and
destroy it, but leave the stump, bound
with iron and bronze, in the grass of
the field, while its roots remain in the
ground. Let him be drenched with
the dew of heaven; let him live with
the wild animals, until seven times
pass by for him.'

24"This is the interpretation, Your
Majesty, and this is the decree the
Most High has issued against my lord
the king: 25You will be driven away
from people and will live with the
wild animals; you will eat grass like
the ox and be drenched with the dew
of heaven. Seven times will pass by
for you until you acknowledge that
the Most High is sovereign over all
kingdoms on earth and gives them
to anyone he wishes. 26The command
to leave the stump of the tree with its
roots means that your kingdom will
be restored to you when you acknowledge that Heaven rules. 27Therefore,
Your Majesty, be pleased to accept my
advice: Renounce your sins by doing
what is right, and your wickedness
by being kind to the oppressed. It
may be that then your prosperity
will continue."

The Dream Is Fulfilled

28All this happened to King Nebuchadnezzar. 29Twelve months later,
as the king was walking on the roof
of the royal palace of Babylon, 30he
said, "Is not this the great Babylon I
have built as the royal residence, by
my mighty power and for the glory
of my majesty?"

31Even as the words were on his
lips, a voice came from heaven, "This
is what is decreed for you, King Nebuchadnezzar: Your royal authority has been taken from you. 32You
will be driven away from people
and will live with the wild animals;
you will eat grass like the ox. Seven
times will pass by for you until you
acknowledge that the Most High is
sovereign over all kingdoms on earth
and gives them to anyone he wishes."

33Immediately what had been said
about Nebuchadnezzar was fulfilled.
He was driven away from people and
ate grass like the ox. His body was
drenched with the dew of heaven
until his hair grew like the feathers of
an eagle and his nails like the claws
of a bird.

34At the end of that time, I, Nebuchadnezzar, raised my eyes toward
heaven, and my sanity was restored.
Then I praised the Most High; I honored and glorified him who lives
forever.

[a] 16 Or *years*; also in verses 23, 25 and 32

His dominion is an eternal dominion;
his kingdom endures from
generation to generation.
35 All the peoples of the earth
are regarded as nothing.
He does as he pleases
with the powers of heaven
and the peoples of the earth.
No one can hold back his hand
or say to him: "What have you
done?"

36 At the same time that my sanity
was restored, my honor and splendor
were returned to me for the glory of
my kingdom. My advisers and nobles
sought me out, and I was restored to
my throne and became even greater
than before. 37 Now I, Nebuchadnezzar, praise and exalt and glorify the
King of heaven, because everything
he does is right and all his ways are
just. And those who walk in pride he
is able to humble.

The Writing on the Wall

5 King Belshazzar gave a great banquet
for a thousand of his nobles and drank
wine with them. 2 While Belshazzar was
drinking his wine, he gave orders to bring
in the gold and silver goblets that Nebuchadnezzar his father[a] had taken from the
temple in Jerusalem, so that the king and
his nobles, his wives and his concubines
might drink from them. 3 So they brought in
the gold goblets that had been taken from
the temple of God in Jerusalem, and the
king and his nobles, his wives and his concubines drank from them. 4 As they drank
the wine, they praised the gods of gold
and silver, of bronze, iron, wood and stone.
5 Suddenly the fingers of a human hand
appeared and wrote on the plaster of the
wall, near the lampstand in the royal
palace. The king watched the hand as it
wrote. 6 His face turned pale and he was
so frightened that his legs became weak
and his knees were knocking.
7 The king summoned the enchanters,
astrologers[b] and diviners. Then he said to
these wise men of Babylon, "Whoever reads
this writing and tells me what it means will
be clothed in purple and have a gold chain
placed around his neck, and he will be made
the third highest ruler in the kingdom."
8 Then all the king's wise men came in,
but they could not read the writing or tell
the king what it meant. 9 So King Belshazzar became even more terrified and his face
grew more pale. His nobles were baffled.
10 The queen,[c] hearing the voices of the
king and his nobles, came into the banquet hall. "May the king live forever!" she
said. "Don't be alarmed! Don't look so pale!
11 There is a man in your kingdom who has
the spirit of the holy gods in him. In the
time of your father he was found to have
insight and intelligence and wisdom like
that of the gods. Your father, King Nebuchadnezzar, appointed him chief of the
magicians, enchanters, astrologers and diviners. 12 He did this because Daniel, whom
the king called Belteshazzar, was found
to have a keen mind and knowledge and
understanding, and also the ability to interpret dreams, explain riddles and solve
difficult problems. Call for Daniel, and
he will tell you what the writing means."
13 So Daniel was brought before the king,
and the king said to him, "Are you Daniel,
one of the exiles my father the king brought
from Judah? 14 I have heard that the spirit of
the gods is in you and that you have insight,
intelligence and outstanding wisdom. 15 The
wise men and enchanters were brought
before me to read this writing and tell me
what it means, but they could not explain
it. 16 Now I have heard that you are able to
give interpretations and to solve difficult
problems. If you can read this writing and
tell me what it means, you will be clothed
in purple and have a gold chain placed
around your neck, and you will be made
the third highest ruler in the kingdom."
17 Then Daniel answered the king, "You
may keep your gifts for yourself and give
your rewards to someone else. Nevertheless, I will read the writing for the king
and tell him what it means.
18 "Your Majesty, the Most High God gave
your father Nebuchadnezzar sovereignty
and greatness and glory and splendor.
19 Because of the high position he gave
him, all the nations and peoples of every
language dreaded and feared him. Those
the king wanted to put to death, he put
to death; those he wanted to spare, he
spared; those he wanted to promote, he
promoted; and those he wanted to humble, he humbled. 20 But when his heart became arrogant and hardened with pride,
he was deposed from his royal throne
and stripped of his glory. 21 He was driven
away from people and given the mind of
an animal; he lived with the wild donkeys
and ate grass like the ox; and his body was
drenched with the dew of heaven, until he
acknowledged that the Most High God is
sovereign over all kingdoms on earth and
sets over them anyone he wishes.

[a] 2 Or *ancestor*; or *predecessor*; also in verses 11, 13 and 18 [b] 7 Or *Chaldeans*; also in verse 11
[c] 10 Or *queen mother*

22"But you, Belshazzar, his son,[a] have not humbled yourself, though you knew all this. 23Instead, you have set yourself up against the Lord of heaven. You had the goblets from his temple brought to you, and you and your nobles, your wives and your concubines drank wine from them. You praised the gods of silver and gold, of bronze, iron, wood and stone, which cannot see or hear or understand. But you did not honor the God who holds in his hand your life and all your ways. 24Therefore he sent the hand that wrote the inscription.

25"This is the inscription that was written:

MENE, MENE, TEKEL, PARSIN

26"Here is what these words mean:

Mene[b]: God has numbered the days of your reign and brought it to an end.

27 *Tekel*[c]: You have been weighed on the scales and found wanting.

28 *Peres*[d]: Your kingdom is divided and given to the Medes and Persians."

29Then at Belshazzar's command, Daniel was clothed in purple, a gold chain was placed around his neck, and he was proclaimed the third highest ruler in the kingdom.

30That very night Belshazzar, king of the Babylonians,[e] was slain, 31and Darius the Mede took over the kingdom, at the age of sixty-two.[f]

Daniel in the Den of Lions

6 [g] It pleased Darius to appoint 120 satraps to rule throughout the kingdom, 2with three administrators over them, one of whom was Daniel. The satraps were made accountable to them so that the king might not suffer loss. 3Now Daniel so distinguished himself among the administrators and the satraps by his exceptional qualities that the king planned to set him over the whole kingdom. 4At this, the administrators and the satraps tried to find grounds for charges against Daniel in his conduct of government affairs, but they were unable to do so. They could find no corruption in him, because he was trustworthy and neither corrupt nor negligent. 5Finally these men said, "We will never find any basis for charges against this man Daniel unless it has something to do with the law of his God."

6So these administrators and satraps went as a group to the king and said: "May King Darius live forever! 7The royal administrators, prefects, satraps, advisers and governors have all agreed that the king should issue an edict and enforce the decree that anyone who prays to any god or human being during the next thirty days, except to you, Your Majesty, shall be thrown into the lions' den. 8Now, Your Majesty, issue the decree and put it in writing so that it cannot be altered — in accordance with the law of the Medes and Persians, which cannot be repealed." 9So King Darius put the decree in writing.

10Now when Daniel learned that the decree had been published, he went home to his upstairs room where the windows opened toward Jerusalem. Three times a day he got down on his knees and prayed, giving thanks to his God, just as he had done before. 11Then these men went as a group and found Daniel praying and asking God for help. 12So they went to the king and spoke to him about his royal decree: "Did you not publish a decree that during the next thirty days anyone who prays to any god or human being except to you, Your Majesty, would be thrown into the lions' den?"

The king answered, "The decree stands — in accordance with the law of the Medes and Persians, which cannot be repealed."

13Then they said to the king, "Daniel, who is one of the exiles from Judah, pays no attention to you, Your Majesty, or to the decree you put in writing. He still prays three times a day." 14When the king heard this, he was greatly distressed; he was determined to rescue Daniel and made every effort until sundown to save him.

15Then the men went as a group to King Darius and said to him, "Remember, Your Majesty, that according to the law of the Medes and Persians no decree or edict that the king issues can be changed."

16So the king gave the order, and they brought Daniel and threw him into the lions' den. The king said to Daniel, "May your God, whom you serve continually, rescue you!"

17A stone was brought and placed over the mouth of the den, and the king sealed it with his own signet ring and with the rings of his nobles, so that Daniel's

[a] 22 Or *descendant*; or *successor* [b] 26 *Mene* can mean *numbered* or *mina* (a unit of money). [c] 27 *Tekel* can mean *weighed* or *shekel*. [d] 28 *Peres* (the singular of *Parsin*) can mean *divided* or *Persia* or *a half mina* or *a half shekel*. [e] 30 Or *Chaldeans* [f] 31 In Aramaic texts this verse (5:31) is numbered 6:1. [g] In Aramaic texts 6:1-28 is numbered 6:2-29.

situation might not be changed. 18Then
the king returned to his palace and spent
the night without eating and without any
entertainment being brought to him. And
he could not sleep.
19At the first light of dawn, the king got
up and hurried to the lions' den. 20When
he came near the den, he called to Daniel
in an anguished voice, "Daniel, servant of
the living God, has your God, whom you
serve continually, been able to rescue you
from the lions?"
21Daniel answered, "May the king live
forever! 22My God sent his angel, and he
shut the mouths of the lions. They have
not hurt me, because I was found innocent in his sight. Nor have I ever done any
wrong before you, Your Majesty."
23The king was overjoyed and gave orders to lift Daniel out of the den. And when
Daniel was lifted from the den, no wound
was found on him, because he had trusted
in his God.
24At the king's command, the men who
had falsely accused Daniel were brought
in and thrown into the lions' den, along
with their wives and children. And before
they reached the floor of the den, the lions overpowered them and crushed all
their bones.
25Then King Darius wrote to all the nations and peoples of every language in
all the earth:

"May you prosper greatly!

26"I issue a decree that in every part
of my kingdom people must fear and
reverence the God of Daniel.

"For he is the living God
  and he endures forever;
his kingdom will not be destroyed,
  his dominion will never end.
27 He rescues and he saves;
  he performs signs and wonders
  in the heavens and on the earth.
He has rescued Daniel
  from the power of the lions."

28So Daniel prospered during the reign
of Darius and the reign of Cyrus[a] the Persian.

Daniel's Dream of Four Beasts

7 In the first year of Belshazzar king of
Babylon, Daniel had a dream, and visions passed through his mind as he was
lying in bed. He wrote down the substance
of his dream.
2Daniel said: "In my vision at night I
looked, and there before me were the four
winds of heaven churning up the great
sea. 3Four great beasts, each different
from the others, came up out of the sea.
4"The first was like a lion, and it had
the wings of an eagle. I watched until its
wings were torn off and it was lifted from
the ground so that it stood on two feet like
a human being, and the mind of a human
was given to it.
5"And there before me was a second
beast, which looked like a bear. It was
raised up on one of its sides, and it had
three ribs in its mouth between its teeth. It
was told, 'Get up and eat your fill of flesh!'
6"After that, I looked, and there before
me was another beast, one that looked
like a leopard. And on its back it had four
wings like those of a bird. This beast had
four heads, and it was given authority
to rule.
7"After that, in my vision at night I
looked, and there before me was a fourth
beast — terrifying and frightening and
very powerful. It had large iron teeth;
it crushed and devoured its victims and
trampled underfoot whatever was left. It
was different from all the former beasts,
and it had ten horns.
8"While I was thinking about the horns,
there before me was another horn, a little
one, which came up among them; and
three of the first horns were uprooted before it. This horn had eyes like the eyes of
a human being and a mouth that spoke
boastfully.
9"As I looked,

"thrones were set in place,
  and the Ancient of Days took his
    seat.
His clothing was as white as snow;
  the hair of his head was white like
    wool.
His throne was flaming with fire,
  and its wheels were all ablaze.
10 A river of fire was flowing,
  coming out from before him.
Thousands upon thousands attended
    him;
  ten thousand times ten thousand
    stood before him.
The court was seated,
  and the books were opened.

11"Then I continued to watch because of
the boastful words the horn was speaking.
I kept looking until the beast was slain
and its body destroyed and thrown into
the blazing fire. 12(The other beasts had
been stripped of their authority, but were
allowed to live for a period of time.)

[a] 28 Or *Darius, that is, the reign of Cyrus*

13"In my vision at night I looked, and there before me was one like a son of man,[a] coming with the clouds of heaven. He approached the Ancient of Days and was led into his presence. 14He was given authority, glory and sovereign power; all nations and peoples of every language worshiped him. His dominion is an everlasting dominion that will not pass away, and his kingdom is one that will never be destroyed.

The Interpretation of the Dream

15"I, Daniel, was troubled in spirit, and the visions that passed through my mind disturbed me. 16I approached one of those standing there and asked him the meaning of all this.

"So he told me and gave me the interpretation of these things: 17'The four great beasts are four kings that will rise from the earth. 18But the holy people of the Most High will receive the kingdom and will possess it forever — yes, for ever and ever.'

19"Then I wanted to know the meaning of the fourth beast, which was different from all the others and most terrifying, with its iron teeth and bronze claws — the beast that crushed and devoured its victims and trampled underfoot whatever was left. 20I also wanted to know about the ten horns on its head and about the other horn that came up, before which three of them fell — the horn that looked more imposing than the others and that had eyes and a mouth that spoke boastfully. 21As I watched, this horn was waging war against the holy people and defeating them, 22until the Ancient of Days came and pronounced judgment in favor of the holy people of the Most High, and the time came when they possessed the kingdom.

23"He gave me this explanation: 'The fourth beast is a fourth kingdom that will appear on earth. It will be different from all the other kingdoms and will devour the whole earth, trampling it down and crushing it. 24The ten horns are ten kings who will come from this kingdom. After them another king will arise, different from the earlier ones; he will subdue three kings. 25He will speak against the Most High and oppress his holy people and try to change the set times and the laws. The holy people will be delivered into his hands for a time, times and half a time.[b]

26" 'But the court will sit, and his power will be taken away and completely destroyed forever. 27Then the sovereignty, power and greatness of all the kingdoms under heaven will be handed over to the holy people of the Most High. His kingdom will be an everlasting kingdom, and all rulers will worship and obey him.'

28"This is the end of the matter. I, Daniel, was deeply troubled by my thoughts, and my face turned pale, but I kept the matter to myself."

Daniel's Vision of a Ram and a Goat

8 In the third year of King Belshazzar's reign, I, Daniel, had a vision, after the one that had already appeared to me. 2In my vision I saw myself in the citadel of Susa in the province of Elam; in the vision I was beside the Ulai Canal. 3I looked up, and there before me was a ram with two horns, standing beside the canal, and the horns were long. One of the horns was longer than the other but grew up later. 4I watched the ram as it charged toward the west and the north and the south. No animal could stand against it, and none could rescue from its power. It did as it pleased and became great.

5As I was thinking about this, suddenly a goat with a prominent horn between its eyes came from the west, crossing the whole earth without touching the ground. 6It came toward the two-horned ram I had seen standing beside the canal and charged at it in great rage. 7I saw it attack the ram furiously, striking the ram and shattering its two horns. The ram was powerless to stand against it; the goat knocked it to the ground and trampled on it, and none could rescue the ram from its power. 8The goat became very great, but at the height of its power the large horn was broken off, and in its place four prominent horns grew up toward the four winds of heaven.

9Out of one of them came another horn, which started small but grew in power to the south and to the east and toward the Beautiful Land. 10It grew until it reached the host of the heavens, and it threw some of the starry host down to the earth and trampled on them. 11It set itself up to be as great as the commander of the army of the LORD; it took away the daily sacrifice from the LORD, and his sanctuary was thrown down. 12Because of rebellion, the LORD's people[c] and the daily sacrifice were given over to it. It prospered in everything it did, and truth was thrown to the ground.

13Then I heard a holy one speaking, and another holy one said to him, "How long

[a] 13 The Aramaic phrase *bar enash* means *human being*. The phrase *son of man* is retained here because of its use in the New Testament as a title of Jesus, probably based largely on this verse.
[b] 25 Or *for a year, two years and half a year*
[c] 12 Or *rebellion, the armies*

will it take for the vision to be fulfilled — the vision concerning the daily sacrifice, the rebellion that causes desolation, the surrender of the sanctuary and the trampling underfoot of the LORD's people?"

14 He said to me, "It will take 2,300 evenings and mornings; then the sanctuary will be reconsecrated."

The Interpretation of the Vision

15 While I, Daniel, was watching the vision and trying to understand it, there before me stood one who looked like a man. 16 And I heard a man's voice from the Ulai calling, "Gabriel, tell this man the meaning of the vision."

17 As he came near the place where I was standing, I was terrified and fell prostrate. "Son of man,"[a] he said to me, "understand that the vision concerns the time of the end."

18 While he was speaking to me, I was in a deep sleep, with my face to the ground. Then he touched me and raised me to my feet.

19 He said: "I am going to tell you what will happen later in the time of wrath, because the vision concerns the appointed time of the end.[b] 20 The two-horned ram that you saw represents the kings of Media and Persia. 21 The shaggy goat is the king of Greece, and the large horn between its eyes is the first king. 22 The four horns that replaced the one that was broken off represent four kingdoms that will emerge from his nation but will not have the same power.

23 "In the latter part of their reign, when rebels have become completely wicked, a fierce-looking king, a master of intrigue, will arise. 24 He will become very strong, but not by his own power. He will cause astounding devastation and will succeed in whatever he does. He will destroy those who are mighty, the holy people. 25 He will cause deceit to prosper, and he will consider himself superior. When they feel secure, he will destroy many and take his stand against the Prince of princes. Yet he will be destroyed, but not by human power.

26 "The vision of the evenings and mornings that has been given you is true, but seal up the vision, for it concerns the distant future."

27 I, Daniel, was worn out. I lay exhausted for several days. Then I got up and went about the king's business. I was appalled by the vision; it was beyond understanding.

Daniel's Prayer

9 In the first year of Darius son of Xerxes[c] (a Mede by descent), who was made ruler over the Babylonian[d] kingdom — 2 in the first year of his reign, I, Daniel, understood from the Scriptures, according to the word of the LORD given to Jeremiah the prophet, that the desolation of Jerusalem would last seventy years. 3 So I turned to the Lord God and pleaded with him in prayer and petition, in fasting, and in sackcloth and ashes.

4 I prayed to the LORD my God and confessed:

"Lord, the great and awesome God, who keeps his covenant of love with those who love him and keep his commandments, 5 we have sinned and done wrong. We have been wicked and have rebelled; we have turned away from your commands and laws. 6 We have not listened to your servants the prophets, who spoke in your name to our kings, our princes and our ancestors, and to all the people of the land.

7 "Lord, you are righteous, but this day we are covered with shame — the people of Judah and the inhabitants of Jerusalem and all Israel, both near and far, in all the countries where you have scattered us because of our unfaithfulness to you. 8 We and our kings, our princes and our ancestors are covered with shame, LORD, because we have sinned against you. 9 The Lord our God is merciful and forgiving, even though we have rebelled against him; 10 we have not obeyed the LORD our God or kept the laws he gave us through his servants the prophets. 11 All Israel has transgressed your law and turned away, refusing to obey you.

"Therefore the curses and sworn judgments written in the Law of Moses, the servant of God, have been poured out on us, because we have sinned against you. 12 You have fulfilled the words spoken against us and against our rulers by bringing on us great disaster. Under the whole heaven nothing has ever been done like what has been done to Jerusalem. 13 Just as it is written in the Law of Moses, all this disaster has come on us, yet we have not sought the favor of the LORD our God by turning from

[a] 17 The Hebrew phrase *ben adam* means *human being*. The phrase *son of man* is retained as a form of address here because of its possible association with "Son of Man" in the New Testament.
[b] 19 Or *because the end will be at the appointed time* [c] 1 Hebrew *Ahasuerus* [d] 1 Or *Chaldean*

our sins and giving attention to your truth. 14The LORD did not hesitate to bring the disaster on us, for the LORD our God is righteous in everything he does; yet we have not obeyed him.

15"Now, Lord our God, who brought your people out of Egypt with a mighty hand and who made for yourself a name that endures to this day, we have sinned, we have done wrong. 16Lord, in keeping with all your righteous acts, turn away your anger and your wrath from Jerusalem, your city, your holy hill. Our sins and the iniquities of our ancestors have made Jerusalem and your people an object of scorn to all those around us.

17"Now, our God, hear the prayers and petitions of your servant. For your sake, Lord, look with favor on your desolate sanctuary. 18Give ear, our God, and hear; open your eyes and see the desolation of the city that bears your Name. We do not make requests of you because we are righteous, but because of your great mercy. 19Lord, listen! Lord, forgive! Lord, hear and act! For your sake, my God, do not delay, because your city and your people bear your Name."

The Seventy "Sevens"

20While I was speaking and praying, confessing my sin and the sin of my people Israel and making my request to the LORD my God for his holy hill— 21while I was still in prayer, Gabriel, the man I had seen in the earlier vision, came to me in swift flight about the time of the evening sacrifice. 22He instructed me and said to me, "Daniel, I have now come to give you insight and understanding. 23As soon as you began to pray, a word went out, which I have come to tell you, for you are highly esteemed. Therefore, consider the word and understand the vision:

24"Seventy 'sevens'[a] are decreed for your people and your holy city to finish[b] transgression, to put an end to sin, to atone for wickedness, to bring in everlasting righteousness, to seal up vision and prophecy and to anoint the Most Holy Place.[c]

25"Know and understand this: From the time the word goes out to restore and rebuild Jerusalem until the Anointed One,[d] the ruler, comes, there will be seven 'sevens,' and sixty-two 'sevens.' It will be rebuilt with streets and a trench, but in times of trouble. 26After the sixty-two 'sevens,' the Anointed One will be put to death and will have nothing.[e] The people of the ruler who will come will destroy the city and the sanctuary. The end will come like a flood: War will continue until the end, and desolations have been decreed. 27He will confirm a covenant with many for one 'seven.'[f] In the middle of the 'seven'[f] he will put an end to sacrifice and offering. And at the temple[g] he will set up an abomination that causes desolation, until the end that is decreed is poured out on him.[h]"[i]

Daniel's Vision of a Man

10 In the third year of Cyrus king of Persia, a revelation was given to Daniel (who was called Belteshazzar). Its message was true and it concerned a great war.[j] The understanding of the message came to him in a vision.

2At that time I, Daniel, mourned for three weeks. 3I ate no choice food; no meat or wine touched my lips; and I used no lotions at all until the three weeks were over.

4On the twenty-fourth day of the first month, as I was standing on the bank of the great river, the Tigris, 5I looked up and there before me was a man dressed in linen, with a belt of fine gold from Uphaz around his waist. 6His body was like topaz, his face like lightning, his eyes like flaming torches, his arms and legs like the gleam of burnished bronze, and his voice like the sound of a multitude.

7I, Daniel, was the only one who saw the vision; those who were with me did not see it, but such terror overwhelmed them that they fled and hid themselves. 8So I was left alone, gazing at this great vision; I had no strength left, my face turned deathly pale and I was helpless. 9Then I heard him speaking, and as I listened to him, I fell into a deep sleep, my face to the ground.

10A hand touched me and set me trembling on my hands and knees. 11He said, "Daniel, you who are highly esteemed, consider carefully the words I am about to speak to you, and stand up, for I have now been sent to you." And when he said this to me, I stood up trembling.

12Then he continued, "Do not be afraid, Daniel. Since the first day that you set your

[a] 24 Or *'weeks'*; also in verses 25 and 26 [b] 24 Or *restrain* [c] 24 Or *the most holy One* [d] 25 Or *an anointed one*; also in verse 26 [e] 26 Or *death and will have no one*; or *death, but not for himself* [f] 27 Or *'week'* [g] 27 Septuagint and Theodotion; Hebrew *wing* [h] 27 Or *it* [i] 27 Or *And one who causes desolation will come upon the wing of the abominable temple, until the end that is decreed is poured out on the desolated city* [j] 1 Or *true and burdensome*

mind to gain understanding and to humble yourself before your God, your words were heard, and I have come in response to them. 13 But the prince of the Persian kingdom resisted me twenty-one days. Then Michael, one of the chief princes, came to help me, because I was detained there with the king of Persia. 14 Now I have come to explain to you what will happen to your people in the future, for the vision concerns a time yet to come."

15 While he was saying this to me, I bowed with my face toward the ground and was speechless. 16 Then one who looked like a man[a] touched my lips, and I opened my mouth and began to speak. I said to the one standing before me, "I am overcome with anguish because of the vision, my lord, and I feel very weak. 17 How can I, your servant, talk with you, my lord? My strength is gone and I can hardly breathe."

18 Again the one who looked like a man touched me and gave me strength. 19 "Do not be afraid, you who are highly esteemed," he said. "Peace! Be strong now; be strong."

When he spoke to me, I was strengthened and said, "Speak, my lord, since you have given me strength."

20 So he said, "Do you know why I have come to you? Soon I will return to fight against the prince of Persia, and when I go, the prince of Greece will come; 21 but first I will tell you what is written in the Book of Truth. (No one supports me against them except Michael, your prince.

11 1 And in the first year of Darius the Mede, I took my stand to support and protect him.)

The Kings of the South and the North

2 "Now then, I tell you the truth: Three more kings will arise in Persia, and then a fourth, who will be far richer than all the others. When he has gained power by his wealth, he will stir up everyone against the kingdom of Greece. 3 Then a mighty king will arise, who will rule with great power and do as he pleases. 4 After he has arisen, his empire will be broken up and parceled out toward the four winds of heaven. It will not go to his descendants, nor will it have the power he exercised, because his empire will be uprooted and given to others.

5 "The king of the South will become strong, but one of his commanders will become even stronger than he and will rule his own kingdom with great power. 6 After some years, they will become allies. The daughter of the king of the South will go to the king of the North to make an alliance, but she will not retain her power, and he and his power[b] will not last. In those days she will be betrayed, together with her royal escort and her father[c] and the one who supported her.

7 "One from her family line will arise to take her place. He will attack the forces of the king of the North and enter his fortress; he will fight against them and be victorious. 8 He will also seize their gods, their metal images and their valuable articles of silver and gold and carry them off to Egypt. For some years he will leave the king of the North alone. 9 Then the king of the North will invade the realm of the king of the South but will retreat to his own country. 10 His sons will prepare for war and assemble a great army, which will sweep on like an irresistible flood and carry the battle as far as his fortress.

11 "Then the king of the South will march out in a rage and fight against the king of the North, who will raise a large army, but it will be defeated. 12 When the army is carried off, the king of the South will be filled with pride and will slaughter many thousands, yet he will not remain triumphant. 13 For the king of the North will muster another army, larger than the first; and after several years, he will advance with a huge army fully equipped.

14 "In those times many will rise against the king of the South. Those who are violent among your own people will rebel in fulfillment of the vision, but without success. 15 Then the king of the North will come and build up siege ramps and will capture a fortified city. The forces of the South will be powerless to resist; even their best troops will not have the strength to stand. 16 The invader will do as he pleases; no one will be able to stand against him. He will establish himself in the Beautiful Land and will have the power to destroy it. 17 He will determine to come with the might of his entire kingdom and will make an alliance with the king of the South. And he will give him a daughter in marriage in order to overthrow the kingdom, but his plans[d] will not succeed or help him. 18 Then he will turn his attention to the coastlands and will take many of them, but a commander will put an end to his

[a] *16* Most manuscripts of the Masoretic Text; one manuscript of the Masoretic Text, Dead Sea Scrolls and Septuagint *Then something that looked like a human hand* [b] *6* Or *offspring*
[c] *6* Or *child* (see Vulgate and Syriac) [d] *17* Or *but she*

insolence and will turn his insolence back on him. 19 After this, he will turn back toward the fortresses of his own country but will stumble and fall, to be seen no more.

20 “His successor will send out a tax collector to maintain the royal splendor. In a few years, however, he will be destroyed, yet not in anger or in battle.

21 “He will be succeeded by a contemptible person who has not been given the honor of royalty. He will invade the kingdom when its people feel secure, and he will seize it through intrigue. 22 Then an overwhelming army will be swept away before him; both it and a prince of the covenant will be destroyed. 23 After coming to an agreement with him, he will act deceitfully, and with only a few people he will rise to power. 24 When the richest provinces feel secure, he will invade them and will achieve what neither his fathers nor his forefathers did. He will distribute plunder, loot and wealth among his followers. He will plot the overthrow of fortresses — but only for a time.

25 “With a large army he will stir up his strength and courage against the king of the South. The king of the South will wage war with a large and very powerful army, but he will not be able to stand because of the plots devised against him. 26 Those who eat from the king’s provisions will try to destroy him; his army will be swept away, and many will fall in battle. 27 The two kings, with their hearts bent on evil, will sit at the same table and lie to each other, but to no avail, because an end will still come at the appointed time. 28 The king of the North will return to his own country with great wealth, but his heart will be set against the holy covenant. He will take action against it and then return to his own country.

29 “At the appointed time he will invade the South again, but this time the outcome will be different from what it was before. 30 Ships of the western coastlands will oppose him, and he will lose heart. Then he will turn back and vent his fury against the holy covenant. He will return and show favor to those who forsake the holy covenant.

31 “His armed forces will rise up to desecrate the temple fortress and will abolish the daily sacrifice. Then they will set up the abomination that causes desolation. 32 With flattery he will corrupt those who have violated the covenant, but the people who know their God will firmly resist him.

33 “Those who are wise will instruct many, though for a time they will fall by the sword or be burned or captured or plundered. 34 When they fall, they will receive a little help, and many who are not sincere will join them. 35 Some of the wise will stumble, so that they may be refined, purified and made spotless until the time of the end, for it will still come at the appointed time.

The King Who Exalts Himself

36 “The king will do as he pleases. He will exalt and magnify himself above every god and will say unheard-of things against the God of gods. He will be successful until the time of wrath is completed, for what has been determined must take place. 37 He will show no regard for the gods of his ancestors or for the one desired by women, nor will he regard any god, but will exalt himself above them all. 38 Instead of them, he will honor a god of fortresses; a god unknown to his ancestors he will honor with gold and silver, with precious stones and costly gifts. 39 He will attack the mightiest fortresses with the help of a foreign god and will greatly honor those who acknowledge him. He will make them rulers over many people and will distribute the land at a price.[a]

40 “At the time of the end the king of the South will engage him in battle, and the king of the North will storm out against him with chariots and cavalry and a great fleet of ships. He will invade many countries and sweep through them like a flood. 41 He will also invade the Beautiful Land. Many countries will fall, but Edom, Moab and the leaders of Ammon will be delivered from his hand. 42 He will extend his power over many countries; Egypt will not escape. 43 He will gain control of the treasures of gold and silver and all the riches of Egypt, with the Libyans and Cushites[b] in submission. 44 But reports from the east and the north will alarm him, and he will set out in a great rage to destroy and annihilate many. 45 He will pitch his royal tents between the seas at[c] the beautiful holy mountain. Yet he will come to his end, and no one will help him.

The End Times

12 “At that time Michael, the great prince who protects your people, will arise. There will be a time of distress such as has not happened from the beginning of nations until then. But at that time your people — everyone whose name is found written in the book — will be delivered.

[a] 39 Or *land for a reward* [b] 43 That is, people from the upper Nile region [c] 45 Or *the sea and*

[2]Multitudes who sleep in the dust of the
earth will awake: some to everlasting
life, others to shame and everlasting contempt. [3]Those who are wise[a] will shine
like the brightness of the heavens, and
those who lead many to righteousness,
like the stars for ever and ever. [4]But you,
Daniel, roll up and seal the words of the
scroll until the time of the end. Many will
go here and there to increase knowledge."

[5]Then I, Daniel, looked, and there before
me stood two others, one on this bank of
the river and one on the opposite bank.
[6]One of them said to the man clothed in
linen, who was above the waters of the
river, "How long will it be before these
astonishing things are fulfilled?"

[7]The man clothed in linen, who was
above the waters of the river, lifted his
right hand and his left hand toward heav-
en, and I heard him swear by him who
lives forever, saying, "It will be for a time,
times and half a time.[b] When the power of
the holy people has been finally broken,
all these things will be completed."

[8]I heard, but I did not understand. So
I asked, "My lord, what will the outcome
of all this be?"

[9]He replied, "Go your way, Daniel, because the words are rolled up and sealed
until the time of the end. [10]Many will be
purified, made spotless and refined, but
the wicked will continue to be wicked.
None of the wicked will understand, but
those who are wise will understand.

[11]"From the time that the daily sacrifice is abolished and the abomination
that causes desolation is set up, there
will be 1,290 days. [12]Blessed is the one
who waits for and reaches the end of the
1,335 days.

[13]"As for you, go your way till the end.
You will rest, and then at the end of the
days you will rise to receive your allotted
inheritance."

[a] 3 Or *who impart wisdom* [b] 7 Or *a year, two years and half a year*

HOSEA

1 The word of the LORD that came to
Hosea son of Beeri during the reigns
of Uzziah, Jotham, Ahaz and Hezekiah,
kings of Judah, and during the reign of
Jeroboam son of Jehoash[a] king of Israel:

Hosea's Wife and Children

2When the LORD began to speak through
Hosea, the LORD said to him, "Go, marry
a promiscuous woman and have children with her, for like an adulterous wife
this land is guilty of unfaithfulness to the
LORD." 3So he married Gomer daughter
of Diblaim, and she conceived and bore
him a son.

4Then the LORD said to Hosea, "Call him
Jezreel, because I will soon punish the
house of Jehu for the massacre at Jezreel, and I will put an end to the kingdom
of Israel. 5In that day I will break Israel's
bow in the Valley of Jezreel."

6Gomer conceived again and gave birth
to a daughter. Then the LORD said to Hosea, "Call her Lo-Ruhamah (which means
"not loved"), for I will no longer show love
to Israel, that I should at all forgive them.
7Yet I will show love to Judah; and I will
save them — not by bow, sword or battle,
or by horses and horsemen, but I, the LORD
their God, will save them."

8After she had weaned Lo-Ruhamah,
Gomer had another son. 9Then the LORD
said, "Call him Lo-Ammi (which means
"not my people"), for you are not my people, and I am not your God.[b]

10"Yet the Israelites will be like the sand
on the seashore, which cannot be measured or counted. In the place where it was
said to them, 'You are not my people,' they
will be called 'children of the living God.'
11The people of Judah and the people of Israel will come together; they will appoint
one leader and will come up out of the
land, for great will be the day of Jezreel.[c]

2[d] "Say of your brothers, 'My people,' and
of your sisters, 'My loved one.'

Israel Punished and Restored

2"Rebuke your mother, rebuke her,
for she is not my wife,
and I am not her husband.
Let her remove the adulterous look
from her face
and the unfaithfulness from
between her breasts.
3Otherwise I will strip her naked
and make her as bare as on the day
she was born;
I will make her like a desert,
turn her into a parched land,
and slay her with thirst.
4I will not show my love to her
children,
because they are the children of
adultery.
5Their mother has been unfaithful
and has conceived them in
disgrace.
She said, 'I will go after my lovers,
who give me my food and my water,
my wool and my linen, my olive oil
and my drink.'
6Therefore I will block her path with
thornbushes;
I will wall her in so that she cannot
find her way.
7She will chase after her lovers but not
catch them;
she will look for them but not find
them.
Then she will say,
'I will go back to my husband as at
first,
for then I was better off than now.'
8She has not acknowledged that I was
the one
who gave her the grain, the new
wine and oil,
who lavished on her the silver and
gold —
which they used for Baal.

9"Therefore I will take away my grain
when it ripens,
and my new wine when it is ready.
I will take back my wool and my
linen,
intended to cover her naked body.
10So now I will expose her lewdness
before the eyes of her lovers;
no one will take her out of my
hands.
11I will stop all her celebrations:
her yearly festivals, her New Moons,
her Sabbath days — all her
appointed festivals.

[a] *1* Hebrew *Joash,* a variant of *Jehoash* [b] *9* Or *your I AM* [c] *11* In Hebrew texts 1:10,11 is numbered 2:1,2. [d] In Hebrew texts 2:1-23 is numbered 2:3-25.

12 I will ruin her vines and her fig trees,
which she said were her pay from her lovers;
I will make them a thicket,
and wild animals will devour them.
13 I will punish her for the days
she burned incense to the Baals;
she decked herself with rings and jewelry,
and went after her lovers,
but me she forgot,"
declares the LORD.

14 "Therefore I am now going to allure her;
I will lead her into the wilderness
and speak tenderly to her.
15 There I will give her back her vineyards,
and will make the Valley of Achor[a] a door of hope.
There she will respond[b] as in the days of her youth,
as in the day she came up out of Egypt.

16 "In that day," declares the LORD,
"you will call me 'my husband';
you will no longer call me 'my master.[c]'
17 I will remove the names of the Baals from her lips;
no longer will their names be invoked.
18 In that day I will make a covenant for them
with the beasts of the field, the birds in the sky
and the creatures that move along the ground.
Bow and sword and battle
I will abolish from the land,
so that all may lie down in safety.
19 I will betroth you to me forever;
I will betroth you in[d] righteousness and justice,
in[d] love and compassion.
20 I will betroth you in[d] faithfulness,
and you will acknowledge the LORD.

21 "In that day I will respond,"
declares the LORD—
"I will respond to the skies,
and they will respond to the earth;
22 and the earth will respond to the grain,
the new wine and the olive oil,
and they will respond to Jezreel.[e]
23 I will plant her for myself in the land;
I will show my love to the one I called 'Not my loved one.[f]'
I will say to those called 'Not my people,[g]' 'You are my people';
and they will say, 'You are my God.'"

Hosea's Reconciliation With His Wife

3 The LORD said to me, "Go, show your
love to your wife again, though she is
loved by another man and is an adulteress. Love her as the LORD loves the Israelites, though they turn to other gods and
love the sacred raisin cakes."
2 So I bought her for fifteen shekels[h] of
silver and about a homer and a lethek[i] of
barley. 3 Then I told her, "You are to live with
me many days; you must not be a prostitute or be intimate with any man, and I
will behave the same way toward you."
4 For the Israelites will live many days
without king or prince, without sacrifice or
sacred stones, without ephod or household
gods. 5 Afterward the Israelites will return
and seek the LORD their God and David
their king. They will come trembling to the
LORD and to his blessings in the last days.

The Charge Against Israel

4 Hear the word of the LORD, you Israelites,
because the LORD has a charge to bring
against you who live in the land:
"There is no faithfulness, no love,
no acknowledgment of God in the land.
2 There is only cursing,[j] lying and murder,
stealing and adultery;
they break all bounds,
and bloodshed follows bloodshed.
3 Because of this the land dries up,
and all who live in it waste away;
the beasts of the field, the birds in the sky
and the fish in the sea are swept away.

4 "But let no one bring a charge,
let no one accuse another,
for your people are like those
who bring charges against a priest.
5 You stumble day and night,
and the prophets stumble with you.
So I will destroy your mother—
6 my people are destroyed from lack of knowledge.

[a] 15 *Achor* means *trouble.* [b] 15 Or *sing* [c] 16 Hebrew *baal* [d] 19,20 Or *with* [e] 22 *Jezreel* means *God plants.* [f] 23 Hebrew *Lo-Ruhamah* (see 1:6) [g] 23 Hebrew *Lo-Ammi* (see 1:9)
[h] 2 That is, about 6 ounces or about 170 grams [i] 2 A homer and a lethek possibly weighed about 430 pounds or about 195 kilograms. [j] 2 That is, to pronounce a curse on

"Because you have rejected
knowledge,
I also reject you as my priests;
because you have ignored the law of
your God,
I also will ignore your children.
7 The more priests there were,
the more they sinned against me;
they exchanged their glorious God[a]
for something disgraceful.
8 They feed on the sins of my people
and relish their wickedness.
9 And it will be: Like people, like priests.
I will punish both of them for their
ways
and repay them for their deeds.

10 "They will eat but not have enough;
they will engage in prostitution but
not flourish,
because they have deserted the LORD
to give themselves 11 to prostitution;
old wine and new wine
take away their understanding.
12 My people consult a wooden idol,
and a diviner's rod speaks to them.
A spirit of prostitution leads them
astray;
they are unfaithful to their God.
13 They sacrifice on the mountaintops
and burn offerings on the hills,
under oak, poplar and terebinth,
where the shade is pleasant.
Therefore your daughters turn to
prostitution
and your daughters-in-law to
adultery.

14 "I will not punish your daughters
when they turn to prostitution,
nor your daughters-in-law
when they commit adultery,
because the men themselves consort
with harlots
and sacrifice with shrine
prostitutes —
a people without understanding
will come to ruin!

15 "Though you, Israel, commit adultery,
do not let Judah become guilty.

"Do not go to Gilgal;
do not go up to Beth Aven.[b]
And do not swear, 'As surely as the
LORD lives!'
16 The Israelites are stubborn,
like a stubborn heifer.
How then can the LORD pasture them
like lambs in a meadow?
17 Ephraim is joined to idols;
leave him alone!
18 Even when their drinks are gone,
they continue their prostitution;
their rulers dearly love shameful
ways.
19 A whirlwind will sweep them away,
and their sacrifices will bring them
shame.

Judgment Against Israel

5 "Hear this, you priests!
Pay attention, you Israelites!
Listen, royal house!
This judgment is against you:
You have been a snare at Mizpah,
a net spread out on Tabor.
2 The rebels are knee-deep in
slaughter.
I will discipline all of them.
3 I know all about Ephraim;
Israel is not hidden from me.
Ephraim, you have now turned to
prostitution;
Israel is corrupt.

4 "Their deeds do not permit them
to return to their God.
A spirit of prostitution is in their heart;
they do not acknowledge the LORD.
5 Israel's arrogance testifies against
them;
the Israelites, even Ephraim,
stumble in their sin;
Judah also stumbles with them.
6 When they go with their flocks and
herds
to seek the LORD,
they will not find him;
he has withdrawn himself from
them.
7 They are unfaithful to the LORD;
they give birth to illegitimate
children.
When they celebrate their New Moon
feasts,
he will devour[c] their fields.

8 "Sound the trumpet in Gibeah,
the horn in Ramah.
Raise the battle cry in Beth Aven[b];
lead on, Benjamin.
9 Ephraim will be laid waste
on the day of reckoning.
Among the tribes of Israel
I proclaim what is certain.
10 Judah's leaders are like those
who move boundary stones.
I will pour out my wrath on them
like a flood of water.

[a] 7 Syriac (see also an ancient Hebrew scribal tradition); Masoretic Text *me; / I will exchange their glory* [b] 15,8 *Beth Aven* means *house of wickedness* (a derogatory name for Bethel, which means *house of God*). [c] 7 Or *Now their New Moon feasts / will devour them and*

11 Ephraim is oppressed,
trampled in judgment,
intent on pursuing idols.[a]
12 I am like a moth to Ephraim,
like rot to the people of Judah.

13 "When Ephraim saw his sickness,
and Judah his sores,
then Ephraim turned to Assyria,
and sent to the great king for help.
But he is not able to cure you,
not able to heal your sores.
14 For I will be like a lion to Ephraim,
like a great lion to Judah.
I will tear them to pieces and go
away;
I will carry them off, with no one
to rescue them.
15 Then I will return to my lair
until they have borne their guilt
and seek my face —
in their misery
they will earnestly seek me."

Israel Unrepentant

6 "Come, let us return to the LORD.
He has torn us to pieces
but he will heal us;
he has injured us
but he will bind up our wounds.
2 After two days he will revive us;
on the third day he will restore us,
that we may live in his presence.
3 Let us acknowledge the LORD;
let us press on to acknowledge him.
As surely as the sun rises,
he will appear;
he will come to us like the winter
rains,
like the spring rains that water the
earth."

4 "What can I do with you, Ephraim?
What can I do with you, Judah?
Your love is like the morning mist,
like the early dew that disappears.
5 Therefore I cut you in pieces with my
prophets,
I killed you with the words of my
mouth —
then my judgments go forth like
the sun.[b]
6 For I desire mercy, not sacrifice,
and acknowledgment of God rather
than burnt offerings.
7 As at Adam,[c] they have broken the
covenant;
they were unfaithful to me there.
8 Gilead is a city of evildoers,
stained with footprints of blood.
9 As marauders lie in ambush for a
victim,
so do bands of priests;
they murder on the road to Shechem,
carrying out their wicked schemes.
10 I have seen a horrible thing in Israel:
There Ephraim is given to
prostitution,
Israel is defiled.

11 "Also for you, Judah,
a harvest is appointed.

"Whenever I would restore the
fortunes of my people,
7 1 whenever I would heal Israel,
the sins of Ephraim are exposed
and the crimes of Samaria
revealed.
They practice deceit,
thieves break into houses,
bandits rob in the streets;
2 but they do not realize
that I remember all their evil
deeds.
Their sins engulf them;
they are always before me.

3 "They delight the king with their
wickedness,
the princes with their lies.
4 They are all adulterers,
burning like an oven
whose fire the baker need not stir
from the kneading of the dough
till it rises.
5 On the day of the festival of our king
the princes become inflamed with
wine,
and he joins hands with the mockers.
6 Their hearts are like an oven;
they approach him with intrigue.
Their passion smolders all night;
in the morning it blazes like a
flaming fire.
7 All of them are hot as an oven;
they devour their rulers.
All their kings fall,
and none of them calls on me.

8 "Ephraim mixes with the nations;
Ephraim is a flat loaf not turned
over.
9 Foreigners sap his strength,
but he does not realize it.
His hair is sprinkled with gray,
but he does not notice.
10 Israel's arrogance testifies against him,
but despite all this
he does not return to the LORD his God
or search for him.

[a] *11* The meaning of the Hebrew for this word is uncertain. [b] *5* The meaning of the Hebrew for this line is uncertain. [c] *7* Or *Like Adam*; or *Like human beings*

11 "Ephraim is like a dove,
easily deceived and senseless —
now calling to Egypt,
now turning to Assyria.
12 When they go, I will throw my net
over them;
I will pull them down like the birds
in the sky.
When I hear them flocking together,
I will catch them.
13 Woe to them,
because they have strayed from me!
Destruction to them,
because they have rebelled against
me!
I long to redeem them
but they speak about me falsely.
14 They do not cry out to me from their
hearts
but wail on their beds.
They slash themselves,[a] appealing to
their gods
for grain and new wine,
but they turn away from me.
15 I trained them and strengthened
their arms,
but they plot evil against me.
16 They do not turn to the Most High;
they are like a faulty bow.
Their leaders will fall by the sword
because of their insolent words.
For this they will be ridiculed
in the land of Egypt.

Israel to Reap the Whirlwind

8 "Put the trumpet to your lips!
An eagle is over the house of the
LORD
because the people have broken my
covenant
and rebelled against my law.
2 Israel cries out to me,
'Our God, we acknowledge you!'
3 But Israel has rejected what is good;
an enemy will pursue him.
4 They set up kings without my consent;
they choose princes without my
approval.
With their silver and gold
they make idols for themselves
to their own destruction.
5 Samaria, throw out your calf-idol!
My anger burns against them.
How long will they be incapable of
purity?
6 They are from Israel!
This calf — a metalworker has made it;
it is not God.
It will be broken in pieces,
that calf of Samaria.

7 "They sow the wind
and reap the whirlwind.
The stalk has no head;
it will produce no flour.
Were it to yield grain,
foreigners would swallow it up.
8 Israel is swallowed up;
now she is among the nations
like something no one wants.
9 For they have gone up to Assyria
like a wild donkey wandering
alone.
Ephraim has sold herself to lovers.
10 Although they have sold themselves
among the nations,
I will now gather them together.
They will begin to waste away
under the oppression of the mighty
king.
11 "Though Ephraim built many altars
for sin offerings,
these have become altars for
sinning.
12 I wrote for them the many things of
my law,
but they regarded them as
something foreign.
13 Though they offer sacrifices as gifts
to me,
and though they eat the meat,
the LORD is not pleased with them.
Now he will remember their
wickedness
and punish their sins:
They will return to Egypt.
14 Israel has forgotten their Maker
and built palaces;
Judah has fortified many towns.
But I will send fire on their cities
that will consume their fortresses."

Punishment for Israel

9 Do not rejoice, Israel;
do not be jubilant like the other
nations.
For you have been unfaithful to your
God;
you love the wages of a prostitute
at every threshing floor.
2 Threshing floors and winepresses will
not feed the people;
the new wine will fail them.
3 They will not remain in the LORD's
land;
Ephraim will return to Egypt
and eat unclean food in Assyria.
4 They will not pour out wine offerings
to the LORD,
nor will their sacrifices please him.

[a] 14 Some Hebrew manuscripts and Septuagint; most Hebrew manuscripts *They gather together*

Such sacrifices will be to them like the
bread of mourners;
all who eat them will be unclean.
This food will be for themselves;
it will not come into the temple of
the LORD.

5 What will you do on the day of your
appointed festivals,
on the feast days of the LORD?
6 Even if they escape from destruction,
Egypt will gather them,
and Memphis will bury them.
Their treasures of silver will be taken
over by briers,
and thorns will overrun their tents.
7 The days of punishment are coming,
the days of reckoning are at hand.
Let Israel know this.
Because your sins are so many
and your hostility so great,
the prophet is considered a fool,
the inspired person a maniac.
8 The prophet, along with my God,
is the watchman over Ephraim,[a]
yet snares await him on all his paths,
and hostility in the house of his God.
9 They have sunk deep into corruption,
as in the days of Gibeah.
God will remember their wickedness
and punish them for their sins.

10 "When I found Israel,
it was like finding grapes in the
desert;
when I saw your ancestors,
it was like seeing the early fruit on
the fig tree.
But when they came to Baal Peor,
they consecrated themselves to
that shameful idol
and became as vile as the thing
they loved.
11 Ephraim's glory will fly away like a
bird —
no birth, no pregnancy, no
conception.
12 Even if they rear children,
I will bereave them of every one.
Woe to them
when I turn away from them!
13 I have seen Ephraim, like Tyre,
planted in a pleasant place.
But Ephraim will bring out
their children to the slayer."

14 Give them, LORD —
what will you give them?
Give them wombs that miscarry
and breasts that are dry.

15 "Because of all their wickedness in
Gilgal,
I hated them there.
Because of their sinful deeds,
I will drive them out of my house.
I will no longer love them;
all their leaders are rebellious.
16 Ephraim is blighted,
their root is withered,
they yield no fruit.
Even if they bear children,
I will slay their cherished
offspring."

17 My God will reject them
because they have not obeyed him;
they will be wanderers among
the nations.

10 Israel was a spreading vine;
he brought forth fruit for himself.
As his fruit increased,
he built more altars;
as his land prospered,
he adorned his sacred stones.
2 Their heart is deceitful,
and now they must bear their guilt.
The LORD will demolish their altars
and destroy their sacred stones.

3 Then they will say, "We have no king
because we did not revere
the LORD.
But even if we had a king,
what could he do for us?"
4 They make many promises,
take false oaths
and make agreements;
therefore lawsuits spring up
like poisonous weeds in a plowed
field.
5 The people who live in Samaria fear
for the calf-idol of Beth Aven.[b]
Its people will mourn over it,
and so will its idolatrous priests,
those who had rejoiced over its
splendor,
because it is taken from them into
exile.
6 It will be carried to Assyria
as tribute for the great king.
Ephraim will be disgraced;
Israel will be ashamed of its
foreign alliances.
7 Samaria's king will be destroyed,
swept away like a twig on the
surface of the waters.
8 The high places of wickedness[c] will
be destroyed —
it is the sin of Israel.

[a] 8 Or *The prophet is the watchman over Ephraim, / the people of my God* [b] 5 *Beth Aven* means *house of wickedness* (a derogatory name for Bethel, which means *house of God*). [c] 8 Hebrew *aven*, a reference to Beth Aven (a derogatory name for Bethel); see verse 5.

Thorns and thistles will grow up
and cover their altars.
Then they will say to the mountains,
"Cover us!"
and to the hills, "Fall on us!"

9 "Since the days of Gibeah, you have
sinned, Israel,
and there you have remained.[a]
Will not war again overtake
the evildoers in Gibeah?
10 When I please, I will punish them;
nations will be gathered against
them
to put them in bonds for their
double sin.
11 Ephraim is a trained heifer
that loves to thresh;
so I will put a yoke
on her fair neck.
I will drive Ephraim,
Judah must plow,
and Jacob must break up the
ground.
12 Sow righteousness for yourselves,
reap the fruit of unfailing love,
and break up your unplowed ground;
for it is time to seek the LORD,
until he comes
and showers his righteousness on
you.
13 But you have planted wickedness,
you have reaped evil,
you have eaten the fruit of
deception.
Because you have depended on your
own strength
and on your many warriors,
14 the roar of battle will rise against
your people,
so that all your fortresses will be
devastated —
as Shalman devastated Beth Arbel on
the day of battle,
when mothers were dashed to the
ground with their children.
15 So will it happen to you, Bethel,
because your wickedness is great.
When that day dawns,
the king of Israel will be completely
destroyed.

God's Love for Israel

11 "When Israel was a child, I loved
him,
and out of Egypt I called my son.
2 But the more they were called,
the more they went away from
me.[b]
They sacrificed to the Baals
and they burned incense
to images.
3 It was I who taught Ephraim to walk,
taking them by the arms;
but they did not realize
it was I who healed them.
4 I led them with cords of human
kindness,
with ties of love.
To them I was like one who lifts
a little child to the cheek,
and I bent down to feed them.

5 "Will they not return to Egypt
and will not Assyria rule over them
because they refuse to repent?
6 A sword will flash in their cities;
it will devour their false prophets
and put an end to their plans.
7 My people are determined to turn
from me.
Even though they call me God
Most High,
I will by no means exalt them.

8 "How can I give you up, Ephraim?
How can I hand you over, Israel?
How can I treat you like Admah?
How can I make you like
Zeboyim?
My heart is changed within me;
all my compassion is aroused.
9 I will not carry out my fierce anger,
nor will I devastate Ephraim again.
For I am God, and not a man —
the Holy One among you.
I will not come against their cities.
10 They will follow the LORD;
he will roar like a lion.
When he roars,
his children will come trembling
from the west.
11 They will come from Egypt,
trembling like sparrows,
from Assyria, fluttering like doves.
I will settle them in their homes,"
declares the LORD.

Israel's Sin

12 Ephraim has surrounded me with
lies,
Israel with deceit.
And Judah is unruly against God,
even against the faithful Holy One.[c]

12[d] 1 Ephraim feeds on the wind;
he pursues the east wind all day
and multiplies lies and violence.
He makes a treaty with Assyria
and sends olive oil to Egypt.

[a] 9 Or *there a stand was taken* [b] 2 Septuagint; Hebrew *them* [c] 12 In Hebrew texts this verse (11:12) is numbered 12:1. [d] In Hebrew texts 12:1-14 is numbered 12:2-15.

2 The LORD has a charge to bring
against Judah;
he will punish Jacob[a] according to
his ways
and repay him according to his deeds.
3 In the womb he grasped his brother's
heel;
as a man he struggled with God.
4 He struggled with the angel and
overcame him;
he wept and begged for his favor.
He found him at Bethel
and talked with him there —
5 the LORD God Almighty,
the LORD is his name!
6 But you must return to your God;
maintain love and justice,
and wait for your God always.

7 The merchant uses dishonest scales
and loves to defraud.
8 Ephraim boasts,
"I am very rich; I have become
wealthy.
With all my wealth they will not find
in me
any iniquity or sin."

9 "I have been the LORD your God
ever since you came out of Egypt;
I will make you live in tents again,
as in the days of your appointed
festivals.
10 I spoke to the prophets,
gave them many visions
and told parables through them."

11 Is Gilead wicked?
Its people are worthless!
Do they sacrifice bulls in Gilgal?
Their altars will be like piles of stones
on a plowed field.
12 Jacob fled to the country of Aram[b];
Israel served to get a wife,
and to pay for her he tended sheep.
13 The LORD used a prophet to bring
Israel up from Egypt,
by a prophet he cared for him.
14 But Ephraim has aroused his bitter
anger;
his Lord will leave on him the guilt
of his bloodshed
and will repay him for his
contempt.

The LORD's Anger Against Israel

13 When Ephraim spoke, people
trembled;
he was exalted in Israel.
But he became guilty of Baal
worship and died.
2 Now they sin more and more;
they make idols for themselves
from their silver,
cleverly fashioned images,
all of them the work of craftsmen.
It is said of these people,
"They offer human sacrifices!
They kiss[c] calf-idols!"
3 Therefore they will be like the
morning mist,
like the early dew that disappears,
like chaff swirling from a threshing
floor,
like smoke escaping through a
window.

4 "But I have been the LORD your God
ever since you came out of Egypt.
You shall acknowledge no God but
me,
no Savior except me.
5 I cared for you in the wilderness,
in the land of burning heat.
6 When I fed them, they were satisfied;
when they were satisfied, they
became proud;
then they forgot me.
7 So I will be like a lion to them,
like a leopard I will lurk by the path.
8 Like a bear robbed of her cubs,
I will attack them and rip them
open;
like a lion I will devour them —
a wild animal will tear them apart.

9 "You are destroyed, Israel,
because you are against me,
against your helper.
10 Where is your king, that he may
save you?
Where are your rulers in all your
towns,
of whom you said,
'Give me a king and princes'?
11 So in my anger I gave you a king,
and in my wrath I took him away.
12 The guilt of Ephraim is stored up,
his sins are kept on record.
13 Pains as of a woman in childbirth
come to him,
but he is a child without wisdom;
when the time arrives,
he doesn't have the sense to come
out of the womb.

14 "I will deliver this people from the
power of the grave;
I will redeem them from death.
Where, O death, are your plagues?
Where, O grave, is your
destruction?

[a] 2 *Jacob* means *he grasps the heel*, a Hebrew idiom for *he takes advantage of* or *he deceives*.
[b] 12 That is, Northwest Mesopotamia [c] 2 Or *"Men who sacrifice / kiss*

"I will have no compassion,
15 even though he thrives among his brothers.
An east wind from the LORD will come,
blowing in from the desert;
his spring will fail
and his well dry up.
His storehouse will be plundered
of all its treasures.
16 The people of Samaria must bear their guilt,
because they have rebelled against their God.
They will fall by the sword;
their little ones will be dashed to the ground,
their pregnant women ripped open."[a]

Repentance to Bring Blessing

14 [b] Return, Israel, to the LORD your God.
Your sins have been your downfall!
2 Take words with you
and return to the LORD.
Say to him:
"Forgive all our sins
and receive us graciously,
that we may offer the fruit of our lips.[c]
3 Assyria cannot save us;
we will not mount warhorses.
We will never again say 'Our gods'
to what our own hands have made,
for in you the fatherless find compassion."

4 "I will heal their waywardness
and love them freely,
for my anger has turned away from them.
5 I will be like the dew to Israel;
he will blossom like a lily.
Like a cedar of Lebanon
he will send down his roots;
6 his young shoots will grow.
His splendor will be like an olive tree,
his fragrance like a cedar of Lebanon.
7 People will dwell again in his shade;
they will flourish like the grain,
they will blossom like the vine —
Israel's fame will be like the wine of Lebanon.
8 Ephraim, what more have I[d] to do with idols?
I will answer him and care for him.
I am like a flourishing juniper;
your fruitfulness comes from me."

9 Who is wise? Let them realize these things.
Who is discerning? Let them understand.
The ways of the LORD are right;
the righteous walk in them,
but the rebellious stumble in them.

[a] 16 In Hebrew texts this verse (13:16) is numbered 14:1. [b] In Hebrew texts 14:1-9 is numbered 14:2-10. [c] 2 Or *offer our lips as sacrifices of bulls* [d] 8 Or Hebrew; Septuagint *What more has Ephraim*

JOEL

1 The word of the LORD that came to Joel son of Pethuel.

An Invasion of Locusts

2 Hear this, you elders;
listen, all who live in the land.
Has anything like this ever happened in your days
or in the days of your ancestors?
3 Tell it to your children,
and let your children tell it to their children,
and their children to the next generation.
4 What the locust swarm has left
the great locusts have eaten;
what the great locusts have left
the young locusts have eaten;
what the young locusts have left
other locusts[a] have eaten.

5 Wake up, you drunkards, and weep!
Wail, all you drinkers of wine;
wail because of the new wine,
for it has been snatched from your lips.
6 A nation has invaded my land,
a mighty army without number;
it has the teeth of a lion,
the fangs of a lioness.
7 It has laid waste my vines
and ruined my fig trees.
It has stripped off their bark
and thrown it away,
leaving their branches white.

8 Mourn like a virgin in sackcloth
grieving for the betrothed of her youth.
9 Grain offerings and drink offerings
are cut off from the house of the LORD.
The priests are in mourning,
those who minister before the LORD.
10 The fields are ruined,
the ground is dried up;
the grain is destroyed,
the new wine is dried up,
the olive oil fails.

11 Despair, you farmers,
wail, you vine growers;
grieve for the wheat and the barley,
because the harvest of the field is destroyed.
12 The vine is dried up
and the fig tree is withered;
the pomegranate, the palm and the apple[b] tree —
all the trees of the field — are dried up.
Surely the people's joy
is withered away.

A Call to Lamentation

13 Put on sackcloth, you priests, and mourn;
wail, you who minister before the altar.
Come, spend the night in sackcloth,
you who minister before my God;
for the grain offerings and drink offerings
are withheld from the house of your God.
14 Declare a holy fast;
call a sacred assembly.
Summon the elders
and all who live in the land
to the house of the LORD your God,
and cry out to the LORD.

15 Alas for that day!
For the day of the LORD is near;
it will come like destruction from the Almighty.[c]

16 Has not the food been cut off
before our very eyes —
joy and gladness
from the house of our God?
17 The seeds are shriveled
beneath the clods.[d]
The storehouses are in ruins,
the granaries have been broken down,
for the grain has dried up.
18 How the cattle moan!
The herds mill about
because they have no pasture;
even the flocks of sheep are suffering.

[a] 4 The precise meaning of the four Hebrew words used here for locusts is uncertain.
[b] 12 Or possibly *apricot* [c] 15 Hebrew *Shaddai* [d] 17 The meaning of the Hebrew for this word is uncertain.

19 To you, LORD, I call,
for fire has devoured the pastures
in the wilderness
and flames have burned up all the
trees of the field.
20 Even the wild animals pant for you;
the streams of water have dried up
and fire has devoured the pastures
in the wilderness.

An Army of Locusts

2 Blow the trumpet in Zion;
sound the alarm on my holy hill.
Let all who live in the land tremble,
for the day of the LORD is coming.
It is close at hand —
2 a day of darkness and gloom,
a day of clouds and blackness.
Like dawn spreading across the
mountains
a large and mighty army comes,
such as never was in ancient times
nor ever will be in ages to come.
3 Before them fire devours,
behind them a flame blazes.
Before them the land is like the
garden of Eden,
behind them, a desert waste —
nothing escapes them.
4 They have the appearance of horses;
they gallop along like cavalry.
5 With a noise like that of chariots
they leap over the mountaintops,
like a crackling fire consuming
stubble,
like a mighty army drawn up for
battle.

6 At the sight of them, nations are in
anguish;
every face turns pale.
7 They charge like warriors;
they scale walls like soldiers.
They all march in line,
not swerving from their course.
8 They do not jostle each other;
each marches straight ahead.
They plunge through defenses
without breaking ranks.
9 They rush upon the city;
they run along the wall.
They climb into the houses;
like thieves they enter through the
windows.
10 Before them the earth shakes,
the heavens tremble,
the sun and moon are darkened,
and the stars no longer shine.
11 The LORD thunders
at the head of his army;
his forces are beyond number,
and mighty is the army that obeys
his command.
The day of the LORD is great;
it is dreadful.
Who can endure it?

Rend Your Heart

12 "Even now," declares the LORD,
"return to me with all your heart,
with fasting and weeping and
mourning."

13 Rend your heart
and not your garments.
Return to the LORD your God,
for he is gracious and
compassionate,
slow to anger and abounding in love,
and he relents from sending
calamity.
14 Who knows? He may turn and relent
and leave behind a blessing —
grain offerings and drink offerings
for the LORD your God.

15 Blow the trumpet in Zion,
declare a holy fast,
call a sacred assembly.
16 Gather the people,
consecrate the assembly;
bring together the elders,
gather the children,
those nursing at the breast.
Let the bridegroom leave his room
and the bride her chamber.
17 Let the priests, who minister before
the LORD,
weep between the portico and the
altar.
Let them say, "Spare your people,
LORD.
Do not make your inheritance an
object of scorn,
a byword among the nations.
Why should they say among the
peoples,
'Where is their God?'"

The LORD's Answer

18 Then the LORD was jealous for his land
and took pity on his people.

19 The LORD replied[a] to them:

"I am sending you grain, new wine
and olive oil,
enough to satisfy you fully;
never again will I make you
an object of scorn to the nations.

[a] 18,19 *Or LORD will be jealous . . . / and take pity . . . / 19The LORD will reply*

20 "I will drive the northern horde far
from you,
pushing it into a parched and
barren land;
its eastern ranks will drown in the
Dead Sea
and its western ranks in the
Mediterranean Sea.
And its stench will go up;
its smell will rise."

Surely he has done great things!
21 Do not be afraid, land of Judah;
be glad and rejoice.
Surely the LORD has done great
things!
22 Do not be afraid, you wild animals,
for the pastures in the wilderness
are becoming green.
The trees are bearing their fruit;
the fig tree and the vine yield their
riches.
23 Be glad, people of Zion,
rejoice in the LORD your God,
for he has given you the autumn
rains
because he is faithful.
He sends you abundant showers,
both autumn and spring rains, as
before.
24 The threshing floors will be filled
with grain;
the vats will overflow with new
wine and oil.

25 "I will repay you for the years the
locusts have eaten —
the great locust and the young
locust,
the other locusts and the locust
swarm[a] —
my great army that I sent among
you.
26 You will have plenty to eat, until you
are full,
and you will praise the name of
the LORD your God,
who has worked wonders for you;
never again will my people be
shamed.
27 Then you will know that I am in
Israel,
that I am the LORD your God,
and that there is no other;
never again will my people be
shamed.

The Day of the LORD

28 "And afterward,
I will pour out my Spirit on all
people.
Your sons and daughters will
prophesy,
your old men will dream dreams,
your young men will see visions.
29 Even on my servants, both men and
women,
I will pour out my Spirit in those
days.
30 I will show wonders in the heavens
and on the earth,
blood and fire and billows of
smoke.
31 The sun will be turned to darkness
and the moon to blood
before the coming of the great and
dreadful day of the LORD.
32 And everyone who calls
on the name of the LORD will be
saved;
for on Mount Zion and in Jerusalem
there will be deliverance,
as the LORD has said,
even among the survivors
whom the LORD calls.[b]

The Nations Judged

3[c] "In those days and at that time,
when I restore the fortunes of
Judah and Jerusalem,
2 I will gather all nations
and bring them down to the Valley
of Jehoshaphat.[d]
There I will put them on trial
for what they did to my
inheritance, my people Israel,
because they scattered my people
among the nations
and divided up my land.
3 They cast lots for my people
and traded boys for prostitutes;
they sold girls for wine to drink.

4 "Now what have you against me, Tyre
and Sidon and all you regions of Philistia? Are you repaying me for something
I have done? If you are paying me back,
I will swiftly and speedily return on your
own heads what you have done. 5 For you
took my silver and my gold and carried off
my finest treasures to your temples.[e] 6 You
sold the people of Judah and Jerusalem
to the Greeks, that you might send them
far from their homeland.

[a] *25* The precise meaning of the four Hebrew words used here for locusts is uncertain. [b] *32* In Hebrew texts 2:28-32 is numbered 3:1-5. [c] In Hebrew texts 3:1-21 is numbered 4:1-21. [d] *2* *Jehoshaphat* means *the LORD judges*; also in verse 12. [e] *5* Or *palaces*

[7]"See, I am going to rouse them out of
the places to which you sold them, and
I will return on your own heads what
you have done. [8]I will sell your sons and
daughters to the people of Judah, and they
will sell them to the Sabeans, a nation far
away." The LORD has spoken.

[9] Proclaim this among the nations:
Prepare for war!
Rouse the warriors!
Let all the fighting men draw near
and attack.
[10] Beat your plowshares into swords
and your pruning hooks into spears.
Let the weakling say,
"I am strong!"
[11] Come quickly, all you nations from
every side,
and assemble there.

Bring down your warriors, LORD!

[12] "Let the nations be roused;
let them advance into the Valley of
Jehoshaphat,
for there I will sit
to judge all the nations on every
side.
[13] Swing the sickle,
for the harvest is ripe.
Come, trample the grapes,
for the winepress is full
and the vats overflow—
so great is their wickedness!"

[14] Multitudes, multitudes
in the valley of decision!
For the day of the LORD is near
in the valley of decision.
[15] The sun and moon will be darkened,
and the stars no longer shine.
[16] The LORD will roar from Zion
and thunder from Jerusalem;
the earth and the heavens will
tremble.
But the LORD will be a refuge for his
people,
a stronghold for the people of
Israel.

Blessings for God's People

[17] "Then you will know that I, the LORD
your God,
dwell in Zion, my holy hill.
Jerusalem will be holy;
never again will foreigners invade
her.

[18] "In that day the mountains will drip
new wine,
and the hills will flow with milk;
all the ravines of Judah will run
with water.
A fountain will flow out of the
LORD's house
and will water the valley of
acacias.[a]
[19] But Egypt will be desolate,
Edom a desert waste,
because of violence done to the
people of Judah,
in whose land they shed innocent
blood.
[20] Judah will be inhabited forever
and Jerusalem through all
generations.
[21] Shall I leave their innocent blood
unavenged?
No, I will not."

The LORD dwells in Zion!

[a] 18 *Or Valley of Shittim*

AMOS

1 The words of Amos, one of the shepherds
of Tekoa — the vision he saw concerning
Israel two years before the earthquake,
when Uzziah was king of Judah and Jeroboam son of Jehoash[a] was king of Israel.
2 He said:

"The LORD roars from Zion
and thunders from Jerusalem;
the pastures of the shepherds dry up,
and the top of Carmel withers."

Judgment on Israel's Neighbors

3 This is what the LORD says:

"For three sins of Damascus,
even for four, I will not relent.
Because she threshed Gilead
with sledges having iron teeth,
4 I will send fire on the house of Hazael
that will consume the fortresses of
Ben-Hadad.
5 I will break down the gate of
Damascus;
I will destroy the king who is in[b]
the Valley of Aven[c]
and the one who holds the scepter in
Beth Eden.
The people of Aram will go into
exile to Kir,"
says the LORD.

6 This is what the LORD says:

"For three sins of Gaza,
even for four, I will not relent.
Because she took captive whole
communities
and sold them to Edom,
7 I will send fire on the walls of Gaza
that will consume her fortresses.
8 I will destroy the king[d] of Ashdod
and the one who holds the scepter
in Ashkelon.
I will turn my hand against Ekron,
till the last of the Philistines are
dead,"
says the Sovereign LORD.

9 This is what the LORD says:

"For three sins of Tyre,
even for four, I will not relent.
Because she sold whole communities
of captives to Edom,
disregarding a treaty of
brotherhood,
10 I will send fire on the walls of Tyre
that will consume her fortresses."

11 This is what the LORD says:

"For three sins of Edom,
even for four, I will not relent.
Because he pursued his brother with
a sword
and slaughtered the women of the
land,
because his anger raged continually
and his fury flamed unchecked,
12 I will send fire on Teman
that will consume the fortresses of
Bozrah."

13 This is what the LORD says:

"For three sins of Ammon,
even for four, I will not relent.
Because he ripped open the pregnant
women of Gilead
in order to extend his borders,
14 I will set fire to the walls of Rabbah
that will consume her fortresses
amid war cries on the day of battle,
amid violent winds on a stormy
day.
15 Her king[e] will go into exile,
he and his officials together,"
says the LORD.

2 This is what the LORD says:

"For three sins of Moab,
even for four, I will not relent.
Because he burned to ashes
the bones of Edom's king,
2 I will send fire on Moab
that will consume the fortresses of
Kerioth.[f]
Moab will go down in great tumult
amid war cries and the blast of the
trumpet.
3 I will destroy her ruler
and kill all her officials with him,"
says the LORD.

4 This is what the LORD says:

"For three sins of Judah,
even for four, I will not relent.
Because they have rejected the law of
the LORD
and have not kept his decrees,

[a] *1* Hebrew *Joash,* a variant of *Jehoash* [b] *5* Or *the inhabitants of* [c] *5* *Aven* means *wickedness.*
[d] *8* Or *inhabitants* [e] *15* Or / *Molek* [f] *2* Or *of her cities*

because they have been led astray by
false gods,[a]
the gods[b] their ancestors followed,
5 I will send fire on Judah
that will consume the fortresses of
Jerusalem."

Judgment on Israel

6 This is what the LORD says:

"For three sins of Israel,
even for four, I will not relent.
They sell the innocent for silver,
and the needy for a pair of sandals.
7 They trample on the heads of the poor
as on the dust of the ground
and deny justice to the oppressed.
Father and son use the same girl
and so profane my holy name.
8 They lie down beside every altar
on garments taken in pledge.
In the house of their god
they drink wine taken as fines.

9 "Yet I destroyed the Amorites before
them,
though they were tall as the cedars
and strong as the oaks.
I destroyed their fruit above
and their roots below.
10 I brought you up out of Egypt
and led you forty years in the
wilderness
to give you the land of the
Amorites.

11 "I also raised up prophets from
among your children
and Nazirites from among your
youths.
Is this not true, people of Israel?"
declares the LORD.
12 "But you made the Nazirites drink
wine
and commanded the prophets not
to prophesy.

13 "Now then, I will crush you
as a cart crushes when loaded with
grain.
14 The swift will not escape,
the strong will not muster their
strength,
and the warrior will not save his
life.
15 The archer will not stand his ground,
the fleet-footed soldier will not get
away,
and the horseman will not save his
life.
16 Even the bravest warriors
will flee naked on that day,"
declares the LORD.

[a] 4 Or *by lies* [b] 4 Or *lies*

Witnesses Summoned Against Israel

3 Hear this word, people of Israel, the
word the LORD has spoken against
you — against the whole family I brought
up out of Egypt:

2 "You only have I chosen
of all the families of the earth;
therefore I will punish you
for all your sins."

3 Do two walk together
unless they have agreed to do so?
4 Does a lion roar in the thicket
when it has no prey?
Does it growl in its den
when it has caught nothing?
5 Does a bird swoop down to a trap on
the ground
when no bait is there?
Does a trap spring up from the
ground
if it has not caught anything?
6 When a trumpet sounds in a city,
do not the people tremble?
When disaster comes to a city,
has not the LORD caused it?

7 Surely the Sovereign LORD does
nothing
without revealing his plan
to his servants the prophets.

8 The lion has roared —
who will not fear?
The Sovereign LORD has spoken —
who can but prophesy?

9 Proclaim to the fortresses of Ashdod
and to the fortresses of Egypt:
"Assemble yourselves on the
mountains of Samaria;
see the great unrest within her
and the oppression among her
people."

10 "They do not know how to do right,"
declares the LORD,
"who store up in their fortresses
what they have plundered and
looted."

11 Therefore this is what the Sovereign
LORD says:

"An enemy will overrun your land,
pull down your strongholds
and plunder your fortresses."

12 This is what the LORD says:

"As a shepherd rescues from the lion's
mouth
only two leg bones or a piece of an
ear,

so will the Israelites living in Samaria
be rescued,
with only the head of a bed
and a piece of fabric[a] from a
couch.[b]"

13 "Hear this and testify against the descendants of Jacob," declares the Lord, the LORD God Almighty.

14 "On the day I punish Israel for her
sins,
I will destroy the altars of Bethel;
the horns of the altar will be cut off
and fall to the ground.
15 I will tear down the winter house
along with the summer house;
the houses adorned with ivory will be
destroyed
and the mansions will be
demolished,"
declares the LORD.

Israel Has Not Returned to God

4 Hear this word, you cows of Bashan
on Mount Samaria,
you women who oppress the poor
and crush the needy
and say to your husbands, "Bring
us some drinks!"
2 The Sovereign LORD has sworn by his
holiness:
"The time will surely come
when you will be taken away with
hooks,
the last of you with fishhooks.[c]
3 You will each go straight out
through breaches in the wall,
and you will be cast out toward
Harmon,[d]"
declares the LORD.
4 "Go to Bethel and sin;
go to Gilgal and sin yet more.
Bring your sacrifices every morning,
your tithes every three years.[e]
5 Burn leavened bread as a thank
offering
and brag about your freewill
offerings —
boast about them, you Israelites,
for this is what you love to do,"
declares the Sovereign LORD.

6 "I gave you empty stomachs in every
city
and lack of bread in every town,
yet you have not returned to me,"
declares the LORD.

7 "I also withheld rain from you
when the harvest was still three
months away.
I sent rain on one town,
but withheld it from another.
One field had rain;
another had none and dried up.
8 People staggered from town to town
for water
but did not get enough to drink,
yet you have not returned to me,"
declares the LORD.

9 "Many times I struck your gardens
and vineyards,
destroying them with blight and
mildew.
Locusts devoured your fig and olive
trees,
yet you have not returned to me,"
declares the LORD.

10 "I sent plagues among you
as I did to Egypt.
I killed your young men with the sword,
along with your captured horses.
I filled your nostrils with the stench of
your camps,
yet you have not returned to me,"
declares the LORD.

11 "I overthrew some of you
as I overthrew Sodom and
Gomorrah.
You were like a burning stick
snatched from the fire,
yet you have not returned to me,"
declares the LORD.

12 "Therefore this is what I will do to
you, Israel,
and because I will do this to you,
Israel,
prepare to meet your God."

13 He who forms the mountains,
who creates the wind,
and who reveals his thoughts to
mankind,
who turns dawn to darkness,
and treads on the heights of the
earth —
the LORD God Almighty is his name.

A Lament and Call to Repentance

5 Hear this word, Israel, this lament I take up concerning you:

2 "Fallen is Virgin Israel,
never to rise again,
deserted in her own land,
with no one to lift her up."

[a] 12 The meaning of the Hebrew for this phrase is uncertain. [b] 12 Or *Israelites be rescued, / those who sit in Samaria / on the edge of their beds / and in Damascus on their couches.* [c] 2 Or *away in baskets, / the last of you in fish baskets* [d] 3 Masoretic Text; with a different word division of the Hebrew (see Septuagint) *out, you mountain of oppression* [e] 4 Or *days*

3 This is what the Sovereign LORD says
to Israel:

"Your city that marches out a thousand strong
will have only a hundred left;
your town that marches out a hundred strong
will have only ten left."

4 This is what the LORD says to Israel:

"Seek me and live;
5 do not seek Bethel,
do not go to Gilgal,
do not journey to Beersheba.
For Gilgal will surely go into exile,
and Bethel will be reduced to nothing.[a]"
6 Seek the LORD and live,
or he will sweep through the tribes of Joseph like a fire;
it will devour them,
and Bethel will have no one to quench it.
7 There are those who turn justice into bitterness
and cast righteousness to the ground.
8 He who made the Pleiades and Orion,
who turns midnight into dawn
and darkens day into night,
who calls for the waters of the sea
and pours them out over the face of the land —
the LORD is his name.
9 With a blinding flash he destroys the stronghold
and brings the fortified city to ruin.
10 There are those who hate the one who upholds justice in court
and detest the one who tells the truth.
11 You levy a straw tax on the poor
and impose a tax on their grain.
Therefore, though you have built stone mansions,
you will not live in them;
though you have planted lush vineyards,
you will not drink their wine.
12 For I know how many are your offenses
and how great your sins.

There are those who oppress the innocent and take bribes
and deprive the poor of justice in the courts.
13 Therefore the prudent keep quiet in such times,
for the times are evil.
14 Seek good, not evil,
that you may live.
Then the LORD God Almighty will be with you,
just as you say he is.
15 Hate evil, love good;
maintain justice in the courts.
Perhaps the LORD God Almighty will have mercy
on the remnant of Joseph.

16 Therefore this is what the Lord, the
LORD God Almighty, says:

"There will be wailing in all the streets
and cries of anguish in every public square.
The farmers will be summoned to weep
and the mourners to wail.
17 There will be wailing in all the vineyards,
for I will pass through your midst,"
says the LORD.

The Day of the LORD

18 Woe to you who long
for the day of the LORD!
Why do you long for the day of the LORD?
That day will be darkness, not light.
19 It will be as though a man fled from a lion
only to meet a bear,
as though he entered his house
and rested his hand on the wall
only to have a snake bite him.
20 Will not the day of the LORD be darkness, not light —
pitch-dark, without a ray of brightness?

21 "I hate, I despise your religious festivals;
your assemblies are a stench to me.
22 Even though you bring me burnt offerings and grain offerings,
I will not accept them.
Though you bring choice fellowship offerings,
I will have no regard for them.
23 Away with the noise of your songs!
I will not listen to the music of your harps.
24 But let justice roll on like a river,
righteousness like a never-failing stream!

[a] 5 Hebrew *aven*, a reference to Beth Aven (a derogatory name for Bethel); see Hosea 4:15.

25 "Did you bring me sacrifices and offerings
forty years in the wilderness,
people of Israel?
26 You have lifted up the shrine of your king,
the pedestal of your idols,
the star of your god[a] —
which you made for yourselves.
27 Therefore I will send you into exile beyond Damascus,"
says the LORD, whose name is God Almighty.

Woe to the Complacent

6 Woe to you who are complacent in Zion,
and to you who feel secure on Mount Samaria,
you notable men of the foremost nation,
to whom the people of Israel come!
2 Go to Kalneh and look at it;
go from there to great Hamath,
and then go down to Gath in Philistia.
Are they better off than your two kingdoms?
Is their land larger than yours?
3 You put off the day of disaster
and bring near a reign of terror.
4 You lie on beds adorned with ivory
and lounge on your couches.
You dine on choice lambs
and fattened calves.
5 You strum away on your harps like David
and improvise on musical instruments.
6 You drink wine by the bowlful
and use the finest lotions,
but you do not grieve over the ruin of Joseph.
7 Therefore you will be among the first to go into exile;
your feasting and lounging will end.

The LORD Abhors the Pride of Israel

8 The Sovereign LORD has sworn by himself — the LORD God Almighty declares:

"I abhor the pride of Jacob
and detest his fortresses;
I will deliver up the city
and everything in it."

9 If ten people are left in one house,
they too will die. 10 And if the relative who
comes to carry the bodies out of the house
to burn them[b] asks anyone who might be
hiding there, "Is anyone else with you?"
and he says, "No," then he will go on to say,
"Hush! We must not mention the name
of the LORD."

11 For the LORD has given the command,
and he will smash the great house into pieces
and the small house into bits.

12 Do horses run on the rocky crags?
Does one plow the sea[c] with oxen?
But you have turned justice into poison
and the fruit of righteousness into bitterness —
13 you who rejoice in the conquest of Lo Debar[d]
and say, "Did we not take Karnaim[e]
by our own strength?"

14 For the LORD God Almighty declares,
"I will stir up a nation against you, Israel,
that will oppress you all the way
from Lebo Hamath to the valley of the Arabah."

Locusts, Fire and a Plumb Line

7 This is what the Sovereign LORD showed
me: He was preparing swarms of locusts after the king's share had been
harvested and just as the late crops were
coming up. 2 When they had stripped the
land clean, I cried out, "Sovereign LORD,
forgive! How can Jacob survive? He is so
small!"
3 So the LORD relented.
"This will not happen," the LORD said.
4 This is what the Sovereign LORD
showed me: The Sovereign LORD was calling for judgment by fire; it dried up the
great deep and devoured the land. 5 Then I
cried out, "Sovereign LORD, I beg you, stop!
How can Jacob survive? He is so small!"
6 So the LORD relented.
"This will not happen either," the Sovereign LORD said.

7 This is what he showed me: The Lord
was standing by a wall that had been built
true to plumb,[f] with a plumb line[g] in his
hand. 8 And the LORD asked me, "What do
you see, Amos?"
"A plumb line," I replied.

[a] 26 Or *lifted up Sakkuth your king / and Kaiwan your idols, / your star-gods*; Septuagint *lifted up the shrine of Molek / and the star of your god Rephan, / their idols* [b] 10 Or *to make a funeral fire in honor of the dead* [c] 12 With a different word division of the Hebrew; Masoretic Text *plow there* [d] 13 *Lo Debar* means *nothing.* [e] 13 *Karnaim* means *horns*; *horn* here symbolizes strength. [f] 7 The meaning of the Hebrew for this phrase is uncertain. [g] 7 The meaning of the Hebrew for this phrase is uncertain; also in verse 8.

Then the Lord said, "Look, I am setting a plumb line among my people Israel; I will spare them no longer.

9 "The high places of Isaac will be destroyed
and the sanctuaries of Israel will be ruined;
with my sword I will rise against the house of Jeroboam."

Amos and Amaziah

10 Then Amaziah the priest of Bethel sent a message to Jeroboam king of Israel: "Amos is raising a conspiracy against you in the very heart of Israel. The land cannot bear all his words. 11 For this is what Amos is saying:

"'Jeroboam will die by the sword,
and Israel will surely go into exile,
away from their native land.'"

12 Then Amaziah said to Amos, "Get out, you seer! Go back to the land of Judah. Earn your bread there and do your prophesying there. 13 Don't prophesy anymore at Bethel, because this is the king's sanctuary and the temple of the kingdom."

14 Amos answered Amaziah, "I was neither a prophet nor the son of a prophet, but I was a shepherd, and I also took care of sycamore-fig trees. 15 But the LORD took me from tending the flock and said to me, 'Go, prophesy to my people Israel.'
16 Now then, hear the word of the LORD. You say,

"'Do not prophesy against Israel,
and stop preaching against the descendants of Isaac.'

17 "Therefore this is what the LORD says:

"'Your wife will become a prostitute in the city,
and your sons and daughters will fall by the sword.
Your land will be measured and divided up,
and you yourself will die in a pagan[a] country.
And Israel will surely go into exile,
away from their native land.'"

A Basket of Ripe Fruit

8 This is what the Sovereign LORD showed me: a basket of ripe fruit.
2 "What do you see, Amos?" he asked.

"A basket of ripe fruit," I answered.

Then the LORD said to me, "The time is ripe for my people Israel; I will spare them no longer.

3 "In that day," declares the Sovereign LORD, "the songs in the temple will turn to wailing.[b] Many, many bodies — flung everywhere! Silence!"

4 Hear this, you who trample the needy
and do away with the poor of the land,

5 saying,

"When will the New Moon be over
that we may sell grain,
and the Sabbath be ended
that we may market wheat?" —
skimping on the measure,
boosting the price
and cheating with dishonest scales,
6 buying the poor with silver
and the needy for a pair of sandals,
selling even the sweepings with the wheat.

7 The LORD has sworn by himself, the Pride of Jacob: "I will never forget anything they have done.

8 "Will not the land tremble for this,
and all who live in it mourn?
The whole land will rise like the Nile;
it will be stirred up and then sink
like the river of Egypt.

9 "In that day," declares the Sovereign LORD,

"I will make the sun go down at noon
and darken the earth in broad daylight.
10 I will turn your religious festivals into mourning
and all your singing into weeping.
I will make all of you wear sackcloth
and shave your heads.
I will make that time like mourning
for an only son
and the end of it like a bitter day.

11 "The days are coming," declares the Sovereign LORD,
"when I will send a famine through the land —
not a famine of food or a thirst for water,
but a famine of hearing the words of the LORD.
12 People will stagger from sea to sea
and wander from north to east,
searching for the word of the LORD,
but they will not find it.

13 "In that day

"the lovely young women and strong young men
will faint because of thirst.

[a] 17 Hebrew *an unclean* [b] 3 Or *"the temple singers will wail*

14 Those who swear by the sin of Samaria —
who say, 'As surely as your god lives, Dan,'
or, 'As surely as the god[a] of Beersheba lives' —
they will fall, never to rise again."

Israel to Be Destroyed

9 I saw the Lord standing by the altar, and he said:

"Strike the tops of the pillars
so that the thresholds shake.
Bring them down on the heads of all the people;
those who are left I will kill with the sword.
Not one will get away,
none will escape.
2 Though they dig down to the depths below,
from there my hand will take them.
Though they climb up to the heavens above,
from there I will bring them down.
3 Though they hide themselves on the top of Carmel,
there I will hunt them down and seize them.
Though they hide from my eyes at the bottom of the sea,
there I will command the serpent to bite them.
4 Though they are driven into exile by their enemies,
there I will command the sword to slay them.

"I will keep my eye on them
for harm and not for good."

5 The Lord, the LORD Almighty —
he touches the earth and it melts,
and all who live in it mourn;
the whole land rises like the Nile,
then sinks like the river of Egypt;
6 he builds his lofty palace[b] in the heavens
and sets its foundation[c] on the earth;
he calls for the waters of the sea
and pours them out over the face of the land —
the LORD is his name.

7 "Are not you Israelites
the same to me as the Cushites[d]?"
declares the LORD.
"Did I not bring Israel up from Egypt,
the Philistines from Caphtor[e]
and the Arameans from Kir?

8 "Surely the eyes of the Sovereign LORD
are on the sinful kingdom.
I will destroy it
from the face of the earth.
Yet I will not totally destroy
the descendants of Jacob,"
declares the LORD.
9 "For I will give the command,
and I will shake the people of Israel
among all the nations
as grain is shaken in a sieve,
and not a pebble will reach the ground.
10 All the sinners among my people
will die by the sword,
all those who say,
'Disaster will not overtake or meet us.'

Israel's Restoration

11 "In that day

"I will restore David's fallen shelter —
I will repair its broken walls
and restore its ruins —
and will rebuild it as it used to be,
12 so that they may possess the remnant of Edom
and all the nations that bear my name,[f]"
declares the LORD,
who will do these things.

13 "The days are coming," declares the LORD,

"when the reaper will be overtaken by the plowman
and the planter by the one treading grapes.
New wine will drip from the mountains
and flow from all the hills,
14 and I will bring my people Israel back from exile.[g]

"They will rebuild the ruined cities
and live in them.
They will plant vineyards and drink their wine;
they will make gardens and eat their fruit.
15 I will plant Israel in their own land,
never again to be uprooted
from the land I have given them,"

says the LORD your God.

[a] 14 Hebrew *the way* [b] 6 The meaning of the Hebrew for this phrase is uncertain. [c] 6 The meaning of the Hebrew for this word is uncertain. [d] 7 That is, people from the upper Nile region [e] 7 That is, Crete [f] 12 Hebrew; Septuagint *so that the remnant of people / and all the nations that bear my name may seek me* [g] 14 Or *will restore the fortunes of my people Israel*

OBADIAH

Obadiah's Vision

[1]The vision of Obadiah.

This is what the Sovereign LORD says about Edom —

We have heard a message from the LORD:
An envoy was sent to the nations to say,
"Rise, let us go against her for battle" —

[2]"See, I will make you small among the nations;
you will be utterly despised.
[3]The pride of your heart has deceived you,
you who live in the clefts of the rocks[a]
and make your home on the heights,
you who say to yourself,
'Who can bring me down to the ground?'
[4]Though you soar like the eagle
and make your nest among the stars,
from there I will bring you down,"
declares the LORD.
[5]"If thieves came to you,
if robbers in the night —
oh, what a disaster awaits you! —
would they not steal only as much as they wanted?
If grape pickers came to you,
would they not leave a few grapes?
[6]But how Esau will be ransacked,
his hidden treasures pillaged!
[7]All your allies will force you to the border;
your friends will deceive and overpower you;
those who eat your bread will set a trap for you,[b]
but you will not detect it.

[8]"In that day," declares the LORD,
"will I not destroy the wise men of Edom,
those of understanding in the mountains of Esau?
[9]Your warriors, Teman, will be terrified,
and everyone in Esau's mountains
will be cut down in the slaughter.
[10]Because of the violence against your brother Jacob,
you will be covered with shame;
you will be destroyed forever.
[11]On the day you stood aloof
while strangers carried off his wealth
and foreigners entered his gates
and cast lots for Jerusalem,
you were like one of them.
[12]You should not gloat over your brother
in the day of his misfortune,
nor rejoice over the people of Judah
in the day of their destruction,
nor boast so much
in the day of their trouble.
[13]You should not march through the gates of my people
in the day of their disaster,
nor gloat over them in their calamity
in the day of their disaster,
nor seize their wealth
in the day of their disaster.
[14]You should not wait at the crossroads
to cut down their fugitives,
nor hand over their survivors
in the day of their trouble.

[15]"The day of the LORD is near
for all nations.
As you have done, it will be done to you;
your deeds will return upon your own head.
[16]Just as you drank on my holy hill,
so all the nations will drink continually;
they will drink and drink
and be as if they had never been.
[17]But on Mount Zion will be deliverance;
it will be holy,
and Jacob will possess his inheritance.
[18]Jacob will be a fire
and Joseph a flame;
Esau will be stubble,
and they will set him on fire and destroy him.
There will be no survivors
from Esau."
The LORD has spoken.

[a] 3 Or *of Sela* [b] 7 The meaning of the Hebrew for this clause is uncertain.

19 People from the Negev will occupy
the mountains of Esau,
and people from the foothills will possess
the land of the Philistines.
They will occupy the fields of Ephraim and Samaria,
and Benjamin will possess Gilead.
20 This company of Israelite exiles who are in Canaan
will possess the land as far as Zarephath;
the exiles from Jerusalem who are in Sepharad
will possess the towns of the Negev.
21 Deliverers will go up on[a] Mount Zion
to govern the mountains of Esau.
And the kingdom will be the LORD's.

[a] 21 Or *from*

JONAH

Jonah Flees From the LORD

1 The word of the LORD came to Jonah
son of Amittai: 2"Go to the great city of
Nineveh and preach against it, because
its wickedness has come up before me."
3But Jonah ran away from the LORD
and headed for Tarshish. He went down
to Joppa, where he found a ship bound
for that port. After paying the fare, he
went aboard and sailed for Tarshish to
flee from the LORD.
4Then the LORD sent a great wind on the
sea, and such a violent storm arose that
the ship threatened to break up. 5All the
sailors were afraid and each cried out to
his own god. And they threw the cargo
into the sea to lighten the ship.
But Jonah had gone below deck, where
he lay down and fell into a deep sleep. 6The
captain went to him and said, "How can
you sleep? Get up and call on your god!
Maybe he will take notice of us so that
we will not perish."
7Then the sailors said to each other,
"Come, let us cast lots to find out who is
responsible for this calamity." They cast
lots and the lot fell on Jonah. 8So they
asked him, "Tell us, who is responsible for
making all this trouble for us? What kind
of work do you do? Where do you come
from? What is your country? From what
people are you?"
9He answered, "I am a Hebrew and I
worship the LORD, the God of heaven, who
made the sea and the dry land."
10This terrified them and they asked,
"What have you done?" (They knew he was
running away from the LORD, because he
had already told them so.)
11The sea was getting rougher and
rougher. So they asked him, "What should
we do to you to make the sea calm down
for us?"
12"Pick me up and throw me into the
sea," he replied, "and it will become calm.
I know that it is my fault that this great
storm has come upon you."
13Instead, the men did their best to row
back to land. But they could not, for the
sea grew even wilder than before. 14Then
they cried out to the LORD, "Please, LORD,
do not let us die for taking this man's life.
Do not hold us accountable for killing an
innocent man, for you, LORD, have done
as you pleased." 15Then they took Jonah
and threw him overboard, and the raging
sea grew calm. 16At this the men greatly
feared the LORD, and they offered a sacrifice to the LORD and made vows to him.

Jonah's Prayer

17Now the LORD provided a huge fish to
swallow Jonah, and Jonah was in the belly
of the fish three days and three nights.
2[a] 1From inside the fish Jonah prayed to
the LORD his God. 2He said:

"In my distress I called to the LORD,
and he answered me.
From deep in the realm of the dead I
called for help,
and you listened to my cry.
3You hurled me into the depths,
into the very heart of the seas,
and the currents swirled about me;
all your waves and breakers
swept over me.
4I said, 'I have been banished
from your sight;
yet I will look again
toward your holy temple.'
5The engulfing waters threatened
me,[b]
the deep surrounded me;
seaweed was wrapped around my
head.
6To the roots of the mountains I sank
down;
the earth beneath barred me in
forever.
But you, LORD my God,
brought my life up from the pit.

7"When my life was ebbing away,
I remembered you, LORD,
and my prayer rose to you,
to your holy temple.

8"Those who cling to worthless idols
turn away from God's love for them.
9But I, with shouts of grateful praise,
will sacrifice to you.
What I have vowed I will make good.
I will say, 'Salvation comes from
the LORD.'"

10And the LORD commanded the fish,
and it vomited Jonah onto dry land.

[a] In Hebrew texts 2:1 is numbered 1:17, and 2:1-10 is numbered 2:2-11. [b] 5 Or *waters were at my throat*

Jonah Goes to Nineveh

3 Then the word of the LORD came to
Jonah a second time: 2"Go to the great
city of Nineveh and proclaim to it the
message I give you."
3Jonah obeyed the word of the LORD and
went to Nineveh. Now Nineveh was a very
large city; it took three days to go through
it. 4Jonah began by going a day's journey
into the city, proclaiming, "Forty more
days and Nineveh will be overthrown."
5The Ninevites believed God. A fast was
proclaimed, and all of them, from the
greatest to the least, put on sackcloth.
6When Jonah's warning reached the king
of Nineveh, he rose from his throne, took
off his royal robes, covered himself with
sackcloth and sat down in the dust. 7This
is the proclamation he issued in Nineveh:

"By the decree of the king and his
nobles:

Do not let people or animals, herds
or flocks, taste anything; do not let
them eat or drink. 8But let people and
animals be covered with sackcloth.
Let everyone call urgently on God. Let
them give up their evil ways and their
violence. 9Who knows? God may yet relent and with compassion turn from his
fierce anger so that we will not perish."

10When God saw what they did and
how they turned from their evil ways, he
relented and did not bring on them the
destruction he had threatened.

Jonah's Anger at the LORD's Compassion

4 But to Jonah this seemed very wrong,
and he became angry. 2He prayed to
the LORD, "Isn't this what I said, LORD,
when I was still at home? That is what I
tried to forestall by fleeing to Tarshish.
I knew that you are a gracious and
compassionate God, slow to anger and
abounding in love, a God who relents
from sending calamity. 3Now, LORD, take
away my life, for it is better for me to die
than to live."
4But the LORD replied, "Is it right for
you to be angry?"
5Jonah had gone out and sat down at
a place east of the city. There he made
himself a shelter, sat in its shade and
waited to see what would happen to the
city. 6Then the LORD God provided a leafy
plant[a] and made it grow up over Jonah
to give shade for his head to ease his
discomfort, and Jonah was very happy
about the plant. 7But at dawn the next
day God provided a worm, which chewed
the plant so that it withered. 8When the
sun rose, God provided a scorching east
wind, and the sun blazed on Jonah's head
so that he grew faint. He wanted to die,
and said, "It would be better for me to
die than to live."
9But God said to Jonah, "Is it right for
you to be angry about the plant?"
"It is," he said. "And I'm so angry I wish
I were dead."
10But the LORD said, "You have been
concerned about this plant, though you
did not tend it or make it grow. It sprang
up overnight and died overnight. 11And
should I not have concern for the great
city of Nineveh, in which there are more
than a hundred and twenty thousand
people who cannot tell their right hand
from their left — and also many animals?"

[a] 6 The precise identification of this plant is uncertain; also in verses 7, 9 and 10.

MICAH

1 The word of the LORD that came to Micah of Moresheth during the reigns of Jotham, Ahaz and Hezekiah, kings of Judah — the vision he saw concerning Samaria and Jerusalem.

2 Hear, you peoples, all of you,
listen, earth and all who live in it,
that the Sovereign LORD may bear witness against you,
the Lord from his holy temple.

Judgment Against Samaria and Jerusalem

3 Look! The LORD is coming from his dwelling place;
he comes down and treads on the heights of the earth.
4 The mountains melt beneath him
and the valleys split apart,
like wax before the fire,
like water rushing down a slope.
5 All this is because of Jacob's transgression,
because of the sins of the people of Israel.
What is Jacob's transgression?
Is it not Samaria?
What is Judah's high place?
Is it not Jerusalem?

6 "Therefore I will make Samaria a heap of rubble,
a place for planting vineyards.
I will pour her stones into the valley
and lay bare her foundations.
7 All her idols will be broken to pieces;
all her temple gifts will be burned with fire;
I will destroy all her images.
Since she gathered her gifts from the wages of prostitutes,
as the wages of prostitutes they will again be used."

Weeping and Mourning

8 Because of this I will weep and wail;
I will go about barefoot and naked.
I will howl like a jackal
and moan like an owl.
9 For Samaria's plague is incurable;
it has spread to Judah.
It has reached the very gate of my people,
even to Jerusalem itself.
10 Tell it not in Gath[a];
weep not at all.
In Beth Ophrah[b]
roll in the dust.
11 Pass by naked and in shame,
you who live in Shaphir.[c]
Those who live in Zaanan[d]
will not come out.
Beth Ezel is in mourning;
it no longer protects you.
12 Those who live in Maroth[e] writhe in pain,
waiting for relief,
because disaster has come from the LORD,
even to the gate of Jerusalem.
13 You who live in Lachish,
harness fast horses to the chariot.
You are where the sin of Daughter Zion began,
for the transgressions of Israel were found in you.
14 Therefore you will give parting gifts
to Moresheth Gath.
The town of Akzib[f] will prove deceptive
to the kings of Israel.
15 I will bring a conqueror against you
who live in Mareshah.[g]
The nobles of Israel
will flee to Adullam.
16 Shave your head in mourning
for the children in whom you delight;
make yourself as bald as the vulture,
for they will go from you into exile.

Human Plans and God's Plans

2 Woe to those who plan iniquity,
to those who plot evil on their beds!
At morning's light they carry it out
because it is in their power to do it.
2 They covet fields and seize them,
and houses, and take them.
They defraud people of their homes,
they rob them of their inheritance.

[a] 10 *Gath* sounds like the Hebrew for *tell.* [b] 10 *Beth Ophrah* means *house of dust.* [c] 11 *Shaphir* means *pleasant.* [d] 11 *Zaanan* sounds like the Hebrew for *come out.* [e] 12 *Maroth* sounds like the Hebrew for *bitter.* [f] 14 *Akzib* means *deception.* [g] 15 *Mareshah* sounds like the Hebrew for *conqueror.*

3 Therefore, the LORD says:

"I am planning disaster against this people,
from which you cannot save yourselves.
You will no longer walk proudly,
for it will be a time of calamity.
4 In that day people will ridicule you;
they will taunt you with this mournful song:
'We are utterly ruined;
my people's possession is divided up.
He takes it from me!
He assigns our fields to traitors.'"

5 Therefore you will have no one in the assembly of the LORD
to divide the land by lot.

False Prophets

6 "Do not prophesy," their prophets say.
"Do not prophesy about these things;
disgrace will not overtake us."
7 You descendants of Jacob, should it be said,
"Does the LORD become[a] impatient?
Does he do such things?"

"Do not my words do good
to the one whose ways are upright?
8 Lately my people have risen up
like an enemy.
You strip off the rich robe
from those who pass by without a care,
like men returning from battle.
9 You drive the women of my people
from their pleasant homes.
You take away my blessing
from their children forever.
10 Get up, go away!
For this is not your resting place,
because it is defiled,
it is ruined, beyond all remedy.
11 If a liar and deceiver comes and says,
'I will prophesy for you plenty of wine and beer,'
that would be just the prophet for this people!

Deliverance Promised

12 "I will surely gather all of you, Jacob;
I will surely bring together the remnant of Israel.
I will bring them together like sheep in a pen,
like a flock in its pasture;
the place will throng with people.
13 The One who breaks open the way
will go up before them;
they will break through the gate
and go out.
Their King will pass through before them,
the LORD at their head."

Leaders and Prophets Rebuked

3 Then I said,

"Listen, you leaders of Jacob,
you rulers of Israel.
Should you not embrace justice,
2 you who hate good and love evil;
who tear the skin from my people
and the flesh from their bones;
3 who eat my people's flesh,
strip off their skin
and break their bones in pieces;
who chop them up like meat for the pan,
like flesh for the pot?"

4 Then they will cry out to the LORD,
but he will not answer them.
At that time he will hide his face from them
because of the evil they have done.

5 This is what the LORD says:

"As for the prophets
who lead my people astray,
they proclaim 'peace'
if they have something to eat,
but prepare to wage war against anyone
who refuses to feed them.
6 Therefore night will come over you,
without visions,
and darkness, without divination.
The sun will set for the prophets,
and the day will go dark for them.
7 The seers will be ashamed
and the diviners disgraced.
They will all cover their faces
because there is no answer from God."
8 But as for me, I am filled with power,
with the Spirit of the LORD,
and with justice and might,
to declare to Jacob his transgression,
to Israel his sin.

9 Hear this, you leaders of Jacob,
you rulers of Israel,
who despise justice
and distort all that is right;
10 who build Zion with bloodshed,
and Jerusalem with wickedness.

[a] 7 Or *Is the Spirit of the LORD*

[11] Her leaders judge for a bribe,
her priests teach for a price,
and her prophets tell fortunes for money.
Yet they look for the LORD's support and say,
"Is not the LORD among us?
No disaster will come upon us."
[12] Therefore because of you,
Zion will be plowed like a field,
Jerusalem will become a heap of rubble,
the temple hill a mound overgrown with thickets.

The Mountain of the LORD

4 In the last days
the mountain of the LORD's temple will be established
as the highest of the mountains;
it will be exalted above the hills,
and peoples will stream to it.

[2] Many nations will come and say,
"Come, let us go up to the mountain of the LORD,
to the temple of the God of Jacob.
He will teach us his ways,
so that we may walk in his paths."
The law will go out from Zion,
the word of the LORD from Jerusalem.
[3] He will judge between many peoples
and will settle disputes for strong nations far and wide.
They will beat their swords into plowshares
and their spears into pruning hooks.
Nation will not take up sword against nation,
nor will they train for war anymore.
[4] Everyone will sit under their own vine
and under their own fig tree,
and no one will make them afraid,
for the LORD Almighty has spoken.
[5] All the nations may walk
in the name of their gods,
but we will walk in the name of the LORD
our God for ever and ever.

The LORD's Plan

[6] "In that day," declares the LORD,
"I will gather the lame;
I will assemble the exiles
and those I have brought to grief.
[7] I will make the lame my remnant,
those driven away a strong nation.
The LORD will rule over them in Mount Zion
from that day and forever.
[8] As for you, watchtower of the flock,
stronghold[a] of Daughter Zion,
the former dominion will be restored to you;
kingship will come to Daughter Jerusalem."

[9] Why do you now cry aloud —
have you no king[b]?
Has your ruler[c] perished,
that pain seizes you like that of a woman in labor?
[10] Writhe in agony, Daughter Zion,
like a woman in labor,
for now you must leave the city
to camp in the open field.
You will go to Babylon;
there you will be rescued.
There the LORD will redeem you
out of the hand of your enemies.

[11] But now many nations
are gathered against you.
They say, "Let her be defiled,
let our eyes gloat over Zion!"
[12] But they do not know
the thoughts of the LORD;
they do not understand his plan,
that he has gathered them like sheaves to the threshing floor.
[13] "Rise and thresh, Daughter Zion,
for I will give you horns of iron;
I will give you hooves of bronze,
and you will break to pieces many nations."
You will devote their ill-gotten gains to the LORD,
their wealth to the Lord of all the earth.

A Promised Ruler From Bethlehem

5[d] Marshal your troops now, city of troops,
for a siege is laid against us.
They will strike Israel's ruler
on the cheek with a rod.

[2] "But you, Bethlehem Ephrathah,
though you are small among the clans[e] of Judah,
out of you will come for me
one who will be ruler over Israel,
whose origins are from of old,
from ancient times."

[a] 8 Or *hill* [b] 9 Or *King* [c] 9 Or *Ruler* [d] In Hebrew texts 5:1 is numbered 4:14, and 5:2-15 is numbered 5:1-14. [e] 2 Or *rulers*

3 Therefore Israel will be abandoned
until the time when she who is in
labor bears a son,
and the rest of his brothers return
to join the Israelites.

4 He will stand and shepherd his flock
in the strength of the LORD,
in the majesty of the name of the
LORD his God.
And they will live securely, for then
his greatness
will reach to the ends of the earth.

5 And he will be our peace
when the Assyrians invade our
land
and march through our fortresses.
We will raise against them seven
shepherds,
even eight commanders,
6 who will rule[a] the land of Assyria
with the sword,
the land of Nimrod with drawn
sword.[b]
He will deliver us from the Assyrians
when they invade our land
and march across our borders.

7 The remnant of Jacob will be
in the midst of many peoples
like dew from the LORD,
like showers on the grass,
which do not wait for anyone
or depend on man.
8 The remnant of Jacob will be among
the nations,
in the midst of many peoples,
like a lion among the beasts of the
forest,
like a young lion among flocks of
sheep,
which mauls and mangles as it goes,
and no one can rescue.
9 Your hand will be lifted up in triumph
over your enemies,
and all your foes will be destroyed.

10 "In that day," declares the LORD,

"I will destroy your horses from
among you
and demolish your chariots.
11 I will destroy the cities of your land
and tear down all your strongholds.
12 I will destroy your witchcraft
and you will no longer cast spells.
13 I will destroy your idols
and your sacred stones from
among you;
you will no longer bow down
to the work of your hands.
14 I will uproot from among you your
Asherah poles[c]
when I demolish your cities.
15 I will take vengeance in anger and
wrath
on the nations that have not
obeyed me."

The LORD's Case Against Israel

6 Listen to what the LORD says:

"Stand up, plead my case before the
mountains;
let the hills hear what you have to
say.

2 "Hear, you mountains, the LORD's
accusation;
listen, you everlasting foundations
of the earth.
For the LORD has a case against his
people;
he is lodging a charge against Israel.

3 "My people, what have I done to you?
How have I burdened you? Answer
me.
4 I brought you up out of Egypt
and redeemed you from the land of
slavery.
I sent Moses to lead you,
also Aaron and Miriam.
5 My people, remember
what Balak king of Moab plotted
and what Balaam son of Beor
answered.
Remember your journey from Shittim
to Gilgal,
that you may know the righteous
acts of the LORD."

6 With what shall I come before the
LORD
and bow down before the exalted
God?
Shall I come before him with burnt
offerings,
with calves a year old?
7 Will the LORD be pleased with
thousands of rams,
with ten thousand rivers of olive
oil?
Shall I offer my firstborn for my
transgression,
the fruit of my body for the sin of
my soul?
8 He has shown you, O mortal, what is
good.
And what does the LORD require of
you?
To act justly and to love mercy
and to walk humbly[d] with your God.

[a] 6 Or *crush* [b] 6 Or *Nimrod in its gates* [c] 14 That is, wooden symbols of the goddess Asherah [d] 8 Or *prudently*

Israel's Guilt and Punishment

[9] Listen! The LORD is calling to the
city —
and to fear your name is wisdom —
"Heed the rod and the One who
appointed it.[a]
[10] Am I still to forget your ill-gotten
treasures, you wicked house,
and the short ephah,[b] which is
accursed?
[11] Shall I acquit someone with dishonest
scales,
with a bag of false weights?
[12] Your rich people are violent;
your inhabitants are liars
and their tongues speak deceitfully.
[13] Therefore, I have begun to destroy
you,
to ruin[c] you because of your sins.
[14] You will eat but not be satisfied;
your stomach will still be empty.[d]
You will store up but save nothing,
because what you save[e] I will give
to the sword.
[15] You will plant but not harvest;
you will press olives but not use the
oil,
you will crush grapes but not drink
the wine.
[16] You have observed the statutes of
Omri
and all the practices of Ahab's
house;
you have followed their traditions.
Therefore I will give you over to ruin
and your people to derision;
you will bear the scorn of the
nations.[f]"

Israel's Misery

7 What misery is mine!
I am like one who gathers summer
fruit
at the gleaning of the vineyard;
there is no cluster of grapes to eat,
none of the early figs that I crave.
[2] The faithful have been swept from
the land;
not one upright person remains.
Everyone lies in wait to shed blood;
they hunt each other with nets.
[3] Both hands are skilled in doing evil;
the ruler demands gifts,
the judge accepts bribes,
the powerful dictate what they
desire —
they all conspire together.
[4] The best of them is like a brier,
the most upright worse than a
thorn hedge.
The day God visits you has come,
the day your watchmen sound the
alarm.
Now is the time of your confusion.
[5] Do not trust a neighbor;
put no confidence in a friend.
Even with the woman who lies in your
embrace
guard the words of your lips.
[6] For a son dishonors his father,
a daughter rises up against her
mother,
a daughter-in-law against her
mother-in-law —
a man's enemies are the members
of his own household.

[7] But as for me, I watch in hope for the
LORD,
I wait for God my Savior;
my God will hear me.

Israel Will Rise

[8] Do not gloat over me, my enemy!
Though I have fallen, I will rise.
Though I sit in darkness,
the LORD will be my light.
[9] Because I have sinned against him,
I will bear the LORD's wrath,
until he pleads my case
and upholds my cause.
He will bring me out into the light;
I will see his righteousness.
[10] Then my enemy will see it
and will be covered with shame,
she who said to me,
"Where is the LORD your God?"
My eyes will see her downfall;
even now she will be trampled
underfoot
like mire in the streets.
[11] The day for building your walls will
come,
the day for extending your
boundaries.
[12] In that day people will come to you
from Assyria and the cities of
Egypt,
even from Egypt to the Euphrates
and from sea to sea
and from mountain to mountain.
[13] The earth will become desolate
because of its inhabitants,
as the result of their deeds.

[a] 9 The meaning of the Hebrew for this line is uncertain. [b] 10 An ephah was a dry measure. [c] 13 Or *Therefore, I will make you ill and destroy you; / I will ruin* [d] 14 The meaning of the Hebrew for this word is uncertain. [e] 14 Or *You will press toward birth but not give birth, / and what you bring to birth* [f] 16 Septuagint; Hebrew *scorn due my people*

Prayer and Praise

14 Shepherd your people with your staff,
the flock of your inheritance,
which lives by itself in a forest,
in fertile pasturelands.[a]
Let them feed in Bashan and Gilead
as in days long ago.

15 "As in the days when you came out of
Egypt,
I will show them my wonders."

16 Nations will see and be ashamed,
deprived of all their power.
They will put their hands over their
mouths
and their ears will become deaf.
17 They will lick dust like a snake,
like creatures that crawl on the
ground.
They will come trembling out of their
dens;
they will turn in fear to the LORD
our God
and will be afraid of you.
18 Who is a God like you,
who pardons sin and forgives the
transgression
of the remnant of his inheritance?
You do not stay angry forever
but delight to show mercy.
19 You will again have compassion on us;
you will tread our sins underfoot
and hurl all our iniquities into the
depths of the sea.
20 You will be faithful to Jacob,
and show love to Abraham,
as you pledged on oath to our ancestors
in days long ago.

[a] 14 Or *in the middle of Carmel*

NAHUM

1 A prophecy concerning Nineveh. The book of the vision of Nahum the Elkoshite.

The LORD's Anger Against Nineveh

2 The LORD is a jealous and avenging God;
the LORD takes vengeance and is filled with wrath.
The LORD takes vengeance on his foes
and vents his wrath against his enemies.
3 The LORD is slow to anger but great in power;
the LORD will not leave the guilty unpunished.
His way is in the whirlwind and the storm,
and clouds are the dust of his feet.
4 He rebukes the sea and dries it up;
he makes all the rivers run dry.
Bashan and Carmel wither
and the blossoms of Lebanon fade.
5 The mountains quake before him
and the hills melt away.
The earth trembles at his presence,
the world and all who live in it.
6 Who can withstand his indignation?
Who can endure his fierce anger?
His wrath is poured out like fire;
the rocks are shattered before him.

7 The LORD is good,
a refuge in times of trouble.
He cares for those who trust in him,
8 but with an overwhelming flood
he will make an end of Nineveh;
he will pursue his foes into the realm of darkness.

9 Whatever they plot against the LORD
he will bring[a] to an end;
trouble will not come a second time.
10 They will be entangled among thorns
and drunk from their wine;
they will be consumed like dry stubble.[b]
11 From you, Nineveh, has one come forth
who plots evil against the LORD
and devises wicked plans.
12 This is what the LORD says:

"Although they have allies and are numerous,
they will be destroyed and pass away.
Although I have afflicted you, Judah,
I will afflict you no more.
13 Now I will break their yoke from your neck
and tear your shackles away."

14 The LORD has given a command concerning you, Nineveh:
"You will have no descendants to bear your name.
I will destroy the images and idols
that are in the temple of your gods.
I will prepare your grave,
for you are vile."

15 Look, there on the mountains,
the feet of one who brings good news,
who proclaims peace!
Celebrate your festivals, Judah,
and fulfill your vows.
No more will the wicked invade you;
they will be completely destroyed.[c]

Nineveh to Fall

2[d] An attacker advances against you, Nineveh.
Guard the fortress,
watch the road,
brace yourselves,
marshal all your strength!

2 The LORD will restore the splendor of Jacob
like the splendor of Israel,
though destroyers have laid them waste
and have ruined their vines.

3 The shields of the soldiers are red;
the warriors are clad in scarlet.
The metal on the chariots flashes
on the day they are made ready;
the spears of juniper are brandished.[e]
4 The chariots storm through the streets,
rushing back and forth through the squares.

[a] 9 Or *What do you foes plot against the LORD? / He will bring it* [b] 10 The meaning of the Hebrew for this verse is uncertain. [c] 15 In Hebrew texts this verse (1:15) is numbered 2:1. [d] In Hebrew texts 2:1-13 is numbered 2:2-14. [e] 3 Hebrew; Septuagint and Syriac *ready; / the horsemen rush to and fro.*

They look like flaming torches;
they dart about like lightning.

5 Nineveh summons her picked troops,
yet they stumble on their way.
They dash to the city wall;
the protective shield is put in place.
6 The river gates are thrown open
and the palace collapses.
7 It is decreed[a] that Nineveh
be exiled and carried away.
Her female slaves moan like doves
and beat on their breasts.
8 Nineveh is like a pool
whose water is draining away.
"Stop! Stop!" they cry,
but no one turns back.
9 Plunder the silver!
Plunder the gold!
The supply is endless,
the wealth from all its treasures!
10 She is pillaged, plundered, stripped!
Hearts melt, knees give way,
bodies tremble, every face grows
pale.

11 Where now is the lions' den,
the place where they fed their
young,
where the lion and lioness went,
and the cubs, with nothing to fear?
12 The lion killed enough for his cubs
and strangled the prey for his
mate,
filling his lairs with the kill
and his dens with the prey.

13 "I am against you,"
declares the LORD Almighty.
"I will burn up your chariots in
smoke,
and the sword will devour your
young lions.
I will leave you no prey on the
earth.
The voices of your messengers
will no longer be heard."

Woe to Nineveh

3 Woe to the city of blood,
full of lies,
full of plunder,
never without victims!
2 The crack of whips,
the clatter of wheels,
galloping horses
and jolting chariots!
3 Charging cavalry,
flashing swords
and glittering spears!
Many casualties,
piles of dead,
bodies without number,
people stumbling over the corpses —
4 all because of the wanton lust of a
prostitute,
alluring, the mistress of sorceries,
who enslaved nations by her
prostitution
and peoples by her witchcraft.

5 "I am against you," declares the LORD
Almighty.
"I will lift your skirts over your face.
I will show the nations your
nakedness
and the kingdoms your shame.
6 I will pelt you with filth,
I will treat you with contempt
and make you a spectacle.
7 All who see you will flee from you and
say,
'Nineveh is in ruins — who will
mourn for her?'
Where can I find anyone to comfort
you?"

8 Are you better than Thebes,
situated on the Nile,
with water around her?
The river was her defense,
the waters her wall.
9 Cush[b] and Egypt were her boundless
strength;
Put and Libya were among her
allies.
10 Yet she was taken captive
and went into exile.
Her infants were dashed to pieces
at every street corner.
Lots were cast for her nobles,
and all her great men were put in
chains.
11 You too will become drunk;
you will go into hiding
and seek refuge from the enemy.

12 All your fortresses are like fig trees
with their first ripe fruit;
when they are shaken,
the figs fall into the mouth of the
eater.
13 Look at your troops —
they are all weaklings.
The gates of your land
are wide open to your enemies;
fire has consumed the bars of your
gates.

14 Draw water for the siege,
strengthen your defenses!
Work the clay,
tread the mortar,
repair the brickwork!

[a] 7 The meaning of the Hebrew for this word is uncertain. [b] 9 That is, the upper Nile region

15 There the fire will consume you;
the sword will cut you down —
they will devour you like a swarm of locusts.
Multiply like grasshoppers,
multiply like locusts!
16 You have increased the number of your merchants
till they are more numerous than the stars in the sky,
but like locusts they strip the land
and then fly away.
17 Your guards are like locusts,
your officials like swarms of locusts
that settle in the walls on a cold day —
but when the sun appears they fly away,
and no one knows where.
18 King of Assyria, your shepherds[a] slumber;
your nobles lie down to rest.
Your people are scattered on the mountains
with no one to gather them.
19 Nothing can heal you;
your wound is fatal.
All who hear the news about you
clap their hands at your fall,
for who has not felt
your endless cruelty?

[a] *18* That is, rulers

HABAKKUK

1 The prophecy that Habakkuk the prophet received.

Habakkuk's Complaint

2 How long, LORD, must I call for help,
but you do not listen?
Or cry out to you, "Violence!"
but you do not save?
3 Why do you make me look at injustice?
Why do you tolerate wrongdoing?
Destruction and violence are before me;
there is strife, and conflict abounds.
4 Therefore the law is paralyzed,
and justice never prevails.
The wicked hem in the righteous,
so that justice is perverted.

The LORD's Answer

5 "Look at the nations and watch —
and be utterly amazed.
For I am going to do something in your days
that you would not believe,
even if you were told.
6 I am raising up the Babylonians,[a]
that ruthless and impetuous people,
who sweep across the whole earth
to seize dwellings not their own.
7 They are a feared and dreaded people;
they are a law to themselves
and promote their own honor.
8 Their horses are swifter than leopards,
fiercer than wolves at dusk.
Their cavalry gallops headlong;
their horsemen come from afar.
They fly like an eagle swooping to devour;
9 they all come intent on violence.
Their hordes[b] advance like a desert wind
and gather prisoners like sand.
10 They mock kings
and scoff at rulers.
They laugh at all fortified cities;
by building earthen ramps they capture them.
11 Then they sweep past like the wind and go on —
guilty people, whose own strength is their god."

Habakkuk's Second Complaint

12 LORD, are you not from everlasting?
My God, my Holy One, you[c] will never die.
You, LORD, have appointed them to execute judgment;
you, my Rock, have ordained them to punish.
13 Your eyes are too pure to look on evil;
you cannot tolerate wrongdoing.
Why then do you tolerate the treacherous?
Why are you silent while the wicked
swallow up those more righteous than themselves?
14 You have made people like the fish in the sea,
like the sea creatures that have no ruler.
15 The wicked foe pulls all of them up with hooks,
he catches them in his net,
he gathers them up in his dragnet;
and so he rejoices and is glad.
16 Therefore he sacrifices to his net
and burns incense to his dragnet,
for by his net he lives in luxury
and enjoys the choicest food.
17 Is he to keep on emptying his net,
destroying nations without mercy?

2 I will stand at my watch
and station myself on the ramparts;
I will look to see what he will say to me,
and what answer I am to give to this complaint.[d]

The LORD's Answer

2 Then the LORD replied:

"Write down the revelation
and make it plain on tablets
so that a herald[e] may run with it.
3 For the revelation awaits an appointed time;
it speaks of the end
and will not prove false.
Though it linger, wait for it;
it[f] will certainly come
and will not delay.

[a] 6 Or *Chaldeans* [b] 9 The meaning of the Hebrew for this word is uncertain.
[c] 12 An ancient Hebrew scribal tradition; Masoretic Text *we* [d] 1 Or *and what to answer when I am rebuked* [e] 2 Or *so that whoever reads it* [f] 3 Or *Though he linger, wait for him; / he*

4 "See, the enemy is puffed up;
his desires are not upright —
but the righteous person will live
by his faithfulness[a] —
5 indeed, wine betrays him;
he is arrogant and never at rest.
Because he is as greedy as the grave
and like death is never satisfied,
he gathers to himself all the nations
and takes captive all the peoples.

6 "Will not all of them taunt him with
ridicule and scorn, saying,

"'Woe to him who piles up stolen goods
and makes himself wealthy by
extortion!
How long must this go on?'
7 Will not your creditors suddenly arise?
Will they not wake up and make
you tremble?
Then you will become their prey.
8 Because you have plundered many
nations,
the peoples who are left will
plunder you.
For you have shed human blood;
you have destroyed lands and
cities and everyone in them.

9 "Woe to him who builds his house by
unjust gain,
setting his nest on high
to escape the clutches of ruin!
10 You have plotted the ruin of many
peoples,
shaming your own house and
forfeiting your life.
11 The stones of the wall will cry out,
and the beams of the woodwork
will echo it.

12 "Woe to him who builds a city with
bloodshed
and establishes a town by injustice!
13 Has not the LORD Almighty determined
that the people's labor is only fuel
for the fire,
that the nations exhaust
themselves for nothing?
14 For the earth will be filled with the
knowledge of the glory of the
LORD
as the waters cover the sea.

15 "Woe to him who gives drink to his
neighbors,
pouring it from the wineskin till
they are drunk,
so that he can gaze on their naked
bodies!
16 You will be filled with shame instead
of glory.
Now it is your turn! Drink and let
your nakedness be exposed[b]!
The cup from the LORD's right hand
is coming around to you,
and disgrace will cover your glory.
17 The violence you have done to
Lebanon will overwhelm you,
and your destruction of animals
will terrify you.
For you have shed human blood;
you have destroyed lands and
cities and everyone in them.

18 "Of what value is an idol carved by a
craftsman?
Or an image that teaches lies?
For the one who makes it trusts in his
own creation;
he makes idols that cannot speak.
19 Woe to him who says to wood,
'Come to life!'
Or to lifeless stone, 'Wake up!'
Can it give guidance?
It is covered with gold and silver;
there is no breath in it."
20 The LORD is in his holy temple;
let all the earth be silent before
him.

Habakkuk's Prayer

3 A prayer of Habakkuk the prophet. On *shigionoth*.[c]

2 LORD, I have heard of your fame;
I stand in awe of your deeds, LORD.
Repeat them in our day,
in our time make them known;
in wrath remember mercy.

3 God came from Teman,
the Holy One from Mount Paran.[d]
His glory covered the heavens
and his praise filled the earth.
4 His splendor was like the sunrise;
rays flashed from his hand,
where his power was hidden.
5 Plague went before him;
pestilence followed his steps.
6 He stood, and shook the earth;
he looked, and made the nations
tremble.
The ancient mountains crumbled
and the age-old hills collapsed —
but he marches on forever.
7 I saw the tents of Cushan in distress,
the dwellings of Midian
in anguish.

[a] 4 Or *faith* [b] 16 Masoretic Text; Dead Sea Scrolls, Aquila, Vulgate and Syriac (see also Septuagint) *and stagger* [c] 1 Probably a literary or musical term [d] 3 The Hebrew has *Selah* (a word of uncertain meaning) here and at the middle of verse 9 and at the end of verse 13.

8 Were you angry with the rivers, LORD?
Was your wrath against the streams?
Did you rage against the sea
when you rode your horses
and your chariots to victory?
9 You uncovered your bow,
you called for many arrows.
You split the earth with rivers;
10 the mountains saw you and writhed.
Torrents of water swept by;
the deep roared
and lifted its waves on high.

11 Sun and moon stood still in the heavens
at the glint of your flying arrows,
at the lightning of your flashing spear.
12 In wrath you strode through the earth
and in anger you threshed the nations.
13 You came out to deliver your people,
to save your anointed one.
You crushed the leader of the land of wickedness,
you stripped him from head to foot.
14 With his own spear you pierced his head
when his warriors stormed out to scatter us,
gloating as though about to devour
the wretched who were in hiding.
15 You trampled the sea with your horses,
churning the great waters.

16 I heard and my heart pounded,
my lips quivered at the sound;
decay crept into my bones,
and my legs trembled.
Yet I will wait patiently for the day of calamity
to come on the nation invading us.
17 Though the fig tree does not bud
and there are no grapes on the vines,
though the olive crop fails
and the fields produce no food,
though there are no sheep in the pen
and no cattle in the stalls,
18 yet I will rejoice in the LORD,
I will be joyful in God my Savior.

19 The Sovereign LORD is my strength;
he makes my feet like the feet of a deer,
he enables me to tread on the heights.

For the director of music. On my stringed instruments.

ZEPHANIAH

1 The word of the LORD that came to
Zephaniah son of Cushi, the son of
Gedaliah, the son of Amariah, the son of
Hezekiah, during the reign of Josiah son
of Amon king of Judah:

Judgment on the Whole Earth in the Day of the LORD

2 "I will sweep away everything
from the face of the earth,"
declares the LORD.
3 "I will sweep away both man and beast;
I will sweep away the birds in the sky
and the fish in the sea —
and the idols that cause the wicked
to stumble."[a]

"When I destroy all mankind
on the face of the earth,"
declares the LORD,
4 "I will stretch out my hand against
Judah
and against all who live in
Jerusalem.
I will destroy every remnant of Baal
worship in this place,
the very names of the idolatrous
priests —
5 those who bow down on the roofs
to worship the starry host,
those who bow down and swear by
the LORD
and who also swear by Molek,[b]
6 those who turn back from following
the LORD
and neither seek the LORD nor
inquire of him."

7 Be silent before the Sovereign LORD,
for the day of the LORD is near.
The LORD has prepared a sacrifice;
he has consecrated those he has
invited.

8 "On the day of the LORD's sacrifice
I will punish the officials
and the king's sons
and all those clad
in foreign clothes.
9 On that day I will punish
all who avoid stepping on the
threshold,[c]
who fill the temple of their gods
with violence and deceit.

10 "On that day,"
declares the LORD,
"a cry will go up from the Fish Gate,
wailing from the New Quarter,
and a loud crash from the hills.
11 Wail, you who live in the market
district[d];
all your merchants will be wiped out,
all who trade with[e] silver will be
destroyed.
12 At that time I will search Jerusalem
with lamps
and punish those who are
complacent,
who are like wine left on its dregs,
who think, 'The LORD will do nothing,
either good or bad.'
13 Their wealth will be plundered,
their houses demolished.
Though they build houses,
they will not live in them;
though they plant vineyards,
they will not drink the wine."
14 The great day of the LORD is near —
near and coming quickly.
The cry on the day of the LORD is
bitter;
the Mighty Warrior shouts his
battle cry.
15 That day will be a day of wrath —
a day of distress and anguish,
a day of trouble and ruin,
a day of darkness and gloom,
a day of clouds and blackness —
16 a day of trumpet and battle cry
against the fortified cities
and against the corner towers.

17 "I will bring such distress on all people
that they will grope about like
those who are blind,
because they have sinned against
the LORD.
Their blood will be poured out like
dust
and their entrails like dung.
18 Neither their silver nor their gold
will be able to save them
on the day of the LORD's wrath."

In the fire of his jealousy
the whole earth will be consumed,
for he will make a sudden end
of all who live on the earth.

[a] *3* The meaning of the Hebrew for this line is uncertain. [b] *5* Hebrew *Malkam*
[c] *9* See 1 Samuel 5:5. [d] *11* Or *the Mortar* [e] *11* Or *in*

Judah and Jerusalem Judged Along With the Nations

Judah Summoned to Repent

2 Gather together, gather yourselves together,
you shameful nation,
2 before the decree takes effect
and that day passes like windblown chaff,
before the LORD's fierce anger
comes upon you,
before the day of the LORD's wrath
comes upon you.
3 Seek the LORD, all you humble of the land,
you who do what he commands.
Seek righteousness, seek humility;
perhaps you will be sheltered
on the day of the LORD's anger.

Philistia

4 Gaza will be abandoned
and Ashkelon left in ruins.
At midday Ashdod will be emptied
and Ekron uprooted.
5 Woe to you who live by the sea,
you Kerethite people;
the word of the LORD is against you,
Canaan, land of the Philistines.
He says, "I will destroy you,
and none will be left."
6 The land by the sea will become pastures
having wells for shepherds
and pens for flocks.
7 That land will belong
to the remnant of the people of Judah;
there they will find pasture.
In the evening they will lie down
in the houses of Ashkelon.
The LORD their God will care for them;
he will restore their fortunes.[a]

Moab and Ammon

8 "I have heard the insults of Moab
and the taunts of the Ammonites,
who insulted my people
and made threats against their land.
9 Therefore, as surely as I live,"
declares the LORD Almighty,
the God of Israel,
"surely Moab will become like Sodom,
the Ammonites like Gomorrah —
a place of weeds and salt pits,
a wasteland forever.
The remnant of my people will plunder them;
the survivors of my nation will inherit their land."
10 This is what they will get in return for their pride,
for insulting and mocking
the people of the LORD Almighty.
11 The LORD will be awesome to them
when he destroys all the gods of the earth.
Distant nations will bow down to him,
all of them in their own lands.

Cush

12 "You Cushites,[b] too,
will be slain by my sword."

Assyria

13 He will stretch out his hand against the north
and destroy Assyria,
leaving Nineveh utterly desolate
and dry as the desert.
14 Flocks and herds will lie down there,
creatures of every kind.
The desert owl and the screech owl
will roost on her columns.
Their hooting will echo through the windows,
rubble will fill the doorways,
the beams of cedar will be exposed.
15 This is the city of revelry
that lived in safety.
She said to herself,
"I am the one! And there is none besides me."
What a ruin she has become,
a lair for wild beasts!
All who pass by her scoff
and shake their fists.

Jerusalem

3 Woe to the city of oppressors,
rebellious and defiled!
2 She obeys no one,
she accepts no correction.
She does not trust in the LORD,
she does not draw near to her God.
3 Her officials within her
are roaring lions;
her rulers are evening wolves,
who leave nothing for the morning.
4 Her prophets are unprincipled;
they are treacherous people.
Her priests profane the sanctuary
and do violence to the law.
5 The LORD within her is righteous;
he does no wrong.
Morning by morning he dispenses his justice,
and every new day he does not fail,
yet the unrighteous know no shame.

[a] 7 Or *will bring back their captives* [b] 12 That is, people from the upper Nile region

Jerusalem Remains Unrepentant

6 "I have destroyed nations;
their strongholds are demolished.
I have left their streets deserted,
with no one passing through.
Their cities are laid waste;
they are deserted and empty.
7 Of Jerusalem I thought,
'Surely you will fear me
and accept correction!'
Then her place of refuge[a] would not
be destroyed,
nor all my punishments come
upon[b] her.
But they were still eager
to act corruptly in all they did.
8 Therefore wait for me,"
declares the LORD,
"for the day I will stand up to
testify.[c]
I have decided to assemble the
nations,
to gather the kingdoms
and to pour out my wrath on them —
all my fierce anger.
The whole world will be consumed
by the fire of my jealous anger.

Restoration of Israel's Remnant

9 "Then I will purify the lips of the
peoples,
that all of them may call on the
name of the LORD
and serve him shoulder to
shoulder.
10 From beyond the rivers of Cush[d]
my worshipers, my scattered
people,
will bring me offerings.
11 On that day you, Jerusalem, will not
be put to shame
for all the wrongs you have done
to me,
because I will remove from you
your arrogant boasters.
Never again will you be haughty
on my holy hill.
12 But I will leave within you
the meek and humble.
The remnant of Israel
will trust in the name of the LORD.
13 They will do no wrong;
they will tell no lies.
A deceitful tongue
will not be found in their mouths.
They will eat and lie down
and no one will make them afraid."

14 Sing, Daughter Zion;
shout aloud, Israel!
Be glad and rejoice with all your
heart,
Daughter Jerusalem!
15 The LORD has taken away your
punishment,
he has turned back your enemy.
The LORD, the King of Israel, is with
you;
never again will you fear any
harm.
16 On that day
they will say to Jerusalem,
"Do not fear, Zion;
do not let your hands hang limp.
17 The LORD your God is with you,
the Mighty Warrior who saves.
He will take great delight in you;
in his love he will no longer
rebuke you,
but will rejoice over you with
singing."

18 "I will remove from you
all who mourn over the loss of your
appointed festivals,
which is a burden and reproach
for you.
19 At that time I will deal
with all who oppressed you.
I will rescue the lame;
I will gather the exiles.
I will give them praise and honor
in every land where they have
suffered shame.
20 At that time I will gather you;
at that time I will bring
you home.
I will give you honor and praise
among all the peoples of the earth
when I restore your fortunes[e]
before your very eyes,"
says the LORD.

[a] 7 Or *her sanctuary* [b] 7 Or *all those I appointed over* [c] 8 Septuagint and Syriac; Hebrew *will rise up to plunder* [d] 10 That is, the upper Nile region [e] 20 Or *I bring back your captives*

HAGGAI

A Call to Build the House of the LORD

1 In the second year of King Darius, on
the first day of the sixth month, the
word of the LORD came through the prophet Haggai to Zerubbabel son of Shealtiel,
governor of Judah, and to Joshua son of
Jozadak,[a] the high priest:
2 This is what the LORD Almighty says:
"These people say, 'The time has not yet
come to rebuild the LORD's house.'"
3 Then the word of the LORD came
through the prophet Haggai: 4 "Is it a
time for you yourselves to be living in
your paneled houses, while this house
remains a ruin?"
5 Now this is what the LORD Almighty
says: "Give careful thought to your ways.
6 You have planted much, but harvested
little. You eat, but never have enough.
You drink, but never have your fill. You
put on clothes, but are not warm. You
earn wages, only to put them in a purse
with holes in it."
7 This is what the LORD Almighty says:
"Give careful thought to your ways. 8 Go
up into the mountains and bring down
timber and build my house, so that I
may take pleasure in it and be honored,"
says the LORD. 9 "You expected much,
but see, it turned out to be little. What
you brought home, I blew away. Why?"
declares the LORD Almighty. "Because of
my house, which remains a ruin, while
each of you is busy with your own house.
10 Therefore, because of you the heavens
have withheld their dew and the earth
its crops. 11 I called for a drought on the
fields and the mountains, on the grain,
the new wine, the olive oil and everything else the ground produces, on people and livestock, and on all the labor
of your hands."

12 Then Zerubbabel son of Shealtiel,
Joshua son of Jozadak, the high priest,
and the whole remnant of the people
obeyed the voice of the LORD their God
and the message of the prophet Haggai,
because the LORD their God had sent him.
And the people feared the LORD.
13 Then Haggai, the LORD's messenger,
gave this message of the LORD to the people: "I am with you," declares the LORD.
14 So the LORD stirred up the spirit of Zerubbabel son of Shealtiel, governor of Judah,
and the spirit of Joshua son of Jozadak,
the high priest, and the spirit of the whole
remnant of the people. They came and
began to work on the house of the LORD
Almighty, their God, 15 on the twenty-fourth
day of the sixth month.

The Promised Glory of the New House

2 In the second year of King Darius,
1 on the twenty-first day of the seventh month, the word of the LORD came
through the prophet Haggai: 2 "Speak to
Zerubbabel son of Shealtiel, governor of
Judah, to Joshua son of Jozadak,[b] the
high priest, and to the remnant of the
people. Ask them, 3 'Who of you is left who
saw this house in its former glory? How
does it look to you now? Does it not seem
to you like nothing? 4 But now be strong,
Zerubbabel,' declares the LORD. 'Be strong,
Joshua son of Jozadak, the high priest. Be
strong, all you people of the land,' declares
the LORD, 'and work. For I am with you,'
declares the LORD Almighty. 5 'This is what
I covenanted with you when you came out
of Egypt. And my Spirit remains among
you. Do not fear.'
6 "This is what the LORD Almighty says:
'In a little while I will once more shake
the heavens and the earth, the sea and
the dry land. 7 I will shake all nations, and
what is desired by all nations will come,
and I will fill this house with glory,' says
the LORD Almighty. 8 'The silver is mine
and the gold is mine,' declares the LORD
Almighty. 9 'The glory of this present house
will be greater than the glory of the former house,' says the LORD Almighty. 'And
in this place I will grant peace,' declares
the LORD Almighty."

Blessings for a Defiled People

10 On the twenty-fourth day of the ninth
month, in the second year of Darius, the
word of the LORD came to the prophet
Haggai: 11 "This is what the LORD Almighty
says: 'Ask the priests what the law says:
12 If someone carries consecrated meat in
the fold of their garment, and that fold

[a] *1* Hebrew *Jehozadak,* a variant of *Jozadak;* also in verses 12 and 14 [b] *2* Hebrew *Jehozadak,* a variant of *Jozadak;* also in verse 4

touches some bread or stew, some wine,
olive oil or other food, does it become
consecrated?'"
The priests answered, "No."
13Then Haggai said, "If a person defiled
by contact with a dead body touches one
of these things, does it become defiled?"
"Yes," the priests replied, "it becomes
defiled."
14Then Haggai said, "'So it is with this
people and this nation in my sight,' declares the LORD. 'Whatever they do and
whatever they offer there is defiled.
15"'Now give careful thought to this
from this day on[a] — consider how things
were before one stone was laid on another in the LORD's temple. 16When anyone
came to a heap of twenty measures, there
were only ten. When anyone went to a
wine vat to draw fifty measures, there
were only twenty. 17I struck all the work of
your hands with blight, mildew and hail,
yet you did not return to me,' declares
the LORD. 18'From this day on, from this
twenty-fourth day of the ninth month,
give careful thought to the day when the
foundation of the LORD's temple was laid.
Give careful thought: 19Is there yet any
seed left in the barn? Until now, the vine
and the fig tree, the pomegranate and the
olive tree have not borne fruit.
"'From this day on I will bless you.'"

Zerubbabel the LORD's Signet Ring

20The word of the LORD came to Haggai
a second time on the twenty-fourth day
of the month: 21"Tell Zerubbabel governor
of Judah that I am going to shake the
heavens and the earth. 22I will overturn
royal thrones and shatter the power of
the foreign kingdoms. I will overthrow
chariots and their drivers; horses and
their riders will fall, each by the sword
of his brother.
23"'On that day,' declares the LORD Almighty, 'I will take you, my servant Zerubbabel son of Shealtiel,' declares the
LORD, 'and I will make you like my signet
ring, for I have chosen you,' declares the
LORD Almighty."

[a] 15 Or *to the days past*

ZECHARIAH

A Call to Return to the LORD

1 In the eighth month of the second year of Darius, the word of the LORD came to the prophet Zechariah son of Berekiah, the son of Iddo:

2“The LORD was very angry with your ancestors. 3Therefore tell the people: This is what the LORD Almighty says: ‘Return to me,’ declares the LORD Almighty, ‘and I will return to you,’ says the LORD Almighty. 4Do not be like your ancestors, to whom the earlier prophets proclaimed: This is what the LORD Almighty says: ‘Turn from your evil ways and your evil practices.’ But they would not listen or pay attention to me, declares the LORD. 5Where are your ancestors now? And the prophets, do they live forever? 6But did not my words and my decrees, which I commanded my servants the prophets, overtake your ancestors?

“Then they repented and said, ‘The LORD Almighty has done to us what our ways and practices deserve, just as he determined to do.’ ”

The Man Among the Myrtle Trees

7On the twenty-fourth day of the eleventh month, the month of Shebat, in the second year of Darius, the word of the LORD came to the prophet Zechariah son of Berekiah, the son of Iddo.

8During the night I had a vision, and there before me was a man mounted on a red horse. He was standing among the myrtle trees in a ravine. Behind him were red, brown and white horses.

9I asked, “What are these, my lord?”

The angel who was talking with me answered, “I will show you what they are.”

10Then the man standing among the myrtle trees explained, “They are the ones the LORD has sent to go throughout the earth.”

11And they reported to the angel of the LORD who was standing among the myrtle trees, “We have gone throughout the earth and found the whole world at rest and in peace.”

12Then the angel of the LORD said, “LORD Almighty, how long will you withhold mercy from Jerusalem and from the towns of Judah, which you have been angry with these seventy years?” 13So the LORD spoke kind and comforting words to the angel who talked with me.

14Then the angel who was speaking to me said, “Proclaim this word: This is what the LORD Almighty says: ‘I am very jealous for Jerusalem and Zion, 15and I am very angry with the nations that feel secure. I was only a little angry, but they went too far with the punishment.’

16“Therefore this is what the LORD says: ‘I will return to Jerusalem with mercy, and there my house will be rebuilt. And the measuring line will be stretched out over Jerusalem,’ declares the LORD Almighty.

17“Proclaim further: This is what the LORD Almighty says: ‘My towns will again overflow with prosperity, and the LORD will again comfort Zion and choose Jerusalem.’ ”

Four Horns and Four Craftsmen

18Then I looked up, and there before me were four horns. 19I asked the angel who was speaking to me, “What are these?”

He answered me, “These are the horns that scattered Judah, Israel and Jerusalem.”

20Then the LORD showed me four craftsmen. 21I asked, “What are these coming to do?”

He answered, “These are the horns that scattered Judah so that no one could raise their head, but the craftsmen have come to terrify them and throw down these horns of the nations who lifted up their horns against the land of Judah to scatter its people.”[a]

A Man With a Measuring Line

2[b] Then I looked up, and there before me was a man with a measuring line in his hand. 2I asked, “Where are you going?”

He answered me, “To measure Jerusalem, to find out how wide and how long it is.”

3While the angel who was speaking to me was leaving, another angel came to meet him 4and said to him: “Run, tell that young man, ‘Jerusalem will be a city without walls because of the great number of people and animals in it. 5And I myself will be a wall of fire around it,’ declares the LORD, ‘and I will be its glory within.’

[a] *21* In Hebrew texts 1:18-21 is numbered 2:1-4.
[b] In Hebrew texts 2:1-13 is numbered 2:5-17.

6"Come! Come! Flee from the land of the north," declares the LORD, "for I have scattered you to the four winds of heaven," declares the LORD.

7"Come, Zion! Escape, you who live in Daughter Babylon!" 8For this is what the LORD Almighty says: "After the Glorious One has sent me against the nations that have plundered you — for whoever touches you touches the apple of his eye — 9I will surely raise my hand against them so that their slaves will plunder them.[a] Then you will know that the LORD Almighty has sent me.

10"Shout and be glad, Daughter Zion. For I am coming, and I will live among you," declares the LORD. 11"Many nations will be joined with the LORD in that day and will become my people. I will live among you and you will know that the LORD Almighty has sent me to you. 12The LORD will inherit Judah as his portion in the holy land and will again choose Jerusalem. 13Be still before the LORD, all mankind, because he has roused himself from his holy dwelling."

Clean Garments for the High Priest

3 Then he showed me Joshua the high priest standing before the angel of the LORD, and Satan[b] standing at his right side to accuse him. 2The LORD said to Satan, "The LORD rebuke you, Satan! The LORD, who has chosen Jerusalem, rebuke you! Is not this man a burning stick snatched from the fire?"

3Now Joshua was dressed in filthy clothes as he stood before the angel. 4The angel said to those who were standing before him, "Take off his filthy clothes."

Then he said to Joshua, "See, I have taken away your sin, and I will put fine garments on you."

5Then I said, "Put a clean turban on his head." So they put a clean turban on his head and clothed him, while the angel of the LORD stood by.

6The angel of the LORD gave this charge to Joshua: 7"This is what the LORD Almighty says: 'If you will walk in obedience to me and keep my requirements, then you will govern my house and have charge of my courts, and I will give you a place among these standing here.

8" 'Listen, High Priest Joshua, you and your associates seated before you, who are men symbolic of things to come: I am going to bring my servant, the Branch. 9See, the stone I have set in front of Joshua! There are seven eyes[c] on that one stone, and I will engrave an inscription on it,' says the LORD Almighty, 'and I will remove the sin of this land in a single day.

10" 'In that day each of you will invite your neighbor to sit under your vine and fig tree,' declares the LORD Almighty."

The Gold Lampstand and the Two Olive Trees

4 Then the angel who talked with me returned and woke me up, like someone awakened from sleep. 2He asked me, "What do you see?"

I answered, "I see a solid gold lampstand with a bowl at the top and seven lamps on it, with seven channels to the lamps. 3Also there are two olive trees by it, one on the right of the bowl and the other on its left."

4I asked the angel who talked with me, "What are these, my lord?"

5He answered, "Do you not know what these are?"

"No, my lord," I replied.

6So he said to me, "This is the word of the LORD to Zerubbabel: 'Not by might nor by power, but by my Spirit,' says the LORD Almighty.

7"What are you, mighty mountain? Before Zerubbabel you will become level ground. Then he will bring out the capstone to shouts of 'God bless it! God bless it!' "

8Then the word of the LORD came to me: 9"The hands of Zerubbabel have laid the foundation of this temple; his hands will also complete it. Then you will know that the LORD Almighty has sent me to you.

10"Who dares despise the day of small things, since the seven eyes of the LORD that range throughout the earth will rejoice when they see the chosen capstone[d] in the hand of Zerubbabel?"

11Then I asked the angel, "What are these two olive trees on the right and the left of the lampstand?"

12Again I asked him, "What are these two olive branches beside the two gold pipes that pour out golden oil?"

13He replied, "Do you not know what these are?"

"No, my lord," I said.

14So he said, "These are the two who are anointed to[e] serve the Lord of all the earth."

[a] 8,9 Or *says after . . . eye:* 9"*I . . . plunder them."* [b] 1 Hebrew *satan* means *adversary.* [c] 9 Or *facets* [d] 10 Or *the plumb line* [e] 14 Or *two who bring oil and*

The Flying Scroll

5 I looked again, and there before me was a flying scroll.

2 He asked me, "What do you see?"

I answered, "I see a flying scroll, twenty cubits long and ten cubits wide.[a]"

3 And he said to me, "This is the curse that is going out over the whole land; for according to what it says on one side, every thief will be banished, and according to what it says on the other, everyone who swears falsely will be banished. 4 The LORD Almighty declares, 'I will send it out, and it will enter the house of the thief and the house of anyone who swears falsely by my name. It will remain in that house and destroy it completely, both its timbers and its stones.' "

The Woman in a Basket

5 Then the angel who was speaking to me came forward and said to me, "Look up and see what is appearing."

6 I asked, "What is it?"

He replied, "It is a basket." And he added, "This is the iniquity[b] of the people throughout the land."

7 Then the cover of lead was raised, and there in the basket sat a woman! 8 He said, "This is wickedness," and he pushed her back into the basket and pushed its lead cover down on it.

9 Then I looked up — and there before me were two women, with the wind in their wings! They had wings like those of a stork, and they lifted up the basket between heaven and earth.

10 "Where are they taking the basket?" I asked the angel who was speaking to me.

11 He replied, "To the country of Babylonia[c] to build a house for it. When the house is ready, the basket will be set there in its place."

Four Chariots

6 I looked up again, and there before me were four chariots coming out from between two mountains — mountains of bronze. 2 The first chariot had red horses, the second black, 3 the third white, and the fourth dappled — all of them powerful. 4 I asked the angel who was speaking to me, "What are these, my lord?"

5 The angel answered me, "These are the four spirits[d] of heaven, going out from standing in the presence of the Lord of the whole world. 6 The one with the black horses is going toward the north country, the one with the white horses toward the west,[e] and the one with the dappled horses toward the south."

7 When the powerful horses went out, they were straining to go throughout the earth. And he said, "Go throughout the earth!" So they went throughout the earth.

8 Then he called to me, "Look, those going toward the north country have given my Spirit[f] rest in the land of the north."

A Crown for Joshua

9 The word of the LORD came to me: 10 "Take silver and gold from the exiles Heldai, Tobijah and Jedaiah, who have arrived from Babylon. Go the same day to the house of Josiah son of Zephaniah. 11 Take the silver and gold and make a crown, and set it on the head of the high priest, Joshua son of Jozadak.[g] 12 Tell him this is what the LORD Almighty says: 'Here is the man whose name is the Branch, and he will branch out from his place and build the temple of the LORD. 13 It is he who will build the temple of the LORD, and he will be clothed with majesty and will sit and rule on his throne. And he[h] will be a priest on his throne. And there will be harmony between the two.' 14 The crown will be given to Heldai,[i] Tobijah, Jedaiah and Hen[j] son of Zephaniah as a memorial in the temple of the LORD. 15 Those who are far away will come and help to build the temple of the LORD, and you will know that the LORD Almighty has sent me to you. This will happen if you diligently obey the LORD your God."

Justice and Mercy, Not Fasting

7 In the fourth year of King Darius, the word of the LORD came to Zechariah on the fourth day of the ninth month, the month of Kislev. 2 The people of Bethel had sent Sharezer and Regem-Melek, together with their men, to entreat the LORD 3 by asking the priests of the house of the LORD Almighty and the prophets, "Should I mourn and fast in the fifth month, as I have done for so many years?"

4 Then the word of the LORD Almighty came to me: 5 "Ask all the people of the land and the priests, 'When you fasted and mourned in the fifth and seventh months for the past seventy years, was it really for me that you fasted? 6 And when you were eating and drinking, were you not just

[a] 2 That is, about 30 feet long and 15 feet wide or about 9 meters long and 4.5 meters wide
[b] 6 Or *appearance* [c] 11 Hebrew *Shinar* [d] 5 Or *winds* [e] 6 Or *horses after them* [f] 8 Or *spirit* [g] 11 Hebrew *Jehozadak*, a variant of *Jozadak* [h] 13 Or *there* [i] 14 Syriac; Hebrew *Helem* [j] 14 Or *and the gracious one, the*

feasting for yourselves? 7Are these not the
words the LORD proclaimed through the
earlier prophets when Jerusalem and its
surrounding towns were at rest and prosperous, and the Negev and the western
foothills were settled?' "

8And the word of the LORD came again
to Zechariah: 9"This is what the LORD Almighty said: 'Administer true justice; show
mercy and compassion to one another.
10Do not oppress the widow or the fatherless, the foreigner or the poor. Do not plot
evil against each other.'

11"But they refused to pay attention;
stubbornly they turned their backs and
covered their ears. 12They made their
hearts as hard as flint and would not listen to the law or to the words that the LORD
Almighty had sent by his Spirit through
the earlier prophets. So the LORD Almighty
was very angry.

13" 'When I called, they did not listen; so
when they called, I would not listen,' says
the LORD Almighty. 14'I scattered them
with a whirlwind among all the nations,
where they were strangers. The land they
left behind them was so desolate that no
one traveled through it. This is how they
made the pleasant land desolate.' "

The LORD Promises to Bless Jerusalem

8 The word of the LORD Almighty came to me.

2This is what the LORD Almighty says:
"I am very jealous for Zion; I am burning
with jealousy for her."

3This is what the LORD says: "I will return to Zion and dwell in Jerusalem. Then
Jerusalem will be called the Faithful City,
and the mountain of the LORD Almighty
will be called the Holy Mountain."

4This is what the LORD Almighty says:
"Once again men and women of ripe old
age will sit in the streets of Jerusalem,
each of them with cane in hand because
of their age. 5The city streets will be filled
with boys and girls playing there."

6This is what the LORD Almighty says: "It
may seem marvelous to the remnant of this
people at that time, but will it seem marvelous to me?" declares the LORD Almighty.

7This is what the LORD Almighty says: "I
will save my people from the countries of
the east and the west. 8I will bring them
back to live in Jerusalem; they will be my
people, and I will be faithful and righteous
to them as their God."

9This is what the LORD Almighty says:
"Now hear these words, 'Let your hands
be strong so that the temple may be built.'
This is also what the prophets said who
were present when the foundation was
laid for the house of the LORD Almighty.
10Before that time there were no wages for
people or hire for animals. No one could
go about their business safely because of
their enemies, since I had turned everyone against their neighbor. 11But now I
will not deal with the remnant of this
people as I did in the past," declares the
LORD Almighty.

12"The seed will grow well, the vine will
yield its fruit, the ground will produce its
crops, and the heavens will drop their
dew. I will give all these things as an inheritance to the remnant of this people.
13Just as you, Judah and Israel, have been
a curse[a] among the nations, so I will save
you, and you will be a blessing.[b] Do not
be afraid, but let your hands be strong."

14This is what the LORD Almighty says:
"Just as I had determined to bring disaster on you and showed no pity when your
ancestors angered me," says the LORD Almighty, 15"so now I have determined to do
good again to Jerusalem and Judah. Do
not be afraid. 16These are the things you
are to do: Speak the truth to each other,
and render true and sound judgment in
your courts; 17do not plot evil against each
other, and do not love to swear falsely. I
hate all this," declares the LORD.

18The word of the LORD Almighty came
to me.

19This is what the LORD Almighty says:
"The fasts of the fourth, fifth, seventh and
tenth months will become joyful and glad
occasions and happy festivals for Judah.
Therefore love truth and peace."

20This is what the LORD Almighty says:
"Many peoples and the inhabitants of
many cities will yet come, 21and the inhabitants of one city will go to another and
say, 'Let us go at once to entreat the LORD
and seek the LORD Almighty. I myself am
going.' 22And many peoples and powerful
nations will come to Jerusalem to seek
the LORD Almighty and to entreat him."

23This is what the LORD Almighty says:
"In those days ten people from all languages and nations will take firm hold
of one Jew by the hem of his robe and
say, 'Let us go with you, because we have
heard that God is with you.' "

[a] *13* That is, your name has been used in cursing (see Jer. 29:22); or, you have been regarded as under a curse. [b] *13* Or *and your name will be used in blessings* (see Gen. 48:20); or *and you will be seen as blessed*

Judgment on Israel's Enemies

9 A prophecy:

The word of the LORD is against the land of Hadrak
and will come to rest on Damascus —
for the eyes of all people and all the tribes of Israel
are on the LORD —[a]
2 and on Hamath too, which borders on it,
and on Tyre and Sidon, though they are very skillful.
3 Tyre has built herself a stronghold;
she has heaped up silver like dust,
and gold like the dirt of the streets.
4 But the Lord will take away her possessions
and destroy her power on the sea,
and she will be consumed by fire.
5 Ashkelon will see it and fear;
Gaza will writhe in agony,
and Ekron too, for her hope will wither.
Gaza will lose her king
and Ashkelon will be deserted.
6 A mongrel people will occupy Ashdod,
and I will put an end to the pride of the Philistines.
7 I will take the blood from their mouths,
the forbidden food from between their teeth.
Those who are left will belong to our God
and become a clan in Judah,
and Ekron will be like the Jebusites.
8 But I will encamp at my temple
to guard it against marauding forces.
Never again will an oppressor overrun my people,
for now I am keeping watch.

The Coming of Zion's King

9 Rejoice greatly, Daughter Zion!
Shout, Daughter Jerusalem!
See, your king comes to you,
righteous and victorious,
lowly and riding on a donkey,
on a colt, the foal of a donkey.
10 I will take away the chariots from Ephraim
and the warhorses from Jerusalem,
and the battle bow will be broken.
He will proclaim peace to the nations.
His rule will extend from sea to sea
and from the River[b] to the ends of the earth.
11 As for you, because of the blood of my covenant with you,
I will free your prisoners from the waterless pit.
12 Return to your fortress, you prisoners of hope;
even now I announce that I will restore twice as much to you.
13 I will bend Judah as I bend my bow
and fill it with Ephraim.
I will rouse your sons, Zion,
against your sons, Greece,
and make you like a warrior's sword.

The LORD Will Appear

14 Then the LORD will appear over them;
his arrow will flash like lightning.
The Sovereign LORD will sound the trumpet;
he will march in the storms of the south,
15 and the LORD Almighty will shield them.
They will destroy
and overcome with slingstones.
They will drink and roar as with wine;
they will be full like a bowl
used for sprinkling[c] the corners of the altar.
16 The LORD their God will save his people on that day
as a shepherd saves his flock.
They will sparkle in his land
like jewels in a crown.
17 How attractive and beautiful they will be!
Grain will make the young men thrive,
and new wine the young women.

The LORD Will Care for Judah

10 Ask the LORD for rain in the springtime;
it is the LORD who sends the thunderstorms.
He gives showers of rain to all people,
and plants of the field to everyone.
2 The idols speak deceitfully,
diviners see visions that lie;
they tell dreams that are false,
they give comfort in vain.
Therefore the people wander like sheep
oppressed for lack of a shepherd.

[a] *1* Or *Damascus. / For the eye of the LORD is on all people, / as well as on the tribes of Israel,*
[b] *10* That is, the Euphrates [c] *15* Or *bowl, / like*

3 "My anger burns against the
shepherds,
and I will punish the leaders;
for the LORD Almighty will care
for his flock, the people of Judah,
and make them like a proud horse
in battle.
4 From Judah will come the cornerstone,
from him the tent peg,
from him the battle bow,
from him every ruler.
5 Together they[a] will be like warriors in
battle
trampling their enemy into the
mud of the streets.
They will fight because the LORD is
with them,
and they will put the enemy
horsemen to shame.

6 "I will strengthen Judah
and save the tribes of Joseph.
I will restore them
because I have compassion on them.
They will be as though
I had not rejected them,
for I am the LORD their God
and I will answer them.
7 The Ephraimites will become like
warriors,
and their hearts will be glad as
with wine.
Their children will see it and be joyful;
their hearts will rejoice in the LORD.
8 I will signal for them
and gather them in.
Surely I will redeem them;
they will be as numerous as before.
9 Though I scatter them among the
peoples,
yet in distant lands they will
remember me.
They and their children will survive,
and they will return.
10 I will bring them back from Egypt
and gather them from Assyria.
I will bring them to Gilead and
Lebanon,
and there will not be room enough
for them.
11 They will pass through the sea of
trouble;
the surging sea will be subdued
and all the depths of the Nile will
dry up.
Assyria's pride will be brought down
and Egypt's scepter will pass away.
12 I will strengthen them in the LORD
and in his name they will live
securely,"
declares the LORD.

11 Open your doors, Lebanon,
so that fire may devour your
cedars!
2 Wail, you juniper, for the cedar has
fallen;
the stately trees are ruined!
Wail, oaks of Bashan;
the dense forest has been
cut down!
3 Listen to the wail of the shepherds;
their rich pastures are destroyed!
Listen to the roar of the lions;
the lush thicket of the Jordan is
ruined!

Two Shepherds

4 This is what the LORD my God says:
"Shepherd the flock marked for slaughter. 5 Their buyers slaughter them and go
unpunished. Those who sell them say,
'Praise the LORD, I am rich!' Their own
shepherds do not spare them. 6 For I will
no longer have pity on the people of the
land," declares the LORD. "I will give everyone into the hands of their neighbors
and their king. They will devastate the
land, and I will not rescue anyone from
their hands."
7 So I shepherded the flock marked for
slaughter, particularly the oppressed of
the flock. Then I took two staffs and called
one Favor and the other Union, and I shepherded the flock. 8 In one month I got rid
of the three shepherds.
The flock detested me, and I grew weary of them 9 and said, "I will not be your
shepherd. Let the dying die, and the perishing perish. Let those who are left eat
one another's flesh."
10 Then I took my staff called Favor
and broke it, revoking the covenant I
had made with all the nations. 11 It was
revoked on that day, and so the oppressed
of the flock who were watching me knew
it was the word of the LORD.
12 I told them, "If you think it best, give
me my pay; but if not, keep it." So they
paid me thirty pieces of silver.
13 And the LORD said to me, "Throw it to
the potter" — the handsome price at which
they valued me! So I took the thirty pieces
of silver and threw them to the potter at
the house of the LORD.
14 Then I broke my second staff called
Union, breaking the family bond between
Judah and Israel.
15 Then the LORD said to me, "Take again
the equipment of a foolish shepherd. 16 For
I am going to raise up a shepherd over the
land who will not care for the lost, or seek

[a] 4,5 Or *ruler, all of them together.* / [5] *They*

the young, or heal the injured, or feed the
healthy, but will eat the meat of the choice
sheep, tearing off their hooves.

17 “Woe to the worthless shepherd,
who deserts the flock!
May the sword strike his arm and his
right eye!
May his arm be completely
withered,
his right eye totally blinded!”

Jerusalem’s Enemies to Be Destroyed

12 A prophecy: The word of the LORD
concerning Israel.

The LORD, who stretches out the heavens, who lays the foundation of the earth,
and who forms the human spirit within
a person, declares: 2“I am going to make
Jerusalem a cup that sends all the surrounding peoples reeling. Judah will be
besieged as well as Jerusalem. 3On that
day, when all the nations of the earth
are gathered against her, I will make Jerusalem an immovable rock for all the
nations. All who try to move it will injure
themselves. 4On that day I will strike every horse with panic and its rider with
madness,” declares the LORD. “I will keep
a watchful eye over Judah, but I will blind
all the horses of the nations. 5Then the
clans of Judah will say in their hearts, ‘The
people of Jerusalem are strong, because
the LORD Almighty is their God.’
6“On that day I will make the clans of
Judah like a firepot in a woodpile, like a
flaming torch among sheaves. They will
consume all the surrounding peoples right
and left, but Jerusalem will remain intact
in her place.
7“The LORD will save the dwellings of
Judah first, so that the honor of the house
of David and of Jerusalem’s inhabitants
may not be greater than that of Judah.
8On that day the LORD will shield those
who live in Jerusalem, so that the feeblest
among them will be like David, and the
house of David will be like God, like the
angel of the LORD going before them. 9On
that day I will set out to destroy all the
nations that attack Jerusalem.

Mourning for the One They Pierced

10“And I will pour out on the house of
David and the inhabitants of Jerusalem a
spirit[a] of grace and supplication. They will
look on[b] me, the one they have pierced, and
they will mourn for him as one mourns for
an only child, and grieve bitterly for him
as one grieves for a firstborn son. 11On that
day the weeping in Jerusalem will be as
great as the weeping of Hadad Rimmon
in the plain of Megiddo. 12The land will
mourn, each clan by itself, with their wives
by themselves: the clan of the house of David and their wives, the clan of the house
of Nathan and their wives, 13the clan of the
house of Levi and their wives, the clan of
Shimei and their wives, 14and all the rest
of the clans and their wives.

Cleansing From Sin

13 “On that day a fountain will be
opened to the house of David and
the inhabitants of Jerusalem, to cleanse
them from sin and impurity.
2“On that day, I will banish the names
of the idols from the land, and they will
be remembered no more,” declares the
LORD Almighty. “I will remove both the
prophets and the spirit of impurity from
the land. 3And if anyone still prophesies,
their father and mother, to whom they
were born, will say to them, ‘You must die,
because you have told lies in the LORD’s
name.’ Then their own parents will stab
the one who prophesies.
4“On that day every prophet will be
ashamed of their prophetic vision. They
will not put on a prophet’s garment of hair
in order to deceive. 5Each will say, ‘I am
not a prophet. I am a farmer; the land has
been my livelihood since my youth.[c]’ 6If
someone asks, ‘What are these wounds on
your body[d]?’ they will answer, ‘The wounds
I was given at the house of my friends.’

The Shepherd Struck, the Sheep Scattered

7 “Awake, sword, against my shepherd,
against the man who is close to me!”
declares the LORD Almighty.
“Strike the shepherd,
and the sheep will be scattered,
and I will turn my hand against the
little ones.
8 In the whole land,” declares the LORD,
“two-thirds will be struck down and
perish;
yet one-third will be left in it.
9 This third I will put into the fire;
I will refine them like silver
and test them like gold.
They will call on my name
and I will answer them;
I will say, ‘They are my people,’
and they will say, ‘The LORD is our
God.’ ”

[a] 10 Or *the Spirit* [b] 10 Or *to* [c] 5 Or *farmer; a man sold me in my youth* [d] 6 Or *wounds between your hands*

The LORD Comes and Reigns

14 A day of the LORD is coming, Jerusalem, when your possessions will be plundered and divided up within your very walls.

[2]I will gather all the nations to Jerusalem to fight against it; the city will be captured, the houses ransacked, and the women raped. Half of the city will go into exile, but the rest of the people will not be taken from the city. [3]Then the LORD will go out and fight against those nations, as he fights on a day of battle. [4]On that day his feet will stand on the Mount of Olives, east of Jerusalem, and the Mount of Olives will be split in two from east to west, forming a great valley, with half of the mountain moving north and half moving south. [5]You will flee by my mountain valley, for it will extend to Azel. You will flee as you fled from the earthquake[a] in the days of Uzziah king of Judah. Then the LORD my God will come, and all the holy ones with him.

[6]On that day there will be neither sunlight nor cold, frosty darkness. [7]It will be a unique day — a day known only to the LORD — with no distinction between day and night. When evening comes, there will be light.

[8]On that day living water will flow out from Jerusalem, half of it east to the Dead Sea and half of it west to the Mediterranean Sea, in summer and in winter.

[9]The LORD will be king over the whole earth. On that day there will be one LORD, and his name the only name.

[10]The whole land, from Geba to Rimmon, south of Jerusalem, will become like the Arabah. But Jerusalem will be raised up high from the Benjamin Gate to the site of the First Gate, to the Corner Gate, and from the Tower of Hananel to the royal winepresses, and will remain in its place. [11]It will be inhabited; never again will it be destroyed. Jerusalem will be secure.

[12]This is the plague with which the LORD will strike all the nations that fought against Jerusalem: Their flesh will rot while they are still standing on their feet, their eyes will rot in their sockets, and their tongues will rot in their mouths. [13]On that day people will be stricken by the LORD with great panic. They will seize each other by the hand and attack one another. [14]Judah too will fight at Jerusalem. The wealth of all the surrounding nations will be collected — great quantities of gold and silver and clothing. [15]A similar plague will strike the horses and mules, the camels and donkeys, and all the animals in those camps.

[16]Then the survivors from all the nations that have attacked Jerusalem will go up year after year to worship the King, the LORD Almighty, and to celebrate the Festival of Tabernacles. [17]If any of the peoples of the earth do not go up to Jerusalem to worship the King, the LORD Almighty, they will have no rain. [18]If the Egyptian people do not go up and take part, they will have no rain. The LORD[b] will bring on them the plague he inflicts on the nations that do not go up to celebrate the Festival of Tabernacles. [19]This will be the punishment of Egypt and the punishment of all the nations that do not go up to celebrate the Festival of Tabernacles.

[20]On that day HOLY TO THE LORD will be inscribed on the bells of the horses, and the cooking pots in the LORD's house will be like the sacred bowls in front of the altar. [21]Every pot in Jerusalem and Judah will be holy to the LORD Almighty, and all who come to sacrifice will take some of the pots and cook in them. And on that day there will no longer be a Canaanite[c] in the house of the LORD Almighty.

[a] 5 Or *[5]My mountain valley will be blocked and will extend to Azel. It will be blocked as it was blocked because of the earthquake* [b] 18 Or *part, then the LORD* [c] 21 Or *merchant*

MALACHI

1 A prophecy: The word of the LORD to
Israel through Malachi.[a]

Israel Doubts God's Love

2“I have loved you,” says the LORD.
“But you ask, ‘How have you loved us?’
“Was not Esau Jacob's brother?” declares the LORD. “Yet I have loved Jacob,
3but Esau I have hated, and I have turned
his hill country into a wasteland and left
his inheritance to the desert jackals.”
4Edom may say, “Though we have been
crushed, we will rebuild the ruins.”
But this is what the LORD Almighty says:
“They may build, but I will demolish. They
will be called the Wicked Land, a people
always under the wrath of the LORD. 5You
will see it with your own eyes and say,
‘Great is the LORD — even beyond the borders of Israel!’

Breaking Covenant Through Blemished Sacrifices

6“A son honors his father, and a slave his
master. If I am a father, where is the hon-
or due me? If I am a master, where is the
respect due me?” says the LORD Almighty.
“It is you priests who show contempt
for my name.
“But you ask, ‘How have we shown contempt for your name?’
7“By offering defiled food on my altar.
“But you ask, ‘How have we defiled you?’
“By saying that the LORD's table is contemptible. 8When you offer blind animals
for sacrifice, is that not wrong? When
you sacrifice lame or diseased animals,
is that not wrong? Try offering them to
your governor! Would he be pleased with
you? Would he accept you?” says the LORD
Almighty.
9“Now plead with God to be gracious to
us. With such offerings from your hands,
will he accept you?” — says the LORD Almighty.
10“Oh, that one of you would shut the
temple doors, so that you would not light
useless fires on my altar! I am not pleased
with you,” says the LORD Almighty, “and I
will accept no offering from your hands.
11My name will be great among the nations, from where the sun rises to where
it sets. In every place incense and pure offerings will be brought to me, because my
name will be great among the nations,”
says the LORD Almighty.
12“But you profane it by saying, ‘The
Lord's table is defiled,’ and, ‘Its food is
contemptible.’ 13And you say, ‘What a burden!’ and you sniff at it contemptuously,”
says the LORD Almighty.
“When you bring injured, lame or diseased animals and offer them as sacrifices,
should I accept them from your hands?”
says the LORD. 14“Cursed is the cheat who
has an acceptable male in his flock and
vows to give it, but then sacrifices a blem-
ished animal to the Lord. For I am a great
king,” says the LORD Almighty, “and my
name is to be feared among the nations.

Additional Warning to the Priests

2 “And now, you priests, this warning is
for you. 2If you do not listen, and if you
do not resolve to honor my name,” says
the LORD Almighty, “I will send a curse on
you, and I will curse your blessings. Yes,
I have already cursed them, because you
have not resolved to honor me.
3“Because of you I will rebuke your descendants[b]; I will smear on your faces
the dung from your festival sacrifices,
and you will be carried off with it. 4And
you will know that I have sent you this
warning so that my covenant with Levi
may continue,” says the LORD Almighty.
5“My covenant was with him, a covenant
of life and peace, and I gave them to him;
this called for reverence and he revered
me and stood in awe of my name. 6True
instruction was in his mouth and nothing
false was found on his lips. He walked with
me in peace and uprightness, and turned
many from sin.
7“For the lips of a priest ought to preserve knowledge, because he is the messenger of the LORD Almighty and people
seek instruction from his mouth. 8But you
have turned from the way and by your
teaching have caused many to stumble;
you have violated the covenant with Levi,”
says the LORD Almighty. 9“So I have caused
you to be despised and humiliated before
all the people, because you have not followed my ways but have shown partiality
in matters of the law.”

[a] 1 *Malachi* means *my messenger.* [b] 3 Or *will blight your grain*

Breaking Covenant Through Divorce

10 Do we not all have one Father[a]? Did
not one God create us? Why do we profane
the covenant of our ancestors by being
unfaithful to one another?

11 Judah has been unfaithful. A detestable thing has been committed in Israel
and in Jerusalem: Judah has desecrated
the sanctuary the LORD loves by marrying women who worship a foreign god.
12 As for the man who does this, whoever
he may be, may the LORD remove him
from the tents of Jacob[b] — even though
he brings an offering to the LORD Almighty.

13 Another thing you do: You flood the
LORD's altar with tears. You weep and wail
because he no longer looks with favor on
your offerings or accepts them with pleasure from your hands. 14 You ask, "Why?"
It is because the LORD is the witness between you and the wife of your youth. You
have been unfaithful to her, though she
is your partner, the wife of your marriage
covenant.

15 Has not the one God made you? You
belong to him in body and spirit. And what
does the one God seek? Godly offspring.[c] So
be on your guard, and do not be unfaithful
to the wife of your youth.

16 "The man who hates and divorces his
wife," says the LORD, the God of Israel,
"does violence to the one he should protect,"[d] says the LORD Almighty.

So be on your guard, and do not be unfaithful.

Breaking Covenant Through Injustice

17 You have wearied the LORD with your
words.

"How have we wearied him?" you ask.

By saying, "All who do evil are good in
the eyes of the LORD, and he is pleased with
them" or "Where is the God of justice?"

3 "I will send my messenger, who will
prepare the way before me. Then suddenly the Lord you are seeking will come
to his temple; the messenger of the covenant, whom you desire, will come," says
the LORD Almighty.

2 But who can endure the day of his coming? Who can stand when he appears? For
he will be like a refiner's fire or a launderer's soap. 3 He will sit as a refiner and
purifier of silver; he will purify the Levites
and refine them like gold and silver. Then
the LORD will have men who will bring
offerings in righteousness, 4 and the offerings of Judah and Jerusalem will be
acceptable to the LORD, as in days gone
by, as in former years.

5 "So I will come to put you on trial. I
will be quick to testify against sorcerers,
adulterers and perjurers, against those
who defraud laborers of their wages, who
oppress the widows and the fatherless,
and deprive the foreigners among you
of justice, but do not fear me," says the
LORD Almighty.

Breaking Covenant by Withholding Tithes

6 "I the LORD do not change. So you, the
descendants of Jacob, are not destroyed.
7 Ever since the time of your ancestors you
have turned away from my decrees and
have not kept them. Return to me, and
I will return to you," says the LORD Almighty.

"But you ask, 'How are we to return?'

8 "Will a mere mortal rob God? Yet you
rob me.

"But you ask, 'How are we robbing you?'

"In tithes and offerings. 9 You are under a curse — your whole nation — because you are robbing me. 10 Bring the
whole tithe into the storehouse, that
there may be food in my house. Test me
in this," says the LORD Almighty, "and see
if I will not throw open the floodgates of
heaven and pour out so much blessing
that there will not be room enough to
store it. 11 I will prevent pests from devouring your crops, and the vines in your
fields will not drop their fruit before it
is ripe," says the LORD Almighty. 12 "Then
all the nations will call you blessed, for
yours will be a delightful land," says the
LORD Almighty.

Israel Speaks Arrogantly Against God

13 "You have spoken arrogantly against
me," says the LORD.

"Yet you ask, 'What have we said
against you?'

14 "You have said, 'It is futile to serve
God. What do we gain by carrying out
his requirements and going about like
mourners before the LORD Almighty?
15 But now we call the arrogant blessed.
Certainly evildoers prosper, and even
when they put God to the test, they get
away with it.' "

[a] 10 Or *father* [b] 12 Or *12May the LORD remove from the tents of Jacob anyone who gives testimony in behalf of the man who does this* [c] 15 The meaning of the Hebrew for the first part of this verse is uncertain. [d] 16 Or *"I hate divorce," says the LORD, the God of Israel, "because the man who divorces his wife covers his garment with violence,"*

The Faithful Remnant

16 Then those who feared the LORD talked
with each other, and the LORD listened and
heard. A scroll of remembrance was written in his presence concerning those who
feared the LORD and honored his name.
17 “On the day when I act,” says the LORD
Almighty, “they will be my treasured possession. I will spare them, just as a father
has compassion and spares his son who
serves him. 18 And you will again see the
distinction between the righteous and the
wicked, between those who serve God and
those who do not.

Judgment and Covenant Renewal

4 [a] “Surely the day is coming; it will burn
like a furnace. All the arrogant and
every evildoer will be stubble, and the day
that is coming will set them on fire,” says
the LORD Almighty. “Not a root or a branch
will be left to them. 2 But for you who revere
my name, the sun of righteousness will
rise with healing in its rays. And you will
go out and frolic like well-fed calves. 3 Then
you will trample on the wicked; they will
be ashes under the soles of your feet on the
day when I act,” says the LORD Almighty.
4 “Remember the law of my servant Moses, the decrees and laws I gave him at
Horeb for all Israel.
5 “See, I will send the prophet Elijah to
you before that great and dreadful day of
the LORD comes. 6 He will turn the hearts
of the parents to their children, and the
hearts of the children to their parents; or
else I will come and strike the land with
total destruction.”

[a] In Hebrew texts 4:1-6 is numbered 3:19-24.

NEW TESTAMENT

MATTHEW

The Genealogy of Jesus the Messiah

1 This is the genealogy[a] of Jesus the Messiah[b] the son of David, the son of Abraham:

2 Abraham was the father of Isaac,
Isaac the father of Jacob,
Jacob the father of Judah and his brothers,
3 Judah the father of Perez and Zerah, whose mother was Tamar,
Perez the father of Hezron,
Hezron the father of Ram,
4 Ram the father of Amminadab,
Amminadab the father of Nahshon,
Nahshon the father of Salmon,
5 Salmon the father of Boaz, whose mother was Rahab,
Boaz the father of Obed, whose mother was Ruth,
Obed the father of Jesse,
6 and Jesse the father of King David.

David was the father of Solomon, whose mother had been Uriah's wife,
7 Solomon the father of Rehoboam,
Rehoboam the father of Abijah,
Abijah the father of Asa,
8 Asa the father of Jehoshaphat,
Jehoshaphat the father of Jehoram,
Jehoram the father of Uzziah,
9 Uzziah the father of Jotham,
Jotham the father of Ahaz,
Ahaz the father of Hezekiah,
10 Hezekiah the father of Manasseh,
Manasseh the father of Amon,
Amon the father of Josiah,
11 and Josiah the father of Jeconiah[c] and his brothers at the time of the exile to Babylon.

12 After the exile to Babylon:
Jeconiah was the father of Shealtiel,
Shealtiel the father of Zerubbabel,
13 Zerubbabel the father of Abihud,
Abihud the father of Eliakim,
Eliakim the father of Azor,
14 Azor the father of Zadok,
Zadok the father of Akim,
Akim the father of Elihud,
15 Elihud the father of Eleazar,
Eleazar the father of Matthan,
Matthan the father of Jacob,
16 and Jacob the father of Joseph, the husband of Mary, and Mary was the mother of Jesus who is called the Messiah.

17 Thus there were fourteen generations in all from Abraham to David, fourteen from David to the exile to Babylon, and fourteen from the exile to the Messiah.

Joseph Accepts Jesus as His Son

18 This is how the birth of Jesus the Messiah came about[d]: His mother Mary was pledged to be married to Joseph, but before they came together, she was found to be pregnant through the Holy Spirit.
19 Because Joseph her husband was faithful to the law, and yet[e] did not want to expose her to public disgrace, he had in mind to divorce her quietly.
20 But after he had considered this, an angel of the Lord appeared to him in a dream and said, "Joseph son of David, do not be afraid to take Mary home as your wife, because what is conceived in
her is from the Holy Spirit. 21 She will give birth to a son, and you are to give him the name Jesus,[f] because he will save his people from their sins."
22 All this took place to fulfill what the
Lord had said through the prophet: 23 "The virgin will conceive and give birth to a son, and they will call him Immanuel"[g] (which means "God with us").
24 When Joseph woke up, he did what the angel of the Lord had commanded him
and took Mary home as his wife. 25 But he did not consummate their marriage until she gave birth to a son. And he gave him the name Jesus.

The Magi Visit the Messiah

2 After Jesus was born in Bethlehem in Judea, during the time of King Herod, Magi[h] from the east came to Jerusalem
2 and asked, "Where is the one who has

[a] *1* Or *is an account of the origin* [b] *1* Or *Jesus Christ. Messiah* (Hebrew) and *Christ* (Greek) both mean *Anointed One*; also in verse 18. [c] *11* That is, Jehoiachin; also in verse 12 [d] *18* Or *The origin of Jesus the Messiah was like this* [e] *19* Or *was a righteous man and* [f] *21* *Jesus* is the Greek form of *Joshua*, which means *the LORD saves.* [g] *23* Isaiah 7:14 [h] *1* Traditionally *wise men*

been born king of the Jews? We saw his
star when it rose and have come to worship him."
3When King Herod heard this he was
disturbed, and all Jerusalem with him.
4When he had called together all the people's chief priests and teachers of the law,
he asked them where the Messiah was to
be born. 5"In Bethlehem in Judea," they
replied, "for this is what the prophet has
written:

6" 'But you, Bethlehem, in the land of
Judah,
are by no means least among the
rulers of Judah;
for out of you will come a ruler
who will shepherd my people
Israel.'[a]"

7Then Herod called the Magi secretly
and found out from them the exact time
the star had appeared. 8He sent them
to Bethlehem and said, "Go and search
carefully for the child. As soon as you find
him, report to me, so that I too may go
and worship him."
9After they had heard the king, they
went on their way, and the star they had
seen when it rose went ahead of them
until it stopped over the place where the
child was. 10When they saw the star, they
were overjoyed. 11On coming to the house,
they saw the child with his mother Mary,
and they bowed down and worshiped him.
Then they opened their treasures and presented him with gifts of gold, frankincense
and myrrh. 12And having been warned in
a dream not to go back to Herod, they returned to their country by another route.

The Escape to Egypt

13When they had gone, an angel of the
Lord appeared to Joseph in a dream. "Get
up," he said, "take the child and his mother
and escape to Egypt. Stay there until I tell
you, for Herod is going to search for the
child to kill him."
14So he got up, took the child and his
mother during the night and left for Egypt,
15where he stayed until the death of Herod.
And so was fulfilled what the Lord had
said through the prophet: "Out of Egypt
I called my son."[b]
16When Herod realized that he had been
outwitted by the Magi, he was furious,
and he gave orders to kill all the boys in
Bethlehem and its vicinity who were two
years old and under, in accordance with
the time he had learned from the Magi.
17Then what was said through the prophet
Jeremiah was fulfilled:

18"A voice is heard in Ramah,
weeping and great mourning,
Rachel weeping for her children
and refusing to be comforted,
because they are no more."[c]

The Return to Nazareth

19After Herod died, an angel of the Lord
appeared in a dream to Joseph in Egypt
20and said, "Get up, take the child and his
mother and go to the land of Israel, for
those who were trying to take the child's
life are dead."
21So he got up, took the child and his
mother and went to the land of Israel.
22But when he heard that Archelaus was
reigning in Judea in place of his father
Herod, he was afraid to go there. Having
been warned in a dream, he withdrew to
the district of Galilee, 23and he went and
lived in a town called Nazareth. So was
fulfilled what was said through the prophets, that he would be called a Nazarene.

John the Baptist Prepares the Way

3 In those days John the Baptist came,
preaching in the wilderness of Judea
2and saying, "Repent, for the kingdom of
heaven has come near." 3This is he who
was spoken of through the prophet Isaiah:

"A voice of one calling in the
wilderness,
'Prepare the way for the Lord,
make straight paths for him.' "[d]

4John's clothes were made of camel's
hair, and he had a leather belt around his
waist. His food was locusts and wild honey.
5People went out to him from Jerusalem
and all Judea and the whole region of
the Jordan. 6Confessing their sins, they
were baptized by him in the Jordan River.
7But when he saw many of the Pharisees and Sadducees coming to where
he was baptizing, he said to them: "You
brood of vipers! Who warned you to flee
from the coming wrath? 8Produce fruit
in keeping with repentance. 9And do not
think you can say to yourselves, 'We have
Abraham as our father.' I tell you that out
of these stones God can raise up children
for Abraham. 10The ax is already at the
root of the trees, and every tree that does
not produce good fruit will be cut down
and thrown into the fire.
11"I baptize you with[e] water for repentance. But after me comes one who is more

[a] *6* Micah 5:2,4 [b] *15* Hosea 11:1 [c] *18* Jer. 31:15 [d] *3* Isaiah 40:3 [e] *11* Or *in*

powerful than I, whose sandals I am not worthy to carry. He will baptize you with[a] the Holy Spirit and fire. 12 His winnowing fork is in his hand, and he will clear his threshing floor, gathering his wheat into the barn and burning up the chaff with unquenchable fire."

The Baptism of Jesus

13 Then Jesus came from Galilee to the Jordan to be baptized by John. 14 But John tried to deter him, saying, "I need to be baptized by you, and do you come to me?"

15 Jesus replied, "Let it be so now; it is proper for us to do this to fulfill all righteousness." Then John consented.

16 As soon as Jesus was baptized, he went up out of the water. At that moment heaven was opened, and he saw the Spirit of God descending like a dove and alighting on him. 17 And a voice from heaven said, "This is my Son, whom I love; with him I am well pleased."

Jesus Is Tested in the Wilderness

4 Then Jesus was led by the Spirit into the wilderness to be tempted[b] by the devil. 2 After fasting forty days and forty nights, he was hungry. 3 The tempter came to him and said, "If you are the Son of God, tell these stones to become bread."

4 Jesus answered, "It is written: 'Man shall not live on bread alone, but on every word that comes from the mouth of God.'[c]"

5 Then the devil took him to the holy city and had him stand on the highest point of the temple. 6 "If you are the Son of God," he said, "throw yourself down. For it is written:

"'He will command his angels
concerning you,
and they will lift you up in their
hands,
so that you will not strike your foot
against a stone.'[d]"

7 Jesus answered him, "It is also written: 'Do not put the Lord your God to the test.'[e]"

8 Again, the devil took him to a very high mountain and showed him all the kingdoms of the world and their splendor. 9 "All this I will give you," he said, "if you will bow down and worship me."

10 Jesus said to him, "Away from me, Satan! For it is written: 'Worship the Lord your God, and serve him only.'[f]"

11 Then the devil left him, and angels came and attended him.

Jesus Begins to Preach

12 When Jesus heard that John had been put in prison, he withdrew to Galilee. 13 Leaving Nazareth, he went and lived in Capernaum, which was by the lake in the area of Zebulun and Naphtali — 14 to fulfill what was said through the prophet Isaiah:

15 "Land of Zebulun and land of
Naphtali,
the Way of the Sea, beyond the
Jordan,
Galilee of the Gentiles —
16 the people living in darkness
have seen a great light;
on those living in the land of the
shadow of death
a light has dawned."[g]

17 From that time on Jesus began to preach, "Repent, for the kingdom of heaven has come near."

Jesus Calls His First Disciples

18 As Jesus was walking beside the Sea of Galilee, he saw two brothers, Simon called Peter and his brother Andrew. They were casting a net into the lake, for they were fishermen. 19 "Come, follow me," Jesus said, "and I will send you out to fish for people." 20 At once they left their nets and followed him.

21 Going on from there, he saw two other brothers, James son of Zebedee and his brother John. They were in a boat with their father Zebedee, preparing their nets. Jesus called them, 22 and immediately they left the boat and their father and followed him.

Jesus Heals the Sick

23 Jesus went throughout Galilee, teaching in their synagogues, proclaiming the good news of the kingdom, and healing every disease and sickness among the people. 24 News about him spread all over Syria, and people brought to him all who were ill with various diseases, those suffering severe pain, the demon-possessed, those having seizures, and the paralyzed; and he healed them. 25 Large crowds from Galilee, the Decapolis,[h] Jerusalem, Judea and the region across the Jordan followed him.

Introduction to the Sermon on the Mount

5 Now when Jesus saw the crowds, he went up on a mountainside and sat down. His disciples came to him, 2 and he began to teach them.

[a] *11* Or *in* [b] *1* The Greek for *tempted* can also mean *tested.* [c] *4* Deut. 8:3 [d] *6* Psalm 91:11,12
[e] *7* Deut. 6:16 [f] *10* Deut. 6:13 [g] *16* Isaiah 9:1,2 [h] *25* That is, the Ten Cities

The Beatitudes

He said:

3 “Blessed are the poor in spirit,
for theirs is the kingdom of heaven.
4 Blessed are those who mourn,
for they will be comforted.
5 Blessed are the meek,
for they will inherit the earth.
6 Blessed are those who hunger and
thirst for righteousness,
for they will be filled.
7 Blessed are the merciful,
for they will be shown mercy.
8 Blessed are the pure in heart,
for they will see God.
9 Blessed are the peacemakers,
for they will be called children
of God.
10 Blessed are those who are persecuted
because of righteousness,
for theirs is the kingdom of heaven.

11 “Blessed are you when people insult you, persecute you and falsely say all kinds of evil against you because of me. 12 Rejoice and be glad, because great is your reward in heaven, for in the same way they persecuted the prophets who were before you.

Salt and Light

13 “You are the salt of the earth. But if the salt loses its saltiness, how can it be made salty again? It is no longer good for anything, except to be thrown out and trampled underfoot.

14 “You are the light of the world. A town built on a hill cannot be hidden. 15 Neither do people light a lamp and put it under a bowl. Instead they put it on its stand, and it gives light to everyone in the house. 16 In the same way, let your light shine before others, that they may see your good deeds and glorify your Father in heaven.

The Fulfillment of the Law

17 “Do not think that I have come to abolish the Law or the Prophets; I have not come to abolish them but to fulfill them. 18 For truly I tell you, until heaven and earth disappear, not the smallest letter, not the least stroke of a pen, will by any means disappear from the Law until everything is accomplished. 19 Therefore anyone who sets aside one of the least of these commands and teaches others accordingly will be called least in the kingdom of heaven, but whoever practices and teaches these commands will be called great in the kingdom of heaven. 20 For I tell you that unless your righteousness surpasses that of the Pharisees and the teachers of the law, you will certainly not enter the kingdom of heaven.

Murder

21 “You have heard that it was said to the people long ago, ‘You shall not murder,[a] and anyone who murders will be subject to judgment.’ 22 But I tell you that anyone who is angry with a brother or sister[b,c] will be subject to judgment. Again, anyone who says to a brother or sister, ‘Raca,’[d] is answerable to the court. And anyone who says, ‘You fool!’ will be in danger of the fire of hell.

23 “Therefore, if you are offering your gift at the altar and there remember that your brother or sister has something against you, 24 leave your gift there in front of the altar. First go and be reconciled to them; then come and offer your gift.

25 “Settle matters quickly with your adversary who is taking you to court. Do it while you are still together on the way, or your adversary may hand you over to the judge, and the judge may hand you over to the officer, and you may be thrown into prison. 26 Truly I tell you, you will not get out until you have paid the last penny.

Adultery

27 “You have heard that it was said, ‘You shall not commit adultery.’[e] 28 But I tell you that anyone who looks at a woman lustfully has already committed adultery with her in his heart. 29 If your right eye causes you to stumble, gouge it out and throw it away. It is better for you to lose one part of your body than for your whole body to be thrown into hell. 30 And if your right hand causes you to stumble, cut it off and throw it away. It is better for you to lose one part of your body than for your whole body to go into hell.

Divorce

31 “It has been said, ‘Anyone who divorces his wife must give her a certificate of divorce.’[f] 32 But I tell you that anyone who divorces his wife, except for sexual immorality, makes her the victim of adultery, and anyone who marries a divorced woman commits adultery.

[a] *21* Exodus 20:13 [b] *22* The Greek word for *brother or sister* (*adelphos*) refers here to a fellow disciple, whether man or woman; also in verse 23. [c] *22* Some manuscripts *brother or sister without cause* [d] *22* An Aramaic term of contempt [e] *27* Exodus 20:14 [f] *31* Deut. 24:1

Oaths

33“Again, you have heard that it was said
to the people long ago, ‘Do not break your
oath, but fulfill to the Lord the vows you
have made.’ 34But I tell you, do not swear
an oath at all: either by heaven, for it is
God’s throne; 35or by the earth, for it is his
footstool; or by Jerusalem, for it is the city
of the Great King. 36And do not swear by
your head, for you cannot make even one
hair white or black. 37All you need to say
is simply ‘Yes’ or ‘No’; anything beyond
this comes from the evil one.[a]

Eye for Eye

38“You have heard that it was said, ‘Eye
for eye, and tooth for tooth.’[b] 39But I tell
you, do not resist an evil person. If anyone slaps you on the right cheek, turn to
them the other cheek also. 40And if anyone wants to sue you and take your shirt,
hand over your coat as well. 41If anyone
forces you to go one mile, go with them
two miles. 42Give to the one who asks you,
and do not turn away from the one who
wants to borrow from you.

Love for Enemies

43“You have heard that it was said, ‘Love
your neighbor[c] and hate your enemy.’ 44But
I tell you, love your enemies and pray for
those who persecute you, 45that you may
be children of your Father in heaven. He
causes his sun to rise on the evil and the
good, and sends rain on the righteous and
the unrighteous. 46If you love those who
love you, what reward will you get? Are not
even the tax collectors doing that? 47And if
you greet only your own people, what are
you doing more than others? Do not even
pagans do that? 48Be perfect, therefore, as
your heavenly Father is perfect.

Giving to the Needy

6 “Be careful not to practice your righteousness in front of others to be seen
by them. If you do, you will have no reward
from your Father in heaven.

2“So when you give to the needy, do not
announce it with trumpets, as the hypocrites do in the synagogues and on the
streets, to be honored by others. Truly I
tell you, they have received their reward
in full. 3But when you give to the needy,
do not let your left hand know what your
right hand is doing, 4so that your giving
may be in secret. Then your Father, who
sees what is done in secret, will reward you.

Prayer

5“And when you pray, do not be like the
hypocrites, for they love to pray standing in the synagogues and on the street
corners to be seen by others. Truly I tell
you, they have received their reward in
full. 6But when you pray, go into your
room, close the door and pray to your
Father, who is unseen. Then your Father,
who sees what is done in secret, will reward you. 7And when you pray, do not
keep on babbling like pagans, for they
think they will be heard because of their
many words. 8Do not be like them, for
your Father knows what you need before
you ask him.

9“This, then, is how you should pray:

“ ‘Our Father in heaven,
hallowed be your name,
10 your kingdom come,
your will be done,
on earth as it is in heaven.
11 Give us today our daily bread.
12 And forgive us our debts,
as we also have forgiven our
debtors.
13 And lead us not into temptation,[d]
but deliver us from the evil one.[e]’

14For if you forgive other people when they
sin against you, your heavenly Father
will also forgive you. 15But if you do not
forgive others their sins, your Father will
not forgive your sins.

Fasting

16“When you fast, do not look somber
as the hypocrites do, for they disfigure
their faces to show others they are fasting. Truly I tell you, they have received
their reward in full. 17But when you fast,
put oil on your head and wash your face,
18so that it will not be obvious to others
that you are fasting, but only to your
Father, who is unseen; and your Father,
who sees what is done in secret, will reward you.

Treasures in Heaven

19“Do not store up for yourselves treasures on earth, where moths and vermin
destroy, and where thieves break in and
steal. 20But store up for yourselves treasures in heaven, where moths and vermin
do not destroy, and where thieves do not
break in and steal. 21For where your treasure is, there your heart will be also.
22“The eye is the lamp of the body. If

[a] *37* Or *from evil* [b] *38* Exodus 21:24; Lev. 24:20; Deut. 19:21 [c] *43* Lev. 19:18 [d] *13* The Greek for *temptation* can also mean *testing.* [e] *13* Or *from evil*; some late manuscripts *one, / for yours is the kingdom and the power and the glory forever. Amen.*

your eyes are healthy,[a] your whole body will be full of light. 23But if your eyes are unhealthy,[b] your whole body will be full of darkness. If then the light within you is darkness, how great is that darkness!

24"No one can serve two masters. Either you will hate the one and love the other, or you will be devoted to the one and despise the other. You cannot serve both God and money.

Do Not Worry

25"Therefore I tell you, do not worry about your life, what you will eat or drink; or about your body, what you will wear. Is not life more than food, and the body more than clothes? 26Look at the birds of the air; they do not sow or reap or store away in barns, and yet your heavenly Father feeds them. Are you not much more valuable than they? 27Can any one of you by worrying add a single hour to your life[c]?

28"And why do you worry about clothes? See how the flowers of the field grow. They do not labor or spin. 29Yet I tell you that not even Solomon in all his splendor was dressed like one of these. 30If that is how God clothes the grass of the field, which is here today and tomorrow is thrown into the fire, will he not much more clothe you — you of little faith? 31So do not worry, saying, 'What shall we eat?' or 'What shall we drink?' or 'What shall we wear?' 32For the pagans run after all these things, and your heavenly Father knows that you need them. 33But seek first his kingdom and his righteousness, and all these things will be given to you as well. 34Therefore do not worry about tomorrow, for tomorrow will worry about itself. Each day has enough trouble of its own.

Judging Others

7 "Do not judge, or you too will be judged. 2For in the same way you judge others, you will be judged, and with the measure you use, it will be measured to you.

3"Why do you look at the speck of sawdust in your brother's eye and pay no attention to the plank in your own eye? 4How can you say to your brother, 'Let me take the speck out of your eye,' when all the time there is a plank in your own eye? 5You hypocrite, first take the plank out of your own eye, and then you will see clearly to remove the speck from your brother's eye.

6"Do not give dogs what is sacred; do not throw your pearls to pigs. If you do, they may trample them under their feet, and turn and tear you to pieces.

Ask, Seek, Knock

7"Ask and it will be given to you; seek and you will find; knock and the door will be opened to you. 8For everyone who asks receives; the one who seeks finds; and to the one who knocks, the door will be opened.

9"Which of you, if your son asks for bread, will give him a stone? 10Or if he asks for a fish, will give him a snake? 11If you, then, though you are evil, know how to give good gifts to your children, how much more will your Father in heaven give good gifts to those who ask him! 12So in everything, do to others what you would have them do to you, for this sums up the Law and the Prophets.

The Narrow and Wide Gates

13"Enter through the narrow gate. For wide is the gate and broad is the road that leads to destruction, and many enter through it. 14But small is the gate and narrow the road that leads to life, and only a few find it.

True and False Prophets

15"Watch out for false prophets. They come to you in sheep's clothing, but inwardly they are ferocious wolves. 16By their fruit you will recognize them. Do people pick grapes from thornbushes, or figs from thistles? 17Likewise, every good tree bears good fruit, but a bad tree bears bad fruit. 18A good tree cannot bear bad fruit, and a bad tree cannot bear good fruit. 19Every tree that does not bear good fruit is cut down and thrown into the fire. 20Thus, by their fruit you will recognize them.

True and False Disciples

21"Not everyone who says to me, 'Lord, Lord,' will enter the kingdom of heaven, but only the one who does the will of my Father who is in heaven. 22Many will say to me on that day, 'Lord, Lord, did we not prophesy in your name and in your name drive out demons and in your name perform many miracles?' 23Then I will tell them plainly, 'I never knew you. Away from me, you evildoers!'

The Wise and Foolish Builders

24"Therefore everyone who hears these words of mine and puts them into practice is like a wise man who built his house on the rock. 25The rain came down, the streams rose, and the winds blew and

[a] *22* The Greek for *healthy* here implies *generous.* [b] *23* The Greek for *unhealthy* here implies *stingy.* [c] *27* Or *single cubit to your height*

beat against that house; yet it did not fall,
because it had its foundation on the rock.
26 But everyone who hears these words of
mine and does not put them into practice
is like a foolish man who built his house on
sand. 27 The rain came down, the streams
rose, and the winds blew and beat against
that house, and it fell with a great crash."

28 When Jesus had finished saying these
things, the crowds were amazed at his
teaching, 29 because he taught as one who
had authority, and not as their teachers
of the law.

Jesus Heals a Man With Leprosy

8 When Jesus came down from the
mountainside, large crowds followed
him. 2 A man with leprosy[a] came and knelt
before him and said, "Lord, if you are willing, you can make me clean."
3 Jesus reached out his hand and
touched the man. "I am willing," he said.
"Be clean!" Immediately he was cleansed
of his leprosy. 4 Then Jesus said to him, "See
that you don't tell anyone. But go, show
yourself to the priest and offer the gift Moses commanded, as a testimony to them."

The Faith of the Centurion

5 When Jesus had entered Capernaum,
a centurion came to him, asking for help.
6 "Lord," he said, "my servant lies at home
paralyzed, suffering terribly."
7 Jesus said to him, "Shall I come and
heal him?"
8 The centurion replied, "Lord, I do not
deserve to have you come under my roof.
But just say the word, and my servant will
be healed. 9 For I myself am a man under
authority, with soldiers under me. I tell
this one, 'Go,' and he goes; and that one,
'Come,' and he comes. I say to my servant,
'Do this,' and he does it."
10 When Jesus heard this, he was amazed
and said to those following him, "Truly I
tell you, I have not found anyone in Israel
with such great faith. 11 I say to you that
many will come from the east and the
west, and will take their places at the feast
with Abraham, Isaac and Jacob in the
kingdom of heaven. 12 But the subjects of
the kingdom will be thrown outside, into
the darkness, where there will be weeping
and gnashing of teeth."
13 Then Jesus said to the centurion,
"Go! Let it be done just as you believed
it would." And his servant was healed at
that moment.

Jesus Heals Many

14 When Jesus came into Peter's house,
he saw Peter's mother-in-law lying in bed
with a fever. 15 He touched her hand and
the fever left her, and she got up and began to wait on him.
16 When evening came, many who were
demon-possessed were brought to him,
and he drove out the spirits with a word
and healed all the sick. 17 This was to fulfill what was spoken through the prophet
Isaiah:

"He took up our infirmities
and bore our diseases."[b]

The Cost of Following Jesus

18 When Jesus saw the crowd around
him, he gave orders to cross to the other
side of the lake. 19 Then a teacher of the
law came to him and said, "Teacher, I will
follow you wherever you go."
20 Jesus replied, "Foxes have dens and
birds have nests, but the Son of Man has
no place to lay his head."
21 Another disciple said to him, "Lord,
first let me go and bury my father."
22 But Jesus told him, "Follow me, and
let the dead bury their own dead."

Jesus Calms the Storm

23 Then he got into the boat and his disciples followed him. 24 Suddenly a furious
storm came up on the lake, so that the waves
swept over the boat. But Jesus was sleeping.
25 The disciples went and woke him, saying,
"Lord, save us! We're going to drown!"
26 He replied, "You of little faith, why
are you so afraid?" Then he got up and
rebuked the winds and the waves, and it
was completely calm.
27 The men were amazed and asked,
"What kind of man is this? Even the winds
and the waves obey him!"

Jesus Restores Two Demon-Possessed Men

28 When he arrived at the other side in
the region of the Gadarenes,[c] two demon-
possessed men coming from the tombs
met him. They were so violent that no
one could pass that way. 29 "What do you
want with us, Son of God?" they shouted.
"Have you come here to torture us before
the appointed time?"
30 Some distance from them a large herd
of pigs was feeding. 31 The demons begged
Jesus, "If you drive us out, send us into the
herd of pigs."

[a] *2* The Greek word traditionally translated *leprosy* was used for various diseases affecting the skin. [b] *17* Isaiah 53:4 (see Septuagint) [c] *28* Some manuscripts *Gergesenes*; other manuscripts *Gerasenes*

32He said to them, "Go!" So they came out and went into the pigs, and the whole herd rushed down the steep bank into the lake and died in the water. 33Those tending the pigs ran off, went into the town and reported all this, including what had happened to the demon-possessed men. 34Then the whole town went out to meet Jesus. And when they saw him, they pleaded with him to leave their region.

Jesus Forgives and Heals a Paralyzed Man

9 Jesus stepped into a boat, crossed over and came to his own town. 2Some men brought to him a paralyzed man, lying on a mat. When Jesus saw their faith, he said to the man, "Take heart, son; your sins are forgiven."

3At this, some of the teachers of the law said to themselves, "This fellow is blaspheming!"

4Knowing their thoughts, Jesus said, "Why do you entertain evil thoughts in your hearts? 5Which is easier: to say, 'Your sins are forgiven,' or to say, 'Get up and walk'? 6But I want you to know that the Son of Man has authority on earth to forgive sins." So he said to the paralyzed man, "Get up, take your mat and go home." 7Then the man got up and went home. 8When the crowd saw this, they were filled with awe; and they praised God, who had given such authority to man.

The Calling of Matthew

9As Jesus went on from there, he saw a man named Matthew sitting at the tax collector's booth. "Follow me," he told him, and Matthew got up and followed him.

10While Jesus was having dinner at Matthew's house, many tax collectors and sinners came and ate with him and his disciples. 11When the Pharisees saw this, they asked his disciples, "Why does your teacher eat with tax collectors and sinners?"

12On hearing this, Jesus said, "It is not the healthy who need a doctor, but the sick. 13But go and learn what this means: 'I desire mercy, not sacrifice.'[a] For I have not come to call the righteous, but sinners."

Jesus Questioned About Fasting

14Then John's disciples came and asked him, "How is it that we and the Pharisees fast often, but your disciples do not fast?"

15Jesus answered, "How can the guests of the bridegroom mourn while he is with them? The time will come when the bridegroom will be taken from them; then they will fast.

16"No one sews a patch of unshrunk cloth on an old garment, for the patch will pull away from the garment, making the tear worse. 17Neither do people pour new wine into old wineskins. If they do, the skins will burst; the wine will run out and the wineskins will be ruined. No, they pour new wine into new wineskins, and both are preserved."

Jesus Raises a Dead Girl and Heals a Sick Woman

18While he was saying this, a synagogue leader came and knelt before him and said, "My daughter has just died. But come and put your hand on her, and she will live." 19Jesus got up and went with him, and so did his disciples.

20Just then a woman who had been subject to bleeding for twelve years came up behind him and touched the edge of his cloak. 21She said to herself, "If I only touch his cloak, I will be healed."

22Jesus turned and saw her. "Take heart, daughter," he said, "your faith has healed you." And the woman was healed at that moment.

23When Jesus entered the synagogue leader's house and saw the noisy crowd and people playing pipes, 24he said, "Go away. The girl is not dead but asleep." But they laughed at him. 25After the crowd had been put outside, he went in and took the girl by the hand, and she got up. 26News of this spread through all that region.

Jesus Heals the Blind and the Mute

27As Jesus went on from there, two blind men followed him, calling out, "Have mercy on us, Son of David!"

28When he had gone indoors, the blind men came to him, and he asked them, "Do you believe that I am able to do this?"

"Yes, Lord," they replied.

29Then he touched their eyes and said, "According to your faith let it be done to you"; 30and their sight was restored. Jesus warned them sternly, "See that no one knows about this." 31But they went out and spread the news about him all over that region.

32While they were going out, a man who was demon-possessed and could not talk was brought to Jesus. 33And when the demon was driven out, the man who had been mute spoke. The crowd was amazed and said, "Nothing like this has ever been seen in Israel."

34But the Pharisees said, "It is by the prince of demons that he drives out demons."

[a] 13 Hosea 6:6

The Workers Are Few

35 Jesus went through all the towns and
villages, teaching in their synagogues,
proclaiming the good news of the kingdom
and healing every disease and sickness.
36 When he saw the crowds, he had compassion on them, because they were harassed
and helpless, like sheep without a shepherd. 37 Then he said to his disciples, "The
harvest is plentiful but the workers are few.
38 Ask the Lord of the harvest, therefore, to
send out workers into his harvest field."

Jesus Sends Out the Twelve

10 Jesus called his twelve disciples to
him and gave them authority to
drive out impure spirits and to heal every
disease and sickness.

2 These are the names of the twelve
apostles: first, Simon (who is called Peter) and his brother Andrew; James son
of Zebedee, and his brother John; 3 Philip
and Bartholomew; Thomas and Matthew
the tax collector; James son of Alphaeus,
and Thaddaeus; 4 Simon the Zealot and
Judas Iscariot, who betrayed him.

5 These twelve Jesus sent out with the
following instructions: "Do not go among
the Gentiles or enter any town of the Samaritans. 6 Go rather to the lost sheep of
Israel. 7 As you go, proclaim this message:
'The kingdom of heaven has come near.'
8 Heal the sick, raise the dead, cleanse
those who have leprosy,[a] drive out demons. Freely you have received; freely
give.

9 "Do not get any gold or silver or copper to take with you in your belts— 10 no
bag for the journey or extra shirt or sandals or a staff, for the worker is worth his
keep. 11 Whatever town or village you enter,
search there for some worthy person and
stay at their house until you leave. 12 As
you enter the home, give it your greeting.
13 If the home is deserving, let your peace
rest on it; if it is not, let your peace return
to you. 14 If anyone will not welcome you
or listen to your words, leave that home
or town and shake the dust off your feet.
15 Truly I tell you, it will be more bearable
for Sodom and Gomorrah on the day of
judgment than for that town.

16 "I am sending you out like sheep
among wolves. Therefore be as shrewd
as snakes and as innocent as doves. 17 Be
on your guard; you will be handed over
to the local councils and be flogged in the
synagogues. 18 On my account you will be
brought before governors and kings as
witnesses to them and to the Gentiles.
19 But when they arrest you, do not worry
about what to say or how to say it. At that
time you will be given what to say, 20 for it
will not be you speaking, but the Spirit of
your Father speaking through you.

21 "Brother will betray brother to death,
and a father his child; children will rebel
against their parents and have them put
to death. 22 You will be hated by everyone
because of me, but the one who stands
firm to the end will be saved. 23 When you
are persecuted in one place, flee to another. Truly I tell you, you will not finish
going through the towns of Israel before
the Son of Man comes.

24 "The student is not above the teacher, nor a servant above his master. 25 It is
enough for students to be like their teachers, and servants like their masters. If
the head of the house has been called
Beelzebul, how much more the members
of his household!

26 "So do not be afraid of them, for there
is nothing concealed that will not be disclosed, or hidden that will not be made
known. 27 What I tell you in the dark, speak
in the daylight; what is whispered in your
ear, proclaim from the roofs. 28 Do not be
afraid of those who kill the body but cannot kill the soul. Rather, be afraid of the
One who can destroy both soul and body
in hell. 29 Are not two sparrows sold for a
penny? Yet not one of them will fall to the
ground outside your Father's care.[b] 30 And
even the very hairs of your head are all
numbered. 31 So don't be afraid; you are
worth more than many sparrows.

32 "Whoever acknowledges me before
others, I will also acknowledge before my
Father in heaven. 33 But whoever disowns
me before others, I will disown before my
Father in heaven.

34 "Do not suppose that I have come to
bring peace to the earth. I did not come
to bring peace, but a sword. 35 For I have
come to turn

"'a man against his father,
  a daughter against her mother,
a daughter-in-law against her
    mother-in-law—
36   a man's enemies will be the
    members of his own
    household.'[c]

37 "Anyone who loves their father or
mother more than me is not worthy of
me; anyone who loves their son or daughter more than me is not worthy of me.

[a] 8 The Greek word traditionally translated *leprosy* was used for various diseases affecting the skin. [b] 29 Or *will*; or *knowledge* [c] 36 Micah 7:6

38Whoever does not take up their cross and
follow me is not worthy of me. 39Whoever
finds their life will lose it, and whoever
loses their life for my sake will find it.

40"Anyone who welcomes you welcomes
me, and anyone who welcomes me welcomes the one who sent me. 41Whoever
welcomes a prophet as a prophet will
receive a prophet's reward, and whoever welcomes a righteous person as a
righteous person will receive a righteous
person's reward. 42And if anyone gives
even a cup of cold water to one of these
little ones who is my disciple, truly I tell
you, that person will certainly not lose
their reward."

Jesus and John the Baptist

11 After Jesus had finished instructing
his twelve disciples, he went on from
there to teach and preach in the towns
of Galilee.[a]

2When John, who was in prison, heard
about the deeds of the Messiah, he sent
his disciples 3to ask him, "Are you the one
who is to come, or should we expect someone else?"

4Jesus replied, "Go back and report to
John what you hear and see: 5The blind
receive sight, the lame walk, those who
have leprosy[b] are cleansed, the deaf hear,
the dead are raised, and the good news is
proclaimed to the poor. 6Blessed is anyone who does not stumble on account
of me."

7As John's disciples were leaving, Jesus
began to speak to the crowd about John:
"What did you go out into the wilderness
to see? A reed swayed by the wind? 8If not,
what did you go out to see? A man dressed
in fine clothes? No, those who wear fine
clothes are in kings' palaces. 9Then what
did you go out to see? A prophet? Yes, I tell
you, and more than a prophet. 10This is the
one about whom it is written:

> "'I will send my messenger ahead of
> you,
> who will prepare your way before
> you.'[c]

11Truly I tell you, among those born of
women there has not risen anyone greater
than John the Baptist; yet whoever is least
in the kingdom of heaven is greater than
he. 12From the days of John the Baptist
until now, the kingdom of heaven has
been subjected to violence,[d] and violent
people have been raiding it. 13For all the
Prophets and the Law prophesied until
John. 14And if you are willing to accept it,
he is the Elijah who was to come. 15Who-
ever has ears, let them hear.

16"To what can I compare this generation? They are like children sitting in the
marketplaces and calling out to others:

> 17"'We played the pipe for you,
> and you did not dance;
> we sang a dirge,
> and you did not mourn.'

18For John came neither eating nor drinking, and they say, 'He has a demon.' 19The
Son of Man came eating and drinking, and
they say, 'Here is a glutton and a drunkard, a friend of tax collectors and sinners.'
But wisdom is proved right by her deeds."

Woe on Unrepentant Towns

20Then Jesus began to denounce the
towns in which most of his miracles had
been performed, because they did not repent. 21"Woe to you, Chorazin! Woe to you,
Bethsaida! For if the miracles that were
performed in you had been performed in
Tyre and Sidon, they would have repented
long ago in sackcloth and ashes. 22But I
tell you, it will be more bearable for Tyre
and Sidon on the day of judgment than
for you. 23And you, Capernaum, will you be
lifted to the heavens? No, you will go down
to Hades.[e] For if the miracles that were
performed in you had been performed
in Sodom, it would have remained to this
day. 24But I tell you that it will be more
bearable for Sodom on the day of judgment than for you."

The Father Revealed in the Son

25At that time Jesus said, "I praise you,
Father, Lord of heaven and earth, because
you have hidden these things from the
wise and learned, and revealed them to
little children. 26Yes, Father, for this is what
you were pleased to do.

27"All things have been committed to
me by my Father. No one knows the Son
except the Father, and no one knows the
Father except the Son and those to whom
the Son chooses to reveal him.

28"Come to me, all you who are weary
and burdened, and I will give you rest.
29Take my yoke upon you and learn from
me, for I am gentle and humble in heart,
and you will find rest for your souls.
30For my yoke is easy and my burden is
light."

[a] *1* Greek *in their towns* [b] *5* The Greek word traditionally translated *leprosy* was used for various diseases affecting the skin. [c] *10* Mal. 3:1 [d] *12* Or *been forcefully advancing* [e] *23* That is, the realm of the dead

Jesus Is Lord of the Sabbath

12 At that time Jesus went through the grainfields on the Sabbath. His disciples were hungry and began to pick some heads of grain and eat them. 2 When the Pharisees saw this, they said to him, "Look! Your disciples are doing what is unlawful on the Sabbath."

3 He answered, "Haven't you read what David did when he and his companions were hungry? 4 He entered the house of God, and he and his companions ate the consecrated bread—which was not lawful for them to do, but only for the priests. 5 Or haven't you read in the Law that the priests on Sabbath duty in the temple desecrate the Sabbath and yet are innocent? 6 I tell you that something greater than the temple is here. 7 If you had known what these words mean, 'I desire mercy, not sacrifice,'[a] you would not have condemned the innocent. 8 For the Son of Man is Lord of the Sabbath."

9 Going on from that place, he went into their synagogue, 10 and a man with a shriveled hand was there. Looking for a reason to bring charges against Jesus, they asked him, "Is it lawful to heal on the Sabbath?"

11 He said to them, "If any of you has a sheep and it falls into a pit on the Sabbath, will you not take hold of it and lift it out? 12 How much more valuable is a person than a sheep! Therefore it is lawful to do good on the Sabbath."

13 Then he said to the man, "Stretch out your hand." So he stretched it out and it was completely restored, just as sound as the other. 14 But the Pharisees went out and plotted how they might kill Jesus.

God's Chosen Servant

15 Aware of this, Jesus withdrew from that place. A large crowd followed him, and he healed all who were ill. 16 He warned them not to tell others about him. 17 This was to fulfill what was spoken through the prophet Isaiah:

18 "Here is my servant whom I have chosen,
the one I love, in whom I delight;
I will put my Spirit on him,
and he will proclaim justice to the nations.
19 He will not quarrel or cry out;
no one will hear his voice in the streets.
20 A bruised reed he will not break,
and a smoldering wick he will not snuff out,
till he has brought justice through to victory.
21 In his name the nations will put their hope."[b]

Jesus and Beelzebul

22 Then they brought him a demon-possessed man who was blind and mute, and Jesus healed him, so that he could both talk and see. 23 All the people were astonished and said, "Could this be the Son of David?"

24 But when the Pharisees heard this, they said, "It is only by Beelzebul, the prince of demons, that this fellow drives out demons."

25 Jesus knew their thoughts and said to them, "Every kingdom divided against itself will be ruined, and every city or household divided against itself will not stand. 26 If Satan drives out Satan, he is divided against himself. How then can his kingdom stand? 27 And if I drive out demons by Beelzebul, by whom do your people drive them out? So then, they will be your judges. 28 But if it is by the Spirit of God that I drive out demons, then the kingdom of God has come upon you.

29 "Or again, how can anyone enter a strong man's house and carry off his possessions unless he first ties up the strong man? Then he can plunder his house.

30 "Whoever is not with me is against me, and whoever does not gather with me scatters. 31 And so I tell you, every kind of sin and slander can be forgiven, but blasphemy against the Spirit will not be forgiven. 32 Anyone who speaks a word against the Son of Man will be forgiven, but anyone who speaks against the Holy Spirit will not be forgiven, either in this age or in the age to come.

33 "Make a tree good and its fruit will be good, or make a tree bad and its fruit will be bad, for a tree is recognized by its fruit. 34 You brood of vipers, how can you who are evil say anything good? For the mouth speaks what the heart is full of. 35 A good man brings good things out of the good stored up in him, and an evil man brings evil things out of the evil stored up in him. 36 But I tell you that everyone will have to give account on the day of judgment for every empty word they have spoken. 37 For by your words you will be acquitted, and by your words you will be condemned."

[a] *7* Hosea 6:6 [b] *21* Isaiah 42:1-4

The Sign of Jonah

[38]Then some of the Pharisees and teachers of the law said to him, "Teacher, we want to see a sign from you."

[39]He answered, "A wicked and adulterous generation asks for a sign! But none will be given it except the sign of the prophet Jonah. [40]For as Jonah was three days and three nights in the belly of a huge fish, so the Son of Man will be three days and three nights in the heart of the earth. [41]The men of Nineveh will stand up at the judgment with this generation and condemn it; for they repented at the preaching of Jonah, and now something greater than Jonah is here. [42]The Queen of the South will rise at the judgment with this generation and condemn it; for she came from the ends of the earth to listen to Solomon's wisdom, and now something greater than Solomon is here.

[43]"When an impure spirit comes out of a person, it goes through arid places seeking rest and does not find it. [44]Then it says, 'I will return to the house I left.' When it arrives, it finds the house unoccupied, swept clean and put in order. [45]Then it goes and takes with it seven other spirits more wicked than itself, and they go in and live there. And the final condition of that person is worse than the first. That is how it will be with this wicked generation."

Jesus' Mother and Brothers

[46]While Jesus was still talking to the crowd, his mother and brothers stood outside, wanting to speak to him. [47]Someone told him, "Your mother and brothers are standing outside, wanting to speak to you."

[48]He replied to him, "Who is my mother, and who are my brothers?" [49]Pointing to his disciples, he said, "Here are my mother and my brothers. [50]For whoever does the will of my Father in heaven is my brother and sister and mother."

The Parable of the Sower

13 That same day Jesus went out of the house and sat by the lake. [2]Such large crowds gathered around him that he got into a boat and sat in it, while all the people stood on the shore. [3]Then he told them many things in parables, saying: "A farmer went out to sow his seed. [4]As he was scattering the seed, some fell along the path, and the birds came and ate it up. [5]Some fell on rocky places, where it did not have much soil. It sprang up quickly, because the soil was shallow. [6]But when the sun came up, the plants were scorched, and they withered because they had no root. [7]Other seed fell among thorns, which grew up and choked the plants. [8]Still other seed fell on good soil, where it produced a crop — a hundred, sixty or thirty times what was sown. [9]Whoever has ears, let them hear."

[10]The disciples came to him and asked, "Why do you speak to the people in parables?"

[11]He replied, "Because the knowledge of the secrets of the kingdom of heaven has been given to you, but not to them. [12]Whoever has will be given more, and they will have an abundance. Whoever does not have, even what they have will be taken from them. [13]This is why I speak to them in parables:

"Though seeing, they do not see;
 though hearing, they do not hear
 or understand.

[14]In them is fulfilled the prophecy of Isaiah:

"'You will be ever hearing but never
 understanding;
 you will be ever seeing but never
 perceiving.
[15]For this people's heart has become
 calloused;
 they hardly hear with their ears,
 and they have closed their eyes.
Otherwise they might see with their
 eyes,
 hear with their ears,
 understand with their hearts
and turn, and I would heal them.'[a]

[16]But blessed are your eyes because they see, and your ears because they hear. [17]For truly I tell you, many prophets and righteous people longed to see what you see but did not see it, and to hear what you hear but did not hear it.

[18]"Listen then to what the parable of the sower means: [19]When anyone hears the message about the kingdom and does not understand it, the evil one comes and snatches away what was sown in their heart. This is the seed sown along the path. [20]The seed falling on rocky ground refers to someone who hears the word and at once receives it with joy. [21]But since they have no root, they last only a short time. When trouble or persecution comes because of the word, they quickly fall away. [22]The seed falling among the thorns refers to someone who hears the word, but the worries of this life and the deceitfulness of wealth choke the word, making it unfruitful. [23]But the seed falling on good soil refers to someone who hears the word and understands it. This is the one who produces a crop, yielding a hundred, sixty or thirty times what was sown."

[a] 15 Isaiah 6:9,10 (see Septuagint)

The Parable of the Weeds

24Jesus told them another parable: "The
kingdom of heaven is like a man who
sowed good seed in his field. 25But while
everyone was sleeping, his enemy came
and sowed weeds among the wheat, and
went away. 26When the wheat sprouted
and formed heads, then the weeds also
appeared.

27"The owner's servants came to him
and said, 'Sir, didn't you sow good seed
in your field? Where then did the weeds
come from?'

28" 'An enemy did this,' he replied.

"The servants asked him, 'Do you want
us to go and pull them up?'

29" 'No,' he answered, 'because while you
are pulling the weeds, you may uproot the
wheat with them. 30Let both grow together
until the harvest. At that time I will tell the
harvesters: First collect the weeds and tie
them in bundles to be burned; then gather
the wheat and bring it into my barn.' "

The Parables of the Mustard Seed and the Yeast

31He told them another parable: "The
kingdom of heaven is like a mustard seed,
which a man took and planted in his field.
32Though it is the smallest of all seeds, yet
when it grows, it is the largest of garden
plants and becomes a tree, so that the
birds come and perch in its branches."

33He told them still another parable:
"The kingdom of heaven is like yeast
that a woman took and mixed into about
sixty pounds[a] of flour until it worked all
through the dough."

34Jesus spoke all these things to the
crowd in parables; he did not say anything to them without using a parable.
35So was fulfilled what was spoken through
the prophet:

"I will open my mouth in parables,
I will utter things hidden since the
creation of the world."[b]

The Parable of the Weeds Explained

36Then he left the crowd and went into
the house. His disciples came to him and
said, "Explain to us the parable of the
weeds in the field."

37He answered, "The one who sowed the
good seed is the Son of Man. 38The field is
the world, and the good seed stands for
the people of the kingdom. The weeds are
the people of the evil one, 39and the enemy
who sows them is the devil. The harvest
is the end of the age, and the harvesters
are angels.

40"As the weeds are pulled up and burned
in the fire, so it will be at the end of the age.
41The Son of Man will send out his angels,
and they will weed out of his kingdom
everything that causes sin and all who do
evil. 42They will throw them into the blazing
furnace, where there will be weeping and
gnashing of teeth. 43Then the righteous will
shine like the sun in the kingdom of their
Father. Whoever has ears, let them hear.

The Parables of the Hidden Treasure and the Pearl

44"The kingdom of heaven is like treasure hidden in a field. When a man found
it, he hid it again, and then in his joy went
and sold all he had and bought that field.

45"Again, the kingdom of heaven is like
a merchant looking for fine pearls. 46When
he found one of great value, he went away
and sold everything he had and bought it.

The Parable of the Net

47"Once again, the kingdom of heaven is
like a net that was let down into the lake
and caught all kinds of fish. 48When it
was full, the fishermen pulled it up on the
shore. Then they sat down and collected
the good fish in baskets, but threw the bad
away. 49This is how it will be at the end of
the age. The angels will come and separate
the wicked from the righteous 50and throw
them into the blazing furnace, where there
will be weeping and gnashing of teeth.

51"Have you understood all these
things?" Jesus asked.

"Yes," they replied.

52He said to them, "Therefore every
teacher of the law who has become a disciple in the kingdom of heaven is like the
owner of a house who brings out of his
storeroom new treasures as well as old."

A Prophet Without Honor

53When Jesus had finished these parables, he moved on from there. 54Coming
to his hometown, he began teaching the
people in their synagogue, and they were
amazed. "Where did this man get this
wisdom and these miraculous powers?"
they asked. 55"Isn't this the carpenter's
son? Isn't his mother's name Mary, and
aren't his brothers James, Joseph, Simon
and Judas? 56Aren't all his sisters with
us? Where then did this man get all these
things?" 57And they took offense at him.

But Jesus said to them, "A prophet is not
without honor except in his own town and
in his own home."

58And he did not do many miracles there
because of their lack of faith.

[a] *33* Or about 27 kilograms   [b] *35* Psalm 78:2

John the Baptist Beheaded

14 At that time Herod the tetrarch heard the reports about Jesus, [2]and he said to his attendants, "This is John the Baptist; he has risen from the dead! That is why miraculous powers are at work in him."

[3]Now Herod had arrested John and bound him and put him in prison because of Herodias, his brother Philip's wife, [4]for John had been saying to him: "It is not lawful for you to have her." [5]Herod wanted to kill John, but he was afraid of the people, because they considered John a prophet.

[6]On Herod's birthday the daughter of Herodias danced for the guests and pleased Herod so much [7]that he promised with an oath to give her whatever she asked. [8]Prompted by her mother, she said, "Give me here on a platter the head of John the Baptist." [9]The king was distressed, but because of his oaths and his dinner guests, he ordered that her request be granted [10]and had John beheaded in the prison. [11]His head was brought in on a platter and given to the girl, who carried it to her mother. [12]John's disciples came and took his body and buried it. Then they went and told Jesus.

Jesus Feeds the Five Thousand

[13]When Jesus heard what had happened, he withdrew by boat privately to a solitary place. Hearing of this, the crowds followed him on foot from the towns. [14]When Jesus landed and saw a large crowd, he had compassion on them and healed their sick.

[15]As evening approached, the disciples came to him and said, "This is a remote place, and it's already getting late. Send the crowds away, so they can go to the villages and buy themselves some food."

[16]Jesus replied, "They do not need to go away. You give them something to eat."

[17]"We have here only five loaves of bread and two fish," they answered.

[18]"Bring them here to me," he said. [19]And he directed the people to sit down on the grass. Taking the five loaves and the two fish and looking up to heaven, he gave thanks and broke the loaves. Then he gave them to the disciples, and the disciples gave them to the people. [20]They all ate and were satisfied, and the disciples picked up twelve basketfuls of broken pieces that were left over. [21]The number of those who ate was about five thousand men, besides women and children.

Jesus Walks on the Water

[22]Immediately Jesus made the disciples get into the boat and go on ahead of him to the other side, while he dismissed the crowd. [23]After he had dismissed them, he went up on a mountainside by himself to pray. Later that night, he was there alone, [24]and the boat was already a considerable distance from land, buffeted by the waves because the wind was against it.

[25]Shortly before dawn Jesus went out to them, walking on the lake. [26]When the disciples saw him walking on the lake, they were terrified. "It's a ghost," they said, and cried out in fear.

[27]But Jesus immediately said to them: "Take courage! It is I. Don't be afraid."

[28]"Lord, if it's you," Peter replied, "tell me to come to you on the water."

[29]"Come," he said.

Then Peter got down out of the boat, walked on the water and came toward Jesus. [30]But when he saw the wind, he was afraid and, beginning to sink, cried out, "Lord, save me!"

[31]Immediately Jesus reached out his hand and caught him. "You of little faith," he said, "why did you doubt?"

[32]And when they climbed into the boat, the wind died down. [33]Then those who were in the boat worshiped him, saying, "Truly you are the Son of God."

[34]When they had crossed over, they landed at Gennesaret. [35]And when the men of that place recognized Jesus, they sent word to all the surrounding country. People brought all their sick to him [36]and begged him to let the sick just touch the edge of his cloak, and all who touched it were healed.

That Which Defiles

15 Then some Pharisees and teachers of the law came to Jesus from Jerusalem and asked, [2]"Why do your disciples break the tradition of the elders? They don't wash their hands before they eat!"

[3]Jesus replied, "And why do you break the command of God for the sake of your tradition? [4]For God said, 'Honor your father and mother'[a] and 'Anyone who curses their father or mother is to be put to death.'[b] [5]But you say that if anyone declares that what might have been used to help their father or mother is 'devoted to God,' [6]they are not to 'honor their father or mother' with it. Thus you nullify the word of God for the sake of your tradition. [7]You hypocrites! Isaiah was right when he prophesied about you:

[a] 4 Exodus 20:12; Deut. 5:16 [b] 4 Exodus 21:17; Lev. 20:9

8 “ ‘These people honor me with their lips,
but their hearts are far from me.
9 They worship me in vain;
their teachings are merely human
rules.’[a]”

10 Jesus called the crowd to him and said,
“Listen and understand. 11 What goes into
someone’s mouth does not defile them,
but what comes out of their mouth, that
is what defiles them.”
12 Then the disciples came to him and
asked, “Do you know that the Pharisees
were offended when they heard this?”
13 He replied, “Every plant that my heavenly Father has not planted will be pulled
up by the roots. 14 Leave them; they are
blind guides.[b] If the blind lead the blind,
both will fall into a pit.”
15 Peter said, “Explain the parable to us.”
16 “Are you still so dull?” Jesus asked
them. 17 “Don’t you see that whatever enters the mouth goes into the stomach and
then out of the body? 18 But the things that
come out of a person’s mouth come from
the heart, and these defile them. 19 For out
of the heart come evil thoughts — murder,
adultery, sexual immorality, theft, false
testimony, slander. 20 These are what defile a person; but eating with unwashed
hands does not defile them.”

The Faith of a Canaanite Woman

21 Leaving that place, Jesus withdrew
to the region of Tyre and Sidon. 22 A Canaanite woman from that vicinity came
to him, crying out, “Lord, Son of David,
have mercy on me! My daughter is demon-
possessed and suffering terribly.”
23 Jesus did not answer a word. So his disciples came to him and urged him, “Send
her away, for she keeps crying out after us.”
24 He answered, “I was sent only to the
lost sheep of Israel.”
25 The woman came and knelt before
him. “Lord, help me!” she said.
26 He replied, “It is not right to take the
children’s bread and toss it to the dogs.”
27 “Yes it is, Lord,” she said. “Even the
dogs eat the crumbs that fall from their
master’s table.”
28 Then Jesus said to her, “Woman, you
have great faith! Your request is granted.” And her daughter was healed at that
moment.

Jesus Feeds the Four Thousand

29 Jesus left there and went along the Sea
of Galilee. Then he went up on a mountainside and sat down. 30 Great crowds
came to him, bringing the lame, the blind,
the crippled, the mute and many others,
and laid them at his feet; and he healed
them. 31 The people were amazed when
they saw the mute speaking, the crippled
made well, the lame walking and the blind
seeing. And they praised the God of Israel.
32 Jesus called his disciples to him and
said, “I have compassion for these people;
they have already been with me three
days and have nothing to eat. I do not
want to send them away hungry, or they
may collapse on the way.”
33 His disciples answered, “Where could
we get enough bread in this remote place
to feed such a crowd?”
34 “How many loaves do you have?”
Jesus asked.
“Seven,” they replied, “and a few small
fish.”
35 He told the crowd to sit down on the
ground. 36 Then he took the seven loaves
and the fish, and when he had given
thanks, he broke them and gave them
to the disciples, and they in turn to the
people. 37 They all ate and were satisfied.
Afterward the disciples picked up seven
basketfuls of broken pieces that were left
over. 38 The number of those who ate was
four thousand men, besides women and
children. 39 After Jesus had sent the crowd
away, he got into the boat and went to the
vicinity of Magadan.

The Demand for a Sign

16 The Pharisees and Sadducees came
to Jesus and tested him by asking
him to show them a sign from heaven.
2 He replied, “When evening comes, you
say, ‘It will be fair weather, for the sky is
red,’ 3 and in the morning, ‘Today it will be
stormy, for the sky is red and overcast.’ You
know how to interpret the appearance of
the sky, but you cannot interpret the signs
of the times.[c] 4 A wicked and adulterous
generation looks for a sign, but none will
be given it except the sign of Jonah.” Jesus
then left them and went away.

The Yeast of the Pharisees and Sadducees

5 When they went across the lake, the
disciples forgot to take bread. 6 “Be careful,” Jesus said to them. “Be on your guard
against the yeast of the Pharisees and
Sadducees.”
7 They discussed this among themselves
and said, “It is because we didn’t bring
any bread.”

[a] 9 Isaiah 29:13 [b] 14 Some manuscripts *blind guides of the blind* [c] 2,3 Some early manuscripts do not have *When evening comes . . . of the times.*

[8]Aware of their discussion, Jesus asked, "You of little faith, why are you talking among yourselves about having no bread? [9]Do you still not understand? Don't you remember the five loaves for the five thousand, and how many basketfuls you gathered? [10]Or the seven loaves for the four thousand, and how many basketfuls you gathered? [11]How is it you don't understand that I was not talking to you about bread? But be on your guard against the yeast of the Pharisees and Sadducees." [12]Then they understood that he was not telling them to guard against the yeast used in bread, but against the teaching of the Pharisees and Sadducees.

Peter Declares That Jesus Is the Messiah

[13]When Jesus came to the region of Caesarea Philippi, he asked his disciples, "Who do people say the Son of Man is?"

[14]They replied, "Some say John the Baptist; others say Elijah; and still others, Jeremiah or one of the prophets."

[15]"But what about you?" he asked. "Who do you say I am?"

[16]Simon Peter answered, "You are the Messiah, the Son of the living God."

[17]Jesus replied, "Blessed are you, Simon son of Jonah, for this was not revealed to you by flesh and blood, but by my Father in heaven. [18]And I tell you that you are Peter,[a] and on this rock I will build my church, and the gates of Hades[b] will not overcome it. [19]I will give you the keys of the kingdom of heaven; whatever you bind on earth will be[c] bound in heaven, and whatever you loose on earth will be[c] loosed in heaven." [20]Then he ordered his disciples not to tell anyone that he was the Messiah.

Jesus Predicts His Death

[21]From that time on Jesus began to explain to his disciples that he must go to Jerusalem and suffer many things at the hands of the elders, the chief priests and the teachers of the law, and that he must be killed and on the third day be raised to life.

[22]Peter took him aside and began to rebuke him. "Never, Lord!" he said. "This shall never happen to you!"

[23]Jesus turned and said to Peter, "Get behind me, Satan! You are a stumbling block to me; you do not have in mind the concerns of God, but merely human concerns."

[24]Then Jesus said to his disciples, "Whoever wants to be my disciple must deny themselves and take up their cross and follow me. [25]For whoever wants to save their life[d] will lose it, but whoever loses their life for me will find it. [26]What good will it be for someone to gain the whole world, yet forfeit their soul? Or what can anyone give in exchange for their soul? [27]For the Son of Man is going to come in his Father's glory with his angels, and then he will reward each person according to what they have done.

[28]"Truly I tell you, some who are standing here will not taste death before they see the Son of Man coming in his kingdom."

The Transfiguration

17 After six days Jesus took with him Peter, James and John the brother of James, and led them up a high mountain by themselves. [2]There he was transfigured before them. His face shone like the sun, and his clothes became as white as the light. [3]Just then there appeared before them Moses and Elijah, talking with Jesus.

[4]Peter said to Jesus, "Lord, it is good for us to be here. If you wish, I will put up three shelters — one for you, one for Moses and one for Elijah."

[5]While he was still speaking, a bright cloud covered them, and a voice from the cloud said, "This is my Son, whom I love; with him I am well pleased. Listen to him!"

[6]When the disciples heard this, they fell facedown to the ground, terrified. [7]But Jesus came and touched them. "Get up," he said. "Don't be afraid." [8]When they looked up, they saw no one except Jesus.

[9]As they were coming down the mountain, Jesus instructed them, "Don't tell anyone what you have seen, until the Son of Man has been raised from the dead."

[10]The disciples asked him, "Why then do the teachers of the law say that Elijah must come first?"

[11]Jesus replied, "To be sure, Elijah comes and will restore all things. [12]But I tell you, Elijah has already come, and they did not recognize him, but have done to him everything they wished. In the same way the Son of Man is going to suffer at their hands." [13]Then the disciples understood that he was talking to them about John the Baptist.

Jesus Heals a Demon-Possessed Boy

[14]When they came to the crowd, a man approached Jesus and knelt before him. [15]"Lord, have mercy on my son," he said. "He has seizures and is suffering greatly.

[a] *18* The Greek word for *Peter* means *rock*. [b] *18* That is, the realm of the dead [c] *19* Or *will have been* [d] *25* The Greek word means either *life* or *soul*; also in verse 26.

He often falls into the fire or into the water. 16I brought him to your disciples, but
they could not heal him.”
17“You unbelieving and perverse generation,” Jesus replied, “how long shall I
stay with you? How long shall I put up with
you? Bring the boy here to me.” 18Jesus rebuked the demon, and it came out of the
boy, and he was healed at that moment.
19Then the disciples came to Jesus in
private and asked, “Why couldn’t we drive
it out?”
20He replied, “Because you have so little
faith. Truly I tell you, if you have faith as
small as a mustard seed, you can say to
this mountain, ‘Move from here to there,’
and it will move. Nothing will be impossible for you.” [21][a]

Jesus Predicts His Death a Second Time

22When they came together in Galilee,
he said to them, “The Son of Man is going
to be delivered into the hands of men.
23They will kill him, and on the third day
he will be raised to life.” And the disciples
were filled with grief.

The Temple Tax

24After Jesus and his disciples arrived in Capernaum, the collectors of the two-drachma
temple tax came to Peter and asked,
“Doesn’t your teacher pay the temple tax?”
25“Yes, he does,” he replied.
When Peter came into the house, Jesus
was the first to speak. “What do you think,
Simon?” he asked. “From whom do the
kings of the earth collect duty and taxes —
from their own children or from others?”
26“From others,” Peter answered.
“Then the children are exempt,” Jesus
said to him. 27“But so that we may not
cause offense, go to the lake and throw
out your line. Take the first fish you catch;
open its mouth and you will find a four-
drachma coin. Take it and give it to them
for my tax and yours.”

The Greatest in the Kingdom of Heaven

18 At that time the disciples came to
Jesus and asked, “Who, then, is the
greatest in the kingdom of heaven?”
2He called a little child to him, and
placed the child among them. 3And he
said: “Truly I tell you, unless you change
and become like little children, you will
never enter the kingdom of heaven.
4Therefore, whoever takes the lowly position of this child is the greatest in the kingdom of heaven. 5And whoever welcomes
one such child in my name welcomes me.

Causing to Stumble

6“If anyone causes one of these little
ones — those who believe in me — to
stumble, it would be better for them to
have a large millstone hung around their
neck and to be drowned in the depths of
the sea. 7Woe to the world because of the
things that cause people to stumble! Such
things must come, but woe to the person
through whom they come! 8If your hand
or your foot causes you to stumble, cut it
off and throw it away. It is better for you
to enter life maimed or crippled than to
have two hands or two feet and be thrown
into eternal fire. 9And if your eye causes
you to stumble, gouge it out and throw
it away. It is better for you to enter life
with one eye than to have two eyes and
be thrown into the fire of hell.

The Parable of the Wandering Sheep

10“See that you do not despise one of
these little ones. For I tell you that their
angels in heaven always see the face of
my Father in heaven. [11][b]
12“What do you think? If a man owns a
hundred sheep, and one of them wanders
away, will he not leave the ninety-nine on
the hills and go to look for the one that
wandered off? 13And if he finds it, truly I
tell you, he is happier about that one sheep
than about the ninety-nine that did not
wander off. 14In the same way your Father
in heaven is not willing that any of these
little ones should perish.

Dealing With Sin in the Church

15“If your brother or sister[c] sins,[d] go
and point out their fault, just between
the two of you. If they listen to you, you
have won them over. 16But if they will not
listen, take one or two others along, so
that ‘every matter may be established by
the testimony of two or three witnesses.’[e]
17If they still refuse to listen, tell it to the
church; and if they refuse to listen even
to the church, treat them as you would a
pagan or a tax collector.
18“Truly I tell you, whatever you bind
on earth will be[f] bound in heaven, and
whatever you loose on earth will be[f] loosed
in heaven.

[a] *21* Some manuscripts include here words similar to Mark 9:29. [b] *11* Some manuscripts include here the words of Luke 19:10. [c] *15* The Greek word for *brother or sister* (*adelphos*) refers here to a fellow disciple, whether man or woman; also in verses 21 and 35. [d] *15* Some manuscripts *sins against you* [e] *16* Deut. 19:15 [f] *18* Or *will have been*

19“Again, truly I tell you that if two of
you on earth agree about anything they
ask for, it will be done for them by my Father in heaven. 20For where two or three
gather in my name, there am I with them.”

The Parable of the Unmerciful Servant

21Then Peter came to Jesus and asked,
“Lord, how many times shall I forgive my
brother or sister who sins against me? Up
to seven times?”
22Jesus answered, “I tell you, not seven
times, but seventy-seven times.[a]
23“Therefore, the kingdom of heaven is
like a king who wanted to settle accounts
with his servants. 24As he began the settlement, a man who owed him ten thousand
bags of gold[b] was brought to him. 25Since
he was not able to pay, the master ordered
that he and his wife and his children and
all that he had be sold to repay the debt.
26“At this the servant fell on his knees
before him. ‘Be patient with me,’ he
begged, ‘and I will pay back everything.’
27The servant’s master took pity on him,
canceled the debt and let him go.
28“But when that servant went out, he
found one of his fellow servants who owed
him a hundred silver coins.[c] He grabbed
him and began to choke him. ‘Pay back
what you owe me!’ he demanded.
29“His fellow servant fell to his knees
and begged him, ‘Be patient with me, and
I will pay it back.’
30“But he refused. Instead, he went off
and had the man thrown into prison until
he could pay the debt. 31When the other
servants saw what had happened, they
were outraged and went and told their
master everything that had happened.
32“Then the master called the servant in.
‘You wicked servant,’ he said, ‘I canceled
all that debt of yours because you begged
me to. 33Shouldn’t you have had mercy on
your fellow servant just as I had on you?’
34In anger his master handed him over to
the jailers to be tortured, until he should
pay back all he owed.
35“This is how my heavenly Father will
treat each of you unless you forgive your
brother or sister from your heart.”

Divorce

19 When Jesus had finished saying
these things, he left Galilee and went
into the region of Judea to the other side
of the Jordan. 2Large crowds followed him,
and he healed them there.
3Some Pharisees came to him to test
him. They asked, “Is it lawful for a man to
divorce his wife for any and every reason?”
4“Haven’t you read,” he replied, “that
at the beginning the Creator ‘made them
male and female,’[d] 5and said, ‘For this reason a man will leave his father and mother
and be united to his wife, and the two will
become one flesh’[e]? 6So they are no longer
two, but one flesh. Therefore what God
has joined together, let no one separate.”
7“Why then,” they asked, “did Moses
command that a man give his wife a certificate of divorce and send her away?”
8Jesus replied, “Moses permitted you to
divorce your wives because your hearts
were hard. But it was not this way from
the beginning. 9I tell you that anyone
who divorces his wife, except for sexual
immorality, and marries another woman
commits adultery.”
10The disciples said to him, “If this is the
situation between a husband and wife, it
is better not to marry.”
11Jesus replied, “Not everyone can accept this word, but only those to whom it
has been given. 12For there are eunuchs
who were born that way, and there are
eunuchs who have been made eunuchs by
others — and there are those who choose
to live like eunuchs for the sake of the
kingdom of heaven. The one who can
accept this should accept it.”

The Little Children and Jesus

13Then people brought little children to
Jesus for him to place his hands on them
and pray for them. But the disciples rebuked them.
14Jesus said, “Let the little children come
to me, and do not hinder them, for the
kingdom of heaven belongs to such as
these.” 15When he had placed his hands
on them, he went on from there.

The Rich and the Kingdom of God

16Just then a man came up to Jesus and
asked, “Teacher, what good thing must I
do to get eternal life?”
17“Why do you ask me about what is
good?” Jesus replied. “There is only One
who is good. If you want to enter life, keep
the commandments.”
18“Which ones?” he inquired.
Jesus replied, “ ‘You shall not murder,
you shall not commit adultery, you shall
not steal, you shall not give false testimony, 19honor your father and mother,’[f] and
‘love your neighbor as yourself.’[g]”

[a] 22 Or *seventy times seven* [b] 24 Greek *ten thousand talents*; a talent was worth about 20 years of a day laborer’s wages. [c] 28 Greek *a hundred denarii*; a denarius was the usual daily wage of a day laborer (see 20:2). [d] 4 Gen. 1:27 [e] 5 Gen. 2:24 [f] 19 Exodus 20:12-16; Deut. 5:16-20 [g] 19 Lev. 19:18

20“All these I have kept,” the young man
said. “What do I still lack?”
21Jesus answered, “If you want to be
perfect, go, sell your possessions and give
to the poor, and you will have treasure in
heaven. Then come, follow me.”
22When the young man heard this, he
went away sad, because he had great
wealth.
23Then Jesus said to his disciples, “Truly I tell you, it is hard for someone who
is rich to enter the kingdom of heaven.
24Again I tell you, it is easier for a camel
to go through the eye of a needle than for
someone who is rich to enter the kingdom of God.”
25When the disciples heard this, they
were greatly astonished and asked, “Who
then can be saved?”
26Jesus looked at them and said, “With
man this is impossible, but with God all
things are possible.”
27Peter answered him, “We have left
everything to follow you! What then will
there be for us?”
28Jesus said to them, “Truly I tell you, at
the renewal of all things, when the Son of
Man sits on his glorious throne, you who
have followed me will also sit on twelve
thrones, judging the twelve tribes of Israel. 29And everyone who has left houses
or brothers or sisters or father or mother
or wife[a] or children or fields for my sake
will receive a hundred times as much and
will inherit eternal life. 30But many who
are first will be last, and many who are
last will be first.

The Parable of the Workers in the Vineyard

20 “For the kingdom of heaven is like
a landowner who went out early
in the morning to hire workers for his
vineyard. 2He agreed to pay them a denarius[b] for the day and sent them into
his vineyard.
3“About nine in the morning he went out
and saw others standing in the marketplace doing nothing. 4He told them, ‘You
also go and work in my vineyard, and I will
pay you whatever is right.’ 5So they went.
“He went out again about noon and
about three in the afternoon and did the
same thing. 6About five in the afternoon
he went out and found still others standing around. He asked them, ‘Why have
you been standing here all day long doing nothing?’
7“ ‘Because no one has hired us,’ they
answered.
“He said to them, ‘You also go and work
in my vineyard.’
8“When evening came, the owner of
the vineyard said to his foreman, ‘Call
the workers and pay them their wages,
beginning with the last ones hired and
going on to the first.’
9“The workers who were hired about
five in the afternoon came and each received a denarius. 10So when those came
who were hired first, they expected to
receive more. But each one of them also
received a denarius. 11When they received
it, they began to grumble against the
landowner. 12‘These who were hired last
worked only one hour,’ they said, ‘and
you have made them equal to us who
have borne the burden of the work and
the heat of the day.’
13“But he answered one of them, ‘I am
not being unfair to you, friend. Didn’t you
agree to work for a denarius? 14Take your
pay and go. I want to give the one who was
hired last the same as I gave you. 15Don’t I
have the right to do what I want with my
own money? Or are you envious because
I am generous?’
16“So the last will be first, and the first
will be last.”

Jesus Predicts His Death a Third Time

17Now Jesus was going up to Jerusalem.
On the way, he took the Twelve aside and
said to them, 18“We are going up to Jerusalem, and the Son of Man will be delivered
over to the chief priests and the teachers of
the law. They will condemn him to death
19and will hand him over to the Gentiles
to be mocked and flogged and crucified.
On the third day he will be raised to life!”

A Mother’s Request

20Then the mother of Zebedee’s sons
came to Jesus with her sons and, kneeling
down, asked a favor of him.
21“What is it you want?” he asked.
She said, “Grant that one of these two
sons of mine may sit at your right and
the other at your left in your kingdom.”
22“You don’t know what you are asking,”
Jesus said to them. “Can you drink the cup
I am going to drink?”
“We can,” they answered.
23Jesus said to them, “You will indeed
drink from my cup, but to sit at my right
or left is not for me to grant. These places
belong to those for whom they have been
prepared by my Father.”
24When the ten heard about this, they

[a] 29 Some manuscripts do not have *or wife*. [b] 2 A denarius was the usual daily wage of a day laborer.

were indignant with the two brothers. 25 Jesus called them together and said, "You know that the rulers of the Gentiles lord it over them, and their high officials exercise authority over them. 26 Not so with you. Instead, whoever wants to become great among you must be your servant, 27 and whoever wants to be first must be your slave — 28 just as the Son of Man did not come to be served, but to serve, and to give his life as a ransom for many."

Two Blind Men Receive Sight

29 As Jesus and his disciples were leaving Jericho, a large crowd followed him. 30 Two blind men were sitting by the roadside, and when they heard that Jesus was going by, they shouted, "Lord, Son of David, have mercy on us!"

31 The crowd rebuked them and told them to be quiet, but they shouted all the louder, "Lord, Son of David, have mercy on us!"

32 Jesus stopped and called them. "What do you want me to do for you?" he asked.

33 "Lord," they answered, "we want our sight."

34 Jesus had compassion on them and touched their eyes. Immediately they received their sight and followed him.

Jesus Comes to Jerusalem as King

21 As they approached Jerusalem and came to Bethphage on the Mount of Olives, Jesus sent two disciples, 2 saying to them, "Go to the village ahead of you, and at once you will find a donkey tied there, with her colt by her. Untie them and bring them to me. 3 If anyone says anything to you, say that the Lord needs them, and he will send them right away."

4 This took place to fulfill what was spoken through the prophet:

5 "Say to Daughter Zion,
'See, your king comes to you,
gentle and riding on a donkey,
and on a colt, the foal of a donkey.' "[a]

6 The disciples went and did as Jesus had instructed them. 7 They brought the donkey and the colt and placed their cloaks on them for Jesus to sit on. 8 A very large crowd spread their cloaks on the road, while others cut branches from the trees and spread them on the road. 9 The crowds that went ahead of him and those that followed shouted,

"Hosanna[b] to the Son of David!"

"Blessed is he who comes in the name of the Lord!"[c]

"Hosanna[b] in the highest heaven!"

10 When Jesus entered Jerusalem, the whole city was stirred and asked, "Who is this?"

11 The crowds answered, "This is Jesus, the prophet from Nazareth in Galilee."

Jesus at the Temple

12 Jesus entered the temple courts and drove out all who were buying and selling there. He overturned the tables of the money changers and the benches of those selling doves. 13 "It is written," he said to them, " 'My house will be called a house of prayer,'[d] but you are making it 'a den of robbers.'[e]"

14 The blind and the lame came to him at the temple, and he healed them. 15 But when the chief priests and the teachers of the law saw the wonderful things he did and the children shouting in the temple courts, "Hosanna to the Son of David," they were indignant.

16 "Do you hear what these children are saying?" they asked him.

"Yes," replied Jesus, "have you never read,

" 'From the lips of children and infants
you, Lord, have called forth your praise'[f]?"

17 And he left them and went out of the city to Bethany, where he spent the night.

Jesus Curses a Fig Tree

18 Early in the morning, as Jesus was on his way back to the city, he was hungry. 19 Seeing a fig tree by the road, he went up to it but found nothing on it except leaves. Then he said to it, "May you never bear fruit again!" Immediately the tree withered.

20 When the disciples saw this, they were amazed. "How did the fig tree wither so quickly?" they asked.

21 Jesus replied, "Truly I tell you, if you have faith and do not doubt, not only can you do what was done to the fig tree, but also you can say to this mountain, 'Go, throw yourself into the sea,' and it will be done. 22 If you believe, you will receive whatever you ask for in prayer."

[a] 5 Zech. 9:9 [b] 9 A Hebrew expression meaning "Save!" which became an exclamation of praise; also in verse 15 [c] 9 Psalm 118:25,26 [d] 13 Isaiah 56:7 [e] 13 Jer. 7:11 [f] 16 Psalm 8:2 (see Septuagint)

The Authority of Jesus Questioned

23 Jesus entered the temple courts, and, while he was teaching, the chief priests and the elders of the people came to him. "By what authority are you doing these things?" they asked. "And who gave you this authority?"

24 Jesus replied, "I will also ask you one question. If you answer me, I will tell you by what authority I am doing these things. 25 John's baptism — where did it come from? Was it from heaven, or of human origin?"

They discussed it among themselves and said, "If we say, 'From heaven,' he will ask, 'Then why didn't you believe him?' 26 But if we say, 'Of human origin' — we are afraid of the people, for they all hold that John was a prophet."

27 So they answered Jesus, "We don't know."

Then he said, "Neither will I tell you by what authority I am doing these things.

The Parable of the Two Sons

28 "What do you think? There was a man who had two sons. He went to the first and said, 'Son, go and work today in the vineyard.'

29 "'I will not,' he answered, but later he changed his mind and went.

30 "Then the father went to the other son and said the same thing. He answered, 'I will, sir,' but he did not go.

31 "Which of the two did what his father wanted?"

"The first," they answered.

Jesus said to them, "Truly I tell you, the tax collectors and the prostitutes are entering the kingdom of God ahead of you. 32 For John came to you to show you the way of righteousness, and you did not believe him, but the tax collectors and the prostitutes did. And even after you saw this, you did not repent and believe him.

The Parable of the Tenants

33 "Listen to another parable: There was a landowner who planted a vineyard. He put a wall around it, dug a winepress in it and built a watchtower. Then he rented the vineyard to some farmers and moved to another place. 34 When the harvest time approached, he sent his servants to the tenants to collect his fruit.

35 "The tenants seized his servants; they beat one, killed another, and stoned a third. 36 Then he sent other servants to them, more than the first time, and the tenants treated them the same way. 37 Last of all, he sent his son to them. 'They will respect my son,' he said.

38 "But when the tenants saw the son, they said to each other, 'This is the heir. Come, let's kill him and take his inheritance.' 39 So they took him and threw him out of the vineyard and killed him.

40 "Therefore, when the owner of the vineyard comes, what will he do to those tenants?"

41 "He will bring those wretches to a wretched end," they replied, "and he will rent the vineyard to other tenants, who will give him his share of the crop at harvest time."

42 Jesus said to them, "Have you never read in the Scriptures:

"'The stone the builders rejected
  has become the cornerstone;
the Lord has done this,
  and it is marvelous in our eyes'[a]?

43 "Therefore I tell you that the kingdom of God will be taken away from you and given to a people who will produce its fruit. 44 Anyone who falls on this stone will be broken to pieces; anyone on whom it falls will be crushed."[b]

45 When the chief priests and the Pharisees heard Jesus' parables, they knew he was talking about them. 46 They looked for a way to arrest him, but they were afraid of the crowd because the people held that he was a prophet.

The Parable of the Wedding Banquet

22 Jesus spoke to them again in parables, saying: 2 "The kingdom of heaven is like a king who prepared a wedding banquet for his son. 3 He sent his servants to those who had been invited to the banquet to tell them to come, but they refused to come.

4 "Then he sent some more servants and said, 'Tell those who have been invited that I have prepared my dinner: My oxen and fattened cattle have been butchered, and everything is ready. Come to the wedding banquet.'

5 "But they paid no attention and went off — one to his field, another to his business. 6 The rest seized his servants, mistreated them and killed them. 7 The king was enraged. He sent his army and destroyed those murderers and burned their city.

8 "Then he said to his servants, 'The wedding banquet is ready, but those I invited did not deserve to come. 9 So go to the street corners and invite to the banquet anyone you find.' 10 So the servants went out into the streets and gathered all the people they could find, the bad as well as

[a] 42 Psalm 118:22,23 [b] 44 Some manuscripts do not have verse 44.

the good, and the wedding hall was filled with guests.

[11]"But when the king came in to see the guests, he noticed a man there who was not wearing wedding clothes. [12]He asked, 'How did you get in here without wedding clothes, friend?' The man was speechless.

[13]"Then the king told the attendants, 'Tie him hand and foot, and throw him outside, into the darkness, where there will be weeping and gnashing of teeth.'

[14]"For many are invited, but few are chosen."

Paying the Imperial Tax to Caesar

[15]Then the Pharisees went out and laid plans to trap him in his words. [16]They sent their disciples to him along with the Herodians. "Teacher," they said, "we know that you are a man of integrity and that you teach the way of God in accordance with the truth. You aren't swayed by others, because you pay no attention to who they are. [17]Tell us then, what is your opinion? Is it right to pay the imperial tax[a] to Caesar or not?"

[18]But Jesus, knowing their evil intent, said, "You hypocrites, why are you trying to trap me? [19]Show me the coin used for paying the tax." They brought him a denarius, [20]and he asked them, "Whose image is this? And whose inscription?"

[21]"Caesar's," they replied.

Then he said to them, "So give back to Caesar what is Caesar's, and to God what is God's."

[22]When they heard this, they were amazed. So they left him and went away.

Marriage at the Resurrection

[23]That same day the Sadducees, who say there is no resurrection, came to him with a question. [24]"Teacher," they said, "Moses told us that if a man dies without having children, his brother must marry the widow and raise up offspring for him. [25]Now there were seven brothers among us. The first one married and died, and since he had no children, he left his wife to his brother. [26]The same thing happened to the second and third brother, right on down to the seventh. [27]Finally, the woman died. [28]Now then, at the resurrection, whose wife will she be of the seven, since all of them were married to her?"

[29]Jesus replied, "You are in error because you do not know the Scriptures or the power of God. [30]At the resurrection people will neither marry nor be given in marriage; they will be like the angels in heaven. [31]But about the resurrection of the dead — have you not read what God said to you, [32]'I am the God of Abraham, the God of Isaac, and the God of Jacob'[b]? He is not the God of the dead but of the living."

[33]When the crowds heard this, they were astonished at his teaching.

The Greatest Commandment

[34]Hearing that Jesus had silenced the Sadducees, the Pharisees got together. [35]One of them, an expert in the law, tested him with this question: [36]"Teacher, which is the greatest commandment in the Law?"

[37]Jesus replied: " 'Love the Lord your God with all your heart and with all your soul and with all your mind.'[c] [38]This is the first and greatest commandment. [39]And the second is like it: 'Love your neighbor as yourself.'[d] [40]All the Law and the Prophets hang on these two commandments."

Whose Son Is the Messiah?

[41]While the Pharisees were gathered together, Jesus asked them, [42]"What do you think about the Messiah? Whose son is he?"

"The son of David," they replied.

[43]He said to them, "How is it then that David, speaking by the Spirit, calls him 'Lord'? For he says,

[44]" 'The Lord said to my Lord:
"Sit at my right hand
until I put your enemies
under your feet." '[e]

[45]If then David calls him 'Lord,' how can he be his son?" [46]No one could say a word in reply, and from that day on no one dared to ask him any more questions.

A Warning Against Hypocrisy

23 Then Jesus said to the crowds and to his disciples: [2]"The teachers of the law and the Pharisees sit in Moses' seat. [3]So you must be careful to do everything they tell you. But do not do what they do, for they do not practice what they preach. [4]They tie up heavy, cumbersome loads and put them on other people's shoulders, but they themselves are not willing to lift a finger to move them.

[5]"Everything they do is done for people to see: They make their phylacteries[f] wide and the tassels on their garments long; [6]they love the place of honor at banquets

[a] 17 A special tax levied on subject peoples, not on Roman citizens [b] 32 Exodus 3:6
[c] 37 Deut. 6:5 [d] 39 Lev. 19:18 [e] 44 Psalm 110:1 [f] 5 That is, boxes containing Scripture verses, worn on forehead and arm

and the most important seats in the synagogues; 7they love to be greeted with respect in the marketplaces and to be called 'Rabbi' by others.

8"But you are not to be called 'Rabbi,' for you have one Teacher, and you are all brothers. 9And do not call anyone on earth 'father,' for you have one Father, and he is in heaven. 10Nor are you to be called instructors, for you have one Instructor, the Messiah. 11The greatest among you will be your servant. 12For those who exalt themselves will be humbled, and those who humble themselves will be exalted.

Seven Woes on the Teachers of the Law and the Pharisees

13"Woe to you, teachers of the law and Pharisees, you hypocrites! You shut the door of the kingdom of heaven in people's faces. You yourselves do not enter, nor will you let those enter who are trying to. [14][a]

15"Woe to you, teachers of the law and Pharisees, you hypocrites! You travel over land and sea to win a single convert, and when you have succeeded, you make them twice as much a child of hell as you are.

16"Woe to you, blind guides! You say, 'If anyone swears by the temple, it means nothing; but anyone who swears by the gold of the temple is bound by that oath.' 17You blind fools! Which is greater: the gold, or the temple that makes the gold sacred? 18You also say, 'If anyone swears by the altar, it means nothing; but anyone who swears by the gift on the altar is bound by that oath.' 19You blind men! Which is greater: the gift, or the altar that makes the gift sacred? 20Therefore, anyone who swears by the altar swears by it and by everything on it. 21And anyone who swears by the temple swears by it and by the one who dwells in it. 22And anyone who swears by heaven swears by God's throne and by the one who sits on it.

23"Woe to you, teachers of the law and Pharisees, you hypocrites! You give a tenth of your spices — mint, dill and cumin. But you have neglected the more important matters of the law — justice, mercy and faithfulness. You should have practiced the latter, without neglecting the former. 24You blind guides! You strain out a gnat but swallow a camel.

25"Woe to you, teachers of the law and Pharisees, you hypocrites! You clean the outside of the cup and dish, but inside they are full of greed and self-indulgence. 26Blind Pharisee! First clean the inside of the cup and dish, and then the outside also will be clean.

27"Woe to you, teachers of the law and Pharisees, you hypocrites! You are like whitewashed tombs, which look beautiful on the outside but on the inside are full of the bones of the dead and everything unclean. 28In the same way, on the outside you appear to people as righteous but on the inside you are full of hypocrisy and wickedness.

29"Woe to you, teachers of the law and Pharisees, you hypocrites! You build tombs for the prophets and decorate the graves of the righteous. 30And you say, 'If we had lived in the days of our ancestors, we would not have taken part with them in shedding the blood of the prophets.' 31So you testify against yourselves that you are the descendants of those who murdered the prophets. 32Go ahead, then, and complete what your ancestors started!

33"You snakes! You brood of vipers! How will you escape being condemned to hell? 34Therefore I am sending you prophets and sages and teachers. Some of them you will kill and crucify; others you will flog in your synagogues and pursue from town to town. 35And so upon you will come all the righteous blood that has been shed on earth, from the blood of righteous Abel to the blood of Zechariah son of Berekiah, whom you murdered between the temple and the altar. 36Truly I tell you, all this will come on this generation.

37"Jerusalem, Jerusalem, you who kill the prophets and stone those sent to you, how often I have longed to gather your children together, as a hen gathers her chicks under her wings, and you were not willing. 38Look, your house is left to you desolate. 39For I tell you, you will not see me again until you say, 'Blessed is he who comes in the name of the Lord.'[b]"

The Destruction of the Temple and Signs of the End Times

24 Jesus left the temple and was walking away when his disciples came up to him to call his attention to its buildings. 2"Do you see all these things?" he asked. "Truly I tell you, not one stone here will be left on another; every one will be thrown down."

3As Jesus was sitting on the Mount of Olives, the disciples came to him privately. "Tell us," they said, "when will this happen, and what will be the sign of your coming and of the end of the age?"

[a] *14* Some manuscripts include here words similar to Mark 12:40 and Luke 20:47.
[b] *39* Psalm 118:26

4Jesus answered: "Watch out that no
one deceives you. 5For many will come in
my name, claiming, 'I am the Messiah,'
and will deceive many. 6You will hear of
wars and rumors of wars, but see to it that
you are not alarmed. Such things must
happen, but the end is still to come. 7Na-
tion will rise against nation, and kingdom
against kingdom. There will be famines
and earthquakes in various places. 8All
these are the beginning of birth pains.

9"Then you will be handed over to be
persecuted and put to death, and you
will be hated by all nations because of
me. 10At that time many will turn away
from the faith and will betray and hate
each other, 11and many false prophets
will appear and deceive many people.
12Because of the increase of wickedness,
the love of most will grow cold, 13but the
one who stands firm to the end will be
saved. 14And this gospel of the kingdom
will be preached in the whole world as
a testimony to all nations, and then the
end will come.

15"So when you see standing in the holy
place 'the abomination that causes desolation,'[a] spoken of through the prophet
Daniel — let the reader understand —
16then let those who are in Judea flee to
the mountains. 17Let no one on the housetop go down to take anything out of the
house. 18Let no one in the field go back to
get their cloak. 19How dreadful it will be
in those days for pregnant women and
nursing mothers! 20Pray that your flight
will not take place in winter or on the
Sabbath. 21For then there will be great
distress, unequaled from the beginning
of the world until now — and never to be
equaled again.

22"If those days had not been cut short,
no one would survive, but for the sake of
the elect those days will be shortened. 23At
that time if anyone says to you, 'Look,
here is the Messiah!' or, 'There he is!' do
not believe it. 24For false messiahs and
false prophets will appear and perform
great signs and wonders to deceive, if
possible, even the elect. 25See, I have told
you ahead of time.

26"So if anyone tells you, 'There he is,
out in the wilderness,' do not go out; or,
'Here he is, in the inner rooms,' do not
believe it. 27For as lightning that comes
from the east is visible even in the west,
so will be the coming of the Son of Man.
28Wherever there is a carcass, there the
vultures will gather.

29"Immediately after the distress of
those days

"'the sun will be darkened,
and the moon will not give its light;
the stars will fall from the sky,
and the heavenly bodies will be
shaken.'[b]

30"Then will appear the sign of the Son
of Man in heaven. And then all the peoples of the earth[c] will mourn when they
see the Son of Man coming on the clouds
of heaven, with power and great glory.[d]
31And he will send his angels with a loud
trumpet call, and they will gather his elect
from the four winds, from one end of the
heavens to the other.

32"Now learn this lesson from the fig
tree: As soon as its twigs get tender and its
leaves come out, you know that summer
is near. 33Even so, when you see all these
things, you know that it[e] is near, right at
the door. 34Truly I tell you, this generation will certainly not pass away until
all these things have happened. 35Heaven
and earth will pass away, but my words
will never pass away.

The Day and Hour Unknown

36"But about that day or hour no one
knows, not even the angels in heaven,
nor the Son,[f] but only the Father. 37As it
was in the days of Noah, so it will be at
the coming of the Son of Man. 38For in the
days before the flood, people were eating
and drinking, marrying and giving in
marriage, up to the day Noah entered
the ark; 39and they knew nothing about
what would happen until the flood came
and took them all away. That is how it
will be at the coming of the Son of Man.
40Two men will be in the field; one will be
taken and the other left. 41Two women will
be grinding with a hand mill; one will be
taken and the other left.

42"Therefore keep watch, because you do
not know on what day your Lord will come.
43But understand this: If the owner of the
house had known at what time of night
the thief was coming, he would have kept
watch and would not have let his house be
broken into. 44So you also must be ready,
because the Son of Man will come at an
hour when you do not expect him.

45"Who then is the faithful and wise servant, whom the master has put in charge
of the servants in his household to give
them their food at the proper time? 46It
will be good for that servant whose master

[a] *15* Daniel 9:27; 11:31; 12:11 [b] *29* Isaiah 13:10; 34:4 [c] *30* Or *the tribes of the land* [d] *30* See Daniel 7:13-14. [e] *33* Or *he* [f] *36* Some manuscripts do not have *nor the Son.*

finds him doing so when he returns. 47Truly I tell you, he will put him in charge of all his possessions. 48But suppose that servant is wicked and says to himself, 'My master is staying away a long time,' 49and he then begins to beat his fellow servants and to eat and drink with drunkards. 50The master of that servant will come on a day when he does not expect him and at an hour he is not aware of. 51He will cut him to pieces and assign him a place with the hypocrites, where there will be weeping and gnashing of teeth.

The Parable of the Ten Virgins

25 "At that time the kingdom of heaven will be like ten virgins who took their lamps and went out to meet the bridegroom. 2Five of them were foolish and five were wise. 3The foolish ones took their lamps but did not take any oil with them. 4The wise ones, however, took oil in jars along with their lamps. 5The bridegroom was a long time in coming, and they all became drowsy and fell asleep.

6"At midnight the cry rang out: 'Here's the bridegroom! Come out to meet him!'

7"Then all the virgins woke up and trimmed their lamps. 8The foolish ones said to the wise, 'Give us some of your oil; our lamps are going out.'

9" 'No,' they replied, 'there may not be enough for both us and you. Instead, go to those who sell oil and buy some for yourselves.'

10"But while they were on their way to buy the oil, the bridegroom arrived. The virgins who were ready went in with him to the wedding banquet. And the door was shut.

11"Later the others also came. 'Lord, Lord,' they said, 'open the door for us!'

12"But he replied, 'Truly I tell you, I don't know you.'

13"Therefore keep watch, because you do not know the day or the hour.

The Parable of the Bags of Gold

14"Again, it will be like a man going on a journey, who called his servants and entrusted his wealth to them. 15To one he gave five bags of gold, to another two bags, and to another one bag,[a] each according to his ability. Then he went on his journey. 16The man who had received five bags of gold went at once and put his money to work and gained five bags more. 17So also, the one with two bags of gold gained two more. 18But the man who had received one bag went off, dug a hole in the ground and hid his master's money.

19"After a long time the master of those servants returned and settled accounts with them. 20The man who had received five bags of gold brought the other five. 'Master,' he said, 'you entrusted me with five bags of gold. See, I have gained five more.'

21"His master replied, 'Well done, good and faithful servant! You have been faithful with a few things; I will put you in charge of many things. Come and share your master's happiness!'

22"The man with two bags of gold also came. 'Master,' he said, 'you entrusted me with two bags of gold; see, I have gained two more.'

23"His master replied, 'Well done, good and faithful servant! You have been faithful with a few things; I will put you in charge of many things. Come and share your master's happiness!'

24"Then the man who had received one bag of gold came. 'Master,' he said, 'I knew that you are a hard man, harvesting where you have not sown and gathering where you have not scattered seed. 25So I was afraid and went out and hid your gold in the ground. See, here is what belongs to you.'

26"His master replied, 'You wicked, lazy servant! So you knew that I harvest where I have not sown and gather where I have not scattered seed? 27Well then, you should have put my money on deposit with the bankers, so that when I returned I would have received it back with interest.

28" 'So take the bag of gold from him and give it to the one who has ten bags. 29For whoever has will be given more, and they will have an abundance. Whoever does not have, even what they have will be taken from them. 30And throw that worthless servant outside, into the darkness, where there will be weeping and gnashing of teeth.'

The Sheep and the Goats

31"When the Son of Man comes in his glory, and all the angels with him, he will sit on his glorious throne. 32All the nations will be gathered before him, and he will separate the people one from another as a shepherd separates the sheep from the goats. 33He will put the sheep on his right and the goats on his left.

34"Then the King will say to those on his right, 'Come, you who are blessed by my Father; take your inheritance,

[a] *15* Greek *five talents . . . two talents . . . one talent*; also throughout this parable; a talent was worth about 20 years of a day laborer's wage.

the kingdom prepared for you since the creation of the world. 35For I was hungry and you gave me something to eat, I was thirsty and you gave me something to drink, I was a stranger and you invited me in, 36I needed clothes and you clothed me, I was sick and you looked after me, I was in prison and you came to visit me.'

37"Then the righteous will answer him, 'Lord, when did we see you hungry and feed you, or thirsty and give you something to drink? 38When did we see you a stranger and invite you in, or needing clothes and clothe you? 39When did we see you sick or in prison and go to visit you?'

40"The King will reply, 'Truly I tell you, whatever you did for one of the least of these brothers and sisters of mine, you did for me.'

41"Then he will say to those on his left, 'Depart from me, you who are cursed, into the eternal fire prepared for the devil and his angels. 42For I was hungry and you gave me nothing to eat, I was thirsty and you gave me nothing to drink, 43I was a stranger and you did not invite me in, I needed clothes and you did not clothe me, I was sick and in prison and you did not look after me.'

44"They also will answer, 'Lord, when did we see you hungry or thirsty or a stranger or needing clothes or sick or in prison, and did not help you?'

45"He will reply, 'Truly I tell you, whatever you did not do for one of the least of these, you did not do for me.'

46"Then they will go away to eternal punishment, but the righteous to eternal life."

The Plot Against Jesus

26 When Jesus had finished saying all these things, he said to his disciples, 2"As you know, the Passover is two days away—and the Son of Man will be handed over to be crucified."

3Then the chief priests and the elders of the people assembled in the palace of the high priest, whose name was Caiaphas, 4and they schemed to arrest Jesus secretly and kill him. 5"But not during the festival," they said, "or there may be a riot among the people."

Jesus Anointed at Bethany

6While Jesus was in Bethany in the home of Simon the Leper, 7a woman came to him with an alabaster jar of very expensive perfume, which she poured on his head as he was reclining at the table.

8When the disciples saw this, they were indignant. "Why this waste?" they asked. 9"This perfume could have been sold at a high price and the money given to the poor."

10Aware of this, Jesus said to them, "Why are you bothering this woman? She has done a beautiful thing to me. 11The poor you will always have with you,[a] but you will not always have me. 12When she poured this perfume on my body, she did it to prepare me for burial. 13Truly I tell you, wherever this gospel is preached throughout the world, what she has done will also be told, in memory of her."

Judas Agrees to Betray Jesus

14Then one of the Twelve—the one called Judas Iscariot—went to the chief priests 15and asked, "What are you willing to give me if I deliver him over to you?" So they counted out for him thirty pieces of silver. 16From then on Judas watched for an opportunity to hand him over.

The Last Supper

17On the first day of the Festival of Unleavened Bread, the disciples came to Jesus and asked, "Where do you want us to make preparations for you to eat the Passover?"

18He replied, "Go into the city to a certain man and tell him, 'The Teacher says: My appointed time is near. I am going to celebrate the Passover with my disciples at your house.'" 19So the disciples did as Jesus had directed them and prepared the Passover.

20When evening came, Jesus was reclining at the table with the Twelve. 21And while they were eating, he said, "Truly I tell you, one of you will betray me."

22They were very sad and began to say to him one after the other, "Surely you don't mean me, Lord?"

23Jesus replied, "The one who has dipped his hand into the bowl with me will betray me. 24The Son of Man will go just as it is written about him. But woe to that man who betrays the Son of Man! It would be better for him if he had not been born."

25Then Judas, the one who would betray him, said, "Surely you don't mean me, Rabbi?"

Jesus answered, "You have said so."

26While they were eating, Jesus took bread, and when he had given thanks, he broke it and gave it to his disciples, saying, "Take and eat; this is my body."

[a] 11 See Deut. 15:11.

27 Then he took a cup, and when he had given thanks, he gave it to them, saying, "Drink from it, all of you. 28 This is my blood of the[a] covenant, which is poured out for many for the forgiveness of sins. 29 I tell you, I will not drink from this fruit of the vine from now on until that day when I drink it new with you in my Father's kingdom."

30 When they had sung a hymn, they went out to the Mount of Olives.

Jesus Predicts Peter's Denial

31 Then Jesus told them, "This very night you will all fall away on account of me, for it is written:

> "'I will strike the shepherd,
> and the sheep of the flock will be scattered.'[b]

32 But after I have risen, I will go ahead of you into Galilee."

33 Peter replied, "Even if all fall away on account of you, I never will."

34 "Truly I tell you," Jesus answered, "this very night, before the rooster crows, you will disown me three times."

35 But Peter declared, "Even if I have to die with you, I will never disown you." And all the other disciples said the same.

Gethsemane

36 Then Jesus went with his disciples to a place called Gethsemane, and he said to them, "Sit here while I go over there and pray." 37 He took Peter and the two sons of Zebedee along with him, and he began to be sorrowful and troubled. 38 Then he said to them, "My soul is overwhelmed with sorrow to the point of death. Stay here and keep watch with me."

39 Going a little farther, he fell with his face to the ground and prayed, "My Father, if it is possible, may this cup be taken from me. Yet not as I will, but as you will."

40 Then he returned to his disciples and found them sleeping. "Couldn't you men keep watch with me for one hour?" he asked Peter. 41 "Watch and pray so that you will not fall into temptation. The spirit is willing, but the flesh is weak."

42 He went away a second time and prayed, "My Father, if it is not possible for this cup to be taken away unless I drink it, may your will be done."

43 When he came back, he again found them sleeping, because their eyes were heavy. 44 So he left them and went away once more and prayed the third time, saying the same thing.

45 Then he returned to the disciples and said to them, "Are you still sleeping and resting? Look, the hour has come, and the Son of Man is delivered into the hands of sinners. 46 Rise! Let us go! Here comes my betrayer!"

Jesus Arrested

47 While he was still speaking, Judas, one of the Twelve, arrived. With him was a large crowd armed with swords and clubs, sent from the chief priests and the elders of the people. 48 Now the betrayer had arranged a signal with them: "The one I kiss is the man; arrest him." 49 Going at once to Jesus, Judas said, "Greetings, Rabbi!" and kissed him.

50 Jesus replied, "Do what you came for, friend."[c]

Then the men stepped forward, seized Jesus and arrested him. 51 With that, one of Jesus' companions reached for his sword, drew it out and struck the servant of the high priest, cutting off his ear.

52 "Put your sword back in its place," Jesus said to him, "for all who draw the sword will die by the sword. 53 Do you think I cannot call on my Father, and he will at once put at my disposal more than twelve legions of angels? 54 But how then would the Scriptures be fulfilled that say it must happen in this way?"

55 In that hour Jesus said to the crowd, "Am I leading a rebellion, that you have come out with swords and clubs to capture me? Every day I sat in the temple courts teaching, and you did not arrest me. 56 But this has all taken place that the writings of the prophets might be fulfilled." Then all the disciples deserted him and fled.

Jesus Before the Sanhedrin

57 Those who had arrested Jesus took him to Caiaphas the high priest, where the teachers of the law and the elders had assembled. 58 But Peter followed him at a distance, right up to the courtyard of the high priest. He entered and sat down with the guards to see the outcome.

59 The chief priests and the whole Sanhedrin were looking for false evidence against Jesus so that they could put him to death. 60 But they did not find any, though many false witnesses came forward.

Finally two came forward 61 and declared, "This fellow said, 'I am able to destroy the temple of God and rebuild it in three days.'"

62 Then the high priest stood up and said to Jesus, "Are you not going to answer?

[a] *28* Some manuscripts *the new* [b] *31* Zech. 13:7 [c] *50* Or *"Why have you come, friend?"*

What is this testimony that these men are bringing against you?" 63But Jesus remained silent.

The high priest said to him, "I charge you under oath by the living God: Tell us if you are the Messiah, the Son of God."

64"You have said so," Jesus replied. "But I say to all of you: From now on you will see the Son of Man sitting at the right hand of the Mighty One and coming on the clouds of heaven."[a]

65Then the high priest tore his clothes and said, "He has spoken blasphemy! Why do we need any more witnesses? Look, now you have heard the blasphemy. 66What do you think?"

"He is worthy of death," they answered.

67Then they spit in his face and struck him with their fists. Others slapped him 68and said, "Prophesy to us, Messiah. Who hit you?"

Peter Disowns Jesus

69Now Peter was sitting out in the courtyard, and a servant girl came to him. "You also were with Jesus of Galilee," she said.

70But he denied it before them all. "I don't know what you're talking about," he said.

71Then he went out to the gateway, where another servant girl saw him and said to the people there, "This fellow was with Jesus of Nazareth."

72He denied it again, with an oath: "I don't know the man!"

73After a little while, those standing there went up to Peter and said, "Surely you are one of them; your accent gives you away."

74Then he began to call down curses, and he swore to them, "I don't know the man!"

Immediately a rooster crowed. 75Then Peter remembered the word Jesus had spoken: "Before the rooster crows, you will disown me three times." And he went outside and wept bitterly.

Judas Hangs Himself

27 Early in the morning, all the chief priests and the elders of the people made their plans how to have Jesus executed. 2So they bound him, led him away and handed him over to Pilate the governor.

3When Judas, who had betrayed him, saw that Jesus was condemned, he was seized with remorse and returned the thirty pieces of silver to the chief priests and the elders. 4"I have sinned," he said, "for I have betrayed innocent blood."

"What is that to us?" they replied. "That's your responsibility."

5So Judas threw the money into the temple and left. Then he went away and hanged himself.

6The chief priests picked up the coins and said, "It is against the law to put this into the treasury, since it is blood money." 7So they decided to use the money to buy the potter's field as a burial place for foreigners. 8That is why it has been called the Field of Blood to this day. 9Then what was spoken by Jeremiah the prophet was fulfilled: "They took the thirty pieces of silver, the price set on him by the people of Israel, 10and they used them to buy the potter's field, as the Lord commanded me."[b]

Jesus Before Pilate

11Meanwhile Jesus stood before the governor, and the governor asked him, "Are you the king of the Jews?"

"You have said so," Jesus replied.

12When he was accused by the chief priests and the elders, he gave no answer. 13Then Pilate asked him, "Don't you hear the testimony they are bringing against you?" 14But Jesus made no reply, not even to a single charge—to the great amazement of the governor.

15Now it was the governor's custom at the festival to release a prisoner chosen by the crowd. 16At that time they had a well-known prisoner whose name was Jesus[c] Barabbas. 17So when the crowd had gathered, Pilate asked them, "Which one do you want me to release to you: Jesus Barabbas, or Jesus who is called the Messiah?" 18For he knew it was out of self-interest that they had handed Jesus over to him.

19While Pilate was sitting on the judge's seat, his wife sent him this message: "Don't have anything to do with that innocent man, for I have suffered a great deal today in a dream because of him."

20But the chief priests and the elders persuaded the crowd to ask for Barabbas and to have Jesus executed.

21"Which of the two do you want me to release to you?" asked the governor.

"Barabbas," they answered.

22"What shall I do, then, with Jesus who is called the Messiah?" Pilate asked.

They all answered, "Crucify him!"

23"Why? What crime has he committed?" asked Pilate.

But they shouted all the louder, "Crucify him!"

[a] *64* See Psalm 110:1; Daniel 7:13. [b] *10* See Zech. 11:12,13; Jer. 19:1-13; 32:6-9. [c] *16* Many manuscripts do not have *Jesus*; also in verse 17.

24 When Pilate saw that he was getting
nowhere, but that instead an uproar was
starting, he took water and washed his
hands in front of the crowd. "I am innocent of this man's blood," he said. "It is
your responsibility!"
25 All the people answered, "His blood is
on us and on our children!"
26 Then he released Barabbas to them.
But he had Jesus flogged, and handed him
over to be crucified.

The Soldiers Mock Jesus

27 Then the governor's soldiers took
Jesus into the Praetorium and gathered
the whole company of soldiers around
him. 28 They stripped him and put a scarlet
robe on him, 29 and then twisted together
a crown of thorns and set it on his head.
They put a staff in his right hand. Then
they knelt in front of him and mocked
him. "Hail, king of the Jews!" they said.
30 They spit on him, and took the staff and
struck him on the head again and again.
31 After they had mocked him, they took off
the robe and put his own clothes on him.
Then they led him away to crucify him.

The Crucifixion of Jesus

32 As they were going out, they met a
man from Cyrene, named Simon, and
they forced him to carry the cross. 33 They
came to a place called Golgotha (which
means "the place of the skull"). 34 There
they offered Jesus wine to drink, mixed
with gall; but after tasting it, he refused
to drink it. 35 When they had crucified him,
they divided up his clothes by casting lots.
36 And sitting down, they kept watch over
him there. 37 Above his head they placed
the written charge against him: THIS IS
JESUS, THE KING OF THE JEWS.
38 Two rebels were crucified with him,
one on his right and one on his left.
39 Those who passed by hurled insults at
him, shaking their heads 40 and saying,
"You who are going to destroy the temple
and build it in three days, save yourself!
Come down from the cross, if you are the
Son of God!" 41 In the same way the chief
priests, the teachers of the law and the
elders mocked him. 42 "He saved others,"
they said, "but he can't save himself! He's
the king of Israel! Let him come down
now from the cross, and we will believe
in him. 43 He trusts in God. Let God rescue
him now if he wants him, for he said, 'I
am the Son of God.'" 44 In the same way
the rebels who were crucified with him
also heaped insults on him.

The Death of Jesus

45 From noon until three in the afternoon
darkness came over all the land. 46 About
three in the afternoon Jesus cried out in
a loud voice, *"Eli, Eli,[a] lema sabachthani?"*
(which means "My God, my God, why have
you forsaken me?").[b]
47 When some of those standing there
heard this, they said, "He's calling Elijah."
48 Immediately one of them ran and got
a sponge. He filled it with wine vinegar,
put it on a staff, and offered it to Jesus
to drink. 49 The rest said, "Now leave him
alone. Let's see if Elijah comes to save
him."
50 And when Jesus had cried out again in
a loud voice, he gave up his spirit.
51 At that moment the curtain of the temple was torn in two from top to bottom.
The earth shook, the rocks split 52 and the
tombs broke open. The bodies of many
holy people who had died were raised to
life. 53 They came out of the tombs after
Jesus' resurrection and[c] went into the
holy city and appeared to many people.
54 When the centurion and those with
him who were guarding Jesus saw the
earthquake and all that had happened,
they were terrified, and exclaimed, "Surely
he was the Son of God!"
55 Many women were there, watching
from a distance. They had followed Jesus
from Galilee to care for his needs. 56 Among
them were Mary Magdalene, Mary the
mother of James and Joseph,[d] and the
mother of Zebedee's sons.

The Burial of Jesus

57 As evening approached, there came a
rich man from Arimathea, named Joseph,
who had himself become a disciple of
Jesus. 58 Going to Pilate, he asked for Jesus'
body, and Pilate ordered that it be given
to him. 59 Joseph took the body, wrapped
it in a clean linen cloth, 60 and placed it in
his own new tomb that he had cut out of
the rock. He rolled a big stone in front of
the entrance to the tomb and went away.
61 Mary Magdalene and the other Mary
were sitting there opposite the tomb.

The Guard at the Tomb

62 The next day, the one after Preparation Day, the chief priests and the Pharisees went to Pilate. 63 "Sir," they said, "we
remember that while he was still alive that
deceiver said, 'After three days I will rise
again.' 64 So give the order for the tomb
to be made secure until the third day.

[a] 46 Some manuscripts *Eloi, Eloi* [b] 46 Psalm 22:1 [c] 53 Or *tombs, and after Jesus' resurrection they* [d] 56 Greek *Joses,* a variant of *Joseph*

Otherwise, his disciples may come and
steal the body and tell the people that he
has been raised from the dead. This last
deception will be worse than the first."
65 "Take a guard," Pilate answered. "Go,
make the tomb as secure as you know
how." 66 So they went and made the tomb
secure by putting a seal on the stone and
posting the guard.

Jesus Has Risen

28 After the Sabbath, at dawn on the
first day of the week, Mary Magdalene and the other Mary went to look
at the tomb.
2 There was a violent earthquake, for an
angel of the Lord came down from heav-
en and, going to the tomb, rolled back
the stone and sat on it. 3 His appearance
was like lightning, and his clothes were
white as snow. 4 The guards were so afraid
of him that they shook and became like
dead men.
5 The angel said to the women, "Do not
be afraid, for I know that you are looking
for Jesus, who was crucified. 6 He is not
here; he has risen, just as he said. Come
and see the place where he lay. 7 Then go
quickly and tell his disciples: 'He has risen
from the dead and is going ahead of you
into Galilee. There you will see him.' Now
I have told you."
8 So the women hurried away from the
tomb, afraid yet filled with joy, and ran
to tell his disciples. 9 Suddenly Jesus met
them. "Greetings," he said. They came
to him, clasped his feet and worshiped
him. 10 Then Jesus said to them, "Do not
be afraid. Go and tell my brothers to go to
Galilee; there they will see me."

The Guards' Report

11 While the women were on their way,
some of the guards went into the city and
reported to the chief priests everything
that had happened. 12 When the chief
priests had met with the elders and devised a plan, they gave the soldiers a large
sum of money, 13 telling them, "You are to
say, 'His disciples came during the night
and stole him away while we were asleep.'
14 If this report gets to the governor, we will
satisfy him and keep you out of trouble."
15 So the soldiers took the money and did
as they were instructed. And this story has
been widely circulated among the Jews to
this very day.

The Great Commission

16 Then the eleven disciples went to Galilee, to the mountain where Jesus had told
them to go. 17 When they saw him, they
worshiped him; but some doubted. 18 Then
Jesus came to them and said, "All authority in heaven and on earth has been given
to me. 19 Therefore go and make disciples
of all nations, baptizing them in the name
of the Father and of the Son and of the
Holy Spirit, 20 and teaching them to obey
everything I have commanded you. And
surely I am with you always, to the very
end of the age."

MARK

John the Baptist Prepares the Way

1 The beginning of the good news about
Jesus the Messiah,[a] the Son of God,[b] 2 as
it is written in Isaiah the prophet:

"I will send my messenger ahead of you,
who will prepare your way"[c] —
3 "a voice of one calling in the
wilderness,
'Prepare the way for the Lord,
make straight paths for him.' "[d]

4 And so John the Baptist appeared in the
wilderness, preaching a baptism of repentance for the forgiveness of sins. 5 The
whole Judean countryside and all the people of Jerusalem went out to him. Confessing their sins, they were baptized by him
in the Jordan River. 6 John wore clothing
made of camel's hair, with a leather belt
around his waist, and he ate locusts and
wild honey. 7 And this was his message:
"After me comes the one more powerful
than I, the straps of whose sandals I am
not worthy to stoop down and untie. 8 I
baptize you with[e] water, but he will baptize you with[e] the Holy Spirit."

The Baptism and Testing of Jesus

9 At that time Jesus came from Nazareth in Galilee and was baptized by John
in the Jordan. 10 Just as Jesus was coming
up out of the water, he saw heaven being
torn open and the Spirit descending on
him like a dove. 11 And a voice came from
heaven: "You are my Son, whom I love;
with you I am well pleased."
12 At once the Spirit sent him out into the
wilderness, 13 and he was in the wilderness
forty days, being tempted[f] by Satan. He
was with the wild animals, and angels
attended him.

Jesus Announces the Good News

14 After John was put in prison, Jesus
went into Galilee, proclaiming the good
news of God. 15 "The time has come," he
said. "The kingdom of God has come near.
Repent and believe the good news!"

Jesus Calls His First Disciples

16 As Jesus walked beside the Sea of
Galilee, he saw Simon and his brother
Andrew casting a net into the lake, for
they were fishermen. 17 "Come, follow me,"
Jesus said, "and I will send you out to fish
for people." 18 At once they left their nets
and followed him.
19 When he had gone a little farther, he
saw James son of Zebedee and his brother John in a boat, preparing their nets.
20 Without delay he called them, and they
left their father Zebedee in the boat with
the hired men and followed him.

Jesus Drives Out an Impure Spirit

21 They went to Capernaum, and when
the Sabbath came, Jesus went into the
synagogue and began to teach. 22 The people were amazed at his teaching, because
he taught them as one who had authority, not as the teachers of the law. 23 Just
then a man in their synagogue who was
possessed by an impure spirit cried out,
24 "What do you want with us, Jesus of
Nazareth? Have you come to destroy us? I
know who you are — the Holy One of God!"
25 "Be quiet!" said Jesus sternly. "Come
out of him!" 26 The impure spirit shook
the man violently and came out of him
with a shriek.
27 The people were all so amazed that
they asked each other, "What is this? A
new teaching — and with authority! He
even gives orders to impure spirits and
they obey him." 28 News about him spread
quickly over the whole region of Galilee.

Jesus Heals Many

29 As soon as they left the synagogue,
they went with James and John to the
home of Simon and Andrew. 30 Simon's
mother-in-law was in bed with a fever,
and they immediately told Jesus about
her. 31 So he went to her, took her hand
and helped her up. The fever left her and
she began to wait on them.
32 That evening after sunset the people
brought to Jesus all the sick and demon-
possessed. 33 The whole town gathered at
the door, 34 and Jesus healed many who
had various diseases. He also drove out
many demons, but he would not let the
demons speak because they knew who
he was.

[a] *1* Or *Jesus Christ. Messiah* (Hebrew) and *Christ* (Greek) both mean *Anointed One.* [b] *1* Some manuscripts do not have *the Son of God.* [c] *2* Mal. 3:1 [d] *3* Isaiah 40:3 [e] *8* Or *in* [f] *13* The Greek for *tempted* can also mean *tested.*

Jesus Prays in a Solitary Place

35Very early in the morning, while it was still dark, Jesus got up, left the house and went off to a solitary place, where he prayed. 36Simon and his companions went to look for him, 37and when they found him, they exclaimed: "Everyone is looking for you!"

38Jesus replied, "Let us go somewhere else — to the nearby villages — so I can preach there also. That is why I have come." 39So he traveled throughout Galilee, preaching in their synagogues and driving out demons.

Jesus Heals a Man With Leprosy

40A man with leprosy[a] came to him and begged him on his knees, "If you are willing, you can make me clean."

41Jesus was indignant.[b] He reached out his hand and touched the man. "I am willing," he said. "Be clean!" 42Immediately the leprosy left him and he was cleansed.

43Jesus sent him away at once with a strong warning: 44"See that you don't tell this to anyone. But go, show yourself to the priest and offer the sacrifices that Moses commanded for your cleansing, as a testimony to them." 45Instead he went out and began to talk freely, spreading the news. As a result, Jesus could no longer enter a town openly but stayed outside in lonely places. Yet the people still came to him from everywhere.

Jesus Forgives and Heals a Paralyzed Man

2 A few days later, when Jesus again entered Capernaum, the people heard that he had come home. 2They gathered in such large numbers that there was no room left, not even outside the door, and he preached the word to them. 3Some men came, bringing to him a paralyzed man, carried by four of them. 4Since they could not get him to Jesus because of the crowd, they made an opening in the roof above Jesus by digging through it and then lowered the mat the man was lying on. 5When Jesus saw their faith, he said to the paralyzed man, "Son, your sins are forgiven."

6Now some teachers of the law were sitting there, thinking to themselves, 7"Why does this fellow talk like that? He's blaspheming! Who can forgive sins but God alone?"

8Immediately Jesus knew in his spirit that this was what they were thinking in their hearts, and he said to them, "Why are you thinking these things? 9Which is easier: to say to this paralyzed man, 'Your sins are forgiven,' or to say, 'Get up, take your mat and walk'? 10But I want you to know that the Son of Man has authority on earth to forgive sins." So he said to the man, 11"I tell you, get up, take your mat and go home." 12He got up, took his mat and walked out in full view of them all. This amazed everyone and they praised God, saying, "We have never seen anything like this!"

Jesus Calls Levi and Eats With Sinners

13Once again Jesus went out beside the lake. A large crowd came to him, and he began to teach them. 14As he walked along, he saw Levi son of Alphaeus sitting at the tax collector's booth. "Follow me," Jesus told him, and Levi got up and followed him.

15While Jesus was having dinner at Levi's house, many tax collectors and sinners were eating with him and his disciples, for there were many who followed him. 16When the teachers of the law who were Pharisees saw him eating with the sinners and tax collectors, they asked his disciples: "Why does he eat with tax collectors and sinners?"

17On hearing this, Jesus said to them, "It is not the healthy who need a doctor, but the sick. I have not come to call the righteous, but sinners."

Jesus Questioned About Fasting

18Now John's disciples and the Pharisees were fasting. Some people came and asked Jesus, "How is it that John's disciples and the disciples of the Pharisees are fasting, but yours are not?"

19Jesus answered, "How can the guests of the bridegroom fast while he is with them? They cannot, so long as they have him with them. 20But the time will come when the bridegroom will be taken from them, and on that day they will fast.

21"No one sews a patch of unshrunk cloth on an old garment. Otherwise, the new piece will pull away from the old, making the tear worse. 22And no one pours new wine into old wineskins. Otherwise, the wine will burst the skins, and both the wine and the wineskins will be ruined. No, they pour new wine into new wineskins."

Jesus Is Lord of the Sabbath

23One Sabbath Jesus was going through the grainfields, and as his disciples walked along, they began to pick some heads of

[a] 40 The Greek word traditionally translated *leprosy* was used for various diseases affecting the skin. [b] 41 Many manuscripts *Jesus was filled with compassion*

grain. 24 The Pharisees said to him, "Look, why are they doing what is unlawful on the Sabbath?"

25 He answered, "Have you never read what David did when he and his companions were hungry and in need? 26 In the days of Abiathar the high priest, he entered the house of God and ate the consecrated bread, which is lawful only for priests to eat. And he also gave some to his companions."

27 Then he said to them, "The Sabbath was made for man, not man for the Sabbath. 28 So the Son of Man is Lord even of the Sabbath."

Jesus Heals on the Sabbath

3 Another time Jesus went into the synagogue, and a man with a shriveled hand was there. 2 Some of them were looking for a reason to accuse Jesus, so they watched him closely to see if he would heal him on the Sabbath. 3 Jesus said to the man with the shriveled hand, "Stand up in front of everyone."

4 Then Jesus asked them, "Which is lawful on the Sabbath: to do good or to do evil, to save life or to kill?" But they remained silent.

5 He looked around at them in anger and, deeply distressed at their stubborn hearts, said to the man, "Stretch out your hand." He stretched it out, and his hand was completely restored. 6 Then the Pharisees went out and began to plot with the Herodians how they might kill Jesus.

Crowds Follow Jesus

7 Jesus withdrew with his disciples to the lake, and a large crowd from Galilee followed. 8 When they heard about all he was doing, many people came to him from Judea, Jerusalem, Idumea, and the regions across the Jordan and around Tyre and Sidon. 9 Because of the crowd he told his disciples to have a small boat ready for him, to keep the people from crowding him. 10 For he had healed many, so that those with diseases were pushing forward to touch him. 11 Whenever the impure spirits saw him, they fell down before him and cried out, "You are the Son of God." 12 But he gave them strict orders not to tell others about him.

Jesus Appoints the Twelve

13 Jesus went up on a mountainside and called to him those he wanted, and they came to him. 14 He appointed twelve[a] that they might be with him and that he might send them out to preach 15 and to have authority to drive out demons. 16 These are the twelve he appointed: Simon (to whom he gave the name Peter), 17 James son of Zebedee and his brother John (to them he gave the name Boanerges, which means "sons of thunder"), 18 Andrew, Philip, Bartholomew, Matthew, Thomas, James son of Alphaeus, Thaddaeus, Simon the Zealot 19 and Judas Iscariot, who betrayed him.

Jesus Accused by His Family and by Teachers of the Law

20 Then Jesus entered a house, and again a crowd gathered, so that he and his disciples were not even able to eat. 21 When his family[b] heard about this, they went to take charge of him, for they said, "He is out of his mind."

22 And the teachers of the law who came down from Jerusalem said, "He is possessed by Beelzebul! By the prince of demons he is driving out demons."

23 So Jesus called them over to him and began to speak to them in parables: "How can Satan drive out Satan? 24 If a kingdom is divided against itself, that kingdom cannot stand. 25 If a house is divided against itself, that house cannot stand. 26 And if Satan opposes himself and is divided, he cannot stand; his end has come. 27 In fact, no one can enter a strong man's house without first tying him up. Then he can plunder the strong man's house. 28 Truly I tell you, people can be forgiven all their sins and every slander they utter, 29 but whoever blasphemes against the Holy Spirit will never be forgiven; they are guilty of an eternal sin."

30 He said this because they were saying, "He has an impure spirit."

31 Then Jesus' mother and brothers arrived. Standing outside, they sent someone in to call him. 32 A crowd was sitting around him, and they told him, "Your mother and brothers are outside looking for you."

33 "Who are my mother and my brothers?" he asked.

34 Then he looked at those seated in a circle around him and said, "Here are my mother and my brothers! 35 Whoever does God's will is my brother and sister and mother."

The Parable of the Sower

4 Again Jesus began to teach by the lake. The crowd that gathered around him was so large that he got into a boat and sat in it out on the lake, while all

[a] 14 Some manuscripts *twelve — designating them apostles —*

[b] 21 Or *his associates*

the people were along the shore at the
water's edge. 2He taught them many
things by parables, and in his teaching
said: 3"Listen! A farmer went out to sow
his seed. 4As he was scattering the seed,
some fell along the path, and the birds
came and ate it up. 5Some fell on rocky
places, where it did not have much soil.
It sprang up quickly, because the soil was
shallow. 6But when the sun came up, the
plants were scorched, and they withered
because they had no root. 7Other seed
fell among thorns, which grew up and
choked the plants, so that they did not
bear grain. 8Still other seed fell on good
soil. It came up, grew and produced a crop,
some multiplying thirty, some sixty, some
a hundred times."

9Then Jesus said, "Whoever has ears to
hear, let them hear."

10When he was alone, the Twelve and
the others around him asked him about
the parables. 11He told them, "The secret
of the kingdom of God has been given to
you. But to those on the outside everything
is said in parables 12so that,

"'they may be ever seeing but never
perceiving,
and ever hearing but never
understanding;
otherwise they might turn and be
forgiven!'[a]"

13Then Jesus said to them, "Don't you
understand this parable? How then will
you understand any parable? 14The farmer sows the word. 15Some people are like
seed along the path, where the word
is sown. As soon as they hear it, Satan
comes and takes away the word that
was sown in them. 16Others, like seed
sown on rocky places, hear the word and
at once receive it with joy. 17But since
they have no root, they last only a short
time. When trouble or persecution comes
because of the word, they quickly fall
away. 18Still others, like seed sown among
thorns, hear the word; 19but the worries
of this life, the deceitfulness of wealth
and the desires for other things come in
and choke the word, making it unfruitful. 20Others, like seed sown on good soil,
hear the word, accept it, and produce a
crop — some thirty, some sixty, some a
hundred times what was sown."

A Lamp on a Stand

21He said to them, "Do you bring in
a lamp to put it under a bowl or a bed?
Instead, don't you put it on its stand?
22For whatever is hidden is meant to be
disclosed, and whatever is concealed is
meant to be brought out into the open. 23If
anyone has ears to hear, let them hear."

24"Consider carefully what you hear," he
continued. "With the measure you use, it
will be measured to you — and even more.
25Whoever has will be given more; whoever
does not have, even what they have will
be taken from them."

The Parable of the Growing Seed

26He also said, "This is what the kingdom of God is like. A man scatters seed
on the ground. 27Night and day, whether
he sleeps or gets up, the seed sprouts and
grows, though he does not know how. 28All
by itself the soil produces grain — first the
stalk, then the head, then the full kernel
in the head. 29As soon as the grain is ripe,
he puts the sickle to it, because the harvest has come."

The Parable of the Mustard Seed

30Again he said, "What shall we say the
kingdom of God is like, or what parable
shall we use to describe it? 31It is like a
mustard seed, which is the smallest of
all seeds on earth. 32Yet when planted, it
grows and becomes the largest of all garden plants, with such big branches that
the birds can perch in its shade."

33With many similar parables Jesus
spoke the word to them, as much as they
could understand. 34He did not say anything to them without using a parable. But
when he was alone with his own disciples,
he explained everything.

Jesus Calms the Storm

35That day when evening came, he said
to his disciples, "Let us go over to the other
side." 36Leaving the crowd behind, they
took him along, just as he was, in the boat.
There were also other boats with him. 37A
furious squall came up, and the waves
broke over the boat, so that it was nearly
swamped. 38Jesus was in the stern, sleeping on a cushion. The disciples woke him
and said to him, "Teacher, don't you care
if we drown?"

39He got up, rebuked the wind and said
to the waves, "Quiet! Be still!" Then the
wind died down and it was completely
calm.

40He said to his disciples, "Why are you
so afraid? Do you still have no faith?"

41They were terrified and asked each
other, "Who is this? Even the wind and
the waves obey him!"

[a] *12* Isaiah 6:9,10

Jesus Restores a Demon-Possessed Man

5 They went across the lake to the region
of the Gerasenes.[a] 2When Jesus got
out of the boat, a man with an impure
spirit came from the tombs to meet him.
3This man lived in the tombs, and no one
could bind him anymore, not even with
a chain. 4For he had often been chained
hand and foot, but he tore the chains
apart and broke the irons on his feet. No
one was strong enough to subdue him.
5Night and day among the tombs and in
the hills he would cry out and cut himself
with stones.

6When he saw Jesus from a distance,
he ran and fell on his knees in front of
him. 7He shouted at the top of his voice,
"What do you want with me, Jesus, Son of
the Most High God? In God's name don't
torture me!" 8For Jesus had said to him,
"Come out of this man, you impure spirit!"

9Then Jesus asked him, "What is your
name?"

"My name is Legion," he replied, "for we
are many." 10And he begged Jesus again
and again not to send them out of the
area.

11A large herd of pigs was feeding on
the nearby hillside. 12The demons begged
Jesus, "Send us among the pigs; allow us to
go into them." 13He gave them permission,
and the impure spirits came out and went
into the pigs. The herd, about two thousand in number, rushed down the steep
bank into the lake and were drowned.

14Those tending the pigs ran off and reported this in the town and countryside,
and the people went out to see what had
happened. 15When they came to Jesus,
they saw the man who had been possessed by the legion of demons, sitting
there, dressed and in his right mind; and
they were afraid. 16Those who had seen
it told the people what had happened to
the demon-possessed man — and told
about the pigs as well. 17Then the people began to plead with Jesus to leave
their region.

18As Jesus was getting into the boat,
the man who had been demon-possessed
begged to go with him. 19Jesus did not
let him, but said, "Go home to your own
people and tell them how much the Lord
has done for you, and how he has had
mercy on you." 20So the man went away
and began to tell in the Decapolis[b] how
much Jesus had done for him. And all the
people were amazed.

Jesus Raises a Dead Girl and Heals a Sick Woman

21When Jesus had again crossed over by
boat to the other side of the lake, a large
crowd gathered around him while he was
by the lake. 22Then one of the synagogue
leaders, named Jairus, came, and when he
saw Jesus, he fell at his feet. 23He pleaded
earnestly with him, "My little daughter is
dying. Please come and put your hands on
her so that she will be healed and live."
24So Jesus went with him.

A large crowd followed and pressed
around him. 25And a woman was there
who had been subject to bleeding for
twelve years. 26She had suffered a great
deal under the care of many doctors and
had spent all she had, yet instead of getting better she grew worse. 27When she
heard about Jesus, she came up behind
him in the crowd and touched his cloak,
28because she thought, "If I just touch
his clothes, I will be healed." 29Immedi-
ately her bleeding stopped and she felt
in her body that she was freed from her
suffering.

30At once Jesus realized that power had
gone out from him. He turned around in
the crowd and asked, "Who touched my
clothes?"

31"You see the people crowding against
you," his disciples answered, "and yet you
can ask, 'Who touched me?' "

32But Jesus kept looking around to see
who had done it. 33Then the woman, knowing what had happened to her, came and
fell at his feet and, trembling with fear,
told him the whole truth. 34He said to her,
"Daughter, your faith has healed you. Go
in peace and be freed from your suffering."

35While Jesus was still speaking, some
people came from the house of Jairus,
the synagogue leader. "Your daughter is
dead," they said. "Why bother the teacher
anymore?"

36Overhearing[c] what they said, Jesus
told him, "Don't be afraid; just believe."

37He did not let anyone follow him except Peter, James and John the brother of
James. 38When they came to the home of
the synagogue leader, Jesus saw a commotion, with people crying and wailing
loudly. 39He went in and said to them,
"Why all this commotion and wailing?
The child is not dead but asleep." 40But
they laughed at him.

After he put them all out, he took the
child's father and mother and the disciples
who were with him, and went in where

[a] *1* Some manuscripts *Gadarenes*; other manuscripts *Gergesenes* [b] *20* That is, the Ten Cities
[c] *36* Or *Ignoring*

the child was. 41He took her by the hand
and said to her, *"Talitha koum!"* (which
means "Little girl, I say to you, get up!").
42Immediately the girl stood up and began
to walk around (she was twelve years old).
At this they were completely astonished.
43He gave strict orders not to let anyone
know about this, and told them to give
her something to eat.

A Prophet Without Honor

6 Jesus left there and went to his hometown, accompanied by his disciples.
2When the Sabbath came, he began to
teach in the synagogue, and many who
heard him were amazed.

"Where did this man get these things?"
they asked. "What's this wisdom that has
been given him? What are these remarkable miracles he is performing? 3Isn't this
the carpenter? Isn't this Mary's son and
the brother of James, Joseph,[a] Judas and
Simon? Aren't his sisters here with us?"
And they took offense at him.

4Jesus said to them, "A prophet is not
without honor except in his own town,
among his relatives and in his own home."
5He could not do any miracles there, except lay his hands on a few sick people
and heal them. 6He was amazed at their
lack of faith.

Jesus Sends Out the Twelve

Then Jesus went around teaching from
village to village. 7Calling the Twelve to
him, he began to send them out two by
two and gave them authority over impure spirits.

8These were his instructions: "Take
nothing for the journey except a staff —
no bread, no bag, no money in your belts.
9Wear sandals but not an extra shirt.
10Whenever you enter a house, stay there
until you leave that town. 11And if any
place will not welcome you or listen to
you, leave that place and shake the dust
off your feet as a testimony against them."

12They went out and preached that people should repent. 13They drove out many
demons and anointed many sick people
with oil and healed them.

John the Baptist Beheaded

14King Herod heard about this, for Jesus'
name had become well known. Some were
saying,[b] "John the Baptist has been raised
from the dead, and that is why miraculous
powers are at work in him."

15Others said, "He is Elijah."

And still others claimed, "He is a prophet, like one of the prophets of long ago."

16But when Herod heard this, he said,
"John, whom I beheaded, has been raised
from the dead!"

17For Herod himself had given orders
to have John arrested, and he had him
bound and put in prison. He did this because of Herodias, his brother Philip's
wife, whom he had married. 18For John
had been saying to Herod, "It is not lawful
for you to have your brother's wife." 19So
Herodias nursed a grudge against John
and wanted to kill him. But she was not
able to, 20because Herod feared John and
protected him, knowing him to be a righteous and holy man. When Herod heard
John, he was greatly puzzled[c]; yet he liked
to listen to him.

21Finally the opportune time came. On
his birthday Herod gave a banquet for his
high officials and military commanders
and the leading men of Galilee. 22When
the daughter of[d] Herodias came in and
danced, she pleased Herod and his dinner guests.

The king said to the girl, "Ask me for
anything you want, and I'll give it to
you." 23And he promised her with an oath,
"Whatever you ask I will give you, up to
half my kingdom."

24She went out and said to her mother,
"What shall I ask for?"

"The head of John the Baptist," she answered.

25At once the girl hurried in to the king
with the request: "I want you to give me
right now the head of John the Baptist
on a platter."

26The king was greatly distressed,
but because of his oaths and his dinner
guests, he did not want to refuse her. 27So
he immediately sent an executioner with
orders to bring John's head. The man
went, beheaded John in the prison, 28and
brought back his head on a platter. He
presented it to the girl, and she gave it to
her mother. 29On hearing of this, John's
disciples came and took his body and
laid it in a tomb.

Jesus Feeds the Five Thousand

30The apostles gathered around Jesus
and reported to him all they had done and
taught. 31Then, because so many people
were coming and going that they did not
even have a chance to eat, he said to them,
"Come with me by yourselves to a quiet
place and get some rest."

[a] 3 Greek *Joses,* a variant of *Joseph* [b] 14 Some early manuscripts *He was saying* [c] 20 Some early manuscripts *he did many things* [d] 22 Some early manuscripts *When his daughter*

32 So they went away by themselves in a
boat to a solitary place. 33 But many who
saw them leaving recognized them and
ran on foot from all the towns and got
there ahead of them. 34 When Jesus landed
and saw a large crowd, he had compassion
on them, because they were like sheep
without a shepherd. So he began teaching
them many things.

35 By this time it was late in the day, so
his disciples came to him. "This is a remote
place," they said, "and it's already very
late. 36 Send the people away so that they
can go to the surrounding countryside
and villages and buy themselves something to eat."

37 But he answered, "You give them
something to eat."

They said to him, "That would take
more than half a year's wages[a]! Are we
to go and spend that much on bread and
give it to them to eat?"

38 "How many loaves do you have?" he
asked. "Go and see."

When they found out, they said, "Five—
and two fish."

39 Then Jesus directed them to have all
the people sit down in groups on the green
grass. 40 So they sat down in groups of hundreds and fifties. 41 Taking the five loaves
and the two fish and looking up to heaven,
he gave thanks and broke the loaves. Then
he gave them to his disciples to distribute
to the people. He also divided the two
fish among them all. 42 They all ate and
were satisfied, 43 and the disciples picked
up twelve basketfuls of broken pieces of
bread and fish. 44 The number of the men
who had eaten was five thousand.

Jesus Walks on the Water

45 Immediately Jesus made his disciples get into the boat and go on ahead of
him to Bethsaida, while he dismissed the
crowd. 46 After leaving them, he went up
on a mountainside to pray.

47 Later that night, the boat was in the
middle of the lake, and he was alone on
land. 48 He saw the disciples straining at
the oars, because the wind was against
them. Shortly before dawn he went out to
them, walking on the lake. He was about
to pass by them, 49 but when they saw him
walking on the lake, they thought he was
a ghost. They cried out, 50 because they all
saw him and were terrified.

Immediately he spoke to them and said,
"Take courage! It is I. Don't be afraid."
51 Then he climbed into the boat with them,
and the wind died down. They were completely amazed, 52 for they had not understood about the loaves; their hearts were
hardened.

53 When they had crossed over, they
landed at Gennesaret and anchored there.
54 As soon as they got out of the boat, people recognized Jesus. 55 They ran throughout that whole region and carried the sick
on mats to wherever they heard he was.
56 And wherever he went—into villages,
towns or countryside—they placed the
sick in the marketplaces. They begged
him to let them touch even the edge of his
cloak, and all who touched it were healed.

That Which Defiles

7 The Pharisees and some of the teachers
of the law who had come from Jerusalem gathered around Jesus 2 and saw some
of his disciples eating food with hands
that were defiled, that is, unwashed. 3 (The
Pharisees and all the Jews do not eat unless they give their hands a ceremonial
washing, holding to the tradition of the
elders. 4 When they come from the marketplace they do not eat unless they wash.
And they observe many other traditions,
such as the washing of cups, pitchers and
kettles.[b])

5 So the Pharisees and teachers of the
law asked Jesus, "Why don't your disciples live according to the tradition of the
elders instead of eating their food with
defiled hands?"

6 He replied, "Isaiah was right when
he prophesied about you hypocrites; as
it is written:

"'These people honor me with their lips,
but their hearts are far from me.
7 They worship me in vain;
their teachings are merely human
rules.'[c]

8 You have let go of the commands of God
and are holding on to human traditions."

9 And he continued, "You have a fine
way of setting aside the commands of God
in order to observe[d] your own traditions!
10 For Moses said, 'Honor your father and
mother,'[e] and, 'Anyone who curses their father or mother is to be put to death.'[f] 11 But
you say that if anyone declares that what
might have been used to help their father
or mother is Corban (that is, devoted to
God)— 12 then you no longer let them do
anything for their father or mother. 13 Thus

[a] 37 Greek *take two hundred denarii* [b] 4 Some early manuscripts *pitchers, kettles and dining couches* [c] 6,7 Isaiah 29:13 [d] 9 Some manuscripts *set up* [e] 10 Exodus 20:12; Deut. 5:16 [f] 10 Exodus 21:17; Lev. 20:9

you nullify the word of God by your tradition that you have handed down. And you do many things like that."

14 Again Jesus called the crowd to him and said, "Listen to me, everyone, and understand this. 15 Nothing outside a person can defile them by going into them. Rather, it is what comes out of a person that defiles them." [16][a]

17 After he had left the crowd and entered the house, his disciples asked him about this parable. 18 "Are you so dull?" he asked. "Don't you see that nothing that enters a person from the outside can defile them? 19 For it doesn't go into their heart but into their stomach, and then out of the body." (In saying this, Jesus declared all foods clean.)

20 He went on: "What comes out of a person is what defiles them. 21 For it is from within, out of a person's heart, that evil thoughts come — sexual immorality, theft, murder, 22 adultery, greed, malice, deceit, lewdness, envy, slander, arrogance and folly. 23 All these evils come from inside and defile a person."

Jesus Honors a Syrophoenician Woman's Faith

24 Jesus left that place and went to the vicinity of Tyre.[b] He entered a house and did not want anyone to know it; yet he could not keep his presence secret. 25 In fact, as soon as she heard about him, a woman whose little daughter was possessed by an impure spirit came and fell at his feet. 26 The woman was a Greek, born in Syrian Phoenicia. She begged Jesus to drive the demon out of her daughter.

27 "First let the children eat all they want," he told her, "for it is not right to take the children's bread and toss it to the dogs."

28 "Lord," she replied, "even the dogs under the table eat the children's crumbs."

29 Then he told her, "For such a reply, you may go; the demon has left your daughter."

30 She went home and found her child lying on the bed, and the demon gone.

Jesus Heals a Deaf and Mute Man

31 Then Jesus left the vicinity of Tyre and went through Sidon, down to the Sea of Galilee and into the region of the Decapolis.[c] 32 There some people brought to him a man who was deaf and could hardly talk, and they begged Jesus to place his hand on him.

33 After he took him aside, away from the crowd, Jesus put his fingers into the man's ears. Then he spit and touched the man's tongue. 34 He looked up to heaven and with a deep sigh said to him, *"Ephphatha!"* (which means "Be opened!"). 35 At this, the man's ears were opened, his tongue was loosened and he began to speak plainly.

36 Jesus commanded them not to tell anyone. But the more he did so, the more they kept talking about it. 37 People were overwhelmed with amazement. "He has done everything well," they said. "He even makes the deaf hear and the mute speak."

Jesus Feeds the Four Thousand

8 During those days another large crowd gathered. Since they had nothing to eat, Jesus called his disciples to him and said, 2 "I have compassion for these people; they have already been with me three days and have nothing to eat. 3 If I send them home hungry, they will collapse on the way, because some of them have come a long distance."

4 His disciples answered, "But where in this remote place can anyone get enough bread to feed them?"

5 "How many loaves do you have?" Jesus asked.

"Seven," they replied.

6 He told the crowd to sit down on the ground. When he had taken the seven loaves and given thanks, he broke them and gave them to his disciples to distribute to the people, and they did so. 7 They had a few small fish as well; he gave thanks for them also and told the disciples to distribute them. 8 The people ate and were satisfied. Afterward the disciples picked up seven basketfuls of broken pieces that were left over. 9 About four thousand were present. After he had sent them away, 10 he got into the boat with his disciples and went to the region of Dalmanutha.

11 The Pharisees came and began to question Jesus. To test him, they asked him for a sign from heaven. 12 He sighed deeply and said, "Why does this generation ask for a sign? Truly I tell you, no sign will be given to it." 13 Then he left them, got back into the boat and crossed to the other side.

The Yeast of the Pharisees and Herod

14 The disciples had forgotten to bring bread, except for one loaf they had with them in the boat. 15 "Be careful," Jesus warned them. "Watch out for the yeast of the Pharisees and that of Herod."

[a] *16* Some manuscripts include here the words of 4:23. [b] *24* Many early manuscripts *Tyre and Sidon* [c] *31* That is, the Ten Cities

16 They discussed this with one another
and said, "It is because we have no bread."
17 Aware of their discussion, Jesus asked
them: "Why are you talking about having
no bread? Do you still not see or understand? Are your hearts hardened? 18 Do
you have eyes but fail to see, and ears but
fail to hear? And don't you remember?
19 When I broke the five loaves for the five
thousand, how many basketfuls of pieces
did you pick up?"
"Twelve," they replied.
20 "And when I broke the seven loaves for
the four thousand, how many basketfuls
of pieces did you pick up?"
They answered, "Seven."
21 He said to them, "Do you still not understand?"

Jesus Heals a Blind Man at Bethsaida

22 They came to Bethsaida, and some
people brought a blind man and begged
Jesus to touch him. 23 He took the blind
man by the hand and led him outside the
village. When he had spit on the man's
eyes and put his hands on him, Jesus
asked, "Do you see anything?"
24 He looked up and said, "I see people;
they look like trees walking around."
25 Once more Jesus put his hands on the
man's eyes. Then his eyes were opened, his
sight was restored, and he saw everything
clearly. 26 Jesus sent him home, saying,
"Don't even go into[a] the village."

Peter Declares That Jesus Is the Messiah

27 Jesus and his disciples went on to the
villages around Caesarea Philippi. On
the way he asked them, "Who do people
say I am?"
28 They replied, "Some say John the Baptist; others say Elijah; and still others, one
of the prophets."
29 "But what about you?" he asked. "Who
do you say I am?"
Peter answered, "You are the Messiah."
30 Jesus warned them not to tell anyone
about him.

Jesus Predicts His Death

31 He then began to teach them that the
Son of Man must suffer many things and
be rejected by the elders, the chief priests
and the teachers of the law, and that he
must be killed and after three days rise
again. 32 He spoke plainly about this, and
Peter took him aside and began to rebuke him.
33 But when Jesus turned and looked at
his disciples, he rebuked Peter. "Get behind
me, Satan!" he said. "You do not have in
mind the concerns of God, but merely
human concerns."

The Way of the Cross

34 Then he called the crowd to him along
with his disciples and said: "Whoever
wants to be my disciple must deny themselves and take up their cross and follow
me. 35 For whoever wants to save their life[b]
will lose it, but whoever loses their life for
me and for the gospel will save it. 36 What
good is it for someone to gain the whole
world, yet forfeit their soul? 37 Or what can
anyone give in exchange for their soul? 38 If
anyone is ashamed of me and my words
in this adulterous and sinful generation,
the Son of Man will be ashamed of them
when he comes in his Father's glory with
the holy angels."
9 And he said to them, "Truly I tell you,
some who are standing here will not
taste death before they see that the kingdom of God has come with power."

The Transfiguration

2 After six days Jesus took Peter, James
and John with him and led them up a
high mountain, where they were all alone.
There he was transfigured before them.
3 His clothes became dazzling white, whiter than anyone in the world could bleach
them. 4 And there appeared before them
Elijah and Moses, who were talking with
Jesus.
5 Peter said to Jesus, "Rabbi, it is good
for us to be here. Let us put up three shelters — one for you, one for Moses and one
for Elijah." 6 (He did not know what to say,
they were so frightened.)
7 Then a cloud appeared and covered
them, and a voice came from the cloud:
"This is my Son, whom I love. Listen to
him!"
8 Suddenly, when they looked around,
they no longer saw anyone with them
except Jesus.
9 As they were coming down the mountain, Jesus gave them orders not to tell
anyone what they had seen until the
Son of Man had risen from the dead.
10 They kept the matter to themselves,
discussing what "rising from the dead"
meant.
11 And they asked him, "Why do the
teachers of the law say that Elijah must
come first?"

[a] *26* Some manuscripts *go and tell anyone in* [b] *35* The Greek word means either *life* or *soul*;
also in verses 36 and 37.

12 Jesus replied, "To be sure, Elijah does come first, and restores all things. Why then is it written that the Son of Man must suffer much and be rejected? 13 But I tell you, Elijah has come, and they have done to him everything they wished, just as it is written about him."

Jesus Heals a Boy Possessed by an Impure Spirit

14 When they came to the other disciples, they saw a large crowd around them and the teachers of the law arguing with them. 15 As soon as all the people saw Jesus, they were overwhelmed with wonder and ran to greet him.

16 "What are you arguing with them about?" he asked.

17 A man in the crowd answered, "Teacher, I brought you my son, who is possessed by a spirit that has robbed him of speech. 18 Whenever it seizes him, it throws him to the ground. He foams at the mouth, gnashes his teeth and becomes rigid. I asked your disciples to drive out the spirit, but they could not."

19 "You unbelieving generation," Jesus replied, "how long shall I stay with you? How long shall I put up with you? Bring the boy to me."

20 So they brought him. When the spirit saw Jesus, it immediately threw the boy into a convulsion. He fell to the ground and rolled around, foaming at the mouth.

21 Jesus asked the boy's father, "How long has he been like this?"

"From childhood," he answered. 22 "It has often thrown him into fire or water to kill him. But if you can do anything, take pity on us and help us."

23 " 'If you can'?" said Jesus. "Everything is possible for one who believes."

24 Immediately the boy's father exclaimed, "I do believe; help me overcome my unbelief!"

25 When Jesus saw that a crowd was running to the scene, he rebuked the impure spirit. "You deaf and mute spirit," he said, "I command you, come out of him and never enter him again."

26 The spirit shrieked, convulsed him violently and came out. The boy looked so much like a corpse that many said, "He's dead." 27 But Jesus took him by the hand and lifted him to his feet, and he stood up.

28 After Jesus had gone indoors, his disciples asked him privately, "Why couldn't we drive it out?"

29 He replied, "This kind can come out only by prayer.[a]"

Jesus Predicts His Death a Second Time

30 They left that place and passed through Galilee. Jesus did not want anyone to know where they were, 31 because he was teaching his disciples. He said to them, "The Son of Man is going to be delivered into the hands of men. They will kill him, and after three days he will rise." 32 But they did not understand what he meant and were afraid to ask him about it.

33 They came to Capernaum. When he was in the house, he asked them, "What were you arguing about on the road?" 34 But they kept quiet because on the way they had argued about who was the greatest.

35 Sitting down, Jesus called the Twelve and said, "Anyone who wants to be first must be the very last, and the servant of all."

36 He took a little child whom he placed among them. Taking the child in his arms, he said to them, 37 "Whoever welcomes one of these little children in my name welcomes me; and whoever welcomes me does not welcome me but the one who sent me."

Whoever Is Not Against Us Is for Us

38 "Teacher," said John, "we saw someone driving out demons in your name and we told him to stop, because he was not one of us."

39 "Do not stop him," Jesus said. "For no one who does a miracle in my name can in the next moment say anything bad about me, 40 for whoever is not against us is for us. 41 Truly I tell you, anyone who gives you a cup of water in my name because you belong to the Messiah will certainly not lose their reward.

Causing to Stumble

42 "If anyone causes one of these little ones — those who believe in me — to stumble, it would be better for them if a large millstone were hung around their neck and they were thrown into the sea. 43 If your hand causes you to stumble, cut it off. It is better for you to enter life maimed than with two hands to go into hell, where the fire never goes out. [44][b] 45 And if your foot causes you to stumble, cut it off. It is better for you to enter life crippled than to have two feet and be thrown into hell. [46][b] 47 And if your eye causes you to stumble, pluck it out. It is better for you to enter the

[a] 29 Some manuscripts *prayer and fasting* [b] 44,46 Some manuscripts include here the words of verse 48.

kingdom of God with one eye than to have
two eyes and be thrown into hell, 48where

"'the worms that eat them do not die,
and the fire is not quenched.'[a]

49Everyone will be salted with fire.
50"Salt is good, but if it loses its saltiness,
how can you make it salty again? Have
salt among yourselves, and be at peace
with each other."

Divorce

10 Jesus then left that place and went
into the region of Judea and across
the Jordan. Again crowds of people came to
him, and as was his custom, he taught them.
2Some Pharisees came and tested him
by asking, "Is it lawful for a man to divorce his wife?"
3"What did Moses command you?" he
replied.
4They said, "Moses permitted a man
to write a certificate of divorce and send
her away."
5"It was because your hearts were hard
that Moses wrote you this law," Jesus replied. 6"But at the beginning of creation
God 'made them male and female.'[b] 7'For
this reason a man will leave his father and
mother and be united to his wife,[c] 8and
the two will become one flesh.'[d] So they
are no longer two, but one flesh. 9There-
fore what God has joined together, let no
one separate."
10When they were in the house again,
the disciples asked Jesus about this. 11He
answered, "Anyone who divorces his wife
and marries another woman commits
adultery against her. 12And if she divorces
her husband and marries another man,
she commits adultery."

The Little Children and Jesus

13People were bringing little children
to Jesus for him to place his hands on
them, but the disciples rebuked them.
14When Jesus saw this, he was indignant.
He said to them, "Let the little children
come to me, and do not hinder them, for
the kingdom of God belongs to such as
these. 15Truly I tell you, anyone who will
not receive the kingdom of God like a little
child will never enter it." 16And he took the
children in his arms, placed his hands on
them and blessed them.

The Rich and the Kingdom of God

17As Jesus started on his way, a man ran
up to him and fell on his knees before him.
"Good teacher," he asked, "what must I
do to inherit eternal life?"
18"Why do you call me good?" Jesus answered. "No one is good — except God
alone. 19You know the commandments:
'You shall not murder, you shall not commit adultery, you shall not steal, you shall
not give false testimony, you shall not
defraud, honor your father and mother.'[e]"
20"Teacher," he declared, "all these I
have kept since I was a boy."
21Jesus looked at him and loved him.
"One thing you lack," he said. "Go, sell
everything you have and give to the poor,
and you will have treasure in heaven.
Then come, follow me."
22At this the man's face fell. He went
away sad, because he had great wealth.
23Jesus looked around and said to his
disciples, "How hard it is for the rich to
enter the kingdom of God!"
24The disciples were amazed at his
words. But Jesus said again, "Children,
how hard it is[f] to enter the kingdom of
God! 25It is easier for a camel to go through
the eye of a needle than for someone who
is rich to enter the kingdom of God."
26The disciples were even more amazed,
and said to each other, "Who then can
be saved?"
27Jesus looked at them and said, "With
man this is impossible, but not with God;
all things are possible with God."
28Then Peter spoke up, "We have left
everything to follow you!"
29"Truly I tell you," Jesus replied, "no one
who has left home or brothers or sisters or
mother or father or children or fields for
me and the gospel 30will fail to receive a
hundred times as much in this present age:
homes, brothers, sisters, mothers, children
and fields — along with persecutions — and
in the age to come eternal life. 31But many
who are first will be last, and the last first."

Jesus Predicts His Death a Third Time

32They were on their way up to Jerusalem, with Jesus leading the way, and the
disciples were astonished, while those
who followed were afraid. Again he took
the Twelve aside and told them what was
going to happen to him. 33"We are going
up to Jerusalem," he said, "and the Son
of Man will be delivered over to the chief
priests and the teachers of the law. They
will condemn him to death and will hand
him over to the Gentiles, 34who will mock
him and spit on him, flog him and kill
him. Three days later he will rise."

[a] *48* Isaiah 66:24 [b] *6* Gen. 1:27 [c] *7* Some early manuscripts do not have *and be united to his wife.* [d] *8* Gen. 2:24 [e] *19* Exodus 20:12-16; Deut. 5:16-20 [f] *24* Some manuscripts *is for those who trust in riches*

The Request of James and John

35Then James and John, the sons of
Zebedee, came to him. "Teacher," they
said, "we want you to do for us whatever
we ask."
36"What do you want me to do for you?"
he asked.
37They replied, "Let one of us sit at your
right and the other at your left in your
glory."
38"You don't know what you are asking," Jesus said. "Can you drink the cup
I drink or be baptized with the baptism I
am baptized with?"
39"We can," they answered.
Jesus said to them, "You will drink the
cup I drink and be baptized with the baptism I am baptized with, 40but to sit at my
right or left is not for me to grant. These
places belong to those for whom they have
been prepared."
41When the ten heard about this, they
became indignant with James and John.
42Jesus called them together and said,
"You know that those who are regarded
as rulers of the Gentiles lord it over them,
and their high officials exercise authority over them. 43Not so with you. Instead,
whoever wants to become great among
you must be your servant, 44and whoever
wants to be first must be slave of all. 45For
even the Son of Man did not come to be
served, but to serve, and to give his life as
a ransom for many."

Blind Bartimaeus Receives His Sight

46Then they came to Jericho. As Jesus
and his disciples, together with a large
crowd, were leaving the city, a blind man,
Bartimaeus (which means "son of Timae-
us"), was sitting by the roadside begging.
47When he heard that it was Jesus of Nazareth, he began to shout, "Jesus, Son of
David, have mercy on me!"
48Many rebuked him and told him to be
quiet, but he shouted all the more, "Son
of David, have mercy on me!"
49Jesus stopped and said, "Call him."
So they called to the blind man, "Cheer
up! On your feet! He's calling you."
50Throwing his cloak aside, he jumped
to his feet and came to Jesus.
51"What do you want me to do for you?"
Jesus asked him.
The blind man said, "Rabbi, I want to
see."
52"Go," said Jesus, "your faith has healed
you." Immediately he received his sight
and followed Jesus along the road.

Jesus Comes to Jerusalem as King

11 As they approached Jerusalem and
came to Bethphage and Bethany at
the Mount of Olives, Jesus sent two of his
disciples, 2saying to them, "Go to the village ahead of you, and just as you enter
it, you will find a colt tied there, which no
one has ever ridden. Untie it and bring it
here. 3If anyone asks you, 'Why are you
doing this?' say, 'The Lord needs it and
will send it back here shortly.'"
4They went and found a colt outside in
the street, tied at a doorway. As they untied it, 5some people standing there asked,
"What are you doing, untying that colt?"
6They answered as Jesus had told them to,
and the people let them go. 7When they
brought the colt to Jesus and threw their
cloaks over it, he sat on it. 8Many people
spread their cloaks on the road, while
others spread branches they had cut in
the fields. 9Those who went ahead and
those who followed shouted,

"Hosanna![a]"

"Blessed is he who comes in the name
of the Lord!"[b]

10 "Blessed is the coming kingdom of
our father David!"

"Hosanna in the highest heaven!"

11Jesus entered Jerusalem and went into
the temple courts. He looked around at
everything, but since it was already late,
he went out to Bethany with the Twelve.

Jesus Curses a Fig Tree and Clears the Temple Courts

12The next day as they were leaving
Bethany, Jesus was hungry. 13Seeing in the
distance a fig tree in leaf, he went to find
out if it had any fruit. When he reached
it, he found nothing but leaves, because
it was not the season for figs. 14Then he
said to the tree, "May no one ever eat fruit
from you again." And his disciples heard
him say it.
15On reaching Jerusalem, Jesus entered
the temple courts and began driving out
those who were buying and selling there.
He overturned the tables of the money
changers and the benches of those selling
doves, 16and would not allow anyone to
carry merchandise through the temple
courts. 17And as he taught them, he said,
"Is it not written: 'My house will be called
a house of prayer for all nations'[c]? But you
have made it 'a den of robbers.'[d]"

[a] 9 A Hebrew expression meaning "Save!" which became an exclamation of praise; also in verse 10 [b] 9 Psalm 118:25,26 [c] 17 Isaiah 56:7 [d] 17 Jer. 7:11

18The chief priests and the teachers of
the law heard this and began looking for
a way to kill him, for they feared him,
because the whole crowd was amazed at
his teaching.
19When evening came, Jesus and his
disciples[a] went out of the city.
20In the morning, as they went along,
they saw the fig tree withered from the
roots. 21Peter remembered and said to
Jesus, "Rabbi, look! The fig tree you cursed
has withered!"
22"Have faith in God," Jesus answered.
23"Truly[b] I tell you, if anyone says to this
mountain, 'Go, throw yourself into the
sea,' and does not doubt in their heart but
believes that what they say will happen,
it will be done for them. 24Therefore I tell
you, whatever you ask for in prayer, believe that you have received it, and it will
be yours. 25And when you stand praying, if
you hold anything against anyone, forgive
them, so that your Father in heaven may
forgive you your sins." [26][c]

The Authority of Jesus Questioned

27They arrived again in Jerusalem, and
while Jesus was walking in the temple
courts, the chief priests, the teachers of the
law and the elders came to him. 28"By what
authority are you doing these things?"
they asked. "And who gave you authority
to do this?"
29Jesus replied, "I will ask you one question. Answer me, and I will tell you by
what authority I am doing these things.
30John's baptism — was it from heaven,
or of human origin? Tell me!"
31They discussed it among themselves
and said, "If we say, 'From heaven,' he will
ask, 'Then why didn't you believe him?'
32But if we say, 'Of human origin' . . ." (They
feared the people, for everyone held that
John really was a prophet.)
33So they answered Jesus, "We don't know."
Jesus said, "Neither will I tell you by
what authority I am doing these things."

The Parable of the Tenants

12 Jesus then began to speak to them
in parables: "A man planted a vineyard. He put a wall around it, dug a pit
for the winepress and built a watchtower. Then he rented the vineyard to some
farmers and moved to another place. 2At
harvest time he sent a servant to the tenants to collect from them some of the fruit
of the vineyard. 3But they seized him, beat
him and sent him away empty-handed.
4Then he sent another servant to them;
they struck this man on the head and
treated him shamefully. 5He sent still another, and that one they killed. He sent
many others; some of them they beat,
others they killed.
6"He had one left to send, a son, whom
he loved. He sent him last of all, saying,
'They will respect my son.'
7"But the tenants said to one another,
'This is the heir. Come, let's kill him, and
the inheritance will be ours.' 8So they took
him and killed him, and threw him out of
the vineyard.
9"What then will the owner of the vineyard do? He will come and kill those tenants
and give the vineyard to others. 10Haven't
you read this passage of Scripture:

" 'The stone the builders rejected
has become the cornerstone;
11the Lord has done this,
and it is marvelous in our eyes'[d]?"

12Then the chief priests, the teachers of
the law and the elders looked for a way
to arrest him because they knew he had
spoken the parable against them. But they
were afraid of the crowd; so they left him
and went away.

Paying the Imperial Tax to Caesar

13Later they sent some of the Pharisees
and Herodians to Jesus to catch him in
his words. 14They came to him and said,
"Teacher, we know that you are a man of
integrity. You aren't swayed by others,
because you pay no attention to who they
are; but you teach the way of God in accordance with the truth. Is it right to pay the
imperial tax[e] to Caesar or not? 15Should
we pay or shouldn't we?"
But Jesus knew their hypocrisy. "Why
are you trying to trap me?" he asked.
"Bring me a denarius and let me look at
it." 16They brought the coin, and he asked
them, "Whose image is this? And whose
inscription?"
"Caesar's," they replied.
17Then Jesus said to them, "Give back to
Caesar what is Caesar's and to God what
is God's."
And they were amazed at him.

Marriage at the Resurrection

18Then the Sadducees, who say there
is no resurrection, came to him with a
question. 19"Teacher," they said, "Moses

[a] *19* Some early manuscripts *came, Jesus* [b] *22,23* Some early manuscripts *"If you have faith in God," Jesus answered, 23"truly* [c] *26* Some manuscripts include here words similar to Matt. 6:15. [d] *11* Psalm 118:22,23 [e] *14* A special tax levied on subject peoples, not on Roman citizens

wrote for us that if a man's brother dies and leaves a wife but no children, the man must marry the widow and raise up offspring for his brother. 20 Now there were seven brothers. The first one married and died without leaving any children. 21 The second one married the widow, but he also died, leaving no child. It was the same with the third. 22 In fact, none of the seven left any children. Last of all, the woman died too. 23 At the resurrection[a] whose wife will she be, since the seven were married to her?"

24 Jesus replied, "Are you not in error because you do not know the Scriptures or the power of God? 25 When the dead rise, they will neither marry nor be given in marriage; they will be like the angels in heaven. 26 Now about the dead rising — have you not read in the Book of Moses, in the account of the burning bush, how God said to him, 'I am the God of Abraham, the God of Isaac, and the God of Jacob'[b]? 27 He is not the God of the dead, but of the living. You are badly mistaken!"

The Greatest Commandment

28 One of the teachers of the law came and heard them debating. Noticing that Jesus had given them a good answer, he asked him, "Of all the commandments, which is the most important?"

29 "The most important one," answered Jesus, "is this: 'Hear, O Israel: The Lord our God, the Lord is one.[c] 30 Love the Lord your God with all your heart and with all your soul and with all your mind and with all your strength.'[d] 31 The second is this: 'Love your neighbor as yourself.'[e] There is no commandment greater than these."

32 "Well said, teacher," the man replied. "You are right in saying that God is one and there is no other but him. 33 To love him with all your heart, with all your understanding and with all your strength, and to love your neighbor as yourself is more important than all burnt offerings and sacrifices."

34 When Jesus saw that he had answered wisely, he said to him, "You are not far from the kingdom of God." And from then on no one dared ask him any more questions.

Whose Son Is the Messiah?

35 While Jesus was teaching in the temple courts, he asked, "Why do the teachers of the law say that the Messiah is the son of David? 36 David himself, speaking by the Holy Spirit, declared:

"'The Lord said to my Lord:
"Sit at my right hand
until I put your enemies
under your feet."'[f]

37 David himself calls him 'Lord.' How then can he be his son?"

The large crowd listened to him with delight.

Warning Against the Teachers of the Law

38 As he taught, Jesus said, "Watch out for the teachers of the law. They like to walk around in flowing robes and be greeted with respect in the marketplaces, 39 and have the most important seats in the synagogues and the places of honor at banquets. 40 They devour widows' houses and for a show make lengthy prayers. These men will be punished most severely."

The Widow's Offering

41 Jesus sat down opposite the place where the offerings were put and watched the crowd putting their money into the temple treasury. Many rich people threw in large amounts. 42 But a poor widow came and put in two very small copper coins, worth only a few cents.

43 Calling his disciples to him, Jesus said, "Truly I tell you, this poor widow has put more into the treasury than all the others. 44 They all gave out of their wealth; but she, out of her poverty, put in everything — all she had to live on."

The Destruction of the Temple and Signs of the End Times

13 As Jesus was leaving the temple, one of his disciples said to him, "Look, Teacher! What massive stones! What magnificent buildings!"

2 "Do you see all these great buildings?" replied Jesus. "Not one stone here will be left on another; every one will be thrown down."

3 As Jesus was sitting on the Mount of Olives opposite the temple, Peter, James, John and Andrew asked him privately, 4 "Tell us, when will these things happen? And what will be the sign that they are all about to be fulfilled?"

5 Jesus said to them: "Watch out that no one deceives you. 6 Many will come in my name, claiming, 'I am he,' and will

[a] 23 Some manuscripts *resurrection, when people rise from the dead,* [b] 26 Exodus 3:6
[c] 29 Or *The Lord our God is one Lord* [d] 30 Deut. 6:4,5 [e] 31 Lev. 19:18 [f] 36 Psalm 110:1

deceive many. 7When you hear of wars and rumors of wars, do not be alarmed. Such things must happen, but the end is still to come. 8Nation will rise against nation, and kingdom against kingdom. There will be earthquakes in various places, and famines. These are the beginning of birth pains.

9"You must be on your guard. You will be handed over to the local councils and flogged in the synagogues. On account of me you will stand before governors and kings as witnesses to them. 10And the gospel must first be preached to all nations. 11Whenever you are arrested and brought to trial, do not worry beforehand about what to say. Just say whatever is given you at the time, for it is not you speaking, but the Holy Spirit.

12"Brother will betray brother to death, and a father his child. Children will rebel against their parents and have them put to death. 13Everyone will hate you because of me, but the one who stands firm to the end will be saved.

14"When you see 'the abomination that causes desolation'[a] standing where it[b] does not belong — let the reader understand — then let those who are in Judea flee to the mountains. 15Let no one on the housetop go down or enter the house to take anything out. 16Let no one in the field go back to get their cloak. 17How dreadful it will be in those days for pregnant women and nursing mothers! 18Pray that this will not take place in winter, 19because those will be days of distress unequaled from the beginning, when God created the world, until now — and never to be equaled again.

20"If the Lord had not cut short those days, no one would survive. But for the sake of the elect, whom he has chosen, he has shortened them. 21At that time if anyone says to you, 'Look, here is the Messiah!' or, 'Look, there he is!' do not believe it. 22For false messiahs and false prophets will appear and perform signs and wonders to deceive, if possible, even the elect. 23So be on your guard; I have told you everything ahead of time.

24"But in those days, following that distress,

"'the sun will be darkened,
and the moon will not give its light;
25the stars will fall from the sky,
and the heavenly bodies will be shaken.'[c]

26"At that time people will see the Son of Man coming in clouds with great power and glory. 27And he will send his angels and gather his elect from the four winds, from the ends of the earth to the ends of the heavens.

28"Now learn this lesson from the fig tree: As soon as its twigs get tender and its leaves come out, you know that summer is near. 29Even so, when you see these things happening, you know that it[b] is near, right at the door. 30Truly I tell you, this generation will certainly not pass away until all these things have happened. 31Heaven and earth will pass away, but my words will never pass away.

The Day and Hour Unknown

32"But about that day or hour no one knows, not even the angels in heaven, nor the Son, but only the Father. 33Be on guard! Be alert[d]! You do not know when that time will come. 34It's like a man going away: He leaves his house and puts his servants in charge, each with their assigned task, and tells the one at the door to keep watch.

35"Therefore keep watch because you do not know when the owner of the house will come back — whether in the evening, or at midnight, or when the rooster crows, or at dawn. 36If he comes suddenly, do not let him find you sleeping. 37What I say to you, I say to everyone: 'Watch!'"

Jesus Anointed at Bethany

14 Now the Passover and the Festival of Unleavened Bread were only two days away, and the chief priests and the teachers of the law were scheming to arrest Jesus secretly and kill him. 2"But not during the festival," they said, "or the people may riot."

3While he was in Bethany, reclining at the table in the home of Simon the Leper, a woman came with an alabaster jar of very expensive perfume, made of pure nard. She broke the jar and poured the perfume on his head.

4Some of those present were saying indignantly to one another, "Why this waste of perfume? 5It could have been sold for more than a year's wages[e] and the money given to the poor." And they rebuked her harshly.

6"Leave her alone," said Jesus. "Why are you bothering her? She has done a beautiful thing to me. 7The poor you will always have with you,[f] and you can help them any time you want. But you will not always have me. 8She did what she could.

[a] 14 Daniel 9:27; 11:31; 12:11 [b] 14,29 Or *he* [c] 25 Isaiah 13:10; 34:4 [d] 33 Some manuscripts *alert and pray* [e] 5 Greek *than three hundred denarii* [f] 7 See Deut. 15:11.

She poured perfume on my body beforehand to prepare for my burial. 9Truly I tell you, wherever the gospel is preached throughout the world, what she has done will also be told, in memory of her."

10Then Judas Iscariot, one of the Twelve, went to the chief priests to betray Jesus to them. 11They were delighted to hear this and promised to give him money. So he watched for an opportunity to hand him over.

The Last Supper

12On the first day of the Festival of Unleavened Bread, when it was customary to sacrifice the Passover lamb, Jesus' disciples asked him, "Where do you want us to go and make preparations for you to eat the Passover?"

13So he sent two of his disciples, telling them, "Go into the city, and a man carrying a jar of water will meet you. Follow him. 14Say to the owner of the house he enters, 'The Teacher asks: Where is my guest room, where I may eat the Passover with my disciples?' 15He will show you a large room upstairs, furnished and ready. Make preparations for us there."

16The disciples left, went into the city and found things just as Jesus had told them. So they prepared the Passover.

17When evening came, Jesus arrived with the Twelve. 18While they were reclining at the table eating, he said, "Truly I tell you, one of you will betray me—one who is eating with me."

19They were saddened, and one by one they said to him, "Surely you don't mean me?"

20"It is one of the Twelve," he replied, "one who dips bread into the bowl with me. 21The Son of Man will go just as it is written about him. But woe to that man who betrays the Son of Man! It would be better for him if he had not been born."

22While they were eating, Jesus took bread, and when he had given thanks, he broke it and gave it to his disciples, saying, "Take it; this is my body."

23Then he took a cup, and when he had given thanks, he gave it to them, and they all drank from it.

24"This is my blood of the[a] covenant, which is poured out for many," he said to them. 25"Truly I tell you, I will not drink again from the fruit of the vine until that day when I drink it new in the kingdom of God."

26When they had sung a hymn, they went out to the Mount of Olives.

Jesus Predicts Peter's Denial

27"You will all fall away," Jesus told them, "for it is written:

"'I will strike the shepherd,
and the sheep will be scattered.'[b]

28But after I have risen, I will go ahead of you into Galilee."

29Peter declared, "Even if all fall away, I will not."

30"Truly I tell you," Jesus answered, "today—yes, tonight—before the rooster crows twice[c] you yourself will disown me three times."

31But Peter insisted emphatically, "Even if I have to die with you, I will never disown you." And all the others said the same.

Gethsemane

32They went to a place called Gethsemane, and Jesus said to his disciples, "Sit here while I pray." 33He took Peter, James and John along with him, and he began to be deeply distressed and troubled. 34"My soul is overwhelmed with sorrow to the point of death," he said to them. "Stay here and keep watch."

35Going a little farther, he fell to the ground and prayed that if possible the hour might pass from him. 36"*Abba*,[d] Father," he said, "everything is possible for you. Take this cup from me. Yet not what I will, but what you will."

37Then he returned to his disciples and found them sleeping. "Simon," he said to Peter, "are you asleep? Couldn't you keep watch for one hour? 38Watch and pray so that you will not fall into temptation. The spirit is willing, but the flesh is weak."

39Once more he went away and prayed the same thing. 40When he came back, he again found them sleeping, because their eyes were heavy. They did not know what to say to him.

41Returning the third time, he said to them, "Are you still sleeping and resting? Enough! The hour has come. Look, the Son of Man is delivered into the hands of sinners. 42Rise! Let us go! Here comes my betrayer!"

Jesus Arrested

43Just as he was speaking, Judas, one of the Twelve, appeared. With him was a crowd armed with swords and clubs, sent from the chief priests, the teachers of the law, and the elders.

44Now the betrayer had arranged a signal with them: "The one I kiss is the man; arrest

[a] *24* Some manuscripts *the new* [b] *27* Zech. 13:7 [c] *30* Some early manuscripts do not have *twice.* [d] *36* Aramaic for *father*

him and lead him away under guard." 45Go-
ing at once to Jesus, Judas said, "Rabbi!"
and kissed him. 46The men seized Jesus and
arrested him. 47Then one of those standing
near drew his sword and struck the servant
of the high priest, cutting off his ear.
48"Am I leading a rebellion," said Jesus,
"that you have come out with swords and
clubs to capture me? 49Every day I was
with you, teaching in the temple courts,
and you did not arrest me. But the Scriptures must be fulfilled." 50Then everyone
deserted him and fled.
51A young man, wearing nothing but a
linen garment, was following Jesus. When
they seized him, 52he fled naked, leaving
his garment behind.

Jesus Before the Sanhedrin

53They took Jesus to the high priest,
and all the chief priests, the elders and
the teachers of the law came together.
54Peter followed him at a distance, right
into the courtyard of the high priest. There
he sat with the guards and warmed himself at the fire.
55The chief priests and the whole Sanhedrin were looking for evidence against
Jesus so that they could put him to death,
but they did not find any. 56Many testified
falsely against him, but their statements
did not agree.
57Then some stood up and gave this false
testimony against him: 58"We heard him
say, 'I will destroy this temple made with
human hands and in three days will build
another, not made with hands.'" 59Yet even
then their testimony did not agree.
60Then the high priest stood up before
them and asked Jesus, "Are you not going
to answer? What is this testimony that
these men are bringing against you?" 61But
Jesus remained silent and gave no answer.
Again the high priest asked him, "Are
you the Messiah, the Son of the Blessed
One?"
62"I am," said Jesus. "And you will see
the Son of Man sitting at the right hand
of the Mighty One and coming on the
clouds of heaven."
63The high priest tore his clothes. "Why
do we need any more witnesses?" he
asked. 64"You have heard the blasphemy. What do you think?"
They all condemned him as worthy of
death. 65Then some began to spit at him;
they blindfolded him, struck him with
their fists, and said, "Prophesy!" And the
guards took him and beat him.

Peter Disowns Jesus

66While Peter was below in the courtyard, one of the servant girls of the high
priest came by. 67When she saw Peter
warming himself, she looked closely at
him.
"You also were with that Nazarene,
Jesus," she said.
68But he denied it. "I don't know or understand what you're talking about," he
said, and went out into the entryway.[a]
69When the servant girl saw him there,
she said again to those standing around,
"This fellow is one of them." 70Again he
denied it.
After a little while, those standing near
said to Peter, "Surely you are one of them,
for you are a Galilean."
71He began to call down curses, and he
swore to them, "I don't know this man
you're talking about."
72Immediately the rooster crowed the
second time.[b] Then Peter remembered the
word Jesus had spoken to him: "Before
the rooster crows twice[c] you will disown
me three times." And he broke down and
wept.

Jesus Before Pilate

15 Very early in the morning, the chief
priests, with the elders, the teachers
of the law and the whole Sanhedrin, made
their plans. So they bound Jesus, led him
away and handed him over to Pilate.
2"Are you the king of the Jews?" asked
Pilate.
"You have said so," Jesus replied.
3The chief priests accused him of many
things. 4So again Pilate asked him, "Aren't
you going to answer? See how many
things they are accusing you of."
5But Jesus still made no reply, and Pilate
was amazed.
6Now it was the custom at the festival
to release a prisoner whom the people
requested. 7A man called Barabbas was
in prison with the insurrectionists who
had committed murder in the uprising.
8The crowd came up and asked Pilate to
do for them what he usually did.
9"Do you want me to release to you the
king of the Jews?" asked Pilate, 10knowing
it was out of self-interest that the chief
priests had handed Jesus over to him.
11But the chief priests stirred up the crowd
to have Pilate release Barabbas instead.
12"What shall I do, then, with the one
you call the king of the Jews?" Pilate asked
them.

[a] *68* Some early manuscripts *entryway and the rooster crowed* [b] *72* Some early manuscripts do not have *the second time.* [c] *72* Some early manuscripts do not have *twice.*

13“Crucify him!” they shouted.

14“Why? What crime has he committed?” asked Pilate.

But they shouted all the louder, “Crucify him!”

15Wanting to satisfy the crowd, Pilate released Barabbas to them. He had Jesus flogged, and handed him over to be crucified.

The Soldiers Mock Jesus

16The soldiers led Jesus away into the palace (that is, the Praetorium) and called together the whole company of soldiers. 17They put a purple robe on him, then twisted together a crown of thorns and set it on him. 18And they began to call out to him, “Hail, king of the Jews!” 19Again and again they struck him on the head with a staff and spit on him. Falling on their knees, they paid homage to him. 20And when they had mocked him, they took off the purple robe and put his own clothes on him. Then they led him out to crucify him.

The Crucifixion of Jesus

21A certain man from Cyrene, Simon, the father of Alexander and Rufus, was passing by on his way in from the country, and they forced him to carry the cross. 22They brought Jesus to the place called Golgotha (which means “the place of the skull”). 23Then they offered him wine mixed with myrrh, but he did not take it. 24And they crucified him. Dividing up his clothes, they cast lots to see what each would get.

25It was nine in the morning when they crucified him. 26The written notice of the charge against him read: THE KING OF THE JEWS.

27They crucified two rebels with him, one on his right and one on his left. [28][a] 29Those who passed by hurled insults at him, shaking their heads and saying, “So! You who are going to destroy the temple and build it in three days, 30come down from the cross and save yourself!” 31In the same way the chief priests and the teachers of the law mocked him among themselves. “He saved others,” they said, “but he can’t save himself! 32Let this Messiah, this king of Israel, come down now from the cross, that we may see and believe.” Those crucified with him also heaped insults on him.

The Death of Jesus

33At noon, darkness came over the whole land until three in the afternoon. 34And at three in the afternoon Jesus cried out in a loud voice, *“Eloi, Eloi, lema sabachthani?”* (which means “My God, my God, why have you forsaken me?”).[b]

35When some of those standing near heard this, they said, “Listen, he’s calling Elijah.”

36Someone ran, filled a sponge with wine vinegar, put it on a staff, and offered it to Jesus to drink. “Now leave him alone. Let’s see if Elijah comes to take him down,” he said.

37With a loud cry, Jesus breathed his last.

38The curtain of the temple was torn in two from top to bottom. 39And when the centurion, who stood there in front of Jesus, saw how he died,[c] he said, “Surely this man was the Son of God!”

40Some women were watching from a distance. Among them were Mary Magdalene, Mary the mother of James the younger and of Joseph,[d] and Salome. 41In Galilee these women had followed him and cared for his needs. Many other women who had come up with him to Jerusalem were also there.

The Burial of Jesus

42It was Preparation Day (that is, the day before the Sabbath). So as evening approached, 43Joseph of Arimathea, a prominent member of the Council, who was himself waiting for the kingdom of God, went boldly to Pilate and asked for Jesus’ body. 44Pilate was surprised to hear that he was already dead. Summoning the centurion, he asked him if Jesus had already died. 45When he learned from the centurion that it was so, he gave the body to Joseph. 46So Joseph bought some linen cloth, took down the body, wrapped it in the linen, and placed it in a tomb cut out of rock. Then he rolled a stone against the entrance of the tomb. 47Mary Magdalene and Mary the mother of Joseph saw where he was laid.

Jesus Has Risen

16 When the Sabbath was over, Mary Magdalene, Mary the mother of James, and Salome bought spices so that they might go to anoint Jesus’ body. 2Very early on the first day of the week, just after sunrise, they were on their way to the tomb 3and they asked each other, “Who will roll the stone away from the entrance of the tomb?”

[a] *28* Some manuscripts include here words similar to Luke 22:37. [b] *34* Psalm 22:1 [c] *39* Some manuscripts *saw that he died with such a cry* [d] *40* Greek *Joses*, a variant of *Joseph*; also in verse 47

4 But when they looked up, they saw
that the stone, which was very large, had
been rolled away. 5 As they entered the
tomb, they saw a young man dressed in
a white robe sitting on the right side, and
they were alarmed.
6 "Don't be alarmed," he said. "You are
looking for Jesus the Nazarene, who was
crucified. He has risen! He is not here. See
the place where they laid him. 7 But go, tell
his disciples and Peter, 'He is going ahead
of you into Galilee. There you will see him,
just as he told you.'"
8 Trembling and bewildered, the women
went out and fled from the tomb. They
said nothing to anyone, because they
were afraid.[a]

[The earliest manuscripts and some other ancient witnesses do not have verses 9 – 20.]

9 When Jesus rose early on the first day of the
week, he appeared first to Mary Magdalene, out
of whom he had driven seven demons. 10 She went
and told those who had been with him and who
were mourning and weeping. 11 When they heard
that Jesus was alive and that she had seen him,
they did not believe it.
12 Afterward Jesus appeared in a different form
to two of them while they were walking in the
country. 13 These returned and reported it to the
rest; but they did not believe them either.
14 Later Jesus appeared to the Eleven as they
were eating; he rebuked them for their lack of
faith and their stubborn refusal to believe those
who had seen him after he had risen.
15 He said to them, "Go into all the world and
preach the gospel to all creation. 16 Whoever be-
lieves and is baptized will be saved, but whoever
does not believe will be condemned. 17 And these
signs will accompany those who believe: In my
name they will drive out demons; they will speak in
new tongues; 18 they will pick up snakes with their
hands; and when they drink deadly poison, it will
not hurt them at all; they will place their hands
on sick people, and they will get well."
19 After the Lord Jesus had spoken to them, he
was taken up into heaven and he sat at the right
hand of God. 20 Then the disciples went out and
preached everywhere, and the Lord worked with
them and confirmed his word by the signs that
accompanied it.

[a] *8* Some manuscripts have the following ending between verses 8 and 9, and one manuscript has it after verse 8 (omitting verses 9-20): *Then they quickly reported all these instructions to those around Peter. After this, Jesus himself also sent out through them from east to west the sacred and imperishable proclamation of eternal salvation. Amen.*

LUKE

Introduction

1 Many have undertaken to draw up an account of the things that have been fulfilled[a] among us, 2just as they were handed down to us by those who from the first were eyewitnesses and servants of the word. 3With this in mind, since I myself have carefully investigated everything from the beginning, I too decided to write an orderly account for you, most excellent Theophilus, 4so that you may know the certainty of the things you have been taught.

The Birth of John the Baptist Foretold

5In the time of Herod king of Judea there was a priest named Zechariah, who belonged to the priestly division of Abijah; his wife Elizabeth was also a descendant of Aaron. 6Both of them were righteous in the sight of God, observing all the Lord's commands and decrees blamelessly. 7But they were childless because Elizabeth was not able to conceive, and they were both very old.

8Once when Zechariah's division was on duty and he was serving as priest before God, 9he was chosen by lot, according to the custom of the priesthood, to go into the temple of the Lord and burn incense. 10And when the time for the burning of incense came, all the assembled worshipers were praying outside.

11Then an angel of the Lord appeared to him, standing at the right side of the altar of incense. 12When Zechariah saw him, he was startled and was gripped with fear. 13But the angel said to him: "Do not be afraid, Zechariah; your prayer has been heard. Your wife Elizabeth will bear you a son, and you are to call him John. 14He will be a joy and delight to you, and many will rejoice because of his birth, 15for he will be great in the sight of the Lord. He is never to take wine or other fermented drink, and he will be filled with the Holy Spirit even before he is born. 16He will bring back many of the people of Israel to the Lord their God. 17And he will go on before the Lord, in the spirit and power of Elijah, to turn the hearts of the parents to their children and the disobedient to the wisdom of the righteous — to make ready a people prepared for the Lord."

18Zechariah asked the angel, "How can I be sure of this? I am an old man and my wife is well along in years."

19The angel said to him, "I am Gabriel. I stand in the presence of God, and I have been sent to speak to you and to tell you this good news. 20And now you will be silent and not able to speak until the day this happens, because you did not believe my words, which will come true at their appointed time."

21Meanwhile, the people were waiting for Zechariah and wondering why he stayed so long in the temple. 22When he came out, he could not speak to them. They realized he had seen a vision in the temple, for he kept making signs to them but remained unable to speak.

23When his time of service was completed, he returned home. 24After this his wife Elizabeth became pregnant and for five months remained in seclusion. 25"The Lord has done this for me," she said. "In these days he has shown his favor and taken away my disgrace among the people."

The Birth of Jesus Foretold

26In the sixth month of Elizabeth's pregnancy, God sent the angel Gabriel to Nazareth, a town in Galilee, 27to a virgin pledged to be married to a man named Joseph, a descendant of David. The virgin's name was Mary. 28The angel went to her and said, "Greetings, you who are highly favored! The Lord is with you."

29Mary was greatly troubled at his words and wondered what kind of greeting this might be. 30But the angel said to her, "Do not be afraid, Mary; you have found favor with God. 31You will conceive and give birth to a son, and you are to call him Jesus. 32He will be great and will be called the Son of the Most High. The Lord God will give him the throne of his father David, 33and he will reign over Jacob's descendants forever; his kingdom will never end."

34"How will this be," Mary asked the angel, "since I am a virgin?"

35The angel answered, "The Holy Spirit will come on you, and the power of the Most High will overshadow you. So the holy one to be born will be called[b] the Son

[a] 1 Or *been surely believed* [b] 35 Or *So the child to be born will be called holy,*

of God. 36 Even Elizabeth your relative is
going to have a child in her old age, and
she who was said to be unable to conceive
is in her sixth month. 37 For no word from
God will ever fail."
38 "I am the Lord's servant," Mary answered. "May your word to me be fulfilled."
Then the angel left her.

Mary Visits Elizabeth

39 At that time Mary got ready and hurried to a town in the hill country of Judea,
40 where she entered Zechariah's home
and greeted Elizabeth. 41 When Elizabeth
heard Mary's greeting, the baby leaped in
her womb, and Elizabeth was filled with
the Holy Spirit. 42 In a loud voice she exclaimed: "Blessed are you among women,
and blessed is the child you will bear! 43 But
why am I so favored, that the mother of
my Lord should come to me? 44 As soon as
the sound of your greeting reached my
ears, the baby in my womb leaped for joy.
45 Blessed is she who has believed that the
Lord would fulfill his promises to her!"

Mary's Song

46 And Mary said:

"My soul glorifies the Lord
47 and my spirit rejoices in God my Savior,
48 for he has been mindful
of the humble state of his servant.
From now on all generations will call me blessed,
49 for the Mighty One has done great things for me—
holy is his name.
50 His mercy extends to those who fear him,
from generation to generation.
51 He has performed mighty deeds with his arm;
he has scattered those who are proud in their inmost thoughts.
52 He has brought down rulers from their thrones
but has lifted up the humble.
53 He has filled the hungry with good things
but has sent the rich away empty.
54 He has helped his servant Israel,
remembering to be merciful
55 to Abraham and his descendants forever,
just as he promised our ancestors."

56 Mary stayed with Elizabeth for about
three months and then returned home.

The Birth of John the Baptist

57 When it was time for Elizabeth to have
her baby, she gave birth to a son. 58 Her
neighbors and relatives heard that the
Lord had shown her great mercy, and they
shared her joy.
59 On the eighth day they came to circumcise the child, and they were going
to name him after his father Zechariah,
60 but his mother spoke up and said, "No!
He is to be called John."
61 They said to her, "There is no one
among your relatives who has that name."
62 Then they made signs to his father,
to find out what he would like to name
the child. 63 He asked for a writing tablet, and to everyone's astonishment he
wrote, "His name is John." 64 Immediately
his mouth was opened and his tongue
set free, and he began to speak, praising
God. 65 All the neighbors were filled with
awe, and throughout the hill country of
Judea people were talking about all these
things. 66 Everyone who heard this wondered about it, asking, "What then is this
child going to be?" For the Lord's hand
was with him.

Zechariah's Song

67 His father Zechariah was filled with
the Holy Spirit and prophesied:

68 "Praise be to the Lord, the God of Israel,
because he has come to his people and redeemed them.
69 He has raised up a horn[a] of salvation for us
in the house of his servant David
70 (as he said through his holy prophets of long ago),
71 salvation from our enemies
and from the hand of all who hate us—
72 to show mercy to our ancestors
and to remember his holy covenant,
73 the oath he swore to our father Abraham:
74 to rescue us from the hand of our enemies,
and to enable us to serve him without fear
75 in holiness and righteousness before him all our days.

76 And you, my child, will be called a prophet of the Most High;
for you will go on before the Lord to prepare the way for him,

[a] 69 *Horn* here symbolizes a strong king.

77 to give his people the knowledge of
salvation
through the forgiveness of their
sins,
78 because of the tender mercy of our God,
by which the rising sun will come to
us from heaven
79 to shine on those living in darkness
and in the shadow of death,
to guide our feet into the path of
peace."

80 And the child grew and became strong
in spirit[a]; and he lived in the wilderness
until he appeared publicly to Israel.

The Birth of Jesus

2 In those days Caesar Augustus issued
a decree that a census should be taken
of the entire Roman world. 2 (This was the
first census that took place while[b] Quirin-
ius was governor of Syria.) 3 And everyone
went to their own town to register.
4 So Joseph also went up from the town
of Nazareth in Galilee to Judea, to Bethlehem the town of David, because he belonged to the house and line of David. 5 He
went there to register with Mary, who was
pledged to be married to him and was expecting a child. 6 While they were there, the
time came for the baby to be born, 7 and
she gave birth to her firstborn, a son. She
wrapped him in cloths and placed him
in a manger, because there was no guest
room available for them.
8 And there were shepherds living out
in the fields nearby, keeping watch over
their flocks at night. 9 An angel of the Lord
appeared to them, and the glory of the
Lord shone around them, and they were
terrified. 10 But the angel said to them,
"Do not be afraid. I bring you good news
that will cause great joy for all the people.
11 Today in the town of David a Savior has
been born to you; he is the Messiah, the
Lord. 12 This will be a sign to you: You will
find a baby wrapped in cloths and lying
in a manger."
13 Suddenly a great company of the
heavenly host appeared with the angel,
praising God and saying,

14 "Glory to God in the highest heaven,
and on earth peace to those on
whom his favor rests."

15 When the angels had left them and
gone into heaven, the shepherds said to
one another, "Let's go to Bethlehem and
see this thing that has happened, which
the Lord has told us about."
16 So they hurried off and found Mary
and Joseph, and the baby, who was lying
in the manger. 17 When they had seen him,
they spread the word concerning what
had been told them about this child, 18 and
all who heard it were amazed at what
the shepherds said to them. 19 But Mary
treasured up all these things and pondered them in her heart. 20 The shepherds
returned, glorifying and praising God for
all the things they had heard and seen,
which were just as they had been told.
21 On the eighth day, when it was time to
circumcise the child, he was named Jesus,
the name the angel had given him before
he was conceived.

Jesus Presented in the Temple

22 When the time came for the purification rites required by the Law of Moses,
Joseph and Mary took him to Jerusalem to
present him to the Lord 23 (as it is written in
the Law of the Lord, "Every firstborn male
is to be consecrated to the Lord"[c]), 24 and
to offer a sacrifice in keeping with what
is said in the Law of the Lord: "a pair of
doves or two young pigeons."[d]
25 Now there was a man in Jerusalem
called Simeon, who was righteous and
devout. He was waiting for the consolation of Israel, and the Holy Spirit was on
him. 26 It had been revealed to him by the
Holy Spirit that he would not die before he
had seen the Lord's Messiah. 27 Moved by
the Spirit, he went into the temple courts.
When the parents brought in the child
Jesus to do for him what the custom of
the Law required, 28 Simeon took him in
his arms and praised God, saying:

29 "Sovereign Lord, as you have
promised,
you may now dismiss[e] your servant
in peace.
30 For my eyes have seen your salvation,
31 which you have prepared in the
sight of all nations:
32 a light for revelation to the Gentiles,
and the glory of your people
Israel."

33 The child's father and mother marveled at what was said about him. 34 Then
Simeon blessed them and said to Mary, his
mother: "This child is destined to cause the
falling and rising of many in Israel, and
to be a sign that will be spoken against,
35 so that the thoughts of many hearts will
be revealed. And a sword will pierce your
own soul too."

[a] 80 Or *in the Spirit* [b] 2 Or *This census took place before* [c] 23 Exodus 13:2,12 [d] 24 Lev. 12:8
[e] 29 Or *promised, / now dismiss*

36There was also a prophet, Anna, the
daughter of Penuel, of the tribe of Asher. She was very old; she had lived with
her husband seven years after her marriage, 37and then was a widow until she
was eighty-four.[a] She never left the temple
but worshiped night and day, fasting and
praying. 38Coming up to them at that very
moment, she gave thanks to God and spoke
about the child to all who were looking
forward to the redemption of Jerusalem.
39When Joseph and Mary had done everything required by the Law of the Lord,
they returned to Galilee to their own town
of Nazareth. 40And the child grew and became strong; he was filled with wisdom,
and the grace of God was on him.

The Boy Jesus at the Temple

41Every year Jesus' parents went to Jerusalem for the Festival of the Passover.
42When he was twelve years old, they went
up to the festival, according to the custom.
43After the festival was over, while his parents were returning home, the boy Jesus
stayed behind in Jerusalem, but they were
unaware of it. 44Thinking he was in their
company, they traveled on for a day. Then
they began looking for him among their
relatives and friends. 45When they did not
find him, they went back to Jerusalem to
look for him. 46After three days they found
him in the temple courts, sitting among
the teachers, listening to them and asking
them questions. 47Everyone who heard
him was amazed at his understanding
and his answers. 48When his parents saw
him, they were astonished. His mother
said to him, "Son, why have you treated
us like this? Your father and I have been
anxiously searching for you."
49"Why were you searching for me?"
he asked. "Didn't you know I had to be in
my Father's house?"[b] 50But they did not
understand what he was saying to them.
51Then he went down to Nazareth with
them and was obedient to them. But his
mother treasured all these things in her
heart. 52And Jesus grew in wisdom and
stature, and in favor with God and man.

John the Baptist Prepares the Way

3 In the fifteenth year of the reign of
Tiberius Caesar — when Pontius Pilate
was governor of Judea, Herod tetrarch of
Galilee, his brother Philip tetrarch of Itu-
rea and Traconitis, and Lysanias tetrarch
of Abilene — 2during the high-priesthood
of Annas and Caiaphas, the word of God
came to John son of Zechariah in the wilderness. 3He went into all the country
around the Jordan, preaching a baptism
of repentance for the forgiveness of sins.
4As it is written in the book of the words
of Isaiah the prophet:

"A voice of one calling in the
wilderness,
'Prepare the way for the Lord,
make straight paths for him.
5Every valley shall be filled in,
every mountain and hill made low.
The crooked roads shall become
straight,
the rough ways smooth.
6And all people will see God's
salvation.' "[c]

7John said to the crowds coming out to
be baptized by him, "You brood of vipers!
Who warned you to flee from the coming
wrath? 8Produce fruit in keeping with repentance. And do not begin to say to yourselves, 'We have Abraham as our father.'
For I tell you that out of these stones God
can raise up children for Abraham. 9The
ax is already at the root of the trees, and
every tree that does not produce good fruit
will be cut down and thrown into the fire."
10"What should we do then?" the crowd
asked.
11John answered, "Anyone who has two
shirts should share with the one who has
none, and anyone who has food should
do the same."
12Even tax collectors came to be baptized. "Teacher," they asked, "what should
we do?"
13"Don't collect any more than you are
required to," he told them.
14Then some soldiers asked him, "And
what should we do?"
He replied, "Don't extort money and
don't accuse people falsely — be content
with your pay."
15The people were waiting expectantly
and were all wondering in their hearts if
John might possibly be the Messiah. 16John
answered them all, "I baptize you with[d]
water. But one who is more powerful than
I will come, the straps of whose sandals
I am not worthy to untie. He will baptize
you with[d] the Holy Spirit and fire. 17His
winnowing fork is in his hand to clear his
threshing floor and to gather the wheat
into his barn, but he will burn up the chaff
with unquenchable fire." 18And with many
other words John exhorted the people
and proclaimed the good news to them.

[a] 37 Or *then had been a widow for eighty-four years.* [b] 49 Or *be about my Father's business*
[c] 6 Isaiah 40:3-5 [d] 16 Or *in*

[19]But when John rebuked Herod the tetrarch because of his marriage to Herodias, his brother's wife, and all the other evil things he had done, [20]Herod added this to them all: He locked John up in prison.

The Baptism and Genealogy of Jesus

[21]When all the people were being baptized, Jesus was baptized too. And as he was praying, heaven was opened [22]and the Holy Spirit descended on him in bodily form like a dove. And a voice came from heaven: "You are my Son, whom I love; with you I am well pleased."

[23]Now Jesus himself was about thirty years old when he began his ministry. He was the son, so it was thought, of Joseph,

the son of Heli, [24]the son of Matthat,
the son of Levi, the son of Melki,
the son of Jannai, the son of Joseph,
[25]the son of Mattathias, the son of Amos,
the son of Nahum, the son of Esli,
the son of Naggai, [26]the son of Maath,
the son of Mattathias, the son of Semein,
the son of Josek, the son of Joda,
[27]the son of Joanan, the son of Rhesa,
the son of Zerubbabel, the son of Shealtiel,
the son of Neri, [28]the son of Melki,
the son of Addi, the son of Cosam,
the son of Elmadam, the son of Er,
[29]the son of Joshua, the son of Eliezer,
the son of Jorim, the son of Matthat,
the son of Levi, [30]the son of Simeon,
the son of Judah, the son of Joseph,
the son of Jonam, the son of Eliakim,
[31]the son of Melea, the son of Menna,
the son of Mattatha, the son of Nathan,
the son of David, [32]the son of Jesse,
the son of Obed, the son of Boaz,
the son of Salmon,[a] the son of Nahshon,
[33]the son of Amminadab, the son of Ram,[b]
the son of Hezron, the son of Perez,
the son of Judah, [34]the son of Jacob,
the son of Isaac, the son of Abraham,
the son of Terah, the son of Nahor,
[35]the son of Serug, the son of Reu,
the son of Peleg, the son of Eber,
the son of Shelah, [36]the son of Cainan,
the son of Arphaxad, the son of Shem,
the son of Noah, the son of Lamech,
[37]the son of Methuselah, the son of Enoch,
the son of Jared, the son of Mahalalel,
the son of Kenan, [38]the son of Enosh,
the son of Seth, the son of Adam,
the son of God.

Jesus Is Tested in the Wilderness

4 Jesus, full of the Holy Spirit, left the Jordan and was led by the Spirit into the wilderness, [2]where for forty days he was tempted[c] by the devil. He ate nothing during those days, and at the end of them he was hungry.

[3]The devil said to him, "If you are the Son of God, tell this stone to become bread."

[4]Jesus answered, "It is written: 'Man shall not live on bread alone.'[d]"

[5]The devil led him up to a high place and showed him in an instant all the kingdoms of the world. [6]And he said to him, "I will give you all their authority and splendor; it has been given to me, and I can give it to anyone I want to. [7]If you worship me, it will all be yours."

[8]Jesus answered, "It is written: 'Worship the Lord your God and serve him only.'[e]"

[9]The devil led him to Jerusalem and had him stand on the highest point of the temple. "If you are the Son of God," he said, "throw yourself down from here. [10]For it is written:

"'He will command his angels concerning you
to guard you carefully;
[11]they will lift you up in their hands,
so that you will not strike your foot against a stone.'[f]"

[12]Jesus answered, "It is said: 'Do not put the Lord your God to the test.'[g]"

[13]When the devil had finished all this tempting, he left him until an opportune time.

Jesus Rejected at Nazareth

[14]Jesus returned to Galilee in the power of the Spirit, and news about him spread through the whole countryside. [15]He was teaching in their synagogues, and everyone praised him.

[16]He went to Nazareth, where he had been brought up, and on the Sabbath day he went into the synagogue, as was his custom. He stood up to read, [17]and the scroll of the prophet Isaiah was handed to him. Unrolling it, he found the place where it is written:

[18]"The Spirit of the Lord is on me,
because he has anointed me
to proclaim good news to the poor.
He has sent me to proclaim freedom for the prisoners
and recovery of sight for the blind,

[a] *32* Some early manuscripts *Sala* [b] *33* Some manuscripts *Amminadab, the son of Admin, the son of Arni*; other manuscripts vary widely. [c] *2* The Greek for *tempted* can also mean *tested.* [d] *4* Deut. 8:3 [e] *8* Deut. 6:13 [f] *11* Psalm 91:11,12 [g] *12* Deut. 6:16

to set the oppressed free,
19 to proclaim the year of the Lord's favor."[a]

20 Then he rolled up the scroll, gave it back to the attendant and sat down. The eyes of everyone in the synagogue were fastened on him. 21 He began by saying to them, "Today this scripture is fulfilled in your hearing."

22 All spoke well of him and were amazed at the gracious words that came from his lips. "Isn't this Joseph's son?" they asked.

23 Jesus said to them, "Surely you will quote this proverb to me: 'Physician, heal yourself!' And you will tell me, 'Do here in your hometown what we have heard that you did in Capernaum.' "

24 "Truly I tell you," he continued, "no prophet is accepted in his hometown. 25 I assure you that there were many widows in Israel in Elijah's time, when the sky was shut for three and a half years and there was a severe famine throughout the land. 26 Yet Elijah was not sent to any of them, but to a widow in Zarephath in the region of Sidon. 27 And there were many in Israel with leprosy[b] in the time of Elisha the prophet, yet not one of them was cleansed — only Naaman the Syrian."

28 All the people in the synagogue were furious when they heard this. 29 They got up, drove him out of the town, and took him to the brow of the hill on which the town was built, in order to throw him off the cliff. 30 But he walked right through the crowd and went on his way.

Jesus Drives Out an Impure Spirit

31 Then he went down to Capernaum, a town in Galilee, and on the Sabbath he taught the people. 32 They were amazed at his teaching, because his words had authority.

33 In the synagogue there was a man possessed by a demon, an impure spirit. He cried out at the top of his voice, 34 "Go away! What do you want with us, Jesus of Nazareth? Have you come to destroy us? I know who you are — the Holy One of God!"

35 "Be quiet!" Jesus said sternly. "Come out of him!" Then the demon threw the man down before them all and came out without injuring him.

36 All the people were amazed and said to each other, "What words these are! With authority and power he gives orders to impure spirits and they come out!" 37 And the news about him spread throughout the surrounding area.

Jesus Heals Many

38 Jesus left the synagogue and went to the home of Simon. Now Simon's mother-in-law was suffering from a high fever, and they asked Jesus to help her. 39 So he bent over her and rebuked the fever, and it left her. She got up at once and began to wait on them.

40 At sunset, the people brought to Jesus all who had various kinds of sickness, and laying his hands on each one, he healed them. 41 Moreover, demons came out of many people, shouting, "You are the Son of God!" But he rebuked them and would not allow them to speak, because they knew he was the Messiah.

42 At daybreak, Jesus went out to a solitary place. The people were looking for him and when they came to where he was, they tried to keep him from leaving them. 43 But he said, "I must proclaim the good news of the kingdom of God to the other towns also, because that is why I was sent." 44 And he kept on preaching in the synagogues of Judea.

Jesus Calls His First Disciples

5 One day as Jesus was standing by the Lake of Gennesaret,[c] the people were crowding around him and listening to the word of God. 2 He saw at the water's edge two boats, left there by the fishermen, who were washing their nets. 3 He got into one of the boats, the one belonging to Simon, and asked him to put out a little from shore. Then he sat down and taught the people from the boat.

4 When he had finished speaking, he said to Simon, "Put out into deep water, and let down the nets for a catch."

5 Simon answered, "Master, we've worked hard all night and haven't caught anything. But because you say so, I will let down the nets."

6 When they had done so, they caught such a large number of fish that their nets began to break. 7 So they signaled their partners in the other boat to come and help them, and they came and filled both boats so full that they began to sink.

8 When Simon Peter saw this, he fell at Jesus' knees and said, "Go away from me, Lord; I am a sinful man!" 9 For he and all his companions were astonished at the catch of fish they had taken, 10 and so were James and John, the sons of Zebedee, Simon's partners.

Then Jesus said to Simon, "Don't be afraid; from now on you will fish for people." 11 So they pulled their boats up on shore, left everything and followed him.

[a] *19* Isaiah 61:1,2 (see Septuagint); Isaiah 58:6 [b] *27* The Greek word traditionally translated *leprosy* was used for various diseases affecting the skin. [c] *1* That is, the Sea of Galilee

Jesus Heals a Man With Leprosy

12 While Jesus was in one of the towns, a man came along who was covered with leprosy.[a] When he saw Jesus, he fell with his face to the ground and begged him, "Lord, if you are willing, you can make me clean."

13 Jesus reached out his hand and touched the man. "I am willing," he said. "Be clean!" And immediately the leprosy left him.

14 Then Jesus ordered him, "Don't tell anyone, but go, show yourself to the priest and offer the sacrifices that Moses commanded for your cleansing, as a testimony to them."

15 Yet the news about him spread all the more, so that crowds of people came to hear him and to be healed of their sicknesses. 16 But Jesus often withdrew to lonely places and prayed.

Jesus Forgives and Heals a Paralyzed Man

17 One day Jesus was teaching, and Pharisees and teachers of the law were sitting there. They had come from every village of Galilee and from Judea and Jerusalem. And the power of the Lord was with Jesus to heal the sick. 18 Some men came carrying a paralyzed man on a mat and tried to take him into the house to lay him before Jesus. 19 When they could not find a way to do this because of the crowd, they went up on the roof and lowered him on his mat through the tiles into the middle of the crowd, right in front of Jesus.

20 When Jesus saw their faith, he said, "Friend, your sins are forgiven."

21 The Pharisees and the teachers of the law began thinking to themselves, "Who is this fellow who speaks blasphemy? Who can forgive sins but God alone?"

22 Jesus knew what they were thinking and asked, "Why are you thinking these things in your hearts? 23 Which is easier: to say, 'Your sins are forgiven,' or to say, 'Get up and walk'? 24 But I want you to know that the Son of Man has authority on earth to forgive sins." So he said to the paralyzed man, "I tell you, get up, take your mat and go home." 25 Immediately he stood up in front of them, took what he had been lying on and went home praising God. 26 Everyone was amazed and gave praise to God. They were filled with awe and said, "We have seen remarkable things today."

Jesus Calls Levi and Eats With Sinners

27 After this, Jesus went out and saw a tax collector by the name of Levi sitting at his tax booth. "Follow me," Jesus said to him, 28 and Levi got up, left everything and followed him.

29 Then Levi held a great banquet for Jesus at his house, and a large crowd of tax collectors and others were eating with them. 30 But the Pharisees and the teachers of the law who belonged to their sect complained to his disciples, "Why do you eat and drink with tax collectors and sinners?"

31 Jesus answered them, "It is not the healthy who need a doctor, but the sick. 32 I have not come to call the righteous, but sinners to repentance."

Jesus Questioned About Fasting

33 They said to him, "John's disciples often fast and pray, and so do the disciples of the Pharisees, but yours go on eating and drinking."

34 Jesus answered, "Can you make the friends of the bridegroom fast while he is with them? 35 But the time will come when the bridegroom will be taken from them; in those days they will fast."

36 He told them this parable: "No one tears a piece out of a new garment to patch an old one. Otherwise, they will have torn the new garment, and the patch from the new will not match the old. 37 And no one pours new wine into old wineskins. Otherwise, the new wine will burst the skins; the wine will run out and the wineskins will be ruined. 38 No, new wine must be poured into new wineskins. 39 And no one after drinking old wine wants the new, for they say, 'The old is better.'"

Jesus Is Lord of the Sabbath

6 One Sabbath Jesus was going through the grainfields, and his disciples began to pick some heads of grain, rub them in their hands and eat the kernels. 2 Some of the Pharisees asked, "Why are you doing what is unlawful on the Sabbath?"

3 Jesus answered them, "Have you never read what David did when he and his companions were hungry? 4 He entered the house of God, and taking the consecrated bread, he ate what is lawful only for priests to eat. And he also gave some to his companions." 5 Then Jesus said to them, "The Son of Man is Lord of the Sabbath."

6 On another Sabbath he went into the synagogue and was teaching, and a man was there whose right hand was shriveled. 7 The Pharisees and the teachers of the law were looking for a reason to accuse Jesus, so they watched him closely to see if he

[a] *12* The Greek word traditionally translated *leprosy* was used for various diseases affecting the skin.

would heal on the Sabbath. 8 But Jesus
knew what they were thinking and said
to the man with the shriveled hand, "Get
up and stand in front of everyone." So he
got up and stood there.
9 Then Jesus said to them, "I ask you,
which is lawful on the Sabbath: to do good
or to do evil, to save life or to destroy it?"
10 He looked around at them all, and
then said to the man, "Stretch out your
hand." He did so, and his hand was completely restored. 11 But the Pharisees and
the teachers of the law were furious and
began to discuss with one another what
they might do to Jesus.

The Twelve Apostles

12 One of those days Jesus went out to a
mountainside to pray, and spent the night
praying to God. 13 When morning came,
he called his disciples to him and chose
twelve of them, whom he also designated
apostles: 14 Simon (whom he named Peter),
his brother Andrew, James, John, Philip,
Bartholomew, 15 Matthew, Thomas, James
son of Alphaeus, Simon who was called the
Zealot, 16 Judas son of James, and Judas
Iscariot, who became a traitor.

Blessings and Woes

17 He went down with them and stood on
a level place. A large crowd of his disciples
was there and a great number of people
from all over Judea, from Jerusalem, and
from the coastal region around Tyre and
Sidon, 18 who had come to hear him and
to be healed of their diseases. Those troubled by impure spirits were cured, 19 and
the people all tried to touch him, because
power was coming from him and healing
them all.
20 Looking at his disciples, he said:

"Blessed are you who are poor,
for yours is the kingdom of God.
21 Blessed are you who hunger now,
for you will be satisfied.
Blessed are you who weep now,
for you will laugh.
22 Blessed are you when people hate you,
when they exclude you and insult
you
and reject your name as evil,
because of the Son of Man.

23 "Rejoice in that day and leap for joy,
because great is your reward in heaven.
For that is how their ancestors treated
the prophets.

24 "But woe to you who are rich,
for you have already received your
comfort.
25 Woe to you who are well fed now,
for you will go hungry.
Woe to you who laugh now,
for you will mourn and weep.
26 Woe to you when everyone speaks
well of you,
for that is how their ancestors
treated the false prophets.

Love for Enemies

27 "But to you who are listening I say:
Love your enemies, do good to those who
hate you, 28 bless those who curse you, pray
for those who mistreat you. 29 If someone
slaps you on one cheek, turn to them the
other also. If someone takes your coat, do
not withhold your shirt from them. 30 Give
to everyone who asks you, and if anyone
takes what belongs to you, do not demand
it back. 31 Do to others as you would have
them do to you.
32 "If you love those who love you, what
credit is that to you? Even sinners love
those who love them. 33 And if you do good
to those who are good to you, what credit
is that to you? Even sinners do that. 34 And
if you lend to those from whom you expect
repayment, what credit is that to you?
Even sinners lend to sinners, expecting to
be repaid in full. 35 But love your enemies,
do good to them, and lend to them without expecting to get anything back. Then
your reward will be great, and you will be
children of the Most High, because he is
kind to the ungrateful and wicked. 36 Be
merciful, just as your Father is merciful.

Judging Others

37 "Do not judge, and you will not be
judged. Do not condemn, and you will not
be condemned. Forgive, and you will be
forgiven. 38 Give, and it will be given to you.
A good measure, pressed down, shaken
together and running over, will be poured
into your lap. For with the measure you
use, it will be measured to you."
39 He also told them this parable: "Can
the blind lead the blind? Will they not both
fall into a pit? 40 The student is not above
the teacher, but everyone who is fully
trained will be like their teacher.
41 "Why do you look at the speck of
sawdust in your brother's eye and pay
no attention to the plank in your own
eye? 42 How can you say to your brother, 'Brother, let me take the speck out of
your eye,' when you yourself fail to see the
plank in your own eye? You hypocrite, first
take the plank out of your eye, and then
you will see clearly to remove the speck
from your brother's eye.

A Tree and Its Fruit

43“No good tree bears bad fruit, nor does a bad tree bear good fruit. 44Each tree is recognized by its own fruit. People do not pick figs from thornbushes, or grapes from briers. 45A good man brings good things out of the good stored up in his heart, and an evil man brings evil things out of the evil stored up in his heart. For the mouth speaks what the heart is full of.

The Wise and Foolish Builders

46“Why do you call me, ‘Lord, Lord,’ and do not do what I say? 47As for everyone who comes to me and hears my words and puts them into practice, I will show you what they are like. 48They are like a man building a house, who dug down deep and laid the foundation on rock. When a flood came, the torrent struck that house but could not shake it, because it was well built. 49But the one who hears my words and does not put them into practice is like a man who built a house on the ground without a foundation. The moment the torrent struck that house, it collapsed and its destruction was complete.”

The Faith of the Centurion

7 When Jesus had finished saying all this to the people who were listening, he entered Capernaum. 2There a centurion’s servant, whom his master valued highly, was sick and about to die. 3The centurion heard of Jesus and sent some elders of the Jews to him, asking him to come and heal his servant. 4When they came to Jesus, they pleaded earnestly with him, “This man deserves to have you do this, 5because he loves our nation and has built our synagogue.” 6So Jesus went with them.

He was not far from the house when the centurion sent friends to say to him: “Lord, don’t trouble yourself, for I do not deserve to have you come under my roof. 7That is why I did not even consider myself worthy to come to you. But say the word, and my servant will be healed. 8For I myself am a man under authority, with soldiers under me. I tell this one, ‘Go,’ and he goes; and that one, ‘Come,’ and he comes. I say to my servant, ‘Do this,’ and he does it.”

9When Jesus heard this, he was amazed at him, and turning to the crowd following him, he said, “I tell you, I have not found such great faith even in Israel.” 10Then the men who had been sent returned to the house and found the servant well.

Jesus Raises a Widow’s Son

11Soon afterward, Jesus went to a town called Nain, and his disciples and a large crowd went along with him. 12As he approached the town gate, a dead person was being carried out — the only son of his mother, and she was a widow. And a large crowd from the town was with her. 13When the Lord saw her, his heart went out to her and he said, “Don’t cry.”

14Then he went up and touched the bier they were carrying him on, and the bearers stood still. He said, “Young man, I say to you, get up!” 15The dead man sat up and began to talk, and Jesus gave him back to his mother.

16They were all filled with awe and praised God. “A great prophet has appeared among us,” they said. “God has come to help his people.” 17This news about Jesus spread throughout Judea and the surrounding country.

Jesus and John the Baptist

18John’s disciples told him about all these things. Calling two of them, 19he sent them to the Lord to ask, “Are you the one who is to come, or should we expect someone else?”

20When the men came to Jesus, they said, “John the Baptist sent us to you to ask, ‘Are you the one who is to come, or should we expect someone else?’ ”

21At that very time Jesus cured many who had diseases, sicknesses and evil spirits, and gave sight to many who were blind. 22So he replied to the messengers, “Go back and report to John what you have seen and heard: The blind receive sight, the lame walk, those who have leprosy[a] are cleansed, the deaf hear, the dead are raised, and the good news is proclaimed to the poor. 23Blessed is anyone who does not stumble on account of me.”

24After John’s messengers left, Jesus began to speak to the crowd about John: “What did you go out into the wilderness to see? A reed swayed by the wind? 25If not, what did you go out to see? A man dressed in fine clothes? No, those who wear expensive clothes and indulge in luxury are in palaces. 26But what did you go out to see? A prophet? Yes, I tell you, and more than a prophet. 27This is the one about whom it is written:

“ ‘I will send my messenger ahead of you,
who will prepare your way before you.’[b]

[a] 22 The Greek word traditionally translated *leprosy* was used for various diseases affecting the skin. [b] 27 Mal. 3:1

28 I tell you, among those born of women
there is no one greater than John; yet the
one who is least in the kingdom of God is
greater than he."
29 (All the people, even the tax collectors,
when they heard Jesus' words, acknowledged that God's way was right, because
they had been baptized by John. 30 But the
Pharisees and the experts in the law rejected God's purpose for themselves, because
they had not been baptized by John.)
31 Jesus went on to say, "To what, then,
can I compare the people of this generation? What are they like? 32 They are like
children sitting in the marketplace and
calling out to each other:

"'We played the pipe for you,
and you did not dance;
we sang a dirge,
and you did not cry.'

33 For John the Baptist came neither eating bread nor drinking wine, and you say,
'He has a demon.' 34 The Son of Man came
eating and drinking, and you say, 'Here
is a glutton and a drunkard, a friend of
tax collectors and sinners.' 35 But wisdom
is proved right by all her children."

Jesus Anointed by a Sinful Woman

36 When one of the Pharisees invited
Jesus to have dinner with him, he went to
the Pharisee's house and reclined at the
table. 37 A woman in that town who lived
a sinful life learned that Jesus was eating
at the Pharisee's house, so she came there
with an alabaster jar of perfume. 38 As she
stood behind him at his feet weeping, she
began to wet his feet with her tears. Then
she wiped them with her hair, kissed them
and poured perfume on them.
39 When the Pharisee who had invited
him saw this, he said to himself, "If this
man were a prophet, he would know who
is touching him and what kind of woman
she is — that she is a sinner."
40 Jesus answered him, "Simon, I have
something to tell you."
"Tell me, teacher," he said.
41 "Two people owed money to a certain
moneylender. One owed him five hundred
denarii,[a] and the other fifty. 42 Neither of
them had the money to pay him back, so
he forgave the debts of both. Now which
of them will love him more?"
43 Simon replied, "I suppose the one who
had the bigger debt forgiven."
"You have judged correctly," Jesus said.
44 Then he turned toward the woman and said to Simon, "Do you see this
woman? I came into your house. You did
not give me any water for my feet, but she
wet my feet with her tears and wiped them
with her hair. 45 You did not give me a kiss,
but this woman, from the time I entered,
has not stopped kissing my feet. 46 You did
not put oil on my head, but she has poured
perfume on my feet. 47 Therefore, I tell you,
her many sins have been forgiven — as her
great love has shown. But whoever has
been forgiven little loves little."
48 Then Jesus said to her, "Your sins are
forgiven."
49 The other guests began to say among
themselves, "Who is this who even forgives sins?"
50 Jesus said to the woman, "Your faith
has saved you; go in peace."

The Parable of the Sower

8 After this, Jesus traveled about from
one town and village to another, proclaiming the good news of the kingdom of
God. The Twelve were with him, 2 and also
some women who had been cured of evil
spirits and diseases: Mary (called Magdalene) from whom seven demons had come
out; 3 Joanna the wife of Chuza, the manager of Herod's household; Susanna; and
many others. These women were helping
to support them out of their own means.
4 While a large crowd was gathering and
people were coming to Jesus from town
after town, he told this parable: 5 "A farmer
went out to sow his seed. As he was scattering the seed, some fell along the path;
it was trampled on, and the birds ate it
up. 6 Some fell on rocky ground, and when
it came up, the plants withered because
they had no moisture. 7 Other seed fell
among thorns, which grew up with it and
choked the plants. 8 Still other seed fell on
good soil. It came up and yielded a crop,
a hundred times more than was sown."
When he said this, he called out, "Whoever has ears to hear, let them hear."
9 His disciples asked him what this parable meant. 10 He said, "The knowledge
of the secrets of the kingdom of God has
been given to you, but to others I speak
in parables, so that,

"'though seeing, they may not see;
though hearing, they may not
understand.'[b]

11 "This is the meaning of the parable:
The seed is the word of God. 12 Those along
the path are the ones who hear, and then
the devil comes and takes away the word
from their hearts, so that they may not

[a] *41* A denarius was the usual daily wage of a day laborer (see Matt. 20:2). [b] *10* Isaiah 6:9

believe and be saved. 13 Those on the rocky
ground are the ones who receive the word
with joy when they hear it, but they have
no root. They believe for a while, but in the
time of testing they fall away. 14 The seed
that fell among thorns stands for those
who hear, but as they go on their way
they are choked by life's worries, riches
and pleasures, and they do not mature.
15 But the seed on good soil stands for those
with a noble and good heart, who hear
the word, retain it, and by persevering
produce a crop.

A Lamp on a Stand

16 "No one lights a lamp and hides it in
a clay jar or puts it under a bed. Instead,
they put it on a stand, so that those who
come in can see the light. 17 For there is
nothing hidden that will not be disclosed,
and nothing concealed that will not be
known or brought out into the open.
18 Therefore consider carefully how you
listen. Whoever has will be given more;
whoever does not have, even what they
think they have will be taken from them."

Jesus' Mother and Brothers

19 Now Jesus' mother and brothers came
to see him, but they were not able to get
near him because of the crowd. 20 Someone
told him, "Your mother and brothers are
standing outside, wanting to see you."

21 He replied, "My mother and brothers
are those who hear God's word and put it
into practice."

Jesus Calms the Storm

22 One day Jesus said to his disciples, "Let
us go over to the other side of the lake." So
they got into a boat and set out. 23 As they
sailed, he fell asleep. A squall came down
on the lake, so that the boat was being
swamped, and they were in great danger.

24 The disciples went and woke him,
saying, "Master, Master, we're going to
drown!"

He got up and rebuked the wind and
the raging waters; the storm subsided,
and all was calm. 25 "Where is your faith?"
he asked his disciples.

In fear and amazement they asked one
another, "Who is this? He commands even
the winds and the water, and they obey
him."

Jesus Restores a Demon-Possessed Man

26 They sailed to the region of the Gerasenes,[a] which is across the lake from
Galilee. 27 When Jesus stepped ashore, he
was met by a demon-possessed man from
the town. For a long time this man had not
worn clothes or lived in a house, but had
lived in the tombs. 28 When he saw Jesus,
he cried out and fell at his feet, shouting
at the top of his voice, "What do you want
with me, Jesus, Son of the Most High God?
I beg you, don't torture me!" 29 For Jesus
had commanded the impure spirit to come
out of the man. Many times it had seized
him, and though he was chained hand
and foot and kept under guard, he had
broken his chains and had been driven
by the demon into solitary places.

30 Jesus asked him, "What is your
name?"

"Legion," he replied, because many
demons had gone into him. 31 And they
begged Jesus repeatedly not to order them
to go into the Abyss.

32 A large herd of pigs was feeding there
on the hillside. The demons begged Jesus
to let them go into the pigs, and he gave
them permission. 33 When the demons
came out of the man, they went into the
pigs, and the herd rushed down the steep
bank into the lake and was drowned.

34 When those tending the pigs saw
what had happened, they ran off and reported this in the town and countryside,
35 and the people went out to see what
had happened. When they came to Jesus,
they found the man from whom the demons had gone out, sitting at Jesus' feet,
dressed and in his right mind; and they
were afraid. 36 Those who had seen it told
the people how the demon-possessed man
had been cured. 37 Then all the people of
the region of the Gerasenes asked Jesus to
leave them, because they were overcome
with fear. So he got into the boat and left.

38 The man from whom the demons had
gone out begged to go with him, but Jesus
sent him away, saying, 39 "Return home
and tell how much God has done for you."
So the man went away and told all over
town how much Jesus had done for him.

Jesus Raises a Dead Girl and Heals a Sick Woman

40 Now when Jesus returned, a crowd
welcomed him, for they were all expecting
him. 41 Then a man named Jairus, a synagogue leader, came and fell at Jesus' feet,
pleading with him to come to his house
42 because his only daughter, a girl of about
twelve, was dying.

As Jesus was on his way, the crowds
almost crushed him. 43 And a woman was

[a] 26 Some manuscripts *Gadarenes*; other manuscripts *Gergesenes*; also in verse 37

there who had been subject to bleeding for
twelve years,[a] but no one could heal her.
44 She came up behind him and touched
the edge of his cloak, and immediately
her bleeding stopped.
45 "Who touched me?" Jesus asked.
When they all denied it, Peter said,
"Master, the people are crowding and
pressing against you."
46 But Jesus said, "Someone touched me;
I know that power has gone out from me."
47 Then the woman, seeing that she
could not go unnoticed, came trembling
and fell at his feet. In the presence of all
the people, she told why she had touched
him and how she had been instantly
healed. 48 Then he said to her, "Daughter,
your faith has healed you. Go in peace."
49 While Jesus was still speaking, someone came from the house of Jairus, the synagogue leader. "Your daughter is dead," he
said. "Don't bother the teacher anymore."
50 Hearing this, Jesus said to Jairus,
"Don't be afraid; just believe, and she
will be healed."
51 When he arrived at the house of Jairus, he did not let anyone go in with him
except Peter, John and James, and the
child's father and mother. 52 Meanwhile,
all the people were wailing and mourning
for her. "Stop wailing," Jesus said. "She is
not dead but asleep."
53 They laughed at him, knowing that
she was dead. 54 But he took her by the
hand and said, "My child, get up!" 55 Her
spirit returned, and at once she stood up.
Then Jesus told them to give her something to eat. 56 Her parents were astonished, but he ordered them not to tell
anyone what had happened.

Jesus Sends Out the Twelve

9 When Jesus had called the Twelve
together, he gave them power and
authority to drive out all demons and to
cure diseases, 2 and he sent them out to
proclaim the kingdom of God and to heal
the sick. 3 He told them: "Take nothing for
the journey — no staff, no bag, no bread,
no money, no extra shirt. 4 Whatever house
you enter, stay there until you leave that
town. 5 If people do not welcome you, leave
their town and shake the dust off your feet
as a testimony against them." 6 So they
set out and went from village to village,
proclaiming the good news and healing
people everywhere.
7 Now Herod the tetrarch heard about all
that was going on. And he was perplexed
because some were saying that John had
been raised from the dead, 8 others that
Elijah had appeared, and still others that
one of the prophets of long ago had come
back to life. 9 But Herod said, "I beheaded
John. Who, then, is this I hear such things
about?" And he tried to see him.

Jesus Feeds the Five Thousand

10 When the apostles returned, they reported to Jesus what they had done. Then
he took them with him and they withdrew
by themselves to a town called Bethsaida,
11 but the crowds learned about it and followed him. He welcomed them and spoke
to them about the kingdom of God, and
healed those who needed healing.
12 Late in the afternoon the Twelve
came to him and said, "Send the crowd
away so they can go to the surrounding
villages and countryside and find food
and lodging, because we are in a remote
place here."
13 He replied, "You give them something
to eat."
They answered, "We have only five
loaves of bread and two fish — unless
we go and buy food for all this crowd."
14 (About five thousand men were there.)
But he said to his disciples, "Have them
sit down in groups of about fifty each."
15 The disciples did so, and everyone sat
down. 16 Taking the five loaves and the two
fish and looking up to heaven, he gave
thanks and broke them. Then he gave
them to the disciples to distribute to the
people. 17 They all ate and were satisfied,
and the disciples picked up twelve basketfuls of broken pieces that were left over.

Peter Declares That Jesus Is the Messiah

18 Once when Jesus was praying in private and his disciples were with him,
he asked them, "Who do the crowds say
I am?"
19 They replied, "Some say John the Baptist; others say Elijah; and still others, that
one of the prophets of long ago has come
back to life."
20 "But what about you?" he asked. "Who
do you say I am?"
Peter answered, "God's Messiah."

Jesus Predicts His Death

21 Jesus strictly warned them not to tell
this to anyone. 22 And he said, "The Son of
Man must suffer many things and be rejected by the elders, the chief priests and
the teachers of the law, and he must be
killed and on the third day be raised to life."

[a] 43 Many manuscripts *years, and she had spent all she had on doctors*

23 Then he said to them all: "Whoever
wants to be my disciple must deny themselves and take up their cross daily and
follow me. 24 For whoever wants to save
their life will lose it, but whoever loses their
life for me will save it. 25 What good is it for
someone to gain the whole world, and yet
lose or forfeit their very self? 26 Whoever
is ashamed of me and my words, the Son
of Man will be ashamed of them when he
comes in his glory and in the glory of the
Father and of the holy angels.
27 "Truly I tell you, some who are standing here will not taste death before they
see the kingdom of God."

The Transfiguration

28 About eight days after Jesus said this,
he took Peter, John and James with him
and went up onto a mountain to pray. 29 As
he was praying, the appearance of his face
changed, and his clothes became as bright
as a flash of lightning. 30 Two men, Moses
and Elijah, appeared in glorious splendor,
talking with Jesus. 31 They spoke about his
departure,[a] which he was about to bring
to fulfillment at Jerusalem. 32 Peter and his
companions were very sleepy, but when
they became fully awake, they saw his
glory and the two men standing with him.
33 As the men were leaving Jesus, Peter said
to him, "Master, it is good for us to be here.
Let us put up three shelters — one for you,
one for Moses and one for Elijah." (He did
not know what he was saying.)
34 While he was speaking, a cloud appeared and covered them, and they were
afraid as they entered the cloud. 35 A voice
came from the cloud, saying, "This is my
Son, whom I have chosen; listen to him."
36 When the voice had spoken, they found
that Jesus was alone. The disciples kept
this to themselves and did not tell anyone
at that time what they had seen.

Jesus Heals a Demon-Possessed Boy

37 The next day, when they came down
from the mountain, a large crowd met
him. 38 A man in the crowd called out,
"Teacher, I beg you to look at my son, for
he is my only child. 39 A spirit seizes him
and he suddenly screams; it throws him
into convulsions so that he foams at the
mouth. It scarcely ever leaves him and is
destroying him. 40 I begged your disciples
to drive it out, but they could not."
41 "You unbelieving and perverse generation," Jesus replied, "how long shall I
stay with you and put up with you? Bring
your son here."
42 Even while the boy was coming, the
demon threw him to the ground in a convulsion. But Jesus rebuked the impure
spirit, healed the boy and gave him back
to his father. 43 And they were all amazed
at the greatness of God.

Jesus Predicts His Death a Second Time

While everyone was marveling at all
that Jesus did, he said to his disciples,
44 "Listen carefully to what I am about
to tell you: The Son of Man is going to be
delivered into the hands of men." 45 But
they did not understand what this meant.
It was hidden from them, so that they did
not grasp it, and they were afraid to ask
him about it.
46 An argument started among the disciples as to which of them would be the
greatest. 47 Jesus, knowing their thoughts,
took a little child and had him stand beside him. 48 Then he said to them, "Whoever welcomes this little child in my name
welcomes me; and whoever welcomes me
welcomes the one who sent me. For it is
the one who is least among you all who
is the greatest."
49 "Master," said John, "we saw someone driving out demons in your name
and we tried to stop him, because he is
not one of us."
50 "Do not stop him," Jesus said, "for
whoever is not against you is for you."

Samaritan Opposition

51 As the time approached for him to be
taken up to heaven, Jesus resolutely set
out for Jerusalem. 52 And he sent messengers on ahead, who went into a Samaritan
village to get things ready for him; 53 but
the people there did not welcome him,
because he was heading for Jerusalem.
54 When the disciples James and John saw
this, they asked, "Lord, do you want us
to call fire down from heaven to destroy
them[b]?" 55 But Jesus turned and rebuked
them. 56 Then he and his disciples went to
another village.

The Cost of Following Jesus

57 As they were walking along the road,
a man said to him, "I will follow you wherever you go."
58 Jesus replied, "Foxes have dens and
birds have nests, but the Son of Man has
no place to lay his head."
59 He said to another man, "Follow me."
But he replied, "Lord, first let me go and
bury my father."

[a] 31 Greek *exodos* [b] 54 Some manuscripts *them, just as Elijah did*

60 Jesus said to him, "Let the dead bury their own dead, but you go and proclaim the kingdom of God."

61 Still another said, "I will follow you, Lord; but first let me go back and say goodbye to my family."

62 Jesus replied, "No one who puts a hand to the plow and looks back is fit for service in the kingdom of God."

Jesus Sends Out the Seventy-Two

10 After this the Lord appointed seventy-two[a] others and sent them two by two ahead of him to every town and place where he was about to go. 2 He told them, "The harvest is plentiful, but the workers are few. Ask the Lord of the harvest, therefore, to send out workers into his harvest field. 3 Go! I am sending you out like lambs among wolves. 4 Do not take a purse or bag or sandals; and do not greet anyone on the road.

5 "When you enter a house, first say, 'Peace to this house.' 6 If someone who promotes peace is there, your peace will rest on them; if not, it will return to you. 7 Stay there, eating and drinking whatever they give you, for the worker deserves his wages. Do not move around from house to house.

8 "When you enter a town and are welcomed, eat what is offered to you. 9 Heal the sick who are there and tell them, 'The kingdom of God has come near to you.' 10 But when you enter a town and are not welcomed, go into its streets and say, 11 'Even the dust of your town we wipe from our feet as a warning to you. Yet be sure of this: The kingdom of God has come near.' 12 I tell you, it will be more bearable on that day for Sodom than for that town.

13 "Woe to you, Chorazin! Woe to you, Bethsaida! For if the miracles that were performed in you had been performed in Tyre and Sidon, they would have repented long ago, sitting in sackcloth and ashes. 14 But it will be more bearable for Tyre and Sidon at the judgment than for you. 15 And you, Capernaum, will you be lifted to the heavens? No, you will go down to Hades.[b]

16 "Whoever listens to you listens to me; whoever rejects you rejects me; but whoever rejects me rejects him who sent me."

17 The seventy-two returned with joy and said, "Lord, even the demons submit to us in your name."

18 He replied, "I saw Satan fall like lightning from heaven. 19 I have given you authority to trample on snakes and scorpions and to overcome all the power of the enemy; nothing will harm you. 20 However, do not rejoice that the spirits submit to you, but rejoice that your names are written in heaven."

21 At that time Jesus, full of joy through the Holy Spirit, said, "I praise you, Father, Lord of heaven and earth, because you have hidden these things from the wise and learned, and revealed them to little children. Yes, Father, for this is what you were pleased to do.

22 "All things have been committed to me by my Father. No one knows who the Son is except the Father, and no one knows who the Father is except the Son and those to whom the Son chooses to reveal him."

23 Then he turned to his disciples and said privately, "Blessed are the eyes that see what you see. 24 For I tell you that many prophets and kings wanted to see what you see but did not see it, and to hear what you hear but did not hear it."

The Parable of the Good Samaritan

25 On one occasion an expert in the law stood up to test Jesus. "Teacher," he asked, "what must I do to inherit eternal life?"

26 "What is written in the Law?" he replied. "How do you read it?"

27 He answered, " 'Love the Lord your God with all your heart and with all your soul and with all your strength and with all your mind'[c]; and, 'Love your neighbor as yourself.'[d]"

28 "You have answered correctly," Jesus replied. "Do this and you will live."

29 But he wanted to justify himself, so he asked Jesus, "And who is my neighbor?"

30 In reply Jesus said: "A man was going down from Jerusalem to Jericho, when he was attacked by robbers. They stripped him of his clothes, beat him and went away, leaving him half dead. 31 A priest happened to be going down the same road, and when he saw the man, he passed by on the other side. 32 So too, a Levite, when he came to the place and saw him, passed by on the other side. 33 But a Samaritan, as he traveled, came where the man was; and when he saw him, he took pity on him. 34 He went to him and bandaged his wounds, pouring on oil and wine. Then he put the man on his own donkey, brought him to an inn and took care of him. 35 The next day he took out two denarii[e] and gave them to the innkeeper. 'Look after him,' he said, 'and when I return, I will reimburse you for any extra expense you may have.'

[a] *1* Some manuscripts *seventy;* also in verse 17 [b] *15* That is, the realm of the dead [c] *27* Deut. 6:5
[d] *27* Lev. 19:18 [e] *35* A denarius was the usual daily wage of a day laborer (see Matt. 20:2).

36 "Which of these three do you think
was a neighbor to the man who fell into
the hands of robbers?"

37 The expert in the law replied, "The one
who had mercy on him."

Jesus told him, "Go and do likewise."

At the Home of Martha and Mary

38 As Jesus and his disciples were on their
way, he came to a village where a woman named Martha opened her home to
him. 39 She had a sister called Mary, who
sat at the Lord's feet listening to what he
said. 40 But Martha was distracted by all
the preparations that had to be made.
She came to him and asked, "Lord, don't
you care that my sister has left me to do
the work by myself? Tell her to help me!"

41 "Martha, Martha," the Lord answered,
"you are worried and upset about many
things, 42 but few things are needed — or
indeed only one.[a] Mary has chosen what
is better, and it will not be taken away
from her."

Jesus' Teaching on Prayer

11 One day Jesus was praying in a certain place. When he finished, one of
his disciples said to him, "Lord, teach us
to pray, just as John taught his disciples."

2 He said to them, "When you pray, say:

"'Father,[b]
hallowed be your name,
your kingdom come.[c]
3 Give us each day our daily bread.
4 Forgive us our sins,
for we also forgive everyone who
sins against us.[d]
And lead us not into temptation.[e]'"

5 Then Jesus said to them, "Suppose
you have a friend, and you go to him at
midnight and say, 'Friend, lend me three
loaves of bread; 6 a friend of mine on a
journey has come to me, and I have no
food to offer him.' 7 And suppose the one
inside answers, 'Don't bother me. The door
is already locked, and my children and I
are in bed. I can't get up and give you anything.' 8 I tell you, even though he will not
get up and give you the bread because of
friendship, yet because of your shameless
audacity[f] he will surely get up and give
you as much as you need.

9 "So I say to you: Ask and it will be giv-
en to you; seek and you will find; knock
and the door will be opened to you. 10 For
everyone who asks receives; the one who
seeks finds; and to the one who knocks,
the door will be opened.

11 "Which of you fathers, if your son asks
for[g] a fish, will give him a snake instead?
12 Or if he asks for an egg, will give him a
scorpion? 13 If you then, though you are evil,
know how to give good gifts to your children,
how much more will your Father in heaven
give the Holy Spirit to those who ask him!"

Jesus and Beelzebul

14 Jesus was driving out a demon that
was mute. When the demon left, the man
who had been mute spoke, and the crowd
was amazed. 15 But some of them said, "By
Beelzebul, the prince of demons, he is driving out demons." 16 Others tested him by
asking for a sign from heaven.

17 Jesus knew their thoughts and said
to them: "Any kingdom divided against
itself will be ruined, and a house divided
against itself will fall. 18 If Satan is divided against himself, how can his kingdom
stand? I say this because you claim that I
drive out demons by Beelzebul. 19 Now if I
drive out demons by Beelzebul, by whom
do your followers drive them out? So then,
they will be your judges. 20 But if I drive
out demons by the finger of God, then
the kingdom of God has come upon you.

21 "When a strong man, fully armed,
guards his own house, his possessions
are safe. 22 But when someone stronger
attacks and overpowers him, he takes
away the armor in which the man trusted
and divides up his plunder.

23 "Whoever is not with me is against
me, and whoever does not gather with
me scatters.

24 "When an impure spirit comes out
of a person, it goes through arid places
seeking rest and does not find it. Then
it says, 'I will return to the house I left.'
25 When it arrives, it finds the house swept
clean and put in order. 26 Then it goes and
takes seven other spirits more wicked than
itself, and they go in and live there. And
the final condition of that person is worse
than the first."

27 As Jesus was saying these things, a
woman in the crowd called out, "Blessed
is the mother who gave you birth and
nursed you."

28 He replied, "Blessed rather are those
who hear the word of God and obey it."

[a] 42 Some manuscripts *but only one thing is needed* [b] 2 Some manuscripts *Our Father in heaven* [c] 2 Some manuscripts *come. May your will be done on earth as it is in heaven.* [d] 4 Greek *everyone who is indebted to us* [e] 4 Some manuscripts *temptation, but deliver us from the evil one* [f] 8 *Or yet to preserve his good name* [g] 11 Some manuscripts *for bread, will give him a stone? Or if he asks for*

The Sign of Jonah

29As the crowds increased, Jesus said,
"This is a wicked generation. It asks for a
sign, but none will be given it except the
sign of Jonah. 30For as Jonah was a sign to
the Ninevites, so also will the Son of Man
be to this generation. 31The Queen of the
South will rise at the judgment with the
people of this generation and condemn
them, for she came from the ends of the
earth to listen to Solomon's wisdom; and
now something greater than Solomon is
here. 32The men of Nineveh will stand
up at the judgment with this generation
and condemn it, for they repented at the
preaching of Jonah; and now something
greater than Jonah is here.

The Lamp of the Body

33"No one lights a lamp and puts it in
a place where it will be hidden, or under
a bowl. Instead they put it on its stand,
so that those who come in may see the
light. 34Your eye is the lamp of your body.
When your eyes are healthy,[a] your whole
body also is full of light. But when they
are unhealthy,[b] your body also is full of
darkness. 35See to it, then, that the light
within you is not darkness. 36Therefore,
if your whole body is full of light, and no
part of it dark, it will be just as full of light
as when a lamp shines its light on you."

Woes on the Pharisees and the Experts in the Law

37When Jesus had finished speaking,
a Pharisee invited him to eat with him;
so he went in and reclined at the table.
38But the Pharisee was surprised when
he noticed that Jesus did not first wash
before the meal.

39Then the Lord said to him, "Now then,
you Pharisees clean the outside of the cup
and dish, but inside you are full of greed
and wickedness. 40You foolish people! Did
not the one who made the outside make
the inside also? 41But now as for what is
inside you — be generous to the poor, and
everything will be clean for you.

42"Woe to you Pharisees, because you
give God a tenth of your mint, rue and
all other kinds of garden herbs, but you
neglect justice and the love of God. You
should have practiced the latter without
leaving the former undone.

43"Woe to you Pharisees, because you
love the most important seats in the synagogues and respectful greetings in the
marketplaces.

44"Woe to you, because you are like un-
marked graves, which people walk over
without knowing it."

45One of the experts in the law answered
him, "Teacher, when you say these things,
you insult us also."

46Jesus replied, "And you experts in the
law, woe to you, because you load people
down with burdens they can hardly carry,
and you yourselves will not lift one finger
to help them.

47"Woe to you, because you build tombs
for the prophets, and it was your ancestors who killed them. 48So you testify that
you approve of what your ancestors did;
they killed the prophets, and you build
their tombs. 49Because of this, God in his
wisdom said, 'I will send them prophets
and apostles, some of whom they will kill
and others they will persecute.' 50Therefore
this generation will be held responsible for
the blood of all the prophets that has been
shed since the beginning of the world,
51from the blood of Abel to the blood of
Zechariah, who was killed between the
altar and the sanctuary. Yes, I tell you,
this generation will be held responsible
for it all.

52"Woe to you experts in the law, because you have taken away the key to
knowledge. You yourselves have not entered, and you have hindered those who
were entering."

53When Jesus went outside, the Pharisees and the teachers of the law began
to oppose him fiercely and to besiege him
with questions, 54waiting to catch him in
something he might say.

Warnings and Encouragements

12 Meanwhile, when a crowd of many
thousands had gathered, so that
they were trampling on one another, Jesus
began to speak first to his disciples, saying: "Be[c] on your guard against the yeast
of the Pharisees, which is hypocrisy. 2There
is nothing concealed that will not be disclosed, or hidden that will not be made
known. 3What you have said in the dark
will be heard in the daylight, and what
you have whispered in the ear in the inner
rooms will be proclaimed from the roofs.

4"I tell you, my friends, do not be afraid
of those who kill the body and after that
can do no more. 5But I will show you whom
you should fear: Fear him who, after your
body has been killed, has authority to
throw you into hell. Yes, I tell you, fear
him. 6Are not five sparrows sold for two

[a] 34 The Greek for *healthy* here implies *generous.* [b] 34 The Greek for *unhealthy* here implies *stingy.* [c] 1 Or *speak to his disciples, saying: "First of all, be*

pennies? Yet not one of them is forgotten by God. 7 Indeed, the very hairs of your head are all numbered. Don't be afraid; you are worth more than many sparrows.

8 "I tell you, whoever publicly acknowledges me before others, the Son of Man will also acknowledge before the angels of God. 9 But whoever disowns me before others will be disowned before the angels of God. 10 And everyone who speaks a word against the Son of Man will be forgiven, but anyone who blasphemes against the Holy Spirit will not be forgiven.

11 "When you are brought before synagogues, rulers and authorities, do not worry about how you will defend yourselves or what you will say, 12 for the Holy Spirit will teach you at that time what you should say."

The Parable of the Rich Fool

13 Someone in the crowd said to him, "Teacher, tell my brother to divide the inheritance with me."

14 Jesus replied, "Man, who appointed me a judge or an arbiter between you?" 15 Then he said to them, "Watch out! Be on your guard against all kinds of greed; life does not consist in an abundance of possessions."

16 And he told them this parable: "The ground of a certain rich man yielded an abundant harvest. 17 He thought to himself, 'What shall I do? I have no place to store my crops.'

18 "Then he said, 'This is what I'll do. I will tear down my barns and build bigger ones, and there I will store my surplus grain. 19 And I'll say to myself, "You have plenty of grain laid up for many years. Take life easy; eat, drink and be merry." '

20 "But God said to him, 'You fool! This very night your life will be demanded from you. Then who will get what you have prepared for yourself?'

21 "This is how it will be with whoever stores up things for themselves but is not rich toward God."

Do Not Worry

22 Then Jesus said to his disciples: "Therefore I tell you, do not worry about your life, what you will eat; or about your body, what you will wear. 23 For life is more than food, and the body more than clothes. 24 Consider the ravens: They do not sow or reap, they have no storeroom or barn; yet God feeds them. And how much more valuable you are than birds! 25 Who of you by worrying can add a single hour to your life[a]? 26 Since you cannot do this very little thing, why do you worry about the rest?

27 "Consider how the wild flowers grow. They do not labor or spin. Yet I tell you, not even Solomon in all his splendor was dressed like one of these. 28 If that is how God clothes the grass of the field, which is here today, and tomorrow is thrown into the fire, how much more will he clothe you — you of little faith! 29 And do not set your heart on what you will eat or drink; do not worry about it. 30 For the pagan world runs after all such things, and your Father knows that you need them. 31 But seek his kingdom, and these things will be given to you as well.

32 "Do not be afraid, little flock, for your Father has been pleased to give you the kingdom. 33 Sell your possessions and give to the poor. Provide purses for yourselves that will not wear out, a treasure in heaven that will never fail, where no thief comes near and no moth destroys. 34 For where your treasure is, there your heart will be also.

Watchfulness

35 "Be dressed ready for service and keep your lamps burning, 36 like servants waiting for their master to return from a wedding banquet, so that when he comes and knocks they can immediately open the door for him. 37 It will be good for those servants whose master finds them watching when he comes. Truly I tell you, he will dress himself to serve, will have them recline at the table and will come and wait on them. 38 It will be good for those servants whose master finds them ready, even if he comes in the middle of the night or toward daybreak. 39 But understand this: If the owner of the house had known at what hour the thief was coming, he would not have let his house be broken into. 40 You also must be ready, because the Son of Man will come at an hour when you do not expect him."

41 Peter asked, "Lord, are you telling this parable to us, or to everyone?"

42 The Lord answered, "Who then is the faithful and wise manager, whom the master puts in charge of his servants to give them their food allowance at the proper time? 43 It will be good for that servant whom the master finds doing so when he returns. 44 Truly I tell you, he will put him in charge of all his possessions. 45 But suppose the servant says to himself, 'My master is taking a long time in coming,' and he then begins to beat the other servants, both men and women, and to eat

[a] 25 Or *single cubit to your height*

and drink and get drunk. 46The master of
that servant will come on a day when he
does not expect him and at an hour he is
not aware of. He will cut him to pieces and
assign him a place with the unbelievers.
47"The servant who knows the master's
will and does not get ready or does not do
what the master wants will be beaten with
many blows. 48But the one who does not
know and does things deserving punishment will be beaten with few blows. From
everyone who has been given much, much
will be demanded; and from the one who
has been entrusted with much, much more
will be asked.

Not Peace but Division

49"I have come to bring fire on the earth,
and how I wish it were already kindled!
50But I have a baptism to undergo, and
what constraint I am under until it is
completed! 51Do you think I came to bring
peace on earth? No, I tell you, but division.
52From now on there will be five in one
family divided against each other, three
against two and two against three. 53They
will be divided, father against son and son
against father, mother against daughter
and daughter against mother, mother-in-
law against daughter-in-law and daughter-
in-law against mother-in-law."

Interpreting the Times

54He said to the crowd: "When you see a
cloud rising in the west, immediately you
say, 'It's going to rain,' and it does. 55And
when the south wind blows, you say, 'It's
going to be hot,' and it is. 56Hypocrites! You
know how to interpret the appearance of
the earth and the sky. How is it that you
don't know how to interpret this present
time?
57"Why don't you judge for yourselves
what is right? 58As you are going with your
adversary to the magistrate, try hard to
be reconciled on the way, or your adversary may drag you off to the judge, and
the judge turn you over to the officer, and
the officer throw you into prison. 59I tell
you, you will not get out until you have
paid the last penny."

Repent or Perish

13 Now there were some present at that
time who told Jesus about the Galileans whose blood Pilate had mixed with
their sacrifices. 2Jesus answered, "Do you
think that these Galileans were worse sinners than all the other Galileans because
they suffered this way? 3I tell you, no! But
unless you repent, you too will all perish.
4Or those eighteen who died when the tower in Siloam fell on them — do you think
they were more guilty than all the others
living in Jerusalem? 5I tell you, no! But
unless you repent, you too will all perish."
6Then he told this parable: "A man had
a fig tree growing in his vineyard, and he
went to look for fruit on it but did not find
any. 7So he said to the man who took care
of the vineyard, 'For three years now I've
been coming to look for fruit on this fig
tree and haven't found any. Cut it down!
Why should it use up the soil?'
8"'Sir,' the man replied, 'leave it alone
for one more year, and I'll dig around it
and fertilize it. 9If it bears fruit next year,
fine! If not, then cut it down.'"

Jesus Heals a Crippled Woman on the Sabbath

10On a Sabbath Jesus was teaching in
one of the synagogues, 11and a woman
was there who had been crippled by a
spirit for eighteen years. She was bent over
and could not straighten up at all. 12When
Jesus saw her, he called her forward and
said to her, "Woman, you are set free from
your infirmity." 13Then he put his hands
on her, and immediately she straightened
up and praised God.
14Indignant because Jesus had healed
on the Sabbath, the synagogue leader said
to the people, "There are six days for work.
So come and be healed on those days, not
on the Sabbath."
15The Lord answered him, "You hypocrites! Doesn't each of you on the Sabbath
untie your ox or donkey from the stall and
lead it out to give it water? 16Then should
not this woman, a daughter of Abraham,
whom Satan has kept bound for eighteen
long years, be set free on the Sabbath day
from what bound her?"
17When he said this, all his opponents
were humiliated, but the people were delighted with all the wonderful things he
was doing.

The Parables of the Mustard Seed and the Yeast

18Then Jesus asked, "What is the kingdom of God like? What shall I compare
it to? 19It is like a mustard seed, which a
man took and planted in his garden. It
grew and became a tree, and the birds
perched in its branches."
20Again he asked, "What shall I compare
the kingdom of God to? 21It is like yeast
that a woman took and mixed into about
sixty pounds[a] of flour until it worked all
through the dough."

[a] *21* Or about 27 kilograms

The Narrow Door

22Then Jesus went through the towns and villages, teaching as he made his way to Jerusalem. 23Someone asked him, "Lord, are only a few people going to be saved?"

He said to them, 24"Make every effort to enter through the narrow door, because many, I tell you, will try to enter and will not be able to. 25Once the owner of the house gets up and closes the door, you will stand outside knocking and pleading, 'Sir, open the door for us.'

"But he will answer, 'I don't know you or where you come from.'

26"Then you will say, 'We ate and drank with you, and you taught in our streets.'

27"But he will reply, 'I don't know you or where you come from. Away from me, all you evildoers!'

28"There will be weeping there, and gnashing of teeth, when you see Abraham, Isaac and Jacob and all the prophets in the kingdom of God, but you yourselves thrown out. 29People will come from east and west and north and south, and will take their places at the feast in the kingdom of God. 30Indeed there are those who are last who will be first, and first who will be last."

Jesus' Sorrow for Jerusalem

31At that time some Pharisees came to Jesus and said to him, "Leave this place and go somewhere else. Herod wants to kill you."

32He replied, "Go tell that fox, 'I will keep on driving out demons and healing people today and tomorrow, and on the third day I will reach my goal.' 33In any case, I must press on today and tomorrow and the next day — for surely no prophet can die outside Jerusalem!

34"Jerusalem, Jerusalem, you who kill the prophets and stone those sent to you, how often I have longed to gather your children together, as a hen gathers her chicks under her wings, and you were not willing. 35Look, your house is left to you desolate. I tell you, you will not see me again until you say, 'Blessed is he who comes in the name of the Lord.'[a]"

Jesus at a Pharisee's House

14 One Sabbath, when Jesus went to eat in the house of a prominent Pharisee, he was being carefully watched. 2There in front of him was a man suffering from abnormal swelling of his body. 3Jesus asked the Pharisees and experts in the law, "Is it lawful to heal on the Sabbath or not?" 4But they remained silent. So taking hold of the man, he healed him and sent him on his way.

5Then he asked them, "If one of you has a child[b] or an ox that falls into a well on the Sabbath day, will you not immediately pull it out?" 6And they had nothing to say.

7When he noticed how the guests picked the places of honor at the table, he told them this parable: 8"When someone invites you to a wedding feast, do not take the place of honor, for a person more distinguished than you may have been invited. 9If so, the host who invited both of you will come and say to you, 'Give this person your seat.' Then, humiliated, you will have to take the least important place. 10But when you are invited, take the lowest place, so that when your host comes, he will say to you, 'Friend, move up to a better place.' Then you will be honored in the presence of all the other guests. 11For all those who exalt themselves will be humbled, and those who humble themselves will be exalted."

12Then Jesus said to his host, "When you give a luncheon or dinner, do not invite your friends, your brothers or sisters, your relatives, or your rich neighbors; if you do, they may invite you back and so you will be repaid. 13But when you give a banquet, invite the poor, the crippled, the lame, the blind, 14and you will be blessed. Although they cannot repay you, you will be repaid at the resurrection of the righteous."

The Parable of the Great Banquet

15When one of those at the table with him heard this, he said to Jesus, "Blessed is the one who will eat at the feast in the kingdom of God."

16Jesus replied: "A certain man was preparing a great banquet and invited many guests. 17At the time of the banquet he sent his servant to tell those who had been invited, 'Come, for everything is now ready.'

18"But they all alike began to make excuses. The first said, 'I have just bought a field, and I must go and see it. Please excuse me.'

19"Another said, 'I have just bought five yoke of oxen, and I'm on my way to try them out. Please excuse me.'

20"Still another said, 'I just got married, so I can't come.'

21"The servant came back and reported this to his master. Then the owner of the house became angry and ordered his servant, 'Go out quickly into the streets and alleys of the town and bring in the poor, the crippled, the blind and the lame.'

[a] *35* Psalm 118:26 [b] *5* Some manuscripts *donkey*

22"'Sir,' the servant said, 'what you ordered has been done, but there is still
room.'
23"Then the master told his servant,
'Go out to the roads and country lanes
and compel them to come in, so that my
house will be full. 24I tell you, not one of
those who were invited will get a taste of
my banquet.'"

The Cost of Being a Disciple

**25Large crowds were traveling with
Jesus, and turning to them he said:** 26"If
anyone comes to me and does not hate
father and mother, wife and children,
brothers and sisters — yes, even their own
life — such a person cannot be my disciple.
27And whoever does not carry their cross
and follow me cannot be my disciple.
28"Suppose one of you wants to build a
tower. Won't you first sit down and esti-
mate the cost to see if you have enough
money to complete it? 29For if you lay the
foundation and are not able to finish it,
everyone who sees it will ridicule you,
30saying, 'This person began to build and
wasn't able to finish.'
31"Or suppose a king is about to go to
war against another king. Won't he first
sit down and consider whether he is able
with ten thousand men to oppose the one
coming against him with twenty thousand? 32If he is not able, he will send a
delegation while the other is still a long
way off and will ask for terms of peace.
33In the same way, those of you who do
not give up everything you have cannot
be my disciples.
34"Salt is good, but if it loses its saltiness,
how can it be made salty again? 35It is fit
neither for the soil nor for the manure
pile; it is thrown out.
"Whoever has ears to hear, let them
hear."

The Parable of the Lost Sheep

**15 Now the tax collectors and sinners
were all gathering around to hear
Jesus. 2But the Pharisees and the teachers
of the law muttered, "This man welcomes
sinners and eats with them."**
3Then Jesus told them this parable:
4"Suppose one of you has a hundred sheep
and loses one of them. Doesn't he leave
the ninety-nine in the open country and
go after the lost sheep until he finds it?
5And when he finds it, he joyfully puts it
on his shoulders 6and goes home. Then he
calls his friends and neighbors together
and says, 'Rejoice with me; I have found
my lost sheep.' 7I tell you that in the same
way there will be more rejoicing in heaven
over one sinner who repents than over
ninety-nine righteous persons who do
not need to repent.

The Parable of the Lost Coin

8"Or suppose a woman has ten silver
coins[a] and loses one. Doesn't she light a
lamp, sweep the house and search carefully until she finds it? 9And when she finds
it, she calls her friends and neighbors together and says, 'Rejoice with me; I have
found my lost coin.' 10In the same way, I
tell you, there is rejoicing in the presence
of the angels of God over one sinner who
repents."

The Parable of the Lost Son

11Jesus continued: "There was a man
who had two sons. 12The younger one said
to his father, 'Father, give me my share
of the estate.' So he divided his property
between them.
13"Not long after that, the younger son
got together all he had, set off for a distant country and there squandered his
wealth in wild living. 14After he had spent
everything, there was a severe famine in
that whole country, and he began to be
in need. 15So he went and hired himself
out to a citizen of that country, who sent
him to his fields to feed pigs. 16He longed
to fill his stomach with the pods that the
pigs were eating, but no one gave him
anything.
17"When he came to his senses, he said,
'How many of my father's hired servants
have food to spare, and here I am starving
to death! 18I will set out and go back to
my father and say to him: Father, I have
sinned against heaven and against you. 19I
am no longer worthy to be called your son;
make me like one of your hired servants.'
20So he got up and went to his father.
"But while he was still a long way off, his
father saw him and was filled with compassion for him; he ran to his son, threw
his arms around him and kissed him.
21"The son said to him, 'Father, I have
sinned against heaven and against you. I
am no longer worthy to be called your son.'
22"But the father said to his servants,
'Quick! Bring the best robe and put it on
him. Put a ring on his finger and sandals
on his feet. 23Bring the fattened calf and
kill it. Let's have a feast and celebrate.
24For this son of mine was dead and is
alive again; he was lost and is found.' So
they began to celebrate.

[a] *8* Greek *ten drachmas,* each worth about a day's wages

25 "Meanwhile, the older son was in the field. When he came near the house, he heard music and dancing. 26 So he called one of the servants and asked him what was going on. 27 'Your brother has come,' he replied, 'and your father has killed the fattened calf because he has him back safe and sound.'

28 "The older brother became angry and refused to go in. So his father went out and pleaded with him. 29 But he answered his father, 'Look! All these years I've been slaving for you and never disobeyed your orders. Yet you never gave me even a young goat so I could celebrate with my friends. 30 But when this son of yours who has squandered your property with prostitutes comes home, you kill the fattened calf for him!'

31 " 'My son,' the father said, 'you are always with me, and everything I have is yours. 32 But we had to celebrate and be glad, because this brother of yours was dead and is alive again; he was lost and is found.' "

The Parable of the Shrewd Manager

16 Jesus told his disciples: "There was a rich man whose manager was accused of wasting his possessions. 2 So he called him in and asked him, 'What is this I hear about you? Give an account of your management, because you cannot be manager any longer.'

3 "The manager said to himself, 'What shall I do now? My master is taking away my job. I'm not strong enough to dig, and I'm ashamed to beg — 4 I know what I'll do so that, when I lose my job here, people will welcome me into their houses.'

5 "So he called in each one of his master's debtors. He asked the first, 'How much do you owe my master?'

6 " 'Nine hundred gallons[a] of olive oil,' he replied.

"The manager told him, 'Take your bill, sit down quickly, and make it four hundred and fifty.'

7 "Then he asked the second, 'And how much do you owe?'

" 'A thousand bushels[b] of wheat,' he replied.

"He told him, 'Take your bill and make it eight hundred.'

8 "The master commended the dishonest manager because he had acted shrewdly. For the people of this world are more shrewd in dealing with their own kind than are the people of the light. 9 I tell you, use worldly wealth to gain friends for yourselves, so that when it is gone, you will be welcomed into eternal dwellings.

10 "Whoever can be trusted with very little can also be trusted with much, and whoever is dishonest with very little will also be dishonest with much. 11 So if you have not been trustworthy in handling worldly wealth, who will trust you with true riches? 12 And if you have not been trustworthy with someone else's property, who will give you property of your own?

13 "No one can serve two masters. Either you will hate the one and love the other, or you will be devoted to the one and despise the other. You cannot serve both God and money."

14 The Pharisees, who loved money, heard all this and were sneering at Jesus. 15 He said to them, "You are the ones who justify yourselves in the eyes of others, but God knows your hearts. What people value highly is detestable in God's sight.

Additional Teachings

16 "The Law and the Prophets were proclaimed until John. Since that time, the good news of the kingdom of God is being preached, and everyone is forcing their way into it. 17 It is easier for heaven and earth to disappear than for the least stroke of a pen to drop out of the Law.

18 "Anyone who divorces his wife and marries another woman commits adultery, and the man who marries a divorced woman commits adultery.

The Rich Man and Lazarus

19 "There was a rich man who was dressed in purple and fine linen and lived in luxury every day. 20 At his gate was laid a beggar named Lazarus, covered with sores 21 and longing to eat what fell from the rich man's table. Even the dogs came and licked his sores.

22 "The time came when the beggar died and the angels carried him to Abraham's side. The rich man also died and was buried. 23 In Hades, where he was in torment, he looked up and saw Abraham far away, with Lazarus by his side. 24 So he called to him, 'Father Abraham, have pity on me and send Lazarus to dip the tip of his finger in water and cool my tongue, because I am in agony in this fire.'

25 "But Abraham replied, 'Son, remember that in your lifetime you received your good things, while Lazarus received bad things, but now he is comforted here and you are in agony. 26 And besides all this, between us and you a great chasm has been set in place, so that those who want to go from here to you cannot, nor can anyone cross over from there to us.'

[a] 6 Or about 3,000 liters [b] 7 Or about 30 tons

27“He answered, ‘Then I beg you, father,
send Lazarus to my family, 28for I have five
brothers. Let him warn them, so that they
will not also come to this place of torment.’
29“Abraham replied, ‘They have Moses
and the Prophets; let them listen to them.’
30“ ‘No, father Abraham,’ he said, ‘but
if someone from the dead goes to them,
they will repent.’
31“He said to him, ‘If they do not listen
to Moses and the Prophets, they will not
be convinced even if someone rises from
the dead.’ ”

Sin, Faith, Duty

17 Jesus said to his disciples: “Things
that cause people to stumble are
bound to come, but woe to anyone through
whom they come. 2It would be better for
them to be thrown into the sea with a
millstone tied around their neck than to
cause one of these little ones to stumble.
3So watch yourselves.
“If your brother or sister[a] sins against
you, rebuke them; and if they repent, forgive them. 4Even if they sin against you
seven times in a day and seven times come
back to you saying ‘I repent,’ you must
forgive them.”
5The apostles said to the Lord, “Increase
our faith!”
6He replied, “If you have faith as small
as a mustard seed, you can say to this
mulberry tree, ‘Be uprooted and planted
in the sea,’ and it will obey you.
7“Suppose one of you has a servant
plowing or looking after the sheep. Will
he say to the servant when he comes in
from the field, ‘Come along now and sit
down to eat’? 8Won’t he rather say, ‘Prepare my supper, get yourself ready and
wait on me while I eat and drink; after
that you may eat and drink’? 9Will he
thank the servant because he did what
he was told to do? 10So you also, when you
have done everything you were told to do,
should say, ‘We are unworthy servants; we
have only done our duty.’ ”

Jesus Heals Ten Men With Leprosy

11Now on his way to Jerusalem, Jesus
traveled along the border between Samaria
and Galilee. 12As he was going into a village,
ten men who had leprosy[b] met him. They
stood at a distance 13and called out in a
loud voice, “Jesus, Master, have pity on us!”
14When he saw them, he said, “Go, show
yourselves to the priests.” And as they
went, they were cleansed.
15One of them, when he saw he was
healed, came back, praising God in a loud
voice. 16He threw himself at Jesus’ feet and
thanked him — and he was a Samaritan.
17Jesus asked, “Were not all ten cleansed?
Where are the other nine? 18Has no one returned to give praise to God except this
foreigner?” 19Then he said to him, “Rise
and go; your faith has made you well.”

The Coming of the Kingdom of God

20Once, on being asked by the Pharisees
when the kingdom of God would come,
Jesus replied, “The coming of the kingdom of God is not something that can be
observed, 21nor will people say, ‘Here it
is,’ or ‘There it is,’ because the kingdom
of God is in your midst.”[c]
22Then he said to his disciples, “The time
is coming when you will long to see one of
the days of the Son of Man, but you will not
see it. 23People will tell you, ‘There he is!’
or ‘Here he is!’ Do not go running off after
them. 24For the Son of Man in his day[d] will
be like the lightning, which flashes and
lights up the sky from one end to the other.
25But first he must suffer many things and
be rejected by this generation.
26“Just as it was in the days of Noah,
so also will it be in the days of the Son
of Man. 27People were eating, drinking,
marrying and being given in marriage
up to the day Noah entered the ark. Then
the flood came and destroyed them all.
28“It was the same in the days of Lot. People were eating and drinking, buying and
selling, planting and building. 29But the
day Lot left Sodom, fire and sulfur rained
down from heaven and destroyed them all.
30“It will be just like this on the day the
Son of Man is revealed. 31On that day no
one who is on the housetop, with possessions inside, should go down to get
them. Likewise, no one in the field should
go back for anything. 32Remember Lot’s
wife! 33Whoever tries to keep their life
will lose it, and whoever loses their life
will preserve it. 34I tell you, on that night
two people will be in one bed; one will be
taken and the other left. 35Two women
will be grinding grain together; one will
be taken and the other left.” [36][e]
37“Where, Lord?” they asked.
He replied, “Where there is a dead body,
there the vultures will gather.”

[a] 3 The Greek word for *brother or sister* (*adelphos*) refers here to a fellow disciple, whether man or woman. [b] 12 The Greek word traditionally translated *leprosy* was used for various diseases affecting the skin. [c] 21 Or *is within you* [d] 24 Some manuscripts do not have *in his day.*
[e] 36 Some manuscripts include here words similar to Matt. 24:40.

The Parable of the Persistent Widow

18 Then Jesus told his disciples a parable to show them that they should
always pray and not give up. 2He said:
"In a certain town there was a judge who
neither feared God nor cared what people thought. 3And there was a widow in
that town who kept coming to him with
the plea, 'Grant me justice against my
adversary.'
4"For some time he refused. But finally
he said to himself, 'Even though I don't
fear God or care what people think, 5yet
because this widow keeps bothering me,
I will see that she gets justice, so that she
won't eventually come and attack me!'"
6And the Lord said, "Listen to what the
unjust judge says. 7And will not God bring
about justice for his chosen ones, who cry
out to him day and night? Will he keep
putting them off? 8I tell you, he will see
that they get justice, and quickly. However,
when the Son of Man comes, will he find
faith on the earth?"

The Parable of the Pharisee and the Tax Collector

9To some who were confident of their
own righteousness and looked down on
everyone else, Jesus told this parable:
10"Two men went up to the temple to pray,
one a Pharisee and the other a tax collector. 11The Pharisee stood by himself and
prayed: 'God, I thank you that I am not
like other people — robbers, evildoers,
adulterers — or even like this tax collector. 12I fast twice a week and give a tenth
of all I get.'
13"But the tax collector stood at a distance. He would not even look up to heav-
en, but beat his breast and said, 'God, have
mercy on me, a sinner.'
14"I tell you that this man, rather than
the other, went home justified before God.
For all those who exalt themselves will be
humbled, and those who humble themselves will be exalted."

The Little Children and Jesus

15People were also bringing babies to
Jesus for him to place his hands on them.
When the disciples saw this, they rebuked
them. 16But Jesus called the children to
him and said, "Let the little children come
to me, and do not hinder them, for the
kingdom of God belongs to such as these.
17Truly I tell you, anyone who will not receive the kingdom of God like a little child
will never enter it."

The Rich and the Kingdom of God

18A certain ruler asked him, "Good
teacher, what must I do to inherit eternal life?"
19"Why do you call me good?" Jesus answered. "No one is good — except God
alone. 20You know the commandments:
'You shall not commit adultery, you shall
not murder, you shall not steal, you shall
not give false testimony, honor your father
and mother.'[a]"
21"All these I have kept since I was a
boy," he said.
22When Jesus heard this, he said to him,
"You still lack one thing. Sell everything
you have and give to the poor, and you
will have treasure in heaven. Then come,
follow me."
23When he heard this, he became very
sad, because he was very wealthy. 24Jesus
looked at him and said, "How hard it is for
the rich to enter the kingdom of God! 25In-
deed, it is easier for a camel to go through
the eye of a needle than for someone who
is rich to enter the kingdom of God."
26Those who heard this asked, "Who
then can be saved?"
27Jesus replied, "What is impossible with
man is possible with God."
28Peter said to him, "We have left all we
had to follow you!"
29"Truly I tell you," Jesus said to them,
"no one who has left home or wife or
brothers or sisters or parents or children
for the sake of the kingdom of God 30will
fail to receive many times as much in this
age, and in the age to come eternal life."

Jesus Predicts His Death a Third Time

31Jesus took the Twelve aside and told
them, "We are going up to Jerusalem, and
everything that is written by the prophets
about the Son of Man will be fulfilled. 32He
will be delivered over to the Gentiles. They
will mock him, insult him and spit on him;
33they will flog him and kill him. On the
third day he will rise again."
34The disciples did not understand any
of this. Its meaning was hidden from
them, and they did not know what he
was talking about.

A Blind Beggar Receives His Sight

35As Jesus approached Jericho, a blind
man was sitting by the roadside begging.
36When he heard the crowd going by, he
asked what was happening. 37They told
him, "Jesus of Nazareth is passing by."
38He called out, "Jesus, Son of David,
have mercy on me!"

[a] *20* Exodus 20:12-16; Deut. 5:16-20

39 Those who led the way rebuked him
and told him to be quiet, but he shouted
all the more, "Son of David, have mercy
on me!"
40 Jesus stopped and ordered the man
to be brought to him. When he came near,
Jesus asked him, 41 "What do you want me
to do for you?"
"Lord, I want to see," he replied.
42 Jesus said to him, "Receive your sight;
your faith has healed you." 43 Immediately
he received his sight and followed Jesus,
praising God. When all the people saw it,
they also praised God.

Zacchaeus the Tax Collector

19 Jesus entered Jericho and was passing through. 2 A man was there by
the name of Zacchaeus; he was a chief tax
collector and was wealthy. 3 He wanted to
see who Jesus was, but because he was
short he could not see over the crowd. 4 So
he ran ahead and climbed a sycamore-fig
tree to see him, since Jesus was coming
that way.
5 When Jesus reached the spot, he looked
up and said to him, "Zacchaeus, come
down immediately. I must stay at your
house today." 6 So he came down at once
and welcomed him gladly.
7 All the people saw this and began to
mutter, "He has gone to be the guest of
a sinner."
8 But Zacchaeus stood up and said to
the Lord, "Look, Lord! Here and now I give
half of my possessions to the poor, and if
I have cheated anybody out of anything,
I will pay back four times the amount."
9 Jesus said to him, "Today salvation
has come to this house, because this man,
too, is a son of Abraham. 10 For the Son of
Man came to seek and to save the lost."

The Parable of the Ten Minas

11 While they were listening to this, he
went on to tell them a parable, because
he was near Jerusalem and the people
thought that the kingdom of God was
going to appear at once. 12 He said: "A man
of noble birth went to a distant country to
have himself appointed king and then to
return. 13 So he called ten of his servants
and gave them ten minas.[a] 'Put this money to work,' he said, 'until I come back.'
14 "But his subjects hated him and sent
a delegation after him to say, 'We don't
want this man to be our king.'
15 "He was made king, however, and
returned home. Then he sent for the servants to whom he had given the money,
in order to find out what they had gained
with it.
16 "The first one came and said, 'Sir, your
mina has earned ten more.'
17 " 'Well done, my good servant!' his
master replied. 'Because you have been
trustworthy in a very small matter, take
charge of ten cities.'
18 "The second came and said, 'Sir, your
mina has earned five more.'
19 "His master answered, 'You take
charge of five cities.'
20 "Then another servant came and said,
'Sir, here is your mina; I have kept it laid
away in a piece of cloth. 21 I was afraid of
you, because you are a hard man. You take
out what you did not put in and reap what
you did not sow.'
22 "His master replied, 'I will judge you
by your own words, you wicked servant!
You knew, did you, that I am a hard man,
taking out what I did not put in, and reap-
ing what I did not sow? 23 Why then didn't
you put my money on deposit, so that
when I came back, I could have collected
it with interest?'
24 "Then he said to those standing by,
'Take his mina away from him and give
it to the one who has ten minas.'
25 " 'Sir,' they said, 'he already has ten!'
26 "He replied, 'I tell you that to everyone who has, more will be given, but as
for the one who has nothing, even what
they have will be taken away. 27 But those
enemies of mine who did not want me to
be king over them — bring them here and
kill them in front of me.' "

Jesus Comes to Jerusalem as King

28 After Jesus had said this, he went on
ahead, going up to Jerusalem. 29 As he approached Bethphage and Bethany at the
hill called the Mount of Olives, he sent two
of his disciples, saying to them, 30 "Go to
the village ahead of you, and as you enter
it, you will find a colt tied there, which no
one has ever ridden. Untie it and bring it
here. 31 If anyone asks you, 'Why are you
untying it?' say, 'The Lord needs it.' "
32 Those who were sent ahead went and
found it just as he had told them. 33 As they
were untying the colt, its owners asked
them, "Why are you untying the colt?"
34 They replied, "The Lord needs it."
35 They brought it to Jesus, threw their
cloaks on the colt and put Jesus on it. 36 As
he went along, people spread their cloaks
on the road.
37 When he came near the place where
the road goes down the Mount of Olives,

[a] *13* A mina was about three months' wages.

the whole crowd of disciples began joyfully to praise God in loud voices for all the miracles they had seen:

38 "Blessed is the king who comes in the
name of the Lord!"[a]

"Peace in heaven and glory in the
highest!"

39 Some of the Pharisees in the crowd said to Jesus, "Teacher, rebuke your disciples!"

40 "I tell you," he replied, "if they keep quiet, the stones will cry out."

41 As he approached Jerusalem and saw the city, he wept over it 42 and said, "If you, even you, had only known on this day what would bring you peace — but now it is hidden from your eyes. 43 The days will come upon you when your enemies will build an embankment against you and encircle you and hem you in on every side. 44 They will dash you to the ground, you and the children within your walls. They will not leave one stone on another, because you did not recognize the time of God's coming to you."

Jesus at the Temple

45 When Jesus entered the temple courts, he began to drive out those who were selling. 46 "It is written," he said to them, "'My house will be a house of prayer'[b]; but you have made it 'a den of robbers.'[c]"

47 Every day he was teaching at the temple. But the chief priests, the teachers of the law and the leaders among the people were trying to kill him. 48 Yet they could not find any way to do it, because all the people hung on his words.

The Authority of Jesus Questioned

20 One day as Jesus was teaching the people in the temple courts and proclaiming the good news, the chief priests and the teachers of the law, together with the elders, came up to him. 2 "Tell us by what authority you are doing these things," they said. "Who gave you this authority?"

3 He replied, "I will also ask you a question. Tell me: 4 John's baptism — was it from heaven, or of human origin?"

5 They discussed it among themselves and said, "If we say, 'From heaven,' he will ask, 'Why didn't you believe him?' 6 But if we say, 'Of human origin,' all the people will stone us, because they are persuaded that John was a prophet."

7 So they answered, "We don't know where it was from."

8 Jesus said, "Neither will I tell you by what authority I am doing these things."

The Parable of the Tenants

9 He went on to tell the people this parable: "A man planted a vineyard, rented it to some farmers and went away for a long time. 10 At harvest time he sent a servant to the tenants so they would give him some of the fruit of the vineyard. But the tenants beat him and sent him away empty-handed. 11 He sent another servant, but that one also they beat and treated shamefully and sent away empty-handed. 12 He sent still a third, and they wounded him and threw him out.

13 "Then the owner of the vineyard said, 'What shall I do? I will send my son, whom I love; perhaps they will respect him.'

14 "But when the tenants saw him, they talked the matter over. 'This is the heir,' they said. 'Let's kill him, and the inheritance will be ours.' 15 So they threw him out of the vineyard and killed him.

"What then will the owner of the vineyard do to them? 16 He will come and kill those tenants and give the vineyard to others."

When the people heard this, they said, "God forbid!"

17 Jesus looked directly at them and asked, "Then what is the meaning of that which is written:

"'The stone the builders rejected
has become the cornerstone'[d]?

18 Everyone who falls on that stone will be broken to pieces; anyone on whom it falls will be crushed."

19 The teachers of the law and the chief priests looked for a way to arrest him immediately, because they knew he had spoken this parable against them. But they were afraid of the people.

Paying Taxes to Caesar

20 Keeping a close watch on him, they sent spies, who pretended to be sincere. They hoped to catch Jesus in something he said, so that they might hand him over to the power and authority of the governor. 21 So the spies questioned him: "Teacher, we know that you speak and teach what is right, and that you do not show partiality but teach the way of God in accordance with the truth. 22 Is it right for us to pay taxes to Caesar or not?"

[a] 38 Psalm 118:26 [b] 46 Isaiah 56:7 [c] 46 Jer. 7:11 [d] 17 Psalm 118:22

23He saw through their duplicity and
said to them, 24"Show me a denarius.
Whose image and inscription are on it?"
"Caesar's," they replied.
25He said to them, "Then give back to
Caesar what is Caesar's, and to God what
is God's."
26They were unable to trap him in what
he had said there in public. And astonished by his answer, they became silent.

The Resurrection and Marriage

27Some of the Sadducees, who say there
is no resurrection, came to Jesus with a
question. 28"Teacher," they said, "Moses
wrote for us that if a man's brother dies
and leaves a wife but no children, the
man must marry the widow and raise up
offspring for his brother. 29Now there were
seven brothers. The first one married a
woman and died childless. 30The second
31and then the third married her, and in
the same way the seven died, leaving no
children. 32Finally, the woman died too.
33Now then, at the resurrection whose wife
will she be, since the seven were married
to her?"
34Jesus replied, "The people of this
age marry and are given in marriage.
35But those who are considered worthy
of taking part in the age to come and
in the resurrection from the dead will
neither marry nor be given in marriage,
36and they can no longer die; for they are
like the angels. They are God's children,
since they are children of the resurrection. 37But in the account of the burning bush, even Moses showed that the
dead rise, for he calls the Lord 'the God
of Abraham, and the God of Isaac, and
the God of Jacob.'[a] 38He is not the God of
the dead, but of the living, for to him all
are alive."
39Some of the teachers of the law responded, "Well said, teacher!" 40And no
one dared to ask him any more questions.

Whose Son Is the Messiah?

41Then Jesus said to them, "Why is it said
that the Messiah is the son of David? 42Da-
vid himself declares in the Book of Psalms:

"'The Lord said to my Lord:
"Sit at my right hand
43until I make your enemies
a footstool for your feet."'[b]

44David calls him 'Lord.' How then can he
be his son?"

Warning Against the Teachers of the Law

45While all the people were listening,
Jesus said to his disciples, 46"Beware of
the teachers of the law. They like to walk
around in flowing robes and love to be
greeted with respect in the marketplaces
and have the most important seats in the
synagogues and the places of honor at
banquets. 47They devour widows' houses
and for a show make lengthy prayers.
These men will be punished most severely."

The Widow's Offering

21 As Jesus looked up, he saw the rich
putting their gifts into the temple
treasury. 2He also saw a poor widow put
in two very small copper coins. 3"Truly I
tell you," he said, "this poor widow has
put in more than all the others. 4All these
people gave their gifts out of their wealth;
but she out of her poverty put in all she
had to live on."

The Destruction of the Temple and Signs of the End Times

5Some of his disciples were remarking
about how the temple was adorned with
beautiful stones and with gifts dedicated
to God. But Jesus said, 6"As for what you
see here, the time will come when not one
stone will be left on another; every one of
them will be thrown down."
7"Teacher," they asked, "when will these
things happen? And what will be the sign
that they are about to take place?"
8He replied: "Watch out that you are not
deceived. For many will come in my name,
claiming, 'I am he,' and, 'The time is near.'
Do not follow them. 9When you hear of
wars and uprisings, do not be frightened.
These things must happen first, but the
end will not come right away."
10Then he said to them: "Nation will
rise against nation, and kingdom against
kingdom. 11There will be great earthquakes, famines and pestilences in various places, and fearful events and great
signs from heaven.
12"But before all this, they will seize you
and persecute you. They will hand you
over to synagogues and put you in prison, and you will be brought before kings
and governors, and all on account of my
name. 13And so you will bear testimony
to me. 14But make up your mind not to
worry beforehand how you will defend
yourselves. 15For I will give you words and
wisdom that none of your adversaries will

[a] 37 Exodus 3:6 [b] 43 Psalm 110:1

be able to resist or contradict. 16You will be betrayed even by parents, brothers and sisters, relatives and friends, and they will put some of you to death. 17Everyone will hate you because of me. 18But not a hair of your head will perish. 19Stand firm, and you will win life.

20"When you see Jerusalem being surrounded by armies, you will know that its desolation is near. 21Then let those who are in Judea flee to the mountains, let those in the city get out, and let those in the country not enter the city. 22For this is the time of punishment in fulfillment of all that has been written. 23How dreadful it will be in those days for pregnant women and nursing mothers! There will be great distress in the land and wrath against this people. 24They will fall by the sword and will be taken as prisoners to all the nations. Jerusalem will be trampled on by the Gentiles until the times of the Gentiles are fulfilled.

25"There will be signs in the sun, moon and stars. On the earth, nations will be in anguish and perplexity at the roaring and tossing of the sea. 26People will faint from terror, apprehensive of what is coming on the world, for the heavenly bodies will be shaken. 27At that time they will see the Son of Man coming in a cloud with power and great glory. 28When these things begin to take place, stand up and lift up your heads, because your redemption is drawing near."

29He told them this parable: "Look at the fig tree and all the trees. 30When they sprout leaves, you can see for yourselves and know that summer is near. 31Even so, when you see these things happening, you know that the kingdom of God is near.

32"Truly I tell you, this generation will certainly not pass away until all these things have happened. 33Heaven and earth will pass away, but my words will never pass away.

34"Be careful, or your hearts will be weighed down with carousing, drunkenness and the anxieties of life, and that day will close on you suddenly like a trap. 35For it will come on all those who live on the face of the whole earth. 36Be always on the watch, and pray that you may be able to escape all that is about to happen, and that you may be able to stand before the Son of Man."

37Each day Jesus was teaching at the temple, and each evening he went out to spend the night on the hill called the Mount of Olives, 38and all the people came early in the morning to hear him at the temple.

Judas Agrees to Betray Jesus

22 Now the Festival of Unleavened Bread, called the Passover, was approaching, 2and the chief priests and the teachers of the law were looking for some way to get rid of Jesus, for they were afraid of the people. 3Then Satan entered Judas, called Iscariot, one of the Twelve. 4And Judas went to the chief priests and the officers of the temple guard and discussed with them how he might betray Jesus. 5They were delighted and agreed to give him money. 6He consented, and watched for an opportunity to hand Jesus over to them when no crowd was present.

The Last Supper

7Then came the day of Unleavened Bread on which the Passover lamb had to be sacrificed. 8Jesus sent Peter and John, saying, "Go and make preparations for us to eat the Passover."

9"Where do you want us to prepare for it?" they asked.

10He replied, "As you enter the city, a man carrying a jar of water will meet you. Follow him to the house that he enters, 11and say to the owner of the house, 'The Teacher asks: Where is the guest room, where I may eat the Passover with my disciples?' 12He will show you a large room upstairs, all furnished. Make preparations there."

13They left and found things just as Jesus had told them. So they prepared the Passover.

14When the hour came, Jesus and his apostles reclined at the table. 15And he said to them, "I have eagerly desired to eat this Passover with you before I suffer. 16For I tell you, I will not eat it again until it finds fulfillment in the kingdom of God."

17After taking the cup, he gave thanks and said, "Take this and divide it among you. 18For I tell you I will not drink again from the fruit of the vine until the kingdom of God comes."

19And he took bread, gave thanks and broke it, and gave it to them, saying, "This is my body given for you; do this in remembrance of me."

20In the same way, after the supper he took the cup, saying, "This cup is the new covenant in my blood, which is poured out for you.[a] 21But the hand of him who is going to betray me is with mine on the table. 22The Son of Man will go as it has been decreed. But woe to that man who betrays him!" 23They began to question among themselves which of them it might be who would do this.

[a] 19,20 Some manuscripts do not have *given for you . . . poured out for you.*

24A dispute also arose among them as to
which of them was considered to be greatest. 25Jesus said to them, "The kings of the
Gentiles lord it over them; and those who
exercise authority over them call themselves Benefactors. 26But you are not to be
like that. Instead, the greatest among you
should be like the youngest, and the one
who rules like the one who serves. 27For
who is greater, the one who is at the table
or the one who serves? Is it not the one who
is at the table? But I am among you as one
who serves. 28You are those who have stood
by me in my trials. 29And I confer on you a
kingdom, just as my Father conferred one
on me, 30so that you may eat and drink at
my table in my kingdom and sit on thrones,
judging the twelve tribes of Israel.

31"Simon, Simon, Satan has asked to sift
all of you as wheat. 32But I have prayed for
you, Simon, that your faith may not fail.
And when you have turned back, strength-
en your brothers."

33But he replied, "Lord, I am ready to go
with you to prison and to death."

34Jesus answered, "I tell you, Peter, before the rooster crows today, you will deny
three times that you know me."

35Then Jesus asked them, "When I sent
you without purse, bag or sandals, did
you lack anything?"

"Nothing," they answered.

36He said to them, "But now if you have
a purse, take it, and also a bag; and if
you don't have a sword, sell your cloak
and buy one. 37It is written: 'And he was
numbered with the transgressors'[a]; and I
tell you that this must be fulfilled in me.
Yes, what is written about me is reaching
its fulfillment."

38The disciples said, "See, Lord, here are
two swords."

"That's enough!" he replied.

Jesus Prays on the Mount of Olives

39Jesus went out as usual to the Mount
of Olives, and his disciples followed him.
40On reaching the place, he said to them,
"Pray that you will not fall into temptation." 41He withdrew about a stone's throw
beyond them, knelt down and prayed,
42"Father, if you are willing, take this cup
from me; yet not my will, but yours be
done." 43An angel from heaven appeared
to him and strengthened him. 44And being
in anguish, he prayed more earnestly, and
his sweat was like drops of blood falling
to the ground.[b]

45When he rose from prayer and went
back to the disciples, he found them asleep,
exhausted from sorrow. 46"Why are you
sleeping?" he asked them. "Get up and pray
so that you will not fall into temptation."

Jesus Arrested

47While he was still speaking a crowd
came up, and the man who was called
Judas, one of the Twelve, was leading
them. He approached Jesus to kiss him,
48but Jesus asked him, "Judas, are you
betraying the Son of Man with a kiss?"

49When Jesus' followers saw what was
going to happen, they said, "Lord, should
we strike with our swords?" 50And one of
them struck the servant of the high priest,
cutting off his right ear.

51But Jesus answered, "No more of this!"
And he touched the man's ear and healed
him.

52Then Jesus said to the chief priests,
the officers of the temple guard, and the
elders, who had come for him, "Am I leading a rebellion, that you have come with
swords and clubs? 53Every day I was with
you in the temple courts, and you did not
lay a hand on me. But this is your hour —
when darkness reigns."

Peter Disowns Jesus

54Then seizing him, they led him away
and took him into the house of the high
priest. Peter followed at a distance. 55And
when some there had kindled a fire in the
middle of the courtyard and had sat down
together, Peter sat down with them. 56A
servant girl saw him seated there in the
firelight. She looked closely at him and
said, "This man was with him."

57But he denied it. "Woman, I don't know
him," he said.

58A little later someone else saw him and
said, "You also are one of them."

"Man, I am not!" Peter replied.

59About an hour later another asserted,
"Certainly this fellow was with him, for he
is a Galilean."

60Peter replied, "Man, I don't know
what you're talking about!" Just as he was
speaking, the rooster crowed. 61The Lord
turned and looked straight at Peter. Then
Peter remembered the word the Lord had
spoken to him: "Before the rooster crows
today, you will disown me three times."
62And he went outside and wept bitterly.

The Guards Mock Jesus

63The men who were guarding Jesus
began mocking and beating him.
64They blindfolded him and demanded,
"Prophesy! Who hit you?" 65And they said
many other insulting things to him.

[a] 37 Isaiah 53:12 [b] 43,44 Many early manuscripts do not have verses 43 and 44.

Jesus Before Pilate and Herod

66At daybreak the council of the elders of the people, both the chief priests and the teachers of the law, met together, and Jesus was led before them. 67"If you are the Messiah," they said, "tell us."

Jesus answered, "If I tell you, you will not believe me, 68and if I asked you, you would not answer. 69But from now on, the Son of Man will be seated at the right hand of the mighty God."

70They all asked, "Are you then the Son of God?"

He replied, "You say that I am."

71Then they said, "Why do we need any more testimony? We have heard it from his own lips."

23 Then the whole assembly rose and led him off to Pilate. 2And they began to accuse him, saying, "We have found this man subverting our nation. He opposes payment of taxes to Caesar and claims to be Messiah, a king."

3So Pilate asked Jesus, "Are you the king of the Jews?"

"You have said so," Jesus replied.

4Then Pilate announced to the chief priests and the crowd, "I find no basis for a charge against this man."

5But they insisted, "He stirs up the people all over Judea by his teaching. He started in Galilee and has come all the way here."

6On hearing this, Pilate asked if the man was a Galilean. 7When he learned that Jesus was under Herod's jurisdiction, he sent him to Herod, who was also in Jerusalem at that time.

8When Herod saw Jesus, he was greatly pleased, because for a long time he had been wanting to see him. From what he had heard about him, he hoped to see him perform a sign of some sort. 9He plied him with many questions, but Jesus gave him no answer. 10The chief priests and the teachers of the law were standing there, vehemently accusing him. 11Then Herod and his soldiers ridiculed and mocked him. Dressing him in an elegant robe, they sent him back to Pilate. 12That day Herod and Pilate became friends — before this they had been enemies.

13Pilate called together the chief priests, the rulers and the people, 14and said to them, "You brought me this man as one who was inciting the people to rebellion. I have examined him in your presence and have found no basis for your charges against him. 15Neither has Herod, for he sent him back to us; as you can see, he has done nothing to deserve death. 16Therefore, I will punish him and then release him." [17][a]

18But the whole crowd shouted, "Away with this man! Release Barabbas to us!" 19(Barabbas had been thrown into prison for an insurrection in the city, and for murder.)

20Wanting to release Jesus, Pilate appealed to them again. 21But they kept shouting, "Crucify him! Crucify him!"

22For the third time he spoke to them: "Why? What crime has this man committed? I have found in him no grounds for the death penalty. Therefore I will have him punished and then release him."

23But with loud shouts they insistently demanded that he be crucified, and their shouts prevailed. 24So Pilate decided to grant their demand. 25He released the man who had been thrown into prison for insurrection and murder, the one they asked for, and surrendered Jesus to their will.

The Crucifixion of Jesus

26As the soldiers led him away, they seized Simon from Cyrene, who was on his way in from the country, and put the cross on him and made him carry it behind Jesus. 27A large number of people followed him, including women who mourned and wailed for him. 28Jesus turned and said to them, "Daughters of Jerusalem, do not weep for me; weep for yourselves and for your children. 29For the time will come when you will say, 'Blessed are the childless women, the wombs that never bore and the breasts that never nursed!' 30Then

> " 'they will say to the mountains, "Fall on us!"
> and to the hills, "Cover us!" '[b]

31For if people do these things when the tree is green, what will happen when it is dry?"

32Two other men, both criminals, were also led out with him to be executed. 33When they came to the place called the Skull, they crucified him there, along with the criminals — one on his right, the other on his left. 34Jesus said, "Father, forgive them, for they do not know what they are doing."[c] And they divided up his clothes by casting lots.

35The people stood watching, and the rulers even sneered at him. They said, "He saved others; let him save himself if he is God's Messiah, the Chosen One."

[a] *17* Some manuscripts include here words similar to Matt. 27:15 and Mark 15:6.
[b] *30* Hosea 10:8 [c] *34* Some early manuscripts do not have this sentence.

36The soldiers also came up and mocked
him. They offered him wine vinegar 37and
said, "If you are the king of the Jews, save
yourself."
38There was a written notice above him,
which read: THIS IS THE KING OF THE JEWS.
39One of the criminals who hung there
hurled insults at him: "Aren't you the Messiah? Save yourself and us!"
40But the other criminal rebuked him.
"Don't you fear God," he said, "since you
are under the same sentence? 41We are
punished justly, for we are getting what
our deeds deserve. But this man has done
nothing wrong."
42Then he said, "Jesus, remember me
when you come into your kingdom.[a]"
43Jesus answered him, "Truly I tell you,
today you will be with me in paradise."

The Death of Jesus

44It was now about noon, and darkness
came over the whole land until three in
the afternoon, 45for the sun stopped shining. And the curtain of the temple was
torn in two. 46Jesus called out with a loud
voice, "Father, into your hands I commit
my spirit."[b] When he had said this, he
breathed his last.
47The centurion, seeing what had happened, praised God and said, "Surely this
was a righteous man." 48When all the
people who had gathered to witness this
sight saw what took place, they beat their
breasts and went away. 49But all those
who knew him, including the women who
had followed him from Galilee, stood at a
distance, watching these things.

The Burial of Jesus

50Now there was a man named Joseph,
a member of the Council, a good and upright man, 51who had not consented to
their decision and action. He came from
the Judean town of Arimathea, and he
himself was waiting for the kingdom of
God. 52Going to Pilate, he asked for Jesus'
body. 53Then he took it down, wrapped it
in linen cloth and placed it in a tomb cut
in the rock, one in which no one had yet
been laid. 54It was Preparation Day, and
the Sabbath was about to begin.
55The women who had come with Jesus
from Galilee followed Joseph and saw
the tomb and how his body was laid in
it. 56Then they went home and prepared
spices and perfumes. But they rested on
the Sabbath in obedience to the commandment.

Jesus Has Risen

24 On the first day of the week, very
early in the morning, the women
took the spices they had prepared and
went to the tomb. 2They found the stone
rolled away from the tomb, 3but when they
entered, they did not find the body of the
Lord Jesus. 4While they were wondering
about this, suddenly two men in clothes
that gleamed like lightning stood beside
them. 5In their fright the women bowed
down with their faces to the ground, but
the men said to them, "Why do you look
for the living among the dead? 6He is not
here; he has risen! Remember how he told
you, while he was still with you in Galilee:
7'The Son of Man must be delivered over
to the hands of sinners, be crucified and
on the third day be raised again.' " 8Then
they remembered his words.
9When they came back from the tomb,
they told all these things to the Eleven and
to all the others. 10It was Mary Magdalene,
Joanna, Mary the mother of James, and
the others with them who told this to the
apostles. 11But they did not believe the
women, because their words seemed to
them like nonsense. 12Peter, however, got
up and ran to the tomb. Bending over, he
saw the strips of linen lying by themselves,
and he went away, wondering to himself
what had happened.

On the Road to Emmaus

13Now that same day two of them were
going to a village called Emmaus, about
seven miles[c] from Jerusalem. 14They were
talking with each other about everything
that had happened. 15As they talked and
discussed these things with each other,
Jesus himself came up and walked along
with them; 16but they were kept from recognizing him.
17He asked them, "What are you discussing together as you walk along?"
They stood still, their faces downcast.
18One of them, named Cleopas, asked him,
"Are you the only one visiting Jerusalem
who does not know the things that have
happened there in these days?"
19"What things?" he asked.
"About Jesus of Nazareth," they replied.
"He was a prophet, powerful in word and
deed before God and all the people. 20The
chief priests and our rulers handed him
over to be sentenced to death, and they
crucified him; 21but we had hoped that
he was the one who was going to redeem
Israel. And what is more, it is the third

[a] *42* Some manuscripts *come with your kingly power* [b] *46* Psalm 31:5 [c] *13* Or about 11 kilometers

day since all this took place. [22]In addition, some of our women amazed us. They
went to the tomb early this morning [23]but
didn't find his body. They came and told
us that they had seen a vision of angels,
who said he was alive. [24]Then some of our
companions went to the tomb and found
it just as the women had said, but they did
not see Jesus."

[25]He said to them, "How foolish you
are, and how slow to believe all that the
prophets have spoken! [26]Did not the Messiah have to suffer these things and then
enter his glory?" [27]And beginning with
Moses and all the Prophets, he explained
to them what was said in all the Scriptures
concerning himself.

[28]As they approached the village to
which they were going, Jesus continued
on as if he were going farther. [29]But they
urged him strongly, "Stay with us, for it is
nearly evening; the day is almost over."
So he went in to stay with them.

[30]When he was at the table with them,
he took bread, gave thanks, broke it and
began to give it to them. [31]Then their eyes
were opened and they recognized him,
and he disappeared from their sight.
[32]They asked each other, "Were not our
hearts burning within us while he talked
with us on the road and opened the Scriptures to us?"

[33]They got up and returned at once to
Jerusalem. There they found the Eleven
and those with them, assembled together
[34]and saying, "It is true! The Lord has risen
and has appeared to Simon." [35]Then the
two told what had happened on the way,
and how Jesus was recognized by them
when he broke the bread.

Jesus Appears to the Disciples

[36]While they were still talking about
this, Jesus himself stood among them and
said to them, "Peace be with you."

[37]They were startled and frightened,
thinking they saw a ghost. [38]He said to
them, "Why are you troubled, and why do
doubts rise in your minds? [39]Look at my
hands and my feet. It is I myself! Touch
me and see; a ghost does not have flesh
and bones, as you see I have."

[40]When he had said this, he showed
them his hands and feet. [41]And while they
still did not believe it because of joy and
amazement, he asked them, "Do you have
anything here to eat?" [42]They gave him a
piece of broiled fish, [43]and he took it and
ate it in their presence.

[44]He said to them, "This is what I told
you while I was still with you: Everything
must be fulfilled that is written about me
in the Law of Moses, the Prophets and
the Psalms."

[45]Then he opened their minds so they
could understand the Scriptures. [46]He told
them, "This is what is written: The Messiah will suffer and rise from the dead
on the third day, [47]and repentance for
the forgiveness of sins will be preached
in his name to all nations, beginning at
Jerusalem. [48]You are witnesses of these
things. [49]I am going to send you what my
Father has promised; but stay in the city
until you have been clothed with power
from on high."

The Ascension of Jesus

[50]When he had led them out to the vicinity of Bethany, he lifted up his hands
and blessed them. [51]While he was blessing them, he left them and was taken up
into heaven. [52]Then they worshiped him
and returned to Jerusalem with great
joy. [53]And they stayed continually at the
temple, praising God.

JOHN

The Word Became Flesh

1 In the beginning was the Word, and
the Word was with God, and the Word
was God. 2 He was with God in the beginning. 3 Through him all things were made;
without him nothing was made that has
been made. 4 In him was life, and that life
was the light of all mankind. 5 The light
shines in the darkness, and the darkness
has not overcome[a] it.

6 There was a man sent from God whose
name was John. 7 He came as a witness
to testify concerning that light, so that
through him all might believe. 8 He himself was not the light; he came only as a
witness to the light.

9 The true light that gives light to everyone was coming into the world. 10 He was in
the world, and though the world was made
through him, the world did not recognize
him. 11 He came to that which was his own,
but his own did not receive him. 12 Yet to all
who did receive him, to those who believed
in his name, he gave the right to become
children of God — 13 children born not of
natural descent, nor of human decision or
a husband's will, but born of God.

14 The Word became flesh and made
his dwelling among us. We have seen his
glory, the glory of the one and only Son,
who came from the Father, full of grace
and truth.

15 (John testified concerning him. He
cried out, saying, "This is the one I spoke
about when I said, 'He who comes after me
has surpassed me because he was before
me.'") 16 Out of his fullness we have all
received grace in place of grace already
given. 17 For the law was given through
Moses; grace and truth came through
Jesus Christ. 18 No one has ever seen God,
but the one and only Son, who is himself
God and[b] is in closest relationship with
the Father, has made him known.

John the Baptist Denies Being the Messiah

19 Now this was John's testimony when
the Jewish leaders[c] in Jerusalem sent
priests and Levites to ask him who he was.
20 He did not fail to confess, but confessed
freely, "I am not the Messiah."

21 They asked him, "Then who are you?
Are you Elijah?"

He said, "I am not."

"Are you the Prophet?"

He answered, "No."

22 Finally they said, "Who are you? Give
us an answer to take back to those who
sent us. What do you say about yourself?"

23 John replied in the words of Isaiah the
prophet, "I am the voice of one calling in
the wilderness, 'Make straight the way
for the Lord.'"[d]

24 Now the Pharisees who had been sent
25 questioned him, "Why then do you baptize if you are not the Messiah, nor Elijah,
nor the Prophet?"

26 "I baptize with[e] water," John replied,
"but among you stands one you do not
know. 27 He is the one who comes after
me, the straps of whose sandals I am not
worthy to untie."

28 This all happened at Bethany on the
other side of the Jordan, where John was
baptizing.

John Testifies About Jesus

29 The next day John saw Jesus coming
toward him and said, "Look, the Lamb of
God, who takes away the sin of the world!
30 This is the one I meant when I said, 'A
man who comes after me has surpassed
me because he was before me.' 31 I myself
did not know him, but the reason I came
baptizing with water was that he might
be revealed to Israel."

32 Then John gave this testimony: "I saw
the Spirit come down from heaven as a
dove and remain on him. 33 And I myself
did not know him, but the one who sent
me to baptize with water told me, 'The
man on whom you see the Spirit come
down and remain is the one who will baptize with the Holy Spirit.' 34 I have seen and
I testify that this is God's Chosen One."[f]

John's Disciples Follow Jesus

35 The next day John was there again
with two of his disciples. 36 When he saw

[a] *5* Or *understood* [b] *18* Some manuscripts *but the only Son, who* [c] *19* The Greek term traditionally translated *the Jews* (*hoi Ioudaioi*) refers here and elsewhere in John's Gospel to those Jewish leaders who opposed Jesus; also in 5:10, 15, 16; 7:1, 11, 13; 9:22; 18:14, 28, 36; 19:7, 12, 31, 38; 20:19. [d] *23* Isaiah 40:3 [e] *26* Or *in*; also in verses 31 and 33 (twice) [f] *34* See Isaiah 42:1; many manuscripts *is the Son of God.*

Jesus passing by, he said, "Look, the Lamb of God!"

37When the two disciples heard him say this, they followed Jesus. 38Turning around, Jesus saw them following and asked, "What do you want?"

They said, "Rabbi" (which means "Teacher"), "where are you staying?"

39"Come," he replied, "and you will see."

So they went and saw where he was staying, and they spent that day with him. It was about four in the afternoon.

40Andrew, Simon Peter's brother, was one of the two who heard what John had said and who had followed Jesus. 41The first thing Andrew did was to find his brother Simon and tell him, "We have found the Messiah" (that is, the Christ). 42And he brought him to Jesus.

Jesus looked at him and said, "You are Simon son of John. You will be called Cephas" (which, when translated, is Peter[a]).

Jesus Calls Philip and Nathanael

43The next day Jesus decided to leave for Galilee. Finding Philip, he said to him, "Follow me."

44Philip, like Andrew and Peter, was from the town of Bethsaida. 45Philip found Nathanael and told him, "We have found the one Moses wrote about in the Law, and about whom the prophets also wrote — Jesus of Nazareth, the son of Joseph."

46"Nazareth! Can anything good come from there?" Nathanael asked.

"Come and see," said Philip.

47When Jesus saw Nathanael approaching, he said of him, "Here truly is an Israelite in whom there is no deceit."

48"How do you know me?" Nathanael asked.

Jesus answered, "I saw you while you were still under the fig tree before Philip called you."

49Then Nathanael declared, "Rabbi, you are the Son of God; you are the king of Israel."

50Jesus said, "You believe[b] because I told you I saw you under the fig tree. You will see greater things than that." 51He then added, "Very truly I tell you,[c] you[c] will see 'heaven open, and the angels of God ascending and descending on'[d] the Son of Man."

Jesus Changes Water Into Wine

2 On the third day a wedding took place at Cana in Galilee. Jesus' mother was there, 2and Jesus and his disciples had also been invited to the wedding. 3When the wine was gone, Jesus' mother said to him, "They have no more wine."

4"Woman,[e] why do you involve me?" Jesus replied. "My hour has not yet come."

5His mother said to the servants, "Do whatever he tells you."

6Nearby stood six stone water jars, the kind used by the Jews for ceremonial washing, each holding from twenty to thirty gallons.[f]

7Jesus said to the servants, "Fill the jars with water"; so they filled them to the brim.

8Then he told them, "Now draw some out and take it to the master of the banquet."

They did so, 9and the master of the banquet tasted the water that had been turned into wine. He did not realize where it had come from, though the servants who had drawn the water knew. Then he called the bridegroom aside 10and said, "Everyone brings out the choice wine first and then the cheaper wine after the guests have had too much to drink; but you have saved the best till now."

11What Jesus did here in Cana of Galilee was the first of the signs through which he revealed his glory; and his disciples believed in him.

12After this he went down to Capernaum with his mother and brothers and his disciples. There they stayed for a few days.

Jesus Clears the Temple Courts

13When it was almost time for the Jewish Passover, Jesus went up to Jerusalem. 14In the temple courts he found people selling cattle, sheep and doves, and others sitting at tables exchanging money. 15So he made a whip out of cords, and drove all from the temple courts, both sheep and cattle; he scattered the coins of the money changers and overturned their tables. 16To those who sold doves he said, "Get these out of here! Stop turning my Father's house into a market!" 17His disciples remembered that it is written: "Zeal for your house will consume me."[g]

18The Jews then responded to him, "What sign can you show us to prove your authority to do all this?"

19Jesus answered them, "Destroy this temple, and I will raise it again in three days."

20They replied, "It has taken forty-six years to build this temple, and you are going to raise it in three days?" 21But the

[a] 42 *Cephas* (Aramaic) and *Peter* (Greek) both mean *rock*. [b] 50 Or *Do you believe . . . ?* [c] 51 The Greek is plural. [d] 51 Gen. 28:12 [e] 4 The Greek for *Woman* does not denote any disrespect. [f] 6 Or from about 75 to about 115 liters [g] 17 Psalm 69:9

temple he had spoken of was his body.
22After he was raised from the dead, his
disciples recalled what he had said. Then
they believed the scripture and the words
that Jesus had spoken.

23Now while he was in Jerusalem at the
Passover Festival, many people saw the
signs he was performing and believed in
his name.[a] 24But Jesus would not entrust
himself to them, for he knew all people.
25He did not need any testimony about
mankind, for he knew what was in each
person.

Jesus Teaches Nicodemus

3 Now there was a Pharisee, a man
named Nicodemus who was a member
of the Jewish ruling council. 2He came to
Jesus at night and said, "Rabbi, we know
that you are a teacher who has come from
God. For no one could perform the signs
you are doing if God were not with him."

3Jesus replied, "Very truly I tell you, no
one can see the kingdom of God unless
they are born again.[b]"

4"How can someone be born when they
are old?" Nicodemus asked. "Surely they
cannot enter a second time into their
mother's womb to be born!"

5Jesus answered, "Very truly I tell you,
no one can enter the kingdom of God unless they are born of water and the Spirit.
6Flesh gives birth to flesh, but the Spirit[c]
gives birth to spirit. 7You should not be
surprised at my saying, 'You[d] must be
born again.' 8The wind blows wherever
it pleases. You hear its sound, but you
cannot tell where it comes from or where
it is going. So it is with everyone born of
the Spirit."[e]

9"How can this be?" Nicodemus asked.

10"You are Israel's teacher," said Jesus,
"and do you not understand these things?
11Very truly I tell you, we speak of what
we know, and we testify to what we have
seen, but still you people do not accept
our testimony. 12I have spoken to you of
earthly things and you do not believe; how
then will you believe if I speak of heavenly things? 13No one has ever gone into
heaven except the one who came from
heaven — the Son of Man.[f] 14Just as Moses
lifted up the snake in the wilderness, so
the Son of Man must be lifted up,[g] 15that
everyone who believes may have eternal
life in him."[h]

16For God so loved the world that he
gave his one and only Son, that whoever
believes in him shall not perish but have
eternal life. 17For God did not send his Son
into the world to condemn the world, but
to save the world through him. 18Who-
ever believes in him is not condemned,
but whoever does not believe stands condemned already because they have not
believed in the name of God's one and only
Son. 19This is the verdict: Light has come
into the world, but people loved darkness
instead of light because their deeds were
evil. 20Everyone who does evil hates the
light, and will not come into the light for
fear that their deeds will be exposed. 21But
whoever lives by the truth comes into the
light, so that it may be seen plainly that
what they have done has been done in
the sight of God.

John Testifies Again About Jesus

22After this, Jesus and his disciples went
out into the Judean countryside, where he
spent some time with them, and baptized.
23Now John also was baptizing at Aenon
near Salim, because there was plenty of
water, and people were coming and being baptized. 24(This was before John was
put in prison.) 25An argument developed
between some of John's disciples and a
certain Jew over the matter of ceremonial
washing. 26They came to John and said to
him, "Rabbi, that man who was with you
on the other side of the Jordan — the one
you testified about — look, he is baptizing,
and everyone is going to him."

27To this John replied, "A person can
receive only what is given them from
heaven. 28You yourselves can testify that
I said, 'I am not the Messiah but am sent
ahead of him.' 29The bride belongs to the
bridegroom. The friend who attends the
bridegroom waits and listens for him,
and is full of joy when he hears the bridegroom's voice. That joy is mine, and it is
now complete. 30He must become greater;
I must become less."[i]

31The one who comes from above is
above all; the one who is from the earth
belongs to the earth, and speaks as one
from the earth. The one who comes from
heaven is above all. 32He testifies to what
he has seen and heard, but no one accepts
his testimony. 33Whoever has accepted it
has certified that God is truthful. 34For the

[a] 23 Or *in him* [b] 3 The Greek for *again* also means *from above*; also in verse 7. [c] 6 Or *but spirit* [d] 7 The Greek is plural. [e] 8 The Greek for *Spirit* is the same as that for *wind*.
[f] 13 Some manuscripts *Man, who is in heaven* [g] 14 The Greek for *lifted up* also means *exalted*.
[h] 15 Some interpreters end the quotation with verse 21. [i] 30 Some interpreters end the quotation with verse 36.

one whom God has sent speaks the words of God, for God[a] gives the Spirit without limit. 35 The Father loves the Son and has placed everything in his hands. 36 Whoever believes in the Son has eternal life, but whoever rejects the Son will not see life, for God's wrath remains on them.

Jesus Talks With a Samaritan Woman

4 Now Jesus learned that the Pharisees had heard that he was gaining and baptizing more disciples than John— 2 although in fact it was not Jesus who baptized, but his disciples. 3 So he left Judea and went back once more to Galilee.

4 Now he had to go through Samaria. 5 So he came to a town in Samaria called Sychar, near the plot of ground Jacob had given to his son Joseph. 6 Jacob's well was there, and Jesus, tired as he was from the journey, sat down by the well. It was about noon.

7 When a Samaritan woman came to draw water, Jesus said to her, "Will you give me a drink?" 8 (His disciples had gone into the town to buy food.)

9 The Samaritan woman said to him, "You are a Jew and I am a Samaritan woman. How can you ask me for a drink?" (For Jews do not associate with Samaritans.[b])

10 Jesus answered her, "If you knew the gift of God and who it is that asks you for a drink, you would have asked him and he would have given you living water."

11 "Sir," the woman said, "you have nothing to draw with and the well is deep. Where can you get this living water? 12 Are you greater than our father Jacob, who gave us the well and drank from it himself, as did also his sons and his livestock?"

13 Jesus answered, "Everyone who drinks this water will be thirsty again, 14 but whoever drinks the water I give them will never thirst. Indeed, the water I give them will become in them a spring of water welling up to eternal life."

15 The woman said to him, "Sir, give me this water so that I won't get thirsty and have to keep coming here to draw water."

16 He told her, "Go, call your husband and come back."

17 "I have no husband," she replied.

Jesus said to her, "You are right when you say you have no husband. 18 The fact is, you have had five husbands, and the man you now have is not your husband. What you have just said is quite true."

19 "Sir," the woman said, "I can see that you are a prophet. 20 Our ancestors worshiped on this mountain, but you Jews claim that the place where we must worship is in Jerusalem."

21 "Woman," Jesus replied, "believe me, a time is coming when you will worship the Father neither on this mountain nor in Jerusalem. 22 You Samaritans worship what you do not know; we worship what we do know, for salvation is from the Jews. 23 Yet a time is coming and has now come when the true worshipers will worship the Father in the Spirit and in truth, for they are the kind of worshipers the Father seeks. 24 God is spirit, and his worshipers must worship in the Spirit and in truth."

25 The woman said, "I know that Messiah" (called Christ) "is coming. When he comes, he will explain everything to us."

26 Then Jesus declared, "I, the one speaking to you—I am he."

The Disciples Rejoin Jesus

27 Just then his disciples returned and were surprised to find him talking with a woman. But no one asked, "What do you want?" or "Why are you talking with her?"

28 Then, leaving her water jar, the woman went back to the town and said to the people, 29 "Come, see a man who told me everything I ever did. Could this be the Messiah?" 30 They came out of the town and made their way toward him.

31 Meanwhile his disciples urged him, "Rabbi, eat something."

32 But he said to them, "I have food to eat that you know nothing about."

33 Then his disciples said to each other, "Could someone have brought him food?"

34 "My food," said Jesus, "is to do the will of him who sent me and to finish his work. 35 Don't you have a saying, 'It's still four months until harvest'? I tell you, open your eyes and look at the fields! They are ripe for harvest. 36 Even now the one who reaps draws a wage and harvests a crop for eternal life, so that the sower and the reaper may be glad together. 37 Thus the saying 'One sows and another reaps' is true. 38 I sent you to reap what you have not worked for. Others have done the hard work, and you have reaped the benefits of their labor."

Many Samaritans Believe

39 Many of the Samaritans from that town believed in him because of the woman's testimony, "He told me everything I ever did." 40 So when the Samaritans came to him, they urged him to stay with them, and he stayed two days. 41 And because of his words many more became believers.

[a] 34 Greek *he* [b] 9 Or *do not use dishes Samaritans have used*

42 They said to the woman, "We no longer believe just because of what you said; now we have heard for ourselves, and we know that this man really is the Savior of the world."

Jesus Heals an Official's Son

43 After the two days he left for Galilee. 44 (Now Jesus himself had pointed out that a prophet has no honor in his own country.) 45 When he arrived in Galilee, the Galileans welcomed him. They had seen all that he had done in Jerusalem at the Passover Festival, for they also had been there.

46 Once more he visited Cana in Galilee, where he had turned the water into wine. And there was a certain royal official whose son lay sick at Capernaum. 47 When this man heard that Jesus had arrived in Galilee from Judea, he went to him and begged him to come and heal his son, who was close to death.

48 "Unless you people see signs and wonders," Jesus told him, "you will never believe."

49 The royal official said, "Sir, come down before my child dies."

50 "Go," Jesus replied, "your son will live."

The man took Jesus at his word and departed. 51 While he was still on the way, his servants met him with the news that his boy was living. 52 When he inquired as to the time when his son got better, they said to him, "Yesterday, at one in the afternoon, the fever left him."

53 Then the father realized that this was the exact time at which Jesus had said to him, "Your son will live." So he and his whole household believed.

54 This was the second sign Jesus performed after coming from Judea to Galilee.

The Healing at the Pool

5 Some time later, Jesus went up to Jerusalem for one of the Jewish festivals. 2 Now there is in Jerusalem near the Sheep Gate a pool, which in Aramaic is called Bethesda[a] and which is surrounded by five covered colonnades. 3 Here a great number of disabled people used to lie — the blind, the lame, the paralyzed. [4][b] 5 One who was there had been an invalid for thirty-eight years. 6 When Jesus saw him lying there and learned that he had been in this condition for a long time, he asked him, "Do you want to get well?"

7 "Sir," the invalid replied, "I have no one to help me into the pool when the water is stirred. While I am trying to get in, someone else goes down ahead of me."

8 Then Jesus said to him, "Get up! Pick up your mat and walk." 9 At once the man was cured; he picked up his mat and walked.

The day on which this took place was a Sabbath, 10 and so the Jewish leaders said to the man who had been healed, "It is the Sabbath; the law forbids you to carry your mat."

11 But he replied, "The man who made me well said to me, 'Pick up your mat and walk.' "

12 So they asked him, "Who is this fellow who told you to pick it up and walk?"

13 The man who was healed had no idea who it was, for Jesus had slipped away into the crowd that was there.

14 Later Jesus found him at the temple and said to him, "See, you are well again. Stop sinning or something worse may happen to you." 15 The man went away and told the Jewish leaders that it was Jesus who had made him well.

The Authority of the Son

16 So, because Jesus was doing these things on the Sabbath, the Jewish leaders began to persecute him. 17 In his defense Jesus said to them, "My Father is always at his work to this very day, and I too am working." 18 For this reason they tried all the more to kill him; not only was he breaking the Sabbath, but he was even calling God his own Father, making himself equal with God.

19 Jesus gave them this answer: "Very truly I tell you, the Son can do nothing by himself; he can do only what he sees his Father doing, because whatever the Father does the Son also does. 20 For the Father loves the Son and shows him all he does. Yes, and he will show him even greater works than these, so that you will be amazed. 21 For just as the Father raises the dead and gives them life, even so the Son gives life to whom he is pleased to give it. 22 Moreover, the Father judges no one, but has entrusted all judgment to the Son, 23 that all may honor the Son just as they honor the Father. Whoever does not honor the Son does not honor the Father, who sent him.

24 "Very truly I tell you, whoever hears my word and believes him who sent me has eternal life and will not be judged but has

[a] 2 Some manuscripts *Bethzatha*; other manuscripts *Bethsaida* [b] 3,4 Some manuscripts include here, wholly or in part, *paralyzed — and they waited for the moving of the waters.* [4] *From time to time an angel of the Lord would come down and stir up the waters. The first one into the pool after each such disturbance would be cured of whatever disease they had.*

crossed over from death to life. [25]Very truly
I tell you, a time is coming and has now
come when the dead will hear the voice
of the Son of God and those who hear will
live. [26]For as the Father has life in himself,
so he has granted the Son also to have life
in himself. [27]And he has given him authority to judge because he is the Son of Man.
[28]"Do not be amazed at this, for a time
is coming when all who are in their graves
will hear his voice [29]and come out — those
who have done what is good will rise to
live, and those who have done what is evil
will rise to be condemned. [30]By myself I
can do nothing; I judge only as I hear,
and my judgment is just, for I seek not
to please myself but him who sent me.

Testimonies About Jesus

[31]"If I testify about myself, my testimony
is not true. [32]There is another who testifies
in my favor, and I know that his testimony
about me is true.
[33]"You have sent to John and he has
testified to the truth. [34]Not that I accept
human testimony; but I mention it that
you may be saved. [35]John was a lamp that
burned and gave light, and you chose for
a time to enjoy his light.
[36]"I have testimony weightier than that
of John. For the works that the Father has
given me to finish — the very works that
I am doing — testify that the Father has
sent me. [37]And the Father who sent me
has himself testified concerning me. You
have never heard his voice nor seen his
form, [38]nor does his word dwell in you, for
you do not believe the one he sent. [39]You
study[a] the Scriptures diligently because
you think that in them you have eternal
life. These are the very Scriptures that
testify about me, [40]yet you refuse to come
to me to have life.
[41]"I do not accept glory from human
beings, [42]but I know you. I know that you
do not have the love of God in your hearts.
[43]I have come in my Father's name, and
you do not accept me; but if someone else
comes in his own name, you will accept
him. [44]How can you believe since you accept
glory from one another but do not seek
the glory that comes from the only God[b]?
[45]"But do not think I will accuse you
before the Father. Your accuser is Moses,
on whom your hopes are set. [46]If you believed Moses, you would believe me, for
he wrote about me. [47]But since you do not
believe what he wrote, how are you going
to believe what I say?"

Jesus Feeds the Five Thousand

6 Some time after this, Jesus crossed to
the far shore of the Sea of Galilee (that
is, the Sea of Tiberias), [2]and a great crowd
of people followed him because they saw
the signs he had performed by healing the
sick. [3]Then Jesus went up on a mountainside and sat down with his disciples. [4]The
Jewish Passover Festival was near.
[5]When Jesus looked up and saw a great
crowd coming toward him, he said to Philip, "Where shall we buy bread for these
people to eat?" [6]He asked this only to test
him, for he already had in mind what he
was going to do.
[7]Philip answered him, "It would take
more than half a year's wages[c] to buy
enough bread for each one to have a bite!"
[8]Another of his disciples, Andrew, Simon Peter's brother, spoke up, [9]"Here is
a boy with five small barley loaves and
two small fish, but how far will they go
among so many?"
[10]Jesus said, "Have the people sit down."
There was plenty of grass in that place,
and they sat down (about five thousand
men were there). [11]Jesus then took the
loaves, gave thanks, and distributed to
those who were seated as much as they
wanted. He did the same with the fish.
[12]When they had all had enough to
eat, he said to his disciples, "Gather the
pieces that are left over. Let nothing be
wasted." [13]So they gathered them and
filled twelve baskets with the pieces of
the five barley loaves left over by those
who had eaten.
[14]After the people saw the sign Jesus
performed, they began to say, "Surely
this is the Prophet who is to come into the
world." [15]Jesus, knowing that they intended to come and make him king by force,
withdrew again to a mountain by himself.

Jesus Walks on the Water

[16]When evening came, his disciples went
down to the lake, [17]where they got into a
boat and set off across the lake for Capernaum. By now it was dark, and Jesus
had not yet joined them. [18]A strong wind
was blowing and the waters grew rough.
[19]When they had rowed about three or
four miles,[d] they saw Jesus approaching
the boat, walking on the water; and they
were frightened. [20]But he said to them,
"It is I; don't be afraid." [21]Then they were
willing to take him into the boat, and
immediately the boat reached the shore
where they were heading.

[a] 39 Or [39]*Study* [b] 44 Some early manuscripts *the Only One* [c] 7 Greek *take two hundred denarii* [d] 19 Or *about 5 or 6 kilometers*

22 The next day the crowd that had
stayed on the opposite shore of the lake realized that only one boat had been there,
and that Jesus had not entered it with his
disciples, but that they had gone away
alone. 23 Then some boats from Tiberias
landed near the place where the people
had eaten the bread after the Lord had
given thanks. 24 Once the crowd realized
that neither Jesus nor his disciples were
there, they got into the boats and went to
Capernaum in search of Jesus.

Jesus the Bread of Life

25 When they found him on the other
side of the lake, they asked him, "Rabbi,
when did you get here?"
26 Jesus answered, "Very truly I tell you,
you are looking for me, not because you
saw the signs I performed but because
you ate the loaves and had your fill. 27 Do
not work for food that spoils, but for food
that endures to eternal life, which the Son
of Man will give you. For on him God the
Father has placed his seal of approval."
28 Then they asked him, "What must we
do to do the works God requires?"
29 Jesus answered, "The work of God is
this: to believe in the one he has sent."
30 So they asked him, "What sign then
will you give that we may see it and believe you? What will you do? 31 Our ancestors ate the manna in the wilderness; as
it is written: 'He gave them bread from
heaven to eat.'[a]"
32 Jesus said to them, "Very truly I tell
you, it is not Moses who has given you the
bread from heaven, but it is my Father
who gives you the true bread from heav-
en. 33 For the bread of God is the bread that
comes down from heaven and gives life
to the world."
34 "Sir," they said, "always give us this
bread."
35 Then Jesus declared, "I am the bread
of life. Whoever comes to me will never
go hungry, and whoever believes in me
will never be thirsty. 36 But as I told you,
you have seen me and still you do not believe. 37 All those the Father gives me will
come to me, and whoever comes to me I
will never drive away. 38 For I have come
down from heaven not to do my will but
to do the will of him who sent me. 39 And
this is the will of him who sent me, that
I shall lose none of all those he has giv-
en me, but raise them up at the last day.
40 For my Father's will is that everyone who
looks to the Son and believes in him shall
have eternal life, and I will raise them up
at the last day."
41 At this the Jews there began to grumble about him because he said, "I am the
bread that came down from heaven."
42 They said, "Is this not Jesus, the son
of Joseph, whose father and mother we
know? How can he now say, 'I came down
from heaven'?"
43 "Stop grumbling among yourselves,"
Jesus answered. 44 "No one can come to
me unless the Father who sent me draws
them, and I will raise them up at the last
day. 45 It is written in the Prophets: 'They
will all be taught by God.'[b] Everyone who
has heard the Father and learned from
him comes to me. 46 No one has seen the
Father except the one who is from God;
only he has seen the Father. 47 Very truly I
tell you, the one who believes has eternal
life. 48 I am the bread of life. 49 Your ancestors ate the manna in the wilderness,
yet they died. 50 But here is the bread that
comes down from heaven, which anyone
may eat and not die. 51 I am the living
bread that came down from heaven. Whoever eats this bread will live forever. This
bread is my flesh, which I will give for the
life of the world."
52 Then the Jews began to argue sharply
among themselves, "How can this man
give us his flesh to eat?"
53 Jesus said to them, "Very truly I tell
you, unless you eat the flesh of the Son
of Man and drink his blood, you have no
life in you. 54 Whoever eats my flesh and
drinks my blood has eternal life, and I
will raise them up at the last day. 55 For
my flesh is real food and my blood is real
drink. 56 Whoever eats my flesh and drinks
my blood remains in me, and I in them.
57 Just as the living Father sent me and I
live because of the Father, so the one who
feeds on me will live because of me. 58 This
is the bread that came down from heav-
en. Your ancestors ate manna and died,
but whoever feeds on this bread will live
forever." 59 He said this while teaching in
the synagogue in Capernaum.

Many Disciples Desert Jesus

60 On hearing it, many of his disciples
said, "This is a hard teaching. Who can
accept it?"
61 Aware that his disciples were grumbling about this, Jesus said to them, "Does
this offend you? 62 Then what if you see the
Son of Man ascend to where he was before!
63 The Spirit gives life; the flesh counts
for nothing. The words I have spoken to
you — they are full of the Spirit[c] and life.
64 Yet there are some of you who do not

[a] *31* Exodus 16:4; Neh. 9:15; Psalm 78:24,25 [b] *45* Isaiah 54:13 [c] *63* Or *are Spirit*; or *are spirit*

believe." For Jesus had known from the
beginning which of them did not believe
and who would betray him. 65He went on
to say, "This is why I told you that no one
can come to me unless the Father has
enabled them."

66From this time many of his disciples
turned back and no longer followed him.

67"You do not want to leave too, do you?"
Jesus asked the Twelve.

68Simon Peter answered him, "Lord, to
whom shall we go? You have the words of
eternal life. 69We have come to believe and
to know that you are the Holy One of God."

70Then Jesus replied, "Have I not chosen
you, the Twelve? Yet one of you is a devil!" 71(He meant Judas, the son of Simon
Iscariot, who, though one of the Twelve,
was later to betray him.)

Jesus Goes to the Festival of Tabernacles

7 After this, Jesus went around in Galilee.
He did not want[a] to go about in Judea
because the Jewish leaders there were
looking for a way to kill him. 2But when the
Jewish Festival of Tabernacles was near,
3Jesus' brothers said to him, "Leave Galilee and go to Judea, so that your disciples
there may see the works you do. 4No one
who wants to become a public figure acts
in secret. Since you are doing these things,
show yourself to the world." 5For even his
own brothers did not believe in him.

6Therefore Jesus told them, "My time
is not yet here; for you any time will do.
7The world cannot hate you, but it hates
me because I testify that its works are evil.
8You go to the festival. I am not[b] going up
to this festival, because my time has not
yet fully come." 9After he had said this, he
stayed in Galilee.

10However, after his brothers had left
for the festival, he went also, not publicly, but in secret. 11Now at the festival the
Jewish leaders were watching for Jesus
and asking, "Where is he?"

12Among the crowds there was widespread whispering about him. Some said,
"He is a good man."

Others replied, "No, he deceives the people." 13But no one would say anything
publicly about him for fear of the leaders.

Jesus Teaches at the Festival

14Not until halfway through the festival
did Jesus go up to the temple courts and begin to teach. 15The Jews there were amazed
and asked, "How did this man get such
learning without having been taught?"

16Jesus answered, "My teaching is not
my own. It comes from the one who sent
me. 17Anyone who chooses to do the will
of God will find out whether my teaching
comes from God or whether I speak on
my own. 18Whoever speaks on their own
does so to gain personal glory, but he who
seeks the glory of the one who sent him
is a man of truth; there is nothing false
about him. 19Has not Moses given you the
law? Yet not one of you keeps the law. Why
are you trying to kill me?"

20"You are demon-possessed," the crowd
answered. "Who is trying to kill you?"

21Jesus said to them, "I did one miracle,
and you are all amazed. 22Yet, because Moses gave you circumcision (though actually it did not come from Moses, but from the
patriarchs), you circumcise a boy on the
Sabbath. 23Now if a boy can be circumcised
on the Sabbath so that the law of Moses
may not be broken, why are you angry
with me for healing a man's whole body
on the Sabbath? 24Stop judging by mere
appearances, but instead judge correctly."

Division Over Who Jesus Is

25At that point some of the people of
Jerusalem began to ask, "Isn't this the
man they are trying to kill? 26Here he is,
speaking publicly, and they are not saying
a word to him. Have the authorities really
concluded that he is the Messiah? 27But we
know where this man is from; when the
Messiah comes, no one will know where
he is from."

28Then Jesus, still teaching in the temple courts, cried out, "Yes, you know me,
and you know where I am from. I am not
here on my own authority, but he who sent
me is true. You do not know him, 29but I
know him because I am from him and
he sent me."

30At this they tried to seize him, but
no one laid a hand on him, because his
hour had not yet come. 31Still, many in the
crowd believed in him. They said, "When
the Messiah comes, will he perform more
signs than this man?"

32The Pharisees heard the crowd whispering such things about him. Then the
chief priests and the Pharisees sent temple
guards to arrest him.

33Jesus said, "I am with you for only a
short time, and then I am going to the
one who sent me. 34You will look for me,
but you will not find me; and where I am,
you cannot come."

35The Jews said to one another, "Where
does this man intend to go that we cannot

[a] *1* Some manuscripts *not have authority* [b] *8* Some manuscripts *not yet*

find him? Will he go where our people live scattered among the Greeks, and teach the Greeks? 36 What did he mean when he said, 'You will look for me, but you will not find me,' and 'Where I am, you cannot come'?"

37 On the last and greatest day of the festival, Jesus stood and said in a loud voice, "Let anyone who is thirsty come to me and drink. 38 Whoever believes in me, as Scripture has said, rivers of living water will flow from within them."[a] 39 By this he meant the Spirit, whom those who believed in him were later to receive. Up to that time the Spirit had not been given, since Jesus had not yet been glorified.

40 On hearing his words, some of the people said, "Surely this man is the Prophet."

41 Others said, "He is the Messiah."

Still others asked, "How can the Messiah come from Galilee? 42 Does not Scripture say that the Messiah will come from David's descendants and from Bethlehem, the town where David lived?" 43 Thus the people were divided because of Jesus. 44 Some wanted to seize him, but no one laid a hand on him.

Unbelief of the Jewish Leaders

45 Finally the temple guards went back to the chief priests and the Pharisees, who asked them, "Why didn't you bring him in?"

46 "No one ever spoke the way this man does," the guards replied.

47 "You mean he has deceived you also?" the Pharisees retorted. 48 "Have any of the rulers or of the Pharisees believed in him? 49 No! But this mob that knows nothing of the law — there is a curse on them."

50 Nicodemus, who had gone to Jesus earlier and who was one of their own number, asked, 51 "Does our law condemn a man without first hearing him to find out what he has been doing?"

52 They replied, "Are you from Galilee, too? Look into it, and you will find that a prophet does not come out of Galilee."

[The earliest manuscripts and many other ancient witnesses do not have John 7:53 — 8:11. A few manuscripts include these verses, wholly or in part, after John 7:36, John 21:25, Luke 21:38 or Luke 24:53.]

8 *53 Then they all went home, 1 but Jesus went to the Mount of Olives.*

2 At dawn he appeared again in the temple courts, where all the people gathered around him, and he sat down to teach them. 3 The teachers of the law and the Pharisees brought in a woman caught in adultery. They made her stand before the group 4 and said to Jesus, "Teacher, this woman was caught in the act of adultery. 5 In the Law Moses commanded us to stone such women. Now what do you say?" 6 They were using this question as a trap, in order to have a basis for accusing him.

But Jesus bent down and started to write on the ground with his finger. 7 When they kept on questioning him, he straightened up and said to them, "Let any one of you who is without sin be the first to throw a stone at her." 8 Again he stooped down and wrote on the ground.

9 At this, those who heard began to go away one at a time, the older ones first, until only Jesus was left, with the woman still standing there. 10 Jesus straightened up and asked her, "Woman, where are they? Has no one condemned you?"

11 "No one, sir," she said.

"Then neither do I condemn you," Jesus declared. "Go now and leave your life of sin."

Dispute Over Jesus' Testimony

12 When Jesus spoke again to the people, he said, "I am the light of the world. Whoever follows me will never walk in darkness, but will have the light of life."

13 The Pharisees challenged him, "Here you are, appearing as your own witness; your testimony is not valid."

14 Jesus answered, "Even if I testify on my own behalf, my testimony is valid, for I know where I came from and where I am going. But you have no idea where I come from or where I am going. 15 You judge by human standards; I pass judgment on no one. 16 But if I do judge, my decisions are true, because I am not alone. I stand with the Father, who sent me. 17 In your own Law it is written that the testimony of two witnesses is true. 18 I am one who testifies for myself; my other witness is the Father, who sent me."

19 Then they asked him, "Where is your father?"

"You do not know me or my Father," Jesus replied. "If you knew me, you would know my Father also." 20 He spoke these words while teaching in the temple courts near the place where the offerings were put. Yet no one seized him, because his hour had not yet come.

Dispute Over Who Jesus Is

21 Once more Jesus said to them, "I am going away, and you will look for me, and you will die in your sin. Where I go, you cannot come."

[a] *37,38* Or *me. And let anyone drink 38 who believes in me." As Scripture has said, "Out of him* (or *them) will flow rivers of living water."*

22This made the Jews ask, "Will he kill himself? Is that why he says, 'Where I go, you cannot come'?"

23But he continued, "You are from below; I am from above. You are of this world; I am not of this world. 24I told you that you would die in your sins; if you do not believe that I am he, you will indeed die in your sins."

25"Who are you?" they asked.

"Just what I have been telling you from the beginning," Jesus replied. 26"I have much to say in judgment of you. But he who sent me is trustworthy, and what I have heard from him I tell the world."

27They did not understand that he was telling them about his Father. 28So Jesus said, "When you have lifted up[a] the Son of Man, then you will know that I am he and that I do nothing on my own but speak just what the Father has taught me. 29The one who sent me is with me; he has not left me alone, for I always do what pleases him." 30Even as he spoke, many believed in him.

Dispute Over Whose Children Jesus' Opponents Are

31To the Jews who had believed him, Jesus said, "If you hold to my teaching, you are really my disciples. 32Then you will know the truth, and the truth will set you free."

33They answered him, "We are Abraham's descendants and have never been slaves of anyone. How can you say that we shall be set free?"

34Jesus replied, "Very truly I tell you, everyone who sins is a slave to sin. 35Now a slave has no permanent place in the family, but a son belongs to it forever. 36So if the Son sets you free, you will be free indeed. 37I know that you are Abraham's descendants. Yet you are looking for a way to kill me, because you have no room for my word. 38I am telling you what I have seen in the Father's presence, and you are doing what you have heard from your father.[b]"

39"Abraham is our father," they answered.

"If you were Abraham's children," said Jesus, "then you would[c] do what Abraham did. 40As it is, you are looking for a way to kill me, a man who has told you the truth that I heard from God. Abraham did not do such things. 41You are doing the works of your own father."

"We are not illegitimate children," they protested. "The only Father we have is God himself."

42Jesus said to them, "If God were your Father, you would love me, for I have come here from God. I have not come on my own; God sent me. 43Why is my language not clear to you? Because you are unable to hear what I say. 44You belong to your father, the devil, and you want to carry out your father's desires. He was a murderer from the beginning, not holding to the truth, for there is no truth in him. When he lies, he speaks his native language, for he is a liar and the father of lies. 45Yet because I tell the truth, you do not believe me! 46Can any of you prove me guilty of sin? If I am telling the truth, why don't you believe me? 47Whoever belongs to God hears what God says. The reason you do not hear is that you do not belong to God."

Jesus' Claims About Himself

48The Jews answered him, "Aren't we right in saying that you are a Samaritan and demon-possessed?"

49"I am not possessed by a demon," said Jesus, "but I honor my Father and you dishonor me. 50I am not seeking glory for myself; but there is one who seeks it, and he is the judge. 51Very truly I tell you, whoever obeys my word will never see death."

52At this they exclaimed, "Now we know that you are demon-possessed! Abraham died and so did the prophets, yet you say that whoever obeys your word will never taste death. 53Are you greater than our father Abraham? He died, and so did the prophets. Who do you think you are?"

54Jesus replied, "If I glorify myself, my glory means nothing. My Father, whom you claim as your God, is the one who glorifies me. 55Though you do not know him, I know him. If I said I did not, I would be a liar like you, but I do know him and obey his word. 56Your father Abraham rejoiced at the thought of seeing my day; he saw it and was glad."

57"You are not yet fifty years old," they said to him, "and you have seen Abraham!"

58"Very truly I tell you," Jesus answered, "before Abraham was born, I am!" 59At this, they picked up stones to stone him, but Jesus hid himself, slipping away from the temple grounds.

Jesus Heals a Man Born Blind

9 As he went along, he saw a man blind from birth. 2His disciples asked him, "Rabbi, who sinned, this man or his parents, that he was born blind?"

[a] 28 The Greek for *lifted up* also means *exalted.* [b] 38 Or *presence. Therefore do what you have heard from the Father.* [c] 39 Some early manuscripts *"If you are Abraham's children," said Jesus, "then*

3“Neither this man nor his parents
sinned,” said Jesus, “but this happened
so that the works of God might be displayed in him. 4As long as it is day, we
must do the works of him who sent me.
Night is coming, when no one can work.
5While I am in the world, I am the light
of the world.”
6After saying this, he spit on the ground,
made some mud with the saliva, and put
it on the man’s eyes. 7“Go,” he told him,
“wash in the Pool of Siloam” (this word
means “Sent”). So the man went and
washed, and came home seeing.
8His neighbors and those who had formerly seen him begging asked, “Isn’t this
the same man who used to sit and beg?”
9Some claimed that he was.
Others said, “No, he only looks like him.”
But he himself insisted, “I am the man.”
10“How then were your eyes opened?”
they asked.
11He replied, “The man they call Jesus
made some mud and put it on my eyes.
He told me to go to Siloam and wash. So
I went and washed, and then I could see.”
12“Where is this man?” they asked him.
“I don’t know,” he said.

The Pharisees Investigate the Healing

13They brought to the Pharisees the
man who had been blind. 14Now the day
on which Jesus had made the mud and
opened the man’s eyes was a Sabbath.
15Therefore the Pharisees also asked him
how he had received his sight. “He put
mud on my eyes,” the man replied, “and
I washed, and now I see.”
16Some of the Pharisees said, “This man
is not from God, for he does not keep the
Sabbath.”
But others asked, “How can a sinner
perform such signs?” So they were divided.
17Then they turned again to the blind
man, “What have you to say about him?
It was your eyes he opened.”
The man replied, “He is a prophet.”
18They still did not believe that he had
been blind and had received his sight until
they sent for the man’s parents. 19“Is this
your son?” they asked. “Is this the one
you say was born blind? How is it that
now he can see?”
20“We know he is our son,” the parents
answered, “and we know he was born
blind. 21But how he can see now, or who
opened his eyes, we don’t know. Ask him.
He is of age; he will speak for himself.”
22His parents said this because they were
afraid of the Jewish leaders, who already
had decided that anyone who acknowledged that Jesus was the Messiah would be
put out of the synagogue. 23That was why
his parents said, “He is of age; ask him.”
24A second time they summoned the
man who had been blind. “Give glory to
God by telling the truth,” they said. “We
know this man is a sinner.”
25He replied, “Whether he is a sinner or
not, I don’t know. One thing I do know. I
was blind but now I see!”
26Then they asked him, “What did he
do to you? How did he open your eyes?”
27He answered, “I have told you already
and you did not listen. Why do you want
to hear it again? Do you want to become
his disciples too?”
28Then they hurled insults at him and
said, “You are this fellow’s disciple! We are
disciples of Moses! 29We know that God
spoke to Moses, but as for this fellow, we
don’t even know where he comes from.”
30The man answered, “Now that is remarkable! You don’t know where he comes
from, yet he opened my eyes. 31We know
that God does not listen to sinners. He
listens to the godly person who does his
will. 32Nobody has ever heard of opening
the eyes of a man born blind. 33If this man
were not from God, he could do nothing.”
34To this they replied, “You were steeped
in sin at birth; how dare you lecture us!”
And they threw him out.

Spiritual Blindness

35Jesus heard that they had thrown him
out, and when he found him, he said, “Do
you believe in the Son of Man?”
36“Who is he, sir?” the man asked. “Tell
me so that I may believe in him.”
37Jesus said, “You have now seen him;
in fact, he is the one speaking with you.”
38Then the man said, “Lord, I believe,”
and he worshiped him.
39Jesus said,[a] “For judgment I have
come into this world, so that the blind will
see and those who see will become blind.”
40Some Pharisees who were with him
heard him say this and asked, “What?
Are we blind too?”
41Jesus said, “If you were blind, you
would not be guilty of sin; but now that
you claim you can see, your guilt remains.

The Good Shepherd and His Sheep

10 “Very truly I tell you Pharisees, anyone who does not enter the sheep
pen by the gate, but climbs in by some
other way, is a thief and a robber. 2The one

[a] *38,39* Some early manuscripts do not have *Then the man said . . . 39Jesus said.*

who enters by the gate is the shepherd of the sheep. 3 The gatekeeper opens the gate for him, and the sheep listen to his voice. He calls his own sheep by name and leads them out. 4 When he has brought out all his own, he goes on ahead of them, and his sheep follow him because they know his voice. 5 But they will never follow a stranger; in fact, they will run away from him because they do not recognize a stranger's voice." 6 Jesus used this figure of speech, but the Pharisees did not understand what he was telling them.

7 Therefore Jesus said again, "Very truly I tell you, I am the gate for the sheep. 8 All who have come before me are thieves and robbers, but the sheep have not listened to them. 9 I am the gate; whoever enters through me will be saved.[a] They will come in and go out, and find pasture. 10 The thief comes only to steal and kill and destroy; I have come that they may have life, and have it to the full.

11 "I am the good shepherd. The good shepherd lays down his life for the sheep. 12 The hired hand is not the shepherd and does not own the sheep. So when he sees the wolf coming, he abandons the sheep and runs away. Then the wolf attacks the flock and scatters it. 13 The man runs away because he is a hired hand and cares nothing for the sheep.

14 "I am the good shepherd; I know my sheep and my sheep know me — 15 just as the Father knows me and I know the Father — and I lay down my life for the sheep. 16 I have other sheep that are not of this sheep pen. I must bring them also. They too will listen to my voice, and there shall be one flock and one shepherd. 17 The reason my Father loves me is that I lay down my life — only to take it up again. 18 No one takes it from me, but I lay it down of my own accord. I have authority to lay it down and authority to take it up again. This command I received from my Father."

19 The Jews who heard these words were again divided. 20 Many of them said, "He is demon-possessed and raving mad. Why listen to him?"

21 But others said, "These are not the sayings of a man possessed by a demon. Can a demon open the eyes of the blind?"

Further Conflict Over Jesus' Claims

22 Then came the Festival of Dedication[b] at Jerusalem. It was winter, 23 and Jesus was in the temple courts walking in Solomon's Colonnade. 24 The Jews who were there gathered around him, saying, "How long will you keep us in suspense? If you are the Messiah, tell us plainly."

25 Jesus answered, "I did tell you, but you do not believe. The works I do in my Father's name testify about me, 26 but you do not believe because you are not my sheep. 27 My sheep listen to my voice; I know them, and they follow me. 28 I give them eternal life, and they shall never perish; no one will snatch them out of my hand. 29 My Father, who has given them to me, is greater than all[c]; no one can snatch them out of my Father's hand. 30 I and the Father are one."

31 Again his Jewish opponents picked up stones to stone him, 32 but Jesus said to them, "I have shown you many good works from the Father. For which of these do you stone me?"

33 "We are not stoning you for any good work," they replied, "but for blasphemy, because you, a mere man, claim to be God."

34 Jesus answered them, "Is it not written in your Law, 'I have said you are "gods"'[d]? 35 If he called them 'gods,' to whom the word of God came — and Scripture cannot be set aside — 36 what about the one whom the Father set apart as his very own and sent into the world? Why then do you accuse me of blasphemy because I said, 'I am God's Son'? 37 Do not believe me unless I do the works of my Father. 38 But if I do them, even though you do not believe me, believe the works, that you may know and understand that the Father is in me, and I in the Father." 39 Again they tried to seize him, but he escaped their grasp.

40 Then Jesus went back across the Jordan to the place where John had been baptizing in the early days. There he stayed, 41 and many people came to him. They said, "Though John never performed a sign, all that John said about this man was true." 42 And in that place many believed in Jesus.

The Death of Lazarus

11 Now a man named Lazarus was sick. He was from Bethany, the village of Mary and her sister Martha. 2 (This Mary, whose brother Lazarus now lay sick, was the same one who poured perfume on the Lord and wiped his feet with her hair.) 3 So the sisters sent word to Jesus, "Lord, the one you love is sick."

4 When he heard this, Jesus said, "This sickness will not end in death. No, it is for God's glory so that God's Son may be

[a] 9 Or *kept safe* [b] 22 That is, Hanukkah [c] 29 Many early manuscripts *What my Father has given me is greater than all* [d] 34 Psalm 82:6

glorified through it." 5Now Jesus loved
Martha and her sister and Lazarus. 6So
when he heard that Lazarus was sick,
he stayed where he was two more days,
7and then he said to his disciples, "Let us
go back to Judea."

8"But Rabbi," they said, "a short while
ago the Jews there tried to stone you, and
yet you are going back?"

9Jesus answered, "Are there not twelve
hours of daylight? Anyone who walks in
the daytime will not stumble, for they see
by this world's light. 10It is when a person
walks at night that they stumble, for they
have no light."

11After he had said this, he went on to
tell them, "Our friend Lazarus has fall-
en asleep; but I am going there to wake
him up."

12His disciples replied, "Lord, if he sleeps,
he will get better." 13Jesus had been speaking of his death, but his disciples thought
he meant natural sleep.

14So then he told them plainly, "Laza-
rus is dead, 15and for your sake I am glad
I was not there, so that you may believe.
But let us go to him."

16Then Thomas (also known as Didy-
mus[a]) said to the rest of the disciples, "Let
us also go, that we may die with him."

Jesus Comforts the Sisters of Lazarus

17On his arrival, Jesus found that Lazarus had already been in the tomb for
four days. 18Now Bethany was less than
two miles[b] from Jerusalem, 19and many
Jews had come to Martha and Mary to
comfort them in the loss of their brother. 20When Martha heard that Jesus was
coming, she went out to meet him, but
Mary stayed at home.

21"Lord," Martha said to Jesus, "if you
had been here, my brother would not have
died. 22But I know that even now God will
give you whatever you ask."

23Jesus said to her, "Your brother will
rise again."

24Martha answered, "I know he will rise
again in the resurrection at the last day."

25Jesus said to her, "I am the resurrection and the life. The one who believes in
me will live, even though they die; 26and
whoever lives by believing in me will never
die. Do you believe this?"

27"Yes, Lord," she replied, "I believe that
you are the Messiah, the Son of God, who
is to come into the world."

28After she had said this, she went back
and called her sister Mary aside. "The
Teacher is here," she said, "and is asking
for you." 29When Mary heard this, she got
up quickly and went to him. 30Now Jesus
had not yet entered the village, but was
still at the place where Martha had met
him. 31When the Jews who had been with
Mary in the house, comforting her, noticed
how quickly she got up and went out, they
followed her, supposing she was going to
the tomb to mourn there.

32When Mary reached the place where
Jesus was and saw him, she fell at his feet
and said, "Lord, if you had been here, my
brother would not have died."

33When Jesus saw her weeping, and the
Jews who had come along with her also
weeping, he was deeply moved in spirit and troubled. 34"Where have you laid
him?" he asked.

"Come and see, Lord," they replied.

35Jesus wept.

36Then the Jews said, "See how he loved
him!"

37But some of them said, "Could not he
who opened the eyes of the blind man
have kept this man from dying?"

Jesus Raises Lazarus From the Dead

38Jesus, once more deeply moved, came
to the tomb. It was a cave with a stone
laid across the entrance. 39"Take away
the stone," he said.

"But, Lord," said Martha, the sister of
the dead man, "by this time there is a
bad odor, for he has been there four days."

40Then Jesus said, "Did I not tell you
that if you believe, you will see the glory
of God?"

41So they took away the stone. Then
Jesus looked up and said, "Father, I thank
you that you have heard me. 42I knew
that you always hear me, but I said this
for the benefit of the people standing
here, that they may believe that you
sent me."

43When he had said this, Jesus called in
a loud voice, "Lazarus, come out!" 44The
dead man came out, his hands and feet
wrapped with strips of linen, and a cloth
around his face.

Jesus said to them, "Take off the grave
clothes and let him go."

The Plot to Kill Jesus

45Therefore many of the Jews who had
come to visit Mary, and had seen what
Jesus did, believed in him. 46But some
of them went to the Pharisees and told
them what Jesus had done. 47Then the
chief priests and the Pharisees called a
meeting of the Sanhedrin.

[a] 16 *Thomas* (Aramaic) and *Didymus* (Greek) both mean *twin*. [b] 18 Or about 3 kilometers

"What are we accomplishing?" they
asked. "Here is this man performing many
signs. 48 If we let him go on like this, everyone will believe in him, and then the
Romans will come and take away both
our temple and our nation."
49 Then one of them, named Caiaphas,
who was high priest that year, spoke up,
"You know nothing at all! 50 You do not
realize that it is better for you that one
man die for the people than that the whole
nation perish."
51 He did not say this on his own, but
as high priest that year he prophesied
that Jesus would die for the Jewish nation, 52 and not only for that nation but
also for the scattered children of God, to
bring them together and make them one.
53 So from that day on they plotted to take
his life.
54 Therefore Jesus no longer moved
about publicly among the people of Judea.
Instead he withdrew to a region near the
wilderness, to a village called Ephraim,
where he stayed with his disciples.
55 When it was almost time for the Jewish
Passover, many went up from the country
to Jerusalem for their ceremonial cleansing before the Passover. 56 They kept looking for Jesus, and as they stood in the
temple courts they asked one another,
"What do you think? Isn't he coming to the
festival at all?" 57 But the chief priests and
the Pharisees had given orders that anyone who found out where Jesus was should
report it so that they might arrest him.

Jesus Anointed at Bethany

12 Six days before the Passover, Jesus
came to Bethany, where Lazarus
lived, whom Jesus had raised from the
dead. 2 Here a dinner was given in Jesus'
honor. Martha served, while Lazarus was
among those reclining at the table with
him. 3 Then Mary took about a pint[a] of pure
nard, an expensive perfume; she poured
it on Jesus' feet and wiped his feet with
her hair. And the house was filled with the
fragrance of the perfume.
4 But one of his disciples, Judas Iscariot,
who was later to betray him, objected,
5 "Why wasn't this perfume sold and the
money given to the poor? It was worth a
year's wages.[b]" 6 He did not say this because he cared about the poor but because
he was a thief; as keeper of the money
bag, he used to help himself to what was
put into it.
7 "Leave her alone," Jesus replied. "It
was intended that she should save this
perfume for the day of my burial. 8 You
will always have the poor among you,[c]
but you will not always have me."
9 Meanwhile a large crowd of Jews found
out that Jesus was there and came, not
only because of him but also to see Lazarus, whom he had raised from the dead.
10 So the chief priests made plans to kill
Lazarus as well, 11 for on account of him
many of the Jews were going over to Jesus
and believing in him.

Jesus Comes to Jerusalem as King

12 The next day the great crowd that
had come for the festival heard that Jesus
was on his way to Jerusalem. 13 They took
palm branches and went out to meet him,
shouting,

"Hosanna![d]"

"Blessed is he who comes in the name
of the Lord!"[e]

"Blessed is the king of Israel!"

14 Jesus found a young donkey and sat on
it, as it is written:

15 "Do not be afraid, Daughter Zion;
see, your king is coming,
seated on a donkey's colt."[f]

16 At first his disciples did not understand all this. Only after Jesus was glorified did they realize that these things had
been written about him and that these
things had been done to him.
17 Now the crowd that was with him
when he called Lazarus from the tomb and
raised him from the dead continued to
spread the word. 18 Many people, because
they had heard that he had performed
this sign, went out to meet him. 19 So the
Pharisees said to one another, "See, this is
getting us nowhere. Look how the whole
world has gone after him!"

Jesus Predicts His Death

20 Now there were some Greeks among
those who went up to worship at the festival. 21 They came to Philip, who was from
Bethsaida in Galilee, with a request. "Sir,"
they said, "we would like to see Jesus."
22 Philip went to tell Andrew; Andrew and
Philip in turn told Jesus.
23 Jesus replied, "The hour has come for
the Son of Man to be glorified. 24 Very truly
I tell you, unless a kernel of wheat falls

[a] *3* Or about 0.5 liter [b] *5* Greek *three hundred denarii* [c] *8* See Deut. 15:11. [d] *13* A Hebrew expression meaning "Save!" which became an exclamation of praise [e] *13* Psalm 118:25,26 [f] *15* Zech. 9:9

to the ground and dies, it remains only a
single seed. But if it dies, it produces many
seeds. 25Anyone who loves their life will
lose it, while anyone who hates their life
in this world will keep it for eternal life.
26Whoever serves me must follow me; and
where I am, my servant also will be. My
Father will honor the one who serves me.
27"Now my soul is troubled, and what
shall I say? 'Father, save me from this
hour'? No, it was for this very reason I
came to this hour. 28Father, glorify your
name!"

Then a voice came from heaven, "I have
glorified it, and will glorify it again." 29The
crowd that was there and heard it said it
had thundered; others said an angel had
spoken to him.
30Jesus said, "This voice was for your
benefit, not mine. 31Now is the time for
judgment on this world; now the prince
of this world will be driven out. 32And I,
when I am lifted up[a] from the earth, will
draw all people to myself." 33He said this to
show the kind of death he was going to die.
34The crowd spoke up, "We have heard
from the Law that the Messiah will remain
forever, so how can you say, 'The Son of
Man must be lifted up'? Who is this 'Son
of Man'?"
35Then Jesus told them, "You are going
to have the light just a little while longer. Walk while you have the light, before
darkness overtakes you. Whoever walks
in the dark does not know where they are
going. 36Believe in the light while you have
the light, so that you may become children
of light." When he had finished speaking,
Jesus left and hid himself from them.

Belief and Unbelief Among the Jews

37Even after Jesus had performed so
many signs in their presence, they still
would not believe in him. 38This was to
fulfill the word of Isaiah the prophet:

"Lord, who has believed our message
and to whom has the arm of the
Lord been revealed?"[b]

39For this reason they could not believe,
because, as Isaiah says elsewhere:

40"He has blinded their eyes
and hardened their hearts,
so they can neither see with their
eyes,
nor understand with their hearts,
nor turn — and I would heal them."[c]

41Isaiah said this because he saw Jesus'
glory and spoke about him.
42Yet at the same time many even
among the leaders believed in him. But
because of the Pharisees they would not
openly acknowledge their faith for fear
they would be put out of the synagogue;
43for they loved human praise more than
praise from God.
44Then Jesus cried out, "Whoever believes in me does not believe in me only,
but in the one who sent me. 45The one
who looks at me is seeing the one who
sent me. 46I have come into the world as
a light, so that no one who believes in me
should stay in darkness.
47"If anyone hears my words but does
not keep them, I do not judge that person.
For I did not come to judge the world, but
to save the world. 48There is a judge for the
one who rejects me and does not accept my
words; the very words I have spoken will
condemn them at the last day. 49For I did
not speak on my own, but the Father who
sent me commanded me to say all that I
have spoken. 50I know that his command
leads to eternal life. So whatever I say is
just what the Father has told me to say."

Jesus Washes His Disciples' Feet

13 It was just before the Passover Festival. Jesus knew that the hour had
come for him to leave this world and go to
the Father. Having loved his own who were
in the world, he loved them to the end.
2The evening meal was in progress,
and the devil had already prompted Judas, the son of Simon Iscariot, to betray
Jesus. 3Jesus knew that the Father had
put all things under his power, and that
he had come from God and was returning to God; 4so he got up from the meal,
took off his outer clothing, and wrapped
a towel around his waist. 5After that, he
poured water into a basin and began to
wash his disciples' feet, drying them with
the towel that was wrapped around him.
6He came to Simon Peter, who said to
him, "Lord, are you going to wash my feet?"
7Jesus replied, "You do not realize now
what I am doing, but later you will understand."
8"No," said Peter, "you shall never wash
my feet."

Jesus answered, "Unless I wash you, you
have no part with me."
9"Then, Lord," Simon Peter replied, "not
just my feet but my hands and my head
as well!"
10Jesus answered, "Those who have had
a bath need only to wash their feet; their
whole body is clean. And you are clean,

[a] *32* The Greek for *lifted up* also means *exalted.*
[b] *38* Isaiah 53:1
[c] *40* Isaiah 6:10

though not every one of you." 11For he knew who was going to betray him, and that was why he said not every one was clean.

12When he had finished washing their feet, he put on his clothes and returned to his place. "Do you understand what I have done for you?" he asked them. 13"You call me 'Teacher' and 'Lord,' and rightly so, for that is what I am. 14Now that I, your Lord and Teacher, have washed your feet, you also should wash one another's feet. 15I have set you an example that you should do as I have done for you. 16Very truly I tell you, no servant is greater than his master, nor is a messenger greater than the one who sent him. 17Now that you know these things, you will be blessed if you do them.

Jesus Predicts His Betrayal

18"I am not referring to all of you; I know those I have chosen. But this is to fulfill this passage of Scripture: 'He who shared my bread has turned[a] against me.'[b]

19"I am telling you now before it happens, so that when it does happen you will believe that I am who I am. 20Very truly I tell you, whoever accepts anyone I send accepts me; and whoever accepts me accepts the one who sent me."

21After he had said this, Jesus was troubled in spirit and testified, "Very truly I tell you, one of you is going to betray me."

22His disciples stared at one another, at a loss to know which of them he meant. 23One of them, the disciple whom Jesus loved, was reclining next to him. 24Simon Peter motioned to this disciple and said, "Ask him which one he means."

25Leaning back against Jesus, he asked him, "Lord, who is it?"

26Jesus answered, "It is the one to whom I will give this piece of bread when I have dipped it in the dish." Then, dipping the piece of bread, he gave it to Judas, the son of Simon Iscariot. 27As soon as Judas took the bread, Satan entered into him.

So Jesus told him, "What you are about to do, do quickly." 28But no one at the meal understood why Jesus said this to him. 29Since Judas had charge of the money, some thought Jesus was telling him to buy what was needed for the festival, or to give something to the poor. 30As soon as Judas had taken the bread, he went out. And it was night.

Jesus Predicts Peter's Denial

31When he was gone, Jesus said, "Now the Son of Man is glorified and God is glorified in him. 32If God is glorified in him,[c] God will glorify the Son in himself, and will glorify him at once.

33"My children, I will be with you only a little longer. You will look for me, and just as I told the Jews, so I tell you now: Where I am going, you cannot come.

34"A new command I give you: Love one another. As I have loved you, so you must love one another. 35By this everyone will know that you are my disciples, if you love one another."

36Simon Peter asked him, "Lord, where are you going?"

Jesus replied, "Where I am going, you cannot follow now, but you will follow later."

37Peter asked, "Lord, why can't I follow you now? I will lay down my life for you."

38Then Jesus answered, "Will you really lay down your life for me? Very truly I tell you, before the rooster crows, you will disown me three times!

Jesus Comforts His Disciples

14 "Do not let your hearts be troubled. You believe in God[d]; believe also in me. 2My Father's house has many rooms; if that were not so, would I have told you that I am going there to prepare a place for you? 3And if I go and prepare a place for you, I will come back and take you to be with me that you also may be where I am. 4You know the way to the place where I am going."

Jesus the Way to the Father

5Thomas said to him, "Lord, we don't know where you are going, so how can we know the way?"

6Jesus answered, "I am the way and the truth and the life. No one comes to the Father except through me. 7If you really know me, you will know[e] my Father as well. From now on, you do know him and have seen him."

8Philip said, "Lord, show us the Father and that will be enough for us."

9Jesus answered: "Don't you know me, Philip, even after I have been among you such a long time? Anyone who has seen me has seen the Father. How can you say, 'Show us the Father'? 10Don't you believe that I am in the Father, and that the Father is in me? The words I say to you I do not

[a] 18 Greek *has lifted up his heel* [b] 18 Psalm 41:9 [c] 32 Many early manuscripts do not have *If God is glorified in him.* [d] 1 Or *Believe in God* [e] 7 Some manuscripts *If you really knew me, you would know*

speak on my own authority. Rather, it is
the Father, living in me, who is doing his
work. [11]Believe me when I say that I am in
the Father and the Father is in me; or at
least believe on the evidence of the works
themselves. [12]Very truly I tell you, whoever
believes in me will do the works I have
been doing, and they will do even greater
things than these, because I am going to
the Father. [13]And I will do whatever you
ask in my name, so that the Father may
be glorified in the Son. [14]You may ask me
for anything in my name, and I will do it.

Jesus Promises the Holy Spirit

[15]"If you love me, keep my commands.
[16]And I will ask the Father, and he will
give you another advocate to help you
and be with you forever— [17]the Spirit of
truth. The world cannot accept him, because it neither sees him nor knows him.
But you know him, for he lives with you
and will be[a] in you. [18]I will not leave you
as orphans; I will come to you. [19]Before
long, the world will not see me anymore,
but you will see me. Because I live, you also
will live. [20]On that day you will realize that
I am in my Father, and you are in me, and
I am in you. [21]Whoever has my commands
and keeps them is the one who loves me.
The one who loves me will be loved by my
Father, and I too will love them and show
myself to them."

[22]Then Judas (not Judas Iscariot) said,
"But, Lord, why do you intend to show
yourself to us and not to the world?"

[23]Jesus replied, "Anyone who loves me
will obey my teaching. My Father will love
them, and we will come to them and make
our home with them. [24]Anyone who does
not love me will not obey my teaching.
These words you hear are not my own;
they belong to the Father who sent me.

[25]"All this I have spoken while still
with you. [26]But the Advocate, the Holy
Spirit, whom the Father will send in my
name, will teach you all things and will
remind you of everything I have said to
you. [27]Peace I leave with you; my peace I
give you. I do not give to you as the world
gives. Do not let your hearts be troubled
and do not be afraid.

[28]"You heard me say, 'I am going away
and I am coming back to you.' If you loved
me, you would be glad that I am going to
the Father, for the Father is greater than
I. [29]I have told you now before it happens,
so that when it does happen you will believe. [30]I will not say much more to you,
for the prince of this world is coming. He
has no hold over me, [31]but he comes so
that the world may learn that I love the
Father and do exactly what my Father has
commanded me.

"Come now; let us leave.

The Vine and the Branches

15 "I am the true vine, and my Father
is the gardener. [2]He cuts off every
branch in me that bears no fruit, while every branch that does bear fruit he prunes[b]
so that it will be even more fruitful. [3]You
are already clean because of the word I
have spoken to you. [4]Remain in me, as I
also remain in you. No branch can bear
fruit by itself; it must remain in the vine.
Neither can you bear fruit unless you remain in me.

[5]"I am the vine; you are the branches.
If you remain in me and I in you, you will
bear much fruit; apart from me you can
do nothing. [6]If you do not remain in me,
you are like a branch that is thrown away
and withers; such branches are picked up,
thrown into the fire and burned. [7]If you
remain in me and my words remain in
you, ask whatever you wish, and it will
be done for you. [8]This is to my Father's
glory, that you bear much fruit, showing
yourselves to be my disciples.

[9]"As the Father has loved me, so have
I loved you. Now remain in my love. [10]If
you keep my commands, you will remain
in my love, just as I have kept my Father's
commands and remain in his love. [11]I have
told you this so that my joy may be in
you and that your joy may be complete.
[12]My command is this: Love each other
as I have loved you. [13]Greater love has
no one than this: to lay down one's life
for one's friends. [14]You are my friends if
you do what I command. [15]I no longer
call you servants, because a servant does
not know his master's business. Instead,
I have called you friends, for everything
that I learned from my Father I have made
known to you. [16]You did not choose me,
but I chose you and appointed you so that
you might go and bear fruit—fruit that
will last—and so that whatever you ask
in my name the Father will give you. [17]This
is my command: Love each other.

The World Hates the Disciples

[18]"If the world hates you, keep in mind
that it hated me first. [19]If you belonged to
the world, it would love you as its own. As
it is, you do not belong to the world, but
I have chosen you out of the world. That
is why the world hates you. [20]Remember

[a] *17* Some early manuscripts *and is*
[b] *2* The Greek for *he prunes* also means *he cleans.*

what I told you: 'A servant is not greater than his master.'[a] If they persecuted me, they will persecute you also. If they obeyed my teaching, they will obey yours also. 21They will treat you this way because of my name, for they do not know the one who sent me. 22If I had not come and spoken to them, they would not be guilty of sin; but now they have no excuse for their sin. 23Whoever hates me hates my Father as well. 24If I had not done among them the works no one else did, they would not be guilty of sin. As it is, they have seen, and yet they have hated both me and my Father. 25But this is to fulfill what is written in their Law: 'They hated me without reason.'[b]

The Work of the Holy Spirit

26"When the Advocate comes, whom I will send to you from the Father — the Spirit of truth who goes out from the Father — he will testify about me. 27And you also must testify, for you have been with me from the beginning.

16 "All this I have told you so that you will not fall away. 2They will put you out of the synagogue; in fact, the time is coming when anyone who kills you will think they are offering a service to God. 3They will do such things because they have not known the Father or me. 4I have told you this, so that when their time comes you will remember that I warned you about them. I did not tell you this from the beginning because I was with you, 5but now I am going to him who sent me. None of you asks me, 'Where are you going?' 6Rather, you are filled with grief because I have said these things. 7But very truly I tell you, it is for your good that I am going away. Unless I go away, the Advocate will not come to you; but if I go, I will send him to you. 8When he comes, he will prove the world to be in the wrong about sin and righteousness and judgment: 9about sin, because people do not believe in me; 10about righteousness, because I am going to the Father, where you can see me no longer; 11and about judgment, because the prince of this world now stands condemned.

12"I have much more to say to you, more than you can now bear. 13But when he, the Spirit of truth, comes, he will guide you into all the truth. He will not speak on his own; he will speak only what he hears, and he will tell you what is yet to come. 14He will glorify me because it is from me that he will receive what he will make known to you. 15All that belongs to the Father is mine. That is why I said the Spirit will receive from me what he will make known to you."

The Disciples' Grief Will Turn to Joy

16Jesus went on to say, "In a little while you will see me no more, and then after a little while you will see me."

17At this, some of his disciples said to one another, "What does he mean by saying, 'In a little while you will see me no more, and then after a little while you will see me,' and 'Because I am going to the Father'?" 18They kept asking, "What does he mean by 'a little while'? We don't understand what he is saying."

19Jesus saw that they wanted to ask him about this, so he said to them, "Are you asking one another what I meant when I said, 'In a little while you will see me no more, and then after a little while you will see me'? 20Very truly I tell you, you will weep and mourn while the world rejoices. You will grieve, but your grief will turn to joy. 21A woman giving birth to a child has pain because her time has come; but when her baby is born she forgets the anguish because of her joy that a child is born into the world. 22So with you: Now is your time of grief, but I will see you again and you will rejoice, and no one will take away your joy. 23In that day you will no longer ask me anything. Very truly I tell you, my Father will give you whatever you ask in my name. 24Until now you have not asked for anything in my name. Ask and you will receive, and your joy will be complete.

25"Though I have been speaking figuratively, a time is coming when I will no longer use this kind of language but will tell you plainly about my Father. 26In that day you will ask in my name. I am not saying that I will ask the Father on your behalf. 27No, the Father himself loves you because you have loved me and have believed that I came from God. 28I came from the Father and entered the world; now I am leaving the world and going back to the Father."

29Then Jesus' disciples said, "Now you are speaking clearly and without figures of speech. 30Now we can see that you know all things and that you do not even need to have anyone ask you questions. This makes us believe that you came from God."

31"Do you now believe?" Jesus replied. 32"A time is coming and in fact has come when you will be scattered, each to your own home. You will leave me all alone. Yet I am not alone, for my Father is with me.

33"I have told you these things, so that in me you may have peace. In this world you will have trouble. But take heart! I have overcome the world."

[a] *20* John 13:16 [b] *25* Psalms 35:19; 69:4

Jesus Prays to Be Glorified

17 After Jesus said this, he looked toward heaven and prayed:

"Father, the hour has come. Glorify
your Son, that your Son may glorify
you. 2For you granted him authority
over all people that he might give
eternal life to all those you have giv-
en him. 3Now this is eternal life: that
they know you, the only true God, and
Jesus Christ, whom you have sent. 4I
have brought you glory on earth by
finishing the work you gave me to do.
5And now, Father, glorify me in your
presence with the glory I had with
you before the world began.

Jesus Prays for His Disciples

6"I have revealed you[a] to those
whom you gave me out of the world.
They were yours; you gave them to
me and they have obeyed your word.
7Now they know that everything you
have given me comes from you. 8For
I gave them the words you gave me
and they accepted them. They knew
with certainty that I came from you,
and they believed that you sent me.
9I pray for them. I am not praying for
the world, but for those you have giv-
en me, for they are yours. 10All I have
is yours, and all you have is mine. And
glory has come to me through them.
11I will remain in the world no longer,
but they are still in the world, and I
am coming to you. Holy Father, protect them by the power of[b] your name,
the name you gave me, so that they
may be one as we are one. 12While I
was with them, I protected them and
kept them safe by[c] that name you
gave me. None has been lost except
the one doomed to destruction so that
Scripture would be fulfilled.

13"I am coming to you now, but I
say these things while I am still in
the world, so that they may have the
full measure of my joy within them.
14I have given them your word and
the world has hated them, for they
are not of the world any more than
I am of the world. 15My prayer is not
that you take them out of the world
but that you protect them from the
evil one. 16They are not of the world,
even as I am not of it. 17Sanctify them
by[d] the truth; your word is truth. 18As
you sent me into the world, I have
sent them into the world. 19For them
I sanctify myself, that they too may
be truly sanctified.

Jesus Prays for All Believers

20"My prayer is not for them alone.
I pray also for those who will believe
in me through their message, 21that
all of them may be one, Father, just
as you are in me and I am in you.
May they also be in us so that the
world may believe that you have sent
me. 22I have given them the glory
that you gave me, that they may
be one as we are one — 23I in them
and you in me — so that they may
be brought to complete unity. Then
the world will know that you sent
me and have loved them even as you
have loved me.

24"Father, I want those you have
given me to be with me where I am,
and to see my glory, the glory you
have given me because you loved
me before the creation of the world.

25"Righteous Father, though the
world does not know you, I know
you, and they know that you have
sent me. 26I have made you[a] known
to them, and will continue to make
you known in order that the love you
have for me may be in them and that
I myself may be in them."

Jesus Arrested

18 When he had finished praying, Jesus
left with his disciples and crossed
the Kidron Valley. On the other side there
was a garden, and he and his disciples
went into it.

2Now Judas, who betrayed him, knew
the place, because Jesus had often met
there with his disciples. 3So Judas came
to the garden, guiding a detachment of
soldiers and some officials from the chief
priests and the Pharisees. They were carrying torches, lanterns and weapons.

4Jesus, knowing all that was going to
happen to him, went out and asked them,
"Who is it you want?"

5"Jesus of Nazareth," they replied.

"I am he," Jesus said. (And Judas the
traitor was standing there with them.)
6When Jesus said, "I am he," they drew
back and fell to the ground.

7Again he asked them, "Who is it you
want?"

"Jesus of Nazareth," they said.

8Jesus answered, "I told you that I am

[a] 6,26 Greek *your name* [b] 11 Or *Father, keep them faithful to* [c] 12 Or *kept them faithful to*
[d] 17 Or *them to live in accordance with*

he. If you are looking for me, then let these
men go." 9 This happened so that the words
he had spoken would be fulfilled: "I have
not lost one of those you gave me."[a]
10 Then Simon Peter, who had a sword,
drew it and struck the high priest's servant, cutting off his right ear. (The servant's name was Malchus.)
11 Jesus commanded Peter, "Put your
sword away! Shall I not drink the cup the
Father has given me?"
12 Then the detachment of soldiers with
its commander and the Jewish officials
arrested Jesus. They bound him 13 and
brought him first to Annas, who was the
father-in-law of Caiaphas, the high priest
that year. 14 Caiaphas was the one who had
advised the Jewish leaders that it would
be good if one man died for the people.

Peter's First Denial

15 Simon Peter and another disciple were
following Jesus. Because this disciple was
known to the high priest, he went with
Jesus into the high priest's courtyard, 16 but
Peter had to wait outside at the door. The
other disciple, who was known to the high
priest, came back, spoke to the servant
girl on duty there and brought Peter in.
17 "You aren't one of this man's disciples
too, are you?" she asked Peter.
He replied, "I am not."
18 It was cold, and the servants and officials stood around a fire they had made to
keep warm. Peter also was standing with
them, warming himself.

The High Priest Questions Jesus

19 Meanwhile, the high priest questioned
Jesus about his disciples and his teaching.
20 "I have spoken openly to the world,"
Jesus replied. "I always taught in synagogues or at the temple, where all the
Jews come together. I said nothing in secret. 21 Why question me? Ask those who
heard me. Surely they know what I said."
22 When Jesus said this, one of the officials nearby slapped him in the face. "Is
this the way you answer the high priest?"
he demanded.
23 "If I said something wrong," Jesus replied, "testify as to what is wrong. But if I
spoke the truth, why did you strike me?"
24 Then Annas sent him bound to Caiaphas
the high priest.

Peter's Second and Third Denials

25 Meanwhile, Simon Peter was still
standing there warming himself. So they
asked him, "You aren't one of his disciples
too, are you?"
He denied it, saying, "I am not."
26 One of the high priest's servants, a
relative of the man whose ear Peter had
cut off, challenged him, "Didn't I see you
with him in the garden?" 27 Again Peter
denied it, and at that moment a rooster
began to crow.

Jesus Before Pilate

28 Then the Jewish leaders took Jesus
from Caiaphas to the palace of the Roman
governor. By now it was early morning, and
to avoid ceremonial uncleanness they did
not enter the palace, because they wanted
to be able to eat the Passover. 29 So Pilate
came out to them and asked, "What charges are you bringing against this man?"
30 "If he were not a criminal," they replied, "we would not have handed him
over to you."
31 Pilate said, "Take him yourselves and
judge him by your own law."
"But we have no right to execute anyone," they objected. 32 This took place to
fulfill what Jesus had said about the kind
of death he was going to die.
33 Pilate then went back inside the palace, summoned Jesus and asked him, "Are
you the king of the Jews?"
34 "Is that your own idea," Jesus asked,
"or did others talk to you about me?"
35 "Am I a Jew?" Pilate replied. "Your own
people and chief priests handed you over
to me. What is it you have done?"
36 Jesus said, "My kingdom is not of
this world. If it were, my servants would
fight to prevent my arrest by the Jewish
leaders. But now my kingdom is from
another place."
37 "You are a king, then!" said Pilate.
Jesus answered, "You say that I am a
king. In fact, the reason I was born and
came into the world is to testify to the truth.
Everyone on the side of truth listens to me."
38 "What is truth?" retorted Pilate. With
this he went out again to the Jews gathered there and said, "I find no basis for a
charge against him. 39 But it is your custom
for me to release to you one prisoner at
the time of the Passover. Do you want me
to release 'the king of the Jews'?"
40 They shouted back, "No, not him! Give
us Barabbas!" Now Barabbas had taken
part in an uprising.

Jesus Sentenced to Be Crucified

19 Then Pilate took Jesus and had him
flogged. 2 The soldiers twisted together a crown of thorns and put it on his
head. They clothed him in a purple robe

[a] 9 John 6:39

3and went up to him again and again,
saying, "Hail, king of the Jews!" And they
slapped him in the face.
4Once more Pilate came out and said
to the Jews gathered there, "Look, I am
bringing him out to you to let you know
that I find no basis for a charge against
him." 5When Jesus came out wearing the
crown of thorns and the purple robe, Pilate
said to them, "Here is the man!"
6As soon as the chief priests and their
officials saw him, they shouted, "Crucify!
Crucify!"
But Pilate answered, "You take him and
crucify him. As for me, I find no basis for
a charge against him."
7The Jewish leaders insisted, "We have a
law, and according to that law he must die,
because he claimed to be the Son of God."
8When Pilate heard this, he was even
more afraid, 9and he went back inside
the palace. "Where do you come from?"
he asked Jesus, but Jesus gave him no
answer. 10"Do you refuse to speak to me?"
Pilate said. "Don't you realize I have power
either to free you or to crucify you?"
11Jesus answered, "You would have no
power over me if it were not given to you
from above. Therefore the one who handed me over to you is guilty of a greater sin."
12From then on, Pilate tried to set Jesus
free, but the Jewish leaders kept shouting,
"If you let this man go, you are no friend
of Caesar. Anyone who claims to be a king
opposes Caesar."
13When Pilate heard this, he brought
Jesus out and sat down on the judge's seat
at a place known as the Stone Pavement
(which in Aramaic is Gabbatha). 14It was
the day of Preparation of the Passover; it
was about noon.
"Here is your king," Pilate said to the Jews.
15But they shouted, "Take him away!
Take him away! Crucify him!"
"Shall I crucify your king?" Pilate asked.
"We have no king but Caesar," the chief
priests answered.
16Finally Pilate handed him over to
them to be crucified.

The Crucifixion of Jesus

So the soldiers took charge of Jesus.
17Carrying his own cross, he went out to
the place of the Skull (which in Aramaic
is called Golgotha). 18There they crucified
him, and with him two others — one on
each side and Jesus in the middle.
19Pilate had a notice prepared and fastened to the cross. It read: JESUS OF NAZA-
RETH, THE KING OF THE JEWS. 20Many of the
Jews read this sign, for the place where
Jesus was crucified was near the city, and
the sign was written in Aramaic, Latin
and Greek. 21The chief priests of the Jews
protested to Pilate, "Do not write 'The King
of the Jews,' but that this man claimed to
be king of the Jews."
22Pilate answered, "What I have written,
I have written."
23When the soldiers crucified Jesus, they
took his clothes, dividing them into four
shares, one for each of them, with the
undergarment remaining. This garment
was seamless, woven in one piece from
top to bottom.
24"Let's not tear it," they said to one another. "Let's decide by lot who will get it."
This happened that the scripture might
be fulfilled that said,

"They divided my clothes among
them
and cast lots for my garment."[a]

So this is what the soldiers did.
25Near the cross of Jesus stood his mother, his mother's sister, Mary the wife of
Clopas, and Mary Magdalene. 26When
Jesus saw his mother there, and the disciple whom he loved standing nearby, he
said to her, "Woman,[b] here is your son,"
27and to the disciple, "Here is your mother." From that time on, this disciple took
her into his home.

The Death of Jesus

28Later, knowing that everything had
now been finished, and so that Scripture would be fulfilled, Jesus said, "I
am thirsty." 29A jar of wine vinegar was
there, so they soaked a sponge in it, put
the sponge on a stalk of the hyssop plant,
and lifted it to Jesus' lips. 30When he had
received the drink, Jesus said, "It is finished." With that, he bowed his head and
gave up his spirit.
31Now it was the day of Preparation, and
the next day was to be a special Sabbath.
Because the Jewish leaders did not want
the bodies left on the crosses during the
Sabbath, they asked Pilate to have the legs
broken and the bodies taken down. 32The
soldiers therefore came and broke the legs
of the first man who had been crucified
with Jesus, and then those of the other.
33But when they came to Jesus and found
that he was already dead, they did not
break his legs. 34Instead, one of the soldiers
pierced Jesus' side with a spear, bringing a
sudden flow of blood and water. 35The man
who saw it has given testimony, and his

[a] *24* Psalm 22:18 [b] *26* The Greek for *Woman* does not denote any disrespect.

testimony is true. He knows that he tells
the truth, and he testifies so that you also
may believe. [36]These things happened so
that the scripture would be fulfilled: "Not
one of his bones will be broken,"[a] [37]and, as
another scripture says, "They will look on
the one they have pierced."[b]

The Burial of Jesus

[38]Later, Joseph of Arimathea asked Pilate for the body of Jesus. Now Joseph was a disciple of Jesus, but secretly because he feared the Jewish leaders. With Pilate's permission, he came and took the body
away. [39]He was accompanied by Nicodemus, the man who earlier had visited Jesus at night. Nicodemus brought a mixture of myrrh and aloes, about seventy-five
pounds.[c] [40]Taking Jesus' body, the two of them wrapped it, with the spices, in strips of linen. This was in accordance with Jewish burial customs.
[41]At the place where Jesus was crucified, there was a garden, and in the garden a new tomb, in which
no one had ever been laid. [42]Because it was the Jewish day of Preparation and since the tomb was nearby, they laid Jesus there.

The Empty Tomb

20 Early on the first day of the week, while it was still dark, Mary Magdalene went to the tomb and saw that the stone had been removed from the
entrance. [2]So she came running to Simon Peter and the other disciple, the one Jesus loved, and said, "They have taken the Lord out of the tomb, and we don't know where they have put him!"

[3]So Peter and the other disciple started
for the tomb. [4]Both were running, but the other disciple outran Peter and reached
the tomb first. [5]He bent over and looked in at the strips of linen lying there but did not
go in. [6]Then Simon Peter came along behind him and went straight into the tomb. He saw the strips of linen lying there,
[7]as well as the cloth that had been wrapped around Jesus' head. The cloth was still lying in its place, separate from the lin-
en. [8]Finally the other disciple, who had reached the tomb first, also went inside.
He saw and believed. [9](They still did not understand from Scripture that Jesus had
to rise from the dead.) [10]Then the disciples went back to where they were staying.

Jesus Appears to Mary Magdalene

[11]Now Mary stood outside the tomb crying. As she wept, she bent over to look into
the tomb [12]and saw two angels in white, seated where Jesus' body had been, one at the head and the other at the foot.

[13]They asked her, "Woman, why are you crying?"

"They have taken my Lord away," she said, "and I don't know where they have
put him." [14]At this, she turned around and saw Jesus standing there, but she did not realize that it was Jesus.

[15]He asked her, "Woman, why are you crying? Who is it you are looking for?"

Thinking he was the gardener, she said, "Sir, if you have carried him away, tell me where you have put him, and I will get him."

[16]Jesus said to her, "Mary."

She turned toward him and cried out in Aramaic, "Rabboni!" (which means "Teacher").

[17]Jesus said, "Do not hold on to me, for I have not yet ascended to the Father. Go instead to my brothers and tell them, 'I am ascending to my Father and your Father, to my God and your God.'"

[18]Mary Magdalene went to the disciples with the news: "I have seen the Lord!" And she told them that he had said these things to her.

Jesus Appears to His Disciples

[19]On the evening of that first day of the week, when the disciples were together, with the doors locked for fear of the Jewish leaders, Jesus came and stood among
them and said, "Peace be with you!" [20]After he said this, he showed them his hands and side. The disciples were overjoyed when they saw the Lord.

[21]Again Jesus said, "Peace be with you! As the Father has sent me, I am sending you."
[22]And with that he breathed on them and said, "Receive the Holy Spirit.
[23]If you forgive anyone's sins, their sins are forgiven; if you do not forgive them, they are not forgiven."

Jesus Appears to Thomas

[24]Now Thomas (also known as Didymus[d]), one of the Twelve, was not with
the disciples when Jesus came. [25]So the other disciples told him, "We have seen the Lord!"

But he said to them, "Unless I see the nail marks in his hands and put my finger where the nails were, and put my hand into his side, I will not believe."

[26]A week later his disciples were in the house again, and Thomas was with them.

[a] *36* Exodus 12:46; Num. 9:12; Psalm 34:20 [b] *37* Zech. 12:10 [c] *39* Or about 34 kilograms
[d] *24* *Thomas* (Aramaic) and *Didymus* (Greek) both mean *twin.*

Though the doors were locked, Jesus came
and stood among them and said, "Peace
be with you!" 27Then he said to Thomas,
"Put your finger here; see my hands. Reach
out your hand and put it into my side. Stop
doubting and believe."
28Thomas said to him, "My Lord and
my God!"
29Then Jesus told him, "Because you
have seen me, you have believed; blessed
are those who have not seen and yet have
believed."

The Purpose of John's Gospel

30Jesus performed many other signs in
the presence of his disciples, which are
not recorded in this book. 31But these are
written that you may believe[a] that Jesus
is the Messiah, the Son of God, and that by
believing you may have life in his name.

Jesus and the Miraculous Catch of Fish

21 Afterward Jesus appeared again to
his disciples, by the Sea of Galilee.[b] It
happened this way: 2Simon Peter, Thomas (also known as Didymus[c]), Nathanael
from Cana in Galilee, the sons of Zebedee,
and two other disciples were together.
3"I'm going out to fish," Simon Peter told
them, and they said, "We'll go with you."
So they went out and got into the boat, but
that night they caught nothing.
4Early in the morning, Jesus stood on
the shore, but the disciples did not realize
that it was Jesus.
5He called out to them, "Friends, haven't
you any fish?"
"No," they answered.
6He said, "Throw your net on the right
side of the boat and you will find some."
When they did, they were unable to haul
the net in because of the large number
of fish.
7Then the disciple whom Jesus loved
said to Peter, "It is the Lord!" As soon as
Simon Peter heard him say, "It is the Lord,"
he wrapped his outer garment around him
(for he had taken it off) and jumped into
the water. 8The other disciples followed
in the boat, towing the net full of fish,
for they were not far from shore, about a
hundred yards.[d] 9When they landed, they
saw a fire of burning coals there with fish
on it, and some bread.
10Jesus said to them, "Bring some of
the fish you have just caught." 11So Simon Peter climbed back into the boat
and dragged the net ashore. It was full
of large fish, 153, but even with so many
the net was not torn. 12Jesus said to them,
"Come and have breakfast." None of the
disciples dared ask him, "Who are you?"
They knew it was the Lord. 13Jesus came,
took the bread and gave it to them, and
did the same with the fish. 14This was now
the third time Jesus appeared to his disciples after he was raised from the dead.

Jesus Reinstates Peter

15When they had finished eating, Jesus
said to Simon Peter, "Simon son of John,
do you love me more than these?"
"Yes, Lord," he said, "you know that I
love you."
Jesus said, "Feed my lambs."
16Again Jesus said, "Simon son of John,
do you love me?"
He answered, "Yes, Lord, you know that
I love you."
Jesus said, "Take care of my sheep."
17The third time he said to him, "Simon
son of John, do you love me?"
Peter was hurt because Jesus asked him
the third time, "Do you love me?" He said,
"Lord, you know all things; you know that
I love you."
Jesus said, "Feed my sheep. 18Very truly I tell you, when you were younger you
dressed yourself and went where you wanted; but when you are old you will stretch
out your hands, and someone else will
dress you and lead you where you do not
want to go." 19Jesus said this to indicate the
kind of death by which Peter would glorify
God. Then he said to him, "Follow me!"
20Peter turned and saw that the disciple whom Jesus loved was following
them. (This was the one who had leaned
back against Jesus at the supper and had
said, "Lord, who is going to betray you?")
21When Peter saw him, he asked, "Lord,
what about him?"
22Jesus answered, "If I want him to remain alive until I return, what is that to
you? You must follow me." 23Because of
this, the rumor spread among the believers that this disciple would not die.
But Jesus did not say that he would not
die; he only said, "If I want him to remain
alive until I return, what is that to you?"
24This is the disciple who testifies to
these things and who wrote them down.
We know that his testimony is true.
25Jesus did many other things as well.
If every one of them were written down, I
suppose that even the whole world would
not have room for the books that would
be written.

[a] 31 Or *may continue to believe* [b] 1 Greek *Tiberias* [c] 2 *Thomas* (Aramaic) and *Didymus* (Greek) both mean *twin.* [d] 8 Or about 90 meters

ACTS

Jesus Taken Up Into Heaven

1 In my former book, Theophilus, I wrote about all that Jesus began to do and to teach 2until the day he was taken up to heaven, after giving instructions through the Holy Spirit to the apostles he had chosen. 3After his suffering, he presented himself to them and gave many convincing proofs that he was alive. He appeared to them over a period of forty days and spoke about the kingdom of God. 4On one occasion, while he was eating with them, he gave them this command: "Do not leave Jerusalem, but wait for the gift my Father promised, which you have heard me speak about. 5For John baptized with[a] water, but in a few days you will be baptized with[a] the Holy Spirit."

6Then they gathered around him and asked him, "Lord, are you at this time going to restore the kingdom to Israel?"

7He said to them: "It is not for you to know the times or dates the Father has set by his own authority. 8But you will receive power when the Holy Spirit comes on you; and you will be my witnesses in Jerusalem, and in all Judea and Samaria, and to the ends of the earth."

9After he said this, he was taken up before their very eyes, and a cloud hid him from their sight.

10They were looking intently up into the sky as he was going, when suddenly two men dressed in white stood beside them. 11"Men of Galilee," they said, "why do you stand here looking into the sky? This same Jesus, who has been taken from you into heaven, will come back in the same way you have seen him go into heaven."

Matthias Chosen to Replace Judas

12Then the apostles returned to Jerusalem from the hill called the Mount of Olives, a Sabbath day's walk[b] from the city. 13When they arrived, they went upstairs to the room where they were staying. Those present were Peter, John, James and Andrew; Philip and Thomas, Bartholomew and Matthew; James son of Alphaeus and Simon the Zealot, and Judas son of James. 14They all joined together constantly in prayer, along with the women and Mary the mother of Jesus, and with his brothers.

15In those days Peter stood up among the believers (a group numbering about a hundred and twenty) 16and said, "Brothers and sisters,[c] the Scripture had to be fulfilled in which the Holy Spirit spoke long ago through David concerning Judas, who served as guide for those who arrested Jesus. 17He was one of our number and shared in our ministry."

18(With the payment he received for his wickedness, Judas bought a field; there he fell headlong, his body burst open and all his intestines spilled out. 19Everyone in Jerusalem heard about this, so they called that field in their language Akeldama, that is, Field of Blood.)

20"For," said Peter, "it is written in the Book of Psalms:

> "'May his place be deserted;
> let there be no one to dwell in it,'[d]

and,

> "'May another take his place of leadership.'[e]

21Therefore it is necessary to choose one of the men who have been with us the whole time the Lord Jesus was living among us, 22beginning from John's baptism to the time when Jesus was taken up from us. For one of these must become a witness with us of his resurrection."

23So they nominated two men: Joseph called Barsabbas (also known as Justus) and Matthias. 24Then they prayed, "Lord, you know everyone's heart. Show us which of these two you have chosen 25to take over this apostolic ministry, which Judas left to go where he belongs." 26Then they cast lots, and the lot fell to Matthias; so he was added to the eleven apostles.

The Holy Spirit Comes at Pentecost

2 When the day of Pentecost came, they were all together in one place. 2Suddenly a sound like the blowing of a violent wind came from heaven and filled the whole house where they were sitting. 3They saw what seemed to be tongues of fire that separated and came to rest on each of them. 4All of them were filled

[a] *5* Or *in* [b] *12* That is, about 5/8 mile or about 1 kilometer [c] *16* The Greek word for *brothers and sisters* (*adelphoi*) refers here to believers, both men and women, as part of God's family; also in 6:3; 11:29; 12:17; 16:40; 18:18, 27; 21:7, 17; 28:14, 15. [d] *20* Psalm 69:25 [e] *20* Psalm 109:8

with the Holy Spirit and began to speak
in other tongues[a] as the Spirit enabled
them.
5 Now there were staying in Jerusalem
God-fearing Jews from every nation under
heaven. 6 When they heard this sound, a
crowd came together in bewilderment,
because each one heard their own language being spoken. 7 Utterly amazed, they
asked: "Aren't all these who are speaking
Galileans? 8 Then how is it that each of
us hears them in our native language?
9 Parthians, Medes and Elamites; residents
of Mesopotamia, Judea and Cappadocia,
Pontus and Asia,[b] 10 Phrygia and Pamphylia, Egypt and the parts of Libya near
Cyrene; visitors from Rome 11 (both Jews
and converts to Judaism); Cretans and
Arabs — we hear them declaring the wonders of God in our own tongues!" 12 Amazed
and perplexed, they asked one another,
"What does this mean?"
13 Some, however, made fun of them
and said, "They have had too much wine."

Peter Addresses the Crowd

14 Then Peter stood up with the Eleven,
raised his voice and addressed the crowd:
"Fellow Jews and all of you who live in Jerusalem, let me explain this to you; listen
carefully to what I say. 15 These people are
not drunk, as you suppose. It's only nine in
the morning! 16 No, this is what was spoken
by the prophet Joel:

17 " 'In the last days, God says,
I will pour out my Spirit on all
people.
Your sons and daughters will
prophesy,
your young men will see visions,
your old men will dream dreams.
18 Even on my servants, both men and
women,
I will pour out my Spirit in those
days,
and they will prophesy.
19 I will show wonders in the heavens
above
and signs on the earth below,
blood and fire and billows of
smoke.
20 The sun will be turned to darkness
and the moon to blood
before the coming of the great and
glorious day of the Lord.
21 And everyone who calls
on the name of the Lord will be
saved.'[c]

22 "Fellow Israelites, listen to this: Jesus
of Nazareth was a man accredited by God
to you by miracles, wonders and signs,
which God did among you through him,
as you yourselves know. 23 This man was
handed over to you by God's deliberate
plan and foreknowledge; and you, with
the help of wicked men,[d] put him to death
by nailing him to the cross. 24 But God
raised him from the dead, freeing him
from the agony of death, because it was
impossible for death to keep its hold on
him. 25 David said about him:

" 'I saw the Lord always before me.
Because he is at my right hand,
I will not be shaken.
26 Therefore my heart is glad and my
tongue rejoices;
my body also will rest in hope,
27 because you will not abandon me to
the realm of the dead,
you will not let your holy one see
decay.
28 You have made known to me the
paths of life;
you will fill me with joy in your
presence.'[e]

29 "Fellow Israelites, I can tell you confidently that the patriarch David died and
was buried, and his tomb is here to this
day. 30 But he was a prophet and knew
that God had promised him on oath that
he would place one of his descendants on
his throne. 31 Seeing what was to come, he
spoke of the resurrection of the Messiah,
that he was not abandoned to the realm of
the dead, nor did his body see decay. 32 God
has raised this Jesus to life, and we are all
witnesses of it. 33 Exalted to the right hand
of God, he has received from the Father the
promised Holy Spirit and has poured out
what you now see and hear. 34 For David
did not ascend to heaven, and yet he said,

" 'The Lord said to my Lord:
"Sit at my right hand
35 until I make your enemies
a footstool for your feet." '[f]

36 "Therefore let all Israel be assured of
this: God has made this Jesus, whom you
crucified, both Lord and Messiah."
37 When the people heard this, they were
cut to the heart and said to Peter and
the other apostles, "Brothers, what shall
we do?"
38 Peter replied, "Repent and be baptized, every one of you, in the name of
Jesus Christ for the forgiveness of your

[a] 4 Or *languages*; also in verse 11 [b] 9 That is, the Roman province by that name
[c] *21* Joel 2:28-32 [d] *23* Or *of those not having the law* (that is, Gentiles) [e] *28* Psalm 16:8-11 (see Septuagint) [f] *35* Psalm 110:1

sins. And you will receive the gift of the Holy Spirit. 39The promise is for you and your children and for all who are far off — for all whom the Lord our God will call."

40With many other words he warned them; and he pleaded with them, "Save yourselves from this corrupt generation." 41Those who accepted his message were baptized, and about three thousand were added to their number that day.

The Fellowship of the Believers

42They devoted themselves to the apostles' teaching and to fellowship, to the breaking of bread and to prayer. 43Everyone was filled with awe at the many wonders and signs performed by the apostles. 44All the believers were together and had everything in common. 45They sold property and possessions to give to anyone who had need. 46Every day they continued to meet together in the temple courts. They broke bread in their homes and ate together with glad and sincere hearts, 47praising God and enjoying the favor of all the people. And the Lord added to their number daily those who were being saved.

Peter Heals a Lame Beggar

3 One day Peter and John were going up to the temple at the time of prayer — at three in the afternoon. 2Now a man who was lame from birth was being carried to the temple gate called Beautiful, where he was put every day to beg from those going into the temple courts. 3When he saw Peter and John about to enter, he asked them for money. 4Peter looked straight at him, as did John. Then Peter said, "Look at us!" 5So the man gave them his attention, expecting to get something from them.

6Then Peter said, "Silver or gold I do not have, but what I do have I give you. In the name of Jesus Christ of Nazareth, walk." 7Taking him by the right hand, he helped him up, and instantly the man's feet and ankles became strong. 8He jumped to his feet and began to walk. Then he went with them into the temple courts, walking and jumping, and praising God. 9When all the people saw him walking and praising God, 10they recognized him as the same man who used to sit begging at the temple gate called Beautiful, and they were filled with wonder and amazement at what had happened to him.

Peter Speaks to the Onlookers

11While the man held on to Peter and John, all the people were astonished and came running to them in the place called Solomon's Colonnade. 12When Peter saw this, he said to them: "Fellow Israelites, why does this surprise you? Why do you stare at us as if by our own power or godliness we had made this man walk? 13The God of Abraham, Isaac and Jacob, the God of our fathers, has glorified his servant Jesus. You handed him over to be killed, and you disowned him before Pilate, though he had decided to let him go. 14You disowned the Holy and Righteous One and asked that a murderer be released to you. 15You killed the author of life, but God raised him from the dead. We are witnesses of this. 16By faith in the name of Jesus, this man whom you see and know was made strong. It is Jesus' name and the faith that comes through him that has completely healed him, as you can all see.

17"Now, fellow Israelites, I know that you acted in ignorance, as did your leaders. 18But this is how God fulfilled what he had foretold through all the prophets, saying that his Messiah would suffer. 19Repent, then, and turn to God, so that your sins may be wiped out, that times of refreshing may come from the Lord, 20and that he may send the Messiah, who has been appointed for you — even Jesus. 21Heaven must receive him until the time comes for God to restore everything, as he promised long ago through his holy prophets. 22For Moses said, 'The Lord your God will raise up for you a prophet like me from among your own people; you must listen to everything he tells you. 23Anyone who does not listen to him will be completely cut off from their people.'[a]

24"Indeed, beginning with Samuel, all the prophets who have spoken have foretold these days. 25And you are heirs of the prophets and of the covenant God made with your fathers. He said to Abraham, 'Through your offspring all peoples on earth will be blessed.'[b] 26When God raised up his servant, he sent him first to you to bless you by turning each of you from your wicked ways."

Peter and John Before the Sanhedrin

4 The priests and the captain of the temple guard and the Sadducees came up to Peter and John while they were speaking to the people. 2They were greatly disturbed because the apostles

[a] *23* Deut. 18:15,18,19 [b] *25* Gen. 22:18; 26:4

were teaching the people, proclaiming in Jesus the resurrection of the dead. 3They seized Peter and John and, because it was evening, they put them in jail until the next day. 4But many who heard the message believed; so the number of men who believed grew to about five thousand.

5The next day the rulers, the elders and the teachers of the law met in Jerusalem. 6Annas the high priest was there, and so were Caiaphas, John, Alexander and others of the high priest's family. 7They had Peter and John brought before them and began to question them: "By what power or what name did you do this?"

8Then Peter, filled with the Holy Spirit, said to them: "Rulers and elders of the people! 9If we are being called to account today for an act of kindness shown to a man who was lame and are being asked how he was healed, 10then know this, you and all the people of Israel: It is by the name of Jesus Christ of Nazareth, whom you crucified but whom God raised from the dead, that this man stands before you healed. 11Jesus is

"'the stone you builders rejected,
which has become the
cornerstone.'[a]

12Salvation is found in no one else, for there is no other name under heaven given to mankind by which we must be saved."

13When they saw the courage of Peter and John and realized that they were unschooled, ordinary men, they were astonished and they took note that these men had been with Jesus. 14But since they could see the man who had been healed standing there with them, there was nothing they could say. 15So they ordered them to withdraw from the Sanhedrin and then conferred together. 16"What are we going to do with these men?" they asked. "Everyone living in Jerusalem knows they have performed a notable sign, and we cannot deny it. 17But to stop this thing from spreading any further among the people, we must warn them to speak no longer to anyone in this name."

18Then they called them in again and commanded them not to speak or teach at all in the name of Jesus. 19But Peter and John replied, "Which is right in God's eyes: to listen to you, or to him? You be the judges! 20As for us, we cannot help speaking about what we have seen and heard."

21After further threats they let them go. They could not decide how to punish them, because all the people were praising God for what had happened. 22For the man who was miraculously healed was over forty years old.

The Believers Pray

23On their release, Peter and John went back to their own people and reported all that the chief priests and the elders had said to them. 24When they heard this, they raised their voices together in prayer to God. "Sovereign Lord," they said, "you made the heavens and the earth and the sea, and everything in them. 25You spoke by the Holy Spirit through the mouth of your servant, our father David:

"'Why do the nations rage
and the peoples plot in vain?
26 The kings of the earth rise up
and the rulers band together
against the Lord
and against his anointed one.[b,c]

27Indeed Herod and Pontius Pilate met together with the Gentiles and the people of Israel in this city to conspire against your holy servant Jesus, whom you anointed. 28They did what your power and will had decided beforehand should happen. 29Now, Lord, consider their threats and enable your servants to speak your word with great boldness. 30Stretch out your hand to heal and perform signs and wonders through the name of your holy servant Jesus."

31After they prayed, the place where they were meeting was shaken. And they were all filled with the Holy Spirit and spoke the word of God boldly.

The Believers Share Their Possessions

32All the believers were one in heart and mind. No one claimed that any of their possessions was their own, but they shared everything they had. 33With great power the apostles continued to testify to the resurrection of the Lord Jesus. And God's grace was so powerfully at work in them all 34that there were no needy persons among them. For from time to time those who owned land or houses sold them, brought the money from the sales 35and put it at the apostles' feet, and it was distributed to anyone who had need.

36Joseph, a Levite from Cyprus, whom the apostles called Barnabas (which means "son of encouragement"), 37sold a field he owned and brought the money and put it at the apostles' feet.

[a] *11* Psalm 118:22 [b] *26* That is, Messiah or Christ [c] *26* Psalm 2:1,2

Ananias and Sapphira

5 Now a man named Ananias, together
with his wife Sapphira, also sold a piece
of property. 2With his wife's full knowledge he kept back part of the money for
himself, but brought the rest and put it
at the apostles' feet.
3Then Peter said, "Ananias, how is it
that Satan has so filled your heart that
you have lied to the Holy Spirit and have
kept for yourself some of the money you
received for the land? 4Didn't it belong to
you before it was sold? And after it was
sold, wasn't the money at your disposal?
What made you think of doing such a
thing? You have not lied just to human
beings but to God."
5When Ananias heard this, he fell down
and died. And great fear seized all who
heard what had happened. 6Then some
young men came forward, wrapped up his
body, and carried him out and buried him.
7About three hours later his wife came
in, not knowing what had happened. 8Pe-
ter asked her, "Tell me, is this the price you
and Ananias got for the land?"
"Yes," she said, "that is the price."
9Peter said to her, "How could you conspire to test the Spirit of the Lord? Listen!
The feet of the men who buried your husband are at the door, and they will carry
you out also."
10At that moment she fell down at his
feet and died. Then the young men came
in and, finding her dead, carried her out
and buried her beside her husband. 11Great
fear seized the whole church and all who
heard about these events.

The Apostles Heal Many

12The apostles performed many signs
and wonders among the people. And all
the believers used to meet together in
Solomon's Colonnade. 13No one else dared
join them, even though they were highly
regarded by the people. 14Nevertheless,
more and more men and women believed
in the Lord and were added to their number. 15As a result, people brought the sick
into the streets and laid them on beds
and mats so that at least Peter's shadow
might fall on some of them as he passed
by. 16Crowds gathered also from the towns
around Jerusalem, bringing their sick and
those tormented by impure spirits, and all
of them were healed.

The Apostles Persecuted

17Then the high priest and all his associates, who were members of the party of
the Sadducees, were filled with jealousy.
18They arrested the apostles and put them
in the public jail. 19But during the night an
angel of the Lord opened the doors of the
jail and brought them out. 20"Go, stand in
the temple courts," he said, "and tell the
people all about this new life."
21At daybreak they entered the temple
courts, as they had been told, and began
to teach the people.
When the high priest and his associates
arrived, they called together the Sanhedrin — the full assembly of the elders of
Israel — and sent to the jail for the apostles. 22But on arriving at the jail, the officers did not find them there. So they went
back and reported, 23"We found the jail
securely locked, with the guards standing
at the doors; but when we opened them,
we found no one inside." 24On hearing this
report, the captain of the temple guard
and the chief priests were at a loss, wondering what this might lead to.
25Then someone came and said, "Look!
The men you put in jail are standing in the
temple courts teaching the people." 26At
that, the captain went with his officers
and brought the apostles. They did not
use force, because they feared that the
people would stone them.
27The apostles were brought in and
made to appear before the Sanhedrin to be
questioned by the high priest. 28"We gave
you strict orders not to teach in this name,"
he said. "Yet you have filled Jerusalem
with your teaching and are determined
to make us guilty of this man's blood."
29Peter and the other apostles replied:
"We must obey God rather than human
beings! 30The God of our ancestors raised
Jesus from the dead — whom you killed
by hanging him on a cross. 31God exalted
him to his own right hand as Prince and
Savior that he might bring Israel to repentance and forgive their sins. 32We are
witnesses of these things, and so is the
Holy Spirit, whom God has given to those
who obey him."
33When they heard this, they were furious and wanted to put them to death. 34But
a Pharisee named Gamaliel, a teacher of
the law, who was honored by all the people, stood up in the Sanhedrin and ordered
that the men be put outside for a little
while. 35Then he addressed the Sanhedrin:
"Men of Israel, consider carefully what
you intend to do to these men. 36Some
time ago Theudas appeared, claiming to
be somebody, and about four hundred
men rallied to him. He was killed, all his
followers were dispersed, and it all came
to nothing. 37After him, Judas the Galilean appeared in the days of the census
and led a band of people in revolt. He

too was killed, and all his followers were scattered. 38Therefore, in the present case I advise you: Leave these men alone! Let them go! For if their purpose or activity is of human origin, it will fail. 39But if it is from God, you will not be able to stop these men; you will only find yourselves fighting against God."

40His speech persuaded them. They called the apostles in and had them flogged. Then they ordered them not to speak in the name of Jesus, and let them go.

41The apostles left the Sanhedrin, rejoicing because they had been counted worthy of suffering disgrace for the Name. 42Day after day, in the temple courts and from house to house, they never stopped teaching and proclaiming the good news that Jesus is the Messiah.

The Choosing of the Seven

6 In those days when the number of disciples was increasing, the Hellenistic Jews[a] among them complained against the Hebraic Jews because their widows were being overlooked in the daily distribution of food. 2So the Twelve gathered all the disciples together and said, "It would not be right for us to neglect the ministry of the word of God in order to wait on tables. 3Brothers and sisters, choose seven men from among you who are known to be full of the Spirit and wisdom. We will turn this responsibility over to them 4and will give our attention to prayer and the ministry of the word."

5This proposal pleased the whole group. They chose Stephen, a man full of faith and of the Holy Spirit; also Philip, Procorus, Nicanor, Timon, Parmenas, and Nicolas from Antioch, a convert to Judaism. 6They presented these men to the apostles, who prayed and laid their hands on them.

7So the word of God spread. The number of disciples in Jerusalem increased rapidly, and a large number of priests became obedient to the faith.

Stephen Seized

8Now Stephen, a man full of God's grace and power, performed great wonders and signs among the people. 9Opposition arose, however, from members of the Synagogue of the Freedmen (as it was called) — Jews of Cyrene and Alexandria as well as the provinces of Cilicia and Asia — who began to argue with Stephen. 10But they could not stand up against the wisdom the Spirit gave him as he spoke.

11Then they secretly persuaded some men to say, "We have heard Stephen speak blasphemous words against Moses and against God."

12So they stirred up the people and the elders and the teachers of the law. They seized Stephen and brought him before the Sanhedrin. 13They produced false witnesses, who testified, "This fellow never stops speaking against this holy place and against the law. 14For we have heard him say that this Jesus of Nazareth will destroy this place and change the customs Moses handed down to us."

15All who were sitting in the Sanhedrin looked intently at Stephen, and they saw that his face was like the face of an angel.

Stephen's Speech to the Sanhedrin

7 Then the high priest asked Stephen, "Are these charges true?"

2To this he replied: "Brothers and fathers, listen to me! The God of glory appeared to our father Abraham while he was still in Mesopotamia, before he lived in Harran. 3'Leave your country and your people,' God said, 'and go to the land I will show you.'[b]

4"So he left the land of the Chaldeans and settled in Harran. After the death of his father, God sent him to this land where you are now living. 5He gave him no inheritance here, not even enough ground to set his foot on. But God promised him that he and his descendants after him would possess the land, even though at that time Abraham had no child. 6God spoke to him in this way: 'For four hundred years your descendants will be strangers in a country not their own, and they will be enslaved and mistreated. 7But I will punish the nation they serve as slaves,' God said, 'and afterward they will come out of that country and worship me in this place.'[c] 8Then he gave Abraham the covenant of circumcision. And Abraham became the father of Isaac and circumcised him eight days after his birth. Later Isaac became the father of Jacob, and Jacob became the father of the twelve patriarchs.

9"Because the patriarchs were jealous of Joseph, they sold him as a slave into Egypt. But God was with him 10and rescued him from all his troubles. He gave Joseph wisdom and enabled him to gain the goodwill of Pharaoh king of Egypt. So Pharaoh made him ruler over Egypt and all his palace.

[a] *1* That is, Jews who had adopted the Greek language and culture [b] *3* Gen. 12:1
[c] *7* Gen. 15:13,14

11"Then a famine struck all Egypt and Canaan, bringing great suffering, and our ancestors could not find food. 12When Jacob heard that there was grain in Egypt, he sent our forefathers on their first visit. 13On their second visit, Joseph told his brothers who he was, and Pharaoh learned about Joseph's family. 14After this, Joseph sent for his father Jacob and his whole family, seventy-five in all. 15Then Jacob went down to Egypt, where he and our ancestors died. 16Their bodies were brought back to Shechem and placed in the tomb that Abraham had bought from the sons of Hamor at Shechem for a certain sum of money.

17"As the time drew near for God to fulfill his promise to Abraham, the number of our people in Egypt had greatly increased. 18Then 'a new king, to whom Joseph meant nothing, came to power in Egypt.'[a] 19He dealt treacherously with our people and oppressed our ancestors by forcing them to throw out their newborn babies so that they would die.

20"At that time Moses was born, and he was no ordinary child.[b] For three months he was cared for by his family. 21When he was placed outside, Pharaoh's daughter took him and brought him up as her own son. 22Moses was educated in all the wisdom of the Egyptians and was powerful in speech and action.

23"When Moses was forty years old, he decided to visit his own people, the Israelites. 24He saw one of them being mistreated by an Egyptian, so he went to his defense and avenged him by killing the Egyptian. 25Moses thought that his own people would realize that God was using him to rescue them, but they did not. 26The next day Moses came upon two Israelites who were fighting. He tried to reconcile them by saying, 'Men, you are brothers; why do you want to hurt each other?'

27"But the man who was mistreating the other pushed Moses aside and said, 'Who made you ruler and judge over us? 28Are you thinking of killing me as you killed the Egyptian yesterday?'[c] 29When Moses heard this, he fled to Midian, where he settled as a foreigner and had two sons.

30"After forty years had passed, an angel appeared to Moses in the flames of a burning bush in the desert near Mount Sinai. 31When he saw this, he was amazed at the sight. As he went over to get a closer look, he heard the Lord say: 32'I am the God of your fathers, the God of Abraham, Isaac and Jacob.'[d] Moses trembled with fear and did not dare to look.

33"Then the Lord said to him, 'Take off your sandals, for the place where you are standing is holy ground. 34I have indeed seen the oppression of my people in Egypt. I have heard their groaning and have come down to set them free. Now come, I will send you back to Egypt.'[e]

35"This is the same Moses they had rejected with the words, 'Who made you ruler and judge?' He was sent to be their ruler and deliverer by God himself, through the angel who appeared to him in the bush. 36He led them out of Egypt and performed wonders and signs in Egypt, at the Red Sea and for forty years in the wilderness.

37"This is the Moses who told the Israelites, 'God will raise up for you a prophet like me from your own people.'[f] 38He was in the assembly in the wilderness, with the angel who spoke to him on Mount Sinai, and with our ancestors; and he received living words to pass on to us.

39"But our ancestors refused to obey him. Instead, they rejected him and in their hearts turned back to Egypt. 40They told Aaron, 'Make us gods who will go before us. As for this fellow Moses who led us out of Egypt — we don't know what has happened to him!'[g] 41That was the time they made an idol in the form of a calf. They brought sacrifices to it and reveled in what their own hands had made. 42But God turned away from them and gave them over to the worship of the sun, moon and stars. This agrees with what is written in the book of the prophets:

"'Did you bring me sacrifices and
    offerings
  forty years in the wilderness,
    people of Israel?
43You have taken up the tabernacle of
    Molek
  and the star of your god Rephan,
    the idols you made to worship.
Therefore I will send you into exile'[h]
    beyond Babylon.

44"Our ancestors had the tabernacle of the covenant law with them in the wilderness. It had been made as God directed Moses, according to the pattern he had seen. 45After receiving the tabernacle, our ancestors under Joshua brought it with them when they took the land from the nations God drove out before them. It remained in the land until the time of David, 46who enjoyed God's favor and asked that

[a] *18* Exodus 1:8 [b] *20* Or *was fair in the sight of God* [c] *28* Exodus 2:14 [d] *32* Exodus 3:6
[e] *34* Exodus 3:5,7,8,10 [f] *37* Deut. 18:15 [g] *40* Exodus 32:1 [h] *43* Amos 5:25-27 (see Septuagint)

he might provide a dwelling place for the
God of Jacob.[a] 47But it was Solomon who
built a house for him.
48"However, the Most High does not live
in houses made by human hands. As the
prophet says:

49 " 'Heaven is my throne,
and the earth is my footstool.
What kind of house will you build
for me?
says the Lord.
Or where will my resting place be?
50 Has not my hand made all these
things?'[b]

51"You stiff-necked people! Your hearts
and ears are still uncircumcised. You are
just like your ancestors: You always resist
the Holy Spirit! 52Was there ever a prophet
your ancestors did not persecute? They
even killed those who predicted the coming of the Righteous One. And now you
have betrayed and murdered him — 53you
who have received the law that was given
through angels but have not obeyed it."

The Stoning of Stephen

54When the members of the Sanhedrin
heard this, they were furious and gnashed
their teeth at him. 55But Stephen, full of
the Holy Spirit, looked up to heaven and
saw the glory of God, and Jesus standing
at the right hand of God. 56"Look," he said,
"I see heaven open and the Son of Man
standing at the right hand of God."
57At this they covered their ears and,
yelling at the top of their voices, they all
rushed at him, 58dragged him out of the
city and began to stone him. Meanwhile,
the witnesses laid their coats at the feet
of a young man named Saul.
59While they were stoning him, Stephen
prayed, "Lord Jesus, receive my spirit."
60Then he fell on his knees and cried out,
"Lord, do not hold this sin against them."
When he had said this, he fell asleep.
8 And Saul approved of their killing him.

The Church Persecuted and Scattered

On that day a great persecution broke
out against the church in Jerusalem, and
all except the apostles were scattered
throughout Judea and Samaria. 2Godly
men buried Stephen and mourned deeply
for him. 3But Saul began to destroy the
church. Going from house to house, he
dragged off both men and women and
put them in prison.

Philip in Samaria

4Those who had been scattered
preached the word wherever they went.
5Philip went down to a city in Samaria and
proclaimed the Messiah there. 6When the
crowds heard Philip and saw the signs he
performed, they all paid close attention
to what he said. 7For with shrieks, impure
spirits came out of many, and many who
were paralyzed or lame were healed. 8So
there was great joy in that city.

Simon the Sorcerer

9Now for some time a man named
Simon had practiced sorcery in the city
and amazed all the people of Samaria.
He boasted that he was someone great,
10and all the people, both high and low,
gave him their attention and exclaimed,
"This man is rightly called the Great Power
of God." 11They followed him because he
had amazed them for a long time with his
sorcery. 12But when they believed Philip
as he proclaimed the good news of the
kingdom of God and the name of Jesus
Christ, they were baptized, both men and
women. 13Simon himself believed and
was baptized. And he followed Philip everywhere, astonished by the great signs
and miracles he saw.
14When the apostles in Jerusalem heard
that Samaria had accepted the word of
God, they sent Peter and John to Samaria. 15When they arrived, they prayed for
the new believers there that they might
receive the Holy Spirit, 16because the Holy
Spirit had not yet come on any of them;
they had simply been baptized in the
name of the Lord Jesus. 17Then Peter and
John placed their hands on them, and
they received the Holy Spirit.
18When Simon saw that the Spirit was
given at the laying on of the apostles'
hands, he offered them money 19and said,
"Give me also this ability so that everyone
on whom I lay my hands may receive the
Holy Spirit."
20Peter answered: "May your money
perish with you, because you thought you
could buy the gift of God with money!
21You have no part or share in this ministry, because your heart is not right before God. 22Repent of this wickedness and
pray to the Lord in the hope that he may
forgive you for having such a thought in
your heart. 23For I see that you are full of
bitterness and captive to sin."
24Then Simon answered, "Pray to the
Lord for me so that nothing you have said
may happen to me."

[a] *46* Some early manuscripts *the house of Jacob*
[b] *50* Isaiah 66:1,2

25After they had further proclaimed the
word of the Lord and testified about Jesus,
Peter and John returned to Jerusalem,
preaching the gospel in many Samaritan villages.

Philip and the Ethiopian

26Now an angel of the Lord said to
Philip, "Go south to the road — the desert road — that goes down from Jerusalem to Gaza." 27So he started out, and on
his way he met an Ethiopian[a] eunuch,
an important official in charge of all the
treasury of the Kandake (which means
"queen of the Ethiopians"). This man had
gone to Jerusalem to worship, 28and on
his way home was sitting in his chariot
reading the Book of Isaiah the prophet.
29The Spirit told Philip, "Go to that chariot
and stay near it."
30Then Philip ran up to the chariot and
heard the man reading Isaiah the prophet.
"Do you understand what you are reading?" Philip asked.
31"How can I," he said, "unless someone
explains it to me?" So he invited Philip to
come up and sit with him.
32This is the passage of Scripture the
eunuch was reading:

"He was led like a sheep to the
slaughter,
and as a lamb before its shearer is
silent,
so he did not open his mouth.
33In his humiliation he was deprived of
justice.
Who can speak of his descendants?
For his life was taken from the
earth."[b]

34The eunuch asked Philip, "Tell me,
please, who is the prophet talking about,
himself or someone else?" 35Then Philip
began with that very passage of Scripture
and told him the good news about Jesus.
36As they traveled along the road, they
came to some water and the eunuch said,
"Look, here is water. What can stand in the
way of my being baptized?" [37][c] 38And he
gave orders to stop the chariot. Then both
Philip and the eunuch went down into the
water and Philip baptized him. 39When
they came up out of the water, the Spirit
of the Lord suddenly took Philip away,
and the eunuch did not see him again,
but went on his way rejoicing. 40Philip,
however, appeared at Azotus and traveled about, preaching the gospel in all the
towns until he reached Caesarea.

Saul's Conversion

9 Meanwhile, Saul was still breathing out murderous threats against
the Lord's disciples. He went to the high
priest 2and asked him for letters to the
synagogues in Damascus, so that if he
found any there who belonged to the Way,
whether men or women, he might take
them as prisoners to Jerusalem. 3As he
neared Damascus on his journey, suddenly a light from heaven flashed around
him. 4He fell to the ground and heard a
voice say to him, "Saul, Saul, why do you
persecute me?"
5"Who are you, Lord?" Saul asked.
"I am Jesus, whom you are persecuting," he replied. 6"Now get up and go into
the city, and you will be told what you
must do."
7The men traveling with Saul stood there
speechless; they heard the sound but did
not see anyone. 8Saul got up from the
ground, but when he opened his eyes he
could see nothing. So they led him by the
hand into Damascus. 9For three days he was
blind, and did not eat or drink anything.
10In Damascus there was a disciple
named Ananias. The Lord called to him
in a vision, "Ananias!"
"Yes, Lord," he answered.
11The Lord told him, "Go to the house
of Judas on Straight Street and ask for a
man from Tarsus named Saul, for he is
praying. 12In a vision he has seen a man
named Ananias come and place his hands
on him to restore his sight."
13"Lord," Ananias answered, "I have
heard many reports about this man and
all the harm he has done to your holy
people in Jerusalem. 14And he has come
here with authority from the chief priests
to arrest all who call on your name."
15But the Lord said to Ananias, "Go!
This man is my chosen instrument to
proclaim my name to the Gentiles and
their kings and to the people of Israel. 16I
will show him how much he must suffer
for my name."
17Then Ananias went to the house and
entered it. Placing his hands on Saul, he
said, "Brother Saul, the Lord — Jesus, who
appeared to you on the road as you were
coming here — has sent me so that you
may see again and be filled with the Holy
Spirit." 18Immediately, something like
scales fell from Saul's eyes, and he could
see again. He got up and was baptized,
19and after taking some food, he regained
his strength.

[a] *27* That is, from the southern Nile region [b] *33* Isaiah 53:7,8 (see Septuagint) [c] *37* Some manuscripts include here *Philip said, "If you believe with all your heart, you may." The eunuch answered, "I believe that Jesus Christ is the Son of God."*

Saul in Damascus and Jerusalem

Saul spent several days with the disciples in Damascus. 20At once he began to preach in the synagogues that Jesus is the Son of God. 21All those who heard him were astonished and asked, "Isn't he the man who raised havoc in Jerusalem among those who call on this name? And hasn't he come here to take them as prisoners to the chief priests?" 22Yet Saul grew more and more powerful and baffled the Jews living in Damascus by proving that Jesus is the Messiah.

23After many days had gone by, there was a conspiracy among the Jews to kill him, 24but Saul learned of their plan. Day and night they kept close watch on the city gates in order to kill him. 25But his followers took him by night and lowered him in a basket through an opening in the wall.

26When he came to Jerusalem, he tried to join the disciples, but they were all afraid of him, not believing that he really was a disciple. 27But Barnabas took him and brought him to the apostles. He told them how Saul on his journey had seen the Lord and that the Lord had spoken to him, and how in Damascus he had preached fearlessly in the name of Jesus. 28So Saul stayed with them and moved about freely in Jerusalem, speaking boldly in the name of the Lord. 29He talked and debated with the Hellenistic Jews,[a] but they tried to kill him. 30When the believers learned of this, they took him down to Caesarea and sent him off to Tarsus.

31Then the church throughout Judea, Galilee and Samaria enjoyed a time of peace and was strengthened. Living in the fear of the Lord and encouraged by the Holy Spirit, it increased in numbers.

Aeneas and Dorcas

32As Peter traveled about the country, he went to visit the Lord's people who lived in Lydda. 33There he found a man named Aeneas, who was paralyzed and had been bedridden for eight years. 34"Aeneas," Peter said to him, "Jesus Christ heals you. Get up and roll up your mat." Immediately Aeneas got up. 35All those who lived in Lydda and Sharon saw him and turned to the Lord.

36In Joppa there was a disciple named Tabitha (in Greek her name is Dorcas); she was always doing good and helping the poor. 37About that time she became sick and died, and her body was washed and placed in an upstairs room. 38Lydda was near Joppa; so when the disciples heard that Peter was in Lydda, they sent two men to him and urged him, "Please come at once!"

39Peter went with them, and when he arrived he was taken upstairs to the room. All the widows stood around him, crying and showing him the robes and other clothing that Dorcas had made while she was still with them.

40Peter sent them all out of the room; then he got down on his knees and prayed. Turning toward the dead woman, he said, "Tabitha, get up." She opened her eyes, and seeing Peter she sat up. 41He took her by the hand and helped her to her feet. Then he called for the believers, especially the widows, and presented her to them alive. 42This became known all over Joppa, and many people believed in the Lord. 43Peter stayed in Joppa for some time with a tanner named Simon.

Cornelius Calls for Peter

10 At Caesarea there was a man named Cornelius, a centurion in what was known as the Italian Regiment. 2He and all his family were devout and God-fearing; he gave generously to those in need and prayed to God regularly. 3One day at about three in the afternoon he had a vision. He distinctly saw an angel of God, who came to him and said, "Cornelius!"

4Cornelius stared at him in fear. "What is it, Lord?" he asked.

The angel answered, "Your prayers and gifts to the poor have come up as a memorial offering before God. 5Now send men to Joppa to bring back a man named Simon who is called Peter. 6He is staying with Simon the tanner, whose house is by the sea."

7When the angel who spoke to him had gone, Cornelius called two of his servants and a devout soldier who was one of his attendants. 8He told them everything that had happened and sent them to Joppa.

Peter's Vision

9About noon the following day as they were on their journey and approaching the city, Peter went up on the roof to pray. 10He became hungry and wanted something to eat, and while the meal was being prepared, he fell into a trance. 11He saw heaven opened and something like a large sheet being let down to earth by its four corners. 12It contained all kinds of four-footed animals, as well as reptiles and birds. 13Then a voice told him, "Get up, Peter. Kill and eat."

[a] 29 That is, Jews who had adopted the Greek language and culture

14“Surely not, Lord!” Peter replied. “I have never eaten anything impure or unclean.”

15The voice spoke to him a second time, “Do not call anything impure that God has made clean.”

16This happened three times, and immediately the sheet was taken back to heaven.

17While Peter was wondering about the meaning of the vision, the men sent by Cornelius found out where Simon’s house was and stopped at the gate. 18They called out, asking if Simon who was known as Peter was staying there.

19While Peter was still thinking about the vision, the Spirit said to him, “Simon, three[a] men are looking for you. 20So get up and go downstairs. Do not hesitate to go with them, for I have sent them.”

21Peter went down and said to the men, “I’m the one you’re looking for. Why have you come?”

22The men replied, “We have come from Cornelius the centurion. He is a righteous and God-fearing man, who is respected by all the Jewish people. A holy angel told him to ask you to come to his house so that he could hear what you have to say.” 23Then Peter invited the men into the house to be his guests.

Peter at Cornelius’s House

The next day Peter started out with them, and some of the believers from Joppa went along. 24The following day he arrived in Caesarea. Cornelius was expecting them and had called together his relatives and close friends. 25As Peter entered the house, Cornelius met him and fell at his feet in reverence. 26But Peter made him get up. “Stand up,” he said, “I am only a man myself.”

27While talking with him, Peter went inside and found a large gathering of people. 28He said to them: “You are well aware that it is against our law for a Jew to associate with or visit a Gentile. But God has shown me that I should not call anyone impure or unclean. 29So when I was sent for, I came without raising any objection. May I ask why you sent for me?”

30Cornelius answered: “Three days ago I was in my house praying at this hour, at three in the afternoon. Suddenly a man in shining clothes stood before me 31and said, ‘Cornelius, God has heard your prayer and remembered your gifts to the poor. 32Send to Joppa for Simon who is called Peter. He is a guest in the home of Simon the tanner, who lives by the sea.’ 33So I sent for you immediately, and it was good of you to come. Now we are all here in the presence of God to listen to everything the Lord has commanded you to tell us.”

34Then Peter began to speak: “I now realize how true it is that God does not show favoritism 35but accepts from every nation the one who fears him and does what is right. 36You know the message God sent to the people of Israel, announcing the good news of peace through Jesus Christ, who is Lord of all. 37You know what has happened throughout the province of Judea, beginning in Galilee after the baptism that John preached — 38how God anointed Jesus of Nazareth with the Holy Spirit and power, and how he went around doing good and healing all who were under the power of the devil, because God was with him.

39“We are witnesses of everything he did in the country of the Jews and in Jerusalem. They killed him by hanging him on a cross, 40but God raised him from the dead on the third day and caused him to be seen. 41He was not seen by all the people, but by witnesses whom God had already chosen — by us who ate and drank with him after he rose from the dead. 42He commanded us to preach to the people and to testify that he is the one whom God appointed as judge of the living and the dead. 43All the prophets testify about him that everyone who believes in him receives forgiveness of sins through his name.”

44While Peter was still speaking these words, the Holy Spirit came on all who heard the message. 45The circumcised believers who had come with Peter were astonished that the gift of the Holy Spirit had been poured out even on Gentiles. 46For they heard them speaking in tongues[b] and praising God.

Then Peter said, 47“Surely no one can stand in the way of their being baptized with water. They have received the Holy Spirit just as we have.” 48So he ordered that they be baptized in the name of Jesus Christ. Then they asked Peter to stay with them for a few days.

Peter Explains His Actions

11 The apostles and the believers throughout Judea heard that the Gentiles also had received the word of God. 2So when Peter went up to Jerusalem, the circumcised believers criticized him

[a] *19* One early manuscript *two*; other manuscripts do not have the number. [b] *46* Or *other languages*

3and said, "You went into the house of
uncircumcised men and ate with them."
4Starting from the beginning, Peter
told them the whole story: 5"I was in the
city of Joppa praying, and in a trance I
saw a vision. I saw something like a large
sheet being let down from heaven by its
four corners, and it came down to where I
was. 6I looked into it and saw four-footed
animals of the earth, wild beasts, reptiles
and birds. 7Then I heard a voice telling me,
'Get up, Peter. Kill and eat.'
8"I replied, 'Surely not, Lord! Nothing
impure or unclean has ever entered my
mouth.'
9"The voice spoke from heaven a second
time, 'Do not call anything impure that
God has made clean.' 10This happened
three times, and then it was all pulled up
to heaven again.
11"Right then three men who had been
sent to me from Caesarea stopped at the
house where I was staying. 12The Spirit told
me to have no hesitation about going with
them. These six brothers also went with
me, and we entered the man's house. 13He
told us how he had seen an angel appear
in his house and say, 'Send to Joppa for
Simon who is called Peter. 14He will bring
you a message through which you and all
your household will be saved.'
15"As I began to speak, the Holy Spirit came on them as he had come on us
at the beginning. 16Then I remembered
what the Lord had said: 'John baptized
with[a] water, but you will be baptized with[a]
the Holy Spirit.' 17So if God gave them the
same gift he gave us who believed in the
Lord Jesus Christ, who was I to think that
I could stand in God's way?"
18When they heard this, they had no further objections and praised God, saying,
"So then, even to Gentiles God has granted
repentance that leads to life."

The Church in Antioch

19Now those who had been scattered
by the persecution that broke out when
Stephen was killed traveled as far as
Phoenicia, Cyprus and Antioch, spreading the word only among Jews. 20Some
of them, however, men from Cyprus and
Cyrene, went to Antioch and began to
speak to Greeks also, telling them the
good news about the Lord Jesus. 21The
Lord's hand was with them, and a great
number of people believed and turned
to the Lord.
22News of this reached the church in
Jerusalem, and they sent Barnabas to
Antioch. 23When he arrived and saw what
the grace of God had done, he was glad
and encouraged them all to remain true
to the Lord with all their hearts. 24He was
a good man, full of the Holy Spirit and
faith, and a great number of people were
brought to the Lord.
25Then Barnabas went to Tarsus to look
for Saul, 26and when he found him, he
brought him to Antioch. So for a whole
year Barnabas and Saul met with the
church and taught great numbers of people. The disciples were called Christians
first at Antioch.
27During this time some prophets came
down from Jerusalem to Antioch. 28One
of them, named Agabus, stood up and
through the Spirit predicted that a severe
famine would spread over the entire Roman world. (This happened during the
reign of Claudius.) 29The disciples, as each
one was able, decided to provide help for
the brothers and sisters living in Judea.
30This they did, sending their gift to the
elders by Barnabas and Saul.

Peter's Miraculous Escape From Prison

12 It was about this time that King Herod arrested some who belonged to
the church, intending to persecute them.
2He had James, the brother of John, put to
death with the sword. 3When he saw that
this met with approval among the Jews,
he proceeded to seize Peter also. This happened during the Festival of Unleavened
Bread. 4After arresting him, he put him in
prison, handing him over to be guarded
by four squads of four soldiers each. Herod
intended to bring him out for public trial
after the Passover.
5So Peter was kept in prison, but the
church was earnestly praying to God for
him.
6The night before Herod was to bring
him to trial, Peter was sleeping between
two soldiers, bound with two chains, and
sentries stood guard at the entrance. 7Sud-
denly an angel of the Lord appeared and
a light shone in the cell. He struck Peter
on the side and woke him up. "Quick, get
up!" he said, and the chains fell off Peter's wrists.
8Then the angel said to him, "Put on
your clothes and sandals." And Peter did
so. "Wrap your cloak around you and follow me," the angel told him. 9Peter followed him out of the prison, but he had
no idea that what the angel was doing
was really happening; he thought he was

[a] 16 Or *in*

seeing a vision. 10They passed the first and
second guards and came to the iron gate
leading to the city. It opened for them by
itself, and they went through it. When
they had walked the length of one street,
suddenly the angel left him.
11Then Peter came to himself and said,
"Now I know without a doubt that the Lord
has sent his angel and rescued me from
Herod's clutches and from everything
the Jewish people were hoping would
happen."
12When this had dawned on him, he
went to the house of Mary the mother
of John, also called Mark, where many
people had gathered and were praying.
13Peter knocked at the outer entrance, and
a servant named Rhoda came to answer
the door. 14When she recognized Peter's
voice, she was so overjoyed she ran back
without opening it and exclaimed, "Peter
is at the door!"
15"You're out of your mind," they told
her. When she kept insisting that it was so,
they said, "It must be his angel."
16But Peter kept on knocking, and when
they opened the door and saw him, they
were astonished. 17Peter motioned with his
hand for them to be quiet and described
how the Lord had brought him out of prison. "Tell James and the other brothers
and sisters about this," he said, and then
he left for another place.
18In the morning, there was no small
commotion among the soldiers as to what
had become of Peter. 19After Herod had a
thorough search made for him and did not
find him, he cross-examined the guards
and ordered that they be executed.

Herod's Death

Then Herod went from Judea to Caesarea and stayed there. 20He had been quarreling with the people of Tyre and Sidon;
they now joined together and sought an
audience with him. After securing the support of Blastus, a trusted personal servant
of the king, they asked for peace, because
they depended on the king's country for
their food supply.
21On the appointed day Herod, wearing his royal robes, sat on his throne and
delivered a public address to the people.
22They shouted, "This is the voice of a god,
not of a man." 23Immediately, because
Herod did not give praise to God, an angel
of the Lord struck him down, and he was
eaten by worms and died.
24But the word of God continued to
spread and flourish.

Barnabas and Saul Sent Off

25When Barnabas and Saul had finished their mission, they returned from[a]
Jerusalem, taking with them John, also
13 called Mark. 1Now in the church at
Antioch there were prophets and
teachers: Barnabas, Simeon called Niger,
Lucius of Cyrene, Manaen (who had been
brought up with Herod the tetrarch) and
Saul. 2While they were worshiping the
Lord and fasting, the Holy Spirit said,
"Set apart for me Barnabas and Saul for
the work to which I have called them."
3So after they had fasted and prayed,
they placed their hands on them and
sent them off.

On Cyprus

4The two of them, sent on their way by
the Holy Spirit, went down to Seleucia and
sailed from there to Cyprus. 5When they
arrived at Salamis, they proclaimed the
word of God in the Jewish synagogues.
John was with them as their helper.
6They traveled through the whole island
until they came to Paphos. There they met
a Jewish sorcerer and false prophet named
Bar-Jesus, 7who was an attendant of the
proconsul, Sergius Paulus. The proconsul,
an intelligent man, sent for Barnabas and
Saul because he wanted to hear the word
of God. 8But Elymas the sorcerer (for that is
what his name means) opposed them and
tried to turn the proconsul from the faith.
9Then Saul, who was also called Paul, filled
with the Holy Spirit, looked straight at
Elymas and said, 10"You are a child of the
devil and an enemy of everything that is
right! You are full of all kinds of deceit and
trickery. Will you never stop perverting the
right ways of the Lord? 11Now the hand of
the Lord is against you. You are going to
be blind for a time, not even able to see
the light of the sun."
Immediately mist and darkness came
over him, and he groped about, seeking
someone to lead him by the hand. 12When
the proconsul saw what had happened,
he believed, for he was amazed at the
teaching about the Lord.

In Pisidian Antioch

13From Paphos, Paul and his companions sailed to Perga in Pamphylia, where
John left them to return to Jerusalem.
14From Perga they went on to Pisidian
Antioch. On the Sabbath they entered
the synagogue and sat down. 15After the
reading from the Law and the Prophets,
the leaders of the synagogue sent word

[a] *25* Some manuscripts *to*

to them, saying, "Brothers, if you have a
word of exhortation for the people, please
speak."
16 Standing up, Paul motioned with his
hand and said: "Fellow Israelites and
you Gentiles who worship God, listen
to me! 17 The God of the people of Israel
chose our ancestors; he made the people
prosper during their stay in Egypt; with
mighty power he led them out of that
country; 18 for about forty years he endured their conduct[a] in the wilderness;
19 and he overthrew seven nations in Canaan, giving their land to his people as
their inheritance. 20 All this took about
450 years.
"After this, God gave them judges until
the time of Samuel the prophet. 21 Then
the people asked for a king, and he gave
them Saul son of Kish, of the tribe of Benjamin, who ruled forty years. 22 After removing Saul, he made David their king.
God testified concerning him: 'I have
found David son of Jesse, a man after
my own heart; he will do everything I
want him to do.'
23 "From this man's descendants God has
brought to Israel the Savior Jesus, as he
promised. 24 Before the coming of Jesus,
John preached repentance and baptism
to all the people of Israel. 25 As John was
completing his work, he said: 'Who do
you suppose I am? I am not the one you
are looking for. But there is one coming
after me whose sandals I am not worthy
to untie.'
26 "Fellow children of Abraham and you
God-fearing Gentiles, it is to us that this
message of salvation has been sent. 27 The
people of Jerusalem and their rulers did
not recognize Jesus, yet in condemning
him they fulfilled the words of the prophets that are read every Sabbath. 28 Though
they found no proper ground for a death
sentence, they asked Pilate to have him
executed. 29 When they had carried out
all that was written about him, they took
him down from the cross and laid him in a
tomb. 30 But God raised him from the dead,
31 and for many days he was seen by those
who had traveled with him from Galilee
to Jerusalem. They are now his witnesses
to our people.
32 "We tell you the good news: What God
promised our ancestors 33 he has fulfilled
for us, their children, by raising up Jesus.
As it is written in the second Psalm:

"'You are my son;
today I have become your father.'[b]

34 God raised him from the dead so that
he will never be subject to decay. As God
has said,

"'I will give you the holy and sure
blessings promised to David.'[c]

35 So it is also stated elsewhere:

"'You will not let your holy one see
decay.'[d]

36 "Now when David had served God's
purpose in his own generation, he fell
asleep; he was buried with his ancestors and his body decayed. 37 But the one
whom God raised from the dead did not
see decay.
38 "Therefore, my friends, I want you to
know that through Jesus the forgiveness
of sins is proclaimed to you. 39 Through
him everyone who believes is set free from
every sin, a justification you were not able
to obtain under the law of Moses. 40 Take
care that what the prophets have said
does not happen to you:

41 "'Look, you scoffers,
wonder and perish,
for I am going to do something
in your days
that you would never believe,
even if someone told you.'[e]"

42 As Paul and Barnabas were leaving
the synagogue, the people invited them
to speak further about these things on
the next Sabbath. 43 When the congregation was dismissed, many of the Jews
and devout converts to Judaism followed
Paul and Barnabas, who talked with them
and urged them to continue in the grace
of God.
44 On the next Sabbath almost the whole
city gathered to hear the word of the Lord.
45 When the Jews saw the crowds, they were
filled with jealousy. They began to contradict what Paul was saying and heaped
abuse on him.
46 Then Paul and Barnabas answered
them boldly: "We had to speak the word
of God to you first. Since you reject it and
do not consider yourselves worthy of eternal life, we now turn to the Gentiles. 47 For
this is what the Lord has commanded us:

"'I have made you[f] a light for the
Gentiles,
that you[f] may bring salvation
to the ends of the earth.'[g]"

48 When the Gentiles heard this, they
were glad and honored the word of the

[a] *18* Some manuscripts *he cared for them* [b] *33* Psalm 2:7 [c] *34* Isaiah 55:3 [d] *35* Psalm 16:10 (see Septuagint) [e] *41* Hab. 1:5 [f] *47* The Greek is singular. [g] *47* Isaiah 49:6

Lord; and all who were appointed for eternal life believed.

49The word of the Lord spread through the whole region. 50But the Jewish leaders incited the God-fearing women of high standing and the leading men of the city. They stirred up persecution against Paul and Barnabas, and expelled them from their region. 51So they shook the dust off their feet as a warning to them and went to Iconium. 52And the disciples were filled with joy and with the Holy Spirit.

In Iconium

14 At Iconium Paul and Barnabas went as usual into the Jewish synagogue. There they spoke so effectively that a great number of Jews and Greeks believed. 2But the Jews who refused to believe stirred up the other Gentiles and poisoned their minds against the brothers. 3So Paul and Barnabas spent considerable time there, speaking boldly for the Lord, who confirmed the message of his grace by enabling them to perform signs and wonders. 4The people of the city were divided; some sided with the Jews, others with the apostles. 5There was a plot afoot among both Gentiles and Jews, together with their leaders, to mistreat them and stone them. 6But they found out about it and fled to the Lycaonian cities of Lystra and Derbe and to the surrounding country, 7where they continued to preach the gospel.

In Lystra and Derbe

8In Lystra there sat a man who was lame. He had been that way from birth and had never walked. 9He listened to Paul as he was speaking. Paul looked directly at him, saw that he had faith to be healed 10and called out, "Stand up on your feet!" At that, the man jumped up and began to walk.

11When the crowd saw what Paul had done, they shouted in the Lycaonian language, "The gods have come down to us in human form!" 12Barnabas they called Zeus, and Paul they called Hermes because he was the chief speaker. 13The priest of Zeus, whose temple was just outside the city, brought bulls and wreaths to the city gates because he and the crowd wanted to offer sacrifices to them.

14But when the apostles Barnabas and Paul heard of this, they tore their clothes and rushed out into the crowd, shouting: 15"Friends, why are you doing this? We too are only human, like you. We are bringing you good news, telling you to turn from these worthless things to the living God, who made the heavens and the earth and the sea and everything in them. 16In the past, he let all nations go their own way. 17Yet he has not left himself without testimony: He has shown kindness by giving you rain from heaven and crops in their seasons; he provides you with plenty of food and fills your hearts with joy." 18Even with these words, they had difficulty keeping the crowd from sacrificing to them.

19Then some Jews came from Antioch and Iconium and won the crowd over. They stoned Paul and dragged him outside the city, thinking he was dead. 20But after the disciples had gathered around him, he got up and went back into the city. The next day he and Barnabas left for Derbe.

The Return to Antioch in Syria

21They preached the gospel in that city and won a large number of disciples. Then they returned to Lystra, Iconium and Antioch, 22strengthening the disciples and encouraging them to remain true to the faith. "We must go through many hardships to enter the kingdom of God," they said. 23Paul and Barnabas appointed elders[a] for them in each church and, with prayer and fasting, committed them to the Lord, in whom they had put their trust. 24After going through Pisidia, they came into Pamphylia, 25and when they had preached the word in Perga, they went down to Attalia.

26From Attalia they sailed back to Antioch, where they had been committed to the grace of God for the work they had now completed. 27On arriving there, they gathered the church together and reported all that God had done through them and how he had opened a door of faith to the Gentiles. 28And they stayed there a long time with the disciples.

The Council at Jerusalem

15 Certain people came down from Judea to Antioch and were teaching the believers: "Unless you are circumcised, according to the custom taught by Moses, you cannot be saved." 2This brought Paul and Barnabas into sharp dispute and debate with them. So Paul and Barnabas were appointed, along with some other believers, to go up to Jerusalem to see the apostles and elders about this question. 3The church sent them on their way, and as they traveled through Phoenicia and Samaria, they told how the Gentiles had been converted. This news made all the believers

[a] 23 Or *Barnabas ordained elders*; or *Barnabas had elders elected*

very glad. 4 When they came to Jerusalem,
they were welcomed by the church and the
apostles and elders, to whom they reported
everything God had done through them.
5 Then some of the believers who belonged to the party of the Pharisees stood
up and said, "The Gentiles must be circumcised and required to keep the law
of Moses."
6 The apostles and elders met to consider
this question. 7 After much discussion, Peter got up and addressed them: "Brothers,
you know that some time ago God made
a choice among you that the Gentiles
might hear from my lips the message of
the gospel and believe. 8 God, who knows
the heart, showed that he accepted them
by giving the Holy Spirit to them, just as
he did to us. 9 He did not discriminate between us and them, for he purified their
hearts by faith. 10 Now then, why do you
try to test God by putting on the necks of
Gentiles a yoke that neither we nor our
ancestors have been able to bear? 11 No! We
believe it is through the grace of our Lord
Jesus that we are saved, just as they are."
12 The whole assembly became silent as
they listened to Barnabas and Paul telling
about the signs and wonders God had done
among the Gentiles through them. 13 When
they finished, James spoke up. "Brothers," he said, "listen to me. 14 Simon[a] has
described to us how God first intervened
to choose a people for his name from the
Gentiles. 15 The words of the prophets are
in agreement with this, as it is written:

16 " 'After this I will return
and rebuild David's fallen tent.
Its ruins I will rebuild,
and I will restore it,
17 that the rest of mankind may seek
the Lord,
even all the Gentiles who bear my
name,
says the Lord, who does these
things'[b] —
18 things known from long ago.[c]

19 "It is my judgment, therefore, that we
should not make it difficult for the Gentiles who are turning to God. 20 Instead
we should write to them, telling them
to abstain from food polluted by idols,
from sexual immorality, from the meat
of strangled animals and from blood.
21 For the law of Moses has been preached
in every city from the earliest times and is
read in the synagogues on every Sabbath."

The Council's Letter to Gentile Believers

22 Then the apostles and elders, with the
whole church, decided to choose some of
their own men and send them to Antioch with Paul and Barnabas. They chose
Judas (called Barsabbas) and Silas, men
who were leaders among the believers.
23 With them they sent the following letter:

The apostles and elders, your brothers,

To the Gentile believers in Antioch, Syria and Cilicia:

Greetings.

24 We have heard that some went
out from us without our authoriza-
tion and disturbed you, troubling your
minds by what they said. 25 So we all
agreed to choose some men and send
them to you with our dear friends Barnabas and Paul — 26 men who have
risked their lives for the name of our
Lord Jesus Christ. 27 Therefore we are
sending Judas and Silas to confirm by
word of mouth what we are writing.
28 It seemed good to the Holy Spirit
and to us not to burden you with anything beyond the following requirements: 29 You are to abstain from food
sacrificed to idols, from blood, from
the meat of strangled animals and
from sexual immorality. You will do
well to avoid these things.

Farewell.

30 So the men were sent off and went
down to Antioch, where they gathered the
church together and delivered the letter.
31 The people read it and were glad for its
encouraging message. 32 Judas and Silas,
who themselves were prophets, said much
to encourage and strengthen the believers. 33 After spending some time there, they
were sent off by the believers with the
blessing of peace to return to those who
had sent them. [34][d] 35 But Paul and Barnabas remained in Antioch, where they
and many others taught and preached
the word of the Lord.

Disagreement Between Paul and Barnabas

36 Some time later Paul said to Barnabas, "Let us go back and visit the believers
in all the towns where we preached the
word of the Lord and see how they are

[a] 14 Greek *Simeon,* a variant of *Simon;* that is, Peter [b] 17 Amos 9:11,12 (see Septuagint)
[c] 17,18 Some manuscripts *things' — / [18]the Lord's work is known to him from long ago*
[d] 34 Some manuscripts include here *But Silas decided to remain there.*

doing." 37 Barnabas wanted to take John, also called Mark, with them, 38 but Paul did not think it wise to take him, because he had deserted them in Pamphylia and had not continued with them in the work. 39 They had such a sharp disagreement that they parted company. Barnabas took Mark and sailed for Cyprus, 40 but Paul chose Silas and left, commended by the believers to the grace of the Lord. 41 He went through Syria and Cilicia, strengthening the churches.

Timothy Joins Paul and Silas

16 Paul came to Derbe and then to Lystra, where a disciple named Timothy lived, whose mother was Jewish and a believer but whose father was a Greek. 2 The believers at Lystra and Iconium spoke well of him. 3 Paul wanted to take him along on the journey, so he circumcised him because of the Jews who lived in that area, for they all knew that his father was a Greek. 4 As they traveled from town to town, they delivered the decisions reached by the apostles and elders in Jerusalem for the people to obey. 5 So the churches were strengthened in the faith and grew daily in numbers.

Paul's Vision of the Man of Macedonia

6 Paul and his companions traveled throughout the region of Phrygia and Galatia, having been kept by the Holy Spirit from preaching the word in the province of Asia. 7 When they came to the border of Mysia, they tried to enter Bithynia, but the Spirit of Jesus would not allow them to. 8 So they passed by Mysia and went down to Troas. 9 During the night Paul had a vision of a man of Macedonia standing and begging him, "Come over to Macedonia and help us." 10 After Paul had seen the vision, we got ready at once to leave for Macedonia, concluding that God had called us to preach the gospel to them.

Lydia's Conversion in Philippi

11 From Troas we put out to sea and sailed straight for Samothrace, and the next day we went on to Neapolis. 12 From there we traveled to Philippi, a Roman colony and the leading city of that district[a] of Macedonia. And we stayed there several days.

13 On the Sabbath we went outside the city gate to the river, where we expected to find a place of prayer. We sat down and began to speak to the women who had gathered there. 14 One of those listening was a woman from the city of Thyatira named Lydia, a dealer in purple cloth. She was a worshiper of God. The Lord opened her heart to respond to Paul's message. 15 When she and the members of her household were baptized, she invited us to her home. "If you consider me a believer in the Lord," she said, "come and stay at my house." And she persuaded us.

Paul and Silas in Prison

16 Once when we were going to the place of prayer, we were met by a female slave who had a spirit by which she predicted the future. She earned a great deal of money for her owners by fortune-telling. 17 She followed Paul and the rest of us, shouting, "These men are servants of the Most High God, who are telling you the way to be saved." 18 She kept this up for many days. Finally Paul became so annoyed that he turned around and said to the spirit, "In the name of Jesus Christ I command you to come out of her!" At that moment the spirit left her.

19 When her owners realized that their hope of making money was gone, they seized Paul and Silas and dragged them into the marketplace to face the authorities. 20 They brought them before the magistrates and said, "These men are Jews, and are throwing our city into an uproar 21 by advocating customs unlawful for us Romans to accept or practice."

22 The crowd joined in the attack against Paul and Silas, and the magistrates ordered them to be stripped and beaten with rods. 23 After they had been severely flogged, they were thrown into prison, and the jailer was commanded to guard them carefully. 24 When he received these orders, he put them in the inner cell and fastened their feet in the stocks.

25 About midnight Paul and Silas were praying and singing hymns to God, and the other prisoners were listening to them. 26 Suddenly there was such a violent earthquake that the foundations of the prison were shaken. At once all the prison doors flew open, and everyone's chains came loose. 27 The jailer woke up, and when he saw the prison doors open, he drew his sword and was about to kill himself because he thought the prisoners had escaped. 28 But Paul shouted, "Don't harm yourself! We are all here!"

29 The jailer called for lights, rushed in and fell trembling before Paul and Silas. 30 He then brought them out and asked, "Sirs, what must I do to be saved?"

[a] *12* The text and meaning of the Greek for *the leading city of that district* are uncertain.

31They replied, "Believe in the Lord
Jesus, and you will be saved — you and
your household." 32Then they spoke the
word of the Lord to him and to all the
others in his house. 33At that hour of the
night the jailer took them and washed
their wounds; then immediately he and
all his household were baptized. 34The
jailer brought them into his house and
set a meal before them; he was filled with
joy because he had come to believe in
God — he and his whole household.

35When it was daylight, the magistrates
sent their officers to the jailer with the
order: "Release those men." 36The jailer
told Paul, "The magistrates have ordered
that you and Silas be released. Now you
can leave. Go in peace."

37But Paul said to the officers: "They
beat us publicly without a trial, even
though we are Roman citizens, and threw
us into prison. And now do they want to
get rid of us quietly? No! Let them come
themselves and escort us out."

38The officers reported this to the magistrates, and when they heard that Paul
and Silas were Roman citizens, they were
alarmed. 39They came to appease them
and escorted them from the prison, re-
questing them to leave the city. 40After
Paul and Silas came out of the prison, they
went to Lydia's house, where they met with
the brothers and sisters and encouraged
them. Then they left.

In Thessalonica

17 When Paul and his companions had
passed through Amphipolis and Ap-
ollonia, they came to Thessalonica, where
there was a Jewish synagogue. 2As was his
custom, Paul went into the synagogue,
and on three Sabbath days he reasoned
with them from the Scriptures, 3explain-
ing and proving that the Messiah had to
suffer and rise from the dead. "This Jesus
I am proclaiming to you is the Messiah,"
he said. 4Some of the Jews were persuaded
and joined Paul and Silas, as did a large
number of God-fearing Greeks and quite
a few prominent women.

5But other Jews were jealous; so they
rounded up some bad characters from the
marketplace, formed a mob and started
a riot in the city. They rushed to Jason's
house in search of Paul and Silas in order
to bring them out to the crowd.[a] 6But when
they did not find them, they dragged Jason and some other believers before the
city officials, shouting: "These men who
have caused trouble all over the world
have now come here, 7and Jason has welcomed them into his house. They are all
defying Caesar's decrees, saying that there
is another king, one called Jesus." 8When
they heard this, the crowd and the city
officials were thrown into turmoil. 9Then
they made Jason and the others post bond
and let them go.

In Berea

10As soon as it was night, the believers
sent Paul and Silas away to Berea. On
arriving there, they went to the Jewish
synagogue. 11Now the Berean Jews were of
more noble character than those in Thessalonica, for they received the message
with great eagerness and examined the
Scriptures every day to see if what Paul
said was true. 12As a result, many of them
believed, as did also a number of prominent Greek women and many Greek men.

13But when the Jews in Thessalonica
learned that Paul was preaching the word
of God at Berea, some of them went there
too, agitating the crowds and stirring
them up. 14The believers immediately sent
Paul to the coast, but Silas and Timothy
stayed at Berea. 15Those who escorted Paul
brought him to Athens and then left with
instructions for Silas and Timothy to join
him as soon as possible.

In Athens

16While Paul was waiting for them in
Athens, he was greatly distressed to see
that the city was full of idols. 17So he reasoned in the synagogue with both Jews
and God-fearing Greeks, as well as in the
marketplace day by day with those who
happened to be there. 18A group of Epi-
curean and Stoic philosophers began to
debate with him. Some of them asked,
"What is this babbler trying to say?" Others remarked, "He seems to be advocating
foreign gods." They said this because Paul
was preaching the good news about Jesus
and the resurrection. 19Then they took him
and brought him to a meeting of the Areopagus, where they said to him, "May we
know what this new teaching is that you
are presenting? 20You are bringing some
strange ideas to our ears, and we would
like to know what they mean." 21(All the
Athenians and the foreigners who lived
there spent their time doing nothing but
talking about and listening to the latest
ideas.)

22Paul then stood up in the meeting of
the Areopagus and said: "People of Athens! I see that in every way you are very

[a] 5 Or *the assembly of the people*

religious. 23For as I walked around and
looked carefully at your objects of worship,
I even found an altar with this inscription:
TO AN UNKNOWN GOD. So you are ignorant
of the very thing you worship — and this
is what I am going to proclaim to you.
24"The God who made the world and
everything in it is the Lord of heaven and
earth and does not live in temples built by
human hands. 25And he is not served by
human hands, as if he needed anything.
Rather, he himself gives everyone life
and breath and everything else. 26From
one man he made all the nations, that
they should inhabit the whole earth; and
he marked out their appointed times in
history and the boundaries of their lands.
27God did this so that they would seek him
and perhaps reach out for him and find
him, though he is not far from any one
of us. 28'For in him we live and move and
have our being.'[a] As some of your own
poets have said, 'We are his offspring.'[b]
29"Therefore since we are God's offspring, we should not think that the divine
being is like gold or silver or stone — an
image made by human design and skill.
30In the past God overlooked such ignorance, but now he commands all people
everywhere to repent. 31For he has set a
day when he will judge the world with justice by the man he has appointed. He has
given proof of this to everyone by raising
him from the dead."
32When they heard about the resurrection of the dead, some of them sneered,
but others said, "We want to hear you
again on this subject." 33At that, Paul left
the Council. 34Some of the people became
followers of Paul and believed. Among
them was Dionysius, a member of the Areopagus, also a woman named Damaris,
and a number of others.

In Corinth

18 After this, Paul left Athens and
went to Corinth. 2There he met a
Jew named Aquila, a native of Pontus,
who had recently come from Italy with
his wife Priscilla, because Claudius had
ordered all Jews to leave Rome. Paul went
to see them, 3and because he was a tent-
maker as they were, he stayed and worked
with them. 4Every Sabbath he reasoned in
the synagogue, trying to persuade Jews
and Greeks.
5When Silas and Timothy came from
Macedonia, Paul devoted himself exclu-
sively to preaching, testifying to the Jews
that Jesus was the Messiah. 6But when
they opposed Paul and became abusive,
he shook out his clothes in protest and
said to them, "Your blood be on your own
heads! I am innocent of it. From now on I
will go to the Gentiles."
7Then Paul left the synagogue and went
next door to the house of Titius Justus,
a worshiper of God. 8Crispus, the synagogue leader, and his entire household
believed in the Lord; and many of the
Corinthians who heard Paul believed and
were baptized.
9One night the Lord spoke to Paul in a
vision: "Do not be afraid; keep on speaking, do not be silent. 10For I am with you,
and no one is going to attack and harm
you, because I have many people in this
city." 11So Paul stayed in Corinth for a year
and a half, teaching them the word of God.
12While Gallio was proconsul of Achaia,
the Jews of Corinth made a united attack
on Paul and brought him to the place of
judgment. 13"This man," they charged, "is
persuading the people to worship God in
ways contrary to the law."
14Just as Paul was about to speak, Gallio
said to them, "If you Jews were making a
complaint about some misdemeanor or serious crime, it would be reasonable for me
to listen to you. 15But since it involves questions about words and names and your
own law — settle the matter yourselves.
I will not be a judge of such things." 16So
he drove them off. 17Then the crowd there
turned on Sosthenes the synagogue leader and beat him in front of the proconsul;
and Gallio showed no concern whatever.

Priscilla, Aquila and Apollos

18Paul stayed on in Corinth for some
time. Then he left the brothers and sisters and sailed for Syria, accompanied by
Priscilla and Aquila. Before he sailed, he
had his hair cut off at Cenchreae because
of a vow he had taken. 19They arrived at
Ephesus, where Paul left Priscilla and Aquila. He himself went into the synagogue
and reasoned with the Jews. 20When they
asked him to spend more time with them,
he declined. 21But as he left, he promised,
"I will come back if it is God's will." Then
he set sail from Ephesus. 22When he landed at Caesarea, he went up to Jerusalem
and greeted the church and then went
down to Antioch.
23After spending some time in Antioch,
Paul set out from there and traveled from
place to place throughout the region of
Galatia and Phrygia, strengthening all
the disciples.

[a] *28* From the Cretan philosopher Epimenides

[b] *28* From the Cilician Stoic philosopher Aratus

24Meanwhile a Jew named Apollos, a
native of Alexandria, came to Ephesus.
He was a learned man, with a thorough
knowledge of the Scriptures. 25He had been
instructed in the way of the Lord, and he
spoke with great fervor[a] and taught about
Jesus accurately, though he knew only
the baptism of John. 26He began to speak
boldly in the synagogue. When Priscilla
and Aquila heard him, they invited him
to their home and explained to him the
way of God more adequately.

27When Apollos wanted to go to Achaia, the brothers and sisters encouraged
him and wrote to the disciples there to
welcome him. When he arrived, he was
a great help to those who by grace had
believed. 28For he vigorously refuted his
Jewish opponents in public debate, proving from the Scriptures that Jesus was
the Messiah.

Paul in Ephesus

19 While Apollos was at Corinth, Paul
took the road through the interior
and arrived at Ephesus. There he found
some disciples 2and asked them, "Did
you receive the Holy Spirit when[b] you
believed?"

They answered, "No, we have not even
heard that there is a Holy Spirit."

3So Paul asked, "Then what baptism
did you receive?"

"John's baptism," they replied.

4Paul said, "John's baptism was a baptism of repentance. He told the people to
believe in the one coming after him, that
is, in Jesus." 5On hearing this, they were
baptized in the name of the Lord Jesus.
6When Paul placed his hands on them, the
Holy Spirit came on them, and they spoke
in tongues[c] and prophesied. 7There were
about twelve men in all.

8Paul entered the synagogue and spoke
boldly there for three months, arguing
persuasively about the kingdom of God.
9But some of them became obstinate; they
refused to believe and publicly maligned
the Way. So Paul left them. He took the disciples with him and had discussions daily
in the lecture hall of Tyrannus. 10This went
on for two years, so that all the Jews and
Greeks who lived in the province of Asia
heard the word of the Lord.

11God did extraordinary miracles
through Paul, 12so that even handker-
chiefs and aprons that had touched him
were taken to the sick, and their illnesses
were cured and the evil spirits left them.

13Some Jews who went around driving
out evil spirits tried to invoke the name
of the Lord Jesus over those who were
demon-possessed. They would say, "In
the name of the Jesus whom Paul preaches, I command you to come out." 14Seven
sons of Sceva, a Jewish chief priest, were
doing this. 15One day the evil spirit answered them, "Jesus I know, and Paul I
know about, but who are you?" 16Then the
man who had the evil spirit jumped on
them and overpowered them all. He gave
them such a beating that they ran out of
the house naked and bleeding.

17When this became known to the Jews
and Greeks living in Ephesus, they were all
seized with fear, and the name of the Lord
Jesus was held in high honor. 18Many of
those who believed now came and openly
confessed what they had done. 19A number
who had practiced sorcery brought their
scrolls together and burned them publicly. When they calculated the value of the
scrolls, the total came to fifty thousand
drachmas.[d] 20In this way the word of the
Lord spread widely and grew in power.

21After all this had happened, Paul decided[e] to go to Jerusalem, passing through
Macedonia and Achaia. "After I have been
there," he said, "I must visit Rome also."
22He sent two of his helpers, Timothy and
Erastus, to Macedonia, while he stayed in
the province of Asia a little longer.

The Riot in Ephesus

23About that time there arose a great
disturbance about the Way. 24A silversmith
named Demetrius, who made silver shrines
of Artemis, brought in a lot of business for
the craftsmen there. 25He called them together, along with the workers in related
trades, and said: "You know, my friends,
that we receive a good income from this
business. 26And you see and hear how this
fellow Paul has convinced and led astray
large numbers of people here in Ephesus
and in practically the whole province of
Asia. He says that gods made by human
hands are no gods at all. 27There is danger not only that our trade will lose its
good name, but also that the temple of the
great goddess Artemis will be discredited;
and the goddess herself, who is worshiped
throughout the province of Asia and the
world, will be robbed of her divine majesty."

28When they heard this, they were furious and began shouting: "Great is Artemis of the Ephesians!" 29Soon the whole
city was in an uproar. The people seized

[a] *25* Or *with fervor in the Spirit* [b] *2* Or *after* [c] *6* Or *other languages* [d] *19* A drachma was a silver coin worth about a day's wages. [e] *21* Or *decided in the Spirit*

Gaius and Aristarchus, Paul's traveling
companions from Macedonia, and all
of them rushed into the theater together. 30Paul wanted to appear before the
crowd, but the disciples would not let him.
31Even some of the officials of the province,
friends of Paul, sent him a message begging him not to venture into the theater.
32The assembly was in confusion: Some
were shouting one thing, some another.
Most of the people did not even know why
they were there. 33The Jews in the crowd
pushed Alexander to the front, and they
shouted instructions to him. He motioned
for silence in order to make a defense before the people. 34But when they realized
he was a Jew, they all shouted in unison
for about two hours: "Great is Artemis of
the Ephesians!"
35The city clerk quieted the crowd and
said: "Fellow Ephesians, doesn't all the
world know that the city of Ephesus is
the guardian of the temple of the great
Artemis and of her image, which fell from
heaven? 36Therefore, since these facts are
undeniable, you ought to calm down and
not do anything rash. 37You have brought
these men here, though they have neither robbed temples nor blasphemed our
goddess. 38If, then, Demetrius and his fellow craftsmen have a grievance against
anybody, the courts are open and there
are proconsuls. They can press charges.
39If there is anything further you want
to bring up, it must be settled in a legal
assembly. 40As it is, we are in danger of being charged with rioting because of what
happened today. In that case we would not
be able to account for this commotion,
since there is no reason for it." 41After he
had said this, he dismissed the assembly.

Through Macedonia and Greece

20 When the uproar had ended, Paul
sent for the disciples and, after encouraging them, said goodbye and set out
for Macedonia. 2He traveled through that
area, speaking many words of encouragement to the people, and finally arrived in
Greece, 3where he stayed three months.
Because some Jews had plotted against
him just as he was about to sail for Syria,
he decided to go back through Macedonia. 4He was accompanied by Sopater
son of Pyrrhus from Berea, Aristarchus
and Secundus from Thessalonica, Gaius
from Derbe, Timothy also, and Tychicus
and Trophimus from the province of Asia.
5These men went on ahead and waited for
us at Troas. 6But we sailed from Philippi
after the Festival of Unleavened Bread,
and five days later joined the others at
Troas, where we stayed seven days.

Eutychus Raised From the Dead at Troas

7On the first day of the week we came
together to break bread. Paul spoke to
the people and, because he intended to
leave the next day, kept on talking until
midnight. 8There were many lamps in
the upstairs room where we were meeting. 9Seated in a window was a young
man named Eutychus, who was sinking
into a deep sleep as Paul talked on and
on. When he was sound asleep, he fell to
the ground from the third story and was
picked up dead. 10Paul went down, threw
himself on the young man and put his
arms around him. "Don't be alarmed,"
he said. "He's alive!" 11Then he went upstairs again and broke bread and ate.
After talking until daylight, he left. 12The
people took the young man home alive
and were greatly comforted.

Paul's Farewell to the Ephesian Elders

13We went on ahead to the ship and sailed
for Assos, where we were going to take Paul
aboard. He had made this arrangement
because he was going there on foot. 14When
he met us at Assos, we took him aboard and
went on to Mitylene. 15The next day we set
sail from there and arrived off Chios. The
day after that we crossed over to Samos,
and on the following day arrived at Miletus.
16Paul had decided to sail past Ephesus to
avoid spending time in the province of Asia,
for he was in a hurry to reach Jerusalem, if
possible, by the day of Pentecost.
17From Miletus, Paul sent to Ephesus
for the elders of the church. 18When they
arrived, he said to them: "You know how I
lived the whole time I was with you, from
the first day I came into the province of
Asia. 19I served the Lord with great humility and with tears and in the midst of
severe testing by the plots of my Jewish
opponents. 20You know that I have not
hesitated to preach anything that would
be helpful to you but have taught you
publicly and from house to house. 21I have
declared to both Jews and Greeks that they
must turn to God in repentance and have
faith in our Lord Jesus.
22"And now, compelled by the Spirit, I
am going to Jerusalem, not knowing what
will happen to me there. 23I only know
that in every city the Holy Spirit warns
me that prison and hardships are facing
me. 24However, I consider my life worth
nothing to me; my only aim is to finish
the race and complete the task the Lord
Jesus has given me — the task of testifying
to the good news of God's grace.

25 "Now I know that none of you among
whom I have gone about preaching the
kingdom will ever see me again. 26 Therefore, I declare to you today that I am innocent of the blood of any of you. 27 For I have
not hesitated to proclaim to you the whole
will of God. 28 Keep watch over yourselves
and all the flock of which the Holy Spirit
has made you overseers. Be shepherds of
the church of God,[a] which he bought with
his own blood.[b] 29 I know that after I leave,
savage wolves will come in among you and
will not spare the flock. 30 Even from your
own number men will arise and distort the
truth in order to draw away disciples after
them. 31 So be on your guard! Remember
that for three years I never stopped warning each of you night and day with tears.

32 "Now I commit you to God and to the
word of his grace, which can build you
up and give you an inheritance among
all those who are sanctified. 33 I have not
coveted anyone's silver or gold or clothing.
34 You yourselves know that these hands of
mine have supplied my own needs and the
needs of my companions. 35 In everything I
did, I showed you that by this kind of hard
work we must help the weak, remembering the words the Lord Jesus himself said:
'It is more blessed to give than to receive.' "

36 When Paul had finished speaking, he
knelt down with all of them and prayed.
37 They all wept as they embraced him and
kissed him. 38 What grieved them most was
his statement that they would never see
his face again. Then they accompanied
him to the ship.

On to Jerusalem

21 After we had torn ourselves away
from them, we put out to sea and
sailed straight to Kos. The next day we
went to Rhodes and from there to Patara.
2 We found a ship crossing over to Phoenicia, went on board and set sail. 3 After
sighting Cyprus and passing to the south
of it, we sailed on to Syria. We landed at
Tyre, where our ship was to unload its cargo. 4 We sought out the disciples there and
stayed with them seven days. Through
the Spirit they urged Paul not to go on to
Jerusalem. 5 When it was time to leave,
we left and continued on our way. All of
them, including wives and children, accompanied us out of the city, and there on
the beach we knelt to pray. 6 After saying
goodbye to each other, we went aboard
the ship, and they returned home.

7 We continued our voyage from Tyre
and landed at Ptolemais, where we greeted the brothers and sisters and stayed with
them for a day. 8 Leaving the next day, we
reached Caesarea and stayed at the house
of Philip the evangelist, one of the Seven.
9 He had four unmarried daughters who
prophesied.

10 After we had been there a number
of days, a prophet named Agabus came
down from Judea. 11 Coming over to us,
he took Paul's belt, tied his own hands
and feet with it and said, "The Holy Spirit says, 'In this way the Jewish leaders in
Jerusalem will bind the owner of this belt
and will hand him over to the Gentiles.' "

12 When we heard this, we and the people
there pleaded with Paul not to go up to
Jerusalem. 13 Then Paul answered, "Why
are you weeping and breaking my heart?
I am ready not only to be bound, but also
to die in Jerusalem for the name of the
Lord Jesus." 14 When he would not be dis-
suaded, we gave up and said, "The Lord's
will be done."

15 After this, we started on our way up to
Jerusalem. 16 Some of the disciples from
Caesarea accompanied us and brought us
to the home of Mnason, where we were to
stay. He was a man from Cyprus and one
of the early disciples.

Paul's Arrival at Jerusalem

17 When we arrived at Jerusalem, the
brothers and sisters received us warmly.
18 The next day Paul and the rest of us
went to see James, and all the elders were
present. 19 Paul greeted them and reported
in detail what God had done among the
Gentiles through his ministry.

20 When they heard this, they praised
God. Then they said to Paul: "You see,
brother, how many thousands of Jews
have believed, and all of them are zealous
for the law. 21 They have been informed
that you teach all the Jews who live among
the Gentiles to turn away from Moses,
telling them not to circumcise their children or live according to our customs.
22 What shall we do? They will certainly
hear that you have come, 23 so do what
we tell you. There are four men with us
who have made a vow. 24 Take these men,
join in their purification rites and pay
their expenses, so that they can have their
heads shaved. Then everyone will know
there is no truth in these reports about
you, but that you yourself are living in
obedience to the law. 25 As for the Gentile
believers, we have written to them our
decision that they should abstain from
food sacrificed to idols, from blood, from

[a] *28* Many manuscripts *of the Lord* [b] *28* Or *with the blood of his own Son*

the meat of strangled animals and from
sexual immorality."
26 The next day Paul took the men and
purified himself along with them. Then he
went to the temple to give notice of the
date when the days of purification would
end and the offering would be made for
each of them.

Paul Arrested

27 When the seven days were nearly over,
some Jews from the province of Asia saw
Paul at the temple. They stirred up the
whole crowd and seized him, 28 shouting,
"Fellow Israelites, help us! This is the man
who teaches everyone everywhere against
our people and our law and this place.
And besides, he has brought Greeks into
the temple and defiled this holy place."
29 (They had previously seen Trophimus
the Ephesian in the city with Paul and
assumed that Paul had brought him into
the temple.)
30 The whole city was aroused, and the
people came running from all directions.
Seizing Paul, they dragged him from the
temple, and immediately the gates were
shut. 31 While they were trying to kill him,
news reached the commander of the Roman troops that the whole city of Jerusalem was in an uproar. 32 He at once took
some officers and soldiers and ran down
to the crowd. When the rioters saw the
commander and his soldiers, they stopped
beating Paul.
33 The commander came up and arrested him and ordered him to be bound
with two chains. Then he asked who he
was and what he had done. 34 Some in
the crowd shouted one thing and some
another, and since the commander could
not get at the truth because of the uproar,
he ordered that Paul be taken into the
barracks. 35 When Paul reached the steps,
the violence of the mob was so great he
had to be carried by the soldiers. 36 The
crowd that followed kept shouting, "Get
rid of him!"

Paul Speaks to the Crowd

37 As the soldiers were about to take Paul
into the barracks, he asked the commander, "May I say something to you?"
"Do you speak Greek?" he replied.
38 "Aren't you the Egyptian who started
a revolt and led four thousand terrorists
out into the wilderness some time ago?"
39 Paul answered, "I am a Jew, from Tarsus in Cilicia, a citizen of no ordinary city.
Please let me speak to the people."
40 After receiving the commander's
permission, Paul stood on the steps and
motioned to the crowd. When they were
all silent, he said to them in Aramaic[a]:
22 1 "Brothers and fathers, listen now
to my defense."
2 When they heard him speak to them in
Aramaic, they became very quiet.
Then Paul said: 3 "I am a Jew, born in
Tarsus of Cilicia, but brought up in this
city. I studied under Gamaliel and was
thoroughly trained in the law of our ancestors. I was just as zealous for God as
any of you are today. 4 I persecuted the
followers of this Way to their death, arresting both men and women and throwing
them into prison, 5 as the high priest and
all the Council can themselves testify. I
even obtained letters from them to their
associates in Damascus, and went there
to bring these people as prisoners to Jerusalem to be punished.
6 "About noon as I came near Damascus, suddenly a bright light from heaven
flashed around me. 7 I fell to the ground
and heard a voice say to me, 'Saul! Saul!
Why do you persecute me?'
8 " 'Who are you, Lord?' I asked.
" 'I am Jesus of Nazareth, whom you are
persecuting,' he replied. 9 My companions
saw the light, but they did not understand
the voice of him who was speaking to me.
10 " 'What shall I do, Lord?' I asked.
" 'Get up,' the Lord said, 'and go into
Damascus. There you will be told all that
you have been assigned to do.' 11 My companions led me by the hand into Damascus, because the brilliance of the light
had blinded me.
12 "A man named Ananias came to see
me. He was a devout observer of the law
and highly respected by all the Jews
living there. 13 He stood beside me and
said, 'Brother Saul, receive your sight!'
And at that very moment I was able to
see him.
14 "Then he said: 'The God of our ancestors has chosen you to know his will and to
see the Righteous One and to hear words
from his mouth. 15 You will be his witness
to all people of what you have seen and
heard. 16 And now what are you waiting
for? Get up, be baptized and wash your
sins away, calling on his name.'
17 "When I returned to Jerusalem and
was praying at the temple, I fell into a
trance 18 and saw the Lord speaking to me.
'Quick!' he said. 'Leave Jerusalem immediately, because the people here will not
accept your testimony about me.'

[a] 40 Or possibly *Hebrew*; also in 22:2

19" 'Lord,' I replied, 'these people know
that I went from one synagogue to another to imprison and beat those who
believe in you. 20And when the blood of
your martyr[a] Stephen was shed, I stood
there giving my approval and guarding
the clothes of those who were killing him.'
21"Then the Lord said to me, 'Go; I will
send you far away to the Gentiles.' "

Paul the Roman Citizen

22The crowd listened to Paul until he
said this. Then they raised their voices
and shouted, "Rid the earth of him! He's
not fit to live!"
23As they were shouting and throwing
off their cloaks and flinging dust into the
air, 24the commander ordered that Paul be
taken into the barracks. He directed that he
be flogged and interrogated in order to find
out why the people were shouting at him
like this. 25As they stretched him out to flog
him, Paul said to the centurion standing
there, "Is it legal for you to flog a Roman
citizen who hasn't even been found guilty?"
26When the centurion heard this, he
went to the commander and reported it.
"What are you going to do?" he asked.
"This man is a Roman citizen."
27The commander went to Paul and
asked, "Tell me, are you a Roman citizen?"
"Yes, I am," he answered.
28Then the commander said, "I had to
pay a lot of money for my citizenship."
"But I was born a citizen," Paul replied.
29Those who were about to interrogate
him withdrew immediately. The commander himself was alarmed when he
realized that he had put Paul, a Roman
citizen, in chains.

Paul Before the Sanhedrin

30The commander wanted to find out
exactly why Paul was being accused by
the Jews. So the next day he released him
and ordered the chief priests and all the
members of the Sanhedrin to assemble.
Then he brought Paul and had him stand
before them.
23 Paul looked straight at the Sanhedrin and said, "My brothers, I
have fulfilled my duty to God in all good
conscience to this day." 2At this the high
priest Ananias ordered those standing
near Paul to strike him on the mouth.
3Then Paul said to him, "God will strike
you, you whitewashed wall! You sit there
to judge me according to the law, yet you
yourself violate the law by commanding
that I be struck!"
4Those who were standing near Paul
said, "How dare you insult God's high
priest!"
5Paul replied, "Brothers, I did not realize
that he was the high priest; for it is written: 'Do not speak evil about the ruler of
your people.'[b]"
6Then Paul, knowing that some of them
were Sadducees and the others Pharisees,
called out in the Sanhedrin, "My brothers,
I am a Pharisee, descended from Pharisees. I stand on trial because of the hope
of the resurrection of the dead." 7When
he said this, a dispute broke out between
the Pharisees and the Sadducees, and the
assembly was divided. 8(The Sadducees
say that there is no resurrection, and that
there are neither angels nor spirits, but
the Pharisees believe all these things.)
9There was a great uproar, and some of
the teachers of the law who were Pharisees stood up and argued vigorously. "We
find nothing wrong with this man," they
said. "What if a spirit or an angel has
spoken to him?" 10The dispute became so
violent that the commander was afraid
Paul would be torn to pieces by them. He
ordered the troops to go down and take
him away from them by force and bring
him into the barracks.
11The following night the Lord stood
near Paul and said, "Take courage! As you
have testified about me in Jerusalem, so
you must also testify in Rome."

The Plot to Kill Paul

12The next morning some Jews formed
a conspiracy and bound themselves with
an oath not to eat or drink until they had
killed Paul. 13More than forty men were involved in this plot. 14They went to the chief
priests and the elders and said, "We have
taken a solemn oath not to eat anything
until we have killed Paul. 15Now then, you
and the Sanhedrin petition the commander to bring him before you on the pretext
of wanting more accurate information
about his case. We are ready to kill him
before he gets here."
16But when the son of Paul's sister heard
of this plot, he went into the barracks and
told Paul.
17Then Paul called one of the centurions and said, "Take this young man to
the commander; he has something to tell
him." 18So he took him to the commander.
The centurion said, "Paul, the prisoner,
sent for me and asked me to bring this
young man to you because he has something to tell you."

[a] 20 Or *witness* [b] 5 Exodus 22:28

19 The commander took the young man by the hand, drew him aside and asked, "What is it you want to tell me?"

20 He said: "Some Jews have agreed to ask you to bring Paul before the Sanhedrin tomorrow on the pretext of wanting more accurate information about him. 21 Don't give in to them, because more than forty of them are waiting in ambush for him. They have taken an oath not to eat or drink until they have killed him. They are ready now, waiting for your consent to their request."

22 The commander dismissed the young man with this warning: "Don't tell anyone that you have reported this to me."

Paul Transferred to Caesarea

23 Then he called two of his centurions and ordered them, "Get ready a detachment of two hundred soldiers, seventy horsemen and two hundred spearmen[a] to go to Caesarea at nine tonight. 24 Provide horses for Paul so that he may be taken safely to Governor Felix."

25 He wrote a letter as follows:

> 26 Claudius Lysias,
>
> To His Excellency, Governor Felix:
>
> Greetings.
>
> 27 This man was seized by the Jews and they were about to kill him, but I came with my troops and rescued him, for I had learned that he is a Roman citizen. 28 I wanted to know why they were accusing him, so I brought him to their Sanhedrin. 29 I found that the accusation had to do with questions about their law, but there was no charge against him that deserved death or imprisonment. 30 When I was informed of a plot to be carried out against the man, I sent him to you at once. I also ordered his accusers to present to you their case against him.

31 So the soldiers, carrying out their orders, took Paul with them during the night and brought him as far as Antipatris. 32 The next day they let the cavalry go on with him, while they returned to the barracks. 33 When the cavalry arrived in Caesarea, they delivered the letter to the governor and handed Paul over to him. 34 The governor read the letter and asked what province he was from. Learning that he was from Cilicia, 35 he said, "I will hear your case when your accusers get here." Then he ordered that Paul be kept under guard in Herod's palace.

Paul's Trial Before Felix

24 Five days later the high priest Ananias went down to Caesarea with some of the elders and a lawyer named Tertullus, and they brought their charges against Paul before the governor. 2 When Paul was called in, Tertullus presented his case before Felix: "We have enjoyed a long period of peace under you, and your foresight has brought about reforms in this nation. 3 Everywhere and in every way, most excellent Felix, we acknowledge this with profound gratitude. 4 But in order not to weary you further, I would request that you be kind enough to hear us briefly.

5 "We have found this man to be a troublemaker, stirring up riots among the Jews all over the world. He is a ringleader of the Nazarene sect 6 and even tried to desecrate the temple; so we seized him. [7][b] 8 By examining him yourself you will be able to learn the truth about all these charges we are bringing against him."

9 The other Jews joined in the accusation, asserting that these things were true.

10 When the governor motioned for him to speak, Paul replied: "I know that for a number of years you have been a judge over this nation; so I gladly make my defense. 11 You can easily verify that no more than twelve days ago I went up to Jerusalem to worship. 12 My accusers did not find me arguing with anyone at the temple, or stirring up a crowd in the synagogues or anywhere else in the city. 13 And they cannot prove to you the charges they are now making against me. 14 However, I admit that I worship the God of our ancestors as a follower of the Way, which they call a sect. I believe everything that is in accordance with the Law and that is written in the Prophets, 15 and I have the same hope in God as these men themselves have, that there will be a resurrection of both the righteous and the wicked. 16 So I strive always to keep my conscience clear before God and man.

17 "After an absence of several years, I came to Jerusalem to bring my people gifts for the poor and to present offerings. 18 I was ceremonially clean when they found me in the temple courts doing this. There was no crowd with me, nor was I involved in any disturbance. 19 But

[a] *23* The meaning of the Greek for this word is uncertain. [b] *6-8* Some manuscripts include here *him, and we would have judged him in accordance with our law. 7 But the commander Lysias came and took him from us with much violence, 8 ordering his accusers to come before you.*

there are some Jews from the province of Asia, who ought to be here before you and bring charges if they have anything against me. 20Or these who are here should state what crime they found in me when I stood before the Sanhedrin— 21unless it was this one thing I shouted as I stood in their presence: 'It is concerning the resurrection of the dead that I am on trial before you today.'"

22Then Felix, who was well acquainted with the Way, adjourned the proceedings. "When Lysias the commander comes," he said, "I will decide your case." 23He ordered the centurion to keep Paul under guard but to give him some freedom and permit his friends to take care of his needs.

24Several days later Felix came with his wife Drusilla, who was Jewish. He sent for Paul and listened to him as he spoke about faith in Christ Jesus. 25As Paul talked about righteousness, self-control and the judgment to come, Felix was afraid and said, "That's enough for now! You may leave. When I find it convenient, I will send for you." 26At the same time he was hoping that Paul would offer him a bribe, so he sent for him frequently and talked with him.

27When two years had passed, Felix was succeeded by Porcius Festus, but because Felix wanted to grant a favor to the Jews, he left Paul in prison.

Paul's Trial Before Festus

25 Three days after arriving in the province, Festus went up from Caesarea to Jerusalem, 2where the chief priests and the Jewish leaders appeared before him and presented the charges against Paul. 3They requested Festus, as a favor to them, to have Paul transferred to Jerusalem, for they were preparing an ambush to kill him along the way. 4Festus answered, "Paul is being held at Caesarea, and I myself am going there soon. 5Let some of your leaders come with me, and if the man has done anything wrong, they can press charges against him there."

6After spending eight or ten days with them, Festus went down to Caesarea. The next day he convened the court and ordered that Paul be brought before him. 7When Paul came in, the Jews who had come down from Jerusalem stood around him. They brought many serious charges against him, but they could not prove them.

8Then Paul made his defense: "I have done nothing wrong against the Jewish law or against the temple or against Caesar."

9Festus, wishing to do the Jews a favor, said to Paul, "Are you willing to go up to Jerusalem and stand trial before me there on these charges?"

10Paul answered: "I am now standing before Caesar's court, where I ought to be tried. I have not done any wrong to the Jews, as you yourself know very well. 11If, however, I am guilty of doing anything deserving death, I do not refuse to die. But if the charges brought against me by these Jews are not true, no one has the right to hand me over to them. I appeal to Caesar!"

12After Festus had conferred with his council, he declared: "You have appealed to Caesar. To Caesar you will go!"

Festus Consults King Agrippa

13A few days later King Agrippa and Bernice arrived at Caesarea to pay their respects to Festus. 14Since they were spending many days there, Festus discussed Paul's case with the king. He said: "There is a man here whom Felix left as a prisoner. 15When I went to Jerusalem, the chief priests and the elders of the Jews brought charges against him and asked that he be condemned.

16"I told them that it is not the Roman custom to hand over anyone before they have faced their accusers and have had an opportunity to defend themselves against the charges. 17When they came here with me, I did not delay the case, but convened the court the next day and ordered the man to be brought in. 18When his accusers got up to speak, they did not charge him with any of the crimes I had expected. 19Instead, they had some points of dispute with him about their own religion and about a dead man named Jesus who Paul claimed was alive. 20I was at a loss how to investigate such matters; so I asked if he would be willing to go to Jerusalem and stand trial there on these charges. 21But when Paul made his appeal to be held over for the Emperor's decision, I ordered him held until I could send him to Caesar."

22Then Agrippa said to Festus, "I would like to hear this man myself."

He replied, "Tomorrow you will hear him."

Paul Before Agrippa

23The next day Agrippa and Bernice came with great pomp and entered the audience room with the high-ranking military officers and the prominent men of the city. At the command of Festus, Paul was brought in. 24Festus said: "King Agrippa, and all who are present with us,

you see this man! The whole Jewish community has petitioned me about him in
Jerusalem and here in Caesarea, shouting
that he ought not to live any longer. 25I
found he had done nothing deserving of
death, but because he made his appeal
to the Emperor I decided to send him to
Rome. 26But I have nothing definite to
write to His Majesty about him. Therefore I have brought him before all of you,
and especially before you, King Agrippa,
so that as a result of this investigation I
may have something to write. 27For I think
it is unreasonable to send a prisoner on
to Rome without specifying the charges
against him."

26 Then Agrippa said to Paul, "You have
permission to speak for yourself."
So Paul motioned with his hand and began his defense: 2"King Agrippa, I consider
myself fortunate to stand before you today
as I make my defense against all the accusations of the Jews, 3and especially so because you are well acquainted with all the
Jewish customs and controversies. Therefore, I beg you to listen to me patiently.
4"The Jewish people all know the way
I have lived ever since I was a child, from
the beginning of my life in my own country, and also in Jerusalem. 5They have
known me for a long time and can testify, if they are willing, that I conformed
to the strictest sect of our religion, living
as a Pharisee. 6And now it is because of
my hope in what God has promised our
ancestors that I am on trial today. 7This is
the promise our twelve tribes are hoping
to see fulfilled as they earnestly serve God
day and night. King Agrippa, it is because
of this hope that these Jews are accusing
me. 8Why should any of you consider it
incredible that God raises the dead?
9"I too was convinced that I ought to do
all that was possible to oppose the name of
Jesus of Nazareth. 10And that is just what
I did in Jerusalem. On the authority of
the chief priests I put many of the Lord's
people in prison, and when they were put
to death, I cast my vote against them.
11Many a time I went from one synagogue
to another to have them punished, and I
tried to force them to blaspheme. I was
so obsessed with persecuting them that I
even hunted them down in foreign cities.
12"On one of these journeys I was going to Damascus with the authority and
commission of the chief priests. 13About
noon, King Agrippa, as I was on the road,
I saw a light from heaven, brighter than
the sun, blazing around me and my companions. 14We all fell to the ground, and I
heard a voice saying to me in Aramaic,[a]
'Saul, Saul, why do you persecute me? It
is hard for you to kick against the goads.'
15"Then I asked, 'Who are you, Lord?'
"'I am Jesus, whom you are persecuting,'
the Lord replied. 16'Now get up and stand
on your feet. I have appeared to you to
appoint you as a servant and as a witness
of what you have seen and will see of me.
17I will rescue you from your own people
and from the Gentiles. I am sending you
to them 18to open their eyes and turn them
from darkness to light, and from the power
of Satan to God, so that they may receive
forgiveness of sins and a place among
those who are sanctified by faith in me.'
19"So then, King Agrippa, I was not disobedient to the vision from heaven. 20First
to those in Damascus, then to those in Jerusalem and in all Judea, and then to the
Gentiles, I preached that they should repent
and turn to God and demonstrate their repentance by their deeds. 21That is why some
Jews seized me in the temple courts and
tried to kill me. 22But God has helped me to
this very day; so I stand here and testify to
small and great alike. I am saying nothing
beyond what the prophets and Moses said
would happen — 23that the Messiah would
suffer and, as the first to rise from the dead,
would bring the message of light to his own
people and to the Gentiles."
24At this point Festus interrupted Paul's
defense. "You are out of your mind, Paul!"
he shouted. "Your great learning is driving
you insane."
25"I am not insane, most excellent Festus," Paul replied. "What I am saying is
true and reasonable. 26The king is familiar
with these things, and I can speak freely
to him. I am convinced that none of this
has escaped his notice, because it was
not done in a corner. 27King Agrippa, do
you believe the prophets? I know you do."
28Then Agrippa said to Paul, "Do you
think that in such a short time you can
persuade me to be a Christian?"
29Paul replied, "Short time or long — I
pray to God that not only you but all who
are listening to me today may become
what I am, except for these chains."
30The king rose, and with him the governor and Bernice and those sitting with
them. 31After they left the room, they began saying to one another, "This man is
not doing anything that deserves death
or imprisonment."
32Agrippa said to Festus, "This man
could have been set free if he had not
appealed to Caesar."

[a] 14 Or *Hebrew*

Paul Sails for Rome

27 When it was decided that we would
sail for Italy, Paul and some other
prisoners were handed over to a centurion
named Julius, who belonged to the Imperial Regiment. 2We boarded a ship from
Adramyttium about to sail for ports along
the coast of the province of Asia, and we
put out to sea. Aristarchus, a Macedonian
from Thessalonica, was with us.
3The next day we landed at Sidon; and
Julius, in kindness to Paul, allowed him
to go to his friends so they might provide
for his needs. 4From there we put out to
sea again and passed to the lee of Cyprus
because the winds were against us. 5When
we had sailed across the open sea off the
coast of Cilicia and Pamphylia, we landed at Myra in Lycia. 6There the centurion
found an Alexandrian ship sailing for
Italy and put us on board. 7We made slow
headway for many days and had difficulty
arriving off Cnidus. When the wind did not
allow us to hold our course, we sailed to
the lee of Crete, opposite Salmone. 8We
moved along the coast with difficulty and
came to a place called Fair Havens, near
the town of Lasea.
9Much time had been lost, and sailing
had already become dangerous because
by now it was after the Day of Atonement.[a]
So Paul warned them, 10"Men, I can see
that our voyage is going to be disastrous
and bring great loss to ship and cargo,
and to our own lives also." 11But the centurion, instead of listening to what Paul
said, followed the advice of the pilot and
of the owner of the ship. 12Since the harbor
was unsuitable to winter in, the majority
decided that we should sail on, hoping to
reach Phoenix and winter there. This was
a harbor in Crete, facing both southwest
and northwest.

The Storm

13When a gentle south wind began to
blow, they saw their opportunity; so they
weighed anchor and sailed along the
shore of Crete. 14Before very long, a wind
of hurricane force, called the Northeaster,
swept down from the island. 15The ship
was caught by the storm and could not
head into the wind; so we gave way to
it and were driven along. 16As we passed
to the lee of a small island called Cauda,
we were hardly able to make the lifeboat
secure, 17so the men hoisted it aboard.
Then they passed ropes under the ship
itself to hold it together. Because they
were afraid they would run aground on
the sandbars of Syrtis, they lowered the
sea anchor[b] and let the ship be driven
along. 18We took such a violent battering
from the storm that the next day they
began to throw the cargo overboard. 19On
the third day, they threw the ship's tackle
overboard with their own hands. 20When
neither sun nor stars appeared for many
days and the storm continued raging, we
finally gave up all hope of being saved.
21After they had gone a long time without food, Paul stood up before them and
said: "Men, you should have taken my
advice not to sail from Crete; then you
would have spared yourselves this damage and loss. 22But now I urge you to keep
up your courage, because not one of you
will be lost; only the ship will be destroyed.
23Last night an angel of the God to whom
I belong and whom I serve stood beside
me 24and said, 'Do not be afraid, Paul. You
must stand trial before Caesar; and God
has graciously given you the lives of all
who sail with you.' 25So keep up your courage, men, for I have faith in God that it will
happen just as he told me. 26Nevertheless,
we must run aground on some island."

The Shipwreck

27On the fourteenth night we were still
being driven across the Adriatic[c] Sea,
when about midnight the sailors sensed
they were approaching land. 28They took
soundings and found that the water was
a hundred and twenty feet[d] deep. A short
time later they took soundings again and
found it was ninety feet[e] deep. 29Fearing
that we would be dashed against the rocks,
they dropped four anchors from the stern
and prayed for daylight. 30In an attempt
to escape from the ship, the sailors let the
lifeboat down into the sea, pretending
they were going to lower some anchors
from the bow. 31Then Paul said to the centurion and the soldiers, "Unless these men
stay with the ship, you cannot be saved."
32So the soldiers cut the ropes that held
the lifeboat and let it drift away.
33Just before dawn Paul urged them all
to eat. "For the last fourteen days," he said,
"you have been in constant suspense and
have gone without food — you haven't
eaten anything. 34Now I urge you to take
some food. You need it to survive. Not
one of you will lose a single hair from his
head." 35After he said this, he took some
bread and gave thanks to God in front
of them all. Then he broke it and began

[a] *9* That is, Yom Kippur [b] *17* Or *the sails* [c] *27* In ancient times the name referred to an area extending well south of Italy. [d] *28* Or about 37 meters [e] *28* Or about 27 meters

to eat. 36They were all encouraged and
ate some food themselves. 37Altogether
there were 276 of us on board. 38When
they had eaten as much as they wanted,
they lightened the ship by throwing the
grain into the sea.

39When daylight came, they did not recognize the land, but they saw a bay with
a sandy beach, where they decided to run
the ship aground if they could. 40Cutting
loose the anchors, they left them in the
sea and at the same time untied the ropes
that held the rudders. Then they hoisted
the foresail to the wind and made for the
beach. 41But the ship struck a sandbar
and ran aground. The bow stuck fast and
would not move, and the stern was broken to pieces by the pounding of the surf.

42The soldiers planned to kill the prisoners to prevent any of them from swimming
away and escaping. 43But the centurion
wanted to spare Paul's life and kept them
from carrying out their plan. He ordered
those who could swim to jump overboard
first and get to land. 44The rest were to
get there on planks or on other pieces of
the ship. In this way everyone reached
land safely.

Paul Ashore on Malta

28 Once safely on shore, we found out
that the island was called Malta.
2The islanders showed us unusual kindness. They built a fire and welcomed us
all because it was raining and cold. 3Paul
gathered a pile of brushwood and, as he
put it on the fire, a viper, driven out by the
heat, fastened itself on his hand. 4When
the islanders saw the snake hanging from
his hand, they said to each other, "This
man must be a murderer; for though he
escaped from the sea, the goddess Justice
has not allowed him to live." 5But Paul
shook the snake off into the fire and suffered no ill effects. 6The people expected
him to swell up or suddenly fall dead; but
after waiting a long time and seeing nothing unusual happen to him, they changed
their minds and said he was a god.

7There was an estate nearby that belonged to Publius, the chief official of the
island. He welcomed us to his home and
showed us generous hospitality for three
days. 8His father was sick in bed, suffering from fever and dysentery. Paul went
in to see him and, after prayer, placed his
hands on him and healed him. 9When this
had happened, the rest of the sick on the
island came and were cured. 10They honored us in many ways; and when we were
ready to sail, they furnished us with the
supplies we needed.

Paul's Arrival at Rome

11After three months we put out to sea in
a ship that had wintered in the island — it
was an Alexandrian ship with the figure-
head of the twin gods Castor and Pollux.
12We put in at Syracuse and stayed there
three days. 13From there we set sail and
arrived at Rhegium. The next day the
south wind came up, and on the following
day we reached Puteoli. 14There we found
some brothers and sisters who invited us
to spend a week with them. And so we
came to Rome. 15The brothers and sisters
there had heard that we were coming,
and they traveled as far as the Forum of
Appius and the Three Taverns to meet us.
At the sight of these people Paul thanked
God and was encouraged. 16When we got to
Rome, Paul was allowed to live by himself,
with a soldier to guard him.

Paul Preaches at Rome Under Guard

17Three days later he called together the local Jewish leaders. When they
had assembled, Paul said to them: "My
brothers, although I have done nothing
against our people or against the customs of our ancestors, I was arrested in
Jerusalem and handed over to the Romans. 18They examined me and wanted
to release me, because I was not guilty
of any crime deserving death. 19The Jews
objected, so I was compelled to make an
appeal to Caesar. I certainly did not intend to bring any charge against my own
people. 20For this reason I have asked to
see you and talk with you. It is because
of the hope of Israel that I am bound
with this chain."

21They replied, "We have not received
any letters from Judea concerning you,
and none of our people who have come
from there has reported or said anything
bad about you. 22But we want to hear
what your views are, for we know that
people everywhere are talking against
this sect."

23They arranged to meet Paul on a
certain day, and came in even larger
numbers to the place where he was staying. He witnessed to them from morning till evening, explaining about the
kingdom of God, and from the Law of
Moses and from the Prophets he tried
to persuade them about Jesus. 24Some
were convinced by what he said, but others would not believe. 25They disagreed
among themselves and began to leave
after Paul had made this final statement: "The Holy Spirit spoke the truth
to your ancestors when he said through
Isaiah the prophet:

26 " 'Go to this people and say,
"You will be ever hearing but never understanding;
you will be ever seeing but never perceiving."
27 For this people's heart has become calloused;
they hardly hear with their ears,
and they have closed their eyes.
Otherwise they might see with their eyes,
hear with their ears,
understand with their hearts
and turn, and I would heal them.'[a]

28 "Therefore I want you to know that
God's salvation has been sent to the Gentiles, and they will listen!" [29] [b]
30 For two whole years Paul stayed there
in his own rented house and welcomed
all who came to see him. 31 He proclaimed
the kingdom of God and taught about the
Lord Jesus Christ — with all boldness and
without hindrance!

[a] 27 Isaiah 6:9,10 (see Septuagint) [b] 29 Some manuscripts include here *After he said this, the Jews left, arguing vigorously among themselves.*

ROMANS

1 Paul, a servant of Christ Jesus, called to be an apostle and set apart for the gospel of God — 2the gospel he promised beforehand through his prophets in the Holy Scriptures 3regarding his Son, who as to his earthly life[a] was a descendant of David, 4and who through the Spirit of holiness was appointed the Son of God in power[b] by his resurrection from the dead: Jesus Christ our Lord. 5Through him we received grace and apostleship to call all the Gentiles to the obedience that comes from[c] faith for his name's sake. 6And you also are among those Gentiles who are called to belong to Jesus Christ.

7To all in Rome who are loved by God and called to be his holy people:

Grace and peace to you from God our Father and from the Lord Jesus Christ.

Paul's Longing to Visit Rome

8First, I thank my God through Jesus Christ for all of you, because your faith is being reported all over the world. 9God, whom I serve in my spirit in preaching the gospel of his Son, is my witness how constantly I remember you 10in my prayers at all times; and I pray that now at last by God's will the way may be opened for me to come to you.

11I long to see you so that I may impart to you some spiritual gift to make you strong — 12that is, that you and I may be mutually encouraged by each other's faith. 13I do not want you to be unaware, brothers and sisters,[d] that I planned many times to come to you (but have been prevented from doing so until now) in order that I might have a harvest among you, just as I have had among the other Gentiles.

14I am obligated both to Greeks and non-Greeks, both to the wise and the foolish. 15That is why I am so eager to preach the gospel also to you who are in Rome.

16For I am not ashamed of the gospel, because it is the power of God that brings salvation to everyone who believes: first to the Jew, then to the Gentile. 17For in the gospel the righteousness of God is revealed — a righteousness that is by faith from first to last,[e] just as it is written: "The righteous will live by faith."[f]

God's Wrath Against Sinful Humanity

18The wrath of God is being revealed from heaven against all the godlessness and wickedness of people, who suppress the truth by their wickedness, 19since what may be known about God is plain to them, because God has made it plain to them. 20For since the creation of the world God's invisible qualities — his eternal power and divine nature — have been clearly seen, being understood from what has been made, so that people are without excuse.

21For although they knew God, they neither glorified him as God nor gave thanks to him, but their thinking became futile and their foolish hearts were darkened. 22Although they claimed to be wise, they became fools 23and exchanged the glory of the immortal God for images made to look like a mortal human being and birds and animals and reptiles.

24Therefore God gave them over in the sinful desires of their hearts to sexual impurity for the degrading of their bodies with one another. 25They exchanged the truth about God for a lie, and worshiped and served created things rather than the Creator — who is forever praised. Amen.

26Because of this, God gave them over to shameful lusts. Even their women exchanged natural sexual relations for unnatural ones. 27In the same way the men also abandoned natural relations with women and were inflamed with lust for one another. Men committed shameful acts with other men, and received in themselves the due penalty for their error.

28Furthermore, just as they did not think it worthwhile to retain the knowledge of God, so God gave them over to a depraved mind, so that they do what ought not to be done. 29They have become filled with every kind of wickedness, evil, greed and depravity. They are full of envy, murder, strife, deceit and malice. They are gossips, 30slanderers, God-haters, insolent, arrogant and boastful; they invent ways

[a] 3 Or *who according to the flesh* [b] 4 Or *was declared with power to be the Son of God* [c] 5 Or *that is* [d] 13 The Greek word for *brothers and sisters* (*adelphoi*) refers here to believers, both men and women, as part of God's family; also in 7:1, 4; 8:12, 29; 10:1; 11:25; 12:1; 15:14, 30; 16:14, 17. [e] 17 Or *is from faith to faith* [f] 17 Hab. 2:4

of doing evil; they disobey their parents; 31 they have no understanding, no fidelity, no love, no mercy. 32 Although they know God's righteous decree that those who do such things deserve death, they not only continue to do these very things but also approve of those who practice them.

God's Righteous Judgment

2 You, therefore, have no excuse, you who pass judgment on someone else, for at whatever point you judge another, you are condemning yourself, because you who pass judgment do the same things. 2 Now we know that God's judgment against those who do such things is based on truth. 3 So when you, a mere human being, pass judgment on them and yet do the same things, do you think you will escape God's judgment? 4 Or do you show contempt for the riches of his kindness, forbearance and patience, not realizing that God's kindness is intended to lead you to repentance?

5 But because of your stubbornness and your unrepentant heart, you are storing up wrath against yourself for the day of God's wrath, when his righteous judgment will be revealed. 6 God "will repay each person according to what they have done."[a] 7 To those who by persistence in doing good seek glory, honor and immortality, he will give eternal life. 8 But for those who are self-seeking and who reject the truth and follow evil, there will be wrath and anger. 9 There will be trouble and distress for every human being who does evil: first for the Jew, then for the Gentile; 10 but glory, honor and peace for everyone who does good: first for the Jew, then for the Gentile. 11 For God does not show favoritism.

12 All who sin apart from the law will also perish apart from the law, and all who sin under the law will be judged by the law. 13 For it is not those who hear the law who are righteous in God's sight, but it is those who obey the law who will be declared righteous. 14 (Indeed, when Gentiles, who do not have the law, do by nature things required by the law, they are a law for themselves, even though they do not have the law. 15 They show that the requirements of the law are written on their hearts, their consciences also bearing witness, and their thoughts sometimes accusing them and at other times even defending them.) 16 This will take place on the day when God judges people's secrets through Jesus Christ, as my gospel declares.

The Jews and the Law

17 Now you, if you call yourself a Jew; if you rely on the law and boast in God; 18 if you know his will and approve of what is superior because you are instructed by the law; 19 if you are convinced that you are a guide for the blind, a light for those who are in the dark, 20 an instructor of the foolish, a teacher of little children, because you have in the law the embodiment of knowledge and truth — 21 you, then, who teach others, do you not teach yourself? You who preach against stealing, do you steal? 22 You who say that people should not commit adultery, do you commit adultery? You who abhor idols, do you rob temples? 23 You who boast in the law, do you dishonor God by breaking the law? 24 As it is written: "God's name is blasphemed among the Gentiles because of you."[b]

25 Circumcision has value if you observe the law, but if you break the law, you have become as though you had not been circumcised. 26 So then, if those who are not circumcised keep the law's requirements, will they not be regarded as though they were circumcised? 27 The one who is not circumcised physically and yet obeys the law will condemn you who, even though you have the[c] written code and circumcision, are a lawbreaker.

28 A person is not a Jew who is one only outwardly, nor is circumcision merely outward and physical. 29 No, a person is a Jew who is one inwardly; and circumcision is circumcision of the heart, by the Spirit, not by the written code. Such a person's praise is not from other people, but from God.

God's Faithfulness

3 What advantage, then, is there in being a Jew, or what value is there in circumcision? 2 Much in every way! First of all, the Jews have been entrusted with the very words of God.

3 What if some were unfaithful? Will their unfaithfulness nullify God's faithfulness? 4 Not at all! Let God be true, and every human being a liar. As it is written:

"So that you may be proved right
when you speak
and prevail when you judge."[d]

5 But if our unrighteousness brings out God's righteousness more clearly, what shall we say? That God is unjust in bringing his wrath on us? (I am using a human argument.) 6 Certainly not! If that were so, how could God judge the world? 7 Someone

[a] 6 Psalm 62:12; Prov. 24:12 [b] 24 Isaiah 52:5 (see Septuagint); Ezek. 36:20,22 [c] 27 Or *who, by means of a* [d] 4 Psalm 51:4

might argue, "If my falsehood enhances God's truthfulness and so increases his glory, why am I still condemned as a sinner?" 8Why not say — as some slanderously claim that we say — "Let us do evil that good may result"? Their condemnation is just!

No One Is Righteous

9What shall we conclude then? Do we have any advantage? Not at all! For we have already made the charge that Jews and Gentiles alike are all under the power of sin. 10As it is written:

"There is no one righteous, not even one;
11 there is no one who understands;
there is no one who seeks God.
12 All have turned away,
they have together become worthless;
there is no one who does good,
not even one."[a]
13 "Their throats are open graves;
their tongues practice deceit."[b]
"The poison of vipers is on their lips."[c]
14 "Their mouths are full of cursing and bitterness."[d]
15 "Their feet are swift to shed blood;
16 ruin and misery mark their ways,
17 and the way of peace they do not know."[e]
18 "There is no fear of God before their eyes."[f]

19Now we know that whatever the law says, it says to those who are under the law, so that every mouth may be silenced and the whole world held accountable to God. 20Therefore no one will be declared righteous in God's sight by the works of the law; rather, through the law we become conscious of our sin.

Righteousness Through Faith

21But now apart from the law the righteousness of God has been made known, to which the Law and the Prophets testify. 22This righteousness is given through faith in[g] Jesus Christ to all who believe. There is no difference between Jew and Gentile, 23for all have sinned and fall short of the glory of God, 24and all are justified freely by his grace through the redemption that came by Christ Jesus. 25God presented Christ as a sacrifice of atonement,[h] through the shedding of his blood — to be received by faith. He did this to demonstrate his righteousness, because in his forbearance he had left the sins committed beforehand unpunished — 26he did it to demonstrate his righteousness at the present time, so as to be just and the one who justifies those who have faith in Jesus.

27Where, then, is boasting? It is excluded. Because of what law? The law that requires works? No, because of the law that requires faith. 28For we maintain that a person is justified by faith apart from the works of the law. 29Or is God the God of Jews only? Is he not the God of Gentiles too? Yes, of Gentiles too, 30since there is only one God, who will justify the circumcised by faith and the uncircumcised through that same faith. 31Do we, then, nullify the law by this faith? Not at all! Rather, we uphold the law.

Abraham Justified by Faith

4 What then shall we say that Abraham, our forefather according to the flesh, discovered in this matter? 2If, in fact, Abraham was justified by works, he had something to boast about — but not before God. 3What does Scripture say? "Abraham believed God, and it was credited to him as righteousness."[i]

4Now to the one who works, wages are not credited as a gift but as an obligation. 5However, to the one who does not work but trusts God who justifies the ungodly, their faith is credited as righteousness. 6David says the same thing when he speaks of the blessedness of the one to whom God credits righteousness apart from works:

7 "Blessed are those
whose transgressions are forgiven,
whose sins are covered.
8 Blessed is the one
whose sin the Lord will never count against them."[j]

9Is this blessedness only for the circumcised, or also for the uncircumcised? We have been saying that Abraham's faith was credited to him as righteousness. 10Under what circumstances was it credited? Was it after he was circumcised, or before? It was not after, but before! 11And he received circumcision as a sign, a seal of the righteousness that he had by faith while he was still uncircumcised. So then,

[a] *12* Psalms 14:1-3; 53:1-3; Eccles. 7:20 [b] *13* Psalm 5:9 [c] *13* Psalm 140:3 [d] *14* Psalm 10:7 (see Septuagint) [e] *17* Isaiah 59:7,8 [f] *18* Psalm 36:1 [g] *22* Or *through the faithfulness of*
[h] *25* The Greek for *sacrifice of atonement* refers to the atonement cover on the ark of the covenant (see Lev. 16:15,16). [i] *3* Gen. 15:6; also in verse 22 [j] *8* Psalm 32:1,2

he is the father of all who believe but have not been circumcised, in order that righteousness might be credited to them. 12And he is then also the father of the circumcised who not only are circumcised but who also follow in the footsteps of the faith that our father Abraham had before he was circumcised.

13It was not through the law that Abraham and his offspring received the promise that he would be heir of the world, but through the righteousness that comes by faith. 14For if those who depend on the law are heirs, faith means nothing and the promise is worthless, 15because the law brings wrath. And where there is no law there is no transgression.

16Therefore, the promise comes by faith, so that it may be by grace and may be guaranteed to all Abraham's offspring — not only to those who are of the law but also to those who have the faith of Abraham. He is the father of us all. 17As it is written: "I have made you a father of many nations."[a] He is our father in the sight of God, in whom he believed — the God who gives life to the dead and calls into being things that were not.

18Against all hope, Abraham in hope believed and so became the father of many nations, just as it had been said to him, "So shall your offspring be."[b] 19Without weakening in his faith, he faced the fact that his body was as good as dead — since he was about a hundred years old — and that Sarah's womb was also dead. 20Yet he did not waver through unbelief regarding the promise of God, but was strengthened in his faith and gave glory to God, 21being fully persuaded that God had power to do what he had promised. 22This is why "it was credited to him as righteousness." 23The words "it was credited to him" were written not for him alone, 24but also for us, to whom God will credit righteousness — for us who believe in him who raised Jesus our Lord from the dead. 25He was delivered over to death for our sins and was raised to life for our justification.

Peace and Hope

5 Therefore, since we have been justified through faith, we[c] have peace with God through our Lord Jesus Christ, 2through whom we have gained access by faith into this grace in which we now stand. And we[d] boast in the hope of the glory of God. 3Not only so, but we[d] also glory in our sufferings, because we know that suffering produces perseverance; 4perseverance, character; and character, hope. 5And hope does not put us to shame, because God's love has been poured out into our hearts through the Holy Spirit, who has been given to us.

6You see, at just the right time, when we were still powerless, Christ died for the ungodly. 7Very rarely will anyone die for a righteous person, though for a good person someone might possibly dare to die. 8But God demonstrates his own love for us in this: While we were still sinners, Christ died for us.

9Since we have now been justified by his blood, how much more shall we be saved from God's wrath through him! 10For if, while we were God's enemies, we were reconciled to him through the death of his Son, how much more, having been reconciled, shall we be saved through his life! 11Not only is this so, but we also boast in God through our Lord Jesus Christ, through whom we have now received reconciliation.

Death Through Adam, Life Through Christ

12Therefore, just as sin entered the world through one man, and death through sin, and in this way death came to all people, because all sinned —

13To be sure, sin was in the world before the law was given, but sin is not charged against anyone's account where there is no law. 14Nevertheless, death reigned from the time of Adam to the time of Moses, even over those who did not sin by breaking a command, as did Adam, who is a pattern of the one to come.

15But the gift is not like the trespass. For if the many died by the trespass of the one man, how much more did God's grace and the gift that came by the grace of the one man, Jesus Christ, overflow to the many! 16Nor can the gift of God be compared with the result of one man's sin: The judgment followed one sin and brought condemnation, but the gift followed many trespasses and brought justification. 17For if, by the trespass of the one man, death reigned through that one man, how much more will those who receive God's abundant provision of grace and of the gift of righteousness reign in life through the one man, Jesus Christ!

18Consequently, just as one trespass resulted in condemnation for all people, so also one righteous act resulted in justification and life for all people. 19For just as through the disobedience of the one

[a] *17* Gen. 17:5 [b] *18* Gen. 15:5 [c] *1* Many manuscripts *let us* [d] *2,3* Or *let us*

man the many were made sinners, so also through the obedience of the one man the many will be made righteous.

20The law was brought in so that the trespass might increase. But where sin increased, grace increased all the more, 21so that, just as sin reigned in death, so also grace might reign through righteousness to bring eternal life through Jesus Christ our Lord.

Dead to Sin, Alive in Christ

6 What shall we say, then? Shall we go on sinning so that grace may increase? 2By no means! We are those who have died to sin; how can we live in it any longer? 3Or don't you know that all of us who were baptized into Christ Jesus were baptized into his death? 4We were therefore buried with him through baptism into death in order that, just as Christ was raised from the dead through the glory of the Father, we too may live a new life.

5For if we have been united with him in a death like his, we will certainly also be united with him in a resurrection like his. 6For we know that our old self was crucified with him so that the body ruled by sin might be done away with,[a] that we should no longer be slaves to sin— 7because anyone who has died has been set free from sin.

8Now if we died with Christ, we believe that we will also live with him. 9For we know that since Christ was raised from the dead, he cannot die again; death no longer has mastery over him. 10The death he died, he died to sin once for all; but the life he lives, he lives to God.

11In the same way, count yourselves dead to sin but alive to God in Christ Jesus. 12Therefore do not let sin reign in your mortal body so that you obey its evil desires. 13Do not offer any part of yourself to sin as an instrument of wickedness, but rather offer yourselves to God as those who have been brought from death to life; and offer every part of yourself to him as an instrument of righteousness. 14For sin shall no longer be your master, because you are not under the law, but under grace.

Slaves to Righteousness

15What then? Shall we sin because we are not under the law but under grace? By no means! 16Don't you know that when you offer yourselves to someone as obedient slaves, you are slaves of the one you obey—whether you are slaves to sin, which leads to death, or to obedience, which leads to righteousness? 17But thanks be to God that, though you used to be slaves to sin, you have come to obey from your heart the pattern of teaching that has now claimed your allegiance. 18You have been set free from sin and have become slaves to righteousness.

19I am using an example from everyday life because of your human limitations. Just as you used to offer yourselves as slaves to impurity and to ever-increasing wickedness, so now offer yourselves as slaves to righteousness leading to holiness. 20When you were slaves to sin, you were free from the control of righteousness. 21What benefit did you reap at that time from the things you are now ashamed of? Those things result in death! 22But now that you have been set free from sin and have become slaves of God, the benefit you reap leads to holiness, and the result is eternal life. 23For the wages of sin is death, but the gift of God is eternal life in[b] Christ Jesus our Lord.

Released From the Law, Bound to Christ

7 Do you not know, brothers and sisters—for I am speaking to those who know the law—that the law has authority over someone only as long as that person lives? 2For example, by law a married woman is bound to her husband as long as he is alive, but if her husband dies, she is released from the law that binds her to him. 3So then, if she has sexual relations with another man while her husband is still alive, she is called an adulteress. But if her husband dies, she is released from that law and is not an adulteress if she marries another man.

4So, my brothers and sisters, you also died to the law through the body of Christ, that you might belong to another, to him who was raised from the dead, in order that we might bear fruit for God. 5For when we were in the realm of the flesh,[c] the sinful passions aroused by the law were at work in us, so that we bore fruit for death. 6But now, by dying to what once bound us, we have been released from the law so that we serve in the new way of the Spirit, and not in the old way of the written code.

[a] 6 Or *be rendered powerless* [b] 23 Or *through* [c] 5 In contexts like this, the Greek word for *flesh* (*sarx*) refers to the sinful state of human beings, often presented as a power in opposition to the Spirit.

The Law and Sin

7What shall we say, then? Is the law sinful? Certainly not! Nevertheless, I would not
have known what sin was had it not been
for the law. For I would not have known
what coveting really was if the law had
not said, "You shall not covet."[a] 8But sin,
seizing the opportunity afforded by the
commandment, produced in me every
kind of coveting. For apart from the law, sin
was dead. 9Once I was alive apart from the
law; but when the commandment came,
sin sprang to life and I died. 10I found that
the very commandment that was intended
to bring life actually brought death. 11For
sin, seizing the opportunity afforded by the
commandment, deceived me, and through
the commandment put me to death. 12So
then, the law is holy, and the commandment is holy, righteous and good.

13Did that which is good, then, become
death to me? By no means! Nevertheless,
in order that sin might be recognized as
sin, it used what is good to bring about my
death, so that through the commandment
sin might become utterly sinful.

14We know that the law is spiritual; but
I am unspiritual, sold as a slave to sin. 15I
do not understand what I do. For what I
want to do I do not do, but what I hate I
do. 16And if I do what I do not want to do,
I agree that the law is good. 17As it is, it is
no longer I myself who do it, but it is sin
living in me. 18For I know that good itself
does not dwell in me, that is, in my sinful
nature.[b] For I have the desire to do what
is good, but I cannot carry it out. 19For I
do not do the good I want to do, but the
evil I do not want to do — this I keep on
doing. 20Now if I do what I do not want to
do, it is no longer I who do it, but it is sin
living in me that does it.

21So I find this law at work: Although I
want to do good, evil is right there with
me. 22For in my inner being I delight in
God's law; 23but I see another law at work
in me, waging war against the law of my
mind and making me a prisoner of the law
of sin at work within me. 24What a wretched man I am! Who will rescue me from this
body that is subject to death? 25Thanks be
to God, who delivers me through Jesus
Christ our Lord!

So then, I myself in my mind am a slave
to God's law, but in my sinful nature[c] a
slave to the law of sin.

Life Through the Spirit

8 Therefore, there is now no condemnation for those who are in Christ Jesus,
2because through Christ Jesus the law of
the Spirit who gives life has set you[d] free
from the law of sin and death. 3For what
the law was powerless to do because it was
weakened by the flesh,[e] God did by sending
his own Son in the likeness of sinful flesh
to be a sin offering.[f] And so he condemned
sin in the flesh, 4in order that the righteous
requirement of the law might be fully met
in us, who do not live according to the flesh
but according to the Spirit.

5Those who live according to the flesh
have their minds set on what the flesh
desires; but those who live in accordance
with the Spirit have their minds set on
what the Spirit desires. 6The mind governed by the flesh is death, but the mind
governed by the Spirit is life and peace.
7The mind governed by the flesh is hostile
to God; it does not submit to God's law, nor
can it do so. 8Those who are in the realm
of the flesh cannot please God.

9You, however, are not in the realm of
the flesh but are in the realm of the Spirit,
if indeed the Spirit of God lives in you. And
if anyone does not have the Spirit of Christ,
they do not belong to Christ. 10But if Christ
is in you, then even though your body is
subject to death because of sin, the Spirit
gives life[g] because of righteousness. 11And
if the Spirit of him who raised Jesus from
the dead is living in you, he who raised
Christ from the dead will also give life to
your mortal bodies because of[h] his Spirit
who lives in you.

12Therefore, brothers and sisters, we
have an obligation — but it is not to the
flesh, to live according to it. 13For if you
live according to the flesh, you will die;
but if by the Spirit you put to death the
misdeeds of the body, you will live.

14For those who are led by the Spirit of
God are the children of God. 15The Spirit you
received does not make you slaves, so that
you live in fear again; rather, the Spirit you
received brought about your adoption to
sonship.[i] And by him we cry, *"Abba,*[j] Father." 16The Spirit himself testifies with our
spirit that we are God's children. 17Now if
we are children, then we are heirs — heirs
of God and co-heirs with Christ, if indeed
we share in his sufferings in order that we
may also share in his glory.

[a] *7* Exodus 20:17; Deut. 5:21 [b] *18* Or *my flesh* [c] *25* Or *in the flesh* [d] *2* The Greek is singular; some manuscripts *me* [e] *3* In contexts like this, the Greek word for *flesh* (*sarx*) refers to the sinful state of human beings, often presented as a power in opposition to the Spirit; also in verses 4-13. [f] *3* Or *flesh, for sin* [g] *10* Or *you, your body is dead because of sin, yet your spirit is alive* [h] *11* Some manuscripts *bodies through* [i] *15* The Greek word for *adoption to sonship* is a term referring to the full legal standing of an adopted male heir in Roman culture; also in verse 23. [j] *15* Aramaic for *father*

Present Suffering and Future Glory

[18]I consider that our present sufferings are not worth comparing with the glory that will be revealed in us. [19]For the creation waits in eager expectation for the children of God to be revealed. [20]For the creation was subjected to frustration, not by its own choice, but by the will of the one who subjected it, in hope [21]that[a] the creation itself will be liberated from its bondage to decay and brought into the freedom and glory of the children of God.

[22]We know that the whole creation has been groaning as in the pains of childbirth right up to the present time. [23]Not only so, but we ourselves, who have the firstfruits of the Spirit, groan inwardly as we wait eagerly for our adoption to sonship, the redemption of our bodies. [24]For in this hope we were saved. But hope that is seen is no hope at all. Who hopes for what they already have? [25]But if we hope for what we do not yet have, we wait for it patiently.

[26]In the same way, the Spirit helps us in our weakness. We do not know what we ought to pray for, but the Spirit himself intercedes for us through wordless groans. [27]And he who searches our hearts knows the mind of the Spirit, because the Spirit intercedes for God's people in accordance with the will of God.

[28]And we know that in all things God works for the good of those who love him, who[b] have been called according to his purpose. [29]For those God foreknew he also predestined to be conformed to the image of his Son, that he might be the firstborn among many brothers and sisters. [30]And those he predestined, he also called; those he called, he also justified; those he justified, he also glorified.

More Than Conquerors

[31]What, then, shall we say in response to these things? If God is for us, who can be against us? [32]He who did not spare his own Son, but gave him up for us all—how will he not also, along with him, graciously give us all things? [33]Who will bring any charge against those whom God has chosen? It is God who justifies. [34]Who then is the one who condemns? No one. Christ Jesus who died—more than that, who was raised to life—is at the right hand of God and is also interceding for us. [35]Who shall separate us from the love of Christ? Shall trouble or hardship or persecution or famine or nakedness or danger or sword? [36]As it is written:

"For your sake we face death all day long;
we are considered as sheep to be slaughtered."[c]

[37]No, in all these things we are more than conquerors through him who loved us. [38]For I am convinced that neither death nor life, neither angels nor demons,[d] neither the present nor the future, nor any powers, [39]neither height nor depth, nor anything else in all creation, will be able to separate us from the love of God that is in Christ Jesus our Lord.

Paul's Anguish Over Israel

9 I speak the truth in Christ—I am not lying, my conscience confirms it through the Holy Spirit— [2]I have great sorrow and unceasing anguish in my heart. [3]For I could wish that I myself were cursed and cut off from Christ for the sake of my people, those of my own race, [4]the people of Israel. Theirs is the adoption to sonship; theirs the divine glory, the covenants, the receiving of the law, the temple worship and the promises. [5]Theirs are the patriarchs, and from them is traced the human ancestry of the Messiah, who is God over all, forever praised![e] Amen.

God's Sovereign Choice

[6]It is not as though God's word had failed. For not all who are descended from Israel are Israel. [7]Nor because they are his descendants are they all Abraham's children. On the contrary, "It is through Isaac that your offspring will be reckoned."[f] [8]In other words, it is not the children by physical descent who are God's children, but it is the children of the promise who are regarded as Abraham's offspring. [9]For this was how the promise was stated: "At the appointed time I will return, and Sarah will have a son."[g]

[10]Not only that, but Rebekah's children were conceived at the same time by our father Isaac. [11]Yet, before the twins were born or had done anything good or bad—in order that God's purpose in election might stand: [12]not by works but by him who calls—she was told, "The older will serve the younger."[h] [13]Just as it is written: "Jacob I loved, but Esau I hated."[i]

[a] 20,21 Or *subjected it in hope.* [21]*For* [b] 28 Or *that all things work together for good to those who love God, who;* or *that in all things God works together with those who love him to bring about what is good—with those who* [c] 36 Psalm 44:22 [d] 38 Or *nor heavenly rulers* [e] 5 Or *Messiah, who is over all. God be forever praised!* Or *Messiah. God who is over all be forever praised!* [f] 7 Gen. 21:12 [g] 9 Gen. 18:10,14 [h] 12 Gen. 25:23 [i] 13 Mal. 1:2,3

14 What then shall we say? Is God unjust?
Not at all! 15 For he says to Moses,

"I will have mercy on whom I have
mercy,
and I will have compassion on
whom I have compassion."[a]

16 It does not, therefore, depend on human
desire or effort, but on God's mercy. 17 For
Scripture says to Pharaoh: "I raised you up
for this very purpose, that I might display
my power in you and that my name might
be proclaimed in all the earth."[b] 18 Therefore God has mercy on whom he wants
to have mercy, and he hardens whom he
wants to harden.

19 One of you will say to me: "Then why
does God still blame us? For who is able
to resist his will?" 20 But who are you, a
human being, to talk back to God? "Shall
what is formed say to the one who formed
it, 'Why did you make me like this?' "[c]
21 Does not the potter have the right to
make out of the same lump of clay some
pottery for special purposes and some for
common use?

22 What if God, although choosing to
show his wrath and make his power
known, bore with great patience the objects of his wrath — prepared for destruction? 23 What if he did this to make the
riches of his glory known to the objects of
his mercy, whom he prepared in advance
for glory — 24 even us, whom he also called,
not only from the Jews but also from the
Gentiles? 25 As he says in Hosea:

"I will call them 'my people' who are
not my people;
and I will call her 'my loved one'
who is not my loved one,"[d]

26 and,

"In the very place where it was said to
them,
'You are not my people,'
there they will be called 'children of
the living God.' "[e]

27 Isaiah cries out concerning Israel:

"Though the number of the Israelites
be like the sand by the sea,
only the remnant will be saved.
28 For the Lord will carry out
his sentence on earth with speed
and finality."[f]

29 It is just as Isaiah said previously:

"Unless the Lord Almighty
had left us descendants,
we would have become like Sodom,
we would have been like
Gomorrah."[g]

Israel's Unbelief

30 What then shall we say? That the Gentiles, who did not pursue righteousness,
have obtained it, a righteousness that is
by faith; 31 but the people of Israel, who
pursued the law as the way of righteousness, have not attained their goal. 32 Why
not? Because they pursued it not by faith
but as if it were by works. They stumbled
over the stumbling stone. 33 As it is written:

"See, I lay in Zion a stone that causes
people to stumble
and a rock that makes them fall,
and the one who believes in him
will never be put to shame."[h]

10 Brothers and sisters, my heart's
desire and prayer to God for the
Israelites is that they may be saved. 2 For
I can testify about them that they are
zealous for God, but their zeal is not based
on knowledge. 3 Since they did not know
the righteousness of God and sought to
establish their own, they did not submit
to God's righteousness. 4 Christ is the culmination of the law so that there may be
righteousness for everyone who believes.

5 Moses writes this about the righteousness that is by the law: "The person who
does these things will live by them."[i] 6 But
the righteousness that is by faith says: "Do
not say in your heart, 'Who will ascend into
heaven?' "[j] (that is, to bring Christ down)
7 "or 'Who will descend into the deep?' "[k]
(that is, to bring Christ up from the dead).
8 But what does it say? "The word is near
you; it is in your mouth and in your heart,"[l]
that is, the message concerning faith that
we proclaim: 9 If you declare with your
mouth, "Jesus is Lord," and believe in your
heart that God raised him from the dead,
you will be saved. 10 For it is with your heart
that you believe and are justified, and it
is with your mouth that you profess your
faith and are saved. 11 As Scripture says,
"Anyone who believes in him will never be
put to shame."[m] 12 For there is no difference
between Jew and Gentile — the same Lord
is Lord of all and richly blesses all who call
on him, 13 for, "Everyone who calls on the
name of the Lord will be saved."[n]

[a] *15* Exodus 33:19 [b] *17* Exodus 9:16 [c] *20* Isaiah 29:16; 45:9 [d] *25* Hosea 2:23 [e] *26* Hosea 1:10
[f] *28* Isaiah 10:22,23 (see Septuagint) [g] *29* Isaiah 1:9 [h] *33* Isaiah 8:14; 28:16 [i] *5* Lev. 18:5
[j] *6* Deut. 30:12 [k] *7* Deut. 30:13 [l] *8* Deut. 30:14 [m] *11* Isaiah 28:16 (see Septuagint) [n] *13* Joel 2:32

14How, then, can they call on the one
they have not believed in? And how can
they believe in the one of whom they have
not heard? And how can they hear without
someone preaching to them? 15And how
can anyone preach unless they are sent?
As it is written: "How beautiful are the feet
of those who bring good news!"[a]

16But not all the Israelites accepted the
good news. For Isaiah says, "Lord, who has
believed our message?"[b] 17Consequently,
faith comes from hearing the message,
and the message is heard through the
word about Christ. 18But I ask: Did they
not hear? Of course they did:

"Their voice has gone out into all
the earth,
their words to the ends of the
world."[c]

19Again I ask: Did Israel not understand?
First, Moses says,

"I will make you envious by those
who are not a nation;
I will make you angry by a nation
that has no understanding."[d]

20And Isaiah boldly says,

"I was found by those who did not
seek me;
I revealed myself to those who did
not ask for me."[e]

21But concerning Israel he says,

"All day long I have held out my
hands
to a disobedient and obstinate
people."[f]

The Remnant of Israel

11 I ask then: Did God reject his people? By no means! I am an Israelite
myself, a descendant of Abraham, from
the tribe of Benjamin. 2God did not reject
his people, whom he foreknew. Don't you
know what Scripture says in the passage
about Elijah — how he appealed to God
against Israel: 3"Lord, they have killed
your prophets and torn down your altars;
I am the only one left, and they are trying
to kill me"[g]? 4And what was God's answer
to him? "I have reserved for myself seven
thousand who have not bowed the knee to
Baal."[h] 5So too, at the present time there
is a remnant chosen by grace. 6And if by
grace, then it cannot be based on works;
if it were, grace would no longer be grace.
7What then? What the people of Israel
sought so earnestly they did not obtain.
The elect among them did, but the others
were hardened, 8as it is written:

"God gave them a spirit of stupor,
eyes that could not see
and ears that could not hear,
to this very day."[i]

9And David says:

"May their table become a snare and
a trap,
a stumbling block and a
retribution for them.
10May their eyes be darkened so they
cannot see,
and their backs be bent forever."[j]

Ingrafted Branches

11Again I ask: Did they stumble so as to
fall beyond recovery? Not at all! Rather,
because of their transgression, salvation
has come to the Gentiles to make Israel
envious. 12But if their transgression means
riches for the world, and their loss means
riches for the Gentiles, how much greater
riches will their full inclusion bring!

13I am talking to you Gentiles. Inasmuch
as I am the apostle to the Gentiles, I take
pride in my ministry 14in the hope that
I may somehow arouse my own people
to envy and save some of them. 15For if
their rejection brought reconciliation to
the world, what will their acceptance be
but life from the dead? 16If the part of the
dough offered as firstfruits is holy, then
the whole batch is holy; if the root is holy,
so are the branches.

17If some of the branches have been
broken off, and you, though a wild olive
shoot, have been grafted in among the
others and now share in the nourishing
sap from the olive root, 18do not consider yourself to be superior to those other
branches. If you do, consider this: You do
not support the root, but the root supports
you. 19You will say then, "Branches were
broken off so that I could be grafted in."
20Granted. But they were broken off because of unbelief, and you stand by faith.
Do not be arrogant, but tremble. 21For if
God did not spare the natural branches,
he will not spare you either.

22Consider therefore the kindness and
sternness of God: sternness to those who fell,
but kindness to you, provided that you continue in his kindness. Otherwise, you also
will be cut off. 23And if they do not persist in
unbelief, they will be grafted in, for God is

[a] *15* Isaiah 52:7 [b] *16* Isaiah 53:1 [c] *18* Psalm 19:4 [d] *19* Deut. 32:21 [e] *20* Isaiah 65:1
[f] *21* Isaiah 65:2 [g] *3* 1 Kings 19:10,14 [h] *4* 1 Kings 19:18 [i] *8* Deut. 29:4; Isaiah 29:10
[j] *10* Psalm 69:22,23

able to graft them in again. [24]After all, if you
were cut out of an olive tree that is wild by
nature, and contrary to nature were grafted
into a cultivated olive tree, how much more
readily will these, the natural branches, be
grafted into their own olive tree!

All Israel Will Be Saved

[25]I do not want you to be ignorant of
this mystery, brothers and sisters, so that
you may not be conceited: Israel has experienced a hardening in part until the
full number of the Gentiles has come in,
[26]and in this way[a] all Israel will be saved.
As it is written:

"The deliverer will come from Zion;
he will turn godlessness away from
Jacob.
[27] And this is[b] my covenant with them
when I take away their sins."[c]

[28]As far as the gospel is concerned, they
are enemies for your sake; but as far as
election is concerned, they are loved on
account of the patriarchs, [29]for God's gifts
and his call are irrevocable. [30]Just as you
who were at one time disobedient to God
have now received mercy as a result of
their disobedience, [31]so they too have now
become disobedient in order that they too
may now[d] receive mercy as a result of
God's mercy to you. [32]For God has bound
everyone over to disobedience so that he
may have mercy on them all.

Doxology

[33] Oh, the depth of the riches of the
wisdom and[e] knowledge of
God!
How unsearchable his judgments,
and his paths beyond tracing out!
[34] "Who has known the mind of the
Lord?
Or who has been his counselor?"[f]
[35] "Who has ever given to God,
that God should repay them?"[g]
[36] For from him and through him and
for him are all things.
To him be the glory forever! Amen.

A Living Sacrifice

12 Therefore, I urge you, brothers and
sisters, in view of God's mercy, to offer your bodies as a living sacrifice, holy
and pleasing to God — this is your true
and proper worship. [2]Do not conform to
the pattern of this world, but be transformed by the renewing of your mind.
Then you will be able to test and approve
what God's will is — his good, pleasing
and perfect will.

Humble Service in the Body of Christ

[3]For by the grace given me I say to every one of you: Do not think of yourself
more highly than you ought, but rather
think of yourself with sober judgment,
in accordance with the faith God has distributed to each of you. [4]For just as each
of us has one body with many members,
and these members do not all have the
same function, [5]so in Christ we, though
many, form one body, and each member
belongs to all the others. [6]We have different gifts, according to the grace given to
each of us. If your gift is prophesying, then
prophesy in accordance with your[h] faith;
[7]if it is serving, then serve; if it is teaching,
then teach; [8]if it is to encourage, then give
encouragement; if it is giving, then give
generously; if it is to lead,[i] do it diligently; if it is to show mercy, do it cheerfully.

Love in Action

[9]Love must be sincere. Hate what is
evil; cling to what is good. [10]Be devoted to
one another in love. Honor one another
above yourselves. [11]Never be lacking in
zeal, but keep your spiritual fervor, serving the Lord. [12]Be joyful in hope, patient
in affliction, faithful in prayer. [13]Share
with the Lord's people who are in need.
Practice hospitality.

[14]Bless those who persecute you; bless
and do not curse. [15]Rejoice with those who
rejoice; mourn with those who mourn.
[16]Live in harmony with one another. Do not
be proud, but be willing to associate with
people of low position.[j] Do not be conceited.

[17]Do not repay anyone evil for evil. Be
careful to do what is right in the eyes of
everyone. [18]If it is possible, as far as it depends on you, live at peace with everyone.
[19]Do not take revenge, my dear friends, but
leave room for God's wrath, for it is written: "It is mine to avenge; I will repay,"[k]
says the Lord. [20]On the contrary:

"If your enemy is hungry, feed him;
if he is thirsty, give him something
to drink.
In doing this, you will heap burning
coals on his head."[l]

[21]Do not be overcome by evil, but overcome
evil with good.

[a] 26 Or *and so* [b] 27 Or *will be* [c] 27 Isaiah 59:20,21; 27:9 (see Septuagint); Jer. 31:33,34
[d] 31 Some manuscripts do not have *now*. [e] 33 Or *riches and the wisdom and the*
[f] 34 Isaiah 40:13 [g] 35 Job 41:11 [h] 6 Or *the* [i] 8 Or *to provide for others* [j] 16 Or *willing to do menial work* [k] 19 Deut. 32:35 [l] 20 Prov. 25:21,22

Submission to Governing Authorities

13 Let everyone be subject to the governing authorities, for there is no authority except that which God has established. The authorities that exist have been established by God. 2Consequently, whoever rebels against the authority is rebelling against what God has instituted, and those who do so will bring judgment on themselves. 3For rulers hold no terror for those who do right, but for those who do wrong. Do you want to be free from fear of the one in authority? Then do what is right and you will be commended. 4For the one in authority is God's servant for your good. But if you do wrong, be afraid, for rulers do not bear the sword for no reason. They are God's servants, agents of wrath to bring punishment on the wrongdoer. 5Therefore, it is necessary to submit to the authorities, not only because of possible punishment but also as a matter of conscience.

6This is also why you pay taxes, for the authorities are God's servants, who give their full time to governing. 7Give to everyone what you owe them: If you owe taxes, pay taxes; if revenue, then revenue; if respect, then respect; if honor, then honor.

Love Fulfills the Law

8Let no debt remain outstanding, except the continuing debt to love one another, for whoever loves others has fulfilled the law. 9The commandments, "You shall not commit adultery," "You shall not murder," "You shall not steal," "You shall not covet,"[a] and whatever other command there may be, are summed up in this one command: "Love your neighbor as yourself."[b] 10Love does no harm to a neighbor. Therefore love is the fulfillment of the law.

The Day Is Near

11And do this, understanding the present time: The hour has already come for you to wake up from your slumber, because our salvation is nearer now than when we first believed. 12The night is nearly over; the day is almost here. So let us put aside the deeds of darkness and put on the armor of light. 13Let us behave decently, as in the daytime, not in carousing and drunkenness, not in sexual immorality and debauchery, not in dissension and jealousy. 14Rather, clothe yourselves with the Lord Jesus Christ, and do not think about how to gratify the desires of the flesh.[c]

The Weak and the Strong

14 Accept the one whose faith is weak, without quarreling over disputable matters. 2One person's faith allows them to eat anything, but another, whose faith is weak, eats only vegetables. 3The one who eats everything must not treat with contempt the one who does not, and the one who does not eat everything must not judge the one who does, for God has accepted them. 4Who are you to judge someone else's servant? To their own master, servants stand or fall. And they will stand, for the Lord is able to make them stand.

5One person considers one day more sacred than another; another considers every day alike. Each of them should be fully convinced in their own mind. 6Whoever regards one day as special does so to the Lord. Whoever eats meat does so to the Lord, for they give thanks to God; and whoever abstains does so to the Lord and gives thanks to God. 7For none of us lives for ourselves alone, and none of us dies for ourselves alone. 8If we live, we live for the Lord; and if we die, we die for the Lord. So, whether we live or die, we belong to the Lord. 9For this very reason, Christ died and returned to life so that he might be the Lord of both the dead and the living.

10You, then, why do you judge your brother or sister[d]? Or why do you treat them with contempt? For we will all stand before God's judgment seat. 11It is written:

> "'As surely as I live,' says the Lord,
> 'every knee will bow before me;
> every tongue will acknowledge
> God.'"[e]

12So then, each of us will give an account of ourselves to God.

13Therefore let us stop passing judgment on one another. Instead, make up your mind not to put any stumbling block or obstacle in the way of a brother or sister. 14I am convinced, being fully persuaded in the Lord Jesus, that nothing is unclean in itself. But if anyone regards something as unclean, then for that person it is unclean. 15If your brother or sister is distressed because of what you eat, you are no longer acting in love. Do not by your eating destroy someone for whom Christ died. 16Therefore do not let what you know is good be spoken of as evil. 17For the kingdom of God is not a matter of eating and drinking, but of righteousness, peace and

[a] *9* Exodus 20:13-15,17; Deut. 5:17-19,21 [b] *9* Lev. 19:18 [c] *14* In contexts like this, the Greek word for *flesh* (*sarx*) refers to the sinful state of human beings, often presented as a power in opposition to the Spirit. [d] *10* The Greek word for *brother or sister* (*adelphos*) refers here to a believer, whether man or woman, as part of God's family; also in verses 13, 15 and 21. [e] *11* Isaiah 45:23

joy in the Holy Spirit, 18because anyone who serves Christ in this way is pleasing to God and receives human approval.

19Let us therefore make every effort to do what leads to peace and to mutual edification. 20Do not destroy the work of God for the sake of food. All food is clean, but it is wrong for a person to eat anything that causes someone else to stumble. 21It is better not to eat meat or drink wine or to do anything else that will cause your brother or sister to fall.

22So whatever you believe about these things keep between yourself and God. Blessed is the one who does not condemn himself by what he approves. 23But whoever has doubts is condemned if they eat, because their eating is not from faith; and everything that does not come from faith is sin.[a]

15 We who are strong ought to bear with the failings of the weak and not to please ourselves. 2Each of us should please our neighbors for their good, to build them up. 3For even Christ did not please himself but, as it is written: "The insults of those who insult you have fallen on me."[b] 4For everything that was written in the past was written to teach us, so that through the endurance taught in the Scriptures and the encouragement they provide we might have hope.

5May the God who gives endurance and encouragement give you the same attitude of mind toward each other that Christ Jesus had, 6so that with one mind and one voice you may glorify the God and Father of our Lord Jesus Christ.

7Accept one another, then, just as Christ accepted you, in order to bring praise to God. 8For I tell you that Christ has become a servant of the Jews[c] on behalf of God's truth, so that the promises made to the patriarchs might be confirmed 9and, moreover, that the Gentiles might glorify God for his mercy. As it is written:

"Therefore I will praise you among
the Gentiles;
I will sing the praises of your
name."[d]

10Again, it says,

"Rejoice, you Gentiles, with his
people."[e]

11And again,

"Praise the Lord, all you Gentiles;
let all the peoples extol him."[f]

12And again, Isaiah says,

"The Root of Jesse will spring up,
one who will arise to rule over the
nations;
in him the Gentiles will hope."[g]

13May the God of hope fill you with all joy and peace as you trust in him, so that you may overflow with hope by the power of the Holy Spirit.

Paul the Minister to the Gentiles

14I myself am convinced, my brothers and sisters, that you yourselves are full of goodness, filled with knowledge and competent to instruct one another. 15Yet I have written you quite boldly on some points to remind you of them again, because of the grace God gave me 16to be a minister of Christ Jesus to the Gentiles. He gave me the priestly duty of proclaiming the gospel of God, so that the Gentiles might become an offering acceptable to God, sanctified by the Holy Spirit.

17Therefore I glory in Christ Jesus in my service to God. 18I will not venture to speak of anything except what Christ has accomplished through me in leading the Gentiles to obey God by what I have said and done— 19by the power of signs and wonders, through the power of the Spirit of God. So from Jerusalem all the way around to Illyricum, I have fully proclaimed the gospel of Christ. 20It has always been my ambition to preach the gospel where Christ was not known, so that I would not be building on someone else's foundation. 21Rather, as it is written:

"Those who were not told about him
will see,
and those who have not heard will
understand."[h]

22This is why I have often been hindered from coming to you.

Paul's Plan to Visit Rome

23But now that there is no more place for me to work in these regions, and since I have been longing for many years to visit you, 24I plan to do so when I go to Spain. I hope to see you while passing through and to have you assist me on my journey there, after I have enjoyed your company for a while. 25Now, however, I am on my way to Jerusalem in the service of the Lord's people there. 26For Macedonia and Achaia were pleased to make a contribution

[a] *23* Some manuscripts place 16:25-27 here; others after 15:33. [b] *3* Psalm 69:9 [c] *8* Greek *circumcision* [d] *9* 2 Samuel 22:50; Psalm 18:49 [e] *10* Deut. 32:43 [f] *11* Psalm 117:1 [g] *12* Isaiah 11:10 (see Septuagint) [h] *21* Isaiah 52:15 (see Septuagint)

for the poor among the Lord's people in
Jerusalem. 27They were pleased to do it,
and indeed they owe it to them. For if the
Gentiles have shared in the Jews' spiritual
blessings, they owe it to the Jews to share
with them their material blessings. 28So
after I have completed this task and have
made sure that they have received this
contribution, I will go to Spain and visit
you on the way. 29I know that when I come
to you, I will come in the full measure of
the blessing of Christ.

30I urge you, brothers and sisters, by
our Lord Jesus Christ and by the love of
the Spirit, to join me in my struggle by
praying to God for me. 31Pray that I may
be kept safe from the unbelievers in Judea
and that the contribution I take to Jerusalem may be favorably received by the
Lord's people there, 32so that I may come
to you with joy, by God's will, and in your
company be refreshed. 33The God of peace
be with you all. Amen.

Personal Greetings

16 I commend to you our sister Phoebe,
a deacon[a,b] of the church in Cenchreae. 2I ask you to receive her in the
Lord in a way worthy of his people and to
give her any help she may need from you,
for she has been the benefactor of many
people, including me.

3 Greet Priscilla[c] and Aquila, my co-workers
in Christ Jesus. 4They risked their
lives for me. Not only I but all the
churches of the Gentiles are grateful to them.

5 Greet also the church that meets at their
house.

Greet my dear friend Epenetus, who
was the first convert to Christ in the
province of Asia.

6 Greet Mary, who worked very hard for
you.

7 Greet Andronicus and Junia, my fellow
Jews who have been in prison with
me. They are outstanding among[d]
the apostles, and they were in Christ
before I was.

8 Greet Ampliatus, my dear friend in the
Lord.

9 Greet Urbanus, our co-worker in Christ,
and my dear friend Stachys.

10 Greet Apelles, whose fidelity to Christ
has stood the test.

Greet those who belong to the household of Aristobulus.

11 Greet Herodion, my fellow Jew.

Greet those in the household of Narcis-
sus who are in the Lord.

12 Greet Tryphena and Tryphosa, those
women who work hard in the Lord.

Greet my dear friend Persis, another
woman who has worked very hard
in the Lord.

13 Greet Rufus, chosen in the Lord, and
his mother, who has been a mother
to me, too.

14 Greet Asyncritus, Phlegon, Hermes, Pat-
robas, Hermas and the other brothers
and sisters with them.

15 Greet Philologus, Julia, Nereus and his
sister, and Olympas and all the Lord's
people who are with them.

16 Greet one another with a holy kiss.

All the churches of Christ send greetings.

17I urge you, brothers and sisters, to
watch out for those who cause divisions
and put obstacles in your way that are
contrary to the teaching you have learned.
Keep away from them. 18For such people are not serving our Lord Christ, but
their own appetites. By smooth talk and
flattery they deceive the minds of naive
people. 19Everyone has heard about your
obedience, so I rejoice because of you; but
I want you to be wise about what is good,
and innocent about what is evil.

20The God of peace will soon crush Satan
under your feet.

The grace of our Lord Jesus be with you.

21Timothy, my co-worker, sends his
greetings to you, as do Lucius, Jason and
Sosipater, my fellow Jews.

22I, Tertius, who wrote down this letter,
greet you in the Lord.

23Gaius, whose hospitality I and the
whole church here enjoy, sends you his
greetings.

Erastus, who is the city's director of public works, and our brother Quartus send
you their greetings. [24][e]

25Now to him who is able to establish
you in accordance with my gospel, the
message I proclaim about Jesus Christ, in
keeping with the revelation of the mystery hidden for long ages past, 26but now
revealed and made known through the
prophetic writings by the command of
the eternal God, so that all the Gentiles
might come to the obedience that comes
from[f] faith — 27to the only wise God be
glory forever through Jesus Christ! Amen.

[a] 1 Or *servant* [b] 1 The word *deacon* refers here to a Christian designated to serve with the overseers/elders of the church in a variety of ways; similarly in Phil. 1:1 and 1 Tim. 3:8,12. [c] 3 Greek *Prisca*, a variant of *Priscilla* [d] 7 Or *are esteemed by* [e] 24 Some manuscripts include here *May the grace of our Lord Jesus Christ be with all of you. Amen.* [f] 26 Or *that is*

1 CORINTHIANS

1 Paul, called to be an apostle of Christ
Jesus by the will of God, and our brother Sosthenes,

2To the church of God in Corinth, to those
sanctified in Christ Jesus and called to be
his holy people, together with all those
everywhere who call on the name of our
Lord Jesus Christ — their Lord and ours:

3Grace and peace to you from God our
Father and the Lord Jesus Christ.

Thanksgiving

4I always thank my God for you because
of his grace given you in Christ Jesus. 5For
in him you have been enriched in every
way — with all kinds of speech and with
all knowledge — 6God thus confirming our
testimony about Christ among you. 7There-
fore you do not lack any spiritual gift as
you eagerly wait for our Lord Jesus Christ
to be revealed. 8He will also keep you firm
to the end, so that you will be blameless
on the day of our Lord Jesus Christ. 9God is
faithful, who has called you into fellowship
with his Son, Jesus Christ our Lord.

A Church Divided Over Leaders

10I appeal to you, brothers and sisters,[a]
in the name of our Lord Jesus Christ, that
all of you agree with one another in what
you say and that there be no divisions
among you, but that you be perfectly united in mind and thought. 11My brothers
and sisters, some from Chloe's household
have informed me that there are quarrels
among you. 12What I mean is this: One of
you says, "I follow Paul"; another, "I follow
Apollos"; another, "I follow Cephas[b]"; still
another, "I follow Christ."

13Is Christ divided? Was Paul crucified
for you? Were you baptized in the name of
Paul? 14I thank God that I did not baptize
any of you except Crispus and Gaius, 15so
no one can say that you were baptized
in my name. 16(Yes, I also baptized the
household of Stephanas; beyond that, I
don't remember if I baptized anyone else.)
17For Christ did not send me to baptize, but
to preach the gospel — not with wisdom
and eloquence, lest the cross of Christ be
emptied of its power.

Christ Crucified Is God's Power and Wisdom

18For the message of the cross is foolishness to those who are perishing, but
to us who are being saved it is the power
of God. 19For it is written:

> "I will destroy the wisdom of the wise;
> the intelligence of the intelligent I
> will frustrate."[c]

20Where is the wise person? Where is the
teacher of the law? Where is the philosopher of this age? Has not God made foolish the wisdom of the world? 21For since
in the wisdom of God the world through
its wisdom did not know him, God was
pleased through the foolishness of what
was preached to save those who believe.
22Jews demand signs and Greeks look for
wisdom, 23but we preach Christ crucified:
a stumbling block to Jews and foolishness to Gentiles, 24but to those whom God
has called, both Jews and Greeks, Christ
the power of God and the wisdom of God.
25For the foolishness of God is wiser than
human wisdom, and the weakness of God
is stronger than human strength.

26Brothers and sisters, think of what you
were when you were called. Not many of
you were wise by human standards; not
many were influential; not many were of
noble birth. 27But God chose the foolish
things of the world to shame the wise;
God chose the weak things of the world
to shame the strong. 28God chose the lowly things of this world and the despised
things — and the things that are not — to
nullify the things that are, 29so that no one
may boast before him. 30It is because of
him that you are in Christ Jesus, who has
become for us wisdom from God — that is,
our righteousness, holiness and redemption. 31Therefore, as it is written: "Let the
one who boasts boast in the Lord."[d]

2 And so it was with me, brothers and
sisters. When I came to you, I did not
come with eloquence or human wisdom as
I proclaimed to you the testimony about
God.[e] 2For I resolved to know nothing while
I was with you except Jesus Christ and him
crucified. 3I came to you in weakness with

[a] *10* The Greek word for *brothers and sisters* (*adelphoi*) refers here to believers, both men and women, as part of God's family; also in verses 11 and 26; and in 2:1; 3:1; 4:6; 6:8; 7:24, 29; 10:1; 11:33; 12:1; 14:6, 20, 26, 39; 15:1, 6, 50, 58; 16:15, 20. [b] *12* That is, Peter [c] *19* Isaiah 29:14
[d] *31* Jer. 9:24 [e] *1* Some manuscripts *proclaimed to you God's mystery*

great fear and trembling. [4]My message and my preaching were not with wise and persuasive words, but with a demonstration of the Spirit's power, [5]so that your faith might not rest on human wisdom, but on God's power.

God's Wisdom Revealed by the Spirit

[6]We do, however, speak a message of wisdom among the mature, but not the wisdom of this age or of the rulers of this age, who are coming to nothing. [7]No, we declare God's wisdom, a mystery that has been hidden and that God destined for our glory before time began. [8]None of the rulers of this age understood it, for if they had, they would not have crucified the Lord of glory. [9]However, as it is written:

"What no eye has seen,
what no ear has heard,
and what no human mind has
conceived"[a] —
the things God has prepared for
those who love him —

[10]these are the things God has revealed to us by his Spirit.

The Spirit searches all things, even the deep things of God. [11]For who knows a person's thoughts except their own spirit within them? In the same way no one knows the thoughts of God except the Spirit of God. [12]What we have received is not the spirit of the world, but the Spirit who is from God, so that we may understand what God has freely given us. [13]This is what we speak, not in words taught us by human wisdom but in words taught by the Spirit, explaining spiritual realities with Spirit-taught words.[b] [14]The person without the Spirit does not accept the things that come from the Spirit of God but considers them foolishness, and cannot understand them because they are discerned only through the Spirit. [15]The person with the Spirit makes judgments about all things, but such a person is not subject to merely human judgments, [16]for,

"Who has known the mind of
the Lord
so as to instruct him?"[c]

But we have the mind of Christ.

The Church and Its Leaders

3 Brothers and sisters, I could not address you as people who live by the Spirit but as people who are still worldly — mere infants in Christ. [2]I gave you milk, not solid food, for you were not yet ready for it. Indeed, you are still not ready. [3]You are still worldly. For since there is jealousy and quarreling among you, are you not worldly? Are you not acting like mere humans? [4]For when one says, "I follow Paul," and another, "I follow Apollos," are you not mere human beings?

[5]What, after all, is Apollos? And what is Paul? Only servants, through whom you came to believe — as the Lord has assigned to each his task. [6]I planted the seed, Apollos watered it, but God has been making it grow. [7]So neither the one who plants nor the one who waters is anything, but only God, who makes things grow. [8]The one who plants and the one who waters have one purpose, and they will each be rewarded according to their own labor. [9]For we are co-workers in God's service; you are God's field, God's building.

[10]By the grace God has given me, I laid a foundation as a wise builder, and someone else is building on it. But each one should build with care. [11]For no one can lay any foundation other than the one already laid, which is Jesus Christ. [12]If anyone builds on this foundation using gold, silver, costly stones, wood, hay or straw, [13]their work will be shown for what it is, because the Day will bring it to light. It will be revealed with fire, and the fire will test the quality of each person's work. [14]If what has been built survives, the builder will receive a reward. [15]If it is burned up, the builder will suffer loss but yet will be saved — even though only as one escaping through the flames.

[16]Don't you know that you yourselves are God's temple and that God's Spirit dwells in your midst? [17]If anyone destroys God's temple, God will destroy that person; for God's temple is sacred, and you together are that temple.

[18]Do not deceive yourselves. If any of you think you are wise by the standards of this age, you should become "fools" so that you may become wise. [19]For the wisdom of this world is foolishness in God's sight. As it is written: "He catches the wise in their craftiness"[d]; [20]and again, "The Lord knows that the thoughts of the wise are futile."[e] [21]So then, no more boasting about human leaders! All things are yours, [22]whether Paul or Apollos or Cephas[f] or the world or life or death or the present or the future — all are yours, [23]and you are of Christ, and Christ is of God.

[a] *9* Isaiah 64:4 [b] *13* Or *Spirit, interpreting spiritual truths to those who are spiritual*
[c] *16* Isaiah 40:13 [d] *19* Job 5:13 [e] *20* Psalm 94:11 [f] *22* That is, Peter

The Nature of True Apostleship

4 This, then, is how you ought to regard us: as servants of Christ and as those entrusted with the mysteries God has revealed. [2]Now it is required that those who have been given a trust must prove faithful. [3]I care very little if I am judged by you or by any human court; indeed, I do not even judge myself. [4]My conscience is clear, but that does not make me innocent. It is the Lord who judges me. [5]Therefore judge nothing before the appointed time; wait until the Lord comes. He will bring to light what is hidden in darkness and will expose the motives of the heart. At that time each will receive their praise from God.

[6]Now, brothers and sisters, I have applied these things to myself and Apollos for your benefit, so that you may learn from us the meaning of the saying, "Do not go beyond what is written." Then you will not be puffed up in being a follower of one of us over against the other. [7]For who makes you different from anyone else? What do you have that you did not receive? And if you did receive it, why do you boast as though you did not?

[8]Already you have all you want! Already you have become rich! You have begun to reign and that without us! How I wish that you really had begun to reign so that we also might reign with you! [9]For it seems to me that God has put us apostles on display at the end of the procession, like those condemned to die in the arena. We have been made a spectacle to the whole universe, to angels as well as to human beings. [10]We are fools for Christ, but you are so wise in Christ! We are weak, but you are strong! You are honored, we are dishonored! [11]To this very hour we go hungry and thirsty, we are in rags, we are brutally treated, we are homeless. [12]We work hard with our own hands. When we are cursed, we bless; when we are persecuted, we endure it; [13]when we are slandered, we answer kindly. We have become the scum of the earth, the garbage of the world — right up to this moment.

Paul's Appeal and Warning

[14]I am writing this not to shame you but to warn you as my dear children. [15]Even if you had ten thousand guardians in Christ, you do not have many fathers, for in Christ Jesus I became your father through the gospel. [16]Therefore I urge you to imitate me. [17]For this reason I have sent to you Timothy, my son whom I love, who is faithful in the Lord. He will remind you of my way of life in Christ Jesus, which agrees with what I teach everywhere in every church.

[18]Some of you have become arrogant, as if I were not coming to you. [19]But I will come to you very soon, if the Lord is willing, and then I will find out not only how these arrogant people are talking, but what power they have. [20]For the kingdom of God is not a matter of talk but of power. [21]What do you prefer? Shall I come to you with a rod of discipline, or shall I come in love and with a gentle spirit?

Dealing With a Case of Incest

5 It is actually reported that there is sexual immorality among you, and of a kind that even pagans do not tolerate: A man is sleeping with his father's wife. [2]And you are proud! Shouldn't you rather have gone into mourning and have put out of your fellowship the man who has been doing this? [3]For my part, even though I am not physically present, I am with you in spirit. As one who is present with you in this way, I have already passed judgment in the name of our Lord Jesus on the one who has been doing this. [4]So when you are assembled and I am with you in spirit, and the power of our Lord Jesus is present, [5]hand this man over to Satan for the destruction of the flesh,[a,b] so that his spirit may be saved on the day of the Lord.

[6]Your boasting is not good. Don't you know that a little yeast leavens the whole batch of dough? [7]Get rid of the old yeast, so that you may be a new unleavened batch — as you really are. For Christ, our Passover lamb, has been sacrificed. [8]Therefore let us keep the Festival, not with the old bread leavened with malice and wickedness, but with the unleavened bread of sincerity and truth.

[9]I wrote to you in my letter not to associate with sexually immoral people — [10]not at all meaning the people of this world who are immoral, or the greedy and swindlers, or idolaters. In that case you would have to leave this world. [11]But now I am writing to you that you must not associate with anyone who claims to be a brother or sister[c] but is sexually immoral or greedy, an idolater or slanderer, a drunkard or swindler. Do not even eat with such people.

[a] *5* In contexts like this, the Greek word for *flesh* (*sarx*) refers to the sinful state of human beings, often presented as a power in opposition to the Spirit. [b] *5* Or *of his body* [c] *11* The Greek word for *brother or sister* (*adelphos*) refers here to a believer, whether man or woman, as part of God's family; also in 8:11, 13.

12What business is it of mine to judge those outside the church? Are you not to judge those inside? 13God will judge those outside. "Expel the wicked person from among you."[a]

Lawsuits Among Believers

6 If any of you has a dispute with another, do you dare to take it before the ungodly for judgment instead of before the Lord's people? 2Or do you not know that the Lord's people will judge the world? And if you are to judge the world, are you not competent to judge trivial cases? 3Do you not know that we will judge angels? How much more the things of this life! 4Therefore, if you have disputes about such matters, do you ask for a ruling from those whose way of life is scorned in the church? 5I say this to shame you. Is it possible that there is nobody among you wise enough to judge a dispute between believers? 6But instead, one brother takes another to court — and this in front of unbelievers!

7The very fact that you have lawsuits among you means you have been completely defeated already. Why not rather be wronged? Why not rather be cheated? 8Instead, you yourselves cheat and do wrong, and you do this to your brothers and sisters. 9Or do you not know that wrongdoers will not inherit the kingdom of God? Do not be deceived: Neither the sexually immoral nor idolaters nor adulterers nor men who have sex with men[b] 10nor thieves nor the greedy nor drunkards nor slanderers nor swindlers will inherit the kingdom of God. 11And that is what some of you were. But you were washed, you were sanctified, you were justified in the name of the Lord Jesus Christ and by the Spirit of our God.

Sexual Immorality

12"I have the right to do anything," you say — but not everything is beneficial. "I have the right to do anything" — but I will not be mastered by anything. 13You say, "Food for the stomach and the stomach for food, and God will destroy them both." The body, however, is not meant for sexual immorality but for the Lord, and the Lord for the body. 14By his power God raised the Lord from the dead, and he will raise us also. 15Do you not know that your bodies are members of Christ himself? Shall I then take the members of Christ and unite them with a prostitute? Never! 16Do you not know that he who unites himself with a prostitute is one with her in body? For it is said, "The two will become one flesh."[c] 17But whoever is united with the Lord is one with him in spirit.[d]

18Flee from sexual immorality. All other sins a person commits are outside the body, but whoever sins sexually, sins against their own body. 19Do you not know that your bodies are temples of the Holy Spirit, who is in you, whom you have received from God? You are not your own; 20you were bought at a price. Therefore honor God with your bodies.

Concerning Married Life

7 Now for the matters you wrote about: "It is good for a man not to have sexual relations with a woman." 2But since sexual immorality is occurring, each man should have sexual relations with his own wife, and each woman with her own husband. 3The husband should fulfill his marital duty to his wife, and likewise the wife to her husband. 4The wife does not have authority over her own body but yields it to her husband. In the same way, the husband does not have authority over his own body but yields it to his wife. 5Do not deprive each other except perhaps by mutual consent and for a time, so that you may devote yourselves to prayer. Then come together again so that Satan will not tempt you because of your lack of self-control. 6I say this as a concession, not as a command. 7I wish that all of you were as I am. But each of you has your own gift from God; one has this gift, another has that.

8Now to the unmarried[e] and the widows I say: It is good for them to stay unmarried, as I do. 9But if they cannot control themselves, they should marry, for it is better to marry than to burn with passion.

10To the married I give this command (not I, but the Lord): A wife must not separate from her husband. 11But if she does, she must remain unmarried or else be reconciled to her husband. And a husband must not divorce his wife.

12To the rest I say this (I, not the Lord): If any brother has a wife who is not a believer and she is willing to live with him, he must not divorce her. 13And if a woman has a husband who is not a believer and he is willing to live with her, she must not divorce him. 14For the unbelieving husband has been sanctified through his wife, and the unbelieving wife has been sanctified through her believing husband. Otherwise

[a] *13* Deut. 13:5; 17:7; 19:19; 21:21; 22:21,24; 24:7 [b] *9* The words *men who have sex with men* translate two Greek words that refer to the passive and active participants in homosexual acts. [c] *16* Gen. 2:24 [d] *17* Or *in the Spirit* [e] *8* Or *widowers*

your children would be unclean, but as it is, they are holy.

15 But if the unbeliever leaves, let it be so. The brother or the sister is not bound in such circumstances; God has called us to live in peace. 16 How do you know, wife, whether you will save your husband? Or, how do you know, husband, whether you will save your wife?

Concerning Change of Status

17 Nevertheless, each person should live as a believer in whatever situation the Lord has assigned to them, just as God has called them. This is the rule I lay down in all the churches. 18 Was a man already circumcised when he was called? He should not become uncircumcised. Was a man uncircumcised when he was called? He should not be circumcised. 19 Circumcision is nothing and uncircumcision is nothing. Keeping God's commands is what counts. 20 Each person should remain in the situation they were in when God called them.

21 Were you a slave when you were called? Don't let it trouble you — although if you can gain your freedom, do so. 22 For the one who was a slave when called to faith in the Lord is the Lord's freed person; similarly, the one who was free when called is Christ's slave. 23 You were bought at a price; do not become slaves of human beings. 24 Brothers and sisters, each person, as responsible to God, should remain in the situation they were in when God called them.

Concerning the Unmarried

25 Now about virgins: I have no command from the Lord, but I give a judgment as one who by the Lord's mercy is trustworthy. 26 Because of the present crisis, I think that it is good for a man to remain as he is. 27 Are you pledged to a woman? Do not seek to be released. Are you free from such a commitment? Do not look for a wife. 28 But if you do marry, you have not sinned; and if a virgin marries, she has not sinned. But those who marry will face many troubles in this life, and I want to spare you this.

29 What I mean, brothers and sisters, is that the time is short. From now on those who have wives should live as if they do not; 30 those who mourn, as if they did not; those who are happy, as if they were not; those who buy something, as if it were not theirs to keep; 31 those who use the things of the world, as if not engrossed in them. For this world in its present form is passing away.

32 I would like you to be free from concern. An unmarried man is concerned about the Lord's affairs — how he can please the Lord. 33 But a married man is concerned about the affairs of this world — how he can please his wife — 34 and his interests are divided. An unmarried woman or virgin is concerned about the Lord's affairs: Her aim is to be devoted to the Lord in both body and spirit. But a married woman is concerned about the affairs of this world — how she can please her husband. 35 I am saying this for your own good, not to restrict you, but that you may live in a right way in undivided devotion to the Lord.

36 If anyone is worried that he might not be acting honorably toward the virgin he is engaged to, and if his passions are too strong[a] and he feels he ought to marry, he should do as he wants. He is not sinning. They should get married. 37 But the man who has settled the matter in his own mind, who is under no compulsion but has control over his own will, and who has made up his mind not to marry the virgin — this man also does the right thing. 38 So then, he who marries the virgin does right, but he who does not marry her does better.[b]

39 A woman is bound to her husband as long as he lives. But if her husband dies, she is free to marry anyone she wishes, but he must belong to the Lord. 40 In my judgment, she is happier if she stays as she is — and I think that I too have the Spirit of God.

Concerning Food Sacrificed to Idols

8 Now about food sacrificed to idols: We know that "We all possess knowledge." But knowledge puffs up while love builds up. 2 Those who think they know something do not yet know as they ought to know. 3 But whoever loves God is known by God.[c]

[a] 36 Or *if she is getting beyond the usual age for marriage* [b] 36-38 Or *36 If anyone thinks he is not treating his daughter properly, and if she is getting along in years* (or *if her passions are too strong*), *and he feels she ought to marry, he should do as he wants. He is not sinning. He should let her get married. 37 But the man who has settled the matter in his own mind, who is under no compulsion but has control over his own will, and who has made up his mind to keep the virgin unmarried — this man also does the right thing. 38 So then, he who gives his virgin in marriage does right, but he who does not give her in marriage does better.* [c] 2,3 An early manuscript and another ancient witness *think they have knowledge do not yet know as they ought to know. 3 But whoever loves truly knows.*

4So then, about eating food sacrificed to
idols: We know that "An idol is nothing at
all in the world" and that "There is no God
but one." 5For even if there are so-called
gods, whether in heaven or on earth (as
indeed there are many "gods" and many
"lords"), 6yet for us there is but one God,
the Father, from whom all things came
and for whom we live; and there is but
one Lord, Jesus Christ, through whom all
things came and through whom we live.

7But not everyone possesses this knowledge. Some people are still so accustomed
to idols that when they eat sacrificial food
they think of it as having been sacrificed
to a god, and since their conscience is
weak, it is defiled. 8But food does not bring
us near to God; we are no worse if we do
not eat, and no better if we do.

9Be careful, however, that the exercise of
your rights does not become a stumbling
block to the weak. 10For if someone with
a weak conscience sees you, with all your
knowledge, eating in an idol's temple,
won't that person be emboldened to eat
what is sacrificed to idols? 11So this weak
brother or sister, for whom Christ died, is
destroyed by your knowledge. 12When you
sin against them in this way and wound
their weak conscience, you sin against
Christ. 13Therefore, if what I eat causes
my brother or sister to fall into sin, I will
never eat meat again, so that I will not
cause them to fall.

Paul's Rights as an Apostle

9 Am I not free? Am I not an apostle?
Have I not seen Jesus our Lord? Are
you not the result of my work in the Lord?
2Even though I may not be an apostle to
others, surely I am to you! For you are the
seal of my apostleship in the Lord.

3This is my defense to those who sit
in judgment on me. 4Don't we have the
right to food and drink? 5Don't we have
the right to take a believing wife along
with us, as do the other apostles and the
Lord's brothers and Cephas[a]? 6Or is it only
I and Barnabas who lack the right to not
work for a living?

7Who serves as a soldier at his own expense? Who plants a vineyard and does
not eat its grapes? Who tends a flock and
does not drink the milk? 8Do I say this
merely on human authority? Doesn't the
Law say the same thing? 9For it is written
in the Law of Moses: "Do not muzzle an
ox while it is treading out the grain."[b]
Is it about oxen that God is concerned?
10Surely he says this for us, doesn't he? Yes,
this was written for us, because whoever
plows and threshes should be able to do
so in the hope of sharing in the harvest.
11If we have sown spiritual seed among
you, is it too much if we reap a material
harvest from you? 12If others have this
right of support from you, shouldn't we
have it all the more?

But we did not use this right. On the
contrary, we put up with anything rather
than hinder the gospel of Christ.

13Don't you know that those who serve
in the temple get their food from the temple, and that those who serve at the altar
share in what is offered on the altar? 14In
the same way, the Lord has commanded
that those who preach the gospel should
receive their living from the gospel.

15But I have not used any of these rights.
And I am not writing this in the hope that
you will do such things for me, for I would
rather die than allow anyone to deprive
me of this boast. 16For when I preach the
gospel, I cannot boast, since I am compelled to preach. Woe to me if I do not
preach the gospel! 17If I preach voluntarily,
I have a reward; if not voluntarily, I am
simply discharging the trust committed
to me. 18What then is my reward? Just this:
that in preaching the gospel I may offer
it free of charge, and so not make full use
of my rights as a preacher of the gospel.

Paul's Use of His Freedom

19Though I am free and belong to no
one, I have made myself a slave to everyone, to win as many as possible. 20To
the Jews I became like a Jew, to win the
Jews. To those under the law I became
like one under the law (though I myself
am not under the law), so as to win those
under the law. 21To those not having the
law I became like one not having the law
(though I am not free from God's law but
am under Christ's law), so as to win those
not having the law. 22To the weak I became
weak, to win the weak. I have become all
things to all people so that by all possible
means I might save some. 23I do all this for
the sake of the gospel, that I may share
in its blessings.

The Need for Self-Discipline

24Do you not know that in a race all
the runners run, but only one gets the
prize? Run in such a way as to get the
prize. 25Everyone who competes in the
games goes into strict training. They do
it to get a crown that will not last, but we
do it to get a crown that will last forever.

[a] 5 That is, Peter [b] 9 Deut. 25:4

26 Therefore I do not run like someone running aimlessly; I do not fight like a boxer
beating the air. 27 No, I strike a blow to my
body and make it my slave so that after I
have preached to others, I myself will not
be disqualified for the prize.

Warnings From Israel's History

10 For I do not want you to be ignorant
of the fact, brothers and sisters, that
our ancestors were all under the cloud and
that they all passed through the sea. 2 They
were all baptized into Moses in the cloud
and in the sea. 3 They all ate the same spiritual food 4 and drank the same spiritual
drink; for they drank from the spiritual
rock that accompanied them, and that
rock was Christ. 5 Nevertheless, God was
not pleased with most of them; their bodies were scattered in the wilderness.

6 Now these things occurred as examples
to keep us from setting our hearts on evil
things as they did. 7 Do not be idolaters, as
some of them were; as it is written: "The
people sat down to eat and drink and got
up to indulge in revelry."[a] 8 We should not
commit sexual immorality, as some of
them did — and in one day twenty-three
thousand of them died. 9 We should not
test Christ,[b] as some of them did — and
were killed by snakes. 10 And do not grumble, as some of them did — and were killed
by the destroying angel.

11 These things happened to them as
examples and were written down as warnings for us, on whom the culmination of
the ages has come. 12 So, if you think you
are standing firm, be careful that you
don't fall! 13 No temptation[c] has overtaken
you except what is common to mankind.
And God is faithful; he will not let you be
tempted[c] beyond what you can bear. But
when you are tempted,[c] he will also provide a way out so that you can endure it.

Idol Feasts and the Lord's Supper

14 Therefore, my dear friends, flee from
idolatry. 15 I speak to sensible people; judge
for yourselves what I say. 16 Is not the cup
of thanksgiving for which we give thanks
a participation in the blood of Christ? And
is not the bread that we break a participation in the body of Christ? 17 Because
there is one loaf, we, who are many, are
one body, for we all share the one loaf.

18 Consider the people of Israel: Do not
those who eat the sacrifices participate
in the altar? 19 Do I mean then that food
sacrificed to an idol is anything, or that an
idol is anything? 20 No, but the sacrifices of
pagans are offered to demons, not to God,
and I do not want you to be participants
with demons. 21 You cannot drink the cup
of the Lord and the cup of demons too;
you cannot have a part in both the Lord's
table and the table of demons. 22 Are we
trying to arouse the Lord's jealousy? Are
we stronger than he?

The Believer's Freedom

23 "I have the right to do anything," you
say — but not everything is beneficial. "I
have the right to do anything" — but not
everything is constructive. 24 No one should
seek their own good, but the good of others.

25 Eat anything sold in the meat market
without raising questions of conscience,
26 for, "The earth is the Lord's, and everything in it."[d]

27 If an unbeliever invites you to a meal
and you want to go, eat whatever is put before you without raising questions of conscience. 28 But if someone says to you, "This
has been offered in sacrifice," then do not
eat it, both for the sake of the one who told
you and for the sake of conscience. 29 I am
referring to the other person's conscience,
not yours. For why is my freedom being
judged by another's conscience? 30 If I take
part in the meal with thankfulness, why
am I denounced because of something I
thank God for?

31 So whether you eat or drink or whatever you do, do it all for the glory of
God. 32 Do not cause anyone to stumble,
whether Jews, Greeks or the church of
God — 33 even as I try to please everyone
in every way. For I am not seeking my
own good but the good of many, so that
11 they may be saved. 1 Follow my example, as I follow the example of Christ.

On Covering the Head in Worship

2 I praise you for remembering me in
everything and for holding to the traditions just as I passed them on to you. 3 But I
want you to realize that the head of every
man is Christ, and the head of the woman
is man,[e] and the head of Christ is God.
4 Every man who prays or prophesies with
his head covered dishonors his head. 5 But
every woman who prays or prophesies
with her head uncovered dishonors her
head — it is the same as having her head
shaved. 6 For if a woman does not cover her
head, she might as well have her hair cut
off; but if it is a disgrace for a woman to
have her hair cut off or her head shaved,
then she should cover her head.

[a] 7 Exodus 32:6 [b] 9 Some manuscripts *test the Lord* [c] 13 The Greek for *temptation* and *tempted* can also mean *testing* and *tested*. [d] 26 Psalm 24:1 [e] 3 Or *of the wife is her husband*

[7]A man ought not to cover his head,[a]
since he is the image and glory of God;
but woman is the glory of man. [8]For man
did not come from woman, but woman
from man; [9]neither was man created for
woman, but woman for man. [10]It is for this
reason that a woman ought to have authority over her own[b] head, because of the
angels. [11]Nevertheless, in the Lord woman
is not independent of man, nor is man
independent of woman. [12]For as woman
came from man, so also man is born of
woman. But everything comes from God.
[13]Judge for yourselves: Is it proper for
a woman to pray to God with her head
uncovered? [14]Does not the very nature of
things teach you that if a man has long
hair, it is a disgrace to him, [15]but that if a
woman has long hair, it is her glory? For
long hair is given to her as a covering. [16]If
anyone wants to be contentious about
this, we have no other practice — nor do
the churches of God.

Correcting an Abuse of the Lord's Supper

[17]In the following directives I have no
praise for you, for your meetings do more
harm than good. [18]In the first place, I hear
that when you come together as a church,
there are divisions among you, and to
some extent I believe it. [19]No doubt there
have to be differences among you to show
which of you have God's approval. [20]So
then, when you come together, it is not
the Lord's Supper you eat, [21]for when you
are eating, some of you go ahead with
your own private suppers. As a result, one
person remains hungry and another gets
drunk. [22]Don't you have homes to eat and
drink in? Or do you despise the church
of God by humiliating those who have
nothing? What shall I say to you? Shall I
praise you? Certainly not in this matter!
[23]For I received from the Lord what I also
passed on to you: The Lord Jesus, on the
night he was betrayed, took bread, [24]and
when he had given thanks, he broke it and
said, "This is my body, which is for you;
do this in remembrance of me." [25]In the
same way, after supper he took the cup,
saying, "This cup is the new covenant in
my blood; do this, whenever you drink it,
in remembrance of me." [26]For whenever
you eat this bread and drink this cup, you
proclaim the Lord's death until he comes.
[27]So then, whoever eats the bread or
drinks the cup of the Lord in an unworthy
manner will be guilty of sinning against
the body and blood of the Lord. [28]Everyone
ought to examine themselves before they
eat of the bread and drink from the cup.
[29]For those who eat and drink without discerning the body of Christ eat and drink
judgment on themselves. [30]That is why
many among you are weak and sick, and
a number of you have fallen asleep. [31]But
if we were more discerning with regard
to ourselves, we would not come under
such judgment. [32]Nevertheless, when we
are judged in this way by the Lord, we are
being disciplined so that we will not be
finally condemned with the world.
[33]So then, my brothers and sisters, when
you gather to eat, you should all eat together. [34]Anyone who is hungry should eat
something at home, so that when you meet
together it may not result in judgment.
And when I come I will give further
directions.

Concerning Spiritual Gifts

12 Now about the gifts of the Spirit,
brothers and sisters, I do not want
you to be uninformed. [2]You know that
when you were pagans, somehow or other you were influenced and led astray
to mute idols. [3]Therefore I want you to
know that no one who is speaking by the
Spirit of God says, "Jesus be cursed," and
no one can say, "Jesus is Lord," except by
the Holy Spirit.
[4]There are different kinds of gifts, but
the same Spirit distributes them. [5]There
are different kinds of service, but the same
Lord. [6]There are different kinds of working, but in all of them and in everyone it
is the same God at work.
[7]Now to each one the manifestation of
the Spirit is given for the common good.
[8]To one there is given through the Spirit
a message of wisdom, to another a message of knowledge by means of the same
Spirit, [9]to another faith by the same Spirit,
to another gifts of healing by that one
Spirit, [10]to another miraculous powers, to
another prophecy, to another distinguishing between spirits, to another speaking
in different kinds of tongues,[c] and to still
another the interpretation of tongues.[c]
[11]All these are the work of one and the
same Spirit, and he distributes them to
each one, just as he determines.

[a] 4-7 Or [4]*Every man who prays or prophesies with long hair dishonors his head.* [5]*But every woman who prays or prophesies with no covering of hair dishonors her head — she is just like one of the "shorn women."* [6]*If a woman has no covering, let her be for now with short hair; but since it is a disgrace for a woman to have her hair shorn or shaved, she should grow it again.* [7]*A man ought not to have long hair* [b] 10 Or *have a sign of authority on her* [c] 10 Or *languages*; also in verse 28

Unity and Diversity in the Body

12 Just as a body, though one, has many
parts, but all its many parts form one
body, so it is with Christ. 13 For we were all
baptized by[a] one Spirit so as to form one
body — whether Jews or Gentiles, slave or
free — and we were all given the one Spirit
to drink. 14 Even so the body is not made
up of one part but of many.

15 Now if the foot should say, "Because
I am not a hand, I do not belong to the
body," it would not for that reason stop
being part of the body. 16 And if the ear
should say, "Because I am not an eye, I do
not belong to the body," it would not for
that reason stop being part of the body. 17 If
the whole body were an eye, where would
the sense of hearing be? If the whole body
were an ear, where would the sense of
smell be? 18 But in fact God has placed the
parts in the body, every one of them, just
as he wanted them to be. 19 If they were all
one part, where would the body be? 20 As
it is, there are many parts, but one body.

21 The eye cannot say to the hand, "I don't
need you!" And the head cannot say to the
feet, "I don't need you!" 22 On the contrary,
those parts of the body that seem to be
weaker are indispensable, 23 and the parts
that we think are less honorable we treat
with special honor. And the parts that are
unpresentable are treated with special mod-
esty, 24 while our presentable parts need no
special treatment. But God has put the body
together, giving greater honor to the parts
that lacked it, 25 so that there should be no
division in the body, but that its parts should
have equal concern for each other. 26 If one
part suffers, every part suffers with it; if one
part is honored, every part rejoices with it.

27 Now you are the body of Christ, and
each one of you is a part of it. 28 And God
has placed in the church first of all apostles, second prophets, third teachers, then
miracles, then gifts of healing, of helping, of guidance, and of different kinds of
tongues. 29 Are all apostles? Are all prophets? Are all teachers? Do all work miracles?
30 Do all have gifts of healing? Do all speak
in tongues[b]? Do all interpret? 31 Now eagerly desire the greater gifts.

Love Is Indispensable

And yet I will show you the most excellent way.

13 If I speak in the tongues[c] of men
or of angels, but do not have love,
I am only a resounding gong or a clang-
ing cymbal. 2 If I have the gift of prophecy and can fathom all mysteries and all
knowledge, and if I have a faith that can
move mountains, but do not have love, I
am nothing. 3 If I give all I possess to the
poor and give over my body to hardship
that I may boast,[d] but do not have love,
I gain nothing.

4 Love is patient, love is kind. It does not
envy, it does not boast, it is not proud. 5 It
does not dishonor others, it is not self-
seeking, it is not easily angered, it keeps
no record of wrongs. 6 Love does not delight in evil but rejoices with the truth.
7 It always protects, always trusts, always
hopes, always perseveres.

8 Love never fails. But where there are
prophecies, they will cease; where there
are tongues, they will be stilled; where
there is knowledge, it will pass away. 9 For
we know in part and we prophesy in part,
10 but when completeness comes, what is
in part disappears. 11 When I was a child,
I talked like a child, I thought like a child,
I reasoned like a child. When I became a
man, I put the ways of childhood behind
me. 12 For now we see only a reflection as
in a mirror; then we shall see face to face.
Now I know in part; then I shall know fully,
even as I am fully known.

13 And now these three remain: faith,
hope and love. But the greatest of these
is love.

Intelligibility in Worship

14 Follow the way of love and eagerly
desire gifts of the Spirit, especially
prophecy. 2 For anyone who speaks in a
tongue[e] does not speak to people but to
God. Indeed, no one understands them;
they utter mysteries by the Spirit. 3 But
the one who prophesies speaks to people
for their strengthening, encouraging and
comfort. 4 Anyone who speaks in a tongue
edifies themselves, but the one who prophesies edifies the church. 5 I would like every one of you to speak in tongues,[f] but
I would rather have you prophesy. The
one who prophesies is greater than the
one who speaks in tongues,[f] unless someone interprets, so that the church may
be edified.

6 Now, brothers and sisters, if I come
to you and speak in tongues, what good
will I be to you, unless I bring you some
revelation or knowledge or prophecy or
word of instruction? 7 Even in the case of
lifeless things that make sounds, such as

[a] *13* Or *with;* or *in* [b] *30* Or *other languages* [c] *1* Or *languages* [d] *3* Some manuscripts *body to the flames* [e] *2* Or *in another language;* also in verses 4, 13, 14, 19, 26 and 27 [f] *5* Or *in other languages;* also in verses 6, 18, 22, 23 and 39

the pipe or harp, how will anyone know what tune is being played unless there is a distinction in the notes? [8]Again, if the trumpet does not sound a clear call, who will get ready for battle? [9]So it is with you. Unless you speak intelligible words with your tongue, how will anyone know what you are saying? You will just be speaking into the air. [10]Undoubtedly there are all sorts of languages in the world, yet none of them is without meaning. [11]If then I do not grasp the meaning of what someone is saying, I am a foreigner to the speaker, and the speaker is a foreigner to me. [12]So it is with you. Since you are eager for gifts of the Spirit, try to excel in those that build up the church.

[13]For this reason the one who speaks in a tongue should pray that they may interpret what they say. [14]For if I pray in a tongue, my spirit prays, but my mind is unfruitful. [15]So what shall I do? I will pray with my spirit, but I will also pray with my understanding; I will sing with my spirit, but I will also sing with my understanding. [16]Otherwise when you are praising God in the Spirit, how can someone else, who is now put in the position of an inquirer,[a] say "Amen" to your thanksgiving, since they do not know what you are saying? [17]You are giving thanks well enough, but no one else is edified.

[18]I thank God that I speak in tongues more than all of you. [19]But in the church I would rather speak five intelligible words to instruct others than ten thousand words in a tongue.

[20]Brothers and sisters, stop thinking like children. In regard to evil be infants, but in your thinking be adults. [21]In the Law it is written:

"With other tongues
  and through the lips of foreigners
I will speak to this people,
  but even then they will not listen
    to me,
      says the Lord."[b]

[22]Tongues, then, are a sign, not for believers but for unbelievers; prophecy, however, is not for unbelievers but for believers. [23]So if the whole church comes together and everyone speaks in tongues, and inquirers or unbelievers come in, will they not say that you are out of your mind? [24]But if an unbeliever or an inquirer comes in while everyone is prophesying, they are convicted of sin and are brought under judgment by all, [25]as the secrets of their hearts are laid bare. So they will fall down and worship God, exclaiming, "God is really among you!"

Good Order in Worship

[26]What then shall we say, brothers and sisters? When you come together, each of you has a hymn, or a word of instruction, a revelation, a tongue or an interpretation. Everything must be done so that the church may be built up. [27]If anyone speaks in a tongue, two — or at the most three — should speak, one at a time, and someone must interpret. [28]If there is no interpreter, the speaker should keep quiet in the church and speak to himself and to God.

[29]Two or three prophets should speak, and the others should weigh carefully what is said. [30]And if a revelation comes to someone who is sitting down, the first speaker should stop. [31]For you can all prophesy in turn so that everyone may be instructed and encouraged. [32]The spirits of prophets are subject to the control of prophets. [33]For God is not a God of disorder but of peace — as in all the congregations of the Lord's people.

[34]Women[c] should remain silent in the churches. They are not allowed to speak, but must be in submission, as the law says. [35]If they want to inquire about something, they should ask their own husbands at home; for it is disgraceful for a woman to speak in the church.[d]

[36]Or did the word of God originate with you? Or are you the only people it has reached? [37]If anyone thinks they are a prophet or otherwise gifted by the Spirit, let them acknowledge that what I am writing to you is the Lord's command. [38]But if anyone ignores this, they will themselves be ignored.[e]

[39]Therefore, my brothers and sisters, be eager to prophesy, and do not forbid speaking in tongues. [40]But everything should be done in a fitting and orderly way.

The Resurrection of Christ

15 Now, brothers and sisters, I want to remind you of the gospel I preached to you, which you received and on which you have taken your stand. [2]By this gospel you are saved, if you hold firmly to the word I preached to you. Otherwise, you have believed in vain.

[a] *16* The Greek word for *inquirer* is a technical term for someone not fully initiated into a religion; also in verses 23 and 24. [b] *21* Isaiah 28:11,12 [c] *33,34* Or *peace. As in all the congregations of the Lord's people, [34]women* [d] *34,35* In a few manuscripts these verses come after verse 40. [e] *38* Some manuscripts *But anyone who is ignorant of this will be ignorant*

3For what I received I passed on to you
as of first importance[a]: that Christ died
for our sins according to the Scriptures,
4that he was buried, that he was raised
on the third day according to the Scriptures, 5and that he appeared to Cephas,[b]
and then to the Twelve. 6After that, he
appeared to more than five hundred of
the brothers and sisters at the same time,
most of whom are still living, though some
have fallen asleep. 7Then he appeared to
James, then to all the apostles, 8and last
of all he appeared to me also, as to one
abnormally born.

9For I am the least of the apostles and
do not even deserve to be called an apostle, because I persecuted the church of
God. 10But by the grace of God I am what
I am, and his grace to me was not without effect. No, I worked harder than all
of them — yet not I, but the grace of God
that was with me. 11Whether, then, it is I
or they, this is what we preach, and this
is what you believed.

The Resurrection of the Dead

12But if it is preached that Christ has
been raised from the dead, how can some
of you say that there is no resurrection of
the dead? 13If there is no resurrection of the
dead, then not even Christ has been raised.
14And if Christ has not been raised, our
preaching is useless and so is your faith.
15More than that, we are then found to be
false witnesses about God, for we have
testified about God that he raised Christ
from the dead. But he did not raise him
if in fact the dead are not raised. 16For if
the dead are not raised, then Christ has
not been raised either. 17And if Christ has
not been raised, your faith is futile; you
are still in your sins. 18Then those also who
have fallen asleep in Christ are lost. 19If
only for this life we have hope in Christ,
we are of all people most to be pitied.

20But Christ has indeed been raised
from the dead, the firstfruits of those
who have fallen asleep. 21For since death
came through a man, the resurrection of
the dead comes also through a man. 22For
as in Adam all die, so in Christ all will be
made alive. 23But each in turn: Christ, the
firstfruits; then, when he comes, those
who belong to him. 24Then the end will
come, when he hands over the kingdom
to God the Father after he has destroyed
all dominion, authority and power. 25For
he must reign until he has put all his enemies under his feet. 26The last enemy to
be destroyed is death. 27For he "has put
everything under his feet."[c] Now when it
says that "everything" has been put under
him, it is clear that this does not include
God himself, who put everything under
Christ. 28When he has done this, then the
Son himself will be made subject to him
who put everything under him, so that
God may be all in all.

29Now if there is no resurrection, what
will those do who are baptized for the
dead? If the dead are not raised at all, why
are people baptized for them? 30And as for
us, why do we endanger ourselves every
hour? 31I face death every day — yes, just
as surely as I boast about you in Christ
Jesus our Lord. 32If I fought wild beasts
in Ephesus with no more than human
hopes, what have I gained? If the dead
are not raised,

> "Let us eat and drink,
> for tomorrow we die."[d]

33Do not be misled: "Bad company corrupts
good character."[e] 34Come back to your
senses as you ought, and stop sinning;
for there are some who are ignorant of
God — I say this to your shame.

The Resurrection Body

35But someone will ask, "How are the
dead raised? With what kind of body will
they come?" 36How foolish! What you sow
does not come to life unless it dies. 37When
you sow, you do not plant the body that
will be, but just a seed, perhaps of wheat
or of something else. 38But God gives it a
body as he has determined, and to each
kind of seed he gives its own body. 39Not
all flesh is the same: People have one kind
of flesh, animals have another, birds another and fish another. 40There are also
heavenly bodies and there are earthly
bodies; but the splendor of the heavenly
bodies is one kind, and the splendor of the
earthly bodies is another. 41The sun has
one kind of splendor, the moon another
and the stars another; and star differs
from star in splendor.

42So will it be with the resurrection of
the dead. The body that is sown is perishable, it is raised imperishable; 43it is
sown in dishonor, it is raised in glory; it
is sown in weakness, it is raised in power;
44it is sown a natural body, it is raised a
spiritual body.

If there is a natural body, there is also
a spiritual body. 45So it is written: "The
first man Adam became a living being"[f];

[a] *3* Or *you at the first* [b] *5* That is, Peter [c] *27* Psalm 8:6 [d] *32* Isaiah 22:13 [e] *33* From the Greek poet Menander [f] *45* Gen. 2:7

the last Adam, a life-giving spirit. 46The spiritual did not come first, but the natural, and after that the spiritual. 47The first man was of the dust of the earth; the second man is of heaven. 48As was the earthly man, so are those who are of the earth; and as is the heavenly man, so also are those who are of heaven. 49And just as we have borne the image of the earthly man, so shall we[a] bear the image of the heavenly man.

50I declare to you, brothers and sisters, that flesh and blood cannot inherit the kingdom of God, nor does the perishable inherit the imperishable. 51Listen, I tell you a mystery: We will not all sleep, but we will all be changed — 52in a flash, in the twinkling of an eye, at the last trumpet. For the trumpet will sound, the dead will be raised imperishable, and we will be changed. 53For the perishable must clothe itself with the imperishable, and the mortal with immortality. 54When the perishable has been clothed with the imperishable, and the mortal with immortality, then the saying that is written will come true: "Death has been swallowed up in victory."[b]

55"Where, O death, is your victory?
Where, O death, is your sting?"[c]

56The sting of death is sin, and the power of sin is the law. 57But thanks be to God! He gives us the victory through our Lord Jesus Christ.

58Therefore, my dear brothers and sisters, stand firm. Let nothing move you. Always give yourselves fully to the work of the Lord, because you know that your labor in the Lord is not in vain.

The Collection for the Lord's People

16 Now about the collection for the Lord's people: Do what I told the Galatian churches to do. 2On the first day of every week, each one of you should set aside a sum of money in keeping with your income, saving it up, so that when I come no collections will have to be made. 3Then, when I arrive, I will give letters of introduction to the men you approve and send them with your gift to Jerusalem. 4If it seems advisable for me to go also, they will accompany me.

Personal Requests

5After I go through Macedonia, I will come to you — for I will be going through Macedonia. 6Perhaps I will stay with you for a while, or even spend the winter, so that you can help me on my journey, wherever I go. 7For I do not want to see you now and make only a passing visit; I hope to spend some time with you, if the Lord permits. 8But I will stay on at Ephesus until Pentecost, 9because a great door for effective work has opened to me, and there are many who oppose me.

10When Timothy comes, see to it that he has nothing to fear while he is with you, for he is carrying on the work of the Lord, just as I am. 11No one, then, should treat him with contempt. Send him on his way in peace so that he may return to me. I am expecting him along with the brothers.

12Now about our brother Apollos: I strongly urged him to go to you with the brothers. He was quite unwilling to go now, but he will go when he has the opportunity.

13Be on your guard; stand firm in the faith; be courageous; be strong. 14Do everything in love.

15You know that the household of Stephanas were the first converts in Achaia, and they have devoted themselves to the service of the Lord's people. I urge you, brothers and sisters, 16to submit to such people and to everyone who joins in the work and labors at it. 17I was glad when Stephanas, Fortunatus and Achaicus arrived, because they have supplied what was lacking from you. 18For they refreshed my spirit and yours also. Such men deserve recognition.

Final Greetings

19The churches in the province of Asia send you greetings. Aquila and Priscilla[d] greet you warmly in the Lord, and so does the church that meets at their house. 20All the brothers and sisters here send you greetings. Greet one another with a holy kiss.

21I, Paul, write this greeting in my own hand.

22If anyone does not love the Lord, let that person be cursed! Come, Lord[e]!

23The grace of the Lord Jesus be with you.

24My love to all of you in Christ Jesus. Amen.[f]

[a] 49 Some early manuscripts *so let us* [b] 54 Isaiah 25:8 [c] 55 Hosea 13:14 [d] 19 Greek *Prisca,* a variant of *Priscilla* [e] 22 The Greek for *Come, Lord* reproduces an Aramaic expression (*Marana tha*) used by early Christians. [f] 24 Some manuscripts do not have *Amen.*

2 CORINTHIANS

1 Paul, an apostle of Christ Jesus by the
will of God, and Timothy our brother,

To the church of God in Corinth, together with all his holy people throughout
Achaia:

2Grace and peace to you from God our
Father and the Lord Jesus Christ.

Praise to the God of All Comfort

3Praise be to the God and Father of our
Lord Jesus Christ, the Father of compassion and the God of all comfort, 4who comforts us in all our troubles, so that we can
comfort those in any trouble with the comfort we ourselves receive from God. 5For
just as we share abundantly in the sufferings of Christ, so also our comfort abounds
through Christ. 6If we are distressed, it is
for your comfort and salvation; if we are
comforted, it is for your comfort, which
produces in you patient endurance of the
same sufferings we suffer. 7And our hope
for you is firm, because we know that just
as you share in our sufferings, so also you
share in our comfort.
8We do not want you to be uninformed,
brothers and sisters,[a] about the troubles
we experienced in the province of Asia. We
were under great pressure, far beyond our
ability to endure, so that we despaired of
life itself. 9Indeed, we felt we had received
the sentence of death. But this happened
that we might not rely on ourselves but on
God, who raises the dead. 10He has delivered us from such a deadly peril, and he
will deliver us again. On him we have set
our hope that he will continue to deliver
us, 11as you help us by your prayers. Then
many will give thanks on our behalf for
the gracious favor granted us in answer
to the prayers of many.

Paul's Change of Plans

12Now this is our boast: Our conscience
testifies that we have conducted ourselves
in the world, and especially in our relations with you, with integrity[b] and godly
sincerity. We have done so, relying not on
worldly wisdom but on God's grace. 13For
we do not write you anything you cannot
read or understand. And I hope that, 14as
you have understood us in part, you will
come to understand fully that you can
boast of us just as we will boast of you in
the day of the Lord Jesus.
15Because I was confident of this, I wanted to visit you first so that you might benefit twice. 16I wanted to visit you on my
way to Macedonia and to come back to
you from Macedonia, and then to have
you send me on my way to Judea. 17Was
I fickle when I intended to do this? Or do
I make my plans in a worldly manner so
that in the same breath I say both "Yes,
yes" and "No, no"?
18But as surely as God is faithful, our
message to you is not "Yes" and "No."
19For the Son of God, Jesus Christ, who was
preached among you by us — by me and
Silas[c] and Timothy — was not "Yes" and
"No," but in him it has always been "Yes."
20For no matter how many promises God
has made, they are "Yes" in Christ. And so
through him the "Amen" is spoken by us to
the glory of God. 21Now it is God who makes
both us and you stand firm in Christ. He
anointed us, 22set his seal of ownership
on us, and put his Spirit in our hearts as
a deposit, guaranteeing what is to come.
23I call God as my witness — and I
stake my life on it — that it was in order
to spare you that I did not return to Corinth. 24Not that we lord it over your faith,
but we work with you for your joy, because
it is by faith you stand firm. 2 1So I made
up my mind that I would not make
another painful visit to you. 2For if I grieve
you, who is left to make me glad but you
whom I have grieved? 3I wrote as I did, so
that when I came I would not be distressed
by those who should have made me rejoice.
I had confidence in all of you, that you
would all share my joy. 4For I wrote you out
of great distress and anguish of heart and
with many tears, not to grieve you but to
let you know the depth of my love for you.

Forgiveness for the Offender

5If anyone has caused grief, he has not
so much grieved me as he has grieved all
of you to some extent — not to put it too
severely. 6The punishment inflicted on
him by the majority is sufficient. 7Now

[a] *8* The Greek word for *brothers and sisters* (*adelphoi*) refers here to believers, both men and women, as part of God's family; also in 8:1; 13:11. [b] *12* Many manuscripts *holiness* [c] *19* Greek *Silvanus*, a variant of *Silas*

instead, you ought to forgive and comfort him, so that he will not be overwhelmed by excessive sorrow. 8I urge you, therefore, to reaffirm your love for him. 9Another reason I wrote you was to see if you would stand the test and be obedient in everything. 10Anyone you forgive, I also forgive. And what I have forgiven — if there was anything to forgive — I have forgiven in the sight of Christ for your sake, 11in order that Satan might not outwit us. For we are not unaware of his schemes.

Ministers of the New Covenant

12Now when I went to Troas to preach the gospel of Christ and found that the Lord had opened a door for me, 13I still had no peace of mind, because I did not find my brother Titus there. So I said goodbye to them and went on to Macedonia.

14But thanks be to God, who always leads us as captives in Christ's triumphal procession and uses us to spread the aroma of the knowledge of him everywhere. 15For we are to God the pleasing aroma of Christ among those who are being saved and those who are perishing. 16To the one we are an aroma that brings death; to the other, an aroma that brings life. And who is equal to such a task? 17Unlike so many, we do not peddle the word of God for profit. On the contrary, in Christ we speak before God with sincerity, as those sent from God.

3 Are we beginning to commend ourselves again? Or do we need, like some people, letters of recommendation to you or from you? 2You yourselves are our letter, written on our hearts, known and read by everyone. 3You show that you are a letter from Christ, the result of our ministry, written not with ink but with the Spirit of the living God, not on tablets of stone but on tablets of human hearts.

4Such confidence we have through Christ before God. 5Not that we are competent in ourselves to claim anything for ourselves, but our competence comes from God. 6He has made us competent as ministers of a new covenant — not of the letter but of the Spirit; for the letter kills, but the Spirit gives life.

The Greater Glory of the New Covenant

7Now if the ministry that brought death, which was engraved in letters on stone, came with glory, so that the Israelites could not look steadily at the face of Moses because of its glory, transitory though it was, 8will not the ministry of the Spirit be even more glorious? 9If the ministry that brought condemnation was glorious, how much more glorious is the ministry that brings righteousness! 10For what was glorious has no glory now in comparison with the surpassing glory. 11And if what was transitory came with glory, how much greater is the glory of that which lasts!

12Therefore, since we have such a hope, we are very bold. 13We are not like Moses, who would put a veil over his face to prevent the Israelites from seeing the end of what was passing away. 14But their minds were made dull, for to this day the same veil remains when the old covenant is read. It has not been removed, because only in Christ is it taken away. 15Even to this day when Moses is read, a veil covers their hearts. 16But whenever anyone turns to the Lord, the veil is taken away. 17Now the Lord is the Spirit, and where the Spirit of the Lord is, there is freedom. 18And we all, who with unveiled faces contemplate[a] the Lord's glory, are being transformed into his image with ever-increasing glory, which comes from the Lord, who is the Spirit.

Present Weakness and Resurrection Life

4 Therefore, since through God's mercy we have this ministry, we do not lose heart. 2Rather, we have renounced secret and shameful ways; we do not use deception, nor do we distort the word of God. On the contrary, by setting forth the truth plainly we commend ourselves to everyone's conscience in the sight of God. 3And even if our gospel is veiled, it is veiled to those who are perishing. 4The god of this age has blinded the minds of unbelievers, so that they cannot see the light of the gospel that displays the glory of Christ, who is the image of God. 5For what we preach is not ourselves, but Jesus Christ as Lord, and ourselves as your servants for Jesus' sake. 6For God, who said, "Let light shine out of darkness,"[b] made his light shine in our hearts to give us the light of the knowledge of God's glory displayed in the face of Christ.

7But we have this treasure in jars of clay to show that this all-surpassing power is from God and not from us. 8We are hard pressed on every side, but not crushed; perplexed, but not in despair; 9persecuted, but not abandoned; struck down, but not destroyed. 10We always carry around in our body the death of Jesus, so that the life of Jesus may also be revealed in our

[a] 18 Or *reflect* [b] 6 Gen. 1:3

body. 11For we who are alive are always
being given over to death for Jesus' sake,
so that his life may also be revealed in our
mortal body. 12So then, death is at work in
us, but life is at work in you.
13It is written: "I believed; therefore I
have spoken."[a] Since we have that same
spirit of[b] faith, we also believe and therefore speak, 14because we know that the one
who raised the Lord Jesus from the dead
will also raise us with Jesus and present
us with you to himself. 15All this is for your
benefit, so that the grace that is reaching
more and more people may cause thanksgiving to overflow to the glory of God.
16Therefore we do not lose heart.
Though outwardly we are wasting away,
yet inwardly we are being renewed day
by day. 17For our light and momentary
troubles are achieving for us an eternal
glory that far outweighs them all. 18So
we fix our eyes not on what is seen, but
on what is unseen, since what is seen is
temporary, but what is unseen is eternal.

Awaiting the New Body

5 For we know that if the earthly tent we
live in is destroyed, we have a building
from God, an eternal house in heaven, not
built by human hands. 2Meanwhile we
groan, longing to be clothed instead with
our heavenly dwelling, 3because when we
are clothed, we will not be found naked.
4For while we are in this tent, we groan
and are burdened, because we do not wish
to be unclothed but to be clothed instead
with our heavenly dwelling, so that what is
mortal may be swallowed up by life. 5Now
the one who has fashioned us for this very
purpose is God, who has given us the Spirit
as a deposit, guaranteeing what is to come.
6Therefore we are always confident
and know that as long as we are at home
in the body we are away from the Lord.
7For we live by faith, not by sight. 8We are
confident, I say, and would prefer to be
away from the body and at home with
the Lord. 9So we make it our goal to please
him, whether we are at home in the body
or away from it. 10For we must all appear
before the judgment seat of Christ, so
that each of us may receive what is due
us for the things done while in the body,
whether good or bad.

The Ministry of Reconciliation

11Since, then, we know what it is to fear
the Lord, we try to persuade others. What
we are is plain to God, and I hope it is also
plain to your conscience. 12We are not trying to commend ourselves to you again,
but are giving you an opportunity to take
pride in us, so that you can answer those
who take pride in what is seen rather than
in what is in the heart. 13If we are "out
of our mind," as some say, it is for God;
if we are in our right mind, it is for you.
14For Christ's love compels us, because we
are convinced that one died for all, and
therefore all died. 15And he died for all,
that those who live should no longer live
for themselves but for him who died for
them and was raised again.
16So from now on we regard no one
from a worldly point of view. Though we
once regarded Christ in this way, we do
so no longer. 17Therefore, if anyone is in
Christ, the new creation has come:[c] The
old has gone, the new is here! 18All this is
from God, who reconciled us to himself
through Christ and gave us the ministry
of reconciliation: 19that God was recon-
ciling the world to himself in Christ, not
counting people's sins against them. And
he has committed to us the message of
reconciliation. 20We are therefore Christ's
ambassadors, as though God were making
his appeal through us. We implore you on
Christ's behalf: Be reconciled to God. 21God
made him who had no sin to be sin[d] for
us, so that in him we might become the
righteousness of God.

6 As God's co-workers we urge you not
to receive God's grace in vain. 2For
he says,

"In the time of my favor I heard you,
and in the day of salvation I helped
you."[e]

I tell you, now is the time of God's favor,
now is the day of salvation.

Paul's Hardships

3We put no stumbling block in anyone's
path, so that our ministry will not be discredited. 4Rather, as servants of God we
commend ourselves in every way: in great
endurance; in troubles, hardships and
distresses; 5in beatings, imprisonments
and riots; in hard work, sleepless nights
and hunger; 6in purity, understanding,
patience and kindness; in the Holy Spirit
and in sincere love; 7in truthful speech
and in the power of God; with weapons
of righteousness in the right hand and
in the left; 8through glory and dishon-
or, bad report and good report; genuine,
yet regarded as impostors; 9known, yet

[a] *13* Psalm 116:10 (see Septuagint) [b] *13* Or *Spirit-given* [c] *17* Or *Christ, that person is a new creation.* [d] *21* Or *be a sin offering* [e] *2* Isaiah 49:8

regarded as unknown; dying, and yet
we live on; beaten, and yet not killed;
10sorrowful, yet always rejoicing; poor,
yet making many rich; having nothing,
and yet possessing everything.
11We have spoken freely to you, Corinthians, and opened wide our hearts to you.
12We are not withholding our affection
from you, but you are withholding yours
from us. 13As a fair exchange — I speak as to
my children — open wide your hearts also.

Warning Against Idolatry

14Do not be yoked together with unbelievers. For what do righteousness and
wickedness have in common? Or what
fellowship can light have with darkness?
15What harmony is there between Christ
and Belial[a]? Or what does a believer have
in common with an unbeliever? 16What
agreement is there between the temple
of God and idols? For we are the temple
of the living God. As God has said:

"I will live with them
and walk among them,
and I will be their God,
and they will be my people."[b]

17Therefore,

"Come out from them
and be separate,
says the Lord.
Touch no unclean thing,
and I will receive you."[c]

18And,

"I will be a Father to you,
and you will be my sons and
daughters,
says the Lord Almighty."[d]

7 Therefore, since we have these promises, dear friends, let us purify ourselves
from everything that contaminates body
and spirit, perfecting holiness out of reverence for God.

Paul's Joy Over the Church's Repentance

2Make room for us in your hearts. We
have wronged no one, we have corrupted
no one, we have exploited no one. 3I do
not say this to condemn you; I have said
before that you have such a place in our
hearts that we would live or die with you. 4I
have spoken to you with great frankness;
I take great pride in you. I am greatly
encouraged; in all our troubles my joy
knows no bounds.
5For when we came into Macedonia, we
had no rest, but we were harassed at every turn — conflicts on the outside, fears
within. 6But God, who comforts the downcast, comforted us by the coming of Titus,
7and not only by his coming but also by
the comfort you had given him. He told
us about your longing for me, your deep
sorrow, your ardent concern for me, so that
my joy was greater than ever.
8Even if I caused you sorrow by my letter, I do not regret it. Though I did regret
it — I see that my letter hurt you, but only
for a little while — 9yet now I am happy,
not because you were made sorry, but because your sorrow led you to repentance.
For you became sorrowful as God intended
and so were not harmed in any way by us.
10Godly sorrow brings repentance that
leads to salvation and leaves no regret,
but worldly sorrow brings death. 11See
what this godly sorrow has produced in
you: what earnestness, what eagerness to
clear yourselves, what indignation, what
alarm, what longing, what concern, what
readiness to see justice done. At every
point you have proved yourselves to be
innocent in this matter. 12So even though
I wrote to you, it was neither on account
of the one who did the wrong nor on account of the injured party, but rather that
before God you could see for yourselves
how devoted to us you are. 13By all this
we are encouraged.
In addition to our own encouragement,
we were especially delighted to see how
happy Titus was, because his spirit has
been refreshed by all of you. 14I had boasted to him about you, and you have not
embarrassed me. But just as everything
we said to you was true, so our boasting
about you to Titus has proved to be true as
well. 15And his affection for you is all the
greater when he remembers that you were
all obedient, receiving him with fear and
trembling. 16I am glad I can have complete
confidence in you.

The Collection for the Lord's People

8 And now, brothers and sisters, we want
you to know about the grace that God
has given the Macedonian churches. 2In
the midst of a very severe trial, their overflowing joy and their extreme poverty
welled up in rich generosity. 3For I testify
that they gave as much as they were able,
and even beyond their ability. Entirely on
their own, 4they urgently pleaded with us
for the privilege of sharing in this service

[a] 15 Greek *Beliar,* a variant of *Belial* [b] 16 Lev. 26:12; Jer. 32:38; Ezek. 37:27 [c] 17 Isaiah 52:11; Ezek. 20:34,41 [d] 18 2 Samuel 7:14; 7:8

to the Lord's people. 5And they exceeded our expectations: They gave themselves first of all to the Lord, and then by the will of God also to us. 6So we urged Titus, just as he had earlier made a beginning, to bring also to completion this act of grace on your part. 7But since you excel in everything — in faith, in speech, in knowledge, in complete earnestness and in the love we have kindled in you[a] — see that you also excel in this grace of giving.

8I am not commanding you, but I want to test the sincerity of your love by comparing it with the earnestness of others. 9For you know the grace of our Lord Jesus Christ, that though he was rich, yet for your sake he became poor, so that you through his poverty might become rich.

10And here is my judgment about what is best for you in this matter. Last year you were the first not only to give but also to have the desire to do so. 11Now finish the work, so that your eager willingness to do it may be matched by your completion of it, according to your means. 12For if the willingness is there, the gift is acceptable according to what one has, not according to what one does not have.

13Our desire is not that others might be relieved while you are hard pressed, but that there might be equality. 14At the present time your plenty will supply what they need, so that in turn their plenty will supply what you need. The goal is equality, 15as it is written: "The one who gathered much did not have too much, and the one who gathered little did not have too little."[b]

Titus Sent to Receive the Collection

16Thanks be to God, who put into the heart of Titus the same concern I have for you. 17For Titus not only welcomed our appeal, but he is coming to you with much enthusiasm and on his own initiative. 18And we are sending along with him the brother who is praised by all the churches for his service to the gospel. 19What is more, he was chosen by the churches to accompany us as we carry the offering, which we administer in order to honor the Lord himself and to show our eagerness to help. 20We want to avoid any criticism of the way we administer this liberal gift. 21For we are taking pains to do what is right, not only in the eyes of the Lord but also in the eyes of man.

22In addition, we are sending with them our brother who has often proved to us in many ways that he is zealous, and now even more so because of his great confidence in you. 23As for Titus, he is my partner and co-worker among you; as for our brothers, they are representatives of the churches and an honor to Christ. 24Therefore show these men the proof of your love and the reason for our pride in you, so that the churches can see it.

9 There is no need for me to write to you about this service to the Lord's people. 2For I know your eagerness to help, and I have been boasting about it to the Macedonians, telling them that since last year you in Achaia were ready to give; and your enthusiasm has stirred most of them to action. 3But I am sending the brothers in order that our boasting about you in this matter should not prove hollow, but that you may be ready, as I said you would be. 4For if any Macedonians come with me and find you unprepared, we — not to say anything about you — would be ashamed of having been so confident. 5So I thought it necessary to urge the brothers to visit you in advance and finish the arrangements for the generous gift you had promised. Then it will be ready as a generous gift, not as one grudgingly given.

Generosity Encouraged

6Remember this: Whoever sows sparingly will also reap sparingly, and whoever sows generously will also reap generously. 7Each of you should give what you have decided in your heart to give, not reluctantly or under compulsion, for God loves a cheerful giver. 8And God is able to bless you abundantly, so that in all things at all times, having all that you need, you will abound in every good work. 9As it is written:

> "They have freely scattered their gifts
> to the poor;
> their righteousness endures
> forever."[c]

10Now he who supplies seed to the sower and bread for food will also supply and increase your store of seed and will enlarge the harvest of your righteousness. 11You will be enriched in every way so that you can be generous on every occasion, and through us your generosity will result in thanksgiving to God.

12This service that you perform is not only supplying the needs of the Lord's people but is also overflowing in many expressions of thanks to God. 13Because of the service by which you have proved yourselves, others will praise God for the obedience

[a] 7 Some manuscripts *and in your love for us* [b] 15 Exodus 16:18 [c] 9 Psalm 112:9

that accompanies your confession of the
gospel of Christ, and for your generosity in
sharing with them and with everyone else.
[14]And in their prayers for you their hearts
will go out to you, because of the surpassing grace God has given you. [15]Thanks be
to God for his indescribable gift!

Paul's Defense of His Ministry

10 By the humility and gentleness of
Christ, I appeal to you — I, Paul, who
am "timid" when face to face with you, but
"bold" toward you when away! [2]I beg you
that when I come I may not have to be as
bold as I expect to be toward some people
who think that we live by the standards
of this world. [3]For though we live in the
world, we do not wage war as the world
does. [4]The weapons we fight with are not
the weapons of the world. On the contrary, they have divine power to demolish
strongholds. [5]We demolish arguments
and every pretension that sets itself up
against the knowledge of God, and we
take captive every thought to make it
obedient to Christ. [6]And we will be ready
to punish every act of disobedience, once
your obedience is complete.

[7]You are judging by appearances.[a] If
anyone is confident that they belong to
Christ, they should consider again that we
belong to Christ just as much as they do. [8]So
even if I boast somewhat freely about the
authority the Lord gave us for building you
up rather than tearing you down, I will not
be ashamed of it. [9]I do not want to seem to
be trying to frighten you with my letters.
[10]For some say, "His letters are weighty and
forceful, but in person he is unimpressive
and his speaking amounts to nothing."
[11]Such people should realize that what we
are in our letters when we are absent, we
will be in our actions when we are present.

[12]We do not dare to classify or compare
ourselves with some who commend themselves. When they measure themselves by
themselves and compare themselves with
themselves, they are not wise. [13]We, however, will not boast beyond proper limits,
but will confine our boasting to the sphere
of service God himself has assigned to us,
a sphere that also includes you. [14]We are
not going too far in our boasting, as would
be the case if we had not come to you, for
we did get as far as you with the gospel
of Christ. [15]Neither do we go beyond our
limits by boasting of work done by others.
Our hope is that, as your faith continues
to grow, our sphere of activity among
you will greatly expand, [16]so that we can
preach the gospel in the regions beyond
you. For we do not want to boast about
work already done in someone else's territory. [17]But, "Let the one who boasts boast
in the Lord."[b] [18]For it is not the one who
commends himself who is approved, but
the one whom the Lord commends.

Paul and the False Apostles

11 I hope you will put up with me in a
little foolishness. Yes, please put up
with me! [2]I am jealous for you with a godly
jealousy. I promised you to one husband,
to Christ, so that I might present you as a
pure virgin to him. [3]But I am afraid that
just as Eve was deceived by the serpent's
cunning, your minds may somehow be led
astray from your sincere and pure devotion to Christ. [4]For if someone comes to
you and preaches a Jesus other than the
Jesus we preached, or if you receive a different spirit from the Spirit you received,
or a different gospel from the one you
accepted, you put up with it easily enough.

[5]I do not think I am in the least inferior
to those "super-apostles."[c] [6]I may indeed
be untrained as a speaker, but I do have
knowledge. We have made this perfectly
clear to you in every way. [7]Was it a sin for
me to lower myself in order to elevate
you by preaching the gospel of God to you
free of charge? [8]I robbed other churches
by receiving support from them so as to
serve you. [9]And when I was with you and
needed something, I was not a burden to
anyone, for the brothers who came from
Macedonia supplied what I needed. I have
kept myself from being a burden to you
in any way, and will continue to do so.
[10]As surely as the truth of Christ is in me,
nobody in the regions of Achaia will stop
this boasting of mine. [11]Why? Because I do
not love you? God knows I do!

[12]And I will keep on doing what I am
doing in order to cut the ground from
under those who want an opportunity to
be considered equal with us in the things
they boast about. [13]For such people are
false apostles, deceitful workers, mas-
querading as apostles of Christ. [14]And no
wonder, for Satan himself masquerades
as an angel of light. [15]It is not surprising,
then, if his servants also masquerade as
servants of righteousness. Their end will
be what their actions deserve.

Paul Boasts About His Sufferings

[16]I repeat: Let no one take me for a fool.
But if you do, then tolerate me just as
you would a fool, so that I may do a little

[a] 7 Or *Look at the obvious facts* [b] 17 Jer. 9:24 [c] 5 Or *to the most eminent apostles*

boasting. 17In this self-confident boasting I am not talking as the Lord would, but as a fool. 18Since many are boasting in the way the world does, I too will boast. 19You gladly put up with fools since you are so wise! 20In fact, you even put up with anyone who enslaves you or exploits you or takes advantage of you or puts on airs or slaps you in the face. 21To my shame I admit that we were too weak for that!

Whatever anyone else dares to boast about — I am speaking as a fool — I also dare to boast about. 22Are they Hebrews? So am I. Are they Israelites? So am I. Are they Abraham's descendants? So am I. 23Are they servants of Christ? (I am out of my mind to talk like this.) I am more. I have worked much harder, been in prison more frequently, been flogged more severely, and been exposed to death again and again. 24Five times I received from the Jews the forty lashes minus one. 25Three times I was beaten with rods, once I was pelted with stones, three times I was shipwrecked, I spent a night and a day in the open sea, 26I have been constantly on the move. I have been in danger from rivers, in danger from bandits, in danger from my fellow Jews, in danger from Gentiles; in danger in the city, in danger in the country, in danger at sea; and in danger from false believers. 27I have labored and toiled and have often gone without sleep; I have known hunger and thirst and have often gone without food; I have been cold and naked. 28Besides everything else, I face daily the pressure of my concern for all the churches. 29Who is weak, and I do not feel weak? Who is led into sin, and I do not inwardly burn?

30If I must boast, I will boast of the things that show my weakness. 31The God and Father of the Lord Jesus, who is to be praised forever, knows that I am not lying. 32In Damascus the governor under King Aretas had the city of the Damascenes guarded in order to arrest me. 33But I was lowered in a basket from a window in the wall and slipped through his hands.

Paul's Vision and His Thorn

12 I must go on boasting. Although there is nothing to be gained, I will go on to visions and revelations from the Lord. 2I know a man in Christ who fourteen years ago was caught up to the third heaven. Whether it was in the body or out of the body I do not know — God knows. 3And I know that this man — whether in the body or apart from the body I do not know, but God knows — 4was caught up to paradise and heard inexpressible things, things that no one is permitted to tell. 5I will boast about a man like that, but I will not boast about myself, except about my weaknesses. 6Even if I should choose to boast, I would not be a fool, because I would be speaking the truth. But I refrain, so no one will think more of me than is warranted by what I do or say, 7or because of these surpassingly great revelations. Therefore, in order to keep me from becoming conceited, I was given a thorn in my flesh, a messenger of Satan, to torment me. 8Three times I pleaded with the Lord to take it away from me. 9But he said to me, "My grace is sufficient for you, for my power is made perfect in weakness." Therefore I will boast all the more gladly about my weaknesses, so that Christ's power may rest on me. 10That is why, for Christ's sake, I delight in weaknesses, in insults, in hardships, in persecutions, in difficulties. For when I am weak, then I am strong.

Paul's Concern for the Corinthians

11I have made a fool of myself, but you drove me to it. I ought to have been commended by you, for I am not in the least inferior to the "super-apostles,"[a] even though I am nothing. 12I persevered in demonstrating among you the marks of a true apostle, including signs, wonders and miracles. 13How were you inferior to the other churches, except that I was never a burden to you? Forgive me this wrong!

14Now I am ready to visit you for the third time, and I will not be a burden to you, because what I want is not your possessions but you. After all, children should not have to save up for their parents, but parents for their children. 15So I will very gladly spend for you everything I have and expend myself as well. If I love you more, will you love me less? 16Be that as it may, I have not been a burden to you. Yet, crafty fellow that I am, I caught you by trickery! 17Did I exploit you through any of the men I sent to you? 18I urged Titus to go to you and I sent our brother with him. Titus did not exploit you, did he? Did we not walk in the same footsteps by the same Spirit?

19Have you been thinking all along that we have been defending ourselves to you? We have been speaking in the sight of God as those in Christ; and everything we do, dear friends, is for your strengthening. 20For I am afraid that when I come I may not find you as I want you to be, and you

[a] *11* Or *the most eminent apostles*

may not find me as you want me to be.
I fear that there may be discord, jealousy, fits of rage, selfish ambition, slander,
gossip, arrogance and disorder. [21]I am
afraid that when I come again my God
will humble me before you, and I will be
grieved over many who have sinned earlier and have not repented of the impurity,
sexual sin and debauchery in which they
have indulged.

Final Warnings

13 This will be my third visit to you.
"Every matter must be established
by the testimony of two or three witnesses."[a] [2]I already gave you a warning when
I was with you the second time. I now repeat it while absent: On my return I will
not spare those who sinned earlier or any
of the others, [3]since you are demanding
proof that Christ is speaking through me.
He is not weak in dealing with you, but is
powerful among you. [4]For to be sure, he
was crucified in weakness, yet he lives
by God's power. Likewise, we are weak in
him, yet by God's power we will live with
him in our dealing with you.
[5]Examine yourselves to see whether you
are in the faith; test yourselves. Do you not
realize that Christ Jesus is in you — unless,
of course, you fail the test? [6]And I trust
that you will discover that we have not
failed the test. [7]Now we pray to God that
you will not do anything wrong — not so
that people will see that we have stood the
test but so that you will do what is right
even though we may seem to have failed.
[8]For we cannot do anything against the
truth, but only for the truth. [9]We are glad
whenever we are weak but you are strong;
and our prayer is that you may be fully
restored. [10]This is why I write these things
when I am absent, that when I come I
may not have to be harsh in my use of
authority — the authority the Lord gave
me for building you up, not for tearing
you down.

Final Greetings

[11]Finally, brothers and sisters, rejoice!
Strive for full restoration, encourage one
another, be of one mind, live in peace. And
the God of love and peace will be with you.
[12]Greet one another with a holy kiss. [13]All
God's people here send their greetings.
[14]May the grace of the Lord Jesus Christ,
and the love of God, and the fellowship of
the Holy Spirit be with you all.

[a] *1* Deut. 19:15

GALATIANS

1 Paul, an apostle — sent not from men
nor by a man, but by Jesus Christ and
God the Father, who raised him from the
dead — 2and all the brothers and sisters[a]
with me,

To the churches in Galatia:

3Grace and peace to you from God our
Father and the Lord Jesus Christ, 4who
gave himself for our sins to rescue us from
the present evil age, according to the will
of our God and Father, 5to whom be glory
for ever and ever. Amen.

No Other Gospel

6I am astonished that you are so quickly
deserting the one who called you to live
in the grace of Christ and are turning
to a different gospel — 7which is really
no gospel at all. Evidently some people
are throwing you into confusion and are
trying to pervert the gospel of Christ. 8But
even if we or an angel from heaven should
preach a gospel other than the one we
preached to you, let them be under God's
curse! 9As we have already said, so now I
say again: If anybody is preaching to you
a gospel other than what you accepted, let
them be under God's curse!
10Am I now trying to win the approval of
human beings, or of God? Or am I trying
to please people? If I were still trying to
please people, I would not be a servant
of Christ.

Paul Called by God

11I want you to know, brothers and sisters, that the gospel I preached is not of
human origin. 12I did not receive it from
any man, nor was I taught it; rather, I received it by revelation from Jesus Christ.
13For you have heard of my previous
way of life in Judaism, how intensely I
persecuted the church of God and tried to
destroy it. 14I was advancing in Judaism
beyond many of my own age among my
people and was extremely zealous for
the traditions of my fathers. 15But when
God, who set me apart from my mother's
womb and called me by his grace, was
pleased 16to reveal his Son in me so that
I might preach him among the Gentiles,
my immediate response was not to consult any human being. 17I did not go up to
Jerusalem to see those who were apostles
before I was, but I went into Arabia. Later
I returned to Damascus.
18Then after three years, I went up to
Jerusalem to get acquainted with Cephas[b]
and stayed with him fifteen days. 19I saw
none of the other apostles — only James,
the Lord's brother. 20I assure you before
God that what I am writing you is no lie.
21Then I went to Syria and Cilicia. 22I was
personally unknown to the churches of
Judea that are in Christ. 23They only heard
the report: "The man who formerly persecuted us is now preaching the faith he
once tried to destroy." 24And they praised
God because of me.

Paul Accepted by the Apostles

2 Then after fourteen years, I went up
again to Jerusalem, this time with
Barnabas. I took Titus along also. 2I went
in response to a revelation and, meeting
privately with those esteemed as leaders, I presented to them the gospel that I
preach among the Gentiles. I wanted to be
sure I was not running and had not been
running my race in vain. 3Yet not even
Titus, who was with me, was compelled
to be circumcised, even though he was a
Greek. 4This matter arose because some
false believers had infiltrated our ranks to
spy on the freedom we have in Christ Jesus
and to make us slaves. 5We did not give in
to them for a moment, so that the truth
of the gospel might be preserved for you.
6As for those who were held in high
esteem — whatever they were makes
no difference to me; God does not show
favoritism — they added nothing to my
message. 7On the contrary, they recognized that I had been entrusted with the
task of preaching the gospel to the uncircumcised,[c] just as Peter had been to the
circumcised.[d] 8For God, who was at work
in Peter as an apostle to the circumcised,
was also at work in me as an apostle to
the Gentiles. 9James, Cephas[e] and John,
those esteemed as pillars, gave me and

[a] *2* The Greek word for *brothers and sisters* (*adelphoi*) refers here to believers, both men and women, as part of God's family; also in verse 11; and in 3:15; 4:12, 28, 31; 5:11, 13; 6:1, 18. [b] *18* That is, Peter [c] *7* That is, Gentiles [d] *7* That is, Jews; also in verses 8 and 9 [e] *9* That is, Peter; also in verses 11 and 14

Barnabas the right hand of fellowship when they recognized the grace given to me. They agreed that we should go to the Gentiles, and they to the circumcised. 10All they asked was that we should continue to remember the poor, the very thing I had been eager to do all along.

Paul Opposes Cephas

11When Cephas came to Antioch, I opposed him to his face, because he stood condemned. 12For before certain men came from James, he used to eat with the Gentiles. But when they arrived, he began to draw back and separate himself from the Gentiles because he was afraid of those who belonged to the circumcision group. 13The other Jews joined him in his hypocrisy, so that by their hypocrisy even Barnabas was led astray.

14When I saw that they were not acting in line with the truth of the gospel, I said to Cephas in front of them all, "You are a Jew, yet you live like a Gentile and not like a Jew. How is it, then, that you force Gentiles to follow Jewish customs?

15"We who are Jews by birth and not sinful Gentiles 16know that a person is not justified by the works of the law, but by faith in Jesus Christ. So we, too, have put our faith in Christ Jesus that we may be justified by faith in[a] Christ and not by the works of the law, because by the works of the law no one will be justified.

17"But if, in seeking to be justified in Christ, we Jews find ourselves also among the sinners, doesn't that mean that Christ promotes sin? Absolutely not! 18If I rebuild what I destroyed, then I really would be a lawbreaker.

19"For through the law I died to the law so that I might live for God. 20I have been crucified with Christ and I no longer live, but Christ lives in me. The life I now live in the body, I live by faith in the Son of God, who loved me and gave himself for me. 21I do not set aside the grace of God, for if righteousness could be gained through the law, Christ died for nothing!"[b]

Faith or Works of the Law

3 You foolish Galatians! Who has bewitched you? Before your very eyes Jesus Christ was clearly portrayed as crucified. 2I would like to learn just one thing from you: Did you receive the Spirit by the works of the law, or by believing what you heard? 3Are you so foolish? After beginning by means of the Spirit, are you now trying to finish by means of the flesh?[c] 4Have you experienced[d] so much in vain — if it really was in vain? 5So again I ask, does God give you his Spirit and work miracles among you by the works of the law, or by your believing what you heard? 6So also Abraham "believed God, and it was credited to him as righteousness."[e]

7Understand, then, that those who have faith are children of Abraham. 8Scripture foresaw that God would justify the Gentiles by faith, and announced the gospel in advance to Abraham: "All nations will be blessed through you."[f] 9So those who rely on faith are blessed along with Abraham, the man of faith.

10For all who rely on the works of the law are under a curse, as it is written: "Cursed is everyone who does not continue to do everything written in the Book of the Law."[g] 11Clearly no one who relies on the law is justified before God, because "the righteous will live by faith."[h] 12The law is not based on faith; on the contrary, it says, "The person who does these things will live by them."[i] 13Christ redeemed us from the curse of the law by becoming a curse for us, for it is written: "Cursed is everyone who is hung on a pole."[j] 14He redeemed us in order that the blessing given to Abraham might come to the Gentiles through Christ Jesus, so that by faith we might receive the promise of the Spirit.

The Law and the Promise

15Brothers and sisters, let me take an example from everyday life. Just as no one can set aside or add to a human covenant that has been duly established, so it is in this case. 16The promises were spoken to Abraham and to his seed. Scripture does not say "and to seeds," meaning many people, but "and to your seed,"[k] meaning one person, who is Christ. 17What I mean is this: The law, introduced 430 years later, does not set aside the covenant previously established by God and thus do away with the promise. 18For if the inheritance depends on the law, then it no longer depends on the promise; but God in his grace gave it to Abraham through a promise.

19Why, then, was the law given at all? It was added because of transgressions until

[a] *16* Or *but through the faithfulness of . . . justified on the basis of the faithfulness of* [b] *21* Some interpreters end the quotation after verse 14. [c] *3* In contexts like this, the Greek word for *flesh* (*sarx*) refers to the sinful state of human beings, often presented as a power in opposition to the Spirit. [d] *4* Or *suffered* [e] *6* Gen. 15:6 [f] *8* Gen. 12:3; 18:18; 22:18 [g] *10* Deut. 27:26 [h] *11* Hab. 2:4 [i] *12* Lev. 18:5 [j] *13* Deut. 21:23 [k] *16* Gen. 12:7; 13:15; 24:7

the Seed to whom the promise referred
had come. The law was given through
angels and entrusted to a mediator. 20 A
mediator, however, implies more than
one party; but God is one.
21 Is the law, therefore, opposed to the
promises of God? Absolutely not! For if
a law had been given that could impart
life, then righteousness would certainly
have come by the law. 22 But Scripture has
locked up everything under the control
of sin, so that what was promised, being
given through faith in Jesus Christ, might
be given to those who believe.

Children of God

23 Before the coming of this faith,[a] we
were held in custody under the law, locked
up until the faith that was to come would
be revealed. 24 So the law was our guardian until Christ came that we might be
justified by faith. 25 Now that this faith has
come, we are no longer under a guardian.
26 So in Christ Jesus you are all children
of God through faith, 27 for all of you who
were baptized into Christ have clothed
yourselves with Christ. 28 There is neither
Jew nor Gentile, neither slave nor free,
nor is there male and female, for you are
all one in Christ Jesus. 29 If you belong to
Christ, then you are Abraham's seed, and
heirs according to the promise.
4 What I am saying is that as long as
an heir is underage, he is no different
from a slave, although he owns the whole
estate. 2 The heir is subject to guardians
and trustees until the time set by his father. 3 So also, when we were underage,
we were in slavery under the elemental
spiritual forces[b] of the world. 4 But when
the set time had fully come, God sent his
Son, born of a woman, born under the
law, 5 to redeem those under the law, that
we might receive adoption to sonship.[c]
6 Because you are his sons, God sent the
Spirit of his Son into our hearts, the Spirit who calls out, "*Abba*,[d] Father." 7 So you
are no longer a slave, but God's child; and
since you are his child, God has made you
also an heir.

Paul's Concern for the Galatians

8 Formerly, when you did not know God,
you were slaves to those who by nature are
not gods. 9 But now that you know God —
or rather are known by God — how is it
that you are turning back to those weak
and miserable forces[e]? Do you wish to be
enslaved by them all over again? 10 You are
observing special days and months and
seasons and years! 11 I fear for you, that
somehow I have wasted my efforts on you.
12 I plead with you, brothers and sisters,
become like me, for I became like you. You
did me no wrong. 13 As you know, it was
because of an illness that I first preached
the gospel to you, 14 and even though my
illness was a trial to you, you did not treat
me with contempt or scorn. Instead, you
welcomed me as if I were an angel of God,
as if I were Christ Jesus himself. 15 Where,
then, is your blessing of me now? I can
testify that, if you could have done so, you
would have torn out your eyes and given
them to me. 16 Have I now become your
enemy by telling you the truth?
17 Those people are zealous to win you
over, but for no good. What they want is
to alienate you from us, so that you may
have zeal for them. 18 It is fine to be zealous, provided the purpose is good, and to
be so always, not just when I am with you.
19 My dear children, for whom I am again
in the pains of childbirth until Christ is
formed in you, 20 how I wish I could be with
you now and change my tone, because I
am perplexed about you!

Hagar and Sarah

21 Tell me, you who want to be under the
law, are you not aware of what the law
says? 22 For it is written that Abraham had
two sons, one by the slave woman and the
other by the free woman. 23 His son by the
slave woman was born according to the
flesh, but his son by the free woman was
born as the result of a divine promise.
24 These things are being taken figuratively: The women represent two covenants. One covenant is from Mount Sinai
and bears children who are to be slaves:
This is Hagar. 25 Now Hagar stands for
Mount Sinai in Arabia and corresponds to
the present city of Jerusalem, because she
is in slavery with her children. 26 But the
Jerusalem that is above is free, and she
is our mother. 27 For it is written:

"Be glad, barren woman,
you who never bore a child;
shout for joy and cry aloud,
you who were never in labor;
because more are the children of the
desolate woman
than of her who has a husband."[f]

[a] 22,23 Or *through the faithfulness of Jesus . . . 23 Before faith came* [b] 3 Or *under the basic principles* [c] 5 The Greek word for *adoption to sonship* is a legal term referring to the full legal standing of an adopted male heir in Roman culture. [d] 6 Aramaic for *Father* [e] 9 Or *principles* [f] 27 Isaiah 54:1

[28]Now you, brothers and sisters, like Isaac, are children of promise. [29]At that time the son born according to the flesh persecuted the son born by the power of the Spirit. It is the same now. [30]But what does Scripture say? "Get rid of the slave woman and her son, for the slave woman's son will never share in the inheritance with the free woman's son."[a] [31]Therefore, brothers and sisters, we are not children of the slave woman, but of the free woman.

Freedom in Christ

5 It is for freedom that Christ has set us free. Stand firm, then, and do not let yourselves be burdened again by a yoke of slavery.

[2]Mark my words! I, Paul, tell you that if you let yourselves be circumcised, Christ will be of no value to you at all. [3]Again I declare to every man who lets himself be circumcised that he is obligated to obey the whole law. [4]You who are trying to be justified by the law have been alienated from Christ; you have fallen away from grace. [5]For through the Spirit we eagerly await by faith the righteousness for which we hope. [6]For in Christ Jesus neither circumcision nor uncircumcision has any value. The only thing that counts is faith expressing itself through love.

[7]You were running a good race. Who cut in on you to keep you from obeying the truth? [8]That kind of persuasion does not come from the one who calls you. [9]"A little yeast works through the whole batch of dough." [10]I am confident in the Lord that you will take no other view. The one who is throwing you into confusion, whoever that may be, will have to pay the penalty. [11]Brothers and sisters, if I am still preaching circumcision, why am I still being persecuted? In that case the offense of the cross has been abolished. [12]As for those agitators, I wish they would go the whole way and emasculate themselves!

Life by the Spirit

[13]You, my brothers and sisters, were called to be free. But do not use your freedom to indulge the flesh[b]; rather, serve one another humbly in love. [14]For the entire law is fulfilled in keeping this one command: "Love your neighbor as yourself."[c] [15]If you bite and devour each other, watch out or you will be destroyed by each other.

[16]So I say, walk by the Spirit, and you will not gratify the desires of the flesh. [17]For the flesh desires what is contrary to the Spirit, and the Spirit what is contrary to the flesh. They are in conflict with each other, so that you are not to do whatever[d] you want. [18]But if you are led by the Spirit, you are not under the law.

[19]The acts of the flesh are obvious: sexual immorality, impurity and debauchery; [20]idolatry and witchcraft; hatred, discord, jealousy, fits of rage, selfish ambition, dissensions, factions [21]and envy; drunkenness, orgies, and the like. I warn you, as I did before, that those who live like this will not inherit the kingdom of God.

[22]But the fruit of the Spirit is love, joy, peace, forbearance, kindness, goodness, faithfulness, [23]gentleness and self-control. Against such things there is no law. [24]Those who belong to Christ Jesus have crucified the flesh with its passions and desires. [25]Since we live by the Spirit, let us keep in step with the Spirit. [26]Let us not become conceited, provoking and envying each other.

Doing Good to All

6 Brothers and sisters, if someone is caught in a sin, you who live by the Spirit should restore that person gently. But watch yourselves, or you also may be tempted. [2]Carry each other's burdens, and in this way you will fulfill the law of Christ. [3]If anyone thinks they are something when they are not, they deceive themselves. [4]Each one should test their own actions. Then they can take pride in themselves alone, without comparing themselves to someone else, [5]for each one should carry their own load. [6]Nevertheless, the one who receives instruction in the word should share all good things with their instructor.

[7]Do not be deceived: God cannot be mocked. A man reaps what he sows. [8]Whoever sows to please their flesh, from the flesh will reap destruction; whoever sows to please the Spirit, from the Spirit will reap eternal life. [9]Let us not become weary in doing good, for at the proper time we will reap a harvest if we do not give up. [10]Therefore, as we have opportunity, let us do good to all people, especially to those who belong to the family of believers.

[a] *30* Gen. 21:10 [b] *13* In contexts like this, the Greek word for *flesh* (*sarx*) refers to the sinful state of human beings, often presented as a power in opposition to the Spirit; also in verses 16, 17, 19 and 24; and in 6:8. [c] *14* Lev. 19:18 [d] *17* Or *you do not do what*

Not Circumcision but the New Creation

11See what large letters I use as I write
to you with my own hand!
12Those who want to impress people by
means of the flesh are trying to compel
you to be circumcised. The only reason
they do this is to avoid being persecuted
for the cross of Christ. 13Not even those
who are circumcised keep the law, yet they
want you to be circumcised that they may
boast about your circumcision in the flesh.
14May I never boast except in the cross of
our Lord Jesus Christ, through which[a]
the world has been crucified to me, and
I to the world. 15Neither circumcision nor
uncircumcision means anything; what
counts is the new creation. 16Peace and
mercy to all who follow this rule — to[b]
the Israel of God.
17From now on, let no one cause me
trouble, for I bear on my body the marks
of Jesus.
18The grace of our Lord Jesus Christ
be with your spirit, brothers and sisters.
Amen.

[a] 14 Or *whom* [b] 16 Or *rule and to*

EPHESIANS

1 Paul, an apostle of Christ Jesus by the
will of God,

To God's holy people in Ephesus,[a] the
faithful in Christ Jesus:

[2]Grace and peace to you from God our
Father and the Lord Jesus Christ.

Praise for Spiritual Blessings in Christ

[3]Praise be to the God and Father of our
Lord Jesus Christ, who has blessed us in
the heavenly realms with every spiritual
blessing in Christ. [4]For he chose us in him
before the creation of the world to be holy
and blameless in his sight. In love [5]he[b]
predestined us for adoption to sonship[c]
through Jesus Christ, in accordance with
his pleasure and will— [6]to the praise of
his glorious grace, which he has freely
given us in the One he loves. [7]In him we
have redemption through his blood, the
forgiveness of sins, in accordance with the
riches of God's grace [8]that he lavished on
us. With all wisdom and understanding,
[9]he[d] made known to us the mystery of
his will according to his good pleasure,
which he purposed in Christ, [10]to be put
into effect when the times reach their fulfillment — to bring unity to all things in
heaven and on earth under Christ.

[11]In him we were also chosen,[e] having
been predestined according to the plan of
him who works out everything in confor-
mity with the purpose of his will, [12]in order
that we, who were the first to put our hope
in Christ, might be for the praise of his glory. [13]And you also were included in Christ
when you heard the message of truth,
the gospel of your salvation. When you
believed, you were marked in him with a
seal, the promised Holy Spirit, [14]who is a
deposit guaranteeing our inheritance until the redemption of those who are God's
possession — to the praise of his glory.

Thanksgiving and Prayer

[15]For this reason, ever since I heard
about your faith in the Lord Jesus and
your love for all God's people, [16]I have not
stopped giving thanks for you, remembering you in my prayers. [17]I keep asking
that the God of our Lord Jesus Christ, the
glorious Father, may give you the Spirit[f]
of wisdom and revelation, so that you
may know him better. [18]I pray that the
eyes of your heart may be enlightened
in order that you may know the hope to
which he has called you, the riches of his
glorious inheritance in his holy people,
[19]and his incomparably great power for
us who believe. That power is the same
as the mighty strength [20]he exerted when
he raised Christ from the dead and seated him at his right hand in the heavenly
realms, [21]far above all rule and authority,
power and dominion, and every name that
is invoked, not only in the present age but
also in the one to come. [22]And God placed
all things under his feet and appointed
him to be head over everything for the
church, [23]which is his body, the fullness
of him who fills everything in every way.

Made Alive in Christ

2 As for you, you were dead in your transgressions and sins, [2]in which you used
to live when you followed the ways of this
world and of the ruler of the kingdom of
the air, the spirit who is now at work in
those who are disobedient. [3]All of us also
lived among them at one time, gratifying
the cravings of our flesh[g] and following its
desires and thoughts. Like the rest, we were
by nature deserving of wrath. [4]But because
of his great love for us, God, who is rich in
mercy, [5]made us alive with Christ even
when we were dead in transgressions — it
is by grace you have been saved. [6]And God
raised us up with Christ and seated us
with him in the heavenly realms in Christ
Jesus, [7]in order that in the coming ages he
might show the incomparable riches of his
grace, expressed in his kindness to us in
Christ Jesus. [8]For it is by grace you have
been saved, through faith — and this is
not from yourselves, it is the gift of God —
[9]not by works, so that no one can boast.
[10]For we are God's handiwork, created in
Christ Jesus to do good works, which God
prepared in advance for us to do.

[a] *1* Some early manuscripts do not have *in Ephesus.* [b] *4,5* Or *sight in love.* [5]*He* [c] *5* The Greek word for *adoption to sonship* is a legal term referring to the full legal standing of an adopted male heir in Roman culture. [d] *8,9* Or *us with all wisdom and understanding.* [9]*And he* [e] *11* Or *were made heirs* [f] *17* Or *a spirit* [g] *3* In contexts like this, the Greek word for *flesh* (*sarx*) refers to the sinful state of human beings, often presented as a power in opposition to the Spirit.

Jew and Gentile Reconciled Through Christ

11 Therefore, remember that formerly
you who are Gentiles by birth and called
"uncircumcised" by those who call themselves "the circumcision" (which is done in
the body by human hands) — 12 remember
that at that time you were separate from
Christ, excluded from citizenship in Israel and foreigners to the covenants of the
promise, without hope and without God
in the world. 13 But now in Christ Jesus
you who once were far away have been
brought near by the blood of Christ.
14 For he himself is our peace, who has
made the two groups one and has destroyed the barrier, the dividing wall of
hostility, 15 by setting aside in his flesh the
law with its commands and regulations.
His purpose was to create in himself one
new humanity out of the two, thus making
peace, 16 and in one body to reconcile both
of them to God through the cross, by which
he put to death their hostility. 17 He came
and preached peace to you who were far
away and peace to those who were near.
18 For through him we both have access to
the Father by one Spirit.
19 Consequently, you are no longer foreigners and strangers, but fellow citizens
with God's people and also members of
his household, 20 built on the foundation
of the apostles and prophets, with Christ
Jesus himself as the chief cornerstone. 21 In
him the whole building is joined together
and rises to become a holy temple in the
Lord. 22 And in him you too are being built
together to become a dwelling in which
God lives by his Spirit.

God's Marvelous Plan for the Gentiles

3 For this reason I, Paul, the prisoner of
Christ Jesus for the sake of you Gentiles —
2 Surely you have heard about the administration of God's grace that was given
to me for you, 3 that is, the mystery made
known to me by revelation, as I have already written briefly. 4 In reading this, then,
you will be able to understand my insight
into the mystery of Christ, 5 which was not
made known to people in other generations as it has now been revealed by the
Spirit to God's holy apostles and prophets.
6 This mystery is that through the gospel
the Gentiles are heirs together with Israel,
members together of one body, and shar-
ers together in the promise in Christ Jesus.
7 I became a servant of this gospel by the
gift of God's grace given me through the
working of his power. 8 Although I am less
than the least of all the Lord's people, this
grace was given me: to preach to the Gentiles the boundless riches of Christ, 9 and to
make plain to everyone the administration
of this mystery, which for ages past was kept
hidden in God, who created all things. 10 His
intent was that now, through the church,
the manifold wisdom of God should be
made known to the rulers and authorities
in the heavenly realms, 11 according to his
eternal purpose that he accomplished in
Christ Jesus our Lord. 12 In him and through
faith in him we may approach God with
freedom and confidence. 13 I ask you, therefore, not to be discouraged because of my
sufferings for you, which are your glory.

A Prayer for the Ephesians

14 For this reason I kneel before the Father, 15 from whom every family[a] in heaven
and on earth derives its name. 16 I pray that
out of his glorious riches he may strength-
en you with power through his Spirit in
your inner being, 17 so that Christ may dwell
in your hearts through faith. And I pray
that you, being rooted and established in
love, 18 may have power, together with all
the Lord's holy people, to grasp how wide
and long and high and deep is the love of
Christ, 19 and to know this love that surpasses knowledge — that you may be filled
to the measure of all the fullness of God.
20 Now to him who is able to do immea-
surably more than all we ask or imagine,
according to his power that is at work
within us, 21 to him be glory in the church
and in Christ Jesus throughout all generations, for ever and ever! Amen.

Unity and Maturity in the Body of Christ

4 As a prisoner for the Lord, then, I urge
you to live a life worthy of the calling
you have received. 2 Be completely humble and gentle; be patient, bearing with
one another in love. 3 Make every effort to
keep the unity of the Spirit through the
bond of peace. 4 There is one body and one
Spirit, just as you were called to one hope
when you were called; 5 one Lord, one faith,
one baptism; 6 one God and Father of all,
who is over all and through all and in all.
7 But to each one of us grace has been
given as Christ apportioned it. 8 This is
why it[b] says:

"When he ascended on high,
he took many captives
and gave gifts to his people."[c]

[a] *15* The Greek for *family* (*patria*) is derived from the Greek for *father* (*pater*). [b] *8* Or *God*
[c] *8* Psalm 68:18

9 (What does "he ascended" mean except that he also descended to the lower, earthly regions[a]? 10 He who descended is the very one who ascended higher than all the heavens, in order to fill the whole universe.) 11 So Christ himself gave the apostles, the prophets, the evangelists, the pastors and teachers, 12 to equip his people for works of service, so that the body of Christ may be built up 13 until we all reach unity in the faith and in the knowledge of the Son of God and become mature, attaining to the whole measure of the fullness of Christ.

14 Then we will no longer be infants, tossed back and forth by the waves, and blown here and there by every wind of teaching and by the cunning and craftiness of people in their deceitful scheming. 15 Instead, speaking the truth in love, we will grow to become in every respect the mature body of him who is the head, that is, Christ. 16 From him the whole body, joined and held together by every supporting ligament, grows and builds itself up in love, as each part does its work.

Instructions for Christian Living

17 So I tell you this, and insist on it in the Lord, that you must no longer live as the Gentiles do, in the futility of their thinking. 18 They are darkened in their understanding and separated from the life of God because of the ignorance that is in them due to the hardening of their hearts. 19 Having lost all sensitivity, they have given themselves over to sensuality so as to indulge in every kind of impurity, and they are full of greed.

20 That, however, is not the way of life you learned 21 when you heard about Christ and were taught in him in accordance with the truth that is in Jesus. 22 You were taught, with regard to your former way of life, to put off your old self, which is being corrupted by its deceitful desires; 23 to be made new in the attitude of your minds; 24 and to put on the new self, created to be like God in true righteousness and holiness.

25 Therefore each of you must put off falsehood and speak truthfully to your neighbor, for we are all members of one body. 26 "In your anger do not sin"[b]: Do not let the sun go down while you are still angry, 27 and do not give the devil a foothold. 28 Anyone who has been stealing must steal no longer, but must work, doing something useful with their own hands, that they may have something to share with those in need.

29 Do not let any unwholesome talk come out of your mouths, but only what is helpful for building others up according to their needs, that it may benefit those who listen. 30 And do not grieve the Holy Spirit of God, with whom you were sealed for the day of redemption. 31 Get rid of all bitterness, rage and anger, brawling and slander, along with every form of malice. 32 Be kind and compassionate to one another, forgiving each other, just as in Christ God forgave you.

5 1 Follow God's example, therefore, as dearly loved children 2 and walk in the way of love, just as Christ loved us and gave himself up for us as a fragrant offering and sacrifice to God.

3 But among you there must not be even a hint of sexual immorality, or of any kind of impurity, or of greed, because these are improper for God's holy people. 4 Nor should there be obscenity, foolish talk or coarse joking, which are out of place, but rather thanksgiving. 5 For of this you can be sure: No immoral, impure or greedy person — such a person is an idolater — has any inheritance in the kingdom of Christ and of God.[c] 6 Let no one deceive you with empty words, for because of such things God's wrath comes on those who are disobedient. 7 Therefore do not be partners with them.

8 For you were once darkness, but now you are light in the Lord. Live as children of light 9 (for the fruit of the light consists in all goodness, righteousness and truth) 10 and find out what pleases the Lord. 11 Have nothing to do with the fruitless deeds of darkness, but rather expose them. 12 It is shameful even to mention what the disobedient do in secret. 13 But everything exposed by the light becomes visible — and everything that is illuminated becomes a light. 14 This is why it is said:

"Wake up, sleeper,
  rise from the dead,
  and Christ will shine on you."

15 Be very careful, then, how you live — not as unwise but as wise, 16 making the most of every opportunity, because the days are evil. 17 Therefore do not be foolish, but understand what the Lord's will is. 18 Do not get drunk on wine, which leads to debauchery. Instead, be filled with the Spirit, 19 speaking to one another with psalms, hymns, and songs from the Spirit. Sing and make music from your heart to the Lord, 20 always giving thanks to God the Father for everything, in the name of our Lord Jesus Christ.

[a] 9 Or *the depths of the earth* [b] 26 Psalm 4:4 (see Septuagint) [c] 5 Or *kingdom of the Messiah and God*

Instructions for Christian Households

21 Submit to one another out of reverence for Christ.

22 Wives, submit yourselves to your own husbands as you do to the Lord. 23 For the husband is the head of the wife as Christ is the head of the church, his body, of which he is the Savior. 24 Now as the church submits to Christ, so also wives should submit to their husbands in everything.

25 Husbands, love your wives, just as Christ loved the church and gave himself up for her 26 to make her holy, cleansing[a] her by the washing with water through the word, 27 and to present her to himself as a radiant church, without stain or wrinkle or any other blemish, but holy and blameless. 28 In this same way, husbands ought to love their wives as their own bodies. He who loves his wife loves himself. 29 After all, no one ever hated their own body, but they feed and care for their body, just as Christ does the church — 30 for we are members of his body. 31 "For this reason a man will leave his father and mother and be united to his wife, and the two will become one flesh."[b] 32 This is a profound mystery — but I am talking about Christ and the church. 33 However, each one of you also must love his wife as he loves himself, and the wife must respect her husband.

6 Children, obey your parents in the Lord, for this is right. 2 "Honor your father and mother" — which is the first commandment with a promise — 3 "so that it may go well with you and that you may enjoy long life on the earth."[c]

4 Fathers,[d] do not exasperate your children; instead, bring them up in the training and instruction of the Lord.

5 Slaves, obey your earthly masters with respect and fear, and with sincerity of heart, just as you would obey Christ. 6 Obey them not only to win their favor when their eye is on you, but as slaves of Christ, doing the will of God from your heart. 7 Serve wholeheartedly, as if you were serving the Lord, not people, 8 because you know that the Lord will reward each one for whatever good they do, whether they are slave or free.

9 And masters, treat your slaves in the same way. Do not threaten them, since you know that he who is both their Master and yours is in heaven, and there is no favoritism with him.

The Armor of God

10 Finally, be strong in the Lord and in his mighty power. 11 Put on the full armor of God, so that you can take your stand against the devil's schemes. 12 For our struggle is not against flesh and blood, but against the rulers, against the authorities, against the powers of this dark world and against the spiritual forces of evil in the heavenly realms. 13 Therefore put on the full armor of God, so that when the day of evil comes, you may be able to stand your ground, and after you have done everything, to stand. 14 Stand firm then, with the belt of truth buckled around your waist, with the breastplate of righteousness in place, 15 and with your feet fitted with the readiness that comes from the gospel of peace. 16 In addition to all this, take up the shield of faith, with which you can extinguish all the flaming arrows of the evil one. 17 Take the helmet of salvation and the sword of the Spirit, which is the word of God.

18 And pray in the Spirit on all occasions with all kinds of prayers and requests. With this in mind, be alert and always keep on praying for all the Lord's people. 19 Pray also for me, that whenever I speak, words may be given me so that I will fearlessly make known the mystery of the gospel, 20 for which I am an ambassador in chains. Pray that I may declare it fearlessly, as I should.

Final Greetings

21 Tychicus, the dear brother and faithful servant in the Lord, will tell you everything, so that you also may know how I am and what I am doing. 22 I am sending him to you for this very purpose, that you may know how we are, and that he may encourage you.

23 Peace to the brothers and sisters,[e] and love with faith from God the Father and the Lord Jesus Christ. 24 Grace to all who love our Lord Jesus Christ with an undying love.[f]

[a] *26* Or *having cleansed* [b] *31* Gen. 2:24 [c] *3* Deut. 5:16 [d] *4* Or *Parents* [e] *23* The Greek word for *brothers and sisters* (*adelphoi*) refers here to believers, both men and women, as part of God's family. [f] *24* Or *Grace and immortality to all who love our Lord Jesus Christ.*

PHILIPPIANS

1 Paul and Timothy, servants of Christ Jesus,

To all God's holy people in Christ Jesus at Philippi, together with the overseers and deacons[a]:

2 Grace and peace to you from God our Father and the Lord Jesus Christ.

Thanksgiving and Prayer

3 I thank my God every time I remember you. 4 In all my prayers for all of you, I always pray with joy 5 because of your partnership in the gospel from the first day until now, 6 being confident of this, that he who began a good work in you will carry it on to completion until the day of Christ Jesus.

7 It is right for me to feel this way about all of you, since I have you in my heart and, whether I am in chains or defending and confirming the gospel, all of you share in God's grace with me. 8 God can testify how I long for all of you with the affection of Christ Jesus.

9 And this is my prayer: that your love may abound more and more in knowledge and depth of insight, 10 so that you may be able to discern what is best and may be pure and blameless for the day of Christ, 11 filled with the fruit of righteousness that comes through Jesus Christ — to the glory and praise of God.

Paul's Chains Advance the Gospel

12 Now I want you to know, brothers and sisters,[b] that what has happened to me has actually served to advance the gospel. 13 As a result, it has become clear throughout the whole palace guard[c] and to everyone else that I am in chains for Christ. 14 And because of my chains, most of the brothers and sisters have become confident in the Lord and dare all the more to proclaim the gospel without fear.

15 It is true that some preach Christ out of envy and rivalry, but others out of goodwill. 16 The latter do so out of love, knowing that I am put here for the defense of the gospel. 17 The former preach Christ out of selfish ambition, not sincerely, supposing that they can stir up trouble for me while I am in chains. 18 But what does it matter? The important thing is that in every way, whether from false motives or true, Christ is preached. And because of this I rejoice.

Yes, and I will continue to rejoice, 19 for I know that through your prayers and God's provision of the Spirit of Jesus Christ what has happened to me will turn out for my deliverance.[d] 20 I eagerly expect and hope that I will in no way be ashamed, but will have sufficient courage so that now as always Christ will be exalted in my body, whether by life or by death. 21 For to me, to live is Christ and to die is gain. 22 If I am to go on living in the body, this will mean fruitful labor for me. Yet what shall I choose? I do not know! 23 I am torn between the two: I desire to depart and be with Christ, which is better by far; 24 but it is more necessary for you that I remain in the body. 25 Convinced of this, I know that I will remain, and I will continue with all of you for your progress and joy in the faith, 26 so that through my being with you again your boasting in Christ Jesus will abound on account of me.

Life Worthy of the Gospel

27 Whatever happens, conduct yourselves in a manner worthy of the gospel of Christ. Then, whether I come and see you or only hear about you in my absence, I will know that you stand firm in the one Spirit,[e] striving together as one for the faith of the gospel 28 without being frightened in any way by those who oppose you. This is a sign to them that they will be destroyed, but that you will be saved — and that by God. 29 For it has been granted to you on behalf of Christ not only to believe in him, but also to suffer for him, 30 since you are going through the same struggle you saw I had, and now hear that I still have.

Imitating Christ's Humility

2 Therefore if you have any encouragement from being united with Christ, if any comfort from his love, if any common sharing in the Spirit, if any tenderness and

[a] *1* The word *deacons* refers here to Christians designated to serve with the overseers/elders of the church in a variety of ways; similarly in Romans 16:1 and 1 Tim. 3:8,12. [b] *12* The Greek word for *brothers and sisters* (*adelphoi*) refers here to believers, both men and women, as part of God's family; also in verse 14; and in 3:1, 13, 17; 4:1, 8, 21. [c] *13* Or *whole palace* [d] *19* Or *vindication*; or *salvation* [e] *27* Or *in one spirit*

compassion, 2then make my joy complete
by being like-minded, having the same
love, being one in spirit and of one mind.
3Do nothing out of selfish ambition or
vain conceit. Rather, in humility value
others above yourselves, 4not looking to
your own interests but each of you to the
interests of the others.
5In your relationships with one another,
have the same mindset as Christ Jesus:

6 Who, being in very nature[a] God,
did not consider equality with God
something to be used to his
own advantage;
7 rather, he made himself nothing
by taking the very nature[b] of a
servant,
being made in human likeness.
8 And being found in appearance as
a man,
he humbled himself
by becoming obedient to death —
even death on a cross!

9 Therefore God exalted him to the
highest place
and gave him the name that is
above every name,
10 that at the name of Jesus every knee
should bow,
in heaven and on earth and under
the earth,
11 and every tongue acknowledge that
Jesus Christ is Lord,
to the glory of God the Father.

Do Everything Without Grumbling

12Therefore, my dear friends, as you
have always obeyed — not only in my
presence, but now much more in my absence — continue to work out your salvation with fear and trembling, 13for it is
God who works in you to will and to act in
order to fulfill his good purpose.
14Do everything without grumbling or
arguing, 15so that you may become blameless and pure, "children of God without
fault in a warped and crooked generation."[c] Then you will shine among them
like stars in the sky 16as you hold firmly to
the word of life. And then I will be able to
boast on the day of Christ that I did not run
or labor in vain. 17But even if I am being
poured out like a drink offering on the sacrifice and service coming from your faith,
I am glad and rejoice with all of you. 18So
you too should be glad and rejoice with me.

Timothy and Epaphroditus

19I hope in the Lord Jesus to send Timothy to you soon, that I also may be cheered
when I receive news about you. 20I have no
one else like him, who will show genuine
concern for your welfare. 21For everyone
looks out for their own interests, not those
of Jesus Christ. 22But you know that Timothy has proved himself, because as a son
with his father he has served with me in
the work of the gospel. 23I hope, therefore,
to send him as soon as I see how things go
with me. 24And I am confident in the Lord
that I myself will come soon.
25But I think it is necessary to send
back to you Epaphroditus, my brother,
co-worker and fellow soldier, who is also
your messenger, whom you sent to take
care of my needs. 26For he longs for all of
you and is distressed because you heard
he was ill. 27Indeed he was ill, and almost
died. But God had mercy on him, and not
on him only but also on me, to spare me
sorrow upon sorrow. 28Therefore I am all
the more eager to send him, so that when
you see him again you may be glad and I
may have less anxiety. 29So then, welcome
him in the Lord with great joy, and honor
people like him, 30because he almost died
for the work of Christ. He risked his life to
make up for the help you yourselves could
not give me.

No Confidence in the Flesh

3 Further, my brothers and sisters, rejoice in the Lord! It is no trouble for
me to write the same things to you again,
and it is a safeguard for you. 2Watch out
for those dogs, those evildoers, those mu-
tilators of the flesh. 3For it is we who are
the circumcision, we who serve God by his
Spirit, who boast in Christ Jesus, and who
put no confidence in the flesh — 4though
I myself have reasons for such confidence.
If someone else thinks they have reasons to put confidence in the flesh, I have
more: 5circumcised on the eighth day, of
the people of Israel, of the tribe of Benjamin, a Hebrew of Hebrews; in regard to the
law, a Pharisee; 6as for zeal, persecuting
the church; as for righteousness based on
the law, faultless.
7But whatever were gains to me I now
consider loss for the sake of Christ. 8What
is more, I consider everything a loss because of the surpassing worth of knowing
Christ Jesus my Lord, for whose sake I have
lost all things. I consider them garbage,
that I may gain Christ 9and be found in
him, not having a righteousness of my
own that comes from the law, but that
which is through faith in[d] Christ — the
righteousness that comes from God on the

[a] 6 Or *in the form of* [b] 7 Or *the form* [c] 15 Deut. 32:5 [d] 9 Or *through the faithfulness of*

basis of faith. 10I want to know Christ — yes, to know the power of his resurrection and participation in his sufferings, becoming like him in his death, 11and so, somehow, attaining to the resurrection from the dead.

12Not that I have already obtained all this, or have already arrived at my goal, but I press on to take hold of that for which Christ Jesus took hold of me. 13Brothers and sisters, I do not consider myself yet to have taken hold of it. But one thing I do: Forgetting what is behind and straining toward what is ahead, 14I press on toward the goal to win the prize for which God has called me heavenward in Christ Jesus.

Following Paul's Example

15All of us, then, who are mature should take such a view of things. And if on some point you think differently, that too God will make clear to you. 16Only let us live up to what we have already attained.

17Join together in following my example, brothers and sisters, and just as you have us as a model, keep your eyes on those who live as we do. 18For, as I have often told you before and now tell you again even with tears, many live as enemies of the cross of Christ. 19Their destiny is destruction, their god is their stomach, and their glory is in their shame. Their mind is set on earthly things. 20But our citizenship is in heaven. And we eagerly await a Savior from there, the Lord Jesus Christ, 21who, by the power that enables him to bring everything under his control, will transform our lowly bodies so that they will be like his glorious body.

Closing Appeal for Steadfastness and Unity

4 Therefore, my brothers and sisters, you whom I love and long for, my joy and crown, stand firm in the Lord in this way, dear friends!

2I plead with Euodia and I plead with Syntyche to be of the same mind in the Lord. 3Yes, and I ask you, my true companion, help these women since they have contended at my side in the cause of the gospel, along with Clement and the rest of my co-workers, whose names are in the book of life.

Final Exhortations

4Rejoice in the Lord always. I will say it again: Rejoice! 5Let your gentleness be evident to all. The Lord is near. 6Do not be anxious about anything, but in every situation, by prayer and petition, with thanksgiving, present your requests to God. 7And the peace of God, which transcends all understanding, will guard your hearts and your minds in Christ Jesus.

8Finally, brothers and sisters, whatever is true, whatever is noble, whatever is right, whatever is pure, whatever is lovely, whatever is admirable — if anything is excellent or praiseworthy — think about such things. 9Whatever you have learned or received or heard from me, or seen in me — put it into practice. And the God of peace will be with you.

Thanks for Their Gifts

10I rejoiced greatly in the Lord that at last you renewed your concern for me. Indeed, you were concerned, but you had no opportunity to show it. 11I am not saying this because I am in need, for I have learned to be content whatever the circumstances. 12I know what it is to be in need, and I know what it is to have plenty. I have learned the secret of being content in any and every situation, whether well fed or hungry, whether living in plenty or in want. 13I can do all this through him who gives me strength.

14Yet it was good of you to share in my troubles. 15Moreover, as you Philippians know, in the early days of your acquaintance with the gospel, when I set out from Macedonia, not one church shared with me in the matter of giving and receiving, except you only; 16for even when I was in Thessalonica, you sent me aid more than once when I was in need. 17Not that I desire your gifts; what I desire is that more be credited to your account. 18I have received full payment and have more than enough. I am amply supplied, now that I have received from Epaphroditus the gifts you sent. They are a fragrant offering, an acceptable sacrifice, pleasing to God. 19And my God will meet all your needs according to the riches of his glory in Christ Jesus.

20To our God and Father be glory for ever and ever. Amen.

Final Greetings

21Greet all God's people in Christ Jesus. The brothers and sisters who are with me send greetings. 22All God's people here send you greetings, especially those who belong to Caesar's household.

23The grace of the Lord Jesus Christ be with your spirit. Amen.[a]

[a] *23* Some manuscripts do not have *Amen.*

COLOSSIANS

1 Paul, an apostle of Christ Jesus by the will of God, and Timothy our brother,

2To God's holy people in Colossae, the faithful brothers and sisters[a] in Christ:

Grace and peace to you from God our Father.[b]

Thanksgiving and Prayer

3We always thank God, the Father of our Lord Jesus Christ, when we pray for you, 4because we have heard of your faith in Christ Jesus and of the love you have for all God's people — 5the faith and love that spring from the hope stored up for you in heaven and about which you have already heard in the true message of the gospel 6that has come to you. In the same way, the gospel is bearing fruit and growing throughout the whole world — just as it has been doing among you since the day you heard it and truly understood God's grace. 7You learned it from Epaphras, our dear fellow servant,[c] who is a faithful minister of Christ on our[d] behalf, 8and who also told us of your love in the Spirit.

9For this reason, since the day we heard about you, we have not stopped praying for you. We continually ask God to fill you with the knowledge of his will through all the wisdom and understanding that the Spirit gives,[e] 10so that you may live a life worthy of the Lord and please him in every way: bearing fruit in every good work, growing in the knowledge of God, 11being strengthened with all power according to his glorious might so that you may have great endurance and patience, 12and giving joyful thanks to the Father, who has qualified you[f] to share in the inheritance of his holy people in the kingdom of light. 13For he has rescued us from the dominion of darkness and brought us into the kingdom of the Son he loves, 14in whom we have redemption, the forgiveness of sins.

The Supremacy of the Son of God

15The Son is the image of the invisible God, the firstborn over all creation. 16For in him all things were created: things in heaven and on earth, visible and invisible, whether thrones or powers or rulers or authorities; all things have been created through him and for him. 17He is before all things, and in him all things hold together. 18And he is the head of the body, the church; he is the beginning and the firstborn from among the dead, so that in everything he might have the supremacy. 19For God was pleased to have all his fullness dwell in him, 20and through him to reconcile to himself all things, whether things on earth or things in heaven, by making peace through his blood, shed on the cross.

21Once you were alienated from God and were enemies in your minds because of[g] your evil behavior. 22But now he has reconciled you by Christ's physical body through death to present you holy in his sight, without blemish and free from accusation — 23if you continue in your faith, established and firm, and do not move from the hope held out in the gospel. This is the gospel that you heard and that has been proclaimed to every creature under heaven, and of which I, Paul, have become a servant.

Paul's Labor for the Church

24Now I rejoice in what I am suffering for you, and I fill up in my flesh what is still lacking in regard to Christ's afflictions, for the sake of his body, which is the church. 25I have become its servant by the commission God gave me to present to you the word of God in its fullness — 26the mystery that has been kept hidden for ages and generations, but is now disclosed to the Lord's people. 27To them God has chosen to make known among the Gentiles the glorious riches of this mystery, which is Christ in you, the hope of glory.

28He is the one we proclaim, admonishing and teaching everyone with all wisdom, so that we may present everyone fully mature in Christ. 29To this end I strenuously contend with all the energy Christ so powerfully works in me.

2 I want you to know how hard I am contending for you and for those at Laodicea, and for all who have not met

[a] 2 The Greek word for *brothers and sisters* (*adelphoi*) refers here to believers, both men and women, as part of God's family; also in 4:15. [b] 2 Some manuscripts *Father and the Lord Jesus Christ* [c] 7 Or *slave* [d] 7 Some manuscripts *your* [e] 9 Or *all spiritual wisdom and understanding* [f] 12 Some manuscripts *us* [g] 21 Or *minds, as shown by*

me personally. 2My goal is that they may be encouraged in heart and united in love, so that they may have the full riches of complete understanding, in order that they may know the mystery of God, namely, Christ, 3in whom are hidden all the treasures of wisdom and knowledge. 4I tell you this so that no one may deceive you by fine-sounding arguments. 5For though I am absent from you in body, I am present with you in spirit and delight to see how disciplined you are and how firm your faith in Christ is.

Spiritual Fullness in Christ

6So then, just as you received Christ Jesus as Lord, continue to live your lives in him, 7rooted and built up in him, strengthened in the faith as you were taught, and overflowing with thankfulness.

8See to it that no one takes you captive through hollow and deceptive philosophy, which depends on human tradition and the elemental spiritual forces[a] of this world rather than on Christ.

9For in Christ all the fullness of the Deity lives in bodily form, 10and in Christ you have been brought to fullness. He is the head over every power and authority. 11In him you were also circumcised with a circumcision not performed by human hands. Your whole self ruled by the flesh[b] was put off when you were circumcised by[c] Christ, 12having been buried with him in baptism, in which you were also raised with him through your faith in the working of God, who raised him from the dead.

13When you were dead in your sins and in the uncircumcision of your flesh, God made you[d] alive with Christ. He forgave us all our sins, 14having canceled the charge of our legal indebtedness, which stood against us and condemned us; he has taken it away, nailing it to the cross. 15And having disarmed the powers and authorities, he made a public spectacle of them, triumphing over them by the cross.[e]

Freedom From Human Rules

16Therefore do not let anyone judge you by what you eat or drink, or with regard to a religious festival, a New Moon celebration or a Sabbath day. 17These are a shadow of the things that were to come; the reality, however, is found in Christ. 18Do not let anyone who delights in false humility and the worship of angels disqualify you. Such a person also goes into great detail about what they have seen; they are puffed up with idle notions by their unspiritual mind. 19They have lost connection with the head, from whom the whole body, supported and held together by its ligaments and sinews, grows as God causes it to grow.

20Since you died with Christ to the elemental spiritual forces of this world, why, as though you still belonged to the world, do you submit to its rules: 21"Do not handle! Do not taste! Do not touch!"? 22These rules, which have to do with things that are all destined to perish with use, are based on merely human commands and teachings. 23Such regulations indeed have an appearance of wisdom, with their self-imposed worship, their false humility and their harsh treatment of the body, but they lack any value in restraining sensual indulgence.

Living as Those Made Alive in Christ

3 Since, then, you have been raised with Christ, set your hearts on things above, where Christ is, seated at the right hand of God. 2Set your minds on things above, not on earthly things. 3For you died, and your life is now hidden with Christ in God. 4When Christ, who is your[f] life, appears, then you also will appear with him in glory.

5Put to death, therefore, whatever belongs to your earthly nature: sexual immorality, impurity, lust, evil desires and greed, which is idolatry. 6Because of these, the wrath of God is coming.[g] 7You used to walk in these ways, in the life you once lived. 8But now you must also rid yourselves of all such things as these: anger, rage, malice, slander, and filthy language from your lips. 9Do not lie to each other, since you have taken off your old self with its practices 10and have put on the new self, which is being renewed in knowledge in the image of its Creator. 11Here there is no Gentile or Jew, circumcised or uncircumcised, barbarian, Scythian, slave or free, but Christ is all, and is in all.

12Therefore, as God's chosen people, holy and dearly loved, clothe yourselves with compassion, kindness, humility, gentleness and patience. 13Bear with each other and forgive one another if any of you has

[a] 8 Or *the basic principles*; also in verse 20 [b] 11 In contexts like this, the Greek word for *flesh* (*sarx*) refers to the sinful state of human beings, often presented as a power in opposition to the Spirit; also in verse 13. [c] 11 Or *put off in the circumcision of* [d] 13 Some manuscripts *us* [e] 15 Or *them in him* [f] 4 Some manuscripts *our* [g] 6 Some early manuscripts *coming on those who are disobedient*

a grievance against someone. Forgive as
the Lord forgave you. 14And over all these
virtues put on love, which binds them all
together in perfect unity.
15Let the peace of Christ rule in your
hearts, since as members of one body you
were called to peace. And be thankful.
16Let the message of Christ dwell among
you richly as you teach and admonish one
another with all wisdom through psalms,
hymns, and songs from the Spirit, singing to God with gratitude in your hearts.
17And whatever you do, whether in word
or deed, do it all in the name of the Lord
Jesus, giving thanks to God the Father
through him.

Instructions for Christian Households

18Wives, submit yourselves to your husbands, as is fitting in the Lord.
19Husbands, love your wives and do not
be harsh with them.
20Children, obey your parents in everything, for this pleases the Lord.
21Fathers,[a] do not embitter your children, or they will become discouraged.
22Slaves, obey your earthly masters in
everything; and do it, not only when their
eye is on you and to curry their favor, but
with sincerity of heart and reverence for
the Lord. 23Whatever you do, work at it
with all your heart, as working for the
Lord, not for human masters, 24since you
know that you will receive an inheritance
from the Lord as a reward. It is the Lord
Christ you are serving. 25Anyone who does
wrong will be repaid for their wrongs, and
there is no favoritism.
4 Masters, provide your slaves with what
is right and fair, because you know
that you also have a Master in heaven.

Further Instructions

2Devote yourselves to prayer, being
watchful and thankful. 3And pray for us,
too, that God may open a door for our
message, so that we may proclaim the
mystery of Christ, for which I am in chains.
4Pray that I may proclaim it clearly, as I
should. 5Be wise in the way you act toward
outsiders; make the most of every opportunity. 6Let your conversation be always
full of grace, seasoned with salt, so that
you may know how to answer everyone.

Final Greetings

7Tychicus will tell you all the news about
me. He is a dear brother, a faithful minister and fellow servant[b] in the Lord. 8I
am sending him to you for the express
purpose that you may know about our[c]
circumstances and that he may encourage
your hearts. 9He is coming with Onesimus,
our faithful and dear brother, who is one
of you. They will tell you everything that
is happening here.
10My fellow prisoner Aristarchus sends
you his greetings, as does Mark, the cousin of Barnabas. (You have received instructions about him; if he comes to you,
welcome him.) 11Jesus, who is called Justus, also sends greetings. These are the
only Jews[d] among my co-workers for the
kingdom of God, and they have proved a
comfort to me. 12Epaphras, who is one of
you and a servant of Christ Jesus, sends
greetings. He is always wrestling in prayer
for you, that you may stand firm in all the
will of God, mature and fully assured. 13I
vouch for him that he is working hard
for you and for those at Laodicea and
Hierapolis. 14Our dear friend Luke, the
doctor, and Demas send greetings. 15Give
my greetings to the brothers and sisters at
Laodicea, and to Nympha and the church
in her house.
16After this letter has been read to you,
see that it is also read in the church of the
Laodiceans and that you in turn read the
letter from Laodicea.
17Tell Archippus: "See to it that you complete the ministry you have received in
the Lord."
18I, Paul, write this greeting in my own
hand. Remember my chains. Grace be
with you.

[a] *21* Or *Parents* [b] *7* Or *slave*; also in verse 12 [c] *8* Some manuscripts *that he may know about your* [d] *11* Greek *only ones of the circumcision group*

1 THESSALONIANS

1 Paul, Silas[a] and Timothy,

To the church of the Thessalonians in God the Father and the Lord Jesus Christ:

Grace and peace to you.

Thanksgiving for the Thessalonians' Faith

2 We always thank God for all of you and continually mention you in our prayers. 3 We remember before our God and Father your work produced by faith, your labor prompted by love, and your endurance inspired by hope in our Lord Jesus Christ.

4 For we know, brothers and sisters[b] loved by God, that he has chosen you, 5 because our gospel came to you not simply with words but also with power, with the Holy Spirit and deep conviction. You know how we lived among you for your sake. 6 You became imitators of us and of the Lord, for you welcomed the message in the midst of severe suffering with the joy given by the Holy Spirit. 7 And so you became a model to all the believers in Macedonia and Achaia. 8 The Lord's message rang out from you not only in Macedonia and Achaia — your faith in God has become known everywhere. Therefore we do not need to say anything about it, 9 for they themselves report what kind of reception you gave us. They tell how you turned to God from idols to serve the living and true God, 10 and to wait for his Son from heaven, whom he raised from the dead — Jesus, who rescues us from the coming wrath.

Paul's Ministry in Thessalonica

2 You know, brothers and sisters, that our visit to you was not without results. 2 We had previously suffered and been treated outrageously in Philippi, as you know, but with the help of our God we dared to tell you his gospel in the face of strong opposition. 3 For the appeal we make does not spring from error or impure motives, nor are we trying to trick you. 4 On the contrary, we speak as those approved by God to be entrusted with the gospel. We are not trying to please people but God, who tests our hearts. 5 You know we never used flattery, nor did we put on a mask to cover up greed — God is our witness. 6 We were not looking for praise from people, not from you or anyone else, even though as apostles of Christ we could have asserted our authority. 7 Instead, we were like young children[c] among you.

Just as a nursing mother cares for her children, 8 so we cared for you. Because we loved you so much, we were delighted to share with you not only the gospel of God but our lives as well. 9 Surely you remember, brothers and sisters, our toil and hardship; we worked night and day in order not to be a burden to anyone while we preached the gospel of God to you. 10 You are witnesses, and so is God, of how holy, righteous and blameless we were among you who believed. 11 For you know that we dealt with each of you as a father deals with his own children, 12 encouraging, comforting and urging you to live lives worthy of God, who calls you into his kingdom and glory.

13 And we also thank God continually because, when you received the word of God, which you heard from us, you accepted it not as a human word, but as it actually is, the word of God, which is indeed at work in you who believe. 14 For you, brothers and sisters, became imitators of God's churches in Judea, which are in Christ Jesus: You suffered from your own people the same things those churches suffered from the Jews 15 who killed the Lord Jesus and the prophets and also drove us out. They displease God and are hostile to everyone 16 in their effort to keep us from speaking to the Gentiles so that they may be saved. In this way they always heap up their sins to the limit. The wrath of God has come upon them at last.[d]

Paul's Longing to See the Thessalonians

17 But, brothers and sisters, when we were orphaned by being separated from you for a short time (in person, not in thought), out of our intense longing we made every effort to see you. 18 For we wanted to come to you — certainly I, Paul, did, again and again — but Satan blocked

[a] *1* Greek *Silvanus,* a variant of *Silas* [b] *4* The Greek word for *brothers and sisters* (*adelphoi*) refers here to believers, both men and women, as part of God's family; also in 2:1, 9, 14, 17; 3:7; 4:1, 10, 13; 5:1, 4, 12, 14, 25, 27. [c] *7* Some manuscripts *were gentle* [d] *16* Or *them fully*

our way. [19]For what is our hope, our joy, or the crown in which we will glory in the presence of our Lord Jesus when he comes? Is it not you? [20]Indeed, you are our glory and joy.

3 So when we could stand it no longer, we thought it best to be left by ourselves in Athens. [2]We sent Timothy, who is our brother and co-worker in God's service in spreading the gospel of Christ, to strengthen and encourage you in your faith, [3]so that no one would be unsettled by these trials. For you know quite well that we are destined for them. [4]In fact, when we were with you, we kept telling you that we would be persecuted. And it turned out that way, as you well know. [5]For this reason, when I could stand it no longer, I sent to find out about your faith. I was afraid that in some way the tempter had tempted you and that our labors might have been in vain.

Timothy's Encouraging Report

[6]But Timothy has just now come to us from you and has brought good news about your faith and love. He has told us that you always have pleasant memories of us and that you long to see us, just as we also long to see you. [7]Therefore, brothers and sisters, in all our distress and persecution we were encouraged about you because of your faith. [8]For now we really live, since you are standing firm in the Lord. [9]How can we thank God enough for you in return for all the joy we have in the presence of our God because of you? [10]Night and day we pray most earnestly that we may see you again and supply what is lacking in your faith.

[11]Now may our God and Father himself and our Lord Jesus clear the way for us to come to you. [12]May the Lord make your love increase and overflow for each other and for everyone else, just as ours does for you. [13]May he strengthen your hearts so that you will be blameless and holy in the presence of our God and Father when our Lord Jesus comes with all his holy ones.

Living to Please God

4 As for other matters, brothers and sisters, we instructed you how to live in order to please God, as in fact you are living. Now we ask you and urge you in the Lord Jesus to do this more and more. [2]For you know what instructions we gave you by the authority of the Lord Jesus.

[3]It is God's will that you should be sanctified: that you should avoid sexual immorality; [4]that each of you should learn to control your own body[a] in a way that is holy and honorable, [5]not in passionate lust like the pagans, who do not know God; [6]and that in this matter no one should wrong or take advantage of a brother or sister.[b] The Lord will punish all those who commit such sins, as we told you and warned you before. [7]For God did not call us to be impure, but to live a holy life. [8]Therefore, anyone who rejects this instruction does not reject a human being but God, the very God who gives you his Holy Spirit.

[9]Now about your love for one another we do not need to write to you, for you yourselves have been taught by God to love each other. [10]And in fact, you do love all of God's family throughout Macedonia. Yet we urge you, brothers and sisters, to do so more and more, [11]and to make it your ambition to lead a quiet life: You should mind your own business and work with your hands, just as we told you, [12]so that your daily life may win the respect of outsiders and so that you will not be dependent on anybody.

Believers Who Have Died

[13]Brothers and sisters, we do not want you to be uninformed about those who sleep in death, so that you do not grieve like the rest of mankind, who have no hope. [14]For we believe that Jesus died and rose again, and so we believe that God will bring with Jesus those who have fallen asleep in him. [15]According to the Lord's word, we tell you that we who are still alive, who are left until the coming of the Lord, will certainly not precede those who have fallen asleep. [16]For the Lord himself will come down from heaven, with a loud command, with the voice of the archangel and with the trumpet call of God, and the dead in Christ will rise first. [17]After that, we who are still alive and are left will be caught up together with them in the clouds to meet the Lord in the air. And so we will be with the Lord forever. [18]Therefore encourage one another with these words.

The Day of the Lord

5 Now, brothers and sisters, about times and dates we do not need to write to you, [2]for you know very well that the day of the Lord will come like a thief in the night. [3]While people are saying, "Peace and safety," destruction will come on them

[a] 4 Or *learn to live with your own wife*; or *learn to acquire a wife* [b] 6 The Greek word for *brother or sister* (*adelphos*) refers here to a believer, whether man or woman, as part of God's family.

suddenly, as labor pains on a pregnant
woman, and they will not escape.
4But you, brothers and sisters, are not in
darkness so that this day should surprise
you like a thief. 5You are all children of
the light and children of the day. We do
not belong to the night or to the darkness.
6So then, let us not be like others, who are
asleep, but let us be awake and sober. 7For
those who sleep, sleep at night, and those
who get drunk, get drunk at night. 8But
since we belong to the day, let us be sober,
putting on faith and love as a breastplate,
and the hope of salvation as a helmet. 9For
God did not appoint us to suffer wrath but
to receive salvation through our Lord Jesus
Christ. 10He died for us so that, whether we
are awake or asleep, we may live together
with him. 11Therefore encourage one another and build each other up, just as in
fact you are doing.

Final Instructions

12Now we ask you, brothers and sisters,
to acknowledge those who work hard
among you, who care for you in the Lord
and who admonish you. 13Hold them in
the highest regard in love because of their
work. Live in peace with each other. 14And
we urge you, brothers and sisters, warn
those who are idle and disruptive, encourage the disheartened, help the weak, be
patient with everyone. 15Make sure that
nobody pays back wrong for wrong, but
always strive to do what is good for each
other and for everyone else.
16Rejoice always, 17pray continually,
18give thanks in all circumstances; for
this is God's will for you in Christ Jesus.
19Do not quench the Spirit. 20Do not treat
prophecies with contempt 21but test them
all; hold on to what is good, 22reject every
kind of evil.
23May God himself, the God of peace,
sanctify you through and through. May
your whole spirit, soul and body be kept
blameless at the coming of our Lord Jesus
Christ. 24The one who calls you is faithful,
and he will do it.

25Brothers and sisters, pray for us.
26Greet all God's people with a holy kiss.
27I charge you before the Lord to have this
letter read to all the brothers and sisters.
28The grace of our Lord Jesus Christ be
with you.

2 THESSALONIANS

1 Paul, Silas[a] and Timothy,

To the church of the Thessalonians in God our Father and the Lord Jesus Christ:

2 Grace and peace to you from God the Father and the Lord Jesus Christ.

Thanksgiving and Prayer

3 We ought always to thank God for you, brothers and sisters,[b] and rightly so, because your faith is growing more and more, and the love all of you have for one another is increasing. 4 Therefore, among God's churches we boast about your perseverance and faith in all the persecutions and trials you are enduring.

5 All this is evidence that God's judgment is right, and as a result you will be counted worthy of the kingdom of God, for which you are suffering. 6 God is just: He will pay back trouble to those who trouble you 7 and give relief to you who are troubled, and to us as well. This will happen when the Lord Jesus is revealed from heaven in blazing fire with his powerful angels. 8 He will punish those who do not know God and do not obey the gospel of our Lord Jesus. 9 They will be punished with everlasting destruction and shut out from the presence of the Lord and from the glory of his might 10 on the day he comes to be glorified in his holy people and to be marveled at among all those who have believed. This includes you, because you believed our testimony to you.

11 With this in mind, we constantly pray for you, that our God may make you worthy of his calling, and that by his power he may bring to fruition your every desire for goodness and your every deed prompted by faith. 12 We pray this so that the name of our Lord Jesus may be glorified in you, and you in him, according to the grace of our God and the Lord Jesus Christ.[c]

The Man of Lawlessness

2 Concerning the coming of our Lord Jesus Christ and our being gathered to him, we ask you, brothers and sisters, 2 not to become easily unsettled or alarmed by the teaching allegedly from us — whether by a prophecy or by word of mouth or by letter — asserting that the day of the Lord has already come. 3 Don't let anyone deceive you in any way, for that day will not come until the rebellion occurs and the man of lawlessness[d] is revealed, the man doomed to destruction. 4 He will oppose and will exalt himself over everything that is called God or is worshiped, so that he sets himself up in God's temple, proclaiming himself to be God.

5 Don't you remember that when I was with you I used to tell you these things? 6 And now you know what is holding him back, so that he may be revealed at the proper time. 7 For the secret power of lawlessness is already at work; but the one who now holds it back will continue to do so till he is taken out of the way. 8 And then the lawless one will be revealed, whom the Lord Jesus will overthrow with the breath of his mouth and destroy by the splendor of his coming. 9 The coming of the lawless one will be in accordance with how Satan works. He will use all sorts of displays of power through signs and wonders that serve the lie, 10 and all the ways that wickedness deceives those who are perishing. They perish because they refused to love the truth and so be saved. 11 For this reason God sends them a powerful delusion so that they will believe the lie 12 and so that all will be condemned who have not believed the truth but have delighted in wickedness.

Stand Firm

13 But we ought always to thank God for you, brothers and sisters loved by the Lord, because God chose you as firstfruits[e] to be saved through the sanctifying work of the Spirit and through belief in the truth. 14 He called you to this through our gospel, that you might share in the glory of our Lord Jesus Christ.

15 So then, brothers and sisters, stand firm and hold fast to the teachings[f] we passed on to you, whether by word of mouth or by letter.

[a] 1 Greek *Silvanus*, a variant of *Silas* [b] 3 The Greek word for *brothers and sisters* (*adelphoi*) refers here to believers, both men and women, as part of God's family; also in 2:1, 13, 15; 3:1, 6, 13. [c] 12 Or *God and Lord, Jesus Christ* [d] 3 Some manuscripts *sin* [e] 13 Some manuscripts *because from the beginning God chose you* [f] 15 Or *traditions*

16 May our Lord Jesus Christ himself and God our Father, who loved us and by his grace gave us eternal encouragement and good hope, 17 encourage your hearts and strengthen you in every good deed and word.

Request for Prayer

3 As for other matters, brothers and sisters, pray for us that the message of the Lord may spread rapidly and be honored, just as it was with you. 2 And pray that we may be delivered from wicked and evil people, for not everyone has faith. 3 But the Lord is faithful, and he will strengthen you and protect you from the evil one. 4 We have confidence in the Lord that you are doing and will continue to do the things we command. 5 May the Lord direct your hearts into God's love and Christ's perseverance.

Warning Against Idleness

6 In the name of the Lord Jesus Christ, we command you, brothers and sisters, to keep away from every believer who is idle and disruptive and does not live according to the teaching[a] you received from us. 7 For you yourselves know how you ought to follow our example. We were not idle when we were with you, 8 nor did we eat anyone's food without paying for it. On the contrary, we worked night and day, laboring and toiling so that we would not be a burden to any of you. 9 We did this, not because we do not have the right to such help, but in order to offer ourselves as a model for you to imitate. 10 For even when we were with you, we gave you this rule: "The one who is unwilling to work shall not eat."

11 We hear that some among you are idle and disruptive. They are not busy; they are busybodies. 12 Such people we command and urge in the Lord Jesus Christ to settle down and earn the food they eat. 13 And as for you, brothers and sisters, never tire of doing what is good.

14 Take special note of anyone who does not obey our instruction in this letter. Do not associate with them, in order that they may feel ashamed. 15 Yet do not regard them as an enemy, but warn them as you would a fellow believer.

Final Greetings

16 Now may the Lord of peace himself give you peace at all times and in every way. The Lord be with all of you.

17 I, Paul, write this greeting in my own hand, which is the distinguishing mark in all my letters. This is how I write.

18 The grace of our Lord Jesus Christ be with you all.

[a] 6 Or *tradition*

1 TIMOTHY

1 Paul, an apostle of Christ Jesus by the
command of God our Savior and of
Christ Jesus our hope,

2To Timothy my true son in the faith:

Grace, mercy and peace from God the
Father and Christ Jesus our Lord.

Timothy Charged to Oppose False Teachers

3As I urged you when I went into Macedonia, stay there in Ephesus so that you
may command certain people not to teach
false doctrines any longer 4or to devote
themselves to myths and endless genealogies. Such things promote controversial
speculations rather than advancing God's
work — which is by faith. 5The goal of this
command is love, which comes from a pure
heart and a good conscience and a sincere
faith. 6Some have departed from these and
have turned to meaningless talk. 7They
want to be teachers of the law, but they do
not know what they are talking about or
what they so confidently affirm.
8We know that the law is good if one
uses it properly. 9We also know that the
law is made not for the righteous but for
lawbreakers and rebels, the ungodly and
sinful, the unholy and irreligious, for those
who kill their fathers or mothers, for murderers, 10for the sexually immoral, for
those practicing homosexuality, for slave
traders and liars and perjurers — and for
whatever else is contrary to the sound
doctrine 11that conforms to the gospel
concerning the glory of the blessed God,
which he entrusted to me.

The Lord's Grace to Paul

12I thank Christ Jesus our Lord, who has
given me strength, that he considered me
trustworthy, appointing me to his service.
13Even though I was once a blasphemer
and a persecutor and a violent man, I was
shown mercy because I acted in ignorance
and unbelief. 14The grace of our Lord was
poured out on me abundantly, along with
the faith and love that are in Christ Jesus.
15Here is a trustworthy saying that deserves full acceptance: Christ Jesus came
into the world to save sinners — of whom
I am the worst. 16But for that very reason I
was shown mercy so that in me, the worst
of sinners, Christ Jesus might display his
immense patience as an example for those
who would believe in him and receive
eternal life. 17Now to the King eternal, immortal, invisible, the only God, be honor
and glory for ever and ever. Amen.

The Charge to Timothy Renewed

18Timothy, my son, I am giving you this
command in keeping with the prophecies once made about you, so that by
recalling them you may fight the battle
well, 19holding on to faith and a good conscience, which some have rejected and so
have suffered shipwreck with regard to
the faith. 20Among them are Hymenaeus
and Alexander, whom I have handed over
to Satan to be taught not to blaspheme.

Instructions on Worship

2 I urge, then, first of all, that petitions,
prayers, intercession and thanksgiving
be made for all people — 2for kings and
all those in authority, that we may live
peaceful and quiet lives in all godliness
and holiness. 3This is good, and pleases
God our Savior, 4who wants all people to
be saved and to come to a knowledge of
the truth. 5For there is one God and one
mediator between God and mankind, the
man Christ Jesus, 6who gave himself as a
ransom for all people. This has now been
witnessed to at the proper time. 7And for
this purpose I was appointed a herald
and an apostle — I am telling the truth,
I am not lying — and a true and faithful
teacher of the Gentiles.
8Therefore I want the men everywhere to
pray, lifting up holy hands without anger
or disputing. 9I also want the women to
dress modestly, with decency and propriety,
adorning themselves, not with elaborate
hairstyles or gold or pearls or expensive
clothes, 10but with good deeds, appropriate
for women who profess to worship God.
11A woman[a] should learn in quietness
and full submission. 12I do not permit a
woman to teach or to assume authority over a man;[b] she must be quiet. 13For
Adam was formed first, then Eve. 14And
Adam was not the one deceived; it was the
woman who was deceived and became a
sinner. 15But women[c] will be saved through
childbearing — if they continue in faith,
love and holiness with propriety.

[a] 11 Or *wife*; also in verse 12 [b] 12 Or *over her husband* [c] 15 Greek *she*

Qualifications for Overseers and Deacons

3 Here is a trustworthy saying: Whoever aspires to be an overseer desires a noble task. 2Now the overseer is to be above reproach, faithful to his wife, temperate, self-controlled, respectable, hospitable, able to teach, 3not given to drunkenness, not violent but gentle, not quarrelsome, not a lover of money. 4He must manage his own family well and see that his children obey him, and he must do so in a manner worthy of full[a] respect. 5(If anyone does not know how to manage his own family, how can he take care of God's church?) 6He must not be a recent convert, or he may become conceited and fall under the same judgment as the devil. 7He must also have a good reputation with outsiders, so that he will not fall into disgrace and into the devil's trap.

8In the same way, deacons[b] are to be worthy of respect, sincere, not indulging in much wine, and not pursuing dishonest gain. 9They must keep hold of the deep truths of the faith with a clear conscience. 10They must first be tested; and then if there is nothing against them, let them serve as deacons.

11In the same way, the women[c] are to be worthy of respect, not malicious talkers but temperate and trustworthy in everything.

12A deacon must be faithful to his wife and must manage his children and his household well. 13Those who have served well gain an excellent standing and great assurance in their faith in Christ Jesus.

Reasons for Paul's Instructions

14Although I hope to come to you soon, I am writing you these instructions so that, 15if I am delayed, you will know how people ought to conduct themselves in God's household, which is the church of the living God, the pillar and foundation of the truth. 16Beyond all question, the mystery from which true godliness springs is great:

He appeared in the flesh,
  was vindicated by the Spirit,[d]
was seen by angels,
  was preached among the nations,
was believed on in the world,
  was taken up in glory.

4 The Spirit clearly says that in later times some will abandon the faith and follow deceiving spirits and things taught by demons. 2Such teachings come through hypocritical liars, whose consciences have been seared as with a hot iron. 3They forbid people to marry and order them to abstain from certain foods, which God created to be received with thanksgiving by those who believe and who know the truth. 4For everything God created is good, and nothing is to be rejected if it is received with thanksgiving, 5because it is consecrated by the word of God and prayer.

6If you point these things out to the brothers and sisters,[e] you will be a good minister of Christ Jesus, nourished on the truths of the faith and of the good teaching that you have followed. 7Have nothing to do with godless myths and old wives' tales; rather, train yourself to be godly. 8For physical training is of some value, but godliness has value for all things, holding promise for both the present life and the life to come. 9This is a trustworthy saying that deserves full acceptance. 10That is why we labor and strive, because we have put our hope in the living God, who is the Savior of all people, and especially of those who believe.

11Command and teach these things. 12Don't let anyone look down on you because you are young, but set an example for the believers in speech, in conduct, in love, in faith and in purity. 13Until I come, devote yourself to the public reading of Scripture, to preaching and to teaching. 14Do not neglect your gift, which was given you through prophecy when the body of elders laid their hands on you.

15Be diligent in these matters; give yourself wholly to them, so that everyone may see your progress. 16Watch your life and doctrine closely. Persevere in them, because if you do, you will save both yourself and your hearers.

Widows, Elders and Slaves

5 Do not rebuke an older man harshly, but exhort him as if he were your father. Treat younger men as brothers, 2older women as mothers, and younger women as sisters, with absolute purity.

3Give proper recognition to those widows who are really in need. 4But if a widow has

[a] 4 Or *him with proper* [b] *8* The word *deacons* refers here to Christians designated to serve with the overseers/elders of the church in a variety of ways; similarly in verse 12; and in Romans 16:1 and Phil. 1:1. [c] *11* Possibly deacons' wives or women who are deacons [d] *16* Or *vindicated in spirit* [e] *6* The Greek word for *brothers and sisters* (*adelphoi*) refers here to believers, both men and women, as part of God's family.

children or grandchildren, these should learn first of all to put their religion into practice by caring for their own family and so repaying their parents and grandparents, for this is pleasing to God. 5The widow who is really in need and left all alone puts her hope in God and continues night and day to pray and to ask God for help. 6But the widow who lives for pleasure is dead even while she lives. 7Give the people these instructions, so that no one may be open to blame. 8Anyone who does not provide for their relatives, and especially for their own household, has denied the faith and is worse than an unbeliever.

9No widow may be put on the list of widows unless she is over sixty, has been faithful to her husband, 10and is well known for her good deeds, such as bringing up children, showing hospitality, washing the feet of the Lord's people, helping those in trouble and devoting herself to all kinds of good deeds.

11As for younger widows, do not put them on such a list. For when their sensual desires overcome their dedication to Christ, they want to marry. 12Thus they bring judgment on themselves, because they have broken their first pledge. 13Besides, they get into the habit of being idle and going about from house to house. And not only do they become idlers, but also busybodies who talk nonsense, saying things they ought not to. 14So I counsel younger widows to marry, to have children, to manage their homes and to give the enemy no opportunity for slander. 15Some have in fact already turned away to follow Satan.

16If any woman who is a believer has widows in her care, she should continue to help them and not let the church be burdened with them, so that the church can help those widows who are really in need.

17The elders who direct the affairs of the church well are worthy of double honor, especially those whose work is preaching and teaching. 18For Scripture says, "Do not muzzle an ox while it is treading out the grain,"[a] and "The worker deserves his wages."[b] 19Do not entertain an accusation against an elder unless it is brought by two or three witnesses. 20But those elders who are sinning you are to reprove before everyone, so that the others may take warning. 21I charge you, in the sight of God and Christ Jesus and the elect angels, to keep these instructions without partiality, and to do nothing out of favoritism.

22Do not be hasty in the laying on of hands, and do not share in the sins of others. Keep yourself pure.

23Stop drinking only water, and use a little wine because of your stomach and your frequent illnesses.

24The sins of some are obvious, reaching the place of judgment ahead of them; the sins of others trail behind them. 25In the same way, good deeds are obvious, and even those that are not obvious cannot remain hidden forever.

6 All who are under the yoke of slavery should consider their masters worthy of full respect, so that God's name and our teaching may not be slandered. 2Those who have believing masters should not show them disrespect just because they are fellow believers. Instead, they should serve them even better because their masters are dear to them as fellow believers and are devoted to the welfare[c] of their slaves.

False Teachers and the Love of Money

These are the things you are to teach and insist on. 3If anyone teaches otherwise and does not agree to the sound instruction of our Lord Jesus Christ and to godly teaching, 4they are conceited and understand nothing. They have an unhealthy interest in controversies and quarrels about words that result in envy, strife, malicious talk, evil suspicions 5and constant friction between people of corrupt mind, who have been robbed of the truth and who think that godliness is a means to financial gain.

6But godliness with contentment is great gain. 7For we brought nothing into the world, and we can take nothing out of it. 8But if we have food and clothing, we will be content with that. 9Those who want to get rich fall into temptation and a trap and into many foolish and harmful desires that plunge people into ruin and destruction. 10For the love of money is a root of all kinds of evil. Some people, eager for money, have wandered from the faith and pierced themselves with many griefs.

Final Charge to Timothy

11But you, man of God, flee from all this, and pursue righteousness, godliness, faith, love, endurance and gentleness. 12Fight the good fight of the faith. Take hold of the eternal life to which you were called when you made your good confession in the presence of many witnesses. 13In the sight of God, who gives life to everything, and of Christ Jesus, who while testifying before Pontius Pilate

[a] *18* Deut. 25:4 [b] *18* Luke 10:7 [c] *2* Or *and benefit from the service*

made the good confession, I charge you
14to keep this command without spot or
blame until the appearing of our Lord
Jesus Christ, 15which God will bring about
in his own time — God, the blessed and
only Ruler, the King of kings and Lord of
lords, 16who alone is immortal and who
lives in unapproachable light, whom no
one has seen or can see. To him be honor
and might forever. Amen.

17Command those who are rich in this
present world not to be arrogant nor to
put their hope in wealth, which is so uncertain, but to put their hope in God, who
richly provides us with everything for our
enjoyment. 18Command them to do good,
to be rich in good deeds, and to be generous and willing to share. 19In this way
they will lay up treasure for themselves
as a firm foundation for the coming age,
so that they may take hold of the life that
is truly life.

20Timothy, guard what has been entrusted to your care. Turn away from godless chatter and the opposing ideas of
what is falsely called knowledge, 21which
some have professed and in so doing have
departed from the faith.

Grace be with you all.

2 TIMOTHY

1 Paul, an apostle of Christ Jesus by the
will of God, in keeping with the promise
of life that is in Christ Jesus,

2To Timothy, my dear son:

Grace, mercy and peace from God the
Father and Christ Jesus our Lord.

Thanksgiving

3I thank God, whom I serve, as my ancestors did, with a clear conscience, as
night and day I constantly remember
you in my prayers. 4Recalling your tears, I
long to see you, so that I may be filled with
joy. 5I am reminded of your sincere faith,
which first lived in your grandmother
Lois and in your mother Eunice and, I am
persuaded, now lives in you also.

Appeal for Loyalty to Paul and the Gospel

6For this reason I remind you to fan
into flame the gift of God, which is in you
through the laying on of my hands. 7For
the Spirit God gave us does not make us
timid, but gives us power, love and self-
discipline. 8So do not be ashamed of the
testimony about our Lord or of me his prisoner. Rather, join with me in suffering for
the gospel, by the power of God. 9He has
saved us and called us to a holy life — not
because of anything we have done but because of his own purpose and grace. This
grace was given us in Christ Jesus before the
beginning of time, 10but it has now been revealed through the appearing of our Savior,
Christ Jesus, who has destroyed death and
has brought life and immortality to light
through the gospel. 11And of this gospel I
was appointed a herald and an apostle and
a teacher. 12That is why I am suffering as I
am. Yet this is no cause for shame, because
I know whom I have believed, and am convinced that he is able to guard what I have
entrusted to him until that day.

13What you heard from me, keep as the
pattern of sound teaching, with faith and
love in Christ Jesus. 14Guard the good deposit that was entrusted to you — guard it with
the help of the Holy Spirit who lives in us.

Examples of Disloyalty and Loyalty

15You know that everyone in the province of Asia has deserted me, including
Phygelus and Hermogenes.

16May the Lord show mercy to the household of Onesiphorus, because he often
refreshed me and was not ashamed of my
chains. 17On the contrary, when he was in
Rome, he searched hard for me until he
found me. 18May the Lord grant that he
will find mercy from the Lord on that day!
You know very well in how many ways he
helped me in Ephesus.

The Appeal Renewed

2 You then, my son, be strong in the grace
that is in Christ Jesus. 2And the things
you have heard me say in the presence of
many witnesses entrust to reliable people
who will also be qualified to teach others.
3Join with me in suffering, like a good soldier of Christ Jesus. 4No one serving as a
soldier gets entangled in civilian affairs,
but rather tries to please his commanding
officer. 5Similarly, anyone who competes
as an athlete does not receive the victor's
crown except by competing according to
the rules. 6The hardworking farmer should
be the first to receive a share of the crops.
7Reflect on what I am saying, for the Lord
will give you insight into all this.

8Remember Jesus Christ, raised from
the dead, descended from David. This
is my gospel, 9for which I am suffering
even to the point of being chained like a
criminal. But God's word is not chained.
10Therefore I endure everything for the
sake of the elect, that they too may obtain
the salvation that is in Christ Jesus, with
eternal glory.

11Here is a trustworthy saying:

If we died with him,
  we will also live with him;
12 if we endure,
  we will also reign with him.
If we disown him,
  he will also disown us;
13 if we are faithless,
  he remains faithful,
  for he cannot disown himself.

Dealing With False Teachers

14Keep reminding God's people of these
things. Warn them before God against
quarreling about words; it is of no value,
and only ruins those who listen. 15Do your
best to present yourself to God as one approved, a worker who does not need to be
ashamed and who correctly handles the

word of truth. 16Avoid godless chatter, because those who indulge in it will become
more and more ungodly. 17Their teaching
will spread like gangrene. Among them
are Hymenaeus and Philetus, 18who have
departed from the truth. They say that the
resurrection has already taken place, and
they destroy the faith of some. 19Neverthe-
less, God's solid foundation stands firm,
sealed with this inscription: "The Lord
knows those who are his," and, "Everyone
who confesses the name of the Lord must
turn away from wickedness."

20In a large house there are articles not
only of gold and silver, but also of wood
and clay; some are for special purposes
and some for common use. 21Those who
cleanse themselves from the latter will be
instruments for special purposes, made
holy, useful to the Master and prepared
to do any good work.

22Flee the evil desires of youth and pursue righteousness, faith, love and peace,
along with those who call on the Lord out
of a pure heart. 23Don't have anything to
do with foolish and stupid arguments,
because you know they produce quarrels.
24And the Lord's servant must not be quarrelsome but must be kind to everyone,
able to teach, not resentful. 25Opponents
must be gently instructed, in the hope that
God will grant them repentance leading
them to a knowledge of the truth, 26and
that they will come to their senses and
escape from the trap of the devil, who has
taken them captive to do his will.

3 But mark this: There will be terrible
times in the last days. 2People will
be lovers of themselves, lovers of money, boastful, proud, abusive, disobedient to their parents, ungrateful, unholy,
3without love, unforgiving, slanderous,
without self-control, brutal, not lovers of
the good, 4treacherous, rash, conceited,
lovers of pleasure rather than lovers of
God — 5having a form of godliness but
denying its power. Have nothing to do
with such people.

6They are the kind who worm their way
into homes and gain control over gullible
women, who are loaded down with sins
and are swayed by all kinds of evil desires, 7always learning but never able to
come to a knowledge of the truth. 8Just
as Jannes and Jambres opposed Moses,
so also these teachers oppose the truth.
They are men of depraved minds, who, as
far as the faith is concerned, are rejected.
9But they will not get very far because, as
in the case of those men, their folly will
be clear to everyone.

A Final Charge to Timothy

10You, however, know all about my
teaching, my way of life, my purpose,
faith, patience, love, endurance, 11perse-
cutions, sufferings — what kinds of things
happened to me in Antioch, Iconium and
Lystra, the persecutions I endured. Yet the
Lord rescued me from all of them. 12In
fact, everyone who wants to live a godly life in Christ Jesus will be persecuted,
13while evildoers and impostors will go
from bad to worse, deceiving and being
deceived. 14But as for you, continue in
what you have learned and have become
convinced of, because you know those
from whom you learned it, 15and how
from infancy you have known the Holy
Scriptures, which are able to make you
wise for salvation through faith in Christ
Jesus. 16All Scripture is God-breathed and
is useful for teaching, rebuking, correcting
and training in righteousness, 17so that
the servant of God[a] may be thoroughly
equipped for every good work.

4 In the presence of God and of Christ
Jesus, who will judge the living and
the dead, and in view of his appearing
and his kingdom, I give you this charge:
2Preach the word; be prepared in season
and out of season; correct, rebuke and encourage — with great patience and careful
instruction. 3For the time will come when
people will not put up with sound doctrine.
Instead, to suit their own desires, they will
gather around them a great number of
teachers to say what their itching ears
want to hear. 4They will turn their ears
away from the truth and turn aside to
myths. 5But you, keep your head in all
situations, endure hardship, do the work
of an evangelist, discharge all the duties
of your ministry.

6For I am already being poured out like
a drink offering, and the time for my departure is near. 7I have fought the good
fight, I have finished the race, I have kept
the faith. 8Now there is in store for me the
crown of righteousness, which the Lord,
the righteous Judge, will award to me on
that day — and not only to me, but also
to all who have longed for his appearing.

Personal Remarks

9Do your best to come to me quickly,
10for Demas, because he loved this world,
has deserted me and has gone to Thessalonica. Crescens has gone to Galatia, and
Titus to Dalmatia. 11Only Luke is with me.
Get Mark and bring him with you, because
he is helpful to me in my ministry. 12I sent

[a] 17 Or *that you, a man of God,*

Tychicus to Ephesus. 13 When you come, bring the cloak that I left with Carpus at Troas, and my scrolls, especially the parchments.

14 Alexander the metalworker did me a great deal of harm. The Lord will repay him for what he has done. 15 You too should be on your guard against him, because he strongly opposed our message.

16 At my first defense, no one came to my support, but everyone deserted me. May it not be held against them. 17 But the Lord stood at my side and gave me strength, so that through me the message might be fully proclaimed and all the Gentiles might hear it. And I was delivered from the lion's mouth. 18 The Lord will rescue me from every evil attack and will bring me safely to his heavenly kingdom. To him be glory for ever and ever. Amen.

Final Greetings

19 Greet Priscilla[a] and Aquila and the household of Onesiphorus. 20 Erastus stayed in Corinth, and I left Trophimus sick in Miletus. 21 Do your best to get here before winter. Eubulus greets you, and so do Pudens, Linus, Claudia and all the brothers and sisters.[b]

22 The Lord be with your spirit. Grace be with you all.

[a] *19* Greek *Prisca*, a variant of *Priscilla* [b] *21* The Greek word for *brothers and sisters* (*adelphoi*) refers here to believers, both men and women, as part of God's family.

TITUS

1 Paul, a servant of God and an apostle of Jesus Christ to further the faith of God's elect and their knowledge of the truth that leads to godliness — [2]in the hope of eternal life, which God, who does not lie, promised before the beginning of time, [3]and which now at his appointed season he has brought to light through the preaching entrusted to me by the command of God our Savior,

[4]To Titus, my true son in our common faith:

Grace and peace from God the Father and Christ Jesus our Savior.

Appointing Elders Who Love What Is Good

[5]The reason I left you in Crete was that you might put in order what was left unfinished and appoint[a] elders in every town, as I directed you. [6]An elder must be blameless, faithful to his wife, a man whose children believe[b] and are not open to the charge of being wild and disobedient. [7]Since an overseer manages God's household, he must be blameless — not overbearing, not quick-tempered, not given to drunkenness, not violent, not pursuing dishonest gain. [8]Rather, he must be hospitable, one who loves what is good, who is self-controlled, upright, holy and disciplined. [9]He must hold firmly to the trustworthy message as it has been taught, so that he can encourage others by sound doctrine and refute those who oppose it.

Rebuking Those Who Fail to Do Good

[10]For there are many rebellious people, full of meaningless talk and deception, especially those of the circumcision group. [11]They must be silenced, because they are disrupting whole households by teaching things they ought not to teach — and that for the sake of dishonest gain. [12]One of Crete's own prophets has said it: "Cretans are always liars, evil brutes, lazy gluttons."[c] [13]This saying is true. Therefore rebuke them sharply, so that they will be sound in the faith [14]and will pay no attention to Jewish myths or to the merely human commands of those who reject the truth. [15]To the pure, all things are pure, but to those who are corrupted and do not believe, nothing is pure. In fact, both their minds and consciences are corrupted. [16]They claim to know God, but by their actions they deny him. They are detestable, disobedient and unfit for doing anything good.

Doing Good for the Sake of the Gospel

2 You, however, must teach what is appropriate to sound doctrine. [2]Teach the older men to be temperate, worthy of respect, self-controlled, and sound in faith, in love and in endurance.

[3]Likewise, teach the older women to be reverent in the way they live, not to be slanderers or addicted to much wine, but to teach what is good. [4]Then they can urge the younger women to love their husbands and children, [5]to be self-controlled and pure, to be busy at home, to be kind, and to be subject to their husbands, so that no one will malign the word of God.

[6]Similarly, encourage the young men to be self-controlled. [7]In everything set them an example by doing what is good. In your teaching show integrity, seriousness [8]and soundness of speech that cannot be condemned, so that those who oppose you may be ashamed because they have nothing bad to say about us.

[9]Teach slaves to be subject to their masters in everything, to try to please them, not to talk back to them, [10]and not to steal from them, but to show that they can be fully trusted, so that in every way they will make the teaching about God our Savior attractive.

[11]For the grace of God has appeared that offers salvation to all people. [12]It teaches us to say "No" to ungodliness and worldly passions, and to live self-controlled, upright and godly lives in this present age, [13]while we wait for the blessed hope — the appearing of the glory of our great God and Savior, Jesus Christ, [14]who gave himself for us to redeem us from all wickedness and to purify for himself a people that are his very own, eager to do what is good.

[15]These, then, are the things you should teach. Encourage and rebuke with all authority. Do not let anyone despise you.

[a] 5 Or *ordain* [b] 6 Or *children are trustworthy* [c] 12 From the Cretan philosopher Epimenides

Saved in Order to Do Good

3 Remind the people to be subject to rulers and authorities, to be obedient, to be ready to do whatever is good, 2to slander no one, to be peaceable and considerate, and always to be gentle toward everyone.

3At one time we too were foolish, disobedient, deceived and enslaved by all kinds of passions and pleasures. We lived in malice and envy, being hated and hating one another. 4But when the kindness and love of God our Savior appeared, 5he saved us, not because of righteous things we had done, but because of his mercy. He saved us through the washing of rebirth and renewal by the Holy Spirit, 6whom he poured out on us generously through Jesus Christ our Savior, 7so that, having been justified by his grace, we might become heirs having the hope of eternal life. 8This is a trustworthy saying. And I want you to stress these things, so that those who have trusted in God may be careful to devote themselves to doing what is good. These things are excellent and profitable for everyone.

9But avoid foolish controversies and genealogies and arguments and quarrels about the law, because these are unprofitable and useless. 10Warn a divisive person once, and then warn them a second time. After that, have nothing to do with them. 11You may be sure that such people are warped and sinful; they are self-condemned.

Final Remarks

12As soon as I send Artemas or Tychicus to you, do your best to come to me at Nicopolis, because I have decided to winter there. 13Do everything you can to help Zenas the lawyer and Apollos on their way and see that they have everything they need. 14Our people must learn to devote themselves to doing what is good, in order to provide for urgent needs and not live unproductive lives.

15Everyone with me sends you greetings. Greet those who love us in the faith.

Grace be with you all.

PHILEMON

[1]Paul, a prisoner of Christ Jesus, and
Timothy our brother,

To Philemon our dear friend and fellow
worker — [2]also to Apphia our sister and
Archippus our fellow soldier — and to the
church that meets in your home:

[3]Grace and peace to you[a] from God our
Father and the Lord Jesus Christ.

Thanksgiving and Prayer

[4]I always thank my God as I remember
you in my prayers, [5]because I hear about
your love for all his holy people and your
faith in the Lord Jesus. [6]I pray that your
partnership with us in the faith may be
effective in deepening your understanding of every good thing we share for the
sake of Christ. [7]Your love has given me
great joy and encouragement, because
you, brother, have refreshed the hearts
of the Lord's people.

Paul's Plea for Onesimus

[8]Therefore, although in Christ I could be
bold and order you to do what you ought
to do, [9]yet I prefer to appeal to you on
the basis of love. It is as none other than
Paul — an old man and now also a prisoner of Christ Jesus — [10]that I appeal to
you for my son Onesimus,[b] who became
my son while I was in chains. [11]Formerly he
was useless to you, but now he has become
useful both to you and to me.

[12]I am sending him — who is my very
heart — back to you. [13]I would have liked
to keep him with me so that he could take
your place in helping me while I am in
chains for the gospel. [14]But I did not want to
do anything without your consent, so that
any favor you do would not seem forced
but would be voluntary. [15]Perhaps the reason he was separated from you for a little
while was that you might have him back
forever — [16]no longer as a slave, but better
than a slave, as a dear brother. He is very
dear to me but even dearer to you, both as
a fellow man and as a brother in the Lord.

[17]So if you consider me a partner, welcome him as you would welcome me. [18]If
he has done you any wrong or owes you
anything, charge it to me. [19]I, Paul, am
writing this with my own hand. I will pay
it back — not to mention that you owe me
your very self. [20]I do wish, brother, that I
may have some benefit from you in the
Lord; refresh my heart in Christ. [21]Confident
of your obedience, I write to you, knowing
that you will do even more than I ask.

[22]And one thing more: Prepare a guest
room for me, because I hope to be restored
to you in answer to your prayers.

[23]Epaphras, my fellow prisoner in Christ
Jesus, sends you greetings. [24]And so do
Mark, Aristarchus, Demas and Luke, my
fellow workers.

[25]The grace of the Lord Jesus Christ be
with your spirit.

[a] *3* The Greek is plural; also in verses 22 and 25; elsewhere in this letter "you" is singular.
[b] *10* *Onesimus* means *useful.*

HEBREWS

God's Final Word: His Son

1 In the past God spoke to our ancestors
through the prophets at many times
and in various ways, 2but in these last days
he has spoken to us by his Son, whom he
appointed heir of all things, and through
whom also he made the universe. 3The Son
is the radiance of God's glory and the exact
representation of his being, sustaining
all things by his powerful word. After he
had provided purification for sins, he sat
down at the right hand of the Majesty in
heaven. 4So he became as much superior
to the angels as the name he has inherited
is superior to theirs.

The Son Superior to Angels

5For to which of the angels did God ever
say,

"You are my Son;
today I have become your Father"[a]?

Or again,

"I will be his Father,
and he will be my Son"[b]?

6And again, when God brings his firstborn
into the world, he says,

"Let all God's angels worship him."[c]

7In speaking of the angels he says,

"He makes his angels spirits,
and his servants flames of fire."[d]

8But about the Son he says,

"Your throne, O God, will last for ever
and ever;
a scepter of justice will be the
scepter of your kingdom.
9 You have loved righteousness and
hated wickedness;
therefore God, your God, has set
you above your companions
by anointing you with the oil of joy."[e]

10He also says,

"In the beginning, Lord, you laid the
foundations of the earth,
and the heavens are the work of
your hands.
11 They will perish, but you remain;
they will all wear out like a
garment.
12 You will roll them up like a robe;
like a garment they will be
changed.
But you remain the same,
and your years will never end."[f]

13To which of the angels did God ever say,

"Sit at my right hand
until I make your enemies
a footstool for your feet"[g]?

14Are not all angels ministering spirits sent
to serve those who will inherit salvation?

Warning to Pay Attention

2 We must pay the most careful attention, therefore, to what we have heard,
so that we do not drift away. 2For since the
message spoken through angels was binding, and every violation and disobedience
received its just punishment, 3how shall we
escape if we ignore so great a salvation?
This salvation, which was first announced
by the Lord, was confirmed to us by those
who heard him. 4God also testified to it
by signs, wonders and various miracles,
and by gifts of the Holy Spirit distributed
according to his will.

Jesus Made Fully Human

5It is not to angels that he has subjected the world to come, about which we
are speaking. 6But there is a place where
someone has testified:

"What is mankind that you are
mindful of them,
a son of man that you care for him?
7 You made them a little[h] lower than
the angels;
you crowned them with glory and
honor
8 and put everything under their
feet."[i,j]

In putting everything under them,[k] God left
nothing that is not subject to them.[k] Yet at
present we do not see everything subject to
them.[k] 9But we do see Jesus, who was made

[a] 5 Psalm 2:7 [b] 5 2 Samuel 7:14; 1 Chron. 17:13 [c] 6 Deut. 32:43 (see Dead Sea Scrolls and Septuagint) [d] 7 Psalm 104:4 [e] 9 Psalm 45:6,7 [f] 12 Psalm 102:25-27 [g] 13 Psalm 110:1 [h] 7 Or *them for a little while* [i] 6-8 Psalm 8:4-6 [j] 7,8 Or *7You made him a little lower than the angels;/ you crowned him with glory and honor/ 8and put everything under his feet."* [k] 8 Or *him*

lower than the angels for a little while, now
crowned with glory and honor because he
suffered death, so that by the grace of God
he might taste death for everyone.
10In bringing many sons and daughters
to glory, it was fitting that God, for whom
and through whom everything exists,
should make the pioneer of their salvation
perfect through what he suffered. 11Both
the one who makes people holy and those
who are made holy are of the same family. So Jesus is not ashamed to call them
brothers and sisters.[a] 12He says,

"I will declare your name to my
brothers and sisters;
in the assembly I will sing your
praises."[b]

13And again,

"I will put my trust in him."[c]

And again he says,

"Here am I, and the children God
has given me."[d]

14Since the children have flesh and
blood, he too shared in their humanity so
that by his death he might break the power of him who holds the power of death—
that is, the devil— 15and free those who
all their lives were held in slavery by their
fear of death. 16For surely it is not angels
he helps, but Abraham's descendants. 17For
this reason he had to be made like them,[e]
fully human in every way, in order that
he might become a merciful and faithful
high priest in service to God, and that he
might make atonement for the sins of
the people. 18Because he himself suffered
when he was tempted, he is able to help
those who are being tempted.

Jesus Greater Than Moses

3 Therefore, holy brothers and sisters,
who share in the heavenly calling,
fix your thoughts on Jesus, whom we acknowledge as our apostle and high priest.
2He was faithful to the one who appointed him, just as Moses was faithful in all
God's house. 3Jesus has been found worthy of greater honor than Moses, just as
the builder of a house has greater honor
than the house itself. 4For every house is
built by someone, but God is the builder
of everything. 5"Moses was faithful as a
servant in all God's house,"[f] bearing witness to what would be spoken by God in
the future. 6But Christ is faithful as the Son
over God's house. And we are his house, if
indeed we hold firmly to our confidence
and the hope in which we glory.

Warning Against Unbelief

7So, as the Holy Spirit says:

"Today, if you hear his voice,
8 do not harden your hearts
as you did in the rebellion,
during the time of testing in the
wilderness,
9 where your ancestors tested and
tried me,
though for forty years they saw
what I did.
10 That is why I was angry with that
generation;
I said, 'Their hearts are always
going astray,
and they have not known my ways.'
11 So I declared on oath in my anger,
'They shall never enter my rest.'"[g]

12See to it, brothers and sisters, that
none of you has a sinful, unbelieving heart
that turns away from the living God. 13But
encourage one another daily, as long as it
is called "Today," so that none of you may
be hardened by sin's deceitfulness. 14We
have come to share in Christ, if indeed we
hold our original conviction firmly to the
very end. 15As has just been said:

"Today, if you hear his voice,
do not harden your hearts
as you did in the rebellion."[h]

16Who were they who heard and rebelled? Were they not all those Moses led
out of Egypt? 17And with whom was he
angry for forty years? Was it not with those
who sinned, whose bodies perished in the
wilderness? 18And to whom did God swear
that they would never enter his rest if not
to those who disobeyed? 19So we see that
they were not able to enter, because of
their unbelief.

A Sabbath-Rest for the People of God

4 Therefore, since the promise of entering his rest still stands, let us be
careful that none of you be found to have
fallen short of it. 2For we also have had
the good news proclaimed to us, just as
they did; but the message they heard was
of no value to them, because they did not
share the faith of those who obeyed.[i] 3Now

[a] *11* The Greek word for *brothers and sisters (adelphoi)* refers here to believers, both men and women, as part of God's family; also in verse 12; and in 3:1, 12; 10:19; 13:22. [b] *12* Psalm 22:22 [c] *13* Isaiah 8:17 [d] *13* Isaiah 8:18 [e] *17* Or *like his brothers* [f] *5* Num. 12:7 [g] *11* Psalm 95:7-11 [h] *15* Psalm 95:7,8 [i] *2* Some manuscripts *because those who heard did not combine it with faith*

we who have believed enter that rest, just as God has said,

> "So I declared on oath in my anger,
> 'They shall never enter my rest.'"[a]

And yet his works have been finished since the creation of the world. 4For somewhere he has spoken about the seventh day in these words: "On the seventh day God rested from all his works."[b] 5And again in the passage above he says, "They shall never enter my rest."

6Therefore since it still remains for some to enter that rest, and since those who formerly had the good news proclaimed to them did not go in because of their disobedience, 7God again set a certain day, calling it "Today." This he did when a long time later he spoke through David, as in the passage already quoted:

> "Today, if you hear his voice,
> do not harden your hearts."[c]

8For if Joshua had given them rest, God would not have spoken later about another day. 9There remains, then, a Sabbath-rest for the people of God; 10for anyone who enters God's rest also rests from their works,[d] just as God did from his. 11Let us, therefore, make every effort to enter that rest, so that no one will perish by following their example of disobedience.

12For the word of God is alive and active. Sharper than any double-edged sword, it penetrates even to dividing soul and spirit, joints and marrow; it judges the thoughts and attitudes of the heart. 13Nothing in all creation is hidden from God's sight. Everything is uncovered and laid bare before the eyes of him to whom we must give account.

Jesus the Great High Priest

14Therefore, since we have a great high priest who has ascended into heaven,[e] Jesus the Son of God, let us hold firmly to the faith we profess. 15For we do not have a high priest who is unable to empathize with our weaknesses, but we have one who has been tempted in every way, just as we are—yet he did not sin. 16Let us then approach God's throne of grace with confidence, so that we may receive mercy and find grace to help us in our time of need.

5 Every high priest is selected from among the people and is appointed to represent the people in matters related to God, to offer gifts and sacrifices for sins. 2He is able to deal gently with those who are ignorant and are going astray, since he himself is subject to weakness. 3This is why he has to offer sacrifices for his own sins, as well as for the sins of the people. 4And no one takes this honor on himself, but he receives it when called by God, just as Aaron was.

5In the same way, Christ did not take on himself the glory of becoming a high priest. But God said to him,

> "You are my Son;
> today I have become your Father."[f]

6And he says in another place,

> "You are a priest forever,
> in the order of Melchizedek."[g]

7During the days of Jesus' life on earth, he offered up prayers and petitions with fervent cries and tears to the one who could save him from death, and he was heard because of his reverent submission. 8Son though he was, he learned obedience from what he suffered 9and, once made perfect, he became the source of eternal salvation for all who obey him 10and was designated by God to be high priest in the order of Melchizedek.

Warning Against Falling Away

11We have much to say about this, but it is hard to make it clear to you because you no longer try to understand. 12In fact, though by this time you ought to be teachers, you need someone to teach you the elementary truths of God's word all over again. You need milk, not solid food! 13Anyone who lives on milk, being still an infant, is not acquainted with the teaching about righteousness. 14But solid food is for the mature, who by constant use have trained themselves to distinguish good from evil.

6 Therefore let us move beyond the elementary teachings about Christ and be taken forward to maturity, not laying again the foundation of repentance from acts that lead to death,[h] and of faith in God, 2instruction about cleansing rites,[i] the laying on of hands, the resurrection of the dead, and eternal judgment. 3And God permitting, we will do so.

4It is impossible for those who have once been enlightened, who have tasted the heavenly gift, who have shared in the Holy Spirit, 5who have tasted the goodness of the word of God and the powers of the coming age 6and who have fallen[j] away,

[a] 3 Psalm 95:11; also in verse 5 [b] 4 Gen. 2:2 [c] 7 Psalm 95:7,8 [d] 10 Or *labor* [e] 14 Greek *has gone through the heavens* [f] 5 Psalm 2:7 [g] 6 Psalm 110:4 [h] 1 Or *from useless rituals* [i] 2 Or *about baptisms* [j] 6 Or *age,* 6*if they fall*

to be brought back to repentance. To their loss they are crucifying the Son of God all over again and subjecting him to public disgrace. 7Land that drinks in the rain often falling on it and that produces a crop useful to those for whom it is farmed receives the blessing of God. 8But land that produces thorns and thistles is worthless and is in danger of being cursed. In the end it will be burned.

9Even though we speak like this, dear friends, we are convinced of better things in your case — the things that have to do with salvation. 10God is not unjust; he will not forget your work and the love you have shown him as you have helped his people and continue to help them. 11We want each of you to show this same diligence to the very end, so that what you hope for may be fully realized. 12We do not want you to become lazy, but to imitate those who through faith and patience inherit what has been promised.

The Certainty of God's Promise

13When God made his promise to Abraham, since there was no one greater for him to swear by, he swore by himself, 14saying, "I will surely bless you and give you many descendants."[a] 15And so after waiting patiently, Abraham received what was promised.

16People swear by someone greater than themselves, and the oath confirms what is said and puts an end to all argument. 17Because God wanted to make the unchanging nature of his purpose very clear to the heirs of what was promised, he confirmed it with an oath. 18God did this so that, by two unchangeable things in which it is impossible for God to lie, we who have fled to take hold of the hope set before us may be greatly encouraged. 19We have this hope as an anchor for the soul, firm and secure. It enters the inner sanctuary behind the curtain, 20where our forerunner, Jesus, has entered on our behalf. He has become a high priest forever, in the order of Melchizedek.

Melchizedek the Priest

7 This Melchizedek was king of Salem and priest of God Most High. He met Abraham returning from the defeat of the kings and blessed him, 2and Abraham gave him a tenth of everything. First, the name Melchizedek means "king of righteousness"; then also, "king of Salem" means "king of peace." 3Without father or mother, without genealogy, without beginning of days or end of life, resembling the Son of God, he remains a priest forever.

4Just think how great he was: Even the patriarch Abraham gave him a tenth of the plunder! 5Now the law requires the descendants of Levi who become priests to collect a tenth from the people — that is, from their fellow Israelites — even though they also are descended from Abraham. 6This man, however, did not trace his descent from Levi, yet he collected a tenth from Abraham and blessed him who had the promises. 7And without doubt the lesser is blessed by the greater. 8In the one case, the tenth is collected by people who die; but in the other case, by him who is declared to be living. 9One might even say that Levi, who collects the tenth, paid the tenth through Abraham, 10because when Melchizedek met Abraham, Levi was still in the body of his ancestor.

Jesus Like Melchizedek

11If perfection could have been attained through the Levitical priesthood — and indeed the law given to the people established that priesthood — why was there still need for another priest to come, one in the order of Melchizedek, not in the order of Aaron? 12For when the priesthood is changed, the law must be changed also. 13He of whom these things are said belonged to a different tribe, and no one from that tribe has ever served at the altar. 14For it is clear that our Lord descended from Judah, and in regard to that tribe Moses said nothing about priests. 15And what we have said is even more clear if another priest like Melchizedek appears, 16one who has become a priest not on the basis of a regulation as to his ancestry but on the basis of the power of an indestructible life. 17For it is declared:

> "You are a priest forever,
>   in the order of Melchizedek."[b]

18The former regulation is set aside because it was weak and useless 19(for the law made nothing perfect), and a better hope is introduced, by which we draw near to God.

20And it was not without an oath! Others became priests without any oath, 21but he became a priest with an oath when God said to him:

> "The Lord has sworn
>   and will not change his mind:
> 'You are a priest forever.'"[b]

22Because of this oath, Jesus has become the guarantor of a better covenant.

[a] 14 Gen. 22:17 [b] 17,21 Psalm 110:4

23 Now there have been many of those
priests, since death prevented them from
continuing in office; 24 but because Jesus
lives forever, he has a permanent priesthood. 25 Therefore he is able to save completely[a] those who come to God through
him, because he always lives to intercede
for them.
26 Such a high priest truly meets our
need — one who is holy, blameless, pure,
set apart from sinners, exalted above the
heavens. 27 Unlike the other high priests,
he does not need to offer sacrifices day
after day, first for his own sins, and then
for the sins of the people. He sacrificed
for their sins once for all when he offered
himself. 28 For the law appoints as high
priests men in all their weakness; but the
oath, which came after the law, appointed the Son, who has been made perfect
forever.

The High Priest of a New Covenant

8 Now the main point of what we are
saying is this: We do have such a high
priest, who sat down at the right hand of
the throne of the Majesty in heaven, 2 and
who serves in the sanctuary, the true tabernacle set up by the Lord, not by a mere
human being.
3 Every high priest is appointed to offer
both gifts and sacrifices, and so it was necessary for this one also to have something
to offer. 4 If he were on earth, he would not
be a priest, for there are already priests
who offer the gifts prescribed by the law.
5 They serve at a sanctuary that is a copy
and shadow of what is in heaven. This is
why Moses was warned when he was about
to build the tabernacle: "See to it that you
make everything according to the pattern
shown you on the mountain."[b] 6 But in fact
the ministry Jesus has received is as superior to theirs as the covenant of which
he is mediator is superior to the old one,
since the new covenant is established on
better promises.
7 For if there had been nothing wrong
with that first covenant, no place would
have been sought for another. 8 But God
found fault with the people and said[c]:

"The days are coming, declares the
Lord,
when I will make a new covenant
with the people of Israel
and with the people of Judah.
9 It will not be like the covenant
I made with their ancestors
when I took them by the hand
to lead them out of Egypt,
because they did not remain faithful
to my covenant,
and I turned away from them,
declares the Lord.
10 This is the covenant I will establish
with the people of Israel
after that time, declares the Lord.
I will put my laws in their minds
and write them on their hearts.
I will be their God,
and they will be my people.
11 No longer will they teach their
neighbor,
or say to one another, 'Know the
Lord,'
because they will all know me,
from the least of them to the
greatest.
12 For I will forgive their wickedness
and will remember their sins no
more."[d]

13 By calling this covenant "new," he has
made the first one obsolete; and what is
obsolete and outdated will soon disappear.

Worship in the Earthly Tabernacle

9 Now the first covenant had regulations
for worship and also an earthly sanctuary. 2 A tabernacle was set up. In its first
room were the lampstand and the table
with its consecrated bread; this was called
the Holy Place. 3 Behind the second curtain
was a room called the Most Holy Place,
4 which had the golden altar of incense
and the gold-covered ark of the covenant.
This ark contained the gold jar of manna,
Aaron's staff that had budded, and the
stone tablets of the covenant. 5 Above the
ark were the cherubim of the Glory, overshadowing the atonement cover. But we
cannot discuss these things in detail now.
6 When everything had been arranged
like this, the priests entered regularly into
the outer room to carry on their ministry.
7 But only the high priest entered the inner room, and that only once a year, and
never without blood, which he offered
for himself and for the sins the people
had committed in ignorance. 8 The Holy
Spirit was showing by this that the way
into the Most Holy Place had not yet been
disclosed as long as the first tabernacle
was still functioning. 9 This is an illustra-
tion for the present time, indicating that
the gifts and sacrifices being offered were
not able to clear the conscience of the
worshiper. 10 They are only a matter of
food and drink and various ceremonial
washings — external regulations applying
until the time of the new order.

[a] *25* Or *forever* [b] *5* Exodus 25:40 [c] *8* Some manuscripts may be translated *fault and said to the people.* [d] *12* Jer. 31:31-34

The Blood of Christ

11 But when Christ came as high priest of the good things that are now already here,[a] he went through the greater and more perfect tabernacle that is not made with human hands, that is to say, is not a part of this creation. 12 He did not enter by means of the blood of goats and calves; but he entered the Most Holy Place once for all by his own blood, thus obtaining[b] eternal redemption. 13 The blood of goats and bulls and the ashes of a heifer sprinkled on those who are ceremonially unclean sanctify them so that they are outwardly clean. 14 How much more, then, will the blood of Christ, who through the eternal Spirit offered himself unblemished to God, cleanse our consciences from acts that lead to death,[c] so that we may serve the living God!

15 For this reason Christ is the mediator of a new covenant, that those who are called may receive the promised eternal inheritance — now that he has died as a ransom to set them free from the sins committed under the first covenant.

16 In the case of a will,[d] it is necessary to prove the death of the one who made it, 17 because a will is in force only when somebody has died; it never takes effect while the one who made it is living. 18 This is why even the first covenant was not put into effect without blood. 19 When Moses had proclaimed every command of the law to all the people, he took the blood of calves, together with water, scarlet wool and branches of hyssop, and sprinkled the scroll and all the people. 20 He said, "This is the blood of the covenant, which God has commanded you to keep."[e] 21 In the same way, he sprinkled with the blood both the tabernacle and everything used in its ceremonies. 22 In fact, the law requires that nearly everything be cleansed with blood, and without the shedding of blood there is no forgiveness.

23 It was necessary, then, for the copies of the heavenly things to be purified with these sacrifices, but the heavenly things themselves with better sacrifices than these. 24 For Christ did not enter a sanctuary made with human hands that was only a copy of the true one; he entered heaven itself, now to appear for us in God's presence. 25 Nor did he enter heaven to offer himself again and again, the way the high priest enters the Most Holy Place every year with blood that is not his own. 26 Otherwise Christ would have had to suffer many times since the creation of the world. But he has appeared once for all at the culmination of the ages to do away with sin by the sacrifice of himself. 27 Just as people are destined to die once, and after that to face judgment, 28 so Christ was sacrificed once to take away the sins of many; and he will appear a second time, not to bear sin, but to bring salvation to those who are waiting for him.

Christ's Sacrifice Once for All

10 The law is only a shadow of the good things that are coming — not the realities themselves. For this reason it can never, by the same sacrifices repeated endlessly year after year, make perfect those who draw near to worship. 2 Otherwise, would they not have stopped being offered? For the worshipers would have been cleansed once for all, and would no longer have felt guilty for their sins. 3 But those sacrifices are an annual reminder of sins. 4 It is impossible for the blood of bulls and goats to take away sins.

5 Therefore, when Christ came into the world, he said:

> "Sacrifice and offering you did not desire,
> but a body you prepared for me;
> 6 with burnt offerings and sin offerings you were not pleased.
> 7 Then I said, 'Here I am — it is written about me in the scroll —
> I have come to do your will, my God.' "[f]

8 First he said, "Sacrifices and offerings, burnt offerings and sin offerings you did not desire, nor were you pleased with them" — though they were offered in accordance with the law. 9 Then he said, "Here I am, I have come to do your will." He sets aside the first to establish the second. 10 And by that will, we have been made holy through the sacrifice of the body of Jesus Christ once for all.

11 Day after day every priest stands and performs his religious duties; again and again he offers the same sacrifices, which can never take away sins. 12 But when this priest had offered for all time one sacrifice for sins, he sat down at the right hand of God, 13 and since that time he waits for his enemies to be made his footstool. 14 For by one sacrifice he has made perfect forever those who are being made holy.

[a] 11 Some early manuscripts *are to come* [b] 12 Or *blood, having obtained* [c] 14 Or *from useless rituals* [d] 16 Same Greek word as *covenant*; also in verse 17 [e] 20 Exodus 24:8 [f] 7 Psalm 40:6-8 (see Septuagint)

[15]The Holy Spirit also testifies to us about this. First he says:

[16]"This is the covenant I will make with them
after that time, says the Lord.
I will put my laws in their hearts,
and I will write them on their minds."[a]

[17]Then he adds:

"Their sins and lawless acts
I will remember no more."[b]

[18]And where these have been forgiven, sacrifice for sin is no longer necessary.

A Call to Persevere in Faith

[19]Therefore, brothers and sisters, since
we have confidence to enter the Most Holy
Place by the blood of Jesus, [20]by a new and
living way opened for us through the curtain, that is, his body, [21]and since we have a
great priest over the house of God, [22]let us
draw near to God with a sincere heart and
with the full assurance that faith brings,
having our hearts sprinkled to cleanse us
from a guilty conscience and having our
bodies washed with pure water. [23]Let us
hold unswervingly to the hope we profess,
for he who promised is faithful. [24]And let
us consider how we may spur one another on toward love and good deeds, [25]not
giving up meeting together, as some are
in the habit of doing, but encouraging one
another — and all the more as you see the
Day approaching.

[26]If we deliberately keep on sinning
after we have received the knowledge of
the truth, no sacrifice for sins is left, [27]but
only a fearful expectation of judgment
and of raging fire that will consume the
enemies of God. [28]Anyone who rejected the
law of Moses died without mercy on the
testimony of two or three witnesses. [29]How
much more severely do you think someone
deserves to be punished who has trampled
the Son of God underfoot, who has treated
as an unholy thing the blood of the covenant that sanctified them, and who has
insulted the Spirit of grace? [30]For we know
him who said, "It is mine to avenge; I will
repay,"[c] and again, "The Lord will judge
his people."[d] [31]It is a dreadful thing to fall
into the hands of the living God.

[32]Remember those earlier days after
you had received the light, when you endured in a great conflict full of suffering.
[33]Sometimes you were publicly exposed to
insult and persecution; at other times you
stood side by side with those who were so
treated. [34]You suffered along with those in
prison and joyfully accepted the confiscation of your property, because you knew
that you yourselves had better and lasting
possessions. [35]So do not throw away your
confidence; it will be richly rewarded.

[36]You need to persevere so that when
you have done the will of God, you will
receive what he has promised. [37]For,

"In just a little while,
he who is coming will come
and will not delay."[e]

[38]And,

"But my righteous[f] one will live by faith.
And I take no pleasure
in the one who shrinks back."[g]

[39]But we do not belong to those who shrink
back and are destroyed, but to those who
have faith and are saved.

Faith in Action

11 Now faith is confidence in what we
hope for and assurance about what
we do not see. [2]This is what the ancients
were commended for.

[3]By faith we understand that the universe was formed at God's command, so
that what is seen was not made out of
what was visible.

[4]By faith Abel brought God a better
offering than Cain did. By faith he was
commended as righteous, when God spoke
well of his offerings. And by faith Abel still
speaks, even though he is dead.

[5]By faith Enoch was taken from this life,
so that he did not experience death: "He
could not be found, because God had tak-
en him away."[h] For before he was taken,
he was commended as one who pleased
God. [6]And without faith it is impossible to
please God, because anyone who comes to
him must believe that he exists and that
he rewards those who earnestly seek him.

[7]By faith Noah, when warned about
things not yet seen, in holy fear built an
ark to save his family. By his faith he condemned the world and became heir of the
righteousness that is in keeping with faith.

[8]By faith Abraham, when called to go
to a place he would later receive as his inheritance, obeyed and went, even though
he did not know where he was going. [9]By
faith he made his home in the promised

[a] *16* Jer. 31:33 [b] *17* Jer. 31:34 [c] *30* Deut. 32:35 [d] *30* Deut. 32:36; Psalm 135:14 [e] *37* Isaiah 26:20; Hab. 2:3 [f] *38* Some early manuscripts *But the righteous* [g] *38* Hab. 2:4 (see Septuagint) [h] *5* Gen. 5:24

land like a stranger in a foreign country;
he lived in tents, as did Isaac and Jacob,
who were heirs with him of the same
promise. 10For he was looking forward to
the city with foundations, whose architect
and builder is God. 11And by faith even
Sarah, who was past childbearing age,
was enabled to bear children because she[a]
considered him faithful who had made the
promise. 12And so from this one man, and
he as good as dead, came descendants as
numerous as the stars in the sky and as
countless as the sand on the seashore.

13All these people were still living by
faith when they died. They did not receive
the things promised; they only saw them
and welcomed them from a distance, ad-
mitting that they were foreigners and
strangers on earth. 14People who say such
things show that they are looking for a
country of their own. 15If they had been
thinking of the country they had left, they
would have had opportunity to return.
16Instead, they were longing for a better
country — a heavenly one. Therefore God
is not ashamed to be called their God, for
he has prepared a city for them.

17By faith Abraham, when God tested him, offered Isaac as a sacrifice. He
who had embraced the promises was
about to sacrifice his one and only son,
18even though God had said to him, "It
is through Isaac that your offspring will
be reckoned."[b] 19Abraham reasoned that
God could even raise the dead, and so in a
manner of speaking he did receive Isaac
back from death.

20By faith Isaac blessed Jacob and Esau
in regard to their future.

21By faith Jacob, when he was dying,
blessed each of Joseph's sons, and worshiped as he leaned on the top of his staff.
22By faith Joseph, when his end was
near, spoke about the exodus of the Israelites from Egypt and gave instructions
concerning the burial of his bones.

23By faith Moses' parents hid him for
three months after he was born, because
they saw he was no ordinary child, and
they were not afraid of the king's edict.

24By faith Moses, when he had grown up,
refused to be known as the son of Pharaoh's daughter. 25He chose to be mistreated
along with the people of God rather than
to enjoy the fleeting pleasures of sin. 26He
regarded disgrace for the sake of Christ
as of greater value than the treasures of
Egypt, because he was looking ahead to his
reward. 27By faith he left Egypt, not fearing
the king's anger; he persevered because he
saw him who is invisible. 28By faith he kept
the Passover and the application of blood,
so that the destroyer of the firstborn would
not touch the firstborn of Israel.

29By faith the people passed through the
Red Sea as on dry land; but when the Egyptians tried to do so, they were drowned.

30By faith the walls of Jericho fell, after
the army had marched around them for
seven days.

31By faith the prostitute Rahab, because
she welcomed the spies, was not killed
with those who were disobedient.[c]

32And what more shall I say? I do not
have time to tell about Gideon, Barak,
Samson and Jephthah, about David and
Samuel and the prophets, 33who through
faith conquered kingdoms, administered
justice, and gained what was promised;
who shut the mouths of lions, 34quenched
the fury of the flames, and escaped the
edge of the sword; whose weakness was
turned to strength; and who became powerful in battle and routed foreign armies.
35Women received back their dead, raised to
life again. There were others who were tortured, refusing to be released so that they
might gain an even better resurrection.
36Some faced jeers and flogging, and even
chains and imprisonment. 37They were put
to death by stoning;[d] they were sawed in
two; they were killed by the sword. They
went about in sheepskins and goatskins,
destitute, persecuted and mistreated —
38the world was not worthy of them. They
wandered in deserts and mountains, living
in caves and in holes in the ground.

39These were all commended for their
faith, yet none of them received what had
been promised, 40since God had planned
something better for us so that only together with us would they be made perfect.

12 Therefore, since we are surrounded
by such a great cloud of witnesses,
let us throw off everything that hinders
and the sin that so easily entangles. And
let us run with perseverance the race
marked out for us, 2fixing our eyes on
Jesus, the pioneer and perfecter of faith.
For the joy set before him he endured the
cross, scorning its shame, and sat down at
the right hand of the throne of God. 3Con-
sider him who endured such opposition
from sinners, so that you will not grow
weary and lose heart.

[a] *11* Or *By faith Abraham, even though he was too old to have children — and Sarah herself was not able to conceive — was enabled to become a father because he* [b] *18* Gen. 21:12 [c] *31* Or *unbelieving* [d] *37* Some early manuscripts *stoning; they were put to the test;*

God Disciplines His Children

4 In your struggle against sin, you have not yet resisted to the point of shedding your blood. 5 And have you completely forgotten this word of encouragement that addresses you as a father addresses his son? It says,

"My son, do not make light of the
 Lord's discipline,
 and do not lose heart when he
 rebukes you,
6 because the Lord disciplines the one
 he loves,
 and he chastens everyone he
 accepts as his son."[a]

7 Endure hardship as discipline; God is treating you as his children. For what children are not disciplined by their father? 8 If you are not disciplined — and everyone undergoes discipline — then you are not legitimate, not true sons and daughters at all. 9 Moreover, we have all had human fathers who disciplined us and we respected them for it. How much more should we submit to the Father of spirits and live! 10 They disciplined us for a little while as they thought best; but God disciplines us for our good, in order that we may share in his holiness. 11 No discipline seems pleasant at the time, but painful. Later on, however, it produces a harvest of righteousness and peace for those who have been trained by it.

12 Therefore, strengthen your feeble arms and weak knees. 13 "Make level paths for your feet,"[b] so that the lame may not be disabled, but rather healed.

Warning and Encouragement

14 Make every effort to live in peace with everyone and to be holy; without holiness no one will see the Lord. 15 See to it that no one falls short of the grace of God and that no bitter root grows up to cause trouble and defile many. 16 See that no one is sexually immoral, or is godless like Esau, who for a single meal sold his inheritance rights as the oldest son. 17 Afterward, as you know, when he wanted to inherit this blessing, he was rejected. Even though he sought the blessing with tears, he could not change what he had done.

The Mountain of Fear and the Mountain of Joy

18 You have not come to a mountain that can be touched and that is burning with fire; to darkness, gloom and storm; 19 to a trumpet blast or to such a voice speaking words that those who heard it begged that no further word be spoken to them, 20 because they could not bear what was commanded: "If even an animal touches the mountain, it must be stoned to death."[c] 21 The sight was so terrifying that Moses said, "I am trembling with fear."[d]

22 But you have come to Mount Zion, to the city of the living God, the heavenly Jerusalem. You have come to thousands upon thousands of angels in joyful assembly, 23 to the church of the firstborn, whose names are written in heaven. You have come to God, the Judge of all, to the spirits of the righteous made perfect, 24 to Jesus the mediator of a new covenant, and to the sprinkled blood that speaks a better word than the blood of Abel.

25 See to it that you do not refuse him who speaks. If they did not escape when they refused him who warned them on earth, how much less will we, if we turn away from him who warns us from heaven? 26 At that time his voice shook the earth, but now he has promised, "Once more I will shake not only the earth but also the heavens."[e] 27 The words "once more" indicate the removing of what can be shaken — that is, created things — so that what cannot be shaken may remain.

28 Therefore, since we are receiving a kingdom that cannot be shaken, let us be thankful, and so worship God acceptably with reverence and awe, 29 for our "God is a consuming fire."[f]

Concluding Exhortations

13 Keep on loving one another as brothers and sisters. 2 Do not forget to show hospitality to strangers, for by so doing some people have shown hospitality to angels without knowing it. 3 Continue to remember those in prison as if you were together with them in prison, and those who are mistreated as if you yourselves were suffering.

4 Marriage should be honored by all, and the marriage bed kept pure, for God will judge the adulterer and all the sexually immoral. 5 Keep your lives free from the love of money and be content with what you have, because God has said,

"Never will I leave you;
 never will I forsake you."[g]

6 So we say with confidence,

"The Lord is my helper; I will not be
 afraid.
 What can mere mortals do to me?"[h]

[a] *5,6* Prov. 3:11,12 (see Septuagint) [b] *13* Prov. 4:26 [c] *20* Exodus 19:12,13 [d] *21* See Deut. 9:19.
[e] *26* Haggai 2:6 [f] *29* Deut. 4:24 [g] *5* Deut. 31:6 [h] *6* Psalm 118:6,7

7Remember your leaders, who spoke the
word of God to you. Consider the outcome
of their way of life and imitate their faith.
8Jesus Christ is the same yesterday and
today and forever.
9Do not be carried away by all kinds
of strange teachings. It is good for our
hearts to be strengthened by grace, not
by eating ceremonial foods, which is of
no benefit to those who do so. 10We have
an altar from which those who minister
at the tabernacle have no right to eat.
11The high priest carries the blood of
animals into the Most Holy Place as a sin
offering, but the bodies are burned outside the camp. 12And so Jesus also suffered
outside the city gate to make the people
holy through his own blood. 13Let us, then,
go to him outside the camp, bearing the
disgrace he bore. 14For here we do not have
an enduring city, but we are looking for
the city that is to come.
15Through Jesus, therefore, let us continually offer to God a sacrifice of praise —
the fruit of lips that openly profess his
name. 16And do not forget to do good and
to share with others, for with such sacrifices God is pleased.
17Have confidence in your leaders and
submit to their authority, because they
keep watch over you as those who must
give an account. Do this so that their work
will be a joy, not a burden, for that would
be of no benefit to you.
18Pray for us. We are sure that we have
a clear conscience and desire to live honorably in every way. 19I particularly urge
you to pray so that I may be restored to
you soon.

Benediction and Final Greetings

20Now may the God of peace, who
through the blood of the eternal covenant
brought back from the dead our Lord
Jesus, that great Shepherd of the sheep,
21equip you with everything good for doing his will, and may he work in us what
is pleasing to him, through Jesus Christ,
to whom be glory for ever and ever. Amen.

22Brothers and sisters, I urge you to bear
with my word of exhortation, for in fact I
have written to you quite briefly.
23I want you to know that our brother
Timothy has been released. If he arrives
soon, I will come with him to see you.
24Greet all your leaders and all the Lord's
people. Those from Italy send you their
greetings.
25Grace be with you all.

JAMES

1 James, a servant of God and of the Lord
Jesus Christ,

To the twelve tribes scattered among
the nations:

Greetings.

Trials and Temptations

2Consider it pure joy, my brothers and
sisters,[a] whenever you face trials of many
kinds, 3because you know that the testing
of your faith produces perseverance. 4Let
perseverance finish its work so that you
may be mature and complete, not lacking
anything. 5If any of you lacks wisdom, you
should ask God, who gives generously to
all without finding fault, and it will be giv-
en to you. 6But when you ask, you must believe and not doubt, because the one who
doubts is like a wave of the sea, blown and
tossed by the wind. 7That person should
not expect to receive anything from the
Lord. 8Such a person is double-minded
and unstable in all they do.
9Believers in humble circumstances
ought to take pride in their high position.
10But the rich should take pride in their
humiliation — since they will pass away
like a wild flower. 11For the sun rises with
scorching heat and withers the plant; its
blossom falls and its beauty is destroyed.
In the same way, the rich will fade away
even while they go about their business.
12Blessed is the one who perseveres under
trial because, having stood the test, that
person will receive the crown of life that the
Lord has promised to those who love him.
13When tempted, no one should say,
"God is tempting me." For God cannot be
tempted by evil, nor does he tempt anyone; 14but each person is tempted when
they are dragged away by their own evil
desire and enticed. 15Then, after desire has
conceived, it gives birth to sin; and sin,
when it is full-grown, gives birth to death.
16Don't be deceived, my dear brothers
and sisters. 17Every good and perfect gift
is from above, coming down from the Father of the heavenly lights, who does not
change like shifting shadows. 18He chose
to give us birth through the word of truth,
that we might be a kind of firstfruits of
all he created.

Listening and Doing

19My dear brothers and sisters, take note
of this: Everyone should be quick to listen,
slow to speak and slow to become angry,
20because human anger does not produce
the righteousness that God desires. 21There-
fore, get rid of all moral filth and the evil
that is so prevalent and humbly accept the
word planted in you, which can save you.
22Do not merely listen to the word, and so
deceive yourselves. Do what it says. 23Any-
one who listens to the word but does not
do what it says is like someone who looks
at his face in a mirror 24and, after looking
at himself, goes away and immediately
forgets what he looks like. 25But whoever
looks intently into the perfect law that
gives freedom, and continues in it — not
forgetting what they have heard, but doing
it — they will be blessed in what they do.
26Those who consider themselves religious and yet do not keep a tight rein on
their tongues deceive themselves, and
their religion is worthless. 27Religion that
God our Father accepts as pure and faultless is this: to look after orphans and widows in their distress and to keep oneself
from being polluted by the world.

Favoritism Forbidden

2 My brothers and sisters, believers in
our glorious Lord Jesus Christ must not
show favoritism. 2Suppose a man comes
into your meeting wearing a gold ring and
fine clothes, and a poor man in filthy old
clothes also comes in. 3If you show special
attention to the man wearing fine clothes
and say, "Here's a good seat for you," but
say to the poor man, "You stand there"
or "Sit on the floor by my feet," 4have you
not discriminated among yourselves and
become judges with evil thoughts?
5Listen, my dear brothers and sisters:
Has not God chosen those who are poor
in the eyes of the world to be rich in faith
and to inherit the kingdom he promised
those who love him? 6But you have dishonored the poor. Is it not the rich who
are exploiting you? Are they not the ones
who are dragging you into court? 7Are they
not the ones who are blaspheming the
noble name of him to whom you belong?

[a] *2* The Greek word for *brothers and sisters* (*adelphoi*) refers here to believers, both men and women, as part of God's family; also in verses 16 and 19; and in 2:1, 5, 14; 3:10, 12; 4:11; 5:7, 9, 10, 12, 19.

8If you really keep the royal law found in Scripture, "Love your neighbor as yourself,"[a] you are doing right. 9But if you show favoritism, you sin and are convicted by the law as lawbreakers. 10For whoever keeps the whole law and yet stumbles at just one point is guilty of breaking all of it. 11For he who said, "You shall not commit adultery,"[b] also said, "You shall not murder."[c] If you do not commit adultery but do commit murder, you have become a lawbreaker.

12Speak and act as those who are going to be judged by the law that gives freedom, 13because judgment without mercy will be shown to anyone who has not been merciful. Mercy triumphs over judgment.

Faith and Deeds

14What good is it, my brothers and sisters, if someone claims to have faith but has no deeds? Can such faith save them? 15Suppose a brother or a sister is without clothes and daily food. 16If one of you says to them, "Go in peace; keep warm and well fed," but does nothing about their physical needs, what good is it? 17In the same way, faith by itself, if it is not accompanied by action, is dead.

18But someone will say, "You have faith; I have deeds."

Show me your faith without deeds, and I will show you my faith by my deeds. 19You believe that there is one God. Good! Even the demons believe that — and shudder.

20You foolish person, do you want evidence that faith without deeds is useless[d]? 21Was not our father Abraham considered righteous for what he did when he offered his son Isaac on the altar? 22You see that his faith and his actions were working together, and his faith was made complete by what he did. 23And the scripture was fulfilled that says, "Abraham believed God, and it was credited to him as righteousness,"[e] and he was called God's friend. 24You see that a person is considered righteous by what they do and not by faith alone.

25In the same way, was not even Rahab the prostitute considered righteous for what she did when she gave lodging to the spies and sent them off in a different direction? 26As the body without the spirit is dead, so faith without deeds is dead.

Taming the Tongue

3 Not many of you should become teachers, my fellow believers, because you know that we who teach will be judged more strictly. 2We all stumble in many ways. Anyone who is never at fault in what they say is perfect, able to keep their whole body in check.

3When we put bits into the mouths of horses to make them obey us, we can turn the whole animal. 4Or take ships as an example. Although they are so large and are driven by strong winds, they are steered by a very small rudder wherever the pilot wants to go. 5Likewise, the tongue is a small part of the body, but it makes great boasts. Consider what a great forest is set on fire by a small spark. 6The tongue also is a fire, a world of evil among the parts of the body. It corrupts the whole body, sets the whole course of one's life on fire, and is itself set on fire by hell.

7All kinds of animals, birds, reptiles and sea creatures are being tamed and have been tamed by mankind, 8but no human being can tame the tongue. It is a restless evil, full of deadly poison.

9With the tongue we praise our Lord and Father, and with it we curse human beings, who have been made in God's likeness. 10Out of the same mouth come praise and cursing. My brothers and sisters, this should not be. 11Can both fresh water and salt water flow from the same spring? 12My brothers and sisters, can a fig tree bear olives, or a grapevine bear figs? Neither can a salt spring produce fresh water.

Two Kinds of Wisdom

13Who is wise and understanding among you? Let them show it by their good life, by deeds done in the humility that comes from wisdom. 14But if you harbor bitter envy and selfish ambition in your hearts, do not boast about it or deny the truth. 15Such "wisdom" does not come down from heaven but is earthly, unspiritual, demonic. 16For where you have envy and selfish ambition, there you find disorder and every evil practice.

17But the wisdom that comes from heaven is first of all pure; then peace-loving, considerate, submissive, full of mercy and good fruit, impartial and sincere. 18Peacemakers who sow in peace reap a harvest of righteousness.

Submit Yourselves to God

4 What causes fights and quarrels among you? Don't they come from your desires that battle within you? 2You desire but do not have, so you kill. You covet but you cannot get what you want, so you quarrel and fight. You do not have because you do not ask God. 3When you ask, you do not receive, because you ask

[a] *8* Lev. 19:18 [b] *11* Exodus 20:14; Deut. 5:18 [c] *11* Exodus 20:13; Deut. 5:17 [d] *20* Some early manuscripts *dead* [e] *23* Gen. 15:6

with wrong motives, that you may spend what you get on your pleasures.

4 You adulterous people,[a] don't you know that friendship with the world means enmity against God? Therefore, anyone who chooses to be a friend of the world becomes an enemy of God. 5 Or do you think Scripture says without reason that he jealously longs for the spirit he has caused to dwell in us[b]? 6 But he gives us more grace. That is why Scripture says:

"God opposes the proud
but shows favor to the humble."[c]

7 Submit yourselves, then, to God. Resist the devil, and he will flee from you. 8 Come near to God and he will come near to you. Wash your hands, you sinners, and purify your hearts, you double-minded. 9 Grieve, mourn and wail. Change your laughter to mourning and your joy to gloom. 10 Humble yourselves before the Lord, and he will lift you up.

11 Brothers and sisters, do not slander one another. Anyone who speaks against a brother or sister[d] or judges them speaks against the law and judges it. When you judge the law, you are not keeping it, but sitting in judgment on it. 12 There is only one Lawgiver and Judge, the one who is able to save and destroy. But you — who are you to judge your neighbor?

Boasting About Tomorrow

13 Now listen, you who say, "Today or tomorrow we will go to this or that city, spend a year there, carry on business and make money." 14 Why, you do not even know what will happen tomorrow. What is your life? You are a mist that appears for a little while and then vanishes. 15 Instead, you ought to say, "If it is the Lord's will, we will live and do this or that." 16 As it is, you boast in your arrogant schemes. All such boasting is evil. 17 If anyone, then, knows the good they ought to do and doesn't do it, it is sin for them.

Warning to Rich Oppressors

5 Now listen, you rich people, weep and wail because of the misery that is coming on you. 2 Your wealth has rotted, and moths have eaten your clothes. 3 Your gold and silver are corroded. Their corrosion will testify against you and eat your flesh like fire. You have hoarded wealth in the last days. 4 Look! The wages you failed to pay the workers who mowed your fields are crying out against you. The cries of the harvesters have reached the ears of the Lord Almighty. 5 You have lived on earth in luxury and self-indulgence. You have fattened yourselves in the day of slaughter.[e] 6 You have condemned and murdered the innocent one, who was not opposing you.

Patience in Suffering

7 Be patient, then, brothers and sisters, until the Lord's coming. See how the farmer waits for the land to yield its valuable crop, patiently waiting for the autumn and spring rains. 8 You too, be patient and stand firm, because the Lord's coming is near. 9 Don't grumble against one another, brothers and sisters, or you will be judged. The Judge is standing at the door!

10 Brothers and sisters, as an example of patience in the face of suffering, take the prophets who spoke in the name of the Lord. 11 As you know, we count as blessed those who have persevered. You have heard of Job's perseverance and have seen what the Lord finally brought about. The Lord is full of compassion and mercy.

12 Above all, my brothers and sisters, do not swear — not by heaven or by earth or by anything else. All you need to say is a simple "Yes" or "No." Otherwise you will be condemned.

The Prayer of Faith

13 Is anyone among you in trouble? Let them pray. Is anyone happy? Let them sing songs of praise. 14 Is anyone among you sick? Let them call the elders of the church to pray over them and anoint them with oil in the name of the Lord. 15 And the prayer offered in faith will make the sick person well; the Lord will raise them up. If they have sinned, they will be forgiven. 16 Therefore confess your sins to each other and pray for each other so that you may be healed. The prayer of a righteous person is powerful and effective.

17 Elijah was a human being, even as we are. He prayed earnestly that it would not rain, and it did not rain on the land for three and a half years. 18 Again he prayed, and the heavens gave rain, and the earth produced its crops.

19 My brothers and sisters, if one of you should wander from the truth and someone should bring that person back, 20 remember this: Whoever turns a sinner from the error of their way will save them from death and cover over a multitude of sins.

[a] 4 An allusion to covenant unfaithfulness; see Hosea 3:1. [b] 5 Or *that the spirit he caused to dwell in us envies intensely;* or *that the Spirit he caused to dwell in us longs jealously* [c] 6 Prov. 3:34 [d] 11 The Greek word for *brother or sister* (*adelphos*) refers here to a believer, whether man or woman, as part of God's family. [e] 5 Or *yourselves as in a day of feasting*

1 PETER

1 Peter, an apostle of Jesus Christ,

To God's elect, exiles scattered throughout the provinces of Pontus, Galatia, Cappadocia, Asia and Bithynia, 2who have been chosen according to the foreknowledge of God the Father, through the sanctifying work of the Spirit, to be obedient to Jesus Christ and sprinkled with his blood:

Grace and peace be yours in abundance.

Praise to God for a Living Hope

3Praise be to the God and Father of our Lord Jesus Christ! In his great mercy he has given us new birth into a living hope through the resurrection of Jesus Christ from the dead, 4and into an inheritance that can never perish, spoil or fade. This inheritance is kept in heaven for you, 5who through faith are shielded by God's power until the coming of the salvation that is ready to be revealed in the last time. 6In all this you greatly rejoice, though now for a little while you may have had to suffer grief in all kinds of trials. 7These have come so that the proven genuineness of your faith — of greater worth than gold, which perishes even though refined by fire — may result in praise, glory and honor when Jesus Christ is revealed. 8Though you have not seen him, you love him; and even though you do not see him now, you believe in him and are filled with an inexpressible and glorious joy, 9for you are receiving the end result of your faith, the salvation of your souls.

10Concerning this salvation, the prophets, who spoke of the grace that was to come to you, searched intently and with the greatest care, 11trying to find out the time and circumstances to which the Spirit of Christ in them was pointing when he predicted the sufferings of the Messiah and the glories that would follow. 12It was revealed to them that they were not serving themselves but you, when they spoke of the things that have now been told you by those who have preached the gospel to you by the Holy Spirit sent from heaven. Even angels long to look into these things.

Be Holy

13Therefore, with minds that are alert and fully sober, set your hope on the grace to be brought to you when Jesus Christ is revealed at his coming. 14As obedient children, do not conform to the evil desires you had when you lived in ignorance. 15But just as he who called you is holy, so be holy in all you do; 16for it is written: "Be holy, because I am holy."[a]

17Since you call on a Father who judges each person's work impartially, live out your time as foreigners here in reverent fear. 18For you know that it was not with perishable things such as silver or gold that you were redeemed from the empty way of life handed down to you from your ancestors, 19but with the precious blood of Christ, a lamb without blemish or defect. 20He was chosen before the creation of the world, but was revealed in these last times for your sake. 21Through him you believe in God, who raised him from the dead and glorified him, and so your faith and hope are in God.

22Now that you have purified yourselves by obeying the truth so that you have sincere love for each other, love one another deeply, from the heart.[b] 23For you have been born again, not of perishable seed, but of imperishable, through the living and enduring word of God. 24For,

"All people are like grass,
and all their glory is like the
flowers of the field;
the grass withers and the flowers fall,
25 but the word of the Lord endures
forever."[c]

And this is the word that was preached to you.

2 Therefore, rid yourselves of all malice and all deceit, hypocrisy, envy, and slander of every kind. 2Like newborn babies, crave pure spiritual milk, so that by it you may grow up in your salvation, 3now that you have tasted that the Lord is good.

The Living Stone and a Chosen People

4As you come to him, the living Stone — rejected by humans but chosen by God and precious to him — 5you also, like living

[a] 16 Lev. 11:44,45; 19:2 (see Septuagint) [b] 22 Some early manuscripts *from a pure heart* [c] 25 Isaiah 40:6-8

stones, are being built into a spiritual house[a] to be a holy priesthood, offering spiritual sacrifices acceptable to God through Jesus Christ. 6 For in Scripture it says:

> "See, I lay a stone in Zion,
> a chosen and precious cornerstone,
> and the one who trusts in him
> will never be put to shame."[b]

7 Now to you who believe, this stone is precious. But to those who do not believe,

> "The stone the builders rejected
> has become the cornerstone,"[c]

8 and,

> "A stone that causes people to stumble
> and a rock that makes them fall."[d]

They stumble because they disobey the message — which is also what they were destined for.

9 But you are a chosen people, a royal priesthood, a holy nation, God's special possession, that you may declare the praises of him who called you out of darkness into his wonderful light. 10 Once you were not a people, but now you are the people of God; once you had not received mercy, but now you have received mercy.

Living Godly Lives in a Pagan Society

11 Dear friends, I urge you, as foreigners and exiles, to abstain from sinful desires, which wage war against your soul. 12 Live such good lives among the pagans that, though they accuse you of doing wrong, they may see your good deeds and glorify God on the day he visits us.

13 Submit yourselves for the Lord's sake to every human authority: whether to the emperor, as the supreme authority, 14 or to governors, who are sent by him to punish those who do wrong and to commend those who do right. 15 For it is God's will that by doing good you should silence the ignorant talk of foolish people. 16 Live as free people, but do not use your freedom as a cover-up for evil; live as God's slaves. 17 Show proper respect to everyone, love the family of believers, fear God, honor the emperor.

18 Slaves, in reverent fear of God submit yourselves to your masters, not only to those who are good and considerate, but also to those who are harsh. 19 For it is commendable if someone bears up under the pain of unjust suffering because they are conscious of God. 20 But how is it to your credit if you receive a beating for doing wrong and endure it? But if you suffer for doing good and you endure it, this is commendable before God. 21 To this you were called, because Christ suffered for you, leaving you an example, that you should follow in his steps.

> 22 "He committed no sin,
> and no deceit was found in his mouth."[e]

23 When they hurled their insults at him, he did not retaliate; when he suffered, he made no threats. Instead, he entrusted himself to him who judges justly. 24 "He himself bore our sins" in his body on the cross, so that we might die to sins and live for righteousness; "by his wounds you have been healed." 25 For "you were like sheep going astray,"[f] but now you have returned to the Shepherd and Overseer of your souls.

3 Wives, in the same way submit yourselves to your own husbands so that, if any of them do not believe the word, they may be won over without words by the behavior of their wives, 2 when they see the purity and reverence of your lives. 3 Your beauty should not come from outward adornment, such as elaborate hairstyles and the wearing of gold jewelry or fine clothes. 4 Rather, it should be that of your inner self, the unfading beauty of a gentle and quiet spirit, which is of great worth in God's sight. 5 For this is the way the holy women of the past who put their hope in God used to adorn themselves. They submitted themselves to their own husbands, 6 like Sarah, who obeyed Abraham and called him her lord. You are her daughters if you do what is right and do not give way to fear.

7 Husbands, in the same way be considerate as you live with your wives, and treat them with respect as the weaker partner and as heirs with you of the gracious gift of life, so that nothing will hinder your prayers.

Suffering for Doing Good

8 Finally, all of you, be like-minded, be sympathetic, love one another, be compassionate and humble. 9 Do not repay evil with evil or insult with insult. On the contrary, repay evil with blessing, because

[a] 5 Or *into a temple of the Spirit* [b] *6* Isaiah 28:16 [c] *7* Psalm 118:22 [d] *8* Isaiah 8:14
[e] *22* Isaiah 53:9 [f] *24,25* Isaiah 53:4,5,6 (see Septuagint)

to this you were called so that you may
inherit a blessing. 10For,

> "Whoever would love life
> and see good days
> must keep their tongue from evil
> and their lips from deceitful
> speech.
> 11 They must turn from evil and do
> good;
> they must seek peace and pursue it.
> 12 For the eyes of the Lord are on the
> righteous
> and his ears are attentive to their
> prayer,
> but the face of the Lord is against
> those who do evil."[a]

13Who is going to harm you if you are
eager to do good? 14But even if you should
suffer for what is right, you are blessed.
"Do not fear their threats[b]; do not be
frightened."[c] 15But in your hearts revere
Christ as Lord. Always be prepared to
give an answer to everyone who asks you
to give the reason for the hope that you
have. But do this with gentleness and
respect, 16keeping a clear conscience, so
that those who speak maliciously against
your good behavior in Christ may be
ashamed of their slander. 17For it is better, if it is God's will, to suffer for doing
good than for doing evil. 18For Christ also
suffered once for sins, the righteous for
the unrighteous, to bring you to God. He
was put to death in the body but made
alive in the Spirit. 19After being made
alive,[d] he went and made proclamation to the imprisoned spirits — 20to
those who were disobedient long ago
when God waited patiently in the days
of Noah while the ark was being built.
In it only a few people, eight in all, were
saved through water, 21and this water
symbolizes baptism that now saves you
also — not the removal of dirt from the
body but the pledge of a clear conscience
toward God.[e] It saves you by the resurrection of Jesus Christ, 22who has gone into
heaven and is at God's right hand — with
angels, authorities and powers in submission to him.

Living for God

4 Therefore, since Christ suffered in his
body, arm yourselves also with the
same attitude, because whoever suffers
in the body is done with sin. 2As a result,
they do not live the rest of their earthly
lives for evil human desires, but rather
for the will of God. 3For you have spent
enough time in the past doing what pagans choose to do — living in debauchery,
lust, drunkenness, orgies, carousing and
detestable idolatry. 4They are surprised
that you do not join them in their reckless, wild living, and they heap abuse on
you. 5But they will have to give account to
him who is ready to judge the living and
the dead. 6For this is the reason the gospel was preached even to those who are
now dead, so that they might be judged
according to human standards in regard
to the body, but live according to God in
regard to the spirit.

7The end of all things is near. Therefore be alert and of sober mind so that
you may pray. 8Above all, love each other
deeply, because love covers over a multitude of sins. 9Offer hospitality to one
another without grumbling. 10Each of
you should use whatever gift you have
received to serve others, as faithful stewards of God's grace in its various forms.
11If anyone speaks, they should do so as
one who speaks the very words of God.
If anyone serves, they should do so with
the strength God provides, so that in all
things God may be praised through Jesus
Christ. To him be the glory and the power
for ever and ever. Amen.

Suffering for Being a Christian

12Dear friends, do not be surprised at the
fiery ordeal that has come on you to test
you, as though something strange were
happening to you. 13But rejoice inasmuch
as you participate in the sufferings of
Christ, so that you may be overjoyed when
his glory is revealed. 14If you are insulted
because of the name of Christ, you are
blessed, for the Spirit of glory and of God
rests on you. 15If you suffer, it should not
be as a murderer or thief or any other
kind of criminal, or even as a meddler.
16However, if you suffer as a Christian, do
not be ashamed, but praise God that you
bear that name. 17For it is time for judgment to begin with God's household; and
if it begins with us, what will the outcome
be for those who do not obey the gospel
of God? 18And,

> "If it is hard for the righteous to be
> saved,
> what will become of the ungodly
> and the sinner?"[f]

[a] 12 Psalm 34:12-16 [b] 14 Or *fear what they fear* [c] 14 Isaiah 8:12 [d] 18,19 Or *but made alive in the spirit, 19in which also* [e] 21 Or *but an appeal to God for a clear conscience* [f] 18 Prov. 11:31 (see Septuagint)

19 So then, those who suffer according
to God's will should commit themselves
to their faithful Creator and continue to
do good.

To the Elders and the Flock

5 To the elders among you, I appeal as
a fellow elder and a witness of Christ's
sufferings who also will share in the glory to be revealed: 2 Be shepherds of God's
flock that is under your care, watching
over them — not because you must, but
because you are willing, as God wants you
to be; not pursuing dishonest gain, but
eager to serve; 3 not lording it over those
entrusted to you, but being examples to
the flock. 4 And when the Chief Shepherd
appears, you will receive the crown of
glory that will never fade away.

5 In the same way, you who are younger, submit yourselves to your elders. All
of you, clothe yourselves with humility
toward one another, because,

> "God opposes the proud
> but shows favor to the humble."[a]

6 Humble yourselves, therefore, under
God's mighty hand, that he may lift you
up in due time. 7 Cast all your anxiety on
him because he cares for you.

8 Be alert and of sober mind. Your enemy
the devil prowls around like a roaring lion
looking for someone to devour. 9 Resist
him, standing firm in the faith, because
you know that the family of believers
throughout the world is undergoing the
same kind of sufferings.

10 And the God of all grace, who called
you to his eternal glory in Christ, after you
have suffered a little while, will himself
restore you and make you strong, firm
and steadfast. 11 To him be the power for
ever and ever. Amen.

Final Greetings

12 With the help of Silas,[b] whom I regard
as a faithful brother, I have written to you
briefly, encouraging you and testifying
that this is the true grace of God. Stand
fast in it.

13 She who is in Babylon, chosen together
with you, sends you her greetings, and so
does my son Mark. 14 Greet one another
with a kiss of love.

Peace to all of you who are in Christ.

[a] *5* Prov. 3:34 [b] *12* Greek *Silvanus*, a variant of *Silas*

2 PETER

1 Simon Peter, a servant and apostle of Jesus Christ,

To those who through the righteousness of our God and Savior Jesus Christ have received a faith as precious as ours:

2 Grace and peace be yours in abundance through the knowledge of God and of Jesus our Lord.

Confirming One's Calling and Election

3 His divine power has given us everything we need for a godly life through our knowledge of him who called us by his own glory and goodness. 4 Through these he has given us his very great and precious promises, so that through them you may participate in the divine nature, having escaped the corruption in the world caused by evil desires.

5 For this very reason, make every effort to add to your faith goodness; and to goodness, knowledge; 6 and to knowledge, self-control; and to self-control, perseverance; and to perseverance, godliness; 7 and to godliness, mutual affection; and to mutual affection, love. 8 For if you possess these qualities in increasing measure, they will keep you from being ineffective and unproductive in your knowledge of our Lord Jesus Christ. 9 But whoever does not have them is nearsighted and blind, forgetting that they have been cleansed from their past sins.

10 Therefore, my brothers and sisters,[a] make every effort to confirm your calling and election. For if you do these things, you will never stumble, 11 and you will receive a rich welcome into the eternal kingdom of our Lord and Savior Jesus Christ.

Prophecy of Scripture

12 So I will always remind you of these things, even though you know them and are firmly established in the truth you now have. 13 I think it is right to refresh your memory as long as I live in the tent of this body, 14 because I know that I will soon put it aside, as our Lord Jesus Christ has made clear to me. 15 And I will make every effort to see that after my departure you will always be able to remember these things.

16 For we did not follow cleverly devised stories when we told you about the coming of our Lord Jesus Christ in power, but we were eyewitnesses of his majesty. 17 He received honor and glory from God the Father when the voice came to him from the Majestic Glory, saying, "This is my Son, whom I love; with him I am well pleased."[b] 18 We ourselves heard this voice that came from heaven when we were with him on the sacred mountain.

19 We also have the prophetic message as something completely reliable, and you will do well to pay attention to it, as to a light shining in a dark place, until the day dawns and the morning star rises in your hearts. 20 Above all, you must understand that no prophecy of Scripture came about by the prophet's own interpretation of things. 21 For prophecy never had its origin in the human will, but prophets, though human, spoke from God as they were carried along by the Holy Spirit.

False Teachers and Their Destruction

2 But there were also false prophets among the people, just as there will be false teachers among you. They will secretly introduce destructive heresies, even denying the sovereign Lord who bought them — bringing swift destruction on themselves. 2 Many will follow their depraved conduct and will bring the way of truth into disrepute. 3 In their greed these teachers will exploit you with fabricated stories. Their condemnation has long been hanging over them, and their destruction has not been sleeping.

4 For if God did not spare angels when they sinned, but sent them to hell,[c] putting them in chains of darkness[d] to be held for judgment; 5 if he did not spare the ancient world when he brought the flood on its ungodly people, but protected Noah, a preacher of righteousness, and seven others; 6 if he condemned the cities of Sodom and Gomorrah by burning them to ashes, and made them an example of what is going to happen to the ungodly; 7 and if he rescued Lot, a righteous man,

[a] 10 The Greek word for *brothers and sisters* (*adelphoi*) refers here to believers, both men and women, as part of God's family. [b] 17 Matt. 17:5; Mark 9:7; Luke 9:35 [c] 4 Greek *Tartarus* [d] 4 Some manuscripts *in gloomy dungeons*

who was distressed by the depraved conduct of the lawless 8(for that righteous
man, living among them day after day,
was tormented in his righteous soul by
the lawless deeds he saw and heard) —
9if this is so, then the Lord knows how to
rescue the godly from trials and to hold
the unrighteous for punishment on the
day of judgment. 10This is especially true
of those who follow the corrupt desire of
the flesh[a] and despise authority.

Bold and arrogant, they are not afraid
to heap abuse on celestial beings; 11yet
even angels, although they are stronger
and more powerful, do not heap abuse
on such beings when bringing judgment
on them from[b] the Lord. 12But these people blaspheme in matters they do not
understand. They are like unreasoning
animals, creatures of instinct, born only
to be caught and destroyed, and like animals they too will perish.

13They will be paid back with harm for
the harm they have done. Their idea of
pleasure is to carouse in broad daylight.
They are blots and blemishes, reveling in
their pleasures while they feast with you.[c]
14With eyes full of adultery, they never
stop sinning; they seduce the unstable;
they are experts in greed — an accursed
brood! 15They have left the straight way
and wandered off to follow the way of Balaam son of Bezer,[d] who loved the wages
of wickedness. 16But he was rebuked for
his wrongdoing by a donkey — an animal without speech — who spoke with a
human voice and restrained the prophet's
madness.

17These people are springs without water and mists driven by a storm. Blackest
darkness is reserved for them. 18For they
mouth empty, boastful words and, by
appealing to the lustful desires of the
flesh, they entice people who are just
escaping from those who live in error.
19They promise them freedom, while they
themselves are slaves of depravity —
for "people are slaves to whatever has
mastered them." 20If they have escaped
the corruption of the world by knowing
our Lord and Savior Jesus Christ and are
again entangled in it and are overcome,
they are worse off at the end than they
were at the beginning. 21It would have
been better for them not to have known
the way of righteousness, than to have
known it and then to turn their backs on
the sacred command that was passed on
to them. 22Of them the proverbs are true:
"A dog returns to its vomit,"[e] and, "A sow
that is washed returns to her wallowing
in the mud."

The Day of the Lord

3 Dear friends, this is now my second
letter to you. I have written both of
them as reminders to stimulate you to
wholesome thinking. 2I want you to recall
the words spoken in the past by the holy
prophets and the command given by our
Lord and Savior through your apostles.

3Above all, you must understand that
in the last days scoffers will come, scoff-
ing and following their own evil desires.
4They will say, "Where is this 'coming'
he promised? Ever since our ancestors
died, everything goes on as it has since
the beginning of creation." 5But they deliberately forget that long ago by God's
word the heavens came into being and
the earth was formed out of water and
by water. 6By these waters also the world
of that time was deluged and destroyed.
7By the same word the present heavens
and earth are reserved for fire, being kept
for the day of judgment and destruction
of the ungodly.

8But do not forget this one thing, dear
friends: With the Lord a day is like a thousand years, and a thousand years are like
a day. 9The Lord is not slow in keeping
his promise, as some understand slow-
ness. Instead he is patient with you, not
wanting anyone to perish, but everyone
to come to repentance.

10But the day of the Lord will come like
a thief. The heavens will disappear with
a roar; the elements will be destroyed by
fire, and the earth and everything done
in it will be laid bare.[f]

11Since everything will be destroyed in
this way, what kind of people ought you
to be? You ought to live holy and godly
lives 12as you look forward to the day
of God and speed its coming.[g] That day
will bring about the destruction of the
heavens by fire, and the elements will
melt in the heat. 13But in keeping with
his promise we are looking forward to
a new heaven and a new earth, where
righteousness dwells.

14So then, dear friends, since you are

[a] *10* In contexts like this, the Greek word for *flesh* (*sarx*) refers to the sinful state of human beings, often presented as a power in opposition to the Spirit; also in verse 18. [b] *11* Many manuscripts *beings in the presence of* [c] *13* Some manuscripts *in their love feasts* [d] *15* Greek *Bosor* [e] *22* Prov. 26:11 [f] *10* Some manuscripts *be burned up* [g] *12* Or *as you wait eagerly for the day of God to come*

looking forward to this, make every effort
to be found spotless, blameless and at
peace with him. [15]Bear in mind that our
Lord's patience means salvation, just as
our dear brother Paul also wrote you with
the wisdom that God gave him. [16]He writes
the same way in all his letters, speaking in
them of these matters. His letters contain
some things that are hard to understand,
which ignorant and unstable people distort, as they do the other Scriptures, to
their own destruction.

[17]Therefore, dear friends, since you have
been forewarned, be on your guard so
that you may not be carried away by the
error of the lawless and fall from your
secure position. [18]But grow in the grace
and knowledge of our Lord and Savior
Jesus Christ. To him be glory both now
and forever! Amen.

1 JOHN

The Incarnation of the Word of Life

1 That which was from the beginning,
which we have heard, which we have
seen with our eyes, which we have looked
at and our hands have touched — this
we proclaim concerning the Word of life.
2 The life appeared; we have seen it and
testify to it, and we proclaim to you the
eternal life, which was with the Father
and has appeared to us. 3 We proclaim
to you what we have seen and heard, so
that you also may have fellowship with
us. And our fellowship is with the Father
and with his Son, Jesus Christ. 4 We write
this to make our[a] joy complete.

Light and Darkness, Sin and Forgiveness

5 This is the message we have heard
from him and declare to you: God is light;
in him there is no darkness at all. 6 If we
claim to have fellowship with him and yet
walk in the darkness, we lie and do not live
out the truth. 7 But if we walk in the light,
as he is in the light, we have fellowship
with one another, and the blood of Jesus,
his Son, purifies us from all[b] sin.

8 If we claim to be without sin, we deceive ourselves and the truth is not in us.
9 If we confess our sins, he is faithful and
just and will forgive us our sins and purify
us from all unrighteousness. 10 If we claim
we have not sinned, we make him out to
be a liar and his word is not in us.

2 My dear children, I write this to you so
that you will not sin. But if anybody
does sin, we have an advocate with the
Father — Jesus Christ, the Righteous One.
2 He is the atoning sacrifice for our sins,
and not only for ours but also for the sins
of the whole world.

Love and Hatred for Fellow Believers

3 We know that we have come to know
him if we keep his commands. 4 Whoever
says, "I know him," but does not do what
he commands is a liar, and the truth is
not in that person. 5 But if anyone obeys
his word, love for God[c] is truly made complete in them. This is how we know we are
in him: 6 Whoever claims to live in him
must live as Jesus did.

7 Dear friends, I am not writing you a
new command but an old one, which you
have had since the beginning. This old
command is the message you have heard.
8 Yet I am writing you a new command; its
truth is seen in him and in you, because
the darkness is passing and the true light
is already shining.

9 Anyone who claims to be in the light
but hates a brother or sister[d] is still in the
darkness. 10 Anyone who loves their brother and sister[e] lives in the light, and there
is nothing in them to make them stumble.
11 But anyone who hates a brother or sister
is in the darkness and walks around in
the darkness. They do not know where
they are going, because the darkness has
blinded them.

Reasons for Writing

12 I am writing to you, dear children,
because your sins have been
forgiven on account of his
name.
13 I am writing to you, fathers,
because you know him who is from
the beginning.
I am writing to you, young men,
because you have overcome the
evil one.

14 I write to you, dear children,
because you know the Father.
I write to you, fathers,
because you know him who is from
the beginning.
I write to you, young men,
because you are strong,
and the word of God lives in you,
and you have overcome the evil one.

On Not Loving the World

15 Do not love the world or anything in
the world. If anyone loves the world, love
for the Father[f] is not in them. 16 For everything in the world — the lust of the
flesh, the lust of the eyes, and the pride

[a] 4 Some manuscripts *your* [b] 7 Or *every* [c] 5 Or *word, God's love* [d] 9 The Greek word for *brother or sister* (*adelphos*) refers here to a believer, whether man or woman, as part of God's family; also in verse 11; and in 3:15, 17; 4:20; 5:16. [e] 10 The Greek word for *brother and sister* (*adelphos*) refers here to a believer, whether man or woman, as part of God's family; also in 3:10; 4:20, 21. [f] 15 Or *world, the Father's love*

of life — comes not from the Father but from the world. 17 The world and its desires pass away, but whoever does the will of God lives forever.

Warnings Against Denying the Son

18 Dear children, this is the last hour; and as you have heard that the antichrist is coming, even now many antichrists have come. This is how we know it is the last hour. 19 They went out from us, but they did not really belong to us. For if they had belonged to us, they would have remained with us; but their going showed that none of them belonged to us.

20 But you have an anointing from the Holy One, and all of you know the truth.[a] 21 I do not write to you because you do not know the truth, but because you do know it and because no lie comes from the truth. 22 Who is the liar? It is whoever denies that Jesus is the Christ. Such a person is the antichrist — denying the Father and the Son. 23 No one who denies the Son has the Father; whoever acknowledges the Son has the Father also.

24 As for you, see that what you have heard from the beginning remains in you. If it does, you also will remain in the Son and in the Father. 25 And this is what he promised us — eternal life.

26 I am writing these things to you about those who are trying to lead you astray. 27 As for you, the anointing you received from him remains in you, and you do not need anyone to teach you. But as his anointing teaches you about all things and as that anointing is real, not counterfeit — just as it has taught you, remain in him.

God's Children and Sin

28 And now, dear children, continue in him, so that when he appears we may be confident and unashamed before him at his coming.

29 If you know that he is righteous, you know that everyone who does what is right has been born of him.

3 See what great love the Father has lavished on us, that we should be called children of God! And that is what we are! The reason the world does not know us is that it did not know him. 2 Dear friends, now we are children of God, and what we will be has not yet been made known. But we know that when Christ appears,[b] we shall be like him, for we shall see him as he is. 3 All who have this hope in him purify themselves, just as he is pure.

4 Everyone who sins breaks the law; in fact, sin is lawlessness. 5 But you know that he appeared so that he might take away our sins. And in him is no sin. 6 No one who lives in him keeps on sinning. No one who continues to sin has either seen him or known him.

7 Dear children, do not let anyone lead you astray. The one who does what is right is righteous, just as he is righteous. 8 The one who does what is sinful is of the devil, because the devil has been sinning from the beginning. The reason the Son of God appeared was to destroy the devil's work. 9 No one who is born of God will continue to sin, because God's seed remains in them; they cannot go on sinning, because they have been born of God. 10 This is how we know who the children of God are and who the children of the devil are: Anyone who does not do what is right is not God's child, nor is anyone who does not love their brother and sister.

More on Love and Hatred

11 For this is the message you heard from the beginning: We should love one another. 12 Do not be like Cain, who belonged to the evil one and murdered his brother. And why did he murder him? Because his own actions were evil and his brother's were righteous. 13 Do not be surprised, my brothers and sisters,[c] if the world hates you. 14 We know that we have passed from death to life, because we love each other. Anyone who does not love remains in death. 15 Anyone who hates a brother or sister is a murderer, and you know that no murderer has eternal life residing in him.

16 This is how we know what love is: Jesus Christ laid down his life for us. And we ought to lay down our lives for our brothers and sisters. 17 If anyone has material possessions and sees a brother or sister in need but has no pity on them, how can the love of God be in that person? 18 Dear children, let us not love with words or speech but with actions and in truth.

19 This is how we know that we belong to the truth and how we set our hearts at rest in his presence: 20 If our hearts condemn us, we know that God is greater than our hearts, and he knows everything. 21 Dear friends, if our hearts do not condemn us, we have confidence before God 22 and receive from him anything we ask, because

[a] 20 Some manuscripts *and you know all things* [b] 2 Or *when it is made known* [c] 13 The Greek word for *brothers and sisters* (*adelphoi*) refers here to believers, both men and women, as part of God's family; also in verse 16.

we keep his commands and do what pleases him. 23And this is his command: to believe in the name of his Son, Jesus Christ, and to love one another as he commanded us. 24The one who keeps God's commands lives in him, and he in them. And this is how we know that he lives in us: We know it by the Spirit he gave us.

On Denying the Incarnation

4 Dear friends, do not believe every spirit, but test the spirits to see whether they are from God, because many false prophets have gone out into the world. 2This is how you can recognize the Spirit of God: Every spirit that acknowledges that Jesus Christ has come in the flesh is from God, 3but every spirit that does not acknowledge Jesus is not from God. This is the spirit of the antichrist, which you have heard is coming and even now is already in the world.

4You, dear children, are from God and have overcome them, because the one who is in you is greater than the one who is in the world. 5They are from the world and therefore speak from the viewpoint of the world, and the world listens to them. 6We are from God, and whoever knows God listens to us; but whoever is not from God does not listen to us. This is how we recognize the Spirit[a] of truth and the spirit of falsehood.

God's Love and Ours

7Dear friends, let us love one another, for love comes from God. Everyone who loves has been born of God and knows God. 8Whoever does not love does not know God, because God is love. 9This is how God showed his love among us: He sent his one and only Son into the world that we might live through him. 10This is love: not that we loved God, but that he loved us and sent his Son as an atoning sacrifice for our sins. 11Dear friends, since God so loved us, we also ought to love one another. 12No one has ever seen God; but if we love one another, God lives in us and his love is made complete in us.

13This is how we know that we live in him and he in us: He has given us of his Spirit. 14And we have seen and testify that the Father has sent his Son to be the Savior of the world. 15If anyone acknowledges that Jesus is the Son of God, God lives in them and they in God. 16And so we know and rely on the love God has for us.

God is love. Whoever lives in love lives in God, and God in them. 17This is how love is made complete among us so that we will have confidence on the day of judgment: In this world we are like Jesus. 18There is no fear in love. But perfect love drives out fear, because fear has to do with punishment. The one who fears is not made perfect in love.

19We love because he first loved us. 20Whoever claims to love God yet hates a brother or sister is a liar. For whoever does not love their brother and sister, whom they have seen, cannot love God, whom they have not seen. 21And he has given us this command: Anyone who loves God must also love their brother and sister.

Faith in the Incarnate Son of God

5 Everyone who believes that Jesus is the Christ is born of God, and everyone who loves the father loves his child as well. 2This is how we know that we love the children of God: by loving God and carrying out his commands. 3In fact, this is love for God: to keep his commands. And his commands are not burdensome, 4for everyone born of God overcomes the world. This is the victory that has overcome the world, even our faith. 5Who is it that overcomes the world? Only the one who believes that Jesus is the Son of God.

6This is the one who came by water and blood—Jesus Christ. He did not come by water only, but by water and blood. And it is the Spirit who testifies, because the Spirit is the truth. 7For there are three that testify: 8the[b] Spirit, the water and the blood; and the three are in agreement. 9We accept human testimony, but God's testimony is greater because it is the testimony of God, which he has given about his Son. 10Whoever believes in the Son of God accepts this testimony. Whoever does not believe God has made him out to be a liar, because they have not believed the testimony God has given about his Son. 11And this is the testimony: God has given us eternal life, and this life is in his Son. 12Whoever has the Son has life; whoever does not have the Son of God does not have life.

Concluding Affirmations

13I write these things to you who believe in the name of the Son of God so that you may know that you have eternal life. 14This is the confidence we have in approaching

[a] 6 Or *spirit* [b] 7,8 Late manuscripts of the Vulgate *testify in heaven: the Father, the Word and the Holy Spirit, and these three are one. 8And there are three that testify on earth: the* (not found in any Greek manuscript before the fourteenth century)

God: that if we ask anything according
to his will, he hears us. 15And if we know
that he hears us — whatever we ask — we
know that we have what we asked of him.
16If you see any brother or sister commit a sin that does not lead to death, you should pray and God will give them life. I refer to those whose sin does not lead to death. There is a sin that leads to death. I am not saying that you should pray about
that. 17All wrongdoing is sin, and there is sin that does not lead to death.
18We know that anyone born of God does not continue to sin; the One who was born of God keeps them safe, and the evil
one cannot harm them. 19We know that we are children of God, and that the whole world is under the control of the evil one.
20We know also that the Son of God has come and has given us understanding, so that we may know him who is true. And we are in him who is true by being in his Son Jesus Christ. He is the true God and eternal life.
21Dear children, keep yourselves from idols.

2 JOHN

1The elder,

To the lady chosen by God and to her
children, whom I love in the truth — and
not I only, but also all who know the
truth — 2because of the truth, which lives
in us and will be with us forever:

3Grace, mercy and peace from God the
Father and from Jesus Christ, the Father's
Son, will be with us in truth and love.

4It has given me great joy to find some
of your children walking in the truth, just
as the Father commanded us. 5And now,
dear lady, I am not writing you a new
command but one we have had from the
beginning. I ask that we love one another.
6And this is love: that we walk in obedience to his commands. As you have heard
from the beginning, his command is that
you walk in love.

7I say this because many deceivers, who
do not acknowledge Jesus Christ as coming in the flesh, have gone out into the
world. Any such person is the deceiver and
the antichrist. 8Watch out that you do not
lose what we[a] have worked for, but that
you may be rewarded fully. 9Anyone who
runs ahead and does not continue in the
teaching of Christ does not have God; whoever continues in the teaching has both
the Father and the Son. 10If anyone comes
to you and does not bring this teaching,
do not take them into your house or welcome them. 11Anyone who welcomes them
shares in their wicked work.
12I have much to write to you, but I do
not want to use paper and ink. Instead,
I hope to visit you and talk with you face
to face, so that our joy may be complete.

13The children of your sister, who is chosen by God, send their greetings.

[a] *8* Some manuscripts *you*

3 JOHN

[1]The elder,

To my dear friend Gaius, whom I love
in the truth.

[2]Dear friend, I pray that you may enjoy
good health and that all may go well with
you, even as your soul is getting along
well. [3]It gave me great joy when some
believers came and testified about your
faithfulness to the truth, telling how you
continue to walk in it. [4]I have no greater joy than to hear that my children are
walking in the truth.

[5]Dear friend, you are faithful in what
you are doing for the brothers and sisters,[a] even though they are strangers to
you. [6]They have told the church about
your love. Please send them on their way
in a manner that honors God. [7]It was for
the sake of the Name that they went out,
receiving no help from the pagans. [8]We
ought therefore to show hospitality to
such people so that we may work together
for the truth.

[9]I wrote to the church, but Diotrephes,
who loves to be first, will not welcome
us. [10]So when I come, I will call attention
to what he is doing, spreading malicious
nonsense about us. Not satisfied with that,
he even refuses to welcome other believers. He also stops those who want to do so
and puts them out of the church.

[11]Dear friend, do not imitate what is evil
but what is good. Anyone who does what
is good is from God. Anyone who does
what is evil has not seen God. [12]Demetri-
us is well spoken of by everyone — and
even by the truth itself. We also speak
well of him, and you know that our testimony is true.

[13]I have much to write you, but I do
not want to do so with pen and ink. [14]I
hope to see you soon, and we will talk
face to face.

[15]Peace to you. The friends here send
their greetings. Greet the friends there
by name.

[a] 5 The Greek word for *brothers and sisters* (*adelphoi*) refers here to believers, both men and women, as part of God's family.

JUDE

1Jude, a servant of Jesus Christ and a brother of James,

To those who have been called, who are loved in God the Father and kept for[a] Jesus Christ:

2Mercy, peace and love be yours in abundance.

The Sin and Doom of Ungodly People

3Dear friends, although I was very eager to write to you about the salvation we share, I felt compelled to write and urge you to contend for the faith that was once for all entrusted to God's holy people. 4For certain individuals whose condemnation was written about[b] long ago have secretly slipped in among you. They are ungodly people, who pervert the grace of our God into a license for immorality and deny Jesus Christ our only Sovereign and Lord.

5Though you already know all this, I want to remind you that the Lord[c] at one time delivered his people out of Egypt, but later destroyed those who did not believe. 6And the angels who did not keep their positions of authority but abandoned their proper dwelling — these he has kept in darkness, bound with everlasting chains for judgment on the great Day. 7In a similar way, Sodom and Gomorrah and the surrounding towns gave themselves up to sexual immorality and perversion. They serve as an example of those who suffer the punishment of eternal fire.

8In the very same way, on the strength of their dreams these ungodly people pollute their own bodies, reject authority and heap abuse on celestial beings. 9But even the archangel Michael, when he was disputing with the devil about the body of Moses, did not himself dare to condemn him for slander but said, "The Lord rebuke you!"[d] 10Yet these people slander whatever they do not understand, and the very things they do understand by instinct — as irrational animals do — will destroy them.

11Woe to them! They have taken the way of Cain; they have rushed for profit into Balaam's error; they have been destroyed in Korah's rebellion.

12These people are blemishes at your love feasts, eating with you without the slightest qualm — shepherds who feed only themselves. They are clouds without rain, blown along by the wind; autumn trees, without fruit and uprooted — twice dead. 13They are wild waves of the sea, foaming up their shame; wandering stars, for whom blackest darkness has been reserved forever.

14Enoch, the seventh from Adam, prophesied about them: "See, the Lord is coming with thousands upon thousands of his holy ones 15to judge everyone, and to convict all of them of all the ungodly acts they have committed in their ungodliness, and of all the defiant words ungodly sinners have spoken against him."[e] 16These people are grumblers and faultfinders; they follow their own evil desires; they boast about themselves and flatter others for their own advantage.

A Call to Persevere

17But, dear friends, remember what the apostles of our Lord Jesus Christ foretold. 18They said to you, "In the last times there will be scoffers who will follow their own ungodly desires." 19These are the people who divide you, who follow mere natural instincts and do not have the Spirit.

20But you, dear friends, by building yourselves up in your most holy faith and praying in the Holy Spirit, 21keep yourselves in God's love as you wait for the mercy of our Lord Jesus Christ to bring you to eternal life.

22Be merciful to those who doubt; 23save others by snatching them from the fire; to others show mercy, mixed with fear — hating even the clothing stained by corrupted flesh.[f]

Doxology

24To him who is able to keep you from stumbling and to present you before his glorious presence without fault and with great joy — 25to the only God our Savior be glory, majesty, power and authority, through Jesus Christ our Lord, before all ages, now and forevermore! Amen.

[a] *1* Or *by*; or *in* [b] *4* Or *individuals who were marked out for condemnation* [c] *5* Some early manuscripts *Jesus* [d] *9* Jude is alluding to the Jewish *Testament of Moses* (approximately the first century A.D.). [e] *14,15* From the Jewish *First Book of Enoch* (approximately the first century B.C.) [f] *22,23* The Greek manuscripts of these verses vary at several points.

REVELATION

Prologue

1 The revelation from Jesus Christ, which God gave him to show his servants what must soon take place. He made it known by sending his angel to his servant John, 2 who testifies to everything he saw — that is, the word of God and the testimony of Jesus Christ. 3 Blessed is the one who reads aloud the words of this prophecy, and blessed are those who hear it and take to heart what is written in it, because the time is near.

Greetings and Doxology

4 John,

To the seven churches in the province of Asia:

Grace and peace to you from him who is, and who was, and who is to come, and from the seven spirits[a] before his throne, 5 and from Jesus Christ, who is the faithful witness, the firstborn from the dead, and the ruler of the kings of the earth.

To him who loves us and has freed us from our sins by his blood, 6 and has made us to be a kingdom and priests to serve his God and Father — to him be glory and power for ever and ever! Amen.

7 "Look, he is coming with the clouds,"[b]
  and "every eye will see him,
 even those who pierced him";
 and all peoples on earth "will
  mourn because of him."[c]
   So shall it be! Amen.

8 "I am the Alpha and the Omega," says the Lord God, "who is, and who was, and who is to come, the Almighty."

John's Vision of Christ

9 I, John, your brother and companion in the suffering and kingdom and patient endurance that are ours in Jesus, was on the island of Patmos because of the word of God and the testimony of Jesus. 10 On the Lord's Day I was in the Spirit, and I heard behind me a loud voice like a trumpet, 11 which said: "Write on a scroll what you see and send it to the seven churches: to Ephesus, Smyrna, Pergamum, Thyatira, Sardis, Philadelphia and Laodicea."

12 I turned around to see the voice that was speaking to me. And when I turned I saw seven golden lampstands, 13 and among the lampstands was someone like a son of man,[d] dressed in a robe reaching down to his feet and with a golden sash around his chest. 14 The hair on his head was white like wool, as white as snow, and his eyes were like blazing fire. 15 His feet were like bronze glowing in a furnace, and his voice was like the sound of rushing waters. 16 In his right hand he held seven stars, and coming out of his mouth was a sharp, double-edged sword. His face was like the sun shining in all its brilliance.

17 When I saw him, I fell at his feet as though dead. Then he placed his right hand on me and said: "Do not be afraid. I am the First and the Last. 18 I am the Living One; I was dead, and now look, I am alive for ever and ever! And I hold the keys of death and Hades.

19 "Write, therefore, what you have seen, what is now and what will take place later. 20 The mystery of the seven stars that you saw in my right hand and of the seven golden lampstands is this: The seven stars are the angels[e] of the seven churches, and the seven lampstands are the seven churches.

To the Church in Ephesus

2 "To the angel[f] of the church in Ephesus write:

These are the words of him who holds the seven stars in his right hand and walks among the seven golden lampstands. 2 I know your deeds, your hard work and your perseverance. I know that you cannot tolerate wicked people, that you have tested those who claim to be apostles but are not, and have found them false. 3 You have persevered and have endured hardships for my name, and have not grown weary.

4 Yet I hold this against you: You have forsaken the love you had at first. 5 Consider how far you have fallen! Repent and do the things you did at first. If you do not repent, I will come to you and remove your

[a] 4 That is, the sevenfold Spirit [b] 7 Daniel 7:13 [c] 7 Zech. 12:10 [d] 13 See Daniel 7:13.
[e] 20 Or *messengers* [f] 1 Or *messenger*; also in verses 8, 12 and 18

lampstand from its place. 6But you have this in your favor: You hate the practices of the Nicolaitans, which I also hate.

7Whoever has ears, let them hear what the Spirit says to the churches. To the one who is victorious, I will give the right to eat from the tree of life, which is in the paradise of God.

To the Church in Smyrna

8"To the angel of the church in Smyrna write:

These are the words of him who is the First and the Last, who died and came to life again. 9I know your afflictions and your poverty — yet you are rich! I know about the slander of those who say they are Jews and are not, but are a synagogue of Satan. 10Do not be afraid of what you are about to suffer. I tell you, the devil will put some of you in prison to test you, and you will suffer persecution for ten days. Be faithful, even to the point of death, and I will give you life as your victor's crown.

11Whoever has ears, let them hear what the Spirit says to the churches. The one who is victorious will not be hurt at all by the second death.

To the Church in Pergamum

12"To the angel of the church in Pergamum write:

These are the words of him who has the sharp, double-edged sword. 13I know where you live — where Satan has his throne. Yet you remain true to my name. You did not renounce your faith in me, not even in the days of Antipas, my faithful witness, who was put to death in your city — where Satan lives.

14Nevertheless, I have a few things against you: There are some among you who hold to the teaching of Balaam, who taught Balak to entice the Israelites to sin so that they ate food sacrificed to idols and committed sexual immorality. 15Likewise, you also have those who hold to the teaching of the Nicolaitans. 16Repent therefore! Otherwise, I will soon come to you and will fight against them with the sword of my mouth.

17Whoever has ears, let them hear what the Spirit says to the churches. To the one who is victorious, I will give some of the hidden manna. I will also give that person a white stone with a new name written on it, known only to the one who receives it.

To the Church in Thyatira

18"To the angel of the church in Thyatira write:

These are the words of the Son of God, whose eyes are like blazing fire and whose feet are like burnished bronze. 19I know your deeds, your love and faith, your service and perseverance, and that you are now doing more than you did at first.

20Nevertheless, I have this against you: You tolerate that woman Jezebel, who calls herself a prophet. By her teaching she misleads my servants into sexual immorality and the eating of food sacrificed to idols. 21I have given her time to repent of her immorality, but she is unwilling. 22So I will cast her on a bed of suffering, and I will make those who commit adultery with her suffer intensely, unless they repent of her ways. 23I will strike her children dead. Then all the churches will know that I am he who searches hearts and minds, and I will repay each of you according to your deeds.

24Now I say to the rest of you in Thyatira, to you who do not hold to her teaching and have not learned Satan's so-called deep secrets, 'I will not impose any other burden on you, 25except to hold on to what you have until I come.'

26To the one who is victorious and does my will to the end, I will give authority over the nations — 27that one 'will rule them with an iron scepter and will dash them to pieces like pottery'[a] — just as I have received authority from my Father. 28I will also give that one the morning star. 29Whoever has ears, let them hear what the Spirit says to the churches.

To the Church in Sardis

3 "To the angel[b] of the church in Sardis write:

These are the words of him who holds the seven spirits[c] of God and the seven stars. I know your deeds; you have a reputation of being alive, but

[a] *27* Psalm 2:9 [b] *1* Or *messenger*; also in verses 7 and 14 [c] *1* That is, the sevenfold Spirit

you are dead. 2Wake up! Strengthen what remains and is about to die, for I have found your deeds unfinished in the sight of my God. 3Remember, therefore, what you have received and heard; hold it fast, and repent. But if you do not wake up, I will come like a thief, and you will not know at what time I will come to you.

4Yet you have a few people in Sardis who have not soiled their clothes. They will walk with me, dressed in white, for they are worthy. 5The one who is victorious will, like them, be dressed in white. I will never blot out the name of that person from the book of life, but will acknowledge that name before my Father and his angels. 6Whoever has ears, let them hear what the Spirit says to the churches.

To the Church in Philadelphia

7"To the angel of the church in Philadelphia write:

These are the words of him who is holy and true, who holds the key of David. What he opens no one can shut, and what he shuts no one can open. 8I know your deeds. See, I have placed before you an open door that no one can shut. I know that you have little strength, yet you have kept my word and have not denied my name. 9I will make those who are of the synagogue of Satan, who claim to be Jews though they are not, but are liars—I will make them come and fall down at your feet and acknowledge that I have loved you. 10Since you have kept my command to endure patiently, I will also keep you from the hour of trial that is going to come on the whole world to test the inhabitants of the earth.

11I am coming soon. Hold on to what you have, so that no one will take your crown. 12The one who is victorious I will make a pillar in the temple of my God. Never again will they leave it. I will write on them the name of my God and the name of the city of my God, the new Jerusalem, which is coming down out of heaven from my God; and I will also write on them my new name. 13Whoever has ears, let them hear what the Spirit says to the churches.

To the Church in Laodicea

14"To the angel of the church in Laodicea write:

These are the words of the Amen, the faithful and true witness, the ruler of God's creation. 15I know your deeds, that you are neither cold nor hot. I wish you were either one or the other! 16So, because you are lukewarm—neither hot nor cold—I am about to spit you out of my mouth. 17You say, 'I am rich; I have acquired wealth and do not need a thing.' But you do not realize that you are wretched, pitiful, poor, blind and naked. 18I counsel you to buy from me gold refined in the fire, so you can become rich; and white clothes to wear, so you can cover your shameful nakedness; and salve to put on your eyes, so you can see.

19Those whom I love I rebuke and discipline. So be earnest and repent. 20Here I am! I stand at the door and knock. If anyone hears my voice and opens the door, I will come in and eat with that person, and they with me.

21To the one who is victorious, I will give the right to sit with me on my throne, just as I was victorious and sat down with my Father on his throne. 22Whoever has ears, let them hear what the Spirit says to the churches."

The Throne in Heaven

4 After this I looked, and there before me was a door standing open in heaven. And the voice I had first heard speaking to me like a trumpet said, "Come up here, and I will show you what must take place after this." 2At once I was in the Spirit, and there before me was a throne in heaven with someone sitting on it. 3And the one who sat there had the appearance of jasper and ruby. A rainbow that shone like an emerald encircled the throne. 4Surrounding the throne were twenty-four other thrones, and seated on them were twenty-four elders. They were dressed in white and had crowns of gold on their heads. 5From the throne came flashes of lightning, rumblings and peals of thunder. In front of the throne, seven lamps were blazing. These are the seven spirits[a] of God. 6Also in front of the throne there was what looked like a sea of glass, clear as crystal.

[a] 5 That is, the sevenfold Spirit

In the center, around the throne, were
four living creatures, and they were covered with eyes, in front and in back. 7The
first living creature was like a lion, the
second was like an ox, the third had a face
like a man, the fourth was like a flying
eagle. 8Each of the four living creatures
had six wings and was covered with eyes
all around, even under its wings. Day and
night they never stop saying:

"'Holy, holy, holy
is the Lord God Almighty,'[a]
who was, and is, and is to come."

9Whenever the living creatures give glory, honor and thanks to him who sits on
the throne and who lives for ever and
ever, 10the twenty-four elders fall down
before him who sits on the throne and
worship him who lives for ever and ever.
They lay their crowns before the throne
and say:

11 "You are worthy, our Lord and God,
to receive glory and honor and
power,
for you created all things,
and by your will they were created
and have their being."

The Scroll and the Lamb

5 Then I saw in the right hand of him
who sat on the throne a scroll with
writing on both sides and sealed with
seven seals. 2And I saw a mighty angel
proclaiming in a loud voice, "Who is worthy to break the seals and open the scroll?"
3But no one in heaven or on earth or under
the earth could open the scroll or even
look inside it. 4I wept and wept because
no one was found who was worthy to open
the scroll or look inside. 5Then one of the
elders said to me, "Do not weep! See, the
Lion of the tribe of Judah, the Root of
David, has triumphed. He is able to open
the scroll and its seven seals."

6Then I saw a Lamb, looking as if it
had been slain, standing at the center of
the throne, encircled by the four living
creatures and the elders. The Lamb had
seven horns and seven eyes, which are
the seven spirits[b] of God sent out into all
the earth. 7He went and took the scroll
from the right hand of him who sat on
the throne. 8And when he had taken it, the
four living creatures and the twenty-four
elders fell down before the Lamb. Each
one had a harp and they were holding
golden bowls full of incense, which are the
prayers of God's people. 9And they sang
a new song, saying:

"You are worthy to take the scroll
and to open its seals,
because you were slain,
and with your blood you purchased
for God
persons from every tribe and
language and people and
nation.
10 You have made them to be a
kingdom and priests to serve
our God,
and they will reign[c] on the earth."

11Then I looked and heard the voice of
many angels, numbering thousands upon
thousands, and ten thousand times ten
thousand. They encircled the throne and
the living creatures and the elders. 12In a
loud voice they were saying:

"Worthy is the Lamb, who was slain,
to receive power and wealth and
wisdom and strength
and honor and glory and praise!"

13Then I heard every creature in heav-
en and on earth and under the earth
and on the sea, and all that is in them,
saying:

"To him who sits on the throne and to
the Lamb
be praise and honor and glory and
power,
for ever and ever!"

14The four living creatures said, "Amen,"
and the elders fell down and worshiped.

The Seals

6 I watched as the Lamb opened the first
of the seven seals. Then I heard one
of the four living creatures say in a voice
like thunder, "Come!" 2I looked, and there
before me was a white horse! Its rider held
a bow, and he was given a crown, and he
rode out as a conqueror bent on conquest.

3When the Lamb opened the second
seal, I heard the second living creature
say, "Come!" 4Then another horse came
out, a fiery red one. Its rider was given
power to take peace from the earth and
to make people kill each other. To him
was given a large sword.

5When the Lamb opened the third
seal, I heard the third living creature say,
"Come!" I looked, and there before me
was a black horse! Its rider was holding
a pair of scales in his hand. 6Then I heard
what sounded like a voice among the four

[a] *8* Isaiah 6:3 [b] *6* That is, the sevenfold Spirit [c] *10* Some manuscripts *they reign*

living creatures, saying, "Two pounds[a] of
wheat for a day's wages,[b] and six pounds[c]
of barley for a day's wages,[b] and do not
damage the oil and the wine!"
7When the Lamb opened the fourth
seal, I heard the voice of the fourth living
creature say, "Come!" 8I looked, and there
before me was a pale horse! Its rider was
named Death, and Hades was following
close behind him. They were given power
over a fourth of the earth to kill by sword,
famine and plague, and by the wild beasts
of the earth.
9When he opened the fifth seal, I saw
under the altar the souls of those who
had been slain because of the word of God
and the testimony they had maintained.
10They called out in a loud voice, "How
long, Sovereign Lord, holy and true, until you judge the inhabitants of the earth
and avenge our blood?" 11Then each of
them was given a white robe, and they
were told to wait a little longer, until the
full number of their fellow servants, their
brothers and sisters,[d] were killed just as
they had been.
12I watched as he opened the sixth seal.
There was a great earthquake. The sun
turned black like sackcloth made of goat
hair, the whole moon turned blood red,
13and the stars in the sky fell to earth, as
figs drop from a fig tree when shaken by a
strong wind. 14The heavens receded like a
scroll being rolled up, and every mountain
and island was removed from its place.
15Then the kings of the earth, the princes, the generals, the rich, the mighty, and
everyone else, both slave and free, hid in
caves and among the rocks of the mountains. 16They called to the mountains and
the rocks, "Fall on us and hide us[e] from
the face of him who sits on the throne
and from the wrath of the Lamb! 17For the
great day of their[f] wrath has come, and
who can withstand it?"

144,000 Sealed

7 After this I saw four angels standing
at the four corners of the earth, holding back the four winds of the earth to
prevent any wind from blowing on the
land or on the sea or on any tree. 2Then
I saw another angel coming up from the
east, having the seal of the living God. He
called out in a loud voice to the four angels who had been given power to harm
the land and the sea: 3"Do not harm the
land or the sea or the trees until we put
a seal on the foreheads of the servants
of our God." 4Then I heard the number of
those who were sealed: 144,000 from all
the tribes of Israel.

5From the tribe of Judah 12,000 were
sealed,
from the tribe of Reuben 12,000,
from the tribe of Gad 12,000,
6from the tribe of Asher 12,000,
from the tribe of Naphtali 12,000,
from the tribe of Manasseh 12,000,
7from the tribe of Simeon 12,000,
from the tribe of Levi 12,000,
from the tribe of Issachar 12,000,
8from the tribe of Zebulun 12,000,
from the tribe of Joseph 12,000,
from the tribe of Benjamin 12,000.

The Great Multitude in White Robes

9After this I looked, and there before me
was a great multitude that no one could
count, from every nation, tribe, people and
language, standing before the throne and
before the Lamb. They were wearing white
robes and were holding palm branches
in their hands. 10And they cried out in a
loud voice:

"Salvation belongs to our God,
who sits on the throne,
and to the Lamb."

11All the angels were standing around the
throne and around the elders and the four
living creatures. They fell down on their
faces before the throne and worshiped
God, 12saying:

"Amen!
Praise and glory
and wisdom and thanks and honor
and power and strength
be to our God for ever and ever.
Amen!"

13Then one of the elders asked me,
"These in white robes — who are they,
and where did they come from?"
14I answered, "Sir, you know."
And he said, "These are they who have
come out of the great tribulation; they
have washed their robes and made them
white in the blood of the Lamb. 15There-
fore,

"they are before the throne of God
and serve him day and night in his
temple;
and he who sits on the throne
will shelter them with his presence.

[a] 6 Or about 1 kilogram [b] 6 Greek *a denarius* [c] 6 Or about 3 kilograms [d] 11 The Greek word for *brothers and sisters* (*adelphoi*) refers here to believers, both men and women, as part of God's family; also in 12:10; 19:10. [e] 16 See Hosea 10:8. [f] 17 Some manuscripts *his*

16 'Never again will they hunger;
never again will they thirst.
The sun will not beat down on them,'[a]
nor any scorching heat.
17 For the Lamb at the center of the
throne
will be their shepherd;
'he will lead them to springs of living
water.'[a]
'And God will wipe away every tear
from their eyes.'[b]"

The Seventh Seal and the Golden Censer

8 When he opened the seventh seal,
there was silence in heaven for about
half an hour.

2And I saw the seven angels who stand
before God, and seven trumpets were giv-
en to them.

3Another angel, who had a golden
censer, came and stood at the altar. He
was given much incense to offer, with
the prayers of all God's people, on the
golden altar in front of the throne. 4The
smoke of the incense, together with the
prayers of God's people, went up before
God from the angel's hand. 5Then the angel took the censer, filled it with fire from
the altar, and hurled it on the earth; and
there came peals of thunder, rumblings,
flashes of lightning and an earthquake.

The Trumpets

6Then the seven angels who had the
seven trumpets prepared to sound them.

7The first angel sounded his trumpet,
and there came hail and fire mixed with
blood, and it was hurled down on the
earth. A third of the earth was burned
up, a third of the trees were burned up,
and all the green grass was burned up.

8The second angel sounded his trumpet,
and something like a huge mountain, all
ablaze, was thrown into the sea. A third
of the sea turned into blood, 9a third of
the living creatures in the sea died, and a
third of the ships were destroyed.

10The third angel sounded his trumpet,
and a great star, blazing like a torch, fell
from the sky on a third of the rivers and
on the springs of water— 11the name of
the star is Wormwood.[c] A third of the waters turned bitter, and many people died
from the waters that had become bitter.

12The fourth angel sounded his trumpet,
and a third of the sun was struck, a third
of the moon, and a third of the stars, so
that a third of them turned dark. A third
of the day was without light, and also a
third of the night.

13As I watched, I heard an eagle that was
flying in midair call out in a loud voice:
"Woe! Woe! Woe to the inhabitants of the
earth, because of the trumpet blasts about
to be sounded by the other three angels!"

9 The fifth angel sounded his trumpet,
and I saw a star that had fallen from
the sky to the earth. The star was given
the key to the shaft of the Abyss. 2When
he opened the Abyss, smoke rose from it
like the smoke from a gigantic furnace.
The sun and sky were darkened by the
smoke from the Abyss. 3And out of the
smoke locusts came down on the earth
and were given power like that of scorpions of the earth. 4They were told not to
harm the grass of the earth or any plant
or tree, but only those people who did not
have the seal of God on their foreheads.
5They were not allowed to kill them but
only to torture them for five months. And
the agony they suffered was like that of
the sting of a scorpion when it strikes.
6During those days people will seek death
but will not find it; they will long to die,
but death will elude them.

7The locusts looked like horses prepared
for battle. On their heads they wore something like crowns of gold, and their faces
resembled human faces. 8Their hair was
like women's hair, and their teeth were like
lions' teeth. 9They had breastplates like
breastplates of iron, and the sound of their
wings was like the thundering of many
horses and chariots rushing into battle.
10They had tails with stingers, like scorpions, and in their tails they had power to
torment people for five months. 11They had
as king over them the angel of the Abyss,
whose name in Hebrew is Abaddon and
in Greek is Apollyon (that is, Destroyer).

12The first woe is past; two other woes
are yet to come.

13The sixth angel sounded his trumpet,
and I heard a voice coming from the four
horns of the golden altar that is before
God. 14It said to the sixth angel who had
the trumpet, "Release the four angels
who are bound at the great river Euphrates." 15And the four angels who had been
kept ready for this very hour and day and
month and year were released to kill a
third of mankind. 16The number of the
mounted troops was twice ten thousand
times ten thousand. I heard their number.

17The horses and riders I saw in my vision looked like this: Their breastplates
were fiery red, dark blue, and yellow as
sulfur. The heads of the horses resembled
the heads of lions, and out of their mouths

[a] *16,17* Isaiah 49:10 [b] *17* Isaiah 25:8 [c] *11* Wormwood is a bitter substance.

came fire, smoke and sulfur. 18A third of mankind was killed by the three plagues of fire, smoke and sulfur that came out of their mouths. 19The power of the horses was in their mouths and in their tails; for their tails were like snakes, having heads with which they inflict injury.

20The rest of mankind who were not killed by these plagues still did not repent of the work of their hands; they did not stop worshiping demons, and idols of gold, silver, bronze, stone and wood — idols that cannot see or hear or walk. 21Nor did they repent of their murders, their magic arts, their sexual immorality or their thefts.

The Angel and the Little Scroll

10 Then I saw another mighty angel coming down from heaven. He was robed in a cloud, with a rainbow above his head; his face was like the sun, and his legs were like fiery pillars. 2He was holding a little scroll, which lay open in his hand. He planted his right foot on the sea and his left foot on the land, 3and he gave a loud shout like the roar of a lion. When he shouted, the voices of the seven thunders spoke. 4And when the seven thunders spoke, I was about to write; but I heard a voice from heaven say, "Seal up what the seven thunders have said and do not write it down."

5Then the angel I had seen standing on the sea and on the land raised his right hand to heaven. 6And he swore by him who lives for ever and ever, who created the heavens and all that is in them, the earth and all that is in it, and the sea and all that is in it, and said, "There will be no more delay! 7But in the days when the seventh angel is about to sound his trumpet, the mystery of God will be accomplished, just as he announced to his servants the prophets."

8Then the voice that I had heard from heaven spoke to me once more: "Go, take the scroll that lies open in the hand of the angel who is standing on the sea and on the land."

9So I went to the angel and asked him to give me the little scroll. He said to me, "Take it and eat it. It will turn your stomach sour, but 'in your mouth it will be as sweet as honey.'[a]" 10I took the little scroll from the angel's hand and ate it. It tasted as sweet as honey in my mouth, but when I had eaten it, my stomach turned sour. 11Then I was told, "You must prophesy again about many peoples, nations, languages and kings."

The Two Witnesses

11 I was given a reed like a measuring rod and was told, "Go and measure the temple of God and the altar, with its worshipers. 2But exclude the outer court; do not measure it, because it has been given to the Gentiles. They will trample on the holy city for 42 months. 3And I will appoint my two witnesses, and they will prophesy for 1,260 days, clothed in sackcloth." 4They are "the two olive trees" and the two lampstands, and "they stand before the Lord of the earth."[b] 5If anyone tries to harm them, fire comes from their mouths and devours their enemies. This is how anyone who wants to harm them must die. 6They have power to shut up the heavens so that it will not rain during the time they are prophesying; and they have power to turn the waters into blood and to strike the earth with every kind of plague as often as they want.

7Now when they have finished their testimony, the beast that comes up from the Abyss will attack them, and overpower and kill them. 8Their bodies will lie in the public square of the great city — which is figuratively called Sodom and Egypt — where also their Lord was crucified. 9For three and a half days some from every people, tribe, language and nation will gaze on their bodies and refuse them burial. 10The inhabitants of the earth will gloat over them and will celebrate by sending each other gifts, because these two prophets had tormented those who live on the earth.

11But after the three and a half days the breath[c] of life from God entered them, and they stood on their feet, and terror struck those who saw them. 12Then they heard a loud voice from heaven saying to them, "Come up here." And they went up to heaven in a cloud, while their enemies looked on.

13At that very hour there was a severe earthquake and a tenth of the city collapsed. Seven thousand people were killed in the earthquake, and the survivors were terrified and gave glory to the God of heaven.

14The second woe has passed; the third woe is coming soon.

The Seventh Trumpet

15The seventh angel sounded his trumpet, and there were loud voices in heaven, which said:

"The kingdom of the world has
become
the kingdom of our Lord and of
his Messiah,
and he will reign for ever and ever."

[a] 9 Ezek. 3:3 [b] 4 See Zech. 4:3,11,14. [c] 11 Or *Spirit* (see Ezek. 37:5,14)

16 And the twenty-four elders, who were
seated on their thrones before God, fell on
their faces and worshiped God, 17 saying:

"We give thanks to you, Lord God
Almighty,
the One who is and who was,
because you have taken your great
power
and have begun to reign.
18 The nations were angry,
and your wrath has come.
The time has come for judging the
dead,
and for rewarding your servants
the prophets
and your people who revere your
name,
both great and small —
and for destroying those who destroy
the earth."

19 Then God's temple in heaven was
opened, and within his temple was seen
the ark of his covenant. And there came
flashes of lightning, rumblings, peals of
thunder, an earthquake and a severe
hailstorm.

The Woman and the Dragon

12 A great sign appeared in heaven: a
woman clothed with the sun, with
the moon under her feet and a crown of
twelve stars on her head. 2 She was pregnant and cried out in pain as she was
about to give birth. 3 Then another sign
appeared in heaven: an enormous red
dragon with seven heads and ten horns
and seven crowns on its heads. 4 Its tail
swept a third of the stars out of the sky
and flung them to the earth. The dragon stood in front of the woman who was
about to give birth, so that it might devour
her child the moment he was born. 5 She
gave birth to a son, a male child, who "will
rule all the nations with an iron scepter."[a]
And her child was snatched up to God and
to his throne. 6 The woman fled into the
wilderness to a place prepared for her by
God, where she might be taken care of
for 1,260 days.

7 Then war broke out in heaven. Michael
and his angels fought against the dragon,
and the dragon and his angels fought
back. 8 But he was not strong enough,
and they lost their place in heaven. 9 The
great dragon was hurled down — that
ancient serpent called the devil, or Satan, who leads the whole world astray.
He was hurled to the earth, and his angels with him.

10 Then I heard a loud voice in heav-
en say:

"Now have come the salvation and
the power
and the kingdom of our God,
and the authority of his Messiah.
For the accuser of our brothers and
sisters,
who accuses them before our God
day and night,
has been hurled down.
11 They triumphed over him
by the blood of the Lamb
and by the word of their testimony;
they did not love their lives so much
as to shrink from death.
12 Therefore rejoice, you heavens
and you who dwell in them!
But woe to the earth and the sea,
because the devil has gone down to
you!
He is filled with fury,
because he knows that his time is
short."

13 When the dragon saw that he had
been hurled to the earth, he pursued the
woman who had given birth to the male
child. 14 The woman was given the two
wings of a great eagle, so that she might
fly to the place prepared for her in the
wilderness, where she would be taken
care of for a time, times and half a time,
out of the serpent's reach. 15 Then from his
mouth the serpent spewed water like a
river, to overtake the woman and sweep
her away with the torrent. 16 But the earth
helped the woman by opening its mouth
and swallowing the river that the dragon had spewed out of his mouth. 17 Then
the dragon was enraged at the woman
and went off to wage war against the rest
of her offspring — those who keep God's
commands and hold fast their testimony
about Jesus.

The Beast out of the Sea

13 The dragon[b] stood on the shore of the
sea. And I saw a beast coming out of
the sea. It had ten horns and seven heads,
with ten crowns on its horns, and on each
head a blasphemous name. 2 The beast I
saw resembled a leopard, but had feet like
those of a bear and a mouth like that of a
lion. The dragon gave the beast his power
and his throne and great authority. 3 One
of the heads of the beast seemed to have
had a fatal wound, but the fatal wound
had been healed. The whole world was
filled with wonder and followed the beast.

[a] 5 Psalm 2:9 [b] 1 Some manuscripts *And I*

4People worshiped the dragon because
he had given authority to the beast, and
they also worshiped the beast and asked,
"Who is like the beast? Who can wage war
against it?"
5The beast was given a mouth to utter
proud words and blasphemies and to exercise its authority for forty-two months. 6It
opened its mouth to blaspheme God, and
to slander his name and his dwelling place
and those who live in heaven. 7It was giv-
en power to wage war against God's holy
people and to conquer them. And it was
given authority over every tribe, people,
language and nation. 8All inhabitants
of the earth will worship the beast — all
whose names have not been written in
the Lamb's book of life, the Lamb who
was slain from the creation of the world.[a]
9Whoever has ears, let them hear.

10"If anyone is to go into captivity,
into captivity they will go.
If anyone is to be killed[b] with the
sword,
with the sword they will be killed."[c]

This calls for patient endurance and faithfulness on the part of God's people.

The Beast out of the Earth

11Then I saw a second beast, coming
out of the earth. It had two horns like a
lamb, but it spoke like a dragon. 12It exercised all the authority of the first beast
on its behalf, and made the earth and its
inhabitants worship the first beast, whose
fatal wound had been healed. 13And it
performed great signs, even causing fire
to come down from heaven to the earth
in full view of the people. 14Because of the
signs it was given power to perform on
behalf of the first beast, it deceived the
inhabitants of the earth. It ordered them
to set up an image in honor of the beast
who was wounded by the sword and yet
lived. 15The second beast was given power to give breath to the image of the first
beast, so that the image could speak and
cause all who refused to worship the image to be killed. 16It also forced all people,
great and small, rich and poor, free and
slave, to receive a mark on their right
hands or on their foreheads, 17so that they
could not buy or sell unless they had the
mark, which is the name of the beast or
the number of its name.
18This calls for wisdom. Let the person
who has insight calculate the number of
the beast, for it is the number of a man.[d]
That number is 666.

The Lamb and the 144,000

14 Then I looked, and there before me
was the Lamb, standing on Mount
Zion, and with him 144,000 who had his
name and his Father's name written on
their foreheads. 2And I heard a sound from
heaven like the roar of rushing waters and
like a loud peal of thunder. The sound I
heard was like that of harpists playing
their harps. 3And they sang a new song
before the throne and before the four living creatures and the elders. No one could
learn the song except the 144,000 who had
been redeemed from the earth. 4These are
those who did not defile themselves with
women, for they remained virgins. They
follow the Lamb wherever he goes. They
were purchased from among mankind
and offered as firstfruits to God and the
Lamb. 5No lie was found in their mouths;
they are blameless.

The Three Angels

6Then I saw another angel flying in
midair, and he had the eternal gospel to
proclaim to those who live on the earth —
to every nation, tribe, language and people. 7He said in a loud voice, "Fear God
and give him glory, because the hour of
his judgment has come. Worship him who
made the heavens, the earth, the sea and
the springs of water."
8A second angel followed and said,
"'Fallen! Fallen is Babylon the Great,'[e]
which made all the nations drink the maddening wine of her adulteries."
9A third angel followed them and said
in a loud voice: "If anyone worships the
beast and its image and receives its mark
on their forehead or on their hand, 10they,
too, will drink the wine of God's fury, which
has been poured full strength into the
cup of his wrath. They will be tormented
with burning sulfur in the presence of
the holy angels and of the Lamb. 11And
the smoke of their torment will rise for
ever and ever. There will be no rest day or
night for those who worship the beast and
its image, or for anyone who receives the
mark of its name." 12This calls for patient
endurance on the part of the people of
God who keep his commands and remain
faithful to Jesus.
13Then I heard a voice from heaven say,
"Write this: Blessed are the dead who die
in the Lord from now on."
"Yes," says the Spirit, "they will rest
from their labor, for their deeds will follow them."

[a] 8 Or *written from the creation of the world in the book of life belonging to the Lamb who was slain*
[b] 10 Some manuscripts *anyone kills* [c] 10 Jer. 15:2 [d] 18 Or *is humanity's number* [e] 8 Isaiah 21:9

Harvesting the Earth and Trampling the Winepress

14I looked, and there before me was a
white cloud, and seated on the cloud was
one like a son of man[a] with a crown of
gold on his head and a sharp sickle in his
hand. 15Then another angel came out of
the temple and called in a loud voice to
him who was sitting on the cloud, "Take
your sickle and reap, because the time
to reap has come, for the harvest of the
earth is ripe." 16So he who was seated on
the cloud swung his sickle over the earth,
and the earth was harvested.

17Another angel came out of the temple
in heaven, and he too had a sharp sickle.
18Still another angel, who had charge of
the fire, came from the altar and called
in a loud voice to him who had the sharp
sickle, "Take your sharp sickle and gather the clusters of grapes from the earth's
vine, because its grapes are ripe." 19The
angel swung his sickle on the earth, gathered its grapes and threw them into the
great winepress of God's wrath. 20They
were trampled in the winepress outside
the city, and blood flowed out of the press,
rising as high as the horses' bridles for a
distance of 1,600 stadia.[b]

Seven Angels With Seven Plagues

15 I saw in heaven another great and
marvelous sign: seven angels with
the seven last plagues — last, because with
them God's wrath is completed. 2And I saw
what looked like a sea of glass glowing
with fire and, standing beside the sea,
those who had been victorious over the
beast and its image and over the number
of its name. They held harps given them
by God 3and sang the song of God's servant
Moses and of the Lamb:

"Great and marvelous are your deeds,
  Lord God Almighty.
Just and true are your ways,
  King of the nations.[c]
4 Who will not fear you, Lord,
  and bring glory to your name?
For you alone are holy.
All nations will come
  and worship before you,
for your righteous acts have been
    revealed."[d]

5After this I looked, and I saw in heaven
the temple — that is, the tabernacle of the
covenant law — and it was opened. 6Out of
the temple came the seven angels with the
seven plagues. They were dressed in clean,
shining linen and wore golden sashes
around their chests. 7Then one of the four
living creatures gave to the seven angels
seven golden bowls filled with the wrath
of God, who lives for ever and ever. 8And
the temple was filled with smoke from
the glory of God and from his power, and
no one could enter the temple until the
seven plagues of the seven angels were
completed.

The Seven Bowls of God's Wrath

16 Then I heard a loud voice from the
temple saying to the seven angels,
"Go, pour out the seven bowls of God's
wrath on the earth."

2The first angel went and poured out his
bowl on the land, and ugly, festering sores
broke out on the people who had the mark
of the beast and worshiped its image.

3The second angel poured out his bowl
on the sea, and it turned into blood like
that of a dead person, and every living
thing in the sea died.

4The third angel poured out his bowl on
the rivers and springs of water, and they
became blood. 5Then I heard the angel in
charge of the waters say:

"You are just in these judgments,
    O Holy One,
  you who are and who were;
6 for they have shed the blood of your
    holy people and your prophets,
  and you have given them blood to
    drink as they deserve."

7And I heard the altar respond:

"Yes, Lord God Almighty,
  true and just are your judgments."

8The fourth angel poured out his bowl
on the sun, and the sun was allowed to
scorch people with fire. 9They were seared
by the intense heat and they cursed the
name of God, who had control over these
plagues, but they refused to repent and
glorify him.

10The fifth angel poured out his bowl
on the throne of the beast, and its kingdom was plunged into darkness. People gnawed their tongues in agony 11and
cursed the God of heaven because of their
pains and their sores, but they refused to
repent of what they had done.

12The sixth angel poured out his bowl
on the great river Euphrates, and its water
was dried up to prepare the way for the

[a] *14* See Daniel 7:13. [b] *20* That is, about 180 miles or about 300 kilometers [c] *3* Some manuscripts *ages* [d] *3,4* Phrases in this song are drawn from Psalm 111:2,3; Deut. 32:4; Jer. 10:7; Psalms 86:9; 98:2.

kings from the East. 13 Then I saw three
impure spirits that looked like frogs; they
came out of the mouth of the dragon, out
of the mouth of the beast and out of the
mouth of the false prophet. 14 They are
demonic spirits that perform signs, and
they go out to the kings of the whole world,
to gather them for the battle on the great
day of God Almighty.

> 15 "Look, I come like a thief! Blessed
> is the one who stays awake and re-
> mains clothed, so as not to go naked
> and be shamefully exposed."

16 Then they gathered the kings together
to the place that in Hebrew is called Ar-
mageddon.
17 The seventh angel poured out his bowl
into the air, and out of the temple came a
loud voice from the throne, saying, "It is
done!" 18 Then there came flashes of lightning, rumblings, peals of thunder and a
severe earthquake. No earthquake like it
has ever occurred since mankind has been
on earth, so tremendous was the quake.
19 The great city split into three parts, and
the cities of the nations collapsed. God
remembered Babylon the Great and gave
her the cup filled with the wine of the fury
of his wrath. 20 Every island fled away and
the mountains could not be found. 21 From
the sky huge hailstones, each weighing
about a hundred pounds,[a] fell on people.
And they cursed God on account of the
plague of hail, because the plague was
so terrible.

Babylon, the Prostitute on the Beast

17 One of the seven angels who had the
seven bowls came and said to me,
"Come, I will show you the punishment
of the great prostitute, who sits by many
waters. 2 With her the kings of the earth
committed adultery, and the inhabitants
of the earth were intoxicated with the
wine of her adulteries."
3 Then the angel carried me away in
the Spirit into a wilderness. There I saw
a woman sitting on a scarlet beast that
was covered with blasphemous names
and had seven heads and ten horns. 4 The
woman was dressed in purple and scarlet,
and was glittering with gold, precious
stones and pearls. She held a golden cup
in her hand, filled with abominable things
and the filth of her adulteries. 5 The name
written on her forehead was a mystery:

BABYLON THE GREAT
THE MOTHER OF PROSTITUTES
AND OF THE ABOMINATIONS OF THE EARTH.

6 I saw that the woman was drunk with the
blood of God's holy people, the blood of
those who bore testimony to Jesus.
When I saw her, I was greatly astonished. 7 Then the angel said to me: "Why
are you astonished? I will explain to you
the mystery of the woman and of the beast
she rides, which has the seven heads and
ten horns. 8 The beast, which you saw, once
was, now is not, and yet will come up out
of the Abyss and go to its destruction. The
inhabitants of the earth whose names
have not been written in the book of life
from the creation of the world will be astonished when they see the beast, because
it once was, now is not, and yet will come.
9 "This calls for a mind with wisdom. The
seven heads are seven hills on which the
woman sits. 10 They are also seven kings.
Five have fallen, one is, the other has not
yet come; but when he does come, he must
remain for only a little while. 11 The beast
who once was, and now is not, is an eighth
king. He belongs to the seven and is going
to his destruction.
12 "The ten horns you saw are ten kings
who have not yet received a kingdom, but
who for one hour will receive authority as
kings along with the beast. 13 They have
one purpose and will give their power and
authority to the beast. 14 They will wage
war against the Lamb, but the Lamb will
triumph over them because he is Lord
of lords and King of kings — and with
him will be his called, chosen and faithful followers."
15 Then the angel said to me, "The waters
you saw, where the prostitute sits, are peoples, multitudes, nations and languages.
16 The beast and the ten horns you saw will
hate the prostitute. They will bring her to
ruin and leave her naked; they will eat her
flesh and burn her with fire. 17 For God has
put it into their hearts to accomplish his
purpose by agreeing to hand over to the
beast their royal authority, until God's
words are fulfilled. 18 The woman you saw
is the great city that rules over the kings
of the earth."

Lament Over Fallen Babylon

18 After this I saw another angel coming down from heaven. He had great
authority, and the earth was illuminated
by his splendor. 2 With a mighty voice he
shouted:

> "'Fallen! Fallen is Babylon the
> Great!'[b]
> She has become a dwelling for
> demons

[a] 21 Or about 45 kilograms [b] 2 Isaiah 21:9

and a haunt for every impure spirit,
a haunt for every unclean bird,
a haunt for every unclean and detestable animal.
3 For all the nations have drunk
the maddening wine of her adulteries.
The kings of the earth committed adultery with her,
and the merchants of the earth grew rich from her excessive luxuries."

Warning to Escape Babylon's Judgment

4 Then I heard another voice from heaven say:

" 'Come out of her, my people,'[a]
so that you will not share in her sins,
so that you will not receive any of her plagues;
5 for her sins are piled up to heaven,
and God has remembered her crimes.
6 Give back to her as she has given;
pay her back double for what she has done.
Pour her a double portion from her own cup.
7 Give her as much torment and grief
as the glory and luxury she gave herself.
In her heart she boasts,
'I sit enthroned as queen.
I am not a widow;[b]
I will never mourn.'
8 Therefore in one day her plagues will overtake her:
death, mourning and famine.
She will be consumed by fire,
for mighty is the Lord God who judges her.

Threefold Woe Over Babylon's Fall

9 "When the kings of the earth who committed adultery with her and shared her
luxury see the smoke of her burning, they
will weep and mourn over her. 10 Terrified at her torment, they will stand far
off and cry:

" 'Woe! Woe to you, great city,
you mighty city of Babylon!
In one hour your doom has come!'

11 "The merchants of the earth will weep
and mourn over her because no one buys
their cargoes anymore — 12 cargoes of
gold, silver, precious stones and pearls;
fine linen, purple, silk and scarlet cloth;
every sort of citron wood, and articles of
every kind made of ivory, costly wood,
bronze, iron and marble; 13 cargoes of cinnamon and spice, of incense, myrrh and
frankincense, of wine and olive oil, of
fine flour and wheat; cattle and sheep;
horses and carriages; and human beings
sold as slaves.

14 "They will say, 'The fruit you longed
for is gone from you. All your luxury and
splendor have vanished, never to be recovered.' 15 The merchants who sold these
things and gained their wealth from her
will stand far off, terrified at her torment.
They will weep and mourn 16 and cry out:

" 'Woe! Woe to you, great city,
dressed in fine linen, purple and scarlet,
and glittering with gold, precious stones and pearls!
17 In one hour such great wealth has been brought to ruin!'

"Every sea captain, and all who travel by ship, the sailors, and all who earn
their living from the sea, will stand far off.
18 When they see the smoke of her burning,
they will exclaim, 'Was there ever a city
like this great city?' 19 They will throw dust
on their heads, and with weeping and
mourning cry out:

" 'Woe! Woe to you, great city,
where all who had ships on the sea
became rich through her wealth!
In one hour she has been brought to ruin!'

20 "Rejoice over her, you heavens!
Rejoice, you people of God!
Rejoice, apostles and prophets!
For God has judged her
with the judgment she imposed on you."

The Finality of Babylon's Doom

21 Then a mighty angel picked up a boul-
der the size of a large millstone and threw
it into the sea, and said:

"With such violence
the great city of Babylon will be thrown down,
never to be found again.
22 The music of harpists and musicians,
pipers and trumpeters,
will never be heard in you again.
No worker of any trade
will ever be found in you again.
The sound of a millstone
will never be heard in you again.

[a] 4 Jer. 51:45 [b] 7 See Isaiah 47:7,8.

23 The light of a lamp
will never shine in you again.
The voice of bridegroom and bride
will never be heard in you again.
Your merchants were the world's
important people.
By your magic spell all the nations
were led astray.
24 In her was found the blood of
prophets and of God's holy
people,
of all who have been slaughtered
on the earth."

Threefold Hallelujah Over Babylon's Fall

19 After this I heard what sounded
like the roar of a great multitude
in heaven shouting:

"Hallelujah!
Salvation and glory and power
belong to our God,
2 for true and just are his judgments.
He has condemned the great
prostitute
who corrupted the earth by her
adulteries.
He has avenged on her the blood of
his servants."

3 And again they shouted:

"Hallelujah!
The smoke from her goes up for ever
and ever."

4 The twenty-four elders and the four
living creatures fell down and worshiped
God, who was seated on the throne. And
they cried:

"Amen, Hallelujah!"

5 Then a voice came from the throne,
saying:

"Praise our God,
all you his servants,
you who fear him,
both great and small!"

6 Then I heard what sounded like a great
multitude, like the roar of rushing waters
and like loud peals of thunder, shouting:

"Hallelujah!
For our Lord God Almighty reigns.
7 Let us rejoice and be glad
and give him glory!
For the wedding of the Lamb has
come,
and his bride has made herself
ready.
8 Fine linen, bright and clean,
was given her to wear."

(Fine linen stands for the righteous acts
of God's holy people.)

9 Then the angel said to me, "Write this:
Blessed are those who are invited to the
wedding supper of the Lamb!" And he
added, "These are the true words of God."
10 At this I fell at his feet to worship him.
But he said to me, "Don't do that! I am a fellow servant with you and with your brothers and sisters who hold to the testimony
of Jesus. Worship God! For it is the Spirit of
prophecy who bears testimony to Jesus."

The Heavenly Warrior Defeats the Beast

11 I saw heaven standing open and there
before me was a white horse, whose rider is called Faithful and True. With justice he judges and wages war. 12 His eyes
are like blazing fire, and on his head are
many crowns. He has a name written on
him that no one knows but he himself.
13 He is dressed in a robe dipped in blood,
and his name is the Word of God. 14 The
armies of heaven were following him,
riding on white horses and dressed in
fine linen, white and clean. 15 Coming out
of his mouth is a sharp sword with which
to strike down the nations. "He will rule
them with an iron scepter."[a] He treads the
winepress of the fury of the wrath of God
Almighty. 16 On his robe and on his thigh
he has this name written:

KING OF KINGS AND LORD OF LORDS.

17 And I saw an angel standing in the
sun, who cried in a loud voice to all the
birds flying in midair, "Come, gather together for the great supper of God, 18 so that
you may eat the flesh of kings, generals,
and the mighty, of horses and their riders,
and the flesh of all people, free and slave,
great and small."
19 Then I saw the beast and the kings
of the earth and their armies gathered
together to wage war against the rider
on the horse and his army. 20 But the beast
was captured, and with it the false prophet who had performed the signs on its
behalf. With these signs he had deluded
those who had received the mark of the
beast and worshiped its image. The two
of them were thrown alive into the fiery
lake of burning sulfur. 21 The rest were
killed with the sword coming out of the
mouth of the rider on the horse, and all
the birds gorged themselves on their flesh.

[a] 15 Psalm 2:9

The Thousand Years

20 And I saw an angel coming down
out of heaven, having the key to
the Abyss and holding in his hand a great
chain. 2He seized the dragon, that ancient
serpent, who is the devil, or Satan, and
bound him for a thousand years. 3He threw
him into the Abyss, and locked and sealed
it over him, to keep him from deceiving
the nations anymore until the thousand
years were ended. After that, he must be
set free for a short time.

4I saw thrones on which were seated
those who had been given authority to
judge. And I saw the souls of those who
had been beheaded because of their testimony about Jesus and because of the
word of God. They[a] had not worshiped the
beast or its image and had not received its
mark on their foreheads or their hands.
They came to life and reigned with Christ a
thousand years. 5(The rest of the dead did
not come to life until the thousand years
were ended.) This is the first resurrection.
6Blessed and holy are those who share in
the first resurrection. The second death
has no power over them, but they will be
priests of God and of Christ and will reign
with him for a thousand years.

The Judgment of Satan

7When the thousand years are over,
Satan will be released from his prison
8and will go out to deceive the nations in
the four corners of the earth — Gog and
Magog — and to gather them for battle. In
number they are like the sand on the seashore. 9They marched across the breadth
of the earth and surrounded the camp of
God's people, the city he loves. But fire
came down from heaven and devoured
them. 10And the devil, who deceived them,
was thrown into the lake of burning sulfur,
where the beast and the false prophet had
been thrown. They will be tormented day
and night for ever and ever.

The Judgment of the Dead

11Then I saw a great white throne and
him who was seated on it. The earth and
the heavens fled from his presence, and
there was no place for them. 12And I saw
the dead, great and small, standing before
the throne, and books were opened. Another book was opened, which is the book
of life. The dead were judged according
to what they had done as recorded in the
books. 13The sea gave up the dead that
were in it, and death and Hades gave up
the dead that were in them, and each
person was judged according to what they
had done. 14Then death and Hades were
thrown into the lake of fire. The lake of
fire is the second death. 15Anyone whose
name was not found written in the book
of life was thrown into the lake of fire.

A New Heaven and a New Earth

21 Then I saw "a new heaven and a new
earth,"[b] for the first heaven and the
first earth had passed away, and there was
no longer any sea. 2I saw the Holy City, the
new Jerusalem, coming down out of heaven
from God, prepared as a bride beautifully
dressed for her husband. 3And I heard a
loud voice from the throne saying, "Look!
God's dwelling place is now among the people, and he will dwell with them. They will
be his people, and God himself will be with
them and be their God. 4'He will wipe every
tear from their eyes. There will be no more
death'[c] or mourning or crying or pain, for
the old order of things has passed away."

5He who was seated on the throne said,
"I am making everything new!" Then he
said, "Write this down, for these words are
trustworthy and true."

6He said to me: "It is done. I am the Alpha and the Omega, the Beginning and
the End. To the thirsty I will give water
without cost from the spring of the water
of life. 7Those who are victorious will inherit all this, and I will be their God and
they will be my children. 8But the cowardly,
the unbelieving, the vile, the murderers,
the sexually immoral, those who practice
magic arts, the idolaters and all liars —
they will be consigned to the fiery lake of
burning sulfur. This is the second death."

The New Jerusalem, the Bride of the Lamb

9One of the seven angels who had the
seven bowls full of the seven last plagues
came and said to me, "Come, I will show
you the bride, the wife of the Lamb."
10And he carried me away in the Spirit to
a mountain great and high, and showed
me the Holy City, Jerusalem, coming down
out of heaven from God. 11It shone with the
glory of God, and its brilliance was like
that of a very precious jewel, like a jasper, clear as crystal. 12It had a great, high
wall with twelve gates, and with twelve
angels at the gates. On the gates were
written the names of the twelve tribes of
Israel. 13There were three gates on the east,
three on the north, three on the south and
three on the west. 14The wall of the city had
twelve foundations, and on them were the
names of the twelve apostles of the Lamb.

[a] 4 Or *God; I also saw those who* [b] 1 Isaiah 65:17 [c] 4 Isaiah 25:8

15 The angel who talked with me had a measuring rod of gold to measure the city, its gates and its walls. 16 The city was laid out like a square, as long as it was wide. He measured the city with the rod and found it to be 12,000 stadia[a] in length, and as wide and high as it is long. 17 The angel measured the wall using human measurement, and it was 144 cubits[b] thick.[c] 18 The wall was made of jasper, and the city of pure gold, as pure as glass. 19 The foundations of the city walls were decorated with every kind of precious stone. The first foundation was jasper, the second sapphire, the third agate, the fourth emerald, 20 the fifth onyx, the sixth ruby, the seventh chrysolite, the eighth beryl, the ninth topaz, the tenth turquoise, the eleventh jacinth, and the twelfth amethyst.[d] 21 The twelve gates were twelve pearls, each gate made of a single pearl. The great street of the city was of gold, as pure as transparent glass.

22 I did not see a temple in the city, because the Lord God Almighty and the Lamb are its temple. 23 The city does not need the sun or the moon to shine on it, for the glory of God gives it light, and the Lamb is its lamp. 24 The nations will walk by its light, and the kings of the earth will bring their splendor into it. 25 On no day will its gates ever be shut, for there will be no night there. 26 The glory and honor of the nations will be brought into it. 27 Nothing impure will ever enter it, nor will anyone who does what is shameful or deceitful, but only those whose names are written in the Lamb's book of life.

Eden Restored

22 Then the angel showed me the river of the water of life, as clear as crystal, flowing from the throne of God and of the Lamb 2 down the middle of the great street of the city. On each side of the river stood the tree of life, bearing twelve crops of fruit, yielding its fruit every month. And the leaves of the tree are for the healing of the nations. 3 No longer will there be any curse. The throne of God and of the Lamb will be in the city, and his servants will serve him. 4 They will see his face, and his name will be on their foreheads. 5 There will be no more night. They will not need the light of a lamp or the light of the sun, for the Lord God will give them light. And they will reign for ever and ever.

John and the Angel

6 The angel said to me, "These words are trustworthy and true. The Lord, the God who inspires the prophets, sent his angel to show his servants the things that must soon take place."

7 "Look, I am coming soon! Blessed is the one who keeps the words of the prophecy written in this scroll."

8 I, John, am the one who heard and saw these things. And when I had heard and seen them, I fell down to worship at the feet of the angel who had been showing them to me. 9 But he said to me, "Don't do that! I am a fellow servant with you and with your fellow prophets and with all who keep the words of this scroll. Worship God!"

10 Then he told me, "Do not seal up the words of the prophecy of this scroll, because the time is near. 11 Let the one who does wrong continue to do wrong; let the vile person continue to be vile; let the one who does right continue to do right; and let the holy person continue to be holy."

Epilogue: Invitation and Warning

12 "Look, I am coming soon! My reward is with me, and I will give to each person according to what they have done. 13 I am the Alpha and the Omega, the First and the Last, the Beginning and the End.

14 "Blessed are those who wash their robes, that they may have the right to the tree of life and may go through the gates into the city. 15 Outside are the dogs, those who practice magic arts, the sexually immoral, the murderers, the idolaters and everyone who loves and practices falsehood.

16 "I, Jesus, have sent my angel to give you[e] this testimony for the churches. I am the Root and the Offspring of David, and the bright Morning Star."

17 The Spirit and the bride say, "Come!" And let the one who hears say, "Come!" Let the one who is thirsty come; and let the one who wishes take the free gift of the water of life.

18 I warn everyone who hears the words of the prophecy of this scroll: If anyone adds anything to them, God will add to that person the plagues described in this scroll. 19 And if anyone takes words away from this scroll of prophecy, God will take away from that person any share in the tree of life and in the Holy City, which are described in this scroll.

20 He who testifies to these things says, "Yes, I am coming soon."

Amen. Come, Lord Jesus.

21 The grace of the Lord Jesus be with God's people. Amen.

[a] *16* That is, about 1,400 miles or about 2,200 kilometers [b] *17* That is, about 200 feet or about 65 meters [c] *17* Or *high* [d] *20* The precise identification of some of these precious stones is uncertain. [e] *16* The Greek is plural.

TABLE OF WEIGHTS & MEASURES

	Biblical Unit	Approximate American Equivalent	Approximate Metric Equivalent
Weights	talent (60 minas)	75 pounds	34 kilograms
	mina (50 shekels)	1 1/4 pounds	560 grams
	shekel (2 bekas)	2/5 ounce	11.5 grams
	pim (2/3 shekel)	1/4 ounce	7.8 grams
	beka (10 gerahs)	1/5 ounce	5.7 grams
	gerah	1/50 ounce	0.6 gram
	daric	1/3 ounce	8.4 grams
Length	cubit	18 inches	45 centimeters
	span	9 inches	23 centimeters
	handbreadth	3 inches	7.5 centimeters
	stadion (pl. stadia)	600 feet	183 meters
Capacity			
Dry Measure	cor [homer] (10 ephahs)	6 bushels	220 liters
	lethek (5 ephahs)	3 bushels	110 liters
	ephah (10 omers)	3/5 bushel	22 liters
	seah (1/3 ephah)	7 quarts	7.5 liters
	omer (1/10 ephah)	2 quarts	2 liters
	cab (1/18 ephah)	1 quart	1 liter
Liquid Measure	bath (1 ephah)	6 gallons	22 liters
	hin (1/6 bath)	1 gallon	3.8 liters
	log (1/72 bath)	1/3 quart	0.3 liter

The figures of the table are calculated on the basis of a shekel equaling 11.5 grams, a cubit equaling 18 inches and an ephah equaling 22 liters. The quart referred to is either a dry quart (slightly larger than a liter) or a liquid quart (slightly smaller than a liter), whichever is applicable. The ton referred to in the footnotes is the American ton of 2,000 pounds. These weights are calculated relative to the particular commodity involved. Accordingly, the same measure of capacity in the text may be converted into different weights in the footnotes.

This table is based upon the best available information, but it is not intended to be mathematically precise; like the measurement equivalents in the footnotes, it merely gives approximate amounts and distances. Weights and measures differed somewhat at various times and places in the ancient world. There is uncertainty particularly about the ephah and the bath; further discoveries may shed more light on these units of capacity.

NOTES

NOTES

NOTES

NOTES

NOTES

NOTES

NOTES

NOTES

NOTES

NOTES

NOTES

NOTES

NOTES

NOTES

NOTES

NOTES

A NOTE REGARDING THE TYPE

This Bible was set in the Zondervan NIV Typeface, commissioned by Zondervan, a division of HarperCollins Christian Publishing, and designed in Aarhus, Denmark, by Klaus E. Krogh and Heidi Rand Sørensen of 2K/DENMARK. The design takes inspiration from the vision of the New International Version (NIV) to be a modern translation that gives the reader the most accurate Bible text possible, reflects the very best of biblical scholarship, and uses contemporary global English. The designers of the Zondervan NIV Typeface sought to reflect this rich, half-century-old tradition of accuracy, readability, and clarity while also embodying the best advancements in modern Bible typography. The result is a distinctive, open Bible typeface that is uncompromisingly beautiful, clear, readable at any size, and perfectly suited to the New International Version.